You've got the contacts — now learn how to use them!

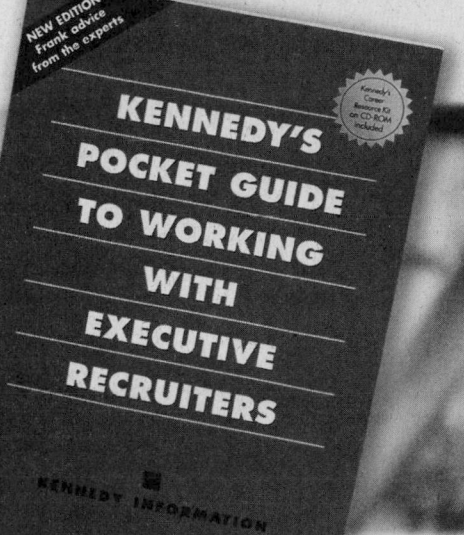

NEW EDITION
Frank advice from the experts

Kennedy's Career Resource Kit on CD-ROM included

KENNEDY'S POCKET GUIDE TO WORKING WITH EXECUTIVE RECRUITERS

KENNEDY INFORMATION

with **Kennedy's Pocket Guide to Working with Executive Recruiters**
— the valuable companion to The Directory of Executive Recruiters!

Packed with the tips, advice and know-how you need to maximize your career opportunities with executive recruiters, including...

How the Industry Works:

- Using an Executive Recruiter
- Working with Job Search Professionals
- The Executive Recruiting Industry
- Types of Executive Recruiters
- Retainer and Contingency Firms

- Specialists and Generalists
- The Client/Recruiter Relationship
- The Executive Recruiting Process
- The Candidate/Recruiter Relationship
- PLUS! Dozens of "Insider" Tips and Techniques

Including: Forming a Recruiter Contact Strategy... Identifying Specific Recruiters... Making Your Achievements Visible... Using the Tools... Cover Letters... Mass mailings... *A glossary of recruiting buzzwords and much more!*

Only $17.95. Check your local bookstore or order direct at www.KennedyInfo.com.

Or get this book free when you subscribe to www.ExecutiveRegistry.com.

KENNEDY INFORMATION

Tel: 800.531.0007 • Fax: 603.924.4034 • bookstore@kennedyinfo.com • www.KennedyInfo.com

35th EDITION

THE

DIRECTORY

OF

EXECUTIVE

RECRUITERS

2007-2008

KENNEDY INFORMATION

Compiled and published by Kennedy Information, Inc.
A BNA Company

1 Phoenix Mill Lane, Fl. 3, Peterborough, NH 03458 USA
Tel: 603.924.1006 • Fax: 603.924.4034
bookstore@kennedyinfo.com • www.KennedyInfo.com
Library of Congress Catalog Card Number 73-642226
ISBN-10: 1-932079-69-6 ISBN-13: 978-1-932079-69-2 Price $59.95

35th edition, ©2006 by Kennedy Information, Inc., Peterborough, New Hampshire.

All rights reserved. This publication is a creative work copyrighted by Kennedy Information, Inc. and is fully protected by all applicable copyright laws, as well as by misappropriation, trade secret, unfair competition, and other applicable laws. The creators, authors and editors of this directory have added value to the underlying factual material herein through one or more of the following: unique and original selection, coordination, expression, arrangement, and classification of the information.

Kennedy Information will vigorously defend all of its rights in this publication.

ISSN 0090-6484
ISBN-10: 1-932079-69-6   ISBN-13: 978-1-932079-69-2

COMMERCIAL USE SPECIFICALLY PROHIBITED.
The price of this directory, and its CD are purposely kept as low as possible as a service to executives seeking a change (and organizations seeking to *hire* an executive search firm). Companies with something to sell to executive recruiters fall within the copyright restriction and must obtain permission and pay a fee for use of all or part of the list.

Foreword

We are proud to present the 35th annual edition of *The Directory of Executive Recruiters*, the most complete listing of executive recruiters available today. The Directory, which we have published since 1971, is continually researched, added to and updated by our full time staff, making it the most in-depth and comprehensive reference available for job seekers.

We've taken *The Directory of Executive Recruiters* online so up-to-date listings are always available. With your purchase you gain access to the entire contents of this edition on the web. Simply visit www.MyRedDER.com, enter your user code, and gain access to the entire *Directory of Executive Recruiters* online.

Whether you're buying this guide in order to manage your career over the long term, or to facilitate an immediate change, you will find 8,245 search firm locations listed with supplementary and comprehensive cross indexes by management function, geography and industry. We also identify 16,564 key recruiters, with their titles and individual areas of specialty in many cases.

To the best of our knowledge, none of the firms listed in this Directory, in either section, charge the individual for **recruiting services**. In today's ever changing career service marketplace, however, the lines between corporate paid recruiting and related services such as career coaching and counseling, resume preparation and critique, outplacement, assessment and many others, have become quite blurred. While it is our understanding that none of the firms in this book, in either section, charge the individual for recruiting services (and indeed it is a requirement for listing), a small percentage of them do accept fees from individuals for **other services** – these firms will be identified with 'Firm offers job seeker paid career services' at the bottom of their listing.

This being said, however, no individual job seeker using this product should expect to be solicited for individual paid services by any of the recruiting firms listed in this book.

If, as a result of contacting a recruiter, you should receive a call, a mailing, an offer to have your resume listed in a database for a fee, or any type of solicitation, PLEASE NOTIFY US AT ONCE. The firm will be removed from the Directory.

Before you dig into this wealth of information, please read the Introduction, which will provide important advice on your search and how to best use this book.

It is our objective to make *The Directory of Executive Recruiters* as complete and easy to use as possible. Accordingly, we always welcome your comments and suggestions on how we can improve the book.

Joe Bremner
Publisher

Brad Smith
COO

Candice Batten
Vice President Operations

Gloria Milburn
Operations Manager, List Management Services

RD Whitney
Vice President, Recruiting and Career Media Group

Note: Every effort has been made to verify the information included in this book. However, we assume no responsibility for errors or omissions and reserve the right to include or eliminate company listings and otherwise edit the contents.

Contact information:
Listings Service, database@kennedyinfo.com
Customer Service, 800.531.0007, 603.924.1006
Commercial Use/Violations, Candice Batten, 603.924.0900 ext. 636

What You Need to Know about Executive Recruiters

There are entire books on how to use executive recruiting services to your best advantage. In the next few pages we give you a brief overview of the subject. This is followed by a question and answer session with tips on why, when and how to interact with recruiters.

We also highly recommend our companion publication, *Kennedy's Pocket Guide to Working with Executive Recruiters*. It contains frank advice, including how and when to contact recruiters and how to respond when a headhunter calls. Visit www.KennedyInfo.com for details.

FOUR FACTS YOU SHOULD KNOW

1) Individuals do not pay fees to search firms.

Executive search firms are paid by the companies that hire them to fill a position, typically a fee of one-third of the job's first year compensation. Search firms are not working for you, but for their paying clients. Therefore, do not expect firms to be overly responsive when you contact them.

If your resume is impressive, they may add you to their database of executives. They may contact you if they have a position that fits your profile or to ask you to recommend other people who might be interested in the job. In either case, you will be starting the process of building a relationship with the recruiter. Every phone call or meeting will probably be noted in the firm's database.

Some companies advertise career counseling and resume mailing services to executives.

2) The difference between retainer and contingency search firms is important.

There are two types of recruiters: Retainer and Contingency. Both charge the client employer a fee and neither should ever charge the prospective employee for recruitment services.

The distinctions between retainer and contingency firms are:

Retainer Firms:

• Retainer recruiters are hired by a client company for an assignment, typically for 90-120 days, and are paid regardless of the results of the search. They may also be kept on retainer by their clients to fill whatever assignments they have.

• One retainer firm is hired by a client company for a given job opening

• They are more often used to fill higher level positions with salaries of $100,000 and above.

• For these assignments they will assemble a short "slate" of candidates. Therefore, if a retainer firm seriously considers you for a position, you will probably be part of a small group of candidates.

• While your file is being used by a retained recruiter for an assignment, no other recruiter at that firm can contact you, even if you would be the perfect candidate. As a result, you are unlikely to be contacted by a firm for more than one or two positions a year, at most.

• If you work for a company that has hired the search firm during the last year or two, you will be "off-limits" for any other position it may have, no matter how well qualified you are. For this reason alone, it is important to be known to multiple search firms.

Contingency Firms:

• Contingency recruiters are more often use for junior and mid-level executives, typically for positions with salaries below $100,000.

• Contingency recruiters receive payment only when their candidate is hired.

• Contingency recruiters do not usually work on an exclusive basis with their clients. Since they are competing with other recruiters to provide candidates for each assignment, they tend to work fast and to submit to the client company as many candidates as they can. This means you may be one of many candidates for a given job.

• Contingency recruiters provide you with a great deal of exposure, since they send many resumes to their clients. This can be useful to you early in your career or if you are unemployed. However, bear in mind that you may not always want your resume widely distributed if you are happy in your current job.

When a headhunter calls you, it can be hard to tell whether they are from a contingency or retainer search firm. This directory helps clarify that information. Even so, contingency firms occasionally work on a retainer basis and some retainer firms do contingency work from time to time. Our advice is to ask explicitly the nature of the assignment before giving your permission to any recruiter to distribute your resume.

3) Some search firms specialize, while others don't. Consider both kinds.

Recruiting firms are often generalists, covering many different management functions (e.g., sales) and industries (e.g., tex-

tiles). Quite a few firms and many individual recruiters, however, do specialize. To make your search as effective as possible, consider recruiters who cover your function and specialize in your industry. Generalist firms should not be ignored, especially at the higher executive ranks. The largest multiple-office search firms tend to cover all functions and industries, but will often have practice areas for particular areas of expertise.

4) **Most recruiters work nationally, so don't limit your search by geography.**
At the lower salary levels, companies may be reluctant to consider out-of-town executives because of the expense of interviewing and relocating them. In these instances, search firms may focus on local candidates. However, for many executive appointments, search firms will look nationally or even internationally. It is in your interest to be known to search firms who fill positions in your industry, function and salary range, no matter where they are. A New York recruiter is as likely to have an assignment in Los Angeles as in Boston.

Question & Answer Session: 14 Valuable Tips

Q: **What's the best way to contact an executive recruiter: phone, fax, e-mail or mail?**

A: Mail or e-mail your resume with a cover letter, and **don't** follow up by phone, e-mail or mail. Executive recruiters are interested only in the job seekers that fit their current openings. Don't risk alienating a recruiter who may find an opening for you later by taking up his or her valuable time now.

Some firms in the directory list Web sites. Most of these give detailed advice on whom to contact. You can also use our online service www.ExecutiveAgent.com and e-mail your resume and cover letter directly to the right recruiters.

Q: **Should I send my resume to retainer firms, contingency firms, or both?**

A: It depends. Early in your career and for mid-level positions, contingency firms are more likely to help you. Contingency firms also tend to be strong in industries with high turnover such as retailing, advertising, EDP, publishing and healthcare. Senior positions are more likely to be handled by retainer firms. If you are unemployed, it is fine to contact many firms of both kinds. If you are happy in your current job but want to actively manage your career, be careful not to contact any retainer firms your employer uses.

Q: **How many resumes should I send out?**

A: Resumes are cheap to send, while *perfect* job openings are scarce. Since different search firms know about different job opportunities, you should send your resume and cover letter widely. It makes sense to cover all of the firms in your industry and function. It's also smart to include leading generalist firms and firms in your area or places you're interested in moving to. Your initial objective is to get into multiple firms' databases so that when they have an assignment that matches your background, your name will come up.

Q: **Should I include a cover letter?**

A: Absolutely. But keep it brief, direct, and adopt a confident tone.

Q: How can I make sure that my resume gets to the right specialist at a recruiting firm?

A: Use the information in this directory wherever possible. Make sure that your resume clearly communicates your employment history and accomplishments. Many recruiters scan resumes into databases. This means you should use standard typefaces and formats, generally following the reverse-chronology model.

Q: How long should I wait before I can expect a response?

A: You won't get a response unless you fit an opening.

Q: Can I count on a headhunter to get me a job?

A: Working with a recruiter should be part of a multi-faceted job search. Recruiters work most effectively for everyone involved when you have made contact before you want to make a job change. They can also be helpful in keeping you abreast of developments within your industry, in newly important skills and specialties you have already or may want to acquire. You can make a good impression with recruiters if you are knowledgeable and helpful to them, possibly recommending other people for positions. Other important steps to take in your job search:

- Network with family, friends, acquaintances and business contacts.
- Contact target firms directly.
- Reply to position listings in newspapers, association and university publications, online services etc.
- Subscribe to services that mail or e-mail you information about job openings.

Q: When is the best time to contact a recruiter?

A: Immediately, and on a continuing basis. We do recommend that executives actively manage their careers whether or not they are looking to change jobs. This includes keeping selected recruiters up-to-date with your career progress and accomplishments. Whenever you do want to make a change, recruiters will already know you and understand what your objectives are.

Q: How do I keep my boss from finding out I'm looking for a job?

A: Tell your boss that you often get calls from headhunters because you have given helpful advice in the past. Be careful not to let any recruiter send your resume to companies unless you give specific approval.

Q: Can I cover a single national or international firm with one resume?

A: Spring for the extra postage or use www.ExecutiveAgent.com to cover your bases. Even large firms vary in the way they handle resumes, so it's best to be on the safe side and send a resume to each office: some firms centralize, others don't.

Q: Should I concentrate on headhunters that specialize in my job function, or go by industry?

A: Normally both. Review both the list of management functions and the list of industries carefully. Some people may be primarily a specialist in a function (such as a Chief Financial Officer) while others

may have general skills but expertise in a particular industry. For many people, both dimensions are relevant. (See recruiter specialty index).

Q: How long can I use my *Directory of Executive Recruiters* book before purchasing a new one?

A: Turnover in this business is high; new firms are constantly being formed, partnerships dissolved, addresses changed. Three-quarters of the listings change in some way. With each update using a current directory pays for itself in time savings alone. For the most up-to-date listings, use www.MyRedDER.com, our electronic version of the directory, which is updated regularly.

Q: I've heard a few horror stories – is there any way to tell whether a headhunting firm is trustworthy?

A: The primary professional association for search firms is the Association of Executive Search Consultants (AESC). Membership in AESC is indicated in the listings and is indicative of a commitment to professionalism in executive recruiting.

International Association of Corporate and Professional Recruitment (IACPR) is an organization of senior-level HR executives and retained executive search consultants. Membership in IACPR is also indicated in the listings.

Q: What other services does Kennedy Information recommend?

A: 1) Your purchase gives you the opportunity to access the Directory online. Visit www.MyRedDER.com.

2) Labels, Reports and PC Disks: If you wish to send letters to a large number of recruiting firms, we have a mailing label service to speed things up.

3) Resume Mailing Service: Send us your resume and we'll print it on high quality paper along with your cover letter, sign and mail out to your targeted list of recruiters.

4) Executive Agent: Quickly emails your resume and cover letter to your selected list of recruiters. More details available at: www.ExecutiveAgent.com/DER07.

5) Executive Registry: Access $100k+ positions filled exclusively by executive recruiters. A membership service, your credentials are posted and you can search a database of active positions confidentially. More details available at: www.ExecutiveRegistry.com/DER07.

How to Use this Directory

The Directory of Executive Recruiters has been designed to be useful in a number of ways:

1. Start by referring to the index of 84 management functions and 121 industries. These indexes enable you to find recruiting firms that specialize in your area(s). They also show whether the firm operates on a retainer or contingency basis. Review generalist firms too, a category that includes many of the largest search firms.

2. In addition, you may search for individual recruiters according to their areas of specialization. Refer to the index of recruiter specialties in this directory.

3. You may want to narrow your search to concentrate on recruiting firms in certain locations. To do this, consult our geographic index. Remember that many firms fill executive positions nationally, so it doesn't pay to limit yourself.

4. Build your own targeted list of executive recruiters by using the various indexes. The directory listings contain a wealth of information about each firm, including contact information, brief descriptions and key individual recruiters.

5. Included with the Directory is an envelope containing the *Directory of Executive Recruiters* Career Resource Kit CD. Simply run the CD from your PC and access helpful articles and advice from today's career experts. You'll also find reviews of other services that put you in contact with the recruiters working in your area of expertise.

How to Read a Listing

Phone, Fax, Email and Web addresses →

ABC Recruiting Inc
10 Any St ◄——————— **Recruiting firm's name and main office mailing address**
Anytown, State, Zip
(555) 123-4567
Fax: (555) 644-2477
Email: recruit@aol.com
Web: www.abcrecruit.com

Summary: Executive recruiters to US and ◄——— **General summary of the firm**
European companies for senior managers.
Special emphasis on banking, insurance
and management consulting.

Whom to contact, title and individual recruiter specialties →

Key Contact, Title - Specialty:
Mr. Joe Green, President - *Senior executives*
Ms. Mary Brown – *Financial services,
    consulting*

Specific functional and industry areas covered by the firm →

Salary minimum: $100,000 ◄——— **Lowest salary for positions handled by this firm**
Functions: Generalist, Directors, CFOs
Industries: Generalist, Banking, Mgmt.
    Consulting, Insurance

Professional Associations: AESC, IACPR ◄——— **Association memberships**

Affiliates →
Affiliates:
DEF Recruiting
Oldtown, State

Branch offices contact information and individual recruiter specialties →

Branches:
200 New St
Newton, State, Zip
(666) 987-6543
Key Contact – Specialty:
Mr. John Gray, Vice President – *CEOs, COOs, CFOs*
Email: abcrecruit@aol.com
Web: www.abcrecruitnewton.com

Retainer Recruiting Firms, A to Z

Firms in this section are retained by the hiring entity and paid at least a portion of their fee immediately to initiate the search. We acknowledge that some executive search firms in this category occasionally accept assignments on a contingency basis. These firms are denoted with the symbol (†).

Full street addresses are listed for all U.S., Canada and Mexico locations, when known.

For firms charging on a contingency basis all or part of the time, please refer to the parallel A to Z listing of Contingency Recruiting firms.

1 Exec Street[†]

201 Post St Ste 401
San Francisco, CA 94108-5063
(415) 982-0555
Email: contactus@1execstreet.com
Web: www.1execstreet.com

Summary: Our firm is a competitive advantage for high-growth companies. We collaborate with our clients to define their hiring needs and strategies, and build successful teams and divisions within their organizations. We create and deliver solutions that meet our clients' evolving hiring.

Key Contact - Specialty:
Mr. Todd Greenhalgh, President & Managing Partner
Mr. George Veh, Senior Partner & Vice President
Mr. John Francis, Senior Partner & Vice President

Salary Minimum: $75,000

Functions: Management, Middle Mgmt., Quality, Sales & Mktg., Engineering

Industries: Generalist (All), Manufacturing, Chemicals, Medical Devices, Plastics, Rubber, Paints, Petro. Products, Machine, Appliance, Computer Equip., Consumer Elect., Misc. Mfg., Electronic, Elec. Components, Mgmt. Consulting, E-commerce, Logistics Svcs., Supply Chain Mgmt, Network Infrastructure

20-20 Foresight Executive Search LLC

1 Lincoln Ctr Ste 1500
Oakbrook Terrace, IL 60181-4272
(708) 246-2100
Email: bcavoto@2020-4.com
Web: www.2020-4.com

Summary: We are a premier retained search firm in the real estate, construction and financial services fields. We hold three basic strengths as the foundation of our firm: expertise, performance and service.

Key Contact - Specialty:
Mr. Robert Cavoto, Managing Principal - *Construction, Financial services, Real estate*
Ms. Cindy Cluzanowski, Principal - *Construction, Real estate*
Mr. Darryl Dougherty, Principal - *Construction, Real estate*
Mr. Ken Nordine, Principal - *Construction, Financial services, Real estate*
Ms. Jan Wojewoski, Principal - *Construction, Real estate*

Salary Minimum: $70,000

Functions: Generalist (All), Management

Industries: Generalist (All), Construction, Finance, Real Estate, Property/Facility Mgmt.

Branches:
4695 Macarthur Ct Ste 1100
Newport Beach, CA 92660-1866
(949) 784-2100
Email: bcavoto@2020-4.com
Key Contact - Specialty:
Mr. Bob Cavoto, Managing Principal - *Construction, Financial services, Real estate*

1201 Pennsylvania Ave NW Ste 300
Washington, DC 20004-2436
(202) 625-2100
Email: scook@2020-4.com

Key Contact - Specialty:
Ms. Stephanie Cook, Principal - *Construction, Real estate*

360 Search Advisors Inc

230 Park Ave Rm 1000
New York, NY 10169-1099
(646) 435-5751
Email: info@360advisors.com
Web: www.360advisors.com

Summary: We are a highly specialized retained executive search boutique that focuses on critical assignments for our clients in: investment banking, capital markets and wealth management. Our firm was founded by a former senior Wall Street executive; who understands first hand, the tangible and intangible needs of clients.

Salary Minimum: $250,000

Functions: Generalist (All), Management, Senior Mgmt., Sales & Mktg., Sales Mgmt., HR Mgmt., M&A, Risk Mgmt., Minorities/Diversity

Industries: Banking, Invest. Banking, Brokers, Venture Cap., Mutual/Hedge Funds

5 Star Hospitality Executive Recruiters[†]

(formerly known as RY Hospitality Executive Search)
136 Middlebury Dr
Jupiter, FL 33458-3006
(561) 799-3085
Fax: (561) 799-0554
Email: sharon@5-starher.com
Web: www.5-starher.com

Summary: We specialize in recruiting mid and upper level management positions in the hospitality/retail industry. Our clients include: fine dining & casual restaurants, hotels/motels, country clubs, convention centers and contract food services quick serve, private estates, resorts and real estate communities.

Key Contact - Specialty:
Ms. Sharon Rowlson, President
Ms. Michelle Grace, Recruiter

Salary Minimum: $40,000

Functions: Generalist (All), Management

Industries: Banking, Hospitality, Hotels, Resorts, Clubs, Restaurants, Quick Service Restaurants, Full Service Restaurants, Inst./Industrial Food Svc., Entertainment, Real Estate, Property/Facility Mgmt.

A la Carte International Inc

3330 Pacific Ave Ste 500
Virginia Beach, VA 23451-2997
(757) 425-6111
(800) 446-3037
Fax: (757) 425-8507
Email: alacarte@wedofood.com
Web: www.wedofood.com

Summary: Boutique retained search firm specializing in the food sector, staffing at the director level and above for general management, operations, sales, marketing and technology.

Key Contact - Specialty:
Mr. Michael J. Romaniw, President - *General management*
Mrs. Kelley P. Nicastro, Senior Vice President - *Technology*
Mr. Terry Forehand, Senior Vice President - *Operations*
Mrs. Lisa James Gollihur, Director, Research
Ms. Cynthia R. Dixon, Systems Administrator
Mr. Michael Glassman, Sommelier

Salary Minimum: $100,000

Functions: Generalist (All), Mfg., Product Dev., Sales & Mktg., Mktg. Research, Mktg. Mgmt., Sales Mgmt., Staffing, R&D, Minorities/Diversity

Industries: Generalist (All), Manufacturing, Food, Bev., Tobacco, Textiles, Apparel, Chemicals, Wholesale, Retail, E-commerce, Hospitality, Hotels, Resorts, Clubs, Restaurants, Quick Service Restaurants, Full Service Restaurants, Inst./Industrial Food Svc., Advertising, Call Centers, Database SW, Industry Specific SW, Mfg. SW, Marketing SW, Women's

A-L Associates LLC[†]

546 5th Ave Fl 6
New York, NY 10036-5000
(212) 878-9000
(800) 292-1390
Fax: (212) 878-9096
Email: general@alassoc.com
Web: www.alassoc.com

Summary: Expedient, value added global executive search. Function specializations include most within financial services as well as a broad spectrum of legal and technical disciplines.

Key Contact - Specialty:
Mr. Curt Miller, Chief Executive Officer - *Financial services, Technical*
Mr. Edward S. Orchant, President & Chief Operating Officer - *Capital markets, Financial services*
Ms. Sandra Manning, Recruiter

Salary Minimum: $100,000

Functions: Management, Finance, CFOs, IT, MIS Mgmt., Attorneys

Industries: Generalist (All), Banking, Invest. Banking, Mutual/Hedge Funds

Abbott Smith Worldwide

(formerly known as Abbott Smith Associates Inc)
PO Box 318
Millbrook, NY 12545-0318
(845) 677-5300
Fax: (845) 677-3315
Email: abbottsmith@prodigy.net

Summary: For many years, we have recruited senior level candidates for general management positions worldwide with a special emphasis on change management, HR, and senior level management

Key Contact - Specialty:
Mr. David W. Brinkerhoff, Managing Partner
Ms. Sara P. McWilliams, Senior Partner

Salary Minimum: $100,000

Functions: Management, HR Mgmt.

Industries: Generalist (All)

Abécassis, Medeiros, Hurtubise Conseil

302-28 Rue Notre-Dame E
Montreal, QC H2Y 1B9
Canada
(514) 842-8213
Fax: (514) 842-8128
Email: info@abecassis.com
Web: www.abecassis.com

Summary: Our firm has solid expertise in filling management positions at intermediary and executive levels. We have built a solid reputation in our province. The strength of our company lies in: our rigorous and efficient approach to exploring the employment market, our commitment to understanding our clients' requirements, and finding the right candidate.

Email your resume to a targeted list of recruiters now at www.ExecutiveAgent.com/DER07

Key Contact - Specialty:
Mrs. Pauline P. Abécassis, CHRA, Recruiter
Ms. Anne-Marie Medeiros, CHRA, Recruiter
Mr. Jean-Pierre Hurtubise, CHRA, Recruiter
Mr. Harry Abécassis, Recruiter

Salary Minimum: $70,000

Functions: Generalist (All), Management, Mfg., Materials, Sales & Mktg., HR Mgmt., Finance, Engineering

Industries: Generalist (All), Food, Bev., Tobacco, Paper, Chemicals, Metal Products, Wholesale, Retail, Finance, Venture Cap., Services, Non-profits, Legal, Accounting, Mgmt. Consulting, Communications, Telecoms, Insurance

Abel Fuller & Zedler LLC

440 Benmar Dr Ste 1085
Houston, TX 77060-3197
(281) 447-3334
Fax: (281) 447-3334
Email: agarcia@execufirm.com
Web: www.execufirm.com

Summary: We are a retained executive search firm conducting searches in senior management. We are a generalist practice versed in bringing the best candidate to our clients.

Key Contact - Specialty:
Mr. Abel R. Garcia, President & Chief Executive Officer
Mr. Bob Rollins, Senior Vice President, Human Capital Dev - *Manufacturing (Management), Marketing, Production, Sales*
Ms. Suzy Houston, Senior Vice President, Talent Acqstn - *Executives*
Ms. Helen Cavazos, Vice President

Salary Minimum: $80,000

Functions: Generalist (All)

Industries: Energy, Utilities, Manufacturing, Transportation, Wholesale, Retail, Finance, Services, Aerospace, Software, Healthcare

Abeln, Magy, Underberg & Associates

800 Wayzata Blvd E Ste 200
Wayzata, MN 55391-1765
(952) 476-4938
Fax: (952) 404-7470
Email: info@abelnmagy.com
Web: www.abelnmagy.com

Summary: Professional retained search consultants with over 100 years of combined experience in a variety of functions.

Key Contact - Specialty:
Mr. David S. Magy
Mr. Kenneth E. Abeln
Mr. Rick Underberg

Functions: Generalist (All)

Industries: Generalist (All)

David Abramson & Asssociates LLC

1660 South Highway 100 Suite 500
Minneapolis, MN 55416-1551
(952) 697-3570
Fax: (952) 6973573
Email: david@abramsonassociates.com
Web: www.davidabramsonassociates.com

Summary: Executive search and leadership development firm focused on helping clients fill positions for Senior Financial Executives and CPA firms' Partners and Senior Managers by helping them maximize their potential. With our founder's extensive experience as a CPA, we know success

in public accounting and financial positions like no one else!

Key Contact - Specialty:
Mr. David Abramson, Chief Executive Officer

Functions: Finance

Industries: Generalist (All)

ADA Executive Search Inc

3716 N Fremont St
Chicago, IL 60613-3912
(312) 933-2135
Email: adaeziman@adaexecutivesearch.com
Web: www.adaexecutivesearch.com

Summary: We are a generalist firm conducting management through executive level search assignments for Fortune 500 companies, emerging businesses, higher educational institutions, association management and not-for-profit organizations. We are committed to developing lasting relationships with diverse and distinguished clients and candidates.

Key Contact - Specialty:
Mr. William C. Wheeler, Jr., JD, CAE, Principal & Chief Executive Officer - *Telecommunications*

Salary Minimum: $75,000

Functions: Generalist (All)

Industries: Generalist (All)

Branches:
4134 Gulf of Mexico Dr Ste 205B
Longboat Key, FL 34228-2642
(941) 387-8700
Email: adaeziman@adaexecutivesearch.com
Key Contact - Specialty:
Ms. Alicia Donn Aeziman, Principal & Founder

Adams & Associates International

PO Box 129
Barrington, IL 60011-0129
(847) 304-5301
(847) 304-5300
Email: search@adamsassoc.com
Web: www.leanthinking.net

Summary: We are an executive recruiting firm of senior and mid-level executives in manufacturing, technology and professional services. Our specialists are in top-level Lean Value Stream, Lean Enterprise and Operational Excellence recruiting.

Key Contact - Specialty:
Mr. Adam Zak, President - *Change management, General management, Operations, Six sigma*
Ms. Sheila Cunningham, Managing Director - *Change management, General management, Operations, Six sigma*
Ms. Joan Bennett, Associate Director - *Change management, General management, Operations, Six sigma*

Salary Minimum: $150,000

Functions: Management, Board Members, Senior Mgmt., Middle Mgmt., Mfg., Production, Plant Mgmt., Quality, Productivity, Purchasing

Industries: Generalist (All), Manufacturing, Venture Cap., Services, Mgmt. Consulting, Aerospace, Healthcare

Adams Executive Search[†]

3416 Fairfield Trl
Clearwater, FL 33761-1111
(727) 772-1536
Email: tla@axsearch.com
Web: www.axsearch.com

Summary: We offer retained and exclusive search services. We specialize in all facets of real estate development, construction, finance and corporate and multi-site operations. We also service those ancillary functions that support the development process, for example legal, finance and HR. Our clients include developers, general contractors and users of commercial, light industrial, residential, hospitality, restaurants and retail.

Key Contact - Specialty:
Mr. Thomas Adams, Chairman
Ms. Elizabeth Adams, Vice President

Salary Minimum: $80,000

Functions: Generalist (All)

Industries: Construction, Retail, Architectural Svcs., Legal, Accounting, HR Services, Hospitality, Real Estate

G Adams Partners

205 W Wacker Dr Ste 810
Chicago, IL 60606-1275
(312) 577-5648
Fax: (312) 673-0390
Email: jerry@adamspartners.com
Web: www.adamspartners.com

Summary: We offer tailored executive search services to the leading construction, architecture, design, engineering and real estate firms.

Key Contact - Specialty:
Mr. Gerald Adams, President - *Construction, Engineering, Real estate*
Ms. Karen O'Shea, Vice President - *Architecture, Built environments, Construction, General contractors, Real estate*

Salary Minimum: $100,000

Functions: Board Members, Senior Mgmt., Middle Mgmt., Engineering, Architects, Int'l.

Industries: Construction, Architectural Svcs., Real Estate

Addison Kelly Ltd

3390 South Service Rd
Burlington, ON L7N 3J5
Canada
(905) 336-5666
Fax: (905) 319-6645
Email: mkelly@addisonkelly.com
Web: www.addisonkelly.com

Summary: Our firm is a retained search firm specializing at the senior technical, management and senior management level in the energy, telecom/cable industries.

Key Contact - Specialty:
Mr. Mike Kelly, President & Principal - *Cable, Communications, Energy, Telecommunications*
Mr. Dave MacPherson, Senior Associate - *Communications, Energy, Telecommunications*

Salary Minimum: $90,000

Functions: Management, Senior Mgmt., Engineering

Industries: Energy, Utilities, Oil & Gas, Manufacturing, Engineering Svcs., Communications, Telecoms, Telephony, Digital, Wireless, Fiber Optic, Network Infrastructure, RF/Microwave, Environmental Svcs., Software

Jerry Adel & Company

1201-3266 Yonge St
First Class Business Stores
Toronto, ON M4N 3P6
Canada
(416) 488-7585
Fax: (416) 481-4065

† occasional contingency assignment

Email: jerry@jerryadel.com
Web: www.jerryadel.com

Summary: We are a professional practice providing executive search and related services to medium and large size firms. About 75 to 80 percent of our clients are in manufacturing. Professional technical and administrative positions are available also.

Key Contact - Specialty:
Mr. Jerry Adel, President

Salary Minimum: $50,000

Functions: Generalist (All), Senior Mgmt., Middle Mgmt., Plant Mgmt., Purchasing, Mktg. Mgmt., Sales Mgmt., CFOs

Industries: Generalist (All)

The Adkins Group Inc†

3105 Manchaca Rd Ste A
Austin, TX 78704-8874
(512) 916-9600
Fax: (512) 916-9665
Email: info@theadkinsgroup.com
Web: www.theadkinsgroup.com

Summary: Our firm is a privately held corporation, specializing in delivering high-quality executive search, research, and recruitment consulting to established and start-up organizations across the U.S.

Key Contact - Specialty:
Mr. Jeff Adkins, PHR, President
Mr. Steve Weigl, Senior Account Executive - *Senior management, Staffing, Start-up companies, Technical (Management), Technology*
Mr. Gil Oakes, Director, Search Operations

Salary Minimum: $100,000

Functions: Management, Senior Mgmt., Middle Mgmt., Mfg., Product Dev., Sales & Mktg., Finance, Engineering, Eng. Design, Mgmt. Consultants

Industries: Generalist (All)

Adkisson Consultants Inc

PO Box 5643
Bloomington, IL 61702-5643
(309) 452-7200
(866) 311-0000
Fax: (309) 452-7204
Email: opportunity@wefinddocs.com
Web: www.wefinddocs.com

Summary: We help healthcare organizations achieve excellence. Our firm strives to be a leader in the medical search consulting industry specializing in the placement of physicians, physician executives, healthcare executives and allied health professionals; serving hospitals, group practices and healthcare systems.

Key Contact - Specialty:
Mr. Billy D. Adkisson, FAAHC, CHE, President & Chief Executive Officer
Ms. Shannon L. McKay, Senior Account Executive & Principal
Ms. Michelle S. Houchin, Senior Account Executive & Principal - *Healthcare*
Ms. Susan E. McGuire, MA, Senior Account Executive - *Healthcare*

Salary Minimum: $60,000

Functions: Healthcare, Physicians, Allied Health

Industries: Healthcare, Hospitals

Adler Management Inc†

(also known as AMI Consulting)
66 Witherspoon St Ste 315
Princeton, NJ 08542-3226
(609) 443-3300
Fax: (609) 443-4439
Email: jadler@amiconsulting.com
Web: www.amiconsulting.com

Summary: Our firm specializes in management consulting in the high-technology markets. We recruit, evaluate and structure management teams for venture backed start-ups, as well as Fortune 500 companies.

Key Contact - Specialty:
Mr. Jack E. Adler, President
Mr. John Sherman, Senior Associate
Mrs. Cheryl Levine, Associate - *Research*

Salary Minimum: $100,000

Functions: Generalist (All), Senior Mgmt., Middle Mgmt., Mktg. Mgmt., Sales Mgmt., IT

Industries: Semiconductors, Venture Cap., Publishing, New Media, Telecoms, Software, Security SW

Advantage Partners Inc

29225 Chagrin Blvd Ste 300
Cleveland, OH 44122-4629
(216) 514-1212
Fax: (216) 514-1213
Email: resume@advantagepartnersinc.com
Web: www.advantagepartnersinc.com

Summary: We are a boutique firm recruiting at the senior management and executive level specializing in privately held companies, investor owned business, and financial services.

Key Contact - Specialty:
Ms. Nikki C. Bondi, Managing Partner - *Business development, CEOs, Closely-held business, Entrepreneurs, Manufacturing*
Mr. James B. McPolin, Partner - *Competitive intelligence, General management*
Ms. Nancy Shaw, Partner - *C-level, CFOs, Manufacturing, Private equity*
Ms. Tiona Thompson, Partner - *Banking, Financial services, Insurance*
Ms. Nikki Madsen Davis, Partner - *Business development, CIOs, Information Technology, Systems (Analysts), Technology*
Ms. Pamela Taubert, Principal

Salary Minimum: $125,000

Functions: Generalist (All)

Industries: Generalist (All)

Aegis Consulting

633 3rd Ave Rm 2700
New York, NY 10017-8159
(212) 687-2200
Fax: (212) 687-0079
Email: info@aegisnet.com
Web: www.aegisnet.com

Summary: Retained executive search firm specializing in information technology and services, professional services, strategic marketing, and business development across various industries. Dedicated to excellence and timeliness of results, we employ a proven, research-based methodology in the execution of searches from top executive hires to rare functional specialists.

Key Contact - Specialty:
Ms. Nancy Caudill, Managing Director - *Business development, General management, Information Technology, Management consulting, Professional services*

Mr. Dante Sucgang, Director - *Business development, General management, Information Technology, Management consulting, Professional services*
Ms. Vered Lieb, Director
Mr. Jeffrey G. Zwiff, Director - *Banking, Banking (Retail), Business development, Direct marketing, Marketing*
Mr. Bradford W. Hoyda, Principal
Ms. Marci B. Pepper, Consulting Associate - *Finance*

Salary Minimum: $120,000

Functions: Management, Senior Mgmt., Sales & Mktg., HR Mgmt., IT, MIS Mgmt., Mgmt. Consultants

Industries: Energy, Utilities, Manufacturing, Transportation, Retail, Finance, Services, Mgmt. Consulting, Media, Communications, Government, Biotech/Life Sciences

Aegis Group Search Consultants LLC

41451 W 11 Mile Rd
Novi, MI 48375-1855
(248) 344-1450
Fax: (248) 347-2231
Email: resume@aegis-group.com
Web: www.aegis-group.com

Summary: We are a minority-owned firm and certified as a Minority Business Enterprise that specializes in the executive recruitment of senior-level management for hospitals, integrated healthcare systems, managed care/health insurance companies, physician group practices and medical schools.

Key Contact - Specialty:
Mr. Timothy Ignash, Founder & Partner - *Healthcare*
Mr. John Green, Jr., President & Partner - *Healthcare*

Salary Minimum: $75,000

Functions: Management, Senior Mgmt., Healthcare, Physicians, Health Admin., CFOs

Industries: Healthcare, Hospitals, Long-term/Home Care

AET Advisors LLC

4875 Olde Towne Pkwy Ste 150
Marietta, GA 30068-5635
(404) 237-8208
Fax: (404) 261-6961
Email: aetadvisors@mindspring.com

Summary: A retained executive search and strategic planning consulting practice, focusing exclusively on the real estate industry. We have firm functions in every aspect of the industry in organizational/strategic planning.

Key Contact - Specialty:
Mr. Arnold E. Taras, President - *Construction, Real estate, Senior management*

Salary Minimum: $75,000

Functions: Management, Board Members, Senior Mgmt., Middle Mgmt., CFOs, Specialized Svcs., Architects

Industries: Construction, Real Estate

Affinity Executive Search

1025 S Shore Dr
Miami Beach, FL 33141-2413
(305) 865-1973
Fax: (305) 865-1972
Email: careers@affinitysearch.com
Web: www.affinitysearch.com

Summary: We provide executive search at all levels of engineering, sales, marketing, finance, manufacturing, operations, purchasing and other levels of corporate operations and management. We serve the following industries: semiconductor capital equipment & high purity materials, power supplies & systems and test & measurement equipment.

Key Contact - Specialty:
Mrs. Renee Kohn, Chief Executive Officer - *Diversity*
Mr. Steven Kohn - *Engineering, Manufacturing, Presidents, Sales*
Ms. Renee Leavy - *Operations, Research & development*

Salary Minimum: $80,000

Functions: Senior Mgmt.

Industries: Generalist (All), Manufacturing, Semiconductors, Retail, Finance, Aerospace, Packaging, Software, Biotech/Life Sciences

AGORA Consulting†

1880 Office Club Pt
Colorado Springs, CO 80920-5002
(719) 219-0360
Email: agora@agoraconsulting.com
Web: www.agoraconsulting.com

Summary: We are an executive retained search firm specializing on placing senior level professionals in high-technology (semiconductors, electronics, software, hardware, eCommerce, internet solutions and services, IT) and non-profit organizations.

Key Contact - Specialty:
Mr. Rob Lauer, President
Mr. Dave Bechtold, Director, Marketing & Operations - *Computers (Hardware,Software), E-business, Internet, Semiconductors*
Ms. Jody Richardson, Executive Director - *Administration, Human resources, Office (Administration), Operations, Research*
Ms. Sandy Prebeck, Director, Research - *Administration, Research*
Ms. Susan Jenkins, Executive Recruiter - *Business development, Computers (Hardware,Software), Electronics, Human resources*

Salary Minimum: $100,000

Functions: Generalist (All)

Industries: Generalist (All)

Ahern Search Partners

3982 Powell Rd Ste 205
Powell, OH 43065-7662
(614) 436-4126
(614) 783-3557
Fax: (614) 436-4125
Email: mahern@ahernsearch.com
Web: www.ahernsearch.com

Summary: We provide executive search specializing in the healthcare market. We have extensive experience in the hospital health system, payer manager care, consulting firms and vendors supporting these verticals. Our emphasis is on leadership positions including: technology, human resources, sales, finance and operations.

Key Contact - Specialty:
Mrs. Mollie M. Ahern, President & Founder

Salary Minimum: $100,000

Functions: Management, Health Admin., MIS Mgmt., Systems Implem., Mgmt. Consultants

Industries: Healthcare, Hospitals

Ahrensdorf & Associates

PO Box 7494
Saint Davids, PA 19087-7494
(610) 971-0500
Fax: (610) 971-9530
Email: leeahrensdorf@att.net

Summary: We are a generalist, retainer search firm that stresses service and quality and recruits with the goal of building partnerships with its client base.

Key Contact - Specialty:
Mr. Lee Ahrensdorf, President - *Biotechnology, Financial services, Healthcare, Pharmaceutical, Transportation*

Salary Minimum: $100,000

Functions: Generalist (All), Management, Senior Mgmt., Mfg., Sales & Mktg., HR Mgmt., Finance, CFOs, IT, R&D

Industries: Generalist (All), Manufacturing, Chemicals, Drugs Mfg., Medical Devices, Plastics, Rubber, Transportation, Finance, Banking, Invest. Banking, Misc. Financial, Non-profits, Pharm Svcs., Legal, Telecoms, Wireless, Insurance, Real Estate, Biotech/Life Sciences, Healthcare, Hospitals

AKS Associates Ltd

175 Derby St Ste 27
Hingham, MA 02043-4054
(781) 740-1704
Fax: (781) 749-5184
Email: sandy@akssearch.com
Web: www.akssearch.com

Summary: Senior-level search focused on general management, financial, IT and operations functions in the professional services, not-for-profit, and financial services industries. We offer a personalized approach using the highest quality standards with competitive fee arrangements.

Key Contact - Specialty:
Mr. Alexander Salmela, President

Salary Minimum: $90,000

Functions: Generalist (All)

Industries: Finance, Non-profits

Cheryl Alexander & Associates

8588 Shadow Creek Dr
Maple Grove, MN 55311-1510
(763) 416-4570
Email: cherylalexander@cherylalexander.com
Web: www.cherylalexander.com

Summary: We are a retained executive search firm specializing in senior level positions in technology, manufacturing, marketing, international, finance, HR and development. Our primary industries include: energy, environmental, telecom and non-profits. We are known as an effective resource for diversity search assignments.

Key Contact - Specialty:
Ms. Cheryl Alexander, Chief Executive Officer

Salary Minimum: $90,000

Functions: Generalist (All)

Industries: Manufacturing, Misc. Financial, Mgmt. Consulting, IT Implementation

Alexander Associates

993 Lenox Dr Ste 200
Lawrenceville, NJ 08648-2316
(609) 844-7597
(609) 844-7589
Email: info@alexassociates.com
Web: www.alexassociates.com

Summary: We are a leading retainer-based firm performing searches for clients. The principals of our firm are practicing consultants who increase the effectiveness and competitiveness of our clients' organizations.

Key Contact - Specialty:
Mr. Richard J. Alexander, Founding Partner - *Sales*
Mr. A. Gregory Phinney, Managing Director - *Sales*

Salary Minimum: $125,000

Functions: Management, Sales Mgmt., CFOs, IT, MIS Mgmt.

Industries: Generalist (All)

Raymond Alexander Associates

97 Lackawanna Ave Ste 102
Totowa, NJ 07512-2332
(973) 256-1000
Fax: (973) 256-5871
Email: raa@raymondalexander.com
Web: www.raymondalexander.com

Summary: We are a recruitment firm specializing in accounting and financial professionals. We place professionals in Fortune 500 companies and privately held corporations throughout the New York/New Jersey metropolitan area.

Key Contact - Specialty:
Mr. Raymond Jezierski, CPA, Founder & President

Salary Minimum: $75,000

Functions: Finance

Industries: Construction, Manufacturing, Printing, Chemicals, Non-profits, Pharm Svcs., Accounting, Hospitality, Insurance, Real Estate

The Alexander Group

2700 Post Oak Blvd Ste 2400
Houston, TX 77056-5793
(713) 993-7900
Fax: (713) 993-7979
Email: info@thealexandergroup.com
Web: www.thealexandergroup.com

Summary: A retained executive search firm specializing in executive and senior management searches across most functional areas in all major industries including financial services, high technology, not-for-profit, energy, biotechnology, legal and healthcare. Experience in start-up and high-growth companies.

Key Contact - Specialty:
Ms. Jane S. Howze, Managing Director
Mr. John C. Lamar, Managing Director

Salary Minimum: $100,000

Functions: Generalist (All), Management, Board Members, Senior Mgmt., Sales Mgmt., HR Mgmt., CFOs, Mgmt. Consultants, Non-profits, Attorneys

Industries: Generalist (All), Energy, Utilities, Banking, Legal, HR Services, Biotech/Life Sciences

Branches:
235 Pine St Ste 1275
San Francisco, CA 94104-2752
(415) 677-8668
Fax: (415) 677-8674
Email: info@thealexandergroup.com

† occasional contingency assignment

Key Contact - Specialty:
Ms. Sarah J. Mitchell - *CEOs, COOs, Financial services, Healthcare*

Alexander Ross
21 E 40th St Ste 1802
New York, NY 10016-0505
(212) 889-9333
Fax: (212) 481-3565
Email: benrl@alexanderross.com
Web: www.alexanderross.com

Summary: We are an executive search firm dedicated solely to change management and learning functions internally and externally (consultants). Known for in-depth assessment and extensive database of professionals in these fields.

Key Contact - Specialty:
Mr. Ben Lichtenstein, President - *Change management, Consulting, Human resources, Organizational development, Training*

Salary Minimum: $100,000

Functions: HR Mgmt., Training, Mgmt. Consultants

Industries: Generalist (All)

Penelope Alexander
(also known as Alexander & Company)
8308 Barber Oak Dr
Plano, TX 75025-4743
(866) 443-4401
Email: penny@prrecruiter.net

Summary: I am a consultant with extensive experience in recruiting public relations, investor relations, marketing communications and corporate communications professionals for all industries. I work with PR agencies and corporations on a nationwide basis. Searches are conducted on contract or retained basis only.

Key Contact - Specialty:
Ms. Penelope Alexander, Consultant - *Public relations*

Salary Minimum: $40,000

Functions: PR

Industries: Generalist (All)

Alexander, Wollman & Stark
1835 Market St Ste 2626
Philadelphia, PA 19103-2931
(267) 256-0721
Fax: (267) 256-0725
Email: alcxwollstark@aol.com

Summary: We are a retainer based search and consulting firm specializing in physician and executive search and consulting for medical schools, academic health centers, teaching hospitals and managed care organizations.

Key Contact - Specialty:
Mr. Raymond Alexander, Principal
Mr. Paul Stark, Principal

Salary Minimum: $100,000

Functions: Senior Mgmt., Healthcare, Physicians

Industries: Non-profits, Healthcare

Branches:
45 Bennington St
Needham, MA 02494-1932
(781) 453-1911
Key Contact - Specialty:
Mr. Arthur A. Beraducci, Principal

13 Hathorn Hl
Woodstock, VT 05091-1238
(802) 457-1582
Fax: (802) 457-1688

Email: hwvt@aol.com
Key Contact - Specialty:
Dr. Harry Wollman, MD, Principal

Alfus Group Inc†
353 Lexington Ave Fl 8
New York, NY 10016-0941
(212) 599-1000
Fax: (212) 599-1523
Email: mail@thealfusgroup.com
Web: www.thealfusgroup.com

Summary: We conduct executive search with a specialty in hotel, restaurant, clubs, real estate, entertainment, in related industries. These include: time-share, gaming, cruise lines, airlines, hospitals, and managed care facilities.

Key Contact - Specialty:
Mr. Phillip Alfus, President - *Hospitality, Hotels, Senior management*
Ms. Amy Falbaum, Director
Ms. Paula Caracappa, Director - *Amusement parks, Gaming, Hotels, Resorts*
Ms. Susan Wilner, Director - *Hotels, Resorts*
Mr. Pat Thompson, Associate - *Real estate*
Ms. Danielle Padwa, Associate - *Sports*
Mr. Thomas Elbe, Director - *Hospitality, Hotels, Marketing, Sales*
Ms. Lisa Vendetti, Associate - *Advertising, Marketing*
Ms. Moira Boag, Director, Research

Salary Minimum: $80,000

Functions: Hospitality, Hotel Mgmt.

Industries: Construction, Finance, Accounting, Mgmt. Consulting, HR Services, Hotels, Resorts, Clubs, Restaurants, Full Service Restaurants, Entertainment, Recreation, Travel

Allegro
1823 W Bay Ave Ste A
Newport Beach, CA 92663-4516
(949) 279-4444
Email: info@allegro1.com
Web: www.allegro1.com

Summary: We specialize in matching the most qualified candidates with the most appropriate positions, creating a productive and positive environment for both employer and employee. We provide candidates to perform specific tasks as an integral part of your team, or as a full team to complete a specific assignment. We offer complete recruitment solutions for both companies and the professionals

Key Contact - Specialty:
Mr. John Grafman, Chief Executive Officer

Functions: Eng. Design

Industries: Motor Vehicles, Defense

Allen Associates
4555 Lake Forest Dr Fl 6
Cincinnati, OH 45242-3785
(513) 563-3040
Email: feedback@allensearch.com
Web: www.allensearch.com

Summary: Executive search consultants exclusively focused on critical assignments for senior decision makers and board members. Typically, assignments are at the officer - CEO level.

Key Contact - Specialty:
Mr. Michael Allen, President

Salary Minimum: $200,000

Functions: Generalist (All), Senior Mgmt.

Industries: Generalist (All), Textiles, Apparel, Consumer Goods, Retail, Venture Cap.,

Entertainment, Media, New Media, Broadcast, Film

David Allen Associates†
PO Box 56
Haddonfield, NJ 08033-0048
(856) 795-6470
Email: david@davidallenassoc.com
Web: www.davidallenassoc.com

Summary: We are a boutique with a focus on risk management, finance, capital markets, marketing and clinical / regulatory affairs. We have enjoyed close working relationships with leaders in the consumer goods, energy, financial services, life sciences and technology industries for many years.

Key Contact - Specialty:
Mr. David Ritchings, Partner - *Asset management, High technology, Investment management, Life Sciences, Petrochemical*
Mr. William Marchand, Partner - *Consumer (Packaged Goods), Energy, Life Sciences*

Salary Minimum: $100,000

Functions: Product Dev., Mktg. Research, Mktg. Mgmt., PR, CFOs, Cash Mgmt., M&A, Risk Mgmt., R&D

Industries: Generalist (All), Oil & Gas, Food, Bev., Tobacco, Drugs Mfg., Medical Devices, Semiconductors, Consumer Goods, Banking, Invest. Banking, Mutual/Hedge Funds, Entertainment, Telecoms, Biotech/Life Sciences

Allen Evans Klein International
60 E 42nd St Rm 2228
New York, NY 10165-2216
(212) 983-9300
Fax: (212) 983-9272
Email: info@allenevans.com
Web: www.allenevans.com

Summary: We are a retainer based executive search and advisory firm for emerging, turnaround and global 1000 companies. Our vertical markets include: technology, internet, electronic information services, financial services, media, consumer goods, distribution, hospitality, retail, education and beyond.

Key Contact - Specialty:
Mr. Robert Klein, Managing Partner

Salary Minimum: $100,000

Functions: Generalist (All), Board Members, Senior Mgmt.

Industries: Generalist (All)

Allerton Heneghan & O'Neill
1 Tower Ln Ste 1700
Oakbrook Terrace, IL 60181-4631
(630) 645-2294
Fax: (630) 645-2298
Email: resume@ahosearch.com
Web: www.ahosearch.com

Summary: Retainer-based search firm with long-standing client relationships with large, multi-national companies and smaller, entrepreneurial organizations. Principal and professional support person work in tandem on each assignment.

Key Contact - Specialty:
Mr. Donald A. Heneghan, Managing Partner
Ms. Jennifer A. Cushing, Partner
Mr. Terrence J. McSherry, Partner

Salary Minimum: $100,000

Functions: Generalist (All), Senior Mgmt., Plant Mgmt., Mktg. Mgmt., Training, CFOs, MIS Mgmt., Minorities/Diversity

Industries: Generalist (All), Drugs Mfg., Motor Vehicles, Finance, Mgmt. Consulting, Telecoms, Software

Alliance Search Management Inc

1717 Woodstead Ct Ste 106
The Woodlands, TX 77380-1448
(281) 367-8630
(800) 444-0573
Email: kathy@alliancesearch.com
Web: www.alliancesearch.com

Summary: A privately held healthcare boutique practice; rich in diversity of assignments, has a relatively small "hands off list" assuring our clients the greatest access to the largest candidate pool. While 88 percent of our engagements are completed in officer ranks, we accept assignments at all levels of the organization, setting no minimum fees for our clients.

Key Contact - Specialty:
Ms. Kathy Powell-Florip, President

Salary Minimum: $80,000

Functions: Board Members, Senior Mgmt., Healthcare, Allied Health, Health Admin., Mktg. Mgmt., Finance, Minorities/Diversity

Industries: Generalist (All), Healthcare

AllianceSource LLC

865 United Nations Plz Apt 13A
New York, NY 10017-1812
(212) 308-1095
Email: execsearch@att.net
Web: www.alliancesource.net

Summary: Personal, flexible, fee-by-arrangement, selective partnering services. Focus is function leaders, senior management, and diversity across industries. Financial services, healthcare, hospitality, IT, management consulting, manufacturing, pharmaceutical and other industries. Hallmarks are far-reaching, unrestricted candidate development, strong communications, culture-fit candidates, and rapid completion. Please note, only emailed resumes are reviewed for qualifications.

Key Contact - Specialty:
Ms. Pamela S. Henry, Managing Principal

Salary Minimum: $85,000

Functions: Senior Mgmt., Mfg., Healthcare, Sales & Mktg., HR Mgmt., Finance, IT, Specialized Svcs., Legal, Hospitality

Industries: Manufacturing, Food, Bev., Tobacco, Lumber, Furniture, Soap, Perf., Cosmtcs., Drugs Mfg., Plastics, Rubber, Metal Products, Machine, Appliance, Consumer Elect., Consumer Goods, Retail, Finance, Services, Hospitality, Hotels, Resorts, Clubs, Restaurants, Entertainment, Recreation, Travel, Communications, Government, Real Estate, Software, Healthcare

Allied Search LLC

388 W Turnberry Dr
West Chester, PA 19382-2370
(610) 793-6859
Fax: (610) 793-0346
Email: info@alliedsearch.com
Web: www.alliedsearch.com

Summary: Our firm is a firm specializing in the recruitment of marketing, sales and executive-level individuals within the information technology industry.

Key Contact - Specialty:
Ms. Karen Woodeshick, President & Chief Executive Officer - *Executives, Marketing, Sales*

Salary Minimum: $75,000

Functions: Sales & Mktg.

Industries: Software, Accounting SW, Database SW, Doc. Mgmt., Production SW, ERP SW, Industry Specific SW, Mfg. SW, Networking, Comm. SW, Security SW, System SW

Almond & Associates

207 Broadway Ste 300
Tacoma, WA 98402-4024
(253) 952-5555
Fax: (253) 952-5560
Email: info@almondsearch.com
Web: www.almondandassociates.com

Summary: Full service employment consulting firm providing quality search and recruiting services for key executive/management positions. The company also provides a broad range of employee assessment products and consulting services.

Key Contact - Specialty:
Mr. John Almond, President
Ms. Shannon French, Executive Recruiter
Mr. Pete Almond, Recruiter
Ms. Le'Anna Roffe, Recruiter
Ms. Janene Bocchi, Lead Administrative Contact

Functions: Generalist (All)

Industries: Construction, Food, Bev., Tobacco, Plastics, Rubber, Non-profits, Accounting, HR Services, Hotels, Resorts, Clubs, Packaging, Software, Long-term/Home Care

Branches:
11911 NE 1st St Ste B305
Bellevue, WA 98005-3057
(425) 455-2224
Email: brett.norris@almondsearch.com
Key Contact - Specialty:
Mr. Brett Norris, Manager
Ms. Nicola Norris, Manager

Ambler Associates

320 Decker Dr
Irving, TX 75062-8162
(972) 404-8712
Email: petera@peopleprograms.com

Summary: Director-level to senior executive-level positions in a wide range of industries.

Key Contact - Specialty:
Mr. Peter W. Ambler, President
Mr. Lawrence Hysinger, Principal - *Finance*

Salary Minimum: $60,000

Functions: Generalist (All)

Industries: Energy, Utilities, Manufacturing, Transportation, Retail, Finance, Services, Media, Environmental Svcs., Packaging

American Executive Management Inc

30 Federal St Ste 102
Salem, MA 01970-3801
(978) 744-5923
Email: execsearch@americanexecutive.us
Web: www.americanexecutive.us

Summary: Extensive experience with major international corporations. Excellent performance and references.

Key Contact - Specialty:
Mr. E.J. Cloutier, Chairman - *General management*
Ms. S. Smith, Office Manager

Salary Minimum: $100,000

Functions: Generalist (All), Senior Mgmt., Middle Mgmt., Sales & Mktg., HR Mgmt., Finance, IT, Engineering

Industries: Generalist (All), Energy, Utilities, Construction, Equip Svcs., Hospitality, Media, Telecoms, Defense

American Group Practice Inc

1016 5th Ave
New York, NY 10028-0132
(212) 371-3091
Email: agp420@aol.com

Summary: Retainer search for practicing physicians, physician executives and senior-level healthcare executives; medical staff planning and medical group practice development, PHOs, MSOs, GPWWs and other physician/hospital relations activities.

Key Contact - Specialty:
Mr. Ralph Herz, Jr., Director, Medical

Salary Minimum: $80,000

Functions: Board Members, Senior Mgmt., Healthcare, Physicians, Nurses, Allied Health, Health Admin.

Industries: Healthcare, Hospitals, Long-term/Home Care, Dental, Physical Therapy, Occupational Therapy, Women's

American Human Resource Associates Ltd (AHRA)

PO Box 18269
Cleveland, OH 44118-0269
(877) 342-5833
(440) 995-7120
Email: inquiry@ahrasearch.com
Web: www.ahrasearch.com

Summary: The real estate transaction industry: title insurance, credit & collection, residential lending and vendor management. Banking: commercial real estate lending, asset based lending and commercial leasing. Commercial building: property management and building and development. Turn around management: searches for CEO, CFO and senior staff. Merger and acquisition support in the above industry niches.

Key Contact - Specialty:
Mr. Ted Howard, Managing Member
Mr. Ryan Anderson, Director
Mr. Eric Biro, Senior Recruiter
Ms. Diana Keis-Miller, Chief Operating Officer - *Accounting (Bookkeeping), Administration, Communications, COOs, Finance*
Mr. John Knotek, Chief Financial Officer - *Accounting (Big 4, Public), CFOs*
Mr. Jim Kaliszewski, Associate Recruiter
Ms. Erin Young, Sourcing Specialist
Mr. Steve Downie, Student Associate - *Marketing, Research*
Mr. Tim Farley, Student Associate - *Research & development*
Ms. Jennifer Howard, Information Technologist
Mrs. Meredith Ashby, PhD, Consulting Scientist - *Mathematics*
Dr. George Nothnagel, Consulting I/O Psychologist

Salary Minimum: $75,000

Functions: Generalist (All)

Industries: Finance, Insurance, Real Estate, Non-Classifiable

Branches:
9371 French Quarters Cir
Weeki Wachee, FL 34613-4213
(877) 322-2987
(352) 597-2501
Email: ltrautvetter@ahrasearch.com

† occasional contingency assignment

Key Contact - Specialty:
Mr. Lee Trautvetter, Regional Manager -
Banking, CEOs, CFOs, COOs, Leasing

American Incite
917 Hillfield Ct Ste 4
Oceanside, CA 92054-7013
(760) 754-2444
Email: search@americanincite.com
Web: www.americanincite.com

Summary: We assist Fortune 500 firms to venture
backed startups in manufacturing, service and
contracting industries. We recruit key executives
in sales, marketing, operations and engineering.

Key Contact - Specialty:
Mr. Brandon R. Ebeling, CPC, Founder & Chief
Executive Officer

Salary Minimum: $100,000

Functions: Management, Senior Mgmt.,
Automation, Mktg. Mgmt., Sales Mgmt.,
Engineering

Industries: Energy, Utilities, Construction,
Manufacturing, Test, Measure Equip., Venture
Cap., Services, Equip Svcs., Mgmt. Consulting,
HR Services, Law Enforcement, Engineering
Svcs., Property/Facility Mgmt., Software, Non-
Classifiable

American Legal Search LLC†
209 10th Ave S Ste 428
Nashville, TN 37203-0778
(615) 251-9600
(888) 220-9111
Fax: (615) 251-8920
Web: www.americanlegalsearch.com

Summary: From law firm mergers and practice
group acquisitions to permanent search and
contract staffing, our principals have been serving
the legal communities throughout the country.

Key Contact - Specialty:
Mr. Joseph D. Freedman, JD, Chief Executive
Officer & Mng Principal

Salary Minimum: $75,000

Functions: Legal

Industries: Energy, Utilities, Construction,
Finance, Services, Media, Communications,
Environmental Svcs., Insurance, Real Estate,
Healthcare

Branches:
1425 Richard Arrington Jr Blvd S Ste 206
Birmingham, AL 35205-3841
(205) 930-9811
Fax: (205) 930-9018
Email: richard@americanlegalsearch.com
Key Contact - Specialty:
Mr. Richard Brock, JD, President

201 W Platt St Ste 364
Tampa, FL 33606-2313
(813) 239-4044
Email: keith@americanlegalsearch.com
Key Contact - Specialty:
Mr. Keith Quinn, JD, Managing Director, Tampa

100 Park Ave Fl 16
New York, NY 10017-5538
(212) 984-1086
Fax: (212) 937-3792
Email: rhonda@americanlegalsearch.com
Key Contact - Specialty:
Ms. Rhonda Singer, JD, Managing Director, East
Coast
Ms. Jeanne Huang Li, Recruiter

588 Harwood Cv
Memphis, TN 38120-3003
(901) 277-2563
Email: kevin@americanlegalsearch.com
Key Contact - Specialty:
Mr. Kevin R. Fisher, Esq.

American Physician Network Inc†
PO Box 222352
West Palm Beach, FL 33422-2352
(561) 688-2999
(800) 245-8227
Fax: (888) 699-5512
Email:
apn12345@bellsouth.net,apn12345@aol.com
Web: www.apn1.com

Summary: Specializing in connecting physicians
with their future, we are dedicated to connecting
physicians and physician executives with prime
placements to assure successful futures for both
the healthcare professional and the medical
practice. We also specialize in medical corporate
development and practice brokerage services.

Key Contact - Specialty:
Dr. Bhopindar Singh, MD, Founder - *Physicians*

Salary Minimum: $120,000

Functions: Healthcare, Physicians, Health
Admin., Mgmt. Consultants

Industries: Healthcare

Ames & Ames LLC
PO Box 267
Burlingame, CA 94011-0267
(650) 218-7404

Summary: We provide key executive searches.

Key Contact - Specialty:
Mr. A.P. Ames, President

Salary Minimum: $225,000

Functions: Senior Mgmt.

Industries: Generalist (All)

Ampersand Associates Inc
3495 Piedmont Rd NE Ste 12-115
Atlanta, GA 30305-1739
(404) 812-8923
Fax: (404) 812-8921
Email: marjorie@ampersandinc.net
Web: www.ampersandinc.net

Summary: We are a recruiting firm for candidates
at the c-level. We also create advisory boards for
companies. We specialize in life sciences,
healthcare, technology and traditional business.

Key Contact - Specialty:
Ms. Marjorie Singley-Hall, Managing Partner -
*Entrepreneurs, Executives, Healthcare, Life
Sciences, Technology*

Salary Minimum: $100,000

Functions: Management, Board Members, Senior
Mgmt., Mfg., Healthcare, Legal

Industries: Generalist (All), Biotech/Life
Sciences, Healthcare, Hospitals, Long-
term/Home Care, Women's

Anderson & Associates
112 S Tryon St
Charlotte, NC 28284-2191
(704) 347-0090
Fax: (704) 347-0064
Email: info@andersonexecsearch.com
Web: www.andersonexecsearch.com

Summary: Retained executive search and related
consulting services. Emphasis in financial
services, healthcare, manufacturing and non-profit

industries. Functional experience: searches for
CEO/CFO, directors and senior executives.

Key Contact - Specialty:
Mr. Douglas K. Anderson, President

Salary Minimum: $100,000

Functions: Management, Mfg., Healthcare, Sales
& Mktg., HR Mgmt., Finance

Industries: Generalist (All)

C Anderson & Associates
(formerly known as Anderson Sales Group)
2136 Ford Pkwy Ste 204
Saint Paul, MN 55116-1863
(651) 695-8555
Email: info@candersonassociates.com
Web: www.candersonassociates.com

Summary: We are a retained executive search and
recruitment services firm that specializes
exclusively in the placement of top sales
professionals. We service our clients and
candidates locally and throughout the country.

Key Contact - Specialty:
Mr. Dan Anderson, Partner - *Sales*
Ms. Carla Anderson, President - *Sales*

Salary Minimum: $75,000

Functions: Sales & Mktg., Sales Reps.

Industries: Manufacturing, Wholesale, Finance,
Services, Pharm Svcs., E-commerce, IT
Implementation, PSA/ASP, Communications,
Software, Biotech/Life Sciences

Anderson Bradshaw Associates Inc
1064 Richelieu Ln
Houston, TX 77018-2034
(713) 869-6789
Email: aba@hal-pc.org
Web: www.andersonbradshaw.com

Summary: Our primary focus is on positions in
the following industries: engineering &
construction/EPC (refineries, chemical/petro-
chem, power plants and upstream oil & gas
facilities), oil & gas (exploration & production and
project development - on/offshore), operations &
maintenance (O&G production, refineries, petro-
chem and power plants), construction/construction
management and architectural/engineering.

Key Contact - Specialty:
Mr. Robert W. Anderson, President -
Construction

Salary Minimum: $75,000

Functions: Generalist (All), Int'l.

Industries: Generalist (All), Energy, Utilities, Oil
& Gas, Construction, Chemicals, Misc. Mfg.,
Equip Svcs., HR Services, IT Implementation,
Engineering Svcs., Defense, Haz. Waste,
Aerospace

Anderson Philips Associates
2800 N 44th St Ste 340
Phoenix, AZ 85008-1560
(602) 553-3800
Fax: (602) 952-8792
Email: sbatisto@andersonphilipsassociates.com
Web: www.andersonphilipsassociates.com

Summary: Anderson Philips Associates is a
generalist recruiting firm and accepts search
assignments on a retainer basis exclusively.

Key Contact - Specialty:
Ms. Ronni R. Anderson, President & Chief
Executive Officer - *Administration, Boards of
Directors, C-level, Hospitality, Insurance*
Mr. Steven P. Batisto, Executive Vice President -
*Amusement parks, High technology, Sales,
Senior management, Venture capital*

Functions: Generalist (All)

Industries: Construction, Manufacturing, Retail,
Finance, Services, Hospitality,
Communications, Insurance, Software,
Biotech/Life Sciences

The Andre Group Inc[†]

1220 Valley Forge Rd Ste 19
Phoenixville, PA 19460-2676
(610) 917-2212
Fax: (610) 917-0551
Email: info@theandregroup.com

Summary: Recognized in national recruitment and
search of HR professionals exclusively. Clients
include Fortune 500 companies. Retainer-based
payment structure.

Key Contact - Specialty:
Mr. Larry Cozzilo, President - *Human resources*

Functions: HR Mgmt., Benefits, Staffing,
Training

Industries: Generalist (All)

Andrew Associates Executive Search Inc[†]

PO Box 2029
Lake Oswego, OR 97035-0016
(503) 635-7222
(866) 294-1301
Fax: (503) 635-5236
Email: kennedy@andysrch.com
Web: www.andysrch.com

Summary: We are an executive search firm
offering: bench strength management, targeted
proactive board member search, and strategic
career planning. Our firm (retained by start-up to
mid-cap companies) aggressively recruits leaders
essential to your corporate success; and offers
counsel and critical assessment of executive staff
structure, succession planning and development.

Key Contact - Specialty:
Mr. Andy Wihtol, President

Salary Minimum: $80,000

Functions: Board Members, Senior Mgmt.,
Finance, CFOs, IT, MIS Mgmt.

Industries: Generalist (All), Agri., Forestry,
Mining, Construction, Manufacturing, Metal
Products, Semiconductors, Transportation,
Wholesale, Services, Hospitality,
Communications, Insurance, Software,
Biotech/Life Sciences, Healthcare

The Angus Group Ltd[†]

250 W Court St Ste 100E
Cincinnati, OH 45202-1046
(513) 961-5575
Fax: (513) 961-5616
Email: angus@angusgroup.com
Web: www.angusgroup.com

Summary: Recruiting services to businesses, most
disciplines. Most professionals in office have
extensive experience.

Key Contact - Specialty:
Mr. David Hartig, President - *C-level,
Engineering, General management*
Mr. Pete Nadherny, Chief Executive Officer -
*Banking, C-level, Finance, General
management*

Mr. Ted Plattenburg, Principal - *Municipal, Non-
profit, Sales*
Mrs. Mary Beth Stewart, Vice President -
Banking
Ms. Karen Kranak, CPC, Vice President - *Human
resources, Marketing*

Salary Minimum: $50,000

Functions: Senior Mgmt., Middle Mgmt., Mfg.,
Materials, Sales & Mktg., HR Mgmt., Finance,
IT, Engineering

Industries: Energy, Utilities, Manufacturing,
Transportation, Retail, Finance, Services,
Accounting, HR Services, Media, Advertising,
Packaging, Biotech/Life Sciences

Anthony Andrew LLC

16633 Dallas Pkwy Ste 600
Addison, TX 75001-6892
(972) 588-1880
Fax: (972) 588-1801
Email: info@anthonyandrew.com
Web: www.anthonyandrew.com

Summary: A personalized retained search firm
created for clients and candidates who demand the
highest standards of principles, performance and
results. Major areas of our retained search include
senior leaders and individual performers of all
functional areas within Information Technology,
Business Process Outsourcing, Sales and
Marketing, and Human Resources.

Key Contact - Specialty:
Mr. Anthony A. Cinello, Founder & President

Salary Minimum: $150,000

Functions: Generalist (All), Management

Industries: HR Services, IT Implementation, Call
Centers, Network Infrastructure

APA Search Inc

1 Byram Brook Pl Ste 104
Armonk, NY 10504-2323
(914) 273-6000
Fax: (914) 273-8025
Email: info@apasearch.com
Web: www.apasearch.com

Summary: We are a highly resourceful, retained
executive level search serving diverse industries.
Our subspecialties are: automotive, retail,
hardware and financial. We offer an extremely
skilled staff. All searches completed. Our finalist
candidates are always the most qualified rather
than the most available.

Key Contact - Specialty:
Mr. Howard Kesten, President

Salary Minimum: $75,000

Functions: Generalist (All)

Industries: Manufacturing, Motor Vehicles,
Consumer Elect., Misc. Mfg., Electronic, Elec.
Components, Transportation

The Arcus Group Inc

5001 Lyndon B Johnson Fwy Ste 875
Dallas, TX 75244-6159
(817) 294-4349
Email: david.gabriel@arcusgroup.com
Web: www.arcusgroup.com

Summary: Our firm focuses on senior level search
for companies focused on leveraging advanced
technology. This includes biotechnology,
software, communications infrastructure and
services, semiconductor and industrial technology.
We take pride on having achieved and maintaining
a 100 percent completion percentage.

Key Contact - Specialty:
Mr. David Gabriel, Managing Director
Ms. Leslie Lucks, Principal

Salary Minimum: $150,000

Argus National Inc

98 Mill Plain Rd Ste 301
Danbury, CT 06811-6101
(203) 790-8420
Email: argusnat@aol.com

Summary: We are a firm that specializes in
customized management search and recruitment.

Key Contact - Specialty:
Mr. Ronald J. Guido, President
Mr. John Kelly, Vice President
Ms. Constance Gruen, Vice President

Salary Minimum: $75,000

Functions: Generalist (All)

Industries: Generalist (All)

ARI International

1501 Ocean Ave
Seal Beach, CA 90740-6546
(562) 795-5111
Email: ari.ron@att.net
Web: www.ariinternationalsearch.com

Summary: Our firm provides exclusive retained
executive search. We service all functions and are
recognized for our industry expertise in
commercial aviation, military, aerospace,
advanced composites, consumer products, medical
device and cosmetics.

Key Contact - Specialty:
Mr. Ronald L. Curci, President & Chief Executive
Officer

Salary Minimum: $100,000

Functions: Generalist (All), Management, Board
Members, Sales & Mktg.

Industries: Soap, Perf., Cosmtcs., Aerospace

Ariail & Associates

210 W Friendly Ave Ste 200
Greensboro, NC 27401-6128
(336) 275-2906
Email: ariailassoc@msn.com
Web: www.ariailassoc.com

Summary: We are a retained search firm
specializing in the procurement of senior-level
executives in the household furniture and
institutional furnishing industry. We have a
successful procurement of CEOs and VPs of
sales/marketing, manufacturing, general
management and CFOs.

Key Contact - Specialty:
Mr. Randolph C. Ariail, President

Salary Minimum: $150,000

Functions: Board Members, Senior Mgmt.

Industries: Lumber, Furniture

Ariel Associates

15934 Riverside Dr W Apt 5J
New York, NY 10032-1016
(212) 923-1155
Email: info@arielassociates.com
Web: www.arielassociates.com

Summary: We specialize in executive search for
professionals in publishing and interactive for
consumer and B2B magazines, journals,
newsletters, electronic publishing, database, and
business information services. We place senior
executives, publishers and managers in editorial &
content, sales, marketing, business development,

circulation, finance and HR. We also place senior sales executives in publishing, interactive, media and business information services.

Key Contact - Specialty:
Mr. Eugene Fixler, President - *Interactive, Media, Publishing, Sales*
Ms. Rona Wexler, Executive Vice President - *Interactive, Media, Publishing, Sales*

Salary Minimum: $100,000

Functions: Management, Senior Mgmt., Sales & Mktg., Sales Mgmt., Direct Mktg., HR Mgmt., Finance

Industries: Media, Publishing, New Media

Charles Aris Inc†
(an affiliate of MRI)
324 W Wendover Ave Ste 230
Greensboro, NC 27408-8439
(336) 378-1818
Fax: (336) 378-0129
Email: info@charlesaris.com
Web: www.charlesaris.com

Summary: Our network targets, recruits and delivers high-impact talent for our clients' critical needs. Our mission is to be the world's preferred and preeminent provider of staffing solutions.

Key Contact - Specialty:
Mr. C. Mitchell Oakley, Jr., President/Managing Director
Mr. Chad M. Oakley, III, Vice President, Business Development - *Business development, Marketing*

Salary Minimum: $40,000

Functions: Generalist (All), Management, Mfg., Sales & Mktg., R&D, Engineering, Specialized Svcs.

Industries: Generalist (All), Textiles, Apparel, Chemicals, Drugs Mfg., Medical Devices, Retail, Finance, Misc. Financial, Services, Hospitality, Media, Communications, Biotech/Life Sciences, Healthcare

Armitage Associates Ltd
1201-100 Yonge St
Toronto, ON M5C 2W1
Canada
(416) 863-0576
Fax: (416) 863-0092
Email: info@armitagesearch.com
Web: www.armitagesearch.com

Summary: Boutique specializing in mid to senior-level assignments.

Key Contact - Specialty:
Mr. John D. Armitage, Managing Partner - *Financial services, High technology*
Ms. Karen Wood, Director, Research - *Financial services, High technology*

Salary Minimum: $80,000

Functions: Generalist (All), Board Members, Senior Mgmt., CFOs, M&A, MIS Mgmt.

Industries: Generalist (All), Finance, Hospitality, Insurance, Real Estate, Software

Branches:
279 Boul Rosemere
Rosemere, QC J7A 2T1
Canada
(450) 965-1441
Email: info@armitagesearch.com

Arnold Associates
60 State St Ste 700
Boston, MA 02109-1894
(617) 988-0403

Email: chris.arnold@esearchfirm.com
Web: www.esearchfirm.com

Summary: We are a retained executive search firm specializing in the recruitment of senior managers and executives within the mutual fund, investment management and financial services industries. Functional areas of expertise include: marketing, sales, distribution, operations, asset management, electronic commerce, administration and technology.

Key Contact - Specialty:
Mr. Christopher Arnold, Principal - *Investment management, Mutual funds*

Salary Minimum: $140,000

Functions: Generalist (All), Management, Senior Mgmt., Middle Mgmt., Product Dev., Sales & Mktg., Mktg. Research, Mktg. Mgmt., Direct Mktg., Finance

Industries: Finance

William B Arnold Associates Inc
2304 S Holly St Unit A
Denver, CO 80222-6275
(303) 393-6662
Web: www.wbarnold.com

Summary: We are a generalist search practice that services all industries and functions, including senior and middle management.

Key Contact - Specialty:
Mr. William B. Arnold, President
Ms. Sheridan J. Arnold, Vice President

Salary Minimum: $100,000

Functions: Generalist (All)

Industries: Generalist (All)

Artgo Inc
6941 Waite Hill Rd
Willoughby, OH 44094-9309
(440) 942-0597
Email: adbaldwin2@earthlink.net

Summary: Executive search for corporate needs including special capabilities in top and middle management assignments.

Key Contact - Specialty:
Mr. Arthur D. Baldwin, II, President

Functions: Generalist (All)

Industries: Generalist (All), Manufacturing, Electronic, Elec. Components, Non-profits, Higher Ed., Hospitality, Aerospace

J Nicholas Arthur
77 Franklin St Fl 10
Boston, MA 02110-1510
(617) 204-9000
Fax: (617) 303-8934
Email: nicholas.bogard@jnicholasarthur.com

Summary: Our firm specializes in recruiting senior management personnel for the financial services industry.

Key Contact - Specialty:
Mr. Nicholas C. Bogard, President
Mr. Arthur P. Beecher, Managing Director
Mr. John Richardson, Managing Director
Ms. Ellen Thurmond, Managing Director - *Human resources, Investment management*
Ms. Anne Rowland, Managing Director - *Financial services, Investment*

Salary Minimum: $100,000

Functions: Generalist (All), Senior Mgmt., Mktg. Mgmt., Sales Mgmt., Direct Mktg., CFOs, Cash Mgmt., M&A

Industries: Generalist (All), Banking, Invest. Banking, Brokers, Venture Cap., Misc. Financial, Insurance, Life, Commercial, Re-Insurance

Ashlar-Stone Management Consultants Inc
401-50 Burnhamthorpe Rd W
Sussex Centre
Mississauga, ON L5B 3C2
Canada
(905) 615-0900
Fax: (905) 615-0917
Web: www.ashlar-stone.com

Summary: Small, responsive firm providing high quality executive search services with superior results in all industries. One consultant covers all aspects of an assignment including research, recruiting, interviewing, and shortlist presentation.

Key Contact - Specialty:
Mr. Stuart K.J. Moore, Principal
Mr. Robert D. Chisholm, Associate

Salary Minimum: $80,000

Functions: Generalist (All)

Industries: Manufacturing, Transportation, Retail, Mgmt. Consulting, Hospitality, Publishing, Packaging

Ashton Tweed
620 Lee Rd Ste 130
Wayne, PA 19087-5636
(610) 725-0290
Fax: (610) 725-0291
Email: info@ashtontweed.com
Web: www.ashtontweed.com

Summary: Our firm is an executive search and interim talent organization that helps companies recruit and retain highly experienced professionals. Our work spans most industries and disciplines, with a major emphasis in Life Sciences.

Key Contact - Specialty:
Mr. Jim Rudman, Partner
Mr. Jim Laird, Partner - *Biotechnology, Executives, Finance, Medical (Devices), Pharmaceutical*
Mr. Jordan Warshafsky, Partner - *Biotechnology, Executives, Finance, Medical (Devices), Pharmaceutical*

Salary Minimum: $100,000

Functions: Senior Mgmt.

Industries: Construction, Manufacturing, Printing, Medical Devices, Finance, Banking, Non-profits, Pharm Svcs., Accounting, Biotech/Life Sciences

Ashworth Consultants Inc
53 Fulton St
Boston, MA 02109-1415
(617) 720-0350
Email: ashworthco@aol.com

Summary: Provides board level consulting in compensation, management planning and personnel selection for start-ups, threshold companies and established organizations.

Key Contact - Specialty:
Mr. Robert I. Ash, President

Salary Minimum: $100,000

Functions: Generalist (All)

Industries: Mgmt. Consulting

Asset Group Inc†
PO Box 211
Verona, NJ 07044-0211
(973) 571-1367
Fax: (973) 571-1387
Email: neilepi@comcast.net
Web: www.assetgroup.biz

Summary: Intensely client-focused, we have a uniquely flexible fee structure, offering clients a fixed fee based on the work involved.

Key Contact - Specialty:
Mr. P. Neil Ralley, President - *International*

Salary Minimum: $80,000

Functions: Generalist (All)

Industries: Manufacturing, Chemicals, Soap, Perf., Cosmtcs., Plastics, Rubber, Paints, Petro. Products, Consumer Elect., Misc. Mfg.

Association Executive Resources Group
PO Box 3880
Gaithersburg, MD 20885-3880
(301) 417-7045
Fax: (301) 417-7049
Email: jhurley@aerg.org
Web: www.aerg.org

Summary: Dedicated exclusively to searches for CEO and professional staff positions for national trade and professional associations and other not-for-profit organizations.

Key Contact - Specialty:
Mr. Gerard F. Hurley, Chairman & Chief Executive Officer
Mr. Charles D. Rumbarger, Past Chairman

Salary Minimum: $100,000

Functions: Generalist (All), Senior Mgmt.

Industries: Non-profits

Association Strategies Inc
1111 N Fairfax St
Alexandria, VA 22314-1484
(703) 683-0580
Email: jim@assnstrategies.com
Web: www.assnstrategies.com

Summary: Retained executive search firm focused on recruiting for association/non-profit organizations.

Key Contact - Specialty:
Ms. Pamela Kaul, President & Founder
Mr. James Zaniello, Vice President
Ms. Laura L. Parrish, Associate
Ms. Elsie Durland, Organization Development Director
Mr. Michael Strand, Executive, Human Resources - *Diversity, Marketing*

Salary Minimum: $85,000

Functions: Minorities/Diversity, Non-profits

Industries: Non-profits, Hospitality, Media

Aster Search Group
555 Madison Ave
New York, NY 10022-3301
(212) 888-6182
Email: ecohen@astersearch.com
Web: www.astersearch.com

Summary: We conduct assignments for hospitals, integrated delivery networks, managed care companies, long-term care facilities, home care companies, and healthcare agencies.

Key Contact - Specialty:
Ms. Eve Cohen, President - *Healthcare*

Salary Minimum: $70,000
Functions: Healthcare
Industries: Generalist (All), Healthcare, Hospitals

Atlanta Executive Partners Inc
PO Box W
Teaticket, MA 02536-0230
(508) 495-4300
Email: aep@mindspring.com

Summary: We take a systematic approach to provide leaders who enhance company performance and competitive standing. We perform benchmarking to establish clear criteria for acquiring or aligning with executives and companies. We provide real world solutions from line-management experienced consultants.

Key Contact - Specialty:
Mr. Robert J. Sweet, President - *Aerospace, Communications, Manufacturing, Technology, Telecommunications*

Salary Minimum: $150,000

Functions: Generalist (All), Management, Mfg., Sales & Mktg., Finance, IT, R&D

Industries: Generalist (All), Computer Equip., Test, Measure Equip., Mgmt. Consulting, Government, Aerospace, Software

Atlantic Pacific Group Inc†
PO Box 4563
Laguna Beach, CA 92652-4563
(949) 376-4938
Fax: (949) 376-4855
Email: lblakemore@apgsearch.com
Web: www.apgsearch.com

Summary: We are an executive search firm specializing in the placement of professionals within human resources, HRIS, organizational development, training and accounting. Specialty includes search for the temporary staffing industry at all levels.

Key Contact - Specialty:
Ms. Linda Blakemore, Owner & Manager - *Human resources*

Salary Minimum: $60,000

Functions: Generalist (All), Middle Mgmt., Sales Mgmt., HR Mgmt., Benefits, Staffing, Training

Industries: Generalist (All), Finance, Banking, Invest. Banking, Services, Pharm Svcs., Accounting, Mgmt. Consulting, HR Services, Advertising, Biotech/Life Sciences, Long-term/Home Care

Atlantic West International†
1289 N Fordham Blvd Ste A200
Chapel Hill, NC 27514-6110
(919) 942-3080
Fax: (919) 942-0190
Email: rvawi@aol.com

Summary: Executive search and recruitment services focused in the medical device, pharmaceutical, and biotechnology industries from multinational corporations to small, privately held domestic firms.

Key Contact - Specialty:
Mr. Richard W. Valenti

Salary Minimum: $75,000

Functions: Generalist (All)

Industries: Drugs Mfg., Medical Devices, Plastics, Rubber, Biotech/Life Sciences

Auerbach Associates Inc
65 Franklin St Ste 400
Boston, MA 02110-1303
(617) 451-0095
Fax: (617) 451-5199
Email: info@auerbach-assc.com
Web: www.auerbach-assc.com

Summary: Specializes in retained executive search for colleges & universities, healthcare organizations, and not-for-profit institutions. We place a special emphasis on recruitment of women and under-represented groups.

Key Contact - Specialty:
Ms. Judith A. Auerbach, President - *Healthcare*

Salary Minimum: $180,000

Functions: Senior Mgmt.

Industries: Non-profits, Higher Ed.

Auguston and Associates Inc
1010 S Ocean Blvd Apt 601
Pompano Beach, FL 33062-6628
(954) 943-0503
(888) 244-5598
Fax: (954) 784-1660
Email: g.auguston@att.net
Web: www.augustonandassociates.com

Summary: We specialize in medical device manufacturers, all functions: general management, engineering, R&D, operations, manufacturing, regulatory, clinical, quality, sales, marketing and HR. With search partners worldwide we help our clients build world class, results-oriented management teams.

Key Contact - Specialty:
Ms. Gail Auguston, President

Salary Minimum: $100,000

Functions: Generalist (All), Management, Mfg., Plant Mgmt., Quality, Sales & Mktg., HR Mgmt., R&D

Industries: Medical Devices

Auster Associates
2131 Deloraine Trl
Maitland, FL 32751-3746
(407) 831-2400
Email: marc@austerassociates.com
Web: www.austerassociates.com

Summary: Generalist search firm with emphasis in manufacturing, employee benefits consulting, insurance and IT. Clients include Fortune 500 companies as well as venture capital startups and private companies.

Key Contact - Specialty:
Mr. Marc Auster, President
Ms. Gail Rogg, Vice President
Mr. Dick Cole, Senior Associate - *Manufacturing*

Salary Minimum: $90,000

Functions: Generalist (All)

Industries: Manufacturing, Food, Bev., Tobacco, Finance, Non-profits, Mgmt. Consulting, Telecoms, Aerospace, Insurance, Networking, Comm. SW, Healthcare

Allen Austin Executive Search Consultants
4543 Post Oak Place Dr Ste 217
Houston, TX 77027-3103
(713) 355-1900
Fax: (713) 355-1901
Email: randrews@allenaustinsearch.com
Web: www.allenaustinsearch.com

Summary: We combine tremendous resources with superior search and selection systems in order to deliver maximum value and 'A' players to our client companies. Our proven track record of expeditious completion of 100 percent of all retained assignments, our performance guarantee and our industry experience make us your obvious choice for conducting your senior level searches.

Key Contact - Specialty:
Mr. Robert L. Andrews, Chairman & Chief Executive Officer - *Retail*
Mrs. S. Caitlin McCall - Baron, Senior Partner - *Education (Higher), Gas, Government, Non-profit, Oil*
Mr. Pat Carlucci, Senior Partner - *Consumer (Packaged Goods), Food, Food service*
Mrs. Natasha Shelyukh, Partner - *Consumer (Packaged Goods), Food, Food & beverage, Food service, Retail*
Ms. Nicole A. Fende, Partner - *Banking, Financial services, Insurance*
Mr. Mark Spillard, Partner - *Finance*
Mr. Bill Adams, Partner - *Energy, Financial services, Healthcare, Life Sciences, Sales*
Ms. Stephanie Scanlan, Partner - *Accounting, Accounting (Big 4, Public), Finance, Financial*
Mr. Doug Ehrenkranz, Partner - *Agriculture, Consumer (Packaged Goods), Retail*
Mr. Mark Gittler, Partner - *Fashion, Retail*

Salary Minimum: $90,000

Functions: Management, Board Members, Senior Mgmt., Middle Mgmt.

Industries: Generalist (All), Energy, Utilities, Oil & Gas, Consumer Goods, Retail, Finance, Non-profits, Higher Ed., Communications, Healthcare

Branches:
54 Danbury Rd Ste 336
Ridgefield, CT 06877-4019
(203) 894-8315
Email: pcarlucci@allenaustinsearch.com
Key Contact - Specialty:
Mr. Pat Carlucci, Partner

PO Box 201166
San Antonio, TX 78220-8166
(210) 310-2528
Email: jgorman@allenaustinsearch.com
Key Contact - Specialty:
Ms. Jackie Gorman-Johnson, Partner - *Communications*

Austin-McGregor

3500 Oak Lawn Ave Ste 550
Dallas, TX 75219-6724
(972) 488-0500
Fax: (972) 488-0535
Email: info@austinmcgregor.com
Web: www.austinmcgregor.com

Summary: Our firm is a boutique by design, Top 30, retained executive search firm that focuses at the VP level through CEO/Board and above in VC/private equity backed high-technology, consumer/industrial and other emerging sectors.

Key Contact - Specialty:
Mr. Chip McCreary, Chairman & Founder - *Entertainment, High technology, Industrial*
Mr. Dru George, Partner - *High technology*
Mrs. Ardell Archer, Senior Vice President

Salary Minimum: $175,000

Functions: Generalist (All), Senior Mgmt., Mfg., Materials, Sales & Mktg., Finance, IT, R&D

Industries: Generalist (All), Manufacturing, Transportation, Wholesale, Retail, Invest. Banking, Venture Cap., Services, Media, Software

Branches:
320 Cowper St
Palo Alto, CA 94301-1501
(650) 3311588
Email: stephen@austinmcgregor.com
Key Contact - Specialty:
Mr. Stephen Sterett, Managing Partner

3685 Schooner Rdg
Alpharetta, GA 30005-4290
(404) 643-7268
Email: scott@austinmcgregor.com
Key Contact - Specialty:
Mr. Scott Brooks, Partner - *High technology*

416 S 17th St
Mattoon, IL 61938-5202
(217) 235-1051
Fax: (217) 235-2053
Email: pbailey@consolidated.net
Key Contact - Specialty:
Mr. Paul Bailey, Senior Vice President & Partner - *Entertainment, High technology, Industrial*

2121 Cooperative Way Ste 210
Herndon, VA 20171-5344
(703) 728-8506
Email: info@austinmcgregor.com
Key Contact - Specialty:
Mr. Jeremy King, Managing Partner

Automotive Recruiters International Inc

PO Box 127
Gladstone, MI 49837-0127
(906) 428-9330
Email: resumes@ketchumassoc.com
Web: www.automotiveexecutives.com

Summary: Our firm is an industry specific executive search firm dedicated to assisting clients in identifying, attracting and hiring leadership within the 90th percentile. Our mission is to perform the most professional, highly ethical search work, which results in the creation of long term value for our clients.

Key Contact - Specialty:
Mr. Jeffrey R. Ketchum, President

Salary Minimum: $100,000

Functions: Generalist (All), Management, Middle Mgmt., Mfg., Production, Quality, Materials

Industries: Motor Vehicles

Avery Associates

3 1/2 N Santa Cruz Ave Ste A
Los Gatos, CA 95030-5964
(408) 399-4424
Fax: (408) 399-4423
Email: jobs@averyassoc.net
Web: www.averyassoc.net

Summary: Public sector practice is focused on city and county government and agencies. Private sector search is focused on administrative positions in technology, communications and financial/general services.

Key Contact - Specialty:
Mr. William Avery, President
Mr. Paul Kimura, Principal
Mr. Gary Brown, Principal

Salary Minimum: $75,000

Functions: Generalist (All), Management, Materials, Sales & Mktg., Benefits, Staffing, Training, Finance

Industries: Generalist (All), Computer Equip., Consumer Elect., Test, Measure Equip., Media, Government, Software

Avery James Inc

6601 Center Dr W Ste 500
Los Angeles, CA 90045-1594
(310) 342-8224
Web: www.averyjames.com

Summary: We specialize in the recruitment of senior executives and middle management. Our clients are publicly traded and privately held companies in the high technology, industrial and financial sectors.

Key Contact - Specialty:
Ms. Michele James, President - *Aerospace, Defense, Environmental*
Mr. Bill James, Managing Principal, Diversity Engagement - *Engineering, Financial services, Technology*

Salary Minimum: $100,000

Functions: Generalist (All), Management, Board Members, Senior Mgmt., Middle Mgmt., Engineering, Minorities/Diversity

Industries: Generalist (All), Construction, Manufacturing, Transportation, Finance, Services, Accounting, Mgmt. Consulting, HR Services, Engineering Svcs., Communications, RF/Microwave, Environmental Svcs., Aerospace

Avondale Search International Inc

3305 Riverside Ave
Jacksonville, FL 32205-8503
(904) 296-4449
Email: margot@avondalesearch.com
Web: www.avondalesearch.com

Summary: High ethical standards and tremendous search capabilities are qualities that our search consultants have come to be known by. Put your most senior level search assignment in our hands and you will be assured that the position will be filled in a timely manner, discreetly and with the best person for that leadership position.

Key Contact - Specialty:
Ms. Margot Finley-Aguilera, President - *General management, Sales*

Salary Minimum: $50,000

Functions: Generalist (All), Management, Board Members, Senior Mgmt., Sales Mgmt., IT, MIS Mgmt.

Industries: Generalist (All), Non-profits, Higher Ed., Software

The Ayers Group

405 Lexington Ave Ste 1601
New York, NY 10174-1699
(212) 889-7788
Fax: (212) 697-0682
Email: annette.rivera@ayers.com
Web: www.ayers.com

Summary: We offer executive search, career transition management, organizational effectiveness consulting and technical consulting services.

Key Contact - Specialty:
Mr. William L. Ayers, Jr., President & Chief Executive Officer
Mr. Robert R. Deissig, President, Staffing Services Division
Mr. Harry Plastik, Managing Director
Mr. Terry Ebert, EdD, Managing Director
Ms. Joan Caruso, Managing Director, Orgn Effectiveness - *Capital markets, Human resources, Technology*

Salary Minimum: $150,000

Functions: Management, HR Mgmt., MIS Mgmt.

Industries: Finance, Banking, Invest. Banking, Services, Media, Insurance, Healthcare

Branches:
101 Merritt 7 Ste 1
Norwalk, CT 06851-1060
(203) 354-7788
Fax: (203) 354-6683
Key Contact - Specialty:
Ms. Joan Learn, Senior Vice President

2001 US Highway 46 Ste 101
Parsippany, NJ 07054-1315
(973) 394-7788
Fax: (973) 394-7783
Key Contact - Specialty:
Mr. Bob Scumaci, Vice President

7 Roszel Rd Fl 5
Princeton, NJ 08540-6205
(609) 720-8670
Fax: (609) 720-7783
Key Contact - Specialty:
Mr. Walter O'Neill, Senior Vice President

The Baer Group
53 Perimeter Ctr E Ste 100
Atlanta, GA 30346-2204
(216) 371-9982
Email: gherbruck@aol.com

Summary: Provides retained search for mid to senior-level executives in most functions and industries with a specialization in healthcare. Other services include search, industry and market research.

Key Contact - Specialty:
Ms. Gretchen S. Herbruck, President - *Healthcare*

Salary Minimum: $90,000

Functions: Generalist (All), Management, Mfg., Healthcare, HR Mgmt., Specialized Svcs., Mgmt. Consultants

Industries: Generalist (All), Drugs Mfg., Medical Devices, Plastics, Rubber, Paints, Petro. Products, Metal Products, Machine, Appliance, Services, Healthcare

Baker Montgomery
980 N Michigan Ave Ste 930
Chicago, IL 60611-4554
(312) 397-8833
(312) 397-8844
Fax: (312) 397-9631
Email: veronica@bakermontgomery.com
Web: www.bakermontgomery.com

Summary: We are a retained search firm focusing on management consulting, professional services and aligned industry clients. The candidates we place are generally at the managing director, CEO, COO, CTO, CFO, VP and partner levels with senior manager/senior principal work for larger clients.

Key Contact - Specialty:
Mr. William W. Baker, Partner
Ms. Sharon I. Baker, Partner
Ms. Nancy Mora, Principal - *Consulting*
Ms. Veronica Cervantes, Manager, Research - *Consulting, Professional services*
Mr. Edward Kress, Principal

Salary Minimum: $100,000

Functions: Management, Board Members, Senior Mgmt., Sales Mgmt., CFOs, Mgmt. Consultants

Industries: Energy, Utilities, Manufacturing, Transportation, Finance, Venture Cap., Services, Mgmt. Consulting, HR Services, E-commerce, IT Implementation, PSA/ASP, Media, Communications, Wireless, Insurance,

Software, ERP SW, Mfg. SW, Biotech/Life Sciences

Baker, Parker & Associates Inc
5 Concourse Pkwy NE Ste 2440
Atlanta, GA 30328-6111
(770) 804-1996
Fax: (770) 804-1917
Email: confidential@bpasearch.com
Web: www.bpasearch.com

Summary: We specialize in value-added senior management searches for most industries and institutions of higher education. Significant experience serving international companies.

Key Contact - Specialty:
Mr. Daniel F. Parker, Sr., Partner
Mr. Jerry H. Baker, Partner
Mr. Gary L. Daugherty, Senior Vice President
Mrs. Laurie Wilder, Vice President
Mr. Martin M. Baker, Vice President
Mrs. Bernie Johnson, Executive Recruiting Coordinator
Mrs. Anya Gray, Principal
Ms. Porsha Bush, Executive Recruiting Coordinator
Ms. Christine Parker, Associate
Ms. Katie Mangum, Associate
Mr. Bryan Hanson, Associate

Salary Minimum: $100,000

Functions: Generalist (All)

Industries: Generalist (All)

Baldwin Associates LLC
3 Goose Cove Rd
Bath, ME 04530-4017
(207) 442-7070
Fax: (207) 442-8995
Email: probohm@aol.com
Web: baldwinsearch@aol.com

Summary: Our executive search practice is focused on introducing gifted senior executive and general management candidates to our prestigious high technology clients. We have remained purposefully small and fiercely independent so that our practice members are integrally involved in every phase of all searches.

Key Contact - Specialty:
Mr. Peter Robohm, Principal

Salary Minimum: $150,000

Functions: Management, Board Members, Senior Mgmt., Middle Mgmt., Sales & Mktg., CFOs, IT, Mgmt. Consultants

Industries: Computer Equip., Mgmt. Consulting, Telecoms, Software

Bales Partners Inc
980 N Michigan Ave Ste 1400
Chicago, IL 60611-7500
(312) 214-3998
Fax: (312) 214-3981
Email: pbales@balespartners.com

Summary: Our general practice encompasses most functions and industries whose assignments are conducted only by experienced principals.

Key Contact - Specialty:
Mr. L. Patrick Bales, Partner

Salary Minimum: $100,000

Functions: Generalist (All)

Industries: Generalist (All)

Allen Ballach Associates Inc
906-255 Simcoe St N
The Paterre Arts
Oshawa, ON L1G 4T4
Canada
(905) 725-0314
Fax: (905) 725-3418
Email: allen@aballach.com
Web: www.aballach.com

Summary: Providing senior management and executive-level search and selection solutions to the advanced technology, microelectronics, engineering, construction, automotive, and aerospace market sectors.

Key Contact - Specialty:
Mr. Allen Ballach, President - *Engineering, Manufacturing*
Ms. Tammy Marrast, BSc, Director, Research & Testing

Salary Minimum: $100,000

Functions: Generalist (All), Senior Mgmt.

Industries: Generalist (All), Energy, Utilities, Oil & Gas, Construction, Manufacturing, Food, Bev., Tobacco, Drugs Mfg., Medical Devices, Motor Vehicles, Robotics, Semiconductors, Media, Communications, Environmental Svcs., Aerospace, Software

Ballein Search Partners
PO Box 5204
Oak Brook, IL 60522-5204
(630) 322-9220
Fax: (630) 322-9221
Email: kathy@balleinsp.com

Summary: Our firm is dedicated to serving only healthcare organizations. We understand current challenges and trends that shape your company's future. We work in partnership with the client to recruit, retain and build a high performing executive team. We can use a long-term approach for organizational continuity and stability. Integrity, objectivity, honesty and communication are the operating principles that guide our work.

Key Contact - Specialty:
Ms. Kathy Ballein, President - *Healthcare*

Salary Minimum: $100,000

Functions: Management, Board Members, Senior Mgmt., Healthcare, Allied Health, Health Admin., HR Mgmt.

Industries: Healthcare, Hospitals, Long-term/Home Care

Ballos & Company Inc
45 Fieldstone Dr
Morristown, NJ 07960-2634
(973) 538-4753
Email: blcisearch@aol.com

Summary: Effective, ethical, professional search firm with a high percentage of repeat business: process, chemical, pharmaceutical, bio-technology, manufacturing and technology driven industries.

Key Contact - Specialty:
Mr. Constantine J. Ballos, President

Salary Minimum: $100,000

Functions: Generalist (All), Management, Mfg., Materials, Sales & Mktg., R&D, Engineering

Industries: Generalist (All), Paper, Chemicals, Drugs Mfg., Plastics, Rubber, Paints, Petro. Products, Environmental Svcs.

James Bangert & Associates Inc

1001 Twelve Oaks Center Dr Ste 1030F
Wayzata, MN 55391-4320
(952) 475-3454
Email: jab@bangertassoc.com

Summary: We serve both large corporate clients
as well as small start-ups. Successful search
assignments range from department/division
manager to officer level positions.

Key Contact - Specialty:
Mr. James Bangert, President

Salary Minimum: $75,000

Functions: Senior Mgmt., Mfg., Plant Mgmt.,
Quality, Sales & Mktg., Mktg. Mgmt., Sales
Mgmt., Engineering

Industries: Manufacturing, Drugs Mfg., Medical
Devices, Computer Equip., Test, Measure
Equip., Electronic, Elec. Components,
Semiconductors, Digital, Wireless, Fiber Optic,
Network Infrastructure

Banyan Group E.S.C., Ltd

6 Courseview Rd
Bronxville, NY 10708-2402
(914) 337-7159
Fax: (914) 337-7164
Email: dkuhns@banyan-group.com
Web: www.banyan-group.com

Summary: Our firm works primarily with small
and mid-sized companies (both for-profit and non-
profit) in defining and developing key leadership.
We are especially skilled in working with
entrepreneurs and their venture capital funding
partners, and also with not-for-profit boards of
directors.

Key Contact - Specialty:
Mr. David L. Kuhns, Managing Director - *Boards
of Directors, CEOs, Entrepreneurs, Non-profit,
Venture capital*
Ms. Claudia Ko, Associate

Functions: Senior Mgmt.

Industries: Generalist (All), Non-profits

The Barack Group Inc

405 Lexington Ave Rm 5002
New York, NY 10174-5003
(212) 867-9700
Fax: (212) 663-9555
Email: rob@barackgroup.com
Web: www.barackgroup.com

Summary: We are a specialized recruiting firm for
consumer goods and services, sports, and
entertainment companies.

Key Contact - Specialty:
Ms. Brianne Barack, President & Chief Executive
Officer
Mr. Robert Strong, Chief Operating Officer &
Mng Partner

Salary Minimum: $100,000

Functions: Senior Mgmt., Sales & Mktg.,
Advertising, Mktg. Mgmt., Sales Mgmt., PR

Industries: Food, Bev., Tobacco, Soap, Perf.,
Cosmtcs., Drugs Mfg., Consumer Goods,
Hotels, Resorts, Clubs, Entertainment, Sports,
Advertising, New Media, Telecoms

Barger & Sargeant Inc

PO Box 1460
Center Harbor, NH 03226-1460
(603) 253-4700

Summary: Noted for thoroughness in consulting,
interviewing and board recruiting.

Key Contact - Specialty:
Mr. H. Carter Barger, President

Salary Minimum: $150,000

Functions: Generalist (All), Board Members,
Senior Mgmt., Plant Mgmt., Mktg. Mgmt.,
Direct Mktg., CFOs

Industries: Generalist (All), Retail, Banking,
Insurance, Healthcare

Barkston Group LLC

PO Box 218
Litchfield, CT 06759-0218
(860) 567-2400
Fax: (860) 567-1466
Email: dpatenge@barkstongroup.com

Summary: Our search firm and consultancy serves
the securities industry. The firm focuses on long-
term partnerships with a limited number of
financial services firms and has front to back
office expertise.

Key Contact - Specialty:
Mr. David W. Patenge, President

Salary Minimum: $400,000

Functions: Cash Mgmt.

Industries: Invest. Banking, Brokers, Venture
Cap., Mutual/Hedge Funds

J W Barleycorn & Associates Inc†

1614 Lancaster Ave
Reynoldsburg, OH 43068-2639
(614) 861-4400
Fax: (614) 861-5558
Email: bcorn@insight.rr.com

Summary: Expertise in small and medium size
companies with concentration in engineering, HR,
legal, sales/marketing, healthcare, finance and
senior-level executives.

Key Contact - Specialty:
Mr. James W. Barleycorn, President
Mrs. Kimberly B. Smith, Executive. Human
Resources
Mrs. Sherry S. Stepleton, Administrator

Salary Minimum: $70,000

Functions: Generalist (All)

Industries: Manufacturing, Chemicals, Misc.
Mfg., Finance, Non-profits, Legal, Accounting,
Mgmt. Consulting, Software, Healthcare

Barnes Development Group LLC

1045 W Glen Oaks Ln Ste 4
Mequon, WI 53092-3477
(262) 241-8468
Fax: (262) 241-8438
Email: resume@barnesdevelopment.com
Web: www.barnesdevelopment.com

Summary: Practice dedicated to retained
executive search consulting with emphasis in
manufacturing, service, health care and nonprofit
industries.

Key Contact - Specialty:
Mr. Richard E. Barnes, President - *Manufacturing*
Ms. Roanne L. Barnes, Executive Vice President -
Long term care, Non-profit

Salary Minimum: $60,000

Functions: Generalist (All)

Industries: Generalist (All)

Barone-O'Hara Associates Inc

34 Fackler Rd
Princeton, NJ 08540-4706
(609) 683-5566
Fax: (609) 683-8077
Email: boha4@yahoo.com
Web: www.baroneohara.com

Summary: We provide executive search
exclusively to manufacturers of healthcare
devices. We are especially successful with small
companies such as startups, restarts and fast
growth. Our consulting is provided as an adjunct
to executive search through CEO resources.

Key Contact - Specialty:
Ms. Marialice Barone, President - *Orthopedics*
Mr. James J. O'Hara, President - *Orthopedics*
Ms. Wendy L. Barone, Vice President, Research
Ms. Catherine Short, Vice President, Medvestors
- *Computers (Software)*
Ms. Alicia DeLorenzo, Vice President, Business
Development - *Telecommunications*

Salary Minimum: $90,000

Functions: Management, Board Members, Senior
Mgmt., Middle Mgmt., Mfg., Materials, Sales &
Mktg., Mktg. Research, Mktg. Mgmt., Sales
Mgmt.

Industries: Medical Devices, Healthcare

Barrack Hill Partners Inc

27 Country Club Rd
Newton, MA 02459-3021
(617) 332-1884
(617) 519-9992
Fax: (617) 332-0208
Email: cmorrill@bhp-us.com
Web: www.bhp-us.com

Summary: We are a boutique retained executive
search firm, generalist practice with a focus on
technology, publishing and media, life sciences,
financial services and non-profit. Clients range
from start-up to large multinational. Certified
Women's Business Enterprise with commitment to
diversity

Key Contact - Specialty:
Ms. Carolyn Morrill, Managing Partner - *C-level,
Diversity, General management*

Salary Minimum: $75,000

Functions: Senior Mgmt.

Industries: Generalist (All)

Barro Global Search Inc

10951 W Pico Blvd Ste 316
Los Angeles, CA 90064-2189
(310) 441-5305
Email: drbarro@barroglobal.com
Web: www.barroglobal.com

Summary: We are a retained healthcare executive
search firm and provider of professional advisory
services for candidates and employers. With speed
and efficiency, candidates who are an exact fit are
selected for the client, saving valuable time. The
right fit contributes to building a strong
relationship between candidate and employer.
Results: stability, long-term growth and
satisfaction for both. Being different makes a
difference.

Key Contact - Specialty:
Dr. Arlene R. Barro, President & Chief Executive
Officer - *Biomedical, Healthcare, Hospital,
Physicians, Publishing*

Salary Minimum: $70,000

Functions: Management, Healthcare, Physicians,
Nurses, Allied Health

Industries: Higher Ed., Publishing, Biotech/Life Sciences, Healthcare, Hospitals

Bartholdi Partners

12020 Sunrise Valley Dr Ste 160
Reston, VA 20191-3482
(703) 476-5519
Fax: (703) 391-0029
Email: cholt@bartholdisearch.com
Web: www.bartholdisearch.com

Summary: We are a boutique retained search firm with focus in technology, health care and financial services. The firm recruits senior-level executives in all functional areas.

Key Contact - Specialty:
Ms. Carol Holt, Partner - *Healthcare, Information Technology, International, Medical (Devices), Wireless*
Mr. Walter Wilowaty, Partner - *Database, Information Technology, Marketing, Telecommunications*
Ms. Ann Caldwell, Partner - *Financial services, Information Technology, Marketing, Sales, Telecommunications*
Mr. Jacques de Labry, Partner - *Information Technology, Telecommunications*

Salary Minimum: $100,000

Functions: Generalist (All)

Industries: Drugs Mfg., Medical Devices, IT Implementation, Communications, Wireless, Network Infrastructure, Government, Software, Biotech/Life Sciences, Healthcare

Barton Associates[†]

121 N Cedar Crest Blvd
Allentown, PA 18104-4664
(610) 439-8751
Fax: (610) 439-1207
Email: barton@fast.net
Web: www.bartonsearch.com

Summary: We are a successful provider of confidential executive search for many years. Experts in finance, accounting human resources, engineering, corporate management and sales and marketing.

Key Contact - Specialty:
Mr. Malcolm Singerman, Principal
Mr. Bernard Harms, Director - *Engineering, Information Technology, Manufacturing*
Ms. Shirley Coffey, Director - *Accounting, Financial, Human resources*
Mr. Gil Tucker, Director - *Marketing, Sales*

Salary Minimum: $50,000

Functions: Generalist (All)

Industries: Energy, Utilities, Oil & Gas, Construction, Manufacturing, Chemicals, Drugs Mfg., Medical Devices, Finance, Banking, Communications

Barton Associates Inc[†]

4314 Yoakum Blvd
Houston, TX 77006-5818
(713) 961-9111
Fax: (713) 993-9399
Email: info@bartona.com
Web: www.bartona.com

Summary: A retainer practice built on strong client relationships and timely execution of projects. Expertise encompasses most industries and functional areas.

Key Contact - Specialty:
Mr. Gary R. Barton, Partner - *General management, Human resources*
Mr. Sean E. Barton, Partner
Ms. Beth A. Barton, Director, Research

Ms. Sue Holzhauser, Consultant
Ms. Courtney Barton, Consultant
Mrs. Heather Marlow, Consultant
Mr. Clark Holzhauser, Video Conference

Salary Minimum: $75,000

Functions: Management, Sales & Mktg., HR Mgmt., Finance, MIS Mgmt.

Industries: Generalist (All), Banking, Invest. Banking, IT Implementation, Higher Ed., Hospitality, New Media, Software, ERP SW

Affiliates:
Mid-Town Video Conferencing
Houston, TX

Carol Bates & Associates Inc

544 24th St
Manhattan Beach, CA 90266-2207
(310) 545-5890
Email: resume@carolbates.com

Summary: Executive recruiting focused on the needs of clients who provide global IT and business consulting services.

Key Contact - Specialty:
Ms. Carol Bates, Owner

Functions: Management, Senior Mgmt., Middle Mgmt., Sales Mgmt., MIS Mgmt.

Industries: Mgmt. Consulting, IT Implementation

Battalia Winston International

(a member of The Amrop Hever Group)
555 Madison Ave
New York, NY 10022-3301
(212) 308-8080
Fax: (212) 308-1309
Email: info@battaliawinston.com
Web: www.battaliawinston.com

Summary: Our firm is one of the top 12 national executive search firms concentrating in seven practice areas: financial services, healthcare, technology, industrial products, consulting/professional services, consumer/retail, including media & entertainment and not-for-profit. Through its diversified staff of experienced professionals our firm has built its practice on long standing relationships and client satisfaction.

Key Contact - Specialty:
Ms. Dale Winston, Chairperson & Chief Executive Officer - *Boards of Directors, CEOs, CFOs, COOs, Non-profit*

Salary Minimum: $150,000

Functions: Board Members, Senior Mgmt., Mktg. Mgmt., HR Mgmt., Benefits, Staffing, CFOs, MIS Mgmt., Mgmt. Consultants, Non-profits

Industries: Food, Bev., Tobacco, Medical Devices, Retail, Invest. Banking, Non-profits, Publishing, Insurance, Software, Biotech/Life Sciences, Healthcare

Branches:
1888 Century Park E Ste 1150
Los Angeles, CA 90067-1727
(310) 284-8080
Fax: (310) 284-3438
Email: mmcclain@battaliawinston.com
Key Contact - Specialty:
Mr. Michael McClain, Partner - *Consumer (Packaged Goods), Entertainment*

718 University Ave Ste 100
Los Gatos, CA 95032-7608
(408) 357-7838
Fax: (408) 357-7801
Email: info@battaliawinston.com

Key Contact - Specialty:
Mr. David R. Mather, Partner - *Boards of Directors, CEOs, Senior management, Technology*

150 S Wacker Dr Ste 1220
Chicago, IL 60606-4201
(312) 704-0050
Fax: (312) 704-0305
Email: rfolts@battaliawinston.com
Key Contact - Specialty:
Mr. Richard W. Folts, Partner - *Automotive, Consumer, Industrial*

65 William St Ste 330
Wellesley, MA 02481-3826
(781) 239-1400
Fax: (781) 239-1415
Email: space@battaliawinston.com
Key Contact - Specialty:
Ms. Sue Pace, Partner - *Finance, Manufacturing, Marketing, Operations, Sales*

379 Thornall St Ste 10
Edison, NJ 08837-2233
(732) 549-8200
Fax: (732) 549-8443
Email: tgallagher@battaliawinston.com
Key Contact - Specialty:
Mr. Terence M. Gallagher, President - *Consulting, Financial services, Industrial, Information Technology, Professional services*

L Battalin & Company[†]

11129 Sandyshell Way
Boca Raton, FL 33498-4914
(561) 477-3441
Fax: (561) 447-5654
Email: larry@lbatco.com
Web: www.lbatco.com

Summary: Specialize in recruitment and placement of marketing management within the consumer packaged goods industry only, while pursuing the equal opportunity objectives.

Key Contact - Specialty:
Mr. Laurence H. Battalin, President - *Marketing*

Salary Minimum: $75,000

Functions: Generalist (All), Mktg. Research, Mktg. Mgmt., Minorities/Diversity

Industries: Generalist (All), Food, Bev., Tobacco, Textiles, Apparel, Soap, Perf., Cosmtcs., Computer Equip., New Media

R Gaines Baty Associates Inc

12750 Merit Dr
Dallas, TX 75251-1214
(972) 386-7900
Fax: (972) 387-2224
Email: gbaty@rgba.com
Web: www.rgba.com

Summary: We are a full-scale, retained search for outsourcing/BPO, IT and consulting management within numerous industries (healthcare, government, etc.) and general and sales management for technology and services/solutions companies. Personal attention, results-orientation and long-term approach are the way that we perform business. Extensive experience in search business, doing it right, with 99 percent repeat/referral clients.

Key Contact - Specialty:
Mr. R. Gaines Baty, President

Salary Minimum: $150,000

Functions: Senior Mgmt., Distribution, Sales Mgmt., IT, MIS Mgmt., Mgmt. Consultants

Industries: Generalist (All), Energy, Utilities, Manufacturing, Computer Equip.,

Transportation, Wholesale, Retail, Finance, Venture Cap., Services, Equip Svcs., Mgmt. Consulting, E-commerce, IT Implementation, Communications, Wireless, Government, Claims, Software, Healthcare, Hospitals

Martin H Bauman Associates LLC

150 E 58th St Fl 37
New York, NY 10155-0002
(212) 752-6580
Fax: (212) 755-1096
Email: mhb@baumanassociates.com
Web: www.martinbaumanassociates.com

Summary: Our firm offers a highly personalized service in executive recruitment. At the core of our recruitment process is our peerless assessment capability.

Key Contact - Specialty:
Mr. Martin H. Bauman, President - *Finance, General management, Transportation, Venture capital*

Salary Minimum: $165,000

Functions: Generalist (All), Management, Board Members, Senior Mgmt., Mfg., Purchasing, Distribution, Sales & Mktg., HR Mgmt., Finance

Industries: Generalist (All)

The Bauman Group

350 2nd St Ste 2
Los Altos, CA 94022-3602
(650) 941-0800
Fax: (650) 941-1729
Email: joann@thebaumangroup.com
Web: www.thebaumangroup.com

Summary: We are a retained search firm that provides senior-level clinical and regulatory expertise to biotechnology and pharmaceutical companies. We work closely with the venture community.

Key Contact - Specialty:
Ms. Ina Bauman, President
Ms. Shari Grande, MSW, Executive Recruiter

Salary Minimum: $100,000

Functions: Healthcare, Physicians

Industries: Medical Devices, Biotech/Life Sciences, Healthcare

BCA Inc†

3525 Del Mar Heights Rd Ste 660
San Diego, CA 92130-2122
(888) 324-8644
Fax: (888) 324-8644
Email: hr@bcasearch.com
Web: www.hrcareerpage.com

Summary: We are one of the few search firms devoted exclusively to HR. Our functional expertise has allowed us to build a reputation for quick and effective delivery, diversity recruitment expertise and continued success with difficult and/or extremely focused requirements.

Key Contact - Specialty:
Mr. Joe Gonzalez, Managing Partner - *Human resources*
Ms. Cecelia Gonzalez, Managing Partner - *Human resources*
Ms. Rosemary Daniels, Staffing Consultant

Salary Minimum: $100,000

Functions: HR Mgmt.

Industries: Generalist (All)

BCGI (Baron Consulting Group Inc)

2306-2 Bloor St E
Royal Bank Building
Toronto, ON M4W 1A8
Canada
(416) 979-2404
Email: resumes@bcgi.ca
Web: www.bcgi.ca

Summary: Our consultants apply industry experience to the searches in their area of specialty.

Key Contact - Specialty:
Mr. Robert Baron, Principal - *Real estate*

Salary Minimum: $75,000

Functions: Generalist (All), Management

Industries: Construction, Banking, Accounting, Real Estate, Property/Facility Mgmt.

Beach Executive Search Inc

11324 NW 12th Ct
Coral Springs, FL 33071-6494
(954) 340-7337
Email: wlbeach@bellsouth.net

Summary: Generalist retained search firm specialized in performing a highly personalized service to client companies.

Key Contact - Specialty:
Mr. William L. Beach, President

Salary Minimum: $75,000

Functions: Generalist (All)

Industries: Generalist (All)

The Beam Group

1835 Market St Ste 502
Philadelphia, PA 19103-2933
(215) 988-2100
Fax: (215) 988-1558
Email: info@beamgroup.com
Web: www.beamgroup.com

Summary: We are a generalist search firm with a diverse group of insurance, financial services, consumer products and high-technology clients. Particular expertise in candidate assessment.

Key Contact - Specialty:
Mr. Russell A. Glicksman, President & Chief Executive Officer
Mr. Tom Kelly, Senior Vice President
Mr. Paul Sampson, Senior Vice President - *Engineering, Manufacturing, Operations*
Mr. Scott McKenna, Vice President
Ms. Sandi Macan, Vice President - *Direct marketing, Financial services, Healthcare, Human resources*
Ms. Suzanne Martin, Vice President
Ms. Karen DiLullo, Office Manager - *Sales, Technology*

Salary Minimum: $125,000

Functions: Management, Senior Mgmt., Materials, Distribution, Healthcare, Sales & Mktg., Direct Mktg., HR Mgmt., Finance, MIS Mgmt.

Industries: Manufacturing, Food, Bev., Tobacco, Paper, Soap, Perf., Cosmtcs., Drugs Mfg., Retail, Finance, Banking, Brokers, Venture Cap., Services, HR Services, Publishing, Insurance, Software, Healthcare

Branches:
600 3rd Ave
New York, NY 10016-1901
(212) 476-4150
Fax: (212) 986-7798

Key Contact - Specialty:
Mr. Howard M. Pines, Chairman
Mr. Richard Coffina, Senior Vice President - *Asset management, Financial services, Human resources*
Mr. Jonathan B. Santamaria, Senior Vice President - *Logistics, Sales*
Mr. Al Swann, Recruiter - *Technology*

Beaudine & Associates, Inc.

9925 Haynes Bridge Rd Ste 200-222
Alpharetta, GA 30022-1913
(770) 685-5500
Email: frank@beaudine.com
Web: www.beaudine.com

Summary: Our firm excels in retained executive search and leadership services providing hands on attention to all components of the search process, from research to presenting candidates to closing the deal in a responsive manner. We recognize the stakes are high when it comes to your leadership team and that you depend upon us to bring you the very best.

Key Contact - Specialty:
Mr. Frank R. Beaudine, Jr., President & Chief Executive Officer

Salary Minimum: $100,000

Functions: Generalist (All), Management

Industries: Generalist (All), Energy, Utilities, Manufacturing, Motor Vehicles, Finance, Services, Environmental Svcs., Aerospace, Marketing SW, Healthcare

J R Bechtle & Company

2300 Glades Rd Ste 460W
Boca Raton, FL 33431-8519
(561) 955-0012
Fax: (561) 955-0091
Email: jrb.miami@jrbechtle.com
Web: www.jrbechtle.com

Summary: We fill positions requiring extensive knowledge of European business practices and/or familiarity with the German language while covering a broad spectrum of industries. We concentrate on technically oriented products, machinery, high-technology components and software and the pharmaceutical and biotech market.

Key Contact - Specialty:
Mr. Egon L. Lacher, Managing Partner

Salary Minimum: $95,000

Functions: Management, Senior Mgmt., Materials, Packaging, Sales & Mktg., Finance, Engineering

Industries: Generalist (All), Manufacturing, Paper, Printing, Medical Devices, Plastics, Rubber, Paints, Petro. Products, Metal Products, Machine, Appliance, Motor Vehicles, Computer Equip., Test, Measure Equip., Electronic, Elec. Components, Robotics, Semiconductors

Branches:
1211 W 22nd St Ste 529
Oak Brook, IL 60523-2170
(630) 203-2120
Fax: (630) 527-1379
Email: jrb.chicago@jrbechtle.com
Key Contact - Specialty:
Mr. Herb Haessig, Partner

67 S Bedford St Ste 400W
Burlington, MA 01803-5177
(781) 229-5804
Fax: (781) 359-1829
Email: jrb.boston@jrbechtle.com

Key Contact - Specialty:
Mr. Thomas Kennedy, Principal

The Bedford Consulting Group Inc

(a Toronto partner of Transearch International)
400-145 Adelaide St W
Toronto, ON M5H 4E5
Canada
(416) 963-9000
Fax: (416) 963-9998
Email: search@bedfordgroup.com
Web: www.bedfordgroup.com

Summary: We reinvented the executive search process with proprietary tools that customize culture, role specific leadership competencies and business deliverables for each assignment. The net gain for our clients is increased competitive advantage through better leadership. No other executive search firm uses this measurement process. We are the largest independently owned executive search firm in Canada.

Key Contact - Specialty:
Mr. Steven Pezim, Managing Director - *Retail*
Mr. Howard J. Pezim, Managing Director - *Healthcare, Manufacturing*

Salary Minimum: $80,000

Functions: Generalist (All), Management, Mfg., Healthcare, Sales & Mktg., HR Mgmt., Finance, CFOs, IT, MIS Mgmt.

Industries: Generalist (All), Manufacturing, Retail, Finance, Media, Communications, Packaging, Insurance, Software, Biotech/Life Sciences, Healthcare

Branches:
132 Reynolds St
Oakville, ON L6J 3K5
Canada
(905) 338-7008
Fax: (905) 338-0662
Email: naturalresources@bedfordgroup.com
Key Contact - Specialty:
Mr. Russell Buckland, Managing Partner

The Bedford Group†

154 Quicksand Pond Rd
Little Compton, RI 02837-1924
(401) 635-8466
Fax: (401) 635-0293
Email: thebedfordgroup@earthlink.net

Summary: Leading specialist in medical device and electronics manufacturing, semiconductor, wireless and network communications industries. We have an outstanding completion record. Off limit recruiting strictly observed.

Key Contact - Specialty:
Mr. John W. Edwards, Managing Director - *Electronics, Semiconductors, Telecommunications*
Ms. Lillian E. Edwards, Director, Research - *Electronics, Healthcare, Telecommunications*

Salary Minimum: $90,000

Functions: Management, Senior Mgmt., Middle Mgmt., Mfg., Product Dev., Quality, Sales & Mktg., R&D, Engineering

Industries: Medical Devices, Robotics, Semiconductors, Transportation, Engineering Svcs., Communications, Telecoms, Wireless, Network Infrastructure, RF/Microwave, Networking, Comm. SW, Security SW, Biotech/Life Sciences

BeechTree Partners LLC

(formerly known as GlobalNet Partners Inc)
875 N Michigan Ave Ste 3100
John Hancock Center
Chicago, IL 60611-1962
(312) 794-7808
Fax: (312) 893-3813
Email: info@beechtreepartners.com
Web: www.beechtreepartners.com

Summary: We are an executive search and consulting firm specializing in managed care, life sciences, behavioral health care, pharmaceutical, prescription benefit management, provider systems, consulting, and health care technology. Our partnering approach, rapid fill times and uncompromising dedication have honored us with executive searches from many of our industry's leading names.

Key Contact - Specialty:
Mr. Brad Newpoff, CPC, Managing Partner - *Biotechnology, Consulting, Managed care*
Mr. Mark Gamboa, Partner - *Biotechnology, Managed care, Pharmaceutical*
Mr. Bryan Nolan, Director, Research

Salary Minimum: $90,000

Functions: Senior Mgmt., Healthcare, Physicians, Sales & Mktg., HR Mgmt., Benefits, Training, CFOs, Mgmt. Consultants, Minorities/Diversity

Industries: Finance, Brokers, Venture Cap., Services, Insurance, Software, Training SW, Biotech/Life Sciences, Healthcare, Hospitals, Long-term/Home Care, Dental

Affiliates:
Working Solutions Inc
Dublin, OH

Branches:
1902 Wright Pl Ste 200
Carlsbad, CA 92008-6583
(760) 431-5109
Email: info@beechtreepartners.com

Harvey Bell & Assoc

700 Lindsay Ave
Rohnert Park, CA 94928-4522
(707) 795-0650
Email: harveybell@aol.com

Summary: Name generation, candidate development, screening and background checks on an hourly basis for positions from individual contributor to upper management in all fields. Long term clients are recruiting organizations and corporations. All new clients were by referral. There is a low cost trial program.

Key Contact - Specialty:
Mr. Harvey Bell, Owner

Salary Minimum: $60,000

Functions: Generalist (All), Management, Senior Mgmt., Middle Mgmt., Mfg., Mktg. Mgmt., Sales Mgmt., CFOs, MIS Mgmt., R&D

Industries: Generalist (All)

David Bell Executive Search†

200-133 Richmond St W
Toronto, ON M5H 2L3
Canada
(416) 597-0188
Fax: (416) 597-0432
Email: info@davidbellsearch.com
Web: www.pub-rels.com

Summary: We are one of the only executive search firms in the country that specializes exclusively in all facets of public relations. We

provide a wide variety of clients with PR professionals at all levels. We collaborate closely with PR associations and schools to help maintain the highest professional standards for the industry.

Key Contact - Specialty:
Mr. David Bell

Salary Minimum: $50,000

Functions: PR

Industries: Generalist (All)

Bell Wishingrad Partners Inc

230 Park Ave Rm 1000
New York, NY 10169-1099
(212) 949-6666
Email: postmaster@bell.wishingrad.com

Summary: A practice focused upon senior management positions in financial services and affiliated industries. Search activities performed only by partners with limited client base avoiding off-limit conflicts.

Key Contact - Specialty:
Ms. Vivian Wishingrad, Partner - *Financial services*

Salary Minimum: $250,000

Functions: Generalist (All), Senior Mgmt., Mktg. Mgmt., Sales Mgmt., Cash Mgmt., M&A

Industries: Generalist (All), Finance, Banking, Invest. Banking, Brokers, Venture Cap., Mutual/Hedge Funds, Misc. Financial

Belle Isle, Djandji Executive Search

1200-1555 Rue Peel
La Tour Peel
Montreal, QC H3A 3L8
Canada
(514) 844-1012
Fax: (514) 844-0539
Email: info@bidi.com
Web: www.bidi.com

Summary: Firm has a broad range of search assignments expertise in the private, public and para-public sectors covering all functional areas and a broad cross-section of industries.

Key Contact - Specialty:
Mr. Charles Belle Isle, Partner
Mr. Guy Djandji, Partner

Salary Minimum: $100,000

Functions: Generalist (All), Senior Mgmt.

Industries: Generalist (All), Food, Bev., Tobacco, Lumber, Furniture, Paper, Printing, Drugs Mfg., Metal Products, Venture Cap., Supply Chain Mgmt, Media, Communications

Bench International Search Inc

120 S Doheny Dr
Beverly Hills, CA 90211-2510
(310) 854-9900
Fax: (310) 854-9000
Web: www.benchinternational.com

Summary: We are one of the oldest retained executive search firms specializing in the pharmaceutical and biotech sectors. Our firm has extensive experience, is broadly and deeply networked, uses innovative approaches to recruiting and has a proven track record of placing highly successful industry leaders.

Key Contact - Specialty:
Ms. Denise DeMan, Founder, Chairman & CEO - *Biopharmaceutical, Biotechnology, Healthcare, Life Sciences, Pharmaceutical*
Dr. Stephen Williams, PhD, President & Chief Business Officer - *Biopharmaceutical,*

Biotechnology, Healthcare, Life Sciences, Pharmaceutical

Dr. William Sigmund, MD, Senior Vice President & CMO - *Biopharmaceutical, Biotechnology, Healthcare, Life Sciences, Pharmaceutical*

Mr. Fred J. McCallum, Vice President - *Biopharmaceutical, Biotechnology, Healthcare, Life Sciences, Pharmaceutical*

Salary Minimum: $150,000

Functions: Board Members, Senior Mgmt., Middle Mgmt., Sales & Mktg., Mktg. Research, R&D, Minorities/Diversity

Industries: Drugs Mfg., Medical Devices, Pharm Svcs., Biotech/Life Sciences, Healthcare

Branches:
115 E 57th St Fl 11
New York, NY 10022-2120
(646) 435-9200
Email: rdunn@benchinternational.com
Key Contact - Specialty:
Ms. Janet Foulkes, MBA, Global Senior Vice President - *Biopharmaceutical, Biotechnology, Healthcare, Life Sciences, Pharmaceutical*

Richard L Bencin & Associates[†]

2616 Hidden Canyon Dr
Brecksville, OH 44141-3530
(440) 526-6726
Fax: (440) 546-1623
Email: rlbencin@netzero.com
Web: www.rlbencin.com

Summary: Dedicated specialist in call center management/sales recruiting.

Key Contact - Specialty:
Mr. Richard L. Bencin, President - *Call centers, Direct marketing*
Mr. David Maggiore, Executive Vice President - *Call centers, Direct marketing*

Salary Minimum: $40,000

Functions: Direct Mktg., Customer Svc.

Industries: Generalist (All)

T H Bender & Partners

500 N Michigan Ave Ste 300
Chicago, IL 60611-3775
(312) 396-4120
(312) 925-1033
Fax: (312) 264-0202
Email: tilman.bender@thbender.com
Web: thbender.com

Summary: Our firm provides executive search and management consulting services. Our offices serve corporate and private equity clients. We also conduct market evaluations as well as compensation and corporate governance related studies that provide a strong, realistic foundation for our recommendations which help clients to successfully navigate and enter their markets.

Key Contact - Specialty:
Mr. Tilman Bender, Managing Partner
Mr. Peter Mayer, Managing Director, Europe

Salary Minimum: $150,000

Bender Executive Search Management Consulting

45 N Station Plz Ste 315
Great Neck, NY 11021-5011
(516) 773-4300
Fax: (516) 482-5355
Email: benderexec@aol.com
Web: www.marketingexecsearch.com

Summary: Our firm provides a tailor made consultative approach by a former marketing executive with extensive success specializing in marketing search nationwide. We are a multi-resource firm with sophisticated research capability. We are known for quality, thoroughness, fast results, proactive personalized service and close collaborative relationships.

Key Contact - Specialty:
Mr. Alan Bender, President - *Market research, Marketing, Sales*
Ms. Robyn Goodman, Consultant

Salary Minimum: $75,000

Functions: Senior Mgmt., Middle Mgmt., Advertising, Mktg. Research, Mktg. Mgmt., Sales Mgmt., Direct Mktg., PR, Mgmt. Consultants, Minorities/Diversity

Industries: Generalist (All), Manufacturing, Retail, Finance, Services, Mgmt. Consulting, Hospitality, Entertainment, Media, Communications

Bennett Search & Consulting Company Inc

285 W Naomi Dr # 1
Naples, FL 34104-9456
(239) 352-0219
(230) 290-2331
Email: robertbennett@comcast.net
Web: bobbennettgroup.com

Summary: We are generalists covering banking, electronics, manufacturing, security, real estate development, restaurant/hotel management, golf and country club staffing. We recruit senior management, general management, sales, manufacturing, engineering and human resources management.

Key Contact - Specialty:
Mr. Robert C. Bennett, Jr., President
Ms. Colleen Shue
Mr. Beirne Brown, Associate - *Hotels, Restaurants*
Mr. Michael McFarland - *Research*

Salary Minimum: $80,000

Functions: Generalist (All), Management, Healthcare, Sales & Mktg., Finance, IT, Engineering, Minorities/Diversity, Legal, Hospitality

Industries: Food, Bev., Tobacco, Finance, Banking, Services, Legal, Accounting, Mgmt. Consulting, Law Enforcement, Hospitality, Environmental Svcs., Real Estate

Bennett Wheelless Group Ltd

33 W Monroe St Ste 2110
Chicago, IL 60603-5414
(312) 252-8883
(312) 252-8884
Fax: (312) 252-8209
Email: nbennett@bennettwheelless.com
Web: www.bennettwheelless.com

Summary: Our firm is a retained executive search firm serving the direct marketing and interactive marketing community. We serve our clients best by developing long-term relationships and partnering with them in order to identify and qualify candidates.

Key Contact - Specialty:
Ms. Neysa Bennett, President - *Database, Direct marketing, Interactive, Marketing*
Ms. Heather Baker, Executive Recruiter - *Database, Direct marketing, Interactive, Marketing*

Salary Minimum: $90,000

Functions: Direct Mktg.

Industries: Retail, Finance, E-commerce, Hotels, Resorts, Clubs, Entertainment, Publishing, Telecoms, Database SW, Marketing SW, Healthcare

Bennett Yarger Associates

23 Doctors Hill Dr
Scituate, MA 02066-3650
(781) 545-7616
Fax: (781) 545-8565
Email: rbennett@bennettyarger.com
Web: www.bennettyarger.com

Summary: We serve government and non-profit organizations by recruiting experienced leaders into positions that improve the capabilities of these institutions.

Key Contact - Specialty:
Mr. Richard T. Bennett, Owner
Mr. Richard M. Kobayashi, Senior Consultant
Mr. Ned Rightor, Senior Consultant
Ms. Susan Rudermand, Senior Consultant
Ms. Pam Antil, Senior Manager

Functions: Generalist (All), Senior Mgmt., Admin. Svcs., Staffing, CFOs, MIS Mgmt., Mgmt. Consultants, Minorities/Diversity

Industries: Generalist (All), Transportation, Services, Non-profits, Law Enforcement, Higher Ed., Government

Branches:
1535 3rd St
Sacramento, CA 95814-5320
(916) 443-2421
Fax: (847) 205-5330
Email: rneher@bennettyarger.com
Key Contact - Specialty:
Mr. Robert Neher

222 Purchase St Ste 282
Rye, NY 10580-2101
(914) 925-0314
Fax: (914) 967-1354
Email: fculross@bennettsearch.com
Key Contact - Specialty:
Mr. Frank Culross

Berardi & Associates

(a division of The Solomon-Page Group LLC)
1140 Avenue of the Americas Fl 8
New York, NY 10036-5803
(212) 403-6180
Fax: (212) 764-9690
Email: jmiranda@spges.com
Web: www.spgjobs.com

Summary: We provide individual executive search in the magazine publishing, book publishing, educational publishing and new media industries by media professionals with experience in the industry.

Key Contact - Specialty:
Ms. Loretta A. Berardi, President
Ms. Susan Gold, Executive Vice President
Mr. David Moran, Vice President
Ms. Laura Zwerlein Cassidy, Vice President

Functions: Generalist (All), Senior Mgmt., Middle Mgmt., Advertising, Mktg. Mgmt., Sales Mgmt., Direct Mktg.

Industries: Generalist (All), Mgmt. Consulting, HR Services, K-12 Ed., Higher Ed., Advertising, Publishing, New Media

Berkhemer Clayton Inc

241 S Figueroa St Ste 300
Los Angeles, CA 90012-2504
(213) 621-2300
Fax: (213) 621-2309
Web: www.berkhemerclayton.com

Summary: We are a senior level retained firm with strong functional practices in corporate

communications, finance, marketing, HR and non-profit leadership. Committed to inclusive process and striving to present a full spectrum of candidates, including men, women and people of color. Firm is multi-ethnic owned.

Key Contact - Specialty:
Ms. Betsy Berkhemer-Credaire, President - *Communications, Marketing, Public relations*
Mr. Fred J. Clayton, Chief Executive Officer - *Finance, General management, Human resources, Marketing*
Ms. Krista J. Grossman, Associate Vice President - *Communications, Marketing, Public relations*
Ms. Janis Avila Swartz, Senior Associate - *Diversity, General management, Human resources*

Salary Minimum: $120,000

Functions: Senior Mgmt., PR, HR Mgmt., Finance, Minorities/Diversity, Non-profits

Industries: Energy, Utilities, Wholesale, Retail, Misc. Financial, Services, Hospitality, Advertising, Software, Entertainment SW, Biotech/Life Sciences, Healthcare

Berman, Larson, Kane[†]

12 N State Rt 17 Ste 209
Paramus, NJ 07652-2644
(800) 640-0126
(201) 909-0906
Fax: (201) 909-0976
Email: ken@jobsbl.com
Web: www.jobsbl.com

Summary: With over 350,000 professionals on file, our experienced staff will isolate a top performer to meet your staffing needs. We have candidates available for both direct hire and contracting.

Key Contact - Specialty:
Mr. Robert Larson, CPC, President - *Accounting (General), Administration, Human resources, Information Technology, Sales*

Salary Minimum: $30,000

Functions: Sales & Mktg., HR Mgmt., Finance, IT

Industries: Generalist (All), Plastics, Rubber, Pharm Svcs., Mgmt. Consulting, HR Services, E-commerce, Full Service Restaurants, Inst./Industrial Food Svc., Software

Best, Coleman and Partners Inc

198 Tremont St Ste 511
Boston, MA 02116
Email: bbest@webmailoutlet.com

Summary: Senior management, sales and marketing positions within the wholesale and retail industries exclusively. Retained search only.

Key Contact - Specialty:
Mr. Benjamin M. Best, III, President - *Marketing, Retail, Sales, Wholesale*
Ms. Anne Coleman, Vice President

Salary Minimum: $90,000

Functions: Senior Mgmt., Mktg. Research, Mktg. Mgmt., Sales Mgmt.

Industries: Wholesale, Retail

BFL Associates Ltd

12 E Greenway Plz Ste 1222
Houston, TX 77046-1296
(713) 965-2112
Fax: (713) 965-2114
Email: bjorn@bflassociates.com
Web: www.bflassociates.com

Summary: Our firm works to locate and secure the resources clients need to succeed. Clients initially engage our services to locate talent for executive positions. But with capabilities that extend far beyond recruiting, we are frequently able to provide the value-added services of employee retention programs, compensation analysis and long-term planning for healthy business growth.

Key Contact - Specialty:
Mr. Bjorn F. Lindgren, Managing Partner

Salary Minimum: $200,000

Functions: Generalist (All)

Industries: Generalist (All)

BH Solutions Group Inc[†]

4040 Embassy Pkwy Ste 200
Akron, OH 44333-8354
(330) 666-6970
Fax: (330) 666-7380
Email: basnett@bhsolutionsgroup.com
Web: www.bhsolutionsgroup.com

Summary: Executive recruiting and consulting. Specializing in the areas of senior level sales and sales management, IT, supply chain and accounting/finance.

Key Contact - Specialty:
Mr. Ben Basnett, Managing Partner
Mr. John Bernatovicz, Vice President, Sales & New Business Dev
Ms. Pam Beran, Office Manager

Salary Minimum: $75,000

Functions: Management, Sales Mgmt., Finance, IT

Industries: Generalist (All), Finance, Accounting

Bialecki Inc

780 3rd Ave Rm 4203
New York, NY 10017-2024
(212) 755-1090
Web: www.bialecki.com

Summary: We are retained only on senior-level positions and perform highly specialized searches for investment banking talent. We have expertise in corporate finance sector heads, M&A, all structured products and risk management. We have had substantial repeat business.

Key Contact - Specialty:
Ms. Linda Bialecki, President

Salary Minimum: $1,000,000

Functions: Management, Board Members, Senior Mgmt.

Industries: Invest. Banking, Venture Cap., Mutual/Hedge Funds

Bialla & Associates Inc

4000 Bridgeway Ste 201
Sausalito, CA 94965-1451
(415) 332-7111
Fax: (415) 332-3964
Web: www.bialla.com

Summary: Handle blue chip clients, CEOs, COOs, CFOs, functional heads (i.e. VP marketing, etc.).

Key Contact - Specialty:
Mr. Vito Bialla, Partner - *CEOs, Consumer, Consumer (Packaged Goods), Entertainment, Sports*
Mr. John McCrea, Partner - *Banking, Consumer (Packaged Goods), Retail, Technology, Tourism*
Mr. Terry Thomas, Partner - *Biotechnology, C-level, Consumer, Consumer (Packaged Goods), Technology*
Ms. Carolyn Carpeneti, Associate - *Fashion, Non-profit*

Mr. John Geoghegan, Associate - *Advertising, Marketing*
Ms. Kris Snodgrass, Manager & Associate, Research - *Research*

Salary Minimum: $150,000

Functions: Senior Mgmt., Mktg. Mgmt., CFOs, Int'l.

Industries: Generalist (All)

Paul J Biestek Associates Inc

800 E Northwest Hwy Ste 700
Palatine, IL 60074-6513
(847) 825-5131
Email: search@biestek-associates.com
Web: www.biestek-associates.com

Summary: We draw on extensive experience of executive search consulting and corporate human recource management experience.

Key Contact - Specialty:
Mr. Paul J. Biestek, President

Salary Minimum: $80,000

Functions: Generalist (All), Mfg., Materials, Sales Mgmt., Finance, IT, R&D, Engineering

Industries: Generalist (All), Energy, Utilities, Manufacturing, Food, Bev., Tobacco, Medical Devices, Machine, Appliance, Defense, Aerospace

bigEARS Inc[†]

PO Box 576
Loveland, CO 80539-0576
(970) 988-8204
Email: david@bigearsinc.com
Web: www.bigearsinc.com

Summary: Concentration is human capital management and recruiting for firms between 20 to 100 employees.

Key Contact - Specialty:
Mr. David Rodgers

Salary Minimum: $75,000

Functions: Generalist (All)

Industries: Manufacturing, Medical Devices, Plastics, Rubber, Paints, Petro. Products, Metal Products, Machine, Appliance, Misc. Mfg., Robotics, Biotech/Life Sciences

Biomedical Search Consultants[†]

PO Box 721
Hawleyville, CT 06440-0721
(203) 426-1445
Email: ta4nabio@cs.com

Summary: We specialize in pharmaceutical, biopharmaceutical, biological, medical devices, diagnostics and cosmetic industries.

Key Contact - Specialty:
Mr. Thomas A. Fornabaio, Professional Recruiter
Mr. James T. Fornabaio, Professional Recruiter - *Engineering*

Functions: Management, Middle Mgmt., Mfg., Product Dev., Production, Plant Mgmt., Quality, Packaging, R&D, Engineering

Industries: Chemicals, Soap, Perf., Cosmtcs., Drugs Mfg., Medical Devices, Biotech/Life Sciences

BioPharmMed[†]

(also known as BPM Resources)
550 N Reo St Ste 300
Tampa, FL 33609-1037
(813) 261-5117
Email: bpm@ix.netcom.com
Web: www.biopharmmed.com

† occasional contingency assignment

Summary: Our firm offers commitment, knowledge, experience and results in our retained partnership with clients ranging from start-up ventures to Fortune 500 corporations. We specialize in biotech, medical device, pharmaceutical and optics/telecommunication. We are computer linked to over 695 search firms worldwide and offer permanent and contract placements.

Key Contact - Specialty:
Ms. Tina Hunter Greene, President
Ms. Margaret Comer - *Bakery, Food & beverage, Hospitality*

Salary Minimum: $80,000

Functions: Generalist (All), Senior Mgmt., Middle Mgmt., Product Dev., Quality, R&D, Engineering

Industries: Drugs Mfg., Medical Devices, Biotech/Life Sciences

BioQuest
100 Spear St Ste 1125
San Francisco, CA 94105-1526
(415) 777-2422
Email: sandmeier@bioquestinc.com
Web: www.bioquestinc.com

Summary: A retained executive search firm serving the healthcare/life sciences industry, we specialize in consulting with venture-backed companies on executive-level positions.

Key Contact - Specialty:
Dr. H. Jurgen Weber, PhD, Founding Partner
Mr. Roger J. Anderson, Managing Partner
Dr. Ruedi Sandmeier, PhD, Managing Director
Ms. Kim Ennis, RN, Vice President
Ms. Gale Richards, Vice President
Mr. Brad Buehler, Senior Consultant
Ms. Mary Letterii, Consultant
Mr. Anthony Smayda, Consultant - *General management*

Salary Minimum: $150,000

Functions: Management, Board Members, Senior Mgmt., CFOs

Industries: Drugs Mfg., Medical Devices, Pharm Svcs., Biotech/Life Sciences, Healthcare

Branches:
34232 Pacific Coast Hwy Ste D
Dana Point, CA 92629-3855
(949) 488-8018
Email: info@bioquestinc.com
Key Contact - Specialty:
Mr. Dave Mildrew, Consultant

Bisck & Associates Inc
300 S Jackson St Ste 100
Denver, CO 80209-3183
(303) 800-4778
Email: resume@bisckandassociates.com
Web: www.bisckandassociates.com

Summary: We are a recruiting firm for sales and marketing professionals at all levels across a wide range of industries.

Key Contact - Specialty:
Ms. Karen Dandridge, President & Chief Executive Officer - *Marketing, Sales*

Salary Minimum: $40,000

Functions: Sales & Mktg.

Industries: Generalist (All)

Bishop Partners
708 3rd Ave Rm 2200
New York, NY 10017-4214
(212) 986-3419
Fax: (212) 986-3350
Email: timoney@bishopnet.com
Web: www.bishoppartners.com

Summary: Our firm is dedicated to excellence in providing executive search consulting to the information, communications and entertainment industries, including both product and service companies in cable, broadcasting, publishing, entertainment, interactive media and related technology.

Key Contact - Specialty:
Ms. Susan Bishop, President - *Entertainment, Media, Publishing, Telecommunications*
Ms. Laura Timoney, Vice President - *Entertainment, Media, Publishing, Telecommunications*
Ms. Holly Haygood, Vice President - *Cable, New media, Publishing*

Salary Minimum: $150,000

Functions: Generalist (All), Management, Board Members, Senior Mgmt., Sales & Mktg., HR Mgmt., CFOs

Industries: Hospitality, Media, Advertising, Publishing, New Media, Broadcast, Film, Telecoms

Blackman Kallick Executive Search[†]
10 S Riverside Plz Ste 900
Chicago, IL 60606-3770
(312) 207-1040
Fax: (312) 207-0939
Web: www.bkadvice.com/search

Summary: Each assignment custom designed and researched for every client. Unique client mix, dedicated staff, outstanding references. Law firm, financial, mid and upper-management specialists. Several clients retained on annual partnership basis.

Key Contact - Specialty:
Mr. Gary M. Wolfson, Managing Partner - *Financial, Legal, Management, Manufacturing, Marketing*
Ms. Kate Augustine, Senior Associate - *Legal, Legal (Attorneys)*

Salary Minimum: $50,000

Functions: Generalist (All)

Industries: Generalist (All), Legal, Accounting

Blackshaw, Olmstead, Lynch & Koenig
3414 Peachtree Rd NE Ste 730
Atlanta, GA 30326-1166
(404) 261-7770
Fax: (404) 261-4469
Email: resumes@bolksearch.com
Web: www.bolksearch.com

Summary: We are a retained only generalist firm, specializing in senior level management.

Key Contact - Specialty:
Mr. Brian Blackshaw, Partner
Mr. George T. Olmstead, Partner - *Non-profit, Organizational development, Product management/development, Senior management, Strategic planning*
Mr. Joel S. Koenig, Partner
Ms. Lisa Shalet, Vice President, Research

Ms. Rhonda Morris, Vice President, Operations
Mr. Mart Kilpatrick, Researcher - *Finance, Franchising, Human resources, International, MBAs*

Salary Minimum: $150,000

Functions: Generalist (All), Board Members, Senior Mgmt.

Industries: Generalist (All)

Branches:
6303 Owensmouth Ave Fl 11
Woodland Hills, CA 91367-2263
(818) 996-5323
Fax: (818) 996-6845
Email: wtsai@leaderscapital.com
Key Contact - Specialty:
Mr. William Tsai, Partner

99 Harbor Rd
Southport, CT 06890-1316
(203) 256-3545
Fax: (203) 256-3537
Key Contact - Specialty:
Mr. John P. Lynch, III, Partner

500 N Michigan Ave Ste 300
Chicago, IL 60611-3775
(312) 924-1300
Key Contact - Specialty:
Mr. Gary Kreutz, Partner

Blair & Company LLC
2 Sound View Dr Ste 100
Greenwich, CT 06830-6471
(203) 661-8790
(800) 247-7750
Fax: (203) 622-0321
Email: gblair@blairandcompany.com
Web: www.blairandcompany.com

Summary: We help pharmaceutical and biotech companies to recruit the highly qualified senior R&D executives needed to implement major strategic initiatives and changes in regulatory requirements.

Key Contact - Specialty:
Ms Gail F. Blair, President

Salary Minimum: $150,000

Functions: Middle Mgmt., R&D

Industries: Drugs Mfg., Biotech/Life Sciences

Blake/Hansen & Schmidt Ltd
(an alliance partner of HansenGroup Ltd)
5514 Ridgeway Ct
Westlake Village, CA 91362-5266
(818) 879-1192
Email: jeri@blakehansenschmidt.com
Web: www.blakehansenschmidt.com

Summary: We specializes in the packaging and plastics industries and focuses on recruiting mid and senior-level managers, corporate officers and board members.

Key Contact - Specialty:
Ms. Jeri E. Schmidt, President

Salary Minimum: $65,000

Functions: Generalist (All)

Industries: Plastics, Rubber, Packaging

J Blakslee International Ltd
336 Bon Air Shopping Ctr Ste 369
Greenbrae, CA 94904-3017
(415) 389-7300
Fax: (415) 389-7302
Email: resumes@jblakslee.com

Summary: Senior-level retained executive search to the pharmaceutical, bio-technology and medical device/instrument industry.

Key Contact - Specialty:
Mr. Jan H. Blakslee, President - *Biotechnology, Pharmaceutical*

Salary Minimum: $150,000

Functions: Generalist (All), Board Members, Senior Mgmt., Product Dev., Mktg. Mgmt., CFOs, R&D

Industries: Drugs Mfg., Medical Devices, Biotech/Life Sciences

Blaney Executive Search

9 Damonmill Sq Ste 2E
Concord, MA 01742-2842
(978) 371-2192
(978) 371-2193
Email: jblaney@blaneyinc.com
Web: www.blaneyinc.com

Summary: Firm specializing in the placement of key individuals in high-technology organizations involved in the computer hardware, software and networking/communications and energy & fuel cell fields. We offer our clients a highly-professional, customized approach to the search process, which results in filling the position with the best possible candidate within a very reasonable time frame.

Key Contact - Specialty:
Mr. John A. Blaney, President - *CEOs, COOs*

Salary Minimum: $150,000

Functions: Senior Mgmt., Sales & Mktg., Mktg. Research, Mktg. Mgmt., Sales Mgmt., CFOs, IT, MIS Mgmt., Engineering

Industries: Generalist (All), Energy, Utilities, Manufacturing, Computer Equip., Test, Measure Equip., Semiconductors, Finance, Services, Non-profits, Mgmt. Consulting, HR Services, Engineering Svcs., Media, Advertising, Communications, Telecoms, Telephony, Digital, Wireless, Network Infrastructure, Environmental Svcs., Software, Industry Specific SW, Security SW, Biotech/Life Sciences, Healthcare

Paula Blank International

520 S El Camino Real Ste 342
San Mateo, CA 94402-1716
(650) 685-6855
Fax: (650) 685-0671
Email: pbint@paulablankinternational.com
Web: www.paulablankinternational.com

Summary: Our firm is a global executive search firm representing emerging and established life science companies in their recruitment of senior management. We have supported the growth of the biotechnology, pharmaceutical and medical device industries.

Key Contact - Specialty:
Ms. Paula Blank, Principal - *Biomedical, Pharmaceutical*
Ms. Annette Pfister, Alliance Partner
Mr. Nick Maczkov, Alliance Partner
Mr. Jerry Beers, Alliance Partners

Salary Minimum: $175,000

Functions: Generalist (All), Board Members, Senior Mgmt., Product Dev., Physicians, Mktg. Mgmt., CFOs, R&D

Industries: Drugs Mfg., Medical Devices, Invest. Banking, Venture Cap., Biotech/Life Sciences, Healthcare

Blanton & Company†

PO Box 43829
Birmingham, AL 35243-0829
(205) 967-5208
Fax: (205) 967-8020
Email: tblanton@blantonco.com

Summary: We are specialists in all disciplines in the biotechnology, paper, industrial process control, medical equipment, semiconductors, computers, telecom and pharmaceutical industries.

Key Contact - Specialty:
Mr. Thomas Blanton, President, Operations
Ms. Julia Blanton, Recruiter, Sales

Salary Minimum: $75,000

Functions: Generalist (All)

Industries: Paper, Chemicals, Drugs Mfg., Medical Devices, Computer Equip., Test, Measure Equip., Electronic, Elec. Components, Pharm Svcs., Telecoms, Software

David Blevins & Associates Inc

(also known as Family Vintners LLC)
2261 Market St Ste 105
San Francisco, CA 94114-1600
(707) 495-3714
Email: daveblevins@earthlink.net

Summary: We are an executive search and recruiting firm serving the wine and luxury beverage industries. We have targeted search for all positions and disciplines in the industry. Clients include Fortune 500 companies to small emerging entities. We have programs for all budgets, off-sight HR for small companies and offer all HR functions and programs. We also offer development of private placement funding for new and existing winery ventures, strategic branding and planning.

Key Contact - Specialty:
Mr. David C. Blevins, Chief Executive Officer & President

Salary Minimum: $40,000

Functions: Sales & Mktg., Specialized Svcs.

Industries: Food, Bev., Tobacco

Blumenthal-Hart Ltd

53 W Jackson Blvd Ste 1307
Chicago, IL 60604-3558
(312) 663-0090
Fax: (312) 663-0405
Email: resumes@blumenthal-hart.com
Web: www.blumenthal-hart.com

Summary: Our primary focus is academic institutions, non-profit organizations, associations and foundations. We concentrate on searches that cross most functional areas. We not only determine the skills, experience, education, style and other characteristics the ideal candidate needs to be successful, but we are thorough in our candidate evaluations. Our firm provides executive talent that fits.

Key Contact - Specialty:
Ms. Joan H. Blumenthal, President - *Associations, Education, Education (Higher), Non-profit, Philanthropy*
Ms. Linda Mesa, Senior Associate - *Associations, Education (Higher), Facilities engineering, Non-profit, Philanthropy*

Salary Minimum: $100,000

Functions: Generalist (All), Management, Admin. Svcs., Sales & Mktg.

Industries: Generalist (All), Services, Non-profits, Higher Ed., Hospitals

Board Search Partners LLC

700 Larkspur Landing Cir Ste 199
Larkspur, CA 94939-1754
(415) 462-8100
Fax: (415) 462-8101
Email: ann@boardsearchpartners.com
Web: www.boardsearchpartners.com

Summary: Board of directors search - We recruit new outside directors with exactly the right skills for the boards of public and private high-technology companies.

Key Contact - Specialty:
Ms. Ann Peckenpaugh, President

Functions: Board Members

Industries: Computer Equip., Consumer Elect., Electronic, Elec. Components, Semiconductors, Communications, Telecoms, Wireless, Software, Database SW

Boardroom Consultants

530 5th Ave Fl 21
New York, NY 10036-5106
(212) 328-0440
Fax: (212) 328-0441
Email: info@boardroomconsultants.com
Web: www.boardroomconsultants.com

Summary: We are a generalist firm, which recruits senior-level management for all industries. In addition, we specialize in the recruitment of corporate board directors and advisory board members.

Key Contact - Specialty:
Mr. Roger M. Kenny, Managing Partner - *Healthcare, High technology*
Mr. Peter A. Kindler, Co-Founder & Partner - *Finance*
Mr. Peter W. Eldredge, Partner - *Media, Publishing, Telecommunications*
Ms. Sarah Stewart, Partner
Mr. John Ingram, Partner
Mr. George Fleck, Consultant
Mr. Glynn Kenny, Consultant & Director of Information

Salary Minimum: $200,000

Functions: Generalist (All), Board Members, Senior Mgmt., CFOs, MIS Mgmt., Engineering, Mgmt. Consultants

Industries: Generalist (All), Motor Vehicles, Finance, Mgmt. Consulting, Media, Healthcare

BoardWalk Consulting LLC

127 Peachtree St NE Ste 200
Atlanta, GA 30303-1800
(404) 262-7392
Fax: (404) 795-0855
Email: info@boardwalkconsulting.com
Web: www.boardwalkconsulting.com

Summary: We provide executive search and board enhancement services to nonprofits, foundations and the institutions that champion them.

Key Contact - Specialty:
Mr. Sam Pettway, Founding Director - *Boards of Directors, C-level, Diversity, Non-profit, Public sector*
Ms. Kim E. Anderson, Director - *Boards of Directors, Diversity, Healthcare, Non-profit, Social work*
Ms. Margaret C. Reiser, Director
Ms. LaDawna Reynolds, Senior Administrative Manager
Mr. Kelly Lee, Manager, Research
Ms. Cynthia Gentry, Research Associate - *Boards of Directors, Non-profit, Public sector, Social work, Strategic planning*

Salary Minimum: $100,000

Functions: Management, Board Members, Senior Mgmt.

Industries: Non-profits, K-12 Ed., Higher Ed., Hospitals

Paul Bodner & Associates Inc

1808 Taos Estates St
Las Vegas, NV 89128-8259
(702) 386-9007
Fax: (702) 386-9016
Email: pbodner@lvcm.com

Summary: Our mission is to find that unique person who has the talent and expertise required by our client, but who also matches their values and culture.

Key Contact - Specialty:
Mr. Paul Bodner, President

Salary Minimum: $60,000

Functions: Generalist (All), Senior Mgmt., Middle Mgmt., Physicians, Sales Mgmt.

Industries: PSA/ASP, K-12 Ed., Healthcare, Hospitals, Long-term/Home Care

Boettcher Associates

120 Bishops Way Ste 126
Brookfield, WI 53005-6214
(262) 782-2205

Summary: We are a generalist executive search firm in all functions in all industries and management consulting in HR areas including outplacement.

Key Contact - Specialty:
Mr. Jack W. Boettcher, President

Salary Minimum: $50,000

Functions: Generalist (All), Management, Mfg., Materials, Sales & Mktg., HR Mgmt., Finance

Industries: Generalist (All), Metal Products, Machine, Appliance, Transportation, HR Services, Software

The Boland Group Inc

207 Elpin Dr E Ste 100
Catonsville, MD 21228-4800
(410) 788-8100
Fax: (410) 788-0778
Email: ann@bolandgroup.com
Web: www.bolandgroup.com

Summary: Performance based retained search firm (portion of fees earned at key milestones) for 4 information intensive industries (IT, life sciences, financial services, professional services) and 4 information sensitive functions (senior execs/GMs, financial officers, technology officers, sales/marketing execs). 100% percent request for repeat business track record on all fully retained searches.

Key Contact - Specialty:
Ms. Ann Boland, President
Mr. Joseph Boland, JD, Chief Operating and Financial Officer - *Computers, Consulting, Engineering, General management, Managed care*

Functions: Management, Senior Mgmt., Middle Mgmt., Sales & Mktg., HR Mgmt., Finance, CFOs, IT, Specialized Svcs., Mgmt. Consultants

Industries: Generalist (All), Manufacturing, Finance, Services, Communications, Insurance, Property/Facility Mgmt., Software, Biotech/Life Sciences, Healthcare

Bonell Ryan Inc

444 Madison Ave Ste 3202
New York, NY 10022-6923
(212) 754-0700
Fax: (702) 995-9935
Email: info@bonellryan.com
Web: www.bonellryan.com

Summary: We are an executive search in financial services, payment systems, eCommerce, and marketing.

Key Contact - Specialty:
Ms. Debra Ryan, President

Salary Minimum: $150,000

Functions: Management, Senior Mgmt., Sales & Mktg., Mktg. Research, Mktg. Mgmt., Sales Mgmt., Direct Mktg., Finance, CFOs, Credit

Industries: Banking, Venture Cap., New Media, Telecoms

Bonnell Associates Ltd

1 Canterbury Grn
Stamford, CT 06901-2032
(203) 319-7214
Fax: (203) 319-7219
Email: info@bonnellassociates.com
Web: www.bonnellassociates.com

Summary: Retained executive search firm offering focus on organizations which are in turnaround, startup and dynamic growth environments. Industry experience includes concentration in insurance and financial services, education and publishing, technology, manufacturing and non-profit.

Key Contact - Specialty:
Mr. William R. Bonnell, President - *Finance, Financial services, Healthcare, Managed care*
Ms. Linda Buggy, Senior Associate
Mr. Bruce Shulan, Managing Director

Salary Minimum: $150,000

Functions: Generalist (All)

Industries: Finance, Services, Publishing, New Media, Telecoms, Insurance, Software, Biotech/Life Sciences, Healthcare

The Bonner Group

PO Box 15
Long Valley, NJ 07853-0015
(908) 876-5200
Fax: (908) 876-9275
Email: bonnergroup@bonnergroup.com

Summary: Retained executive search services for senior-level management, technical and professional positions in the pharmaceutical and bio-technology industries.

Key Contact - Specialty:
Mr. Bernard J. Bonner, President

Salary Minimum: $100,000

Functions: Generalist (All), Senior Mgmt., Product Dev., Quality

Industries: Chemicals, Drugs Mfg., Medical Devices, Biotech/Life Sciences

Boone-Scaturro Associates Inc†

1122 Cambridge Sq Ste A
Alpharetta, GA 30004-1858
(770) 740-9737
(800) 749-1884
Fax: (770) 475-5055
Email: mes@boone-scaturro.com
Web: www.boone-scaturro.com

Summary: We are a physician search firm serving the hybrid and retained search. Full search or

choose from array of services. Guaranteed to exceed expectations.

Key Contact - Specialty:
Ms. Mary Ellen Scaturro, President & Chief Executive Officer - *Executives, Physicians*
Mr. Charles C. Boone, Chairman of the Board
Mr. Leonard Scaturro, Secretary & Treasurer
Ms. Vaughn Armstrong, Research Associate
Ms. Mindy Kelchner, Search Consultant - *Healthcare, Physicians*

Salary Minimum: $55,000

Functions: Healthcare, Physicians

Industries: Healthcare, Hospitals

The Borton Wallace Company

PO Box 17849
Asheville, NC 28816-7849
(828) 258-1831
Fax: (828) 251-0989
Email: info@bortonwallace.com
Web: www.bortonwallace.com

Summary: We help select clients build strong organizations. Our founding principals foster longstanding partnerships, lead clients to hire for superior performance and promote strategic recruitment. We continue to identify and adopt new pathways to create value.

Key Contact - Specialty:
Mr. Murray B. Parker, President
Ms. Kitty Reusch, Director, Web & Research
Ms. Claudia Harrelson, Executive Admin & Corp Secretary

Salary Minimum: $75,000

Functions: Generalist (All), Board Members

Industries: Chemicals, Soap, Perf., Cosmtcs., Drugs Mfg., Medical Devices, Plastics, Rubber, Consumer Goods, Compliance, Biotech/Life Sciences

Bosch & Associates LLC

PO Box 1030
Greens Farms, CT 06838-1030
(203) 255-8700
Fax: (203) 259-4959
Email: human.resources@boschllc.com
Web: www.boschllc.com

Summary: Our clients' surveys repeatedly tell us that we are the best search firm they've used. Our placement retention rates are some of the best in the search industry. We subscribe to a proven executive search methodology, consistently delivering executives of superior performance. We are extremely well networked in our chosen industries and functional areas.

Key Contact - Specialty:
Mr. Eric E. Bosch, President - *Finance, General management, Human resources, Marketing, Sales*
Mr. Brian Gardner - *Marketing, Public relations, Risk management*
Ms. Diane Bosch, Vice President - *General management, Market research, Strategic planning*
Ms. Patricia A. Spodnick - *Finance, Human resources, Sales*
Mr. Robert Beres - *Competitive intelligence, Finance, General management, Marketing*
Ms. Amy J. Matthews - *Business development, Consumer, Consumer (Packaged Goods), Diversity, Marketing*

Salary Minimum: $80,000

Functions: Management, Product Dev., Sales & Mktg., HR Mgmt., Finance, Risk Mgmt., Mgmt. Consultants, Minorities/Diversity, Security Personnel, Int'l.

Email your resume to a targeted list of recruiters now at www.ExecutiveAgent.com/DER07

Industries: Generalist (All), Food, Bev., Tobacco, Drugs Mfg., Computer Equip., Consumer Elect., Finance, Pharm Svcs., Equip Svcs., Mgmt. Consulting, HR Services, Advertising, Publishing, New Media, Communications, Telecoms, Insurance, Software, Non-Classifiable

Bosland Gray Associates

2001 US Highway 46 Ste 310
Parsippany, NJ 07054-1315
(973) 402-4964
Email: agray@boslandgray.com

Summary: Fee fixed at beginning of search; proven expertise within technical and specialized areas; each assignment commands the direct and personal attention of one of the firm's principals.

Key Contact - Specialty:
Mr. Andrew Gray, Managing Director
Mr. Richard Bosland, Managing Director

Salary Minimum: $80,000

Functions: Generalist (All)

Industries: Generalist (All), Manufacturing, Chemicals, Drugs Mfg., Consumer Elect., Test, Measure Equip., Misc. Mfg., Retail, Mgmt. Consulting, Biotech/Life Sciences

Boston Search†

224 Clarendon St Ste 41
Boston, MA 02116-3793
(617) 266-4333
Fax: (781) 735-0562
Email: rprotsik@bostonsearchgroup.com
Web: www.bostonsearchgroup.com

Summary: Our firm is a national leader in retained executive search for emerging companies. We specialize in providing leaders for technology-driven startups. Our principals have been engaged to fill more than 100 senior-management positions at the VP level and above, for a slate of clients that includes venture capitalists and private investors, their portfolio companies and public companies with a strong commitment to entrepreneurship and technology.

Key Contact - Specialty:
Mr. Ralph Protsik, Co-Founder & Managing Director - *Education, Information service, Media, Publishing, Technology*
Mr. Clark Waterfall, Co-Founder & Managing Director - *Biotechnology, Computers (Software), Technology*

Salary Minimum: $120,000

Functions: Board Members, Senior Mgmt.

Industries: Generalist (All), Venture Cap., E-commerce, IT Implementation, K-12 Ed., Higher Ed., New Media, Telecoms, Wireless, Software, Biotech/Life Sciences

The Boulware Group Inc

625 N Michigan Ave Ste 422
Chicago, IL 60611-3172
(312) 322-0088
Email: info@boulwareinc.com
Web: www.boulwareinc.com

Summary: A retained executive search firm, we find visionary leaders who shape our clients' futures and have recruited leadership for a range of organizations in public, private, and non-profit sectors. We are committed to developing diverse candidate pools for every search and engage our clients in learning about candidates who are different.

Key Contact - Specialty:
Ms. Christine Boulware, Managing Director - *C-level, Diversity, Legal, Non-profit, Public sector*

Mr. Ed Letchinger, Manager, Business
Mr. Dan Nevez, Director, Research
Ms. Anna Koivisto, Candidate Relations

Salary Minimum: $120,000

Functions: Management, Senior Mgmt., Minorities/Diversity, Non-profits, Environmentalists, Health & Safety, Legal

Industries: Energy, Utilities, Banking, Non-profits, Legal, HR Services, Higher Ed., Women's

Bowman & Associates†

1660 S Amphlett Blvd Ste 245
San Mateo, CA 94402-2508
(650) 573-0188
Fax: (650) 573-8209
Email: contact@bowmansearch.com
Web: www.bowmansearch.com

Summary: Staffed by senior professionals completing mid and senior-level management assignments exclusively for hospitality and leisure industry employers. Primarily retained assignments.

Key Contact - Specialty:
Mr. Daniel P. Bowman, Managing Partner - *Hospitality*
Mr. Alfred J. Domenico, Executive Vice President
Mr. Robert J. Dahl, Vice President - *Hospitality, Hotels*
Mr. Robert H. Rodgers, Recruiter - *Hospitality*

Salary Minimum: $80,000

Functions: Generalist (All)

Industries: Hospitality

Bowman & Associates Inc

PO Box 450149
Atlanta, GA 31145-0149
(404) 329-9314
Fax: (404) 320-3114
Email: admin@bowmanassociates.com
Web: www.bowmanassociates.com

Summary: Specialize in venture-funded start-up companies in medical devices, diagnostics and biotechnology.

Key Contact - Specialty:
Ms. Mary Bowman, President - *Biotechnology, Diagnostics, Start-up companies*

Salary Minimum: $150,000

Functions: Board Members, Senior Mgmt.

Industries: Medical Devices

Boyce Cunnane Inc

PO Box 19064
Baltimore, MD 21284-9064
(410) 583-5511
Email: bc@cunnane.com
Web: www.cunnane.com

Summary: We specialize exclusively in recruiting mid and upper-level tax professionals for corporations, CPA firms and law firms. Searches have targeted lawyers, accountants and economists in all tax specialties: compliance, research and planning, IRS audit, employee benefits, personal financial planning, state and local, international, (including transfer pricing, customs, international assignment tax services and multi-lingual tax consultants).

Key Contact - Specialty:
Mr. William Cunnane - *Tax*

Salary Minimum: $100,000

Functions: Taxes

Industries: Generalist (All)

Boyden

50 Broadway
Hawthorne, NY 10532-1245
(914) 747-0093
Fax: (914) 747-0108
Web: www.boyden.com

Summary: Our firm is a pioneering executive search firm that recruits at the senior management and director level across a broad range of specialty practices and multiple levels of functional expertise. Our firm is committed to continued growth in its industry, while providing the benefit of adaptation by local offices to meet individual needs and requirements.

Key Contact - Specialty:
Mr. Chris Clarke, President
Ms. Theresa Flynn, Manager, Group Marketing - *Marketing*
Mr. John Papagni, Quality Assurance & Training Manager - *Quality, Training*
Ms. Lydia Reitano, Financial Controller - *Accounting*

Salary Minimum: $100,000

Functions: Generalist (All), Board Members, Senior Mgmt., Mfg., Distribution, HR Mgmt., CFOs, Risk Mgmt., IT, Non-profits

Industries: Generalist (All), Agri., Forestry, Mining, Energy, Utilities, Construction, Manufacturing, Drugs Mfg., Consumer Goods, Transportation, Finance, Mgmt. Consulting, HR Services, IT Implementation, Hospitality, Government, Aerospace, Packaging

Branches:
248 E Vera Ln
Tempe, AZ 85284-4034
(480) 705-7269
Email: reinsel@boyden.com
Key Contact - Specialty:
Mr. Ray Einsel, Managing Director - *Banking (Corporate, Retail), Boards of Directors, Financial services, Real estate*

275 Battery St Ste 420
San Francisco, CA 94111-3358
(415) 981-7900
Fax: (415) 981-0644
Email: boydensf@boyden.com
Key Contact - Specialty:
Mr. Frederick J. Greene, Managing Director - *Advertising, Boards of Directors, Consumer (Durables, Packaged Goods), Non-profit*
Mr. Robert Concannon, II, Managing Director - *.com, Communications, Networking, Systems, Technology*
Mr. Richard Kampmann, Managing Director - *Construction, Financial services, Leasing, Mergers & acquisitions, Risk management*
Ms. Meredith Moore, Managing Director - *Agriculture, Consumer (Products), Human resources, Non-profit, Transportation*
Mr. Ross Blanchard, Managing Director - *Consumer (Products), Financial services, Human resources, Life Sciences, Management consulting*
Mr. Roger Norton, Managing Director - *Consumer, Government, Human resources, Life Sciences*

1200 G St NW Ste 800
Washington, DC 20005-6705
(202) 331-3390
Email: baltimore-washington@boyden.com
Key Contact - Specialty:
Mr. Timothy McNamara, Managing Director - *Aviation, Financial services, Government, Risk management*

2859 Paces Ferry Rd SE Ste 2100
Atlanta, GA 30339-5767
(770) 955-9550
Fax: (770) 980-9367
Email: atlanta@boyden.com
Key Contact - Specialty:
Mr. Jeff McKinnis, Managing Director - *Boards of Directors, Communications, Financial services, Technology, Venture capital*
Mr. Charles Chalk, Managing Director - *Aviation, Boards of Directors, Communications, Industrial, Pharmaceutical*
Mr. Dave Gallagher, Managing Director - *Boards of Directors, Consumer (Durables,Packaged Goods,Products), Food & beverage*
Mr. Dan Grassi, Managing Director - *Boards of Directors, Communications, Financial services, Management consulting, Technology*

180 N Stetson Ave Ste 2500
Chicago, IL 60601-6777
(312) 565-1300
Fax: (312) 565-2117
Email: chicago@boyden.com
Key Contact - Specialty:
Mr. Richard A. McCallister, Managing Director - *Biotechnology, Boards of Directors, Financial services, Industrial, Professional services*
Ms. Trina D. Gordon, Managing Director - *Consumer (Products), Human resources, Industrial, Life Sciences, Technology*
Mr. John S. Gude, Managing Director - *Biotechnology, Diversity, Food & beverage, Industrial, Technology*
Mr. Kellogg Fairbank, Managing Director - *Chemical, Education, Financial services, Non-profit, Outsourcing*
Ms. Trisha Hutchison, Principal - *Consumer (Products), Industrial, Non-profit*

217 E Redwood St Ste 1600
Baltimore, MD 21202-3363
(410) 625-3800
Fax: (410) 625-3801
Email: baltimore-washington@boyden.com
Key Contact - Specialty:
Mr. Daniel Hobbs, Principal - *Consumer (Durables,Packaged Goods), Government, Human resources, Industrial*
Mr. Joseph Kirby, Principal - *Aviation, Consumer (Products), Industrial, Technology, Transportation*
Mr. Douglas Norton, Managing Director - *Industrial, Life Sciences, Technology*

344 N Old Woodward Ave Ste 304
Birmingham, MI 48009-5351
(248) 258-0616
Fax: (248) 258-2823
Email: det.info@boyden.com
Key Contact - Specialty:
Mr. Dennis B. Sullivan, Managing Director - *Consumer (Products), Education, Financial services, Industrial, Non-profit*
Mr. Jeffrey A. Evans, Managing Director - *Diversity, Education, Human resources, Non-profit*
Mr. Douglas R. Allen, Managing Director - *Consumer (Durables), Diversity, Financial services, Industrial, Technology*
Ms. Cynthia F. Kinney, Managing Director - *Education, Non-profit, Outsourcing, Technology*
Mr. Damian Zikakis, Managing Director - *Automotive, Non-profit, Professional services*

10 S 5th St Ste 700
Lumber Exchange Bldg
Minneapolis, MN 55402-1033
(612) 338-3335
Fax: (612) 305-4353
Email: amyers@boyden.com

Key Contact - Specialty:
Ms. Ann Myers, Managing Director - *Consumer (Products), Financial services, Industrial, Life Sciences, Technology*

1390 Timberlake Manor Pkwy Ste 260
Chesterfield, MO 63017-6041
(636) 519-7400
Fax: (636) 519-7410
Email: stlouis@boyden.com
Key Contact - Specialty:
Mr. George Zamborsky, Managing Director - *Consumer (Products), Human resources, Industrial, Life Sciences, Non-profit*

33 Union Pl Ste 3
Summit, NJ 07901-3650
(908) 598-0400
Fax: (908) 598-0331
Email: summit@boyden.com
Key Contact - Specialty:
Mr. Carlyle Newell, Managing Director - *Chemical, Food & beverage, Manufacturing, Professional services, Technology*
Mr. Jeffrey Stark, Managing Director - *Chemical, Government, Manufacturing*

360 Lexington Ave Ste 1300
New York, NY 10017-6502
(212) 949-9400
Fax: (212) 949-5905
Email: jrice@boyden.com
Key Contact - Specialty:
Ms. Jeanne Branthover, Managing Director - *Consumer (Products), Financial services, Human resources, Technology*
Mr. Richard Lipstein, Managing Director - *Financial services*

1000 Gamma Dr Ste 600
Pittsburgh, PA 15238-2928
(412) 756-1000
Fax: (412) 756-1010
Email: pittsburgh@boyden.com
Key Contact - Specialty:
Mr. Thomas T. Flannery, Managing Director - *Boards of Directors, Financial services, Industrial, International, Life Sciences*
Mr. E. Wade Close, Jr., Managing Director - *Automotive, Manufacturing, Metals*
Mr. John Howard, Managing Director - *Construction, Manufacturing, Metals, Mining*
Mr. William Coleman, Jr., Managing Director - *Consumer (Packaged Goods,Products)*
Mr. John Hamilton, Principal - *Human resources, Life Sciences*

5847 San Felipe St Ste 3940
Houston, TX 77057-3008
(713) 655-0123
Fax: (713) 655-0107
Email: info@boydenhou.com
Key Contact - Specialty:
Mr. Thomas C. Zay, Jr., Managing Director - *Chemical, Consumer (Packaged Goods), Education, Energy, Food & beverage*
Mr. James N.J. Hertlein, Managing Director - *Boards of Directors, Energy, Human resources, Industrial, Technology*
Mr. Charlie Rhoads, Managing Director - *Chemical, Non-profit*
Ms. Cheryl Smith, Managing Director - *Energy, Human resources, Private equity, Utilities, Venture capital*

1060-144 4 Ave SW
SunLife Plaza 1
Calgary, AB T2P 3N4
Canada
(403) 237-6603
Fax: (403) 237-5551
Email: calgary@boyden.ca

Key Contact - Specialty:
Mr. Robert Travis, Managing Partner - *Consumer (Products), Energy, Technology, Transportation, Utilities*
Mr. Brent Shervey, Managing Partner - *Education, Non-profit, Professional services, Travel, Utilities*
Mr. Andy Sharman, Senior Associate - *Financial services*

700-110 Yonge St
Canada Trust Building
Toronto, ON M5C 1T4
Canada
(416) 640-1300
Fax: (416) 214-0147
Email: infotoronto@boyden.com
Key Contact - Specialty:
Ms. Sussannah Kelly, Managing Director
Mr. Michael McInerney, Managing Director
Dr. Louis Stokes, Managing Director - *Boards of Directors, Human resources, Management consulting, Professional services*
Mr. Philip Drouillard, Managing Director
Ms. Judy Hunter, Managing Director
Mr. Bill McNamee-Lamb, Managing Director

Boyle & Associates Retained Search Corp

PO Box 16658
Saint Paul, MN 55116-0658
(651) 223-5050
Fax: (651) 699-5378
Email: paul@talenthunt.com
Web: www.talenthunt.com

Summary: We specialize in finding and securing the best fit for your company's needs through a disciplined retained search process. We provide direct recruiting from an agreed upon list of source or target companies. We work for our client companies to draw the best of the doers to your firm.

Key Contact - Specialty:
Mr. Paul R. Boyle, President

Salary Minimum: $65,000

Functions: Generalist (All), Quality, Materials Plng., Distribution, Mktg. Mgmt., CFOs, Network Admin., Engineering

Industries: Generalist (All), Agri., Forestry, Mining, Construction, Manufacturing, Transportation, Services, Media

Boyle Ogata Bregman

17461 Derian Ave Ste 202
Irvine, CA 92614-5820
(949) 474-0115
Fax: (949) 474-2204
Email: mrb@bobsearch.com
Web: www.bobsearch.com

Summary: Using our performance-based search system, we recruit and place "A" players based on their ability to produce specific results critical to your company's success. We also feature organizational consulting, diversity recruiting, executive coaching and compensation analysis.

Key Contact - Specialty:
Mr. Michael Boyle, Principal - *Aerospace, High technology, Telecommunications, Venture capital*
Mr. Mark Bregman, MA Psych, Principal - *High technology, Manufacturing, Marketing, Organizational development, Sales*

Salary Minimum: $80,000

Functions: Management, Mfg., Materials, Sales & Mktg., HR Mgmt., Finance, R&D, Engineering, Specialized Svcs.

Industries: Construction, Manufacturing, Transportation, Wholesale, Services, Communications, Aerospace, Software, Biotech/Life Sciences

J Brad Herbeck Inc

3 W Hawthorn Pkwy Ste 265
Vernon Hills, IL 60061-1448
(847) 247-1400
Fax: (847) 247-1576
Email: brad@jbradherbeck.com
Web: www.jbradherbeck.com

Summary: We are a generalist firm representing all major industries.

Key Contact - Specialty:
Mr. J. Brad Herbeck, President

Salary Minimum: $150,000

Functions: Generalist (All)

Industries: Generalist (All)

The Bradbury Group

2112 Vizcaya Way Ste 200
Campbell, CA 95008-5662
(408) 377-5400
Fax: (408) 377-1112
Email: paul@ifindem.com
Web: www.thebradburygroup.net

Summary: We have a high track record of success clarifying and creating corporate culture and realistic position profiles, identifying, attracting & evaluating non-active candidates. Industries include: high-tech (hardware, software, Internet), semiconductor (ICs and capital equipment), bio-technology (medical devices, diagnostics, systems, healthcare and pharmaceuticals), telecom (networking and software) and engineering/environmental consulting firms.

Key Contact - Specialty:
Mr. Paul W. Bradbury, Jr., Managing Principal

Salary Minimum: $100,000

Functions: Management, Board Members, Admin. Svcs., Int'l.

Industries: Manufacturing, Medical Devices, Computer Equip., Consumer Elect., Test, Measure Equip., Robotics, Semiconductors, Venture Cap., Media, Communications, Telecoms, Environmental Svcs., Haz. Waste, Software, Biotech/Life Sciences

JT Brady & Associates[†]

10900 Perry Hwy # 12203
Wexford, PA 15090-8370
(724) 934-2228
Email: jtbrady@nauticom.net
Web: www.jtbrady.net

Summary: Created to provide a more cost effective, personalized and timely solution to address clients' recruiting needs. We offer a full-service comprehensive process custom tailored for each client.

Key Contact - Specialty:
Mr. Jack Brady, President - *Human resources, Marketing, Operations, Sales*

Salary Minimum: $60,000

Functions: Management, Sales & Mktg., Direct Mktg.

Industries: Generalist (All), Food, Bev., Tobacco, Paper, Printing, Drugs Mfg., Banking, Services, Advertising, Publishing, New Media, Broadcast, Film

Brady Associates International Inc

PO Box 1892
New York, NY 10021-0049
(212) 396-4950

Summary: Executive search consultant for the diversified utility and financial services industries.

Key Contact - Specialty:
Ms. Susan E. Harbers, President - *Energy, Financial services, Middle management, Senior management*

Salary Minimum: $100,000

Functions: Generalist (All), Management, Board Members, Senior Mgmt., Middle Mgmt., Sales & Mktg., IT

Industries: Generalist (All), Energy, Utilities

The Brand Company

(formerly known as The Brand Company Inc)
219 Driftwood Dr Unit J
Greenwood, SC 29649-9717
(864) 223-9857
Email: brandexec@earthlink.net

Summary: Responsive and personalized client focus on senior level searches for board directors, general management executives, functional heads and critical technology specialists. Generalist practice with particular experience in manufacturing, distribution and service businesses.

Key Contact - Specialty:
Mr. J. Brand Spangenberg, Chairman - *High technology, Marketing, Operations, Senior management, Technical*

Salary Minimum: $100,000

Functions: Senior Mgmt., Plant Mgmt., Mktg. Mgmt., Sales Mgmt., HR Mgmt., CFOs, Engineering

Industries: Energy, Utilities, Metal Products, Machine, Appliance, Misc. Mfg., Packaging

Brandywine Consulting Group

5 Great Valley Pkwy Ste 356
Malvern, PA 19355-1426
(610) 407-4600
(800) 555-1668
Fax: (610) 407-4605
Email: ann.sheara@brandywineconsult.com
Web: www.brandywineconsult.com

Summary: We are a broad-based practice with some specialization in chemical process, pulp & paper, packaging, pharmaceuticals, consumer products and healthcare. Senior-level retained assignments include behavioral-based interview design and psychological assessment.

Key Contact - Specialty:
Mr. Richard H. Beatty, President & Chief Executive Officer

Salary Minimum: $75,000

Functions: Generalist (All), Board Members, Senior Mgmt., Middle Mgmt., Production, Plant Mgmt., Healthcare, Mktg. Mgmt., Sales Mgmt.

Industries: Generalist (All), Paper, Drugs Mfg., Medical Devices, Pharm Svcs., Healthcare

Affiliates:
Brandywine Management Group
Berlin, MD

Brandywine Management Group

8 Drawbridge Rd
Berlin, MD 21811-1823
(410) 208-9791
Fax: (410) 208-9792

Summary: Retained search, consulting and outplacement firm engaged in technical, general and senior-level management practices.

Key Contact - Specialty:
Mr. Jeffrey A. Morse, President - *Healthcare, Technical*
Mr. Stewart Schwartz
Mr. F. William Gaw - *Technical*
Ms. Patty Grady

Salary Minimum: $55,000

Functions: Generalist (All), Senior Mgmt., Production, Plant Mgmt., Packaging, Healthcare, Sales & Mktg., HR Mgmt.

Industries: Generalist (All), Lumber, Furniture, Chemicals, Drugs Mfg., Metal Products, Misc. Mfg., Healthcare

Branches:
82 Pocono Rd
Mountain Lakes, NJ 07046-1650
(800) 860-8812
(973) 394-0018
Key Contact - Specialty:
Mrs. Sally Harrison

Brault & Associates Ltd

18417 Lanier Island Sq
Leesburg, VA 20176-3937
(703) 771-0200
Fax: (703) 771-0270
Email: jean-pierre@mindspring.com

Summary: We are an executive search firm specializing in the high-technology industry and intelligence community, IT and security, DoD and intelligence systems, systems engineering and integration, and Internet and network security.

Key Contact - Specialty:
Mr. Jean-Pierre Brault, President - *High technology*

Salary Minimum: $125,000

Functions: Senior Mgmt., IT, MIS Mgmt., Int'l.

Industries: Generalist (All), Non-profits, Mgmt. Consulting, Defense

The Bray Group[†]

354 Brush Hill Rd
Milton, MA 02186-1031
(617) 696-9594
Fax: (617) 696-9593
Email: rbray@thebraygroup.com
Web: www.thebraygroup.com

Summary: An executive search practice that focuses on serving financial services companies and non-profit organizations.

Key Contact - Specialty:
Mr. Bob Bray, Partner
Ms. Diane McGwin, Senior Vice President

Salary Minimum: $75,000

Functions: Generalist (All), Middle Mgmt., Finance

Industries: Generalist (All), Printing, Finance, Banking, Invest. Banking, Brokers, Venture Cap., Mutual/Hedge Funds, Misc. Financial, Non-profits, Logistics Svcs., Insurance

The Brazik Group LLC

1060 Borghese Ln Apt 1702
Naples, FL 34114-7881
(239) 394-2433
(239) 394-2433
Email: questions@brazikgroup.com
Web: www.brazikgroup.com

Summary: We are a retained executive search and consulting firm. We specialize in retail and wholesale with carefully selected consultants in marketing, operations and HR.

Key Contact - Specialty:
Mr. Charles Brazik, President

Salary Minimum: $70,000

Functions: Generalist (All), Board Members, Senior Mgmt., Production, Materials Plng., Nurses, HR Mgmt., CFOs, MIS Mgmt.

Industries: Generalist (All), Manufacturing, Metal Products, Misc. Mfg., Wholesale, Retail, HR Services, IT Implementation, Healthcare, Hospitals

The Brentwood Group Inc†

170 Kinnelon Rd Rm 7
Kinnelon, NJ 07405-2323
(973) 283-1000
Fax: (973) 283-1220
Email: info@thebrentwoodgroup.com
Web: www.thebrentwoodgroup.com

Summary: Our firm of nine professionals provides experience, consistency, quality and results. We are a cohesive team that understands, executes and actually fills your search.

Key Contact - Specialty:
Ms. Doris Banach-Osenni, President - *Direct marketing, Financial services, Management consulting, Publishing, Senior management*
Ms. Pat Pagana, Senior Manager - *Engineering, Financial services, Operations, Publishing*
Ms. Ivy Tessler, Senior Manager - *Consumer, Consumer (Products), Direct marketing, Financial services, Pharmaceutical*
Ms. Lori Micciche, Manager - *Design, Financial services, Operations, Retail*

Salary Minimum: $50,000

Functions: Generalist (All)

Industries: Food, Bev., Tobacco, Textiles, Apparel, Chemicals, Drugs Mfg., Banking, Mgmt. Consulting, HR Services, Insurance, Biotech/Life Sciences, Healthcare

The Brentwood Group Ltd

4949 Meadows Rd Ste 140
Lake Oswego, OR 97035-3156
(503) 697-8136
Fax: (503) 697-8161
Email: contact@brentwoodgroup.com
Web: www.brentwoodgroup.com

Summary: We are a results driven, client focused, retained executive search firm exclusively dedicated to serving high technology clients for their senior executive requirements working exclusively with founders, executive leadership, the venture capital community and corporations focused on building great technology companies.

Key Contact - Specialty:
Mr. Frank Moscow, President - *High technology, Senior management*

Salary Minimum: $100,000

Functions: Board Members, Senior Mgmt., Middle Mgmt., Product Dev., Sales & Mktg., Mktg. Mgmt., CFOs

Industries: Computer Equip., Consumer Elect., Test, Measure Equip., Electronic, Elec.

Components, Semiconductors, Venture Cap., Telecoms, Digital, Wireless, Network Infrastructure, Software

Brentwood International

9841 Airport Blvd Ste 420
Los Angeles, CA 90045-5416
(310) 338-5480
Fax: (310) 338-5484
Email: postmaster@brentwoodintl.com
Web: www.brentwoodintl.com

Summary: Exclusively executive search specializing in high-technology, aerospace, financial services, higher education, engineering, marketing and consumer products.

Key Contact - Specialty:
Mr. James E. Keenan, President
Ms. Seda Aksut, MA, CC, Partner - *Aerospace, High technology*
Mr. Kevin Keenan, Managing Consultant
Ms. Clare Finnigan Ellinger, Managing Consultant - *Advertising, Direct marketing, Marketing, New media*
Ms. Robyn Whittaker, Associate - *Marketing, Sales*
Ms. Linda Barr, Associate - *High technology*
Ms. Cynthia Jones, Managing Consultant - *Aerospace, High technology*
Mr. Ed Rardin, Consultant - *Manufacturing, Marketing*
Mr. Tom Simpson, Consultant
Mr. Philip Selvey, Consultant

Salary Minimum: $75,000

Functions: Generalist (All), Management, IT

Industries: Generalist (All), Services, Mgmt. Consulting, HR Services, IT Implementation, Digital, Wireless, Aerospace, Software, Security SW, System SW

Branches:
4147 Rowland Dr
Fairfield, CA 94533-9799
(707) 426-5424
Key Contact - Specialty:
Mr. Lawrence Broe

1928 Graham Ave Unit A
Redondo Beach, CA 90278-1921
(310) 940-1188
Fax: (310) 937-2957
Email: saksut@brentwoodintl.com
Key Contact - Specialty:
Ms. Samantha Sutherland

Briant Associates Inc

18-2 E Dundee Rd Ste 202
Barrington, IL 60010-5274
(847) 382-5725
Fax: (847) 382-7265
Email: recruiter@briantassociates.com
Web: www.briantassociates.com

Summary: We are a boutique firm specializing in consumer package goods and durable goods (building products, hardware, house wares, and office products), and food industries. Partners are fully engaged in each step of the recruitment process. We utilize consultative methodologies, conducting searches for senior sales, marketing, public relations, manufacturing, engineering, supply chain/logistics, and general management positions.

Key Contact - Specialty:
Ms. Larissa Klavins, Partner - *Consumer (Durables,Packaged Goods), Hardware, Housewares*
Mr. Rick Bingham, Partner - *Bakery, Consumer, Dairy, Food, Food service*

Salary Minimum: $85,000

Functions: Generalist (All), Management, Senior Mgmt., Mfg., Plant Mgmt., Materials, Distribution, Sales & Mktg., PR, Engineering

Industries: Manufacturing, Food, Bev., Tobacco, Soap, Perf., Cosmtcs., Paints, Petro. Products, Metal Products, Machine, Appliance, Misc. Mfg., Electronic, Elec. Components, Consumer Goods, HR Services, Inst./Industrial Food Svc., Communications, Packaging

BrickWork Consulting Inc

230 W 13th St
New York, NY 10011-7746
(212) 741-9669
Fax: (212) 741-9681
Email: info@bwcon.com
Web: www.bwcon.com

Summary: Woman-owned boutique strategic talent management firm specializing in retained forward and reverse searches, recruiting and career transitional services. Specializing in financial services, banking, investment banking, diversity, asset management, legal, management consulting, venture capital, marketing, information security and technology. Proprietary search software and proprietary database of more than 40,000 candidates.

Key Contact - Specialty:
Ms. Christine Debany, President
Mr. Ralph J. Westerhoff, Executive Vice President
Ms. Dorothy B. Cunnigham, Chief Staff Psychologist
Ms. Olivia DeBunny, Director, Facilities

Functions: Management, Senior Mgmt., Middle Mgmt., Mktg. Mgmt., HR Mgmt., Staffing, Finance, Cash Mgmt., Minorities/Diversity, Legal

Industries: Finance, Banking, Invest. Banking, Brokers, Venture Cap., Mutual/Hedge Funds, Mgmt. Consulting, HR Services, IT Implementation, Communications, Call Centers, Insurance, Software

BridgeGate LLC

17701 Cowan Ste 240
Irvine, CA 92614-6840
(949) 553-9200
Email: info@bridgegate.com
Web: www.bridgegate.com

Summary: We build high performance leadership teams for emerging and established companies across all industries. Internally, we support multiple functional specialties in order to provide a complete executive recruitment solution to our clients.

Key Contact - Specialty:
Mr. Kevin Rosenberg, Managing Partner - *CIOs, Controllers, Executives, General management, Information Technology*
Mr. Joel May, Partner - *Computers (Sales), Senior management, Start-up companies, Technology, Venture capital*
Mr. John DiSanto, Partner - *Computers (Sales), Emerging growth, High technology, Senior management, Start-up companies*
Mr. Jim Beaky, Director - *Computers (Hardware,Networking,Sales,Software), Field engineering*
Mr. Steve Brown, Director - *Computers (Software), Engineering, Start-up companies, Technology, Venture capital*
Mr. Josh Goodman, Director - *Accounting, CFOs, Finance, Human resources, Operations*

Salary Minimum: $100,000

Email your resume to a targeted list of recruiters now at www.ExecutiveAgent.com/DER07

Functions: Generalist (All), Management, Senior Mgmt., Middle Mgmt., Sales & Mktg., HR Mgmt., Finance, IT, Mgmt. Consultants

Industries: Generalist (All), Services, E-commerce, IT Implementation, Communications, Software

Bridgestar

(an initiative of the Bridgespan Group)
535 Boylston St Fl 10
Boston, MA 02116
(617) 572-2833
Email: info@bridgestar.org
Web: www.bridgestar.org

Summary: We are a nonprofit providing talent-matching services, content and tools to help nonprofits build strong leadership teams and individuals pursue career paths as nonprofit leaders.

Key Contact - Specialty:
Mr. Jeffrey L. Bradach, Co-Founder & Managing Partner
Ms. Janet Albert, Regional Director, Talent & Recruiting
Ms. Kathleen Yazbak-Chartier, Director, Talent and Recruiting

Functions: Non-profits

Industries: Non-profits

Brigham Hill Consultancy

2909 Cole Ave Ste 220
Dallas, TX 75204-1373
(214) 871-8700
Fax: (214) 871-6004
Email: brigham@brighamhill.com
Web: www.brighamhill.com

Summary: Our firm provides retained executive search and related management consulting services by combining the rigorous search protocols of the business world with sensitivity to the unique mission of not-for-profits.

Key Contact - Specialty:
Mr. L. Lincoln Eldredge, President
Ms. Deborah Tunnell, Consultant
Ms. Susana Rabel, Consultant

Salary Minimum: $90,000

Functions: Generalist (All), Non-profits

Industries: Generalist (All), Non-profits, Higher Ed.

Brill Neumann Associates Inc

312 Stuart St
Boston, MA 02116-5242
(617) 753-1800
Fax: (617) 753-9330
Email: liz@brillneumann.com
Web: www.brillneumann.com

Summary: We specialize in consulting and executive search for leading colleges and universities, economic and community development initiatives and health care organizations.

Key Contact - Specialty:
Mr. Nicholas S. Brill, President
Ms. Elizabeth A. Neumann, Vice President
Ms. Jackie Rosenthal, Recruiter
Mr. Branden F. Grimmett, Recruiter
Ms. Marsha Miller, Recruiter
Ms. Rebecca Kennedy, Recruiter
Ms. Ora Smith, Recruiter - *Engineering, Marketing*

Functions: Generalist (All)

Industries: Services, Non-profits, Higher Ed., Biotech/Life Sciences, Healthcare

The Brimeyer Group Inc

50 9th Ave S
Hopkins, MN 55343-6702
(952) 945-0246
Fax: (952) 945-0102
Email: brimgroup@aol.com
Web: www.brimgroup.com

Summary: We provide executive search for local government and non-profit clients. We provide management consulting services to select clients.

Key Contact - Specialty:
Mr. James Brimeyer, President - *Non-profit, Public sector*
Ms. Pam Wunderlich, Vice President - *Associations*

Salary Minimum: $50,000

Functions: Generalist (All), Engineering

Industries: Generalist (All), Hospitality, Government

Brindisi Search

10751 Falls Rd Ste 250
Lutherville, MD 21093-4552
(410) 339-7673
(410) 442-5887
Fax: (410) 823-0146
Email: tbrindisi@aol.com
Web: www.brindisisearch.com

Summary: We identify and secure results-focused: human resource, organization development, and change management leaders, for dynamic, progressive organizations. Our client driven search process emphasizes: cultural fit, talent, and leadership quotient. Our comprehensive approach produces outstanding results. Our clients are industry leaders.

Key Contact - Specialty:
Mr. Thomas J. Brindisi, President - *Change management, Human resources, Organizational development, Strategic planning*

Salary Minimum: $90,000

Functions: Senior Mgmt., Quality, Productivity, HR Mgmt., Benefits, Staffing, Training, e-HR, Pension/Ret. Planning, Mgmt. Consultants

Industries: Generalist (All)

Brooke Chase Associates Inc

1543 2nd St Ste 201
Sarasota, FL 34236-8541
(941) 358-3111
(877) 374-0039
Fax: (941) 358-3311
Email: jmcelmeel@brookechase.com
Web: www.brookechase.com

Summary: We are specialists in the recruitment of sales, marketing, manufacturing, operations & general management professionals within the building materials, homebuilders, lawn & garden, automotive and kitchen & bath industries.

Key Contact - Specialty:
Mr. Joseph J. McElmeel, Chairman & Chief Executive Officer - *General management, Marketing, Sales*
Mr. Richard Miller, Managing Director - *Engineering, Executives, Hardware, Home and building controls, HVAC*
Mr. Michael Roach, Executive Recruiter - *Building products, Production, Quality, Senior management, Six Sigma*

Salary Minimum: $50,000

Functions: Generalist (All), Senior Mgmt., Middle Mgmt., Plant Mgmt., Quality, Mktg. Research, Mktg. Mgmt., Sales Mgmt.

Industries: Generalist (All), Construction, Manufacturing, Lumber, Furniture, Paper, Plastics, Rubber, Paints, Petro. Products, Metal Products, Consumer Elect., Consumer Goods, HR Services, Environmental Svcs., Packaging

Branches:
4040 Civic Center Dr Ste 200
San Rafael, CA 94903-4187
(415) 892-0077
Fax: (415) 892-2345
Email: jgnussbaum@brookechase.com
Key Contact - Specialty:
Mr. Jack Nussbaum, President

6000 Fairview Rd Ste 1200
Charlotte, NC 28210-2253
(704) 852-4050
Fax: (704) 852-9922
Email: hsharpe@brookechase.com
Key Contact - Specialty:
Mr. Howard Sharpe, President - *Hardware*

Polly Brown Associates Inc

230 Park Ave Rm 1152
New York, NY 10169-1161
(212) 661-7575 x225
Email: pbrown@pollybrownassociates.com
Web: www.pollybrownassociates.com

Summary: Our clients are the leaders in luxury products/consumer goods, in the categories of cosmetics, fragrances, jewelry and accessories. We primarily focus on searches in the fields of marketing, sales, merchandising, public relations, product development and generalist practices and HR positions in all industries.

Key Contact - Specialty:
Ms. Polly M. Brown, President - *Cosmetics*

Salary Minimum: $100,000

Functions: Generalist (All), Management, Product Dev., Sales & Mktg., HR Mgmt., Finance

Industries: Food, Bev., Tobacco, Soap, Perf., Cosmtcs., Retail, HR Services, Packaging

Brown Venture Associates Inc

2500 Sand Hill Rd Ste 215
Menlo Park, CA 94025-7073
(650) 233-0205
Fax: (650) 233-1902
Email: info@bva.com
Web: www.bva.com

Summary: Search firm specializing in CEO and VP level searches for high-technology companies and recruitment of venture capital general partners.

Key Contact - Specialty:
Mr. Jerry Brown, President
Ms. Aloka R. Naskar, Managing Partner
Mr. Dan Lankford, Partner

Salary Minimum: $200,000

Functions: Board Members, Senior Mgmt.

Industries: Test, Measure Equip., Semiconductors, Communications, Software

Brownson & Associates LP

2825 Wilcrest Dr Ste 530
Houston, TX 77042-6006
(713) 626-4790
Fax: (713) 877-1745
Email: brownsonassoc@brownson.com
Web: www.brownson.com

Summary: Our firm is a leading retained executive search consulting firm with specialty practices encompassing energy, energy services, chemical & petrochemical, engineering,

† occasional contingency assignment

manufacturing, financial, healthcare, pharmaceutical, environmental, transportation, consumer goods and retail industries in all functional managerial areas. Exceeding client expectations is our only measure of success.

Key Contact - Specialty:
Mr. Bruce Brownson, President & Chief Executive Officer - *Six Sigma, Supermarkets, Treasury, Wall Street, Wireless*
Mr. Carl Stover, Vice President - *Chemical, Manufacturing, Petrochemical, Pharmaceutical*
Mrs. Christina Davis, Vice President, Research - *Geology, Human resources, Information service, Information Systems, Information Technology*
Mr. Paul Giddens, Senior Vice President & Practice Direct - *Forest industry/products, Foundries, Home and building controls, Human resources, Manufacturing (Management)*

Salary Minimum: $75,000

Functions: Generalist (All)

Industries: Generalist (All), Energy, Utilities, Manufacturing, Transportation, Retail, Finance, Hospitality, Environmental Svcs., Biotech/Life Sciences, Healthcare

BrownThompson Executive Search

5080 Shoreham Pl Ste 204
San Diego, CA 92122-5932
(858) 452-0100
Fax: (858) 623-5910
Email: tom@brownthompson.us.com
Web: www.brownthompson.us.com

Summary: We specialize in working with corporations and not-for-profit organizations in the selection of senior-level financial management and audit committee director appointments in all industries.

Key Contact - Specialty:
Mr. Thomas Brown, President
Ms. Judy Thompson, Managing Director

Salary Minimum: $150,000

Functions: Board Members, CFOs

Industries: Generalist (All), Energy, Utilities, Construction, Manufacturing, Electronic, Elec. Components, Semiconductors, Finance, Communications, Software, Biotech/Life Sciences

Brush Creek Partners

14512 Horton St
Overland Park, KS 66223-2693
(816) 228-9192
(913) 402-0259
Email: jlunn@brushcreekpartners.com

Summary: We conduct senior level searches, serving a wide variety of client needs. Our client base ranges from small privately owned businesses to Fortune 100 multinationals in virtually all major industry sectors. Our approach to strategy development, candidate sourcing and screening has enabled us to remain client centered versus industry specific.

Key Contact - Specialty:
Mr. Jerry D. Lunn, President & Chief Executive Officer

Salary Minimum: $100,000

Functions: Generalist (All), Senior Mgmt., Sales & Mktg., HR Mgmt., CFOs, MIS Mgmt., R&D

Industries: Generalist (All), Chemicals, Computer Equip., Misc. Mfg., Finance, Telecoms, Biotech/Life Sciences

Buffkin & Associates LLC

730 Cool Springs Blvd Ste 120
Franklin, TN 37067-7290
(615) 771-0098
Fax: (615) 771-0099
Email: info@buffkinassociates.com
Web: www.buffkinassociates.com

Summary: We are a retained search firm with the following practices: direct marketing/printing, entertainment/media, technology and general management. Searches have been completed at the board, executive and senior levels.

Key Contact - Specialty:
Mr. Craig Buffkin, Managing Partner - *Direct marketing, Technology*
Mr. Roland Lundy, Senior Parnter - *Entertainment*

Salary Minimum: $125,000

Functions: Management, Sales & Mktg., CFOs

Industries: E-commerce, IT Implementation, Entertainment, Media

J Burkey Associates

900 Laurel Ave
River Edge, NJ 07661-1611
(201) 262-7990
Fax: (201) 262-7955
Email: jburkey@erols.com

Summary: We offer executive search services at an hourly-based or fixed fee; it's the clients' choice. Our practice is devoted to the placement of executives in pharmaceuticals, both human and animal. Our functional expertise has always been and continues to be varied, but our most frequent search activity has been in marketing and business development, product management, regulatory affairs, HR and general management.

Key Contact - Specialty:
Ms. Julie V. Burkey, Principal - *Pharmaceutical*

Salary Minimum: $100,000

Functions: Generalist (All), Management

Industries: Drugs Mfg., Medical Devices, Pharm Svcs., Non-Classifiable

Burkholder Group Inc

985 Pico Pt
Colorado Springs, CO 80906-1380
(719) 867-1222
Fax: (719) 623-0033
Email: info@burkholdergroup.com
Web: www.burkholdergroup.com

Summary: We are property and casualty insurance specialists with a national practice encompassing general management and all functional disciplines. Our primary focus is on management and executive level searches.

Key Contact - Specialty:
Mr. John Burkholder, President

Salary Minimum: $75,000

Functions: Generalist (All)

Industries: Insurance

The Burling Group Ltd

191 N Wacker Dr Ste 2300
Chicago, IL 60606-1615
(312) 346-0888
Email: web@burlinggroup.com
Web: www.burlinggroup.com

Summary: We are a generalist firm serving entrepreneurial clients experiencing growth and expansion.

Key Contact - Specialty:
Mr. Ronald Deitch, President

Salary Minimum: $100,000

Functions: Senior Mgmt.

Industries: Medical Devices, Metal Products, Misc. Mfg., Accounting, Mgmt. Consulting, HR Services, Logistics Svcs., Publishing, Packaging

Joseph R Burns & Associates Inc

8 Stafford Dr
Madison, NJ 07940-2005
(973) 377-1350
(973) 377-1450
Fax: (973) 377-9350
Email: burnsassc@aol.com

Summary: We are an executive search firm with excellent recruitment skills and a demonstrated record of success in servicing our clients with the highest degree of professionalism.

Key Contact - Specialty:
Mr. Joseph R. Burns, President

Salary Minimum: $90,000

Functions: Generalist (All), Management, Mfg., Healthcare, Sales & Mktg., HR Mgmt., CFOs, Cash Mgmt., M&A, IT

Industries: Generalist (All), Food, Bev., Tobacco, Computer Equip., Invest. Banking, Non-profits, New Media, Telecoms, Healthcare

Burns & Young Executive Search[†]

3740 Caymus Dr
Sparks, NV 89436-7155
(775) 626-4405
Email: kburns@burnsandyoung.com
Web: www.myspace.com/burnsandyoung

Summary: Full service staffing company specializing in Aerospace, Data Storage and various high-tech industries. Highly successful track record securing the placement of mid to upper level positions, including Purchasing, Production Control, Operations, Quality and Test, Warehouse Management, and Sales and Marketing.

Key Contact - Specialty:
Mr. Kelly J. Burns, Executive Recruiter & President

Salary Minimum: $50,000

Functions: Mfg., Production, Quality, Materials, Purchasing, Materials Plng., Sales & Mktg., Engineering

Industries: Manufacturing, Computer Equip., Logistics Svcs., Supply Chain Mgmt, Government, Defense, Aerospace

Burton and Grove Executive Search

1320 Tower Rd
Schaumburg, IL 60173-4309
(847) 919-8880
Email: support@burtonandgrove.com
Web: www.burtonandgrove.com

Summary: Primary focus is on sales & marketing positions within software, document management, printing and select business-to-business clients.

Key Contact - Specialty:
Mr. Steve Crothers, President - *Business to business, Printing*

Salary Minimum: $70,000

Functions: Management, Senior Mgmt., Middle Mgmt., Sales & Mktg.

Industries: Printing, Services, Communications, Software, Doc. Mgmt., Production SW

Busch International

5150 El Camino Real Ste A30
Los Altos, CA 94022-1546
(650) 623-0990
Email: olga@buschint.com
Web: www.buschint.com

Summary: Our firm consists of senior consultants specializing in high-technology electronics exclusively. Assignments are with growth companies requiring CEOs, VPs, COOs in marketing, sales, engineering and operations.

Key Contact - Specialty:
Mr. Jack Busch, President
Mrs. Olga Ocon, Partner
Mr. Bertrand Smith, Partner

Salary Minimum: $150,000

Functions: Senior Mgmt., Sales & Mktg.

Industries: Computer Equip., Consumer Elect., Test, Measure Equip., Venture Cap., New Media, Telecoms

Business Systems of America Inc[†]

566 W Lake St Ste 450
Chicago, IL 60661-5203
(312) 559-9222
Fax: (312) 559-9299
Email: recruiter@bsofa.com
Web: www.bsofa.com

Summary: We provide tested IT professions to Fortune 500 companies. We discover, empower and support the career of the best IT professionals.

Key Contact - Specialty:
Mr. Bennett Santana, President
Mr. Freddie Torres, Branch Manager

Salary Minimum: $50,000

Functions: IT, MIS Mgmt., Systems Analysis, Systems Dev., Systems Implem., Systems Support, Network Admin.

Industries: Generalist (All)

Butterfass, Pepe & MacCallan Inc

PO Box 721
Mahwah, NJ 07430-0721
(201) 560-9500
Fax: (201) 560-9506
Email: staff@bpmi.com
Web: www.bpmi.com

Summary: We are a retained search firm specializing in the financial services industry, recruiting financial professionals to asset managers, commercial & investment banks, insurance companies and other financial institutions.

Key Contact - Specialty:
Mr. Stanley W. Butterfass, Principal
Ms. Leonida R. Pepe, Principal
Ms. Deirdre MacCallan, Principal

Salary Minimum: $200,000

Functions: Generalist (All), HR Mgmt., Finance, CFOs, Cash Mgmt., M&A, Risk Mgmt., Minorities/Diversity

Industries: Generalist (All), Banking, Invest. Banking, Brokers, Venture Cap., HR Services, Insurance

Byron Leonard International Inc

99 Long Ct Ste 201
Thousand Oaks, CA 91360-7401
(805) 373-7500

Email: bli@bli-inc.com
Web: www.bli-inc.com

Summary: We have search experience in growth industries, emphasizing custom fit of candidates to the enterprise, disciplined recruitment methodology, exceptional research. Satisfied clients: start-ups to multinationals.

Key Contact - Specialty:
Mr. Stephen M. Wolf, Principal
Mr. Leonard M. Linton, Principal & Co-Founder
- *Banking, Banking (Investment), Buyout funds, Private equity, Venture capital*

Salary Minimum: $80,000

Functions: Generalist (All), Senior Mgmt., Product Dev., Mktg. Research, Mktg. Mgmt., CFOs, MIS Mgmt.

Industries: Generalist (All), Computer Equip., Non-profits, Legal, Mgmt. Consulting, IT Implementation, New Media, Software

C P Consulting[†]

674 The Hideout
Lake Ariel, PA 18436-9797
(570) 698-8321
Fax: (570) 698-8321

Summary: We are an HR consulting, specializing in the sourcing and screening of middle and upper management candidates. We do not generate names. Unsolicited resumes cannot be responded to.

Key Contact - Specialty:
Ms. Catherine Phillips, Owner - *Financial services*

Salary Minimum: $100,000

Functions: Generalist (All), Management, Mktg. Mgmt., Benefits, Staffing, Training, CFOs

Industries: Generalist (All), Finance, Banking, Misc. Financial, Non-profits, Pharm Svcs., Legal, HR Services, Media

C-suite Inc

2 Elm Sq
Andover, MA 01810-3668
(978) 475-1511
(212) 966-1383
Email: bmarch@c-suiteinc.com
Web: www.c-suiteinc.com

Summary: We are a retained executive search firm catering to both fashion and retail (apparel, luxury items, footwear, action sports,).

Key Contact - Specialty:
Ms. Barbara Marchetti, President

Salary Minimum: $150,000

Functions: Senior Mgmt.

Industries: Retail

CAA Search

(a division of CAAS International)
5469 Sunbird Dr
Loves Park, IL 61111-7117
(815) 654-8535
(815) 654-3569
Fax: (815) 654-0469
Email: christian@caasearch.com
Web: www.caasearch.com

Summary: Executive search for manufacturing companies for executive, sales, operations and technical management people. Record of success with technology industries includes capital equipment like machine tools, fabrication, automation, automotive, appliance, hardware and recreational products. With expert experience in

all levels of sales, marketing, engineering and operations positions. We make the right fit.

Key Contact - Specialty:
Mr. Christian A. Anderson, Chief Executive Officer

Salary Minimum: $40,000

Functions: Generalist (All), Admin. Svcs.

Industries: Manufacturing, Printing, Medical Devices, Metal Products, Machine, Appliance, Motor Vehicles, Computer Equip., Electronic, Elec. Components, Consumer Goods, Mgmt. Consulting

The Cadman Consulting Group Inc

500-666 Burrard St
Vancouver, BC V6C 3P6
Canada
(604) 689-4345
Fax: (604) 676-2458
Email: info@cadman.ca
Web: www.cadman.ca

Summary: Our firm is a Vancouver based leading provider of information technology professionals. We specialize in providing IT professionals for full time and contract positions throughout the lower mainland. Our clients include companies in both the public and private sectors.

Key Contact - Specialty:
Mr. Gary Cadman, President & Chief Executive Officer

Functions: Product Dev., IT

Industries: Generalist (All), Software, Database SW, Development SW, Doc. Mgmt., Production SW, Industry Specific SW, Mfg. SW, Networking, Comm. SW, Security SW, System SW, Training SW

Cadmus International[†]

1001 S Dairy Ashford St Ste 100
Houston, TX 77077-2341
(713) 977-1900
Email: stc@cadmusint.com
Web: www.cadmusint.com

Summary: We are a high-technology search and consulting firm that performs retainer/container, on-site/off-site, business unit or client company development and industry intelligence.

Key Contact - Specialty:
Mr. Stephen T. Cadmus, President - *Computers (Software), Hardware, High technology*
Ms. Wendy Veggeberg
Mr. Ed Boe

Functions: Generalist (All), Management

Industries: Generalist (All), Computer Equip., Consumer Elect., Test, Measure Equip., Venture Cap., Mgmt. Consulting, Telecoms, Software

The Caldwell Partners International

165 Avenue Rd
Toronto, ON M5R 3S4
Canada
(416) 920-7702
Fax: (416) 922-8646
Email: leaders@caldwell.ca
Web: www.caldwellpartners.com

Summary: We are Canada's only publicly traded executive search firm. We maintain the largest database of premier career opportunities from the nation's top organizations.

Key Contact - Specialty:
Ms. Kelly A. Blair
Mr. Christopher J. Laubitz

Mr. Marty Parker
Mr. Ronald D. Charles
Mr. Jack Penaligon
Mr. Francis W.H. Brunelle
Mr. C. Douglas Caldwell
Mr. Ralph A. Chauvin
Ms. Anne M. Fawcett
Ms. Catherine Lepard

Functions: Generalist (All)

Industries: Generalist (All)

Branches:
850-1095 Pender St W
Vancouver, BC V6E 2M6
Canada
(604) 669-3550
Fax: (604) 669-5095
Email: vancouver@caldwell.ca
Key Contact - Specialty:
Mr. Don Prior, Partner
Mr. Harry Parslow

500-5657 Spring Garden Rd
Parklane Mall
Halifax, NS B3J 3R4
Canada
(902) 429-5909
Fax: (902) 429-5606
Email: halifax@caldwell.ca
Key Contact - Specialty:
Ms. Susan Letson, Partner
Ms. Lois Dyer Mann, Partner

161-1 Place Ville-Marie
Immeuble Commercial
Montreal, QC H3B 2B6
Canada
(514) 908-2954
Fax: (514) 908-2953
Email: montreal@caldwell.ca
Key Contact - Specialty:
Mr. Andre Vincent
Mr. Denis Trudeau

The Caler Group[†]

23337 Lago Mar Cir
Boca Raton, FL 33433-7235
(561) 394-8045
Fax: (561) 394-4645
Email: caler@calergroup.com
Web: www.calergroup.com

Summary: Certified minority/women business
enterprise, international retained executive
recruiting company specializing in high-
technology, Internet, data networking, telecom,
financial services and energy industries.
Functional areas of sales, marketing,
manufacturing, product
development/management/marketing, marketing,
quality, Six Sigma, customer service, system
engineers, etc. CEOs to individual contributors.

Key Contact - Specialty:
Ms. Colleen Perrone, President
Mr. Chris Genske, Vice President

Salary Minimum: $100,000

Functions: Management, Senior Mgmt., Mfg.,
Quality, Sales & Mktg., Mktg. Research, Sales
Mgmt., Finance, IT, Hardware

Industries: Generalist (All), Manufacturing,
Electronic, Elec. Components, Wholesale,
Finance, Banking, Invest. Banking, Misc.
Financial, Call Centers, Wireless, Network
Infrastructure, Software

Lee Calhoon & Company Inc

PO Box 201
1621 Birchrun Rd
Birchrunville, PA 19421-0201
(610) 469-9000
(800) 469-0896
Fax: (610) 469-0398
Email: info@leecalhoon.com
Web: www.leecalhoon.com

Summary: We are a retained executive search
firm which specializes exclusively in the
healthcare industry. We have conducted numerous
searches in the payer, provider, pharma,
information systems and technology, managed
care, service, medical device, disease and
population health management, behavioral,
workers' comp and disability, consulting, and e-
Health sectors.

Key Contact - Specialty:
Mr. Lee Calhoon, President & Chief Executive
Officer - *Healthcare, Managed care*
Mrs. Patricia Calhoon, Principal
Mr. Bill Fedora, Principal
Mr. Christopher Calhoon, Consultant

Salary Minimum: $150,000

Functions: Senior Mgmt., Middle Mgmt.,
Healthcare, Physicians, Nurses, Health Admin.

Industries: Drugs Mfg., Medical Devices, Pharm
Svcs., E-commerce, IT Implementation,
Insurance, Software, Biotech/Life Sciences,
Healthcare, Hospitals, Women's

Caliber Associates

5090 Shoreham Pl
San Diego, CA 92122-5933
(858) 551-7880
Fax: (858) 551-7887
Email: info@caliberassociates.com
Web: www.caliberassociates.com

Summary: Finding the leaders who find the cure.
We specialize in retained executive search
services exclusively for the life sciences, both
emerging organizations and major pharmaceutical
companies. Our focus areas include: regulatory
affairs, QA/QC, clinical research/medical affairs,
discovery R&D, development,
operations/manufacturing, project management,
and sales/marketing management/business
development.

Key Contact - Specialty:
Mr. Steven P. Hochberg, Founder & President
Ms. Patricia Riley, Executive Search Consultant
Ms. Juliana Mozi, Administrative Manager -
*CIOs, High technology, Information
Technology, Management, Start-up companies*

Salary Minimum: $125,000

Functions: Management, Product Dev., Plant
Mgmt., Quality, Sales & Mktg., CFOs, R&D

Industries: Drugs Mfg., Medical Devices, Pharm
Svcs., Biotech/Life Sciences

Branches:
125 Strafford Ave Ste 112
Wayne, PA 19087-3335
(610) 971-1880
Email: info@caliberassociates.com
Key Contact - Specialty:
Ms. Anna Casetta, Principal

Callaghan International Inc[†]

119 W 57th St Ste 1220
New York, NY 10019-2401
(212) 265-9200
(212) 242-5284
Fax: (212) 262-0024

Email: kmc@callaghan-international.com
Web: www.callaghan-international.com

Summary: We are a full service retained search
firm specializing in diversity placement of senior
level executives. We have a multilingual staff,
with international experience. We are generalists
with a background in most industries and
functions.

Key Contact - Specialty:
Ms. Kathryn M. Callaghan, President & Chief
Executive Officer - *Advertising, Automation,
Biopharmaceutical, Consumer (Products),
Diversity*
Mr. John Lovet, Senior Vice President -
Information Technology
Ms. Stephanie Whelan, Vice President -
*Biopharmaceutical, Executives, Financial
services, Human resources, Staffing*
Ms. Elaine Kennedy, Director, Research -
*Advertising, Biotechnology, Consumer
(Products), Fashion, Finance*
Mr. Bud Courtney, Associate - *Administration,
Research*

Salary Minimum: $100,000

Functions: Senior Mgmt., Mfg., Sales & Mktg.,
IT, Engineering, Minorities/Diversity, Int'l.

Industries: Generalist (All), Construction,
Manufacturing, Food, Bev., Tobacco, Soap,
Perf., Cosmtcs., Drugs Mfg., Medical Devices,
Computer Equip., Consumer Elect., Misc. Mfg.,
Wholesale, Retail, Finance, Misc. Financial,
Non-profits, Accounting, Law Enforcement, IT
Implementation, Hospitality, Government,
Insurance, Software, Biotech/Life Sciences

Callan Associates Ltd

2215 York Rd Ste 510
Oak Brook, IL 60523-2379
(630) 574-9300
Fax: (630) 574-3099
Email: info@callanassociates.com
Web: www.callanassociates.com

Summary: We are a leading retained search firm
that provides high quality, personalized senior-
level recruiting services to a prestigious group of
public and private manufacturing, industrial and
professional service organizations in all functions.

Key Contact - Specialty:
Mr. Robert M. Callan, Partner - *General
management*
Ms. Elizabeth C. Beaudin, Partner - *General
management, Manufacturing, Procurement,
Purchasing, Sales*
Ms. Marianne C. Ray, Partner - *Finance, General
management, Manufacturing*
Mr. Robert M. Callan, Jr., Partner - *Finance,
General management, Operations*
Ms. Caren R. Truhlar, Director, Research

Salary Minimum: $100,000

Functions: Management, Senior Mgmt., Mfg.,
Purchasing, Packaging, Sales & Mktg., Finance,
CFOs, IT, Mgmt. Consultants

Industries: Generalist (All), Energy, Utilities,
Manufacturing, Metal Products, Test, Measure
Equip., Electronic, Elec. Components, Banking,
Venture Cap., Mgmt. Consulting,
Communications, Packaging

Cambridge Forbes Retained Search

702 N Division St
Carson City, NV 89703-3921
(775) 450-3924
Fax: (949) 443-2313

Email: edprovost@cambridge-forbesretainedsearch.com
Web: www.cambridge-forbesretainedsearch.com

Summary: Only vice president level or higher i.e. C-level and boards.

Key Contact - Specialty:
Mr. Ed Provost, Chief Executive Officer

Salary Minimum: $85,000

Functions: Management, Board Members, Senior Mgmt., Plant Mgmt., Distribution, Sales & Mktg., CFOs, Risk Mgmt., MIS Mgmt., Mgmt. Consultants

Industries: Construction, Food, Bev., Tobacco, Motor Vehicles, Transportation, Finance, HR Services, Logistics Svcs., Supply Chain Mgmt, Homeland Security, Software

Cambridge Management Planning Inc

(an affiliate of IIC Partners)
203-2323 Yonge Street
Toronto, ON M4P 2C9
Canada
(416) 484-8408
Fax: (416) 484-0151
Email: mail@cambridgemgmt.com
Web: www.cambridgemgmt.com

Summary: We offer executive searches: mid to senior-management searches for a wide range of corporations. Emphasis placed on highly targeted, in-house market research capabilities.

Key Contact - Specialty:
Mr. Graham Carver, President
Mr. David Howes, Partner
Mr. Peter Shrive, Partner
Mr. Chris Poole, Partner
Ms. Elesha Browne, Partner

Salary Minimum: $100,000

Functions: Generalist (All)

Industries: Generalist (All)

Cameron Craig Group[†]

19831 Henderson Rd Apt M
Cornelius, NC 28031-5882
(704) 655-1352
Email: jobs@cameroncraig.com
Web: www.cameroncraig.com

Summary: Retained search firm focused on the architectural design industry. We find architects, designers, planners, and construction administrators for clients nationwide.

Key Contact - Specialty:
Mr. Trey Cameron, Principal - *Architecture, Construction, Design, Engineering, Interior design*
Mrs. Karen Craig, Principal - *Architecture, Construction, Engineering, Information Technology, Interior design*
Mrs. Betty Billy, Principal - *Architecture, Construction, Design, Engineering, Interior design*
Mr. Chris Surratt, Recruiter - *Architecture, Construction, Engineering, Healthcare, Interior design*

Salary Minimum: $50,000

Functions: Management, Structural, Eng. Design, Architects, Technicians, Bldg. Contractors, Design

Industries: Architectural Svcs., HR Services, Engineering Svcs., Non-Classifiable

Campa & Associates

1801-1 Yonge St
Toronto Star Building
Toronto, ON M5E 1E5
Canada
(416) 407-7777
Email: carl@campasearch.com

Summary: We recruit high performance management talent for world-class engineered products manufacturers.

Key Contact - Specialty:
Mr. Carl Campa, President

Salary Minimum: $90,000

Functions: Generalist (All), Management, Mfg., Plant Mgmt., Materials, Sales & Mktg., Engineering, Mgmt. Consultants

Industries: Generalist (All), Plastics, Rubber, Metal Products, Machine, Appliance, Motor Vehicles, Misc. Mfg., Aerospace

Campbell/Carlson LLC

831 E Morehead St Ste 750
Charlotte, NC 28202-2731
(704) 373-0234
Email: recruiting@campbellcarlson.com
Web: www.campbellcarlson.com

Summary: We are a retained executive search firm that specializes in recruiting senior-level executives in a wide range of industries. Our partners have spent a considerable portion of their careers working as senior managers in various businesses, where they were responsible for making key personnel decisions.

Key Contact - Specialty:
Mr. Dan Campbell, Principal - *Distribution, Finance, Manufacturing, Technology*
Ms. Cynthia Carlson, Principal - *Marketing, Sales, Technology, Training*

Salary Minimum: $100,000

Functions: Management

Industries: Generalist (All)

Candidates on Demand Group Inc

433 5th Ave Fl 6
New York, NY 10016-2207
(212) 213-0982
Fax: (212) 213-3891
Email: mw@codgi.com
Web: www.codgi.com

Summary: We are a full service firm specializing in sales, IT/engineering, medical, office support, marketing, legal, accounting/finance and creative services.

Key Contact - Specialty:
Mr. Michael Woloshin, President

Salary Minimum: $100,000

Functions: Generalist (All)

Industries: Generalist (All), Medical Devices, Finance, Banking, Invest. Banking, Brokers, IT Implementation, Publishing, Software, Accounting SW

Branches:
140 Glastonbury Blvd
Glastonbury, CT 06033-4402
(860) 659-2220 x10
Email: danw@codgi.com
Key Contact - Specialty:
Mr. Dan Weinick, Director, Human Resources and Recruiting

35 Pinelawn Rd Ste 209W
Melville, NY 11747-3177
(516) 293-2933 x16
Key Contact - Specialty:
Mr. David Rivard, Recruiter

433 5th Ave Fl 6
New York, NY 10016-2207
(212) 213-0982 x103
Email: efishkind@codgi.com

17440 Dallas Pkwy Ste 214
Dallas, TX 75287-7308
(972) 267-6666 x111
Fax: (972) 692-6625
Email: nic@coddallas.com
Key Contact - Specialty:
Mr. Spencer Hartstein, Senior Vice President

Cannellos-Smartt Associates[†]

23 Davenport Way
Hillsborough, NJ 08844-2923
(908) 359-8319
(908) 369-0041
Email: rudysmartt@csa-search.com
Web: www.csa-search.com

Summary: We are a retained executive search firm specializing in all areas of the pharmaceutical, medical devices and life sciences industries. Our areas of expertise are: all R&D functions, sales, marketing, finance, business development, manufacturing and supply chain searches.

Key Contact - Specialty:
Mr. Rudy Smartt, Partner & Search Consultant - *Business development, Manufacturing, Sales*

Salary Minimum: $100,000

Functions: Generalist (All), Management, Admin. Svcs.

Industries: Generalist (All), Food, Bev., Tobacco, Drugs Mfg., Medical Devices, Misc. Financial, Pharm Svcs., Accounting, Mgmt. Consulting, Supply Chain Mgmt, Healthcare

Branches:
30 Wagner Ln
Hillsborough, NJ 08844-3327
(908) 369-0041
Email: rcannellos@csa-cearch.com
Key Contact - Specialty:
Mr. Rick Cannellos, Partner & Executive Search Consultant - *Finance*

Canny, Bowen Inc

280 Park Ave Rm 3000W
New York, NY 10017-1245
(212) 949-6611
Fax: (212) 949-5191
Email: main@cannybowen.com
Web: www.cannybowen.com

Summary: We are a retainer-based executive search firm specializing in senior executive search.

Key Contact - Specialty:
Mr. David R. Peasback, President & Chief Executive Officer
Mr. Greg Gabel, Managing Director
Mr. Eric P. Gustafson, Managing Director
Mr. Jeffrey Wilkens, Principal
Mr. Brian Kelley, Managing Director

Salary Minimum: $175,000

Functions: Generalist (All)

Industries: Generalist (All)

Canpro Executive Search

302-7321 Victoria Park Ave
Markham, ON L3R 2Z8
Canada
(905) 475-3115
Fax: (905) 475-2849
Email: aboyle@canpro.com
Web: www.canpro.com

Summary: We provide executive searches to the country's leading corporations.

Key Contact - Specialty:
Mr. Art Boyle, President

Salary Minimum: $50,000

Functions: Management, Mfg., Materials, Sales & Mktg., HR Mgmt., Finance

Industries: Generalist (All)

Cantor Executive Search Solutions Inc[†]

250 W 57th St Ste 1632
New York, NY 10107-1609
(212) 333-3000
Fax: (212) 245-1012
Email: requests@cantorconcern.com
Web: www.cantorconcern.com

Summary: A search firm with professional staff experienced in business, government, not-for-profit and management consulting search. Company serves all industries and specializes in public affairs, public relations, corporate communications and IR.

Key Contact - Specialty:
Ms. Marie T. Raperto, President & Chief Executive Officer - *Investor relations, Public relations*

Salary Minimum: $50,000

Functions: PR

Industries: Generalist (All)

Branches:
424 Tahmore Dr
Fairfield, CT 06825-2517
(203) 372-2662
Fax: (203) 372-2618
Email: rlferrante@cantorconcern.com
Key Contact - Specialty:
Mr. Robert Ferrante, Managing Director

Caplan Associates Inc

PO Box 4227
East Hampton, NY 11937-0257
(631) 907-9700
Fax: (631) 907-0444
Email: info@caplanassoc.com
Web: www.caplanassoc.com

Summary: We are a retained executive-level search firm servicing only pharmaceutical and bio-technology companies: executive, general & senior management, business development, marketing, sales, healthcare, clinical regulatory, pharmaceutical publishing, medical education and advertising.

Key Contact - Specialty:
Ms. Shellie Caplan, President - *Biotechnology, Business development, General management, Marketing, Pharmaceutical*

Salary Minimum: $100,000

Functions: Healthcare

Industries: Pharm Svcs., Advertising, Biotech/Life Sciences, Healthcare

Capodice & Associates

1243 S Tamiami Trl
Sarasota, FL 34239-2219
(941) 906-1990
Fax: (941) 906-1991
Email: peter@capodice.com
Web: www.capodice.com

Summary: Retained executive search firm specializing in the restaurant/hospitality, entertainment, franchising, consumer products, healthcare and pharmaceutical industries. Senior-level executive placements are across all disciplines.

Key Contact - Specialty:
Mr. Peter Capodice, President - *Entertainment, Franchising, Hospitality*

Salary Minimum: $50,000

Functions: Generalist (All)

Industries: Manufacturing, Food, Bev., Tobacco, Retail, Services, HR Services, Hospitality, Biotech/Life Sciences, Healthcare

Caprio & Associates Inc

1415 W 22nd St Ste Tower
Oak Brook, IL 60523-2031
(630) 705-9101
Fax: (630) 705-9102
Email: jerry@caprioassociates.com
Web: www.caprioassociates.com

Summary: We are specialists in recruiting senior-level management, marketing and sales, for the Food, Packaging, Packaging Machinery & Printing Industries.

Key Contact - Specialty:
Mr. Jerry Caprio, President - *Flexographic printing, Food & beverage, Packaging, Printing*

Salary Minimum: $75,000

Functions: Generalist (All), Senior Mgmt., Plant Mgmt., Packaging, Sales Mgmt., Direct Mktg.

Industries: Generalist (All), Manufacturing, Food, Bev., Tobacco, Paper, Printing, Equip Svcs., Inst./Industrial Food Svc., Packaging

Capstone Consulting Group

723 S Dearborn St
Chicago, IL 60605-1837
(312) 922-9556
Fax: (312) 922-9558
Email: capstone@capstoneconsulting.com
Web: www.capstoneconsulting.com

Summary: We are a highly focused search-driven consultancy offering a wide range of strategic business planning services. Committed to the highest level of client partnership; detailed, methodical and personalized attention are our hallmarks.

Key Contact - Specialty:
Mr. Mark R. Ormond, Founder & Principal
Ms. Lori K. Pedelty, President & Co-Founder - *Manufacturing, Tax*

Salary Minimum: $75,000

Functions: Generalist (All), Senior Mgmt., Middle Mgmt., Mfg., Taxes, Systems Implem., Engineering

Industries: Generalist (All), Manufacturing, Metal Products, Consumer Elect., Misc. Mfg., Services, Legal, Accounting, Mgmt. Consulting, HR Services

Capstone Inc

971 Albany Shaker Rd
Latham, NY 12110-1409
(518) 783-9300
Fax: (518) 783-9328
Email: amyj@capstone-inc.com
Web: www.capstone-inc.com

Summary: We offer a turnkey approach to retained search including organizational analysis, position definition, compensation surveys, interview training and final candidate selection as requested.

Key Contact - Specialty:
Ms. Amy M. Johnson, President

Salary Minimum: $70,000

Functions: Generalist (All), Senior Mgmt., Mfg., Automation, Sales & Mktg., CFOs, Systems Dev., Engineering

Industries: Generalist (All), Paper, Chemicals, Plastics, Rubber, Software

Cardinal Mark Inc

601 Carlson Pkwy Ste 1050
Minnetonka, MN 55305-5219
(952) 449-3005
Email: jimz@cardinalmark.com
Web: www.cardinalmark.com

Summary: We concentrate our search efforts in the telecom and data communications industries. Areas of placement in software have included LANs, WANs, optical networking and storage.

Key Contact - Specialty:
Mr. Jim Zuehlke

Functions: Board Members, Mktg. Research, Mktg. Mgmt., Sales Mgmt., Direct Mktg.

Industries: Media, Network Infrastructure, Networking, Comm. SW, Security SW, System SW

Cardwell Enterprises Inc

PO Box 59418
Chicago, IL 60659-0418
(773) 273-5774
Fax: (847) 475-6792

Summary: Expertise in corporate communications, investor relations, public relations, government and public affairs on behalf of corporations and public relations agencies.

Key Contact - Specialty:
Ms. Jean Cardwell, President - *Investor relations, Public relations*

Salary Minimum: $80,000

Functions: PR, Minorities/Diverslty

Industries: Generalist (All)

Career and Professional Development Resources

4900 Boxwood Cir
Boynton Beach, FL 33436-4724
(561) 734-0775
(561) 561-596-3656
Email: tbcareer@bellsouth.net
Web: www.tobycareer.com

Summary: Full service career management specializing in not profit recruiting for experienced development directors and executive directors in Southeast Florida.

Key Contact - Specialty:
Ms. Toby Chabon-Berger, Principal - *COOs, Education, Entertainment, Management, Non-profit*

Salary Minimum: $50,000

Functions: Non-profits

Industries: Non-profits

Career Specialists Inc

155 108th Ave NE Ste 200
Bellevue, WA 98004-5957
(425) 455-0582
(425) 455-2508
Fax: (425) 646-9738
Email: prolfe@qwest.net

Summary: Executive search, specifically CEOs
and their direct reports.

Key Contact - Specialty:
Ms. Pamela Rolfe, President - *CEOs, Senior
management*
Ms. Susan Chapman, Vice President

Salary Minimum: $100,000

Functions: Generalist (All), Board Members,
Senior Mgmt., Healthcare, CFOs, IT, Attorneys

Industries: Generalist (All), Manufacturing,
Textiles, Apparel, Wholesale, Retail, Finance,
Banking, Invest. Banking, Non-profits, Legal,
E-commerce, Insurance, Healthcare, Hospitals

CareerSMITH Inc

537 Newport Center Dr Ste 364
Newport Beach, CA 92660-6937
(949) 760-8666
Email: ebsmith@careersmith.com
Web: www.careersmith.com

Summary: We are dedicated to offering first class
employment opportunities with top flight
engineering and construction companies for E & C
professionals, from entry level engineers to the
most senior executives.

Key Contact - Specialty:
Mr. E. Brian Smith, President
Ms. Samantha Shuller, Senior Search Consultant
Mr. Tony Bolliger, Senior Search Consultant

Functions: CFOs, Engineering, Eng. Design,
Health & Safety

Industries: Construction, Transportation,
Engineering Svcs., Environmental Svcs.

CareerStrategies LLC

(formerly known as STRATA Performance Group
Inc)
400 Chesterfield Ctr Ste 400
Chesterfield, MO 63017-4800
(636) 537-7849
Email: rwolf@cscpi.net
Web: www.careerstrategies.us

Summary: Our firm offers a unique approach in
successfully identifying and recruiting the best
talent for our client organizations. We have
completed challenging senior level search
assignments in the manufacturing, healthcare,
construction, financial services and service
industries. Our experienced professionals each
have in-depth industry experience.

Key Contact - Specialty:
Mr. Robert J. Wolf, CPBA, Managing Partner -
*Finance, Financial, General management,
Manufacturing, Marketing*

Salary Minimum: $75,000

Functions: Generalist (All)

Industries: Generalist (All)

Carlsen Resources Inc†

800 Belford Ave Ste 200
Grand Junction, CO 81501-3100
(970) 242-9462
Fax: (970) 242-9074
Email: criinfo@carlsenresources.com
Web: www.carlsenresources.com

Summary: Executive-level management positions
across all functions in cable TV, telephone,
cellular, DBS, wireless, entertainment,
multimedia, online and IT.

Key Contact - Specialty:
Ms. Ann R. Carlsen, Founder & Chief Executive
Officer
Mr. Dan Washington, Chief Operating Officer
Ms. Laurni Blanchard, Research Associate
Ms. Dolores Miles, Customer Care Associate

Salary Minimum: $200,000

Functions: Generalist (All), Mktg. Mgmt.,
Staffing, CFOs, MIS Mgmt.,
Minorities/Diversity, Int'l.

Industries: Generalist (All), Media, Advertising,
New Media, Broadcast, Film, Telecoms

Branches:
3621 Fillmore Ave
Brooklyn, NY 11234-4833
(718) 998-7722
Fax: (718) 998-8159

Carlson Food Careers

3486 Rice St
Saint Paul, MN 55126-3079
(651) 766-1081
Email: jobs@foodcareers.com
Web: www.foodcareers.com

Summary: We specialize in the placement of
personnel at all levels for the food manufacturing
industry. We work with national and multi-
national food manufacturers in retail packaged
goods as well as food ingredients. We serve
publicly and privately-owned clients who pay all
fees. We specialize in the fields of finance,
culinary, nutraceuticals, human resources, and
technical services.

Key Contact - Specialty:
Mr. Van Carlson, Recruiter

Functions: Generalist (All), Management

Industries: Food, Bev., Tobacco, Mgmt.
Consulting, Engineering Svcs., Logistics Svcs.,
Supply Chain Mgmt, Packaging

Carlson Research Group

5051 Castello Dr Ste 211
Naples, FL 34103-8985
(239) 649-7576
Fax: (239) 649-8058
Email: bc@carlsonresearch.com
Web: www.carlsonresearch.com

Summary: We are a nationally recognized
recruiting firm offering complete and cost
effective recruitment and research solutions to our
clients. We pride ourselves on the accuracy,
reliability and timeliness of our services.

Key Contact - Specialty:
Mr. Bob Carlson

Salary Minimum: $75,000

Functions: Management, HR Mgmt., Finance,
R&D

Industries: Manufacturing, Medical Devices,
Retail, Banking, Pharm Svcs., Hospitality,
Insurance, Hospitals

Carlyle Group LTD

625 N Michigan Ave Ste 2100
Chicago, IL 60611-3180
(312) 587-3030
Fax: (312) 587-0491
Email: research@carlylesearch.com
Web: www.carlylesearch.com

Summary: We have distinguished ourselves as a
premier retained executive search firm. We
provide recruiting services at every organizational
level from middle through top level executive
professionals. Areas of expertise include: financial
services, management consulting, real estate,
electronic commerce and strategy recruiting.

Key Contact - Specialty:
Mr. Max DeZara, President & Chief Executive
Officer
Mr. Larry S. Loubet, Managing Director
Mr. Ward P. Feste, Managing Director - *Real
estate*
Mr. Jon Schultz, Managing Director - *Real estate*
Ms. Samantha Whitney-Ulane, Managing
Director
Mr. Michael Wyman, Managing Director -
*Consumer, Financial services, Industrial,
Professional services, Technology*
Mr. Todd Justic, Principal - *Real estate*

Salary Minimum: $90,000

Functions: Management, Senior Mgmt., Middle
Mgmt., Finance, CFOs, Mgmt. Consultants

Industries: Manufacturing, Drugs Mfg., Medical
Devices, Finance, Banking, Misc. Financial,
Equip Svcs., Mgmt. Consulting, Real Estate,
Property/Facility Mgmt.

Carnegie Partners Inc†

3941 Park Dr Ste 20 PMB 353
El Dorado Hills, CA 95762-4549
(916) 941-9053
Fax: (916) 290-0312
Email: info@carnegiepartners.com
Web: www.carnegiepartners.com

Summary: Professional executive search firm
specializing in sales & marketing, recycling,
resource management, metals and senior
management positions.

Key Contact - Specialty:
Mr. Robert W. Hollis, President & Chief
Executive Officer - *Business development,
Environmental, Sales, Senior management*
Mr. Mark Lukacs, Partner - *Business
development, Construction, Environmental,
Healthcare*
Mr. Gary Liss, Partner - *Business development,
Environmental, Facilities engineering,
Government*
Dr. Jon Gelbard, PhD, Partner - *Business
development, Entertainment, Environmental,
Forest industry/products, Non-profit*
Mrs. Elizabeth Hollis, Partner & Chief Financial
Officer - *Environmental*

Salary Minimum: $50,000

Functions: Generalist (All), Management,
Distribution, Sales & Mktg., Attorneys

Industries: Generalist (All), Agri., Forestry,
Mining, Energy, Utilities, Construction,
Manufacturing, Metal Products, Electronic,
Elec. Components, Retail, Non-profits,
Environmental Svcs., Haz. Waste, Packaging,
Real Estate, Healthcare

Carpenter, Shackleton & Company

58 Foxwood Lane Ste 100
Barrington, IL 60010-1615
(847) 381-2555

Summary: We are a retainer search firm specializing in recruiting for public and private clients for all functions and industries.

Key Contact - Specialty:
Mr. George M. Shackleton, CMC, Managing Partner
Ms. DL Shackleton, Partner - *Marketing, Sales*
Ms. R. Allyn, Partner - *Healthcare, Information Technology*

Functions: Generalist (All)

Industries: Generalist (All)

Branches:
1720 S Indiana Ave
Chicago, IL 60616-1302
(312) 583-0800
Email: m.shackleton@sbcglobal.net
Key Contact - Specialty:
Mr. Michael Shackleton, Managing Partner, Chicago - *Distribution, Diversity, Education (Higher), Human resources, Management*
Mr. Eric Carpenter, Founding Partner - *General management*
Ms. L. Rodriguez, Partner - *Diversity, Marketing, Sales*

Carrington & Carrington Ltd
39 S La Salle St Ste 700
Chicago, IL 60603-1606
(312) 606-0015
Fax: (312) 606-0501
Email: wcarrington@cclltd.com
Web: www.cclltd.com

Summary: We are a full-service executive search firm that specializes in the recruitment and placement of African-American, Hispanic and other diverse professionals. We work across all functional and industry lines. We are considered specialists in diversity and earned our reputation by successfully placing senior executives in specialized areas.

Key Contact - Specialty:
Ms. Marian H. Carrington, Principal
Mr. Willie E. Carrington, Principal

Salary Mlnimum: $100,000

Functions: Generalist (All), Materials, Healthcare, Sales & Mktg., HR Mgmt., Finance, IT, Minorities/Diversity

Industries: Generalist (All), Food, Bev., Tobacco, Drugs Mfg., Finance, Telecoms

Carris, Jackowitz Associates
201 E 79th St
New York, NY 10021-0830
(212) 879-5482

Summary: We are generalists.

Key Contact - Specialty:
Mr. S. Joseph Carris, Partner

Salary Minimum: $75,000

Functions: Generalist (All), Management, Board Members, Senior Mgmt., Middle Mgmt.

Industries: Generalist (All)

Branches:
PO Box 54
Andover, NJ 07821-0054
(973) 786-5884

Key Contact - Specialty:
Mr. Ronald N. Jackowitz, Partner

Carson Kolb Healthcare Group Inc
20301 SW Birch St Ste 101
Newport Beach, CA 92660-1754
(949) 476-2988
(800) 606-9439
Fax: (949) 476-2155
Email: info@carsonkolb.com
Web: www.carsonkolb.com

Summary: We strive to provide the most professional and competent representation for healthcare organizations at the greatest value.

Key Contact - Specialty:
Mr. Matthew A. Kolb, President & Co-Founder - *Healthcare*
Ms. Sally C. Kolb, Chief Executive Officer & Co-Founder - *Healthcare*
Mr. Sam Couch, Recruiter

Salary Minimum: $80,000

Functions: Physicians

Industries: Healthcare

Carson-Thomas & Associates†
3550 Wilshire Blvd Ste 916
Los Angeles, CA 90010-2410
(213) 249-9040
Fax: (213) 249-9041
Email: carsonthomas@earthlink.net
Web: www.carsonthomas.com

Summary: We have many years worth of search, recruitment and placement experience. We have high quality applicant and client pools at all levels, including: college graduates with and without experience, administrative support, management through executive, professional and technical.

Key Contact - Specialty:
Ms. Sandra Carson, Partner
Mr. Frank Thomas, Partner
Ms. Jule Steingrueber-Worrell, MA, Partner & Office Manager

Functions: Generalist (All), Management, Sales & Mktg., HR Mgmt., Finance, IT, Specialized Svcs.

Industries: Generalist (All)

Carter Executive Search LLP
PO Box 702605
Dallas, TX 75370-2605
(972) 625-3345
Fax: (972) 625-3347
Email: chris@carterexecutivesearch.com
Web: www.carterexecutivesearch.com

Summary: We specialize in meeting our clients needs to find the best people in the industry. With experience in the retail supermarket industry, our principal has worked in retail operations, sales, HR and recruiting.

Key Contact - Specialty:
Mr. Chris Carter, President & Chief Executive Officer

Salary Minimum: $100,000

Functions: Generalist (All)

Industries: Generalist (All), Construction, Manufacturing, Transportation, Wholesale, Retail, Services, Accounting, HR Services, Logistics Svcs.

The Carter Group LLC
6321 Piccadilly Square Dr
Mobile, AL 36609-5103
(251) 342-0999
Email: larry.lemke@thecartergroup.com
Web: www.thecartergroup.com

Summary: We place senior level, all functions, GM, CEO and board. We have extensive candidate sourcing, rigorous assessment, presentation and process management in order to bring searches to a rapid successful conclusion with hires of the highest quality. We are averaging four weeks to source and identify person hired.

Key Contact - Specialty:
Mr. Guy W. Carter, President
Ms. Janice Spiker, Vice President
Mr. Jerome L. Haynesworth, Vice President - *Financial services*
Mr. Larry Lemke, Vice President

Salary Minimum: $150,000

Functions: Management, Mfg., Materials, Healthcare, Sales & Mktg., HR Mgmt., Finance, IT, Engineering, Int'l.

Industries: Agri., Forestry, Mining, Energy, Utilities, Construction, Manufacturing, Food, Bev., Tobacco, Motor Vehicles, Computer Equip., Transportation, Wholesale, Retail, Services, Higher Ed., Hospitality, Media, Communications, Telecoms, Aerospace, Real Estate, Software, Healthcare

CarterBaldwin
200 Mansell Ct E Ste 450
Roswell, GA 30076-4842
(678) 448-0000
Fax: (770) 552-1088
Email: info@carterbaldwin.com
Web: www.carterbaldwin.com

Summary: Ours is a retained executive search firm, managed by a partnership team with extensive search consulting experience. We conduct searches for positions ranging from CEO and board members to vice presidents and directors. We have partnered with companies ranging from pre-profit startups to Fortune 500 companies across multiple industries.

Key Contact - Specialty:
Mrs. Jennifer Poole Sobocinski, Managing Partner
Mr. Price Harding, Partner - *Boards of Directors, C-level, CEOs, CFOs, COOs*
Mr. David Sobocinski, Partner - *C-level, CEOs, CFOs, CIOs, COOs*
Mrs. Maggie Bellville, Partner - *Boards of Directors, C-level, Cable, Cellular, CEOs*

Salary Minimum: $125,000

Functions: Generalist (All), Management, Board Members, Senior Mgmt., Mfg., Sales & Mktg., HR Mgmt., Finance, CFOs, MIS Mgmt.

Industries: Generalist (All), Manufacturing

Caruso & Associates Inc
1509 N Military Trl Ste 216
West Palm Beach, FL 33409-4765
(561) 683-2336
Email: info@carusoassociates.com
Web: www.carusoassociates.com

Summary: Searches are performed by partners of firm and not handed off to other recruiters, a personal hands-on approach to develop a close working relationship with our clients.

Key Contact - Specialty:
Mr. Dennis J. Caruso, Managing Director - *Construction, Finance, Real estate, Resorts*

Salary Minimum: $75,000

Functions: Generalist (All)

Industries: Real Estate

Caruthers & Company LLC

1175 Post Rd E
Westport, CT 06880-5431
(203) 221-3234
(203) 454-0414
Fax: (203) 221-7300

Summary: Practice focused on senior-level corporate communications, public affairs, marketing services, advertising and marketing assignments. We have special expertise in pharmaceutical and biotechnology categories.

Key Contact - Specialty:
Mr. Robert D. Caruthers, Principal - *Marketing, Public relations*

Salary Minimum: $75,000

Functions: Advertising, Mktg. Research, Mktg. Mgmt., PR

Industries: Generalist (All)

Cary & Associates

PO Box 2043
Winter Park, FL 32790-2043
(407) 647-1145
Email: concary@caryassociates.com
Web: www.caryassociates.com

Summary: Our principal was a SVP of operations and HR for a retail/wholesale company. He also achieved significant success with a recognized search firm prior to starting the firm.

Key Contact - Specialty:
Mr. Con Cary, Owner - *Manufacturing, Retail, Wholesale*

Salary Minimum: $50,000

Functions: Generalist (All), Senior Mgmt., Middle Mgmt., Distribution, Sales Mgmt., CFOs, MIS Mgmt.

Industries: Generalist (All), Food, Bev., Tobacco, Transportation, Wholesale, Retail, Finance, Equip Svcs., Logistics Svcs., Restaurants, Quick Service Restaurants

Rosemary Cass Ltd

175 Post Rd W
Westport, CT 06880-4643
(203) 454-2920
Fax: (203) 454-4643
Email: resumes@rosemarycassltd.com
Web: www.rosemarycassltd.com

Summary: Specializes in pharmaceutical, biotechnology, medical devices and related healthcare industries. We perform searches in all disciplines within these industries.

Key Contact - Specialty:
Ms. Rosemary Cass, President

Salary Minimum: $150,000

Functions: Generalist (All)

Industries: Drugs Mfg., Medical Devices

The Cassie Shipherd Group LLC

26 Main St
Toms River, NJ 08753-7436
(732) 473-1779
Fax: (732) 473-1023
Email: cassiegroup@cassie.com
Web: www.cassie.com

Summary: Building management teams for the healthcare industry, more specifically: biotechnology, pharmaceuticals, diagnostics and medical devices. We have a major focus on emerging technology companies. We work across all functions including, but not limited to: general management, marketing, sales, R&D, operations, HR, QA/QC and regulatory.

Key Contact - Specialty:
Mr. Ronald L. Cassie, President
Dr. Richard Lutes, MD, Vice President
Dr. Sam Gallucci, SPHR, EdD, Vice President

Salary Minimum: $100,000

Functions: Board Members, Senior Mgmt., Quality, Mktg. Mgmt., Sales Mgmt., HR Mgmt., CFOs, R&D

Industries: Drugs Mfg., Medical Devices, Biotech/Life Sciences, Healthcare

Branches:
12809 Anthony Ln
Valley Center, CA 92082-5015
(760) 751-2174
Email: chuckh@cassie.com
Key Contact - Specialty:
Mr. Chuck Heiser, Vice President - *Medical (Devices), Pharmaceutical*

4 Middle St Ste 213
Newburyport, MA 01950-2764
(978) 462-5441
Email: jimm@cassie.com
Key Contact - Specialty:
Mr. Jim Myhre, Vice President - *Medical, Medical (Devices)*

12 Running Brook Rd
Bridgewater, NJ 08807-1412
(908) 429-1335
Fax: (908) 218-0213
Email: fredh@cassie.com
Key Contact - Specialty:
Dr. Fred P. Hauck, PhD, Vice President - *Biotechnology, Pharmaceutical*

PO Box 1674
New Bern, NC 28563-1674
(252) 634-9355
Fax: (252) 634-3090
Email: johns@cassie.com
Key Contact - Specialty:
Mr. John T. Shipherd, Managing Partner - *Biotechnology, Pharmaceutical*

PO Box 521125
Salt Lake City, UT 84152-1125
(801) 272-4668
Email: pingf@cassie.com
Key Contact - Specialty:
Ping Fong, Vice President - *Biotechnology, Pharmaceutical*

Catalyst Search Group

100 Tri State Intl Ste 230
Lincolnshire, IL 60069-4403
(847) 573-1967
Fax: (847) 367-8673
Email: talent@cooltechjobs.com
Web: www.cooltechjobs.com

Summary: We're a boutique search firm specializing in IT and high technology companies, helping companies identify, evaluate, and hire top performing technology managers and executives. We offer the benefits of large firm experience, and small firm attention. Our reputation is built upon: service, dedication, quality and results.

Key Contact - Specialty:
Mr. Greg Ambrose, Managing Director
Mr. Don Kinney, Vice President & IT Practice Leader - *CIOs, Information Technology, Systems, Technical, Technology*

Salary Minimum: $100,000

Functions: Management, Board Members, Senior Mgmt., Sales Mgmt., IT, MIS Mgmt., Systems Analysis, Systems Dev., Network Admin., DB Admin.

Industries: Generalist (All), Manufacturing, Finance, Services, Media, Communications, Insurance, Software, Biotech/Life Sciences

Catalyx Group

303 W 42nd St Ste 607
New York, NY 10036-6908
(212) 956-3525
Email: lposter@catalyx.com
Web: www.catalyx.com

Summary: We provide industry expertise in biotechnology, high technology and select consumer and industrial sectors. Our firm conducts searches for CEOs and management teams for private-equity buyouts and venture capital portfolio companies. We recruit exceptional CEOs, senior executives, board members and senior R&D leaders. We also recruit entire management teams for promising startups.

Key Contact - Specialty:
Mr. Lawrence D. Poster, Managing Director - *Biotechnology, Venture capital*
Mr. Karl C. Alorbi, PhD, Vice President - *Biopharmaceutical, Boards of Directors, C-level, International, Marketing*
Mr. Yossi Almoni, Vice President - *Biomedical, Biopharmaceutical, Biotechnology, High technology, Information Technology*

Salary Minimum: $100,000

Functions: Board Members, Senior Mgmt., Middle Mgmt., Sales & Mktg., Mktg. Mgmt., CFOs, M&A, IT, MIS Mgmt., R&D

Industries: Generalist (All), Manufacturing, Food, Bev., Tobacco, Chemicals, Soap, Perf., Cosmtcs., Drugs Mfg., Medical Devices, Retail, Finance, Banking, Invest. Banking, Venture Cap., E-commerce, Restaurants, New Media, Communications, Wireless, Software, Entertainment SW, Biotech/Life Sciences, Healthcare, Hospitals

Branches:
100-20 Stonepark Lane
Nepean, ON K2H 9P4
Canada
(613) 726-7379
Email: pwinter@catalyx.com
Key Contact - Specialty:
Mr. Peter Winter, MS, Director - *Clinical, Management*

Michael J Cavanagh & Associates Inc

213-250 Eglinton Ave W
Toronto, ON M4R 1A7
Canada
(416) 324-9661
Email: cavsearch@sympatico.ca

Summary: We are one of Canada's most experienced recruiters, established in the aerospace, automotive, industrial engineered products, medical equipment, and packaged goods industries, to name a few. Our firm operates at the senior executive level. We also have served a number of US-based aerospace and telecommunications companies, including multi-billion dollar clients.

Key Contact - Specialty:
Mr. Michael Cavanagh, President
Mr. Bill McKinlay, Partner

Salary Minimum: $100,000

† occasional contingency assignment

Functions: Generalist (All), Senior Mgmt., Plant Mgmt., Purchasing, Mktg. Mgmt., Sales Mgmt., CFOs, MIS Mgmt.

Industries: Generalist (All), Drugs Mfg., Motor Vehicles, Hospitality, Aerospace, Healthcare

CBI Group Inc[†]

1298 Rockbridge Rd Ste B
Stone Mountain, GA 30087-3165
(770) 925-2915
(800) 875-1292
Fax: (770) 925-2601
Email: cbinc@mindspring.com
Web: www.cbisearch.com

Summary: We are nationwide executive search and recruiting professionals in the consulting and engineering disciplines. Our firm provides civil, mechanical, electrical, structural engineering and planning design specialists. Clients include outstanding firms representing a variety of project types and employing from 15 to 3000 employees from coast to coast.

Key Contact - Specialty:
Mr. Phil Collins, President
Mr. Bob Bowers, Executive Vice President - *Electrical, Mechanical*
Mr. Greg George, Vice President

Functions: Generalist (All), Engineering

Industries: Transportation, Services, Architectural Svcs., Engineering Svcs., Environmental Svcs.

CCL Contracts Consultancy Inc[†]

11490 Westheimer Rd Ste 850
Houston, TX 77077-6845
(713) 425-6304
Fax: (713) 783-0067
Email: chris.maltby@ccl.us.com
Web: www.cclglobal.com

Summary: Our firm is a leading company in the recruitment and provision of personnel to the oil and gas industry to projects worldwide.

Key Contact - Specialty:
Mr. Chris Maltby, Operations Manager

Functions: Generalist (All), Middle Mgmt., Production, Staffing, Eng. Design

Industries: Energy, Utilities, Oil & Gas, Construction

Cedrone & O'Neill[†]

1 Technology Park Dr Unit B
Bourne, MA 02532-8336
(800) 693-2074
(508) 759-8305
Fax: (617) 332-3343
Email: dsugar@co-consulting.com
Web: www.co-consulting.com

Summary: We specialize in placing mid to senior level manager in the building products and construction channels.

Key Contact - Specialty:
Mr. Matt Cedrone, President
Mr. Dave Sugar, Vice President

Salary Minimum: $80,000

Functions: Sales & Mktg., Sales Mgmt.

Industries: Construction, Consumer Goods

Cejka Search

(a Cross Country Healthcare Inc company)
222 S Central Ave Ste 400
Saint Louis, MO 63105-3509
(314) 726-1603
(800) 678-7858
Fax: (314) 726-0026

Email: lrobertson@cejkasearch.com
Web: www.cejkasearch.com

Summary: We are a nationally recognized executive and physician search firm providing recruitment services exclusively to the healthcare industry. Partnering with organizations in pursuit of the nation's best healthcare talent, our firm completes over 500 assignments annually across all levels of the healthcare continuum.

Key Contact - Specialty:
Ms. Carol Westfall, President - *Healthcare*
Ms. Mary Scholz Barber, Vice President, Marketing
Mr. Mike Calcagno, Senior Vice President, Client & Mkt Dev
Ms. Karen Ensor, Director, Human Resources
Ms. Karen Robbins, Controller
Mr. Mark Ross, Director, Technology
Ms. Lori Schutte, Vice President, Client Services
Mr. Paul Smallwood, Vice President, Physician Search
Ms. Debbie Biggs, Director, Client Services
Mr. Allan Cacanindin, Associate Director, Marketing
Ms. Michelle Phillips, Director, Candidate Acquistion

Salary Minimum: $90,000

Functions: Management, Senior Mgmt., Middle Mgmt., Healthcare, CFOs, Mgmt. Consultants

Industries: Insurance, Biotech/Life Sciences, Healthcare

Cendea

13740 N Highway 183 Ste O1
Austin, TX 78750-1835
(512) 219-6000
Email: info.kd@cendea.com
Web: www.cendea.com

Summary: We are a senior-level executive search firm. Different by design, our proprietary processes and methodologies, along with our senior staff only policy, allows us to get the information you need to make an informed decision for your company.

Key Contact - Specialty:
Mr. Wade Allen, President & Chief Executive Officer

Salary Minimum: $150,000

Functions: Management, Board Members, Senior Mgmt., Middle Mgmt., Mfg., Healthcare, Sales & Mktg., Mktg. Mgmt., Sales Mgmt., CFOs

Industries: Generalist (All), Energy, Utilities, Oil & Gas, Manufacturing, Printing, Computer Equip., Banking, Services, Telecoms, Call Centers, Software, Healthcare, Hospitals

Cenera Inc

1015 4 St SW
Office Building
Calgary, AB T2R 1J4
Canada
(403) 290-0466
(800) 387-8797
Fax: (403) 294-0513
Email: debra.johnstone@cenera.ca
Web: www.cenera.ca

Summary: Successfully conduct searches in a broad range of industries and government. Treat every engagement as a partnership with our client, determining the best way to streamline the process without compromising thoroughness.

Key Contact - Specialty:
Ms. Debra J. Johnstone, Partner
Mr. Gary R. Agnew, Partner
Mr. Bruce Green, Partner

Mr. Bruce Wade, Partner
Mr. Jerry Stilson, Partner

Salary Minimum: $80,000

Functions: Generalist (All)

Industries: Generalist (All)

CEO Resources Inc

1616 Walnut St Ste 1605
Philadelphia, PA 19103-5304
(215) 209-3065
Email: resume2@ceoresources.com
Web: www.ceoresources.com

Summary: We match candidates who fit the cultures of organizations and bring the ability to catapult companies to significant business growth. Companies in the technology, biotech/pharmaceutical, service, and other industries have retained us for search services. We have been recognized for fostering communications with clients and providing intimate customer service.

Key Contact - Specialty:
Ms. R. Linda Resnick, President

Salary Minimum: $150,000

Functions: Generalist (All), Board Members, Senior Mgmt.

Industries: Generalist (All), Manufacturing, Drugs Mfg., Computer Equip., Consumer Elect., Misc. Mfg., Semiconductors, Finance, Services, Non-profits, E-commerce, Communications, Software, Biotech/Life Sciences

CES Partners Ltd

53 W Jackson Blvd Ste 1526
Chicago, IL 60604-4169
(312) 987-4505
(866) 987-4505
Fax: (312) 386-1557
Email: bcesafsky@cespartners.net
Web: www.cespartners.net

Summary: Our firm is a premier executive search firm dedicated to assisting progressive organizations fulfill their recruitment needs. We are specially suited for and committed to the health care industry.

Key Contact - Specialty:
Mr. Barry Cesafsky, President & Chief Executive Officer
Mr. Scott Smith
Ms. Pamela Andrews
Mr. Thomas W. Burke
Mr. Edward F. Otto
Ms. Rita Wall
Ms. Sarita Gilligan

Salary Minimum: $100,000

Functions: Generalist (All), Management, Senior Mgmt., Healthcare

Industries: Non-profits, Insurance, Healthcare, Hospitals, Long-term/Home Care

CFOheadhunter LLC[†]

1212 Brightwaters Blvd NE
Saint Petersburg, FL 33704-3728
(727) 821-3380
Email: pat@cfoheadhunter.com
Web: www.cfoheadhunter.com

Summary: Our firm is a recruitment business focused on bringing together CFOs and private equity backed companies that seek them. Our practice includes senior level executive search, board services - especially audit committee members and pre-acquisition management assessment.

Key Contact - Specialty:
Mr. Patrick M. Jennings, Managing Partner

Salary Minimum: $175,000

Functions: CFOs

Industries: Generalist (All)

cFour Partners Worldwide

100 Wilshire Blvd Ste 1840
Santa Monica, CA 90401-3601
(310) 394-2639
Fax: (310) 394-2669
Email: info@cfour.com
Web: www.cfour.com

Summary: We offer services for semiconductor, networking & telecom, digital media & entertainment, private equity practice and venture capital markets across all functional roles.

Key Contact - Specialty:
Mr. Robert W. Bellano, Founder & Managing Director
Mr. John Emery, Director
Ms. Christina Ramstein, Director
Mr. Andy Riabokin, Director
Mr. David Shotland, Director - *Administration, Information Technology, Operations*

Salary Minimum: $100,000

Functions: Senior Mgmt.

Industries: Energy, Utilities, Computer Equip., Venture Cap., E-commerce, New Media, Broadcast, Film, Telecoms, Wireless, Fiber Optic, Software

Branches:
7825 Fay Ave Ste 200
La Jolla, CA 92037-4270
(619) 595-3800
(858) 456-3585
Fax: (619) 334-7782
Email: info@cfour.com
Key Contact - Specialty:
Mr. Donald Parker, Director - *Biotechnology, Computers (Software), Telecommunications*

Chaitin & Associates Inc†

22543 Ventura Blvd Ste 220
Woodland Hills, CA 91364-1403
(818) 225-8655
Fax: (818) 225-8660
Email: execpro2@aol.com

Summary: We are an executive search firm with experience working for major corporate clients. We conduct careful searches for all clients from the background of personality, technical background and education for all of our clients.

Key Contact - Specialty:
Mr. Chuck Hayes, Vice President - *Finance, Manufacturing*
Mr. Dick Chaitin, Vice President

Salary Minimum: $25,000

Functions: Senior Mgmt., Middle Mgmt., Plant Mgmt., Sales & Mktg., Advertising, Sales Mgmt., Staffing, CFOs

Industries: Generalist (All), Textiles, Apparel, Wholesale, Retail, Misc. Financial, HR Services

Chaloner Associates Inc†

36 Milford St
Boston, MA 02118-3612
(617) 451-5170
Fax: (617) 451-8160
Email: info@chaloner.com
Web: www.chaloner.com

Summary: We work in the fields of corporate communications, marketing, public relations,
advertising, investor relations, internal, organizational and marketing communications.

Key Contact - Specialty:
Mr. Edward H. Chaloner, President
Mr. Tom Lutrzy, Executive Vice President - *Communications*
Mr. Scott White, Senior Associate
Ms. Amy Lafond, Associate - *Public relations*
Mr. Rich Young, Associate
Ms. Sally Burke, Associate - *Advertising, Marketing*
Ms. Mary Harman, Associate
Ms. Jenn Marcotte, Project Manager
Ms. Jeanne MacMillan, Associate

Salary Minimum: $75,000

Functions: Advertising, Mktg. Research, Mktg. Mgmt., Direct Mktg., PR, Graphic Designers

Industries: Generalist (All)

Chandler Group

4165 Shoreline Dr Ste 220
Spring Park, MN 55384-9613
(952) 471-3000
Fax: (952) 471-3021
Email: bchandler@chandgroup.com
Web: www.chandgroup.com

Summary: We are a retained executive search firm with a singular focus on the success of our clients. By forming true partnerships, we provide client organizations with the commitment and expertise to identify, acquire and retain top talent that will ensure organizational success in today's challenging business environment. We do this with unwavering integrity, respect for all individuals and total dedication to our long-term professional relationships.

Key Contact - Specialty:
Mr. Brad J. Chandler, Principal - *Healthcare, HMOs, Hospital, Managed care, Medical (Devices)*
Ms. Cynthia A. Chandler, Principal - *Communications, Finance, Manufacturing, Non-profit, Transportation*
Mr. Thom B. Telfer, Partner - *Associations, Consumer (Packaged Goods), Finance, Manufacturing (Management), Organizational development*
Ms. Nancy M. Hovren, Senior Consultant - *Financial services, Healthcare, Hospital, Information Systems, Non-profit*
Mr. Mark A. Klingsheim, Vice President - *Financial services, Information Technology, Manufacturing (Management), Medical, Medical (Devices)*

Salary Minimum: $90,000

Functions: Board Members, Senior Mgmt., Middle Mgmt., Mgmt. Consultants

Industries: Generalist (All), Medical Devices, Misc. Mfg., Consumer Goods, Mutual/Hedge Funds, Non-profits, Mgmt. Consulting, HR Services, Media, Government, Insurance, Healthcare, Hospitals

ChangeBridge International

(an affiliate of MRI)
150 River Rd Ste H-1
Montville, NJ 07045-9441
(973) 316-9371
Fax: (973) 316-9373
Email: kit@changebridgeinternational.com
Web: www.changebridgeinternational.com

Summary: Our firm is dedicated to working together with a common focus on delivering the top talent in a focused market in order to provide our clients with the total staffing solution resource. We bring a wide and varied range of market experience, complementing our respective markets
and objectives enabling us to team as necessary on the full range of services.

Key Contact - Specialty:
Ms. Kit Welge, Managing Partner
Mr. Keith Allen, Project Coordinator
Mr. Andy Kazi, Project Coordinator
Ms. Kelly Nadar, Research Associate - *Aerospace, Management, Military, Technical, Training*

Functions: Mfg.

Industries: Soap, Perf., Cosmtcs., Drugs Mfg., Medical Devices, Plastics, Rubber, Metal Products

Chanko-Ward Ltd

2 W 45th St
New York, NY 10036-4212
(212) 869-4040
Email: info@chankoward.com
Web: www.chankoward.com

Summary: For many years we have focused on the identification and selection of financial, accounting, planning, HR and IT professionals in all industries. Our consulting business format is based upon a practiced philosophy of one-to-one personal service.

Key Contact - Specialty:
Mr. Jim Chanko, President

Salary Minimum: $150,000

Functions: HR Mgmt., Finance, CFOs, Budgeting, Cash Mgmt., M&A, IT

Industries: Generalist (All), Banking, Invest. Banking, Mutual/Hedge Funds, Misc. Financial

Robert B Channing Consulting

1099 Rebecca St
Oakville, ON L6L 1Y6
Canada
(905) 338-9981
Fax: (905) 338-9982
Email: rbcc@cogeco.ca

Summary: We are small firm working in all sectors.

Key Contact - Specialty:
Mr. Robert B. Channing, Founder

Salary Minimum: $75,000

Functions: Generalist (All)

Industries: Generalist (All)

The Chapman Group Inc†

8151 E Evans Rd Ste 4
Scottsdale, AZ 85260-3648
(480) 483-8833
Fax: (480) 483-6750
Email: jeffc@thechapmangroup.com
Web: www.thechapmangroup.com

Summary: We conduct searches for mission-critical individual contributors, managers and executives for technology companies with an emphasis on manufacturing automation technology companies.

Key Contact - Specialty:
Mr. Jeff H. Chapman, President & Chief Search Consultant - *Executives, Factories, Factories (Automation), Marketing, Robotics*

Salary Minimum: $55,000

Functions: Generalist (All), Senior Mgmt., Middle Mgmt., Automation, Sales Mgmt., Systems Implem., Engineering

Industries: Generalist (All), Machine, Appliance, Test, Measure Equip., Mgmt. Consulting, Software

Charleston Partners
2 Bellevue Ave
Rumson, NJ 07760-1105
(732) 842-5015
Fax: (732) 842-0993
Email: info@charlestonpartners.com
Web: www.charlestonpartners.com

Summary: A retained "boutique" executive search firm that exclusively recruits human resource executives globally.

Key Contact - Specialty:
Mr. Francis Luisi, Principal - *Human resources*
Ms. Jill Krumholz, Principal - *Communications, Human resources, Media, Printing, Publishing*

Salary Minimum: $150,000

Functions: HR Mgmt., Benefits, Staffing, Training

Industries: HR Services

Branches:
13 Seagrass Ln
Isle of Palms, SC 29451-2838
(843) 886-0608
Fax: (208) 575-6018
Email: nherron@charlestonpartners.com
Key Contact - Specialty:
Ms. Nan Herron

The Chase Group Inc
10955 Lowell Ave Ste 500
Overland Park, KS 66210-2326
(913) 663-3100
Fax: (913) 663-3131
Email: chase@chasegroup.com
Web: www.chasegroup.com

Summary: We offer an unparalleled level of professional recruiting service to our clients. Our staffing experts work exclusively in the substantive areas of the life sciences industry including: global pharmaceuticals, biotechnology, diagnostics and medical devices; allowing us to remain focused on identifying the highest quality personnel for these markets.

Key Contact - Specialty:
Ms. Karen Leathers, President - *Biotechnology, Diagnostics, Pharmaceutical*
Mr. Ken Allison, Chief Operating Officer - *Biotechnology, Diagnostics, Pharmaceutical*

Functions: Management, Senior Mgmt., Mfg., Materials, Sales & Mktg., HR Mgmt., M&A, IT, R&D, Int'l.

Industries: Drugs Mfg., Medical Devices, Pharm Svcs., Media, Advertising, Biotech/Life Sciences, Healthcare

Chase Hunter Group Inc
1143 W North Shore Ave
Chicago, IL 60626-4617
(773) 338-7865
(773) 338-1389
Email: bdouglas@chase-hunter.com
Web: www.chase-hunter.com

Summary: Our firm is healthcare's partner in retained executive search, focusing on the clinical and administrative placements from the director level to the CEO. We place the right people in the right roles in the right organization. We are a boutique firm that is quality, and not number, driven.

Key Contact - Specialty:
Mr. Bob Douglas, Managing Partner
Mr. Jim Schneider, ACHE, Senior Parnter - *Operations, Systems*
Ms. Diana Monier, Associate Partner

Salary Minimum: $50,000

Functions: Generalist (All), Middle Mgmt., Healthcare, Allied Health, Health Admin., MIS Mgmt.

Industries: Generalist (All), Drugs Mfg., Services, HR Services, Insurance, Healthcare

ChaseAmerica Inc
3931 RCA Blvd Ste 3106
Northcorp Center
Palm Beach Gardens, FL 33410-4215
(561) 491-5000
Fax: (561) 491-5001
Email: dstefan@chaseamericainc.com
Web: www.chaseamericainc.com

Summary: Our firm is a retained executive search firm, which has recruited and placed senior level management for homebuilders, land developers, commercial real estate, multifamily, hotels, resorts and golf course communities and high net worth individuals in real estate.

Key Contact - Specialty:
Mr. David E. Stefan, President - *Apparel, Sports*
Mr. Mike Williams, Managing Partner - *Construction, General contractors, Real estate*
Mrs. Ceil Schiavo, Manager - *Entertainment, Hotels, Resorts, Sports*

Salary Minimum: $100,000

Functions: Generalist (All), Board Members, Senior Mgmt., Hospitality

Industries: Generalist (All), Construction, Manufacturing, Finance, Services, Hospitality, Hotels, Resorts, Clubs, Restaurants, Media, Communications, Environmental Svcs., Aerospace, Insurance, Real Estate, Property/Facility Mgmt., Entertainment SW, Biotech/Life Sciences, Healthcare

AD Check Associates Inc
204 S Franklin St
Wilkes Barre, PA 18701-1101
(570) 829-5066
Fax: (570) 820-8293
Email: check204@aol.com

Summary: Near 100 percent completion rate; deep, long term client commitments, 75 percent of volume is repeat business; performance-based contracts; competitively favorable fee and expense structures.

Key Contact - Specialty:
Mr. Andrew D. Check, President - *Healthcare, Manufacturing*

Salary Minimum: $60,000

Functions: Generalist (All)

Industries: Manufacturing, Accounting, Mgmt. Consulting, HR Services, Advertising, Telecoms, Healthcare

The Cherbonnier Group Inc
(a division of TCG International Inc)
1 Riverway Ste 1700
Houston, TX 77056-1997
(713) 688-4701
Email: mikec@chergroup.com
Web: www.thecherbonniergroup.com

Summary: Searches have crossed most industry lines and most senior positions both line and staff. Many years of executive search experience. Provide in-depth candidate evaluations.

Key Contact - Specialty:
Mr. L. Michael Cherbonnier, President

Salary Minimum: $150,000

Functions: Generalist (All), Management, Board Members, Senior Mgmt.

Industries: Generalist (All), Energy, Utilities, Oil & Gas, Construction, Manufacturing, Chemicals, Medical Devices, Paints, Petro. Products, Finance, Invest. Banking, Venture Cap., Services, Legal, Mgmt. Consulting, HR Services, Engineering Svcs., Government, Environmental Svcs., Biotech/Life Sciences

The Cheyenne Group
60 E 42nd St Rm 2821
New York, NY 10165-2814
(212) 471-5000
Fax: (212) 471-5050
Email: candidates@cheyennegroup.com
Web: www.cheyennegroup.com

Summary: We are an executive search firm that has built a global reputation for having the scope and reach of some of the larger firms with the attention to detail, industry expertise and care of a specialized boutique.

Key Contact - Specialty:
Ms. Pat Mastandrea, Partner & Chief Executive Officer
Mr. Jeff Schon, Partner - *Education, Publishing*
Ms. Regina Angeles, Principal, Mosaic - *Diversity*
Mr. Peter Herrick, Controller & CAO
Ms. Elizabeth Gaines, Executive Assistant - *Communications, Entertainment, Media, New media, Publishing*

Salary Minimum: $150,000

Functions: Generalist (All), Middle Mgmt.

Industries: Mgmt. Consulting, HR Services, E-commerce, Media, Advertising, Publishing, New Media, Broadcast, Film

Branches:
1875 Century Park E Ste 600
Los Angeles, CA 90067-2507
(310) 284-3230
Key Contact - Specialty:
Ms. Franca Virgili, Founding Partner
Ms. Sonia Norville, Executive Assistant

23676 N Mcgraw Ct
Port Barrington, IL 60010-1025
(847) 277-1141
Key Contact - Specialty:
Ms. Anne Bishop, Senior Associate

Chicago Consulting Partners Ltd
930 S 4th Ave Unit 7
Libertyville, IL 60048-3429
(847) 680-0416
Email: morganpierce@morganpierce.com
Web: www.ccpltd.com

Summary: Search firm specializing in managerial, senior technical and executive level positions. Principals experienced in industries of specialty.

Key Contact - Specialty:
Mr. Brett P. Lichty, Principal - *Benefits, Communications, Consulting, Insurance, Non-profit*
Mr. Robert Pugh, Principal - *Benefits, Communications, Compensation, Financial services, Management consulting*

Salary Minimum: $70,000

Functions: Generalist (All), Senior Mgmt., Product Dev., Sales & Mktg., Benefits, Actuaries, Graphic Designers

Industries: Generalist (All), Finance, Services, Non-profits, Architectural Svcs., Legal, Accounting, Mgmt. Consulting, HR Services, Media, Communications, Insurance, Casualty, Claims, Life, Commercial, Re-Insurance, Software, Doc. Mgmt., Production SW, Entertainment SW, Healthcare

Chicago Research Group Inc

PO Box 3757
Chapel Hill, NC 27515-3757
(919) 968-0120
Email: admin@chicagoresearch.com
Web: www.chicagoresearch.com

Summary: Boutique generalist firm

Key Contact - Specialty:
Ms. Deborah Marshall, President
Mr. Bob Ross, Vice President

Salary Minimum: $75,000

Functions: Generalist (All)

Industries: Generalist (All)

Chiron Advisors Inc

420 Lexington Ave Rm 2736
New York, NY 10170-2799
(212) 867-6969
Fax: (212) 867-7449
Email: mstone@chironadvisors.com
Web: www.chironadvisors.com

Summary: Executive search firm focused exclusively on financial services industry.

Key Contact - Specialty:
Ms. Margaret Stone, President - *Financial services*

Salary Minimum: $100,000

Functions: Management, Healthcare, Finance, Risk Mgmt.

Industries: Finance

Chisholm & Partners International Inc[†]

2600-161 Bay St
B C E Place
Toronto, ON M5J 2S1
Canada
(416) 777-6800
Email: info@chisintl.com
Web: www.chisintl.com

Summary: Our firm is committed to an uncompromised level of service, wherein each search is tailored to meet the needs of our clients in a timely manner. Every search is carefully planned and executed to identify and attract the best candidates available in today's professional arena. A distinguishing factor of our firm is the ability to understand and analyze a client's organizational needs.

Key Contact - Specialty:
Mr. Timothy J. Chisholm, Principal
Ms. Sherrilynn Chisholm, Principal

Salary Minimum: $75,000

Functions: Generalist (All), Management

Industries: Generalist (All), Soap, Perf., Cosmtcs., Banking, Invest. Banking, Brokers, Venture Cap., Mutual/Hedge Funds, Misc. Financial, Life, Re-Insurance

CHM Partners International LLC

466 Southern Blvd
Chatham, NJ 07928-1462
(973) 966-1600
Fax: (973) 966-6933
Email: solutions@chm-partners.com
Web: www.chm-partners.com

Summary: We have partner management of all assignments. Our practice serves large public corporations and small privately held organizations in professional services, biotechnology/pharmaceutical, academia/research centers, non-profit and manufacturing industries.

Key Contact - Specialty:
Mr. Robert N. McDowell, Managing Partner - *Education, Financial services, Manufacturing, Non-profit, Professional services*
Mr. Paul H. Sartori, Partner - *Biotechnology, Diagnostics, Management consulting, Pharmaceutical, Start-up companies*
Mr. James J. Welch, Partner - *Biotechnology, Executives, Management consulting, Pharmaceutical, Research & development*

Salary Minimum: $120,000

Functions: Generalist (All), Board Members, Senior Mgmt., Mktg. Mgmt., Sales Mgmt., HR Mgmt., CFOs, MIS Mgmt., Mgmt. Consultants, Int'l.

Industries: Generalist (All), Manufacturing, Finance, Banking, Services, Non-profits, Pharm Svcs., Legal, Higher Ed., Telecoms, Insurance, Biotech/Life Sciences, Healthcare

Choi & Burns LLC

152 W 57th St Fl 32
Carnegie Hall Tower
New York, NY 10019-3310
(212) 755-7051
Fax: (212) 355-2610
Email: info@choiburns.com
Web: www.choiburns.com

Summary: We are completely client driven, very consultative boutique search firm with exclusive focus on financial services, primarily investment banking and private equity.

Key Contact - Specialty:
Ms. Julie A. Choi, President & Chief Executive Officer
Ms. Bethany E. Burns, Managing Director
Ms. Sumi W. Kang, Managing Director - *Banking, Banking (Investment), Buyout funds, Private equity, Venture capital*

Salary Minimum: $500,000

Functions: Generalist (All), Management, Board Members, M&A

Industries: Generalist (All), Invest. Banking, Venture Cap.

CHRIS Kauffman & Company[†]

PO Box 53218
Atlanta, GA 30355-1218
(404) 233-3530
Fax: (404) 262-7960
Email: chris@restaurantallstars.com
Web: www.restaurantallstars.com

Summary: Specializing in the nationwide placement of restaurant industry professionals including corporate restaurant industry executives, culinary professionals, field & unit operations management.

Key Contact - Specialty:
Mr. Christopher C. Kauffman, President

Salary Minimum: $50,000

Functions: Generalist (All), Senior Mgmt.

Industries: Generalist (All), Hospitality

Chrisman & Company Inc

350 S Figueroa St Ste 550
Los Angeles, CA 90071-1300
(213) 620-1192
Email: info@chrismansearch.com
Web: www.chrismansearch.com

Summary: Our firm provides board member, mid and upper-echelon executive searches.

Key Contact - Specialty:
Mr. Timothy Chrisman, President

Salary Minimum: $150,000

Functions: Generalist (All), Board Members, Senior Mgmt., Middle Mgmt., HR Mgmt., Finance, CFOs

Industries: Generalist (All), Finance, Banking, Invest. Banking, Brokers, Misc. Financial, Insurance, Real Estate

Christian & Timbers

1177 Avenue of the Americas Fl 18
New York, NY 10036-2714
(212) 588-3500
(800) 380-9444
Fax: (212) 688-5754
Email: comments@ctnet.com
Web: www.ctnet.com

Summary: Executive search firm focusing on CEO, board of directors and senior-level executive assignments.

Key Contact - Specialty:
Mr. Brian Sullivan, Chairman & Chief Executive Officer
Mr. David Nocifora, Chief Operating and Financial Officer
Mr. Burke St. John, Vice Chair
Mr. Brendan Burnett-Stohner, Vice Chair - *Private equity*
Ms. Kerry Allison-Gaines
Mr. Daniel C. Barr
Mr. Craig Bower
Mr. Barry Bregman
Ms. Cynthia M. Brunjes
Ms. Rosemarie Bruno
Mr. Glenn M. Buggy
Ms. Samantha Carey
Kari Chachkes
Mr. Jim DiFilippo
Ms. Jennifer Edwards
Mr. William B. Feehan
Mr. Hugo Fueglein
Mr. Marc Gasperino
Ms. Rebecca Glasman
Mr. Dennis Grant
Mr. Paul J. Groce
Mr. Douglas G. Hanslip
Mr. Daniel A. Kaplan
Ms. Jeneane Kee
Mr. Gary I. Klein
Sandy Li
Ms. Helga Long
Mr. Keith S. Macomber
Ms. Andrea (Ang) Norod
Mr. Steven Payne
Mr. Ronald Porter
Mr. Adam J. Prager
Mr. Jeffrey I. Shapiro
Mr. Serguei Zaychenko

Salary Minimum: $225,000

Functions: Board Members, Senior Mgmt.

Industries: Generalist (All)

Branches:
2180 Sand Hill Rd Ste 300
Menlo Park, CA 94025-6947
(650) 798-0980
Fax: (650) 854-8026
Key Contact - Specialty:
Mr. Craig G. Smith, Managing Partner
Mr. Ben Anderson
Mr. William A. Domann, Jr.
Mr. Robert L. Forman
Mr. Simon J. Francis
Mr. Louis J. La Rocca
Mr. Dimitri Tsamados

875 15th St NW Ste 901
Washington, DC 20005-2236
(202) 730-7910

Key Contact - Specialty:
Mr. Danny Gillis
Mr. Richard W. Herman
Mr. Martin Mendelsohn
Mr. Peter Metzger
Kerry Moynihan
Ms. Beth Solomon
Mr. Bradley Webb
Mr. Stephen Winings

10211 Wincopin Cir Ste 480
Columbia, MD 21044-3428
(443) 393-0001
Fax: (410) 872-0208
Key Contact - Specialty:
Mr. William (Buster) C. Houchins, Vice Chair
Mr. Richard Alexander
Stacy A. Braun
Mr. Ernest W. Brittingham
Mr. Steve Cornacchia
Mr. Gregory J. Lovas

24 New England Executive Park Ste 2
Burlington, MA 01803-5206
(781) 229-9515
Fax: (781) 229-8608
Key Contact - Specialty:
Mr. Stephen P. Mader, Vice Chair
Ms. Jennifer M. Burgess
Ms. Jennifer M. Condon
Ms. Carol Corley
Mr. Peter Dube
Mr. Jeff Leopold
Mr. David J. Merwin
Mr. William J. Michaud
Mr. Peter Witt

25825 Science Park Dr Ste 100
Beachwood, OH 44122-7315
(216) 464-8710
Fax: (216) 464-6160
Key Contact - Specialty:
Ms. Helen Briggs
Mr. James C. Carter
Mr. Tony Charles
Mr. Christopher J. Conti
Ms. Monica Hill
Mr. Adam P. Kohn, Vice Chair
Mr. Geoffrey P. Loree
Mr. John H. Moon
Mr. Umesh Ramakrishnan, Vice Chair
Nawf Tannous
Mr. Robert F. Voth
Mr. John K. Westropp

William J Christopher Associates Inc

307 N Walnut St
West Chester, PA 19380-2623
(610) 696-4397
Fax: (610) 692-5177
Email: wjc@wjca.com
Web: www.wjca.com

Summary: We have many years of successful executive search experience at corporate and operating levels with companies large, small, public and private with business in diversified industries, such as distribution, manufacturing and service companies.

Key Contact - Specialty:
Mr. John Jeffrey Bole, President

Salary Minimum: $50,000

Functions: Board Members, Senior Mgmt., Middle Mgmt., Plant Mgmt.

Industries: Generalist (All), Manufacturing, Paper, Printing, Services, Packaging

Christopher-Westmont & Associates Inc

PO Box 470188
Broadview Heights, OH 44147-0188
(440) 877-0510
Fax: (440) 877-0511
Email: cwestmont@aol.com

Summary: Firm is focused on high technology including manufacturing, engineering and operations in automotive and general industry.

Key Contact - Specialty:
Mr. John R. Donnelly, Consultant
Mr. Patrick Donnelly, Consultant - *Financial services*
Mr. Christopher Donnelly, Consultant - *Manufacturing*
Mr. Randy Letsch, Partner

Salary Minimum: $100,000

Functions: Senior Mgmt., Mfg., Plant Mgmt., Quality, Materials, Sales & Mktg., Sales Mgmt., HR Mgmt., CFOs, Engineering

Industries: Generalist (All), Metal Products, Motor Vehicles, Aerospace, Packaging, Biotech/Life Sciences

CHS & Associates†

PO Box 5581
Evanston, IL 60204-5581
(847) 328-0095
Email: chuck@chscreativesearch.com
Web: www.chscreativesearch.com

Summary: We offer a range of customized recruitment and search services and fee structures to meet the needs of our clients. We have experience in a wide range of management functions and industries with an emphasis in, but not limited too, marketing, branding, direct marketing, events planning, advertising, creative management and design. We also provide selective career, executive coaching and customized outplacement services.

Key Contact - Specialty:
Mr. Charles Silverstein, Principal

Salary Minimum: $40,000

Functions: Generalist (All), Management, Advertising, Mktg. Research, Mktg. Mgmt., Direct Mktg., Staffing, Training, Graphic Designers

Industries: Generalist (All), Textiles, Apparel, Retail, Non-profits, HR Services, E-commerce, Higher Ed., Advertising, Publishing, New Media, Broadcast, Film, Wireless, Fiber Optic, Packaging, Marketing SW

Churchill & Affiliates Inc

1200 Bustleton Pike Ste 3
Feasterville Trevose, PA 19053-4108
(215) 421-1740
Fax: (215) 322-4391
Email: hwasserman@churchillsearch.com
Web: www.churchillsearch.com

Summary: We are an executive search and recruitment for the telecom industry. Specialize in sales, marketing, engineering and support from senior management to field sales and support.

Key Contact - Specialty:
Mr. Harvey Wasserman, President

Salary Minimum: $75,000

Functions: Senior Mgmt., Middle Mgmt., Production

Industries: Equip Svcs., Advertising, Telecoms, Call Centers, Telephony, Digital, Wireless, Fiber Optic, Network Infrastructure, Software, Networking, Comm. SW

Cizek Associates Inc

2415 E Camelback Rd Ste 700
Phoenix, AZ 85016-4245
(602) 553-1066
Fax: (602) 553-1166
Email: phx@cizekassociates.com
Web: www.cizekassociates.com

Summary: Generalist national retained executive search firm with strength in manufacturing, consumer products, technology, higher education, non-profit and banking/financial services. We also provide executive assessment, management audit, and leadership development.

Key Contact - Specialty:
Ms. Marti J. Cizek, President

Salary Minimum: $100,000

Functions: Generalist (All), Management, Senior Mgmt., Mfg., Materials, Sales & Mktg., HR Mgmt., Finance, CFOs, IT

Industries: Generalist (All), Manufacturing, Paper, Printing, Soap, Perf., Cosmtcs., Leather, Stone, Glass, Metal Products, Machine, Appliance, Consumer Goods, Finance, Services, Higher Ed., Communications, Aerospace

Branches:
3212 Jefferson Way Ste 475
Napa, CA 94558-3436
(650) 343-2600
Fax: (650) 340-8830
Email: bayarea@cizekassociates.com
Key Contact - Specialty:
Mr. Edward G. Linskey, Jr., Senior Vice President - *Finance, Technology*

2021 Midwest Rd Ste 200
Oak Brook, IL 60523-1370
(708) 534-7860
Email: chgo@cizekassociates.com
Key Contact - Specialty:
Mr. John T. Cizek, Principal - *Manufacturing*

CJA Executive Search

24811 Hendon St
Laguna Hills, CA 92653-4603
(714) 573-1820
(800) 559-2559
Fax: (714) 731-3952
Email: lindas@cjapower.com
Web: www.cjapower.com

Summary: Creators of power hiring, the five-step recruiting and assessment process now used by thousands of managers. Also, offer half-day power hiring workshops to all clients. Includes performance profiles and unique new assessment tools.

Key Contact - Specialty:
Mr. Louis S. Adler, Chairman - *High technology, Manufacturing, Sales*
Mr. Brad M. Remillard, President - *Distribution*

Salary Minimum: $100,000

Functions: Generalist (All), Senior Mgmt., Plant Mgmt., Purchasing, Materials Plng., Mktg. Research, Sales Mgmt., CFOs

Industries: Generalist (All), Manufacturing, Plastics, Rubber, Computer Equip., Transportation, Retail, Finance, Hospitality, Telecoms, Software

Branches:
5757 W Century Blvd Ste 700
Los Angeles, CA 90045-6409
(310) 378-4571
Fax: (310) 791-4434

Email: barryd@cjapower.com
Key Contact - Specialty:
Mr. Barry A. Deutsch, Managing Director & Sr
  Vice President

Claddagh Resources America†

3169 Holcomb Bridge Rd Ste 700
Norcross, GA 30071-1367
(678) 405-4400
Email: awood@claddaghresources.net
Web: www.claddaghresources.net

Summary: Premier outsourced recruiting,
executive search and market research firm. Cross-
industry expertise in the following sectors:
financial services, aerospace, consulting,
manufacturing, technology and pharmaceutical.
Introduce our clients to leading edge web
technologies and methodologies guaranteeing an
improvement in the efficiency of hiring processes
at a reduced cost.

Key Contact - Specialty:
Mr. Peter Casey, Founder & Chief Executive
  Officer
Ms. April Wood, Chief Operating Officer
Mr. Timeyo Banda, Director, Information
  Technology
Mr. Jim Scapin, Director

Salary Minimum: $40,000

Functions: Generalist (All)

Industries: Generalist (All), Energy, Utilities,
  Manufacturing, Retail, Finance, Services,
  Communications, Government, Aerospace,
  Software

Arlene Clapp Ltd

4250 Park Glen Rd
Minneapolis, MN 55416-4758
(952) 928-7474
Fax: (952) 928-7475
Email: aclapp@mn.rr.com
Web: www.arleneclapp.com

Summary: We specialize in placements in
commercial real estate (office, retail and
industrial) and construction industries.

Key Contact - Specialty:
Ms. Arlene Clapp, President - *Construction, Real
  estate*

Functions: Management

Industries: Construction, Real Estate

Clarey Andrews & Klein Inc

(a Penrhyn International company)
1200 Shermer Rd Ste 108
Northbrook, IL 60062-4563
(847) 498-2870
Email: chicago@penrhyn.com
Web: www.penrhyn.com

Summary: Our firm is a generalist executive
search consultancy specializing in filling senior
executive positions, primarily GMs and their
direct reports, for a broad range of public and
private companies. Principals of the firm conduct
all searches.

Key Contact - Specialty:
Mr. Jack R. Clarey, Principal
Mr. Gregory A. Klein, Principal

Salary Minimum: $150,000

Functions: Generalist (All), Management, Mfg.,
  Sales & Mktg., HR Mgmt., Finance

Industries: Generalist (All), Manufacturing

Clarey/Napier International

(an IIC company)
1221 McKinney St Ste 3112
Houston, TX 77010-2008
(713) 238-6705
Fax: (713) 236-4778
Email: cni@cnintl.com
Web: www.iicpartners.com

Summary: Executive search specializing in all
phases of the energy industry including oil & gas,
chemicals, power, refining, marketing,
petrochemicals, engineering & construction,
environmental, alternative, renewable and
management consulting services.

Key Contact - Specialty:
Mr. William A. Clarey, II, Partner
Ms. Ginger L. Napier, Partner

Salary Minimum: $100,000

Functions: Generalist (All)

Industries: Energy, Utilities, Construction,
  Manufacturing, Mgmt. Consulting, HR Services

Clark Executive Search Inc

PO Box 560
Shelter Island, NY 11964-0560
(631) 749-3540
Email: mail@clarksearch.com
Web: www.clarksearch.com

Summary: We specialize in executive search for
the pharmaceutical and biotechnology industries
as well as related life science technology platform
companies and nonprofits. Our clients retain us to
find mid-level to senior-level candidates for a
wide variety of functions within the industry.

Key Contact - Specialty:
Ms. Ellen H. Clark, President -
  *Biopharmaceutical, Biotechnology,
  Pharmaceutical, Start-up companies*

Salary Minimum: $100,000

Functions: Generalist (All)

Industries: Pharm Svcs., Biotech/Life Sciences

Ken Clark International

2000 Lenox Dr Ste 200
Lawrenceville, NJ 08648-2314
(609) 308-5200
Fax: (609) 308-5250
Email: info-princeton@kenclark.com
Web: www.kenclark.com

Summary: As a global firm with numerous
offices, practices, consultants and support staff, we
serve only one or two clients in each industry to
provide virtually unlimited recruiting targets to
our select clients. We specialize in life sciences,
materials & chemicals, consumer and scientific
products industries.

Key Contact - Specialty:
Mr. Kenneth Clark, Chairman & Chief Executive
  Officer
Mr. Robert Chandis, Vice President
Mr. Guy Sava, President, Global Industrial
  Practice

Salary Minimum: $100,000

Functions: Generalist (All), Management, Board
  Members, Senior Mgmt., Mfg., Materials, Sales
  & Mktg., IT, R&D, Engineering

Industries: Generalist (All), Manufacturing, Food,
  Bev., Tobacco, Chemicals, Soap, Perf.,
  Cosmtcs., Drugs Mfg., Medical Devices, Test,
  Measure Equip., Consumer Goods, Pharm Svcs.,
  HR Services, Supply Chain Mgmt, Biotech/Life
  Sciences, Healthcare

Branches:
660 Newport Center Dr Ste 770
Newport Beach, CA 92660-8027
(949) 219-0900
Fax: (949) 219-9800
Email: info-newportbeach@kenclark.com
Key Contact - Specialty:
Mr. Jeffrey Clark, Regional President

400 Perimeter Center Ter NE Ste 900
Atlanta, GA 30346-1236
(770) 804-6400
Fax: (770) 804-6401
Email: info-atlanta@kenclark.com
Key Contact - Specialty:
Ms. Elizabeth Bicknese, Vice President

500 Lake Cook Rd Ste 250
Deerfield, IL 60015-4959
(847) 282-5150
Fax: (847) 282-5160
Email: info-chicago@kenclark.com
Key Contact - Specialty:
Mr. James Crawford, Regional President

1050 Winter St Ste 1000
Waltham, MA 02451-1406
(781) 839-7200
Fax: (781) 839-7203
Email: info-boston@kenclark.com
Key Contact - Specialty:
Mr. William O'Callaghan, Regional President

328 Conestoga Rd Ste 100
Wayne, PA 19087-4759
(610) 995-2249
Email: info-philadelphia@kenclark.com
Key Contact - Specialty:
Ms. Cheryl Johnson, Managing Director

Classic Consultants Inc

8051 N Tamiami Trl
Sarasota, FL 34243-2032
(941) 351-3500
(800) 949-6107
Email: cci3513500@aol.com
Web: www.classicconsultants.com

Summary: We are an executive search recruitment
firm partnering with private equity healthcare and
special need population providers, including
special education, child & adolescent mental
health, mental retardation and developmental
disabilities.

Key Contact - Specialty:
Ms. Edith Young, Chief Executive Officer

Functions: Management

Industries: Logistics Svcs., Supply Chain Mgmt,
  Telecoms, Call Centers, Compliance,
  Environmental Svcs., Doc. Mgmt., Production
  SW, Healthcare, Long-term/Home Care

Claude Vézina Conseil

(an EMA Partners International company)
1100-1100 Rue de la Gauchetiere O
Montreal, QC H3B 2S2
Canada
(514) 849-2333
Fax: (514) 849-5619
Email: isa@cvez.com
Web: www.ema-partners.com

Summary: We are a leader in our region in senior
executive search and members of board of
directors.

Key Contact - Specialty:
Mr. Claude Vézina, Senior Parnter -
  Biotechnology, Finance, Sales

Mr. Andréc de Billy, Consultant
Ms. Isabelle Belley, Research Coordinator -
*Executives, Finance, Human resources,
Management, Senior management*

Salary Minimum: $80,000

Functions: Generalist (All)

Industries: Energy, Utilities, Manufacturing,
Finance, Services, Media, Communications,
Government, Aerospace, Real Estate,
Biotech/Life Sciences

CMM & Associates Inc

4145 Reflections Pkwy
Sarasota, FL 34233-1452
(941) 342-6345
Email: info@cmm-associates.com
Web: www.cmm-associates.com

Summary: As a world class legal search firm, our
firm helps clients find talent and leadership for
their organizations. Our goal is to further our
clients' success by attracting exceptional
professionals. We are with them every step of the
way, providing boardroom level counsel,
addressing management issues, and offering
retention advice.

Key Contact - Specialty:
Mr. Casey McCormick, President & Chief
Executive Officer - *CEOs, Legal, Legal
(Attorneys,Lawyers), Senior management*

Salary Minimum: $100,000

Functions: Board Members, Senior Mgmt., Legal,
Attorneys

Industries: Generalist (All), Legal

CNR Group†

(formerly known as CNR Search & Services)
30752 Via Conquista
San Juan Capistrano, CA 92675-1735
(949) 488-0065
Email: cnrkenmiller@juno.com
Web: www.cnrsearch.com

Summary: Experienced search firm with expertise
in our specialty areas. Extensive industry
databascs. Our primary method of operation is
networking and direct recruiting on a confidential
basis.

Key Contact - Specialty:
Mr. Kenneth Miller, President - *Healthcare, High
technology*

Salary Minimum: $85,000

Functions: Advertising, Mktg. Research, PR, IT

Industries: Services, Pharm Svcs., Media,
Advertising, Publishing, New Media, Insurance,
Software, Biotech/Life Sciences, Healthcare

COBA Executive Search

14947 E Wagontrail Pl
Aurora, CO 80015-2118
(303) 693-8382
Email: mekiken43256@comcast.net

Summary: We fill positions in industries ranging
from biotech to high tech, energy and banking, to
manufacturing and distribution, both domestically
and internationally. Our candidates are selected
not only for skill sets but their ability to blend into
the cultural environment of our clients.

Key Contact - Specialty:
Dr. Mark E. Kiken, PhD, President - *Banking,
Biotechnology, Computers, Food,
Manufacturing*
Mr. Ed Sears, Managing Principal - *Financial,
Manufacturing, Systems*

Salary Minimum: $85,000

Functions: Management, Board Members, Senior
Mgmt.

Industries: Agri., Forestry, Mining, Energy,
Utilities, Manufacturing, Wholesale, Finance,
Communications, Software, Biotech/Life
Sciences

Cochran, Cochran & Yale LLC

955 E Henrietta Rd
Rochester, NY 14623-1409
(585) 424-6060
Fax: (585) 424-6069
Email: roch@ccy.com
Web: www.ccy.com

Summary: We provide retained search with
specialized divisions, which include: finance, HR,
software, electronics, process manufacturing and
consumer products marketing & sales. The
industries that we serve include: pharmaceuticals,
plastics, high technology electronics, aerospace,
consumer products, banking, biotechnology and
wine/spirits.

Key Contact - Specialty:
Mr. Gary M. Baker, Partner - *Finance, Human
resources, Manufacturing*
Mr. David Call, CPC, Vice President

Salary Minimum: $60,000

Functions: Generalist (All), Management, Mfg.,
Materials, Sales & Mktg., HR Mgmt., Finance,
IT

Industries: Energy, Utilities, Food, Bev.,
Tobacco, Chemicals, Soap, Perf., Cosmtcs.,
Medical Devices, Plastics, Rubber, Machine,
Appliance, Consumer Elect., Electronic, Elec.
Components, Consumer Goods, Banking,
Venture Cap., Accounting, Packaging

Branches:
5900 Main St
Williamsville, NY 14221-5714
(716) 631-1300
Fax: (716) 631-1319
Email: buff@ccy.com
Key Contact - Specialty:
Mr. Walter Y. Critchley, President - *Human
resources, Manufacturing, Operations*

The Coelyn Group

1 Park Plz Ste 600
Irvine, CA 92614-5987
(949) 553-8855
Fax: (949) 363-0837
Email: contact@coelyngroup.com
Web: www.coelyngroup.com

Summary: Retainer-based executive search firm
specializing in senior-level executive positions
strictly in life sciences, medical device,
pharmaceutical, biotechnology, eCommerce and
diagnostics.

Key Contact - Specialty:
Mr. Ronald H. Coelyn, Partner - *Life Sciences*
Ms. Carol L. Moson, Partner - *Life Sciences*
Ms. Lynn S. Nishimoto, Partner - *Life Sciences*

Salary Minimum: $200,000

Functions: Generalist (All)

Industries: Drugs Mfg., Medical Devices,
Biotech/Life Sciences

Coffou Partners Inc

330 N Wabash Ave Ste 2111
Chicago, IL 60611-7620
(312) 464-0896
Fax: (312) 464-0322
Email: info@coffou.com
Web: www.coffou.com

Summary: Our firm is a woman-owned, full-
service, retainer-based executive search and
business consulting firm. We conduct mid and
senior-level executive searches for a variety of
industries, including healthcare, high technology,
consumer products, e-business, finance and
manufacturing.

Key Contact - Specialty:
Ms. Sara Coffou, President

Salary Minimum: $75,000

Functions: Generalist (All), Management,
Healthcare, Sales & Mktg., HR Mgmt., Finance,
IT

Industries: Generalist (All), Finance, Banking,
Invest. Banking

Cole, Warren & Long Inc

1500 John F Kennedy Blvd Ste 312
Philadelphia, PA 19102-1733
(215) 563-0701
(800) 394-8517
Fax: (215) 563-2907
Email: cwlserch@cwl-inc.com
Web: www.cwl-inc.com

Summary: We are an executive search and general
management consulting firm. Broad range of
clients including: financial services, insurance,
banking, manufacturing, IT, electronics, utilities,
healthcare, etc. Unique hourly rate offers many
options to clients.

Key Contact - Specialty:
Mr. Ronald Cole, Chairman of the Board &
President
Mr. Richard Lewis, Vice President -
Manufacturing, Technical
Mr. Craig Cole, Vice President - *Middle
management*
Ms. Karen Dydak, Director, Research

Salary Minimum: $100,000

Functions: Management, Senior Mgmt., Mfg.,
Materials, Sales & Mktg., HR Mgmt., IT, MIS
Mgmt., Engineering, Mgmt. Consultants

Industries: Energy, Utilities, Manufacturing,
Finance, Mgmt. Consulting, HR Services,
Hospitality, Telecoms, Insurance, Software,
Healthcare

Coleman Lew & Associates Inc

326 W 10th St
Charlotte, NC 28202-1712
(704) 377-0362
Email: awhitlock@colemanlew.com
Web: www.colemanlew.com

Summary: Generalist search firm specializing in
the recruitment of board and senior level
executives for public, private, academic, non-
profit, and international organizations.

Key Contact - Specialty:
Mr. Charles E. Lew, Principal - *Boards of
Directors, CEOs, COOs, Presidents, Senior
management*
Mr. Kenneth D. Carrick, Jr., Principal - *Banking,
Education (Higher), Manufacturing
(Management), Non-profit, Retail*
Mr. Thomas M. Brinkley, Principal - *Banking,
Construction, Manufacturing (Management),
Non-profit*
Mr. Frank W. Sherman, Principal - *Food service,
Restaurants, Retail, Wholesale*

Functions: Board Members, Senior Mgmt.

Industries: Generalist (All), Energy, Utilities,
Construction, Manufacturing, Wholesale, Retail,
Finance, Non-profits, Higher Ed., Restaurants

Colton Bernard Inc

870 Market St Ste 822
San Francisco, CA 94102-2921
(415) 399-8700
Fax: (415) 399-0750
Email: inquiry@coltonbernard.com
Web: www.coltonbernard.com

Summary: We provide a full range of marketing, information, organizational and management recruiting services for the fashion industry exclusively. We also offer licensing, sales training programs, image development, seminars & workshops and interactive consumer testing.

Key Contact - Specialty:
Mr. Harry Bernard, Executive Vice President & CMO - *Senior management*
Mr. Roy C. Colton, President & Chief Executive Officer - *Senior management*
Mr. Brad Smith, Senior Vice President - *Senior management*

Salary Minimum: $200,000

Functions: Generalist (All), Board Members, Senior Mgmt., Mktg. Mgmt., CFOs, MIS Mgmt., Mgmt. Consultants, Int'l.

Industries: Textiles, Apparel, Retail

Colucci, Blendow & Johnson

PO Box 10
Half Moon Bay, CA 94019-0010
(650) 712-0103
Email: exsearch@ix.netcom.com

Summary: We have retained search experience in medical technology including pharmaceuticals, diagnostics, biotechnology, medical devices and instrumentation.

Key Contact - Specialty:
Mr. Bart A. Colucci, President

Salary Minimum: $80,000

Functions: Generalist (All)

Industries: Generalist (All), Drugs Mfg., Medical Devices, Pharm Svcs., Biotech/Life Sciences

Columbia Consulting Group

5525 Twin Knolls Rd Ste 331
Columbia, MD 21045-3207
(443) 276-2525
Fax: (443) 276-2536
Email: info@ccgsearch.com
Web: www.ccgsearch.com

Summary: Client-retained executive search consultants serving most industries and functions.

Key Contact - Specialty:
Mr. Lawrence J. Holmes, Managing Director
Mr. Robert C. Gauthier, Managing Director
Ms. Jan Molino-Bem, Managing Director - *Healthcare, Human resources, Non-profit*

Salary Minimum: $150,000

Functions: Generalist (All)

Industries: Energy, Utilities, Manufacturing, Transportation, Retail, Finance, Services, Non-profits, Communications, Insurance, Healthcare

Branches:
16952 Freshwind Cir
Jupiter, FL 33477-1202
(561) 748-0232
Email: info@ccgsearch.com
Key Contact - Specialty:
Mr. Larry D. Mingle, Managing Director

1 Southgate Ct
Annapolis, MD 21401-2729
(410) 280-8858
Email: info@ccgsearch.com

Key Contact - Specialty:
Ms. Christine A. Pettingill, Managing Director - *Healthcare, Human resources, Information Technology, Management, Management consulting*

36 S Charles St Ste 2410
Baltimore, MD 21201-3108
(410) 385-2525
Fax: (410) 385-0044
Email: info@ccgsearch.com
Key Contact - Specialty:
Ms. Julie Mercer, Managing Director - *CEOs, CFOs, Financial services, Human resources, Non-profit*
Mr. Philip H. Grantham, Managing Director - *CEOs, CFOs, Finance, Financial services, Insurance*
Mr. Thomas J. McMahon, Managing Director - *CEOs, CFOs, Healthcare, Manufacturing, Manufacturing (Management)*

67 Wall St Ste 2100
New York, NY 10005-3113
(212) 832-2525
Fax: (212) 832-7722
Email: info@ccgsearch.com
Key Contact - Specialty:
Mr. Noboru Kobayashi, Managing Director - *Banking, Compliance, Financial services*
Mr. Tilghman G. Pitts, Managing Director - *Financial services*

Combined Resources Inc

12252 Moss Point Rd
Strongsville, OH 44136-3506
(440) 570-2285
(877) 236-9789
Fax: (440) 572-2000
Email: halawan@searchamerica.cc
Web: www.cri-search.com

Summary: Our firm provides comprehensive human capital management services to meet the unique needs of law firms and corporate legal departments. We have distinguished our firm by providing excellent, cost-effective service to our clients and confidential, respectful service to our candidates. We guarantee the success of our executive search assignments for one full year.

Key Contact - Specialty:
Mr. Gilbert Sherman, President
Mr. Haider Alawan, Vice President, Legal Search - *Engineering, Manufacturing, Six sigma*

Functions: Senior Mgmt., HR Mgmt., Finance, CFOs, IT, MIS Mgmt., Legal, Attorneys

Industries: Generalist (All), Legal

Comforce Staffing Services[†]

40 E Midland Ave
Paramus, NJ 07652-2923
(201) 599-9100
(888) 535-5533
Fax: (201) 599-1947
Email: staffing@comforcestaffing.com
Web: www.comforcestaffing.com

Summary: We specialize in office, medical, human resources, information technology, and scientific full time and temp jobs.

Key Contact - Specialty:
Ms. Linda Schnierer, President & Chief Executive Officer
Mr. Henry Schnierer, Executive Vice President
Ms. Leigh Kaloustian, Branch Manager, Office Division
Ms. Maryann Brogan, Manager, Medical Office/Clinical Div
Mr. Scott Schnierer, Director, Marketing & Business Develop

Ms. Suzanne Larson, Resource Manager, Human Resource Div
Ms. Karen O'Dell, Office Supervisor

Functions: Generalist (All)

Industries: Medical Devices, Consumer Elect., Pharm Svcs., Mgmt. Consulting, HR Services, IT Implementation, Network Infrastructure, Hospitals, Physical Therapy

Branches:
145 US Highway 46
Wayne Interchange Plaza
Wayne, NJ 07470-6830
(973) 890-8700
Fax: (973) 890-9697
Email: labforce@comforcestaffing.com
Key Contact - Specialty:
Ms. Lin Poulsen, Manager
Ms. Joan Miller, Branch Manager
Mr. Brian Morris, Manager, Business Development

Commonwealth Resources Inc[†]

262 Washington St Ste 8
Boston, MA 02108-4607
(617) 250-1100
Fax: (617) 250-1199
Email: info@crijobs.com
Web: www.crijobs.com

Summary: We are an executive search firm specializing in construction placement within the construction management and general contracting industries. We have extensive experience placing VPs, construction managers, project managers, estimators, field engineers, project engineers, schedulers, sales & marketing and business development individuals.

Key Contact - Specialty:
Mr. Tim Fraser, President & Co-Founder
Mr. Aaron Green, Co-Founder
Mr. Thomas Quinn, Partner
Mr. Phil Falzone, Recruiter
Mr. Peter Moorman, Recruiter
Mr. Jonathan Factor, Recruiter

Functions: Middle Mgmt., Bldg. Contractors

Industries: Construction, Real Estate

Compass Group Ltd

401 S Old Woodward Ave Ste 460
Birmingham, MI 48009-6622
(248) 540-9110
Fax: (248) 647-8288
Email: executivesearch@compassgroup.com
Web: www.compassgroup.com

Summary: We are a generalist firm, specializing in recruitment for senior-level executive positions. Emphasis is in automotive, manufacturing, healthcare, technology, not-for-profit and service industries. We also place senior executives on an interim basis.

Key Contact - Specialty:
Mr. Paul W. Czamanske, President & Chief Executive Officer - *Automotive, CEOs, COOs, Industrial, Non-profit*
Ms. Christina L. Balian-Mehren, Vice President - *Education (Higher), Finance, General management, Marketing, Non-profit*
Ms. Krista L. Fish, Consultant - *Financial services, Human resources, Management, Manufacturing, Strategic planning*
Mr. James W. Sturtz, Vice President - *Engineering, Financial, Human resources, Manufacturing, Marketing*
Ms. Lois A. Duerk, Director, Research

Salary Minimum: $100,000

Functions: Senior Mgmt., Mfg., Materials, Sales & Mktg., HR Mgmt., Finance, Engineering, Non-profits, Legal, Int'l.

Industries: Generalist (All)

Branches:
2021 Spring Rd Ste 750
Oak Brook, IL 60523-1880
(630) 645-9110
Fax: (630) 571-7771
Email: executivesearch@compassgroup.com
Key Contact - Specialty:
Mr. Peter M. Czamanske, Vice President - *Automotive, Engineering, Human resources, Industrial, Information Technology*
Mr. Jerold L. Lipe, Vice President - *Automotive, Human resources, Manufacturing, Purchasing, Senior management*

Comprehensive Search[†]
(a division of Jeffrey W Brown Inc)
316 S Lewis St
LaGrange, GA 30240-3144
(706) 884-3232
Fax: (706) 884-4106
Email: merritt@comp-search.com
Web: www.comp-search.com

Summary: We are a retainer, contingency, recruitment research, and contract employers. Synergistically, we also offer contract employees, testing, outplacement and spousal assistance. We also have a strategic partner; a job board specializing in the interior furnishings and building products industry.

Key Contact - Specialty:
Mr. Jeffrey W. Brown, President
Mr. Greg Brown, Account Developer
Ms. Gail W. Standard, Vice President
Ms. Gail Morin, Vice President - *Building products*
Ms. Marilyn McSweeney, Senior Search Consultant
Mr. Kevin Franks, Operations Manager - *Information Technology*
Ms. Sherry Kwintner, Senior Resource Strategist - *Architecture, Building products, Built environments, Electrical, Engineering*
Ms. Merritt Shelton, Talent Manager
Mr. Jim Wissler, Account Developer - *Consumer (Products), Furniture*

Salary Minimum: $50,000

Functions: Generalist (All), Mfg., Sales Mgmt., Architects

Industries: Construction, Manufacturing, Textiles, Apparel, Lumber, Furniture, Leather, Stone, Glass, Computer Equip., Architectural Svcs., Hospitality, Hotels, Resorts, Clubs, Advertising, Government

Compton Graham International Inc
9986 Horse Creek Rd
Fort Myers, FL 33913-2000
(239) 433-4660
Email: jac@comptongraham.com
Web: www.comptongraham.com

Summary: Provides executive search and recruiting research services, specializing in mid and senior-level positions for progressive organizations. Key benefits include target research resulting in high quality, cost effective results quickly.

Key Contact - Specialty:
Ms. Jo Ann L. Compton, CMC, President

Salary Minimum: $75,000
Functions: Generalist (All)
Industries: Generalist (All)

The Comwell Company Inc[†]
227 US Highway 206
Flanders, NJ 07836-9110
(973) 927-9400
Fax: (973) 927-0372
Email: mailman@comwellconsultants.com
Web: www.comwellconsultants.com

Summary: As we help give people dignity and align their skills, abilities, values and interests with current tasks and future strategies, client organizations become more competitive, productive and profitable.

Key Contact - Specialty:
Mr. John F. Sobecki, President
Mr. David Gavin, Executive Vice President

Salary Minimum: $75,000

Functions: Generalist (All), Board Members, Senior Mgmt., Middle Mgmt., Mktg. Research, Staffing, Training

Industries: Generalist (All), Chemicals, Misc. Mfg., Finance, HR Services, Media, Healthcare

Conard Associates Inc
74 Northeastern Blvd Ste 22A
Nashua, NH 03062-3194
(603) 886-0600
Fax: (603) 886-8886
Email: rod@conard.com
Web: www.conard.com

Summary: We help companies develop high performance cultures through customer focused, bottom line process improvement and behavior change initiatives and we use a consultative approach to help them acquire leaders who are aligned with the company's business and cultural goals and who demonstrate core competencies essential to world-class (Lean) competition.

Key Contact - Specialty:
Dr. Rodney J. Conard, President

Salary Minimum: $100,000

Functions: Senior Mgmt.

Industries: Generalist (All)

Conboy, Sur & Associates Inc
(an afflicate of Morice Consulting LLP)
15 E Churchville Rd Ste 170
Bel Air, MD 21014-3837
(410) 925-4122
Email: conboysur@aol.com
Web: www.conboysur.com

Summary: Generalist retained executive search firm that selects, evaluates and recruits senior management across a broad spectrum of industries and functional specialties.

Key Contact - Specialty:
Mr. William K. Sur, Managing Director
Mr. James Morice, Managing Director - *Biotechnology, CFOs, Consumer, Consumer (Products), General management*

Salary Minimum: $150,000

Functions: Management, Board Members, Senior Mgmt., Mfg., Distribution, Sales & Mktg., PR, HR Mgmt., CFOs, IT

Industries: Generalist (All), Manufacturing, Food, Bev., Tobacco, Paper, Chemicals, Soap, Perf., Cosmtcs., Drugs Mfg., Medical Devices, Metal Products, Computer Equip., Retail, Supply Chain Mgmt, Telecoms, Packaging, Software, Biotech/Life Sciences

Affiliates:
Deininger Unternehmensberatung GmbH
Frankfurt
Germany

CONEX Incorporated
575 Madison Ave Fl 10
New York, NY 10022-8511
(212) 371-3737
Email: mail@conex-usa.com
Web: www.conex-usa.com

Summary: We are a generalist firm with broad client base in most industries and functions.

Key Contact - Specialty:
Mr. Fred Siegel, Founder, President & CEO
Mr. Declan Maguire, Senior Partner
Ms. Christina Lopez, Vice President
Ms. Naomi Laks, Vice President
Mr. Brynne Levy, Assistant Vice President
Ms. Jessica Hollander, Researcher

Salary Minimum: $120,000

Functions: Generalist (All)

Industries: Generalist (All)

Robert Connelly & Associates Inc
5200 Willson Rd Ste 150
Minneapolis, MN 55424-1300
(952) 925-3039
Fax: (952) 922-5762
Email: olsen@robertconnelly.com
Web: www.robertconnelly.com

Summary: A generalist firm with expertise in medium and large corporations at the mid and upper-management ranks. Specializing in architectural/engineering, real estate, construction, facilities management, environmental engineering and agribusiness.

Key Contact - Specialty:
Mr. Robert F. Olsen, President - *Construction, Real estate*

Salary Minimum: $50,000

Functions: Generalist (All), Management, Board Members, Senior Mgmt., Product Dev.

Industries: Agri., Forestry, Mining, Construction, Food, Bev., Tobacco, Architectural Svcs., Legal, Engineering Svcs., Real Estate, Property/Facility Mgmt., Healthcare

Conroy Ross Partners Limited
(an IIC company)
830-255 5 Ave SW
Bow Valley Square 3
Calgary, AB T2P 3G6
Canada
(403) 261-8080
Fax: (403) 261-8085
Email: mail@conroyross.com
Web: www.conroyross.com

Summary: Areas of specialization include energy, both upstream and downstream, as well as pipelines, refinery, commodity marketing and power. Other strengths include: manufacturing, transportation, retail, distribution and financial services.

Key Contact - Specialty:
Mr. M.J. Conroy, Chairman & Founding Partner - *Financial, General management*
Mr. S. Scott Doupe, Partner - *Finance, General management, Manufacturing, Real estate, Utilities*
Ms. Noranne Dickin, Partner - *Energy, Financial, Utilities*
Mr. Mark Hopkins, Partner - *Professional services, Utilities*
Ms. Catherine Bell, Principal
Ms. Lesley Ann Dunne, Principal

Functions: Generalist (All), Senior Mgmt., Sales & Mktg., Mktg. Mgmt., CFOs, MIS Mgmt., Specialized Svcs., Non-profits

Industries: Generalist (All), Energy, Utilities, Manufacturing, Finance, HR Services, Government, Software

Branches:
10303 Jasper Ave NW
Metropolitan Place
Edmonton, AB T5J 3N6
Canada
(780) 432-5490
Email: mail@conroyross.com
Key Contact - Specialty:
Mr. Michael Ross, Managing Partner
Mr. Andrew Ross, Partner
Ms. Antara Wosnak, Principal

Conspectus Inc

222 Purchase St Ste 318
Rye, NY 10580-2101
(914) 925-0600
Email: resume@conspectusinc.com
Web: www.conspectusinc.com

Summary: Specializing in security analysts, portfolio managers and investment bankers.

Key Contact - Specialty:
Mr. Eric Stieglitz, Managing Director - *Asset management, Brokerage, Investor relations, Wall Street*

Salary Minimum: $125,000

Functions: Finance, Cash Mgmt.

Industries: Finance, Banking, Invest. Banking, Venture Cap., Misc. Financial

Construction Executives Inc

PO Box 231360
New Orleans, LA 70183-1360
(888) 800-6952
Email: info@constructionexecutive.com
Web: www.constructionexecutive.com

Summary: Our firm provides senior level, retained executive search exclusively for general contractors, specialty contactors, heavy contractors, design builders, construction managers, real estate developers, owners and other firms that require construction talent. The positions that we service are senior level executives such as CEOs, CFOs, COOs, presidents, divisional managers and other officers or emerging leaders.

Key Contact - Specialty:
Mr. Kent Arendt, Director - *Construction*

Salary Minimum: $100,000

Functions: Management, Board Members, Senior Mgmt., HR Mgmt., CFOs

Industries: Construction

Construction Resources Group Inc[†]

(also known as CRG Inc)
466 94th Ave N
Saint Petersburg, FL 33702-2522
(727) 578-1962
Fax: (727) 578-9982
Email: charris@crgexecutivesearch.com
Web: www.crgexecutivesearch.com

Summary: Specialize in identifying and recruiting project and staff-level managers and executives exclusively for engineering and construction organizations.

Key Contact - Specialty:
Ms. Cheryl P. Harris, President - *Architecture, Construction, Engineering, General contractors*
Mr. Brad W. Barker, Professional Recruiter - *Architecture, Built environments, Construction, Engineering, General contractors*

Salary Minimum: $50,000

Functions: Generalist (All)

Industries: Construction

The Consulting Group

(a Marlar International company)
366 Madison Ave Fl 10
New York, NY 10017-3196
(212) 751-8484
Fax: (212) 980-5935
Email: tcgny@aol.com
Web: www.consultinggroupny.com

Summary: Our firm is a specialist in the global securities markets with a subspecialty in real estate. Clients include banks, investment banks, insurance companies, pension managers and other institutional money sources.

Key Contact - Specialty:
Mr. J. Michael Mitchell, Managing Director - *Real estate, Securities*
Ms. Jessica S. Flagg, Managing Director - *Real estate, Securities*
Ms. Kate Debold, Director, Research - *Real estate, Securities*
Mr. Tim Christy, Senior Vice President
Mr. Terry Ware, Research

Salary Minimum: $150,000

Functions: Generalist (All), Senior Mgmt., Middle Mgmt., Admin. Svcs., CFOs, M&A, Risk Mgmt., MIS Mgmt.

Industries: Generalist (All), Construction, Finance, Invest. Banking, Brokers, Venture Cap., Misc. Financial, Real Estate

The Continuum Group

2095 Hidden Ridge Ln
Highland Park, IL 60035-2867
(847) 831-5200
(800) 261-4632
Fax: (847) 831-2246
Email: jrobbins@the-continuum-group.com
Web: the-continuum-group.com

Summary: Our president has developed extensive experience within several industries, including healthcare systems, major academic medical centers, community hospitals, healthcare associations, e-publishing, consumer packaged goods, professional service firms and not-for-profit. This ranges from participation in research assignment activities and consulting in executive search with major executive search firms and corporations.

Key Contact - Specialty:
Ms. Joni Robbins, MS, President

Salary Minimum: $70,000

Functions: Senior Mgmt., Middle Mgmt., Healthcare

Industries: Generalist (All), Food, Bev., Tobacco, Soap, Perf., Cosmtcs., Drugs Mfg., Wholesale, Services, Non-profits, Pharm Svcs., Mgmt. Consulting, HR Services, K-12 Ed., Higher Ed., Engineering Svcs., Publishing, New Media, Marketing SW, Healthcare, Hospitals, Long-term/Home Care, Women's

Contract Recruiters International Inc[†]

PO Box 668
Longs, SC 29568-0668
(843) 399-9461
Fax: (843) 399-9480
Email: gunner@contractrecruitersinc.com
Web: www.contractrecruitersinc.com

Summary: We supply professional contract recruiters to companies on an hourly basis. We have very reasonable rates with no minimum contract term. The recruiter can either work onsite at your location or work off site, you can decide. Industries include, defense, IT, telecom, engineering, manufacturing, finance, sales, semiconductor, aerospace and consulting.

Key Contact - Specialty:
Mr. Gunner Beery, President
Ms. Mary Ann Geiger

Functions: Staffing

Industries: Energy, Utilities, Manufacturing, Finance, Services, Communications, Government, Aerospace, Insurance, Software, Healthcare

Conway & Greenwood Inc

(also known as Executive Search Consultants)
1122 Oberlin Rd Ste 310
Raleigh, NC 27605-1137
(919) 833-9000
Email: searchinquiry@conwaygreenwood.com
Web: www.conwaygreenwood.com

Summary: Our firm is a national executive search firm specializing in the management of retained search assignments for the purpose of recruiting senior level executives. We have developed successful, long-term relationships with many of the nation's leading companies, covering a wide range of industries. We provide both temporary and permanent placement opportunities across the nation.

Key Contact - Specialty:
Mr. Luther Snyder, Recruiter - *CEOs, General management, Government, High technology, Non-profit*

Functions: Generalist (All)

Industries: Generalist (All)

Conway + Associates

1007 Church St Ste 307
Evanston, IL 60201-5912
(847) 866-6832
Fax: (847) 866-6265
Email: conway@sisna.com

Summary: Provide industry research, candidate identification, screening and recommendations to corporate clients. Services range from research to full search services with in-depth personal interviews and reference checks.

Key Contact - Specialty:
Ms. Maureen Conway, President

Functions: Generalist (All)

Industries: Generalist (All)

† occasional contingency assignment

Philip Conway Management
320 Hampton Pl
Hinsdale, IL 60521-3823
(630) 655-4566
Summary: Specialists in the recruitment of senior and middle-managers. Each assignment is handled by one designated professional from research through final negotiations and follow up.
Key Contact - Specialty:
Mr. Philip A. Conway
Salary Minimum: $60,000
Functions: Generalist (All), Senior Mgmt., Middle Mgmt., Plant Mgmt., Quality, Sales Mgmt., Staffing, CFOs
Industries: Generalist (All)

Conyngham Partners LLC
PO Box 94
Ridgewood, NJ 07451-0094
(201) 652-3444
Email: beth@conynghampartners.com
Web: www.conynghampartners.com
Summary: A client-focused firm dedicated to providing high-level consulting service to the pharmaceutical industry. A boutique firm specializing in executive search assignments resulting in the identification of corporate leaders.
Key Contact - Specialty:
Ms. Beth Conyngham, President - *Healthcare*
Ms. Patricia Feichtel, Executive Recruiter - *Healthcare*
Ms. Linda Pierro, Director, Administrative Operations - *Accounting, Accounting (Bookkeeping), Administration*
Salary Minimum: $100,000
Functions: Generalist (All), Management, Mfg., Sales & Mktg., HR Mgmt., Finance, IT, R&D
Industries: Generalist (All), Drugs Mfg., Pharm Svcs., Biotech/Life Sciences, Healthcare

Cook & Company
12 Masterton Rd
Bronxville, NY 10708-4804
(914) 779-4838
Email: search@cook-co.com
Web: www.cook-co.com
Summary: A gold standard boutique firm specializing in the recruitment of A+ players for top management in the consumer and financial services industries.
Key Contact - Specialty:
Dr. Patricia S. Cook, Chairman & Chief Executive Officer - *Financial services, General management*
Mr. William C. Bush, President & Chief Operating Officer - *Financial services, General management*
Salary Minimum: $150,000
Functions: Board Members, Senior Mgmt., Sales & Mktg., CFOs
Industries: Food, Bev., Tobacco, Consumer Elect., Consumer Goods, Banking, Venture Cap., K-12 Ed., Entertainment, Recreation, Publishing, New Media

Cook Associates
(an AEA International Search company)
212 W Kinzie St Fl 1
Chicago, IL 60610-4695
(312) 329-0900
Fax: (312) 329-2422
Email: info@cookassociates.com
Web: www.cookassociates.com

Summary: We provide executive search services to many industries. We focus on senior-level assignments across all functional areas. Our long-term relationships with our clients are built on integrity, performance and follow-through.
Key Contact - Specialty:
Mr. John Kins, Chairman
Mr. Arnie Kins, President - *Mergers & acquisitions*
Ms. Mary Kier, Executive Vice President & Managing Dir - *Executives*
Mr. Walter Rach, Vice President - *Food & beverage*
Mr. Chuck Meek, Vice President, Family Practice
Ms. Mary Jane Shermer, Vice President - *Retail, Wholesale*
Salary Minimum: $150,000
Functions: Generalist (All), Management, Board Members, Senior Mgmt.
Industries: Generalist (All)

Branches:
1711 Pearl St Ste 203
Boulder, CO 80302-5577
(303) 247-1177
Fax: (303) 544-5806
Email: info@cookassociates.com
Key Contact - Specialty:
Mr. John Olson, Vice President, Managing Director - *Industrial*

1225 19th St NW Ste 800
Washington, DC 20036-2489
(202) 251-9877
Email: llozada@cookassociates.com
Key Contact - Specialty:
Ms. Lori Lozada, Vice President & Mng Director, Legal

7 New England Executive Park Ste 7
Burlington, MA 01803-5008
(781) 565-1144
Key Contact - Specialty:
Mr. Seth Harris, Managing Director

560 Lexington Ave
New York, NY 10022-6828
(212) 308-5399
Email: info@cookassociates.com
Key Contact - Specialty:
Mr. Gary Klein, Vice President, Managing Director - *Communications, Entertainment, Media*
Ms. Susan Denison, Vice President - *Communications, Entertainment, Media*
Mr. Serguei Zaychenko, Director - *Communications, Entertainment, Media*
Mr. Jim DiFilippo, Vice President & Mng Director, Retail
Ms. Ann MacCarthy, Vice President, Retail & Consumer

12438 Elmont Rd Ste 101
Ashland, VA 23005-7607
(804) 798-9131
Key Contact - Specialty:
Ms. Carolyn Peart, Vice President - *Architecture, Construction, Engineering*

The Cooke Group Inc
1001 W Glen Oaks Ln Ste 102
Mequon, WI 53092-3366
(262) 241-9842
Fax: (262) 241-1004
Email: rmarshall@cookegroup.net
Web: www.cookegroup.net
Summary: We specialize in transactional and strategic business planning, capital and operational restructuring, executive and organizational development, interim executive and financial

management services and retained executive search. Our clients include small, mid and large market businesses with annual revenues from $5 million to over $2 billion.
Key Contact - Specialty:
Mr. Jeffrey R. Cooke, President - *CEOs, Closely-held business, Mergers & acquisitions, Organizational development, Strategic planning*
Mr. James A. Kettinger, Consultant - *Accounting, Business development, Finance, Management consulting, Start-up companies*
Mr. George Schneider, Consultant - *Management consulting, Manufacturing, Manufacturing (Management), Mergers & acquisitions, Senior management*
Mr. Jerry Kozik, Consultant - *Business development, Finance, Management consulting, Operations, Senior management*
Mr. Joe Terranova, Consultant - *Manufacturing, Materials, Production, Quality, Re-engineering*
Mr. William R. Frederick, CPA, Consultant - *Accounting, Business development, Finance, Mergers & acquisitions, Start-up companies*
Mr. Frederick G. Luehrs, PE, Consultant - *Automation, Engineering, Manufacturing, Materials, Operations*
Mr. Robert H. Marshall, Consultant - *Human resources, Organizational development, Public sector*
Salary Minimum: $75,000
Functions: Generalist (All), Management, Senior Mgmt., Mfg., Plant Mgmt., Productivity, CFOs
Industries: Generalist (All), Manufacturing, Printing, Metal Products, Misc. Mfg., Wholesale, Finance, Misc. Financial, Accounting, Mgmt. Consulting

The Cooper Executive Search Group Inc
PO Box 375
Wales, WI 53183-0375
(262) 968-9049
Fax: (262) 968-9059
Email: cesgroup@aol.com
Summary: We are a full-service firm with particular strengths in transitional and middle market and high growth companies. Significant client-side experience provides for unusual sensitivity to client needs.
Key Contact - Specialty:
Mr. Robert M. Cooper, President
Salary Minimum: $90,000
Functions: Generalist (All)
Industries: Food, Bev., Tobacco, Chemicals, Metal Products, Machine, Appliance, Wholesale, Non-profits, Biotech/Life Sciences, Healthcare

Coors Executive Resources Ltd
1095 Nimitzview Dr Ste 100
Cincinnati, OH 45230-4341
(513) 233-0443
(800) 507-6917
Fax: (513) 233-0877
Email: ccoors@coorsrecruiters.com
Web: www.coorsrecruiters.com
Summary: We are a search and consulting firm dedicated exclusively to the recruitment and placement of senior level healthcare executives, physicians, nurse executives and hospital based HR executives in for-profit and not-for-profit health systems, hospitals and medical practices.
Key Contact - Specialty:
Ms. Cheryl Coors, MHA, NAPR, President - *Healthcare*

Mr. Michael Hartz, Recruiter - *Healthcare, Physicians*
Mr. Russell Dean, Senior Search Consultant - *Healthcare*
Ms. Alison Iobst, Office Manager, Business
Ms. Sarah Weber, Research Associate - *Healthcare*

Salary Minimum: $80,000

Functions: Healthcare

Industries: HR Services, Healthcare, Hospitals

The Corban Group
5050 Research Ct Ste 600
Suwanee, GA 30024-6606
(678) 638-6000
(866) 426-7226
Fax: (678) 638-6001
Email: brodgers@corbangroup.com
Web: www.corbangroup.com

Summary: We are a total human capital solutions provider.

Key Contact - Specialty:
Mr. Bob Rodgers, President

Functions: Board Members, Senior Mgmt.

Industries: Generalist (All), Services

Branches:
235 3rd St S
Saint Petersburg, FL 33701-4242
(727) 803-1800
Key Contact - Specialty:
Mr. Bob Rodgers, President

Core Management Search LLC†
5130 Saratoga Ln N Ste 201
Minneapolis, MN 55442-3227
(763) 559-0977
Fax: (763) 559-1664
Email: jlentner@coremanage.com
Web: www.coremanage.com

Summary: We are a retained and contingency search firm specializing in identifying and building your organization's core management team. We place mid to senior level management positions. We help you hire the core competencies that you need to take your organization to the next level.

Key Contact - Specialty:
Ms. Julie Lentner, Principal

Salary Minimum: $60,000

Functions: Generalist (All)

Industries: Generalist (All), Medical Devices, Electronic, Elec. Components, Robotics, Semiconductors, Transportation, Accounting, Logistics Svcs., Supply Chain Mgmt, Mfg. SW

Cornell Global LLC†
PO Box 7113
Wilton, CT 06897-7113
(203) 762-0730
Fax: (203) 761-9507
Email: info@cornellglobal.com
Web: www.cornellglobal.com

Summary: Our firm is a team of professionals with extensive business and search experience. Our success is predicated on our commitment to understand each client's business, strategy, culture and competitive marketplace. Armed with this knowledge, we are able to recruit the type of individual most likely to help the client best the competition.

Key Contact - Specialty:
Mr. John F. Weidner, Jr., Partner - *Business development, Finance, Financial services, General management, Information Technology*
Mr. William H. Perry, Partner - *Financial services, Technology*
Ms. Lynne Sebastian, Partner - *Financial services, General management, Human resources, Technology*
Mr. John A. Luce, Partner - *Financial services, Investor relations, Sales*
Mr. James R. Hocking, Partner - *Financial services, Investment management*
Ms. Barbara A. Joyce, Partner - *Banking, Financial services, General management, Sales*

Functions: Senior Mgmt., Middle Mgmt., Sales & Mktg., HR Mgmt , Finance, Cash Mgmt., Risk Mgmt., Pension/Ret. Planning, MIS Mgmt., Mgmt. Consultants

Industries: Generalist (All), Banking, Invest. Banking, Brokers, Venture Cap., Mutual/Hedge Funds, Misc. Financial, Mgmt. Consulting, IT Implementation

Cornell Group International Consulting Inc
2 Park 80 Plz W Ste 9A
Saddle Brook, NJ 07663-5822
(201) 843-0006
(845) 565-8905
Fax: (201) 845-4576
Email: cornell@cornellinternational.com
Web: www.cornellinternational.com

Summary: We are the only retained executive search firm with a fully integrated set of recruiting solutions in middle management, leadership and consulting. We offer retained executive search services, as well as innovative, lower cost recruiting solutions through our unique, proprietary solution systems. We offer …the Power of Options.

Key Contact - Specialty:
Mr. Alan Guarino, Chief Executive Officer
Mr. Donald Kilinski, Chief Operating Officer - *Finance, Financial services*
Mr. Steven Davis, Division President, Execution Services - *Financial services*
Mr. David Mather, Division President - *Executives, Industrial, Information Technology, International, Telecommunications*

Salary Minimum: $80,000

Functions: Management, Board Members, Senior Mgmt., Middle Mgmt., Admin. Svcs., Mfg., Sales & Mktg., Pension/Ret. Planning, IT

Industries: Generalist (All), Medical Devices, Finance, Banking, Invest. Banking, Brokers, Venture Cap., Mutual/Hedge Funds, Misc. Financial, Non-profits, Mgmt. Consulting, HR Services, Entertainment, Media, Advertising, Publishing, New Media, Telecoms, Network Infrastructure, Software, Healthcare

Affiliates:
Shore Asociados Ejecutivos S A de CV
Mexico City, DF
Mexico

Branches:
350 Sansome St Ste 220
San Francisco, CA 94104-1306
(415) 693-0407
Key Contact - Specialty:
Ms. Jennifer Colosi, Managing Director, Executive Search - *Audits, Finance, Financial services, Industrial*

1 Landmark Sq
Stamford, CT 06901-2603
(914) 472-3171

Key Contact - Specialty:
Mai Keklak, Partner - *Healthcare, Information Technology, Media, Publishing*

800 Boylston St Ste 1550
Prudential Tower
Boston, MA 02199-8111
(617) 425-4661
Key Contact - Specialty:
Mr. Andrew Zaleta, Managing Partner - *Boards of Directors, C-level, Life Sciences, Non-profit, Technology*

9 Ivy Ridge Ct
Mount Kisco, NY 10549-3949
(914) 244-1129
Key Contact - Specialty:
Ms Susan Sachs, Partner - *Advertising, Human resources, Media, Printing, Publishing*

200 Park Ave Rm 2600
New York, NY 10166-2699
(203) 733-6168
Key Contact - Specialty:
Mr. Robert Neal, Partner - *Financial services, Information Technology*

372 Route 52 Ste 4
Newburgh, NY 12550
(845) 565-8905
Key Contact - Specialty:
Mr. Dan Gonzalez, Managing Director, Executive Search - *Brokerage, Financial services, Venture capital*
Ms. Tami Mazzarelli, Executive Assistant

Corporate Advisors Inc†
250 NE 27th St
Miami, FL 33137-4522
(305) 573-7753
Web: www.corporateadvisors.com

Summary: Serving global multinationals, regional top 200 public/private employers in the eCommerce, consumer, high-technology, telecom and financial services industries. Confidential searches in all business functional disciplines at the mid through senior management levels.

Key Contact - Specialty:
Mr. Jerry Kurtzman, Managing Director

Salary Minimum: $75,000

Functions: Senior Mgmt., Middle Mgmt., Sales & Mktg., HR Mgmt., Finance, Int'l.

Industries: Generalist (All)

Corporate Connections International
14286 Beach Blvd Ste 19
Jacksonville, FL 32250-1568
(904) 223-3567
(508) 945-7741
Fax: (904) 992-9220
Email: info@medicalsalesrecruiter.net
Web: www.medicalsalesrecruiter.net

Summary: We are medical sales recruiters specializing in the placement of B2B, medical, and management professionals.

Key Contact - Specialty:
Ms. Debra Duggan, President

Salary Minimum: $30,000

Functions: Sales & Mktg., Sales Mgmt.

Industries: Drugs Mfg., Pharm Svcs., Healthcare, Long-term/Home Care

Corporate Environment Ltd
PO Box 798
Crystal Lake, IL 60039-0798
(815) 455-6070
Fax: (815) 455-0124
Email: tomsearch@consultant.com

Summary: We specialize in the process capital
equipment markets including environmental water
and wastewater equipment/services: irrigation
industry and the metal finishing systems industry.
Positions/functions: engineering, operations, sales
& marketing, key technical specialist, middle &
senior level managers and executives.

Key Contact - Specialty:
Mr. Tom McDermott, President - *Environmental,
Technical*

Salary Minimum: $65,000

Functions: Generalist (All), Management, Senior
Mgmt., Middle Mgmt., Mktg. Mgmt.,
Engineering, Environmentalists

Industries: Generalist (All), Agri., Forestry,
Mining, Energy, Utilities, Manufacturing,
Machine, Appliance, Misc. Mfg., Equip Svcs.,
Engineering Svcs., Environmental Svcs., Haz.
Waste

Corporate Moves Inc[†]
PO Box 1638
Williamsville, NY 14231-1638
(716) 633-0234
Email: info@cmisearch.com
Web: www.cmisearch.com.com

Summary: We are an Executive Search Firm
specializing in Retained and Engaged Search in
Senior level Management positions. Markets
include: Medical, Dental, Biotechnology,
Scientific, Industrial and B2B.

Key Contact - Specialty:
Ms. Leslie Wilcox Hughes, CRPC, President,
CEO & Recruiter

Functions: Senior Mgmt., Middle Mgmt., Sales &
Mktg., Mktg. Mgmt., Sales Mgmt., R&D,
Specialized Svcs., Int'l.

Industries: Generalist (All), Drugs Mfg., Medical
Devices, Plastics, Rubber, Computer Equip.,
Mgmt. Consulting, Packaging, Software,
Biotech/Life Sciences, Women's, Non-
Classifiable

Corporate Search Consultants[†]
800 5th Ave Ste 101-124
Seattle, WA 98104-3191
(206) 332-0233
Email: info@cssearch.com

Summary: Boutique executive search firm
offering flexible, custom designed retained
services and established network of Associate
Firms.

Key Contact - Specialty:
Ms. M.B. Barbour, Principal

Salary Minimum: $70,000

Functions: Senior Mgmt., Middle Mgmt.,
Distribution, Mktg. Mgmt., Sales Mgmt., HR
Mgmt., Int'l.

Industries: Food, Bev., Tobacco, Drugs Mfg.,
Medical Devices, Consumer Elect., Retail,
Banking, Invest. Banking, Brokers, Pharm
Svcs., Logistics Svcs., Quick Service
Restaurants, Inst./Industrial Food Svc., New
Media, Telecoms, Wireless, Hospitals

Corporate Search Consultants International
(formerly known as R J Dishaw & Associates)
12865 County Road 577
Anna, TX 75409-7431
(972) 924-5000
Email: exsearch@msn.com

Summary: A generalist firm specializing in
quality service. MS, PhD level in technical,
managerial, financial, engineering and
manufacturing fields.

Key Contact - Specialty:
Mr. Raymond J. Dishaw - *Engineering,
Manufacturing*

Salary Minimum: $100,000

Functions: Management, Board Members, Mfg.,
Automation, Materials Plng., HR Mgmt., IT,
R&D, Engineering

Industries: Generalist (All), Energy, Utilities,
Construction, Manufacturing, Chemicals, Drugs
Mfg., Metal Products, Motor Vehicles,
Computer Equip., Consumer Elect., Wholesale,
Finance, Services, Accounting, Equip Svcs.,
Media, Telecoms, Defense, Haz. Waste,
Aerospace, Packaging, Software, Biotech/Life
Sciences, Healthcare

The Corporate Source Group Inc
280 S Main St
Andover, MA 01810-4929
(978) 475-6400
Fax: (978) 475-6800
Email: csginquiry@csg-search.com
Web: www.csg-search.com

Summary: Broad based, professional firm
specializing in targeted search for difficult
assignments.

Key Contact - Specialty:
Mr. Dana Willis, President

Salary Minimum: $150,000

Functions: Generalist (All), Senior Mgmt.,
Finance, IT, Engineering, Int'l.

Industries: Generalist (All), Finance, Media,
Software

Branches:
521 W Holly St
Phoenix, AZ 85003-1118
(602) 253-0976
Key Contact - Specialty:
Mr. John VonKaenel

5420 Bay Center Dr Ste 105
Tampa, FL 33609-3425
(813) 286-4422
Key Contact - Specialty:
Mr. Mark Hausherr

13920 Grey Colt Dr
North Potomac, MD 20878-3817
(301) 294-8866
Key Contact - Specialty:
Ms. Tara Stotz

Corporate Staffing Group Inc[†]
3655 Route 202 Ste 115
Doylestown, PA 18902-6602
(215) 345-1100
Fax: (215) 348-8177
Email: cbaker@corporatestaffing.com
Web: www.corporatestaffing.com

Summary: Our firm's charter is to provide
professional customized results to clients by
gaining an in depth understanding of their
particular technology and culture. Over the years
we have focused on technology, aerospace and
process control and more recently
medical/pharmaceutical, financial services,
consumer goods and legal services.

Key Contact - Specialty:
Mr. Chuck Baker, Founder - *Financial services,
Pharmaceutical*
Mr. Jason Baker, Partner
Ms. Laurie Carey, Partner - *Financial services*

Salary Minimum: $60,000

Functions: Generalist (All), Board Members,
Middle Mgmt., Mktg. Mgmt., Systems Dev.,
Systems Implem., R&D, Engineering

Industries: Generalist (All), Semiconductors,
Misc. Financial, Telecoms, Wireless, Fiber
Optic, RF/Microwave, Government, Defense,
Development SW, Healthcare

Corso, Mizgala + French
(an InterSearch company)
800-2 St Clair Ave E
Colonial Place
Toronto, ON M4T 2T5
Canada
(416) 488-4111
Fax: (416) 488-3111
Email: cmf@intersearchcanada.com
Web: www.intersearch-canada.com

Summary: Serve private, public sector clients and
non-profit organizations. Broad experience: with
combined success of mid to senior-recruiting
assignments.

Key Contact - Specialty:
Mr. John J. Corso, Partner
Mr. Anthony B. Mizgala, Partner
Mr. Guy P. French, Partner
Mr. Ralph G. Hansen, Partner
Ms. Ana Sekesan, Administrator

Salary Minimum: $90,000

Functions: Senior Mgmt.

Industries: Generalist (All)

The Counsel Network[†]
885 Georgia St W
HSBC Building
Vancouver, BC V6C 3E8
Canada
(604) 643-1755
(877) 826-8262
Fax: (604) 575-9156
Email: lal@headhunt.com
Web: www.headhunt.com

Summary: We are one of the country's
independent leading lawyer recruitment firms. We
have an unrivalled track record of successful
assignments on behalf of blue chip law firms and
major corporations. All recruiters are former
lawyers and the firm is the national preferred
supplier to The Canadian Bar Association and the
national recognized supplier to The Canadian
Corporate Counsel Association.

Key Contact - Specialty:
Mr. Stephen Nash, President & General Counsel
Ms. Dal Bhathal, Managing Director
Mr. G. Sean Dunnigan, QC, Managing Director -
Legal
Ms. Laurie A. Larabie, Manager, National
Operations
Mr. Marcus Bolda, Recruiter
Ms. Candace Elston, Recruiter

Salary Minimum: $50,000

Functions: Management, Legal

Industries: Generalist (All), Legal

Branches:
2600-144 4 Ave SW
SunLife Plaza 1
Calgary, AB T2P 3N4
Canada
(403) 264-3838
Fax: (403) 264-3819
Email: sdunnigan@headhunt.com
Key Contact - Specialty:
Mr. Sean Dunnigan, QC, Managing Director
Mrs. Sameera Sereda, Senior Consultant

2600-161 Bay St
B C E Place
Toronto, ON M5J 2S1
Canada
(416) 360 1080
(877) 826-8686
Fax: (416) 360-1082
Email: snash@headhunt.com
Key Contact - Specialty:
Mr. Daryn Salo, Senior Consultant
Mr. David Sciuk, Managing Director
Ms. Laurie Ann Larabie, National Operations
  Manager

Courtright & Associates Inc

PO Box 236
Scranton, PA 18504-0236
(570) 961-5450
Email: rjcx@adelphia.net
Web: www.courtrightassoc.com

Summary: We specialize in recruiting for
biotechnology and pharmaceutical firms nationally
and general management positions.

Key Contact - Specialty:
Mr. Robert J. Courtright, President -
  Biotechnology, Management, Pharmaceutical

Salary Minimum: $80,000

Functions: Generalist (All), Management

Industries: Drugs Mfg., Pharm Svcs.,
  Biotech/Life Sciences

Cowell & Associates Ltd

819 Keystone Ave
River Forest, IL 60305-1319
(708) 771-8989
Fax: (708) 771-1788
Email: roycowell@aol.com

Summary: Provide specialized highly focused
services in organization development and
evaluation/recruitment of executive talent.
Consultative approach coupled with limited
number of concurrent assignments yields timely
quality results and meaningful relationships.

Key Contact - Specialty:
Mr. Roy A. Cowell, President - *General
  management*

Salary Minimum: $75,000

Functions: Generalist (All), Management, Board
  Members, Senior Mgmt., Mktg. Mgmt., CFOs,
  Mgmt. Consultants

Industries: Generalist (All), Manufacturing,
  Retail, Services, Communications, Telecoms,
  Software

The Coxe Group Inc

1218 3rd Ave Ste 1700
Seattle, WA 98101-3037
(206) 467-4040
Fax: (206) 467-4038
Email: consultants@coxegroup.com
Web: www.coxegroup.com

Summary: We are a comprehensive firm, which
exclusively serves the design community,
including: architects, engineers, planners, interior

designers and landscape architects. Our 11
consultants offer a broad base of experience and a
wide range of expertise. Our services include:
general management, marketing, ownership
transition, firm valuation, merger & acquisition,
financial planning, organizational development,
conflict management and executive search.

Key Contact - Specialty:
Mr. Hugh Hochberg, Principal
Mr. Peter Piven, Principal
Mr. Bob Mattox, Principal
Mr. Thomas Kvan, Principal
Ms. Sharlene Silverman, Principal

Functions: Engineering, Architects, Graphic
  Designers

Industries: Construction, Environmental Svcs

CraigSearch[†]

1130 E Arapaho Rd Ste 180
Richardson, TX 75081-2348
(972) 644-3264
Fax: (972) 644-3265
Email: search@craigsearch.com
Web: www.craigsearch.com

Summary: We are an Executive search firm
specializing in placement of mid and senior-level
management within the retail grocery, wholesale
grocery and food service distribution industries.

Key Contact - Specialty:
Mr. Edward C. Nemec, Managing Partner - *Retail*

Salary Minimum: $75,000

Functions: Management, Senior Mgmt.

Industries: Food, Bev., Tobacco, Transportation,
  Wholesale, Retail, Finance, Real Estate

Crawford deMunnik Inc

1910-390 Bay St
Toronto, ON M5H 2Y2
Canada
(416) 863-0153
Email: toronto@crawforddemunnik.com
Web: www.crawforddemunnik.com

Summary: We are a partnership of human
resources consultants. We work with clients to
help them build senior management and executive
teams with the leadership skills, abilities and
potential to achieve the corporation's goals, not
just today, but into the future.

Key Contact - Specialty:
Mr. John D. Crawford, PhD, CMC, Partner

Salary Minimum: $125,000

Functions: Generalist (All)

Industries: Generalist (All)

Creative-Leadership Inc

445 Hutchinson Ave Ste 800
Columbus, OH 43235-8615
(614) 410-6505
(800) 875-5323
Fax: (614) 760-0737
Email: resumes@clci.com
Web: www.clci.com

Summary: We are hiring specialist, training
people who wish to upgrade their skills in people
selection, and providing executive search services,
using a 5 step systematic approach to people
selection.

Key Contact - Specialty:
Mr. Bob Spence, President & Chief Executive
  Officer - *Senior management*
Ms. Noni Clayton, Director, Sales & Marketing
Ms. Susan Collins, Senior Executive Search
  Consultant
Mr. Brian Dobler, Executive Search Coordinator

Ms. Kristen Newman, Executive Search
  Coordinator
Ms. Christina Sloane, Executive Search Associate
Ms. Adrienne Astengo, Receptionist & Assistant

Salary Minimum: $50,000

Functions: Generalist (All)

Industries: Generalist (All)

Crest Associates Inc

366 Crest Ave
Alamo, CA 94507-2639
(925) 945-7374
Fax: (925) 935-9170
Email: bmannas@aol.com

Summary: We have conducted retained searches
for both companies and search firms. For search
firms, we typically charge on an hourly basis; for
companies, the charge is a 25 percent fee based on
annual compensation. We do not specialize but do
focused, targeted research and candidate
development.

Key Contact - Specialty:
Ms. Barbara Annas, Principal

Salary Minimum: $100,000

Functions: Management

Industries: Paper, Computer Equip., Finance, IT
  Implementation, Telecoms, Software,
  Development SW, ERP SW, Mfg. SW,
  Marketing SW

Crist Associates

21 W 2nd St Ste 3
Hinsdale, IL 60521-1783
(630) 321-1110
Fax: (630) 321-1112
Web: www.cristassociates.com

Summary: Our firm is a senior level executive
search firm. We limit ourselves to 30 searches per
year and focus exclusively on CEO, COO, CFO
and board level engagements.

Key Contact - Specialty:
Mr. Peter D. Crist, Chairman
Mr. Thomas R. Kolder, President
Mr. Scott W. Simmons, Vice President
Ms. Jackie Boyd, Vice President

Salary Minimum: $450,000

Functions: Board Members, Senior Mgmt., CFOs

Industries: Generalist (All)

Criterion Search Group Inc

PO Box 466
Wayne, PA 19087-0466
(610) 581-0590
Fax: (610) 581-0594
Email: hare@criterionsg.com
Web: www.criterionsg.com

Summary: Ours is a boutique firm respected for
its personalized service and success in finding
world-class executives for a range of
organizations. We specialize in the fields of
financial services, pharmaceuticals,
telecommunications, packaging, and the legal and
non-profit communities. We specialize in both
temporary and permanent placements.

Key Contact - Specialty:
Ms. Beth C. Hare, Principal - *Financial, Human
  resources*

Salary Minimum: $90,000

Functions: Management, Sales & Mktg., HR
  Mgmt., Benefits, Training, Finance, IT, MIS
  Mgmt.

Industries: Manufacturing, Finance, Services,
  Media, Software, Healthcare

Cromwell Partners Inc

305 Madison Ave
New York, NY 10165-0006
(212) 953-3220
Fax: (212) 953-4688
Email: recruiters@cromwell-partners.com
Web: www.cromwell-partners.com

Summary: We provide executive search services
in the following areas: investment management,
investment banking, commercial banking, private
equity, capital markets, sales & trading, equity
research, manufacturing/consumer products, legal,
and compliance.

Key Contact - Specialty:
Mr. Joseph Ziccardi, Chief Executive Officer -
  Financial services
Mr. Paul Heller, President - *Financial services*

Salary Minimum: $100,000

Functions: Generalist (All)

Industries: Energy, Utilities, Manufacturing,
  Consumer Goods, Finance, Banking, Invest.
  Banking, Mutual/Hedge Funds, Misc. Financial,
  Services, Pharm Svcs.

Cross Hill Partners LLC

245 Park Ave Fl 24
New York, NY 10167-2499
(212) 672-1604
Fax: (212) 202-6316
Email: info@crosshillpartners.com
Web: www.crosshillpartners.com

Summary: We are a retained search firm founded
by career search professionals who together
possess over 400 assignments of combined
experience.

Key Contact - Specialty:
Mr. Christopher Shea, Managing Partner -
  *Brokerage, C-level, Capital markets, E-
  business, Senior management*
Ms. Diane Shea, Managing Partner - *Banking,
  Banking (Investment), Capital markets,
  Insurance, Private equity*

Salary Minimum: $150,000

Functions: Generalist (All), Senior Mgmt.

Industries: Finance, Banking, Invest. Banking,
  Brokers, Venture Cap., Mutual/Hedge Funds,
  Misc. Financial, Media, Publishing, New Media,
  Insurance, Software

Crowder & Company

40950 Woodward Ave Ste 335
Bloomfield Hills, MI 48304-5129
(248) 645-0909
Fax: (248) 645-2366
Email: ewc@crowdercompany.com
Web: www.crowdercompany.com

Summary: We are a results-driven consulting firm
providing multi-disciplinary executive search at
the senior management level.

Key Contact - Specialty:
Mr. Edward W. Crowder, President
Ms. Leticia C. Delos Santos, Database
  Administrator

Salary Minimum: $90,000

Functions: Generalist (All), Management, Senior
  Mgmt., Mfg., Sales & Mktg., HR Mgmt.,
  Finance, Engineering

Industries: Manufacturing, Chemicals, Plastics,
  Rubber, Metal Products, Machine, Appliance,
  Motor Vehicles, Misc. Mfg., Electronic, Elec.
  Components, Transportation, Packaging

Timothy D Crowe Jr

26 Higate Rd
Chelmsford, MA 01824-4440
(978) 256-2008

Summary: Our firm is a small consulting
organization dedicated to providing service to only
a few companies.

Key Contact - Specialty:
Mr. Timothy D. Crowe, Jr., President

Salary Minimum: $50,000

Functions: Generalist (All)

Industries: Manufacturing, Computer Equip.,
  Test, Measure Equip., Aerospace, Software

Crowe-Innes & Associates LLC

1120 Mar West St Ste D
Tiburon, CA 94920-1880
(415) 789-1422
Fax: (415) 435-6867
Email: info@croweinnes.com
Web: www.croweinnes.com

Summary: Our firm conducts senior-level
searches within a variety of industries and
functional disciplines with a significant emphasis
in technology, retail/apparel, consumer products
and financial services. Our clients range in size
from newly emerging growth companies to
Fortune 500 companies.

Key Contact - Specialty:
Ms. Jenny Crowe-Innes, President & Chief
  Executive Officer
Ms. Beth Logan, Vice President

Salary Minimum: $150,000

Functions: Senior Mgmt., Sales & Mktg., PR, HR
  Mgmt., Finance, IT

Industries: Generalist (All)

Crown Advisors Inc

30 Isabella St Ste 203
Pittsburgh, PA 15212-5862
(412) 566-1100
Fax: (412) 566-1256
Email: info@crownsearch.com
Web: www.crownsearch.com

Summary: A leader in commercial real estate
executive search, our reputation for excellence
makes us your first choice for all CRE positions.
We work with owners, developers, investors,
lenders, advisors, borrowers, constructors and all
CRE service providers.

Key Contact - Specialty:
Mr. John Cigna, Partner
Mr. Philip Canzian, Partner
Mr. Bert McDermott, Partner
Mr. Kevin Jones, Partner - *Construction, Real
  estate*
Mr. Tom Callahan, Partner - *Construction, Real
  estate*

Salary Minimum: $100,000

Functions: Generalist (All), Senior Mgmt.

Industries: Energy, Utilities, Construction,
  Finance, Banking, Invest. Banking, Brokers,
  Services, Hospitality, Real Estate,
  Property/Facility Mgmt.

Branches:
800 E Northwest Hwy Ste 612
Palatine, IL 60074-6512
(847) 221-2213
(847) 830-6998
Fax: (847) 221-2219
Email: jdimare@crownsearch.com

Key Contact - Specialty:
Mr. John DiMare, Partner

CSI Consulting[†]

1820-150 York St
National Bank Tower
Toronto, ON M5H 3S5
Canada
(416) 364-6376
Fax: (416) 364-2735
Email: csi@csican.com
Web: www.csican.com

Summary: We are a dynamic IT consulting
practice, providing customized project resources,
and technology solutions addressing the unique
needs of clients.

Key Contact - Specialty:
Ms. Shylee Holla
Mr. Ajit Someshwar

Salary Minimum: $40,000

Functions: IT

Industries: Generalist (All)

The CSO Board

PO Box 130863
Dallas, TX 75313-0863
(214) 291-5885
(877) 405-6300
Fax: (214) 291-5885
Email: info@csoboard.com
Web: www.csoboard.com

Summary: We are a strategic management and
technology-consulting firm helping top
management with their most important problems.
We help leading corporations, organizations,
professionals, and executives make distinctive,
lasting and substantial improvements in their
performance.

Key Contact - Specialty:
Mr. Jaime Chanaga, CISSP, CISA, Managing
  Director - *E-business, Information Technology,
  Management consulting, Professional services,
  Senior management*

CTR

581 Bellwood Dr Ste 100
Santa Clara, CA 95054-2106
(408) 980-8082

Summary: We are a mid-level to executive-level
recruitment services to corporate clients in high-
technology environments.

Key Contact - Specialty:
Mr. Timothy J. Outman, President & Founder -
  High technology

Functions: Management, Senior Mgmt.,
  Production, Healthcare, Sales & Mktg.,
  Engineering

Industries: Generalist (All), HR Services,
  Software, Biotech/Life Sciences

Cullen International Executive Search Inc

50 Northcrest Dr
Newnan, GA 30265-1200
(678) 230-5475
Fax: (770) 252-5648
Email: richardcullen@bellsouth.net

Summary: Retained Executive Search Firm
placing company President's & CEO's.

Key Contact - Specialty:
Mr. Richard R. Cullen, Chairman & Chief
  Executive Officer
Ms. Kimberly G. Cullen, President

Mr. Adam R. Cullen, Vice President
Ms. Ashley N. Cullen, Vice President

Salary Minimum: $1,000,000

Functions: Generalist (All), Board Members, Senior Mgmt., Healthcare, Sales & Mktg., HR Mgmt., Finance, CFOs, Int'l.

Industries: Generalist (All)

Curran Partners Inc

(a US partner of Eurosearch Consultants International)
1 Landmark Sq Ste 525
Stamford, CT 06901-2601
(203) 363-5350
Fax: (203) 363-5353
Email: research@curranpartners.com
Web: www.curranpartners.com

Summary: Executive search firm working exclusively on retained assignments.

Key Contact - Specialty:
Mr. Michael N. Curran, Managing Partner
Mr. Eric A. Montgomery, Partner
Mrs. Nancy D. Hintze, Associate

Salary Minimum: $150,000

Functions: Generalist (All)

Industries: Generalist (All)

Curry Company

25 Eastfield Rd
Mount Vernon, NY 10552-1307
(914) 667-5735
Email: curryco@nyc.rr.com

Summary: A boutique retained executive search firm. Our strength is in the identification and recruitment of highly talented candidates who will outperform in the present position and build bench strength for the future success of both the client and the individual.

Key Contact - Specialty:
Ms. Joan Gagan, Managing Director
Mr. William E. Halpin, Managing Director

Salary Minimum: $100,000

Functions: Generalist (All), Management, Senior Mgmt., Mfg., Product Dev., Materials, Sales & Mktg., HR Mgmt., Finance, Security Personnel

Industries: Energy, Utilities, Manufacturing, Food, Bev., Tobacco, Paper, Chemicals, Drugs Mfg., Medical Devices, Metal Products, Motor Vehicles, Computer Equip., Consumer Elect., Electronic, Elec. Components, Consumer Goods, Transportation, Retail, Finance, Misc. Financial, Services, Equip Svcs., Mgmt. Consulting, Communications, Aerospace, Packaging, Healthcare

Judith Cushman & Associates[†]

1275 12th Ave NW Ste 14
Issaquah, WA 98027-8993
(425) 392-8660
Fax: (425) 391-9190
Email: jcushman@jc-a.com
Web: www.jc-a.com

Summary: Our firm provides added value recruiting and consulting solutions for the communications, investor relations and marcom functions. We facilitate and manage the search process, enabling the organization to make the best selection, saving time and adding value throughout the course of a search.

Key Contact - Specialty:
Ms. Judith Cushman, President

Salary Minimum: $55,000

Functions: Board Members, Senior Mgmt., PR

Industries: Media, Communications, Biotech/Life Sciences

The Custer Group

6005 Tattersall Ct
Brentwood, TN 37027-5728
(615) 309-0577
Email: research@custergroup.com
Web: www.custergroup.com

Summary: A generalist firm providing intelligent solutions for the recruitment, assessment and selection of exceptional executive talent for our clients.

Key Contact - Specialty:
Mr. J. Dwight Custer, President - *Healthcare, Senior management, Technology*
Mr. Bryce W. Custer, Vice President - *General management, Healthcare*
Ms. Leslie Rule, Research Associate - *Research*

Salary Minimum: $100,000

Functions: Senior Mgmt.

Industries: Generalist (All)

Custom Research Solutions[†]

16400 Pacific Coast Hwy Ste 221
Huntington Beach, CA 92649-1823
(888) 722-6697
Fax: (800) 829-5870
Email: arodrigue@custom-research.com
Web: www.custom-research.com

Summary: Our firm provides HR, market/sales and association membership research for our customers. We work with our clients to identify specific candidates from their target competitors and industries for their key positions.

Key Contact - Specialty:
Mr. Jon Cianci, National Account Manager

Functions: Generalist (All)

Industries: Generalist (All), Manufacturing, Retail, Finance, Services, Hospitality, Communications, Government, Packaging, Insurance

Cuthbertson Associates Inc

3 Park Ave Fl 30
New York, NY 10016
(212) 984-0747
Fax: (212) 972-7036
Email: bcuthbertsoninc@webmailoutlet.com

Summary: Retained search firm nationally placing high technology, publishing professionals and management consultants.

Key Contact - Specialty:
Mr. Chris Cuthbertson, Principal

Salary Minimum: $75,000

Functions: Sales Mgmt., Direct Mktg., Mgmt. Consultants

Industries: Mgmt. Consulting, Media, Publishing, Telecoms

CXO Executive Search Ltd

1560 Sawgrass Corporate Pkwy Fl 4
Sunrise, FL 33323-2858
(954) 331-8091
Fax: (954) 331-4601
Email: clee@cxoexecutivesearch.com
Web: www.cxoexecutivesearch.com

Summary: Our firm offers leadership solutions for the technology, security, energy, consumer, media, entertainment, sports, logistics, life sciences and financial services industries. We recruit chief executive officers, chief operating officers, chief financial officers, chief human resources officers as well as other executives for senior operations and staff positions.

Key Contact - Specialty:
Mr. Conrad Lee, President
Mr. Walter Birch, Partner - *Boards of Directors, Healthcare, Hospital, Investor relations, Life Sciences*

Salary Minimum: $200,000

Functions: Generalist (All), Senior Mgmt.

Industries: Energy, Utilities, Transportation, Retail, Venture Cap., Logistics Svcs., Hospitality, Sports, Media, Communications, Government, Real Estate, Software, Healthcare, Hospitals

Cyntal International Ltd

405 Lexington Ave Fl 26
New York, NY 10174-2699
(917) 368-8181
Email: cynthia@cyntal.com

Summary: We are a generalist firm for upper-middle and senior-executive leadership roles. Our expertise covers: General Management, Marketing, Product and Sales Management, Corporate Communications and other disciplines.

Key Contact - Specialty:
Ms. Cynthia D. Vroom, President

Salary Minimum: $125,000

Functions: Management, Senior Mgmt., Middle Mgmt., Sales & Mktg., Advertising, Mktg. Research, Mktg. Mgmt., PR, Specialized Svcs., Minorities/Diversity

Industries: Generalist (All), Manufacturing, Food, Bev., Tobacco, Misc. Mfg., Consumer Goods, Finance, Services, Non-profits, Hospitality, Entertainment, Media, Communications

D'Antoni Partners Inc

122 W John Carpenter Fwy Ste 525
Irving, TX 75039-2022
(972) 719-4400
Fax: (972) 719-4401
Email: richard@dantonipartners.com
Web: www.dantonipartners.com

Summary: Retained by clients in healthcare services, IT and life sciences to search for board members, C-level executives and VPs of all functional areas. Our experience as CEO/COO of several private and public companies in services and biotechnology add to our rare value proposition.

Key Contact - Specialty:
Mr. Richard D'Antoni, President - *Healthcare*
Ms. Kay K. Tieman, Vice President - *Healthcare*

Salary Minimum: $150,000

Functions: Generalist (All)

Industries: Drugs Mfg., Medical Devices, Pharm Svcs., Biotech/Life Sciences, Healthcare

Dahl-Morrow International[†]

608 S King St Ste 103
Leesburg, VA 20175-3924
(703) 779-5600
Fax: (703) 779-5678
Email: dmi@dahl-morrowintl.com
Web: www.dahl-morrowintl.com

Summary: Our firm provides both permanent and interim executives to client companies worldwide. We work in the extensive industry verticals of high technology and communications. Our expertise includes the systems integrators who service the government and intelligence community. We work in all functional areas.

Key Contact - Specialty:
Ms. Barbara Steinem, President
Ms. Andy Steinem, Chief Executive Officer
Ms. Kimberly Armour, Vice President
Ms. Phoebe Henderson, Senior Consultant

Salary Minimum: $100,000

Functions: Sales & Mktg., Finance, IT, Engineering, Int'l.

Industries: Services, Communications, Government, Software

DAL Partners

4 Corporate Dr Ste 482
Shelton, CT 06484-6263
(203) 256-3777
Fax: (203) 225-7807
Email: dalsearch@aol.com
Web: www.dalpartners.com

Summary: A generalist executive-management retainer search firm. Experienced in multi-industries and multi-functions.

Key Contact - Specialty:
Mr. Donald A. Lotufo, Partner
Mr. Michael E. Rush, Managing Partner
Mr. Jack Barwis, Senior Vice President
Dr. Mary McGrath

Salary Minimum: $80,000

Functions: Generalist (All)

Industries: Generalist (All)

The Dalley Hewitt Company

3075 Howell Mill Rd NW Unit 11
Atlanta, GA 30327-1657
(404) 605-9070
Fax: (404) 355-6136
Email: rives@dalleyhewitt.com
Web: www.dalleyhewitt.com

Summary: We are a management recruiting and consulting firm that provides clients with a flexible package of executive search services.

Key Contact - Specialty:
Ms. Rives D. Hewitt, President
Mr. Werner Boel, Principal
Ms. Mirla Bigda, Senior Associate

Salary Minimum: $50,000

Functions: Generalist (All)

Industries: Manufacturing, Printing, Medical Devices, Computer Equip., Misc. Mfg., Services, Higher Ed., Biotech/Life Sciences

Daly & Company Inc

175 Federal St
Boston, MA 02110-2210
(617) 262-2800
Fax: (617) 728-4477
Email: info@dalyco.com
Web: www.dalyco.com

Summary: Our industry focus is venture capital financed technology start-ups filling senior requirements, CEO, COO, CFO, VP and CTO.

Key Contact - Specialty:
Mr. Dan Daly, President

Salary Minimum: $125,000

Functions: Senior Mgmt.

Industries: Medical Devices, Consumer Elect., Test, Measure Equip., Electronic, Elec. Components, Venture Cap., Mutual/Hedge Funds, Non-profits, Telecoms, Wireless, Software

The Damase Group

PO Box 1833
Framingham, MA 01701-0033
(508) 879-2300
Email: resumes@damasegroup.com
Web: www.damasegroup.com

Summary: Our firm partners with successful boutique and mid-tier retained executive search firms conducting senior level assignments, while simultaneously offering competitively priced retained search service (at fixed fees) to our corporate clients for mid-level assignments. We work within two industry verticals: technology and manufacturing.

Key Contact - Specialty:
Mr. Randy Cyr, President - *CFOs, Controllers, General management, Marketing, Sales*

Salary Minimum: $100,000

Functions: Generalist (All), Management, Senior Mgmt., Middle Mgmt., Sales & Mktg., Mktg. Mgmt., Sales Mgmt., Sales Reps., Finance, CFOs

Industries: Manufacturing, Communications, Software

Alfred Daniels & Associates Inc

5795 Waverly Ave
La Jolla, CA 92037-7336
(858) 459-4009
Web: www.alfreddaniels.com

Summary: We specialize in placing equity and debt capital markets professionals. We have extensive experience in equity, fixed income and credit derivatives; convertible sales, trading & origination; stat, risk and other arbitrage trading. Clients include prominent securities firms and hedge funds.

Key Contact - Specialty:
Mr. Alfred Daniels, President
Ms. Lynn Scullion Reisfeld, Director

Salary Minimum: $50,000

Functions: Management, Senior Mgmt., Middle Mgmt., Sales & Mktg., Mktg. Mgmt., Sales Mgmt.

Industries: Finance, Banking, Invest. Banking, Brokers, Venture Cap., Misc. Financial

Dankowski & Associates Inc[†]

13089 Root Rd Ste 200
The Woods SE
Columbia Station, OH 44028-9590
(440) 236-3088
(800) 326-5694
Email: info@dankowskiassociates.com
Web: www.dankowskiassociates.com

Summary: Recruiter of HR professionals. Experience in recruiting as well as a specialist in HR recruiting.

Key Contact - Specialty:
Mr. Tom Dankowski, President - *Human resources*

Salary Minimum: $50,000

Functions: HR Mgmt., Benefits, Staffing, Training, Minorities/Diversity

Industries: Generalist (All)

Alan Darling Consulting

374 Dover Rd Ste 18
South Newfane, VT 05351-9711
(802) 348-6365

Summary: Private executive search driven by original research, complete with an extensive research survey and written report.

Key Contact - Specialty:
Mr. Alan Darling

Salary Minimum: $100,000

Functions: Generalist (All), Senior Mgmt., Healthcare, Sales & Mktg., Engineering

Industries: Manufacturing, Electronic, Elec. Components, Non-profits, Legal, Defense, Aerospace, Healthcare

Daubenspeck and Associates Ltd

401 N Michigan Ave Ste 730
Chicago, IL 60611-4231
(312) 828-0400
Email: rd@daubenspeck.com
Web: www.daubenspeck.com

Summary: The firm specializes in providing executive search and executive team building, for example, placing entire management teams. Additionally, the firm trains its clients in building staffing mechanisms.

Key Contact - Specialty:
Mr. Kenneth Daubenspeck, Chief Executive Officer
Mrs. Rima Daubenspeck - *General management, Professional services*

Salary Minimum: $150,000

Functions: Generalist (All), Senior Mgmt., Distribution, Staffing, CFOs, IT, Mgmt. Consultants, Minorities/Diversity

Industries: Generalist (All), Finance, Hospitality, Media, Insurance, Software, Healthcare

Daudlin, De Beaupre & Company Inc

18530 Mack Ave Ste 315
Grosse Pointe Farms, MI 48236-3254
(313) 885-1235
Fax: (313) 885-1247

Summary: Search consultants specializing in the recruitment of executives and professionals in the healthcare field.

Key Contact - Specialty:
Mr. Paul T. Daudlin, President - *Healthcare*
Ms. Mary Anne De Beaupre, Executive Vice President - *Healthcare*
Ms. Mary Jane Langlois, Senior Associate - *Healthcare*
Mr. James Delmotte, EdD, Vice President - *Healthcare*
Dr. Thomas Dakoske, PhD, Senior Associate - *Healthcare*

Salary Minimum: $60,000

Functions: Nurses, Allied Health, Health Admin.

Industries: Healthcare

Andre David & Associates Inc

PO Box 700967
Dallas, TX 75370-0967
(972) 250-1986
Fax: (972) 250-2243
Email: tpatch@andredavid.com

Summary: We are a management consulting firm engaging in executive search. We perform searches with a high degree of professionalism, a sense of urgency and a commitment to excellence. We bring client and external expertise to search engagements.

Key Contact - Specialty:
Mr. Terry Patch, President - *Human resources*

Salary Minimum: $100,000

Functions: Mktg. Mgmt., Benefits, Staffing, Mgmt. Consultants, Minorities/Diversity

Industries: Generalist (All), Food, Bev., Tobacco

Davidson Associates

50 California St Ste 502
San Francisco, CA 94111-4624
(415) 563-1152
Fax: (415) 567-5920
Email: dmd@ddavidson.com
Web: www.ddavidson.com

Summary: Our principal and founder extensive experience recruiting senior level executives in the high technology, consumer products, retail and financial services industries. She has filled senior positions in marketing, finance, communications, operations and HR. We are passionate about delivering results while providing personalized service to each client.

Key Contact - Specialty:
Ms. Donna Davidson, Principal

Salary Minimum: $100,000

Functions: Generalist (All), Management

Industries: Generalist (All), Food, Bev., Tobacco, Consumer Goods, Retail, Finance, Non-profits, Hospitality, Entertainment, Media, New Media, Call Centers, Wireless

Davies Park

1505-10060 Jasper Ave NW
Scotia Bank Tower
Edmonton, AB T5J 3R8
Canada
(780) 420-9900
Fax: (780) 426-2936
Email: search@daviespark.com
Web: www.daviespark.com

Summary: Our principals have experience in executive search and we operate in two major centers, Edmonton and Calgary, Alberta, Canada. Our services are retainer based and we serve only clients in western Canada.

Key Contact - Specialty:
Mr. A. Gerry Davies, Partner - *Executives, Financial, General management, Healthcare, Senior management*
Ms. Elizabeth Hurley, Partner - *Education, Education (Higher), Executives, Non-profit, Senior management*
Mr. Anurag Shourie, Partner - *Education, Education (Higher), Logistics, Senior management, Technology*

Salary Minimum: $80,000

Functions: Generalist (All), Senior Mgmt., Materials, Physicians, Health Admin., HR Mgmt., CFOs, Engineering

Industries: Generalist (All), Energy, Utilities, Manufacturing, Transportation, Wholesale, Retail, Finance, Hospitality, Communications, Government, Biotech/Life Sciences, Healthcare

Branches:
2930-300 5 Ave SW
Alberta Stock Exhange Tower
Calgary, AB T2P 3C4
Canada
(403) 263-0600
Fax: (403) 269-1080
Email: consult@daviespark.com

Key Contact - Specialty:
Mr. Allan C. Nelson, Partner - *Accounting, Executives, Marketing, Oil, Senior management*
Mr. Mike Kerr, Partner - *Education, Executives, Government, Oil, Operations*

John J Davis & Associates Inc

521 5th Ave Ste 1740
New York, NY 10175-0003
(212) 286-9489
Fax: (973) 467-3706
Email: jack.davis@jdavisassoc.com
Web: www.johnjdavisandassoc.com

Summary: A highly specialized firm focused exclusively in the senior and middle management areas of IS and telecommunications.

Key Contact - Specialty:
Mr. John J. Davis, President
Mr. Thomas D. Bell, Vice President
Mr. Jack P. Long, Vice President
Mr. Jack Davis, Vice President
Mr. John D. Simon, Managing Director

Salary Minimum: $150,000

Functions: Generalist (All), Board Members, Admin. Svcs., MIS Mgmt.

Industries: Generalist (All), Energy, Utilities, Manufacturing, Drugs Mfg., Transportation, Retail, Finance, Services, Legal, Mgmt. Consulting, E-commerce, IT Implementation, Media, Publishing, Communications, Insurance, Security SW, Healthcare

Alan Davis & Associates Inc

Boîte 750 de PO
Rue de 538 forces
Hudson Heights, QC J0P 1J0
Canada
(450) 458-3535
Fax: (450) 458-3530
Email: adavis@alandavis.com
Web: www.alandavis.com

Summary: We are an executive and professional search firm providing highly innovative solutions for difficult-to-fill positions. We provide a range of professional services to an impressive list of long-standing clients, many of who are world leaders in their respective industries. We specialize in management, engineering, scientific and IT specialists.

Key Contact - Specialty:
Mr. Alan Davis, President
Ms. Diane Bates, Vice President, Operations
Ms. Laurie O'Donnell, Senior Consultant
Ms. Glenda Newton, Senior Consultant

Functions: Board Members, Senior Mgmt., Middle Mgmt., Product Dev., HR Mgmt., R&D, Engineering, Technicians, Int'l.

Industries: Generalist (All), Energy, Utilities, Construction, Manufacturing, Finance, Pharm Svcs., HR Services, Communications, Aerospace, Software, Biotech/Life Sciences

Joseph A Davis Consultants Inc

104 E 40th St Rm 203
New York, NY 10016-1801
(212) 682-4006
Fax: (212) 661-0846
Email: jadci@compuserve.com

Summary: We are an African-American firm specializing in recruiting diverse professionals. We are generalists and work on retained search assignments.

Key Contact - Specialty:
Mr. Joseph A. Davis, President
Ms. Winifred R. Davis, Vice President

Salary Minimum: $90,000

Functions: Generalist (All), Management, Sales & Mktg., HR Mgmt., Finance, IT, Specialized Svcs.

Industries: Generalist (All), Energy, Utilities, Finance, HR Services, Media, Communications

Day & Associates

(an EMA Partners International company)
577 Airport Blvd Ste 130
Burlingame, CA 94010-2021
(650) 343-2660
Fax: (650) 344-8460
Email: jkday@dayassociates.net
Web: www.dayassociates.net

Summary: We are consultants in executive search, assisting client organizations in the life science/healthcare, including biotechnology, pharmaceuticals, device, diagnostic & medical OTC and high technology, including software, internet and wireless communication. We have high technology segments to identify and attract senior executives, senior management teams and board positions. Our focus is on start-ups, early stage and mid-size organizations.

Key Contact - Specialty:
Mr. J. Kevin Day, Managing Director - *Healthcare*

Salary Minimum: $150,000

Functions: Board Members, Senior Mgmt.

Industries: Drugs Mfg., Medical Devices, Venture Cap., New Media, Communications, Software, Biotech/Life Sciences, Healthcare

DBL Associates[†]

1334 Park View Ave Ste 100
Manhattan Beach, CA 90266-3788
(310) 545-8121
Email: dlong@dblsearch.com
Web: www.dblsearch.com

Summary: We specialize in the placement of CPAs and MBAs in financial, accounting, tax and IT positions. Our client base includes financial services, high technology, healthcare, manufacturing, distribution, entertainment and internet companies. We have extensive experience placing executives.

Key Contact - Specialty:
Mr. David B. Long, President - *MBAs*

Salary Minimum: $80,000

Functions: Management, Senior Mgmt., Middle Mgmt., Mktg. Mgmt., HR Mgmt., Finance, IT

Industries: Generalist (All), Manufacturing, Retail, Finance, Services, Software, Healthcare

Dean Associates

PO Box 1079
Santa Cruz, CA 95061-1079
(831) 423-2931
Email: dean@deanassociates.com
Web: www.deanassociates.com

Summary: Specialists in finding executive talent who are best suited to your culture, management style and values. We offer retained executive search and consultation services and focus on the successful placement of board members, executive management and VP level talent for high technology companies, professional service firms and non-profit organizations.

Key Contact - Specialty:
Ms. Mary Dean, Managing Director

Salary Minimum: $45,000

Functions: Generalist (All)

Industries: Misc. Mfg., Electronic, Elec. Components, Semiconductors, Services, Telecoms, Wireless, Fiber Optic, Network Infrastructure

Deerfield Associates

572 Washington St Ste 15
Wellesley, MA 02482-6437
(781) 237-2800
Fax: (781) 237-5600
Email: doug@deerfieldassociates.com
Web: www.deerfieldassociates.com

Summary: Retained executive search firm focusing on executive-level positions in the education sectors. Our approach is that of a highly customer service oriented firm offering personalized attention, high quality work and a cost effective method in a timely manner.

Key Contact - Specialty:
Mr. Douglas C. Cooney, President
Ms. Joan Grzybowski, Managing Director

Salary Minimum: $100,000

Functions: Board Members, Senior Mgmt., CFOs

Industries: Non-profits, Higher Ed.

Deffet Group Inc†

7801 Marysville Rd
Ostrander, OH 43061-9703
(740) 666-7600
Fax: (740) 666-7610
Email: info@deffetgroup.com
Web: www.deffetgroup.com

Summary: Specializing in executive search within the long-term care and retirement housing industries.

Key Contact - Specialty:
Mr. G. Daniel Deffet

Salary Minimum: $50,000

Functions: Healthcare

Industries: Non-profits, Mgmt. Consulting, HR Services, Hospitals, Long-term/Home Care

Patrick Delaney & Associates Inc

70 W Madison Ste 1400
#14038A
Chicago, IL 60602-4267
(888) 797-0070
Email: pdelaney@pdelaney.us
Web: www.pdelaney.us

Summary: We have built a history of success in working with executive leaders when they must make an addition, or shift, in their senior management team. Our focus is on leadership. We are focused, at every facet, on making your search project produce the right results. To this end, we commit to accomplishing only 6 high quality search projects per year.

Key Contact - Specialty:
Mr. Patrick J. Delaney, Principal

Salary Minimum: $150,000

Functions: Generalist (All), Management, Board Members, Senior Mgmt., Healthcare, Sales & Mktg., HR Mgmt., Finance, IT, Mgmt. Consultants

Industries: Generalist (All), Manufacturing, Transportation, Finance, Services, Media, Software, Biotech/Life Sciences, Healthcare, Non-Classifiable

Edward Dellon Associates Inc

450 N Brand Blvd Ste 600
Glendale, CA 91203-2349
(310) 286-0625
Fax: (818) 291-6205
Email: edward_dellon@yahoo.com

Summary: Especially proficient in the selection and recruitment of development and construction teams for large, complex and high profile projects.

Key Contact - Specialty:
Mr. Edward Dellon, President - *Construction, Real estate*

Salary Minimum: $100,000

Functions: Generalist (All), Senior Mgmt., Middle Mgmt., CFOs, Budgeting, Engineering, Architects, Int'l.

Industries: Generalist (All), Construction, Invest. Banking, Hospitality, Real Estate

Dellosso and Greenberg

525 E 82nd St
New York, NY 10028-7116
(212) 570-5350
Fax: (212) 327-0613
Email: esearch@dellossoandgreenberg.com
Web: www.dellossoandgreenberg.com

Summary: A boutique executive search firm, specializing in the placement of accountants, financial executives and in-house counsel in top public accounting firms, financial services and primarily technology-based Fortune 500 businesses. We place candidates in public accounting and target a transition from traditional accounting and law firms to senior financial and in-house counsel positions.

Key Contact - Specialty:
Mr. Bernard Dellosso, Managing Partner & CFO - *Accounting (Big 4), CFOs, Finance, Legal, Tax*
Ms. Amy Jo Greenberg, Managing Partner & Director, Recruitment - *Accounting (Big 4), Financial services, Human resources, Legal, Wall Street*

Salary Minimum: $75,000

Functions: HR Mgmt., Finance, CFOs, Budgeting, Cash Mgmt., Taxes, M&A, Risk Mgmt., Legal, Attorneys

Industries: Generalist (All), Finance, Banking, Invest. Banking, Mutual/Hedge Funds, Legal, Accounting, HR Services, Media, New Media, Software

Delphi Systems Ltd

6740 Pennsylvania Ave
Kansas City, MO 64113-1966
(816) 333-6944
Fax: (816) 333-6944
Email: delphi@kc.rr.com
Web: www.macrae.net/ires/search/primer.html

Summary: We conduct a retained general practice limited to positions commanding $200K or more. Our competitive distinctions are our use of WingSpread, an internet mediated, skills-based decision support system to define our clients needs and Knowbot based hyper search technologies for discovering our candidates.

Key Contact - Specialty:
Mr. P. Wayne Reagan, Chief Executive Officer
Mr. Karl Moeller, President
Mr. Mike Yinger, Vice President, Systems
Mr. Tom Lewin, PhD, Vice President, WingSpread
Mr. Mike Gersten, Vice President, Sales
Mr. George Roletter, Vice President, Affinity Groups

Salary Minimum: $200,000

Functions: Generalist (All), Senior Mgmt.

Industries: Generalist (All)

Delta ExSearch†

(formerly known as ExSearch Latinoamerica)
Seneca 47
Col. Polanco
11560 Mexico City, DF
Mexico
55 9171 2800
55 9171 2839
Fax: 55 9171 2801
Email: servicioalcliente@deltaexsearch.com
Web: www.deltaexsearch.com

Summary: We are an executive search firm specialized in four functions: top level and middle management executives in sales and marketing, information technology, financial and human resources.

Key Contact - Specialty:
Mr. Salvador Elizaga, Managing Partner

Salary Minimum: $60,000

Functions: Management, Senior Mgmt.

Industries: Generalist (All), Manufacturing, Transportation, Wholesale, Retail, Finance, Services, Communications, Insurance, Software, Biotech/Life Sciences, Non-Classifiable

Delta Services

PO Box 1294
Sugar Land, TX 77487-1294
(281) 494-9300
Email: resumes@thesearchfirm.com
Web: www.thesearchfirm.com

Summary: The leading global energy retained executive search firm. Our Expertise: high impact business leader retained search. Results: long term legendary employee leadership and performance. Risk: none. Guarantee: outperform your expectations and all previous retained search experiences. Mission: develop united recruiting partnerships through understanding the character, culture, capability and chemistry that defines success in each organization.

Key Contact - Specialty:
Mr. John F. Jansen, President - *C-level, Engineering, Management, Oil, Petrochemical*
Mr. Joel Ray, Vice President - *CIOs, Consulting, Geology, Human resources, Information Technology*

Salary Minimum: $150,000

Functions: Board Members, Senior Mgmt., Mfg., Sales & Mktg., Finance, IT, R&D, Engineering, Geotechnical, Int'l.

Industries: Generalist (All), Oil & Gas, Construction, Chemicals, Banking, Invest. Banking, Venture Cap., Services, Non-profits, Mgmt. Consulting, HR Services, E-commerce, IT Implementation, Engineering Svcs., Supply Chain Mgmt., Software, Security SW

Denell-Archer International Executive Search†

300-4999 Rue Sainte-Catherine O
Chateau Maisonneuve
Westmount, QC H3Z 1T3
Canada
(514) 282-9855
Fax: (514) 282-1643
Email: general@denell-archer.com
Web: www.denell-archer.com

Summary: Our unique ability to identify and find top-caliber candidates and then guide the selection

process to a successful offer is the direct result of our 'strategic search solution' - a powerful tool that ensures a solid hire and a firm commitment.

Key Contact - Specialty:
Mr. Daniel Ascher, President - *Business development, Consumer (Packaged Goods), General management, Market research, Marketing*
Mr. Michael Vice, Senior Associate - *Diagnostics, Life Sciences, Medical, Packaging, Pharmaceutical*

Salary Minimum: $90,000

Functions: Management, Board Members, Senior Mgmt., Middle Mgmt., Sales & Mktg., Advertising, Mktg. Research, Mktg. Mgmt., Sales Mgmt., CFOs

Industries: Manufacturing, Printing, Chemicals, Drugs Mfg., Medical Devices, Plastics, Rubber, Venture Cap., Pharm Svcs., Media, Advertising, Publishing, New Media, Packaging, Marketing SW, Biotech/Life Sciences, Healthcare, Women's

Denney & Company Inc
PO Box 22156
Pittsburgh, PA 15222-0156
(412) 517-8084
Fax: (412) 517-8085
Email: tldenney@msn.com

Summary: Generalist practice: director, CEO, COO and only senior executive-levels. Clients include financial services, industries, consumer durable/non-durable goods and medical products. We also offer strategic acquisition search practice.

Key Contact - Specialty:
Mr. Thomas L. Denney, President - *General management*
Mr. Edward B. Denney, Vice President - *General management*

Salary Minimum: $300,000

Functions: Generalist (All), Int'l.

Industries: Generalist (All), Food, Bev., Tobacco

Derba & Derba[†]
7 Whispering Pines Dr
Andover, MA 01810-3421
(978) 470-8270
Fax: (978) 470-4592
Email: bobderb@aol.com
Web: www.shoppersworld.com/derba

Summary: Executive search and personnel consulting firm specializing in the private club/resort sector of the hospitality industry for: GMs, COOs, clubhouse managers, directors of golf, golf course superintendents, executive chefs and controllers.

Key Contact - Specialty:
Mr. Robert Derba, President & Partner
Mr. Peter Derba, Vice President
Mr. Matthew Derba, Vice President

Salary Minimum: $100,000

Functions: Senior Mgmt.

Industries: Hospitality, Hotels, Resorts, Clubs, Restaurants, Full Service Restaurants

Derek Associates Inc[†]
PO Box 13
Mendon, MA 01756-0013
(508) 883-2289
Fax: (508) 883-2264
Email: joren@derekassociates.com
Web: www.derekassociates.com

Key Contact - Specialty:
Mr. Joren Fishback, Senior Consultant - *Engineering, Environmental, Geology, Transportation*

Salary Minimum: $40,000

Functions: Generalist (All), Engineering, Geotechnical, Environmentalists

Industries: Generalist (All), Oil & Gas, Architectural Svcs., Engineering Svcs., Compliance, Environmental Svcs., Haz. Waste

Derhak Ireland & Partners Inc
100-65 International Blvd
Etobicoke, ON M9W 6L9
Canada
(416) 675-7600
Fax: (416) 675-7833
Email: info@derhak-ireland.com
Web: www.derhak-ireland.com

Summary: We are a retained firm of senior executive recruitment professionals, all of whom have extensive management experience in pharmaceuticals, high-tech, automotive, telecom, consumer goods, and market research.

Key Contact - Specialty:
Mr. Allen R. Derhak, BA, MBA, Partner & President - *Aerospace, Associations, Automotive, Consumer (Packaged Goods), Engineering*
Mr. Murray W. Clarke, BPhm, MBA, Partner - *Biotechnology, Healthcare, Pharmaceutical*
Mr. William M. Derhak, BComm, MA, Partner - *Aerospace, Automation, Automotive, Fiber-optics, High technology*
Mr. Howard Kleiman, BA, Partner - *Administration, Finance, General management, Manufacturing*
Mr. David E. Van Schaik, CPP, CIM, Partner - *Aerospace, Automotive, Engineering, High technology, Manufacturing*
Mr. Wayne Percy, BA, Partner - *Consumer (Packaged Goods), Market research*
Mr. Frank Tancredi, BA, CHRP, Partner - *Consumer (Products), Engineering, Finance, General management, Human resources*

Salary Minimum: $75,000

Functions: Generalist (All), Management, Mfg., Healthcare, Sales & Mktg., Finance, Engineering

Industries: Generalist (All), Manufacturing, Finance, Aerospace, Packaging, Healthcare

DerrJones Inc[†]
355 Lancaster Ave Ste A205
Haverford, PA 19041-7500
(610) 645-4160
Email: mcgeever@derrjones.com
Web: www.derrjones.com

Summary: Our firm specializes in executive level sales and sales management opportunities across a wide range of industries. We work extensively with service related businesses that focus on: consultative, relationship driven, solution based selling strategies. It is not unusual to find us working on assignments outside our area of specialization as we continue to support long standing clients.

Key Contact - Specialty:
Ms. Cynthia McGeever, Principal

Functions: Sales & Mktg., Sales Mgmt., Sales Reps.

Industries: Generalist (All)

Despres & Associates Inc[†]
(an Alliance Partnership International company)
117 S Cook St Ste 304
Barrington, IL 60010-4311
(847) 382-0625
Fax: (847) 382-1705
Email: rdespres@despres.net
Web: www.despres.net

Summary: We specialize in sales and sales management people. We place directors and VPs and other executives in any industry and focus on high-technology companies.

Key Contact - Specialty:
Mr. Raoul Despres, President - *General management, Sales*

Salary Minimum: $75,000

Functions: Senior Mgmt., Sales & Mktg., Sales Mgmt.

Industries: Generalist (All), Printing, E-commerce, New Media, Telecoms, Wireless, Software, Doc. Mgmt., Production SW, ERP SW

Development Resource Group Inc (DRG)
104 E 40th St Rm 304
New York, NY 10016-1801
(212) 983-1600
Fax: (212) 983-1687
Email: search@drgnyc.com
Web: www.drgnyc.com

Summary: Specialist in retained search for all not-for-profit CEOs, CFOs, COOs, senior managers and development specialists.

Key Contact - Specialty:
Mr. David E. Edell, President
Mr. David Hinsley Cheng, Managing Director
Ms. Mary Wheeler, Senior Vice President
Mr. Daniel Ripps, Vice President

Functions: Generalist (All), Senior Mgmt., Non-profits

Industries: Non-profits, Higher Ed., Government, Development SW, Healthcare

DGL Consultants[†]
PO Box 450
189 S Main St
Richford, VT 05476-0450
(802) 848-7764
Fax: (802) 848-3117
Email: resumes@dglconsultants.com
Web: www.dglconsultants.com

Summary: Our firm is a retained executive search and management consulting firm that helps clients nationwide. Our clients are exclusively investment management and Wall Street firms, insurance companies, mutual fund and annuity distributors.

Key Contact - Specialty:
Mr. Donald Lariviere, President
Ms. Pam Zappala, Executive Vice President

Salary Minimum: $125,000

Functions: Sales & Mktg., Mktg. Research, Mktg. Mgmt., Sales Mgmt., Cash Mgmt., Pension/Ret. Planning

Industries: Finance, Invest. Banking, Mutual/Hedge Funds, Life

DHR International
10 S Riverside Plz Ste 2220
Chicago, IL 60606-3707
(312) 782-1581
Fax: (312) 782-2096
Web: www.dhrinternational.com

† occasional contingency assignment

Summary: With offices worldwide, DHR Consultants recruit leaders in all industries and functions including, but not limited to: board services, diversity, education, industrial, healthcare and life sciences, retail/consumer, financial services, technology, nonprofit, media and entertainment.

Key Contact - Specialty:
Mr. David H. Hoffmann, Chairman & Chief Executive Officer
Mr. Steve Ethington, Executive Vice President
Ms. Mary Lee Montague, Executive Vice President
Mr. Larry Poore, Executive Vice President
Mr. Craig Randall, Executive Vice President & Managing Dir
Ms. Marcey Rubin Stamas, Executive Vice President
Mr. Glenn Sugiyama, Executive Vice President
Mr. John Quinn, Executive Vice President
Ms. Michelle Smead, Executive Vice President
Mr. Dan Burns, Executive Vice President
Mr. Tom Goodrich, Executive Vice President
Mr. Jim Shroeder, Executive Vice President

Salary Minimum: $100,000

Functions: Generalist (All)

Industries: Generalist (All)

Branches:
11811 N Tatum Blvd Ste 3031
Phoenix, AZ 85028-1621
(602) 992-7810
Fax: (602) 953-7811
Key Contact - Specialty:
Mr. David Bruno, Vice Chairman - *Retail*
Mr. Bill Franquemont, Executive Vice President

19200 Von Karman Ave Ste 500
Irvine, CA 92612-8513
(949) 622-5483
Fax: (949) 622-5512
Key Contact - Specialty:
Mr. Larry Cabaldon, Executive Vice President
Mr. Ron LaGrow, Executive Vice President
Dr. Gary Hegenbart

28202 Cabot Rd Ste 300
Laguna Niguel, CA 92677-1249
(949) 365-5690
Fax: (949) 365-5691
Key Contact - Specialty:
Mr. David Kurrasch, Executive Vice President & Managing Dir

2029 Century Park E Ste 1010
Los Angeles, CA 90067-2911
(310) 789-7333
Fax: (310) 789-7350
Key Contact - Specialty:
Ms. Gabriella Colantoni, Executive Vice President & Managing Dir
Mr. Bob Marchant, Executive Vice President
Ms. Julia Eakes, EVP
Mr. Ronald Hendrixson, EVP
Ms. Colleen Hulce, EVP

11455 El Camino Real Ste 210
San Diego, CA 92130-2088
(858) 792-7654
Fax: (858) 792-6340
Key Contact - Specialty:
Mr. Joel T. Grushkin, Executive Vice President & Managing Dir
Mr. Robert Jones, EVP

50 California St. Ste 1500
San Francisco, CA 94111-4612
(415) 277-5416
Fax: (415) 358-4497
Key Contact - Specialty:
Mr. Bouren Brian, EVP

1200 17th St Ste 2175
Denver, CO 80202-5865
(303) 629-0730
Fax: (303) 629-0724
Key Contact - Specialty:
Mr. David S. Conner, Executive Vice President
Mr. Martin M. Pocs, Vice Chairman & Managing Director
Ms. Amy St. Denis, EVP

519 Heritage Rd Ste 2J
Southbury, CT 06488-1699
(203) 264-0810
Fax: (203) 262-8742
Key Contact - Specialty:
Mr. Ralph B. DeCristoforo, Executive Vice President - *Healthcare*

263 Tresser Blvd
Stamford, CT 06901-3236
(203) 564-1483
Fax: (203) 564-1754
Key Contact - Specialty:
Ms. Gayle Mattson, EVP

5335 Wisconsin Ave NW Ste 800
Washington, DC 20015-2073
(202) 362-2700
Fax: (202) 237-0111
Key Contact - Specialty:
Mr. Stephen Hayes, Vice Chairman
Mr. Nick Visser, EVP

1165 Ansley Ave SW
Vero Beach, FL 32968-5081
(772) 569-7959
Key Contact - Specialty:
Mr. Jerry Frenzel, EVP

100 Galleria Pkwy SE Ste 1150
Atlanta, GA 30339-5955
(678) 385-5000
Fax: (678) 385-5019
Key Contact - Specialty:
Mr. Robert Chandler, FACHE, Executive Vice President & Ntl Prac Ldr
Mr. Norman Morgan, Executive Vice President

24 Sloan St
Roswell, GA 30075-4920
(770) 640-1533
Fax: (770) 643-6743
Key Contact - Specialty:
Mr. David Reddick, Executive Vice President & Managing Dir
Mr. Rick Meyer, EVP

7300 W 110th St Fl 7
Overland Park, KS 66210-2330
(913) 317-1600
Fax: (913) 317-1601
Key Contact - Specialty:
Mr. Michael Klockenga, Executive Vice President & Managing Dir

3940 Olympic Blvd Ste 400
Erlanger, KY 41018-3593
(859) 372-6664
Key Contact - Specialty:
Mr. Ken Norris, EVP

7 New England Executive Park Ste 700
Burlington, MA 01803-5010
(781) 222-1022
Fax: (781) 222-1028
Key Contact - Specialty:
Mr. John Baker, Executive Vice Presiden & Co-Leader
Mr. Michael DeSimone, EVP

6639 Centurion Dr Ste 140
Lansing, MI 48917-8273
(517) 886-9010
Fax: (517) 886-9042

Key Contact - Specialty:
Mr. C. Keith Groty, Assistant Vice President, Education
Mr. Dennis Muchmore, Executive Vice President
Mr. Merritt Norvell, President, Education
Mr. Gordon S. White, Jr., Executive Vice President & Managing Dir

100 W Big Beaver Rd Ste 200
Troy, MI 48084-5283
(248) 680-6716
Fax: (248) 680-6732
Key Contact - Specialty:
Mr. David Sidlar, EVP

701 4th Ave S Ste 500
Minneapolis, MN 55415-1810
(612) 337-9030
Fax: (612) 338-0359
Key Contact - Specialty:
Ms. Terri Naughtin, Executive Vice President
Mr. Eric Sivertson, Managing Director
Mr. John McLean, EVP

7800 Forsyth Blvd Ste 750
Saint Louis, MO 63105-3311
(314) 727-2000
Fax: (314) 727-2903
Key Contact - Specialty:
Mr. Michael Burroughs, Executive Vice President & Managing Dir
Mr. Scott Harris, Executive Vice President
Mr. Larry Munson, Executive Vice President
Mr. Denny Taylor, Executive Vice President

1 Newark Ctr Fl 14
1085 Raymond Blvd
Newark, NJ 07102-5236
(973) 792-1710
Fax: (973) 791-1539
Key Contact - Specialty:
Mr. James Abruzzo, Executive Vice President & Managing Dir - *Non-profit*
Mr. Mark Velten, Senior Vice President
Mr. Donald Pizzi, EVP
Mr. Laure Lee White

280 Park Ave Rm 4301W
New York, NY 10017-1216
(212) 883-6800
Fax: (212) 883-9507
Key Contact - Specialty:
Mr. Sigmund Ginsburg, Executive Vice President - *Non-profit*
Ms. Debra Graf, Executive Vice President
Mr. Lawrence Noble, Executive Vice President
Ms. Olivia Quatrone, Executive Vice President
Mr. Frank T. Spencer, Vice Chairman & Regional Mng Director
Ms. Suzie Stewart, Executive Vice President
Mr. John Tarbell, Executive Vice President
Ms. Lauren Lee White, EVP
Mr. Lawrence Poster, EVP
Ms. Laurie Rosenfield, EVP

2000 Auburn Dr Ste 200
Beachwood, OH 44122-4328
(216) 378-7595
Fax: (216) 378-7505
Key Contact - Specialty:
Mr. John Thornton, Managing Director & Vice President
Mr. Dan Carney, EVP

312 Walnut St Ste 1600
Cincinnati, OH 45202-4038
(513) 762-7690
Fax: (513) 721-4628
Key Contact - Specialty:
Mr. Ted Plattenburg, EVP

1101 Montclair Cir
Westlake, OH 44145-1448
(440) 871-5458
Fax: (440) 871-5438
Key Contact - Specialty:
Mr. Richard Stanislaw, EVP

1500 Market St Fl 12
East Tower
Philadelphia, PA 19102-2107
(215) 665-5683
Fax: (215) 665-5711
Key Contact - Specialty:
Ms. Carolyn Oakley Lowe, Executive Vice
President
Mr. Michael Volpe, Executive Vice President &
Managing Dir

603 Stanwix St Ste 1350
Pittsburgh, PA 15222-1497
(412) 261-1492
Fax: (412) 261-1702
Key Contact - Specialty:
Mr. Joseph Christman, Executive Vice President
& Managing Dir
Mr. Robert Kirkpatrick, Executive Vice President
Mr. Barry Rowland, Executive Vice President
Mr. David Smith, Executive Vice President
Ms. Alexandra Hendrickson, EVP

PO Box 22502
50 Laurens St
Charleston, SC 29413-2502
(917) 992-4769
Fax: (843) 723-1857
Key Contact - Specialty:
Mr. Franklin Key Brown, Executive Vice
President & Managing Dir

1221 S Mo Pac Expy Ste 170
Austin, TX 78746-7651
(512) 328-6363
Fax: (512) 328-6337
Key Contact - Specialty:
Mr. Richard Beal, Executive Vice President &
Managing Dir
Mr. Lance Winn, Executive Vice President

901 S Mo Pac Expy Ste I300
Austin, TX 78746-5785
(512) 329-2120
Fax: (512) 329-2001
Key Contact - Specialty:
Mr. Ted Balistreri, EVP/Managing Director

7502 Greenville Ave Ste 610
Dallas, TX 75231-3829
(214) 574-4044
Fax: (214) 574-4048
Key Contact - Specialty:
Mr. Fred Halstead, Executive Vice President
Mr. Tim Feaster, EVP
Ms. Melinda Semurdy, EVP

1300 Post Oak Blvd Ste 1100
Houston, TX 77056
(713) 626-9494
Fax: (713) 626-8585
Key Contact - Specialty:
Mr. Jeffrey Smith, EVP
Mr. Rick Walter, EVP

601 Union St Ste 4200
Seattle, WA 98101-4036
(206) 652-3540
Fax: (206) 652-3539
Key Contact - Specialty:
Mr. Scott Rabinowitz, EVP

300 N Corporate Dr Ste 290
Brookfield, WI 53045-5865
(262) 879-0850
Fax: (262) 879-0855

Key Contact - Specialty:
Mr. Dennis Hood, Vice Chairman & Managing
Director
Mr. Robert Stanislaw, Executive Vice President
& Managing Dir
Mr. Justin Strom

833 Kings Way
Madison, WI 53704-6046
(608) 262-4962
Fax: (608) 212-4000
Key Contact - Specialty:
Pat Richter, Executive Vice President -
Education, Sports

DHR International

130 Peaceful Valley
Vine Grove, KY 40175
(270) 828-6601
Fax: (270) 828-6609
Email: cgidcumb@dhrinternational.com
Web: www.dhrinternational.com

Summary: We are the fastest growing and most
innovative retained executive search firm of the
nation's "Top 5." With over 40 offices worldwide,
we recruit leaders in all industries and functions
including, but not limited to: Board Services,
Diversity, Education, Aerospace, Industrial,
Healthcare and Life Sciences, Retail/Consumer,
Financial Services, Technology, Nonprofit, Media
and Entertainment.

Key Contact - Specialty:
Ms. Cathy Gidcumb, Senior Associate

Functions: Senior Mgmt.

Industries: Generalist (All)

Arthur Diamond Associates Inc

4630 Montgomery Ave Ste 200
Bethesda, MD 20814-3436
(301) 657-8866
Fax: (301) 657-8876
Email: bribakow@arthurdiamond.com
Web: www.arthurdiamond.com

Summary: Focused on executive, senior and
middle management positions in all major
industries and not for profit associations and
foundations. We firmly believe that an
organization's culture, industry and dynamics
often determine the best candidate criteria.

Key Contact - Specialty:
Mr. Barton R. Ribakow, President - *Energy, Real
estate, Technology*
Ms. Beth Gibbs, Senior Vice President -
Associations, Non-profit

Functions: Board Members, Senior Mgmt.,
Middle Mgmt., Sales & Mktg., HR Mgmt.,
CFOs, Non-profits

Industries: Generalist (All), Construction, Non-
profits, HR Services, Real Estate,
Property/Facility Mgmt., Security SW

Diamond Management Group Ltd†

1924 N Maud Ave Ste B
Chicago, IL 60614-4908
(773) 935-7757
(312) 719-4631
Fax: (773) 409-5900
Email: rlandman@rcn.com
Web: www.dmgexecutivesearch.com

Summary: We are a professional
recruitment/executive search firm with extensive
contacts in senior management/leadership, IT,
sales, operations, manufacturing and finance
functions. We provide client companies and not-
for-profit organizations and associations with

exclusive search services for identifying and
recruiting high-performing management and
technical professionals that will lead organizations
to higher levels of success and performance.

Key Contact - Specialty:
Mr. Richard Landman, CPC, President -
*Associations, Financial, Management,
Manufacturing, Private equity*

Salary Minimum: $60,000

Functions: Management, Senior Mgmt., Middle
Mgmt., Sales Mgmt., CFOs, Non-profits

Industries: Manufacturing, Printing, Metal
Products, Motor Vehicles, Misc. Mfg., Non-
profits, Accounting, Mgmt. Consulting, IT
Implementation, Higher Ed., Logistics Svcs.,
Supply Chain Mgmt., Real Estate,
Property/Facility Mgmt.

Dieck Group Inc

114 W Monroe St
Mauston, WI 53948-1130
(608) 847-3400
Fax: (608) 847-5799
Email: regina@dieckgroup.com
Web: www.dieckgroup.com

Summary: Executive search firm focusing
exclusively on the biotechnology, medical device,
and related industries.

Key Contact - Specialty:
Mr. Dan Dieck, President
Ms. Regina K. Nelson, Director, Research &
Administration - *Biomaterials, Biomedical,
Biopharmaceutical, Biotechnology, Life
Sciences*

Salary Minimum: $100,000

Functions: Board Members, Senior Mgmt.

Industries: Drugs Mfg., Medical Devices,
Biotech/Life Sciences

The Diestel Group

2755 E Cottonwood Pkwy Ste 580
Salt Lake City, UT 84121-6965
(801) 365-0400
Fax: (801) 365-0401
Email: info@diestel.com
Web: www.diestel.com

Summary: Skilled consultants utilizing a
collaborative, partnering approach to executive
search and organizational consulting. We place a
focus on general management positions for
leading companies.

Key Contact - Specialty:
Mr. Brent Jespersen, Principal
Ms. Jill Perelson, Principal
Mr. Paul Jespersen, Partner - *Healthcare,
Pharmaceutical*

Salary Minimum: $80,000

Functions: Generalist (All), Management

Industries: Generalist (All)

Differential Partners

233 N Michigan Ave Ste 2333
Chicago, IL 60601-5710
(312) 819-5919
(312) 819-5906
Email: sjablo@differ-ential.com
Web: www.differentialpartners.com

Summary: We execute our own searches with no
handoff to junior level personnel. Our practice is
national in scope and our references impeccable.

Key Contact - Specialty:
Mr. Steven A. Jablo, Managing Partner

Salary Minimum: $120,000

Functions: Generalist (All), Senior Mgmt.

Industries: Generalist (All), Finance, Services, Non-profits, Legal, Accounting, HR Services, Hospitality, Insurance, Real Estate, Non-Classifiable

DillonGray

1796 Equestrian Dr Ste 112
Pleasanton, CA 94588-2621
(925) 846-9396
Fax: (925) 846-4972
Email: larry@dillongray.com
Web: www.dillongray.com

Summary: Our firm developed a unique internet executive search process, allowing the delivery of candidates to the client through the internet. We conduct executive searches for technology related companies from startups to Fortune 500 companies. We utilize advance candidate assessment technology, which has not experienced a hiring failure after matching candidates to clients in ten years.

Key Contact - Specialty:
Mr. Larry Dillon, Managing Director -
Biotechnology, Business development, CEOs, CFOs, CIOs
Ms. Helen Schultz, Managing Director -
Biotechnology, CEOs, CFOs, CIOs, Technology

Salary Minimum: $150,000

Functions: Management, Senior Mgmt., Sales & Mktg.

Industries: Computer Equip., Consumer Elect., Electronic, Elec. Components, Semiconductors, Communications, Software, Accounting SW, Database SW, Development SW, Marketing SW, Networking, Comm. SW, Security SW, System SW

Dimension 11 Ltd†

2301 15th Ave
Regina, SK S4P 1A3
Canada
(306) 586-2315
(800) 303-2315
Email: information@dimension11.com
Web: www.dimension11.com

Summary: We make looking for the right person for a position easier and worry free. Together we will guide the process in preparing a job description and analyzing the best person for the job. Then we follow up with a profile of the selected individual, comprehensive interviews and thorough reference checks, as well as a six-month guarantee of suitability.

Key Contact - Specialty:
Ms. Sherry Knight, CHRP, CMC, President
Ms. Annette Ghebremichael

Salary Minimum: $25,000

Functions: Generalist (All)

Industries: Generalist (All)

Branches:
2-1115 Grosvenor Ave
Saskatoon, SK S7H 4G2
Canada
(306) 955-1209
(800) 303-2315
Email: saskatoon@dimension11.com
Key Contact - Specialty:
Mr. Robert Graham, CHRP, MBA, Human Resources Specialist

The Dinerstein Group

45 Rockefeller Plz
New York, NY 10111-0100
(212) 332-3200

Email: jm@dinerstcingroup.com
Web: www.dinersteingroup.com

Summary: We are a results oriented executive search and management consulting firm with focus on emerging growth companies. Client base includes: media/new media, information services, telecom, consumer products, advertising, public relations, technology, venture capital and private equity companies. Additional experience in not-for-profit.

Key Contact - Specialty:
Ms. Jan Dinerstein, President
Ms. JoAnn Murray, Vice President

Salary Minimum: $150,000

Functions: Senior Mgmt., Sales & Mktg., Advertising, Mktg. Mgmt., Direct Mktg., PR, HR Mgmt., CFOs, M&A, IT

Industries: Generalist (All)

Robert W Dingman Company Inc

650 Hampshire Rd Ste 116
Westlake Village, CA 91361-2538
(805) 778-1777
Fax: (805) 778-9288
Email: info@dingman.com
Web: www.dingman.com

Summary: Senior management level assignments where need emphasizes a compatible management style, values, personality and goals between the candidates and the client.

Key Contact - Specialty:
Mr. Robert W. Dingman, Chairman of the Board
Mr. Bruce Dingman, President - *Education, Hospitality, Non-profit, Transportation*

Salary Minimum: $100,000

Functions: Management, Board Members, Senior Mgmt., Mktg. Mgmt., Sales Mgmt., HR Mgmt., CFOs, MIS Mgmt., Non-profits

Industries: Generalist (All), Manufacturing, Transportation, Finance, Services, Non-profits, Hospitality, Media, Healthcare

Dinte Resources Inc

8300 Greensboro Dr Ste 750
Mc Lean, VA 22102-3663
(703) 448-3300
Fax: (703) 448-0215
Email: pdinte@dinte.com
Web: www.dinte.com

Summary: High quality retained firm providing executive search and interim executive solutions to corporations and associations thereby assisting them in meeting business objectives.

Key Contact - Specialty:
Mr. Paul Dinte, Chief Executive Officer
Mr. Mike Humenik, President & Chief Operating Officer
Mr. Christopher Sunday, Vice President

Salary Minimum: $150,000

Functions: Senior Mgmt.

Industries: Energy, Utilities, Manufacturing, Finance, Services, Communications, Government, Environmental Svcs., Aerospace, Software, Biotech/Life Sciences

The Directorship Search Group Inc

8 Sound Shore Dr Ste 250
Greenwich, CT 06830-7259
(203) 618-7000
Fax: (203) 618-7007
Email: bstephens@directorshipsearch.com
Web: www.directorship.com

Summary: We are consultants in executive and director search, management succession planning and corporate governance. Clients range from Fortune 20 to emerging companies.

Key Contact - Specialty:
Mr. Russell S. Reynolds, Jr., Chairman & Chief Executive Officer - *CEOs, Financial services*
Mr. Thomas L. McLane, Vice Chairman & Head, Corp. Gov. Pract - *CEOs, COOs, Manufacturing*
Mr. Carter L. Burgess, Jr., Managing Director - *CFOs, Financial services*

Salary Minimum: $150,000

Functions: Generalist (All), Management, Board Members, Senior Mgmt., Healthcare, Sales & Mktg., HR Mgmt.

Industries: Generalist (All), Agri., Forestry, Mining, Manufacturing, Retail, Finance, Services, Packaging

Branches:
230 Park Ave Rm 964
New York, NY 10169-0913
(212) 973-9200
Fax: (212) 973-1975
Key Contact - Specialty:
Mr. Michael P. Kelly, Managing Director
Mr. Robin H. Prince, Jr., Vice President - *Marketing*

Dise & Company Inc

20600 Chagrin Blvd Ste 925
Cleveland, OH 44122-5353
(216) 752-1700
Email: support@diseco.com
Web: www.diseco.com

Summary: Our strength is the rapid identification of the most appropriate candidates given the client's strategic objectives and corporate culture. Our search practitioners have many years of experience in a broad base of industries and functions.

Key Contact - Specialty:
Mr. John Donnelly, Managing Director - *Closely-held business, Consumer (Marketing,Products), General management, Management consulting*
Mr. P. William Marshall, Vice President - *Finance*
Ms. Susan Paley Zak, Director, Executive Search - *General management, Manufacturing (Management), Market research, Marketing, Social work*
Mr. Ralph A. Dise, Jr., President

Salary Minimum: $75,000

Functions: Generalist (All), Management, Mfg., Sales & Mktg., HR Mgmt., Finance, Engineering, Specialized Svcs.

Industries: Generalist (All), Construction, Manufacturing, Food, Bev., Tobacco, Wholesale, Finance, Services, Aerospace, Packaging, Healthcare, Non-Classifiable

Diverse Connections

7545 Irvine Center Dr Ste 200
Irvine, CA 92618-2933
(949) 888-4862
Fax: (949) 888-4852
Email: iortiz@diverseconnections.net
Web: www.diverseconnections.net

Summary: We specialize in executive search providing women and minority candidates for executive, professional, and director levels. We serve a broad base of industries including: consumer products and services, media/entertainment, technology and healthcare.

Key Contact - Specialty:
Ms. Irene Ortiz-Glass, President - *Diversity*
Ms. Kelly Martinez, Principal

Salary Minimum: $70,000

Functions: Management

Industries: Generalist (All)

Diversified Management Resources Inc

PO Box 108
Belmont, MA 02478-0002
(617) 484-0074
Email: positions@dmrfinancial.com
Web: www.dmrfinancial.com

Summary: We work on searches for sales, marketing and operations professionals in financial services. Our clients include mutual fund, insurance and banking firms. We are a retained executive search firm.

Key Contact - Specialty:
Mr. Charles A. O'Neill, Principal
Mr. Gordon Evans, Recruiter
Mr. Robert Goldberg, Recruiter
Ms. Laura McCoy, Recruiter

Salary Minimum: $100,000

Functions: Generalist (All), Management, Board Members

Industries: Finance, Banking, Invest. Banking, Brokers, Venture Cap., Mutual/Hedge Funds, Misc. Financial, Services

Diversified Search Ray & Berndtson

(formerly known as Ray & Berndtson)
405 Lexington Ave Fl 26
New York, NY 10174-2699
(212) 907-6501
(866) 729-2376
Fax: (212) 907-6502
Email: diversfied@
Web: www.diversifiedsearch.com

Summary: Retained executive search and management consulting firm serving major companies across all industries and functions.

Key Contact - Specialty:
Mr. Gerard Cattie, Managing Director - *CIOs, Education (Higher), Information Technology, Non-profit, Philanthropy*
Mr. Michael Wellman, Sector Leader, Technology - *CEOs, CFOs, Industrial, Private equity, Technology*

Salary Minimum: $150,000

Functions: Generalist (All)

Industries: Generalist (All), Energy, Utilities, Food, Bev., Tobacco, Chemicals, Soap, Perf., Cosmtcs., Drugs Mfg., Medical Devices, Metal Products, Machine, Appliance, Motor Vehicles

Diversified Search Ray & Berndtson

(formerly known as Ray & Berndtson)
2005 Market St Ste 3300
Philadelphia, PA 19103-7041
(215) 732-6666
(800) 423-3932
Fax: (215) 568-8399
Email: diversified@divsearch.com
Web: www.diversifiedsearch.com

Summary: Global, generalist search firm committed to diversity. Partnering with our clients to identify and attract visionary leadership to propel organizations forward. We are consistently recognized as a leader in the industry. We are

dedicated to the highest standards as evidenced by our long-term client relationships and internal quality initiatives.

Key Contact - Specialty:
Ms. Judith M. von Seldeneck, President, CEO & Chairman
Ms. Cynthia Barth, Managing Director - *Healthcare, Hospital, Life Sciences, Non-profit, Physicians*
Ms. Judy Boreham, Managing Director - *Biopharmaceutical, Biotechnology, C-level, Diversity, Pharmaceutical*
Mr. Keith Gaspard, Practice Leader, Life Sciences - *Biotechnology, Life Sciences, Medical (Devices), Pharmaceutical, Technology*
Ms. Cynthia P. Heckscher, Sector Leader, Healthcare - *Boards of Directors, C-level, CEOs, Diversity, Healthcare*
Mr. B.A. (Mackie) MacLean, Jr., Sector Leader, Professional Services - *C-level, Financial services, Management consulting, Manufacturing, Venture capital*
Ms. Kim M. Morrisson, PhD, Sector Leader, Education & NFP - *Associations, Education, Education (Higher), Non-profit, Philanthropy*
Mr. Ronald L. Stemphoski, Managing Director - *Administration, CEOs, Diversity, Healthcare, Physicians*
Mr. Andrew Wheeler, Managing Director - *Biotechnology, Education, Medical (Devices), Pharmaceutical, Research & development*

Salary Minimum: $120,000

Functions: Generalist (All), Senior Mgmt., Mfg., Healthcare, Sales & Mktg., HR Mgmt., IT, R&D, Engineering, Int'l.

Industries: Generalist (All), Energy, Utilities, Manufacturing, Retail, Finance, Services, New Media, Insurance, Software, Biotech/Life Sciences, Healthcare

Affiliates:
Diversified Search Ray & Berndtson
New York, NY

DK Search Inc†

1124 Highway 315
Wilkes Barre, PA 18702-6943
(570) 696-5630
(570) 970-1622
Fax: (570) 825-7790
Email: tom.dksearch@epix.net
Web: dksearchinc.com

Summary: A boutique retained search firm known for its ability to make the right fit for clients and candidates.

Key Contact - Specialty:
Mr. Thomas Dimmick, President - *Business to business, Chemical, Healthcare, Insurance, Manufacturing*
Ms. Christine Sompel, Senior Researcher - *Manufacturing (Management), Marketing, Mechanical, MIS, Operations*

Salary Minimum: $80,000

Functions: Generalist (All), Mktg. Research, Sales Mgmt.

Industries: Manufacturing, Medical Devices, Plastics, Rubber, Metal Products, Electronic, Elec. Components, Consumer Goods, Finance, Brokers, Services, Environmental Svcs., Insurance, Commercial, Software, Biotech/Life Sciences, Healthcare, Dental

DLB Associates

271 Madison Ave Ste 1406
New York, NY 10016-1001
(212) 953-6460
Fax: (212) 953-6764

Email: info@dlb-associates.com

Summary: Boutique firm specializing in the recruitment of general management, marketing, advertising, direct response, interactive, corporate communications and new media professionals for consumer and service industries.

Key Contact - Specialty:
Mr. Lawrence E. Brolin, President - *Advertising, Consulting, Direct marketing, General management, Marketing*

Salary Minimum: $125,000

Functions: Senior Mgmt., Advertising, Mktg. Research, Mktg. Mgmt., Direct Mktg., PR, Mgmt. Consultants

Industries: Food, Bev., Tobacco, Soap, Perf., Cosmtcs., Banking, Misc. Financial, Mgmt. Consulting, Entertainment, Media, Advertising, Publishing, New Media

DLG Associates Inc

1515 Mockingbird Ln Ste 560
Charlotte, NC 28209-3300
(704) 522-9993
Fax: (704) 522-7730
Email: info@dlgassociates.com
Web: www.dlgassociates.com

Summary: Specialize in financial services, real estate and MIS/DP custom search; senior officers of the company have combined executive management experience in banking and/or MIS.

Key Contact - Specialty:
Mr. David J. Guilford, President - *Accounting, Banking, Banking (Commercial,Mortgage), Capital markets*
Mr. W. Kenneth Goodson, Jr., Executive Vice President - *Banking, Banking (Mortgage), Capital markets, Information Technology, Real estate*

Salary Minimum: $75,000

Functions: Senior Mgmt., Sales & Mktg., Finance, CFOs, Risk Mgmt., IT, MIS Mgmt., Attorneys

Industries: Finance, Banking, Invest. Banking, Misc. Financial, Services

DMR Global Inc†

10230 W Sample Rd
Coral Springs, FL 33065-3940
(954) 796-5043
(954) 796-0032
Fax: (954) 796-5044
Email: rdaratany@dmrglobal.com
Web: www.dmrglobal.com

Summary: We are a national/international, retained/exclusive contingency executive search and career-counseling firm. We accommodate clients in many areas, and have divisions that specialize in the home building construction, financial services, aviation, manufacturing & retail industries. We complete search assignments from staff to senior and executive management positions across all functional areas.

Key Contact - Specialty:
Mr. Ron Daratany, President - *Aviation, Business development, Management consulting, Real estate, Senior management*
Ms. Emily Maynard, Director, Recruiting - *Construction, Engineering, Financial services, Information Technology, Management*
Mr. Jose Montesino, Manager, Recruiting - *Aviation, Business development, Construction, Financial services, Manufacturing (Management)*

Salary Minimum: $50,000

Functions: Generalist (All), Management

Industries: Construction, Misc. Mfg., Transportation, Finance, Architectural Svcs., Aerospace, Insurance, Real Estate, Accounting SW, Mfg. SW

DNPitchon Associates

60 W Ridgewood Ave
Ridgewood, NJ 07450-3197
(201) 612-8350
Email: resume@dnpitchon.com
Web: www.dnpitchon.com

Summary: Our firm is a consultative executive recruiting practice, focusing on selected industries and positions that complement our approach, capabilities, and experience.We enhance the quality of management for companies seeking to improve their operating performance and competitive global position. Our experience also includes mid-to executive-level positions across an array of functions and industries, both technical and traditional.

Key Contact - Specialty:
Mr. Daniel N. Pitchon, President

Salary Minimum: $100,000

Functions: Generalist (All)

Industries: Generalist (All)

Doherty International Inc

899 Skokie Blvd Ste 406
Northbrook, IL 60062-4024
(847) 564-1753
Fax: (847) 564-1763
Email: doherty_int@ameritech.net

Summary: Our success is dramatically reflected in our energized, comprehensive approach to the total search process, which reflects in our enviable completion rate in the areas of general management and supply chain recruiting. With extensive experience in the transition field, the leadership of the organization feels professionally comfortable and competent in delivering effective programs to a growing list of clients.

Key Contact - Specialty:
Mr. John J. Doherty, President - *Human resources, Logistics, Marketing*

Salary Minimum: $100,000

Functions: Generalist (All), Senior Mgmt., Plant Mgmt., Materials, Mktg. Research, Mktg. Mgmt., HR Mgmt., IT

Industries: Logistics Svcs.

Doleman Enterprises[†]

1151 Water Pointe Ln
Reston, VA 20194-1035
(703) 742-5454
Web: www.patriot.net/users/doleman

Summary: We are an executive search and professional recruitment, logistics management & research analysis, IT, fiber optics marketing and engineering.

Key Contact - Specialty:
Ms. Linda J. Howard, Principal - *Pharmaceutical*
Mr. Robert J. Doleman, Principal - *Engineering*
Mr. Howard Miller, Senior Executive

Salary Minimum: $40,000

Functions: Generalist (All)

Industries: Manufacturing, Chemicals, Computer Equip., Misc. Mfg., Finance, Services, Pharm Svcs., Government, Software, Biotech/Life Sciences

The Domann Organization Inc

1 Market St Fl 35
San Francisco, CA 94105-1521
(800) 923-6626
Email: info@domann.net
Web: www.domann.net

Summary: Industry sectors: biopharmaceuticals, biotechnology, diagnostics, genomics, medical devices, pharmaceuticals and proteomics. Positions: board members, CEOs, presidents, EVPs, COOs, CBOs, CSOs, CMOs, VPs/senior executives (business development, clinical research, HR, medical affairs, product development, regulatory affairs, R&D, quality assurance/control and operations/manufacturing).

Key Contact - Specialty:
Mr. William A. Domann, Jr., Founder & Chief Executive Officer
Ms. Jovanna Bost, Vice President, Business Development - *Business development, Marketing*

Salary Minimum: $125,000

Functions: Management, Board Members, Senior Mgmt.

Industries: Drugs Mfg., Medical Devices, Pharm Svcs., Biotech/Life Sciences

Donahue/Patterson Associates

33 N La Salle St Ste 2600
Chicago, IL 60602-3399
(312) 732-0999
Email: info@donahuepatterson.com
Web: www.donahuepatterson.com

Summary: We are a retained executive search-consulting firm. The firm is driven by its core values of integrity, excellence, quality service and sensitivity. Services are provided to clients in all industries and all assignments are fully and thoroughly conducted by firm principals. The firm follows a process-based methodology resulting in consistent high feedback from our clients.

Key Contact - Specialty:
Mr. E.M. Donahue, Partner - *Agriculture, Food, Human resources, Mining, Sales*
Mr. H.S. Patterson, Partner - *Accounting (Public), Finance, Insurance, Legal, Professional services*

Salary Minimum: $80,000

Functions: Mfg., Production, Sales & Mktg., HR Mgmt., Finance, CFOs, Risk Mgmt., IT, Legal

Industries: Food, Bev., Tobacco, Lumber, Furniture, Printing, Chemicals, Medical Devices, Paints, Petro. Products, Metal Products, Finance, Legal, Accounting, Mgmt. Consulting, E-commerce, Advertising, Publishing, Insurance, Database SW, Development SW, Doc. Mgmt., Production SW, HR SW, Networking, Comm. SW

Dotson & Associates

412 E 55th St Apt 8A
New York, NY 10022-5114
(212) 593-4274

Summary: Specializing in placement of mid and senior-level marketing, communications, sales and service quality professionals. Expertise in financial services, technology and general communications including direct mail and telemarketing.

Key Contact - Specialty:
Ms. M. Ileen Dotson, Principal

Salary Minimum: $75,000

Functions: Generalist (All), Health Admin., Advertising, Mktg. Research, Mktg. Mgmt.,

Sales Mgmt., Direct Mktg., Finance, Minorities/Diversity

Industries: Generalist (All), Banking, Hospitality, New Media, Broadcast, Film, Telecoms, Healthcare

Douglas-Allen Inc

1500 Main St
Tower Square
Springfield, MA 01115-1000
(413) 739-0900
Email: research@douglas-allen.com
Web: www.douglas-allen.com

Summary: Serving the nation's top investment firms in the recruitment of portfolio managers, analysts and sales & marketing professionals.

Key Contact - Specialty:
Mr. Robert D. Stevens, CFA, Principal - *Investment management*
Ms. Kimberly A. Leask, Director, Research

Salary Minimum: $100,000

Functions: Cash Mgmt.

Industries: Finance, Venture Cap., Mutual/Hedge Funds

DPSI Medical One

(a subsidiary of Diversified Placement Services Inc)
5105 Clinton St Ste 2
Erie, PA 16509-2533
(814) 868-0961
Email: werglobal@onesourcenetwork.com

Summary: We are a primarily a physician recruiting and consulting firm networking with other recruiters, serving both facilities groups and individual physicians.

Key Contact - Specialty:
Mr. Ron Spero, President & Owner - *Physicians*
Mrs. Gerry Spero, Vice President
Mr. Joseph B. Spero, Esq., Vice President - *Communications*
Ms. Ronette Schneider, PT, Vice President
Mr. Ben Schneider, Vice President - *Sales, Technical*

Functions: Generalist (All), Management, Materials, Healthcare, Sales & Mktg., Finance, IT, Attorneys

Industries: Energy, Utilities, Manufacturing, Services, Media, Software, Healthcare

Drake & Andrews International

PO Box 1272
Euless, TX 76039-1272
(877) 212-2600
Fax: (214) 291-5885
Email: info@drakeandrews.com
Web: www.drakeandrews.com

Summary: Drake & Andrews is an international retained executive search firm. We are dedicated to helping clients solve business problems and build effective top leadership teams. Our philosophy in all we do is to help clients make lasting and substantial improvements in their performance in the acquisition, development, and retention of extraordinary talent. Our work is based on an unconditional client satisfaction guarantee. If when the work is done, the client does not feel that full value was received, then the client decides how much it was worth and how much to pay (if anything).

Key Contact - Specialty:
Mr. Jaime Chanaga, Managing Director

Salary Minimum: $100,000

Functions: Board Members, Senior Mgmt., MIS Mgmt., Mgmt. Consultants

Industries: Generalist (All), Energy, Utilities, Manufacturing, Transportation, Finance, Services, Mgmt. Consulting, Law Enforcement, E-commerce, IT Implementation, Media, Communications, Government, Software, Security SW, System SW, Biotech/Life Sciences, Healthcare

Dressler Associates

624 University Ave
Palo Alto, CA 94301-2019
(650) 323-0456
Fax: (650) 323-2904
Email: search@cdressler.com
Web: www.dresslerassociates.com

Summary: A fully retained executive search firm specializing in CEO searches for early stage technology based, venture funded companies and partner searches for venture capital firms.

Key Contact - Specialty:
Ms. Carol F. Dressler, President - *CEOs, High technology*

Salary Minimum: $150,000

Functions: Generalist (All), Senior Mgmt., Mktg. Mgmt., Engineering

Industries: Generalist (All), Venture Cap.

Robert Drexler Associates Inc†

PO Box 151
Saddle River, NJ 07458-0151
(201) 760-2300
Fax: (201) 760-2301
Email: drexler@engineeringemployment.com
Web: www.engineeringemployment.com

Summary: Individual retained and group search terms are available. We are engineering, technical, and executive search consultants. Our clients include pharmaceutical, biotechnology, chemical, petrochemical, petroleum, fuel cell, industrial, commercial, environmental, bridge & highway, engineering construction, transportation and aerospace.

Key Contact - Specialty:
Mr. Robert C. Drexler, President

Salary Minimum: $65,000

Functions: Generalist (All), Product Dev., Automation, Plant Mgmt., Sales Mgmt., Engineering, Environmentalists, Architects

Industries: Generalist (All), Energy, Utilities, Construction, Chemicals, Pharm Svcs., Environmental Svcs., Aerospace, Biotech/Life Sciences

Drinkwater & Associates

167 West St
Beverly, MA 01915-2244
(978) 922-3676
Email: wendydrinkwater@comcast.net

Summary: We conduct executive search engagements for many of the premier retained executive search firms, boutique search firms, private and public corporations and start-ups across numerous industries worldwide.

Key Contact - Specialty:
Ms. Wendy A. Drinkwater, Managing Partner
Ms. Ashley B. Ullstein, Senior Associate
Mr. Brian McElroy, Senior Associate
Ms. Diane P. Esecson, Senior Associate
Ms. Cindy Morton, Senior Associate
Mrs. Susan Gittins, Senior Associate

Salary Minimum: $100,000

Functions: Senior Mgmt.

Industries: Generalist (All), Manufacturing, Finance, Services, Mgmt. Consulting, Hospitality, Communications, Government, Software, Healthcare

James Drury Partners

875 N Michigan Ave Ste 3805
Chicago, IL 60611-1903
(312) 654-6708
Fax: (312) 654-6710
Email: jdrury@jdrurypartners.com
Web: www.jdrurypartners.com

Summary: We are an executive search specializing in recruitment of CEOs, board directors and chief functional officers. Corporate governance counsel including board evaluations and management assessment.

Key Contact - Specialty:
Mr. Jim Drury, Chairman & Chief Executive Officer - *CEOs*

Salary Minimum: $175,000

Functions: Generalist (All), Board Members

Industries: Generalist (All)

Ducharme Group Inc

157 Bowood Ave
Toronto, ON M4N 1Y3
Canada
(416) 481-7221
Fax: (416) 481-5641
Email: ducharmegroup@sympatico.ca
Web: www.ducharmegroup.ca

Summary: We are a boutique firm offering responsive, rigorous and personalized recruiting services. We can draw on an extensive network of HR and research professionals, compensation and career counseling to compliment and enhance process.

Key Contact - Specialty:
Ms. Lynda Ducharme, President - *Finance, Non-profit, Professional services, Senior management*

Salary Minimum: $60,000

Functions: Management, Senior Mgmt., Middle Mgmt., HR Mgmt., Finance, Non-profits

Industries: Services, Media

J.H. Dugan & Company

130 E San Fernando St PH 18
San Jose, CA 95112-7419
(408) 920-7700
Fax: (408) 920-7701
Email: registry@jhdugan.com
Web: www.jhdugan.com

Summary: We are a client driven plastics industry, human capital, search and search research firm. Our clients include world class, as well as start-up companies.

Key Contact - Specialty:
Mr. John H. Dugan, President - *Plastics*

Salary Minimum: $60,000

Functions: Generalist (All), Management, Mfg., Packaging, Sales & Mktg., M&A, R&D, Engineering

Industries: Generalist (All), Medical Devices, Plastics, Rubber, Computer Equip., Misc. Mfg., Electronic, Elec. Components, Packaging, Industry Specific SW

Ronald Dukes Associates LLC

20 N Wacker Dr Ste 2010
Chicago, IL 60606-3002
(312) 357-2895
Fax: (312) 357-2897
Email: ron@rdukesassociates.com
Web: www.rdukesassociates.com

Summary: Provide executive search consulting to companies in the general industrial sector to include general management and officer positions in all functional areas with a concentration in industrial and automotive.

Key Contact - Specialty:
Mr. Ronald Dukes, President - *General management*

Salary Minimum: $150,000

Functions: Generalist (All), Board Members

Industries: Generalist (All), HR SW, Mfg. SW, Marketing SW

Michael Dunford Associates LLC

2400 E Commercial Blvd Ste 309
Fort Lauderdale, FL 33308-4022
(954) 492-1928
Fax: (954) 492-1926
Email: retainer@dunfordassociates.com
Web: www.dunfordassociates.com

Summary: Our firm is a boutique retained executive search firm. We are a high quality, client focused and service oriented provider of senior executive recruitment solutions. The team includes seasoned professionals from top ten global retained search firms experienced in providing successful specialized service for cross-functional senior management needs.

Key Contact - Specialty:
Mr. Michael S. Dunford, Managing Member - *Consumer, Hospital, Information service, Medical (Devices), Pharmaceutical*
Ms. Lori A. Deibel, Senior Director - *Consumer, Hospital, Information service, Medical (Devices), Pharmaceutical*
Ms. Beth Anne Dreher, Senior Associate - *Consumer, Hospital, Information service, Medical (Devices), Pharmaceutical*

Salary Minimum: $150,000

Functions: Generalist (All)

Industries: Manufacturing, Transportation, Retail, Services, Hospitality, Media, Communications, Software, Biotech/Life Sciences, Healthcare

Dunlap & Sullivan Associates

29 Pearl St NW Ste 227
Grand Rapids, MI 49503-3039
(616) 458-4142
Fax: (616) 458-4203
Email: dunsul@aol.com

Summary: We offer executive search concentrating on senior executive appointments, across a wide spectrum of industries. Building a personal relationship with clients, creating a high percentage of repeat business.

Key Contact - Specialty:
Mr. John P. Sullivan, Co-Principal

Salary Minimum: $75,000

Functions: Management, Senior Mgmt., Middle Mgmt., Mktg. Mgmt., Sales Mgmt., HR Mgmt., CFOs, MIS Mgmt.

Industries: Lumber, Furniture, Printing, Plastics, Rubber, Metal Products, Machine, Appliance, Motor Vehicles

Dunn Associates

229 Limberline Dr
Greensburg, PA 15601-9028
(724) 832-9822
(877) 586-2538
Fax: (724) 832-9836
Email: maddunn@aol.com
Web: www.dunnassociatesinc.com

Summary: We provide quality recruiting for substantially less. For any industry, honesty, integrity, timeliness, attention to details. Telephone screening, full search except face-to-face interviews. We offer 'unbundled' research services as well.

Key Contact - Specialty:
Ms. Margaret A. Dunn, President
Ms. Jean Pistentis, Research & Recruiting
  Consultant
Ms. Eileen Vehon, Researcher & Recruiter

Salary Minimum: $60,000

Functions: Management

Industries: Higher Ed.

Dupont White & Stone LLC†

45 S Park Pl Ste 264
Morristown, NJ 07960-3924
(973) 984-6425
(201) 315-5300
Email: managingdirector@dupontws.com
Web: www.dupontws.com

Summary: Our firm recruits senior management executives, board of director members and professionals on behalf of corporations and professional firms. We are a retained search firm.

Key Contact - Specialty:
Mr. William Trautman, Managing Director

Salary Minimum: $120,000

Functions: Generalist (All)

Industries: Manufacturing, Transportation, Finance, Pharm Svcs., Legal, E-commerce, IT Implementation, Supply Chain Mgmt, Communications, Software

Durakis Executive Search

PO Box 1382
Brooklandville, MD 21022-1382
(410) 252-2055
Email: resumes@durakis.com
Web: www.durakis.com

Summary: General executive search practice. Middle and senior management. Most functions; all industries.

Key Contact - Specialty:
Mr. Charles A. Durakis, Jr., President

Salary Minimum: $150,000

Functions: Senior Mgmt., Advertising, Mktg. Mgmt., Sales Mgmt., CFOs, MIS Mgmt., Non-profits

Industries: Drugs Mfg., Computer Equip., Consumer Elect., Pharm Svcs., Insurance, Healthcare

Duran Human Capital Partners Inc†

300 Orchard City Dr, Ste 142
Campbell, CA 95008-2945
(408) 540-0070
Fax: (408) 540-0069
Email: jimf@duranhcp.com
Web: www.duranhcp.com

Summary: We are a staffing company specializing in contract recruiting in the hardware, software, networking, telecommunications and semiconductor industries. We offer fully customized staffing solutions, both on site and off. We place special emphasis on identifying technical talent that adds maximum value and provide a unique partnering experience to our clients.

Key Contact - Specialty:
Mr. James Duran, President & Founder
Mr. Jim Foster, Vice President, Operations
Ms. Tracee Tulloh, Director, Accounts
  Management
Mr. Mark Tortorici, Lead Trainer

Functions: Generalist (All)

Industries: Generalist (All)

DuVall & Associates

4203 Costa Salada
San Clemente, CA 92673-6409
(949) 488-8790
Fax: (949) 488-8793
Email: karen@duvall.com
Web: www.duvall.com

Summary: We are a retained executive search firm with extensive experience in the high technology industry. We are recognized for our success in recruiting top executives and also known for recruiting entire start up teams from the C-level (across all functions) to the sales, marketing and support teams.

Key Contact - Specialty:
Ms. Karen DuVall, President
Mr. Rick Westcott, Vice President - *High technology*

Salary Minimum: $100,000

Functions: Management, Board Members, Senior Mgmt., Middle Mgmt., Product Dev., Sales & Mktg., Mktg. Mgmt., Sales Mgmt., Sales Reps., CFOs

Industries: Computer Equip., E-commerce, Communications, Telecoms, Telephony, Digital, Wireless, Fiber Optic, Network Infrastructure, Software, Networking, Comm. SW, Security SW

Dynamic Synergy Corp

600 Entrada Dr Fl 2
Santa Monica, CA 90402-1308
(310) 573-7300
Email: info@dynamicsynergy.com
Web: www.dynamicsynergy.com

Summary: Our corporation's special talent is to find the best candidate to fulfill the requirements. We provide an extremely high-level of service, quickly generating a short list of qualified candidates. Our short turnaround time results in cost effectiveness. We work with VC-funded, pre-IPO, start-ups and high-growth companies. As partners with our clients, we offer unique options to exchange equity for our professional search services.

Key Contact - Specialty:
Mr. Mark J. Landay, Managing Director

Salary Minimum: $100,000

Functions: Management, Senior Mgmt.

Industries: Communications, Network Infrastructure, Software, Biotech/Life Sciences

Early Cochran & Olson LLC

1 E Wacker Dr Ste 2510
Chicago, IL 60601-1843
(312) 595-4200
Fax: (312) 595-4209
Email: eco94@aol.com
Web: www.ecollc.com

Summary: Practice limited to retained searches for lawyers to fill senior corporate and law firm positions. Experienced consultants serve Fortune 500 corporations and major law firms. References furnished.

Key Contact - Specialty:
Ms. Corinne Cochran, Principal
Mr. B. Tucker Olson, Principal
Ms. Laura J. Hagen
Mr. Bruce R. LeMar
Mr. A. Andrew Olson, III

Salary Minimum: $150,000

Functions: Legal, Attorneys

Industries: Generalist (All)

Eastman & Beaudine Inc

7201 Bishop Rd Ste 220
Plano, TX 75024-3648
(972) 312-1012
Fax: (972) 312-1020
Email: info@eastman-beaudine.com
Web: www.eastman-beaudine.com

Summary: We are consultants to management in executive selection.

Key Contact - Specialty:
Mr. Robert E. Beaudine, President & Chief
  Executive Officer - *Real estate, Retail, Sports*
Ms. Nancy Berg, Chief Financial & Operating
  Officer
Mrs. Katy Sheehan, Associate

Salary Minimum: $100,000

Functions: Generalist (All), Board Members, Senior Mgmt., Mktg. Mgmt., Sales Mgmt., CFOs, MIS Mgmt.

Industries: Generalist (All), Food, Bev., Tobacco, Venture Cap., HR Services, Hospitality, Insurance, Real Estate

Echelon SA de CV

(a member of The Amrop Hever Group)
Calzada Del Desierto de los Leones 46
Colonia San Angel
Alvaro Obregon
01000 Mexico City, DF
Mexico
55 5616 4498
Fax: 55 5550 8173
Email: francis@ai.com.mx
Web: www.amrop.com/contact/mexico_city.html

Summary: Our firm is committed to helping private and public sector client organizations achieve greater profitability, performance and efficiency through the engagement of outstanding chief executives and senior managers.

Key Contact - Specialty:
Mr. José Luis Newman, Managing Partner
Mr. Pablo Francis, Managing Partner - *Finance, Financial services, Human resources, Investment management, Marketing*

Salary Minimum: $80,000

Functions: Generalist (All)

Industries: Generalist (All)

Ecruiters.net†

(an Advanced Marketing Team Inc company)
PO Box 1086
Chanhassen, MN 55317-1086
(952) 233-5750
Email: headhunter@ecruiters.net
Web: www.ecruiters.net

Summary: We are a retained executive search firm that specializes in the areas of internet technology, e-commerce and specialty and mass market retail executives. We work with the best

retail merchants, internet managers and technology executives in the country. Our clients range from startup internet companies to Fortune 500 companies and the largest retailers in the world.

Key Contact - Specialty:
Mr. David Happe, President & Chief Executive Officer

Functions: Generalist (All)

Industries: Wholesale, Retail

Edelman & Associates[†]

3 Virginia Dr Ste 200
Lakeville, MA 02347-1724
(508) 947-5300
Email: paul@edeltech.com
Web: www.edeltech.com

Summary: We are an executive search and technical recruiting firm serving software, biotechnology, and other technology based companies. Our software clients are comprised of supply chain management, CRM, marketing campaign automation, enterprise application infrastructure, database, search engine, and data storage companies. Our biotech clients are involved in drug discovery, clinical research, and medical devices.

Key Contact - Specialty:
Mr. Paul Edelman, Sole Proprietor - *Computers (Software), Internet*
Ms. Michelle Leonard, Manager, Research - *Business development, Marketing, Sales*

Salary Minimum: $80,000

Functions: Generalist (All)

Industries: Manufacturing, Services, Media, Communications, Aerospace, Software, Biotech/Life Sciences

Edgewood International

3018 Edgewood Pkwy
Woodridge, IL 60517-3720
(630) 985-6067
(630) 985-6780
Fax: (630) 985-6069
Email: wocatedgewood@aol.com

Summary: Our firm conducts domestic and international retained executive searches in high technology, financial services, healthcare and commercial industries. Our disciplines include: general management, engineering, IT, manufacturing, sales & marketing, finance, supply chain management, strategic planning, R&D, medical and health care.

Key Contact - Specialty:
Mr. William O'Connor, Managing Partner - *Electronics, High technology, Telecommunications*

Salary Minimum: $75,000

Functions: Board Members, Senior Mgmt., Middle Mgmt., Healthcare, Mktg. Mgmt., Sales Mgmt., Pension/Ret. Planning, MIS Mgmt.

Industries: Drugs Mfg., Medical Devices, Metal Products, Computer Equip., Electronic, Elec. Components, Semiconductors, Invest. Banking, Misc. Financial, Pharm Svcs., IT Implementation, Telephony, Fiber Optic, Aerospace, Insurance, Software, Biotech/Life Sciences, Hospitals

Edward W Kelley & Partners, Ltd.

(formerly known as A.T. Kearney Executive Search)
222 W Adams St
Chicago, IL 60606-5312
(312) 648-0111
Fax: (312) 223-6369
Web: www.ewkp.com

Summary: We are a broad line firm serving most industries and all functions. A division of a global management consulting firm and a wholly owned subsidiary of an international information services company. Emphasis is on quality, tangible results and value-added service.

Key Contact - Specialty:
Mr. Steve Fisher, President
Mr. Benjamin DeBerry, Vice President & Geographic Leader - *Consumer, Industrial, Retail*

Salary Minimum: $150,000

Functions: Generalist (All)

Industries: Generalist (All), Agri., Forestry, Mining, Energy, Utilities, Construction, Manufacturing, Food, Bev., Tobacco, Textiles, Apparel, Lumber, Furniture, Paper, Printing

Branches:
600 Anton Blvd Fl 11
Plaza Tower
Costa Mesa, CA 92626-7100
(714) 445-6819
Fax: (714) 371-4001
Key Contact - Specialty:
Mr. Matt Pierce, Vice President - *Technology*

1111 Corporate Center Dr Ste 106
Monterey Park, CA 91754-7649
(323) 260-5040
Key Contact - Specialty:
Mr. Alberto Pimentel

3945 Freedom Cir Ste 1100
Santa Clara, CA 95054-1276
(408) 330-3500
Fax: (408) 330-3503
Key Contact - Specialty:
Ms. Maggie Yen Smith, Principal

200 S Biscayne Blvd Ste 3500
Wachovia Financial Center
Miami, FL 33131-5303
(305) 577-0046
Fax: (305) 577-3837
Key Contact - Specialty:
Mr. John Mestepey, Vice President - *Industrial*

3399 Peachtree Rd NE Ste 820
Atlanta, GA 30326-1149
(404) 475-1240
Fax: (404) 475-1249
Key Contact - Specialty:
Mr. Steve Dezember, Vice President & Geographic Leader - *Healthcare*

153 E 53rd St
New York, NY 10022-4611
(212) 705-1500
Fax: (212) 350-1569
Key Contact - Specialty:
Mr. Mark McMahon, Vice President & Geographic Leader - *Industrial*

13951 Trinity Blvd Ste 3325
Fort Worth, TX 76155-2547
(817) 355-8430
Fax: (817) 355-8401
Key Contact - Specialty:
Mr. Paul Ray, Jr., Vice Chairman & Practice & Region Leader - *Industrial*

333 John Carlyle St
Alexandria, VA 22314-5767
(703) 836-6210
Fax: (703) 519-0391
Key Contact - Specialty:
Ms. Shelly Storbeck, Vice President, Geographic & Prac Leader - *Education (Higher)*

2300-20 Queen St W
Cadillac Fairview Tower MS 68
Toronto, ON M5H 3R3
Canada
(416) 947-1990
Fax: (416) 947-0255
Key Contact - Specialty:
Ms. Virginia Murray, Vice President & Geographic Leader - *Industrial*

Bruce Edwards & Associates Inc

PO Box 51206
Durham, NC 27717-1206
(919) 489-5368
(919) 604-3157
Email: brucedwar@aol.com

Summary: We are a 100 percent retained search firm. We specialize in president, CEO, VP and director level searches. Life sciences, technology, manufacturing and retail segments.

Key Contact - Specialty:
Mr. S. Bruce Edwards, President - *CEOs, COOs, Presidents*
Ms. Jacqueline Edwards, Executive Search Consultant
Mr. George D. Smith, Secretary
Ms. Peggy Musselwhite, Search Consultant

Functions: Generalist (All), Senior Mgmt., Plant Mgmt., Mktg. Mgmt., Sales Mgmt., CFOs, MIS Mgmt., Systems Analysis

Industries: Generalist (All), Computer Equip., Venture Cap., Telecoms

EFL Associates

(a TranSearch International company)
7101 College Blvd Ste 550
Overland Park, KS 66210-2075
(913) 451-8866
Fax: (913) 491-7490
Email: eflinfo@eflassociates.com
Web: www.eflassociates.com

Summary: Executive search practice specializing in the most senior-levels of executive leadership for a broad base of client companies.

Key Contact - Specialty:
Mr. Peter K. Lemke, Chairman & Chief Executive Officer
Mr. Jason M. Meschke, President & Chief Operating Officer
Ms. Evelyn C. Davis, Senior Vice President
Mr. Rick Shull, Managing Director, Adv Tech Practice
Dr. Gordon Lamb, PhD, Senior Vice President & Founding Mng Dir
Mr. David Horner, Senior Vice President, Higher Education - *Education (Higher)*

Salary Minimum: $100,000

Functions: Generalist (All), Management, Senior Mgmt.

Industries: Generalist (All)

Branches:
7951 E Maplewood Ave Ste 280
Greenwood Village, CO 80111-4778
(303) 779-1724
Fax: (303) 694-6866
Email: info@eflcol.com
Key Contact - Specialty:
Ms. Mary Hobson, Senior Vice President

2275 Half Day Rd Ste 350
Bannockburn, IL 60015-1277
(847) 821-2797
Email: jbyrne@eflassociates.com
Key Contact - Specialty:
Ms. Joan Byrne, Manager, Administration -
General management

570 Greenway Dr
Lake Forest, IL 60045-4801
(847) 234-2796
Fax: (847) 821-2799
Email: mferrari@eflassociates.com
Key Contact - Specialty:
Dr. Michael Ferrari, DBA, Senior Vice President
& Mng Director

Egan & Associates Inc

1784 Barton Ave Ste 10
West Bend, WI 53090-5418
(262) 335-0707
Fax: (262) 335-0625
Email: info@eganassociates.com
Web: www.eganassociates.com

Summary: Perform executive searches on a
retainer basis only. No contingency work
performed. The vast majority of clients are
manufacturers with searches being performed for
all major disciplines within manufacturing.

Key Contact - Specialty:
Mr. Daniel K. Egan, President
Ms. Shelly Gladbach, Office Manager -
Management, Telecommunications
Ms. Joy V. Massar, Recruiter

Salary Minimum: $70,000

Functions: Generalist (All), Mfg.

Industries: Generalist (All), Manufacturing,
Paper, Printing, Metal Products, Retail,
Accounting, HR Services, Engineering Svcs.

Egret Consulting Group[†]

383 N Seymour Ave
Mundelein, IL 60060-2322
(847) 970-5949
Email: info@egretconsulting.com
Web: www.egretconsulting.com

Summary: We are a retained search firm
specializing in the electrical and industrial
industries. Our value proposition is finding talent
with key industry understanding and relationships.
We serve manufacturers and wholesale
distributors in all functional disciplines requiring
industry expertise.

Key Contact - Specialty:
Mr. Ted Konnerth, President - *Design,
Distribution, Industrial, Manufacturing, Sales*
Ms. Prudence Thompson, Vice President,
Business Development - *Distribution,
Management, Sales, Wholesale*
Mr. Shawn Randazzo, Project Coordinator -
*Electrical, Engineering, Management,
Manufacturing, Manufacturing (Management)*
Ms. Diane Duncan, Director, Manufacturing -
Electrical, Manufacturing (Management)

Salary Minimum: $50,000

Functions: Generalist (All), Management, Sales
& Mktg.

Industries: Manufacturing, Misc. Mfg.,
Electronic, Elec. Components, Supply Chain
Mgmt, Non-Classifiable

EHR Consulting[†]

200 Rosehall Dr Unit 220
Lake Zurich, IL 60047-6250
(847) 726-7229
Email: rikr7@yahoo.com

Summary: Ten years in Human Resources,
specializing in Staffing. Experience working in
various industries including Insurance, Printing,
Office Automation, IT, and Pharmaceutical.

Key Contact - Specialty:
Ms. Erica H. Reiner, PHR, Consultant -
*Consulting, Diversity, Sales, Staffing, Strategic
planning*

Functions: Generalist (All)

Industries: Paper, Printing, Drugs Mfg., Non-
profits, HR Services, Insurance, Claims,
Healthcare

Electronic Careers

21355 Pacific Coast Hwy Ste 100
Malibu, CA 90265-5251
(310) 317-6115
Fax: (310) 317-6119
Email: ecareers@electroniccareers.com
Web: www.electroniccareers.com

Summary: We provide executive and professional
search for sales and engineering in the electronics
industry.

Key Contact - Specialty:
Mr. Tom Myers, President - *Engineering*
Mr. Robert Alexander, Senior Recruiter

Functions: Sales Mgmt., Engineering

Industries: Electronic, Elec. Components

Elinvar[†]

1804 Hillsborough St
Raleigh, NC 27605-1643
(919) 878-4454
Email: info@elinvar.com
Web: www.elinvar.com

Summary: Recruiting and consulting specializing
in accounting, finance, HR and other key positions.
Our focus is mid-market and emerging growth
companies who recognize the importance of hiring
top talent.

Key Contact - Specialty:
Ms. Patti Gillenwater, President & Chief
Executive Officer - *Finance, Human resources*
Ms. Melissa Necaise, Principal
Ms. Kim Foster, Principal

Salary Minimum: $35,000

Functions: Senior Mgmt., HR Mgmt., Finance

Industries: Generalist (All)

Elite Resources Group[†]

PO Box 13113
Fairlawn, OH 44334-8513
(330) 867-9412
Fax: (330) 867-0468
Email: search@elite-rg.com
Web: www.elite-rg.com

Summary: We are a full-service HR consulting
and staffing based business. We focus on
conducting executive/management/professional
searches in the context of your mission, culture
and direction. We specialize in all positions within
trucking, logistics, distribution and allied
industries.

Key Contact - Specialty:
Mr. Gary T. Suhay, President - *Engineering,
Quality, Research & development,
Transportation*

Salary Minimum: $50,000

Functions: Generalist (All), Production,
Materials, Purchasing, Materials Plng.,
Distribution, R&D, Engineering

Industries: Generalist (All), Lumber, Furniture,
Chemicals, Plastics, Rubber, Machine,

Appliance, Misc. Mfg., Wholesale, Retail,
Finance

Elite Staffing Solutions Inc

210-190 Robert Speck Pky
Sherwood Business Centre
Mississauga, ON L4Z 3K3
Canada
(905) 803-8045
Fax: (905) 803-8676
Email: sean@elitestaffing.ca
Web: www.elitestaffingsolutionsinc.com

Summary: The number one objective of our firm
is providing our clients with the quality applicants
they so much deserve. The foundation of our
success is our ability to develop long-term
relationships with our clients and applicants. We
are the leading provider of human resources
services by continually surpassing the expectations
of our clients and applicants. We address
permanent, temporary, or contract placements in a
prompt, professional and personable manner.

Key Contact - Specialty:
Ms. Camy McConachie, President
Mr. Sean McConachie, Vice President

Salary Minimum: $28,000

Functions: Generalist (All)

Industries: Generalist (All)

Elite-Minds

7184 White Pine Crt
Gooderham Estates
Mississauga, ON L5W 1W6
Canada
(905) 670-8008
(866) 242-3796
Fax: (905) 670-7505
Email: info@elite-minds.com
Web: www.elite-minds.com

Summary: Our firm is recognized as a specialized
Canada boutique executive search and
professional services firm. Our experience
encompasses a broad spectrum of industries
including, manufacturing, distribution, consumer
package goods, financial services,
telecommunications, automotive, multimedia,
utilities, and food services in every functional area
including, CFO, COO, and CEOs.

Key Contact - Specialty:
Ms. Kim White, Founder
Mr. Mark Robinson, General Manager -
*Communications, E-business, Professional
services, Sales, Technology*

Functions: Generalist (All), Management, Senior
Mgmt.

Industries: Energy, Utilities, Manufacturing,
Food, Bev., Tobacco, Chemicals, Consumer
Goods, Finance, Banking, Invest. Banking,
Pharm Svcs., HR Services, E-commerce,
Publishing, Communications, Healthcare

Elliot Group

(also known as Elliot Associates Inc)
505 White Plains Rd Ste 228
Tarrytown, NY 10591-5143
(914) 631-4904
Fax: (914) 631-6481
Web: www.theelliotgroup.com

Summary: We provide executive search and
strategic consulting to the hospitality, foodservice,
retail and manufacturing industries.

Key Contact - Specialty:
Ms. Alice Elliot, CPC, President & Chief
Executive Officer - *Hospitality, Manufacturing*

Salary Minimum: $100,000

Functions: Generalist (All), Management, Board Members, Senior Mgmt., Middle Mgmt.

Industries: Manufacturing, Food, Bev., Tobacco, Retail, Services, HR Services, Hospitality

Affiliates:
The Elliot Executive Source
Tarrytown, NY

Branches:
9720 Wilshire Blvd Fl 6
Beverly Hills, CA 90212-2025
(310) 205-2240
Fax: (310) 205-2241
Email: don@theelliotgroup.com
Key Contact - Specialty:
Mr. Don Fitzgerald, Vice President

1080 Cambridge Sq Ste A
Alpharetta, GA 30004-1878
(770) 664-5354
Fax: (770) 664-0233
Email: joan@theelliotgroup.com
Key Contact - Specialty:
Ms. Joan Ray, Executive Vice President

22 Chase St
Amesbury, MA 01913-2926
(978) 388-1515
Fax: (978) 388-6277
Email: connie@theelliotgroup.com
Key Contact - Specialty:
Ms. Connie Newkirk, Regional Manager

3970 Via Siena
Poland, OH 44514-5337
(330) 707-1094
Email: greg@theelliotgroup.com
Key Contact - Specialty:
Mr. Greg Palmer, Vice President

1417 W 51st St Ste A
Austin, TX 78756-2654
(512) 454-0477
Fax: (512) 454-0936
Email: troy@theelliotgroup.com
Key Contact - Specialty:
Mr. Troy Erb, Vice President

The Elliott Company
439 Church St
Mount Pleasant, SC 29464-5303
(843) 388-0900
Email: staff@elliottco.net
Web: www.elliottco.net
Summary: We are an executive resource dedicated to serving companies and supporting clients' profitable growth through retained leadership acquisition, as well as our merchant banking and business development activities. We practice no conflict of interest.
Key Contact - Specialty:
Mr. Roger S. Elliott, President
Salary Minimum: $150,000
Functions: Management, Board Members, Senior Mgmt., Mfg., Sales & Mktg., HR Mgmt., CFOs, M&A, Int'l.
Industries: Energy, Utilities, Manufacturing, Transportation, Finance, Services, Media, Biotech/Life Sciences

Steve Ellis & Associates†
10100 Santa Monica Blvd Ste 950
Los Angeles, CA 90067-4125
(310) 829-0611
Fax: (310) 829-2024
Email: steve@searchellis.com
Web: www.searchellis.com

Summary: We provide individualized executive search for commercial and corporate banking. We specialize in banking and financial services. We place relationship managers, regional managers, business development officers and credit officers. We conduct searches on both a retainer basis as well as exclusive contingency.
Key Contact - Specialty:
Mr. Steve Ellis, President
Salary Minimum: $100,000
Functions: Senior Mgmt., Middle Mgmt.
Industries: Banking

Elwell & Associates Inc
31920 Nottingwood St
Farmington Hills, MI 48334-2870
(248) 488-9750
Fax: (248) 488-9751
Email: elwellas@elwellassociates.com
Web: www.elwellassociates.com
Summary: Specializing in searches for high impact senior executives, across functions in demanding manufacturing and service industries.
Key Contact - Specialty:
Mr. Stephen R. Elwell, President
Ms. K. Gowman, Director, Research - Manufacturing
Salary Minimum: $90,000
Functions: Generalist (All), Senior Mgmt., Middle Mgmt., Mfg., Materials, Sales & Mktg., HR Mgmt., Finance, MIS Mgmt., Engineering
Industries: Generalist (All), Manufacturing, Finance, Venture Cap., Mgmt. Consulting, HR Services, Engineering Svcs., Logistics Svcs., Supply Chain Mgmt., Defense, Aerospace, Packaging, Biotech/Life Sciences

Mark Elzweig Company Ltd
183 Madison Ave Ste 1704
New York, NY 10016-4501
(212) 685-7070
Fax: (212) 685-7761
Email: elzweig@elzweig.com
Web: www.elzweig.com
Summary: We are specialists in the asset management industry. We handle a variety of searches in the marketing, administration and investment arenas. Our clients are money management firms and major investment banks.
Key Contact - Specialty:
Mr. Mark Elzweig, President
Salary Minimum: $150,000
Functions: Senior Mgmt., Middle Mgmt., Product Dev., Sales & Mktg., Cash Mgmt.
Industries: Finance, Banking, Misc. Financial, Services

Emerging Medical Technologies Inc
7784 S Addison Way
Aurora, CO 80016-7044
(303) 699-1990
Email: tcmemt@aol.com
Summary: We serve companies and investors in the fields of medical devices, biotechnology and pharmaceuticals. Specializing in research, product development, marketing, sales, quality and regulatory affairs.
Key Contact - Specialty:
Mr. Thomas C. Miller, President - *Engineering, Marketing, Senior management*
Ms. Susan Osborn, Director - *MIS, Product management/development, Sales*

Salary Minimum: $75,000
Functions: Management, Mfg., Sales & Mktg., Specialized Svcs.
Industries: Drugs Mfg., Medical Devices, Pharm Svcs., Biotech/Life Sciences, Non-Classifiable

Empire International
1147 Lancaster Ave
Berwyn, PA 19312-1243
(610) 647-7976
Fax: (610) 647-8488
Email: info@empire-internl.com
Web: www.empire-internl.com
Summary: We are a generalist retained search firm addressing senior-level management engagements throughout the English-speaking world.
Key Contact - Specialty:
Mr. Charles V. Combe, II, President
Mr. M.J. Stanford, Vice President
Mr. Paul Lange, Managing Director
Mr. Howard W. Imhof, Senior Consultant
Ms. Jessica E. Bye, Manager, Research
Mr. Kevin O'Keefe, Associate
Ms. Melinda Combe, Vice President
Mr. Thomas MacCarthy, Director, Research
Ms. Christina Flynn, Consultant - *Chemical, Process equipment, Quality*
Salary Minimum: $100,000
Functions: Generalist (All)
Industries: Generalist (All), Manufacturing, Medical Devices, Metal Products, Electronic, Elec. Components, E-commerce, Publishing, New Media, Packaging, Biotech/Life Sciences

Emplex Associates†
PO Box 2497
Southfield, MI 48037-2497
(248) 352-6362
(888) 203-1010
Web: www.emplexcorp.com
Summary: Serving food processors, aggregate mining, automotive components and general manufacturing.
Key Contact - Specialty:
Mr. George Hayes, President
Functions: Middle Mgmt., Plant Mgmt., HR Mgmt.
Industries: Generalist (All), Agri., Forestry, Mining, Food, Bev., Tobacco, Plastics,,Rubber, Metal Products, Machine, Appliance, Motor Vehicles, Misc. Mfg., Engineering Svcs.

EmployeeROI/ Wilcox & Associates†
575 Madison Ave Ste 1006
New York, NY 10022-2511
(212) 937-8413
(203) 483-1097
Email: wilcoassociates@aol.com
Web: www.employeeroi.com
Summary: Our firm is an executive education and management-consulting firm offering organizational development and leadership development consulting services.
Key Contact - Specialty:
Mr. Clark Wilcox, Partner & Sr Managing Dir, Exec Search - *Boards of Directors, CEOs, CFOs, CIOs, Diversity*
Salary Minimum: $120,000
Functions: Board Members, Senior Mgmt., Sales & Mktg., Sales Mgmt., HR Mgmt., CFOs, MIS Mgmt., Security Personnel

Industries: Generalist (All), Energy, Utilities, Transportation, Finance, Venture Cap., Misc. Financial, Services, Mgmt. Consulting, HR Services, Law Enforcement, Engineering Svcs., Hospitality, Communications, Defense, Compliance, Homeland Security, Aerospace, Property/Facility Mgmt., Software, Development SW, Security SW, Biotech/Life Sciences, Women's, Non-Classifiable

The Energists

10260 Westheimer Rd Ste 300
Houston, TX 77042-3108
(713) 781-6881
Fax: (713) 781-2998
Email: search@energists.com
Web: www.energists.com

Summary: Specialists (each consultant has many years of technical/business energy industry and search experience) in executive search to the upstream and midstream energy industry.

Key Contact - Specialty:
Mr. Alex Preston, President - *Production*

Salary Minimum: $80,000

Functions: Management, Senior Mgmt., Middle Mgmt., Production, Mktg. Mgmt., Sales Mgmt., Engineering, Geotechnical

Industries: Oil & Gas

The Enfield Company

3005 S Lamar Blvd Ste 109D
Austin, TX 78704-4785
(512) 444-9921
Web: www.silverdevelopment.com

Summary: We maintain a special focus on the issues and people affecting traditional and new-media educational publishing, as well as professional services operating in these areas.

Key Contact - Specialty:
Mr. Herbert E. Smith, Managing Partner
Ms. Kim MacIntosh, Associate - *Training*

Salary Minimum: $60,000

Functions: Senior Mgmt., Mktg. Research, Mktg. Mgmt., Sales Mgmt., Sales Reps., Training, Mgmt. Consultants

Industries: Generalist (All), Venture Cap., K-12 Ed., Higher Ed., Publishing, New Media, Entertainment SW

Enns Partners Inc

(a member of The Amrop Hever Group)
601-100 University Ave
Toronto, ON M5J 1V6
Canada
(416) 598-0012
Fax: (416) 598-4328
Email: info@ennspartners.com
Web: www.ennspartners.com

Summary: Experienced consulting firm serving senior executive search requirements.

Key Contact - Specialty:
Mr. George Enns, Partner
Ms. Rita Eskudt, Partner
Mr. Jock McGregor, Partner
Mr. Bob Dolan, Partner
Ms. Judi Bradette, Partner
Ms. Anne Marie Turnbull, Partner

Salary Minimum: $100,000

Functions: Generalist (All), Management, Senior Mgmt.

Industries: Generalist (All), Energy, Utilities, Manufacturing, Food, Bev., Tobacco, Drugs Mfg., Motor Vehicles, Misc. Mfg.,

Transportation, Retail, Finance, Legal, Supply Chain Mgmt, Communications

EPIC Business Strategies LLC[†]

1115 Oscar Sq
Celebration, FL 34747-4043
(407) 574-5769
(414) 755-1728
Fax: (321) 939-4032
Email: info@epicstrategies.com
Web: www.epicstrategies.com

Summary: We specialize in providing business solutions in executive recruiting, contract recruiting, mid-management placement, personal career marketing plans, and management consulting. We have extensive experience holding positions in executive management with major companies in a variety of areas and assignments.

Key Contact - Specialty:
Mr. Doug Franklin, Principal

Salary Minimum: $50,000

Functions: Generalist (All), Senior Mgmt., Middle Mgmt., Sales & Mktg., Engineering

Industries: Manufacturing, Wholesale, Services, Government, Healthcare

Epsen Fuller IMD Ineternational Search Group

10 N Park Pl Ste 420
Morristown, NJ 07960-7101
(973) 359-9929
Fax: (973) 359-9928
Email: info@epsenfuller.com
Web: www.epsenfuller.com

Summary: Our firm is the world's 9th largest executive search and consulting firm. With global reach and borderless search capability, we are dedicated to serving the strategic human resource needs of multi-national Fortune 500 corporations as well as mid-cap and venture-backed, emerging growth companies.

Key Contact - Specialty:
Mr. Thomas J. Fuller, General Managing Partner - *Consumer (Products), Emerging growth, Fashion, Financial services, International*
Mr. John P. GIlbert, Partner - *Biomedical, Biopharmaceutical, Biotechnology, Life Sciences, Medical (Devices)*
Mr. Jason L. Mitterwager, Partner - *Banking, Consumer (Products), Financial services*
Mr. Mark J. Williams, Partner - *Aerospace, Automotive, Defense, Healthcare, Hospital*
Mr. Wayne A. Newell, Managing Director, Diversity Practice - *Diversity*
Mr. Mark Rich, MBA, Managing Director, Leadership Consulting
Mr. Joseph W. Ryan, Principal - *Biotechnology, High technology, Life Sciences, Medical (Devices), Pharmaceutical*
Ms. Allison P. Foullois, Marketing & Public Relations Manager

Salary Minimum: $150,000

Functions: Generalist (All)

Industries: Manufacturing, Consumer Goods, Retail, Finance, Services, Communications, Defense, Software, Biotech/Life Sciences, Healthcare

Branches:
230 Park Ave Rm 1000
New York, NY 10169-1099
(212) 551-1734
Email: tfuller@epsenfuller.com

Key Contact - Specialty:
Mr. Thomas Fuller, General Managing Partner - *Consumer (Products), Fashion, Financial services, Life Sciences, Technology*

Erickson-Pearson Search

8008 S Madison Way
Centennial, CO 80122-3631
(303) 703-6165
Fax: (303) 773-3284
Email: epdavid@earthlink.net

Summary: An independent practitioner with many years of search experience, primarily in the nonprofit sector. A particularly strong experience base in community development.

Key Contact - Specialty:
Mr. David Erickson-Pearson, President

Salary Minimum: $60,000

Functions: Management, CFOs, Non-profits

Industries: Misc. Financial, Non-profits

ERx-Executive Recruitment in Healthcare Marketing & Comm[†]

5340 Alla Rd Ste 200
Los Angeles, CA 90066-7050
(310) 578-7373
Fax: (310) 578-5005
Email: healthcare@erx.net

Summary: We serve the recruitment needs of our healthcare public relations and marketing communication clients from middle to senior level management. Our clients include private and public companies, emerging growth companies, national non-profit organizations and PR/marketing communication firms with healthcare practices.

Key Contact - Specialty:
Ms. Deborah Kaufman, Principal - *Healthcare, High technology*

Salary Minimum: $75,000

Functions: Advertising, Mktg. Research, Mktg. Mgmt., Direct Mktg., PR

Industries: Healthcare

ESA

141 Durham Rd Ste 16
Madison, CT 06443-2655
(203) 245-1983
Fax: (203) 245-8428
Email: esa.search@snet.net
Web: www.esa-search.com

Summary: Concentration in high-technology industries. Specializing in the full range of functional areas found in most high-technology manufacturing companies, biotechnology companies and pharmaceutical companies.

Key Contact - Specialty:
Mr. Barry L. Dicker, Managing Partner - *High technology*
Mr. Cas Hill, Partner

Salary Minimum: $75,000

Functions: Generalist (All), Board Members, Senior Mgmt., Mktg. Mgmt., MIS Mgmt., Systems Analysis, Systems Dev., Engineering

Industries: Generalist (All), Manufacturing, Aerospace, Software

Essex Consulting Group

PO Box 550
Essex, MA 01929-0010
(978) 337-6633
Email: brad@essexsearch.com

Summary: We provide management recruitment services to organizations seeking strategically important leaders and professionals who will accelerate the realization of specific and time-sensitive business objectives resulting in enhanced enterprise value and performance.

Key Contact - Specialty:
Mr. J. Bradley Hildt, Principal - *Financial services, Management consulting, Technology*

Salary Minimum: $125,000

Functions: Generalist (All), Senior Mgmt.

Industries: Generalist (All), Finance, Banking, Invest. Banking, Brokers, Venture Cap., Mutual/Hedge Funds, Services, Media, Real Estate, Software

ET Search Inc
1250 Prospect St Ste 101
La Jolla, CA 92037-3618
(858) 459-3443
Fax: (858) 459-4147
Email: ets@etsearch.com
Web: www.etsearch.com

Summary: We are an internationally recognized executive search firm that specializes in placing tax executives with our client organizations. We are unique because we have a long standing track record of placing tax executives.

Key Contact - Specialty:
Ms. Kathleen Jennings, President - *Tax*

Functions: Taxes

Industries: Generalist (All)

Ethos Consulting Inc
3219 Camelback Rd Ste 515
Phoenix, AZ 85018-2307
(480) 296-3801
Fax: (602) 955-5939
Email: resumes@ethosconsulting.com
Web: www.ethosconsulting.com

Summary: Highly personalized, senior-level executive search practice that concentrates on delivering results to clients in a timely and professional manner.

Key Contact - Specialty:
Mr. Conrad E. Prusak, President - *General management*
Ms. Julie J. Prusak, Vice President - *Consulting, Marketing*

Salary Minimum: $120,000

Functions: Board Members, Senior Mgmt., Sales & Mktg., HR Mgmt., CFOs

Industries: Energy, Utilities, Manufacturing, Retail, Finance, Services, Hospitality, Media, Communications, Software, Biotech/Life Sciences

R J Evans & Associates Inc†
26949 Chagrin Blvd Ste 300
Beachwood, OH 44122-4230
(216) 464-5100
Fax: (216) 464-8276
Email: resume@rjevans.com
Web: www.rjevans.com

Summary: We have a passion for our clients. We are a boutique search firm that goes beyond expectation. Our innovative model utilizes a consultative approach, working with companies at a strategic level to evaluate, assess, and meet both the near and long-term human capital needs of our clients.

Key Contact - Specialty:
Mr. Robert Evans, President
Ms. Betty L. Evans, Vice President

Mr. Alfred L. Stroman, III, Managing Director
Mr. Paul A. Brown, Managing Director - *Financial services, Technology*

Salary Minimum: $100,000

Functions: Generalist (All)

Industries: Manufacturing, Finance, Services, Communications, Defense, Aerospace, Software

Evenium†
110 Cheshire Ln Ste 100
Minnetonka, MN 55305-1009
(952) 697-6100
Fax: (952) 697-6100
Email: info@eveniumgroup.com
Web: www.eveniumgroup.com

Summary: We are a retained executive search firm. We function on the belief that success is built on quality people. We focus on national sales, general management, HR and finance roles.

Key Contact - Specialty:
Mr. John McGeady, Founder & Chief Executive Officer - *General management, Human resources*
Ms. Angela Dohmen, Director, Executive Client Services

Salary Minimum: $70,000

Functions: Generalist (All)

Industries: Manufacturing, Food, Bev., Tobacco, Paper, Printing, Medical Devices, Finance

ExecuGroup Inc
PO Box 5040
Grenada, MS 38901-6040
(662) 226-9025
Fax: (662) 226-9090
Email: tray@execugroup.com
Web: www.execugroup.com

Summary: We are an executive search firm specializing in customized recruiting for mid to senior level management positions across most industries. Our staff of professionals works with companies in the banking, financial services and manufacturing sectors as business partners to meet staffing, outplacement and management coaching needs.

Key Contact - Specialty:
Mr. Robert T. Ray, President - *Management*

Salary Minimum: $75,000

Functions: Senior Mgmt., Plant Mgmt., Sales & Mktg., Mktg. Mgmt., HR Mgmt.

Industries: Generalist (All), Manufacturing, Finance, Banking, Brokers, Misc. Financial, Mgmt. Consulting, HR Services, Insurance, HR SW, Marketing SW

Branches:
961 Marcon Blvd Ste 106
Allentown, PA 18109-9371
(610) 264-7566
Fax: (610) 264-7567
Email: jnorwine@execugroup.com
Key Contact - Specialty:
Mr. James O. Norwine, Partner

ExecuQuest Inc
PO Box 6405
Grand Rapids, MI 49516-6405
(616) 949-1800
Fax: (616) 949-1801
Email: execuquest@aol.com

Summary: Executive search firm focused on mid-level and senior management positions in manufacturing, banking and financial services

industries. Also handle CFO, controller and treasurer searches in all industries.

Key Contact - Specialty:
Mr. William L. Waanders, President
Ms. Patricia J. Waanders, Research Associate

Salary Minimum: $100,000

Functions: Management, Senior Mgmt., HR Mgmt., Finance, CFOs

Industries: Generalist (All), Manufacturing, Finance, Banking, Services, Non-profits, HR Services

ExecuTech
PO Box 707
Kent, OH 44240-0013
(330) 677-0010
Fax: (330) 677-0148
Email: executech@sbcglobal.net

Summary: We perform customized search in chemical, manufacturing, and electronics industries with emphasis in key executives who impact the organization with favorable significance. We have specialty practice groups in pharmaceutical, polymers, IT, building, finance, HR, operations, technical and hard-to-find.

Key Contact - Specialty:
Mr. J. Mark Seaholts, President

Salary Minimum: $60,000

Functions: Generalist (All)

Industries: Generalist (All), Manufacturing, Electronic, Elec. Components, Finance, Services, HR Services, Law Enforcement, Hospitality, Packaging, Software

Branches:
2046 Waller Rd
Nathalie, VA 24577-3590
(434) 349-1200
Key Contact - Specialty:
Mr. Marshal Molliver, General Manager

Executive Careers Ltd
1801 Century Park E Ste 2400
Los Angeles, CA 90067-2326
(310) 552-3455
(310) 306-0360
Fax: (310) 578-7524
Email: eclresumes@att.net

Summary: We are a generalist practice with strong specializations in retail, middle market, family and emerging businesses. Managed by industrial psychologist.

Key Contact - Specialty:
Ms. Annette R. Segil - *C-level, Non-profit, Retail*

Salary Minimum: $85,000

Functions: Generalist (All), Management

Industries: Generalist (All), Manufacturing, Wholesale, Retail, Finance, Services, Non-profits, Accounting, HR Services, Advertising, Broadcast, Film, Packaging, Entertainment SW, HR SW, Healthcare, Non-Classifiable

Executive Dimensions
PO Box 801
Williamsville, NY 14231-0801
(716) 632-9034
Fax: (716) 632-2889
Email: execsearch@executivedimensions.com
Web: www.executivedimensions.com

Summary: We are an executive search and consulting firm that offers a spectrum of services to an array of industries and organizations. Our searches are innovative, yet approached within a practical framework to address the ever-changing

needs of your marketplace. Client satisfaction is the ultimate goal of every executive search we conduct. We deliver the highest level of expertise and experience in each executive search engagement.

Key Contact - Specialty:
Ms. Gwen Arcara, President & Principal
Ms. Colleen Gau, Director, Administration - *Administration, Executives, Healthcare*
Mr. David Arcara, Recruiter - *Information Technology*

Salary Minimum: $100,000

Functions: Generalist (All), Senior Mgmt.

Industries: Finance, Healthcare

Executive Directions & Pinnacle International[†]

PO Box 3006
North Canton, OH 44720-8006
(330) 499-1001
Fax: (330) 499-2579
Email: executive@staffing.net
Web: www.executive-directions.com

Summary: The firm provides small, medium, and large corporations with executive search, team building, strategic staffing, interim/contracting and corporate consulting services while requiring only a minimal initial investment/retainer. The four broad industry specializations include: automotive systems & components; plastic molding & assembly; resins, compounds and converting; and packaging & converting.

Key Contact - Specialty:
Mr. Paul E. Richards, President & Chief Executive Officer - *Automotive, Consumer, Converting, Equipment, Molding*
Mr. R. Glenn Richards, Executive Vice President - *Automotive, Consumer, Converting, Molding, Plastics*
Mr. Sean R. Broom, Division Manager - *Automotive, Consumer, Consumer (Packaged Goods), Converting, Equipment*

Salary Minimum: $75,000

Functions: Generalist (All)

Industries: Manufacturing, Food, Bev., Tobacco, Textiles, Apparel, Paper, Printing, Chemicals, Soap, Perf., Cosmtcs., Plastics, Rubber, Misc. Mfg., Packaging

Executive Directions Inc

PO Box 223
Foxboro, MA 02035-0223
(508) 698-3030
Fax: (508) 543-6047
Email: info@execdir.com
Web: www.executivedirections.com

Summary: We have many years experience in assisting technology and manufacturing companies with their staffing needs in a wide variety of functions at senior and executive-level.

Key Contact - Specialty:
Mr. Eric Greenstein, President - *Executives*

Salary Minimum: $100,000

Functions: Generalist (All)

Industries: Manufacturing, Computer Equip., Test, Measure Equip., Software

Executive HealthSearch Inc[†]

109 Croton Ave
Ossining, NY 10562-4219
(888) 471-3244
(914) 944-8314
Fax: (914) 206-5490

Email: info@executivehealthsearch.com
Web: www.executivehealthsearch.com

Summary: We are a retained search firm in the healthcare industry. We focus our highly specialized talents and experience to provide the right executives to fit within the culture of our client's organization.

Key Contact - Specialty:
Mr. Kenneth Kruger, President
Mr. Alan Gordon, Executive Vice President
Mr. Adam M. Stern, Vice President, Search Operations - *Healthcare, Home health, Hospital, Human resources, Physicians*
Ms. Laila Sobel, Manager, Research - *E-business, Healthcare, Hospital*

Functions: Senior Mgmt., Healthcare

Industries: Finance, Accounting, HR Services, Healthcare, Hospitals, Long-term/Home Care, Dental, Physical Therapy, Occupational Therapy, Women's

The Executive Management Consulting Organization (TEMCO)

PO Box 303
Oconomowoc, WI 53066-0303
(262) 567-2069

Summary: We are HR management consultants with a broad range of services including executive search, personnel management, organization analysis, management training/development, employee/supervisory counseling, team-building workshops and personnel function audits.

Key Contact - Specialty:
Mr. Thomas E. Masson, President

Salary Minimum: $50,000

Functions: Generalist (All)

Industries: Generalist (All)

The Executive Network Inc

203-612 View Street
Royal Trust Building
Victoria, BC V8W 1J5
Canada
(250) 389-2848
Fax: (250) 389-2988
Email: inquiries@executivenetwork.ca
Web: www.executivenetwork.ca

Summary: Our search consultants utilize their outstanding networking resources, combined with professional excellence to search for, and secure key people for our clients.

Key Contact - Specialty:
Mr. Walter J. Donald, RPR, CMP, President - *Boards of Directors, CEOs, Education (Higher), Government, Human resources*
Mr. Brad Colbert, BA, Senior Search Consultant - *Accounting, Advertising, Boards of Directors, Finance, Manufacturing*
Mr. John Affleck, BA, Search Consultant - *Accounting, Government, Insurance (Life), Non-profit, Real estate*
Ms. Alexandra Griffith, BA, Corporate Services Manager - *Administration, Executives, Hospitality, Information Technology, Non-profit*

Salary Minimum: $50,000

Functions: Generalist (All), Senior Mgmt.

Industries: Generalist (All), Manufacturing, Transportation, Retail, Finance, Services, Hospitality, Media, Government, Real Estate

Executive Recruiting & Search Consulting LLC

PO Box 678
1029 Broad St
Grinnell, IA 50112-0678
(641) 236-1901
(515) 205-0010
Email: execrecruiter@iowatelecom.net
Web: www.erscllc.com

Summary: Professional third party recruiter, with specific expertise in recruiting accounting and finance professionals, representing the companies that have engaged us as a resource to assist them in attracting the best available candidate to enhance the company's performance in their accounting & finance function.

Key Contact - Specialty:
Mr. Dean T. O'Regan, Executive Recruiter

Salary Minimum: $50,000

Functions: Finance, CFOs

Industries: Generalist (All), Agri., Forestry, Mining, Construction, Manufacturing, Transportation, Wholesale, Retail

Executive Recruiting Inc

201 Montglen Ct
Greenville, SC 29607-6083
(864) 329-1858
Fax: (864) 752-1758
Email: mark@erigreenville.com
Web: www.erigreenville.com

Summary: Specialize in placing professional, managerial, and executive people of accomplishment and expertise. Comprehensive search and screening techniques are utilized ensuring that candidate selection comes from the best skill sets available.

Key Contact - Specialty:
Mr. Mark Martin, President

Salary Minimum: $75,000

Functions: Generalist (All)

Industries: Energy, Utilities, Manufacturing, Food, Bev., Tobacco, Paper, Printing, Medical Devices, Consumer Goods, K-12 Ed., Higher Ed., Database SW

Executive Resource Group Inc

2470 Windy Hill Rd SE Ste 300
Marietta, GA 30067-8621
(770) 955-1811
Email: dbalunas@aol.com

Summary: Our mission is to provide the highest quality, custom tailored, research based retained executive search services to clients in manufacturing and distribution, consulting, healthcare and retailing.

Key Contact - Specialty:
Mr. David A. Balunas, President - *Operations*

Salary Minimum: $75,000

Functions: Generalist (All), Senior Mgmt., Mfg., Materials, Sales Mgmt., HR Mgmt., IT, Mgmt. Consultants

Industries: Generalist (All), Manufacturing, Plastics, Rubber, Retail, Mgmt. Consulting, Software, Healthcare

Executive Resource Group Inc

29 Oakhurst Rd
Cape Elizabeth, ME 04107-1407
(207) 871-5527
Fax: (207) 799-8624
Email: sibyl@mediahunter.com
Web: www.mediahunter.com

Summary: We are our newspaper client's representatives in the marketplace. Qualified women are always included in the final presentation of each search. We represent the character of the client and handle all actions professionally.

Key Contact - Specialty:
Ms. Sibyl Masquelier, President - *Publishing*

Salary Minimum: $75,000

Functions: Generalist (All)

Industries: Publishing, New Media, Broadcast, Film

Affiliates:
Graphic Search Associates
Newtown Square, PA

Executive Resources International LLC

(formerly known as Organization Resources Inc.)
63 Atlantic Ave
Boston, MA 02110-3722
(617) 742-8970
Email: resumes@erisearch.net
Web: www.erisearch.net

Summary: One of Boston's oldest retained executive search firms, specializing in custom tailored search work for emerging businesses; financial services companies, the non-profit sector and board appointments. Working with private or family owned companies and VC/PE portfolio companies, we are known for our quality, teamwork and long-term relationships as 80 percent of our business is repeat or referral.

Key Contact - Specialty:
Mr. John C. Jay, Managing Director, Emerging Bus Search
Mr. John C. Mechem, Director, Financial Services Search
Mr. Michael S. Massey, Vice President, Financial Servs Search
Mr. David L. Kuhns, Director, IT Search Practice
Mr. Larry Blumsack, Vice President, Emerging Bus Search Prac - *Clinical, Medical, Medical (Devices), Regulatory*

Salary Minimum: $150,000

Functions: Generalist (All), Management, Board Members, Senior Mgmt., Middle Mgmt., Mfg., Sales & Mktg., HR Mgmt., Finance, IT

Industries: Generalist (All), Manufacturing, Medical Devices, Retail, Finance, Non-profits, Government, Insurance, Software, Biotech/Life Sciences

The Executive Roundtable

PO Box 64421
Souderton, PA 18964-0421
(888) 721-1650
(215) 721-1650
Fax: (215) 721-8650
Email: execrt@verizon.net

Summary: We are an executive search firm specializing in the recruiting of general management, marketing & sales, manufacturing and financial executives in various industries. We use an extensive consultative approach throughout the entire hiring process to ensure that an excellent candidate is hired that will match the requirements of the company.

Key Contact - Specialty:
Mr. Barry Hartzell, President

Salary Minimum: $80,000

Functions: Management, Senior Mgmt., Middle Mgmt., Mfg., Sales & Mktg., Mktg. Mgmt., Sales Reps., HR Mgmt., Finance, MIS Mgmt.

Industries: Generalist (All)

Executive Search International

1525 Centre St
Newton, MA 02461-1200
(617) 527-8787
Email: info@execsearchintl.com
Web: www.execsearchintl.com

Summary: A boutique firm, we deliver best practice search and recruiting service for client organizations, ranging from multinational corporations to small entrepreneurial businesses. Leveraging strong, established relationships we recruit leadership talent for clients in multi-channel marketing (catalog, online, retail and B2B merchants), small business, consumer products, professional services, technology, among other industries.

Key Contact - Specialty:
Mr. Les Gore, Managing Partner

Salary Minimum: $150,000

Functions: Management, Senior Mgmt.

Industries: Generalist (All), Food, Bev., Tobacco, Textiles, Apparel, Printing, Misc. Mfg., Wholesale, Retail, Banking, Venture Cap., Services, Non-profits, Mgmt. Consulting, E-commerce, Media

Executive Search Inc

5401 Gamble Dr Ste 275
Minneapolis, MN 55416-1572
(952) 541-9153
Fax: (952) 541-9979

Summary: We are dedicated to identifying and tracking high performers in many areas of business. Dedication to results gives us the unique ability to effectively conclude the most demanding assignments.

Key Contact - Specialty:
Mr. James G. Gresham, President

Salary Minimum: $75,000

Functions: Generalist (All)

Industries: Generalist (All)

Executive Search Services (ESS)

2925 4th St Apt 11
Santa Monica, CA 90405-5518
(310) 392-3244
Email: ess@exec.nu
Web: www.exec.nu

Summary: We offer retained search with a special emphasis on the corporate officer and executive. Additionally, our next generation recruiting strategy affords clients the leverage of proprietary web assets with the service of retained search.

Key Contact - Specialty:
Mr. Matthew M. Susleck, Managing Director - *Engineering, Management, Marketing*

Salary Minimum: $125,000

Functions: Generalist (All), Management, Board Members, Senior Mgmt., Middle Mgmt., Sales & Mktg., CFOs, MIS Mgmt., Engineering, Int'l.

Industries: Generalist (All), Energy, Utilities, Construction, Manufacturing, Services, Media, Communications, Environmental Svcs., Biotech/Life Sciences, Healthcare, Non-Classifiable

Executive Search World†

66 Queen St Ste 1802
Honolulu, HI 96813-4408
(808) 526-3812
Email: info@executivesearchworld.com
Web: www.executivesearchworld.com

Summary: We are an executive search in all industries and all functions with focus at mid and senior-executive level. We are driven by results with high integrity.

Key Contact - Specialty:
Mr. James P. Ellis, President - *CIOs, Construction, Senior management, Technology, Tourism*

Salary Minimum: $50,000

Functions: Generalist (All), Management, Senior Mgmt., Middle Mgmt., Sales & Mktg., Finance, CFOs, IT, MIS Mgmt., Systems Implem.

Industries: Generalist (All), Construction, Retail, Finance, Services, Hospitality, Hotels, Resorts, Clubs, Communications, Insurance, Real Estate, Biotech/Life Sciences, Healthcare

Executive Solutions

PO Box 1974
Cupertino, CA 95015-1974
(408) 364-1399
Email: pobox1974@sbcglobal.net

Summary: We have a proven track record recruiting in semiconductor, computers, software, networking, finance, biotechnology, entertainment and board member searches. Exceptional experience recruiting and sourcing of candidates in marketing, engineering, sales, finance and operations. Designed and led programs of diversity. Work effectively in complex matrix environments with virtual teams located worldwide.

Key Contact - Specialty:
Mr. Gary Barnes, President & Chief Executive Officer
Ms. Aida Regina, Chief Operating Officer
Dr. R. Bijoux, Executive Vice President, Client Serv

Salary Minimum: $150,000

Functions: Generalist (All), Management, Senior Mgmt., Middle Mgmt., Product Dev., Sales & Mktg., Mktg. Mgmt., PR, CFOs, Minorities/Diversity

Industries: Generalist (All), Energy, Utilities, Manufacturing, Finance, Venture Cap., Services, Engineering Svcs., Hospitality, Media, Communications, Government, Aerospace, Software, Biotech/Life Sciences, Non-Classifiable

Executive Solutions International

2203 N Lois Ave Ste M350
Tampa, FL 33607-2367
(813) 879-9700
(877) 959-9700
Fax: (813) 879-9090
Email: jbabbitt@executive-solutions.biz
Web: www.executive-solutions.biz

Summary: Our firm is an executive search firm that specializes in the insurance industry. Whether you are an employer or a candidate, we welcome the opportunity to listen to your needs and guide you through the process.

Key Contact - Specialty:
Mr. Josh Babbitt, Managing Director
Ms. Lila Robertson, Executive Recruiter

Mr. Jim Brooks, Executive Recruiter - *Insurance (Health,Life,Property,Reinsurance,Workers Compensation)*
Mr. Mike Gay, Researcher - *Insurance*

Functions: Generalist (All)

Industries: Insurance, Casualty, Claims, Life, Commercial, Re-Insurance

Executive Source
200-2150 Scarth St
Y & D Building
Regina, SK S4P 2H7
Canada
(306) 359-2550
Fax: (306) 359-2555
Email: search@executivesource.ca
Web: www.executivesource.ca

Summary: An executive recruitment firm serving clients filling senior level positions. Our firm offers an extensive toolkit for identifying and recruiting key talent as successors in senior roles and assisting board-level search processes. Cross-functional assignments in public and private sector industries: agriculture, resource sector, telecom, financial services, education, health and government.

Key Contact - Specialty:
Ms. Holly Hetherington, MBA, CMC, President
Ms. Theresa Lauzon, Manager, Business
Ms. Carla Bortolotto, Manager, Search Services

Functions: Generalist (All), Management, Senior Mgmt.

Industries: Generalist (All)

Executive Source
55 5th Ave Ste 1900
New York, NY 10003-4399
(212) 691-5505
Fax: (212) 691-9839
Email: tes@executivesource.com
Web: www.executivesource.com

Summary: Our firm is a retained search firm with a primary focus in Human Resources specializing in financial and professional services.

Key Contact - Specialty:
Ms. Sarah J. Marks, Principal & Founder
Mr. Richard C. Plazza, Principal & Founder - *Financial services, Human resources*
Ms. Cara Vera, Recruiter

Salary Minimum: $125,000

Functions: HR Mgmt.

Industries: Finance, Mgmt. Consulting, HR Services

Executive Strategies Inc[†]
701 Macy Dr
Roswell, GA 30076-6332
(770) 552-3085
Fax: (770) 552-1043
Email: esi@esisearch.com
Web: www.esisearch.com

Summary: Our firm has extensive senior management experience in a multitude of industries. We have the understanding of internal and external recruiting processes. Work with clients through the entire process: position description, reference checking and follow-up after placement. Principal is former corporate executive.

Key Contact - Specialty:
Mr. Holland R. Earle, Managing Principal - *General management*

Salary Minimum: $75,000

Functions: Senior Mgmt., HR Mgmt., IT

Industries: Energy, Utilities, Mgmt. Consulting, HR Services, Advertising, New Media

Executives Unlimited Inc
5000 E Spring St Ste 395
Long Beach, CA 90815-5228
(562) 627-3800
(866) 957-4466
Email: resumes@executives-unlimited.com
Web: www.executives-unlimited.com

Summary: A premier provider of highly accomplished senior level executives. We successfully support more than 300 clients from start-up companies to global corporations with their direct hire, try-out to hire and interim executive needs.

Key Contact - Specialty:
Ms. Tomilee Gill, President

Salary Minimum: $115,000

Functions: Generalist (All), Management, Board Members, Senior Mgmt., CFOs

Industries: Generalist (All), Energy, Utilities, Manufacturing, Food, Bev., Tobacco, Textiles, Apparel, Plastics, Rubber, Consumer Goods, Wholesale, Retail, Finance, Services, Non-profits, Pharm Svcs., IT Implementation, Communications, Telecoms, Aerospace, Packaging, Real Estate, Software, Mfg. SW, Biotech/Life Sciences, Healthcare, Hospitals

Branches:
4700 Gilbert Ave Ste 47
Western Springs, IL 60558-1666
(708) 784-0891
Email: resumes@executives-unlimited.com
Key Contact - Specialty:
Mr. Walter Halatek, Managing Director

2560 US Highway 22 Ste 201
Scotch Plains, NJ 07076-1529
(908) 233-3519
Email: resumes@executives-unlimited.com
Key Contact - Specialty:
Mr. Michael Michalisin, CPA, Managing Director, Northeast Regional

7605 Leesburg Dr
Colleyville, TX 76034-6917
(817) 849-1211
Key Contact - Specialty:
Mr. James Nadeau, Regional Managing Director

Explore Company
1054 31st St NW Ste 330
Washington, DC 20007-6042
(202) 333-3473
Email: explorecompany@aol.com
Web: www.explorecompany.com

Summary: A retained executive search and management consulting firm specializing in recruitment for nonprofit and philanthropic organizations. Our firm is committed to strengthening leadership and governance of nonprofit organizations.

Key Contact - Specialty:
Mr. Daniel Sherman, Founder & President
Mr. Steven Sherman, Vice President
Ms. Dalia Johnson, Assistant to President

Functions: Senior Mgmt.

Industries: Non-profits

Eyler Associates Inc
PO Box 65638
West Des Moines, IA 50265-0638
(515) 245-4244
Email: mreyler@msn.com

Summary: We have completed in excess of 450 senior-level assignments. We have broad exposure to manufacturing, banking, financial services, insurance and healthcare.

Key Contact - Specialty:
Mr. Richard N. Eyler, President

Salary Minimum: $75,000

Functions: Management, Mfg., Sales & Mktg., Finance, IT

Industries: Lumber, Furniture, Metal Products, Machine, Appliance, Motor Vehicles, Banking, Invest. Banking, Venture Cap., Insurance, Healthcare

J Fabri Associates LLC[†]
1515 N Lake George Dr
Mishawaka, IN 46545-4062
(574) 277-0812
Fax: (574) 277-0826
Email: jfabri@sbcglobal.net

Summary: Senior level retained executive search organization with major emphasis in the industrial and hi-tech industries. We have a strong concentration on mid-size senior level or equity positions throughout the USA. Our major focus in on sales/marketing positions.

Key Contact - Specialty:
Mr. John Fabri, President

Salary Minimum: $75,000

Functions: Board Members, Senior Mgmt., Mfg., Sales & Mktg.

Industries: Manufacturing, Wholesale, Software

Fagan & Company
PO Box 611
Ligonier, PA 15658-0611
(724) 238-9571
Email: faganco@laurelweb.net

Summary: Full range executive search in industrial areas and financial services. Search and appraisal-related consulting (i.e. organizational development and competitive analysis).

Key Contact - Specialty:
Mr. Charles A. Fagan, III - *Administration, Financial services, Senior management*
Ms. Stephanie L. Bronder - *Human resources, Non-profit*
Mr. Alfred N. Pilz

Salary Minimum: $100,000

Functions: Board Members, Senior Mgmt., Admin. Svcs., Int'l.

Industries: Generalist (All), Manufacturing, Finance, Services, Non-profits

Faircastle Technology Group LLC
27 Wells Rd Ste 1117
Monroe, CT 06468-1266
(203) 459-0631
Email: info@faircastle.com
Web: www.faircastle.com

Summary: Established, high technology only; specialists in finding the best company executives and bringing them to your table. Often retained when large search firms fail. Clients are industry leading and leading edge information and niche technology firms. Full or customized retained search plus aggressive interviewing/hiring processes.

Key Contact - Specialty:
Ms. Ann Rice Banno, President - *C-level, Computers (Software), High technology, Semiconductors, Senior management*

Email your resume to a targeted list of recruiters now at www.ExecutiveAgent.com/DER07

Salary Minimum: $150,000

Functions: Board Members, Senior Mgmt., Product Dev., Mktg. Mgmt., Sales Mgmt., CFOs, MIS Mgmt., Mgmt. Consultants, Mgmt. Consultants, Homeland Security

Industries: Manufacturing, Medical Devices, Computer Equip., Test, Measure Equip., Electronic, Elec. Components, Semiconductors, Consumer Goods, Services, Mgmt. Consulting, E-commerce, IT Implementation, PSA/ASP, Communications, Wireless, Homeland Security, Environmental Svcs., Software, Security SW, Healthcare

Fairfax Group[†]

9800 Shelard Pkwy Ste 110
Minneapolis, MN 55441-6451
(763) 541-9898
Email: careers@fairfaxgroup.com
Web: www.fairfaxgroup.com

Summary: We are specialists in senior level IT and financial executive search. Our sub-specialties include HR management and engineering management.

Key Contact - Specialty:
Mr. Mark Campbell, Managing Partner - *Tax*
Mr. David Campbell, Partner

Salary Minimum: $90,000

Functions: HR Mgmt., Finance, CFOs, Budgeting, Cash Mgmt., IT, MIS Mgmt., Systems Analysis, Systems Dev.

Industries: Generalist (All)

Fairfaxx Corp

338 Commerce Dr
Fairfield, CT 06825-5510
(203) 337-3900
Fax: (203) 337-3910
Email: fairfaxxse@aol.com

Summary: Executive search with heavy emphasis in the apparel and wellness products industries

Key Contact - Specialty:
Mr. Jeffrey Thomas - *Apparel, Retail*
Mr. Joseph Tucci - *High technology*

Salary Minimum: $75,000

Functions: Generalist (All), Management

Industries: Textiles, Apparel, Soap, Perf., Cosmtcs., Wholesale, Retail

Fairfield

721 5th Ave
New York, NY 10022-2523
(212) 838-0220
Email: newyork@fairfield.ch
Web: www.fairfield.ch

Summary: We specialize in placing executive in retail and wholesale apparel manufacturing. Client inquiries invited. E-mailed executive CVs welcome. We don't accept unsolicited hard copy resumes; they will be returned unopened.

Key Contact - Specialty:
Dr. Bruce Barton Buchholtz, MD, Chairman & Managing Director - *Retail, Wholesale*

Salary Minimum: $75,000

Functions: Management, Senior Mgmt., Sales & Mktg., HR Mgmt., Finance, Textile/Fashion

Industries: Textiles, Apparel, Wholesale, Retail

Branches:
9663 Santa Monica Blvd
Beverly Hills, CA 90210-4303
(310) 858-5250
Email: beverlyhills@fairfield.ch

Key Contact - Specialty:
Mr. Todd Clinton Buchholtz, Principal

Paul Falcone Associates

PO Box 115
Mount Freedom, NJ 07970-0115
(973) 895-5200
Fax: (973) 895-5266
Email: pfasearch@yahoo.com

Summary: Specializing in consumer packaged goods primarily in human recources, sales, supply chain/logistics, and marketing.

Key Contact - Specialty:
Mr. Paul Falcone, Managing Director

Salary Minimum: $90,000

Functions: Distribution, Sales & Mktg., Sales Mgmt., HR Mgmt., Staffing, Training

Industries: Food, Bev., Tobacco, Soap, Perf., Cosmtcs., Consumer Goods, Logistics Svcs., Supply Chain Mgmt

James Farris Associates

909 NW 63rd St
Oklahoma City, OK 73116-7605
(405) 525-5061
Fax: (405) 525-5069
Email: james@jamesfarris.com
Web: www.jamesfarris.com

Summary: Retained searches for mid to top-level in finance, management, healthcare, insurance, manufacturing, HR, IS & technical professions, sales & marketing, along with outplacement and consulting services.

Key Contact - Specialty:
Mr. James W. Farris, President
Ms. Susan Litchfield, Office Manager - *Accounting, Finance*

Salary Minimum: $40,000

Functions: Generalist (All), HR Mgmt.

Industries: Generalist (All), Oil & Gas, Non-profits, Healthcare

Fathom Human Capital Solutions

312 Crest Pointe S
Bremen, GA 30110-2360
(678) 921-0167
(888) 302-6652
Fax: (678) 528-7042
Email: info@fathomhcs.com
Web: www.fathomhcs.com

Summary: Our fundamental business is identifying and assessing the very best talent within the healthcare industry and those professional service organizations serving it. We actively recruit the following healthcare professionals: physicians, healthcare executives, allied nursing, pharmaceutical, technical, and management consultants.

Key Contact - Specialty:
Mr. Jeff Williams, Managing Principal - *Executives, Healthcare, Management consulting, Medical, Physicians*
Ms. Janice Williams, Director, Recruiting - *C-level, CEOs, CFOs, Psychiatry, Surgical*

Salary Minimum: $80,000

Functions: Management, Senior Mgmt., Healthcare, Physicians, Nurses, Allied Health, HR Mgmt., CFOs

Industries: Non-profits, Pharm Svcs., Mgmt. Consulting, HR Services, Biotech/Life Sciences, Healthcare, Hospitals, Long-term/Home Care, Physical Therapy, Occupational Therapy, Women's

James Feerst & Associates Inc[†]

6613 N Eagle Ridge Dr Ste 200
Tucson, AZ 85750-0931
(520) 529-1594
Fax: (520) 529-1314
Email: judithemiller@msn.com

Summary: Executive search firm specializing in the pharmaceutical, biotechnology, diagnostics and medical device fields. Broad range of functional experience. Expert in recruiting physicians.

Key Contact - Specialty:
Mr. James E. Feerst, President - *Pharmaceutical*
Ms. Judith E. Miller, Executive Vice President - *Pharmaceutical*

Salary Minimum: $80,000

Functions: Product Dev., Plant Mgmt., Quality, Physicians, Health Admin., Mktg. Mgmt., R&D, Engineering

Industries: Generalist (All), Drugs Mfg., Medical Devices, Pharm Svcs., Biotech/Life Sciences, Healthcare

K Fehling & Associates

2902 Isabella Blvd Ste 30
Jacksonville Beach, FL 32250-8006
(904) 280-0035
Fax: (904) 246-5613
Email: resumes@kfasearch.com
Web: www.kfasearch.com

Summary: Retainer-based executive search firm dedicated to senior level positions in the healthcare and life science industries (medical devices, biotechnology, diagnostics, distribution and pharmaceutical).

Key Contact - Specialty:
Ms. Kathleen H. Fehling, President
Ms. Martha Z. Stachitas, Executive Search Consultant
Ms. Antonia M. Sandoval, Administrative Assistant
Ms. Christy Loman, Research Associate

Salary Minimum: $150,000

Functions: Board Members, Senior Mgmt., Healthcare

Industries: Drugs Mfg., Medical Devices, Pharm Svcs., Equip Svcs., Biotech/Life Sciences

Feldman Gray & Associates Inc[†]

700-45 St Clair Ave W
I A C Building
Toronto, ON M4V 1K9
Canada
(416) 515-7600
Email: general@feldman-gray.com
Web: www.feldman-gray.com

Summary: One of the country's largest executive search practices providing services to a broad range of industries.

Key Contact - Specialty:
Mr. Fred Feldman, Senior Parnter - *Senior management*
Mr. Ron Meyers, Partner - *Senior management*
Mr. Warren Lundy, Partner - *Senior management*
Mr. Corey Daxon, Partner - *Middle management, Senior management*

Salary Minimum: $60,000

Functions: Generalist (All)

Industries: Generalist (All)

Ferguson & Burke Associates

5204 Remington Dr
Alexandria, VA 22309-3342
(703) 360-2323
(800) 401-2323
Fax: (703) 360-7615
Email: careers@fergburke.com
Web: www.fergburke.com

Summary: We are a global retained executive search firm that specializes in senior level financial vertical. Our noted expertise is in auditing accounting, finance, and consulting assignments. Of special interest is the knowledge we have in recruiting executives with an expertise tailored to meet the demands of today's global businesses. We are also noted for our expertise within the business risk consulting community, internal auditing, enterprise risk consulting.

Key Contact - Specialty:
Ms. Mary Anne Burke, Managing Director

Salary Minimum: $100,000

Ferguson Partners Ltd

191 N Wacker Dr Ste 2850
Chicago, IL 60606-1880
(312) 368-5040
Web: www.fergusonpartners.com

Summary: We provide executive and director recruiting, CEO succession planning, and board assessments to clients in the real estate, financial services and related industries. The firm primarily serves the commercial real estate ownership and brokerage, homebuilding, commercial mortgage finance (CMBS), residential mortgage finance, hospitality, and senior housing sectors.

Key Contact - Specialty:
Mr. William J. Ferguson, Chief Executive Officer & Chairman
Mr. Wayne (Jay) J. Costley, Jr., Senior Managing Director & COO
Mr. Richard J. Lovett, Managing Director
Mr. Jonathan A. Boba, Director

Salary Minimum: $100,000

Functions: Board Members, Senior Mgmt., CFOs, Minorities/Diversity

Industries: Construction, Finance, Hospitality, Real Estate, Long-term/Home Care

Branches:
10100 Santa Monica Blvd Ste 300
Los Angeles, CA 90067-4107
(310) 772-2235
Fax: (310) 772-2236
Key Contact - Specialty:
Ms. Debra S. Barbanel, Vice Chairman & Senior Managing Director
Mr. Robert W. Mayes, Senior Director
Ms. Kara C. Sugimoto, Director

50 California St Ste 1650
San Francisco, CA 94111-4611
(415) 439-5367
Key Contact - Specialty:
Ms. Stephanie K. Pearson, Senior Director

1120 Avenue of the Americas Ste 1512
New York, NY 10036-6700
(212) 626-6950
Fax: (212) 626-6959
Key Contact - Specialty:
Mr. James D. Dell'Olio, President & Senior Managing Director
Ms. Karen Gaucher, Director
Mr. Oren D. Klaber, Director
Mr. George Gilmartin, Director

5430 Lbj Fwy Ste 1200
Dallas, TX 75240-2639
(972) 455-9250
Fax: (972) 455-9251
Key Contact - Specialty:
Mr. David N. Konker, Managing Director
Mr. Larry W. Mendez, Director

Ferneborg & Associates Inc

160 Bovet Rd Ste 403
San Mateo, CA 94402-3114
(650) 577-0100
Fax: (650) 577-0122
Email: mailbox@execsearch.com
Web: www.execsearch.com

Summary: We are an independently owned retained executive search firm dedicated to identifying and recruiting premier senior-level management executives for our corporate clients.

Key Contact - Specialty:
Mr. John R. Ferneborg, President
Mr. J. William (JW) Ferneborg, Vice President

Salary Minimum: $125,000

Functions: Generalist (All), Management, Board Members, Senior Mgmt., Sales & Mktg., Finance

Industries: Generalist (All), Manufacturing, Food, Bev., Tobacco, Computer Equip., Consumer Elect., Transportation, Wholesale, Retail, Finance, Services, Hospitality, Media, Real Estate, Software

Ferrari Search Group[†]

4560 Sunrise Dr
Bemus Point, NY 14712-9637
(716) 386-2398
Email: ferrarisearch@hotmail.com

Summary: We perform executive search on a proactive basis serving the financial community. We maintain an active computerized database of executives in investment firms, banks, investment banking institutions and corporate financial executives.

Key Contact - Specialty:
Mr. S. Jay Ferrari - *Financial services*

Salary Minimum: $60,000

Functions: Management, Senior Mgmt., Middle Mgmt., M&A, Risk Mgmt., Attorneys

Industries: Generalist (All), Finance, Banking, Invest. Banking, Venture Cap., Mutual/Hedge Funds, Misc. Financial

Filcro Media Staffing

(also known as Broadcasting Executive Search)
521 5th Ave Fl 18
Reception
New York, NY 10175-1801
(212) 599-0909
Email: mail@executivesearch.tv
Web: www.executivesearch.tv

Summary: Broadcasting and media executive search. Business, technical and creative recruitment. Retainer based.

Key Contact - Specialty:
Mr. Tony Filson, President - *Cable, Communications, Film, Media, New media*
Ms. Maxine Paul, Director, Research
Ms. Helene Crocitto, Executive Vice President - *Banking, Finance, Financial services, International, Investment*

Salary Minimum: $75,000

Functions: Generalist (All), Management, Sales & Mktg., Advertising, Sales Mgmt., Finance, Engineering

Industries: Finance, Entertainment, Media, Advertising, New Media, Broadcast, Film, Communications, Digital, Government, Entertainment SW

Financial Plus Management Solutions Inc[†]

1901-372 Bay St
Sterling Tower
Toronto, ON M5H 2W9
Canada
(416) 594-9232
Email: roman@financialplus.net

Summary: We are a firm, which has built a reputation of providing high-caliber individuals who bring added value to our clients.

Key Contact - Specialty:
Mr. Roman M. Skrypuch, President & Owner - *Financial services, Sales*

Salary Minimum: $40,000

Functions: Generalist (All), Management, Sales & Mktg., HR Mgmt., Finance, IT

Industries: Generalist (All), Finance, Accounting, Equip Svcs., HR Services, Software

Eileen Finn & Associates Inc

230 Park Ave Fl 10
New York, NY 10169-1099
(212) 687-1260
Fax: (212) 551-1473
Email: eileen@eileenfinn.com
Web: www.eileenfinn.com

Summary: We are a retained executive search firm specializing in the sourcing and placement of senior HR professionals for major corporate, institutional and not-for-profit clients.

Key Contact - Specialty:
Ms. Eileen Finn, President - *Financial services, Human resources*

Salary Minimum: $100,000

Functions: HR Mgmt.

Industries: Finance, Non-profits, Pharm Svcs., Accounting, Mgmt. Consulting, Hospitality, Publishing, New Media, Insurance, Entertainment SW

First Choice Search

PO Box 946
Danville, CA 94526-0946
(206) 632-0050
(206) 919-8892
Email: info@firstchoicesearch.com
Web: www.firstchoicesearch.com

Summary: Partner with select group of clients to act as an extension of their HR function for the term of a project. Assists in analyzing, researching and recommending organizational changes and needs in relation to the search assignment.

Key Contact - Specialty:
Ms. Michele J. Sarlat, President

Salary Minimum: $50,000

Functions: Mfg., Finance, MIS Mgmt.

Industries: Generalist (All), Agri., Forestry, Mining, Chemicals, Soap, Perf., Cosmtcs., Medical Devices, Plastics, Rubber, Paints, Petro. Products, Engineering Svcs., Packaging

Howard Fischer Associates International Inc

1800 John F Kennedy Blvd Fl 7
Philadelphia, PA 19103-7404
(215) 568-8363
Fax: (215) 568-4815

Email: search@hfischer.com
Web: www.hfischer.com

Summary: Board and executive search in technology, media, cable & entertainment, manufacturing, financial services and bio-pharm.

Key Contact - Specialty:
Mr. Howard Fischer, Chief Executive Officer - *CEOs, COOs, Presidents*
Mr. Adam Fischer, Partner - *CEOs, CFOs, CIOs, COOs*

Salary Minimum: $255,000

Functions: Generalist (All)

Industries: Computer Equip., Electronic, Elec. Components, Venture Cap., New Media, Communications, Telecoms, Wireless, Fiber Optic, Network Infrastructure, Software

Branches:
1688 Dell Ave Ste 200
Campbell, CA 95008-6926
(408) 374-0580
Key Contact - Specialty:
Mr. Jeff Markowitz, Partner

1050 Winter St Ste 1000
Waltham, MA 02451-1406
(781) 839-7272
Key Contact - Specialty:
Mr. Jeffrey J. DiSandro, Principal

Fischer Group International Inc

296 Country Club Rd Fl 2
Avon, CT 06001-2508
(860) 404-7700
Fax: (860) 404-7799
Email: info@fischergroupintl.com
Web: www.fischergroupintl.com

Summary: Our firm was founded by seasoned search professionals. The firm conducts senior level retained executive search and provides HR consulting.

Key Contact - Specialty:
Mr. John C. Fischer, General Management
Mr. C. Edward Snyder, Human Resources
Ms. Laurie Kritzer - *Financial services, Manufacturing*
Mr. Jerome P. Kane, Power Generation & Distribution
Ms. Diane Beir - *Banking*
Mr. Joseph F. Keiser, Principal, Southeast Asia
Ms. Pamela Richardson
Mr. Sunit Mehra, MD, India
Mr. Alfred Shum, MD, Greater China
Mr. Philip Mayer, MD, Western Europe

Salary Minimum: $150,000

Functions: Management

Industries: Generalist (All)

Fisher & Associates

1063 Lenor Way
San Jose, CA 95128-4111
(408) 554-0156
Fax: (408) 246-7807
Email: fisherassoc@aol.com

Summary: We are a retained executive search firm specializing in the placement of high-technology marketing, sales and engineering executives.

Key Contact - Specialty:
Mr. Gary E. Fisher, President - *CEOs, Marketing*

Salary Minimum: $100,000

Functions: Senior Mgmt., Middle Mgmt., Product Dev., Sales & Mktg., Mktg. Mgmt., Sales Mgmt., Engineering

Industries: Computer Equip., Consumer Elect., E-commerce, Communications, Telecoms, Digital, Wireless, Fiber Optic, Network Infrastructure, Software, Industry Specific SW, Networking, Comm. SW, Security SW, System SW

Fisher Personnel Management Services

2351 N Filbert Rd
Exeter, CA 93221-9781
(559) 594-5774
Fax: (559) 594-5777
Email: hookme@fisheads.net
Web: www.fisheads.net

Summary: Our firm works with mid and senior-level management primarily for manufacturing companies. Industries we specialize in are aerospace, aircraft, automotive, consumer products, defense, electronics, high technology, industrial/manufacturing, packaging, transportation and truck equipment.

Key Contact - Specialty:
Mr. Neal Fisher, Principal
Ms. Judy Gibson, Principal - *Aerospace, Automotive*

Salary Minimum: $100,000

Functions: Generalist (All), Management, Mfg., Materials, Sales & Mktg., IT, Engineering

Industries: Generalist (All), Metal Products, Machine, Appliance, Motor Vehicles, Computer Equip., Consumer Elect., Aerospace

Fitzgerald Associates

21 Muzzey St
Lexington, MA 02421-5259
(781) 863-1945
Email: info@fitzsearch.com
Web: www.fitzsearch.com

Summary: We have extensive, exclusive experience recruiting for the healthcare industry. Clients include MCOs, ASPs, healthcare information management, demand/disease management, e-health and pharmaceutical marketing services companies and vendors to those organizations.

Key Contact - Specialty:
Mr. Geoffrey Fitzgerald, Principal - *Internet, Managed care*
Ms. Diane Fitzgerald, Principal - *Managed care*

Salary Minimum: $80,000

Functions: Generalist (All), Healthcare

Industries: Generalist (All)

Fitzgibbon & Associates

PO Box 1108
Media, PA 19063-0808
(610) 565-7566
Email: ffitzz@comcast.net

Summary: We are specialists in sensitive searches requiring highest standards of professional representation of the corporation's image in retail and direct response/catalog industries.

Key Contact - Specialty:
Mr. Michael T. Fitzgibbon, Principal

Salary Minimum: $80,000

Functions: Generalist (All), Senior Mgmt., Middle Mgmt., Distribution, Customer Svc., MIS Mgmt.

Industries: Generalist (All), Communications

Flagship Global Inc[†]

197 8th St Apt 623
Charlestown, MA 02129-4233
(617) 241-9000
Email: ac@flagshipboston.com

Summary: We are committed to providing our clients with extraordinary, customized service that produces exceptional hires.

Key Contact - Specialty:
Ms. Anna Coppola, President - *Financial services, Investment management*

Salary Minimum: $150,000

Functions: Generalist (All), Cash Mgmt., Risk Mgmt.

Industries: Generalist (All), Invest. Banking, Brokers, Venture Cap., Mutual/Hedge Funds, Misc. Financial

Flannery & Associates, LLC

N27 W23953 Paul Rd Ste 204
West Wind III
Pewaukee, WI 53072-6244
(262) 523-1206
Fax: (262) 523-1873
Email: shari@flannerysearch.com
Web: www.flannerysearch.com

Summary: We are a generalist practice with clients nationwide. We have particular expertise in health care and manufacturing. We have completed searches in marketing and sales, operations, finance, HR, general management, IS, and regulatory affairs.

Key Contact - Specialty:
Mr. Peter Flannery, President - *Biotechnology, Communications, Healthcare, Manufacturing, Sales*

Salary Minimum: $60,000

Functions: Generalist (All)

Industries: Generalist (All), Manufacturing, Medical Devices, Metal Products, Finance, Pharm Svcs., HR Services, Healthcare, Hospitals, Long-term/Home Care

Florapersonnel Inc

1740 Lake Markham Rd
Sanford, FL 32771-8964
(407) 320-8177
Fax: (407) 320-8083
Email: hortsearch@aol.com
Web: www.florapersonnel.com

Summary: We are an international search firm for the greater horticulture industry. Retained only.

Key Contact - Specialty:
Mr. Robert F. Zahra, General Manager
Mr. Jack Ferrell, Account Executive
Ms. Judy Devine, Recruiter

Functions: Senior Mgmt., Mktg. Mgmt., Specialized Svcs.

Industries: Agri., Forestry, Mining, Construction, Wholesale, Property/Facility Mgmt.

Agustin Flores

(A TranSearch International company)
Periférico Sur 4194 1o Piso Suite C
Jardines del Pedregal
01900 Mexico City, DF
Mexico
55 5578 8866
55 5568 8871
Email: transearchaf@mexis.com
Web: www.transearch.com

Summary: Generalist consultant.

Key Contact - Specialty:
Mr. Agustin Flores

Functions: Generalist (All)

Industries: Generalist (All)

J G Flynn & Associates Inc

8-4100 Gallaghers Parkland Dr
Kelowna, BC V1W 3Z8
Canada
(604) 689-7202
Fax: (250) 860-3186
Email: recruit@jgflynn.com
Web: www.jgflynn.com

Summary: We are an established boutique executive search firm. We enjoy an international reputation as one of the premier direct sourcing firms in North America. We are generalists although we are best known in the areas of engineering, mining, forestry, energy, technology-driven, and IS organizations. We don't rely on advertising; instead, our research-based approach is thorough, efficient and discreet.

Key Contact - Specialty:
Mr. Jerry Flynn, President - *General management, Senior management*
Mr. John English, BA, MBA, Associate - *Chemical, Energy*

Salary Minimum: $70,000

Functions: Generalist (All), Management, Mfg., HR Mgmt., IT, R&D, Engineering, Int'l.

Industries: Generalist (All), Agri., Forestry, Mining, Energy, Utilities, Construction, Manufacturing, Aerospace

Flynn, Hannock Inc

(a Taplow Group company)
41 Crossroads Plz # 115
West Hartford, CT 06117-2402
(860) 521-5005
Fax: (860) 561-5294
Email: search@flynnhannock.com
Web: www.flynnhannock.com

Summary: We provide executive searches in banking/finance, insurance, manufacturing, healthcare, utilities and non-profit. The firm has a general practice. We also provide interim management services. We provide international retained search services as well as other human capital services through our membership in The Taplow Group.

Key Contact - Specialty:
Mr. Elwin (Terry) Hannock, III, President - *Hospital, Management consulting, Manufacturing, Manufacturing (Management), Marketing*
Mr. Richard Handel, Managing Director
Ms. Astrid Bigham, Consultant
Ms. Glenna McNally, Consultant - *Banking, Finance, General management, Human resources, Management*
Ms. Pamela Hannock, Administrator - *General management, Insurance, Interim, Management, Manufacturing (Management)*

Salary Minimum: $100,000

Functions: Generalist (All), Management, Senior Mgmt., Sales & Mktg., HR Mgmt., Finance

Industries: Energy, Utilities, Manufacturing, Finance, Services, Insurance, Healthcare, Hospitals

FM Industries Inc

10125 Crosstown Cir Ste 300
Eden Prairie, MN 55344-3318
(952) 941-0966
Fax: (952) 941-4462

Email: fmindustries@fmindustries.net
Web: www.fmindustries.net

Summary: We are a multi-disciplined executive search and Human Resouces consulting organization representing client companies and their positions.

Key Contact - Specialty:
Mr. Fred A. Montana, Owner & President
Ms. Karen Miller, Chief Financial Officer - *C-level*

Salary Minimum: $50,000

Functions: Generalist (All), Senior Mgmt., Middle Mgmt., Mfg., Production, CFOs

Industries: Generalist (All)

Fogec Consultants Inc

PO Box 28806
Milwaukee, WI 53228-0806
(414) 427-0690
Email: tfogec@fogec.com
Web: www.fogec.com/fci/

Summary: Specialize in executive, managerial and professional positions across industry lines. Extensive client-side experience provides for highly personalized service and strong sensitivity to client needs.

Key Contact - Specialty:
Mr. Thomas G. Fogec, President - *Human resources*

Salary Minimum: $50,000

Functions: Generalist (All), HR Mgmt., Finance, Cash Mgmt.

Industries: Generalist (All), Banking, Invest. Banking, Brokers, Accounting

Foley Proctor Yoskowitz LLC

1 Cattano Ave
Morristown, NJ 07960-6860
(973) 605-1000
(800) 238-1123
Fax: (973) 605-1020
Email: fpy@fpysearch.com
Web: www.fpysearch.com

Summary: All of the partners are trained hospital administrators and seasoned healthcare search executives with long term client relationships in recruiting CEOs, senior administrators, physician chairmen/executives, product line/department managers, managed care/practice administrators and staff physicians.

Key Contact - Specialty:
Mr. Thomas Foley, FACHE, Senior Parnter

Salary Minimum: $70,000

Functions: Generalist (All), Board Members, Senior Mgmt., Middle Mgmt., Physicians, Nurses, Health Admin.

Industries: Healthcare, Hospitals, Long-term/Home Care, Dental, Physical Therapy, Occupational Therapy, Women's

Branches:
24 E 39th St
New York, NY 10016-2555
(212) 928-1110
(800) 238-1123
Fax: (973) 605-1020
Email: fpy@fpysearch.com

Key Contact - Specialty:
Mrs. Reggie Yoskowitz, MPH, Partner
Ms. Patricia Turiello, Partner

L W Foote Company

110 110th Ave NE Ste 603
Bellevue, WA 98004-5890
(425) 451-1660
Fax: (425) 451-1535
Email: email@lwfoote.com
Web: www.lwfoote.com

Summary: We have recruited exceptional individuals for clients in a broad range of industries with emphasis in technology (both hardware and software), consumer products and telecom.

Key Contact - Specialty:
Mr. Leland W. Foote, President
Mr. James E. Bloomer, Vice President & General Manager
Ms. Valerie Rosman, Director, Research

Salary Minimum: $85,000

Functions: Generalist (All)

Industries: Generalist (All), Food, Bev., Tobacco, Textiles, Apparel, Computer Equip., Telecoms, Software

Forager

1516 Sudeenew Dr
Johnsburg, IL 60050-0918
(815) 344-0006
Email: aaforager@comcast.net

Summary: Each search is personally managed by a senior partner with deep industry knowledge and a broad network of contacts.

Key Contact - Specialty:
Ms. Anita Artner, President

Salary Minimum: $100,000

Functions: Generalist (All), Management, Materials, HR Mgmt., Finance, R&D, Minorities/Diversity

Industries: Generalist (All), Food, Bev., Tobacco, Drugs Mfg., Medical Devices, Metal Products, Consumer Elect., Misc. Mfg., Logistics Svcs., Packaging, Healthcare

Branches:
9124 Hidden Farm Rd
Alta Loma, CA 91737-1534
(909) 980-0120
Email: jmforager@cs.com
Key Contact - Specialty:
Ms. Jackie Muhr, Vice President - *Logistics, Sales*

1623 Brookside Dr
Littleton, CO 80126-3430
(303) 346-2819
Email: toforager@aol.com
Key Contact - Specialty:
Ms. Tonya Artner, Account Executive - *Sales*

The Ford Group Inc

295 E Swedesford Rd # 282
Wayne, PA 19087-1462
(610) 296-5205
Email: info@thefordgroup.com
Web: www.thefordgroup.com

Summary: We are a national, boutique firm, specializing in retained executive search for selected general management positions in leading corporations and global management consulting firms. Our focus and expertise includes human resources, finance/accounting and management consulting.

Key Contact - Specialty:
Ms. Sandra D. Ford, Chief Executive Officer &
Mng Director - *Accounting (Big 4), Change
management, Financial services, Human
resources, Management consulting*

Salary Minimum: $125,000

Functions: Management, HR Mgmt., Finance,
CFOs, Mgmt. Consultants, Minorities/Diversity

Industries: Generalist (All), Drugs Mfg., Finance,
Services, Non-profits, Accounting, Mgmt.
Consulting, HR Services, Telecoms,
Biotech/Life Sciences, Healthcare

Ford Webb Associates Inc

27 Main St
Concord, MA 01742-2560
(978) 371-4900
Email: info@fordwebb.com
Web: www.fordwebb.com

Summary: We apply a rigorous management
consultancy to a chief executive search, which
assures a thoughtful process and certain result. We
have recruited Fortune 500 and private company
CEOs, over 70 government cabinet secretaries,
university and college presidents and 100's of
chief executives for foundation, service, advocacy,
research, and membership organizations.

Key Contact - Specialty:
Mr. Ted Webb
Ms. Jean Ford

Functions: Management, Board Members, Senior
Mgmt.

Industries: Non-profits, Law Enforcement, Higher
Ed., Government, Healthcare

Foster/Searing Ltd

1750 Tysons Blvd Ste 250
Mc Lean, VA 22102-4252
(703) 584-3220
Email: info@fostersearing.com
Web: www.fostersearing.com

Summary: We are a boutique executive search
firm created to provide highly customized service
to select clients. By limiting the number of
engagements conducted, we are able to dedicate
the type of attention to each search that our senior
level clients expect. Based on our extensive
experience with both established and start-up
businesses, our firm brings to its clients
exceptional search expertise.

Key Contact - Specialty:
Mr. James Searing, Partner - *Biotechnology, Non-
profit, Pharmaceutical, Technology*
Ms. Bonnie Foster, Partner - *Biotechnology,
Information Technology, Pharmaceutical,
Telecommunications*
Ms. Vickie Moore, Partner - *Biotechnology,
Energy, Pharmaceutical, Professional services*
Mr. Greg Moyer, Partner - *Human resources,
Professional services*
Ms. Laurie Harrison, Director
Ms. Gretchen Spiro, Director

Salary Minimum: $150,000

Functions: Generalist (All)

Industries: Generalist (All), Energy, Utilities,
Non-profits, Pharm Svcs., Mgmt. Consulting,
New Media, Communications, Government,
Aerospace, Biotech/Life Sciences

Fowler & Associates†

6427 Laurel Valley Rd
Dallas, TX 75248-3904
(972) 490-5096
Fax: (972) 490-5096

Email: fowlerassoc@aol.com
Web: www.fowler-assoc.com

Summary: We are a retained executive search
firm specializing in recruiting executive,
management and technical employees in medium
to heavy manufacturing, HVAC & refrigeration,
building products and power
generation/distribution industries.

Key Contact - Specialty:
Mr. Thomas A. Fowler, President

Salary Minimum: $70,000

Functions: Generalist (All)

Industries: Generalist (All)

Foy, Schneid & Daniel Inc

575 Madison Ave Fl 10
New York, NY 10022-8511
(212) 980-2525
Web: www.fsdsearch.com

Summary: Professional executive search practice
with targeted experience in most industries. The
ability and experience of our consultants ensures
that clients achieve efficient and quality results.

Key Contact - Specialty:
Ms. Beverly Daniel, Partner

Salary Minimum: $75,000

Functions: Senior Mgmt., Mfg., Distribution,
Mktg. Mgmt., HR Mgmt., IT, Mgmt.
Consultants, Non-profits

Industries: Generalist (All), Manufacturing,
Consumer Goods, Transportation, Retail, Non-
profits, Mgmt. Consulting

FPA-US

(formerly known as Foster Partners)
2146 Hemlock Farms
Lords Valley, PA 18428-9074
(570) 775-1898
(888) 775-1899
Fax: (570) 775-2989
Email: foster.fpa@earthlink.net
Web: www.fosterpartners.biz

Summary: Primary client service emphasis in the
financial services industry. We serve US
corporations with executive staffing in Asia and
in-bound global companies with senior
management recruiting for US operations.
Industry emphasis ranges from consumer goods,
specialty retailing to engineered durable goods
products.

Key Contact - Specialty:
Mr. Dwight E. Foster, Chairman - *CEOs, CFOs,
Financial services, General management,
Insurance (Casualty)*

Salary Minimum: $100,000

Functions: Management, Board Members, Senior
Mgmt., Mfg., Distribution, Sales & Mktg.,
Finance, CFOs, Taxes, IT

Industries: Manufacturing, Computer Equip.,
Consumer Elect., Wholesale, Retail, Finance,
Banking, Invest. Banking, Insurance, Healthcare

Franchise Recruiters Ltd ®

3500 Innsbruck Ln
Lincolnshire Country Club
& Toronto Office Crete, IL 60417-1126
(708) 757-5595
Email: franchise@att.net
Web: www.franchiserecruiters.com

Summary: We have experience hiring qualified
franchise management professionals in the
disciplines of president/CEO/COO, franchise
sales, international development, operations, board

members, marketing, legal, finance, training, real
estate and consulting. Replacement guarantee on
candidates with competitive search fees. Client
references provided. Offices in the U.S. & Canada.

Key Contact - Specialty:
Mr. Jerry C. Wilkerson, President & Founder -
Executives

Salary Minimum: $100,000

Functions: Board Members, Senior Mgmt.,
Middle Mgmt., Automation, Sales Mgmt., IT,
Int'l.

Industries: Generalist (All), Law Enforcement,
Hospitality, Hotels, Resorts, Clubs, Restaurants,
Quick Service Restaurants, Full Service
Restaurants, Entertainment, Recreation, Sports,
Travel

Branches:
203-20 Holly St
Toronto, ON M4S 3B1
Canada
(416) 322-5730
Email: franchise@att.net
Key Contact - Specialty:
Mr. George Kinzie, President

Franchot & Associates Inc

700 Twelve Oaks Center Dr Ste 267
Wayzata, MN 55391-4441
(952) 253-0080
Fax: (952) 253-0081
Email: doug@franchotassociates.com
Web: www.franchotassociates.com

Summary: We are a general practice firm with
particular expertise in small and mid-cap
companies and not-for-profits. We offer a unique
process that transitions past the hire to ensure
successful integration of the new hire.

Key Contact - Specialty:
Mr. Douglas Franchot, President - *General
management*

Salary Minimum: $80,000

Functions: Management, Senior Mgmt., Non-
profits

Industries: Generalist (All), Food, Bev., Tobacco,
Finance, Services, Non-profits, Legal, Media,
Advertising, Publishing, Government

Francis & Associates

6923 Vista Dr
West Des Moines, IA 50266-9309
(515) 221-9800
Fax: (515) 221-9806
Email: dfrancis@fa-search.com
Web: www.fa-search.com

Summary: We are a very professional, generalist
retained search firm, known for high quality,
timely work with extreme customer service.
Clients range from start-up, venture capital funded
entities to Fortune 100 companies.

Key Contact - Specialty:
Mr. Dwaine Francis, Managing Partner
Ms. Karen Novak, Executive Vice President

Salary Minimum: $125,000

Functions: Generalist (All)

Industries: Generalist (All)

Neil Frank & Company

PO Box 3570
Redondo Beach, CA 90277-1570
(310) 543-1611
Fax: (310) 540-2639
Email: neilnick@aol.com
Web: www.neilfrank.com

Summary: We are functional specialist in public relations, corporate communications and marketing communications. Retained solo practice.

Key Contact - Specialty:
Mr. Neil Frank, Principal - *Public relations*

Salary Minimum: $50,000

Functions: PR

Industries: Advertising

Frank Palma Associates

110 S Jefferson Rd
Whippany, NJ 07981-1038
(973) 884-1498
Fax: (973) 884-1499
Email: fpalma@fpalmaassoc.com
Web: www.fpalmaassoc.com

Summary: Our principal has been recognized as one of the leading practitioners in the field of executive search and as one of North America's top 200 executive recruiters. He has successfully completed hundreds of key searches within a diversified number of industries and functional disciplines.

Key Contact - Specialty:
Mr. Frank Palma, President
Ms. Macky Whalen, Vice President, Operations - *High technology, Industrial*

Salary Minimum: $100,000

Functions: Management, Mfg., Distribution, Sales & Mktg., HR Mgmt., Finance, IT, R&D, Health & Safety, Legal

Industries: Construction, Manufacturing, Food, Bev., Tobacco, Chemicals, Motor Vehicles, Transportation, Retail, Banking, Pharm Svcs., Telecoms, Insurance

Franklin Allen Consultants Ltd

1205 Franklin Ave Ste 350
Garden City, NY 11530-1629
(516) 248-4511
Fax: (516) 294-6646
Email: hroher@franklinallen.com

Summary: We are a generalist search firm. We recruit for professionals, scientists, middle & senior management, up to and including president/CEO and board level positions. We specialize in healthcare, pharmaceutical, biotechnology & medtech companies, hospitals, general manufacturing and consumer & industrial product companies.

Key Contact - Specialty:
Mr. Howard F. Roher, President
Mr. Allen B. Kupchik, Senior Vice President

Salary Minimum: $75,000

Functions: Generalist (All)

Industries: Generalist (All)

K S Frary & Associates Inc

16 Schooner Rdg Ste 301
Marblehead, MA 01945-1556
(781) 631-2464
Fax: (781) 631-2465
Email: ksfrary@comcast.net
Web: www.ksfrary.com

Summary: We are a full-service firm with proven assessment skills, strong customer focus and in-depth research capabilities with a record of recruiting leaders who produce results. We place a heavy focus on small to mid-size manufacturing and technology companies in eastern New England.

Key Contact - Specialty:
Mr. Kevin S. Frary, President
Mr. Ted L. Hubbard, Vice President - *Financial services, Publishing*

Salary Minimum: $90,000

Functions: Generalist (All)

Industries: Generalist (All), Manufacturing, Publishing, Biotech/Life Sciences

A W Fraser & Associates

10303 Jasper Ave NW
Metropolitan Place
Edmonton, AB T5J 3N6
Canada
(780) 428-8578
Fax: (780) 426-2933
Email: edmonton@awfraser.com
Web: www.awfraser.com

Summary: Originating from one of the first national practice of industrial psychology, we have been continuously staffed by chartered psychologists and, from the beginning of certification, certified management consultants.

Key Contact - Specialty:
Mr. Larry Pelensky
Mr. Ross Hill

Functions: Generalist (All)

Industries: Generalist (All)

Valerie Frederickson & Company

800 Menlo Ave Ste 220
Menlo Park, CA 94025-4732
(650) 614-0220
Fax: (650) 614-0223
Email: resumes@vfandco.com
Web: www.vfandco.com

Summary: Our firm is a leading full-service HR management, executive search and outplacement consulting firm serving both emerging technology companies and large multinational corporations.

Key Contact - Specialty:
Ms. Valerie Frederickson, CMP, Managing Principal & Founder - *Biotechnology, CEOs, Financial services, Government, Technology*
Mr. Bryan Power, Director, Client Services - *Administration, CFOs, Compensation, COOs, Product management/development*

Salary Minimum: $100,000

Functions: Board Members, Senior Mgmt., Sales Mgmt., HR Mgmt., CFOs, Int'l.

Industries: Generalist (All), Services, Software

M A French Associates

PO Box 63613
Colorado Springs, CO 80962-3613
(719) 440-1118
Email: mafrench@adelphia.net

Summary: At our firm we specialize in matching the most qualified candidates with the most appropriate positions, creating a productive and positive environment for both employer and employee.

Key Contact - Specialty:
Ms. Margaret A. French, Gerontolog, Managing Director - *Assisted living, Banking (Commercial), Boards of Directors, CEOs, CFOs*

Salary Minimum: $75,000

Functions: Generalist (All)

Industries: Generalist (All), Agri., Forestry, Mining, Banking, Invest. Banking, HR Services, Engineering Svcs., Hospitality, Advertising, Wireless, Healthcare

P N French Associates Inc

126 Nowell Farme Rd
Carlisle, MA 01741-1830
(978) 369-4569

Summary: Retained search for colleges, universities and related not-for-profit organizations. We have completed assignments in a variety of functional areas and specialize in searches for senior administrators.

Key Contact - Specialty:
Mr. Peter N. French, President - *Non-profit*

Salary Minimum: $70,000

Functions: Management, Senior Mgmt., Middle Mgmt., Admin. Svcs., Purchasing, Distribution, IT, Specialized Svcs., Minorities/Diversity, Non-profits

Industries: Transportation, Non-profits, Accounting, Higher Ed., New Media, Broadcast, Film, Compliance, Property/Facility Mgmt.

The Fritzsche Dunn Roth Group

9801 Fall Creek Rd Ste 312
Indianapolis, IN 46256-4802
(317) 575-8605
Fax: (317) 575-8606
Email: info@fdrgroup.net
Web: www.fdrgroup.net

Summary: We have been successfully providing management and HR services for many years. Our clients range in size from Fortune 500 companies to small, entrepreneurial firms in a variety of market sectors including manufacturing, finance, distribution, retail and non-profit.

Key Contact - Specialty:
Mr. Andy Roth, Managing Partner
Mr. Mike Fritzsche, Managing Partner
Mr. Jerry Dunn, Managing Partner

Salary Minimum: $80,000

Functions: Generalist (All)

Industries: Generalist (All)

Frontier Partners Inc

155 Wickford Point Rd
North Kingstown, RI 02852-4049
(401) 267-9092
Fax: (401) 267-9078
Email: mwarter@frontiersearch.com
Web: www.frontiersearch.com

Summary: A full service firm dedicated to matching the requirements of its clients with the life goals of its candidates. Focus is on finding top management and entire teams for high-growth, start-up and early-stage companies and leading municipal and not-for-profit institutions.

Key Contact - Specialty:
Mr. Mark Warter, President

Salary Minimum: $85,000

Functions: Generalist (All), Management

Industries: Generalist (All), Computer Equip., Finance, Venture Cap., Non-profits, Higher Ed., Media, Communications, Government, Software, Healthcare

Fulcrum Resource Group Inc

171 Dorset Rd
Waban, MA 02468-1452
(617) 964-1855
Fax: (617) 964-8377
Email: info@fulcrumgroup.com
Web: www.fulcrumgroup.com

Summary: Our clients are business owners and managers from manufacturing or other traditional industries who ask us to help them strengthen their

organizations by recruiting GMs or VPs, improving teamwork or developing compensation programs. We provide specialized assistance for owners and managers seeking executive talent who have limited experience successfully recruiting senior managers; or integrating top talent into your team.

Key Contact - Specialty:
Mr. Harvey Wigder, President

Salary Minimum: $100,000

Functions: Generalist (All), Management

Industries: Generalist (All)

C F Furr & Company

6308 Hawks Bill Dr
Wilmington, NC 28409-9280
(910) 452-2217
Email: cffurrco@mindspring.com

Summary: History of achieving excellent results for clients; commitment to successful search completion, principal involvement in every search, exceptional research capabilities, thorough sourcing & screening, comprehensive candidate reports, disciplined communications & follow through and replacement search guarantee.

Key Contact - Specialty:
Mr. C. Franklin Furr, Principal - *Financial services, Healthcare*

Salary Minimum: $70,000

Functions: Production

Industries: Finance, Banking, Invest. Banking, Brokers, Misc. Financial

Furst Group/MPI

555 S Perryville Rd
Rockford, IL 61108-2530
(815) 229-9111
Fax: (815) 229-8926
Web: www.furstgroup.com

Summary: Specialists in medical management, cost containment and health insurance markets including HMOs, PPOs, medical group practices, indemnity, hospital, pharmaceutical, hospice & palliative care and ancillary markets.

Key Contact - Specialty:
Ms. Sherrie L. Barch, Principal - *Healthcare*
Mr. Dennis L. Pankratz, Vice President - *Healthcare*
Mr. David Appino, Vice President - *Healthcare*

Salary Minimum: $100,000

Functions: Board Members, Senior Mgmt., Admin. Svcs., Mktg. Research, Mktg. Mgmt., Sales Mgmt., HR Mgmt., CFOs, MIS Mgmt., Minorities/Diversity

Industries: Healthcare

Branches:
3131 E Camelback Rd
Phoenix, AZ 85016-4500
(520) 742-0004
Fax: (520) 742-0005
Email: dford@furstgroup.com
Key Contact - Specialty:
Mr. Dan Ford, Vice President - *Healthcare*

7500 Flying Cloud Dr Ste 765
Eden Prairie, MN 55344-3779
(952) 914-0060
Fax: (952) 914-0084
Email: tfrischmon@furstgroup.com
Key Contact - Specialty:
Mr. Timothy Frischmon, Vice President - *Healthcare*

1735 Market St Ste A607
Philadelphia, PA 19103-7502
(610) 430-6884
Fax: (610) 430-6885
Email: dbanks@furstgroup.com
Key Contact - Specialty:
Ms. Deanna L. Banks, Vice President - *Healthcare*

1431 Greenway Dr Ste 800
Irving, TX 75038-2574
(972) 910-7438
Key Contact - Specialty:
Mr. Bob Clarke, Principal - *Healthcare*

601 Union St Ste 4200
Seattle, WA 98101-4036
(206) 652-3270
Key Contact - Specialty:
Mr. J. Robert Clarke, Principal - *Healthcare*

Furst Search Group

6870 Rote Rd Ste 100
Rockford, IL 61107-2690
(815) 229-7800
(866) 463-8778
Fax: (815) 394-0239
Email: info@furstsearch.com
Web: www.furstsearch.com

Summary: Retained management recruiting and within manufacturing, banking, financial services and service sector.

Key Contact - Specialty:
Mr. Thomas C. Furst, President
Dr. Martin E. Pschirrer, Senior Vice President
Mr. Kevin Logterman, Vice President

Salary Minimum: $100,000

Functions: Generalist (All), Management, Board Members, Senior Mgmt., Middle Mgmt., Mfg.

Industries: Manufacturing, Banking, Misc. Financial, Services, Non-profits, Accounting, Mgmt. Consulting, HR Services, Engineering Svcs., Advertising

GAAP Inc

1524 Av Summerhill
Montreal, QC H3H 1B9
Canada
(514) 935-3253
(800) 363-7196
Email: ehughes@gaapsearch.com
Web: www.gaapsearch.com

Summary: We are a boutique senior-level retained executive search firm serving a select list of Fortune 500 companies.

Key Contact - Specialty:
Mr. Emerson Hughes, President
Mr. Frank Connor, Partner
Mr. Shawn Davidson, Partner
Mr. Steve Johnstone, Partner
Ms. Jennifer Young, Partner
Mr. Normand Turgeon, Partner
Ms. Aggie Wybraniec, Consultant
Mr. Kent Fraser, Consultant

Salary Minimum: $90,000

Functions: Board Members, Senior Mgmt., CFOs

Industries: Generalist (All), Paper, Drugs Mfg., Pharm Svcs., Accounting, Mgmt. Consulting, HR Services, New Media, Telecoms, Commercial, Biotech/Life Sciences

Affiliates:
Phase V Search
Boston, MA

Gaffney Management Consultants Inc

1701 E Woodfield Rd Ste 430
Schaumburg, IL 60173-5129
(847) 592-3220
Fax: (847) 592-3219
Email: kg@gaffneyinc.com
Web: www.gaffneyinc.com

Summary: Retained executive search firm servicing the needs of major manufacturing and industrial related organizations both public and private. Effective recruitment in the areas of: general management, manufacturing operations, quality, purchasing/materials, finance/accounting, IT/MIS, product engineering, HR and sales/marketing.

Key Contact - Specialty:
Mr. Keith Gaffney, Managing Director - *Middle management*
Mr. William Gaffney, President & Chief Executive Officer - *CEOs, Presidents*

Salary Minimum: $80,000

Functions: Management, Mfg., Materials, Sales & Mktg., HR Mgmt., Finance, IT, Int'l.

Industries: Generalist (All), Agri., Forestry, Mining, Construction, Manufacturing, Defense, Environmental Svcs., Aerospace, Software

Gage & Associates

5170 Palisade Cir
Riverside, CA 92506-1521
(951) 684-4200
Fax: (951) 684-6138
Email: amgage@charter.net

Summary: We specialize in the placement and recruitment of executives in the Inland Region of Southern California. Our primary clients are manufacturing companies that are looking to expand or reorganize.

Key Contact - Specialty:
Mr. Arthur M. Gage, President - *Sales*
Ms. Erin Perets, Executive Vice President - *Sales*

Salary Minimum: $100,000

Functions: Mfg., Sales & Mktg.

Industries: Generalist (All), Manufacturing

Gaines & Associates International Inc

650 N Dearborn St Ste 450
Chicago, IL 60610-3757
(312) 654-2900
Fax: (312) 654-2903
Email: wsresearch@gainesintl.com
Web: www.gainesintl.com

Summary: We are a professional search firm specializing in the design and building industries. We conduct in-depth searches with a level of expertise founded on years of experience. We dedicate ourselves to providing timely effective solutions by assessing needs, finding the right individuals and facilitating communications that benefit both employer and candidate.

Key Contact - Specialty:
Ms. Donna Gaines, President - *Construction, Engineering, Interior design, Real estate*

Salary Minimum: $70,000

Functions: Generalist (All)

Industries: Construction, Real Estate

Branches:
1825 'I' St NW Ste 400
Washington, DC 20006-5415
(202) 244-6929
Key Contact - Specialty:
Ms. Cathie Kempf, Vice President

2221 Peachtree Rd NE Ste P33
Atlanta, GA 30309-1106
(404) 355-7008
Email: gheath@gainesintl.com
Key Contact - Specialty:
Mr. Grant Heath, Vice President

Jay Gaines & Company Inc

450 Park Ave Ste 500
New York, NY 10022-2752
(212) 308-9222
Fax: (212) 308-5146
Email: jgandco@jaygaines.com
Web: www.jaygaines.com

Summary: Major concentrations of activities are general management, financial services with heavy emphasis on the financial markets and investment management, eCommerce, IT, information based businesses, insurance and manufacturing.

Key Contact - Specialty:
Mr. Jay Gaines, President
Mr. Terry (Tarin) Anwar, Managing Director - *Capital markets, CFOs, Finance, Investment management, Risk management*
Ms. Anne Crowley, Managing Director
Ms. Marie Rice, Managing Director
Ms. Olga Prod, Vice President - *General management, Information service, Information Systems, Information Technology*

Salary Minimum: $250,000

Functions: Generalist (All)

Industries: Generalist (All), Manufacturing, Finance, Banking, Invest. Banking, Mutual/Hedge Funds, Mgmt. Consulting, Publishing, Insurance, Software

Galgay Search Associates[†]

62 Vernon Rd
Belmont, MA 02478-1015
(617) 489-4364
Email: pamela@galgaysearch.com
Web: www.galgaysearch.com

Summary: Executive search firm serving retailers and developers in corporate and regional real estate, construction, store planning & design, acquisition, development, leasing, asset management, real estate legal and real estate finance.

Key Contact - Specialty:
Ms. Pamela Galgay, Principal

Functions: Generalist (All)

Industries: Real Estate

Gary Galyean

PO Box 644393
Vero Beach, FL 32964
(772) 559-3382
Email: galyean@gmail.com

Summary: Specializing in the search for and placement of PGA golf professionals, GCSAA superintendents, and golf and country club managers for leading resort, hotel and private club properties.

Key Contact - Specialty:
Mr. Gary A. Galyean, President

Salary Minimum: $100,000

Functions: Senior Mgmt.

Industries: Hotels, Resorts, Clubs

Gans, Gans & Associates Inc

7445 Quail Meadow Rd
Plant City, FL 33565-3314
(813) 986-4441
Fax: (813) 986-4775
Email: simone@gansgans.com
Web: www.gansgans.com

Summary: We specialize in recruiting individuals of diverse backgrounds, including women and people of various ethnic and racial backgrounds, for executive, management, professional and technical positions within all industries. Also, specializing in public housing, city governments and the legal profession.

Key Contact - Specialty:
Ms. Simone Gans Barefield, President & Chief Executive Officer

Salary Minimum: $75,000

Functions: Generalist (All), Management, Senior Mgmt., Healthcare, CFOs, IT, MIS Mgmt., Specialized Svcs., Mgmt. Consultants, Minorities/Diversity

Industries: Generalist (All), Non-profits, Pharm Svcs., HR Services, E-commerce, IT Implementation, Communications, Network Infrastructure, Government, Insurance, Software, Biotech/Life Sciences, Healthcare, Long-term/Home Care

W N Garbarini & Associates

961 Cherokee Ct
Westfield, NJ 07090-2611
(908) 232-2737
Fax: (908) 232-2326
Email: wngarbarini@comcast.net

Summary: Boutique general search firm with unique personalized service approach.

Key Contact - Specialty:
Mr. William N. Garbarini, President
Ms. Linda Lauchiere, Vice President, Research

Salary Minimum: $100,000

Functions: Management, Healthcare, Sales & Mktg., Mktg. Mgmt., Sales Mgmt., HR Mgmt., Finance, CFOs, IT

Industries: Food, Bev., Tobacco, Drugs Mfg., Medical Devices, Computer Equip., Biotech/Life Sciences, Healthcare

Gardiner International

645 5th Ave Fl 18
New York, NY 10022-5910
(212) 546-6263

Summary: We provide our clients with the best available candidates for top level recruitment regardless of geographic location with a single consultant in charge from start to finish, using advanced IT, global industry expertise and cross-cultural judgment.

Key Contact - Specialty:
Mr. E. Nicholas P. Gardiner, President - *CEOs, CFOs, CIOs, COOs, Presidents*
Ms. Sharon Mancini, Director

Salary Minimum: $180,000

Functions: Senior Mgmt., Int'l.

Industries: Generalist (All)

Gardner-Ross Associates Inc

232 Madison Ave
New York, NY 10016-2901
(212) 689-1133
Fax: (212) 689-4893

Email: gardnrxl@earthlink.net

Summary: We are a firm, which specializes in packaging, P.O.P. displays, publishing, trade shows, new media and IT. Our assignments range from CEO, COO, marketing/sales management, operations and most upper-management positions.

Key Contact - Specialty:
Mr. Marvin Gardner, President
Ms. Elsa Ross, Executive Vice President - *New media, Publishing*

Salary Minimum: $100,000

Functions: Generalist (All), IT, MIS Mgmt., Mgmt. Consultants

Industries: Generalist (All), Paper, Printing, Misc. Mfg., Mgmt. Consulting, Publishing, New Media, Packaging, Non-Classifiable

Garfield & Associates[†]

(formerly known as Growth Strategies Inc)
5448 Estate Oak Cir
Fort Lauderdale, FL 33312-6280
(954) 989-2425
Email: vaxa1@bellsouth.net

Summary: We have international experience in working with many segments of the high-technology industry to provide senior and middle management leadership with functional expertise in sales, marketing, corporate development and management consulting.

Key Contact - Specialty:
Mr. John Garfield, Managing Director - *General management, High technology*

Salary Minimum: $60,000

Functions: Generalist (All), Senior Mgmt., Middle Mgmt., Product Dev., Mktg. Mgmt., Sales Mgmt., M&A, MIS Mgmt., Mgmt. Consultants, Int'l.

Industries: Generalist (All), Manufacturing, Drugs Mfg., Medical Devices, Computer Equip., Consumer Elect., Semiconductors, Mgmt. Consulting, Entertainment, Communications, Telecoms, Software, Biotech/Life Sciences

The Garms Group Inc

830 W Main St Ste 250
Lake Zurich, IL 60047-2349
(847) 382-7200
(312) 953-7200
Email: dangarms@garms.com
Web: www.garms.com

Summary: We provide executive consulting and business development advisory services. Our practice includes conducting executive searches for technology based businesses, leveraging strategic relationships that enable growth businesses to identify new channels to market and additional sources of capital. We have successfully recruited board members, CEOs, VPs of business development and sales.

Key Contact - Specialty:
Mr. Daniel S. Garms, Managing Partner - *Business development, C-level, CEOs, Communications, Computers (Sales)*
Ms. Jeanne M. Garms, President

Salary Minimum: $90,000

Functions: Management, Senior Mgmt., Middle Mgmt., Product Dev., Sales & Mktg., Mktg. Mgmt., Sales Mgmt., IT, Engineering, Mgmt. Consultants

Industries: Energy, Utilities, Construction, Manufacturing, Computer Equip., Venture Cap., Services, Equip Svcs., Mgmt. Consulting, Media, Publishing, New Media, Broadcast, Film, Telecoms, Government, Aerospace, Software

The Garret Group[†]

(also known as Skurnik, Stecker & Wharton)
342 Parsippany Rd
Parsippany, NJ 07054-1275
(973) 884-0711
Fax: (973) 884-1307
Email: jwharton@staffing.net

Summary: Specialists in recruiting engineering, operations, quality assurance and regulatory affairs professionals for the pharmaceutical, medical device and consumer packaged goods industries.

Key Contact - Specialty:
Mr. John P. Wharton, Partner - *Engineering, Operations*
Mr. Bernd Stecker, Partner - *Engineering, Operations*
Mr. James N. Finn, Partner - *Consumer (Packaged Goods), Cosmetics, Engineering, Manufacturing (Management), Medical (Devices)*

Salary Minimum: $90,000

Functions: Management, Middle Mgmt., Mfg., Product Dev., Quality, Packaging, R&D, Engineering

Industries: Food, Bev., Tobacco, Soap, Perf., Cosmtcs., Drugs Mfg., Medical Devices, Plastics, Rubber, Consumer Elect., Consumer Goods, Engineering Svcs., Logistics Svcs., Supply Chain Mgmt, Packaging, Biotech/Life Sciences

Branches:
1323 Asher Ct
Ormond Beach, FL 32174-2872
(386) 672-4345
Fax: (386) 672-4346
Email: jnfinn@earthlink.net
Key Contact - Specialty:
Mr. Jim Finn, Partner

Garrett Associates Inc

PO Box 53359
Atlanta, GA 30355-1359
(404) 364-0001
Email: garrett@gaisearch.com
Web: www.garrettassociatesinc.com

Summary: Our firm is a retained executive search firm providing services exclusively to the healthcare industry.

Key Contact - Specialty:
Ms. Linda M. Garrett, Principal - *Healthcare*

Salary Minimum: $50,000

Functions: Management, Healthcare

Industries: Healthcare, Hospitals, Long-term/Home Care

Garrett Search Partners LLC

4037 N Mozart St Ste 1
Chicago, IL 60618-2706
(312) 224-8417
Fax: (312) 224-8033
Email: info@garrettsearch.com
Web: www.garrettsearch.com

Summary: With offices in Dallas and Chicago, Garrett Search Partners is a boutique executive search firm serving North American clients on a retained basis. Our expertise reaches across all functional disciplines in the professional services, technology, and manufacturing sectors.

Key Contact - Specialty:
Ms. Chelsea A. Garrett, President & Chief Executive Officer
Mr. Kevin P. Teschner, Vice President

Salary Minimum: $75,000

Functions: Generalist (All), Middle Mgmt.

Industries: Generalist (All), Energy, Utilities, Manufacturing, Transportation, Finance, Services, Mgmt. Consulting, E-commerce, Supply Chain Mgmt, Hospitality, Communications, Packaging, Software

Garrison-Randall

480 2nd St Ste 304
San Francisco, CA 94107-1429
(415) 995-8400
Fax: (415) 995-8422
Email: rfornino@earthlink.net

Summary: Our expertise lies in placing administrative professionals in the health care industry whose areas of specialization include executive administration, patient care, finance, business development, ancillary services, case management, practice management and medical staff recruitment, and acute care. We do not work with medical sales, pharmaceuticals or biotechnology firms.

Key Contact - Specialty:
Ms. Rita M. Fornino, President - *Healthcare*

Salary Minimum: $90,000

Functions: Management, Board Members, Senior Mgmt., Middle Mgmt., Healthcare, Physicians, Nurses, Health Admin., PR, HR Mgmt.

Industries: Healthcare

Garthwaite Partners International LLC

13 Arcadia Rd Ste 14
Old Greenwich, CT 06870-1743
(203) 698-0015
(203) 834-1070
Fax: (203) 698-3001
Email: info2@garthwaitepartners.com
Web: www.garthwaitepartners.com

Summary: We specialize in C-level and senior management entrepreneurs, senior sales & marketing executives, and finance executives. We have particular expertise in consumer products, media, entertainment, communications, new media, e-learning, health/medical devices. We produce a diverse slate of candidates.

Key Contact - Specialty:
Ms. Candace Garthwaite, PhD, Managing Partner - *C-level, Closely-held business, Diversity, Entrepreneurs, Financial services*
Ms. Linda Buggy, Partner - *Consumer (Products), E-business, Education (Higher), Media, New media*

Salary Minimum: $100,000

Functions: Senior Mgmt., Middle Mgmt., Sales & Mktg., Mktg. Mgmt., Sales Mgmt., Finance, Int'l.

Industries: Generalist (All), Medical Devices, Consumer Goods, Finance, Misc. Financial, Mgmt. Consulting, E-commerce, K-12 Ed., Higher Ed., Entertainment, Media, Publishing, New Media, Communications, Call Centers, Healthcare

Gauthier Conseils[†]

510-1001 Rue Sherbrooke E
Montreal, QC H2L 1L3
Canada
(514) 528-9089
Fax: (514) 274-2242
Email: info@gauthier.com
Web: www.gauthier.com

Summary: Our firm specializes in the recruitment (headhunting) of mid-and-senior management personnel as well as professionals.

Key Contact - Specialty:
Ms. Jean R. Gauthier, President

Functions: Generalist (All)

Industries: Generalist (All)

GCI & Associates[†]

(also known as GCI Inc)
21 Eastbrook Bnd Ste 210
Peachtree City, GA 30269-1546
(770) 486-3393
Fax: (610) 629-3377
Email: incgci@bellsouth.net
Web: www.radiusequity.com

Summary: We place executives with private equity firms, as well as managers, engineers and sales candidates with manufacturing companies. We also act as intermediaries for healthy and distressed mid-market manufacturing companies that wish to be or that must be sold.

Key Contact - Specialty:
Mr. Gary Corcoran, Senior Parnter - *Engineering, Executives, Manufacturing, Mergers & acquisitions, Private equity*
Mr. Frank Oakley, Partner - *Engineering, Molding, Molding (Injection), Sales*
Ms. Kelly Corcoran, Researcher

Salary Minimum: $80,000

Functions: Management, Senior Mgmt., Mfg., Plant Mgmt., Sales & Mktg., Sales Mgmt., M&A, Engineering

Industries: Manufacturing, Finance

Murray Geddes & Associates

513-283 Danforth Ave
Toronto, ON M4K 1N2
Canada
(416) 998-1374
Email: mg@mgagrowth.com
Web: www.mgagrowth.com

Summary: Improving human capital potential through executive search, assessments and related services for senior management and board of directors. Promoting excellence in the assessment, selection and development process for board of directors and senior management.

Key Contact - Specialty:
Mr. Murray Geddes, MBA, Managing Director - *Boards of Directors, C-level, Executives, General management*

Salary Minimum: $50,000

Functions: Generalist (All)

Industries: Generalist (All), Motor Vehicles, Transportation, Finance, Misc. Financial, Services, Non-profits, Mgmt. Consulting, Wireless, Dental

General Engineering Tectonics

(also known as GET, Inc.).
PO Box 1076
601 N Loma Dr
Lodi, CA 95241-1076
(209) 333-2000
Fax: (209) 333-7982
Email: info@getstaffing.com
Web: www.getstaffing.com

Summary: We are a recruiting and search consulting firm specializing in finding and placing high-technology industry personnel. We find the right people.

Key Contact - Specialty:
Mr. Gary Kroll, Staffing Manager - *Research*
Ms. Linda Kneen, Recruiter

Functions: Engineering

† occasional contingency assignment

Industries: Computer Equip., Consumer Elect., Misc. Mfg., Accounting, HR Services, Telecoms, Software

Genesis Corporate Search Ltd

1800-520 5 Ave SW
Northland Bank Tower
Calgary, AB T2P 3R7
Canada
(403) 237-8622
Fax: (403) 233-7622
Email: genesis@genesiscorporatesearch.com
Web: www.genesiscorporatesearch.com

Summary: We are a permanent search and placement of oil and gas professionals, specifically in the areas of engineering, geology, geophysics and finance.

Key Contact - Specialty:
Ms. P.F. Hines, President - *Engineering*

Functions: Middle Mgmt., CFOs, Engineering, Geotechnical

Industries: Energy, Utilities, Oil & Gas

Geneva Group International Inc

4 Embarcadero Ctr Ste 1400
San Francisco, CA 94111-4164
(415) 433-4646
Email: isill@aol.com
Web: www.genevagroup.com

Summary: Specializes in president, CEO, board member and officer level searches for enterprise software, Internet, wireless and eCommerce companies. Special emphasis on key officers for venture capital backed, privately held emerging technologies.

Key Contact - Specialty:
Mr. Igor M. Sill, Managing Partner - *Computers (Software), Internet*
Mr. Bob Jacobs, Partner & Vice President
Mr. Grant MacFarlane, Partner & Vice President - *Marketing, Professional services*

Salary Minimum: $100,000

Functions: Generalist (All), Board Members, Senior Mgmt.

Industries: Generalist (All), Venture Cap., New Media, Software

Gerald Walsh Associates Inc[†]

200-1801 Hollis Street
Central Trust Tower
Halifax, NS B3J 3N4
Canada
(902) 421-1676
Fax: (902) 491-1300
Email: apply@geraldwalsh.com
Web: www.geraldwalsh.com

Summary: Our firm specializes in executive search, career transition and executive coaching services.

Key Contact - Specialty:
Mr. Gerald Walsh, President
Ms. Adrien Alder, Director, Business Development
Ms. Sylvie Lagace, Office Manager - *Telecommunications*

Functions: Generalist (All), Management, Mfg., Sales & Mktg., HR Mgmt., Finance, IT, Engineering

Industries: Generalist (All)

J. Gernetzke & Associates[†]

PO Box 307331
Columbus, OH 43230-7331
(614) 856-1480
Fax: (614) 856-1491
Email: info@gernetzke.com
Web: www.gernetzke.com

Summary: We are quality conscious and provide a highly individualized level of service to our clients. Since our beginning, we have been involved in recruiting management personnel at all levels – manager, director and executive level – and across all functional organizational lines. Our clients are in a variety of industries and have operations locally, regionally and all across the United States.

Key Contact - Specialty:
Mr. Jim Gernetzke, President
Mr. Don Jensen, Director

Functions: Middle Mgmt., Distribution, HR Mgmt., Finance

Industries: Generalist (All), Manufacturing, Retail, Banking, Hospitality

GES Services Inc

45 Rockefeller Plz Fl 20
Rockefeller Center
New York, NY 10111-2099
(212) 332-3260
Fax: (212) 332-3261
Email: information@gesservices.com
Web: www.gesservices.com

Summary: We recruit senior and middle management professionals for personal trust, private banking, financial planning, investment management and related wealth management disciplines.

Key Contact - Specialty:
Ms. Christy Guzzetta, President
Ms. Abby J. Norris, Vice President & Sr Search Consultant

Salary Minimum: $100,000

Functions: Management, Senior Mgmt., Middle Mgmt., Admin. Svcs., Sales Mgmt., Cash Mgmt.

Industries: Finance, Banking, Invest. Banking, Brokers, Misc. Financial, Services, Accounting, Mgmt. Consulting, HR Services

Gibson & Company Inc

250 N Sunny Slope Rd Ste 300
Brookfield, WI 53005-4824
(262) 785-8100

Summary: The firm specializes in CEO searches and CEO succession assignments, also covering all direct reports to the CEO: COO, CFO, CIO, CMO, CTO and Chief Human Resources Officer.

Key Contact - Specialty:
Mr. Bruce Gibson

Salary Minimum: $375,000

Functions: Generalist (All)

Industries: Generalist (All)

Gielow Associates Inc

5590 N Berkeley Blvd
Milwaukee, WI 53217-5139
(800) 969-7715
(414) 964-4121
Fax: (414) 964-6410
Email: curt@gielowassociates.com
Web: www.gielowassociates.com

Summary: We are a generalist firm with special expertise in non-profit organizations, trade

associations, hospitals, insurance and general healthcare. The principal has many years of search experience.

Key Contact - Specialty:
Mr. Curtis C. Gielow, President & Chief Executive Officer - *Healthcare, Sports*

Salary Minimum: $50,000

Functions: Generalist (All)

Industries: Drugs Mfg., Medical Devices, Non-profits, Pharm Svcs., Legal, Accounting, Hospitality, Healthcare

Tom Gilbert Associates[†]

9 Duarte Ct
Novato, CA 94949-6616
(415) 883-7026
Email: tomgilbert94949@yahoo.com

Summary: Search firm that specializes in IT, software development, security and high-technology HR searches for client companies that range from pre-IPO start-ups to established companies.

Key Contact - Specialty:
Mr. Tom Gilbert, Owner

Salary Minimum: $50,000

Functions: Quality, HR Mgmt., Benefits, Staffing, IT, Systems Analysis, Systems Implem., Systems Support, Network Admin., DB Admin.

Industries: Generalist (All), Manufacturing, Finance, Banking, Invest. Banking, Brokers, Venture Cap., Equip Svcs., Media, Telecoms, Insurance, Software, Biotech/Life Sciences

Gilbert Tweed Associates Inc

415 Madison Ave Fl 20
New York, NY 10017-7939
(212) 758-3000
Fax: (212) 832-1040
Email: hrdprt@covad.net
Web: www.gilberttweed.com

Summary: Generalist search practice providing a broad range of support services to ensure successful completion of every search. Strong track record recruiting female and minority candidates. Also provides organizational profiling service and seminars.

Key Contact - Specialty:
Ms. Janet Tweed, Chief Executive Officer
Ms. Stephanie Pinson, President
Ms. Karen DelPrete, Managing Partner
Ms. Maureen Alphonse-Charles, Managing Director
Ms. Melissa Henderson, Managing Director
Mr. Ira Shapiro, Managing Director
Mr. Abram Claude, Jr., Managing Director
Mr. Ravi Bhatia, President, GTA India
Ms. Kathy Murphy, Managing Director
Mr. John Gillespie, Vice President
Mr. Randy Cyr, Vice President
Ms. Patricia Britton, Vice President
Mr. Stephen Humphreys, Vice President
Mr. Howard Leifman, Vice President
Ms. Paula Marks, Vice President

Salary Minimum: $150,000

Functions: Generalist (All), Management, Senior Mgmt., Mfg., Sales & Mktg., CFOs

Industries: Generalist (All), Construction, Manufacturing, Transportation, Banking, Government, Aerospace, Software, Biotech/Life Sciences, Healthcare

Branches:
68 Southfield Ave Ste 100
2 Stamford Landing
Stamford, CT 06902-7223
(203) 921-0363
Email: pbrowne-zak@gilberttweed.com
Key Contact - Specialty:
Ms. Patricia Browne-Zak, Managing Director

65 William St Fl 3
Wellesley Hills, MA 02481-3802
(781) 431-0400
Email: chill@gilberttweed.com
Key Contact - Specialty:
Mr. Steve Garfinkle, Managing Director

Gilreath Consultantcy

PO Box 310
8 College Rd
Concord, MA 01742-0310
(978) 287-4432
Fax: (978) 287-4431
Email: jim@gilreathsearch.com
Web: www.gilreathsearch.com

Summary: Utilizing a diligent screening process, we recruit primarily investor CEOs, COOs, GMs, heads of operations, finance and engineering for midsized manufacturing companies owned by prestigious private equity firms. Our clients prefer "skin in the game" hires. We also recruit operating partners for private equity firms.

Key Contact - Specialty:
Mr. James M. Gilreath, President
Mrs. Diane C. Gilreath, Vice President

Salary Minimum: $100,000

Functions: Senior Mgmt., Middle Mgmt.

Industries: Manufacturing, Textiles, Apparel, Lumber, Furniture, Medical Devices, Plastics, Rubber, Metal Products, Machine, Appliance, Motor Vehicles, Consumer Elect., Misc. Mfg., Electronic, Elec. Components, Consumer Goods, Venture Cap., Aerospace

Glazin/Sisco Executive Search Consultants Inc

(an EMA Partners International company)
2200-4950 Yonge St
Office Building
North York, ON M2N 6K1
Canada
(416) 203-3004
Fax: (416) 203-3007
Email: search@glazinsisco.com
Web: www.glazinsisco.com

Summary: We are a fully retained executive search firm with an enviable client base, conducting interesting senior-level assignments. Our industry specialties include real estate, resort, hospitality, retail and food service.

Key Contact - Specialty:
Ms. Lynne Glazin, Partner - *Entertainment, Hospitality, Real estate, Sports, Tourism*
Ms. Carol Sisco, Partner - *Entertainment, Hospitality, Real estate, Sports*
Ms. Shelly Silbernagel, Associate

Salary Minimum: $80,000

Functions: Generalist (All), Management, Mfg., Sales & Mktg., HR Mgmt., Finance, IT

Industries: Generalist (All), Construction, Retail, Services, Real Estate, Healthcare

Branches:
12540-1066 Hastings St W
Oceanic Plaza Towers
Vancouver, BC V6E 3X2
Canada
(604) 687-3828
Fax: (604) 687-3875
Email: shall@glazinsisco.com
Key Contact - Specialty:
Ms. Sue Hall, Researcher

J P Gleason Associates Inc

18 Spring St
Cary, IL 60013-2815
(847) 516-8900
Email: info@jpgleason.com
Web: www.jpgleason.com

Summary: We are a higher-level search in marketing, sales, finance, HR and operations for clients in transportation, manufacturing, retail and other industries. Personal, consultative approach with limited number of clients.

Key Contact - Specialty:
Mr. James P. Gleason, President - *Finance, Human resources, Manufacturing, Marketing, Sales*
Ms. Jennifer E. Feit, Director, Research - *Banking*

Salary Minimum: $100,000

Functions: Generalist (All), Management, Mfg., Sales & Mktg., HR Mgmt., Finance

Industries: Generalist (All), Manufacturing, Food, Bev., Tobacco, Consumer Goods, Transportation, Pharm Svcs., Hospitality, Restaurants, Full Service Restaurants, Insurance

Glines Associates Inc

39 S La Salle St Ste 714
Chicago, IL 60603-1619
(312) 580-0646
Email: search@glinesassociates.com
Web: www.glinesassociates.com

Summary: We are a retained executive search firm devoted to acquiring executives for the healthcare and life sciences industry. Our clients gain from our industry expertise, precision search and recruitment, and hands-on involvement.

Key Contact - Specialty:
Mr. Larry Glines, President - *Orthopedics, Pharmaceutical, Prosthetic devices, Regulatory, Surgical*
Mr. Adam Chavarria, Director, Research - *Operating rooms, Pharmaceutical, Prosthetic devices, Regulatory, Surgical*

Salary Minimum: $90,000

Functions: Generalist (All)

Industries: Drugs Mfg., Medical Devices, Biotech/Life Sciences, Healthcare

Global Hospitality Search Consultants Ltd

107-2430 Meadowpine Blvd
Mississauga, ON L5N 6S2
Canada
(905) 814-5701
Fax: (905) 814-5702
Email: torontomail@globalhospitality.com
Web: www.globalhospitality.com

Summary: A search firm you can trust.

Key Contact - Specialty:
Mr. Richard Mirosolin

Functions: Hotel Mgmt.

Industries: Hotels, Resorts, Clubs, Restaurants, Quick Service Restaurants, Full Service Restaurants, Inst./Industrial Food Svc., Entertainment, Recreation

Global Research

444 E 82nd St Apt 34A
New York, NY 10028-5944
(212) 980-3800
Fax: (212) 650-1732
Email: info@globalresearchnet.com
Web: www.globalresearchnet.com

Summary: Clients provide us with a job description and a list of companies that they would like researched, then we look to find the relevant contacts. We then prepare a customized resume on each appropriatcly positioned candidate. We also provide companies' contact information to clients requesting them.

Key Contact - Specialty:
Mr. Richard R. Wolf, President

Salary Minimum: $30,000

Functions: Generalist (All)

Industries: Banking, Invest. Banking, Brokers, Pharm Svcs., Accounting, HR Services, Advertising, Insurance, Biotech/Life Sciences, Healthcare

Global Research Partnership Inc

127 Garth Rd Ste 2A
Scarsdale, NY 10583-3768
(914) 723-4229
Email: gai@grpi.com
Web: www.grpi.com

Summary: We un-bundle the executive search process offering whatever part of the process the client wishes to outsource. We have language capabilities in Japanese, French and Spanish and over 50% of our revenues come from international searches in Asia, Russia, Europe and Latin America.

Key Contact - Specialty:
Ms. Gai Galitzine, Managing Director
Ms. Betty Wong Tomita, Managing Director

Functions: Generalist (All)

Industries: Manufacturing, Food, Bev., Tobacco, Chemicals, Consumer Goods, Retail, Services, Media, Communications, Software, Healthcare

Global Search Associates[†]

(also know as GlobalHunt.com)
6135 E Pershing Ave
Scottsdale, AZ 85254-3838
(480) 609-2855
Email: kf@globalhunt.com
Web: www.globalhunt.com

Summary: Clients rely upon us for the candidate that meets the firms current and future goals setting the trend of long-term tenure and significant internal growth. Candidates rely upon us for integrity, dignity and confidentiality.

Key Contact - Specialty:
Mrs. Katrina Fowler, Chief Executive Officer

Salary Minimum: $50,000

Functions: Generalist (All)

Industries: Construction, Consumer Goods, Finance, Banking, Legal, Insurance, Life, Commercial, Real Estate, Property/Facility Mgmt.

Glocap Search LLC[†]

152 W 57th St Fl 15
New York, NY 10019-3310
(212) 333-6400
Fax: (212) 333-6401
Email: comments@glocap.com
Web: www.glocap.com

Summary: Our firm places investment professionals into private equity, leveraged buyout, venture capital, hedge fund and asset management firms. We recruit at all levels, from analyst to general partner.

Key Contact - Specialty:
Mr. Adam Zoia, Managing Partner
Mr. Brian Korb, Partner
Mr. Theodore Petrara, Partner

Salary Minimum: $100,000

Functions: Management, Finance, IT

Industries: Finance

F Gloss International

1309 Vincent Pl
Mc Lean, VA 22101-3615
(703) 847-0010
Email: fred_gloss@fgloss.com

Summary: Clientele includes firms in the global IT, aviation, transportation, travel/hospitality, aerospace, national defense and intelligence, and satellite-telecom-wireless sectors. Clients provide products, systems and professional services to federal government agencies. We support major international consulting firms, airlines and software solution providers. We assist clients in facilitating merger & acquisition, partnering agreements and JVs.

Key Contact - Specialty:
Mr. Fred C. Gloss, Chief Executive Officer

Salary Minimum: $100,000

Functions: Generalist (All), Management, Board Members, Senior Mgmt., Mktg. Mgmt., Sales Mgmt., IT, Mgmt. Consultants, Int'l.

Industries: Generalist (All), Transportation, Mgmt. Consulting, HR Services, E commerce, IT Implementation, Supply Chain Mgmt., Hospitality, Hotels, Resorts, Clubs, Travel, Communications, Telecoms, Wireless, Defense, Homeland Security, Aerospace, Software, Marketing SW, Security SW

Glou International Inc

687 Highland Ave
Needham Heights, MA 02494-2232
(781) 449-3310
Fax: (781) 449-3358
Email: alan@glou.com
Web: www.glou.com

Summary: Relationship building, retained search, mentoring/coaching. Talent assessments and networking.

Key Contact - Specialty:
Mr. Alan Glou, President - *Executives, Management*

Salary Minimum: $80,000

Functions: Senior Mgmt.

Industries: Generalist (All)

The Gobbell Company

25001 Via Bonita
Laguna Niguel, CA 92677-1540
(949) 476-2258
Fax: (949) 476-2258
Email: john@gobbellcompany.com
Web: www.gobbellcompany.com

Summary: Small, high quality retainer firm. Emphasize senior management in telecom, engineering, construction, healthcare, food, aerospace, investment, financial services and real estate.

Key Contact - Specialty:
Mr. John J. Gobbell, Managing Director - *Senior management*

Salary Minimum: $100,000

Functions: Generalist (All), Senior Mgmt., Admin. Svcs., HR Mgmt., CFOs, R&D, Engineering

Industries: Generalist (All), Computer Equip., Consumer Elect., Transportation, Finance, Hospitality, Aerospace

Robert G Godfrey Associates Ltd

PO Box 3392
Oak Park, IL 60303-3392
(708) 771-2374
Fax: (708) 771-2615
Email: r.godfrey@sbcglobal.net

Summary: Highly personalized executive search practice with an emphasis on efficient, high quality and professional service. Firm has reputation for long-term placements. Also offers recruitment consulting services to include contract recruitment.

Key Contact - Specialty:
Mr. Robert G. Godfrey, President - *Healthcare, Market research*
Ms. Laura J. Godfrey, Vice President

Functions: Generalist (All)

Industries: Finance, Non-profits, Accounting, Higher Ed., Insurance, Biotech/Life Sciences, Long-term/Home Care

The Gogates Group Inc

228 French Hill Rd
Wayne, NJ 07470-3934
(973) 694-3643
Email: info@gogatesgrp.com
Web: www.gogatesgrp.com

Summary: Our emphasis is on quantitatively oriented research analysts, traders and money managers for investment banks, hedge funds and private investment firms.

Key Contact - Specialty:
Mr. Andrew Gogates, President & Founder

Salary Minimum: $100,000

Functions: Generalist (All), Risk Mgmt.

Industries: Generalist (All), Finance, Banking, Invest. Banking, Brokers, Misc. Financial

Gold Partners

100 S Main St Ste 200
Doylestown, PA 18901-4882
(215) 230-7774
Email: goldpartners@searchgold.com
Web: www.searchgold.com

Summary: We offer pharmaceutical and bio-technology physician search.

Key Contact - Specialty:
Mr. Jacob Gold, Consultant
Mr. Mark Gold, President
Mr. Bryan Shea, Senior Vice President & COO - *Pharmaceutical, Physicians*
Ms. Lauren Adams, Vice President, Pharmaceuticals
Mr. Jean Boutin, Vice President, Research - *Pharmaceutical, Physicians*

Salary Minimum: $150,000

Functions: Senior Mgmt., Healthcare, Physicians

Industries: Drugs Mfg., Pharm Svcs., Biotech/Life Sciences

The Goldman Group Advantage

11654 Plaza America Dr Ste 735
Reston, VA 20190-4700
(703) 729-7066
(888) 858-8518
Fax: (703) 470-4653
Email: shelly@thegoldmangroupadvantage.com
Web: www.thegoldmangroupadvantage.com

Summary: We are a unique firm specializing in retained executive search services, career agent/career management services and executive coaching services.

Key Contact - Specialty:
Ms. Shelly Goldman, CEIP, CPCC, President

Functions: Generalist (All)

Industries: Generalist (All), Construction, Manufacturing, Medical Devices, Pharm Svcs., Communications, Defense, Homeland Security

Fred J Goldsmith Associates

14056 Margate St
Sherman Oaks, CA 91401-5747
(818) 783-3931
Fax: (818) 907-9724
Email: fjgoldsmith@adelphia.net

Summary: Executive search - technology, consumer products, distribution, oil & exploration industries, food services and IIR services.

Key Contact - Specialty:
Mr. Fred J. Goldsmith, President - *Distribution, Food, Natural resources, Technology*

Salary Minimum: $80,000

Functions: Senior Mgmt., Quality, Distribution, Sales Mgmt., Benefits, CFOs, Mgmt. Consultants

Industries: Chemicals, Computer Equip., Mgmt. Consulting, HR Services, Software

Gomez Fregoso y Asociados

Av. Chapultepec Sur # 223 int. 69
Colonia Americana
44140 Guadalajara, JAL
Mexico
33 3825 1414
33 3826 1289
Email: gomezfre@orbinet.com.mx

Summary: Executive search consultants. Serving clients in most functions and industries.

Key Contact - Specialty:
Mr. Miguel Gomez, President
Ms. Monica Vazquez, Partner

Salary Minimum: $35,000

Functions: Generalist (All)

Industries: Generalist (All)

Gonzer Associates[†]

1225 Raymond Blvd
Newark, NJ 07102-2978
(973) 624-5600
(800) 631-4218
Fax: (973) 624-7170
Email: ljga@gonzer.com
Web: www.gonzer.com

Summary: We are a professional search firm with concentration on corporations producing technical or engineered products. Although recruiting is done on an individual basis per associate, the selection process is by consensus.

Key Contact - Specialty:
Mr. Lawrence J. Gonzer, President - *Engineering*
Mr. Daniel J. Muhlfelder, Executive Vice
President - *Engineering*

Salary Minimum: $25,000

Functions: Generalist (All), Production, Systems
Dev., Systems Support, Engineering, Mgmt.
Consultants, Technicians, Graphic Designers

Industries: Generalist (All), Energy, Utilities,
Machine, Appliance, Mgmt. Consulting, Media,
Aerospace, Software

Goodwin & Company

1150 Connecticut Ave NW Ste 615
Washington, DC 20036-4135
(202) 785-9292
Fax: (202) 785-9297
Email: mail@goodwinco.com
Web: www.goodwinco.com

Summary: An executive search firm serving
corporate and not-for-profit clients in finance,
environmental, advocacy, education and
philanthropy.

Key Contact - Specialty:
Mr. Tom Goodwin, President

Salary Minimum: $90,000

Functions: Generalist (All), Senior Mgmt., PR,
CFOs, Minorities/Diversity, Non-profits,
Environmentalists

Industries: Generalist (All)

GordonSugar Associates Inc[†]

1300 W Belmont Ave Ste 108
Chicago, IL 60657-3200
(312) 943-2800
Fax: (773) 880-2353
Email: contact@gordonsugar.com
Web: www.gordonsugar.com

Summary: We specialize in areas of Six Sigma,
particularly for companies focused on developing
or expanding world class continuous improvement
programs.

Key Contact - Specialty:
Mr. Daniel Gordon, President - *Six Sigma*

Salary Minimum: $100,000

Functions: Senior Mgmt.

Industries: Generalist (All)

GordonTyler

2220 Brandywine St
Philadelphia, PA 19130-3109
(215) 569-2344
Email: fpolaski@gordontyler.com
Web: www.gordontyler.com

Summary: Specialists in research and
development, technical services and engineering
for consumer products and services companies.

Key Contact - Specialty:
Dr. Fern Polaski

Salary Minimum: $85,000

Functions: Product Dev., R&D, Engineering

Industries: Food, Bev., Tobacco, Soap, Perf.,
Cosmtcs., Drugs Mfg., Packaging, Biotech/Life
Sciences

Gossage Sager Associates LLC

351 Town Place Cir Apt 508
Buffalo Grove, IL 60089-2426
(312) 961-5536
Fax: (847) 419-7743
Email: dsager@gossagesager.com
Web: www.gossagesager.com

Summary: We are exclusively devoted to
executive search in academic, public, school,
special and state libraries, in addition to
organizations (non-profits and businesses) that
serve libraries.

Key Contact - Specialty:
Mr. Donald J. Sager, President
Ms. Sarah Long, Vice President
Mr. Daniel Bradbury, Associate
Ms. Muriel Regan, Associate
Mr. Wayne Gossage, Chairman

Salary Minimum: $80,000

Functions: Generalist (All)

Industries: Non-profits, Higher Ed., Government,
Non-Classifiable

Branches:
25 W 43rd St Ste 812
New York, NY 10036-7414
(212) 417-9468
Fax: (212) 997-1127
Key Contact - Specialty:
Ms. Sarah Warner, Associate

Gosselin Associates LLC[†]

99 Anna Farm Rd W
North Stonington, CT 06359-1034
(860) 204-0560
(860) 974-3398
Fax: (860) 889-2805
Email: kevin@gosselin-associates.com
Web: www.gosselin-associates.com

Summary: With an extensive history of expertise
in our field, we specialize in the recruitment of
facilities management professionals in the
healthcare industry. Specifically, our areas of
emphasis include general facilities leadership
positions, plant operations, renovation &
construction program management, safety &
security, bio-medical and project management.
Our hospital clients are nationwide.

Key Contact - Specialty:
Mr. Jack Gosselin, FASHE, Principal
Mr. Kevin Benton, Senior Search Consultant -
*Construction, Environmental, Facilities
engineering, Healthcare, Hospital*

Salary Minimum: $70,000

Functions: Healthcare

Industries: Hospitals

Gould, McCoy, Chadick, Ellig

300 Park Ave
New York, NY 10022-7402
(212) 688-8671
Email: resume@gmce-search.com
Web: www.gmce-search.com

Summary: Executive search firm providing
comprehensive services to corporations in the
identification, assessment and selection of their
management personnel. Known for our
thoroughness, our assessment ability and quality
of our service.

Key Contact - Specialty:
Ms. Susan L. Chadick, Chief Executive Officer -
Financial services, Human resources
Ms. Janice Reals Ellig, President - *Financial
services*
Ms. Stacy Lauren, Managing Director - *Financial
services, Marketing, Restaurants*
Ms. Paula Weiner, Managing Director -
*Advertising, Consumer, Consumer
(Marketing,Packaged Goods), Direct marketing*
Ms. Millington F. McCoy, Co-Founder - *Boards
of Directors*

Salary Minimum: $150,000

Functions: Generalist (All)

Industries: Generalist (All)

The Governance Group Inc

(a Taplow Group company)
33 Union Pl Ste 3
Summit, NJ 07901-3650
(908) 277-1800
Fax: (908) 277-4445
Email: tgg4u@aol.com
Web: www.governancegroup.com

Summary: Generalist firm, committed to
diversity. Emphasizes executive resources
consulting approach supporting relocation,
merger, acquisition, divestiture, or restructuring.
Exceptional expertise in consulting, investment
managers, real estate, telecom, energy, utilities,
technology, investment banking, recruitment for
retirement and benefit plan service providers as
well as consumer products.

Key Contact - Specialty:
Mr. Steven N. Schrenzel, Managing Director -
*Asset management, Marketing, Minorities,
Technology*
Mr. Robert I. Gandel, Managing Director -
Finance, International, Marketing, Sales
Ms. Katrin Dambrot, Managing Director -
Financial services, Marketing
Ms. Cindy Pelham-Webb, Director, Research
Ms. Judy Lerner, Recruiter
Ms. Nana K. Joyner, Recruiter - *CIOs*

Salary Minimum: $90,000

Functions: Board Members, Senior Mgmt., Mktg.
Mgmt., Sales Mgmt., HR Mgmt., Finance,
Minorities/Diversity

Industries: Generalist (All), Construction,
Manufacturing, Food, Bev., Tobacco, Finance,
Accounting, Mgmt. Consulting, HR Services,
Communications, Telecoms, Insurance, Real
Estate, Software, HR SW, Marketing SW

Graham & Company

PO Box 239
Monmouth Beach, NJ 07750-0239
(732) 263-0088
Fax: (732) 222-0804
Email: hscott35@aol.com

Summary: Executive search firm with a
diversified portfolio of clients in traditional and
technology driven organizations handling
executive management assignments in most
functional areas. Considerable activity in precision
metal manufacturing, plastics industry, specialty
chemicals, & finished wood systems.

Key Contact - Specialty:
Mr. Harold Scott, President - *Manufacturing*

Salary Minimum: $75,000

Functions: Generalist (All), Middle Mgmt.,
Admin. Svcs., Production, Plant Mgmt., Quality,
Productivity, Purchasing, Materials Plng., Allied
Health

Industries: Generalist (All), Chemicals, Plastics,
Rubber, Metal Products, Machine, Appliance,
Motor Vehicles, Accounting, Logistics Svcs.,
Supply Chain Mgmt

Grand Roads Executive Search

641 W Lake St Ste 100
Chicago, IL 60661-1055
(312) 207-1190
Fax: (312) 207-1192
Email: info@grandroads.com
Web: www.grandroads.com

Summary: Retained search recruiting with focus on senior management positions.

Key Contact - Specialty:
Mr. Ken Gaebler, President

Salary Minimum: $150,000

Functions: Board Members, Senior Mgmt., Distribution, HR Mgmt., M&A, IT, Engineering

Industries: Energy, Utilities, Retail, Finance, Non-profits, E-commerce, Entertainment, Media, Telecoms, Healthcare

A Davis Grant & Company
13 Lake Park Dr
Piscataway, NJ 08854-5123
(732) 463-1414
Email: info@adg.net
Web: www.adg.net

Summary: Our firm was designed from its inception to be a value added resource for the hiring company to depend on in its selection and staffing of IT professionals. Our clients are some of the most recognized and respected names in industry.

Key Contact - Specialty:
Mr. Allan D. Grossman, Senior Partner

Salary Minimum: $100,000

Functions: IT, MIS Mgmt., Systems Analysis, Systems Dev., Systems Implem., Systems Support

Industries: Generalist (All)

Grant Cooper & Associates Inc
222 S Meramec Ave Ste 202
Saint Louis, MO 63105-3514
(314) 726-5290
(800) 886-4690
Email: resume@grantcooper.com
Web: www.grantcooper.com

Summary: Executive search consultants specializing in upper and middle management searches. Broad experience in most industries including: healthcare, financial services, technology, bio-technology, manufacturing, retail and not-for-profit, including most investment banking and capital markets disciplines.

Key Contact - Specialty:
Mr. James Schmidt, Managing Partner
Mr. Michael Taylor, Managing Partner
Ms. Susan Cejka, Managing Partner
Mr. J. Dale Meier, Managing Partner
Mr. Kent Rapp, Partner
Ms. Carrie Hackett, Partner
Ms. Nancy Williams, Consultant
Ms. Ginny Gittemeier, Consultant
Ms. Terry Spink, Consultant
Ms. Kimberly Ratier, Associate Consultant
Ms. Beth Gordon, Associate Consultant

Salary Minimum: $100,000

Functions: Senior Mgmt.

Industries: Manufacturing, Wholesale, Retail, Finance, Services, Hospitality, Media, Aerospace, Biotech/Life Sciences, Healthcare

Grantham, Griffin & Buck Inc
121 Steeplechase Rd
Chapel Hill, NC 27514-1425
(919) 942-8185
Email: info@ggbinc.com
Web: www.integritycareers.com

Summary: We are a small, intensive generalist firm that is highly responsive to client needs. We have strong, long-term relationships with our clients. We offer solid experience with service, healthcare, pharmaceutical, manufacturing

industries, non-profit organizations, as well as universities and colleges. We have long-term professional relationships with Fortune 500 Corporations as well as small privately/family held corporations.

Key Contact - Specialty:
Mr. John Buck, Vice President

Salary Minimum: $100,000

Functions: Generalist (All), Senior Mgmt., Purchasing, Mktg. Research, Benefits, Staffing, CFOs, R&D

Industries: Generalist (All), Textiles, Apparel, Lumber, Furniture, Drugs Mfg., Medical Devices, Retail, Finance, Non-profits, Pharm Svcs., Healthcare

Graphic Arts Employment Specialists
409 N Pacific Coast Hwy Ste 455
Redondo Beach, CA 90277-2870
(818) 499-9722
(888) 712-0857
Email: career@gaes.com
Web: www.gaes.com

Summary: Our firm is a professional recruiting and placement operation. We provide the printing and publishing industries with the finest management and production personnel available.

Key Contact - Specialty:
Ms. Barbara Wolford, General Manager
Ms. Jolene Caruso-Soares, Executive Associate, Publishing - *Editorial*

Functions: Management, Graphic Designers

Industries: Printing, Media, Publishing

Grasslands Group†
(also known as Western Canadian Search)
5-244 1st Ave NE
Swift Current, SK S9H 2B4
Canada
(306) 778-0570
(888) 778-0570
Fax: (306) 778-6403
Email: info@grasslandsgroup.com
Web: www.grasslandsgroup.com

Summary: We are a private Employment Services firm that provides Executive Search, RPO and Testing and Assessment services to international employers and job placement services to candidates throughout Western Canada and the Prairie Provinces.

Key Contact - Specialty:
Mr. Blair Clark, General Manager - *Controllers, Engineering, Executives, Manufacturing, Sales*
Ms. Susan McLaughlin, Administrator & Executive Assistant

Salary Minimum: $75,000

Functions: Generalist (All), Management, Sales Mgmt., Sales Reps.

Industries: Generalist (All)

Annie Gray Associates Inc
225 S Meramec Ave Ste 425T
Saint Louis, MO 63105-5801
(314) 721-0205
Email: resume-ag@anniegray.com
Web: www.anniegray.com

Summary: We are a boutique firm exclusive to representing the leading corporations and non-profits. Our Electuaries by our division is a service for CEOs only. It brings the executive and the crème de la crème executive secretary together. All assignments are on retainer.

Key Contact - Specialty:
Ms. Annie Gray, President & Chief Executive Officer

Salary Minimum: $60,000

Functions: Generalist (All), Board Members, Senior Mgmt., Mfg., CFOs, Non-profits

Industries: Generalist (All), Non-profits

Grech Associates Executive Search Inc
(formerly known as Grech Associates)
1205-20 Bay St
WaterPark Place
Toronto, ON M5J 2N8
Canada
(416) 862-9987
Email: growthleaders@grechexec.com
Web: www.grechexec.com

Summary: We deliver a new approach to research-based, retained search. We're the only firm in North America to guarantee the performance of a placed executive within their first year on board.

Key Contact - Specialty:
Mr. Peter Grech, Managing Director

Salary Minimum: $90,000

Functions: Management, Senior Mgmt.

Industries: Banking, Invest. Banking, Venture Cap., Mutual/Hedge Funds, Accounting, Mgmt. Consulting, Telecoms, Call Centers, Wireless, Insurance, Software

Sheila Greco Associates LLC†
174 State Highway 67
Amsterdam, NY 12010-7310
(518) 843-4611
(888) 400-8049
Fax: (518) 843-5498
Email: info@sheilagreco.com
Web: www.sheilagreco.com

Summary: We are a full service recruiting firm. We specialize in executive search, research and competitive analysis. We partner with our clients to develop long term relationships. We work within your budget. Our new division allows our customers to purchase the most accurate executive names in the Fortune 1000.

Key Contact - Specialty:
Ms. Sheila Greco, President
Mr. Joseph Morse, Senior Vice President
Mr. Stephen Coffey, Executive Recruiter

Salary Minimum: $50,000

Functions: Generalist (All), Senior Mgmt., Mktg. Research, CFOs, IT, Mgmt. Consultants

Industries: Generalist (All), Manufacturing, Finance, Banking, Pharm Svcs., IT Implementation, Hospitality, Media, Advertising, Telecoms

A Greenstein & Company
20 Vernon St
Norwood, MA 02062-2184
(781) 769-4966

Summary: We provide unbundled services, including: research and/or telephone screening, as well as full-service search. Our clients are primarily in the high-technology, biomedical and defense industries.

Key Contact - Specialty:
Ms. Arlene Bachant, President - *Engineering, General management*

Functions: Management

Industries: Computer Equip., Consumer Elect., Robotics, Semiconductors, Mgmt. Consulting, Defense, Aerospace, Software

Greger/Peterson Associates Inc

22208 Skyview Dr
West Linn, OR 97068-8232
(503) 655-4100
Fax: (503) 655-4600
Email: confidential@gregerpeterson.com

Summary: Culture-sensitive, organizational approach dedicated to quality results and client service. Principals have national firm backgrounds. Specialists in the following verticals: eBusiness, technology, entertainment, hospitality and leisure. Senior-level searches only. Exclusively-retained.

Key Contact - Specialty:
Mr. Kenneth R. Greger, Managing Director - *E-business, Entertainment*
Ms. Donna Daniels, Assistant to Managing Director

Salary Minimum: $150,000

Functions: Generalist (All), Senior Mgmt., Healthcare, Mktg. Mgmt., Sales Mgmt.

Industries: Generalist (All), Medical Devices, Consumer Elect., Mgmt. Consulting, E-commerce, Hospitality, Media, New Media, Communications, Software, Biotech/Life Sciences, Healthcare

Branches:
582 27th St
Manhattan Beach, CA 90266-2210
(310) 546-8555
Fax: (310) 546-8550
Email: confidential@gregerpeterson.com
Key Contact - Specialty:
Mr. John S. Peterson, Managing Director

Greywolf Consulting Service Inc

1613 S Capital of Texas Hwy Ste 202
Austin, TX 78746-6545
(512) 732-0700 x205
Fax: (512) 732-0716
Email: talktous@greywolfconsulting.com
Web: www.greywolfconsulting.com

Summary: Retained search firm practice specializing in mid to senior-level management/executive assignments in leading edge technology industries, including semiconductor, capital equipment, communications and CAE.

Key Contact - Specialty:
Mr. Kim Butler, Owner

Functions: Senior Mgmt., Middle Mgmt., Product Dev., Mktg. Mgmt., Sales Mgmt., HR Mgmt., Finance, MIS Mgmt.

Industries: Electronic, Elec. Components, Communications, Telecoms, Call Centers, Network Infrastructure, Software

Griffith & Werner Inc

(a Taplow Group company)
PO Box 165134
Miami, FL 33116-5134
(305) 598-5600
(786) 249-0575
Email: geo@griff-wern.com
Web: www.taplowgroup.com

Summary: Senior executive and upper-management search consulting services, as well as senior-level assignments.

Key Contact - Specialty:
Mr. Warland Griffith, III, President
Mr. George Griffith, Managing Partner - *Latin America*

Salary Minimum: $100,000

Functions: Senior Mgmt., Plant Mgmt., Materials Plng., Mktg. Mgmt., HR Mgmt., CFOs, Int'l.

Industries: Drugs Mfg., Medical Devices, Consumer Goods, Pharm Svcs.

C John Grom Executive Search Inc

868 Thelma Dr
Wadsworth, OH 44281-9253
(330) 336-2213
Fax: (330) 336-2035
Email: ribrom@aol.com
Web: www.cjohngrom.webpointusa.com

Summary: We recruit at the CEO, COO, CFO and VP level for a variety of industries. Some of our most recent active clients are private equity firms looking for leadership for new acquisitions.

Key Contact - Specialty:
Mr. C. John Grom, Principal

Salary Minimum: $100,000

Functions: Generalist (All), Management, Senior Mgmt., Middle Mgmt., Plant Mgmt., Sales & Mktg., HR Mgmt., CFOs

Industries: Generalist (All), Telecoms

Richard Gros & Associates

35 Mason St
Greenwich, CT 06830-5433
(203) 861-9726
Fax: (203) 618-1828
Email: rgros83@aol.com
Web: www.richardgros.com

Summary: Our firm specializes in senior-level searches in the communications, consumer products, pharmaceutical/medical, retail and venture capital sectors.

Key Contact - Specialty:
Mr. Richard Roger Gros, Founder & President

Salary Minimum: $300,000

Functions: Generalist (All), Board Members

Industries: Generalist (All), Food, Bev., Tobacco, Chemicals, Retail, HR Services, Advertising

Grossberg & Associates

805 W Fitzhenry Ct
Glenwood, IL 60425-1114
(708) 755-0385
Email: bobgsearch@aol.com
Web: www.card.netscape.com/bobgsearch

Summary: Human recources professionals whose sole function is to assist clients in developing a talented management staff.

Key Contact - Specialty:
Mr. Robert M. Grossberg, Managing Partner

Salary Minimum: $80,000

Functions: Mfg., Materials, Sales & Mktg., HR Mgmt., Finance, Engineering

Industries: Manufacturing, Chemicals, Plastics, Rubber, Paints, Petro. Products, Metal Products, Machine, Appliance, Motor Vehicles, Misc. Mfg., Services, Packaging, Marketing SW

Groton Planning Group

4 Otter Trce
Brunswick, ME 04011-7379
(207) 373-0467
Email: stevek@suscom-maine.net

Summary: Sole practitioner.

Key Contact - Specialty:
Mr. Stephan J. Kornacki, Principal

Functions: Middle Mgmt., Physicians, Sales & Mktg., Mktg. Research, Mktg. Mgmt., Sales Mgmt., Sales Reps.

Industries: Drugs Mfg., Medical Devices, Pharm Svcs., Biotech/Life Sciences, Healthcare

Groupe Ranger Inc†

1411 Rue Peel
Edifice Marine
Montreal, QC H3A 1S5
Canada
(514) 844-1746
Fax: (514) 844-6996
Email: info@groupe-ranger.com
Web: www.groupe-ranger.com

Summary: We are very active in searches for companies established in francophone countries, by supplying French speaking outstanding MIS candidate.

Key Contact - Specialty:
Mr. Jean-Jacques Ranger, President
Ms. Lise Hebert, Senior Parnter
Mr. Normand Leduc, Senior Parnter

Salary Minimum: $65,000

Functions: Generalist (All), Management, Mfg., Materials, HR Mgmt., IT

Industries: Generalist (All)

Groupe SFP

3343 Rue Foucher
Trois-Rivieres, QC G8Z 1M8
Canada
(819) 373-8208
(877) 373-8208
Fax: (819) 373-8165
Email: resshum@groupe-sfp.com
Web: www.groupe-sfp.com

Summary: Selection, human resources, consultant, health and safety in the workplace, labor relations, mediation, and training.

Key Contact - Specialty:
Mr. Francois Massicotte, Chief Executive Officer - *Human resources*
Ms. Tracey Ann Powers, Personnel Coordinator - *Human resources*

Functions: Generalist (All)

Industries: Generalist (All)

Branches:
193 Rue Lindsay
Drummondville, QC J2C 1N8
Canada
(819) 474-6898
Fax: (819) 474-5011
Email: fmassicotte@groupe-sfp.com

450 Boul Sainte-Anne
Joliette, QC J6E 4Z9
Canada
(450) 753-3052
Fax: (450) 753-7938
Email: atousignant@groupe-sfp.com
Key Contact - Specialty:
Mr. Andree Tousignant, Consultant, Human Resources

Groves & Partners Inc

1401 Daniel Creek Rd
Mississauga, ON L5V 1V3
Canada
(905) 567-9247
Fax: (905) 567-9469

Email: barry@grovesintl.com
Web: www.grovesintl.com

Summary: We recruit for all of the strategic requirements of today's logistics, distribution and transportation fields. We recruit for private and public corporations, third party/distribution providers and major transportation companies.

Key Contact - Specialty:
Mr. Barry Groves, Partner - *Logistics, Transportation*

Salary Minimum: $40,000

Functions: Generalist (All), Management, Materials, Sales & Mktg., HR Mgmt., Finance

Industries: Generalist (All), Manufacturing, Transportation, Retail, Equip Svcs., Mgmt. Consulting, HR Services, Non-Classifiable

Wolf Gugler & Associates Ltd

300-1370 Don Mills Rd
North York, ON M3B 3N7
Canada
(888) 848-3006
Email: resumes@wolfgugler.com
Web: www.wolfgugler.com

Summary: Our firm has expertise in retainer based executive search and management appraisals of top performers. We have in depth knowledge of home improvement, hardware and housewares, retailers, and their suppliers in both the US and Canada. Significant work is also performed in the sales & marketing disciplines. We also utilize online testing.

Key Contact - Specialty:
Mr. Wolf Gugler, President - *Building products, Consumer (Durables,Hard Goods), Hardware, Housewares*
Ms. Lesley Fulton, Senior Associate - *Building products, Consumer (Durables,Hard Goods), Hardware, Housewares*
Ms. Maria Vieria, Manager, Business, Canada - *Human resources, Retail*

Salary Minimum: $55,000

Functions: Management, Senior Mgmt., Middle Mgmt., Sales Mgmt

Industries: Lumber, Furniture, Paints, Petro. Products, Machine, Appliance, Consumer Elect., Consumer Goods, Retail

Branches:
1530 N Harrison Ste 168
Shawnee, OK 74804-4021
(405) 848-3006
Email: resumes@wolfgugler.com
Key Contact - Specialty:
Ms. Linn Henderson, Manager, Business - *Hardware, Housewares, Human resources*

Guidry & East Healthcare Search Consultants[†]

2951 Marina Bay Dr Ste 130
League City, TX 77573-4078
(281) 535-2001
Fax: (281) 535-2010
Email: jim@guidryeast.com
Web: www.guidryeast.com

Summary: Client-retained medical and healthcare searches and related consulting services in recruiting executives and middle-management.

Key Contact - Specialty:
Mr. Jim Guidry, President - *Healthcare*

Salary Minimum: $50,000

Functions: Management, Senior Mgmt., Middle Mgmt., Healthcare

Industries: Healthcare, Hospitals, Physical Therapy, Occupational Therapy, Women's

Gundersen Partners LLC

655 Montgomery St Ste 860
San Francisco, CA 94111-2628
(415) 441-3777
Fax: (415) 775-4925
Email: nfink@gpllc.com
Web: www.gpllc.com

Summary: We are an executive search consultancy servicing the media, entertainment, communications and technology industries. Our expertise is cross functional in the industry verticals served. We are retained to complete senior level searches in every function, including C-level general management, marketing, sales, finance, engineering and creative.

Key Contact - Specialty:
Mr. Neil Fink, Managing Partner
Ms. Katy Scott, Consultant - *Manufacturing*

Salary Minimum: $150,000

Functions: Generalist (All), Senior Mgmt., Product Dev., Mktg. Mgmt., Sales Mgmt., Engineering, Int'l.

Industries: Generalist (All), Computer Equip., Consumer Elect., Misc. Financial, E-commerce, Media, Communications, Wireless, Software

Gundersen Partners LLC

30 Irving Pl Fl 2
New York, NY 10003-2303
(212) 677-7660
Fax: (212) 358-0275
Email: jgundersen@gpllc.com
Web: www.gundersenpartners.com

Summary: Specializes in all facets of consumer marketing. Blue chip client base includes multinational corporations and advertising, direct marketing, marketing services agencies.

Key Contact - Specialty:
Mr. Steven G. Gundersen, Chief Executive Officer - *Advertising, General management*
Ms. Tina Moore, Managing Partner
Mr. Peter Fitzpatrick, President - *Financial services, International*
Mr. Jon Gundersen, Operations Manager
Mr. Leo Parente, Senior Parnter

Salary Minimum: $100,000

Functions: Management, Sales & Mktg., Advertising

Industries: Generalist (All), Manufacturing, Consumer Elect., Retail, Finance, Services, Media, Advertising, New Media, Communications, Packaging, Insurance

Branches:
100 W Long Lake Rd Ste 121
Bloomfield Hills, MI 48304-2773
(248) 258-3800
Fax: (248) 258-9747
Email: edtazzia@mindspring.com
Key Contact - Specialty:
Mr. Ed Tazzia, Managing Director - *Technology*
Ms. Susan Storts, Consultant

Gustin Partners

2276 Washington St
Newton Lower Falls, MA 02462-1440
(617) 332-0800
Fax: (617) 332-0882
Email: info@gustinpartners.com
Web: www.gustinpartners.com

Summary: Our executive search, team building and market alignment capabilities give boards of directors, CEOs and private-equity investors the talent and the knowledge required to create measurable value in the most challenging of markets.

Key Contact - Specialty:
Mr. Charles Gustin, Managing Partner

Salary Minimum: $150,000

Functions: Generalist (All), Senior Mgmt., Mktg. Mgmt., Sales Mgmt., CFOs, MIS Mgmt., Systems Implem., Int'l.

Industries: Generalist (All), Energy, Utilities, Computer Equip., Finance, Venture Cap., Mgmt. Consulting, Telecoms, Wireless, Software, Networking, Comm. SW, Security SW

Gynn Associates Inc

2207 Bay Club Cir
Tampa, FL 33607-5941
(813) 282-7480
Fax: (813) 282-7330
Email: gynnsearch@aol.com
Web: www.gynncorp.com

Summary: Proven ability to interpret the operational and organizational needs of clients while attracting, assessing and acquiring the human solution required attaining the business objectives of the client.

Key Contact - Specialty:
Mr. Walter T. Gynn, President - *Construction, Manufacturing, Real estate*

Salary Minimum: $100,000

Functions: Generalist (All), Management, Board Members, Senior Mgmt., Middle Mgmt., Sales & Mktg., Mktg. Mgmt., Sales Mgmt., HR Mgmt., CFOs

Industries: Construction, Real Estate

Haddad Associates

PO Box 462
Tarpon Springs, FL 34688-0462
(727) 939-8078
Email: rjhaddad@gte.net
Web: www.haddadassociates.com

Summary: Small executive search firm providing retained search services for mid and senior management positions. General practice. We place an emphasis in consulting industries.

Key Contact - Specialty:
Mr. Ronald J. Haddad, President

Salary Minimum: $75,000

Functions: Generalist (All)

Industries: Generalist (All), Mgmt. Consulting

Hadley Lockwood Inc

17 State St Fl 38
New York, NY 10004-1537
(212) 785-4405
Fax: (212) 785-4415
Email: info@hadleylockwood.com
Web: www.hadleylockwood.com

Summary: Executive search and recruitment for financial and investment companies, with concentration in investment banking, alternative investments, capital markets, securities research, retail regional and branch management. Consulting services regarding entire reorganizations, additional departments and new businesses for the same client.

Key Contact - Specialty:
Mr. Irwin Brandon, President - *Securities*
Mr. George McGough, Executive Vice President - *Securities*

Salary Minimum: $100,000

Functions: Generalist (All)

Industries: Finance, Invest. Banking, Brokers, Venture Cap., Misc. Financial

Haggerman & Associates
3447 S Campbell Ave
Springfield, MO 65807-5101
(417) 881-8639
(800) 378-3554
Fax: (417) 889-6176
Email: lynne@haggermanandassociates.com
Web: www.haggermanandassociates.com

Summary: We are a human resources consulting firm providing four primary services: retained search, outplacement, public and in-house group and one-on-one management training programs, and human resource consulting.

Key Contact - Specialty:
Ms. Lynne Haggerman, President & Owner
Mrs. Tonya Eddington, BS, Consultant, Human Resources
Ms. Joyce Vanhook, BS, Consultant, Human Resources

Functions: Generalist (All)

Industries: Generalist (All)

Halbrecht Lieberman Associates Inc
32 Surf Rd Ste A
Westport, CT 06880-6733
(203) 222-4890
Fax: (203) 222-4895
Email: infor@hlassoc.com
Web: www.hlassoc.com

Summary: We specialize in the field of IT across all industries. Most often, we recruit CIOs, CTOs and senior IT executives who report to the CIO.

Key Contact - Specialty:
Ms. Beverly Lieberman, President - *Executives*
Mr. Roger Rowell, Vice President & CIO - *Operations*

Salary Minimum: $175,000

Functions: IT, MIS Mgmt.

Industries: Generalist (All)

Hale & Estrada LLC
3553A Atlantic Ave Ste 326
Long Beach, CA 90807-4515
(562) 424-6868
Email: info@hale-estrada.com
Web: www.hale-estrada.com

Summary: Extensive years of executive recruiting in high technology and public sector. Search capabilities includes assessment tools and ability to deliver the broadest pool of candidates representing today's diverse marketplace.

Key Contact - Specialty:
Ms. Barbara Estrada, Senior Parnter - *Diversity, High technology, Senior management*
Mr. Dick Hale, Senior Parnter - *High technology, Senior management*

Salary Minimum: $100,000

Functions: Management

Industries: Finance, Digital, Wireless, Government, Software, HR SW, Marketing SW, Networking, Comm. SW, Biotech/Life Sciences, Healthcare

Hale Associates
1816 N Sedgwick St
Chicago, IL 60614-5306
(312) 337-3288
Fax: (312) 337-3451

Email: mdhale@ameritech.net

Summary: We service the executive search industry and specialize in research and sourcing services. The firm customizes these services to meet client needs.

Key Contact - Specialty:
Ms. Maureen D. Hale, President - *General management*

Salary Minimum: $50,000

Functions: Generalist (All), Senior Mgmt., Mktg. Mgmt., Sales Mgmt., CFOs, Cash Mgmt., Mgmt. Consultants

Industries: Generalist (All), Metal Products, Banking, Invest. Banking, Brokers, Accounting, Mgmt. Consulting

K C Hale Inc
PO Box 1215
Avon, CT 06001-1215
(860) 675-7511
Fax: (860) 677-0354
Email: kathyd@kchale.com
Web: www.kchale.com

Summary: We have extensive search capability and experience in management, retirement services and healthcare. We focus on sales, marketing and operations positions.

Key Contact - Specialty:
Ms. Kathryn H. Dumanis, President
Ms. Kathleen M. McCormack, Vice President

Salary Minimum: $100,000

Functions: Generalist (All), Board Members, Senior Mgmt., Sales & Mktg., Mktg. Research, Sales Mgmt., Risk Mgmt.

Industries: Invest. Banking, Brokers, Mutual/Hedge Funds, Misc. Financial, Accounting, HR Services, Insurance, Healthcare

Michael J Hall & Company†
19578 10th Ave NE
Poulsbo, WA 98370-7332
(360) 598-3700
(800) 583-0379
Fax: (360) 697-3744
Email: krysten@aejob.com
Web: www.aejob.com

Summary: We provide Recruiting Consulting, Insurance Brokerage, and Management Consulting firm to the A/E industry.

Key Contact - Specialty:
Mr. Michael J. Hall, President
Mrs. Krysten Wilder, Recruiter

Functions: CFOs, Engineering, Environmentalists, Architects, Technicians

Industries: Generalist (All)

The Halyburton Company Inc
6201 Fairview Rd Ste 200
Charlotte, NC 28210-3297
(704) 556-9892
Email: bob@halyburtonco.com
Web: www.halyburtonco.com

Summary: We offer many years of search experience in most industries and disciplines. We strive for excellence in representing our clients and in evaluating prospective candidates.

Key Contact - Specialty:
Mr. Robert R. Halyburton, President

Salary Minimum: $80,000

Functions: Senior Mgmt., Plant Mgmt., Sales & Mktg., HR Mgmt., CFOs, Non-profits

Industries: Generalist (All), Agri., Forestry, Mining, Manufacturing, Lumber, Furniture, Plastics, Rubber, Metal Products, Misc. Mfg., Non-profits, Higher Ed., Logistics Svcs., Supply Chain Mgmt

The Hamilton Group
198 Waterton
Williamsburg, VA 23188-8400
(301) 530-9407
Email: boguski@cox.net
Web: www.hamiltongroup.com

Summary: Clients consist of Fortune 500, venture capital funded/emerging companies in the high-technology industry. Partners, former executives from industry, serve as advisors to board of directors, presidents, CEOs and senior management.

Key Contact - Specialty:
Mr. Ronald T. Boguski, Partner - *Professional services, Telecommunications*

Salary Minimum: $150,000

Functions: Generalist (All), Board Members, Senior Mgmt., Mfg., Sales & Mktg., CFOs, MIS Mgmt.

Industries: Generalist (All), Computer Equip., Test, Measure Equip., Electronic, Elec. Components, Telecoms, Digital, Wireless, Fiber Optic, Aerospace, Software, Mfg. SW

Hamilton Partners
1 Gorham Island Rd
Westport, CT 06880-3212
(203) 221-9111
Fax: (203) 221-9190
Email: research@hamiltonpartners.cc
Web: www.hamiltonpartners.cc

Summary: We have built our firm one stone at a time, ensuring that each new principal shares similar philosophies and has complementary skills and experience. Our firm's principals possess a diverse set of experiences and expertise in executive search, strategy development, HR practices, leadership and change management consulting, as well as broad operational and HR line management.

Key Contact - Specialty:
Mr. Peter F. Murphy, Managing Partner
Mr. James Calvan, Partner
Mr. Michael Murphy, Partner
Mr. Fred Lane, Partner

Salary Minimum: $250,000

Functions: Generalist (All), Management, Senior Mgmt., Sales & Mktg., HR Mgmt., CFOs, M&A, IT

Industries: Generalist (All), Manufacturing, Finance, Venture Cap., Services, Publishing, Communications, Telecoms, Wireless, Network Infrastructure

Hamilton-Chase & Associates Inc
PO Box 237
Gloucester, MA 01931-0237
(978) 281-1759
Email: jrusso@hamilton-chase.com
Web: www.hamilton-chase.com

Summary: We are an executive and technical search firm working across multiple industries including high technology. Client organizations range in size from start-ups to Fortune 500. We employ quantitative interviewing/reference checking methodology, significantly improving candidate selection.

Key Contact - Specialty:
Mr. Joseph E. Russo, President

Salary Minimum: $100,000

Functions: Generalist (All), Management, Mfg., Sales & Mktg., HR Mgmt., Finance, IT, Engineering

Industries: Generalist (All), Manufacturing, Finance, Media, Aerospace, Software, Biotech/Life Sciences

Hamilton-Ryker

PO Box 1068
947 E Main St
Martin, TN 38237-1068
(731) 587-3161
Fax: (731) 587-3195
Email: bcollins@hamilton-ryker.com
Web: www.hamilton-ryker.com

Summary: Firm specializes in search activities for engineers and manufacturing, data processing, banking & finance, personnel and all disciplines. Also outplacement, management consulting and temp staffing.

Key Contact - Specialty:
Mr. Wayne McCreight, Owner
Ms. Shannon Holleran, Regional Vice President

Salary Minimum: $40,000

Functions: Generalist (All), Senior Mgmt., Mfg., Purchasing, Mktg. Mgmt., HR Mgmt., Finance

Industries: Generalist (All), Motor Vehicles, Finance, Accounting, HR Services, Media, Insurance

Hammann & Associates[†]

3540 Blue Rock Rd Ste 2
Cincinnati, OH 45239-5107
(513) 385-2528
Fax: (513) 385-2512
Email: edhammann@fuse.net

Summary: We are a retained executive search firm. We serve clients in multiple industries with emphasis on legal, management and senior technical positions.

Key Contact - Specialty:
Mr. Ed Hammann, Owner - *Management*

Salary Minimum: $50,000

Functions: Generalist (All), Management

Industries: Generalist (All), Manufacturing, Semiconductors, Finance, Services, Legal, Mgmt. Consulting, E-commerce, Call Centers, Software, Entertainment SW, Security SW, Healthcare, Physical Therapy, Occupational Therapy

Hampton Consulting, LLC

6080 Center Dr Ste 600
Los Angeles, CA 90045-1540
(310) 823-1850
Fax: (310) 822-1216
Web: www.hamptonsearch.com

Summary: Executive search and consulting firm specializing in senior-level assignments within the financial services industry. Member of the AESC and IACPR.

Key Contact - Specialty:
Ms. Lynn A. Williams, President - *Banking (Investment), Competitive intelligence, Consumer (Products), Middle management, Senior management*

Salary Minimum: $175,000

Functions: Generalist (All)

Industries: Generalist (All), Manufacturing, Finance, Banking, Invest. Banking, Brokers, Venture Cap., Mutual/Hedge Funds, Communications, Insurance

Handler & Associates

(a World Search Group company)
2255 Cumberland Pkwy SE Ste 1500
Atlanta, GA 30339-4534
(770) 805-5000
Fax: (770) 805-5011
Email: info@handler.com
Web: www.handler.com

Summary: Our firm serves the business community; we have grown from a small generalist executive search firm into a mid-sized firm with a large national reach. We are known throughout the industry for our rapid response rate and customer attention, unique fee schedule, high percent of completion and ethical standards. All of the firm's search assignments are backed by a satisfaction and length of employment guarantee.

Key Contact - Specialty:
Mr. William L. Handler, Founder & Chief Executive Officer

Salary Minimum: $100,000

Functions: Generalist (All), Management, Mfg., Materials, Sales & Mktg., HR Mgmt., Finance, IT

Industries: Generalist (All), Energy, Utilities, Oil & Gas, Paper, Chemicals, Metal Products, Consumer Elect., Banking, Telecoms, Packaging, Healthcare

Handley Group Inc

3655 Route 202 Ste 105
Doylestown, PA 18902-6602
(215) 340-1820
Fax: (215) 340-1846
Email: rrodenbaugh@hgsearch.com
Web: www.hgsearch.com

Summary: Senior executive search for the healthcare industry. Specializing in medical devices, diagnostics, biotechnology, life sciences, biopharmaceuticals and pharmaceuticals.

Key Contact - Specialty:
Mr. Robert Rodenbaugh, Managing Partner - *Healthcare*

Salary Minimum: $100,000

Functions: Generalist (All), Management, Board Members, Senior Mgmt., Sales & Mktg., Mktg. Mgmt.

Industries: Generalist (All), Drugs Mfg., Medical Devices, Biotech/Life Sciences, Healthcare

Hands-on Broadcast[†]

124 W 24th St Ste 6B
New York, NY 10011-1922
(212) 924-5036
Fax: (212) 604-9036
Email: bgspeed@aol.com
Web: www.jobopts.com

Summary: We offer senior creative management as well as executive marketing and sales executives for television and entertainment. We also place designers and producers for TV and after effects and special effects artists for television, film and animation. Senior creative management is our specialty.

Key Contact - Specialty:
Ms. Lorraine Bege, President - *Cable, Entertainment*

Salary Minimum: $40,000

Functions: Generalist (All), Middle Mgmt., Advertising, Mktg. Mgmt., Direct Mktg., Graphic Designers, Int'l.

Industries: Generalist (All), Hospitality, Media, Advertising, Publishing, New Media, Broadcast, Film

Handy Associates Corp

(also known as Handy Partners)
420 Lexington Ave Rm 1644
New York, NY 10170-1699
(212) 697-5600
Fax: (212) 697-8547
Email: pbrennan@handypartners.com
Web: www.handypartners.com

Summary: We serve all major industries including advertising, consumer packaged goods, publishing, finance/investment banking, insurance, manufacturing, pharmaceuticals, telecom, eCommerce, the international maritime & transportation industries and IT.

Key Contact - Specialty:
Mr. Patrick J. Brennan, Managing Partner - *Finance*
Mr. Gaffney J. Feskoe, Partner - *Finance*
Mr. Chester A. Hopkins, Partner - *General management, Marketing*

Salary Minimum: $100,000

Functions: Management, Senior Mgmt., Mfg., Production, Mktg. Mgmt., CFOs, IT, MIS Mgmt., Network Admin., Minorities/Diversity

Industries: Generalist (All)

Hanley & Associates

1101 Pennsylvania Ave NW Ste 600
Washington, DC 20004-2544
(202) 756-4952
Email: hanleyassoc@aol.com

Summary: Our firm has special strengths in placing mid and upper-management, IT managers in medical/healthcare, financial services and high-technology industries.

Key Contact - Specialty:
Ms. Dorothy Hanley-Lowrie, President

Salary Minimum: $100,000

Functions: Management, Healthcare, Finance, IT, MIS Mgmt.

Industries: Generalist (All), Banking, Mgmt. Consulting, IT Implementation, Software, Healthcare

The Hanover Consulting Group[†]

11707 Hunters Run Dr
Hunt Valley, MD 21030-1986
(410) 785-1912
Fax: (410) 785-1913
Email: info@thehanovergroup.net
Web: www.thehanovergroup.net

Summary: Our firm specializes in finding and evaluating top talent for the banking and trust industries. Our evaluation process matches the likes, dislikes and personality of the individual with the goals, activities and culture of the company. Our process helps people to further their career with more job satisfaction and enable companies to achieve their business goals with more consistent performance and lower turnover.

Key Contact - Specialty:
Mr. Thomas D.B. Graff, CSAM, President - *Banking, Banking (Commercial, Corporate, Retail), Investment management*

Salary Minimum: $50,000

Functions: Senior Mgmt., Middle Mgmt., Productivity, Sales & Mktg., Cash Mgmt., Pension/Ret. Planning

Industries: Finance, Banking, Invest. Banking, Brokers, Mutual/Hedge Funds, Misc. Financial

Bente Hansen Executive Search

12707 High Bluff Dr Fl 2
San Diego, CA 92130-2223
(858) 350-4330
Fax: (760) 634-1533
Email: bente@bentehansen.com
Web: www.bentehansen.com

Summary: Our firm is a retained executive search firm specializing in start-up and mid-sized research and technology based companies. The managing directors are experts at conducting retained searches in the fields of: bioscience, telecom, software, hardware, eCommerce and non-profit service industries at senior management levels.

Key Contact - Specialty:
Dr. Bente Hansen, PhD, Principal
Dr. Mary Colacicco, PhD, Managing Director, Research

Salary Minimum: $100,000

Functions: Generalist (All), Management, Board Members, Senior Mgmt., Physicians, Sales & Mktg.

Industries: Biotech/Life Sciences

Hansen Executive Search Inc

12206 Charles Plz Apt 6
Omaha, NE 68154-1365
(402) 697-7960
Fax: (402) 697-7959

Summary: Executive recruitment in consumer packaged goods, specializing in sales/marketing management, MIS, manufacturing and general management.

Key Contact - Specialty:
Mr. James P. Hansen, President

Salary Minimum: $50,000

Functions: Generalist (All), Management, Plant Mgmt., Sales & Mktg., Advertising, Mktg. Research, Mktg. Mgmt., Sales Mgmt.

Industries: Generalist (All), Food, Bev., Tobacco, Paper, Soap, Perf., Cosmtcs., Drugs Mfg., Consumer Goods, Transportation, Finance, Media

Ronald B Hanson Associates†

N9620 Beach Ln
Merrillan, WI 54754-8037
(715) 333-7020
(715) 333-8602
Fax: (715) 333-2811
Email: rbhassoc@aol.com

Summary: We are a specialized financial services boutique search firm targeting primarily the insurance industry. Our smaller client list allows us expansive access to quality candidate sources.

Key Contact - Specialty:
Mr. Ron Hanson, Owner

Salary Minimum: $60,000

Functions: Generalist (All)

Industries: Insurance

Hanzel & Company Inc

420 Lexington Ave Rm 400
New York, NY 10170-0499
(212) 972-1832

Summary: Principal area of practice is in senior management for revenue producing functions of investment banking.

Key Contact - Specialty:
Mr. Bruce S. Hanzel, Principal
Mr. Robert T. Anderson, Principal

Salary Minimum: $80,000

Functions: Management, M&A

Industries: Invest. Banking, Brokers

Harcor Quest & Associates†

27389 Detroit Rd Apt J23
Westlake, OH 44145-2217
(440) 871-5177
Fax: (440) 871-5185
Email: harcorquest@yahoo.com

Summary: We are a full-service executive search and recruitment firm meeting the wide range of management needs of client companies from both the service and industrial sectors.

Key Contact - Specialty:
Ms. Rachel Taylor, Managing Director - *Senior management*

Salary Minimum: $60,000

Functions: Management, Mfg., Product Dev., Production, Plant Mgmt., Mktg. Research, R&D, Engineering

Industries: Chemicals, Soap, Perf., Cosmtcs., Drugs Mfg., Medical Devices, Plastics, Rubber, Paints, Petro. Products, Metal Products, Motor Vehicles, Test, Measure Equip., Misc. Mfg., Electronic, Elec. Components, Biotech/Life Sciences, Healthcare

Harcourt Group Ltd

2178 Harcourt Dr
Cleveland Heights, OH 44106-4613
(216) 791-6000
(216) 791-6205
Fax: (216) 795-1522
Email: jkh@harcourtgroup.com
Web: www.harcourtgroup.com

Summary: Together the principals combine the highest level of achievement in research and search methodology. A boutique format has allowed them to deliver the quality and attention which clients deserve.

Key Contact - Specialty:
Mr. James P. Herget, Co-Owner - *Financial services, Industrial*
Mrs. Jane K. Herget, Co-Owner

Salary Minimum: $100,000

Functions: Generalist (All)

Industries: Energy, Utilities, Manufacturing, Transportation, Wholesale, Finance, Services, Communications, Aerospace, Software, Healthcare

Harmon/Watson/DeGross International†

7397 Danbury Dr
West Bloomfield, MI 48322-3582
(248) 737-8227
Fax: (248) 737-8229
Email: hwdharmon@aol.com

Summary: We are an international retained executive search firm focused on industrial manufacturing in automotive, aerospace and other diversified manufacturing businesses. This partnership combines the executive experience of three seasoned professionals dedicated to an innovative and hands on approach to executive search.

Key Contact - Specialty:
Mr. Sam Harmon, Principal
Mr. Marc Watson, Principal
Mr. Doug DeGross, Principal

Salary Minimum: $100,000

Functions: Generalist (All)

Industries: Manufacturing

Harris & Associates / iic Partners

(formerly known as Harris & Associates)
4236 Tuller Rd
Dublin, OH 43017-2090
(614) 798-8500
Email: mail@harrisandassociates.com
Web: www.harrisandassociates.com

Summary: Our firm is the eighth largest global executive search and board advisory consulting firm with offices worldwide. On behalf of organizations that range from emerging corporations to Fortune 500 companies, we provide clients with direct access to world class leadership talent.

Key Contact - Specialty:
Mr. Jeffrey Harris, Managing Partner
Mr. Richard Westerfield, Partner

Salary Minimum: $150,000

Functions: Generalist (All)

Industries: Generalist (All), Manufacturing, Transportation, Finance, Misc. Financial, Accounting, Mgmt. Consulting, Communications, Insurance, Real Estate

The Harris Consulting Corp

1400-444 St Mary Ave
Centra Gas Building
Winnipeg, MB R3C 3T1
Canada
(204) 942-8735
Fax: (204) 944-8941
Email: resumes@harrisconsult.com
Web: www.harrisconsult.com

Summary: A Canadian firm, we offer proactive and research driven search for management, professional and executive positions with particular depth of experience in manufacturing, healthcare, financial services, agribusiness and not-for-profit sectors.

Key Contact - Specialty:
Mr. Keith Sinclair, BA, CHRP, President & Chief Executive Officer - *Change management, Executives, Human resources, Interim, Organizational development*
Mr. David S. Morgan, MSc, CHRP, Vice President - *Change management, Executives, Human resources, Interim, Organizational development*
Ms. Alora Sinclair, Director, Corporate Services - *Staffing*
Ms. Vishera Trush, Recruitment Specialist

Salary Minimum: $60,000

Functions: Generalist (All), Management, Board Members, Senior Mgmt., Mfg., Materials, Healthcare, Sales & Mktg., HR Mgmt., Finance

Industries: Generalist (All)

Harris Heery & Associates Inc

40 Richards Ave
Norwalk, CT 06854-2319
(203) 857-0808
Fax: (203) 857-0822
Email: bheery@harrisheery.com
Web: www.harrisheery.com

Summary: We are a specialized firm for consumer goods and services companies recruiting

marketing and sales executives on a domestic and international basis.

Key Contact - Specialty:
Mr. William J. Heery, Senior Vice President
Mr. Andrew S. Harris, President

Salary Minimum: $80,000

Functions: Management, Sales & Mktg., Mktg. Mgmt., Direct Mktg.

Industries: Food, Bev., Tobacco, Textiles, Apparel, Soap, Perf., Cosmtcs., Drugs Mfg., Consumer Elect., Banking, Venture Cap., Non-profits, Hospitality, Hotels, Resorts, Clubs, Restaurants, Entertainment, New Media, Telecoms, Wireless, Insurance, Healthcare

A E Harrison & Partners Inc

209-190 Robert Speck Pky
Sherwood Business Centre
Mississauga, ON L4Z 3K3
Canada
(905) 615-1577
Email: mail@aeharrison.com
Web: www.aeharrison.com

Summary: A retainer based search company that specializes in the recruitment of sales, marketing and general management executives in most industry sectors.

Key Contact - Specialty:
Mr. Rick Harrison

Functions: Management, Sales & Mktg., Sales Mgmt.

Industries: Generalist (All)

Hartman Personnel

4504 Starkey Rd Ste 207
Roanoke, VA 24014-4040
(540) 776-8571
(877) 523-4351
Email: inform@hartman-personnel.com
Web: www.hartman-personnel.com

Summary: We are a personnel placement agency that specializes in IS.

Key Contact - Specialty:
Ms. June Hartman, President
Mr. Kevin Hartman, Recruiter
Mr. Forrest Lavinder, Recruiter

Functions: Board Members, Sales Mgmt., IT, MIS Mgmt., Systems Analysis, Systems Dev., Systems Implem., Engineering

Industries: Generalist (All), Manufacturing, Services, IT Implementation, PSA/ASP, New Media, Communications, Telecoms, Call Centers, Network Infrastructure, Software, ERP SW, Industry Specific SW

Hartsfield Advisors Inc

PO Box 28489
Atlanta, GA 30358-0489
(770) 901-9711
Email: bdee_hartsfield@bellsouth.net

Summary: Extensive year record of improving clients' competitiveness through leadership selection at the CEO and key functional officer levels only. Clients range from Fortune 1000 to mid-cap companies in manufacturing and service sectors.

Key Contact - Specialty:
Mr. Vincent Dee - *Boards of Directors, C-level, COOs, General management, Sales*
Ms. Perri Wagner

Salary Minimum: $200,000

Functions: Management, Board Members, Senior Mgmt.

Industries: Generalist (All), Manufacturing, Food, Bev., Tobacco, Motor Vehicles, Test, Measure Equip., Consumer Goods, Invest. Banking, Venture Cap., Telecoms

Harvard Aimes Group

6 Holcomb St
West Haven, CT 06516-7211
(203) 933-1976
Email: jdg@riskmanagementsearch.com
Web: www.riskmanagementsearch.com

Summary: Retained search for risk management (including safety and claims), benefits and insurance professionals in corporate environment only. All consultants have extensive experience working in the field in which they now recruit.

Key Contact - Specialty:
Mr. James J. Gunther, Principal
Ms. Carole Olderman, Research Associate

Salary Minimum: $50,000

Functions: Risk Mgmt.

Industries: Generalist (All)

Harvard Group International[†]

1640 Powers Ferry Rd SE Bldg 25
Marietta, GA 30067-1444
(404) 459-9045
Fax: (404) 459-9044
Email: resume@hgi1.com
Web: www.hgi1.com

Summary: We have a unique search process, which produces rapid performance-driven results. Recruiting at all levels and functions, best-in-class candidates are presented within 30 Days with a 100 percent completion guarantee. The firm also has a well-known performance driven diversity practice.

Key Contact - Specialty:
Mr. Thomas Gordy, Senior Partner - *Automotive, Aviation, Consumer (Products), Manufacturing, Technology*
Mr. Jeff McMahon, Recruiter - *CFOs, Financial services*

Salary Minimum: $75,000

Functions: Generalist (All), Management, Mfg., Materials, Sales & Mktg., HR Mgmt., Finance, IT

Industries: Generalist (All), Manufacturing, Transportation, Retail, Finance, Services, Hospitality, Government, Aerospace, Healthcare

The Harvard Group

2407 Indian Pony Ct
Henderson, NV 89052-0427
(702) 270-7759
Email: dbutler@harvardgrp.net

Summary: We are a boutique search firm focusing on the placement of high achieving mid to senior level executives. We search the industry looking for people who meet our client's requirements, matching the candidates' requirements and preferences with our client's needs. We provide cost effective services to meet the specific needs of each of our clients nationwide.

Key Contact - Specialty:
Mr. Donald Butler, Managing Partner

Salary Minimum: $50,000

Functions: Generalist (All)

Industries: Generalist (All), Retail, Finance, Banking, Invest. Banking, Brokers, Venture Cap., Mutual/Hedge Funds, Misc. Financial, Non-profits, Accounting, Mgmt. Consulting, HR Services, Real Estate

Hastings & Associates Inc

PO Box 2028
Sausalito, CA 94966-2028
(415) 307-7972
Email: jeff@hastingssearch.com
Web: hastingsassociatesinc.com

Summary: We are a management consulting and executive search firm, specializing in general management and marketing.

Key Contact - Specialty:
Mr. Jeff Hastings, President - *General management, Marketing*

Salary Minimum: $100,000

Functions: Management, Board Members, Sales & Mktg., Advertising, Mktg. Mgmt., Sales Mgmt., Direct Mktg., HR Mgmt., CFOs, Minorities/Diversity

Industries: Manufacturing, Food, Bev., Tobacco, Consumer Goods, Retail, Finance, Banking, Services, Media, Communications, Software, Healthcare

The Hawkins Company

600 Corporate Pt Ste 1120
Culver City, CA 90230-7668
(310) 348-8800
Fax: (310) 348-8844
Email: resumebank@thehawkinscompany.com
Web: www.thehawkinscompany.com

Summary: Retained executive search firm specializing in public and private sector recruitment with strong emphasis on diversity recruitment. Accounting/finance, marketing/sales, HR and general management.

Key Contact - Specialty:
Mr. William D. Hawkins, President

Salary Minimum: $100,000

Functions: Generalist (All), Senior Mgmt.

Industries: Consumer Elect., Finance, Non-profits, Accounting, Law Enforcement, Higher Ed., Hospitality, Media, Advertising, Broadcast, Film, Government, Healthcare

William E Hay & Company

20 S Clark St Ste 2305
Chicago, IL 60603-1807
(312) 782-6510
Fax: (312) 795-0490
Email: wehay20@yahoo.com

Summary: We are a generalist firm representing equal time in the private sector manufacturing, service and not-for-profit sectors across all functional categories.

Key Contact - Specialty:
Mr. William E. Hay, President

Salary Minimum: $75,000

Functions: Management, Senior Mgmt., Healthcare, Health Admin., Sales & Mktg., HR Mgmt., Finance, CFOs, Mgmt. Consultants

Industries: Construction, Banking, Mgmt. Consulting, Healthcare

Hayden Group Inc

11 Newbury St
Boston, MA 02116-3131
(617) 927-0015

Summary: Senior level executive search boutique specializing exclusively in all components of the investment management (institutional, retail and private wealth management) and banking industries. Extensive track record in CEO/COO, sales/marketing/client service/distribution, portfolio management (including lift-outs) and

staff (finance, operations, technology, compliance) assignments.

Key Contact - Specialty:
Mr. Robert E. Hawley, Partner - *Financial services*
Mr. Harry B. McCormick, Partner - *Financial services*

Functions: Generalist (All), Senior Mgmt., Sales & Mktg., Finance, IT

Industries: Finance, Banking, Mutual/Hedge Funds, Misc. Financial

Lee Heagy & Company

1420 Spring Hill Rd Ste 600
Mc Lean, VA 22102-3030
(703) 442-5302
Fax: (508) 590-8784
Email: dlee@leeheagy.com
Web: www.leeheagy.com

Summary: Intensely focused, respected, bio-technology/biomedical/diagnostics/pharmaceutical retained executive search consultants. Additional sector experience includes agriculture and agricultural biotechnology, animal health and associations. Principal has extensive executive search experience. A 'Rites-Honored' recruiter featured in the Wall Street Journal's Career Journal.

Key Contact - Specialty:
Ms. Donna N. Lee, President - *Biotechnology*

Salary Minimum: $150,000

Functions: Generalist (All)

Industries: Agri., Forestry, Mining, Food, Bev., Tobacco, Chemicals, Drugs Mfg., Medical Devices, Finance, Pharm Svcs., Biotech/Life Sciences, Healthcare

HCPG Healthcare Professional Group[†]

356 New Byhalia Rd Ste 2
First Fedral Place
Collierville, TN 38017-3742
(901) 853-6696
Fax: (901) 853-1137
Email: info@hcpg.net
Web: www.hcpg.net

Summary: Our focus includes pharmacy services, PBM, Specialty Pharmacy, healthcare professionals, and medical device. We are dedicated to excelling in these areas of our expertise. Our services are provided with the utmost consultative professionalism, confidentiality, and innovation.

Key Contact - Specialty:
Mr. Jeb Blanchard, CPC, Owner - *Business development, C-level, Executives, Healthcare, Managed care*
Ms. Kay Gammill, Dph, CPC, Account Executive - *Executives, Healthcare, Managed care, Medical, Pharmaceutical*
Ms. Laura Cordera, MA, Recruiter
Ms. Margaret Blackwell, Recruiter & Researcher

Salary Minimum: $70,000

Functions: Senior Mgmt., Middle Mgmt., Healthcare

Industries: Drugs Mfg., Medical Devices, Pharm Svcs., Marketing SW, Healthcare, Hospitals

F P Healy & Company Inc

PO Box 446
Bronxville, NY 10708-0446
(212) 661-0366
(800) 374-3259
Fax: (914) 793-6590

Email: fphealy@aol.com

Summary: We are an executive search firm that serves all industries including computer, eCommerce, commercial & industrial technologies, financial services, banking, insurance, aerospace, defense, energy, pharmaceutical and telemarketing operations.

Key Contact - Specialty:
Mr. Frank P. Healy, President
Mr. Richard P. Healy
Mr. George Saqqal, Managing Director

Salary Minimum: $75,000

Functions: Generalist (All)

Industries: Energy, Utilities, Paper, Printing, Chemicals, Drugs Mfg., Computer Equip., Electronic, Elec. Components, Semiconductors, Venture Cap., Misc. Financial

Heath/Norton Associates Inc

301 Crocus Ct Ste 7L
Dayton, NJ 08810-1456
(732) 329-4663
Email: hnsearch@aol.com

Summary: As a retainer firm we specializes in sales, marketing and general management.

Key Contact - Specialty:
Mr. Richard S. Stoller, Senior Vice President, Managing Partner - *General management, Marketing, Sales*

Salary Minimum: $75,000

Functions: Generalist (All), Management, Materials, Sales & Mktg., Mktg. Mgmt., HR Mgmt.

Industries: Generalist (All), Manufacturing, Food, Bev., Tobacco, Medical Devices, Metal Products, Machine, Appliance, Consumer Elect., Test, Measure Equip., Misc. Mfg., Consumer Goods, Inst./Industrial Food Svc., Aerospace

Hechkoff Executive Search Inc

444 Madison Ave Ste 710
New York, NY 10022-6969
(212) 935-2100
Fax: (212) 935-2199
Email: search@hechkoff.com
Web: www.hechkoff.com

Summary: We are a retained executive search firm specializing in challenging assignments for the consulting, outsourcing, technology services, mergers & acquisitions, big 4 professional services, and public relations arenas.

Key Contact - Specialty:
Mr. Robert B. Hechkoff, President - *Accounting, Accounting (Big 4), Management consulting, Mergers & acquisitions, Professional services*
Ms. Maria Pellicione, Managing Director - *Biotechnology, Investor relations, Pharmaceutical, Public relations*

Salary Minimum: $125,000

Functions: Senior Mgmt., PR, M&A, IT, Systems Implem., Mgmt. Consultants

Industries: Services, Accounting, Mgmt. Consulting, IT Implementation, Biotech/Life Sciences

Hedman & Associates[†]

3312 Woodford Dr Ste 200
Arlington, TX 76013-1139
(817) 277-0888
Email: 1khedman@comcast.net

Summary: Extensive recruiting experience; strictly confidential; emphasis on identification and assessment of high impact performers and

matching candidates with client needs; special competence identifying profit center management talent. High performance talent identification. Clients include those seeking or doing business in the Peoples Republic of China where Mandarin and other Chinese dialects, and experience is required.

Key Contact - Specialty:
Mr. Kent R. Hedman, President - *General management*

Salary Minimum: $50,000

Functions: Generalist (All), Int'l.

Industries: Generalist (All)

Hedquist International Inc

230 Florence St
Crystal Lake, IL 60014-5702
(815) 479-1700
Fax: (815) 444-1701
Email: info@hedquistintl.com
Web: www.hedquistintl.com

Summary: We are a retained executive search firm specializing in the recruitment, selection and placement of officers, presidents, vice presidents, directors and board of directors.

Key Contact - Specialty:
Mr. Jeff Hedquist, Founder & President

Functions: Senior Mgmt.

Industries: Healthcare

Heffelfinger Associates Inc[†]

PO Box 323
Norfolk, MA 02056-0323
(508) 528-7440
Email: heffone@wn.net

Summary: We specialize in the computer/communication industry, both vendor and corporate IS management positions. Coverage through NASA (North American Search Alliance partners).

Key Contact - Specialty:
Mr. Thomas V. Heffelfinger, President - *C-level, CEOs, CIOs*

Salary Minimum: $150,000

Functions: Generalist (All), Management, Senior Mgmt., Sales & Mktg., IT, R&D

Industries: Generalist (All), Computer Equip., Test, Measure Equip., Electronic, Elec. Components, Semiconductors, IT Implementation, Telecoms, Software

JH Hegeler Company

1285 Avenue of the Americas Fl 35
New York, NY 10019-6028
(212) 687-8600
Email: info@jhegeler.com
Web: www.jhegeler.com

Summary: We are a retainer executive search firm specializing in the financial services industry. The firm recruits senior-level executives in equity & fixed income research, portfolio management, investment banking, sales, trading and marketing.

Key Contact - Specialty:
Ms. Julia H. Hegeler

Salary Minimum: $300,000

Functions: Generalist (All)

Industries: Finance

Heidrick & Struggles

233 S Wacker Dr Ste 7000
Chicago, IL 60606-6350
(312) 496-1200
(312) 496-1000
Fax: (312) 496-1048
Email: chicago@heidrick.com
Web: www.heidrick.com

Summary: We provide senior level executive search and leadership consulting services, including: talent management, board building, executive on-boarding and M&A effectiveness. We focus on quality service and build strong leadership teams through our relationships with clients and individuals worldwide.

Key Contact - Specialty:
Ms. Linda H. Heagy, Managing Partner - *Banking (Investment), Consumer, Financial services*
Ms. Caroline B. Ballantin, Practice Leader - *Asset management, Banking (Investment), Finance, Financial services*
Mr. Gregory T. Carrott, Partner - *Consumer*
Mr. Carlos F. Cata, Principal
Ms. Lynn K. Cherney, Partner - *Asset management, Banking (Investment), Financial services*
Mr. Robert Chrismer, Principal - *Professional services*
Mr. Scott Cuellar, Partner - *Aerospace, Aviation, Defense, Energy, Materials*
Mr. Torrey N. Foster, Jr., Managing Partner - *Communications, Consumer, Media, Private equity, Venture capital*
Mr. John T. Gardner, Vice Chairman - *Aerospace, Aviation, Boards of Directors, Defense, Energy*
Mr. Richard P. Gustafson, Vice Chairman - *Hospital, Life Sciences, Managed care*
Mr. Bruce Halbeck, Practice Leader - *Financial services, Insurance*
Mr. Bo Herbst, Principal - *Industrial*
Mr. Timothy C. Hicks, Practice Leader - *Industrial*
Mr. Bradley J. Holden, Partner - *Aerospace, Aviation, Defense, Energy, Materials*
Mr. Miles L. McKie, Partner - *Consumer*
Mr. Michael R. Miller, Partner - *Industrial, Private equity, Venture capital*
Mr. David S. Moore, Partner - *Aerospace, Aviation, Communications, Defense, Media*
Mr. Dale M. Visokey, Managing Partner - *Aerospace, Aviation, Boards of Directors, Defense, Finance*
Mr. David C. Brown, Partner
Mr. Jeff W. Dodson, Partner
Mr. Theodore L. Dysart, Managing Partner
Thames Fulton, Principal
Mr. Richard W. Greene, Partner
Mr. Daniel E. Kepler, Partner
Ms. Betsy Tilkemeier, Partner

Salary Minimum: $180,000

Functions: Generalist (All)

Industries: Generalist (All)

Branches:
633 W 5th St Ste 3300
Los Angeles, CA 90071-2052
(213) 625-8811
Fax: (213) 617-7216
Email: losangeles@heidrick.com
Key Contact - Specialty:
Mr. Paul Legvold, Managing Partner - *Asset management, Banking (Investment), Financial services, Private equity, Venture capital*
Ms. Kelley L. Brack, Partner - *Aerospace, Aviation, Boards of Directors, Consumer, Defense*
Ms. Joy Chen, Principal - *Consumer, Financial services, Professional services, Technology*

Mr. Richard N. Eidinger, Managing Partner - *Finance, Hospital, Life Sciences, Managed care, Private equity*
Mr. Ronald E. Gerevas, Partner - *Consumer, Energy, Industrial, Materials*
Ms. Stephanie M. Gold, Principal - *Boards of Directors, Financial services, Private equity, Venture capital*
Mr. David L. Vied, Partner - *Life Sciences*
Mr. John Wasley, Managing Partner
Mr. Donald T. Sagolla, Partner
Mr. Stephen D. Tibbs, Partner

2740 Sand Hill Rd
Menlo Park, CA 94025-7020
(650) 234-1500
Fax: (650) 233-7582
Email: menlopark@heidrick.com
Key Contact - Specialty:
Mr. Pravesh Mehra, Managing Partner
Mr. Thomas J. Friel, Chairman & Chief Executive Officer - *Boards of Directors, Private equity, Venture capital*
Mr. Kevin A. Gaunt, Principal - *Communications, Finance, Media, Private equity, Venture capital*
Mr. John M. Hewins, Principal
Mr. R. Andrew Holtvedt, Practice Leader - *Communications, Finance, Hardware, Media, Professional services*
Mr. Jason A. Kranz, Principal - *Hardware, Private equity, Semiconductors, Systems, Venture capital*
Mr. Tim O'Shea, Practice Leader - *Boards of Directors, Hardware, Semiconductors, Systems, Technology*
Mr. Jeffrey S. Sanders, Partner - *Boards of Directors, Finance, Hardware, Private equity, Systems*
Ms. Lucia B. Steinhilber, Partner - *Private equity, Venture capital*
Mr. John Thompson, Vice Chairman - *Boards of Directors, Communications, Hardware, Media, Systems*
Ms. Kyung H. Yoon, Vice Chairman - *Boards of Directors, Communications, Financial services, Media, Professional services*
Mr. Michael Hickcox, Principal
Mr. Rick Mirabile, Partner

1 California St Ste 2400
San Francisco, CA 94111-5435
(415) 981-2854
Fax: (415) 981-0482
Email: sanfrancisco@heidrick.com
Key Contact - Specialty:
Mr. Jack Scott, Managing Partner - *Consumer, Hardware, Private equity, Systems, Venture capital*
Mr. Terry Chuah, Partner - *Aerospace, Aviation, Defense, Industrial, Real estate*
Ms. Lauren M. Doliva, Partner - *Boards of Directors, Consumer, Human resources, Private equity, Venture capital*
Ms. Katherine M. Graham, Principal - *CIOs*
Mr. Peter V. Hall, Partner - *Financial services, Real estate*
Ms. Lee Hanson, Managing Partner - *Asset management, Boards of Directors, Communications, Media, Professional services*
Ms. Lisa W. Maibach, Partner - *Consumer, Private equity, Venture capital*
Ms. Karen D. Quint, Partner - *Consumer, Finance, Insurance, Life Sciences, Private equity*
Mr. Kelvin Thompson, Partner - *CIOs, Consumer, Financial services*
Mr. Kelly O. Kay, Partner
Mr. Erik R. Lundh, Principal

281 Tresser Blvd Fl 7
Stamford, CT 06901-3238
(203) 252-2900
Fax: (203) 252-2828

Email: greenwich@heidrick.com
Key Contact - Specialty:
Mr. Bruce Robertson, Partner - *Consumer, Finance, Private equity, Venture capital*
Ms. Wendelyne C.H. Murphy, Partner

601 Brickell Key Dr Ste 1000
Miami, FL 33131-2649
(305) 262-2606
Fax: (305) 262-6697
Email: miami@heidrick.com
Key Contact - Specialty:
Mr. Guy M. Cote, Partner - *Consumer, Real estate, Technology*
Ms. Carla V. Palazio, Partner - *Consumer, Supply Chain, Technology*

303 Peachtree St NE Ste 4300
Atlanta, GA 30308-3266
(404) 577-2410
Fax: (404) 577-4048
Email: atlanta@heidrick.com
Key Contact - Specialty:
Mr. Dale E. Jones, Managing Partner - *Boards of Directors, Communications, Consumer, Human resources, Media*
Ms. Michelle Betts, Principal - *Life Sciences, Research & development*
Ms. J. Veronica Biggins, Managing Partner - *Boards of Directors, Financial services*
Ms. Ellen E. Brown, Principal - *Legal*
Ms. Mary R. Buckle, Partner - *Financial services, Life Sciences*
Mr. Charles E. Commander, Partner - *Aerospace, Aviation, Defense, Energy, Materials*
Mr. Graham W. Galloway, Managing Partner
Mr. Robert J. Gallagher, Principal - *Communications, Hardware, Media, Private equity, Systems*
Mr. M. Evan Lindsay, Vice Chairman - *Boards of Directors, Financial services, Insurance*
Mr. William A. Matthews, III, Partner - *Life Sciences*
Mr. J. Rucker McCarty, Partner - *Finance, Financial services*
Mr. Stephen A. Miles, Partner - *Boards of Directors, Finance, Industrial*
Mr. George F. Norton, Partner - *CIOs, Communications, Consumer, Media, Professional services*
Ms. Jane M. Stevenson, Managing Partner - *Communications, Consumer, Media, Private equity, Professional services*
Mr. Clifford F. Wright, Managing Partner - *Consumer, Industrial, Supply Chain*
Ms. Euris E. Belle, Principal

150 Federal St Fl 27
Boston, MA 02110-1745
(617) 737-6300
Fax: (617) 737-1888
Email: boston@heidrick.com
Key Contact - Specialty:
Mr. Stuart H. Sadick, Managing Partner - *Aerospace, Aviation, Defense, Private equity, Professional services*
Mr. Fred Adair, Partner
Ms. Debra Germaine, Partner - *Communications, Financial services, Hardware, Media, Systems*
Mr. Robert F. Gorog, Partner - *Asset management, Banking (Investment), Financial services, Insurance*
Mr. Robert E. Hallagan, Vice Chairman - *Aerospace, Aviation, Boards of Directors, Defense, Energy*
Mr. Joseph McCabe, Managing Partner - *Asset management, Financial services, Human resources, Insurance*
Ms. Emmelyn M. O'Meara, Principal - *Consumer*
Mr. Richard A. von Ruede, Partner - *Life Sciences*

245 Park Ave Fl 43
New York, NY 10167-0152
(212) 867-9876
Fax: (212) 370-9035
Email: newyork@heidrick.com
Key Contact - Specialty:
Mr. Jory J. Marino, Managing Partner - *Asset management, CIOs, Finance, Financial services, Insurance*
Mr. Jean-Louis Alpeyrie, Partner - *Communications, Hardware, Media, Private equity, Systems*
Mr. Timothy B. Boerkoel, Partner - *Consumer, Human resources*
Mr. Roger H. Chen, Principal - *Aerospace, Aviation, Boards of Directors, Communications, Defense*
Ms. June Eichbaum, Partner - *Financial services, Industrial, Legal, Professional services*
Mr. Len Greer, Principal - *Life Sciences, Managed care*
Ms. Joie A. Gregor, Vice Chairman - *Aerospace, Aviation, Boards of Directors, Communications, Defense*
Ms. Erin M. Hamrick, Partner - *CIOs, Financial services*
Mr. Theodore Jadick, Vice Chairman - *Boards of Directors, Communications, Consumer, Finance, Media*
Mr. David S. Joys, Vice Chairman - *Banking (Investment), Boards of Directors, Consumer, Financial services, Private equity*
Mr. Daniel S. Kelley, Principal - *Consumer*
Mr. George Manderlink, Partner
Ms. Melanie Kusin, Vice Chairman - *Boards of Directors, Consumer, Private equity, Venture capital*
Ms. Filomena Leonardi, Practice Leader - *Life Sciences, Managed care, Professional services*
Ms. Alison J. Weil, Principal
Ms. Anne Lim O'Brien, Partner - *Boards of Directors, Consumer, Finance, Private equity, Venture capital*
Mr. Vincent C. Perro, Managing Partner
Mr. Bryan L. Proctor, Principal - *Energy, Finance, Financial services, Industrial, Materials*
Ms. Victoria S. Reese, Partner - *Consumer, Financial services, Legal, Life Sciences, Professional services*
Mr. Gerard R. Roche, Senior Chairman - *Boards of Directors, Private equity, Venture capital*
Mr. Rich Rosen, Partner
Mr. Peter J. Ross, Partner - *Human resources*
Mr. Michael J. Speck, Practice Leader - *Consumer, Private equity, Technology, Venture capital*
Mr. Nathaniel J. Sutton, Managing Partner
Ms. Anne Wyser-Pratte, Managing Partner
Mr. Kevin Umeh, Principal
Mr. Jeffrey C. Weirichs, Partner
Mr. James Thomas Penny, Principal

40 Wall St Fl 48
New York, NY 10005-1312
(212) 699-3000
Fax: (212) 699-3100
Email: wallstreet@heidrick.com
Key Contact - Specialty:
Mr. Daniel Edwards, Managing Partner
Ms. Michelle DeSena, Principal - *Banking (Investment), Financial services*
Mr. Michael Franzino, Managing Partner - *Asset management, Banking (Investment), Boards of Directors, Financial services, Insurance*
Ms. Valerie E. Germain, Partner - *CIOs*
Ms. Jennifer M. Gomez, Principal
Mr. Ted Gregory, Partner - *Asset management, Banking (Investment), Financial services, Human resources, Real estate*
Mr. Gavin Holland, Principal - *CIOs, Financial services, Human resources*

Mr. Timothy Holt, Jr., Principal - *Banking (Investment), Finance, Financial services, Insurance, Private equity*
Mr. Todd R. Monti, Partner - *Asset management, Banking (Investment), Finance, Financial services, Private equity*
Mr. Eric V. Pikus, Principal - *Finance, Financial services, Insurance, Real estate*
Mr. Leslie W. Stern, Partner - *Asset management, Banking (Investment), Financial services, Insurance, Private equity*
Mr. Roger W. Stoy, Jr., Practice Leader - *Asset management, Finance, Financial services, Insurance, Real estate*
Mr. Alex Alcott, Principal
Mr. David Boehmer, Principal
Ms. Jane B. Marcus, Practice Leader
Ms. Allison C.F. Walker, Partner

600 Superior Ave E Ste 2500
Cleveland, OH 44114-2600
(216) 241-7410
Fax: (216) 241-2217
Email: cleveland@heidrick.com
Key Contact - Specialty:
Ms. Judy Klein, Managing Partner - *Aerospace, Aviation, Boards of Directors, Communications, Defense*
Mr. Jonathan Graham, Partner - *Energy, Industrial, Materials, Professional services, Supply Chain*
Ms. Bonnie W. Gwin, President, Regional - *Boards of Directors, Communications, Consumer, Media, Professional services*
Mr. Michael Nieset, Practice Leader - *Boards of Directors, Communications, Hardware, Media, Systems*
Mr. Timothy W. O'Brien, Partner - *Industrial*
Ms. Ann K. Smith, Principal - *Industrial, Legal*
Mr. Charles E. Wallace, Partner - *Aerospace, Aviation, Boards of Directors, Defense, Energy*
Mr. John Abele, Principal

1 Logan Sq Ste 3075
Philadelphia, PA 19103-6902
(215) 988-1000
Fax: (215) 988-9496
Email: philadelphia@heidrick.com
Key Contact - Specialty:
Mr. Kenneth L. Kring, Managing Partner
Mr. Robert J. Atkins, Partner - *Life Sciences*
Ms. Michael J. DeSantis, Partner - *Finance, Life Sciences*
Ms. Elizabeth R. Ewing, Principal - *Finance, Financial services, Industrial*
Ms. Michele C. Heid, Managing Partner - *Aerospace, Aviation, Defense, Finance, Industrial*
Mr. John P. Strackhouse, Partner - *Boards of Directors, Communications, Hardware, Media, Systems*
Mr. Fran Van Kirk, Partner - *Boards of Directors, Financial services*

5950 Sherry Ln Ste 400
Dallas, TX 75225-6552
(214) 706-7700
Fax: (214) 987-4047
Email: dallas@heidrick.com
Key Contact - Specialty:
Mr. Victor Arias, Jr., Partner - *Boards of Directors, Consumer, Financial services, Real estate*
Ms. Matrice Ellis Kirk, Partner - *Consumer, Private equity, Venture capital*
Ms. Shannon Knox, Principal
Mr. John Scott Petty, Partner - *CIOs, Financial services, Industrial, Real estate*
Ms. Madelaine Pfau, Managing Partner - *Consumer, Finance, Human resources, Professional services*

Mr. Michael D. Taylor, Partner - *CIOs, Hardware, Private equity, Systems, Venture capital*
Mr. Michael Thompson, Partner - *Communications, Media, Professional services, Technology*

600 Travis St Ste 6875
Houston, TX 77002-3014
(713) 237-9000
Fax: (713) 751-3018
Email: houston@heidrick.com
Key Contact - Specialty:
Mr. David A. Morris, Partner - *Asset management, Finance, Financial services*
Mr. Les T. Csorba, Partner - *Energy, Industrial, Materials, Supply Chain*
Mr. Andrew W. Talkington, Managing Partner - *Asset management, Energy, Human resources, Industrial, Materials*
Ms. Heather J. Kopecky, Partner
Mr. Mark H. Livingston, Principal

1750 Tysons Blvd Ste 300
Mc Lean, VA 22102-4243
(703) 848-2500
Fax: (703) 905-8900
Email: tysonscorner@heidrick.com
Key Contact - Specialty:
Mr. Randy Jayne, Managing Partner - *Aerospace, Aviation, Boards of Directors, Communications, Defense*
Mr. Krishnan Rajagopalan, Managing Partner - *Private equity, Professional services, Venture capital*
Mr. Donald S. Biskin, Partner - *Life Sciences, Managed care, Private equity, Venture capital*
Mr. Michael J. Flagg, Managing Partner - *Boards of Directors, Communications, Finance, Hardware, Media*
Mr. J. Eric Joseph, Managing Partner - *Computers (Software), Private equity, Professional services, Technology, Venture capital*
Mr. Gerard P. McNamara, Partner - *CIOs, Communications, Financial services, Industrial, Media*
Mr. Chris Cantarella, Principal
Ms. Teresa J. Hollans, Principal

PO Box 601
2310-161 Bay St
Etobicoke, ON M8Z 5Y9
Canada
(416) 361-4700
Fax: (416) 361-4770
Email: toronto@heidrick.com
Key Contact - Specialty:
Mr. Robert L. Hines, Managing Partner - *Asset management, Boards of Directors, Consumer, Finance, Professional services*
Ms. Catherine Lepard, Partner - *Computers (Software), Hardware, Systems*
Ms. Alyson M. Soko, Principal - *Financial services, Private equity, Real estate, Venture capital*
Ms. Andrea Waines, Partner - *Human resources*

Ruben Dario 281 Ofna 700
Torre Chapultepec
Col Bosques de Chapultepec
11580 Mexico City, DF
Mexico
55 9138 0370
Fax: 55 5280 5230
Email: hsmexico@heidrick.com

Key Contact - Specialty:
Mr. Miguel A. Onofrietti, Jr., Partner

† occasional contingency assignment

Ms. Carla Ormsbee, Partner
Mr. Juan Ignacio Perez, Managing Partner

Heinze & Associates Inc

6125 Blue Circle Dr Ste 218
Hopkins, MN 55343-9108
(952) 938-2828
Fax: (952) 933-9089

Summary: Custom designed search strategy
conducted by experienced professionals.

Key Contact - Specialty:
Mr. David Heinze, President - *General
management*

Salary Minimum: $75,000

Functions: Generalist (All), Senior Mgmt., Plant
Mgmt., Mktg. Mgmt., Sales Mgmt., HR Mgmt.,
CFOs

Industries: Generalist (All), Medical Devices,
Machine, Appliance, Consumer Elect., Misc.
Mfg., Insurance

Helbling & Associates Inc

117 VIP Dr Ste 210
Wexford, PA 15090-6934
(724) 935-7500
Fax: (724) 935-7531
Email: helbling@helblingsearch.com
Web: www.helblingsearch.com

Summary: Retained executive search and
management consulting firm exclusively serving
the construction, real estate and facilities
management industries. Majority of experience
with construction-related firms but possess
extensive work with owners and large institutions.
Our professional staff offers clients extensive
recruiting and consulting experience within the
aforementioned industries.

Key Contact - Specialty:
Mr. Thomas J. Helbling, President - *Construction,
Real estate*
Mr. James Lord, Senior Consultant

Functions: Generalist (All), Management, Middle
Mgmt., Purchasing, Sales & Mktg., HR Mgmt.,
CFOs, Engineering, Architects, Health & Safety

Industries: Construction, Non-profits,
Architectural Svcs., Higher Ed., Publishing,
Environmental Svcs., Real Estate, Healthcare,
Hospitals, Long-term/Home Care

Helffrich International

PO Box 1695
Oldsmar, FL 34677-1695
(813) 855-6465
Fax: (813) 855-6625
Email: helffrichintl@mindspring.com
Web: www.higlobalsearch.com

Summary: International "modified retained"
search firm that specializes in sourcing
management, sales, marketing and senior level
technical professionals for domestic and
international positions. The company works
primarily for clients in the advanced materials,
energy, health care, manufacturing, mining, and
nanotechnology industries. Resumes from
candidates with international experience and
foreign language capabilities are welcome.

Key Contact - Specialty:
Mr. Alan B. Helffrich, Jr., CPC, President
Mr. Michael D. Helffrich, CPC, Vice President
Ms. Henrietta Helffrich, Office Manager

Salary Minimum: $100,000

Functions: Management, Mfg., Materials,
Healthcare, Sales & Mktg., HR Mgmt., Finance,
Engineering, Int'l.

Industries: Generalist (All), Healthcare

The Helms International Group

(also known as CoachWise)
22 Bayberry Ln
Rehoboth Beach, DE 19971-1221
(302) 226-2389
Email: mhelms@coachwise.com
Web: www.coachwise.com

Summary: We coach business and nonprofit
executives as they add key people to their
organizations.

Key Contact - Specialty:
Ms. Mary P. Helms, President - *Human resources*

The Hennessy Group Inc

115 Pheasant Run Ste 214
Newtown, PA 18940-1886
(215) 497-9950
Fax: (215) 497-9951
Email: info@thehennessygroup.com
Web: www.thehennessygroup.com

Summary: We provide executive search
consulting to companies in the healthcare,
chemical, industrial and consumer industries. The
firm was founded based on a perceived need in the
industry for an executive search firm that focused
exclusively on delivery and results. The firm's
mission is to help clients create and sustain a
competitive advantage through executive
leadership.

Key Contact - Specialty:
Mr. Robert Hennessy, President - *Pharmaceutical*
Mr. Malcolm Kinnaird, Managing Director -
Chemical, Consumer (Marketing), Industrial

Salary Minimum: $100,000

Functions: Generalist (All)

Industries: Chemicals, Drugs Mfg., Pharm Svcs.

Bruce Henry Associates Inc

1975 E Sunrise Blvd Ste 825
Fort Lauderdale, FL 33304-1446
(954) 763-5966
(800) 780-6540
Fax: (954) 763-5988
Email: bruce@brucehenry.com
Web: www.brucehenry.com

Summary: We are dentistry's executive search
firm. Our business is based on integrity,
professionalism, timeliness and attention to detail.

Key Contact - Specialty:
Mr. Bruce Henry, President
Ms. Cynthia Smith, Managing Director - *Dental*

Salary Minimum: $50,000

Functions: Generalist (All)

Industries: Dental

The Hensge Company

2100 Manchester Rd Ste 900
Wheaton, IL 60187-4521
(630) 871-1818
Email: info@hensge.com
Web: www.hensge.com

Summary: Our practice is aimed at helping clients
achieve superior strategic results by better
alignment of their organization with their strategic
objectives and culture.

Key Contact - Specialty:
Mr. Bill Hensge, President - *Senior management*

Salary Minimum: $100,000

Functions: Generalist (All), Management

Industries: Generalist (All), Paper, Printing,
Plastics, Rubber, Metal Products, Machine,
Appliance, Consumer Elect., Mgmt. Consulting,
HR Services, Fiber Optic

Herd Freed Hartz

601 Union St Ste 4200
Seattle, WA 98101-4036
(206) 525-9700
Fax: (206) 374-3067
Email: execjobs@herdfreedhartz.com
Web: www.herdfreedhartz.com

Summary: We are a nationwide, retained search in
Technology, Life Science, Manufacturing and
Consumer industries.

Key Contact - Specialty:
Mr. Paul Freed, Founding Partner
Mr. Jim Herd, Founding Partner
Mr. Kevin Hartz, Founding Partner

Salary Minimum: $100,000

Functions: Senior Mgmt., Middle Mgmt., Mfg.

Industries: Generalist (All), Venture Cap.,
Services, Mgmt. Consulting, Advertising, New
Media, Digital, Wireless, Network
Infrastructure, Software, Biotech/Life Sciences

Hergenrather & Company

21 Hillside Dr
Rancho Santa Margarita, CA 92688-5554
(949) 635-1200
Fax: (949) 635-1201
Email: rah@hergenrather.com
Web: www.hergenrather.com

Summary: Executive search firm engaged in
senior-level searches in every functional area and
in most industries.

Key Contact - Specialty:
Dr. Richard A. Hergenrather, Chairman & Chief
Executive Officer

Salary Minimum: $80,000

Functions: Management, Senior Mgmt., Mfg.,
Product Dev., Materials, Purchasing,
Distribution, Sales & Mktg., HR Mgmt.,
Engineering

Industries: Construction, Manufacturing, Printing,
Computer Equip., Consumer Elect., Electronic,
Elec. Components, Transportation, HR Services,
Defense, Aerospace

Heritage Partners International

278 Orange St
New Haven, CT 06510-1716
(203) 789-0000
Fax: (203) 789-0022
Email: info@heritageleaders.com
Web: www.heritagepartnersintl.com

Summary: Ours is a senior level executive search
firm that focuses on delivering superior work to a
select group of clients globally in the life sciences
industry. Our clients include several of the top ten
pharmaceutical and biotechnology companies.

Key Contact - Specialty:
Mr. Kevin Butler, Co-Founder, President &
Managing Partner
Mr. Tig Conger, Partner
Mr. Peter J.M. Goosens, Senior Partner
Terri Angotto, Partner
Mr. Matthew J. Vossler, Partner
Mr. Charles Grebenstein, PhD, Partner

Functions: Board Members, Senior Mgmt.

Industries: Drugs Mfg., Medical Devices,
Biotech/Life Sciences

Heritage Recruiting Group LLC

39 Old Ridgebury Rd Ste 6
Danbury, CT 06810-5100
(203) 794-1495
Email: resumes@heritagerecruiting.com
Web: www.heritagerecruiting.com

Summary: A boutique retained executive search firm with experience across many disciplines including senior management, HR, marketing, sales, finance, engineering, customer retention, call center management, IT and others. Industries include, but are not limited to: consumer products, pharmaceuticals, paper, high-technology and manufacturing.

Key Contact - Specialty:
Mr. Jeffry E. Muthersbaugh, President - *Human resources, Marketing, Presidents, Sales, Senior management*
Ms. Marie Minei, Senior Recruiter - *Consumer (Products), Hardware, Pharmaceutical, Printing*

Salary Minimum: $65,000

Functions: Generalist (All), Management, Senior Mgmt., Mfg., Sales & Mktg., HR Mgmt., Finance, IT

Industries: Generalist (All), Food, Bev., Tobacco, Textiles, Apparel, Printing, Drugs Mfg., Medical Devices, Metal Products, Computer Equip., Consumer Elect., Banking, Invest. Banking, Pharm Svcs., Publishing, Software, Biotech/Life Sciences

A Herndon & Associates Inc

5100 Westheimer Rd Ste 200
Houston, TX 77056-5597
(713) 968-6577
Fax: (281) 589-7151
Email: info@aherndon.com
Web: www.aherndon.com

Summary: This firm provides performance based recruiting utilizing retention maximization strategies under a unique hourly pricing model designed for today's marketplace. The firm also provides HR and management training seminars on hiring and retention.

Key Contact - Specialty:
Ms. Angela Herndon, President

Salary Minimum: $95,000

Functions: Management, Board Members, Middle Mgmt., Sales & Mktg., Finance, IT, Legal, Attorneys, Int'l.

Industries: Generalist (All), E-commerce, Communications, Software

The Herrmann Group Ltd

1100-60 Bloor St W
Toronto, ON M4W 3B8
Canada
(416) 922-4242
Fax: (416) 922-4366
Email: info@herrmanngroup.com
Web: www.herrmanngroup.com

Summary: Specialize in building and retaining strong business alliances with our clients. We become an integral part of their organizations and are thereby able to offer valuable support and services. We go beyond supplying people.

Key Contact - Specialty:
Ms. Gerlinde Herrmann, President

Salary Minimum: $60,000

Functions: Generalist (All), Senior Mgmt., Mktg. Research, Staffing, Cash Mgmt., Systems Analysis, Mgmt. Consultants

Industries: Generalist (All)

Hersher Associates Ltd

3000 Dundee Rd Ste 314
Northbrook, IL 60062-2434
(847) 272-4050
Fax: (847) 272-1998
Email: hersher@hersher.com
Web: www.hersher.com

Summary: Healthcare retained executive search and consulting firm that recruits chief medical information officers and other key directors & managers. Clients include integrated delivery networks, academic medical centers, managed care organizations and IT vendors. We have an established track record in clinical redesign, finance, and other areas of executive leadership.

Key Contact - Specialty:
Ms. Betsy S. Hersher, President - *Healthcare*

Salary Minimum: $75,000

Functions: Board Members, Senior Mgmt., Physicians, Nurses, Health Admin., Sales & Mktg., CFOs, IT, MIS Mgmt., Specialized Svcs.

Industries: Higher Ed., Healthcare

Stanley Herz & Company

293 Route 100 Ste 103
Somers, NY 10589-3215
(914) 277-7500
Fax: (914) 277-7749
Email: search@stanleyherz.com
Web: www.stanleyherz.com

Summary: Retained executive search. Senior management. There is an emphasis on middle market companies.

Key Contact - Specialty:
Mr. Stanley Herz, Managing Principal - *Senior management*

Salary Minimum: $125,000

Functions: Management, Mfg., Sales & Mktg., Finance, R&D, Engineering

Industries: Generalist (All)

Robert Hess & Associates LLC†

2610 Park Cove Way
Broomfield, CO 80020-9399
(303) 410-6589
Fax: (303) 410-0046
Email: chanda@robhess.com
Web: www.robhess.com

Summary: We serve the homebuilding industry on a national basis placing middle through senior managers in every functional area of responsibility including, but not limited to, division and regional management, acquisitions, architecture, development, construction, purchasing, accounting, sales, and marketing.

Key Contact - Specialty:
Mrs. Chanda Sloat, Principal
Ms. Mist Ladd, Recruiter
Ms. Carrie Kucinski, Recruiter
Mrs. Celia Ross, Recruiter

Salary Minimum: $60,000

Functions: Generalist (All)

Industries: Construction, Finance, Architectural Svcs., Accounting, Real Estate, Accounting SW, Marketing SW

Heyman Associates Inc

11 Penn Plz Ste 1105
New York, NY 10001-2006
(212) 784-2717
Fax: (212) 244-9648
Email: info@heymanassociates.com
Web: www.heymanassociates.com

Summary: We are a leading executive search firm placing mid-and senior-level executives in corporate & marketing communications, public affairs, internal communications, public relations, investor relations, & other closely related positions in the US and Europe. Searches cover every communications discipline. Clients include prominent corporations, public relations agencies, universities & nonprofit organizations.

Key Contact - Specialty:
Mr. William C. Heyman, President & Chief Executive Officer - *Investor relations, Philanthropy, Public relations*
Ms. Maryanne B. Rainone, Senior Vice President & Mng Director - *Communications, Investor relations, Public relations*
Ms. Elisabeth A. Ryan, Senior Vice President & Mng Director - *Investor relations, Public relations*
Ms. Julie Jarrett, Vice President - *Public relations*

Salary Minimum: $150,000

Functions: PR

Industries: Generalist (All)

Higdon Partners LLC

230 Park Ave Rm 951
New York, NY 10169-0951
(212) 986-4662
Fax: (212) 986-5002
Email: info@higdonpartners.com
Web: www.higdonpartners.com

Summary: A boutique executive search firm with a sole focus on senior placements in investment management. We place CEOs, CIOs, COOs, PMs, and analysts, as well as marketing, sales, operational and risk management professionals at buy-side firms.

Key Contact - Specialty:
Mr. Henry G. Higdon, Partner - *Asset management*
Ms. Maryann Bovich, Partner - *Asset management, Financial services, Investment management, Private equity*
Ms. Jane Bierwirth, Managing Director - *Asset management, Investment management*
Mr. Derek Braddock, Managing Director - *Asset management*
Mr. David M. Cochran, Jr., Vice President - *Asset management*
Ms. Leslie R. Meyers, Managing Director - *Financial services, Investment management, Private equity*
Ms. Laurie Anne Eamma, Director, Research
Ms. Lorraine Brennan, Vice President, Operations

Salary Minimum: $150,000

Functions: Board Members, Senior Mgmt., Product Dev., CFOs, Risk Mgmt.

Industries: Mutual/Hedge Funds

Higgins Group Inc

1000 Westlakes Dr Ste 295
Berwyn, PA 19312-2409
(610) 640-2660
Fax: (610) 640-2672
Email: donna@higgins-group.com
Web: www.higgins-group.com

Summary: We are a boutique firm focused on providing exceptional levels of quality and attention to selected clients. Our process emphasizes urgency, outstanding fit and communication. We work exclusively with pharmaceutical and bio-technology companies filling senior level positions across all functions. We also have a particular strength recruiting physicians at all levels.

† occasional contingency assignment

Key Contact - Specialty:
Ms. Donna Higgins, President - *Biopharmaceutical, Biotechnology, Pharmaceutical*
Mr. Carol Cottone, Partner - *Biopharmaceutical, Biotechnology, Pharmaceutical*
Ms. Wendi Pratt, Operations Manager

Salary Minimum: $150,000

Functions: Management, Board Members, Senior Mgmt., Middle Mgmt., Physicians

Industries: Drugs Mfg., Medical Devices, Biotech/Life Sciences

---

High Desert Executive Search LLC

PO Box 80714
Albuquerque, NM 87198-0714
(505) 232-9561
Email: resume@highdesertsearch.com
Web: www.highdesertsearch.com

Summary: We are a retained executive search firm. Our areas of concentration include finance, HR and sales & marketing. We place directors and above.

Key Contact - Specialty:
Mr. Jim McCaskill, CPC, President

Salary Minimum: $80,000

Functions: Senior Mgmt., Middle Mgmt., Sales Mgmt., HR Mgmt., Finance, CFOs

Industries: Manufacturing, Drugs Mfg., Medical Devices, Computer Equip., Consumer Elect., Test, Measure Equip., Electronic, Elec. Components, Semiconductors, Retail, Services, Hospitality, Real Estate, Software, Biotech/Life Sciences

---

Highland Concord

(a subsidiary of Mitchell/Wolfson Associates)
600 Central Ave Ste 375
Highland Park, IL 60035-3257
(847) 266-1100
Web: www.highlandconcord.com

Summary: Within the insurance industry, we work with primary carriers, reinsurers, brokerage firms, consultants and corporate risk management.

Key Contact - Specialty:
Mr. Robert H. Wolfson, President - *Risk management*

Salary Minimum: $100,000

Functions: Generalist (All), Benefits, Risk Mgmt.

Industries: Generalist (All), Insurance

Highland Partners

622 3rd Ave Fl 38
New York, NY 10017-6707
(212) 351-7300
Fax: (646) 658-0552
Email: contact_highland@hhgroup.com
Web: www.highlandpartners.com

Summary: Our firm is a leading retained executive search boutique. We conduct search assignments at the top end of the recruiting spectrum (CEO, COO, CFO, CIO, CTO, CMO, CAO, and Board of director level).

Key Contact - Specialty:
Mr. Gerard G. Cameron, Managing Partner
Mr. Ted Eastwick, Partner - *Financial services*
Mr. Matthew Faber, Partner - *Healthcare, Life Sciences*
Ms. Abbe Goldfarb, Consultant - *Asset management, Financial services*
Mr. Jim Johnston, Partner - *Financial services, Insurance*

Mr. Joel Millonzi, Partner - *Asset management, Boards of Directors, Financial services*
Mr. Robert A. Molnar, Partner - *CIOs, Information Technology*
Mr. Martin D. Nass, Practice Leader, Global Real Estate - *Financial services, Real estate*
Mr. Thomas A. Rowe, Practice Leader - *CFOs, Financial services, Insurance*
Mr. Michael J. Sullivan, Partner - *CFOs, Financial services, Information Technology, Insurance, Technology*
Ms. Dorathea I. Zoppo, Consultant - *Healthcare, Life Sciences*

Salary Minimum: $150,000

Functions: Management, Board Members, HR Mgmt., Finance, IT, Legal

Industries: Manufacturing, Consumer Goods, Finance, Services, Legal, HR Services, Communications, Insurance, Software, Biotech/Life Sciences

Branches:
15849 N 71st St Ste 100
Scottsdale, AZ 85254-2179
(480) 281-1530
Fax: (480) 281-1500
Key Contact - Specialty:
Mr. Hugh Illsley, Partner - *Boards of Directors, Consumer, Financial services, Insurance, Retail*

222 N Sepulveda Blvd Ste 1780
El Segundo, CA 90245-5639
(310) 321-3220
Fax: (310) 321-0166
Email: pam.smith@highlandpartners.com
Key Contact - Specialty:
Mr. Robert Rollo, Vice Chairman & Global Leader Specialty - *Boards of Directors, Industrial*
Mr. Peter Kelly, Practice Co-Leader, Global Banking - *Banking, Financial services*
Ms. Bethany George, Consultant - *Boards of Directors, Consumer, Human resources, Retail*

16255 Ventura Blvd Ste 400
Encino, CA 91436-2308
(818) 905-6010
Fax: (818) 905-3330
Email: janet.christensen@highlandpartners.com
Key Contact - Specialty:
Mr. Neal Maslan, Practice Leader, Global Healthcare Servi - *Boards of Directors, Healthcare, Life Sciences*
Mr. Martin J. Hewett, Partner - *Industrial, Information Technology, Technology*
Mr. Darin DeWitt, Consultant - *Healthcare, Life Sciences*

595 Market St Ste 2500
San Francisco, CA 94105-2838
(415) 356-5000
Fax: (415) 356-5001
Email: kathy.fry@highlandpartners.com
Key Contact - Specialty:
Mr. Michael Ballenger, Partner - *Boards of Directors, Healthcare, Life Sciences*
Ms. Mercedes Chatfield-Taylor, Partner - *Information Technology, Technology*
Ms. Kristin Herbert, Practice Leader, Legal - *Legal*
Ms. Karen Bertrand, Consultant - *Healthcare, Life Sciences*
Mr. Stephen P. Van Liere, Consultant - *Legal*

281 Tresser Blvd Fl 10
Stamford, CT 06901-3222
(203) 326-4640
Fax: (203) 326-4641
Email: katherine.nomack@highlandpartners.com

Key Contact - Specialty:
Mr. Darren G. Romano, Practice Leader, Global Human Resources - *Human resources, Industrial*
Mr. Phil Schneidermeyer, Practice Leader, CIO - *CIOs, Information Technology, Technology*
Mr. Chris Berger, Consultant - *Human resources*
Ms. Jodie Emery, Partner - *Life Sciences, Private equity*
Ms. Nancy Schwartz, Consultant - *Boards of Directors, Senior management*

191 Peachtree St NE Ste 800
Atlanta, GA 30303-1747
(404) 688-0800
Fax: (404) 688-0133
Email: onalia.russell@highlandpartners.com
Key Contact - Specialty:
Mr. Bud Wright, Managing Partner - *Boards of Directors, CFOs, Consumer, Retail*
Mr. Jeff Lemming, Partner - *Fashion, Retail*
Mr. J. Michael Allred, Partner - *Boards of Directors, Consumer, Information Technology, Retail, Technology*
Mr. Bruce MacLane, Jr., Consultant - *Consumer, Retail, Technology*

225 W Wacker Dr Ste 2100
Chicago, IL 60606-1299
(312) 782-3113
Fax: (312) 782-1743
Email: dore.lacny@highlandpartners.com
Key Contact - Specialty:
Mr. Patrick Corey, Managing Partner - *Insurance*
Mr. Michael J. Corey, Vice Chairman, Co-Leader Fin Svcs Sector - *CFOs, Financial services, Insurance*
Ms. Hilary Jambor, Partner - *Consumer, Retail*
Mr. Tom Moran, Partner - *CFOs, Financial services, Insurance*
Mr. John Rothschild, Partner - *Boards of Directors, CFOs, Financial services, Information Technology, Technology*
Mr. Paul D. Hanson, Consultant - *Financial services, Insurance*
Mr. Liam Lawrence, Consultant - *Financial services, Insurance*
Mr. Brian Schnepff, Consultant - *Financial services, Insurance*

230 3rd Ave Ste 3
Waltham, MA 02451-7542
(781) 902-6000
Fax: (781) 902-6001
Email: samantha.conroy@highlandpartners.com
Key Contact - Specialty:
Ms. Deidre Allison, Partner - *Healthcare, Life Sciences*
Ms. Rachel Hamlin, Consultant - *Asset management, Financial services*

225 S 6th St Ste 4925
Minneapolis, MN 55402-4646
(612) 215-6900
Fax: (612) 215-6901
Email: diane.simondi@highlandpartners.com
Key Contact - Specialty:
Mr. Michael T. Kelly, Chairman - *Boards of Directors, CFOs, Healthcare, Life Sciences*
Mr. Jeremy Hanson, Managing Partner
Ms. Karen Bair, Consultant - *Healthcare, Life Sciences*
Ms. Catherine Robinson, Consultant - *Healthcare, Life Sciences*
Mr. Jason Waterman, Consultant - *Information Technology, Technology*

5956 Sherry Ln Ste 1800
Dallas, TX 75225-8029
(214) 754-0019
Fax: (214) 754-0615
Email: sandy.shepherd@highlandpartners.com

Key Contact - Specialty:
Ms. Judy Neal Stubbs, Partner - *CFOs, Consumer, Financial services, Human resources, Industrial*
Mr. James M. Bethmann, Vice Chairman - *Boards of Directors, Industrial, Information Technology, Technology*
Mr. David M. Love, II, Partner - *Consumer, Industrial, Retail*
Mr. Wayne Mitchell, Partner - *Information Technology, Technology*
Mr. Dave Palmlund, Partner - *CIOs, Consumer, Human resources, Industrial, Retail*
Mr. Keith A. Tibbits, Jr., Consultant - *Industrial, Information Technology, Technology*
Mr. Dave Winston, Consultant - *Information Technology, Technology*
Mr. Steve Ingram, Partner - *CIOs, Technology*

600-155 University Ave
Toronto, ON M5H 3B7
Canada
(416) 862-1273
Fax: (416) 363-5720
Email: rachel.hing@highlandpartners.com
Key Contact - Specialty:
Mr. John Wallace, President & Chief Executive Officer - *Information Technology, Technology*
Mr. Marcelo MacKinlay, Partner - *Boards of Directors, Human resources, Industrial, Legal*
Mr. Patrick McMahon, Partner - *Information Technology, Technology*
Mr. Bill Probert, Partner - *Healthcare, Life Sciences*
Ms. Sheila Ross, Partner - *Asset management, Consumer, Financial services, Retail*
Ms. Janice Detta Colli, Consultant - *Financial services, Information Technology, Technology*
Mr. Derek Roberts, Co-Leader, Global Insurance Practice - *Financial services, Insurance*
Ms. France Simard, Practice Leader, Communs & Converge - *Healthcare, Information Technology, Life Sciences, Technology*

Highlander Search†
PO Box 4163
Greensboro, NC 27404-4163
(336) 333-9886
Email: jphighlander@mindspring.com
Summary: Our extensive experience in executive search, technical recruiting and outplacement consulting has yielded wide industry knowledge and understanding of modern business challenges and goals. We provide: experienced organizational consultants, operational modeling, manpower assessment, wage and benefit surveys, and organizational chart development and evaluation.
Key Contact - Specialty:
Mr. Jeffrey M. Penley, CPC, President
Salary Minimum: $50,000
Functions: Generalist (All), Management, Materials
Industries: Lumber, Furniture, Transportation, Logistics Svcs.

Higley, Hall & Company Inc
45 Lyman St Ste 17
Westborough, MA 01581-2628
(508) 836-4292
Fax: (508) 836-4294
Email: donhall@higleyhall.com
Web: www.higleyhall.com
Summary: We have an executive banking background on part of principal - quality firm.
Key Contact - Specialty:
Mr. Donald L. Hall, President - *Financial*
Salary Minimum: $50,000

Functions: Management, Senior Mgmt.
Industries: Finance

Hill & Associates†
(a division of Melfur International Inc Corp)
15332 Antioch St Ste 719
Pacific Palisades, CA 90272-3603
(310) 230-7663
(310) 925-1241
Email: thill29832@aol.com
Summary: Extensive industry knowledge and contacts; outstanding ability to build management teams; an ex-carnation company sales manager with experience in management consulting and executive search; specializes in the food, beverage, wine and spirits industries.
Key Contact - Specialty:
Mr. Tom Hill, President
Salary Minimum: $60,000
Functions: Generalist (All), Management, Sales & Mktg., Mktg. Mgmt., Sales Mgmt.
Industries: Food, Bev., Tobacco, Drugs Mfg.

The Himmelfarb Group
1119 Pleasant St
Oak Park, IL 60302-3009
(708) 848-0086
Fax: (708) 848-8001
Email: info@himmelfarbgroup.com
Web: www.himmelfarbgroup.com
Summary: We are a small executive search firm working on a retained basis for not-for-profit organizations and foundations.
Key Contact - Specialty:
Ms. Susan Himmelfarb, Principal - *Non-profit, Philanthropy*
Functions: Senior Mgmt., Non-profits
Industries: Non-profits

The Hindman Group Inc†
17295 Chesterfield Airport Rd
Chesterfield, MO 63005-1423
(800) 800-9220
(636) 777-7850
Fax: (800) 241-9220
Email: thgsearch@thehindmangroup.com
Web: www.thehindmangroup.com
Summary: We are executive search consultants to the food distribution, manufacturing and logistics industries specializing in the recruitment of mid to top-level executives.
Key Contact - Specialty:
Mr. Jeffrey J. Hindman, CPC, CSP, President - *Food service, Logistics, Manufacturing, Manufacturing (Management), Supply Chain*
Salary Minimum: $90,000
Functions: Generalist (All), Management, Board Members, Mfg., Materials, Sales & Mktg., Finance, Minorities/Diversity
Industries: Generalist (All), Agri., Forestry, Mining, Manufacturing, Food, Bev., Tobacco, Transportation, Wholesale, Retail, Finance, Accounting, Mgmt. Consulting, Hospitality, Software, Biotech/Life Sciences

Hire Consulting Services LLC
PO Box 230299
Encinitas, CA 92023-0299
(760) 230-4301
Email: mjames@hireconsultant.com
Web: www.hireconsultant.com
Summary: Retained based executive search firm specializing in recruiting senior level management

executives and professionals in most functions and industries. We partner with companies that require a competitive recruiting edge to hire top talent.
Key Contact - Specialty:
Mr. Mark S. James, CPC, President & Founder - *C-level, CEOs, CFOs, CIOs, COOs*
Salary Minimum: $100,000
Functions: Management, Board Members, Senior Mgmt., Middle Mgmt., Sales & Mktg., Mktg. Mgmt., Sales Mgmt., Sales Reps., HR Mgmt.
Industries: Generalist (All)

The Hire Net Work Inc†
1500-5650 Yonge St
The Xerox Tower
North York, ON M2M 4G3
Canada
(416) 410-4430
(800) 628-3736
Fax: (416) 512-8304
Email: louis@hire-network.com
Web: www.hire-network.com
Summary: We provide search, assessments, executive coaching and consulting services for management and executives, both permanent and contract.
Key Contact - Specialty:
Mr. Louis Noorden, Partner
Functions: Generalist (All), Management, Mfg., Healthcare, HR Mgmt., MIS Mgmt., Engineering, Mgmt. Consultants, Int'l.
Industries: Generalist (All), Manufacturing, Retail, Finance, Mgmt. Consulting, Environmental Svcs., Aerospace, Healthcare

Hitchcock & Associates
2064 Antioch Ct Ste A
Oakland, CA 94611-2928
(510) 339-8675
Fax: (510) 339-8674
Email: nhsearch@earthlink.net
Summary: Research and retained executive search services in the areas of biotechnology, pharmaceutical, high technology, e-commerce and retail. We have Spanish and Japanese language capabilities. Available to provide on-site consulting and recruiting services.
Key Contact - Specialty:
Ms. Nancy Hitchcock, BA, MA, President - *Management consulting, Retail*
Salary Minimum: $75,000
Functions: Management, Sales & Mktg., HR Mgmt., Finance, MIS Mgmt., R&D, Engineering, Int'l.
Industries: Drugs Mfg., Retail, Finance, Pharm Svcs., Mgmt. Consulting, Publishing, Biotech/Life Sciences

The Hobart West Solutions
1608 Walnut St Ste 1702
Philadelphia, PA 19103-5410
(215) 735-9440
Fax: (215) 735-9430
Email: pmcgowan@hobartwest.com
Web: www.hobartwest.com
Summary: We take a personalized approach to every search. We specialize in legal, medical RN (insurance), finance, accounting, project management, etc.
Key Contact - Specialty:
Ms. Pat McGowan, General Manager
Functions: Generalist (All), Admin. Svcs., Nurses, HR Mgmt., Finance, Technicians, Legal

Industries: Generalist (All), Computer Equip., Finance, Misc. Financial, Legal, Accounting, HR Services, Insurance, Claims, Healthcare

Hobbs & Towne Inc

PO Box 987
1288 Valley Forge Rd Ste 88
Valley Forge, PA 19482-0987
(610) 783-4600
Fax: (610) 783-4511
Email: kkennedy@hobbstowne.com
Web: www.hobbstowne.com

Summary: We are a retained search firm focused in the energy technology and life science industries. We specialize in working with venture capital and private equity portfolio companies.

Key Contact - Specialty:
Mr. Andrew Towne, President - *Biotechnology, C-level, Energy, High technology, Utilities*
Mr. Robert Hobbs, Managing Partner - *CEOs, CFOs, Manufacturing, Pharmaceutical, Printing*
Mr. Roland Olsen, Vice President, Technical Resources
Mr. Don Titus, Senior Vice President

Salary Minimum: $100,000

Functions: Management

Industries: Generalist (All), Energy, Utilities, Manufacturing, Printing, Drugs Mfg., Medical Devices, Packaging, Biotech/Life Sciences

Hochman & Associates Inc†

1801 Avenue of the Stars Ste 1250
Los Angeles, CA 90067-5906
(310) 552-0662
Email: jhochman@earthlink.net
Web: www.hochmanassociates.com

Summary: Networking and disciplined search methodologies have consistently allowed us to efficiently find and prepare the perfect match candjdates to fill client needs. Extensive, hands-on experience has enhanced our ability to complete successful job placements.

Key Contact - Specialty:
Ms. Judith L. Hochman, President

Salary Minimum: $60,000

Functions: Generalist (All), Senior Mgmt., Sales Mgmt., HR Mgmt., Finance, Cash Mgmt., M&A

Industries: Generalist (All), Finance, Banking, Invest. Banking, Brokers, Venture Cap., Mutual/Hedge Funds, Accounting, Insurance

Hockett Associates Inc

PO Box 1765
Los Altos, CA 94023-1765
(650) 941-8815
Fax: (650) 941-8817
Email: bill@hockettinc.com
Web: www.hockettinc.com

Summary: Senior management search for life science, technology and other companies, characterized by comprehensive targeting and networking, personal contact, a limited practice size, high quality and an unusual success rate.

Key Contact - Specialty:
Mr. Bill Hockett, Managing Partner - *Education, Technology, Venture capital*

Salary Minimum: $150,000

Functions: Management, Board Members, Senior Mgmt., Mfg., Sales & Mktg., CFOs

Industries: Drugs Mfg., Medical Devices, Venture Cap., New Media, Biotech/Life Sciences

The Hocquet Group

191 Washington St
Keene, NH 03431-3131
(603) 721-1714
Email: info@hocquetgroup.com
Web: www.hocquetgroup.com

Summary: We are an executive recruiting firm focused exclusively on the consulting industry. Our mission is to align high-caliber individuals with exceptional opportunities at leading firms.

Key Contact - Specialty:
Mr. Tim Bourgeois, Partner
Mr. Tom Rodenhauser, Partner

Functions: Mgmt. Consultants

Industries: Services

Hoglund & Associates Inc

33 N La Salle St Ste 2600
Chicago, IL 60602-3399
(312) 357-1037
Fax: (312) 732-0990
Email: jhoglund@hoglundassociates.com

Summary: Search firm; results-oriented, takes great pride in providing superior client service and committed to unwavering professional ethics and standards.

Key Contact - Specialty:
Mr. Gerald C. Hoglund, President - *Engineering, Human resources, Marketing, Sales*

Salary Minimum: $70,000

Functions: Generalist (All)

Industries: Generalist (All), Manufacturing, Drugs Mfg., Medical Devices, Machine, Appliance, Misc. Financial, Services, Mgmt. Consulting, Insurance, Healthcare

Harvey Hohauser & Associates LLC

5600 New King Dr Ste 355
Troy, MI 48098-2603
(248) 641-1400
Fax: (248) 641-1929
Email: information@hohauser.com
Web: www.hohauser.com

Summary: We are management consultants specializing in executive recruitment, management appraisals and organization analysis.

Key Contact - Specialty:
Mr. Harvey Hohauser, President
Mr. Barry Nayler, Vice President - *International*
Mr. Todd Hohauser, Vice President
Ms. Debra Schlutow, Director, Research Services

Salary Minimum: $90,000

Functions: Management, Senior Mgmt., Mfg., Sales & Mktg., HR Mgmt., Finance, Engineering, Int'l.

Industries: Generalist (All), Manufacturing, Chemicals, Plastics, Rubber, Machine, Appliance, Motor Vehicles, Finance, Non-profits, Government, Insurance, Real Estate, Hospitals

Branches:
2843 E Grand River Ave Ste 220
East Lansing, MI 48823-6722
(517) 339-9009
Fax: (517) 339-0034
Email: glickman@hohauser.com

Key Contact - Specialty:
Mr. Kenneth S. Glickman, Senior Vice President

Holden Management Search

1201 N Orange St Ste 747
Wilmington, DE 19801-1186
(302) 351-4929
Fax: (302) 351-2441
Email: info@onlineconstructionrecruiter.com
Web: www.holdensearch.com

Summary: Retained executive search firm specializing in construction recruitment for professional and management level positions. Client companies include general contractors, specialty contractors, highway contractors, civil contractors, construction managers, home builders (residential contractors), engineering contractors (design build), as well as real estate developers and owners who employ construction talent.

Key Contact - Specialty:
Mr. Ken Shaw, Director - *C-level, CEOs, CFOs, Construction, Human resources*

Salary Minimum: $100,000

Functions: Generalist (All)

Industries: Construction, Hotels, Resorts, Clubs

Holland & Associates Inc†

PO Box 488
Chelsea, MI 48118-0488
(734) 475-3701
Fax: (734) 475-7032
Email: general@hollandsearch.com
Web: www.hollandsearch.com

Summary: We provide professional and personalized service to clients involved in the design, development, manufacture and marketing & sales of technologically advanced products for consumer and commercial markets.

Key Contact - Specialty:
Mr. Thomas A. Parr, President - *Manufacturing, Operations, Sales*
Mr. Paul D. Alman, Vice President - *General management*

Salary Minimum: $50,000

Functions: Generalist (All), Board Members, Senior Mgmt., Mfg., Product Dev., Mktg. Mgmt., Sales Mgmt., Engineering

Industries: Food, Bev., Tobacco, Computer Equip., Finance, Telecoms, Telephony, Digital, Wireless, Network Infrastructure, RF/Microwave, Software, Doc. Mgmt., Production SW, ERP SW, Security SW, System SW, Training SW

Branches:
2700 Porter Rd
Plover, WI 54467-2503
(715) 344-6646
Fax: (715) 344-1674
Key Contact - Specialty:
Mr. Daniel O. Holland, Senior Consultant

Hollander Horizon International

1617 S Pacific Coast Hwy Ste C
Redondo Beach, CA 90277-5612
(310) 540-3231
Fax: (310) 540-4230
Email: azimmerman@hhisearch.com
Web: www.hhisearch.com

Summary: Executive search to the food and consumer products industries. Our practice is limited to and highly accomplished in the areas of R&D, manufacturing, engineering and quality control.

Key Contact - Specialty:
Mr. Arnold Zimmerman, Senior Parnter - *Food, Technical*

Salary Minimum: $75,000

Functions: Generalist (All), Plant Mgmt., Quality, Purchasing, Distribution, Packaging, R&D, Engineering

Industries: Generalist (All), Food, Bev., Tobacco, Soap, Perf., Cosmtcs., Drugs Mfg.

Branches:
16 Wall St
Princeton, NJ 08540-1513
(800) 743-9175
Key Contact - Specialty:
Mr. Michael Hollander, Senior Parnter - *Food*

HollandRusk & Associates

211 E Ontario St Ste 1110
Chicago, IL 60611-3277
(312) 266-9595
Fax: (312) 266-8650
Email: srholland@hollandrusk.com

Summary: We provide a highly personalized, customized search methodology in order to accurately and professionally serve clients. Our owner has nurtured diverse networks within senior management to offer an array of talented finalists. We are 100 percent woman-owned.

Key Contact - Specialty:
Ms. Susan R. Holland, President
Mr. Kyle R. Holland, Director, Research

Salary Minimum: $125,000

Functions: Generalist (All), Management, Board Members, Senior Mgmt., Mfg., Sales & Mktg., Finance, Specialized Svcs., Minorities/Diversity, Int'l.

Industries: Generalist (All), Energy, Utilities, Construction, Manufacturing, Transportation, Non-profits, Legal, HR Services, Defense, Compliance, Environmental Svcs., Packaging

The Hollins Group Inc

225 W Wacker Dr Ste 1575
Chicago, IL 60606-1274
(312) 606-8000
Fax: (312) 606-0213
Email: search@thehollinsgroup.com
Web: www.thehollinsgroup.com

Summary: Provides senior and board of director-level search services to major corporations, privately held firms, educational institutions and non-profit organizations across a wide range of industries and functional disciplines.

Key Contact - Specialty:
Mr. Lawrence I. Hollins, President

Salary Minimum: $90,000

Functions: Management, Board Members, Mfg., Health Admin., Sales & Mktg., HR Mgmt., Finance, MIS Mgmt., Minorities/Diversity, Non-profits

Industries: Generalist (All)

Branches:
1720 Mars Hill Rd Ste 8
MSC 307
Acworth, GA 30101-8084
(770) 420-9506
Email: search@thehollinsgroup.com

Key Contact - Specialty:
Dr. Charles Taylor, Vice President & Managing Director

The Holman Group Inc

1592 Union St
San Francisco, CA 94123-4531
(415) 751-2700
Email: jsh@holmangroup.net
Web: www.holmangroup.net

Summary: We are one of the most experienced and accomplished executive recruiting firm in two areas of specialization within the information technology industries: ceo and general partner searches. Generally we work on searches in the $200K+ category.

Key Contact - Specialty:
Mr. Jonathan S. Holman, Founder & President

Salary Minimum: $200,000

Functions: Senior Mgmt.

Industries: Computer Equip., Test, Measure Equip., Electronic, Elec. Components, Semiconductors, Venture Cap., E-commerce, Communications, Software

Holohan Group Ltd

755 S New Ballas Rd Ste 260
Saint Louis, MO 63141-8744
(314) 997-3393
Email: info@holohangroup.com
Web: www.holohangroup.com

Summary: Executive, management, scientific, technical, and healthcare recruitment management consulting firm uniquely composed of a professional staff of primarily Ph.D. senior consultants, serving a core group of technology driven Fortune 500 companies. The firm concentrates on a persistent focus for each assignment and the development of long-term client relationships.

Key Contact - Specialty:
Mr. Barth A. Holohan, Jr., President - *Compliance, Quality, Regulatory*
Dr. James A. Miles, Senior Consultant, Science & Technology - *Agriculture, Biopharmaceutical, Biotechnology, Pharmaceutical, Research & development*
Mr. Rick Bearden, Senior Consultant - *Healthcare, Human resources, Information Technology, Marketing, Supply Chain*
Dr. Jack Kennedy, Senior Consultant, Science & Technology - *Agriculture, Biotechnology, Business development, Marketing, Product management/development*
Dr. Robert E.W. Jansson, Senior Consultant, Science & Technology - *Chemical, Materials, Research & development, Science, Technology*
Mr. Bruce J. Robb, Senior Consultant, Pharmaceuticals - *Business development, Compliance, Marketing, Pharmaceutical, Quality*

Salary Minimum: $100,000

Functions: Management, Mfg., Product Dev., Quality, Physicians, Sales & Mktg., IT, R&D, Engineering, Legal

Industries: Agri., Forestry, Mining, Food, Bev., Tobacco, Chemicals, Drugs Mfg., Medical Devices, Retail, Travel, Communications, Biotech/Life Sciences, Healthcare, Hospitals

J B Homer Associates Inc

708 3rd Ave Fl 22
New York, NY 10017-4201
(212) 697-3300
Email: jhomer@jbhomer.com
Web: www.jbhomer.com

Summary: We are dedicated to the principle that a corporation's executives hold the key to the success of any enterprise. Our total focus is specialized executive recruitment for senior-level IT and operations executives across all industries.

Key Contact - Specialty:
Ms. Judy B. Homer, President
Mr. Fred Weber, Managing Director
Ms. Gina Schiller, Senior Vice President, Tech Recruit - *Banking (Retail), Consumer (Products), Financial, Financial services*
Mr. Allan Einhorn, Vice President, Technology Recruitment - *Banking (Retail), Brokerage, Consumer (Products), Financial services*

Salary Minimum: $150,000

Functions: Generalist (All), IT, MIS Mgmt., Systems Implem., Systems Support

Industries: Generalist (All), Food, Bev., Tobacco, Drugs Mfg., Medical Devices, Finance, Brokers, Misc. Financial, Services, Pharm Svcs., Accounting, Mgmt. Consulting, HR Services, IT Implementation, Media, Communications, Network Infrastructure, Networking, Comm. SW, Security SW

Horgan Splaine Partners

2155 S Bascom Ave Ste 110
Campbell, CA 95008-3200
(408) 626-4852
Email: sean@horgansplaine.com
Web: www.horgansplaine.com

Summary: Our firm conducts retained executive search assignments (director level and above) for companies in high-technology industries, for example: storage, SAN, NAS, internet, clean energy, enterprise software, software as a service, systems, networking, semiconductor.

Key Contact - Specialty:
Mr. Tom Horgan
Mr. Sean P. Splaine

Salary Minimum: $150,000

Functions: Management, Senior Mgmt.

Industries: Computer Equip., Semiconductors, E-commerce, Communications, Digital, Wireless, Fiber Optic, Network Infrastructure, Software, Doc. Mgmt., Production SW, Industry Specific SW, Networking, Comm. SW, System SW

Hornberger Management Company

1201 N Orange St Ste 747
Wilmington, DE 19801-1186
(302) 573-2541
Fax: (302) 213-9195
Email: hmc@hmc.com
Web: www.hmc.com

Summary: We offer board and executive search exclusively for the construction industry (general & specialty contractors, design-build, construction management and real estate developer). Specializing in CEO, COO, CFO and officer level positions. In addition we find outside board directors and executives for contract positions.

Key Contact - Specialty:
Mr. Frederick C. Hornberger, Jr., President - *Construction*

Salary Minimum: $200,000

Functions: Management, Senior Mgmt., Sales & Mktg., HR Mgmt., CFOs

Industries: Construction

Horton International LLC

433 S Main St Ste 327
West Hartford, CT 06110-2822
(860) 521-0101
Fax: (860) 521-0140
Email: hartford@horton-usa.com
Web: www.horton-intl.com

Summary: A generalist firm that recruits senior-level management for all industries.

Key Contact - Specialty:
Mr. Larry C. Brown, Managing Partner
Mr. Robert Gilchrist, Managing Partner
Ms. Patricia Racz, Managing Director
Ms. Susan Hay, Managing Director
Mr. James Bond, Managing Director
Mr. Terry McCarthy, Managing Director - *Asset management, Banking (Investment), C-level, Financial services, Media*
Ms. Molly Robb, Managing Director - *Biomedical, Biotechnology, Life Sciences, Medical (Devices), Pharmaceutical*

Salary Minimum: $120,000

Functions: Generalist (All), Senior Mgmt., Mfg., Healthcare, Sales & Mktg., HR Mgmt., Finance, IT, Engineering, Int'l.

Industries: Generalist (All), Energy, Utilities, Manufacturing, Food, Bev., Tobacco, Chemicals, Drugs Mfg., Medical Devices, Metal Products, Machine, Appliance, Motor Vehicles, Computer Equip., Consumer Elect., Test, Measure Equip., Transportation, Finance, Banking, Invest. Banking, Venture Cap., Services, Media, Communications, Aerospace, Insurance, Software, Biotech/Life Sciences, Healthcare

Branches:
Av Santa Fe 495 Piso 4
Col Cruz Manca (Sta Fe)
05349 Mexico City, DF
Mexico
55 5093 2936
Fax: 55 5093 2910
Email: cepeda@horton-intl.com
Key Contact - Specialty:
Mr. Guillermo Cepeda, Managing Partner

Hospitality Career Services[†]

5035 E Barwick Dr Ste 213
Cave Creek, AZ 85331-5981
(480) 585-0707
(480) 585-0347
Email: mitch@hotelheadhunter.com
Web: www.hotelheadhunter.com

Summary: We represent the candidates that hotel owners and operators want to hire. We have a staff of seven full time recruiters working in hospitality management and a database of over 15,000. We do not place candidates with less than three years of management experience in the hospitality industry.

Key Contact - Specialty:
Mr. Mitchell T. Prager, CHA, President - *Gaming, Hospitality, Hotels*

Salary Minimum: $40,000

Functions: Generalist (All), Management, Board Members, Senior Mgmt., Middle Mgmt., Sales & Mktg., HR Mgmt., Finance, Hospitality, Hotel Mgmt.

Industries: Hospitality, Hotels, Resorts, Clubs, Restaurants, Full Service Restaurants, Entertainment

Hospitality Executive Search Inc

729 Boylston St Ste 303
Boston, MA 02116-2650
(617) 266-7000
Fax: (617) 267-2033
Email: jspatt@jspatt.com
Web: www.jspatt.com

Summary: We undertake retained hospitality search projects for senior-level and board level; executive selection and placement.

Key Contact - Specialty:
Mr. Jonathan M. Spatt, President

Salary Minimum: $65,000

Functions: Management, Board Members, Senior Mgmt., Middle Mgmt., Product Dev., Sales & Mktg., HR Mgmt., CFOs, MIS Mgmt.

Industries: Food, Bev., Tobacco, Hospitality, Hotels, Resorts, Clubs, Restaurants, Entertainment

Hotard & Associates

5640 Six Forks Rd Ste 202
Raleigh, NC 27609-8613
(919) 866-0792
Fax: (919) 866-0794
Email: resumes@hotard-assoc.com
Web: www.hotard-assoc.com

Summary: We are a retained executive search firm open to assignments in any leadership area but focus on accounting, finance and tax management positions.

Key Contact - Specialty:
Mr. Joseph Hotard, President
Mr. Carol Reed, Recruiter

Salary Minimum: $100,000

Functions: Generalist (All), Senior Mgmt., CFOs, Cash Mgmt., Taxes, M&A, IT

Industries: Generalist (All), Oil & Gas, Finance, HR Services, Telecoms, Accounting SW

The Howard-Sloan-Koller Group[†]

300 E 42nd St Fl 15
New York, NY 10017-5925
(212) 661-5250
Fax: (212) 557-9178
Email: hsk@hsksearch.com
Web: www.hsksearch.com

Summary: We do retained search and consulting for the publishing, media, advertising and entertainment media. Our specialties are in all forms of print publishing including magazine, newspapers, newsletters and books, as well as all forms of digital communications, including online, interactive, internet and streaming and multimedia. We have strong practices in direct marketing, public relations, advertising (creative and account sides), conferences and cable.

Key Contact - Specialty:
Mr. Edward R. Koller, Jr., President & Chief Executive Officer - *CEOs, Publishing, Sales*
Ms. Karen Danziger, Executive Vice President - *Boards of Directors, Creative, Editorial*

Salary Minimum: $100,000

Functions: Management, Senior Mgmt., Middle Mgmt., Sales & Mktg., Advertising, Mktg. Mgmt., Sales Mgmt., Direct Mktg., PR, CFOs

Industries: Advertising, Publishing, New Media, Broadcast, Film, Telecoms

Howe and Associates

919 Conestoga Rd Ste 3-214
Bryn Mawr, PA 19010-1354
(610) 527-3100
Fax: (610) 527-3184
Email: execsearch@howe-assoc.com
Web: www.howe-assoc.com

Summary: Serves financial services companies, mid-size and large corporations. Clients represent a variety of industries including financial services, manufacturing, consumer products, healthcare management, and technology.

Key Contact - Specialty:
Mr. I.H. (Chip) Clothier, Managing Partner - *Manufacturing, Marketing, Sales*
Mr. John R. Fell, III, Managing Partner - *Asset management, Banking (Corporate), Finance, Financial services, Sales*

Salary Minimum: $100,000

Functions: Senior Mgmt., Middle Mgmt., Mfg., Materials, Sales & Mktg., HR Mgmt., Finance, Cash Mgmt., IT

Industries: Generalist (All), Manufacturing, Food, Bev., Tobacco, Textiles, Apparel, Consumer Goods, Transportation, Wholesale, Retail, Finance, Banking, Invest. Banking, Services, E-commerce, IT Implementation, Supply Chain Mgmt, Media, Communications, Telecoms, Insurance, Software

HPI Executive Search & HR Consulting[†]

700 Mill St Ste 14
Half Moon Bay, CA 94019-1781
(650) 726-8500
Email: staffing@hpiconsulting.com
Web: www.hpiconsulting.com

Summary: We are a full service executive search firm that specializes in human recources, finance, and marketing executives.

Key Contact - Specialty:
Mr. James Holley, President
Ms. Shirley Holley, Principal

Salary Minimum: $90,000

Functions: Management, Mktg. Research

Industries: Finance, Banking, Legal, HR Services, Telecoms, Wireless, Network Infrastructure, Software, Development SW, Marketing SW

HQ Search Inc

40 Shuman Blvd Ste 160
Naperville, IL 60563-8650
(630) 778-3416
Email: info@hqsearch.com
Web: www.hqsearch.com

Summary: Specializing globally in all areas of financial services in: corporations, domestic & international banks, investment banks, private equity/venture capital, hedge funds/sales & trading, consulting, pension funds, money management and insurance companies.

Key Contact - Specialty:
Mr. Don Graham, Principal

Salary Minimum: $100,000

Functions: Finance, CFOs, Cash Mgmt., Credit, M&A, Risk Mgmt.

Industries: Finance, Banking, Invest. Banking, Brokers, Venture Cap., Misc. Financial

HRCG Inc (The Human Resource Consulting Group Inc)

7907 S Dover St
Littleton, CO 80128-5320
(303) 933-6164

Summary: An executive search practice with highly-experienced business executives and consultants with backgrounds in consumer goods, high-technology, telecom, healthcare, advertising and diversified multinational corporations.

Key Contact - Specialty:
Mr. Joseph L. Zaccaro, President - *Management*
Mr. John F. Kane, Principal - *Management*

Salary Minimum: $100,000

Functions: Generalist (All)

Industries: Generalist (All)

Branches:
6496 Ivarene Ave
Hollywood, CA 90068-2824
(323) 462-6967
Fax: (323) 467-1438
Key Contact - Specialty:
Ms. Megan F. Barnett - *Management*

800 Turnpike St Ste 300
North Andover, MA 01845-6156
(978) 686-5338
Fax: (978) 685-1048
Key Contact - Specialty:
Mr. Al Zink, Principal

8330 Corporate Dr Stop 3
Racine, WI 53406-3773
(262) 884-8674
Fax: (262) 884-8679
Key Contact - Specialty:
Ms. Terri Ladzinski, Principal

HRCS (Human Resources Contract Services Inc)†

11845 W Olympic Blvd Ste 540W
Los Angeles, CA 90064-5082
(310) 235-2880
Fax: (310) 235-2881
Email: info@hrcs.com
Web: www.hrcs.com

Summary: Our firm is a premier provider of HR professionals. Servicing all industries, we provide HR consultants for interim, long term and contract to hire projects. We provide HR permanent placement search and client HR payroll services. We offer an industry competitive fee structure.

Key Contact - Specialty:
Mr. Donald A. Lumpkin, President

Salary Minimum: $60,000

Functions: HR Mgmt., Benefits, Staffing, Training

Industries: Generalist (All)

HRD Consultants Inc

60 Walnut Ave Ste 100
Clark, NJ 07066-1635
(732) 815-7825
Fax: (732) 815-7810
Email: hrd@aol.com
Web: www.hrdconsultants.com

Summary: We offer our clients a long history in HR recruitment, an extensive network, information regarding trends in HR and a commitment to excellence.

Key Contact - Specialty:
Ms. Marcia Glatman, President

Salary Minimum: $150,000

Functions: HR Mgmt.

Industries: Generalist (All)

Arnold Huberman Associates Inc†

51 E 25th St Ste 501
New York, NY 10010-8209
(212) 545-9033
Fax: (212) 779-9641
Email: arnie@huberman.com
Web: www.huberman.com

Summary: Our firm provides specialists in management recruiting in the areas of corporate communications and public relations across all industries. Specific expertise in finding public relations agencies for corporations.

Key Contact - Specialty:
Mr. Arnold M. Huberman, President - *Public relations*

Functions: PR

Industries: Generalist (All)

Hudepohl & Associates Inc

150 W Wilson Bridge Rd Ste 203
Worthington, OH 43085-2287
(614) 854-7300
Email: info@hudepohl.com
Web: www.hudepohl.com

Summary: We specialize in accounting, finance, HR, investment management and IT positions. Our team has extensive experience in search. Our clients include public pension funds, financial institutions, insurance companies, manufacturing, and higher education institutions.

Key Contact - Specialty:
Mr. Gary L. Hudepohl, Principal & Managing Director
Ms. Debbie Roche, Principal

Salary Minimum: $75,000

Functions: HR Mgmt., Finance, CFOs, Cash Mgmt., IT, MIS Mgmt.

Industries: Chemicals, Banking, Invest. Banking, Venture Cap., Higher Ed., Call Centers, Insurance

Hudson Consulting Group†

1376 Meadowood Ln
Hudson, OH 44236-2155
(216) 533-5249
Email: skiel@hudgrp.com
Web: www.hudgrp.com

Summary: Hudson Consulting Group conducts professional, fixed priced executive and middle management searches for the manufacturing, retail and healthcare sectors. The Firm also provides buy-side advisory support to executives seeking transition from a corporate to private equity setting.

Key Contact - Specialty:
Mr. Stephen J. Kiel, CPA, Managing Director - *Consumer (Products), Finance, Private equity, Restaurants, Retail*
Mr. Robert O. Harvey, MHA, Director - *Engineering, Healthcare, Information Technology, Long term care, Medical (Devices)*
Mr. Van P. Carter, JD, Director - *Banking, Distribution, Legal, Manufacturing, Regulatory*

Salary Minimum: $70,000

Functions: Senior Mgmt., Middle Mgmt.

Industries: Food, Bev., Tobacco, Medical Devices, Machine, Appliance, Motor Vehicles, Misc. Mfg., Wholesale, Retail, Legal, Mgmt. Consulting, Supply Chain Mgmt., Restaurants, Real Estate, Hospitals, Long-term/Home Care

Hudson Gain Corp

1 Penn Plz Fl 36
New York, NY 10119-3699
(212) 835-1600
Email: careers@hudsongain.com
Web: www.hudsongain.com

Summary: Our firm offers leadership change solutions. We help clients attract the best leadership quickly and we invest in the lasting success of each placement. We specialize in senior level executive search, new leader acquisition and new hire integration, as well as succession planning and leadership development.

Key Contact - Specialty:
Mr. James Celentano, President & Managing Partner - *Financial services, Retail, Technology*

Salary Minimum: $150,000

Functions: Generalist (All), Management, Board Members, Senior Mgmt., Mktg. Mgmt., Sales Mgmt., Direct Mktg., HR Mgmt., CFOs, MIS Mgmt.

Industries: Generalist (All), Manufacturing, Retail, Banking, Venture Cap., E-commerce, Entertainment, Media, Communications, Software

Huey Enterprises Inc†

273 Clarkson Executive Park
Ellisville, MO 63011-2173
(636) 394-9393
Fax: (636) 794-3100
Email: art@huey.com
Web: www.huey.com

Summary: Our firm has particular strength in direct recruiting of executive and professional level candidates with highly specialized skills. We have an extensive database of industry talent/contacts in specialization areas supplemented by in-depth knowledge of Internet search and recruiting techniques.

Key Contact - Specialty:
Mr. Arthur T. Huey, President

Salary Minimum: $100,000

Functions: Generalist (All)

Industries: Construction, Retail, Real Estate

Hughes & Company

PO Box 7365
Alexandria, VA 22307-0365
(703) 765-8853
Fax: (703) 765-6828
Email: info@hughessearch.com

Summary: We are a specialized search firm offering highly personalized, responsive service within the consumer packaged goods and services industry. Our focus is on building management teams. We are known for quality, team-work and long-term relationships. We concentrate on recruiting exceptional management talent for sales, marketing, financial and general management positions.

Key Contact - Specialty:
Mr. Donald J. Hughes, Managing Partner - *Accounting, Consumer (Marketing,Packaged Goods,Products), Exports*
Mr. Martin Smith, Managing Partner - *Boards of Directors, CEOs, Consumer (Products), Convenience stores, Dairy*
Mr. J. Reid Johnston, Managing Partner - *CFOs, Convenience stores, Finance, Financial services, International*

† occasional contingency assignment

Mr. John Rodgers, Vice President - *Consumer (Packaged Goods), Diversity, Food, Sales, Seafood*

Mr. William B. Casey, Vice President - *Citrus, Consumer, Consumer (Products), Floriculture, Marketing*

Salary Minimum: $75,000

Functions: Board Members, Senior Mgmt., Middle Mgmt., Allied Health, Sales & Mktg., Advertising, Sales Mgmt., Finance, Int'l.

Industries: Generalist (All), Manufacturing, Food, Bev., Tobacco, Paper, Soap, Perf., Cosmtcs., Drugs Mfg., Consumer Elect., Retail, Pharm Svcs., Legal, Healthcare, Hospitals, Long-term/Home Care

E A Hughes & Company Inc

245 5th Ave Rm 901
New York, NY 10016-8728
(212) 689-4600
Fax: (212) 689-4975
Email: hr@eahughes.com
Web: www.eahughes.com

Summary: We conduct our business by supporting our client's in assembling the best executive teams to suit their company's culture and strategies. Our team is dedicated to our clients, supporting their every need to guarantee the best possible future for their company. We are arguably one of the most respected and talented search firms in the retail/wholesale apparel, home fashion, textile and direct marketing industries.

Key Contact - Specialty:
Ms. Elaine A. Hughes, President - *Apparel, Retail*
Mr. Marvin Lord, Executive Vice President - *Apparel, Retail*
Ms. Carolyn Wojcik, Vice President - *Apparel, Design*
Ms. Cheryl Slinko, Senior Associate - *Apparel, Design, Retail*
Mrs. Mary Wahlig, Senior Consultant - *Retail*

Salary Minimum: $100,000

Functions: Board Members, Senior Mgmt., Product Dev., Mktg. Research, Mktg. Mgmt., Sales Mgmt., Direct Mktg., Textile/Fashion

Industries: Textiles, Apparel, Consumer Goods, Wholesale, Retail

Human Capital Partners, LLC

2325 Sumter Lake Dr
Marietta, GA 30062-5435
(770) 971-3007
Fax: (770) 971-1101
Email: nom@humancapitalptrs.com
Web: www.humancapitalptrs.com

Summary: Human Capital Partners (HCP) is a small, boutique retained executive search firm based in Atlanta, GA. We conduct searches for professionals and mid/senior level executives for a broad range of clients throughout the U.S. HCP works in most functional arenas with special emphasis in finance/accounting; human resources; professional services/sales; and marketing.

Key Contact - Specialty:
Ms. Nancy O'Brien May, Managing Principal - *Accounting (Public), Benefits, Compensation, Consulting, Controllers*

Salary Minimum: $100,000

Functions: Middle Mgmt., Mktg. Mgmt., Sales Mgmt., HR Mgmt., Benefits, Finance, Pension/Ret. Planning

Industries: Generalist (All)

The Human Resource Advantage Inc

702 Laurel Ln
Wyckoff, NJ 07481-1029
(201) 848-7333
Fax: (201) 847-9325
Email: pzapka@bellatlantic.net

Summary: A retained executive search consulting firm focused on providing exceptional people to our client partners, as well as innovative, just-in-time organizational solutions.

Key Contact - Specialty:
Mr. Paul Zapka, President

Salary Minimum: $130,000

Functions: Generalist (All)

Industries: Generalist (All)

Branches:
21 Feather Sound Dr
Anthem Country Club
Henderson, NV 89052-6614
(702) 361-8416
Key Contact - Specialty:
Mr. Joe Tuschman, Chief Operating Officer

Human Resource Management Services

5314 S Yale Ave Ste 400
Tulsa, OK 74135-6271
(918) 495-1988
Email: rjmesser@hrmgt.org

Summary: We are a boutique firm specializing in assisting our clients to fill senior financial, HR, administrative and technical officer and managerial positions.

Key Contact - Specialty:
Mr. Richard Messer, SPHR, CMC, President

Salary Minimum: $80,000

Functions: Generalist (All), Management

Industries: Generalist (All), Manufacturing, Retail, Finance, Services, Non-profits, HR Services

Human Resources Group Inc

2912 Marketplace Dr Ste 105
Fitchburg, WI 53719-5324
(608) 233-5491
(800) 817-8597
Fax: (608) 233-4090
Email: info@hrgroup.com
Web: www.hrgroup.com

Summary: We conduct retained executive, management, technical and sales/marketing searches across a variety of industries. We are a focused firm with extensive search experience providing comprehensive, value-added client services, including tailored search strategies and detailed candidate evaluations and reporting.

Key Contact - Specialty:
Mr. Daniel Stahl, SPHR, President
Ms. Mila Stahl, Vice President & Principal
Mr. Kevin Peternel, Vice President & Principal

Salary Minimum: $50,000

Functions: Board Members, Senior Mgmt., Middle Mgmt., Mfg., Mktg. Research, Mktg. Mgmt., Sales Mgmt., Engineering

Industries: Generalist (All), Agri., Forestry, Mining, Energy, Utilities, Oil & Gas, Construction, Manufacturing, Drugs Mfg., Medical Devices, Transportation, Wholesale, Retail, Services, Non-profits, Legal, Mgmt. Consulting, HR Services, Media, Communications, Telecoms, Environmental

Svcs., Packaging, Insurance, Biotech/Life Sciences, Healthcare

Human Resources Personnel Agency[†]

PO Box 3161
Little Rock, AR 72203-3161
(501) 376-4622
Fax: (501) 376-6416
Email: jobs@employment4u.com
Web: www.employment4u.com

Summary: Firm works only with manufacturing related positions. Plant start-ups a specialty. Staff offers hands-on manufacturing experience.

Key Contact - Specialty:
Mr. Brett Walker, President & Chief Executive Officer - *Human resources, Manufacturing, Materials, Purchasing*
Mr. Lance Click, Vice President

Functions: Generalist (All), Automation, Productivity, HR Mgmt., Benefits, Systems Dev., Engineering

Industries: Generalist (All), Textiles, Apparel, Printing, Plastics, Rubber, Metal Products, Machine, Appliance, Consumer Elect.

The Humbert Group LLC[†]

PO Box 514
Marion, IA 52302-0514
(319) 373-4434
Email: recruiterguy@msn.com
Web: www.recruiterguy.com

Summary: Our firm has a very different business model than most recruitment firms. We focus on one firm at a time and partner with our client to identify and deliver the best available candidates at all levels, including executive.

Key Contact - Specialty:
Mr. Bill Humbert, Principal

Functions: Generalist (All), Management, Middle Mgmt., Mfg., Plant Mgmt., Sales & Mktg., HR Mgmt., Finance, IT, Engineering

Industries: Generalist (All), Manufacturing, Food, Bev., Tobacco, Test, Measure Equip., Misc. Mfg., Electronic, Elec. Components, Semiconductors, Consumer Goods, Communications, Telecoms, Call Centers, Telephony, Defense, Aerospace, Software, Accounting SW, Database SW, Development SW, ERP SW, HR SW, Mfg. SW, Marketing SW, System SW

HumCap LP[†]

14875 Landmark Blvd Ste 150
Dallas, TX 75254-1413
(214) 520-0760
Fax: (214) 520-8839
Email: info@humcapinc.com
Web: www.humcapinc.com

Summary: We are a retained executive search and technical contract placement firm specializing in recruiting services for technical, professional, and executive positions. We provide candidates to perform specific tasks as an integral part of your team, or as a full team to complete a specific assignment.

Key Contact - Specialty:
Mr. Tad McIntosh, President
Mr. Kelly Guy, Director, Recruiting Services
Mr. Rorry Phillips, Director, Human Resource Services

Salary Minimum: $50,000

Functions: Management, Middle Mgmt., Sales Reps., HR Mgmt., Staffing, Finance, Engineering

Industries: Manufacturing, Medical Devices, Computer Equip., Test, Measure Equip., Electronic, Elec. Components, Semiconductors, Communications, Telecoms, Call Centers, Telephony, Digital, Wireless, Fiber Optic, Network Infrastructure, RF/Microwave, Aerospace, Networking, Comm. SW, Security SW, Biotech/Life Sciences, Non-Classifiable

HI Hunt & Company Ltd

2 Avery St Apt 30G
Boston, MA 02111-1017
(617) 261-1611
Fax: (617) 350-0999
Email: hihunt@hihunt.net

Summary: Executive search firm specializing in the areas of investment banking, structured finance, and fund management businesses.

Key Contact - Specialty:
Mr. Herbert I. Hunt, III, Principal - *Financial services*

Salary Minimum: $100,000

Functions: Senior Mgmt., Finance, CFOs

Industries: Invest. Banking, Venture Cap., Mutual/Hedge Funds, Misc. Financial

The Hunt Group Inc

(also known as J B Hunt Executive Search Inc)
21235 Catawba Ave
Cornelius, NC 28031-8504
(704) 895-2600
Fax: (704) 895-2665
Email: joehunt@huntsearch.com
Web: www.huntsearch.com

Summary: Executive search and recruiting firm with practices specializing in the consumer goods, life sciences, industrial products and professional services. We conduct searches for executives and professionals in general management, supply chain/logistics, manufacturing/operations, sales/marketing, scientific affairs and key administrative positions including corporate counsel, finance and HR.

Key Contact - Specialty:
Mr. Joseph B. Hunt, Senior Parnter - *Senior management*

Salary Minimum: $150,000

Functions: Generalist (All), Management, Board Members, Senior Mgmt.

Industries: Generalist (All), Manufacturing, Food, Bev., Tobacco, Chemicals, Soap, Perf., Cosmtcs., Drugs Mfg., Medical Devices, Consumer Goods, Services, Mgmt. Consulting, Packaging, Biotech/Life Sciences

Hunt Howe Partners LLC

1 Dag Hammarskjold Plz
New York, NY 10017-2201
(212) 758-2800
Fax: (212) 758-7710
Email: info@hunthowe.com
Web: www.hunthowe.com

Summary: We specialize in finding leaders who can steer through a turbulent present while creating the future by discovering and skillfully pursuing new routes to success. We think about tomorrow's organization and not just the current structure keeping in mind longer-term possibilities as well as predictable near-term scenarios. We are experts in emerging business models as well as today's patterns and practices.

Key Contact - Specialty:
Mr. William S. Howe, Managing Director - *Biotechnology, Financial services, Media, Pharmaceutical*

Mr. James E. Hunt, Managing Director - *Financial services, High technology, Professional services*
Mr. Jeffrey G. Neuberth, Managing Director
Ms. Sandra Rupp, Managing Director - *Financial services, Marketing, Professional services*
Mr. John W. Johnson, Jr., Consultant
Ms. Carol McCullough, Consultant - *Finance*

Salary Minimum: $200,000

Functions: Generalist (All)

Industries: Chemicals, Drugs Mfg., Medical Devices, Computer Equip., Consumer Elect., Electronic, Elec. Components, Banking, Services, Communications, Biotech/Life Sciences

Hunt, Patton & Brazeal Inc[†]

7170 S Braden Ave Ste 185
Tulsa, OK 74136-6324
(918) 492-6910
Fax: (918) 492-7023
Email: hpb@huntpatton.com
Web: www.huntpatton.com

Summary: We are recruiting specialists for executive, professional and technical engineering positions in environmental, construction, oil & gas, petroleum, chemical, medical and laboratory industries.

Key Contact - Specialty:
Dr. Pat Patton, President
Mr. John Williams, Vice President

Salary Minimum: $50,000

Functions: Generalist (All), Senior Mgmt., Middle Mgmt., Production, Plant Mgmt., Purchasing, Mktg. Mgmt., Engineering

Industries: Energy, Utilities, Oil & Gas, Construction, Manufacturing, Chemicals, Paints, Petro. Products, Metal Products, Machine, Appliance, Test, Measure Equip., Misc. Mfg., Equip Svcs., Environmental Svcs., Haz. Waste

Branches:
3 Riverway Ste 170
Houston, TX 77056-1991
(713) 355-8350
Fax: (713) 355-8352
Email: hpbhouston@huntpatton.com
Key Contact - Specialty:
Ms. Missy Pangelinan, Recruiter, Executive & Technical

The Hunter Group Inc[†]

33 Bloomfield Hills Pkwy Ste 242
Bloomfield Hills, MI 48304-2946
(248) 645-1551
Fax: (248) 645-6130
Email: renee@huntergroup.com
Web: www.huntergroup.com

Summary: We offer combined executive recruiting expertise. One of Michigan's fastest growing executive search firms.

Key Contact - Specialty:
Mr. James Lionas, Principal
Ms. Sherry Muir Irwin, Principal - *Automotive, Technical*
Mr. Charles Biggs, Principal
Ms. Renee Sakmar, Principal
Ms. Ellen Letourneau, Principal

Functions: Generalist (All), Senior Mgmt., Mfg., Health Admin., HR Mgmt., CFOs, Engineering

Industries: Generalist (All), Plastics, Rubber, Metal Products, Motor Vehicles, Misc. Mfg., Healthcare

Branches:
4065 Riverglen Cir Ste 100
Suwanee, GA 30024-1858
(678) 931-0117
Email: renee@huntergroup.com
Key Contact - Specialty:
Dr. Rudieger Mueller

33 Bloomfield Hills Pkwy Ste 242
Bloomfield Hills, MI 48304-2946
(615) 236-1500
Email: renee@huntergroup.com
Key Contact - Specialty:
Mr. John Radebaugh

Hunter, Rowan & Crowe[†]

9843 Treasure Cay Ln
Bonita Springs, FL 34135-6810
(239) 495-1389
Fax: (239) 992-7517
Email: crowehrc@earthlink.net

Summary: Management consulting experience provides unique expertise for quick study and understanding of client organization culture to better match candidate styles. Proprietary network and research database.

Key Contact - Specialty:
Mr. Thomas H. Crowe, President - *General management, Manufacturing, Marketing, Sales*
Ms. Carol Rowan, Director, Research

Salary Minimum: $100,000

Functions: Generalist (All), Management, Mfg., Sales & Mktg., Finance

Industries: Generalist (All), Oil & Gas, Construction, Manufacturing, Food, Bev., Tobacco, Paper, Drugs Mfg., Plastics, Rubber, Metal Products, Machine, Appliance, Misc. Mfg., Consumer Goods, Wholesale, Finance, Mgmt. Consulting, E-commerce, Media, Advertising, Publishing, Real Estate

Hunter Search Group Inc

PO Box 27108
West Des Moines, IA 50265-9416
(515) 256-4440
Fax: (515) 287-0707
Email: debra@huntersearchgroup.com
Web: www.huntersearchgroup.com

Summary: We specialize in executive management, CFOs & SVPs, senior sales & marketing people, and engineers. We consider ourselves generalists with much of our work in the past in the following industries: financial services, manufacturing, and non-profit organizations. We also offer consulting services in leadership development, executive coaching, career coaching and executive assessments.

Key Contact - Specialty:
Ms. Debra S. Habr, President - *Financial services, Manufacturing*

Salary Minimum: $70,000

Functions: Senior Mgmt., Sales & Mktg., CFOs

Industries: Generalist (All), Manufacturing, Finance, Banking, Misc. Financial, Services, Non-profits

Hunter Sterling LLC[†]

PO Box 3296
Saratoga, CA 95070-1296
(831) 277-1628
Email: john@huntersterling.com
Web: www.huntersterling.com

Summary: We are a retained search firm specializing in c-level searches in information technology, Internet, software, and IS.

Key Contact - Specialty:
Dr. John Webster, PhD, President & Chief
Executive Officer
Dr. Pat Templin, Senior Vice President
Mr. Mark S. Webster, Chief Operating Officer -
Networking, Wireless

Salary Minimum: $120,000

Functions: Generalist (All)

Industries: Computer Equip., Electronic, Elec.
Components, Services, Communications,
Software, Biotech/Life Sciences

Hunter-Stiles Associates
PO Box 164313
Austin, TX 78716-4313
(512) 347-7708
Email: crl4009@yahoo.com

Summary: We are a high-technology focused,
executive search firm. Our search work focuses on
senior executives, CEOs, COOs, presidents,
CFOs, CTOs and VP level sales and marketing
positions. The markets we serve include
biotechnology, telecom, hardware and software.

Key Contact - Specialty:
Mr. Charles Leadford, Chief Executive Officer &
Founder - *Senior management*

Salary Minimum: $150,000

Functions: Senior Mgmt.

Industries: Computer Equip., E-commerce,
Communications, Software, Marketing SW,
Biotech/Life Sciences, Healthcare

Huntress Real Estate Executive Search[†]
PO Box 8667
Kansas City, MO 64114-1058
(913) 383-8180
Fax: (913) 383-8184
Email: info@huntress.net
Web: www.huntress.net

Summary: We offer real estate related consulting
advisory services. We specialize in management
consultants to the real estate, finance and
construction industry including organizational
planning, compensation studies and senior
executive staffing. We spend major activity on
executive search.

Key Contact - Specialty:
Mr. Stan Stanton, President - *Construction,
Finance, Industrial, Retail*

Salary Minimum: $50,000

Functions: Generalist (All), Board Members,
Senior Mgmt., Admin. Svcs., CFOs, M&A,
Architects, Legal, Attorneys, Int'l.

Industries: Real Estate

Hutchinson Smiley Ltd[†]
1002-890 Yonge St
Toronto, ON M4W 3P4
Canada
(416) 967-6654
Email: hsl@pathcom.com

Summary: We are a management and IS
consulting firm that specializes in contract and
permanent placement of skilled systems resources
and business consultants. Our focus has been the
IT and systems areas for a number of years.

Key Contact - Specialty:
Mr. Robert W. Sydia, President
Mr. Robert A. Sydia, Vice President
Mr. John Nakashima, Resource Consulting

Functions: Management, IT, MIS Mgmt.,
Systems Analysis, Systems Dev., Systems

Implem., Systems Support, Network Admin.,
DB Admin., Mgmt. Consultants

Industries: Generalist (All)

Hutton Merrill & Associates
3333 Bowers Ave Ste 130
Santa Clara, CA 95054-2928
(408) 919-2999
Email: tom@huttonllc.com
Web: www.huttonllc.com

Summary: We are a high-technology executive
search firm with a primary focus on
semiconductors, software and communications.
We conduct extensive, original research for every
assignment.

Key Contact - Specialty:
Mr. Thomas J. Hutton
Ms. Barbara Merrill
Ms. Vera Wong

Salary Minimum: $150,000

Functions: Generalist (All), Management, Mfg.,
Sales & Mktg., Engineering

Industries: Generalist (All), Computer Equip.,
Test, Measure Equip., Software

HVS Executive Search
372 Willis Ave
Mineola, NY 11501-1818
(516) 248-8828
Fax: (516) 742-3059
Email: kkefgen@hvsinternational.com
Web: www.hvsinternational.com

Summary: We are a retainer search firm
specializing in the recruitment of senior-level
executives in the hospitality industry.

Key Contact - Specialty:
Mr. Keith Kefgen, President
Ms. Dena Blum-Rothman, Vice President
Mr. Stephen Rushmore, Secretary & Treasurer
Mr. Dave Mansbach, Vice President -
Restaurants
Mr. Stephen Goebel, Managing Director, Las
Vegas - *Hospitality*
Mr. Christopher Mumford, Managing Director,
London
Mr. Mark Keith, Managing Director, Hong Kong
Mr. Manav Thadani, Managing Director, India
Mr. Michael Wurster, Vice President - *Gaming,
Hospitality, Technology*

Salary Minimum: $75,000

Functions: Generalist (All)

Industries: Hospitality

Hyde, Danforth & Company[†]
10670 N Central Expy Ste 450
Dallas, TX 75231-1075
(214) 691-5966
(888) 887-0990
Fax: (214) 369-7317
Email: resume@hydedanforth.com
Web: www.hydedanforth.com

Summary: Over 85 percent of engagements
performed for existing or referred clients. A
quality boutique practice serving industry,
attorneys, professionals and academia. Also
provide H/R career and transition consulting.

Key Contact - Specialty:
Mr. W. Michael Danforth, President
Mr. W. Jerry Hyde, Executive Vice President &
Founder
Mr. Michael R. McGee, SPHR, Vice President
Mr. George Neary, Vice President

Salary Minimum: $75,000

Functions: Generalist (All), Healthcare, Sales &
Mktg., HR Mgmt., Finance, Attorneys

Industries: Generalist (All), Banking, Legal,
Accounting, HR Services, Hospitality, Hotels,
Resorts, Clubs, Advertising, Insurance, Real
Estate, Healthcare, Hospitals

Identify Inc
99 S Lake Ave Ste 201
Pasadena, CA 91101-4751
(626) 395-0444
Email: info@identifyinc.com
Web: www.identifyinc.com

Summary: As executive search and contract
recruiters, our firms' services focus on a broad
range of positions and industries. Our recruiting
methodology and service replicates the
thoroughness of retained search without incurring
costly search fees because our bills are on an hourly
basis.

Key Contact - Specialty:
Ms. Christine Teeple, Executive Vice President
Ms. Dianne McGee, Executive Vice President

Salary Minimum: $50,000

Functions: Generalist (All), Management, Middle
Mgmt., Admin. Svcs., HR Mgmt.

Industries: Generalist (All), Finance, Banking,
Services, Non-profits, Accounting, HR Services,
Higher Ed., Media, Telecoms, Software,
Marketing SW, Healthcare

IMA Search Inc
106 Peninsula Dr Ste A
Babylon, NY 11702-3336
(631) 422-3900
Fax: (631) 587-3556
Email: imasearch@aol.com
Web: www.ima-search.com

Summary: We provide confidential services such
as worldwide executive search and career
counseling. As generalists we cover most areas
and disciplines and offer executive assessment,
background checks. We offer clients a more
effective approach to succession planning.

Key Contact - Specialty:
Mr. Paul D. Steinberg, President & Chief
Executive Officer - *High technology, Retail,
Social work, Telecommunications*
Dr. Steven A. Martello, Vice President & General
Counsel - *COOs, Executives, Investor relations,
Legal, Legal (Attorneys)*
Ms. Suzanne Welling, Vice President -
*Marketing, Middle management, Non-profit,
Philanthropy, Sales*
Mr. Dante J. Laurino, Vice President -
*Professional services, Retail, Sales, Sports,
Telecommunications*

Salary Minimum: $85,000

Functions: Generalist (All)

Industries: Generalist (All)

John Imber Associates Ltd
310 Busse Hwy
Park Ridge, IL 60068-3251
(847) 692-8000
Email: rebmi@aol.com

Summary: Utilizing a search process designed to
attract, select and retain individuals fittingly
prepared and motivated to thrive within your
unique corporate environment.

Key Contact - Specialty:
Mr. John Imber, President

Salary Minimum: $90,000

Functions: Mfg., Sales & Mktg.

Industries: Manufacturing

The IMC Group

230 Park Ave Fl 10
New York, NY 10169-1099
(212) 838-9535
Email: info@the-imc.com
Web: www.the-imc.com

Summary: We have experience as senior-level retained executive search consultants for hospitality, leisure and entertainment companies.

Key Contact - Specialty:
Mr. Herbert Regehly, President
Mr. Howard Chamberlain, Director

Salary Minimum: $100,000

Functions: Generalist (All), Management, Senior Mgmt., Int'l.

Industries: Services, Hospitality, Hotels, Resorts, Clubs, Restaurants, Full Service Restaurants, Inst./Industrial Food Svc., Entertainment, Recreation, Sports, Travel, Hospitals

Incerca International[†]

501 N Riverside Dr Ste 103
Gurnee, IL 60031-5918
(847) 775-1390
Fax: (847) 775-1394
Email: incerca@incerca.com
Web: www.incerca.com

Summary: Our firm provides quality global executive search services to the building materials and consumer durables industries. We specialize in the marketing, sales, operations and general management functions for manufacturers and retailers within these two industry segments. We can provide your firm with an individual or a whole operations' marketing, sales or general management team.

Key Contact - Specialty:
Mr. Rinaldo Manago, President & Owner - *Retail, Wholesale*
Ms. Jenny Slifko, Senior Executive Recruiter
Ms. Kathy Foy, Executive Recruiter
Mr. James Pillars, Research Analyst
Ms. Amilie Dubois, Research Analyst

Salary Minimum: $100,000

Functions: Generalist (All)

Industries: Construction, Manufacturing, Wholesale, Retail, Real Estate

Independent Power Consultants[†]

2100 Tanglewilde St Apt 191
Houston, TX 77063-1283
(832) 252-6250
(713) 540-5655
Fax: (832) 252-6250
Email: lahjr2003@houston.rr.com
Web: www.ipcsearch.com

Summary: Firm specializing in the power industry executive search. Assignments include positions in trading, business development, project development, project management, operations and asset management.

Key Contact - Specialty:
Mr. Luis A. Hernandez, Jr., President - *Energy, Engineering, Human resources, Power, Strategic planning*
Mrs. Alejandra Gonzalez, Research Assistant

Salary Minimum: $75,000

Functions: Generalist (All), Board Members

Industries: Generalist (All), Energy, Utilities, Mgmt. Consulting, HR Services

Infinger & Associates[†]

4764 Homestead Pl
Matthews, NC 28104-8905
(704) 845-0521
Email: roninfinger@carolina.rr.com

Summary: We are a retained executive search firm that assists its clients in recruiting qualified, available individuals for most disciplines and functional areas.

Key Contact - Specialty:
Mr. Ronald Infinger, Principal

Salary Minimum: $50,000

Functions: Generalist (All)

Industries: Energy, Utilities, Manufacturing, Transportation, Finance, Banking, Non-profits, Insurance, Real Estate, Healthcare

Infinity Resources LLC

1200 US Highway 22 Ste 2000
Bridgewater, NJ 08807-2943
(732) 502-9518
Email: hmaphet@infinity-resources.com
Web: www.infinity-resources.com

Summary: Retained executive search and HR consulting firm with a strong commitment to value added search model. Specialists in talent management.

Key Contact - Specialty:
Ms. Harriet Maphet, President

Salary Minimum: $100,000

Functions: Generalist (All)

Industries: Generalist (All), Manufacturing, Chemicals, Drugs Mfg., Medical Devices, Finance, Services, Pharm Svcs., Entertainment, Biotech/Life Sciences

Branches:
1419 Waters Edge Dr
Toms River, NJ 08753-2660
(732) 722-8723
Email: wmorgan@infinity-resources.com
Key Contact - Specialty:
Mr. Wyman Morgan, DR - *Biotechnology, Chemical, Life Sciences, Research & development, Technology*

2013 Crompond Rd Ste 100
Yorktown Heights, NY 10598-4235
(914) 245-0800
Fax: (914) 245-7795
Key Contact - Specialty:
Mr. Marc Roberts, Senior Vice President

Infonet Resources LLC[†]

30 Partridge Lndg
Glastonbury, CT 06033-2850
(860) 652-8000
Fax: (860) 633-4203
Email: tim@infonet.bz
Web: www.infonet.bz

Summary: We are an executive search for IT executives and leaders for capital markets and Fortune 500 companies. We have particular strength in banking, brokerage and diversified financial sectors.

Key Contact - Specialty:
Mr. Timothy J. McIntyre, Chief Executive Officer

Salary Minimum: $120,000

Functions: MIS Mgmt.

Industries: Finance, Banking, Invest. Banking, Brokers, E-commerce, Media, Insurance, Real Estate, Software, Healthcare

Ingenium Partners Inc

2 Cityplace Dr Ste 200
Saint Louis, MO 63141-7055
(314) 991-8007
Fax: (314) 991-8710
Email: sgoldenberg@ingeniumpartners.com
Web: www.ingeniumpartners.com

Summary: We provide comprehensive executive search consulting services to organizations in the financial services, retail, real estate, manufacturing, service, healthcare and nonprofit industries. Specific functional areas include finance, HR, sales & marketing, operations and general management.

Key Contact - Specialty:
Ms. Susan Goldenberg, President
Ms. Linda Bearman, Senior Search Consultant
Ms. Judy Iffrig, Research Assistant

Salary Minimum: $100,000

Functions: Senior Mgmt., Middle Mgmt., Admin. Svcs., Sales & Mktg., HR Mgmt., Benefits, Finance, CFOs, Non-profits

Industries: Generalist (All)

Innovative Research Worlwide Inc

400 Frandorson Cir Ste 204
Apollo Beach, FL 33572-2692
(813) 645-4646
(877) 479-9462
Fax: (813) 645-4636
Email: jwilkson@irworldwide.com
Web: www.irworldwide.com

Summary: Retaining our firm ensures that you will receive confidentiality, passion, performance and efficiency. We recruit talent that has a proven track record for their distinguished performance.

Key Contact - Specialty:
Mr. James Wilkson, President
Mr. Philip Harrell, Senior Managing Partner
Mr. Steve McQuinn, Managing Partner

Functions: Generalist (All)

Industries: Generalist (All), Energy, Utilities, Manufacturing, Finance, Services, Hospitality, Media, Communications, Software, Biotech/Life Sciences

InSearch Management Consultants Inc

PO Box 2036
Novato, CA 94948-2036
(415) 884-2700
Email: info@insearchinc.com
Web: www.insearchinc.com

Summary: Retain search and consultant. Specializing in newly created and succession searches and strategies. Typical assignments include culture building and behavior based sourcing. Governance and BOD expert.

Key Contact - Specialty:
Mr. Michael Huskins, President - *Management, Senior management, Start-up companies*
Mr. John McLaughlin, Executive Recruiter - *C-level, CFOs, Information Technology, Telecommunications, Wireless*

Salary Minimum: $150,000

Functions: Board Members, Senior Mgmt., Middle Mgmt., Materials, Sales & Mktg., Mktg. Mgmt., Sales Mgmt., Direct Mktg., MIS Mgmt., Minorities/Diversity

Industries: Generalist (All), Manufacturing, Food, Bev., Tobacco, Drugs Mfg., Retail, Misc. Financial, E-commerce, K-12 Ed., Supply Chain Mgmt, Entertainment, Media, Publishing, Communications, Insurance, Software, ERP SW, Biotech/Life Sciences, Healthcare

InSearch Worldwide Corp

1 Landmark Sq
Stamford, CT 06901-2603
(203) 355-3000
Fax: (203) 355-3100
Email: info@insearchworldwide.com
Web: www.insearchworldwide.com

Summary: We are a leading talent acquisition firm specializing in recruitment process outsourcing, retained executive and middle management search, and human resource consultancy. Our business is based on performance, strategic vision and dedicated partnerships. This approach has given us a long and documented history of recruiting top talent, which positively impacts our clients' corporate framework.

Key Contact - Specialty:
Mr. Randolph Gulian, President & Managing Director
Mr. James Perry, Senior Vice President & Mng Director
Mr. Phil Thawley, Senior Vice President & Mng Director - *Consumer (Marketing), Credit cards, Human resources, Professional services, Strategic planning*
Mrs. Rebecca Bleiman, Vice President & National Acct Director - *Change management, Consumer (Marketing), Credit cards, Financial services, Staffing*
Mr. John T. Markey, IV, Vice President & National Acct Director - *Consumer (Packaged Goods), Human resources, Insurance, Minorities, Staffing*

Salary Minimum: $80,000

Functions: Management, Sales & Mktg., Mktg. Mgmt., Direct Mktg., Finance, IT, MIS Mgmt., DB Admin., Mgmt. Consultants, Int'l.

Industries: Generalist (All), Energy, Utilities, Manufacturing, Food, Bev., Tobacco, Computer Equip., Retail, Finance, Invest. Banking, Brokers, Services, Mgmt. Consulting, Hospitality, Media, Publishing, New Media, Communications, Aerospace, Packaging, Insurance, Real Estate, Software, Biotech/Life Sciences, Healthcare

Branches:
19925 Stevens Creek Blvd
Cupertino, CA 95014-2300
(408) 725-7147
Fax: (408) 725-8885
Email: landberg@insearchworldwide.com
Key Contact - Specialty:
Mr. Steven Landberg, Senior Vice President & Mng Director

445 Park Ave
New York, NY 10022-2606
(212) 836-4855
Fax: (212) 836-4840
Email: smith@insearchworldwide.com
Key Contact - Specialty:
Ms. Millie Mashal, Senior Vice President & Mng Director

Insight Recruiters

301 S Elm St Ste 818
Greensboro, NC 27401-2680
(336) 698-4571
Fax: (336) 201-5141
Email: robinmanley@insightrecruiters.com
Web: www.insightrecruiters.com

Summary: Our firm specializes in the national search of better human resource professionals for world class companies and companies that are on their way for being known as a great place to work. We utilize our website to provide information about our firm and our practice.

Key Contact - Specialty:
Ms. Robin Manley, President & Executive HR Recruiter - *Human resources*

Salary Minimum: $80,000

Functions: HR Mgmt.

Industries: Generalist (All)

Institute for Quality Employment Inc

(also known as IQExec Job Creations)
PO Box 22481
100 S Broad St
Philadelphia, PA 19110-2481
(215) 496-0987
(609) 313-1283
Fax: (215) 964-9506
Email: iqexec@yahoo.com

Summary: We focus on job creation via advisory coaching for boardroom presentations. Industries we specialize in include: architecture, engineering, construction, finance, consulting, public works, insurance, chemical, food service, science & research, utilities, manufacturing, transportation, publishing, and health care.

Key Contact - Specialty:
Mr. Jerry Conti, President

Salary Minimum: $225,000

Functions: Management, Senior Mgmt.

Industries: Generalist (All), Construction, Transportation, Venture Cap., Services, Architectural Svcs., Legal, HR Services, Engineering Svcs., Government, Environmental Svcs., Real Estate

Insurance Headhunters Inc[†]

19029 US Highway 19 N Apt 18E
Clearwater, FL 33764-3041
(727) 531-1600
Email: ws@i-hh.com
Web: www.insurance-headhunters.com

Summary: There is confidentiality and trust in what we do, know, and say. We form the bond between our clients and our candidates. By headhunting, our team identifies ideal candidates, preserving your time for only key interviews. From the first handshake, we are facilitator and resource, guiding the complex negotiations that transform strangers to prospects and finally to team partners. That is how relationships are built. Insurance recruiting is our only specialty.

Key Contact - Specialty:
Mr. William Sullivan

Salary Minimum: $50,000

Functions: Generalist (All), Management, Purchasing

Industries: Generalist (All), Insurance, Casualty, Claims, Life, Commercial, Re-Insurance

Intech Summit Group Inc

5075 Shoreham Pl Ste 280
San Diego, CA 92122-5960
(858) 452-2100
Fax: (858) 452-8500
Email: resume@isgsearch.com
Web: www.isgsearch.com

Summary: Principals have extensive combined professional search experience at all levels of executive recruitment in healthcare & life

sciences, technology, government, HR, telecom, finance, legal, professional services, supply chain and consulting.

Key Contact - Specialty:
Mr. Michael R. Cohen, Chief Executive Officer - *Consulting*
Mr. Chris Chaney, President - *Technology, Venture capital*

Salary Minimum: $80,000

Functions: Board Members, HR Mgmt., Finance, Taxes, M&A, Mgmt. Consultants

Industries: Generalist (All), Energy, Utilities, Manufacturing, Drugs Mfg., Misc. Mfg., Finance, Invest. Banking, Brokers, Venture Cap., Misc. Financial, Services, Pharm Svcs., Legal, Accounting, Mgmt. Consulting, HR Services, Telecoms, Government, Insurance, Software, Biotech/Life Sciences, Healthcare

Branches:
2774 Jefferson St Ste A
Carlsbad, CA 92008-1703
(760) 720-2120
Fax: (760) 720-2121
Email: hr@isgsearch.com
Key Contact - Specialty:
Ms. Kathy Kinley, Senior Vice President - *Human resources*

Integrated Search Solutions Group LLC (ISSG)

33 Main St
Port Washington, NY 11050-2916
(516) 767-3030
Email: janis@issg.net
Web: www.issg.net

Summary: We are a retainer based executive search firm with experience in successfully attracting top talent in the areas of outsourcing (IT, BPO, and BPM), consulting (strategy and technology), and traditional IT functions (CIO, CTO). We have worked successfully for major corporations and venture capitalized start-ups.

Key Contact - Specialty:
Mr. Laurence Janis, Managing Partner
Mr. Vincent J. Sessa, Partner
Mr. John Seebold, Associate Partner
Mr. Guy Kirkwood, Associate Partner, Europe
Mr. Andrew Kris, Partner, Europe

Salary Minimum: $150,000

Functions: Senior Mgmt., IT

Industries: Energy, Utilities, Food, Bev., Tobacco, Consumer Elect., Banking, Invest. Banking, Brokers, Venture Cap., Mgmt. Consulting, HR Services, IT Implementation, Telecoms, Software

Integrity Network Inc

9800 Pyramid Ct Ste 400
Englewood, CO 80112-2669
(303) 663-2050
Fax: (720) 895-1999
Email: judy@integritynetworkinc.com
Web: www.integritynetworkinc.com

Summary: We are a retained executive search firm that specializes in the high-technology industry placing sales & marketing executives. Our typical search is with a software/Internet company where we place a Vice President of sales, marketing, or business development candidates.

Key Contact - Specialty:
Mrs. Judith A. Kennelley, President
Mr. Thomas H. Hickey, Vice President

Salary Minimum: $150,000

Functions: Sales & Mktg., Mktg. Mgmt., Sales Mgmt.

Industries: Software

Integrity Search Inc

17 Veterans Sq Fl 2
Media, PA 19063-3217
(610) 543-8590
Fax: (610) 543-3668
Email: jlong@integritysearchinc.com
Web: www.integritysearchinc.com

Summary: Offering a conclusive, strategic approach to executive search and management coaching on interviewing and hiring process, plus an unrivaled reputation for treating both candidates and clients with respect and integrity.

Key Contact - Specialty:
Ms. Janet R. Long, President - *Communications, Management consulting, Marketing*
Ms. Robin Lebow, Director, Client Services
Mr. Marvin Melnikoff, Division President, BrandLeaders

Salary Minimum: $90,000

Functions: Mktg. Mgmt., PR, Mgmt. Consultants

Industries: Generalist (All), Consumer Goods, HR Services, Entertainment, Media

InteliSearch Inc

60 Long Ridge Rd
Stamford, CT 06902-1838
(203) 325-1389
Fax: (203) 325-1678
Email: executivesolutions@intelisearch-inc.com
Web: www.intelisearch-inc.com

Summary: We are an executive search and leadership advisory firm with broad industry and multi-functional expertise offering measurable ROI and metrics-backed accountability. Our integrated approach and world-class assessment methodologies have earned the firm The Connecticut Quality Improvement Award. Methodologies are inspired by the client side experiences of its founder, a former Global 25 top HR/ethics executive.

Key Contact - Specialty:
Mr. George L. Rodriguez, Managing Principal
Mr. Paul Feeny, Managing Partner - *CFOs, Controllers, COOs, Financial services, Insurance*

Salary Minimum: $125,000

Functions: Generalist (All), Management, Senior Mgmt., Middle Mgmt., Sales & Mktg., HR Mgmt., Finance, CFOs, Taxes, Minorities/Diversity

Industries: Generalist (All), Chemicals, Consumer Goods, Transportation, Finance, Services, Insurance, Re-Insurance, Software

IntelliSource†

PO Box 1355
Bristol, TN 37621-1355
(877) 223-4730
Email: eg@theintellisource.com
Web: www.theintellisource.com

Summary: A full service executive recruiting firm offering tradition executive search along with state of the art options like unbundled search, and web search. Along with this we provide outplacement, online assessments, temporary professionals, dual career assistance, and employment outsourcing.

Key Contact - Specialty:
Mr. E.G. Souder, Jr., President - *Accounting, C-level, Engineering, Healthcare, Human resources*

Salary Minimum: $50,000

Functions: Senior Mgmt., Plant Mgmt., Quality, Materials, Purchasing, Healthcare, Sales & Mktg., HR Mgmt., Finance, Engineering

Industries: Generalist (All), Printing, Chemicals, Plastics, Rubber, Motor Vehicles, Banking, Non-profits, Fiber Optic, Hospitals, Long-term/Home Care

Inter Link Technology Solutions Inc†

4606 S Clyde Morris Blvd Ste 2D
Port Orange, FL 32129-7454
(386) 322-5440
(800) 713-9207
Fax: (386) 322-9970
Email: recruiting@interlink-inc.net
Web: www.interlink-inc.net

Summary: Our firm is comprised of a consortium of specialists who for years were employed in several technical fields and in many capacities. This insight offers us the unique competitive advantage of having worked on the inside, understanding what motivates the employer, how the employment process really works and foremost, the trials and tribulations of standing in the job seeker's shoes.

Key Contact - Specialty:
Mr. John Gould, Chief Executive Officer

Salary Minimum: $30,000

Functions: Senior Mgmt., Middle Mgmt., Production, IT, Engineering

Industries: Computer Equip., IT Implementation, Communications, Software

Interchange Personnel Inc†

1403 Joliet Ave SW
Calgary, AB T2T 1S3
Canada
(403) 216-1520

Summary: Our corporate objective is to provide an objective picture of applicants' positive and negative personality and work traits based on comprehensive behavioral based interviewing and an intuitive sense.

Key Contact - Specialty:
Ms. Karen L. Aiken, President - *CFOs, Engineering, Gas, Middle management, Oil*

Salary Minimum: $30,000

Functions: Generalist (All), Senior Mgmt., Middle Mgmt., Admin. Svcs., Training, CFOs, Engineering

Industries: Generalist (All), Energy, Utilities, Construction, Invest. Banking, Misc. Financial, HR Services, Real Estate

Interlangue Group†

90 Park Ave Rm 1600
New York, NY 10016-1301
(212) 687-5050
Fax: (212) 687-4645
Email: general@interlangue.com
Web: www.interlangue.com

Summary: Devoted exclusively to the foreign banking sector (executive search and compensation issues) with emphasis on treasury: risk management (middle & front office): VaR, RAROC, overall risk policy structuring and corporate finance: corporate bank transacting, credit, work-out, auditing/comptrollership.

Key Contact - Specialty:
Ms. Danelle Dann, Managing Director

Salary Minimum: $100,000

Functions: Management

Industries: Finance, Banking, Invest. Banking

International Management Advisors Inc

PO Box 174
New York, NY 10150-0174
(212) 758-7770

Summary: Quality, medium size generalist firm serving multinational and national organizations. We conduct searches in most functional areas. Results through teamwork.

Key Contact - Specialty:
Ms. Constance W. Klages, President
Mr. Paul J. Harbaugh, Jr., Executive Vice President - *Chemical, Marketing, Retail*

Salary Minimum: $100,000

Functions: Generalist (All), Senior Mgmt., Mktg. Mgmt., HR Mgmt., IT, Engineering, Minorities/Diversity

Industries: Generalist (All), Energy, Utilities, Misc. Financial, Non-profits, Mgmt. Consulting, HR Services, Biotech/Life Sciences

Interquest Inc

98 Cuttermill Rd Ste 337S
Great Neck, NY 11021-3009
(516) 482-2330
Fax: (516) 482-2114
Email: meyer@mhaberman.com

Summary: We offer extensive years of experience in retained legal searches for corporations and law firms. We cover all industries and all legal disciplines. Our specialization is general counsel and partner searches plus law firm mergers.

Key Contact - Specialty:
Mr. Meyer Haberman, President

Salary Minimum: $150,000

Functions: Attorneys

Industries: Generalist (All)

InterSource Executive Search Inc

PO Box 161987
Austin, TX 78716-1987
(512) 457-0883
Email: vl@intersourcesearch.com
Web: www.intersourcesearch.com

Summary: Our firm is an executive search, contract services, research and executive coaching firm. We specialize in HR, accounting/finance and marketing disciplines. In addition to search we also conduct executive level assessment and coaching. While our client list includes the Fortune 500 we love working with mid-size and start-up companies as well. We work as an integral part of your team, committed to making a notable positive impact.

Key Contact - Specialty:
Ms. Vikki Loving, Chief Executive Officer - *Finance, Human resources*

Salary Minimum: $75,000

Functions: Board Members, Senior Mgmt., Mktg. Mgmt., HR Mgmt., Finance, CFOs, Int'l.

Industries: Generalist (All), Legal, HR Services

Branches:
1675 Friendship Church Rd
Murphy, NC 28906-4921
(828) 644-9558
Email: vl@intersourcesearch.com

Key Contact - Specialty:
Ms. Lisa Waggoner, Principal - *Finance, Human resources*

Intrepid Consulting Group

1415 W 22nd St Fl Tower
Oak Brook, IL 60523-2031
(630) 986-9900
Fax: (630) 986-8950
Email: admin@intrepidcg.com
Web: intrepidcg.com

Summary: Our firm is a retainer based executive search and management assessment firm focused on senior level positions in the technology industry, as well as CIO and CTO positions across industries. The firm is based on the following core principles: critical industry experience, war for talent methodology, exclusively fixed fees, and unmatched focus.

Key Contact - Specialty:
Mr. Karl Aavik, Managing Director - *CIOs, Consulting, E-business, Engineering, General management*

Functions: Management, Senior Mgmt., Product Dev., IT, MIS Mgmt., Engineering, Mgmt. Consultants

Industries: Generalist (All), Manufacturing, Computer Equip., Test, Measure Equip., Misc. Mfg., Electronic, Elec. Components, Semiconductors, Consumer Goods, Mgmt. Consulting, E-commerce, IT Implementation, Communications, Call Centers, Aerospace, Packaging, Software, Biotech/Life Sciences

IPS Search Inc

980 N Michigan Ave Ste 1400
Chicago, IL 60611-7500
(312) 214-4983
Fax: (312) 214-4949
Email: info@ipssearch.com
Web: www.ipssearch.com

Summary: We have specialized in delivering effective global retained search solutions specifically to the insurance industry. Our US subsidiary based in Chicago works with specialty carriers, regional carriers and reinsurers recruiting executive level and senior management positions nationally

Key Contact - Specialty:
Mr. James W. Evan-Cook, President
Ms. Betty Moy, Vice President - *Research*

Salary Minimum: $100,000

Functions: Generalist (All), Senior Mgmt.

Industries: Insurance, Casualty, Claims, Commercial, Re-Insurance

IQ Partners Inc

(formerly known as IQ Partners Executive Search Consultants)
650-99 Spadina Ave
Toronto, ON M5V 3P8
Canada
(416) 599-4700
Email: info@iqpartners.com
Web: www.iqpartners.com

Summary: Our firm helps intelligent companies hire better, hire less and retain more. Our services include executive search, qualification & assessment, employee development & retention, career management, and contract HR services. We specialize in marketing, communications, media, technology and financial services, and operate at the mid to senior management level.

Key Contact - Specialty:
Mr. Randy Quarin, Senior Partner - *Advertising, Finance, Management, Marketing, Media*
Mr. Bruce Powell, Managing Partner - *Communications, Management, Marketing, Media, Technology*

Functions: Generalist (All), Senior Mgmt., Middle Mgmt.

Industries: Generalist (All), Finance, Services, HR Services, Media, Advertising, Publishing, New Media, Communications, Software

IR Search†

8146 Greenback Ln Ste 102
Fair Oaks, CA 95628-2539
(916) 721-5511
Fax: (916) 721-5007
Email: info@irgroupco.com
Web: www.irgroupco.com

Summary: A strategic consulting, M&A and executive search firm specializing in services to the insurance industry.

Key Contact - Specialty:
Mr. Richard Shoemaker, President - *CEOs, CFOs, COOs*
Ms. Sandra Simmons, CPC, Managing Director - *Annuities, HMOs*
Mr. Gene Boscacci, Managing Director - *Construction*

Salary Minimum: $100,000

Functions: Senior Mgmt.

Industries: Insurance, Healthcare

Branches:
498 Palm springs Dr Ste 100
Altamonte Springs, FL 32701-7849
(407) 261-9162
Email: bruce.fernandez@irgroupco.com
Key Contact - Specialty:
Mr. Bruce Fernandez, Managing Director - *Financial services, Insurance, Insurance (Casualty,Reinsurance)*

Isaacson Miller Inc

334 Boylston St Fl 5
Boston, MA 02116-3492
(617) 262-6500
Fax: (617) 262-6509
Email: resumes@imsearch.com
Web: www.imsearch.com

Summary: A national retained firm serving mission-driven organizations in senior-level searches. Fields of expertise include education (both higher education and K-12), research institutes, healthcare (both community care and academic medical centers), foundations, human and social services, community and economic development, advocacy, conservation and environment, arts and culture, and public management.

Key Contact - Specialty:
Mr. John Isaacson, President & Managing Director

Salary Minimum: $135,000

Functions: Generalist (All), Senior Mgmt., Healthcare, CFOs, Minorities/Diversity, Non-profits

Industries: Generalist (All), Non-profits, Higher Ed., Government, Healthcare

Branches:
533 Airport Blvd Ste 400
Burlingame, CA 94010-2013
(650) 685-2475
Email: resumes@imsearch.com

Key Contact - Specialty:
Mr. David Bellshaw

1875 Connecticut Ave NW Ste 710
Washington, DC 20009-5740
(202) 682-1504
Email: resumes@imsearch.com
Key Contact - Specialty:
Ms. Barbara Stevens
Ms. Jane Gruenebaum
Ms. Ericka Miller

iScout Inc

309 E Rand Rd Ste 275
Arlington Heights, IL 60004-3103
(877) 472-6880
Fax: (847) 556-9513
Email: info@iscoutnow.com
Web: www.iscoutnow.com

Summary: We are a consulting firm that works with high tech start-ups to build teams and teach them how to become self-sufficient to eliminate the dependency on staffing agencies. Within 6 months of working with our firm, you will never have to pay a placement fee again.

Key Contact - Specialty:
Ms. Christy Carter, President & Founder - *Consulting, Information Technology, Staffing, Start-up companies, Technology*
Mr. Michael Biersma, Sales & Business Development - *Competitive intelligence, Information Technology, Staffing, Start-up companies, Technology*
Mrs. Julie Caruso, Director, Operations - *Administration, Consulting, Information Technology, Staffing, Start-up companies*
Mrs. Victoria Casey, Principal Consultant - *Consulting, Information Technology, Organizational development, Staffing, Start-up companies*
Mr. Sharath Kumar, Lead Researcher - *Consulting, Information Technology, Research, Staffing, Start-up companies*

Functions: Management, Senior Mgmt., Sales & Mktg., Sales Reps., Staffing, IT, Systems Analysis, Mgmt. Consultants, Architects, Technicians

Industries: Generalist (All), Finance, Services, Mgmt. Consulting, E-commerce, IT Implementation, Engineering Svcs., Communications, Software

Jackowitz & Company Inc

40 Grove St Ste 427
Wellesley, MA 02482-7772
(781) 237-7250
Fax: (781) 237-7850
Email: info@jackowitzco.com
Web: www.jackowitzco.com

Summary: We are a retainer based, full service executive search firm specializing in the financial services, IT, life sciences and direct marketing industries. The firm recruits senior executives across all functions.

Key Contact - Specialty:
Mr. Todd Jackowitz, President - *Direct marketing, Financial services, Information Technology*
Mr. Tom Valle, Senior Vice President - *Financial services, Life Sciences*
Ms. Susanne Talbot, Principal - *Financial services, Information Technology*

Salary Minimum: $150,000

Functions: Senior Mgmt.

Industries: Finance, Banking, Mutual/Hedge Funds, Misc. Financial, Services, Communications, Insurance, Software, Biotech/Life Sciences, Healthcare

S H Jacobs & Associates Inc[†]

93 York Rd Ste 204
Jenkintown, PA 19046-3925
(215) 886-2700
Email: shjresume@aol.com
Web: www.jacobsexecutivesearch.com

Summary: Executive search firm dedicated to the marketing, marketing communications and advertising sectors of industry, service companies and ad agencies.

Key Contact - Specialty:
Mr. Saul H. Jacobs, President - *Market research, Media, New media, Pharmaceutical, Public relations*
Ms. Susan Rosenthal, Executive Recruiter - *Market research, Marketing, Medical (Devices), Pharmaceutical, Public relations*

Salary Minimum: $50,000

Functions: Management, Senior Mgmt., Middle Mgmt., Advertising, Mktg. Research, Mktg. Mgmt., Direct Mktg., PR

Industries: Food, Bev., Tobacco, Textiles, Apparel, Drugs Mfg., Medical Devices, Computer Equip., Consumer Elect., Pharm Svcs., Hospitality, Advertising, New Media, Broadcast, Film, Hospitals

Jacobs Scott Ltd

1027 Pandora Ave
Victoria, BC V8V 3P6
Canada
(250) 413-3140
(250) 655-6402
Fax: (250) 655-6486
Email: mail@jacobsscott.com
Web: www.jacobsscott.com

Summary: Jacobs Scott sources, selects and places skill sets in most sectors and specializes in the selection of talent that enhances organizational success. We provide value-added services such as team building, executive coaching and psychometric assessments. Through our international affiliate offices, we are able to source the best available talent, worldwide.

Key Contact - Specialty:
Mr. Shawn L. Jacobs, SAIPM, Managing Partner - *CEOs, Energy, Engineering, Finance, High technology*
Dr. Dominique Surel, BA MBA Doc, Partner - *Accounting (Big 4), Human resources, Manufacturing, Marketing, Research & development*
Mr. Cassie Hamman, BComm, MBA, Partner - *Automation, Change management, Engineering, General management, Manufacturing*

Salary Minimum: $75,000

Functions: Generalist (All), Senior Mgmt., Sales Mgmt., PR, HR Mgmt., CFOs, Actuaries, IT, Engineering, Geotechnical

Industries: Agri., Forestry, Mining, Energy, Utilities, Oil & Gas, Construction, Manufacturing, Food, Bev., Tobacco, Textiles, Apparel, Chemicals, Computer Equip., Consumer Elect., Misc. Mfg., Electronic, Elec. Components, Robotics, Consumer Goods, Retail, Finance, Banking, Non-profits, HR Services, IT Implementation, Engineering Svcs., Logistics Svcs., Supply Chain Mgmt, Hospitality, Entertainment, Recreation, Communications, Telecoms, Wireless, Network Infrastructure, RF/Microwave, Government, Defense, Environmental Svcs., Aerospace,

Insurance, Life, Re-Insurance, Software, ERP SW, HR SW, Marketing SW

Jacobson Executive Search

(a division of The Jacobson Group)
120 S La Salle St Ste 1410
Chicago, IL 60603-3579
(312) 726-1580
(800) 466-1578
Fax: (312) 726-2295
Email: info@jacobsononline.com
Web: www.jacobsononline.com

Summary: The executive search practice for a national professional and human capital services firm dedicated to insurance, healthcare and financial services, we offer a consultative approach to talent acquisition for C-level, VP, and board assignments. Leverage our time-tested search methodology, unparalleled market intelligence, and extensive industry network.

Key Contact - Specialty:
Mr. Gregory P. Jacobson, Chief Executive Officer - *Boards of Directors, C-level, Executives, Financial services, Healthcare*
Mrs. Margaret Resce Milkint, Partner - *Actuarial, Boards of Directors, C-level, Executives, Financial services*
Mr. Douglas E. Terry, Vice President - *Boards of Directors, C-level, Executives, Financial services, Healthcare*
Mr. Jay D'Aprile, Executive Search Consultant - *Actuarial, Boards of Directors, C-level, Executives, Financial services*
Ms. Courtney Cremens, Project Manager, Business Development - *Boards of Directors, C-level, Executives, Financial services, Healthcare*
Ms. Mary K. Watts, Assistant Vice President, Search Project - *Actuarial, Boards of Directors, C-level, Executives, Financial services*

Salary Minimum: $75,000

Functions: Generalist (All), Board Members, Senior Mgmt., Mktg. Mgmt., HR Mgmt., Benefits, CFOs, Risk Mgmt., Actuaries, MIS Mgmt.

Industries: Finance, Insurance, Healthcare

Branches:
1600 Parkwood Cir SE Ste 350
Atlanta, GA 30339-2147
(770) 952-3877
Fax: (770) 952-0061
Email: atlanta@jacobsononline.com
Key Contact - Specialty:
Mr. Marty Murphy, Senior Vice President - *Actuarial, Financial services, Healthcare, Insurance, Managed care*

5 Neshaminy Interplex Ste 113
Trevose, PA 19053-6967
(215) 639-5860
Fax: (215) 639-8096
Email: philly@jacobsononline.com
Key Contact - Specialty:
Mr. Nate Bass, Partner - *Financial services, Healthcare, Insurance, Managed care*

Devon James Associates Inc

15600 NE 8th St Ste B1-672
Bellevue, WA 98008-3900
(425) 378-1682
Fax: (425) 378-1683
Email: resumes@devonjames.com
Web: www.devonjames.com

Summary: In addition to their retained executive search practice, the firm provides a full suite of recruiting services. Including research, sourcing, screening, assessment and hard skills testing, group training, interviewing, reporting, offer

negotiation, org. chart/salary budgeting, and HR consulting.

Key Contact - Specialty:
Ms. Colleen Aylward, Founder & Chairman - *High technology, Senior management, Staffing, Start-up companies, Technology*

Salary Minimum: $75,000

Functions: Generalist (All)

Industries: HR Services, E-commerce, New Media, Wireless, Network Infrastructure, Software, Development SW, HR SW, Networking, Comm. SW, Biotech/Life Sciences

Branches:
325M Sharon Park Dr Ste 113
Menlo Park, CA 94025-6805
(650) 207-6573
Email: resumes@devonjames.com
Key Contact - Specialty:
Mr. Michael Grabham, Chief Executive Officer - *CEOs, Presidents, Senior management, Telecommunications, Wireless*
Mr. Paul Westmoreland, Partner, Research

R I James Executive Search Consultants

4320 S Centinela Ave Apt 302
Los Angeles, CA 90066-7132
(310) 572-1616
Email: search@rijames.com
Web: www.rijames.com

Summary: We are specialists in mid to senior-level placement in supply chain business logistics and materials management. Our client references reflect the highest standards of excellence. Recognized for professional logistics recruitment.

Key Contact - Specialty:
Ms. Rhoda Isaacs, President - *Logistics, Supply Chain*

Salary Minimum: $65,000

Functions: Management, Senior Mgmt., Middle Mgmt., Materials, Distribution

Industries: Generalist (All), Consumer Goods, Transportation, Wholesale, Retail, Logistics Svcs., Supply Chain Mgmt

JBK Associates Inc

25 Bergen St
Englewood, NJ 07631-2907
(201) 567-9070
Fax: (201) 567-9078
Email: jobs@jbkassociates.net
Web: www.jbkassociates.net

Summary: We are an established fully retained executive search firm with an outstanding candidate completion and retention track record. We specialize in the placement of mid to senior management in all sales, marketing and finance functions in healthcare and consumer products.

Key Contact - Specialty:
Ms. Julie Kampf, President

Salary Minimum: $100,000

Functions: Generalist (All), Management, Senior Mgmt., Mfg., Sales & Mktg., Finance

Industries: Manufacturing, Food, Bev., Tobacco, Textiles, Apparel, Soap, Perf., Cosmtcs., Drugs Mfg., Medical Devices, Pharm Svcs., Mgmt. Consulting, Biotech/Life Sciences, Healthcare

JDG Associates Ltd[†]

1700 Research Blvd
Rockville, MD 20850-3156
(301) 340-2210
Fax: (301) 762-3117

† occasional contingency assignment

Email: degioia@jdgsearch.com
Web: www.jdgsearch.com

Summary: Recruiters serving the disciplines of IT, finance/accounting, engineering, management science and association and non-profit management.

Key Contact - Specialty:
Mr. Joseph DeGioia, President

Salary Minimum: $85,000

Functions: Generalist (All), Board Members, Healthcare, IT, MIS Mgmt., Systems Analysis, Systems Implem., Non-profits

Industries: Non-profits, Accounting, Mgmt. Consulting, IT Implementation, Logistics Svcs., Supply Chain Mgmt, Government, Defense, Homeland Security, Haz. Waste, Software, Security SW, Biotech/Life Sciences, Healthcare

JDG y Asociados SA de CV

Blvd A L Rodriguez 78
83000 Hermosillo, SON
Mexico
66 2214 2875
66 2214 7781
Fax: 66 2214 8276
Email: jdg@jdgyasociados.com
Web: www.jdgyasociados.com

Summary: Serves a select number of national and multinational companies, granting the competitive advantage of a broad search universe. Specializes in locating the best-qualified bilingual (English/Spanish) executive for each position, and willing to relocate throughout Mexico and the USA. Emphasis on searching for high performers and also career counseling.

Key Contact - Specialty:
Mr. Jose D. Gurrola, Principal & General Manager
Ing. Laura G. Ciscomani, Partner

Salary Minimum: $60,000

Functions: Generalist (All), Management, Mfg., Product Dev., Materials, Sales & Mktg., HR Mgmt., Finance, IT, Engineering

Industries: Generalist (All), Agri., Forestry, Mining, Construction, Manufacturing, Food, Bev., Tobacco, Plastics, Rubber, Consumer Elect., Transportation, Retail, Finance, Services, Communications, Packaging, Software

Jefferson Partners LLC

29 Arrowhead Way
Darien, CT 06820-5506
(203) 655-3230
Email: mwellman@jeffersonsearch.com
Web: www.jeffersonsearch.com

Summary: Our firm is a retainer executive search firm focused only on the assessment, acquisition and retention of senior executive leadership talent for our clients. Our firm was formed to provide clients with the same level of professionalism historically available only through the major search firms.

Key Contact - Specialty:
Mr. Michael A. Wellman, Chairman & Managing Partner - *Boards of Directors, Finance, General management, High technology, Marketing*

Salary Minimum: $150,000

Functions: Generalist (All), Management, Board Members, Senior Mgmt., Sales & Mktg., Mktg. Mgmt., Sales Mgmt., Finance, Mgmt. Consultants

Industries: Generalist (All), Agri., Forestry, Mining, Energy, Utilities, Manufacturing, Computer Equip., Consumer Elect., Electronic, Elec. Components, Semiconductors, Consumer

Goods, Retail, Finance, Services, Media, Communications, Packaging, Software

The Jeremiah Group LLC

35 Cross Neck Rd
Marion, MA 02738-1256
(508) 748-2718
Email: mccoy.daniel@worldnet.att.net

Summary: Our success is tied to our ability to evaluate and present candidates who are the best fit to the company and the job. This is based on knowledge of the client's culture, business and work style.

Key Contact - Specialty:
Mr. Daniel McCoy, Managing Director & CEO
Ms. Carol Knipper, Principal Search Consultant

Salary Minimum: $65,000

Functions: Generalist (All), Management, Board Members, Production, Direct Mktg., R&D

Industries: Generalist (All), Consumer Elect., Services, Mgmt. Consulting, HR Services, Higher Ed., Publishing, New Media

G M Jerolman & Associates LLC

175 N Main St
Branford, CT 06405-3019
(203) 483-4342
Fax: (781) 459-0476
Email: gregg@retailithunter.com
Web: www.retailithunter.com

Summary: Boutique executive search firm specializing in senior-level IT assignments for the retail and apparel trade industries. This specialization allows us to surface larger pools of qualified candidates in shorter periods of time.

Key Contact - Specialty:
Mr. Gregory M. Jerolman, President

Salary Minimum: $80,000

Functions: Generalist (All), Management, Board Members, Systems Analysis, Systems Dev., Systems Implem., Systems Support, Network Admin., DB Admin., Mgmt. Consultants

Industries: Generalist (All), Food, Bev., Tobacco, Textiles, Apparel, Consumer Goods, Wholesale, Retail, Venture Cap., Mgmt. Consulting, Hospitality, Hotels, Resorts, Clubs, Restaurants, Call Centers, Software

JG Consultants Inc

(also known as JGConsultantsInc.)
8150 N Central Expy Ste 220
Dallas, TX 75206-1878
(214) 696-9196
Email: jandg@flash.net

Summary: We perform CFO, CEO, COO, CMO, and VP level retained search work in the technology industry. We provide ongoing management assessment consulting work and assist with hiring and talent retention for existing clients. We selectively perform many multi-location, multi-country and multi-hire searches within our area of expertise.

Key Contact - Specialty:
Ms. Jay Stephenson, President - *Biotechnology, Boards of Directors, CEOs, COOs, Presidents*
Ms. Ginnie Bellville, Senior Consultant - *Business development, Cellular, Change management, CIOs, Communications*
Mr. Mark England, Independent Consultant - *General management, High technology, Information Technology, International, Internet*

Salary Minimum: $134,000

Functions: Generalist (All), Management, Board Members, Senior Mgmt., Product Dev., Sales &

Mktg., Mktg. Mgmt., Sales Mgmt., Systems Support

Industries: Computer Equip., Robotics, Semiconductors, Finance, Venture Cap., Mgmt. Consulting, IT Implementation, Supply Chain Mgmt, Communications, Wireless, Network Infrastructure, RF/Microwave, Software, Industry Specific SW, Networking, Comm. SW, Security SW, Healthcare

JK Consultants†

1257 Sanguinetti Rd Ste 300
Sonora, CA 95370-6215
(209) 532-7772
Email: resume@jksuccess.com
Web: www.jksuccess.com

Summary: Our firm is committed to helping our clients strengthen their leadership capabilities through unsurpassed executive sourcing and business solutions. Our services include executive coaching, corporate relocation services and much more.

Key Contact - Specialty:
Mr. Fred Khachi, President

Salary Minimum: $50,000

Functions: Generalist (All), Management, Board Members, Senior Mgmt., Middle Mgmt., Sales & Mktg., Mktg. Mgmt., Sales Mgmt., Attorneys, Int'l.

Industries: Generalist (All), Agri., Forestry, Mining, Energy, Utilities, Construction, Manufacturing, Wholesale, Retail, Finance, Banking, Invest. Banking, Brokers, Venture Cap., Services, Communications, Aerospace, Software, Biotech/Life Sciences, Healthcare

JL & Company†

3020 Bridgeway Ste 330
Sausalito, CA 94965-1439
(415) 383-9464
Email: jon@jlsearch.com
Web: www.jlsearch.com

Summary: Retained executive search for VC-funded start-ups. VP/SVP and director level marketing, product management, business development and sales.

Key Contact - Specialty:
Mr. Jon R. Love, Principal

Salary Minimum: $100,000

Functions: Mktg. Mgmt.

Industries: Finance, Entertainment, Media, Communications

JLI-Boston

230 Commercial St
Boston, MA 02109-1308
(617) 227-4030
Email: contact@jli-boston.com
Web: www.jli-boston.com

Summary: We are exclusively in the plastics, packaging and medical device industries. Conducts critical searches for best-in-class executives, managers and technical specialists who can significantly impact its clients' capabilities, profits and market position.

Key Contact - Specialty:
Mr. N.G. Fountas, Managing Director - *Plastics*
Mr. J. Desisto, Research Associate

Salary Minimum: $70,000

Functions: Generalist (All), Management, Mfg., Sales & Mktg., R&D, Engineering

Industries: Chemicals, Medical Devices, Plastics, Rubber, Mgmt. Consulting, Packaging

JM & Company

1045 1St Ave Ste 110
King of Prussia, PA 19406-1309
(610) 964-0200
Fax: (610) 964-8596
Web: www.jmsearch.com

Summary: Our firm works on a retained basis with private equity and venture capital firms to help ensure the profitability and success of their portfolio companies. This work is accomplished through extensive due diligence and very detailed recruitment and assessment of A+ players in their industries.

Key Contact - Specialty:
Mr. John C. Marshall, President - *CEOs, Manufacturing, Packaging, Private equity*
Mr. John D. Hildebrand, Partner - *Building products, CEOs, Manufacturing (Management), Plastics*
Mr. Robert A. Sargent, Partner - *CEOs, CFOs, Technology, Venture capital*
Mr. Chuck Egoville, Partner - *RF microwave, Storage, Supply Chain, Technology, Venture capital*
Mr. Jim McGinley, Partner - *Food service, Manufacturing (Management), Packaging, Plastics, Thermoforming*
Mr. Hayden Tewell, Partner - *Consumer (Packaged Goods), Packaging, Paper, Pharmaceutical*
Mr. Craig Baker, Partner - *Molding (Injection), Packaging, Paper*
Ms. Michelle A. Tague, Office Manager

Salary Minimum: $125,000

Functions: Board Members, Senior Mgmt., Plant Mgmt., Materials, Purchasing, Mktg. Mgmt., Sales Mgmt., CFOs

Industries: Generalist (All), Manufacturing, Paper, Plastics, Rubber, Consumer Goods, Finance, E-commerce, PSA/ASP, Telecoms, Packaging, Software

The Job Dr Inc

(also known as KenInfo Group)
PO Box 3012
Dana Point, CA 92629-8012
(949) 360-1800
Email: contact@thejobdr.com
Web: www.thejobdr.com

Summary: Specializing in software engineering and development positions: C#, C++, .Net, Linux, JNI, Java, J2EE, VB, VB. Net, SQL and Oracle technologies. We staff permanent positions in software development, architecture, database, network, and enterprise environments. We service clients in the MIS/IT, software or software product, firmware and other technology fields. From coders to CTOs.

Key Contact - Specialty:
Mr. Roger Howland, President
Mr. Fred Winslow, Director, Recruiting - *Computers (Software)*
Mr. Chuck Shay, Recruitment Manager - *Computers (Programming)*

Salary Minimum: $75,000

Functions: IT, MIS Mgmt., Systems Analysis, Systems Dev., Systems Implem., DB Admin.

Industries: Generalist (All), Wireless, RF/Microwave, Defense, Aerospace, Insurance, Software, Development SW, Biotech/Life Sciences, Healthcare

JobPlex Inc

(an affiliate of DHR International)
10 S Riverside Plz Ste 2250
Chicago, IL 60606-3847
(312) 627-9301
Fax: (312) 831-1071
Web: www.jobplex.com

Summary: We focus on the recruiting needs for middle management positions worldwide. We were created to serve the middle management market; thereby complimenting the retained executive search services provided by our affiliate DHR International. We combine proprietary databases, technology sourcing, direct sourcing, and the strength of a core research group in a tailored approach for every client. Additionally, we have now increased the depth of our service offering to include Enterprise Solutions and On-Site Solutions.

Key Contact - Specialty:
Mr. Robert Aylsworth, President & Chief Executive Officer
Mr. Robert Miller, President, Retail Consumer Products - *Consumer (Products), Retail*
Mr. Terry Shade, Vice President
Mr. Jamie Baisley, Vice President
Mr. Steve Goering, Vice President
Mr. Lou Canellis, Executive Vice President

Functions: Generalist (All)

Industries: Generalist (All)

Branches:
2029 Century Park E Ste 1010
Los Angeles, CA 90067-2911
(310) 789-7343
Key Contact - Specialty:
Mr. Steve Aylsworth, Managing Director
Mrs. Leslie Button, Executive Vice President
Ms. Annemarie Curry, Executive Vice President
Mr. Martin Byrne, Executive Vice President

50 California St Ste 1500
San Francisco, CA 94111-4612
(415) 227-5416
Key Contact - Specialty:
Ms. Danielle Glynn, Vice President
Mr. Steve Scheier, Executive Vice President

1200 17th St Ste 2180
Denver, CO 80202-5855
(303) 629-9199
Key Contact - Specialty:
Mr. Kevin Hahn, Managing Director
Mr. Steve Ziegler, Executive Vice President

5335 Wisconsin Ave NW Ste 800
Washington, DC 20015-2073
(202) 544-7854
Key Contact - Specialty:
Mr. Will Caggiano, Vice President

3201 W Parkland Blvd
Tampa, FL 33609-4637
(813) 348-0931
Key Contact - Specialty:
Mr. John Watters, Vice President

12820 Briar Dr
Leawood, KS 66209-1890
(913) 207-7238
Key Contact - Specialty:
Mr. Rod Cooper, Vice President

9900 Corporate Campus Dr Ste 3000
Louisville, KY 40223-4060
(502) 657-6348
Key Contact - Specialty:
Mr. Chad Smith, Executive Vice President
Mr. Chad Pinkston, Director of Development

601 Carlson Pkwy Ste 1050
Minnetonka, MN 55305-5219
(952) 449-6011
Key Contact - Specialty:
Mr. Scott Coleman, President, Upper Midwest Region

6100 NE Woodmont St
Lees Summit, MO 64064-2423
(816) 582-6409
Key Contact - Specialty:
Mr. Scott Eckley, Practice Leader, Energy Practice Group - *Energy*

1 Newark Ctr Fl 14
Newark, NJ 07102-5236
(312) 919-9301
Key Contact - Specialty:
Mr. Bill Chaney, Vice President

280 Park Ave Fl 43W
New York, NY 10017-1216
(212) 867-0453
Fax: (212) 883-9507
Key Contact - Specialty:
Mrs. Allison Sinert, Executive Vice President
Mr. Lawrence Vasell, Executive Vice President
Mr. Gregg Aprahamian, Executive Vice President
Mr. Steve Saperstein, Executive Vice President

12377 Merit Dr Ste 870
Dallas, TX 75251-2262
(214) 750-6111
Key Contact - Specialty:
Mr. Robert Elam, President, Southwest Region
Dr. Mark Moore, Executive Vice President
Ms. Josie Johnson, Executive Vice President

300 N Corporate Dr Ste 290
Brookfield, WI 53045-5865
(262) 879-0554
Key Contact - Specialty:
Mr. Ray Thurber, Managing Director

John & Powers Inc

14323 S Outer 40 Ste 206
Chesterfield, MO 63017-5734
(314) 453-0080

Summary: Consulting firm which exclusively specializes in executive search to all industries. Clients represented include Fortune 500 companies, medium size organizations and turnaround situations.

Key Contact - Specialty:
Mr. Harold A. John, President

Salary Minimum: $125,000

Functions: Generalist (All), Management

Industries: Generalist (All)

John H Johnson & Associates Inc

310 S Michigan Ave Ste 1400
Chicago, IL 60604-4296
(312) 663-4176
Email: coach@johnjosephgroup.com
Web: www.johnjosephgroup.com

Summary: Professional retainer-based executive search firm for all industries and functional areas.

Key Contact - Specialty:
Mr. John H. Johnson, Chief Executive Officer

Salary Minimum: $75,000

Functions: Mfg., Sales & Mktg., HR Mgmt., Finance, Engineering

Industries: Generalist (All), Construction, Lumber, Furniture, Medical Devices, Plastics, Rubber, Metal Products, Machine, Appliance, Electronic, Elec. Components, Wholesale, HR

Services, Supply Chain Mgmt, Restaurants, Quick Service Restaurants, Inst./Industrial Food Svc., Defense, Aerospace, Packaging, Property/Facility Mgmt., Healthcare

Johnson & Company

1962 Elm St
Stratford, CT 06615-6331
(203) 377-7800
Email: info@johnsonsearch.com
Web: www.johnsonsearch.com

Summary: We have a quality reputation for recruiting functional heads and GMs as well as helping organizations evaluate and upgrade their Executive talent.

Key Contact - Specialty:
Mr. Stanley C. Johnson, President
Mr. Steve Rexford, Director - *Administration, Consumer (Hard Goods), Human resources, Organizational development, Senior management*

Salary Minimum: $100,000

Functions: Management, Senior Mgmt., Mfg., Sales & Mktg., HR Mgmt., Finance, CFOs, MIS Mgmt.

Industries: Generalist (All), Food, Bev., Tobacco, Textiles, Apparel, Paper, Printing, Soap, Perf., Cosmtcs., Drugs Mfg., Paints, Petro. Products, Motor Vehicles, Computer Equip., Consumer Elect.

L J Johnson & Company[†]

PO Box 2023
Ann Arbor, MI 48106-2023
(734) 663-6446
Email: jjohnson@a2mail.net

Summary: We retained searches for management, logistics, technical and administrative personnel. We provide financial and management consultants. There is a strong emphasis on manufacturing, engineering and automotive tier 1.

Key Contact - Specialty:
Mr. L.J. Johnson, President - *Manufacturing*

Salary Minimum: $40,000

Functions: Generalist (All)

Industries: Generalist (All), Manufacturing, Finance, Engineering Svcs., Logistics Svcs.

Ronald S Johnson Associates Inc

44360 Lakeside Dr
Indian Wells, CA 92210-7643
(310) 612-6953
Fax: (760) 779-1902
Email: searchrsj@aol.com

Summary: Retainer search firm specializing in senior management for medium to high-technology, venture backed companies in hardware, software, network/telecom and transportation.

Key Contact - Specialty:
Mr. Ronald S. Johnson, President

Salary Minimum: $150,000

Functions: Generalist (All)

Industries: Generalist (All), Computer Equip., Venture Cap., Hospitality, Hotels, Resorts, Clubs, Telecoms, Digital, Wireless, Network Infrastructure, Software

Johnson Sinish Group[†]

10826 Coldwater Rd
Fort Wayne, IN 46845-1241
(260) 490-1777
Fax: (260) 490-1888
Email: glenn@techedgecorp.com

Summary: Our firm offers retained executive search in all industries. The company is systematic in approach and uses the executive position planning system to help clients define executive or key knowledge worker positions and ideal candidate characteristics. The firm maintains a substantial research function.

Key Contact - Specialty:
Mr. Glenn Johnson, President
Mr. Bill Sinish, Executive Vice President
Mr. Russell Swing, Search Manager
Mr. Michael Sinish, Sports Search Specialist

Salary Minimum: $75,000

Functions: Board Members, Senior Mgmt., Middle Mgmt., Mfg., Materials, Sales & Mktg., HR Mgmt., Finance, IT, Engineering

Industries: Generalist (All)

Roye Johnston Associates

2680 Mary Lane Pl
Escondido, CA 92025-7754
(760) 432-8080
(800) 886-6619
Email: royj@juno.com

Summary: Specialists in occupational medicine, physicians and nurses.

Key Contact - Specialty:
Mr. Roye Johnston, President - *Physicians*
Mr. Brian Johnston, Secretary

Salary Minimum: $100,000

Functions: Physicians

Industries: Call Centers, Occupational Therapy

Jonas, Walters & Associates Inc

1110 N Old World 3rd St Ste 410
Milwaukee, WI 53203-1121
(414) 291-2828
Fax: (414) 291-2822
Email: info@jonaswalters.com
Web: www.jonaswalters.com

Summary: Focus on the recruitment of senior executives for major U.S. manufacturers. Significant experience in Eastern Europe and Latin America. All corporate functions. Outstanding retention record. Separate board search division. Highly skilled consultants with extensive search experience.

Key Contact - Specialty:
Mr. William F. Walters, President - *CEOs, CFOs, COOs, Presidents, Private equity*
Mr. Donald S. Hucko, Senior Vice President - *Finance, Manufacturing, Marketing, Sales, Supply Chain*

Salary Minimum: $100,000

Functions: Generalist (All), Management, Board Members, Senior Mgmt., Mfg., Sales & Mktg., HR Mgmt., Finance

Industries: Generalist (All), Construction, Manufacturing, Food, Bev., Tobacco, Metal Products, Machine, Appliance, Misc. Mfg., Electronic, Elec. Components, Consumer Goods, Retail, Finance, Venture Cap.

Jones & Egan Inc

521 5th Ave Rm 1700
New York, NY 10175-1799
(212) 292-5070
Fax: (212) 292-5071
Email: info@jonesegan.com
Web: www.jonesegan.com

Summary: Many years of specialty search experience within financial services plus a deliberate effort to work with a limited number of clients in order to provide a more personalized and focused service.

Key Contact - Specialty:
Mr. John F. Egan, Principal - *Financial services*
Mr. Jonathan C. Jones, Principal - *Financial services*

Salary Minimum: $125,000

Functions: Generalist (All)

Industries: Banking, Invest. Banking, Misc. Financial

Jones Management Company

1 Dock St Ste 412
Stamford, CT 06902-5897
(203) 353-1140
Email: info@jones-mgt.com
Web: www.jones-mgt.com

Summary: We are a quality provider of executive search and professional consulting services. We offer full service solutions backed by years of experience and proven methodologies. Our professional approach proves that partnering with us is the most time efficient and cost effective method of successfully fulfilling critical staffing requirements.

Key Contact - Specialty:
Mr. Francis E. Jones, Chief Executive Officer
Ms. Denise Guest, Senior Research Associate - *Finance*
Mr. William Ceyrnik, Managing Director
Mr. Cory Visi, Managing Director
Mr. John Murray, Vice President
Mr. Gary Rogers, Vice President - *Manufacturing (Management), Production, Quality, Training, Transportation*

Salary Minimum: $100,000

Functions: Generalist (All), Management, Quality, Finance, Budgeting, Credit, M&A, IT, Mgmt. Consultants

Industries: Generalist (All), Manufacturing, Plastics, Rubber, Consumer Goods, Transportation, Finance, Invest. Banking, Venture Cap., Mutual/Hedge Funds, Misc. Financial, Logistics Svcs., Supply Chain Mgmt, Media, Government, Environmental Svcs., Packaging, Real Estate, Software, Healthcare

Jones-Parker/Starr

11312 US Highway 15 501 N Ste 107
PMB 307
Chapel Hill, NC 27517-6377
(919) 542-5977
(919) 542-5887
Fax: (919) 542-1622
Email: jonespark1@aol.com
Web: www.jonesparkerstarr.com

Summary: We provide consulting services to the executive search profession and act as a resource for multi-national corporations setting up in house search firms and recruiting HR executives. We undertake only assignments that allow us to add value to an organization. This usually involves organizations undergoing change.

Key Contact - Specialty:
Ms. Janet Jones-Parker, Managing Director - *Professional services*
Mr. Jonathan Starr, Managing Director - *Professional services*
Mr. Andrew MacLean, Vice President

Salary Minimum: $150,000

Functions: Board Members, Senior Mgmt., HR Mgmt., Staffing, Mgmt. Consultants

Industries: Generalist (All)

John Jordan and Company†

PO Box 641
Stafford, TX 77497-0641
(281) 277-9313
Fax: (877) 772-5329
Email: resumes@johnjordan.biz
Web: www.johnjordan.biz

Summary: A full-service executive recruiting service offering high-level services in executive search and HR consulting.

Key Contact - Specialty:
Mr. John Jordan, Managing Director

Salary Minimum: $85,000

Functions: Sales & Mktg., Mktg. Mgmt., Finance, Mgmt. Consultants, Minorities/Diversity

Industries: Generalist (All), Computer Equip., Consumer Elect., Test, Measure Equip., Retail, Finance, Equip Svcs., Mgmt. Consulting, HR Services, Telecoms, Software

Jordan-Sitter Associates

23995 Bat Cave Rd Ste 200
San Antonio, TX 78266-2680
(210) 651-5561
Fax: (210) 651-5562
Email: chris@jordansitter.com
Web: www.jordansitter.com

Summary: Construction, mining, industrial & agricultural equipment manufacturers, dealers, rental companies and related businesses on an exclusive and retained basis only. All disciplines.

Key Contact - Specialty:
Mr. William P. Sitter, Owner - *Construction, Industrial, Mining*
Mr. Christopher W. Sitter, Vice President

Salary Minimum: $90,000

Functions: Generalist (All), Management, Senior Mgmt., Middle Mgmt., Mfg., Sales & Mktg., Engineering, Int'l.

Industries: Agri., Forestry, Mining, Energy, Utilities, Construction, Manufacturing, Metal Products, Machine, Appliance, Misc. Mfg., Equip Svcs.

Joseph Michaels Inc

1 Market St Ste 3600
San Francisco, CA 94105-1420
(415) 434-1099
(800) 786-1099
Email: ftreadwell@josephmichaels.com
Web: www.josephmichaels.com

Summary: Executive search of financial executives public and private CFO - also controller, treasurer, tax, general accounting manager, CPA etc.

Key Contact - Specialty:
Mr. Joe Pelayo, CPC, President - *Accounting, CFOs, Executives, Financial*
Mr. Fred Treadwell, Director, Recruiting - *Accounting, Accounting (Big 4,General), CFOs, Finance*

Salary Minimum: $100,000

Functions: Finance, CFOs
Industries: Generalist (All)

JP Resources†

26 Bermuda Inlet Dr
Saint Helena Island, SC 29920-6675
(843) 838-0100
Fax: (843) 838-1128
Email: skyjones@islc.net

Summary: We provide recruitment research for hard to find and mid to upper-level management. We specialize in manufacturing, engineering and sales & marketing.

Key Contact - Specialty:
Ms. Carolyn Jones, Research Consultant

Salary Minimum: $60,000

Functions: Generalist (All)

Industries: Manufacturing, Retail, Services, Media

JSG Group Management Consultants

400-178 Main St
Unionville, ON L3R 2G9
Canada
(905) 477-3625
(905) 477-4215
Email: admin@jsggroup.com
Web: www.jsggroup.com

Summary: Retainer based executive search firm, specializing in the automotive, technology and energy sectors. Clients include: general manufacturing, automotive manufacturers, vehicles & parts distributors, engineering, construction; major power/energy services utility organizations, software, services companies and professional services firms.

Key Contact - Specialty:
Mr. Richard W. Birarda, Managing Partner - *Automotive, Finance, General management, Sales, Technology*
Ms. Nancy L. Birarda, PEng, Partner & Director Client Communications - *Consulting, Engineering*
Mr. Peter Cooper, Partner
Mr. Arnie Teolis, Partner

Salary Minimum: $70,000

Functions: Management, Senior Mgmt., Plant Mgmt., Mktg. Research, Mktg. Mgmt., Sales Mgmt., CFOs, MIS Mgmt., Engineering, Int'l.

Industries: Generalist (All), Energy, Utilities, Construction, Chemicals, Plastics, Rubber, Metal Products, Motor Vehicles, Computer Equip., Retail, Services, Accounting, Mgmt. Consulting, Engineering Svcs., Logistics Svcs., Supply Chain Mgmt., Advertising, Aerospace

Judd Associates

85 Greenwood Rd
Morganville, NJ 07751-4021
(732) 970-0234
Fax: (732) 970-0017
Email: heidi@judd.net

Summary: We never take on more than two to three assignments at a time - allowing every client to be our #1 priority. The president of our company personally conducts every assignment.

Key Contact - Specialty:
Ms. Heidi Judd, President

Salary Minimum: $80,000

Functions: Board Members, Senior Mgmt., Middle Mgmt., Mfg., Sales & Mktg., HR Mgmt., Finance, CFOs, R&D, Engineering

Industries: Generalist (All), Manufacturing, Chemicals, Soap, Perf., Cosmtcs., Drugs Mfg., Medical Devices, Computer Equip., Consumer Elect., Mgmt. Consulting, Software

Julian-Soper & Associates Inc

645 N Michigan Ave
Chicago, IL 60611-2826
(312) 274-0430
Email: jsasearch@aol.com

Summary: We are management consultants specializing in executive search for mid to senior-level positions.

Key Contact - Specialty:
Ms. Gracemarie Soper, President

Salary Minimum: $50,000

Functions: Generalist (All), Mfg.

Industries: Generalist (All), Misc. Financial, Non-profits, Accounting, Mgmt. Consulting, HR Services, Publishing, Telecoms, Packaging, Insurance, Mfg. SW, Healthcare

K&P International

4343 Commerce Ct Ste 102
Lisle, IL 60532-3614
(630) 577-1560
Fax: (630) 577-1563
Email: holke@konstroffer.com
Web: www.konstroffer.com

Summary: We are an executive search firm serving all industries for mid and upper-management positions.

Key Contact - Specialty:
Mr. Oluf F. Konstroffer, President
Ms. Christiane Holke, Senior Executive Search Consultant
Ms. Heidi Rehner, Executive Search Consultant

Salary Minimum: $100,000

Functions: Generalist (All), Senior Mgmt., Middle Mgmt., Mfg., Purchasing, Sales & Mktg., HR Mgmt., CFOs, Budgeting, Int'l.

Industries: Generalist (All), Drugs Mfg., Medical Devices, Plastics, Rubber, Metal Products, Misc. Mfg., Aerospace

Kacevich, Lewis & Brown Inc

300 W Main St Bldg B
Northborough, MA 01532-2132
(508) 393-6002
Fax: (508) 393-9527
Email: joek@klbinc.com
Web: www.klbinc.com

Summary: We specialize in the search and placement of senior-level executives in the collegiate and professional ranks, including athletic directors, GMs and head coaches. We also provide resume writing and interview preparation services for high-level executives in the sports industry.

Key Contact - Specialty:
Mr. Joseph B. Kacevich, Jr., President - *Internet*

Salary Minimum: $120,000

Functions: Management

Industries: Sports

Randy S Kahn & Associates

812 Wallberg Ave
Westfield, NJ 07090-2336
(908) 654-1927
Fax: (908) 654-8575

Summary: Our firm provides high quality 'unbundled' search services. Because of the breadth and depth of the corporate staff, line and

external consulting experience, we can offer uncommon insight into the position/candidate matching process. Unfortunately, we cannot always respond to unsolicited resumes.

Key Contact - Specialty:
Mr. Randy S. Kahn, President - *Accounting*

Salary Minimum: $50,000

Functions: Management, Mfg., Materials, Sales & Mktg., HR Mgmt., Finance

Industries: Construction, Manufacturing, Food, Bev., Tobacco, Finance, Services, Mgmt. Consulting, HR Services, Healthcare

Kalish & Associates Inc

145 E 84th St Apt 5A
New York, NY 10028-2057
(212) 717-8935
Email: kalishinc@aol.com

Summary: Specialists in mid and senior-level development personnel for colleges, medical centers, Jewish philanthropies and other not-for-profit organizations.

Key Contact - Specialty:
Mr. Mark Kalish, CFRE, President

Salary Minimum: $80,000

Functions: Generalist (All)

Industries: Non-profits

Kanzer Associates Inc

500 N Michigan Ave Ste 500
Chicago, IL 60611-3755
(312) 464-0893
(312) 464-0831
Fax: (312) 464-3719
Email: wkanzer@kanzer.com
Web: www.kanzer.com

Summary: Provides clients with quality focus, aggressive timing, technical competence and commitment to communication, follow-through and delivery of a quality product.

Key Contact - Specialty:
Mr. William F. Kanzer, Principal - *Audits, Banking, Compliance, Credit cards, Database*

Salary Minimum: $125,000

Functions: Generalist (All), Board Members, Senior Mgmt., Mfg., Mktg. Mgmt., Customer Svc., PR, HR Mgmt., Finance, Risk Mgmt.

Industries: Generalist (All), Retail, Finance, Banking, Misc. Financial, Services, Non-profits, Accounting, Mgmt. Consulting, Media, Advertising, New Media, Communications, Telecoms, Call Centers, Insurance, Casualty, Re-Insurance

Gary Kaplan & Associates

201 S Lake Ave Ste 600
Pasadena, CA 91101-3016
(626) 796-8100
Fax: (626) 796-1003
Email: info@gkasearch.com
Web: www.gkasearch.com

Summary: We are an international executive search firm committed to quality of effort, service and timely completion of assignments. Diversified clients include financial services, entertainment, high technology, consumer products, education, non-profits, healthcare, hospitality and natural resources.

Key Contact - Specialty:
Mr. Gary Kaplan, President
Mr. Walter B. McNichols, Senior Vice President

Salary Minimum: $100,000

Functions: Generalist (All)

Industries: Generalist (All)

Kaplan & Associates Inc

1220 Wyngate Rd
Wynnewood, PA 19096-2427
(610) 642-5644
Web: www.kasearch.com

Summary: We partner with CEOs, boards and investors to help companies reach a new level of success through the acquisition of superior leadership. We are a generalist firm with particular expertise working with growth companies & venture-backed firms; banks, investment managers & financial institutions; and technology firms in software, IT services & telecom and life sciences.

Key Contact - Specialty:
Mr. Alan J. Kaplan, President & Chief Executive Officer
Ms. Dara Klein, Principal - *Banking, Finance, Marketing, Sales, Technology*
Ms. Ellen Mallin, Principal - *Banking, CEOs, Finance, Investment management, Technology*
Ms. Karen M. Kane, Principal - *Banking, Biopharmaceutical, Healthcare, Information Technology, Telecommunications*

Salary Minimum: $150,000

Functions: Generalist (All), Management, Board Members, Senior Mgmt., Mfg., Sales & Mktg., HR Mgmt., Finance, CFOs, IT

Industries: Finance, Banking, Invest. Banking, Venture Cap., Mutual/Hedge Funds, HR Services, E-commerce, Media, New Media, Communications, Real Estate, Software, Biotech/Life Sciences

Karel & Company / Executive Search

20 Rices Ln
Westport, CT 06880-1922
(203) 341-9911
Email: inquiries@karelco.com
Web: www.karelco.com

Summary: We place C-level executives and senior managers in the following industries: Architecture, construction, engineering, environmental consulting, facilities/property/asset management, real estate, real estate development, and the energy, power & utilities industries.

Key Contact - Specialty:
Mr. Stephen A. Karel, President & Chief Executive Officer - *Construction, Engineering, Environmental, Facilities engineering, Real estate*

Salary Minimum: $100,000

Functions: Generalist (All), Management, Senior Mgmt., Engineering

Industries: Energy, Utilities, Construction, Textiles, Apparel, Retail, Architectural Svcs., Mgmt. Consulting, Engineering Svcs., Environmental Svcs., Haz. Waste, Real Estate, Property/Facility Mgmt.

Branches:
13522 Delano St
Van Nuys, CA 91401-3032
(818) 785-6700
Key Contact - Specialty:
Mr. H.E. Greer, Vice President

2 Herrada Rd
Santa Fe, NM 87508-2114
(505) 466-6631

Key Contact - Specialty:
Mr. Lawrence Heon, Esq., Vice President & Associate

Karr Scheffel LLC

PO Box 3755
Los Altos, CA 94024-0755
(650) 574-5277
Fax: (650) 574-0310
Email: search@karrscheffel.com
Web: www.karrscheffel.com

Summary: Specialized retained executive search firm recruiting CFOs, controllers, VPs of finance and other senior financial positions including COOs and board of directors when financial experience is important. We work in all industries.

Key Contact - Specialty:
Ms. Cynthia Karr, Partner - *CFOs, Controllers*
Ms. Liz Karr, Partner - *CFOs, Controllers*
Mr. Cliff Scheffel, Partner
Ms. Gayle Rydinski, Partner - *Accounting, CFOs, Controllers, Finance, Treasury*

Salary Minimum: $125,000

Functions: CFOs

Industries: Generalist (All)

Martin Kartin & Company Inc

211 E 70th St
New York, NY 10021-5205
(212) 628-7676
Fax: (212) 628-8838
Email: mkartin@martinkartin.com
Web: www.martinkartin.com

Summary: We offer retained searches done within a customized boutique environment. Extensive experience serving clients and candidates in consumer products in the disciplines of marketing, sales, finance, operations, HR and general management. Efficient search at reasonable fees with personal service and attention.

Key Contact - Specialty:
Mr. Martin C. Kartin, President

Salary Minimum: $100,000

Functions: Generalist (All), Senior Mgmt., Mfg., Materials, Sales & Mktg., Finance, R&D

Industries: Generalist (All), Food, Bev., Tobacco, Textiles, Apparel, Soap, Perf., Cosmtcs., Drugs Mfg., Retail, Media

Leslie Kavanagh Associates Inc[†]

36 W 44th St Ste 711
New York, NY 10036-8105
(212) 661-0670
Fax: (212) 599-8316
Email: corp@lkasearch.com
Web: www.lkasearch.com

Summary: We are a talent management firm specializing in human capital, strategic procurement/global logistics, and information technology.

Key Contact - Specialty:
Mr. Will Pleva, President - *Operations*

Salary Minimum: $60,000

Functions: Senior Mgmt., Quality, Materials, Purchasing, HR Mgmt., Benefits, Training, IT, Systems Dev., Network Admin.

Industries: Energy, Utilities, Manufacturing, Transportation, Finance, Services, Media, Communications, Aerospace, Packaging, Insurance, Software, Biotech/Life Sciences

Kazan International Inc

5 Cold Hill Rd S Ste 26
Mendham, NJ 07945-3208
(973) 543-0300
Fax: (973) 543-4235
Email: info@kazansearch.com
Web: www.kazansearch.com

Summary: We are a retainer-based executive search firm dedicated to the healthcare industry. Our specialization includes senior management positions in medical devices, diagnostics, biotechnology, and pharmaceuticals.

Key Contact - Specialty:
Mr. J. Neil Kazan, President - *Biotechnology, Diagnostics, Healthcare, Pharmaceutical*
Mr. Brian Kazan, Managing Director
Mr. Gary Resnick, Vice President

Salary Minimum: $150,000

Functions: Generalist (All), Management, Board Members, Senior Mgmt., Mfg., Quality, Sales & Mktg., Finance, R&D, Int'l.

Industries: Generalist (All), Drugs Mfg., Medical Devices, Venture Cap., Pharm Svcs., Supply Chain Mgmt, Biotech/Life Sciences

Branches:
601 108th Ave NE Fl 19
Bellevue, WA 98004-4376
(425) 943-7709
Email: jrt@kazansearch.com
Key Contact - Specialty:
Mr. Robert Tassone, Managing Director

John Keister & Associates

374 E Marseilles St
Vernon Hills, IL 60061-4151
(847) 955-0540
Email: jk@johnkeister.com
Web: www.johnkeister.com

Summary: We are a nationwide executive search firm specializing in library management and administrative positions. We provide executive search services and board consulting services to public, academic, and special libraries.

Key Contact - Specialty:
Mr. John Keister, President - *Non-profit, Public sector*

Functions: Management, Board Members, Senior Mgmt.

Industries: Non-profits, Mgmt. Consulting, Higher Ed., Government

S D Kelly & Associates Inc

182 Forbes Rd Ste 224
Braintree, MA 02184-2636
(781) 794-9800
Fax: (781) 794-9809
Email: info@sdkelly.com
Web: www.sdkelly.com

Summary: We specialize in retained and exclusive search within the technology sector. Primary industries: electronic components & subassemblies, test & measurement, manufacturing equipment, advanced materials, chemicals & plastics, factory automation, defense, and medical devices. Search assignments are conducted at mid & executive management levels in R&D, engineering, sales, marketing and operations (mfg, SCM, quality, test).

Key Contact - Specialty:
Ms. Susan D. Kelly, President - *Business development, Design, Engineering, International, Marketing*
Miss Renee Selden, Research
Mr. Matthew Kelly, Research - *Technology*

Salary Minimum: $100,000

Functions: Senior Mgmt., Middle Mgmt., Mfg., Product Dev., Quality, Materials, Sales & Mktg., R&D, Engineering, Int'l.

Industries: Manufacturing, Chemicals, Medical Devices, Plastics, Rubber, Computer Equip., Test, Measure Equip., Electronic, Elec. Components, Robotics, Semiconductors, Communications, Fiber Optic, RF/Microwave, Aerospace, ERP SW, Mfg. SW, Biotech/Life Sciences

Kelly & Company

1285 Avenue of the Americas Fl 35
New York, NY 10019-6028
(212) 554-4170
Fax: (212) 554-4171
Email: bkelly@kellyandco.com
Web: www.kellyandco.com

Summary: We are a retained executive search firm with expertise in the identification, recruitment, selection and retention of senior executives within Human Resources.

Key Contact - Specialty:
Mr. William J. Kelly, President

Salary Minimum: $150,000

Functions: HR Mgmt., Benefits, Staffing, DB Admin., Mgmt. Consultants

Industries: Mgmt. Consulting, HR Services

Kelly Associates

4021 Monona Dr Apt B
Monona, WI 53716-1147
(608) 222-5330
(760) 324-2466
Fax: (608) 222-5330
Email: kellyassociates@webtv.net

Summary: The company targets existing private golf clubs as well as new golf courses and associated golf clubs that are searching for a club manager, head golf professional or a golf course superintendent.

Key Contact - Specialty:
Mr. Ronald Kelly, President
Ms. Mary K. Kelly, Secretary & Treasurer

Salary Minimum: $75,000

Functions: Management, Senior Mgmt.

Industries: Hospitality, Hotels, Resorts, Clubs, Entertainment, Recreation

Kendrick Executive Resources Inc

17950 Preston Rd Ste 760
Dallas, TX 75252-5666
(972) 713-6000
Email: steve@kerinc.com
Web: www.kerinc.com

Summary: We are a highly focused specialty-boutique retained executive search firm specializing in the recruitment of IT leadership. Our experience includes years of both proven large firm global executive search and corporate recruiting expertise.

Key Contact - Specialty:
Mr. Steve Kendrick, President
Mr. Mitch Heinemann, Consultant
Ms. Donna Walker, Administration

Salary Minimum: $150,000

Functions: MIS Mgmt.

Industries: Generalist (All)

David Warwick Kennedy & Associates

500-666 Burrard St
Vancouver, BC V6C 3P6
Canada
(604) 685-9494
Fax: (604) 535-3044
Email: david@dwksearch.com
Web: www.dwksearch.com

Summary: We are a management-consulting firm. Our firm has one main specialty area: executive search.

Key Contact - Specialty:
Mr. David Kennedy, Certified Management Consultant

Salary Minimum: $50,000

Functions: Generalist (All), Finance, CFOs, Taxes, MIS Mgmt., Mgmt. Consultants

Industries: Generalist (All), Agri., Forestry, Mining, Paper, Printing, Wholesale, Retail, Finance, Accounting, Logistics Svcs., Supply Chain Mgmt

Kennedy & Company

20 N Wacker Dr Ste 3820
Chicago, IL 60606-3103
(312) 372-0099
Fax: (312) 372-0629
Email: info@kennedycompanyinc.com
Web: www.kennedycompanyinc.com

Summary: Executive search practice serving clients in most functions and industries with expertise in finance, healthcare, technology manufacturing and service industries.

Key Contact - Specialty:
Mr. Thomas J. Moran, President & Managing Director
Ms. Lenore Meyer, Vice President, Administration
Ms. Mary Ann Bartoli, Vice President
Ms. Susan Zander, Project Manager

Salary Minimum: $75,000

Functions: Generalist (All), Board Members, Senior Mgmt., CFOs, Cash Mgmt., M&A, MIS Mgmt., Non-profits

Industries: Generalist (All), Manufacturing, Finance, Banking, Invest. Banking, Brokers, Misc. Financial, Non-profits, HR Services, Healthcare

Branches:
10151 Deerwood Park Blvd Ste 250-213
Jacksonville, FL 32256-0589
(904) 361-0255
Email: info@kennedycompanyinc.com
Key Contact - Specialty:
Ms. Diane Dombeck, Senior Vice President

Kennedy Personnel Solutions Inc

23-5012 49 St
Atrium Centre
Lloydminster, AB T9V 0K2
Canada
(780) 875-4275
Fax: (780) 875-0998
Email: kennedypersonnelsolutions@telus.net
Web: www.kennedypersonnelsolutions.com

Summary: Our mission is to provide exceptional quality and service to our clients in a confidential and professional manner, to provide our employees with opportunities, development, and a positive and supportive work environment and to seek opportunities and always approach our projects with a continuous improvement

methodology. Our agency has staff has years of experience within the oil and gas industry and the human resource management area at senior working levels.

Key Contact - Specialty:
Ms. Kathy Kennedy, RPR, President

Functions: Generalist (All)

Industries: Generalist (All)

Kensington International

PO Box 4153
Burlingame, CA 94011-4153
(650) 697-1030
Email: kisearch@pacbell.net

Summary: We are a retained search. Client base includes: high technology, bio-technology, life sciences, consumer package goods, food & beverage, financial services, professional services, technical (engineering and software) operations, IT, marketing/sales, accounting/finance, manufacturing and production.

Key Contact - Specialty:
Mr. Holland Kensington, President - *Biotechnology, Financial services, Food & beverage, High technology, Hospitality*

Salary Minimum: $150,000

Functions: Generalist (All), Sales & Mktg., HR Mgmt., Finance, IT

Industries: Generalist (All), Food, Bev., Tobacco, Finance, Accounting, Engineering Svcs., Logistics Svcs., Wireless, Fiber Optic, Network Infrastructure, Software, ERP SW, Biotech/Life Sciences, Healthcare

Kensington International

(an affiliate of Career Partners International)
1415 W 22nd St Ste 500
Oak Brook, IL 60523-2084
(630) 571-0123
Fax: (630) 571-3139
Email: info@kionline.com
Web: www.kionline.com

Summary: We are a privately held, retained executive search firm with a focus on finding executives for privately held and mid-sized companies and emerging leaders for public companies. We deliver the best candidates, not merely the best available candidates.

Key Contact - Specialty:
Mr. Brian G. Clarke, Partner & Director - *Human resources, Marketing, Sales*
Mr. Richard George, Partner & Director
Mr. Scott Robinson, Partner & Director - *Human resources, Manufacturing*
Ms. Karolyn Leonard, Director, Search Operations - *C-level, Consumer, Human resources, Manufacturing, Research*

Salary Minimum: $110,000

Functions: Generalist (All), Senior Mgmt., Middle Mgmt.

Industries: Generalist (All), Manufacturing, Transportation, Wholesale, Retail, Finance, Services

Kenzer Corp

(also known as Kenzer Corp.)
450 7th Ave Ste 2604
New York, NY 10123-2690
(212) 308-4300
Fax: (212) 6951681
Email: ny@kenzer.com
Web: www.kenzer.com

Summary: We are a full-service executive search firm with computer-integrated offices. We have

many years worth of history of operating with a high air of urgency and the highest standard of professionalism.

Key Contact - Specialty:
Mr. Robert D. Kenzer, Chairman & Chief Executive Officer - *C-level, CEOs, CFOs, CIOs, COOs*
Ms. Elaine Erickson, President & Chief Operating Officer - *Apparel, CEOs, CFOs, CIOs, Retail*
Mr. Marc Moskowitz, Chief Financial Officer
Ms. Kitty Keane, Vice President & Administration
Mr. Lou Jankovic, Vice President, Information Technology

Salary Minimum: $50,000

Functions: Management, Mfg., Materials, Sales & Mktg., HR Mgmt., Finance, IT, R&D, Engineering, Specialized Svcs.

Industries: Manufacturing, Transportation, Wholesale, Retail, Finance, Services, Hospitality, Media, Telecoms, Software

Branches:
210 Interstate North Cir SE Ste 700
Atlanta, GA 30339-2179
(770) 955-7210
Fax: (770) 955-6504
Email: atlanta@kenzer.com
Key Contact - Specialty:
Mr. Neil Schor, Vice President - *Financial services, Hospitality, Manufacturing, Retail*

5001 Lyndon B Johnson Fwy Ste 717
Dallas, TX 75244-6131
(972) 620-7776
Fax: (972) 243-7570
Email: dallas@kenzer.com
Key Contact - Specialty:
Ms. Linda Clark

Kershner & Co[†]

PO Box 341181
Bethesda, MD 20827-1181
(301) 258-7475
Email: bk@kershnerandco.com
Web: www.kershnerandco.com

Summary: We specialize in helping leading financial institutions find the right people to execute profitable strategies. We focus exclusively in the financial services industry, while remaining a generalist by function. Our longevity and success is based on our ability to deliver fast and accurate results while always maintaining the highest level of ethical standards and confidentiality.

Key Contact - Specialty:
Mr. Bruce Kershner, President - *Banking, Capital markets, Finance, Financial services*

Salary Minimum: $75,000

Functions: Generalist (All)

Industries: Finance, Banking, Invest. Banking, Brokers, Venture Cap.

Ketchum & Associates Inc

PO Box 127
Gladstone, MI 49837-0127
(906) 428-9330
Email: eresumes@ketchumassoc.com
Web: www.ketchumassoc.com

Summary: We are a national recruiting firm specializing in manufacturing. 70% of our placements occur in executive management, plant engineering and quality. Our experience spans across a number of manufacturing processes including: assembly, automation, casting, electrical, electronics, forging, machinery, machining, molding (blow, compression,

injection), paint, roll forming, stamping and welding.

Key Contact - Specialty:
Mr. J. Ronald Ketchum

Functions: Senior Mgmt., Production, Plant Mgmt., Quality, Engineering

Industries: Plastics, Rubber, Metal Products, Motor Vehicles

Michael L Ketner & Associates Inc

100 N Braddock Ave Ste 301
Pittsburgh, PA 15208-2563
(412) 731-8100
Fax: (412) 731-9224
Email: ketner@ketner.com
Web: www.ketner.com

Summary: With many years experience and more than 4,500 successful search assignments under our belt, we are uniquely qualified to fill any senior level construction executive need.

Key Contact - Specialty:
Mr. Michael L. Ketner, CPC, President - *Construction*

Salary Minimum: $80,000

Functions: Senior Mgmt.

Industries: Construction

KeyStone Search

105 5th Ave S Ste 512
Minneapolis, MN 55401-2537
(612) 375-8898
Email: info@keystonesearch.com
Web: www.keystonesearch.com

Summary: Executive search firm incorporating a core values and corporate culture identification process in order to provide higher quality matches between candidates and clients.

Key Contact - Specialty:
Mr. Michael Frommelt, Principal & Co-Founder
Mr. Bob Schoenbaum, Principal & Co-Founder
Ms. Marcia Ballinger, Principal - *High technology*
Ms. Rebecca Yanisch, Principal

Salary Minimum: $100,000

Functions: Generalist (All)

Industries: Generalist (All)

Kilcullen & Company[†]

150 N Radnor Chester Rd Ste C210
Radnor Financial Center
Radnor, PA 19087-5254
(484) 598-2100
Fax: (484) 598-2101
Email: kilcullenco@executivesearcher.com
Web: www.executivesearcher.com

Summary: Ours is a retainer-based search and consulting firm specializing in diversified recruiting services for the global financial services industry. Since founded, we have been retained by top tier global money managers in the selection of a broad range of investment professionals. Positions recruited have included national sales managers, defined contribution specialists, institutional sales representatives, product managers and domestic/international wholesalers.

Key Contact - Specialty:
Mr. Brian A. Kilcullen, President
Mr. Jason J. Cominsky, Consultant
Miss Theresa Volpe, Consultant
Miss Karen Donohue, Consultant

Salary Minimum: $75,000

Functions: Management, Senior Mgmt., Middle Mgmt., Product Dev., Sales & Mktg., Mktg. Mgmt., Sales Mgmt., CFOs, Cash Mgmt., Pension/Ret. Planning

Industries: Mutual/Hedge Funds, Misc. Financial

Kiley, Owen & McGovern Inc

PO Box 68
Blackwood, NJ 08012-0068
(856) 228-4865
Fax: (856) 227-1225
Email: reo@kilowen.com
Web: www.kilowen.com

Summary: Retainer search firm specializing in sales & marketing management, software, engineering in the computer, telecom, and data communications industries.

Key Contact - Specialty:
Ms. Sheila M. McGovern, President - *Sales*
Mr. Tom Vandegrift, Secretary & Treasurer - *Computers*
Mr. Ralph Owen, Consultant - *Sales*
Mr. Ed Bryant, Consultant

Salary Minimum: $75,000

Functions: Senior Mgmt., Middle Mgmt., Product Dev., Sales & Mktg., IT

Industries: Computer Equip., Telecoms, Software

The Kilman Advisory Group[†]

406 Farmington Ave
Farmington, CT 06032-1964
(860) 676-7817
Fax: (860) 676-7839
Email: contact@kilman.com
Web: www.kilman.com

Summary: Provide search and customized outplacement services to corporations and law firms. We are most valuable in searches where a thorough approach to finding the best attorney is essential. Particularly experienced at building in-house legal departments.

Key Contact - Specialty:
Mr. Paul H. Kilman, Principal

Salary Minimum: $100,000

Functions: HR Mgmt., Legal, Attorneys

Industries: Generalist (All)

Kincannon & Reed

2106 Gallows Rd Ste C
Vienna, VA 22182-3961
(703) 761-4046
Fax: (703) 790-1533
Email: krcontact@krsearch.net
Web: www.krsearch.com

Summary: The firm provides senior executive and board level recruitment services in agribusiness, food and life sciences.

Key Contact - Specialty:
Mr. Kelly Kincannon, Chief Executive Officer - *Agriculture, Boards of Directors, CEOs, Food & beverage, Life Sciences*
Ms. Diana Braak, Vice President
Ms. Suzanne Cox, Vice President
Mr. Greg Duerksen, Vice President - *Food*
Mr. Michael Cooper, Vice President - *Agriculture, Boards of Directors, CFOs, Food & beverage, Life Sciences*
Ms. Julie Kanak, MD - *Agriculture, Banking (Corporate), Boards of Directors, Food & beverage, Life Sciences*

Salary Minimum: $120,000

Functions: Generalist (All)

Industries: Agri., Forestry, Mining, Food, Bev., Tobacco, Non-profits, Pharm Svcs., Hospitality, Biotech/Life Sciences, Healthcare

Branches:
111 Chestnut St Apt 603
San Francisco, CA 94111-1034
(415) 834-0828
Fax: (415) 834-0828
Email: fmedero@krsearch.net
Key Contact - Specialty:
Mr. Fred Medero

P Jason King Associates Inc

PO Box 819
Canadensis, PA 18325-0819
(212) 697-7899
Email: info@yoursintravel.com
Web: www.pjasonkingassociates.com

Summary: We are a recruitment source exclusively for the travel industry. Our firm consists of executive search, corporate services, international, management consulting all exclusively for the travel industry. Candidates must apply online only.

Key Contact - Specialty:
Mr. P. Jason King, President & Chief Executive Officer - *Tourism, Transportation, Travel*

Salary Minimum: $75,000

Functions: Management, Senior Mgmt., Middle Mgmt., Sales & Mktg., Sales Mgmt., Direct Mktg., Customer Svc., HR Mgmt., Minorities/Diversity, Hotel Mgmt.

Industries: Mgmt. Consulting, Hospitality, Hotels, Resorts, Clubs, Call Centers, Women's

Kingsbury Wax Bova LLC[†]

60 Hamilton St
Cambridge, MA 02139-4525
(617) 868-6166
Fax: (617) 868-0817
Email: research@kwb.com
Web: www.kwb.com

Summary: We provide middle and senior management search and corporate advisory services to assist our clients to meet financial and operational goals while expanding internationally.

Key Contact - Specialty:
Mr. Robert M. Wax, President - *Leasing*
Mr. David Lane, Partner - *Data processing, Manufacturing, Printing*

Salary Minimum: $100,000

Functions: Generalist (All), Senior Mgmt., Middle Mgmt., Plant Mgmt., Mktg. Mgmt., Sales Mgmt., Finance, CFOs, Taxes, Attorneys

Industries: Generalist (All), Paper, Printing, Finance, Legal

Branches:
230 Park Ave Rm 1000
New York, NY 10169-1099
(212) 297-0300
Fax: (212) 297-0331
Email: bbova@kwb.com
Key Contact - Specialty:
Mr. Barry Bova, Senior Managing Partner - *Finance, Human resources, Legal*

Kingsley Allen Executive Search

7-120 Newkirk Rd
Richmond Hill, ON L4C 9S7
Canada
(905) 884-1633
Fax: (905) 884-7079
Email: office@esearchzone.com
Web: www.kitsearch.com

Summary: We are a dynamic bilingual executive search firm specializing in eCommerce, direct marketing and general practice.

Key Contact - Specialty:
Mr. Gerry Merovitz

Salary Minimum: $70,000

Functions: Generalist (All), Sales & Mktg., Finance, IT, Specialized Svcs.

Industries: Generalist (All)

Kinkead Partners

703 Hebron Ave Ste 6
Glastonbury, CT 06033-5001
(860) 659-4664
Fax: (860) 659-4658
Email: dkinkead@kinkeadsearch.com
Web: www.kinkeadsearch.com

Summary: We are an executive search firm specializing in general management and marketing leadership within consumer and industrial market spaces.

Key Contact - Specialty:
Mr. David N. Kinkead, Principal

Salary Minimum: $125,000

Functions: Mktg. Mgmt.

Industries: Food, Bev., Tobacco, Machine, Appliance, Consumer Elect., Electronic, Elec. Components, Equip Svcs., E-commerce, Marketing SW, Non-Classifiable

The Kinlin Company Inc

749 Main St Unit I
Osterville, MA 02655-1944
(508) 420-1165
Fax: (508) 428-8525
Email: info@kinlin.com
Web: www.kinlin.com

Summary: Firm specializes in the recruitment of senior executives within the asset and wealth management industry.

Key Contact - Specialty:
Ms. Ellen C. Kinlin, President
Ms. Molly Lee, Consultant
Ms. Karen Morison, Office Manager
Ms. Lynn Voccola, Director, Research

Salary Minimum: $500,000

Functions: Management, Sales & Mktg., Mktg. Mgmt., Sales Mgmt., Cash Mgmt., M&A

Industries: Generalist (All), Finance, Invest. Banking, Brokers, Misc. Financial

Kinser & Baillou LLC

590 Madison Ave Fl 21
New York, NY 10022-2524
(212) 588-8801
Fax: (212) 588-8802
Email: search@kinserbaillou.com
Web: www.kinserbaillou.com

Summary: Assignments done by experienced search professionals. We have successful search experience with top corporations and new ventures. Our firm provides extensive candidate source contacts. We offer board of directors and management searches.

Key Contact - Specialty:
Ms. Astrid von Baillou, Partner

Salary Minimum: $100,000

Functions: Board Members, Senior Mgmt.

Industries: Generalist (All), Energy, Utilities, Transportation, Banking, Venture Cap., HR Services, Communications, Healthcare

The Kinsley Group

3815 River Crossing Pkwy Ste 100
Indianapolis, IN 46240-7766
(317) 569-2256
Fax: (317) 569-2259
Email: tkginfo@kinsleygroup.com
Web: www.kinsleygroup.com

Summary: Organizational success depends on
effective leadership. We are a professional
services firm dedicated to helping our client
organizations achieve exceptional performance
through the acquisition and development of strong
leadership talent. Specializing in executive
assessment, leadership development, retained
executive search and strategic human capital
consulting, we are setting a new industry standard
by combining the discipline of experienced
executives with proven, best-practice professional
expertise.

Key Contact - Specialty:
Mr. Richard J. Kinsley, President - *C-level,
Executives, General management, Presidents,
Senior management*
Mr. Jonathan D. Sarn, Vice President - *C-level,
Executives, General management, Presidents,
Senior management*

Salary Minimum: $100,000

Functions: Generalist (All), Management, Board
Members, Senior Mgmt., Middle Mgmt.

Industries: Generalist (All)

Kiradjieff & Goode Inc

57 River St Ste 202
River Place
Wellesley Hills, MA 02481-2039
(781) 489-6777
Fax: (781) 489-6767
Email: cgoode@kg-inc.com
Web: www.kg-inc.com

Summary: Board member, upper level executive
searches. Extensive experience and track record
with a passionate commitment to personalized
service, consistent results and successful long-
term client relationships/strategic partnerships.

Key Contact - Specialty:
Mr. Richard W. Goode, Jr., Chief Executive
Officer & Mng Director - *Healthcare, Private
equity, Venture capital*
Ms. Laura K. Goode, Managing Director -
*Manufacturing, Real estate, Retail, Venture
capital*

Salary Minimum: $150,000

Functions: Generalist (All), Management, Board
Members, Mfg., Sales & Mktg., HR Mgmt.,
Finance, CFOs, IT

Industries: Generalist (All), Energy, Utilities,
Manufacturing, Retail, Finance, Services, Real
Estate, Software, Biotech/Life Sciences,
Healthcare

Kittleman & Associates LLC

300 S Wacker Dr Ste 1710
Chicago, IL 60606-6601
(312) 986-1166
Fax: (312) 986-0895
Email: search@kittleman.net
Web: www.kittleman.net

Summary: Executive search, management
consulting and leadership development
exclusively for non-profit organizations including
professional associations and private foundations.

Key Contact - Specialty:
Mr. Richard M. King, President
Mr. Edward Rivera, Principal
Ms. Rhyan Zweifler, Principal

Salary Minimum: $90,000

Functions: Generalist (All), Senior Mgmt.

Industries: Non-profits, K-12 Ed., Higher Ed.

Branches:
200 E Broward Blvd Ste 1920
Fort Lauderdale, FL 33301-1934
(954) 712-1101
Key Contact - Specialty:
Ms. Jane Luiso, Principal - *Non-profit*
Ms. Jan Caldwell, Executive Associate - *Non-
profit*

The Kleinstein Group

33 Wood Ave S
Iselin, NJ 08830-2735
(732) 494-7500
Fax: (732) 494-7579
Email: jkleinstein@kleinsteingroup.com
Web: www.kleinsteingroup.com

Summary: The firm's unique research approach
enables us to present candidates within three to
four weeks from the initiation of assignment. The
firm works on a retainer basis with a wide range of
clients, from emerging growth-oriented
organizations, to specialty industries, to Fortune
100 companies.

Key Contact - Specialty:
Mr. Jonathan Kleinstein, President
Mrs. Connie Bernardo, Managing Director

Salary Minimum: $100,000

Functions: Generalist (All)

Industries: Generalist (All)

Lillian Kloock & Associates LLC†

24 Perimeter Ctr E Ste 2414
Atlanta, GA 30346-1707
(770) 351-0500
(800) 540-9666
Fax: (770) 351-0400
Email: resumes@lkassociates.biz
Web: www.lkassociates.biz

Summary: Providing comprehensive search
services at all management levels. Focused in
healthcare, IT and consulting, as well as
entrepreneurial and early growth stage companies.
Dedicated to serving our clients and candidates
with integrity.

Key Contact - Specialty:
Mrs. Lillian Kloock, CPAR, CPC, Owner
Ms. Patty Maddox, Staffing Manager

Salary Minimum: $45,000

Functions: Generalist (All), Senior Mgmt.,
Middle Mgmt., Product Dev., Sales Mgmt.

Industries: Software, Healthcare

Knapp Consultants

PO Box 505
Westport Point, MA 02791-0505
(508) 636-8882
Fax: (508) 636-7253
Email: consultantknapp@aol.com

Summary: We are an executive
search/management consulting firm specializing in
aerospace, electronics, general manufacturing and
gas turbine industries.

Key Contact - Specialty:
Mr. Ronald A. Knapp, President - *Aerospace,
Manufacturing*

Salary Minimum: $90,000

Functions: Generalist (All), Management, Board
Members, Senior Mgmt., Mfg.

Industries: Manufacturing, Metal Products,
Aerospace

Knightsbridge Executive Search

2 Bloor St E
Royal Bank Building Floor 30
Toronto, ON M4W 1A8
Canada
(647) 777-3111
Fax: (647) 777-3169
Email: executivesearch@knightsbridge.ca
Web: www.knightsbridge.ca

Summary: We provide full service, retained
executive search for middle management through
senior level executive positions.

Key Contact - Specialty:
Mr. Brad Beveridge, Managing Director
Ms. Janice N. Kussner, Partner
Ms. Angela Eckford, Partner
Ms. Lisa Knight, Partner
Mr. Jack Penaligon, Partner
Mr. Ed Perkovic, Director, Research
Ms. Sharon Neelin, Partner

Salary Minimum: $75,000

Functions: Generalist (All), Senior Mgmt.,
Middle Mgmt., Mfg., Sales & Mktg., HR
Mgmt., CFOs, MIS Mgmt.

Industries: Generalist (All), Manufacturing,
Transportation, Retail, Finance, Government

The Knutson Group LLC

3370 N Hayden Rd Ste 123 PMB 588
Scottsdale, AZ 85251-6632
(480) 984-0077
Fax: (877) 496-9011
Email: dave@knutsongroup.com

Summary: Executive search firm that conducts
retained searches at the director level and above in
a variety of industries.

Key Contact - Specialty:
Mr. David Knutson, CPC, President - *Financial
services, General management, Human
resources, Management, Treasury*

Salary Minimum: $100,000

Functions: Management, Senior Mgmt., Mfg.,
Sales Mgmt., CFOs

Industries: Generalist (All), Energy, Utilities,
Manufacturing, Finance, Communications,
Aerospace

Koehler & Company

700 Pilgrim Pkwy
Elm Grove, WI 53122-2063
(262) 796-8010
Email: search@koehlerco.us

Summary: We are a well established, broadly
experienced, retainer search firm. We focus on
recruiting mid and upper level executives for a
diversified client base and have conducted
searches in general management, operations, sales
& marketing, engineering, HR and finance. We
are committed to finding high quality, proven
management talent for the clients we serve.

Key Contact - Specialty:
Mr. Jack Koehler, President - *CEOs, COOs,
Human resources, Manufacturing, Senior
management*
Ms. Wanda Felber, Associate

Salary Minimum: $100,000

Functions: Management, Board Members, Senior
Mgmt., Product Dev., Plant Mgmt., Sales &
Mktg., Sales Mgmt.

Industries: Generalist (All), Manufacturing,
Plastics, Rubber, Metal Products, Machine,

Appliance, Consumer Elect., Test, Measure Equip., Misc. Mfg., Electronic, Elec. Components, Robotics, Semiconductors, Consumer Goods

Lee Koehn Associates Inc

4380 SW Macadam Ave Ste 185
Portland, OR 97239-6426
(503) 224-9067
Fax: (503) 224-8122
Email: koehn@lkassociates.com
Web: www.lkassociates.com

Summary: A boutique retained search firm known for quality, timeliness and results. We place a major emphasis in financial services,internet marketing/media, high technology, telecom, manufacturing.

Key Contact - Specialty:
Mr. Lee Koehn, President
Ms. Nancy King, Director & Vice President, Research

Salary Minimum: $100,000

Functions: Generalist (All)

Industries: Generalist (All), Manufacturing, Finance, Banking, Misc. Financial, New Media, Software, Marketing SW

T J Koellhoffer & Associates

250 State Route 28 Ste 206
Bridgewater, NJ 08807-1979
(908) 526-6880
(610) 982-5959
Fax: (610) 982-9111
Email: tkoell@aol.com

Summary: Specializing in technical and executive recruiting of senior management, manufacturing, R&D, business development and engineering talent for applied research, medical device, scientific instrumentation, electronics, manufacturing and biotechnology clients.

Key Contact - Specialty:
Mr. Thomas J. Koellhoffer, President - *Biomedical, Engineering, Telecommunications*
Mr. Bruce Campelia, Senior Consultant

Salary Minimum: $95,000

Functions: Management, Board Members, Senior Mgmt., Production, Sales & Mktg., IT, MIS Mgmt., R&D, Engineering, Mgmt. Consultants

Industries: Manufacturing, Drugs Mfg., Medical Devices, Plastics, Rubber, Metal Products, Machine, Appliance, Computer Equip., Consumer Elect., Test, Measure Equip., Misc. Mfg., Electronic, Elec. Components, Semiconductors, Consumer Goods, Venture Cap., Engineering Svcs., Media, New Media, Broadcast, Film, RF/Microwave, Government, Defense, Homeland Security, Aerospace, Packaging, Software, Database SW, Entertainment SW, ERP SW, Mfg. SW, Security SW, Biotech/Life Sciences

Koenig & Associates

(an affiliate of Lincolnshire Intl)
402 Queen St
Saskatoon, SK S7K 0M3
Canada
(306) 934-1743
Fax: (306) 934-1630
Email: info@koenig.ca
Web: www.koenig.ca

Summary: We work with senior executives and organizations that want to maximize business performance through HR, recruitment, communication and organizational design.

Key Contact - Specialty:
Ms. Peggie Koenig, CMC, CHRP, President & Principal
Mr. Jason Aebig, MA, Senior Consultant - *Finance, Management*
Ms. Shauna Wilkinson, Senior Consultant - *Management*

Functions: Generalist (All)

Industries: Generalist (All)

Koltnow & Company

152 W 36th St Rm 505
New York, NY 10018-8762
(212) 594-5700
Fax: (212) 594-5577
Email: myresume@koltnow.com

Summary: Specializing in apparel related services including design, sales, production and senior management. We have additional expertise in accessories, catalog and specialty retailers. We work closely with clients to identify needs and find candidates who match specific profiles.

Key Contact - Specialty:
Ms. Emily Koltnow, Principal & Owner

Salary Minimum: $75,000

Functions: Mfg.

Industries: Textiles, Apparel

Koppen & Associates LLC

8025 Forsyth Blvd
Saint Louis, MO 63105-1706
(314) 721-9770
(800) 984-9774
Fax: (314) 721-9760
Email: koppen@koppenllc.com
Web: www.koppenllc.com

Summary: Retained executive search, recruiting research and human recources consulting services.

Key Contact - Specialty:
Ms. Kristin Koppen, President & Owner

Salary Minimum: $70,000

Functions: Board Members, Senior Mgmt., Middle Mgmt., Mfg., Health Admin., Sales & Mktg., HR Mgmt., Finance, Engineering

Industries: Generalist (All), Higher Ed.

Korban Associates

PO Box 322
Pocopson, PA 19366-0322
(610) 444-8611
(541) 593-8611
Email: rokorban@korban.com

Summary: We are a mid-size retained firm specializing in the pharmaceutical, biopharmaceutical, medical device and healthcare industries. We have extensive experience in other aspects of the life sciences, as well as food and nutritional, consumer products and certain technology based manufacturing industries.

Key Contact - Specialty:
Mr. Michael MacNamara, Principal - *Biopharmaceutical, Pharmaceutical, Physicians, Regulatory, Research & development*
Ms. Nancy Kovach, Principal - *Diagnostics, Medical (Devices), Pharmaceutical, Regulatory, Research & development*

Salary Minimum: $150,000

Functions: Generalist (All)

Industries: Drugs Mfg., Medical Devices, Biotech/Life Sciences, Healthcare

Branches:
18160 Cottonwood Rd
Sunriver, OR 97707-9317
(541) 593-8611
Email: rokorban@korban.com
Key Contact - Specialty:
Mr. Richard O. Korban, President - *Biomedical, Biopharmaceutical, C-level, Medical (Devices), Pharmaceutical*

Koren, Rogers Associates Inc†

701 Westchester Ave Ste 212W
White Plains, NY 10604-3078
(914) 686-5800
Fax: (914) 686-4116
Email: mkoren@korenrogers.com
Web: www.korenrogers.com

Summary: Provide finance, technology, marketing, life sciences and HR executive recruiting services with emphasis in consumer/pharmaceutical, Internet, entertainment, media, communication industries and financial services.

Key Contact - Specialty:
Mr. Michael Koren, President & Chief Executive Officer - *Finance, General management*
Ms. Ilene Z. Heller, Chief Operating Officer
Ms. Andrea R. Pollak, Marketing & Strategy Director
Ms. Diane Jarett, Manager, Business
Mr. Michael Moenter, Senior Search Consultant
Ms. Ann Perry, Search Consultant
Mr. Jason M. Jobe, Search Consultant
Ms. Susan J. Polese, Consultant, Recruitment
Ms. Denise L. Malfa, Search Consultant
Ms. Ann Miressi, Office Manager

Salary Minimum: $100,000

Functions: Generalist (All), Senior Mgmt., Healthcare, CFOs, Cash Mgmt., Taxes, M&A, IT, MIS Mgmt., Minorities/Diversity

Industries: Food, Bev., Tobacco, Drugs Mfg., Motor Vehicles, Computer Equip., Finance, Pharm Svcs., Hospitality, Telecoms, Software, Biotech/Life Sciences, Healthcare

Korn/Ferry International

1900 Avenue of the Stars Ste 2600
Los Angeles, CA 90067-4507
(310) 552-1834
Fax: (310) 553-6452
Web: www.kornferry.com

Summary: We provide executive human capital solutions internationally. The firm works closely with clients to deliver customized executive search, management assessment and mid-level search services, including the identification of CEOs, COOs, CFOs, board members and other senior-level executives; the formal evaluation of senior management teams; and the recruitment of middle managers.

Key Contact - Specialty:
Mr. Paul Reilly, Chairman & Chief Executive Officer
Mr. Gary Burnison, Chief Financial & Operating Officer
Mr. Gary Hourihan, President, Global Leadership Solutions
Mr. Robert McNabb, Chief Executive Officer, Futurestep
Mr. Peter Dunn, General Counsel
Mr. Don Spetner, Chief Marketing Officer
Mr. Dan Demeter, CIO
Mr. L. Parker Harrell, Jr., Managing Director, Global Financial Mkt - *Financial services*
Mr. Robert Damon, President, North America
Ms. Caroline Nahas, Office Head

Salary Minimum: $150,000

Functions: Generalist (All), Management, Board Members, Senior Mgmt., Healthcare, Sales & Mktg., Finance, CFOs, IT, Int'l.

Industries: Generalist (All), Energy, Utilities, Consumer Goods, Retail, Services, Entertainment, Telecoms, Government, Software, Biotech/Life Sciences

Affiliates:
Korn/Ferry International
Mexico City, DF
Mexico

Branches:
2600 Michelson Dr Ste 720
Irvine, CA 92612-6527
(949) 851-1834
Fax: (949) 833-7608
Key Contact - Specialty:
Mr. Peter Santora

3 Lagoon Dr Ste 280
Redwood City, CA 94065-5158
(650) 632-1834
Fax: (650) 632-1835
Key Contact - Specialty:
Mr. Wes Richards, Office Head

1 Sansome St Fl 32
San Francisco, CA 94104-4436
(415) 956-1834
Fax: (415) 956-8265
Key Contact - Specialty:
Mr. Jeff Hocking, Office Managing Director

1600 Broadway Ste 2400
Denver, CO 80202-4921
(303) 542-1880
Fax: (303) 542-1885
Key Contact - Specialty:
Mr. Fred Thompson, Office Managing Principal

695 East Main St
Financial Centre
Stamford, CT 06901-2141
(203) 359-3350
Fax: (203) 327-2044
Key Contact - Specialty:
Mr. Tim Friar, Office Managing Director
Ms. Julie Goldberg, Office Head

1700 K St NW Ste 700
Washington, DC 20006-3812
(202) 822-9444
Fax: (202) 822-8127
Key Contact - Specialty:
Mr. Nels Olson, Office Managing Director

200 S Biscayne Blvd Ste 4620
Miami, FL 33131-2303
(305) 377-4121
Fax: (305) 377-4428
Key Contact - Specialty:
Ms. Bonnie Crabtree, Office Managing Director

1230 Peachtree St NE Ste 2000
Atlanta, GA 30309-3595
(404) 577-7542
Fax: (404) 892-8955
Key Contact - Specialty:
Mr. Craig Dunlevie, Office Managing Director

233 S Wacker Dr Ste 3300
Sears Tower
Chicago, IL 60606-6387
(312) 466-1834
Fax: (312) 466-0451
Key Contact - Specialty:
Mr. Mark Pierce, Office Managing Director
Ms. Tierney Remick, Global Managing Director, Consumer

Mr. Scott Kingdom, Global Managing Director, Industrial
Mr. Thomas Giella, Sector Leader, Healthcare Services

265 Franklin St Ste 1701
Boston, MA 02110-3113
(617) 345-0200
Fax: (617) 345-0544
Key Contact - Specialty:
Mr. Robert K. Sullivan, Jr., Office Managing Director

5051 Highway 7 Ste 100
Minneapolis, MN 55416-2291
(952) 345-3600
Key Contact - Specialty:
Mr. Bob Eichinger, Office Head

80 S 8th St Ste 4816
IDS Center
Minneapolis, MN 55402-5301
(612) 333-1834
Fax: (612) 333-8971
Key Contact - Specialty:
Mr. Lee Artimovich, Office Managing Director

7 Roszel Rd Fl 5
Princeton, NJ 08540-6205
(609) 452-8848
Fax: (609) 452-9699
Key Contact - Specialty:
Mr. Richard Arons, Office Managing Director
Ms. Cheryl Buxton, Global Managing Director
Mr. Glen Schostak, Global Leader - *Amusement parks, Food service, Gaming, Hospitality*

200 Park Ave Fl 37
New York, NY 10166-3799
(212) 687-1834
Fax: (212) 986-5684
Key Contact - Specialty:
Mr. Charles Wardell, Regional Managing Director
Ms. Leslie Gordon, Global Leader
Mr. Brooks Chamberlin, Leader, North American - *Risk management*
Mr. Stephen Israel, Global Leader, Biotechnology

1835 Market St Ste 2000
Philadelphia, PA 19103-2932
(215) 496-6666
Fax: (215) 568-9911
Key Contact - Specialty:
Mr. David Shabot, Office Managing Director - *Healthcare*

2100 McKinney Ave Ste 1800
Dallas, TX 75201-6991
(214) 954-1834
Fax: (214) 954-1849
Key Contact - Specialty:
Mr. Bill Funk, Office Managing Director & Sector Leader - *Education*

1100 Louisiana St Ste 2850
Houston, TX 77002-5237
(713) 651-1834
Fax: (713) 651-0848
Key Contact - Specialty:
Mr. Greg Barnes, Office Managing Director
Mr. John McKay, Global Leader, Energy - *Energy, Gas, Oil*
Mr. Eric Nielsen, Office Head - *Minorities*

11710 Plaza America Dr Ste 450
Reston, VA 20190-4738
(703) 761-7020

Key Contact - Specialty:
Ms. Lorraine Lavet, Office Head

719 2nd Ave Ste 801
Seattle, WA 98104-1733
(206) 447-1834
Fax: (206) 447-9261
Key Contact - Specialty:
Mr. Robert Ferguson, Office Managing Director
Mr. Shelly Jones, Global Leader, Aerospace

910-401 9 Ave SW
Gulf Canada Square
Calgary, AB T2P 3C5
Canada
(403) 269-3277
Fax: (403) 262-9347
Key Contact - Specialty:
Mr. Bob Sutton, Office Managing Director

PO Box 49206 Van Stn Bentall Centre
3300-1055 Dunsmuir St
Vancouver, BC V7X 1K8
Canada
(604) 684-1834
Fax: (604) 684-1884
Key Contact - Specialty:
Mr. Grant Spitz, Office Managing Director

PO Box 763
3320-181 Bay St
Etobicoke, ON M8Z 5P9
Canada
(416) 365-1841
Fax: (416) 365-0851
Key Contact - Specialty:
Mr. Jeff Rosin, Regional Managing Director, Canada

3125-630 Boul Rene-Levesque O
Edifice C I L
Montreal, QC H3B 1S6
Canada
(514) 397-9655
Fax: (514) 397-0410
Key Contact - Specialty:
Mr. Jean-Claude Lauzon, Office Managing Director

Kostmayer Associates Inc
111 Hamlet Hill Rd Unit 1410
Baltimore, MD 21210-1518
(410) 435-2288
Email: roger@kostmayerassociates.com
Web: www.kostmayerassociates.com

Summary: We are an executive search consulting firm. Our firm specializes in senior financial services positions with high quality, fast results, effective communications and unusually thorough methodology.

Key Contact - Specialty:
Mr. Roger C. Kostmayer, Principal - *Annuities, Asset management, Financial services, Mutual funds*

Salary Minimum: $100,000

Functions: Senior Mgmt., CFOs, Cash Mgmt.

Industries: Finance, Banking, Invest. Banking, Brokers, Venture Cap., Mutual/Hedge Funds, Misc. Financial, Mgmt. Consulting, Insurance

Branches:
16 Merrymount Rd
Baltimore, MD 21210-1909
(410) 323-3303
Email: matt@kostmayerassociates.com

Key Contact - Specialty:
Mr. Matthew C. Kostmayer, Principal - *401(K), Analysts, Annuities, Asset management, Banking (Investment)*

The J Kovach Group
201 Penn Center Blvd Ste 460
Pittsburgh, PA 15235-5435
(412) 825-5168
Web: www.jkovachgroup.com

Summary: We have many years of experience in executive search for the real estate and construction industry. Recently added healthcare specialty doing administrative and physician recruiting.

Key Contact - Specialty:
Mr. Jerry Kovach, Principal - *Construction, Real estate*

Salary Minimum: $60,000

Functions: Generalist (All)

Industries: Construction, Real Estate, Healthcare, Hospitals

Kramer Executive Resources Inc
909 3rd Ave Fl 5
New York, NY 10022-4764
(212) 832-1122
(646) 495-3100
Fax: (646) 495-3118
Email: info@kramerexec.com
Web: www.kramerexec.com

Summary: We are a retainer search firm specializing in the recruitment of accounting, tax and financial professionals for placement in public or private accounting, CFO or controller type individuals, turnaround/workout professionals litigation support, and business valuation professionals.

Key Contact - Specialty:
Ms. Chloe Almour, Senior Vice President
Mr. M.T. Ozwald, Vice President

Salary Minimum: $75,000

Functions: Finance, CFOs

Industries: Manufacturing, Textiles, Apparel, Wholesale, Retail, Banking, Services, Legal, Accounting, Advertising, Publishing, Broadcast, Film, Telecoms, Government, Insurance, Real Estate

Krauthamer & Associates
5530 Wisconsin Ave Ste 1202
Chevy Chase, MD 20815-4301
(301) 654-7533
Fax: (301) 654-0136
Email: gkrauthamer@krauthamerinc.com
Web: www.krauthamerinc.com

Summary: Our firm is a retained executive search consultant. We are generalists who place senior to executive level management including board of directors. Our clients cover a broad range of industries including aerospace, real estate, healthcare, professional services, technology, power/energy, private equity, manufacturing, transportation, economic development, construction and not-for-profit industries.

Key Contact - Specialty:
Mr. Gary L. Krauthamer, Principal
Ms. Ellen S. Dorfman, Principal
Mr. Todd A. Dorfman, Principal

Salary Minimum: $125,000

Functions: Generalist (All)

Industries: Generalist (All), Energy, Utilities, Manufacturing, Transportation, Finance, Services, Aerospace, Real Estate, HR SW, Healthcare

Krecklo International Inc
(formerly known as BDK Global Search Inc)
2200-1250 Boul René-Lévesque O
Le 1250 Rene-Levesque
Montreal, QC H3B 4W8
Canada
(514) 281-9999
Email: info@krecklo.com
Web: www.krecklo.com

Summary: We are a retained senior executive search practice, specializing in the functional level of CIO and their direct reports, such as VP, director and manager level positions. Through our president, we have extensive experience in satisfying client requirements by serving all industries.

Key Contact - Specialty:
Mr. Brian D. Krecklo, CHRP, President - *C-level, CEOs, CFOs, CIOs, Hospitality*
Mr. Vijay P. Mathur, Executive Vice President - *CIOs, High technology, Information Systems, Information Technology*
Mr. Brian W. Powell, Vice President - *CIOs, Information Systems, Information Technology*
Mr. Michael J. Timmons, Senior Consultant - *Engineering, Human resources, Technology*

Salary Minimum: $90,000

Functions: IT, MIS Mgmt.

Industries: Generalist (All)

Branches:
1844 Pilgrims Way
Oakville, ON L6M 1X1
Canada
(877) 573-2556
Email: info@krecklo.com
Key Contact - Specialty:
Mr. Wayne Hussey, Senior Associate - *CIOs, Information Systems, Information Technology, Sports*

Evie Kreisler & Associates Inc†
(also known as Kreisler & Associates LLC)
2575 Peachtree Rd NE Ste 300
Atlanta, GA 30305-3686
(404) 262-0599
Fax: (404) 262-0699
Email: kreisler5d@aol.com
Web: www.kreisler-associates.com

Summary: Specialists, all disciplines, retail; apparel wholesale/manufacturing and consumer products. Our consultants have related industry background. We take pride in finding the perfect fit.

Key Contact - Specialty:
Ms. Debbi Kreisler, President - *Consumer, Retail*
Ms. Angela Maier, Director, Recruitment - *Consumer, Retail*

Salary Minimum: $50,000

Functions: Generalist (All), Board Members, Senior Mgmt., Middle Mgmt., Product Dev., Advertising, Sales Mgmt., CFOs

Industries: Generalist (All), Textiles, Apparel, Wholesale, Retail, Services, Media

Branches:
255 1/2 Newport Ave
Long Beach, CA 90903-5922
(213) 622-8994
Email: kreisler5d@aol.com
Key Contact - Specialty:
Ms. Robin Breit - *Consumer, Retail*

215 Sunset Dr
Libertyville, IL 60048-2147
(312) 251-0077
Fax: (312) 251-0289
Key Contact - Specialty:
Mr. Jeff Mateer, General Manager - *Consumer, Retail*

1 W 34th St Rm 201
New York, NY 10001-3011
(212) 279-8999
Fax: (212) 268-9660
Key Contact - Specialty:
Ms. Kathy Gross, Vice President & General Manager - *Consumer, Manufacturing, Retail*

Kremple & Meade Inc
PO Box 426
Pacific Palisades, CA 90272-0426
(310) 459-4221
Email: tomnet@gte.net

Summary: Boutique search firm engaged for senior executive searches in various industries. Emphasize medium-size companies. VP, CEO, CO and management teams.

Key Contact - Specialty:
Mr. Thomas M. Meade, Partner
Ms. Jeannette Clemens, Director, Research

Salary Minimum: $125,000

Functions: Management, Mfg., Materials, Sales & Mktg., Finance, IT

Industries: Manufacturing, Aerospace

Kremple Consulting Group
222 Reward St
Nevada City, CA 95959-2930
(530) 265-5688
Fax: (530) 265-4648
Email: jkremple@kcgresearch.com
Web: www.kcgresearch.com

Summary: We are a national firm serving our clients with the highest degree of integrity and the optimum amount of personal attention by a partner of the firm. Research and candidate development services are also available.

Key Contact - Specialty:
Mr. Jeffrey Kremple, Managing Partner
Mr. Robert Kremple, Senior Parnter

Salary Minimum: $80,000

Functions: Generalist (All)

Industries: Manufacturing, Retail, Mgmt. Consulting, HR Services, IT Implementation, Hospitality, New Media, Broadcast, Film, Communications, Software

D A Kreuter Associates Inc
555 E North Ln Ste 5020R
Conshohocken, PA 19428-2233
(610) 834-1100
Web: www.dakassociates.com

Summary: Executive search and selection consultants for the diversified, financial services sector and ibid. Handle all functions; specialize in investment management, marketing, sales and senior management.

Key Contact - Specialty:
Mr. Daniel A. Kreuter, President
Mr. Steven M. Clark, Managing Director

Salary Minimum: $100,000

Functions: Generalist (All), Senior Mgmt., Sales & Mktg.

Industries: Generalist (All), Finance

Kristan International Inc

12 E Greenway Plz Ste 1100
Houston, TX 77046-1201
(713) 961-3040
Fax: (713) 961-3626
Email: executivesearch@kristan.com
Web: www.kristan.com

Summary: We are a retained executive search
firm. We conduct retained assignments for global
corporations, service organizations, consulting
firms, start-ups and private enterprises.

Key Contact - Specialty:
Mr. Robert P. Kristan, President - *General
management*

Salary Minimum: $75,000

Functions: Generalist (All), Management, Senior
Mgmt., Mfg., Plant Mgmt., Sales & Mktg.,
Sales Mgmt., Finance, CFOs, Design

Industries: Generalist (All), Energy, Utilities,
Construction, Manufacturing, Textiles, Apparel,
Lumber, Furniture, Finance, Services,
Architectural Svcs., Call Centers

Sharon Krohn Consulting[†]

100 W Monroe St Ste 312
Chicago, IL 60603-1902
(312) 251-0039
Fax: (312) 251-0036
Email: info@realestateexecutivesearch.com
Web: www.realestateexecutivesearch.com

Summary: We are an executive search and HR
consulting specializing in real estate, construction,
architecture and related industries.

Key Contact - Specialty:
Ms. Sharon Krohn, Principal - *Property
management, Real estate*

Functions: Generalist (All), Management, Senior
Mgmt.

Industries: Construction, Real Estate,
Property/Facility Mgmt.

Kulper & Company LLC

PO Box 1445
Morristown, NJ 07962-1445
(973) 285-3850
Fax: (973) 285-3851
Email: resumes@kulpercompany.com
Web: www.kulpercompany.com

Summary: We are a high quality boutique ISO
9002-registered retained firm. C-level search
assignments is our specialty.

Key Contact - Specialty:
Mr. Keith D. Kulper, President - *Financial
services, High technology, Telecommunications*
Dr. Denise M. Kenny-Kulper, EdD, Partner
Mr. Sloan Kulper, Technology Manager &
Webmaster - *Technology*

Salary Minimum: $100,000

Functions: Management, Senior Mgmt.

Industries: Generalist (All), Manufacturing, Food,
Bev., Tobacco, Computer Equip., Finance,
Services, Non-profits, Mgmt. Consulting, IT
Implementation, Higher Ed., Media,
Communications, Telecoms, Wireless, Network
Infrastructure, Packaging, Insurance, Healthcare

John Kurosky & Associates

3 Corporate Park Ste 210
Irvine, CA 92606-5162
(949) 851-6370
Email: jk@execjka.com
Web: www.execjka.com

Summary: Generalist retained practice
specializing in placement of C-level, and direct
reports in all disciplines within technology driven
firms, manufacturing, financial services, security
access control industry, biotech, and pharma. In
addition, dedicated legal search group places
partners and senior associates.

Key Contact - Specialty:
Mr. John Kurosky, Managing Partner - *C-level,
CEOs, General management, Management,
Manufacturing*
Mr. William Mason, Managing Partner - *C-level,
CEOs, General management, Home and
building controls, Management*
Ms. Karen Kissinger, Vice President - *Legal
(Attorneys,Lawyers)*
Mr. Dick Israel, Partner - *Accounting, Aerospace,
Biopharmaceutical, Financial services*

Salary Minimum: $150,000

Functions: Generalist (All), Production, Legal,
Attorneys

Industries: Generalist (All), Manufacturing,
Finance, Banking, Invest. Banking, Services,
Legal, Communications, Government,
Homeland Security, Aerospace, Software,
Security SW, Biotech/Life Sciences

Mark J Kussman and Associates

3255 Blackhawk Meadow Dr Ste 1
Danville, CA 94506-5881
(925) 648-1683
(925) 389-1387
Fax: (925) 648-1683
Email: mark@markjkussman.com
Web: www.markjkussman.com

Summary: We have extensive search experience.
Venture capital backed to Fortune 500 clients.

Key Contact - Specialty:
Mr. Mark Kussman, President

Salary Minimum: $100,000

Functions: Generalist (All)

Industries: Drugs Mfg., Medical Devices, Test,
Measure Equip., Venture Cap., Pharm Svcs.,
Software, Biotech/Life Sciences, Healthcare,
Hospitals, Women's

The Kuypers Company

7717 Watson Dr
Plano, TX 75025-6128
(972) 527-9450
Fax: (972) 527-9451
Email: contact@thekuyperscompany.com
Web: www.thekuyperscompany.com

Summary: Our firm assists both private and public
provider and payor healthcare clients in the
recruitment and selection of senior level
executives. The exceptional experience and track
record of our founder assists in search at the CEO
and next lower executive level and in working
with search committees.

Key Contact - Specialty:
Mr. Arnie Kuypers, President

Salary Minimum: $120,000

Functions: Generalist (All)

Industries: Healthcare

L & B Resources[†]

6374 S Lamar Ct Ste 210
Littleton, CO 80123-3857
(303) 798-4005
Email: ryer@l-b-resources.com
Web: www.l-b-resources.com

Summary: We offer senior level retained searches.

Key Contact - Specialty:
Mr. Edward C. Ryer, Principal

Salary Minimum: $60,000

Functions: Generalist (All)

Industries: Generalist (All)

Marvin Laba & Associates

16030 Ventura Blvd Ste 660
Encino, CA 91436-4470
(818) 808-0072
Fax: (818) 808-0057
Email: resumes@mlasearch.com

Summary: The company specializes in
department, specialty stores, mass retailers and
their vendors & suppliers. Wholesale, retail and
eCommerce management positions of all
descriptions are worked on.

Key Contact - Specialty:
Mr. Marvin Laba, President - *Retail*

Salary Minimum: $75,000

Functions: Generalist (All), Board Members,
Senior Mgmt., Middle Mgmt., Product Dev.,
Sales & Mktg., Mktg. Research, Sales Mgmt.,
HR Mgmt., CFOs

Industries: Manufacturing, Textiles, Apparel,
Soap, Perf., Cosmtcs., Wholesale, Retail,
Finance, Accounting, Mgmt. Consulting, HR
Services, E-commerce, Accounting SW,
Marketing SW

Lambert Group International LLC

191 Post Rd W
Westport, CT 06880-4625
(203) 221-2899
Fax: (203) 834-0922
Email: jerry.lambert@lambert-group.com

Summary: Senior executive search solutions and
consulting services. Highly customized approach
to each assignment. Services include recruiting,
leadership transition, succession planning,
outplacement counseling and senior level private
consulting/executive coaching. Retained only.

Key Contact - Specialty:
Mr. Gerald M. Lambert, President - *General
management*

Salary Minimum: $125,000

Functions: Senior Mgmt., Sales Mgmt., Customer
Svc.

Industries: Generalist (All), Paper, Packaging,
Insurance, Healthcare

Lane Partners, Inc.[†]

12 Alfred St Ste 300
Woburn, MA 01801-1915
(781) 932-6208
Email: david@lanepartners.com
Web: www.lanepartners.com

Summary: We optimize our search effectiveness
by focusing on a few select industry sectors. This
approach leverages our specialized knowledge and
experience accumulated over many years, as well
as our global network of top industry players. We
specialize in the following practice areas:
Document Solutions, Business Process
Outsourcing, Supply Chain Management and Print
Communications.

Key Contact - Specialty:
Mr. David M. Lane, President - *Data processing,
E-business, Logistics, Outsourcing, Packaging*

Salary Minimum: $125,000

Functions: Management, Senior Mgmt., Middle
Mgmt., Plant Mgmt., Quality, Sales & Mktg.,
Sales Reps.

Email your resume to a targeted list of recruiters now at www.ExecutiveAgent.com/DER07

Industries: Printing, E-commerce, Logistics Svcs., Supply Chain Mgmt, Call Centers, Packaging, Doc. Mgmt., Production SW

Langley & Associates Inc

PO Box 261606
Highlands Ranch, CO 80163-1606
(303) 694-2228
Fax: (303) 694-2216
Email: cmlangley@earthlink.net

Summary: We specialize in filling senior-level management positions within the utility industry (CEO, COO, President, GM, SVP, etc.) We work in all areas of the utility industry (i.e.: electric, gas, nuclear power, IOUs, RECs, G&Ts, municipal utilities and PPDs).

Key Contact - Specialty:
Ms. Carol M. Langley, President

Functions: Generalist (All), Management, Board Members, Senior Mgmt.

Industries: Generalist (All), Energy, Utilities, Oil & Gas, Finance, Mgmt. Consulting, Government

The Lapham Group Inc

80 Park Ave Apt 3K
New York, NY 10016-2542
(212) 599-0644
Fax: (212) 697-2688
Email: info@thelaphamgroup.com
Web: www.thelaphamgroup.com

Summary: We specialize in diversified financial services and general management for the healthcare, high-technology and retail industries.

Key Contact - Specialty:
Mr. Lawrence L. Lapham
Mr. Craig L. Lapham - *Private equity*

Salary Minimum: $100,000

Functions: Generalist (All)

Industries: Retail, Finance, Misc. Financial, Insurance

Stephen Laramee & Associates Inc[†]

1801-1 Yonge St
Telsec Business Centre
Toronto, ON M5E 1W7
Canada
(877) 897-1474
Fax: (413) 369-0515
Email: slaramee@on.aibn.com
Web: www.larameeassociates.com

Summary: We provide mid management to and including senior executive search for manufacturing and/or distributor-based organizations.

Key Contact - Specialty:
Mr. Stephen Laramee, President

Salary Minimum: $40,000

Functions: Senior Mgmt., Product Dev., Production, Plant Mgmt., Mktg. Mgmt., Sales Mgmt., CFOs

Industries: Food, Bev., Tobacco, Textiles, Apparel, Lumber, Furniture, Paper, Chemicals, Drugs Mfg., Metal Products

Larsen & Lee Inc[†]

(an affiliate of Larsen International Inc)
4807 Chevy Chase Blvd
Chevy Chase, MD 20815-5339
(301) 718-4280
Email: info@llisearch.com

Summary: Search specialists for financial planners, wealth/investment advisors, and ultra-HNW relationship managers.

Key Contact - Specialty:
Mr. Joseph J. Lee, Principal - *Tax*

Salary Minimum: $80,000

Functions: Generalist (All), Taxes, Specialized Svcs., Attorneys

Industries: Generalist (All), Finance, Banking, Invest. Banking, Brokers, Venture Cap., Mutual/Hedge Funds, Misc. Financial, Legal, Accounting, Life

Larsen International Inc

9901 Valley Ranch Pkwy E Ste 2000
Irving, TX 75063-6787
(972) 830-9050
(800) 338-7475
Fax: (972) 830-9049
Email: larsenintl@comcast.net
Web: www.larseninternational.com

Summary: We have experience representing client companies in the recruitment of mid-to-upper-level professionals and executives. We accept senior level assignments, with a strong expertise in the consulting engineering, architectural and electronic security industries.

Key Contact - Specialty:
Mr. Donald J. Larsen, Principal
Ms. Celia Towsey, Director, Research

Salary Minimum: $70,000

Functions: Generalist (All)

Industries: Construction, Test, Measure Equip., Architectural Svcs., Mgmt. Consulting, Engineering Svcs., Homeland Security, Environmental Svcs., Haz. Waste, Property/Facility Mgmt., Security SW

Affiliates:
Larsen & Lee Inc[†]
Chevy Chase, MD

Larsen, Whitney, Blecksmith & Zilliacus, Inc.

888 W 6th St Ste 500
Los Angeles, CA 90017-2734
(213) 243-0033
Fax: (213) 243-0030
Email: lwbz1@mindspring.com

Summary: Generalist firm, retainer based.

Key Contact - Specialty:
Mr. William A. Whitney, Principal - *Entertainment, Hospitality, Non-profit*
Mr. Edward L. Blecksmith, Principal - *Hospitality, Real estate*

Salary Minimum: $300,000

Functions: Management, Mfg., Healthcare, Sales & Mktg., HR Mgmt., Finance, Engineering

Industries: Energy, Utilities, Construction, Drugs Mfg., Medical Devices, Plastics, Rubber, Motor Vehicles, Computer Equip., Transportation, Finance, Banking, Invest. Banking, Brokers, Venture Cap., Misc. Financial, Services, Non-profits, Pharm Svcs., Accounting, Mgmt. Consulting, Hospitality, Media, Wireless, Fiber Optic, Government, Defense, Aerospace, Packaging, Insurance, Real Estate, Software, Biotech/Life Sciences, Healthcare

Larson Associates

1440 N Harbor Blvd Ste 800
Fullerton, CA 92835-4121
(714) 449-3312
(714) 529-4121

Email: ray@consultlarson.com
Web: www.consultlarson.com

Summary: Executive and professional search for chemical, electronics, high-technology, industrial firms, management, marketing, sales and technical people. Also, management consulting for HR and organizational development functions.

Key Contact - Specialty:
Mr. Ray Larson, President - *Industrial, Management, Sales*

Salary Minimum: $50,000

Functions: Generalist (All), Senior Mgmt., Middle Mgmt., Mktg. Mgmt., Sales Mgmt., Mgmt. Consultants

Industries: Generalist (All), Chemicals, Plastics, Rubber, Metal Products, Computer Equip., Test, Measure Equip., Misc. Mfg.

LarsonAllen Search LLC[†]

(a division of Larson, Allen, Weishair & Co LLP)
220 S 6th St Ste 300
Minneapolis, MN 55402-1418
(612) 376-4500
Fax: (612) 376-4850
Email: tenger@larsonallen.com
Web: www.larsonallen.com/search

Summary: We are a full-service executive search and staffing company. Our firm serves all industries and management level positions and above.

Key Contact - Specialty:
Mr. Terry Enger, Principal in Charge - *Technical*
Mr. Tim Voller, Executive Search Consultant - *Management*
Mr. David Bares, Consultant, Professional Search
Ms. Deni Toomey, Consultant, Professional Search
Ms. Melissa Butenschoen, Consultant, Professional Search - *Accounting, Banking, Consulting, Controllers, Financial*

Salary Minimum: $60,000

Functions: Management, Senior Mgmt., Mfg.

Industries: Construction, Food, Bev., Tobacco, Medical Devices, Misc. Mfg., Finance, Misc. Financial, Non-profits, Legal, Accounting, Mgmt. Consulting, Accounting SW, Healthcare, Hospitals

Lasher Associates

1565 N Park Dr Ste 104
Weston, FL 33326-3229
(954) 217-5081
Email: mick@lasherassociates.com
Web: www.lasherassociates.com

Summary: Boutique firm, serving the largest corporations to emerging companies in most industries. Committed to the highest level of performance, confidentiality and professionalism. Specialties in technology, life sciences, emerging companies, consumer products, manufacturing and financial services.

Key Contact - Specialty:
Mr. Charles M. Lasher
Ms. Susan Hawkins, Vice President
Ms. Marjorie Kean, Vice President - *International*
Mr. James Schepp, Vice President - *Biomedical, Biopharmaceutical, Biotechnology, C-level, Life Sciences*

Salary Minimum: $125,000

Functions: Generalist (All), Admin. Svcs.

Industries: Generalist (All), Manufacturing, Drugs Mfg., Wholesale, Finance, Services, Non-profits, Media, Communications, Insurance, Software, Biotech/Life Sciences

---

† occasional contingency assignment

Branches:
8083 S Syracuse St
Centennial, CO 80112-3226
(720) 488-8678
Key Contact - Specialty:
Mr. Dan Bronson

Michael Latas & Associates Inc

1311 Lindbergh Plaza Ctr
Saint Louis, MO 63132-1630
(314) 993-6500
Email: latas@latas.com
Web: www.latas.com

Summary: We are dedicated exclusively to
serving the construction, A/E/P and real estate
industries. Your premier source for senior
management, middle management and
professional level needs. We are organized into
division specialization, which is backed up by our
research director, exhaustive research library,
multiple databases and our support staff of
research, sourcing and recruiting specialists. Our
work is strictly confidential.

Key Contact - Specialty:
Mr. Michael Latas
Mr. Richard L. Latas
Mr. Gary H. Jesberg - *General contractors*
Mr. Edward L. Nickels - *Telecommunications,
    Utilities*
Mr. William E. Ragan - *Telecommunications,
    Utilities*
Mr. Daniel J. Conroy - *General contractors*
Mr. Rodney L. Robinson - *Materials, Utilities*
Mr. Kent L. Lawrence
Mr. William C. Leonard - *General contractors*
Mr. Philip S. Aleman - *Mechanical*
Ms. Kathie N. Foster - *General contractors*
Mr. James P. Fox - *Property management*
Mr. Gary K. Stepanek
Mr. John H. Patterson
Mr. Roy Wurst - *Bridges, Highways, Materials,
    Utilities*
Mr. Shane Twenhafel - *Bridges, Highways,
    Materials, Utilities*
Mr. Robert Nagy - *Bridges, Highways, Materials,
    Utilities*

Salary Minimum: $60,000

Functions: Generalist (All), Senior Mgmt.,
    Middle Mgmt., Materials, Purchasing, CFOs,
    Engineering, Environmentalists, Architects

Industries: Generalist (All), Construction, Haz.
    Waste, Real Estate

Branches:
PO Box 4503
Youngstown, OH 44515-0503
(440) 799-9445
Fax: (216) 799-7612
Email: srusnov@latas.com
Key Contact - Specialty:
Mr. Samuel Rusnov

Latham Executive Search, LLC

9144 Shadow Glen Way
Fort Myers, FL 33913-6603
(239) 645-5854
Email: alynn@latham.us
Web: www.latham.us

Summary: Specialize in positions targeting
candidates with an MBA from a top school. Areas
of expertise include equity research, institutional
sales, strategic planning and management
consulting. Clients include Fortune 500 industry
leaders as well as smaller, more entrepreneurial
companies. Sub-specialties include health care and
the financial services industry as well as board of
director searches.

Key Contact - Specialty:
Ms. Audrey Lynn, Sole Proprietor

Salary Minimum: $100,000

Functions: Board Members, Senior Mgmt.

Industries: Finance, Healthcare

Latin America Search Associates

2805 E Oakland Park Blvd Ste 377
Fort Lauderdale, FL 33306-1813
(954) 564-6110
Fax: (954) 489-1484
Email: info@latamsearch.com
Web: www.latamsearch.com

Summary: We are a boutique search firm
specializing in the recruitment of bilingual
executives with international experience for
transnational companies.

Key Contact - Specialty:
Mr. Victor P. Viglino, President - *Latin America*

Salary Minimum: $60,000

Functions: Generalist (All)

Industries: Food, Bev., Tobacco, Soap, Perf.,
    Cosmtcs., Drugs Mfg., Medical Devices,
    Computer Equip., Consumer Elect., Banking,
    Services, Logistics Svcs., Telecoms

Lauer, Sbarbaro Associates

(an EMA Partners International company)
30 N La Salle St Ste 4030
Chicago, IL 60602-2533
(312) 372-7050
Fax: (312) 704-4393
Email: sbarbs@aol.com
Web: www.lauersbarbaro-ema.com

Summary: Medium size generalist firm with
principal participation on every assignment.
Known for its long-term client relationships and
professional approach to clients and candidates
alike. Excellent placement success record.

Key Contact - Specialty:
Mr. Richard D. Sbarbaro, Chairman
Mr. William J. Yacullo, President

Salary Minimum: $80,000

Functions: Generalist (All)

Industries: Generalist (All)

Lawrence Corporate Resources

PO Box 381
Mundelein, IL 60060-0381
(847) 275-8934
Fax: (847) 689-8231
Email: edla@edlawrence.com
Web: www.edlawrence.com

Summary: Recruitment process outsourcing firm
with notable successes in IT, manufacturing, sales,
telecom, accounting/financial, engineering and
pharmaceutical/life sciences disciplines. We
provide high end, senior level leadership to a
company's recruiting processes. We do contract
work exclusively. Our firm is a high-volume
recruiter best known for achieving outstanding
hiring results with inexperienced hiring managers.

Key Contact - Specialty:
Mr. Ed Lawrence, Contract Recruiter
Mr. Luq Latif, Contract Recruiter - *Accounting,
    Accounting (General), Finance, Maintenance,
    Manufacturing*
Ms. Barbara Moreth, Coordinator, Recruiting -
    *Accounting, Finance, Information Systems,
    Information Technology, Manufacturing*

Functions: Senior Mgmt., Middle Mgmt., Mfg.,
    Sales & Mktg., Mktg. Mgmt., HR Mgmt.,

Finance, Taxes, Engineering,
    Minorities/Diversity

Industries: Generalist (All), Electronic, Elec.
    Components, Wholesale, Logistics Svcs., Call
    Centers, Wireless

W R Lawry Inc†

PO Box 832
6 Tolland Cir Ste 7
Simsbury, CT 06070-7132
(860) 651-0281
(866) 651-0281
Fax: (800) 945-4153
Email: info@wrlawry.com
Web: www.wrlawry.com

Summary: Technical recruiting firm specializing
in locating specific, highly qualified individuals or
managers. We specialize in high-level healthcare
professionals and executives.

Key Contact - Specialty:
Mr. William R. Lawry, President - *Engineering,
    Plastics, Quality, Telecommunications*

Salary Minimum: $50,000

Functions: Generalist (All), Mfg., Product Dev.,
    Plant Mgmt., Quality, Healthcare, R&D,
    Engineering

Industries: Generalist (All), Energy, Utilities,
    Manufacturing, Printing, Chemicals, Drugs
    Mfg., Medical Devices, Plastics, Rubber, Paints,
    Petro. Products, Misc. Mfg., Electronic, Elec.
    Components, Robotics, Semiconductors,
    Telecoms, RF/Microwave, Defense, Aerospace,
    Healthcare

Leader Search Inc

4247 Passchendaele Rd SW
Calgary, AB T2T 6E6
Canada
(403) 262-8545
(877) 814-1131
Fax: (403) 262-8549
Email: recruiting@leadersearch.com
Web: www.leadersearch.com

Summary: We are a retainer firm specializing in
fitting right character candidates to the right
culture of our clients.

Key Contact - Specialty:
Mr. R.W. Johnson, President
Ms. Kendra Koss, Partner

Functions: Generalist (All), Management, Mfg.,
    Materials, Sales & Mktg., Finance, Engineering,
    Specialized Svcs.

Industries: Generalist (All), Energy, Utilities,
    Manufacturing, Finance, Hospitality, Non-
    Classifiable

Branches:
10101 N Arabian Trl Unit 1001
Scottsdale, AZ 85258-6218
(480) 368-5155

Leaders Trust International

Pico de Verapaz 449-A D 101
Col Jardines en la Montana
14210 Mexico City, DF
Mexico
55 5630 0132
55 5630 0265
Fax: 55 5645 7745
Email: elizabeth.falcon@leaderstrust.com.mx
Web: www.leaderstrust.com

Summary: We are an executive search firm,
which provides excellent professional counsel to
firms in top executives search. We build a
successful management organization that can fully
understand top companies culture, needs and goals

in order to link them to top performer individuals who will contribute to their goals.

Key Contact - Specialty:
Mrs. Elizabeth Falcon, Managing Partner - *Consumer, Manufacturing, Retail*
Mr. Jorge Segovia, Senior Consultant - *Financial services, Telecommunications*

Salary Minimum: $60,000

Functions: Generalist (All), Board Members, Plant Mgmt., Mktg. Mgmt., HR Mgmt., Credit, MIS Mgmt., Mgmt. Consultants

Industries: Generalist (All), Construction, Manufacturing, Food, Bev., Tobacco, Printing, Plastics, Rubber, Motor Vehicles, Retail, Banking, Pharm Svcs., Telecoms

Leadership Capital Group LLC

2025 E Beltline Ave SE Ste 101
Grand Rapids, MI 49546-7676
(616) 954-2722
(616) 954-2715
Fax: (616) 954-2732
Email: info@leadershipcg.com
Web: www.leadershipcg.com

Summary: We are a professional services organization offering retained corporate psychology, organization development and executive search functions. Our firm works with organizations of all sizes helping them to not only identify, but also develop their leadership capital. We are generalists and work across industries.

Key Contact - Specialty:
Mr. Roger Jansen, PhD, CAND, Partner
Ms. Heidi Frye, Partner
Mr. Michael Kelly, Partner & Chief Operating Officer
Mr. James McLean, Executive Consultant
Mr. Ken Pederson, Organizational Consultant

Salary Minimum: $110,000

Functions: Generalist (All), Management

Industries: Generalist (All)

Leadership Group Executive Search (LGES)

(formally known as Lautz, Grotte, Engler & Swimley LLC)
2682 Bishop Dr Ste 122
San Ramon, CA 94583-4450
(888) 278-9500
Email: resume@lges.com
Web: www.lges.com

Summary: A senior executive search firm with several offices in the San Francisco, New York, and Washington, D.C. areas. Founded by experienced business executives who have been partners at leading search firms, our practice is focused on top-level executive searches including C-level executives, board members, and VP-level executives in all functional areas for a broad range of national, regional, and local companies.

Key Contact - Specialty:
Mr. Lindsay A. Lautz, Principal - *Consumer, Electronics, Entertainment, New media, Telecommunications*
Mr. Bob Currie, Principal - *Boards of Directors, C-level, CEOs, CIOs, Computers (Software)*

Salary Minimum: $150,000

Functions: Senior Mgmt., Mktg. Mgmt., Sales Mgmt., CFOs

Industries: Generalist (All), Computer Equip., Consumer Elect., Venture Cap., E-commerce, IT Implementation, Entertainment, Media, Communications, Software

The Leadership Group

7047 E Greenway Pkwy Ste 250
Scottsdale, AZ 85254-8113
(480) 473-9088
Fax: (480) 473-9089
Email: admin@tlgsearch.com
Web: www.tlgsearch.com

Summary: Retained executive search exclusively within the commercial building construction industry. Our core values include integrity and honesty, relationships with authenticity and win/win business scenarios. Our core competency is to recruit the elite within the industry.

Key Contact - Specialty:
Mr. Scott T. Love, President & Chief Executive Officer

Salary Minimum: $100,000

Functions: Management, Board Members, Senior Mgmt., CFOs

Industries: Construction

The Leadership Search Group

19 Lakeside Ln Ste 220
North Barrington, IL 60010-6956
(847) 277-0008
Fax: (847) 277-0436
Email: rwk@lsg-search.com
Web: www.lsg-search.com

Summary: We are an organization of management professionals from industry, distribution and supply chain, services, retail and financial services with executive line management responsibility including recruiting and hiring. Our extensive experience assures our clients of the highest level of talent assessment and selection. Although the industrial practice is exclusive retained search, the financial services practice does offer a contingency service.

Key Contact - Specialty:
Mr. Gary Spahn, Managing Partner

Salary Minimum: $65,000

Functions: Generalist (All), Management

Industries: Generalist (All), Construction, Manufacturing, Metal Products, Machine, Appliance, Wholesale, Retail, Finance, Banking, Invest. Banking, Logistics Svcs., Supply Chain Mgmt

Branches:
1111 S Waukegan Rd Unit 5
Lake Forest, IL 60045-3758
(847) 295-5724
Fax: (847) 295-5724
Email: gfs@lsg-search.com
Key Contact - Specialty:
Mr. Robert W. Knopik, Managing Director
Mr. Alvis Saleniaks, Director, Research

Leadership Solutions

4502 Floradale Ct
Rocklin, CA 95677-4539
(916) 791-5533
Fax: (916) 791-5828
Email: jbaker@lssearch.com
Web: www.lssearch.com

Summary: Specialists in recruiting and evaluating CEOs, COOs, CFOs, presidents, and functional VPs for growth oriented companies in the food manufacturing sector. We are also an excellent source for sales, marketing, finance and operations professionals at the director level. All placements resulting from a comprehensive and methodical search are guaranteed for one full year.

Key Contact - Specialty:
Mr. Jake Baker, President & Chief Executive Officer
Mr. Robert Behney, Recruiter
Ms. Linda Sloan, Senior Research Associate
Mr. John Harris, Senior Associate
Mr. Jason Bradley Baker, Research Associate

Salary Minimum: $90,000

Functions: Management, Board Members, Senior Mgmt., Middle Mgmt., Mfg., Sales & Mktg., Mktg. Mgmt., Sales Mgmt., CFOs, Attorneys

Industries: Generalist (All), Agri., Forestry, Mining, Manufacturing, Food, Bev., Tobacco, Consumer Goods, Wholesale, Venture Cap.

The Lear Group Inc

578 Dover Center Rd Ste 2
Bay Village, OH 44140-2361
(440) 892-9828
Fax: (440) 892-9757
Email: leargroup@aol.com
Web: www.learrecruit.com

Summary: We offer executive search and recruitment services to a wide variety of industrial, financial and professional service clients. Areas of concentration include: partner/principal, C-levels, general management, attorneys, accounting, commercial banking, finance, sales, marketing, engineering, manufacturing and professional service. We are active in Lean enterprise, supply chain and global procurement areas.

Key Contact - Specialty:
Mr. Larry Gregg, Managing Director - *General management, Manufacturing, Manufacturing (Management), Research & development, Senior management*
Mr. Michael Ginley, Director - *Banking, General management, Manufacturing, Senior management, Six sigma*

Salary Minimum: $100,000

Functions: Generalist (All), Management, Senior Mgmt., Mfg., Production, Productivity, Purchasing, Finance, Legal

Industries: Manufacturing, Medical Devices, Plastics, Rubber, Metal Products, Machine, Appliance, Motor Vehicles, Misc. Mfg., Electronic, Elec. Components, Finance, Banking, Legal, Accounting, Mgmt. Consulting, Supply Chain Mgmt, Aerospace, Packaging, Biotech/Life Sciences

LedbetterStevens Inc

58 Thomas St PH
New York, NY 10013-3861
(212) 687-6600
Fax: (212) 687-1113
Email: lsi@ledbetterstevens.com
Web: www.ledbetterstevens.com

Summary: To serve our clients, the goal of our firm is to function as the superior provider of unparalleled executive and scientific management teams. Our ultimate responsibility is to contribute to client objectives by adhering to an exceptional work ethic and the professional standards required to build and maintain long term relationships.

Key Contact - Specialty:
Ms. Charlene Ledbetter, Principal
Ms. Jennifer Stevens, Principal
Mr. Thomas Green, Principal

Salary Minimum: $150,000

Functions: Senior Mgmt.

Industries: Drugs Mfg., Venture Cap., Pharm Svcs., Biotech/Life Sciences

The Leis Group

7255 Poppy Hills Ct
Blacklick, OH 43004-9007
(614) 755-4530
Email: blake_leis@theleisgroup.com
Web: www.theleisgroup.com

Summary: Our firm is an executive search firm specializing in the health care industry. Our firm is committed to the strategic executive recruiting success of our clients while representing unparalleled integrity and due diligence in our provision of executive search services.

Key Contact - Specialty:
Mr. Blake Leis, President

Salary Minimum: $100,000

Functions: Generalist (All), Management, Senior Mgmt., Health Admin., Sales & Mktg., Mktg. Mgmt., Sales Mgmt., HR Mgmt., CFOs, M&A

Industries: Drugs Mfg., Medical Devices, Pharm Svcs., Biotech/Life Sciences, Healthcare, Hospitals, Long-term/Home Care, Physical Therapy, Occupational Therapy

LePage International Inc

(a World Search Group company)
2200-1250 Boul René-Lévesque O
Le 1250 Rene-Levesque
Montreal, QC H3B 4W8
Canada
(514) 879-8700
Fax: (514) 879-8701
Email: reception@lepageintl.com
Web: www.lepageintl.com

Summary: We are a bilingual firm (French & English) with search experience, research-based generalist firm senior and middle management searches across most functions and industries.

Key Contact - Specialty:
Mr. Jacques LePage, President & Managing Director

Salary Minimum: $65,000

Functions: Generalist (All), Management, Mfg., Materials, Sales & Mktg., HR Mgmt., Engineering, Int'l.

Industries: Generalist (All), Agri., Forestry, Mining, Energy, Utilities, Manufacturing, Media, Aerospace, Software

The LeROI Group

(formerly known as Special Markets Group Inc)
4732 Old Countryside Cir S
Stone Mountain, GA 30083-5833
(888) 245-2150
(404) 508-0834
Fax: (404) 296-7999
Email: kennethlee@specialmarketsgroup.com
Web: www.specialmarketsgroup.com

Summary: Retained firm dedicated to providing executive search and HR consulting to both small entrepreneurial organizations as well as large corporate entities. Expertise in diversity/minority positions and general business.

Key Contact - Specialty:
Mr. Kenneth D. Lee, President - *Minorities*
Mr. Craig Triplett, Managing Partner

Salary Minimum: $50,000

Functions: Generalist (All), Senior Mgmt., Mktg. Mgmt., Sales Mgmt., CFOs, MIS Mgmt., Minorities/Diversity

Industries: Generalist (All), Food, Bev., Tobacco, Computer Equip., Finance, Non-profits, Higher Ed., Hospitality, Media, Insurance

J E Lessner Associates Inc

2143 E Newark Rd
Lapeer, MI 48446-9473
(810) 667-9335
Fax: (810) 667-3470
Email: jack@jelessner.com
Web: www.jelessner.com

Summary: We perform executive searches, organizational development and outplacement activities.

Key Contact - Specialty:
Mr. Jack Lessner, President - *Organizational development*
Ms. Mary Ann Lessner, Vice President, Staff Admin.
Mr. Mark Lessner, Search Consultant - *Engineering, Manufacturing, Sales*
Ms. Jan Roodvoets, Search Consultant - *Manufacturing, Materials, Sales*

Salary Minimum: $65,000

Functions: Generalist (All), Management, Mfg., Materials, Sales & Mktg., HR Mgmt., Finance, Engineering, Int'l.

Industries: Generalist (All), Manufacturing, Chemicals, Plastics, Rubber, Metal Products, Motor Vehicles, Transportation, Aerospace

Levin & Company Inc

28 State St Ste 1100
Boston, MA 02109-5717
(617) 573-5258
Fax: (617) 573-5259
Email: maureen@levinandcompany.com
Web: www.levinandcompany.com

Summary: We look beyond resumes to character and build complementary teams with special emphasis on workplace diversity. We focus on life sciences, biotechnology, pharmaceuticals and biomedical companies.

Key Contact - Specialty:
Ms. Becky Levin, Founder & Chief Executive Officer - *Biomedical, Biotechnology*
Ms. Tamara Davis, Head, Corporate Governance Practice - *Biopharmaceutical, Biotechnology, Boards of Directors, Medical (Devices), Pharmaceutical*
Ms. Maureen Salkin, Vice President, Research - *Biomedical, Biopharmaceutical, Biotechnology, Medical (Devices), Pharmaceutical*

Salary Minimum: $150,000

Functions: Generalist (All), Board Members, Senior Mgmt., CFOs, MIS Mgmt.

Industries: Generalist (All), Drugs Mfg., Medical Devices, Pharm Svcs., Biotech/Life Sciences, Healthcare

Branches:
1800 Century Park E Ste 600
Los Angeles, CA 90067-1509
(310) 229-5915
Fax: (310) 229-5916
Key Contact - Specialty:
Mr. Christos Richards, President - *Biomedical, Biopharmaceutical, Biotechnology, High technology, Medical*

425 Market St Ste 2200
San Francisco, CA 94105-2434
(415) 912-2860
Fax: (415) 912-2861
Email: evan@levinandcompany.com

Key Contact - Specialty:
Mr. Evan Fishel, Vice President - *Biomedical, Biopharmaceutical, Biotechnology, Pharmaceutical*

Alan Levine Associates[†]

180 Wells Ave Ste 105
Newton Center, MA 02459-3328
(617) 928-1900
Email: info@alanlevineassociates.com
Web: www.alanlevineassociates.com

Summary: We are a specialized, personalized, quality search firm with many years of service to the retail, wholesale, direct mail and consumer packaged goods industries.

Key Contact - Specialty:
Mr. Alan C. Levine, Managing Principal - *Manufacturing, Retail*

Salary Minimum: $75,000

Functions: Generalist (All), Management, Senior Mgmt., Sales & Mktg., Mktg. Mgmt., Sales Mgmt.

Industries: Generalist (All), Food, Bev., Tobacco, Textiles, Apparel, Soap, Perf., Cosmtcs., Consumer Elect., Consumer Goods, Wholesale, Retail, Misc. Financial, Supply Chain Mgmt., Hotels, Resorts, Clubs

Michael Levine Search Consultants

11 E 44th St Fl 5
New York, NY 10017-3608
(212) 328-1940
Fax: (212) 328-1950
Web: www.mlsearch.com

Summary: A boutique firm who can guarantee personalized care in every search. Our contacts are wide and we can find people in places not normally covered by a large firm.

Key Contact - Specialty:
Mr. Michael Levine, President
Mr. Steven Spector, Recruiter

Salary Minimum: $100,000

Functions: Generalist (All), Senior Mgmt., Middle Mgmt., Advertising, Mktg. Research, PR, Int'l.

Industries: Generalist (All), Soap, Perf., Cosmtcs., Retail, Hospitality, Advertising, New Media, Broadcast, Film

Levison Search Associates

PO Box 1133
El Dorado, CA 95623-1133
(800) 538-4766
Fax: (530) 626-5604
Email: rlevison@levisonsearch.com
Web: www.levisonsearch.com

Summary: Specialize in recruiting physicians, mid-level practitioners and executives for hospitals, HMOs, medical groups and clinics.

Key Contact - Specialty:
Ms. Regina Levison, President - *Healthcare*
Mr. Michael Levison, Executive Vice President - *Healthcare*

Salary Minimum: $80,000

Functions: Generalist (All), Physicians, Health Admin.

Industries: Generalist (All), Healthcare

Lewis Companies Inc

305-162 Cumberland St
Renaissance Court
Toronto, ON M5R 3N5
Canada
(416) 929-1506
Fax: (416) 929-8470
Email: lorraine.lewis@lewiscos.com
Web: www.lewiscos.com

Summary: We are an executive search practice
that has developed an extensive network of
corporate contacts and professional affiliations.
The firm's search process is determined, creative
and thorough, blending a wealth of professional
experience, style and ethics. It is provided at
reasonable cost.

Key Contact - Specialty:
Ms. Lorraine Lewis, Managing Partner

Salary Minimum: $100,000

Functions: Generalist (All)

Industries: Generalist (All), Agri., Forestry,
Mining, Energy, Utilities, Transportation,
Finance, Engineering Svcs., Government,
Environmental Svcs., Aerospace, Biotech/Life
Sciences

Lexington Associates

1177 High Ridge Rd
Stamford, CT 06905-1221
(203) 321-1298
Fax: (203) 321-2122
Email: dshufelt@lexassoc.com
Web: www.lexassoc.com

Summary: We specialize in retained executive
searches for high technology and financial
services firms. We are uniquely positioned to
address major issues facing corporations in these
turbulent times. We offer a concierge level of
service in order to meet or exceed our clients'
expectations.

Key Contact - Specialty:
Mr. Douglas G. Shufelt, Managing Partner

Salary Minimum: $100,000

Functions: Management, Senior Mgmt., Sales &
Mktg., CFOs

Industries: Finance, Banking, Venture Cap.,
Mutual/Hedge Funds, Communications,
Telecoms, Call Centers, Telephony, Network
Infrastructure, Software, Networking, Comm.
SW

Leyendecker Executive Search†

(also known as Leyendecker & Associates)
5847 San Felipe St Ste 1700
Houston, TX 77057-3073
(713) 680-1299
Email: inquiry@leyendecker.com
Web: www.leyendecker.com

Summary: The primary focus of our firm is the
field of corporate finance. Clients include Wall
Street and regional investment banks, money
center & foreign banks, equity investor groups,
mezzanine funds, institutional investors, corporate
treasury and M&A departments.

Key Contact - Specialty:
Mr. Douglas Leyendecker, Principal
Mr. Jeffery Smith, Principal - *Energy*
Mr. James Ford, Principal
Ms. Pat Bajenski, Principal
Mr. David A. Prodoehl, Principal
Ms. Colleen Curran, Director, Research

Salary Minimum: $75,000

Functions: Generalist (All), CFOs, M&A

Industries: Energy, Utilities, Oil & Gas,
Chemicals, Finance, Banking, Invest. Banking,
Venture Cap., Mutual/Hedge Funds, Misc.
Financial

The Libra Group Ltd

PO Box 32424
Charlotte, NC 28232-2424
(704) 334-0476
Fax: (704) 334-7186
Email: partners@thelibragroup.com

Summary: We are an African American search
firm that specializes in diversity. We have 100
percent success at placing mid to upper-level
managers.

Key Contact - Specialty:
Grazell R. Howard, Esq., Chief Executive Officer
& President - *Diversity*
Mr. Frank G. Chester, Chief Operating Officer &
Executive VP - *Human resources, Marketing*

Salary Minimum: $75,000

Functions: Generalist (All), Management, Senior
Mgmt., Mfg., HR Mgmt., Finance, Engineering,
Minorities/Diversity

Industries: Generalist (All), Manufacturing,
Paints, Petro. Products, Retail, Finance, Brokers,
Misc. Financial, Services, Legal, Defense

Lightworld Enterprises LLC

PO Box 18754
Cleveland Heights, OH 44118-0754
(216) 932-0101
Email: jobs@lightworldenterprises.com
Web: www.lightworldenterprises.com

Summary: We specialize in executive recruiting,
high-volume research, consulting and education.
Our firm supports corporations that value
diversity. We provide professional search services,
targeted research and training with a focus on
people of color and women.

Key Contact - Specialty:
Ms. Kelly Chapman, President

Salary Minimum: $100,000

Functions: Minorities/Diversity

Industries: Generalist (All), Manufacturing,
Motor Vehicles, Retail, Finance, Banking, HR
Services, Telecoms, Call Centers, Wireless

Lois L Lindauer Searches

437 Boylston St
Boston, MA 02116-3307
(617) 262-1102
Fax: (617) 262-1106
Email: llindauer@lllsearches.com
Web: www.lllsearches.com

Summary: We are a retained executive search
firm that supports the non-profit sector by filling
mid to executive-level positions. Our specialty is
development.

Key Contact - Specialty:
Ms. Lois L. Lindauer, Director - *Management*
Ms. Jill Lasman, Associate Director
Ms. Nicole Gakidis, Assistant Director
Ms. Leenie Glickman, Candidate Development
Specialist
Ms. Maureen Huminik, Search Director
Ms. Layla Stevenson, Director, Marketing &
Operations
Ms. Jodi-Joy O'Keefe, Search Director
Ms. Audrey H. Paek, Search Director
Ms. Teresa A. Ward, Search Director

Salary Minimum: $50,000

Functions: Middle Mgmt., Non-profits

Industries: Non-profits, Higher Ed.

David Lindemer Associates Inc†

PO Box 2827
Ann Arbor, MI 48106-2827
(734) 663-0070
Email: david@lindemer.com
Web: www.lindemer.com

Summary: Our concentration is at senior and
middle management levels where managerial
ability is as critical to success as industry
experience. Our industry specialization includes:
life-sciences, medical devices, manufacturing,
healthcare data management/decision support and
bio-technology. We also have functional
specialties in marketing, product management, HR
and organization development.

Key Contact - Specialty:
Mr. David Lindemer, President

Salary Minimum: $75,000

Functions: Senior Mgmt., Middle Mgmt., Mktg.
Research, Mktg. Mgmt., HR Mgmt.

Industries: Generalist (All), Construction,
Medical Devices, Software, Biotech/Life
Sciences, Hospitals

Lindsey & Company Inc

PO Box 1273
Darien, CT 06820-1273
(203) 655-1590
Fax: (203) 655-3798
Email: info@lindseycompany.com
Web: www.lindseycompany.com

Summary: We are a general search firm in all
industries and functions.

Key Contact - Specialty:
Mr. Lary L. Lindsey, President
Mr. Thomas K. McInerney, Managing Partner
Mr. Paul Bova, Managing Partner
Mr. David Verner, Managing Partner
Mr. Brian Curry, Managing Partner
Mrs. Mary Moore, Director, Recruiting
Ms. Tami Dupuis, Associate, Recruiting

Salary Minimum: $120,000

Functions: Generalist (All)

Industries: Generalist (All)

Lipsky Group Inc†

220 Nice Ln Apt 112
Newport Beach, CA 92663-2602
(949) 645-4300
Fax: (949) 645-4522
Email: lipsky@ix.netcom.com
Web: www.lipskygroup.com

Summary: We are a boutique executive search,
coaching and consulting firm. We specialize in
start-ups and turnarounds, specifically in the
computer communications and telecom
marketplace. We do everything from complete
executive staff to full departments (i.e. sales &
marketing).

Key Contact - Specialty:
Ms. Marla J. Lipsky, President - *Sales*

Salary Minimum: $75,000

Functions: Generalist (All), Management, Senior
Mgmt., Sales & Mktg., Mktg. Research, Sales
Mgmt.

Industries: Generalist (All), Computer Equip.,
Venture Cap., Communications, Telecoms,
Software, Marketing SW, Networking, Comm.
SW, Security SW

† occasional contingency assignment

Lipson & Co

1900 Avenue of the Stars Ste 2810
Los Angeles, CA 90067-4509
(310) 277-4646
Fax: (310) 277-8585
Email: howard@lipsonco.com
Web: www.lipsonco.com

Summary: A boutique firm servicing the
executive needs of the entertainment (television,
film and video games), high technology and
consumer goods industries. The company's
principals, with firsthand experience in their
specialized industries, have completed senior level
searches (CEO, president, SVP, etc.) throughout
the world.

Key Contact - Specialty:
Mr. Howard R. Lipson, President - *Entertainment,
Multimedia*
Ms. Harriet L. Lipson, Senior Vice President -
Entertainment, Multimedia

Salary Minimum: $125,000

Functions: Senior Mgmt.

Industries: E-commerce, Entertainment, Sports,
Media, Advertising, Publishing, New Media,
Broadcast, Film, Digital, Wireless

Litchfield & Willis Inc

PO Box 271482
Houston, TX 77277-1482
(713) 528-8885
Fax: (713) 528-8895
Email: lw@litchwillis.com
Web: www.litchwillis.com

Summary: A retained search firm, we also provide
consulting services in succession and
organizational management. Special expertise for
clients in: professional services industry, oil &
gas/energy, emerging companies, manufacturing,
public sector organizations and large national
corporations.

Key Contact - Specialty:
Ms. Barbara H. Litchfield, Principal -
*Engineering, General management, Public
sector*
Mr. Jim Davenport, Vice President - *Engineering,
Healthcare*
Mrs. Jacqueline Allen, Accountant

Functions: Generalist (All), Health Admin.,
Customer Svc., Engineering

Industries: Generalist (All), Non-profits,
Architectural Svcs., Mgmt. Consulting,
Healthcare

Livingston, Robert & Co

209 Bruce Park Ave
Greenwich, CT 06830-2703
(203) 618-8400
Email: peter@prlsearch.com

Summary: Small, research oriented, general
management oriented, clients are both large
corporations and start-ups. Only the principals'
work on the assignments.

Key Contact - Specialty:
Mr. Peter R. Livingston, Principal - *Financial
services, General management, Marketing,
Sales, Wall Street*
Mr. Bill Runquist, Principal - *Asset management,
COOs, General management, Manufacturing,
Marketing*

Salary Minimum: $150,000

Functions: Generalist (All), Management, Mfg.,
Materials, Sales & Mktg., HR Mgmt., Finance,
M&A, IT, Non-profits

Industries: Generalist (All), Oil & Gas,
Manufacturing, Food, Bev., Tobacco, Textiles,
Apparel, Chemicals, Drugs Mfg., Medical
Devices, Computer Equip., Consumer Elect.,
Transportation, Invest. Banking, Brokers,
Venture Cap., Mutual/Hedge Funds, Non-
profits, New Media, Packaging, Software,
Biotech/Life Sciences

Lloyd Associates[†]

12725 Morris Rd Ext Ste 185
Alpharetta, GA 30004-5025
(770) 754-1528
Email: ctlloyd@mindspring.com

Summary: Our practice emphasizes commercial
banks, including: community, regional and money
center banks and consulting firms serving these
banks. Our specialties are CEO, CFO, Senior Loan
Officers and Senior Credit Officers, Managers of
retail delivery channels and payment systems.

Key Contact - Specialty:
Ms. Carolyn T. Lloyd, Principal & Owner

Salary Minimum: $50,000

Functions: Generalist (All), Senior Mgmt., Cash
Mgmt., Risk Mgmt.

Industries: Finance, Banking

The Lloyd Group

6916 Prestonshire Ln
Dallas, TX 75225-1740
(214) 361-7411
Email: glloyd@tlgusa.com
Web: www.tlgusa.com

Summary: Executive search and research
consulting group specializing in start-up and
emerging business teams as well as strategic
partners. Industries serviced include consulting,
IT, architectural/design services and creative
shops.

Key Contact - Specialty:
Ms. Gwyneth Lloyd, Principal - *Consulting,
Emerging growth, Information Technology,
Management consulting, Marketing*

Salary Minimum: $75,000

Functions: Generalist (All)

Industries: Generalist (All), Services, Media,
Communications

Locke and KEY Executive Search

PO Box 6746
Oakland, CA 94603-0746
(510) 533-2005
Fax: (510) 533-2055
Email: lklocke@lockeandkey.com
Web: www.lockeandkey.com

Summary: Retained executive search and
consulting firm focused on recruiting key senior
level executives for growing and profitable
companies. We partner with companies going
through rapid changes: start up, fast growth, re-
engineering, re-structuring, re-positioning, re-
funding, new leadership and mergers &
acquisitions. We also conduct partial unbundled
searches and hourly work.

Key Contact - Specialty:
Ms. Lisa K. Locke, President
Mr. John Tincu, Partner
Ms. Karen Iacano, Director, Research

Salary Minimum: $50,000

Functions: Management, Mfg., Materials, Sales &
Mktg., HR Mgmt., Finance, IT, R&D,
Engineering, Legal

Industries: Generalist (All), Construction,
Manufacturing, Food, Bev., Tobacco, Medical

Devices, Metal Products, Machine, Appliance,
Test, Measure Equip., Misc. Mfg., Electronic,
Elec. Components, Transportation, Wholesale,
Retail, Finance, Services, Insurance, Real
Estate, Software, Marketing SW

Loewenstein & Associates Inc

5847 San Felipe St Ste 1250
Houston, TX 77057-3285
(713) 952-1840
Fax: (713) 952-4534
Email: executivesearch@loewenstein.com
Web: www.loewenstein.com

Summary: Our clients include established,
emerging, and start-up companies that provide
products and services to the energy, industrial and
manufacturing industries. Our proven
methodology and professional staff provide clients
with predictable results that have become our
trademark. Successful searches include C-level
executives, principals, VPs, directors and
individual contributors.

Key Contact - Specialty:
Mr. Ron Loewenstein, President - *Information
Technology, Sales, Technology*

Salary Minimum: $100,000

Functions: Generalist (All), Board Members,
Senior Mgmt., Middle Mgmt., Production,
Automation, Sales & Mktg., MIS Mgmt.,
Systems Implem., Mgmt. Consultants

Industries: Generalist (All), Energy, Utilities,
Chemicals, Computer Equip., Mgmt.
Consulting, Software

Logan, Chace LLC

420 Lexington Ave Rm 845
New York, NY 10170-0038
(212) 949-2500
Fax: (212) 949-5212
Email: admin@loganchace.com

Summary: We specialize in consultants to
management in executive selection. We are a
generalist firm specializing in strategically critical
assignments.

Key Contact - Specialty:
Mr. James P. Logan, III
Mr. Christopher D. Chace

Salary Minimum: $100,000

Functions: Generalist (All)

Industries: Generalist (All)

The Logan Group Inc

PO Box 170105
Saint Louis, MO 63117-7805
(314) 565-2828
Email: loganstl@earthlink.net
Web: www.advr.com/logan

Summary: Search firm engaged in quality search
and surveys. Activity tailored to clients' needs.

Key Contact - Specialty:
Mr. Brian Ryan, President

Salary Minimum: $60,000

Functions: Management, Board Members, Senior
Mgmt., Middle Mgmt., Mfg., Healthcare, Sales
& Mktg., HR Mgmt., Finance, IT

Industries: Manufacturing, Services, Media,
Government

Logic Associates Inc[†]

67 Wall St Fl 22
New York, NY 10005-3111
(212) 227-8000
Fax: (212) 766-0188

Email your resume to a targeted list of recruiters now at www.ExecutiveAgent.com/DER07

Email: bperry@logicassociates.com
Web: www.logicassociates.com

Summary: Regarded as one of the national leaders in corporate insurance/risk management recruiting.

Key Contact - Specialty:
Mr. Bill Perry, President
Mr. Worth Fiers, Vice President, Risk
  Management
Mr. John Gallo, Vice President

Salary Minimum: $50,000

Functions: Board Members, Senior Mgmt., Middle Mgmt., Health Admin., Benefits, Budgeting, Risk Mgmt.

Industries: Generalist (All), Insurance

Logistics Management Resources Inc

PO Box 2014
New City, NY 10956-8614
(845) 638-4224
Fax: (845) 638-4621
Email: info@logisticsresources.com
Web: www.logisticsresources.com

Summary: Our firm is a boutique executive search organization. Our client base impressive is smaller than that of large search firms, allowing greater service to client options. We specialize in operational analysis, network analysis and optimization, strategic sourcing, strategic planning, supply chain management and logistics.

Key Contact - Specialty:
Ms. Marjorie Slater, President - *General management, Logistics, Purchasing*

Functions: Generalist (All), Board Members, Senior Mgmt., Middle Mgmt., Admin. Svcs., Materials, Purchasing, Distribution, Customer Svc.

Industries: Generalist (All), Manufacturing, Food, Bev., Tobacco, Paper, Soap, Perf., Cosmtcs., Drugs Mfg., Medical Devices, Paints, Petro. Products, Consumer Goods, Transportation, Wholesale, Retail, Services, Logistics Svcs., Supply Chain Mgmt, Hospitality, Biotech/Life Sciences, Non-Classifiable

Cathryn Lohrisch & Company Inc

1201-3266 Yonge St
First Class Business Stores
Toronto, ON M4N 3P6
Canada
(416) 222-3063
Email: lohrisch@sympatico.ca

Summary: We are a search firm that provides personalized service tailored to clients' needs. Our firm conducts searches for senior staff positions in the private, public and not-for-profit sectors.

Key Contact - Specialty:
Ms. Cathryn Lohrisch, President

Salary Minimum: $50,000

Functions: Generalist (All), Management, PR, HR Mgmt., Finance, CFOs, Non-profits

Industries: Generalist (All), Finance, Non-profits, HR Services, Higher Ed., Government, Insurance

Longshore. Simmons. Garofolo

625 W Ridge Pike Ste E410
Conshohocken, PA 19428-3201
(610) 941-3400
Fax: (610) 941-2424
Email: info@thelsggroup.com
Web: www.thelsggroup.com

Summary: Healthcare executive search including managed care, recruitment for physician

leadership, hospital & community based specialists, primary care, healthcare consulting specializing in compensation, hospital based practice, market studies, hospital/physician strategies, practice valuation and sales.

Key Contact - Specialty:
Mr. Frank Garofolo, Senior Vice President
Mr. Robert Carper, Principal

Salary Minimum: $75,000

Functions: Generalist (All), Senior Mgmt., Physicians, Health Admin., CFOs, IT, MIS Mgmt.

Industries: Generalist (All), Drugs Mfg., HR Services, Insurance, Doc. Mgmt., Production SW, Healthcare

Lord & Albus Company†

10314 Sweetwood Dr
Houston, TX 77070-5221
(281) 955-5673
Email: jpalbus@earthlink.net
Web: www.home.earthlink.net/~jpalbus

Summary: Personalized approach to each search assignment, we will assist in defining the client's needs, coordinate all interviewing, reference checks and salary negotiations. Serve as an extension of your company EEO employer.

Key Contact - Specialty:
Mr. John P. Albus, Owner & Principal

Salary Minimum: $40,000

Functions: Generalist (All)

Industries: Energy, Utilities, Construction, Manufacturing, Finance, Services, Communications, Environmental Svcs., Packaging, Software, Biotech/Life Sciences

J S Lord & Company Inc

266 Main St Ste 7B
Medfield, MA 02052-2018
(508) 359-5100
Fax: (508) 359-5660
Email: jslandco@aol.com

Summary: Firm founded to provide clients with the focus, commitment and communications necessary to complete searches in a timely manner. Original research and candidate development will be undertaken on each assignment with the goal of presenting final candidates within three to five weeks.

Key Contact - Specialty:
Mr. J. Scott Lord, President - *Biotechnology*

Salary Minimum: $150,000

Functions: Generalist (All)

Industries: Food, Bev., Tobacco, Soap, Perf., Cosmtcs., Drugs Mfg., Medical Devices, Biotech/Life Sciences

Louis Heyden Group

5031 E Karen Dr
Scottsdale, AZ 85254-2286
(602) 652-8627
Email: contact@louisheyden.com
Web: www.louisheyden.com

Summary: Retained executive search focused on the leadership needs of the manufacturing and durable good sector with emphasis on the global automotive industry. Our engagement activities and client relationships represent the full spectrum of leadership for publicly traded Fortune companies, as well as privately held and select venture-backed organizations.

Key Contact - Specialty:
Mr. Jeff Heyden, Chief Executive Officer & Mng Partner - *C-level, Executives, Industrial, Manufacturing, Manufacturing (Management)*

Salary Minimum: $120,000

Functions: Generalist (All), Board Members, Senior Mgmt., Middle Mgmt., Mfg., CFOs

Industries: Energy, Utilities, Manufacturing, Motor Vehicles, Consumer Elect., Electronic, Elec. Components, Consumer Goods, Mgmt. Consulting, E-commerce, Aerospace

LSK Group

1653 Little Meadow Rd
Pittsburgh, PA 15241-2055
(412) 831-4810
Fax: (615) 468-5719
Email: brian@lskgroup.com
Web: www.lskgroup.com

Summary: Retained executive search firm providing recruiting services for leadership positions on behalf of corporate clients in manufacturing, retail, consumer products, education and professional services. Functional experience in general management, marketing, business development, supply chain, operations, HR, finance, real estate/construction. Typical assignments are director level and above.

Key Contact - Specialty:
Mr. Brian McKeever, President

Salary Minimum: $125,000

Functions: Generalist (All), Management

Industries: Generalist (All), Consumer Goods, Retail, Finance, Services

LSM Consulting (Lamon, Stuart, Michaels)

502-67 Yonge St
Montreal Trust
Toronto, ON M5E 1J8
Canada
(416) 361-7033
Fax: (416) 361-0728
Web: www.lsmconsulting.com

Summary: We are a management-consulting firm that works with individual and organizational goals to increase employee contribution, commitment and satisfaction. In partnership with our clients, we develop practical solutions in the areas of recruitment services, workplace & people effectiveness, supply chain & operations, process consulting and e-business solutions.

Key Contact - Specialty:
Mr. Wayne Lamon, President
Mr. Robert Stuart, Partner

Salary Minimum: $50,000

Functions: Generalist (All), Mfg., Sales & Mktg., Finance, IT, Engineering, Mgmt. Consultants

Industries: Generalist (All), Energy, Utilities, Manufacturing, Finance, Insurance, Software

Lubawski & Associates

1765 Maple St Ste 15
Northfield, IL 60093-3026
(847) 441-7300
Fax: (847) 441-7532
Email: info@lubawski.com
Web: www.lubawski.com

Summary: Retained search firm specializing in senior-level health care and science assignments.

Key Contact - Specialty:
Mr. James Lubawski, President

Functions: Management

---

† occasional contingency assignment

Industries: Medical Devices, Non-profits, Pharm Svcs., Higher Ed., Biotech/Life Sciences, Hospitals, Long-term/Home Care, Dental

The John Lucht Consultancy Inc

350 W 50th St Apt 8B
New York, NY 10019-6671
(212) 259-9211
Email: resumes@luchtconsultancy.com
Web: www.luchtconsultancy.com

Summary: We are an outstanding generalist firm. We recruit CEOs, outside board members and senior management in virtually every function. We also assess current staff. We serve nearly all industries and functions and are noted for the thoroughness of our searching, referencing and documentation. We are also noted for exclusively serving only one client per industry.

Key Contact - Specialty:
Mr. John Lucht, President - *Senior management*
Ms. Jean Sanders, Office Manager

Salary Minimum: $300,000

Functions: Generalist (All), Board Members, Senior Mgmt., Mktg. Mgmt., HR Mgmt., CFOs, MIS Mgmt.

Industries: Generalist (All), Drugs Mfg., Publishing, New Media, Broadcast, Film, Insurance

The Luciani Group†

171 Las Vegas Rd
Orinda, CA 94563-1956
(925) 258-5070
Email: tom@lucianigroup.com
Web: www.lucianigroup.com

Summary: We are a search, consulting organization that does retained searches. We specialize in financial executive placement exclusively. Our firm's clients are in the high-technology industry.

Key Contact - Specialty:
Mr. Thomas G. Luciani, Founder & President - *High technology, Treasury*
Ms. Stacey McGurk, Research Consultant - *High technology*

Functions: Generalist (All), CFOs, Budgeting, Cash Mgmt., Taxes, M&A, Risk Mgmt., Mgmt. Consultants

Industries: Generalist (All), Computer Equip., Electronic, Elec. Components, New Media, Broadcast, Film, Communications, Telecoms, Software

Charles Luntz & Associates Inc

1734 Clarkson Rd # 223
Chesterfield, MO 63017-4976
(636) 787-7992
Email: chuck@charlesluntz.com
Web: www.charlesluntz.com

Summary: Veteran owned generalist firm representing companies in urban and rural locations. Fill positions considered key to employer. Will un-bundled search with hourly billing. Guarantee placements. Have a 30 percent maximum with a 15% minimum and no penalty for cancellation. Excellent completion record.

Key Contact - Specialty:
Mr. Charles E. Luntz, President
Ms. Joy P. Brother, Executive Vice President
Ms. Mary Ahearn, Vice President & Secretary
Ms. Courtney Starmer, Associate
Ms. Genine Whitney, Associate

Salary Minimum: $50,000

Functions: Generalist (All), Management, Board Members, Senior Mgmt., Middle Mgmt., Admin. Svcs., Mfg., Healthcare

Industries: Generalist (All), Energy, Utilities, Manufacturing, Food, Bev., Tobacco, Chemicals, Medical Devices, Metal Products, Consumer Elect., Test, Measure Equip., Misc. Mfg., Electronic, Elec. Components, Transportation, Finance, Services, Non-profits, Media, Communications, Government, Defense, Environmental Svcs., Haz. Waste, Aerospace, Software, Mfg. SW, Marketing SW, Biotech/Life Sciences, Healthcare, Hospitals, Non-Classifiable

P J Lynch Associates

PO Box 967
Ridgefield, CT 06877-8967
(203) 438-8475
Email: patlynch@pjlynch.com
Web: www.pjlynch.com

Summary: We are a quality organization matching highly skilled managers to performance driven organizations. We use a timely and effective search process. We provide value added service to our clients, through our understanding of their requirement and culture.

Key Contact - Specialty:
Mr. Patrick J. Lynch, Managing Partner - *Publishing*
Dr. Arlene McSweeney, Senior Parnter - *Organizational development*
Mr. Paul Rohrmann, Senior Parnter

Salary Minimum: $80,000

Functions: Generalist (All), Management, Sales & Mktg.

Industries: Finance, Publishing, New Media, Digital, Software, Database SW, Biotech/Life Sciences

Lynrow Associates LLC

18 Tobacco Rd
Weston, CT 06883-1612
(203) 226-4464
Fax: (203) 226-5764
Email: lynrow@mindspring.com

Summary: Senior and middle management searches focusing in consumer products and financial services.

Key Contact - Specialty:
Ms. Lynn O'Donnell, President - *Asset management, Consumer (Marketing,Packaged Goods,Products), Financial services*
Mr. Thomas O'Donnell, Partner - *Asset management, Banking (Mortgage), Financial services, Marketing, Mutual funds*
Ms. Tracey Michaels, Director, Research - *Consumer (Products), Financial services*

Functions: Senior Mgmt., Middle Mgmt., Product Dev., Advertising, Mktg. Research, Mktg. Mgmt., Direct Mktg., HR Mgmt., IT

Industries: Food, Bev., Tobacco, Soap, Perf., Cosmtcs., Drugs Mfg., Retail, Finance, Banking, Mutual/Hedge Funds, Media, Communications

Lyons Associates†

PO Box 984
Saratoga Springs, NY 12866-0984
(518) 583-0444
Fax: (518) 583-0421
Email: info@i-lyons.com
Web: www.i-lyons.com

Summary: A generalist retained search firm exclusively to the hospitality industry. Emphasizing the recruitment of mid and upper-level management.

Key Contact - Specialty:
Mr. Sean J. Lyons, Managing Director - *Hospitality*

Salary Minimum: $40,000

Functions: Management, Middle Mgmt.

Industries: Hospitality, Hotels, Resorts, Clubs, Restaurants, Entertainment, Recreation

Lyons Black & Associates Ltd

500-666 Burrard St
Insignia International Inc
Vancouver, BC V6C 3P6
Canada
(604) 632-4084
Fax: (604) 632-4085
Email: alyons@lyonsblack.com
Web: www.lyonsblack.com

Summary: Our firm is a retained executive search firm providing consulting services to a diversified, international client base that includes companies in many industries across four continents. The firm's clients range from large multinationals to many smaller and medium-sized companies; its projects likewise extend from technical roles to presidential and board of directors searches.

Key Contact - Specialty:
Mr. Arthur Lyons, BBA, MBA, Partner

Salary Minimum: $50,000

Functions: Generalist (All)

Industries: Generalist (All), Agri., Forestry, Mining, Energy, Utilities, Oil & Gas, Retail, Higher Ed.

M-Pact Inc

PO Box 1592
Brentwood, TN 37024-1592
(615) 376-0154
Fax: (615) 376-0891
Email: resumes@m-pactinc.com
Web: www.m-pactinc.com

Summary: Retained executive search firm serving manufacturing sector clients with divisions, facilities and subsidiaries.

Key Contact - Specialty:
Mr. Bruce MacDonald, Principal

Salary Minimum: $100,000

Functions: Generalist (All), Senior Mgmt.

Industries: Manufacturing, Food, Bev., Tobacco, Printing, Chemicals, Plastics, Rubber, Paints, Petro. Products, Leather, Stone, Glass, Metal Products, Motor Vehicles, Aerospace

MacArthur, Church & Keres

PO Box 45155
Omaha, NE 68145-0155
(402) 333-8333
Email: director@mckusa.com
Web: www.mckusa.com

Summary: Offered are a variety of highly focused and advanced services addressing the difficult task of identifying, attracting, recruiting, and retaining those talented individuals who have the greatest impact on their company's success.

Key Contact - Specialty:
Ms. Beverly Scheuble, Managing Director - *Capital goods, Manufacturing (Management), Senior management, Six Sigma, Supply Chain*
Mr. James Keres, Principal - *Financial services, Product management/development, Risk management, Senior management, Technical (Management)*

Salary Minimum: $95,000

Functions: Generalist (All), Management, Senior Mgmt., Mfg., Plant Mgmt., Purchasing, Sales & Mktg., CFOs, Risk Mgmt., Actuaries

Industries: Generalist (All), Services, Re-Insurance

The Macdonald Group Inc

112 Plymouth Rd Ste 1B
Hillsdale, NJ 07642-1120
(201) 696-5446
Email: macdgrp@aol.com

Summary: We are a generalist firm, offering personal service with cost effective and quality results.

Key Contact - Specialty:
Mr. G. William Macdonald, President

Salary Minimum: $75,000

Functions: Generalist (All)

Industries: Generalist (All), Drugs Mfg., Machine, Appliance, Misc. Mfg., Pharm Svcs., Healthcare

Machlowitz Consultants Inc

445 Park Ave Fl 9
New York, NY 10022-8632
(212) 213-2435
Fax: (212) 213-3923
Email: mm@machlowitz.com
Web: www.machlowitz.com

Summary: Boutique firm known for results: resourceful research, diverse slates, creative solutions, speedy client service, repeat business and success in unique searches.

Key Contact - Specialty:
Dr. Marilyn M. Machlowitz, PhD, President

Salary Minimum: $100,000

Functions: Generalist (All), Management

Industries: Finance, Non-profits

Mackenzie Eason & Associates

3023 S University Dr Ste 230
Fort Worth, TX 76109-5608
(800) 450-5165
Fax: (888) 596-7943
Email: info@mackenzieeason.com
Web: www.mackenzieeason.com

Summary: MEA is a boutique recruiting firm specializing in healthcare recruiting and consultation. We offer a variety of recruiting and consulting services to systems, hospitals, clinics, and practice groups.

Key Contact - Specialty:
Mr. J. Darien George, Managing Partner - *Consulting, Marketing*
Mr. Duke F. Ashley-Lassen, Partner - *Consulting*
Mr. Myles Bruce, Partner - *Consulting, Marketing*
Mr. Roy R. Shelden, Consultant - *Consulting*

Functions: Senior Mgmt., Healthcare, Physicians, Allied Health

Industries: Biotech/Life Sciences, Healthcare, Hospitals, Long-term/Home Care, Dental, Physical Therapy, Occupational Therapy, Women's

MacKenzie Gray Management Inc

2900-350 7 Ave SW
First Canadian Tower
Calgary, AB T2P 3N9
Canada
(403) 264-8906
Email: info@mackenziegray.ca
Web: www.mackenziegray.ca

Summary: We are a retainer-based executive search firm. Our clients include corporations and organizations varying in size from small, local based companies to large multinationals, encompassing a broad range of industries.

Key Contact - Specialty:
Mr. Douglas G. MacKenzie, Managing Partner
Ms. Elaine L.R. Lee, Partner, Corporate Directorships - *C-level, Capital markets, CEOs, CFOs, Construction*

Salary Minimum: $100,000

Functions: Generalist (All), Management, Senior Mgmt., Middle Mgmt.

Industries: Agri., Forestry, Mining, Energy, Utilities, Oil & Gas, Construction, Manufacturing, Food, Bev., Tobacco, Finance, Misc. Financial, Non-profits, Legal, Accounting, Mgmt. Consulting, HR Services, Law Enforcement, Hospitality, Recreation, Real Estate, Software

Mackenzie Search

429 Timonium Ct
Havre de Grace, MD 21078-2568
(410) 942-0096
Fax: (410) 942-0094
Email: info@msgsearch.com
Web: www.msgsearch.com

Summary: We are a bioscience and technology executive search and search research firm. Our consultants offer real world business experience in our niche markets serving a broad cross section of companies. Being a boutique firm, we are not concerned with blockage issues and can target and recruit from a greater number of sources.

Key Contact - Specialty:
Mr. Keith Barkley, Principal & Managing Director - *Biopharmaceutical, Healthcare, High technology, Managed care, Medical*

Salary Minimum: $75,000

Functions: Board Members, Senior Mgmt.

Industries: Chemicals, Drugs Mfg., Medical Devices, Misc. Mfg., Venture Cap., Pharm Svcs., Mgmt. Consulting, HR Services, E-commerce, IT Implementation, Software, Biotech/Life Sciences, Healthcare

Maczkov-Biosciences Inc

126 Harvard Dr
Larkspur, CA 94939-1110
(415) 924-9360
Fax: (415) 924-5508
Email: info@maczkov-biosciences.com
Web: www.maczkov-biosciences.com

Summary: Twenty years of recruiting senior-level executives in life sciences and biotechnology.

Key Contact - Specialty:
Mr. Nicholas Maczkov, President & Chief Executive Officer - *Healthcare*

Salary Minimum: $125,000

Functions: Board Members, Senior Mgmt.

Industries: Biotech/Life Sciences

Bob Maddox Associates†

3134 W Roxboro Rd NE Ste 300
Atlanta, GA 30324-2542
(404) 231-0558
Fax: (404) 231-1074
Email: robertmaddox@mindspring.com

Summary: We provide executive search in two divisions: regional sales & sales management personnel, and development & senior director/manager for non-profit (501C3) organizations. Our services include candidate profiling, sourcing, evaluation, presentation and final selection presentation tailored for the client's board of directors and/or staff.

Key Contact - Specialty:
Mr. Robert E. Maddox, Partner - *Marketing*

Salary Minimum: $70,000

Functions: Generalist (All), Management, Board Members, Senior Mgmt., Middle Mgmt., Sales & Mktg., Mktg. Mgmt., Sales Mgmt., Non-profits

Industries: Generalist (All), Construction, Medical Devices, Computer Equip., Test, Measure Equip., Electronic, Elec. Components, Services, Non-profits, Equip Svcs., Mgmt. Consulting, HR Services, Higher Ed., Hospitality, Communications, Telecoms, Call Centers, Government, Defense, Compliance, Homeland Security, Marketing SW, Healthcare, Hospitals, Long-term/Home Care

The Madeira Group

(a division of HR Unlimited Inc)
PO Box 3928
Cottonwood, AZ 86326-2565
(928) 634-0584
Fax: (928) 634-0597
Email: rvierra@madeiragroup.com
Web: www.madeiragroup.com

Summary: We are committed to providing a quality executive search service to our clients in a cost effective manner. Our success is defined by one factor... client satisfaction. We specialize in the healthcare industry.

Key Contact - Specialty:
Mr. Ronald Vachon-Vierra, President - *Healthcare*

Salary Minimum: $80,000

Functions: Generalist (All)

Industries: Healthcare, Hospitals

Branches:
PO Box 37
Huntington Mills, PA 18622-0037
(570) 864-2028
Fax: (570) 864-2025
Email: gkauffman@madeiragroup.com
Key Contact - Specialty:
Ms. Gail Kauffman, Vice President, Research & Recruiting - *Healthcare, Home health, Hospital, Insurance (Health), Managed care*

The Madison Group

342 Madison Ave
New York, NY 10173-0002
(212) 599-0032
Email: inquiries@themadisongroup.net
Web: www.themadisongroup.net

Summary: Committed to quality service and unblocked access to candidates in each market served. We strive to provide very personal service to a select group of clients.

Key Contact - Specialty:
Mr. David Soloway, Managing Director
Ms. Lynn Fernandez, Director, Research
Ms. Ruth Miller, Associate Director
Mr. Philip Tesoriero, Associate Director

Salary Minimum: $75,000

Functions: Management, Senior Mgmt., Middle Mgmt., Sales & Mktg., Mktg. Mgmt., Finance, CFOs, Taxes

Industries: Generalist (All), Manufacturing, Finance, Venture Cap., Services, Legal, Accounting, Hospitality, Software, Biotech/Life Sciences

Madison MacArthur Inc

33 Madison Ave
Toronto, ON M5R 2S2
Canada
(416) 920-0092
Fax: (416) 920-0099
Email: info@mmsearch.com
Web: www.mmsearch.com

Summary: We work with our clients to enhance their workforce. Our firm delivers professional services to the following industries: consumer goods manufacturing, entertainment & news services, IT, marketing & communications, financial & professional services, retail & hospitality services, publishing & broadcasting, telecom, new media & architecture design, utilities/commodities, not-for-profit & public sector and health wellness & life sciences.

Key Contact - Specialty:
Mr. Ian MacArthur, Director & Owner - *Financial services, Hospitality, Retail, Sales*
Ms. Sylvia MacArthur, Director & Owner - *Advertising, Communications, Marketing, Telecommunications*
Mr. Robert Bellamy, Managing Director - *Financial services, Healthcare*

Salary Minimum: $75,000

Functions: Generalist (All)

Industries: Manufacturing, Retail, Finance, Hospitality, Media, Communications, Insurance, Software, Healthcare

The Magellan Group

100 Overlook Ctr Fl 2
Princeton, NJ 08540-7814
(609) 375-2390
Email: krice@magellangroupllc.com
Web: www.magellangroupllc.com

Summary: We specialize in senior and middle management search and work with venture capital, pharmaceutical, bio-technology and other healthcare-related organizations.

Key Contact - Specialty:
Ms. Kimberley Rice, President - *Healthcare*
Mrs. Bridget Madden, Director, Research - *Biopharmaceutical, Pharmaceutical, Research*

Salary Minimum: $130,000

Functions: Senior Mgmt., Sales & Mktg., R&D, Int'l.

Industries: Manufacturing, Drugs Mfg., Medical Devices, Venture Cap., Pharm Svcs., HR SW, Industry Specific SW, Biotech/Life Sciences

Magellan International LP

333 Clay St Ste 3680
Houston, TX 77002-4107
(713) 439-7485
Fax: (713) 439-7489
Email: milp@milp.com
Web: www.milp.com

Summary: Our firm is a privately held, US-based executive search firm specializing in the professional services. We advise top professional services and Fortune 500 firms who seek guidance and counsel on senior leadership needs. We enhance our clients' business and our candidates' careers by providing searches of the highest quality.

Key Contact - Specialty:
Mr. Jonathan H. Phillips, CPC, Managing Director - *Consulting, Consumer (Durables, Packaged Goods), Energy, Engineering*
Mr. Steve M. Tatar, Managing Director

Mr. Clark R. Beecher, Director - *Information Technology, Management consulting, Operations, Professional services, Strategic planning*
Ms. Carey Ibrahimbegovic, Director - *Audits, Tax*
Ms. Candice R. Meade, Office Manager - *Office*

Salary Minimum: $125,000

Functions: Generalist (All), Management, Board Members, Purchasing, CFOs, IT, MIS Mgmt., Mgmt. Consultants, Legal, Attorneys

Industries: Generalist (All), Energy, Utilities, Oil & Gas, Chemicals, Drugs Mfg., Invest. Banking, Venture Cap., Pharm Svcs., Mgmt. Consulting, IT Implementation, Biotech/Life Sciences

Maglio & Clark Inc

500 Elm Grove Rd Ste 209
Elm Grove, WI 53122-2546
(262) 784-6020
Fax: (262) 784-6046
Email: consulting@maglioandclark.com
Web: www.maglioandclark.com

Summary: Executive search consultants with a focus on partnering with a diverse base of clients. Extensive experience establishing North American staff for global corporations.

Key Contact - Specialty:
Mr. Charles J. Maglio
Mr. Wayne B. Clark
Mr. Robert Swanson, Vice President

Salary Minimum: $75,000

Functions: Generalist (All), Management, Mfg., Materials, Sales & Mktg., HR Mgmt., Finance, Engineering

Industries: Generalist (All), Construction, Food, Bev., Tobacco, Paper, Printing, Chemicals, Drugs Mfg., Medical Devices, Plastics, Rubber, Paints, Petro. Products, Motor Vehicles, Electronic, Elec. Components, Semiconductors, Pharm Svcs., Legal, Accounting, Equip Svcs., HR Services, Law Enforcement, IT Implementation, Engineering Svcs., Telecoms, Digital, Fiber Optic, Hospitals, Long-term/Home Care

RJ Maglio LLC

PO Box 915213
Longwood, FL 32791-5213
(407) 671-8400
Email: info@maglioinc.com
Web: www.maglioinc.com

Summary: Extensive experience in senior level assignments in all functional areas within the hospitality, travel, and leisure industries.

Key Contact - Specialty:
Mr. Richard Maglio, Principal

Salary Minimum: $100,000

Functions: Generalist (All)

Industries: Hospitality, Hotels, Resorts, Clubs, Restaurants

Maiorino & Weston Associates Inc

4250 Galt Ocean Dr Apt 3U
Fort Lauderdale, FL 33308-6145
(954) 568-7826
Email: bobm@mwasearch.com

Summary: We offer corporate structuring and re-structuring counsel and individual career counseling. Our executive search services encompass the consumer goods, entertainment, sports, communications and hospitality industries. Concentrations in marketing & sales management, finance, HR and general management.

Key Contact - Specialty:
Mr. Robert Maiorino, President

Salary Minimum: $100,000

Functions: Generalist (All), Management, Mfg., HR Mgmt., Finance, Minorities/Diversity, Int'l.

Industries: Generalist (All), Food, Bev., Tobacco, Soap, Perf., Cosmtcs., Consumer Elect., HR Services, Hospitality, Media

Malcolm Preston & Huggins Search Partners

2201-200 Front St W
Toronto, ON M5V 3K2
Canada
(416) 979-4069
Fax: (416) 979-8418
Email: cathy@mphsearch.com
Web: www.mphsearch.com

Summary: Our firm is a senior executive and officer level search firm that specializes in building senior management teams. Our focus on senior level search leverages our experience as both successful business leaders as well as search consultants. Our experience-based approach produces the best possible fit for both client and candidate.

Key Contact - Specialty:
Mrs. Cathy Preston, Managing Partner
Mr. Rod Malcolm, Managing Partner
Mr. Gary Huggins, Managing Partner

Salary Minimum: $100,000

Functions: Management

Industries: Generalist (All)

T Malouf & Company

2020 Arapahoe St Unit 1110
Denver, CO 80205-2549
(303) 295-9599
Email: info@tmalouf.com
Web: www.tmalouf.com

Summary: We are a retained firm with two partners, representing many years in the search industry. Our practice areas are high technology and sports/fitness/health. We do searches for non-profit as well as commercial clients.

Key Contact - Specialty:
Ms. Terry Malouf, President & Chief Executive Officer

Salary Minimum: $80,000

Functions: Generalist (All)

Industries: Non-profits, E-commerce, IT Implementation, Recreation, Sports, Communications, Software

Management Advice International Ltd

400-6 Adelaide St E
Dynamic Building
Toronto, ON M5C 1H6
Canada
(416) 916-6800
(877) 574-6800
Email: resume@madvice.com

Summary: We are a firm with a personal touch who specializes in recruiting generalists who will fit our clients' firms. We help firms improve their executive team.

Key Contact - Specialty:
Mr. David Sprague, President
Mr. Peter Crawford, Principal - *Marketing*
Mr. David Sherrington, Principal

Salary Minimum: $90,000

Functions: Generalist (All), Management, Mfg., Materials, Sales & Mktg., Finance

Industries: Generalist (All)

Management Architects

6484 Washington St Ste B
Yountville, CA 94599-1451
(707) 945-1340
(707) 945-1343
Email: doug@managementarchitects.net
Web: www.managementarchitects.net

Summary: We are a retained search firm that specializes in recruiting executive management teams for high technology start-ups and emerging growth companies.

Key Contact - Specialty:
Mr. Doug Griffith, Principal & Owner

Salary Minimum: $150,000

Functions: Management

Industries: Communications

Management Executive Services Associates Inc (MESA)

6019 N Belmont Way
Parker, CO 80134-5503
(303) 841-4512

Summary: Emphasis in diversified industrial, engineered products and systems in non-regulated and regulated industries. Place corporate general management and senior executives and professionals in all operations management and staff functions. Firm's principals personally execute search engagements and are seasoned former industrial executives. Placements have superior retention and promotional records in client companies.

Key Contact - Specialty:
Mr. Dennis F. Cook, President - *High technology, Manufacturing*

Salary Minimum: $100,000

Functions: Generalist (All)

Industries: Generalist (All), Agri., Forestry, Mining, Energy, Utilities, Construction, Manufacturing, Communications, Aerospace, Packaging

MR of Laguna Hills-Orange County[†]

(an affiliate of MRI)
25381 Commercentre Dr Ste 250
Lake Forest, CA 92630-8882
(949) 768-9112
Email: info@mriorangecounty.com
Web: www.mriorangecounty.com

Summary: We rank in the top 5 percent of all offices within our franchise. We are national specialists in bio-technology, pharmaceutical, automotive aftermarket, retail, chemical, finance, food, hospitality, manufacturing, architecture and construction. Through our franchise, we have access to video conferencing and branch offices in 900 cities.

Key Contact - Specialty:
Mr. Thomas J. Toole, President & Chief Executive Officer - *Executives, General management*

Salary Minimum: $50,000

Functions: Generalist (All), Senior Mgmt., Mfg., Sales & Mktg., HR Mgmt., Finance, Architects

Industries: Generalist (All), Agri., Forestry, Mining, Construction, Manufacturing, Food, Bev., Tobacco, Chemicals, Drugs Mfg., Medical Devices, Plastics, Rubber, Paints, Petro.

Products, Transportation, Wholesale, Finance, Venture Cap., Architectural Svcs., Pharm Svcs., Engineering Svcs., Hospitality, Hotels, Resorts, Clubs, Restaurants, Quick Service Restaurants, Entertainment, Environmental Svcs., Real Estate, Property/Facility Mgmt., Biotech/Life Sciences, Healthcare, Hospitals, Long-term/Home Care

MR of San Jose-Metro[†]

(an affiliate of MRI)
17415 Monterey St Ste 200
Morgan Hill, CA 95037-3668
(408) 779-9050
Email: jrosica@mrisanjose.com
Web: www.mrisanjose.com

Summary: We specialize in the computer & electronic, systems engineering, IS & IT consulting, semiconductor, semiconductor capital equipment, eCommerce infrastructure, wireless, broadband, telecom/data communications, ERP, MRP software and ASP industries. Also specializing in telecom, datacom and wireless.

Key Contact - Specialty:
Mr. John Rosica, Principal & Manager - *High technology*

Salary Minimum: $50,000

Functions: Generalist (All)

Industries: Venture Cap., Equip Svcs., Mgmt. Consulting, HR Services, IT Implementation, Telecoms, RF/Microwave, Defense, Security SW, Biotech/Life Sciences

The Millard Group

(also known as SC of Middlesex)
109 Broad St
Middletown, CT 06457-3264
(860) 344-5920
Email: info@themillardgroup.com
Web: www.themillardgroup.com

Summary: We are dedicated to providing results based recruiting in the high-technology industry. We have two areas of expertise in the application software industry and the networking industry.

Key Contact - Specialty:
Mr. Craig A. Millard, Managing Partner - *Networking, Wireless*
Mr. Paul R. Millard, Managing Partner - *E-business, ERP*

Salary Minimum: $100,000

Functions: Senior Mgmt., Sales & Mktg.

Industries: E-commerce, IT Implementation, Communications, Telecoms, Telephony, Digital, Wireless, Fiber Optic, Network Infrastructure, Software, Accounting SW, Database SW, ERP SW, HR SW, Mfg. SW, Networking, Comm. SW, Security SW

Weber & Company

(an affiliate of MRI)
255 Alhambra Cir Ste 520
Coral Gables, FL 33134-7408
(305) 444-1200
Fax: (305) 444-2266
Email: email@webco.cc
Web: www.webco.cc

Summary: We fulfill positions in the medical device, pharmaceutical and bio-technology industries. As a highly-specialized firm, we work with start-ups and Fortune 500 companies in need of change. Our firm is made unique by our proven track record of developing strategic client relationships.

Key Contact - Specialty:
Mr. James K. Weber, Managing Partner

Salary Minimum: $80,000

Functions: Management, Mfg., Product Dev., Production, Plant Mgmt., Quality, Healthcare, Sales & Mktg.

Industries: Medical Devices, Electronic, Elec. Components, Mfg. SW, Biotech/Life Sciences, Healthcare

Medical Device Recruiters Inc[†]

(an affiliate of MRI)
2745 E Oakland Park Blvd Ste 200
Fort Lauderdale, FL 33306-1638
(954) 958-0255
Fax: (954) 958-0253
Email: tjohasky@mdrsource.com
Web: www.medicaldeviceheadhunter.com

Summary: We are experts in finding and placing talented people. Each account executive's desk is specialized for the industry it services. In our office we specialize in the medical device industry.

Key Contact - Specialty:
Mr. Tom K. Johasky, Manager, Owner - *Business development, Competitive intelligence, Regulatory, Research, Six Sigma*
Mr. Eric Johasky, Account Executive - *Management, Marketing, Medical (Devices,Sales), Orthopedics*
Mr. Navin Deendyal, Account Executive - *Engineering, Healthcare, Medical, Medical (Devices), Research*
Ms. Lucy Vedramis, Account Executive
Ms. Jusell Louis, Researcher & Assistant
Mrs. Jennifer White, Account Executive
Mr. Herb Goldman, Account Executive
Mr. Michael Williams, Account Executive

Functions: Senior Mgmt., Product Dev., Quality, Healthcare, Mktg. Research, Sales Reps.

Industries: Medical Devices, HR Services, Biotech/Life Sciences, Healthcare, Dental

The Halcyon Group[†]

(an affiliate of MRI)
233 12th St Ste 818A
Columbus, GA 31901-2420
(706) 571-9611
Email: michael@halcyongroup.net
Web: www.halcyongroup.net

Summary: Our firm specializes in the recruitment of upper and middle management positions for durable consumer goods manufacturers whose products are sold through the mass, home centers, specialty, independent and alternate retail channels.

Key Contact - Specialty:
Mr. Michael L. Silverstein, President

Functions: Generalist (All), Product Dev., Production, Engineering

Industries: Generalist (All), Manufacturing, Metal Products, Consumer Elect., Consumer Goods, Banking

SC of Fort Wayne

(an affiliate of MRI)
126 W Columbia St Ste 208
Fort Wayne, IN 46802-1719
(260) 426-2805
Email: recruiter@dentalheadhunter.com
Web: www.dentalheadhunter.com

Summary: We specialize in finding and placing sales & marketing talent in the dental industry; from the individual contributor to the director or VP level.

Key Contact - Specialty:
Mr. Nick Harris, Vice President & General Manager

Functions: Sales & Mktg.

Industries: Medical Devices, Biotech/Life Sciences, Healthcare

Protis Executive Innovations[†]

(an affiliate of MRI)
6650 Telecom Dr Ste 260
Indianapolis, IN 46278-2016
(317) 275-5400
Fax: (317) 275-5401
Email: protisei@protisei.com
Web: www.protisei.com

Summary: We use a blend of technology, expertise and insight as a leading executive search firm that adds measurable value with each search and each point of contact. We provide total human capital solutions geared around traditional search, e-search and organizational development. Our clients are form the Fortune 100 to e-business and emerging technology start-ups.

Key Contact - Specialty:
Mr. Bert Miller, President
Mr. Michael Bitar, Vice President
Ms. Laura Gonzalez-Miller, Vice President, Marketing
Mr. Vernon Davis, Senior Vice President - *Financial services*
Ms. Cheryl Carter Jones, Vice President

Salary Minimum: $45,000

Functions: Senior Mgmt., Quality, Sales & Mktg., Mktg. Research

Industries: Food, Bev., Tobacco, Banking

Lowell Johnson Associates LLC

(an affiliate of MRI)
20902 Mack Ave Ste 201
Grosse Pointe Woods, MI 48236-1076
(313) 886-0880
Fax: (313) 886-0850
Email: lowell.johnson@recruitco.com
Web: www.recruitco.com

Summary: We are dedicated to achieving the highest level of client satisfaction in conducting accounting, audit, tax and M&A retained searches. We employ the latest technology while maintaining strict confidentiality, professionalism and personal integrity.

Key Contact - Specialty:
Mr. Lowell D. Johnson, CPA, President
Mr. Kenneth Johnson, Senior Associate - *Treasury*
Mr. Jack C. Donnelly, Senior Associate - *Accounting (Big 4), Analysts, Audits, Controllers, Tax*

Salary Minimum: $100,000

Functions: Finance, CFOs, Budgeting, Cash Mgmt., Taxes, M&A, Attorneys

Industries: Generalist (All)

MR of Lincoln

(also known as The Elam Group)
1633 Normandy Ct Ste C
Lincoln, NE 68512-1473
(402) 467-5534
Email: contact@mrilincoln.com
Web: www.elamgroup.com

Summary: Group of professionals out of industry, with extensive management background. Focus on mid to top-level assignments. Concentrates in insurance industry.

Key Contact - Specialty:
Ms. Kimarra Elam, Chief Executive Officer - *Executives, Insurance (Health,Life), Managed care, Underwriting*
Mr. William J. Elam, Jr., Chairman

Salary Minimum: $100,000

Functions: Management, Senior Mgmt., Middle Mgmt., Admin. Svcs., Sales Mgmt., Sales Reps., Benefits, Actuaries, Pension/Ret. Planning

Industries: Generalist (All), Insurance, Casualty, Claims, Life, Commercial, Re-Insurance

PrincetonOne[†]

(also known as MRI PrincetonOne)
88 Orchard Rd Ste 2
Skillman, NJ 08558-2642
(908) 281-6023
Fax: (908) 281-6052
Email: info@princetonone.com
Web: www.PrincetonOne.com

Summary: We recruit only the highest quality candidates, those with business savvy and technological know-how. We go beyond filling your immediate needs to positioning ourselves as your partner. Knowing your company culture and long-term goals allows us to help you navigate your future with the best and brightest at the helm.

Key Contact - Specialty:
Mr. Josh Suskin

Salary Minimum: $50,000

Functions: Generalist (All), Management, Mfg., Healthcare, Sales & Mktg., HR Mgmt., IT, Specialized Svcs.

Industries: Energy, Utilities, Construction, Manufacturing, Wholesale, Services, Communications, Packaging, Software, Biotech/Life Sciences, Healthcare

Branches:
591 Redwood Hwy Ste 2225
Mill Valley, CA 94941-6003
(415) 383-7044
Fax: (415) 383-1426
Email: millvalley@princetonone.com
Key Contact - Specialty:
Mr. Eric Wheel, Managing Partner - *Internet*

7750 Pardee Ln Ste 100
Oakland, CA 94621-1492
(510) 635-7901
Fax: (510) 562-7237
Email: oakland@princetonone.com
Key Contact - Specialty:
Mr. Steve Swanson, Managing Partner

1 City Blvd W Ste 300
Orange, CA 92868-3686
(714) 978-0500
Fax: (714) 978-8064
Email: orange@princetonone.com
Key Contact - Specialty:
Ms. Chris Wuebbens, Managing Partner - *E-business*
Mr. Ray Stayer, CSAM, Senior Account Manager - *Building products*

7995 E Prentice Ave Ste 101
Greenwood Village, CO 80111-2710
(303) 706-0123
(800) 875-6165
Fax: (303) 331-4147
Email: denver@princetonone.com
Key Contact - Specialty:
Mr. Frank Leonard

---

401 E Jackson St Ste 1430
Tampa, FL 33602-5226
(813) 224-0550
(888) 289-3555
Fax: (813) 224-0549
Email: tampa@princetonone.com
Key Contact - Specialty:
Mr. Dan Smith, CSAM, Managing Partner
Mr. Wayne Coonan, Director, National Accounts

36 Pennsylvania St Fl 7
Indianapolis, IN 46204-3626
(317) 257-5411
Fax: (317) 259-6886
Email: bill.kuntz@princetonone.com
Key Contact - Specialty:
Mr. Bill Kuntz, Managing Partner
Mr. Mark Haering, CSAM, Senior Parnter - *Finance*

5151 Edina Industrial Blvd Ste 600
Edina, MN 55439-3024
(952) 830-1420
Fax: (952) 893-9254
Email: minneapolis@princetonone.com
Key Contact - Specialty:
Mr. Richard Fox, Managing Partner
Mr. Jim Delebo, Account Executive

145 Pinelawn Road
Suite 345N
Melville, NY 11747
(631) 777-2710
Fax: (631) 777-2714
Key Contact - Specialty:
Mr. Harris Cohen, Managing Partner

7550 Lucerne Dr Ste 110
Cleveland, OH 44130-6503
(440) 243-5151
Fax: (440) 243-4868
Email: cleveland@princetonone.com
Key Contact - Specialty:
Mr. Jeff DiPaolo, Managing Partner
Mr. Tom McGuire, CSAM, Executive Recruiter - *Sales*

503 S Front St Ste 240
Columbus, OH 43215-5666
(614) 252-6200
Fax: (614) 252-4744
Email: columbus@princetonsearch.com
Key Contact - Specialty:
Mr. Jeff Hawn, CSAM, Managing Partner
Mr. Gerry E. Harris, CSAM, Director, National Accounts
Ms. Susan M. Kessel, CSAM, Account Executive - *Healthcare*
Mr. Drew Merrels, Account Executive
Mr. Jim Windle, CSAM, Account Executive - *Management, Sales, Technical*

1835 Market St Ste 910
Philadelphia, PA 19103-1607
(215) 789-3450
Fax: (215) 789-3459
Email: philadelphia@princetonone.com
Key Contact - Specialty:
Ms. Lauren Williams, Managing Partner

40 24th St Fl 5
Crane Building
Pittsburgh, PA 15222-4657
(412) 566-2100
Fax: (412) 566-2229
Email: pittsburgh@princetonone.com
Key Contact - Specialty:
Mr. Jonathan Bender, Managing Partner - *Human resources*

1360 Post Oak Blvd Ste 2015
Houston, TX 77056-3049
(713) 850-9850
(800) 878-0995
Fax: (281) 754-4615
Email: houston@princetonone.com
Key Contact - Specialty:
Mr. Jim Maranto, Managing Partner

1250 S Capital Of Texas Hwy Ste III390
West Lake Hills, TX 78746-6522
(512) 327-8292
(877) 906-6051
Email: austin@princetonone.com
Key Contact - Specialty:
Mrs. Lisa Kojis, Managing Parnter

WorldBridge Partners of New York[†]

(an affiliate of MRI)
2303 Grand Ave Ste 200
Baldwin, NY 11510-3144
(516) 771-1200
Email: wbpny@worldbridgepartners.com
Web: www.worldbridgepartners.com

Summary: We provide customized solutions to the complex issue of talent acquisition. Understanding that every company is unique, utilizing maximum flexibility in designing a mutually beneficial relationship with our clients.

Key Contact - Specialty:
Mr. Thomas Wieder, Senior Managing Partner
Mr. Warren Harvey, Senior Vice President - *Asset management, Investment management, Mutual funds*

Functions: Management, Senior Mgmt., Middle Mgmt., Sales & Mktg., Mktg. Mgmt., Sales Mgmt., HR Mgmt., Finance, CFOs, IT

Industries: Generalist (All), Finance, Banking, Invest. Banking, Brokers, Venture Cap., Mutual/Hedge Funds, Misc. Financial, HR Services, E-commerce, Telecoms, Software, Non-Classifiable

MR/SC of Nassau[†]

(also known as Jacobs Executive Advisors)
363 Hempstead Ave Ste 200
Malverne, NY 11565-1233
(516) 599-5824
Fax: (516) 599-2066
Email: info@mriscn.com
Web: www.mriscn.com

Summary: Specializing in all aspects of the insurance, agricultural, specialty chemicals and electrical industries. Search devoted to board directors, "C-level" positions, or capacities of utmost strategic significance to an enterprise.

Key Contact - Specialty:
Mr. James F. Jacobs, Managing Director & Practice Ldr, Ins - *Insurance, Insurance (Casualty, Claims, Property, Reinsurance)*
Mr. Joseph J. Janik, Practice Leader, Ind & Agriculture - *Agriculture, Chemical, Electrical*

Salary Minimum: $75,000

Functions: Generalist (All)

Industries: Agri., Forestry, Mining, Chemicals, Electronic, Elec. Components, Insurance, Casualty, Claims, Commercial, Re-Insurance

The Landstone Group

(an affiliate of MRI)
295 Madison Ave Fl 36
New York, NY 10017-6344
(212) 972-7300
Fax: (212) 972-7309

Email: mail@landstonegroup.com
Web: www.landstonegroup.com

Summary: "Helping our clients grow through the acquisition of talent." Our purpose is to assist our clients in defining executive positions, identifying well-qualified and motivated candidates, and selecting those best suited through comprehensive, quality assured search processes. Our process will also provide information and feedback that not only helps direct your search for executive talent, but also can be utilized to manage your business more effectively.

Key Contact - Specialty:
Mr. Jeffrey A. Heath, MBA, President - *Computers, Consumer, E-business, Franchising, Wireless*
Mr. Dwight Hall, Vice President - *Internet, Multimedia, Peripherals, Retail, Telecommunications*

Salary Minimum: $85,000

Functions: Generalist (All), Management, Board Members, Senior Mgmt., Middle Mgmt., Product Dev., Sales & Mktg., Mgmt. Consultants, Mgmt. Consultants, Homeland Security

Industries: Medical Devices, Computer Equip., Consumer Elect., Consumer Goods, Retail, Venture Cap., Services, Mgmt. Consulting, HR Services, E-commerce, Communications, Telecoms, Digital, Wireless, Software, Database SW, Industry Specific SW, Networking, Comm. SW, Security SW, Biotech/Life Sciences

MR of Manhattan[†]

(also known as The Jonas Group)
54 W 21st St Rm 1005
New York, NY 10010-7327
(212) 979-5902
Fax: (212) 979-5903
Email: info@jonasgrp.com
Web: www.mrinetwork.com

Summary: We are an independently owned office that specializes exclusively in the retail and wholesale sectors. We work mid to senior-level positions in (store) operations, merchandising, finance, sales, marketing, supply chain and HR.

Key Contact - Specialty:
Mr. John Jonas, Managing Director & President

Salary Minimum: $100,000

Functions: Board Members, Senior Mgmt., Middle Mgmt., Product Dev., Advertising, Mktg. Mgmt., Sales Mgmt., HR Mgmt., Finance, Textile/Fashion

Industries: Textiles, Apparel, Lumber, Furniture, Soap, Perf., Cosmtcs., Consumer Elect., Consumer Goods, Wholesale, Retail

Carlyle & Conlan Inc

(also known as MR of Park Central)
630 Davis Dr Ste 260
Morrisville, NC 27560-6506
(919) 474-0771
Fax: (919) 474-0682
Email: resume@ccesearch.com
Web: www.ccesearch.com

Summary: We are a high integrity, retained search and consulting firm with specialty practices in IT, life sciences, sales, marketing, professional services, finance/HR and corporate officers. Our clients range from emerging growth organizations through Fortune 1000 companies. Our approach is both strategic and tactical, as a collaborative business partner offering both recruitment services and an alliance network.

Key Contact - Specialty:
Ms. Anastasia C. Pucci, President

Mr. Kirk Sears, Vice President & Partner
Mr. Donald M. Alexander, Director
Ms. Erica Langdon, Director, Information Technology
Ms. Megan Lisiecki, Senior Account Executive
Ms. Brandy Ellis, Account Executive
Ms. Jean Marie Small, Office Manager
Ms. Chris Conlan, Controller - *Biomedical, Engineering, Manufacturing, Medical (Devices,Sales)*

Salary Minimum: $100,000

Functions: Board Members, Senior Mgmt., Middle Mgmt.

Industries: Venture Cap., Pharm Svcs., E-commerce, IT Implementation, PSA/ASP, Media, Communications, Software, Biotech/Life Sciences, Healthcare

The Mayberry Group[†]

(an affiliate of MRI)
PO Box 688
143 Ellis Acres Ln Ste 2
Mount Airy, NC 27030-6850
(336) 789-3200
(800) 893-7772
Fax: (336) 719-2227
Email: rellis@mrmayberry.com
Web: www.mrmayberry.com

Summary: In textiles, apparel, retail and IS, we have successfully completed searches for companies ranging from Fortune 500 to small growth companies in manufacturing, engineering, sourcing, quality, MIS, sales, merchandising and design.

Key Contact - Specialty:
Mr. Ron Ellis, President
Ms. Diana Ellis, Senior Account Executive
Mr. Jeffrey Ellis, Associate, Research & Recruitment - *Private equity*

Functions: Generalist (All), Middle Mgmt., Plant Mgmt., Quality, MIS Mgmt., Systems Implem., Network Admin., DB Admin.

Industries: Generalist (All), Textiles, Apparel, Retail, Software

Banister International[†]

(also known as MR of Cherry Hill)
2005 Market St Ste 820
Philadelphia, PA 19103-7025
(267) 256-2300
Fax: (267) 330-0333
Email: emamrak@banister.cc
Web: www.banister.cc

Summary: We have consistently been a key performer among the numerous offices within our franchise. The key to our success has been our ability to partner with our clients to provide a single source for all of their staffing needs. Whether it is a critical management position or a multiple hire staffing project, we have the specialists to get the job done.

Key Contact - Specialty:
Mr. Patrick Sylvester, Chief Executive Officer
Mr. Ed Mamrak, Chief Operating Officer - *Medical, Start-up companies, Surgical*
Mr. Jim Parker, Managing Director
Mr. Shari Ober, Managing Director, Human Resources - *Financial services, Insurance, Medical, Medical (Devices)*

Functions: Generalist (All), Management, Materials, Sales & Mktg., HR Mgmt., Finance, IT, Specialized Svcs.

Industries: Generalist (All), Manufacturing, Textiles, Apparel, Medical Devices, Transportation, Retail, Finance, Misc. Financial, Mgmt. Consulting, HR Services, Hospitality

---

MR/SC of Chattanooga-Brainerd[†]

(an affiliate of MRI)
6005 Century Oaks Dr Ste 400
Chattanooga, TN 37416-3686
(423) 894-5500
Fax: (423) 894-1177
Email: myresume@mrichattanooga.com
Web: www.mrichattanooga.com

Summary: We offer full-service recruitment, contract, outplacement and video-conference center, both retained and contingency search. Our specialties include: technical, management, IT/IS, medical & pharmaceutical sales & pharmaceutical marketing, and chemical/scientist/research.

Key Contact - Specialty:
Mr. Bill Cooper, President - *Chemical, Technical*
Mr. Al Clark, Managing Partner - *Business to business, Executives, Management, Manufacturing (Management), Senior management*
Mrs. Sue Killian, Office Manager
Mr. David Stephens, Vice President, National Accounts - *Marketing, Pharmaceutical, Sales*
Mr. Thomas Clark, Senior Account Manager
Mr. David Rievley, Senior Account Manager - *Chemical, Information Technology, Manufacturing, Research & development, Staffing*
Ms. Jennifer Mullins, Senior Account Manager

Salary Minimum: $45,000

Functions: Generalist (All), Senior Mgmt., Product Dev., Healthcare, Sales & Mktg., Mktg. Mgmt., Sales Mgmt., Sales Reps., R&D

Industries: Generalist (All), Chemicals, Drugs Mfg., Medical Devices, Plastics, Rubber, Consumer Elect., Misc. Mfg., Accounting, Mgmt. Consulting, Biotech/Life Sciences, Healthcare

MR of Frisco[†]

(also known as The Frisco Group)
18723 Everwood Ct
Dallas, TX 75252-2690
(972) 407-9197
Email: fred@thefriscogroup.com
Web: www.thefriscogroup.com

Summary: We are a leading executive search firm focusing on the following industries: specialty chemicals, pharmaceutical manufacturing and semiconductors. Our firm holds a reputation for dedicated client service, uncompromising ethics, timeliness and successful results. We apply a consultative approach, investing time with our clients to thoroughly understand the organization's culture, business strategy and leadership needs.

Key Contact - Specialty:
Mr. Frederick Williams, MBA, Managing Principal - *Energy*

Salary Minimum: $75,000

Functions: Plant Mgmt.

Industries: Chemicals, Medical Devices, Plastics, Rubber, Paints, Petro. Products

Kaye/Bassman International Corp

(also known as MR of Plano North)
4965 Preston Park Blvd Ste 400
Plano, TX 75093-5141
(972) 931-5242
Fax: (972) 931-9683
Email: recruiting@kbic.com
Web: www.kbic.com

Summary: Our organization was founded with a mission of positively impacting companies and enhancing careers by providing the finest

professional, executive, technical and scientific search.

Key Contact - Specialty:
Mr. Jeff Kaye, President & Chief Executive Officer

Salary Minimum: $75,000

Functions: Generalist (All), Healthcare, Physicians, Nurses, Finance, M&A, R&D, Attorneys

Industries: Generalist (All), Oil & Gas, Construction, Manufacturing, Retail, Finance, Banking, Legal, Higher Ed., Call Centers, Insurance, Real Estate, Biotech/Life Sciences, Healthcare, Hospitals, Long-term/Home Care

Sloane & Associates Inc[†]

(an affiliate of MRI)
250 N Sunny Slope Rd Ste 127
Brookfield, WI 53005-4802
(262) 790-8820
Email: resumes@sloaneassociates.com
Web: www.sloaneassociates.com

Summary: We are search consultants to the real estate, design, contract furniture, EPC, and construction industries. We know these industries well and our candidates are all proven performers. Because of our established reputation and industry experience, we are widely recognized by both client companies and candidates seeking change. Both retained and contingency search.

Key Contact - Specialty:
Mr. Ronald Sloane, CPA, President - *Construction, Design, Owner reps, Property management, Real estate*
Ms. Margaret Wotruba, Director, Recruiting - *Architecture, Construction, Engineering, Facilities engineering, Interior design*
Ms. Linda Graebner-Smith, NCIDQ, Director, Business Development - *Architecture, Business development, Furniture, Interior design, Professional services*

Salary Minimum: $75,000

Functions: Generalist (All), Senior Mgmt., Sales Mgmt., Architects

Industries: Generalist (All), Construction, Architectural Svcs., Accounting, Engineering Svcs., Real Estate, Property/Facility Mgmt.

Management Resource Group Ltd

2805 Eastern Ave
Davenport, IA 52803-2088
(563) 323-3333
(800) 249-2443
Fax: (563) 326-0682
Email: mrgdavenport@mrgpeople.com
Web: www.mrgpeople.com

Summary: We are a multi-office HR consulting firm dedicated to increasing organizational effectiveness through creative and customized approaches to the identification, assessment, selection, development and transition of people.

Key Contact - Specialty:
Ms. Lynn Gibson, Senior Executive Search Consultant - *Finance, Senior management*
Mr. Daniel Portes, President - *Finance, Senior management*
Mr. William Wilke, Senior Consultant

Salary Minimum: $70,000

Functions: Generalist (All), Senior Mgmt., Mfg., Finance, Non-profits

Industries: Generalist (All), Construction, Manufacturing, Banking, Non-profits, Healthcare

Branches:
800 N Compton Dr Ste 2
Hiawatha, IA 52233-2215
(319) 294-9499
Fax: (319) 378-1217
Email: mrogers@mgpeople.com
Key Contact - Specialty:
Ms. Marcia Rogers, President, Cedar Rapids Office

Management Resources Group Inc[†]

106 Mission Ct Ste 202
Franklin, TN 37067-6441
(615) 837-0082
Email: dan@m-r-g.net

Summary: Our firm is a privately held professional recruitment and consulting firm. Health care is the primary industry focus. Retained searches and consulting engagements range from executive to mid-level management assignments and are mainly targeted in the functional areas of administration, finance, operations, clinical management, and sales management/business development.

Key Contact - Specialty:
Mr. Dan McDonald, Managing Principal
Mr. Bob Bicsak, Managing Principal - *Creative, Executives, Healthcare, Marketing, Retail*

Functions: Senior Mgmt.

Industries: Manufacturing, Drugs Mfg., Medical Devices, Misc. Mfg., Finance, Pharm Svcs., Mgmt. Consulting, Healthcare, Hospitals, Long-term/Home Care

Management Search & Consulting Inc

1001 Bishop St Ste 1540
ASB Tower
Honolulu, HI 96813-3408
(808) 533-4423
Fax: (808) 545-2435
Email: mgmtsearch@hawaii.rr.com

Summary: Executive search and recruitment focused on upper-mid and senior-level positions. Retainer required.

Key Contact - Specialty:
Mr. Peter Glick, President

Salary Minimum: $65,000

Functions: Generalist (All), CFOs

Industries: Generalist (All), Agri., Forestry, Mining, Energy, Utilities, Construction, Finance, Misc. Financial, Services, Pharm Svcs., Accounting, Mgmt. Consulting, HR Services, Hotels, Resorts, Clubs, Real Estate, Healthcare

Management Search of RI[†]

1 State St Ste 501
Providence, RI 02908-5000
(401) 273-5511
(800) 405-1152
Fax: (401) 273-5573
Email: jmeyer@ri.msi1.com
Web: www.msi1.com

Summary: Privately held professional search firms - team focused search; multi-disciplined, corporately mandated minimal industry blacklists. Specialists in mid-level search.

Key Contact - Specialty:
Mr. James L. Meyer, CPC, Partner
Mr. Stephen E. Judge, CPC, Partner

Salary Minimum: $65,000

Functions: Generalist (All), Senior Mgmt., Middle Mgmt., Plant Mgmt., Materials, Sales Mgmt., Finance, IT, Engineering

Industries: Generalist (All), Manufacturing, Drugs Mfg., Medical Devices, Finance, Architectural Svcs., Aerospace, Insurance, Software, Biotech/Life Sciences

Branches:
50 Founders Plz Ste 304
East Hartford, CT 06108-6508
(860) 289-1581
Key Contact - Specialty:
Mr. Sean Murphy, CPC, General Manager

Mancino Burfield Edgerton

12 Roszel Rd Ste C101
Princeton, NJ 08540-6234
(609) 520-8400
Fax: (609) 520-8993
Email: mbe@mbels.com
Web: www.mbels.com

Summary: We provide retained executive search services for the life sciences industry including pharmaceuticals, biotechnology, medical device, diagnostics and healthcare services. Clients include major and developing corporations.

Key Contact - Specialty:
Mr. Gene Mancino, Partner - *Biopharmaceutical, Biotechnology, Boards of Directors, CEOs, CFOs*

Salary Minimum: $150,000

Functions: Management, Board Members, Senior Mgmt., Materials, Sales & Mktg., Mktg. Mgmt., HR Mgmt., CFOs, M&A

Industries: Drugs Mfg., Medical Devices, Venture Cap., Pharm Svcs., Biotech/Life Sciences, Healthcare

Branches:
404 Harrison Ave
Westfield, NJ 07090-2439
(908) 232-3274
Fax: (908) 654-5202
Email: elaine@mbels.com
Key Contact - Specialty:
Ms. Elaine Burfield, Partner

100 S Main St Ste 200
Doylestown, PA 18901-4882
(215) 230-8999
Email: paul@mbels.com
Key Contact - Specialty:
Mr. Paul Edgerton, Practice Leader

Mannard & Associates Inc

1600 Golf Rd Ste 1200
Rolling Meadows, IL 60008-4229
(847) 981-5170
Fax: (847) 981-5189

Summary: Boutique firm focused on manufacturing companies. Principle markets are machinery, part fabrication and packaging. Metal and plastic materials are typical. Firm characterized by quality, service, flexibility; strong repeat client base.

Key Contact - Specialty:
Mr. Thomas B. Mannard, President - *Manufacturing*
Ms. Kathleen Weinrauch, Vice President
Mr. James Ryan, Associate

Salary Minimum: $70,000

Functions: Generalist (All), Senior Mgmt., Plant Mgmt., Materials, Sales & Mktg., HR Mgmt., Finance, Engineering

Industries: Generalist (All), Food, Bev., Tobacco, Paper, Plastics, Rubber, Metal Products, Machine, Appliance, Packaging

The Manning Group

700 W Saint Clair Ave Ste 218
Cleveland, OH 44113-1274
(216) 664-1857
Fax: (216) 664-1855
Email: barbara@themanninggrp.com

Summary: Our firm is a retained executive search firm whose practice is focused on a select group of companies for whom we execute a wide variety of searches. Most of our assignments are in the manufacturing, financial services and not-for-profit sectors.

Key Contact - Specialty:
Ms. Barbara Behn Deeds, President

Salary Minimum: $70,000

Functions: Generalist (All)

Industries: Construction, Manufacturing, Chemicals, Finance, Services, Defense, Aerospace, Packaging

Michael E Marion & Associates Inc

98 Floral Ave
New Providence, NJ 07974-1542
(908) 771-9330
Fax: (908) 665-9380
Email: info@marionsearch.com
Web: www.marionsearch.com

Summary: We are regularly retained to conduct individual and group searches in healthcare and consumer products worldwide by Fortune 100 firms as well as emerging companies.

Key Contact - Specialty:
Mr. Michael E. Marion, President
Ms. Nicole Newell, Recruiter

Salary Minimum: $75,000

Functions: Generalist (All), Management

Industries: Generalist (All), Drugs Mfg., Medical Devices, Consumer Goods, Venture Cap., Pharm Svcs., Biotech/Life Sciences, Healthcare

Mariposa Search

370 27th St Ste A
San Francisco, CA 94131-2012
(415) 641-9011
Fax: (650) 745-1129
Email: info@mariposasearch.com
Web: www.mariposasearch.com

Summary: We are an executive search firm. Our search professionals combine many years of experience in the executive search and research industry. Our innovative, flexible approach is focused on providing the candidates most suited to your position requirements, corporate culture and technological needs. We work extensively with our clients to ensure good communication, relevant candidates and excellent results.

Key Contact - Specialty:
Ms. Alison Raby, Search Consultant

Salary Minimum: $75,000

Functions: Management, Board Members, Senior Mgmt., Mktg. Mgmt., R&D

Industries: PSA/ASP, Software, Accounting SW, Database SW, Development SW, Doc. Mgmt., Production SW, Entertainment SW, Networking, Comm. SW, Security SW, System SW

The Mark Method

311 4th Ave Apt 615
San Diego, CA 92101-6977
(619) 234-9494
Email: cmark@markmethod.com
Web: www.markmethod.com

Summary: Sales & Sales Management, Specializing in the contract furnishings and office supplies industries. Specializing in Sales Compensation consulting.

Key Contact - Specialty:
Mr. Cary Mark, President

Salary Minimum: $75,000

Functions: Senior Mgmt., Product Dev., Sales & Mktg., Sales Mgmt., Finance

Industries: Lumber, Furniture, Drugs Mfg., Medical Devices, Machine, Appliance, Transportation, Accounting SW, Healthcare

Brad Marks International

15233 Ventura Blvd PH 16
Sherman Oaks, CA 91403-2291
(818) 382-6300
Fax: (818) 386-0050
Email: info@bradmarks.com
Web: www.bradmarks.com

Summary: A specialist firm which recruits senior-level management for the entertainment and new media industries. The firm's practice currently includes nine recruiters with combined search experience.

Key Contact - Specialty:
Mr. Brad Marks, Chairman & Chief Executive Officer
Ms. Chanda Smith, Director, Recruiting
Mr. Bob Miggins - *Sales*
Mr. Justin Marks
Mr. Chris Monjoy
Ms. Monica Chalk, Head of Operations & Client Relations
Mr. Michael Cassara, Managing Director

Salary Minimum: $100,000

Functions: Senior Mgmt.

Industries: Non-profits, Hospitality, Media, Advertising, Publishing, New Media, Broadcast, Film, Telecoms

Markt & Markworth Ltd

20600 Chagrin Blvd Ste 1100
Cleveland, OH 44122-5327
(216) 491-3120
Fax: (216) 491-3121
Email: jmarkworth@markt-markworth.com
Web: www.markt-markworth.com

Summary: The foundation of our search practice is based on the highest level of professionalism while using technology to shorten response times to fill positions and keeping the client apprised of all activity.

Key Contact - Specialty:
Mr. John H. Markt, Principal - *Distribution, Manufacturing, Supply Chain, Technical (Management), Wholesale*
Ms. Jennifer I. Markworth, Principal - *Executives, Financial services, Human resources, Legal, Management consulting*
Ms. Michelle Davis, Office Manager

Salary Minimum: $125,000

Functions: Generalist (All), Management, Senior Mgmt., Mfg., Distribution, Sales & Mktg., HR Mgmt., Finance, IT, Attorneys

Industries: Generalist (All), Manufacturing, Transportation, Wholesale, Retail, Services, Media, Communications, Aerospace, Healthcare

The Marlow Group

PO Box 812707
Wellesley, MA 02482-0023
(781) 237-7012
Email: marlowgroup@aol.com

Summary: We are a generalist firm serving emerging high-technology companies - sales, marketing, operations and technical.

Key Contact - Specialty:
Mr. Paul M. Jones, Managing Director

Salary Minimum: $100,000

Functions: Senior Mgmt., Sales & Mktg., Mktg. Mgmt., Sales Mgmt., CFOs

Industries: Computer Equip., New Media, Telecoms, Software, Biotech/Life Sciences

Marra Peters & Partners

99 Morris Ave
Springfield, NJ 07081-1425
(973) 376-8999
Email: info@marrapeters.com
Web: www.marrapeters.com

Summary: Clients are assured of their importance as they receive a sophisticated service in a highly personalized and responsive manner. We provide a consultative approach to retain the executive who will impact your business in the most contributory way.

Key Contact - Specialty:
Mr. John Marra, Jr., President - *Finance, General management, Marketing*
Mr. Charles J. Pelisson, Vice President - *Human resources, Marketing, Research & development*
Mr. Philip Masin, Vice President - *General management*

Salary Minimum: $125,000

Functions: Generalist (All), Management, Mfg., Sales & Mktg., HR Mgmt., Finance, IT, Specialized Svcs.

Industries: Generalist (All), Construction, Retail, Mgmt. Consulting, Media, Government, Real Estate

The Marshall Group†

31 Cambridge Ln
Lincolnshire, IL 60069-3104
(847) 940-0021
Fax: (847) 940-7031
Email: don@donmarshallgroup.com
Web: www.donmarshallgroup.com

Summary: We provide personal retained search designed to locate and provide management and non-management personnel to high-growth clients in all industries and services.

Key Contact - Specialty:
Mr. Don Marshall, President

Functions: Generalist (All)

Industries: Generalist (All)

Marsteller Wilcox Associates†

PO Box 473
Streamwood, IL 60107-0473
(630) 241-5213
(630) 241-5214
Fax: (413) 473-6075
Email: mwilcox@mwaltd.com
Web: www.mwaltd.com

Summary: We offer non-traditional search programs to meet clients' changing needs. Our specialty markets are lean/sigma, operations leadership and global supply chain. Secondary markets include business development, technology and marketing.

Key Contact - Specialty:
Mr. Mark Wilcox, Partner - *Manufacturing, Manufacturing (Management), Materials, Operations, Six Sigma*
Ms. Linda Marsteller, Partner - *Facilities engineering, Factories (Automation), Finance, Forest industry/products, Human resources*

Salary Minimum: $100,000

Functions: Generalist (All), Management, Mfg., Plant Mgmt., Materials, Sales & Mktg., Finance, R&D, Engineering

Industries: Generalist (All), Paper, Printing, Chemicals, Paints, Petro. Products, Motor Vehicles, HR Services, Software

Donovan Martin & Associates

1000 Elwell Ct Ste 217
Palo Alto, CA 94303-4306
(650) 969-8235

Summary: We provide executive and professional search services for a variety of companies, from large, long-established firms to the newest start-ups.

Key Contact - Specialty:
Mr. Donovan Martin, Principal - *CEOs, CFOs, Executives*

Salary Minimum: $100,000

Functions: Generalist (All), Board Members, Senior Mgmt., Middle Mgmt.

Industries: Computer Equip., Consumer Elect.

J Martin & Associates

10820 Holman Ave Apt 103
Los Angeles, CA 90024-5782
(310) 475-5380
Email: jmexecsrch@aol.com
Web: www.martinexecsearch.com

Summary: Specialization computer/high-technology, healthcare, venture capital backed start-up, emerging, high-growth, Fortune 500, CEO to senior sales & marketing levels. We believe in quick results, high quality.

Key Contact - Specialty:
Ms. Judy R. Martin, President - *High technology*

Salary Minimum: $75,000

Functions: Generalist (All)

Industries: Services, Hospitality, New Media, Software

Martin Partners LLC†

(an Alliance Partnership International company)
224 S Michigan Ave Ste 620
Chicago, IL 60604-2533
(312) 922-1800
Email: resume@martinpartners.com
Web: www.martinpartners.com

Summary: We are a retained executive search firm providing senior level recruiting and leadership development services to clients. The firm's clients range in size from private equity-backed firms to Fortune 500 corporations, from all sectors of technology, biotechnology and financial services.

Key Contact - Specialty:
Mr. Theodore B. Martin, Jr., Founder & Chief Executive Officer
Mr. Thomas A. Jagielo, Partner - *Diagnostics, Healthcare, Marketing, Pharmaceutical*
Mr. Paul W. Schmidt, Partner - *General management, Retail*
Mrs. Kathleen L. Hajek, Partner - *Consulting, General management, Healthcare, Technology*

Mr. Brad E. Nassar, Partner - *Banking, Financial services, Investment management, Mergers & acquisitions*
Ms. Laura Andrews, Chief Administrative Officer
Ms. Viann P. Stroup, Executive Assistant & Research Director - *Administration, Research, Technology*
Ms. Christine Mortell, Corporate Reception & Administration - *Administration*
Mr. Steve DeCoster, Partner - *Financial services, General management, Healthcare, Technology*

Salary Minimum: $130,000

Functions: Generalist (All), Management, Mfg., Sales & Mktg., HR Mgmt., Finance, Mgmt. Consultants

Industries: Generalist (All), Manufacturing, Drugs Mfg., Medical Devices, Consumer Elect., Retail, Finance, Venture Cap., Misc. Financial, Services, Pharm Svcs., Mgmt. Consulting, E-commerce, Media, New Media, Communications, Insurance, Real Estate, Software, Biotech/Life Sciences

George R Martin

PO Box 673
Doylestown, PA 18901-0673
(215) 348-8146
Email: exsearch@comcat.com

Summary: Concentrate on marketing, sales, technical and operations functions. Completion rate is high, with excellent stick and promotion ratios. Highly qualified research staff.

Key Contact - Specialty:
Mr. George R. Martin

Salary Minimum: $60,000

Functions: Generalist (All)

Industries: Manufacturing, Chemicals, Drugs Mfg., Medical Devices, Plastics, Rubber, Test, Measure Equip., Non-profits, Biotech/Life Sciences, Long-term/Home Care

Masserman & Associates Inc†

10 Morningside Ct
Ossining, NY 10562-3003
(914) 373-4677
(914) 941-3869
Email: bruce@masserman.com/bruce masserman@aol.com

Summary: We are a search firm specializing exclusively in the technology marketplace. Our focus is the middle to senior level executive within the financial services and pharmaceutical industries. Our ability to understand how technology fits within the business structure is a key factor to our success.

Key Contact - Specialty:
Mr. Bruce Masserman, Principal - *Financial services, Publishing*

Salary Minimum: $85,000

Functions: IT, MIS Mgmt., Systems Analysis, Systems Dev., Systems Implem., Systems Support, Network Admin., DB Admin.

Industries: Finance, Banking, Invest. Banking, Brokers, Misc. Financial, Services, Pharm Svcs., Insurance, Development SW

Louis Thomas Masterson & Company

1422 Euclid Ave Ste 706
Cleveland, OH 44115-2001
(216) 621-2112
Fax: (216) 621-7320
Email: ltmasterson@ltmco.com
Web: www.ltmco.com

Summary: We provide high quality, responsive executive recruiting service. Searches cover many industries and multiple disciplines.

Key Contact - Specialty:
Mr. Louis T. Masterson, President - *General management*
Ms. Jonny Kmiec, Office Administrator

Salary Minimum: $70,000

Functions: Generalist (All), Senior Mgmt., Mfg., Healthcare, Physicians, Health Admin., HR Mgmt.

Industries: Generalist (All), Manufacturing, Chemicals, Paints, Petro. Products, Finance, Services, Healthcare

Matlin Partners LLC
12 Rebecca Rd
Newton, MA 02465-1418
(617) 969-9198
Fax: (617) 218-7004
Email: tmccarthy@matlinpartners.com
Web: www.matlinpartners.com

Summary: Our firm provides executive search consulting services, primarily to emerging, venture-backed and larger technology companies in the enterprise software, e-business, IT services and healthcare IT sectors. We have successfully completed searches across a broad spectrum of senior executive-level assignments, including: CEO, COO, CFO, CTO and heads of sales, marketing, business development and product development.

Key Contact - Specialty:
Mr. Todd J. McCarthy, III, Managing Partner
Mr. Daniel E. O'Connor, Managing Partner - *Management*

Salary Minimum: $125,000

Functions: Generalist (All), Senior Mgmt.

Industries: Generalist (All), E-commerce, IT Implementation, New Media, Software

Matté & Company Inc
124 W Putnam Ave
Greenwich, CT 06830-5317
(203) 661-2224
Fax: (203) 661-5927
Email: nmatte8985@aol.com

Summary: Consulting services in executive search and leadership and organizational assessment for Fortune 500 companies. All searches are completed within ten weeks of commencement.

Key Contact - Specialty:
Mr. Norman E. Matté, Chairman - *Distribution, International, Technology*

Salary Minimum: $200,000

Functions: Generalist (All), Management, Middle Mgmt., Mfg., Distribution, HR Mgmt., Finance, IT, Int'l.

Industries: Generalist (All), Food, Bev., Tobacco, Drugs Mfg., Paints, Petro. Products, Computer Equip., Finance, Pharm Svcs., HR Services, Logistics Svcs., Supply Chain Mgmt, Restaurants, Government, Defense, Homeland Security

Matte Consulting Group
(an IIC company)
1550-2001 Rue University
Immeuble Commercial
Montreal, QC H3A 2A6
Canada
(514) 848-1008
Fax: (514) 848-9157

Email: admin@matteiic.com
Web: www.matteiic.com

Summary: We are a highly dynamic executive search firm specializing in senior recruitments.

Key Contact - Specialty:
Mr. Richard M. Matte, Managing Partner - *General management, Manufacturing*
Mr. Michael St-Louis, Partner - *General management*

Salary Minimum: $100,000

Functions: Generalist (All), Management, Mfg., Healthcare, Sales & Mktg., Finance, IT

Industries: Generalist (All), Energy, Utilities, Manufacturing, Finance, Media, Packaging, Healthcare

Matthews & Stephens Associates Inc†
1344 Silas Deane Hwy Ste 303
Rocky Hill, CT 06067-1342
(860) 258-1995
Fax: (860) 258-1998
Email: sbaskowski@matthews-stephens.com
Web: www.matthews-stephens.com

Summary: We have a practice with unique customized approach and alternatives. We have an extremely personalized seasoned staff that listens to you and then develops a search plan. We specialize in healthcare (administration, finance and compliance) and insurance.

Key Contact - Specialty:
Mr. Stephen A. Baskowski, CPC, President

Salary Minimum: $75,000

Functions: Generalist (All), Management, Senior Mgmt., Health Admin., Finance, CFOs

Industries: Generalist (All), Retail, Insurance, Life, Healthcare, Hospitals

MAXIMUS Executive Search Services
10474 Santa Monica Blvd Ste 208
Los Angeles, CA 90025-6930
(310) 475-8001
Fax: (310) 475-8007
Email: searchla@maximus.com
Web: www.maximus.com/recruit

Summary: One of the nation's leading public sector recruiting firm. Specialize in: public sector/not-for-profit, transportation, utilities, engineering, healthcare and education. Recruit in all functional areas within these industries.

Key Contact - Specialty:
Mr. Eric J. Middleton
Ms. Sherrill A. Uyeda
Ms. Marsha R. Noble

Functions: Generalist (All), Senior Mgmt., Health Admin., HR Mgmt., Finance, IT, Engineering, Non-profits

Industries: Generalist (All), Energy, Utilities, Transportation, Non-profits, Higher Ed., Telecoms, Government, Healthcare

Affiliates:
MAXIMUS
Reston, VA

K Maxin & Associates
10 Allegheny Ctr Apt 421
Pittsburgh, PA 15212-5222
(412) 322-2595
(800) 867-8447
Fax: (412) 322-7027
Email: kmaxin@usa.net

Summary: We perform executive searches in the construction and real estate industries.

Key Contact - Specialty:
Mr. Keith A. Maxin, President - *Construction, Real estate*

Salary Minimum: $70,000

Functions: Generalist (All), Management, Board Members, Senior Mgmt., Middle Mgmt., Mktg. Mgmt., CFOs, M&A, Engineering, Architects

Industries: Construction, Real Estate, Property/Facility Mgmt.

Maxson Group LLC†
11701 Gold Parke Ln Ste 100
Gold River, CA 95670-8351
(916) 852-6769
Email: resumes@maxsonsearch.com
Web: www.maxsonsearch.com

Summary: A generalist executive search firm providing comprehensive services to clients in identification, assessment and selection of key executives and board members across a wide range of industries and functions.

Key Contact - Specialty:
Mr. Geof lambert, Partner
Ms. Gillian Parrillo, Partner

Salary Minimum: $100,000

Functions: Generalist (All)

Industries: Generalist (All), Food, Bev., Tobacco, Computer Equip., Finance, Hotels, Resorts, Clubs, Full Service Restaurants, Communications, Real Estate, Software, Biotech/Life Sciences

The Mazzitelli Grp
500 Lake St Ste 212
Excelsior, MN 55331-2516
(952) 476-5449
Fax: (952) 475-4932
Email: tm@mazzsearch.com
Web: www.mazzsearch.com

Summary: We are a generalist retainer search firm.

Key Contact - Specialty:
Ms. Teresa Mazzitelli, President

Functions: Senior Mgmt.

Industries: Manufacturing, Higher Ed., Inst./Industrial Food Svc., Defense

MBA Management Inc†
14900 Conference Center Dr Ste 300
Chantilly, VA 20151-3835
(703) 273-0028
Fax: (703) 961-7950
Web: www.mbamgmt.com

Summary: We are a leading executive search firm in the markets of architecture, civil engineering, commercial & residential construction and IT. Additionally we provide merger and acquisition assistance to firms seeking expansion into new markets, interim executives and contract employment services.

Key Contact - Specialty:
Mr. James Mugnolo, Chairman - *Construction, Mergers & acquisitions*
Mrs. Susan Yoder, President

Salary Minimum: $60,000

Functions: Finance, CFOs, IT, MIS Mgmt., Engineering, Environmentalists, Architects

Industries: Generalist (All), Energy, Utilities, Construction, Transportation, Architectural Svcs., Engineering Svcs., Environmental Svcs., Haz. Waste, Real Estate, Property/Facility

Mgmt., Industry Specific SW, Security SW, System SW

Branches:
35 Technology Pkwy S Ste 170
Norcross, GA 30092-2945
(770) 613-5305
Fax: (770) 613-2304
Email: gblair@mbamgmt.com
Key Contact - Specialty:
Mr. George Blair, Senior Associate - *Accounting (General), CFOs, Comptrollers, Construction, Real estate*

76-6344 Leone St
Kailua Kona, HI 96740-2271
(808) 329-5119
Fax: (808) 326-7908
Email: phamilton@mbamgmt.com
Key Contact - Specialty:
Mr. Philip Hamilton, Executive Vice President - *Bridges, Construction, Engineering, Highways, HVAC*

2715 Carrington Dr
Dundee, IL 60118-1755
(847) 836-8598
Fax: (847) 836-8614
Email: kgrimes@mbamgmt.com
Key Contact - Specialty:
Mr. Kent Grimes, Senior Associate - *Construction, General contractors, Home, Real estate*

1872 Pratt Dr Ste 1650
Blacksburg, VA 24060-6156
(540) 552-2900
Fax: (540) 961-3602
Email: asiegel@mbamgmt.com
Key Contact - Specialty:
Mr. Alec Siegel, Director, Operations, Blacksburg - *CIOs, Client/server, Computers, Database, Information Technology*

MC2 Executive Search[†]

10 Silver Lake Rd
Newtown, PA 18940-1846
(215) 504-5488
Fax: (215) 504-5538
Email: info@mc2execsearch.com
Web: www.mc2execsearch.com
Summary: Our firm is a premier executive search firm serving select clients in healthcare and life sciences including: device, diagnostic, imaging, equipment, pharmaceutical and biotechnology segments. Our innovative efforts focus on quality and measurable results to meet our clients' leadership challenges.

Key Contact - Specialty:
Ms. Joan L. Scala, Managing Partner - *Executives, Medical, Medical (Devices), Presidents, Senior management*
Mr. Guy Scala, Vice President - *Instrumentation, Management, Marketing, Medical, Medical (Sales)*
Ms. Kathy Siegel, Director
Ms. Carolyn Maye - *Biopharmaceutical, Business development, Pharmaceutical, Quality, Regulatory*
Ms. Elizabeth (Sue) Rosko, Manager - *Compliance, Financial, Manufacturing, Manufacturing (Management), Surgical*
Ms. Arlene Ricker, Director - *Biotechnology, Human resources, Management consulting, Operations, Orthopedics*

Functions: Management, Senior Mgmt., Middle Mgmt.

Industries: Drugs Mfg., Medical Devices, Packaging, Biotech/Life Sciences

The McAulay Firm

100 N Tryon St Ste 5220
Charlotte, NC 28202-4001
(704) 342-1880
Fax: (704) 342-0825
Email: bholland@mcaulay.com
Web: www.mcaulay.com
Summary: We are a generalist company that provides services in all functions and industries.

Key Contact - Specialty:
Mr. Albert L. McAulay, Jr., President
Mr. Charles C. Lucas, III, Vice President
Mr. Steven B. Smith, Vice President

Salary Minimum: $100,000

Functions: Generalist (All)

Industries: Agri., Forestry, Mining, Energy, Utilities, Construction, Textiles, Apparel, Venture Cap., Non-profits, Mgmt. Consulting, Packaging, Insurance, Real Estate

K E McCarthy & Associates

431 E Grand Ave
El Segundo, CA 90245-3904
(310) 760-0030
Email: kemassoc@aol.com
Summary: Our firm has experience serving financial institutions, technology firms and consulting organizations in general management emphasizing finance, treasury, capital markets and IT executives. We have expertise in search and consultation to growth companies in high technology and financial services. Our national education policy and reform practice covers K-12 through higher education with search and advisory services.

Key Contact - Specialty:
Mr. Kevin E. McCarthy, Principal

Salary Minimum: $75,000

Functions: Generalist (All), Board Members, Senior Mgmt., Middle Mgmt., Admin. Svcs., Finance, CFOs, Systems Implem., Mgmt. Consultants

Industries: Generalist (All), Finance, Banking, Invest. Banking, Brokers, Venture Cap., Mutual/Hedge Funds, Misc. Financial, Services, Non-profits, Accounting, Mgmt. Consulting, IT Implementation, K-12 Ed., Higher Ed., Government, Aerospace, Software

McCooe & Associates Inc

615 Franklin Tpke
Ridgewood, NJ 07450-1903
(201) 445-3161
Fax: (201) 445-8958
Email: mccooe@mcsearch.net
Web: www.mcsearch.net
Summary: Specializes in executive recruitment of strategic HR. Exceptional discernment of best candidate fit in an organization. Offers management consulting in compensation planning, job evaluation, organization development, training and career development.

Key Contact - Specialty:
Mr. John J. McCooe, President - *Senior management*
Mr. Sean J. McCooe, Senior Consultant & Vice President - *Business development, Senior management*

Salary Minimum: $80,000

Functions: Generalist (All), Management, Senior Mgmt., Plant Mgmt., Distribution, HR Mgmt., R&D, Engineering, Int'l.

Industries: Generalist (All), Oil & Gas, Construction, Textiles, Apparel, Paper, Chemicals, Medical Devices, Plastics, Rubber, Non-profits, Higher Ed., Healthcare, Hospitals

McCormack & Associates

10061 Riverside Dr Ste 890
Toluca Lake, CA 91602-2560
(323) 549-9200
Fax: (323) 549-9222
Email: search@mccormackassociates.com
Web: www.mccormackassociates.com
Summary: We provide specialty practice in diversity recruiting for corporations, service providers and not-for-profit organizations. Recruit people of color and alternative sexual orientation for boards of directors and senior management. Secondary focus on healthcare, higher education and associations.

Key Contact - Specialty:
Mr. Joseph A. McCormack, Managing Partner

Salary Minimum: $100,000

Functions: Senior Mgmt., Minorities/Diversity

Industries: Drugs Mfg., Non-profits, HR Services, Higher Ed., Advertising, Publishing, Healthcare

McCormack & Farrow

949 S Coast Dr Ste 620
Costa Mesa, CA 92626-7786
(714) 549-7222
Email: resumes@mfsearch.com
Web: www.mfsearch.com
Summary: We are a general practice, retained search firm, conducting searches in most industries and functions, with special emphasis on high-technology, start-up & emerging companies, manufacturing, healthcare and healthcare products.

Key Contact - Specialty:
Mr. Jerry M. Farrow, Managing Partner
Mr. Kenneth L. Thompson, Partner
Ms. Helen E. Friedman, Partner
Mr. Kenneth Bertok, Partner
Ms. Heather S. Linehan, Partner

Salary Minimum: $150,000

Functions: Generalist (All), Management, Senior Mgmt., Mfg., Distribution, Sales & Mktg., HR Mgmt., Finance, IT

Industries: Generalist (All), Medical Devices, Computer Equip., Retail, Banking, HR Services, Aerospace, Healthcare

Branches:
19426 N 87th Dr
Peoria, AZ 85382-8648
(623) 566-2142
Key Contact - Specialty:
Mr. Gene Phelps, Partner

McCracken & Partners Executive Search Inc

(also known as McCracken & Partners)
2210-120 Adelaide St W
Richmond Adelaide Ctr Phase 1
Toronto, ON M5H 1T1
Canada
(416) 363-8900 x222
Email: md@mccracken-partners.com
Web: www.mccracken-partners.com
Summary: We are an executive search firm experienced in assignments spanning organizations and companies in a wide range of industries and executive functions—particularly executives and professionals in the financial services and real estate development industries. In

addition, we are also proficient in senior level public sector search work.

Key Contact - Specialty:
Mr. Gary W. McCracken, MBA, President & Managing Partner - *Boards of Directors, CEOs, CFOs, Consulting, Entrepreneurs*
Mr. Robert E. Millward, MCIP, RPP, Associate Partner - *Municipal, Real estate*
Ms. Diane E. Armstrong, RN, CSC, Principal - *Accounting, Banking, Controllers, Entrepreneurs, Finance*
Ms. Sara R. Bingaman, MMH, Principal - *Banking (Investment), Financial services, Hospitality, Investment management, Private equity*
Lee J. Davidson, Administrative Assistant

Salary Minimum: $100,000

Functions: Generalist (All), Management, Board Members, Senior Mgmt., Sales & Mktg., HR Mgmt., Finance, CFOs, Hospitality, Hotel Mgmt.

Industries: Generalist (All), Construction, Manufacturing, Finance, Services, Hospitality, Communications, Government, Environmental Svcs., Insurance, Real Estate

McCray Sheweloff & Associates Inc

(formerly known as McCray, Shriver, Eckdahl & Associates Inc)
10940 Wilshire Blvd Ste 2100
Los Angeles, CA 90024-3955
(310) 479-7667
Fax: (310) 479-8608
Email: principal@mccray-inc.com
Web: www.mccray-inc.com

Summary: We provide board-level, presidential and general management solutions in high-technology, industrial and consumer industries. We have many years of proven success.

Key Contact - Specialty:
Mr. William J. Sheweloff, Executive Vice President & Partner - *Biotechnology, Boards of Directors, C-level, High technology, Manufacturing*
Mr. Harold McCray, President - *C-level, Communications, Defense, Manufacturing, Wireless*

Salary Minimum: $125,000

Functions: Generalist (All), Board Members, Mfg., Sales & Mktg., HR Mgmt., CFOs, IT, Engineering, Int'l.

Industries: Construction, Manufacturing, Consumer Elect., Robotics, Retail, Services, Media, Communications, Defense, Aerospace, Software

M W McDonald & Associates Inc†

286 El Dorado St Ste B
Monterey, CA 93940-2923
(831) 646-0300
(831) 646-0300
Email: pamela@mwmsearch.com
Web: www.mwmsearch.com

Summary: Offering full-service executive-level search and information services to high-technology companies from start-up companies to those with over $25 billion in assets.

Key Contact - Specialty:
Mr. Michael W. McDonald, President - *High technology*
Ms. Pamela Neidermeier, Recruiter

Salary Minimum: $50,000

Functions: Mfg., Sales & Mktg., Finance, IT, R&D, Specialized Svcs., Mgmt. Consultants

Industries: Generalist (All)

G E McFarland & Company

535 Colonial Park Dr
Roswell, GA 30075-3782
(770) 992-0900
Fax: (770) 640-0067
Email: gemcfarland@mindspring.com
Web: www.mcfarlandpartners.com

Summary: We serve a broad cross-section of client organizations representing most industries, with a particular emphasis on basic manufacturing, information & communication systems, electronics, biomedical technology, aerospace, construction/construction materials and financial services.

Key Contact - Specialty:
Mr. Charles P. Beall, Chairman

Salary Minimum: $100,000

Functions: Generalist (All)

Industries: Generalist (All), Construction, Manufacturing, Aerospace, Packaging, Insurance

McGrath & Associates Inc

481 Franklin Cir Ste 200
Yardley, PA 19067-7230
(215) 493-4190
Fax: (215) 689-3899
Email: contactus@mcgrathassociates.com
Web: www.mcgrathassociates.com/dra5.htm

Summary: We are a retainer based search firm. Our firm is a boutique with a functional specialization. We focus on IT, financial planning & control, sales & marketing, security, operations and consulting. The primary industries served are: telecom, IT, pharmaceutical, insurance, financial services and consulting.

Key Contact - Specialty:
Mr. Steven L. McGrath, Founder & Managing Director - *Finance, Sales*
Mr. Alex Hraur, Partner - *Telecommunications*
Mr. Fred Viskovich, Associate Partner - *Human resources, Manufacturing*

Salary Minimum: $75,000

Functions: Generalist (All), Management, Mfg., Sales & Mktg., HR Mgmt., Finance, IT, Mgmt. Consultants

Industries: Generalist (All), Manufacturing, Finance, Pharm Svcs., Telecoms, Software, Healthcare

McIntyre Associates

5 Essex Ct
Farmington, CT 06032-1433
(860) 284-1000
Fax: (860) 284-1111
Email: jeff@mcassoc.com
Web: www.mcassoc.com

Summary: We specialize in the recruitment of high-technology security, wireless technology, enterprise software start-up/turn-around executives and board members with specific expertise in scaling intriguing e-security and biometrics technology assets into profitable operating companies.

Key Contact - Specialty:
Mr. Jeffrey F. McIntyre, President - *Wireless*

Salary Minimum: $150,000

Functions: Generalist (All)

Industries: Computer Equip., Robotics, Law Enforcement, IT Implementation, Wireless, Defense, Software, Database SW, Security SW, System SW

The McIntyre Company

1490 Manning Pkwy
Powell, OH 43065-7350
(614) 318-8000
Fax: (614) 318-8037
Web: www.mcintyreco.com

Summary: Retained executive search; C-suite. Particular expertise in retail, grocery, distribution and logistics. Focus on corporate culture and business philosophy synergies.

Key Contact - Specialty:
Ms. Cookie Anne McIntyre, Chief Executive Officer - *Distribution, Logistics, Retail*
Ms. Kristy Keyes, Director, Recruiting

Salary Minimum: $150,000

Functions: Senior Mgmt.

Industries: Retail

McKinley • Arend International

3200 Southwest Fwy Ste 3300
Houston, TX 77027-7526
(713) 623-6400
(713) 623-6487
Email: jmmckinley@mckinleyarend.com
Web: www.mckinleyarend.com

Summary: We are a firm conducting technical, non-technical and support searches. We have several affiliations throughout the world including London, Brussels, and Bombay.

Key Contact - Specialty:
Mr. James M. McKinley, Principal
Mr. Lewis Arend, Principal

Functions: Generalist (All)

Industries: Generalist (All)

McKinley Group Inc†

601 Carlson Pkwy Ste 950
Minnetonka, MN 55305-5230
(952) 767-1130
Fax: (952) 476-2123
Email: info@mckinleygroupinc.com
Web: www.mckinleygroupinc.com

Summary: We are an executive search firm with broad industry and functional expertise. We have global capabilities both permanent and contract.

Key Contact - Specialty:
Mr. Kurt Rakos, Senior Parnter - *Food service, Management*
Ms. Pat O'Donnell

Salary Minimum: $40,000

Functions: Management, Sales & Mktg., Mktg. Mgmt., HR Mgmt., Finance, Engineering

Industries: Generalist (All), Manufacturing, Food, Bev., Tobacco, Paper, Printing, Medical Devices, Misc. Mfg., Consumer Goods, Finance, Misc. Financial, Services, Accounting, Mgmt. Consulting, HR Services, Hospitality, Communications, Packaging, Software

McNamara Search Associates Inc†

2280 Guilford Ln
Lexington, KY 40513-1825
(859) 296-2828
(866) 296-2828
Fax: (859) 273-9944
Email: mcsearch@insightbb.com
Web: www.mcnamarasearch.com

Summary: We provide expert executive, professional and technical search and recruitment services. Our exclusive search process is streamlined to deliver maximal results while saving you time and money. Utilizing our extensive experience, our firm partners with companies to hire outstanding professionals in a variety of fields.

Key Contact - Specialty:
Ms. Lynda Hook McNamara, President
Mr. Greg M. Byrne, Consultant, Senior Search & Recruiting
Ms. Elaine Brush Kaiser, Senior Recruiting Consultant
Ms. Kate Phillips, Consultant, Recruitment

Salary Minimum: $45,000

Functions: Management, Senior Mgmt.

Industries: Generalist (All), Energy, Utilities, Manufacturing, Transportation, Finance, Non-profits, HR Services, Hospitality, Communications, Environmental Svcs., Insurance

McQuoid & Associates Inc

8400 Normandale Lake Blvd Ste 920
Minneapolis, MN 55437-3843
(952) 921-2363
Fax: (952) 921-2361
Email: irene@mcquoidassociates.com
Web: www.mcquoidassociates.com

Summary: Our firm is a generalist retained search firm with broad experience in general management, sales and marketing, financial, operations, human resources, board and IT searches. Industries served range from Fortune 500 to start-up with special expertise in the financial services, manufacturing, telecom, publishing, and high tech sectors.

Key Contact - Specialty:
Mr. David McQuoid, President

Salary Minimum: $75,000

Functions: Generalist (All)

Industries: Generalist (All)

Jon McHae & Associates Inc

3333 Riverwood Pkwy SE Ste 310
Atlanta, GA 30339
(770) 272-9040
Fax: (770) 272-9204
Email: jma@jonmcrae.com
Web: www.jonmcrae.com

Summary: We are a boutique firm providing executive search counsel for governing boards and presidents of not-for-profit institutions, with a focus in private education. We offer expertise in presidential and cabinet level searches, a professional and comprehensive approach with proven wisdom in the identification and evaluation of exceptional leaders. We enable you to make a better selection based on professionally developed information.

Key Contact - Specialty:
Mr. O. Jon McRae, President & Senior Consultant
Dr. Kenneth B. Orr, PhD, Senior Associate
Gen. David M. Gring, PhD, Senior Associate

Functions: Management

Industries: Non-profits, Higher Ed.

MCS Associates

18881 Von Karman Ave Ste 1175
Irvine, CA 92612-1569
(949) 263-8700
Fax: (949) 263-0770
Email: info@mcsassociates.com
Web: www.mcsassociates.com

Summary: Consulting and litigation support firm that specializes in banking, real estate, insurance and financial services. Clients include large and small organizations nationwide.

Key Contact - Specialty:
Mr. Norman Katz, Managing Partner - *Finance*
Mr. Thomas J. Haupert, Managing Director - *Finance, Real estate*

Salary Minimum: $75,000

Functions: Board Members, Senior Mgmt., Finance, CFOs, Cash Mgmt., Risk Mgmt., Legal

Industries: Generalist (All), Finance, Banking, Invest. Banking, Misc. Financial, Accounting, Insurance, Casualty, Claims, Life, Commercial, Re-Insurance, Real Estate

McSherry & Associates 2 Inc

1 Westbrook Corporate Ctr Ste 300
Westchester, IL 60154-5709
(708) 449-4004
Fax: (630) 416-7653
Email: jmcsherry@mchserryassoc2.com
Web: www.mcsherryassoc2.com

Summary: Client centered, guaranteed performance on every search. Specialists in serving mid-market companies, insurance companies, professional services firms, manufacturers, financial services firms, private equity owned firms, family-owned businesses and educational organizations with operations worldwide. Customized sourcing strategy implemented on every assignment.

Key Contact - Specialty:
Mr. Jim McSherry, Managing Partner - *C-level, Insurance, Manufacturing, Professional services*
Mr. Jim O'Neill, Senior Parnter - *Financial services, Management consulting, Private equity, Professional services, Venture capital*
Ms. Jane Conroy, Vice President, Research & Sourcing - *Associations, Banking, CIOs, Consumer, Human resources*
Ms. Peggy Prunty, Director, Administration - *Administration, Asset management, Boards of Directors, Credit cards, Education (Higher)*

Salary Minimum: $100,000

Functions: Generalist (All), Board Members, Senior Mgmt., Distribution, Sales & Mktg., HR Mgmt., MIS Mgmt.

Industries: Generalist (All), Energy, Utilities, Paper, Paints, Petro. Products, Finance, Services, Media, Aerospace, Insurance, ERP SW

James Mead & Co

15 Old Danbury Rd Ste 202
Wilton, CT 06897-2524
(203) 834-6300
Fax: (203) 834-6301
Email: mailbox@jmeadco.com

Summary: The vertically integrated source for clients seeking executive solutions in consumer oriented brand-building businesses. Each recruiter has extensive packaged goods general management, sales, marketing and organizational development experience with some of the world's best companies, enabling us to provide significant marketplace advantage and an unmatched value-added consultative relationship.

Key Contact - Specialty:
Mr. James D. Mead, President - *General management, Sales*
Mr. Arthur S. Brown, Executive Vice President & Partner - *General management, Sales*

Mr. Thomas G. Hardy, Senior Vice President
Ms. Laura T. Putnam, Senior Vice President - *Business development, Cellular, CEOs, Consumer (Durables,Marketing)*

Salary Minimum: $140,000

Functions: Management, Senior Mgmt., Middle Mgmt., Sales & Mktg., Advertising, Mktg. Research, Mktg. Mgmt., Sales Mgmt.

Industries: Food, Bev., Tobacco, Textiles, Apparel, Soap, Perf., Cosmtcs., Drugs Mfg., Consumer Elect., Consumer Goods, Retail, Mgmt. Consulting, Quick-Service Restaurants

PMeder&Associates

100 N Field Dr Ste 125
Lake Forest, IL 60045-2596
(847) 615-8798
Email: pmeder@mederassociates.com
Web: www.mederassociates.com

Summary: The firm engages in senior and executive-level search for a wide variety of companies and professional service firms.

Key Contact - Specialty:
Mr. Peter F. Meder, President
Ms. Jane McCarthy, Vice President
Ms. Jill Kovacs, Associate

Salary Minimum: $150,000

Functions: Generalist (All), Senior Mgmt., Production, Health Admin., Mktg. Mgmt., CFOs, Mgmt. Consultants

Industries: Generalist (All), Energy, Utilities, Food, Bev., Tobacco, Motor Vehicles, Finance, Mgmt. Consulting, New Media

Branches:
245 Park Ave Fl 40
New York, NY 10167-4099
(212) 557-4663
Fax: (847) 914-0253
Key Contact - Specialty:
Ms. Nichole Florjancic, Principal

The Medfall Group

103-6453 Morrison St
Niagara Falls, ON L2E 7H1
Canada
(905) 357-6644
Fax: (905) 357-2601
Email: medfall@medfall.com
Web: www.medfall.com

Summary: We are a healthcare management company specializing in physician leadership and healthcare executive search. Our website identifies our client base and the subject matter addressed by our consulting division. Our expertise is available to Canadian and international clients.

Key Contact - Specialty:
Dr. Patrick Gibney, President

Salary Minimum: $80,000

Functions: Management, Senior Mgmt., Healthcare, Physicians, Allied Health, CFOs, Mgmt. Consultants

Industries: Healthcare, Hospitals

Melancon & Company

PO Box 2383
McKinney, TX 75070-8169
(972) 231-9963
Email: info@melanconcompany.com
Web: www.melanconcompany.com

Summary: We are a retainer-based executive search firm specializing in the identification and recruitment of key executive talent for high-performance organizations. The company is one of

the oldest and most highly regarded search firms in the Southwest.

Key Contact - Specialty:
Mr. Robert M. Melancon, Managing Principal

Salary Minimum: $100,000

Functions: Generalist (All)

Industries: Generalist (All)

Menard International Search

4 Springhurst Dr Ste 211
East Greenbush, NY 12061-2233
(518) 477-8123
Fax: (518) 477-7574
Email: kmenard@menardintl.com
Web: www.menardintl.com

Summary: We are an executive search firm specializing in filling senior level management, scientific and technical positions for pharmaceutical, biotechnology and medical device companies. Our expertise includes all areas of drug discovery and development including R&D management, clinical research, regulatory affairs, QA/QC, project management and business development.

Key Contact - Specialty:
Mr. Kirk Menard, President
Mr. William Sheldon, Search Consultant
Mr. John Harvey, Search Consultant

Salary Minimum: $100,000

Functions: Board Members, Senior Mgmt., Mfg., Product Dev., Quality, Physicians, Sales & Mktg., HR Mgmt., MIS Mgmt.

Industries: Drugs Mfg., Medical Devices, Pharm Svcs., Biotech/Life Sciences

Meng, Finseth & Associates Inc

3858 W Carson St Ste 202
Torrance, CA 90503-6705
(310) 316-0706
Fax: (310) 316-1064
Email: info@mengfinseth.com
Web: www.mengfinseth.com

Summary: We are a retained executive search practice serving a broad range of clientele, in both the public and private sectors. The firm is committed to providing candidate excellence in a timely and cost effective manner, while protecting the confidentiality, trust and integrity of all parties.

Key Contact - Specialty:
Mr. Charles M. Meng, Chairmen & President
Mr. Carl L. Finseth, Founder
Ms. Marlene M. Rafferty, Vice President
Ms. Cameron E. Wisowaty, Vice President
Ms. Malissa Mannila, Associate
Mrs. Dana Trotter, Associate
Mr. Todd Trotter, Research Associate

Functions: Generalist (All), Management, Senior Mgmt., Purchasing, Sales & Mktg., HR Mgmt., Finance, Engineering, Non-profits

Industries: Generalist (All), Drugs Mfg., Electronic, Elec. Components, Misc. Financial, Non-profits, Pharm Svcs., Higher Ed., Full Service Restaurants, Media, Government, Defense, Environmental Svcs., Aerospace, Healthcare

The Mercer Group Inc

5579B Chamblee Dunwoody Rd Ste 511
Atlanta, GA 30338-4128
(770) 551-0403
Fax: (770) 399-9749
Email: mercer@mindspring.com
Web: www.mercergroupinc.com

Summary: Specialize in public sector. Full-fledged management consulting firm offering services in executive search, strategy, market research, organization studies, organization development and compensation.

Key Contact - Specialty:
Mr. James L. Mercer, CMC, President & Chief Executive Officer - *Government*

Salary Minimum: $50,000

Functions: Generalist (All), Senior Mgmt., Staffing, Mgmt. Consultants

Industries: Generalist (All), Mgmt. Consulting, HR Services, Higher Ed., Government

MercerMorgan LLC

PO Box 26958
Scottsdale, AZ 85255-0132
(800) 383-4542
(480) 281-1833
Fax: (480) 281-1832
Email: info@mercermorgan.com
Web: www.mercermorgan.com

Summary: We offer retained executive search services focused on placing leaders in the healthcare, insurance and benefits, financial services and technology industries.

Key Contact - Specialty:
Mr. Sal DiGiuseppi, Managing Partner
Mr. David Nelson, Managing Partner

Salary Minimum: $160,000

Functions: Generalist (All), Management, Senior Mgmt., Healthcare

Industries: Generalist (All), Finance, Services, Mgmt. Consulting, Communications, Insurance, Casualty, Claims, Life, Biotech/Life Sciences, Healthcare, Hospitals, Long-term/Home Care, Dental

Meridian Executive Resources[†]

(also known as Sherwood Meridian Resources)
328 Tampico
Walnut Creek, CA 94598-2917
(925) 946-0566
Fax: (925) 946-0566
Email: sandys@meridianer.com
Web: www.meridianer.com

Summary: We provide retained search services to source mission-critical executives for world-class management teams. Our only focus is on the unique aspects of building winning entrepreneurial management teams.

Key Contact - Specialty:
Mr. Sandy Sanderson, Founder
Ms. Alena Pierce, Partner
Ms. Sherrie Thorpe, Partner - *Science*
Ms. Claudia Lindquist, Partner

Salary Minimum: $100,000

Functions: Board Members, Senior Mgmt., Mgmt. Consultants

Industries: Computer Equip., Test, Measure Equip., Electronic, Elec. Components, Mgmt. Consulting, HR Services, E-commerce, Communications, Telephony, Digital, Wireless, Fiber Optic, Software, Security SW, System SW

Branches:
342 Remington Loop
Danville, CA 94526-3734
(415) 235-3513
Fax: (925) 838-9948

Key Contact - Specialty:
Mr. David Manion, Senior Parnter

Merritt, Hawkins & Associates

(a division of The MHA Group)
5001 Statesman Dr
Irving, TX 75063-2414
(800) 876-0500
(469) 524-1400
Fax: (469) 524-1422
Email: info@mhagroup.com
Web: www.merritthawkins.com

Summary: We are a large physician staffing firm, performing 2,600 search assignments each year. We also specialize in the permanent recruitment of advanced practice allied health care professionals, and conduct educational seminars nationwide to a variety of health care associations.

Key Contact - Specialty:
Mr. Jim Merritt, President - *Physicians*
Mr. Joe Hawkins, Chief Executive Officer - *Physicians*

Functions: Physicians

Industries: Generalist (All)

Branches:
3500 Barranca Pkwy Ste 240
Irvine, CA 92606-8231
(800) 288-1210
(949) 757-7750
Fax: (949) 757-7756
Email: info@mhagroup.com
Key Contact - Specialty:
Mr. Steven Thomas - *Physicians*

5901 Peachtree Dunwoody Rd NE Ste A450
Atlanta, GA 30328-7184
(800) 306-1330
(770) 396-4800
Fax: (770) 481-1115
Email: info@mhagroup.com
Key Contact - Specialty:
Mr. Mark Smith - *Physicians*

310 E 4500 S Ste 300
Salt Lake City, UT 84107-4240
(800) 211-4971
(801) 264-0260
Fax: (801) 264-0255
Email: info@mhagroup.com
Key Contact - Specialty:
Mr. Joseph Caldwell - *Physicians*

Messett Associates Inc

7700 N Kendall Dr Ste 304
Miami, FL 33156-7559
(305) 275-1000
Fax: (305) 274-4462
Email: messett@messett.com
Web: www.messett.com

Summary: We undertake top-level executive searches, acquisitions, mergers, plus joint venture partner identification on a worldwide basis.

Key Contact - Specialty:
Mr. William J. Messett III, President
Mr. William J. Messett IV, Vice President

Salary Minimum: $100,000

Functions: Generalist (All), Int'l.

Industries: Generalist (All), Agri., Forestry, Mining, Energy, Utilities, Manufacturing, Transportation, Retail, Finance, Brokers, Pharm Svcs., Hospitality, Insurance, Software

Meticulum, Inc.

31 High St
Vinalhaven, ME 04863-3802
(207) 863-9309

Email: mcticulum@gmail.com
Web: www.meticulum.com

Summary: We specialize in the strategic placement of tough-to-find professionals within biotechnology, pharmaceuticals and environmental health sciences. The common threads that run through our searches are their well-defined focus and level of complexity. Our areas of expertise are: R&D, toxicology, pathology, nanotechnology (including nanotoxicology), ecological risk assessment, drug safety and bioinformatics.

Key Contact - Specialty:
Mr. John A. Gasbarre, President - *Biotechnology, Environmental, Pharmaceutical*
Mr. Kip E. Kipson, Vice President - *Administration, General management, Operations*

Salary Minimum: $100,000

Functions: Management, Quality, Physicians, R&D, Engineering, Process, Environmentalists

Industries: Drugs Mfg., Pharm Svcs., Compliance, Environmental Svcs., Haz. Waste, Biotech/Life Sciences

Metlife
2701 Queens Plz N
Long Island City, NY 11101-4007
(212) 578-5261
Email: idecker@metlife.com
Web: www.metlife.com

Summary: We are a major force in financial services: investments, financial advise, banking and insurance. Through our products and services, our ultimate goal is simple in concept to build financial freedom for everyone.

Key Contact - Specialty:
Mr. Ian Decker, Director, Executive Recruiting

Functions: Management

Industries: Finance, Misc. Financial

Meyer Associates Inc
5079 Riverhill Rd NE
Marietta, GA 30068-4859
(770) 565-2020

Summary: Since our inception, the goal has been straightforward - to give clients real value. We recognize that use of executive recruiting services is an investment that must produce exceptional returns and tangible benefits.

Key Contact - Specialty:
Mr. Rick M. Meyer - *Finance, Management consulting, Manufacturing, Sales*

Salary Minimum: $75,000

Functions: Senior Mgmt., Middle Mgmt., Mfg., Plant Mgmt., Mktg. Mgmt., Sales Mgmt., Mgmt. Consultants

Industries: Manufacturing, Mgmt. Consulting, IT Implementation

David Meyers Associates Ltd
1600 Burning Bush Ln
Hoffman Estates, IL 60192-1209
(847) 705-6700
Fax: (847) 705-6705
Email: meyersdgm@comcast.net
Web: www.meyersassociates.com

Summary: Consultants to the private club and resort markets with forte placing top level Executive Chefs. Firm is strategically allied with the Master Club Advisors, a firm comprised of four (4) Master Club Managers further substantiating operational insight, industry leadership and presence.

Key Contact - Specialty:
Mr. David Meyers, President

Salary Minimum: $80,000

Functions: Chefs

Industries: Hospitality, Hotels, Resorts, Clubs

mf Branch Associates, Inc.
PO Box 18105
Asheville, NC 28814-0105
(828) 658-0055
Fax: (345) 948-0418
Email: minnie@mfbranch.com
Web: www.mfbranch.com

Summary: We conduct a search for clients in the telecommunication and advanced data communication networking industries for both the vendor as well as the service provider. The positions represented include executive management, advanced R&D, marketing, product management and sales.

Key Contact - Specialty:
Ms. Minnie Branch, President

Salary Minimum: $80,000

Functions: Generalist (All), Board Members, Senior Mgmt., Middle Mgmt., Mktg. Mgmt., Sales Mgmt., Systems Dev., R&D

Industries: Telecoms, Telephony, Wireless, Fiber Optic, Network Infrastructure, Software, Networking, Comm. SW

mfg/Search Inc
431 E Colfax Ave Ste 120
South Bend, IN 46617-2790
(574) 282-2547
(800) 782-7976
Email: mfg@mfgsearch.com
Web: www.mfgsearch.com

Summary: We are a generalist retained fee search firm. We have particular strength in manufacturing industries but are not limited to those fields.

Key Contact - Specialty:
Ms. Christine Austin

Salary Minimum: $75,000

Functions: Generalist (All)

Industries: Manufacturing

Branches:
104 Alsace Cv Ste 300
Little Rock, AR 72223-9573
(800) 782-7976 x16
Key Contact - Specialty:
Mr. T. Evan Moore

1170 Peachtree St NE Ste 1200
Atlanta, GA 30309-7673
(800) 782-7976 x15
Email: amitry@mfgsearch.com
Key Contact - Specialty:
Mr. Alfred Mitry

203 N La Salle St Ste 2100
Chicago, IL 60601-1226
(800) 782-7976 x11
Key Contact - Specialty:
Mr. Walter Pollock

50 Main St
White Plains, NY 10606-1901
(800) 782-7976 x19

Key Contact - Specialty:
Mr. Arthur Forrest

Anthony Michael & Company
60 State St Ste 700
Boston, MA 02109-1894
(800) 565-5578
Fax: (508) 242-9590
Email: info@anthonymichaelco.com
Web: www.anthonymichaelco.com

Summary: Our assignments span middle to senior management in the following areas: portfolio management & research, sales & marketing and investment banking.

Key Contact - Specialty:
Mr. Michael J. Kulesza, Senior Managing Director
Ms. Toni L. Knights, Information Manager

Salary Minimum: $100,000

Functions: Generalist (All), Management, Board Members, Senior Mgmt., Sales & Mktg., Mktg. Mgmt., Sales Mgmt., Attorneys, Int'l.

Industries: Generalist (All), Finance, Banking, Invest. Banking, Brokers, Misc. Financial

Michael Associates
613 S Poplar Ave
Elmhurst, IL 60126-4061
(630) 832-2550
Email: msg5758@aol.com

Summary: We offer searches for general management, specializing in manufacturing management, technical & engineering, personnel & engineering management, materials management and IT.

Key Contact - Specialty:
Mr. Michael S. Golding, Principal - *Engineering, Management, Manufacturing, MIS*

Salary Minimum: $40,000

Functions: Management, Senior Mgmt., Middle Mgmt., Mfg., Materials, HR Mgmt., MIS Mgmt., R&D, Engineering

Industries: Generalist (All), Manufacturing, Plastics, Rubber, Metal Products, Motor Vehicles, Misc. Mfg., Electronic, Elec. Components, Architectural Svcs., Equip Svcs., HR Services, Engineering Svcs., Packaging

John Michael Associates[†]
PO Box 17130
Washington, DC 20041-7130
(703) 471-6300
Fax: (703) 471-4064
Email: gf@searchjma.com
Web: www.searchjma.com

Summary: We are a retained search company that represents law firms and corporations seeking legal talent. Our experience includes work with over 100 law firms and corporations.

Key Contact - Specialty:
Mr. Gary J. Fossett, Chief Executive Officer - *Capital markets, Healthcare, Intellectual property, Securities, Technology*
Mr. Brad J. Toynbee, Principal - *Energy, Intellectual property, Securities, Tax*

Salary Minimum: $300,000

Functions: Generalist (All), Senior Mgmt.

Industries: Legal, Mgmt. Consulting

Gregory Michaels & Associates Inc

804 N Dearborn St
Chicago, IL 60610-3317
(312) 377-2100
Fax: (312) 377-2121
Email: wesearch4@gregorymichaels.com
Web: www.gregorymichaels.com

Summary: We are a boutique executive search firm recruiting upper-level management.

Key Contact - Specialty:
Mr. Gregory P. Crecos, Managing Partner
Mr. Joseph J. Scodius, Manager
Ms. Kambrea R. Wendler, Manager
Ms. Mary K. Simon, Senior Consultant
Ms. Lorrie A. Hopp, Senior Consultant
Ms. Heather L. McCarthy, Consultant
Ms. Erin Cook, Senior Research Associate
Ms. Jacklyn Correa, Research Associate

Salary Minimum: $275,000

Functions: Generalist (All), Board Members, Senior Mgmt., Sales & Mktg., Mktg. Mgmt., HR Mgmt., Finance, MIS Mgmt.

Industries: Generalist (All), Services

Michigan Consulting Group[†]

49945 Streamwood Dr
Novi, MI 48374-2148
(989) 386-2219
(248) 376-4202
Fax: (989) 386-2219
Email: mcg@provide.net

Summary: We are a privately owned world-class executive search firm. We are seasoned executive search professionals with a reputation for adding value to our clients. Delivering top senior and mid level executive talent. Our executive search practice serves a broad base of corporate clients. Our commitment: To serve our clients with optimum cost effectiveness and efficiency reflected in the consistent delivery of exceptional candidates.

Key Contact - Specialty:
Mr. David E. Southworth, President - *Aerospace, Automotive, Defense, Middle management, Senior management*
Mr. David Southworth, II, Executive Vice President - *Automotive, Engineering, Human resources, Legal (Attorneys), Middle management*
Mr. Douglas Kramer, Vice President - *Engineering, Foundries, Machining, Manufacturing (Management), Quality*
Mr. Pedro Salinas Gasga, Vice President, Mexico & Central America
Miss Kathy Palazzolo, Vice President - *Aerospace, Engineering, Manufacturing (Management), Middle management, Senior management*
Mr. Jun Tanaka, Vice President

Salary Minimum: $65,000

Functions: Generalist (All), Management, Senior Mgmt., Mfg., Product Dev., Sales & Mktg., Sales Mgmt., Finance, CFOs, Engineering

Industries: Generalist (All), Manufacturing, Chemicals, Drugs Mfg., Medical Devices, Plastics, Rubber, Leather, Stone, Glass, Metal Products, Machine, Appliance, Motor Vehicles, Computer Equip., Consumer Elect., Misc. Mfg., Electronic, Elec. Components, Transportation, Defense, Aerospace, Healthcare

Branches:
4000 Fayette Ct
Jackson, MI 49203-5309
(517) 784-9856

Email: e52560@cs.com
Key Contact - Specialty:
Mr. Edward Southworth, Executive Vice President - *Hospital, Medical, Plastics, Rubber*

2612 Avonhurst Dr
Troy, MI 48084-1028
(248) 646-6600
Fax: (248) 646-8022
Email: cindyparsons@comcast.net
Key Contact - Specialty:
Ms. Cindy Parsons, Vice President - *Pharmaceutical*

Millbrook Partners LLC

PO Box 66
3290 Franklin Ave
Millbrook, NY 12545-0066
(845) 677-2500
Fax: (845) 677-3315
Email: research@millbrooksearch.com
Web: www.millbrooksearch.com

Summary: Focused on building highly consultative partnering client relationships. Our search scope spans business leaders across multiple industries including diversified industrial, management consulting, financial services, energy, high tech, consumer; covering product as well as services businesses. Roles include all C-level, general management, sales and marketing, finance, HR and IT.

Key Contact - Specialty:
Mr. Robert Whaley, Managing Partner
Mr. David Brinkerhoff, Strategic Partner - *Human resources, Organizational development, Senior management*
Ms. Joyce Edwards, Director, Research - *Benefits, Compensation, Human resources, Organizational development, Training*
Mr. Mark Nevins, Strategic Partner - *C-level, Senior management*
Ms. Kathryn C. Mayer, Recruiter
Mr. Alan Hack, Strategic Partner

Salary Minimum: $150,000

Functions: Generalist (All), Senior Mgmt., Sales & Mktg., HR Mgmt., Finance, Risk Mgmt., MIS Mgmt.

Industries: Generalist (All), Finance, Mgmt. Consulting

The Millenia Group Inc[†]

7700 Irvine Center Dr Ste 800
Irvine, CA 92618-3047
(949) 851-0000
Fax: (949) 851-0001
Email: rh@themilleniagroup.com
Web: www.themilleniagroup.com

Summary: We are a boutique firm specializing in senior-level and mid-management accounting, finance, HR, and shared services placement with expertise in consumer products, financial services, manufacturing and high-technology for Fortune 500 and privately-held companies for nationwide search.

Key Contact - Specialty:
Ms. Rhonda Hamade, Principal - *Accounting (Big 4), Controllers, Investor relations, Semiconductors, Treasury*

Salary Minimum: $75,000

Functions: HR Mgmt., Benefits, Finance, CFOs

Industries: Generalist (All), Food, Bev., Tobacco, Consumer Elect., Misc. Mfg., Electronic, Elec. Components, Semiconductors, Consumer Goods, Wholesale, Mgmt. Consulting, Logistics Svcs., Telecoms, Wireless

Millennium Search Group Inc

4025 Camino Del Rio S Ste 300
San Diego, CA 92108-4108
(619) 542-7777
Web: www.msgiusa.com

Summary: We are an executive search firm specializing exclusively in placement of senior-level executives (partners, VPs, directors, principals and senior managers) in management consulting, audit, tax, M&A and risk management.

Key Contact - Specialty:
Mr. David M. Ferrara, President - *Management consulting, Tax*
Mr. Stephen J. Abkin, Executive Vice President - *Management consulting, Tax*

Salary Minimum: $150,000

Functions: Sales Mgmt., M&A, Risk Mgmt., IT, Systems Implem., Mgmt. Consultants

Industries: Generalist (All), Accounting, Mgmt. Consulting, E-commerce, IT Implementation, Network Infrastructure, Software, ERP SW, Security SW

Miller, Abramson & Company Inc

21 NW 2nd St
Delray Beach, FL 33444-2613
(561) 330-8500
Email: maci@macnet.net
Web: www.macnet.net

Summary: For every assignment we: provide a target list of companies to recruit from; source candidates who fit your job specifications; contact candidates and discuss their qualifications; send you resumes and comments on interested candidates. Our clients enjoy substantial savings based upon our unique hourly fee structure. Spanish language capability.

Key Contact - Specialty:
Ms. Lisa Miller, Partner - *Building products, Controllers, Product management/development*
Ms. Cheryl Abramson, Partner - *Purchasing, Textiles*

Salary Minimum: $40,000

Functions: Mfg., Plant Mgmt., Materials, Sales & Mktg., Sales Mgmt., Finance, CFOs, MIS Mgmt., Engineering, Design

Industries: Generalist (All), Manufacturing, Textiles, Apparel, Lumber, Furniture, Plastics, Rubber, Metal Products, Misc. Mfg., Wholesale, Finance, Banking, Misc. Financial, Logistics Svcs.

Craig Miller Associates

1720 E Garry Ave Ste 207
Santa Ana, CA 92705-5832
(949) 261-7247
(949) 261-6246
Fax: (949) 261-9539
Email: cmiller@cmasearch.com
Web: www.cmasearch.com

Summary: Retained executive search firm with a concentration in senior management search in all key functional departments. We have significant success in attracting high impact executives for leading both high-growth and turnaround situations.

Key Contact - Specialty:
Mr. Craig N. Miller, President
Mr. Scott Seabaugh, Vice President
Mr. Richard Pantuliano, Vice President

Salary Minimum: $100,000

Functions: Generalist (All), Senior Mgmt., Mfg., Sales & Mktg., HR Mgmt., Finance, IT, Engineering

Industries: Generalist (All), Manufacturing, Medical Devices, Computer Equip., Aerospace, Software

Miller-Hall HRISearch†

23 Vista Toscana
Lake Elsinore, CA 92532-0215
(909) 245-4116
(914) 834-9697
Email: hrisearch@aol.com
Web: www.hrisearch.com

Summary: Search firm exclusively focused on HRIS (HR information system) mid to high-level positions. We will price your HRIS position using industry benchmarks; prepare your job description or job specifications and present pre-screened qualified candidates.

Key Contact - Specialty:
Mr. Larry Hall, Managing Director

Salary Minimum: $75,000

Functions: HR Mgmt., Systems Analysis, Systems Implem.

Industries: Generalist (All), Software, ERP SW, HR SW

Branches:
50 Woodlawn Ave
New Rochelle, NY 10804-4619
(914) 834-9697
Email: msmilleras@aol.com
Key Contact - Specialty:
Mr. Marc Miller, Founder

Miller.Miller LLC†

PO Box 3088
Kirkland, WA 98083-3088
(425) 822-3145
(800) 820-1055
Fax: (425) 827-9194
Email: info@millermiller.com
Web: www.millermiller.com

Summary: We represent biotechnology, medical device and pharmaceutical companies ranging from start-ups to major international corporations. We place individuals in: senior management, marketing, research, product development, quality assurance, regulatory and clinical affairs and manufacturing positions.

Key Contact - Specialty:
Ms. Shirley M. Miller, President - *Biotechnology*

Functions: Generalist (All), Senior Mgmt., Middle Mgmt., Product Dev., Quality, Mktg. Research, Mktg. Mgmt., R&D

Industries: Generalist (All), Biotech/Life Sciences

Herbert Mines Associates Inc

(a Globe Search Group company)
375 Park Ave Ste 801
New York, NY 10152-0801
(212) 355-0909
Fax: (212) 223-2186
Email: hma@herbertmines.com
Web: www.herbertmines.com

Summary: Retainer search for senior management for retail, direct marketing, eCommerce, textiles, apparel, specialty food, supermarkets, cosmetics, fashion manufacturing and consumer businesses. Clients range from small to multi-billion dollar conglomerates. Over 80 percent of assignments are from existing clients.

Key Contact - Specialty:
Mr. Harold Reiter, Chief Executive Officer & Chairman
Mr. Dave Hardie, Managing Director
Mr. Gene Manheim, Managing Director
Mr. Brian M. Meany, Managing Director

Mr. Robert Nahas, Managing Director
Ms. Mary Saxon, Managing Director
Ms. Kristin Dennehy, Vice President
Ms. Heidi Rustin, Vice President
Ms. Gail Winans, Principal
Mr. Dan Searby, Principal
Ms. Ruth Raisman, Principal
Ms. Jennifer Snapp, Senior Associate
Ms. Virginia Sisson, Senior Associate
Ms. Patricia Accarino, Senior Associate
Ms. Tania Cross, Senior Associate

Salary Minimum: $150,000

Functions: Generalist (All), Board Members, Senior Mgmt., Product Dev., Advertising, Mktg. Mgmt., Sales Mgmt., Direct Mktg., HR Mgmt., CFOs

Industries: Generalist (All), Food, Bev., Tobacco, Textiles, Apparel, Soap, Perf., Cosmtcs., Consumer Goods, Wholesale, Retail, Mgmt. Consulting, HR Services, Hospitality, Media

Laurie Mitchell & Company Inc†

(also known as Marketing Communications Executive Search)
25018 Hazelmere Rd
Cleveland, OH 44122-3241
(216) 292-9936
Email: mitchelladsearch@aol.com
mitchellprsearch@aol.com
Web: www.lauriemitchellcompany.com

Summary: Serving corporate, agency and individual needs with discretion and integrity. Retained search services in public relations, marketing communications, financial communications, advertising, marketing and sales promotion.

Key Contact - Specialty:
Ms. Laurie Mitchell, CPC, President - *Advertising, Public relations*

Salary Minimum: $35,000

Functions: Advertising, Mktg. Research, Mktg. Mgmt., Direct Mktg., PR

Industries: Generalist (All)

Mitroff Consulting†

945 Hunt Ave
Saint Helena, CA 94574-1115
(707) 963-8410
(415) 307-7806
Email: norman@normanmitroff.com
Web: www.normanmitroff.com

Summary: Specialize in recruitment, on a retained basis, for the restaurant and wine industry. We commit ourselves to your specific search needs on a confidential basis and guarantee timely results. We bring forth top-notch candidates.

Key Contact - Specialty:
Dr. Norman Mitroff, President

Functions: Management, Board Members, Senior Mgmt., Hospitality

Industries: Agri., Forestry, Mining, Wholesale, Retail, HR Services, Hospitality, Hotels, Resorts, Clubs, Restaurants, Quick Service Restaurants, Full Service Restaurants, Inst./Industrial Food Svc., Entertainment, Recreation, Healthcare

MIXTEC Group LLC†

709 E Colorado Blvd Ste 250
Pasadena, CA 91101-2159
(626) 440-7077
Fax: (626) 440-1557
Email: mixtec@mixtec.net
Web: www.mixtec.net

Summary: We specialize in searches for senior executives in the produce, food, food service, and agricultural industries. We base our search efforts on our in-depth knowledge of these industry sectors and on our top management and consulting experience.

Key Contact - Specialty:
Mr. Christopher C. Nelson, President & Chief Executive Officer
Mr. Jerry Butt, Vice President
Mrs. Mary Sanburn, Principal
Mr. Joe Stubbs, Managing Director, Foodservice
Dr. Ward A. Fredericks, Chairman - *Life Sciences*

Salary Minimum: $80,000

Functions: Generalist (All)

Industries: Food, Bev., Tobacco

MJS Executive Search

500 Mamaroneck Ave Ste 314
Harrison, NY 10528-1600
(914) 798-7750
Email: matt@mjsearch.com
Web: www.mjsearch.com

Summary: We are a unique retained executive search firm specializing in the placement of marketing, sales, and general management professionals in the consumer goods and service industries. We deliver highly qualified candidates using industry expertise, a disciplined process, and strong client relationships.

Key Contact - Specialty:
Mr. Matthew Schwartz, President - *Consumer, Consumer (Marketing), CRM, Direct marketing, Sales*

Salary Minimum: $100,000

Functions: Generalist (All), Management, Sales & Mktg.

Industries: Generalist (All), Consumer Goods, Services, HR Services, E-commerce, Hospitality, Hotels, Resorts, Clubs, Entertainment, Sports, Media, Advertising, New Media

Molloy Partners

340 Broadway
Saratoga Springs, NY 12866-3141
(518) 581-2532
Fax: (518) 581-2832
Email: tom@molloypartners.com

Summary: Both corporate clients and colleges/universities engage us. On the corporate side we specialize in sales, marketing, finance and HR. In higher education we are retained for senior-level assignments in fundraising, IT, public relations/marketing, finance/investments, HR and administration.

Key Contact - Specialty:
Mr. Thomas F. Molloy, President - *Administration, CFOs, Education, Information Technology, Non-profit*

Salary Minimum: $100,000

Functions: Generalist (All), Board Members, Senior Mgmt., Sales Mgmt., HR Mgmt., CFOs, MIS Mgmt., Non-profits

Industries: Generalist (All), Finance, Non-profits, HR Services, Higher Ed., Software, Healthcare

Oscar Montano Inc

1223 Wilshire Blvd Ste E
Santa Monica, CA 90403-5400
(310) 394-0555
Fax: (310) 496-0301
Email: owm@oscarmontano.com
Web: www.oscarmontano.com

Summary: Specializing in consumer and automotive finance, we provide the complete search process plus industry knowledge. We also do salary surveys, organizational consulting and specialized outplacement.

Key Contact - Specialty:
Mr. Oscar W. Montano, President - *Automotive*
Ms. Linda Gossard, Research & Candidate Development
Ms. Diana Carter, Recruiter, Strategic Marketing
Ms. Kathy McGuire, Internal Management & Technology

Salary Minimum: $80,000

Functions: Senior Mgmt., Sales & Mktg.

Industries: Finance, Banking, Venture Cap., Misc. Financial, Commercial

C A Moore & Associates Inc[†]

801 Twelve Oaks Center Dr Ste 803C
Wayzata, MN 55391-4610
(952) 473-0990
Fax: (952) 473-7080
Email: camoore@camoore.net
Web: www.camoore.net

Summary: Our firm has a strong network of contacts and expertise in many areas, with a concentration in financial services.

Key Contact - Specialty:
Ms. Connie Moore, CPCU, President - *Direct marketing, Financial services, Risk management*
Mrs. Linda Thomas, Search Associate

Salary Minimum: $75,000

Functions: Generalist (All), Management

Industries: Generalist (All), Finance, Banking, Invest. Banking, Brokers, Misc. Financial, Services, HR Services, Law Enforcement, Insurance, Casualty, Claims, Life, Commercial, Re-Insurance

Thomas R Moore Executive Search LLC

2000 E Lamar Blvd Ste 600
Bank of America Building
Arlington, TX 76006-7340
(817) 548-8766
(817) 446-1441
Fax: (817) 472-8293
Email: trm@trmexecsearch.com
Web: www.trmexecsearch.com

Summary: We provide an executive recruiting service specializing in fund development personnel. This service is offered to not-for-profit institutions seeking executive staff personnel in development, public relations, planned giving, alumni affairs, annual support and foundation management.

Key Contact - Specialty:
Mr. Thomas R. Moore, President

Salary Minimum: $60,000

Functions: Generalist (All), Direct Mktg., Non-profits

Industries: Generalist (All), Non-profits, Higher Ed., Healthcare

Morgan Howard Worldwide

62 Southfield Ave Ste 208
Stamford, CT 06902-7229
(203) 324-3355
Fax: (203) 967-3923
Web: www.morganhoward.com

Summary: Morgan Howard is a leading globally-oriented consultancy that provides human capital advice on the most senior, sensitive and confidential client matters where true insight is highly valued. Clients are served worldwide by partners who are experienced and culturally sensitive, whether the client's requirements are in the Americas, Asia Pacific or in Europe.

Key Contact - Specialty:
Mr. Alister Wellesley, Chairman

Salary Minimum: $175,000

Functions: Board Members, Senior Mgmt.

Industries: Generalist (All), Manufacturing, Transportation, Retail, Finance, Hospitality, Media, Communications, Insurance, Software

Moriarty Fox Inc

20 N Wacker Dr Ste 2410
Chicago, IL 60606-3059
(312) 332-4600
Email: mfsearch1@aol.com

Summary: For many years, our firm has prided itself on establishing long and productive professional relationships with its many and varied client organizations. The firm's partners are well acquainted with many of the country's business and professional leaders.

Key Contact - Specialty:
Mr. Philip S.J. Moriarty, President & Founder
Mr. J. Thomas Kenny, Partner

Salary Minimum: $100,000

Functions: Generalist (All)

Industries: Generalist (All)

Morris & Berger

500 N Brand Blvd Ste 2150
Glendale, CA 91203-3318
(818) 507-1234
Fax: (818) 507-4770
Email: mb@morrisberger.com
Web: www.morrisberger.com

Summary: Retained, generalist executive search firm with specialty practice in nonprofit sector including academic, arts, social services and foundations.

Key Contact - Specialty:
Ms. Kristine A. Morris, Partner - *Non-profit*
Dr. Jay V. Berger, Partner - *Non-profit*
Ms. Karin Berger Stellar, Vice President & Partner - *Non-profit*

Salary Minimum: $120,000

Functions: Generalist (All)

Industries: Non-profits, Higher Ed., Government, Healthcare

Morton, Doyle Associates[†]

26 Bellevue Rd
Arlington, MA 02476-7920
(781) 641-1100
Fax: (781) 641-1151
Email: mortondoyle@rcn.com

Summary: Specializing in high-technology, IT and manufacturing industries. Functional specialties in engineering and other technical areas as well as sales & marketing and general management.

Key Contact - Specialty:
Mr. John F. Doyle, Principal

Salary Minimum: $100,000

Functions: Management, Sales & Mktg., IT, Engineering

Industries: Generalist (All), Computer Equip., Test, Measure Equip., Software

Morton, McCorkle & Associates Inc

2190 S Mason Rd Ste 309
Saint Louis, MO 63131-1639
(314) 984-9494
Fax: (314) 984-9460
Email: mmacnslt@aol.com

Summary: We are an upper-level retained search firm encompassing most all functions and industries. Our emphasis is on general management, marketing and key line positions. We have had many years of exceptional performance. Our clients range in size (revenues) from 10s-of-millions to over 50-billion.

Key Contact - Specialty:
Mr. Sam B. McCorkle, President

Salary Minimum: $75,000

Functions: Generalist (All), Management, Senior Mgmt., Plant Mgmt., Materials, R&D, Engineering, Int'l.

Industries: Generalist (All), Agri., Forestry, Mining, Manufacturing, Food, Bev., Tobacco, Chemicals, Machine, Appliance, Wholesale, Non-profits, HR Services, Inst./Industrial Food Svc., Packaging, Biotech/Life Sciences

Moss & Company Executive Search LLC

21481 N 78th St
Scottsdale, AZ 85255-7718
(480) 538-0665
Email: info@mossandco.com
Web: www.mossandco.com

Summary: We are a retained executive search firm specializing in the real estate development, construction, banking, architecture and property management fields.

Key Contact - Specialty:
Ms. Barbara Moss, President - *Construction, Property management*

Salary Minimum: $50,000

Functions: Generalist (All)

Industries: Construction, Banking, Architectural Svcs., Real Estate, Property/Facility Mgmt.

Branches:
456 Eakin Dr NW
Bainbridge Island, WA 98110-1758
(206) 855-8100
Email: ttorseth@mossandco.com
Key Contact - Specialty:
Ms. Theresa Torseth, Senior Associate Recruiter - *Construction, Finance, Property management*

Moyer, Sherwood Associates Inc

1285 Avenue of the Americas Fl 35
New York, NY 10019-6028
(212) 554-4008
Email: research@moyersherwood.com
Web: www.moyersherwood.com

Summary: We offer highly professional service, combining three strong elements: traditional, thorough, confidential executive search consulting; modern, computer-based methodology; and a commitment to creativity in our search execution.

Key Contact - Specialty:
Mr. David S. Moyer - *Public relations*
Ms. Christina Campanella, Research Associate

Salary Minimum: $125,000

Functions: PR

Industries: Generalist (All)

Branches:
65 High Ridge Rd Ste 502
Stamford, CT 06905-3800
(203) 656-2220
Key Contact - Specialty:
Ms. Margaret L. O'Donnell

MPA Executive Search Inc

204-7900 Boul Taschereau
MS A
Brossard, QC J4X 1C2
Canada
(514) 875-3996
(450) 465-6998
Fax: (450) 465-9215
Email: courrier@5148753996.ca
Web: www.m-p-a.qc.ca

Summary: We specialize in the search of
intermediate and executive-level personnel. Strong
experience in engineering and manufacturing.

Key Contact - Specialty:
Mr. Marc Paquet, President

Salary Minimum: $40,000

Functions: Generalist (All), Management, Mfg.,
Materials, Sales & Mktg., HR Mgmt., Finance,
Engineering

Industries: Generalist (All), Agri., Forestry,
Mining, Manufacturing, Packaging,
Biotech/Life Sciences, Healthcare

Mruk & EMA Partners

(an EMA Partners International company)
230 Park Ave Rm 1000
New York, NY 10169-1099
(212) 808-3076

Summary: We place board members, senior
management, sales & marketing, MIS
management and HR management professionals in
the manufacturing, financial services, publishing,
packaging, insurance, real estate,
biotechnology/life sciences and healthcare
industries.

Key Contact - Specialty:
Mr. Edwin S. Mruk, Senior Parnter - *Financial
services, General management, Healthcare,
Manufacturing*

Salary Minimum: $100,000

Functions: Board Members, Senior Mgmt., Mfg.,
Health Admin., Sales & Mktg., HR Mgmt.,
Benefits, CFOs, MIS Mgmt., Int'l.

Industries: Manufacturing, Services, Hospitality,
Publishing, Packaging, Insurance, Real Estate,
Biotech/Life Sciences, Healthcare

MSA Executive Search|Clark Consulting-Healthcare Group

700 W 47th St Ste 400
Kansas City, MO 64112-1805
(816) 795-1947
Fax: (816) 478-1929
Email: jane.groves@mgmtscience.com
Web: www.mgmtscience.com

Summary: We are a leading healthcare HR
consulting firm. The executive search practice
provides retained executive level searches
including CEO, COO, CFO, CNO, CMO, CHRO,
VPs and directors. Search methodology includes
national sourcing, in-depth candidate interviews
and profiles, including executive assessment.

Key Contact - Specialty:
Ms. Jane Groves, Managing Senior Vice
President - *C-level, Healthcare, Hospital,
Human resources, Organizational development*

Ms. Kathy Hall, Senior Vice President - *C-level,
Healthcare, Hospital, Human resources,
Organizational development*
Mr. Mark Madden, Senior Vice President - *C-
level, Healthcare, Hospital, Human resources,
Organizational development*
Mr. Roger Samuel, Vice President - *Boards of
Directors, C-level, Healthcare, Hospital,
Human resources*
Mr. Mick Ruel, Senior Associate - *Healthcare,
Hospital, Human resources, Long term care*

Salary Minimum: $100,000

Functions: Senior Mgmt., Middle Mgmt.

Industries: Healthcare, Hospitals, Long-
term/Home Care, Women's

MTA Partners

11555 Stephenville Dr Ste 101
Frisco, TX 75035-9009
(972) 335-1882
(972) 380-1988
Email: mtucker@mtapartners.com
Web: www.mtapartners.com

Summary: We are a retained firm specializing in
the medical and non-profit industries. We offer
unequalled client service based on a minimal
number of searches conducted at a time. Over 90
percent of our candidates go to second interviews
with our clients.

Key Contact - Specialty:
Mr. Michael Tucker, Managing Partner -
Healthcare, Non-profit
Ms. Brooke Myers, Associate
Mrs. Carol Reince, Associate
Mrs. Stephanie Franklin, Associate
Ms. Peggy L. Fritz, Program Facilitator

Salary Minimum: $100,000

Functions: Senior Mgmt., Sales & Mktg., Mktg.
Mgmt., Sales Mgmt.

Industries: Drugs Mfg., Medical Devices, Pharm
Svcs., Biotech/Life Sciences, Healthcare

Much & Co Inc

25 Broad St
The Exchange
New York, NY 10004-2517
(212) 217-0600
Fax: (212) 217-0613
Email: muchandco@aol.com

Summary: Financial services: specializing in
investment management, investment research and
investment banking in all the major financial
capitals and in the emerging markets.

Key Contact - Specialty:
Mr. Isaac Much, President

Salary Minimum: $20,000

Functions: Finance

Industries: Finance, Banking, Invest. Banking,
Brokers, Venture Cap., Telecoms, Biotech/Life
Sciences, Healthcare

Mullen Associates Inc

230 Westchester Cir
Pinehurst, NC 28374-9529
(910) 295-0077
Email: jj@jmullen.com

Summary: We are a retained, boutique firm with
many years of experience in executive search. Our
specialties are paint & coatings, ink and adhesives
industries. We also have a strong background in
the power industry.

Key Contact - Specialty:
Mr. James J. Mullen, President - *Coatings, Paint*

Salary Minimum: $100,000

Functions: Generalist (All), Management, Senior
Mgmt., Middle Mgmt., Product Dev., Plant
Mgmt., Mktg. Mgmt., Sales Mgmt., HR Mgmt.,
R&D

Industries: Generalist (All), Chemicals, Plastics,
Rubber, Paints, Petro. Products

Pamela L Mulligan Inc

5 Hayward Brook Dr
Concord, NH 03301-1837
(603) 226-9900
Fax: (603) 226-9933
Email: plmulligan@comcast.net
Web: www.mulligansearch.com

Summary: Recruiting expertise in managed care,
health care and insurance (to include direct
marketing, TPA, special risk and employee
benefits). Functional titles and areas include: sales,
marketing, underwriting, claims, systems, HR,
medical directors, CFO, psychiatrists, utilization
& care management and operations.

Key Contact - Specialty:
Ms. Pamela L. Mulligan, President - *Healthcare,
Managed care*

Salary Minimum: $60,000

Functions: Generalist (All), Senior Mgmt.,
Product Dev., Nurses, Mktg. Research, Mktg.
Mgmt., Sales Mgmt., CFOs, MIS Mgmt.,
Systems Implem.

Industries: Generalist (All), Insurance, Healthcare

The Mullings Group†

220 Congress Park Dr Ste 245
Delray Beach, FL 33445-4605
(561) 243-8883
Fax: (561) 243-1622
Email: info@mullingsgroup.com
Web: www.mullingsgroup.com

Summary: We are a search firm with practices in
the medical device, healthcare, pharmaceutical,
automation and systems integration industry.

Key Contact - Specialty:
Ms. Holly Scott, Partner & Vice President
Mr. James Hall, Vice President
Ms. Patricia Sheehan, Director, Nursing and
Healthcare
Mr. Lorne Yaffe, Vice President
Mr. Joseph Mullings, President & Chief
Executive Officer
Mr. Matt Kaufman, Search Consultant
Ms. Michelle DeRogatis, Search Consultant
Ms. Suzanne Bohen, Search Consultant
Ms. Renee Fitzgerald, Operations Manager
Ms. Nancy Gennell, Office Assistant
Mr. Chris Cook, Search Consultant

Salary Minimum: $60,000

Functions: Healthcare, Engineering

Industries: Energy, Utilities, Drugs Mfg., Medical
Devices, Computer Equip., Consumer Elect.,
Aerospace, Packaging, Biotech/Life Sciences,
Healthcare

The Mulshine Company Ltd

24 Fox Hollow Ln
Queensbury, NY 12804-1139
(518) 743-9301
Email: mail@mulshinecompany.com
Web: www.mulshinecompany.com

Summary: Extensive experience in specialized
R&D and engineering searches, including
packaging, product & process
development/engineering, product
design/engineering, equipment
development/automation and technical

services/validation oriented searches from senior individual contributor to VP levels for the consumer brands, pharmaceutical and food industries.

Key Contact - Specialty:
Mr. Michael G. Mulshine, President

Salary Minimum: $70,000

Functions: Management, Middle Mgmt., Product Dev., Automation, Packaging, R&D, Engineering, Eng. Design, Process

Industries: Food, Bev., Tobacco, Soap, Perf., Cosmtcs., Drugs Mfg., Machine, Appliance, Consumer Goods, Packaging, Biotech/Life Sciences

Murgence

(formerly known asPearson & Associates)
7400 E McDonald Dr Ste 120
Scottsdale, AZ 85250-6099
(480) 368-9100
(800) 541-3384
Fax: (480) 778-1777
Email: chuck@pearson-assoc.com
Web: www.pearson-assoc.com

Summary: We are a retained firm with focused, committed professionals who offer unique benefits on a principle-to-principle basis.

Key Contact - Specialty:
Mr. Chuck Pearson, Chief Executive Officer
Mr. Dick Nosky, President
Mr. Brandon Coates, Managing Director, Worldwide Practice
Mr. Fred Hammett, Managing Partner
Mr. Lawrence Liakos, Director, Display Practice
Mr. Norb Mendleski, Director, Wireless practice

Salary Minimum: $100,000

Functions: Generalist (All), Management, Senior Mgmt., CFOs

Industries: Energy, Utilities, Paper, Consumer Elect., Semiconductors, Transportation, Finance, Venture Cap., Services, Non-profits, Communications, Digital, Wireless, Fiber Optic, RF/Microwave, Software, Development SW, ERP SW, Marketing SW, Networking, Comm. SW, Biotech/Life Sciences

P J Murphy & Associates Inc

735 N Water St
Milwaukee, WI 53202-4100
(414) 277-9777
Fax: (414) 277-7626
Email: pjmurphy@pjmurphy.com
Web: www.pjmurphy.com

Summary: Established firm; retainer only; considerable work with boards in selecting senior people.

Key Contact - Specialty:
Dr. Patrick J. Murphy, President - *General management*
Mr. Craig S. Zaffrann, Vice President

Salary Minimum: $80,000

Functions: Generalist (All)

Industries: Generalist (All)

Murphy Partners International

956 Shoreline Rd
Lake Barrington, IL 60010-3815
(847) 304-1599
Fax: (847) 304-1144
Email: murphy@mpivips.com

Summary: High level, high quality executive search practice with focus on personal service.

Key Contact - Specialty:
Mr. Bob Murphy, President
Ms. V. Kolacia, Managing Director - *Entertainment, Hospitality*
Ms. K. Froelich, Managing Director - *Food, Paper*
Ms. C. Liota, Managing Director - *Finance, Management consulting, New media*

Salary Minimum: $100,000

Functions: Management, Senior Mgmt., Mfg., Healthcare, Sales & Mktg., HR Mgmt., Finance, CFOs, IT, Int'l.

Industries: Generalist (All), Manufacturing, Retail, Finance, Services, Pharm Svcs., Hospitality, Insurance, Real Estate, Software, Biotech/Life Sciences, Healthcare

MVC Associates International

3001 N Rocky Point Dr E Ste 200
PMB 2034
Tampa, FL 33607-5806
(813) 600-5259
Email: mark@mvcinternational.com
Web: www.mvcinternational.com

Summary: Leading firm in organization design and search in information based marketing, CRM and e-business.

Key Contact - Specialty:
Mr. Mark Van Clieaf, Managing Director

Salary Minimum: $80,000

Functions: Generalist (All), Sales & Mktg.

Industries: Generalist (All)

Mycoff & Associates

26689 Pleasant Park Rd Ste 206
Conifer, CO 80433-7740
(303) 838-7445
(800) 525-9082
Fax: (303) 838-7428
Email: mail@mycoffassociates.com
Web: www.mycoffassociates.com

Summary: We have specialists in executive search for electric, natural gas, telecommunications, and water industries.

Key Contact - Specialty:
Mr. Carl A. Mycoff, President
Mr. Steve C. Dowdy, Principal & Senior Associate
Mr. Eric B. Dolven, Principal & Senior Associate
Mr. Scott A. Fry, Principal & Senior Associate
Mrs. Lanie Prouse, Principal & Senior Associate

Salary Minimum: $70,000

Functions: Generalist (All), Senior Mgmt., Middle Mgmt., Mktg. Mgmt., CFOs, Cash Mgmt., MIS Mgmt., Engineering

Industries: Generalist (All), Energy, Utilities, Telecoms

Nadzam & Associates

PO Box 1426
Bodega Bay, CA 94923-1426
(408) 838-7654
Fax: (408) 371-3513
Email: rjnadzam@nadzam.com
Web: www.nadzam.com

Summary: Consultants to corporate management in executive search, primarily for technology companies (i.e.: electronics, IT, manufacturing and aerospace). Clients range from Fortune 500 to start-up new technology companies.

Key Contact - Specialty:
Mr. Richard J. Nadzam, Principal

Salary Minimum: $150,000

Functions: Generalist (All), Management, Mfg., Sales & Mktg., HR Mgmt., IT, Engineering, Int'l.

Industries: Generalist (All), Manufacturing, Finance, Media, Aerospace, Software, Biotech/Life Sciences

Nagle & Associates[†]

4401 Shallowford Rd Ste 162-202
Roswell, GA 30075-3199
(678) 781-5200
Fax: (770) 973-0552
Web: www.nagleandassociates.net

Summary: Our search services are wholly focused on the healthcare industry. Our clients include hospitals and health systems, medical groups, consulting firms and managed care entities.

Key Contact - Specialty:
Mr. Chip Nagle, CHC, President

Salary Minimum: $90,000

Functions: Senior Mgmt.

Industries: Healthcare, Hospitals

Branches:
611 Cricklewood Rd
West Chester, PA 19382-8507
(484) 888-5577
Email: bwilson@nagleandassociates.net
Key Contact - Specialty:
Mr. Bill Wilson, Senior Vice President - *Healthcare, Hospital*

Nagler Robins Partners

61 Prentice Rd Ste 100
Newton Center, MA 02459-1325
(617) 969-0405
Email: info@nrpinc.com
Web: www.nrpinc.com

Summary: With a long-standing record of quickly meeting client needs, coupled with a high success rate, we focus on providing individualized attention and developing close client relationships.

Key Contact - Specialty:
Ms. Jeri N. Robins, Managing Director
Mr. Leon G. Nagler, Managing Director
Ms. Carol Willett, Research & Candidate Development - *Transportation*

Salary Minimum: $150,000

Functions: Generalist (All), Senior Mgmt.

Industries: Manufacturing, Computer Equip., Venture Cap., Mgmt. Consulting, E-commerce, IT Implementation, Supply Chain Mgmt., New Media, Communications, Telecoms, Digital, Software

Jim Nalepa & Associates

900 S Madison St Ste 1000
Hinsdale, IL 60521-4365
(630) 986-7000
Email: jim@jimnalepa.com
Web: www.jimnalepa.com

Summary: We have successfully delivered the key ingredient of executive success, leadership, to our clients. Seeing the search industry decimated with mergers, IPOs and false technical solutions and believing that the biggest firms in the search industry are now shareholder focused rather than client focused, our firm was founded to recapture a client centric vision.

Key Contact - Specialty:
Mr. Jim Nalepa, President

Salary Minimum: $125,000

Functions: Management, Senior Mgmt., Mfg., Materials, Sales & Mktg., HR Mgmt., Finance, CFOs, IT, Engineering

Industries: Generalist (All)

Thomas Nam Associates

16220 SW Whistling Swan Ln
Beaverton, OR 97007-7263
(503) 530-1514
Email: tkn@thomasnam.com
Web: www.thomasnam.com

Summary: Specializing in executive-level and professional recruitment.

Key Contact - Specialty:
Mr. Thomas Nam, Managing Director

Salary Minimum: $80,000

Functions: Senior Mgmt., Middle Mgmt., Sales & Mktg.

Industries: Generalist (All), Semiconductors, Wireless

National Recruiting Service†

PO Box 218
Dyer, IN 46311-0218
(219) 865-2373
Fax: (219) 865-2375
Email: stanhen@jorsm.com
Web: www.nationalrecruitingservice.com

Summary: We are exclusive search and professional recruiters for the steel, ferrous & nonferrous pipe and tubular products industries. Basic metals experienced candidates are also accepted. We specialize in operations management, engineering/technical management and sales management positions.

Key Contact - Specialty:
Mr. Stanley M. Hendricks, II, Owner - *Management, Metals, Sales, Technical*
Mrs. Anna Yurkovich, Administrative Assistant - *Metals*

Salary Minimum: $50,000

Functions: Management

Industries: Manufacturing, Metal Products, Misc. Mfg.

National Restaurant Search Inc†

555 Sun Valley Dr Ste J1
Roswell, GA 30076-5608
(770) 650-1800
Fax: (770) 650-1801
Email: john@restauranteadhunter.com
Web: www.restauranteadhunter.com

Summary: We specialize in corporate search exclusively in the restaurant/hospitality industry. Assignments include president, CEO, COO, finance, franchising, real estate & construction, marketing, HR and operations at the executive-level. Our executives have restaurant/hotel operations experience.

Key Contact - Specialty:
Mr. John W. Chitvanni, President
Mr. Ron Stockman, Vice President - *CEOs, Food & beverage, General contractors, Hospitality, Hotels*
Mr. Steve Samata, Vice President - *Culinary, Food & beverage, Healthcare, Hospitality, Hotels*

Salary Minimum: $50,000

Functions: Generalist (All), Board Members, Senior Mgmt.

Industries: Hospitality, Hotels, Resorts, Clubs, Restaurants, Quick Service Restaurants, Full Service Restaurants, Inst./Industrial Food Svc.

Branches:
143 First St Ste 209
Batavia, IL 60510-3102
(630) 482-2900
Fax: (630) 482-2922
Email: ron@restauranteadhunter.com
Key Contact - Specialty:
Mr. Ronald F. Stockman, Vice President
Mr. Dennis Minchella, Division Vice President

Nativesun Inc

4110 N Scottsdale Rd Ste 115
Scottsdale, AZ 85251-3939
(602) 697-5620
Email: trudyware@indiannativesun.com
Web: www.indiannativesun.com

Summary: We are a Native American executive search firm that promotes visibility and employment of American Indian and other professionals with both academic degrees and technical certifications in mid to upper level positions in management and technology for labor hour contracts and permanent hire in business and government.

Key Contact - Specialty:
Ms. Trudy Jo Ware, President & Chief Executive Officer

Functions: Minorities/Diversity

Industries: Energy, Utilities, Computer Equip., Electronic, Elec. Components, Semiconductors, IT Implementation, Engineering Svcs., Government, Defense, Acrospace, Software

NDH Search

444 N Larchmont Blvd Ste 108
Los Angeles, CA 90004-3030
(323) 464-6494
Fax: (323) 464-8494
Email: info@ndhsearch.com
Web: www.ndhsearch.com

Summary: Architectural search and placement firm.

Key Contact - Specialty:
Ms. Nancy Horne, President - *Interior design*

Functions: Architects

Industries: Generalist (All)

The Neil Michael Group Inc

9 Park Pl
Great Neck, NY 11021-5030
(516) 482-8810
Fax: (516) 482-3343
Email: neil@nmgsearch.com
Web: www.nmgsearch.com

Summary: Senior executive retained search firm exclusively to the life sciences, specifically in biotechnology and pharmaceuticals. Extensive focus on emerging growth companies.

Key Contact - Specialty:
Dr. Neil M. Solomon, President - *Biopharmaceutical, Biotechnology, Boards of Directors, CEOs, Pharmaceutical*

Functions: Generalist (All), Management

Industries: Drugs Mfg., Medical Devices, Biotech/Life Sciences, Healthcare

The Nema Group†

15537 Sullivan Ridge Dr
Charlotte, NC 28277-2352
(704) 542-8007
Email: info@nemagroup.com
Web: www.nemagroup.com

Summary: We interact globally with a wide variety of industries as a premier alliance partner.

We specialize in a variety of in-depth and proven consulting capabilities, offering international candidate search expertise to start ups, emerging companies, and high-growth middle-market companies, both private and publicly traded.

Key Contact - Specialty:
Mr. Nils DePui Martinsen, President & Chief Executive Officer - *Biopharmaceutical, Biotechnology, Boards of Directors, Change management, Executives*
Ms. Michelle Robinson, Chairperson - *Boards of Directors, Executives*

Salary Minimum: $100,000

Functions: Management, Senior Mgmt., Mfg., Sales & Mktg., Mktg. Mgmt., Sales Mgmt., HR Mgmt., CFOs, M&A, R&D

Industries: Energy, Utilities, Oil & Gas, Manufacturing, Soap, Perf., Cosmtcs., Drugs Mfg., Medical Devices, Consumer Goods, Services, Pharm Svcs., Engineering Svcs., Biotech/Life Sciences

New Directions Search Inc

PO Box 88
1127 Wheaton Oaks Ct
Wheaton, IL 60189-0088
(630) 462-1840
Fax: (630) 462-1862
Email: dalefrank@ndsearch.com
Web: www.ndsearch.com

Summary: Our firm has expertise in senior leadership searches, primarily large and small, public and private manufacturing firms. Our experience in retained search has been marked by long term client relationships based on integrity, trust, hard work and loyalty. Disciplines include: corporate leadership, manufacturing operations, supply chain, purchasing, HR, engineering, sales, marketing, finance and IT.

Key Contact - Specialty:
Mr. Dale A. Frank, President
Mr. John M. Morton, Executive Vice President
Mr. Richard L. Santarelli, Senior Vice President
Mr. Douglas W. Scott, Senior Vice President
Mr. James Owens, Vice President
Mr. Nate Frank, Vice President
Mr. Jeff Crowley, Vice President
Mr. Timothy Sezonov, Vice President

Salary Minimum: $100,000

Functions: Senior Mgmt., Middle Mgmt.

Industries: Manufacturing

New World Healthcare Solutions Inc

13 N Liberty Dr Ste 1
Stony Point, NY 10980-1501
(845) 429-8888
Fax: (845) 429-2958
Email: info@newworldhealthcare.com
Web: www.newworldhealthcare.com

Summary: We specialize in healthcare and provide a unique hiring process, which will ensure the hiring of the right candidate. Our organization actively participates in the evaluation process and truly understands the healthcare industry. We are offering new additional services of resume preparation and career coaching.

Key Contact - Specialty:
Mr. Ira E. Shapiro, Co-Founder & Chief Executive Officer - *Healthcare*
Mr. Matthew B. Smith, Executive Vice President & COO
Mr. Charles C. Wilhelm, Co-Founder & Board Member
Mr. George K. Anderson, Board Member
Mr. James B. Couch, Chief Medical Officer

Ms. Ellen Oldfield, Vice President, Operations
Ms. Crystal Martinez, Managing Director
Ms. Keri A. Wolfe, Operations Manager
Ms. Amy S. Nunn, Research Analyst - *Hospitality*

Salary Minimum: $100,000

Functions: Healthcare, Customer Svc.

Industries: Generalist (All), Insurance, Healthcare

Newlin Associates

10 Elm Ave
Larkspur, CA 94939-2059
(415) 381-1545
Email: resumes@newlinassociates.com
Web: www.newlinassociates.com

Summary: We are a national retained search firm
specializing in the wine, hospitality, and CPG
food/beverage industries.

Key Contact - Specialty:
Mr. David Newlin, Chief Executive Officer

Salary Minimum: $100,000

Functions: Senior Mgmt., Sales & Mktg., Mktg.
Mgmt., Sales Mgmt., HR Mgmt., Finance,
CFOs

Industries: Food, Bev., Tobacco

Newman Tucker Group, Inc.

(formerly known as Medley Newman Tucker
Group)
2800 N Central Ave Ste 1740
Phoenix, AZ 85004-1048
(602) 595-8600
Email: management@newmantuckergroup.com
Web: www.newmantuckergroup.com

Summary: We are one of the premier West Coast
based executive search firms. The principal
partners have extensive experience in diversity,
executive search and recruitment, working with
senior-level management, elected officials and
community groups.

Key Contact - Specialty:
Mr. Charles Newman, President
Mr. Willie Tucker, Vice President
Ms. Vivian W. Martell, Chief Operating Officier -
*Aerospace, Banking (Commercial), Business
development, C-level, Defense*

Salary Minimum: $80,000

Functions: Generalist (All)

Industries: Energy, Utilities, Manufacturing,
Finance, Services, Media, Communications,
Aerospace, Insurance, Software, Biotech/Life
Sciences

Newport O'Connor

444 Madison Ave Ste 3202
New York, NY 10022-6923
(212) 754-6860
Email: info@newport-oconnor.com
Web: www.newport-oconnor.com

Summary: Boutique executive search and HR
consulting firm that specializes in senior level
search and services corporations and professional
service firms (specifically strategic, operational
and IT management consultancies) in a number of
sectors, including: financial services,
energy/utilities, pharmaceutical/healthcare sectors,
etc.

Key Contact - Specialty:
Ms. Maria Newport, President
Ms. Lorrie Hamlin, Executive Search Consultant

Functions: Mgmt. Consultants

Industries: Energy, Utilities, Banking, Pharm
Svcs., Mgmt. Consulting, HR Services,
Aerospace

Next Level Executive Search

(a division of Next Level Sports Inc)
24 Cathedral Pl Ste 500
Saint Augustine, FL 32084-4459
(904) 810-5177
Fax: (904) 810-6855
Email: info@nextlevelexecutive.com
Web: www.nextlevelexecutive.com

Summary: We place mid-to-senior level
executives in the sports and leisure-time industry.
Our focus is on identifying and recruiting
candidates with experience in senior management,
sales and marketing, finance, and law. Our clients
are companies and organizations who market and
sell consumer products or hospitality services in
the sports industry.

Key Contact - Specialty:
Mr. Michael L. Garnes, President - *Legal
(Attorneys), Manufacturing, Marketing, Sales,
Sports*

Salary Minimum: $100,000

Functions: Management, Senior Mgmt., Mfg.,
Sales & Mktg., Mktg. Mgmt., Sales Mgmt.,
Customer Svc., HR Mgmt., Finance, Attorneys

Industries: Consumer Goods, Higher Ed.,
Hospitality, Hotels, Resorts, Clubs,
Entertainment, Recreation, Sports, Travel

Nicholaou & Company

56 Pier Dr
Westmont, IL 60559-3269
(630) 960-2382

Summary: Our firm provides personalized search
service, mid to upper-management.

Key Contact - Specialty:
Ms. Jean Nicholaou, Recruiter

Salary Minimum: $75,000

Functions: Generalist (All), Management, Mfg.,
Sales & Mktg.

Industries: Generalist (All), Manufacturing

Nichols & Company

PO Box 3561
Boulder, CO 80307-3561
(303) 494-3383
Email: chnicholsii@comcast.net
Web: www.imarcllc.com

Summary: We are a retained executive search
firm working with international network of clients
in industrial and technological specialties.
Recruiting senior management and board
members.

Key Contact - Specialty:
Mr. Charles H. Nichols, President

Salary Minimum: $90,000

Functions: Management, Senior Mgmt., Middle
Mgmt.

Industries: Generalist (All)

P J Nicholson & Associates[†]

1301 W 22nd St Ste 606
Oak Brook, IL 60523-2076
(630) 574-0555
Fax: (630) 574-0559
Email: pjnassc@aol.com

Summary: We are a boutique firm that specializes
in financial, operations and general management.
Our firm has represented automotive, chemical,
consumer, financial services and technology
companies.

Key Contact - Specialty:
Mr. Philip J. Nicholson, Principal - *Finance,
General management, Operations*

Salary Minimum: $80,000

Functions: Generalist (All), Senior Mgmt.,
Product Dev., Mktg. Mgmt., CFOs, M&A,
Minorities/Diversity

Industries: Generalist (All), Chemicals, Medical
Devices, Metal Products, Misc. Mfg.

Nolan Associates Inc

1510-320 Bay St
Toronto, ON M5H 4A6
Canada
(416) 868-9991
Email: resumes@nolanassociates.ca
Web: www.nolanassociates.ca

Summary: We are a seven person executive
search firm focusing primarily on financial
services.

Key Contact - Specialty:
D.R. Nolan

Salary Minimum: $80,000

Functions: Finance

Industries: Finance

W D Nolte & Company

6 Middlesex Rd
Darien, CT 06820-3709
(203) 323-5858
(800) 785-5858
Fax: (203) 323-0164
Email: wdn.global@att.net

Summary: Our company has many years as a
management consultant serving public and private
businesses. Recent focus has been securities
industry and middle market businesses.

Key Contact - Specialty:
Mr. William D. Nolte, Jr., Principal

Salary Minimum: $100,000

Functions: Generalist (All), Management, Mfg.,
Materials, Sales & Mktg., CFOs, MIS Mgmt.

Industries: Manufacturing, Finance, Invest.
Banking, Brokers, Venture Cap., Misc.
Financial, Services, Accounting, Mgmt.
Consulting, Telecoms, Software

Nomadic Consulting Inc

200 E Ohio St Ste 300
Chicago, IL 60611-7270
(312) 664-1732
Fax: (312) 664-1738
Email: info@nomadicconsulting.com
Web: www.nomadicconsulting.com

Summary: We provide workforce diversity
solutions, including retained executive search and
related talent sourcing and marketing services. Our
purpose is to help each client attract and develop
leadership that reflects its business commitments,
clients and communities.

Key Contact - Specialty:
Ms. Karen Chung, Managing Director
Mr. John Blanchet-Ruth, Vice President, Bus.
Dev. and Sales - *Administration, Information
Systems, Operations, Sales*
Ms. Peggy Jackson-Turner, Practice Leader,
Retained Exec Search - *Diversity, General
management, Human resources, Middle
management, Senior management*
Ms. Sharon Carney, Practice Leader, Cont Talent
Sourcing - *CIOs, Clinical, Hospital, Systems,
Technical (Management)*

Salary Minimum: $100,000

† occasional contingency assignment

Functions: Generalist (All), Mfg., Healthcare, Sales & Mktg., HR Mgmt., Finance, IT, Engineering, Minorities/Diversity, Legal

Industries: Generalist (All)

Nordeman Grimm Inc

65 E 55th St Fl 33
New York, NY 10022-3314
(212) 935-1000
Fax: (212) 980-1443
Email: resume@nordemangrimm.com
Web: www.nordemangrimm.com

Summary: We specialize in recruiting exceptional senior executives. We are known for quality, team work and long-term relationships.

Key Contact - Specialty:
Mr. Jacques C. Nordeman, Chairman - *E-business, Finance*

Salary Minimum: $150,000

Functions: Generalist (All), Senior Mgmt.

Industries: Generalist (All), Manufacturing, Non-profits, Healthcare

Norman Broadbent International Inc

11555 Heron Bay Blvd
Coral Springs, FL 33076-3360
(954) 603-0419
Email: florida@normabroadbent.com
Web: www.normanbroadbent.com

Summary: We serve clients primarily in the manufacturing, communications, technology, hospitality and leisure sectors, helping them to build outstanding organizations through executive search.

Key Contact - Specialty:
Mr. Charles J. Chalk, Chief Executive Officer
Mr. David W. Gallagher, President
Mr. Steven D. Godwin, Senior Vice President

Salary Minimum: $150,000

Functions: Board Members, Senior Mgmt., Sales & Mktg., Finance, IT, DB Admin., Mgmt. Consultants

Industries: Construction, Manufacturing, Finance, Non-profits, Legal, Accounting, Media, Communications, Government, Biotech/Life Sciences

Nosal Partners LLC

100 1st St Ste 2200
San Francisco, CA 94105-2653
(415) 369-2200
Fax: (415) 369-2202
Email: info@nosalpartners.com
Web: www.nosalpartners.com

Summary: Nosal Partners LLC is the first and only executive leadership solutions™ firm. Headquartered in San Francisco and with capabilities around the globe, the company delivers flexible, customized executive search, executive development and interim executive leadership solutions to a worldwide clientele.

Key Contact - Specialty:
Mr. David Nosal, Chief Executive Officer

Salary Minimum: $150,000

Functions: Generalist (All)

Industries: Generalist (All)

NPF Associates Ltd Inc[†]

2417 N University Dr
Coral Springs, FL 33065-5123
(954) 753-8560
Fax: (954) 753-8611
Email: npfassociates@aol.com

Summary: Executive search firm specializing in human recources, with a client base of Fortune 500 companies.

Key Contact - Specialty:
Mr. Nick P. Fischler, President - *Human resources*

Salary Minimum: $60,000

Functions: HR Mgmt.

Industries: Manufacturing, Retail, Finance, Services, Hospitality, Communications, Aerospace, Insurance

Branches:
888 8th Ave Apt 2U
New York, NY 10019-5706
(212) 757-5126
Fax: (212) 757-5127
Email: bdfischler@aol.com
Key Contact - Specialty:
Mr. Brian Fischler, Vice President - *Human resources*

NR Search Inc[†]

505 Sheridan Rd Apt 2W
Evanston, IL 60202-4710
(847) 475-3100
Fax: (847) 475-3131
Email: nrsearch@sbcglobal.net
Web: www.nrsearch.com

Summary: We've taken the retail search process to a new level from merchandise planning, allocation and replenishment; to buying, design and product development. Our clients are sent the right candidates the first time and not a bundle of resumes. Our executive search and recruitment services allow you to meet tomorrow's challenges today.

Key Contact - Specialty:
Ms. Nancy Shikoff, President

Salary Minimum: $70,000

Functions: Generalist (All), Senior Mgmt., Product Dev., Purchasing, Distribution, Mktg. Mgmt., CFOs

Industries: Retail, Non-profits

Nucci Consulting Group

324 Augusta Dr
Blue Bell, PA 19422-1275
(610) 272-7773
Fax: (610) 278-0488
Email: evnucci@nucciconsultinggroup.com
Web: www.nucciconsultinggroup.com

Summary: We are a retained consulting firm that specializes in the asset management industry with expertise in lift-outs, mergers and the placement of investment management professionals. We only work on a retained basis. Our clients are the most prestigious money management firms in the world.

Key Contact - Specialty:
Ms. Ev Nucci, Chairman & Chief Executive Officer

Salary Minimum: $100,000

Functions: Management, Senior Mgmt., Product Dev., Specialized Svcs.

Industries: Finance, Mutual/Hedge Funds, Misc. Financial

O'Brien Consulting Services

171 Swanton St Unit 72
Winchester, MA 01890-1965
(781) 721-4404
Fax: (781) 721-5890
Email: jim@ocs-executivesearch.com
Web: www.ocs-executivesearch.com

Summary: Our previous line management experience in both technology and manufacturing/distribution industries combined with earlier partner level positions in two major search firms makes us the top choice for clients' executive recruiting needs. We service the senior level retained executive search industry only.

Key Contact - Specialty:
Mr. James J. O'Brien, Jr., President - *Boards of Directors, C-level, CEOs, Presidents, Senior management*

Salary Minimum: $100,000

Functions: Generalist (All), Board Members, Senior Mgmt.

Industries: Generalist (All), Manufacturing, Paper, Medical Devices, Computer Equip., Misc. Mfg., Semiconductors, Finance, Venture Cap., Services, Communications, Digital, Wireless, Network Infrastructure, Software

O'Connor Advisors LLC[†]

401 N Michigan Ave Ste 2910 c/o Aquent
Chicago, IL 60611-5517
(312) 334-6956
Fax: (312) 913-9291
Email: fred@oconnoradvisors.com
Web: www.oconnoradvisors.com

Summary: Our firm is a boutique executive search firm working hand-in-hand with clients to solve key business challenges. We concentrate on leadership positions, notably those in senior management, technology, finance, and human resources. We are differentiated by our highly personalized service, thorough methodology and client focus.

Key Contact - Specialty:
Mr. Fred O'Connor, Founder & Managing Director

Salary Minimum: $50,000

Functions: Generalist (All)

Industries: Generalist (All), Energy, Utilities, Finance, Venture Cap., Mutual/Hedge Funds, Services, Mgmt. Consulting, Insurance

O'Connor, O'Connor, Lordi Ltd

707 Grant St Ste 2727
Pittsburgh, PA 15219-1945
(412) 261-4020
Fax: (412) 261-4480
Email: ool@oolltd.com
Web: www.oolltd.com

Summary: Our firm is recognized as a leader in Operations, Sales/Marketing, Finance and General Management search. We actively pursue emerging leaders and executives in consumer, industrial and service sectors. Our clients range from Fortune 100 to start-up and venture capital.

Key Contact - Specialty:
Mr. Thomas F. O'Connor, President
Mr. Richard E. Brown, Executive Vice President & COO
Mr. Timothy J. Tetrick, Vice President, Recruit & Strategic Sltn

Salary Minimum: $125,000

Functions: Generalist (All), Mfg.

Industries: Construction, Manufacturing, Food, Bev., Tobacco, Chemicals, Medical Devices,

Plastics, Rubber, Paints, Petro. Products, Metal Products, Consumer Elect., Consumer Goods, Finance, Venture Cap., Services, Communications, Biotech/Life Sciences

O'Keefe & Associates Inc

PO Box 1092
Southport, CT 06890-2092
(203) 254-2544
Fax: (203) 254-2126
Email: okeefeinc@okeefeinc.com
Web: www.okeefeinc.com

Summary: We are a retainer-based firm focused on recruiting outstanding talent for consumer products, foodservice, restaurants, OTC drug & pharmaceuticals, medical devices, IT, telecom and management consulting organizations across a variety of functions. We are unique in that our principals take an active role in every search, we build long-term client relationships, and we've been able to maintain continuity within our recruiting staff.

Key Contact - Specialty:
Mr. John O'Keefe, Chairman & Chief Executive Officer
Ms. Kathy O'Keefe, Principal - *Research*
Mr. Bill Tohill, Vice President - *Finance, Restaurants*
Mr. Tom Wilzinski, Vice President - *Manufacturing, Operations*
Mr. William Sawyer, Director
Mr. David Woodward, Vice President - *Direct marketing*
Ms. Susan Moore, Associate

Salary Minimum: $100,000

Functions: Generalist (All), Management, Mfg., Materials, Sales & Mktg., HR Mgmt., Finance, IT

Industries: Generalist (All), Food, Bev., Tobacco, Soap, Perf., Cosmtcs., Drugs Mfg., Medical Devices, Mgmt. Consulting, Restaurants, Quick Service Restaurants, Publishing, Wireless, HR SW

Branches:
503 Begonia Ave
Corona Del Mar, CA 92625-2012
(949) 723-0596
Email: jokeefe@okeefeinc.com
Key Contact - Specialty:
Mr. Robert Wallace, Principal

O'Shea, Divine & Company Inc

(a member of EMA Partners International)
363 San Miguel Dr Ste 200
Newport Beach, CA 92660-7891
(949) 720-9070
Fax: (949) 720-9628
Email: info@divinesearch.com
Web: www.divinesearch.com

Summary: We are a generalist firm recruiting senior-level management, primarily manufacturing, distribution, healthcare, financial services, telecom and not-for-profit. Partners in the major industrial nations.

Key Contact - Specialty:
Mr. Robert S. Divine
Mr. John C. Wallin - *Education, High technology, Information Technology, Manufacturing, Non-profit*
Mr. Francis J. Madden - *Banking, Brokerage, Finance, Investment management, Securities*
Ms. Julie W. Bammer - *Administration, Research*

Salary Minimum: $100,000

Functions: Generalist (All)

Industries: Generalist (All)

Dennis P O'Toole & Associates Inc

102 Laurel Ave
Larchmont, NY 10538-2317
(914) 833-3712
Email: dpotooleassoc@aol.com

Summary: We are a select executive search firm known for personalized service and in-depth recruitment of senior management. Also we provide hard-to-find specialists for resort, hotel, club and entertainment industries.

Key Contact - Specialty:
Mr. Dennis P. O'Toole, President - *Entertainment, Hospitality*

Salary Minimum: $90,000

Functions: Generalist (All), Senior Mgmt., Middle Mgmt., Purchasing, Mktg. Mgmt., Sales Mgmt., HR Mgmt., CFOs

Industries: Generalist (All), Hospitality, Hotels, Resorts, Clubs, Restaurants, Entertainment, Recreation

Oak Hill Consultants LLC

701 S Bedford Rd
Bedford Corners, NY 10549-4851
(914) 234-3802
(914) 234-3806
Fax: (914) 234-9416
Email: info@oakhillconsultants.com
Web: www.oakhillconsultants.com

Summary: Retainer firm focused on top level management searches for industrial/manufacturing companies ranging in size from start up to Fortune 500.

Key Contact - Specialty:
Mr. Robert A. Proctor, III, Founder - *Industrial, Manufacturing*
Ms. Darcy Ytterdahl, Consultant - *Industrial, Manufacturing*
Ms. Gaele McCully, Consultant - *Industrial, Manufacturing*

Salary Minimum: $300,000

Functions: Board Members, Senior Mgmt., Materials, HR Mgmt., CFOs

Industries: Generalist (All), Energy, Utilities, Construction, Manufacturing

Oak Technology Partners LLC

900 Larkspur Landing Cir Ste 165
Larkspur, CA 94939-1760
(415) 464-4555
Fax: (415) 464-4550
Email: mraggio@oakllc.com
Web: www.oakllc.com

Summary: We are a retained executive search firm specializing in the recruitment of key management talent in the technology industry. Areas of focus include general management, engineering and sales & marketing in the software industry.

Key Contact - Specialty:
Mr. Matthew G. Raggio, Partner - *Computers (Software)*
Mr. E. Scott Swimley, Partner

Salary Minimum: $150,000

Functions: Senior Mgmt., Mktg. Mgmt., Sales Mgmt.

Industries: Venture Cap., Software

OakBridge Inc

910 16th St Ste 1160
Denver, CO 80202-2921
(303) 670-0788
Fax: (303) 670-0769
Email: info@oakbridge-global.com
Web: www.oakbridge-global.com

Summary: We are an executive search firm specializing in management search in the healthcare, IT, legal and industrial industries. We focus on helping your company build its international operations through the identification and recruitment of experienced global business leaders.

Key Contact - Specialty:
Ms. Charlotte Kennedy-Takahashi, Chairman
Mr. Andy Levine, Managing Partner

Salary Minimum: $100,000

Functions: Generalist (All)

Industries: Manufacturing, Drugs Mfg., Medical Devices, Pharm Svcs., Legal, Communications, Telecoms, Software, Biotech/Life Sciences, Healthcare

Branches:
425 Market St Ste 2200
San Francisco, CA 94105-2434
(415) 753-0788
Email: info@oakbridge-global.com
Key Contact - Specialty:
Ms. Laurie Flippen, Recruiter

60 State St Ste 700
Boston, MA 02109-1894
(617) 367-0788
Email: info@oakbridge-global.com
Key Contact - Specialty:
Mr. Grant Underhill, Recruiter

OakLeaf Search Partners LLC

1880 Westview Rd Ste 210
Charlottesville, VA 22903-1649
(434) 977-0061
Email: efowler@oakleafsearch.com
Web: www.oakleafsearch.com

Summary: OakLeaf is a boutique firm specializing in financial services with particular expertise in the investment management industry. We have worked with traditional firms, hedge funds, endowments and foundations and recruit at all levels, from: analyst to portfolio manager; marketing associate to head of institutional sales; and general counsel to COO.

Key Contact - Specialty:
Mr. Edward Fowler, Managing Director
Ms. Wendy Carlton, Director, Research

Salary Minimum: $150,000

Functions: Management, Senior Mgmt., Sales & Mktg., Cash Mgmt.

Industries: Finance, Invest. Banking, Venture Cap., Mutual/Hedge Funds, Misc. Financial

Ober & Company

4549 Alla Rd Apt 6
Marina Del Rey, CA 90292-6338
(310) 207-1127

Summary: Broad based executive search practice with expertise in high technology, financial services, aerospace, IT, consumer products, manufacturing, healthcare and consulting.

Key Contact - Specialty:
Ms. Lynn W. Ober, President

Salary Minimum: $100,000

Functions: Generalist (All), Management, Mfg., Healthcare, Sales & Mktg., HR Mgmt., Finance, IT

Industries: Generalist (All), Manufacturing, Finance, Services, Software, Biotech/Life Sciences, Healthcare

Oberlander & Co Inc
PO Box 232
Barnard, VT 05031-0232
(802) 234-6900
Fax: (802) 234-6903
Email: hiosearch@aol.com

Summary: Specialize in providing professional, confidential guidance in management selection.

Key Contact - Specialty:
Mr. Howard I. Oberlander, President

Salary Minimum: $100,000

Functions: Generalist (All)

Industries: Generalist (All)

The Ogdon Partnership
(a division of The Ogdon Group Inc)
375 Park Ave Ste 2409
New York, NY 10152-2499
(212) 308-1600
Fax: (212) 755-3819
Email: info@ogdon.com
Web: www.ogdon.com

Summary: Firm provides general recruiting. We specialize in advertising, PR, publishing, broadcast, new media, editorial, direct response, partner-to-partner legal, general counsel, compliance, financial services, club management, top management and board positions for venture-owned companies. Full recruiting support is also offered to family owned businesses. We separately offer training in presentation skills to C-level executives.

Key Contact - Specialty:
Mr. Thomas H. Ogdon - *C-level, Communications, Publishing, Venture capital*
Ms. Cathy N. Hughes - *Communications, Hospitality, Publishing*
Mr. Edward C. Mattes, Jr. - *Asset management, Compliance, General management, Legal, Publishing*
Ms. Kristin A. Ogdon - *Advertising, Compliance, Financial services, Publishing*
Mr. Kevin Daley

Salary Minimum: $100,000

Functions: Management, Board Members, Senior Mgmt., Sales Mgmt., HR Mgmt., CFOs, Attorneys

Industries: Generalist (All), Manufacturing, Finance, Venture Cap., Services, Legal, Hospitality, Entertainment, Media, Advertising, Publishing, Broadcast, Film, Communications

Olschwanger Partners LLC
7522 Campbell Rd Ste 113-196
Dallas, TX 75248-1726
(972) 931-9144
(214) 535-5721
Fax: (972) 931-9194
Email: pfo@osearch.org
Web: www.osearch.org

Summary: We offer a unique perspective and approach as an executive search and business consultant focusing exclusively within the money management industry.

Key Contact - Specialty:
Mr. Paul F. Olschwanger, Managing Director - *Investment management, Marketing, Sales*
Ms. Debra L. Olschwanger, Vice President - *Investment management, Research*

Functions: Generalist (All), Senior Mgmt., Admin. Svcs., Product Dev., Sales & Mktg., Sales Mgmt., CFOs, Cash Mgmt.

Industries: Finance, Mutual/Hedge Funds, Misc. Financial

Jeanne Omlor
60 W 14th St Apt 4B
New York, NY 10011-7500
(646) 641-4884
Fax: (646) 641-4884
Email: jomlette@yahoo.com

Summary: I specialize in recruiting in all areas of asset management, investment banking, corporate banking, finance. I also work as a consultant on site in other recruiting firms. Will locate and recruit the appropriate person quickly when others have failed. Open to short term assignments.

Key Contact - Specialty:
Ms. Jeanne Omlor, Consultant, Executive Recruiting

Salary Minimum: $150,000

Functions: Generalist (All), Management, Board Members, Senior Mgmt., Finance, Cash Mgmt., Mgmt. Consultants

Industries: Generalist (All), Agri., Forestry, Mining, Energy, Utilities, Oil & Gas, Construction, Manufacturing, Retail, Finance, Banking, Invest. Banking, Brokers, Venture Cap., Mutual/Hedge Funds, Misc. Financial

OnPoint Partners Inc
666 Old Country Rd Ste 207
Garden City, NY 11530-2013
(516) 470-0747
Fax: (516) 470-6030
Email: info@onpointpartners.com
Web: www.onpointpartners.com

Summary: Innovative, executive search practice organized around healthcare, multi-employer, Taft-Hartley and labor, financial services, and insurance disciplines.

Key Contact - Specialty:
Mr. Scott R. Stern, Chief Executive Officer
Mr. John R. Schoonmaker, President
Mrs. Tara J. Quinn, Managing Partner, Operations
Mrs. JoAnn Porcelli, Director, Finance
Mr. Matthew Heinze, Director, Research
Mr. Carmine Asparro, Partner

Salary Minimum: $75,000

Functions: Generalist (All)

Industries: Venture Cap., Misc. Financial, Services, Mgmt. Consulting, HR Services, Insurance, Software, Healthcare

Onstott
(a World Search Group company)
60 William St Ste 250
Wellesley Hills, MA 02481-3823
(781) 235-3050
Fax: (781) 235-8653
Email: info@onstott.com
Web: www.onstott.com

Summary: Retained search firm specializing in recruiting executives for most functional disciplines and industries. Concentration in high-technology, telecom, manufacturing, consumer goods, financial and other service businesses and growth industries.

Key Contact - Specialty:
Mr. Ben Beaver, Managing Director
Ms. Patricia Campbell, Managing Director
Mr. Joe Onstott, Managing Director

Salary Minimum: $150,000

Functions: Generalist (All)

Industries: Generalist (All)

Open Technologies
333 Washington Ave N Ste 300
Minneapolis, MN 55401-1353
(612) 386-0299
Email: isaac@opentechnologies.com
Web: www.opentechnologies.com

Summary: We help new and growing companies hire technology savvy senior business executives. We have an extensive national network of executive contacts in supply chain, outsourcing, eCommerce and business intelligence. Our principal writes a monthly column for the local newspaper on business/technology trends.

Key Contact - Specialty:
Mr. Isaac Cheifetz, President

Salary Minimum: $150,000

Functions: Management

Industries: Manufacturing, Banking, Mgmt. Consulting, E-commerce, IT Implementation, PSA/ASP, Software, ERP SW, Industry Specific SW, Marketing SW

Oppedisano & Company Inc
370 Lexington Ave Rm 1200
New York, NY 10017-6584
(212) 696-0144
Fax: (212) 686-3006
Email: eo@oppedisanoco.com
Web: www.oppedisanoco.com

Summary: Our firm provides executive search services exclusively to the investment management industry.

Key Contact - Specialty:
Mr. Edward Oppedisano, Chairman & Chief Executive Officer - *Investment management*

Functions: Senior Mgmt., Sales & Mktg., Cash Mgmt.

Industries: Mutual/Hedge Funds, Misc. Financial

Opportunity Resources Inc
196 E 75th St Apt 14H
New York, NY 10021-3265
(212) 744-4409
Fax: (212) 744-5004
Email: search@opportunityresources.net

Summary: We are a retained, full-service executive search firm. Our practice is devoted to not-for-profit cultural/educational/human service institutions. We take on a finite number of search assignments at one time to better serve each client. We are results oriented and tailor each search assignment to meet our clients' specific needs.

Key Contact - Specialty:
Ms. Freda Mindlin, President - *Non-profit*

Salary Minimum: $75,000

Functions: Senior Mgmt., Non-profits

Industries: Non-profits

Options Group[†]
121 E 18th St
New York, NY 10003-2148
(212) 982-0900
Fax: (212) 982-5577

Email: mkarp@optionsgroup.com
Web: www.optionsgroup.com

Summary: We are a global search and strategic consulting firm in the financial services industry, specializing in global markets, alternative investments/hedge funds, investment banking, private equity, asset management, quantitative research and technology.

Key Contact - Specialty:
Mr. Gene Shen, Vice Chairman - *Capital markets, Private equity*
Mr. Michael Karp, Chief Executive Officer - *Financial services*
Mr. Bob Reed, Co-Chief Operating Officer - *Financial services*

Salary Minimum: $100,000

Functions: Generalist (All), Cash Mgmt., MIS Mgmt., Systems Analysis, Systems Implem., Systems Support, Attorneys, Int'l.

Industries: Generalist (All), Oil & Gas, Finance, Banking, Invest. Banking, Brokers, Mutual/Hedge Funds, Misc. Financial, Legal, Mgmt. Consulting

Branches:
620 Newport Center Dr Ste 370
Newport Beach, CA 92660-8015
(949) 706-6500
Fax: (949) 706-6501
Key Contact - Specialty:
Mr. Ike Suri, Managing Partner - *Financial services*

Organization Consulting Ltd

5-156 Duncan Mill Rd
Toronto, ON M3B 3N2
Canada
(416) 385-9972
(416) 385-9975
Email: resumes@organizationconsulting.ca
Web: www.organizationconsulting.ca

Summary: We are a retainer based firm with extensive experience at the executive and board levels. Our mission is to be a distinguished executive search practice. Although we are small in size, we are large in scope. We are noted for service excellence and building long term relationships with our clients.

Key Contact - Specialty:
Mr. Robert F. Johnston, CMC, President
Mr. Terry MacGorman, Principal
Mr. Hugh Farrell, Principal
Ms. Cora Allegranza, Manager, Research

Salary Minimum: $150,000

Functions: Board Members, Senior Mgmt.

Industries: Generalist (All)

Organizational Capability Services LLC

PO Box 4560
Cary, NC 27519-4560
(919) 816-0999
Fax: (919) 854-0766
Email: jacksmith@ocsllc.com
Web: www.ocsllc.com

Summary: We provide a portfolio of executive, managerial professional, technical and scientific staffing solutions to both the public and private sector, utilizing truly innovative approaches and leveraging our extensive database and experienced research resources.

Key Contact - Specialty:
Mr. Jack Smith, CCP, Managing Partner - *C-level, Executives, Municipal, Senior management, Staffing*

Salary Minimum: $75,000

Functions: Management

Industries: Generalist (All), Energy, Utilities, Manufacturing, Textiles, Apparel, Lumber, Furniture, Electronic, Elec. Components, Semiconductors, Transportation, Government, Insurance

Branches:
PO Box 648
Naperville, IL 60566-0648
(630) 548-0999
Email: markbidlake@ocsllc.com
Key Contact - Specialty:
Mr. Mark Bidlake, Managing Partner

Orion Consulting Inc

115 US Highway 46 Bldg B
Mountain Lakes, NJ 07046-1672
(973) 402-8866
Fax: (973) 402-9258
Email: oci@orionconsultinginc.com
Web: www.orionconsultinginc.com

Summary: Management consulting firm providing retained executive search, organizational development, training, and general on- and off-site HR services.

Key Contact - Specialty:
Mr. James V. Dromsky, Chief Executive Officer
Mr. William Mann, Senior Vice President - *Consulting, Human resources*

Salary Minimum: $60,000

Functions: Generalist (All), Senior Mgmt.

Industries: Generalist (All), Chemicals, Drugs Mfg., Plastics, Rubber, Paints, Petro. Products, Invest. Banking, Accounting, Telecoms, Defense, Aerospace

Osprey Partners

868 Riverview Dr
Brielle, NJ 08730-1642
(732) 292-0982
Email: osprey57@optonline.net

Summary: Dedicated to search for senior leadership professionals and directors for engineering and technology based companies.

Key Contact - Specialty:
Mr. Michael A. Mulshine, President & Consultant

Salary Minimum: $90,000

Functions: Generalist (All), Management, Sales & Mktg., Finance, IT, R&D, Engineering, Specialized Svcs.

Industries: Generalist (All), Chemicals, Computer Equip., Finance, Communications, Aerospace, Software

Outside the Box, LLC†

20810 Pierceton Ct
Katy, TX 77494-7558
(281) 395-6530
(281) 381-1560
Email: bob@greattalent.net
Web: greattalent.net

Summary: Our team, with its years of human capital experience teamed with an uncanny ability will find the best fit for your company. We identify, attract and retain superior caliber motivated professionals that are capable of making a difference; talents that will help your company grow. Our client partners have come to expect fast turnaround, legendary client service and an unparalleled 18 month performance guarantee.

Key Contact - Specialty:
Miss Suzy Houston, Chief Talent Officer

Mr. Robert Rollins, Senior Vice President, Human Cap Devel
Mr. Albert Hurtado, Vice President, Talent Acquisition - *Boards of Directors, CEOs*

Salary Minimum: $50,000

Functions: Generalist (All), Management, Mfg., Sales & Mktg.

Industries: Generalist (All)

Ovca Associates Inc

16872 Baruna Ln
Huntington Beach, CA 92649-3020
(714) 840-6607
Fax: (714) 840-6672

Summary: We are a generalist practice delivering high value-added services to clients in a wide range of industries.

Key Contact - Specialty:
Mr. William J. Ovca, Jr., President

Salary Minimum: $90,000

Functions: Generalist (All)

Industries: Generalist (All)

Merle W Owens & Associates

401 Harwood Rd Ste B
Bedford, TX 76021-4183
(817) 281-3876
Fax: (817) 281-0475
Email: search@merle-owens.com
Web: www.merle-owens.com

Summary: We are a true generalist executive search firm with a large long-time client base. Our senior consultants have broad industry and search experience.

Key Contact - Specialty:
Mr. Jesse W. Owens, Principal - *Banking, Defense, Engineering, High technology, Manufacturing*
Mr. Merle Owens, Principal - *Energy, Finance, Healthcare, Insurance, Manufacturing*

Salary Minimum: $50,000

Functions: Generalist (All)

Industries: Generalist (All)

The Owens Group LLC

7720 Wisconsin Ave Ste 208
Bethesda, MD 20814-3577
(301) 229-2700
Email: tgo@owenssearch.com
Web: www.owenssearch.com

Summary: We are focused on mid to senior level postings in eCommerce, educational institutions, energy, engineering, finance, life sciences, non-profits, technology, real estate, construction and associations. We believe the most important decisions organizations make are about people.

Key Contact - Specialty:
Mr. Thomas Owens, President

Salary Minimum: $100,000

Functions: Senior Mgmt., Middle Mgmt., Sales & Mktg., Sales Mgmt., HR Mgmt., Finance, CFOs, MIS Mgmt., Engineering, Bldg. Contractors

Industries: Energy, Utilities, Construction, Finance, Services, Non-profits, E-commerce, Higher Ed., Media, Communications, Real Estate, Property/Facility Mgmt., Biotech/Life Sciences, Healthcare

LaMonte Owens Inc
PO Box 27742
Philadelphia, PA 19118-0742
(215) 836-2700
Fax: (215) 836-4167
Email: lowens@voicenet.com
Web: www.lo-diversityrecruiting.com

Summary: Our firm is specialized in Diversity Recruiting of professional, managerial and executive placement nationally.

Key Contact - Specialty:
Mr. LaMonte Owens, President

Salary Minimum: $65,000

Functions: Generalist (All)

Industries: Generalist (All), Drugs Mfg., Finance, HR Services, Software

Oxenham Consultants Inc
1104-1200 Bay St
Toronto, ON M5R 2A5
Canada
(416) 967-3932
(877) 586-4918
Fax: (416) 967-3931
Email: roger@oxenham.com
Web: www.oxenham.com

Summary: We are a full-service, retainer-based executive search firm focused on middle to senior management level recruitment. Our recruiters are generalists with broad industry sector knowledge, successfully managing senior search assignments throughout our market.

Key Contact - Specialty:
Mr. Roger Oxenham, Managing Director - *C-level, Executives, Marketing, Operations, Sales*
Ms. Leanna Macdonnell, Director, Planning - *Energy, Government, Logistics, Non-profit, Regulatory*
Mr. Paul Bruner, Director - *Communications, Finance, Hospitality, Human resources, Real estate*

Salary Minimum: $80,000

Functions: Generalist (All)

Industries: Generalist (All), Energy, Utilities, Manufacturing, Finance, Services, Hospitality, Media, Communications, Government, Real Estate

Oxford Global Resources Inc
100 Cummings Ctr Ste 206L
Beverly, MA 01915-6104
(978) 236-1182
(800) 426-9196
Fax: (978) 236-1077
Email: custserv@oxfordcorp.com
Web: www.oxfordcorp.com

Summary: Our firm is a talent-driven consulting firm providing individual consultants, project teams, and strategic outsourcing services in information technology and software, hardware, mechanical, electrical, validation, and telecommunications engineering. We serve our clients through an integrated network of offices throughout the U.S. and Europe.

Key Contact - Specialty:
Mr. Michael McGowan, President & Chief Operating Officer
Mr. Scott Beyer, Vice President, Marketing
Mr. Ed Kelly, Chief Financial Officer
Mr. James Jandl, Vice President, Human Resources
Ms. Lina Gallotto, Consultant, Information Technology

Mr. Marc Mirabella, Consultant, Software/Hardware
Mr. Jeff Perilli, Consultant, Telecommunication

Functions: Generalist (All), IT, Engineering

Industries: Energy, Utilities, Manufacturing, Drugs Mfg., Medical Devices, Computer Equip., Electronic, Elec. Components, IT Implementation, Telecoms, Aerospace, Software

Branches:
2105 S Bascom Ave Ste 255
Campbell, CA 95008-3293
(408) 369-8054
Email: mail_campbell@oxfordcorp.com
Key Contact - Specialty:
Mr. Adam Smith

P R Management Consultants Inc†
601 Ewing St
Princeton, NJ 08540-2757
(609) 921-6565
Email: findem6565@aol.com

Summary: Specialists in targeted executive search for: plastics, biomedical, chemical, paper and all related industries. Typical recent searches: division president, CFO, director/VP, R&D, VP marketing, European country managers and many others from plant management to engineering, environmental and clinical and regulatory management.

Key Contact - Specialty:
Mr. Jerrold Koenig, President

Salary Minimum: $85,000

Functions: Generalist (All)

Industries: Paper, Chemicals, Soap, Perf., Cosmtcs., Drugs Mfg., Medical Devices, Plastics, Rubber, Misc. Mfg.

P•A•R• Associates Inc
23 W Bay Rd
Osterville, MA 02655-2430
(508) 420-2372
(617) 680-6162
Fax: (508) 420-9268
Email: peter@parassoc.com
Web: www.parassoc.com

Summary: We provide general business search practice. We place heavy emphasis on most senior corporate positions, in particular pre-IPO healthcare related companies, telemedicine, medical device equipment and biotechnology.

Key Contact - Specialty:
Mr. Peter A. Rabinowitz, President - *Healthcare, Operations, Technology*

Salary Minimum: $175,000

Functions: Management, Senior Mgmt., Healthcare, Physicians, Sales & Mktg., Mktg. Mgmt., Finance, CFOs

Industries: Generalist (All), Drugs Mfg., Medical Devices, Venture Cap., Services, Non-profits, Pharm Svcs., Mgmt. Consulting, Insurance, Biotech/Life Sciences, Healthcare

Pacific Advisory Service†
1111 N Plaza Dr Ste 690
Schaumburg, IL 60173-4999
(847) 995-1705
Fax: (847) 995-1710
Email: pasinc@paschgo.com
Web: www.paschgo.com

Summary: Specializing in the recruitment and placement of bilingual (Japanese/English) professionals for US multinational corporations.

Key Contact - Specialty:
Mr. Mitsukuni Baba, President

Salary Minimum: $20,000

Functions: Generalist (All), Management, Senior Mgmt., Middle Mgmt., Product Dev., Production, Plant Mgmt., Purchasing, Sales Mgmt.

Industries: Generalist (All), Construction, Manufacturing, Medical Devices, Plastics, Rubber, Machine, Appliance, Motor Vehicles, Test, Measure Equip., Misc. Mfg., Electronic, Elec. Components, Robotics, Transportation, Finance, Accounting, Healthcare

The Pacific Firm†
2607 7th St Ste G
Berkeley, CA 94710-2571
(510) 647-1000
Fax: (510) 647-1010
Email: sblair@pacfirm.com
Web: www.pacfirm.com

Summary: We specialize in identifying and attracting senior-level executives for emerging companies.

Key Contact - Specialty:
Ms. Stacie Blair, Chief Executive Officer

Salary Minimum: $60,000

Functions: Management, Mfg., Materials, Healthcare, Sales & Mktg., HR Mgmt., Finance, MIS Mgmt.

Industries: Generalist (All)

Branches:
15350 W National Ave Ste 201
New Berlin, WI 53151-5158
(262) 796-1600
Fax: (262) 521-2747
Email: debbie@pacfirm.com
Key Contact - Specialty:
Ms. Debbie Gale, Managing Director

Pacific First Systems†
161 Bay St
B C E Place Floor 27
Toronto, ON M5J 2S1
Canada
(416) 350-2050
Fax: (416) 572-2201
Email: mail@pacificfirst.com
Web: www.pacificfirst.com

Summary: We recruit and place IT consultants.

Key Contact - Specialty:
Mr. Roger Rajkumar, President & Chief Executive Officer
Mr. John Thompson, Director, Recruiting Services
Ms. Mary Dray, Manager, Recruitment Services

Salary Minimum: $50,000

Functions: Management, IT, MIS Mgmt., Systems Dev.

Industries: Generalist (All), Paper, Chemicals, Computer Equip., Banking, Invest. Banking, Brokers, Accounting, Mgmt. Consulting, HR Services, IT Implementation, Telecoms, Accounting SW, Database SW, Development SW, System SW

Page-Wheatcroft & Company Ltd
14131 Midway Rd Ste 680
Addison, TX 75001-3640
(214) 696-4333
Fax: (214) 696-9595
Email: spage@p-wco.com
Web: www.p-wco.com

Summary: We do senior level executive search. We focus on the identification of CEOs and the development of leadership teams for professional services and technology companies. Our focus includes general management consulting & law firms, strategy & technology consulting firms and technology driven Global 2000 companies. Additionally we recruit CEOs and leadership teams for VC and private equity portfolio companies.

Key Contact - Specialty:
Mr. Stephen J.L. Page, Chairman & Chief Executive Officer
Mr. Carl L. Blonkvist, President & Chief Operating Officer - *Consulting*
Mr. Charles P. Campbell, Managing Partner - *Consulting*
Ms. Patricia D. McNicholas, Managing Partner - *Consulting*
Mrs. Julie Bell, Executive Assistant to CEO - *General management*

Salary Minimum: $300,000

Functions: Generalist (All), Senior Mgmt., Mktg. Mgmt., MIS Mgmt., Mgmt. Consultants, Legal, Attorneys

Industries: Generalist (All), Finance, Services, Legal, Mgmt. Consulting, E-commerce, IT Implementation, Communications, Network Infrastructure, Software, Mfg. SW

Palacios & Associates Inc[†]

PO Box 362437
San Juan, PR 00936-2437
(787) 761-8160
Fax: (787) 761-8180
Email: jpa2@jpalacios.com
Web: www.jpalacios.com

Summary: We are a professional executive search firm with a strong emphasis on ethics and confidentiality. We are generalists for the pharmaceutical, biotechnology, chemical, electronic, and medical device manufacturing industries. Our recruiters are certified consultants on the Myers Briggs type psychological indicators and its applications. We have over 85 percent repeated business every year.

Key Contact - Specialty:
Ms. Jeannette C. De Palacios, CPC, President
Ms. Myrgia M. Palacios Cabrera, CPC, Vice President

Salary Minimum: $50,000

Functions: Generalist (All)

Industries: Generalist (All), Manufacturing, Chemicals, Drugs Mfg., Medical Devices, Finance, Engineering Svcs., Compliance, Biotech/Life Sciences

Kirk Palmer & Associates Inc

500 5th Ave Ste 1500
New York, NY 10110-1501
(212) 983-6477
Fax: (212) 599-2597
Email: resume@kirkpalmer.com
Web: www.kirkpalmer.com

Summary: Recognized authorities in the retail and apparel industries. Client base includes many of the top retail and apparel companies. Proven expertise in senior management searches within all functional areas.

Key Contact - Specialty:
Mr. Kirk Palmer, Chief Executive Officer

Salary Minimum: $100,000

Functions: Senior Mgmt., Product Dev., Sales & Mktg., Mktg. Mgmt., Sales Mgmt., Direct Mktg., HR Mgmt., Finance, CFOs, IT

Industries: Textiles, Apparel, Wholesale, Retail, Finance

Branches:
122 Maumell St
Hinsdale, IL 60521-3525
(630) 321-0535
Fax: (630) 321-0537
Key Contact - Specialty:
Ms. Anna Worner, Vice President

306 Moulton St
South Hamilton, MA 01982-1229
(978) 468-2485
Fax: (978) 468-4663
Key Contact - Specialty:
Ms. Leslie Cook, Senior Vice President

Palmer & Company Executive Recruitment Inc

310-69 Bloor St E
Toronto, ON M4W 1A9
Canada
(416) 975-9595
Fax: (416) 975-9068
Email: execsearch@palmerco.ca
Web: www.palmerco.ca

Summary: Our practice spans most sectors and industries and we conduct searches at the senior or officer level.

Key Contact - Specialty:
Mr. Mark Palmer, President

Salary Minimum: $90,000

Functions: Senior Mgmt.

Industries: Retail, Finance, Non-profits, Pharm Svcs., Legal, Higher Ed., Publishing, Communications, Biotech/Life Sciences, Healthcare

Pamenter, Pamenter, Brezer & Deganis Ltd

406-1 Eva Rd
Etobicoke, ON M9C 4Z5
Canada
(416) 620-5980
Fax: (416) 620-5074
Email: ppbdconsulting@aol.com

Summary: Our search work is usually performed in conjunction with reorganization projects. Recently we conducted a major HR restructuring project for a leading business school using our employment model.

Key Contact - Specialty:
Mr. Fred Pamenter, President
Mr. Craig Pamenter, Recruiter

Salary Minimum: $50,000

Functions: Generalist (All), Management, Senior Mgmt., Middle Mgmt., Mktg. Mgmt., PR, HR Mgmt., CFOs

Industries: Generalist (All), Food, Bev., Tobacco, Printing, Misc. Mfg., Higher Ed., Packaging, Healthcare

Pappas DeLaney LLC

4811 S 76th St Ste 110
Greenfield, WI 53220-4351
(414) 271-1967
Fax: (414) 271-1981
Email: pdl@pappasdelaney.com
Web: www.pappasdelaney.com

Summary: Specializes in highly targeted recruiting for employer clients including board directorships and senior management positions.

Key Contact - Specialty:
Mr. Timothy C. Pappas, Principal
Mr. Michael Moore, Principal

Salary Minimum: $100,000

Functions: Generalist (All), Management, Mfg., Materials, Health Admin., Sales & Mktg., Risk Mgmt.

Industries: Generalist (All), Construction, Manufacturing, Food, Bev., Tobacco, Chemicals, Banking, Insurance, Healthcare

The PAR Group - Paul A Reaume Ltd

100 N Waukegan Rd Ste 211
Lake Bluff, IL 60044-1660
(847) 234-0005
Fax: (847) 234-8309
Email: info@pargroupltd.com
Web: www.pargroupltd.com

Summary: Searches for top management and senior staff in local government and related organizations and not-for-profit associations (i.e. city manager, police chief, public works director; executive director and association managers).

Key Contact - Specialty:
Mr. Robert A. Beezat, President - *Government, Non-profit*
Mr. G. Stevens Bernard, Vice President - *Government, Non-profit*
Ms. Heidi J. Voorhees, Vice President - *Government, Non-profit*
Mr. Karl F. Nollenberger, Vice President - *Government, Non-profit*
Mr. Gerald E. Hagman, Vice President - *Government, Non-profit*
Dr. Gregory T. Kuhn, PhD, Adjunct Specialist & Advisor - *Government, Non-profit*

Salary Minimum: $45,000

Functions: Senior Mgmt., HR Mgmt., CFOs, IT, Engineering, Minorities/Diversity

Industries: Law Enforcement, Government

Paradigm Technologies Inc[†]

4706 Alton Dr
Troy, MI 48085-5002
(248) 524-9762
Fax: (248) 524-0347
Email: jbeyer@paradigmtechweb.com
Web: www.paradigmtechweb.com

Summary: We are at the forefront of recruiting automotive executives who are the pioneers at world-class organizations.

Key Contact - Specialty:
Mr. Joe Beyer, President - *Automotive, Engineering*
Ms. Melissa Beyer, Vice President
Mr. Dan Beyer, Recruiter - *Automotive, Engineering, Manufacturing, Materials*
Mr. O'Hara Near, Recruiter
Mr. Joe Heffernan, Recruiter - *Operations*

Salary Minimum: $70,000

Functions: Generalist (All)

Industries: Motor Vehicles

Parallax Ventures Inc

132 Porto Bello Rd
Arden, NC 28704-8613
(828) 654-9790
Email: brads@parallaxventures.net
Web: www.parallaxventures.net

Summary: We perform executive-level searches across major functional units in most industries nationwide. We guarantee our clients, efficient,

ethical, effective, personal and professional service in attracting top talent.

Key Contact - Specialty:
Mr. Bradford W. Shaffer, President

Salary Minimum: $120,000

Functions: Generalist (All), Management, Mfg., Sales & Mktg., HR Mgmt., Finance, IT, Engineering

Industries: Generalist (All), Manufacturing, Semiconductors, Services, Non-profits, Communications, Aerospace, Software, Security SW, Biotech/Life Sciences, Healthcare

Jim Parham & Associates Inc[†]

PO Box 6529
Lakeland, FL 33807-6529
(863) 644-7097
Fax: (863) 644-3766
Email: resumes@jimparham.com
Web: www.jimparham.com

Summary: Specialized executive search for the motor freight industry (LTL, T/L, hazardous haulers, flatbed, tank carriers, refrigerated, van and logistics).

Key Contact - Specialty:
Mr. Jim Parham, President - *Transportation*

Salary Minimum: $35,000

Functions: Board Members, Senior Mgmt., Middle Mgmt., Distribution, Sales Mgmt., CFOs, MIS Mgmt.

Industries: Transportation

Frank Parillo & Associates

2267 N Rockridge Pl
Orange, CA 92867-2134
(714) 921-8008
Email: frank@frankparillo.com
Web: www.frankparillo.qpg.com

Summary: We are serving large, middle and small companies in the biotechnology, pharmaceutical, biopharmaceuticals medical diagnostics (in vivo and in vitro), medical device industries, as well as venture capital-based start-ups. We are focused on middle and senior management. We conduct searches for all executive functions, including general management, R&D, manufacturing, marketing, sales, regulatory affairs, quality assurance, quality control, HR and engineering.

Key Contact - Specialty:
Mr. Frank Parillo, President

Salary Minimum: $60,000

Functions: Generalist (All), Senior Mgmt., Middle Mgmt., Product Dev., Production, Mktg. Mgmt., Sales Mgmt., R&D

Industries: Chemicals, Drugs Mfg., Medical Devices, Biotech/Life Sciences

The Park Group & Associates Inc

4 Evergreen Rd
Severna Park, MD 21146-3802
(410) 384-9120
Fax: (410) 384-9923
Email: info@tpgassociates.com
Web: www.tpgassociates.com

Summary: Specialize in healthcare, insurance, banking and technology. Services include executive search and management consulting in the healthcare and banking industry.

Key Contact - Specialty:
Ms. Lise Perunovich, Principal - *Financial services, Healthcare*
Ms. Katherine Ryan - *Healthcare*

Salary Minimum: $60,000

Functions: Generalist (All), Management, Healthcare, Sales & Mktg., HR Mgmt., Finance, IT, Specialized Svcs.

Industries: Generalist (All), Finance, Services, Insurance, Software, Healthcare

D P Parker & Associates Inc

372 Washington St
Wellesley Hills, MA 02481-6202
(781) 237-1220
Fax: (781) 237-4702
Email: info@dpparker.com
Web: www.dpparker.com

Summary: Specialize in R&D, marketing, operations and general management in specialty materials and chemicals, biotechnology, aerospace, electronics and other technically based industries.

Key Contact - Specialty:
Dr. David P. Parker, President

Salary Minimum: $100,000

Functions: Senior Mgmt.

Industries: Chemicals, Drugs Mfg., Medical Devices, Plastics, Rubber, Metal Products, Electronic, Elec. Components, Semiconductors, Telephony, Biotech/Life Sciences

Parker Business Solutions Inc[†]

PO Box 86
14 Fernald Ave
Corinna, ME 04928-0086
(877) 871-3800
(207) 278-3800
Fax: (877) 780-4777
Email: jack@parkerbusiness.com
Web: www.parkerbusiness.com

Summary: A retained executive search firm with a strong focus in the document imaging industry, placement of sales, sales management, senior service technicians and executive management opportunities.

Key Contact - Specialty:
Mr. Jack A. Parker, President & Chief Executive Officer - *Copiers, Office (Products), Sales, Technicians*
Mrs. Tammy A. Parker, Vice President - *Copiers, Office (Products), Sales, Technicians*
Mr. Alan Bishop, Director, Recruiting - *Copiers, Office (Products), Sales, Technicians*
Mr. Hunter Miles, Senior Recruiter - *Copiers, Office (Products), Sales, Technicians*
Mr. Adam R. Chandler, Client Coordinator - *Copiers, Office (Products), Sales, Technicians*
Ms. Sara Lowe, Director, Candidate Affairs - *Copiers, Office (Products), Sales, Technicians*

Functions: Management, Sales & Mktg., Sales Mgmt., Technicians

Industries: Printing, Electronic, Elec. Components, Equip Svcs., Doc. Mgmt., Production SW, Industry Specific SW

Parker Remick Inc

PO Box 368
Bellingham, WA 98227-0368
(360) 527-2555
Fax: (360) 395-6000
Email: contact@parkerremick.com
Web: www.parkerremick.com

Summary: Our firm manages the complex, time consuming process of executive search for a select group of public and private companies that offer enterprise software, retail technology and consulting, and supply chain technology and consulting. An established leader, we place CEOs and key executives who manage departments, markets, and international regions.

Key Contact - Specialty:
Mr. Robert Healy, JD, Managing Partner - *.com, Boards of Directors, C-level, CEOs, CFOs*
Mr. Kevin Williamson, Managing Partner - *C-level, CEOs, CFOs, Computers (Hardware, Software)*
Ms. Charlotte Remick, Director, Research - *Finance, Tax*

Functions: Board Members, Senior Mgmt., Mktg. Mgmt., Sales Mgmt.

Industries: Computer Equip., E-commerce, Logistics Svcs., Supply Chain Mgmt., Software, Database SW, Doc. Mgmt., Production SW, ERP SW, Industry Specific SW, Mfg. SW, Marketing SW

MD Parkin & Associates[†]

1 Apple Hill Dr
Natick, MA 01760-2072
(508) 647-0221
Email: info@mdparkin.com
Web: www.mdparkin.com

Summary: We specialize in retained search and recruitment within the semiconductor capital equipment, electronic component and contract manufacturing. Our assignments are conducted for senior executives across all functional areas.

Key Contact - Specialty:
Ms. Myrna Parkin, President
Ms. Jean Nolan, Vice President

Salary Minimum: $70,000

Functions: Generalist (All)

Industries: Test, Measure Equip., Electronic, Elec. Components, Robotics, Semiconductors

Parsons Associates Inc

980 N Michigan Ave Ste 1400
Chicago, IL 60611-7500
(312) 475-9660
Fax: (312) 475-9661
Email: sueparsons@ameritech.net

Summary: Our firm provides distinctive service in retained search and is designed to provide a select group of client companies with exceptional quality and performance in the recruitment of highly talented executives.

Key Contact - Specialty:
Ms. Sue N. Parsons, President
Mr. John W. Parsons, Vice President

Salary Minimum: $100,000

Functions: Board Members, Senior Mgmt., Middle Mgmt., Mfg., Materials, Mktg. Mgmt., Sales Mgmt., HR Mgmt., CFOs, MIS Mgmt.

Industries: Generalist (All), Agri., Forestry, Mining, Manufacturing, Food, Bev., Tobacco, Medical Devices, Plastics, Rubber, Metal Products, Machine, Appliance, Computer Equip., Consumer Elect., Test, Measure Equip., Electronic, Elec. Components, Transportation, Wholesale, Retail, Finance, Services, Hospitality, Communications, Packaging, Insurance, Healthcare

Partnervision Consulting Group Inc

PO Box 73
Niagara on the Lake, ON L0S 1J0
Canada
(905) 468-7008
Email: info@partnervision.net
Web: www.partnervision.net

Summary: We bring a consultative approach to the search process. With the existing business climate, your business solution is best arrived at

by bringing in the right leadership and talent at the right time. Technologically driven, we use a multi-pronged search strategy to source and identify the best candidates.

Key Contact - Specialty:
Ms. Lynn Lefebvre, President

Salary Minimum: $85,000

Functions: Management, Middle Mgmt., HR Mgmt.

Industries: Generalist (All)

Partridge Associates Inc[†]

1200 Providence Hwy
Sharon, MA 02067-1656
(781) 784-4144
Email: robert@partridgeassociates.com
Web: www.partridgeassociates.com

Summary: Executive search organization specializing in recruitment for corporate and unit level positions in the hospitality industry. Many years of industry experience in hotels, restaurants and food service.

Key Contact - Specialty:
Mr. Robert J. Partridge, President

Salary Minimum: $50,000

Functions: Generalist (All), Management, Engineering

Industries: Consumer Elect., Electronic, Elec. Components, Hospitality, Hotels, Resorts, Clubs

Paschal•Murray Executive Search

82782 Matthau Dr
Indio, CA 92201-8594
(760) 863-4512
Fax: (760) 863-4513
Email: murrayr@paschalmurray.com
Web: www.paschalmurray.com

Summary: Working on retainer, we assist universities, hospitals, corporations and non-profit organizations in placing senior and mid-level executives in fundraising and executive director/CEO positions.

Key Contact - Specialty:
Ms. Colette Murray, JD, President & Chief Executive Officer - *Associations, Boards of Directors, Education (Higher), Non-profit, Philanthropy*
Ms. Monica Padilla, Executive Assistant - *Non-profit, Philanthropy*

Salary Minimum: $80,000

Functions: Management, Non-profits

Industries: Non-profits, Higher Ed., Healthcare

L Patrick & Steeple LLP

16772 W Bell Rd Ste 110
Surprise, AZ 85374-9702
(623) 544-2548
Fax: (623) 975-4283

Summary: Our firm offers full-retained search services. We are a generalist firm serving most industries and functions.

Key Contact - Specialty:
Mr. Louis P. Giordano, Partner
Ms. Dianne Eden, Partner

Salary Minimum: $75,000

Functions: Senior Mgmt., Middle Mgmt., Mfg., Materials, MIS Mgmt., Engineering

Industries: Generalist (All)

Paul-Tittle Search Group

1485 Chain Bridge Rd Ste 304
Mc Lean, VA 22101-4501
(703) 442-0500
Fax: (703) 893-3871
Email: pta@paul-tittle.com
Web: www.paul-tittle.com

Summary: Executive search and enterprise recruiting services for a broad range of clients. Particular focus on clients in federal systems integration, IT, professional services, telecom and internet/e-commerce. Specialize in mid and senior level management and key individual contributors in: sales, marketing, customer care, technology, engineering, operations, finance, accounting and HR.

Key Contact - Specialty:
Mr. David M. Tittle, President - *Business development, CEOs, Information Technology, Management consulting, Public sector*
Mr. Burt Heacock, Executive Vice President - *CIOs, Engineering, Information Technology, Non-profit, Telecommunications*
Mr. Allan Paul, Senior Vice President - *Accounting, C-level, Finance, Human resources, Management consulting*
Mr. Bruce Phinney, Vice President
Ms. Becky Nolton, Vice President - *Business development, Defense, Marketing, Sales, Telecommunications*
Ms. Stephanie Brunhofer, Vice President - *Accounting, Accounting (Public), Aerospace, CFOs, Controllers*
Ms. Debbie Ratliff, Principal - *Healthcare, Human resources, Information Technology, Middle management, Non-profit*

Salary Minimum: $80,000

Functions: Generalist (All), Senior Mgmt., Middle Mgmt., Sales & Mktg., HR Mgmt., CFOs, IT, Mgmt. Consultants

Industries: Finance, Services, New Media, Telecoms, Government, Defense, Software

Pawlik/Dorman Partners

(a Taplow Group company)
2639 N Southport Ave Ste B
Chicago, IL 60614-1227
(773) 296-0950
Email: bernadettepawlik@cs.com
Web: www.pawlikdorman.com

Summary: Eighty percent of our business is from repeat clients. We intentionally limit the number of engagements we conduct to ensure a thorough understanding of our clients' needs and rapid search completion.

Key Contact - Specialty:
Ms. Bernadette M. Pawlik, Managing Partner

Salary Minimum: $70,000

Functions: Generalist (All)

Industries: Manufacturing, Computer Equip., Consumer Elect., Mgmt. Consulting, HR Services, Advertising, New Media, Telecoms, Software

Peachtree Executive Search

10800 Alpharetta Hwy Ste 481
Roswell, GA 30076-1490
(770) 998-2272

Summary: A small firm focusing on quality service to clients, with a broad client base.

Key Contact - Specialty:
Mr. Mark F. Snoddy, Jr., President

Salary Minimum: $70,000

Functions: Generalist (All), Senior Mgmt., Plant Mgmt., Mktg. Mgmt., Sales Mgmt., HR Mgmt., MIS Mgmt., R&D, Technicians

Industries: Generalist (All), Chemicals, Drugs Mfg., Consumer Goods, Logistics Svcs., Advertising, Environmental Svcs., Packaging, Insurance, Software

Pearson Partners International Inc

8080 N Central Expy Ste 1200
Dallas, TX 75206-3766
(214) 292-4130
Fax: (214) 292-4140
Email: response@pearsonpartnersintl.com
Web: www.pearsonpartnersintl.com

Summary: We have a long history of successful performance in the retained executive search industry. We maintain a global alliance network with offices in Asia, Canada, Europe and the United States. We are focused on providing retained executive recruiting services to clients, on a global basis, across all industries and disciplines, from the middle management level to the boardroom.

Key Contact - Specialty:
Mr. Robert L. Pearson, President & Chief Executive Officer
Mr. William D. Rowe, II, Managing Partner
Mr. Keith D. Pearson, Vice President
Ms. Renee B. Arrington, Vice President
Mr. Stephen P. Konstans, Vice President
Ms. Jill C. Pearson, Vice President
Mr. Mark C. Levy, Chief Financial Officer
Mr. Sandford C.G. Boyce, Director, Research
Ms. Lori Selby, Office Manager

Salary Minimum: $150,000

Functions: Generalist (All), Management, Board Members, Senior Mgmt., Middle Mgmt.

Industries: Generalist (All), Energy, Utilities, Construction, Manufacturing, Transportation, Retail, Finance, Services, Hospitality, Healthcare

Peck & Associates Ltd

250 S Main St
Thiensville, WI 53092-1905
(262) 238-8700
Fax: (262) 238-9525
Email: julie@peckltd.com
Web: www.peckltd.com

Summary: A consulting intensive executive search firm focusing on defining and resolving organizational issues around newly created positions in closely held companies. Particular expertise in succession planning for the individual and the company. We are specialists in non-reversible executive transitions.

Key Contact - Specialty:
Mr. Jim Peck, Partner
Ms. Julie Peck, Partner

Functions: Generalist (All), Board Members, Senior Mgmt., Benefits, Mgmt. Consultants

Industries: Generalist (All), Finance

Pedley-Richard & Associates Inc[†]

7719 Wood Hollow Dr Ste 216
Austin, TX 78731-1634
(512) 418-8848
Fax: (512) 418-8851
Email: drichard@pedley-richard.com
Web: www.pedley-richard.com

Summary: We are a visionary provider of executive technology professionals to leading edge

companies. We provide retained search for executive and technology professionals and contract recruitment services.

Key Contact - Specialty:
Ms. Sally Pedley, Chief Executive Officer
Ms. Deborah Richard, President
Mr. Tom Schable, Operations Manager - *Human resources, Operations*
Ms. Dee Dee Dial, Senior Recruiter

Functions: Senior Mgmt.

Industries: Computer Equip., Electronic, Elec. Components, Consumer Goods, E-commerce, IT Implementation, Engineering Svcs., RF/Microwave, Database SW, Development SW, Networking, Comm. SW

Paul S Pelland PC

51 Charlotte St
Charleston, SC 29403-6635
(843) 853-2757
Fax: (843) 853-2990
Email: pelland@bellsouth.net

Summary: We are foundry and secondary machining/forming specialists. Our emphasis is on executive and senior foundry management, marketing and technological professionals in most metal working areas. Our firm places an emphasis on foundry clients industry.

Key Contact - Specialty:
Mr. Paul S. Pelland, Senior Parnter
Ms. Jane A. Taylor, Research Administrator

Salary Minimum: $60,000

Functions: Management, Middle Mgmt., Mfg., Production, Automation, Plant Mgmt., Quality, Sales & Mktg., Sales Mgmt., Engineering

Industries: Manufacturing, Metal Products, Misc. Mfg.

Penn Associates

1500 John F Kennedy Blvd Ste 200
Philadelphia, PA 19102-1754
(215) 854-6336
Email: rg@pennassociates.net

Summary: Consulting firm specializing in the recruitment of middle and upper-level HR executives. We handle retained search assignments worldwide and provide executive search research services for corporate clients. We bring innovative solutions to staffing problems.

Key Contact - Specialty:
Mr. Joseph A. Dickerson, Principal - *Human resources*

Salary Minimum: $85,000

Functions: HR Mgmt., Benefits, Staffing, Training, e-HR, Mgmt. Consultants

Industries: Generalist (All), Manufacturing, Transportation, Retail, Finance, Mgmt. Consulting, HR Services, Hospitality, Media, Communications, Packaging

The Penn Partners Inc

230 S Broad St Fl 19
Philadelphia, PA 19102-4121
(215) 568-9285
Fax: (215) 568-1277

Summary: Generalist retainer based search practice. Specializing at the senior and middle management level.

Key Contact - Specialty:
Ms. Kathleen M. Shea, President
Mr. John F. Smith, Vice President
Ms. Karen M. Swartz, Manager
Ms. Cheryl L. Littman, Manager

Salary Minimum: $75,000

Functions: Generalist (All), Management, Senior Mgmt., Middle Mgmt., Sales & Mktg., HR Mgmt., Finance

Industries: Generalist (All), Manufacturing, Food, Bev., Tobacco, Drugs Mfg., Machine, Appliance, Consumer Elect., Finance, Mgmt. Consulting

People First Executive Search

(a World Search Group company)
1800-360 Main Street
Comodity Exchange Tower
Winnipeg, MB R3C 3Z3
Canada
(204) 940-3900
Email: careers@peoplefirsthr.com
Web: www.peoplefirsthr.com

Summary: We are a large full-service human resource provider. Our comprehensive approach results in strategically-aligned solutions customized to meet the changing needs of your organization.

Key Contact - Specialty:
Dr. John McFerran, Chief Operating Officer - *C-level, Human resources, Retail*
Ms. Terry-Lynn Lozinski, Senior Consultant - *Accounting, Finance, Non-profit*
Ms. Karen Palmer, Consultant

Salary Minimum: $65,000

Functions: Management, Board Members, Senior Mgmt.

Industries: Generalist (All)

People Management International Inc

1 Darling Dr
Avon, CT 06001-4252
(860) 678-8900
Email: epoff@peoplemanagement.org
Web: www.peoplemanagement.org

Summary: Our functional focus is on CEO, CFO, CTO and comparable leadership positions. The industries we serve are software, professional services, financial services and healthcare. We have a deep expertise in start-up organizations.

Key Contact - Specialty:
Mr. Ronald R. Evans, Managing Director
Mr. Ed Poff, Executive Director
Mr. Robert J. Stevenson, Managing Director
Mr. Tony L. Kroening, Managing Director

Functions: Generalist (All), Senior Mgmt., Mktg. Mgmt., PR, CFOs, M&A, MIS Mgmt.

Industries: Generalist (All), Invest. Banking, Accounting, Advertising, Software

People Management Mid-South LLC

2021 21st Ave S Ste 304
Nashville, TN 37212-4349
(615) 463-2800
Fax: (615) 463-2944
Email: info@jobfitmatters.com
Web: www.jobfitmatters.com

Summary: We specialize in retained executive search, selection, and consultation on issues related to job fit.

Key Contact - Specialty:
Mr. Tommy Thomas, President & Chief Executive Officer

Salary Minimum: $75,000

Functions: Generalist (All)

Industries: Generalist (All), Non-profits, Mgmt. Consulting, Higher Ed., Marketing SW

People Management Rocky Mountains Inc

1373 Regatta Ln
Monument, CO 80132-9007
(719) 488-4433
Fax: (877) 780-2431
Email: rpeters@peoplemanagement.org
Web: www.peoplemanagement.org

Summary: Our mission is to facilitate the success of individuals and organizations by focusing on fitting people to professions, endeavors and relationships that will accommodate the best use of their innate strengths and motivational drives. We are committed to the great good and vitality that occurs when people are matched to the setting that fits them and unveils what they do best.

Key Contact - Specialty:
Mr. Robert W. Peters, President & Chief Executive Officer

Salary Minimum: $75,000

Functions: Non-profits

Industries: Non-profits

People Management SMD LLC

(formerly known as People Management Northeast Inc)
16 Judge Ln
Newington, CT 06111-4223
(860) 667-2633
Email: pmsmdresume@cox.net
Web: www.peoplemanagementsmd.com

Summary: Our focus is on achieving a sound job fit.

Key Contact - Specialty:
Mr. Steven M. Darter, President

Salary Minimum: $180,000

Functions: Senior Mgmt.

Industries: Generalist (All)

Perez-Arton Consultants Inc

23 Spring St Ste 204B
Ossining, NY 10562-4762
(914) 762-2100

Summary: Higher education administration at the presidential, VP, dean and director level. Presidential and board evaluations, board development and institutional assessments. All programmatic and operational areas are in higher education.

Key Contact - Specialty:
Ms. Maria M. Perez, President

Salary Minimum: $75,000

Functions: Senior Mgmt., Middle Mgmt., Admin. Svcs., CFOs

Industries: Higher Ed.

The Perkins Group[†]

10701 McMullen Creek Pkwy Ste D
Charlotte, NC 28226-1633
(704) 543-1111
Email: perkchar@perkinsgroup.com
Web: www.perkinsgroup.com

Summary: We are a nationally recognized retained search firm focused primarily in all facets of manufacturing, consumer industries, medical devices, and banking. We provide our clients with innovative and proven staffing programs designed to "Topgrade" thru succession planning and upgrading your executive team.

Key Contact - Specialty:
Mr. R. Patrick Perkins, CPC, Chief Executive Officer - *Distribution, Manufacturing, Six sigma*

Salary Minimum: $95,000

Functions: Generalist (All), Management, Senior Mgmt., Middle Mgmt., Mfg., Materials, Sales & Mktg., HR Mgmt., Finance

Industries: Generalist (All), Paper, Chemicals, Medical Devices, Paints, Petro. Products, Metal Products, Machine, Appliance, Misc. Mfg., Consumer Goods, Retail

---

Perma, Willits Langone Inc[†]

(also known as Perman Willits Langone)
142 NE Whitney St Ste 100
Camas, WA 98607-2325
(360) 835-2205
Email: resumes@permanwillits.com
Web: www.permantech.com

Summary: We are a retained search and recruitment firm specializing in executives to engineers. OEM industries include: aviation, plastic products design, plastics and composites, and OEMS

Key Contact - Specialty:
Mr. Gary Perman, CRM, Senior Parnter - *Aviation, Building products, Consumer (Durables), Engineering, Plastics*
Mr. Scott Pyper, Senior Recruiter - *Engineering, Manufacturing*
Ms. Rachel Jackson, SRM, Recruiter - *Agriculture, Biomaterials, Factories (Automation), Manufacturing, Manufacturing (Management)*

Salary Minimum: $90,000

Functions: Management, Product Dev., R&D, Engineering

Industries: Agri., Forestry, Mining, Manufacturing, Food, Bev., Tobacco, Plastics, Rubber, Consumer Elect., Misc. Mfg., Electronic, Elec. Components, Consumer Goods, Recreation, Aerospace, Software, Development SW, Doc. Mgmt., Production SW, Industry Specific SW, Mfg. SW, System SW, Biotech/Life Sciences, Non-Classifiable

Branches:
13235 SE 246th Ct
Kent, WA 98042-5129
(253) 638-6780
Fax: (253) 638-6781
Email: carrie@permanwillits.com
Key Contact - Specialty:
Ms. Carrie Langone, Partner - *Engineering, Executives, Information Technology, Operations, Sales*

Perras Consulting Inc

504-100 Allstate Pky
Markham, ON L3R 6H3
Canada
(416) 481-5548 x223
Email: pperras@perrasconsulting.com
Web: www.perrasconsulting.com

Summary: Our firm is an independently owned, retained executive search firm. Utilizing our team's executive search, operations and HR consulting expertise, we subscribe to an overriding commitment to our clients characterized by high quality work, client satisfaction, value for fees, integrity, innovation and teamwork. Clients tell us that our approach is highly creative, proactive, and effective.

Key Contact - Specialty:
Mr. Paul Perras, President

Salary Minimum: $85,000

Functions: Generalist (All)

Industries: Generalist (All)

R H Perry & Associates Inc

(also known as The Registry for College & Univ Presidents)
2607 31st St NW
Washington, DC 20008-3519
(202) 965-6464
Fax: (202) 338-3953
Email: matt@rhperry.net
Web: www.rhperry.net

Summary: Search and personnel consulting firm.

Key Contact - Specialty:
Mr. Robert H. Perry, President
Mr. Neil A. Stein, Vice President
Ms. Sandra Ellis, Director, Research

Functions: Generalist (All), Board Members, Senior Mgmt., HR Mgmt., CFOs

Industries: Generalist (All), Misc. Financial, Higher Ed., Insurance

Branches:
1127 Rosebank Dr
Columbus, OH 43235-2186
(614) 798-0583
Fax: (614) 798-0540
Email: akoenig@worldnet.att.net
Key Contact - Specialty:
Dr. Allen E. Koenig, Senior Consultant

Perry-Martel International Inc[†]

200-440 Laurier Ave W
Bradson Business Centre
Ottawa, ON K1R 7X6
Canada
(613) 236-6995
Email: dperry@perrymartel.com
Web: www.perrymartel.com

Summary: We are in business with our clients to win. Our managing partner has completed 915 searches totaling $150 million in salaries with a 99.6 percent success rate. Our work is backed by a one-year guarantee. Two to three year extended guarantees available.

Key Contact - Specialty:
Mr. David Perry, BA, MM, Managing Partner
Ms. Anita Martel, Partner

Salary Minimum: $100,000

Functions: Generalist (All), Board Members, Senior Mgmt., Sales Mgmt., PR, CFOs, MIS Mgmt., Systems Analysis, Systems Dev.

Industries: Generalist (All), Computer Equip., Electronic, Elec. Components, Semiconductors, E-commerce, Engineering Svcs., Supply Chain Mgmt, New Media, Communications, Wireless, Defense, Homeland Security, Aerospace, Software, Mfg. SW, Biotech/Life Sciences

---

The Persichetti Group[†]

5758 Havensport Rd
Carroll, OH 43112-9643
(740) 756-1301
Fax: (740) 756-1302
Email: kp@pgroup.net
Web: www.pgroup.net

Summary: Professional and executive-level retained generalist search partner supporting a select client base. Research/sourcing services available on hourly basis.

Key Contact - Specialty:
Ms. Kelly Persichetti, President

Salary Minimum: $100,000

Functions: Management, Board Members, Senior Mgmt., Middle Mgmt., Plant Mgmt., Sales & Mktg., IT

Industries: Generalist (All), Manufacturing, Food, Bev., Tobacco, Metal Products, Consumer Elect., Misc. Mfg., HR Services, Packaging

---

Barry Persky & Company Inc

256 Post Rd E
Westport, CT 06880-3620
(203) 454-4500
Fax: (203) 454-3318
Email: bpersky@perskysearch.com
Web: www.barrypersky.com

Summary: The firm specializes in the recruitment of senior executives and managers for its clients in capital equipment, industrial systems & processes, technology, manufacturing, public services, consumer products and communications industries.

Key Contact - Specialty:
Mr. Barry Persky, Founder & President
Mr. Edward Ryan, Practice Director
Ms. Jackie Nette, Director, Research

Salary Minimum: $100,000

Functions: Generalist (All), Senior Mgmt., Mfg., Sales & Mktg., CFOs, Engineering, Int'l.

Industries: Generalist (All), Energy, Utilities, Construction, Manufacturing, Transportation, Services, Media, Environmental Svcs., Aerospace, Biotech/Life Sciences

---

Personal Business Advisors[†]

14008 B Antonio Dr
Helotes, TX 78023-3942
(561) 799-3184
Fax: (210) 568-4439
Email: dirhrpba@bellsouth.net
Web: www.personalbusinessadvisors.com

Summary: Personal Business Advisors offers alternatives to traditional employment for senior level executives.

Key Contact - Specialty:
Ms. Doris Fink, VP Human Resources - *Computers (Software), Hardware, Metals, Plastics*

Functions: Generalist (All)

Industries: Generalist (All)

Personnel Dynamics Inc

879 Sumac Rd
Highland Park, IL 60035-3840
(847) 831-1259
Email: kaplan@personneldynamics.com
Web: www.personneldynamics.com

Summary: We conduct executive search assignments in marketing, sales, accounting, finance and human resources. Additionally, we consult in all facets of HR including strategic planning, compensation, training, development and compliance.

Key Contact - Specialty:
Mr. Edward A. Kaplan, President - *Finance, Human resources, Marketing, Sales*

Salary Minimum: $60,000

Functions: Generalist (All), Senior Mgmt., Plant Mgmt., Purchasing, Sales Mgmt., Customer Svc., HR Mgmt., CFOs, Credit

Industries: Generalist (All), Manufacturing, Printing, Plastics, Rubber, Metal Products, Machine, Appliance, Misc. Financial, Accounting, Mgmt. Consulting, HR Services, Logistics Svcs.

---

† occasional contingency assignment

The Personnel Group Inc
5821 Cedar Lake Rd S
Minneapolis, MN 55416-1487
(952) 525-1557
Fax: (952) 525-1088
Email: mail@thepersonnelgroup.com

Summary: Executives from the Fortune 100 enhance our search practices. Practice has internal psychological/behavioral assessment capability. Provides customer with a variety of services including retained search, on-site recruiters and strategic recruiting/search consulting.

Key Contact - Specialty:
Mr. David G. Nelson, President - *Finance, Manufacturing, Sales*

Salary Minimum: $75,000

Functions: Generalist (All), Management, Mfg., Healthcare, Sales & Mktg., HR Mgmt., Finance, IT, Engineering

Industries: Manufacturing, Chemicals, Computer Equip., Misc. Mfg., Finance, Services, Communications, Telephony, Government, Aerospace, Software, Healthcare

The Personnel Perspective LLC
575 W College Ave Ste 101
Santa Rosa, CA 95401-5079
(707) 576-7653
Fax: (707) 576-8190
Email: info@personnelperspective.com
Web: www.personnelperspective.com

Summary: We are the premier provider of full-range HR consulting, management training and recruitment services in the North Bay and beyond. Our team of HR professionals offers support centered on HR consulting, compliance, compensation, performance management, organizational design, training, recruitment and placement.

Key Contact - Specialty:
Ms. Carolyn Silvestri, Founding Principal - *Business development*
Ms. Jeannette Feldman, Principal
Ms. Carol Comini, Senior Recruiting Consultant
Ms. Shelley Broll, Senior Consultant
Ms. Anne Heron, Senior Consultant
Ms. Kim Dixon, Director, Marketing & Sales
Ms. Arlene Smith, Consultant, Recruiting
Ms. Mimi Lemanski, Associate, Bi-lingual
Ms. Andrea Salvemini, Director, Business Development - *Finance*

Salary Minimum: $50,000

Functions: Management, Admin. Svcs., Mfg., Sales & Mktg.

Industries: Generalist (All), Construction, Manufacturing, Wholesale, Finance, Services, Hospitality, Media, Communications, Packaging, Insurance, Software, Biotech/Life Sciences, Healthcare

Peters, Dalton & Graham Inc
2 Concourse Pkwy NE Ste 155
Atlanta, GA 30328-6192
(770) 650-9707
Fax: (770) 650-9710
Email: resume@pdgsearch.com
Web: www.pdgsearch.com

Summary: Our firm offers specialty search practices: Retained search for all senior-levels and specialties specifically for the staffing industry only.

Key Contact - Specialty:
Mr. Alec Peters, Chairman & Chief Executive Officer
Mr. Thomas Dalton, Executive Vice President

Mr. Jackson Graham, Senior Vice President
Mr. John Egan, Vice President
Mr. Katena Pursuit, Vice President, Director

Salary Minimum: $100,000

Functions: Staffing

Industries: Generalist (All)

Petrie Partners Inc
PO Box 618663
Orlando, FL 32861-8663
(407) 521-7703
Fax: (407) 521-6080

Summary: Our firm combines an exceptionally successful track record with highly personalized service. We have outstanding references from clients and candidates over the past decade.

Key Contact - Specialty:
Mr. Christopher J. Petrie, President
Ms. Colleen Gavigan, Recruiter

Salary Minimum: $100,000

Functions: Generalist (All), Senior Mgmt., Middle Mgmt., Distribution, HR Mgmt., Staffing, Training

Industries: Generalist (All), Drugs Mfg., Medical Devices, HR Services, Hospitality

Phase II Management
25 Stonybrook Rd
Westport, CT 06880-2913
(203) 226-7252
Fax: (203) 226-7252
Email: rpfphaseii@sbcglobal.net
Web: www.phaseiimgmt.com

Summary: Generalist recruiting firm with successful placements from first line supervisory to CEO level, customers range from start-ups and closely held corporations to major multinational firms. Nearly all business disciplines covered.

Key Contact - Specialty:
Mr. Richard P. Fincher, President

Salary Minimum: $80,000

Functions: Generalist (All)

Industries: Food, Bev., Tobacco, Paper, Printing, Soap, Perf., Cosmtcs., Medical Devices, Plastics, Rubber, Metal Products, New Media, Packaging

J R Phillip & Associates Inc
555 Twin Dolphin Dr Ste 120
Redwood City, CA 94065-2102
(650) 631-6700
Fax: (650) 631-6710
Email: info@jrphillip.com
Web: www.jrphillip.com

Summary: We have exstensive search experience. Our clients are venture capital backed startups to Fortune 500.

Key Contact - Specialty:
Mr. John R. Phillip - *Senior management*

Salary Minimum: $175,000

Functions: Generalist (All)

Industries: Drugs Mfg., Medical Devices, Venture Cap., Pharm Svcs., Biotech/Life Sciences, Healthcare, Hospitals, Long-term/Home Care, Dental, Women's

Phillips, DiPisa & Associates Inc
62 Derby St Ste 1
Hingham, MA 02043-3718
(781) 740-9699
Email: dphillips@phillipsdipisa.com
Web: www.phillipsdipisa.com

Summary: Our firm recruits leaders for healthcare providers, managed care organizations and life sciences firms. The firm's roots are in Greater Boston, a historical center of medical innovation and excellence. We now serve clients along the East Coast and throughout the Midwest. We draw on a national pool of candidates.

Key Contact - Specialty:
Mr. Daniel J. Phillips, Managing Partner
Mr. Ralph DiPisa, Senior Parnter
Mr. Tom Lynch, Executive Search Consultant
Ms. Denise Trammel, Executive Search Consultant

Salary Minimum: $90,000

Functions: Management, Senior Mgmt.

Industries: Non-profits, Pharm Svcs., Biotech/Life Sciences, Healthcare, Hospitals, Long-term/Home Care

Phoenix Search
Prol Rio San Angel 35-3
Col Atlamaya
01760 Mexico City, DF
Mexico
55 5681 0877
Email: contact@phoenix-search.com
Web: www.phoenix-search.com

Summary: We are a leading generalist firm covering Latin America from offices in Mexico & Brazil. Our practice is well rounded with successful searches in many industries.

Key Contact - Specialty:
Mr. L. Ignacio Garrote Arango, General Director

Salary Minimum: $45,000

Functions: Generalist (All), Board Members, Senior Mgmt., Mktg. Mgmt., Sales Mgmt., CFOs, MIS Mgmt., Int'l.

Industries: Generalist (All), Energy, Utilities, Manufacturing, Transportation, Wholesale, Retail, Services, Communications, Software

Physician Executive Management Center
3403 W Fletcher Ave
Tampa, FL 33618-2813
(813) 963-1800
Fax: (813) 264-2207
Email: david@physicianexecutive.com
Web: www.physicianexecutive.com

Summary: We are the only firm specializing in physician executives. Our clients include: health care systems, hospitals, group practices, managed care organizations and insurance companies who ask us to find physician-only CEOs, VPs of medical affairs/chief medical officers, medical directors and department chiefs.

Key Contact - Specialty:
Mr. David R. Kirschman, President
Ms. Jennifer R. Grebenschikoff, Vice President

Salary Minimum: $200,000

Functions: Healthcare, Physicians

Industries: Hospitals

Picard International Ltd
101 Park Ave Rm 1800
New York, NY 10178-1702
(212) 252-1620
Fax: (212) 252-0973
Email: office@picardintl.com
Web: www.picardintl.com

Summary: Senior executive searches in a broad range of functions including general management, corporate strategy, technology, capital markets in financial services, management consulting,

healthcare, and high-technology industries. Specialists in asset management lift outs.

Key Contact - Specialty:
Mr. Daniel A. Picard, Principal - *Financial services, Healthcare, Management consulting, Technology*

Salary Minimum: $150,000

Functions: Generalist (All), Health Admin., HR Mgmt., CFOs, Cash Mgmt., Risk Mgmt., MIS Mgmt., Consultants

Industries: Generalist (All), Banking, Invest. Banking, Mgmt. Consulting, HR Services, Software, Healthcare

Nick Pierce & Associates Inc

2475 NorthWinds Pkwy Ste 200
Alpharetta, GA 30004-4808
(678) 624-1111
Email: npierce@npierce.com
Web: www.nickpierceassociates.com

Summary: We are a retained executive search firm focusing primarily in the transaction processing/technology sector. Our concentration is on CEO, COO and upper management assignments starting with base/bonus of $200K+.

Key Contact - Specialty:
Mr. Nicholas Pierce, President

Salary Minimum: $200,000

Functions: Generalist (All), Management, Senior Mgmt.

Industries: Generalist (All), Finance, Banking, Invest. Banking, Brokers, Venture Cap., Mutual/Hedge Funds, Misc. Financial, E-commerce

Pierce & Crow

500 Drakes Landing Rd Ste 300
Greenbrae, CA 94904-2492
(415) 925-1191
Email: info@piercecrow.com
Web: www.piercecrow.com

Summary: We are an award-winning executive search firm specializing in the recruitment of executive management for the emerging technologies industry. Our clients include venture-backed start-ups and Fortune 500 companies. You will recognize the names of our clients and partners as those revolutionizing the business of technology. Our strengths and expertise is in recruiting presidents/CEOs, COOs, VP marketing, sales and business development.

Key Contact - Specialty:
Mr. Dennis Crow, Managing Partner
Ms. Rosanna Ortisi, Principal
Mr. Bill Jennings, Principal

Functions: Senior Mgmt., Sales & Mktg.

Industries: Software

Pinnacle Executive Group Inc†

1025 NE Queens Cir
Lees Summit, MO 64064-1771
(816) 582-6409
Email: scott@1pinnacle.com
Web: www.1pinnacle.com

Summary: We utilize progressive recruitment methods to secure candidates that meet the challenges of major transition and accelerating change found in corporate America today. We have found it extremely important to place the identification of chemistry between candidate and client near the top of our search methodology.

Key Contact - Specialty:
Mr. Scott Eckley, Managing Partner

Salary Minimum: $70,000

Functions: Generalist (All), Management, Senior Mgmt., Middle Mgmt., CFOs, Credit, M&A, Risk Mgmt., Legal, Attorneys

Industries: Energy, Utilities, Oil & Gas, Finance, Invest. Banking, Venture Cap., Mutual/Hedge Funds, Legal, Restaurants

Pinsker & Company Inc

508 Ojai
Granite Bay, CA 95746-6765
(916) 797-9166
Fax: (916) 797-9168
Email: pinskerandco@rcsis.com

Summary: Retained executive selection consultants for board members, presidents and CEOs and the executive team reporting to the president. One on one executive coach to corporate management on how to make more objective and predictable hiring decisions.

Key Contact - Specialty:
Mr. Richard J. Pinsker, CMC, FIMC, President

Salary Minimum: $125,000

Functions: Generalist (All), Board Members, Senior Mgmt., Middle Mgmt.

Industries: Generalist (All), Construction, Food, Bev., Tobacco, Computer Equip., Test, Measure Equip., Misc. Mfg., Architectural Svcs.

Pinton Forrest & Madden

(an EMA Partners International company)
2020-1055 Hastings St W
Guinness Tower
Vancouver, BC V6E 2E9
Canada
(604) 689-9970
(800) 864-9970
Email: pfm@pfmsearch.com
Web: www.pfmsearch.com

Summary: We build long term client relationships through the partners' extensive recruitment and business management experience plus their direct involvement in each search assignment. A thorough, efficient and timely search process delivers quality candidates to our valued private and public sector clients.

Key Contact - Specialty:
Mr. Garth Pinton, Partner
Mr. Casey Forrest, Partner
Mr. George Madden, Partner

Salary Minimum: $70,000

Functions: Senior Mgmt., Middle Mgmt.

Industries: Generalist (All), Agri., Forestry, Mining, Energy, Utilities, Manufacturing, Finance, Services, Communications, Government, Aerospace, Software, Healthcare

Planigestion A Choquette Inc

(formerly known as Adapt Inc)
1060 Crois Augusta
Mascouche, QC J7L 4H1
Canada
(450) 474-4999
Fax: (450) 474-4446
Email: plani-ac@dsuper.net
Web: www.adapt.qc.ca

Summary: We are active in all fields with the exception of data processing. All senior consultants have managed a business at the executive level.

Key Contact - Specialty:
Mr. Andre Choquette, President
Mr. Daniel Lewis, Senior Consultant

Mr. Jean-Pierre Laberge, Senior Consultant
Mrs. Hélène Cadieux, Researcher

Salary Minimum: $60,000

Functions: Generalist (All), Senior Mgmt., Middle Mgmt.

Industries: Generalist (All), Oil & Gas, Construction, Manufacturing, Food, Bev., Tobacco, Textiles, Apparel, Lumber, Furniture, Paper, Drugs Mfg., Medical Devices, Retail, Finance, Banking, Pharm Svcs., Media, Communications, Haz. Waste, Packaging, Software, Biotech/Life Sciences, Healthcare

Rene Plessner Associates Inc

200 E 74th St PH A
New York, NY 10021-3611
(212) 421-3490
Fax: (212) 421-3999
Web: www.rene.plessner.com

Summary: A boutique executive search firm specializing in cosmetics, accessories, apparel and fashion-related areas, also consumer packaged goods, retail and high-technology, with an emphasis on entrepreneurial companies. In addition, we offer a reference checking service whereby we can provide you with in-depth references on someone you may consider hiring but about whom you may not know enough because they come to you from outside the normal search process.

Key Contact - Specialty:
Mr. Rene Plessner, President

Salary Minimum: $75,000

Functions: Generalist (All), Management, Mfg., Sales & Mktg., Advertising, Mktg. Mgmt., Sales Mgmt., PR

Industries: Generalist (All), Textiles, Apparel, Soap, Perf., Cosmtcs., Computer Equip., Advertising, Aerospace

Gerald Plock Associates Inc

101 E Park Blvd Ste 600 PMB 634
Plano, TX 75074-8818
(817) 464-4610
(866) 748-7704
Email: geraldplock@geraldplockassoc.com
Web: www.geraldplockassoc.com

Summary: We are a management consulting firm providing executive recruitment to public sector and non-profit organizations worldwide. Our president is one of the most experienced executive search professionals serving local government/non-profit institutions in the country.

Key Contact - Specialty:
Mr. Gerald Plock, President

Salary Minimum: $75,000

Functions: Generalist (All), Mgmt. Consultants, Non-profits

Industries: Non-profits, Mgmt. Consulting, HR Services, Law Enforcement, Higher Ed., Government, Environmental Svcs.

Branches:
134 Green Bay Rd
Winnetka, IL 60093-4003
(847) 441-5626
Email: wendy@geraldplockassoc.com
Key Contact - Specialty:
Ms. Wendy Lewis, Associate

Plummer & Associates Inc

65 Rowayton Ave
Norwalk, CT 06853-1600
(203) 899-1233
Fax: (203) 838-0887

Email: resume@plummersearch.com
Web: www.plummersearch.com

Summary: We specialize in CEO, COO, senior officer level assignments for the retail industry, wholesale trade, retail services, eCommerce, quick serve/casual dining, catalogs/direct marketing and manufacturers for the retail industry (toys, cosmetics and apparel) and retail consulting firms..

Key Contact - Specialty:
Mr. John Plummer, President
Ms. Kathy Mackenna, Consultant
Ms. Heidi Plummer, Consultant & Administration
Ms. Dina Lokets, Consultant & Research

Salary Minimum: $150,000

Functions: Generalist (All), Senior Mgmt.

Industries: Food, Bev., Tobacco, Textiles, Apparel, Consumer Goods, Wholesale, Retail, Venture Cap., Mgmt. Consulting, Hospitality, Hotels, Resorts, Clubs

PMB Executive Recruiters Inc†

1971 Sandcreek Dr SW
Atlanta, GA 30331-8404
(404) 748-1639
Email: erresumes@pmbgroup.com
Web: www.pmbgroup.com

Summary: Based on our experience and continuous research, we provide an in-depth knowledge of the targeted discipline, industry and career opportunity. We fulfill our ethical and professional commitment to our clients-candidates and companies.

Key Contact - Specialty:
Mr. Patrick M. Bradshaw, SPHR, Executive Placement Coordinator - *Human resources, Legal (Attorneys)*
Ms. Heather Johnson, Senior Recruitment Specialist - *Accounting, Audits, CFOs, Controllers, Finance*
Ms. Paula Stewart, Recruitment Specialist - *Office (Administration)*

Salary Minimum: $50,000

Functions: Management, Senior Mgmt., Admin. Svcs., HR Mgmt., Finance, CFOs

Industries: Generalist (All), Banking, Misc. Financial, Mgmt. Consulting, HR Services, Call Centers

PMcareers

11902 Keating Dr
Tampa, FL 33626-2530
(516) 672-2714
Email: paul@pmcareers.com
Web: www.pmcareers.com

Summary: We perform recruiting assignments in the field of information technology. These searches require finding professionals with the right combination of business and technology skills. We recruit individuals for positions in executive management, project management, business analysis, systems analysis, applications development, systems engineering and support, sales & marketing, and consulting.

Key Contact - Specialty:
Mr. Paul R. Misarti, President & Chief Executive Officer - *Securities*

Salary Minimum: $100,000

Functions: Senior Mgmt., Middle Mgmt., Sales Mgmt., MIS Mgmt., Systems Analysis, Systems Dev., Systems Implem., Systems Support, Network Admin., DB Admin.

Industries: Finance, Mgmt. Consulting, E-commerce, IT Implementation, Communications, Software

PMO Partners Inc

33 N Dearborn St Ste 1400
Chicago, IL 60602-4078
(312) 726-1143
Fax: (312) 726-1145
Email: pashley@pmopartners.com
Web: www.pmopartners.com

Summary: We are a retained executive search firm specializing in banking and financial services.

Key Contact - Specialty:
Ms. Patricia Ashley, President & Chief Executive Officer
Ms. Deanna Drew, Managing Director
Ms. Melissa Osuch, Senior Consultant

Salary Minimum: $75,000

Functions: Generalist (All)

Industries: Finance, Banking, Invest. Banking, Misc. Financial

Pointe Watch Recruiting†

PO Box 757
Moorestown, NJ 08057-0757
(856) 866-2846
Fax: (856) 866-2812
Email: djberr@pointewatchrecruiting.com
Web: www.pointewatchrecruiting.com

Summary: We were established to guide employers and candidates through the search process with a focus on corporate culture; the first step in employee retention. We accept search domestic and international assignments in marketing, finance, legal counsel, operations and HR.

Key Contact - Specialty:
Mr. Douglas Berr, President

Salary Minimum: $75,000

Functions: Generalist (All)

Industries: Food, Bev., Tobacco, Textiles, Apparel, Soap, Perf., Cosmtcs., Plastics, Rubber, Paints, Petro. Products, Leather, Stone, Glass, Machine, Appliance, Consumer Elect., Consumer Goods, Sports

Poirier, Hoevel & Company

12400 Wilshire Blvd Ste 915
Los Angeles, CA 90025-1044
(310) 207-3427
Email: info@phandco.com
Web: www.phandco.com

Summary: A retained generalist executive search firm. Fortune 1000 base with emphasis on manufacturing, financial institutions, entertainment, public accounting, consumer products, aerospace, service and high technology. Please note: we only accept resumes that are submitted electronically through our web site.

Key Contact - Specialty:
Mr. Michael J. Hoevel, Partner
Mr. Roland L. Poirier, Partner

Salary Minimum: $85,000

Functions: Generalist (All), Board Members, Middle Mgmt., Admin. Svcs.

Industries: Generalist (All), Manufacturing, Electronic, Elec. Components, Finance, Banking, Invest. Banking, Mutual/Hedge Funds, Non-profits, E-commerce, Entertainment, Telecoms, Defense, Aerospace, Software

Polachi & Company Inc

(an ITP Worldwide company)
10 Speen St
Framingham, MA 01701-4661
(508) 650-9993
Fax: (508) 650-1503
Email: info@polachi.com
Web: www.polachi.com

Summary: Our firm is focused exclusively within the high technology sector, specifically on high technology firms and venture capital funds. Our team is composed of seasoned search industry veterans who have collaborated on, and completed hundreds of search projects together for years. Our successful track record is predicated on experience, and experience counts.

Key Contact - Specialty:
Mr. Charley Polachi, Managing Partner
Mr. Peter V. Polachi, Managing Partner
Mr. Hale Cochran, Senior Partner
Mr. Jim Poe, Partner
Mr. Paul Moran, Partner
Ms. Maura D. McShane, Partner
Ms. Deb Colgan, Director, Research

Polhill Associates

PO Box 470653
Charlotte, NC 28247-0653
(704) 552-8800
Email: rpolhill@polhillassociates.com
Web: www.polhillassociates.com

Summary: Principals with strong industry credentials provide searches for CEO, sales, marketing and product support management. Focus: construction equipment, material handling, engine/power generation, forestry and mining equipment for manufacturer and dealer clients. We take pride in having high standards, and high client satisfaction.

Key Contact - Specialty:
Mr. Ray L. Polhill, President

Salary Minimum: $60,000

Functions: Generalist (All)

Industries: Energy, Utilities, Construction, Manufacturing, Finance

David Powell Inc

3190 Clearview Way Ste 100
San Mateo, CA 94402-3751
(650) 357-6000
Fax: (650) 357-6001
Email: dpi@davidpowell.com
Web: www.davidpowell.com

Summary: Our primary focus is officer-level searches for emerging and established companies in high-technology industries.

Key Contact - Specialty:
Mr. David Powell, Sr., Chairman & Chief Executive Officer
Mr. David L. Powell, Jr., Managing Partner
Ms. Jean Bagileo, Managing Partner
Ms. Kelly O. Kay, Managing Partner
Mr. Gary Rockow, Partner
Mr. Ray A. Fortney, Partner - *Non-profit, Technology*
Ms. Tiffany Raymond, Associate - *Computers (Software)*

Salary Minimum: $150,000

Functions: Generalist (All), Board Members, Senior Mgmt., CFOs

Industries: Computer Equip., Semiconductors, Venture Cap., Communications, Software, Biotech/Life Sciences, Healthcare

Power Search†

2235 Ridge Rd Ste 107
Rockwall, TX 75087-5142
(972) 772-5577
Fax: (928) 223-9099
Email: moon@mypowersearch.com
Web: www.mypowersearch.com

Summary: We perform retained executive level searches for the high-tech software market. We seek sales professionals, managers, and vice-presidents. In addition, we recruit directors and VPs of marketing, business development, systems operations and product managers. Our clients include venture-backed start-ups and Fortune 500 software corporations.

Key Contact - Specialty:
Mr. Thomas A. Moon, President

Salary Minimum: $85,000

Functions: Generalist (All), Mktg. Mgmt., Sales Mgmt.

Industries: Generalist (All), Software

Powers Consultants Inc†

22 Oak Bend Ct
Saint Louis, MO 63124-1435
(314) 961-8787
(314) 961-6437
Fax: (314) 962-3584
Email: powconinc@aol.com

Summary: We serve many of the largest and smallest professional service firms within the design/build and construction industries, providing clients with a unique two-year performance guarantee on placements plus an extremely high (87 percent) retention stick ratio.

Key Contact - Specialty:
Mr. William D. Powers, President & Chief Executive Officer - *Construction, Engineering, Hospitality*

Salary Minimum: $50,000

Functions: Management, Senior Mgmt., Middle Mgmt., Structural, Eng. Design, Architects, Bldg. Contractors

Industries: Construction, Architectural Svcs., Engineering Svcs., Property/Facility Mgmt.

Prairie Resource Group Inc†

413 Wisconsin Ave Ste B
Oak Park, IL 60302-3076
(708) 445-3456
(866) 582-9567
Email: kent@prgchicago.com
Web: www.prgchicago.com

Summary: 'Specialized to provide organizational consulting for recruiting for demanding positions in multiple industries on a fee for service basis. Particularly effective on unique personnel specifications. We follow an open information model where all information developed is shared with and remains the property of the client.

Key Contact - Specialty:
Mr. M. Kent Taylor, Founder & President - *Competitive intelligence, High technology, Non-profit, Organizational development, Research & development*
Ms. Kathryn A. Garmes, Executive Vice President & Corp Treas - *Computers, General management, ISO 9000, Mergers & acquisitions, Telecommunications*

Salary Minimum: $100,000

Functions: Generalist (All), Management, Senior Mgmt., Mfg., Mktg. Mgmt., Sales Mgmt., HR Mgmt., M&A, R&D, Engineering

Industries: Generalist (All), Manufacturing, Medical Devices, Metal Products, Computer Equip., Test, Measure Equip., Electronic, Elec. Components, Robotics, Semiconductors, Services, Non-profits, Architectural Svcs., Mgmt. Consulting, HR Services, Engineering Svcs., Supply Chain Mgmt, Communications, Telecoms, Software, Accounting SW, Development SW, ERP SW, Industry Specific SW, Networking, Comm. SW

PRAXIS Partners†

PO Box 35232
5004 Monument Ave Ste 102
Richmond, VA 23235-0232
(804) 763-5050
(804) 338-2134
Fax: (804) 763-1523
Email: info@praxispartners.com
Web: www.praxispartners.com

Summary: We are a boutique firm offering partner involvement in all aspects of retained search for senior leadership positions. Complementary consulting services in executive compensation, organization development and employee retention. Client base ranges from family-owned businesses to Fortune 200.

Key Contact - Specialty:
Mr. David H. DeBaugh, SPHR, CMC, Managing Partner - *Engineering, General management, Human resources, Manufacturing, Physicians*
Mr. Gregory E. Best, Principal
Mr. Ken Newton, Recruiter, Physician - *Clinical, Hospital, Insurance, Physicians*
Mrs. Jan DeBaugh, Senior Consultant
Mr. Don Pliszka, Partner

Salary Minimum: $70,000

Functions: Generalist (All), Management, Mfg., Plant Mgmt., Materials, Physicians, Sales & Mktg., HR Mgmt., CFOs, Engineering

Industries: Generalist (All), Construction, Manufacturing, Lumber, Furniture, Printing, Chemicals, Medical Devices, Plastics, Rubber, Metal Products, Machine, Appliance, Motor Vehicles, Misc. Mfg., Finance, Biotech/Life Sciences, Healthcare, Hospitals

Preng & Associates

2925 Briarpark Dr Ste 1111
Houston, TX 77042-3734
(713) 266-2600
Fax: (713) 266-3070
Web: www.preng.com

Summary: Specializes in global energy industry including oil & gas, chemicals, power, refining, water & wastewater management, energy services, eCommerce, manufacturing, natural resources, petrochemicals, EPC and environmental services.

Key Contact - Specialty:
Mr. David E. Preng - *Energy, Management consulting, Natural resources*
Mr. Charles L. Carpenter - *Energy, Manufacturing, Petrochemical*
Mr. George M. Rickus - *Power, Utilities*
Mr. Ralph W. Stevens - *Energy, Management consulting, Manufacturing*
Mr. Tom Slaughter, Director, Research

Salary Minimum: $100,000

Functions: Generalist (All), Board Members, Senior Mgmt., Middle Mgmt., CFOs, Engineering

Industries: Energy, Utilities, Oil & Gas, Mgmt. Consulting, Environmental Svcs.

Prestige Personnel Inc†

999 Old Eagle School Rd Ste 106
Wayne, PA 19087-1707
(610) 995-1066
Fax: (610) 995-1080
Email: chris@prestigepersonnel.com
Web: www.prestigepersonnel.com

Summary: We are a full service recruiting firm with experience in placing professionals in: engineering, manufacturing, production and operations management positions; in local, regional and national forums. We serve companies seeking professionals for growth, and quality candidates looking for a company that needs their skills.

Key Contact - Specialty:
Mr. Chris Hooven, President & Owner - *Engineering, Fastener, Manufacturing, Medical, Plastics*
Mr. Jay Messina, Senior Consultant - *Engineering, Maintenance, Manufacturing, Operations, Production*
Mrs. Nicole Hooven, Vice President, Operations

Functions: Management, Board Members, Mfg., Product Dev., Plant Mgmt., Quality, Engineering, Eng. Design, Process

Industries: Generalist (All), Manufacturing, Food, Bev., Tobacco, Lumber, Furniture, Paper, Printing, Chemicals, Soap, Perf., Cosmtcs., Drugs Mfg., Medical Devices, Plastics, Rubber, Paints, Petro. Products, Leather, Stone, Glass, Metal Products, Misc. Mfg., Consumer Goods, Engineering Svcs., Packaging

Prestonwood Associates

266 Main St Ste 12A
Medfield, MA 02052-2056
(508) 359-7100
Email: dcoletti@prestonwoodassoc.com
Web: www.prestonwoodassociates.com

Summary: Our expertise spans numerous industries including: high technology, healthcare, professional services, law firms and consumer products. We have a history of continuous access to the highest caliber talent in the following executive leadership positions, including CEOs, presidents, board members, marketing, sales, HR and business development executives.

Key Contact - Specialty:
Ms. Diane Coletti, President & Chief Executive Officer
Mr. Craig Greaves, Managing Director
Mr. James McClure, Managing Director

Salary Minimum: $100,000

Functions: Generalist (All), Board Members, Senior Mgmt., Mktg. Research, Sales Mgmt., PR, MIS Mgmt., Mgmt. Consultants

Industries: Generalist (All), Computer Equip., Mgmt. Consulting, HR Services, Telecoms, Software

PRH Management Inc

PO Box 17238
Stamford, CT 06907-7238
(203) 327-3900
Email: peter@prhmanagement.com
Web: www.prhmanagement.com

Summary: We offer a personal service giving professionals the attention needed to attain their unique career objectives. Eighty percent of our candidates are promoted in two years.

Key Contact - Specialty:
Mr. Peter R. Hendelman, President

Salary Minimum: $125,000

Functions: Generalist (All), Management, Board Members, Senior Mgmt., Middle Mgmt.

Industries: Generalist (All), Manufacturing, Computer Equip., Consumer Goods, Venture Cap., E-commerce, IT Implementation, Media, Publishing, New Media, Communications, Telecoms, Telephony, Digital, Wireless, Network Infrastructure, RF/Microwave, Software, Accounting SW, Entertainment SW, ERP SW, HR SW, Marketing SW, Networking, Comm. SW, System SW

PricewaterhouseCoopers Executive Search

200-250 Howe St
PriceWaterhouse Building
Vancouver, BC V6C 3S7
Canada
(604) 806-7000
Fax: (604) 806-7749
Email: execsearch.vancouver@ca.pwc.com
Web: www.pwc.com/executive/ca

Summary: Senior-level consultants work with public, private, government and not-for-profit clients on a broad range of middle management and senior executive searches. Fixed fee arrangement ensures complete objectivity throughout the process.

Key Contact - Specialty:
Mr. Bob McMillin
Mr. Grant Smith

Salary Minimum: $70,000

Functions: Generalist (All), Senior Mgmt., Middle Mgmt., Plant Mgmt., Health Admin., Sales & Mktg., Finance, MIS Mgmt.

Industries: Generalist (All), Energy, Utilities, Manufacturing, Finance, Media, Healthcare

Prichard Kymen Inc

4706 90A Ave NW
MS M
Edmonton, AB T6B 2P9
Canada
(780) 448-0128
Fax: (780) 453-5246
Email: pkymen@telusplanet.net
Web: www.pkymen.cjb.net

Summary: We recruit in the technical, engineering and mid-senior management areas.

Key Contact - Specialty:
Mr. Pat McKinney, Principal

Functions: Generalist (All), Senior Mgmt., Production, Distribution, Allied Health, Mktg. Mgmt., HR Mgmt., Engineering

Industries: Generalist (All), Agri., Forestry, Mining, Construction, Lumber, Furniture, Drugs Mfg., Machine, Appliance, Transportation

The Primary Group Inc

PO Box 916160
Longwood, FL 32791-6160
(407) 869-4111
Fax: (407) 682-3321
Email: primarygroup@pgsearch.com
Web: www.theprimarygroup.com

Summary: We offer executive search and consulting for mutual fund companies, insurance companies, broker-dealers, financial institutions and institutional investment management companies. We have expertise in management and sales from senior to regional levels.

Key Contact - Specialty:
Mr. Ken Friedman, President - *Mutual funds*
Mr. Fabio Duran
Mr. Michael Maron, Vice President

Mr. James Morgan, Vice President
Ms. Barbara Bontempo, Director, Recruiting - *CFOs, Finance, Financial services*
Ms. Cindy Real, Managing Vice President - *CFOs, Finance, Financial services*
Ms. Brooke Mann, Director, Recruiting - *CFOs, Finance*
Mr. Luis Fernandez, Senior Vice President - *CFOs, Finance, Financial services*

Salary Minimum: $50,000

Functions: Generalist (All), Sales & Mktg.

Industries: Finance, Banking, Invest. Banking, Brokers, Venture Cap., Mutual/Hedge Funds, Misc. Financial, Insurance, Life

Prime Objective Inc[†]

16 South Ave W Ste 217
Cranford, NJ 07016-2650
(908) 272-4421
Fax: (908) 272-4525
Email: info@prime-objective.com
Web: www.prime-objective.com

Summary: We are a niche search firm specializing in the recruitment and placement of professionals in the fields of accounting, finance & IT. We are networked with our other member agencies, this provides additional nationwide contacts through networked affiliates' specializing in accounting, finance and IT recruitment.

Key Contact - Specialty:
Mr. Adam Fitzer, President & Founder

Salary Minimum: $40,000

Functions: Finance

Industries: Manufacturing, Consumer Goods, Retail, Finance, Mutual/Hedge Funds, Legal, Accounting, Mgmt. Consulting, Advertising, Software

Primus Associates LC

1111 N I H 35 Ste 240
Round Rock, TX 78664-4244
(512) 246-2266
(512) 615-5678
Email: info@primusassociates.com
Web: www.primusassociates.com

Summary: Our high-technology sector specialization enables us to identify and contact target candidates faster and more effectively than generalist firms. Our client companies range from start-ups to $22B companies.

Key Contact - Specialty:
Mr. Sam Gassett, Chief Executive Officer

Salary Minimum: $100,000

Functions: Generalist (All), Senior Mgmt.

Industries: Computer Equip., Semiconductors, Communications, Telecoms, Digital, Network Infrastructure, Software, Development SW

PrinceGoldsmith LLC

420 Lexington Ave Rm 2048
New York, NY 10170-2003
(212) 313-9891
Email: recruit@princegoldsmith.com

Summary: We are a highly focused executive search firm specializing in investment management and alternatives recruiting. We have extensive experience in the recruitment of senior managers (CEOs, COOs, CFOs) as well as portfolio managers, research analysts and sales & marketing professionals. Our partners are hands on not only in developing client relationships, but more importantly, in executing search assignments.

Key Contact - Specialty:
Ms. Marylin L. Prince, Partner - *Financial services, Investment management*
Mr. Joseph B. Goldsmith, Partner - *Financial services, Investment management*
Ms. Megan Murray Steele, Vice President - *Financial services, Investment management*
Mr. Vincent J. Talamo, Vice President - *Financial services, Investment management*
Ms. Jenalee Doustou, Associate - *Financial services, Investment management*
Mr. Joel C. Wheatley, Director, Research - *Financial services, Investment management, Research*

Salary Minimum: $150,000

Functions: Senior Mgmt., Sales & Mktg., Sales Mgmt., Customer Svc., HR Mgmt., Finance, CFOs, Risk Mgmt., Pension/Ret. Planning, Minorities/Diversity

Industries: Finance, Banking, Mutual/Hedge Funds, Misc. Financial

Princeton Search Partners Inc

19 Andrews Ln
Princeton, NJ 08540-7633
(609) 430-9600
Fax: (609) 613-9776
Email: psp@latinipartners.com

Summary: Our firm is a generalist boutique executive search firm providing highly personalized and responsive service to prestigious clients.

Key Contact - Specialty:
Mr. Anthony A. Latini, Executive Search Consultant - *Financial services, Healthcare, Technology*
Dr. M. Katherine Kraft, Executive Search Consultant - *Human resources*
Mr. William J. Bricker, Executive Search Consultant - *Healthcare*

Salary Minimum: $75,000

Functions: Generalist (All)

Industries: Finance, Services, Legal, Accounting, Mgmt. Consulting, Call Centers, Insurance, Re-insurance, Software, Healthcare

The Principal Group LLC

PO Box 6234
Lancaster, PA 17607-6234
(717) 393-3000
(717) 396-9111
Fax: (717) 396-9786
Email: info@principalgroup.net
Web: www.principalgroup.net

Summary: Our focus is on general management and technology management in the manufacturing, plastics and materials industries. Responsibility levels are VP and president/CEO only.

Key Contact - Specialty:
Mr. Al Rossi, President - *Senior management*
Ms. Laurie Warner, Senior Counselor - *Plastics*
Mr. Bob Nichol, Senior Counselor - *Information Technology, Plastics*
Ms. Patricia Thayer, Research Assistant - *Technology*

Salary Minimum: $100,000

Functions: Generalist (All), Senior Mgmt., IT, R&D, Engineering

Industries: Generalist (All), Manufacturing, Chemicals, Plastics, Rubber, Computer Equip., Packaging

Printlink

620 Park Ave
Rochester, NY 14607-2943
(716) 856-5054
(800) 867-3463
Fax: (716) 856-8500
Email: usjobs@printlink.com
Web: www.printlink.com

Summary: We are a graphic arts professional staffing service for senior/middle print management and all digital prepress positions. Our staff is composed of veterans of the printing and prepress industry. We have dedicated databases to facilitate the placement of employees who are actively employed and seeking a change or better opportunity.

Key Contact - Specialty:
Mr. Arnold N. Kahn, President
Ms. Joanne Kahn, Co-Founder
Mr. Michael Grasso, Manager
Mr. Kit Tang, Recruiter, Information Technology
Ms. Donna Monaco, Operations Manager
Ms. Victoria Gaitskell, Recruiter
Mr. Alphonse Valenti, Recruiter - *MIS*

Functions: Generalist (All)

Industries: Printing, Advertising, Publishing, New Media, Packaging, Doc. Mgmt., Production SW

Branches:
314-466 Speers Rd
Oakville, ON L6K 3W9
Canada
(905) 842-2600
(877) 413-2600
Fax: (800) 856-8501
Email: cdnjobs@printlink.com
Key Contact - Specialty:
Ms. Myrna Penny, Managing Director

The Prior Resource Group Inc

120-50 Queen St N
Commerce House
Kitchener, ON N2H 6P4
Canada
(519) 570-1100
Fax: (519) 570-1144
Email: kitchener@priorresource.com
Web: www.priorresource.com

Summary: Our firm is a full service HR firm offering professional, executive and IT search services and placing administrative and industrial job candidates for permanent, contract or temp positions in a broad range of industries.

Key Contact - Specialty:
Mr. Mark Reno, President

Functions: Generalist (All)

Industries: Generalist (All), Manufacturing, Finance, Services, Communications, Software

Priority Recruiting Solutions, Inc.

2450 Hollywood Blvd Ste 201
Hollywood, FL 33020-6620
(888) 392-3272
(954) 920-8814
Fax: (954) 301-2211
Email: info@priorityrecruiting.com
Web: www.priorityrecruiting.com

Summary: At Priority Recruiting Solutions, our recruiters specialize in finding and delivering exceptional candidates for your company's difficult to fill management and executive-level positions. So whether you're looking to find that one individual with the ability to make an immediate impact or an entire team to launch a new business strategy, we can help.

Key Contact - Specialty:
Mr. Thad Greer, Manager, Business Development
Mrs. Kate Fiorvante, Corporate Recruitment Manager
Mr. Banning Hendriks, Corporate Accounts Manager

Salary Minimum: $50,000

Functions: Management

Industries: Construction, Food, Bev., Tobacco, Medical Devices, Computer Equip., Architectural Svcs., E-commerce, Media, Communications, Real Estate, Software

PROACT Search Inc

126 N Jefferson St Ste 360
Milwaukee, WI 53202-6120
(414) 347-0200
(414) 347-0201
Fax: (414) 347-0202
Email: resumes@proactsearchinc.com
Web: www.proactsearchinc.com

Summary: Retained executive search firm offering tailored recruitment services at executive and director-levels. Strength in academics, preschool, K-12 education, non-profits, colleges & universities, foundations, financial services, and HR services. Full in-house research capabilities, delivering high value added services to clients in a wide range of industries and organizations.

Key Contact - Specialty:
Dr. Nancy R. Noeske, PhD, President & Chief Executive Officer

Salary Minimum: $70,000

Functions: Board Members, Senior Mgmt., Middle Mgmt., HR Mgmt., Finance, Mgmt. Consultants, Minorities/Diversity, Non-profits, Environmentalists

Industries: Energy, Utilities, Transportation, Finance, Banking, Non-profits, Legal, Mgmt. Consulting, HR Services, Higher Ed.

Professional Research Services Inc

PO Box 819
Lake Zurich, IL 60047-0819
(847) 487-8100
(800) 777-4488
Fax: (847) 589-2305
Email: tom@prs1.com
Web: www.prs1.com

Summary: Firm providing name generation for search unbundled employment research and search. We provide services in most industries and functions. We primarily deal with mid-level positions.

Key Contact - Specialty:
Mr. Tom DeBourcy, President
Mr. Mike Silber, Senior Consultant

Salary Minimum: $40,000

Functions: Generalist (All), Middle Mgmt., Physicians, Sales & Mktg., Advertising, HR Mgmt., Finance, R&D, Minorities/Diversity, Hospitality

Industries: Generalist (All), Construction, Manufacturing, Food, Bev., Tobacco, Chemicals, Soap, Perf., Cosmtcs., Drugs Mfg., Medical Devices, Retail, Finance, Banking, Invest. Banking, Venture Cap., Misc. Financial, Services, Pharm Svcs., Hospitality, Hotels, Resorts, Clubs, Restaurants, Quick Service Restaurants, Full Service Restaurants, Inst./Industrial Food Svc., Entertainment, Recreation, Sports, Travel, Media, Advertising, Publishing, New Media, Broadcast, Film,

Communications, Insurance, Software, Biotech/Life Sciences

Professional Services Consultants

1811 Weir Dr Ste 190
Woodbury, MN 55125-2292
(651) 738-8561
Fax: (651) 730-6657
Email: terry@tpetra.com
Web: www.tpetra.com

Summary: Our firm has worked with hundreds of firms ranging in size from one person operations to multiple office conglomerates with national and international locations. The services provided by these firms extend from niche specialties through full service operations in: temp/contract professional, search and permanent placement.

Key Contact - Specialty:
Mr. Terry Petra, CPC, CIPC, President

Functions: Generalist (All)

Industries: Generalist (All)

Professional Team Search Inc[†]

PO Box 30185
Phoenix, AZ 85046-0185
(602) 482-3600
Fax: (602) 788-0710
Email: denise@ww-web.com

Summary: Our company search efforts are targeted toward engineering and executive-level professionals in the high-technology industry.

Key Contact - Specialty:
Ms. Denise M. Chaffin, President

Salary Minimum: $75,000

Functions: Senior Mgmt., Systems Analysis, Systems Dev., Systems Implem., Systems Support, Engineering

Industries: Generalist (All), Computer Equip., Consumer Elect., Electronic, Elec. Components, Semiconductors, Telecoms, Digital, Wireless, RF/Microwave, Government, Aerospace

Project Search Inc

11523-100 Ave NW
Rene Le Marchand
Edmonton, AB T5K 0J8
Canada
(780) 628-5100
(780) 628-5101
Fax: (780) 628-5104
Email: schellb@projectsearch.ca
Web: www.projectsearch.ca

Summary: We specialize in sales, marketing and management recruitment projects. As placement and recruitment experts, finding businesses and people who share the same vision is our greatest challenge and our greatest strength.

Key Contact - Specialty:
Mr. Bill Schell, Managing Director
Miss Jill Nickerson, BMGT, Project Manager - *Chemical, Equipment, Human resources, Manufacturing (Management), Medical (Devices)*

Functions: Management, Senior Mgmt., Middle Mgmt., Sales & Mktg., Mktg. Mgmt., Sales Mgmt.

Industries: Generalist (All)

ProLinks Inc

PO Box 7365
Alexandria, VA 22307-0365
(703) 765-6873
Email: golf@hughessearch.com

Summary: We are a highly regarded specialized recruiting firm, which works exclusively in the golf industry. We are small, cohesive and results oriented. This allows us to provide highly personalized service to a limited clientele.

Key Contact - Specialty:
Mr. Don Hughes, President - *Sports*
Ms. J. Reilly Hughes, Vice President - *Sports*

Salary Minimum: $75,000

Functions: Generalist (All), Specialized Svcs., Mgmt. Consultants, Int'l.

Industries: Generalist (All), Mgmt. Consulting, Hospitality, Hotels, Resorts, Clubs, Recreation, Sports, Non-Classifiable

ProSearch Inc
3555 Welsh Rd
Willow Grove, PA 19090-3857
(215) 659-9005
Email: info@prosearch.com
Web: www.prosearch.com

Summary: We specialize in retained search of IT professionals, from CIO to VP and Director levels. We pride ourselves in quality long standing placements and clients.

Key Contact - Specialty:
Ms. Suzanne F. Fairlie, CPC, President - *Client/server, MIS*

Salary Minimum: $120,000

Functions: Senior Mgmt., IT, MIS Mgmt., Systems Analysis, Systems Dev., Systems Implem., Network Admin., Minorities/Diversity

Industries: Generalist (All), Finance, Network Infrastructure, Software, Accounting SW, Database SW, Development SW, Doc. Mgmt., Production SW, Entertainment SW, ERP SW, HR SW, Industry Specific SW, Mfg. SW, Marketing SW, Networking, Comm. SW, Security SW, System SW, Training SW

Pure Bioscience Recruiting LLC
2623 Allerton Cir SW
Decatur, AL 35603-4465
(954) 237-3141
Email: sfuller@purebioscience.com

Summary: Our firm is a retained, boutique search firm working exclusively with biotechs and pharma.

Key Contact - Specialty:
Mr. David A. Fuller, President
Ms. Sondra Fuller, Vice President

Salary Minimum: $65,000

Functions: Generalist (All), Management

Industries: Drugs Mfg., Medical Devices, Pharm Svcs., Biotech/Life Sciences

Pursuant Legal Consultants
1426 Harvard Ave Ste 236
Seattle, WA 98122-3813
(206) 682-2599
Email: plclawrs@ix.netcom.com

Summary: Our firm is a premier legal recruiting firm specializing in professional personnel matters. We have a high-end retainer-based clientele. Our standards for experience and credentials are extremely high; therefore, we seek to procure stellar candidates for exceptional opportunities. Confidentiality and professionalism are the hallmark of this firm. Our office concentrates on law partners in transition and the general counsel needs of corporate law departments.

Key Contact - Specialty:
Mr. Allen G. Norman, President

Salary Minimum: $100,000

Functions: Legal, Attorneys

Industries: Legal

QSPP Group
1956 Rachael Dr
Lancaster, PA 17601-3628
(717) 569-6579
Email: recruiting@qspp.com
Web: www.qspp.com

Summary: Our firm is a strategy and results consulting firm. We advise our clients on the most effective methods to align their business strategies, processes and people to achieve and sustain desired results. We also handle recruiting projects for our clients.

Key Contact - Specialty:
Mr. Stan Telson, President

Functions: Generalist (All)

Industries: Manufacturing, Communications, Packaging, Software, Biotech/Life Sciences

Quantum International Ltd
1915 E Bay Dr Ste B4
Largo, FL 33771-2203
(727) 587-0000
Fax: (727) 587-0015
Email: quantumnct@pipcline.com

Summary: Boutique retained search; may include specialties (such as sales, finance, training, IT, R&D, engineering, manufacturing, etc.) designated by clients.

Key Contact - Specialty:
Mr. Douglas L. Anderson, Senior Principal
Ms. Carol D. Small, Senior Principal

Salary Minimum: $60,000

Functions: Generalist (All), Senior Mgmt., Middle Mgmt., Product Dev., Mktg. Mgmt., R&D, Engineering, Mgmt. Consultants

Industries: Generalist (All), Construction, Manufacturing, Textiles, Apparel, Chemicals, Plastics, Rubber, Accounting, Mgmt. Consulting

The Quest Organization†
1 Penn Plz Ste 5330
New York, NY 10119-5399
(212) 971-0033
Fax: (212) 971-6256
Email: info@questorg.com
Web: www.questorg.com

Summary: We function as an extension of our client management. We have CPAs with CFO experience in public companies on our staff and we provide personalized high quality business consulting along with every search assignment.

Key Contact - Specialty:
Mr. Michael F. Rosenblatt, President - *Accounting (Big 4), Asset management, Financial services, Human resources, Operations*
Ms. Donna Kelly, Director - *Accounting, Accounting (Big 4,Public), Financial services, Real estate*
Mr. Steven Rosenblatt, Associate - *Financial services, Real estate*

Salary Minimum: $100,000

Functions: Finance, CFOs

Industries: Generalist (All), Construction, Retail, Finance, Brokers, Mutual/Hedge Funds, Services, Entertainment, Media, Telecoms, Real Estate

Quick Job Search
28 Rock Hill Rd
Bala Cynwyd, PA 19004-2132
(610) 668-3223
Fax: (610) 668-0213
Email: recruitsmart@comcast.net
Web: quickjobsearch.com

Summary: We job search for you. 1) Empower job seekers with information. 2) Market your resume to employer targets. 3) Provide job hunting expertise. Engage us for complete career management, or pay as you go for specific services.

Key Contact - Specialty:
Mr. Gary Ames, Managing Director

Functions: Generalist (All)

Industries: Generalist (All)

Quick Leonard Kieffer
555 W Jackson Blvd Fl 2
Chicago, IL 60661-5715
(312) 876-9800
Fax: (312) 876-9264
Email: info@qlksearch.com
Web: www.qlksearch.com

Summary: Our goal is to serve our clients beyond their immediate recruitment needs. We want to be their partners for long-term success, based on our ability to build trusting and lasting relationships. We truly view our clients and our candidates as partners in search for exceptional leaders

Key Contact - Specialty:
Mr. Roger Quick, President & Chief Executive Officer
Mr. Michael Kieffer, Chairman
Dr. Robert Kuramoto, MD, Managing Partner
Ms. Martha Bermingham, RN, MBA, Managing Partner
Mr. Ronald Aldrich, Managing Director
Mr. Scott Sammon, PHR, Managing Director
Ms. Patricia Ahern, Principal
Ms. Sharman W. McGurn, Principal

Functions: Management, Board Members, Senior Mgmt, Productivity, Materials, Healthcare, Health Admin., HR Mgmt., CFOs, MIS Mgmt.

Industries: Generalist (All), Healthcare, Hospitals

Branches:
100 Park Ave Fl 34
New York, NY 10017-5564
(646) 290-6164
Email: info@qlksearch.com
Key Contact - Specialty:
Ms. Kathleen J. Galvin, Managing Partner

Quigley Associates
2845 Post Rd Ste 106
Warwick, RI 02886-3145
(401) 732-7622

Summary: Personalized, high quality firm serving all segments of the healthcare field. Emphasis on senior management and physician search. Practice backed by many years experience.

Key Contact - Specialty:
Mr. Jack Quigley, President

Salary Minimum: $70,000

Functions: Nurses, Allied Health, Health Admin., HR Mgmt., Benefits, Staffing, Training

Industries: HR Services, Insurance, Healthcare

L J Quinn & Associates Inc

(a Stanton Chase International company)
151 S El Molino Ave Ste 303
Pasadena, CA 91101-2562
(626) 793-6044
Fax: (626) 793-7183
Email: ljq@pacbell.net

Summary: Our firm performs senior level executive search and management assessment for both large and small corporations. The firm is rather small and, as a result, provides clients a very personal and professional service. Most of the firms' clients are growth oriented and dynamic organizations in need of creative, line and staff management.

Key Contact - Specialty:
Mr. Leonard J. Quinn, President

Salary Minimum: $100,000

Functions: Board Members, Senior Mgmt., Mktg. Mgmt., Staffing, M&A, MIS Mgmt.

Industries: Computer Equip., Misc. Mfg., Finance, Venture Cap., Telecoms, Real Estate, Software

Quorum Associates†

12 W 57th St Ste 901
New York, NY 10019-3900
(212) 308-6888
Email: info@quorumpartners.com
Web: www.quorumpartners.com

Summary: Our firm provides world class senior management recruitment capability to global financial institutions, investment banks and private equity firms. We combine the global experience of larger search firms with the personalized service and senior partner attention to clients, which characterizes the smaller, niche firms.

Key Contact - Specialty:
Mr. John (Tony) H. Barnes, III, Managing Director, New York
Mr. Francis S.H. Goldwyn, Managing Directory, New York
Ms. Andrea Lowndes, Principal, New York
Mr. Anthony G. Mecca, Senior Vice President, New York
Mr. Carlos Parajon, Principal, New York
Ms. Lisa O'Hara, Office Manager, New York
Ms. Phyllis Oki, Associate, New York & Tokyo
Mr. Benjamin B. Rauch, Managing Directory, New York
Mr. Tim Wilkes, Principal, London

Salary Minimum: $100,000

Functions: Generalist (All), Senior Mgmt., Middle Mgmt., Staffing, CFOs, Cash Mgmt., Systems Analysis, Int'l.

Industries: Generalist (All), Finance, Invest. Banking, Venture Cap.

QVS International

3005 River Dr Apt 501
Savannah, GA 31404-5079
(912) 353-7773
Fax: (912) 353-7133
Email: qvsconsult@aol.com

Summary: We are a retained generalist firm. We have executive search and support staff divisions. Our firm also provides management consulting in marketing, HR, policy & procedure development, flowcharting of operations, mergers/acquisitions and organizational development.

Key Contact - Specialty:
Mr. B.V. Cooper, President - *Middle management, Senior management*
Mr. Eric W. Robyn, Senior Vice President - *Middle management, Senior management*

Salary Minimum: $75,000

Functions: Generalist (All)

Industries: Generalist (All), Construction, Manufacturing, Services, Environmental Svcs., Aerospace, Packaging

R & L Associates Ltd

145 W 67th St Apt 5E
New York, NY 10023-5930
(212) 496-6066
Fax: (212) 496-5807
Email: rlassociate@aol.com

Summary: We specialize in staffing for the executive search industry and corporate HR. The 'go getters' of executive search, we go that extra mile. As management consultants in executive search, we help firms grow their businesses. Partnering with our clients in achieving their business objectives, we recruit consultants, help to open new offices and establish new industry practices. We structure a business development plan with an overview of each search's value.

Key Contact - Specialty:
Ms. Rochelle Schumer, President & Chief Executive Officer - *Executives, Human resources, Management consulting, Professional services*
Mr. Leonard Rehner, Chief Operating Officer & Sr VP - *Banking, Financial services, Venture capital, Wall Street*
Mr. Marvin Schumer, Senior Vice President - *Computers, Executives, Internet, Research, Research & development*
Mr. David Schumer, CIO - *Banking (Investment), CIOs, Computers, Computers (Networking), Finance*

Functions: Management, Senior Mgmt.

Industries: Generalist (All), Finance, Venture Cap., Mgmt. Consulting, HR Services, Higher Ed., New Media

R L R Group

2611 Fm 1960 Rd W Ste F124
Houston, TX 77068-3738
(281) 893-6128
Fax: (281) 893-0162
Email: info@rlrgroup.com
Web: www.rlrgroup.com/

Summary: We are full service retained executive search firm. We perform senior level searches in a broad cross section of industries. We partner with each client, using extensive research to secure the best possible candidates for every position. We have extensive, up-to-date intelligence and knowledge on a variety of industries.

Key Contact - Specialty:
Mr. Robert Hebert, Partner
Mr. Kent Richter, Partner

Salary Minimum: $80,000

Functions: Generalist (All)

Industries: Generalist (All), Energy, Utilities, Oil & Gas, Construction, Manufacturing, Chemicals, Venture Cap., Equip Svcs., Engineering Svcs., Environmental Svcs.

R&P Group†

3300 E 26th St Ste 103
Sioux Falls, SD 57103-4135
(605) 274-8800
(605) 274-8801
Email: janet@randpgroup.com
Web: www.randpgroup.com

Summary: Card industry recruiters; your company's searches are completed by industry insiders with experience in credit, debit, prepaid,

commercial, and smart cards. When you depend on us, you benefit from our extensive card work experience as well as our industry recruiting experience. Recruitment. Redefined.

Key Contact - Specialty:
Ms. Amy DeBerg-Ferwerda, President & Executive Search Pro - *ATM, CEOs, COOs, Credit cards, Presidents*
Ms. Stacey Koopman, Vice President & Exec Search Pro - *ATM, Credit cards, Market research, Marketing, Product management/development*
Mr. David Johnson, Director, Optimism - *ATM, CIOs, COOs, Credit cards, Risk management*
Mr. Ian Horsted, Project Coordinator - *ATM, Credit cards, Sales, Six Sigma, Treasury*

Salary Minimum: $55,000

Functions: Generalist (All), Management, Senior Mgmt., Product Dev., Sales & Mktg., Mktg. Research, Mktg. Mgmt., Sales Mgmt., Finance, IT

Industries: Banking, Misc. Financial

R/K International Inc

1720 Post Rd Ste 222
East-Post House
Westport, CT 06880-5643
(203) 255-9490
Fax: (203) 255-9633
Email: info@rkinternational.com
Web: www.rkinternational.com

Summary: We bring extensive years of experience to the search process in a collaborative effort with our clients. All assignments are managed from start to finish by the principals. Integrity and performance is the key to our success

Key Contact - Specialty:
Mr. Kenneth A. Walsh, President
Mr. Richard M. Dubrow, Executive Vice President - *Technology*

Salary Minimum: $75,000

Functions: Generalist (All)

Industries: Generalist (All)

Frank A Rac & Associates

72 Kings Hwy S
Westport, CT 06880-4712
(203) 226-1390
Fax: (203) 226-0667
Email: far53@aol.com

Summary: We are a retained executive search firm that has been in business for many years. We place senior executives in new economy, as well as the traditional Fortune 1000 companies.

Key Contact - Specialty:
Mr. Frank A. Rac, Founder
Ms. Barbara Pearson, Managing Director - *Technology*

Salary Minimum: $200,000

Functions: Management, Senior Mgmt., Middle Mgmt., Sales & Mktg., HR Mgmt., Finance, Minorities/Diversity

Industries: Generalist (All), Energy, Utilities, Manufacturing, Finance, Communications, Government, Aerospace, Insurance, Software, Biotech/Life Sciences, Healthcare

DB Radden & Co Inc

76084 Via Chianti
Indian Wells, CA 92210-7803
(760) 772-4331
Email: dave@dbradden.com

Summary: We are a boutique search firm focusing on the placement of high achieving mid to senior

level executives. We focus on identifying our clients specific needs based on their growth objective and we fulfill those needs with established professionals who have proven history of success.

Key Contact - Specialty:
Mr. David Radden, President

Salary Minimum: $150,000

Functions: Generalist (All)

Industries: Generalist (All)

Radosevic Associates

12658 Carmel Country Rd Apt 88
San Diego, CA 92130-3186
(858) 350-0050
Email: franjo@adnc.com
Web: www.radosevicassociates.com

Summary: We are a boutique firm with experience in recruiting specialized professionals, upper management and board members in the high-tech and biomedical fields. With multilingual capabilities and search assignments in North America, South America, Europe, Australia and Asia, we have an extensive contact database.

Key Contact - Specialty:
Mr. Frank Radosevic, Founder & President
Ms. Tanya C. Radosevic, Director, Research

Salary Minimum: $90,000

Functions: Generalist (All)

Industries: Generalist (All), Medical Devices, Computer Equip., Consumer Elect., Test, Measure Equip., New Media, Communications, Telecoms, Software, Biotech/Life Sciences

Rafey & Company

2246 Seaford Dr
Wellington, FL 33414-6227
(561) 422-3804
Fax: (561) 422-3803
Email: info@rafeyandcompany.com
Web: www.rafeyandcompany.com

Summary: We are a national boutique retained search firm with emphasis on consulting, communications, IT, software, general technology and HR.

Key Contact - Specialty:
Mr. Andrew M. Rafey, President - *Banking (Retail), C-level, CEOs, CFOs, Communications*
Ms. Mary L. Hoch, Consultant - *Consulting, Technology*

Salary Minimum: $50,000

Functions: Generalist (All), Management, Senior Mgmt.

Industries: Generalist (All), Semiconductors, Venture Cap., Mgmt. Consulting, HR Services, E-commerce, IT Implementation, Communications, Wireless, Fiber Optic

Raines International Inc

250 Park Ave Fl 17
New York, NY 10177-1703
(212) 997-1100
Fax: (212) 997-0196
Email: contact@rainesinternational.com
Web: www.rainesinternational.com

Summary: Executive search organization focused on assignments for senior level management & upwardly mobile executives. We specialize in strategy & corporate development, financial services, consumer products, healthcare, and retail & industrial sectors. Our financial services practice includes searches for research analysts, investment bankers, and related functions for major buy/sells side organizations.

Key Contact - Specialty:
Mr. Bruce R. Raines, President
Ms. Mary O'Keefe, Vice President

Salary Minimum: $150,000

Functions: Generalist (All), Management, Senior Mgmt., Mfg., Sales & Mktg., Finance, CFOs, M&A, IT, Mgmt. Consultants

Industries: Generalist (All), Manufacturing, Food, Bev., Tobacco, Drugs Mfg., Finance, Invest. Banking, Venture Cap., Mutual/Hedge Funds, Misc. Financial, Software, Healthcare

Ramming & Associates†

3 Thackery Ln
Cherry Hill, NJ 08003-1925
(856) 428-7172
Fax: (856) 428-7173
Email: ghr21@comcast.net
Web: www.members.tripod.com/~ramming/index.html

Summary: Most industries served. Extensive executive search and Internet recruiting experience.

Key Contact - Specialty:
Mr. George Ramming, Principal

Salary Minimum: $50,000

Functions: Generalist (All)

Industries: Generalist (All)

Rand Associates

204 Lafayette Ctr
Kennebunk, ME 04043-6869
(207) 985-7700
Fax: (207) 985-7879
Email: candidatemail@aol.com

Summary: Generalist with a concentration within manufacturing and financial services firms.

Key Contact - Specialty:
Mr. Rand W. Gesing, President - *Financial services, Manufacturing*

Functions: Generalist (All), Management, Materials, Sales & Mktg., Engineering

Industries: Generalist (All), Manufacturing, Food, Bev., Tobacco, Textiles, Apparel, Soap, Perf., Cosmtcs., Medical Devices, Plastics, Rubber, Metal Products, Motor Vehicles, Consumer Elect., Test, Measure Equip., Electronic, Elec. Components, Wholesale, Finance, Biotech/Life Sciences

The Rangeley Group

109 Stony Hill Vlg
Brookfield, CT 06804-3958
(203) 775-1865
Email: kennedy@rangeleygroup.com
Web: www.rangeleygroup.com

Summary: Executive search for client companies; corporate senior management; strong practice in SAP, ERP, BW, CRM and data warehousing from functional and technical consultants to CIOs; change management and Six Sigma executives. Industries include: spirits, wines, beers, water beverages, cosmetics/fragrances and aviation.

Key Contact - Specialty:
Mr. William C. Cooper, Chief Executive Officer - *Aviation, Change management, ERP, Liquor, SAP*

Salary Minimum: $70,000

Functions: Management, Senior Mgmt., Mktg. Mgmt., Sales Mgmt., CFOs, IT, MIS Mgmt., Attorneys

Industries: Manufacturing, Food, Bev., Tobacco, Soap, Perf., Cosmtcs., Consumer Goods,

Transportation, Mgmt. Consulting, HR Services, IT Implementation, Travel, Aerospace, Software, Development SW, ERP SW, HR SW, Industry Specific SW, Security SW

The Rankin Group Ltd

PO Box 1120
Lake Geneva, WI 53147-6120
(262) 248-5005
Fax: (262) 248-6035
Email: info@trgsearch.com
Web: www.trgsearch.com

Summary: Search firm specializing in the recruitment of wealth management professionals for institutional and personal trust, private banking, investment and family office positions.

Key Contact - Specialty:
Mr. Jeffrey A. Rankin, Chairman
Ms. M.J. Rankin, President

Salary Minimum: $150,000

Functions: Senior Mgmt., Mktg. Mgmt., Sales Mgmt., CFOs, Non-profits

Industries: Banking

The Ransford Group

808 Travis St Ste 1200
Houston, TX 77002-5758
(713) 722-7281
Email: info@ransford.com
Web: www.ransford.com

Summary: We are built upon three concepts: in-depth research, methodical search and industry specialty.

Key Contact - Specialty:
Mr. Dean E. McMann, Chief Executive Officer
Mr. Thomas W. Smith, Co-Chairman - *Management consulting, Tax*
Mr. Mark A. Malinski
Mr. Douglas H. Dickey, Managing Partner, Cnslt & M&A Practice - *Management consulting, Tax*
Mr. David R. Chyla, Managing Partner, Executive Search - *Management consulting*
Mr. William L. Hayes - *Management consulting*
Ms. Kimberly Turner
Mr. Richard A. Whittier - *Change management, Management consulting*

Salary Minimum: $200,000

Functions: Generalist (All), Management, Board Members, Senior Mgmt., Mktg. Mgmt., CFOs, Taxes, Mgmt. Consultants

Industries: Generalist (All), Accounting, Mgmt. Consulting, Telecoms, Software

The Ransom Group Inc

6956 E Broad St Ste 250
Columbus, OH 43213-1517
(614) 866-7821
Fax: (614) 866-7541
Email: ransom@theransomgroup.com
Web: www.theransomgroup.com

Summary: We are a retained executive search firm specializing in senior-level recruitment within the healthcare and managed care industry.

Key Contact - Specialty:
Mr. David Ransom, President - *Healthcare, Managed care*
Mr. Kevin O'Brien, Partner - *Healthcare, Managed care*
Mr. David Reusser, Partner - *Healthcare, Managed care*

Salary Minimum: $100,000

Functions: Generalist (All)

Industries: Insurance, Healthcare

Edward Rast & Company†

235 Montgomery St Ste 901
San Francisco, CA 94104-3000
(415) 986-1710
Email: er-kires@edwardrast.com
Web: www.edwardrast.com

Summary: Focused executive search to improve client operational results, revenues, profitability and reduce costs in logistics, distribution, supply chain, warehousing, transportation, catalog operations, customer service, tech support and IS. Additional management searches for accounting/finance, business development/marketing/sales, board of directors, compensation, HR, diversity/EEOC, and direct mail marketing.

Key Contact - Specialty:
Mr. Edward Rast, Managing Director

Salary Minimum: $80,000

Functions: Senior Mgmt., Distribution, Direct Mktg., Minorities/Diversity

Industries: Generalist (All), Manufacturing, Computer Equip., Consumer Elect., Transportation, Retail, Finance, Banking, Services, Pharm Svcs., E-commerce, Logistics Svcs., Supply Chain Mgmt, Hospitality, Communications, Call Centers, Packaging, Insurance, Software, Database SW

Ratliff & Taylor Inc

24950 Country Club Blvd Ste 300
North Olmsted, OH 44070-5333
(440) 801-7300
Fax: (440) 801-7400
Email: rtaylor@rtcpi.com
Web: www.ratliffandtaylor.com

Summary: We are providers of retained executive search focusing on building partnerships with our clients' business and cultural requirements. Continuous communication is emphasized by us to ensure ongoing satisfaction.

Key Contact - Specialty:
Mr. Frederick E. Taylor, President - *Finance, General management, Human resources, Information Technology, Marketing*
Mr. David Pack, Vice President, Search Operations

Salary Minimum: $100,000

Functions: Management, Senior Mgmt., Mfg., Materials, Sales & Mktg., HR Mgmt., Finance, IT

Industries: Generalist (All), Energy, Utilities, Construction, Manufacturing, Plastics, Rubber, Paints, Petro. Products, Motor Vehicles, Misc. Mfg., Retail, Banking, Accounting, Equip Svcs., Mgmt. Consulting, Telecoms

Rauenhorst Recruiting Company†

6800 France Ave S Ste 710
Minneapolis, MN 55435-2018
(952) 897-1420
Fax: (952) 897-1445
Email: resumes@rauenhorst.com
Web: www.rauenhorst.com

Summary: We focus on finding highly qualified individuals who are not actively seeking career opportunities. We match your required business needs, as well as the necessary personality style, to ensure a successful placement. We offer complete recruitment solutions for both companies and the professionals, providing both temporary and permanent placements.

Key Contact - Specialty:
Mr. Chuck Rauenhorst, President & Chief Executive Officer

Salary Minimum: $75,000

Functions: Generalist (All), Management

Industries: Agri., Forestry, Mining, Construction, Food, Bev., Tobacco, Misc. Mfg., Non-profits, Architectural Svcs., Engineering Svcs.

Ray & Berndtson/Lovas Stanley

(an affiliate of Ray & Berndtson)
PO Box 125 Stn Royal Bank
200 Bay St
Toronto, ON M5J 2J3
Canada
(416) 366-1990
Fax: (416) 366-7353
Email: managingpartner@raybern.ca
Web: www.rayberndtson.ca

Summary: Retained executive search and management consulting firm serving major worldwide companies across all industries and functions.

Key Contact - Specialty:
Mr. W. Carl Lovas, Managing Partner - *C-level, Senior management*
Mr. Paul R.A. Stanley, Senior Parnter - *C-level, Senior management*
Ms. Sue Banting, Partner - *CIOs, Information Technology*
Ms. Margaret Campbell, Partner - *Government, Municipal, Public sector*
Mr. Joel Fatum, Partner - *C-level, Consumer, Food service, Manufacturing (Management), Retail*
Mr. Larry Ross, Partner
Mr. Alan Small, Partner - *CFOs, Financial services*
Mr. Tony Small, Partner - *Automotive, Industrial, Manufacturing (Management)*
Mr. James H. Stonehouse, Partner - *Healthcare, Hospital*
Ms. Louise Sidky, Principal
Ms. Debbie Dimoff, Principal - *E-business, Financial services, Human resources*
Ms. Marilynne Dunbar, Principal - *Credit, Energy, Financial services, Insurance*
Mr. Andrew Norrie, Principal - *Business development, C-level, Executives, General management, Marketing*
Ms. Kelly Farrell, Principal - *Consumer, Food service, General management*

Salary Minimum: $60,000

Functions: Generalist (All), Senior Mgmt., Product Dev., Sales Mgmt., Benefits, CFOs, MIS Mgmt.

Industries: Generalist (All), Manufacturing, Finance, Media, Government, Healthcare

Ray and Associates Inc

4403 1st Ave SE Ste 407
Cedar Rapids, IA 52402-3221
(319) 393-3115
Fax: (319) 393-4931
Email: rayassoc@netins.net
Web: www.rayandassociatesonline.com

Summary: We are a firm specializing in school personnel matters. We have been recruiting and placing school superintendents, principals and municipal administrators for years. Our professional search team and our services are unmatched and our fees are very competitive, especially when the quality of service is taken into consideration.

Key Contact - Specialty:
Mr. Gary L. Ray, President
Dr. William Newman, Director

Functions: CFOs
Industries: Higher Ed.

Ray Partners Inc

301 Commerce St Ste 1350
Fort Worth, TX 76102-4121
(817) 806-2020
Fax: (817) 870-2908
Web: www.raypartners.com

Summary: We are a client-focused executive search firm that was formed in 2002 by four experienced search professionals. Our experience includes attracting senior level executives in all disciplines, including CEO, COO, CFO, and CIO, as well as heads of marketing, sales, human resources, investor relations, finance, technology, engineering, manufacturing and operations.

Key Contact - Specialty:
Mr. Breck Ray, President
Mr. Tim Bostick, Partner - *Aerospace, Banking, Consumer (Packaged Goods), Defense, Energy*
Mr. Mark Magruder, Partner - *Aerospace, Engineering, Environmental, Senior management, Six Sigma*
Ms. Debbie Smith, Manager, Office Administration - *Accounting, Office (Administration,Support)*

Salary Minimum: $150,000

Functions: Board Members, Senior Mgmt., Quality, CFOs

Industries: Generalist (All), Energy, Utilities, Oil & Gas, Food, Bev., Tobacco, Chemicals, Transportation, Venture Cap., Mutual/Hedge Funds, Misc. Financial, Supply Chain Mgmt, Defense, Aerospace

Raynak Search

PO Box 1566
Soquel, CA 95073-1566
(650) 472-2270
Fax: (831) 479-1799
Email: laura@raynaksearch.com
Web: www.raynaksearch.com

Summary: We perform results-oriented retained executive search for C-level, vice president and director level positions. We serve clients both large and small and lead workshops to identify, interview and evaluate candidates on competency and chemistry. Our specialties include biotechnology, financial services, medical devices, pharmaceutical, software, telecom, electronics, and real estate.

Key Contact - Specialty:
Ms. Laura Raynak, Principal Consultant

Functions: Senior Mgmt.

Industries: Generalist (All)

RCE Associates

24 Jefferson Plz
Princeton, NJ 08540-9542
(732) 329-1601
(609) 918-9183
Fax: (732) 329-1603
Email: rceconsulting@verizon.net
Web: www.plasticsearch.com

Summary: We have completed hundreds of technical and hard to find senior and middle-level executive searches for a variety of manufacturing technologies i.e., scientific instruments, plastics, metal components, tooling, retail and many others.

Key Contact - Specialty:
Mr. John W. Guarniere, President - *Manufacturing*

Functions: Generalist (All), Management, Mfg., Plant Mgmt., Sales & Mktg.

Industries: Generalist (All), Chemicals, Plastics, Rubber, Metal Products, Misc. Mfg., Electronic, Elec. Components, Services, Mgmt. Consulting, HR Services

The RDC Group LLC†
N77W15540 Crossway Dr
Menomonee Falls, WI 53051-4295
(414) 915-5846
Email: bob@rdcrecruiting.com
Web: www.rdcrecruiting.com

Summary: We are a full service executive search firm with a specialization in the power and energy industry. We pride ourselves in experience, proven results, integrity and quality.

Key Contact - Specialty:
Mr. Robert Cutler, President

Salary Minimum: $75,000

Functions: Generalist (All)

Industries: Energy, Utilities

Reaction Search International Inc†
2682 Bishop Dr Ste 208
San Ramon, CA 94583-4450
(800) 280-5092
(800) 280-5092
Email: info@reactionsearch.com
Web: www.reactionsearch.com

Summary: Our clients' success is our primary mission. We are devoted to reacting to their needs, while enhancing each diverse corporate culture. Executive search is the cornerstone of our services. The managing partners of our firm have been involved with placing CEOs to staffing national sales forces.

Key Contact - Specialty:
Mr. Robert Boroff, CSAM, Managing Director - *Biotechnology, Finance, Human resources, Sales*
Mr. Jason Dowling, Project Dir, San Francisco Bay Area - *Finance, Human resources, Operations, Sales*
Mr. Mike Northrop, Project Director - *Human resources, Sales*
Mr. Joe St. Leger, Project Director - *Biotechnology, Electronics, Sales*
Mr. Bill Davis, Project Director

Salary Minimum: $75,000

Functions: Generalist (All), Sales Mgmt.

Industries: Manufacturing, Retail, Finance, Services, Non-profits, Accounting, E-commerce, IT Implementation, Hotels, Resorts, Clubs, Media, Communications, Aerospace, Packaging, Software, Accounting SW, Biotech/Life Sciences

Recruiting Options
PO Box 2448
Staunton, VA 24402-2448
(540) 248-2300
Fax: (540) 248-5530
Email: mail@recruitingoptions.net
Web: www.recruitingoptions.net

Summary: We are a candidate sourcing firm specializing in all functional areas of HR. We identify, source, pre-qualify and refer candidates to our client companies. We operate on a consulting basis with none of the after-hire fees associated with traditional search firms. Our services are a more cost effective HR sourcing alternative to contingency and retained search firms.

Key Contact - Specialty:
Ms. Leah Zimmerman, Managing Principal - *Human resources*
Mr. Steve Zimmerman, SPHR, Senior Consultant - *Human resources*

Salary Minimum: $50,000

Functions: HR Mgmt., Benefits, Staffing, Training, Pension/Ret. Planning

Industries: Generalist (All)

Recruiting Options Inc
1375 Northview Ave NE
Atlanta, GA 30306-3230
(404) 874-1003
Fax: (404) 872-5164
Email: martha@coachmartha.com
Web: www.recruitingoptions.com

Summary: We offer caliber service without the high cost of a retained search firm. Options include a holistic search process for a flat fee including organization assessment, search execution, on boarding coaching; or for hourly fees; candidate interviews & referencing, organizational consulting, team building, leadership development and executive vision coaching.

Key Contact - Specialty:
Ms. Martha Eskew, President - *Advertising, Media, Public relations*

Salary Minimum: $75,000

Functions: Generalist (All), Sales & Mktg., Advertising, Mktg. Research, Mktg. Mgmt., PR, Graphic Designers

Industries: Generalist (All), Media, Advertising, New Media, Government

Recruiting Solutions Worldwide LLC
905 W 7th St Ste 228
Frederick, MD 21701-8527
(301) 524-9295
Email: margo@rsworldwide.com
Web: www.rsworldwide.com

Summary: Our firm was established on the principles of providing ethical, timely and cost effective fixed fee retained executive search services. Our firm is recognized as a valued business partner to a diverse register of emerging Fortune 500 and non-profit organizations with extensive experience seeking executives and professionals.

Key Contact - Specialty:
Ms. Margo L. McInerney Tully, President - *Accounting, Finance, Hospitality, Human resources, Information Technology*
Ms. Maggie Hucke, Vice President - *Accounting, Apparel, Brokerage, Finance, Hospitality*

Salary Minimum: $50,000

Functions: Generalist (All), Management, Senior Mgmt., Sales & Mktg., HR Mgmt., Finance, Cash Mgmt., MIS Mgmt., Minorities/Diversity, Hospitality

Industries: Generalist (All), Manufacturing, Wholesale, Retail, Finance, Services, HR Services, Hospitality, Media, Communications, Government, Aerospace, Insurance, Software, Healthcare

Mary Rector & Associates Inc†
40 S Prospect St Ste 200
Roselle, IL 60172-2064
(630) 894-5060
Fax: (630) 894-5607

Email: dcherdron@aol.com
Web: www.mrector.com

Summary: Our niche firm specializes in placement of mid and senior level management professionals in sales, marketing, education, operations and general management for the professional beauty industry, for example: hair care, skincare and nail care manufacturers, distributors and national chain accounts. We also work with day and destination spas with regard to general management and/or spa director levels.

Key Contact - Specialty:
Ms. Debra Cherdron, President

Salary Minimum: $50,000

Functions: Senior Mgmt., Training

Industries: Generalist (All), Manufacturing, Soap, Perf., Cosmtcs., Consumer Goods

Redden & McGrath Associates Inc
427 Bedford Rd
Pleasantville, NY 10570-3029
(914) 747-3900
Fax: (914) 747-3984
Email: reddenmcgrath@aol.com

Summary: Our boutique firm specializes in direct marketing (customer acquisition, retention and promotion), online/internet, product development, business analysis, and creative services among others for consumer and business-to-business products and service industries. A partner with an emphasis on service and quality directly manages all of our searches.

Key Contact - Specialty:
Ms. Laura McGrath Faller, President

Salary Minimum: $100,000

Functions: Mktg. Mgmt., Direct Mktg.

Industries: Generalist (All)

Redden, Foy & Associates LLC
71 Manor Rd
Ridgefield, CT 06877-4909
(203) 438-4846
Fax: (203) 438-0294
Email: searchrm@aol.com
Web: www.reddenfoy.com

Summary: Newly formed general practice firm by partners with extensive combined experience. Specializing in marketing, direct marketing, marketing research, business analysis and eCommerce. Industries include consumer & B2B products & services, pharmaceutical, retail & consulting. All searches directly managed by a partner emphasizing client satisfaction.

Key Contact - Specialty:
Mr. James Foy, Partner - *E-business, Human resources, Marketing, Non-profit, Retail*
Ms. Mary Redden, Partner - *Competitive intelligence, Consumer (Packaged Goods), Financial services, Market research, Pharmaceutical*

Salary Minimum: $80,000

Functions: Middle Mgmt., Mktg. Mgmt.

Industries: Manufacturing, Retail, Services

Redmond Research
703 S Bay Shore Dr Ste 9
Sister Bay, WI 54234-9485
(920) 854-6555
Fax: (920) 854-7557
Email: feedback@redmondresearch.com
Web: www.redmondresearch.com

Summary: We are a generalist firm known for our specialty practices in semiconductors, enterprise software, manufacturing, medical devices, pharmaceuticals and consumer goods. Our proprietary research methodology is designed to provide select clients with highly talented mid & executive level professionals. We conduct national/international searches for companies large and small.

Key Contact - Specialty:
Mr. Steven Diedrick, Chief Executive Officer & Founder - *Computers (Software), Consumer (Packaged Goods), Manufacturing, Start-up companies, Supply Chain*

Salary Minimum: $120,000

Functions: Management, Senior Mgmt., Mfg., Materials, Sales & Mktg., Finance, CFOs, R&D, Engineering, Int'l.

Industries: Generalist (All), Manufacturing, Chemicals, Medical Devices, Metal Products, Electronic, Elec. Components, Robotics, Semiconductors, Consumer Goods, Mgmt. Consulting, Logistics Svcs., Communications, Packaging, Software, Development SW, Doc. Mgmt., Production SW, ERP SW, Security SW, Biotech/Life Sciences

Redwood Partners Ltd

441 Lexington Ave Rm 702
New York, NY 10017-3922
(212) 843-8585
Fax: (212) 843-9093
Email: info@redwoodpartners.com
Web: www.redwoodpartners.com

Summary: Redwood Partners is a retained executive search firm that works with companies across North America, Europe, Asia and the emerging markets.

Key Contact - Specialty:
Mr. Michael Flannery, Senior Managing Partner - *.com, Entertainment, Media, Technology, Wireless*

Salary Minimum: $150,000

Functions: Board Members, Senior Mgmt.

Industries: Media, Communications, Telephony, Digital, Wireless, Software

Reeder & Associates Ltd

1095 Old Roswell Rd Ste F
Roswell, GA 30076-1665
(770) 649-7523
Fax: (770) 649-7543
Email: research@reederassoc.com
Web: www.reederassoc.com

Summary: We are a nationally known and recognized for expertise in the managed care/health care industry. We have an extensive database and research library of company/organization files and information on key executives and industry profiles. Seventy percent of assignments conducted are for the roles of COO and/or president/CEO.

Key Contact - Specialty:
Mr. Michael S. Reeder, President - *Healthcare, Managed care*

Salary Minimum: $250,000

Functions: Generalist (All), Board Members, Senior Mgmt., Physicians, Health Admin., Mktg. Mgmt., CFOs

Industries: Healthcare

Reffett & Associates

10900 NE 4th St Ste 2300
Bellevue, WA 98004-5882
(425) 637-2993
Fax: (425) 869-5347
Email: info@reffettassociates.com
Web: www.reffettassociates.com

Summary: We do executive search for the following industries: technology/e-commerce, specialty retail/apparel, sourcing & manufacturing and supermarkets/consumer products. When you retain our firm, you will have working for you a team of professionals with experience and expertise in your industry. That team always includes senior members of our firm. We don't delegate something this important.

Key Contact - Specialty:
Mr. William M. Reffett, Managing Partner - *Retail*
Ms. Mary King, Research & Recruitment
Ms. Molly Bell, Research & Recruitment
Ms. Carrie Giebelhaus, Research & Recruitment
Ms. Jeannie Forrest, Administration Director

Salary Minimum: $125,000

Functions: Generalist (All), Management, Board Members, Senior Mgmt., Product Dev., CFOs, MIS Mgmt., Mgmt. Consultants

Industries: Generalist (All), Manufacturing, Textiles, Apparel, Retail, Venture Cap., Mgmt. Consulting, Hospitality

Branches:
3200 Northline Ave Ste 130
Greensboro, NC 27408-7600
(336) 856-8128
Fax: (336) 851-9741
Key Contact - Specialty:
Ms. Deb Hamm, Research and Recruitment

Reifel & Associates

617 Riford Rd
Glen Ellyn, IL 60137-3923
(630) 469-6651
Fax: (630) 469-6659
Email: reifelassociates@aol.com

Summary: Search firm specializing in retained recruiting and industry researching. Search work emphasis in manufacturing operations, operational process improvements, Lean manufacturing management and Six Sigma leadership roles.

Key Contact - Specialty:
Ms. Laurie L. Reifel

Salary Minimum: $75,000

Functions: Management, Production, Plant Mgmt., Quality, Mgmt. Consultants

Industries: Generalist (All), Manufacturing, Services, Healthcare

Daniel F Reilly & Associates Inc

1175 Burbee Pond Rd
West Townshend, VT 05359-9640
(802) 874-8201
(802) 874-8202
Fax: (802)
Email: dfreilly@mindspring.com

Summary: We provide retained search only: (majority of searches are currently related to hedge funds). We have specialized in all technical needs of hedge funds. We also work with software publishers. We place in all positions, including: programmers, statistical analysts, statistical modeling, traders, presales, sales, regional sales, national sales managers, management, project leaders, project managers, software architects, CIOs, CEOs and CFOs.

Key Contact - Specialty:
Mr. Daniel F. Reilly, Jr., President

Salary Minimum: $60,000

Functions: Generalist (All), Management, Product Dev., MIS Mgmt., Systems Analysis, Systems Dev., Systems Implem., Network Admin., DB Admin.

Industries: Brokers, Venture Cap., Mutual/Hedge Funds, Misc. Financial, Software, Database SW, Development SW

The Douglas Reiter Company Inc

PO Box 947
Lake Oswego, OR 97034-0103
(503) 699-6916
Fax: (503) 296-2219
Email: info@reiterco.com
Web: www.reiterco.com

Summary: Our firm specializes in the forest products industry. With many years experience, we possess extensive industry expertise, contacts and demonstrated track record of success.

Key Contact - Specialty:
Mr. Douglas Reiter, President & Chief Executive Officer

Functions: Generalist (All), Mfg.

Industries: Agri., Forestry, Mining, Manufacturing, Lumber, Furniture, Paper, Chemicals, Mgmt. Consulting, Packaging, Mfg. SW

Remedy Search and Placement†

1030 Monarch St Ste 300
Lexington, KY 40513-1844
(859) 224-4455
Fax: (859) 223-2979
Email: lynnb@remedystaff.com
Web: www.remedystaff.com

Summary: Successfully placing professionals in accounting, engineering, finance, human resources, logistics, management, manufacturing, and sales/marketing.

Key Contact - Specialty:
Ms. Lynn Braker, Senior Partner & Vice President

Salary Minimum: $40,000

Functions: Generalist (All)

Industries: Generalist (All)

The Remington Group

200 Applebee St Ste 213
Barrington, IL 60010-3060
(847) 577-2000
Fax: (847) 577-2066
Email: sweet@theremingtongroup.com
Web: www.theremingtongroup.com

Summary: We specialize in the consumer products area concentrating in the house ware and hardware industries. Our expertise covers all non-food consumer goods (this encompasses consumer packaged goods to hard good durables) in the marketing and sales executive area.

Key Contact - Specialty:
Ms. Eleanor Anne Sweet, President

Salary Minimum: $60,000

Functions: Management, Sales & Mktg., Mktg. Research, Mktg. Mgmt., Sales Mgmt.

Industries: Food, Bev., Tobacco, Textiles, Apparel, Lumber, Furniture, Soap, Perf., Cosmtcs., Plastics, Rubber, Paints, Petro. Products, Machine, Appliance, Consumer Elect., Consumer Goods

Renaissance Resources LLC

9100 Arboretum Pkwy Ste 270
Richmond, VA 23236-3493
(804) 330-3088
Fax: (804) 330-7188
Email: dambruster@rrsearch.com
Web: www.rrsearch.com

Summary: We specialize in providing exceptional search consulting across a spectrum of industries and disciplines. The firm also provides specific guarantees to ensure the 100 percent satisfaction of client searches.

Key Contact - Specialty:
Mr. David L. Ambruster, SPHR, Executive Vice President & Managing Dir - *Engineering, General management, Human resources, Manufacturing, Process equipment*
Mr. Thomas Askew, MBA, Executive Vice President & Sr Consultant - *Engineering, Logistics, Manufacturing, Packaging, Quality*
Mr. David O. Seaward, PE, Vice President & Senior Consultant - *Energy, Engineering, Equipment, Finance, Manufacturing*
Ms. Brenda Frierson, MSE, Director, Business Development - *Banking, Business development, Diversity, Marketing, Minorities*
Ms. Sara Gaba, Senior Consultant - *Associations, Change management, Closely-held business, Consulting, Marketing*
Mr. Stuart Leinenbach, MBA, Senior Consultant - *Banking, Benefits, Change management, Compensation, Human resources*
Mr. Michael Steele, MBA, Senior Consultant - *Financial, General management, Logistics, Strategic planning, Technology*
Mr. Ron Witcher, MBA, Senior Consultant, Testing & Assess - *Change management, Organizational development, Senior management, Strategic planning, Training*
Mr. Alec D. Berol, MBA, Senior Consultant - *Human resources, Labor, Logistics, Manufacturing, Manufacturing (Management)*

Salary Minimum: $70,000

Functions: Generalist (All), Management, Senior Mgmt., Middle Mgmt., Mfg., Materials, Sales & Mktg., HR Mgmt., Finance, Engineering

Industries: Generalist (All), Energy, Utilities, Manufacturing, Finance, Services, Software

Renaissance Unlimited Inc

33 Flying Point Rd Ste 200
Southampton, NY 11968-5281
(631) 287-1507
Fax: (631) 287-2428
Email: jharmon@renaissanceunlimited.com
Web: www.renaissanceunlimited.com

Summary: Private client services, we place stockbrokers in various locations nationwide.

Key Contact - Specialty:
Mr. James Harmon, President

Functions: Finance

Industries: Brokers, Misc. Financial

The Renascent Group LLC

PO Box 6446
Fair Haven, NJ 07704-6446
(732) 576-8758
Fax: (732) 219-6642
Email: tberiont@rgroupus.com
Web: www.rgroupus.com

Summary: We are a premier executive search firm specializing exclusively in the search and placement of exemplary executives for some of the country's leading pharmacy/biotech and medical communications companies. We place senior executives including president, director of marketing, senior VP, product director, and PR director.

Key Contact - Specialty:
Mr. Trenton Beriont, President
Ms. Donna Beriont, Recruiter

Functions: Senior Mgmt., Mktg. Mgmt.

Industries: Biotech/Life Sciences, Healthcare

Renaud Foster Management Consultants Inc

550-100 Sparks St
Montreal Trust Building
Ottawa, ON K1P 5B7
Canada
(613) 231-6666
(800) 513-8117
Fax: (613) 231-6663
Email: ottawa@renaudfoster.com
Web: www.renaudfoster.com

Summary: We are recognized as one of the leading providers of expert advice in corporate governance, offering bilingual services to boards, CEOs and senior management in the fields of executive search, board and leadership services.

Key Contact - Specialty:
Mr. Tom Foster, Senior Vice President - *Boards of Directors, CEOs, CFOs, Human resources, Non-profit*

Salary Minimum: $80,000

Functions: Generalist (All), Board Members, Senior Mgmt., Int'l.

Industries: Generalist (All), Agri., Forestry, Mining, Manufacturing, Transportation, Finance, Media, Government, Aerospace

Branches:
1800-130 King St W
Toronto Exchange Tower
Toronto, ON M5X 1X1
Canada
(416) 860-6241
Email: toronto@renaudfoster.com
Key Contact - Specialty:
Ms. Lynda Naveda

The Repovich-Reynolds Group (TRRG Inc)

199 S Hudson Ave Ste 110
Pasadena, CA 91101-2917
(626) 585-9455
Email: behunted@trrg.com
Web: www.trrg.com

Summary: A highly respected executive search and management consulting firm specializing in corporate communications, investor relations and brand marketing searches across all industries and with corporations ranging from pre-IPO to large-cap organizations.

Key Contact - Specialty:
Ms. Smooch S. Repovich Reynolds, Chief Executive Officer - *Communications, Investor relations*
Mr. Tom Ekman, Vice President & Executive Recruiter - *Communications, Investor relations*
Ms. Arelys Rico-Acevedo, Vice President, Business Development - *Administration, Business development, Human resources*
Ms. Cathy Taylor, Vice President & Executive Recruiter - *Communications, Marketing, Public relations*
Ms. Susan San Martin, Vice President & Executive Recruiter - *Communications, Marketing*
Ms. Dawn Hanson, Vice President & Executive Recruiter - *Communications, Marketing, Public relations*

Mr. Joseph Bunning, Director & Executive Recruiter - *Communications, Investor relations*
Ms. Janine Zanelli, Executive Recruiter - *Communications, Investor relations*

Salary Minimum: $100,000

Functions: Generalist (All), Management, Middle Mgmt., Mktg. Mgmt., PR, CFOs

Industries: Generalist (All)

Reserve Technology Institute[†]

2610A Dunlavy St
Houston, TX 77006-3702
(713) 521-7977
Email: info@rti-hou.com
Web: www.rti-hou.com

Summary: We place energy/process (downstream & upstream, offshore and power) engineering specialists, senior management, Project Mgmt, business/project development and engineering management). Refining, chemical, topsides, gas processing, power and process control.

Key Contact - Specialty:
Ms. Mary Needham, President - *Engineering, Senior management*

Salary Minimum: $100,000

Functions: Generalist (All), Management

Industries: Energy, Utilities, Oil & Gas, Construction, Environmental Svcs.

Resolve Associates International

440 SE 13th Ave
Pompano Beach, FL 33060-7618
(954) 942-8344
Email: resolve@gate.net
Web: www.resolveassociates.com

Summary: We are an executive search firm that specializes in the recruitment of senior-level executives. Our Fortune 500, multi-national clientele are leaders in Internet/multi-media, IT, telecom, pharmaceutical, electronics, manufacturing, business services, distribution and retail.

Key Contact - Specialty:
Mr. John Juanito Finch, President

Salary Minimum: $75,000

Functions: Generalist (All), Int'l.

Industries: Generalist (All)

Resource Development Company Inc

925 Harvest Dr Ste 190
Blue Bell, PA 19422-1956
(215) 628-2293
Fax: (215) 628-2780
Email: rdc@rdcinc.com
Web: www.rdcinc.com

Summary: We provide services, which help companies build progressive, high performance organizations that attract and retain talented individuals, acknowledge individual greatness and reward their contributions.

Key Contact - Specialty:
Mr. Craig Toedtman, SPHR, Chairman
Ms. Dana Toedtman, Managing Director - *Education, Education (Higher), General management*
Mr. Kevin McClellan, Recruiter - *Pharmaceutical, Research & development, Six Sigma, Technology, Telecommunications*

Salary Minimum: $75,000

Functions: Management

Industries: Generalist (All), Drugs Mfg., Plastics, Rubber, Metal Products, Machine, Appliance, Misc. Mfg., Venture Cap., HR Services, Telecoms, Insurance

Branches:
9800 Richmond Ave Ste 240
Houston, TX 77042-4521
(713) 465-1118
Fax: (713) 465-9249
Email: chrisb@rdcinc.com
Key Contact - Specialty:
Mr. Christopher Bilotta, President - *Executives, General management, Management*

The Resource Group
99611 Overseas Hwy Ste 302
Key Largo, FL 33037-4344
(305) 852-1779
(360) 432-1117
Fax: (305) 852-1714
Email: ralph@eresourcegrp.com
Web: www.eresourcegrp.com
Summary: We are one of the largest search firm specializing in the direct marketing, catalog, eCommerce and telemarketing arenas. Work at the manager, director and VP level.

Key Contact - Specialty:
Mr. Ralph P. Peragine, President - *Call centers, Circulation management, CRM, Direct marketing, Internet*
Ms. Margaret McClung, Senior Vice President - *Database, Direct marketing, E-business, Internet, Marketing*

Salary Minimum: $80,000

Functions: Generalist (All), Board Members, Senior Mgmt., Middle Mgmt., Mktg. Research, Mktg. Mgmt., Direct Mktg., Customer Svc.

Industries: Generalist (All), Non-Classifiable

The Resource Group†
PO Box 331
Red Bank, NJ 07701-0331
(732) 842-6555
Summary: We fill key sales and management positions with companies involved in the sales of equipment and services for cogeneration, power generation, resource recovery and process industries. We have set up business development groups for utilities, oil/gas companies and equipment suppliers. We have recently been focused on distributed generation and alternative energy (wind, solar, low nox engines, etc).

Key Contact - Specialty:
Mr. Timothy L. Howe, Senior Parnter - *Business development*

Salary Minimum: $100,000

Functions: Generalist (All), Senior Mgmt., Middle Mgmt., Mktg. Mgmt., Sales Mgmt., Engineering, Int'l.

Industries: Energy, Utilities, Machine, Appliance

Resource Inc
PO Box 420
Marshfield Hills, MA 02051-0420
(781) 837-8113
Fax: (781) 837-8063
Email: tom@tchresource.com
Web: www.tchresource.com
Summary: Highly specialized within the foods and consumer product industries. Clients range from Fortune 200 to small rapidly growing privately held companies. Placement of senior and mid level management in the disciplines of manufacturing, quality and R&D, sales &

marketing, engineering & technical, supply chain/logistics and finance.

Key Contact - Specialty:
Mr. Thomas C. Healy, President - *Senior management*
Mr. Edward J. Hanafin, Vice President - *Sales*
Mr. Robert Knapp, Vice President
Ms. Dana Healy, Director, Business Development

Salary Minimum: $70,000

Functions: Management, Senior Mgmt., Mfg., Production, Plant Mgmt., Sales & Mktg., R&D, Engineering

Industries: Manufacturing, Food, Bev., Tobacco, Consumer Goods, Packaging

Resource Management Consultants
12239 Tildenwood Dr
Rockville, MD 20852-4161
(301) 984-4290
Fax: (301) 984-4292
Email: info@rmconsultants.net
Web: www.rmconsultants.net
Summary: As a professional search and recruiting firm we handle sales/marketing professionals, regional/national sales mangers and federal/state government professionals. We have clients that will back the management team of companies to buy the business and allow them to earn equity via a vesting period and performance. We help owners who want to sell their business but want to make sure the business maintains its culture and own identity.

Key Contact - Specialty:
Mr. Brian Hoffman, General Manager
Mr. Thomas Murphy, Director - *Construction, Sales*
Mr. Bob McDonald, Partner
Mr. Matt Hoffman, Research Coordinator
Mr. Pete Borman, Senior Partner
Mr. Patrick O'Brien, Associate
Mr. John Maskney, Associate

Salary Minimum: $80,000

Functions: Senior Mgmt., Middle Mgmt., Sales & Mktg., Mktg. Mgmt., Sales Mgmt., Sales Reps., Training, Mgmt. Consultants, Homeland Security, Non-profits, Bldg. Contractors

Industries: Generalist (All)

Resource Perspectives Inc†
PO Box 2010
Mission Viejo, CA 92690-0010
(949) 282-0042
(949) 635-9741
Email: delany@rpisearch.com, mcherney1@earthlink.net
Summary: With extensive experience in executive search, we serve the consumer packaged goods and related industries. We are specialists in R&D, supply chain, operations/manufacturing, marketing/sales, safety, regulatory, engineering and general management for personal care, cosmetics, foods, beverages, OTC pharmaceuticals, household, paper and related bio-technology categories.

Key Contact - Specialty:
Mr. Donald F. DeLany, Principal - *Consumer, Consumer (Packaged Goods), Marketing, Operations, Sales*
Dr. Steven D. Cherney, Principal - *Consumer, Consumer (Packaged Goods), Engineering, Management, Manufacturing*
Mr. Mark Cherney, Executive Recruiter - *Consumer, Consumer (Packaged Goods), Engineering, Food & beverage, Manufacturing*

Salary Minimum: $60,000

Functions: Management, Middle Mgmt., Mfg., Product Dev., Plant Mgmt., Quality, Packaging, Mktg. Research, R&D, Engineering

Industries: Manufacturing, Food, Bev., Tobacco, Paper, Soap, Perf., Cosmtcs., Biotech/Life Sciences

Results Consulting†
1550 Terrell Mill Rd SE Apt 12N
Marietta, GA 30067-8410
(770) 367-5444
Fax: (770) 988-8802
Email: recruit@resultsconsulting.net
Web: www.resultsconsulting.net
Summary: We specialize in architectural, constsruction, engineering, finance, information technology, sales, marketing and human resources recruiting.

Key Contact - Specialty:
Ms. Lepora Manigault, PhD, Principal

Salary Minimum: $40,000

Functions: Generalist (All)

Industries: Generalist (All)

Retis Associates Inc†
1550 N Lake Shore Dr Apt 11A
Chicago, IL 60610-1689
(312) 337-3077
Fax: (312) 337-3177
Email: retis123@aol.com
Summary: Professional, effective recruitment services for healthcare executives and physicians.

Key Contact - Specialty:
Ms. Lillian Retis, President - *Healthcare*

Functions: Generalist (All), Physicians, Nurses, Allied Health, Health Admin., MIS Mgmt.

Industries: Generalist (All), Healthcare

The Revere Associates Inc
PO Box 498
Bath, OH 44210-0498
(330) 659-0351
Fax: (330) 659-2108
Email: mike@fremon.com
Summary: Our search firm specializes in plastics, polymer, rubber, chemical, adhesives, coatings and packaging industries. We work with small, privately owned companies, as well as Fortune 500s and we are adept at high-technology searches.

Key Contact - Specialty:
Mr. Michael W. Fremon, President - *Chemical, Management, Plastics*

Salary Minimum: $60,000

Functions: Generalist (All), Product Dev., Plant Mgmt., Quality, Mktg. Mgmt., Sales Mgmt., R&D

Industries: Generalist (All), Manufacturing, Textiles, Apparel, Chemicals, Medical Devices, Plastics, Rubber, Paints, Petro. Products, Motor Vehicles, Test, Measure Equip., Electronic, Elec. Components, Robotics, Consumer Goods, Engineering Svcs., Packaging

Reyman Associates
20 N Michigan Ave Ste 520
Chicago, IL 60602-4824
(312) 580-0808
Fax: (312) 580-1181
Email: sreyman@reymanassoc.com
Web: www.reymanassociates.com
Summary: Each consultant dedicates exclusive efforts to one client's recruitment needs at a time,

producing extremely thorough and expeditious results. Our average turnaround time is five to six weeks. Our goal is to meet and exceed our clients' expectations. We believe individual client focus along with our search expertise is what makes that possible.

Key Contact - Specialty:
Ms. Susan Reyman, President

Salary Minimum: $100,000

Functions: Management, Mfg., Sales & Mktg., HR Mgmt., Finance, IT, Engineering, Mgmt. Consultants, Attorneys, Int'l.

Industries: Generalist (All), Manufacturing, Food, Bev., Tobacco, Paper, Chemicals, Drugs Mfg., Plastics, Rubber, Metal Products, Consumer Elect., Misc. Mfg., Transportation, Wholesale, Retail, Finance, Banking, Services, Mgmt. Consulting, Packaging, Insurance, Software

Rhodes Associates

555 5th Ave
New York, NY 10017-2416
(212) 983-2000
Fax: (212) 983-8333
Email: info@rhodesassociates.com
Web: www.rhodesassociates.com

Summary: Our firm is a global retained executive search firm with specialty practices in Real Estate, Asset Management, and Global Banking & Markets.

Key Contact - Specialty:
Mr. Steven Littman, Managing Partner - *Real estate*

Salary Minimum: $200,000

Functions: Generalist (All)

Industries: Finance, Banking, Invest. Banking, Brokers, Venture Cap., Mutual/Hedge Funds, Real Estate, Property/Facility Mgmt.

Richardson Search Group Inc

2313 Coit Rd Ste D PMB 114
Plano, TX 75075-3793
(972) 867-3323
Fax: (972) 608-0936
Email: rsearchgrp@aol.com

Summary: We are a retainer-only executive search firm that is experienced in handling financial, health care and IT positions for a diverse clientele. Our goal is to always be responsive, selective and productive.

Key Contact - Specialty:
Mr. James P. Richardson, President - *Finance*

Salary Minimum: $85,000

Functions: Generalist (All), Senior Mgmt., Middle Mgmt., Mktg. Mgmt., Sales Mgmt., HR Mgmt., CFOs, MIS Mgmt.

Industries: Generalist (All), Banking, Invest. Banking, Telecoms, Real Estate

W F Richer Associates Inc[†]

52 Deerfield Ln S
Pleasantville, NY 10570-1840
(212) 682-4000
(914) 747-3441
Email: wfr@wfricher.com

Summary: We are experts in advanced and emerging technologies. Profiles include CIOs, CTOs, risk management, quantitative finance, system architects, program managers, strategic technology planners and senior hands-on technical developers.

Key Contact - Specialty:
Mr. William F. Richer, President
Ms. Joyce E. Richer, Senior Vice President

Salary Minimum: $100,000

Functions: Generalist (All), IT, MIS Mgmt., Systems Analysis, Systems Dev., Systems Implem., Systems Support, DB Admin., Mgmt. Consultants

Industries: Generalist (All), Finance, Banking, Invest. Banking, Brokers, Venture Cap., Mutual/Hedge Funds, Misc. Financial, Media, New Media, Communications, Software, Database SW, Development SW, System SW

Riddle & McGrath LLC

1040 Crown Pointe Pkwy Ste 310
Atlanta, GA 30338-4777
(770) 804-3190
Fax: (770) 804-3194
Email: info.request@riddle-mcgrath.com
Web: www.riddle-mcgrath.com

Summary: We were established by two veterans of the executive search business to provide the highest level of professional service to a select list of clients. Client needs outside the US are met through our network of correspondent firms.

Key Contact - Specialty:
Mr. James E. Riddle, Principal - *Engineering, General management, Manufacturing, Sales*
Mr. Patrick McGrath, Principal - *Logistics, Transportation*
Mr. William H. Leslie, Managing Director - *Finance, General management, International, Marketing, Operations*

Salary Minimum: $90,000

Functions: Senior Mgmt., Mfg., Distribution, Sales & Mktg., HR Mgmt., Finance, MIS Mgmt.

Industries: Generalist (All), Manufacturing, Consumer Goods, Transportation, Services, Packaging

Ridenour & Associates

(a Taplow Group company)
1555 N Sandburg Ter Apt 602
Chicago, IL 60610-6324
(312) 787-8228
(312) 925-0990
Fax: (312) 787-8528
Email: ssridenour@aol.com
Web: www.ridenourandassociates.com

Summary: Executive search specializing in the recruitment of direct marketing and integrated communications professionals.

Key Contact - Specialty:
Ms. Suzanne S. Ridenour, President - *CRM, Direct marketing, New media*

Salary Minimum: $75,000

Functions: Management, Sales & Mktg., IT, Specialized Svcs., Mgmt. Consultants, Minorities/Diversity, Non-profits, Graphic Designers, Int'l.

Industries: Retail, Hospitality, Media, Insurance, Software, Healthcare

Riley Grainger Executive Search

8500 N Mopac Expy Ste 815
Austin, TX 78759-8347
(512) 467-9900
Email: brian@rgsearch.com
Web: www.rgsearch.com

Summary: Talent is the true source of competitive advantage and ultimately determines the worth of an organization. Companies have retained our services to identify, attract, and secure the "A-

Player" executives who are strong industry leaders and difference makers. These leaders continually impact, create value, and accelerate the success of their business.

Key Contact - Specialty:
Mr. Brian Riley, President

Salary Minimum: $100,000

Functions: Sales & Mktg., Mktg. Research, Mktg. Mgmt., Sales Mgmt.

Industries: Medical Devices, Computer Equip., Consumer Elect., E-commerce, Wireless, Software, Marketing SW, Security SW, System SW, Biotech/Life Sciences

Riotto-Jones & Company LLC

230 Park Ave
New York, NY 10169-0005
(212) 697-4575
Fax: (212) 370-9395
Email: ariotto@riottojones.com
Web: www.riottojones.com

Summary: We are a retained-search firm that recruits senior-level executives in wealth management and financial services.

Key Contact - Specialty:
Mr. Anthony R. Riotto, Founder - *Asset management, Financial services, Trust*

Salary Minimum: $150,000

Functions: Senior Mgmt.

Industries: Finance, Banking, Mutual/Hedge Funds, Misc. Financial

RitaSue Siegel Resources

(an Aquent company)
20 E 46th St
New York, NY 10017-2417
(212) 682-2100
Fax: (212) 682-2946
Email: ritasues@ritasue.com
Web: www.ritasue.com

Summary: Global searches for design managers and senior design staff. Industrial/product design; automotive, consumer, medical, toy and furniture; brand design; visual communications, packaging, interaction, usability, experience design; interior design; retail, hospitality, corporate, labs and healthcare; architecture. Strategic brand identity consultants, sales and marketing specialists for design companies.

Key Contact - Specialty:
Ms. RitaSue Siegel, President

Salary Minimum: $85,000

Functions: Specialized Svcs., Architects, Graphic Designers

Industries: Generalist (All), New Media, Non-Classifiable

Valletta Ritson & Company

20 Hawley St Fl 4
Binghamton, NY 13901-3216
(800) 844-1738 x1
Fax: (607) 786-8301
Email: vallritco@aol.com
Web: www.vallettaritson.com

Summary: Retained executive search focusing on senior leadership and technology professionals.

Key Contact - Specialty:
Mr. Frank L. Valletta, Chief Executive Officer
Ms. Stephanie Andacht, President
Mr. W. Michael Sabitus, Partner
Ms. Heidi J. Bowne, Partner

Salary Minimum: $50,000

Functions: Management, Automation, Sales & Mktg., R&D, Engineering

Industries: Drugs Mfg., Medical Devices, Computer Equip., Test, Measure Equip., Electronic, Elec. Components, Banking, Communications, Telecoms, Telephony, Digital, Wireless, Fiber Optic, Aerospace, Software, Biotech/Life Sciences

RLR Resources†

56 Calle Conejo
Corrales, NM 87048-8622
(505) 897-1201
Fax: (505) 897-1246
Email: rlrr@rlrresources.com
Web: www.rlrresources.com

Summary: We utilize a proactive approach to identify candidates who will best fit your company's job requirements. By developing the job specifications, we will focus in on the key talent in the energy industry.

Key Contact - Specialty:
Ms. Rita Longino, President
Mr. Roy Soto, Vice President

Salary Minimum: $40,000

Functions: Staffing

Industries: Energy, Utilities, Food, Bev., Tobacco, Misc. Financial, Non-profits, Mgmt. Consulting, HR Services, Higher Ed., Call Centers, Government, Homeland Security

RMA Search

101 Continental Pl Ste 105
Brentwood, TN 37027-5033
(615) 377-9603
Fax: (615) 370-5768
Email: rmaoi@bellsouth.net
Web: www.oiworldwide.com

Summary: Consultants specializing in executive search, corporate outplacement, executive coaching, employee appraisal, attitude surveys and operational consulting projects.

Key Contact - Specialty:
Ms. Angela B. Horn, President

Salary Minimum: $30,000

Functions: Generalist (All)

Industries: Generalist (All)

Branches:
633 Chestnut St
Chattanooga, TN 37450-4000
(423) 265-4855
Email: rmljt1@aol.com
Key Contact - Specialty:
Mr. Larry J. Trabucco, Principal

110 Reed Cir
Johnson City, TN 37601-2981
(423) 282-3393
Email: tminatra@naxs.net
Key Contact - Specialty:
Ms. Terri Minatra

301 S Gallaher View Rd Ste 111
Knoxville, TN 37919-5303
(615) 691-4733
Fax: (615) 691-4787
Email: rmaknox@bellsouth.net
Key Contact - Specialty:
Ms. Ellen E. Bowling, Vice President

5050 Poplar Ave Ste 2121
Memphis, TN 38157-2121
(901) 763-1818
Fax: (901) 763-1828
Email: rreilly@oipartners.net

Key Contact - Specialty:
Ms. Lynn Jackson, Senior Vice President

Roberts & Ryan†

150 S Wacker Dr Ste 3010
Chicago, IL 60606-4206
(312) 327-1000
Fax: (312) 327-1020
Email: info@robertsryan.com
Web: www.robertsryan.com

Summary: We are a retained search firm specializing in the selection of senior management. We focus exclusively on placing these often overlooked professionals at the manager, director and VP levels. We employ an exhaustive, research-intensive process that ensures our clients will receive a truly diverse candidate slate.

Key Contact - Specialty:
Mr. Robert Mittenthal, Partner - *Business development, General management, Sales*
Mr. Lawrence Ryan, Partner - *Finance, General management, Manufacturing, Tax*
Mr. Gregg Orloff, Partner - *Advertising, CRM, Public relations*
Mr. CorDell Larkin, Principal - *General management, Private equity, Sales, Technology*

Salary Minimum: $100,000

Functions: Senior Mgmt., Middle Mgmt.

Industries: Manufacturing, Consumer Goods, Finance, Services, Advertising, Insurance, Healthcare

Roberts Ryan & Bentley Inc

PO Box 36612
Towson, MD 21286-6612
(410) 321-6600
(800) 899-0399
Fax: (410) 321-1347
Email: rrb@rrbentley.com
Web: www.rrbentley.com

Summary: Research based retained executive search for mid and upper-management. Operates within most functional areas with emphasis on general management, finance, marketing and industrial/manufacturing practice.

Key Contact - Specialty:
Mr. Richard R. Cappe, President

Salary Minimum: $150,000

Functions: Generalist (All), Management, Staffing, Taxes, Systems Dev., Mgmt. Consultants, Minorities/Diversity

Industries: Generalist (All), Banking, Mgmt. Consulting, Insurance, Casualty, Claims, Life, Commercial

Branches:
3206 Sandy Ridge Dr
Clearwater, FL 33761-1933
(727) 786-1312
Fax: (727) 786-3349
Email: rrb@rrbentley.com
Key Contact - Specialty:
Ms. Sue Ann Whitley, Vice President

J S Robertson - Retained Search

2 N 2nd St Ste 1388
San Jose, CA 95113-1304
(408) 292-9292
Fax: (408) 292-4555
Email: info@jsrobertson.com
Web: www.jsrobertson.com

Summary: Full-service search firm with specialized skill in the semiconductor and related capital equipment industries and the Internet and related systems industries. Very strong emphasis

on ensuring cultural and organizational fit in addition to skill and competence matching.

Key Contact - Specialty:
Mr. Jim Robertson, Principal - *General management*
Ms. Sandy Mrykalo, Director, Research & Administration
Ms. Pamela Hart, Senior Search Consultant
Mr. Greg Goodere, Principal - *Computers (Software)*
Ms. Kay Lovegrove, Recruiter
Mr. Mike Paradis, Recruiter

Salary Minimum: $160,000

Functions: Management, Senior Mgmt., Middle Mgmt., Product Dev., Plant Mgmt., Materials, Sales & Mktg., HR Mgmt., CFOs, MIS Mgmt.

Industries: Manufacturing, Computer Equip., Consumer Elect., Test, Measure Equip., Electronic, Elec. Components, Semiconductors, Software

Robinson Consulting Group

8 Harmon Cove Tower
Secaucus, NJ 07094-1753
(201) 617-9595
Fax: (201) 617-1434
Email: eric@rcgsearch.com
Web: www.rcgsearch.com

Summary: We recruit top-flight minority and female talent on an executive search basis and work successfully with major Fortune 500 companies in all areas of search.

Key Contact - Specialty:
Mr. Bruce Robinson, President
Mr. Eric Robinson, Partner & Vice President
Mr. John Robinson, Senior Consultant

Salary Minimum: $100,000

Functions: Generalist (All), Mfg., Materials, Sales & Mktg., HR Mgmt., Finance, IT, R&D, Minorities/Diversity, Non-profits

Industries: Generalist (All), Manufacturing, Chemicals, Drugs Mfg., Invest. Banking, Brokers, Services, Non-profits, Accounting, Media, Insurance, Healthcare, Non-Classifiable

Robinson, Fraser Group Ltd

400-1235 Bay St
Scrivener Building
Toronto, ON M5R 3K4
Canada
(416) 977-9174
Email: es@robinsonfraser.com

Summary: We specialize in building executive teams.

Key Contact - Specialty:
Mr. Stephen Robinson, President
Dr. Floyd Babcock, Vice President, Not-For-Profit Division
Ms. Alexandra Ross, Director, Client Relations
Ms. Marj Shaw, Executive Assistant

Salary Minimum: $80,000

Functions: Generalist (All), Management, Board Members, Senior Mgmt., HR Mgmt., CFOs, MIS Mgmt.

Industries: Generalist (All), Finance, Misc. Financial, Services, Non-profits, Mgmt. Consulting, Non-Classifiable

Robsham & Associates

4 S Market Place Fl 4
Boston, MA 02109-6201
(617) 742-2944
Fax: (617) 523-0464

Email: bhr@robshamgroup.com
Web: www.robshamgroup.com

Summary: Generous and complete involvement in each client's search; detailed screening and interviewing - extensive candidate reports. We work with a sense of urgency.

Key Contact - Specialty:
Ms. Beverly H. Robsham, President & Founder - *Finance, Marketing*
Mr. Frank Faggiano, Head, Human Resources
Mr. Jason Dalrymple, Database Administrator - *Convenience stores, Data processing, Engineering, Information Technology, Wholesale*

Salary Minimum: $75,000

Functions: Generalist (All)

Industries: Finance, Mgmt. Consulting, HR Services, Advertising, Publishing, New Media, Broadcast, Film

Rodzik & Associates Inc

8601 Six Forks Rd Ste 400
Raleigh, NC 27615-2965
(919) 846-8150
Fax: (919) 846-9130

Summary: We are a full-service firm with optional services and customized pricing to meet client requirements.

Key Contact - Specialty:
Mr. Gerald F. Rodzik, Managing Director
Ms. C.L. Rodzik, President
Mr. T.A. Rodzik, Esq., Secretary & General Counsel
Dr. S.M. Rodzik, PhD, Treasurer

Salary Minimum: $75,000

Functions: Generalist (All)

Industries: Energy, Utilities, Manufacturing, Finance, Services, Software, Biotech/Life Sciences, Healthcare

Rogers - McManamon Executive Search

33781 Via Cascada
San Juan Capistrano, CA 92675-5036
(949) 496-1614
Fax: (949) 496-2305
Email: rogers@mcmanamon.com
Web: www.mcmanamon.com

Summary: Our strength is our easy grasp of technology. We are ideally suited to place team leaders within marketing and engineering roles at today's high technology and biotechnology companies. We are also skilled at recruiting chief information officers, because we understand today's networks, applications and IS.

Key Contact - Specialty:
Mr. Tim McManamon, Partner
Ms. Gay Rogers, Partner - *Engineering, Marketing*

Salary Minimum: $100,000

Functions: Mktg. Mgmt., MIS Mgmt., R&D

Industries: Generalist (All), Test, Measure Equip., Semiconductors, E-commerce, IT Implementation, Communications, Software, Biotech/Life Sciences

ROI International Inc

336 Park Ave N
Renton, WA 98057-5715
(425) 264-2100
Email: hr@roi-intl.com
Web: www.roi-intl.com

Summary: We embarked on a quest to develop a superior process and assemble a team of great recruiters who could identify and place candidates, while consistently outperforming their peers. By exceeding this goal, we add real measurable value to the search process and provide our clients with above average returns on their investment in people.

Key Contact - Specialty:
Mr. Marc Goyette, President - *E-business, Telecommunications*
Ms. Margo Goyette, Vice President - *Telecommunications*

Salary Minimum: $125,000

Functions: Generalist (All)

Industries: Telecoms, Call Centers, Telephony, Digital, Wireless, Network Infrastructure, Insurance, Healthcare

Rolland Consulting Group Inc

1405-1 Car Westmount
One Westmount Square
Westmount, QC H3Z 2P9
Canada
(514) 937 7112
Fax: (514) 937-9738
Email: rgc@videotron.ca

Summary: We specialize in executive recruiting for each client, a specific search strategy.

Key Contact - Specialty:
Ms. Denise Rolland, President
Ms. Jasmine Asselin, Vice President

Functions: Generalist (All), Board Members, Senior Mgmt., Mfg., Sales & Mktg., HR Mgmt., CFOs, MIS Mgmt.

Industries: Generalist (All), Manufacturing, Retail, Media, Aerospace, Healthcare

Rolland Resources Humaines Inc

620-1600 Boul Henri-Bourassa O
Le 1600 Ouest Henri-Bourassa
Montreal, QC H3M 3E2
Canada
(514) 333-6619
Email: rolland@rrh.qc.ca

Summary: We provide recruiting services mostly specializing in the financial sector.

Key Contact - Specialty:
Mr. Guy Rolland, President - *Financial services, Manufacturing, Telecommunications*

Salary Minimum: $60,000

Functions: Generalist (All), Management, Mfg., Materials, Sales & Mktg., HR Mgmt., Finance, Minorities/Diversity

Industries: Generalist (All), Manufacturing, Paper, Chemicals, Drugs Mfg., Invest. Banking, Venture Cap., Telecoms

Rooney Associates Inc

501 Pennsylvania Ave
Glen Ellyn, IL 60137-4456
(630) 469-7102
Fax: (630) 469-0749
Email: jrooney@rooneyassociates.net
Web: rooneyassociates.net

Summary: Boutique firm, highly personalized service. Practice adept in aiding cultural changes or assignments requiring sensitivity, along with creativity.

Key Contact - Specialty:
Mr. Joseph J. Rooney, President - *General management, High technology, Telecommunications*
Mr. Matthew Rooney, Associate

Salary Minimum: $90,000

Functions: Management, Board Members, Senior Mgmt., Middle Mgmt., Mfg., Healthcare, Mktg. Mgmt., Sales Mgmt., Finance, CFOs

Industries: Food, Bev., Tobacco, Computer Equip., Consumer Elect., Banking, Invest. Banking, Venture Cap., Misc. Financial, Telecoms, Software, Healthcare, Hospitals

Ropella & Associates

6480 Highway 90 Ste A
Milton, FL 32570-4560
(850) 983-4777
Fax: (850) 983-1627
Email: ropella@ropella.com
Web: www.ropella.com

Summary: The chemical and allied industries are our focus every day. We track business and employment trends and monitor current developments within commodity, specialty, organic and inorganic chemical manufacturers, distributors and the allied industries.

Key Contact - Specialty:
Mr. Patrick B. Ropella, President & Chief Executive Officer

Salary Minimum: $50,000

Functions: Management, Board Members, Senior Mgmt., Middle Mgmt., Mktg. Research, Mktg. Mgmt., Sales Mgmt.

Industries: Chemicals

Ropes Associates Inc

333 N New River Dr E Ste 3000
Fort Lauderdale, FL 33301-2269
(954) 525-6600
Fax: (954) 779-7279
Email: info@ropesassociates.com
Web: www.ropesassociates.com

Summary: We specialize in real estate industry including developers, builders and operators of residential, resort, commercial and industrial properties.

Key Contact - Specialty:
Mr. John Ropes, President - *Real estate*
Ms. Morgan P. Smith, Associate Partner
Ms. Tara Kriss, Associate - *Financial services*

Salary Minimum: $150,000

Functions: Generalist (All), Senior Mgmt., Middle Mgmt., Mktg. Mgmt., Sales Mgmt., CFOs

Industries: Generalist (All), Construction, Hospitality, Real Estate

Rosebud Research Inc

21 Van Ct
Waldwick, NJ 07463-1614
(201) 612-1055
Email: coreyr@optonline.net

Summary: We work specifically for corporations and retained executive search firms on difficult searches by providing customized cost-effective candidate ID and development. We are a results-driven firm with a proven track record of success. Utilizing creative, concrete sourcing methods and working a strong business network we present on target, interested candidates.

Key Contact - Specialty:
Ms. Corey Rose, Principal - *Consulting, Financial services, Marketing, Non-profit, Sales*

Salary Minimum: $85,000

Functions: Management, Board Members, Senior Mgmt., Middle Mgmt., Sales & Mktg., IT, MIS

Mgmt., Systems Implem., Mgmt. Consultants, Minorities/Diversity

Industries: Drugs Mfg., Medical Devices, Banking, Non-profits, Mgmt. Consulting, HR Services, Hospitality, New Media, Real Estate, Software, Entertainment SW

Rosenthal Associated Intl LLC

230 Park Ave Rm 1000
New York, NY 10169-1099
(212) 268-6300
(908) 389-0505
Fax: (908) 389-0511
Email: abbe@raisearch.com
Web: www.raisearch.com

Summary: We are a boutique search firm specializing in female and diversity research and talent acquisition for all levels and most functional areas on a global basis. We also offer alternative fee solutions.

Key Contact - Specialty:
Ms. Abbe L. Weissman, Principal - *Diversity*
Ms. Randi Fonseca, Vice President
Ms. Heidi Teiko Casimir Finley, Vice President

Salary Minimum: $100,000

Functions: Generalist (All), Minorities/Diversity

Industries: Generalist (All)

Ross & Company Inc

49 John St
Southport, CT 06890-1436
(203) 254-9800
Fax: (203) 254-9801
Email: lr@rosssearch.com
Web: www.rosssearch.com

Summary: We are one of the leading executive recruiting firms, specializing in senior management searches that target various sectors of the healthcare, IT and communications industries.

Key Contact - Specialty:
Mr. H. Lawrence Ross, Managing Director
Mr. James MacDonald, Managing Director
Ms. Diane McIntyre, Managing Director
Ms. Celeste Goodhue, Managing Director
Ms. Heather Beliveau, Senior Associate

Salary Minimum: $150,000

Functions: Senior Mgmt.

Industries: Drugs Mfg., Medical Devices, Venture Cap., Pharm Svcs., Mgmt. Consulting, E-commerce, Media, Software, Biotech/Life Sciences, Healthcare

The Rottman Group Inc

1 Seven Acres Dr Ste 200
Little Rock, AR 72223-4294
(501) 228-4433
Fax: (501) 228-4466
Email: don@rottmangroup.com
Web: www.rottmangroup.com

Summary: Retained healthcare services oriented firm that seeks to maximize an organization's human system by strategically understanding and approaching recruitment.

Key Contact - Specialty:
Mr. Don Rottman, President

Salary Minimum: $60,000

Functions: Generalist (All), Materials, Nurses, Health Admin., Mktg. Mgmt., HR Mgmt., Finance, CFOs, MIS Mgmt., Mgmt. Consultants

Industries: Healthcare, Hospitals

Rovner & Associates Inc[†]

PO Box 835
New Buffalo, MI 49117-0835
(773) 262-5111
Fax: (773) 262-5199
Email: consultant@rovner.com
Web: www.rovner.com

Summary: We specialize in IT professionals from CIO, CTO, VP, high level strategists and architects, including their immediate teams, project and program managers. We also sub-specialize in high-level HR professionals. We pride ourselves in building long term relationships by providing quality search services with uncompromising thoroughness, high integrity, confidentiality and delivery.

Key Contact - Specialty:
Ms. Bettyann Rovner, President - *Technology*

Salary Minimum: $90,000

Functions: Board Members, Sales & Mktg., HR Mgmt., IT, MIS Mgmt., Mgmt. Consultants

Industries: Energy, Utilities, Finance, Services, Mgmt. Consulting, HR Services, New Media, Telecoms, Software

Rowan & Ruggles LLC

11710 Plaza America Dr Ste 2000
Reston, VA 20190-4743
(703) 871-5235
Fax: (703) 871-5111
Email: info@rowrug.com
Web: www.rowrug.com

Summary: We are an executive search, leadership and organizational consultancy committed to helping you achieve a successful future for your enterprise or career.

Key Contact - Specialty:
Mr. Larry Dilworth, Managing Director

Salary Minimum: $100,000

Functions: Management, HR Mgmt., Mgmt. Consultants

Industries: Generalist (All), Energy, Utilities, Manufacturing, Services, Non-profits, Mgmt. Consulting, HR Services, IT Implementation, Media, Communications, Government

David Rowe & Associates Inc

9021 Monroe Ave
Brookfield, IL 60513-1313
(708) 387-1000

Summary: Our firm conducts searches for all executive and management levels in hospitals, hospital systems, organized physician group practices and managed care companies. We conduct searches for deeply skilled networking consultants and engineers, especially those with a communications service provider background.

Key Contact - Specialty:
Mr. David E. Rowe, President
Ms. Lydia Imler-Diskin, Vice President
Ms. Tiffany P. Stoner, Associate

Salary Minimum: $80,000

Functions: Senior Mgmt., Middle Mgmt., Health Admin.

Industries: Healthcare, Hospitals

RSM McGladrey Inc

221 3rd Ave Se Ste 300
Cedar Rapids, IA 52401-1525
(319) 298-5333
Fax: (319) 366-6970
Email: iowaexecutivesearch@rsmi.com
Web: www.rsmmcgladrey.com

Summary: We use a proven sequence of steps to place the best candidate for our clients. We offer a full service to our clients where only the top three to four candidates are presented with their references checked and background verified. We have performed numerous industry-specific and specialized functional searches that have helped hundreds of organizations find the right individual. We focus on mid-size companies in Iowa, KC and Omaha.

Key Contact - Specialty:
Ms. Julie Linderman, Practice Leader & Consulting Manager - *Information Technology, Manufacturing*
Ms. Brandi Adam, Search Consultant - *Manufacturing*

Salary Minimum: $40,000

Functions: Generalist (All), Management, Middle Mgmt., Mfg., Healthcare, Sales & Mktg., HR Mgmt., Finance, IT, Non-profits

Industries: Generalist (All), Construction, Manufacturing, Plastics, Rubber, Metal Products, Computer Equip., Finance, Mutual/Hedge Funds, Non-profits, Mfg. SW, Marketing SW

Affiliates:
Creative Financial Staffing
Des Moines, IA

Branches:
20 N Martingale Rd Ste 500
Schaumburg, IL 60173-2420
(847) 413-6900
Fax: (847) 517-7067
Email: steve.callisher@rsmi.com
Key Contact - Specialty:
Mr. Steve Callisher

400 Locust St Ste 640
Des Moines, IA 50309-2372
(515) 558-6600
Email: iowaexecutivesearch@rsmi.com
Key Contact - Specialty:
Mr. Jeff Judkins, Search Consultant - *Accounting, Financial, Investment, Manufacturing (Management), Middle management*

801 Nicollet Mall Ste 1300
Minneapolis, MN 55402-5703
(612) 573-8750
Fax: (612) 376-9876
Email: michael.sears@rsmi.com
Key Contact - Specialty:
Mr. Michael Sears

RSMR Global Resources Inc

219 W Chicago Ave Fl 2
Chicago, IL 60610-3100
(312) 957-0337
Fax: (312) 957-0335
Email: kellogg@rsmr.com
Web: www.rsmr.com

Summary: We assist our clients with senior management, executive and board level assignments in our areas of expertise. Our consultative approach, commitment to excellence and wealth of industry relationships set us apart in the areas of: power & energy, architecture/engineering/construction, banking & finance, manufacturing and software.

Key Contact - Specialty:
Mr. Christopher Swan, Chief Executive Officer - *Construction, Energy, Engineering, Operations, Utilities*
Mr. John Ryan, President
Mr. Michael Morrow, Executive Vice President - *Equipment, Manufacturing*

Mr. Mitchell Bassler, Vice President - *Construction, Instrumentation*
Ms. Nicole Morgan, Associate
Ms. Ann Marie Melgard, Vice President - *Architecture*

Salary Minimum: $100,000

Functions: Generalist (All), Management, Mfg., Materials, Sales Mgmt., Cash Mgmt., Risk Mgmt., Engineering

Industries: Generalist (All), Energy, Utilities, Construction, Machine, Appliance, Finance, Telecoms, Environmental Svcs., Real Estate

Rurak & Associates Inc

1776 Massachusetts Ave NW Ste 806
Washington, DC 20036-1915
(202) 293-7603
Email: resumes@rurakassociates.com

Summary: We are a generalist practice serving senior management in executive search, selection and development. Our clients range from venture-capitalized start-ups to multinational corporations.

Key Contact - Specialty:
Mr. Zbigniew T. Rurak, Recruiter
Mrs. Caroline Bouhdili, Recruiter

Salary Minimum: $150,000

Functions: Generalist (All)

Industries: Generalist (All)

Rusher, Loscavio & LoPresto

(a Globe Search Group company)
100 Spear St Ste 935
San Francisco, CA 94105-1534
(415) 765-6600
Fax: (415) 546-2201
Email: loscavio@rll.com
Web: www.rll.com

Summary: Retained executive search in financial services, high technology, biotechnology, healthcare, venture backed staffing, manufacturing, non-profit and service industries. Function specialties in board members, general management, manufacturing, distribution, finance, marketing & sales, MIS, HR, engineering & technical management, executive directors and fund development managers.

Key Contact - Specialty:
Mr. William H. Rusher, Jr., Chairman of the Board & CEO - *Boards of Directors, Financial services, High technology, Insurance, Management consulting*
Mr. Michael J. Loscavio, Partner
Mr. Robert M. Fisher, PhD, President, Non Profit & Higher Education - *Education, Non-profit*
Mr. James A. McFadzean, Jr., Vice President, Technology - *Boards of Directors, C-level, General management, High technology, Venture capital*
Mr. Bart Penfold, President, Emerging, Accelerating Growth - *Banking, Biotechnology, C-level, Entrepreneurs, Healthcare*
Mr. Bob LoPresto, Partner - *Banking, C-level, Financial services, High technology, Non-profit*

Salary Minimum: $120,000

Functions: Generalist (All), Management, Board Members, Mfg., Sales & Mktg., HR Mgmt., Finance, MIS Mgmt., Engineering, Non-profits

Industries: Generalist (All), Manufacturing, Computer Equip., Finance, Venture Cap., Non-profits, Insurance, Software, Biotech/Life Sciences

Branches:
2483 E Bayshore Rd Ste 210
Palo Alto, CA 94303-3208
(650) 494-0883
Fax: (650) 494-7231
Email: dnelms@rll.com
Key Contact - Specialty:
Mr. Robert L. LoPresto, President, High Technology - *C-level, High technology, Information Technology, Semiconductors, Telecommunications*

9 Skylar Dr
Southborough, MA 01772-1745
(508) 624-7291
Fax: (508) 624-7521
Key Contact - Specialty:
Mr. Elson Hung, Vice President - *Financial services, Insurance (Life)*

Russell Reynolds Associates Inc

200 Park Ave Fl 23
New York, NY 10166-0002
(212) 351-2000
Fax: (212) 370-0896
Email: info@russellreynolds.com
Web: www.russellreynolds.com

Summary: The firm provides executive recruiting and executive assessment services through a global network of wholly owned offices. The firm's recruiting professionals provide industry expertise to clients world wide through highly specialized practice areas that focus on particular industries, geographies and functions.

Key Contact - Specialty:
Mr. Hobson Brown, Jr., President & Chief Executive Officer
Mr. Clarke Murphy, Managing Director
Mr. Ron Lumbra, Managing Director
Mr. John Archer
Mr. James Bagley
Mr. Shawn Banerji
Mr. Jon Barney
Mr. Marcus Brauer
Ms. Debra Brown
Mr. James Carpenter
Mr. Marshall Crane
Ms. Candi Dalipe
Mr. James Davis
Mr. Patrick Delhougne
Ms. Darleen DeRosa
Mr. Benjamin Dewar
Ms. Barbara Dolgin
Mr. Peter Drummond-Hay
Ms. Mary Helen Dunn
Mr. Stephen Fitzgibbons
Mr. Gordon Grand, III
Ms. Lorraine Hack
Ms. Courtney Hagen
Ms. Heather Hammond
Mr. William Henderson
Ms. Soo J. Hong
Mr. James Houston
Ms. Ann Jung
Ms. Cornelia Kiley
Mr. Christopher Langhoff
Mr. Malcolm MacKay - *Non-profit*
Ms. Carrie Mandel
Mr. Alex Martin
Mr. Graham Michener
Ms. Joanna Miller
Ms. Nancy Mistretta
Ms. Mary Price
Mr. Peter Reichman
Mr. Alan Renne
Mr. John Rogan
Mr. Stephen Scroggins
Mr. Gena A. Smith
Ms. Robyn Soto
Mr. Andrew Tagliabue
Ms. Susan Walser

Mr. Charles Watson
Mr. George Wilbanks

Salary Minimum: $180,000

Functions: Generalist (All), Board Members, Senior Mgmt., Mfg., Healthcare, Sales & Mktg., HR Mgmt., Finance, CFOs, IT

Industries: Generalist (All)

Branches:
300 S Grand Ave Ste 1110
Los Angeles, CA 90071-3121
(213) 253-4400
Fax: (213) 253-4444
Email: jwarren@russellreynolds.com
Key Contact - Specialty:
Mr. Jeffrey M. Warren, Managing Director
Ms. Ilene Nagel

2500 Sand Hill Rd Ste 105
Menlo Park, CA 94025-7063
(650) 233-2400
Fax: (650) 233-2499
Email: bobrand@russellreynolds.com
Key Contact - Specialty:
Mr. Barry Obrand, Managing Director - *Technology*
Mr. David Finke
Mr. Charley Geoly
Mr. Jay Hussey
Mr. Brian Kasser
Mr. Mark Ryan

101 California St Ste 2900
San Francisco, CA 94111-5858
(415) 352-3300
Fax: (415) 781-7690
Email: aadlerman@russellreynolds.com
Key Contact - Specialty:
Ms. Abby Adlerman, Managing Director
Ms. Barbara Anderman
Mr. Keith Anderson
Mr. Jamed Audet, M.D.
Mr. Stephen Cohen
Ms. Carol Emmott
Ms. Jenna Fisher
Ms. Annabel George
Ms. Gabrielle Lajoie
Ms. Margot McShane
Mr. P. Anthony Price
Ms. Jana Rich
Mr. Jeff Rosenthal
Mr. Katie Solomon

1701 Pennsylvania Ave NW Ste 400
Washington, DC 20006-5810
(202) 654-7800
Email: evautour@russellreynolds.com
Key Contact - Specialty:
Mr. Eric L. Vautour, Managing Director - *Associations*
Mr. Matthew Aiello
Ms. Kimberly Archer
Ms. Veronica Fiore
Ms. Denise Grant
Mr. Harry Greenspun
Mr. Clarke Havener
Mr. Gren Millard
Mr. Michael Patino
Mr. Allen Reed
Ms. Anne Martin Simonds
Ms. Mary Tydings
Ms. Nalini Vasagarn

50 Hurt Plz SE Ste 600
Atlanta, GA 30303-2915
(404) 577-3000
Fax: (404) 577-2832
Email: rperkey@russellreynolds.com
Key Contact - Specialty:
Mr. Richard C. Perkey, Managing Director
Ms. Susan Boyd
Mr. Douglas Edwards

Mr. John Farish
Ms. Amy Hayes
Mr. Timothy Henn
Ms. Crystal Holmes Stephens
Mr. Matthew Mooney
Mr. G. Christopher Nunn - *Financial services*
Mr. Dean Stamoulis
Mr. Rory Verrett

200 S Wacker Dr Fl 2900
Chicago, IL 60606-5866
(312) 993-9696
Fax: (312) 876-1919
Email: lklock@russellreynolds.com
Key Contact - Specialty:
Mr. Larry Klock, Managing Director
Mr. Constantine Alexandrakis
Mr. Jack Costello
Ms. Carolyn Doud
Mr. M. Jason Hanold
Ms. Heidi Hoffman
Mr. Clem Johnson
Ms. Seema Kathuria
Ms. Bobbie Lenga
Mr. Bradford McLane
Ms. Laurie O'Shea
Mr. Thomas Putrim
Ms. Andrea Redmond
Mr. David Selby
Mr. Eric Sigurdson
Mr. Frank Smeekes
Ms. Melanie Steinbach
Mr. Lyndon Taylor
Mr. Charles Tribbett, III
Mr. Paul Zellner

1 Federal St Fl 25
Boston, MA 02110-2012
(617) 523-1111
Fax: (617) 523-7305
Email: bostonresearch@russellreynolds.com
Key Contact - Specialty:
Mr. J. Nicholas Hurd, Managing Director
Mr. Thomas Carey
Mr. F. Christopher Davis
Mr. Jeff Garrity
Ms. Laura Pollock
Ms. Jennifer Potter-Brotman
Mr. Dean Profis
Mr. Tuck Rickards
Mr. Alexander Thomson
Ms. Lynn Tidd
Mr. Lenny Vairo - *Financial services*

225 S 6th St Ste 2550
Minneapolis, MN 55402-4653
(612) 332-6966
Fax: (612) 332-2629
Email: bmacdonald@russellreynolds.com
Key Contact - Specialty:
Mr. Robert W. Macdonald, Jr., Managing
   Director
Ms. Kathryn Mitchell Ramstad
Mr. Erik Wordelman

8401 N Central Expy Ste 650
Dallas, TX 75225-4404
(214) 220-2033
Fax: (214) 220-3998
Email: dlove@russellreynolds.com
Key Contact - Specialty:
Mr. David M. Love, III, Managing Director
Ms. Cynthia Graser
Mr. Stuart Guthrie
Mr. Jay Kizer
Mr. Gregory Konstans
Mr. Donald Lieb
Mr. David Long
Mr. Bradley Pierce - *Technology*

600 Travis St Ste 2200
Houston, TX 77002-2910
(713) 754-5995
Fax: (713) 754-5997
Email: snewton@russellreynolds.com
Key Contact - Specialty:
Mr. Stephen Newton, Managing Director
Ms. Lisa Coleman
Mr. John Freud
Mr. Ed Fry
Mr. Stephen Morse
Mr. Ted Orner
Mr. Steve Raben
Mr. Ryan Rainwater
Mr. Curt Ross

3410-40 King St W
Scotia Plaza
Toronto, ON M5H 3Y2
Canada
(416) 364-3355
Fax: (416) 364-5174
Key Contact - Specialty:
Mr. Shawn Cooper, Managing Director
Mr. Paul Cantor
Ms. Lisa Porlier
Mr. Antonella Vergati

Paseo de las Palmas 405-4
Torre Optima I
Lomas de Chapultepec
11000 Mexico City, DF
Mexico
55 5540 0119
Fax: 55 5540 3659
Email: ryturbe@russellreynolds.com
Key Contact - Specialty:
Mr. Rafael Yturbe, Managing Director -
   Industrial
Mr. Jose Denogean
Mr. Cesar Muniz
Mr. Eugenio Riquelme

Russillo/Gardner

60 State St Ste 700
Boston, MA 02109-1894
(617) 350-8600
(617) 345-0700
Fax: (617) 973-5745
Email: tom@russillogardner.com
Web: www.russillogardner.com

Summary: Our firm serves insurance, risk
management, employee benefits, and IT/software
engineering and investment technology industries
for executive level management and senior level
technical specialists. All the firm's consultants
have substantial experience in the fields they
represent.

Key Contact - Specialty:
Mr. Thomas P. Russillo, Partner - *C-level,
   Insurance, Loss Control, Risk management,
   Underwriting*
Mr. Richard E. Gardner, Partner - *CIOs,
   Financial, Information Systems, Information
   Technology, Investment*
Ms. Pamela Marion, Director, Research -
   *Benefits, Brokerage, C-level, Insurance, Risk
   management*

Salary Minimum: $100,000

Functions: Management, Mktg. Mgmt., Sales
   Mgmt., Benefits, Finance, CFOs, Risk Mgmt.,
   IT, Mgmt. Consultants, Environmentalists

Industries: Generalist (All), Insurance, Software

Rust & Associates Inc

PO Box 3829
Suwanee, GA 30024-0996
(678) 388-9895
(888) 835-7878
Fax: (678) 921-0597
Email: john@rustassociates.com
Web: www.rustassociates.com

Summary: International generalist firm: guarantee
search filled or money back; unconditional two-
year guarantee on retention; off limits, lifetime
candidates, two-year clients. Our trademark is
'Executive Search Guaranteed.'

Key Contact - Specialty:
Mr. John R. Rust, President

Salary Minimum: $60,000

Functions: Generalist (All), Board Members,
   Senior Mgmt., Mfg., Materials, Sales & Mktg.,
   Finance, IT, Engineering, Specialized Svcs.

Industries: Generalist (All), Construction,
   Manufacturing, Retail, Finance, Services,
   Communications, Software, Biotech/Life
   Sciences, Healthcare

Rutherford International Executive Search Group Inc

1201-120 Adelaide St W
Richamond Adelaide Ctr Phase 1
Toronto, ON M5H 1T1
Canada
(416) 250-6300
Email: resume@rutherfordinternational.com
Web: www.rutherfordinternational.com

Summary: Our firm is an integrated executive
resources firm providing advice on a broad range
of management-based human affairs. We possess a
keen interest in issues related to executive
leadership, corporate governance, organizational
effectiveness, staffing, and performance
measurement. Our core competency is to assist
clients to identify, evaluate, attract, apply and
retain superior board, executive and management
talent.

Key Contact - Specialty:
Mr. Forbes Rutherford, President - *Banking
   (Commercial, Investment, Mortgage),
   Biotechnology, Boards of Directors*
Mr. Jon Hayhurst, Recruiter
Mr. Georges Renaud, CPM, FRI, Managing
   Director, Western Canada - *Construction,
   Leasing, Property management, Real estate*
Mr. Andrew Ainslie, Director, Business
   Development
Ms. Barb Turner, Recruiter & Administration

Salary Minimum: $80,000

Functions: Management, Board Members, Senior
   Mgmt., R&D, Legal, Int'l.

Industries: Construction, Retail, Finance, Invest.
   Banking, Venture Cap., Mutual/Hedge Funds,
   Services, Legal, Hospitality, Real Estate,
   Property/Facility Mgmt., Biotech/Life Sciences,
   Hospitals, Long-term/Home Care

W A Rutledge & Associates

6 Meadow Crest Dr
Woodbury, CT 06798-2214
(203) 266-0200
Fax: (203) 266-0213

Summary: We provide senior/executive
management search across most functional areas
in technology based consumer and industrial
product companies heavy pharmaceutical,
chemicals, electronics and communications.

Key Contact - Specialty:
Mr. William A. Rutledge, President

Functions: Management, Senior Mgmt., Middle Mgmt.

Industries: Chemicals, Drugs Mfg., Consumer Elect., Misc. Financial, Aerospace, Biotech/Life Sciences

RWS Partners in Search

5549 County Road 327
Buffalo, TX 75831-3977
(903) 322-2159
Fax: (903) 322-7209
Email: rolands@starband.net

Summary: We are a generalist retained executive search firm with extensive successful experience offering our clients a very personalized, responsive and professional service performed only by a senior partner. Over 80 percent of our assignments come from repeat clients. Our experience covers most sectors of the economy for both for-profit and not-for-profit organizations at senior management levels.

Key Contact - Specialty:
Mr. Roland W. Stuebner, Jr., Managing Partner

Salary Minimum: $60,000

Functions: Generalist (All)

Industries: Generalist (All), Metal Products, Computer Equip., Misc. Mfg., Electronic, Elec. Components, Non-profits, Accounting

Saeges†

(a division of IOMA)
29 W 35th St Fl 6
New York, NY 10001-2299
(212) 929-2000
Fax: (212) 244-8723
Email: pdamon@saeges.com
Web: www.saeges.com

Summary: We are the human capital consulting and recruitment firm. We help companies improve performance by building, managing and maximizing their human and intellectual assets. Combining our functional expertise and network of executives, our clients can recruit, develop and maintain a culture of knowledge-based leadership.

Key Contact - Specialty:
Ms. Cheryl Eisen, President

Functions: Senior Mgmt., HR Mgmt., Finance, CFOs, Legal

Industries: Generalist (All), Finance, Pharm Svcs., Legal, Accounting, HR Services, Hospitals

Saenger Associates

23920 Valencia Blvd Ste 270
Santa Clarita, CA 91355-5315
(661) 284-3818
Fax: (661) 284-7555
Email: info@saengerassociates.com
Web: www.saengerassociates.com

Summary: On behalf of corporate retained clients, our firm identifies and recruits candidates for executive, managerial and professional positions in manufacturing, distribution and professional services companies.

Key Contact - Specialty:
Mr. Gary L. Saenger, President
Ms. Karen Milliken, Vice President, Client Services
Ms. Katherine Hayes, Vice President, Client Services
Ms. Paula Triggs, Associate
Ms. Barbara Gorkis, Vice President, Client Services

Salary Minimum: $100,000

Functions: Generalist (All), Management

Industries: Generalist (All), Manufacturing, Medical Devices, Consumer Goods, Transportation, Wholesale, Finance, Services, Non-profits, Pharm Svcs., Aerospace, Packaging, Insurance, Software, Healthcare

The Sagacity Group

7 Sherman Ct
Plainsboro, NJ 08536-2332
(609) 799-7944
Fax: (609) 275-1755
Email: info@sagacitygroup.com
Web: www.sagacitygroup.com

Summary: Specialists in meeting the unique needs of smaller organizations.

Key Contact - Specialty:
Mr. Randall Brett, Managing Director
Ms. Deborah L. Brett, Senior Associate

Functions: Management

Industries: Generalist (All)

Sage Search Partners

19 Hawthorne Ave
Auburndale, MA 02466-2805
(617) 964-0406
Email: pherzog@sagelansing.com
Web: www.sagesearch.com

Summary: Executive search firm specializing in higher education and related not-for-profits. Partners conduct each search in its entirety, without relying on junior associates. Before founding this firm, partners were senior managers at search firms.

Key Contact - Specialty:
Dr. Patricia Herzog, Partner
Ms. Paula Fazli, Partner
Ms. Margot S. Lansing, Administrator & Consultant

Functions: Generalist (All)

Industries: Non-profits, Higher Ed.

Sager Company

9540 Midwest Ave
Cleveland, OH 44125-2463
(216) 475-9900
(800) 459-1307
Fax: (216) 475-9910
Email: info@sagercompany.com
Web: www.sagercompany.com

Summary: Multi-discipline practice identifying talent for senior and executive-level opportunities in general management, sales, marketing, production, operations and finance.

Key Contact - Specialty:
Mr. Christopher Calogeras, Consultant
Mr. Michael Gerbasi, Consultant
Mr. James Simon, CPA, Controller
Ms. Lourdes Maldonado, Administration

Salary Minimum: $150,000

Functions: Generalist (All)

Industries: Generalist (All)

Saito & Associates†

620 Newport Center Dr Ste 1100
Newport Beach, CA 92660-8011
(949) 721-6655
Fax: (949) 721-6656
Email: scott@saitoassociates.com
Web: www.saitoassociates.com

Summary: We are real estate specialists in homebuilding, apartments/multifamily, commercial office, industrial, retail, and land development. We focus on assisting organizations identify, attract and retain top candidates for mid and senior-level management opportunities.

Key Contact - Specialty:
Mr. Scott T. Saito, Owner - *Industrial, Retail*

Salary Minimum: $100,000

Functions: Generalist (All), Board Members, Senior Mgmt., Middle Mgmt., Finance, CFOs

Industries: Construction, Invest. Banking, Accounting, Real Estate, Property/Facility Mgmt.

Sales Executives Inc†

9005 Overlook Blvd
Brentwood, TN 37027-5269
(615) 236-1110
Fax: (866) 516-3460
Email: chazen@sales-executives.com
Web: www.salesexecutivesinc.com

Summary: We specialize in sales only. We work with business-to-business sales reps and sales management professionals. We partner with companies in all industries from small to Fortune 500 companies. The industries that we specialize in include medical/pharmaceutical, transportation, logistics, manufacturing, printing, industrial, consumer goods, IT, telecom, non-profit, office furnishings, etc. We work on a contingency basis with our clients.

Key Contact - Specialty:
Mrs. Cindy Houston Hazen, President

Salary Minimum: $45,000

Functions: Management, Sales & Mktg.

Industries: Generalist (All), Manufacturing, Soap, Perf., Cosmtcs., Medical Devices, Consumer Goods, Transportation, Finance, Services, HR Services, Logistics Svcs., Supply Chain Mgmt

Saleskingdom

(also known as Sales Kingdom of America)
525 N Tryon St Ste 1700
Charlotte, NC 28202-0203
(704) 331-6560
Email: joe@saleskingdom.cc
Web: www.saleskingdom.cc

Summary: Our firm is dedicated to the advancement of the sales professional. Over the years our staff has done nothing but coach, motivate and assist sales professionals in the pursuit of their own goals and dreams. We match up professional salespeople in transition with the organizations who have opportunities.

Key Contact - Specialty:
Mr. Joe Miller, Co-Founder - *Administration, Clinical, Healthcare, Middle management, Systems*

Functions: Sales & Mktg., Advertising, Mktg. Mgmt., Sales Mgmt., Sales Reps.

Industries: Generalist (All)

Eric Salmon & Partners

245 Park Ave Fl 24
New York, NY 10167-2499
(212) 372-8800
Fax: (212) 372-8778
Email: info.usa@ericsalmon.com
Web: www.ericsalmon.com

Summary: We are a retained executive search firm specializing in the recruitment of senior-level executives.

Key Contact - Specialty:
Ms. Susan Landon
Fabrizio Panzeri
Mr. William Venable

Salary Minimum: $150,000

Functions: Generalist (All)

Industries: Generalist (All)

Salovey & Associates[†]

(a division of ExecuFind Recruiting)
360 Brook Ave
Passaic, NJ 07055-2439
(973) 472-4840
(877) 444-3613
Fax: (973) 472-6775
Email: alfarrell@execufind.com
Web: www.execufind.com

Summary: Our retained search firm represents clients in manufacturing and commercial real estate. We distinguish ourselves through in depth knowledge of our demanding clients and cutting edge candidates. All facets are covered, including: operations, engineering, finance, sales & marketing and HR. Bilingual (English-French) services are provided.

Key Contact - Specialty:
Mr. Al Farrell, MBA, Managing Partner - *Chemical*
Ms. Vivian Rabin, MBA, Vice President, US Operations - *Manufacturing*

Salary Minimum: $50,000

Functions: Generalist (All)

Industries: Food, Bev., Tobacco, Lumber, Furniture, Paper, Chemicals, Soap, Perf., Cosmtcs., Plastics, Rubber, Paints, Petro. Products, Metal Products, Real Estate

Salveson Stetson Group Inc

150 N Radnor Chester Rd Ste F100
Radnor, PA 19087-5265
(610) 341-9020
Fax: (610) 341-9025
Email: salveson@ssgsearch.com
Web: www.ssgsearch.com

Summary: We are highly consultative in our approach to search. We perform an in-depth organization assessment to begin a search and remain after the search to help the new executive assimilate.

Key Contact - Specialty:
Mr. John Salveson
Ms. Sally Stetson

Salary Minimum: $100,000

Functions: Generalist (All)

Industries: Generalist (All)

Salzmann Gay Associates Inc

275 Commerce Dr Ste 222
Fort Washington, PA 19034-2409
(215) 654-0285

Key Contact - Specialty:
Ms. Martha Gay, President - *Finance, Marketing, Senior management*

Salary Minimum: $100,000

Functions: Senior Mgmt.

Industries: Generalist (All)

Morgan Samuels Company LLC

9171 Wilshire Blvd Ste 320
Beverly Hills, CA 90210-5542
(310) 205-2200
Fax: (310) 205-2201
Email: resume@morgansamuels.com
Web: www.morgansamuels.com

Summary: We are a specialty firm, which recruits senior-level management for the Internet, financial services, heavy construction and IT industries.

Key Contact - Specialty:
Mr. Bert C. Hensley, Chairman & Chief Executive Officer
Mr. Lewis J. Samuels, Founder - *Construction, Energy, Engineering, Environmental, Utilities*
Mr. F. Michael Budd, Chief Operating Officer
Mr. Carlos Garcia, Principal
Ms. Nancy J. Schlect, Principal
Ms. Jennifer Happillon, Senior Engagement Director
Mr. Matthew P. Lozinski, Senior Engagement Director
Mr. Struan W. Scott, Senior Engagement Director
Mr. Richard A. Skoff, DMD, Senior Associate
Ms. Monica Bua, Senior Associate
Ms. Eddie Clay, Senior Associate
Mr. Mark R. Zoeckler, Vice President, Knowledge Management
Mr. Christian J. Bezick, Senior Engagement Director
Ms. Stephaine L. Conway, Senior Consultant
Ms. Lisa Hochberg, Consultant
Ms. Ann Montgomery, Consultant
Mr. David Dumbroski, Director, Research - *Engineering, Manufacturing, Technology*

Salary Minimum: $150,000

Functions: Generalist (All), Senior Mgmt., Sales & Mktg., HR Mgmt., Finance, IT, Engineering, Mgmt. Consultants

Industries: Generalist (All), Energy, Utilities, Construction, Manufacturing, Finance, Services, Environmental Svcs.

J Sanders Associates LLC[†]

2001 Us Highway 46 Ste 310
Parsippany, NJ 07054-1315
(973) 402-4090
Email: careers@sandersassociates.com
Web: www.sandersassociates.com

Summary: We are a retained executive search firm specializing in the recruitment of senior level management consulting and IT professionals. We place top executives at the intersection of business and IT. We have completed searches for practice leaders, consulting partners, directors, senior managers and business developers, as well as CIOs, CTOs and other technology executives.

Key Contact - Specialty:
Mr. Jason Sanders, Managing Director
Mr. Mal Lazinsk, Managing Director

Salary Minimum: $150,000

Functions: Management, Sales Mgmt., IT, MIS Mgmt., Mgmt. Consultants

Industries: Generalist (All), Mgmt. Consulting, E-commerce, IT Implementation, Software

The Sandler Group LLC

1836 Lackland Hill Pkwy
Saint Louis, MO 63146-3572
(314) 989-3789
(866) 724-6649
Fax: (314) 810-1390
Email: info@sandlergroupllc.com
Web: www.sandlergroupllc.com

Summary: We are a leading boutique executive search firm specializing in the recruitment of senior level professionals in the healthcare industry. We offer comprehensive recruiting and consulting solutions to: health systems, hospitals, managed care organizations, surgery centers, physician practices and long term care facilities.

Key Contact - Specialty:
Mr. Andrew Sandler, CPC, President

Functions: Senior Mgmt., Middle Mgmt., Health Admin., Finance, CFOs

Industries: Healthcare

Sanford Rose Associates - Silicon Valley

228 Hamilton Ave Fl 3
Palo Alto, CA 94301-2583
(650) 798-5270
Fax: (650) 618-8666
Email: info@srasv.com
Web: www.srasv.com

Summary: We are a retained executive search firm focused on serving the needs of early-stage to mid-sized life science companies.

Key Contact - Specialty:
Mr. Roy Fiebiger, Managing Partner

Salary Minimum: $150,000

Functions: Senior Mgmt.

Industries: Drugs Mfg., Medical Devices, Biotech/Life Sciences

Sanford Rose Associates - San Francisco[†]

1415 Oakland Blvd Ste 215
Walnut Creek, CA 94596-4395
(925) 974-1760
Fax: (925) 974-1763
Email: info@srasf.com
Web: www.srasf.com

Summary: We are an executive/key employee search firm specializing in the medical diagnostics/device, biotechnology and pharmaceuticals industries. Our clients span a wide range of companies from start-ups to international conglomerate corporations. Our placements range from the senior scientist to chief executive/general management levels.

Key Contact - Specialty:
Dr. Richard Carter, President & Owner

Functions: Generalist (All), Board Members, Senior Mgmt., Middle Mgmt., Product Dev., Automation, Quality, Sales & Mktg., R&D, Engineering

Industries: Biotech/Life Sciences

Sanford Rose Associates - Pensacola

3 W Garden St Ste 349
Pensacola, FL 32502-5682
(850) 438-8178
Web: www.sra-pensacola.com

Summary: We are executive search consultants specializing in executive and senior management positions to a broad range of functional areas in the banking, financial services, call center services, food processing and closely aligned support industries.

Key Contact - Specialty:
Mr. David A. Purkerson, President - *Call centers, Financial services*

Salary Minimum: $100,000

Functions: Senior Mgmt.

Industries: Food, Bev., Tobacco, Banking, Invest. Banking, Misc. Financial, Higher Ed., Call Centers

Sanford Rose Associates - Alpharetta[†]

1516 Dartmouth Rd Ste 112
Alpharetta, GA 30004-8073
(770) 667-6359
Fax: (770) 667-6118
Email: rmhealy@sanfordrose.com
Web: www.sanfordrose.com/alpharetta

Summary: We are a full-service executive search organization with a primary focus on placing senior level positions including sales, business development, marketing, IT and operations management within the security industry.

Key Contact - Specialty:
Mr. Ray M. Healy

Functions: Senior Mgmt., Sales & Mktg.

Industries: Defense, Compliance, Homeland Security, Marketing SW, Security SW

Sanford Rose Associates - Cumming

(also known as Healthcare IT Practice)
2300 Bethelview Rd Ste 112
Cumming, GA 30040-9475
(770) 888-4734
(678) 642-6467
Fax: (678) 807-1995
Email: tjtolan@sanfordrose.com
Web: www.sanfordrose.com/cumming

Summary: We have a primary focus in locating and placing senior level positions including sales, business development, marketing and product management within the healthcare services, insurance and software/services industries.

Key Contact - Specialty:
Mr. Timothy J. Tolan, Partner - *Business development, Healthcare, Information Technology, Sales, Senior management*

Salary Minimum: $100,000

Functions: Senior Mgmt., Sales & Mktg.

Industries: Non-Classifiable

Sanford Rose Associates - Florissant

7321 S Lindbergh Blvd Ste 110
Saint Louis, MO 63125-4500
(888) 258-9082
(314) 831-1600 x301
Email: sramitch@sbcglobal.net
Web: www.sanfordrose.com/florissant

Summary: We are an executive level retained search firm.

Key Contact - Specialty:
Mr. Mitch Ellis, Principal
Ms. Mary Ellis, Office Manager

Salary Minimum: $100,000

Functions: Management, Board Members, Senior Mgmt.

Industries: Generalist (All)

Sanford Rose Associates - Winston-Salem[†]

1338 Ashley Sq
Winston Salem, NC 27103-2949
(336) 774-6690
Fax: (336) 774-6691
Email: hwrush@sanfordrose.com
Web: www.sanfordrose.com/winstonsalem

Summary: We specialize in food, agribusiness and manufacturing consistent with the managing directors prior experience as a financial executive in these industries.

Key Contact - Specialty:
Mr. Howard W. Rush

Salary Minimum: $100,000

Functions: Management, Board Members, Senior Mgmt., Middle Mgmt., HR Mgmt., Finance, CFOs, M&A, Risk Mgmt., IT

Industries: Agri., Forestry, Mining, Manufacturing, Food, Bev., Tobacco

Sanford Rose Associates - Cincinnati South[†]

4355 Ferguson Dr Ste 210
Cincinnati, OH 45245-5137
(513) 752-5100
Fax: (513) 752-5490
Email: dlittleton@sanfordrose.com

Summary: Retained search for mid to upper level executives for all functions within manufacturing businesses. Continuous improvement (Lean/Six Sigma) of the enterprise is our primary focus and our distinctive competence.

Key Contact - Specialty:
Mr. Darryl Littleton, President - *Manufacturing*

Salary Minimum: $100,000

Functions: Senior Mgmt., Middle Mgmt., Plant Mgmt., Productivity, Purchasing, Mktg. Mgmt., Sales Mgmt., HR Mgmt.

Industries: Manufacturing

Sanford Rose Associates - Westerville[†]

5645 Innisbrook Ct
Westerville, OH 43082-8161
(614) 901-4269
Email: mjfowler@sanfordrose.com
Web: www.sanfordrose.com/westerville

Summary: Performs mid and upper level executive searchs for manufacturing companies.

Key Contact - Specialty:
Mr. M. John Fowler, Jr.

Functions: Generalist (All), Admin. Svcs., Mfg., Plant Mgmt., Quality, Materials, Purchasing, Engineering

Industries: Manufacturing

Sanford Rose Associates - Singapore Pte Ltd[†]

78 Shenton Way 29-02
Singapore 079120
Singapore
622 31088
Fax: 6223 7388
Email: search@sanfordrose.com.sg
Web: www.sanfordrose.com.sg

Summary: Our Singapore office is one of our top three offices around the world in terms of annual billings for successful placements. We have specialist search capabilities in the following industries: finance, technology, industrial and consumer products & services, healthcare.

Key Contact - Specialty:
Mr. Norman Yeow, Managing Director
Mr. Edwin Ng, Executive Director

Salary Minimum: $80,000

Sanford Rose Associates - Korea[†]

#903, Dae Woo Utopia B/D
Bang-I Dong-22
Song-Pa Ku
Seoul 138-050
South Korea
2 2202 3578
Fax: 2 220 1576
Email: kjhan@srakorea.co.kr
Web: www.srakorea.co.kr

Summary: Executive search and management consulting in the field of education.

Key Contact - Specialty:
Kee J. Han, Chief Executive Officer & President - *Information Systems, Information Technology, Telecommunications*

Sanford Rose Associates - Spain[†]

Fco. Grevas 17 Fl 4 Ste E
ES-28020 Madrid
Spain
915 678 481
Fax: 916 309 092
Email: spain@sanfordrose.com
Web: www.sanfordrose.com/spain

Summary: Our firm specializes in Wireless/LD/LEC/CLEC, telecommunications, data communications, electronics, biotechnology, healthcare support, manufacturing, data processing, healthcare, supply chain management, and building products.

Key Contact - Specialty:
Mr. Carlos del Cerro, CMC, Senior Search Consultant - *Biotechnology, Business to business, Capital markets, Consulting*
Mrs. Elena del Cerro, Principal - *Computers (Software), CRM, Data processing, Database (Warehousing)*
Mr. Oscar Roca, Senior Search Consultant - *Networking, Professional services, Sales, Senior management*
Mrs. Dolores Hernandez, Search Consultant - *Construction, General management, Management consulting, Market research*
Mr. John Oxemberg, Senior Partner - *Information Technology, Manufacturing, Outsourcing*

Salary Minimum: $50,000

Functions: Generalist (All), Management, Int'l.

Industries: Construction, Manufacturing, Textiles, Apparel, Machine, Appliance, Test, Measure Equip., Electronic, Elec. Components, Semiconductors, Brokers, Pharm Svcs., Law Enforcement, E-commerce, Higher Ed., Supply Chain Mgmt, Sports, Telecoms, Digital, Wireless, Claims, Database SW, Development SW, Mfg. SW, Networking, Comm. SW, Security SW, Training SW, Biotech/Life Sciences, Healthcare, Hospitals, Physical Therapy

Sathe Executive Search Inc

5821 Cedar Lake Rd S
Minneapolis, MN 55416-1487
(952) 546-2100
(800) 848-4912
Fax: (952) 546-6930
Email: info@sathe.com
Web: www.sathe.com

Summary: Our industry specialties include financial services, manufacturing, banking, construction, medical products, healthcare, hospitality and high-technology.

Key Contact - Specialty:
Mr. Mark Sathe, Founder
Mr. Chandler McCoy, President

Salary Minimum: $85,000

Functions: Generalist (All)

Industries: Generalist (All)

Satterfield & Associates Inc

7875 Annesdale Dr
Cincinnati, OH 45243-4055
(513) 561-3679
Email: info@satterfield3.com
Web: www.satterfield3.com

Summary: We are a retained search firm that specializes in consumer package goods, technology (including internet and web-enabled companies), and healthcare industries. Our focus is on senior marketing, sales, and business development management or, general management with primary functional experience in marketing or sales.

Key Contact - Specialty:
Mr. Richard Satterfield, Jr., Managing Partner - *General management, Telecommunications*

Salary Minimum: $125,000

Functions: Management, Board Members, Senior Mgmt., Healthcare, Sales & Mktg., Advertising, Mktg. Research, Mktg. Mgmt., Sales Mgmt., Direct Mktg.

Industries: Generalist (All), Drugs Mfg., Medical Devices, Retail, Invest. Banking, New Media, Telecoms, Call Centers, Wireless, Insurance, Marketing SW, Biotech/Life Sciences, Healthcare

Branches:
16 Hart Ln
Weston, CT 06883-1533
(203) 222-1977
Email: sheryl@satterfield3.com
Key Contact - Specialty:
Ms. Sheryl Wengel, Senior Partner - *Consumer, Consumer (Durables,Marketing,Packaged Goods,Products)*

14433 Hawthorne Dr
Carmel, IN 46033-8432
(317) 844-8295
Email: john@satterfield3.com
Key Contact - Specialty:
Mr. John Kuklinski, Senior Partner - *Consumer (Marketing,Products), Marketing, New media, Sales*

31 Saint Andrews
North Bend, OH 45052-9786
(513) 467-0014
Email: paul@satterfield3.com
Key Contact - Specialty:
Mr. Paul Renzenbrink, Senior Partner - *Consumer, Consumer (Packaged Goods,Products), General management, Sales*

Savage Consultants Inc

12540-1066 Hastings St W
Oceanic Plaza Towers
Vancouver, BC V6E 3X2
Canada
(604) 601-8222
Email: jws@savageconsultants.com
Web: www.savageconsultants.com

Summary: We provide exclusive search services for senior and mid-level management positions in industrial firms. In addition, a full range of HR and labor relations consulting services are provided to our clients.

Key Contact - Specialty:
Mr. John W. Savage, President

Salary Minimum: $50,000

Functions: Generalist (All)

Industries: Agri., Forestry, Mining, Energy, Utilities, Lumber, Furniture, Paper, Chemicals, Metal Products, Transportation, Mgmt. Consulting, HR Services, HR SW

Savoy Partners Ltd

1620 L St NW Ste 801
Washington, DC 20036-5629
(202) 887-0666
Email: client@savoypartners.com
Web: www.savoypartners.com

Summary: We are an independent, highly regarded, senior-level boutique executive search firm, with extensive executive search experience. Our partners, never by associates or researchers, conduct all searches. We are among the top ten firms in Washington with national practice. We commit to completing our assignment, regardless of the difficulty or length of search.

Key Contact - Specialty:
Mr. Robert J. Brudno, Managing Director
Ms. Elizabeth Clauhsen, Managing Director
Mr. Christopher A. Kidd, Managing Director

Salary Minimum: $150,000

Functions: Generalist (All), Senior Mgmt.

Industries: Generalist (All), Manufacturing, Finance, Services, Non-profits, Mgmt. Consulting, Media, Communications, Telecoms, Defense, Aerospace, Software, Healthcare

David Saxner & Associates Inc

(also known as DSA Inc)
70 W Madison St Ste 1400
Chicago, IL 60602-4267
(312) 214-3360
Email: dsaxner@dsainc.net
Web: www.dsainc.net

Summary: We recruit senior-level and executive management professionals in the real estate industry. We work closely with our clients to facilitate and bring continuity to the recruitment process.

Key Contact - Specialty:
Mr. David Saxner, Principal
Ms. Rikke Vognsen, Principal

Salary Minimum: $125,000

Functions: Management

Industries: Hospitality, Real Estate

SBS Consulting Group (Scott B Smith)

11610 2nd St
Huntley, IL 60142-7114
(847) 669-9151
Fax: (847) 669-3549
Email: scottbsmith@comcast.net

Summary: Retainer based executive search firm with significant recruiting experience in the insurance & hospital/healthcare provider industries.

Key Contact - Specialty:
Mr. Scott Smith, Managing Partner

Salary Minimum: $80,000

Functions: Generalist (All)

Industries: Insurance, Casualty, Claims, Life, Healthcare, Hospitals, Long-term/Home Care, Dental, Physical Therapy, Women's

SC Search Consultants[†]

1100 Beecher Xing N Ste A
Columbus, OH 43230-4565
(614) 939-4240
Fax: (614) 939-4250
Email: info@scsearchconsultants.com
Web: www.scsearchconsultants.com

Summary: We are an executive search firm committed to actively communicating with our clients and understanding their organizational culture to enable us to successfully identify qualified individuals who will impact our clients' business performance and enhance their competitive advantage in the marketplace. Experience reaffirms that a company is as good as the people they hire.

Key Contact - Specialty:
Ms. Cindy Hilsheimer, Principal

Functions: Generalist (All), Management, Middle Mgmt., HR Mgmt., Finance, CFOs, Specialized Svcs.

Industries: Generalist (All), Energy, Utilities, Construction, Manufacturing, Retail, Finance, Services, Non-profits, Logistics Svcs., Hospitality, Media, Communications, Insurance, Real Estate, Property/Facility Mgmt., Healthcare

Schaffer Associates Inc[†]

7621 Little Ave Ste 100
Charlotte, NC 28226-8371
(704) 535-9939
Fax: (704) 535-9699
Email: priority@consultsa.com
Web: www.consultsa.com

Summary: We are a broad-based search and consulting firm serving all sectors of the home improvement, home building and hardware industries. Our executive search practice focuses on mid and senior-level management positions.

Key Contact - Specialty:
Mr. Jim Schaffer, President
Mr. Mark Fisher, Vice President, Business Development - *Building products, Consumer (Products), Manufacturing (Management), Marketing, Sales*

Salary Minimum: $50,000

Functions: Generalist (All), Management, Senior Mgmt., Middle Mgmt., Mfg., Sales & Mktg., Mktg. Mgmt., Hardware

Industries: Generalist (All), Construction, Manufacturing, Lumber, Furniture, Paints, Petro. Products, Metal Products, Consumer Goods, Wholesale, Retail

Schall Lyman & Company Inc

800 Nicollet Mall Ste 2890
Minneapolis, MN 55402-7006
(612) 338-3119
(888) 808-5000
Fax: (612) 336-4509
Email: khamilton@slci.com
Web: www.slci.com

Summary: Generalist retained firm, with excellent track record in manufacturing, consumer packaged goods, retail, financial and real estate services, nonprofit, and other industries. Customized searches in sales & marketing, finance, operations, senior management, human resources, R&D, IT.

Key Contact - Specialty:
Mr. David R. Schall, Managing Partner
Mr. David Lyman, Partner
Kay Hamilton - *C-level*

Salary Minimum: $110,000

Functions: Board Members, Senior Mgmt., Plant Mgmt., Materials, Packaging, Healthcare, Sales & Mktg., HR Mgmt., CFOs, Risk Mgmt.

Industries: Generalist (All), Manufacturing, Wholesale, Retail, Finance, Services, Non-profits, Hospitality, New Media, Communications, Packaging, Insurance, Software, Healthcare, Hospitals

The Schattle Group
PO Box 115
Saunderstown, RI 02874-0115
(401) 739-0500
Summary: We specialize in executive and senior management.
Key Contact - Specialty:
Mr. Donald J. Schattle, Chairman - *Finance, Senior management*
Salary Minimum: $100,000
Functions: Senior Mgmt.
Industries: Generalist (All)

Schneider, Hill & Spangler LLP
PO Box 472
Newtown Square, PA 19073-0472
(610) 240-9500
Fax: (610) 240-9576
Email: info@s-h-s.com
Web: www.s-h-s.com
Summary: A retained C-Level boutique search firm. Our practice is limited exclusively to representing clients in their search for CEOs, COO's, and members of the board with specialist experience for start-up, turnaround, IPO, and emerging growth companies, along with the traditional CEO, & COO roles.
Key Contact - Specialty:
Mr. Steven A. Schneider, Chairman & Chief Executive Officer
Salary Minimum: $125,000
Functions: Board Members, Senior Mgmt., HR Mgmt., CFOs
Industries: Generalist (All), Food, Bev., Tobacco, Soap, Perf., Cosmtcs., Drugs Mfg., Medical Devices, Consumer Goods, Finance, Banking, Media, Insurance, Healthcare

Schuyler Associates Ltd
400 Perimeter Center Ter NE Ste 900
Atlanta, GA 30346-1236
(770) 352-9414
Email: bert@schuyler-associates.com
Web: www.schuyler-associates.com
Summary: The recognized leader in academic medicine and healthcare.
Key Contact - Specialty:
Mr. Lambert Schuyler, President - *Healthcare*
Ms. Sally McDowell, Vice President - *Healthcare*
Salary Minimum: $100,000
Functions: Board Members, Senior Mgmt., Physicians
Industries: Medical Devices, Non-profits, Higher Ed., Biotech/Life Sciences, Healthcare

Schweichler Price & Partners Inc
(also known as Schweichler Associates, Inc.)
1100 Larkspur Landing Cir Ste 340
Larkspur, CA 94939-1880
(415) 924-7200
Fax: (415) 924-9152
Email: search@schweichler.com
Web: www.schweichler.com

Summary: We have the reputation for locating exceptional individuals for organizations undergoing rapid growth or change. We focus on recruiting President, CEO, COO, VP and director-levels. Our firm is particularly effective in entrepreneurial (high-technology) environments.
Key Contact - Specialty:
Mr. Lee Schweichler, President & Partner - *High technology*
Mr. Andrew Price, Partner - *High technology*
Mr. Dave Mullarkey, Partner - *High technology*
Mr. Kevin Barry, Partner - *High technology*
Salary Minimum: $125,000
Functions: Management, Board Members, Senior Mgmt., Sales & Mktg., IT
Industries: Energy, Utilities, Computer Equip., Communications, Telecoms, Software, Biotech/Life Sciences

The Schwimmer Group Ltd
1673 46th St
Brooklyn, NY 11204-1123
(212) 668-1414
Fax: (718) 633-5891
Email: drshs@sprintmail.com
Summary: We serve the industry by focusing on technology and IS asessment, selection and placement. We fulfill client's consulting and full-time needs at senior and technical-levels.
Key Contact - Specialty:
Dr. Samuel Schwimmer, President
Salary Minimum: $150,000
Functions: Senior Mgmt., MIS Mgmt., Systems Analysis
Industries: Generalist (All), Energy, Utilities, Finance, Services, Hospitality, Media, Communications, Government, Software, Biotech/Life Sciences, Healthcare

Scott Executive Search Inc
61 Woodbury Pl Ste 200
Rochester, NY 14618-3445
(585) 264-0330
Email: eannscott@worldnet.att.net
Summary: We are a quality retainer-based executive recruiting for management positions. We focus on service and results. Additionally we offer candidates the option of retaining us to be their executive agent.
Key Contact - Specialty:
Ms. E. Ann Scott, President - *Food, Interactive*
Salary Minimum: $150,000
Functions: Management, Senior Mgmt.
Industries: Food, Bev., Tobacco, Banking, New Media, Packaging, Software

Evan Scott Group International
600 W Germantown Pike Ste 400
Plymouth Meeting, PA 19462-1046
(202) 842-0441
Fax: (610) 843-9845
Email: escott@evanscottgroup.com
Web: www.evanscottgroup.com
Summary: We are a retainer based executive search firm with offices in Washington and Philadelphia. We focus on recruiting senior level executives for clients selling technology solutions to federal, state, and local governments. Our average search takes under 45 days to complete. We are 100% retained by clients to find specific talent.
Key Contact - Specialty:
Mr. Evan Scott, President

Ms. Dani De Leo, Senior Consultant - *Marketing, Sales*
Mr. Donald Jansen, Managing Director - *Consulting*
Salary Minimum: $150,000
Functions: Board Members, Senior Mgmt., CFOs
Industries: Computer Equip., Venture Cap., New Media, Software, Security SW

J Robert Scott
(a Fidelity Investments company)
260 Franklin St Ste 620
Boston, MA 02110-3180
(617) 563-2770
Fax: (617) 723-1282
Email: info@j-robert-scott.com
Web: www.j-robert-scott.com
Summary: We offer a process-based approach, proven commitment and dedication to clients. Exceptionally strong research capability and performance based billing. Quality of work is guaranteed.
Key Contact - Specialty:
Mr. William A. Holodnak, President - *Biotechnology, Financial services, Venture capital*
Mr. Aaron Lapat, Managing Director - *High technology, Information Technology, Semiconductors, Telecommunications, Wireless*
Ms. Nancy Archer-Martin, Practice Leader - *Associations, Education, Education (Higher), Non-profit*
Mr. Jonathan Fortescue, PhD, Managing Director - *Education, Education (Higher), High technology, Information Systems, Non-profit*
Mr. Bruce Rychlik, Managing Director - *Biopharmaceutical, Biotechnology, Healthcare, Start-up companies, Technology*
Ms. Kathryn Seni, Account Manager
Salary Minimum: $150,000
Functions: Management
Industries: Generalist (All), Manufacturing, Finance, Services, Non-profits, Higher Ed., Communications, Software, Biotech/Life Sciences, Healthcare

Search Alliance
750 Menlo Ave Ste 100
Menlo Park, CA 94025-4735
(650) 328-6400
Fax: (650) 328-6460
Email: admin@s3execs.com
Summary: With many years of experience, we achieve client satisfaction acting as your advocate in the marketplace. We conduct high-quality retained searches and manage the process through negotiation and close.
Key Contact - Specialty:
Ms. Fran Safier, Principal
Functions: Generalist (All)
Industries: Biotech/Life Sciences

The Search Alliance Inc
31 S 4th St
Amelia Island, FL 32034-4218
(904) 277-2535
Fax: (904) 277-7924
Web: www.tsainc.net
Summary: Industry specific executive search with an exemplary record of success and repeat business. Extensive experience in executive team evaluation for restructuring, building bench strength and succession planning.

Key Contact - Specialty:
Mr. Thomas Byrnes, Managing Director
Ms. Jocelyn Scrudato, Director, Research

Salary Minimum: $100,000

Functions: Generalist (All), Management, Sales & Mktg., HR Mgmt., Finance, IT, R&D, Engineering

Industries: Generalist (All), Finance, Pharm Svcs., Insurance, Software, Healthcare

Search America Inc[†]

7001 E Fish Lake Rd
Maple Grove, MN 55311-2841
(610) 259-2800
Fax: (610) 259-6110
Email: mail@searchamericainc.com
Web: www.searchamericainc.com

Summary: We specialize in market research with a lot of recruiting experience and extensive training in the behavioral aspects, sensitivity and art of recruiting. Our goal is to partner with our clients by increasing trust, loyalty and continued mutual success.

Key Contact - Specialty:
Mr. Thomas V. Giacoponello, President & Executive Recruiter - *Management consulting, Market research*

Salary Minimum: $100,000

Functions: Mktg. Research

Industries: Generalist (All)

Search America®

5908 Meadowcreek Dr
Dallas, TX 75248-5451
(972) 233-3302
Fax: (775) 368-0040
Email: searchamerica1@aol.com
Web: www.searchamericanow.com

Summary: The firm represents directors, developers and municipalities seeking senior management for golf, country, in-town and yacht clubs. Extensive club industry database; two-year guarantee; interim management available overnight; board consensus-building and orientation workshops/retreats, operational and incumbent management evaluation services; discreet, well connected, credible.

Key Contact - Specialty:
Mr. Harvey M. Weiner, President & Sr Mgt Search Consultant - *Boards of Directors, Club, Executives, Food & beverage, Hospitality*

Salary Minimum: $90,000

Functions: Management, Board Members, Senior Mgmt., Hospitality, Int'l.

Industries: Venture Cap., Services, Mgmt. Consulting, HR Services, Hospitality, Hotels, Resorts, Clubs, Restaurants, Full Service Restaurants, Inst./Industrial Food Svc., Recreation, Real Estate, Training SW

Branches:
8852 Bella Vista Dr
Boca Raton, FL 33433-1842
(561) 479-4787
Fax: (775) 368-0040
Email: searchamerica1@aol.com

Key Contact - Specialty:
Mr. Mark Weiner, Recruiter & Researcher - *Club, Controllers, Culinary, Food & beverage, Recreations*

The Search Company

(a division of Strategic Search Solutions Inc)
8 Oriole Gdns
Toronto, ON M4V 1V7
Canada
(416) 315-8594
Fax: (416) 960-3590

Summary: A full-service agency made up of experienced HR, business and communications professionals; we focus on the development of effective executive teams with a specialty practice in communications, public affairs and corporate research disciplines.

Key Contact - Specialty:
Ms. Rosemary Kaczanowski, President

Salary Minimum: $60,000

Functions: Generalist (All), Senior Mgmt., Middle Mgmt., Advertising, Mktg. Research, PR, Risk Mgmt., Int'l.

Industries: Generalist (All), Energy, Utilities, Manufacturing, Finance, Media, Government

Search Innovations Inc

1328 Arthur Ave
Maple Glen, PA 19002-3201
(215) 643-2300
(215) 643-7415
Email: resumes@searchinnovations.com
Web: www.searchinnovations.com

Summary: Our firm was founded to meet corporate America's need for a highly responsive and creative search partner. We close searches quickly, typically in one-third less time than traditional retained firms. We assess candidates effectively utilizing a blend of behavioral interviewing, sophisticated reference checking and industry expertise.

Key Contact - Specialty:
Ms. Vivian Kessler, President
Mr. Ehud Israel, Executive Vice President
Mr. Joe Caso, Managing Director

Salary Minimum: $120,000

Functions: Generalist (All)

Industries: Manufacturing, Chemicals, Drugs Mfg., Banking, Brokers, Mutual/Hedge Funds, Services, Insurance, Software, Healthcare

Search International[†]

PO Box 81
Newburyport, MA 01950-0181
(603) 473-8900
Fax: (603) 473-8222
Email: resume@searchinternationalinc.com
Web: www.searchinternationalinc.com

Summary: We are a retained Executive Search Firm. We maintain a wide-area network relational database of leading technical and hospitality industry professionals and client companies throughout our five internationally located offices equipped with state-of-the-art optical scanning capability, allowing us to identify highly qualified and extraordinarily suitable talent for our significant client company roster in assignments that we undertake for them.

Key Contact - Specialty:
Mr. Brian Eagar, Chief Executive Officer - *Culinary, Hospitality, Training*
Mr. Michael Schweiger, CHA, Senior Vice President - *Consulting, General management, Technology*

Ms. Christine Hawthorne, Executive Director
Mrs. Maria Johnson, Director
Mr. Andrew Lowery, Director - *Hospitality*
Mr. John Stanley, Vice President - *Culinary*
Mr. Elliott Wade, Associate Director - *Consulting, Management*
Mr. Jack Gasnier, Executive Vice President - *Culinary, Hotels, Resorts*
Mr. Joseph Laite, Director, Convention & Conference - *Sales*

Salary Minimum: $70,000

Functions: Generalist (All), Middle Mgmt., Sales Mgmt., CFOs, MIS Mgmt., Systems Dev., Systems Support, Int'l.

Industries: Generalist (All), Food, Bev., Tobacco, Computer Equip., Invest. Banking, Services, Hospitality

Branches:
16 NE 17th St
Delray Beach, FL 33444-4136
(561) 330-6665
Fax: (561) 330-0696
Email: jamber@searchinternationalinc.com
Key Contact - Specialty:
Mr. John Amber, Vice President

Search Link Inc

19500 Sun Valley Rd
Colfax, CA 95713-9666
(530) 878-0895
Email: info@search-link.net
Web: www.search-link.net

Summary: Ours is a Northern California based contract research and executive level candidate identification firm. Our research experience spans multiple industries including technology, retail, industrial, health care, higher education and consumer, to name a few. This firm was founded to consistently assist executive search professionals and corporate recruiters with their need for on-target candidates.

Key Contact - Specialty:
Ms. Amber Jantz, President

Functions: Generalist (All)

Industries: Generalist (All)

Search Masters International[†]

111 W Washington St Ste 711
Chicago, IL 60602-2809
(312) 346-6581
(866) 839-7836
Fax: (312) 332-4170
Email: info@searchmastersinternational.com
Web: www.searchmastersinternational.com

Summary: We are a scientific executive consulting firm offering services to the biotechnology, pharmaceutical and life science industries that range from project-based solutions to executive retained searches.

Key Contact - Specialty:
Ms. Crystal Tinucci, Senior Executive Consultant - *Biotechnology, Healthcare, Life Sciences, Pharmaceutical*
Mr. Mark Hartwig, Executive Consultant - *Biotechnology, Life Sciences, Pharmaceutical, Quality, Regulatory*
Ms. Theresa Gadbois, Research Associate - *Biopharmaceutical, Biotechnology, Pharmaceutical*

Salary Minimum: $50,000

Functions: Generalist (All), Management, Board Members

Industries: Generalist (All), Chemicals, Drugs Mfg., Medical Devices, Pharm Svcs., Biotech/Life Sciences, Healthcare

Search Research Associates Inc

(also known as The Gordon Scott Group)
400 W Cummings Park Ste 6900
Woburn, MA 01801-6518
(781) 938-0990
(877) 938-0990
Fax: (781) 933-5385
Email: gordon@search-research.com
Web: www.search-research.com

Summary: We recruit healthcare and real estate professionals for our clients, nationwide.

Key Contact - Specialty:
Mr. Gordon Scott, President - *Healthcare, Real estate*
Ms. Noelle Dailey, CPC, Vice President, Operations - *Healthcare*
Mr. Richard Gerding, CPC, Senior Associate - *Real estate*
Mr. Timothy D'Elia, Senior Associate - *Healthcare*
Mr. Mark Digby, Associate - *Real estate*
Ms. Sheri Lefman, Senior Recruiter

Salary Minimum: $50,000

Functions: Management, Middle Mgmt., Healthcare

Industries: Generalist (All), Construction, Real Estate, Property/Facility Mgmt., Hospitals, Long-term/Home Care

Affiliates:
Search Research Associates Inc
Wilmington, NC

Search Strategies Inc

PO Box 776
Moneta, VA 24121-0776
(540) 721-9029
Email: edtalley@hrprosearch.com
Web: www.hrprosearch.com

Summary: Dedicated exclusively to the recruitment and sourcing of human recources and compensation executives.

Key Contact - Specialty:
Mr. Ed Talley, President

Salary Minimum: $50,000

Functions: Senior Mgmt.

Industries: HR Services

search synergy inc

3004 NE 26th Ave
Portland, OR 97212-3547
(503) 288-2400
Email: ross@searchsynergy.com
Web: www.searchsynergy.com

Summary: Specialize in the sporting goods, outdoor and action sports industries. Middle to senior level positions.

Key Contact - Specialty:
Mr. Ross Regis, Founder & President

Functions: Generalist (All)

Industries: Textiles, Apparel

Search4um

4909 Stockdale Hwy Ste 289
Bakersfield, CA 93309-2637
(661) 831-0149
(661) 8310149
Fax: (661) 831-1839
Email: search4um@search4um.com
Web: www.search4um.com

Summary: We are an executive search firm recruiting professionals in the fields of: Legal, oil & gas, agribusiness, construction, financial

institutions, manufacturing, health care, independent power production and environmental. We specialize in matching the most qualified candidates with the most appropriate positions, creating a productive and positive environment for both employer and employee.

Key Contact - Specialty:
Mr. Larry V. Combs, Esq., Founder

Functions: Generalist (All)

Industries: Generalist (All)

The SearchAmerica Group Inc†

(also known as SearchAmericas)
18511 Heritage Trl
Strongsville, OH 44136-7083
(440) 572-0450
Email: tsnow@searchamericas.com
Web: www.searchamericas.com

Summary: We service manufacturers' needs for key management executives mid-level and above in the consumer, home improvement, builder and industrial marketplaces. We specialize in sales, marketing and general management positions but also perform searches in operations, IT and HR. We also have a mergers & acquisitions division and can perform the full M&A process or work in partnership with an investment banker and/or broker to complete the transaction.

Key Contact - Specialty:
Mr. Thomas J. Snow, Chief Executive Officer - *General management, Human resources, Marketing, Operations, Sales*
Mr. Eric J. Sted, Executive Vice President - *General management, Human resources, Marketing, Operations, Sales*
Mr. Michael D. Reilly, President, Mergers & Acquisitions Div. - *Mergers & acquisitions*

Salary Minimum: $40,000

Functions: Generalist (All), Management, Product Dev., Advertising, Mktg. Research, Mktg. Mgmt., Direct Mktg., Customer Svc., M&A

Industries: Food, Bev., Tobacco, Lumber, Furniture, Paints, Petro. Products, Leather, Stone, Glass, Consumer Elect., Wholesale, Retail, Services, Mgmt. Consulting, HR Services

SearchCom Inc

PO Box 671144
Dallas, TX 75367-1144
(972) 490-0300
(214) 783-9578
Email: searchcom@sbcglobal.net

Summary: Executive search for marketing, advertising and public relations talent for corporations and their agencies, across all industries. Also conduct searches in the nonprofit arena. Additional services include performance and career coaching.

Key Contact - Specialty:
Ms. Susan Abrahamson, President - *Advertising, Marketing, Public relations*

Salary Minimum: $70,000

Functions: Senior Mgmt., Middle Mgmt., Healthcare, Sales & Mktg., Advertising, Mktg. Research, Mktg. Mgmt., Direct Mktg., PR, Graphic Designers

Industries: Generalist (All)

SearchManagement†

3003 Briggs Ct
Pleasanton, CA 94588-3142
(925) 461-7040

Email: lherbst@searchmgmnt.com
Web: www.searchmgmnt.com

Summary: We are a leading provider of executive search services to technology companies seeking senior personnel in core disciplines including sales, marketing, engineering, operations and finance.

Key Contact - Specialty:
Ms. Lisa C. Herbst, CPA, President - *Engineering, Finance, High technology, Marketing, Operations*

Salary Minimum: $85,000

Functions: Sales & Mktg., Finance

Industries: Computer Equip., Test, Measure Equip., Services, Media, Software, Biotech/Life Sciences, Healthcare

SearchWide

320 Myrtle St W
Stillwater, MN 55082-4701
(651) 275-1370
(888) 386-6390
Email: info@searchwide.com
Web: www.searchwide.com

Summary: We specialize in recruiting executives for the hospitality industry, convention and visitors bureaus, along with associations and not-for-profit organizations around the country. Our firm offers its clients personalized service within the client's time frame and budget.

Key Contact - Specialty:
Mr. Mike Gamble, President & Chief Executive Officer
Ms. Tara Farrington, Office Manager

Salary Minimum: $75,000

Functions: Management, Board Members, Senior Mgmt., Sales & Mktg., Advertising, Mktg. Mgmt., Sales Mgmt., Customer Svc., PR, Finance

Industries: Services, Non-profits, Hospitality, Hotels, Resorts, Clubs, Entertainment, Recreation, Travel

Branches:
109 S Union St Ste 305
Traverse City, MI 49684-2575
(231) 995-0567
Email: info@searchwide.com
Key Contact - Specialty:
Mr. Jim Carra, Executive Vice President

SeBA International LLC

305 Madison Ave Rm 2508
New York, NY 10165-1215
(212) 370-7000
Email: sebateam@sebasearch.com
Web: www.sebasearch.com

Summary: We are a retained executive search firm specializing in the recruitment of strategy, finance and marketing professionals at the upper and executive management levels. We serve clients in the financial services, technology, manufacturing and life science industries.

Key Contact - Specialty:
Mr. Paul Bond, Principal - *Capital markets, Financial services, Manufacturing, Risk management, Senior management*
Ms. Kate Bullis, Principal - *Diversity, Finance, Marketing, Strategic planning, Technology*

Salary Minimum: $125,000

Functions: Management, Senior Mgmt., Middle Mgmt., Quality, Mktg. Mgmt., CFOs, M&A, Risk Mgmt., Mgmt. Consultants, Int'l.

Industries: Generalist (All)

Secura Burnett Company LLC

599 Bridgeway
Sausalito, CA 94965-2248
(415) 332-8777
Fax: (415) 331-4404
Email: resume@securaburnettco.com
Web: www.securaburnettco.com

Summary: We are a firm specializing in strategy, M&A advisory and consulting on executive search. We are also committed to providing quality search execution for senior executives in financial services and technology.

Key Contact - Specialty:
Mr. William M. Issac, Chairman, The Secura Group
Mr. Louis C. Burnett, Managing Director
Ms. Kathleen G. Ursin, Principal
Ms. Deborah Hodson, Principal
Mr. William R. Donnelly, Principal - *Finance*

Salary Minimum: $150,000

Functions: Generalist (All)

Industries: Wholesale, Retail, Finance, Services, Mgmt. Consulting, HR Services, Insurance, Real Estate, Software, Biotech/Life Sciences

Branches:
2410 Executive Dr Ste D
Indianapolis, IN 46241-5000
(317) 241-2400
Fax: (317) 241-5080
Key Contact - Specialty:
Mr. Lee D. Ashton, Manager, Midwest Region

Security & Investigative Placement Consultants

7707 Westfield Dr
Bethesda, MD 20817-6631
(301) 229-6360
Fax: (301) 263-0907
Email: klavinder@siplacement.com
Web: www.siplacement.com

Summary: Specializing in high-level corporate and industrial security management positions, including chief security officers, as well as financial investigators, such as anti-fraud and anti-money laundering personnel, forensic accountants, and anti-counterfeiting and cyber investigation experts.

Key Contact - Specialty:
Ms. Kathy Lavinder, Executive Director

Salary Minimum: $50,000

Functions: Senior Mgmt., Security Personnel

Industries: Generalist (All)

Seeliger y Conde Miami LLC

(a member of The Amrop Hever Group)
2121 Ponce de Leon Blvd Ste 422
Coral Gables, FL 33134-5221
(305) 442-1160
Fax: (305) 402-0977
Email: mcastanon@sycmiami.com
Web: www.sycmiami.com

Summary: Focused on coordinating regional relationships with multinationals and on performing local search assignments arising from these.

Key Contact - Specialty:
Mr. Martin Castanon, Managing Partner

Salary Minimum: $100,000

Functions: Generalist (All), Senior Mgmt.

Industries: Generalist (All)

Seiden Krieger Associates Inc

375 Park Ave
New York, NY 10152-0002
(212) 688-8383
Fax: (212) 688-5289
Web: www.seidenkrieger.com

Summary: We specialize in CEOs and professionals who report to CEOs. Frequently, such searches are for companies in transition. We have particular expertise in recruiting executives with hands-on experience building telecoms, software and high-technology businesses.

Key Contact - Specialty:
Mr. Steven A. Seiden, President - *CEOs*
Mr. Edwin H. Stern, III, Executive Vice President - *Education, Education (Higher), Non-profit, Philanthropy*
Mr. Steven A. Heller, Executive Vice President - *Healthcare, Insurance, Senior management*

Salary Minimum: $100,000

Functions: Generalist (All), Board Members, Senior Mgmt.

Industries: Generalist (All), Non-profits, Higher Ed., Insurance, Healthcare

Seitchik Corwin & Seitchik Inc

3443 Clay St
San Francisco, CA 94118-2008
(415) 928-5717
(800) 438-0279
Fax: (415) 928-8075
Email: blade@seitchikcorwin.com
Web: www.seitchikcorwin.com

Summary: We specialize in apparel, textile, footwear, handbag, accessories, home fashions and related industries, both wholesale and retail.

Key Contact - Specialty:
Mr. J. Blade Corwin, Partner - *Apparel, Retail, Textiles*

Salary Minimum: $50,000

Functions: Generalist (All)

Industries: Textiles, Apparel, Retail

Branches:
330 E 38th St Apt 5P
New York, NY 10016-2762
(212) 370-3592
Fax: (212) 286-0754
Key Contact - Specialty:
Mr. William Seitchik, Partner - *Apparel, Retail, Textiles*

Selection Resource Inc

3231 Central Park W Ste 109
Toledo, OH 43617-3009
(419) 893-8905
(888) 674-0021
Fax: (419) 893-8512
Email: info@selectionresource.com
Web: www.selectionresource.com

Summary: A retained search firm team of licensed psychologists and certified HR professionals. Our offering combines retained search services with a one year executive coaching engagement on each assignment.

Key Contact - Specialty:
Mr. Eric Summons, DABPS, President & Consulting Psychologist

Salary Minimum: $50,000

Functions: Generalist (All)

Industries: Generalist (All), Manufacturing, Transportation, Finance, Services, Media, Communications, Insurance, Software, Healthcare

Seligman & Herrod[†]

201 W Big Beaver Rd Ste 380
Troy, MI 48084-4116
(248) 457-2161
Email: vh@seligmanherrod.com
Web: www.seligmanherrod.com

Summary: High quality, individualized service to both clients and executives in a broad range of industry and disciplines.

Key Contact - Specialty:
Ms. Vicki Herrod, President

Salary Minimum: $70,000

Functions: Generalist (All)

Industries: Manufacturing, Transportation, Retail, Services, Media, Telecoms, Packaging, Biotech/Life Sciences, Healthcare, Non-Classifiable

Robert Sellery Associates Ltd

1050 Connecticut Ave NW Ste 10
Washington, DC 20036-5350
(202) 331-0090
Fax: (202) 772-3101
Email: sellery@sellery.com
Web: www.sellery.com

Summary: Our practice is in the not-for-profit sector. We find: presidents, CEOs, executive directors, deans, chief development, communication, government relations and financial officers, including corporate social responsibility and investment officers, along with the people reporting to these positions.

Key Contact - Specialty:
Mr. Robert A. Sellery, Jr., Managing Director
Ms. Kathryn B. Wilson, Vice President

Functions: Generalist (All), Senior Mgmt., Non-profits

Industries: Invest. Banking, Misc. Financial, Non-profits, Higher Ed., Government, Healthcare

Setren, Smallberg & Associates

3871 Piedmont Ave Ste 359
Oakland, CA 94611-5378
(510) 208-0310
(510) 208-0311
Fax: (510) 208-0321
Email: larry@setrensmallberg.com
Web: www.setrensmallberg.com

Summary: Our firm is a unique, full-service provider of HR services to biopharmaceutical companies and other dynamic, emerging industries and companies. We provide management consulting, executive search, compensation, training and organizational development. Our clients include many prominent and emerging biopharmaceutical companies.

Key Contact - Specialty:
Mr. Larry Setren, Partner - *Biopharmaceutical*
Mr. Victor Smallberg, Partner - *Biopharmaceutical*

Salary Minimum: $120,000

Functions: Generalist (All), Board Members

Industries: Chemicals, Drugs Mfg., Medical Devices, Pharm Svcs., HR Services, Biotech/Life Sciences, Healthcare

Shannahan & Company Inc

655 Redwood Hwy Ste 133
Mill Valley, CA 94941-3009
(415) 381-3613
Email: peter@shannahan.com
Web: www.shannahan.com

† occasional contingency assignment

Summary: We specialize in the recruitment of investment professionals. We work with investment management firms, mutual funds, insurance companies, banks and consulting firms. We help firms recruit professionals in marketing, sales, client services, consulting and portfolio management.

Key Contact - Specialty:
Mr. Peter Shannahan, President - *Financial services*
Ms. Suzanne Danileson, Project Manager

Salary Minimum: $100,000

Functions: Sales & Mktg., Sales Mgmt.

Industries: Finance, Banking, Invest. Banking, Venture Cap., Mutual/Hedge Funds, Misc. Financial, Mgmt. Consulting, HR Services

Sharp Placement Professionals Inc[†]

PO Box 788
Westbury, NY 11590-0788
(516) 334-1120
Fax: (516) 908-3504
Email: recruit@sharpsearch.com
Web: www.sharpsearch.com

Summary: We specialize in filling those difficult positions that fall between full-service retained search and general contingency search. We will work out a customized program to fill your recruitment needs.

Key Contact - Specialty:
Mr. Donald Levine, CPC, President

Salary Minimum: $60,000

Functions: Management, Board Members, Senior Mgmt., Sales & Mktg., HR Mgmt., IT

Industries: Generalist (All), Manufacturing, Medical Devices, Computer Equip., Consumer Elect., Test, Measure Equip., Accounting, Equip Svcs., Mgmt. Consulting, HR Services, Media, Communications, Telecoms, Aerospace, Software, Biotech/Life Sciences

Shasteen Medical Search[†]

4180 Fairgreen Dr NE
Marietta, GA 30068-4108
(770) 565-1191

Summary: Clinical physician searches. Retained (hourly) or contingency firm. Physician search is our business.

Key Contact - Specialty:
Mr. Steve Shasteen, MA, Owner
Mrs. Martha Shasteen, Co-Owner

Salary Minimum: $110,000

Functions: Management, Physicians

Industries: Telecoms, Wireless, Healthcare

Branches:
4321 Donnybrook Pl
El Paso, TX 79902-1312
(915) 253-9534
Email: dbdoubleu@aol.com
Key Contact - Specialty:
Mr. David Wierson

Peter Shenfield & Associates Inc

507 Douglas Ave
North York, ON M5M 1H6
Canada
(416) 783-6390
Fax: (416) 783-8931
Email: peter@petershenfieldandassociates.com
Web: www.petershenfieldandassociates.com

Summary: Boutique generalist firm with in-depth knowledge of our marketplace. Particular

expertise in HR, manufacturing, high-technology engineering, not for profit and sales & marketing area.

Key Contact - Specialty:
Mr. Peter Shenfield, President

Salary Minimum: $75,000

Functions: Generalist (All), Management, Senior Mgmt.

Industries: Generalist (All), Manufacturing, Drugs Mfg., Metal Products, Motor Vehicles, Misc. Mfg., Electronic, Elec. Components, Wholesale, Retail, Services, Non-profits, Travel, Communications, Software, Healthcare

Shepherd Bueschel & Provus Inc

4146 N Harding Ave Ste 3230
Chicago, IL 60618-1943
(773) 588-3230
Fax: (773) 588-3227
Email: sbp@sbpsearch.com

Summary: Our firm consists of two founding partners with extensive executive search experience as well as prior diverse industry experience. We conduct assignments for a wide range of clients at the $150,000 level and up. Both of the principals are recognized in our industry. The firm has been cited for its work quality.

Key Contact - Specialty:
Mr. David A. Bueschel, Principal
Mr. Daniel M. Shepherd, Principal

Salary Minimum: $150,000

Functions: Generalist (All), Board Members, Senior Mgmt., Mfg., Sales & Mktg., HR Mgmt., CFOs, MIS Mgmt., Mgmt. Consultants, Non-profits

Industries: Generalist (All), Manufacturing, Lumber, Furniture, Medical Devices, Services, Government, Insurance, Biotech/Life Sciences

Sherriff & Associates Inc[†]

4200 Somerset Dr Ste 256
Prairie Village, KS 66208-5213
(913) 341-7117
Fax: (913) 341-2992
Email: bsherriff@sherriff.com
Web: www.sherriff.com

Summary: We provide quality, ethical physician and physician executive search. We are also founders and a member of First Choice, Inc., a consortium of select physician recruitment and locum tenens companies with a vast nationwide presence.

Key Contact - Specialty:
Mr. William W. Sherriff, Vice President - *Physicians*
Ms. Julie A. Sherriff, President - *Physicians*
Mr. Grant Strohm, Researcher
Ms. Shilpa Jandhyala, Assistant, Marketing

Functions: Physicians

Industries: Generalist (All)

Sherwood Lehman Massucco Inc[†]

3455 W Shaw Ave Ste 110
Fresno, CA 93711-3201
(559) 276-8572
Fax: (559) 276-2351
Email: slinc@employmentexpert.com
Web: www.employmentexpert.com

Summary: We are a full-service executive search and employment consulting firm. We leverage our industry experience and knowledge to work as a strategic partner with our clients to help them maximize their human capital investments.

The firm specializes in retained searches for talented, top senior executives, managers and specialized or unique technical talent in the Agriculture, Banking, Healthcare and Manufacturing industries.

Key Contact - Specialty:
Mr. Harry A. Massucco, President - *General management*
Mr. Neal G. Lehman, Vice President - *Financial, General management*
Mr. Jeff Oliver, Vice President, Sales & Marketing - *Agriculture*

Salary Minimum: $60,000

Functions: Generalist (All), Management, CFOs, Engineering

Industries: Agri., Forestry, Mining, Construction, Manufacturing, Food, Bev., Tobacco, Plastics, Rubber, Metal Products, Machine, Appliance, Computer Equip., Misc. Mfg., Electronic, Elec. Components, Finance, Banking, Misc. Financial, Non-profits, Accounting, HR Services, Media, Telecoms, Software

Shirley Associates

200 N Larchmont Blvd
Los Angeles, CA 90004-3707
(323) 460-6202
Email: martin@shirleyassociates.com
Web: www.shirleyassociates.com

Summary: Senior-level executive search practice serving the non-profit sector and semiconductor industry(including equipment manufacturing) clients.

Key Contact - Specialty:
Mr. Martin R. Shirley, Managing Partner - *Finance, Manufacturing*
Ms. Jennifer Arundale, Partner
Ms. Mercedes Paz, Partner - *Education (Higher), Non-profit*

Salary Minimum: $90,000

Functions: Generalist (All), Senior Mgmt., Non-profits

Industries: Generalist (All), Computer Equip., Test, Measure Equip., Electronic, Elec. Components, Semiconductors, Non-profits, K-12 Ed., Higher Ed.

Michael Shirley Associates Inc

5250 W 94th Ter Ste 109
Prairie Village, KS 66207-2502
(913) 341-7655
Fax: (913) 341-7657
Email: michael@mshirleyassociates.com
Web: www.mshirleyassociates.com

Summary: Founder has completed more than 1400 retained searches. We are a generalist firm with significant expertise in banking, financial services, insurance and healthcare. Searches have been completed in 46 states as well as in international locations.

Key Contact - Specialty:
Mr. Michael R. Shirley, President
Ms. Michelle Anderson, Senior Consultant
Ms. Lisa Bruemmer, Director, Administration & Client Servs
Ms. Jenni Leaton, Manager, Research & Accounting

Salary Minimum: $75,000

Functions: Generalist (All)

Industries: Energy, Utilities, Manufacturing, Finance, Banking, Invest. Banking, Accounting, HR Services, Insurance, Healthcare, Hospitals

Shoemaker & Associates

1862 Independence Sq Ste A
Atlanta, GA 30338-5136
(770) 395-7225
Email: lcs@shoemakersearch.com
Web: www.shoemakersearch.com

Summary: We are a highly professional generalist practice conducting a broad range of executive searches at senior-levels and middle management levels in general management, marketing, sales, finance, research, quality, manufacturing and operations. Our firm uses in-depth interviewing techniques to focus on the candidate's fit into the culture of the client's organization.

Key Contact - Specialty:
Mr. Larry Shoemaker, President
Ms. Tami Fitzpatrick, Associate

Salary Minimum: $120,000

Functions: Generalist (All), Mfg., HR Mgmt., Finance

Industries: Generalist (All)

E L Shore & Associates Ltd

1201-2 St Clair Ave E
Colonial Place
Toronto, ON M4T 2T5
Canada
(416) 928-9399
Fax: (416) 928-6509
Email: info@elshore.com
Web: www.elshore.com

Summary: Most industries covered with an emphasis on senior management. Typical searches include retail management, financial services, marketing and manufacturing. Dedicated to providing personalized, professional service having a track record of superior results.

Key Contact - Specialty:
Mr. Earl Shore, Founder

Salary Minimum: $75,000

Functions: Generalist (All), Management, Sales & Mktg., HR Mgmt., Finance, IT

Industries: Generalist (All), Manufacturing, Transportation, Retail, Finance, Services

Shore Asociados Ejecutivos S A de CV

(an InterSearch company)
Av Constituyentes 117 Piso 5
Col San Miguel Chapultepec
11850 Mexico City, DF
Mexico
55 5089 8800
Fax: 55 5515 3979
Email: info@shore.com.mx
Web: www.shore.com.mx

Summary: One of the largest and most important retained executive search and HR consultancy firms in the country.

Key Contact - Specialty:
Mr. Fernando Fernandez De Cordova, Chief Executive Officer
Ms. Linda Shore, General Director
Ms. Virginia Franco, Executive Director
Ms. Susan Shore, Corporate Director
Mr. Auren Lopez, Director, Business Development

Salary Minimum: $25,000

Functions: Generalist (All), Management, Materials, Sales & Mktg., HR Mgmt., Finance, IT

Industries: Generalist (All), Construction, Food, Bev., Tobacco, Transportation, Finance, Hospitality, Media

Branches:
Av Lázaro Cárdenas Pte 2400
Edif Losoles Piso 1 Ofna A-14
Col San Agustin, San Pedro
66270 Garza Garcia, NL
Mexico
81 8363 2769
Fax: 81 8363 2768
Email: fdominguez@shore.com.mx
Key Contact - Specialty:
Mr. Alfonso Calderon
Mr. Francisco Dominguez, Director

Av Lázaro Cárdenas 4145-501 PH
Fracc Camino Real
45040 Guadalajara, JAL
Mexico
33 3647 9012
Fax: 33 3647 7916
Email: jcoello@shore.com.mx
Key Contact - Specialty:
Mr. Jorge Coello, Director

Shore Paralax LLC

212 Carnegie Ctr Ste 206
Princeton, NJ 08540-6236
(609) 844-7504
(732) 295-9503
Fax: (888) 295-9503
Email: search@shoreparalax.com
Web: www.shoreparalax.com

Summary: We offer a unique search process designed to ensure cultural as well as technical fit. Our proprietary rules of leadership program aids candidates in designing a quick entry strategy in house research.

Key Contact - Specialty:
Mr. Edward J. Hopkins, President - *General management, Marketing, Sales*
Mr. Russell Glover, Partner - *General management*
Mr. Mark Hopkins, Partner - *Marketing*
Ms. Agnes Snyder, Partner
Ms. Deborah Kane, Director, Candidate Research Team
Dr. Raymond Harrison, PhD, Principal
Ms. Karen L. Kirchner, Principal
Ms. Marcella Schuyler, Principal
Mr. Lawrence A. Schmieder, Principal

Salary Minimum: $100,000

Functions: Management, Board Members, Mfg., Materials Plng., Mktg. Mgmt., Sales Mgmt., CFOs, M&A, MIS Mgmt.

Industries: Generalist (All), Food, Bev., Tobacco, Soap, Perf., Cosmtcs., Drugs Mfg., Medical Devices, Consumer Goods, Finance, Banking, Venture Cap., Pharm Svcs., HR Services, Media, Advertising, Marketing SW, Biotech/Life Sciences

The Shotland Group

2283 Westshore Ln
Westlake Village, CA 91361-1951
(805) 497-8494
Fax: (805) 497-9504
Email: dshotland@adelphia.net

Summary: We are a generalist practice emphasizing recruitment of mid and upper-level management. Our primary areas of specialization include disciplines within manufacturing and distribution companies.

Key Contact - Specialty:
Mr. David R. Shotland, President - *Engineering, Manufacturing, Marketing*

Salary Minimum: $50,000

Functions: Generalist (All), Senior Mgmt., Middle Mgmt., Materials Plng., Distribution, Sales Mgmt., CFOs, Engineering

Industries: Generalist (All), Soap, Perf., Cosmtcs., Drugs Mfg., Medical Devices, Plastics, Rubber, Metal Products, Consumer Elect., Misc. Mfg.

M Shulman Inc

563 Vermont St
San Francisco, CA 94107-2327
(415) 437-6756
Fax: (415) 437-6755
Email: mel@shulmaninc.com
Web: www.shulmaninc.com

Summary: Generalist practice concentrates on CEO, COO and senior executive-level positions. Clients include high-technology, biotechnology, conglomerates, electronic goods, entertainment, broadcasting, new venture start-ups and retail.

Key Contact - Specialty:
Ms. Mel Shulman, Partner

Salary Minimum: $225,000

Functions: Senior Mgmt.

Industries: Medical Devices, Retail, Pharm Svcs., Mgmt. Consulting, HR Services, Telecoms, Software, Biotech/Life Sciences, Healthcare

John Sibbald Associates Inc

7701 Forsyth Blvd Ste 1095
Saint Louis, MO 63105-1843
(314) 727-0227
Email: jsibbald@sibbaldassociates.com
Web: www.sibbaldassociates.com

Summary: We are small, by design, to provide highly personalized service to limited clientele with emphasis on clubs, resorts, hotels and related hospitality industry employers.

Key Contact - Specialty:
Mr. John R. Sibbald, President
Mr. Scott McNett, Vice President - *Hospitality*
Mr. Randall Martin, Vice President - *Hospitality*
Mr. W. Red Steger, CCM, Senior Vice President
Mr. Daniel Denehy, CCM, President, Consulting Group

Salary Minimum: $100,000

Functions: Generalist (All), Management, Board Members, Senior Mgmt.

Industries: Hospitality, Hotels, Resorts, Clubs, Restaurants, Entertainment, Recreation

Larry Siegel & Associates Inc

1111 3rd Ave Ste 2880
Seattle, WA 98101-3293
(206) 622-4282
Fax: (206) 622-4058
Email: admin@siegel-associates.com
Web: www.siegel-associates.com

Summary: We are a highly experienced generalist firm specializing in recruitment of senior-level management in most functional disciplines with expertise in a wide range of manufacturing and distribution industries.

Key Contact - Specialty:
Mr. Larry Siegel, President
Ms. Carrie Reid, Manager, Research & Administration

Salary Minimum: $100,000

Functions: Generalist (All), Senior Mgmt., Mfg., Distribution, Sales & Mktg., Finance, CFOs, M&A

Industries: Manufacturing, Food, Bev., Tobacco, Metal Products, Electronic, Elec. Components,

Consumer Goods, Transportation, Supply Chain Mgmt, Aerospace

Signature Search

4650 W Spencer St Ste 22
Appleton, WI 54914-9106
(920) 749-9300
Email: mmueller@signaturesearch.com
Web: www.signaturesearch.com

Summary: We are a well established search firm. Functional expertise includes: sales, marketing, top leadership, finance, operations, HR and R&D. Industries include: manufacturing, financial management, travel and healthcare.

Key Contact - Specialty:
Mr. Michael S. Mueller, President

Salary Minimum: $100,000

Functions: Generalist (All)

Industries: Paper, Printing, Chemicals, Plastics, Rubber, Misc. Mfg., Finance, Services, Non-profits, Packaging, Healthcare

Branches:
3737 Glenwood Ave Ste 100
Raleigh, NC 27612-5515
(919) 573-6116
Email: cmagee@signaturesearch.com
Key Contact - Specialty:
Mr. Charles R. Magee, Vice President

Signium International Inc

(formerly known as Meridian Partners)
100 S Ashley Dr Ste 800
Tampa, FL 33602-5348
(813) 866-7600
Fax: (813) 866-8856
Email: info@signiummeridian.com
Web: www.signiummeridian.com

Summary: Our quality focus has allowed us to build deep, long term client partnerships. Our boutique approach combines strong management consulting skills, a dedication to original research, customized technology, and a targeted process. We enable organizations to build "Best in Market" management teams that result in long term market advantages.

Key Contact - Specialty:
Mrs. Charlotte Tinsley, Associate - *C-level, Human resources, Industrial, Senior management, Technology*
Ms. Elizabeth Hatch, Associate - *Management, Manufacturing, Manufacturing (Management), Re-engineering, Senior management*
Ms. Nancy Brereton, Associate - *Administration, Retail, Telecommunications, Training*

Salary Minimum: $125,000

Functions: Generalist (All), Management, Senior Mgmt., Sales & Mktg., HR Mgmt., CFOs, MIS Mgmt., Engineering, Non-profits, Int'l.

Industries: Generalist (All), Manufacturing, Machine, Appliance, Motor Vehicles, Computer Equip., Misc. Mfg., Electronic, Elec. Components, Consumer Goods, Transportation, Retail, Finance, Services, Non-profits, Mgmt. Consulting, HR Services, Communications, Government, Aerospace

Branches:
5201 Blue Lagoon Dr Fl 8
Miami, FL 33126-2092
(305) 718-3330
Fax: (305) 718-3300
Email: wbaker@signium.com
Key Contact - Specialty:
Mr. Walter Baker, Managing Partner - *General management, Industrial, International, Latin America*

1422 Euclid Ave Ste 217
Cleveland, OH 44115-1901
(216) 241-0158
Fax: (216) 241-0172
Email: ganderson@signium.com
Key Contact - Specialty:
Mr. Glenn Anderson, Jr., Managing Partner

Signium International Inc

360 Memorial Dr Ste 120
Crystal Lake, IL 60014-6291
(815) 479-9415
Email: contact@signium.com
Web: www.signium.com

Summary: We are a retained executive search firm, committed to providing a select, demanding client base with A-level, executive talent. We achieve this through a quantitative and disciplined approach, utilizing a synergy of original research, advanced technology and strong management consulting skills.

Key Contact - Specialty:
Dr. Bernd Prasuhn, Chairman of the Board
Mrs. Suzanne M. Speight, Corporate Secretary

Salary Minimum: $100,000

Functions: Generalist (All), Board Members, Senior Mgmt., CFOs, Int'l.

Industries: Generalist (All), Manufacturing, Transportation, Wholesale, Retail, Finance, Services, Media, Communications, Aerospace, Software

Daniel A Silverstein Associates Inc

777 NW 51st St Ste 100
Boca Raton, FL 33431-4406
(561) 981-1801
Fax: (561) 998-7073
Email: dsilverstein@dassearch.com
Web: www.dassearch.com

Summary: Executive search for pharmaceuticals, biotechnology, diagnostics and medical devices. Company directors, CEOs and top management team for life sciences companies.

Key Contact - Specialty:
Mr. Daniel A. Silverstein, President - *Healthcare*

Salary Minimum: $200,000

Functions: Generalist (All)

Industries: Drugs Mfg., Medical Devices, Venture Cap., Pharm Svcs., Mgmt. Consulting, Biotech/Life Sciences

Simpson Associates

2068 Tenoga Dr
Mississauga, ON L5H 3K2
Canada
(905) 271-3332
(800) 419-7473
Fax: (905) 271-2788
Email: info@djsimpson.com
Web: www.djsimpson.com

Summary: We combine search with one of the most powerful assessment tools available today to ensure our clients outperform there most worthy opponents. And we have the track record to prove it.

Key Contact - Specialty:
Mr. David Simpson, General Manager
Ms. Jeanne Gilbert, Recruiter - *Engineering, Technical*

Salary Minimum: $80,000

Functions: Generalist (All), Management, Senior Mgmt.

Industries: Manufacturing, Retail, IT Implementation, Engineering Svcs.

Spelman Johnson Group

193 Northampton St Ste 1
Easthampton, MA 01027-1576
(413) 529-2895
(800) 827-6208
Fax: (413) 527-6881
Email: info@spelmanandjohnson.com
Web: www.spelmanandjohnson.com

Summary: We are the hire authority for higher education. Specializing in executive search, consulting and training, and committed to furthering our clients' institutional objectives. Utilized by over 300 colleges and universities, offering services focused on administrative and academic areas including academic affairs, enrollment, student affairs, financial administration and advancement.

Key Contact - Specialty:
Ms. Katherine Schneider, Partner
Ms. Ellen Heffernan, Partner

Functions: Board Members, Senior Mgmt.

Industries: Higher Ed.

Ruth Sklar Associates Inc[†]

(also known as RSA Executive Search)
475 Park Ave S Fl 10
New York, NY 10016-6901
(212) 213-2929
Fax: (212) 779-9617
Email: info@rsaexecsearch.com
Web: www.rsaexecutivesearch.com

Summary: We emphasize on principal involvement in all phases of search. Recruitment of key executives from finance, healthcare, consumer products, services, microwave electronics and aerospace industries. Specializing in entrepreneurial environments.

Key Contact - Specialty:
Ms. Ruth Sklar, President - *Finance, Healthcare*
Mr. Daniel R. Mazziota, Chairman - *Biotechnology, High technology*

Salary Minimum: $80,000

Functions: Generalist (All)

Industries: Manufacturing, Finance, Pharm Svcs., Accounting, HR Services, Media, Telecoms, Aerospace, Biotech/Life Sciences, Healthcare

Skott/Edwards Consultants

(a Penrhyn International company)
7 Royal Dr
Brick, NJ 08723-6730
(732) 920-1883
Fax: (732) 477-1541
Email: burkland@skottedwards.com
Web: www.skottedwards.com

Summary: Industry expertise emphasizing emerging life science, medical devices, healthcare and pharmaceuticals. All functions including management, finance, HR, manufacturing, sales & marketing, legal, procurement and board of directors.

Key Contact - Specialty:
Mr. Skott B. Burkland, President

Salary Minimum: $100,000

Functions: Board Members, Healthcare

Industries: Generalist (All), Healthcare

Slate Personnel Ltd

1410-10130 103 St NW
Coopers Lybrand Building
Edmonton, AB T5J 3N9
Canada
(780) 424-7528
Fax: (780) 426-7528
Email: info@slatepersonnel.com
Web: www.slatepersonnel.com

Summary: Our firm is one of today's leading agencies servicing Edmonton and surrounding areas with permanent, temporary, and contract placements to a wide-variety of occupations, including but not limited to, accountants, administrative/secretarial, call centre associates, computer/IT specialists, credit/collections, engineering, human resources/managers, legal, sales/marketing, technicians/technologists, and warehouse/inventory. We are dedicated to bringing people and companies together in a positive working relationship.

Key Contact - Specialty:
Mr. Robert C. Slaght, President
Ms. Margaret Slate, General Manager

Functions: Management, Senior Mgmt., Admin. Svcs., Production, Plant Mgmt., Materials, Purchasing, Distribution, Engineering, Legal

Industries: Generalist (All)

Slayton International

200 W Madison St Ste 2800
Chicago, IL 60606-3498
(312) 456-0080
Fax: (312) 456-0089
Email: slayton@slatonintl.com
Web: www.slaytonintl.com

Summary: We are a top retained executive search firm serving some of America's most recognized companies in the consumer products, industrial, life sciences and technology industries.

Key Contact - Specialty:
Mr. Richard S. Slayton, Chief Executive Officer
Mr. Roy F. Hebard, Managing Director
Mr. Brad Berke, Vice President
Mr. John D. Nimesheim, Vice President

Salary Minimum: $150,000

Functions: Generalist (All)

Industries: Generalist (All), Energy, Utilities, Manufacturing, Consumer Goods, Retail, Communications, Environmental Svcs., Software, Biotech/Life Sciences

Branches:
10901 W 120th Ave Ste 300
Broomfield, CO 80021-3418
(303) 415-9800
Email: pdimarchi@slaytonintl.com
Key Contact - Specialty:
Mr. Paul DiMarchi, Vice President
Mr. Eric D. Pringle

1177 High Ridge Rd Ste 216
Stamford, CT 06905-1221
(203) 321-1262
Email: slayton@slaytonintl.com
Key Contact - Specialty:
Mr. Robert Benson, Chairman

1737 H St NW Ste 300
Washington, DC 20006-3956
(202) 293-8030
Key Contact - Specialty:
Ms. Kathryn Griffin

Mr. Tony Hudgins
Mr. Derek Wilkinson

Slone & Associates†

400 Alton Rd Apt 710
Miami Beach, FL 33139-6736
(888) 424-7800
(305) 531-4733
Fax: (202) 318-4302
Email: aslone@sloneandassociates.com
Web: www.sloneandassociates.com

Summary: Our firm is a leading national healthcare consultancy specializing in the healthcare industry. We primarily focus on placing top notch business development and operations professionals with quality companies.

Key Contact - Specialty:
Mr. Adam Slone, President

Salary Minimum: $50,000

Functions: Healthcare, Sales & Mktg.

Industries: Biotech/Life Sciences, Healthcare, Hospitals

Branches:
5705 Locust Branch Ct
Centreville, VA 20120-2885
(877) 416-0681
Email: tara@sloneandassociates.com
Key Contact - Specialty:
Ms. Tara Kochis, Vice President

Christopher Smallhorn Executive Recruiting Inc

55 Cambridge Pkwy Ste 301
Cambridge, MA 02142-1234
(617) 723-8180

Summary: Recruiting senior managers, CEO, COO, CFO, primarily for early stage and emerging companies.

Key Contact - Specialty:
Mr. Christopher Smallhorn, President

Salary Minimum: $150,000

Functions: Generalist (All), Management, Board Members, Healthcare, Health Admin., Mktg. Mgmt., CFOs

Industries: Generalist (All), Drugs Mfg., Medical Devices, Venture Cap., Biotech/Life Sciences, Healthcare

Smith & Laue Search

3244 NE Glisan St
Portland, OR 97232-2523
(503) 460-9181
Email: chuck@smithlaue.com

Summary: A growing influence in executive placement, we place highly qualified Plant Managers in the food processing industry. Reasons for our growth: quality of candidate, thoroughness of process, and positive representation of your company.

Key Contact - Specialty:
Mr. Charles D. Smith, President
Ms. Elizabeth V. Smith, Vice President

Salary Minimum: $100,000

Functions: Management, Board Members, Senior Mgmt., Production, Plant Mgmt., Mktg. Mgmt., Sales Mgmt., CFOs

Industries: Food, Bev., Tobacco, Drugs Mfg., Venture Cap., Pharm Svcs., Packaging

Smith & Partners Inc

1324 Larchmont Dr
Buffalo Grove, IL 60089-1132
(847) 634-2304

Summary: A single professional generalist retained executive recruiting firm where the owner is totally responsible for all aspects of every assignment. The firm offers no magical solutions; it simply gets the job done.

Key Contact - Specialty:
Mr. Richard J. Smith, President & Owner

Salary Minimum: $100,000

Functions: Generalist (All)

Industries: Generalist (All)

Smith & Sawyer LLC

295 Coconut Palm Rd
Indian River Shores, FL 32963-3708
(772) 234-0607
Email: pat@smithsawyer.com
Web: www.smithsawyer.com

Summary: We specialize in senior general management positions, such as: CEO, president and COO in information industries such as: computers, software, telecom, e-commerce and IT services. We also place CIOs and CTOs in all industries, partner/practice leaders in strategy or IT consulting and general partners in VC firms. We are also engaged for CEO and board advisory consulting projects.

Key Contact - Specialty:
Ms. Patricia L. Sawyer, Partner
Mr. Robert L. Smith, Partner

Salary Minimum: $150,000

Functions: Board Members, Senior Mgmt., MIS Mgmt., Mgmt. Consultants

Industries: Computer Equip., Retail, Finance, Venture Cap., Misc. Financial, Services, Mgmt. Consulting, Media, New Media, Communications, Insurance, Software, Healthcare

Smith & Syberg Inc

505 Washington St Ste 2A
Columbus, IN 47201-1905
(812) 372-7254
Fax: (812) 372-7275
Email: mail@smithandsyberg.com
Web: www.smithandsyberg.com

Summary: Our search expertise is utilized for senior and executive management level positions. Clients range from small, entrepreneurial growth companies to Fortune 500 corporations and represent a variety of industries, including manufacturing, airlines, service and distribution.

Key Contact - Specialty:
Mr. Joseph E. Smith, Partner - *Finance, Manufacturing, Transportation*
Mr. Keith A. Syberg, Partner - *Manufacturing*

Salary Minimum: $100,000

Functions: Senior Mgmt., Middle Mgmt., Mfg., Plant Mgmt., Quality, Materials, Purchasing, HR Mgmt., Finance, Engineering

Industries: Manufacturing, Transportation, Banking, Logistics Svcs.

R M Smith Associates

100 E Bellevue Pl Apt 15D
Chicago, IL 60611-1123
(312) 649-5955
Email: ronsmith@rcn.com
Web: www.rmsmithassociates.com

Summary: A boutique firm that specializes in executive search at senior and upper-middle management levels in all management functions for the airline, aerospace, and other travel and tourism industry segments, including cruise lines, large travel companies, tour operators, hotels, travel associations, etc.

Key Contact - Specialty:
Mr. Ronald Smith, President

Salary Minimum: $100,000

Functions: Generalist (All)

Industries: Transportation, Hospitality, Hotels, Resorts, Clubs, Travel, Aerospace

Adam Smith Executive Search Consulting

2434 S Walter Reed Dr Apt D
Arlington, VA 22206-1181
(703) 998-8118
Email: adamsmith@adamsmithsearch.com
Web: www.adamsmithsearch.com

Summary: We are a client-centered management-consulting firm. The firm's management consulting services include: executive search and compensation.

Key Contact - Specialty:
Mr. Adam M. Smith, Managing Director

Salary Minimum: $90,000

Functions: Senior Mgmt.

Industries: Generalist (All), Agri., Forestry, Mining, Manufacturing, Retail, Non-profits, Architectural Svcs., Mgmt. Consulting, IT Implementation, Biotech/Life Sciences, Healthcare

Smith James Group Inc

10800 Alpharetta Hwy Ste 208-520
Roswell, GA 30076-1474
(770) 667-0212
Email: resumes@smithjames.com
Web: www.smithjames.com

Summary: Expertise in telecom, high-technology, manufacturing, defense, banking, service and utilities industry. Concentration is on senior/middle management and key technical positions.

Key Contact - Specialty:
Mr. James Soutouras, Senior Parnter
Mr. Michael Smith, Senior Parnter

Salary Minimum: $75,000

Functions: Generalist (All)

Industries: Generalist (All)

H C Smith Ltd

20600 Chagrin Blvd Ste 101
Shaker Heights, OH 44122-5344
(216) 752-9966
Fax: (216) 752-9970
Email: info@hcsmith.com
Web: www.hcsmith.com

Summary: Professionally managed generalist practice with broad range of global resources. Recognized ability to evaluate and recruit talented minorities and women for executive and board positions.

Key Contact - Specialty:
Dr. Herbert C. Smith, Chairman
Ms. Rebecca Ruben Smith, Executive Vice President

Salary Minimum: $75,000

Functions: Generalist (All)

Industries: Generalist (All)

Smith Roth Squires & Ritter

(formerly known as Smith, Roth & Squires)
230 Park Ave Fl 10
PMB 1095
New York, NY 10169-1099
(516) 767-9480
(503) 675-5324
Email: rrothsrs@aol.com
Web: www.smithrothsquires.com

Summary: We are a senior-level boutique firm serving most industries and all functions. We are hands on, principal directed firm. Our demonstrated track record of repetitive business is indicative of our high personal commitment and the strong relationships that we have built and maintain.

Key Contact - Specialty:
Mr. Ronald P. Roth, Principal
Mr. R. James Squires, Principal

Salary Minimum: $150,000

Functions: Generalist (All)

Industries: Generalist (All)

Branches:
885 10th St Ste 300
Lake Oswego, OR 97034-1711
(503) 675-5324
Email: mrittersrs@comcast.net
Key Contact - Specialty:
Mr. Mark Ritter, Principal

Smith, Scott & Associates[†]

PO Box 38475
Colorado Springs, CO 80937-8475
(719) 538-4404
Email: gary.smith@smithscott.com
Web: www.smithscott.com

Summary: We are an executive search firm focused on recruiting in the areas of human recources, information technology, and management consulting.

Key Contact - Specialty:
Mr. Gary J. Smith, Managing Partner - *Human resources, Management consulting*

Salary Minimum: $80,000

Functions: Senior Mgmt., HR Mgmt., Mgmt. Consultants

Industries: Generalist (All), Mgmt. Consulting, HR Services

Smith Search SC

Barranca de Muerto 472
Col Alpes Del A Obregon
01010 Mexico City, DF
Mexico
55 5593 8036
Fax: 55 5593 8969
Email: smith@smithsearch.com
Web: www.smithsearch.com

Summary: We are an independent executive recruitment firm, specializing in the cross-cultural, bilingual executive for companies.

Key Contact - Specialty:
Mr. John E. Smith, Jr., President
Ms. Maria Elena Pardo, Executive Recruiter
Ms. Ana Luz Smith, Executive Recruiter

Salary Minimum: $75,000

Functions: Generalist (All), Board Members, Plant Mgmt., Mktg. Mgmt., CFOs, MIS Mgmt.

Industries: Generalist (All), Food, Bev., Tobacco, Chemicals, Banking, Invest. Banking, Telecoms

SMR Inc[†]

3320 S Whitepost Way
Eagle, ID 83616-6418
(208) 938-9001
(208) 484-9645
Fax: (208) 938-8098
Email: kalmberg@smrinc.org
Web: www.smrinc.org

Summary: We are an executive search firm founded on the basic principles of value, ethics and responsibility to our clients and candidates. Our staff has worked on both the client side as well as the staffing side of the business. We boast low averages for turnover of the candidates we place.

Key Contact - Specialty:
Mr. Ken Almberg, President

Salary Minimum: $75,000

Functions: Generalist (All)

Industries: Generalist (All)

A William Smyth Inc

PO Box 380
Ross, CA 94957-0380
(415) 457-8383

Summary: Our experience includes related categories (i.e.: consumer packaged goods, high technology and software where sophisticated marketing is required). We are uniquely involved civil engineering community. We specialize in management consulting, M&A, organzation planning, salary surveys and channel planning.

Key Contact - Specialty:
Mr. William Smyth, President

Salary Minimum: $125,000

Functions: Generalist (All), Management, Sales & Mktg., Finance, IT, Int'l.

Industries: Generalist (All), Food, Bev., Tobacco, Soap, Perf., Cosmtcs., Computer Equip., Finance, Hospitality, Software

Snowden Associates

200 International Dr Ste 157
Portsmouth, NH 03801-6833
(603) 431-1553
Fax: (603) 431-3809
Email: portsmouth@snowdenassociates.com
Web: www.snowdenassociates.com

Summary: We use a very personal and thorough search process to identify, screen, interview, access and recommend highly qualified key impact candidates for critical positions at our client firms.

Key Contact - Specialty:
Mr. Len Rishkofski, President & Chief Executive Officer

Salary Minimum: $65,000

Functions: Generalist (All)

Industries: Energy, Utilities, Manufacturing, Wholesale, Finance, Services, Media, Insurance, Biotech/Life Sciences, Healthcare

Branches:
477 Congress St
Portland, ME 04101-3427
(207) 523-3478
Fax: (603) 4313809
Email: silva@snowdenassociates.com
Key Contact - Specialty:
Mr. Steve Silva, Vice President, Search - *Accounting, Banking, CFOs, Financial, Manufacturing*

15 Constitution Dr Ste 127
Bedford, NH 03110-6029
(603) 589-8043
Fax: (603) 589-8044
Email: bedford@snowdenassociates.com
Key Contact - Specialty:
Mr. Al Egan, Vice President, Search

20 Trafalgar Sq Ste 407
Nashua, NH 03063-1996
(603) 589-4026
Fax: (603) 431-3809
Email: portsmouth@snowdenassociates.com
Key Contact - Specialty:
Mr. Will Conway, Vice President, Search

Snyder & Company LLC

35 E Main St Ste 185
Avon, CT 06001-3805
(860) 521-9760
Fax: (860) 521-2495
Email: jamessnyder@compuserve.com

Summary: Characterized by our exhaustive
sourcing methodology and in-depth candidate
assessment skill.

Key Contact - Specialty:
Mr. James F. Snyder, Jr., President

Salary Minimum: $150,000

Functions: Generalist (All)

Industries: Food, Bev., Tobacco, Drugs Mfg.,
Medical Devices, Finance, Pharm Svcs., HR
Services, Insurance, Biotech/Life Sciences,
Healthcare

Socius Search LLC

1220 W 6th St Ste 604
Cleveland, OH 44113-1328
(216) 344-5500
(888) 762-4871
Fax: (216) 344-1607
Email: confidential@socius.com
Web: www.socius.com

Summary: Socius provides Retained Executive
Search Solutions at such superior levels that our
client-partners are rewarded with a significant and
ongoing competitive advantage over their
marketplace rivals.

Key Contact - Specialty:
Mr. Robert C. Huxtable, Managing Partner -
*Banking, Capital markets, CEOs, CFOs,
Financial services*
Mr. Jason Peterson, Managing Partner - *Banking,
Banking (Corporate,Mortgage,Retail),
Financial services*
Mr. Rick Amburgey, Senior Search Executive -
*Banking, Banking (Investment,Mortgage),
CEOs, CFOs*
Mr. Rich Sinatra, Senior Search Executive -
*Biomedical, Biotechnology, CEOs, CFOs,
Healthcare*
Mr. Joseph M. Orlando, Senior Search Executive
- *Actuarial, Insurance, Insurance
(Casualty,Claims,Life)*

Salary Minimum: $150,000

Functions: Board Members, Senior Mgmt.,
Middle Mgmt.

Industries: Generalist (All)

Sockwell Partners, Inc.

(a TranSearch International company)
800 East Blvd
Charlotte, NC 28203-5116
(704) 372-1865
Fax: (704) 372-8960
Email: lhorton@sockwell.com
Web: www.sockwell.com

Summary: We perform senior-level functional
search for clients in for-profit and not-for-profit
sectors; most assignments at CEO/COO/CFO or
division executive-level; client-focus and internal
quality initiatives.

Key Contact - Specialty:
Mr. Robert B. Sherrill, Partner
Mr. Gary Green, Partner
Ms. Susan N. Jernigan, Partner
Ms. Lyttleton Rich, Partner
Mr. Richard L. Campbell, Partner - *Sales*
Ms. Linda Horton, Professional

Salary Minimum: $150,000

Functions: Senior Mgmt.

Industries: Lumber, Furniture, Finance, Services,
Hospitality, Real Estate, Software, Biotech/Life
Sciences, Healthcare

Söderlund Associates Inc

1100 Cleveland Ave
Park Hills, KY 41011-1908
(513) 703-5271
Fax: (859) 581-5355
Email: eric@soderlund.com
Web: www.soderlund.com

Summary: We recruit senior executives for the
computer industry in product development,
marketing, sales, finance, operations and service.

Key Contact - Specialty:
Mr. Eric Soderlund, President - *High technology*
Ms. Terri Ross, Manager, Technology - *High
technology*
Ms. Paige Sutkamp, Manager, Finance - *High
technology*
Ms. Natalie Ruppert, Executive Recruiter - *High
technology*
Ms. Judi Becker, Director, Research - *High
technology*
Ms. Ruth Ullman, Executive Recruiter
Ms. Brit Soderlund-Roberts, Executive Recruiter
Mr. Scott Bruno, Designer
Ms. Janet Nickum

Salary Minimum: $150,000

Functions: Board Members, Mfg., Materials,
Sales & Mktg., R&D, Engineering, Int'l.

Industries: Generalist (All), Manufacturing,
Computer Equip., Electronic, Elec.
Components, Venture Cap., Mgmt. Consulting,
Engineering Svcs., Supply Chain Mgmt,
Wireless, Database SW, Mfg. SW

Solomon-Page Healthcare and Life Sciences Group LLC

1140 Avenue of the Americas Fl 7
New York, NY 10036-5803
(212) 403-6166
Fax: (212) 824-1505
Email: mgouran@spges.com
Web: www.spgjobs.com

Summary: We are a highly focused, retained
executive search firm in most functional areas for
managed healthcare and HMOs, pharmaceutical
and biotechnology, e-health, group insurance,
employee benefits, hospitals and related healthcare
companies and institutions.

Key Contact - Specialty:
Mr. Marc S. Gouran, Group President -
Healthcare

Salary Minimum: $125,000

Functions: Senior Mgmt., Middle Mgmt.,
Physicians, Sales & Mktg., Mktg. Mgmt.,
Benefits, DB Admin.

Industries: Pharm Svcs., Mgmt. Consulting,
Insurance, HR SW, Healthcare

Branches:
7676 Hazard Center Dr Ste 1320
San Diego, CA 92108-4516
(619) 291-2300
Email: dbleau@spgeswest.com
Key Contact - Specialty:
Mr. Donn E. Bleau, Managing Director -
Healthcare

50 S US Highway 1 Ste 204
Jupiter, FL 33477-5114
(561) 741-4454
Fax: (561) 741-4474
Email: vkleinman@spges.com
Key Contact - Specialty:
Mr. Victor Kleinman, Executive Vice President &
Managing Dir - *Biotechnology, Pharmaceutical*

Soltis Management Services

876 Brower Rd
Radnor, PA 19087-2208
(610) 687-4200
Email: soltis@earthlink.net

Summary: Management consultants in retained
executive search, executive assessment,
organization issues and management development.
An inimitable reputation for confidential, results
oriented service to corporate clients. Search
assignments 98 percent successful.

Key Contact - Specialty:
Mr. Charles W. Soltis, President

Salary Minimum: $125,000

Functions: Generalist (All), Senior Mgmt.

Industries: Generalist (All), Construction,
Manufacturing, Drugs Mfg., Medical Devices,
Electronic, Elec. Components, Non-profits,
Higher Ed., Engineering Svcs., Property/Facility
Mgmt.

Solutions Group - Birmingham

PO Box 360805
Birmingham, AL 35236-0805
(205) 663-1301
Fax: (205) 663-1306
Email: sgsearch@aol.com

Summary: We are a generalist firm with
experience in manufacturing, healthcare and
service industries.

Key Contact - Specialty:
Mr. Hinky Verchot, Principal
Ms. Kathy Williams, Recruiter - *Healthcare*

Salary Minimum: $50,000

Functions: Management, Senior Mgmt., Middle
Mgmt., Production, Plant Mgmt., Materials,
Nurses, Sales Mgmt., HR Mgmt., Finance

Industries: Agri., Forestry, Mining,
Manufacturing, Lumber, Furniture, Chemicals,
Plastics, Rubber, Metal Products, Machine,
Appliance, Motor Vehicles, Misc. Mfg.,
Hospitals

Stephen M Sonis Associates[†]

46 Barefoot Hill Rd
Sharon, MA 02067-2830
(781) 784-7738
Fax: (425) 648-4421
Email: smsonis@aol.com

Summary: We specialize in focused, personalized
service for both start-ups and major companies.
We represent a creative, intelligent, cost and time
effective search alternative.

Key Contact - Specialty:
Mr. Stephen M. Sonis, Principal

Salary Minimum: $50,000

Functions: Management, Materials, Sales & Mktg., HR Mgmt., Finance

Industries: Generalist (All)

Spano Pratt
625 N Broadway Ste 200
Milwaukee, WI 53202-5002
(414) 283-9533
Fax: (414) 291-8957
Email: rspano@spanopratt.com
Web: www.spanopratt.com

Summary: Our firm is an executive search and HR consulting group that utilizes a strategic partnership and relationship model with the finest employers. Recognizing the need to identify and personally match our services to the organization's culture is one of the keys that sets us apart.

Key Contact - Specialty:
Mrs. Rose Iannelli, SPHR, Partner - *Financial, Human resources, Marketing, Non-profit, Technical*
Ms. Jamie Pratt, SPHR, Partner - *Financial, Human resources, Marketing, Non-profit*

Functions: Management, Mktg. Mgmt., IT

Industries: Motor Vehicles, Misc. Mfg., Non-profits, HR Services, Accounting SW

SPANUSA†
1415 Boston Post Rd
Larchmont, NY 10538-3935
(800) 479-8599
(914) 381-5555
Fax: (914) 381-0811
Email: info@spanusa.net
Web: www.spanusa.net

Summary: We are primarily focused on the recruitment of bilingual (Spanish-English and Portuguese-English) multicultural executives and professionals (Hispanic and non-Hispanic), across a variety of industries and disciplines. Our expertise, however, need not be confined to searches requiring bilingual, multicultural skills as our industry and functional expertise transcends these increasingly important requirements.

Key Contact - Specialty:
Mr. Manuel S. Boado, Founder, President & CEO - *Consumer, Credit cards, Human resources, International, Manufacturing*
Ms. Carol Coleman, Senior Search Consultant - *Banking, Financial services, Investment management*
Ms. Suzanne Coleman, Senior Search Consultant - *Administration, Advertising, Credit cards, Financial services*
Mr. Joel Gray, Senior Search Consultant - *Entertainment, Financial services, Food & beverage, Insurance, Non-profit*

Salary Minimum: $70,000

Functions: Generalist (All), Management, Minorities/Diversity, Int'l.

Industries: Generalist (All), Drugs Mfg., Finance, Banking, E-commerce, Recreation, Advertising, Telecoms, Mfg. SW, Marketing SW

Branches:
440 N Wabash Ave Apt 2607
Chicago, IL 60611-7648
(312) 828-9229
Fax: (312) 828-9227
Email: jszurek@spanusa.net
Key Contact - Specialty:
Mr. Jim Szurek, Director

3544 Eastham Rd
Dearborn, MI 48120-1106
(313) 436-9366
Fax: (313) 436-9367

Email: fespino@spanusa.net
Key Contact - Specialty:
Ms. Fern Espino, Director

Specialty Consultants
320 Fort Duquesne Blvd
Pittsburgh, PA 15222-1189
(412) 355-8200
Fax: (412) 355-0498
Email: info@specialtyconsultants.com
Web: www.specialtyconsultants.com

Summary: We are a construction and real estate talent resource management organization, offering executive search, staff recruiting, HR consulting and capital placement services.

Key Contact - Specialty:
Mr. Paul J. Lewis, Managing Director - *Real estate*
Mr. Thomas G. Williams, Managing Director - *Real estate*
Mr. Paul Marchionna, Managing Director - *Construction*
Mr. Mark A. Carney, Director - *Real estate*
Wesley P. Easly, Director - *Private equity, Real estate*
Mr. Daniel S. Pauletich, Director - *Construction*
Mr. Nickolas P. Vuckovich, Director - *Real estate*

Salary Minimum: $75,000

Functions: Generalist (All)

Industries: Construction, Real Estate

Spectrum Consultants
1104 Camino Del Mar Ste 3
Del Mar, CA 92014-2644
(858) 259-3232
Fax: (858) 630-3200
Email: spectcon@pacbell.net

Summary: We specialize in telecom, high-technology, aerospace, golf industry, engineering, scientists, advanced materials, general management and marketing.

Key Contact - Specialty:
Mr. G.W. Christiansen, Partner
Mr. Stanley Bass, Partner

Salary Minimum: $100,000

Functions: Generalist (All), Senior Mgmt., Middle Mgmt., Product Dev., CFOs, MIS Mgmt., R&D

Industries: Medical Devices, Motor Vehicles, Misc. Mfg., Electronic, Elec. Components, Robotics, Telecoms, Wireless, RF/Microwave, Defense, Aerospace, Software, Development SW, Biotech/Life Sciences

Spencer Stuart
401 N Michigan Ave Ste 3400
Chicago, IL 60611-4249
(312) 822-0080
Fax: (312) 822-0116
Email: contact@spencerstuart.com
Web: www.spencerstuart.com

Summary: We are the foremost privately held, global executive search firm. The firm conducts nearly 4,000 assignments each year, partnering effectively with clients ranging from the Fortune 500, to mid-cap, to emerging growth companies across a broad range of industries and sectors.

Key Contact - Specialty:
Mr. Thomas J. Snyder, Office Manager - *Boards of Directors, CFOs, Consumer (Durables), Direct marketing, Retail*
Mr. Richard J. Brennen - *CIOs, Technology*
Ms. Virginia Clarke - *Diversity, Real estate*
Ms. Susan Coffin - *Agriculture, Chemical, Industrial, Logistics, Paper*

Ms. Patricia Coleman - *Biotechnology, Healthcare, Legal, Medical (Devices), Pharmaceutical*
Mr. Kevin M. Connelly, Managing Director, North America - *Asset management, CFOs, Insurance, Private equity, Securities*
Mr. Michael J. Corey - *CIOs, Diversity, Healthcare*
Mr. John P. Doyle - *Diversity, Financial services, Human resources*
Mr. Paul W. Earle - *Biotechnology, Boards of Directors, Healthcare, Medical (Devices), Pharmaceutical*
Mr. Charles M. Falcone - *Biotechnology, Diversity, Healthcare, Medical (Devices), Pharmaceutical*
Ms. Amanda C. Fox - *Healthcare, Insurance*
Mr. Joseph M. Kopsick - *Boards of Directors, Consumer, Consumer (Durables, Packaged Goods)*
Mr. Stewart Lumsden - *Consumer*
Ms. Brenda A. Malloy - *Consumer, Direct marketing, Diversity, Retail*
Mr. Eric J. Melulis - *Logistics, Retail, Transportation*
Mr. Christopher C. Nadherny - *Direct marketing, Hospitality, Industrial, Internet, Retail*
Mr. Don Render - *Communications, Computers (Software), Technology*
Mr. Robert G. Shields - *Boards of Directors, Energy, Utilities*
Mr. Gilbert R. Stenholm - *Boards of Directors, Consumer (Durables, Packaged Goods), Industrial*
Mr. H. Alvan Turner - *Automotive, Electrical, Industrial*
Mr. Patrick Walsh - *Agriculture, Chemical, Computers (Software), Industrial, Technology*
Mr. Greg W. Welch - *Communications, Consumer, Direct marketing, Healthcare, Retail*

Salary Minimum: $150,000

Functions: Management, Board Members, Senior Mgmt.

Industries: Generalist (All)

Branches:
2020 Main St Ste 350
Irvine, CA 92614-8233
(949) 930-8000
Fax: (949) 930-8001
Key Contact - Specialty:
Ms. Brigitte Frankel - *Biotechnology, Life Sciences, Medical (Devices), Pharmaceutical*
Mr. Bruce Lachenauer - *Communications, Computers, Computers (Software), Semiconductors, Technology*
Romasha Nath
Mr. Gary Walburger - *Aviation, Boards of Directors, Electrical, Industrial*

10900 Wilshire Blvd Ste 800
Los Angeles, CA 90024-6528
(310) 209-0610
Fax: (310) 209-0912
Key Contact - Specialty:
Mr. Michael C. Bruce, Office Manager - *Asset management, Boards of Directors, CFOs, Financial services, Insurance*
Ms. Stephanie Davis - *Communications, Computers (Software), Technology*
Ms. Judy Havas - *Consumer, Consumer (Products), Direct marketing, Media, Retail*
Mr. Tarun Inuganti - *Diversity, Technology*
Mr. Jack Schlosser - *Healthcare, Life Sciences*

525 Market St Ste 3700
San Francisco, CA 94105-2776
(415) 495-4141
Fax: (415) 495-7524

Email your resume to a targeted list of recruiters now at www.ExecutiveAgent.com/DER07

Key Contact - Specialty:
Mr. Phil Johnston, Office Manager - *Boards of Directors, Communications, Computers (Software), Human resources, Life Sciences*
Mr. T. Christopher Butler - *CFOs, Financial services, Private equity, Securities, Technology*
Ms. Liz Fisher - *Financial services*
Mr. E.C. Grayson - *Energy, Industrial, Metals, Mining*
Ms. Mimi Hancock - *Biotechnology, Life Sciences, Medical (Devices), Pharmaceutical*
Mr. Ben Holzemer - *Life Sciences, Technology*
Ms. Lisa Pieper - *Biotechnology, Healthcare, Life Sciences, Medical (Devices), Pharmaceutical*
Mr. William Schutte - *Communications, Consumer, Consumer (Products), Media, Technology*
Mr. Thomas Seclow - *Communications, Consumer, Consumer (Products), Media, Technology*
Mr. Jonathan O. White - *Aviation, Communications, Computers (Software), Industrial, Technology*
Mr. Mark Yowe - *Biotechnology, Healthcare, Life Sciences, Medical (Devices)*

2988 Campus Dr Fl 3
San Mateo, CA 94403-2531
(650) 356-5500
Fax: (650) 356-5501
Key Contact - Specialty:
Mr. Jonathan Visbal, Office Manager - *Communications, Computers (Software), Semiconductors, Storage, Technology*
Ms. Cathy Anterasian - *Communications, Computers (Software), Consumer, Consumer (Products), Technology*
Mr. James Buckley - *Boards of Directors, Communications, Computers (Software), Technology*
Mr. Adam Charlson - *Communications, Computers (Software), Technology*
Mr. Al Climent - *Communications, Technology*
Mr. Scott Gordon - *Communications, Computers (Software), Marketing, Media, Technology*
Mr. Richard Gostyla - *Boards of Directors, Communications, Computers (Software), Media, Technology*
Mr. Michael Lynch - *Communications, Computers (Software), Semiconductors, Technology*
Ms. Nayla Rizk - *Boards of Directors, Communications, Computers (Software), Technology*
Mr. John H. Ware - *Boards of Directors, Communications, Computers (Software), Semiconductors, Technology*

695 Main St Ste 201
Financial Centre
Stamford, CT 06901-2138
(203) 324-6333
Fax: (203) 326-3737
Key Contact - Specialty:
Mr. Harold K. Somerdyk, Office Manager - *Communications, Consumer, Consumer (Products), Diversity, Technology*
Ms. Lisa Baird - *Asset management, Financial services*
Ms. Ann Blinkhorn - *Boards of Directors, Communications, Marketing, Media, Technology*
Mr. James M. Citrin - *Boards of Directors, Communications, Consumer, Media, Technology*
Mr. Bill Clemens, III - *Biotechnology, Life Sciences, Pharmaceutical*
Mr. John de Regt - *Aviation, Boards of Directors, Electrical, Equipment, Industrial*
Mr. Michael E. Haertel -
Ms. Valerie Harper - *Asset management, Financial services*

Ms. Susan S. Hart - *Boards of Directors, Consumer, Consumer (Products), Retail*
Mr. George Jamison - *Consumer, Consumer (Products)*
Ms. Claudia Lacy Kelly - *Boards of Directors, Consumer, Consumer (Products), Financial services, Human resources*
Mr. Dayton Ogden, Chairman - *Aviation, Boards of Directors, CFOs, Financial services, Industrial*
Mr. J. Rick Richardson - *Consumer, Consumer (Products), Direct marketing, Financial services, Legal*
Mr. Richard M. Routhier - *Communications, Consumer, Consumer (Products), Diversity, Media*
Mr. Thomas Scanlan - *Communications, Computers (Software), Human resources, Media, Technology*
Mr. Thomas W. Wasson - *CIOs, Communications, Computers (Software), Storage, Technology*

1440 New York Ave NW Ste 400
Washington, DC 20005-6201
(202) 639-8111
Fax: (202) 639-8222
Key Contact - Specialty:
Ms. Leslie Hortum, Office Manager - *Education, Non-profit*
Mr. J. Michael Kirkman - *Boards of Directors, Consumer, Education, Financial services, Non-profit*
Ms. Jacqueline G. Arends - *Aviation, Education, Industrial, Non-profit*
Ms. Hypatia Kingsley - *Education, Financial services, Non-profit*
Ms. Sally Sterling - *Diversity, Education, Non-profit*

355 Alhambra Cir Ste 1300
Coral Gables, FL 33134-5038
(305) 443-9911
Fax: (305) 443-2180
Key Contact - Specialty:
Mr. Michael Bell - *Aviation, Industrial*
Mr. David MacEachern - *Aviation, Communications, Industrial, Logistics, Media*
Mr. Kenneth V. Eckhart
Mr. Robert L. Heidrick
Mr. Robert S. DeVries

945 E Paces Ferry Rd NE Ste 2600
Atlanta, GA 30326-1379
(404) 504-4400
Fax: (404) 504-4401
Key Contact - Specialty:
Ms. Sharon Hall, Office Manager - *Consumer, Consumer (Packaged Goods,Products), Diversity, Human resources*
Mr. Lee Esler - *Communications, Computers (Software), Consumer, Consumer (Products), Technology*
Mr. Carl Gilchrist - *CIOs, Communications, Computers (Software), Industrial, Technology*
Mr. Ira Isaacson - *Biotechnology, Healthcare, Life Sciences, Medical (Devices), Pharmaceutical*
Mr. John Mitchell - *Biotechnology, Boards of Directors, Healthcare, Life Sciences, Pharmaceutical*
Mr. William B. Reeves - *Boards of Directors, CFOs, Financial services, Insurance*
Mr. Scott Walker - *Consumer, Consumer (Products), Diversity, Education, Financial services*
Mr. Simmons I. Patrick, Jr.

21 Custom House St Ste 800
Boston, MA 02110-3525
(617) 531-5731
Fax: (617) 531-5732

Key Contact - Specialty:
Mr. Jerry Noonan, Office Manager - *Communications, Consumer, Consumer (Products), Media, Technology*
Mr. Michael Anderson - *Asset management, Financial services*
Mr. Jason C.W. Hancock - *Communications, Computers (Software), Technology*
Ms. Kristine Langdon - *CFOs, Communications, Life Sciences, Pharmaceutical, Technology*
Mr. Tom H. Robinson - *Biotechnology, Life Sciences, Medical (Devices), Pharmaceutical*
Mr. Brian E. Adamik

225 S 6th St Ste 2750
Minneapolis, MN 55402-5633
(612) 313-2000
Fax: (612) 313-2001
Key Contact - Specialty:
Ms. Susan Boren - *Boards of Directors, Consumer, Education, Life Sciences, Non-profit*
Mr. Simon Foster - *Consumer, Consumer (Products), Retail*

277 Park Ave Fl 29
New York, NY 10172-2998
(212) 336-0200
Fax: (212) 336-0296
Key Contact - Specialty:
Mr. William Clemens, Jr., Office Manager - *Consumer, Consumer (Products), Education, Financial services, Human resources*
Mr. Joseph H. Boccuzi - *Biotechnology, Boards of Directors, Life Sciences, Medical (Devices), Pharmaceutical*
Ms. Jennifer Bol - *Biotechnology, Diversity, Education, Life Sciences, Non-profit*
Ms. Sarah E. Burley
Mr. David S. Daniel, Chief Executive Officer - *Boards of Directors, Consumer, Consumer (Products)*
Mr. Tom Daniels - *CFOs, Consumer, Consumer (Products), Diversity, Financial services*
Ms. Julie H. Daum - *Boards of Directors, Diversity, Financial services, Human resources, Industrial*
Ms. Andrea de Cholnoky - *Financial services, Private equity, Real estate, Securities*
Mr. Charles Delman - *Asset management, Financial services*
Mr. Peter K. Gonye - *Boards of Directors, Financial services, Insurance, Private equity, Securities*
Ms. Dionne Hosten - *Communications, Diversity, Financial services, Technology*
Mr. Jed Hughes - *Boards of Directors, Consumer, Education, Industrial, Non-profit*
Mr. John Keller - *Communications, Technology*
Mr. Richard Lannamann - *Asset management, Boards of Directors, Financial services*
Mr. Anthony T. Laudico
Ms. Catherine Nathan - *Legal*
Mr. Thomas J. Neff - *Boards of Directors, Consumer, Consumer (Products), Financial services, Industrial*
Ms. Robin Soren - *Asset management, Financial services*
Mr. Joel von Ranson - *CFOs*
Ms. Kristin Wait - *CIOs, Financial services*
Mr. John Wood - *Communications, Consumer, Consumer (Packaged Goods,Products), Technology*
Mr. Nick Young - *Agriculture, Boards of Directors, Chemical, Energy, Industrial*

2005 Market St Ste 2350
Philadelphia, PA 19103-7076
(215) 814-1600
Fax: (215) 814-1681
Key Contact - Specialty:
Mr. Franklin D. Marsteller, Office Manager - *Boards of Directors, Financial services, Insurance*

† occasional contingency assignment

Mr. Jeff Constable - *Asset management, CFOs, Communications, Financial services, Technology*
Ms. Jennifer Herrmann - *Financial services, Legal*
Ms. Connie B. McCann - *Asset management, Financial services, Private equity, Securities*
Mr. Peter E. McLean - *Boards of Directors, CFOs, Financial services, Private equity, Securities*
Ms. Alexis H. Stiles

13355 Noel Rd Ste 1200
Dallas, TX 75240-5002
(214) 672-5200
Fax: (214) 672-5299
Key Contact - Specialty:
Mr. David Beuerlein, Office Manager - *CIOs, Communications, Industrial, Semiconductors, Technology*
Mr. O.D. Cruse - *Boards of Directors, Communications, Industrial, Technology*
Mr. Randall Kelley - *CFOs, Communications, Technology*
Mr. M. Steven Kendrick
Mr. Bret A. Kidd
Mr. Terry W. Price - *Communications, Computers (Software), Industrial, Technology*
Mr. Steven Rivard - *Automotive, Electrical, Equipment, Industrial, Logistics*
Mr. Ronald Zera - *Consumer, Education, Human resources, Industrial, Life Sciences*

1000 Main St Ste 2700
Houston, TX 77002-2594
(713) 225-1621
Fax: (713) 658-8336
Key Contact - Specialty:
Mr. Thomas M. Simmons, Office Manager - *Boards of Directors, CFOs, Energy, Financial services, Industrial*
Ms. Mary Bass - *Communications, Diversity, Industrial, Life Sciences, Technology*
Mr. Peter K.E. Boerner - *Energy, Industrial, Legal*
Mr. Victor A. Burk
Mr. Brad Farnsworth - *Communications, Consumer, Energy, Industrial, Technology*
Mr. Clay A. Jackson

1900-1 University Ave
One University Avenue
Toronto, ON M5J 2P1
Canada
(416) 361-0311
Fax: (416) 361-6118
Key Contact - Specialty:
Mr. Jeffrey M. Hauswirth, Office Manager - *Aviation, Communications, Computers (Software), Financial services, Technology*
Mr. Jerry Bliley - *Boards of Directors, Consumer, Consumer (Products), Industrial, Metals*
Mr. Roger Clarkson - *Consumer, Consumer (Products), Marketing, Media, Technology*
Mr. John Koopman - *CFOs, Industrial*
Mr. Andrew J. MacDougall - *Boards of Directors, Financial services, Industrial, Insurance, Securities*
Mr. Carter Powis - *Consumer, Consumer (Packaged Goods,Products)*
Ms. Sharon Rudy - *Communications, Consumer, Consumer (Products), Media, Technology*
Mr. Peter Simon - *Asset management, CFOs, Financial services*
Ms. Tanya van Biesen

2500-1002 Rue Sherbrooke O
La Tour Scotia
Montreal, QC H3A 3L6
Canada
(514) 288-3377
Fax: (514) 288-4626

Key Contact - Specialty:
Mr. Robert Nadeau, Office Manager - *Aviation, Industrial, Legal, Life Sciences, Pharmaceutical*
Mr. Jérôme Piché - *Communications, Computers (Software), Consumer, Consumer (Products), Technology*

Edificio Omega
Campos Eliseos 345 Piso 6
11560 Colonia Polanco, DF
Mexico
55 5281 4050
Fax: 55 5281 4184
Key Contact - Specialty:
Mr. Javier Valle, Office Manager - *Life Sciences, Medical (Devices), Pharmaceutical*
Ms. Angeles Fernandez - *Asset management, Financial services*
Mr. Rafael Rojo - *Automotive, Communications, Consumer, Industrial, Technology*

Spilman & Associates Inc[†]
14001 Dallas Pkwy Ste 1200
Dallas, TX 75240-7369
(972) 788-4044
Email: mary@spilmanassociates.com
Web: www.spilmanassociates.com

Summary: Specialization in retail, distribution, direct marketing, transportation services as well as professional services to these market sectors. Additional service offerings in career transition, executive coaching and career services.

Key Contact - Specialty:
Ms. Mary Spilman, Managing Director
Ms. Paula Asinof, MBA, Managing Director

Salary Minimum: $60,000

Functions: Management

Industries: Generalist (All), Food, Bev., Tobacco, Textiles, Apparel, Transportation, Retail, Non-profits, Mgmt. Consulting, Supply Chain Mgmt., Media, Communications

Sports Group International
8601 Six Forks Rd Ste 400
Raleigh, NC 27615-2965
(919) 855-0226
Fax: (919) 855-0793
Email: sgisearch@aol.com
Web: www.sgisearch.com

Summary: We are specialists in recruiting general management, marketing and sales professionals for sporting goods and recreational products companies. Our clients include, equipment, performance footwear, active-wear, and accessories companies. Our firm conducts searches for best practices professionals who consistently demonstrate exceptional results.

Key Contact - Specialty:
Mr. Joseph A. White, CPC, President - *Design, General management, Marketing, Product management/development, Sales*

Salary Minimum: $50,000

Functions: Senior Mgmt., Product Dev., Sales & Mktg.

Industries: Consumer Goods, Sports

Branches:
8601 Six Forks Rd Ste 400
Raleigh, NC 27615-2965
(413) 587-0022
Fax: (413) 587-9248
Email: dkreinhart@aol.com

Key Contact - Specialty:
Mr. Dave Reinhart, CPC, Vice President

SportSearch[†]
2990 E Northern Ave Ste D107
Phoenix, AZ 85028-4840
(602) 485-5555
(888) 834-5627
Fax: (602) 485-5556
Email: mt@sportsearch.net
Web: www.sportsearch.net

Summary: Our firm is a premiere executive search/recruiting and HR consulting firm, sourcing the critical layer of management, completely focused in the sports, recreation and entertainment industries. Led by highly-seasoned, proven executives, our firm provides the following full-service solutions: retained executive search, customized recruiting assignments, online employment resource program and sports & entertainment and HR forum (SEHRF).

Key Contact - Specialty:
Mr. Mark A. Tudi, President
Mr. Josh Margulies, Marketing & Operations Coordinator

Salary Minimum: $75,000

Functions: Generalist (All)

Industries: Manufacturing, Retail, Mgmt. Consulting, HR Services, Hospitality, Entertainment, Recreation, Media, Communications, Entertainment SW

Branches:
200 5th Ave Ste 850
New York, NY 10010-3050
(212) 647-8500
(888) 834-5627
Email: mt@sportsearch.net
Key Contact - Specialty:
Mrs. Jodie Kerchansky

Spring Associates Inc[†]
10 E 23rd St
New York, NY 10010-4402
(212) 473-0013
Fax: (212) 777-5627
Email: info@springassociates.com
Web: www.springassociates.com

Summary: A leader in the PR, marketing and corporate communications fields for over many years. Our clients are both communications and marketing departments of major corporations and the public relations and marketing firms which serve them.

Key Contact - Specialty:
Mr. Dennis Spring, President - *Public relations*

Salary Minimum: $75,000

Functions: PR

Industries: Generalist (All)

Springbrook Partners Inc
16 North St
Hingham, MA 02043-2234
(781) 749-7075
Fax: (781) 749-7599
Email: info@springbrookpartners.com
Web: www.springbrookpartners.com

Summary: A generalist retainer firm, we conduct searches in all functional areas, with a focus on the high-technology market.

Key Contact - Specialty:
Mr. Neal O. George, President - *High technology*

Functions: Generalist (All), Senior Mgmt., Middle Mgmt., Mktg. Mgmt., Sales Mgmt., CFOs, Cash Mgmt., MIS Mgmt.

Industries: Generalist (All), Computer Equip., Finance, New Media, Telecoms, Software

M H Springer & Associates

2660 Townsgate Rd Ste 210
Thousand Oaks, CA 91361-5722
(805) 446-0090
Fax: (805) 446-6490

Summary: Small retained firm specializing in financial services (i.e. banks, savings & loans, and mortgage banking).

Key Contact - Specialty:
Mr. Mark H. Springer, President - *Financial services*

Salary Minimum: $100,000

Functions: Generalist (All), Senior Mgmt., CFOs, Risk Mgmt.

Industries: Generalist (All), Finance, Invest. Banking, Misc. Financial

SSA Executive Search International

4350 E Camelback Rd Ste B200
Phoenix, AZ 85018-8357
(480) 998-1744
Email: mail@ssaexec.com
Web: www.ssaexec.com

Summary: Retained search firm completing board and C-level assignments nationally and internationally.

Key Contact - Specialty:
Ms. Susan F. Shultz, President

Salary Minimum: $100,000

Functions: Generalist (All)

Industries: Generalist (All)

Staffing Consultants Inc

1 Washington St
Norwich, CT 06360-5021
(860) 859-0844
(888) 449-9993
Fax: (860) 859-0784
Email: bill@staffingconsultants.net
Web: www.staffingconsultants.net

Summary: We provide our clients with the most qualified professionals available. We are dedicated to providing our employees with safe, compatible work sites.

Key Contact - Specialty:
Mr. William M. Richardson, President

Functions: Management, Board Members

Industries: Manufacturing, Textiles, Apparel, Paper, Printing, Drugs Mfg., Medical Devices, Plastics, Rubber, Metal Products, Machine, Appliance, Consumer Elect., Misc. Mfg., Electronic, Elec. Components

Staffing Corp†

PO Box 11777
Santa Rosa, CA 95406-1777
(707) 837-7100
Email: email@mail.staffingcorp.com
Web: www.staffingcorp.com

Summary: Our firm specializes in providing employers with managed HR and Recruiting Services which employers need to successfully build and maintain their business here.

Key Contact - Specialty:
Mrs. Jennifer Laxton, Senior Partner

Functions: Engineering

Industries: Software, Accounting SW, Database SW, Development SW, ERP SW, Mfg. SW, Marketing SW, Networking, Comm. SW, Security SW, System SW

Staffing Now Inc†

4600 Westown Pkwy Ste 113
West Des Moines, IA 50266-1000
(515) 222-6350
Fax: (515) 222-6360
Email: corporate@staffingnow.com
Web: www.staffingnow.com

Summary: We are a premier employment firm, specializing in the placement of permanent and temp accounting, office clerical, IT and legal professionals within organizations. We are directed by professionals with years of experience in the management of multi-state temp and permanent placement companies. This experience and professionalism contributes to our company's success.

Key Contact - Specialty:
Mr. Mark Schaul, Chief Financial Officer
Mr. Ron Smith, Chief Executive Officer

Functions: Management, Materials, Sales & Mktg., HR Mgmt., Finance, IT, Legal, Attorneys, Paralegals

Industries: Generalist (All)

Branches:
98 Mill Plain Rd
Danbury, CT 06811-6101
(203) 744-6020
Fax: (203) 744-6270
Email: dantemps@cssit.com
Key Contact - Specialty:
Mr. Jeff Schneider, Regional Manager

1101 Connecticut Ave NW Ste 1250
Washington, DC 20036-4343
(202) 429-2244
Fax: (202) 429-8717
Email: dc@friendsandcompany.com
Key Contact - Specialty:
Mr. Mark Roush, Regional Manager
Ms. Melody Speaker, Division Manager

7000 W Palmetto Park Rd Ste 110
Boca Raton, FL 33433-3429
(561) 392-0202
Fax: (561) 362-6448
Email: boca@staffingnow.com
Key Contact - Specialty:
Mr. Harland Medford, Regional Manager

750 W Lake Cook Rd Ste 200
Buffalo Grove, IL 60089-2084
(847) 325-2980
Fax: (847) 325-2984
Email: buffalogrove@staffingnow.com
Key Contact - Specialty:
Ms. Bonny Koffler, Regional Manager

5440 N Cumberland Ave Ste A135
Chicago, IL 60656-1452
(773) 693-8510
Fax: (773) 693-8515
Email: ohare@staffingnow.com
Key Contact - Specialty:
Ms. Jane Garner, Branch Manager

699 Boylston St Ste 8
Boston, MA 02116-2836
(617) 451-5900
Fax: (617) 451-3825
Email: boston@staffingnow.com
Key Contact - Specialty:
Ms. Moira Hagan, Manager
Ms. Stephanie Hanna, Manager, Recruiting

100 Erdman Way Ste S-202
Leominster, MA 01453-1841
(978) 534-2422
Fax: (978) 534-2424
Email: leominster@staffingnow.com
Key Contact - Specialty:
Ms. Jenna Kidder

125 Village Blvd Ste 330
Princeton, NJ 08540-5753
(609) 452-0287
Fax: (609) 452-0289
Email: njtemps@staffingnow.com
Key Contact - Specialty:
Ms. Laurie Knafo, Regional Manager

Staffing Strategists International†

(an InterSearch company)
5945 Spring Garden Rd
Halifax, NS B3H 1Y4
Canada
(902) 423-1657
Fax: (902) 423-0277
Email: info@staffingstrategists.com
Web: www.staffingstrategists.com

Summary: We are a professional services organization providing innovative retention and recruitment solutions for client organizations. Our portfolio of services includes executive recruitment, retention consulting and response management. Through branch offices and network memberships, we are well positioned to serve our clients needs.

Key Contact - Specialty:
Mr. Jim Wilson, President
Mr. Chris Schulz, Vice President
Ms. Sonja Erman, Staffing Strategist

Salary Minimum: $70,000

Functions: Generalist (All), Board Members

Industries: Generalist (All), Energy, Utilities, Manufacturing, Transportation, Retail, Finance, Government, Aerospace, Software, Healthcare

Branches:
2150-333 7 Ave SW
Toronto Dominion Sq Tower I
Calgary, AB T2P 2Z1
Canada
(403) 262-7476
Fax: (403) 262-9091
Email: calgary@ssalberta.com
Key Contact - Specialty:
Ms. Jill Couillard, General Manager - *Energy*

C J Stafford & Associates†

501-2323 Yonge St
Toronto, ON M4P 2C9
Canada
(416) 484-1960
Fax: (416) 484-0626
Email: tara@cjstafford.com
Web: www.cjstafford.com

Summary: Industry focused search and recruitment specialists for mining, minerals, engineering and construction industries. From engineering and technical through operations management and executive staff we provide clients with the best available talent in a cost effective manner.

Key Contact - Specialty:
Mr. Chris Stafford, President - *Construction, Engineering, Metals, Mining*
Mr. Vince Keenan, Senior Recruiting Consultant - *Construction*
Ms. Tara Brydges, Senior Recruiting Consultant - *Metals, Mining*
Ms. Kellee Miller, Consultant, Recruiting - *Construction*

Mr. Jim Divizio, Consultant, Recruiting - *Construction*
Mr. Rick Hutson, Senior Recruiting Consultant - *Mining*

Salary Minimum: $60,000

Functions: Generalist (All), IT, Engineering, Int'l.

Industries: Generalist (All), Agri., Forestry, Mining, Energy, Utilities, Oil & Gas, Construction, Manufacturing, Brokers

Affiliates:
Downing Teal Inc
Denver, CO

Morgan Stampfl Inc†

2 Penn Plz Rm 1500
New York, NY 10121-1590
(212) 292-5098
Fax: (212) 292-5097
Web: www.morganstampfl.com

Summary: We are an executive search firm specializing in mid and senior-level assignments in investment and commercial banking.

Key Contact - Specialty:
Mr. David G. Morgan, Principal - *Capital markets*
Mr. Eric Stampfl, Principal - *Capital markets*

Salary Minimum: $50,000

Functions: Generalist (All)

Industries: Banking, Invest. Banking

Stanton Chase International

100 E Pratt St Ste 2530
Baltimore, MD 21202-1074
(410) 528-8400
Fax: (410) 528-8409
Email: baltimore@stantonchase.com
Web: www.stantonchase.com

Summary: We are a medium-sized firm with offices in 36 countries. We employ professionals worldwide. Strengths are banking/financial services, high technology, distribution, mining/natural resources, healthcare, and general manufacturing.

Key Contact - Specialty:
Mr. H. Edward Muendel, Chairman, International - *Engineering, Financial services, Manufacturing, Professional services*
Mr. James Mickey Matthews, Managing Director, Reginoal VP
Mr. Bryon Lundell, Director - *Engineering, Healthcare, Manufacturing*
Mr. Brian Thomas, Associate Principal - *Engineering, Manufacturing, Technology*

Salary Minimum: $70,000

Functions: Generalist (All), Management, Board Members, Plant Mgmt., Distribution, Sales & Mktg., CFOs, IT, R&D

Industries: Drugs Mfg., Computer Equip., Misc. Mfg., Retail, Finance, Services, Non-profits, Higher Ed., Telecoms, Healthcare

Branches:
10866 Wilshire Blvd Ste 870
Los Angeles, CA 90024-4365
(310) 474-1029
Fax: (310) 474-6747
Email: losangeles@stantonchase.com
Key Contact - Specialty:
Mr. Edward J. Savage, Managing Director
Mr. Steve Duffy, Director - *Financial services*
Mr. William L. Ross, Principal
Mr. Michael Visbal, Director
Mr. Mike Hagerthy, Consultant
Mr. Barry Wilder, Managing Director

2232 Santa Barbara St Ste 101
Santa Barbara, CA 93105-3546
(805) 682-9800
Fax: (805) 569-9876
Email: santabarbara@stantonchase.com
Key Contact - Specialty:
Mr. Brandt Handley, Director

3350 Riverwood Pkwy SE Ste 1900
Atlanta, GA 30339-3372
(404) 252-3677
Email: atlanta@stantonchase.com
Key Contact - Specialty:
Mr. Dean Bare, Managing Director
Mr. James L. Harvey, Jr., Principal
Mr. Brian Ray, Principal
Mr. Tony Palmer, Principal

123 W Madison St Ste 1700
Chicago, IL 60602-4517
(312) 863-6165
Fax: (312) 863-6166
Email: chicago@stantonchase.com
Key Contact - Specialty:
Mr. James R. Piper, Jr., Managing Director - *Financial services, Non-profit*
Mr. Jeff Levitt, Director

52 Vanderbilt Ave Rm 501
New York, NY 10017-3848
(212) 808-0040
Fax: (212) 983-7499
Email: newyork@stantonchase.com
Key Contact - Specialty:
Mr. Charles D. Wright, Managing Director
Mr. Andrew Sherwood, Managing Director
Mr. Peter Hallock, Principal - *Engineering, Manufacturing, Professional services, Technology*
Mr. Ted Boreman, Director
Mr. Dewey Raymond, Senior Director
Mr. Robert T. Keane, Jr., Director, Recruiting, Financial Advisory
Mr. Mike Schwager, Director

8760A Research Blvd Ste 214
Austin, TX 78758-6420
(512) 502-9833
Fax: (512) 795-8259
Email: d.harap@stantonchase.com
Key Contact - Specialty:
Mr. David Harap, Director - *Healthcare, Technology*

5005 LBJ Fwy Ste 810
Dallas, TX 75244-6144
(972) 404-8411
Fax: (972) 404-8415
Email: dallas@stantonchase.com
Key Contact - Specialty:
Mr. Ed H. Moerbe, Managing Director - *Engineering, Manufacturing, Professional services*
Mr. Stephen B. Watson, Managing Director - *Professional services, Technology*
Ms. Carole Campbell, Director - *Healthcare*
Mr. Jerry McFarland, Director - *Engineering, Manufacturing*
Ms. Nancy Keene, Director - *Engineering, Manufacturing, Professional services*
Mr. Fred Reed, Director - *Engineering, Hospitality, Manufacturing, Travel*
Mr. Rick Davis, Director - *Financial services*
Mr. Roger Toney, Director - *Healthcare, Technology*
Mr. Jon A. Lewis, Director

21206 Park Brook Dr
Katy, TX 77450-4147
(281) 646-1892
Fax: (281) 646-1897
Email: houston@stantonchase.com

Key Contact - Specialty:
Mr. Robert Lueck, Director

404-111 Richmond St W
Toronto, ON M5H 2G4
Canada
(416) 362-5959
Fax: (416) 214-1632
Email: toronto@stantonchase.com
Key Contact - Specialty:
Ms. Gillian Lansdowne, Managing Director - *Consumer (Products), Financial services, Manufacturing, Professional services*
Mr. Martin Furman, Principal
Mr. Benjie Cherniak, Principal
Kylin Cheong, Researcher

1524 Av Summerhill
Montreal, QC H3H 1B9
Canada
(514) 935-3468
Email: montreal@stantonchase.com
Key Contact - Specialty:
Mr. Emerson Hughes, Managing Partner
Mr. Steve Johnstone, Partner
Mr. Shawn Davidson, Partner
Ms. Aggie Wybraniec, Consultant

Amsterdam 289
Col Hipodromo Condesa
06100 Mexico City, DF
Mexico
55 5564 5650
Fax: 55 5564 3084
Email: mexico@stantonchase.com
Key Contact - Specialty:
Mr. Jose Brogeras Oliva, Managing Director - *Engineering, Manufacturing*
Dr. Carmen Suarez, Principal - *Engineering, Manufacturing, Technology*
Ms. Gabriela Robles, Principal - *Engineering, Healthcare, Manufacturing*

Stark Cornwall Group Inc†

3035 Washtenaw Ave Ste 305
Ann Arbor, MI 48104-5119
(734) 474-2447
(517) 332-4100
Fax: (517) 332-2733
Email: mary@starkcornwall.com
Web: www.starkcornwall.com

Summary: The Stark Cornwall Group partners with its clientele to build management teams for the global business environment. We specialize in placing management in the following functions: Finance, Marketing, Operations, Consulting and General Management. The majority of our candidates have Top 10 School MBA's, along with a history of progressing upward in their fields. The Stark Cornwall Group is a boutique executive search and consulting practice. We pride ourselves on our hands on approach to search and consulting services.

Key Contact - Specialty:
Ms. Mary Stark, Director

Salary Minimum: $100,000

Functions: Generalist (All)

Industries: Drugs Mfg., Medical Devices, Plastics, Rubber, Finance, Invest. Banking, Venture Cap., Services, Publishing, New Media, Real Estate

The Stark Wilton Group

PO Box 4924
East Lansing, MI 48826-4924
(517) 332-4100
Fax: (517) 332-2733
Email: starkwiltongroup@comcast.net
Web: www.starkwilton.com

Summary: We are a highly personalized firm. All hiring companies have the opportunity to meet our professional staff, which has worked in industry, banking or management consulting before joining the firm. The firm prides itself in developing and maintaining long-term partnerships with its clients. We specialize in placing top school MBAs, MDs and senior engineering staff with a select group of industry leaders.

Key Contact - Specialty:
Ms. Mary Stark, Director - *Healthcare*
Mr. Wilton Smith, Director - *High technology, Manufacturing, Telecommunications*

Salary Minimum: $100,000

Functions: Generalist (All), Senior Mgmt., Physicians, Mktg. Research, Mktg. Mgmt., M&A, Mgmt. Consultants

Industries: Generalist (All), Drugs Mfg., Medical Devices, Finance, Banking, Invest. Banking, Mgmt. Consulting, Media, Publishing, Biotech/Life Sciences

Staub, Warmbold & Associates Inc

575 Madison Ave
New York, NY 10022-2511
(212) 605-0554
Fax: (212) 759-7304
Email: rstaub@staubwarmbold.com
Web: www.staubwarmbold.com

Summary: We provide executive search services to corporations and the not-for-profit sector. Functional areas include general management, finance, marketing and manufacturing.

Key Contact - Specialty:
Mr. Robert A. Staub, President
Ms. Margot Staub, Vice President
Mr. Robert A. Staub, Jr., Senior Associate - *Consumer (Marketing), General management, Information Technology, Manufacturing (Management), Marketing*

Salary Minimum: $150,000

Functions: Generalist (All)

Industries: Generalist (All)

Stearns Group

401 Waterside Ln
Nokomis, FL 34275-1485
(941) 918-0929
Fax: (941) 918-2820
Email: beth@stearnsgroup.com
Web: www.stearnsgroup.com

Summary: A full service professional research and recruiting firm, we provide services in a discreet, timely manner. We customize our executive searches and research information projects to meet the needs of our client companies because client satisfaction is our only goal. Additionally, we undertake research projects for other recruiting firms.

Key Contact - Specialty:
Ms. Elizabeth Stearns, Partner - *Banking, Healthcare, Management, Manufacturing*
Mr. John Christoffel, Partner - *Financial, Information service, Information Systems, Information Technology, Manufacturing*

Salary Minimum: $50,000

Functions: Generalist (All), Management, Middle Mgmt., Mfg., Healthcare, Physicians, Nurses, Health Admin., CFOs, MIS Mgmt.

Industries: Generalist (All), Energy, Utilities, Manufacturing, Wholesale, Finance, Banking, Invest. Banking, Services, Pharm Svcs., IT Implementation, Hospitality, Packaging, Biotech/Life Sciences, Healthcare, Hospitals,

Long-term/Home Care, Physical Therapy, Occupational Therapy, Women's

Stephen-Bradford Search

1140 Avenue of the Americas Ste 1000
New York, NY 10036-5800
(212) 221-6333
(800) 720-0922
Fax: (212) 391-7826
Email: info@stephenbradford.com
Web: www.stephenbradford.com

Key Contact - Specialty:
Mr. Mitchell L. Berger, Chief Executive Officer
Ms. Erika Weinstein, Managing Director
Ms. Nannette Willner, Senior Director
Ms. Linda Schaler, Senior Director
Ms. Joan Segal, Director
Mr. Don Leon, Senior Director

Salary Minimum: $75,000

Functions: Sales & Mktg., IT

Industries: Food, Bev., Tobacco, Soap, Perf., Cosmtcs., Finance, Services, Entertainment, Recreation, Media, Communications, Software

Stephens Associates Ltd Inc

5186 Blazer Pkwy
Dublin, OH 43017-1339
(614) 766-7900
Fax: (614) 766-7990
Email: saltd@stephensassoc.com
Web: www.stephensassoc.com

Summary: An industry-focused, full-service, all functions, retainer-based firm, with a strong concentration in aerospace & defense, heavy industrial manufacturing, energy/chemical/petrochemical, research/technology, telecom, financial services (banking and investment banking) and venture capital.

Key Contact - Specialty:
Mr. Stephen A. Martinez, Managing Director - *High technology*
Ms. Judith Mitchell, Associate
Ms. Denise Fooce, Director, Research
Ms. Pam Oeffler, Associate

Salary Minimum: $100,000

Functions: Senior Mgmt.

Industries: Generalist (All), Energy, Utilities, Manufacturing, Chemicals, Finance, Services, Telecoms, Aerospace, Insurance, Biotech/Life Sciences

Sterling Global Executive Search[†]

PO Box 25096
Sarasota, FL 34277-2096
(941) 952-9555
Fax: (941) 952-9520
Email: mail@sterlingglobalsearch.com
Web: sterlingglobalexecutivesearch.com

Summary: We are recruiters for executive level and middle management talent for franchise organizations in all stages of growth. We have an impressive list of references and a solid track record of placing exceptional candidates in all disciplines including: franchise sales, operations, training, marketing, real estate/site selection, design and construction, and international development.

Key Contact - Specialty:
Mrs. Nancy Estep-Critchett, President

Salary Minimum: $50,000

Functions: Management, Senior Mgmt., Sales & Mktg.

Industries: Retail, Hospitality, Real Estate

Sterling Global Human Resource Consulting[†]

2415 E Camelback Rd Ste 1090
Phoenix, AZ 85016-9283
(602) 470-8012
(800) 350-8012
Fax: (602) 470-8099
Email: info@sterlingstaffing.com
Web: www.sterlingstaffing.com

Summary: We are an executive search and personnel consulting firm offering recruitment services and competitor research to rapidly expanding multinational firms in the global market place. A multi-cultural organization that shares a single philosophy; commitment to cooperation, quality and thoroughness of our work.

Key Contact - Specialty:
Mr. Robert Macdonald, President & Chief Executive Officer

Salary Minimum: $100,000

Functions: Management, Senior Mgmt., Middle Mgmt., Mfg., Healthcare, Sales & Mktg., HR Mgmt., IT, R&D

Industries: Drugs Mfg., Medical Devices, Electronic, Elec. Components, Retail, Finance, Banking, Invest. Banking, E-commerce, Communications, Software, Biotech/Life Sciences

Sterling Staffing[†]

70 James St Ste 129B
Worcester, MA 01603-1040
(877) 793-1991
Fax: (508) 793-9085
Email: kevin@sterlingstaffing.net
Web: www.sterlingstaffing.net

Summary: The strength behind our firm comes from its founder's unique ability to offer the company extensive experience in the recruitment and staffing. His industry experience also includes years of recruiting for some the nation's largest recruiting companies.

Key Contact - Specialty:
Mr. Kevin O'Malley, SPHR, President & Chief Executive Recruiter - *Banking, CEOs, CFOs, COOs, Diversity*
Mr. Jeffrey Locke, Executive Recruiter - *Asset management, Audits, Banking, Business development, Compliance*
Mr. Julio Vega, Executive Recruiter - *Analysts, Assets & liabilities, Banking, Credit, Financial services*
Mr. Larry Berestka, Executive Vice President - *Banking (Commercial,Corporate,Investment,Mortgage,Retail)*

Salary Minimum: $40,000

Functions: Generalist (All), Management, Senior Mgmt.

Industries: Finance, Banking, Invest. Banking, Brokers, Venture Cap., Mutual/Hedge Funds, Misc. Financial, Accounting, Mgmt. Consulting, HR Services

Michael Stern Associates Inc

1205-20 Bay St
WaterPark Place
Toronto, ON M5J 2N8
Canada
(416) 593-0100
Fax: (416) 593-0100
Email: search@michaelstern.com
Web: www.michaelstern.com

† occasional contingency assignment

Summary: Customized approach and quality results with personal service. Using state-of-the-art research and in-depth assessment methods, we have been successfully recruiting corporate leaders for many years.

Key Contact - Specialty:
Mr. Michael I. Stern, President & Chief Executive Officer
Mr. James Parr, Vice President
Ms. Margaret Vanwyck, Senior Consultant
Ms. Charron Laufer, Senior Consultant

Salary Minimum: $100,000

Functions: Generalist (All), Senior Mgmt., Mktg. Mgmt., Sales Mgmt., HR Mgmt., CFOs, MIS Mgmt.

Industries: Generalist (All), Manufacturing, Retail, Services, Supply Chain Mgmt, Hospitality, Restaurants, Quick Service Restaurants, Communications, Real Estate, Healthcare

The Stevens Group

4612 Willow Bend Dr Ste 101
Arlington, TX 76017-1369
(817) 483-2700
Fax: (817) 887-5946
Email: info@thestevensgroup.com
Web: www.thestevensgroup.com

Summary: We recruit superior executive, administrative and technical talent for corporations and management worldwide. Our competitor organizational intelligence and recruitment services team provides corporate senior management and HRM recruiting clients with advanced tools that can be utilized for a variety of purposes.

Key Contact - Specialty:
Mr. Ken G. Stevens, Managing Director - *Accounting (Public), Banking (Mortgage), Closely-held business, Financial services, Pharmaceutical*
Mr. Brian Stevens, Director, Organizational Intelligence - *Competitive intelligence*
Ms. Mary Morse, Senior Consultant - *Banking (Mortgage), Information Technology, Sales*

Salary Minimum: $90,000

Functions: Generalist (All)

Industries: Generalist (All), Oil & Gas, Drugs Mfg., Finance, Banking, Accounting, IT Implementation, Real Estate, Biotech/Life Sciences

Stevens, Valentine & McKeever

300 Kings Hwy E Ste 8
Haddonfield, NJ 08033-1223
(856) 795-7222
Email: smv@execusearchresources.com
Web: www.execusearchresources.com

Summary: Responsive, consultative search and assessment for all functions within a broad spectrum of industries.

Key Contact - Specialty:
Mr. Leonard W. Stevens, Principal - *Financial services, Human resources*
Mr. Donald Murphy, Affiliate
Ms. Mary Ellen Westbay, Vice President

Salary Minimum: $80,000

Functions: Generalist (All)

Industries: Drugs Mfg., Finance, Services, HR Services, E-commerce, Insurance, Biotech/Life Sciences

The Stevenson Group

1530 Palisade Ave Ste 5
Fort Lee, NJ 07024-5470
(201) 302-0866
Fax: (201) 302-9350
Email: info@stevensongroup.com
Web: www.stevensongroup.com

Summary: Global retained executive search services on a cross-industry basis. Emphasis on general management; sales & marketing; commercial development, research & development and technical management positions within pharmaceuticals, healthcare, information technology, consumer and personal care industries.

Key Contact - Specialty:
Mr. Stephen M. Steinman, President & Chief Executive Officer - *Business to business, Chemical, Consumer, High technology, Pharmaceutical*
Ms. Jennifer Kay, Vice President & Principal - *Biotechnology, High technology, Information Technology, Pharmaceutical*

Salary Minimum: $150,000

Functions: Generalist (All), Senior Mgmt., Middle Mgmt., Mktg. Mgmt., CFOs, MIS Mgmt., R&D, Int'l.

Industries: Generalist (All), Manufacturing, Textiles, Apparel, Chemicals, Soap, Perf., Cosmtcs., Drugs Mfg., Medical Devices, Consumer Goods, Mgmt. Consulting, Supply Chain Mgmt., Software, Biotech/Life Sciences, Healthcare

Stewart Search Inc[†]

222 Lakeview Ave Ste 160
West Palm Beach, FL 33401-6101
(516) 818-1007
Email: howardstewart@stewartsearchinc.com
Web: www.stewartsearchinc.com

Summary: One of the nations leading executive search firm/headhunters in real estate, construction, development, and property management.

Key Contact - Specialty:
Mr. Howard Stewart, Managing Partner - *Construction, Human resources, Property management*

Salary Minimum: $75,000

Functions: Management

Industries: Construction, Real Estate, Property/Facility Mgmt.

Stewart, Stein & Scott Ltd

1000 Shelard Pkwy Ste 200
Minneapolis, MN 55426-4918
(952) 545-8151
Fax: (952) 545-8464
Email: research@stewartstein.net
Web: www.stewartstein.net

Summary: We provide consultants to management in executive recruitment and selection. Our firm is a generalist practice serving a broad base of clients. Partners have many years of diverse executive search experience.

Key Contact - Specialty:
Mr. Terry W. Stein, Partner
Mr. Jeffrey O. Stewart, Partner

Salary Minimum: $100,000

Functions: Generalist (All), Senior Mgmt., Health Admin., Mktg. Mgmt., HR Mgmt., CFOs, MIS Mgmt.

Industries: Generalist (All)

Stewart/Laurence Associates Inc[†]

118 Us Highway 9
Englishtown, NJ 07726-8231
(732) 972-8000
(561) 241-6113
Fax: (561) 241-6974
Email: mel@stewartlaurence.com
Web: www.stewartlaurence.com

Summary: We provide professional recruitment, executive search and outplacement for all areas of hi-tech plus life sciences/bio-tech and medical device industries including: executive, marketing, finance and medical directors (venture capital/IPOs), CEOs/presidents, VPs sales, marketing, business development, R&D and engineering.

Key Contact - Specialty:
Ms. Mel Stewart Klein, President - *International*
Mr. Eric Freer, Vice President

Salary Minimum: $100,000

Functions; Generalist (All), Management, Senior Mgmt.

Industries: Generalist (All), Printing, Drugs Mfg., Medical Devices, Computer Equip., Consumer Elect., Venture Cap., Publishing, New Media, Telecoms, Digital, Wireless, Fiber Optic, Network Infrastructure, Software, Biotech/Life Sciences

Charles Stickler Associates Inc

PO Box 5312
Lancaster, PA 17606-5312
(717) 569-2881
Web: www.charlesstickler.com

Summary: Our firm specializes in finding the top talent available to satisfy the people needs of Metal Service Centers, Processors, Mills, and other clients across the nation.

Key Contact - Specialty:
Mr. Charles W. Stickler, III, CPC, Owner - *Metals*

Salary Minimum: $50,000

Stiles Associates LLC

276 Newport Rd Ste 208
New London, NH 03257-5469
(603) 526-6566
(800) 322-5185
Fax: (603) 526-6185
Email: tberio@leanexecs.com
Web: www.leanexecs.com

Summary: We specialize in recruiting executives in a variety of functions with experience. A principal who is experienced in helping clients build high performance teams manages every assignment of ours.

Key Contact - Specialty:
Mr. Linford E. Stiles, President
Mr. Jason S. Stiles, Vice President - *Operations*
Ms. Sabine Fischer, Director
Mr. Andrew Spiegel, Executive Search Consultant
Mr. Matthew Ayers, Finance & Marketing

Salary Minimum: $70,000

Functions: Management, Senior Mgmt., Plant Mgmt., Materials, Sales & Mktg., HR Mgmt., Finance, Mgmt. Consultants

Industries: Manufacturing, Metal Products, Machine, Appliance, Motor Vehicles, Electronic, Elec. Components, Finance, Aerospace, Insurance, Healthcare

STM Associates

320 S 400 E
Salt Lake City, UT 84111-2905
(801) 531-6500
Fax: (801) 531-6062
Email: stm@stmassociates.com
Web: www.stmassociates.com

Summary: Specialize in natural resources, including mining, metals, pulp & paper, chemicals, as well as energy companies and utilities. Many years repeat business record based on extensive database, original research and personal service.

Key Contact - Specialty:
Mr. Gerald W. Cooke, Principal - *Energy, Mining, Natural resources, Utilities*
Mr. Robert L. Roylance, Principal - *Energy, Mining, Natural resources, Utilities*

Salary Minimum: $75,000

Functions: Management, Senior Mgmt., Mfg., Plant Mgmt., Materials, Sales & Mktg., HR Mgmt., Finance, IT, Int'l.

Industries: Agri., Forestry, Mining, Energy, Utilities, Manufacturing, Chemicals, Transportation, Environmental Svcs.

Stone & Youngblood†

304 Newbury St
Boston, MA 02115-2839
(781) 647-0070
Fax: (781) 647-0460
Email: information@stoneandyoungblood.com
Web: www.stoneandyoungblood.com

Summary: Our consultants are best known for executive searches conducted for clients in traditional & online media, communications, advertising, public relations, and sales & marketing. We are affiliated with offices coast to coast.

Key Contact - Specialty:
Mr. Stephen Sarkis, General Manager

Functions: Generalist (All), Management, Advertising, Mktg. Research, Mktg. Mgmt., Sales Mgmt., Direct Mktg., PR, Sales Reps., HR Mgmt.

Industries: Generalist (All), Manufacturing, Services, Entertainment, Media, Advertising, Publishing, New Media, Broadcast, Film, Communications, Telecoms, Real Estate, Software

Stone Murphy

5500 Wayzata Blvd Ste 1020
Minneapolis, MN 55416-3551
(763) 591-2300
Fax: (763) 591-2301
Email: sm@stonemurphy.com
Web: www.stonemurphy.com

Summary: We are a retained executive search firm engaged in general practice and committed to serving the best interest of our clients.

Key Contact - Specialty:
Ms. Toni Barnum, Partner - *Finance, Financial services, Investment management*
Mr. Gary Murphy, Partner - *Human resources*
Mr. Allan Raymond, Partner - *General management*
Mr. Al Giesen, Managing Director - *Finance, General management, Operations*
Ms. Helen Getzkin, Managing Director - *Finance, General management, Human resources, Information Technology, Sales*
Mr. Bob Cowan, Senior Consultant - *Financial services, Healthcare, Investment management, Technology*

Salary Minimum: $100,000

Functions: Management, Senior Mgmt., Middle Mgmt., Mfg., Sales & Mktg., HR Mgmt., Finance, M&A, Risk Mgmt., IT

Industries: Manufacturing, Finance, Banking, Invest. Banking, Mutual/Hedge Funds, Services, Non-profits, Hospitality, Communications, Government, Insurance, Real Estate, Software, Healthcare

Stone Recruiters

140 Broadway Fl 46
New York, NY 10005-1107
(646) 240-4150
Fax: (212) 208-1410
Email: info@stonerecruiters.com
Web: www.stonerecruiters.com

Summary: We specialize in finding the best skills set to fill a senior role in business can be a key determinant of organizational success. We place special emphasis on identifying executive talent that adds maximum value and provide a unique partnering experience to our clients.

Key Contact - Specialty:
Ms. Catherine E. Reyes, Partner
Mr. Karim M. Guessous, Partner - *Asset management, Banking (Corporate,Investment,Merchant), Brokerage*
Mr. Ariel B. Reyes, Senior Consultant - *Computers (Hardware,Programming,Sales,Science, Software)*

Functions: Management, Senior Mgmt., Middle Mgmt., Sales & Mktg., PR

Industries: Generalist (All), Finance, Invest. Banking, Brokers, Venture Cap., Mutual/Hedge Funds, Media, Advertising, Publishing, New Media, Communications, Software, Biotech/Life Sciences

Stoopen Asociados SC

(an EMA Partners International company)
Minerva 92-702
01030 Mexico City, DF
Mexico
55 5661 6862
55 5661 8119
Fax: 55 5661 5872
Email: crm@stoopen.com.mx
Web: www.stoopen.com.mx

Summary: We are involved in the executive search of all professions. Our company policy stresses quality not volume. We keep the organization at a size that allows the partners to get involved personally in every assignment.

Key Contact - Specialty:
Ms. Josefina Stoopen, President
Ms. Lucia Trueba, Vice President
Ms. Cecilia Hubard

Salary Minimum: $60,000

Functions: Generalist (All), Senior Mgmt., Plant Mgmt., Materials Plng., Sales & Mktg., HR Mgmt., CFOs, IT

Industries: Generalist (All), Construction, Manufacturing, Banking, Mgmt. Consulting, Hospitality, Telecoms

Straight & Company

1002 Brown Thrasher Pt
Saint Marys, GA 31558-4105
(912) 882-3480
(678) 366-3367
Fax: (912) 882-3487
Email: resume@straightco.com
Web: www.straightco.com

Summary: Search specialists for financial services, investment management, insurance and banking. Strengths in general management, finance, marketing and information processing, call center management and Internet based eCommerce.

Key Contact - Specialty:
Mr. Gary R. Straight, President - *Financial services*
Ms. Carla Herron, Vice President - *Research*

Salary Minimum: $75,000

Functions: Generalist (All), Management

Industries: Finance, Banking, Invest. Banking, Misc. Financial, Telecoms, Call Centers, Insurance, Healthcare

Strategic Advancement Inc

242 Old New Brunswick Rd Ste 100
Piscataway, NJ 08854-3754
(732) 562-1222
Fax: (732) 562-9448
Email: aborkin@sai-hr.com
Web: www.sai-hr.com

Summary: We have created a network of contacts that can assist you in finding the right candidate for the position you wish to fill in the shortest amount of time.

Key Contact - Specialty:
Mr. Andrew Borkin, President
Ms. Annette Trenkler, Vice President

Salary Minimum: $60,000

Functions: Generalist (All)

Industries: Generalist (All), Food, Bev., Tobacco, Drugs Mfg., Electronic, Elec. Components, Retail, Finance, Banking

Strategic Alliance Group LLC†

500 W Cypress Creek Rd Ste 420
Fort Lauderdale, FL 33309-6156
(954) 332-3004
Email: info@stratalliance.com
Web: www.stratalliance.com

Summary: From middle-market capitalization firms to top Fortune Global 100 firms, our seasoned staff focuses on providing personal attention to each client, while utilizing sophisticated research capabilities. Offering national exposure and local expertise, our firm has the unique ability to transcend boundaries to target and deliver your industry's most talented executives.

Key Contact - Specialty:
Mr. Arthur Drago, Managing Principal
Mr. Bobby Lloyd, Director, Sales & Marketing - *Asset management, Banking (Investment), Brokerage, Financial services, Investment management*
Mr. Samuel Wiser, Director, Legal & Compliance - *Asset management, Brokerage, Compliance, Financial services, Legal*
Mr. Tom Kulpa, Director, C-level & Information Tech - *Asset management, C-level, Financial services, Information Technology, Investment management*
Mr. Mark Young, Director, Generalist

Salary Minimum: $100,000

Functions: Generalist (All), Management, Senior Mgmt., Middle Mgmt., Sales Mgmt., Cash Mgmt., M&A, Minorities/Diversity, Non-profits, Legal

Industries: Generalist (All), Agri., Forestry, Mining, Transportation, Finance, Services, Communications, Insurance, Biotech/Life Sciences, Healthcare

Strategic Alternatives Executive Search[†]

31 Woodhaven Dr
Laguna Niguel, CA 92677-2819
(650) 851-2211
Email: info@strategicalternatives.com
Web: www.strategicalternatives.com

Summary: Retained boutique executive search firm specializing in senior executive to mid level searches for start-ups to mature companies in high technology and medical fields. We have expertise in R&D, HW/SW product development, sales/marketing, process engineering. Team members were founders and senior executives in start-ups through major corporations and have first hand operational experience. Offices in northern & southern California.

Key Contact - Specialty:
Mr. Ira M. Marks, Principal - *High technology*
Mr. Bob White, Director, Search
Ms. Karen Saucier, Executive Recruiter

Salary Minimum: $120,000

Functions: Board Members, Senior Mgmt., Middle Mgmt., Product Dev., Sales & Mktg., CFOs, IT, R&D, Engineering

Industries: Generalist (All), Drugs Mfg., Medical Devices, Computer Equip., Consumer Elect., Semiconductors, E-commerce, IT Implementation, PSA/ASP, Engineering Svcs., New Media, Communications, Software, Biotech/Life Sciences

Strategic Performance Partners

PO Box 3881
Dublin, OH 43016-0457
(614) 932-0655
Email: tbraden@marketleadership.net
Web: www.marketleadership.net

Summary: Our consulting firm focuses on providing executive search services to the emerging technology markets. We provide our client with a strategic partner who understands the challenges of growing a organization to the next level.

Key Contact - Specialty:
Mr. Tripp Braden, Managing Director
Ms. Patricia Sadler, Director, Research & Development

Salary Minimum: $100,000

Functions: Senior Mgmt., Product Dev., Sales Mgmt., CFOs, R&D

Industries: Software, Accounting SW, Database SW, Development SW, Doc. Mgmt., Production SW, ERP SW, HR SW, Industry Specific SW, Mfg. SW, Marketing SW, Networking, Comm. SW, Security SW, Biotech/Life Sciences, Healthcare

Strategic Search Corp

645 N Michigan Ave Ste 800
Chicago, IL 60611-2890
(312) 944-4000
Email: info@strategicsearch.com
Web: www.strategicsearch.com

Summary: Specialists in R&D, scientific, engineering, manufacturing and technical executive search.

Key Contact - Specialty:
Mr. Scott R. Sargis, Managing Director - *Manufacturing, Technical*

Salary Minimum: $50,000

Functions: Board Members, Senior Mgmt., Middle Mgmt., Mfg., Product Dev., Automation, Materials, IT, R&D, Design

Industries: Generalist (All), Manufacturing, Food, Bev., Tobacco, Chemicals, Soap, Perf., Cosmtcs., Drugs Mfg., Medical Devices, Plastics, Rubber, Machine, Appliance, Computer Equip., Electronic, Elec. Components, Robotics, Semiconductors, Communications, Packaging, Software, Database SW, Development SW, Doc. Mgmt., Production SW, Entertainment SW, Industry Specific SW, Mfg. SW, Security SW, Biotech/Life Sciences, Healthcare

StrategicHire

1851 Alexander Bell Dr Ste 301
Reston, VA 20191-4394
(703) 467-9093
Email: info@strategichire.com
Web: www.strategichire.com

Summary: We are a leading-edge retained executive search firm specializing in senior executive and diversity recruiting. We accomplish our goal by being smarter, faster and better networked than our competition.

Key Contact - Specialty:
Mr. Joe Watson, President & Chief Executive Officer

Salary Minimum: $100,000

Functions: Management

Industries: Computer Equip., Consumer Elect., Venture Cap., Services, Mgmt. Consulting, HR Services, Hospitality, New Media, Telecoms, Software

Stratum Executive Search Group (Stratum ESG)

202-1614 Dundas St E
Whitby, ON L1N 8Y8
Canada
(866) 720-0660
Email: resume1@stratumesg.com
Web: www.stratumesg.com

Summary: We offer the professionalism, process and experience of a large international search firm combined with the personal service and flexibility of a boutique. Working on a retained basis in the technology sector, our clients include large industry leaders as well as smaller entrepreneurial start-ups.

Key Contact - Specialty:
Mr. Patrick Galpin, Managing Director - *Information Technology, Management consulting, Start-up companies, Technology, Venture capital*

Salary Minimum: $125,000

Functions: Management

Industries: Computer Equip., Semiconductors, Mgmt. Consulting, IT Implementation, Communications, Software

Straube Associates

853 Turnpike St
North Andover, MA 01845-6105
(978) 687-1993
Fax: (978) 687-1886
Email: sstraube@straubeassociates.com
Web: www.straubeassociates.com

Summary: We are a retained executive search firm, with experience in sourcing and recruiting candidates for executive level positions, including expanded services in HR consulting. Our primary purpose is to be flexible to the client's needs and provide the highest quality service in the most cost effective manner.

Key Contact - Specialty:
Mr. Stan Straube, President

Ms. Kathy Kelley, Vice President, Business Development
Mr. William Marlow, Vice President, Eng & IT Searches - *Engineering, Medical, Medical (Devices), Military, Plastics*
Mr. John Kellogg, Vice President, Executive Strategy
Ms. Laurie Levy, Director, Research
Ms. Mary Frongillo, Director, Marketing
Ms. Lynda Ferren, Director, Research
Mr. Ed O'Brien, Consultant, Human Resources
Ms. Mary Beth Nason, Senior Staffing Consultant
Mr. Paul Miller, Senior Staffing Consultant

Salary Minimum: $85,000

Functions: Generalist (All)

Industries: Generalist (All)

Strawn Arnold Leech & Ashpitz Inc

2508 Ashley Worth Blvd Ste 150
Austin, TX 78738-5306
(512) 263-1131
Fax: (512) 263-4149
Email: genmail@salainc.com
Web: www.salainc.com

Summary: We place senior-level assignments with pharmaceutical, bio-technology, medical device and health care services companies. We recruit for major corporations and venture capital start-ups.

Key Contact - Specialty:
Mr. William M. Strawn, President - *Biotechnology, Pharmaceutical*
Mr. Jerome M. Arnold, Executive Vice President - *Biotechnology, Pharmaceutical*
Mr. David M. Leech, Executive Vice President - *Biotechnology, Pharmaceutical*
Mr. Jeff Ashpitz, Executive Vice President - *Biotechnology, Pharmaceutical*

Salary Minimum: $150,000

Functions: Generalist (All), Senior Mgmt., Product Dev., Mktg. Mgmt., Sales Mgmt., CFOs, R&D, Mgmt. Consultants

Industries: Generalist (All), Drugs Mfg., Medical Devices, Pharm Svcs., Biotech/Life Sciences

Strelcheck & Associates Inc

1009 W Glen Oaks Ln Ste 211
Mequon, WI 53092-3383
(262) 241-9500
Fax: (262) 241-5559
Email: strelcheck@strelcheck.com

Summary: Physician search: occupational health and most other specialties.

Key Contact - Specialty:
Mr. Robert R. Strzelczyk, President

Functions: Healthcare

Industries: Healthcare, Hospitals, Women's

J Stroll Associates Inc[†]

980 Post Rd E
Westport, CT 06880-5300
(203) 227-3688
Fax: (203) 222-0180
Email: stroll@snet.net
Web: www.jstrollassociates.com

Summary: Identifies suitable candidates for corporate law EEO, general, contracts, patents, civil and partnerships.

Key Contact - Specialty:
Mr. Joseph Stroll, President
Mr. Ray Peters, Executive Vice President

Salary Minimum: $80,000

Functions: Generalist (All), Senior Mgmt., R&D

Industries: Drugs Mfg., Pharm Svcs., Biotech/Life Sciences

The STS Group

307 Orchard City Dr Ste 206
Campbell, CA 95008-2948
(408) 540-1800
Fax: (408) 540-1815
Email: info@stecs.com
Web: www.thestsgroup.com

Summary: Our firm provides executive search and management consulting services for a wide and diverse client base covering executive management, sales & marketing, HR and senior technology positions.

Key Contact - Specialty:
Mr. Ron Anderson, Director
Ms. Farri Ouraie, Co-Founder
Mr. Jon Christensen, Co-Founder
Mr. Bill Minnery, Senior Consultant
Mr. Bill Romero, Senior Consultant

Salary Minimum: $100,000

Functions: Senior Mgmt., Middle Mgmt., Product Dev., IT

Industries: Communications, Software

Sullivan Associates

175 Derby St Ste 25
Hingham, MA 02043-4060
(781) 749-2242
Email: info@sullivanassoc.com
Web: www.sullivanassoc.com

Summary: We were built on the principle of the modified search concept, which delivers outstanding candidates at substantial savings in fees, expenses and turnaround time. Our account managers provide seamless coordination throughout the assignment.

Key Contact - Specialty:
Mr. Michael H. Sullivan, President & Owner
Mr. Rick Kirkendall, Partner - *Consumer (Products), Financial services, Healthcare, Investment management, Technology*

Salary Minimum: $100,000

Functions: Generalist (All)

Industries: Generalist (All)

SullivanKreiss, Inc.†

1 E Main St Ste 206
Northborough, MA 01532-1662
(508) 393-4933
Fax: (508) 393-0076
Email: info@sullivankreiss.com
Web: www.sullivankreiss.com

Summary: We are the premier search firm that serves the building and design industries exclusively. "We build companies."

Key Contact - Specialty:
Ms. Kim McLean, Director, East Coast Operations

Salary Minimum: $50,000

Functions: Generalist (All), Engineering

Industries: Transportation, Architectural Svcs., Engineering Svcs.

Summit Executive Search Group†

38799 Autumn Woods Rd
Murrieta, CA 92563-6244
(951) 600-4886
Fax: (949) 767-5927
Email: ken@summitexecutivesearch.com
Web: www.summitexecutivesearch.com

Summary: We specialize in conducting targeted local and national searches for CxO executive positions, board of director members and manager, director and VP level positions in the following areas: accounting, finance, marketing, sales, human resources, IT/MIS, operations, research and development, strategy, and business development.

Key Contact - Specialty:
Mr. Ken DeWitt, Chief Executive Officer

Salary Minimum: $75,000

Functions: Board Members, Senior Mgmt., Middle Mgmt., Sales & Mktg., Sales Mgmt., Sales Reps., Finance, CFOs

Industries: Generalist (All)

Summit Executive Search Consultants Inc

25 SE 2nd Ave Ste 338
Miami, FL 33131-1543
(305) 379-5008
Fax: (305) 379-5150
Email: ajh@summit-search.com
Web: www.summit-search.com

Summary: We offer highly personalized retainer based search assignments in all functions and industries. Two basic specialties are: manufacturing sector/automotive industry, and diversity/minority/targeted searches for all professions and industries. We also have an ever growing practice in public sector/local govt./not-for-profit.

Key Contact - Specialty:
Mr. Alfred J. Holzman, President

Salary Minimum: $70,000

Functions: Mfg., Production, Quality, Purchasing, Materials Plng., Systems Dev., Engineering, Minorities/Diversity

Industries: Generalist (All), Manufacturing, Plastics, Rubber, Metal Products, Machine, Appliance, Motor Vehicles, Misc. Mfg., Non-profits, Engineering Svcs., Government

Summit Partners Inc

PO Box 543
West Boothbay Harbor, ME 04575-0543
(207) 633-5655
Fax: (207) 633-5735
Email: spi@gwi.net

Summary: We are a retained search-consulting firm serving clients in a number of industries. One in three searches involve COO or CEOs, the balance, officer-level functional heads to include marketing, finance, development, HR, etc.

Key Contact - Specialty:
Mr. Thomas Patrick, Founding Partner & President

Salary Minimum: $100,000

Functions: Senior Mgmt., Sales & Mktg.

Industries: Generalist (All), Finance, HR Services

Superior Search LTD

332 Minnesota St Ste W-1800
Saint Paul, MN 55101-1357
(651) 225-4000
Fax: (651) 225-4403
Email: info@superior-search.com
Web: www.superior-search.com

Summary: Our team has more than 45 years of experience in the industry. We have worked as recruiters, managers and business owners for Fortune 500 and start-up companies. Traditional executive search is the foundation of all of our services.

Key Contact - Specialty:
Mr. Robert A. Duncan, Principal
Mr. Steve T. Mathews, Principal

Salary Minimum: $60,000

Functions: Generalist (All)

Industries: Generalist (All), Travel

Superior Staffing Inc - Professional Placement Division

120 E Mill St Ste 420
Akron, OH 44308-1721
(330) 253-8080
(800) 783-8081
Fax: (330) 253-5374
Email: lkehn@superiorstaffing.com
Web: www.superiorstaffing.com

Summary: Modified contingency search firm specializing in recruiting and placing management and director level candidates.

Key Contact - Specialty:
Ms. Fran Doll, Founder
Ms. Sheri Witte, Chief Executive Officer
Mr. Tom Doll, President
Ms. Liz Kehn, Executive Recruiter

Salary Minimum: $50,000

Functions: Generalist (All), Middle Mgmt., Finance

Industries: Generalist (All), Manufacturing, Transportation, Retail, Finance, Services, Aerospace

Swartz & Associates Inc

PO Box 14167
Scottsdale, AZ 85267-4167
(480) 998-9159
Fax: (480) 596-1960
Email: bill@swartz.com
Web: www.swartz.com

Summary: We provide retained search with a particular focus on board of directors, CEO, CFO and VPs in all functional categories on behalf of high-technology companies.

Key Contact - Specialty:
Mr. William K. Swartz, President
Ms. Pamela L. Swartz, Executive Vice President

Salary Minimum: $100,000

Functions: Generalist (All), Board Members, Senior Mgmt., CFOs, Int'l.

Industries: Generalist (All), Computer Equip., New Media, Software

SWBi International

(formally known as SWBi International (Sink, Walker, Boltrus)
PO Box 57033
Babson Park, MA 02457-0033
(781) 237-1199
Email: dwalker@swbi.com
Web: www.swbi.com

Summary: Our primary search assignments are for private equity firms (VC/LBO) investing in important executive leaders in high-technology markets including communications for public and private networks, software, professional services and internet infrastructure.

Key Contact - Specialty:
Mr. Douglas G. Walker, Executive Managing Director - *Boards of Directors, CEOs, CFOs, CIOs, Financial services*
Mr. Ken Petkunas, MBA, Principal - *High technology, RF microwave, Sales, Semiconductors*

Mr. Cliff Sink, Managing Director
Mr. Sushila Desai, Principal - *Diversity, Human resources, Private equity, Professional services*

Salary Minimum: $225,000

Functions: Generalist (All), Management, Board Members, Mfg., Sales & Mktg., Finance, CFOs, Specialized Svcs.

Industries: Generalist (All), Manufacturing, Computer Equip., Test, Measure Equip., Misc. Mfg., Semiconductors, Finance, Services, Mgmt. Consulting, Media, Communications, Telecoms, Real Estate, Software, Biotech/Life Sciences, Healthcare

Synapse Human Resource Consulting Group

2 Braewick Ct
Dallas, TX 75225-1802
(214) 384-8877
(214) 890-4434
Email: synapsecon@aol.com

Summary: We are a small, high quality retained search firm with experience in multiple industries. We have a limited size of practice to insure high quality work with no conflicts of interest. We seek to become strategic business partner with clients. We also offer HR consulting services.

Key Contact - Specialty:
Mr. Michael Schwartz, President - *Senior management*

Salary Minimum: $75,000

Functions: Generalist (All), Management, Senior Mgmt., Middle Mgmt., Sales & Mktg., Finance, CFOs, IT, MIS Mgmt., Int'l.

Industries: Generalist (All), Retail, Finance, Services, Accounting, Mgmt. Consulting, HR Services, Media, Advertising, New Media, Real Estate, Software, Healthcare

Synergistics Associates Ltd

400 N State St Ste 400
Chicago, IL 60610-4624
(312) 467-5450
Fax: (312) 822-0246
Email: ajbsynerg@aol.com
Web: www.synergisticsassociates.com

Summary: Specialists in data processing executives, particularly CIOs. Founder was a top computer executive.

Key Contact - Specialty:
Mr. Alvin J. Borenstine, President - *CIOs*

Salary Minimum: $150,000

Functions: MIS Mgmt.

Industries: Generalist (All)

The Synergy Organization

3070 Bristol Pike Ste 2-209
Bensalem, PA 19020-5361
(215) 638-9777
Email: synergy@synergyorg.com
Web: www.synergyorg.com

Summary: Innovative executive search/leadership consulting firm founded by experienced organizational psychologists. Our proven system helps progressive employers maximize productivity and profitability by selecting, developing, and retaining the right people. Also, we conduct independent executive assessments of internal/external candidates to help ensure their success.

Key Contact - Specialty:
Dr. Kenneth R. Cohen, PhD, President & Founder - *Biotechnology, C-level, Healthcare, Human resources, Pharmaceutical*

Salary Minimum: $100,000

Functions: Board Members, Senior Mgmt., Middle Mgmt., Nurses

Industries: Non-profits, Pharm Svcs., Mgmt. Consulting, HR Services, HR SW, Biotech/Life Sciences, Healthcare, Hospitals, Long-term/Home Care

Tabb & Associates†

PO Box 340888
Columbus, OH 43234-0888
(614) 880-0000
Email: info@tabbsearch.com
Web: www.tabbsearch.com

Summary: We specialize in placing senior executives in a diverse group of industries. Additionally, have a strong practice in strategy consulting and Transportation.

Key Contact - Specialty:
Mr. Roosevelt Tabb, President & Chief Executive Officer - *General management*

Salary Minimum: $100,000

Functions: Generalist (All), Management, Board Members, Senior Mgmt., Mgmt. Consultants

Industries: Generalist (All), Manufacturing, Chemicals, Metal Products, Consumer Elect., Transportation, Wholesale, Finance, Invest. Banking, Services, Mgmt. Consulting, Logistics Svcs., Supply Chain Mgmt., Restaurants, Quick Service Restaurants, Insurance

Talent Acquisition Services LLC

(formerly known as New Media Staffing LLC)
64 Arlington St N Ste 200
Meriden, CT 06450-4730
(203) 237-3000
Fax: (203) 634-6860
Email: info@nmstaffing.com
Web: www.talentacquisitionservices.com

Summary: Full-service executive search firm, also offering unbundled search, with specific skills with Internet sourcing, technology based searches and creative executive staffing campaigns.

Key Contact - Specialty:
Mr. Robert Simon, Managing Director

Salary Minimum: $150,000

Functions: Generalist (All)

Industries: Venture Cap., Telecoms, Software

Talent Connections LLC

602 Gettysburg Pl
Atlanta, GA 30350-3034
(770) 992-3701
Fax: (770) 992-3521
Email: toptalent2@talentconnections.net
Web: www.talentconections.net

Summary: We are a professional services firm that specializes in recruiting—including recruitment process outsourcing (RPO), executive search, process consulting, and contract recruiting. Making the connections to recruit top talent is the mainstay of the company. We offer a full continuum of talent acquisition solutions whether it's revamping the hiring process, acquiring executive leaders or building a network of contract recruiters to pull from at a moment's notice.

Key Contact - Specialty:
Mr. Tom Darrow, Principal & Founder - *C-level, Consulting, Executives, Human resources, Outsourcing*
Ms. Teela Jackson, Senior Talent Consultant - *Executives, Human resources, Management, Staffing*
Ms. Ginger Wallis, Senior Talent Consultant - *Executives, Human resources, Management, Staffing*
Mr. Lee Perrett, Director - *C-level, Executives, Human resources, Management, Outsourcing*

Functions: Senior Mgmt., Middle Mgmt., Sales & Mktg., HR Mgmt., Benefits, Staffing, Training, Finance, CFOs

Industries: Generalist (All)

TalentFusion

15 Hawley St
Northampton, MA 01060-3348
(413) 584-2552
Email: info@talentfusion.com
Web: www.talentfusion.com

Summary: We provide project based recruitment programs designed to improve our clients critical recruiting metrics. Focused approach to improve recruiter productivity, minimize recruiting cycle times and reduce cost per hire.

Key Contact - Specialty:
Mr. John Laporta, President

Salary Minimum: $60,000

Functions: Generalist (All), Sales Mgmt., MIS Mgmt., Systems Analysis, Systems Dev., Systems Implem., Systems Support, Network Admin.

Industries: Generalist (All), Software

Branches:
1228 W Barry Ave # 1
Chicago, IL 60657-4210
(888) 777-5757
Fax: (773) 388-0287
Email: mhamacher@augustineinc.com
Key Contact - Specialty:
Mr. Mike Hamacher

The Talon Group

16801 Addison Rd Ste 300
Addison, TX 75001-5122
(972) 931-8223
Fax: (972) 931-8063
Email: contact@thetalongroup.com
Web: www.thetalongroup.com

Summary: We assist home building and real estate development clients through quality-driven retained executive search.

Key Contact - Specialty:
Mr. Bob Piper, President - *Real estate*
Mr. Rodney Hall, Senior Parnter - *Real estate*
Mr. Tony Cleveland, Senior Parnter - *Real estate*
Ms. Jean Mason, Partner - *Real estate*
Mr. Stacy Pennington, Research - *Construction, Presidents, Real estate, Senior management*

Salary Minimum: $125,000

Functions: Senior Mgmt., Middle Mgmt.

Industries: Construction, Real Estate

Tandy, Morrison & LaTour LLC

1321 Quarry Ln
Lancaster, PA 17603-2423
(717) 299-5900
Fax: (717) 299-2897
Email: ctandy@tmlsearch.com
Web: www.tmlsearch.com

Summary: We are a small, quality firm by design doing handcrafted work to place executives with significant senior management experience and diverse professional backgrounds. We have a strong commitment to understanding clients' needs and cultures and providing excellent service.

Key Contact - Specialty:
Mr. Charles W. Tandy, Principal - *Finance,*
Healthcare, Senior management
Ms. Catherine J. Morrison, Principal -
Healthcare, Senior management

Salary Minimum: $60,000

Functions: Senior Mgmt., Middle Mgmt.,
Healthcare, HR Mgmt., CFOs, Non-profits

Industries: Generalist (All), Finance, Misc.
Financial, Non-profits, Accounting, HR
Services, E-commerce, Higher Ed.,
Environmental Svcs., Healthcare, Hospitals,
Long-term/Home Care

Branches:
2525 Gross Point Rd
Evanston, IL 60201-4928
(847) 864-4200
Fax: (847) 864-9512
Email: slatour@tmlsearch.com
Key Contact - Specialty:
Dr. Stephen A. LaTour, Principal - *Marketing*

Ned Tannebaum & Partners

9200 S Dadeland Blvd Ste 516
Miami, FL 33156-2713
(305) 670-0100
Fax: (305) 670-3022

Summary: We are a high-quality, very
personalized one-on-one boutique committed to
delivering results as specifically defined by the
client and the client's timeframe because anything
less than results are excuses.

Key Contact - Specialty:
Mr. Ned Tannebaum, President

Salary Minimum: $150,000

Functions: Generalist (All), Management, Sales
& Mktg., HR Mgmt., Finance, Mgmt.
Consultants, Int'l.

Industries: Generalist (All), Energy, Utilities,
Finance, Mgmt. Consulting, HR Services,
Media

Tannura & Associates Inc

13517 Marissa Ct Ste 202
Homer Glen, IL 60491-6617
(708) 645-6666
Fax: (708) 301-7381
Email: rtannura@tannura.com
Web: www.tannura.com

Summary: We specialize in IS and IT ranging
from high-level technical through executive
management including leading edge technology,
traditional systems, telecom, sales and customer
support.

Key Contact - Specialty:
Mr. Robert P. Tannura, President

Salary Minimum: $85,000

Functions: Generalist (All), Sales & Mktg., IT

Industries: Generalist (All), Computer Equip.,
Mgmt. Consulting, IT Implementation,
Communications, Software

Tarnow Associates

7 Elm St
Westfield, NJ 07090-2147
(908) 654-2400
Fax: (908) 654-2499
Email: info@tarnow.com
Web: www.tarnow.com

Summary: We are a generalist firm working at
senior-levels with established market niches in a
select range of industries.

Key Contact - Specialty:
Mr. Emil Vogel, President - *Senior management*
Mr. William A. Myers, Senior Vice President -
Senior management
Ms. Karen Gordon, Vice President - *Senior*
management
Ms. Barbara Mendoza, Manager, Research

Salary Minimum: $100,000

Functions: Generalist (All), Management, Board
Members, Senior Mgmt., Mfg., Healthcare,
Sales & Mktg., HR Mgmt., Finance

Industries: Generalist (All)

Tarzian Search Consultants Inc

401 N Michigan Ave Ste 1200
Chicago, IL 60611-4264
(312) 867-0001
Fax: (312) 867-0004
Email: consult@tarziansearch.com
Web: www.tarziansearch.com

Summary: We are dedicated to helping our clients
achieve greater efficiency and better meet their
business objectives through the offering of
recruitment and retention solutions, specifically:
aligned executive search initiatives, customized
and established training programs, as well as need
and market analysis consulting.

Key Contact - Specialty:
Ms. Wendy Tarzian, President - *Communications,*
Public relations

Salary Minimum: $65,000

Functions: Senior Mgmt., Sales & Mktg., Mktg.
Research, Mktg. Mgmt., Direct Mktg., PR,
Training, Non-profits, Graphic Designers

Industries: Generalist (All), Energy, Utilities,
Construction, Manufacturing, Finance, Misc.
Financial, Services, Non-profits, HR Services,
Media, Advertising, Publishing,
Communications, Telecoms, Wireless,
Government, Environmental Svcs., Packaging,
Insurance, Real Estate, Software, Biotech/Life
Sciences, Non-Classifiable

Tate & Associates Inc

60 Walnut Ave Ste 100
Clark, NJ 07066-1635
(732) 815-7830

Summary: We are a highly successful retained
search firm recognized for timeliness,
customization and quality service. We are
dedicated to results, professional integrity and
commitment to success reflected by 90 percent
repeat business. Specialization includes
healthcare, consumer and industrial
manufacturers.

Key Contact - Specialty:
Mr. Gene M. Tate, President - *Healthcare,*
Industrial

Salary Minimum: $65,000

Functions: Generalist (All)

Industries: Manufacturing, Medical Devices,
Healthcare

TaxSearch Inc

7050 S Yale Ave Ste 310
Tulsa, OK 74136-5720
(918) 281-3300
Fax: (918) 281-3301
Email: taxsearch@taxsearchinc.com
Web: www.taxsearchinc.com

Summary: We have become the search firm of
choice for organizations who are committed to
building and retaining 'world class' tax
departments.

Key Contact - Specialty:
Mr. Tony Santiago, President - *Tax*

Salary Minimum: $90,000

Functions: Taxes

Industries: Generalist (All), Energy, Utilities,
Manufacturing, Finance, Services, Media

Branches:
2205 Middle St Ste 207
Sullivans Island, SC 29482-9766
(843) 883-5100
Fax: (843) 883-5200
Email: tony@taxsearchinc.com

Carl J Taylor & Company

13419 Hughes Ln
Dallas, TX 75240-5330
(972) 490-7697
Fax: (972) 386-5136
Email: ctaylor@carltaylorco.com
Web: carltaylorco.com

Summary: Personalized executive search practice
serving professional service firms and selected
corporate clients. Our success has been attributed
to the satisfactory completion of difficult searches,
an in depth knowledge of our clients' working
environment, and the requests of our client's to
conduct searches for positions throughout their
organizations.

Key Contact - Specialty:
Mr. Carl J. Taylor, President

Salary Minimum: $75,000

Functions: Generalist (All), Mktg. Mgmt., HR
Mgmt., Engineering, Mgmt. Consultants

Industries: Generalist (All), Energy, Utilities,
Construction, Accounting, Mgmt. Consulting,
HR Services, Engineering Svcs.

Taylor Search Partners

8000 Ravines Edge Ct
Columbus, OH 43235-5422
(614) 436-6650
Fax: (614) 848-8033
Email: info@taylorsearchpartners.com
Web: www.taylorsearchpartners.com

Summary: We provide retained search services
for professional, management and executive-level
employees. We assist our clients in addressing
their strategic hiring issues, specifically positions
of greatest importance or sensitivity.

Key Contact - Specialty:
Mr. William Taylor, President
Mr. Jon DeWitt, Executive Vice President
Mr. Mick Shimp, Senior Vice President
Mr. James Cain, Vice President
Ms. Bonnie Trail, Search Project Manager -
Healthcare

Salary Minimum: $100,000

Functions: Generalist (All), Mfg., Materials,
Health Admin., Sales & Mktg., Finance, MIS
Mgmt., Mgmt. Consultants

Industries: Generalist (All), Drugs Mfg., Misc.
Mfg., Finance, Pharm Sycs., Advertising,
Healthcare

Taylor Winfield

5430 LBJ Fwy Ste 1635
3 Lincoln Center
Dallas, TX 75240-2603
(972) 392-1400
Fax: (972) 392-1455
Email: info@taylorwinfield.com
Web: www.taylorwinfield.com

Summary: Through key relationships with premier venture capital firms, our maturing client companies and our executive network of visionary industry leaders; we have conducted retained searches to create hundreds of high technology core management teams in: enterprise software, wireless, networking, computer hardware, services and semiconductors.

Key Contact - Specialty:
Mrs. Connie Adair, Chief Executive Officer
Ms. Nadine North, Managing Director
Mrs. Gerri Kies, Managing Director
Ms. Amy Vernetti, Managing Director

Salary Minimum: $200,000

Functions: Senior Mgmt.

Industries: Venture Cap., Mgmt. Consulting, Telecoms, Software

Taylor, Rodgers & Associates LLC

62 Southfield Ave Ste 208
Stamford, CT 06902-7229
(203) 323-6080
(203) 323-8645
Fax: (203) 327-1479
Email: taylor@taylor-rodgers.com
Web: www.taylor-rodgers.com

Summary: We are a retained executive search firm specializing in the placement of candidates who understand the business value of technology.

Key Contact - Specialty:
Mr. Richard Taylor, Managing Partner & CEO
Mr. James R.L. Holdsworth, Jr., Director

Salary Minimum: $150,000

Functions: Management, Middle Mgmt., Sales & Mktg., Finance

Industries: Generalist (All), Communications, Software

Taylor/Haley Search Partners LLC

5 Bessom St Ste 315
Marblehead, MA 01945-2372
(781) 592-1411
Fax: (603) 484-5821
Email: information@taylorhaley.com
Web: www.taylorhaley.com

Summary: A boutique, exclusivity-based retained search firm specializing in the permanent and interim placement of entrepreneurial senior executives. Our principals have expertise in software/Internet, professional services, communications, emerging technology, direct marketing/retail and pharmaceutical/bio-technology across a variety of functional disciplines. We work with startups, mid-tier and venture-backed companies.

Key Contact - Specialty:
Mr. Kenneth Plasz, Principal & Co-Founder - *Defense, High technology, Senior management, Start-up companies, Telecommunications*
Mr. Steven LaKind, Principal & Co-Founder - *C-level, High technology, Professional services, Senior management, Start-up companies*

Salary Minimum: $60,000

Functions: Senior Mgmt., Sales & Mktg., Sales Mgmt., Direct Mktg., Finance, CFOs, M&A, R&D, Engineering, Minorities/Diversity

Industries: Manufacturing, Retail, Finance, Services, Media, Communications, Government, Defense, Homeland Security, Software, Biotech/Life Sciences

Affiliates:
Threshold Partners
New Brunswick, NJ

Tech International†

PO Box 634
Wyoming, RI 02898-0634
(401) 539-2191
Email: general@techintl-bio.com
Web: www.techintl-bio.com

Summary: We specialize in the following industries: optics, biotechnology, bioprocess, pharmaceutical, medical device, analytical instrumentation and aerospace. Positions include: engineering, scientists, marketing, sales, contract managers, logistics and executive level.

Key Contact - Specialty:
Ms. Helen M. Brophy, Chief Executive Officer
Mr. Sean K. Smith, Vice President, Marketing - *Engineering, Science*
Mr. Howard A. Smith, Vice President - *Optics*

Salary Minimum: $50,000

Functions: Generalist (All), Senior Mgmt., Sales & Mktg., Sales Mgmt., Engineering

Industries: Chemicals, Drugs Mfg., Medical Devices, Test, Measure Equip., Robotics, Venture Cap., Pharm Svcs., Equip Svcs., Mgmt. Consulting, Engineering Svcs., Defense, Aerospace, Biotech/Life Sciences

TechFind Inc†

PO Box 626
Natick, MA 01760-0006
(508) 647-0111
Fax: (508) 647-0110
Email: info@techfind.com
Web: www.techfind.com

Summary: We specialize in the placement of highly trained scientists, business development, technical sales and medical professionals. Our recruiters are trained scientists in the life science area. We have all worked in a chemical, biotechnology or pharmaceutical company and have experience in placing scientists.

Key Contact - Specialty:
Ms. Amy B. Lurier, President - *Biotechnology*

Salary Minimum: $80,000

Functions: Generalist (All), Healthcare, Sales & Mktg., IT, R&D

Industries: Pharm Svcs., Biotech/Life Sciences

Technical Skills Consulting Inc†

800-2 St Clair Ave E
Colonial Place
Toronto, ON M4T 2T5
Canada
(416) 586-7971
Email: tscinc@tscinc.on.ca
Web: www.tscinc.on.ca

Summary: We specialize in the recruitment of engineering, technology and manufacturing professionals.

Key Contact - Specialty:
Mr. Paul MacBean, Senior Consultant - *Engineering, Science, Technology*
Ms. Roxanne Mars, Consultant - *Engineering, Science, Technology*
Mr. Don Phaneuf, Consultant - *Engineering, Science, Technology*

Salary Minimum: $70,000

Functions: Generalist (All), Management, Mfg., Product Dev., Production, Sales & Mktg., HR Mgmt., Finance, R&D, Engineering

Industries: Generalist (All), Agri., Forestry, Mining, Construction, Manufacturing, Aerospace, Packaging, Biotech/Life Sciences

Technifind International†

5959 Gateway Blvd W Ste 601
El Paso, TX 79925-3320
(915) 775-1176
(512) 340-0200
Fax: (915) 778-9314
Email: tvida@technifind.com
Web: www.technifind.com

Summary: We have an extensive network that is very familiar with demographics in various markets and industries. Clientele in the Fortune 1000.

Key Contact - Specialty:
Mr. Tim Vida, Chief Executive Officer
Mr. Bruce Steiner, President

Salary Minimum: $50,000

Functions: Generalist (All), Management, Mfg., Materials, Sales & Mktg., Finance, Engineering, Int'l.

Industries: Generalist (All), Energy, Utilities, Manufacturing, Environmental Svcs., Packaging, Software

Branches:
8310 N Capital of Texas Hwy Ste 305
Austin, TX 78731-1077
(512) 340-0200
Fax: (512) 418-0819
Email: bsteiner@technifind.com

Technology Consultants International

7720 El Camino Real Ste 2N
Carlsbad, CA 92009-8511
(513) 489-2327
Fax: (760) 436-8900
Email: tom@techconsultants.com
Web: www.techconsultants.com

Summary: We serve the high-end computer hardware and software vendor community whose applications consist of scientific, engineering, manufacturing, intranet and enterprise wide business applications. The positions we place are in the areas of executive management, sales & marketing & sales support.

Key Contact - Specialty:
Mr. Thomas Conway, Senior Parnter
Mr. Ed Neenan, Partner

Salary Minimum: $100,000

Functions: Generalist (All), Sales Mgmt., Systems Implem.

Industries: Venture Cap., Call Centers, Digital, Wireless, Network Infrastructure, Compliance, Software

Technology Management Partners

9215 Silverwood Ct
Granite Bay, CA 95746-7244
(650) 948-2100
Email: larry@tmpartners.net

Summary: We specialize in executive and management placement for venture-financed start-up and emerging growth technology based companies.

Key Contact - Specialty:
Mr. Larry Webster, President - *Communications, Executives, New media*

Salary Minimum: $90,000

Functions: Generalist (All), Senior Mgmt., Middle Mgmt., Mktg. Research, Sales Mgmt., Systems Dev., R&D, Engineering

Industries: Generalist (All), Computer Equip., Consumer Elect., New Media, Telecoms, Software

techVenture Inc

1143 Noel Dr
Menlo Park, CA 94025-3348
(408) 275-3000
Fax: (650) 322-3225
Email: info@techventure.com
Web: www.techventure.com

Summary: Our firm is a specialized high stake hire search firm that places executive, managerial and technical staff with early growth technology companies. Our mission is to provide a relationship based recruiting service, one that meets the needs of both pre-public new technology companies and the top notch talent that powers them.

Key Contact - Specialty:
Mr. Fadi Bishara, President

Salary Minimum: $120,000

Functions: Management, Senior Mgmt., Middle Mgmt., IT

Industries: Invest. Banking, Venture Cap., Services, E-commerce, IT Implementation, Media, New Media, Communications, Telecoms, Digital, Network Infrastructure, Government, Software, Biotech/Life Sciences, Healthcare, Non-Classifiable

TEG Solutions†

1400 Lincoln Dr W Ste 103
Marlton, NJ 08053-3408
(856) 985-5368
Email: info@tegsolutions.net
Web: www.tegsolutions.net

Summary: We specialize in executive search assignments in the telecom and technology industries. Our nationwide capability enables clients to enjoy our telecom and technology recruitment expertise anywhere in the continental US.

Key Contact - Specialty:
Mr. Rick DeRose, President - *Technology, Telecommunications*
Mr. Scott Carberry, Vice President - *Technology, Telecommunications*
Mr. Andy Richards, Vice President - *Technology, Telecommunications*

Salary Minimum: $100,000

Functions: Management, Senior Mgmt., Middle Mgmt., Sales & Mktg., Mktg. Mgmt., Sales Mgmt.

Industries: IT Implementation, Telecoms, Telephony, Digital, Wireless, Fiber Optic, Network Infrastructure, RF/Microwave, Software, Security SW

Branches:
4110 Auston Way
Palm Harbor, FL 34685-4003
(727) 781-7544
Fax: (727) 781-1825
Email: vicki@tegsolutions.net
Key Contact - Specialty:
Ms. Vicki Devlin

6400 Goldsboro Rd Ste 400
Bethesda, MD 20817-5846
(240) 235-2144
Fax: (240) 235-2174
Email: sarah@tegsolutions.net

Key Contact - Specialty:
Ms. Sarah McCullough, Vice President, Managed Solutions - *Telecommunications*

104 Loretta Way
Forest Hill, MD 21050-3028
(410) 836-0249
Fax: (775) 256-2071
Email: carol@tegsolutions.net
Key Contact - Specialty:
Ms. Carol Barker

2968 Bayview Ave
Wantagh, NY 11793-4323
(516) 679-3768
Fax: (516) 826-5185
Email: jayne@tegsolutions.net
Key Contact - Specialty:
Ms. Jayne Lynch - *Technology, Telecommunications*

TERHAM Management Consultants

1805-2 Bloor St W
Toronto, ON M4W 3E2
Canada
(416) 968-3636
Fax: (416) 968-6617
Email: consultants@terham.com
Web: www.terham.com

Summary: We specialize in mid-senior level searches in the areas of marketing, advertising (management, account service, creative, media and production), direct marketing (direct mail, database and telemarketing) and new media.

Key Contact - Specialty:
Mr. Terry Hammond, President - *Advertising, Direct marketing, Marketing*

Salary Minimum: $50,000

Functions: Board Members, Senior Mgmt., Middle Mgmt., Healthcare, Sales & Mktg., Advertising, Direct Mktg., Int'l.

Industries: Banking, Restaurants, Sports, Advertising, Publishing, New Media, Broadcast, Film, Telecoms, Marketing SW, Healthcare

Tesar-Reynes Inc

500 N Michigan Ave Ste 1400
Chicago, IL 60611-3759
(312) 661-0700
Fax: (312) 661-1598
Email: tony@tesar-reynes.com
Web: www.tesar-reynes.com

Summary: We specialize in advertising, media, sales promotion, direct marketing, interactive marketing, public relations, research and integrated marketing management. We will fill most searches in 60 to 90 days.

Key Contact - Specialty:
Mr. Tony Reynes, Partner
Mr. Bob Tesar, Partner

Salary Minimum: $50,000

Functions: Advertising, Mktg. Mgmt., Direct Mktg., PR, Minorities/Diversity

Industries: Generalist (All)

James E Thomas & Assoc

1110-383 Richmond St
Royal Bank Building
London, ON N6A 3C4
Canada
(519) 661-0476
Fax: (519) 661-0478
Email: jethomas@thomas-hrconsultants.com
Web: www.thomas-hrconsultants.com

Summary: We are an executive search firm specializing in senior management searches in manufacturing.

Key Contact - Specialty:
Mr. James Thomas, President

Functions: Management

Industries: Manufacturing, Services

Richard Thompson Associates Inc

701 4th Ave S Ste 500
Minneapolis, MN 55415-1810
(612) 339-6060
Email: rpt@rthompassoc.com
Web: www.rthompassoc.com

Summary: We provide senior management and board of directors search consulting services for both nonprofit and for profit organizations.

Key Contact - Specialty:
Mr. Richard P. Thompson, President

Salary Minimum: $60,000

Functions: Board Members, Senior Mgmt., Mfg., HR Mgmt., CFOs, Non-profits

Industries: Generalist (All), Banking, Non-profits, Higher Ed.

Thorne, Brieger Associates Inc

511A Opa Ln
Stratford, CT 06614-8271
(203) 377-3030
Email: sbrieger@thornebrieger.com

Summary: We are skilled recruiters and assessors bringing a consultant's approach to solving organizational problems. Assignments carried out by principals only, each with extensive years of successful generalist experience.

Key Contact - Specialty:
Mr. Steven M. Brieger, Principal

Salary Minimum: $100,000

Functions: Generalist (All)

Industries: Textiles, Apparel, Chemicals, Soap, Perf., Cosmtcs., Drugs Mfg., Medical Devices, Plastics, Rubber, Paints, Petro. Products, Media, Advertising, Software

Thorne, Jacobs Associates Inc

377 Chatham Dr
Chapel Hill, NC 27516-8690
(919) 960-8037
Email: mikejacobs@thornejacobs.com

Summary: A facilitator's approach that strives to ensure a shared, common understanding and agreement among those who will be part of the hiring decision as to what is needed to ensure success. Strong recruiting and assessing skills honed by our extensive experience driven by a sense of urgency. Assignments carried out by principals.

Key Contact - Specialty:
Mr. Mike Jacobs, Principal

Salary Minimum: $100,000

Functions: Senior Mgmt., Middle Mgmt.

Industries: Generalist (All)

Tierney Consulting Group LLC

60 Public Sq Ste 100
Alltel Building
Wilkes Barre, PA 18701-2610
(570) 825-9500
Email: gtierney@ptd.net
Web: www.tierneycg.com

Summary: Our client base focuses largely in aerospace, automotive, and telecom markets. Our clients range from job shops to OEMs manufacturing elex components and systems including connectors, sensors, switches, power elex, SMT assembly, etc. to complex machined, fabricated, stamped or cast components. We perform searches for GMs/presidents, as well as VPs and directors of all disciplines.

Key Contact - Specialty:
Mr. George F. Tierney, President & Chief Executive Officer - *Aerospace, Automotive, Closely-held business, Electronics, Machining*
Mr. Paul J. Argenio, Managing Partner - *Consumer, Electronics, Paper, Professional services, Real estate*
Mr. Robert A. Pace, Managing Partner - *Capital goods, Closely-held business, Electronics, Engineering, Fastener*
Mr. Paul Pace, Managing Partner, Acquisitions - *Aerospace, Closely-held business*
Mr. Donald Symanski, Managing Partner, Acquisitions - *Aerospace, CEOs, Closely-held business, General management, Metals*
Mr. Robert R. Faux, Consultant - *Electronics, Factories, Factories (Automation), High technology, Power*

Salary Minimum: $80,000

Functions: Generalist (All), Senior Mgmt.

Industries: Food, Bev., Tobacco, Paper, Printing, Plastics, Rubber, Metal Products, Motor Vehicles, Computer Equip., Test, Measure Equip., Electronic, Elec. Components, Aerospace

TKW Search

(also known as THELMA.COM)
PO Box 65
219 Railroad Ave.
Woodacre, CA 94973-0065
(415) 488-4440
Email: thelma@thelma.com
Web: www.thelma.com

Summary: We are an executive search and recruitment firm specializing in healthcare information systems. We specialize in matching the most qualified candidates with the most appropriate positions, creating a productive and positive environment for both employer and employee. We offer our clients further value by providing advice and intensive guidance for both the employer and the career seeker.

Key Contact - Specialty:
Ms. Thelma Kay-Weiss, President

Functions: Management, Middle Mgmt.

Industries: Software, Accounting SW, Database SW, Development SW, ERP SW, Industry Specific SW, Healthcare, Hospitals

TNS Partners Inc

6688 N Central Expy Ste 1150
Dallas, TX 75206-3953
(214) 369-3565
Fax: (214) 369-9865
Web: www.tnspartners.com

Summary: We are a generalist firm with an emphasis on senior management positions in high-technology, manufacturing consulting, IT, consumer & industrial products, supply chain management, financial services and non-profit.

Key Contact - Specialty:
Mr. John K. Semyan, Partner - *Financial services, Information Technology, Management consulting, Senior management*
Mr. Craig C. Neidhart, Partner - *CFOs, General management, Human resources, Manufacturing, Marketing*

Mr. James M. Peters, Vice President - *Consulting, Finance, Human resources, Manufacturing, Supply Chain*
Mr. Mike Porter, Vice President - *Finance, General management, Human resources, Marketing, Operations*
Mr. Bob Diers, Vice President - *Cement/concrete, Consumer (Durables), Finance, Marketing, Operations*
Mr. Brian G. Trueblood, Vice President - *Finance, High technology, Marketing, Operations, Senior management*
Mr. James H. Chambers, Vice President - *Aerospace, Education, Non-profit, Operations, Senior management*
Ms. Paula Harrison, Director - *Chemical, Diversity, General management, High technology, Telecommunications*
Mr. Cable Neidhart, Consultant - *Finance, General management, Human resources, Manufacturing, Operations*

Salary Minimum: $100,000

Functions: Generalist (All), Management, Board Members, Senior Mgmt., Mfg., Materials, HR Mgmt., Finance, CFOs

Industries: Generalist (All), Manufacturing, Lumber, Furniture, Services, Non-profits, Mgmt. Consulting, Logistics Svcs.

Madeleine Todd Executive Recruiting

1329 Taylor St Apt 1
San Francisco, CA 94108-1007
(415) 441-7010
Fax: (415) 441-7173
Email: mter@madeleinetodd.com

Summary: With a high-level of personalized attention and service, we have a commitment to recruiting only people who will make a lasting impact to your company. All clients are repeat clients.

Key Contact - Specialty:
Mrs. Madeleine Todd, President

Salary Minimum: $230,000

Functions: Management, Board Members, Senior Mgmt.

Industries: Computer Equip., Test, Measure Equip., Electronic, Elec. Components, Semiconductors, Venture Cap., Communications, Software

Top Gun Ventures LLC

15305 Dallas Pkwy Ste 300
Addison, TX 75001-6470
(972) 980-1616
Fax: (972) 980-1689
Email: don@topgunventures.com
Web: www.topgunventures.com

Summary: We work with corporate clients, venture capitalists and entrepreneurs to meet their global human capital needs through retained executive search.

Key Contact - Specialty:
Mr. Donald E. Tuttle, Managing General Partner
Mr. Peter Donovan, Managing General Partner

Salary Minimum: $125,000

Functions: Generalist (All)

Industries: Manufacturing, Transportation, Retail, Venture Cap., Communications, Government, Defense, Aerospace, Software, Biotech/Life Sciences

Torch Group Inc[†]

33595 Bainbridge Rd Ste 200
Solon, OH 44139-2942
(440) 519-1822
Fax: (440) 519-1823
Email: torchgroup@torchgroup.com
Web: www.torchgroup.com

Summary: We are a highly specialized professional services firm that supplies human capital for the marketing, sales and communications disciplines. We will fill strategic, tactical, permanent, interim and project needs with highly-specialized talent available through our core services - executive recruiting, interim staffing, strategic consulting, and project outsourcing.

Key Contact - Specialty:
Mr. Ron Torch, President & Chief Executive Officer
Ms. Donna Antenucci, Recruiting Specialist

Salary Minimum: $50,000

Functions: Sales & Mktg.

Industries: Generalist (All)

Torstaff Personnel

503-67 Yonge St
Montreal Trust
Toronto, ON M5E 1J8
Canada
(416) 866-8855
Email: jobs@torstaff.com
Web: www.torstaff.com

Summary: We are specialists in accounting, financial and administrative staffing.

Key Contact - Specialty:
Ms. Kathy Reynolds, Partner
Mr. Frank Lubertino, Partner
Ms. Deirdre Arzheimer, Partner

Functions: Admin. Svcs., Customer Svc., HR Mgmt., Finance

Industries: Manufacturing, Retail, Entertainment, Telecoms, Real Estate, Software

Tower Consultants Ltd

203 Exton Cmns
Exton, PA 19341-2449
(484) 875-0999
Fax: (484) 875-0990
Email: dehart@towerconsultants.com
Web: www.towerconsultants.com

Summary: We search behind corporate lines, identify the best candidates and recruit them. We do not resource from our own clients.

Key Contact - Specialty:
Ms. Donna Friedman, Founder & Chief Executive Officer
Ms. Donna DeHart, President

Salary Minimum: $100,000

Functions: HR Mgmt., Benefits, Staffing, Training, e-HR

Industries: Generalist (All)

Branches:
943 SE Central Pkwy
Stuart, FL 34994-3904
(772) 288-3590
Fax: (772) 288-3540
Email: friedman@towerconsultants.com

Key Contact - Specialty:
Mr. Thomas J. Regan, Vice President - *Human resources*
Ms. Christine Rose, Partner - *Human resources*

TowerHunter

4727 E Union Hills Dr Ste 200
Phoenix, AZ 85050-3387
(602) 861-5907
(202) 857-9768
Fax: (602) 861-5876
Email: info@towerhunter.com
Web: www.towerhunter.com

Summary: Built on years of success in executive search, we produce the right talent, in accelerated timeframes, with a results-based retained fee structure. Each search is led by a firm principal. All principals are former corporate executives.

Key Contact - Specialty:
Mr. Terry Hindmarch, Managing Partner - *C-level, Healthcare, HMOs, Hospital, Six Sigma*
Mr. Scott Smith, Managing Partner - *Biomedical, CEOs, CFOs, Diversity, Financial*
Mr. Richard Booton, Vice President - *C-level, Change management, Quality, Senior management, Six Sigma*
Ms. Colleen Neese, Vice President - *Banking, Financial services, Healthcare, HMOs, Hospital*
Mr. Jeff Heyden, Vice President - *Automotive, Manufacturing*

Salary Minimum: $125,000

Functions: Senior Mgmt.

Industries: Manufacturing, Motor Vehicles, Semiconductors, Finance, Banking, HR Services, Telecoms, Healthcare, Hospitals

Branches:
1025 Connecticut Ave NW Ste 1012
Washington, DC 20036-5417
(202) 857-9768
Email: sdavis@towerhunter.com
Key Contact - Specialty:
Mr. Stanley Davis, Executive Vice President - *C-level, Executives, Senior management*

Trac One†

(a subsidiary of Team One Inc)
239 US Highway 22
Green Brook, NJ 08812-1916
(732) 474-1000
Fax: (732) 968-9437
Email: hr@tekwood.com
Web: www.tekwood.com

Summary: We conduct executive searches for MIS professionals exclusively as a subsidiary of a family of companies dedicated to data processing recruitment, search and consulting services.

Key Contact - Specialty:
Mr. Thomas C. Wood, President - *Data processing*

Salary Minimum: $75,000

Functions: Generalist (All), MIS Mgmt., Systems Analysis, Systems Dev., Systems Implem., Systems Support, Engineering

Industries: Generalist (All), Mgmt. Consulting, HR Services, Telecoms, Software

Transplant Management Group LLC

PO Box 10388
Bedford, NH 03110-0388
(603) 424-1476
Fax: (603) 218-6147
Email: frankgreaney@transplantmanagement.com
Web: www.transplantmanagement.com

Summary: Specialists in organ transplant leadership searches, including Organ Procurement Organizations. Administrators, physicians, surgeons. Managed care leadership.

Key Contact - Specialty:
Mr. Francis J. Greaney, Senior Consultant

Salary Minimum: $100,000

Functions: Senior Mgmt., Physicians

Industries: Healthcare, Hospitals

Travaille Executive Search†

1730 Rhode Island Ave NW Ste 401
Washington, DC 20036-3118
(202) 463-6342
Fax: (202) 331-7922
Email: benlong@travaille.com

Summary: We have an in depth understanding of corporate communications, investor relations and marketing communications, plus national and international public affairs. We are excellent in finding financial communicators for start-up companies as well as major corporations. We offer our clients a one year guarantee on all placements.

Key Contact - Specialty:
Mr. Benjamin H. Long, President - *Communications*

Salary Minimum: $45,000

Functions: Generalist (All), Admin. Svcs., PR, Graphic Designers

Industries: Generalist (All), Advertising, Publishing, New Media

Travis & Company Inc

PO Box 366
Ashby, MA 01431-0366
(978) 878-3232
Email: resumes@travisandco.com
Web: www.travisandco.com

Summary: We have expertise in recruiting executives for biotechnology, medical devices, pharmaceuticals, and high technology companies. We have clients of all sizes, from venture-backed start-ups to Fortune 100 companies.

Key Contact - Specialty:
Ms. Mary K. Morse, Principal
Mr. Michael J. Travis, Principal

Salary Minimum: $150,000

Functions: Generalist (All), Senior Mgmt.

Industries: Drugs Mfg., Medical Devices, Computer Equip., Communications, Software, Biotech/Life Sciences

Trendl Associates Ltd

941 W Winona St Ste 1W
Chicago, IL 60640-3228
(773) 728-6973
(773) 728-6974
Fax: (773) 728-6976
Email: info@trendl.net
Web: www.trendl.net

Summary: Our firm was founded as an executive search firm to support the ever expanding human capital needs of our clients. The founding principals of the firm together bring extensive experience in executive search serving the best in class organizations domestically as well as internationally.

Key Contact - Specialty:
Mr. Joseph R. Trendl, President & Chief Executive Officer - *Asset management, Banking, Boards of Directors, Brokerage, C-level*
Ms. Barbara Kauffman, Managing Principal - *C-level, Closely-held business, Consumer, Design, Professional services*

Salary Minimum: $100,000

Functions: Generalist (All), Board Members, Senior Mgmt., Middle Mgmt., CFOs

Industries: Generalist (All), Oil & Gas, Food, Bev., Tobacco, Textiles, Apparel, Retail, Finance, Banking, Invest. Banking, Brokers, Misc. Financial, Non-profits, HR Services, IT Implementation, Hospitality, Software

J C Trident Inc†

65 Sunset Hills Dr
Edwardsville, IL 62025-3633
(618) 659-0045
Fax: (618) 659-0302
Email: dan@jctrident.com
Web: www.jctrident.com

Summary: We specialize in three primary areas. One is assisting in building broker dealer distribution with senior wholesalers, sales managers and key account development. The second is increasing performance through portfolio manager lift-outs. The third is the capital markets area recruiting senior investment bankers and analysts.

Key Contact - Specialty:
Mr. Dan Baccarini, President - *Asset management, Banking (Investment), Financial services, Investment management, Wall Street*

Salary Minimum: $75,000

Functions: Management, Senior Mgmt., Sales & Mktg., Mktg. Mgmt., Sales Mgmt., Attorneys

Industries: Invest. Banking, Brokers, Venture Cap., Mutual/Hedge Funds, Misc. Financial, Life, Re-Insurance, Real Estate

Trilogy Venture Search

840 Hinckley Rd Ste 233
Burlingame, CA 94010-1509
(650) 259-8100
Fax: (650) 259-8110
Email: info@trilogysearch.com
Web: www.trilogysearch.com

Summary: We are a retained firm specializing in C-level searches for: manufacturing, retail, technology, professional services, and life sciences clients. We have a rich history as a trusted partner in building executive management teams, and of advancing candidates that reflect principled leadership and personal integrity.

Key Contact - Specialty:
Mr. Charles Pappalardo, Managing Director

Salary Minimum: $200,000

Functions: Generalist (All)

Industries: Chemicals, Drugs Mfg., Medical Devices, Test, Measure Equip., Healthcare

Trimarc Resources LLC

100 E San Marcos Blvd Ste 400
San Marcos, CA 92069-2988
(888) 874-6272 x150
Fax: (949) 498-5504
Email: gthomas@trimarcresources.com
Web: www.trimarcresources.com

Summary: We are an executive search firm whose clients require the time, attention to detail, and dedication to delivering results, that we provide. We help companies identify, select, and hire

leaders with track records of making great things happen. We specialize in filling key senior level positions in executive management (CXO), sales, finance, engineering, IT, professional services and HR.

Key Contact - Specialty:
Mr. Gordon Thomas, President
Mr. Cliff West, Executive Vice President - *Media, Publishing*
Mr. Mark Blahnik, Vice President - *Outsourcing, Publishing, Sales, Staffing, Technology*
Ms. Christina Champagne, Senior Associate - *Human resources, Marketing, Media, Staffing, Technology*

Salary Minimum: $100,000

Functions: Senior Mgmt.

Industries: Manufacturing, Finance, Services, Hospitality, Media, Communications, Government, Software, Biotech/Life Sciences

TriQuest†

6237 Guadalupe Mines Rd
San Jose, CA 95120-5001
(408) 268-8777
(408) 891-7700
Fax: (408) 927-8777
Email: mredburn@tri-quest.com
Web: www.tri-quest.com

Summary: Professional, technical and executive-level search firm with experience as an established leader in the recruiting industry.

Key Contact - Specialty:
Mr. Mark C. Redburn, President
Ms. Karyn B. McClelland, Director, Operations
Ms. Hayley B. Redburn, Manager, Staffing

Salary Minimum: $65,000

Functions: Generalist (All), Management, Sales & Mktg., HR Mgmt., Finance, IT, R&D, Engineering

Industries: Generalist (All), Computer Equip., Consumer Elect., Test, Measure Equip., Electronic, Elec. Components, Accounting, HR Services, E-commerce, IT Implementation, Media, Communications, Telecoms, Aerospace, Software

Triumph Consulting Inc

(an OI Partners Inc company)
2550 Middle Rd Ste 600
Bettendorf, IA 52722-3291
(563) 355-3313
Fax: (563) 355-3633
Email: tc@triumphconsulting.com
Web: www.triumphconsulting.com

Summary: Practice concentrating in accounting/financial services, manufacturing, technology and healthcare. The principals have extensive prior senior management experience. Each assignment is specifically handled by a designated functional professional throughout all phases of the search process.

Key Contact - Specialty:
Mr. Daniel G. DePuydt, President
Mr. Scott M. White, Executive Vice President
Mr. Michael Avgenackis, Vice President

Salary Minimum: $65,000

Functions: Generalist (All), Senior Mgmt., Plant Mgmt., Health Admin., Mktg. Mgmt., HR Mgmt., CFOs, MIS Mgmt.

Industries: Generalist (All), Chemicals, Plastics, Rubber, Machine, Appliance, Consumer Elect., Finance, Banking, Publishing, Healthcare

Branches:
4600 S Syracuse St Ste 200
Denver, CO 80237-2768
(720) 489-0100
Fax: (720) 489-1525
Email: denver@triumphconsulting.com
Key Contact - Specialty:
Ms. Diane Johnson

2700 Westown Pkwy Ste 200
West Des Moines, IA 50266-1411
(515) 453-9477
Fax: (515) 222-0565
Email: bwigger@triumphconsulting.com
Key Contact - Specialty:
Mr. Bob Wigger

7500 College Blvd Ste 500
Overland Park, KS 66210-4043
(913) 693-7933
Key Contact - Specialty:
Mr. Harold Brannon

Trowbridge&Company Inc

105 Chestnut St Ste 22
Needham, MA 02492-2520
(781) 444-4200
(617) 513-5358
Fax: (603) 886-9595
Email: rlt@trowbridgeandcompany.com
Web: www.trowbridgeandcompany.com

Summary: Our consultants specialize in retained executive search and selection. Our advanced technology products and services clients call upon us to specialize in identifying and attracting senior level executives across all disciplines. Recently expanded our practice to search out key executives in China and South Asia for clients deployed to those regions.

Key Contact - Specialty:
Mr. Robert L. Trowbridge, President - *High technology*
Ms. Alexis L. Scavetta, Principal Consultant

Salary Minimum: $90,000

Functions: Management, Board Members, Mfg., Sales & Mktg., HR Mgmt., CFOs, Systems Analysis, Network Admin., Engineering, Attorneys

Industries: Energy, Utilities, Chemicals, Computer Equip., Test, Measure Equip., Banking, Invest. Banking, Venture Cap., Misc. Financial, Legal, Mgmt. Consulting, Engineering Svcs., Telecoms, Defense, Aerospace, Software, Development SW, Biotech/Life Sciences

The Troyanos Group Ltd

500 Mamaroneck Ave Ste 314
Harrison, NY 10528-1600
(914) 798-7725
(914) 798-7740
Fax: (914) 993-9554
Email: dennis@troyanosgroup.com
Web: www.troyanosgroup.com

Summary: We are a highly specialized firm which recruits senior level professionals in the direct marketing, database and analytics arena. Our client portfolio is corporate as well as agency-based.

Key Contact - Specialty:
Mr. Dennis Troyanos, Chief Executive Officer - *CRM, Direct marketing*

Salary Minimum: $125,000

Functions: Mktg. Mgmt.

Industries: Retail, Finance, Services, Non-profits, Pharm Svcs., Mgmt. Consulting, Advertising, Call Centers, Wireless, Database SW

TRS Associates†

9769 Chaucer Ct
Pickerington, OH 43147-9849
(614) 864-2270
Email: nicklang@trsassociates.com
Web: www.trsassociates.com

Summary: We are a professional firm with extensive years of industry experience placing sales, marketing, senior-level management and technical personnel with companies in the metals and materials industries. We offer permanent and contract placement.

Key Contact - Specialty:
Mr. Nick Lang, President - *Materials, Metals*
Ms. Kristen Dulin, Manager, Research

Salary Minimum: $40,000

Functions: Generalist (All)

Industries: Metal Products, Misc. Mfg.

Tryon & Heideman LLC

8301 State Line Rd
Kansas City, MO 64114-2025
(816) 822-1976
(888) 822-1976
Email: resumes@tryonheideman.com
Web: www.tryonheideman.com

Summary: Our firm emphasizes consensus building on the criteria for executive positions before initiating a search. We develop an in-depth understanding of the client's organizational culture to ensure the best possible match.

Key Contact - Specialty:
Ms. Katey Tryon, Partner
Ms. Mary Marren Heideman, Partner

Salary Minimum: $65,000

Functions: Generalist (All), Management, Board Members, Senior Mgmt., Mfg., Healthcare, Sales & Mktg., HR Mgmt., Finance, Non-profits

Industries: Generalist (All), Non-profits, Women's

TSA Executive Recruiters†

10116 36th Ave Ct SW Ste 200
Lakewood, WA 98499-4792
(253) 588-1216
Fax: (253) 588-2528
Email: tsa@tsacareers.com
Web: www.tsacareers.com

Summary: We are an executive search and technical recruiting firm serving the scientific and enginnering communities in both the private and government sectors. We specialize in finding talented scientific and engineering professionals.

Key Contact - Specialty:
Mr. Mike Dolan, Chief Operating Officer - *Aerospace, Electronics, Engineering, Instrumentation, Optics*
Mr. Tony Hoss, Chief Financial Officer - *Engineering, Manufacturing, Manufacturing (Management), Photonics, Research & development*
Mr. Dan Lynch, Chief Executive Officer - *BSME, Engineering, Mechanical, Product management/development, Research & development*
Ms. Katie Grindley, Office Manager - *Administration*

Salary Minimum: $50,000

Functions: Generalist (All), Middle Mgmt., Product Dev., Production, Quality, Materials, Mktg. Research, Mktg. Mgmt., R&D, Engineering

Industries: Generalist (All), Energy, Utilities, Chemicals, Medical Devices, Plastics, Rubber,

Metal Products, Computer Equip., Test, Measure Equip., Misc. Mfg., Electronic, Elec. Components, Robotics, Semiconductors, Communications, Digital, Fiber Optic, Defense, Aerospace

Tschudin Inc

2125 Center Ave Ste 500
Fort Lee, NJ 07024-5874
(201) 302-6000
Fax: (201) 302-6062
Email: info@tschudin.com
Web: www.tschudin.com

Summary: We specialize in searches for executives who are crucial for company success. We are especially strong in assignments requiring extraordinary care/depth.

Key Contact - Specialty:
Dr. Hugo Tschudin, President
Mr. Richard Danoff, Chief Operating Officer

Salary Minimum: $70,000

Functions: Management, Mfg., Plant Mgmt., Sales & Mktg., Mktg. Mgmt., Sales Mgmt., HR Mgmt., Finance, CFOs, R&D

Industries: Generalist (All)

W G Tucker & Associates Inc

4240 Greensburg Pike Ste L100
Franklin Centre
Pittsburgh, PA 15221-4297
(412) 351-9309
Fax: (412) 351-9195
Email: corporate@wgtucker.com
Web: www.wgtucker.com

Summary: Our firm is an executive search and HR consulting firm. We are recognized for our ability to recruit qualified diversified candidates to fill executive level and key management positions. We also have a HR consulting division.

Key Contact - Specialty:
Ms. Weida G. Tucker, President & Chief Executive Officer

Salary Minimum: $60,000

Functions: Generalist (All), Management, Materials, Health Admin., Sales & Mktg., HR Mgmt., Finance, IT

Industries: Generalist (All), Energy, Utilities, Chemicals, Drugs Mfg., Transportation, Banking, Non-profits, Accounting, HR Services, Telecoms, Healthcare

Tuft & Associates Inc

1209 N Astor St
Chicago, IL 60610-2655
(312) 642-8889
Fax: (312) 642-8883
Email: matuft@tuftassoc.com
Web: www.tuftassoc.com

Summary: We are a specialized executive search firm. The firm focuses on CEO and key management staff of not-for-profit associations, philanthropic and academic nursing institutions.

Key Contact - Specialty:
Ms. Mary Ann Tuft, CAE, President
Ms. Cecile Margulies, Director, Research
Dr. Patricia Estok, Associate
Dr. Billy Brown, Associate
Ms. Carole Badger, JD, Associate
Dr. Edythe Hough, Associate
Ms. Miriam Letchinger, Associate
Ms. Linda Campbell, Associate
Ms. Kathleen Henrichs, Associate
Ms. Jill Christie, Associate

Salary Minimum: $75,000

Functions: Senior Mgmt.

Industries: Non-profits

TWC

2570 Boulevard of the Generals Ste 110
Audubon, PA 19403-3678
(610) 635-0101 x127
Fax: (610) 635-0304
Email: m.sweeny@twilliams.com
Web: www.twilliams.com

Summary: We are a provider of recruitment process outsourcing (RPO) solutions that enable our clients to build a competitive advantage through workforce recruitment and retention. With a focus on human capital management, we provide a single point of contact for on-demand and project recruitment, executive search, and human resources consulting. Our experience includes biotech, energy, financial services, healthcare, information technology, manufacturing, optics, pharmaceuticals, telecommunications, and wireless.

Key Contact - Specialty:
Mr. Mike Sweeny, Vice President, Recruiting Serivces - *Biopharmaceutical, Computers (Software), Engineering, Information Technology, Manufacturing*
Mr. Kevin McCormick, Director, Executive Search Practice - *Biopharmaceutical, C-level, Executives, Sales, Technology*
Ms. Leslie Hafter, Director, Outsourced Recruitment Service - *Biopharmaceutical, Pharmaceutical, Sales, Technology, Telecommunications*

Functions: Senior Mgmt., Middle Mgmt., Product Dev., Sales & Mktg., Mktg. Mgmt., Engineering

Industries: Manufacturing, Finance, Media, Communications, Software

Tyler & Company

375 Northridge Rd Ste 400
Atlanta, GA 30350-3299
(770) 396-3939
Fax: (770) 396-6693
Email: info@tylerandco.com
Web: www.tylerandco.com

Summary: We conduct searches for executive talent in healthcare, pharmaceuticals, insurance, biotechnology and life sciences.

Key Contact - Specialty:
Mr. J. Larry Tyler, President & Chief Executive Officer
Ms. Robin Singleton, Senior Vice President
Mr. Bruce McClearen, Vice President
Mr. Kirk Durossette, Consultant - *Healthcare, HMOs, Home health, Hospital, Physicians*
Ms. Roberta Levine, Senior Consultant
Mr. Nelson Mann, Vice President
Mrs. Marcia Champagne, Senior Vice President

Salary Minimum: $100,000

Functions: Management, Senior Mgmt., Healthcare, Health Admin., HR Mgmt., Finance, CFOs

Industries: Generalist (All), Manufacturing, Food, Bev., Tobacco, Non-profits, Pharm Svcs., Accounting, Mgmt. Consulting, Packaging, Insurance, Biotech/Life Sciences, Healthcare, Hospitals, Long-term/Home Care

Branches:
6800 Old Providence Rd
Charlotte, NC 28226-7738
(704) 366-4499
Fax: (770) 396-6693
Key Contact - Specialty:
Dr. George Linney, Jr., MD, Vice President

5 Christy Dr Ste 108
Chadds Ford, PA 19317-9667
(610) 558-6100
Fax: (610) 558-6101
Email: phoffmeir@tylerandco.com
Key Contact - Specialty:
Ms. Patti Hoffmeir, Senior Vice President
Mr. Dennis Kain, Senior Vice President
Ms. Stephanie Underwood, Vice President

Paul Unger NBS Search Inc

1750 Tysons Blvd Ste 400
Mc Lean, VA 22102-4231
(703) 744-1050
Fax: (703) 716-0584
Email: punger@cox.net
Web: www.paulunger.com

Summary: We are focused on assignments at the C and VP levels for companies ranging from VC backed to Global 2000. Industries served include: telecom, satellite communications, IT, SW, nanotechnology, insurance and health care.

Key Contact - Specialty:
Mr. Paul Unger, Chief Executive Officer

Salary Minimum: $150,000

Functions: Generalist (All), Management, Board Members, Senior Mgmt.

Industries: Generalist (All), Computer Equip., Consumer Elect., Venture Cap., IT Implementation, Communications, Telecoms, Telephony, Wireless, Fiber Optic, RF/Microwave, Government, Aerospace, Insurance, Software, Security SW, Healthcare

Unisource NTC

1560 Holly Court, Suite 200
Thousand Oaks, CA 91360
(805) 241-4357
(800) 736-8470
Fax: (310) 919-3541
Email: info@unisourcentc.com
Web: www.unisourcentc.com

Summary: Ours is a human resource consulting firm that offers a cost-effective alternative to traditional methods of recruiting. We specialize in all industries on a national and international basis. We provide on-staff project management for start-ups and roll-outs. We consult with firms on reducing average cost per hire.

Key Contact - Specialty:
Mr. Christian D. Schilling, Vice President, Research

Salary Minimum: $80,000

Functions: Senior Mgmt., Sales & Mktg.

Industries: Energy, Utilities, Oil & Gas, Construction, Manufacturing, Semiconductors, Mgmt. Consulting, E-commerce, IT Implementation, Logistics Svcs., Supply Chain Mgmt, Network Infrastructure, RF/Microwave, Defense, Aerospace, Software, Biotech/Life Sciences

Van Dyke Associates

PO Box 4475
Wheaton, IL 60189-4475
(630) 221-0191

Summary: We are an owner-operated firm providing high quality professional executive search consulting services to Christian organizations, manufacturing companies and service companies/organizations.

Key Contact - Specialty:
Mr. Roger Van Dyke, Owner & President

Salary Minimum: $75,000

† occasional contingency assignment

Functions: Generalist (All), Senior Mgmt.,
Middle Mgmt., Health Admin., HR Mgmt.,
CFOs, Non-profits

Industries: Generalist (All), Food, Bev., Tobacco

Peter Van Leer & Associates

26546 N Alma School Rd Ste 110
Scottsdale, AZ 85255-8094
(800) 473-3793
Email: insurancesearch@aol.com

Summary: We are a retainer search firm
specializing in the insurance industry with
emphasis on recruitment of senior executives in
the property and casualty industry.

Key Contact - Specialty:
Mr. Peter Van Leer, Owner

Salary Minimum: $60,000

Functions: Generalist (All), Senior Mgmt., Direct
Mktg., Risk Mgmt.

Industries: Generalist (All), Insurance

Vanderzee & Associates Inc[†]

8149 N 87th Pl
Scottsdale, AZ 85258-4399
(480) 563-8150
Email: info@vanderzee.net
Web: www.vanderzee.net

Summary: Retained search assignments
exclusively for senior level positions. Unique
strength: international management skills.
Functional areas: general management, finance,
human resources, sales & marketing, and
operations. Main industries: technology, life
sciences and consumer products.

Key Contact - Specialty:
Mr. Siebe Vanderzee, President
Mr. Massimo Paolillo, Senior Associate
Mr. Eric Bettelheim, Senior Associate
Mr. Peter Trompetter, Senior Associate

Salary Minimum: $100,000

Functions: Generalist (All), Board Members,
Senior Mgmt.

Industries: Generalist (All), Manufacturing,
Medical Devices, Electronic, Elec. Components,
Semiconductors, Consumer Goods,
Transportation, Finance, Services, Hospitality,
Media, Communications, Software, Biotech/Life
Sciences

Vantage Point Associates

75 Spring St Fl 6
New York, NY 10012-4020
(212) 966-3088
Fax: (212) 857-4848
Email: info@vanatgepointassociates.com
Web: www.vantagepointassociates.com

Summary: We are a retained executive
recruitment firm specializing in placing senior
level candidates for companies in the information
technology industries. We place special emphasis
on identifying executive talent that adds maximum
value and provide a unique partnering experience
to our clients.

Key Contact - Specialty:
Mr. Gregg Grossman, President & Founder
Ms. Hannah Corbett, Research

Salary Minimum: $150,000

Functions: Senior Mgmt.

Industries: Venture Cap., E-commerce, New
Media, Digital

Verkamp-Joyce Associates Inc

4320 Winfield Rd Ste 200
Warrenville, IL 60555-4023
(630) 836-8030

Summary: We are a management consulting firm
specializing in executive selection. We assist
clients in identifying upper and middle executive
management talent for every major industry.

Key Contact - Specialty:
Ms. Sheila M. Joyce, Partner
Mr. J. Frank Verkamp, Partner

Salary Minimum: $100,000

Functions: Generalist (All)

Industries: Construction, Manufacturing, Finance,
Accounting, Mgmt. Consulting, HR Services,
Haz. Waste, Packaging, Healthcare

The Verriez Group Inc

203-252 Pall Mall St
London, ON N6A 5P6
Canada
(519) 673-3463
Fax: (519) 673-4748
Email: verriez@verriez.com
Web: www.verriez.com

Summary: Our firm is widely known and
respected for its expertise in the search and
placement of professionals. We have the
experience and capacity to provide a full range of
management recruiting services.

Key Contact - Specialty:
Mr. Paul M. Verriez, President - *Finance*
Miss Tara Forster, Research Associate

Salary Minimum: $75,000

Functions: Finance, CFOs, Budgeting, Taxes,
Risk Mgmt.

Industries: Generalist (All)

Verus Partners LLC

11001 W 120th Ave Ste 400
Broomfield, CO 80021-3493
(303) 410-4250
Fax: (303) 600-9901
Email: resumes@veruspartners.net
Web: www.veruspartners.net

Summary: Executive search firm that specializes
in placing mid to senior level managers and
executives who provide exceptional and long
lasting value to your business. Our emphasis is in
the following industries: financial services, life
sciences, advanced technology, and industrial
products.

Key Contact - Specialty:
Mr. Chet Marino, CPC, President

Salary Minimum: $75,000

Functions: Generalist (All), Senior Mgmt.,
Middle Mgmt., Healthcare, Sales & Mktg.,
Mktg. Mgmt., Sales Mgmt., Finance,
Engineering

Industries: Generalist (All), Manufacturing,
Finance, Mgmt. Consulting, Biotech/Life
Sciences

Vick & Associates[†]

3325 Landershire Ste 1001
Plano, TX 75023-6218
(800) 364-8425
(972) 612-8425
Email: bill@billvick.com
Web: www.billvick.com

Summary: We are a search firm working with
high technology and software companies staffing
mid and senior level sales & marketing positions.

Key Contact - Specialty:
Mr. Bill Vick, Chief Executive Officer

Salary Minimum: $100,000

Functions: Management, Sales & Mktg.

Industries: Soap, Perf., Cosmtcs., Consumer
Elect., Consumer Goods, Misc. Financial,
Services, Accounting, Media, Packaging,
Insurance, Software

Victory & Associates.com Inc

1609 Yellowstone Ave
Lewisville, TX 75077-2461
(972) 966-0251
(877) 966-0251
Fax: (972) 966-0252
Email: victory@victoryandassociates.com
Web: www.victoryandassociates.com

Summary: Our firm's unique niche is that we take
your recruiting project on an hourly basis, so that
your cost per hire is dramatically reduced. We
deliver four to six candidates for each project.

Key Contact - Specialty:
Ms. LuAnn Victory, President

Salary Minimum: $40,000

Functions: Technicians

Industries: Medical Devices, Non-profits, Pharm
Svcs., HR Services, Higher Ed., Biotech/Life
Sciences, Healthcare, Hospitals, Long-
term/Home Care, Women's

Victory Search Group

20701 N Scottsdale Rd Ste 107
Scottsdale, AZ 85255-6413
(480) 585-0073
Fax: (480) 718-7832
Email: info@victorysearchgroup.com
Web: www.victorysearchgroup.com

Summary: Retained executive search firm
specializing in financial function, human
resources, marketing, and general management.

Key Contact - Specialty:
Ms. Amy Frink, Managing Director - *CFOs,
Finance, Financial*
Ms. Julie Doman, Director - *Consumer,
Marketing, Supply Chain*

Salary Minimum: $110,000

Functions: Senior Mgmt.

Industries: Manufacturing, Finance, Banking,
Aerospace, Biotech/Life Sciences

Villareal & Associates Inc

427 S Boston Ave Ste 215
Tulsa, OK 74103-4107
(918) 584-0808
Fax: (918) 584-6281
Email: morey@villarealassociates.com
Web: www.villarealassociates.com

Summary: We are a human recources consulting
firm specializing in compensation, organization
analysis, and executive search.

Key Contact - Specialty:
Mr. Morey J. Villareal - *General management*

Functions: Generalist (All), Management

Industries: Generalist (All)

Villeneuve Associates Inc

1420 5th Ave Ste 2200
Seattle, WA 98101-1346
(425) 836-8445
Web: www.villeneuveassociates.com

Summary: We are a retained officer-level search
firm serving the retail and food service industries.

We recruit top talent and create favorable cultures. As a search partner, we provide succession planning, placement and retention strategies.

Key Contact - Specialty:
Ms. Kim Villeneuve, President & Chief Executive Officer - *CEOs, CFOs, Finance, Food service, Retail*

Salary Minimum: $150,000

Functions: Generalist (All), Board Members, Senior Mgmt., Advertising, Mktg. Mgmt., Direct Mktg., HR Mgmt., CFOs, MIS Mgmt.

Industries: Generalist (All), Retail, Finance, Hospitality, Media

Branches:
100 Park Ave Fl 16
New York, NY 10017-5538
(212) 928-6658
Key Contact - Specialty:
Ms. Liz Etkin, Senior Vice President - *CEOs, CFOs, Finance, Food service, Retail*
Ms. Cindy Fratarcangeli, Senior Vice President - *CEOs, CFOs, Finance, Food service, Retail*

Vlcek & Company Inc

620 Newport Center Dr Ste 1100
Newport Beach, CA 92660-8011
(949) 752-0661
Fax: (949) 752-5205
Email: mail2@vlcekco.com

Summary: We are a boutique retained search/consulting firm serving a variety of firms throughout the U.S. and internationally. We are general search consultants, but we also have strong practice specialties in operations, human resources, finance and general management and have strong experience in the food, healthcare, and consumer services industries.

Key Contact - Specialty:
Mr. Thomas J. Vlcek, President & Lead Consultant - *General management, Human resources, Operations*
Ms. Suzanne M. Galante, Vice President & Senior Consultant - *Financial services*

Salary Minimum: $100,000

Functions: Senior Mgmt., Middle Mgmt., Mfg., HR Mgmt., Finance

Industries: Generalist (All)

Vogel Associates[†]

PO Box 576
Longport, NJ 08403-0576
(609) 487-7099
Fax: (309) 215-3609
Email: resumes@vogelassociates.com
Web: www.vogelassociates.com

Summary: We are a professional recruiting and search specializing exclusively in all areas of HR: employment, training, MD/OD, compensation, benefits, labor & employee relations, EEO/AA, HRIS, etc.

Key Contact - Specialty:
Mr. Michael S. Vogel, President - *Human resources*

Salary Minimum: $60,000

Functions: HR Mgmt.

Industries: Generalist (All)

Vogrinc & Short[†]

429 Phelps Ave Ste 708
Rockford, IL 61108-2459
(815) 394-1001
Fax: (815) 394-1046
Email: brianv@vogshort.com

Summary: Retained search firm representing companies primarily in the manufacturing and distribution industries. Specialties in filtration, hydraulics, power transmission/engine, and home building products. We offer an hourly based recruiting program that has allowed our client companies to cost effectively outsource their recruitment function saving hundreds of thousands of dollars over traditional search methods.

Key Contact - Specialty:
Mr. Brian Vogrinc, Partner
Mr. Thomas Short, Partner

Salary Minimum: $60,000

Functions: Generalist (All), Management, Mfg.

Industries: Generalist (All), Manufacturing, Food, Bev., Tobacco, Plastics, Rubber, Metal Products, Machine, Appliance, Consumer Elect., Misc. Mfg., Electronic, Elec. Components, Banking, Packaging

Vojta & Associates

102 Hobson St
Stamford, CT 06902-8130
(203) 357-8022
Fax: (203) 425-9899
Email: resume@optonline.net

Summary: We are a small boutique search firm that offers high-level recruiting, personalized service and a closely monitored search process to deliver the most qualified candidates.

Key Contact - Specialty:
Ms. Marilyn B. Vojta, Principal - *Consumer (Packaged Goods), Human resources, Organizational development, Sales*

Salary Minimum: $60,000

Functions: Middle Mgmt., Mktg. Mgmt., Sales Mgmt.

Industries: Food, Bev., Tobacco, Drugs Mfg., Mgmt. Consulting, Advertising, Publishing, New Media, Broadcast, Film, Telecoms, Non-Classifiable

The Volkman Group LLC

8197 S Newport Ct
Centennial, CO 80112-3103
(720) 493-5541
Fax: (720) 493-5542
Email: artv@volkmangroup.com
Web: www.volkmangroup.com

Summary: We provide senior level and mid level executive search services to the healthy living and wellness markets. Business expertise spans a wide range of allied industries including manufacturing (food, beverage, supplements, consumer product and personal care), distribution and retailing. Clients benefit from our undivided focus on these niche markets.

Key Contact - Specialty:
Mr. Art Volkman, President

Salary Minimum: $100,000

Functions: Management, Board Members, Senior Mgmt., Middle Mgmt., Mfg., Sales & Mktg., Mktg. Mgmt., Sales Mgmt., HR Mgmt., CFOs

Industries: Food, Bev., Tobacco, Textiles, Apparel, Soap, Perf., Cosmtcs., Drugs Mfg., Retail, Non-profits, Entertainment, Broadcast, Film, Biotech/Life Sciences

Wakefield Talabisco International

11 E 44th St Rm 1206
New York, NY 10017-0056
(212) 661-8600
Fax: (212) 661-8832

Email: info@wtali.com
Web: www.wtali.com

Summary: We are a boutique retained search firm focusing on senior-level positions in marketing, sales, financial management & services, retail, beauty and fashion.

Key Contact - Specialty:
Ms. Barbara Talabisco, President & Chief Executive Officer - *Fashion, Financial services, Marketing*
Ms. Lindy Evans, Vice President

Salary Minimum: $125,000

Functions: Generalist (All), Senior Mgmt., Middle Mgmt., Mktg. Mgmt., Direct Mktg., Staffing, CFOs, Minorities/Diversity

Industries: Generalist (All), Soap, Perf., Cosmtcs., Drugs Mfg., Non-profits, HR Services, Hospitality, Advertising, New Media

Wakefield Talabisco International Inc

13 US Route 4 Ste 8
Mendon, VT 05701-9706
(802) 747-5901
Fax: (802) 747-4473
Email: jaw@wakefieldtalabisco.com
Web: www.wakefieldtalabisco.com

Summary: Minority and female owned, boutique executive search firm that specializes in consumer products, especially direct selling and direct marketing; and not-for-profit, especially foundations and community service organizations.

Key Contact - Specialty:
Mr. J. Alvin Wakefield - *Industrial, Non-profit*
Mr. Donald Hunt, Associate - *Executives, Human resources, Senior management, Staffing*

Salary Minimum: $100,000

Functions: Generalist (All)

Industries: Generalist (All), Food, Bev., Tobacco, Transportation, Retail, Non-profits, Mgmt. Consulting, HR Services, Publishing, Call Centers

Waken & Associates[†]

327 Dahlonega St Ste B303
Cumming, GA 30040-2485
(877) 877-0900
(770) 889-5570
Email: info@wakenassociates.com
Web: www.wakenassociates.com

Summary: Our firm provides executive search for industries such as investment & commercial banking, commercial finance, equity investment, 'Big 5' corporate finance, accounting, insurance and other diverse industries. Search emphasis has been given to sectors such corporate finance, capital markets, lending, wealth management, treasury management, portfolio management, etc.

Key Contact - Specialty:
Mr. Ron Van Weelde, President

Salary Minimum: $75,000

Functions: Generalist (All), Finance

Industries: Banking, Invest. Banking, Brokers, Venture Cap., Mutual/Hedge Funds, Misc. Financial, Accounting, Mgmt. Consulting

J D Walsh & Company

456 Lost District Dr
New Canaan, CT 06840-2016
(203) 972-4359

Summary: We specialize in telecommunication and information services (Internet) industries.

Key Contact - Specialty:
Mr. John Walsh - *Telecommunications*

Salary Minimum: $75,000

Functions: Management

Industries: Mgmt. Consulting, Media, Telecoms, Software

Deborah Snow Walsh Inc

1000 Skokie Blvd Ste 400
Wilmette, IL 60091-1166
(847) 920-0089
Fax: (847) 920-0884
Email: srexec@dswalsh.com
Web: www.dswalsh.com

Summary: We are a retained, executive search firm focusing on senior-level candidates covering all functions and industries, with the reputation for presenting a diverse slate of candidates.

Key Contact - Specialty:
Ms. Deborah Snow Walsh, President

Salary Minimum: $200,000

Functions: Management, Senior Mgmt., Sales & Mktg., HR Mgmt., CFOs, IT, Legal

Industries: Generalist (All)

Lee H Walton & Associates

379 Jeffrey Pl
Valley Cottage, NY 10989-1507
(845) 268-0292
Fax: (845) 268-0293
Email: leehwalton@aol.com

Summary: We offer executive recruiting services for clients in a wide range of industries and functions. We have extensive experience and expertise with Fortune 500, consumer, industrial & service organizations, financial services, consumer products, management consulting/strategic planning, privately held and venture capital backed small companies are areas of strength.

Key Contact - Specialty:
Ms. Lee H. Walton

Salary Minimum: $200,000

Functions: Generalist (All), Middle Mgmt., Sales & Mktg., Advertising, Customer Svc., HR Mgmt., Finance, MIS Mgmt., Mgmt. Consultants, Attorneys

Industries: Generalist (All), Energy, Utilities, Oil & Gas, Construction, Manufacturing, Food, Bev., Tobacco, Drugs Mfg., Consumer Elect., Transportation, Finance, Brokers, Venture Cap., Services, Insurance, Healthcare

Ward & Associates†

800 W 5th Ave
Naperville, IL 60563-8965
(630) 717-6111
Email: bmw@robertward.com
Web: www.robertward.com

Summary: We are a boutique search firm focusing on service to middle market companies. Our past searches have involved management positions in finance, accounting, tax, HR, marketing, sales and operations.

Key Contact - Specialty:
Mr. Robert M. Ward, Principal - *Finance, Tax*

Salary Minimum: $100,000

Functions: Management, HR Mgmt., Finance

Industries: Generalist (All), Food, Bev., Tobacco, Drugs Mfg., Medical Devices, Plastics, Rubber, Venture Cap., Architectural Svcs., Pharm Svcs., Legal, Accounting, Accounting SW

E K Ward & Associates†

(an OI Partners Inc company)
4455 Transit Rd Ste 3B
Buffalo, NY 14221-6030
(716) 626-1389
Fax: (716) 626-1430
Email: email@ekward.com
Web: www.ekward.com

Summary: We conduct executive search services. We specialize in locating hard-to-find talent for a variety of functions/industries including finance, consumer services, engineering, manufacturing, healthcare, as well as professional services at mid to senior executive-levels.

Key Contact - Specialty:
Ms. Eileen K. Ward, Senior Consultant, Executive Search - *Engineering, General management, Human resources, Manufacturing*

Salary Minimum: $50,000

Functions: Generalist (All)

Industries: Manufacturing, Food, Bev., Tobacco, Medical Devices, Banking, Misc. Financial, Accounting, HR Services, Call Centers, Biotech/Life Sciences, Healthcare

The Ward Group

8 Cedar St Ste 68
Woburn, MA 01801-6362
(781) 938-4000
Fax: (781) 938-4100
Email: info@wardgroup.com
Web: www.wardgroup.com

Summary: Our consultative approach to executive search enables us to successfully recruit talented marketing and communications professionals in a timely manner. Our expertise in assessing the professional and personal variables of both clients and candidates has been the cornerstone of our success.

Key Contact - Specialty:
Mr. James M. Ward, President - *Communications, Marketing*
Mr. Jerry Grady, Vice President - *Communications, Marketing*
Mr. Lou Nagy, Vice President - *Communications, Marketing*
Ms. Julie Ried, Director - *Communications, Marketing*
Ms. Colleen E. Lantz, Office Manager

Functions: Sales & Mktg.

Industries: Media, Advertising, New Media

Branches:
345 State Rt 17
Upper Saddle River, NJ 07458-2307
(201) 934-4220
Fax: (201) 934-8509
Email: tjago@wardgroup.com
Key Contact - Specialty:
Mr. Thomas R. Jago, Managing Director - *Communications, Marketing*

Ward Liebelt Associates Inc

19 Ludlow Rd Ste 302
Westport, CT 06880-3040
(203) 454-0414
Fax: (203) 221-7300
Email: wardliebelt@yahoo.com

Summary: We specialize in highly-specialized consumer packaged goods, general management, senior marketing management, sales management and recruitment of management consultants.

Key Contact - Specialty:
Mr. Anthony C. Ward, Partner
Mr. Bob Caruthers, Associate

Salary Minimum: $100,000

Functions: Senior Mgmt., Mktg. Mgmt., Sales Mgmt.

Industries: Food, Bev., Tobacco, Soap, Perf., Cosmtcs., Consumer Goods

Waring & Associates Ltd†

10 Wind Ridge Rd Ste 100
South Barrington, IL 60010-5333
(847) 428-5300
Fax: (847) 428-7857
Email: mail@waring.net
Web: www.waring.net

Summary: Retained firm. Expertise: manufacturing, industrial, technology, chemical and biotechnology companies (all positions), technology functional heads (R&D, operations, engineering, supply chain, MIS, etc).

Key Contact - Specialty:
Mr. David Waring, President
Ms. Alexandra Shahan, Research Specialist
Ms. Nancy Plum, Administration

Salary Minimum: $125,000

Functions: Management, Senior Mgmt., Mfg., Automation, Materials, Sales & Mktg., MIS Mgmt., R&D, Engineering, Int'l.

Industries: Generalist (All), Agri., Forestry, Mining, Energy, Utilities, Construction, Manufacturing, Equip Svcs., Communications, Environmental Svcs., Packaging, Software, Mfg. SW, Biotech/Life Sciences

Warren & Morris Ltd

132 Chapel St
Portsmouth, NH 03801-3848
(603) 431-7929
Fax: (603) 431-3460
Email: info@warrenmorrisltd.com
Web: www.warrenmorrisltd.com

Summary: Our firm provides executive search services to selected clients in the communications industry convergence, including carriers, associated new technology and new media ventures. If you are a services or infrastructure provider for the internet, telephony, wireless or broadband industries or a supplier of technology, software or content to these industries, we know and understand your space.

Key Contact - Specialty:
Mr. Scott C. Warren, Senior Partner
Mr. David J. Higgins, Senior Partner
Mr. Charles Cossitt, Partner
Mr. Arlon A. Chaffee, Partner
Mr. Gary Smetana, Partner
Ms. Amy McCoy, Associate Partner

Functions: Generalist (All)

Industries: Services, Media, Communications, Telecoms, Call Centers, Telephony, Digital, Wireless, Fiber Optic, Software

Branches:
2190 Carmel Valley Rd
Del Mar, CA 92014-3766
(858) 481-3388
Fax: (858) 481-6221
Email: michelle@warrenmorrisltd.com
Key Contact - Specialty:
Mr. Charles C. Morris, Senior Partner
Mr. Robert A. Sweetser, Partner

115 W California Blvd Ste 268
Pasadena, CA 91105-3005
(626) 584-1155
Email: info@warrenmorrisltd.com

Key Contact - Specialty:
Ms. Carolyn Cason, Account Director

Warren Consulting Partners Inc

115 Perimeter Center Pl NE Ste 150
Atlanta, GA 30346-1284
(404) 308-1381
Email: warrenco@bellsouth.net
Web: www.warrenconsult.com

Summary: Executive recruiters specializing in
high technology, financial services, consumer
products, and manufacturing.

Key Contact - Specialty:
Mr. Gregg Warren, Partner

Salary Minimum: $100,000

Functions: Generalist (All)

Industries: Telecoms

Waters Consulting Group Inc

(also known as Waters-Oldani Executive
Recruitment)
2695 Villa Creek Dr Ste 104
Dallas, TX 75234-7310
(972) 481-1950
(800) 899-1669
Fax: (972) 481-1951
Email: support@watersconsulting.com
Web: www.watersconsulting.com

Summary: Our firm has a long-standing tradition
of excellence in HR consulting and executive
search for both the public and private sectors.
Specializing in total compensation systems,
performance appraisal, executive search and
training & development.

Key Contact - Specialty:
Ms. Stacy Layton, Director, Operations &
Business Dev - *Accounting (General),
Administration, Business development, Closely-
held business, Consulting*
Mr. Rollie O. Waters, CMC, President -
*Incentives, Management consulting,
Professional services, Public sector, Senior
management*
Mr. Chris Hartung, Director, Public Sector Search
- *Compensation, General management, Human
resources, Management consulting, Public
sector*

Salary Minimum: $60,000

Functions: Senior Mgmt., HR Mgmt.

Industries: Generalist (All), Construction,
Transportation, Non-profits, Accounting, HR
Services, IT Implementation, K-12 Ed., Higher
Ed., Engineering Svcs., Government

Branches:
10900 NE 4th St Ste 2030
Bellevue, WA 98004-8360
(425) 451-3938
Email: support@watersconsulting.com
Key Contact - Specialty:
Mr. Jerry Oldani, Senior Vice President

R J Watkins & Company Ltd

2515 Brant St
San Diego, CA 92101-1325
(619) 299-3094
Fax: (619) 725-4950
Email: info@rjwatkins.com
Web: www.rjwatkins.com

Summary: Since our inception, we have created
value by attracting high-impact candidates for
growth-oriented firms. Our practice groups focus
on bioscience and technology.

Key Contact - Specialty:
Mr. Robert J. Watkins, President & Chairman -
*Biotechnology, Boards of Directors, CEOs,
High technology, Medical (Devices)*
Mr. Bradley J. Little, Recruiter

Salary Minimum: $125,000

Functions: Generalist (All), Board Members,
Senior Mgmt., Product Dev., Mktg. Research,
CFOs, IT, MIS Mgmt., R&D

Industries: Generalist (All), Drugs Mfg., Medical
Devices, Computer Equip., Finance, Pharm
Svcs., Mgmt. Consulting, Biotech/Life Sciences

Branches:
2155 S Bascom Ave Ste 110
Campbell, CA 95008-3200
(408) 626-4850
Email: thorgan@rjwatkins.com
Key Contact - Specialty:
Mr. Thomas Horgan, Director
Mr. Sean Splaine, Recruiter

152 Lombard St Apt 606
San Francisco, CA 94111-1171
(415) 350-8775
Email: vmulder@rjwatkins.com
Key Contact - Specialty:
Mr. Vaughn Mulder, Corporate Development
Services

Scott Watson & Associates Inc[†]

4301 32nd St W Ste B7
Bradenton, FL 34205-2747
(941) 751-2962
Email: s.watson@scottwatson.com
Web: www.scottwatson.com

Summary: We are an executive search firm
specializing in commercial banking.

Key Contact - Specialty:
Mr. Scott Watson, President
Ms. Martha Watson, Director, Research -
*Banking, Banking
(Commercial, Corporate, Investment, Mortgage)*

Salary Minimum: $70,000

Functions: Generalist (All)

Industries: Banking

Waveland International Inc

(formerly known as Waveland International,
L.L.C.)
1 E Wacker Dr Ste 2900
Chicago, IL 60601-1902
(312) 739-9600
Fax: (312) 739-0250
Web: www.wavelandsearch.com

Summary: Our firm is a relationship driven and
preferred provider focused organization dedicated
to long-term partnerships with our clients and
providing a high-level of customer service.

Key Contact - Specialty:
Mr. Phillip D. Greenspan, Partner
Mr. Louis A. Freda, Partner
Mr. Jeffrey M. Posselt, Partner
Mr. Nelson Rodriguez, Partner
Mr. Philip J. Nicholson, Partner
Mr. Bradley S. Curtis, Managing Director -
Hospitality

Salary Minimum: $125,000

Functions: Generalist (All), Management, Mfg.,
Materials, Sales & Mktg., HR Mgmt., Finance

Industries: Manufacturing, Food, Bev., Tobacco,
Retail, Finance, Software, Biotech/Life Sciences

Branches:
50 N Franklin Tpke Ste 104
Ho Ho Kus, NJ 07423-1562
(201) 444-7704
Fax: (201) 444-7703
Email: info@wavelandsearch.com
Key Contact - Specialty:
Mr. Michael J. Koeller, Partner

5315 Oak Lake Dr Ste 915
Dallas, TX 75287-7512
(972) 931-0332
Fax: (972) 931-0338
Email: swoffice@weavelandsearch.com
Key Contact - Specialty:
Mr. Thomas J. Bolger, Partner

Waverly Partners LLC

400 Powell Dr
Cleveland, OH 44140-1652
(440) 892-5961
Email: info@waverly-partners.com
Web: www.waverly-partners.com

Summary: We are a generalist search firm,
serving clients including Fortune 1000 service and
manufacturing corporations, privately held
entrepreneurial growth companies, chambers of
commerce, economic development organizations
& business associations, hospitals & healthcare
systems, nonprofit organizations, colleges &
universities and professional service firms.

Key Contact - Specialty:
Mr. Eric Peterson, Managing Director & Principal
Ms. Heidi Geiger Milosovic, Managing Director
& Principal
Mr. Matthew Clemens, Managing Director

Salary Minimum: $90,000

Functions: Generalist (All)

Industries: Generalist (All), Manufacturing,
Retail, Finance, Services, Non-profits, Higher
Ed., Healthcare

Branches:
2020 Liberty Ln
Roswell, GA 30075-7902
(770) 645-9066
Key Contact - Specialty:
Mr. Richard Dean, Managing Director &
Principal

4100 Carmel Rd Ste B
Charlotte, NC 28226-6151
(704) 643-9394
Key Contact - Specialty:
Mr. Harrison Turnbull, Managing Director &
Principal
Mr. Clayton Woodard, Managing Director

3434 Granite Cir
Toledo, OH 43617-1160
(419) 842-6192
Key Contact - Specialty:
Mr. Joel Epstein, Managing Director & Principal

3434 Granite Cir
Toledo, OH 43617-1160
(801) 395-9570
Key Contact - Specialty:
Mr. Herbert Scales, Managing Director

13 Seagrass Ln
Isle of Palms, SC 29451-2838
(843) 886-0608

Key Contact - Specialty:
Ms. Nan Herron, Managing Director & Principal

Weber Executive Search

(a division of Weber Management Consultants Inc)
300 E 40th St Apt 26K
New York, NY 10016-2148
(212) 941-0499
Fax: (212) 661-3632
Email: webermanagement@att.com

Summary: We are a executive search firm specializing in consumer products, food, beverage, restaurant and hospitality industries.

Key Contact - Specialty:
Mr. Ronald R. Weber, President

Salary Minimum: $90,000

Functions: Generalist (All), Board Members

Industries: Generalist (All), Food, Bev., Tobacco, Soap, Perf., Cosmtcs., Consumer Goods, Non-profits, Engineering Svcs., Hospitality, Media

Weingarth Group Inc

5901 Treetop Rdg
Durham, NC 27705-8555
(919) 403-6103
(919) 260-7766
Fax: (919) 403-6107
Email: gweingarth@weingarthgroup.com
Web: www.weingarthgroup.com

Summary: A global retained executive search firm with a personalized service approach. We serve companies and organizations in manufacturing, life sciences, general industry and academics.

Key Contact - Specialty:
Mr. Glenn K. Weingarth, President

Salary Minimum: $100,000

Functions: Generalist (All)

Industries: Manufacturing, Drugs Mfg., Medical Devices, Machine, Appliance, Misc. Mfg., Banking, Misc. Financial, Pharm Svcs., Higher Ed., Dental

Weinstein & Company

14 Front St
Exeter, NH 03833-2730
(603) 772-2747
Email: lewweinstein@yahoo.com

Summary: Founder handles all work, taking on only a few searches at a time and providing a high level of service. Clients include consulting firms, LBO firms, VC firms and companies involved in high technology, consumer products, financial services and health care products/services..

Key Contact - Specialty:
Mr. Lewis R. Weinstein, President - *Consulting, High technology, Life Sciences, Private equity, Venture capital*

Salary Minimum: $125,000

Functions: Generalist (All)

Industries: Manufacturing, Retail, Finance, Mgmt. Consulting, Hospitality, Media, Communications, Software, Biotech/Life Sciences, Healthcare

S E Weinstein Company

1830 2nd Ave Ste 240
Rock Island, IL 61201-8003
(309) 794-1992
(800) 258-1701
Fax: (309) 794-1993
Email: hunter1830@sbcglobal.net
Web: www.seweinstein.com

Summary: We are a client-retained executive search firm. We are generalists specializing in 'Rural America' and 'Family Owned' companies. Our specialties are engineering, CEO, COO, CFO, board of directors, IT, food, steel fabrication, sales/marketing, manufacturing, medical, etc. We offer a highly personalized, detailed approach with experience in the development of long-term client-company working relationships.

Key Contact - Specialty:
Mr. Stanley E. Weinstein, President - *International*

Salary Minimum: $100,000

Functions: Generalist (All)

Industries: Manufacturing, Wholesale, Retail, Finance, Media, Aerospace, Insurance, Software, Healthcare

The Weir Group Inc

401-4 King St W
Toronto, ON M5H 1B6
Canada
(416) 440-1033
Fax: (416) 440-1957
Email: reception@theweirgroup.ca
Web: www.theweirgroup.ca

Summary: Our firm builds high-performance executive teams for users and vendors of computing and telecommunications products and services. Areas of specialization include government, financial services, telecommunications, software and biotechnology. Service offerings include executive search, recruitment process management, management assessment, executive coaching, and leadership development.

Key Contact - Specialty:
Mr. Douglas Weir, President
Ms. Nancy Lismer, Associate - *Information Technology, Professional services, Research & development*

Salary Minimum: $105,000

Functions: Senior Mgmt., Product Dev., Mktg. Mgmt., Sales Mgmt., MIS Mgmt., Systems Dev., Systems Implem.

Industries: Generalist (All), Transportation, Wholesale, Retail, Finance, Mgmt. Consulting, IT Implementation, PSA/ASP, Communications, Government, Aerospace, Insurance, Software, Mfg. SW, Marketing SW, Networking, Comm. SW, Security SW, System SW, Biotech/Life Sciences, Healthcare

D L Weiss & Associates

18201 Von Karman Ave Ste 310
Irvine, CA 92612-1067
(949) 833-5001
(800) 862-7743
Fax: (949) 833-5073
Email: mail@dlweiss.com
Web: www.dlweiss.com

Summary: Our firm provides comprehensive search services and leadership solutions for a select group of clients in strategically related industries conducted in a specialized, yet personalized manner.

Key Contact - Specialty:
Mr. David L. Weiss, President - *Aerospace, Automotive, Manufacturing*
Mr. Neal Green, Vice President

Salary Minimum: $100,000

Functions: Generalist (All)

Industries: Energy, Utilities, Manufacturing, Motor Vehicles, Transportation, Retail, Finance, Services, Media, Communications, Aerospace

The Weldon Group

204 E 38th St
New York, NY 10016-2705
(212) 490-2400
Email: gayle@theweldongroup.com
Web: www.theweldongroup.com

Summary: The Weldon Group is a retained search consultancy specializing in the Market Information Industry, including Market Research, Database Marketing, Sales Information, and Statistical Modeling. Clients include major corporations and research and consulting firms. Assignments range from Director to CEO positions with salary beginning at $150K.

Key Contact - Specialty:
Ms. Gayle Parker, Managing Partner - *Competitive intelligence, Market research*
Mr. William T. Applegate, Partner - *Competitive intelligence, Market research*

Salary Minimum: $150,000

Functions: Mktg. Research

Industries: Generalist (All), Retail, Finance, Services, Hospitality, Media, Communications, Software, Biotech/Life Sciences, Healthcare

Wellington Management Group

1500 John F Kennedy Blvd Ste 605
Philadelphia, PA 19102-1744
(215) 569-8900
Fax: (215) 569-4902
Email: resumes@wellingtonmg.com
Web: www.wellingtonmg.com

Summary: A management-consulting firm that provides retained executive search and organizational assessment services for clients. Our retained search practice focuses on C-level, divisional general management and senior functional leadership (EVP, SVP, VP) assignments for clients varying in size from F100 to early-stage across a wide range of industries.

Key Contact - Specialty:
Mr. Robert S. Campbell, Managing Partner - *C-level, CFOs, Management consulting, Professional services, Telecommunications*
Mr. Matthew J. Simeone, Managing Director - *Consumer, Manufacturing (Management), Marketing, Retail, Supply Chain*

Functions: Generalist (All), Management, Board Members, Senior Mgmt., Sales & Mktg., Finance, CFOs, Mgmt. Consultants, Int'l.

Industries: Generalist (All), Manufacturing, Retail, Finance, Services, Mgmt. Consulting, Supply Chain Mgmt., Communications, Software, Biotech/Life Sciences

Wells Inc

4200 Dublin Rd
Columbus, OH 43221-5005
(614) 876-0651
Fax: (614) 876-4038
Email: mwells@wellsinc.com

Summary: We are a management consulting firm specializing in the identification and selection of executives and key personnel for client organizations ranging in size from sole proprietorships to billion dollar corporations.

Key Contact - Specialty:
Mr. Mark Wells, President

Salary Minimum: $150,000

Functions: Generalist (All)

Industries: Generalist (All), Manufacturing, Drugs Mfg., Medical Devices, Finance, Banking, Accounting, Mgmt. Consulting, Telecoms, Healthcare

Welzig, Lowe & Associates†

761 W Birch Ct
Louisville, CO 80027-1151
(303) 666-4195
Email: fwelzig@comcast.net

Summary: We specialize in management and senior engineers for fast-growth companies in all industries.

Key Contact - Specialty:
Mr. Frank E. Welzig, President - *High technology*
Ms. Geraldine Welzig, Owner

Salary Minimum: $80,000

Functions: Generalist (All)

Industries: Computer Equip., Mgmt. Consulting, New Media, Aerospace, Software

The Wentworth Company Inc

(also known as Wentworth Recruiting)
479 W 6th St Ste 108
San Pedro, CA 90731-2657
(310) 732-2301
(800) 995-9678 x301
Email: johnwentworth@wenteo.com
Web: www.wentco.com

Summary: We specialize in recruiting department management, on-site contract recruiting and mid-range single position searches. Training for recruiters. We offer consulting regarding employment department operations and hiring manager satisfaction.

Key Contact - Specialty:
Mr. John Wentworth, President

Salary Minimum: $45,000

Functions: Generalist (All)

Industries: Generalist (All)

Jude M Werra & Associates LLC

205 Bishops Way Ste 226
Brookfield, WI 53005-6272
(262) 797-9166
Fax: (262) 797-9540
Email: jmwa@execpc.com

Summary: We are HR consultants, working exclusively under retainer in executive search of directors and officers, assisting clients in selection, succession planning, performance management and assessment. The firm's client base includes owner-managed, family-owned and venture capital firms, as well as not-for-profits and publicly-held corporations.

Key Contact - Specialty:
Mr. Jude M. Werra, CMC, President

Salary Minimum: $135,000

Functions: Generalist (All), Management, Board Members, Senior Mgmt., Sales & Mktg., HR Mgmt., Finance, CFOs, Engineering, Non-profits

Industries: Generalist (All), Manufacturing, Food, Bev., Tobacco, Printing, Chemicals, Plastics, Rubber, Metal Products, Machine, Appliance, Motor Vehicles, Venture Cap., Non-profits

Affiliates:
Messett Associates Inc
Miami, FL

Wert & Company Inc†

222 5th Ave Fl 5
New York, NY 10001-7700
(212) 684-2796
Fax: (212) 685-4859
Email: info@wertco.com
Web: www.wertco.com

Summary: We are an executive recruitment and consulting firm specializing in recruiting design innovators for mid to senior executive positions, building award-winning creative teams and consulting on strategic organizational growth. Focused on retained search, we represent dynamic brands across a diverse range of industry from entertainment, television, fashion and retail to architecture, design, academia, interactive, and publishing.

Key Contact - Specialty:
Ms. Judy Wert, President - *Design, Marketing*

Salary Minimum: $85,000

Functions: Specialized Svcs.

Industries: Retail, Architectural Svcs., Media, Advertising, Publishing, New Media, Broadcast, Film, Communications, Digital

AT Wertheimer Inc

99 Main St
Nyack, NY 10960-3109
(845) 947-1120
Fax: (845) 947-8253
Email: online@atwertheimer.com
Web: www.atwertheimer.com

Summary: We are an executive search firm, which provides recruitment services for banking and financial professionals. Our specialized areas of recruitment include: HR; sales, trading and research (equity); IT (MIS and CIOs) and public speaking.

Key Contact - Specialty:
Ms. Amy S. Toneatti, Executive Recruiter - *Human resources*

Salary Minimum: $60,000

Functions: HR Mgmt., Finance, IT

Industries: Finance

Wesley, Brown & Bartle Company Inc

152 Madison Ave Fl 20
New York, NY 10016-5424
(212) 684-6900
Fax: (212) 889-8597
Email: info@wbbusa.com
Web: www.wbbusa.com

Summary: A pioneer in management diversity recruitment and the originator of strategic pipelining, our mission has always been to induce and court across the threshold diverse high performers, inclusive of women, military and people of color, for opportunities within the Fortune 500, academia and the non-profit sector.

Key Contact - Specialty:
Mr. Kenneth Arroyo Roldan, Chief Executive Officer
Mr. Wesley Poriotis, Chairman - *Telecommunications*
Ms. Barbara Mendez-Tucker, Senior Parnter - *Manufacturing*
Mr. Jeff Greene, Senior Partner - *Diversity, Executives, Financial services, Manufacturing, Retail*

Salary Minimum: $80,000

Functions: Board Members, Middle Mgmt., Plant Mgmt., Mktg. Mgmt., PR, MIS Mgmt., Minorities/Diversity

Industries: Paper, Drugs Mfg., Consumer Elect., Finance, Advertising, Telecoms

Western Management Consultants

(a World Search Group company)
2000-1188 Georgia St W
Georgia Place
Vancouver, BC V6E 4A2
Canada
(604) 687-0391
Email: vancouver@wmc.bc.ca
Web: www.wmc.ca

Summary: We specialize in executive search, strategic planning, human recources, management assessment, and coaching.

Key Contact - Specialty:
Mr. Brian M. Morrison
Mr. Gerry Humphries
Ms. Tazeem Nathoo
Mr. Richard Savage

Salary Minimum: $80,000

Functions: Generalist (All)

Industries: Generalist (All)

Branches:
800-333 5 Ave SW
British Petroleums Building
Calgary, AB T2P 3B6
Canada
(403) 531-8200
Fax: (403) 531-8218
Email: calgary@wmc.ca
Key Contact - Specialty:
Mr. Allen Snart

400-4 King St W
Toronto, ON M5H 1B6
Canada
(416) 362-6863
Fax: (416) 362-0761
Email: toronto@wmc.ca
Key Contact - Specialty:
Mr. George Toner
Mr. Jim Carlisle

Western Technical Resources

15890 Viewfield Rd
Monte Sereno, CA 95030-3139
(408) 358-8533
(800) 600-5351
Fax: (800) 600-8970
Email: bmw@wtrusa.com
Web: www.wtrusa.com

Summary: We are a temp placement, staffing and consulting firm limited to the engineering and computer disciplines.

Key Contact - Specialty:
Mr. Bruce Weinstein, Principal

Salary Minimum: $50,000

Functions: Generalist (All), Automation, Systems Dev., Systems Implem., R&D, Engineering

Industries: Generalist (All), New Media, Telecoms, Aerospace, Software, Biotech/Life Sciences

The Westminster Group Inc

38 Congdon St
Providence, RI 02906-1352
(401) 273-9300
Fax: (401) 273-6951

Summary: Experienced executive search consultants working in most industries and functions on senior management and board of directors search. Retained search only.

Key Contact - Specialty:
Mr. James King, Founder & Managing Partner - *Financial services, Manufacturing, Transportation*
Ms. Karen Cox, Senior Vice President - *Financial services, Human resources, Manufacturing*
Mr. James Carrington, Senior Vice President - *Business development, Market research, Marketing, Sales*

Salary Minimum: $125,000

Functions: Generalist (All)

Industries: Generalist (All), Manufacturing, Transportation, Finance, Services, Communications, Packaging, Insurance, Healthcare, Non-Classifiable

The Westwood Group†

3737 Glenwood Ave Ste 100
Raleigh, NC 27612-5515
(919) 573-6130
Web: www.westwoodgp.com

Summary: Healthcare executive search firm specializing in the managed care industry. Primary focus is director to senior vice president level positions.

Key Contact - Specialty:
Mr. Mark Freifeld, Executive Director

Functions: Generalist (All)

Industries: Healthcare

S J Wexler Associates Inc

1120 Avenue of the Americas Fl 4
New York, NY 10036-6700
(212) 626-6599
Fax: (212) 626-6598
Email: sjwexler@earthlink.net

Summary: We specialize in placing human resources and communications executives in the mid-and senior management levels.

Key Contact - Specialty:
Ms. Suzanne Wexler, President - *Human resources*

Salary Minimum: $85,000

Functions: HR Mgmt.

Industries: Generalist (All), Communications

Wheeler Associates

30 Surf Rd Ste 30A
Westport, CT 06880-6733
(203) 454-1632
Fax: (203) 454-3380
Email: ctara@wheelerassociates.com
Web: www.wheelerassociates.com

Summary: We are a focused boutique specializing in leading edge technology executives, consultants and business leaders. Specialty in Internet and eBusiness development.

Key Contact - Specialty:
Ms. Susan Tracy-Wheeler, Partner - *Consulting, Human resources*
Ms. Tess Lander, Senior Vice President
Ms. Mary C. Eagan, Recruiter

Salary Minimum: $125,000

Functions: Board Members, Product Dev., Sales & Mktg., HR Mgmt., CFOs, IT, Engineering, Mgmt. Consultants

Industries: Software

Wheeler, Moore & Elam Company

3449 Sheffield Cir
Plano, TX 75075-3437
(972) 567-5413
Fax: (972) 867-8591
Email: drmark@msn.com

Summary: We are a comprehensive, retained national search firm with in-depth research capabilities. A general search practice with broad-based expertise in middle and senior management assignments.

Key Contact - Specialty:
Dr. Mark H. Moore, Partner
Mr. Robert W. Elam, Partner

Salary Minimum: $60,000

Functions: Generalist (All)

Industries: Generalist (All), Energy, Utilities, Oil & Gas, Food, Bev., Tobacco, Drugs Mfg., Medical Devices, Machine, Appliance, Motor Vehicles, Finance, Healthcare

Victor White International (VWI)†

PO Box 3318
Laguna Hills, CA 92654-3318
(949) 380-4800
Fax: (949) 380-7477
Email: vic@victorwhite.com
Web: www.victorwhite.com

Summary: Our firm is a medical research recruitment firm. Our firm also assists established medical firms seeking technology or specialist in specific technologies. Our strength lies with our expertise in medical early stage technology/startup companies, along with our experience in the industry in general..

Key Contact - Specialty:
Mr. Victor Chapa, Managing Partner
Ms. Kate Maurina, Vice President, Technical Recruitment - *Clinical, Marketing*
Ms. Susan Williams, Director, Research
Mr. Diarmuid Ryan, Operations Manager & Web Development
Mr. Gary Davis, Vice President, Tech Transf & Sr Recruit

Salary Minimum: $90,000

Functions: Management, Board Members, Senior Mgmt., Middle Mgmt., Automation, Healthcare

Industries: Manufacturing, Drugs Mfg., Medical Devices, Plastics, Rubber, Computer Equip., Electronic, Elec. Components, Invest. Banking, Venture Cap., Pharm Svcs., Mgmt. Consulting, HR Services, Telecoms, Government, Insurance, Software, Biotech/Life Sciences, Healthcare

White, Roberts & Stratton Inc

211 E Ontario St Ste 1850
Chicago, IL 60611-3598
(312) 644-5554
Fax: (312) 644-4853
Email: wrsinc2975@aol.com
Web: www.wrssearch.com

Summary: We are functional and industry generalist. Our searches are for director and above level positions. Our largest practice areas are finance/accounting, HR, marketing, general management and operations (manufacturing, distribution, supply chain and retail). Our specialty is diversity search.

Salary Minimum: $100,000

Functions: Generalist (All)

Industries: Manufacturing, Retail, Finance, Services, Accounting, Mgmt. Consulting, HR Services, Hospitality

The Whitefox Group

1837 NW 156th Ave
Beaverton, OR 97006-5666
(503) 533-5311
Email: info@whitefoxgroup.com
Web: www.whitefoxgroup.com

Summary: We specialize in recruiting and executive search for mid-level to senior management in the following areas: finance/accounting, HR, IT and nonprofits (executive directors and development directors).

Key Contact - Specialty:
Mr. Peter Wendel, President - *Accounting, CFOs, Finance, Human resources, Non-profit*

Salary Minimum: $40,000

Functions: Management

Industries: Services, Non-profits, Accounting, HR Services, Advertising

Whitehead Mann

(a Whitehead Mann Group company)
280 Park Ave Fl 25E
New York, NY 10017-1275
(212) 894-8300
Email: usa@wmann.com
Web: www.wmann.com

Summary: We recruit, evaluate and develop world class executive talent. We provide an integrated range of leadership services including board and senior executive search, executive assessment and executive coaching. Our expertise covers the major business sectors and functions. Meeting the need for corporate diversity is a core value and practice.

Key Contact - Specialty:
Mr. E. Pendleton James, Director, Non-Executive
Ms. Marsha Paske, Recruiter - *Business development*

Salary Minimum: $250,000

Functions: Generalist (All), Board Members, Senior Mgmt., Mktg. Mgmt., Sales Mgmt., CFOs, Cash Mgmt., MIS Mgmt., Minorities/Diversity

Industries: Generalist (All), Manufacturing, Retail, Finance, Services, Media, Government, Aerospace, Real Estate, Software, Biotech/Life Sciences

Branches:
1 International Pl Ste 1100
Boston, MA 02110-2618
(617) 598-1200
Fax: (617) 261-9697
Email: usa@wmann.com
Key Contact - Specialty:
Mr. Durant A. Hunter, President & Chief Executive Officer - *Senior management*

Whitehouse Pimms

13455 Noel Rd Ste 1000
Dallas, TX 75240-6814
(972) 774-4468
Web: www.whitehousepimms.com

Summary: We recruit for select opportunities with premier management consulting and technology services clients.

Key Contact - Specialty:
Mr. Mark E. Rich, Vice President
Mr. Ralph P. Stow, Vice President
Mr. David B. Rich, Vice President
Mr. Steven K. Boykin, Vice President

Salary Minimum: $120,000

Functions: Generalist (All)

Industries: Mgmt. Consulting, IT Implementation

The WhiteRock Group LLC†

145 W 57th St Fl 9
New York, NY 10019-2220
(212) 258-2780
Fax: (212) 258-2784
Email: gdolfino@whiterockgroup.com
Web: www.whiterockgroup.com

Summary: The WhiteRock Group offers a complete suite of specialized professional staffing, executive search and other human capital solutions worldwide to companies in the financial services industry.

Key Contact - Specialty:
Mr. Gustavo G. Dolfino, BBA, MBA, President - *Boards of Directors, Capital markets, CEOs, Executives, Presidents*
Mr. Paul Gravelle, BS,JD, MBA, Managing Director - *Asset management, Banking (Investment), Boards of Directors, Brokerage, Competitive intelligence*
Mr. Brendan O'Brien, BS, MBA, Managing Director - *Capital markets, Derivatives, Financial services, Securities, Wall Street*

Salary Minimum: $500,000

Functions: Management, Board Members, Senior Mgmt., Middle Mgmt., Finance, Cash Mgmt., M&A, Risk Mgmt., Mgmt. Consultants, Minorities/Diversity

Industries: Finance, Banking, Invest. Banking, Brokers, Venture Cap., Mutual/Hedge Funds, Misc. Financial

Whitney Group

850 3rd Ave
New York, NY 10022-6222
(212) 508-3500
Fax: (212) 508-3589
Email: recruiter@whitneygroup.com
Web: www.whitneygroup.com

Summary: We are a specialist firm with core competencies in financial services industry. Specialties include: global banking & finance, global markets, global research, asset management and insurance/actuarial.

Key Contact - Specialty:
Mr. Gary S. Goldstein, Chief Executive Officer & President
Mr. Jeffrey T. Sussman, Chief Financial & Operating Officer
Ms. Alicia C. Lazaro, Managing Director

Salary Minimum: $150,000

Functions: Senior Mgmt., Risk Mgmt.

Industries: Finance, Banking, Invest. Banking, Brokers, Venture Cap., Mutual/Hedge Funds, Misc. Financial, Real Estate

Branches:
101 Federal St Ste 1900
Boston, MA 02110-1861
(617) 342-7332
Fax: (617) 342-7265
Key Contact - Specialty:
Ms. Ellen Heller, Managing Director

2005 Market St Ste 2340
Philadelphia, PA 19103-7015
(215) 568-5363
Fax: (215) 568-5365
Key Contact - Specialty:
Mr. Jeffrey Bell, Managing Director

Whitridge Associates Inc†

744 E Squantum St
Quincy, MA 02171-1253
(617) 472-2292
Fax: (617) 773-5521

Email: j.cerri@whitridge.com
Web: www.whitridge.com

Summary: Information Technology and Software Engineering staffing services. Supplemental Staffing/Consulting, Contingent/Executive Search.

Key Contact - Specialty:
Mr. Kevin Grassa, President & Chief Executive Officer - *Financial services, Information Technology, Management, Staffing*
Mr. John Cerri, Partner, Search Division - *Information Systems, Information Technology*

Functions: IT, MIS Mgmt.

Industries: Generalist (All), Retail, Finance, Services, Government, Insurance, Software, Biotech/Life Sciences, Healthcare

The Whittaker Group Inc

PO Box 2993
Ann Arbor, MI 48106-2993
(734) 475-9300
Fax: (866) 740-1395
Email: mwhittaker@wgsearch.com
Web: www.wgsearch.com

Summary: Our firm provides retained recruiting and executive search services exclusively within the healthcare specialty. Our referral-based practice has been built through reputation, integrity and personal commitment. Our clients include hospitals, health care organizations, consulting firms, home health, managed care and physician group practices.

Key Contact - Specialty:
Mrs. Michelle A. Whittaker-McCracken, CPC, SPHR, Healthcare Managing Partner - *Healthcare*
Ms. Irene Yasenetskaya, CPC, Director - *Healthcare*
Mr. Robert McCracken, Director

Salary Minimum: $60,000

Functions: Management, Senior Mgmt., Middle Mgmt., Healthcare, Health Admin., Finance, CFOs, Budgeting

Industries: Generalist (All), Finance, Misc. Financial, Healthcare, Hospitals, Long-term/Home Care, Dental

Whittlesey & Associates Inc

159 Chattooga Run
Hendersonville, NC 28739-8109
(828) 697-7373
Email: jimhogg@searchleaders.com

Summary: Primary focus is on the identification and recruitment of dynamic executive leadership for small to medium size companies. Firm also has the expertise and passion for helping management build high performance sales teams. Will only work with organizations that have strong core values and desire to be industry leaders. Clients are a Who's Who of American Industry.

Key Contact - Specialty:
Mr. James G. Hogg, Jr., President - *CEOs, Change management, Competitive intelligence, Organizational development, Senior management*

Salary Minimum: $100,000

Functions: Senior Mgmt., Product Dev., Mktg. Research, Sales Mgmt.

Industries: Generalist (All), Manufacturing, Food, Bev., Tobacco, Paper, Chemicals, Soap, Perf., Cosmtcs., Medical Devices, Misc. Mfg., Consumer Goods, Services, Mgmt. Consulting, Inst./Industrial Food Svc.

The Whyte Group Inc†

5214 Parkway Dr
Chevy Chase, MD 20815-6620
(301) 657-3970
Fax: (301) 657-5076
Email: rwhyte@thewhytegroup.com
Web: www.thewhytegroup.com

Summary: We are a well-established firm whose principal goal is to assist clients in obtaining and sustaining the competitive edge. Our focus is in marketing, HRD and general management in the hospitality, banking and IT industries.

Key Contact - Specialty:
Mr. Roger J. Whyte, President
Ms. Deborah McCarthy, Senior Vice President - *Construction, General management*
Ms. Kathy Brooks, Senior Associate - *General management*

Salary Minimum: $50,000

Functions: Senior Mgmt., Middle Mgmt., Healthcare, Advertising, Direct Mktg., Customer Svc., Staffing, CFOs, MIS Mgmt., Mgmt. Consultants

Industries: Construction, Drugs Mfg., Medical Devices, Banking, Services, Pharm Svcs., Accounting, Mgmt. Consulting, HR Services, Hospitality, Advertising, Biotech/Life Sciences

Daniel Wier & Associates

251 S Lake Ave Ste 930
Pasadena, CA 91101-4873
(626) 356-1725
Fax: (626) 356-2285
Email: dancwier@aol.com

Summary: We have significant experience in placement of director and senior management in profit and not-for-profit sector. Personal attention is given to every assignment. Documented exceptional placement results. We have a global specialty in human capital consulting including executive compensation, broad base pay, etc.

Key Contact - Specialty:
Mr. Daniel C. Wier, President & Chief Executive Officer - *Professional services*

Salary Minimum: $75,000

Functions: Generalist (All), Board Members, Senior Mgmt., Mfg., Sales & Mktg., HR Mgmt., Finance, Mgmt. Consultants

Industries: Energy, Utilities, Food, Bev., Tobacco, Misc. Mfg., Banking, Invest. Banking, Mgmt. Consulting, HR Services, Higher Ed.

Wilcox, Miller & Nelson†

100 Howe Ave Ste 155N
Sacramento, CA 95825-8200
(916) 977-3700
Fax: (916) 977-3733
Email: wilcoxcareer@wilcoxcareer.com
Web: www.wilcoxcareer.com

Summary: We provide premier executive search, consulting and outplacement services to the public and private sectors, for-profit and not-for-profit industries. We create value for our clients and candidates by providing an exceptional customer experience in talent acquisition, retention and transition.

Key Contact - Specialty:
Ms. Diane D. Miller, President - *Associations, Boards of Directors, C-level, Non-profit, Senior management*
Mr. Raymond Nelson, Vice President - *C-level, Finance, Healthcare, Senior management*
Mr. Fred T. Wilcox, Founder - *Financial, Healthcare*

Mr. Charles Dalldorf, Vice President, Public Sector Search - *Associations, Government, Public sector*
Ms. Marilyn L. Nelson, Vice President, Car. Mgmt.& Outplacement
Ms. Lauren Morgan, SPHR, Manager, Business & Administrator
Ms. Blanca Lopez-Topper, Client Services Manager
Mr. Tomm Hoffman, Vice President, Public Safety Sear
Mr. Robert C. Greeley, Consulting Associate - *Administration, Boards of Directors, CEOs, Investment, Management*

Salary Minimum: $50,000

Functions: Generalist (All), Management

Industries: Banking, Non-profits, Legal, Accounting, Mgmt. Consulting, HR Services, Higher Ed., Advertising, Government, Healthcare

The Wilkie Group International
400-90 Adelaide St W
Buss Building
Toronto, ON M5H 3V9
Canada
(416) 214-1979
Fax: (416) 214-1980
Email: careers@wilkiegroup.com
Web: www.wilkiegroup.com

Summary: We are a mid-size firm who provide executive search and selection services.

Key Contact - Specialty:
Mr. Glenn A. Wilkie, President & Chief Executive Officer

Salary Minimum: $120,000

Functions: Generalist (All)

Industries: Food, Bev., Tobacco, Textiles, Apparel, Printing, Chemicals, Retail, Invest. Banking, Mgmt. Consulting, Entertainment, Publishing, Insurance

The Willard Group†
3575 Autumnleaf Cres
Mississauga, ON L5L 1K6
Canada
(905) 607-5777
(905) 607-4411
Email: thewillardgroup@rogers.com

Summary: We specialize in the recruitment and placement of professionals and executives within the private sector. Integrity and confidentiality are our hallmarks.

Key Contact - Specialty:
Ms. Julie Willard, President - *Sales*
Mrs. Jocelyne Willard, Executive Recruiter

Salary Minimum: $50,000

Functions: Generalist (All), Management, Mfg., Materials, Sales & Mktg., HR Mgmt., Engineering, Graphic Designers

Industries: Generalist (All), Construction, Manufacturing, Food, Bev., Tobacco, Lumber, Furniture, Printing, Plastics, Rubber, Metal Products, Motor Vehicles, Transportation, Architectural Svcs., HR Services, Engineering Svcs., Advertising, Packaging

Robert J Williams & Associates
1621 S Garden St
Palatine, IL 60067-7537
(847) 397-9205
Fax: (847) 397-9204
Email: bob@rjwassoc.com
Web: rjwassoc.com

Summary: Generalist, retained executive search firm serving all industries and most executive positions with particular expertise in financial positions in manufacturing and financial services industries.

Key Contact - Specialty:
Mr. Robert Williams, President

Salary Minimum: $120,000

Functions: Generalist (All), Senior Mgmt., Sales & Mktg., HR Mgmt., Finance, CFOs, IT

Industries: Generalist (All), Construction, Manufacturing, Finance, Services, Hospitality, Insurance, Real Estate, Biotech/Life Sciences, Healthcare

Williams Executive Search Inc
90 S 7th St
Wells Fargo Center
Minneapolis, MN 55402-3903
(612) 339-2900
Fax: (612) 305-5040
Email: dubbs@williams-exec.com
Web: www.williams-exec.com

Summary: We are a highly regarded firm representing clients requiring national searches. Recent searches include: CEO, CFO, CTO, CIO, VP of Development, SVP of Sales & Marketing, VP of Finance, several senior & director level sales, marketing, business development positions and several corporate controller positions.

Key Contact - Specialty:
Mr. Bill Dubbs, President
Ms. Diane Fewer, Executive Search Consultant

Salary Minimum: $100,000

Functions: Generalist (All), Senior Mgmt., Sales & Mktg., HR Mgmt., Finance, CFOs, IT

Industries: Manufacturing, Medical Devices, Venture Cap., Misc. Financial, New Media, Telecoms, Software, Healthcare

Williams Roth & Hanley Inc
(formerly known as Williams, Roth & Krueger Inc)
7 S Lincoln St
Hinsdale, IL 60521-3464
(630) 887-7771
Email: wrkinc@aol.com

Summary: We specialize in upper-mid and senior-level searches in all industries and functions. We have extensive experience in general management, sales/marketing, operations, engineering, finance and technical. We have specific expertise in banking/financial services, electronics, plastics, electromechanical, computer hardware/software/services, telecom and consumer products.

Key Contact - Specialty:
Mr. Alan P. Hanley, Partner
Mr. Robert J. Roth, Partner

Salary Minimum: $100,000

Functions: Generalist (All)

Industries: Energy, Utilities, Construction, Manufacturing, Finance, Legal, Equip Svcs., Law Enforcement, Telecoms, Defense, Software

Williger & Associates
290 Lake Vista Dr Ste 1000
Chesterton, IN 46304-8845
(219) 926-9898
Email: dwilliger@comcast.net
Web: www.willigerassociates.com

Summary: We are a boutique firm with national reach. We serve our clients as an advocate of their recruitment objectives with the utmost

professionalism. Please contact David Williger to learn how we can help you achieve your recruitment goals.

Key Contact - Specialty:
Mr. David Williger, Managing Partner - *Advertising, Financial services, Healthcare, Legal, Management consulting*
Ms. Carmen Morales, Partner - *Banking, Consulting, Financial services, Professional services, Senior management*
Mr. Peter Pajakowski, Associate - *Accounting (General), Actuarial, Business to business, Professional services, Securities*
Mr. Ronald Pejril, Associate - *Banking, Financial services, Legal, Management consulting, Wall Street*

Salary Minimum: $100,000

Functions: Management, Senior Mgmt., Middle Mgmt., Production, Purchasing, Healthcare, HR Mgmt., CFOs, Mgmt. Consultants, Legal

Industries: Generalist (All), Manufacturing, Finance, Services, Media, Insurance, Real Estate, Healthcare

Wills Consulting Associates Inc
2 Sound View Dr Ste 100
Greenwich, CT 06830-6471
(203) 622-4930
Fax: (203) 622-4931
Email: jcw@wca-search.com
Web: www.wca-search.com

Summary: We have a long history of success in recruiting public relations and communications professionals for Fortune 500 corporations, professional services firms, public relations agencies and associations. The founder brings to each engagement pre-search experience in public relations, corporate communications and management consulting.

Key Contact - Specialty:
Mr. James C. Wills, President - *Communications, Public relations*

Salary Minimum: $120,000

Functions: PR

Industries: Generalist (All)

The Wilmington Group†
(an affiliate of MRI)
7040 Wrightsville Ave Ste 201
Wilmington, NC 28403-3610
(910) 256-1056
Fax: (910) 256-1057
Email: kirks@wilmingtongroup.com
Web: www.wilmingtongroup.com

Summary: We are a global leader in executive recruitment, conducting thousands of senior-level searches for exclusive clients worldwide. Based in 5 offices across North America and networked with partners in Europe and Asia, we work closely with clients and candidates to craft successful human capital strategies and solutions.

Key Contact - Specialty:
Mr. Kirk Sears, President - *Accounting, CEOs, CFOs, Finance, Manufacturing (Management)*
Mr. Richard Babb, Managing Partner - *Pharmaceutical*
Mr. Brian McMerty, MBA, CPA, Managing Partner - *Information Technology, Pharmaceutical*

Salary Minimum: $60,000

Functions: Generalist (All), Management, Senior Mgmt., Middle Mgmt., Mfg., Healthcare, Sales Mgmt., IT, Engineering, Int'l.

Industries: Generalist (All), Manufacturing, Textiles, Apparel, Chemicals, Drugs Mfg.,

Medical Devices, Metal Products, Machine, Appliance, Motor Vehicles, Pharm Svcs., Legal, Accounting, IT Implementation, Media, Advertising, Publishing, Telecoms, Government, Packaging, Software, Biotech/Life Sciences, Healthcare

J C Wilson Associates

50 California St Ste 1500
San Francisco, CA 94111-4612
(415) 277-5488
(415) 990-5388
Fax: (415) 277-5490
Email: john@jcwilsonassociates.com
Web: www.jcwilsonassociates.com

Summary: We are a boutique executive search firm specializing in the recruitment of CFOs and senior executives for the financial services sector. Amongst our principals, we have extensive recruiting experience at top-tier search firms and in the financial services sector.

Key Contact - Specialty:
Mr. John C. Wilson, President & Chief Executive Officer
Mr. Seiki Murono, Managing Director - *Financial services*
Ms. Vickie Johnston, Consultant, Financial Services - *Asset management, Banking (Investment)*
Mr. Charles H. Adams, Managing Director
Ms. Wendy Gries, Senior Manager, Client Services - *CFOs, Financial services, Senior management*

Salary Minimum: $150,000

Functions: Management, CFOs, Taxes, M&A, IT, Mgmt. Consultants, Int'l.

Industries: Semiconductors, Finance, Services, Mgmt. Consulting, Hospitality, Communications, Insurance, Software, Biotech/Life Sciences, Healthcare

Patricia Wilson Associates

(a Penrhyn International company)
425 Market St Ste 2200
San Francisco, CA 94105-2434
(415) 984-3112
Fax: (415) 984-3150
Email: patty@patriciawilson.net
Web: www.patriciawilson.net

Summary: We are a retained executive search firm. We specialize in conducting senior-level searches for GMs and their key reports across almost all industries.

Key Contact - Specialty:
Ms. Patricia Wilson, Managing Partner

Salary Minimum: $300,000

Functions: Management

Industries: Generalist (All), Non-profits, Legal

Wilson Smith Associates

PO Box 12463
Mill Creek, WA 98082-0463
(425) 486-2900
Email: kennedyinfo@wilsonsmith.com
Web: www.wilsonsmith.com

Summary: We provide On-Demand Recruiting Services (ODRS) when an organization needs to hire a team of talented technical pros. Our services can be delivered either as an external resource "virtually," or as an embedded "onsite internal resource."

Key Contact - Specialty:
Mr. Marvin Smith, Founding Principal

Salary Minimum: $85,000

Functions: Generalist (All)

Industries: Construction, Manufacturing, Services, Media, Communications, Government, Aerospace, Packaging, Software, Biotech/Life Sciences

Wimbledon Group, Inc.†

3009 Madison Ave Suite I 308
Boulder, CO 80303-2041
(720) 234-4180
Fax: (303) 604-6281
Email: jack.welber@wimbledongroup.com
Web: www.wimbledongroup.com

Summary: Ours is a retained search firm focusing on recruiting physicians and related professionals in the pharmaceutical industry. Specialties include but are not limited to oncology, immunology, and neuroscience.

Key Contact - Specialty:
Mr. Jack N. Welber, President & Executive Recruiter
Mr. Andrew Meseck, Vice President

Salary Minimum: $150,000

Functions: Physicians

Industries: Biotech/Life Sciences

Wine-Pro†

PO Box 1776
Rohnert Park, CA 94927-1776
(707) 571-0400
Fax: (707) 576-1320
Email: info@winepro.com
Web: www.winepro.com

Summary: We have many years of successful experience hiring wine industry personnel. We place winemakers, vineyard managers, financial executives, CEO's and International professionals.

Key Contact - Specialty:
Ms. Donna Parker, President

Salary Minimum: $25,000

Functions: Senior Mgmt.

Industries: Generalist (All)

Winguth, Grant & Co

(a Taplow Group company)
505 Montgomery St Fl 11
San Francisco, CA 94111-2585
(415) 283-1970
Email: sgrant@winguthgrant.com
Web: www.winguthgrant.com

Summary: We have a generalist practice which focuses on emerging growth companies and larger corporations going through rapid change. In practice our clients are private, public and not-for-profit ranging from start-up to a billion in revenues.

Key Contact - Specialty:
Ms. Susan G. Grant, President

Salary Minimum: $100,000

Functions: Generalist (All)

Industries: Manufacturing, Transportation, Non-profits, Telecoms, Software

Winston Personnel Group

253 Executive Park Blvd
Winston Salem, NC 27103-1503
(336) 768-4040
Fax: (336) 765-1865
Email: wpgroup@wpgroup.com
Web: www.wpgroup.com

Summary: We are professional recruiters with expertise in engineering, accounting, IT, office support, payroll, clerical temp and industrial temporaries.

Key Contact - Specialty:
Ms. Shirley Shouse, President
Ms. Cannon Simpson, Vice President

Functions: Admin. Svcs., Sales & Mktg., HR Mgmt., Finance, IT

Industries: Generalist (All), Manufacturing, Finance, Services, Communications, Software

Winston Search Inc

2631 Moore Ln
Fort Collins, CO 80526-2161
(970) 494-0400
Fax: (970) 494-0102
Email: tom@winstonsearch.com
Web: www.winstonsearch.com

Summary: We conduct board, senior management and technical search for clients. We also have a mergers & acquisitions division and outplacement for our clients that desire this added value.

Key Contact - Specialty:
Mr. Thomas Winston, President - *Senior management, Technical*
Mr. T.W. Winston, Corporate Recruitment & Research - *Telecommunications*

Salary Minimum: $50,000

Functions: Management, Board Members, Senior Mgmt., Middle Mgmt., Sales & Mktg., Engineering, Int'l.

Industries: Manufacturing, Motor Vehicles, Computer Equip., Finance, Legal, Accounting, Mgmt. Consulting, HR Services, Media, Advertising, New Media, Broadcast, Film, Telecoms, Aerospace, Insurance, Software

Winthrop Partners

108 Corporate Park Dr Ste 220
White Plains, NY 10604-3808
(914) 253-8282
Fax: (914) 253-6440
Email: winthrop@winthroppartners.com
Web: www.winthroppartners.com

Summary: We are a generalist firm with practice leaders in marketing, IS, human reources, general management, and financial functions.

Key Contact - Specialty:
Mr. Steven Goldshore, President - *Financial, Human resources, Marketing*
Mr. Vincent Battipaglia, President
Ms. Evelyn Sirena, President

Salary Minimum: $100,000

Functions: Generalist (All), Board Members, Senior Mgmt., HR Mgmt., CFOs, IT

Industries: Food, Bev., Tobacco, Drugs Mfg., Medical Devices, Misc. Mfg., Pharm Svcs., IT Implementation, Publishing, Accounting SW, HR SW, Healthcare

The Wise Group LLC

2490 Black Rock Tpke Ste 290
Fairfield, CT 06825-2400
(203) 650-2449
Fax: (909) 498-9852
Email: brian@wisesearchgroup.com
Web: www.wisesearchgroup.com

Summary: Specializing in marketing in the medical device, pharmaceutical, and biotechnology industries.

Key Contact - Specialty:
Mr. Brian D. Walker, President
Mr. Charles Carino, Managing Director
Mr. Thomas W. Gerrity, Director, Finance Practice

Mr. Michael Bennis, Senior Search Agent
Mr. Joseph Kirkland, Senior Search Agent
Ms. Renee Morabito, Senior Researcher

Salary Minimum: $100,000

Functions: Senior Mgmt., Middle Mgmt., Sales & Mktg.

Industries: Generalist (All), Chemicals, Drugs Mfg., Medical Devices, Pharm Svcs., Communications, Telecoms, Aerospace, Biotech/Life Sciences, Healthcare

Witt/Kieffer

2015 Spring Rd Ste 510
Oak Brook, IL 60523-3903
(630) 990-1370
Fax: (630) 990-1382
Web: www.wittkieffer.com

Summary: We are a large executive recruiting firm that specializes in leadership for health care, education and community service/cultural organizations. We conduct searches for hospitals, health systems, managed care organizations, commercial insurers, and specialty and venture-capital-based companies, as well as for colleges, universities and community service and cultural organizations.

Key Contact - Specialty:
Mr. Jordan M. Hadelman, Chairman & Chief Executive Officer - *Healthcare*
Mr. Dennis Barden, Vice President, Practice Leader - *Education*
Mr. Manny Berger, Senior Vice President - *Education*
Mr. Paul Bohne, Vice President - *Healthcare*
Ms. Sally DelBeccaro, Chief Financial Officer
Mr. Mike Doody, Senior Vice President, Regional Director - *Healthcare*
Ms. Jean Dowdall, Vice President - *Education*
Mr. Carson Dye, Senior Vice President - *Healthcare*
Ms. Kathleen Gillespie, Vice President - *Healthcare*
Ms. Martha Hauser, Senior Vice President, Regional Director - *Healthcare*
Mr. Howard Jessamy, Diversity Practice Leader - *Healthcare*
Ms. Linda Hodges, Vice President - *Information Technology*
Mr. Mike Meyer, Senior Vice President - *Managed care*
Ms. Susan Nalepa, Vice President
Ms. Karen Otto, Vice President - *Healthcare*
Ms. Anna Wharton Phillips, Senior Vice President, Regional Director - *Healthcare*
Mr. Alexander (Sandy) Williams, Vice President - *Healthcare*
Ms. Anne Zenzer, Senior Vice President - *Healthcare*

Salary Minimum: $90,000

Functions: Senior Mgmt., Healthcare, HR Mgmt., CFOs, MIS Mgmt.

Industries: Non-profits, Higher Ed., Insurance, Biotech/Life Sciences, Healthcare, Hospitals, Long-term/Home Care

Branches:
7272 E Indian School Rd Ste 405
Scottsdale, AZ 85251-3951
(480) 603-4700
Fax: (480) 248-1602
Key Contact - Specialty:
Mr. Michael F. Meyer, Senior Vice President

2200 Powell St Ste 890
Emeryville, CA 94608-1879
(510) 420-1370
Fax: (510) 420-0363

Key Contact - Specialty:
Ms. Elaina Spitaels Genser, Senior Vice President, Regional Director

2 Park Plaza Ste 1625
Irvine, CA 92614-8561
(949) 851-5070
Fax: (949) 851-2412
Key Contact - Specialty:
Mr. Jim Gauss, Executive Vice President

3414 Peachtree Rd NE Ste 452
Atlanta, GA 30326-1165
(404) 233-1370
Fax: (404) 261-1371
Key Contact - Specialty:
Mr. Andrew Chastain, Vice President & Regional Director
Mr. Steve Kratz, Vice President

4550 Montgomery Ave Ste 615N
Bethesda, MD 20814-3366
(301) 654-5070
Fax: (301) 654-1318
Key Contact - Specialty:
Ms. Anna Wharton Phillips, Senior Vice President & Reg Director

25 Mall Rd Ste 608
Burlington, MA 01803-4154
(781) 272-8899
Fax: (781) 272-6677
Key Contact - Specialty:
Mr. Emanuel Berger, Senior Vice President

8000 Maryland Ave Ste 1080
Saint Louis, MO 63105-3752
(314) 862-1370
Fax: (314) 727-5662
Key Contact - Specialty:
Dr. Mary Frances Lyons, Senior Vice President & Practice Leader
Ms. Christine Mackey-Ross, Vice President

5420 Lyndon B Johnson Fwy Ste 460
2 Lincoln Center
Dallas, TX 75240-6292
(972) 490-1370
Fax: (972) 490-3472
Key Contact - Specialty:
Mr. Keith Southerland, Executive Vice President

10375 Richmond Ave Ste 1625
Houston, TX 77042-4183
(713) 266-6779
Fax: (713) 266-8133
Key Contact - Specialty:
Ms. Marvene Eastham, Vice President

WJM Associates Inc

201 E 42nd St Rm 1601
New York, NY 10017-5704
(212) 972-7400
(800) 515-8372
Fax: (212) 972-0695
Email: jfinnerty@wjmassoc.com
Web: www.wjmassoc.com

Summary: Our unique executive search process ties assessment and coaching into success on the job. We focus on culture, change and specific performance profiles that match the competencies required of corporations.

Key Contact - Specialty:
Mr. John P. Finnerty, Vice Chairman

Salary Minimum: $150,000

Functions: Management, Sales & Mktg., HR Mgmt., Int'l.

Industries: Generalist (All), Food, Bev., Tobacco, Printing, Finance, Services, Media

Woessner & Associates

222 S 9th St Ste 4050
Minneapolis, MN 55402-3814
(612) 252-9306
Fax: (612) 343-0305
Email: ron@woessner.com
Web: www.woessner.com

Summary: We support the growth and leadership of excellent organizations in a wide range of industries on a national basis.

Key Contact - Specialty:
Mr. Bradford W. Johnson, Vice President
Mr. Ronald T. Woessner, CPA, President
Mr. Greg A. Fouks, Vice President
Ms. Deborah L. Moorre, CPA, Vice President - *Finance, General management, Marketing, Medical, Operations*
Ms. Marisa Hinnenkamp, Associate
Ms. Tamara Daggett, Recruiter
Mr. Shawn P. Woessner, Recruiter

Salary Minimum: $75,000

Functions: Generalist (All)

Industries: Generalist (All)

Wojdula & Associates Ltd

N7645 E Lakeshore Dr Ste 200
Whitewater, WI 53190-4251
(262) 473-3023
Email: search@wojdula.com
Web: www.wojdula.com

Summary: We are a retainer based search firm with specialization in service, manufacturing and distribution companies. We have expertise in all functions at the middle to upper management of client companies.

Key Contact - Specialty:
Mr. Andy Wojdula, President
Mr. Keith Hofmann, Vice President
Ms. Ann Gallagher, Director, Research
Ms. Donna Wojdula, Vice President

Salary Minimum: $75,000

Functions: Generalist (All)

Industries: Construction, Food, Bev., Tobacco, Soap, Perf., Cosmtcs., Machine, Appliance, Wholesale, Venture Cap., Services, Hospitality, Telecoms

DS Wolf Group International

(formerly known as D S Wolf Associates Inc)
330 Madison Ave Rm 2000
New York, NY 10017-5028
(212) 692-9400
Fax: (212) 692-9221
Email: frothberg@dswolf.com

Summary: Specialization in senior level executive search within investment banking, capital markets, sales & trading, corporate banking, prime brokerage, wealth management (private banking, high net worth brokerage, financial advisory), accounting & finance, healthcare, venture capital, consumer goods & services and legal/general counsel appointments.

Key Contact - Specialty:
Mr. David A. Wolf, President

Functions: Generalist (All), Management, Board Members

Industries: Retail, Finance, Banking, Invest. Banking, Brokers, Venture Cap., Mutual/Hedge Funds, Misc. Financial, Legal, Accounting, Biotech/Life Sciences

M Wood Company

135 S La Salle St Ste 4005
Chicago, IL 60603-4811
(312) 368-0633
Fax: (312) 368-5052
Email: resume@mwoodco.com
Web: www.mwoodco.com

Summary: We are a global retained executive search and consulting firm that recruits mid and senior level management executives in various industries. To candidates and clients, we bring industry knowledge and business perspective that is embedded in a consultative process developed over years of helping companies find the right talent for key executive positions.

Key Contact - Specialty:
Mr. John W. Poracky, Partner
Mr. Milton M. Wood, President & Chief Executive Officer

Salary Minimum: $90,000

Functions: Senior Mgmt., Middle Mgmt., Plant Mgmt., Healthcare, Sales & Mktg., Finance, CFOs, MIS Mgmt.

Industries: Generalist (All), Manufacturing, Healthcare

The Wood Group Inc

1550 Utica Ave S Ste 425
Minneapolis, MN 55416-3679
(952) 546-6997
Fax: (952) 546-6743
Email: info@thewoodgroupinc.com
Web: www.thewoodgroupinc.com

Summary: Our partners draw on a broad range of experience, most notably extensive senior line management in both large and small companies. We recognize our most important responsibility is to represent the client company with discretion, insight and professionalism.

Key Contact - Specialty:
Mr. Michael D. Wood, Chairman - *Finance, General management, Marketing*

Salary Minimum: $125,000

Functions: Generalist (All)

Industries: Generalist (All)

Wood-Snodgrass Inc

12980 Metcalf Ave Ste 130
Overland Park, KS 66213-2646
(913) 681-2200
(800) 207-1958
Fax: (913) 647-1201
Email: steve@woodsnodgrass.com
Web: www.woodsnodgrass.com

Summary: Our firm conducts retained search assignments for organizations beginning at the $75k compensation range. Although we are 'generalists,' providing recruiting services to our clients for senior level management (CFOs, COOs, IT, marketing VPs, etc.), we also specialize in executive search consulting for not-for-profit organizations, associations, foundations and institutes. We are members of the American Society of Association Executives (ASAE).

Key Contact - Specialty:
Mr. Stephen E. Snodgrass, Partner
Mr. William M. Wood, Partner

Salary Minimum: $75,000

Functions: Generalist (All), Senior Mgmt.

Industries: Generalist (All), Energy, Utilities, Finance, Non-profits, Mgmt. Consulting, HR Services, Advertising, Publishing, New Media, Telecoms, Healthcare

Woodhouse Associates Inc

1255 Treat Blvd Ste 300
Walnut Creek, CA 94597-7965
(925) 942-0400
Email: kennedy-inquiry@woodhous.com
Web: www.woodhous.com

Summary: Our firm has developed a fresh, innovative approach to the human asset industry. We are not in the business of finding people jobs. Rather, our business is to completely understand our client's environment, then provide aggressive, energetic and viable solutions to drive that client's future.

Key Contact - Specialty:
Mr. Dave Ventura, Manager, Business Development
Mr. Eric Holzheimer, Managing Director
Mr. Jim Rivers, Director, Research & Assets

Functions: Generalist (All), Management, Sales & Mktg., Finance, Hospitality

Industries: Generalist (All)

Bruce G Woods Executive Search

25 Highland Park Vlg Ste 171
Dallas, TX 75205-2789
(214) 522-9888
Email: search1@airmail.net
Web: www.brucegwoodsexecutivesearch.com

Summary: We are a privately owned firm offering professional and personal attention to clientele. Our specialties include: senior level consulting, eBusiness, CRM, supply chain, healthcare, residential mortgage lending and startups.

Key Contact - Specialty:
Mr. Bruce Gilbert Woods, Principal - *Accounting (Big 4), Consulting, Information Technology, Insurance, Managed care*

Salary Minimum: $250,000

Functions: Mgmt. Consultants

Industries: Accounting, Mgmt. Consulting, IT Implementation, Insurance, Real Estate, Healthcare

Woollett Associates

78 Leeds Ct E
Danville, CA 94526-4351
(925) 838-1372
Fax: (925) 838-8829
Email: jwoolletts@aol.com
Web: www.waexecsearch.com

Summary: We partner in building companies through key management placements in technology and venture-backed companies.

Key Contact - Specialty:
Mr. James S. Woollett, President

Salary Minimum: $70,000

Functions: Generalist (All), Management, Mfg., Sales & Mktg., HR Mgmt., Finance, IT, Engineering

Industries: Generalist (All), Computer Equip., Media, Defense, Aerospace, Software

Work&Partners LLC

(formerly known as Work&Partners Executive Search LLC)
701 Westchester Ave Ste 212W
White Plains, NY 10604-3078
(914) 328-2100
Fax: (914) 328-1693
Email: results@workandpartners.com
Web: www.workandpartners.com

Summary: We take a different approach to executive search. We consider the challenge of recruiting, qualifying and closing candidates an executive-level function. Only professionals with years of experience, substantial networks and a mature sense of a company's requirements research and screen prospects. Only they have the ability to find the best people expertly, aggressively and efficiently.

Key Contact - Specialty:
Mr. Alan J. Work, President & Founder
Mr. Jon R. Work, Managing Director - *Computers (Science), Consulting, Financial services, Professional services, Technology*
Ms. Joan Boyle, Director, Research & Operations
Ms. Victoria Jacobson, Director, Administration - *Telecommunications*

Salary Minimum: $150,000

Functions: Senior Mgmt., Sales Mgmt., MIS Mgmt., Mgmt. Consultants

Industries: Finance, Services, Mgmt. Consulting, E-commerce, IT Implementation, Supply Chain Mgmt, Media, Communications, Insurance, Software, Healthcare

Dick Wray & Consultants Inc

3123 Hannan Ln
Soquel, CA 95073-2525
(831) 464-5577
(800) 525-9729
Fax: (800) 525-9697
Email: dick.wray@dickwray.com
Web: www.dickwray.com

Summary: We conduct retained searches for corporate retail restaurant and retail business.

Key Contact - Specialty:
Mr. Dick Wray, President & Chief Executive Officer

Salary Minimum: $50,000

Functions: Generalist (All), Board Members, Mktg. Mgmt., HR Mgmt., Hospitality, Hotel Mgmt., Chefs

Industries: Retail, HR Services, Hospitality, Hotels, Resorts, Clubs, Restaurants, Quick Service Restaurants, Full Service Restaurants, Entertainment

Branches:
2211 Brighton Bay Trl
Jacksonville, FL 32246-4096
(800) 710-9729
Fax: (800) 711-9729
Email: jim.osborn@dickwray.com
Key Contact - Specialty:
Mr. Jim Osborn, Vice President

2479 Peachtree Rd NE Apt 1804
Atlanta, GA 30305-4100
(800) 846-9729
Fax: (800) 953-9729
Email: jim.weber@dickwray.com
Key Contact - Specialty:
Mr. Jim Webber, COO

Janet Wright & Associates Inc (JWA)

300-21 Bedford Rd
Toronto, ON M5R 2J9
Canada
(416) 923-3008
Fax: (416) 923-8311
Email: admin@jwasearch.com
Web: www.jwasearch.com

Summary: Our firm specializes in senior-level recruiting in the public and not-for-profit sectors. Clients include arts and cultural organizations, social service agencies, crown agencies, hospitals,

independent schools, community colleges and universities.

Key Contact - Specialty:
Ms. Janet Wright, Principal

Salary Minimum: $100,000

Functions: Senior Mgmt.

Industries: Services, Non-profits, K-12 Ed., Higher Ed., Government, Healthcare, Hospitals, Long-term/Home Care

WTW Associates Inc

(an IIC company)
201 E 42nd St Rm 2808
New York, NY 10017-5704
(212) 972-6990
Fax: (212) 297-0546
Email: n.mchugh@wtwassociates.com
Web: www.wtwassociates.com

Summary: Our firm has deep roots in the entertainment industry. We have successfully concluded engagements in nearly all facets of business including finance, legal, marketing & sales, strategic planning, HR, IT, operation and general management. In order to insure our clients the greatest access to possible candidates, we limit the number of clients in each industry. Our industry expertise includes entertainment, new media, digital media and professional services.

Key Contact - Specialty:
Mr. Warren T. Wasp, Jr., President - *Communications, Entertainment, New media*
Ms. Nancy W. Lombardi, Senior Vice President - *Communications, Finance, Human resources*
Mr. Thomas P. Schneider, Senior Vice President - *Entertainment, New media, Publishing*

Salary Minimum: $100,000

Functions: Generalist (All), Senior Mgmt.

Industries: Legal, HR Services, Entertainment, Media, Publishing, New Media, Broadcast, Film, Digital, Software, Entertainment SW

Wyatt Jaffe

4999 France Ave S Ste 260
Minneapolis, MN 55410-2111
(612) 285-2858
Fax: (612) 285-2786
Email: info@wyattjaffe.com
Web: www.wyattjaffe.com

Summary: We are known for engaging high-level management talent that the marketplace perceives as unattainable.

Key Contact - Specialty:
Mr. Mark Jaffe, President

Salary Minimum: $180,000

Functions: Generalist (All)

Industries: Generalist (All), Communications, Software

Wyndham Mills International Inc[†]

2309 W Cone Blvd Ste 200
Greensboro, NC 27408-4047
(336) 275-2622
Fax: (336) 275-3811
Email: contactus@wyndmill.com
Web: www.wyndmill.com

Summary: We are search consultants providing executive, managerial and professional level search services to our client organizations.

Key Contact - Specialty:
Mr. Cabell M. Poindexter, Chief Executive Officer & President - *Energy, Human resources, Utilities*

Mr. Clay Poindexter, Senior Vice President - *Energy, Human resources, Risk management, Utilities*
Mr. Rich Fisher, Director - *Energy, Manufacturing, Sales, Utilities*

Functions: Management, Board Members, Senior Mgmt., Middle Mgmt., Mfg., Plant Mgmt., Packaging, Finance, CFOs, Engineering

Industries: Energy, Utilities, Construction, Manufacturing, Food, Bev., Tobacco, Paper, Paints, Petro. Products, Metal Products, Finance, Banking, Invest. Banking, Services, Equip Svcs., Haz. Waste, Packaging

The Wynkoop Group

2796 Long Lake Dr NE
Roswell, GA 30075-5433
(770) 993-3779
Email: marywynkoop@thewynkoopgroup.com
Web: www.thewynkoopgroup.com

Summary: We provide executive search services for healthcare organizations seeking mid and senior level healthcare executives.

Key Contact - Specialty:
Ms. Mary Wynkoop, President - *Healthcare*

Salary Minimum: $65,000

Functions: Management, Senior Mgmt., Middle Mgmt., Healthcare

Industries: Pharm Svcs., Biotech/Life Sciences, Healthcare, Hospitals, Long-term/Home Care, Dental, Physical Therapy, Occupational Therapy, Women's

Xagas & Associates

1127 Fargo Blvd Ste 1
Geneva, IL 60134-2949
(630) 232-7044

Summary: We specialize in the recruitment of individual contributors, middle managers and senior executives in world-class quality initiatives.

Key Contact - Specialty:
Mr. Steve Xagas, President & Founder - *Operations, Quality*

Salary Minimum: $65,000

Functions: Senior Mgmt., Middle Mgmt., Automation, Materials Plng., Mktg. Mgmt., Benefits, Finance, MIS Mgmt., Engineering, Mgmt. Consultants

Industries: Food, Bev., Tobacco, Soap, Perf., Cosmtcs., Drugs Mfg., Medical Devices, Plastics, Rubber, Metal Products, Machine, Appliance, Motor Vehicles, Computer Equip., Consumer Elect., Test, Measure Equip., Mgmt. Consulting, HR Services, Defense, Aerospace, Software

Xavier Associates Inc

266 Main St Ste 24
Medfield, MA 02052-2056
(508) 359-8294
Fax: (508) 359-5902
Email: bmaynard@gattiihr.com
Web: www.xavierassociates.com

Summary: We recruit for all disciplines in all industries on a retained basis. Our research company can also be engaged to provide customized research to client companies and recruiting firms. Our firm is known for its diversity search capability.

Key Contact - Specialty:
Mr. Robert D. Gatti, President
Mrs. Betty Maynard, Vice President, Operations

Salary Minimum: $70,000

Functions: Generalist (All)

Industries: Generalist (All)

XEC Solutions Inc[†]

5655 Lindero Canyon Rd Ste 521
Westlake Village, CA 91362-4048
(818) 991-1400
Fax: (818) 575-8099
Email: xecsolutions@xecsolutions.com
Web: www.xecsolutions.com

Summary: XEC Solutions is a leading authority in executive acquisition serving the Consumer Product industry. We are not a "personnel agency." Instead, we are executive bounty hunters and strategic planning partners. Our expertise and experience in Personal Care and Cosmetics has made us the go to firm in the HBA industry.

Key Contact - Specialty:
Mr. Michael Schulman, President & Chief Executive Officer
Ms. Mary Lindenmuth, Department Manager

Salary Minimum: $75,000

Functions: Generalist (All)

Industries: Manufacturing, Food, Bev., Tobacco, Soap, Perf., Cosmtcs., Consumer Goods

Yaekle & Company

PO Box 615
Granville, OH 43023-0615
(740) 587-7366
Fax: (740) 587-1973
Email: gary@yaekleco.com
Web: www.yaekleco.com

Summary: We are a specialized and targeted executive search firm. The focus of our firm is on advertising, marketing, sales, retail operations and HR management.

Key Contact - Specialty:
Mr. Gary Yaekle, Senior Vice President

Salary Minimum: $70,000

Functions: Management, Senior Mgmt., Sales & Mktg., Advertising, Mktg. Research, Mktg. Mgmt., Sales Mgmt., Direct Mktg., PR, Staffing

Industries: Generalist (All), Food, Bev., Tobacco, Soap, Perf., Cosmtcs., Motor Vehicles, Retail, Services, Hospitality, Restaurants, Advertising, New Media

YES Partners

325 Sharon Park Dr Ste 221
Menlo Park, CA 94025-6805
(650) 726-8733
Email: rose@yespartners.com
Web: www.yespartners.com

Summary: International Executive search firm helping U.S. companies to expand locally and internationally and International companies to expand in the U.S.

Key Contact - Specialty:
Ms. Rose Mortilla, Vice President

Functions: Board Members, Senior Mgmt.

Industries: Generalist (All), Manufacturing, Semiconductors, Retail, Finance, Services, Media, Communications, Telecoms, Digital, Wireless, Fiber Optic, RF/Microwave, Software, Biotech/Life Sciences

Yetka Management Group

3554 Brecksville Rd Ste 500
Richfield, OH 44286-9157
(330) 659-0841
Fax: (330) 659-7028

Email your resume to a targeted list of recruiters now at www.ExecutiveAgent.com/DER07

Email: ed.miller@yetkagroup.com
Web: www.yetkagroup.com

Summary: Our firm partners with business owners and corporate executives and provides them with comprehensive HR consulting, executive search and career transition services designed to enhance individual and corporate excellence. Our goal is to create a richly satisfying and productive work environment for both the individual and the corporation.

Key Contact - Specialty:
Mr. Edward Miller, Director, Executive Search

Salary Minimum: $100,000

Functions: Generalist (All)

Industries: Chemicals, Plastics, Rubber, Paints, Petro. Products, Metal Products, Motor Vehicles, Misc. Mfg., Wholesale, Supply Chain Mgmt, RF/Microwave, Insurance

The Yorkshire Group Ltd[†]
182 W Central St
Natick, MA 01760-3756
(508) 653-1222
(800) 452-9610
Fax: (508) 653-2631
Email: info@yorkshireltd.com
Web: www.insurancejobchannel.com

Summary: Specializing in the selection of insurance industry professionals. Fees are either retained or contingency, depending on the level of professional being sought. Testing for major traits that match the function is available. Our history includes presidential, mid-management and multi sales search assignments.

Key Contact - Specialty:
Mr. Michael P. Tornesello, President

Salary Minimum: $100,000

Functions: Generalist (All)

Industries: Insurance

Bill Young & Associates Inc
6901A Baltimore National Pike
Frederick, MD 21702-3610
(301) 639-4395
Email: byoung@billyoung.com
Web: www.billyoung.com

Summary: Retained searches for IS, telecom and non-profit executives. Our firm has corporate executive search recruiting expertise.

Key Contact - Specialty:
Mr. William H. Young, President

Salary Minimum: $75,000

Youngblood Executive Search Inc
445 E Ohio St Ste 440
Chicago, IL 60611-4676
(800) 518-1912
Fax: (312) 201-1153
Email: info@yngbloodexecsrch.com
Web: www.yngbloodexecsrch.com

Summary: We recruit high impact executive leadership talent for our clients who trust our broad experience and ability to recruit diverse talent. We focus on identifying and attracting highly qualified leadership talent who will not only enhance immediate performance but also innovate existing organizations and build new ones.

Key Contact - Specialty:
Ms. Ava D. Youngblood, President & Chief Executive Officer
Ms. Tanya Burks, Vice President

Salary Minimum: $130,000

Functions: Generalist (All)

Industries: Energy, Utilities, Construction, Manufacturing, Transportation, Finance, Services, Communications, Environmental Svcs., Software, Biotech/Life Sciences

Youngs, Walker & Company
1605 W Colonial Pkwy Ste 200
Inverness, IL 60067-1224
(847) 991-6900
Fax: (847) 934-6607
Email: info@youngswalker.com
Web: www.youngswalker.com

Summary: Management consulting firm assisting newspaper and broadcast companies of all sizes in the recruitment of corporate executives and all top and middle-level management.

Key Contact - Specialty:
Mr. Carl Youngs, President
Mr. Mike Walker, Vice President

Salary Minimum: $85,000

Functions: Generalist (All), Board Members, Senior Mgmt., Middle Mgmt., Production, Mktg. Mgmt., Sales Mgmt., CFOs, MIS Mgmt.

Industries: Generalist (All), Mgmt. Consulting, Publishing, Broadcast, Film

Steven Yungerberg Associates Inc
4670 Old Kent Rd
Excelsior, MN 55331-9267
(952) 470-2288
Fax: (952) 474-3185

Summary: Management consulting firm specializing in executive selection and recruitment.

Key Contact - Specialty:
Mr. Steven A. Yungerberg, President - *Financial services, Investment management*

Salary Minimum: $100,000

Functions: Generalist (All), Management, Senior Mgmt., Automation, Benefits, CFOs, Cash Mgmt., M&A, Int'l.

Industries: Generalist (All), Finance

Yungner & Associates, LLC[†]
2300 Lukewood Dr
Chanhassen, MN 55317-9370
(952) 975-4981
Email: syungner@mchsi.com

Summary: We specialize in placing top executives in the medical industry. Our clients are medical device, pharmaceutical, biotechnology, and other companies selling a product or service into the healthcare industry. Client size ranges from Fortune 100's to mid-size, small and start-up organizations.

Key Contact - Specialty:
Mr. Steven Yungner, Chief Financial Officer & Director

Salary Minimum: $75,000

Functions: Senior Mgmt., Middle Mgmt., Product Dev., Healthcare, Mktg. Mgmt., Sales Mgmt.

Industries: Drugs Mfg., Medical Devices, Pharm Svcs., Biotech/Life Sciences, Healthcare, Hospitals, Long-term/Home Care, Dental

Z = mc²
PO Box 421423
Atlanta, GA 30342-8423
(404) 705-9206

Email: jobs@zmc2.com
Web: www.zmc2.com

Summary: We are a boutique executive search firm focused on the healthcare, international and technology sectors. We are typically hired to fill senior executive positions for which there are a small group of qualified candidates. We work with clients and candidates throughout the United States.

Key Contact - Specialty:
Ms. Vicki Lauter, Principal

Salary Minimum: $100,000

Functions: Management, Senior Mgmt., Sales Mgmt.

Industries: Medical Devices, Services, Mgmt. Consulting, HR Services, Logistics Svcs., Supply Chain Mgmt, Insurance, Healthcare, Hospitals, Long-term/Home Care

ZanExec LLC
2063 Madrillon Rd
Vienna, VA 22182-3782
(703) 734-7070
Fax: (703) 734-9440
Email: zan@zanexec.com
Web: www.zanexec.com

Summary: We are a firm involved in executive retained search efforts, specializing in the recruitment of senior executive line management with a focus across most industries and verticals. Our clients include the Fortune 500, federal government contractors and systems integrators, management consultants, software/hardware product, web/Internet and manufacturing companies.

Key Contact - Specialty:
Ms. Zan Vourakis, President - *Aviation, Defense, Government, High technology, Senior management*
Mr. Peter Johnson, Executive Vice President - *Aerospace, Business development, C-level, Defense, Engineering*

Salary Minimum: $120,000

Functions: Management, Senior Mgmt., Mfg., Sales & Mktg., Sales Mgmt., Finance, IT, DB Admin., Engineering, Mgmt. Consultants

Industries: Generalist (All), Manufacturing, Transportation, Finance, Media, Publishing, Communications, Defense, Aerospace, Biotech/Life Sciences, Healthcare

The Zarkin Group Inc
22 James Dr
New Rochelle, NY 10804-1715
(914) 235-8100
(800) 977-0509
Fax: (914) 235-8150
Email: nzarkin@aol.com

Summary: We are primarily a retained search firm that recruits nationally with great east coast contacts. Our principals are involved in every search. Quick response and personal attention offering very competitive fee arrangements with depth in chain store retail, DIY and sales/marketing for consumer products manufacturers selling to big box retail chains in hard lines.

Key Contact - Specialty:
Mr. Norman Zarkin, President - *Construction, Distribution, Real estate, Retail*
Ms. Antonella Russo, Manager, Research

Salary Minimum: $65,000

Functions: Generalist (All), Management, Board Members, Mfg., Sales & Mktg., Sales Mgmt.

Industries: Generalist (All), Manufacturing, Consumer Goods, Wholesale, Retail

Zatkovich & Associates

3700 Newbury Ct
Santa Rosa, CA 95404-7672
(707) 577-8317
Email: zakassoc@aol.com
Web: www.zakassoc.com

Summary: We specialize in telecom, networking and information processing, fiber optic start-ups and emerging technology companies. True search value is the difference between 'the best candidate and the best person known to be looking.'

Key Contact - Specialty:
Mr. Gary A. Zatkovich, Principal & Founder - *Sales*
Mr. Jay Latona, Search Consultant & Partner - *Internet*

Salary Minimum: $100,000

Functions: IT

Industries: Telecoms, Telephony, Digital, Wireless, Fiber Optic, Network Infrastructure, RF/Microwave, Marketing SW, Networking, Comm. SW, Security SW

Zay & Company International

(an IIC company)
3353 Peachtree Rd NE Ste M30
Atlanta Financial Center
Atlanta, GA 30326-1053
(404) 876-9986
Email: zaymail@zaycointl.com
Web: www.zaycointl.com

Summary: We were founded to conduct a highly consultative executive search practice, in which; a principal of the firm works directly with each client on every search engagement. The validity of this concept and philosophy has been proven by the continuity of the firm's client base and the consistently successful performance of the executives placed.

Key Contact - Specialty:
Mr. Thomas C. Zay, Sr., Chairman - *Apparel, Asset management, Boards of Directors, CEOs, CFOs*

Salary Minimum: $150,000

Functions: Board Members, Senior Mgmt., Mfg., Mktg. Mgmt., HR Mgmt., CFOs, Attorneys

Industries: Generalist (All), Agri., Forestry, Mining, Energy, Utilities, Construction, Food, Bev., Tobacco, Textiles, Apparel, Printing, Soap, Perf., Cosmtcs., Drugs Mfg., Consumer Goods, Finance, Invest. Banking, Legal, Supply Chain Mgmt, Hospitality, Packaging, Insurance, Real Estate

Egon Zehnder International Inc

350 Park Ave Ste 801
New York, NY 10022-6013
(212) 519-6000
Fax: (212) 519-6060
Web: www.zehnder.com

Summary: Privately-held search firm specializing in senior level executive search, board consulting & director search, management appraisals and talent management.

Key Contact - Specialty:
Mr. A. Daniel Meiland, Executive Chairman
Mr. Russell E. Boyle
Mr. Alan D. Hilliker
Mr. Neil Hindle
Mr. Justus J. O'Brien
Ms. Celeste Rodgers

Mr. Marc P. Schappell, Managing Partner, New York
Mr. Robert Sloan
Ms. Kimberley Van Der Zon
Ms. Juliana A. Zinger
Ms. Anne-Claire Monod - *Industrial*
Mr. Murari Rajan - *Financial services*
Mr. Francisco Paret
Mr. Douglas Rosenberg - *Consumer (Products, Products), Industria,)*
Mr. Alfred Prieto

Salary Minimum: $200,000

Functions: Generalist (All), Management, Board Members, Senior Mgmt.

Industries: Generalist (All), Energy, Utilities, Manufacturing, Retail, Finance, Services, Communications, Insurance, Biotech/Life Sciences, Healthcare

Branches:
350 S Grand Ave
Los Angeles, CA 90071-3406
(213) 337-1500
Fax: (213) 621-8901
Email: ezilosangeles@ezi.net
Key Contact - Specialty:
Mr. Gary J. Matus, Office Manager
Mr. Sid Valluri

1290 Page Mill Rd
Palo Alto, CA 94304-1122
(650) 847-3000
Fax: (650) 847-3050
Email: ezipaloalto@ezi.net
Key Contact - Specialty:
Mr. Jon F. Carter
Ms. Martha Josephson
Mr. Reynold H. Lewke
Ms. Karena Strella
Mr. Pavan Vohra, Office Manager
Mr. Todd Hutchings
Mr. Ravi Srivastava

100 Spear St Ste 920
San Francisco, CA 94105-1534
(415) 228-5200
Key Contact - Specialty:
Mr. S. Ross Brown

121 Alhambra Plz Ste 1130
Coral Gables, FL 33134-4522
(305) 569-1000
Fax: (305) 446-1136
Email: ezimiami@ezi.net
Key Contact - Specialty:
Ms. Angel V. Gallinal
Mr. German Herrera
Mr. Gabriel Sanchez-Zinny, Managing Partner

3475 Piedmont Rd NE Ste 430
Atlanta, GA 30305-2981
(404) 836-2800
Fax: (404) 876-4578
Email: eziatlanta@ezi.net
Key Contact - Specialty:
Ms. Laura Lee Gentry, Office Manager
Mr. Eric Anderson
Mr. Tom Reynolds

1 N Wacker Dr Ste 2300
Chicago, IL 60606-2824
(312) 260-8800
Fax: (312) 782-2846
Email: ezichicagoj@ezi.net
Key Contact - Specialty:
Mr. Karl W. Alleman
Mr. Louis J. Kacyn, Managing Partner
Mr. Kai Lindholst
Mr. Ronald O. Tracy
Mr. Mike Matella
Mr. Michael Portland

45 Milk St Ste 4
Boston, MA 02109-5172
(617) 535-3500
Fax: (617) 457-4949
Email: eziboston@ezi.net
Key Contact - Specialty:
Mr. George L. Davis, Jr., Managing Partner
Mr. Gilbert E. Forest
Mr. Greg T. Schneider
Mr. Jamie Satterthwaite
Mr. Dan Slavin
Mr. Arnaud Tesson

13455 Noel Rd Ste 1400
Dallas, TX 75240-6690
(972) 728-5910
Fax: (972) 728-5915
Email: ezidallas@ezi.net
Key Contact - Specialty:
Mr. Sanjay Gupta
Chris B. Patrick
Mr. Brian C. Reinken, Office Manager
Mr. Chris Pfeiffer
Mr. Brent Magnuson
Ms. Selena LaCroix

3920-181 Bay St
BCE Place
Toronto, ON M5J 2T3
Canada
(416) 364-0222
Fax: (416) 364-0955
Email: ezitoronto@ezi.net
Key Contact - Specialty:
Mr. David P. Harris
Mr. Thomas Long
Mr. Jon N.G. Martin
Ms. Valerie Spriet
Ms. Jan J. Stewart, Managing Partner
Ms. Pamela A. Warren
Mr. Rashid Wasti

3310-1 Place Ville-Marie
Immeuble Commercial
Montreal, QC H3B 3N2
Canada
(514) 876-4249
Email: ezimontreal@ezi.net
Key Contact - Specialty:
Mr. Andre Le Comte
Mr. Pierre Payette
Mr. J. Robert Swidler, Managing Partner
Mr. Marc Normandin

Paseo de las Palmas 405
Edificio Torre Optima Desp 703
Col Lomas de Chapultepec
11000 Mexico City, DF
Mexico
55 5540 7635
Fax: 55 5520 9108
Email: ezimexico@ezi.net
Key Contact - Specialty:
Mr. Dario Pastrana, Managing Partner
Mr. Jose Sanchez Padilla
Mr. Antonio Puron
Mr. Ricardo Weihmann
Mr. Salvador Malo Guzman

Zingaro & Company

21936 Briarcliff Dr
Briarcliff, TX 78669-2012
(512) 327-7277
Fax: (512) 327-1774
Email: search@zingaro.com
Web: www.zingaro.com

Summary: An executive search firm specializing in the retained search and selection of senior management for the healthcare industry, including: pharmaceuticals, devices, diagnostics, venture/biotechnology and pharmaceutical services.

Key Contact - Specialty:
Dr. Ronald J. Zingaro, PhD, President -
  Biotechnology, Diagnostics, Pharmaceutical
Ms. Tracy Wolfe, Vice President - *Healthcare*

Salary Minimum: $100,000

Functions: Management, Mfg., Healthcare, Sales
  & Mktg., Finance, IT, R&D, Engineering,
  Specialized Svcs., Int'l.

Industries: Drugs Mfg., Medical Devices, Pharm
  Svcs., Biotech/Life Sciences, Healthcare

Michael D Zinn & Associates Inc

993 Lenox Dr Ste 200
Princeton Professional Park
Lawrenceville, NJ 08648-2316
(609) 921-8755
Web: www.zinnassociates.com

Summary: Retainer based search firm,
distinguished by our strong commitment to client
service. Focus is senior level positions in
technology, health care, financial services and
industrial.

Key Contact - Specialty:
Mr. Michael D. Zinn, President - *Healthcare,
  Industrial, Medical (Devices), Pharmaceutical,
  Technology*

Salary Minimum: $100,000

Functions: Generalist (All)

Industries: Manufacturing, Chemicals, Drugs
  Mfg., Medical Devices, Finance, Venture Cap.,
  Pharm Svcs., Communications, Software,
  Biotech/Life Sciences

Zurick Davis Inc

10 Tower Office Park Ste 401
Woburn, MA 01801-2120
(781) 938-1975
Fax: (781) 938-0599
Email: leean@zurickdavis.com
Web: www.zurickdavis.com

Summary: Practice serving healthcare clients
including integrated networks,
teaching/community hospitals, medical groups,
insurance companies, service companies, PHOs,
MSOs, rehab/nursing homes, sub-acute, home
health, assisted living, managed care companies
and academic medical centers. Also serve not-for-
profit social services organizations.

Key Contact - Specialty:
Mr. Jeffrey M. Zegas, Founding Principal -
  Healthcare
Mr. Tom Sager, Principal - *Healthcare*
Ms. Myranne Janoff, Principal - *Healthcare*
Mr. Bob Mitchell, Principal - *Healthcare*

Salary Minimum: $90,000

Functions: Generalist (All), Healthcare

Industries: Non-profits, Healthcare, Hospitals,
  Long-term/Home Care

ZweigWhite

1 Apple Hill Dr Ste 2
Natick, MA 01760-2080
(508) 651-1559
Fax: (508) 653-6522
Email: info@zweigwhite.com
Web: www.zweigwhite.com

Summary: Executive search consultants serving
the construction industry exclusively.

Key Contact - Specialty:
Mr. Jerry Deane, Associate, Operations
Ms. Claire Roderick Keerl, Vice President,
  Events
Mr. Christopher J. Klein, Principal, Research -
  Research

Mr. David Lacy, Associate, Consulting
Ms. Laura Rothman, Associate, Research -
  Research
Mr. Ian Rusk, Senior Vice President
Mr. Fred White, Executive Vice President
Mr. Mark C. Zweig, Vice Chairman

Salary Minimum: $75,000

Functions: Generalist (All)

Industries: Construction

Zwell International

35 E Wacker Dr Ste 500
Chicago, IL 60601-2105
(312) 551-0404
Fax: (312) 551-0574
Email: info@zwell.com
Web: www.zwell.com

Summary: We are a professional and executive
recruiting with a special emphasis on core
competency assessment.

Key Contact - Specialty:
Dr. Michael Zwell, President & Chief Executive
  Officer
Mr. Michael Grant, Vice President - *Financial
  services, Publishing*

Salary Minimum: $80,000

Functions: Generalist (All), Board Members,
  Senior Mgmt., Middle Mgmt., Plant Mgmt.,
  CFOs, MIS Mgmt., Int'l.

Industries: Generalist (All), Manufacturing,
  Motor Vehicles, Retail, Finance, Accounting,
  Hospitality

Contingency Recruiting Firms, A to Z

Agencies and other firms in executive recruiting operating all or part of the time on a fee-paid basis payable on placement are in this section. Percentages of retainer and contingency work vary; check with individual firms.

11th Hour Recruiting
(also known as Life Sciences Staffing)
4900 Westwood Way
Antioch, CA 94531-8134
(925) 522-0991
Fax: (925) 775-7027
Email: joe@11thhourrecruiting.biz
Web: www.11thhourrecruiting.biz

Summary: Our firm specializes in IT staffing.

Key Contact - Specialty:
Mr. Joe Cassell, Principal

Salary Minimum: $60,000

Functions: Generalist (All)

Industries: Drugs Mfg., Telecoms, Call Centers, Telephony, Wireless, Development SW, Doc. Mgmt., Production SW, ERP SW, Biotech/Life Sciences, Healthcare

3RSearch Consultants
304 Webster St Apt 2359
Houston, TX 77002-8559
(832) 476-8728
Fax: (713) 456-2477
Email: will@3rsearch.com
Web: www.3rsearch.com

Summary: We offer services in the following areas: contingency search, hr consulting, industry reports, resume writing, retained searches and web design.

Key Contact - Specialty:
Mr. William Dangerfield, Principal

Salary Minimum: $40,000

Functions: Middle Mgmt., Purchasing, Architects, Hospitality

Industries: Oil & Gas, Construction, Retail, Hotels, Resorts, Clubs, Restaurants, Quick Service Restaurants, Full Service Restaurants, Property/Facility Mgmt.

A D & Associates Executive Search Inc
5589 Woodsong Dr Ste 100
Atlanta, GA 30338-2933
(770) 393-0021
Fax: (770) 393-9060
Email: hawks@mindspring.com
Web: www.adaexecsearch.com

Summary: As a generalist firm recognizing human importance, we are committed to excellence. We offer resources and networks from which to draw leadership talent to fill critical positions. Our creative approach leads to getting the right people in the right jobs in a timely and economical manner (the first time). "...Finding the best," includes assessment and after placement coaching (if invited) to perpetuate success in beating your competition.

Key Contact - Specialty:
Mr. A. Dwight Hawksworth, President

Salary Minimum: $50,000

Functions: Generalist (All), Senior Mgmt., Middle Mgmt., Sales & Mktg., HR Mgmt., Finance, IT, Engineering, Minorities/Diversity, Attorneys

Industries: Generalist (All), Finance, Banking, Legal, Accounting, Mgmt. Consulting, HR Services, Communications, Telecoms, Government, Aerospace, Insurance, Software, Accounting SW, Marketing SW

A First Resource
301 Foxcroft Dr
Winston Salem, NC 27103-6117
(336) 765-3969
Email: siburt@a1stresource.com

Summary: Providing excellence in candidate selection to those companies who expect no less. Specializing in manufacturing management, engineering, safety, etc.

Key Contact - Specialty:
Ms. Karen L. Siburt, CPC, President - *Apparel, Engineering, Manufacturing, Textiles*

Salary Minimum: $45,000

Functions: Generalist (All)

Industries: Manufacturing, Textiles, Apparel, Lumber, Furniture, Paper, Drugs Mfg., Medical Devices, Metal Products, Misc. Mfg., HR Services, Publishing

A V Search Consultants
674 US Highway 202/206
Bridgewater, NJ 08807-1748
(908) 429-7800
Fax: (908) 704-9898
Email: info@avsearchconsultants.com
Web: www.avsearchconsultants.com

Summary: Specialize in attorney search on behalf of law firms and corporations.

Key Contact - Specialty:
Ms. Arlene M. Sengstack, President
Ms. Stella Stelzik Feldman, Esq.
Mr. James C. Jacobus, Esq.

Salary Minimum: $100,000

Functions: Attorneys

Industries: Legal

A&S Resources Staffing Inc
3235 Satellite Blvd Ste 300
Duluth, GA 30096-8688
(770) 469-1858
Email: info@asresources.net
Web: www.asresources.net

Summary: Our firm is a female owned and operated contingency professional staffing firm. We place professional candidates within finance, accounting, management, sales, administrative, information technology, supply chain management, logistics, human resources and healthcare opportunities locally and nationally for direct hire and contract positions.

Key Contact - Specialty:
Mrs. Brenda Mitchell, President & Chief Executive Officer - *Direct marketing, Human resources, Staffing, Training*

Salary Minimum: $47,000

Functions: Management, Admin. Svcs., Nurses, Allied Health, Sales & Mktg., Customer Svc., Finance, IT

Industries: Generalist (All), Paper, Printing, Plastics, Rubber, Logistics Svcs., Supply Chain Mgmt, Packaging, Hospitals, Physical Therapy, Occupational Therapy

AAE Group Inc
4697 Bali Hai Ln
Bonita Springs, FL 34134-7143
(239) 947-2977
(828) 743-5850
Email: ralph@aaegroup.com
Web: www.aaegroup.com

Summary: Our sole focus is the automotive specialty and aftermarkets. Services include both retained and contingent searches. Sales,

marketing, engineering and operations, from mid to executive levels, is our specialty.

Key Contact - Specialty:
Mr. Ralph Schroeder, President

Salary Minimum: $75,000

Functions: Management, Senior Mgmt., Middle Mgmt., Product Dev., Purchasing, Sales & Mktg., Engineering

Industries: Motor Vehicles

Aaron Consulting Inc
PO Box 4757
Saint Louis, MO 63108-0757
(314) 367-2627
Fax: (314) 367-2919
Email: aaron@aaronlaw.com
Web: www.aaronlaw.com

Summary: Our firm exclusively represents attorney employers and candidates. Since we were founded, 80 to 100 percent of each year's placements have been with corporate law departments. Our opportunities include Fortune 100 to small companies and general counsel to staff attorney positions.

Key Contact - Specialty:
Mr. Aaron Williams, CPC, President

Salary Minimum: $100,000

Functions: Legal, Attorneys

Industries: Generalist (All)

Aaron Epps Rayle & Wise Inc
17 Lakewood Ln
Seabrook, TX 77586-3432
(713) 827-1150
Fax: (713) 827-1150
Email: rdefee@aerwsearch.com
Web: www.aerwsearch.com

Summary: We specialize in upper to middle management placements in the retail and wholesale food services industries and in information technology for all industries.

Key Contact - Specialty:
Mr. Roy DeFee, Partner & Practice Leader

Salary Minimum: $80,000

Functions: Generalist (All), Middle Mgmt.

Industries: Generalist (All), Food, Bev., Tobacco, Wholesale, Retail, Finance, Restaurants, Full Service Restaurants, Entertainment, Recreation, Travel, Wireless, Fiber Optic, Network Infrastructure, RF/Microwave, Software, Accounting SW

ABA Search & Staffing
(formerly known as ABA Staffing Inc)
33 New Montgomery St Ste 800
San Francisco, CA 94105-4525
(415) 434-4222
(650) 349-9200
Fax: (415) 434-3958
Email: info@abastaff.com
Web: www.abastaff.com

Summary: Our firm specializes in the placement of attorneys, legal administrators, litigation support, paralegals, legal secretaries and office support staff. We are dedicated to providing the highest level of recruiting services on a direct hire or contract basis, to both law firms and corporate legal departments.

Key Contact - Specialty:
Ms. Mandy Farmaian, CSP, Managing Partner - *Human resources, Intellectual property, Legal (Attorneys), Temporary*
Mr. Valli Farmaian, Partner - *Legal, Legal (Attorneys,Lawyers), Office (Administration,Support)*

Salary Minimum: $60,000

Functions: Generalist (All), Admin. Svcs., HR Mgmt., Legal, Attorneys, Paralegals

Industries: Generalist (All), Legal, Real Estate, Biotech/Life Sciences, Healthcare

Abacus Employment

1800 Roswell Rd Ste 3020
Marietta, GA 30062-3980
(770) 509-2490
Fax: (770) 620-3801
Email: info@abacusjobs.com
Web: www.abacusjobs.com

Summary: A full service permanent placement firm for sales, engineering and restaurant management.

Key Contact - Specialty:
Mr. Ron Hickman

Salary Minimum: $30,000

Functions: Sales & Mktg.

Industries: Generalist (All)

Abacus Group LLC

225 W 34th St Ste 1600
New York, NY 10122-1690
(212) 812-8444
Fax: (212) 812-8448
Email: info@abacusnyc.com
Web: www.abacusnyc.com

Summary: Our firm is an executive recruitment firm specializing in the permanent and temporary placement of accounting & finance and accounting support professionals. Industries include (but are not limited to): brokerage, banking, media, entertainment, consumer products, real estate, insurance and public accounting.

Key Contact - Specialty:
Mr. Brian Bereck, Partner
Mr. Len Frankel, CPA, Partner
Ms. Laurie Kotton, CPA, Principal, Accounting & Finance
Mr. Howard Weisberger, Director, Accounting Support

Salary Minimum: $40,000

Functions: Middle Mgmt., Finance, CFOs, Budgeting, Credit, Taxes

Industries: Generalist (All), Construction, Manufacturing, Transportation, Finance, Services, Media, Communications, Insurance, Software, Healthcare

Abacus Growth Group Inc

799 W Boylston St
Worcester, MA 01606-3071
(508) 853-5700
Fax: (508) 853-5766
Email: info@abacus-growth.com
Web: www.abacus-growth.com

Summary: Full service consulting firm offering fast and comprehensive search and staffing solutions.

Key Contact - Specialty:
Mr. Michael Toro, President

Salary Minimum: $40,000

Functions: Generalist (All), Product Dev., Sales & Mktg.

Industries: Generalist (All), Manufacturing, Leather, Stone, Glass, Computer Equip., Consumer Elect., Test, Measure Equip., Electronic, Elec. Components, Semiconductors, Communications, Telecoms, Wireless, Fiber Optic, Network Infrastructure, RF/Microwave, Software

Glen Abbey Executive Search Inc

11-1155 North Service Rd W
Oakville, ON L6M 3E3
Canada
(905) 847-0560
Fax: (905) 847-9592
Email: art@execuprolink.com
Web: www.execuprolink.com

Summary: We provide personalized and comprehensive search services across all industries with a primary focus on technical sales & marketing positions from entry level to senior management. With an impressive track record of success in identifying only the very best and suitable candidates, we will never compromise our extensive screening and selection process.

Key Contact - Specialty:
Mr. Arthur Rivard, CMC

Salary Minimum: $50,000

Functions: Generalist (All), Sales & Mktg.

Industries: Generalist (All), Construction, Food, Bev., Tobacco, Paints, Petro. Products, Machine, Appliance, Consumer Elect., Wholesale, Aerospace, Packaging

Abbott Executive Search

250 Commercial St Ste 3009
Manchester, NH 03101-1118
(603) 669-9909
Fax: (603) 606-5502
Email: info@abbottsearch.com
Web: www.abbottsearch.com

Summary: We're a firm that functions as generalists within the financial services and insurance industries placing middle to senior management. From marketing to operations, from HR to desktop publishing, call center technology to call center supervisors, compliance and beyond.

Key Contact - Specialty:
Ms. Siobhan Tautkus, MBA, Owner - *Financial, Healthcare*
Ms. Miriam Diamond, Research - *Manufacturing, Presidents*

Functions: Generalist (All), IT

Industries: Generalist (All), Manufacturing, Brokers, Misc. Financial, Services, HR Services, Call Centers, Insurance, Software, ERP SW, Training SW, Healthcare, Hospitals, Long-term/Home Care

Ryan Abbott Search Associates Inc

250 W Main St
Branford, CT 06405-4032
(203) 488-7245
Email: mcgetric@rcn.com
Web: www.ryanabbott.com

Summary: We specialize in recruiting for pharmaceutical clients.

Key Contact - Specialty:
Mr. Eugene McGetrick, President
Mr. Ryan McGetrick, MBA, Vice President

Salary Minimum: $50,000

Functions: Board Members, Senior Mgmt., Health Admin., R&D

Industries: Finance, Pharm Svcs., Biotech/Life Sciences, Healthcare

Abel Placement Consultants Inc

100-7030 Woodbine Ave
Markham, ON L3R 6G2
Canada
(905) 513-1515
(905) 764-6274
Fax: (905) 513-2769
Email: ja@abelplacement.com
Web: www.abelplacement.com

Summary: As a generalist recruitment firm, we provide services to a wide range of businesses. Our service is provided to large/medium sized corporate organizations and privately owned companies. We place highly qualified candidates across the board on a permanent basis only.

Key Contact - Specialty:
Mr. John Abel, President

Salary Minimum: $50,000

Functions: Generalist (All)

Industries: Generalist (All), Construction, Manufacturing, Consumer Goods, Wholesale, Accounting, Packaging, Real Estate, Accounting SW, Development SW

Abelson Legal Search

1600 Market St Ste 505
Philadelphia, PA 19103-7220
(215) 561-3010
Fax: (215) 561-3001
Email: abelson@abelsonlegalsearch.com
Web: www.abelsonlegalsearch.com

Summary: We will identify, screen and supply attorneys, paralegals and other legal professionals matched to the needs of our client law firms and corporations in a cost and time efficient manner, while recognizing the career objectives of all candidates.

Key Contact - Specialty:
Ms. Cathy B. Abelson, President
Ms. Sandra G. Mannix, Senior Attorney Search Consultant
Ms. Jessica Abelson, Contract Attorney Search Consultant
Ms. Susan Rubinovitz, Esq., Attorney Search Consultant
Ms. Joyce Feinstein, Attorney Search Consultant
Ms. Pamela Peery, Esq., Attorney Search Consultant
Ms. Peggy Dixon, Recruiter, Legal & Marketing Director
Ms. Erica Engstenberg, Recruiter, Paralegal

Functions: Legal, Attorneys, Paralegals

Industries: Generalist (All), Legal

Ability Search Group Inc.

30400 Telegraph Rd Ste 474
Bingham Farms, MI 48025-4554
(248) 594-2100
Fax: (248) 594-2121
Email: info@abilitysearch.com
Web: www.abilitysearch.com

Summary: Our firm was founded to consult, search and assist companies in hiring highly qualified IT and engineering professionals, who through their expertise and experience have a history of furthering the business goals of their employers.

Key Contact - Specialty:
Dr. Dany Saar, Recruiter

Functions: IT

Industries: Generalist (All)

ABL Logistics Group LLC

124 Park Place Dr
Sinking Spring, PA 19608-9778
(610) 927-1611
Email: ncurrie@abllogistics.com
Web: www.abllogistics.com

Summary: Our firm does logistics recruiting for companies on an exclusive basis. Clients include 3PL, transportation and manufacturers. We work only on mid to upper level opportunities. Five experienced recruiting professionals that have executive level logistics operational backgrounds.

Key Contact - Specialty:
Mr. Ned Currie, Partner - *Distribution, Logistics*

Salary Minimum: $60,000

Functions: Distribution

Industries: Generalist (All), Food, Bev., Tobacco, Chemicals, Drugs Mfg., Medical Devices, Paints, Petro. Products, Consumer Elect., Misc. Mfg., Logistics Svcs., Supply Chain Mgmt

Branches:
557 Willowcreek Ct
Clarendon Hills, IL 60514-1658
(630) 734-0361
Email: jduzinski@abllogistics.com
Key Contact - Specialty:
Mr. Jerry Duzinski, Partner

ABP Personnel Consultants Inc

640-4333 Rue Sainte-Catherine O
Immeuble Commercial
Westmount, QC H3Z 1P9
Canada
(514) 939-3399
Fax: (514) 939-0241
Email: gilbert@abppers.com
Web: www.abppers.com

Summary: Our mission to employers is to participate in locating those hard to find resources and doing it professionally, ethically, honestly and with integrity. From the candidate's point of view, we are dedicated in providing them with accurate info about prospective employers and help them reach their professional goals.

Key Contact - Specialty:
Mr. Gilbert Pigeon, President & Consultant
Ms. Isabelle Munger, Consultant - *Accounting, Analysts, Business development, Business to business*
Ms. Patricia Allioux, Consultant - *Information Technology*

Salary Minimum: $40,000

Functions: Generalist (All), Sales & Mktg., Advertising, Mktg. Research, Mktg. Mgmt., Sales Mgmt., Direct Mktg., Customer Svc., PR

Industries: Generalist (All), Agri., Forestry, Mining, Energy, Utilities, Construction, Manufacturing, Transportation, Wholesale, Retail, Finance, Services, Hospitality, Media, Communications, Haz. Waste, Packaging, Software

Abraham & London Ltd

7 Old Sherman Tpke Ste 209
Danbury, CT 06810-4174
(203) 730-4000
Fax: (203) 798-1784
Email: stu@abrahamlondon.com
Web: www.abrahamlondon.com

Summary: Middle management through executive-level appointments with emphasis in staffing sales, marketing and tech support professionals. Specializing in the converging telecoms, computer and related high-technology industries.

Key Contact - Specialty:
Mr. Stuart R. Laub, President - *Telecommunications*
Ms. Connie Goebel, Executive Recruiter
Ms. Patty Walsh, Executive Recruiter
Ms. Sandra Grenier, Executive Recruiter
Ms. Eileen Bednarz, Executive Recruiter
Mr. Greg Bollaro, Executive Recruiter - *Marketing, Sales, Telecommunications*
Ms. Sandi Marotti, Office Manager

Salary Minimum: $45,000

Functions: Management, Senior Mgmt., Sales & Mktg., Mktg. Mgmt., Sales Mgmt., Engineering

Industries: Generalist (All), Computer Equip., Equip Svcs., Advertising, New Media, Telecoms, Software

B J Abrams & Associates Inc

540 W Frontage Rd Ste 3255
Northfield, IL 60093-1283
(847) 446-2966
Email: babrams@bjabrams.com
Web: www.bjabrams.com

Summary: Can handle searches in manufacturing, front door to back. We place particular manufacturing emphasis in operations and materials management. Healthcare searches also active. Recruit in all disciplines except IT. We are active in the financial and HR side of business and sales & marketing.

Key Contact - Specialty:
Mr. Burton J. Abrams, President - *Human resources, Manufacturing, Sales*
Ms. Carolyn Potter, Senior Associate

Salary Minimum: $50,000

Functions: Generalist (All), Mfg., Materials, Healthcare, Sales & Mktg., HR Mgmt., Finance

Industries: Generalist (All), Manufacturing, Media, Healthcare

ACC Consultants Inc

9008 Washington St NE
Albuquerque, NM 87113-2704
(800) 856-6528
(505) 323-1300
Fax: (505) 323-1400
Email: info@accdental.com
Web: www.accdental.com

Summary: We offer contingent and retained searches in dental field. Administration, management and clinical dental functions covered temp and permanent placement of dentists, dental hygienists, dental assistants and front office management & staff.

Key Contact - Specialty:
Mr. Jerry Berger, President
Mr. Larry Seebinger - *Dental*
Ms. Virginia Berger, RDH, Vice President

Functions: Generalist (All), Allied Health, Health Admin.

Industries: Generalist (All), Healthcare

Accelerated Data Decision Inc

PO Box 152
Augusta, NJ 07822-0152
(973) 726-5060
Fax: (973) 726-5929
Email: search@addinc.net
Web: www.addinc.net

Summary: Our firm is an elite executive search firm, specializing in permanent placement. Our client list spans the globe with large Fortune 100 and 500 companies as well as smaller manufacturers.

Key Contact - Specialty:
Mr. Walter M. Sullivan, President
Ms. Linda Price, Director, Research
Mr. Russell M. Sullivan, Managing Director

Salary Minimum: $50,000

Functions: Generalist (All)

Industries: Manufacturing, Services, Accounting, HR Services, Government, Defense, Aerospace, Software

Accelerated Search LLC

63 Tom Harvey Rd # RD2
Westerly, RI 02891-3617
(401) 348-8899
Email: info@xlsearch.com
Web: www.xlsearch.com

Summary: We are an executive search firm placing IT and sales & marketing professionals in emerging technology companies.

Key Contact - Specialty:
Mr. Scott Gardner, Director, Staffing - *Sales*
Mr. Reed Bocchino, Director, Sales & Marketing
Mr. Chris Messina, Chief Financial Officer
Mr. Steve Givens, President

Salary Minimum: $75,000

Functions: Middle Mgmt., Sales & Mktg., IT

Industries: Computer Equip., Consumer Elect., E-commerce, IT Implementation, New Media, Fiber Optic, Network Infrastructure, Software, Accounting SW, Database SW, Development SW, ERP SW, Industry Specific SW, Mfg. SW, Networking, Comm. SW

The Accent Group

10988 N Harrells Ferry Rd Ste 17
Baton Rouge, LA 70816-8361
(225) 272-1392
(225) 272-1032
Email: freeadvice@theaccentgroup.com
Web: www.theaccentgroup.com

Summary: Our firm, with its international staff, enjoys a long history of executive staffing. Our firm is the executive recruiting division of a HR consulting firm.

Key Contact - Specialty:
Ms. Virginia Pickering, CPC, President
Mr. Jose Campoblanco, Executive Director

Salary Minimum: $50,000

Functions: Board Members, Senior Mgmt., Mfg., Sales & Mktg., HR Mgmt., Finance, CFOs, IT, Engineering, Int'l.

Industries: Generalist (All)

Access Financial

700 Canal St
Stamford, CT 06902-5921
(203) 328-3030
Fax: (203) 328-3098
Email: acc.fin@snet.net
Web: www.accfin.com

Summary: Highly regarded firm specializing in accounting, finance, tax, auditing, and treasury professionals.

Key Contact - Specialty:
Mr. Anthony E. Granger, CPA, Principal Founder & Managing Director
Mr. Ted Smith, Associate Director - *Financial*

Functions: Finance

Industries: Generalist (All)

Access Search Group

181 Metro Dr Ste 290
San Jose, CA 95110-1344
(408) 436-8496
Fax: (408) 573-7479
Email: dmartin@access-search1.com
Web: www.access-search1.com

Summary: With many years of staffing experience our firm is a leader in providing staffing solutions. Our firm partners with companies ranging from Fortune 500 to emerging start-ups providing a full line of staffing solutions so our clients can focus their time on their business.

Key Contact - Specialty:
Ms. Donna Martin, Director, Business Development
Mr. Jeff Lemmo, Director, Recruitment

Functions: Generalist (All)

Industries: Computer Equip., HR Services, IT Implementation, Software

Access Staffing Inc

PO Box 741714
Boynton Beach, FL 33474-1714
(561) 963-3232
Fax: (561) 423-7997
Email: accessit@aol.com

Summary: Our firm specializes in search, recruitment and placement for the IT field, primarily for positions in Florida. Our company president has extensive IT recruiting experience, plus programming, marketing of computer systems and management experience, personally coordinates all of our searches.

Key Contact - Specialty:
Mr. James J. Scimone, President

Functions: IT, MIS Mgmt., Systems Analysis, Systems Dev., Systems Implem., Systems Support, Network Admin., DB Admin.

Industries: Generalist (All)

Access Systems

101 Gibraltar Dr Ste 2D
Morris Plains, NJ 07950-1287
(973) 984-7960
Email: jpalzer@att.net

Summary: Extensive sales and sales management recruiting experience, over 75 percent of the candidates are interviewed in person. High-level of candidates are referrals. Positions are in sales and sales management in information technology.

Key Contact - Specialty:
Ms. Joanne Palzer, President

Salary Minimum: $80,000

Functions: Sales & Mktg., Sales Mgmt.

Industries: Network Infrastructure, Software, Accounting SW, Database SW, Development SW, Doc. Mgmt., Production SW, ERP SW, Mfg. SW, Networking, Comm. SW, Security SW, System SW

Access Tech Search

106 Cobblestone Ct Ste 205
Victor, NY 14564-1045
(585) 924-9946
Email: swhite@accesstechsearch.com

Summary: Working confidentially with talented professionals and client companies nationally. We specialize in recruiting and placing engineers, managers and executives in optical, photonics, RF, ASIC, electronic, defense, digital/analog, aerospace, semiconductor and other high-technology markets.

Key Contact - Specialty:
Ms. Stacey White, Senior Recruiter
Ms. Amy Bronwin, Recruiter
Mr. Stephen Tinkham, Recruiter - *Cellular, Communications, Engineering, Sales*

Salary Minimum: $75,000

Functions: Generalist (All), Management, Middle Mgmt., Mfg., Product Dev., Automation, Packaging, Engineering, Process, Minorities/Diversity

Industries: Generalist (All), Plastics, Rubber, Test, Measure Equip., Electronic, Elec. Components, Robotics, Semiconductors, Engineering Svcs., Communications, Digital, Wireless, Fiber Optic, RF/Microwave, Defense, Aerospace, Packaging, Software, Development SW, Mfg. SW

Access/Resources Inc

248 Olde Homestead Dr Ste 1
Marstons Mills, MA 02648-1756
(508) 428-8897
Email: arirecruit@aol.com

Summary: Our firm offers middle and upper-management recruiting for industrial clients with special capabilities in financial and general management assignments.

Key Contact - Specialty:
Mr. Peter V. Vangel, CPA, Principal - *Financial, General management*

Salary Minimum: $100,000

Functions: Generalist (All), Purchasing, Mktg. Research, Benefits, CFOs, Budgeting, Cash Mgmt., M&A

Industries: Generalist (All), Manufacturing, Medical Devices, Plastics, Rubber, Machine, Appliance, Motor Vehicles, Computer Equip., Accounting

Branches:
37450 Schoolcraft Rd Ste 150
Livonia, MI 48150-1000
(734) 462-3214
Email: arirecruit@aol.com
Key Contact - Specialty:
Ms. Julie Pawlusiak, Associate - *Financial, General management*

Accountant Profile Inc

1700 Highway 36 W Ste 122
Saint Paul, MN 55113-4015
(651) 636-7760
Fax: (651) 636-7728
Email: starhires@accountantprofile.com

Summary: We are a staffing solutions provider in finance/accounting permanent placement. We create value for our customers through commitment (90% placement fill), long term relationships (97% customer retention) and executing a process that delivers unparalleled results (100% placement retention). We partner with employers and job seekers.

Key Contact - Specialty:
Ms. Suzanne Roberts, CPC, President & Executive Recruiter

Salary Minimum: $50,000

Functions: Finance, CFOs, Budgeting, Cash Mgmt., Credit, Taxes, M&A, Risk Mgmt.

Industries: Generalist (All)

Accountants Inc

111 Anza Blvd Ste 400
Burlingame, CA 94010-1932
(650) 579-1111
(800) 430-3111
Fax: (650) 579-1927
Email: hr@accountantsinc.com
Web: www.accountantsinc.com

Summary: Our company provides staffing solutions for accounting and finance departments in companies large and small. By integrating project, project to direct hire, and direct hire services, we provide flexible options for our clients staffing and candidates career needs.

Key Contact - Specialty:
Mr John P. Unroe, President & Chief Executive Officer
Mrs. Ursula Williams, Senior Vice President

Salary Minimum: $100,000

Accounting & Finance Personnel Inc

1702 E Highland Ave Ste 200
Phoenix, AZ 85016-4665
(602) 277-3700
Fax: (602) 926-2629
Web: www.afpersonnel.com

Summary: Firm is owned and operated by accountants. We specialize in placing accountants in full time or temp positions in all industries.

Key Contact - Specialty:
Mr. Michael Nolan, President - *Finance*
Ms. Barbara Meyers, Manager, Recruiting
Mr. Jeffrey Silvia, Manager, Recruiting
Ms. Denise Garcia, Administration Manager

Salary Minimum: $40,000

Functions: Finance, CFOs, Budgeting, Cash Mgmt., Credit, Taxes, M&A, Risk Mgmt.

Industries: Generalist (All)

Branches:
4400 E Broadway Blvd Ste 600
Tucson, AZ 85711-3554
(602) 323-3600
Fax: (602) 795-4753
Key Contact - Specialty:
Mr. Duane Etter, Manager - *Accounting*

Accounting Advantage

(a division of The Howroyd Group)
12400 Wilshire Blvd Ste 1460
Los Angeles, CA 90025-1060
(310) 445-4111
Fax: (310) 312-8722
Email: brentwoodaa@career-rocket.com
Web: www.actadv.com

Summary: Our firm specializes in placing all levels of accounting and financial staff, including investment banking, on a permanent, contract and temp basis.

Key Contact - Specialty:
Mr. Bernard Howroyd
Ms. Penny Haberman

Functions: Finance

Industries: Generalist (All)

Branches:
1295 N Euclid St
Anaheim, CA 92801-1954
(714) 284-5245
Fax: (714) 284-5247
Email: anaheim@actadv.com
Key Contact - Specialty:
Ms. Angela Kim

3900 Kilroy Airport Way Ste 180
Long Beach, CA 90806-6807
(562) 637-4989
Fax: (562) 637-1017
Email: acctngadvlongbeach@actadv.com
Key Contact - Specialty:
Mr. Bob Thompson

230 S Lake Ave
Pasadena, CA 91101-4823
(626) 796-7009
Fax: (626) 796-9706
Email: acctadvsantafesprings@actadv.com
Key Contact - Specialty:
Mr. Josee Minero

12215 Telegraph Rd Ste 111
Santa Fe Springs, CA 90670-3344
(562) 777-1700
Fax: (562) 777-1617
Email: acctadvsantafesprings@actadv.com
Key Contact - Specialty:
Ms. Amber Martinez, Branch Manager

Accounting Assets Inc

8300 Boone Blvd Ste 310
Tysons Corner
Vienna, VA 22182-2626
(703) 883-2123
Fax: (703) 506-4743
Email: positions@accountingassets.com
Web: www.accountingassets.com

Summary: We provide full service Financial and
Accounting career placement in the Washington
Metropolitan Area. We are a locally owned,
privately held company that places a premium on
the importance of providing outstanding personal
service to our clients and candidates.

Key Contact - Specialty:
Mr. Michael Jacobs, Principal
Ms. Dina Jacobs, Principal

Salary Minimum: $60,000

Functions: Generalist (All), Finance

Industries: Generalist (All), Accounting

Accounting Career Consultants

1001 Craig Rd Ste 391
Saint Louis, MO 63146-6213
(314) 569-9898
Fax: (314) 569-9856
Email: info@careeradvancers.com
Web: www.careeradvancers.com

Summary: We are a full service firm that works
on accounting, finance and HR positions at all
levels from CFOs and HR directors to accounting
clerks and HR assistants. We can provide staffing
services ranging from consulting, payroll, or temp
services to direct-hire, executive search or retained
search.

Key Contact - Specialty:
Mr. Melvin Weinberg, CPA, President
Mr. Larry Weinberg, CPA, CPC, CSP, CTS, Vice
President
Ms. Jeune Cruz, Office Manager

Functions: HR Mgmt., Finance

Industries: Generalist (All)

Accounting Connections

1839 NW 24th Ave
Portland, OR 97210-2537
(503) 228-2335
(866) 956-2748
Fax: (503) 228-2175
Email: info@staff4u.com
Web: www.accountingconnections.com

Summary: The most effective and cost-efficient
accounting and financial staffing available. We are
large enough to have the exposure to meet your
needs, yet small enough to maintain the
relationships that are vital to our clients and
candidates. Our goal is to maintain our leadership
position while we continue providing the area's
finest companies with the area's finest employees.

Key Contact - Specialty:
Ms. Pamela A. Ake, Account Manager -
 Accounting, CFOs, Controllers, Finance
Mr. Scott Rugh, Account Manager - *Accounting,
 Accounting (Bookkeeping), Finance*
Mr. Mike Brackenbrough, Account Manager -
 Finance, Human resources
Ms. Layla Bauder, Account Manager -
 Accounting, Finance

Functions: Finance

Industries: Generalist (All)

Accounting Principals Ltd

1 Independent Dr Ste 215
Jacksonville, FL 32202-5007
(904) 360-2400
(800) 981-3849
Fax: (904) 360-2394
Email: jacksonville@accountingprincipals.com
Web: www.accountingprincipals.com

Summary: Our firm is a leader in the recruitment
and placement of accounting and finance
professionals. We offer a complete range of
workforce solutions in accounting, finance,
mortgage and banking through our nationwide
branch network and team of experienced
professionals.

Key Contact - Specialty:
Mr. Jeff Jackovich, President
Mr. Robert P. Crouch, Senior Vice President,
 CFO & Treasurer
Ms. Tyra Tutor, Senior Vice President, Corporate
 Dev
Ms. Kim Wygle, Managing Director -
 Pharmaceutical

Salary Minimum: $40,000

Functions: CFOs, Budgeting, Cash Mgmt.,
 Credit, Taxes, M&A

Industries: Generalist (All)

Branches:
1 Technology Dr Ste I811
Irvine, CA 92618-5319
(949) 788-0209
Fax: (949) 788-0598
Email: irvine@accountingprincipals.com
Key Contact - Specialty:
Ms. Linda McCluskey, Regional Vice President

1 Centerpointe Dr Ste 430
La Palma, CA 90623-1077
(714) 521-4499
Fax: (714) 521-6788
Email: lapalma@accountingprincipals.com
Key Contact - Specialty:
Mr. Ashish Sardo, Area Managing Director

1333 Broadway Ste 225
Oakland, CA 94612-1918
(510) 251-2010
Fax: (510) 251-2028
Email: oakland@accountingprincipals.com
Key Contact - Specialty:
Mr. Jeffrey Taylor, Managing Director

1 Sansome St Ste 1895
San Francisco, CA 94104-4432
(415) 392-2227
Fax: (415) 392-2255
Email: cajobs@accountingprincipals.com

Key Contact - Specialty:
Ms. Linda McClusky, Regional Vice President

410 17th St Ste 1700
Denver, CO 80202-4430
(303) 534-1950
Email: denver@accountingprincipals.com
Key Contact - Specialty:
Ms. Kristin Middleton, Area Manager

2963 Gulf to Bay Blvd Ste 265
Clearwater, FL 33759-4255
(727) 210-1589
Fax: (727) 210-1608
Email: stpetersburg@accountingprincipals.com
Key Contact - Specialty:
Ms. Linda Bowman, Managing Director

1900 Summit Tower Blvd Ste 140
Orlando, FL 32810-5911
(407) 875-0660
Fax: (407) 660-8189
Email: orlando@accountingprincipals.com
Key Contact - Specialty:
Ms. Amy Montenegro, Area Manager

4830 W Kennedy Blvd Ste 600
Tampa, FL 33609-2584
(813) 289-8549
Fax: (813) 289-9466
Email: tampa@accountingprincipals.com
Key Contact - Specialty:
Ms. Joyce McAleer, Area Manager

1050 Crown Pointe Pkwy Ste 1700
Atlanta, GA 30338-7704
(770) 671-9647
Fax: (770) 671-1341
Email: atlanta@accountingprincipals.com
Key Contact - Specialty:
Ms. Kim LaBadia, Managing Director

4860 S Lewis Ave Ste 102
Tulsa, OK 74105-5171
(918) 744-9900
Fax: (918) 744-9994
Email: tulsa@accountingprincipals.com
Key Contact - Specialty:
Ms. Kimberly Nation, Managing Director

8200 Greensboro Dr Ste 1175
Mc Lean, VA 22102-3872
(703) 761-7001
Fax: (703) 761-4248
Key Contact - Specialty:
Ms. Annette McGough, Managing Director

ACHIEVE Technical Services

9110B Alcosta Blvd Ste 313
San Ramon, CA 94583-3801
(925) 803-1080
Fax: (925) 803-9454
Email: resumes@achieve1.com
Web: www.achieve1.com

Summary: We specialize in providing staffing
services for talented medical, legal, regulatory and
scientific professionals looking to work in the
pharmaceutical, biotechnology or medical device
industry.

Key Contact - Specialty:
Mr. Lonnie Barish, MBA, SPHR, President &
 Principal

Salary Minimum: $60,000

Functions: Generalist (All), Management, Middle
 Mgmt., Product Dev., Healthcare, Mktg.
 Research, Mktg. Mgmt., R&D

Industries: Biotech/Life Sciences, Healthcare

Email your resume to a targeted list of recruiters now at www.ExecutiveAgent.com/DER07

Ackerman Johnson Inc

26 E Amberglow Cir Ste 201
Spring, TX 77381-6108
(936) 321-0320
Email: jobs@aj-inc.net
Web: www.ackermanjohnson.com

Summary: We specialize in sales, sales
management, and senior management in medical,
pharmaceutical, voice & data communications,
consulting, computer hardware/software, business
products/services, industrial, consumer products
and energy.

Key Contact - Specialty:
Mr. Frederick W. Stang, President

Salary Minimum: $45,000

Functions: Generalist (All), Sales & Mktg., Sales
Reps.

Industries: Energy, Utilities, Oil & Gas,
Manufacturing, Food, Bev., Tobacco, Drugs
Mfg., Medical Devices, Test, Measure Equip.,
Services, Pharm Svcs., Mgmt. Consulting, K-12
Ed., Logistics Svcs., Inst./Industrial Food Svc.,
Telecoms, Wireless, Government, Packaging,
Software, Biotech/Life Sciences

Acquis Associates Inc

PO Box 1288
Wall, NJ 07719-1288
(732) 280-8425
Email: sharkus@acquis.com
Web: www.acquis.com

Summary: Technical/executive recruiting for the
chemical, pharmaceutical, biotechnology, and
materials industries.

Key Contact - Specialty:
Dr. Linda C. Sharkus, PhD, President - *Chemical*

Salary Minimum: $75,000

Functions: Management, Mktg. Research, R&D,
Engineering

Industries: Chemicals

ACSYS Inc

1300 N Market St Ste 501
Wilmington, DE 19801-1810
(302) 658-6181
Fax: (302) 658-6244
Email: wilmington@acsysinc.com
Web: www.acsysinc.com

Summary: Permanent/temp/contract specialists in
accounting, finance, banking, and human
resources - contingency and retainer.

Key Contact - Specialty:
Mr. Domenic L. Vacca, Managing Director

Salary Minimum: $20,000

Functions: Generalist (All), Senior Mgmt., Mktg.
Research, Sales Mgmt., HR Mgmt., Finance,
CFOs, Taxes

Industries: Generalist (All), Drugs Mfg., Banking,
Invest. Banking, Brokers, Accounting,
Broadcast, Film, Telecoms

Branches:
1850 M St NW Ste 950
Washington, DC 20036-5836
(202) 463-7210
Email: dc@acsysinc.com
Key Contact - Specialty:
Mr. Michael Reamy

100 N Tampa St Ste 1950
Tampa, FL 33602-5855
(813) 221-7930
Email: tampa@acsysinc.com

Key Contact - Specialty:
Lari Blaylock

11675 Rainwater Dr Ste 575
Alpharetta, GA 30004-8693
(678) 393-2100
Email: alpharetta@acsysinc.com
Key Contact - Specialty:
L. Howell

2600 Tower Oaks Blvd Ste 610
Rockville, MD 20852-4251
(240) 221-0455
Email: bethesdahotjobs@acsysinc.com
Key Contact - Specialty:
Ms. Lisa Hull

1820 Chapel Ave W Ste 168
Cherry Hill, NJ 08002-4611
(856) 910-1824
Fax: (856) 910-1939
Email: cherryhill@acsysinc.com
Key Contact - Specialty:
Mr. Michael Shedroff - *Finance, Financial
services*

379 Thornall St Ste 7
Edison, NJ 08837-2226
(732) 205-1900
Email: edison@acsysinc.com
Key Contact - Specialty:
Ms. Christina Navarro

201 S College St Ste 1660
Charlotte, NC 28244-0065
(704) 377-6447
Email: charlotte@acsysinc.com
Key Contact - Specialty:
Ms. Peggy King

4400 Deer Path Rd Ste 103
Harrisburg, PA 17110-3908
(717) 232-5602
Email: harrisburg@acsysinc.com
Key Contact - Specialty:
Mr. William Marshall

1850 William Penn Way Ste 106
Lancaster, PA 17601-6740
(717) 390-0888
Fax: (717) 390-2012
Email: lancaster@acsysinc.com
Key Contact - Specialty:
Ms. Monica Yasgur, Senior Consultant - *Finance,
Financial services*

1700 Market St Ste 1720
Philadelphia, PA 19103-3911
(215) 568-6810
Fax: (215) 977-0362
Email: philadelphia@acsysinc.com
Key Contact - Specialty:
Mr. David Laderman, Director - *Finance,
Financial services*

500 E Swedesford Rd Ste 100
Wayne, PA 19087-1614
(610) 687-6107
Fax: (610) 687-9456
Email: wayne@acsysinc.com
Key Contact - Specialty:
Ms. Susan Sein-Lwin, Director
Ms. Paige McCrossin, Regional Manager

12120 Sunset Hills Rd Ste 400
Reston, VA 20190-5829
(703) 715-2100
Email: reston@acsysinc.com

Key Contact - Specialty:
Mr. Sheridan D. King, CPA

ACT

25492 Hillsboro Dr
Laguna Niguel, CA 92677-1458
(949) 365-9090
Email: weact4u@actsearch.com
Web: www.actsearch.com

Summary: We specialize in executive and
technical recruitment for pre-IPO and Fortune 500
companies developing technologies for wireless,
multimedia and broadband communications.

Key Contact - Specialty:
Mr. John Kratz, Owner

Functions: Generalist (All), Product Dev., Mktg.
Mgmt., R&D, Engineering

Industries: Computer Equip., Consumer Elect.,
Electronic, Elec. Components, Consumer
Goods, Engineering Svcs., Telecoms,
Telephony, Digital, Wireless, Fiber Optic,
Network Infrastructure, RF/Microwave

Action Employment Resources

5140 Main St Unit 303-348
Williamsville, NY 14221-5204
(716) 689-8139
Email: staff@actionemployment.com
Web: www.actionemployment.jobthread.com

Summary: Full service, professional placement
and recruiting firm. Areas of specialization include
engineering (all disciplines), manufacturing
(maintenance, production and quality control) and
sales & marketing. Affiliated with many national
recruiting firms.

Key Contact - Specialty:
Mr. Les Matthews, President

Salary Minimum: $75,000

Functions: Mfg., Product Dev., Plant Mgmt.,
Quality, Packaging, Sales & Mktg., R&D,
Engineering, Architects

Industries: Generalist (All), Oil & Gas,
Manufacturing, Food, Bev., Tobacco,
Chemicals, Drugs Mfg., Medical Devices,
Plastics, Rubber, Metal Products, Machine,
Appliance, Motor Vehicles, Consumer Elect.,
Electronic, Elec. Components, Semiconductors,
Consumer Goods, Non-profits, Architectural
Svcs., Equip Svcs., Mgmt. Consulting,
Engineering Svcs., Environmental Svcs.,
Packaging, Biotech/Life Sciences, Hospitals

Action International

155 E Columbus St Ste 125
Pickerington, OH 43147-1468
(614) 833-3211
Fax: (614) 410-1676
Email: craighohnberger@getn2action.com
Web: www.action-international.com

Summary: Business coaching and consulting firm
specializing in placement of franchised business
coaches in all 50 states and abroad. Seeking high
income earners desiring business ownership and
having a passion both to help others and for
business development.

Key Contact - Specialty:
Mr. Craig Hohnberger, President & Director of
Recruitment
Mrs. Annette Hohnberger, Director, Support

Salary Minimum: $100,000

Functions: Generalist (All), Senior Mgmt., Sales
& Mktg., Direct Mktg.

Industries: Generalist (All), Mgmt. Consulting,
Call Centers

Action Management Services
6055 Rockside Woods Blvd Ste 160
Cleveland, OH 44131-2302
(440) 642-8777
Fax: (216) 642-1294
Email: dale@actionmgmt.com
Web: www.actionmgmt.com

Summary: We are a permanent placement firm which handles both contingency and retained searches. We serve companies in manufacturing, banking, healthcare, distribution and service industries.

Key Contact - Specialty:
Mr. Dale C. Chorba, President & Owner - *Finance, Tax*
Mr. Dale M. Chorba, Executive Vice President & Principal - *Finance, Healthcare, Physicians*

Salary Minimum: $50,000

Functions: Healthcare, HR Mgmt., Finance, CFOs, Budgeting, Cash Mgmt., Credit, Taxes, IT

Industries: Generalist (All), Misc. Mfg., Wholesale, Retail, Finance, Banking, Real Estate, Hospitals, Long-term/Home Care

Action Medical Search
511 W Sprague Rd
Roca, NE 68430-4273
(800) 579-8986
Fax: (413) 778-1899
Email: jobs@actionmedicalsearch.com
Web: www.actionmedicalsearch.com

Summary: A leading medical and healthcare recruitment agency.

Key Contact - Specialty:
Ms. Lia Langston, President - *Healthcare, Medical, OB/GYN, Operating rooms, Orthopedics*

Salary Minimum: $100,000

Functions: Healthcare, Physicians

Industries: Generalist (All), HR Services, Healthcare, Hospitals, Long-term/Home Care, Dental, Physical Therapy, Occupational Therapy, Women's

Active Search and Placement
2298 Tattler St
Arroyo Grande, CA 93420-5526
(805) 474-5611
Fax: (805) 474-5612
Email: nada@investmentemployment.com
Web: www.investmentemployment.com

Summary: We conduct targeted searches for portfolio managers, business development officers, research analysts, trust and operations administrators for clients who are investment management, mutual funds and trust companies.

Key Contact - Specialty:
Ms. Nada D. Williston, Partner - *Investment management, Mutual funds, Trust*

Salary Minimum: $45,000

Functions: Cash Mgmt.

Industries: Finance, Banking, Invest. Banking, Brokers, Venture Cap., Mutual/Hedge Funds, Misc. Financial

Adam-Bryce Inc
10516 Beckridge Ln
Raleigh, NC 27615-2080
(919) 841-1230
Email: jobs@adambryce.com
Web: www.adambryce.com

Summary: We have been involved in staffing and identifying high potential candidates who through the use of technology have moved their IT organizations into the forefront of their industries.

Key Contact - Specialty:
Ms. Nadine Rubin, President - *Information Technology*
Ms. Phyllis Reiss, Executive Recruiter - *Information Technology, Telecommunications*

Salary Minimum: $80,000

Functions: Generalist (All), Management, IT, MIS Mgmt.

Industries: Telecoms, Call Centers, Network Infrastructure, Security SW

Adams & Associates
2132 Briarfield St
Camarillo, CA 93010-3302
(805) 484-8815
Fax: (805) 484-7345
Email: lynnsadams@aol.com

Summary: We specialize in civil engineering. Placing qualified men and women in the fields of transportation, engineering, architecture and management. Covering all levels from design to top management.

Key Contact - Specialty:
Ms. Lynn Adams, Owner

Functions: Engineering, Structural, Architects

Industries: Construction, Transportation, Architectural Svcs., Engineering Svcs.

J N Adams & Associates Inc
26 Overbrook Rd
Madison, CT 06443-1834
(203) 421-5429
Email: jnadams@jnadams.com
Web: www.jnadams.com

Summary: We are an executive placement firm specializing in the recruitment of top professionals in industries such as automotive, medical device and consumer products. Our professionals work in the areas of quality assurance, Six Sigma, engineering and manufacturing.

Key Contact - Specialty:
Mr. Eric M. Berg, President - *Engineering, Manufacturing, Quality, Six sigma*

Functions: Generalist (All), Management, Mfg., Engineering

Industries: Manufacturing, Chemicals, Drugs Mfg., Medical Devices, Plastics, Rubber, Metal Products, Machine, Appliance, Motor Vehicles, Consumer Elect., Test, Measure Equip., Misc. Mfg., Electronic, Elec. Components, Robotics, Consumer Goods, Packaging

Adams & Ryan Inc
60 E 42nd St Rm 465
New York, NY 10165-0467
(212) 697-7087
Email: sherry@adamsandryan.com
Web: www.adamsandryan.com

Summary: Each candidate is met personally, fully screened and informed of your company prior to their CV being sent out. All levels from CEOs to sales are interviewed for your approval.

Key Contact - Specialty:
Ms. Sherry Koski, President - *Management, Operations, Sales, Telecommunications*

Salary Minimum: $35,000

Functions: Generalist (All), Sales Mgmt.

Industries: Invest. Banking, Brokers, Mutual/Hedge Funds, Misc. Financial, Accounting, New Media, Telecoms

Adams Consulting Group LLC
(also known as ACG Resources)
147 W 35th St Rm 1400
New York, NY 10001-2110
(212) 566-7600
Fax: (212) 566-7877
Email: lenadams@acgresources.com
Web: www.acgresources.com

Summary: Our goal is to make available, a full range of executive search and staffing services in the most ethical, cost effective and efficient manner.

Key Contact - Specialty:
Mr. Len Adams, CPC, Chief Executive Officer
Ms. Heather Eidlen, Vice President - *Accounting, Administration, Banking, Banking (Commercial,Corporate)*
Ms. Franca Diona, Vice President - *Banking (Commercial,Corporate,Investment,Mortgage,Retail)*

Salary Minimum: $50,000

Functions: Generalist (All)

Industries: Banking, Invest. Banking, Brokers, Venture Cap., Mutual/Hedge Funds, Misc. Financial, Services, Legal, Accounting

Adams Gardner Executive Search
1177 West Loop S
Houston, TX 77027-9006
(281) 556-6890
(800) 816-7593
Fax: (281) 556-0672
Email: conniek@adamsgardner.com
Web: www.adamsgardner.com

Summary: We are a search firm that specializes in the tax accounting arena that places primarily applicants in VPs of finance, CFOs, directors of tax, controller and senior accountant/tax positions. Our advisors are Big 4 CPAs, CFPs or CPCs. Each candidate is subjected to an investigative interview by a psychotherapist and by CPA advisors. We perform retained and contingent searches.

Key Contact - Specialty:
Ms. Constance A. Kelley, CPC, Chief Executive Officer & President
Mr. Donald Kelley, CPA, Chief Financial Officer & Vice President
Ms. Heather Adams, MSW, Secretary

Salary Minimum: $100,000

Functions: CFOs

Industries: Energy, Utilities, Construction, Manufacturing, Finance, Services, Recreation, Media, Communications, Software, Healthcare

Adams Inc
17330 Wright St Ste 101
Omaha, NE 68130-2157
(402) 333-3009
Fax: (402) 333-3448
Email: jobs@adams-inc.com
Web: www.adams-inc.com

Summary: We specialize in banking, credit card, trust, investment, brokerage insurance and mortgage industries placements. We maintain a database of over 70,000 contacts and track over 1,200 job openings.

Key Contact - Specialty:
Mr. Jay Adams, CPC, President & Owner - *Trust*
Ms. Roxane Adams, CPC, Executive Vice President - *Trust*

Salary Minimum: $40,000

Functions: Generalist (All), Mktg. Research, CFOs, Cash Mgmt., Credit

Industries: Generalist (All), Finance, Banking, Misc. Financial

Addition 2000 Inc

585-550 Rue Sherbrooke O
Immeuble Commercial
Montreal, QC H3A 1B9
Canada
(514) 842-1021
Fax: (514) 842-3458
Email: g.lamontagne@addition2000.com

Summary: Recruitment specialist involved in sales, upper and middle management, accounting, and production fields.

Key Contact - Specialty:
Mr. Gilles Lamontagne, President

Functions: Generalist (All)

Industries: Generalist (All)

Adel-Lawrence Associates Inc

1208 State Route 34 Ste 18
Matawan, NJ 07747-1966
(732) 566-4914
Fax: (732) 566-9326
Email: larryr@alajobs.com
Web: www.alajobs.com

Summary: We are a search/recruitment of engineering and technical personnel. Specializing in field service, biomedical, medical x-ray/imaging, engineers, electronics, IT, management and other related technical disciplines. We offer full-time, temp-to-perm and contracting.

Key Contact - Specialty:
Mr. Larry Radzely, President - *Computers (Software), Engineering, Technical*

Salary Minimum: $40,000

Functions: Systems Dev.

Industries: Medical Devices, Computer Equip., Consumer Elect., Test, Measure Equip., Electronic, Elec. Components, Biotech/Life Sciences

Adept Tech Recruiting Inc

219 Glendale Rd
Scarsdale, NY 10583-1533
(914) 523-5857

Summary: We focus primarily on placement of experienced personnel in the Internet start-up arena. Secondarily, we work on placement of personnel in all areas of home health care.

Key Contact - Specialty:
Mr. Fredrick R. Press, President - *Advertising, Healthcare*

Functions: Nurses, Systems Dev.

Industries: Software, Long-term/Home Care

Administrative Employer Services

42140 Van Dyke Ave Ste 205
Sterling Heights, MI 48314-3676
(586) 997-3377
(877) 423-7736
Fax: (586) 997-3378
Email: info@aespeo.com
Web: www.aespeo.com

Summary: Specializing in the surgical recruitment and placement of all professionals in the PEO and staffing industries.

Key Contact - Specialty:
Mr. Don Onesi, Managing Partner

Functions: Generalist (All)

Industries: Generalist (All), HR Services

Adolfson & Associates

7910 E 29th Ave
Denver, CO 80238-2436
(303) 290-0240
Email: eadolfson@qwest.net

Summary: We are a contingency search firm specializing in the areas of sales and sales management in the medical industry. We also place operations and general management positions in the healthcare service arena, for example: home healthcare services, physical therapy services and O&P services.

Key Contact - Specialty:
Mr. Edwin Adolfson, Owner - *Management, Sales*

Functions: Management, Sales Mgmt., Sales Reps.

Industries: Healthcare, Hospitals, Long-term/Home Care, Physical Therapy

ADOW Professionals

36 E 4th St Ste 1308
Cincinnati, OH 45202-3804
(888) 645-8800
(513) 721-2369
Fax: (513) 721-3724
Email: nationalsearch@adow.com
Web: www.adow.com

Summary: Our firm is a woman owned executive search firm recruiting and providing top talent. Our unique four key elements: the profile, the identification process, the assessment, and the future, guarantee a rapid and complete search with a systematic process. We use technology and the human touch. Through our specialized divisions and numerous affiliate offices we provide the overall market at a glance.

Key Contact - Specialty:
Ms. Kathleen G. Kern, President & Executive Consultant - *Engineering, Marketing, Research & development*
Mr. Jerry L. Kern, Vice President & Executive Consultant - *Healthcare, Materials, Purchasing*
Ms. Tiffany Spencer, Manager, Executive Consultant - *Clerical*
Ms. Jessica Eades

Salary Minimum: $65,000

Functions: Management, Mfg., Packaging, Mktg. Research, Mktg. Mgmt., Minorities/Diversity, Non-profits

Industries: Generalist (All), Non-profits, Higher Ed., Aerospace

ADV Advanced Technical Services Inc

200-1037 McNicoll Ave
Scarborough, ON M1W 3W6
Canada
(416) 502-2545
(800) 933-1883
Fax: (416) 502-2544
Email: contact@advtechnical.com
Web: www.advtechnical.com

Summary: Hi-tech recruitment firm, specializing in placing electrical and computer engineers (software, hardware, telecom, datacom, defense/aerospace and advanced manufacturing). We build long-term relationships with candidates and client companies.

Key Contact - Specialty:
Mr. Paul Hill, President
Mr. John Penturn
Ms. Celia Lee
Ms. Sahin Jivraj
Mr. Cameron Gausby
Mr. Nigel Buck

Salary Minimum: $45,000

Functions: Generalist (All), Mfg., Product Dev., Engineering

Industries: Generalist (All), Manufacturing, Computer Equip., Media, Telecoms, Software

Advance Career Tech

1804 Denison Rd
Naperville, IL 60565-6761
(630) 479-3801
(630) 369-3800
Fax: (630) 369-4228
Email: sam@actrecruiters.com
Web: www.actrecruiters.com

Summary: Ours is a nationwide executive search firm. We are dedicated to serve our pharmaceutical, medical, biotechnology, diagnostic, and biological and process automation and validation industry clients in the placement of acknowledged achievers with their research, clinical research affairs, regulatory affairs, quality and engineering departments.

Key Contact - Specialty:
Mr. Sam Mehta, President

Functions: Healthcare

Industries: Drugs Mfg., Medical Devices, Plastics, Rubber, Biotech/Life Sciences, Healthcare, Hospitals

Advance Consulting Services Inc

1495 Rymco Dr Ste 102
Winston Salem, NC 27103-2947
(336) 774-8778
Email: ysanborn@aol.com

Summary: We are a small business enterprise offering professional recruiting services. We are committed to conducting our clients' search assignments with the highest standard of confidentiality, discretion and integrity.

Key Contact - Specialty:
Ms. Yevonne Sanborn, President - *Public relations, Sales*

Salary Minimum: $40,000

Functions: Senior Mgmt., Sales & Mktg., Sales Mgmt., Engineering

Industries: Manufacturing, Services, Mgmt. Consulting

Advance Employment Inc

2546 E Jolly Rd Unit 3
Lansing, MI 48910-8219
(517) 887-0377
Fax: (517) 887-9944
Web: www.advanceteam.com

Summary: We are a full-service employment firm serving the temp, contract, leasing and executive recruiting needs of our client-partners.

Key Contact - Specialty:
Mr. Mark Taylor - *Engineering, MIS*

Salary Minimum: $40,000

Functions: Generalist (All), Production, Sales Mgmt., Cash Mgmt., Systems Dev., Systems Support, Engineering

Industries: Generalist (All), Construction, Manufacturing, Finance, Accounting, HR Services

Branches:
506 W Carleton Rd Ste A
Hillsdale, MI 49242-9341
(517) 439-4494
Email: hillsdale@advanceteam.com
Key Contact - Specialty:
Ms. Kristen Maze, Account Manager

1711 N West Ave
Jackson, MI 49202-2032
(517) 787-3333
Email: jackson@advanceteam.com
Key Contact - Specialty:
Ms. Dawn Waagner, Director, Business
   Development

6180 Stadium Dr
Kalamazoo, MI 49009-2010
(269) 353-1100
Email: kalamazoo@advanceteam.com
Key Contact - Specialty:
Ms. Lesa Strausbaugh, Director, Business
   Development

4407 W St Joe Hwy
Lansing, MI 48917-4120
(517) 321-4765
(800) 772-4125
Key Contact - Specialty:
Mr. David R. Shockey, Director, Business
   Development

2300 S Mission St
Mount Pleasant, MI 48858-4433
(989) 773-2275
(800) 707-1020
Email: mtpleasant@advanceteam.com
Key Contact - Specialty:
Mr. Andrew Lee, Director, Business
   Development

1519 N Main St
Three Rivers, MI 49093-1377
(616) 279-7222
Email: threerivers@advanceteam.com
Key Contact - Specialty:
Ms. Gorgena Shaw, Manager

Advanced Career Solutions Inc
13352 Silver Lake Dr
Poway, CA 92064-4414
(858) 668-3111
Fax: (858) 668-3011
Email: acssearch@prodigy.net
Web: www.acssearch.com

Summary: We specialize in the placement of
exceptionally qualified and marketable sales,
management engineering, installation, service and
maintenance candidates in today's competitive
mechanical, commercial and industrial HVAC,
refrigeration and construction markets.

Key Contact - Specialty:
Ms. Karen Mattonen, CAC, President

Salary Minimum: $60,000

Functions: Generalist (All), Board Members,
Environmentalists, Bldg. Contractors, Security
Personnel

Industries: Generalist (All), Energy, Utilities,
Construction, Manufacturing, Test, Measure
Equip., Electronic, Elec. Components, Services,
Equip Svcs., Engineering Svcs., Environmental
Svcs., Property/Facility Mgmt., Industry
Specific SW, Security SW

Advanced Corporate Search
3275 Forest Ave
Medford, OR 97501-1917
(541) 773-2162
Email: jgibson@advcorpsearch.com
Web: www.advcorpsearch.com

Summary: We specialize in the satellite, GPS,
RF/microwave, antenna industries and some
aerospace. Sales & management, business
development, program management, engineering
& management, and systems integration are what
we do. Our reputation is one of honesty and
integrity. We have a long proven ability to secure
the 'absolute best'. We are flexible and have a
'win-win' attitude.

Key Contact - Specialty:
Ms. Jan Gibson, President

Salary Minimum: $80,000

Functions: Sales Mgmt., Systems Implem.,
Systems Support, R&D, Engineering

Industries: Electronic, Elec. Components,
Telephony, Digital, Wireless, Fiber Optic,
RF/Microwave, Defense

Advanced HR Solutions Inc
10127 Northwestern Ave
Franksville, WI 53126-9206
(262) 909-4370
Email: vivian@advancedhrsolutions.com
Web: www.advancedhrsolutions.com

Summary: We are dedicated to exceeding client
expectations by providing outstanding quality,
solid results and operating with the highest of
integrity and ethical procedures. The firm
specializes in utilities and manufacturing firms
and places candidates in executive, board-level,
managerial and technical/professional positions. In
addition, psychometrician, candidate/employee
assessment and contract recruiting services are
provided.

Key Contact - Specialty:
Ms. Vivian Rodriguez Krenzke, President

Salary Minimum: $50,000

Functions: Management, Board Members, Senior
Mgmt., Middle Mgmt., Plant Mgmt., Materials
Plng., HR Mgmt., Engineering,
Minorities/Diversity

Industries: Energy, Utilities, Construction,
Manufacturing

Advanced Recruiters Inc
630 E State St Ste 300
Jacksonville, IL 62650-2152
(217) 479-8088
Email: mls@advancedrecruiters.com
Web: www.advancedrecruiters.com

Summary: Our firm specializes in the placement
of sales, marketing, operations, clinical and
healthcare professionals. These professionals are
employed by major pharmaceutical/medical
device companies and hospital systems.

Key Contact - Specialty:
Mr. Mike Strieker, President
Ms. Julie Brewer, Vice President - *Biotechnology*
Mr. Luke Crawford, Vice President -
   *Biopharmaceutical, Biotechnology,
   Distribution, Medical (Devices),
   Pharmaceutical*
Ms. Kiley Vinyard, Vice President -
   *Biopharmaceutical, Biotechnology, Marketing,
   Medical (Devices), Pharmaceutical*
Ms. Sara Logue, Vice President -
   *Biopharmaceutical, Biotechnology, Marketing,
   Medical (Devices), Pharmaceutical*

Salary Minimum: $100,000

Functions: Senior Mgmt.

Industries: Drugs Mfg., Medical Devices, Supply
Chain Mgmt., Marketing SW, Biotech/Life
Sciences, Healthcare

Advanced Recruiting Techniques
2413 Swales Dr
Lawrenceburg, IN 47025-9703
(800) 579-5201
(812) 656-8118
Fax: (866) 837-1285
Email: estes@fuse.net
Web: www.advancedrecruiting.org

Summary: Healthcare recruiting firm well known
for their exceptional ethics, capabilities, and
recruitment strategies. Predominantly specialize in
clinical positions.

Key Contact - Specialty:
Ms. Barbara Estes, Chief Executive Officer

Functions: Healthcare, Physicians

Industries: Hospitals, Long-term/Home Care,
Non-Classifiable

Advanced Resources Group Inc
15450 S Outer 40
Chesterfield, MO 63017-2066
(636) 777-4141
Fax: (636) 777-4142
Email: staffing@advr.com
Web: www.advancedresources.net

Summary: We provide IT consulting services and
direct placement servies to Fortune 1000
companies.

Key Contact - Specialty:
Mr. Frank J. Ehlers, President - *Information
Technology*

Functions: Generalist (All), IT, Systems Analysis,
Systems Dev., Systems Implem., Systems
Support, Network Admin., DB Admin.

Industries: Generalist (All), Energy, Utilities,
Manufacturing, Transportation, Retail, Finance,
Communications, Insurance, Software,
Accounting SW, Healthcare

Advanced Search Group Inc
625 Plainfield Rd Ste 426
Willowbrook, IL 60527-5384
(630) 734-1010
Fax: (630) 734-1011
Email: charlie@advancedsearch.com
Web: www.advancedsearch.com

Summary: Specializing in ChemE, ME, EE and
chemists, operations, technical management and
technical sales and marketing, with the chemical,
pharmaceuticals, petrochems, biotechnology, and
consumer products.

Key Contact - Specialty:
Mr. Charles Diana, President

Salary Minimum: $50,000

Functions: Engineering

Industries: Manufacturing, Food, Bev., Tobacco,
Printing, Chemicals, Soap, Perf., Cosmtcs.,
Drugs Mfg., Plastics, Rubber, Paints, Petro.
Products

Advanced Technology Consultants Inc (ATC)
544 E Weddell Dr Ste 11
Sunnyvale, CA 94089-2123
(650) 692-2485
Fax: (650) 697-1222
Email: reza@atcsearch.com
Web: www.atcsearch.com

Summary: We specializes in software and
emerging technologies, communication &
convergence, professional & IT services, systems
& electronics and bio-informatics.

Key Contact - Specialty:
Mr. Reza Vakili, Senior Partner
Mrs. Annabelle Villa, Principal - *Financial services*
Mr. Tony Morshedi, General Manager
Mr. David Aghighi, Senior Account Executive - *Sales, Staffing, Start-up companies, Storage*

Salary Minimum: $70,000

Functions: Generalist (All), Middle Mgmt., Mktg. Mgmt., Systems Analysis, Systems Dev., Systems Implem., Network Admin., DB Admin.

Industries: Generalist (All), Venture Cap., E-commerce, IT Implementation, Engineering Svcs., Supply Chain Mgmt, Wireless, Software, Development SW, ERP SW, Networking, Comm. SW

Advancement Inc

721 Fair Links Way
Gurnee, IL 60031-4706
(847) 247-2100
Email: reply@advancement.com
Web: www.advancement.com

Summary: Our expertise is focused on semiconductor and wireless technologies in the commercial sector and radar, optics, avionics and communications in the defense sector. We place engineering candidates at all levels from design engineer to executive management. We represent startup venture growth firms to large OEM manufacturing organizations.

Key Contact - Specialty:
Mr. Scott Hall, President - *Semiconductors, Wireless*

Salary Minimum: $60,000

Functions: Product Dev., Engineering

Industries: Computer Equip., Consumer Elect., Semiconductors, Telecoms, Telephony, Digital, Wireless, Fiber Optic, Network Infrastructure, RF/Microwave, Defense, Homeland Security, Aerospace, Development SW, Networking, Comm. SW

Advertising Recruitment Specialists

16700 Sequoia St
Fountain Valley, CA 92708-2333
(714) 775-3910
Fax: (714) 775-3911
Email: kathy@adrecruiters.com
Web: www.adrecruiters.com

Summary: We are a contingency executive search firm that specializes in recruiting for advertising agencies nationwide. Our focus is mainly on account services positions, however we also recruit for media and creative.

Key Contact - Specialty:
Mrs. Kathleen Nomura, Managing Partner
Mrs. Deborah Strobel, Managing Partner

Salary Minimum: $100,000

Functions: Senior Mgmt., Advertising, PR

Industries: Media, Advertising

Branches:
35 Sycamore Dr
Waldwick, NJ 07463-1024
(201) 652-8062
Email: debbie@adrecruiters.com

Key Contact - Specialty:
Ms. Deborah Strobel, Managing Partner

Advice Personnel Inc

230 Park Ave Rm 860
New York, NY 10169-0933
(212) 682-4400
Fax: (212) 697-0343
Email: aschwartz@adviceny.com
Web: www.adviceny.com

Summary: We are a professional recruiting firm specializing in permanent and temporary placement of accounting, finance, tax and administrative support positions.

Key Contact - Specialty:
Mr. Alan Schwartz, CPA, Principal - *Accounting, Accounting (Big 4,Bookkeeping,General,Public)*
Mr. Aaron Greenberg, Principal - *Advertising, Apparel, Brokerage, CFOs, Consumer (Products)*

Salary Minimum: $40,000

Functions: Finance, CFOs, Budgeting, Cash Mgmt., Credit, Taxes, M&A, Risk Mgmt.

Industries: Generalist (All)

Advocate Placement Ltd

200-1200 Bay St
Toronto, ON M5R 2A5
Canada
(416) 927-9222
(800) 461-1275
Fax: (416) 927-8772
Email: alerek@advocateplacement
Web: www.advocateplacement.com

Summary: We are a recruitment company providing diverse legal staffing solutions for companies and law firms in the form of lawyers and law clerks. Our competitive edge is our superior screening process and attention to fit. We specialize in high level partner moves to other law firms and into industry.

Key Contact - Specialty:
Ms. Anita Lerek, President & General Counsel
Mr. Eric Singer, Director, Development & Client Solutions
Mr. Trevor Branion, Manager, Candidate Development
Mr. Michaela Krell, Recruiter

Functions: Legal

Industries: Legal

The Advocates Group Inc

90 New Montgomery St Ste 310
San Francisco, CA 94105-4551
(415) 957-1102
Email: info@advocatesgroup.com
Web: www.advocatesgroup.com

Summary: Our firm is one of the nation's top attorney search and consulting firms, representing top law firms and corporations. Our candidates consistently possess top professional and academic credentials and we have been repeatedly recommended by top legal journals as one of state's premier headhunters.

Key Contact - Specialty:
Mr. Jeffrey S. Stillman, Esq., JD, President - *Legal (Attorneys)*
Ms. Linnette Lum, Search Consultant - *Legal (Attorneys)*
Dr. Helene D. Colaizzi, Search Consultant - *Legal (Attorneys)*

Salary Minimum: $120,000

Functions: Legal, Attorneys

Industries: Generalist (All), Finance, Invest. Banking, Legal, Biotech/Life Sciences

Branches:
11601 Wilshire Blvd Ste 500
Brentwood Center
Los Angeles, CA 90025-1741
(310) 556-0332
Key Contact - Specialty:
Mr. David Popky, Vice President

Aerospace Solutions LLC

308 E Ocotillo Rd Ste 104
Phoenix, AZ 85012-1043
(602) 722-2571
Fax: (602) 265-8979
Email: aerosolutions@qwest.net

Summary: Our firm is a professional search and recruitment contingency firm. We work exclusively in the aerospace sector and related disciplines. This singular focus also allows us to be responsive, disciplined, cost effective and successful in meeting our clients' needs.

Key Contact - Specialty:
Mr. Charles K. Jonkosky, President
Mrs. Kristine Zimmerman, Director

Salary Minimum: $50,000

Functions: Generalist (All)

Industries: Aerospace

Affinity Options

PO Box 507
Vista, CA 92085-0507
(760) 295-0824
Fax: (760) 295-0823
Email: questions@affinityoptions.com
Web: www.affinityoptions.com

Summary: We are an executive search firm focusing in the nationwide placement of allied health professionals, nurses, research workers, scientific and medical sales professionals. We address and solve the hiring needs required by the diverse industries of biomedical, biotech, pharmaceuticals and medical, among others.

Key Contact - Specialty:
Ms. Laura White, Owner, Search Consultant - *Healthcare, Home health, Hospital, Long term care, Medical*

Functions: Healthcare, Nurses, Allied Health

Industries: Drugs Mfg., Pharm Svcs., Healthcare, Hospitals, Long-term/Home Care, Physical Therapy, Occupational Therapy, Women's

Affordable Executive Recruiters

5518 Lemona Ave
Sherman Oaks, CA 91411-3638
(818) 782-8554
Fax: (818) 779-0395
Email: fggerson@earthlink.net

Summary: Specializing in CFOs, CEOs, CPAs, controllers, accountants and payroll personnel. Also HR, credit managers, IT and attorneys.

Key Contact - Specialty:
Mr. Fred Gerson, Owner - *Financial*

Salary Minimum: $30,000

Functions: Generalist (All), Management, Mfg., Sales & Mktg., HR Mgmt., Finance, CFOs, Taxes, Legal, Attorneys

Industries: Generalist (All)

AgentHR

562 W 1675 S
Lehi, UT 84043-5498
(801) 766-5523
Fax: (801) 665-1688
Email: amcomber@agenthr.com
Web: www.agenthr.com/amcomber

Summary: Executive Recruiter specializing in
Marketing, Advertising, PR and Sales

Key Contact - Specialty:
Ms. Andrea McOmber, Executive Recruiter

Salary Minimum: $50,000

Functions: Management, Senior Mgmt., Middle
Mgmt., Sales & Mktg., Advertising, Mktg.
Research, Mktg. Mgmt., Sales Mgmt., Direct
Mktg., Graphic Designers

Industries: Generalist (All), Finance, Services, E-
commerce, Hospitality, Media, Advertising,
Publishing, New Media, Broadcast, Film,
Communications, Insurance, Real Estate,
Software, Entertainment SW, Industry Specific
SW, Marketing SW, Networking, Comm. SW,
Healthcare

Aggressive Partners

4701 Auvergne Ave Ste 101
Lisle, IL 60532-1914
(630) 852-3400
Fax: (630) 852-5072
Email: resume@aggressivecorp.com
Web: www.aggressivecorp.com

Summary: We are dedicated to assisting our
clients through the arduous task of searching for
key team members. Our practice ranges from
middle through senior leadership roles in
companies that manufacture.

Key Contact - Specialty:
Mr. Adam Gaspar, Partner
Mr. Thomas J. Lane, Partner
Mr. Raymond J. Kagee, Vice President

Salary Minimum: $70,000

Functions: Generalist (All), Management, Mfg.,
Materials, Sales & Mktg., HR Mgmt., Finance,
Engineering

Industries: Generalist (All), Manufacturing,
Lumber, Furniture, Medical Devices, Metal
Products, Machine, Appliance, Motor Vehicles,
Computer Equip., Misc. Mfg.

AGI Search

2921 Canal Dr
Panama City, FL 32405-1641
(850) 763-4490
(850) 625-0205
Email: joan@agisearch.com
Web: www.agisearch.com

Summary: We are specialists in recruiting sales
and marketing executive talent for growing and
established high tech companies. Clients may opt
for hourly search rates or more traditional
percentage based fees. We offer extensive in
house research services from a team that has
extensive experience working together in the high
tech industry.

Key Contact - Specialty:
Ms. Joan Holley, Executive Recruiter - *Computers
(Hardware,Sales), Information Technology,
Marketing, Sales*
Ms. Mary Boadwine, Office Manager

Functions: Sales & Mktg.

Industries: Computer Equip.

Agra Placements Ltd

8187 University Blvd
Clive, IA 50325-1122
(515) 225-6563
Fax: (515) 225-7733
Email: iowa@agraplacements.com
Web: www.agraplacements.com

Summary: One of the nation's leading firm
specializing in the recruitment, screening &
selection of management, marketing and technical
professionals for agribusiness, horticultural, food
and commercial firms.

Key Contact - Specialty:
Mr. Doug Rice, President

Salary Minimum: $25,000

Functions: Generalist (All), Mfg., Materials,
Sales & Mktg., Engineering

Industries: Generalist (All), Agri., Forestry,
Mining, Food, Bev., Tobacco, Consumer Elect.,
Test, Measure Equip., Misc. Mfg., Electronic,
Elec. Components, Wholesale, Retail, Finance

Branches:
105 S Andover Rd Ste A
Andover, KS 67002-7867
(316) 733-7701
Fax: (316) 733-7706
Email: kansas@agraplacements.com
Key Contact - Specialty:
Mr. Gary Goodwin, Manager

PO BOx 275
Madison, SD 57042-0275
(605) 256-3880
Fax: (605) 256-3645
Email: south_dakota@agraplacements.com
Key Contact - Specialty:
Mr. Rob Fox, Manager

AGRI-associates, Inc.

116 W 47th St Ste 205
Kansas City, MO 64112-1615
(816) 531-7980
(800) 550-7980
Fax: (816) 531-7982
Email: gjp@agriassociates.com
Web: www.agriassociates.com

Summary: Specialist in personnel search and
recruiting for agribusiness, including suppliers of
agricultural production inputs, agricultural
commodity processors and agricultural production
enterprises.

Key Contact - Specialty:
Mr. Glenn J. Person, President & Principal - *Food*
Dale Feitz, Principal
Ms. Connie Pierce, Principal
Mr. Paul J. Person, Principal

Salary Minimum: $35,000

Functions: Management, Production, Plant
Mgmt., Quality, Sales & Mktg., Finance, R&D,
Engineering

Industries: Agri., Forestry, Mining

Branches:
700 Colorado Blvd #279
Denver, CO 80206-4084
(720) 261-1571
(800) 354-8039
Email: agridenver@cox.net
Key Contact - Specialty:
Mr. Bernie Gross, Principal

1627 Red Cedar Dr Apt 14
Fort Myers, FL 33907-7610
(941) 240-0122
Email: consult@agriassociatesflorida.com

Key Contact - Specialty:
Nat Natarajan, Director
Mr. Rodney J. Huisman, Principal

5665 Highway 9 N Ste 103 PMB 311
Alpharetta, GA 30004-3932
(770) 475-2201
(800) 562-1590
Fax: (770) 475-1136
Email: mtd_agri@bellsouth.net
Key Contact - Specialty:
Mr. Michael T. Deal, Manager

3475 Jersey Ridge Rd Ste 2
Davenport, IA 52807-2293
(563) 344-6974
(800) 728-0363
Fax: (563) 344-9199
Email: agridav@earthlink.net
Key Contact - Specialty:
Mr. Michael S. Vinzenz, Manager

2458 Leyland Draw
Woodbury, MN 55125-3451
(651) 731-3211
(888) 731-9196
Fax: (651) 501-2262
Email: dhansen@bisworks.net
Key Contact - Specialty:
Mr. Dana Hansen, Manager

PO Box 24046
Omaha, NE 68124-0046
(402) 397-4410
Fax: (402) 397-4411
Email: agriomaha@cox.net
Key Contact - Specialty:
Mr. Richard W. Robertson, Manager

2632 Maplewood Dr
Columbus, OH 43231-4852
(614) 891-3362
Fax: (614) 891-3382
Email: jmcgregor@columbus.rr.com
Key Contact - Specialty:
Ms. Jill E. McGregor, Manager

20120 Route 19 Ste 105
PMB 152
Cranberry Township, PA 16066-6209
(724) 741-0800
(866) 318-0800
Email: agriassocpa@cs.com
Key Contact - Specialty:
Mr. Terry Glenister, Principal

PO Box 14
Memphis, TN 38101-0014
(901) 757-8787
(800) 792-2474
Fax: (901) 751-1639
Email: agrimemphis@bellsouth.net
Key Contact - Specialty:
Mr. Robert E. Thompson, Manager
Mr. Gene Pope

131 Degan Ave Ste 203
Lewisville, TX 75057-3664
(972) 221-7568
(800) 561-7568
Fax: (972) 221-1409
Email: agridallas@ev1.net
Key Contact - Specialty:
Mr. Lawrence W. Pete Keeley, Manager
Ms. Karen Carlson, Assistant

Agri-Tech Personnel Inc

4444 N Belleview Ave Ste 209
Kansas City, MO 64116-1507
(816) 873-3636
Fax: (816) 453-6001
Email: corp@agri-techpersonnel.com
Web: www.agri-techpersonnel.com

Email your resume to a targeted list of recruiters now at www.ExecutiveAgent.com/DER07

Summary: Agri-business recruiters for the grain storage & processing, food manufacturing, drug and chemical industries, finding candidates to fill positions in management, manufacturing, engineering, marketing, R&D, Q.C., administration, etc.

Key Contact - Specialty:
Mr. Steve Rice, President
Mr. Dale Pickering
Mr. Brend King, Director, Technical Placement - *Food*
Mr. Jim Hunt, Director. Agriculture & Coop Placement
Ms. Rita Pickering
Ms. Heidi L. Romang

Salary Minimum: $30,000

Functions: Generalist (All)

Industries: Agri., Forestry, Mining, Food, Bev., Tobacco, Accounting, Equip Svcs., Mgmt. Consulting, HR Services, Engineering Svcs., Packaging

Agriesti & Associates

16291 Country Day Rd
Poway, CA 92064-1455
(858) 451-7766
Fax: (858) 451-7843
Email: salesjob@san.rr.com

Summary: We are a search firm specializing in consumer products, sales & marketing professionals, also medical & pharmaceuticals sales. We are affiliated with partners across the country to facilitate our searches.

Key Contact - Specialty:
Ms. Kay Agriesti, President - *Pharmaceutical, Sales*

Functions: Middle Mgmt., Mktg. Research, Mktg. Mgmt., Sales Mgmt.

Industries: Drugs Mfg., Medical Devices, Biotech/Life Sciences, Healthcare, Dental

Agro Quality Search Inc

595 119th Ln NW
Minneapolis, MN 55448-2271
(763) 572-3737
Fax: (763) 572-3738
Email: agroqualsearch@qwest.net
Web: www.agroqualitysearch.com

Summary: We have been successful providing quality searches. Agriculture is our strength: food related areas are second. We provide a full range from CEOs to production supervisors, with sales & marketing a strong area. Strong integrity is our foundation.

Key Contact - Specialty:
Mr. Jerry Olson

Functions: Generalist (All)

Industries: Generalist (All)

AIM Consultants

HC 1 Box 4109
Shell Knob, MO 65747-9408
(417) 858-8801
(800) 586-2499
Fax: (636) 600-5055
Email: brenda@aimcareers.com
Web: www.aimcareers.com

Summary: We are a physician recruitment firm that specializes in the recruitment and placement of primary care and specialty physicians for facilities nationwide. Our clients include single and multiple specialty groups, hospitals, clinics and government providers.

Key Contact - Specialty:
Ms. Brenda Buck, Owner

Functions: Physicians

Industries: Generalist (All)

AIM Recruiting

6635 Wagner Way
San Antonio, TX 78256-2009
(210) 698-4300
Fax: (206) 212-8237
Email: info@aimjobs.net
Web: www.aimjobs.net

Summary: Physician recruitment firm with an extensive network.

Key Contact - Specialty:
Ms. Debbie Smith, Principal

Functions: Physicians

Industries: Healthcare

AJ Associates

635 N 151st Cir
Omaha, NE 68154-1823
(402) 445-9150
Fax: (402) 445-9150
Email: dlockett5@cox.net

Summary: Our firm has experience in the staffing industry covering permanent, contract to hire and contract opportunities in the information technology, and engineering fields. We are a woman owned small business company.

Key Contact - Specialty:
Ms. DeAnn Lockett, President
Mr. Dean Stevens, Recruiter

Functions: Management, Senior Mgmt., IT, Engineering

Industries: Software

AJC Search Associates Ltd

15 Grand Ave
Baldwin, NY 11510-3109
(516) 766-1699
Fax: (516) 766-3889
Email: jayajc@aol.com

Summary: Boutique search firm servicing the employee benefits community. Product lines include retirement plans, life & health insurance, long term care, managed care, capital markets and investments. Specialties include legal, actuarial, consulting, underwriting, sales, computer professionals, marketing, accounting and customer service. Service is our best policy.

Key Contact - Specialty:
Mr. Jay Cohen, Recruiter

Salary Minimum: $50,000

Functions: Generalist (All), Healthcare, Physicians, Nurses, Benefits, Actuaries, Pension/Ret. Planning

Industries: Legal, Accounting, Insurance, Casualty, Claims, Life, Software, Healthcare

Ajilon Communications

402-2255 Carling Ave
Halldon House Building
Ottawa, ON K2B 7Z5
Canada
(613) 232-4744
Fax: (613) 232-1199
Email: ott@ajiloncom.com
Web: www.ajiloncom.com

Summary: Our firm is the leader in the provision of cabling products & services, professional staffing resources and managed services to clients with significant investments in their communications infrastructure. We customize our solutions to meet your needs, whether for contract 'just-in-time' resources, fully outsourced options or, permanent workforce augmentation.

Key Contact - Specialty:
Ms. Coleen Harrigan, Manager, Office Administration
Ms. Lynne Martel, Account Executive
Ms. Maureen McDonald, Technical Recruiter

Salary Minimum: $50,000

Functions: Generalist (All), Board Members, Senior Mgmt., Training, IT, Systems Analysis, Systems Dev., R&D, Engineering, Specialized Svcs.

Industries: Telecoms

Branches:
805-8 Ave SW
Floor 5
Calgary, AB T2P 1H7
Canada
(403) 215-1280
Fax: (403) 215-1288
Email: cal@ajilon.com
Key Contact - Specialty:
Mr. Ken Kyswaty, Branch Manager
Ms. Jill Druery, Director, Western Canada

1600 Bedford Hwy
Sunnyside Place
Bedford, NS B4A 1E8
Canada
(902) 832-0306
Email: hfx@ajilon.com
Key Contact - Specialty:
Mr. Peter Landry, Branch Manager

7-6685 Millcreek Dr
Mississauga, ON L5N 5M5
Canada
(905) 821-3500
Fax: (905) 821-3688
Email: tor@ajilon.com
Key Contact - Specialty:
Mr. Rick Peace, Director, Network Services
Ms. Jo-Ann Attwell, Manager, Office Administration
Mr. Colin Steele, Account Executive
Mr. Chris Zanella, Account Executive - *International*

100-4025 Boul Industriel
Laval, QC H7L 4S3
Canada
(450) 628-6677
(877) 978-7576
Fax: (450) 628-9714
Email: mtl@ajilon.com
Key Contact - Specialty:
Mr. Benoit Chalifoux, General Manager

Ajilon Finance

(formerly known as Accountants On Call (AOC))
2 Park 80 Plz W Ste 9
Saddle Brook, NJ 07663-5822
(201) 843-0006
Fax: (201) 712-1033
Email: staffing@ajilonfinance.com
Web: www.ajilonfinance.com

Summary: We are specialists in the placement of temp and permanent accounting, bookkeeping, data entry and other financial personnel.

Key Contact - Specialty:
Mr. Neil Lebovits, President & Chief Operating Officer
Mr. Robert Mahan, CPA, Chief Financial Officer
Mr. Ed Blust, CMO
Ms. Debbie Buchsbaum, Vice President, Comms. & Administration

Mr. Alexander deGreve, Vice President, Staff Development
Ms. Doris J. Fitzsimmons, Senior Vice President & CFO
Ms. Pam Hoffman
Mr. Patrick Lyons, Chief Financial Officer
Ms. Diane O'Meally, President
Mr. Larry Saltzman, Senior Vice President
Mr. Brad Violette, Executive Vice President

Functions: Finance, CFOs, Budgeting, Cash Mgmt., Credit, Taxes, M&A, Risk Mgmt., Actuaries, Pension/Ret. Planning

Industries: Generalist (All)

Branches:
1201 S Alma School Rd Ste 6750
Mesa, AZ 85210-2101
(480) 644-0500
Fax: (480) 644-9550
Email: mesa@ajilonfinance.com
Key Contact - Specialty:
Ms. Stacy Boase, Branch Manager

2111 E Highland Ave Ste 431
Phoenix, AZ 85016-4735
(602) 957-1200
Fax: (602) 957-1222
Email: phoenix@ajilonfinance.com
Key Contact - Specialty:
Ms. Carol McBride, Branch Manager
Mr. Rodney Griffin, Principal
Mr. David Bolar, Principal
Ms. Christine Sewell-Longtin, Principal
Ms. Bernadette Grattan, Principal
Ms. Robin Bumgarner, Area Manager

3500 W Olive Ave Ste 550
Burbank, CA 91505-5524
(818) 845-6600
Fax: (818) 845-6330
Email: burbank@ajilonfinance.com
Key Contact - Specialty:
Mr. William DeMario, Senior Vice President
Ms. Tisha Cuyugan, Branch Manager

17700 Castleton St Ste 558
City of Industry, CA 91748-5708
(626) 912-0090
Fax: (626) 912-8292
Email: cityofindustry@ajilonfinance.com
Key Contact - Specialty:
Ms. Janette Marx, Branch Manager

4180 La Jolla Village Dr Ste 200
La Jolla, CA 92037-1471
(858) 455-7888
Fax: (858) 453-3373
Email: sandiego@ajilonfinance.com
Key Contact - Specialty:
Ms. Cyndi McDermott, Area Manager

6 Centerpointe Dr Ste 250
La Palma, CA 90623-1098
(714) 739-1300
Fax: (714) 521-6500
Email: lapalma@ajilonfinance.com
Key Contact - Specialty:
Ms. Kira Bruno, Area Vice President
Ms. Merry White, Branch Manager
Ms. Janet Tyler, Senior Recruiter

10940 Wilshire Blvd Ste 850
Los Angeles, CA 90024-3909
(310) 443-8610
Fax: (310) 443-8650
Email: lawest@ajilonfinance.com
Key Contact - Specialty:
Ms. Laurie Matthews, Vice President, Sales Training
Ms. Victoria Kaleta, Area Vice President
Dana Conaway, Executive Recruiter
Ms. Alissa Grand, Branch Manager

800 Wilshire Blvd Ste 850
Los Angeles, CA 90017-2644
(213) 689-4606
Fax: (213) 689-5046
Email: ladowntown@ajilonfinance.com
Key Contact - Specialty:
Mr. David Smachetti, Principal
Ms. Adrineh Safarian, Principal
Ms. Lisa Stell, Principal
Ms. Denise Gardella, Principal
Peace Kim, Principal
Ms. Susan Nowak, Principal
Ms. Mia Husfield, Branch Manager

4590 Macarthur Blvd Ste 350
Newport Beach, CA 92660-2073
(949) 955-0100
Fax: (949) 955-1347
Email: newportbeach@ajilonfinance.com
Key Contact - Specialty:
Ms. Kathleen Gans, Area Vice President
Ms. Cathy Eldridge, Branch Manager
Ms. Traci Duffy, Branch Manager

1 Kaiser Plz Ste 1030
Oakland, CA 94612-3601
(510) 986-1800
Fax: (510) 986-8760
Email: oakland@ajilonfinance.com
Key Contact - Specialty:
Mr. Vito LoGrasso, Branch Manager

4141 Inland Empire Blvd Ste 303
Ontario, CA 91764-5001
(909) 466 8880
Fax: (909) 466-5470
Email: ontario@ajilonfinance.com
Key Contact - Specialty:
Ms. Julie Daignault, Branch Manager
Ms. Viola Penny

285 Hamilton Ave Ste 280
Palo Alto, CA 94301-2538
(650) 328-8400
Fax: (650) 328-8570
Email: paloalto@ajilonfinance.com
Key Contact - Specialty:
Ms. Lynda Galliano

6140 Stoneridge Mall Rd Ste 360
Pleasanton, CA 94588-3235
(925) 734-8666
Fax: (925) 734-5550
Email: pleasanton@ajilonfinance.com
Key Contact - Specialty:
Ms. Julia Holian, Branch Manager
Mr. David Walker, Area Manager

1435 River Park Dr Ste 310
Sacramento, CA 95815-4510
(916) 923-5555
Fax: (916) 923-1662
Email: sacramento@ajilonfinance.com
Key Contact - Specialty:
Mr. Ernesto Uriarto, Branch Manager
Mr. Ron Garner, Owner
Ms. Ann Garner, Owner

44 Montgomery St Ste 2310
San Francisco, CA 94104-4711
(415) 398-3366
Fax: (415) 398-2618
Email: sanfrancisco@ajilonfinance.com
Key Contact - Specialty:
Ms. Anne Pasquier, Branch Vice President

970 W 190th St Ste 210
Torrance, CA 90502-1026
(310) 527-2777
Fax: (310) 527-0109
Email: torrance@ajilonfinance.com
Key Contact - Specialty:
Mr. Steve Shapiro, Branch Vice President
Mr. Randy Wagaman, Branch Manager

2175 N California Blvd Ste 775
Walnut Creek, CA 94596-3574
(925) 937-1000
Fax: (925) 939-3716
Email: walnutcreek@ajilonfinance.com
Key Contact - Specialty:
Ms. Anne Silveira, Branch Manager
Ms. Lynda Langlinais, Area Director

21700 Oxnard St Ste 850
Woodland Hills, CA 91367-7566
(818) 992-7676
Fax: (818) 992-1360
Email: woodlandhills@ajilonfinance.com
Key Contact - Specialty:
Mr. David Sprinkle
Ms. Erin Spitzer, Branch Manager

1099 18th St Ste 2820
Denver, CO 80202-1936
(303) 291-1212
Fax: (303) 291-1055
Email: denver@ajilonfinance.com
Key Contact - Specialty:
Mr. Monte Merz, Area Vice President
Mr. Jeff Higgins, Executive Recruiter

8400 E Prentice Ave Ste 1420
Greenwood Village, CO 80111-2926
(303) 804-5300
Fax: (303) 804-9616
Email: englewood@ajilonfinance.com
Key Contact - Specialty:
Ms. Erin Greenlee

1150 17th St NW Ste 408
Washington, DC 20036-4606
(202) 452-0002
Fax: (202) 452-0992
Email: washingtondc@ajilonfinance.com
Key Contact - Specialty:
Ms. Kelly Bergenstock, Branch Manager
Mr. Tony Zambrano, Branch Manager
Ms. Valarie Green, Staffing Manager

2 Alhambra Plz Ste 640
Coral Gables, FL 33134-5214
(305) 443-9333
Fax: (305) 443-6589
Email: miami@ajilonfinance.com
Key Contact - Specialty:
Ms. Stacy Calderone, Branch Manager

5900 N Andrews Ave Ste 627
Fort Lauderdale, FL 33309-2373
(954) 771-0333
Fax: (954) 492-9699
Email: fortlauderdale@ajilonfinance.com
Key Contact - Specialty:
Mr. Dave Watson, Area Director
Ms. Sharon Maffei, Branch Manager

2180 Satellite Blvd Ste 320
Duluth, GA 30097-4927
(678) 474-9944
Fax: (678) 474-9414
Email: duluth@ajilonfinance.com
Key Contact - Specialty:
Mr. Wade Roberts, Branch Manager

10 S La Salle St Ste 1310
Chicago, IL 60603-1081
(312) 782-7788
Fax: (312) 782-0171
Email: chicago@ajilonfinance.com
Key Contact - Specialty:
Ms. Bridget O'Connell, Senior Vice President

3400 Dundee Rd Ste 150
Northbrook, IL 60062-2333
(847) 205-0800
Fax: (847) 205-1230
Email: northbrook@ajilonfinance.com

Email your resume to a targeted list of recruiters now at www.ExecutiveAgent.com/DER07

Key Contact - Specialty:
Ms. Colleen Craig, Branch Manager

1 Lincoln Ctr Ste 1108
Oakbrook Terrace, IL 60181-4268
(630) 261-1300
Fax: (630) 261-1334
Email: oakbrook@ajilonfinance.com
Key Contact - Specialty:
Ms. Alison Gentry, Branch Vice President

1750 E Golf Rd Ste 200
Schaumburg, IL 60173-5040
(847) 413-8800
Fax: (847) 413-9066
Email: schaumburg@ajilonfinance.com
Key Contact - Specialty:
Mr. Carl Barnard, Branch Manager

111 Monument Cir Ste 3940
Indianapolis, IN 46204-5175
(317) 686-0001
Fax: (317) 686-0007
Email: indianapolis@ajilonfinance.com
Key Contact - Specialty:
Mr. George Lessmeister, Area Vice President
Ms. Crystal Whitacre, Branch Manager

101 Bullitt Ln Ste 206
Louisville, KY 40222-5444
(502) 339-9007
Fax: (502) 339-9646
Email: louisville@ajilonfinance.com
Key Contact - Specialty:
Ms. Leslie Goldhill, Branch Manager

201 N Charles St Ste 300
Baltimore, MD 21201-4114
(410) 685-5700
Fax: (410) 685-5736
Email: baltimore@ajilonfinance.com
Key Contact - Specialty:
Mrs. Lisa Witt, Branch Manager

111 Rockville Pike Ste 420
Rockville, MD 20850-5168
(301) 984-8999
Fax: (301) 984-8680
Email: rockville@ajilonfinance.com
Key Contact - Specialty:
Mr. John Ryder, Area Manager

10 High St Ste 710
Boston, MA 02110-1662
(617) 345-0440
Fax: (617) 345-0423
Email: boston@ajilonfinance.com
Key Contact - Specialty:
Mr. Kyle Swift, Branch Manager

300 Granite St Ste 411
Braintree, MA 02184-3950
(781) 794-5100
Fax: (781) 356-2225
Email: braintree@ajilonfinance.com

161 Worcester Rd Ste 407
Framingham, MA 01701-5300
(508) 872-7800
Fax: (508) 879-9898
Email: framingham@ajilonfinance.com
Key Contact - Specialty:
Ms. Patricia Couch, Area Vice President
Ms. Ann Hamel, Branch Manager

28411 Northwestern Hwy Ste 910
Southfield, MI 48034-5534
(248) 356-0660
Fax: (248) 356-8740
Email: detroit@ajilonfinance.com
Key Contact - Specialty:
Ms. Lynn Moyer, Branch Manager

100 S 5th St Ste 420
Minneapolis, MN 55402-1232
(952) 884-9900
Fax: (952) 884-2446
Email: bloomington@ajilonfinance.com
Key Contact - Specialty:
Ms. Betty Abelson, Area Manager

911 Main St Ste 701
Kansas City, MO 64105-5360
(816) 421-7774
Fax: (816) 421-8224
Email: kansascity@ajilonfinance.com
Key Contact - Specialty:
Mr. Steve Davee, Branch Manager

101 S Hanley Rd Ste 210
Saint Louis, MO 63105-3445
(314) 436-0500
Fax: (314) 436-0833
Email: stlouis@ajilonfinance.com
Key Contact - Specialty:
Mr. Clark Young, Branch Manager
Mr. Louis Hanses

10805 Sunset Office Dr Ste 208
Saint Louis, MO 63127-1026
(314) 966-4900
Fax: (314) 966-6663
Email: sunsethills@ajilonfinance.com
Key Contact - Specialty:
Mr. Stan Carr, Branch Manager

6787 W Tropicana Ave Ste 103
Las Vegas, NV 89103-4758
(702) 284-7112
Fax: (702) 284-7191
Email: ajilonlasvegas@aol.com
Key Contact - Specialty:
Ms. Donna Kelly, Licensee

72 Eagle Rock Ave
East Hanover, NJ 07936-3151
(973) 781-0034
Fax: (973) 781-0658
Email: livingston@ajilonfinance.com
Key Contact - Specialty:
Mr. Richard Scott, Branch Manager

379 Thornall St Ste 10
Edison, NJ 08837-2233
(732) 321-1700
Fax: (732) 494-4386
Email: edison@ajilonfinance.com
Key Contact - Specialty:
Mr. Ted Fitzgerald, Area Manager

30 Montgomery St Ste 120
Jersey City, NJ 07302-3821
(201) 333-4227
Fax: (201) 333-4248
Email: jerseycity@ajilonfinance.com
Key Contact - Specialty:
Ms. Mary Hutchins, Branch Manager

80 E Route 4 Ste 230
The Atrium
Paramus, NJ 07652-2620
(201) 843-8882
Fax: (201) 843-8572
Email: paramus@ajilonfinance.com
Key Contact - Specialty:
Ms. Donna Mahan, Division Manager
Mr. Jamey Myers, Executive Recruiter

119 Cherry Hill Rd Ste 320
Parsippany, NJ 07054-1126
(973) 331-3890
Fax: (973) 331-3891
Email: parsippany@ajilonfinance.com
Key Contact - Specialty:
Mr. Rory Sakin, Senior Vice President
Ms. Rita Silverstein, Branch Vice President

125 Village Blvd Ste 240
Princeton, NJ 08540-5753
(609) 452-7117
Fax: (609) 987-0681
Email: princeton@ajilonfinance.com

1200 Veterans Hwy Ste 300
Hauppauge, NY 11788-3052
(631) 273-8552
Fax: (631) 273-8599
Email: longisland@ajilonfinance.com
Key Contact - Specialty:
Ms. Alana Graceffo

227 W Trade St Ste 1810
Charlotte, NC 28202-1699
(704) 376-0006
Fax: (704) 376-4787
Email: charlotte@ajilonfinance.com
Key Contact - Specialty:
Ms. Jennifer Stuebbe, Branch Manager

1801 Stanley Rd Ste 206
Greensboro, NC 27407-2643
(336) 292-3800
Fax: (336) 292-2245
Email: greensboro@ajilonfinance.com
Key Contact - Specialty:
Mr. Larry Basel, Area Director
Ms. Krista Akins, Branch Manager

4807 Rockside Rd Ste 530
Cleveland, OH 44131-2162
(216) 328-0888
Fax: (216) 328-1709
Email: cleveland@ajilonfinance.com
Key Contact - Specialty:
Ms. Michelle Reynolds, Branch Manager

5110 S Yale Ave Ste 412
Tulsa, OK 74135-7483
(918) 481-3332
Fax: (918) 499-2226
Email: tulsa@ajilonfinance.com
Key Contact - Specialty:
Ms. Jana Rugg, Branch Manager

1260 NW Waterhouse Ave Ste 160
Beaverton, OR 97006-5794
(503) 439-1555
Fax: (503) 533-2385
Email: beavertonfinance@ajilon.com
Key Contact - Specialty:
Ms. Meegan Thye-Walker, Branch Manager
Ayelet Loran

601 SW 2nd Ave Ste 1620
Portland, OR 97204-3124
(503) 228-0300
Fax: (503) 220-2529
Email: portland@ajilonfinance.com
Key Contact - Specialty:
Ms. Cathy Presjak, Branch Manager

1150 1st Ave Ste 960
King Of Prussia, PA 19406-1334
(610) 337-8500
Fax: (610) 227-7344
Email: kingofprussia@ajilonfinance.com
Key Contact - Specialty:
Mr. Michael Goldstein

437 Grant St Ste 800
Pittsburgh, PA 15219-6109
(412) 391-0900
Fax: (412) 391-8288
Email: pittsburgh@ajilonfinance.com
Key Contact - Specialty:
Ms. Laura DeRosa, Branch Manager

250 Commonwealth Dr Ste 100
Greenville, SC 29615-4846
(864) 987-0123
Fax: (864) 288-3044

Email: grccnvillc@ajilonfinance.com
Key Contact - Specialty:
Mr. Keith LoCascio, Branch Manager

6075 Poplar Ave Ste 121
Memphis, TN 38119-0109
(901) 761-1416
Fax: (901) 374-0421
Email: memphis@ajilonfinance.com
Key Contact - Specialty:
Ms. Luanne Hearn, Staffing Consultant
Mr. Buddy Daves, Branch Manager
Ms. Ann Conn, Executive Recruiter

1612 Summit Ave Ste 420
Fort Worth, TX 76102-5916
(817) 870-1800
Fax: (817) 870-1890
Email: fortworth@ajilonfinance.com
Key Contact - Specialty:
Mr. Paul Smith, Principal
Ms. Jaime Headlee, Principal
Mr. Anthony Caggiano, Area Vice President

170 S Main St Ste 550
Salt Lake City, UT 84101-1664
(801) 328-3338
Fax: (801) 328-3324
Email: saltlakecity@ajilonfinance.com
Key Contact - Specialty:
Ms. Laurie Smith, Branch Manager

2325 Dulles Corner Blvd Ste 675
Herndon, VA 20171-4684
(703) 464-4888
Fax: (703) 464-4884
Email: northernvirginia@ajilonfinance.com
Key Contact - Specialty:
Mr. Darryl Patton, Branch Manager

600 108th Ave NE Ste 650
Bellevue, WA 98004-5110
(425) 635-0700
Fax: (425) 635-0315
Email: bellevue@ajilonfinance.com
Key Contact - Specialty:
Ms. Sue Danbom, Branch Manager

601 Union St Ste 2434
Seattle, WA 98101-3914
(206) 467-0700
Fax: (206) 467-9986
Email: seattle@ajilonfinance.com
Key Contact - Specialty:
Ms. Lisa Pleiss, Branch Manager
Mr. Paul Donion, Area Vice President

950 Pacific Ave Ste 510
Tacoma, WA 98402-4410
(253) 274-8822
Fax: (253) 274-9216
Email: tacoma@ajilonfinance.com
Key Contact - Specialty:
Mr. Anthony Caputo, Branch Manager

3333 N Mayfair Rd Ste 213
Milwaukee, WI 53222-3219
(414) 771-1900
Fax: (414) 771-2586
Email: milwaukee@ajilonfinance.com
Key Contact - Specialty:
Ms. Dottie Mahnke, Branch Manager

402-10 Kingsbridge Garden Cir
Emerald Business Centre
Mississauga, ON L5R 3K6
Canada
(905) 501-8878
Fax: (905) 501-8054
Email: mississauga@ajilonfinance.com
Key Contact - Specialty:
Ms. Sara-Jane Gibney, Staffing Manager

2500-1 Adelaide St E
One Financial Place
Toronto, ON M5C 2V9
Canada
(416) 932-1566
Fax: (416) 932-2766
Email: toronto@ajilonfinance.com
Key Contact - Specialty:
Ms. Katherine Ciccariarella, Area Manager

Ajilon Finance

111 N Orange Ave Ste 1020
Orlando, FL 32801-2399
(407) 648-0036
Fax: (407) 835-0995
Email: orlando@ajilonfinance.com
Web: www.ajilonfinance.com

Summary: Specialized recruiting in accounting
and finance.

Key Contact - Specialty:
Mr. Donald F. Phillips, President - *Finance*

Functions: Generalist (All), CFOs, Budgeting,
Cash Mgmt., Credit, Taxes, M&A, Risk Mgmt.

Industries: Generalist (All)

Ajilon Finance

100 S 5th St Ste 420
Minneapolis, MN 55402-1232
(612) 341-9900
Fax: (612) 341-3284
Email: minneapolis@ajilonfinance.com

Summary: Specialize in the placement of financial
and accounting professionals.

Key Contact - Specialty:
Mr. Scott Foley, Area Manager
Mr. Scott Gramstad, Recruiter
Mr. Jason Peterson, Executive Recruiter
Mr. Jason Berglund, Account Manager
Mr. Brian Carlson, Executive Recruiter
Mr. Rich Surprise, Account Manager
Mr. Michael Greenlee, Executive Recruiter

Salary Minimum: $45,000

Functions: Finance

Industries: Finance

Ajilon Finance

5400 Trinity Rd Ste 204
Raleigh, NC 27607-6001
(919) 859-5550
Fax: (919) 859-5575
Email: raleigh@ajilonfinance.com
Web: www.ajilonfinance.com

Summary: Specialists in direct hire and temp
placements of accounting and finance
professionals.

Key Contact - Specialty:
Ms. Sue Durphy, CPA, Branch Manager
Ms. Julie Clark, Regional Sales Manager
Ms. Karen McGee, Division Manager

Functions: Finance

Industries: Generalist (All)

Ajilon Finance

2005 Market St Ste 1930
One Commerce Square
Philadelphia, PA 19103-7011
(215) 568-5600
Fax: (215) 569-2211
Email: philadelphia@ajilonfinance.com
Web: www.ajilonfinance.com

Summary: Through professional memberships,
long-term relationships and constant recruiting, we
maintain regular contact with professionals who

have the experience, skills and bottom-line
accomplishments employers are seeking.
Key Contact - Specialty:
Mr. Mark S. Libes, President - *Accounting*

Functions: Generalist (All), Middle Mgmt.,
CFOs, Budgeting, Cash Mgmt., Credit, Taxes,
Specialized Svcs.

Industries: Generalist (All)

Ajilon Finance

2000 Post Oak Blvd Ste 1970
Houston, TX 77056-4415
(713) 961-5603
Fax: (713) 961-3256
Email: houston@ajilonfinance.com
Web: www.ajilonfinance.com

Summary: We are financial consulting and
recruiting specialists.

Key Contact - Specialty:
Mr. Mathew Parker, Branch Manager

Functions: Finance

Industries: Generalist (All)

Ajilon Finance

1150-505 Burrard St
Bentall Tower 1
Vancouver, BC V7X 1M5
Canada
(604) 669-9096
Fax: (604) 669-9196
Email: vancouver@ajilonfinance.com
Web: www.ajilonfinance.com

Summary: With numerous franchises, and a
international presence, we are uniquely qualified
to help you attract outstanding accounting and
finance professionals to your organization. We
specialize in recruiting and placing a wide range
of high-level accounting and finance personnel
including controllers, accounting managers, cost
accountants, credit managers, staff accountants
and more.

Key Contact - Specialty:
Ms. Paula Hollander, Branch Manager -
Accounting, Clerical

Salary Minimum: $25,000

Functions: Generalist (All), CFOs, Budgeting,
Cash Mgmt., Credit, Taxes, M&A, Risk Mgmt.

Industries: Generalist (All), Energy, Utilities,
Manufacturing, Finance, Services, Media,
Packaging

AJM Professional Services

803 W Big Beaver Rd Ste 357
Troy, MI 48084-4734
(248) 244-2222
Fax: (248) 244-2233
Email: ajminfo@ajmps.com
Web: www.ajmps.com

Summary: Specialists in contingency and retained
search for IS and software engineering
professionals at managerial and staff levels. We
offer access to a national candidate and client base
through various networks and affiliations.

Key Contact - Specialty:
Mr. Charles A. Muller, CPC, Principal
Mr. Jeffrey Jones, Principal

Salary Minimum: $50,000

Functions: IT, MIS Mgmt., Systems Analysis,
Systems Dev., Systems Implem., Systems
Support, Network Admin., DB Admin.

Industries: Generalist (All), Computer Equip., IT
Implementation, Network Infrastructure

AJR Recruiting

13 Center St
Keene, NH 03431-3351
(603) 358-1037
Email: ajrjobs@ne.rr.com

Summary: Specializing in search in the grocery and supermarket industry including search in logistics and warehousing,procurement,retail and the executive level.

Key Contact - Specialty:
Mr. Anthony Rosinski, Recruiter

Functions: Management, Purchasing, Distribution, Sales Mgmt.

Industries: Food, Bev., Tobacco, Wholesale, Retail

Akechi

563 Hampshire Rd Apt 274G
Westlake Village, CA 91361-2234
(805) 494-6467
(805) 469-6008
Fax: (818) 704-7924
Email: jamesrolland@hotmail.com

Summary: Executive search company focusing within the sap arena R3/BW/SEM/APO. We place candidates within the permanent/contract and CTH areas.

Key Contact - Specialty:
Mr. James Rolland, Manager

Salary Minimum: $50,000

Functions: IT

Industries: Generalist (All), Construction, Transportation, Services, Hospitality, Media, Communications, Real Estate, Software, Non-Classifiable

Akin & Associates

PO Box 350
Carlsbad, CA 92018-0350
(760) 929-9897
Fax: (760) 929-0026
Email: comments@akinassoc.com
Web: www.akinassoc.com

Summary: We are full service Human Resources consulting firm in technology market serving western United States. We are in the business of assisting large and small companies achieve their people initiatives. We offer full staffing support from identifying current and future talent needs to sourcing and evaluating candidates to extending offers, HR department creation and more.

Key Contact - Specialty:
Mr. William J. Akin, President

Functions: Middle Mgmt., Product Dev., Healthcare

Industries: Medical Devices, Metal Products, Machine, Appliance, Consumer Elect., Misc. Mfg., Electronic, Elec. Components, Robotics, Pharm Svcs., Equip Svcs., ERP SW, Mfg. SW, Security SW, Biotech/Life Sciences, Healthcare

Helen Akullian Associates

280 Madison Ave Rm 604
New York, NY 10016-0801
(212) 532-3210
Fax: (212) 889-8631
Email: helen.akullian@haainc.com

Summary: We are a highly selective organization with extensive experience and an outstanding reputation. We have gained our reputation by understanding the complexities of varied personnel needs and then carefully applying company criteria to the proper candidates. We

specialize in marketing, public relations, advertising and editorial placements.

Key Contact - Specialty:
Ms. Helen Akullian, President

Salary Minimum: $50,000

Functions: Senior Mgmt., Middle Mgmt., Healthcare, Sales & Mktg., PR

Industries: Finance, Banking, Invest. Banking, Misc. Financial, Advertising, Publishing

Alaska Executive Search Inc

821 N St Ste 204
Anchorage, AK 99501-3285
(907) 276-5707
Fax: (907) 276-5708
Email: anne_b@akexec.com
Web: www.akexec.com

Summary: We specialize in Executive Search: CEO/COO, CFO & Accountants, Engineering & Technical, Sales/Marketing, IT & Software Development, Administrative Staffing, Medical & Nurse search, Temp services placements.

Key Contact - Specialty:
Mr. Robert E. Bulmer, President & Owner - *Banking, Engineering, Executives, General management, Management*
Ms. Laura Bain, Senior Executive Search Consultant - *Accounting (General), CEOs, CFOs, COOs*
Miss Laura Rogers, Technical Recruiter - *BSME, Engineering, Environmental, HVAC, Pipeline*
Miss Elizabeth Howe, Senior Search Consultant, High Tech - *Computers (Programming), Database, ERP, High technology, Information Technology*
Miss Anne Bulmer, Executive Search Consultant - *Communications, Controllers, Finance, Human resources, Insurance*

Salary Minimum: $30,000

Functions: Generalist (All), IT

Industries: Generalist (All), Oil & Gas, Construction, Finance, HR Services, Engineering Svcs., Logistics Svcs., Environmental Svcs., Insurance, Software

The Albo Group Inc

2917 Sylvan Dr
Sterling Heights, MI 48310-3080
(586) 264-9958
Fax: (586) 264-9968
Email: erickson@acd.net
Web: www.thealbogroup.com

Summary: Our firm is an executive recruiting and contract organization that specializes in the placement of qualified personnel. We work in areas that include various engineering disciplines such as design, electrical, manufacturing, and mechanical, accounting & finance, legal, management information systems, quality assurance, sales & marketing and healthcare.

Key Contact - Specialty:
Mr. Dale Erickson, President

Functions: Middle Mgmt.

Industries: Manufacturing, Medical Devices, Pharm Svcs., Biotech/Life Sciences, Healthcare

The Albrecht Group

140 Iowa Ln Ste 204
Cary, NC 27511-4495
(919) 468-8484
(800) 632-9676
Fax: (919) 468-8126
Email: rgalbrecht@agroupnc.com
Web: www.agroupnc.com

Summary: Specializing in searches for senior executives, management, sales, marketing, and engineering professionals.

Key Contact - Specialty:
Mr. Robert Albrecht, President
Mr. Richard Duley, Vice President

Salary Minimum: $50,000

Functions: Management, Mfg., Product Dev., Production, Sales & Mktg., Engineering

Industries: Generalist (All), Manufacturing, Medical Devices, Plastics, Rubber, Metal Products, Machine, Appliance, Motor Vehicles, Consumer Elect., Test, Measure Equip., Misc. Mfg., Packaging

Alexander & Collins

9190 W Olympic Blvd Ste 323
Beverly Hills, CA 90212-3540
(310) 277-8006
Fax: (310) 277-7098
Email: law@alexander-collins.com
Web: www.alexander-collins.com

Summary: We enjoy a longstanding reputation in providing attorney recruitment services of the highest quality to corporate law departments. While serving a wide range of corporate industries, including Fortune 100 companies, we offer particular expertise in the recruitment of minority and general counsel. Our consultants have hands-on-industry experience and have successfully placed attorneys in every discipline within our practice specialties.

Key Contact - Specialty:
Ms. Sara E. Collins, Principal

Functions: Legal, Attorneys, Paralegals

Industries: Legal

Alexander & Sterling

2000 S Dairy Ashford St Ste 610
Houston, TX 77077-5743
(713) 935-3333
(877) 935-3300
Fax: (713) 935-3374
Email: info@alexanderandsterling.com
Web: www.alexanderandsterling.com

Summary: We place partner level attorneys as well as O&G geophysicists, geologists, reservoir engineers and drilling engineers.

Key Contact - Specialty:
Mr. Bill Sonne, Chief Executive Officer - *Energy*

Functions: R&D, Engineering, Attorneys

Industries: Agri., Forestry, Mining, Energy, Utilities, Paints, Petro. Products, Legal

Alexander Consulting Inc

2701 W Busch Blvd Ste 205
Tampa, FL 33618-4578
(813) 935-5100
Fax: (813) 251-6256
Email: info@alexconsult.com
Web: www.alexconsult.com

Summary: We are the premier executive search and recruitment firm to call for placement within the healthcare communications industry. Our unique structure of a dedicated team working together producing superior results over that of an independent lone recruiter allows us intensive search focus in both consumer and business-to-business agencies for all departments.

Key Contact - Specialty:
Mr. James Wagner, Managing Director
Mr. Rick Glaesser, Economic Analyst

Ms. Kris House, Director, Account Services
Ms. Stacy Wagner, Director, Business
Development - *Sales*

Salary Minimum: $50,000

Functions: Healthcare, Advertising, Direct Mktg.

Industries: Medical Devices, Pharm Svcs.,
Advertising, Marketing SW, Healthcare

Alexander Enterprises Inc

1511 Erbs Mill Rd
Blue Bell, PA 19422-3511
(610) 279-0100
Fax: (610) 279-0124
Email: stephyoung@comcast.net

Summary: We conduct recruitment searches for
all types of pharmaceutical professionals (MDs,
PhDs, quality, regulatory, safety, data
management, IT/IS, medical writers,
manufacturing, marketing, etc.).

Key Contact - Specialty:
Ms. Florence D. Young, President -
Pharmaceutical
Ms. Stephanie Young, Vice President -
Pharmaceutical
Mr. W. Michael Young, Vice President,
Marketing - *Pharmaceutical*

Salary Minimum: $65,000

Functions: Generalist (All), Management

Industries: Manufacturing, Drugs Mfg., Pharm
Svcs., Biotech/Life Sciences

The Alicon Group Inc

5405 Alton Pkwy Ste A
Irvine, CA 92604-3718
(949) 559-0344
Fax: (888) 522-6413
Email: info@alicongroup.com
Web: www.alicongroup.com

Summary: We are a woman and minority owned
firm specializing in the placement of oracle
applications related resources. We work with
direct employers and first-tier integration firms to
implement oracle applications on a national basis.

Key Contact - Specialty:
Ms. Debbie Ward, Chief Executive Officer -
Consulting, CRM, ERP, Oracle, Systems
Ms. Kathryn Knox, Partner - *CRM, ERP,
Information Systems, Oracle, Systems*

Functions: IT, Mgmt. Consultants

Industries: Mgmt. Consulting, Software

All Seasons Staffing Services Inc

2875 S Main St
Salt Lake City, UT 84115-3569
(801) 487-8127
(800) 872-6646
Fax: (801) 487-2749
Email: mdodge@dectorininc.com
Web: www.allseasonsstaffing.com

Summary: We work in the electronics, IT and
medical areas.

Key Contact - Specialty:
Mr. Mark Dodge, Recruiting Manager

Salary Minimum: $65,000

Functions: Middle Mgmt.

Industries: Generalist (All)

Don Allan Associates Inc

PO Box 12988
La Jolla, CA 92039-2988
(800) 291-6900 x82
(760) 918-0400

Email: resume@globalstaffing.com
Web: www.globalstaffing.com

Summary: We provide executive search to the
information technology, biometrics, security,
software, interactive/multimedia, e-learning and
medical/healthcare industries. Our primary focus
is on management, marketing, sales, tech support
and consulting. We have an unbundled approach
to the entire search process.

Key Contact - Specialty:
Mr. David Adler, President - *Marketing, Sales,
Technical*

Salary Minimum: $75,000

Functions: Generalist (All), Sales & Mktg., Sales
Mgmt., IT

Industries: Mgmt. Consulting, HR Services,
Media, Publishing, Communications, Telecoms,
Software, HR SW, Security SW, System SW,
Training SW, Healthcare

Jeffrey Allan Company Inc

3209 Rancho Milagro
Carlsbad, CA 92009-2232
(800) 886-1522
(760) 804-1824
Fax: (760) 929-1282
Email: jeff@jeffreyallan.com
Web: www.jeffreyallan.com

Summary: Our firm is a recruiting firm that has
built a reputation for integrity and professionalism.
Discover why companies across the country select
us as their preferred search firm.

Key Contact - Specialty:
Mr. Jeffrey Conners, President
Ms. Norma Conners, Executive Vice President

Salary Minimum: $70,000

Functions: Management, Senior Mgmt.,
Purchasing, Sales & Mktg., HR Mgmt., CFOs,
IT, Int'l.

Industries: Generalist (All), Machine, Appliance,
Consumer Elect., Retail, Government

Allard Associates Inc

(Allard Institute)
425 Market St Ste 2200
San Francisco, CA 94105-2434
(800) 291-5279
Fax: (800) 526-7791
Email: resourcing@allardinstitute.com
Web: www.allardinstitute.com

Summary: Our clients are companies that depend
on data-driven strategies for their success in
industries as financial services, payments, health
care, telecommunications & retailing. We are
experts in risk management, applied analytics,
customer lifecycle optimization, data mining,
marketing, & operations. We provide perm
placement, interim executives, & expert
consultants.

Key Contact - Specialty:
Ms. Susan Allard, Chief Executive Officer &
Founder - *Consulting, Credit cards, Direct
marketing, Risk management*
Mr. Vince Bowey, Chief Marketing Officer &
Head of Consul - *Consulting, Marketing*
Ms. Nina Bates, Senior Associate - *Consulting,
Credit cards, Direct marketing, Risk
management*
Ms. Sue Daugherty, Senior Associate -
*Consulting, Credit cards, Direct marketing, Risk
management*
Ms. Lucie Fox, Senior Associate - *Consulting,
Credit cards, Direct marketing, Risk
management*

Salary Minimum: $90,000

Functions: Senior Mgmt., Product Dev., Sales &
Mktg., Mktg. Mgmt., Direct Mktg., Credit, Risk
Mgmt., DB Admin., Mgmt. Consultants,
Minorities/Diversity

Industries: Retail, Finance, Banking, Venture
Cap., Misc. Financial, Mgmt. Consulting, E-
commerce, New Media, Telecoms, Call Centers,
Homeland Security, Insurance, Software,
Database SW, Marketing SW

Bill Allen & Associates

PO Box 60039
Worcester, MA 01606-0039
(508) 795-1010
Fax: (508) 795-0204
Email: billallen@charter.net

Summary: We specialize in working with over 50
year old candidates in the biotech and life science
areas, with engineering, field sales in service, in
middle to upper management.

Key Contact - Specialty:
Mr. Bill Allen, President

Salary Minimum: $50,000

Functions: Senior Mgmt., Sales & Mktg., Sales
Mgmt., Sales Reps., Engineering, Eng. Design,
Specialized Svcs., Technicians

Industries: Medical Devices, Biotech/Life
Sciences

Frank E Allen & Associates Inc

15 James St
Florham Park, NJ 07932-1346
(973) 966-1606
Fax: (973) 966-9749
Email: hrjobs@att.net
Web: www.frankallen.com

Summary: An executive search resource
specializing in executive human resources
placement.

Key Contact - Specialty:
Mr. Frank Allen, President
Mr. Mark E. Allen, Vice President - *Human
resources*

Salary Minimum: $85,000

Functions: Senior Mgmt., HR Mgmt.

Industries: Generalist (All)

Allen & Associates Inc

1700 E Desert Inn Rd Ste 118
Las Vegas, NV 89169-3206
(702) 731-2066
Fax: (702) 731-5734
Email: recruiter@allenandassoc.com
Web: www.allenandassoc.com

Key Contact - Specialty:
Ms. Marla Allen, Vice President - *Gaming,
Hospitality*
Mr. Bob Allen, Headhunter - *CEOs, CFOs,
COOs*
Ms. Erin McCaslin, Headhunter - *Construction,
Legal, Legal (Attorneys,Lawyers)*

Salary Minimum: $80,000

Functions: Generalist (All), Senior Mgmt., Mfg.,
Mktg. Mgmt., Sales Mgmt., CFOs, Legal,
Attorneys, Hospitality, Hotel Mgmt.

Industries: Generalist (All), Manufacturing, Food,
Bev., Tobacco, Computer Equip., Misc.
Financial, Hospitality, Software

Pat Allen Associates Inc

PO Box 716
Goldens Bridge, NY 10526-0716
(914) 232-1545
Fax: (914) 232-8026
Email: dennis@patallen.com
Web: www.patallen.com

Summary: Years of nationwide exclusive
specialization, safety and loss control for the
insurance industry, including fire protection
engineers. Corporate, industrial and construction
safety for private industry. If you are not a safety
or loss control specialist we cannot help you.

Key Contact - Specialty:
Ms. Pat Allen, CPC, President

Functions: Risk Mgmt.

Industries: Insurance

D S Allen Associates

135 Main St
Flemington, NJ 08822-1622
(908) 653-9500
Email: dsaresumes@dsallen.com
Web: www.dsallen.com

Summary: Specializing in the IT, high technology
and communications industries for corporate and
major consulting organizations. Areas of
expertise: CEO, president, VP, partner and
manager levels plus leading sales/marketing
executives.

Key Contact - Specialty:
Mr. Don Allen, President
Ms. Mary Ann Ulrich, Partner - *Information
Technology, Management consulting*

Salary Minimum: $75,000

Functions: Management, Board Members, Senior
Mgmt., Middle Mgmt., Sales & Mktg., Mktg.
Mgmt., Sales Mgmt., IT, MIS Mgmt., Mgmt.
Consultants

Industries: Generalist (All), Computer Equip.,
Mgmt. Consulting, HR Services, Telecoms,
Software

Allen Consulting Group Inc

2429 Clarjon Dr
Manchester, MO 63021-7822
(314) 984-9909
Fax: (314) 984-9909
Email: tom@allencg.com
Web: www.allencg.com

Summary: Company is an IT consulting and
executive recruiting firm. We provide experienced
IT personnel to client companies for consulting
assignments and permanent placement.

Key Contact - Specialty:
Mr. Thomas R. Allen, President - *Data
processing*

Functions: MIS Mgmt., Systems Analysis,
Systems Dev., Systems Implem., Systems
Support, Network Admin., DB Admin.

Industries: Generalist (All)

Allen Personnel

(a division of Design Group Staffing Inc)
362 Dufferin Ave
London, ON N6B 1Z4
Canada
(519) 672-7040
Fax: (519) 672-7044
Email: research@allenpersonnel.com
Web: www.allenpersonnel.com

Summary: We offer a full-service agency that has
experienced, knowledgeable and professional

consultants who are recruitment experts in their
field.

Key Contact - Specialty:
Ms. Tamara Dahl, Consultant - *Engineering,
Human resources, Manufacturing, Technology*
Ms. Judy Diamond, Consultant - *Accounting,
Banking, Finance, Information Technology*
Mr. Gerri Teal, Consultant - *Construction,
Healthcare, Manufacturing*
Ms. Ana Batista, Recruiter - *Insurance,
Manufacturing*
Ms. Dawn Adams, Recruiter - *Accounting,
Clerical*
Ms. Lee Reaume, Recruiter - *Labor*

Salary Minimum: $25,000

Functions: Generalist (All), Admin. Svcs., Mfg.,
Materials, HR Mgmt., Finance, IT, Engineering,
Design

Industries: Generalist (All), Oil & Gas,
Manufacturing, Plastics, Rubber, Metal
Products, Machine, Appliance, Motor Vehicles,
Transportation, Finance, Banking, Invest.
Banking, Accounting, Communications,
Software

Allen Thomas Associates Inc

518 Prospect Ave
Little Silver, NJ 07739-1438
(732) 219-5353
Fax: (732) 219-5805
Email: recruit@allenthomas.com
Web: www.allenthomas.com

Summary: We are an executive search firm
specializing in mid to upper-management
positions in the healthcare industry. This includes
all management positions in the hospital, home
care, managed care and pharmaceutical fields.

Key Contact - Specialty:
Ms. Linda Forrest, Director - *Healthcare,
Pharmaceutical*
Mr. Thomas Benoit, FACHE, President -
Healthcare
Ms. Dee Galluccio, Recruiter - *Healthcare*

Salary Minimum: $55,000

Functions: Generalist (All)

Industries: Healthcare

Allen-Jeffers Associates

28512 Las Arubas
Laguna Niguel, CA 92677-7558
(949) 643-2146
(949) 858-0807
Fax: (309) 416-2920
Email: contact@allen-jeffersassoc.com
Web: www.allen-jeffersassoc.com

Summary: We are an executive and technical
search firm specializing in the medical device,
pharmaceutical and allied electronics industries.
The measure of our search firm is in the quality
and suitability of our candidates.

Key Contact - Specialty:
Mr. Robert Jeffers, Owner

Salary Minimum: $75,000

Functions: Generalist (All), Product Dev.

Industries: Drugs Mfg., Medical Devices, Misc.
Mfg., Venture Cap., Pharm Svcs., Engineering
Svcs., Fiber Optic, Database SW, Development
SW, Biotech/Life Sciences

Allgood Associates Inc

PO Box 310399
Enterprise, AL 36331-0399
(334) 393-3334
Fax: (334) 347-7829

Email: allgoodjobs@adelphia.net
Web: www.allgoodjobs.com

Summary: We are an executive search and
recruiting firm for the manufacturing sector.

Key Contact - Specialty:
Mr. H. Allgood, President

Salary Minimum: $40,000

Functions: Management, Senior Mgmt., Mfg.,
Quality, Materials, Purchasing, HR Mgmt.,
Finance, Engineering, Environmentalists

Industries: Generalist (All), Manufacturing,
Textiles, Apparel, Paper, Chemicals, Plastics,
Rubber, Metal Products, Motor Vehicles,
Electronic, Elec. Components, Pharm Svcs.,
Telecoms, Aerospace, Development SW

Alliance Enterprise Group LLC

2895 Highway 190 Ste 236
Mandeville, LA 70471-3255
(985) 626-5112
(800) 392-5902
Email: info@allianceenterprisegroup.com
Web: www.allianceenterprisegroup.com

Summary: We serve a wide variety of multi-
disciplinary firms that design, construct and
maintain the country's complex infrastructure
system. We specialize in the permanent placement
of senior management, engineers, architects,
environmental scientists, geologists, health &
safety professionals and business development
talent for A&E firms, consulting companies,
construction firms, municipal, state and federal
agencies.

Key Contact - Specialty:
Ms. Suzanne Villar, Principal - *C-level,
Consulting, Engineering, Environmental,
Executives*

Salary Minimum: $100,000

Functions: Management, Senior Mgmt., Middle
Mgmt., Engineering, Geotechnical, Structural,
Environmentalists, Architects, Health & Safety

Industries: Transportation, Services, Architectural
Svcs., Mgmt. Consulting, Engineering Svcs.,
Environmental Svcs., Haz. Waste

Alliance of Professionals & Consultants Inc

(formerly known as APC Medical Resouces LLC)
9201 Leesville Rd Ste 201
Raleigh, NC 27613-7540
(919) 510-9696
Fax: (919) 510-9668
Email: mgmt@apc-services.com
Web: www.apc-services.com

Summary: Our firm is a responsive professional
services and staffing company. We are a Native
American minority owned company; recognized
for our outstanding success. We provide
information technology, engineering, and business
professionals.

Key Contact - Specialty:
Mr. Roy Roberts, President & Chief Executive
Officer - *Engineering, Professional services,
Technical*
Mrs. Michele Scollard, Manager, Business
Development
Ms. Debbie Bucher, Manager, Human Resources
- *Investment management*

Salary Minimum: $40,000

Functions: MIS Mgmt.

Industries: Generalist (All)

The Alliance Search Group Inc

1309 Oakwood Dr
Polk City, IA 50226-1217
(515) 984-9211
Fax: (515) 984-9187
Email:
wendyjespersen@alliancesearchgroupinc.com
Web: www.alliancesearchgroupinc.com

Summary: We are a full service contingency
search firm specializing in the recruitment and
permanent or contract placement of candidates in
the manufacturing industry.

Key Contact - Specialty:
Mrs. Wendy Jespersen, President
Ms. Allison Frampton, Executive Assistant -
Entertainment

Salary Minimum: $25,000

Functions: Mfg.

Industries: Agri., Forestry, Mining, Construction,
Manufacturing, Transportation, Aerospace,
Packaging, Insurance, Mfg. SW

Branches:
330 Phaeton Dr
Robins, IA 52328-9519
(319) 743-3478
Fax: (319) 378-3566
Key Contact - Specialty:
Ms. Mary Jones, Vice President

Allied Search Inc

2030 Union St Ste 206
San Francisco, CA 94123-4116
(415) 921-2200
(415) 921-1971
Fax: (415) 921-5309
Email: donmay@alliedsearchinc.com
Web: www.alliedsearchinc.com

Summary: Recruit professionals and executives in
all industries. Divisions: executive (CEOs, CIOs,
CTOs, CFOs, COOs, etc.), consulting
(management, IT, ERP, operational, litigation, IT
risk, business risk, etc.), IT, financial (accounting,
etc.), audit (IS, IT, internal, financial, operational,
etc.), tax and HR.

Key Contact - Specialty:
Mr. Donald C. May, Managing Director -
Executives, Management, Middle management

Salary Minimum: $40,000

Functions: Generalist (All), Management, Board
Members, Senior Mgmt., Middle Mgmt., HR
Mgmt., Finance, IT, Mgmt. Consultants, Int'l.

Industries: Generalist (All)

Branches:
3699 Wilshire Blvd Ste 850
Los Angeles, CA 90010-2737
(213) 680-4000
Fax: (213) 680-4080
Email: donmay@alliedsearchinc.com
Key Contact - Specialty:
Mr. Jack Anderson, Manager

Allman & Company Inc

384 John S Mosby Dr
Wilmington, NC 28412-7167
(910) 395-5219
Email: sallman@ec.rr.com

Summary: Executive search for the investment
banking industry.

Key Contact - Specialty:
Mr. Steven L. Allman, CPC, President

Salary Minimum: $75,000

Functions: Sales & Mktg., Pension/Ret. Planning

Industries: Banking, Invest. Banking,
Mutual/Hedge Funds

Alpert Executive Search Inc

420 Lexington Ave Rm 2024
New York, NY 10170-2099
(212) 297-9009
Fax: (212) 297-0818
Email: jobs@alpertsearch.com
Web: www.alpertsearch.com

Summary: Our firm specializes in account
planning, brand planning and strategic planning
recruitment for advertising agencies, brand
consultancies and interactive firms.

Key Contact - Specialty:
Mrs. Ada Alpert, President
Ms. Hilary Moor, Vice President & Senior
Recruit Manager
Ms. Michelle Schenker, Recruitment Manager -
Engineering, Marketing, Sales

Functions: Management, Senior Mgmt., Middle
Mgmt., Advertising, PR

Industries: Advertising

Alpha Resource Group Inc

1916 Brabant Dr
Plano, TX 75025-3325
(972) 527-1616
Fax: (972) 527-4244

Summary: Through our worldwide recruitment
network, we specialize in professional executive
search and placement to many of the industry's
finest hotels, resorts, clubs and casinos.

Key Contact - Specialty:
Mr. Sewell B. Pappas, Managing Director

Salary Minimum: $45,000

Functions: Generalist (All), Hospitality

Industries: Hotels, Resorts, Clubs, Restaurants,
Full Service Restaurants, Entertainment,
Recreation

Alpha Resources

5122 Alfingo St
Las Vegas, NV 89135-3215
(888) 271-7070
(702) 227-4300
Fax: (702) 257-5291
Email: alpharesou@aol.com

Summary: Specializes in marketing and sales for
semiconductor, integrated circuit, analog, digital
and RF.

Key Contact - Specialty:
Mr. Daniel P. Cook, General Manager - *Sales,
Semiconductors*

Salary Minimum: $80,000

Functions: Sales & Mktg.

Industries: Semiconductors

Alpha Systems Inc

3325 Sweetwater Dr
Cumming, GA 30041-6641
(678) 889-6059
Email: wgriffin@adelphia.net
Web: www.jobbs.com/alpha.html

Summary: We place in design, engineering,
automation, controls, instrumentation, software,
systems, distribution, logistics, sales & marketing,
operations, purchasing, robotics, materials,
components, test engineering, general
management in high-technology industries,
chemical, food, drug, bio-technology, plastics,
metal fabrication, films, capital equipment, digital
electronics, RF microwave, optics, photonics,
electronic automation, electro optics and medical
devices.

Key Contact - Specialty:
Mr. William W. Griffin, Owner

Salary Minimum: $50,000

Functions: Management, Senior Mgmt., Middle
Mgmt., Automation, Plant Mgmt., Materials,
Distribution, Sales Mgmt., Engineering

Industries: Generalist (All), Energy, Utilities, Oil
& Gas, Manufacturing, Food, Bev., Tobacco,
Chemicals, Drugs Mfg., Medical Devices,
Plastics, Rubber, Paints, Petro. Products, Metal
Products, Test, Measure Equip., Electronic,
Elec. Components, Robotics, Mgmt. Consulting,
Communications, RF/Microwave, Aerospace,
Packaging, Software, Biotech/Life Sciences

Alphanumeric Group Inc

2464 El Camino Real Ste 221
Santa Clara, CA 95051-3002
(408) 954-1600
Fax: (775) 522-8839
Email: info@alphanugroup.com
Web: www.alphanugroup.com

Summary: Executive retained search firm
specializing in senior level management and
technology specialist for pharmaceutical,
biotechnology, and high-technology companies.

Key Contact - Specialty:
Mr. Robert Sanders, Chief Executive Officer &
President

Salary Minimum: $100,000

Functions: Management, Board Members, Senior
Mgmt., Sales & Mktg., R&D, Engineering,
Technicians

Industries: Drugs Mfg., Pharm Svcs.,
Communications, Telecoms, Digital, Wireless,
Fiber Optic, Network Infrastructure,
RF/Microwave, Aerospace, Software,
Development SW, Biotech/Life Sciences

ALS Group

104 Mount Joy Rd
Milford, NJ 08848-1752
(908) 995-9500
Fax: (908) 995-7032
Email: staff@alsgroup.com
Web: www.alsgroup.com

Summary: Specializing in corporate lending,
commercial lending, credit administration, small
business lending, commercial real estate lending,
asset based, loan work-out, investment banking,
private banking, trust, retail lending, foreign
exchange, indirect lending and finance. Place
portfolio, underwriting, originations and
operations positions within each discipline.

Key Contact - Specialty:
Mr. Scott Lysenko, Partner - *Banking, Banking
(Commercial,Corporate,Investment), Finance*
Ms. Lisa Lysenko, Partner - *Banking, Banking
(Commercial,Corporate,Merchant), Finance*

Salary Minimum: $50,000

Functions: Senior Mgmt., Middle Mgmt., Sales &
Mktg., Finance, Cash Mgmt., Credit, M&A,
Int'l.

Industries: Finance, Banking, Invest. Banking,
Brokers, Venture Cap., Misc. Financial

Alta Search

3600 Montlake Dr
Knoxville, TN 37920-2847
(865) 573-1626
Fax: (865) 579-2524
Email: altasearch@mindspring.com

Summary: Sole practitioner with emphasis in, but not limited to, sales & marketing in the electrical and HVAC markets. Executive-level assignments accepted in industry specialty.

Key Contact - Specialty:
Mr. Mark Hill, CRM - *Technical*

Salary Minimum: $70,000

Functions: Sales & Mktg., Mktg. Research, Mktg. Mgmt., Sales Mgmt.

Industries: Misc. Mfg.

AltcoSearch
655 Amboy Ave Ste C
Woodbridge, NJ 07095-3161
(732) 283-2722
Fax: (732) 283-3666
Email: admin@altcosearch.com
Web: www.altcosearch.com

Summary: We specialize in engineering, operations and scientific positions for consumer packaged goods and pharmaceutical/medical device companies. Our experience, extensive database and industry contacts allow us to quickly identify the best candidates.

Key Contact - Specialty:
Mr. John Shea, CPC, Principal

Salary Minimum: $60,000

Functions: Production, Automation, Plant Mgmt., Quality, Materials, Purchasing, Distribution, Packaging, Engineering

Industries: Food, Bev., Tobacco, Soap, Perf., Cosmtcs., Drugs Mfg., Medical Devices, Consumer Goods

Alternate Route
350 K St Unit 215
San Diego, CA 92101-6992
(800) 379-7463
Email: doug@alternateroute.net
Web: www.alternateroute.net

Summary: We are an executive search firm specializing in the placement of healthcare, sales & marketing and IT professionals.

Key Contact - Specialty:
Mr. Douglas Pajak, President

Functions: Healthcare, Sales & Mktg., IT

Industries: Generalist (All), Healthcare

Alynco Inc
10709 Platte Valley Dr
Little Rock, AR 72212-3629
(501) 221-0066
Fax: (501) 221-0068
Email: fausett@swbell.net

Summary: Prior to starting the firm, its founders' background was in distribution and transportation. As a result, we are uniquely positioned to assist both clients and candidates in this area.

Key Contact - Specialty:
Mr. A. Smith Fausett, President - *Logistics*

Salary Minimum: $50,000

Functions: Distribution

Industries: Generalist (All)

Amato & Associates LLC Insurance Recruiters
28 W Eagle Rd Ste 204
Havertown, PA 19083-1445
(610) 853-9696
Fax: (610) 853-9797
Email: resume@amatorecruits.com
Web: www.amatorecruits.com

Summary: Commercial property/casualty/workers compensation, insurance underwriters, account executives, producers, claims, loss control for carriers, agents/brokers, reinsurers and risk management.

Key Contact - Specialty:
Ms. Bobbi Amato, CPC, President & Owner

Salary Minimum: $30,000

Functions: Generalist (All)

Industries: Insurance

Amber Systems Group LLC
104 S Main St Ste 513
Fond du Lac, WI 54935-4245
(920) 322-9011
Fax: (920) 322-9013
Email: amber@powercom.net
Web: www.ambersystemsgroup.com

Summary: We are a leading professional and technical recruiting firm specializing in information technology, telecommunications, engineering, sales and marketing.

Key Contact - Specialty:
Ms. Celeste Christ, Vice President - *ERP, Healthcare, Information Technology, Sales, SAP*
Mr. Fred Christ, RCDD, President - *Cellular, Engineering, Fiber-optics, Telecommunications, Wireless*

Functions: Management, Healthcare, Sales Mgmt., IT, MIS Mgmt.

Industries: Generalist (All), Telecoms, Call Centers, Telephony, Digital, Wireless, Fiber Optic, Network Infrastructure, RF/Microwave, ERP SW, Networking, Comm. SW, Security SW

Ambiance Personnel Inc
7990 SW 117th Ave Ste 125
Miami, FL 33183-3845
(305) 274-7419
Fax: (305) 598-8071
Email: email@ambiancepersonnel.com
Web: www.ambiancepersonnel.com

Summary: We are a search and staffing firm specializing in international trade, transportation and logistics. We handle Supply Chain, logistics sales, operations/traffic/documentation, accounting, administrative and management positions.

Key Contact - Specialty:
Mr. Robert Maier, Vice President
Mr. John White, Consultant
Ms. Fran Pollack, President - *Distribution, Exports, Supply Chain, Traffic*

Salary Minimum: $30,000

Functions: Management, Senior Mgmt., Sales & Mktg., Sales Reps.

Industries: Generalist (All), Transportation, Services, Non-Classifiable

America at Work
PO Box 812
Reading, PA 19603-0812
(610) 372-9675
Fax: (610) 372-9675
Email: ameriwork@aol.com
Web: www.americaatwork.com

Summary: We are a professional search firm specializing in the recruitment and placement of bilingual (Spanish or Portuguese) professionals. We also assist our clients in attracting qualified high-end Hispanic/Latino candidates.

Key Contact - Specialty:
Mr. Nelson A. De Leon, Owner

Salary Minimum: $50,000

Functions: Generalist (All), Minorities/Diversity

Industries: Generalist (All), Energy, Utilities, Manufacturing, Consumer Elect., Finance, Services, Non-profits, Accounting, HR Services, Healthcare, Hospitals, Non-Classifiable

American Engineering Corp
25 6th Ave SW
Ronan, MT 59864-2632
(406) 676-5026
(866) 200-8905
Fax: (775) 258-7641
Email: ritters@ronan.net

Summary: A new firm built on experience. Although originally focused in industrial automation, we have branched out into land development and other areas of civil engineering. We believe that quality is better than quantity and have constantly out-performed our much larger competitors because of that belief.

Key Contact - Specialty:
Mr. W. Scott Ritter, Owner & Manager - *Electrical, Mechanical*

Salary Minimum: $30,000

Functions: Engineering

Industries: Generalist (All), Construction, Manufacturing, Electronic, Elec. Components, Robotics, Transportation, Architectural Svcs., Biotech/Life Sciences, Occupational Therapy

Branches:
PO Box 266
Calais, ME 04619-0266
(506) 529-1188
Key Contact - Specialty:
Mr. Scott McKay, Agent

1695 MT Highway 35 Trlr 27
Kalispell, MT 59901-2480
(406) 257-3680
Key Contact - Specialty:
Mr. Jay Ringel, Agent

PO Box 22
Tuttle, OK 73089-0022
(405) 381-3589
Fax: (360) 358-1214
Key Contact - Specialty:
Mr. David Walthall, Manager

American Heritage Group Inc
32670 Concord Dr
Madison Heights, MI 48071-1110
(248) 577-1170
(248) 577-1171
Fax: (248) 577-1176
Email: jh@ahgco.com.com
Web: www.ahgco.com

Summary: Executive search, staffing, professional services, vendor management firm. Computer, IT, automotive, engineering, medical devices and pharmaceutical fields.

Key Contact - Specialty:
Mr. John Holliday, President

Functions: Mfg., Plant Mgmt., Healthcare, Sales Mgmt., IT, MIS Mgmt., Systems Dev., DB Admin., Engineering, Mgmt. Consultants

Industries: Generalist (All), Construction, Manufacturing, Drugs Mfg., Medical Devices, Plastics, Rubber, Paints, Petro. Products, Leather, Stone, Glass, Metal Products, Machine, Appliance, Motor Vehicles, Computer Equip., Test, Measure Equip., Robotics, Pharm Svcs., Mgmt. Consulting, E-commerce, IT Implementation, Software, Biotech/Life Sciences, Healthcare

American Medical Consultants Inc

11625 SW 110th Rd
Miami, FL 33176-3152
(305) 271-9225
(800) 510-2157
Fax: (305) 271-8664
Email: amcmo@bellsouth.net
Web: www.americanmedicalconsultants.com

Summary: A physician and healthcare recruitment organization that assists hospitals, group practices, HMOs and solo practitioners in meeting their physician and physician extender needs.

Key Contact - Specialty:
Mr. Martin H. Osinski, MBA, AVA, Principal - *Healthcare, Physicians*
Ms. Patsy Anders, Principal - *Healthcare, Medical*

Salary Minimum: $100,000

Functions: Board Members, Physicians

Industries: Healthcare

American Medical Recruiters

325 Krameria St
Denver, CO 80220-5945
(303) 393-0791
Fax: (303) 393-0683
Email: gmberquist@aol.com

Summary: Recruit for hospitals and medical companies.

Key Contact - Specialty:
Ms. Gailmarie Berquist, President - *Healthcare*

Salary Minimum: $60,000

Functions: Generalist (All), Nurses, Health Admin.

Industries: Generalist (All), Healthcare, Hospitals

American Professional Search Inc

6805 Arno Allisona Rd
College Grove, TN 37046-9216
(615) 368-7979

Summary: Many years of experience as a manager and engineer plus my years of experience as a recruiter, allowing a thorough understanding of client requirements, resulting in the ability to select individuals who will have an immediate positive impact on the hiring organization.

Key Contact - Specialty:
Mr. Ray O'Steen, President
Mrs. Gloria O'Steen, Vice President

Functions: Mfg., Materials, HR Mgmt., Engineering

Industries: Machine, Appliance, Motor Vehicles

American Recruiters Consolidated Inc

6400 N Andrews Ave Ste 100
Fort Lauderdale, FL 33309-9109
(954) 492-4651
Fax: (954) 492-4602
Email: info@arcimail.com
Web: www.americanrecruiters.com

Summary: We provide contingency and retained recruitment services for physicians, imaging professionals, pharmaceuticals, pharmaceutical, nursing, long term care, HR, engineering, manufacturing, HVAC, food equipment and technical/high technology positions. Middle and upper level positions are our focus. We also offer HR training and consulting.

Key Contact - Specialty:
Mr. Gino Scialdone, President & Owner
Mr. Carl Carieri, Chairman of the Board
Mr. Roy Lantz, CCP, SPHR, Executive Vice President
Mr. D.R. Richards, Director, Operations
Mr. Michael Goldberg

Salary Minimum: $50,000

Functions: Management, Senior Mgmt., Middle Mgmt., Mfg., Healthcare, Physicians, Sales & Mktg., HR Mgmt., Finance, Engineering

Industries: Manufacturing, Pharm Svcs., Accounting, Mgmt. Consulting, HR Services, Hospitality, Hotels, Resorts, Clubs, Restaurants, Inst./Industrial Food Svc., Wireless, Packaging, Biotech/Life Sciences, Healthcare, Hospitals, Long-term/Home Care

Branches:
7936 E Arapahoe Ct Ste 2800
Englewood, CO 80112-6825
(720) 346-5000
Fax: (877) 704-5627
Email: denver@arcimail.com
Key Contact - Specialty:
Ms. Renee Owens, Franchise Owner - *Assisted living, Long term care*

119 S Palmetto Ave Ste 155
Daytona Beach, FL 32114-4327
(386) 238-8998
Email: rogers@arcimail.com

1100 Circle 75 Pkwy SE Ste 210
Atlanta, GA 30339-3093
(770) 690-9800
Fax: (770) 690-9850
Email: iphillip@arcimail.com
Key Contact - Specialty:
Ms. Ina Phillip-Jolis, Franchise Owner

1622 E Algonquin Rd Ste J
Schaumburg, IL 60173-4156
(847) 303-0560
Fax: (847) 303-0559
Email: chicagooffice@arcimail.com
Key Contact - Specialty:
Mr. Craig Wilson, Franchise Owner

6 Oriole Ter
Newton, NJ 07860-1484
(973) 300-4886
Fax: (973) 300-5905
Email: gnomer@arcimail.com
Key Contact - Specialty:
Mr. Gary Nomer, Franchise Owner - *Engineering, Food, Manufacturing*

2820 Hollymead Dr
Charlottesville, VA 22911-7505
(434) 974-7259
(888) 813-5980
Email: ktobias@arcimail.com
Key Contact - Specialty:
Ms. Kim Tobias, Vice President, Mid-Atlantic

American Recruiting & Consulting

(formerly known as AR International)
6625 Miami Lakes Dr E Ste 231
Hialeah, FL 33014-2761
(954) 342-0550
Fax: (954) 301-7965
Email: reneed@arcgonline.com
Web: www.arcgonline.com

Summary: We are a national recruiting firm that employs over 25 full time recruiters. We have two divisions, which are high technology and generalist. We place at all levels including executive. ARC Group is a contingency and retained search firm with permanent and contract openings.

Key Contact - Specialty:
Ms. Renee Dixon, Manager, Bus Dev & Recruiting - *Marketing, Operations, Sales*
Mr. Gregg Podalsky, President - *Management, Operations, Sales*

Salary Minimum: $25,000

Functions: Generalist (All)

Industries: Construction, Manufacturing, Finance, Services, Communications, Insurance, Software, Non-Classifiable

American Software & Global Technology

1650 W 82nd St Ste 1070
Minneapolis, MN 55431-1400
(952) 885-5640
Fax: (952) 885-5692
Email: dhalepet@asgt.com
Web: www.asgt.com

Summary: We are a project-based information technology consulting and outsourcing firm. Our mission is to maximize your organization's competitive position and improve your bottom line results by providing skilled IT professionals you need in many key technology areas.

Key Contact - Specialty:
Mrs. Debbie Halepet, Senior Technical Recruiter - *Database (Administration, Warehousing), ERP, Information Systems, Information Technology*

Functions: Production, Systems Dev.

Industries: Aerospace, Software, Database SW, Development SW, ERP SW, HR SW, Industry Specific SW, Networking, Comm. SW, System SW

Americas Project Management Services LLC

741 Riversville Rd
Greenwich, CT 06831-2626
(203) 863-9168
Email: contact_us@americaspms.com
Web: www.americaspms.com

Summary: Our company is designed to provide technical assistance and project management services to any company in the development or extension of projects.

Key Contact - Specialty:
Ms. Laurent Martinez, Managing Director

Salary Minimum: $50,000

Functions: Board Members, Production, Budgeting, Engineering, Int'l.

Industries: Energy, Utilities, Oil & Gas, Construction, Manufacturing, Chemicals, Finance, Banking, Invest. Banking, Mgmt. Consulting, Engineering Svcs., Telecoms, Telephony, Defense, Aerospace, Industry Specific SW, System SW, Biotech/Life Sciences, Hospitals

Americruit

1205 N State Highway 123 Ste 304
San Marcos, TX 78666-7756
(512) 805-7848
Fax: (512) 805-7852
Email: judy@americruit.com

Summary: Our firm specializes in the consumer products industry working with manufacturers to locate sales & marketing professionals. We are particularly knowledgeable in the office products industry.

Key Contact - Specialty:
Mrs. Judy Aswell, Owner & President

Salary Minimum: $50,000

Functions: Product Dev., Sales & Mktg., Mktg. Research, Mktg. Mgmt., Sales Mgmt., Sales Reps.

Industries: Computer Equip., Consumer Elect., Consumer Goods

AmeriPro Search Inc

190 River Birch Cir
Mooresville, NC 28115-5758
(704) 737-6001
Fax: (704) 660-6822
Email: ameripro@bigfoot.com

Summary: Contingency search firm with emphasis on technical (engineering, design,controls, manufacturing and QA/QC/QE), sales (industrial), marketing (industrial), financial (corporate and plant), and IS (midrange and mainframe).

Key Contact - Specialty:
Mr. John C. Brauninger, General Manager - *Manufacturing, Marketing, MIS, Sales, SAP*

Salary Minimum: $50,000

Functions: Generalist (All), Mfg., Materials, Sales & Mktg., Finance, IT, Engineering

Industries: Generalist (All), Manufacturing, Medical Devices, Plastics, Rubber, Machine, Appliance, Motor Vehicles, Software

AmeriResource Group Inc

2525 NW Expressway St Ste 532
Oklahoma City, OK 73112-7222
(405) 842-5900
(800) 583-7823
Fax: (405) 843-9879
Email: staffing@ameriresource.com
Web: www.ameriresource.com

Summary: We are a fully integrated HR company. We provide employees (permanent, contract and temp) to companies from entry level to executive management.

Key Contact - Specialty:
Mr. Nick Martire, National Account Manager - *Engineering, Finance, Human resources, MIS*

Salary Minimum: $30,000

Functions: Generalist (All), Management, Healthcare, HR Mgmt., Finance, IT, Engineering

Industries: Generalist (All), Energy, Utilities, Construction, Manufacturing, Finance, Accounting, HR Services, IT Implementation, Communications, Aerospace, Software

Branches:
5840 S Memorial Dr Ste 212
Tulsa, OK 74145-9081
(918) 627-4900
Fax: (918) 627-4984
Email: argtulsa@ameriresource.com
Key Contact - Specialty:
Mr. Charles Saner, Branch Manager

AmeriSearch Group Inc

227 N Dixie Way Ste 310
South Bend, IN 46637-3300
(574) 271-6040
Fax: (574) 271-6041
Email: hrmgr@amersch.com
Web: www.amersch.com

Summary: We are a firm that specializes in management, technical & professional positions - primarily financial, information technology,

engineering, and manufacturing management. Also provide resume development by certified professional resume writers (CPRW) and an interview coaching class.

Key Contact - Specialty:
Mr. Chuck Daniels, President

Salary Minimum: $60,000

Functions: Management, Mfg., Finance, IT, Engineering

Industries: Generalist (All)

Ames-O'Neill Associates Inc

PO Box 841
Syosset, NY 11791-0841
(516) 921-4488
Email: ames@globalcrossing.net

Summary: We specialize in the recruitment of high-technology specialists in electronics, avionics, aerospace, telecom, software engineering and related support functions for commercial and military clients.

Key Contact - Specialty:
Mr. George C. Ames, President

Salary Minimum: $40,000

Functions: Mfg., Materials, Purchasing, Sales & Mktg., R&D, Engineering, Structural, Eng. Design, Hardware, Systems

Industries: Computer Equip., Consumer Elect., Test, Measure Equip., Electronic, Elec. Components, Semiconductors, RF/Microwave, Defense, Aerospace, Software

Amherst Personnel Group Inc

(also known as Amherst Placement)
77 Fox Pl
Hicksville, NY 11801-5750
(516) 433-7610
Fax: (516) 433-7848
Email: amherstplacement@aol.com

Summary: Specializing in sales (medical, pharmaceutical, consumer and industrial) retail management (store managers and assistant managers) and office support.

Key Contact - Specialty:
Mr. Donald Porter, President - *Sales*
Ms. Pat Breen, Executive Recruiter - *Sales*

Salary Minimum: $20,000

Functions: Generalist (All), Sales & Mktg., Advertising, Mktg. Mgmt., Sales Mgmt.

Industries: Generalist (All), Food, Bev., Tobacco, Soap, Perf., Cosmtcs., Drugs Mfg., Medical Devices, Retail, Healthcare

AMINEX Corp

67 Broad St Fl 3
Boston, MA 02109-4826
(617) 248-6883
Fax: (617) 248-8650
Email: info@aminex.com
Web: www.aminex.com

Summary: We have devoted our full resources and capabilities to provide the insurance industry with talented executives. We believe that attracting leadership talent is of paramount importance to a company's success.

Key Contact - Specialty:
Mr. Lucius F. Sinks, Jr., Partner - *Management, Marketing, Technical*
Mr. Richard Tolstrup, Partner - *Management, Marketing, Technical*
Ms. Lisa Lepore, Partner - *Managed care, Management, Marketing, Technical*

Salary Minimum: $50,000

Functions: Generalist (All), Board Members, Middle Mgmt., Mktg. Mgmt., Sales Mgmt., Customer Svc., Benefits, Staffing, Risk Mgmt.

Industries: Generalist (All), Insurance

Analog Solutions

298 Village Square Dr Ste 140
Loudon, TN 37774-2807
(865) 458-4421
Email: resume@analogsolutions.com
Web: www.analogsolutions.com

Summary: We set ourselves apart from other recruiting firms in the semiconductor industry by offering a specialized service to a select group of growing companies. We focus on analog and mixed signal design and management. We offer our clients the opportunity to work with the industry's very best, low volume, high service organization.

Key Contact - Specialty:
Mr. Gary Fowler, President

Salary Minimum: $90,000

Functions: Generalist (All), Management, R&D, Engineering

Industries: Generalist (All), Computer Equip., Consumer Elect., Electronic, Elec. Components, Semiconductors, Wireless, Fiber Optic, Software

Analytic Recruiting Inc

12 E 41st St Fl 9
New York, NY 10017-6295
(212) 545-8511
Fax: (212) 545-8520
Email: email@analyticrecruiting.com
Web: www.analyticrecruiting.com

Summary: We specialize in recruiting people with strong analytical skills. We cover all major business areas including finance, marketing, operations, manufacturing, planning and systems. Our expertise is in positions that emphasize superior analytical talent and the use of advanced quantitative/modeling techniques and technology in business decision-making. We like to work closely with our clients and are very deliberate in matching skills, career goals and positions.

Key Contact - Specialty:
Mr. Daniel Raz, Principal - *Finance, Financial services, Investment management, Wall Street*
Ms. Rita Raz, Principal - *Credit cards, CRM, Direct marketing, Market research, Marketing*

Salary Minimum: $45,000

Functions: Generalist (All), Product Dev., Mktg. Research, Direct Mktg., Cash Mgmt., Credit, Risk Mgmt., IT, R&D, Mgmt. Consultants

Industries: Generalist (All), Soap, Perf., Cosmtcs., Drugs Mfg., Finance, Banking, Invest. Banking, Brokers, Venture Cap., Mutual/Hedge Funds, Misc. Financial, Mgmt. Consulting, E-commerce, Media, Insurance, Mfg. SW, Marketing SW, Biotech/Life Sciences, Healthcare

Ancilla Resource Corp

3333 Warrenville Rd Ste 200
Lisle, IL 60532-1999
(630) 724-0700
Fax: (630) 724-0777
Email: info@ancillaco.com
Web: www.ancillaco.com

Summary: Our firm is an executive search and management-consulting firm that specializes in the high/IT industry. Our core market begins at the help desk or computer operator level up to the chief information officer and encompasses

everything in between the IT corporate infrastructure.

Key Contact - Specialty:
Mr. Mark P. Conway, President, Regional Operations, Tech P. - *Technical, Technical (Management), Technicians, Technology, Wireless*

Salary Minimum: $30,000

Functions: MIS Mgmt., Systems Analysis, Systems Dev., Systems Implem., Systems Support, Network Admin., DB Admin.

Industries: Generalist (All)

Andersen & Associates

PO Box 1628
Marshalltown, IA 50158-7628
(641) 752-6152
Fax: (641) 752-6287
Email: info@andersenassociates.com
Web: www.andersenassociates.com

Summary: Our firm is a family owned and operated professional recruiting and placement group specializing in executive, IT and telecom positions. Our objective is to ensure a satisfying match of skills, expertise and career goals.

Key Contact - Specialty:
Mrs. Lou Ann Andersen, Owner
Mrs. Leigh Ann Andersen, Executive Recruiter
Mr. Erik Andersen, Technical Recruiter
Mr. Don Tiernan, Senior Associate

Functions: Sales Mgmt., IT, MIS Mgmt., Systems Analysis, Systems Dev., Network Admin., DB Admin., Engineering, Mgmt. Consultants

Industries: Generalist (All), Agri., Forestry, Mining, Manufacturing, Plastics, Rubber, Metal Products, Machine, Appliance, Computer Equip., Electronic, Elec. Components, Finance, Services, IT Implementation, Media, Communications, Insurance, Software, Healthcare

Andersen Career Consultants Inc

5018 Country Club Dr N
Wilson, NC 27896-9122
(252) 246-9909
Email: andersen@nc.rr.com
Web: www.andersencareers.com

Summary: Technical and professional recruiting in manufacturing serving the automotive, plastic, rubber, metal, consumer and industrial products industries.

Key Contact - Specialty:
Mr. Ken Andersen, President & Recruiter

Salary Minimum: $45,000

Functions: Generalist (All), Mfg.

Industries: Manufacturing, Chemicals, Medical Devices, Plastics, Rubber, Paints, Petro. Products, Metal Products, Machine, Appliance, Motor Vehicles, Consumer Elect., Misc. Mfg., Electronic, Elec. Components, Robotics

J P Anderson & Associates Inc

241 Amberly Blvd
Ancaster, ON L9G 3Y4
Canada
(905) 648-4583
Email: careers@jpanderson.com
Web: www.jpanderson.com

Summary: Employment and careers in logistics, engineering, IT and operations management.

Key Contact - Specialty:
Mr. Jeff Anderson, President

Functions: Generalist (All)

Industries: Generalist (All)

Anderson Executive Search Inc

1460 Woodland Trce
Cumming, GA 30041-9340
(678) 455-0691
Email: tammy@aexsearch.com
Web: www.aexsearch.com

Summary: We are a retained, generalist search firm with expertise that includes consulting, telecom, broadband, manufacturing, logistics, procurement, distribution, insurance, IT, CRM, ERP, civil engineering, tax, audit, operations, legal, pharmaceutical, healthcare, nursing, and collections. We assist clients fill their executive and professional level positions in all functional areas across the country.

Key Contact - Specialty:
Mrs. Tammy Anderson Dutremble, President & Chief Executive Officer - *Audits, Change management, Information Technology, SAP, Tax*

Salary Minimum: $65,000

Functions: Generalist (All)

Industries: Generalist (All), Manufacturing, Medical Devices, Misc. Mfg., Mgmt. Consulting, IT Implementation, Engineering Svcs., Environmental Svcs., Software, Biotech/Life Sciences

Anderson Network Group

PO Box 274
Dayton, OH 45409-0274
(937) 299-7601
Email: ang@core.com

Summary: Contingency and retained search services serving manufacturing, construction and distribution clients having needs for exceptional financial, operational and HR professionals.

Key Contact - Specialty:
Mr. Wayne F. Anderson, CPC, Principal - *Accounting, Construction, Distribution, Human resources, Manufacturing*

Salary Minimum: $50,000

Functions: Management, Senior Mgmt., Plant Mgmt., Materials, Distribution, HR Mgmt., Finance, CFOs, Budgeting

Industries: Generalist (All), Construction, Manufacturing, Textiles, Apparel, Motor Vehicles, Misc. Mfg., Transportation, Wholesale, Retail, Services, Mgmt. Consulting, Logistics Svcs.

Anderson Young and Associates Inc

172 Broadway
Woodcliff Lake, NJ 07677-8077
(201) 358-0200
Fax: (201) 782-1852
Email: info@andersonyoungassoc.com
Web: www.andersonyoungassoc.com

Summary: We are an executive search firm that recruits on a retained and contingency basis in the areas of financial services and HR.

Key Contact - Specialty:
Mr. Barry Geister, President
Mr. Michael McManamon, Senior Search Consultant - *Human resources*
Mr. Jonathan Gould, Vice President & Marketing Director

Functions: Generalist (All), Sales Mgmt., HR Mgmt., Benefits, Staffing, Finance, Cash Mgmt., Credit

Industries: Generalist (All), Finance, Banking, Venture Cap., Services, Accounting, Equip Svcs.

Andiamo! Group

44 Montgomery St Ste 1250
San Francisco, CA 94104-4614
(415) 374-8181
Fax: (415) 781-4200
Email: jobs@andiamo-group.com
Web: www.andiamo-group.com

Summary: We are a staffing company committed to matching exceptional talent with extraordinary companies. With our emphasis on candidate advocacy and pipeline to leading-edge companies, we are well positioned to help you successfully navigate the entire recruiting process by providing direct-hire, temp and payroll only services in the sales, administrative and technical arenas.

Key Contact - Specialty:
Mr. Mark Gambirasi, Principal
Ms. Jessica Gambirasi, Recruiter - *Technology*

Salary Minimum: $30,000

Functions: Senior Mgmt., Middle Mgmt., Admin. Svcs., Sales & Mktg., Sales Mgmt., Customer Svc., Sales Reps., HR Mgmt., Finance

Industries: Generalist (All)

Andrews & Associates

4424 Atleigh Ct
Charlotte, NC 28226-5025
(704) 364-2421
Email: dwight@andrewssearch.com

Summary: We have extensive experience in assisting companies in locating CFOs and senior-level financial managers.

Key Contact - Specialty:
Mr. Dwight L. Andrews, CPA, Principal - *Financial*

Functions: CFOs, Budgeting, Taxes

Industries: Generalist (All), Motor Vehicles, Computer Equip., Consumer Elect., Test, Measure Equip., Misc. Mfg., Electronic, Elec. Components, Robotics, Semiconductors, Consumer Goods

Robert Andrews & Co

PO Box 270008
Tampa, FL 33688-0008
(813) 792-0000
Fax: (813) 920-3756

Summary: Our firm specializes in the placement of senior executives in bank and trust companies. It is both a retained and contingency search firm.

Key Contact - Specialty:
Mr. Robert Andrews, President
Mr. Mark Andrews, Vice President

Salary Minimum: $50,000

Functions: Senior Mgmt., Finance

Industries: Finance, Banking, Invest. Banking

Ethan Andrews Associates

PO Box 883362
Steamboat Springs, CO 80488-3362
(970) 870-0391
(877) 288-8735
Email: headhunterpro@gmail.com
Web: www.headhunterpro.com

Summary: We are a recruiting firm specializing in placing early to mid career professionals with growing companies and law firms.

Key Contact - Specialty:
Mr. Lee Cosgrove, JD, Owner

Salary Minimum: $50,000

Functions: Generalist (All)

Industries: Generalist (All), Manufacturing, Food, Bev., Tobacco, Printing, Drugs Mfg., Medical Devices, Computer Equip., Misc. Mfg., Legal, Telecoms

Angel Group LLC

PO Box 7215
Louisville, KY 40257-0215
(502) 897-0333
(888) 236-0333
Email: steve@angel-group.com
Web: www.angel-group.com

Summary: Our company knows how to find talented well-trained professionals who will lead your company to greater success and market share. Industry, trade or craft does not limit the scope of our service. We serve high profile, global companies from every enterprise.

Key Contact - Specialty:
Mr. Steve Angel, CPA, Member - *Administration, Financial*
Mr. Jim Bradshaw, Member - *Aerospace, Defense*
Ms. Barbara Beard, Member - *MIS*
Ms. Jennifer Dudley, CPA, Member - *Accounting, Accounting (Public), Finance*
Mrs. Pam Rogers, Associate - *Legal*

Salary Minimum: $50,000

Functions: Generalist (All), Production, Plant Mgmt., Distribution, Benefits, Cash Mgmt., Systems Dev., Int'l.

Industries: Generalist (All), Manufacturing, Transportation, Retail, Banking, Accounting, Media

Tryg R Angell Ltd

354 Shelton Rd
Trumbull, CT 06611-5162
(203) 377-4541
Fax: (203) 377-4545
Email: tryg@snet.net

Summary: We offer senior positions in the pulp and paper industry. Sales & marketing positions as well as technical and production positions for paper, chemical and other industrial companies.

Key Contact - Specialty:
Mr. Tryg R. Angell, Principal - *Paper, Sales, Technical*

Salary Minimum: $30,000

Functions: Generalist (All), Product Dev., Plant Mgmt., Sales & Mktg., Mktg. Research, Sales Mgmt., Engineering

Industries: Generalist (All), Agri., Forestry, Mining, Energy, Utilities, Construction, Manufacturing, Textiles, Apparel, Lumber, Furniture, Paper, Printing, Chemicals, Plastics, Rubber, Paints, Petro. Products, Metal Products, Machine, Appliance, Misc. Mfg., Equip Svcs., Packaging, Non-Classifiable

Angus Employment Ltd

1100 Burloak Dr
Reimer Tower Floor 5
Burlington, ON L7L 6B2
Canada
(905) 319-0773
Fax: (905) 336-9445
Email: executivesearch@angusemployment.com
Web: www.angusemployment.com

Summary: We recruit on behalf of many high-profile firms in all industries for professional occupations at every level.

Key Contact - Specialty:
Mr. Evan Stewart, President

Functions: Generalist (All), Management, Mfg., Sales & Mktg., Finance, IT, Engineering

Industries: Generalist (All), Manufacturing, Transportation, Finance, IT Implementation, Aerospace, Software

Anita's Careers

100 York Rd Apt E714
Jenkintown, PA 19046-3632
(215) 517-8089
Fax: (215) 517-8556
Email: anitascareers@aol.com
Web: www.anitascareers.com

Summary: An executive search/recruitment firm providing placements for all industries and all for all positions. Additional services include outplacement, resume and career counseling services. We help candidates toward 'star track' careers. Privacy, attention to detail and true customer service are the true values in working with our firm.

Key Contact - Specialty:
Ms. Anita Klein, President

Salary Minimum: $50,000

Functions: Generalist (All), Board Members, Senior Mgmt.

Industries: Generalist (All), Textiles, Apparel, Chemicals, Drugs Mfg., Medical Devices, Finance, Misc. Financial, Services, Non-profits, Pharm Svcs., Legal, Accounting, HR Services, Advertising, Telecoms, Casualty, Claims, Software, Entertainment SW, Marketing SW

Ankenbrandt Group

20281 SW Birch St Ste 200
Newport Beach, CA 92660-1776
(949) 955-1455
Fax: (949) 955-2029
Email: info@ankgrp.com
Web: www.ankgrp.com

Summary: We recruit the people you want. We place senior level managers to CEOs in accounting, finance, marketing, sales, IS and real estate.

Key Contact - Specialty:
Mr. Max Smith

Functions: Management, Board Members, Senior Mgmt., Mfg., Sales & Mktg., Finance, IT, Engineering, Hospitality

Industries: Generalist (All), Real Estate, Property/Facility Mgmt.

Fred Anthony Associates

PO Box 372
Lake Geneva, WI 53147-0372
(262) 245-1940
Fax: (262) 364-2513
Email: fanthony@genevaonline.com

Summary: Focus on Sales, Marketing and Technical Service positions in the Specialty Chemical Industry. Main support industries are paint, coatings, inks, and adhesives.

Key Contact - Specialty:
Mr. Fred Anthony, President

Salary Minimum: $50,000

Functions: Generalist (All), Management, Sales & Mktg.

Industries: Chemicals, Paints, Petro. Products

David Anthony Personnel Associates Inc

64 E Ridgewood Ave
Paramus, NJ 07652-3624
(201) 262-6100
Fax: (201) 262-7744
Email: info@davidanthony.com
Web: www.davidanthony.com

Summary: We specialize in mid to senior level banking opportunities. Our firm concentrates on commercial bank recruiting that focuses on credit and lending. The typical positions that we place are: senior credit analysts, commercial loan officers, relationship managers, commercial real estate, chief credit officer, branch managers, etc.

Key Contact - Specialty:
Mr. David K. Ferrara, President

Salary Minimum: $40,000

Functions: Generalist (All)

Industries: Banking

AP Associates (APA)

1222 Lakefront Dr
Charleston, SC 29412-8267
(908) 371-0066
(843) 278-0504
Email: apa@apassociates.com
Web: www.apassociates.com

Summary: We are an executive and high-tech placement firm meeting staffing requirements within the communication, semiconductor, bio-tech, pharmaceutical, automotive and construction industries. Also the IT/IS, healthcare, legal (patent, import/export, real estate, investment, IPO, M&A, VC), business development, supply chain, hotel/hospitality management, education, environmental, emergency response and quality control professions.

Key Contact - Specialty:
Mr. Alex Palyo, Vice President, Operations - *Manufacturing, Research & development, Semiconductors, Senior management, Venture capital*

Salary Minimum: $50,000

Functions: Generalist (All), Senior Mgmt.

Industries: Manufacturing, Electronic, Elec. Components, Finance, Venture Cap., Hospitality, Media, Communications, Homeland Security, Environmental Svcs., Software, Biotech/Life Sciences, Healthcare

APA Employment Agency Inc

1001 SW 5th Ave Ste 1100
Portland, OR 97204-1127
(503) 233-1200
(800) 715-4562
Fax: (503) 762-6065
Email: les@apaemployment.com
Web: www.apaemployment.com

Summary: We have one of the largest client bases in our area. We place many new candidates weekly. Our name would be a good lead for someone trying to relocate.

Key Contact - Specialty:
Ms. Felicia Hintzue, Manager, Industrial - *Industrial*
Mr. Dave Knox, Administrative Manager - *Human resources, Management*
Mr. Jeff Voigt, Professional Manager - *Management, Sales*
Mr. Les Swanson, Recruiter - *Human resources, Technology*

Salary Minimum: $25,000

Functions: Generalist (All), Management, Admin. Svcs., Plant Mgmt., Productivity, Customer Svc., Staffing, Training

Industries: Generalist (All), Manufacturing, Misc. Mfg., Transportation, Retail, Services, Non-Classifiable

APB Executive Consulting

PO Box 170914
Milwaukee, WI 53217-8081
(866) 964-3003
Email: gthomas@apbexecutiveconsulting.com
Web: www.apbexecutiveconsulting.com

Summary: An executive search consulting firm specializing in the permanent placement of mid to senior level food manufacturing, food processing and technical food ingredient professionals.

Key Contact - Specialty:
Mr. George Thomas
Ms. Anita Kapczynski, Vice President

Salary Minimum: $50,000

Functions: Senior Mgmt., Middle Mgmt., Quality, Purchasing, Sales & Mktg., R&D

Industries: Food, Bev., Tobacco

Apex Executive Recruiting Inc

27520 Hawthorne Blvd Ste 295
Rolling Hills Estates, CA 90274-3515
(310) 265-9996
Fax: (310) 265-9997
Email: mark@apex-careers.com
Web: www.apex-careers.com

Summary: We are a national search firm focused on the medical device and pharmaceutical industry. We provide top talent for the sales, clinical specialists, marketing, sales management and executive level positions. We specialize in the development of world class sales and marketing organizations at both established and start-up companies.

Key Contact - Specialty:
Mr. Mark Cannistraro, Partner & Founder
Mr. Bill White, Vice President

Functions: Healthcare, Sales & Mktg.

Industries: Medical Devices, Pharm Svcs., Healthcare

Apex Search Inc

900-45 Sheppard Ave E
North York, ON M2N 5W9
Canada
(416) 226-2828
Fax: (416) 226-1417
Email: karen@apexsearch.com
Web: www.apexsearch.com

Summary: We are in a strong position of being able to spend time to get to know our clients' environments, technical needs as well as the soft skills necessary to make the proper match.

Key Contact - Specialty:
Ms. Karen Agulnik, Owner
Ms. Joanne Bloye, Senior Consultant

Functions: IT, MIS Mgmt., Systems Analysis, Systems Dev., Systems Implem., Systems Support, Network Admin., DB Admin., Mgmt. Consultants

Industries: Manufacturing, Drugs Mfg.

David Aplin Recruiting

2300-10235 101 St NW
Oxford Tower
Edmonton, AB T5J 3G1
Canada
(780) 428-6663
Fax: (780) 421-4680
Email: edmonton@aplin.com
Web: www.aplin.com

Summary: We are one of the country's leading professional search organizations offering clients and candidates a full range of recruitment services in: IT, accounting/finance, sales/marketing, engineering/technical, supply chain management, HR, legal and office personnel; from intermediate to executive levels.

Key Contact - Specialty:
Mr. David Aplin, Chief Executive Officer
Mr. Mike Bacchus, President - *Sales*
Mr. Mike Corbett, Vice President, Edmonton Region

Salary Minimum: $40,000

Functions: Management, Admin. Svcs., Mfg., Sales & Mktg., HR Mgmt., Finance, IT, Engineering, Legal

Industries: Generalist (All)

Branches:
3850-700 2 St SW
Scotia Centre
Calgary, AB T2P 2W2
Canada
(403) 261-9000
Fax: (403) 266-7195
Email: calgary@aplin.com
Key Contact - Specialty:
Mr. Jeff Aplin, Vice President, Calgary Region

11518-650 Georgia St W
Vancouver Centre
Vancouver, BC V6B 4N7
Canada
(604) 648-2799
Fax: (604) 648-2787
Email: vancouver@aplin.com
Key Contact - Specialty:
Mr. Greg Ford, Vice President, Vancouver Region

602-1 Lombard Pl
Richardson Building
Winnipeg, MB R3B 0X3
Canada
(204) 235-0000
Fax: (204) 235-0002
Email: winnipeg@aplin.com
Key Contact - Specialty:
Mr. Mark Shayna, Branch Manager

303-1791 Barrington St
Toronto Dominion Tower
Halifax, NS B3J 3K9
Canada
(902) 461-1616
Fax: (902) 435-6300
Email: halifax@aplin.com
Key Contact - Specialty:
Mr. Craig Coady, Senior Consultant

1208-350 Sparks St
Ottawa, ON K1R 7S8
Canada
(613) 288-2211
Fax: (613) 288-0213
Email: ottawa@aplin.com
Key Contact - Specialty:
Mr. Chris Duffield, Senior Consultant
Ms. Stéphanie Bolduc, Senior Consultant

905-123 Front St W
Citibank Place
Toronto, ON M5J 2M2
Canada
(416) 367-9700
Fax: (416) 367-1577
Email: toronto@aplin.com
Key Contact - Specialty:
Mr. Barrie Carlyle, Vice President, Toronto Region
Mr. Eddy Gerek, Regional Practice Manager
Mr. Don Green, Regional Practice Manager

The Apollo Group

1210 Millennium Pkwy Ste 1045
Brandon, FL 33511-4858
(813) 685-7272
Fax: (813) 681-3680
Email: bill@apollogroupus.com
Web: www.apollogroupus.com

Summary: We work both contingency and retained in medical device, pharmaceutical, manufacturing, engineering, quality and regulatory in metals, plastics and injection molding. We provide engineers, sales, quality, human resources, R&D, and production management from entry level to executive level vice presidents.

Key Contact - Specialty:
Mr. Bill Handley, Owner & Manager - *Biotechnology, General management, Manufacturing (Management), Medical (Devices), Pharmaceutical*
Mr. Jon Matteson, Senior Account Executive - *Biotechnology, CEOs, CIOs, COOs, Medical (Devices)*
Mr. Shawn Schantz, Senior Account Executive - *Biotechnology, C-level, Manufacturing (Management), Medical (Devices), Pharmaceutical*

Salary Minimum: $40,000

Functions: Generalist (All)

Industries: Drugs Mfg., Medical Devices, Plastics, Rubber, Metal Products, Misc. Mfg., Pharm Svcs., Biotech/Life Sciences

APP Consulting

PO Box 6055
Monroe Township, NJ 08831-6055
(732) 583-1000
(609) 409-1411
Fax: (609) 860-9079
Email: peter@appconsultants.com

Summary: Our firm has been a leader in recruiting middle and upper-level management personnel for growing companies in the pharmaceutical, cosmetic and chemical industries.

Key Contact - Specialty:
Mr. Peter Provda, President - *Consumer, Consumer (Packaged Goods), Engineering, Manufacturing, Materials*
Mr. Norm Phillips, Vice President - *Biopharmaceutical, Medical, Medical (Devices), Pharmaceutical, Research*

Salary Minimum: $35,000

Functions: Generalist (All), Middle Mgmt.

Industries: Manufacturing, Food, Bev., Tobacco, Printing, Chemicals, Soap, Perf., Cosmtcs., Drugs Mfg., Medical Devices, Plastics, Rubber, Paints, Petro. Products, HR Services, Packaging

Apple & Associates Inc

PO Box 996
Chapin, SC 29036-0996
(803) 932-2000
Fax: (803) 932-2006

Email: dapple@appleassoc.com
Web: appleassoc.com

Summary: We are a nationwide executive search firm specializing in recruitment for manufacturing industries, specifically: medical device, pharmaceutical, banking, automotive and consumer products. We place salaried professionals in manufacturing, engineering, Six Sigma, procurement, human resources, sales & marketing, continuous improvement and quality positions from entry level to VP.

Key Contact - Specialty:
Ms. Debi Apple, President

Salary Minimum: $40,000

Functions: Management, Mfg., HR Mgmt., R&D, Engineering

Industries: Generalist (All), Manufacturing, Food, Bev., Tobacco, Chemicals, Soap, Perf., Cosmtcs., Drugs Mfg., Medical Devices, Plastics, Rubber, Motor Vehicles, Misc. Mfg., Robotics, HR Services, Packaging

Apple One Employment Serv

18538 Hawthorne Blvd
Torrance, CA 90504-4585
(310) 370-0708
Email: torrance-ca@appleone.com
Web: www.appleone.com

Summary: A Forbes Private 500 company, our firm combines extensive expertise with formidable resources to offer temp, temp-to-hire and direct hire services. Our vast network, powerful proprietary technology and robust recruitment and referral results deliver best-of-breed solutions for diverse staffing needs, including clerical, administrative, sales & marketing and light industrial.

Key Contact - Specialty:
Mr. Marc Goldman, Vice President, Sales & Marketing
Ms. Christine Duque, Director, Communications

Functions: Generalist (All)

Industries: Generalist (All), Computer Equip., Consumer Elect., Misc. Financial, Legal, Accounting, Mgmt. Consulting, Telecoms, Call Centers, Accounting SW

Application Design Group, Inc.

4227 Earth City Expy Ste 150
Earth City, MO 63045-1397
(314) 298-1850
(888) 470-7499
Fax: (314) 298-1899
Email: jrowan@adg-us.com
Web: www.adg-us.com

Summary: Our firm is a regional IT consulting and placement firm that also develops staffing metrics tools and other HR related software. Our goal is to "Always Help People."

Key Contact - Specialty:
Mr. Jay Rowan, President - *Human resources, Information Technology, Sales*

Salary Minimum: $60,000

Functions: IT, MIS Mgmt., Systems Analysis, Systems Dev., Systems Implem., Systems Support, Network Admin., DB Admin.

Industries: Generalist (All)

Applied Resources Inc

7200 Hemlock Ln N Ste 112
Osseo, MN 55369-5586
(612) 424-4006
Fax: (612) 424-4843

Email: ari@winternet.com
Web: www.winternet.com/~ari

Summary: We provide specialists in identifying engineering and manufacturing professionals. Dedicated to serving technology driven growth companies. Have developed extensive networks in: metal fabrication, data communications software, hardware and medical device industries. We do not normally participate in relocations.

Key Contact - Specialty:
Mr. Michael G. Weiss, CPC, Chief Executive Officer - *Engineering, Management, Manufacturing*

Salary Minimum: $40,000

Functions: Generalist (All), Product Dev., Purchasing, Mktg. Research, Staffing, Systems Implem., R&D, Engineering

Industries: Generalist (All), Manufacturing, Medical Devices, Plastics, Rubber, HR Services, Packaging, Software

Applied Search Associates Inc

PO Box 1207
Dawsonville, GA 30534-0023
(706) 265-2530
Email: applied_search@alltel.net

Summary: Our specialty is direct recruiting and placement of hard to find personnel with specific backgrounds, talent and education. We produce results through experience, preparation and individualized attention to all project details.

Key Contact - Specialty:
Mr. Richard B. Rockwell, Sr., President - *Management, Manufacturing, Marketing, Process equipment, Sales*

Salary Minimum: $50,000

Functions: Generalist (All), Middle Mgmt., Sales & Mktg., Sales Mgmt.

Industries: Energy, Utilities, Manufacturing, Paper, Metal Products, Test, Measure Equip., Robotics, Equip Svcs., Engineering Svcs., Industry Specific SW, Mfg. SW, Marketing SW

April International Inc

200 North Ave Ste 6
New Rochelle, NY 10801-6447
(914) 632-2333
Fax: (914) 632-3582
Email: ken@aprilinternational.com
Web: www.aprilinternational.com

Summary: Executive search for the financial services industry, specializing in accounting, audit, operations and other finance areas.

Key Contact - Specialty:
Mr. Kenneth April, President - *Accounting, Accounting (Big 4), Audits, Banking, Financial*
Mr. Kevin Collins, Vice President
Mr. Fred Stang, Vice President
Ms. Valerie Bowser, Vice President
Mr. Michael Roach, Vice President
Mr. Al Rooney, Vice President
Ms. Keiko Hirano, Vice President - *Accounting, Accounting (Big 4,Public), Audits, Banking*
Mr. Ian Greene, Vice President - *Accounting, Accounting (Big 4,Public), Audits, Banking*

Salary Minimum: $50,000

Functions: Generalist (All), Management, Finance, Risk Mgmt.

Industries: Finance, Banking, Invest. Banking, Brokers, Venture Cap., Mutual/Hedge Funds, Misc. Financial, Services, Accounting, Mgmt. Consulting, HR Services, IT Implementation, Media, Communications, Accounting SW, HR SW

APS Recruiting

12011 Huebner Rd Ste 207
San Antonio, TX 78230-1234
(210) 690-3888
Fax: (210) 690-3836
Email: solutions@apsrecruiting.com
Web: www.apsrecruiting.com

Summary: We are a personnel consulting services firm that focuses on accounting, finance, administrative support and HR professionals. In addition to our direct hire services, we also offer contract, temp and temp-to-hire services.

Key Contact - Specialty:
Ms. Vanessa L. Burk, CPC
Toni D'Onofrio, CPC
Mr. Richard J. Zielinski, CPA, CPC - *Accounting*

Salary Minimum: $20,000

Functions: Admin. Svcs., HR Mgmt., Finance

Industries: Generalist (All)

ARC Associates

75 Gilcreast Rd Unit 305
Londonderry, NH 03053-3567
(603) 425-2488
Fax: (603) 432-2533
Email: kim@arc-associates.com
Web: www.arc-associates.com

Summary: Specialized in finance and accounting search. Selective target search on both contingency and retained basis.

Key Contact - Specialty:
Ms. Kim C. Scoggins, Senior Parnter

Functions: Finance

Industries: Generalist (All)

Branches:
8 Faneuil Hall Market Pl Ste 300
Boston, MA 02109-6111
(617) 973-6488

ARC Partners Inc

6339 E Greenway Rd Ste 102
Scottsdale, AZ 85254-6524
(480) 951-6004
Fax: (480) 951-2082
Email: cynthia@arcsearch.com
Web: www.arcsearch.com

Summary: We offer experience in the healthcare field. Full-service recruitment firm offering both retained and contingency clients.

Key Contact - Specialty:
Ms. Cynthia Allen, President - *Healthcare*

Salary Minimum: $70,000

Functions: Generalist (All), Management, Healthcare, Physicians, Nurses

Industries: Generalist (All), Healthcare, Hospitals

ARC Staffing Inc

9220 NW 38th Dr
Coral Springs, FL 33065-4302
(954) 344-2240
Fax: (412) 422-8682
Email: alan@arcstaffing.net
Web: www.arcstaffing.net

Summary: We are specialists in working within industrial, medical and food distribution.

Key Contact - Specialty:
Mr. Alan Raeburn, President - *Industrial*

Salary Minimum: $50,000

Functions: Sales & Mktg.

Industries: Generalist (All)

John Arceri Group

309 Philadelphia Ave
Massapequa Park, NY 11762-1818
(516) 510-5463

Summary: We are an executive recruiters specializing in sales; servicing Fortune 1000 companies.

Key Contact - Specialty:
Mr. John Mark Arceri, Director - *Brokerage, Client/server, Data processing*

Salary Minimum: $40,000

Functions: Generalist (All), Board Members, MIS Mgmt., Systems Analysis, Systems Dev., Systems Implem., Systems Support, Mgmt. Consultants

Industries: Generalist (All), Banking, Invest. Banking, Brokers, Mgmt. Consulting, HR Services

Architechs

PO Box 119
Prides Crossing, MA 01965-0119
(978) 524-8180
Email: bob@architechs.net

Summary: Our firm is a dynamic technical search and recruiting firm with an excellent reputation for providing quality service to distinguished clients and candidates. Our clientele consists of many of the top organizations from small start-ups to Fortune 500 firms. We have specialized in developing long term, mutually beneficial relationships with some of the best technical professionals in the field.

Key Contact - Specialty:
Mr. Bob Jones, Principal

Salary Minimum: $50,000

Functions: IT, Systems Dev., Engineering

Industries: E-commerce, IT Implementation, Software, Accounting SW, Database SW, Development SW

The Argus Group Corp

302-160 Erskine Ave
Upper Canada Court Right Wing
Toronto, ON M4P 1Z3
Canada
(416) 238-5859
Fax: (416) 932-9387
Email: alec@argusgroupcorp.com
Web: www.argussearchgroup.com

Summary: Like the multi-eyed monster of mythical fame, we always keep our watchful eyes out for your best interest: selecting appropriately trained people who can immediately benefit your corporation.

Key Contact - Specialty:
Mr. Alec Reed, President

Functions: Generalist (All), Senior Mgmt., Advertising, Mktg. Research, Mktg. Mgmt., Sales Mgmt., Direct Mktg., IT

Industries: Generalist (All)

ARI (Axcel Recruiting Inc)

3126 W Cary St Ste 403
Richmond, VA 23221-3504
(888) 766-0144
(804) 781-1800
Fax: (804) 781-1802
Email: info@iaxcel.com
Web: www.iaxcel.com

Summary: We specialize in recruitment for management and senior level opportunities in the consumer packaged goods industry. Our executive search capabilities, proprietary technology and our personal touch offer an unparalleled recruiting experience. Areas of expertise include sales management, national account management, category management, trade marketing, brand marketing, marketing research, and consumer/shopper insights.

Key Contact - Specialty:
Mr. Robert Richards, Vice President & Senior Consultant - *Consumer, Consumer (Marketing, Packaged Goods), Diversity, Sales*
Mr. Charles Robertson, Associate Recruiter - *Consumer*
Mrs. Meghan Richards, Vice President, Business Development - *Consumer (Marketing, Packaged Goods), Diversity, Food & beverage, Market research*

Salary Minimum: $50,000

Functions: Sales & Mktg., Advertising, Mktg. Research, Mktg. Mgmt., Sales Mgmt.

Industries: Food, Bev., Tobacco, Textiles, Apparel, Soap, Perf., Cosmtcs., Computer Equip., Consumer Elect., Consumer Goods, Wholesale, Retail

ARI Summit Search Specialists

12202 Whittington Dr
Houston, TX 77077-4913
(281) 497-5840
Fax: (281) 902-5195
Email: dave@arisummit.com
Web: www.arisummit.com

Summary: Extensive experience specializing in the placement of quality insurance professionals.

Key Contact - Specialty:
Mr. David S. Bunce, Senior Parnter

Salary Minimum: $50,000

Functions: Generalist (All)

Industries: Insurance

Aries Search Group LLC

9925 Haynes Bridge Rd Ste 200
Alpharetta, GA 30022-1913
(770) 569-4708
Fax: (770) 569-4709
Email: ariessearch@bellsouth.net
Web: www.us-recruiters.com

Summary: We specialize in search and recruitment exclusively to the medical industry. We strive towards a commitment to becoming partners in strategic planning with our client companies. We specialize in placement of sales and sales management professionals. We do not recruit healthcare professionals, or clinical positions within medical companies.

Key Contact - Specialty:
Ms. Cindy McAndrew, President - *Marketing, Sales*

Functions: Sales Mgmt., Sales Reps.

Industries: Medical Devices

ARJay & Associates Inc

598 S Milledge Ave Ste 4
Athens, GA 30605-1262
(706) 548-6799
Fax: (706) 548-0356
Email: arjayga@mindspring.com
Web: www.arjaysearch.com

Summary: We engage to facilitate client company growth in a number of ways. We advise on and provide services related to building companies by units via mergers & acquisitions, strategic partnering and strategic unit acquisition; and we engage to recruit key executives, managers and professionals. Our clients are mostly technology-based companies ranging in size from part-startup to Fortune 100.

Key Contact - Specialty:
Mr. Ronald Jones, President

Salary Minimum: $75,000

Functions: Generalist (All)

Industries: Generalist (All)

Arlington Resources Inc

(also known as Casey Accounting & Finance Resources, Inc.)
5105 Tollview Dr Ste 265
Rolling Meadows, IL 60008-3786
(847) 590-9490
Fax: (847) 590-9498
Email: hr@arlingtonresources.com
Web: www.arlingtonresources.com

Summary: Our firm specializes in identifying, locating and evaluating some of the strongest HR professionals for our client companies. We are dedicated to quality, professionalism and excellent customer service. We place HR professionals in executive level positions, contract and temporary positions.

Key Contact - Specialty:
Ms. Patricia Casey, President - *Human resources*

Functions: HR Mgmt.

Industries: Generalist (All)

J Arnold & Associates

PO Box 26123
Austin, TX 78755-0123
(512) 342-1966
Email: janet@jarnoldsearch.com
Web: www.jarnoldsearch.com

Summary: Our firm specializes in the recruitment and placement of consumer marketing and marketing services professionals. By acknowledging the value of strong education and classical training, we are able to provide exceptional marketing talent to large and small companies with both traditional and non-traditional product lines and services.

Key Contact - Specialty:
Ms. Janet Arnold

Salary Minimum: $70,000

Functions: Generalist (All), Advertising, Mktg. Research, Mktg. Mgmt., Direct Mktg.

Industries: Food, Bev., Tobacco, Soap, Perf., Cosmtcs., Consumer Goods, Travel

Aronow Associates Inc

6923 Fairway Lakes Dr
Boynton Beach, FL 33437-6804
(561) 732-6008

Summary: Management recruiting for the financial services industry specializing in sales, product management, strategic planning and all marketing functions. Global finance and treasury management for the corporate market.

Key Contact - Specialty:
Mr. Lawrence E. Aronow, President - *Financial services*

Salary Minimum: $60,000

Functions: Generalist (All), Management, Sales & Mktg., Finance

Industries: Generalist (All), Finance

Arrowhead Executive Search

2160 N 4th St Ste 210
Flagstaff, AZ 86004-4255
(928) 526-8400
(877) 526-8400
Fax: (928) 526-8401
Email: mglemser@arrowheadsearch.com
Web: www.arrowheadsearch.com

Summary: Working in the medical device arena, we focus our teams within the areas of interventional cardiology, endovascular surgery, electrophysiology, urology, general surgery and related areas. We have teams that specifically focus on clinical research and regulatory affairs, field clinical specialists, R&D and manufacturing, product management and sales & marketing.

Key Contact - Specialty:
Mr. Michael Glemser, President & Search Specialist
Mr. Jim Gilliland, Vice President, Operation & Search Spec
Mr. Niles Love, Search Specialist
Ms. Tamara Warner, Search Specialist - *Physicians*
Mr. Tom Hoffman, Search Specialist
Ms. Wendy Velasquez, Sourcing and Research - *Computers, Computers (Programming), Healthcare, Information Technology, Physicians*

Salary Minimum: $40,000

Functions: Generalist (All)

Industries: Drugs Mfg., Medical Devices, Pharm Svcs., Engineering Svcs., Hospitals, Dental

Branches:
1234 S Power Rd Ste 207
Mesa, AZ 85206-3700
(480) 830-6800
Key Contact - Specialty:
Mr. Brad Blue, Recruiter - *Pharmacists*

Arrowhead Physician Recruiting & Placement

466 Orange St Ste 361
Redlands, CA 93274-3240
(909) 792-6883
(888) 792-5669
Fax: (909) 498-7378
Email: arrowone@arrowone.com
Web: www.arrowone.com

Summary: We specialize in timely and cost effective services for our clients and work to find positive matches for both client and physician in a professional, confidential manner. We work on a contingency based agreement.

Key Contact - Specialty:
Ms. Kathleen Reid, Owner

Functions: Physicians

Industries: Healthcare

The Artemis Group Ltd

420 Lexington Ave Rm 300
New York, NY 10170-0399
(212) 297-6155
Fax: (212) 479-2514
Email: info@artemisexecsearch.com
Web: www.artemisexecsearch.com

Summary: We place individual attorneys and practice groups from all practice areas into law firms all over the world, including two-tier, full-service as well as boutique law firms; investment banks; and corporations in a wide range of industries, such as financial, pharmaceutical, technology and telecom. We also handle law firm mergers.

Key Contact - Specialty:
Ms. Nancy D. Zehner, Esq., President & Founder
Mr. Donald M. Kleban, Esq., Senior Managing Director
Ms. Keira A. Chassman, MSW, Managing Director
Mr. Benjamin M. Dewar, Esq., Director
Ms. Carolyn A. Woodberry, MBA, Consultant, Business
Ms. Gina Nations, Administrator & Research Manager

Functions: Attorneys

Industries: Manufacturing, Invest. Banking, Misc. Financial, Pharm Svcs., Mgmt. Consulting, Hospitality, Entertainment, Media, Communications, Insurance

Artemis HRC LLC

281 Norlynn Dr
Howell, MI 48843-9026
(810) 494-0300 x102
Fax: (810) 494-0200
Email: artemis@artemishrc.com
Web: www.artemishrc.com

Summary: Assessment, development and management of custom recruiting solutions to accommodate clients through all stages of growth. Services range from individual searches through corporate acquisition search.

Key Contact - Specialty:
Mr. James Pantelas, President - *Communications, Management, Manufacturing, Sales, Technology*

Salary Minimum: $40,000

Functions: Generalist (All), Management, Mfg., Sales & Mktg., HR Mgmt., Finance, IT, Mgmt. Consultants

Industries: Generalist (All), Manufacturing, Services, Media, Communications, Telecoms, Call Centers, Network Infrastructure, Insurance, Software

Arthur-Blair Associates Inc

11 Beacon St Ste 910
Boston, MA 02108-3013
(617) 723-8135
Fax: (617) 723-8140
Email: tom@aba-inc.com
Web: www.aba-inc.com

Summary: We are dedicated to the placement of lending professionals ranging from loan processors to senior executives in the residential and commercial mortgage banking sector throughout New England and serve skilled professionals in marketing, accounting, administrative and other office support positions in Downtown Boston and throughout the Eastern Massachusetts area.

Key Contact - Specialty:
Mr. Thomas Phinney, Senior Recruiter - *Banking, Finance*
Ms. Rachel Richard, Senior Recruiter
Ms. Courtney Greene, Recruiter

Salary Minimum: $40,000

Functions: Generalist (All)

Industries: Finance, Banking, Venture Cap.

The Artisan Group

15636 Britenbush Ct Ste 200
Waterford, VA 20197-1001
(540) 882-9077
Email: info@theartisangroup.com
Web: www.theartisangroup.com

Summary: Our firm is a premium executive search firm that has built an established track record of success in the identification and recruitment of talented executives, and individual contributors within the non-profit arena. We possess specific expertise in the areas of development of fundraising.

Key Contact - Specialty:
Mr. Paul Siker, Managing Partner

Salary Minimum: $90,000

Functions: Management, Non-profits

Industries: Non-profits

ASAP Search & Recruiters

16 Berryhill Rd Ste 120
Columbia, SC 29210-6433
(803) 772-6751
Fax: (803) 798-0874
Email: work@asapsearch.com
Web: www.asapsearch.com

Summary: Our strength is specializing in the metal working areas such as: stamping, grinding, metallurgy etc. of automotive, manufacturing and power tools in engineering and management professionals.

Key Contact - Specialty:
Mr. Richard V. Bramblett, President - *Automotive*
Ms. Jeanette Bramblett, Vice President
Mr. Nick Stoia, CPC, Technical Staffing Consultant - *Computers (Software)*

Salary Minimum: $30,000

Functions: Generalist (All), Product Dev., Production, Automation, Plant Mgmt., Quality, Purchasing, Sales & Mktg., Engineering

Industries: Generalist (All), Metal Products, Machine, Appliance, Motor Vehicles, Test, Measure Equip., Misc. Mfg., Aerospace

Ash & Associates Executive Search

PO Box 862
Pompano Beach, FL 33061-0862
(954) 946-3395
Fax: (954) 946-3531
Email: ashassoc9@aol.com

Summary: We specialize in all areas of pharmaceutical recruitment including validation. We recruit for clinical trials, clinical research, physician, pharmacist/techs, HR, telecom and IS. We do not work with entry level, non-profit, publishing, advertising, government or public relations fields. We prefer using salary requirements and relocation preferences from the start.

Key Contact - Specialty:
Mr. J. DeRiso, Vice President - *Engineering, Finance, Management, Operations*

Salary Minimum: $60,000

Functions: Generalist (All), Management, Sales & Mktg., HR Mgmt., Finance, IT, MIS Mgmt., Systems Analysis, Systems Dev., Systems Implem.

Industries: Manufacturing, Soap, Perf., Cosmtcs., Drugs Mfg., Medical Devices, Consumer Elect., Pharm Svcs., HR Services, Database SW, Development SW, ERP SW, HR SW, Mfg. SW, Biotech/Life Sciences, Hospitals

The Asheville Group

PO Box 8466
Asheville, NC 28814-8466
(828) 258-9646
Fax: (828) 658-9215
Email: paul@theashevillegroup.com
Web: www.theashevillegroup.com

Summary: We are search and recruitment specialists for upper and middle management professionals.

Key Contact - Specialty:
Mr. Paul M. Rumson, Co-Manager - *BSME, Consumer, Engineering, HVAC, Manufacturing*
Ms. Barbara A. Rumson, Co-Manager - *Design, Engineering, HVAC, Manufacturing, Medical*

Salary Minimum: $50,000

Functions: Generalist (All), Management, Product Dev., Automation, Plant Mgmt., Quality, Purchasing, Engineering, Int'l.

Industries: Generalist (All), Manufacturing, Drugs Mfg., Medical Devices, Plastics, Rubber, Metal Products, Machine, Appliance, Motor Vehicles, Computer Equip., Consumer Elect., Electronic, Elec. Components, Robotics, Consumer Goods

Asheville Search & Consulting

PO Box 549
Arden, NC 28704-0549
(828) 884-3311
Fax: (208) 693-0155
Email: vspinc@citcom.net

Summary: We offer client companies a partnered relationship and the expertise of its principal, who has management experience in both entrepreneurial and established business environments.

Key Contact - Specialty:
Mr. Vincent Putiri, President - *Design, Manufacturing*

Salary Minimum: $25,000

Functions: Middle Mgmt., Product Dev., Production, Automation, Plant Mgmt., Quality, Materials, HR Mgmt., Finance, Engineering

Industries: Metal Products, Machine, Appliance, Motor Vehicles, Test, Measure Equip., Misc. Mfg., Mgmt. Consulting

E.J. Ashton & Associates Ltd

PO Box 1048
Lake Zurich, IL 60047-1048
(847) 842-9727
Fax: (847) 842-9728
Email: ejaltd@aol.com
Web: www.insurancerecruiters.com

Summary: We are executive recruiters exclusively for the insurance industry nationwide. Specialize in accounting, financial, tax, audit, and treasury positions.

Key Contact - Specialty:
Mr. Edmund C. Lipinski, President - *Financial*

Salary Minimum: $40,000

Functions: Finance

Industries: Insurance

Ashworth Group Inc

3066 Landmark Blvd Apt 1305
Palm Harbor, FL 34684-5035
(727) 781-3656
Fax: (727) 771-6361
Email: bill@erpjobcenter.net
Web: www.erpjobcenter.com

Summary: We are an executive recruiting firm working with major and second tier Fortune companies to provide top level IT professionals with career opportunities on a permanent basis. We work with the professionals to find the right career opportunity on a proactive basis rather than fit them into a specific slot.

Key Contact - Specialty:
Mr. William S. Lee, Senior Vice President
Mrs. Emily J. Lee, President

Salary Minimum: $100,000

Functions: Management, IT

Industries: Generalist (All), Services

Asian Diversity Inc

1270 Broadway Rm 703
New York, NY 10001-3211
(212) 465-8777
Fax: (212) 465-8396
Email: jino.ahn@adiversity.com
Web: www.adiversity.com

Summary: We are a diversity, recruiting firm with special emphasis on searching Americans with Asian background in various industries such as computers, investment, banking, sales and apparel.

Key Contact - Specialty:
Mr. Jino Ahn, Executive Director

Salary Minimum: $40,000

Functions: Generalist (All)

Industries: HR Services

Ask Guy Tucker Inc

4990 High Point Rd NE
Atlanta, GA 30342-2311
(404) 303-7177
Fax: (404) 303-0136
Email: resume@askguy.com
Web: www.askguy.com

Summary: We are a recruiting and headhunting firm for advertisers.

Key Contact - Specialty:
Mr. Guy Tucker, President - *Advertising*

Salary Minimum: $35,000

Functions: Senior Mgmt., Middle Mgmt., Advertising

Industries: Advertising

The Asquith Group

PO Box 862
Brunswick, ME 04011-0862
(207) 725-0900
Fax: (270) 569-0427
Email: info@asquithgroup.net
Web: www.asquithgroup.net

Summary: Services offered in retained and contingency search with a focus on engineering, manufacturing and sales. Certified personnel consultant.

Key Contact - Specialty:
Mr. Peter Asquith, CPC, Owner

Functions: Generalist (All), Mfg., Product Dev., Production, Sales & Mktg., Sales Mgmt., Engineering, Structural, Health & Safety

Industries: Generalist (All), Energy, Utilities, Manufacturing, Textiles, Apparel, Paper, Printing, Chemicals, Machine, Appliance, Misc. Mfg., Transportation, Architectural Svcs., Mgmt. Consulting, Engineering Svcs., Compliance, Environmental Svcs., Packaging

Asset Resource Group

50 California St Ste 1500
San Francisco, CA 94111-4612
(415) 434-8800
Fax: (415) 434-8833
Email: arg@assetresource.net
Web: www.assetresource.net

Summary: We are a professional recruiting and consulting practice catering to the executive

staffing needs of the real estate and financial services industries.

Key Contact - Specialty:
Ms. Elizabeth Creger, Principal - *Real estate*

Salary Minimum: $75,000

Functions: Generalist (All), Finance

Industries: Finance, Real Estate, Property/Facility Mgmt.

Asset Resource Inc

15 Alicante Aisle
Irvine, CA 92614-5926
(949) 756-1600
Fax: (949) 756-1661
Email: fbailin@assetresourceinc.com

Summary: We have specializations in data communications, computer networking industries, disciplines in software and hardware development engineering. Clients include start-up, emerging growth and mature companies in Silicon Valley, California. History of repeat business based on referrals and ability to fill requirements.

Key Contact - Specialty:
Mr. Fred Bailin, Senior Consultant - *Communications, Engineering*
Ms. Fran Shulman, Consultant - *Communications, Engineering*

Salary Minimum: $90,000

Functions: IT, Systems Dev., Systems Implem., Engineering, Hardware, Systems

Industries: Network Infrastructure, Software, Development SW, Networking, Comm. SW, Security SW, System SW

ASSIST - Consulting and Business Management Solutions Inc

PO Box 421423
Indianapolis, IN 46242-1423
(317) 821-8750
Fax: (317) 856-5942
Email: kmongonia@assistmanagement.com
Web: www.assistmanagement.com

Summary: Through our work as a leading consulting firm in the healthcare industry, a need was identified to support our clients in the recruitment of individuals to meet their organizations expectations. From experience levels to personality traits, we have developed a proficiency in creating a match to assist our clients in their pursuit of excellence.

Key Contact - Specialty:
Mr. Kevin Mongonia, President

Salary Minimum: $50,000

Functions: Generalist (All)

Industries: Generalist (All), Healthcare, Hospitals, Long-term/Home Care, Physical Therapy, Occupational Therapy

Associated Recruiters LLC

PO Box 4760
Emerald Isle, NC 28594-4760
(252) 670-5537
Fax: (910) 401-1733
Email: diane@nc-itrecruit.com
Web: www.nc-itrecruit.com

Summary: Placement agency for physicians, CRNA, allied health and technology individuals.

Key Contact - Specialty:
Ms. Diane Wallace, President & Senior Consultant

Functions: Generalist (All), Healthcare, Physicians, Nurses, Allied Health, IT, Systems Analysis, Systems Dev., Systems Implem., DB Admin.

Industries: Generalist (All), IT Implementation, Aerospace, Software, Accounting SW, Database SW, Development SW, Doc. Mgmt., Production SW, ERP SW, Industry Specific SW, Healthcare

Associated Recruiters

7144 N Park Manor Dr
Milwaukee, WI 53224-4642
(414) 353-1933
Fax: (414) 353-9418
Email: maury@associatedrecruiters.com
Web: www.associatedrecruiters.com

Summary: We serve the Corrugated Packaging and Folding Carton Industries. All salaried positions from the Executive Suite to the Shop Floor.

Key Contact - Specialty:
Mr. Maurice A. Pettengill, CPC, President

Salary Minimum: $45,000

Functions: Generalist (All), Management, Mfg., Packaging, Sales Mgmt., Sales Reps.

Industries: Manufacturing, Packaging

Associated Staffing Services

(formerly known as Flowers & Associates)
2100 W Alexis Rd
Toledo, OH 43613-5445
(419) 472-6900
Fax: (419) 472-6902
Email: hdhunter@aol.com

Summary: Experience in assisting companies in their hard-to-fill positions. We are experienced in working with all levels of management with enthusiasm.

Key Contact - Specialty:
Mr. William J. Ross, President - *Engineering, Manufacturing*
Mr. Eric W. Ross, Recruiter

Salary Minimum: $55,000

Functions: Generalist (All), Management

Industries: Manufacturing, Medical Devices, Plastics, Rubber, Metal Products, Machine, Appliance, Motor Vehicles, Computer Equip., Consumer Elect., Test, Measure Equip., Electronic, Elec. Components

Associates

222 Franklin Ave
Grand Haven, MI 49417-1336
(616) 842-8596
Fax: (616) 842-6647
Email: associates@talkamerica.net

Summary: We specialize in the automotive supply industry primarily at the management and engineering levels in product development and manufacturing.

Key Contact - Specialty:
Mr. Robert Clark, Owner

Functions: Generalist (All), Senior Mgmt., Quality, Materials Plng., Sales Mgmt., Systems Dev., R&D, Engineering

Industries: Generalist (All), Plastics, Rubber, Paints, Petro. Products, Metal Products, Machine, Appliance, Motor Vehicles, Test, Measure Equip.

ATA Healthcare Recruiters

707 S Kenmore St
Anaheim, CA 92804-3210
(800) 606-5627
(714) 827-2282
Fax: (714) 828-8963
Email: info@atarecruiters.com
Web: www.atarecruiters.com

Summary: We offer a total approach to healthcare recruitment. Our firm is a full service, national e-service recruitment organization. Our recruiters are all medical professionals with rich experience in healthcare. Our firm was created to focus on alleviating staffing problems for the organizations. We partner with some of the nations best employers to provide experienced healthcare professional for key positions within their organizations.

Key Contact - Specialty:
Ms. Donna Arbogast, Principal
Ms. Debra Carey, Professional Healthcare Recruiter

Salary Minimum: $50,000

Functions: Board Members, Senior Mgmt., Middle Mgmt., Quality, Healthcare, Physicians, Nurses, Allied Health, HR Mgmt.

Industries: Pharm Svcs., Accounting, Mgmt. Consulting, HR Services, Logistics Svcs., Call Centers, Insurance, Claims, System SW, Biotech/Life Sciences, Healthcare, Hospitals, Long-term/Home Care, Dental, Physical Therapy, Occupational Therapy, Women's

W R Atchison & Associates Inc

PO Box 10498
Greensboro, NC 27404-0498
(336) 855-5943
Email: recruiter-1@triad.rr.com
Web: www.watchison.com

Summary: We are a specialized and creative service for many years in recruiting pharmaceutical manufacturing, quality assurance, engineering professionals and managerial personnel for growth and major firms.

Key Contact - Specialty:
Mr. W.R. Atchison, President & Treasurer - *Engineering, Financial, Human resources, Operations*
Ms. Ann G. Atchison, Vice President & Secretary

Salary Minimum: $50,000

Functions: Generalist (All), Automation, Plant Mgmt., Quality, Materials, HR Mgmt., Finance, R&D, Engineering

Industries: Generalist (All), Manufacturing, Food, Bev., Tobacco, Pharm Svcs.

Atlantic Management Resources Inc

5 Mountain Blvd Ste 9
Warren, NJ 07059-2625
(908) 791-9000
Fax: (908) 791-9001
Email: support@amrjobs.com
Web: www.amrjobs.com

Summary: We are an executive search firm specializing the recruitment of pharmaceutical and medical sales professionals. We cover the entire sales vertical from entry-level positions to VPs of sales & marketing.

Key Contact - Specialty:
Mr. Lloyd Mandel, President
Mr. Owen Nochimson, Recruiter - *Sales*
Ms. Barbara O'Rourke, Researcher
Mr. David Moore, Recruiter - *Sales*
Ms. Isabel Torres, Office Manager

Mr. Juan Mayor, Senior Consultant
Mr. Clinton Smith, Operations Manager

Salary Minimum: $45,000

Functions: Management, Middle Mgmt., Sales & Mktg., Sales Mgmt.

Industries: Pharm Svcs., Biotech/Life Sciences, Healthcare

Atlantic Search Group Inc

88 Broad St
Boston, MA 02110-3407
(617) 426-9700
Fax: (617) 426-9013
Email: jobs@atlanticsearch.com
Web: www.atlanticsearch.com

Summary: Specializing in accounting, finance, tax and auditing in all industries. All principals are experienced professional accountants and experienced in the personnel/recruiting business. Committed to arranging only quality interviews.

Key Contact - Specialty:
Mr. Daniel F. Jones, Principal
Ms. Gayla K. Hensley, Principal

Functions: Generalist (All), CFOs, Budgeting, Cash Mgmt., Credit, Taxes

Industries: Generalist (All)

Atlantic Systems Group

PO Box 235
Conshohocken, PA 19428-0235
(856) 232-8675
Fax: (856) 232-8624
Email: careers@asgjobs.com
Web: www.asgjobs.com

Summary: Our firm specializes in IT, pharmaceutical, medical device and financial recruiting.

Key Contact - Specialty:
Mr. Jim Smiarowski, Owner
Ms. Jeri Kappler, Executive Recruiter

Salary Minimum: $70,000

Functions: Generalist (All), Senior Mgmt., IT, MIS Mgmt., Systems Dev., Network Admin., DB Admin.

Industries: Generalist (All), Manufacturing, Drugs Mfg., Medical Devices, Transportation, Wholesale, Retail, Finance, Services, Pharm Svcs., Accounting, E-commerce, IT Implementation, Logistics Svcs., Communications, Insurance, Software, Biotech/Life Sciences, Healthcare

Atomic Personnel Inc

PO Box 11244
Elkins Park, PA 19027-0244
(215) 885-4223
Email: atomic@dca.net

Summary: We are a professional recruitment for all engineering, technical and scientific fields and industries. Staffed by experienced graduate technical professionals.

Key Contact - Specialty:
Mr. Arthur L. Krasnow, President - *Manufacturing, Research & development, Science, Technical, Technical (Management)*

Salary Minimum: $40,000

Functions: Mfg., Packaging, R&D, Engineering

Industries: Generalist (All), Energy, Utilities, Construction, Manufacturing, Chemicals, Medical Devices, Leather, Stone, Glass, Metal Products, Test, Measure Equip., Misc. Mfg., Transportation, Equip Svcs., Fiber Optic,

Defense, Haz. Waste, Aerospace, Packaging, Industry Specific SW, Biotech/Life Sciences

ATS Applied Technology Solutions Inc

(a division of Sigma Group of Companies)
1100-55 York St
Prudential House
Toronto, ON M5J 1R7
Canada
(416) 369-0008
Fax: (416) 369-0199
Email: info@atsglobal.com
Web: www.atsglobal.com

Summary: We are an IT solutions and staffing firm dedicated to providing cost effective, professional services and resources. Our ISO 9001:2000 certification is testimony to the high quality standards we adhere to and we have an unyielding commitment to provide service excellence to every customer, on every project, every time.

Key Contact - Specialty:
Mr. Dave Chanchlani, President
Mr. Felix Bedard, Executive Vice President

Salary Minimum: $40,000

Functions: IT

Industries: Generalist (All)

ATS Executive Search

9700 Philips Hwy Ste 108
Jacksonville, FL 32256-1362
(904) 224-1375
Email: misrael@ats-executivesearch.com
Web: www.ats-executivesearch.com

Summary: Our firm partners with top global organizations to deliver the human capital they need to remain leaders. We accomplish this by, first, understanding its client's culture and secondly, by implementing its proprietary benchmark methodology and thirdly, by achieving productive and value-added partnerships that prove its performance standards are the industry's highest.

Key Contact - Specialty:
Mr. Michael Israel, President - *Executives*

Functions: Generalist (All), Management, Senior Mgmt., Sales & Mktg., IT, Legal

Industries: Generalist (All), Finance, Banking, Invest. Banking, Brokers, Misc. Financial, Accounting, E-commerce, IT Implementation, Software, ERP SW, HR SW, Mfg. SW, Marketing SW

Branches:
1000 Holcomb Woods Pkwy Ste 280
Bldg 200
Roswell, GA 30076-2587
(800) 572-2596
Email: ataylor@ats-executivesearch.com
Key Contact - Specialty:
Ms. Adrian Powell-Taylor, Operations Manager

ATS Reliance Technical Group

600-200 Yorkland Blvd
North York, ON M2J 5C1
Canada
(416) 482-8002
(585) 325-1399
Fax: (416) 482-1210
Email: ats@atsrecruitment.com
Web: www.atsrecruitment.com

Summary: Expert executive recruitment in aerospace, manufacturing, railcar, locomotive, automotive, petrochemical, oil & gas, mining, consulting engineering, drafting, architecture,

materials management, skilled trades and industrial labor.

Key Contact - Specialty:
Mr. Philip McDougall, Sales Consultant, Toronto
- *Engineering, Manufacturing*
Mr. Dave Maynard, Sales Consultant, Toronto -
Consulting, Manufacturing
Mr. Jeremy Goldberg, Consultant, Recruitment,
Toronto - *Electrical, Pharmaceutical*
Mr. David Graham, Branch Manager, Toronto &
Industrial - *Skilled trades*
Mr. Joe Bonellos, Sales Representative,
Brampton - *Skilled trades*
Mr. Michael Grew, Consultant, Recruitment,
Toronto & Ind - *Industrial, Skilled trades*

Functions: Generalist (All), Mfg., Product Dev., Automation, Materials, HR Mgmt., IT, Engineering, Architects, Technicians

Industries: Generalist (All), Agri., Forestry, Mining, Energy, Utilities, Oil & Gas, Construction, Manufacturing, Food, Bev., Tobacco, Chemicals, Medical Devices, Plastics, Rubber, Paints, Petro. Products, Metal Products, Machine, Appliance, Motor Vehicles, Test, Measure Equip., Misc. Mfg., Electronic, Elec. Components, Architectural Svcs., Pharm Svcs., Equip Svcs., Software

Branches:
400 Andrews St Ste 405
Rochester, NY 14604-1412
(585) 325-1170
Fax: (585) 325-1375
Email: rochester.office@atsreliance.com
Key Contact - Specialty:
Ms. Connie Tramonto, Recruitment Coordinator -
Engineering, Manufacturing
Ms. Carrie Casale, Recruitment Coordinator -
Aerospace, Information Technology
Mr. Tim Kolb, Branch Manager - *Engineering,
Manufacturing*

730-10655 Southport Rd SW
Calgary, AB T2W 4Y1
Canada
(403) 261-4600
(888) 818-4600
Fax: (403) 265-2909
Email: calgary@atsrecruitment.com
Key Contact - Specialty:
Mr. Stephen McCrum, Recruitment Manager -
Engineering, Information Technology

607-10117 Jasper Ave NW
Royal Bank Building
Edmonton, AB T5J 1W8
Canada
(780) 462-1815
Fax: (780) 461-9968
Email: edmonton@atsrecruitment.com
Key Contact - Specialty:
Mr. Jason Wahl, Branch Manager - *Engineering*

300-1501 Broadway W
Granville Clocktower Centre
Vancouver, BC V6J 4Z6
Canada
(604) 915-9333
Fax: (604) 915-9339
Email: van.bc@atsrecruitment.com
Key Contact - Specialty:
Mr. Paul Dusome, Consultant, Recruitment -
Engineering
Mr. Ian McDougall, Branch Manager -
Engineering

307-3310 South Service Rd
Burlington, ON L7N 3M6
Canada
(905) 333-9632
Fax: (905) 333-9326
Email: burlington@atsrecruitment.com

Key Contact - Specialty:
Ms. Darlene Vitorino, Recruitment Coordinator -
Engineering
Mr. Martin Belanger, Branch Manager -
Engineering

27-260 Holiday Inn Dr
Cambridge, ON N3C 4E8
Canada
(519) 658-5535
Email: cambridge@atsrecruitment.com
Key Contact - Specialty:
Mr. John Rose, Branch Manager -
Manufacturing, Skilled trades

601-171 Queens Ave
171 Queens Ave
London, ON N6A 5J7
Canada
(519) 679-2886
Fax: (519) 679-1483
Email: london@atsrecruitment.com
Key Contact - Specialty:
Mr. Mike Abbott, Branch Manager
Mr. Brad Austin, Sales Representative -
Engineering, Manufacturing

The Atticus Graham Group

3529 Craftsbury Dr
Highlands Ranch, CO 80126-7534
(303) 471-4780
(303) 471-4782
Email: janet@atticusgraham.com

Summary: Partnered with numerous recruitment firms allows us full access to a broad array of opportunities and candidates within advertising, public relations, sales promotion and direct marketing.

Key Contact - Specialty:
Ms. Janet M. Harberth, Senior Parnter -
Advertising
Mr. Peter W. Gagliardi, Senior Parnter -
Advertising

Salary Minimum: $45,000

Functions: Advertising

Industries: Generalist (All), Advertising

Atwater Consulting Inc

5179 Browning Way SW
Lilburn, GA 30047-7042
(770) 806-0864
Email: contact@atwaterconsulting.com
Web: www.atwaterconsulting.com

Summary: Recruiting personnel who speak English, German, Spanish, Italian, Japanese and/or other languages is common. Niche areas include accounting, sales, engineering, management consulting, administrative, management, industrial and manufacturing, healthcare, skilled labor, information technology, etc. We also recruit military officers upon honorable discharge or later. Our staff speaks multiple languages.

Key Contact - Specialty:
Mr. Bob Atwater, CPC, CMSR, President &
Chief Executive Officer

Functions: Generalist (All)

Industries: Generalist (All), Construction, Manufacturing, Wholesale, Services, Hospitality, Real Estate

Audit Recruiters

(formerly known as Stone Enterprises Ltd)
645 N Michigan Ave Ste 800
Chicago, IL 60611-2890
(773) 404-9300
Email: mail@auditrecruiters.com

Summary: We are a successful boutique recruitment firm catering to Fortune 2000, accounting, hardware, software, distribution, healthcare, manufacturing firms and not-for-profit. We specialize in the placement of audit, accounting and tax professionals throughout the U.S. Rely on us and our nationwide network of recruiters.

Key Contact - Specialty:
Ms. Chloe Kidman, Firm Administrator - *Accounting (General), Audits, Finance, Risk management, Tax*

Salary Minimum: $45,000

Functions: Generalist (All)

Industries: Generalist (All), Manufacturing, Transportation, Finance, Services, Accounting, Mgmt. Consulting, Software, Networking, Comm. SW, Healthcare

JG Auerbach & Associates
77 Graeagle
Oakland, CA 94605-4201
(510) 562-9907
Email: joanne@jgauerbach.com
Web: www.jgauerbach.com

Summary: Recruit executive and management corporate and product marketing, sales, business development & professional services for software, Internet and communications companies. Provide consulting services on strategy, organization and people issues relating to company growth.

Key Contact - Specialty:
Ms. JoAnne G. Auerbach, Founder - *E-business, Executives, Marketing, Sales, Start-up companies*

Salary Minimum: $125,000

Functions: Management, Senior Mgmt., Sales & Mktg., Mktg. Mgmt., Sales Mgmt., Mgmt. Consultants, Attorneys

Industries: Venture Cap., Legal, E-commerce, Communications, Telephony, Wireless, Software, Industry Specific SW, Networking, Comm. SW, Security SW

August Associates
24 Torrey Rd
East Sandwich, MA 02537-1130
(508) 833-9622
Email: karenm@augustassociates.net
Web: www.augustassociates.net

Summary: We provide a full range of inside and outside sales recruiting services. Our clients include emerging companies to the Fortune 500.

Key Contact - Specialty:
Ms. Karen Murphy, Managing Director - *Business development, Consumer (Packaged Goods,Products), Sales, Supply Chain*

Salary Minimum: $60,000

Functions: Packaging, Direct Mktg., Sales Reps.

Industries: Generalist (All), Printing, Medical Devices, Banking, Media, Publishing, Software

Auraya Consulting LLC
2620 Regatta Dr Ste 102
Las Vegas, NV 89128-6892
(702) 365-5627
Fax: (775) 703-1368
Email: info@auraya.com
Web: www.auraya.com

Summary: Premier executive search firm specializing in full-time placement and staff augmentation of IT, finance and management professionals.

Key Contact - Specialty:
Mr. Santi Suthisak, Managing Director - *Technology*

Salary Minimum: $35,000

Functions: Generalist (All)

Industries: Manufacturing, Services, Communications, Government, Aerospace, Software, Healthcare

Aureus Executive
(a division of Aureus Group)
11825 Q St
Omaha, NE 68137-3503
(800) 273-6679
(402) 891-6940
Fax: (402) 891-1290
Email: exec@aureusgroup.com
Web: www.aureusexec.com

Summary: We are a generalist firm that recruits mid-to senior-level executives for all industries. By function, we place executives in accounting/finance, operations, marketing, technology, engineering, construction and other related areas.

Key Contact - Specialty:
Ms. Chris Carlson, CPC, Regional Manager
Mr. Bob Giddings, Executive Recruiter

Salary Minimum: $75,000

Functions: Management, Middle Mgmt., Finance, CFOs, Budgeting, MIS Mgmt.

Industries: Generalist (All), Manufacturing, Finance, Banking, Defense, Aerospace, Insurance, Accounting SW, Hospitals

The Aurora Group
8 Sasqua Trl
Weston, CT 06883-1025
(203) 544-8601
Email: info@docjobsearch.com
Web: www.docjobsearch.com

Summary: Our firm deals with all specialties. Our clients and candidates are coast to coast and we pay close attention to the needs of each.

Key Contact - Specialty:
Mr. David Lonis, Chief Executive Officer
Mr. Jim Hemmingway, Executive Vice President
Mr. Samuel Geragi, President
Ms. Katie Whittaker, Senior Recruiter

Functions: Physicians

Industries: Hospitals, Women's

Austin Allen
8127 Walnut Grove Rd
Cordova, TN 38018-7270
(901) 756-0900
Email: jobs@austinallen.com
Web: www.austinallen.com

Summary: We specialize in engineering, manufacturing and human recource positions for manufacturing firms.

Key Contact - Specialty:
Mr. C.A. Cupp, President

Salary Minimum: $45,000

Functions: Engineering

Industries: Manufacturing

Austin, Hill & Associates
1816 Robert Ln
Naperville, IL 60564-4129
(630) 922-6740
Fax: (630) 922-6739

Email: austinhillassoc@aol.com
Web: www.austinhillassociates.com

Summary: Search firm principal has extensive personal experience in sales, marketing, HR and finance. We deliver superior results for our clients.

Key Contact - Specialty:
Mr. Michael Hill, President

Salary Minimum: $50,000

Functions: Management, Senior Mgmt., Mfg., Plant Mgmt., Sales & Mktg., HR Mgmt., Finance, IT, Legal, Attorneys

Industries: Generalist (All), Energy, Utilities, Construction, Manufacturing, Food, Bev., Tobacco, Soap, Perf., Cosmtcs., Drugs Mfg., Consumer Goods, Transportation, Retail, Finance, Misc. Financial, Services, Legal, Communications, Packaging, Software

Austin Park Management Group Inc
103-164 Eglinton Ave E
Glencoe Building
Toronto, ON M4P 1G4
Canada
(416) 488-9565
Fax: (416) 488-9601
Email: austin@austinpark.com
Web: www.austinpark.com

Summary: We are a leader in placing permanent and contract technical professionals. We specialize in Business Intelligence, CRM, ERP and Internet technologies.

Key Contact - Specialty:
Mr. Earl Gardiner, President - *Professional services*

Salary Minimum: $50,000

Functions: Sales & Mktg., IT

Industries: Generalist (All), Finance, Services, Mgmt. Consulting, E-commerce, IT Implementation, Supply Chain Mgmt, Media, Communications, Software

Automation Technology Search
7309 Del Cielo Way
Modesto, CA 95356-9629
(209) 545-4500
Email: atsearch@pc-intouch.com

Summary: We are Recruiters of managers and engineers in design and development involving s/w, firmware in the food, metals, plastics, medical, packaging, and construction industries. Specialties are mechanical, electronic, chemical and computer science engineers.

Key Contact - Specialty:
Mr. Ralph L. Becker, President - *Construction, Engineering, Manufacturing*

Salary Minimum: $30,000

Functions: Middle Mgmt., Mfg., Materials, HR Mgmt., Systems Implem., R&D, Engineering, Technicians

Industries: Agri., Forestry, Mining, Manufacturing, Food, Bev., Tobacco, Plastics, Rubber, Metal Products, Machine, Appliance

Automotive Management Search Inc
2145 Resort Dr Ste 225
Steamboat Springs, CO 80487-8839
(970) 879-4743
Fax: (970) 879-3710
Email: info@autorecruiters.com
Web: www.autorecruiters.com

Summary: Automotive Management Search, Inc. is a executive search firm specializing in the automotive industry. Our focus is in the retail entity.

Key Contact - Specialty:
Mr. David Miller, President - *Automotive*

Salary Minimum: $40,000

Functions: Generalist (All), Management

Industries: Transportation

Automotive Personnel LLC

(also known as SearchPro1)
14701 Detroit Ave Ste 430
Cleveland, OH 44107-4109
(216) 226-7958
Fax: (216) 226-7987
Email: don@searchpro1.com

Summary: Specialize in recruiting personnel for automotive manufacturers and automotive financial corporations, banks and automotive lending areas for finance companies.

Key Contact - Specialty:
Mr. Donald Jasensky, President - *Automotive, Financial*

Salary Minimum: $50,000

Functions: Generalist (All), Management

Industries: Motor Vehicles, Transportation, Wholesale, Retail, Finance, Banking, Misc. Financial, Call Centers

AutoPeople

23 North St
Brattleboro, VT 05301-3496
(802) 257-5678
(972) 788-1988
Fax: (802) 257-2769
Email: ericb@autopeople.com
Web: www.autopeople.com

Summary: Founded by a former automobile dealer, our only specialty is providing management to automobile dealerships.

Key Contact - Specialty:
Mr. Eric L. Blaushild, President

Functions: Generalist (All), Senior Mgmt.

Industries: Motor Vehicles, Retail

Branches:
13355 Noel Rd Ste 500
Dallas, TX 75240-6836
(972) 788-1988
Email: ericb@autopeople.com
Key Contact - Specialty:
Ms. Elisabeth Brown, Vice President, Research

Autorecruit Inc

2-390 Steelcase Rd E
Markham, ON L3R 1G2
Canada
(905) 946-0777
Fax: (416) 946-1340
Email: info@blconsultants.com
Web: www.blconsultants.com/aboutauto.htm

Summary: We are a recruitment firm specializing in the automotive industry. We are all RPR certified recruiters with automotive experience.

Key Contact - Specialty:
Mr. Farid Ahmad

Functions: Management, Mfg., Sales & Mktg., Customer Svc., Int'l.

Industries: Motor Vehicles

availABILITY Personnel Consultants

169 S River Rd Unit 12
Bedford, NH 03110-6972
(603) 669-4440
Email: resumes@availability.org
Web: www.availability.org

Summary: Contingency search specialists in all aspects of professional staffing for manufacturing and service industries from 5MM to Fortune 500 firms and their divisions.

Key Contact - Specialty:
Mr. Walter D. Kilian, CPC, President

Salary Minimum: $40,000

Functions: Generalist (All)

Industries: Manufacturing, Accounting

Avalon Search Group Inc

PO Box 3234
Newberg, OR 97132-5234
(503) 538-7976
Email: tammi@avalonsearchgroup.com
Web: www.avalonsearchgroup.com

Summary: Executive recruiter for the construction, design, architecture, engineering, and real estate industry. Intermediate level to president/CEO positions. Offering experience working with general contractors, heavy highway contractors, construction management firms, consulting firms, developers and owners. Honest and professional search firm that puts your needs first.

Key Contact - Specialty:
Mrs. Tammi McClain-Young, Manager - *Agriculture, Business development, Design, Engineering, Sales*

Salary Minimum: $45,000

Functions: Board Members, Senior Mgmt., Middle Mgmt., Production, Sales Mgmt., Eng. Design, Architects, Bldg. Contractors, Design

Industries: Generalist (All), Construction, Transportation, Architectural Svcs., Equip Svcs., Engineering Svcs., Real Estate

Avant Solutions Inc

58 Maryland Dr
Decatur, AL 35603-5366
(248) 652-1240
(256) 612-0050
Fax: (248) 498-6370
Email: avant@charter.net

Summary: We serve a wide range of clients at the national level, placing some of the nation's top candidates in the following positions: sales and marketing, management, operations, finance, and logistics. We are distinguished by our professional judgment, commitment to quality, consistency, and excellent client relations.

Key Contact - Specialty:
Mr. Daniel Cowan, President - *Computers (Software), Legal, Management, Presidents, Sales*
Ms. Kandy Lee, Vice President - *Executives, Financial services, General management, Legal, Sales*
Mrs. Sandy L. Austin, Database Administrator - *Administration, Business development, Competitive intelligence, Database (Administration)*
Mrs. Irene Daniels, Website Admin. & Research Consultant - *Client/server, Information Systems, Technical (Management)*

Salary Minimum: $60,000

Functions: Senior Mgmt., Sales & Mktg., Sales Mgmt.

Industries: Misc. Financial, Legal, Mgmt. Consulting, HR Services, Supply Chain Mgmt, Software, Accounting SW, Database SW, Doc. Mgmt., Production SW, ERP SW, HR SW

The Avery Group Inc

5130 Central Sarasota Pkwy Apt 208
Sarasota, FL 34238-7620
(941) 921-4578
(800) 838-5494
Fax: (941) 921-1563
Email: sjacobs@theaverygroupinc.com
Web: www.theaverygroupinc.com

Summary: We are located in sunny Sarasota, Florida and provide professional recruiting services nation wide. We specialize in the following areas: Engineering, Construction, Surveyors, Architects, Sales/Marketing.

Key Contact - Specialty:
Mr. Stephen Jacobs, President

Functions: Engineering, Geotechnical, Design

Industries: Generalist (All), Food, Bev., Tobacco, Chemicals, Transportation, Architectural Svcs., Engineering Svcs., Communications, Environmental Svcs., Haz. Waste, Software

Avestruz & Associates Inc

23 Japonica
Irvine, CA 92618-3986
(949) 651-8721
(719) 481-6603
Email: avestruzassoc@cox.net
Web: www.avestruzinc.com

Summary: Specializing in the placement of personnel in marketing, sales, administration and biomedical engineering in the radiology, cardiology, IT and surgery industries.

Key Contact - Specialty:
Mr. Alner Avestruz, President

Salary Minimum: $80,000

Functions: Generalist (All), Healthcare, Sales & Mktg.

Industries: Medical Devices, Biotech/Life Sciences, Healthcare

Branches:
18125 Flowered Meadow Ln
Monument, CO 80132-8715
(719) 481-6603
Email: mike@avestruz.org
Key Contact - Specialty:
Mr. Michael Ochsner, General Manager

The B & B Group Inc

65 Sunset Hills Dr
Edwardsville, IL 62025-3633
(618) 288-1372
Fax: (618) 659-0302
Email: ron@bnbgrp.com
Web: www.bnbgrp.com

Summary: We are financial industry specialists. We provide superior candidates in a time effective manner utilizing networking, referrals, a database of over 20,000 financial professionals and plain old-fashioned hard work.

Key Contact - Specialty:
Mr. Daniel J. Baccarini, President
Mr. Glenn J. Smith, Senior Vice President
Mr. Ron Smith, Vice President
Ms. Angie Grote, Recruiting Specialist - *Analysts*
Ms. Stacy Bowling, Recruiting Specialist - *Analysts*

Salary Minimum: $50,000

Functions: Generalist (All), Management, Sales & Mktg.

Industries: Finance, Banking, Invest. Banking, Brokers, Venture Cap., Mutual/Hedge Funds, Misc. Financial, Insurance

BA Search Group

3388 Ravinia Cir
Aurora, IL 60504-3142
(630) 710-0200
Web: www.basearchgroup.com

Summary: We specialize in finding the best skills set to fill a senior role in business can be a key determinant of organizational success. We place special emphasis on identifying executive talent that adds maximum value and provide a unique partnering experience to our clients.

Key Contact - Specialty:
Mr. Brian Anderson, President

Salary Minimum: $100,000

Functions: Senior Mgmt.

Industries: Retail, Telecoms

Babson Professional Search Inc

(formerly known as Dunhill Professional Search of Raleigh)
975 Walnut St Ste 260
Cary, NC 27511-4216
(919) 460-9988
(800) 783-9933
Fax: (919) 460-9931
Email: info@babsonsearch.com
Web: www.babsonsearch.com

Summary: We are committed to the highest ethical standards and work on a nationwide basis. Please visit our website for a complete description of our services.

Key Contact - Specialty:
Ms. Lelia Babson, Chief Executive Officer
Mr. Jay Babson, President
Ms. Rose Welch, Senior Consultant - *Healthcare*

Functions: Generalist (All), Senior Mgmt., Nurses, Allied Health, Finance, CFOs

Industries: Generalist (All), Healthcare, Hospitals

Bader Research Corp.

(also known as Bader Legal Search)
60 E 42nd St Rm 565
New York, NY 10165-0567
(212) 682-4750
(212) 317-7786
Fax: (212) 682-4758

Summary: We are specialists in the recruitment of highly qualified attorneys for the nation's leading law firms. We also effect mergers & acquisitions of law firms in major cities worldwide.

Key Contact - Specialty:
Mr. Sam Bader, President - *Legal*

Salary Minimum: $100,000

Functions: Attorneys

Industries: Legal

Badon's Employment Inc

5422 Galeria Dr
Baton Rouge, LA 70816-6007
(225) 295-1240
(800) 769-7708
Email: recruiting@badon.com
Web: www.badon.com

Summary: We are a recruiting firm with jobs for degreed engineers with experience in the chemical, petrochemical and refinery industries. We need chemical engineers, mechanical

engineers, electrical engineers among others with experience in: oil refining, chemicals, specialty chemicals, plastics, polymers, packaging, etc.

Key Contact - Specialty:
Ms. Barbara Badon, President - *Refining, Rubber, Six sigma, Technical, Textiles*
Ms. Cheri Badon
Ms. Lisa Arbour, Medical Recruiting Specialist - *Medical (Devices,Sales), Research & development, Respiratory therapy, Subacute healthcare*

Functions: Management, Mfg., Product Dev., Production, Plant Mgmt., Quality, Productivity, IT

Industries: Generalist (All), Energy, Utilities, Oil & Gas, Manufacturing, Paper, Chemicals, Soap, Perf., Cosmtcs., Drugs Mfg., Medical Devices, Plastics, Rubber, Paints, Petro. Products, Packaging, Healthcare, Hospitals, Long-term/Home Care

W G Baird & Associates

15044 Clementine Way
Haymarket, VA 20169-3318
(703) 754-2310
Email: wbaird@comcast.net

Summary: We are a company whose principals have spent many years in large and medium sized companies and who will devote the time it takes to help either clients or candidates to obtain the right fit.

Key Contact - Specialty:
Mr. William G. Baird, President - *Engineering, Human resources, Manufacturing, Technical*

Functions: Generalist (All), Senior Mgmt., Middle Mgmt., Plant Mgmt., Sales & Mktg., HR Mgmt., Engineering

Industries: Generalist (All), Metal Products, Machine, Appliance, Misc. Mfg.

The Baird Group

79 Winne Rd
Delmar, NY 12054-4012
(518) 475-9734
Email: davidbaird@verizon.net

Summary: Specializing in manufacturing for professional positions, finance, purchasing, supply chain, materials science, R&D, operations, management, engineering, health & safety and quality.

Key Contact - Specialty:
Mr. David Baird, President

Salary Minimum: $40,000

Functions: Management, Admin. Svcs., Mfg.

Industries: Generalist (All), Manufacturing, Food, Bev., Tobacco, Textiles, Apparel, Paper, Chemicals, Drugs Mfg., Plastics, Rubber, Metal Products, Consumer Elect., Misc. Mfg., Robotics, Finance, HR Services, Engineering Svcs., Healthcare

Baker, Ellerd & Associates Inc

16200 Ventura Blvd Ste 219
Encino, CA 91436-4917
(818) 995-4311
(800) 486-4311
Fax: (818) 783-9839
Email: bakerellerd@bakerellerd.com
Web: www.bakerellerd.com

Summary: We specialize in the placement of medical doctors, physician assistants and nurse practitioners. Full time, part time or locum tenens.

Key Contact - Specialty:
Mr. Ken Ellerd, President - *Physicians*
Ms. Rosemary Harper, Recruitment, Physician - *Physicians*

Functions: Physicians

Industries: Mgmt. Consulting, Healthcare

Baker Scott & Co

1259 US Highway 46
Parsippany, NJ 07054-4913
(973) 263-3355
Fax: (973) 263-9255
Email: exec.search@bakersscott.com
Web: www.bakerscott.com

Summary: We are a full-service executive search firm specializing in assignments in telecom, cable, broadcasting and emerging technologies across functional disciplines.

Key Contact - Specialty:
Ms. Judy Bouer, Principal
Mr. David Allen, Principal

Salary Minimum: $75,000

Functions: Generalist (All), Senior Mgmt., Middle Mgmt., Advertising, HR Mgmt., CFOs, MIS Mgmt., Int'l.

Industries: Generalist (All), Media, New Media, Broadcast, Film, Telecoms, Software

Baldwin Executive Search Ltd

1411 1 St SE
Calgary, AB T2G 2J3
Canada
(403) 228-1999
Fax: (403) 228-5533
Email: info@baldwinexecutive.ca
Web: www.baldwinexecutive.ca

Summary: We have had a reputation for quick, efficient service of a confidential nature. Niche markets include IT professionals, Administration, and other proven professionals.

Key Contact - Specialty:
Mr. Stephen Baldwin, President & Chief Executive Officer - *Engineering, Financial, Management*

Functions: Generalist (All), Management, Admin. Svcs., Sales Mgmt., Finance, MIS Mgmt., Systems Dev., Systems Implem., Engineering, Attorneys

Industries: Generalist (All), Energy, Utilities, Oil & Gas, Services, Non-profits, Accounting, HR Services, Communications, Telecoms, Call Centers, Software, Healthcare, Hospitals

Baldwin Gilman LLC

4760 Red Bank Rd Ste 216
Cincinnati, OH 45227-1549
(513) 272-2400
(800) 745-2373
Web: www.baldwingilman.com

Summary: Search generalists serving client companies in their search requirements ranging from executive management to key individual contributors. Services are tailored to clients' search or large-scale project needs.

Key Contact - Specialty:
Mr. W. Keith Baldwin, Founder - *Management, Technical*
Mr. Thomas Gilman, President - *Consulting*
Ms. Janice F. Seymour, Vice President - *Manufacturing, Sales*
Mr. William W. Schrepferman, Vice President - *Human resources, Management*
Ms. Nancy Foster, Associate - *Finance*
Mr. Thomas Pharr, Associate - *MIS*
Mr. Stephen Krentz, Associate - *MIS*

Ms. Kathy Phillips, Associate
Mr. Philip Morris, Associate
Ms. Marcianne Lauber, Associate - *Consulting*
Mr. Patrick Smith, Associate - *Consulting,
Information Systems, Information Technology*
Mr. Frank Ilcin, Associate
Ms. Julie George, Associate

Salary Minimum: $50,000

Functions: Management

Industries: Manufacturing, Finance, Services,
Media, Software, Healthcare

Baldwin Recruiting and Consulting

400 Putnam Pike Ste D # 223
Smithfield, RI 02917-2442
(401) 949-1093
(877) 787-8239
Fax: (401) 949-0577
Email: tjack@baldwinrecruiting.com
Web: www.baldwinrecruiting.com

Summary: Searches performed in the fields of
pharmaceutical, medical device, packaging,
consumer goods, transportation, distribution and
healthcare services & distribution.

Key Contact - Specialty:
Mr. Tom Jack, CPC, President

Salary Minimum: $25,000

Functions: Generalist (All)

Industries: Oil & Gas, Chemicals, Drugs Mfg.,
Medical Devices, Plastics, Rubber, Machine,
Appliance, Electronic, Elec. Components,
Consumer Goods, Aerospace, Packaging

The Bales Company

13400 Sutton Park Dr S Ste 1601
Jacksonville, FL 32224-0237
(904) 398-9080
Fax: (904) 398-8121
Email: info@balescompany.com
Web: www.balescompany.com

Summary: Our firm specializes in executive
search and sales recruiting for the medical and
pharmaceutical industry. Members of a network of
35 retained search firms.

Key Contact - Specialty:
Ms. Sally Bales, President - *International*

Salary Minimum: $70,000

Functions: Management, Board Members, Senior
Mgmt., Healthcare, Sales & Mktg., Mktg.
Mgmt., Sales Mgmt., CFOs, Int'l.

Industries: Drugs Mfg., Medical Devices, Venture
Cap., Telecoms, Biotech/Life Sciences,
Healthcare

BallResources

(also known as Power'N Motion)
PO Box 480391
Kansas City, MO 64148-0391
(816) 322-2727
Email: ron9@kc.rr.com

Summary: A no frills, get-the-job-done search
service for all industrial sales and sales
management areas. Specializing in power
transmission, motion control, factory automation
and all metalworking related industries.

Key Contact - Specialty:
Mr. Ronald D. Ball, Owner

Salary Minimum: $25,000

Functions: Generalist (All), Mktg. Mgmt., Sales
Mgmt.

Industries: Generalist (All), Manufacturing,
Plastics, Rubber, Metal Products, Machine,
Appliance, Computer Equip., Test, Measure
Equip., Electronic, Elec. Components, Robotics,
Semiconductors, Packaging

BancSearch Inc

PO Box 700516
Tulsa, OK 74170-0516
(918) 496-9477
Fax: (918) 494-2003
Email: recruiters@bancsearch.com
Web: www.bancsearch.com

Summary: We are a premier recruiting firm that
specializes in discovering and placing extremely
skilled candidates in the banking and financial
industries. We provide the management areas of
banking, trust/wealth management, commercial
banking, marketing and credit cards.

Key Contact - Specialty:
Ms. Maggie Cunningham, CPC, Managing
Director - *Asset management, Banking,
Investment management, Trust*
Mr. Don Cunningham, CPC, President - *Banking,
Credit cards, Financial services*

Salary Minimum: $75,000

Functions: Generalist (All)

Industries: Finance, Banking, Invest. Banking,
Brokers, Misc. Financial

The Bandish Group LLC

755 York Rd Ste 201
Warminster, PA 18974-2076
(215) 444-9002
(800) 881-9976
Email: jobs@bandishgroup.com
Web: www.bandishgroup.com

Summary: We are a pharmaceutical search firm
specializing in the recruitment of clinical research,
clinical and project management, clinical
development and operations, and medical affairs
professionals. We measure our record of success
against our personal standards, which are built
upon an approach hallmarked by professionalism
and integrity. Our search is your success.

Key Contact - Specialty:
Ms. Jackie Bandish, Founder - *Research &
development*
Ms. Sandy Spencer, Recruiter, Clinical &
Medical Affairs - *Clinical, Medical*
Ms. Janene Cleary, Recruitment Manager -
Clinical, Medical
Ms. Natasha Adomov, Staffing Specialist
Ms. Ellen Downey, Staffing Specialist

Salary Minimum: $95,000

Functions: R&D

Industries: Biotech/Life Sciences

The Bankers Register

1140 Avenue of the Americas
New York, NY 10036-5803
(212) 840-0800
Fax: (212) 840-7039
Email: bankers@tbrspg.com

Summary: Specialists in the recruitment and
placement of banking personnel: commercial,
corporate, international, thrift, and mortgage/real
estate.

Key Contact - Specialty:
Mr. Steven Moss, Associate Director

Functions: Generalist (All)

Industries: Banking

Bankers Search LLC

PO Box 854
Madison, CT 06443-0854
(203) 245-0694
Fax: (203) 245-9567
Email: tloughlin@bankerssearch.com
Web: www.bankerssearch.com

Summary: For many years we have been
providing superior executive recruiting services.
We cater to all disciplines of banking, focusing on
the placement of middle and senior management.

Key Contact - Specialty:
Mr. Timothy M. Loughlin, President

Salary Minimum: $90,000

Functions: Generalist (All)

Industries: Banking

BankResources

1 Pioneer Ct
Novato, CA 94945-2119
(415) 209-6160

Summary: We were founded exclusively to
provide financial institutions with highly qualified
executives, managers and professionals from all
banking disciplines to fill staffing requirements on
a permanent or project basis.

Key Contact - Specialty:
Mr. Patrick J. Duncan, Principal

Salary Minimum: $75,000

Functions: Generalist (All)

Industries: Banking

Banner Professional Staffing

125 S Wacker Dr Ste 1250A
Chicago, IL 60606-4402
(312) 580-2500
Fax: (312) 580-2515
Email: contactus@bannerpersonnel.com
Web: www.bannerpersonnel.com

Summary: Banner is a full service placement firm
specializing in Academic, Administrative,
Customer Service / Sales, Insurance, Legal and
Light Industrial staffing. We do it all - temporary,
temp-to-hire and direct hire.

Key Contact - Specialty:
Ms. Emel Singer, President & Chief Executive
Officer - *Administration, Insurance, Legal*

Functions: Generalist (All)

Industries: Generalist (All), Legal, Accounting,
HR Services, Higher Ed., Hospitality, Telecoms,
Call Centers, Insurance

Branches:
1580 S Milwaukee Ave Ste 103
Libertyville, Il 60048-3770
(847) 247-2200
Email: contactus@bannerpersonnel.com
Key Contact - Specialty:
Ms. Singer - *Administration, Insurance, Legal*

Barbachano International Inc (BIP)

2531 Windward Way
Chula Vista, CA 91914-4526
(619) 427-2310
Fax: (619) 427-2312
Email: barbachano@bipsearch.com
Web: www.bipsearch.com

Summary: We specialize in recruiting executive
and staff management for multi-nationals with the
need for diversity or bilingual professionals for
their operations. Our practice specialties are
manufacturing, high technology, logistics, retail,

energy and telecom. We have experience with Fortune 1000 companies and have helped over 60 corporations start-up. We also offer training, HR, productivity consulting and outplacement.

Key Contact - Specialty:
Mr. Fernando O. Barbachano, CPC, General Manager & Vice President - *Accounting, Finance, Management, Marketing, Sales*
Ms. Berenice Barbachano, CPC, President - *Management, Manufacturing, Operations*
Mr. Jorge Roldan, Search Director - *Logistics, Marketing, Materials, Purchasing, Sales*
Mr. Ricardo Lopez, Technical Search Manager - *Engineering, Information Technology, Management, Production, Quality*
Ms. Carmina Flores, Consultant - *Human resources, Management, Organizational development*
Francisco Glennie, Search Manager - *Executives, Human resources*
Mr. Israel Huerta, Database Administrator - *Information Systems, Information Technology*

Salary Minimum: $45,000

Functions: Management, Mfg., Plant Mgmt., Materials, Purchasing, Sales Mgmt., HR Mgmt., Finance, Engineering, Int'l.

Industries: Manufacturing, Medical Devices, Plastics, Rubber, Metal Products, Motor Vehicles, Consumer Elect.

Stanley Barber & Associates

181 Metro Dr Ste 290
San Jose, CA 95110-1344
(408) 501-2111
Fax: (408) 573-7479
Email: info@stanleybarber.com
Web: www.stanleybarber.com

Summary: Specializing in mid to senior level professionals and executives living in San Francisco Bay Area. Not industry specific.

Key Contact - Specialty:
Ms. Nancy Bergman, Vice President, Client Relations
Ms. Kathryn Hicks, Recruiter
Mr. Kevin Dincher, Recruiter
Mr. Al Chiara, Recruiter - *International, Marketing, Telecommunications*

Salary Minimum: $75,000

Functions: Generalist (All)

Industries: Generalist (All)

Barcus Associates

PO Box 1059
Van Alstyne, TX 75495-1059
(903) 482-1362
Email: moreinfo@barcusassociates.com
Web: www.barcusassociates.com

Summary: We focus primarily on revenue related roles in the high technology industry. Our clients typically address the Fortune 1000 or financial industry markets offering core products or services. We offer retained and contingency search at individual contributor through senior management levels, contracting, recruiting training and outplacement seminars.

Key Contact - Specialty:
Ms. Carolyn Barcus, President
Mr. Keith Laursen, Senior Vice President - *Management, Sales*
Mr. Jim Barcus, Vice President

Functions: Management, Sales & Mktg., Mktg. Mgmt., Sales Mgmt.

Industries: Generalist (All), Services, Mgmt. Consulting, Software

Barkbridge Staffing Group LLC

(formerly known as Barkbridge Staffing LLC)
PO Box 8651
Turnersville, NJ 08012-8651
(856) 401-9100
Fax: (856) 228-8585
Email: info@barkbridge.com
Web: www.barkbridge.com

Summary: Whether you are a Fortune 500 company or a startup firm - we can help you build your team. We specialize in the recruitment and placement of IT, finance, engineering, sales/marketing, retail and administrative professionals.

Key Contact - Specialty:
Mr. Joseph Chelston, Managing Recruiter

Functions: Generalist (All), Senior Mgmt., Finance, IT, MIS Mgmt., Systems Dev., Systems Support, Network Admin., DB Admin., Technicians

Industries: Generalist (All), Finance, Banking

Barnes & Associates Executive Search

205 S Ocean Grande Dr Unit 201
Ponte Vedra Beach, FL 32082-4587
(904) 513-6715
(949) 633-6750
Email: msbarnes@ix.netcom.com
Web: www.barnesandassociates.com

Summary: Our firm specializes in recruiting sales and technical consultants in the software industry. A close relationship and expertise in the SAP Business One product line.

Key Contact - Specialty:
Ms. Meredith Barnes Schwarz, Principal - *Information Technology, Sales*

Salary Minimum: $60,000

Functions: Sales & Mktg.

Industries: Computer Equip., New Media, Telecoms, Software, Accounting SW, Database SW, Entertainment SW, ERP SW, HR SW, Mfg. SW

Barr Associates

1000 E Walnut St Ste 521
Perkasie, PA 18944-5463
(215) 258-6944
Fax: (215) 258-6977
Email: sbarr@barr-associates.com
Web: www.barr-associates.com

Summary: Specialized recruiting firm with in-depth knowledge in the semiconductor industry. Custom recruiting focusing on long-term relationships.

Key Contact - Specialty:
Mr. Charly Barr, Director - *Semiconductors*
Ms. Sharon A. Barr, Director - *Semiconductors*
Mr. Tom Ozoroski, Senior Consultant - *Engineering*

Functions: Generalist (All), Engineering

Industries: Computer Equip., Electronic, Elec. Components, Semiconductors, Digital, Wireless, Fiber Optic, RF/Microwave

Barrett & Company Inc

59 Stiles Rd Ste 105
Salem, NH 03079-2886
(603) 890-1111
Fax: (603) 890-1118
Email: info@barrettcompany.com
Web: www.barrettcompany.com

Summary: Extensive experience placing sales and management personnel at all levels. We deal exclusively in the healthcare arena (medical, dental and pharmaceutical). We work on retained and contingency searches with established and start-up organizations.

Key Contact - Specialty:
Mr. Bill Barrett, President - *Medical (Devices,Sales), Pharmaceutical, Sales, Surgical*
Mr. Frank Dion, Executive Vice President
Ms. LeeAnne Martino, Account Executive - *Medical, Medical (Sales), Pharmaceutical, Sales, Surgical*

Salary Minimum: $40,000

Functions: Management, Senior Mgmt., Product Dev., Healthcare, Sales & Mktg., Sales Mgmt.

Industries: Drugs Mfg., Medical Devices, Dental

Barrett Business Services

4724 SW Macadam Ave
Portland, OR 97239-4225
(800) 494-5669
Fax: (503) 220-0987
Web: www.barrettbusiness.com

Summary: Our services provide outsourced solutions to the costs and complexities of a broad array of employment-related issues for businesses of all sizes.

Key Contact - Specialty:
Mr. William W. Sheretz, President & Chief Executive Officer
Mr. Michael D. Mulholland, Vice President, Finance & Secretary
Mr. Gregory R. Vaughn, Vice President - *Consulting, Energy, Finance, Human resources*

Salary Minimum: $70,000

Functions: Senior Mgmt., Middle Mgmt., Sales & Mktg., Sales Mgmt., CFOs, Systems Analysis, Systems Dev., DB Admin., Engineering

Industries: Generalist (All), Construction, Finance, Accounting, Communications, Telecoms, Real Estate, Software

Branches:
19033 68th Ave S Ste D102
Kent, WA 98032-2109
(425) 291-9570
(800) 494-5716
Email: ben.schrenzel@bbsihq.com
Key Contact - Specialty:
Mr. Ben Schrenzel, Practice Manager - *Executives, Sales*
Mr. Douglas Younts, Manager, Recruiting - *Executives, Sales*

Barrett Partners

205 W Wacker Dr Ste 512
Chicago, IL 60606-1482
(312) 443-8877
Fax: (312) 443-8866
Email: resumes@barrettpartners.com
Web: www.barrettpartners.com

Summary: We are professional search consultants specializing in the placement of accounting/financial, engineering/technical and IT candidates for permanent and contract/temp opportunities.

Key Contact - Specialty:
Mr. Joseph Thielman, CPC, President
Mr. Sam Kovacevic, CPC, Vice President
Mr. Kenneth Watkins, CTS - *Engineering, Finance, Technical*
Mr. Tom Watson, Manager

Salary Minimum: $50,000

Functions: Generalist (All), Finance, IT, Engineering

Industries: Generalist (All), Manufacturing, Finance, Services, Media, Insurance, Biotech/Life Sciences

Barrett Rose & Lee Inc

610-5915 Airport Rd
Inducon Airway Centre 2
Toronto, ON L4V 1T1
Canada
(416) 363-9700
(866) 917-9700
Fax: (905) 678-8899
Email: sbyrd@barrettrose.com
Web: www.barrettrose.com

Summary: Our technology vendor clients are creators and vendors of software, hardware, and related service providers. We recruit for sales, marketing, pre-sales, service delivery and finance. Our manufacturing clients produce automotive parts; consumer packaged goods, food and related services. We recruit for production, engineering, materials management, finance and HR.

Key Contact - Specialty:
Mr. J. Arthur Clark, President
Mr. H. Peter Heinemann, General Manager

Salary Minimum: $60,000

Functions: Middle Mgmt., Mfg., Production, Purchasing, Mktg. Mgmt., Sales Mgmt., HR Mgmt., Finance

Industries: Food, Bev., Tobacco, Motor Vehicles, Computer Equip., Consumer Elect., Electronic, Elec. Components, Consumer Goods, Software

Manny Barrientos

13400 Sutton Park Dr S Ste 1601
Jacksonville, FL 32224-0237
(904) 398-9080 x210
Email: manuelb1@aol.com
Web: www.wolfganggroup.com

Summary: We specialize in executive search for medical device, pharmaceutical and biotechnology companies in the areas of sales, marketing, engineering and R&D. We are affiliated with over 300 search firms.

Key Contact - Specialty:
Mr. Manny Barrientos, Founder & Executive Recruiter - *Pharmaceutical*

Salary Minimum: $85,000

Functions: Management, Senior Mgmt., Middle Mgmt., Automation, Healthcare, Sales & Mktg., Mktg. Research, Mktg. Mgmt., Sales Mgmt., CFOs

Industries: Drugs Mfg., Medical Devices, Biotech/Life Sciences, Healthcare

Bartl & Evins

(a division of Fidelity Employment Group Inc)
420 Jericho Tpke Ste 333
Jericho, NY 11753-1319
(516) 433-3333
Fax: (516) 433-2692
Email: mailbox@bartlandevins.com
Web: www.bartlandevins.com

Summary: Our long history of financial recruiting experience means that we know many CFOs and controllers. These relationships translate into a superior resource for our clients. We now also specialize in the placement of public accounting professionals with audit, tax, valuation and forensic backgrounds.

Key Contact - Specialty:
Ms. Susan Evins, President - *CFOs*
Mr. Frank Bartl, Vice President - *Controllers*

Salary Minimum: $75,000

Functions: Senior Mgmt., Finance, CFOs, Budgeting, Cash Mgmt., Credit, Taxes, M&A, DB Admin.

Industries: Generalist (All), Energy, Utilities, Construction, Manufacturing, Accounting

The Barton Group Inc

33050 5 Mile Rd
Livonia, MI 48154-3091
(734) 458-7555
Fax: (734) 458-5176
Email: bgi@mich.com
Web: www.thebartongroup.com

Summary: We are a professional and technical search firm specializing in executive, managerial, electronics/electrical/mechanical engineering, embedded software, sales & marketing, wireless communication, IS, manufacturing, industrial, architectural & engineering, product development, purchasing, quality and executive coaching. All searches focus on placing top candidates in top companies.

Key Contact - Specialty:
Mr. Barton T. Foster, President, CEO & Executive Recruiter - *Automotive*
Mr. Larry Gipson, Executive Recruiter

Salary Minimum: $40,000

Functions: Management, Mfg., Purchasing, Mktg. Mgmt., Sales Mgmt., Engineering, Minorities/Diversity, Int'l.

Industries: Manufacturing, Plastics, Rubber, Metal Products, Motor Vehicles, Transportation

Bartz & Partners

5353 Wayzata Blvd Ste 403
Minneapolis, MN 55416-1333
(952) 417-2500
(970) 252-8400
Email: career@bartz-partners.com
Web: www.bartz-partners.com

Summary: We provide our clients quality and timely search and consulting services specializing in IT recruitment from the senior technical level to the CIO. We also conduct executive level searches in the healthcare provider area.

Key Contact - Specialty:
Mr. Douglas Bartz, Partner

Salary Minimum: $65,000

Functions: Generalist (All), Senior Mgmt., IT, MIS Mgmt., Systems Analysis, Systems Dev., Systems Implem., Systems Support, Network Admin., DB Admin.

Industries: Generalist (All), Healthcare, Hospitals

Branches:
24205 V 66 Trl
Montrose, CO 81401-9014
(970) 252-8400
Email: career@bartz-partners.com
Key Contact - Specialty:
Mr. Doug Bartz, President - *Hospital, Information Systems, Information Technology, Systems (Analysts), Technical (Management)*

Basilone-Oliver Executive Search

4840 McKnight Rd Ste 101
Pittsburgh, PA 15237-3413
(412) 369-9501
Fax: (412) 369-9502
Email: email@basilone-oliver.com
Web: www.basilone-oliver.com

Summary: We have career opportunities nationwide in accounting, Finance, IS, Engineering, HR, Purchasing and Office Support.

Key Contact - Specialty:
Mr. Larry Basilone, Shareholder - *Finance*
Mr. William Brundage, Shareholder - *Engineering, Human resources*

Salary Minimum: $30,000

Functions: Mfg., Purchasing, HR Mgmt., Finance, CFOs, Taxes, IT, MIS Mgmt., Network Admin., Engineering

Industries: Agri., Forestry, Mining, Energy, Utilities, Construction, Manufacturing, Food, Bev., Tobacco, Textiles, Apparel, Lumber, Furniture, Printing, Chemicals, Plastics, Rubber, Paints, Petro. Products, Metal Products, Test, Measure Equip., Misc. Mfg., Electronic, Elec. Components, Transportation, Wholesale, Finance, Banking, Invest. Banking, Brokers, Venture Cap., Misc. Financial, Services, Accounting, Equip Svcs., HR Services, E-commerce, IT Implementation, Hospitality, Hotels, Resorts, Clubs, Entertainment, Recreation, Publishing, Communications, Telecoms, Digital, Wireless, Network Infrastructure, Environmental Svcs., Haz. Waste, Aerospace, Software, Database SW, Development SW, HR SW, Industry Specific SW, Mfg. SW, Networking, Comm. SW, Security SW, Biotech/Life Sciences, Healthcare

Branches:
201 S Tryon St Ste 925
Charlotte, NC 28202-3240
(704) 373-2240
Fax: (704) 373-2243
Key Contact - Specialty:
Mr. Warren Deutsch, Manager

Martyn Bassett Associates Inc

701-1 Richmond St W
One Richmond Street West
Toronto, ON M5H 3W4
Canada
(416) 935-1400
Fax: (416) 935-1106
Email: info@mbassett.com
Web: www.mbassett.com

Summary: We are dedicated to helping emerging technology and software companies build their sales & marketing teams. Our mission is to build dream teams that change the world.

Key Contact - Specialty:
Mr. Martyn Bassett, Founder & Partner
Ms. Heidi Ram, Managing Director, Sales & Marketing - *Accounting, C-level, Human resources*

Salary Minimum: $35,000

Functions: Sales & Mktg.

Industries: Wireless, Software

Bay Search Group

PO Box 259
Barrington, RI 02806-0259
(401) 245-3100
(800) 637-5499
Fax: (401) 245-3117
Email: ford@baysearch.com
Web: www.baysearch.com

Summary: Retained/contingency search firm specializing in IS/IT, web & internet related skills, system & network security, disaster recovery & contingency planning, data communications and applications development. Also, manufacturing and electrical engineering, optics, program and product management, logistics, Six Sigma, lean manufacturing, production control.

Key Contact - Specialty:
Mr. Ford K. Sayre, CPC, President - *Computers (Software), Database, Embedded microprocessor, Information Technology, Product management/development*
Ms. Sally Parsons, CPC, Vice President & Recruiter - *AS/400, Database, Information Technology, Oracle, Systems (Integration)*

Salary Minimum: $90,000

Functions: IT, MIS Mgmt., Systems Analysis, DB Admin.

Industries: Generalist (All), Manufacturing, Metal Products, Electronic, Elec. Components, Transportation, Wholesale, Retail, Finance, Banking, Telecoms

Bayland Associates

4460 Redwood Hwy Ste 16
San Rafael, CA 94903-1953
(415) 499-8111
Email: baylandtjk@aol.com

Summary: Specializes in conducting executive searches exclusively within medical manufacturing, sales and services environments. Medical diagnostic, therapeutic, instrumentation, equipment, device and service marketplaces are where we have the greatest expertise.

Key Contact - Specialty:
Mr. Thomas J. Kunkel, Principal - *Instrumentation*

Salary Minimum: $85,000

Functions: Generalist (All), Senior Mgmt., Mfg., Mktg. Mgmt., Sales Mgmt., IT, R&D, Engineering

Industries: Drugs Mfg., Medical Devices

Baysinger Search & Associates Inc

3275 NW Dockage Way
Palm City, FL 34990-4901
(772) 223-7147
Fax: (772) 223-7150
Email: mary@baysingersearch.com
Web: www.baysingersearch.com

Summary: Our firm specializes in medical search and recruiting for sales, marketing and management positions. Our primary focus is corporations specializing in medical devices with an emphasis in interventional cardiology, radiology and cardiovascular plus implantable arenas.

Key Contact - Specialty:
Ms. Mary M. Baysinger, President
Ms. Jennifer Ruprecht, Executive Medical Recruiter
Ms. Dee McIntosh, Recruiter
Ms. Mimi Hoff, Recruiter

Functions: Healthcare

Industries: Drugs Mfg., Medical Devices, Robotics, Biotech/Life Sciences, Healthcare, Long-term/Home Care, Dental

Branches:
2392 SW Longwood Dr
Palm City, FL 34990-4733
(772) 287-9689
Fax: (772) 287-9603
Key Contact - Specialty:
Ms. Lois Hollinger, Vice President

Baytech Solutions Inc

1032 Irving St Ste 431
San Francisco, CA 94122-2200
(415) 401-6500
Fax: (415) 401-6510

Email: jerald@baytechsol.com
Web: www.baytechsol.com

Summary: Our firm has been established by the best qualified and trained recruiters who want to make a dramatic change for those in need of excellence.

Key Contact - Specialty:
Mr. Jerald Baker, Director

Functions: R&D

Industries: Consumer Goods, Telecoms, Telephony, Digital, Wireless, Fiber Optic, Network Infrastructure, RF/Microwave, Database SW, Development SW

BCG Attorney Search

1111 Brickell Ave Ste 1100
Miami, FL 33131-3122
(305) 415-9900
(800) 709-3090
Fax: (305) 415-9609
Email: jobs@bcgsearch.com
Web: www.bcgsearch.com

Summary: We believe that there is no other group of recruiters that can consistently get the results we do in the law firm market. Our recruiters are all attorneys who practiced with major US law firms and approach their work with a level of passion, insight and thoroughness that is unsurpassed in the industry. We are accomplishing something for the candidates we represent and realize that the course of our candidates' lives will be affected by how well we do our work.

Key Contact - Specialty:
Mr. Evan Jowers, Managing Director
Mr. Scott Weaver, Recruiter

Salary Minimum: $80,000

Functions: Attorneys

Industries: Legal

Branches:
369 San Miguel Dr Ste 320
Newport Beach, CA 92660-7814
(949) 717-6676
(800) 819-6676
Fax: (949) 717-6686
Email: jobs@bcgsearch.com
Key Contact - Specialty:
Mr. Ted Bavly, Managing Director
Ms. Jean Law, Recruiter

175 S Lake Ave Unit 200
Pasadena, CA 91101-2629
(213) 895-7300
(800) 298-6440
Fax: (213) 895-7306
Email: jobs@bcgsearch.com
Key Contact - Specialty:
Mr. Harrison A. Barnes, Chief Executive Officer
Mr. Peter Wilkniss, Chief Operating Officer
Mr. Doug Spaulding, Director, Research & Development
Ms. Claudia Spielman, Recruiter
Mr. Robin Le Grand, Recruiter
Mr. Jamie Barnes, Director, Marketing
Mr. Jefferson Byrd, Writer
Mr. Jason Drew, Researcher
Mr. Michael Garcia, Researcher
Mr. Tom Horne, Writer
Ms. Karen Kupetz, Recruiter
Ms. Brillana Leyba, Administrative Assistant
Ms. Jennifer McKee, Recruiter
Ms. Lisa Orlandi, Recruiter
Mr. Kevin Quinn, Researcher
Mr. Skyler Ramirez, Researcher
Mr. Frank Riela, Recruiter
Mr. Jeff Sketeris, Director, Operations
Ms. Shante Tillett, Production Assistant

Mr. Askia Toure, Production Coordinator
Ms. Carina Zaragoza, Researcher

175 S Lake Ave Unit 200
Pasadena, CA 91101-2629
(213) 895-7300
(800) 298-6440
Email: jobs@bcgsearch.com
Key Contact - Specialty:
Mr. Simon Cairns, Manager

555 California St Ste 300
San Francisco, CA 94111-1505
(415) 568-2204
Fax: (415) 568-2104
Email: jobs@bcgsearch.com
Key Contact - Specialty:
Mr. James Fant, Managing Director
Mr. Eamonn Markham, Managing Director

1400 16th St Ste 400
16 Market Square
Denver, CO 80202-5995
(303) 825-1199
Email: jobs@bcgsearch.com
Key Contact - Specialty:
Mr. Melanie Farancis, Managing Director

1050 Connecticut Ave NW Ste 1000
Washington, DC 20036-5334
(202) 955-5585
(800) 210-5743
Fax: (202) 955-5596
Email: jobs@bcgsearch.com
Key Contact - Specialty:
Mr. Dan Binstock, Managing Director
Ms. Alyson Todd, Recruiter

1170 Peachtree St NE Ste 1200
Atlanta, GA 30309-7673
(404) 249-8588
(888) 581-8588
Fax: (404) 581-5888
Email: jobs@bcgsearch.com
Key Contact - Specialty:
Mr. Raffaele Murdocca, Managing Director
Ms. Jenny Wallace, Recruiter

200 S Wacker Dr Fl 3100
Chicago, IL 60606-5877
(312) 321-9411
(800) 285-9937
Fax: (312) 321-9421
Email: jobs@bcgsearch.com
Key Contact - Specialty:
Ms. Jamie Bailey, Managing Director
Ms. Vanessa Alvarez, Recruiter
Ms. Mel Kinfe, Production Cooodinator

225 Franklin St Ste 2600
Boston, MA 02110-2817
(617) 443-1155
(800) 807-9056
Email: jobs@bcgsearch.com
Key Contact - Specialty:
Mr. Stephen E. Seckler, Managing Director

1560 Broadway Fl 10
New York, NY 10036-1518
(212) 232-0400
(800) 285-9254
Fax: (212) 232-0111
Email: jobs@bcgsearch.com
Key Contact - Specialty:
Ms. Carey Bertolet, Managing Director
Ms. Helen Kwon, Recruiter

525 N Tryon St Fl 16
Charlotte, NC 28202-0216
(704) 334-8000
(888) 581-8588
Email: jobs@bcgsearch.com
Key Contact - Specialty:
Mr. Raffaele Murdocca, Managing Director

1200 Smith St Ste 1600
Houston, TX 77002-4403
(713) 270-1199
(800) 536-5025
Email: jobs@bcgsearch.com
Key Contact - Specialty:
Mr. Robert Kinney, Managing Director

Be Your Best Inc

2771 Georgian Ter
Marietta, GA 30068-3625
(770) 565-0979
Email: missy@beyourbestinc.com
Web: www.beyourbestinc.com

Summary: We are highly skilled recruiters with a reputation for integrity and building great client relationships. Our firm is a woman-owned and family run business, which is a preferred vendor for several Fortune 100 Companies. Experienced in consulting, IT, executive, accounting/auditing and medical field searches.

Key Contact - Specialty:
Ms. Melissa Bowers, President
Mr. David Sillman, Vice President, Recruiting

Salary Minimum: $60,000

Functions: Generalist (All)

Industries: Generalist (All), Finance, Communications, Government, Software, Networking, Comm. SW, Healthcare

Beacon Career Management, LLC

PO Box 1271
Hightstown, NJ 08520-0780
(800) 758-9747
Fax: (609) 490-1599
Email: pwatson@beaconcareermgmt.com
Web: www.beaconcareermgmt.com

Summary: The goal of Beacon Career Management is placement of qualified Executive, Management, and Supervisory talent, including Health Care professionals. We guarantee a strategic and tactical Search Plan will be implemented one day after our initial meeting. We utilize a variety of search processes – networking, referrals, postings – to achieve results.

Key Contact - Specialty:
Ms. Pamela Watson, President - *Executives, Healthcare, Management*

Functions: Management, Middle Mgmt.

Industries: Generalist (All), Energy, Utilities, Manufacturing, Finance, Services, Communications, Insurance, Healthcare

Beacon Professional Search

26 30th Ave
Isle of Palms, SC 29451-2409
(843) 886-4515
Fax: (843) 886-4730
Email: mikeloftus@beaconsearch.com

Summary: Contingency recruiting firm specializing in manufacturing, distribution/logistics/supply chain, engineering, HR and accounting.

Key Contact - Specialty:
Mr. Mike Loftus, Owner

Salary Minimum: $50,000

Functions: Generalist (All)

Industries: Manufacturing, Transportation, Wholesale, Retail, Engineering Svcs., Logistics Svcs., Supply Chain Mgmt

Thomas Beck Inc

PO Box 789
Sausalito, CA 94966-0789
(415) 381-1555
Email: tbimail@aol.com
Web: www.thomasbeck.com

Summary: Our firm specializes in microelectronics executive search. We recruit senior management and professional staff for semiconductor, sub-system manufacturers as well as OEMs. This includes sales & marketing, engineering, R&D, manufacturing and operations professionals. Our scope in this area applies to companies in communications, consumer and computing.

Key Contact - Specialty:
Mr. Thomas Beck

Functions: Generalist (All), Management

Industries: Computer Equip., Consumer Elect., Electronic, Elec. Components, Semiconductors, Digital, Wireless, Fiber Optic, Network Infrastructure

Beck/Eastwood Recruitment Solutions

28170 Avenue Crocker Ste 202
Valencia, CA 91355-1287
(661) 295-6666
Fax: (661) 295-5153
Email: info@beckeastwood.com
Web: www.beckeastwood.com

Summary: We raise the level of commitment to satisfy our clients' needs through innovative strategic partnerships, expert direct recruiting and our recruiting network. We serve clients in medical/healthcare, B2B hw/sw, infrastructure/networks, supply chain, fulfillment/digital print, call center, pharmaceutical, industrial and procurement markets.

Key Contact - Specialty:
Mr. Steven Beck, Senior Parnter - *Computers (Sales), Medical (Devices,Sales), Sales, Surgical*
Mr. Gary Eastwood, Partner - *Procurement, Purchasing, Sales, Supply Chain*

Salary Minimum: $50,000

Functions: Generalist (All), Mktg. Mgmt., Sales Mgmt.

Industries: Generalist (All), Printing, Drugs Mfg., Medical Devices, Plastics, Rubber, Computer Equip., E-commerce, Telecoms, Call Centers, Network Infrastructure, Software, Networking, Comm. SW

Hans Becker Associates LLC

2110 15 Mile Rd
Sterling Heights, MI 48310-4806
(586) 978-0550
Fax: (586) 978-0572
Email: hansbec@aol.com

Summary: We offer services in the engineering, manufacturing, sales, quality, industrial, and automotive industries. Contingency fee basis.

Key Contact - Specialty:
Mr. B. Hans Becker, Owner - *Engineering, Manufacturing, Marketing, Sales*

Salary Minimum: $60,000

Functions: Generalist (All), Middle Mgmt., Quality, Engineering

Industries: Manufacturing, Chemicals, Plastics, Rubber, Metal Products, Motor Vehicles, Misc. Mfg., Mgmt. Consulting

Becker Professional Services

7805 SW 6th Ct
Plantation, FL 33324-3203
(954) 776-5554
Fax: (954) 776-5855
Email: mbecker@beckerpro.com

Summary: We analyze the specific needs of our clients to execute a customized search for executive talent but our strongest focus is accounting and finance professionals.

Key Contact - Specialty:
Mr. Matthew Becker, Chief Executive Officer - *Finance, Human resources*

Salary Minimum: $80,000

Functions: Board Members, Senior Mgmt., Sales Mgmt., HR Mgmt., Finance, CFOs, Taxes

Industries: Generalist (All)

Becker Staffing Services Inc

3 Bala Plz Ste 119W
Bala Cynwyd, PA 19004-3402
(610) 667-3010
(877) 543-9013
Email: jobs@beckerstaffing.com
Web: www.beckerstaffing.com

Summary: We were founded with the mission of providing recruitment and staffing services through long-term client relationships. We offer candidates a broad spectrum of consultation services. We provide retained and contingency search as well as contract and temp staffing.

Key Contact - Specialty:
Mr. Daniel Becker, CPC, President
Ms. Renee Becker, Senior Vice President

Functions: Management, Sales & Mktg.

Industries: Generalist (All), Insurance

Branches:
1919 Chestnut St
Philadelphia, PA 19103-3401
(215) 563-0415
Fax: (610) 934-0221
Email: jobs@beckerstaffing.com
Key Contact - Specialty:
Mr. Harvey Becker, Owner

Robert Beech West Inc

1691 Ponderosa Way
Palm Springs, CA 92264-3535
(760) 864-1380
Email: careers@beechinc.com
Web: www.beechinc.com

Summary: Place sales management and senior level sales personnel in software, solutions, consulting, outsourcing, and financial industries.

Key Contact - Specialty:
Mr. Robert Beech, President

Salary Minimum: $85,000

Functions: Sales & Mktg., Sales Mgmt., Systems Support

Industries: Finance, Invest. Banking, Supply Chain Mgmt., Telecoms, Software, Accounting SW, Database SW, Doc. Mgmt., Production SW, ERP SW, HR SW, Industry Specific SW, Mfg. SW, Marketing SW, Networking, Comm. SW, Security SW, System SW, Training SW

Behrens and Company

PO Box 831
Lake Stevens, WA 98258-0831
(360) 658-6054
Email: rick@behrensco.com
Web: www.behrensco.com

Summary: We provide recruitment in medical device, medical packaging, RFID software & hardware, manufacturing management, packaging machine systems and related industries. Experience in the recruitment of engineering, sales, marketing, executive management, sales management and human resource professionals. Contract placement available in all areas of experience.

Key Contact - Specialty:
Mr. Rick Behrens, Managing Partner

Salary Minimum: $70,000

Functions: Management, Automation, Packaging, Sales & Mktg., Sales Mgmt., CFOs, MIS Mgmt., R&D, Engineering

Industries: Generalist (All), Manufacturing, Food, Bev., Tobacco, Paper, Printing, Chemicals, Drugs Mfg., Medical Devices, Plastics, Rubber, Metal Products, Computer Equip., Test, Measure Equip., Robotics, Semiconductors, Pharm Svcs., Accounting, Equip Svcs., HR Services, Packaging, Mfg. SW, Security SW, Biotech/Life Sciences

Peter Bell & Associates LLC

444 Madison Ave Ste 710
New York, NY 10022-6969
(212) 371-0992
Fax: (212) 371-1368
Email: peter@peterbellassociates.com
Web: www.peterbellassociates.com

Summary: We are a contingency/retained executive search firm specializing in public relations, investor relations, corporate communications and marketing.

Key Contact - Specialty:
Mr. Peter Bell, President
Mr. Barry Piatoff, Vice President

Salary Minimum: $50,000

Functions: PR

Industries: Generalist (All)

Tom Bell & Associates

PO Box 623
New Canaan, CT 06840-0623
(203) 972-7786
Fax: (203) 972-7765
Email: tbell@bellmetro.com
Web: www.bellmetro.com

Summary: We are an executive recruiting firm with an emphasis on senior level, sales management and sales positions. Our candidate pool has an abundance of senior level management experience.

Key Contact - Specialty:
Mr. Tom Bell, President

Salary Minimum: $75,000

Functions: Generalist (All)

Industries: Generalist (All), Printing, Brokers, Non-profits, Pharm Svcs., Legal, Telecoms, Call Centers, Wireless

Gary S Bell Associates Inc

1360 N Lake Shore Dr Apt 1015
Chicago, IL 60610-8456
(312) 335-9086
Fax: (312) 335-9186
Email: gsbassoc@comcast.net

Summary: We concentrate on laboratory products and services, pharmaceuticals, medical devices, clinical and research instrumentation.

Key Contact - Specialty:
Mr. Gary S. Bell, President
Mr. Andrew Bell

Salary Minimum: $65,000

Functions: Healthcare

Industries: Medical Devices, Pharm Svcs., Biotech/Life Sciences

William Bell Associates Inc

605 Candlewood Commons
Howell, NJ 07731-2173
(732) 901-6000
Fax: (732) 901-2299
Email: info@williambellassociates.com
Web: www.williambellassociates.com

Summary: We are specialists in placement of cosmetic chemists and management. Additional areas include purchasing, planning, quality control, quality assurance, packaging and manufacturing.

Key Contact - Specialty:
Mr. Steven Neidenberg, Vice President - *Chemical, Cosmetics*
Ms. Phyllis Kay, Office Manager
Mr. Ken Lesenko, Director, Technical Recruiting

Functions: Mfg., Product Dev., Production, Quality, Purchasing, Materials Plng., Packaging, Sales & Mktg., Customer Svc., R&D

Industries: Soap, Perf., Cosmtcs.

Edward Bell Associates

50 1st St Ste 320
San Francisco, CA 94105-2411
(415) 442-0270
Email: pres@ebajobs.com
Web: www.ebajobs.com

Summary: We specialize in placing accounting, finance and computer professionals in full time and contract positions. As a local recruiting firm, our recruiters have developed strong business relations with our clients. If any questions or concerns arise, our clients have immediate access to our account managers with authority to resolve all issues.

Key Contact - Specialty:
Mr. Edward Bell, CPA, MBA, Owner - *Finance*
Mr. Luigi Favero, Senior Technical Recruiter - *Data processing*
Mr. John Postlethwaite, Financial Recruiter - *Clerical, Finance*

Functions: Generalist (All), Finance, IT

Industries: Generalist (All), Finance, Accounting, Real Estate, Software

Bell Oaks Company Inc

1 Glenlake Pkwy NE Ste 1000
Atlanta, GA 30328-7245
(678) 287-2000
Fax: (678) 287-2001
Email: info@belloaks.com
Web: www.belloaks.com

Summary: Performs executive searches on a retained, contingency or contract basis in the fields of finance/accounting, IT, engineering and manufacturing/operations. We have more than 7,000 completed searches.

Key Contact - Specialty:
Mr. Price Harding, President
Mr. Randy Hain, Regional Vice President

Salary Minimum: $50,000

Functions: Generalist (All), Management, Mfg., Materials, Sales & Mktg., Finance, IT, Engineering

Industries: Generalist (All), Manufacturing, Finance, Media, Government, Software

Belmon Technology Consulting Company

(also known as Belmon Technology Consulting LLC)
20072 Inverness Sq
Ashburn, VA 20147-4106
(703) 728-3202
Email: afbucciero@belmontcc.com
Web: www.belmontech.com

Summary: Our firm is your business partner dedicated to optimizing the staffing requirements of high technology enterprises. We provide customized services in the searching and placement of high technology candidates. We have subject matter expertise in federal and commercial business development, federal & commercial sales, software & hardware engineers, networking and network management systems.

Key Contact - Specialty:
Mr. Tony Bucciero, President - *Engineering, Sales*

Salary Minimum: $100,000

Functions: Management, Product Dev., Sales & Mktg., IT, R&D, Engineering

Industries: Telecoms, Telephony, Digital, Wireless, Fiber Optic, Network Infrastructure, Government, Defense, Aerospace, Database SW, Development SW, Networking, Comm. SW, Security SW, System SW

Joy Reed Belt Search Consultants Inc

PO Box 54410
Oklahoma City, OK 73154-1410
(405) 842-5155
Web: www.joyreedbeltsearch.com

Summary: We are a human resources consulting firm specializing in executive search for national, regional and local corporations and nonprofit organizations with extensive years successful experience in executive search.

Key Contact - Specialty:
Dr. Joy Reed Belt, PhD, President - *CEOs, COOs, Healthcare, Human resources*
Mrs. Carolyn Stuart, Vice President - *CFOs, Finance*
Ms. Robin Nauman, Client Services Coordinator

Salary Minimum: $75,000

Functions: Senior Mgmt., Middle Mgmt., Healthcare, Health Admin., Benefits, M&A, MIS Mgmt., Attorneys, Paralegals

Industries: Generalist (All), Energy, Utilities, Services, HR Services, Advertising, Real Estate, Healthcare

Benamati & Associates

6059 Wright St
Arvada, CO 80004-3947
(303) 467-7885
Email: nben@att.net
Web: www.benamatiassociates.com

Summary: We are a full-service engineering recruiting firm specializing in A/E consulting, MEP, design/build, oil & gas, refining and petrochemical industries. Our specialties are engineering, chemical, electrical, mechanical, and metallurgy. We place staff upward to management positions.

Key Contact - Specialty:
Ms. Nancy Benamati, Owner - *Engineering*

Salary Minimum: $60,000

Functions: Mfg., Engineering, Architects, Design

Industries: Energy, Utilities, Oil & Gas, Construction, Manufacturing, Chemicals, Paints, Petro. Products, Haz. Waste, Biotech/Life Sciences

N L Benke & Associates Inc

1422 Euclid Ave Ste 872
Cleveland, OH 44115-2012
(216) 771-6822
Fax: (216) 771-3568
Email: benke@voyager.net

Summary: Our recruiters have prior experience as accountants, bankers, financial or computer professionals.

Key Contact - Specialty:
Mr. Norman L. Benke, President - *Finance, Human resources*

Salary Minimum: $50,000

Functions: Generalist (All)

Industries: Generalist (All), Finance, Banking, Invest. Banking, Venture Cap., Accounting, HR Services, Call Centers, Network Infrastructure, Database SW

Bennett & Associates

2732 Palo Verde Dr
Odessa, TX 79762-5139
(432) 550-9096
Fax: (432) 362-3211
Email: mark.bennett@grandecom.net

Summary: Specializing in business brokerage and professional search. We have placed thousands of candidates with hundreds of companies as well as assisted many successful people and corporations buy and sell small companies.

Key Contact - Specialty:
Mr. Mark Bennett, Owner

Salary Minimum: $60,000

Functions: Generalist (All), Management, Senior Mgmt., Middle Mgmt.

Industries: Generalist (All), Energy, Utilities, Oil & Gas, Chemicals, Plastics, Rubber, Paints, Petro. Products, Haz. Waste

Bennett & Co Consulting Group

2135 Manzanita Dr Ste 1
Oakland, CA 94611-1134
(510) 339-3175
(510) 913-2053
Fax: (510) 339-2161
Email: lindabennett@earthlink.net
Web: www.interviewconsultant.com

Summary: We specialize in recruiting for all disciplines of HR executive, HR management and logistics/operations search. Clients include manufacturing, biotechnology, software, retail, non-profit and start-up companies. We are experienced in providing half-day interview training workshops with role playing exercises for managers to ensure they make the best hiring decisions.

Key Contact - Specialty:
Ms. Linda E. Bennett, Principal - *Human resources*

Salary Minimum: $85,000

Functions: Materials, HR Mgmt.

Industries: Generalist (All), Manufacturing, Food, Bev., Tobacco, Textiles, Apparel, Consumer Elect., Misc. Mfg., Electronic, Elec. Components, Semiconductors, Retail, Banking, Services, Legal, Logistics Svcs., Software

Bennett Allen & Associates

7422 Carmel Executive Park Dr
Charlotte, NC 28226-8273
(704) 541-5891
Email: ben@bennettallen.com
Web: www.bennettallen.com

Summary: Recruit mechanical engineers for manufacturing industry.

Key Contact - Specialty:
Mr. Ben Liebstein, President

Salary Minimum: $50,000

Functions: Board Members, Product Dev.

Industries: Plastics, Rubber, Metal Products, Machine, Appliance, Motor Vehicles, Computer Equip., Consumer Elect.

Robert Bennett Associates

PO Box 261
Little Neck, NY 11363-0261
(718) 428-5455
(212) 949-2355
Fax: (718) 428-1714
Email: jobs@robertbennettassociates.com
Web: www.robertbennettassociates.com

Summary: Our firm places attorneys in the legal industry.

Key Contact - Specialty:
Ms. Mary Bloom, President
Mr. Robert Bennett, Partner

Salary Minimum: $50,000

Functions: Attorneys

Industries: Legal

Bennett-Pryor

703 Market St Ste 1400
San Francisco, CA 94103-2124
(510) 238-8972
Fax: (510) 238-8364
Email: careers@pryorsearch.com
Web: www.pryorsearch.com

Summary: Our firm provides specialized search and recruitment services for the insurance industry.

Key Contact - Specialty:
Ms. Jo-Ann Pryor, Managing Partner

Salary Minimum: $40,000

Functions: Generalist (All), Senior Mgmt., Middle Mgmt., Admin. Svcs., Product Dev., Sales & Mktg., HR Mgmt., Finance, IT

Industries: Insurance

Benson Associates

280 Madison Ave Rm 703
New York, NY 10016-0801
(212) 683-5962
Fax: (212) 679-2724

Summary: Our principals have extensive experience in executive recruitment.

Key Contact - Specialty:
Mr. Mark Hatten, Partner
Mr. Laurence Rutkovsky, Partner

Salary Minimum: $75,000

Functions: Finance

Industries: Generalist (All)

The Bentley Group Inc

9090 Alexandra Cir
Wellington, FL 33414-6442
(561) 734-3550
(866) 734-3550
Fax: (561) 734-3449
Email: bennett@bentleygrp.com
Web: www.bentleygrp.com

Summary: We have a long-standing commitment to the medical, pharmaceutical and healthcare industries. Our firm was founded with a goal to provide high quality cost effective search services. We focus our attention on best suiting the needs of our clients and candidates with a consistent goal of growing a long-term partnership.

Key Contact - Specialty:
Mr. Bennett S. Vivona, CPC, President - *Operating rooms, Prosthetic devices, Risk management, Sales, Surgical*

Salary Minimum: $50,000

Functions: Generalist (All), Healthcare, Allied Health, Sales Reps.

Industries: Medical Devices, Pharm Svcs., Biotech/Life Sciences, Healthcare, Hospitals, Long-term/Home Care, Dental, Physical Therapy, Occupational Therapy, Women's

Bentley Price Associates Inc

3541 W Oak Trail Rd
Santa Ynez, CA 93460-9310
(805) 686-1234
Fax: (805) 688-1428
Email: drizzo@bentleyprice.com
Web: www.bentleyprice.com

Summary: Management consultants with a long history in the hospitality industry

Key Contact - Specialty:
Mr. Dennis P. Rizzo, President & Chief Executive Officer

Functions: Management, Board Members, Mgmt. Consultants

Industries: Hospitality, Hotels, Resorts, Clubs, Restaurants, Full Service Restaurants, Inst./Industrial Food Svc., Entertainment, Recreation

Berg Recruiting Naturally Inc

95 Yesler Way Fl 2
Seattle, WA 98104-2530
(206) 938-2008
(866) 641-7018
Fax: (206) 938-2176
Email: info@bergrecruiting.com
Web: www.bergrecruiting.com

Summary: Placing c-level, senior execs to sales managers in the healthy lifestyles industry.

Key Contact - Specialty:
Ms. Heather Berg, President - *Food*
Ms. Joan Gulbrandson, Executive Sourcing - *Change management*
Ms. Debbie Maxwell, Orgn Dev & Mgmt Conslnt & Corp Trainer
Ms. Toni Thomas, Treasurer - *Finance, Financial services, Human resources, Investment management, Manufacturing*

Salary Minimum: $75,000

Functions: Management, Senior Mgmt., Mfg., Quality, Healthcare, Allied Health, Sales & Mktg., Sales Mgmt.

Industries: Manufacturing, Food, Bev., Tobacco, Chemicals, Soap, Perf., Cosmtcs., Drugs Mfg., Medical Devices, Services, Pharm Svcs., Hospitality, Environmental Svcs., Packaging, Biotech/Life Sciences, Healthcare, Hospitals, Occupational Therapy, Women's, Non-Classifiable

Berger and Leff Inc

1 Sansome St Ste 2100
San Francisco, CA 94104-4432
(415) 951-4750
Fax: (415) 951-4751
Email: taxjobs@aol.com
Web: www.lisaleff.com

Summary: We are an executive search firm specializing in the recruitment of corporate tax professionals, accountants and attorneys for a variety of industries.

Key Contact - Specialty:
Ms. Lisa A. Leff, Owner

Salary Minimum: $75,000

Functions: Taxes

Industries: Manufacturing, Drugs Mfg., Medical Devices, Computer Equip., Accounting, Telecoms, Software, Mfg. SW, Networking, Comm. SW

C Berger Group Inc

PO Box 274
327 Gundersen Dr
Wheaton, IL 60189-0274
(630) 653-1115
(800) 382-4222
Fax: (630) 653-1691
Email: cberger@cberger.com
Web: www.cberger.com

Summary: Our firm conducts searches for managers and subject specialists in business, academic, public and government libraries, and research, competitive intelligence and knowledge management operations. We supply contract and temp personnel and provide library management consulting and project support services. Our firm is a woman-owned small business.

Key Contact - Specialty:
Ms. Carol A. Berger, Founder - *Competitive intelligence, Consulting, Information service, Market research*
Mr. Joel Patrick Berger, President - *Competitive intelligence, Consulting, Information service, Market research*
Ms. Kimberly Filip, Assistant, Business Operations
Ms. Linda Jourdan, Manager, Client Services
Ms. Julianna Kloeppel, Client Services Specialist
Ms. Mary Lyn Pfeiffer, Manager, Business Operations - *High technology*

Salary Minimum: $50,000

Functions: Management, Sales & Mktg., HR Mgmt., IT, Specialized Svcs., Mgmt. Consultants

Industries: Generalist (All), Manufacturing, Finance, Services, Non-profits, Higher Ed., Media, Communications, Government, Software, Healthcare, Non-Classifiable

Bergeris & Company Inc

PO Box 341
Larchmont, NY 10538-0341
(914) 833-0519
Email: bergeris@aol.com

Summary: Executive search for sales professionals in commercial and investment banking. Special, but not exclusive, focus on credit and private banking. A truly individualized approach.

Key Contact - Specialty:
Mr. Jim Bergeris

Salary Minimum: $100,000

Functions: Generalist (All), Cash Mgmt., Credit, M&A, Risk Mgmt.

Industries: Generalist (All), Finance, Banking, Invest. Banking, Brokers, Venture Cap., Misc. Financial, Mgmt. Consulting

Judith Berinsky Co.

1675 York Ave
New York, NY 10128-6752
(212) 348-8185
(917) 583-7322
Email: jbco95@aol.com

Summary: Middle to senior level management for retail, apparel, accessories & home furnishings companies; specialization in luxury goods firms. National searches on a contingency & retainer basis, research projects & compensation surveys. Functions include: Store & Regional Management, Operations, Sales & Marketing, Public Relations, Merchandising, Design, Human Resources, Finance.

Key Contact - Specialty:
Ms. Judith S. Berinsky, Executive Recruiter - *Consumer (Durables), Management, Marketing, Sales*

Salary Minimum: $75,000

Functions: Senior Mgmt., Middle Mgmt., Product Dev., Purchasing, Sales & Mktg., Advertising, Mktg. Mgmt., Sales Mgmt., Direct Mktg.

Industries: Textiles, Apparel, Lumber, Furniture, Soap, Perf., Cosmtcs., Leather, Stone, Glass, Consumer Goods, Wholesale, Retail, Supply Chain Mgmt

Bernard, Frigon & Associates Inc

34 Av de Beaujolais
Candiac, QC J5R 4B6
Canada
(450) 444-1389
Fax: (450) 444-4349
Email: bfrigon@globetrotter.net

Summary: Our team is well known for efficient interventions based on extensive knowledge acquired through previous practical management responsibilities in the fields of IS, management consulting as well as sales management for a major computer manufacturer.

Key Contact - Specialty:
Mr. Bernard Frigon, President

Functions: Automation, MIS Mgmt., Systems Analysis, Systems Dev., Systems Support, Mgmt. Consultants

Industries: Generalist (All)

Bernhart Associates Executive Search LLC

2068 Greenwood Dr Ste 220
Owatonna, MN 55060-1370
(507) 451-4270
Fax: (507) 451-9433
Email: bgb@bernhart.com
Web: www.bernhart.com

Summary: We are a search firm focusing exclusively in direct marketing, database marketing, CRM and quantitative analysis. Client firms include all industries, start-up to Fortune 500 as well as agencies and service providers.

Key Contact - Specialty:
Mr. Jerry Bernhart, President - *Direct marketing*

Salary Minimum: $75,000

Functions: Sales & Mktg., Mktg. Research, Mktg. Mgmt., Sales Mgmt., Direct Mktg.

Industries: Printing, Retail, Banking, Services, Mgmt. Consulting, E-commerce, Hospitality, Hotels, Resorts, Clubs, Insurance, Database SW, Marketing SW, Healthcare

Berry & Associates

144 N 44th St Ste 200
Lincoln, NE 68503-3701
(402) 434-0460
Fax: (402) 434-0462
Email: mail@berrysrp.com
Web: www.berrysrp.com

Summary: Recruiting only in service line administration and management in maternal/child and women's ambulatory services.

Key Contact - Specialty:
Ms. Debra Berry Miller, President - *Administration*
Mr. Mike Miller, Vice President - *Administration*
Mr. Lyle Working, Assistant Vice President
Ms. Kathy Schultz, Office Manager

Salary Minimum: $50,000

Functions: Healthcare

Industries: Women's

Berry & Associates LLC

2855 S Oakland Pl
Aurora, CO 80014-3111
(303) 752-0478
Fax: (303) 752-1014
Email: berry@rmi.net

Summary: Specializing in real estate finance, development, acquisition, construction, and property management.

Key Contact - Specialty:
Ms. Sandy Berry, Principal - *Banking, Construction, Engineering, Finance, Property management*

Functions: Management

Industries: Real Estate

Besen Associates Inc

PO Box 57
Lake Hiawatha, NJ 07034-0057
(973) 334-5533
Fax: (973) 334-4810
Email: info@besen.com
Web: www.besen.com

Summary: Research and engineering for the pharmaceutical industry. Physicians, pharmaceutical scientists, internal medicine, infectious disease, cardio/pulmonary respiratory, rheumatology, endocrinology, general & biotechnological engineers, marketing sales & manufacturing support personnel, regulatory and quality assurance control.

Key Contact - Specialty:
Mr. Douglas Besen, President - *Physicians, Presidents*

Functions: Generalist (All), Senior Mgmt., Middle Mgmt.

Industries: Drugs Mfg., Call Centers, Digital, Biotech/Life Sciences, Healthcare

Besner EJ Consultant Inc

300-417 Rue Saint-Nicolas
Montreal, QC H2Y 2P4
Canada
(514) 987-9522
Fax: (514) 844-1841

Email: besner@bellnet.ca

Summary: Recruiting specialists for the transportation and logistics industries.

Key Contact - Specialty:
Mr. Elliott J. Besner, President
Yves Pelletier, Consultant

Salary Minimum: $20,000

Functions: Management, Senior Mgmt., Middle Mgmt., Materials, Materials Plng., Sales Mgmt., Customer Svc., Sales Reps., M&A

Industries: Transportation, Logistics Svcs.

Best Fit Recruiting

PO Box 2428 PMB 5942
Pensacola, FL 32513-2428
(813) 969-0619
Email: mac@bestfitrecruiting.com
Web: www.bestfitrecruiting.com

Summary: Recruiting firm engaged in direct hire recruiting, and contract staffing, of healthcare and therapy professionals; PT, OT, SLP.

Key Contact - Specialty:
Mr. Mac McClellan, MBA, PHR, President - *Healthcare, Occupational therapy*
Mr. Don Bryant, MA, MBA, Senior Consultant - *Healthcare*
Mrs. Chris McClellan, Researcher - *Healthcare, Occupational therapy*

Salary Minimum: $40,000

Functions: Allied Health

Industries: Healthcare, Hospitals, Long-term/Home Care, Physical Therapy, Occupational Therapy

Best Personnel Services

211 S Federal Hwy Ste 12
Boynton Beach, FL 33435-4917
(561) 752-9888
(561) 752-9894
Fax: (561) 752-9899
Email: info@bestpersonnelonline.com
Web: www.besthealthandhomecare.com

Summary: Carrying 12 health system contracts, with a reach of 321 hospitals, clinics and their affiliates. Our firm averages 200 job opportunities per month. Our opportunities are with reputable health systems; which offer hospital sponsored solo practices, multi-specialty, single-specialty, group, etc. Our firm further extends its reach by working with over 40 other headhunting companies. This allows optimal results for our candidates.

Key Contact - Specialty:
Mr. Peter Beichman
Ms. Wanda Francis Barr, Healthcare Recruiter - *Physicians*

Salary Minimum: $65,000

Functions: Healthcare

Industries: Hospitals, Long-term/Home Care, Non-Classifiable

BEST Search Inc

PO Box 596
Geneva, IL 60134-0596
(630) 365-3200
(866) 365-3200
Fax: (630) 365-3201
Email: audry@bestsearchinc.com
Web: www.bestsearchinc.com

Summary: Commercial insurance recruiting. Property and casualty only. Clients include insurers, reinsurers, brokers and less frequently, law firms and corporate risk management

departments. Functions include claims/legal, underwriting/marketing, product development, operations and HR. Senior professional through management positions.

Key Contact - Specialty:
Ms. Audry Buchanan, President

Salary Minimum: $60,000

Functions: Generalist (All), Middle Mgmt., Product Dev., Sales & Mktg., Mktg. Mgmt., HR Mgmt., Risk Mgmt., Legal, Attorneys

Industries: Insurance

Beta Consulting Services

4760 Lightkeepers Way Unit 20H
Little River, SC 29566-7956
(877) 281-8331
(843) 280-8321
Email: gbsc@sc.rr.com

Summary: Specializes in printing, graphic arts, direct mail production, and related direct marketing areas.

Key Contact - Specialty:
Mr. Greig Burdick, President & Owner

Functions: Generalist (All)

Industries: Printing, Chemicals, Packaging

James Betts Associates

3975 Oran Gulf Rd
Manlius, NY 13104-9347
(315) 682-3289
(888) 237-5200
Email: jbetts@bettsassociates.com
Web: www.bettsassociates.com

Summary: We offer professional recruitment specializing in both permanent placements and consulting assignments with firms using Cognos tools for business intelligence development projects.

Key Contact - Specialty:
Mr. James Betts, Principal - *Analysts, Competitive intelligence, Computers (Programming), Consulting, Database (Warehousing)*

Salary Minimum: $50,000

Functions: Systems Analysis, Systems Dev., Systems Implem., Systems Support

Industries: Generalist (All), Database SW, Development SW, Doc. Mgmt., Production SW, ERP SW, HR SW

BeyondTech Solutions Inc

300-3665 Kingsway
Vancouver, BC V5R 5W2
Canada
(604) 433-0617
Fax: (604) 433-0627
Email: info@beyond-tech.com
Web: www.beyond-tech.com

Summary: We are a provider of technical recruitment services to clients across industry sectors. We believe in making recruitment simple for employers and job seekers. With our convenient contract and permanent staffing options, you can exercise knowledge and freedom in choosing your career or personnel solution.

Key Contact - Specialty:
Ms. Stella Kuan, Account Manager

Functions: Quality, IT, Systems Analysis, Systems Dev., Systems Implem., Network Admin., DB Admin.

Industries: Generalist (All), Computer Equip., Communications, Telecoms, Software

BG & Associates

10112 Langhorne Ct Ste B
Bethesda, MD 20817-1250
(301) 365-4046
Fax: (301) 365-0435
Email: bg.associates@verizon.net.

Summary: Once given a search assignment we most often find the appropriate candidates within five weeks, through sourcing and cold calling. Once placed our clients and candidates enjoy a job success and retention rate in excess of 95 percent. We work primarily with large companies on contingency and retained searches.

Key Contact - Specialty:
Mr. Brian A. Gray, SPHR, President & Recruiter - *Diversity, Executives, Human resources, Minorities, Staffing*
Ms. Linda Cooper, Researcher & Recruiter - *Human resources*
Ms. Phyllis Washington, Researcher & Recruiter - *General management, Minorities*

Salary Minimum: $60,000

Functions: Management, Mfg., Sales & Mktg., HR Mgmt., Staffing, Finance, IT, Specialized Svcs., Minorities/Diversity

Industries: Generalist (All)

BG Search Associates

2110 Powers Ferry Rd SE Ste 160
Atlanta, GA 30339-5051
(770) 303-0900
Fax: (770) 303-0909
Email: careers@bgsearch.com
Web: www.bgsearch.com

Summary: Provides permanent and contract placement of attorneys and paralegal to corporations and law firms. Certified as a WBE by the Women's Business Enterprise National Council.

Key Contact - Specialty:
Ms. Barbara Goldman, Founder
Ms. Sherie Holmes Bush, Esq., Recruiter
Mr. Brian D. Poe, Esq., Recruiter
Mr. Joel Goldman, Recruiter
Ms. Felicity Watkins, Recruiter
Ms. Kamila Aghazada, Recruiter
Ms. Jessica Goldman, Recruiter
Ms. Ellen Weisbord Feinsand, PhD, Consultant

Functions: Legal

Industries: Generalist (All)

BGR Technologies Inc

1995 Tremainsville Rd
Toledo, OH 43613-4037
(419) 475-8412
Fax: (419) 475-8539
Email: jmbach@bgrcompanies.com
Web: www.bgrcompanies.com

Summary: Our firm offers retained search, contract employment and direct hire of professionals in the folding carton and corrugated industries and IT specialists.

Key Contact - Specialty:
Mr. Dennis Vowles, Executive Recruiter - *Design, Packaging, Sales*
Mr. Morris Lewis, Executive Recruiter - *Computers (Programming), Design, Packaging, Sales*
Mr. Steven Kapela, Executive Recruiter - *Packaging, Sales*
Mr. Jason Bach, Executive Recruiter

Salary Minimum: $48,000

Functions: Packaging, IT

Industries: Generalist (All), Manufacturing, Paper, Printing, Packaging

Big 6 Search International Inc

1695 Pinellas Bayway S Apt E4
Saint Petersburg, FL 33715-2544
(727) 906-0580
Fax: (727) 906-0581
Email: ken@big6jobs.net
Web: www.big6jobs.com

Summary: We specialize in top tier consulting firms, B2B product vendors, software companies, pre-IPO and industry opportunities. Our core focuses are: business development, business intelligence, CRM, data warehousing, EAI, ERP, engineering, IT, networking, SCM, strategy, telecom (telephony and wireless) and web.

Key Contact - Specialty:
Mr. Kenneth Kubicki, CPA, President

Salary Minimum: $100,000

Functions: Generalist (All), Management, Senior Mgmt., Sales & Mktg., IT, MIS Mgmt., Systems Implem., Mgmt. Consultants

Industries: Services, Non-profits, Mgmt. Consulting, HR Services, E-commerce, IT Implementation, New Media, Telecoms, Telephony, Wireless, Government, Software, Accounting SW, Database SW, Development SW, Doc. Mgmt., Production SW, ERP SW, HR SW, Industry Specific SW, Networking, Comm. SW, Security SW

BilingualPro

11601 Wilshire Blvd Ste 500
Los Angeles, CA 90025-1741
(310) 575-1875
Fax: (310) 507-0272
Email: info@bilingualpro.com
Web: www.bilingualpro.com

Summary: We synergize top professional bilingual talent with the world's leading organizations. Specializing in recruiting and placing English speaking professionals fluent in one or more of the following languages: Spanish, Chinese, French, German, Italian, Japanese, Korean, Portuguese, Russian and more in positions that range from entry-level to middle and upper management.

Key Contact - Specialty:
Mr. Luis Massieu, Partner

Salary Minimum: $50,000

Functions: Generalist (All), Management, Senior Mgmt.

Industries: Generalist (All), Agri., Forestry, Mining, Construction, Manufacturing, Transportation, Wholesale, Retail, Finance, Services, Hospitality, Media, Communications, Government, Environmental Svcs., Aerospace, Packaging, Insurance, Real Estate, Software, Healthcare

Binder Hospitality

526 Silverbrook Dr
Danville, KY 40422-1076
(859) 239-0096
(859) 238-0046
Email: binder@mis.net

Summary: We work exclusively within the hospitality industry recruiting and placing executive and middle management for hotels, resorts, country clubs and restaurants. We have extensive executive operations experience in all phases of hospitality management.

Key Contact - Specialty:
Ms. Jan Binder, Executive Recruiter

Salary Minimum: $30,000

Functions: Senior Mgmt., Middle Mgmt., Sales & Mktg., HR Mgmt., Finance, Hospitality

Industries: Hospitality, Hotels, Resorts, Clubs, Restaurants, Full Service Restaurants

BioPharmaceutical, Medical Recruiters (BPM Recruiters)

PO Box 3738
Silverdale, WA 98383-3738
(360) 308-0038
(360) 830-4001
Email: bpm-recruiters@msn.com

Summary: Contingency search firm concentrating on specialty sales positions, sales force expansions, initial start-up hiring, management, managed care, marketing, medical liaison, clinical, scientific and regulatory affair positions. Industries include biopharmaceutical, pharmaceutical and medical device manufacturers. Candidates must have current industry experience.

Key Contact - Specialty:
Ms. Joan Maynard, Partner - *Pharmaceutical*
Ms. Lisa Ward, Partner - *Pharmaceutical*

Functions: Senior Mgmt., Middle Mgmt., Product Dev., Sales & Mktg., Mktg. Mgmt., Sales Mgmt., Sales Reps.

Industries: Drugs Mfg., Medical Devices

BioTech Solutions

791 Broadway
Kingston, NY 12401-5042
(914) 882-3407
Email: robert@biotechexecutivesearch.com
Web: www.biotechexecutivesearch.com

Summary: We are a placement firm dedicated to information technology within the financial, pharmaceutical, and consulting industries.

Key Contact - Specialty:
Mr. Robert Azzara, Principal - *Financial, Pharmaceutical*

Salary Minimum: $60,000

Functions: Generalist (All), IT

Industries: Generalist (All), Pharm Svcs., Haz. Waste, Aerospace, Software, Database SW, Development SW, ERP SW

Birch & Associés

740-2155 Rue Guy
Tour Guy
Montreal, QC H3H 2R9
Canada
(514) 846-1878
Fax: (514) 846-9395
Email: info@birch.ca
Web: www.birch.ca

Summary: We are specialists in executive recruiting. We carefully investigate each of our clients' needs and provide them with qualified candidates who have been rigorously evaluated. An attentive after hiring follow up ensures that the needs of our clients and candidates have been met. We also have another division involved in high technology recruiting.

Key Contact - Specialty:
Mr. Jerry Birch, President
Mr. Stanley Birch, Vice President

Salary Minimum: $65,000

Functions: Generalist (All)

Industries: Generalist (All), Wholesale, Retail, Finance, Software, Biotech/Life Sciences

Bishop Executive Services LLC

434 3rd St N
Jacksonville Beach, FL 32250-7029
(904) 241-1187
Email: jdevice@bellsouth.net
Web: www.besdevice.com

Summary: Our firm is a full service medical sales recruiting firm with a mission centered on establishing, building and strengthening partnerships with medical sales organizations as well as help, counsel and coach respective qualified candidates in their pursuit of obtaining a career in the medical sales industry.

Key Contact - Specialty:
Mr. Jim Bishop, Founder - *Biotechnology, Healthcare, Medical (Devices,Sales), Pharmaceutical*
Mrs. Liz Nadeau, Executive Search Consultant - *Biotechnology, Healthcare, Medical (Devices,Sales), Pharmaceutical*
Mrs. Elke O'Brien-Kletti, Executive Search Consultant - *Biotechnology, Healthcare, Medical (Devices,Sales), Pharmaceutical*

Functions: Healthcare, Sales & Mktg.

Industries: Healthcare

Bishop Partners LLC

8029 Forsyth Blvd
Saint Louis, MO 63105-1723
(314) 863-7755
Fax: (314) 863-7765
Email: bob@bishop-partners.com
Web: www.bishop-partners.com

Summary: We specialize in creative business, including trade shows and event marketing, with experience in advertising, marketing, graphic design and visual communications. Our specialization, expertise and experience targets creative and marketing-related organizations, including advertising agencies, design and sales promotion firms, along with trade show exhibit builders and client side marketing professionals.

Key Contact - Specialty:
Mr. G. Robert Bishop, Managing Member - *Advertising, Marketing*
Ms. Barbara Bishop, Member - *Administration, Advertising, Associations*

Salary Minimum: $50,000

Functions: Sales & Mktg., Advertising

Industries: Generalist (All), Mgmt. Consulting, Media, Advertising, Publishing, New Media, Broadcast, Film, Network Infrastructure, Packaging, Biotech/Life Sciences, Hospitals

Bishop Placement Service LLC

1321 Murfreesboro Pike Ste 600
Nashville, TN 37217-2648
(615) 367-6177
(800) 357-4504
Fax: (800) 769-1787
Email: tina@bishopplacement.com
Web: www.bishopplacement.com

Summary: Specializing in the search and placement of executives and mid-level management in the retail and restaurant industry. General managers to CEO's, and Human Resources Manager to Vice presidents of HR.

Key Contact - Specialty:
Ms. Tina Bishop, CPC, FMP, Owner & Recruiter
Mr. Otis H. Bishop, CPC - *Food service, Hospitality, Human resources, Management, Retail*

Salary Minimum: $35,000

Functions: Generalist (All), Management, HR Mgmt., Hospitality, Chefs

Industries: Generalist (All), Food, Bev., Tobacco, Textiles, Apparel, Retail, Hospitality, Restaurants, Quick Service Restaurants, Full Service Restaurants, Inst./Industrial Food Svc., Sports

Bismarck Executive Search Group

3715 Bismarck Cir
Sheboygan, WI 53083-2654
(920) 457-0798
Email: jim@bismarcksearch.com
Web: www.bismarcksearch.com

Summary: Our philosophy is to deliver only the highest level of value to our clients. Our goal is to develop long-term partnerships with both our clients and candidates by providing exceptional personal, professional, confidential and ethical service.

Key Contact - Specialty:
Mr. Jim Schwiner, President

Functions: Management

Industries: Plastics, Rubber, Metal Products, Misc. Mfg.

The Bixler Group

11502 NE 34th Ave Ste D
Vancouver, WA 98686-3942
(360) 574-7995
Fax: (360) 576-0189
Email: bixlergrp@comcast.net

Summary: Extensive experience in executive and professional search. We specialize in all aspects of the following industries: manufacturing, electronics, food, service and distribution. Positions we specialize in are as follows: GM, VP, CFO, CIO, IT manager, controller, cost, production, and sales & marketing.

Key Contact - Specialty:
Mr. Gary Bixler, Owner

Salary Minimum: $60,000

Functions: Generalist (All)

Industries: Generalist (All), Manufacturing, Food, Bev., Tobacco, Metal Products, Machine, Appliance, Computer Equip., Test, Measure Equip., Electronic, Elec. Components, Accounting, Packaging

BJB Associates

3750 Gateshead Dr
Annapolis, MD 21403-5027
(410) 268-0156
Fax: (410) 265-0545
Email: bjbrecruit@earthlink.net

Summary: Recruit for clients involved in the manufacture of plastic, non-woven or paper disposable consumer products, including medical disposables, paper converters, packaging and supporting chemical and engineering firms to these industries.

Key Contact - Specialty:
Ms. Bobbi Bauman, President & Owner - *Manufacturing*

Salary Minimum: $30,000

Functions: Generalist (All)

Industries: Manufacturing, Food, Bev., Tobacco, Paper, Soap, Perf., Cosmtcs., Medical Devices, Plastics, Rubber

BKG Inc

4 Sawgrass Village Dr Ste 150D
Ponte Vedra Beach, FL 32082-5022
(904) 273-5010
Fax: (888) 467-2169
Email: knipperbkg@prodigy.net

Summary: Attorneys wanted. We only place lawyers. Our clients are law firms.

Key Contact - Specialty:
Mr. William Knipper, President

Salary Minimum: $70,000

Functions: Legal, Attorneys

Industries: Legal

Edward Black Associates Inc

2 Saint Andrews Ter
Westerly, RI 02891-3672
(401) 348-6616
Fax: (401) 348-0882
Email: recruiters@edwardblack.com
Web: www.edwardblack.com

Summary: Specialists in medical device and life sciences recruiting. We understand the relationship between successful companies and successful people: they are one in the same. Our mission: bring them together.

Key Contact - Specialty:
Mr. Gerry Burns, Manager, Biotech & Pharmaceutical Div
Mr. Larry Burns, Manager, Medical Device Division

Salary Minimum: $50,000

Functions: Senior Mgmt., Mfg., Product Dev., Quality, Purchasing, Sales & Mktg., Sales Mgmt., MIS Mgmt., R&D, Engineering

Industries: Drugs Mfg., Medical Devices, Biotech/Life Sciences

Black Leopard Inc

29948 Rose Blossom Dr
Murrieta, CA 92563-4734
(800) 360-4191
(951) 461-4888
Fax: (951) 461-4868
Email: blackleopardinc@aol.com
Web: www.blackleopard.com

Summary: We provide executive search to the media industry with a special emphasis in newspaper publishing and secondly the meat and poultry processing industry. We identify top-tier talent from manager to senior executive in editorial, production, circulation, advertising, sales & marketing, operations, finance, HR, purchasing, quality assurance, R&D, maintenance and engineering.

Key Contact - Specialty:
Mr. Jerry Kurbatoff, President
Ms. Lauren Kurbatoff, Treasurer

Salary Minimum: $50,000

Functions: Generalist (All)

Industries: Food, Bev., Tobacco, Publishing

Blackhawk Executive Search Inc

PO Box 73005
San Clemente, CA 92673-0100
(435) 655-9000
(949) 940-9000
Email: resume@blackhawkusa.com
Web: www.blackhawkusa.com

Summary: Both principals are CPAs with extensive consulting and banking experience.

Key Contact - Specialty:
Mr. Phil Andersen, CPA, Director - *Financial services*
Ms. Phyllis Busser-Andersen, CPA, Director

Salary Minimum: $60,000

Functions: Sales & Mktg., CFOs

Industries: Generalist (All), Misc. Financial

Blackwood Associates Inc

883 Main St
Torrington, CT 06790-3349
(860) 489-0494
Fax: (860) 489-1534
Email: info@blackwoodassoc.com
Web: www.blackwoodassoc.com

Summary: We are an executive contingency search firm with clients throughout the country.

Key Contact - Specialty:
Mr. Jeffrey B. Blackwood, President
Lenni-Lee Nilsson, Office Manager
Ms. Allison Blackwood, Researcher, Marketing

Functions: Generalist (All), Nurses, Finance, Engineering, Architects, Legal, Attorneys, Paralegals

Industries: Generalist (All), Construction, Misc. Mfg., Banking, Misc. Financial, Architectural Svcs., Engineering Svcs., Healthcare, Hospitals, Long-term/Home Care

Michael Blair & Associates

950 Northgate Dr Ste 305
San Rafael, CA 94903-3436
(415) 492-8200
Fax: (415) 492-8288
Email: mike@michaelblair.com
Web: www.michaelblair.com

Summary: Our firm specializes in recruiting sales, sales management, pre-sales and pre-sales management professionals for high tech companies. Our concentration is within the Software Industry. Client's range from early stage companies to the largest most established companies.

Key Contact - Specialty:
Mr. Michael Hanna, President - *Information Technology, Sales*
Ms. Malka Hanna, Vice President - *Information Technology, Sales*

Salary Minimum: $50,000

Functions: Sales & Mktg.

Industries: Accounting SW, Database SW, Development SW, Doc. Mgmt., Production SW, ERP SW, HR SW, Mfg. SW, Marketing SW, Security SW, System SW

Blau & Associates

PO Box 1066
Fond du Lac, WI 54936-1066
(920) 923-5354
Email: jblau@charter.net
Web: webpages.charter.net/jblau

Summary: Our firm is the premier executive search firm servicing the packaging machinery, materials handling and conveyor manufacturing industry.

Key Contact - Specialty:
Mr. Jeffrey Blau, President & Chief Executive Officer

Salary Minimum: $40,000

Functions: Generalist (All)

Industries: Generalist (All), Construction, Manufacturing, Packaging

BLB Consulting Inc

230 Park Ave Rm 665
New York, NY 10169-0665
(212) 808-0577
(212) 808-0578
Fax: (212) 338-9696
Email: hr@blbco.com
Web: www.blbco.com

Summary: Known for our professional but personal approach to placement. Companies range from start up firms to major investment, law and Fortune 500 companies.

Key Contact - Specialty:
Ms. Barbara Bartell, CPC, President - *Human resources*

Salary Minimum: $50,000

Functions: HR Mgmt.

Industries: Generalist (All)

BLH Recruiting

3030 W Salt Creek Ln Ste 121
Arlington Heights, IL 60005-5000
(630) 779-7312
(847) 577-0300
Fax: (847) 577-8131
Email: bryan@blhrecruiting.com
Web: www.blhrecruiting.com

Summary: We are an executive search firm, providing service to Fortune 500 companies. Focusing on management, IT, Financial, and Marketing.

Key Contact - Specialty:
Mr. Bryan Hearn,, AIRS, CIR, Executive Recruiter - *Biomedical, Executives, High technology, Information Systems, Information Technology*

Salary Minimum: $60,000

Functions: HR Mgmt., Finance, IT

Industries: Generalist (All)

Barbara Bliss Co Ltd

1465 Post Rd E
Westport, CT 06880-5528
(203) 256-3593
Fax: (203) 256-3594
Email: bbliss2@optonline.com

Summary: Comprehensive management selection and consultation for all disciplines of direct marketing, database and interactive media, particularly adept at building staff and professional teams for new or expanding direct marketing activities.

Key Contact - Specialty:
Ms. Barbara P. Bliss, President - *Direct marketing*

Salary Minimum: $50,000

Functions: Management, Senior Mgmt., Middle Mgmt., Sales & Mktg., Advertising, Sales Mgmt., Direct Mktg., Customer Svc., DB Admin.

Industries: Banking, Media, Advertising, Publishing, New Media, Broadcast, Film, Telecoms

Bliss Pierce & Associates / Hopson Professional Search

301 Gallaher View Rd Ste 106
Knoxville, TN 37919-5302
(865) 963-1100
Fax: (865) 690-8815
Email: bliss@phrecruiting.com
Web: www.phrecruiting.com

Summary: We specialize in restaurant, hospitality, retail product development, mortgage banking and security industry retail broker positions.

Key Contact - Specialty:
Mr. Bliss Pierce
Mr. Scott Hopson

Functions: Management, Senior Mgmt., Sales & Mktg.

Industries: Retail, Finance, Brokers, Mutual/Hedge Funds, Misc. Financial, Hospitality, Restaurants

Michael Bloch Associates Inc

PO Box 555
Penfield, NY 14526-0555
(585) 388-6440
Email: mbloch@rochester.rr.com
Web: www.michaelblochsearch.com

Summary: We work exclusively in the recruitment of attorneys for law firms. Our understanding of the intricacies of legal recruiting makes it possible for us to produce superior results for our clients. Our searches are conducted in an attentive, ethical and professional manner. We are very selective about the clients we work with and therefore, are unable to work with every law firm or company that requests our services.

Key Contact - Specialty:
Mr. Michael Bloch, President

Salary Minimum: $75,000

Functions: Attorneys

Industries: Legal, Non-Classifiable

Blonstein & Associates Executive Placement

412 Spring Valley Ct
Chesterfield, MO 63017-2721
(314) 220-8801
Fax: (501) 641-3038
Email: steve@thatismyjob.com
Web: www.thatismyjob.com

Summary: We provide placement services to our clients seeking Sales people and Sales Management in many fields but mainly in the pharmaceutical, biotech, and medical sales markets.We are not restricted to specialize in one geographic area.

Key Contact - Specialty:
Mr. Steve Blonstein, President

Functions: Sales & Mktg.

Industries: Generalist (All), Services, Pharm Svcs.

The Howard C Bloom Company

3308 Preston Rd Ste 350
173
Plano, TX 75093-7471
(972) 208-6600
Email: hbloom@bloomlegalsearch.com
Web: www.bloomlegalsearch.com

Summary: Our firm places attorneys including partners, senior associates, practice areas, law firm mergers and in-house counsel.

Key Contact - Specialty:
Mr. Howard Bloom, President
Ms. Joyce Bloom, Vice President

Functions: Attorneys

Industries: Legal

Bloom, Gross & Associates

625 N Michigan Ave Ste 200
Chicago, IL 60611-3162
(312) 654-4550
Fax: (312) 654-4551
Email: kbloom@bloomgross.com
Web: www.bloomgross.com

Summary: Our firm specializes in mid to upper-level searches in four areas: marketing and market research; public relations; advertising, and sales promotion/direct marketing. We work with Fortune 500 companies and agencies of all sizes.

Key Contact - Specialty:
Ms. Karen Bloom, Principal

Salary Minimum: $60,000

Functions: Advertising, Mktg. Mgmt., Direct Mktg., PR, Graphic Designers

Industries: Manufacturing, Food, Bev., Tobacco, Soap, Perf., Cosmtcs., Consumer Elect., Misc. Financial, Pharm Svcs., Hospitality, Restaurants, Media, Advertising, New Media, Telecoms, Real Estate, Healthcare

Blue Moon Recruiting Company

PO Box 3
Port Gamble, WA 98364-0003
(360) 765-3800
(888) 777-8179
Fax: (360) 765-3808
Email: riggsv@bluemoonrecruiting.com
Web: www.bluemoonrecruiting.com

Summary: A contingency based physician recruitment company, working to fill the needs of hospital, clinics and doctors in perfectly matched placements.

Key Contact - Specialty:
Ms. Vanessa Riggs

Functions: Physicians

Industries: Healthcare, Hospitals, Women's, Non-Classifiable

Blue Rock Consulting

9 Woodmont St
Portland, ME 04102-2708
(207) 780-0960
(888) 780-9751
Email: bluerock@maine.rr.com
Web: www.bluerock-maine.com

Summary: Property casualty recruiting by experienced insurance professionals who match the performance needs of our clients with tailored candidate solutions.

Key Contact - Specialty:
Mr. Paul F. Stulgaitis, President

Functions: Senior Mgmt.

Industries: Insurance, Casualty, Commercial

Blue Suit Consulting Inc

1700 Park St Ste 206
Naperville, IL 60563-2370
(630) 369-9300
Fax: (630) 369-7698
Web: www.bluesuit.com

Summary: We provide contract, contract for hire and direct placement with core competencies, including: web enabling, e-business and eCommerce, distributed systems, network, legacy, application development, engineering, project management, system support, troubleshooting and outsourcing.

Key Contact - Specialty:
Mr. Mark McGee, President

Salary Minimum: $40,000

Functions: IT

Industries: Generalist (All), Energy, Utilities, Food, Bev., Tobacco, Finance, Banking, Invest. Banking, Telecoms, Insurance, Software, Healthcare

BluePrint

3500 American Blvd W Ste 680
Minneapolis, MN 55431-4415
(952) 830-4111
Fax: (952) 830-4044
Email: jane.salmen@blueprintpeople.com
Web: www.blueprintpeople.com

Summary: We are a generalist firm with national coverage. We conduct contingency and retained searches. Our staff has combined search experience. We focus on developing long term relationships with our clients.

Key Contact - Specialty:
Ms. Jane Salmen, President
Ms. Susan M. Flagler, Consultant
Ms. Kristi Haselman, Search Consultant
Ms. Marni Sampair, Search Consultant
Ms. Sara Strauss, Search Consultant

The BMW Group Inc

40 Exchange Pl Ste 700
New York, NY 10005-2767
(212) 943-8800
Fax: (212) 943-8852
Email: partner@careerobject.com
Web: www.careerobject.com

Summary: We are a full-service organization specializing in the placement of IT professionals. We place both employees and consultants.

Key Contact - Specialty:
Mr. Alan Burke, Principal - *Technical*
Mr. Ronald Weiss, Principal - *Technical*

Salary Minimum: $75,000

Functions: Generalist (All), IT

Industries: Generalist (All), Database SW, Development SW, System SW

Bodner Inc

372 5th Ave Apt 9K
New York, NY 10018-8110
(212) 714-0371
Email: mail@bodnerinc.com

Summary: Specialize in placement of accounting and finance professionals.

Key Contact - Specialty:
Ms. Marilyn S. Bodner, President - *Finance*

Salary Minimum: $60,000

Functions: Middle Mgmt., Finance

Industries: Generalist (All)

Bogle & Associates

PO Box 9347
Denver, CO 80209-0347
(720) 570-1888
Fax: (720) 489-3810
Email: john@bogleassociates.com
Web: www.bogleassociates.com

Summary: Our firm is focused on sales, service and marketing positions within the medical imaging market to bring exceptional talent to the medical imaging industry while encouraging personal, consultative relationships with the companies and candidates that we represent. We pride ourselves on matching the strengths of candidates to the demands of key positions within leading medical imaging manufacturers.

Key Contact - Specialty:
Mr. Tom Bogle, Managing Principal - *Sales*
Ms. Cindy Windsor, Associate, Chicago - *Management, Marketing*
Mr. Carter Morgan, Associate
Mr. Craig Messick, Associate, Sales

Salary Minimum: $45,000

Functions: Sales & Mktg., Mktg. Mgmt., Sales Mgmt., IT

Industries: Medical Devices, Biotech/Life Sciences, Healthcare

Branches:
508 14th St
Huntington Beach, CA 92648-4042
(714) 949-4163
Fax: (208) 439-7375

PO Box 1750
Palm Springs, CA 92263-1750
(760) 327-9002
Email: andrew@bogleassociates.com
Key Contact - Specialty:
Mr. Andrew Archdale, Partner Associate

814 Durham Rd
Madison, CT 06443-8005
(203) 676-4165
Fax: (203) 421-0695
Email: tierney@bogleassociates.com
Key Contact - Specialty:
Mr. Tom Tierney, Managing Partner

236 Arbor Woods Cir
Oldsmar, FL 34677-4655
(813) 569-7778
Email: carl@bogleassociates.com
Key Contact - Specialty:
Mr. Carl Newcomb

205 Wellington St
Traverse City, MI 49686-2609
(231) 947-7304
Email: randy@bogleassociates.com

153 Cannongate III
Nashua, NH 03063-1954
(603) 595-7392
Fax: (603) 880-8221
Email: brian@bogleassociates.com
Key Contact - Specialty:
Mr. Brian LaBonte, Associate

Bohan & Bradstreet Inc

741 Boston Post Rd Ste 101
Concept Park
Guilford, CT 06437-2743
(203) 453-5535
Fax: (203) 453-5545
Email: info@bohan-bradstreet.com
Web: www.bohan-bradstreet.com

Summary: Specialize in filling management to executive-level within emerging business to Fortune 1000 corporations.

Key Contact - Specialty:
Mr. Edward B. Bradstreet, CPC, President
Mr. Peter M. Cahill, Vice President - *Engineering, Marketing*
Ms. Victoria M. Pallotto, CPC, Vice President - *Engineering, Marketing*
Mr. Philip H. Pearlman, CPA, Vice President
Ms. Julie A. Hipp, Vice President - *Consumer, Market research, Marketing, Sales, Supply Chain*
Ms. Kristi T. Baxter, Search Consultant
Mr. William J. Mack, III, CPC, Search Consultant
Mr. Jay C. Corsaut, Search Consultant
Ms. Jennifer C. Worcester, Search Consultant
Mr. William H. Mooney, Search Consultant
Ms. Amy L. Lemon, Search Consultant

Salary Minimum: $60,000

Functions: Generalist (All), Senior Mgmt., Mfg., Materials, Sales & Mktg., Finance, IT, Engineering

Industries: Generalist (All), Manufacturing, Wholesale, Retail, Finance, Services, Insurance

Dan Bolen & Associates LLC

9741 N 90th Pl Ste 200
Scottsdale, AZ 85258-5065
(480) 767-9000
Fax: (480) 767-0100
Email: danbolen@mindspring.com
Web: www.danbolenassoc.com

Summary: Our firm specializes in executive search and recruiting for the rotating and industrial equipment industry, i.e.: pumps, compressors, motors, turbines, valves, etc. We recruit for all disciplines: general management, sales & marketing, engineering and manufacturing.

Key Contact - Specialty:
Mr. Dan Bolen, Owner - *Engineering, General management, Manufacturing, Sales*
Mr. Dan Marshall, Account Executive - *Engineering, General management, Sales*

Functions: Generalist (All), Senior Mgmt., Middle Mgmt., Product Dev., Production, Plant Mgmt., Sales Mgmt., Engineering

Industries: Generalist (All), Energy, Utilities, Oil & Gas, Manufacturing, Food, Bev., Tobacco, Chemicals, Machine, Appliance, Misc. Mfg., Engineering Svcs.

Mark Bolno & Associates Inc

4910 14th St W Ste 307
Bradenton, FL 34207-2481
(941) 751-2276
Email: bolno@earthlink.net

Summary: We recruit upper-management professionals in the food and beverage manufacturing industries. We specialize in plant management, R&D, quality assurance, quality control, HR, sales & marketing and corporate hotel operations.

Key Contact - Specialty:
Mr. Mark Bolno, President

Salary Minimum: $50,000

Functions: Generalist (All), Senior Mgmt., Middle Mgmt., Product Dev., Production, Plant Mgmt., HR Mgmt., R&D

Industries: Generalist (All), Food, Bev., Tobacco, Hospitality, Hotels, Resorts, Clubs

Bolton Group

PO Box 278551
Sacramento, CA 95827-8551
(916) 362-5000
(800) 820-9115
Fax: (800) 820-9115
Email: sherryj@boltongrp.com
Web: www.boltongrp.com

Summary: We specialize in the telecom/datacom industries, placing engineers. We will cold call into companies, looking for the candidate you specify. We also network with other recruiters for a larger selection of candidates.

Key Contact - Specialty:
Ms. Sherry Junker, Senior Recruiter - *Networking, Telecommunications*

Functions: Generalist (All), Middle Mgmt., Product Dev., Production, Systems Analysis, Systems Dev., Engineering

Industries: Communications, Telecoms, Telephony, Digital, Wireless, Fiber Optic,

Network Infrastructure, RF/Microwave, Industry Specific SW, Mfg. SW, Networking, Comm. SW, System SW

The Bolton Group LLC

3500 Piedmont Rd NE Ste 625
Atlanta, GA 30305-1503
(404) 228-4280
Fax: (404) 228-2060
Email: info@boltongroup.com
Web: www.boltongroup.com

Summary: An executive search firm specializing in accounting and finance placements. We offer placement assistance for a variety of disciplines and positions - ranging from temp A/P clerks to executive level, as well as consulting services.

Key Contact - Specialty:
Mr. Ralph Jones, CPA, MTX, Principal
Mr. Thomas J. Nims, Principal

Salary Minimum: $25,000

Functions: Finance

Industries: Generalist (All)

Branches:
2202 N West Shore Blvd Ste 200
Tampa, FL 33607-5749
(813) 288-4648

7400 Carmel Executive Park Dr Ste 332
Charlotte, NC 28226-0502
(704) 552-3678

Bond & Company

10 Saugatuck Ave
Westport, CT 06880-5720
(203) 221-3233
Fax: (203) 341-7729
Email: richard.bond@snet.net
Web: www.snetyp.com/bondcompany

Summary: We are a boutique recruiting firm doing mostly financial, with some marketing and logistics. We specialize in treasury positions and marketing/financial controller slots. We have done a lot of work for companies with sales in the $200 million to $1 billion ranges.

Key Contact - Specialty:
Mr. Richard Bond, Principal

Functions: Finance

Industries: Generalist (All)

Ann Bond Associates Inc

PO Box 8529
Erie, PA 16505-0529
(814) 838-2936
Email: annbondassociates@earthlink.net
Web: www.annbondassociates.com

Summary: We represent well-known major food manufacturers, distributors and brokers who seek sales and marketing managers nationwide in foodservice and retail positions.

Key Contact - Specialty:
Mr. Gary Smith, President
Mrs. Barbara Smith, Vice President

Salary Minimum: $100,000

Functions: Sales & Mktg.

Industries: Food, Bev., Tobacco

Bond Technologies

1650 W Farm Rd
Chaska, MN 55318-9507
(952) 403-9303
Email: mcline@bondtechnologies.com
Web: www.bondtechnologies.com

Summary: Bond Technologies is a national search firm specializing in software engineering, real-time/embedded systems, controls, and circuit design. Our numerous succesful search assignments include positions ranging from senior engineer through president. We have sucessfully recruited candidates from as far away as Australia, and have filled US GM/President positions for foreign companies.

Key Contact - Specialty:
Mr. Mark Cline, CPC, Founder

Functions: R&D

Industries: Medical Devices, Motor Vehicles, Computer Equip., Consumer Elect., Test, Measure Equip., Telephony, Digital, Wireless, Defense

Bone Personnel Inc

6424 Lima Rd
Fort Wayne, IN 46818-1424
(260) 489-3350
(888) 808-1081
Fax: (260) 490-5866
Email: info@bonepersonnel.com
Web: www.bonepersonnel.com

Summary: Full service licensed employment agency specializing in manufacturing, engineering, HR, accounting, sales & marketing and IT marketplace.

Key Contact - Specialty:
Mr. Bruce A. Bone, CPC, Owner

Functions: Generalist (All)

Industries: Mfg. SW

Bonifield Associates

1 Eves Dr Ste 115
Marlton, NJ 08053-8105
(856) 596-3300
Fax: (856) 596-8866
Email: info@bonifield.com
Web: www.bonifield.com

Summary: All of our professional consultants have experience and background in the insurance industry. We experience specializing for clients ranging from $2 billion to $90 billion in assets. We have served over 300 clients.

Key Contact - Specialty:
Mr. Richard L. Tyson, CLU, President

Salary Minimum: $40,000

Functions: Generalist (All), Management

Industries: Insurance, Casualty, Claims, Life, Commercial, Re-Insurance

The Bontempo Group Inc

(formerly known as Dunhill Professional Search of Bucks-Mont)
801 W Street Rd
Feasterville Trevose, PA 19053-7335
(215) 357-6590
Fax: (215) 953-1612
Email: dave@bontempogroup.com
Web: www.bontempogroup.com

Summary: Specializing in the permanent placement of lawyers, paralegals, sales, business development, marketing, accounting & finance professionals. We handle administrative assistants and office support on a temporary and permanent basis.

Key Contact - Specialty:
Ms. Mary F. Bontempo, President

Mr. David Bontempo, CPC, Vice President - *Accounting, Consulting, Education (Higher), Executives, Marketing*
Ms. Dale Decker, Staffing Manager - *Accounting (Bookkeeping), Administration, Non-profit, Office (Administration,Support)*

Salary Minimum: $35,000

Functions: Sales & Mktg., Finance, Legal, Attorneys, Paralegals

Industries: Generalist (All), Energy, Utilities, Manufacturing, Finance, Banking, Pharm Svcs., Legal, Accounting, Advertising, Publishing, Telecoms, Packaging, Software

Borchert Associates

973 Fall Crk
Grapevine, TX 76051-8248
(817) 424-3193
(888) 818-2801
Fax: (972) 999-4600
Email: greg@glborchert.com
Web: www.glborchert.com

Summary: We have experience in completing mid-management through executive-level assignments in the metal casting field.

Key Contact - Specialty:
Mr. Gregory L. Borchert, President
Ms. Linda Borchert, CPA, Manager, Business

Salary Minimum: $65,000

Functions: Generalist (All)

Industries: Metal Products

Born & Bicknell Inc

5605 NW 29th St
Margate, FL 33063-1531
(954) 956-0000
(800) 376-2676
Fax: (954) 956-9940
Email: info@bornbicknell.com
Web: www.bornbicknell.com

Summary: We offer premium physician recruitment services which are personalized, efficient and cost effective for today's growth oriented healthcare provider organizations.

Key Contact - Specialty:
Ms. Jane E. Born, Chief Executive Officer
Mr. Samuel J. Born, Chief Operating Officer

Functions: Generalist (All), Physicians

Industries: Generalist (All), Healthcare

Branches:
128 Marlou Cir
Ruston, LA 71270-3067
(800) 374-2676
(318) 254-8481
Fax: (318) 254-8335
Key Contact - Specialty:
Ms. Helen M. Bicknell, RN, President

Bornholdt Shivas & Friends Executive Recruiters

33 Concord Rd
Port Washington, NY 11050-4326
(516) 767-1849
Fax: (516) 767-6727
Email: jbornhol@optonline.net
Web: www.bsandf.com

Summary: We are an executive search firm that concentrates in packaged goods marketing and sales; prescription/OTC pharmaceutical drugs marketing and sales, as well as software development marketing and sales.

Key Contact - Specialty:
Mr. John N. Bornholdt, President & Chief
  Executive Officer
Ms. Elizabeth Bornholdt, Placement Counselor -
  Pharmaceutical

Salary Minimum: $60,000

Functions: Generalist (All), Management, Middle
  Mgmt.

Industries: Manufacturing, Food, Bev., Tobacco,
  Soap, Perf., Cosmtcs., Drugs Mfg., Medical
  Devices, Computer Equip., Services, Non-
  profits, Pharm Svcs., Mgmt. Consulting,
  Restaurants, Media, Communications,
  Telecoms, Digital, Wireless, Fiber Optic,
  Network Infrastructure, Software, Biotech/Life
  Sciences

Bos Business Consultants

6925 E Quaker St
Orchard Park, NY 14127-2532
(800) 836-4220
(716) 662-0800
Email: careers@recruitstaff.com
Web: www.recruitstaff.com

Summary: Recruiting firm working with
manufacturing companies helping them locate
qualified engineering, marketing, finance, quality,
manufacturing engineering, R&D and IT
personnel. Industries are medical device,
automotive, consumer durables, aerospace,
electronics, plus others.

Key Contact - Specialty:
Mr. John Bos, Director - *Engineering,
  Manufacturing, Marketing*

Salary Minimum: $40,000

Functions: Mfg., Product Dev., Production, Plant
  Mgmt., Quality, Finance, Engineering

Industries: Generalist (All), Manufacturing,
  Medical Devices, Plastics, Rubber, Metal
  Products, Machine, Appliance, Motor Vehicles,
  Defense, Compliance, Aerospace, Packaging,
  ERP SW, Industry Specific SW, Mfg. SW,
  Marketing SW

Bosworth Field Associates

404-111 Richmond St W
Toronto, ON M5H 2G4
Canada
(416) 362-2151
Fax: (416) 214-1632
Email: resumes@bosworthfield.com
Web: www.bosworthfield.com

Summary: We have considerable expertise in
positions within finance, accounting, tax and risk
management in both the financial services and
general industry sectors.

Key Contact - Specialty:
Ms. Gillian Lansdowne, President

Salary Minimum: $50,000

Functions: Finance, CFOs, Taxes, Risk Mgmt.

Industries: Generalist (All), Finance, Misc.
  Financial, Accounting

BOWEN

(formerly known as BOWEN Workforce Solutions
Inc)
101-525 7 Ave SW
Transcanada Pipelines Tower- R
Calgary, AB T2P 3V5
Canada
(403) 262-1156
Fax: (403) 537-6952
Email: info@bowenworks.ca
Web: www.bowenworks.ca

Summary: Our company is Canada's leading
provider of flexible workforce management
solutions with a portfolio that spans recruitment,
outsourced HR, contractor payment and reporting
services.

Key Contact - Specialty:
Ms. Shannon Bowen-Smed, Chief Executive
  Officer & President
Ms. Laverne Bowen, Chairman
Ms. Anna Nelson, BComm, CA, Vice President,
  Financial Services
Mr. Ken Vinge, Vice President, Sales -
  Marketing, Sales

Ms. Debbie Wershler, Vice President, Flexible
  Workforce Sltns

Howard Bowen Consulting

977 Vineridge Run Ste 14-203
Altamonte Springs, FL 32714-1775
(407) 445-3644
Email: hbowcon@bellsouth.net

Summary: We service management consulting
firms and corporations on the cutting-edge of
business processes and technologies. Our firm is a
provider of high/mid-level professionals
experienced with strategic and tactical-business
issues (i.e. business development, supply chain,
re-engineering, ERP IT infrastructure, strategic
sourcing, transition to web e-commerce, integrated
systems, applications management, and
outsourcing).

Key Contact - Specialty:
Mr. Howard Bowen, President

Salary Minimum: $90,000

Functions: Generalist (All), Management, Senior
  Mgmt., Admin. Svcs., Mfg., MIS Mgmt.,
  Systems Analysis, Mgmt. Consultants

Industries: Generalist (All), Energy, Utilities, Oil
  & Gas, Manufacturing, Drugs Mfg., Motor
  Vehicles, Misc. Mfg., Electronic, Elec.
  Components, Robotics, Consumer Goods,
  Transportation, Pharm Svcs., Mgmt. Consulting,
  E-commerce, IT Implementation, Engineering
  Svcs., Logistics Svcs., Supply Chain Mgmt.,
  Software, Accounting SW, Development SW,
  ERP SW, HR SW, Industry Specific SW, Mfg.
  SW, Networking, Comm. SW

BowersThomas

PO Box 361418
Los Angeles, CA 90036-9388
(323) 938-4236
Email: bowersthomas@earthlink.net

Summary: We are an attorney search and
placement for corporations and law firms. We
provide ethical, qualitative and insightful search
services for all levels of attorneys in commercial
practice areas. All have JD/LL.B and US Bar.

Key Contact - Specialty:
Ms. Pat Thomas

Salary Minimum: $80,000

Functions: Generalist (All), Attorneys

Industries: Generalist (All), Manufacturing,
  Finance, Legal, Media, Real Estate,
  Biotech/Life Sciences

Bowie & Associates Inc

100 N Beechwood Ave Ste 200
Baltimore, MD 21228-4927
(410) 747-1919
Email: abowie@us.net

Summary: Management recruitment services to
third party logistics and supply chain management
clients.

Key Contact - Specialty:
Mr. Andrew Bowie

Salary Minimum: $60,000

Functions: Generalist (All)

Industries: Transportation

James T Boyce & Associates

2 Tansley Terr
Carlisle, ON L0R 1H2
Canada
(905) 690-8394
Email: james.boyce@3web.net

Summary: Search and placement services,
specializing primarily within the life insurance
industry and employee benefit fields.

Key Contact - Specialty:
Mr. James T. Boyce

Functions: Generalist (All)

Industries: HR Services, Insurance

Boylston Search Associates

745 Boylston St Ste 407
Boston, MA 02116-2636
(617) 587-3000
Fax: (617) 587-3030
Email: careers@boylstonsearch.com
Web: www.boylstonsearch.com

Summary: Financial and Managerial Placement
specializes in the recruitment and placement of
Accounting and Finance professionals at the
senior, managerial, and executive levels in eastern
New England.

Key Contact - Specialty:
Mr. R. Steven Dow, Principal - *Finance*
Mr. Barry Zeff, Principal
Mr. Mark Sullivan, Principal

Salary Minimum: $70,000

Functions: Management, Finance, CFOs

Industries: Generalist (All)

BPM International

5559 Cactus Cir
Spring Hill, FL 34606-5514
(352) 686-9936
Email: brianmor@tampabay.rr.com

Summary: We provide executive search to the
healthcare industry; plus, we recruit foreign nurses
and LPNs. We specialize in managed
care/HMOs/pharmaceuticals for human and
veterinary/biotechnology/health
insurance/hospitals/health network systems. We
recruit for all senior-level positions, including:
boards, CEOs, CFOs, COOs, CIOs, VPs, directors
and managers.

Key Contact - Specialty:
Mr. Brian P. Moore, Principal

Salary Minimum: $60,000

Functions: Healthcare, Nurses, Int'l.

Industries: Generalist (All), Drugs Mfg., Medical
  Devices, Non-profits, Pharm Svcs., Mgmt.
  Consulting, Biotech/Life Sciences, Healthcare,
  Hospitals, Long-term/Home Care, Occupational
  Therapy

Braam & Associates

845 Chardonnay Cir
Petaluma, CA 94954-7408
(707) 765-9090
Fax: (707) 765-9190
Email: braam10@aol.com

Summary: We take pride in locating exceptional candidates with specific qualifications to fill the needs of outstanding clients.

Key Contact - Specialty:
Ms. Christine White, General Partner - *Construction, Engineering, Sales*

Functions: Generalist (All), Advertising, Mktg. Mgmt., Sales Mgmt., MIS Mgmt., Systems Implem., Engineering

Industries: Generalist (All), Construction, Media, Telecoms, Software

Brackin & Sayers Associates Inc
1000 McKnight Park Dr Ste 1001
Pittsburgh, PA 15237-6531
(412) 367-4644
Fax: (412) 367-3512
Email: jbrackin@brackinandsayers.com
Web: www.brackinandsayers.com

Summary: Specialize in HR, finance & accounting, sales, manufacturing/engineering and IT, utilizing our resources and those of affiliate recruiting firms.

Key Contact - Specialty:
Mr. Jim Brackin, Partner - *Human resources*
Mr. Bruce Sayers, Partner

Salary Minimum: $50,000

Functions: Mfg., HR Mgmt., Finance

Industries: Generalist (All)

Bradford & Galt Inc
4 Cityplace Dr Ste 100
Saint Louis, MO 63141-7062
(314) 997-4644
(800) 997-4644
Fax: (314) 991-5053
Email: bcl@bgcs.com
Web: www.bradfordandgalt.com

Summary: Our services include IS contracting/consulting temp staffing.

Key Contact - Specialty:
Mr. Bradford Layton, President & Chief Executive Officer

Salary Minimum: $30,000

Functions: Generalist (All), IT, MIS Mgmt., Systems Analysis, Systems Dev., Systems Implem., Systems Support

Industries: Generalist (All)

Branches:
207 Main St Ste 405
Peoria, IL 61602-1397
(309) 674-2000
Fax: (309) 674-8300
Email: webpeo@bgcs.com
Key Contact - Specialty:
Mr. David Voloto, Chief Operating Officer

9200 Indian Creek Pkwy Ste 570
Overland Park, KS 66210-2017
(913) 663-1264
Fax: (913) 345-9742
Email: webkc@bgcs.com

Bradford Consulting
12305 Water Oak Dr
Keller, TX 76248-6760
(817) 741-0854
Email: jobs@bradfordconsulting.com
Web: www.bradfordconsulting.com

Summary: We provide executive and professional search as well as performing staffing consulting for corporate HR departments. We also perform audits of the staffing departments, including an evaluation of the recruiting process, career

websites and related applicant tracking systems and the selection methods. We specialize in performance-based hiring. We also develop customized interviewing and evaluation guides for individual positions as well as for families of jobs.

Key Contact - Specialty:
Mr. Carl Bradford, President - *Management*
Mr. Carter Bradford, Vice President - *Technology*

Salary Minimum: $100,000

Functions: Management, Middle Mgmt., Sales & Mktg., HR Mgmt., Staffing, Training, Mgmt. Consultants

Industries: Generalist (All), Manufacturing, Finance, Services, Mgmt. Consulting, HR Services, IT Implementation, Supply Chain Mgmt, Communications, Telecoms, Software, Accounting SW, ERP SW, HR SW, Mfg. SW, Marketing SW, System SW, Training SW

Bradgate Associates Recruiting
141 Main St Ste 1
Metuchen, NJ 08840-2743
(732) 452-9041
(404) 839-4351
Fax: (206) 309-7153
Email: kplummer@bradgateassciates.com
Web: www.bradgateassociates.com

Summary: We are a placement firm, dedicated to providing exemplary permanent staffing services to a broad base of clients and applicants alike. We provide successful recruitment solutions for clients throughout the USA, Canada and United Kingdom.

Key Contact - Specialty:
Ms. Kiandra Plummer, Executive Recruiter
Mr. John Abey, Executive Recruiter

Functions: Generalist (All)

Industries: Generalist (All)

Bradley & Associates
10006 Russwill Ln
Union, KY 41091-9518
(859) 657-6149
Fax: (859) 657-6159
Email: kenneth.bradley@insightbb.com

Summary: We are a small, high-quality firm specializing in technology, finance and engineering positions.

Key Contact - Specialty:
Mr. Ken Bradley, Owner - *Engineering, Finance*

Salary Minimum: $50,000

Functions: Generalist (All)

Industries: Generalist (All)

Doug Bradley & Associates LLC
108 Poplar Pl
Manitou Springs, CO 80829-2518
(719) 685-5499
(866) 322-2733
Fax: (719) 685-5504
Email: doug.bradley@dbcareer.com
Web: www.dbcareer.com

Summary: We are an executive search firm specializing in IT, healthcare, sales & marketing and eCommerce. Our clientele consist of the top professionals who demand the best from the executive search process. Our consultants believe in cultivating a relationship that leaves no stone unturned.

Key Contact - Specialty:
Mr. Douglas Bradley, General Manager

Salary Minimum: $75,000

Functions: Senior Mgmt., Middle Mgmt., Sales & Mktg., Sales Mgmt., CFOs, MIS Mgmt., Mgmt. Consultants

Industries: Energy, Utilities, Manufacturing, Computer Equip., Electronic, Elec. Components, Services, Mgmt. Consulting, E-commerce, IT Implementation, Hospitality, Telecoms, Government, Software, Database SW, ERP SW, Healthcare, Hospitals, Long-term/Home Care

Bradshaw & Associates
1850 Parkway Pl SE Ste 420
Marietta, GA 30067-8265
(770) 426-5600
(770) 993-1600
Fax: (770) 993-6777
Email: rod@baserver.com
Web: www.baserver.com

Summary: Our career development services specialize in the recruitment and placement of entry to upper level professional talent. Over half of our applicants possess technical degrees and/or MBAs. Our entire staff has extensive experience and has attained a minimum of a bachelor's degree.

Key Contact - Specialty:
Mr. Rod Bradshaw, CPC, MHRM, Manager, Consulting
Mr. Orlando Rodriguez, CPC, Manager, Recruiting - *Hospitality*

Functions: Generalist (All)

Industries: Generalist (All)

BranCo Search Inc
PO Box 488
Niwot, CO 80544-0488
(303) 652-8370
Fax: (303) 652-8369
Email: f.boruff@comcast.net

Summary: We are a privately owned recruiting company specializing in the placement of engineers and management positions in the food manufacturing industry. Ownership of the business has extensive experience (supervisors to VPs of operations) in the industry.

Key Contact - Specialty:
Mr. Fran Boruff, President - *Food, Manufacturing*
Ms. Bettie Boruff, Administrative Assistant

Functions: Generalist (All), Senior Mgmt., Production, Plant Mgmt., Quality, Productivity, Purchasing, Materials Plng.

Industries: Generalist (All), Food, Bev., Tobacco, Chemicals, Drugs Mfg., Transportation

Brandjes Associates
PO Box 5971
Baltimore, MD 21282-5971
(410) 484-5423
Fax: (410) 484-6140
Email: michael@brandjes.us

Summary: A small, very specialized financial services recruiting firm, primarily banking.

Key Contact - Specialty:
Mr. Michael Brandjes, Principal
Ms. Suzanne Frock, Principal

Salary Minimum: $75,000

Functions: Generalist (All), Management, Senior Mgmt., Middle Mgmt., CFOs, Cash Mgmt., Credit, Risk Mgmt.

Industries: Finance, Banking, Invest. Banking, Brokers, Venture Cap., Mutual/Hedge Funds, Misc. Financial

Brandt Associates

PO Box 189
Dalton, PA 18414-0189
(570) 563-2058
Fax: (570) 563-2058
Email: wb4cape@aol.com

Summary: We are a recruiting firm for mid and senior-level management positions with a greater than average success rate. Effective and efficient is the way we do business.

Key Contact - Specialty:
Mr. William E. Brandt, President

Salary Minimum: $50,000

Functions: Generalist (All), Mfg., HR Mgmt., Finance, IT, MIS Mgmt., Systems Analysis

Industries: Generalist (All), Finance, Accounting, HR Services, Telecoms, Environmental Svcs.

Brandywine Technology Partners

2005 Concord Pike Ste 210
Wilmington, DE 19803-2982
(302) 656-6100
(866) 656-6100
Fax: (302) 656-9100
Email: careers@btpartners.net
Web: www.btpartners.net

Summary: We recruit and place IT professionals in contract and career positions with companies that range from 'pre-IPO' to Fortune 100.

Key Contact - Specialty:
Mr. Joel K. Pierson, Partner
Mr. Nate Sharp, CPC, SPHR, Partner -
Administration, Information Technology, Operations
Mr. Dick Burkhard, Partner
Mr. Rich Collins, Recruiter Consultant -
Computers, Computers (Networking,Programming,Science), Information Technology

Salary Minimum: $35,000

Functions: Generalist (All), IT

Industries: Generalist (All), Manufacturing, Finance, Services, Communications, Government, Environmental Svcs., Packaging, Insurance, Real Estate, Software, Healthcare

Brantley Communications

1112 Goodwin Dr
Plano, TX 75023-4909
(972) 509-8979
(877) 832-3583
Email: larry@brantleycommunications.com
Web: www.brantleycommunications.com

Summary: We specialize in the full time placement of professionals in the advertising and communications industries on a contingency basis.

Key Contact - Specialty:
Mr. Larry Brantley, Principal

Salary Minimum: $30,000

Functions: Generalist (All)

Industries: Advertising, Publishing, New Media

Bratland & Associates

PO Box 743
McHenry, IL 60051-9012
(815) 385-7665
Fax: (815) 344-6424
Email: al@bratlandcareers.com
Web: www.bratlandcareers.com

Summary: It is our mission to provide the highest quality service to those within the optical fiber,

optoelectronic and related industries. We pride ourselves in our ability to meet the needs of both the individual and the corporation when it comes time to finding the ideal person or position. We share a genuine concern for the future of all parties involved in the search process. We have to. It's our business.

Key Contact - Specialty:
Mr. A.J. Bratland, President -
Telecommunications
Ms. Dolores Bratland, Vice President
Ms. Mary Zwaan, Research Analyst

Functions: Management, Mfg., Plant Mgmt., Quality, R&D, Engineering

Industries: Telecoms, Fiber Optic

Jerold Braun & Associates

PO Box 67523
Century City Station
Los Angeles, CA 90067-0523
(310) 203-0515
Email: braunsearch@prodigy.net

Summary: We specialize in executive search in retail, eCommerce, manufacturers that supply retailers, telemarketing, TV shopping, and allied fields. Also specializes in all areas of HR management.

Key Contact - Specialty:
Mr. Jerold Braun, Principal
Ms. Joyce Davis, Principal

Salary Minimum: $50,000

Functions: Generalist (All), Management, Board Members, Senior Mgmt.

Industries: Textiles, Apparel, Consumer Elect., Wholesale, Retail, HR Services, Logistics Svcs., Supply Chain Mgmt, Call Centers

Braun-Valley Associates

(also known as Braun Associates Limited)
PO Box 2168 Stn Main
405-201 Front St N
Sarnia, ON N7T 7L7
Canada
(519) 336 4590
(519) 336-4591
Fax: (519) 336-8164
Email: mbraun@mnsi.net

Summary: We are suppliers of temporary and long-term contract personnel to the industrial sector.

Key Contact - Specialty:
Mr. Mark Braun, Contracts Manager
Ms. Kathy Furlotte, Manager - *Engineering*
Mrs. Shelly Weir, Technical Recruiter -
Accounting (Bookkeeping), Administration, Clerical, Human resources, Information Technology

Salary Minimum: $25,000

Functions: Generalist (All), Production, Automation, Plant Mgmt., Quality, Sales Mgmt., Systems Support, Engineering

Industries: Generalist (All), Chemicals, Drugs Mfg., Plastics, Rubber, Paints, Petro. Products, Machine, Appliance, Motor Vehicles, Misc. Mfg.

Breen Group LLC

298 Wallingford Rd
Cheshire, CT 06410-2859
(203) 271-2597
Fax: (203) 272-6897
Email: tbrimberg@breengroup.com
Web: www.breengroup.com

Summary: Search firm specializing in information technology, engineering, sales/marketing, finance/accounting and manufacturing.

Key Contact - Specialty:
Mr. Toby Brimberg, President

Salary Minimum: $65,000

Functions: Sales & Mktg., Finance, IT, Engineering

Industries: Generalist (All), Manufacturing, Finance

Breitner Clark & Hall Inc

1017 Turnpike St Ste 22A
Canton, MA 02021-2855
(781) 828-6411 x221
(800) 331-7004 x221
Fax: (781) 828-6431
Email: owen@breitner.com

Summary: Healthcare specialists concentrating in the permanent placement of physicians and clinical leaders.

Key Contact - Specialty:
Mr. Owen Breitner, Chief Operating Officer
Ms. Ann Breitner, Chief Executive Officer

Salary Minimum: $100,000

Functions: Healthcare, Physicians, Health Admin.

Industries: Healthcare, Hospitals, Long-term/Home Care, Dental, Physical Therapy, Occupational Therapy, Women's

Brethet, Barnum & Associates Inc

300-703 Evans Ave
Toronto, ON M9C 5E9
Canada
(416) 621-4900
(888) 284-8465
Fax: (416) 621-9818
Email: bob@brethetbarnum.com
Web: www.brethetbarnum.com

Summary: As specialists in healthcare, we are committed to excellence in both the quality of our service and the superior people we recruit. Our reputation for integrity and responsiveness to our clients' needs is second to none. We get results.

Key Contact - Specialty:
Mr. Bob Shiley, CPC, Associate - *Biotechnology, Healthcare, Marketing, Medical (Sales), Pharmaceutical*
Ms. Phyllis Chrzan, Associate - *Biotechnology, Marketing, Medical (Devices), Pharmaceutical, Sales*
Ms. Anne Brethet, CPC, General Manager - *Biotechnology, Marketing, Medical (Devices), Pharmaceutical, Sales*

Salary Minimum: $50,000

Functions: Sales & Mktg.

Industries: Drugs Mfg., Medical Devices, Biotech/Life Sciences, Healthcare

Brett Associates, LLC

2184 Morris Ave
Union, NJ 07083-5902
(908) 687-7772

Summary: We have expertise in the recruitment of engineering, maintenance, manufacturing and scientific personnel within the pharmaceutical, chemical, electro-mechanical and consumer products industries.

Key Contact - Specialty:
Mr. Gene Reight, Manager

Salary Minimum: $25,000

Functions: Generalist (All), Middle Mgmt., Production, Plant Mgmt., Quality, Productivity, R&D, Engineering

Industries: Generalist (All), Chemicals, Soap, Perf., Cosmtcs., Drugs Mfg., Medical Devices, Plastics, Rubber, Paints, Petro. Products, Leather, Stone, Glass

Briand Fiorella Search Inc

5144 Sheridan Dr Ste 2
Williamsville, NY 14221-4648
(716) 626-5520
(800) 201-8203
Fax: (716) 626-0042
Web: www.bfisearch.com

Summary: We are a national executive search firm specializing in the medical, pharmaceutical and biotech industries. We are in the business of evaluating and isolating only the strongest professionals for our clients. We are hired by some of the finest corporations to insure they get exposure to candidates who clearly stand out in the top 20% of their peer groups. We then ultimately align the strongest players to our client companies who won't hire anything but the best.

Key Contact - Specialty:
Mr. Paul Briand, President - *Biopharmaceutical, Biotechnology, Medical (Devices,Sales), Pharmaceutical*
Ms. Nicole Fiorella, Vice President - *Biopharmaceutical, Biotechnology, Medical (Devices,Sales), Pharmaceutical*

Salary Minimum: $50,000

Brickell Personnel Consultants

1110 Brickell Ave Ste 512
Miami, FL 33131-3136
(305) 371-6187
Fax: (305) 358-9615
Email: employment@brickellpersonnel.com
Web: www.brickellpersonnel.com

Summary: We have been connecting top talent with the most prestigious businesses in our market for years. We have been consistently successful in servicing the business community and have earned a reputation for generating top tier candidates and solid client relationships based on candor and confidentiality.

Key Contact - Specialty:
Ms. Nidia Torres, President
Ms. Carolina Hickey, Executive Recruiter

Salary Minimum: $50,000

Functions: Management

Industries: Finance, Banking, Invest. Banking, Brokers, Venture Cap., Mutual/Hedge Funds, Misc. Financial, Services

Bridgepoint Search

313 N Brooke Dr
Canton, GA 30114-9403
(770) 479-2450
Email: jdrohan@bridgepointsearch.com
Web: www.bridgepointsearch.com

Summary: We are one of the nations premier software sales recruiting companies. We specialize in the placement of sales, pre-sales and sales management professionals in the software industry.

Key Contact - Specialty:
Mr. John Drohan, Partner

Salary Minimum: $125,000

Functions: Management, Sales & Mktg., Sales Mgmt., Sales Reps.

Industries: Software, Accounting SW, Database SW, Development SW, Doc. Mgmt., Production SW, ERP SW, HR SW, Industry Specific SW, Mfg. SW, System SW, Training SW

BrightStar Talent Group

(formerly known as Big Builder Careers)
3455 Peachtree Rd NE Ste 500
Atlanta, GA 30326-3236
(404) 995-6935
Fax: (678) 669-2728
Email: jwebb@brightstartalentgroup.com
Web: www.brightstartalentgroup.com

Summary: As previous executives for big builders, we understand that to have a leading edge within the industry it is important to find the most talented and qualified individuals. We pride ourselves in offering candidates and builder clients' exceptional professional service, absolute confidentiality, and the most ethical values in the executive recruiting business.

Key Contact - Specialty:
Mr. Mark Matyanowski, Chief Operating Officer
Mr. Justin Webb, Executive Vice President
Mrs. Marci Saunders, Vice President, Marketing

Salary Minimum: $50,000

Functions: Management

Industries: Construction, Architectural Svcs., Real Estate

R A Briones & Company

(also known as R.A. Briones & Co.)
11200 Montwood Dr
El Paso, TX 79936-4252
(915) 629-7222
Email: briones@whc.net
Web: www.brionessearch.com

Summary: General manufacturing with emphasis in bilingual (Spanish) professionals, management, accounting, quality, materials, IT, sales & marketing and maquiladoras.

Key Contact - Specialty:
Mr. Roberto A. Briones, CPC, Owner & Manager
Ms. Lorraine Rocha, Account Executive
Ms. Christina Briones, Account Executive - *Manufacturing*

Salary Minimum: $15,000

Functions: Generalist (All), Management, Senior Mgmt., Mfg.

Industries: Manufacturing, Food, Bev., Tobacco, Textiles, Apparel, Medical Devices, Plastics, Rubber, Metal Products, Machine, Appliance, Motor Vehicles, Consumer Elect., Misc. Mfg., Electronic, Elec. Components, Accounting, Call Centers, Software, Biotech/Life Sciences, Healthcare

Bristol Associates Inc

5757 W Century Blvd Ste 628
Los Angeles, CA 90045-6404
(310) 670-0525
Fax: (310) 670-4075
Email: jbright@bristolassoc.com
Web: www.bristolassoc.com

Summary: We perform executive searches in hospitality, food & beverage industries, direct & interactive marketing, hospitals and casino/gaming. We have depth of experience and professional knowledge and use sophisticated sourcing techniques. Our firm is focused on personal service and is results-oriented.

Key Contact - Specialty:
Mr. James J. Bright, Jr., President - *Gaming*
Ms. Lucy Farber, Vice President - *Gaming*

Ms. Roberta Borer, Executive Vice President - *Healthcare*
Mr. Lee Candiotti, Vice President - *Direct marketing*
Mr. Peter Stern, Vice President
Ms. Kelly Nelson, Vice President - *Hospitality, Travel*

Salary Minimum: $100,000

Functions: Generalist (All), Senior Mgmt.

Industries: Food, Bev., Tobacco, E-commerce, Hospitality, Entertainment, Travel, Media, Advertising, New Media, Call Centers, Healthcare, Hospitals

Britt Associates Inc

3533 Lake Shore Dr
Joliet, IL 60431-8820
(815) 436-8300
Fax: (815) 436-9617
Email: brittassoc@aol.com

Summary: Recruitment/placement of logistics/distribution and supply chain/materials management professionals. Activity is conducted with all of industrial goods and consumer products manufacturers along with wholesale and retail firms.

Key Contact - Specialty:
Mr. William E. Lichtenauer, CPC, President

Salary Minimum: $40,000

Functions: Production, Materials, Purchasing, Materials Plng., Distribution

Industries: Generalist (All)

The Brixton Group Inc

310 Arlington Ave Unit 428
Charlotte, NC 28203-5234
(704) 376-2700
Email: asobel@brixton.net
Web: www.brixton.net

Summary: We work across all industries helping managers achieve their goals on or ahead of schedule, and within budget.

Key Contact - Specialty:
Mr. Andrew Sobel, President

Salary Minimum: $50,000

Functions: Generalist (All)

Industries: Generalist (All)

Broad, Waverly & Associates

PO Box 741
200 Broad St
Red Bank, NJ 07701-0741
(732) 741-1010
Fax: (732) 219-9644
Email: staffing@broadwaverly.com
Web: www.broadwaverly.com

Summary: We are 100% focused on the Monmouth and Ocean County areas to serve their communities, people, and businesses. We've maintained a commitment to high-performance and possess unsurpassed local business knowledge. We offer client companies and candidates a personal service and as a result, we have placed thousands of individuals in a variety of positions in the area's leading companies.

Key Contact - Specialty:
Mr. Bill I. Saloukas, CPC, CTS, President

Salary Minimum: $50,000

Functions: Generalist (All)

Industries: Generalist (All), Accounting

BroadBand HR Consulting

(formerly known as Broadband Resource Group)
320 Greenfield Ave
San Mateo, CA 94403-5012
(650) 312-8138
Email: info@broadbandhr.com
Web: www.broadbandhr.com

Summary: Our firm provides executive and niche specialty search to technology, life science and other firms. We also provide a broad range of Organizational Development, Compensation, and HR Consulting services to our clients.

Key Contact - Specialty:
Ms. Deb McClanahan, Principal - *Biotechnology, Computers (Software), Marketing, Sales, Senior management*

Salary Minimum: $85,000

Functions: Senior Mgmt., Middle Mgmt., Sales & Mktg.

Industries: Generalist (All)

Broadband Media Communications, Inc.

PO Box 639
31892 Via De Linda Ste 100
San Juan Capistrano, CA 92693-0639
(949) 488-8855
(877) 329-6600
Email: recruiters@broadbandrecruiters.com
Web: www.broadbandcareers.com

Summary: We are the leading career center for the broadband-IP professional. Browse 8,000 linked companies, search career opportunities and post your resume or confidential profile and job agents. Employers reach over 250K candidates with unlimited job postings, resume database and candidate agents.

Key Contact - Specialty:
Mr. Mark Clancey, Director, Sales & Business Development - *Engineering, Management, Technical*
Ms. Darcie Renee, Director, Administration & Research

Functions: Generalist (All)

Industries: IT Implementation, Telecoms, Telephony, Digital, Wireless, Fiber Optic, Network Infrastructure, RF/Microwave, HR SW, Networking, Comm. SW

Dan B Brockman

620 Old Barn Rd
Lake Barrington, IL 60010-6203
(847) 382-6015
Email: danbrockman@comcast.net
Web: www.trainingjob.com

Summary: We are specialists in degreed safety engineering practitioners, industrial hygienists, agronomists, compliance managers (OSHA, EPA and MSHA) and environmental affairs managers, training, learning, on-line, instruction, teaching, CBT, OD, Kaizen, Six Sigma and educational specialists.

Key Contact - Specialty:
Mr. Dan B. Brockman, Owner
Ms. Trowby Brockman, Partner

Salary Minimum: $45,000

Functions: Mfg., Training, Engineering, Environmentalists, Health & Safety

Industries: Generalist (All)

Brooks Placement Network

808 E Homer St
Michigan City, IN 46360-5124
(800) 704-9614
Fax: (219) 879-6030
Email: brooks.ed@comcast.net

Summary: Corporate recruiting firm specializing in the die casting, plastic injection molding and machine tool industries.

Key Contact - Specialty:
Mr. Ed Brooks, Owner & Corporate Recruiter

Salary Minimum: $50,000

Functions: Management

Industries: Manufacturing, Plastics, Rubber, Metal Products

Broward Dobbs Inc.

1532 Dunwoody Village Pkwy Ste 200
Atlanta, GA 30338-4136
(770) 399-0744
Fax: (770) 393-8185
Email: luke@broward-dobbs.com
Web: www.broward-dobbs.com

Summary: We are a client-oriented executive recruiting firm specializing in engineering, environmental, telecom, technical sales, manufacturing and real estate. Our clients rang from Fortune 100 to small local companies. Personal attention is our emphasis.

Key Contact - Specialty:
Mr. W. Luke Greene, Jr., President - *Engineering, Manufacturing*
Mr. Milnor Kessler, Executive Vice President - *Manufacturing*

Salary Minimum: $40,000

Functions: Mfg., Production, Automation, Quality, Materials, Purchasing, Packaging, Systems Analysis, Engineering, Environmentalists

Industries: Generalist (All), Food, Bev., Tobacco, Paper, Chemicals, Medical Devices, Plastics, Rubber, Motor Vehicles, Electronic, Elec. Components, Robotics, Telecoms

D Brown & Associates Inc

610 SW Alder St Ste 1111
Portland, OR 97205-3612
(503) 224-6860
(800) 769-8552
Email: info@dbrown.net
Web: www.dbrown.net

Summary: Search and recruitment organization serving clientele in the IT, IS, healthcare reimbursement, accounting, civil & nuclear engineering, forest/paper products and construction fields.

Key Contact - Specialty:
Mr. Dennis S. Brown, President - *Financial, Healthcare*

Salary Minimum: $50,000

Functions: Generalist (All), Senior Mgmt., Mfg., Finance, Budgeting, Systems Dev., Systems Implem., Network Admin., DB Admin.

Industries: Generalist (All), Construction, Lumber, Furniture, Printing, Computer Equip., Mgmt. Consulting, Software, Healthcare, Hospitals

Pat Brown & Associates

PO Box 6211
Mesa, AZ 85216-6211
(480) 503-4275
Fax: (480) 503-4329

Email: ladyhunter@cox.net

Summary: Extensive experience in the insurance industry.

Key Contact - Specialty:
Ms. Pat Brown, President

Salary Minimum: $30,000

Functions: Generalist (All), Board Members

Industries: Insurance, Casualty, Claims

Jim Brown Associates

15 Southwind Cir
Richmond, CA 94804-7405
(510) 235-4472
Fax: (510) 235-4482
Email: jim@jimbrownassociates.com
Web: www.jimbrownassociates.com

Summary: Our firm does middle management through senior-level executive search, all functions, within the pharmaceutical, biotechnology and medical device industries. Primary concentration is with marketing communications agencies specializing in healthcare.

Key Contact - Specialty:
Mr. Jim Brown, Owner - *Pharmaceutical*

Salary Minimum: $90,000

Functions: Generalist (All), Middle Mgmt., Advertising, Mktg. Research, Mktg. Mgmt., Graphic Designers

Industries: Drugs Mfg., Medical Devices, Pharm Svcs., Engineering Svcs., Biotech/Life Sciences

Brown, Bernardy, Van Remmen Inc

1500 Rosecrans Ave Ste 210
Manhattan Beach, CA 90266-3721
(310) 536-0777
Fax: (310) 536-0606
Email: info@bvksearch.com
Web: bvksearch.com

Summary: Specialists in advertising, publishing, marketing, direct marketing and new media.

Key Contact - Specialty:
Mr. Roger Van Remmen, President
Ms. Cathie Kanuit, Partner - *Advertising, New media, Publishing*
Mr. Chris Cochran, Account Executive
Mr. Tom Knaphurst, Account Executive

Salary Minimum: $30,000

Functions: Generalist (All), Advertising, Mktg. Research, Mktg. Mgmt., Sales Mgmt., Direct Mktg.

Industries: Generalist (All), Advertising, Publishing, New Media

Browning Search Group

3267 Bee Cave Rd Ste 107 PMB 68
Austin, TX 78746-6773
(512) 330-9143
Fax: (512) 330-9170
Email: info@browningsearchgroup.com
Web: www.browningsearchgroup.com

Summary: Executive search firm specializing in the traditional and alternative investment management universes. Firm partners with hedge funds, private equity, venture capital and investment management firms both domestically and internationally. Search professionals possess industry specific experience and knowledge to facilitate the most productive and efficient search for all parties involved.

Key Contact - Specialty:
Mr. Simms Browning, Managing Director

Salary Minimum: $50,000

Functions: Generalist (All)

Industries: Venture Cap., Mutual/Hedge Funds, Misc. Financial

Brownstone Sales & Marketing Group Inc

632 Broadway Ph
New York, NY 10012-2614
(646) 654-2118
Email: jr@b-stone.com
Web: www.b-stone.com

Summary: We place sales candidates in the IT arena. We offer a mix of contingency and retained work for sales professionals. We are highly ethical and hard working on behalf of the corporation and candidate. We have seen over 50 percent growth in the past four years.

Key Contact - Specialty:
Mr. James A. Riely, President - *Sales*
Mr. Christopher K. Doyle, Managing Partner

Salary Minimum: $35,000

Functions: Generalist (All), Management, Sales & Mktg., Advertising, Sales Mgmt., Direct Mktg., IT, Network Admin., DB Admin.

Industries: Generalist (All), Computer Equip., IT Implementation, Network Infrastructure, Software

Brunel Multec Canada Ltd

200-200 Ronson Dr
Office Building
Etobicoke, ON M9W 5Z9
Canada
(416) 244-2402
(888) 244-8466
Fax: (416) 244-6883
Email: toronto@multec.ca
Web: www.multec.ca

Summary: We are a search firm specializing in engineering and technical positions, IT, finance, sales, marketing, and senior management placements. We are committed to offering exceptional service.

Key Contact - Specialty:
Mr. Rick Randell, President - *Accounting, Automotive, Healthcare, Manufacturing, Pharmaceutical*
Ms. Anne Andrews, General Manager - *Accounting, Human resources, Sales*
Mr. Jody Leavoy, Director, Technical Staffing Operations - *Aerospace, Design, Engineering, Maintenance, Manufacturing*

Functions: Senior Mgmt., Sales & Mktg., Finance, IT, Engineering

Industries: Generalist (All)

Bryan, Jason & Associates Inc

1200-111 Richmond St W
Toronto, ON M5H 2G4
Canada
(416) 867-9295
Fax: (416) 867-3067
Email: careers@bryan-jason.ca
Web: www.bryan-jason.ca

Summary: We are a well-established search firm that locates and identifies candidates in the accounting/finance sectors of business. Our emphasis is geared towards the real estate, construction, development and property management field. Our consultants also work with clients looking for professionals that have experience on the operational side of real estate.

Key Contact - Specialty:
Ms. Rickie Bryan, President - *Real estate*
Ms. Bonnie Jason, Vice President - *Real estate*

Salary Minimum: $25,000

Functions: Generalist (All), Middle Mgmt., Admin. Svcs., Benefits, Staffing, Training, Cash Mgmt., Credit

Industries: Generalist (All), Real Estate

Bryan Research

14055 Cedar Rd Ste 302
Cleveland, OH 44118-3333
(216) 321-9760

Summary: We are specialists in our chosen industries of chemical and MRO.

Key Contact - Specialty:
Mr. Les Snider, Executive Vice President - *Plastics*

Salary Minimum: $30,000

Functions: Management, Plant Mgmt., Advertising, Sales Mgmt., Customer Svc., Engineering, Architects, Graphic Designers

Industries: Oil & Gas, Textiles, Apparel, Printing, Chemicals, Plastics, Rubber, Paints, Petro. Products, Metal Products, Electronic, Elec. Components, Retail, Engineering Svcs., Logistics Svcs., Advertising, Packaging

Branches:
25820 Hurlingham Rd
Beachwood, OH 44122-2438
(440) 464-6304
Email: lbso1@visn.net
Key Contact - Specialty:
Mr. Bryan Snider

Bryant Bureau

18600 Florence St
Roseville, MI 48066-6600
(586) 772-6452
Fax: (586) 772-6788
Email: jackie@bryantbureau.net
Web: www.bryantbureau.net

Summary: Technical and executive search firm specializing in direct, contract, and temp to direct opportunities. We work in industries such as automotive and manufacturing to assist our clients in finding qualified individuals for positions ranging from general clerical, financial, sales/marketing, design, testing, production, management, to executive level leaders.

Key Contact - Specialty:
Ms. Jackie Nabat, CPC, MBA, Vice President, Eng & Tech Recruitment - *Engineering, Executives, ISO 9000, Logistics, Manufacturing (Management)*
Mr. Ron Daiza, Owner & President - *Accounting, Accounting (Big 4), Administration, Clerical, Legal*
Mrs. Sue Daiza, Chief Financial Officer - *Accounting (Bookkeeping), Finance*

Salary Minimum: $65,000

Functions: Senior Mgmt., Mfg., Production, Plant Mgmt., Engineering, Design

Industries: Manufacturing, Plastics, Rubber, Metal Products, Motor Vehicles, Test, Measure Equip., Misc. Mfg., Electronic, Elec. Components, Robotics, Semiconductors, Misc. Financial, Engineering Svcs., ERP SW, Mfg. SW, System SW

Bryant Bureau Sales Recruiters

(also known as Snelling Personnel Services)
2435 Kimberly Rd Ste 110N
Bettendorf, IA 52722-3521
(563) 355-4411
(800) 873-4411
Fax: (563) 355-3635
Email: bbureau@netexpress.net
Web: www.bbureau.com

Summary: Recruiting and placing sales/sales mgmt candidates with industrial, medical, office/computer and business services. We provide services for Fortune 1000 companies.

Key Contact - Specialty:
Mr. Douglas W. Ryan, CPC, Owner & Sales Recruiting Specialist - *Business to business, Computers (Sales,Software), Medical (Sales), Sales*
Ms. Lisa Britt, Recruiting Specialist, Sales
Mr. Phil Rotman, CPC, Recruiting Specialist, Sales
Ms. Tanya Duncan, Recruiting Specialist, Sales

Salary Minimum: $35,000

Functions: Sales & Mktg., Sales Mgmt.

Industries: Generalist (All), Drugs Mfg., Medical Devices, Metal Products, Machine, Appliance, Equip Svcs., Wireless

Bryant Research

466 Old Hook Rd Ste 32
Emerson, NJ 07630-1372
(201) 599-0590
Fax: (201) 599-2423
Email: resumes@bryantresearch.com
Web: www.bryantresearch.com

Summary: We offer pharmaceutical industry clinical R&D executive recruitment. Our primary emphasis on placing physicians, scientists and professional level R&D personnel in the clinical drug development process. Also biostatistics, regulatory affairs, clinical pharmacology, pk/pd, data management, medical liaisons, drug safety and health economics/outcomes research.

Key Contact - Specialty:
Ms. Lisa Billotti, President

Salary Minimum: $60,000

Functions: Generalist (All), Physicians, R&D

Industries: Drugs Mfg., Medical Devices, Pharm Svcs.

BSA Hospitality/Bonne Smith Associates

7807 E Oakshore Dr
Scottsdale, AZ 85258-3470
(480) 483-5400
Fax: (480) 483-5401
Email: recruit@bsahospitality.com
Web: www.bsahospitality.com

Summary: We are a hospitality executive recruiters specializing in senior and mid-level management positions in the hospitality industry. Retained search and contingency recruiting. Serving hospitality management companies, fine hotels, resorts, country clubs, restaurants and attractions.

Key Contact - Specialty:
Ms. Bonne B. Smith, Founder & President
Ms. Debra Hieber-Kudar, Vice President
Ms. Shannon Beardsley, Research Associate - *Engineering, Human resources, Sales, Tax*

Salary Minimum: $80,000

Functions: Generalist (All)

Industries: Hospitality, Hotels, Resorts, Clubs, Restaurants

BSC Inc
3231 Marcia Louise Dr
Southaven, MS 38672-6751
(662) 449-5662
Email: wes@roadrunnerpm.com
Web: roadrunnerpm.com

Summary: IT from management through developers.

Key Contact - Specialty:
Mr. Wes Johnson, PMP, President - *Information Technology, Management, Marketing, Senior management, Systems (Integration)*

Salary Minimum: $35,000

Functions: Management, IT, MIS Mgmt.

Industries: Generalist (All), IT Implementation, Communications, Software

BSI Management Search & Consulting
1192 Old Kings Bridge RD
Nicholson, GA 30565-2419
(770) 639-5096
Fax: (706) 757-0088
Email: charlie@bsiconsult.com
Web: www.bsiconsult.com

Summary: We assist companies to find, hire and retain sales engineers, sales managers, applications engineers, design engineers, project engineers, project managers, field service engineers & technicians and operations managers. We are a value added search company because we work with candidates who add revenue, increase productivity or decrease costs.

Key Contact - Specialty:
Mr. Charles Schrauth, Account Executive - *Product management/development, Robotics, Sales, Supply Chain, Utilities*

Salary Minimum: $50,000

Functions: Management, Mfg., Plant Mgmt., Sales Mgmt., Engineering

Industries: Manufacturing, Food, Bev., Tobacco, Chemicals, Plastics, Rubber, Metal Products, Test, Measure Equip., Misc. Mfg., Electronic, Elec. Components, Robotics, Consumer Goods, Services, RF/Microwave, Industry Specific SW, Mfg. SW, Security SW, System SW

Benavides Technical Staffing Inc
(formerly known as Riccione & Associates Inc)
17194 Preston Rd Ste 102 PMB 390
Dallas, TX 75248-1227
(972) 407-1900
(866) 794-0287
Fax: (972) 407-1908
Email: nick@riccione.com
Web: www.riccione.com

Summary: We specialize in executive search and placement in engineering, marketing, sales and information technology fields.

Key Contact - Specialty:
Mr. Nicholas Riccione, President

Salary Minimum: $50,000

Functions: Senior Mgmt., Middle Mgmt., Product Dev., Sales & Mktg., Systems Dev., Engineering

Industries: Communications, Telecoms, Digital, Wireless, Fiber Optic, Network Infrastructure, RF/Microwave, Defense, Software,

Development SW, Industry Specific SW, Networking, Comm. SW, Security SW, System SW, Biotech/Life Sciences, Healthcare

BTS Consultants Inc
PO Box 372311
Satellite Beach, FL 32937-0311
(321) 773-7303
(321) 508-0053
Fax: (321) 773-7239
Email: pete@btsconsultants.net

Summary: With experience in health care practice management our focus is the evaluation of medical billing and collection systems and retraining of the staff for physician offices. We do physician and executive recruiting.

Key Contact - Specialty:
Ms. Debbie Giorgio, President
Mr. Peter Giorgio, Sales & Marketing - *Administration, Chiropractic, OB/GYN, Physicians, Psychiatry*

Functions: Physicians

Industries: Claims, Healthcare, Hospitals

btsn, inc.
1-20 Cameron St N
Kitchener, ON N2H 3A1
Canada
(877) 287-6462
(519) 745-2393
Email: search@btsn.com
Web: www.btsn.com

Summary: Search and recruitment firm specializing in bio-technology, telecom, semiconductor and network industries globally.

Key Contact - Specialty:
Ms. Leslie Stallard, President

Salary Minimum: $95,000

Functions: Management, Mfg., R&D, Engineering

Industries: Drugs Mfg., Medical Devices, Test, Measure Equip., Electronic, Elec. Components, Semiconductors, Telecoms, Telephony, Wireless, Fiber Optic, Environmental Svcs., Networking, Comm. SW, Biotech/Life Sciences

Buckman, Enochs & Coss Inc
590 Enterprise Dr
Lewis Center, OH 43035-9427
(614) 825-6215
Fax: (614) 825-6242
Email: senochs@becsearch.com
Web: www.becsearch.com

Summary: We provide corporate search work, specializing in medical, pharmaceutical and bio-technology with an emphasis on sales & marketing.

Key Contact - Specialty:
Mr. Steve Enochs, President - *Pharmaceutical, Sales*

Salary Minimum: $60,000

Functions: Healthcare, Sales & Mktg.

Industries: Drugs Mfg., Medical Devices, Pharm Svcs.

Builders Search Group LLC
1805 SW Regional Airport Blvd Ste 1
Bentonville, AR 72712-7756
(479) 464-9444
(888) 268-1100
Fax: (479) 464-9445
Email: c.leslie@builderssearch.com
Web: www.builderssearch.com

Summary: We are an exclusive provider of executive, management, and professional level recruiting services to employers in the construction industry. We offer clients extensive experience in construction & recruitment. Our commitment is to the construction industry. With our industry expertise and powerful network of construction industry recruiters, we are strategically positioned to provide recruitment services to builders.

Key Contact - Specialty:
Ms. Christi Leslie, SPHR, Founder & Managing Partner
Mr. Scott Leslie, Partner

Salary Minimum: $50,000

Functions: Generalist (All)

Industries: Generalist (All), Construction, Real Estate

Builders Staffing Group
754 Mays Blvd Ste 11
Incline Village, NV 89451-9633
(800) 809-6164
(775) 832-9700
Fax: (775) 832-9703
Email: loanne@buildersstaffinggroup.com
Web: www.buildersstaffinggroup.com

Summary: Executive search specializing in the residential homebuilding industry. We place executive management, mid level management and support staff. Must have prior homebuilding industry experience. Only qualified candidates will be contacted.

Key Contact - Specialty:
Ms. Loanne Kuller, Partner
Ms. Teresa James, Partner

Functions: Senior Mgmt.

Industries: Construction

Building Industry Associates
774 Mays Blvd # 10-369
Incline Village, NV 89451-9604
(949) 631-7471
(775) 831 4358
Email: info@biaca.com

Summary: Executive search firm specializing in the residential home construction industry in the states of California, Nevada, and Arizona; placing presidents, VPs operations, VPs of construction, forward planning, land acquisition, purchasing agents, project managers, superintendents, options coordinators and customer service personnel.

Key Contact - Specialty:
Ms. Bob Schoonmaker, President, Southern CA
Mr. Guy Thurman, Senior Account Executive, N CA, NV - *Construction*
Ms. Tracy Taylor, Senior Account Executive, AZ, NM - *Construction*

Salary Minimum: $75,000

Functions: Management, Senior Mgmt., Middle Mgmt., Purchasing, CFOs, Engineering

Industries: Construction

Building Resources
4201 38th St S Ste 208
Fargo, ND 58104-7535
(701) 281-1087
(877) 365-4038
Fax: (701) 298-7738
Email: info@buildingresources.biz
Web: www.buildingresources.biz

Summary: Ours is an executive search firm specializing in finding excellent sales and upper-management candidates for our clients within the

building and building products industries. We are client-centered, and believe strongly in doing the right thing at all times.

Key Contact - Specialty:
Ms. Rikka Brandon, Founder & President
Ms. Erin Mayer, Director, Business Development - *Building products, Business development, CEOs, Construction, COOs*
Ms. Michele Rhoten, Director, Recruiting Services - *Building products, CEOs, Executives, Management consulting, Marketing*

Functions: Management, Middle Mgmt., Sales Mgmt., Sales Reps.

Industries: Construction, Manufacturing, Lumber, Furniture, Paper, Paints, Petro. Products, Leather, Stone, Glass, Metal Products, Architectural Svcs., Property/Facility Mgmt., Marketing SW

Burchard & Associates Inc

12977 N 40 Dr Ste 315
Saint Louis, MO 63141-8656
(314) 878-2270
(888) 273-5882
Fax: (314) 878-1337
Email: srb@exechunter.com
Web: www.exechunter.com

Summary: Our firm is a full-service retained search and contingent practice. We are exclusively in accounting & financial recruitment experience. Extensive clientele base covering all business sectors.

Key Contact - Specialty:
Mr. Stephen Burchard, President - *Finance*
Ms. Ronda Burchard, General Manager - *Finance*

Salary Minimum: $75,000

Functions: Finance, CFOs, Budgeting, Cash Mgmt., Taxes, M&A

Industries: Manufacturing, Wholesale, Retail, Finance, Telecoms, Insurance, Real Estate, Healthcare

The Burgess Group-Corporate Recruiters International Inc

626 Riverside Dr Apt 11M
New York, NY 10031-7216
(212) 939-9200
(203) 746-6629
Fax: (212) 939-9300
Email: resumes@theburgessgroup.com
Web: www.theburgessgroup.com

Summary: Entry to senior level diversity recruiting, executive search, management training and development consulting specializing in: corporate board governance, sales, marketing, financial services and insurance, real estate, construction, engineering, facilities and purchasing, human and security resources, non-profit management and fundraising, advertising, public, media, investor and external relations, legal, and IT.

Key Contact - Specialty:
Mr. William H. Burgess, III, President & Chief Executive Officer - *Consumer, Diversity, Marketing, Non-profit, Sales*

Salary Minimum: $50,000

Functions: Management, Board Members, Sales & Mktg., Minorities/Diversity

Industries: Consumer Goods, Services, Non-profits, Communications, Insurance, Healthcare

Branches:
5 Almargo Rd
New Fairfield, CT 06812-3416
(203) 746-6629
Fax: (203) 746-3777
Email: resumes@theburgessgroup.com

Burke & Associates

(a division of The Westfield Group)
1010 Washington Blvd
Stamford, CT 06901-2202
(203) 406-2300
Fax: (203) 406-2315
Email: admin@westfieldgroup.com
Web: www.westfieldgroup.com

Summary: We are a contingency and retained search firm specializing in HR, accounting and finance. We have a Fortune 500 and a national client base.

Key Contact - Specialty:
Mr. T. Michael Burke, President
Mr. John Burke, Senior Vice President
Mr. Smith, Recruiter

Salary Minimum: $80,000

Functions: HR Mgmt., Benefits, Staffing, Training, Budgeting, Cash Mgmt., Mgmt. Consultants

Industries: Generalist (All)

Branches:
1 N Broadway
White Plains, NY 10601-2310
(914) 761-4333
Key Contact - Specialty:
Ms. Nila Arrington, Administrator

J Burke & Associates Inc

2000 E Lamar Blvd Ste 600
Arlington, TX 76006-7340
(817) 588-3024
Fax: (817) 274-6763
Email: stoney@jburkeassoc.com
Web: www.jburkeassoc.com

Summary: We are an executive search firm specializing in packaging industry sales, marketing and management. With a network of client companies and a national candidate database we have the competitive edge. Confidentiality, efficient service and industry knowledge are key elements. Let us share success with you.

Key Contact - Specialty:
Mr. Stoney Burke, President
Ms. Kaye Burke, Vice President
Ms. Gayle Smith, Associate - *Chemical*

Salary Minimum: $35,000

Functions: Senior Mgmt., Plant Mgmt., Sales & Mktg., Mktg. Mgmt., Sales Mgmt.

Industries: Packaging

The Burke Group

204-63 Church St
Saint Catharines, ON L2R 3C4
Canada
(905) 641-3070
(888) 896-3618
Fax: (905) 641-0478
Email: tbg@theburkegroup.com
Web: www.theburkegroup.com

Summary: We offer extensive HR expertise in executive search, professional search, HR consulting, outplacement and outsourcing. We provide solutions in areas of assessment, training and development, temporary/contract staffing.

Key Contact - Specialty:
Ms. Diane Chivers, CHRP, Director, Staffing & Operations

Functions: Generalist (All), Senior Mgmt., Middle Mgmt., Plant Mgmt., Health Admin., Sales & Mktg., HR Mgmt., Engineering, Health & Safety

Industries: Generalist (All), Energy, Utilities, Manufacturing, Finance, Services, Hospitality, Media, Communications, Government, Software, Biotech/Life Sciences

Branches:
316-2289 Fairview St
Burlington, ON L7R 2E3
Canada
(905) 634-3570
(888) 330-3490
Fax: (905) 634-0791
Email: tbg@theburkegroup.com
Key Contact - Specialty:
Mrs. Lynn Thomas, Director, Marketing & Sales - *Marketing, Sales*
Miss Jennifer Brisson, Coordinator, Marketing - *Marketing, Sales*

David S Burt Associates

991 Dixon Cir
Billings, MT 59105-2209
(406) 245-9500
(800) 840-4801
Fax: (406) 245-9570
Email: dburtsearch@bresnan.net
Web: www.usaheadhunters.com

Summary: We have extensive chemical industry experience. We have several exclusive agreements with large chemical companies. Our large database of candidates, our comprehensive network and our recruiting capabilities maintain and increase our value to employers. Our affiliations with the top chemical and environmental companies make us invaluable to our candidates.

Key Contact - Specialty:
Mr. David S. Burt, President - *Chemical, Sales*

Salary Minimum: $50,000

Functions: Generalist (All)

Industries: Energy, Utilities, Oil & Gas, Food, Bev., Tobacco, Paper, Chemicals, Soap, Perf., Cosmtcs., Drugs Mfg., Plastics, Rubber, Paints, Petro. Products, Environmental Svcs.

Business Answers International

4440 PGA Blvd Ste 505
Palm Beach Gardens, FL 33410-6543
(561) 775-6110
(800) 583-4726
Fax: (561) 775-0520
Email: rrappaport@plasticlink.com
Web: www.baintl.com

Summary: We are an executive and sales recruitment firm focusing on plastics and related industries.

Key Contact - Specialty:
Mr. Richard Rappaport, President & Principal - *Plastics*
Mr. Michael Batky, Executive Vice President - *Plastics*
Mr. Walter Schnieder, Vice President - *Plastics*

Salary Minimum: $35,000

Functions: Management, Board Members, Senior Mgmt., Middle Mgmt., Plant Mgmt., Mktg. Mgmt., Sales Mgmt.

Industries: Generalist (All), Chemicals, Plastics, Rubber

Business Recruiters Group

7161 Carriage Hills Ln
Cedar Hill, MO 63016-3513
(800) 551-1074
(636) 285-1074
Fax: (636) 285-1084
Email: busrecrgrp@aol.com
Web: www.businessrecruitersgroup.com

Summary: We are a full service executive search
and recruiting firm. Our clients range from multi-
billion dollar conglomerates to small and medium
sized companies. We have a full team on each
search to get the best and fastest results in the
industry.

Key Contact - Specialty:
Ms. Jill Minor, Senior Parnter
Ms. Cindi Love, Senior Associate

Salary Minimum: $50,000

Functions: Generalist (All)

Industries: Generalist (All)

Business System Technologies Corp

125 Half Mile Rd Ste 200
Red Bank, NJ 07701-6749
(732) 671-0589
Fax: (646) 390-8583
Email: bstc@e-businesssystem.com
Web: www.e-businesssystem.com

Summary: Our firm recruits top-performing sales,
marketing, information technology, engineering
and executive candidates.

Key Contact - Specialty:
Mr. Albert J. Siano, President - *Executives,
Information Technology, Marketing, Sales*

Salary Minimum: $40,000

Functions: Senior Mgmt., Sales & Mktg., IT,
Engineering

Industries: Generalist (All), Electronic, Elec.
Components, Services, Mgmt. Consulting, E-
commerce, IT Implementation,
Communications, Digital, Wireless, Fiber Optic,
Network Infrastructure, Database SW,
Development SW, Doc. Mgmt., Production SW,
ERP SW, HR SW, Industry Specific SW, Mfg.
SW, Marketing SW, Networking, Comm. SW,
Security SW, System SW

The Butlers Company Insurance Recruiters

2451 N McMullen Booth Rd Ste 200
Oakbrook Tower
Clearwater, FL 33759-1362
(727) 725-1065
Fax: (727) 725-0389
Email: kbutler@topechelon.com
Web: www.butlerscompany.com

Summary: Search specializing in the insurance
industry only, technical through executive;
actuarial, accounting, financial, underwriting, loss
control, marketing, claims, administrative, DP and
sales.

Key Contact - Specialty:
Mr. Kirby B. Butler, Jr., CPC, President
Mrs. Judi Crenshaw, Senior Executive Recruiter -
Administration, Sales
Mr. Aaron Sakevich, Executive Recruiter - *Sales*

Salary Minimum: $50,000

Functions: Generalist (All)

Industries: Insurance

Buxton & Associates

12501 County Road 74
Eaton, CO 80615-8605
(303) 948-1487
Fax: (970) 454-9122
Email: buxtonassocltd@aol.com
Web: www.buxtonandassociates.com

Summary: Our specialty is financial institutions.
Most of our searches have been for presidents,
senior lenders, commercial lenders, cashiers and
trust professionals.

Key Contact - Specialty:
Mr. Gary Buxton, Principal
Mrs. Stacia Walter, Senior Associate - *Banking,
Banking
(Commercial,Corporate,Investment,Mortgage)*

Salary Minimum: $40,000

Functions: Finance

Industries: Banking

BVM International Inc

PO Box 15073
Bradenton, FL 34280-5073
(941) 792-4209
Fax: (941) 798-9351
Email: consultant@bvm.net
Web: www.bvm.net

Summary: We are a specialty staffing firm
providing retained and contingency searches in the
automotive, consumer electronics, medical device
and telecom industries. We are specialists in
quality assurance/continuous improvement, Six
Sigma, lean manufacturing, supply chain
management, purchasing, supplier development
and materials management.

Key Contact - Specialty:
Mr. Bill Van Mater, President

Salary Minimum: $70,000

Functions: Middle Mgmt., Plant Mgmt., Quality,
Materials, Purchasing, Minorities/Diversity

Industries: Medical Devices, Plastics, Rubber,
Metal Products, Machine, Appliance, Motor
Vehicles, Computer Equip., Consumer Elect.,
Electronic, Elec. Components, Transportation,
Telecoms, Digital, Wireless, Fiber Optic

Thomas Byrne Associates

7 Melrose Dr
Farmington, CT 06032-2255
(860) 676-2468
Fax: (860) 676-0272
Email: info@thomasbyrne.com
Web: www.thomasbyrne.com

Summary: We are a financial and accounting
recruitment firm focused on placement of former
Big 4 CPAs and other high potential individuals.
The firm has a second specialty focused on
staffing high-end rotational programs with CPA
and MBA talent being groomed for senior
management.

Key Contact - Specialty:
Mr. Thomas Byrne, CPC, Principal
Ms. Carmela Campbell, Recruiter - *Accounting*

Salary Minimum: $50,000

Functions: Finance, Budgeting, Taxes, Actuaries

Industries: Generalist (All)

Byrnes & Rupkey Inc

3356 Kimball Ave
Waterloo, IA 50702-5700
(319) 234-6201
Email: weplace@byrnesandrupkey.com
Web: www.byrnesandrupkey.com

Summary: We are dedicated to the recruitment
and placement of executive, manufacturing,
engineering, human resource, food & beverage,
and IT industry professionals. We are part of the
National Network of Executive Search Firms.

Key Contact - Specialty:
Ms. Lois Rupkey, President - *Automation, Food
& beverage, Human resources, Maintenance,
Technical (Management)*
Ms. Kay Gienger, Executive Vice President -
*Design, Information Technology, Manufacturing
(Management), Sales, Systems (Analysts)*
Ms. Kristy Staggs, Executive Vice President -
*Capital goods, HVAC, Manufacturing,
Purchasing, Quality*
Ms. Linda Modderman, Vice President,
Operations

Functions: Generalist (All)

Industries: Manufacturing, Food, Bev., Tobacco,
Machine, Appliance, Misc. Mfg., Consumer
Goods, Finance, Services, Accounting,
Packaging, Software

C and P Marketing Ltd

(also known as Midwest Financial Service Co)
285 Country Pointe Ct Ste 100
Wentzville, MO 63385-5430
(636) 332-8877
Email: pgk77@hotmail.com

Summary: We have exclusive representation of
community banks in all types of lending positions
and senior loan officers.

Key Contact - Specialty:
Mr. Paul G. Krienke, President

Salary Minimum: $40,000

Functions: Credit

Industries: Agri., Forestry, Mining, Finance,
Banking, Misc. Financial

C G & Company

5050 E University Blvd Ste 9B
Odessa, TX 79762-8100
(915) 362-7681
Fax: (915) 362-3578
Email: cgcompany@aol.com
Web: www.cgcompany.com

Summary: Our firm specializes in the placement
of top-level executives and managers, as well as
professionals, in the IT, engineering and health
care industries.

Key Contact - Specialty:
Ms. Cathy George, Owner & Senior Recruiter

Salary Minimum: $70,000

Functions: Generalist (All), Senior Mgmt., Plant
Mgmt., Healthcare, Physicians, Nurses, HR
Mgmt., Benefits, IT, Engineering

Industries: Generalist (All), Energy, Utilities, Oil
& Gas, Computer Equip., Consumer Elect.,
Venture Cap., Pharm Svcs., Accounting, HR
Services, E-commerce, IT Implementation,
Wireless, Fiber Optic, Software, HR SW,
Networking, Comm. SW, Healthcare, Hospitals,
Physical Therapy, Occupational Therapy

C G S Executive Search

6808 Portage Glen Ave NW
North Canton, OH 44720-9407
(330) 244-1845
Email: recruiter1330@yahoo.com

Summary: Companies have relied on us to locate,
identify and attract top candidates for rubber and
plastics professional and executive opportunities.

Key Contact - Specialty:
Mr. Jake Dragomire, Principal
Mr. Randy Knight, Recruiter

Salary Minimum: $80,000

Functions: Generalist (All), Management, Board Members, Senior Mgmt., Middle Mgmt., Mfg., Product Dev., Production, Plant Mgmt., Quality

Industries: Plastics, Rubber, Engineering Svcs., Aerospace

Angeline Cadenhead Associates

7 Bailey Hill Ln
Asheville, NC 28805-6200
(828) 298-6741
(800) 625-4083
Fax: (704) 973-0032
Email: acadenhead@medjobsmatch.com
Web: www.medjobsmatch.com

Summary: We offer physician recruitment. Our firm has an extensive network with other recruiting firms across the country for faster placement.

Key Contact - Specialty:
Ms. Angeline Cadenhead, BSN, President

Functions: Physicians

Industries: Higher Ed., Healthcare, Hospitals, Long-term/Home Care

Cadre Cache LLC

PO Box 25
Severance, NY 12872-0025
(973) 762-2092
Email: cadrecache@cadrecache.com
Web: www.cadrecache.com

Summary: Executive search for officer level banking positions using a disciplined search methodology, combining the development of a comprehensive search profile with original research and regular communication with the hiring manager to ensure efficient, appropriate results.

Key Contact - Specialty:
Ms. Kathleen Kargoll, Principal - *Financial*

Salary Minimum: $75,000

Functions: Generalist (All)

Industries: Finance, Banking, Invest. Banking, Misc. Financial

CAI Personnel Search Group

PO Box 962
Brentwood, TN 37024-0962
(615) 373-8263
(615) 373-4009
Fax: (615) 371-8215
Email: jobs@caipersonnel.com
Web: www.caipersonnel.com

Summary: Recruiting for manufacturing and healthcare industries.

Key Contact - Specialty:
Mr. Stephen Cook, CPC, Manager, Recruiting
Mrs. Diana Stewart, Recruiter - *Manufacturing*
Ms. Rebecca Carroll, Recruiter - *Engineering, Information Technology, Manufacturing*
Ms. Sumathy Krishnamurthy, Recruiter - *Engineering, Manufacturing, Production, Quality*
Ms. Aniko Balzer, Recruiter - *Engineering, Manufacturing, Production, Quality*
Mr. James Webb, Recruiter - *Engineering, Manufacturing, Materials, Production, Purchasing*
Mr. P. Gene Cook, PHR, CPC, Recruiter - *Operations, Technical*

Salary Minimum: $45,000

Functions: Generalist (All), Mfg., Quality, Healthcare, Sales Mgmt., HR Mgmt., Finance, IT, Engineering

Industries: Generalist (All), Construction, Manufacturing, Motor Vehicles, Misc. Mfg., Finance, Pharm Svcs., Biotech/Life Sciences, Healthcare

The Caldwell Group of San Marino

1613 Chelsea Rd Ste 237
San Marino, CA 91108-2419
(626) 281-6450
Fax: (626) 281-7901
Email: rickcaldwell@caldwellgroup.org

Summary: Our specialties include accounting, banking (general and operations), call centers, distribution, engineering, finance, HR, IT and manufacturing.

Key Contact - Specialty:
Mr. Rick Caldwell, Managing Director - *Finance, Information Technology*

Salary Minimum: $30,000

Functions: Generalist (All)

Industries: Generalist (All), Finance, Banking, Services, Accounting, Mgmt. Consulting, HR Services, Call Centers, Software, Accounting SW

Caldwell Legal Recruiting Consultants

PO Box 418
Northport, ME 04849-0418
(207) 338-9500
Fax: (207) 338-9502
Email: iplaw@caldwellrecruiting.com
Web: www.caldwellrecruiting.com

Summary: We are an intellectual property attorney and patent agent placement service. Our clients include both law firms and the corporate sector. We place all levels of attorneys from associate to chief patent counsel positions.

Key Contact - Specialty:
Ms. Kate Caldwell, Principal - *Biotechnology, Intellectual property, Pharmaceutical*

Functions: Legal, Attorneys

Industries: Chemicals, Drugs Mfg., Medical Devices, Plastics, Rubber, Semiconductors, Pharm Svcs., Legal, Telecoms, Fiber Optic

Caliber Business Solutions Inc

3319 West End Ave Ste 110
Nashville, TN 37209-1059
(866) 279-2386
(615) 279-3644
Email: caliber@4caliber.com
Web: www.4caliber.com

Summary: In today's complex business environment, corporations need more than basic recruiting. Our firm answers the demand by servicing clients with up to date information on the current and future changes taking place in today's business environment. As a result we offer corporations professionals on a part-time, temp or permanent basis. We specialize in financial recruiting.

Key Contact - Specialty:
Ms. Nancy McGrath, Director, Sales

Salary Minimum: $50,000

Functions: Finance, CFOs, Taxes

Industries: Services, Communications, Insurance, Casualty, Claims, Life, Commercial, Re-Insurance, Real Estate, Healthcare

California Executive Search Inc

7545 Irvine Center Dr Ste 200
Irvine, CA 92618-2933
(949) 600-7581
(949) 600-7582
Fax: (949) 600-7583
Email: caexec@caexec.com
Web: www.caexec.com

Summary: We are an executive search and consulting firm specialized in the strategic recruitment and placement of legal professionals. Through our commitment and dedication to our clients and candidates as well as our specific experience and knowledge of the legal market (both in-house and private practice) we take the time to understand your individual needs and find the right fit for you through specific and strategic recruiting and marketing.

Key Contact - Specialty:
Ms. Kimberley Harrison, Director, Recruiting
Mr. Matthew Crochet, President & Chief Executive Officer

Functions: Attorneys

Industries: Generalist (All)

California Management Search

(a division of R Marsh & Associates Inc)
881 11th St
Lakeport, CA 95453-4118
(707) 263-6000
(707) 286-8380
Fax: (707) 286-5700
Email: careers@cmsearch.net
Web: www.cmsearch.net

Summary: We pride ourselves on prompt, courteous service to our clients.

Key Contact - Specialty:
Mr. Norman R. Marsh, President - *Healthcare*
Mr. Randy Marsh, Executive Recruiter

Functions: Risk Mgmt., Health & Safety

Industries: Insurance, Casualty, Claims, Commercial, Re-Insurance

California Search Agency Inc

(formerly known as Crane Search Agency)
2603 Main St Ste 550
Irvine, CA 92614-6232
(714) 475-0790
Fax: (714) 475-0796
Email: dcrane@jobagency.com
Web: www.jobagency.com

Summary: We provide technical recruiting for small, medium and large manufacturing and R&D (commercial, industrial, aerospace and military) companies. Firm specializes in all disciplines of engineering and manufacturing personnel.

Key Contact - Specialty:
Mr. Don Crane, President - *Engineering, Manufacturing*

Salary Minimum: $25,000

Functions: Generalist (All)

Industries: Energy, Utilities, Construction, Manufacturing, Transportation, Services, Environmental Svcs., Aerospace, Packaging, Software, Biotech/Life Sciences

California Search Consultants Corp (CSC)

PO Box 2075
Oceanside, CA 92051-2075
(760) 439-5511
Fax: (760) 434-1430
Email: marshall@csccorp.com

Summary: We are a professional management-consulting firm that recruits people who design, market, manufacture and sell electronics from components through complete systems. This includes people in the semiconductor business, telecom, networking, power electronics and some defense related work.

Key Contact - Specialty:
Mr. Marshall Mack, President - *Electronics, Sales, Telecommunications*

Salary Minimum: $40,000

Functions: Management, Product Dev., Plant Mgmt., Quality, Materials, Packaging, Sales & Mktg., R&D, Engineering, Architects

Industries: Generalist (All), Medical Devices, Computer Equip., Test, Measure Equip., Electronic, Elec. Components, Semiconductors, Digital, Wireless, Fiber Optic, Defense, Packaging

The Call Center Network LLC

(also known as The Call Center Group)
3401 Enterprise Pkwy Ste 340
Beachwood, OH 44122-7340
(216) 766-5751
Fax: (216) 766-5752
Email: jobs@thecallcentergroup.com
Web: www.thecallcentergroup.com

Summary: We offer management and executive recruiting for the call center industry. This includes operations management, multi-site management, management of the forecasting & scheduling functions, etc.

Key Contact - Specialty:
Mr. Jeffrey B. Brown, Chief Executive Officer
Ms. Valerie Saunders, Manager, Research - *Call centers, Human resources*

Salary Minimum: $60,000

Functions: Generalist (All), Management, Board Members, Senior Mgmt., Middle Mgmt., Direct Mktg., Customer Svc.

Industries: Generalist (All), Call Centers

The Callos Companies

5083 Market St
Youngstown, OH 44512-2128
(800) 422-5567
(330) 788-4001
Fax: (330) 783-3966
Email: ytown@callos.com
Web: www.callos.com

Summary: We have the ability to access a pool of talent and placement expertise to help you select the best possible candidate, in the right location. We provide an experienced staff with the technical capability to perform effectively. Our network of offices, computer linked, provides access to specialists in nearly every career field.

Key Contact - Specialty:
Mr. Eric Sutton, Vice President, Search & Recruiting
Mr. John G. Callos, Chief Executive Officer
Mr. Thomas Walsh, President

Salary Minimum: $50,000

Functions: Generalist (All), Management, Mfg., Materials, Engineering

Industries: Generalist (All), Plastics, Rubber, Metal Products, Machine, Appliance, Motor Vehicles, Computer Equip., Consumer Elect., Test, Measure Equip., Misc. Mfg., Banking, Invest. Banking

Branches:
3340 W Market St Ste 101
Fairlawn, OH 44333-3306
(800) 344-7091
(330) 864-1220
Fax: (330) 864-1080
Email: akron@callos.com
Key Contact - Specialty:
Mr. Jim Miller, Regional Vice President

239 4th Ave Ste 1917
Pittsburgh, PA 15222-1712
(412) 281-8235
Fax: (412) 281-9417
Email: pittsburgh@callos.com
Key Contact - Specialty:
Mr. Jeff McGraw

Calvert & Associates Inc

PO Box 2982
Kill Devil Hills, NC 27948-2982
(252) 449-8657
Fax: (530) 504-6453
Email: randy@choicerecruiter.com
Web: www.choicerecruiter.com

Summary: We are a search firm specializing exclusively in healthcare placements for executive and director level positions. Utilizing experience in both the not-for-profit and for-profit arenas, both in administration and finance administration, the staff is very knowledgeable of the ever changing and challenging healthcare industry.

Key Contact - Specialty:
Mrs. Karen Calvert, Vice President
Mr. Randy Calvert, President

Functions: Generalist (All), Healthcare

Industries: Generalist (All), Healthcare, Hospitals, Long-term/Home Care

Cambridge Careers Inc

610 32nd Ave SW Ste A
Cedar Rapids, IA 52404-3910
(319) 366-7771
Fax: (319) 861-3514
Email: perm@cambridge-staffing.com
Web: www.cambridge-staffing.com

Summary: Specialize in data processing, design, engineering, medical, accounting, insurance, banking, sales & marketing and office support positions. We also provide outplacement services for companies along with an excellent resume service.

Key Contact - Specialty:
Mr. Mike Cambridge, CPC, Chief Executive Officer & President
Mr. Chuck Roe, General Manager

Salary Minimum: $40,000

Functions: Generalist (All)

Industries: Generalist (All)

Cambridge Group

1175 Post Rd E Ste 6
Westport, CT 06880-5437
(203) 226-4243
Fax: (203) 226-3856
Email: info@cambridgegroup.com
Web: www.cambridgegroup.com

Summary: Our seasoned staff and state of the art database affords our clients the most efficient and expedient searches available. Our permanent specialties include: information technology, physicians and pharmaceutical recruitment. Our contract recruitment services include information technology and pharmaceutical specialties.

Key Contact - Specialty:
Mr. Mike Salvagno, President

Salary Minimum: $60,000

Functions: Generalist (All), Senior Mgmt., Physicians, IT, MIS Mgmt., Systems Implem., Network Admin., DB Admin.

Industries: Generalist (All), Drugs Mfg., Misc. Mfg., Accounting, Mgmt. Consulting, Software, Healthcare

Branches:
1819 John F Kennedy Blvd Ste 475
Philadelphia, PA 19103-1739
(800) 295-0332
Key Contact - Specialty:
Mr. Spiro Michas, General Manager - *Biopharmaceutical, Biotechnology, Pharmaceutical, Regulatory, Staffing*

M Campbell Associates

PO Box 41022
Philadelphia, PA 19127-0022
(215) 482-1790
Email: mcampbel@bellatlantic.net
Web: www.mcampbell.net

Summary: As a premier executive recruitment firm for the placement of finance professionals, we concentrate our expertise primarily on the recruitment of treasury and cash management candidates. Our specialization has given us exceptional access to place talented finance professionals in every business segment; corporate as well as banking and financial services.

Key Contact - Specialty:
Ms. Donna K. Campbell, Recruiter, Researcher & Principal

Salary Minimum: $50,000

Functions: Senior Mgmt., Middle Mgmt., Product Dev., Sales Mgmt., Finance, CFOs, Cash Mgmt., Taxes, M&A, Risk Mgmt.

Industries: Generalist (All), Banking, Invest. Banking

Campbell, Edgar Inc

4388 49 St
Delta, BC V4K 2S7
Canada
(604) 946-8535
(888) 367-3131
Fax: (604) 946-2384
Email: info@retailcareers.com
Web: www.retailcareers.com

Summary: We are the largest recruitment firm in Canada, committed to the retail industry. Placement of only highest quality personnel in temporary, contract and permanent placements

Key Contact - Specialty:
Ms. Sherrie Littler, Senior Consultant
Ms. Cathy Fard, Consultant
Mr. Mike Reeves, Consultant

Salary Minimum: $20,000

Functions: Generalist (All), Management, Senior Mgmt., Middle Mgmt., Purchasing, Distribution, Sales & Mktg., Customer Svc.

Industries: Retail, Restaurants, Quick Service Restaurants, Full Service Restaurants, Inst./Industrial Food Svc., Entertainment, Recreation, Travel

Branches:
1-9059 Shaughnessy St
Vancouver, BC V6P 6R9
Canada
(604) 321-8515
(888) 367-3131
Fax: (604) 321-8541
Email: info@retailcareers.com

THE DIRECTORY OF EXECUTIVE RECRUITERS

Key Contact - Specialty:
Ms. Elaine Hay, CPC, President - *Outsourcing, Professional services, Purchasing, Retail, Sales*

The CAMPO Group

3110 Fairview Dr Ste 106
Owensboro, KY 42303-2175
(270) 685-2820
Email: resume@campogroup.com
Web: www.campogroup.com

Summary: We offer nationwide staffing solutions in the pharmaceutical, biotech, and medical device markets. We specialize in challenging markets: Managed Care, Specialty Field Sales, Medical/Clinical, Marketing, and Executive Leadership.

Key Contact - Specialty:
Mr. John Campo, Business Development, Talent Acquisition - *Biopharmaceutical, Biotechnology, Pharmaceutical*

Salary Minimum: $65,000

Functions: Healthcare

Industries: Healthcare

Canadian Executive Consultants Inc

400-1111 Finch Ave W
North York, ON M3J 2E5
Canada
(416) 665-7577
Fax: (416) 665-8509
Email: info@cdnexec.com
Web: www.cdnexec.com

Summary: We have served presidents, managers, boards of directors and personnel managers. We work with organizations of every size, type and structure, from two-people partnerships to multinational corporations.

Key Contact - Specialty:
Mr. Jay Herberman

Functions: Generalist (All)

Industries: Generalist (All)

CanMed Consultants Inc

659 Mississauga Cres
Mississauga, ON L5H 1Z9
Canada
(905) 274-0707
Fax: (905) 274-0067
Email: mraheja@canmed.com
Web: www.canmed.com

Summary: We provide consultants to executives and professionals in the pharmaceutical and healthcare sector. Services include executive and professional search, locum/contract employees and an online careers service.

Key Contact - Specialty:
Dr. Marc C. Raheja, President - *Senior management*

Salary Minimum: $50,000

Functions: Healthcare

Industries: Generalist (All)

Cannibal Central

26450 Bautista
Mission Viejo, CA 92692-4198
(949) 305-5873
Fax: (949) 305-5874
Email: ksmith@cannibalcentral.com
Web: www.cannibalcentral.com

Summary: We are a boutique search firm specializing in the building/construction industry. With hands on industry experience, we are able to place mid to senior level executive in all positions within the industry.

Key Contact - Specialty:
Ms. Kathee Smith, Headhunter

Salary Minimum: $60,000

Functions: Generalist (All)

Industries: Construction

Cannon And Associates

225 Broadway Rm 3602
New York, NY 10007-3480
(888) 233-3131

Summary: We specialize in the recruitment and placement of supply chain management professionals.

Key Contact - Specialty:
Mr. James Rohan, Partner
Ms. Paula Blumenthal, Partner - *Materials*
Mr. Kevin Rohan - *Purchasing*

Salary Minimum: $50,000

Functions: Materials, Purchasing, Materials Plng., Distribution, Packaging, Customer Svc., Systems Implem., Mgmt. Consultants

Industries: Generalist (All)

Canyon Search

1611 NW Laurel Way
Albany, OR 97321-1529
(541) 791-1236
(949) 589-8524
Fax: (541) 791-8337
Email: canyonsearch@aol.com

Summary: An executive search firm with experience specializing in attracting and referring top sales and sales management talent nationally, with particular emphasis in the printing, packaging and business products industries.

Key Contact - Specialty:
Ms. Pat Gregg, Owner - *Printing*

Salary Minimum: $50,000

Functions: Senior Mgmt., Middle Mgmt., Packaging, Sales & Mktg., Advertising, Sales Mgmt., Direct Mktg., Sales Reps.

Industries: Agri., Forestry, Mining, Manufacturing, Food, Bev., Tobacco, Paper, Printing, Plastics, Rubber, Metal Products, Consumer Goods, Transportation, Services, Advertising, Packaging, Marketing SW

Capital Markets Recruiting Partners, Inc

PO Box 510502
Saint Louis, MO 63151-0502
(877) 281-6797
Fax: (312) 264-0110
Email: huffman.matt@capital-markets.net
Web: www.capital-markets.net

Summary: An executive search firm specializing in the recruitment of mid to senior level professionals in the US and global capital markets. The firm accepts mandates in the areas of asset management, private equity, investment banking, research, and institutional sales and trading.

Key Contact - Specialty:
Mr. Matt Huffman, President - *Analysts, Asset management, Banking (Investment), Capital markets, Private equity*

Salary Minimum: $100,000

Functions: Finance, M&A

Industries: Generalist (All), Finance, Invest. Banking, Venture Cap., Mutual/Hedge Funds, Misc. Financial, Real Estate

Capitol Recruiting

451 Arrowhead Trl
Vero Beach, FL 32963-3925
(772) 231-8650
Email: goodjobs@bellsouth.net

Summary: We specialize in the consumer packaged good industry. We are an executive recruiting firm that specializes in sales & marketing. Our recruiting capabilities include: sales, brand management, broker management, category management, beverage sales, and operations management.

Key Contact - Specialty:
Mr. Buford Sims

Salary Minimum: $65,000

Functions: Senior Mgmt., Middle Mgmt., Sales & Mktg., Advertising, Mktg. Research, Minorities/Diversity

Industries: Food, Bev., Tobacco, Paper, Soap, Perf., Cosmtcs., Consumer Goods, Logistics Svcs., Supply Chain Mgmt., Entertainment, Sports, Advertising

Capitol Staffing Inc

460 Briarwood Dr Ste 110
Jackson, MS 39206-3053
(601) 957-1755
Fax: (601) 957-3880
Email: capitolstaffing@capitolstaffing.com
Web: www.capitolstaffing.com

Summary: We have built relationships through the years with our market area businesses in the: telecom, healthcare, legal, financial services and computer science industries. Accordingly, we attract job applicants with a variety of backgrounds, experience and skill sets. This enables us to provide you with top-notch candidates from which to select.

Key Contact - Specialty:
Ms. Carolyn Harrison, CPC, President - *Engineering, Information Technology, Sales*

Functions: Management, Admin. Svcs., Health Admin., Mktg. Mgmt., Sales Mgmt.

Industries: Generalist (All), Construction, Manufacturing, Retail, Finance, Services, Legal, Accounting, HR Services, Software, Healthcare

CAPPS Global Staffing Inc

13720 Pembroke Cir
Overland Park, KS 66224-4201
(913) 685-0430
Fax: (913) 685-3229
Email: ncapps@kc.rr.com

Summary: We specialize in IT placements and contracting with emphasis on software developers, package implementers, database administrators, software implementers, programmers/analysts, CIOs and system programmers. We place aerospace engineers and CATIA designers. We also place linguists who speak Arabic and Pashto and are willing to work internationally.

Key Contact - Specialty:
Mr. Norm Capps, President - *Client/server*

Salary Minimum: $70,000

Functions: Generalist (All), MIS Mgmt., Systems Analysis, Systems Dev., Systems Implem., Systems Support, Network Admin., DB Admin.

Industries: Generalist (All), Oil & Gas, Banking, Mgmt. Consulting, Telecoms, Telephony, Wireless, Defense, Homeland Security, Aerospace

Capri Resource Group Inc

1904 Capri Ln Ste 100
Schaumburg, IL 60193-2345
(847) 352-4340
Fax: (847) 352-6441

Summary: We specialize in the food and food manufacturing industries.

Key Contact - Specialty:
Ms. Cindy Caravello, President - *Food & beverage, Food service, Manufacturing, Manufacturing (Management), Packaging*

Salary Minimum: $45,000

Functions: Generalist (All)

Industries: Food, Bev., Tobacco

Capstone Search Group

1401 50th St Ste 300
West Des Moines, IA 50266-5938
(515) 273-9991
Fax: (515) 440-2347
Email: careers@insurance-csg.com
Web: www.csgrecruiting.com

Summary: We are a search firm built by two experienced CPC professionals who have run successful recruiting practices in their specific industry niches for many years. We specialize within the insurance and manufacturing industries.

Key Contact - Specialty:
Mr. Scot Dickerson, CPC, President, Insurance Division
Mr. Dennis Leininger, CPC, President, Manufacturing Division
Ms. Diane Quirk, CPC, Business Unit Manager
Mr. Chris Winterboer, CPC, RHU, Search Associate
Mr. Jeff Dorn, Search Associate
Ms. Mary Newgard, AU, Search Associate
Ms. Tara Erpelding, Search Associate, Manufacturing Division
Ms. Allison Wood, Search Associate
Mr. Jake Shapansky, Associate Consultant
Ms. Colleen Sites, Operations Specialist

Functions: Generalist (All)

Industries: Plastics, Rubber, Paints, Petro. Products, Metal Products, Machine, Appliance, Consumer Elect., Misc. Mfg., Engineering Svcs., Insurance

Card Resource Group Inc

2155 2nd Concession
RR 1
Lynden, ON L0R 1T0
Canada
(519) 647-2199
(614) 475-7745
Fax: (519) 647-2099
Email: daina@cardresourcegroup.com
Web: www.cardresourcegroup.com

Summary: We are a management and executive search firm servicing the US based credit card and electronic payments industries. We have expertise in finance, marketing, modeling, product management, database management, credit policy, risk management, collections, customer service, operations and sales.

Key Contact - Specialty:
Ms. Daina Di Veto, Managing Director - *Credit, Finance, Marketing, Operations, Risk management*
Ms. Andria Case, Director - *Call centers, Credit, Marketing, Operations, Sales*
Ms. Cheryl Antoski, Recruiter

Salary Minimum: $75,000

Functions: Management, Product Dev., Quality, Sales & Mktg., Direct Mktg., Finance, Credit, Risk Mgmt., Mgmt. Consultants

Industries: Finance, Banking, Misc. Financial, E-commerce, New Media, Call Centers

Career Advancement Services

7 Michigan Ave
East Dundee, IL 60118-1131
(847) 428-9255
(847) 903-1022
Email: greg@careeradvancementservices.com
Web: www.careeradvancementservices.com

Summary: Recruiting for: graphic design, animation, game software development, Web design, IT networking, biotechnology, criminal justice, medical office, interior design and architectural CAD drafting. We provide outplacement services and individual career coaching.

Key Contact - Specialty:
Mr. Greg Norton, CPC, Principal - *Hotels*

Salary Minimum: $40,000

Functions: IT

Industries: Manufacturing, Transportation, Retail, Finance, Architectural Svcs., Pharm Svcs., Media, Environmental Svcs., Software, Industry Specific SW

Career Advantage Personnel

1215 E Airport Dr Ste 125
Ontario, CA 91761-2018
(909) 466-9232
(512) 310-9095
Email: info@careeradvantage.net
Web: www.careeradvantage.net

Summary: We provide executive search, placement and career coaching.

Key Contact - Specialty:
Ms. Brynda Woods, President

Functions: Generalist (All), Management

Industries: Generalist (All), Manufacturing, Food, Bev., Tobacco, Paper, Drugs Mfg., Medical Devices, Plastics, Rubber, Consumer Elect., Electronic, Elec. Components, Consumer Goods

Career Alternatives Executive Search

5310 Tulip Ave Ste B
Lansing, MI 48911-3766
(517) 882-0234
Email: p.j.burns@sbcglobal.net
Web: N/A

Summary: We are an executive search firm specializing in the sales & marketing areas. Our primary clients are consumer product companies.

Key Contact - Specialty:
Mr. Patrick J. Burns, President - *Sales*

Salary Minimum: $50,000

Functions: Generalist (All), Sales & Mktg., Mktg. Research, Mktg. Mgmt., Sales Mgmt.

Industries: Generalist (All), Food, Bev., Tobacco, Textiles, Apparel, Paper, Soap, Perf., Cosmtcs., Drugs Mfg., Consumer Elect.

Career Associates

21 SE 3rd St Ste 500
Evansville, IN 47708-1421
(812) 423-7263
Fax: (812) 428-0059
Email: gene@career-associates.com
Web: www.career-associates.com

Summary: Our firm offers professional recruiting services which are based upon a contingency fee. We are recruiting generalists working multiple discipline positions.

Key Contact - Specialty:
Mr. Gene Whorl, President

Salary Minimum: $45,000

Functions: Generalist (All)

Industries: Generalist (All)

Career Center Inc

194 Passaic St
Hackensack, NJ 07601-3532
(800) 227-3379
(201) 342-1777
Fax: (201) 342-1776
Email: career@careercenterinc.com
Web: www.careercenterinc.com

Summary: The mission of our staff is to know customers' needs and supply high quality candidates at competitive rates with dependable service. Our dedicated team of professional certified personnel consultants has developed a carefully trained, highly selective talent pool, which we can tap to quickly meet any staffing challenge. We find 'people' solutions.

Key Contact - Specialty:
Mr. Barry Franzino, Jr., CPC, CTS, President
Ms. Connie Powers, CPC, Manager
Mr. James Chambers, Account Executive - *Food, Sales*
Mr. Nick Malefyt, Manager

Salary Minimum: $50,000

Functions: Generalist (All), Management, Admin. Svcs., Materials, Nurses, Sales & Mktg., HR Mgmt., Finance, Minorities/Diversity

Industries: Generalist (All), Food, Bev., Tobacco, Finance, Insurance, Healthcare, Hospitals, Long-term/Home Care

Branches:
2184 Morris Ave
Union, NJ 07083-5902
(908) 687-1812
Key Contact - Specialty:
Mr. Rigoberto Salas, Manager

Career Centers, Inc.

4600 Vine St Ste 1
Cincinnati, OH 45217-1259
(513) 641-0900
Fax: (513) 641-0204
Email: jobs@careercentersinc.com
Web: www.careercentersinc.com

Summary: We are a nationwide recruiting and staffing firm specializing in permanent placements across the nation. We specialize in the fields of mechanical, manufacturing, production, industrial, electrical, metallurgical, software/hardware, electronics, aerospace/defense, chemical, management, support personnel, applications, automation/robotics, packaging, istrumentation, process controls, painting/coatings, test/evaluation, tooling, foundry/casting, and steel aluminum.

Key Contact - Specialty:
Mr. Robert Wick, Principal

Mr. Dave Wick, Principal
Mr. Jim Mahon, Recruiter

Salary Minimum: $40,000

Functions: Mfg.

Industries: Construction, Manufacturing, Food, Bev., Tobacco, Medical Devices, Plastics, Rubber, Paints, Petro. Products, Logistics Svcs., Supply Chain Mgmt, Defense, Environmental Svcs.

Career Choice Inc

1 Purlieu Pl Ste 240
Winter Park, FL 32792-4406
(407) 679-5150
Fax: (407) 679-0998
Email: info@careerchoice.cc

Summary: Our success is driven by the research capability to attract top talent for our clients. Our growth is accomplished through innovative strategies, results-oriented associates, quality services and personal attention to detail. Our focus industry is the Hospitality industry.

Key Contact - Specialty:
Ms. Colleen Herrick, President & Partner - *Finance, Hospitality, Marketing, Research & development*

Salary Minimum: $35,000

Functions: Generalist (All), Product Dev., Purchasing

Industries: Food, Bev., Tobacco, HR Services, Hospitality, Hotels, Resorts, Clubs, Restaurants, Quick Service Restaurants, Full Service Restaurants, Entertainment

Career Concepts Executive Options, Inc.

(formerly known as Career Concepts & Associates Inc)
5601 N.W. 72nd Street, Suite 324
Fifty-Six Expressway Place building
Oklahoma City, OK 73132
(405) 603-7027
Fax: (405) 603-5121
Email: search@careerconceptseo.com
Web: www.careerconceptseo.com

Summary: Career Concepts is a career management firm for executives and professionals. Our services address the needs of both employers and individuals. We specialize in: Executive Search, Corporate Outplacement, Career Transition Counseling, Spousal Relocation, and Professional Resume writing. Our business clients are extremely diversified and range from small, family-owned firms to Fortune 500 corporations.

Key Contact - Specialty:
Mr. David O. Ferguson, President
Mrs. Sharon Ferguson, Executive Search - *Engineering, Executives, Finance, Human resources, Manufacturing*
Mr. Rick Thompson, Director, Executive Search - *Accounting, Banking, Comptrollers, Data processing, Engineering*

Salary Minimum: $40,000

Functions: Generalist (All), Senior Mgmt.

Industries: Generalist (All)

Career Consociates Inc

(also known as CCI Staffing)
220 Montgomery St
San Francisco, CA 94104-3402
(415) 398-3894
Email: sharron@ccistaffing.com
Web: www.ccistaffing.com

Summary: Our company's secret to success has been our unwavering commitment to each client's and candidate's needs. Successful staffing is our first priority. We don't just fill jobs; we match people, skills and personalities.

Key Contact - Specialty:
Ms. Sharron Long, President
Ms. Carol Foster, Recruiter
Ms. Paula Sharpe, Recruiter
Mr. George Matthews, Recruiter
Mr. John Merrell, Recruiter

Functions: Admin. Svcs., PR, Legal, Paralegals

Industries: Generalist (All), Misc. Financial, Legal, Media, Advertising, Publishing, New Media, Broadcast, Film, Biotech/Life Sciences

Career Consultants Staffing Services Inc

7320 N Mo Pac Expy Ste 400
Austin, TX 78731-2347
(512) 346-6660
Fax: (512) 346-6714
Email: career@careeraustin.com
Web: www.careeraustin.com

Summary: Full service staffing from executive search to temp and contract staffing. Tenured professional recruiters handling search activities and separate staff to handle contract/temp placement.

Key Contact - Specialty:
Mrs. Pamela Bratton, Vice President
Mrs. Debra Freeman, CPC, Professional Recruiter - *Administration, Clerical, Middle management, Office (Administration)*
Mr. Larry Escamilla, Professional Recruiter - *Engineering, Field engineering, Logistics, Manufacturing (Management), Six Sigma*
Ms. Kamron Lunsford, Professional Recruiter - *Benefits, Compensation, Diversity, Human resources, Organizational development*
Mr. James Russell, Professional Technical Recruiter - *Client/server, Computers, Database, Technical, Technology*

Functions: Generalist (All), Management, Admin. Svcs., Sales & Mktg., Sales Mgmt., HR Mgmt., Benefits

Industries: Generalist (All), Misc. Mfg., Legal, HR Services, E-commerce, IT Implementation, Engineering Svcs., Logistics Svcs., Supply Chain Mgmt., Telecoms, Call Centers, Software, Database SW, Development SW

Career Counseling Inc (CCI)

(also known as CCI Executive Search)
5760 US Highway 60 W
Owensboro, KY 42301-9281
(941) 355-7006
Fax: (270) 684-1079
Email: syoung17@bellsouth.net

Summary: Our firm has search experience in engineering, operations and sales placement into the manufacturing and store fixture industry.

Key Contact - Specialty:
Mr. Steven J. Young, President - *Chemical*

Salary Minimum: $35,000

Functions: Generalist (All), Senior Mgmt., Mfg., Sales & Mktg.

Industries: Manufacturing, Lumber, Furniture, Plastics, Rubber, Metal Products, Non-Classifiable

Career Enterprises

4807 Rockside Rd Ste 730
Independence, OH 44131-2166
(216) 901-7200

Email: info@careerenterprises.com
Web: www.careerenterprises.com

Summary: Privately-owned contingency and executive search firm. Fully automated database including access to Internet, capable of management and senior executive-level search as well as staff technical placement.

Key Contact - Specialty:
Mr. Stuart Taylor, President

Salary Minimum: $50,000

Functions: IT

Industries: Generalist (All)

Career Forum Inc

165 S Union Blvd Ste 1020
Lakewood, CO 80228-2237
(303) 279-9200
Fax: (303) 279-9296
Email: inquiries@careerforum.com
Web: www.careerforum.com

Summary: Executive search consultants specializing in sales, sales management, technical and management positions in high growth industries including: telecom, software, engineering, IT, printing, print management, advertising sales, construction management, general & operations management, eCommerce, mortgage lending and direct mail.

Key Contact - Specialty:
Mr. Stan Grebe, CPC, President - *Construction, HVAC*
Ms. Jennifer Price, Executive Administrator - *Accounting (General), Administration, Benefits, Human resources*
Mr. David Young, Senior Account Executive
Mr. Chris DuChane, Account Executive, Construction Division - *Construction, Management, Sales*
Mr. Todd Taylor, National Account Executive - *Engineering, Information Technology, Sales*
Ms. Julie Rojas, Account Executive - *Direct marketing, Healthcare, Printing, Sales*
Ms. Kori Hazlett, Account Executive, Oil & Gas Division - *Business development, Gas, Oil, Sales*
Ms. Julie Knox, Account Executive - *Advertising, Business development, Executives, Management, Sales*

Functions: Generalist (All)

Industries: Generalist (All), Construction, Printing, Computer Equip., IT Implementation, Advertising, Publishing, Digital, Network Infrastructure, HR SW

The Career Group Ltd

PO Box 96
Nahant, MA 01908-0096
(781) 596-3322
Fax: (781) 693-6499
Email: judy@careergroup.com
Web: www.careergroup.com

Summary: A boutique placement firm specializing in software development, hardware development and product management as well as executive-level positions in these areas.

Key Contact - Specialty:
Ms. Judy Walsh, President
Mr. Barry Katz, Vice President

Functions: Management, Senior Mgmt., Engineering

Industries: Software

Career Image Inc

12784 Panhandle Rd
Hampton, GA 30228-2282
(770) 897-9115
Email: theheadhunters@comcast.net

Summary: We are a generalist firm specializing in the retail industry. We also have a research division, in which we bill hourly. This division is designed to supplement a client's classified advertising program.

Key Contact - Specialty:
Mr. Ellison C. Day, President - *Retail*
Ms. Sherri Hunter, Account Executive - *Retail*
Mr. Paul Greeve, Account Executive

Salary Minimum: $30,000

Functions: Middle Mgmt.

Industries: Retail

Career Insights

1873 SW Oakwater Pt
Palm City, FL 34990-7753
(772) 286-3084
Email: credentials@careerinsights.net
Web: www.careerinsights.net/default.asp

Summary: We are one of the most effective, successful search firms in the United States. Our search consultants hold the highest standard of professional and personal integrity in the search industry.

Key Contact - Specialty:
Mr. Keith Mills

Salary Minimum: $60,000

Functions: Generalist (All)

Industries: Generalist (All)

Career Logix

PO Box 59563
Schaumburg, IL 60159-0563
(847) 240-2000
Email: jobs@careerlogix.com
Web: webmaster@careerlogix.com

Summary: With today's economy, the traditional methods of both job placement and job hunting have been transformed. Our firm was formed with the goal of providing new, more efficient and cost effective methods of bringing businesses and candidates together. Our services include: job placement, career counseling, resume writing, outplacement and outsourcing.

Key Contact - Specialty:
Mr. Richard Gucwa, President & Chief Executive Officer
Ms. Kristen Boggs, Vice President, Operations

Salary Minimum: $30,000

Functions: Generalist (All)

Industries: Retail, Finance, Banking, Services, Hospitality, Restaurants, Media, Telecoms, Wireless, Marketing SW

Career Management Associates

3737 Woodland Ave Ste 225
West Des Moines, IA 50266-1941
(515) 309-5530
Fax: (515) 309-9049
Email: info@cmacareerhelp.com
Web: www.cmacareerhelp.com

Summary: Operates in over 80 different industry categories. Federal contractor. GSA certified. Contingency Recruiting of Perm, Contract, and contract to hire.

Key Contact - Specialty:

Mr. Bill Grimes, President - *Accounting, Architecture, Consulting, Engineering, Financial*
Mr. William Grimes, Senior Vice President - *Government, Industrial, Labor, Manufacturing, Sales*
Mr. Russell Baugh, Vice President - *Information Technology, Technical, Telecommunications*
Mr. Steve Walter, Vice President - *Government, Science*
Mrs. Connie Ly-barksdale, Staffing Director - *Medical*
Mrs. Pamela Baugh, Staffing Director - *Banking, Engineering, Staffing*
Mrs. Crystal Metheny, Staffing Support Director - *Staffing*

Functions: Management, Mfg., Materials, Healthcare, Sales & Mktg., Finance, IT, R&D, Architects, Health & Safety

Industries: Generalist (All)

Career Management Group LLC

434 Ridgedale Ave Ste 11
East Hanover, NJ 07936-1450
(973) 428-5239
Fax: (973) 428-5084
Email: careermanage@optonline.net
Web: www.careermgmtgroup.com

Summary: We provide candidates in areas such as engineering, healthcare and pharmaceutical, IT, general management, sales & marketing and administration. Our firm tailors recruiting services for both employers and job seekers, keeping abreast of changing job market trends.

Key Contact - Specialty:
Ms. Toni Donofrio, Managing Member

Salary Minimum: $30,000

Functions: Generalist (All)

Industries: Generalist (All), Misc. Mfg., Retail, Legal, Accounting, Engineering Svcs., Telecoms, Telephony, Aerospace, Biotech/Life Sciences

Career Marketing Associates Inc

7100 E Belleview Ave Ste 203
Greenwood Village, CO 80111-1643
(303) 779-8890
(800) 638-8903
Fax: (303) 779-8139
Email: cma@cmagroup.com
Web: www.cmagroup.com

Summary: Since inception our only business has been to provide capable personnel to companies. Each of our recruiters specializes in a field utilizing his or her background.

Key Contact - Specialty:
Mr. Jan Sather, President
Mr. Terry Leyden
Mr. Chip Doro, Vice President - *Marketing*

Salary Minimum: $35,000

Functions: Generalist (All), Product Dev., Production, MIS Mgmt., Systems Analysis, Systems Dev., Systems Support

Industries: Generalist (All), Medical Devices, Computer Equip., Test, Measure Equip., Telecoms, Software, Biotech/Life Sciences

Career Placement Network, LLC

23 Harding Rd
West Caldwell, NJ 07006-7949
(973) 403-9381
Email: rspadaro@cpnjoblink.com
Web: www.cpnjoblink.com

Summary: CPN is a professional staffing firm specializing in recruitment and placement of talented professionals in permanent positions. We place highly-skilled job candidates at all levels in the areas of Information Technology, Telecommunications, Financial & Accounting, Sales & Marketing, and Customer Service.

Key Contact - Specialty:
Mr. Ron Spadaro, Managing Director

Salary Minimum: $50,000

Functions: Sales & Mktg., Finance, IT

Industries: Generalist (All)

Career Profiles

PO Box 11
Portsmouth, NH 03802-0011
(603) 433-3355
Fax: (603) 433-8678
Email: jobnexus@aol.com

Summary: We place individuals with sales, sales management and marketing backgrounds in medical, pharmaceutical, publishing and industrial sales positions. We also place professionals in other disciplines as well.

Key Contact - Specialty:
Ms. Leanne P. Gray, CPC - *Sales*
Mr. Norman G. Gray, RN, CPC - *Sales*

Functions: Healthcare, Sales & Mktg., Sales Mgmt.

Industries: Drugs Mfg., Medical Devices, Consumer Goods, Pharm Svcs., Biotech/Life Sciences, Healthcare, Hospitals, Long-term/Home Care, Dental, Physical Therapy, Occupational Therapy

Career Pros International

PO Box 1631
Charleston, WV 25326-1631
(304) 389-2907
Email: janhensleycmp@careerpros.biz
Web: www.careerpros.biz

Summary: Executive recruitment, outplacement programs from seminars to executive coaching packages, career coaching and career development for executives.

Key Contact - Specialty:
Ms. Janice Hensley, President & Chief Executive Officer

Salary Minimum: $60,000

Functions: Generalist (All)

Industries: Generalist (All)

Career Resources Inc

PO Box 1091
Harrisonburg, VA 22803-1091
(540) 433-2115
Email: tlr@newcareers.com
Web: www.newcareers.com

Summary: Our firm is a full-service recruiting firm with access to thousands of currently available job openings currently available qualified candidates.

Key Contact - Specialty:
Ms. Terry Rhodes, Principal

Salary Minimum: $50,000

Functions: Generalist (All)

Industries: Generalist (All), Manufacturing, Food, Bev., Tobacco, Printing, Medical Devices, Plastics, Rubber, Paints, Petro. Products, Metal Products, Machine, Appliance, Motor Vehicles, Consumer Elect., Misc. Mfg., Electronic, Elec. Components, Robotics

Career Search Associates

13523 University Ave
Clive, IA 50325-8263
(515) 440-5605
(515) 440-5600
Fax: (515) 440-0963
Email: careers@careersearchassoc.com
Web: www.careersearchassoc.com

Summary: Ours is a client driven, specialized
search firm. Our recruiters each focus on separate
areas of expertise. Our areas of specialization
include: accounting, administrative support,
transportation/logistics/supply chain/distribution
management, retail management, HR,
medical/pharmaceutical sales and inside/outside
sales.

Key Contact - Specialty:
Ms. Cheryl Campbell, Manager, Recruiting -
*Distribution, Human resources, Logistics,
Retail, Transportation*
Ms. Tammy Cline, CPC, President & Owner -
Sales

Salary Minimum: $20,000

Functions: Generalist (All), Admin. Svcs., Mfg.,
Distribution, Sales & Mktg., Sales Mgmt.

Industries: Generalist (All), Manufacturing,
Transportation, Retail, Logistics Svcs., Supply
Chain Mgmt, Call Centers

Career Search Consultants LLC

962 E Remington Dr
Chandler, AZ 85249-1021
(480) 814-0855
Email: paul@cscrecruiters.com
Web: www.cscrecruiters.com

Summary: A specialty search firm focused on
positions in paint, coatings and allied chemicals.
We recruit pro-actively, directly contacting
candidates rather than advertising.

Key Contact - Specialty:
Mr. Paul Jentlie, President - *Coatings, Paint*

Functions: Generalist (All), Product Dev.,
Production, Distribution, Sales Mgmt., R&D,
Engineering, Architects

Industries: Energy, Utilities, Construction,
Manufacturing, Printing, Chemicals, Paints,
Petro. Products, Packaging, Real Estate

Career Solutions Group Inc

55 Monument Cir Ste 1000
Indianapolis, IN 46204-5901
(317) 466-9740
Fax: (317) 465-9742
Email: info@csgsearch.com
Web: www.csgsearch.com

Summary: We are a HR consulting firm, which
specializes in executive & technical search. We
work with clients in industries ranging from
banking and accounting to engineering and sales.
All eligible recruiters at our firm are CPC
certified.

Key Contact - Specialty:
Mr. D. Mark Barnhart, Partner
Mr. Steven R. Fero, CPC, Partner

Salary Minimum: $50,000

Functions: Generalist (All)

Industries: Generalist (All), Manufacturing,
Medical Devices, Misc. Mfg., Finance, Banking,
Invest. Banking, Misc. Financial, Services, HR
Services

Career Solutions International

400 Lexington Green Ln
Sanford, FL 32771-1007
(866) 484-4752
(407) 688-6727
Fax: (407) 688-4330
Email: resumes@csigroup.net
Web: www.csigroup.net

Summary: We are a leading authority in executive
talent acquisition for organizations worldwide,
both large and small. Whether you need to hire
one key leader or staff an entire organization, we
are dedicated to helping you make the best
possible hiring decision.

Key Contact - Specialty:
Ms. Suzette DiMascio, CHE, CMCE, President &
Chief Executive Officer - *Biomedical,
Biopharmaceutical, Biotechnology, Business
development, C-level*
Mr. Sean Ramdial, Vice President, Finance &
Banking - *ATM, Banking, C-level, Finance,
Legal*
Mr. Timothy Cooley, Vice President, Technology
& Food Serv - *E-business, Food & beverage,
Hospitality, Information Systems, Restaurants*
Ms. Jessica Eve, Senior Director, Talent
Acquistion - *Biomedical, Biopharmaceutical,
Biotechnology, Boards of Directors, Business
development*
Mr. Fernando Tovar, Director, Talent Acquisition
- *Architecture, Asset management, Building
products, Construction, Engineering*
Ms. Amy Harder, WBE, Director, Diversity,
WBE
Ms. Janine Klein, Director, Talent Acquisition -
Biotechnology, Pharmaceutical

Salary Minimum: $50,000

Functions: Generalist (All), Senior Mgmt.,
Middle Mgmt., Healthcare, Sales & Mktg.,
Finance, Hospitality

Industries: Generalist (All), Finance, Pharm
Svcs., Legal, Accounting, HR Services,
Hospitality, Insurance, Biotech/Life Sciences,
Healthcare, Hospitals, Long-term/Home Care

Career+Plus

488 White Springs Rd
Geneva, NY 14456-3024
(315) 789-3023
Fax: (315) 789-3108
Email: careerop@telenet.net
Web: www.opticsatcareerplus.com

Summary: We specialize in professional sales
management and field reps, as well as all aspects
of engineering management and hands-on
engineers in the optics and laser science industries.
Engineering includes management, design, testing
and research. Sales include management, sales
engineers and field reps.

Key Contact - Specialty:
Mr. James M. Keyser, Owner & Recruiter -
*Engineering, Optics, Photonics, Sales,
Semiconductors*

Salary Minimum: $35,000

Functions: Management, Senior Mgmt., Middle
Mgmt., Sales & Mktg., Mktg. Mgmt., Sales
Mgmt., Engineering

Industries: Semiconductors

CareerConnections USA Inc

12827 Westledge Ln
Saint Louis, MO 63131-2237
(314) 909-8510
(314) 909-7011
Fax: (314) 909-8513

Email: deb@careerconnectionsusa.com
Web: www.careerconnectionsusa.com

Summary: Medical recruitment firm specializing
in the placement of sales, sales management,
marketing and applications personnel in radiology
and IT.

Key Contact - Specialty:
Mrs. Debra Hill, Chief Executive Officer
Mr. Brian Hill, President

Functions: Generalist (All), Sales & Mktg.

Industries: Medical Devices, Software,
Biotech/Life Sciences, Healthcare

Careers for Women and Men Inc

799 Broadway Ste 402
New York, NY 10003-6811
(212) 777-4646
Fax: (212) 777-5949
Email: careers@careersforwomen.com
Web: www.careersforwomen.com

Summary: Applicants must presently live in our
market area to be considered. Executive sales:
from entry level to senior management,
specializing in media plus all other major
industries.

Key Contact - Specialty:
Mr. David W. King, President

Functions: Sales & Mktg., Sales Mgmt.

Industries: Generalist (All)

Careers Inc

208 Ave Ponce De Leon Ste 1100
San Juan, PR 00918-1036
(787) 764-2298
Fax: (787) 764-2530
Email: careers@careersincpr.com
Web: www.careersincpr.com

Summary: Executive recruiting firm with a
professional staff of 29 employees servicing the
manufacturing, construction, finance, sales &
marketing, HR, IT, banking and administrative
personnel positions.

Key Contact - Specialty:
Mr. Rupert R. Amy, President, CEO & Owner
Ms. Ruth Gonzalez, CPC, General Manager &
Partner - *Manufacturing*
Ms. Carla Deyo, CPC, Partner & Vice President -
Sales
Ms. Clara Amiama, Senior Consultant & Partner -
Finance, Information Technology

Salary Minimum: $30,000

Functions: Generalist (All), Management, Mfg.,
Healthcare, Sales & Mktg., HR Mgmt., Finance,
IT

Industries: Generalist (All), Construction,
Manufacturing, Finance, Services, Software

CareersPro Inc

4625 Virginia Ave
Fort Wayne, IN 46808-1267
(260) 482-1200
Fax: (260) 483-1630
Email: andy@careerspro.com
Web: www.careerspro.com

Summary: Headquartered in Fort Wayne, IN, we
are a leading provider of strategic staffing and
career transition services. We partner with
companies of all sizes in virtually every industry
to optimize their business by matching talented
professionals with companies in need of services
or technical expertise. We have over 10 years
experience providing high quality services to
clients throughout the United States, Canada, and
Mexico.

Key Contact - Specialty:
Mr. Andy Gilbert, President

Functions: Quality, Materials, Purchasing, Distribution, Engineering

Industries: Generalist (All), Manufacturing, Communications, Aerospace, Biotech/Life Sciences, Healthcare

CareerTrac Professional Group Inc

250 Bishops Way Ste 101
Brookfield, WI 53005-6222
(262) 754-1414
Fax: (262) 754-1416
Email: cindy@careertrac.com
Web: www.careertrac.com

Summary: Professional search firm specializing in the placement of legal, manufacturing, financial and professional sales personnel. Providing recruitment of attorneys, including associate levels to senior partners; banking executives to mid level operations and support personnel; sales managers/representatives and mid and upper manufacturing management.

Key Contact - Specialty:
Ms. Cindy Johnson, CPC, President - *Advertising, Clerical, Legal, Legal (Attorneys), Office (Administration)*
Mr. Edward R. Buchholz, Vice President - *Banking (Corporate), Executives, General management, Sales, Senior management*

Functions: Admin. Svcs., Sales Mgmt., HR Mgmt., Benefits, Staffing, Finance, Legal, Attorneys, Paralegals

Industries: Generalist (All), Finance, Legal, HR Services

Careerxchange

10689 N Kendall Dr Ste 209
Miami, FL 33176-1594
(305) 595-3800
Fax: (305) 279-8903
Email: jobs@careerxchange.com
Web: www.careerxchange.com

Summary: We place full-time, temp and temp to hire employees in all industries in the clerical, administrative and professional areas. We service large Fortune 500 companies as well as small to medium size family owned businesses.

Key Contact - Specialty:
Ms. Sue Romanos, CPC, CTS, President
Ms. Suzanne Hodes, CPC, CTS, Vice President
Ms. Jessica Diaz, Recruiter

Salary Minimum: $24,900

Functions: Admin. Svcs., Sales & Mktg., Direct Mktg., Customer Svc., Paralegals

Industries: Generalist (All), Legal, Accounting, Call Centers

Branches:
9050 Pines Blvd Ste 150
Pembroke Pines, FL 33024-6400
(954) 437-0070
Fax: (954) 431-3699
Email: jobs@careerxchange.com
Key Contact - Specialty:
Mr. Nick Alonso, Jr., Vice President

Peter N Carey & Associates Inc

1010 Jorie Blvd Ste 400
Oak Brook, IL 60523-2239
(630) 573-4260
(877) 762-2739
Fax: (630) 573-0529
Email: pncarey1@sbcglobal.net

Summary: We are an executive search firm specializing in direct marketing, eCommerce, and the graphic arts industries.

Key Contact - Specialty:
Mr. Peter N. Carey, President - *Direct marketing*

Salary Minimum: $60,000

Functions: Generalist (All)

Industries: Paper, Printing, Non-profits, Mgmt. Consulting, Advertising, Telecoms, Database SW, Doc. Mgmt., Production SW, Marketing SW

Caringly Be All

7301 Blue Heron Cv
Volente, TX 78641-6140
(512) 219-0224
(512) 258-1236
Fax: (512) 258-6024
Email: kbeall@austin.rr.com

Summary: Independent search consultant specializing in healthcare and well-being. Offers highly personalized services for a wide variety of disciplines and settings. Particular focus is personal, professional and organizational development.

Key Contact - Specialty:
Ms. Karen Lee Beall, Owner - *Healthcare*

Functions: Management, Senior Mgmt., Mfg., Healthcare, Physicians, Nurses, Allied Health, Sales & Mktg., CFOs, Mgmt. Consultants

Industries: Generalist (All), Drugs Mfg., Medical Devices, Non-profits, Pharm Svcs., Mgmt. Consulting, Biotech/Life Sciences, Healthcare, Hospitals, Long-term/Home Care, Physical Therapy, Occupational Therapy

Carion Resource Group Inc

6790 Davand Dr
Mississauga, ON L5T 2G5
Canada
(905) 795-9187
Email: jobs@carionresource.com
Web: www.carionresource.com

Summary: We are executive management and support staff recruiters. Career transition and outplacement services are offered to companies restructuring or down sizing.

Key Contact - Specialty:
Mr. Harvey Carey, President - *Distribution, Manufacturing*

Salary Minimum: $30,000

Functions: Middle Mgmt., Admin. Svcs., Production, Plant Mgmt., Purchasing, Distribution, CFOs, Systems Analysis, Systems Implem., Systems Support

Industries: Generalist (All)

Carlson, Bentley Associates

3889 Promontory Ct
Boulder, CO 80304-1053
(303) 443-6500
Email: dlmiller84@comcast.net
Web: www.ptrecruiter.com

Summary: Specializing in the recruitment of healthcare professionals; this includes nursing managers and allied health professionals.

Key Contact - Specialty:
Mr. Don Miller, Owner - *Data processing*

Functions: Management, Board Members, Senior Mgmt., Middle Mgmt., Healthcare, Nurses, Allied Health

Industries: Physical Therapy

Carnegie Executive Search Inc

2 Carnegie Rd
Lawrenceville, NJ 08648-3302
(609) 883-8900
Fax: (609) 883-6644
Web: www.carnegiesearch.com

Summary: We work with integrated marketing communications 'production companies'. We also work with sales, executive producers, technical directors, creative directors, management executives and interactive multimedia technicians and designers.

Key Contact - Specialty:
Mr. William Argust

Functions: Senior Mgmt.

Industries: E-commerce, Entertainment, Advertising, New Media, Broadcast, Film, Non-Classifiable

Carnegie Resources Inc

821 Baxter St Ste 306
Charlotte, NC 28202-2713
(704) 375-7701
Fax: (704) 375-7727
Email: jobs2000@bellsouth.net
Web: www.carnegieresources.com

Summary: We have experience in recruiting serving the engineering, manufacturing and technical sectors. We work with managers, supervisors, engineers, designers, maintenance and technicians in manufacturing, quality and design roles.

Key Contact - Specialty:
Mr. Thomas Shearer, President - *Engineering, Manufacturing*
Mr. Lee Holland, Vice President - *HVAC, Product management/development*
Mr. Rick Linstead, Manager, Engineering - *Machining, Plastics*
Mr. Ron McDowell, Engineering Supervisor - *Materials, Quality*

Salary Minimum: $30,000

Functions: Generalist (All), Management, Mfg., Product Dev., Engineering

Industries: Construction, Manufacturing, Medical Devices, Plastics, Rubber, Metal Products, Machine, Appliance, Motor Vehicles, Computer Equip., Consumer Elect., Test, Measure Equip., Misc. Mfg.

Carney, Sandoe & Associates

136 Boylston St
Boston, MA 02116-4608
(617) 542-0260
(800) 225-7986
Fax: (617) 542-9400
Email: recruitment@carneysandoe.com
Web: www.carneysandoe.com

Summary: We are an educational recruitment, executive search and strategic consulting firm that places teachers and administrators in private, independent schools across the US and overseas. We have placed over 16,000 teachers and administrators in independent schools. We have thousands of positions available in all primary and secondary subjects each year.

Key Contact - Specialty:
Mr. James H. Carney, II, Chairman
Mr. Devereaux McClatchey, President
Ms. Agnes C. Underwood, Vice President & Director, Search
Ms. Kathleen Johnson, Vice President & Senior Associate
Mr. John Faubert, Managing Associate & Director, Placement

Email your resume to a targeted list of recruiters now at www.ExecutiveAgent.com/DER07

Mr. Jonathan Ball, Managing Associate & Director, Sch Serv
Mr. Scott Roy, Managing Associate & Director, Tech
Mr. Ryan Irwin, Senior Associate & Director, Bus Applic
Mr. Rice Bryan, Placement Assoc/Dir, Internal Hiring
Ms. Jessica Clark, Placement Associate
Mr. Todd Gochman, Placement Associate
Ms. H. Burke Rathbun, Placement Associate
Mr. Gary Gruber, Senior Search Consultant
Ms. Rayna Loeb, Senior Search Consultant
Ms. Trina Secor, Senior Search Consultant
Mr. H. Boni Nam, Director, Operations

Functions: Staffing

Industries: Non-profits

Carpenter Legal Search Inc

301 Grant St Ste 3030
Pittsburgh, PA 15219-6406
(412) 255-3770
Fax: (412) 255-3780
Email: lcarpenter@carpenterlegalsearch.com
Web: www.carpenterlegalsearch.com

Summary: We have legal recruiting experience. Our firm is one of the leading legal search firms, with experienced attorneys in full-time, permanent positions with law firms and corporations locally and nationally.

Key Contact - Specialty:
Ms. Lori J. Carpenter, President

Functions: Legal, Attorneys

Industries: Generalist (All)

Carr Management Services Inc

211 Harvey Rd
Chadds Ford, PA 19317-9747
(610) 358-5630
Fax: (610) 358-5696
Email: carrms@aol.com
Web: www.carrms.com

Summary: We offer recruiting services in the areas of biotechnology, biopharmaceuticals, life sciences, research products and diagnostics.

Key Contact - Specialty:
Dr. Denise Carr, President
Dr. James Lowry, Vice President

Functions: Middle Mgmt., Product Dev., Sales & Mktg., Mktg. Research, Mktg. Mgmt., Sales Mgmt.

Industries: Medical Devices, Biotech/Life Sciences

Cars Group International

22540 Manor St Ste 200
Saint Clair Shores, MI 48081-2358
(586) 445-0488
Fax: (586) 445-0489
Email: lmartin@carsgroup.com
Web: www.carsgroup.com

Summary: We are an executive search, contract staffing and consulting practice. We accept retained, contingency or contract assignments. We place senior management, sales, business development, sales management, strategic alliances, channels, pre-sales, consultants, engineers, IT and network professionals primarily for the technology, manufacturing and medical industries.

Key Contact - Specialty:
Ms. Linda D. Martin, Chairman - *Business development, Industrial, Sales, Technology*
Mr. Joseph S. Martin, President & Chief Executive Officer - *Business development, Industrial, Robotics, Technology*

Salary Minimum: $65,000

Functions: Generalist (All), Management, Senior Mgmt., Automation, Sales & Mktg., Mktg. Mgmt., IT, Engineering, Mgmt. Consultants

Industries: Generalist (All), Manufacturing, Wholesale, Finance, Services, Hospitality, Communications, Government, Software, Biotech/Life Sciences

Carter McKenzie Inc

271 US Highway 46 Ste A206
Fairfield, NJ 07004-2400
(973) 244-6060
Fax: (973) 224-6070
Email: recruiter@carter-mckenzie.com
Web: www.cartermckenzie.com

Summary: We are an organization whose principle function is the identification and recruitment of professional staff within the field of IS/technology and HR.

Key Contact - Specialty:
Mr. John Capo, President

Salary Minimum: $50,000

Functions: Generalist (All), Board Members, MIS Mgmt., Systems Analysis, Systems Dev., Systems Implem., Systems Support, Mgmt. Consultants

Industries: Generalist (All), Drugs Mfg., Finance, Brokers, Media, Communications, Insurance, Software, Healthcare

Carter Mckay

777 Terrace Ave Ste 3B
Hasbrouck Heights, NJ 07604-3123
(201) 288-5100
Fax: (201) 288-2660
Email: info.nj@cartermackay.com
Web: www.cartermackay.com

Summary: We specialize in sales, sales management, marketing and senior management within the healthcare, IT and business-to-business sectors. In addition, we place chemists, scientists, QC, and RA personnel within the pharmaceutical/biotechnology industry. Client companies ranging in size from pre-IPO start-up to Fortune 100.

Key Contact - Specialty:
Mr. Bruce Green, Principal - *Healthcare, Marketing, Sales, Senior management*
Mr. George Villano, Principal - *Business to business, Sales, Senior management*

Salary Minimum: $50,000

Functions: Senior Mgmt., Middle Mgmt., Quality, Mktg. Mgmt., Sales Mgmt., Sales Reps., Systems Implem., Systems Support, R&D

Industries: Drugs Mfg., Medical Devices, Computer Equip., Services, Pharm Svcs., New Media, Communications, Software, Biotech/Life Sciences, Healthcare

Branches:
50 Braintree Hill Park Ste 205
Braintree, MA 02184-8710
(781) 535-6161
Fax: (781) 535-6767
Email: info.ma@cartermackay.com
Key Contact - Specialty:
Mr. Michael Rowell, Vice President - *Business to business, Healthcare*

1979 Marcus Ave Ste 210
New Hyde Park, NY 11042-1022
(516) 616-7700
Email: info.ny@cartermackay.com
Key Contact - Specialty:
Mr. Larry Orbach, Principal - *Business to business, Healthcare*

2000 Regency Pkwy Ste 495
Cary, NC 27518-7727
(919) 380-1200
Fax: (919) 380-1267
Email: info.nc@cartermackay.com
Key Contact - Specialty:
Mr. Al Hertz, Vice President - *Business to business, Healthcare*

The Carvir Group Inc

PO Box 125
Fayetteville, GA 30214-0125
(770) 631-3029
Fax: (770) 486-0636
Email: recruiting@carvir.com
Web: www.carvir.com

Summary: We have worked with a broad spectrum of clients - multinational corporations, as well as start-up companies. We focus on clients in the financial services, technology, manufacturing, consumer products, energy, food and pharmaceutical industries.

Key Contact - Specialty:
Mr. Virgil L. Fludd, President - *Finance, General management, Human resources, Marketing, Sales*
Ms. Carolyn Kelley, Vice President

Salary Minimum: $50,000

Functions: Generalist (All), Sales & Mktg., HR Mgmt., Finance, IT, Specialized Svcs.

Industries: Generalist (All), Finance, Services, Media

CAS Comsearch Inc

950 3rd Ave Ste 1600
New York, NY 10022-2770
(212) 593-0861
Fax: (212) 755-4597
Email: comsearch@aol.com

Summary: We are a New York search firm supplying sales, operations and marketing people to companies both large and small. The clients range from telecommunications giants to small furniture dealers. Our firm provides specialized personal service both to applicants and companies.

Key Contact - Specialty:
Ms. Gail Kleinberg Koch, President - *New media, Sales, Telecommunications*
Ms. Amy Sherman, Recruiter - *Sales*
Ms. Margaret Luca, Recruiter - *Administration*

Salary Minimum: $60,000

Functions: Board Members, Senior Mgmt., Middle Mgmt., Admin. Svcs., Sales & Mktg., IT, MIS Mgmt., Systems Analysis, Systems Implem., Systems Support

Industries: Construction, Computer Equip., Architectural Svcs., Legal, E-commerce, IT Implementation, New Media, Communications, Telecoms, Call Centers, Telephony, Digital, Wireless, Network Infrastructure, Software, Biotech/Life Sciences

Casey Accounting & Finance Resources

5105 Tollview Dr Ste 263
Rolling Meadows, IL 60008-3725
(847) 253-9030
Fax: (847) 253-9545

Email: casey@caseyresources.com
Web: www.caseyresources.com

Summary: Specialists in executive placement, contract staffing and project consulting for accounting and finance professionals.

Key Contact - Specialty:
Mr. Pete McTague, CPC, Branch Manager

Salary Minimum: $45,000

Functions: Finance

Industries: Generalist (All)

CasinoRecruiter.com

(also known as Navegante Search)
4255 Dean Martin Dr Ste J
Las Vegas, NV 89103-4161
(702) 798-0180
Fax: (702) 798-1060
Email: marc@casinorecruiter.com
Web: www.casinorecruiter.com

Summary: An executive recruiting firm specializing in the gaming & hospitality industry. We recruit and place experienced executives for Land-Based casinos, Tribal Properties, River Boats and Gaming Manufacturers. Our reputation and integrity are paramount. Marc Weiswasser and Rick Latini head up the department for Larry Woolf, Chairman & CEO.

Key Contact - Specialty:
Mr. Marc Weiswasser, Director - *Gaming, Hospitality*
Mr. Rick Latini, Executive Recruiter - *Gaming, Hospitality*

Salary Minimum: $80,000

Functions: Management, Senior Mgmt., Middle Mgmt.

Industries: Hotels, Resorts, Clubs, Restaurants, Entertainment, Recreation

Cast Metals Personnel Inc

PO Box 2367
Joliet, IL 60434-2367
(815) 725-9111
Fax: (815) 725-9333

Summary: An independent full-service placement organization offering the metal casting industry access to management and technical personnel.

Key Contact - Specialty:
Mr. Chuck Lundeen, President - *Engineering, Management, Technical*

Salary Minimum: $40,000

Functions: Generalist (All), Management, Middle Mgmt., Production, Plant Mgmt., Quality, Sales Mgmt., Engineering

Industries: Generalist (All), Manufacturing, Metal Products, Motor Vehicles

Castleton Consulting Inc

4199 Campus Dr Ste 550
Irvine, CA 92612-4694
(949) 509-0980
Email: info@castleton-inc.com
Web: www.castletonexecutivesearch.com

Summary: We are a management consulting firm specializing in finding full-time and interim management talent for technology-based companies. Our industry expertise includes software, IT and telecom companies, as well as technology consulting services and 'old-economy' industrial sectors like pharmaceuticals, automotive and manufacturing. Our functional emphasis is on executive, sales, marketing and business development management.

Key Contact - Specialty:
Ms. Christina Savich, CAC, President

Salary Minimum: $80,000

Functions: Management, Sales & Mktg., IT

Industries: Computer Equip., Consumer Elect., Electronic, Elec. Components, Robotics, Semiconductors, Mgmt. Consulting, E-commerce, IT Implementation, Telecoms, Network Infrastructure, RF/Microwave, Government, Defense, Software, Accounting SW, Development SW, Doc. Mgmt., Production SW, Entertainment SW, ERP SW, HR SW, Industry Specific SW, Marketing SW, Networking, Comm. SW, Security SW, System SW

Catalina Medical Recruiters Inc

2020 N Central Ave Ste 1080
Phoenix, AZ 85004-4572
(602) 331-1655
(800) 657-0354
Fax: (602) 331-1933
Email: tonya@catalinarecruiters.com
Web: www.catalinarecruiters.com

Summary: We provide temp and permanent physician placement to healthcare facilities. All specialties.

Key Contact - Specialty:
Ms. Joan Pearson, President
Ms. Tonya Pearson, Recruiter
Ms. Dawn Golden, Recruiter
Ms. Rhonda Bishop, Recruiter - *Physicians*

Functions: Physicians

Industries: Healthcare

Catalyst Resource Group LLC

6120 Windward Pkwy Ste 170
Alpharetta, GA 30005-4185
(678) 366-3500
(877) 566-3400
Fax: (678) 366-2511
Email: rcarle@catalystresourcegroup.com
Web: www.catalystresourcegroup.com

Summary: Our firm is a full service strategic search firm that specializes in finance and accounting staffing. We manage both direct hire and contract searches ranging from entry level to CFO positions. Founded by former accounting and finance professionals with both mid-size and Fortune 500 experience.

Key Contact - Specialty:
Mr. Rory Carle, Managing Director
Mr. Irwin Solomom, Managing Director

Salary Minimum: $40,000

Functions: Finance

Industries: Accounting SW

Catapult Search Group Inc

3401 Enterprise Pkwy Ste 340
Beachwood, OH 44122-7340
(216) 766-5705
Fax: (216) 274-9859
Email: mrossen@catapultsearch.com
Web: www.catapultsearch.com

Summary: Specializes in placing salespeople, engineers and project managers in the Automation, Packaging and Material Handling industries.

Key Contact - Specialty:
Mr. Michael Rossen, President

Salary Minimum: $60,000

Functions: Senior Mgmt., Production, Packaging, Sales & Mktg.

Industries: Printing, Machine, Appliance, Test, Measure Equip., Misc. Mfg., Robotics, Equip Svcs., Logistics Svcs., Supply Chain Mgmt., Packaging

CBC Resources Inc

1300 W Belmont Ave Ste 304
Chicago, IL 60657-3241
(773) 880-1309
Email: kconvery@cbcresources.com
Web: www.cbcresources.com

Summary: We offer our clients superior customer service in placing candidates with an HRIS, HR and mechanical engineering.

Key Contact - Specialty:
Ms. Karen Convery, President

Functions: Generalist (All), Sales Mgmt., HR Mgmt., IT, Systems Implem., Mgmt. Consultants

Industries: Generalist (All), Finance, Misc. Financial, Mgmt. Consulting, HR Services, Software

CBS (Compensation & Benefits Search)

31 Lexington Rd
West Hartford, CT 06119-1748
(860) 236-7422
Email: warseck@ntplx.net

Summary: Specializing in the analytical side of health and social policy research-stats/biostats, survey, epidemiology, outcomes, health and pharmacoeconomics, etc.

Key Contact - Specialty:
Mr. Robert Johnson

Salary Minimum: $80,000

Functions: R&D

Industries: Services, Non-profits, Pharm Svcs., Law Enforcement, K-12 Ed., Government

CCL Medical Search

71 Schriever Ln
New City, NY 10956-3313
(845) 634-0111
Fax: (845) 634-0126
Email: cclsearch@aol.com
Web: www.cclmedicalsearch.com

Summary: We are a search firm specializing in healthcare. We have been instrumental in the growth of many hospitals, nursing homes, health centers and private practices. We are placing administrators, physicians, PA, PT, OT nurses, practitioners and other healthcare personnel, to include nursing homes.

Key Contact - Specialty:
Ms. H.M. Richter, President & Chief Executive Officer
Ms. Karen Chafetz, Associate Vice President - *Physicians*

Functions: Board Members, Healthcare, Physicians, Nurses, Allied Health, Health Admin., Finance, CFOs, Credit, Network Admin.

Industries: Generalist (All), Healthcare

CCT Inc Engineering Personnel

218-151 Frobisher Dr
Frobisher Office Centre
Waterloo, ON N2V 2C9
Canada
(519) 743-4894
(800) 982-9436
Email: people@cctinc.org
Web: www.cctinc.org

Summary: We supply engineering personnel to manufactures in our market. We have contract and permanent opportunities for mechanical, electrical, structural/civil engineers, technologists and technician with leading manufacturers.

Key Contact - Specialty:
Mr. James Van Slyck, BA, MBA, Executive Recruitment
Mr. David Varley, Search Consultant - *Engineering, Government, Manufacturing, Manufacturing (Management)*
Mr. Bryce Kipfer, BA, Search Consultant - *Automotive, Engineering, Factories (Automation), Manufacturing*

Salary Minimum: $35,000

Functions: Mfg., Production

Industries: Manufacturing, Medical Devices, Plastics, Rubber, Metal Products, Motor Vehicles, Test, Measure Equip., Misc. Mfg., Electronic, Elec. Components, Robotics, Consumer Goods, Transportation

Branches:
202-3425 Harvester Rd
Burlington, ON L7N 3N1
Canada
(905) 631-9709
Fax: (800) 546-4483
Email: people@cctinc.org
Key Contact - Specialty:
Mr. Robert H. Van Slyck

151 York St
London, ON N6A 1A8
Canada
(519) 858-8369
Fax: (800) 546-4483
Email: people@cctinc.org
Key Contact - Specialty:
Mr. Rob B. Van Slyck, BA, CHRP, Sales

119-2550 Argentia Rd
The Penyagon
Mississauga, ON L5N 5R1
Canada
(905) 858-1481
Fax: (800) 546-4483
Email: people@cctinc.org

CE Insurance Services

2802 W Azeele St
Tampa, FL 33609-3108
(800) 229-4473
(813) 348-9733
Fax: (813) 348-0554
Email: jeff@ceinsurance.com
Web: www.ceinsurance.com

Summary: Search of insurance executives, insurance legal professionals, managerial and professional personnel for insurance companies, agencies, brokers and risk managers.

Key Contact - Specialty:
Mr. Jeffrey M. Carter, President & Chief Executive Officer

Salary Minimum: $45,000

Functions: Generalist (All)

Industries: Insurance

CEC Search LLC

(also known as Chapman Executive Searc LLC)
10025 Twingate Dr
Alpharetta, GA 30022-5586
(770) 447-6471
Email: info@cecsearch.com
Web: www.cecsearch.com

Summary: Executive search firm specializing in operations positions and corporate support roles for the restaurant industry. USA/nationwide.

Key Contact - Specialty:
Mr. Carl E. Chapman, Sr., Principal & Managing Partner - *Food service, Franchising, Hospitality, Restaurants*
Mrs. Julie A. Chapman, Chief Financial Officer

Salary Minimum: $28,000

Functions: Generalist (All), Management, Senior Mgmt., Middle Mgmt., Distribution, HR Mgmt., Benefits, Staffing, Training, Cash Mgmt.

Industries: Generalist (All), Restaurants, Quick Service Restaurants, Full Service Restaurants

Centennial Inc

8044 Montgomery Rd Ste 260
Cincinnati, OH 45236-2929
(513) 366-3760
Email: info@centennialinc.com
Web: www.centennialinc.com

Summary: We bring time-tested principles and cutting-edge practices to help our clients recruit top leadership and professional talent. Our mission is to help our clients solve their ongoing strategic recruiting challenges, so they can better achieve their business, team and personal goals.

Key Contact - Specialty:
Mr. Mike Sipple, Sr., President & Chief Executive Officer - *Boards of Directors, C-level, CEOs, CFOs, CIOs*
Mr. Mike A. Sipple, Jr., Vice President - *Advertising, CIOs, Consumer (Packaged Goods), Creative, Diversity*
Mr. T.J. Bugg, Vice President - *Accounting, Accounting (General,Public), Automotive, CFOs*

Salary Minimum: $65,000

Functions: Generalist (All), Management, Senior Mgmt., Middle Mgmt., Sales & Mktg., HR Mgmt., Finance, CFOs, IT

Industries: Generalist (All), Manufacturing, Transportation, Finance, Packaging

Central Executive Search Inc

6151 Wilson Mills Rd Ste 240
Highland Heights, OH 44143-2134
(440) 461-5400
Fax: (440) 461-8442
Email: stacey@centraljobs.com
Web: www.centraljobs.com

Summary: Specializing in the paper, printing, packaging, converting and adhesives industry. Positions range from manufacturing, R&D, engineering, sales/management and marketing. Good reputation and very experienced in specialized industries.

Key Contact - Specialty:
Mr. Gary Giallombardo, President
Ms. Toni Graziano, General Manager
Ms. Stacey Herbert, Director, Operations
Mr. Angelo Giallombardo, National Account Manager
Mr. Phil Costanzo, National Account Executive - *Printing*

Salary Minimum: $50,000

Functions: Management, Mfg., Product Dev., Plant Mgmt., Materials, Packaging, Sales & Mktg., Sales Reps., R&D

Industries: Manufacturing, Food, Bev., Tobacco, Paper, Printing, Chemicals, Plastics, Rubber, Paints, Petro. Products, Machine, Appliance, Consumer Goods, Packaging

Centre Street Associates Inc

1462 Centre St
Newton Center, MA 02459-2446
(617) 795-0306
Fax: (617) 830-0400
Email: fertig@cstreetsearch.com
Web: www.cstreetsearch.com

Summary: Our firm engages in both retained and contingency recruiting for professional/executive positions in the fields of: finance and audit, pharmaceuticals and biotechnology. We also offer unbundled search services including: candidate sourcing, screening, and reference checking on an hourly consulting basis.

Key Contact - Specialty:
Mr. Arnold Fertig, President

Salary Minimum: $70,000

Functions: Management, Middle Mgmt., Quality

Industries: Generalist (All), Chemicals, Drugs Mfg., Medical Devices, Banking, Invest. Banking, Software, Accounting SW, ERP SW, Marketing SW, Biotech/Life Sciences

CENTREX Human Resource Centre

200-124 James St S
Hamilton, ON L8P 2Z4
Canada
(905) 528-5141
Fax: (905) 528-5147
Email: centrex@allstream.net
Web: www.centrexstaff.com

Summary: We offer temporary & Permanent Placement Service specializing in administrative, accounting, sales and marketing, clerical positions.

Key Contact - Specialty:
Mr. Len Falco, Manager, Business Development

Functions: Board Members, Admin. Svcs.

Industries: Generalist (All)

Centrus Group Inc

1653 Merriman Rd Ste 211
Akron, OH 44313-5276
(330) 864-5800
Fax: (330) 865-9222
Email: hlipton@centrusgroup.com
Web: www.centrusgroup.com

Summary: We are 50 percent contingent and 50 percent retained. We specialize in consumer durables, automotive manufacturing (all positions), cutting tools, telecom, plant and division controllers. We work with all manufacturing positions. We have extensive recruiting experience. Our other focus is crisis management.

Key Contact - Specialty:
Mr. Harvey Lipton, Director, Recruitment

Century Associates Inc

1420 Walnut St Ste 1402
Philadelphia, PA 19102-4014
(215) 732-4311 x18
Fax: (215) 735-1804
Email: dallen@centuryassociates.com
Web: www.centuryassociates.com

Summary: We are involved in the recruitment of Sales, Pre/Post Sales and Marketing professionals in the Information Technology, Medical and Pharmaceutical arenas.

Key Contact - Specialty:
Mr. David Allen, President - *Computers (Software)*

Mr. Tom Jarrett, Senior Account Executive - *Medical (Devices,Sales), Pharmaceutical, Sales*
Ms. Krista Stepanik, Senior Account Executive - *Computers (Sales), Database, Information Technology, Office (Products)*

Salary Minimum: $60,000

Functions: Generalist (All), Management, Board Members, Senior Mgmt., Sales & Mktg., Mktg. Research, Mktg. Mgmt., Sales Mgmt.

Industries: Generalist (All), Medical Devices, Pharm Svcs., Mgmt. Consulting, Supply Chain Mgmt, Wireless, Software, Doc. Mgmt., Production SW, Mfg. SW, Marketing SW, Networking, Comm. SW, Security SW, Biotech/Life Sciences

The Century Group

222 N Sepulveda Blvd Ste 2150
El Segundo, CA 90245-5644
(310) 216-2100
Email: century@century-group.com
Web: www.century-group.com

Summary: Our firm specializes in accounting, finance, tax, audit, controllers, CFOs and searches in a broad range of industries.

Key Contact - Specialty:
Mr. Harry Boxer, Chief Executive Officer - *CFOs, Controllers, Finance*
Mr. Ron Proul, President & Chief Operating Officer - *CFOs, Controllers, Finance*

Salary Minimum: $50,000

Functions: Finance

Industries: Generalist (All)

Branches:
575 Anton Blvd Ste 600
Costa Mesa, CA 92626-7657
(714) 708-5100
(800) 564-0010
Fax: (714) 708-5111
Email: century@century-group.com
Key Contact - Specialty:
Mr. Jeff Lassiter, Vice President, Orange County - *Finance*

550 N Brand Blvd Ste 2150
Glendale, CA 91203-1934
(818) 240-5200
Email: century@century-group.com
Key Contact - Specialty:
Mr. John Hawley, Director, Executive Search

Cerebral Connections

325 La Costa Ave
Encinitas, CA 92024-1112
(760) 487-1323
(408) 265-6856
Fax: (877) 477-1332
Email: doug@cerebralconnections.com
Web: www.cerebralconnections.com

Summary: Our firm is a focused recruiting organization whose charter is: To expose top talent to exciting career opportunities within its customer organizations while providing the highest levels of integrity and service.

Key Contact - Specialty:
Mr. Doug Wierenga, Principal
Mr. Keith Swartz, Principal

Salary Minimum: $60,000

Functions: Management, IT, Network Admin., Engineering, Hardware

Industries: IT Implementation, Engineering Svcs., Software

Michael Cerino Recruiting Associates

PO Box 1294
Willow Grove, PA 19090-0994
(215) 672-6586
Fax: (215) 672-6586
Email: mike@mikecerino.com
Web: www.mikecerino.com

Summary: Specializing in grocery, frozen food, HBC/GM, confections, beverages, meat and perishable, private label & branded sales, food service and retail trades.

Key Contact - Specialty:
Mr. Michael R. Cerino, Owner & Recruiter - *Consumer (Marketing,Packaged Goods), Marketing, Sales*

Salary Minimum: $75,000

Functions: Mktg. Mgmt., Sales Mgmt.

Industries: Food, Bev., Tobacco, Soap, Perf., Cosmtcs.

CFI Resources Inc

7 Clover Dr
Great Neck, NY 11021-1817
(516) 466-1221
(415) 359-0635
Email: careers@cfires.com
Web: www.cfires.com

Summary: Focus on high-technology electronics, semiconductor front-/back-end capital equipment, hardware, software, design automation, robotics, test & measurement, sales, marketing, engineering, applications and field service positions.

Key Contact - Specialty:
Mr. Leo Cohen, Principal - *High technology, Sales*

Functions: Generalist (All), Board Members

Industries: Computer Equip., Test, Measure Equip., Misc. Mfg., Electronic, Elec. Components, Robotics, Semiconductors, Telecoms, Fiber Optic, Software, Industry Specific SW

Branches:
2269 Chestnut St Ste 919
San Francisco, CA 94123-2600
(415) 359-0635
Email: careers@cfires.com
Key Contact - Specialty:
Mr. Dan Friedman

CFOs2GO

3470 Mt Diablo Blvd Ste A125
Lafayette, CA 94549-3978
(925) 299-4450
Email: recruiter@cfos2go.com
Web: www.cfos2go.com

Summary: We are a full-service senior financial executive placement firm that customizes staffing and consulting solutions to a broad group of client companies including emerging high growth and established Fortune 500. Our services include: direct hire, directorships, contract staffing and consulting. We utilize Internet technologies and a network of consulting CFOs and CPAs that provide local representation in virtually every venture capital community in the country.

Key Contact - Specialty:
Mr. Robert Weis, President

Functions: Generalist (All), Finance

Industries: Generalist (All)

CFR Executive Search Inc

175 W Jackson Blvd Ste 2215
Chicago, IL 60604-2704
(312) 435-0990
Fax: (312) 435-1333
Email: jbarry@cfrsearch.com
Web: www.cfrsearch.com

Summary: We assure quality, prescreened accounting and corporate finance professionals who will meet our clients' specifications. They will possess the appropriate management style and work ethic to fit our clients' culture.

Key Contact - Specialty:
Mr. James Barry, President - *Finance*
Mr. Joseph Sexton, Vice President - *Finance*

Salary Minimum: $50,000

Functions: Generalist (All), CFOs, Budgeting, Cash Mgmt., Credit, Taxes, M&A, Risk Mgmt.

Industries: Generalist (All), Manufacturing, Transportation, Wholesale, Retail, Misc. Financial, Services, Insurance

Chacra, Belliveau & Associates Inc

1005-625 Ave du President-Kennedy
Edifice Union Kennedy
Montreal, QC H3A 1K2
Canada
(514) 931-8801
Fax: (514) 931-1940
Email: info@chacra.com
Web: www.chacra.com

Summary: Specializing exclusively in the information technology and systems sector. Managed and staffed by information technology and human resources professionals.

Key Contact - Specialty:
Mr. Steven Chacra, President

Salary Minimum: $40,000

Functions: IT, MIS Mgmt., Systems Analysis, Systems Dev., Systems Support, Network Admin., DB Admin.

Industries: Generalist (All)

Chad Management Group

1000-21 St Clair Ave E
Unicorp Building
Toronto, ON M4T 1L9
Canada
(416) 968-1000
Fax: (416) 968-7754
Email: jobs@chadman.com
Web: www.chadman.com

Summary: We are a leader in marketing and sales recruitment with long-term success in identifying and delivering the top performers promptly and effectively.

Key Contact - Specialty:
Mr. Rick A. Chad, President - *General management, Marketing*
Ms. Laurie Hart, Consultant - *Direct marketing, Public relations*
Mr. Gary Rudson, Consultant
Ms. Silvia Butterworth, Consultant

Functions: Generalist (All), Management, Product Dev., Materials, Sales & Mktg., Finance, IT, Graphic Designers

Industries: Generalist (All), Manufacturing, Food, Bev., Tobacco, Drugs Mfg., Finance, Hospitality, Media, Database SW

Chadwell & Associates Inc

PO Box 1028
Portage, MI 49081-1028
(269) 353-7805
Fax: (269) 353-7802
Email: chadwell@chadwell.com
Web: www.chadwell.com

Summary: We follow our recruiter's code of ethics. Within it, we explain how crucial it is to follow the three R's of recruiting: respect, response and reliability. We specialize in working with the OEMs that manufacture the equipment that goes into food and beverage plants as well as the processors themselves.

Key Contact - Specialty:
Ms. Rebecca A. Chadwell, Engineering Specialist - *Engineering, Technical*

Functions: Management, Senior Mgmt., Mfg., Product Dev., Production, Automation, Plant Mgmt., Packaging, Sales & Mktg., Engineering

Industries: Manufacturing, Food, Bev., Tobacco, Plastics, Rubber, Machine, Appliance, Robotics, Inst./Industrial Food Svc., Packaging

Wayne S Chamberlain & Associates

25835 Narbonne Ave Ste 280C
Lomita, CA 90717-7206
(310) 534-4840
Fax: (310) 539-9885
Email: wayne@waynechamberlain.com
Web: www.waynechamberlain.com

Summary: Our specialization is in the technical placement of professionals in the electronic connector and cable fields. Our typical searches are for sales & marketing managers, design engineers, manufacturing/industrial/quality engineers and technical management.

Key Contact - Specialty:
Mr. Wayne Chamberlain, Owner - *Electronics*

Salary Minimum: $50,000

Functions: Generalist (All), Board Members, Middle Mgmt., Product Dev., Automation, Plant Mgmt., Quality, Mktg. Mgmt., Sales Mgmt.

Industries: Generalist (All), Manufacturing, Plastics, Rubber, Computer Equip., Consumer Elect., Test, Measure Equip., Electronic, Elec. Components, Telecoms, Wireless, Fiber Optic, Mfg. SW, Marketing SW

Chamberlain Associates

121 Greenwood Pl
Decatur, GA 30030-3620
(800) 877-9631
Fax: (404) 378-3079
Email: careers@chamberlainassoc.com
Web: www.chamberlainassoc.com

Summary: We place clinical and management candidates in the hospital, biotechnology and pharmaceutical industries. We provide the highest level of confidentiality with no fee to the candidate.

Key Contact - Specialty:
Ms. Inga Chamberlain, President - *Healthcare, Pharmaceutical*

Salary Minimum: $70,000

Functions: Quality, Nurses, Sales & Mktg., R&D

Industries: Drugs Mfg., Pharm Svcs., Biotech/Life Sciences, Healthcare, Hospitals

Vickers Chambless Managed Search

400 Perimeter Center Ter NE Ste 900
Atlanta, GA 30346-1236
(404) 365-0030
Fax: (404) 231-1351
Email: vcms@vcmssearch.com
Web: www.vcmssearch.com

Summary: We are an executive search services exclusively in the healthcare financial and healthcare administrative areas. Financial: CFO, controller, assistant controller, reimbursement, patient financial services and auditors. Administrative: CEO, COO, medical records and IS.

Key Contact - Specialty:
Mr. Vickers Chambless, President
Ms. Jane Leader, Recruiter - *Communications, Information Technology*

Salary Minimum: $40,000

Functions: Generalist (All), Health Admin., Taxes, M&A

Industries: Accounting, Healthcare, Hospitals, Long-term/Home Care

Chapman & Associates

480-505 Burrard St
Bentall Tower 1
Vancouver, BC V7X 1M3
Canada
(604) 682-7764
Fax: (604) 682-8746
Email: resumes@chapmanassociates.ca
Web: www.chapmanassociates.ca

Summary: With many years of experience recruiting and selecting mid-level to senior personnel, our firm enjoys a proven track record for professionalism, confidentiality and success.

Key Contact - Specialty:
Mr. Gary W. Fumano, President - *Administration, Engineering, Finance, Marketing, Sales*
Mr. Bruce J. MacKenzie, Managing Partner - *Engineering, High technology, Marketing, Sales*
Ms. Lynn Armstrong, Associate
Ms. Kate Pawlett, Associate

Salary Minimum: $50,000

Functions: Generalist (All), Management, Mfg., Materials, Sales & Mktg., HR Mgmt., IT, Engineering

Industries: Generalist (All), Agri., Forestry, Mining, Construction, Manufacturing, Hospitality, Media

R F Chapman & Company

PO Box 1155
Kihei, HI 96753-1155
(808) 874-8470
Fax: (808) 874-5779
Email: chapman@mauigateway.com

Summary: Our firm specializes in the hotel, restaurant and tourism industries. Our focus is on middle and upper-management and the majority of our work is done on a contingency basis.

Key Contact - Specialty:
Mr. Bob Chapman

Functions: Management, Middle Mgmt.

Industries: Hospitality

Charet & Associates

PO Box 435
Cresskill, NJ 07626-0435
(201) 894-5197
Fax: (201) 894-9095

Email: sandy@charet.com
Web: www.charet.com

Summary: We are a well-established firm with a sterling reputation. The firm has an extensive network of marketing, PR and corporate communications professionals and a true understanding of these fields. Company services the public relations, corporate communications, public affairs, investor relations, sales promotion and marketing fields for all industries.

Key Contact - Specialty:
Ms. Sandra Charet, President
Mr. Gary Epstein, Vice President, Recruiting Services
Ms. Vanessa Harries, Director, Administration & Research - *Administration, Advertising, Research*

Salary Minimum: $80,000

Functions: Advertising, Mktg. Mgmt., PR

Industries: Generalist (All)

The Charitable Resources Group

400 9th St Ste A
Conway, PA 15027-1663
(724) 876-0460
Email: tcrgroup@attglobal.net
Web: www.tcrgroup.com

Summary: We provide executive search services for colleges, universities, private schools, hospitals, churches and social service agencies; also VPs for development, enrollment, academic affairs and business, deans, department chairs and presidents.

Key Contact - Specialty:
Mr. Dennis F. Vest, Chairman
Ms. Cheryl A. Hyatt, President & Chief Operating Officer
Mr. Stuart M. Strait, Senior Counsel
Mr. Patrick McDonough, PhD, Executive Vice President, Strategic Plan
Ms. Cher Thomas, Senior Counsel, Strategic Planning - *Computers, Consulting, Information Technology, Professional services, Technology*

Functions: Senior Mgmt.

Industries: Non-profits, K-12 Ed., Higher Ed.

Charles & Associates Inc

827 E 48th St
Kearney, NE 68847-8427
(308) 236-8891
Fax: (308) 236-8893
Email: chasassoc@nebi.com

Summary: Specialists in the outdoor power/lawn and garden equipment industry covering sales & marketing, engineering, manufacturing, production, quality control and material handling.

Key Contact - Specialty:
Mr. Charles F. Dummer, CPC, President
Mrs. Joan Dummer, Vice President

Functions: Middle Mgmt., Product Dev., Mktg. Research, Mktg. Mgmt., Sales Mgmt., R&D, Engineering

Industries: Generalist (All)

Charter Resources International LLC

9396 Charter Crossing Dr
Mechanicsville, VA 23116-5114
(804) 550-1395
Fax: (804) 550-9454
Email: mbilodeau@jobseeker.net
Web: www.jobseeker.net

Summary: We are real estate, legal search and web services specialists.

Key Contact - Specialty:
Mr. Michael Bilodeau, Principal - *Transportation*

Functions: Generalist (All), Board Members, Sales & Mktg.

Industries: Transportation, Retail, Services, Legal, E-commerce, Real Estate

The Chase Research Group Inc

6542 Hypoluxo Rd Ste 108
Lake Worth, FL 33467-7678
(888) 810-7133
(561) 742-1161
Fax: (561) 742-4878
Email: ehaber@chaseresearchgroup.com
Web: www.chaseresearchgroup.com

Summary: The Chase Research Group is a full service Recruiting, Research and Sourcing firm with clients throughout the country. When your company makes the decision to hire the best talent available, The Chase Research Group is ready to respond. We assist companies in locating and hiring the hard to find candidates that often elude typical recruiting organizations.

Key Contact - Specialty:
Mr. Eric Haber, President & Chief Executive Officer

Functions: Generalist (All)

Industries: Retail, Pharm Svcs., Restaurants, Quick Service Restaurants, Full Service Restaurants, Biotech/Life Sciences

Chelsea Resources Inc

18 Oneco St
Norwich, CT 06360-3434
(860) 886-4110
Fax: (860) 886-2210
Email: pat@chelsearesources.com
Web: www.chelsearesources.com

Summary: Recognized leaders in medical device and instrumentation recruiting. We are responsive and successful. Excel at staffing critical positions quickly. Experienced with venture start-up operations. Clients include Fortune 50 and emerging technology companies.

Key Contact - Specialty:
Mr. Patrick J. Soo Hoo, President
Mr. Leo F. Bawza, Vice President

Salary Minimum: $50,000

Functions: Generalist (All), Mfg.

Industries: Medical Devices, Plastics, Rubber

Garry Chesla and Associates LLC

2722 Longview Dr Ste B
Lisle, IL 60532-4201
(630) 369-5700
Fax: (630) 369-5757
Email: gchesla@comcast.net

Summary: I was formerly with Executive Referral Services in Chicago for 10 years. I have started my own Search firm where I continue to recruit in all areas of Retail including grocery, furniture, apparel, service companies, hardlines, and sales.

Key Contact - Specialty:
Mr. Garry Chesla, CPC, President

Salary Minimum: $30,000

Functions: Generalist (All)

Industries: Generalist (All), Construction, Lumber, Furniture, Wholesale, Retail, Services, HR Services, Restaurants, Real Estate

Chicago Financial Search Inc

200 S Wacker Dr Fl 3100
Chicago, IL 60606-5877
(312) 207-0400
Fax: (262) 537-3073
Email: info@chicagofinancial.com
Web: www.chicagofinancial.com

Summary: We recruit and place people in the commodities, securities and banking industries. We specialize in accounting, operations, sales and IT positions within the financial industry.

Key Contact - Specialty:
Mr. Michael P. Kelly, President

Salary Minimum: $30,000

Functions: Management, Finance

Industries: Finance, Brokers, Venture Cap., Mutual/Hedge Funds, Misc. Financial, Accounting, HR Services

Branches:
245 Park Ave Fl 24
New York, NY 10167-2499
(212) 209-7318
Email: resume@chicagofinancial.com

Chicago Legal Search Ltd

180 N La Salle St Ste 3525
Chicago, IL 60601-3128
(312) 251-2580
Fax: (312) 251-0223
Email: attorneys@chicagolegalsearch.com
Web: www.chicagolegalsearch.com

Summary: We strive to service our clients by focusing on the Chicago legal market. We have consistently recruited highly qualified and culturally compatible attorneys at all levels for our law firm and in-house clients.

Key Contact - Specialty:
Mr. Gary A. D'Alessio, Esq., President
Ms. Chris Percival, Senior Legal Search Consultant
Mr. Alan J. Rubenstein, Esq., Executive Vice President
Ms. Eden L. Mandrell, Esq., Senior Legal Search Consultant

Salary Minimum: $90,000

Functions: Legal

Industries: Generalist (All)

Chicagoland Recruiters

645 N Michigan Ave Ste 800
Chicago, IL 60611-2890
(773) 404-9300
Email: mail@chicagolandrecruiters.com
Web: www.chicagolandrecruiters.com

Summary: Our firm is a 100% women-owned business, has operated for many years. We are a boutique search firm proud of our long-term relationships and one consultant per client approach.

Key Contact - Specialty:
Ms. Jennifer Pascia, Administrator

Salary Minimum: $50,000

Functions: Generalist (All)

Industries: Generalist (All), Manufacturing, Transportation, Finance, Services, Accounting, Real Estate, Software, Healthcare

Childs, Smith & Associates

PO Box 298
Welcome, NC 27374-0298
(336) 764-5458
Fax: (336) 793-4978

Email: smith@accounting-jobs.com
Web: www.accounting-jobs.com

Summary: We are a professional search firm specializing in the placement of permanent and temporary accounting, audit, tax and consulting service professionals. We have over 20 years experience providing personalized service to many of the leading public accounting firms and fortune 500 companies in the country.

Key Contact - Specialty:
Mr. Robert Smith, Principal

Salary Minimum: $75,000

Functions: Finance

Industries: Generalist (All)

Ken Chin

PO Box 1881
Brookline, MA 02446-0015
(617) 233-8338
Email: kenchin@job4u.com

Summary: We are an Executive search firm. We specialize in Contingent and Retained, Focus in Biotechnology and Power in Asia, Africa, and the Middle East.

Key Contact - Specialty:
Mr. Ken Chin, Master Recruiter

Salary Minimum: $90,000

Functions: Generalist (All)

Industries: Energy, Utilities, Services, Accounting SW, Database SW, Development SW, Biotech/Life Sciences

Joseph Chris Partners

900 Rockmead Dr Ste 101
Kingwood, TX 77339-2117
(281) 359-0060
Fax: (281) 359-0067
Email: joeramirez@josephchris.com
Web: www.josephchris.com

Summary: We are a leading executive search firm exclusively serving the real estate, development and construction industries. We specialize in executive and senior level management assignments for the single family, multifamily, real estate and construction industries. We have successfully developed a comprehensive professional network in each facet of the real estate industry.

Key Contact - Specialty:
Mr. Joe Ramirez, President - *Real estate*
Ms. Susan Bulick, National Partner & JCR Executive Search
Ms. Debbie Watson, Corporate Marketing Director - *Real estate*

Salary Minimum: $75,000

Functions: Management, Board Members, Senior Mgmt., Middle Mgmt., Finance, Specialized Svcs.

Industries: Construction, Real Estate

Mark Christian & Associates Inc

5844 E Marconi Ave
Scottsdale, AZ 85254-1888
(602) 494-9522
Email: mchrisassc@aol.com

Summary: We offer the IT industry a recruiting service to find key people for their organization. Each principal has many years of experience in the IT industry. Our extensive network of contacts is utilized in all recruiting activity.

Key Contact - Specialty:
Mr. Gary Alexander, Chairman - *Management, Sales*

Ms. Myra Alexander, President - *Sales, Technical*
Mr. Phil Batisto, Associate - *Sales*
Mr. Dave Daggett, Associate - *Sales*

Salary Minimum: $60,000

Functions: Generalist (All), Senior Mgmt., Middle Mgmt., Sales Mgmt., Systems Dev., Systems Support

Industries: Computer Equip.; Services, Mgmt. Consulting, HR Services, E-commerce, IT Implementation, Communications, Software, Database SW, Development SW, Mfg. SW

Christian Recruiters Affiliated LLC

3201 Chimneyrock Dr
Plano, TX 75023-5621
(972) 519-0863
Fax: (972) 964-8696
Email: info@christianrecruiters.com
Web: www.christianrecruiters.com

Summary: Affiliation of healthcare recruiters placing physicians and healthcare professionals across the USA.

Key Contact - Specialty:
Mr. David J. Elliott Fache, Managing Affiliate - *Healthcare, Medical*

Salary Minimum: $35,000

Functions: Generalist (All)

Industries: Non-profits, Pharm Svcs., Healthcare, Hospitals, Long-term/Home Care, Physical Therapy, Occupational Therapy

R Christine Associates

183 Palmers Mill Rd
Media, PA 19063-1037
(610) 565-3310
Fax: (610) 565-3313
Email: rcarich@aol.com

Summary: We have specialized in personal one-on-one service, recruiting technical and executive professionals. High-technology to smoke stack.

Key Contact - Specialty:
Mr. Rich Christine, CPC, Owner - *Engineering, Manufacturing, Sales*

Salary Minimum: $40,000

Functions: Mfg., Materials, Sales Mgmt., HR Mgmt., Engineering

Industries: Medical Devices, Metal Products, Machine, Appliance, Test, Measure Equip.

Christopher Group Executive Search

12 Hawk View Dr
Asheville, NC 28804-1971
(828) 225-4348
Fax: (828) 225-4349
Email: chrisgroup@bellsouth.net
Web: www.christophergroup.com

Summary: Our firm focuses exclusively on the placement of experienced real estate and mortgage professionals. Our clients include: financial institutions, developers, brokerage/property management organizations, corporate real estate entities, REITS/pension funds and valuation/consulting firms.

Key Contact - Specialty:
Mr. J. Christopher Sprehe, President

Salary Minimum: $70,000

Functions: Management

Industries: Banking, Real Estate, Property/Facility Mgmt.

Branches:
7833 Signal Station Rd
Knoxville, TN 37920-9592
(828) 225-4348
Email: chrisgroup3@charter.net
Key Contact - Specialty:
Mr. Nicholas Sprehe, Senior Consultant

M A Churchill & Associates Inc

75 Poplar Dr
Richboro, PA 18954-1645
(215) 968-2233
Email: stu@machurchill.com
Web: www.machurchill.com

Summary: We are a highly focused search firm for the IT, banking/Wall Street/financial systems vendors. Recruiting disciplines are sales, marketing, management, support, pre/post-sales support, product/marketing management, project management and senior systems development.

Key Contact - Specialty:
Mr. Stuart S. Borden, President
Mr. Lawrence Sher, Managing Director
Mr. Brian M. Hochberg, Division Manager
Mr. Jeffrey Michaels, Manager, Business Development
Mr. David Caplan, National Account Manager
Mr. Jack Warrington, National Account Manager

Salary Minimum: $50,000

Functions: Generalist (All), Management, Sales & Mktg., Finance, IT, Int'l.

Industries: Generalist (All), Computer Equip., Finance, Accounting, Media, Software

The Churchill Group

1801-1 Yonge St
Telsec Business Centre
Toronto, ON M5E 1W7
Canada
(416) 368-1358
Fax: (416) 369-0515
Email: churchill@bmts.com
Web: www.churchillstaffing.com

Summary: Our firm is made up of experienced managers who are familiar with the issues facing organizations today. Each of our consultants has many years of recruitment experience in the manufacturing sector.

Key Contact - Specialty:
Mr. Murray Fullerton, President - *Manufacturing*

Salary Minimum: $45,000

Functions: Generalist (All), Mfg.

Industries: Manufacturing, Printing, Metal Products, Machine, Appliance, Motor Vehicles, Misc. Mfg.

The Cisar Group Inc

114 Carriage Dr
Mcknight, PA 15237-2054
(412) 367-5859
Fax: (412) 367-2778
Email: cdcisar@comcast.net
Web: www.thecisargroup.com

Summary: Our strengths are in sales, sales management, marketing, product management, environmental & health & safety, purchasing and engineering. Functions: generalist, directors, middle and senior management.

Key Contact - Specialty:
Mr. Carl D. Cisar, President & Owner - *Engineering, Marketing, Product management/development, Purchasing, Sales*

Salary Minimum: $50,000

Functions: Sales & Mktg., Sales Mgmt.

Industries: Generalist (All)

Civil Search International LLC

7810 S Hardy Dr Ste 108
Tempe, AZ 85284-1119
(480) 820-8663
(800) 737-8182
Fax: (480) 820-8709
Email: mcatena@csijobs.com
Web: www.csijobs.com

Summary: Specialize in civil engineering placements, and all subsets like mechanical, structural, electrical, transportation, enviro, etc.

Key Contact - Specialty:
Mr. Michael A. Catena, President & Co-Founder

Salary Minimum: $75,000

Functions: Management, Engineering, Geotechnical, Structural, Architects

Industries: Energy, Utilities, Oil & Gas, Construction, Paper, Chemicals, Pharm Svcs., Engineering Svcs., Wireless, Network Infrastructure, Healthcare

Civilized People

130 West Beech St Ste 205
Long Beach, NY 11561-3520
(516) 897-3025
Fax: (516) 706-3190
Email: ilana@civilizedpeople.com
Web: www.civilizedpeople.com

Summary: We match great people with great opportunities.

Key Contact - Specialty:
Ms. Ilana Austin, Executive Recruiter

Functions: Hospitality, Chefs

Industries: Generalist (All), Construction, Food, Bev., Tobacco, Retail, Hospitality, Hotels, Resorts, Clubs, Restaurants, Quick Service Restaurants, Full Service Restaurants, Real Estate

CKR Associates LLC

2430 Highway 34 Bldg B
Manasquan, NJ 08736-1806
(732) 292-1022
Email: info@ckrsearch.com
Web: www.ckrsearch.com

Summary: Direct and temp placement in the pharmaceutical/biotech industry.

Key Contact - Specialty:
Mr. Kevin Cox, Owner

Functions: Management, Product Dev., Quality, Materials, Physicians, Mktg. Mgmt., Engineering

Industries: Drugs Mfg., Medical Devices, Biotech/Life Sciences, Healthcare

Clanton & Company

2204 E Vista Canyon Rd
Orange, CA 92867-1746
(714) 282-7980
Fax: (714) 282-0291
Email: fssearch@aol.com

Summary: We were established by a trained psychologist to identify personality factors as well as job qualifications in placement of sales managers with food and non-food manufacturers that sell to the food service industry.

Key Contact - Specialty:
Ms. Diane Clanton, President

Salary Minimum: $50,000

Functions: Sales Mgmt.

Industries: Food, Bev., Tobacco

Clark Associates International Inc

4470 W Sunset Blvd Ste 115
Los Angeles, CA 90027-6305
Fax: (914) 698-8857
Email: tclark@webmailoutlet.com

Key Contact - Specialty:
Mr. Thomas J. Clark, Principal - *Accounting*
Mr. Andrew Crosby, Principal - *Computers*

Salary Minimum: $50,000

Functions: Generalist (All), Management, Sales
& Mktg., Mktg. Mgmt., Direct Mktg.

Industries: Generalist (All), Manufacturing,
Telecoms, Software

Toby Clark Associates Inc

405 E 54th St
New York, NY 10022-5123
(212) 752-5670
Email: tclarkinc@aol.com

Summary: High caliber recruitment for marketing
communications, investor relations and public
relations for corporations, PR firms and investor
relations firms.

Key Contact - Specialty:
Ms. Toby Clark, President
Ms. Sharon Davis, Executive Vice President

Salary Minimum: $75,000

Functions: PR

Industries: Generalist (All)

Howard Clark Associates

PO Box 423
Bellmawr, NJ 08099-0423
(856) 467-3725
Fax: (856) 467-3384
Email: hclark@voicenet.com
Web: www.howardclarkassociates.com

Summary: We provide recruitment of professional
candidates for placement with major corporations
nationwide contingency/search. Also involved in
diversity/female/disadvantaged and military
recruitment.

Key Contact - Specialty:
Mr. Howard L. Clark, President - *Data
processing, Human resources, MIS, Sales*
Mr. Jim Anderson, Manager - *Distribution,
Engineering, Product
management/development, Science*
Mr. Matt Ruffin, Senior Recruiter
Mr. Bob Miller, Recruiter

Salary Minimum: $50,000

Functions: Generalist (All), Senior Mgmt.

Industries: Generalist (All), Food, Bev., Tobacco,
Paper, Chemicals, Soap, Perf., Cosmtcs., Drugs
Mfg., Plastics, Rubber, Consumer Elect.,
Finance, Banking, Accounting, HR Services,
Advertising, Call Centers, Accounting SW

R A Clark Consulting Ltd

3400 Peachtree Rd NE Ste 645
Atlanta, GA 30326-1107
(404) 231-0005
(800) 251-0041
Fax: (404) 231-1030
Email: resume@raclark.com
Web: www.raclark.com

Summary: We are an executive search and
contract services firm specializing exclusively in
the field of human resources. We are committed to
the business success of our clients, advancing the
careers of our candidates and enriching the human
resource profession.

Key Contact - Specialty:
Mr. Richard Clark, President - *Human resources*
Mrs. Robyn Brennaman, Account Manager -
Human resources
Mr. Chad Belk, Account Manager - *Human
resources*
Mr. Chris Daffin, Account Manager - *Boards of
Directors, Non-profit, Senior management*

Functions: HR Mgmt., Benefits, Staffing,
Training, e-HR

Industries: Generalist (All), HR Services

LS Clark Executive Search & Staffing Solutions Inc

14 Bond St Ste 187
Great Neck, NY 11021-2045
(917) 697-9666
(877) 815-0340
Fax: (877) 815-0340
Email: lsc@lsclark.com
Web: www.lsclark.com

Summary: We assist HR and other hiring
professionals by providing recruitment support to
help achieve organizational staffing objectives.
We serve financial, and banking industries. The
firm conducts both contingent and retained
searches.

Key Contact - Specialty:
Ms. Lisa Smith-Clark, President & Owner

Functions: Generalist (All), Admin. Svcs.

Industries: Finance, Banking, Invest. Banking,
Brokers, Venture Cap., Mutual/Hedge Funds,
Misc. Financial, Services, Accounting, HR
Services

The Clark Group

679 S Lake Shore Dr
Harbor Springs, MI 49740-9117
(231) 526-3210
Fax: (231) 526-3212
Email: info@theclarkgroup.net
Web: www.theclarkgroup.net

Summary: We specialize in recruiting sales, sales
support and marketing executives in the food,
beverage, health & beauty aids, consumer health
care and general merchandise segments of the
consumer products industry.

Key Contact - Specialty:
Mr. Larry A. Clark, Owner - *Sales*

Salary Minimum: $50,000

Functions: Sales & Mktg.

Industries: Food, Bev., Tobacco, Drugs Mfg.,
Consumer Goods

Clark Personnel Service

315 S Sage Ave Ste D
Mobile, AL 36606-3604
(251) 471-6777
Fax: (251) 471-4123
Email: office.mobile@clarkpersonnel.com
Web: www.clarkpersonnel.com

Summary: We are a full-service staffing firm
including professional recruiting and temp
staffing.

Key Contact - Specialty:
Mr. Bob Alston, President

Functions: Generalist (All), Senior Mgmt.,
Middle Mgmt., Production, Plant Mgmt.,
Materials Plng., Sales Mgmt., Engineering

Industries: Generalist (All), Food, Bev., Tobacco,
Textiles, Apparel, Lumber, Furniture, Paper,
Chemicals, Metal Products

Branches:
1203 US Highway 98 Ste 1A
Daphne, AL 36526-4255
(251) 625-0790
Fax: (251) 625-0777
Email: office.daphne@clarkpersonnel.com
Key Contact - Specialty:
Ms. Linda Darnell

S R Clarke Inc

3554 Chain Bridge Rd Ste 201
Fairfax, VA 22030-2709
(703) 934-4200
Fax: (703) 934-4201
Email: contact@srclarke.com
Web: www.srclarke.com

Summary: We are an executive search team who
focuses on placing VPs and other executives in the
following arenas: architects/engineers,
mechanical/electrical contractors, commercial
construction, law, real estate development and
management and residential
development/construction.

Key Contact - Specialty:
Mr. Spencer R. Clarke, Chairman & Chief
Executive Officer
Mr. George Clarke, Vice President,
Subcontracting & Design
Ms. Sheryl Clarke, Corporate Secretary & Vice
President
Mr. John Aragona, Advisor
Mr. Don De Mers, President, Western Region
Mr. Greg Brazier, Vice President, Commercial
Construction
Mr. Randy DiBartola, Vice President, Real Estate
Development
Ms. Anne Knudsen, Vice President, Commercial
Construction
Mr. Rod Shapard, Vice President, Residential
Development
Mr. Dennis J. Knox, Director, Finance,
Accounting, Admin
Mr. Jerry Byers, Director, Communications -
CFOs

Functions: Management, Board Members, Senior
Mgmt., Middle Mgmt., Engineering, Architects,
Attorneys

Industries: Generalist (All), Construction,
Transportation, Invest. Banking, Architectural
Svcs., Legal, Accounting, HR Services,
Engineering Svcs., Real Estate,
Property/Facility Mgmt.

Branches:
3 Corporate Park Ste 160
Irvine, CA 92606-
(949) 608-5051
Fax: (703) 934-4201
Email: executiveservices@srclarke.com
Key Contact - Specialty:
Mr. Donald De Mers, Director, Development,
Western US

The Clayton Edward Group Inc

1851 R W Berends Dr SW Ste A
Grand Rapids, MI 49519-4955
(616) 336-8066
Fax: (616) 336-7680
Email: cegrp@cegrp.com
Web: www.cegrp.com

Summary: We are an executive and mid-level
search and recruiting firm serving the automotive
metal-forming/stamping industry as well as
serving manufacturing industries within our local

market. We conduct searches on a retained and contingency-retainer basis.

Key Contact - Specialty:
Mr. Ronald Meadley, President

Salary Minimum: $60,000

Functions: Generalist (All), Senior Mgmt., Middle Mgmt., Mfg., Production, Plant Mgmt., Quality

Industries: Manufacturing, Plastics, Rubber, Metal Products, Motor Vehicles, Transportation

Clear Point Consultants Inc

PO Box 9
Beverly, MA 01915-0001
(978) 524-1900
(888) 524-4004
Fax: (978) 927-7015
Email: info@clearpnt.com
Web: www.clearpnt.com

Summary: Staffing and placement services for information design and delivery professionals. This includes: technical writers, information architects, technical editors, blended learning specialists, course developers, instructional designers, technical trainers, web based trainers, and user interface designers.

Key Contact - Specialty:
Ms. Carol Szatkowski, President

Functions: Product Dev., Training, IT

Industries: Generalist (All)

Cleary Consultants Inc

21 Merchants Row Ste 22
Faneuil Hall
Boston, MA 02109-2011
(617) 367-7189
Fax: (617) 367-3202
Web: www.clearyconsultants.com

Summary: We are a full service professional placement firm located in the Faneuil Hall district of Metropolitan Boston. We specialize in the selection and placement of qualified candidates in the fields of banking/finance, insurance, accounting, investments, MIS/IT, administrative/secretarial, word processing, office support, legal, medical, personnel/human resources, travel, sales/marketing, advertising, and publishing.

Key Contact - Specialty:
Ms. Mary Cleary, President & Chief Executive Officer

Functions: Admin. Svcs.

Industries: Generalist (All)

The Clertech Group Inc

15 N Polk Creek Rd
Norman, AR 71960-8392
(870) 334-3180
Email: gad2@ieee.org

Summary: We specialize in technical searches for senior engineering, technical and management professionals for utilities and related industries: generation/T&D planning & reliability, automation consulting and marketing support. Also recruit in areas of automotive/metals manufacturing.

Key Contact - Specialty:
Mr. George A. Dorko, Director

Salary Minimum: $50,000

Functions: Generalist (All), Mfg., Engineering

Industries: Generalist (All), Energy, Utilities, Construction, Manufacturing, Metal Products, Machine, Appliance, Motor Vehicles, Computer

Equip., Electronic, Elec. Components, IT Implementation, Engineering Svcs., Supply Chain Mgmt, Defense, Aerospace, Property/Facility Mgmt., Database SW, Development SW, Industry Specific SW, Networking, Comm. SW, System SW

Cleveland Business Consultants

1148 Euclid Ave Ste 416
Cleveland, OH 44115-1604
(216) 781-5300
Fax: (216) 348-6396
Email: search@clevelandbusinessconsultants.com
Web: www.clevelandbusinessconsultants.com

Summary: Regional Search Firm wtih focus in engineering, technology, chemistry, sciences, quality control, manufacturing/management, accounting/financial and IT. Over 10,000 searches completed. Evening interviews.

Key Contact - Specialty:
Mr. Don Tillery, Owner & Manager - *Engineering, Manufacturing, Technical*

Functions: Generalist (All), Middle Mgmt., Mfg., Materials, IT, Engineering, Architects, Technicians

Industries: Generalist (All), Manufacturing, Aerospace

CLG Consulting

5765F Burke Centre Pkwy Ste 354
Burke, VA 22015-2233
(703) 495-8002
(877) 254-9361
Fax: (757) 884-9362
Email: cgaskins@clgconsulting.com
Web: www.clgconsulting.com

Summary: Our firm is a group of expert personnel consultants that provide individualized recruitment services, career transition counseling and expert advice on human relations to select companies and professionals. Our search efforts include the use of specialized referral services, extensive networking and direct nationwide recruitment.

Key Contact - Specialty:
Ms. Crystal Gaskins, CPC, President

Salary Minimum: $60,000

Functions: Management, Middle Mgmt., Admin. Svcs., Legal, Paralegals

Industries: Finance, Misc. Financial, Legal, Accounting, Mgmt. Consulting, HR Services, Marketing SW

Client Service Systems Inc

2204 S Sheffield Ave
Sioux Falls, SD 57106-0516
(605) 362-8176
Email: css@team-national.com

Summary: We are a search and placement firm specializing in the food manufacturing industry. The major thrust of business involves, but is not limited to, the recruitment of key individuals for engineering, manufacturing, quality, R&D and HR management roles.

Key Contact - Specialty:
Mr. Russ Hovendick, President

Salary Minimum: $40,000

Functions: Generalist (All)

Industries: Manufacturing, Food, Bev., Tobacco, Transportation, Wholesale, HR Services, Engineering Svcs., Logistics Svcs., Supply Chain Mgmt, Inst./Industrial Food Svc.

Clin Force Inc

4815 Emperor Blvd Ste 300
Durham, NC 27703-8470
(919) 941-0844
(800) 964-2877
Fax: (919) 941-5235
Email: response@clinforce.com
Web: www.clinforce.com

Summary: Our firm has one of the largest network of qualified professionals in the clinical research industry for contract assignments and direct placement across all disciplines and at all levels including: clinical operations, clinical data sciences, medical review & writing, pharmacoeconomics, regulatory affairs, MDs & PhDs and pre-clinical.

Key Contact - Specialty:
Mr. Tony Sims, President - *Clinical, Pharmaceutical*
Mr. Rob Stallings, Vice President, Operations - *Clinical, Pharmaceutical*

Functions: Generalist (All)

Industries: Drugs Mfg., Medical Devices, Pharm Svcs., Environmental Svcs., Biotech/Life Sciences, Healthcare

Branches:
3333 Warrenville Rd Ste 200
Lisle, IL 60532-1999
(866) 310-2193
(708) 229-2192
Fax: (708) 229-9628
Email: response@clinforce.com
Key Contact - Specialty:
Ms. Michelle Hadley, Manager, Business Development

800 Hingham St Ste 200N
Rockland, MA 02370-1079
(877) 776-6002
(781) 681-4310
Fax: (781) 681-4312
Email: response@clinforce.com
Key Contact - Specialty:
Mr. Mike McDermott, Clinical Sciences Recruiter - *Pharmaceutical*

7 Headquarters Plz
Morristown, NJ 07960-3976
(877) 254-6367
(973) 538-1900
Fax: (973) 538-1976
Email: response@clinforce.com
Key Contact - Specialty:
Ms. Kimberly Orlando, Team Lead, Data Sciences

PO Box 460
Spring House, PA 19477-0460
(800) 219-0301
(215) 653-0599
Email: response@clinforce.com
Key Contact - Specialty:
Ms. Diane Nicholas, Manager, Business Development - *Pharmaceutical*

Clinical One

60 Harvard Mill Sq
Wakefield, MA 01880-3208
(781) 876-6400
(800) 919-9100
Fax: (877) 747-9300
Email: peter.reticker@clinicalone.com
Web: www.clinicalone.com

Summary: Healthcare staffing firm offering permanent placement services with nationwide clients, including hospitals. Placements in a variety of clinical disciplines, with a special focus

on allied health, life sciences, and financial personnel.

Key Contact - Specialty:
Mr. Greg Coir, Co-Founder & President
Ms. Cynthia Kinnas, Co-Founder & Chief Operating Officer
Mr. Peter Reticker, Director, Permanent Placement - *Biomedical, Biotechnology, Healthcare, Hospital*

Functions: Generalist (All)

Industries: Healthcare, Hospitals, Long-term/Home Care, Physical Therapy, Occupational Therapy, Women's

Clinical Staffing Associates LLC (CSA)

407 Main St Ste 204
Metuchen, NJ 08840-1850
(732) 321-0088
Fax: (732) 321-0394
Email: csa@clinicalstaffing.com
Web: www.clinicalstaffing.com

Summary: We are a full-service organization with expertise in both the permanent and contractual staffing arena. We specialize in providing experienced clinical research professionals to the pharmaceutical and biotechnology industry.

Key Contact - Specialty:
Ms. Carole Ornstein, President
Ms. Susan Lynn Brenner, Vice President

Functions: Healthcare

Industries: Drugs Mfg., Medical Devices, Pharm Svcs., Biotech/Life Sciences

Clinton, Charles, Wise & Company

931 N State Road 434 Ste 1201
Altamonte Springs, FL 32714-7050
(407) 682-6790
Fax: (407) 682-1697
Email: sales@recruitersofccwc.com
Web: www.recruitersofccwc.com

Summary: We are a firm that recruits sales, marketing and management talent in the high-technology, financial and healthcare industries.

Key Contact - Specialty:
Mr. Craig D. Wise, President - *Sales*
Mr. Omari Clinton, Executive Recruiter
Mr. Kamal Charles, Executive Recruiter
Ms. Annette C. Wise, Vice President - *Sales*

Functions: Senior Mgmt., Middle Mgmt., Sales & Mktg., Mktg. Research, Mktg. Mgmt., Sales Mgmt., Systems Implem., Systems Support, Mgmt. Consultants, Minorities/Diversity

Industries: Drugs Mfg., Medical Devices, Computer Equip., Banking, Software, Healthcare

CM Executive Search, Inc.

(fomerly known as Contractor Marketing)
346 Dayton St
Yellow Springs, OH 45387-1704
(937) 767-1077
Fax: (937) 767-7281
Email: cm@cmexec.com
Web: www.cmexec.com

Summary: We conduct construction industry searches nationwide. We have placed candidates in the following categories: business development / sales, project management, estimating, preconstruction, superintendent, project engineer, marketing support, and others per client request. We conduct contingency and retained searches and our clients range in size from $10M to over $1B in revenue.

Key Contact - Specialty:
Mr. Larry Silver, President - *Business development, Marketing, Sales*
Mr. Jeff Enix, Vice President & Exec Search Consultant - *Construction*
Ms. Tiffany Salter, Executive Search Consultant - *Construction*
Mr. Ben Arthungal, Executive Search Consultant - *Construction*
Ms. Cheryl Blair, Executive Search Consultant - *Construction*
Ms. Doreen Salter, Executive Search Consultant - *Construction*

Salary Minimum: $65,000

Functions: Generalist (All), Sales & Mktg., Advertising, Mktg. Research, Mktg. Mgmt., Sales Mgmt., Direct Mktg., PR

Industries: Construction

CMB Financial Inc

5064 Roswell Rd NE Ste 301D
Atlanta, GA 30342-2278
(404) 591-2305
(800) 536-6005
Fax: (404) 252-9821
Email: mbillings@cmbfinance.com
Web: www.cmbfinance.com

Summary: We are a full service permanent placement recruiting firm. We work in accounting, finance, and audit.

Key Contact - Specialty:
Mrs. Maria Billings Schneider, CPC, Managing Partner, Financial Division - *Accounting, Accounting (Big 4,Public), Audits, Controllers*

Salary Minimum: $30,000

Functions: Finance, CFOs, Budgeting, Cash Mgmt., Credit, Taxes, M&A, Risk Mgmt.

Industries: Generalist (All)

CMC Consultants Inc

500 N Michigan Ave Ste 1940
Chicago, IL 60611-3794
(312) 670-5300
Fax: (312) 670-5333
Email: carolm@cmcconsult.com
Web: www.cmcconsult.com

Summary: Specialists in the professional recruitment of executive-level positions in fields that include accounting, finance, sales, marketing and HR.

Key Contact - Specialty:
Ms. Carol Marcovich, President
Ms. Melissa Murphy, Research Coordinator, Human Resources - *Consulting, Human resources, Outsourcing, Professional services*

Salary Minimum: $50,000

Functions: Board Members, Middle Mgmt., Mfg., Sales & Mktg., HR Mgmt., Finance

Industries: Generalist (All), Manufacturing, Retail, Finance, Accounting, HR Services, Insurance

CMD and Associates LTD

8362 Tamarack Vlg Ste 150
Woodbury, MN 55125-3392
(651) 501-2422
Fax: (651) 501-3946
Email: twanda@cmdandassociates.com
Web: www.cmdandassociates.com

Summary: We are an executive search firm specializing in operations, human resource, financial, manufacturing, sales, marketing, logistics, retail management. We specialize in

recruiting highly talented candidates that will add value to the needs identified by your company.

Key Contact - Specialty:
Mrs. Twanda DeBorde, Principal - *Human resources, Manufacturing (Management), Minorities, Operations, Production*

Salary Minimum: $50,000

Functions: Generalist (All), Senior Mgmt.

Industries: Generalist (All)

CMI Consulting LLC

2800 Palumbo Dr Ste 202
Lexington, KY 40509-1309
(859) 296-2800
Fax: (859) 296-2801
Email: beverly@cmiconsulting.com
Web: www.cmiconsulting.com

Summary: Our staff is dedicated to searching out the management-level employees who are the most highly qualified for the positions you are seeking to fill.

Key Contact - Specialty:
Mrs. Beverly Clemons, President

Salary Minimum: $25,000

Functions: Generalist (All)

Industries: Construction, Manufacturing, Food, Bev., Tobacco, Textiles, Apparel, Lumber, Furniture, Chemicals, Drugs Mfg., Medical Devices, Plastics, Rubber, Paints, Petro. Products

CMW & Associates Inc

PO Box 3004
Springfield, IL 62708-3004
(217) 522-0452
Fax: (217) 241-5974
Email: cmw@topechelon.com
Web: www.cmwassoc.com

Summary: We do consulting in the areas of IT, accounting/finance, engineering & science. We perform executive placement in the areas of engineering, the food industry, healthcare, sales, finance & IT. Our area of expertise is healthcare, technical placements in the IT fields, technical & healthcare sales, and degreed engineering fields.

Key Contact - Specialty:
Ms. Charlene Turczyn, Senior Principal - *Accounting, Business development, C-level, CIOs, Computers (Sales)*
Mr. Michael Turczyn, Senior Recruiter
Mrs. Jill Schroeder, Sales - *Government, Information Systems, Information Technology, Senior management, Treasury*
Mr. Deldon Krueger, Director, Recruiting - *Culinary, Dairy, Food & beverage, Food service*
Mr. Dan Harris, Government Business Development

Salary Minimum: $45,000

Functions: Sales & Mktg., MIS Mgmt., Systems Dev., Engineering

Industries: Generalist (All), Energy, Utilities, Construction, Architectural Svcs., Mgmt. Consulting, Engineering Svcs., Logistics Svcs., Government, Environmental Svcs., Haz. Waste, Software, ERP SW, Industry Specific SW, Security SW, System SW, Training SW, Healthcare, Hospitals, Women's

CN Associates

PO Box 5307
Novato, CA 94948-5307
(415) 883-1114
Fax: (415) 883-3321

Email: chasn@earthlink.net
Web: www.cnassociates.com

Summary: We are a high-technology executive search firm with a strong focus in sales, marketing, tech support and health care staffing (software). We specialize in software, telecomm/datacom and Internet based applications.

Key Contact - Specialty:
Mr. Charles Nicolosi, Principal - *Computers (Software), Sales, Telecommunications*

Salary Minimum: $70,000

Functions: Board Members, Sales & Mktg., MIS Mgmt., Systems Analysis, Systems Dev., Systems Implem., Systems Support, Network Admin., DB Admin., Mgmt. Consultants

Industries: Computer Equip., Mgmt. Consulting, Software, Doc. Mgmt., Production SW, ERP SW, Healthcare

CNI Career Networks

800 Seagate Dr Ste 303
Naples, FL 34103-2809
(800) 562-5465
(239) 262-0184
Fax: (305) 513-5747
Email: info@cnijoblink.com
Web: www.cnijoblink.com

Summary: We specialize in wireless, telecom and financial industries. We have one of the most targeted audiences available on the web.

Key Contact - Specialty:
Ms. Monique Hernandez, President - *Executives*
Mr. Mark Hamdan, Chairman - *Executives*

Functions: Management, Mfg., Purchasing, Sales & Mktg., HR Mgmt., Training, Finance, IT, Engineering, Technicians

Industries: Invest. Banking, Telecoms

Coast to Coast Executive Search

9769 W 119th Dr Ste 14
Broomfield, CO 80021-2560
(303) 464-1704
Fax: (303) 464-1553
Email: exsrch1@aol.com
Web: www.execsearch1.com

Summary: Specializing in the hospitality, restaurant, club, food service and food manufacturing industry, we offer our clients prompt and efficient closure to their important management openings.

Key Contact - Specialty:
Mr. Dennis Updyke, CPC, Owner - *Food service, Hospitality*

Functions: Generalist (All), Board Members, Senior Mgmt., Mfg., Hospitality

Industries: Generalist (All), Food, Bev., Tobacco, Hospitality, Hotels, Resorts, Clubs, Restaurants, Quick Service Restaurants, Full Service Restaurants, Inst./Industrial Food Svc., Entertainment, Recreation, Sports

Cobb Professional Services Ltd

PO Box 568
Carmel, IN 46082-0568
(317) 580-0552
Email: cps@cobbservices.com
Web: www.cobbservices.com

Summary: We provide services to our clients through retained search, contingency and engagement fee methods. Our guiding principles of integrity, teamwork and honest commitment are applied to each project we undertake.

Key Contact - Specialty:
Mr. Mark Cobb, President - *Engineering, Executives, Management, Marketing, Pharmaceutical*

Salary Minimum: $45,000

Functions: Management, Senior Mgmt., Mfg., Product Dev., Production, Quality, Purchasing, Mktg. Mgmt., R&D, Engineering

Industries: Generalist (All), Construction, Manufacturing, Food, Bev., Tobacco, Chemicals, Drugs Mfg., Medical Devices, Motor Vehicles, Misc. Mfg., Consumer Goods, Finance, Services, Non-profits, Pharm Svcs., Accounting, Mgmt. Consulting, Engineering Svcs., Biotech/Life Sciences, Healthcare

Ann Coe & Associates

2033 Sherman Ave
Evanston, IL 60201-3282
(847) 864-0668
Email: anncoe@aol.com

Summary: We provide professional and executive search specializing in IT.

Key Contact - Specialty:
Ms. Ann Coe, President & Owner - *Life Sciences*

Salary Minimum: $50,000

Functions: Product Dev., Customer Svc., IT, MIS Mgmt., Systems Analysis, Systems Implem., Systems Support, Network Admin., DB Admin., Technicians

Industries: Generalist (All)

Riley Cole

PO Box 10635
Oakland, CA 94610-0635
(510) 336-2333
Email: riled@pacbell.net

Summary: We have had extensive years of successful, in-depth recruiting experience. Competitive knowledge, organizational design understanding, as well as proven integrity and discretion allow us to individualize each search assignment.

Key Contact - Specialty:
Mr. Jim Riley, Partner - *Retail, Sales*
Mr. Don Cole, Partner - *Engineering, Research & development*

Salary Minimum: $50,000

Functions: Generalist (All)

Industries: Manufacturing, Food, Bev., Tobacco, Soap, Perf., Cosmtcs., Wholesale, Retail

Coleman Legal

1500 John F Kennedy Blvd Ste 1010
Philadelphia, PA 19102-1741
(215) 864-2700
Fax: (215) 864-2709
Email: cls@colemanlegal.com
Web: www.colemanlegal.com

Summary: We specialize in recruiting lawyers, partners & associates and paralegals for law firms and general counsels, staff attorneys, paralegals and contract specialists for corporations. We also assist in law firm mergers and opening of satellite offices. In addition, we provide temp attorneys, paralegals and contract specialists.

Key Contact - Specialty:
Mr. Michael M. Coleman, Principal
Ms. Tali Perlman, Recruiter
Ms. Marcie Friedman, Recruiter
Ms. Stacy Flickstein, Recruiter
Ms. Natalia Kedves, Recruiter
Mr. Mark Ligos, Recruiter

Functions: Legal, Attorneys, Paralegals

Industries: Legal

Branches:
116 Village Blvd Ste 200
Princeton, NJ 08540-5700
(856) 234-1946
Fax: (800) 200-4414
Email: cls@colemanlegal.com
Key Contact - Specialty:
Tersa Valls

PO Box 746
919 Conestoga Rd Ste 3-210
Bryn Mawr, PA 19010-0746
(610) 527-5007
Email: ccpd@colemancounsel.com
Key Contact - Specialty:
Mr. Robert Nourian, Esq., Principal
Ms. Elizabeth Nourian, Esq., Principal - *Legal*
Ms. Monica R. Buck

Cole's Paper Industry Recruiters Inc

3419 Winter Wheat Rd
Kalamazoo, MI 49004-4307
(269) 341-4495
Fax: (269) 341-4598
Email: jcole@staffing.net
Web: www.colerecruiting.com

Summary: We are a full service independent recruiting firm specializing in the pulp and paper Industries.

Key Contact - Specialty:
Mr. Jim Cole, President

Salary Minimum: $40,000

Functions: Generalist (All)

Industries: Paper

College Executives

(also known as CE Recruiters)
5155 Martinique Dr
Lakeland, FL 33812-5001
(863) 646-6471
Email: info@collegeexecutives.com
Web: www.collegeexecutives.com

Summary: We are executive recruiting firm specializing in mid and upper management recruitment and placement in the private/proprietary education sector. We specialize in mid and upper management recruitment and placement in health care industry.

Key Contact - Specialty:
Dr. Frances J. Morris, PhD, Owner & President
Mr. Michael Schledorn, Senior Vice President, Recruit & Place.
Ms. Kaye M. Simpson, Vice President, Midwest Recruitment - *Physicians*

Functions: Generalist (All), Management, Board Members, Senior Mgmt., Middle Mgmt., Sales & Mktg., Sales Mgmt.

Industries: Retail, Higher Ed., Hospitality, Non-Classifiable

Collins & Associates

10188 W H Ave
Kalamazoo, MI 49009-8506
(269) 372-3275
Fax: (269) 372-3921
Email: pcollins@collins-associates.com
Web: www.collins-associates.com

Summary: We perform services for all areas of computers and computer professionals. All disciplines in engineering, operations and management in the manufacturing industries. Focus in the automotive industry.

Key Contact - Specialty:
Mr. Philip M. Collins, Principal - *Computers, Manufacturing*

Salary Minimum: $40,000

Functions: Management, Mfg., MIS Mgmt., Systems Analysis, Systems Dev., Systems Implem., Network Admin.

Industries: Generalist (All), Plastics, Rubber, Paints, Petro. Products, Metal Products, Machine, Appliance, Motor Vehicles, Computer Equip., Test, Measure Equip., Misc. Mfg., Electronic, Elec. Components, IT Implementation, RF/Microwave, Development SW, Mfg. SW

Branches:
1550 E Beltline SE Ste 200
Grand Rapids, MI 49506-4362
(616) 977-5726
Fax: (616) 977-5728
Email: gina@collins-associates.com
Key Contact - Specialty:
Mr. Peter A. Collins, CPC, Principal -
Manufacturing
Ms. Gina Jonker, Office Coordinator

S L Collins Associates Inc

PO Box 78945
Charlotte, NC 28271-7044
(704) 321-2400
Email: collins@slcollins.com
Web: www.slcollins.com

Summary: We recruit for companies in locations throughout the United States. We are well known in the pharmaceutical, medical device and biotechnology industries for our professionalism, integrity and service to both client companies and candidates. Positions are up to the level of CEO, CFO, SVP, etc.

Key Contact - Specialty:
Mr. Steve L. Collins, President - *Biotechnology, Pharmaceutical*
Mr. David Collins, Vice President -
Pharmaceutical

Salary Minimum: $90,000

Functions: Generalist (All), Senior Mgmt., Middle Mgmt., Plant Mgmt., Quality, Sales & Mktg., Mktg. Mgmt., R&D

Industries: Drugs Mfg., Medical Devices, Pharm Svcs., Biotech/Life Sciences, Healthcare

Colorado Corporate Search LLC

283 Columbine St Ste 125
Denver, CO 80206-4707
(303) 333-6464
Fax: (720) 528-8169
Email: amy@coloradosearch.com
Web: www.coloradosearch.com

Summary: We know the accounting and finance community in our market inside out and backwards.

Key Contact - Specialty:
Ms. Amy C. Duclos, President - *Finance*

Salary Minimum: $90,000

Functions: Finance

Industries: Generalist (All)

Command Consultants Inc

834 Sanctuary Cove Dr
West Palm Beach, FL 33410-4537
(561) 627-1745
Email: mlondon@staffing.net
Web: www.commandconsultants.com

Summary: We are a well established executive search firm who recruits and places senior level sales & marketing professionals within several industries including healthcare, bio-technology and consulting services.

Key Contact - Specialty:
Mr. Mark London, President - *Healthcare, Information Systems, Marketing, Medical (Sales), Sales*
Ms. Maria Basilone, Vice President, Business Development - *Biomedical, Healthcare, Home health, Management, Medical*

Salary Minimum: $75,000

Functions: Generalist (All), Management, Board Members, Sales & Mktg., Sales Mgmt.

Industries: Generalist (All), Medical Devices, Computer Equip., Test, Measure Equip., Digital, Biotech/Life Sciences, Healthcare, Hospitals

Commercial Programming Systems Inc

3575 Cahuenga Blvd W Ste 222
Los Angeles, CA 90068-1341
(323) 851-2681
(888) 277-4562
Fax: (323) 851-5681
Email: cps@cpsinc.com
Web: www.cpsinc.com

Summary: We are the contract service of choice for IT professionals in our market. We provide contract, lease to hire, and executive placement opportunities.

Key Contact - Specialty:
Mr. Alan Strong, Chief Executive Officer
Mr. Philip Sawyer, President
Mr. Brad Eastland, Executive Recruiter
Mrs. Donna Preston, Vice President
Ms. Bonnie Maechler, MSMath, Senior Account Manager - *Information Technology*

Salary Minimum: $120,000

Functions: MIS Mgmt., Systems Analysis, Systems Dev., Systems Implem., Systems Support, Network Admin., DB Admin.

Industries: Generalist (All), Motor Vehicles, Finance, Hospitality, Media, Broadcast, Film, Telecoms, Government

Branches:
2375 E Camelback Rd Ste 500
Phoenix, AZ 85016-3489
(602) 667-7766
(888) 812-5961
Fax: (602) 912-8514
Email: chiara.hughes@cpsinc.com
Key Contact - Specialty:
Ms. Chiara Hughes, Branch Manager

20955 Pathfinder Rd Ste 200
Diamond Bar, CA 91765-4045
(714) 674-0100
(888) 812-5960
Fax: (714) 672-3545
Email: cattman@cpsinc.com
Key Contact - Specialty:
Mr. Steve Catt, Vice President

Common Agenda LLP

PO Box 711
Brielle, NJ 08730-0711
(732) 223-7114
Fax: (732) 223-7116
Email: resume@commonagenda.com
Web: www.commonagenda.com

Summary: Our philosophy is to employ the search industry's best practices (solid strategy, in-depth research, strict adherence to ethical recruitment and confidentiality standards and strong

knowledge management) as the means to identify and recruit exceptional professionals and executives for our clients. We apply proven recruiting methodologies across numerous functions and industries.

Key Contact - Specialty:
Mr. Matthew Reaves, CPC, Managing Director & Founder - *C-level, Technology, Telecommunications, Underwriting, Wireless*
Ms. Darlene Corrubia, Executive Director - *Product management/development, Technical, Technical (Management), Technology, Telecommunications*

Salary Minimum: $100,000

Functions: Management, Senior Mgmt.

Industries: Communications, Telecoms, Telephony, Digital, Wireless, Fiber Optic, Network Infrastructure, RF/Microwave, Re-Insurance, Software, Biotech/Life Sciences

Commonwealth Consultants

5064 Roswell Rd NE Ste 101B
Atlanta, GA 30342-2252
(404) 256-0000
Fax: (404) 256-3625
Email: mailtimp@yahoo.com

Summary: Our firm supplies software vendors with high-level technical sales, sales management and support people.

Key Contact - Specialty:
Mr. David Aiken, Partner
Mr. Tim Panetta, Partner

Salary Minimum: $60,000

Functions: Sales & Mktg.

Industries: Software, Database SW, Development SW, Doc. Mgmt., Production SW, ERP SW, HR SW, Industry Specific SW, Mfg. SW, Security SW, System SW

Compass Run LLC

19111 Saint Abrahams Ct
Hampstead, MD 21074-2742
(443) 921-2943
Fax: (410) 374-9663
Email: info@compassrun.com
Web: www.compassrun.com

Summary: We are an executive search firm specializing is professional recruitment in HR, engineering, IT, accounting/finance and sales/marketing. We develop relationships with the people in our client companies and strive to fill their professional recruitment needs.

Key Contact - Specialty:
Mrs. Barbara Barrett, President - *Engineering, Finance, Human resources, Marketing*

Functions: Generalist (All), Management, Senior Mgmt., Product Dev., Quality, HR Mgmt., R&D, Engineering, Eng. Design

Industries: Generalist (All), Chemicals, Drugs Mfg., Medical Devices, Machine, Appliance, Computer Equip., Robotics, HR Services, IT Implementation, Defense, Aerospace, Software, Industry Specific SW, Biotech/Life Sciences

Compass Search Group LLC

16140 Sand Canyon Ave Ste 102
Irvine, CA 92618-3715
(949) 910-0110
Fax: (949) 910-0703
Email: info@compass-search.net
Web: www.compass-search.net

Summary: Our firm was founded on the most basic personal principles of integrity, respect, honesty, commitment and loyalty. Created to

assist our clients with their changing accounting & finance concerns; we recognize the market requires first-class, trustworthy, ethical partnerships with both clients and candidates.

Key Contact - Specialty:
Ms. Debbie Neal, Principal
Mr. Kevin Tougas, Senior Search Consultant
Mr. Mark Fisher, Senior Search Consultant
Mrs. Marisa Winkle, Research Support Consultant
Ms. Marci Simmons, Research Consultant
Ms. Katie Stenton, Research Consultant
Mr. Robert Wright, Managing Director, WFY
Mr. Scott Young, Accounting & Audit Director, WFY

Salary Minimum: $50,000

Functions: Generalist (All)

Industries: Construction, Manufacturing, Transportation, Finance, Services, Entertainment, Broadcast, Film, Real Estate, Property/Facility Mgmt., Security SW

ComPeople Source Inc

17W070 Burr Oak Ln
Willowbrook, IL 60527-6035
(630) 789-0088
Fax: (630) 789-9950
Email: jack@compeoplesource.com

Summary: Our principal has been heading up perm IT search firms for many years. Our clients range in size from small IT consulting organizations to multi-billion dollar corporations. We handle any IT-related search, from recruiters, to sales, to technical and management candidates.

Key Contact - Specialty:
Mr. Jack Hillon, President

Salary Minimum: $45,000

Functions: Management, Sales & Mktg., IT

Industries: Generalist (All), Computer Equip., New Media, Communications, Software

The Comperio Group

12295 Oracle Blvd Ste 340
Colorado Springs, CO 80921-3902
(719) 785-4888
Email: info@comperiogroup.com
Web: www.comperiogroup.com

Summary: Our firm is an executive recruiting firm that focuses solely on the computer and communications industries. Through specialization, we have gained a broad and deep understanding of both business sectors. As a result, we recruit quickly and efficiently. This kind of focus is critical in industries where competition for talented managers is fierce and unrelenting.

Key Contact - Specialty:
Mr. John Taylor, Managing Director

Salary Minimum: $75,000

Functions: Senior Mgmt., Product Dev., Sales & Mktg.

Industries: Computer Equip., Electronic, Elec. Components, E-commerce, IT Implementation, Communications, Software

CompHealth Group

PO Box 57915
4021 S 700 E Ste 300
Salt Lake City, UT 84157-0915
(801) 264-6400
(800) 453-3030
Fax: (801) 264-6464
Email: info@comphealth.com
Web: www.comphealth.com

Summary: Our firm is a provider of healthcare staffing services. The company provides temp staffing and permanent placement services for healthcare professionals of all types.

Key Contact - Specialty:
Mr. John Genna, Vice President
Mr. Don DeCamp, CPC, Chief Operating Officer
Ms. Mary Biljanic, Public Relations Specialist

Salary Minimum: $80,000

Functions: Healthcare, Physicians, Nurses, Allied Health

Industries: Healthcare, Hospitals, Long-term/Home Care, Physical Therapy, Occupational Therapy, Women's

Affiliates:
CompHealth Group
Norwalk, CT

CompHealth Group
Fort Lauderdale, FL

CompHealth Group
Grand Rapids, MI

CompHealth Group
Dallas, TX

Compton & Associates

737 Blackmoor Gate Ln Ste 200
Saint Augustine, FL 32084-1881
(904) 824-8422
Fax: (904) 823-0755
Email: jcompton@se.rr.com
Web: www.comptonsearch.com

Summary: Our affiliation with networks provides databases of a million candidates and thousands of job orders. While we are classified as generalists, our focus is on the manufacturing sector and IT.

Key Contact - Specialty:
Mr. John W. Compton, Principal

Salary Minimum: $50,000

Functions: Generalist (All), Management, Senior Mgmt., Product Dev., Automation

Industries: Generalist (All), Manufacturing, Motor Vehicles, Computer Equip., Consumer Elect., Misc. Mfg., Electronic, Elec. Components, Supply Chain Mgmt., Communications, Defense, Database SW, Development SW

Computech Corp

4375 N 75th St
Scottsdale, AZ 85251-3590
(480) 947-7534
Fax: (480) 947-7537
Email: jobs@computech-az.com
Web: www.computech-az.com

Summary: Search and consulting firm specializing in various proprietary HR software, Internet, web development, HTML, Java, B2B, J2EE, .Net, eCommerce, client server and other IT positions.

Key Contact - Specialty:
Mr. Bob Dirickson

Functions: Generalist (All), IT, Systems Dev., Systems Implem.

Industries: Generalist (All), Computer Equip., Banking, HR Services, IT Implementation

Computer Careers

PO Box 1613
Joplin, MO 64802-1613
(417) 781-2929
(800) 689-5627
Fax: (800) 689-1622

Email: itcareers@computercareers.net
Web: www.computercareers.net

Summary: We offer permanent and temp IT staffing, including employer of record service for part-time and contract employees.

Key Contact - Specialty:
Mr. Larry Baker, President
Mr. Ryan Baker, Recruiter
Mr. David Spencer, Recruiter

Salary Minimum: $30,000

Functions: IT

Industries: Generalist (All)

Computer Futures

5870 Green Valley Cir Unit 101
Culver City, CA 90230-6908
(310) 641-2283
Fax: (310) 641-2376
Email: computerfutures@comcast.net

Summary: We specialize in positions in the IT arena, covering all levels and disciplines; from programmers, systems engineers, network, PC & web specialists, systems programmers & administrators, to consultants, project managers, directors and VPs.

Key Contact - Specialty:
Ms. Joy Evans, Owner

Salary Minimum: $50,000

Functions: IT

Industries: Generalist (All)

Computer Horizons Canada

701-2700 Matheson Blvd E
Mississauga, ON L4W 4V9
Canada
(905) 602-6085
Fax: (905) 602-6091
Email: toronto@computerhorizons.ca
Web: www.computerhorizons.ca

Summary: We provide IT services including; IT staffing (contract and permanent), project management, outsourcing and CVM solutions.

Key Contact - Specialty:
Mr. Frank Vrabel, Senior Vice President, Business Devel
Mr. Paul Bottero, President
Mr. Bob Pridding, Vice President, Sales

Functions: IT, MIS Mgmt., Systems Analysis, Systems Dev., Systems Implem., Systems Support, Network Admin., DB Admin., Graphic Designers

Industries: Generalist (All)

Branches:
900-805 8 Ave SW
Calgary, AB T2P 1H7
Canada
(403) 265-3380
Fax: (403) 265-3301
Email: calgary@computerhorizons.ca
Key Contact - Specialty:
Mr. Philip Purnell, Vice President, Western Canada

101-1770 Woodward Dr
Ottawa, ON K2C 0P8
Canada
(613) 228-0010
Fax: (613) 228-9022
Email: ottawa@computerhorizons.ca
Key Contact - Specialty:
Mr. Warren Pickering, Vice President, Sales

830-650 Boul de Maisonneuve O
Montreal, QC H3A 3T2
Canada
(514) 840-6100
Fax: (514) 840-6238
Email: montreal@computerhorizons.ca

Computer International Consultants Inc

109 5th St E
Saint Petersburg, FL 33715-2242
(727) 865-9701
Fax: (727) 865-3503
Email: jobs@cictampa.com
Web: www.cictampa.com

Summary: Recruitment experience and competence by a staff of former Fortune 500 executives that understand corporate structure, culture and requirements. Staff experience in IT.

Key Contact - Specialty:
Ms. Linda M. Mitchell, Chief Executive Officer

Salary Minimum: $50,000

Functions: IT, MIS Mgmt., Systems Analysis, Systems Dev., Systems Implem., Systems Support, Network Admin., DB Admin.

Industries: Generalist (All)

Computer Management Inc

7982 Honeygo Blvd Ste 23
Baltimore, MD 21236-4919
(410) 679-7000
Fax: (443) 836-1440
Email: recruiter@technicaljobs.com
Web: www.technicaljobs.com

Summary: We are a technical recruiting firm with experience providing contract and permanent placement services to our clients in defense and private industry. We specialize in IT and engineering.

Key Contact - Specialty:
Ms. Janet Miller, President

Salary Minimum: $45,000

Functions: IT, Systems Analysis, Systems Dev., Systems Implem., Systems Support, Network Admin., DB Admin., Engineering

Industries: Manufacturing, Consumer Elect., Electronic, Elec. Components, Finance, Services, E-commerce, IT Implementation, Hospitality, Media, Communications, Government, Defense, Compliance, Homeland Security, Aerospace, Insurance, Real Estate, Software, Healthcare

Computer Personnel Inc

8224 15th Ave NE
Seattle, WA 98115-4340
(206) 985-0282
(888) 890-0318
Fax: (206) 770-1939
Email: cpi@cpirecruiting.com
Web: www.cpirecruiting.com

Summary: Our practice is focused on IT professionals and on those disciplines related to IT, for example: those professionals with expertise in specific business applications such as SAP, CRS, B2B, eCommerce, etc. We have extensive experience with eCommerce and business-to-business entities.

Key Contact - Specialty:
Mr. Ron Meints, President

Salary Minimum: $30,000

Functions: Generalist (All), IT

Industries: HR Services, E-commerce, IT Implementation, Software, Accounting SW,

Database SW, Development SW, Doc. Mgmt., Production SW, Entertainment SW, ERP SW, HR SW

Computer Recruiters Inc

22276 Buena Ventura St
Woodland Hills, CA 91364-5006
(818) 704-7722
(888) 918-5518
Fax: (818) 704-7724
Email: bob@tekjobs.com
Web: www.tekjobs.com

Summary: We are IT specialists for PC (client server), internet, ERP, CRM, data warehouse, midrange and mainframe. We place positions such as programmer analysts, functional analysts, database administrators, network administrators, systems programmers, systems engineers, EDI analysts, EDI coordinators and all managers. We place full time employees and contractors but not entry-level positions, operators, data entry, technician or sales positions.

Key Contact - Specialty:
Mr. Bob Moore, Manager - *Data processing*

Salary Minimum: $70,000

Functions: Generalist (All), MIS Mgmt., Systems Analysis, Systems Dev., Systems Implem., Systems Support, Network Admin., DB Admin., Architects

Industries: Generalist (All), Software, Accounting SW, Database SW, Development SW, ERP SW, HR SW, Industry Specific SW, Mfg. SW, Networking, Comm. SW, Security SW

Computer Staffing Solutions Inc

(also known as Comprehensive Staffing Solutions Inc)
1841 Piedmont Rd Ste 102
Marietta, GA 30066-4299
(770) 578-6677
Fax: (770) 578-6653
Email: jobs@staffingsolutions.biz
Web: www.staffingsolutions.biz

Summary: We assist clients with IT/technical staffing (programmers, network, software engineers, etc.); assist mortgage lenders staff loan processor, closers, underwriters, team leader and sales positions; and assist hospitals, medical and healthcare centers staff nurses, x-ray technicians, etc. We staff temp positions, permanent positions or temp to perm.

Key Contact - Specialty:
Ms. Jill Freeman, President
Mr. Terry Freeman, Chief Financial Officer
Ms. Jill Hunter, Technical Recruiter
Mr. Jason Donnelly, Administrator
Ms. Kim Moyer, Account Representative

Functions: Healthcare, Physicians, Nurses, Allied Health, HR Mgmt., Finance, IT

Industries: Generalist (All), Finance, Banking, Invest. Banking, Brokers, Misc. Financial, Mgmt. Consulting, HR Services, IT Implementation, Communications, Telecoms, Call Centers, Telephony, Digital, Wireless, Fiber Optic, Network Infrastructure, Government, ERP SW, HR SW, Security SW, Healthcare, Hospitals, Long-term/Home Care, Dental, Physical Therapy, Occupational Therapy, Women's, Non-Classifiable

Computer Strategies Inc

5620 N Kolb Rd Ste 225
Tucson, AZ 85750-0749
(520) 577-7117
(800) 952-9544
Fax: (520) 577-2772

Email: recruiters@computerstrategies.com
Web: www.computerstrategies.com

Summary: We are a professional search firm that specializes in the recruitment of IT professionals for major corporations. We deal with many clients including Fortune 500, mid-sized and dot-com.

Key Contact - Specialty:
Ms. Debby Brodie, Owner & President
Mr. Joshua Small, Vice President, Corporate Recruiting
Ms. Maria Robinson, Recruiter - *Computers (Software), Technology, Telecommunications, Venture capital*

Salary Minimum: $65,000

Functions: Board Members, Senior Mgmt., Middle Mgmt., IT, MIS Mgmt., Systems Analysis, Systems Implem., Network Admin., DB Admin.

Industries: Generalist (All), IT Implementation, Database SW, Development SW

Computer Technology Staffing

(a division of Bio-Pharma Group)
3 Denson Rd
Lincoln, RI 02865-2301
(401) 230-8191
(401) 257-5115
Email: bpencarski@ctstaff.com
Web: www.ctstaff.com

Summary: We provide retained search and contingency technical placement and contract placement at all levels in system engineering, hardware engineering, software engineering, IS/IT, communications, process/manufacturing, defense, bio-technology, and medical device at all levels.

Key Contact - Specialty:
Mr. Robert Pencarski, Managing Partner - *Pharmacists, Process equipment, Quality, Technical, Technology*
Mr. Charles Ostiguy, Partner - *Analysts, Defense, Engineering, Information Technology, Pharmacists*
Dr. James Shelnut, PhD, Affiliate & Technical Consultant - *Biomaterials, Chemical, Coatings, Electronics, High technology*

Salary Minimum: $60,000

Functions: Generalist (All), Management

Industries: Generalist (All), Manufacturing, Electronic, Elec. Components, Semiconductors, Communications, Defense, Aerospace, Packaging, Software, System SW, Biotech/Life Sciences

Concept II Employment Service

412-236 Saint George St
Commerce House
Moncton, NB E1C 1W1
Canada
(506) 388-9675
(877) 385-9675
Fax: (506) 388-9674
Email: resumes@concept2employment.com
Web: www.concept2employment.com

Summary: Providing exceptional staffing and recruiting services to our market community.

Key Contact - Specialty:
Mr. John Alexander, President

Functions: Generalist (All), Management

Industries: Generalist (All), IT Implementation

Concord Search Group

600 W Germantown Pike Ste 400
Plymouth Meeting, PA 19462-1046
(610) 940-0550
Fax: (610) 940-0711
Email: equinn@concordsearch.com
Web: www.concordsearch.com

Summary: Our group specializes in recruiting and compensation consulting in the fields of sales, management and executive positions for technology driven organizations. With extensive combined experience, we have successfully partnered with Fortune 500, most of the Mid-Atlantic region's fastest growing companies.

Key Contact - Specialty:
Mr. Brian Filippini, President
Mrs. Leigh Filippini, Partner
Mr. Adam Bennett, Director, Recruiting
Ms. Alicia Filippini, Director, Recruiting
Ms. Jen Valciukas, Manager, Research - *Internet*
Mrs. Phyllis Hilkert, Executive Recruiter
Miss Jacqui Gary, Executive Recruiter
Miss Lynn Wilson, Executive Recruiter

Salary Minimum: $100,000

Functions: Generalist (All), Management

Industries: Mgmt. Consulting, E-commerce, New Media, Telecoms, Call Centers, Digital, Fiber Optic, Software, Database SW, Development SW, Doc. Mgmt., Production SW, Biotech/Life Sciences

Concorde Search Associates

1 N Broadway Ste 400
White Plains, NY 10601-2321
(914) 428-0700
Fax: (914) 428-4865
Email: jobs@concordepersonnel.com
Web: www.concordepersonnel.com

Summary: We are a 100 percent client-driven search firm. Our total thrust is fulfilling and maximizing the corporate staffing goals of our clients. We provide extra commitment and work ethic.

Key Contact - Specialty:
Mr. Rich Greenwald, President
Mr. William Bernstein, Vice President - *Automotive, Manufacturing, Pharmaceutical*
Ms. Jill Davidson, Recruiter
Ms. Gail Davis, Recruiter
Ms. Ann LaSorsa, Recruiter
Ms. Linda Ragusa, Recruiter
Mr. Robert Weeks, Recruiter - *Accounting, Tax, Transportation*

Salary Minimum: $25,000

Functions: HR Mgmt., Finance

Industries: Generalist (All), Finance, Banking, Accounting

ConcreteCareers.com/Vineyard & Partners

PO Box 900
Bremen, GA 30110-0900
(770) 537-3237
(877) 594-6946
Fax: (770) 537-1488
Email: integrity@concretecareers.com
Web: www.concretecareers.com

Summary: As an industry specific search and recruiting firm, we supplement the concrete industry's HR expertise by locating and matching individual talents, abilities and experiences to specific staffing requirements. Our primary market areas are the pre-cast/pre-stress, concrete masonry and ready mix disciplines. We also serve the cement, aggregate, additive, form, wire and concrete construction industry as opportunities arise.

Key Contact - Specialty:
Mr. Gene Vineyard, President

Salary Minimum: $50,000

Functions: Management, Board Members, Senior Mgmt., Middle Mgmt., Mfg., Production, Plant Mgmt., Quality, Sales & Mktg.

Industries: Construction

Confisa International Group

San Juanico No 128
Col Juriquilla CP
76230 Queretaro, QRO
Mexico
44 2234 0411
Fax: 44 2234 0411
Email: jcmorones@confisagroup.com
Web: www.confisagroup.com

Summary: Highly professional executive search firm that finds talent for top leading companies including Fortune 500s.

Key Contact - Specialty:
Mr. Juan-Carlos Morones, Partner
Mr. Juan Carlos Jaramillo, President
Mr. Fernando Morones, Executive, Key Account - *Automotive*
Ms. Carmen Soto, Senior Consultant - *Automotive, Electronics*

Functions: Generalist (All)

Industries: Food, Bev., Tobacco, Textiles, Apparel, Chemicals, Soap, Perf., Cosmtcs., Plastics, Rubber, Metal Products, Motor Vehicles, Electronic, Elec. Components, Entertainment, Advertising

ConnectCentral

1817 State Route 83 Unit 381
Millersburg, OH 44654-9402
(330) 674-9969
Email: kay@connectcentral.com
Web: www.connectcentral.com

Summary: We service the high-tech industry throughout the U.S., from executive to sales and technical positions. Includes web-based and enterprise-wide solutions, with emphasis on the following: customer relationship management, customer information systems, enterprise content management, human capital management, and IT compliance. Serving all industries, with expertise in energy/utilities, software and consulting.

Key Contact - Specialty:
Ms. Kay Mullins, Principal & Search Consultant

Salary Minimum: $90,000

Functions: Senior Mgmt., Product Dev., Sales & Mktg., Sales Mgmt., Sales Reps., e-HR, Risk Mgmt., IT, MIS Mgmt.

Industries: Generalist (All), Energy, Utilities, Oil & Gas, Construction, Manufacturing, Mgmt. Consulting, HR Services, E-commerce, IT Implementation, Logistics Svcs., Compliance, Software

Conner Recruiting

PO Box 711362
Salt Lake City, UT 84171-1362
(801) 244-0398
Fax: (801) 944-6294
Email: suzanne@connerrecruiting.com
Web: www.connerrecruiting.com

Summary: Specializing in the placement of professionals with expertise in the life science industries, including engineers, marketing, and regulatory professionals as well as accounting and finance professionals, including bank-related industries.

Key Contact - Specialty:
Ms. Suzanne H. Conner, CPA, President

Salary Minimum: $45,000

Functions: Generalist (All)

Industries: Drugs Mfg., Medical Devices, Finance, Banking, Misc. Financial, Accounting, Commercial, Biotech/Life Sciences

Connexion Systems & Engineering

490 Boston Post Rd
Sudbury, MA 01776-3367
(978) 579-0030
Fax: (978) 443-3789
Email: resumes@csetalent.com
Web: www.csetalent.com

Summary: Our firm was founded by several very experienced recruiting professionals. We have recruiters covering engineering, IT/systems, scientific, sales and executive positions.

Key Contact - Specialty:
Mr. Daniel Cushing, Managing Partner - *Acoustics, Aerospace, Automation, Automotive, Aviation*
Mr. Robert Collins, Managing Partner - *Defense, Engineering, Systems, Technical*
Mr. Kenneth DiMaggio, Managing Partner - *Engineering, Information Technology, Systems*
Ms. Cindy Vogel, Resource Manager
Mr. M. James Hunt, Resource Manager - *Engineering, Sales, Systems*
Mr. Scott Cooper, Resource Manager - *Engineering, Sales, Systems*
Ms. Helena Veranian, Office Manager
Mr. Jason Wegiel, Resource Manager - *Biomedical, Biotechnology, Embedded microprocessor, Engineering*
Mr. Mike Chapman, Resource Manager - *Oracle, PeopleSoft, Professional services, SAP, Technology*
Ms. Danielle McGrath, Resource Manager - *Computers, Computers (Automation,Hardware,Networking,Sales)*
Mr. Bobby Hanson, Resource Manager - *Computers, Design, E-business, Electrical, Engineering*
Ms. Amy Patnode, Resource Manager - *Executives, High technology, Middle management*

Salary Minimum: $50,000

Functions: Generalist (All), Senior Mgmt., Mfg., Sales & Mktg., IT, R&D, Engineering, Systems

Industries: Generalist (All), Communications, Aerospace, Software, Biotech/Life Sciences, Healthcare

Connexions Staffing LLC

PO Box 1234
Green Bay, WI 54305-1234
(920) 430-7305
Fax: (920) 430-3072
Email: rsolano@connexions-staffing.com
Web: www.connexions-staffing.com

Summary: We are a professional permanent placement agency serving clients and candidates throughout the United States. Our client focus includes middle market and emerging growth companies across diverse industries, specializing in accounting and financial services, information technology, manufacturing and sales.

Key Contact - Specialty:
Mr. Ralph Solano, Director, Business Development - *Accounting, Sales, Senior management, Technology*

Salary Minimum: $40,000

Functions: Generalist (All), Management, Senior Mgmt., Middle Mgmt., Sales & Mktg., Sales Mgmt., Sales Reps., Finance, IT, Minorities/Diversity

Industries: Generalist (All), Energy, Utilities, Construction, Manufacturing, Misc. Mfg., Finance, Services, Accounting, Communications, Aerospace, Packaging, Insurance, Software, Biotech/Life Sciences, Healthcare, Non-Classifiable

Connexus Group LLC

225 W 34th St Ste 1800
New York, NY 10122-1800
(212) 563-3382
(732) 671-9407
Fax: (732) 671-0656
Email: rbilotta@connexusgrp.com
Web: www.connexusgrp.com

Summary: Specializing in finance, treasury, risk management, marketing, business development and sales within financial, professional services, manufacturing and consumer products. All staff members are experienced professionals within their disciplines. We have extensive experience in executive search.

Key Contact - Specialty:
Mr. Robert Bilotta, Principal

Functions: Management, Board Members

Industries: Manufacturing, Finance, Banking, Invest. Banking, Brokers, Venture Cap., Mutual/Hedge Funds, Misc. Financial, Services, Pharm Svcs., Advertising

Construction Search Partners, LLC

1816 Robert Ln
Naperville, IL 60564-4129
(630) 922-6740
Fax: (630) 922-6739
Email: mike@csp-recruiters.com
Web: www.csp-recruiters.com

Summary: An executive search firm focused against the construction and homebuilding industries. The firm's Principal has previously worked for a national homebuilder, and we actively recruit for positions in all functional areas (Operations, Land, Legal, HR, Marketing, Sales, Accounting & Finance, etc).

Key Contact - Specialty:
Mr. Michael Hill - *Building products, Construction, Home and building controls, Human resources, Sales*

Salary Minimum: $60,000

Functions: Management

Industries: Generalist (All), Construction, Architectural Svcs., Legal, Accounting, HR Services, Engineering Svcs., Logistics Svcs., Supply Chain Mgmt, Real Estate

Construction Search Specialists Inc

115 5th Ave S Ste 407
La Crosse, WI 54601-4096
(608) 784-4711
Fax: (608) 784-4904
Email: css@csssearch.com
Web: www.csssearch.com

Summary: Executive search firm for the construction industry. Mid-management to executive level. Construction management, architecture, and related construction & engineering positions. Professional and confidential.

Key Contact - Specialty:
Mr. Duane McClain, President

Salary Minimum: $50,000

Functions: Generalist (All), Board Members, Senior Mgmt., Middle Mgmt., Engineering, Architects, Bldg. Contractors

Industries: Generalist (All), Construction, Transportation, Architectural Svcs., Real Estate

ConsulPro

650-4141 Rue Sherbrooke O
Westmount Life Building
Westmount, QC H3Z 1B8
Canada
(514) 932-9523
Email: dbrowne@cam.org

Summary: We provide searches in the fields of healthcare and IT.

Key Contact - Specialty:
Mr. David Browne

Salary Minimum: $50,000

Functions: Healthcare

Industries: Generalist (All), Healthcare

Consulting Resource Group Inc

1100 5th Ave S Ste 201
Naples, FL 34102-6407
(239) 285-5575
(888) 285-5575
Fax: (678) 623-5403
Email: mailbox@careersinconsulting.com
Web: www.careersinconsulting.com

Summary: Specialize in search assignments for boutique, specialty and 'niche' management consulting firms. Focus on a variety of management consulting competency areas, including strategy, process reengineering, performance improvement, technology consulting, and organizational change management.

Key Contact - Specialty:
Mr. P. Andrew Robinson, Managing Principal

Salary Minimum: $75,000

Functions: Senior Mgmt., Mgmt. Consultants

Industries: Manufacturing, Drugs Mfg., Medical Devices, Retail, Banking, Accounting, Mgmt. Consulting, HR Services, Logistics Svcs., Supply Chain Mgmt, Advertising, ERP SW, Mfg. SW, Biotech/Life Sciences, Healthcare

Consultis

4401 N Federal Hwy Ste 100
Boca Raton, FL 33431-5164
(561) 362-9104
(800) 275-2667
Fax: (561) 367-9802
Email: southflorida@consultis.com
Web: www.consultis.com

Summary: Our firm is an IT and F&A staff augmentation firm. We provide contract, contract to hire and direct placement services.

Key Contact - Specialty:
Ms. Barbara Fleming, President & Chief Executive Officer
Mr. Jeff A. Fleming, Vice President
Ms. Jamie Delsing, Managing Partner - *Information Technology*
Mr. Bob Hageman, Chief Financial Officer

Salary Minimum: $65,000

Functions: IT, MIS Mgmt., Systems Analysis, Systems Dev., Systems Implem., Systems Support, Network Admin., DB Admin.

Industries: Generalist (All)

Consumer Connection Inc

1200 Whitman Ct NE
Renton, WA 98059-4084
(425) 455-2770
Fax: (425) 454-1702
Email: recruiter@ccinc.org
Web: www.ccinc.org

Summary: One-stop shopping for the world of consumer products. Specializing in sales, sales management, marketing-brand and product management, finance and operations.

Key Contact - Specialty:
Mr. Gary Chatwin, President, Group I
Mr. Howard P. Robboy, President, Group II - *Sales*
Ms. Susan Eastern, Vice President - *Sales*
Ms. Adrien L. Agoado, Vice President, Marketing Specialist - *Marketing*
Mr. Todd King, Senior Account Executive - *Sales*
Mr. Peter Koeck, Senior Account Executive - *Marketing*
Ms. Tiffany A. Pruett, Senior Account Executive - *Marketing*
Mr. Justin Armintrout, Senior Account Executive - *Sales*
Mr. Michael McGowan, Account Executive
Ms. Megan Leverson, Account Executive
Mr. Aaron Blower, Account Executive - *Manufacturing, Operations*
Mr. Jerry Goldberg, Account Executive - *Finance*
Mr. Jeff Heiberg, Researcher
Mr. Steve Bruce, Researcher - *Accounting*

Salary Minimum: $50,000

Functions: Mfg., Sales & Mktg., HR Mgmt.

Industries: Manufacturing, Food, Bev., Tobacco, Textiles, Apparel, Paper, Soap, Perf., Cosmtcs., Drugs Mfg., Machine, Appliance, Consumer Elect., Mfg. SW

Consumer Search Inc

300 W Main St
Northborough, MA 01532-2132
(508) 393-8506
Fax: (508) 393-7458
Email: conniemcsi@aol.com

Summary: Health & beauty care, over-the-counter pharmaceuticals and sales & marketing executives.

Key Contact - Specialty:
Ms. Connie Musso, President

Salary Minimum: $75,000

Functions: Board Members, Mktg. Research, Mktg. Mgmt., Sales Mgmt.

Industries: Generalist (All)

Contemporary Personnel Staffing

105 Kreischer Rd
North Syracuse, NY 13212-3256
(315) 458-2100
(866) 757-2525
Fax: (315) 458-5899
Email: msherman@cpsprofessionals.com
Web: www.cpsprofessionals.com

Summary: We have experience in recruitment and placement of professionals in: accounting, financial management, computer systems, programming and operations, IS management, computer hardware/software sales and banking.

Key Contact - Specialty:
Ms. Karen A. Salcido, Recruiter
Ms. Meg Sherman, Manager, Sales
Ms. Ellen Mable, CTS, Senior Staffing Supervisor
Mr. Matt Biswanger, Staffing Coordinator

Mr. Mark Ruzekowicz, CTS, Staffing Supervisor
Ms. Michele Carey, Staffing Coordinator - *Banking (Mortgage)*

Salary Minimum: $20,000

Functions: Generalist (All)

Industries: Finance, Services, Accounting, Software

Contemporary Services Inc

1701 E Woodfield Rd Ste 1030
Schaumburg, IL 60173-5141
(847) 619-4000
(800) 474-9200
Fax: (847) 619-1077
Email: resumes@mortgagestaff.com
Web: www.mortgagestaff.com

Summary: We are a staffing service providing temp, contract, temp to hire and direct hire placements in all areas of the mortgage industry. We work with all levels of positions from entry level to executive-level.

Key Contact - Specialty:
Ms. Sandra Hansen, Founder
Mr. James Hansen, Regional Operations Manager - *Product management/development*
Ms. Robyn Lemmer, National Production Manager
Ms. Rose Rizzi, Branch Manager - *Banking (Mortgage)*
Ms. Sandy Wettergren, CPC, Area Manager - *Banking (Mortgage)*

Functions: Management

Industries: Banking

Continental Design & Engineering

2710 Enterprise Dr
Anderson, IN 46013-9670
(765) 778-9999
(800) 875-4557
Fax: (765) 778-8590
Email: cdcin@continental-design.com
Web: www.continental-design.com

Summary: We are dedicated to providing technical resources to manufacturing firms that enhance and expand their own design and engineering capabilities. Contract and/or permanent employment searches.

Key Contact - Specialty:
Mr. Tom Epply, President
Ms. Judy Nagengast, Chief Executive Officer - *Manufacturing*
Mr. Bill Nagengast, Chief Operating Officer - *Automotive*
Ms. Cathy Mellinger, Director, Recruitment
Ms. Patty Wikle, Senior Executive Recruiter
Mr. Jim Ballentine, Manager, Design Center

Functions: Mfg.

Industries: Motor Vehicles, Mgmt. Consulting

Continental Search & Outplacement Inc

PO Box 43873
Baltimore, MD 21236-0873
(410) 529-7000
(888) 276-6789
Email: dan@consearch.com
Web: www.consearch.com

Summary: We provide direct hire and contract staffing solutions. We recruit sales, technical and management professionals in a variety of industries including the animal sciences, information technology and manufacturing across the nation. We are an award winning and top

producing recruiting firm in America's most successful recruiting network.

Key Contact - Specialty:
Mr. Daniel C. Simmons, CPC, President - *Agriculture, Dairy, Information Technology, Management, Sales*

Salary Minimum: $40,000

Functions: Middle Mgmt., Sales & Mktg.

Industries: Agri., Forestry, Mining, Inst./Industrial Food Svc., Software, Development SW

Continental Search Associates

PO Box 14
Pickerington, OH 43147-0014
(614) 837-1300
Fax: (614) 837-4860
Email: jimallen@continentaljobs.com
Web: www.continentaljobs.com

Summary: Strong ethics are the guiding principle of our firm. Complete trust is of the utmost importance in relationships between recruiter and client and between recruiter and candidate.

Key Contact - Specialty:
Mr. James R. Allen, President - *Healthcare, Manufacturing, Manufacturing (Management), Medical, Medical (Devices)*

Salary Minimum: $70,000

Functions: Generalist (All), Management, Mfg., Product Dev., Plant Mgmt., Quality, Sales & Mktg., Sales Mgmt., Engineering

Industries: Generalist (All), Manufacturing, Medical Devices, Metal Products, Robotics, Consumer Goods, Legal, Healthcare

Continental Search Associates Inc

PO Box 413
Birmingham, MI 48012-0413
(248) 458-1983
Fax: (248) 644-0461
Email: csaresume@aol.com

Summary: We are a premier search firm specializing exclusively in real estate development.

Key Contact - Specialty:
Mr. William L. Dewey, President
Mr. William R. Dewey, Executive Vice President - *Construction, Engineering*

Salary Minimum: $60,000

Functions: Senior Mgmt.

Industries: Real Estate

Kim Finch Cook Executive Recruiter Inc

9805 NE 116th St Ste 7404
Kirkland, WA 98034-4245
(425) 882-3000
Fax: (425) 882-3000
Email: kim@kfcook..com
Web: www.kfcook.com

Summary: When looking for specific experience in your industry, a candidate with a great track record and outstanding in their field, we can assist you in that process. We match your company with the right candidate. Areas of success have been candidates with a finance & accounting, HR, and sales & marketing background.

Key Contact - Specialty:
Ms. Kim Finch Cook, Principal - *Finance*
Ms. Andrea Graham, Recruiter

Salary Minimum: $50,000

Functions: Generalist (All), Management, Board Members, Middle Mgmt., Mktg. Mgmt., HR Mgmt., CFOs, MIS Mgmt., R&D, Engineering

Industries: Generalist (All), Finance, Venture Cap., Accounting, E-commerce, IT Implementation, Communications, Telecoms, Digital, Wireless, Fiber Optic, Network Infrastructure, Software, Accounting SW, Biotech/Life Sciences

Cook Partners International

1726 Winton Rd N
Rochester, NY 14609-3359
(585) 749-3437
Fax: (585) 288-7937
Email: cpi-jobs@cookpartnersintl.com
Web: www.cookpartnersintl.com

Summary: We focus on searches for positions from professional level to senior executive, CEO & board level management. We specialize in professional & executive searches, management consulting, career advisement and assessment & evaluation. Technical areas of focus: photonics, microelectronics, semiconductor, defense/aerospace and biotechnology (medical devices & equipment).

Key Contact - Specialty:
Mr. Douglas Cook, Chief Executive Officer & President - *Executives, Photonics, Semiconductors, Staffing, Telecommunications*
Mr. Cory Mau, MBA, Vice President, Finance - *Finance*
Mr. Michael Rudd, MBA, Vice President, Sales & Marketing - *Marketing, Sales*

Salary Minimum: $80,000

Functions: Management, Board Members, Senior Mgmt.

Industries: Chemicals, Medical Devices, Computer Equip., Electronic, Elec. Components, Robotics, Semiconductors, Venture Cap., Communications, RF/Microwave, Government, Aerospace, Packaging, Biotech/Life Sciences, Healthcare

Cooper Management Associates Inc

8460 Grand Messina Cir
Boynton Beach, FL 33437-7104
(561) 740-3011
Fax: (561) 740-7538
Email: mcpr@aol.com

Summary: Our firm has executive recruitment experience for the retail industry. Serving clients in department stores, mass merchandisers, hard & soft goods specialty chains, catalog, home centers and eCommerce.

Key Contact - Specialty:
Mr. Michael Cooper, President - *Retail*

Salary Minimum: $100,000

Functions: Generalist (All), Management

Industries: Retail

Copier Careers

PO Box 300140
Minneapolis, MN 55403-5140
(888) 733-4868
(612) 332-4888
Fax: (800) 464-3434
Email: mail@copiercareers.com
Web: www.copiercareers.com

Summary: Exclusive recruiters to the document imaging industry.

Key Contact - Specialty:
Mr. Robert Anderson, Vice President, Recruiting
- *Copiers*

Salary Minimum: $35,000

Functions: Generalist (All), Sales & Mktg.,
Technicians

Industries: Non-Classifiable

Corbin Packaging Professionals

7536 Monterey Bay Dr Unit 3
Mentor on the Lake, OH 44060-9004
(440) 257-5601
Email: corpak@sbcglobal.net

Summary: Specializing in all functions for the
food processing industries.

Key Contact - Specialty:
Mr. Earl Corbin

Salary Minimum: $45,000

Functions: Generalist (All), Middle Mgmt.,
Quality, Packaging, Engineering

Industries: Food, Bev., Tobacco, Engineering
Svcs., Packaging, Biotech/Life Sciences

Core Staffing Inc

59 Maiden Ln Fl 23
New York, NY 10038-4649
(212) 766-1222
Fax: (212) 766-9024
Email: aconnors@employcore.com
Web:
www.employcore.com/employees/fin_jobs.html

Summary: We are a top financial executive
recruiting firm based in New York. Amongst our
client roster are top-tier investment banks, hedge
funds and financial institutions on Wall Street. We
are exclusively dedicated to placing professionals
in corporate finance, accounting, private
equity/hedge funds, treasury, credit, risk, tax,
sales, trading and operations.

Key Contact - Specialty:
Mr. Adam Connors, Director
Mr. Dennis Grady, Recruiter - *Accounting,
Analysts, Asset management, Banking,
Compliance*

Salary Minimum: $35,000

Functions: HR Mgmt., Finance, CFOs,
Budgeting, Cash Mgmt., Credit, Taxes, M&A,
Risk Mgmt., Minorities/Diversity

Industries: Generalist (All), Finance, Banking,
Invest. Banking, Brokers, Venture Cap.,
Mutual/Hedge Funds, Misc. Financial,
Accounting, HR Services, E-commerce,
Accounting SW

Joe Corey Associates LLC

(formerly known as Industry Consultants Inc)
11 Beacon Dr
North Kingstown, RI 02852-4601
(401) 667-2660
Email: info@joecoreyjobs.com
Web: www.joecoreyjobs.com

Summary: Engineering and quality control
recruiting within the disciplines of food science,
chemistry, quality systems/lean manufacturing,
chemical/industrial/mechanical and electrical
engineering. Primarily for food, beverage,
personal care and healthcare manufacturers. Also
cover fields of logistics, materials management
and quality engineering.

Key Contact - Specialty:
Mr. Joe Corey, General Manager

Salary Minimum: $65,000

Functions: Generalist (All), Quality, Distribution,
Engineering, Minorities/Diversity

Industries: Generalist (All), Food, Bev., Tobacco,
Soap, Perf., Cosmtcs., Drugs Mfg., Metal
Products

Cornell Associates

68 N Plank Rd
Newburgh, NY 12550-2109
(845) 565-8860
Fax: (845) 565-0084
Email: resumes@cornellassociates.com
Web: www.cornellassociates.com

Summary: We are an executive search firm with
exceptional record of success in technical search,
manufacturing, chemical, pharmaceutical, finance,
manufacturing and more. Training and HR
consulting division also offers wide range of
services.

Key Contact - Specialty:
Ms. Janet Giannetta, SPHR, Director, Human
Resources
Ms. Denise Monnat, Recruiter

Salary Minimum: $45,000

Functions: Generalist (All), Middle Mgmt., Mfg.,
Materials, Sales & Mktg., Finance, Engineering

Industries: Generalist (All), Food, Bev., Tobacco,
Chemicals, Soap, Perf., Cosmtcs., Drugs Mfg.,
Medical Devices, Plastics, Rubber, Metal
Products, Machine, Appliance, Electronic, Elec.
Components, Transportation, Services,
Hospitality, Media, Communications, Real
Estate, Biotech/Life Sciences

Branches:
2 Canterbury Ct
Danbury, CT 06811-4246
(888) 565-0088
Fax: (845) 565-0084
Email: resumes@cornellassociates.com
Key Contact - Specialty:
Mr. Ryan Cornell, Vice President

2300 Lakeview Pkwy Ste 700
Alpharetta, GA 30004-7966
(888) 565-0088
Fax: (845) 565-0084
Email: resumes@cornellassociates.com
Key Contact - Specialty:
Ms. Donna Cornell, President

Cornerstone Search Associates Inc

45 Warner Way
Canton, MA 02021-1867
(781) 821-2787
Email: rich@cornerstonesearch.com
Web: www.cornerstonesearch.com

Summary: We are a full service placement firm
specializing in software sales and business
development positions. Our typical placements are
for senior sales rep and VP of sales to CEO and
board members. Clients are generally software
companies that are pre-IPO with live products,
solid financing and management.

Key Contact - Specialty:
Mr. Richard Rosen, President - *Finance, Sales*

Salary Minimum: $75,000

Functions: Generalist (All), Sales & Mktg.

Industries: HR Services, E-commerce, Software,
Accounting SW, Doc. Mgmt., Production SW,
ERP SW, HR SW, Industry Specific SW, Mfg.
SW, Marketing SW, Security SW

Cornerstone Search Group LLC

9 Sylvan Way
Parsippany, NJ 07054-3816
(973) 656-0220
Fax: (973) 656-0228
Email: cmiras@cornerstonesg.com
Web: www.cornerstonesg.com

Summary: We help our clients hire experienced
pharmaceutical professionals from the staff
through management (director/VP) levels for full
time and contract positions. We provide our
professional recruiting services on a contingency,
or on a performance based retained search basis to
best suit the hiring needs of our clients.

Key Contact - Specialty:
Mr. Cliff Miras, Managing Partner - *Biomedical,
Biopharmaceutical, Biotechnology, Medical
(Devices), Pharmaceutical*
Mr. Corey Ackerman, Esq., Senior Parnter -
*Biomedical, Biopharmaceutical, Biotechnology,
Medical (Devices), Pharmaceutical*
Mr. Steve Raz, Managing Partner - *Biomedical,
Biopharmaceutical, Biotechnology,
Pharmaceutical, Physicians*

Salary Minimum: $75,000

Functions: Generalist (All), Management, Senior
Mgmt., Middle Mgmt., Product Dev.,
Physicians, Nurses, Mktg. Research, R&D

Industries: Drugs Mfg., Pharm Svcs.,
Biotech/Life Sciences

Corporate Careers Inc

7755 Center Ave Fl 11
Huntington Beach, CA 92647-3007
(714) 372-2220
Fax: (714) 372-2245
Email: ccinfo@corporatecareers.com
Web: www.corporatecareers.com

Summary: We offer mid to senior-level sales and
executive placement within the staffing and
recruiting industry including branch, regional
managers and area VPs.

Key Contact - Specialty:
Ms. Dolores Cronin, President

Salary Minimum: $40,000

Functions: Senior Mgmt., Sales & Mktg., Sales
Mgmt., Staffing, IT

Industries: HR Services

The Corporate Connection Ltd

PO Box 5804
Glen Allen, VA 23058-5804
(804) 562-8457
Email: tcc44@comcast.net

Summary: Full-service recruiting firm with
combined experience in contingency and retained
search placements.

Key Contact - Specialty:
Mr. Marshall W. Rotella, President - *Engineering,
Financial*

Salary Minimum: $25,000

Functions: Generalist (All)

Industries: Generalist (All)

Corporate Consultants

1910-155 University Ave
Toronto, ON M5H 3B7
Canada
(416) 862-1259
Email: info@corporateconsultants.com
Web: www.corporateconsultants.com

Summary: We are a search practice. We place
from executive to specialist, operating in:

accounting & finance exclusively. Our firm is efficient, professional, proven since it's founding.

Key Contact - Specialty:
Mr. Fred Goldi, President
Mr. Gordon Brown, Vice President

Salary Minimum: $75,000

Functions: Finance

Industries: Generalist (All)

Corporate Consulting Associates Inc

33 Bloomfield Hills Pkwy Ste 225
Bloomfield Hills, MI 48304-2946
(248) 955-0000
Fax: (248) 955-0001
Email: response@corpconsulting.com
Web: www.corpconsulting.com

Summary: Executive and senior management level search services specializing in the areas of: IT, healthcare, engineering, accounting/finance, purchasing/supply chain management, sales/marketing and HR. Industries we service include: manufacturing, high technology, service, banking, healthcare, automotive, non-profit, entertainment, real estate, advertising, consumer products, insurance and consulting.

Key Contact - Specialty:
Mr. John Bukowicz, MBA, MSCS, Founder, President & CEO - *Accounting, Accounting (Big 4), Actuarial, Boards of Directors, C-level*
Mr. Ruediger Mueller, PhD, Managing Director - *C-level, Consulting, Consumer, Human resources, Manufacturing*
Mrs. Colleen Geyer, Director, Operations - *Accounting, Audits, Banking, Healthcare, Human resources*
Mr. Matthew Pidek, Director, Engineering Practice - *Distribution, Embedded microprocessor, Engineering, High technology, Manufacturing*
Mr. Anthony Joseph, CPA, MST, Director, Recruitment - *CFOs, Change management, Controllers, Trust, Underwriting*
Ms. Linda Gadde, Director, Healthcare Recruitment Pract - *C-level, Healthcare, Hospital, Human resources, Staffing*
Ms. Julie Ward, Senior Consultant - *Actuarial, C-level, Consulting, Diversity, Healthcare*
Ms. Mandie Panski, Consultant - *Administration, Banking, Marketing, Sales, Senior management*
Ms. Sarah Toney, Research Analyst - *Research*

Salary Minimum: $50,000

Functions: Management, Mfg., Materials, Healthcare, Sales & Mktg., HR Mgmt., Finance, IT, Engineering, Minorities/Diversity

Industries: Generalist (All), Manufacturing, Plastics, Rubber, Paints, Petro. Products, Motor Vehicles, Electronic, Elec. Components, Robotics, Semiconductors, Finance, IT Implementation, Communications, Telephony, Digital, Wireless, Fiber Optic, Network Infrastructure, RF/Microwave, Packaging, Software, ERP SW, HR SW, Security SW, Hospitals

Branches:
4065 Riverglen Cir Ste 100
Suwanee, GA 30024-1858
(678) 931-0117 x810
Email: rmueller@corpconsulting.com

Key Contact - Specialty:
Mr. Rudi Mueller, PhD, Managing Director - *Accounting, Automotive, Boards of Directors, Business development, C-level*

Corporate Consulting Group Inc

105 Braunlich Dr Ste 350B
Pittsburgh, PA 15237-3351
(412) 364-8300
(888) 735-8300
Fax: (412) 364-8539
Email: info@ccgroupinc.net
Web: www.ccgroupinc.net

Summary: We are an executive search firm, specializing exclusively in recruiting executive talent for the construction and real estate industries.

Key Contact - Specialty:
Mr. Charles Groom, President - *Construction, Electrical, Engineering, General contractors, Mechanical*
Mr. Carl Takacs, Vice President, Business Development
Mr. Jason Laratonda, Director, Information Systems
Mr. Dan Hattrup, Director
Mr. Rich Churchfield, Construction Consultant
Mrs. Sandra DalDosso, Executive Assistant
Ms. Maria Simonic, Construction Consultant
Mrs. Diane Coyne, Construction Consultant
Mr. John Martin, Construction Consultant
Ms. Kathy Walter, Consultant
Mr. Gene Trusky, Construction Consultant
Mrs. Kim Early, Consultant

Salary Minimum: $60,000

Functions: Generalist (All)

Industries: Construction, Real Estate

Corporate Dimensions Inc

999 9th St S Ste 200
Naples, FL 34102-8200
(239) 430-1900
Fax: (239) 430-0998
Email: info@corporatedimensionsinc.com
Web: www.corporatedimensionsinc.com

Summary: Our staff of executive recruiters places professionals in sales, marketing, accounting, administrative and executive positions. Its client companies come from the banking, finance, real estate, hospitality, manufacturing, retail, engineering, telecom and IT industries.

Key Contact - Specialty:
Ms. C.J. Hueston, President & Chief Executive Officer

Functions: Management, Sales & Mktg., Finance, IT, Engineering

Industries: Manufacturing, Retail, Finance, Hospitality, Telecoms, Real Estate

Corporate DNA

7700 Irvine Center Dr Ste 800
Irvine, CA 92618-3047
(949) 851-1500
Fax: (949) 851-0001
Email: mf@corp-dna.com
Web: www.corp-dna.com

Summary: Our company offers high caliber finance, accounting and human resources consultants. Whether for short-term projects such as audits, Sarbanes-Oxley work, financial analysis and human resources staffing or long-term assignments to fill in for employees on extended leaves, we can fill your needs. Consultants work under the guidance of company management to ensure a work product that meets your requirements.

Key Contact - Specialty:
Mr. Martin Foxman, President - *Compensation, Compliance, Controllers, Finance, Human resources*
Mr. Josh Miller, Vice President, Business Development - *Accounting, Accounting (Big 4), Controllers, Finance*

Functions: Management

Industries: Finance, Accounting, HR Services

Corporate Dynamix

6619 N Scottsdale Rd
Scottsdale, AZ 85250-4421
(480) 607-0040
(310) 662-4770
Fax: (480) 607-0054
Email: david@cdynamix.com
Web: www.cdynamix.com

Summary: We specialize in the placement of sales, sales management pre/post sales support and marketing personnel in the high-technology industry.

Key Contact - Specialty:
Mr. David Sterenfeld, Principal - *Sales, Technology*

Salary Minimum: $50,000

Functions: Management, Senior Mgmt., Middle Mgmt., Healthcare, Sales & Mktg., Sales Mgmt.

Industries: Software, Accounting SW, Database SW, Development SW, Doc. Mgmt., Production SW, ERP SW, HR SW, Mfg. SW, Marketing SW, Networking, Comm. SW, Security SW, System SW

Branches:
222 N Sepulveda Blvd Ste 2000
El Segundo, CA 90245-5616
(310) 662-4770
Fax: (310) 662-4771
Email: carolyn@cdynamix.com
Key Contact - Specialty:
Ms. Carolyn Stokes, Principal - *Sales*
Ms. Kim Kohn, Researcher

Corporate Growth Specialists

PO Box 2094
Redondo Beach, CA 90278-7694
(310) 921-2979
Email: doug.cgs@verizon.net

Summary: We operate throughout the USA, locating and qualifying candidates for staff through executive level positions in the fields of accounting & finance, procurement & supply chain management, marketing & product management, IT, and management & engineering positions in manufacturing, distribution, construction and energy.

Key Contact - Specialty:
Mr. Doug Boswell, Principal - *Accounting, Construction, Manufacturing, Marketing, Procurement*

Functions: Management, Mfg., Materials, Mktg. Research, Mktg. Mgmt., Finance, IT, R&D, Engineering, Specialized Svcs.

Industries: Generalist (All)

Corporate Image Group

2215 West St Fl 2
Germantown, TN 38138-3885
(901) 360-8091
(800) 823-5100
Fax: (901) 360-0813
Email: mathews@corpimg.com
Web: www.corpimg.com

Summary: Recognized for placement successes, we are a full-service search firm with clients in Fortune 1000, Big 6 and fast growth firms. Concentration is manufacturing and distribution sectors.

Key Contact - Specialty:
Mr. Joseph M. Knose, II, President - *Finance*
Mr. Barry C. Mathews, Vice President - *Engineering*

Functions: Generalist (All), Product Dev., Plant Mgmt., Purchasing, Staffing, Finance, IT

Industries: Generalist (All), Energy, Utilities, Food, Bev., Tobacco, Chemicals, Plastics, Rubber, Metal Products, Machine, Appliance, Consumer Elect.

Branches:
PO Box 5765
Pearl, MS 39288-5765
(601) 420-6869
Fax: (601) 420-6870
Email: judy@corpimg.com
Key Contact - Specialty:
Ms. Judy Presley-Caron, Principal

279 N Zinns Mill Rd Ste F
Lebanon, PA 17042-9576
(717) 274-5733
Email: tdabich@corpimg.com
Key Contact - Specialty:
Mr. Tom Dabich, CPC, Vice President - *Finance, Information Technology*

Corporate Information Systems Inc

71 Union Ave Ste 103
Rutherford, NJ 07070-1274
(201) 896-0600
Fax: (201) 896-8009
Email: ksorge@cisrecruiters.com
Web: www.cisrecruiters.com

Summary: We specialize in the recruitment of software sales people, sales managers, and sales support.

Key Contact - Specialty:
Mr. Carmine Marinaro, President & Chief Executive Officer
Mrs. Kathy Piekarz, Manager, Human Resources

Salary Minimum: $50,000

Functions: Sales Mgmt., Sales Reps.

Industries: Software

Corporate Leads Inc

2009 Mara Park Pl
Williamsburg, VA 23185-2110
(757) 220-8215
Email: careers@corporateleads.com
Web: www.corporateleads.com

Summary: We provide professional search and placement of junior military officers and degreed staff non-commissioned officers in management, engineering, distribution, sales, IT and consulting careers.

Key Contact - Specialty:
Mr. Luis Long, President

Functions: Generalist (All), Middle Mgmt., Plant Mgmt., Distribution, Sales Mgmt., IT, Engineering

Industries: Generalist (All), Telecoms

Branches:
4552 Carriage Crossing Dr
Jacksonville, FL 32258-1372

14506 Bladenboro Dr
Cypress, TX 77429-3441
(281) 256-3313
Email: careernet@corporateleads.com
Key Contact - Specialty:
Mr. Rod Long, Recruiter

Corporate Management Advisors Inc

785 Douglas Ave
Altamonte Springs, FL 32714-2566
(407) 869-1817
Fax: (407) 869-0749
Email: lrudnicki@cmainc.com
Web: www.cmainc.com

Summary: Executive search and consulting for the financial services industry.

Key Contact - Specialty:
Mr. Brad Hollingsworth, Chairman & Chief Executive Officer - *Finance, Real estate, Senior management*
Mr. Gordon Christian, President - *Finance, Real estate, Senior management*
Mr. Thom Hollingsworth, Managing Director - *Senior management*
Mr. Michael Prosser, Executive Vice President
Mr. Bob Skalstad, Executive Vice President
Ms. Gwen Straka, Executive Vice President
Ms. Lakisha Rudnicki, Administrative Assistant

Functions: Senior Mgmt., Sales & Mktg., Sales Mgmt., Finance, CFOs, Cash Mgmt., Risk Mgmt.

Industries: Construction, Wholesale, Retail, Finance, Banking, Invest. Banking, Brokers, Venture Cap., Mutual/Hedge Funds, Real Estate

Corporate Management Solutions Inc

PO Box 288
Auburn, IN 46706-0288
(260) 436-3355
Email: cmsi@cmsrecruiting.com
Web: www.cmsrecruiting.com

Summary: Our firm is a direct hire, company fee paid, recruiting firm of technical and professional talent. The disciplines we have worked are accounting, engineering, I/S, manufacturing, HR and sales & marketing. Our specialty areas include sensors, electronics, automotive, rubber, plastics, metal fabrication, engineering, manufacturing and operations management.

Key Contact - Specialty:
Mr. Thomas R. Havey, CPC, President - *Automotive, Engineering, Human resources, Manufacturing, Production*
Mr. Roger B. Miller, CPC, Past President - *Accounting, Electronics, Engineering, Human resources, Manufacturing*

Salary Minimum: $50,000

Functions: Management, Mfg., Quality, HR Mgmt., Finance, R&D, Engineering

Industries: Generalist (All), Manufacturing, Food, Bev., Tobacco, Paper, Chemicals, Plastics, Rubber, Metal Products, Machine, Appliance, Motor Vehicles, Computer Equip., Consumer Elect., Electronic, Elec. Components, Accounting, HR Services, Software

Corporate Plus Ltd

3145 Tucker Norcross Rd Ste 206
Tucker, GA 30084-2125
(770) 934-5101
Fax: (770) 934-5127
Email: info@corporateplusltd.com
Web: www.corporateplusltd.com

Summary: Executive search and management consulting firm that specializes in the area of diversity talent acquisition. We specialize in sales, marketing, finance, accounting, HR, MIS and engineering.

Key Contact - Specialty:
Mr. Walter McGlawn, Principal - *Engineering, Human resources, MIS, Sales*
Mr. Shawn Menefee, Principal - *Finance, Manufacturing, Sales*

Salary Minimum: $45,000

Functions: Generalist (All), Management, Production, Distribution, Sales Mgmt., HR Mgmt., Systems Dev., Minorities/Diversity

Industries: Generalist (All), Food, Bev., Tobacco, Transportation, HR Services, Hospitality, Telecoms, Insurance

Corporate Recruiters Ltd

490-1140 Pender St W
Vancouver, BC V6E 4G1
Canada
(604) 713-0900
(877) 687-5993
Fax: (604) 687-2427
Email: careers@corporate.bc.ca
Web: www.corporate.bc.ca

Summary: Specialized recruitment services focused specifically on the needs of the technology industries, including board members, executive management, technical professionals, sales & marketing professionals and contract consultants. Areas of expertise: information and communications technology, wireless, biotechnology, and alternative energy.

Key Contact - Specialty:
Mr. Don Safnuk, President & Chief Executive Officer
Mr. Bruce Edmond, Recruiter, Sales & Marketing
Ms. Kimberllay Brooks, Manager, Electronics/Sftwr. Engineering - *Engineering*

Salary Minimum: $40,000

Functions: Generalist (All), Product Dev., Sales Mgmt., MIS Mgmt., Systems Analysis, Systems Dev.

Industries: Generalist (All), Computer Equip., Digital, Wireless, Fiber Optic, Network Infrastructure, Software, Biotech/Life Sciences

Corporate Resources Inc

10016 Taylor Drive
Overland Park, KS 66212-5422
(913) 599-5445
(800) 953-5445
Fax: (913) 599-5455
Email: cri@staffing.net

Summary: A Executive & Technical Search & Consulting Firm serving Industry & nationally recognized for accomplishment in the Electric Rotating Machines & the related Electronics for the Power & Control sectors.

Key Contact - Specialty:
Mr. Thomas B. Windsor, Managing Partner - *Electrical motor, Electronics, Embedded microprocessor, Hardware, Power*
Ms. Molly Cunningham

Salary Minimum: $50,000

Functions: Generalist (All)

Industries: Manufacturing, Misc. Mfg., Electronic, Elec. Components, Engineering Svcs., Aerospace, Software, Development SW, Non-Classifiable

Corporate Resources LLC

10999 Reed Hartman Hwy Ste 333
Cincinnati, OH 45242-8300
(513) 985-9200 x203
Fax: (513) 793-5981
Email: ccordell@eos.net
Web: www.corpresources.com

Summary: Each of our partners/consultants has extensive experience in recruitment of technical personnel. We were ranked the Top Producing Recruiting Firm by Top Echelon network of recruiters in 2003. We are engaged by clients to fill positions or find candidates in the specialty areas of IT, engineering, healthcare, accounting, finance and HR. We effectively handle search, contingency and contracting services.

Key Contact - Specialty:
Ms. Cindy Andrew Cordell, Partner & Consultant
- *Finance, Human resources*

Salary Minimum: $50,000

Functions: Generalist (All), Materials, Staffing, Finance, IT, Engineering

Industries: Generalist (All), Motor Vehicles, Consumer Goods, HR Services, Accounting SW, ERP SW, Healthcare, Long-term/Home Care

Corporate Resources, Stevens Inc

110 N Potomac St
Hagerstown, MD 21740-4810
(301) 797-3434
Fax: (301) 797-3331
Email: jgocha1@aol.com

Summary: Strong in the HVAC arena.

Key Contact - Specialty:
Ms. Jane Stevens, President & Owner - *HVAC, Manufacturing, Sales*

Functions: Generalist (All), Mfg., Healthcare, Sales & Mktg., Engineering

Industries: Generalist (All), Construction, Telecoms

Corporate Search America Inc

365 Wekiva Springs Rd Ste 201
Longwood, FL 32779-3690
(407) 678-3991
Fax: (866) 391-9846
Email: resume@csasearch.com
Web: www.csasearch.com

Summary: Strictly mortgage banking industry recruitment. Our firm can shortcut your effort in finding the most qualified candidate for your company. We recruited in 96 markets last year. We recruit the nation's best, the candidates that aren't found by running an ad or using Internet search engines.

Key Contact - Specialty:
Mr. James G. Boghos, President & Chief Executive Officer
Mr. Jeff Jackson, Executive Vice President - *Financial services*
Mr. Mike Bowdoin, Vice President, Recruiting
Mr. Terry Penn, Vice President, Recruiting
Mr. Scott Dorsett, Vice President, Recruiting
Mr. Randy Winter, Vice President, Recruiting
Mr. Tom Ratcliff, Vice President, Recruiting
Mr. Britt Nichols, Vice President, Recruiting
Mr. Rick Smith, Vice President, Recruiting
Mr. Mike Kyle, Vice President, Recruiting

Salary Minimum: $50,000

Functions: Senior Mgmt.

Industries: Banking, Venture Cap., Misc. Financial, Call Centers

Corporate Search Associates

4105 Rio Bravo St Ste 110
El Paso, TX 79902-1011
(915) 534-2583
Fax: (915) 534-2585
Email: csa01@csajobs.com
Web: www.csajobs.com

Summary: We are specialists in medical device sales & engineers, healthcare and automotive manufacturing. We offer specialists in Latin America, Spanish speaking and manufacturing professionals including plant managers and controllers.

Key Contact - Specialty:
Mr. Thomas Furnival, CPC, CTS, Owner - *Engineering, Sales*
Mr. Jack Bunn, CPC, Senior Executive Recruiter
Ms. Rose Portillo, Account Executive - *Accounting, Accounting (General), CFOs, Medical (Devices), Molding (Injection)*

Salary Minimum: $48,000

Functions: Generalist (All)

Industries: Medical Devices, Plastics, Rubber, Motor Vehicles, Consumer Elect., Consumer Goods, Logistics Svcs., Healthcare, Hospitals, Long-term/Home Care, Occupational Therapy

Corporate Search Consultants

19 S 6th St Ste 200
Terre Haute, IN 47807-3531
(812) 235-2992
Email: jobs@csccareers.com
Web: www.csccareers.com

Summary: We are connecting talented people with Fortune 500 and emerging growth companies. We are one of the nation's leading search firms in food, beverage and dairy manufacturing and distribution. We place people in plant management, production, materials, logistics, engineering, maintenance, HR, QA/QC, sanitation, and executive positions.

Key Contact - Specialty:
Mr. Scott Myers, President - *Bakery, Dairy, Food, Food & beverage*

Salary Minimum: $50,000

Functions: Board Members, Senior Mgmt., Middle Mgmt., Mfg., Plant Mgmt., Materials, Distribution, HR Mgmt., Engineering, Minorities/Diversity

Industries: Food, Bev., Tobacco, Chemicals, Soap, Perf., Cosmtcs., Drugs Mfg.

Corporate Search Consultants Inc

509 W Colonial Dr
Orlando, FL 32804-6803
(800) 800-7231
(407) 578-3888
Fax: (407) 578-5153
Email: mail@corpsearch.com
Web: www.corpsearch.com

Summary: Our firm specializes in healthcare, information technology, finance and insurance.

Key Contact - Specialty:
Mr. Anthony Ciaramitaro, President - *Healthcare*
Mr. Paul Ciaramitaro, Managing Partner - *Information Technology*

Salary Minimum: $60,000

Functions: Healthcare, Allied Health

Industries: Generalist (All)

Corporate Search Group

(formerly known as Ron Pines)
25 Rockcastle Dr
Toronto, ON M9R 2V2
Canada
(416) 235-2554
Fax: (416) 614-3806
Email: csgpines@idirect.ca
Web: www.corporatesearchgroup.org

Summary: We are dedicated in assisting our clients in finding their greatest asset - people. We provide a comprehensive service to corporations who are undertaking initiatives in improvement and organizational change.

Key Contact - Specialty:
Mr. Ron Pines, President

Salary Minimum: $35,000

Functions: Generalist (All), Sales & Mktg.

Industries: Generalist (All), Manufacturing, Food, Bev., Tobacco, Textiles, Apparel, Paper, Chemicals, Drugs Mfg., Plastics, Rubber, Consumer Elect., Consumer Goods, Wholesale, Retail, Inst./Industrial Food Svc., Packaging, Doc. Mgmt., Production SW, Marketing SW

Corporate Search Inc

200 Willow Ln Apt C201
Willow Springs, IL 60480-1547
(800) 408-6423
Fax: (800) 735-6394
Email: mark@corporatesearchinc.com
Web: corporatesearchinc.com

Summary: We specialize in executive staffing of sales and finance positions in all industries. We place operations positions in the metals industries.

Key Contact - Specialty:
Mr. Mark Dyer, General Manager

Salary Minimum: $40,000

Functions: Management, Plant Mgmt., Quality, Materials, Sales Mgmt., Finance

Industries: Manufacturing, Metal Products, Electronic, Elec. Components, Banking, Misc. Financial, Services, Accounting, Equip Svcs.

Corporate Search Inc

6800 Jericho Tpke Ste 111E
Syosset, NY 11791-4401
(516) 496-3200
Fax: (516) 496-3165
Email: jobs@corporatesearch.com
Web: www.corporatesearch.com

Summary: Permanent placement/direct hire firm involved in the search and recruitment of accounting & finance, human resources, office administration, attorneys, paralegals and legal secretaries, sales & marketing, customer service, purchasing, operations and Wall Street traders & brokers. Industries serviced include: manufacturing, distribution, service, real estate, legal, financial services, and insurance.

Key Contact - Specialty:
Ms. Claire Zukerman, CPC, President - *Accounting, Accounting (Big 4), Administration, Finance, Human resources*
Ms. Diane Gerard, Vice President, Administrative Services - *Accounting (Bookkeeping), Administration, Human resources, Marketing, Office (Administration)*
Ms. Corinne Camacho, Vice President, Marketing - *Accounting (Bookkeeping), Administration, Human resources, Legal, Marketing*
Mr. Lewis Leonardi, Vice President, Recruitment

Salary Minimum: $35,000

Functions: Generalist (All), Admin. Svcs., Materials, Sales & Mktg., Sales Mgmt., HR Mgmt., Finance, Credit, Non-profits, Paralegals

Industries: Generalist (All), Construction, Manufacturing, Transportation, Wholesale, Retail, Finance, Banking, Invest. Banking, Brokers, Venture Cap., Mutual/Hedge Funds, Misc. Financial, Services, Legal, Accounting, HR Services, Real Estate, Healthcare

Branches:
100 Park Ave Fl 16
New York, NY 10017-5538
(212) 351-5006
Fax: (212) 351-5055
Email: lorid@corporatesearch.com
Key Contact - Specialty:
Ms. Lori Davis, MD, Financial Services - *Banking, Banking (Investment,Mortgage), Brokerage, Capital markets*
Mr. Michael Fishkin, MD, Accounting & Finance - *Accounting, Accounting (Big 4), CFOs, Controllers, Finance*

Corporate Search of California

(also known as Scott Storch & Associates)
15720 Ventura Blvd Ste 104
Encino, CA 91436-2960
(818) 788-8853
Email: scottstorch@hotmail.com

Summary: Placement and recruiting of medical and pharmaceutical sales representatives and sales managers.

Key Contact - Specialty:
Mr. Scott Storch, President

Salary Minimum: $30,000

Functions: Sales Mgmt., Sales Reps.

Industries: Drugs Mfg., Medical Devices, Pharm Svcs., Biotech/Life Sciences, Healthcare, Hospitals, Long-term/Home Care, Dental, Physical Therapy, Occupational Therapy

Corporate Search Partners

5910 N Central Expy Ste 1625
Dallas, TX 75206-5148
(214) 361-0082
Fax: (214) 361-5587
Web: www.cspjobs.com

Summary: We are a retained and contingent executive search firm specializing in finance, accounting, tax, treasury, investment banking, venture capital, money management and banking professionals.

Key Contact - Specialty:
Mr. Paxson Glenn, Jr., Principal - *Financial services, Investment management*
Mr. Mark Falvo, Principal - *Finance, Technology*
Mr. Brian Finch, Principal - *Finance, Technology*

Salary Minimum: $80,000

Functions: Generalist (All), CFOs, Budgeting, Cash Mgmt., Taxes, M&A

Industries: Generalist (All), Banking, Invest. Banking, Venture Cap.

Corporate Search Technologies LLC

95 Summit Ave
Summit, NJ 07901-3633
(908) 522-0069
Email: info@cstllc.com
Web: www.cstllc.com

Summary: We are an executive search firm that specializes in diversity and interim placement.

Key Contact - Specialty:
Mr. Wayne A. Newell, Founder & President

Mr. Dan Honig, Vice President & Managing Director
Mr. Steve Jeffries, Managing Director - *Minorities, Research & development*
Ms. Ann Dilailo, Managing Director - *Human resources*
Mr. Gordon S. Metsky, Managing Director
Mrs. Debbie Miccolis, Director, Recruiting

Salary Minimum: $60,000

Functions: Generalist (All), Packaging, Mktg. Research, Mktg. Mgmt., M&A, Network Admin., R&D, Minorities/Diversity

Industries: Generalist (All), Soap, Perf., Cosmtcs., Drugs Mfg., Consumer Elect., Venture Cap., Misc. Financial, HR Services, Biotech/Life Sciences

Corporate Select International

401 N Michigan Ave Ste 1200
Chicago, IL 60611-4549
(312) 616-6672
Fax: (312) 616-6678
Email: jobs@corporateselect.com
Web: www.corporateselect.com

Summary: We specialize in recruiting professionals and support staff for companies doing business in increasingly international and multicultural environments.

Key Contact - Specialty:
Ms. Mayumi Cochran, Senior Consultant

Salary Minimum: $30,000

Functions: Generalist (All), Purchasing, Sales & Mktg., HR Mgmt., Finance, IT, Engineering, Int'l.

Industries: Generalist (All), Chemicals, Medical Devices, Plastics, Rubber, Machine, Appliance, Motor Vehicles, Computer Equip., Misc. Financial

Corporate Software Solutions LLC

108 Barrack Hill Rd
Ridgefield, CT 06877-3106
(203) 431-7631
Email: maiolo@corp-soft.com
Web: www.corp-soft.com

Summary: We are an executive placement and IT consulting firm which specializes in skilled professionals. We realize that it is just as important to find our candidates the positions they want, as it is to find our clients the perfect candidate.

Key Contact - Specialty:
Ms. Dee Dee Maiolo, Chief Executive & Operating Officer
Mr. Rick Maiolo, Director, Information Technology

Functions: Management, Board Members

Industries: Software, Accounting SW, Database SW, Development SW, ERP SW, HR SW, Industry Specific SW, Mfg. SW, Security SW, System SW, Biotech/Life Sciences

Corporate Solutions

PO Box 1974
Simpsonville, SC 29681-7374
(864) 228-9508
Email: resume@corp-sol.com
Web: www.corp-sol.com

Summary: Professional recruiting, search and Human Resource consulting firm. Specialize in accounting, engineering, quality, IT and HR.

Key Contact - Specialty:
Mr. James R. Webb, CPC, President - *Accounting, Engineering, Executives, Manufacturing, Middle management*

Salary Minimum: $50,000

Functions: Senior Mgmt., Mfg., Quality, Materials, HR Mgmt., Finance, IT, Engineering

Industries: Manufacturing, Finance, Services, Accounting, Equip Svcs., Mgmt. Consulting, Media, Communications, Packaging, Insurance

Leonard Corwen Corporate Recruiting Services

27850 Solamint Rd Apt 421
Canyon Country, CA 91387-4313
(661) 252-5645
Fax: (661) 252-5645
Email: lencor@msn.com

Summary: Serving the personnel needs of companies and organizations in the recruitment and placement of corporate communications, public relations, advertising, publishing, marketing communications and marketing.

Key Contact - Specialty:
Mr. Leonard Corwen, President - *Advertising, Marketing, Public relations, Publishing*

Salary Minimum: $50,000

Functions: Management, Advertising, Mktg. Mgmt., Direct Mktg., PR, Benefits, Training, Graphic Designers

Industries: Printing, Consumer Elect., Banking, Pharm Svcs., Accounting, Mgmt. Consulting, HR Services, Advertising, Publishing, New Media

J D Cotter Search Inc

2999 E Dublin Granville Rd Ste 301
Columbus, OH 43231-4030
(614) 895-2065
Fax: (614) 895-3071
Email: joe@jdcotter.com
Web: www.jdcotter.com

Summary: We provide permanent or contract; references; fast, thorough, guaranteed; client list available. Or firm prides itself on having peak performance and results.

Key Contact - Specialty:
Mr. Joe Cotter, CPC, President
Mr. Danny Cotter, Vice President
Mr. Doug Boyce, Recruiter
Mr. John L. Cokinos, III, Recruiter
Mr. Barry Miller, Recruiter
Mr. Steve A. Moore, Recruiter
Mr. Dennis Greene, Recruiter
Mr. Randy Gibson, Recruiter
Mr. Richard Washington, Recruiter
Ms. Alicia Rowland, Recruiter - *Advertising, Communications, Healthcare*

Salary Minimum: $50,000

Functions: Generalist (All), Middle Mgmt., Mfg., Materials, HR Mgmt., Finance, IT, Engineering

Industries: Generalist (All)

Coughlin & Associates

PO Box 6902
Monroe, NJ 08831-6902
(609) 409-3380
Fax: (609) 409-3382
Email: jack@jcoughlin.com
Web: www.jcoughlin.com

Summary: Our firm specializes in the food, retail, wholesale, manufacturing and foodservice distributors fields. We have positions ranging from

president to assistant, store manager to sales manager.

Key Contact - Specialty:
Mr. Jack Coughlin, President - *Food*

Salary Minimum: $70,000

Functions: Senior Mgmt., Middle Mgmt., Specialized Svcs.

Industries: Food, Bev., Tobacco, Paper, Soap, Perf., Cosmtcs., Wholesale, Retail, Restaurants

CountryHouse Hotels Executive Search

1 Morton Dr Ste 504
Charlottesville, VA 22903-6807
(434) 977-5029
Email: info@chhsearch.com
Web: www.chhsearch.com

Summary: Major client base consists of four and five star hotels and resorts.

Key Contact - Specialty:
Mr. Grant Howlett, President - *Hospitality*
Mr. Steve Samuels, Director, US Recruitment - *Hospitality*

Salary Minimum: $30,000

Functions: Senior Mgmt., Middle Mgmt., Sales Mgmt., CFOs

Industries: Hotels, Resorts, Clubs

Coverage Incorporated

PO Box 341
Cedarhurst, NY 11516-0341
(516) 374-4406
Email: ajs@coveragesearch.com
Web: www.coveragesearch.com

Summary: Our firm specializes in the recruitment and selection of logistics and supply chain professionals. Our philosophy, which is based upon expertise and integrity, is to bring a rational and realistic approach to the recruitment process.

Key Contact - Specialty:
Mr. Arnold Saxe, Director

Salary Minimum: $85,000

Functions: Management

Industries: Transportation, Logistics Svcs., Supply Chain Mgmt

Cowan Search Group

897 S Chiques Rd
Manheim, PA 17545-9166
(717) 892-4646
(717) 892-4647
Fax: (717) 892-4645
Email: resume@cowansearch.com
Web: www.cowansearch.com

Summary: We specialize in recruitment of top quality sales, management and marketing personnel. Corporate areas of concentration include advertising, telecom, building industry, call center management and computer technology.

Key Contact - Specialty:
Mr. Ken Cowan, President - *Sales*
Ms. Shanda Teague, Vice President - *Advertising, Financial, Marketing, Sales*

Salary Minimum: $40,000

Functions: Generalist (All), Sales & Mktg., Sales Reps.

Industries: Generalist (All), Equip Svcs., Mgmt. Consulting, Media, Advertising, Publishing, New Media, Communications, Telecoms, Call Centers, Telephony, Wireless, Real Estate, Software, Marketing SW

Franklin Cox Associates Inc

(also known as FCA Healthcare Division)
5347 Winding Glen Dr
Lithonia, GA 30038-2398
(770) 593-9678
(770) 593-9054
Fax: (770) 322-9984
Email: info@franklincox.com;
recruiter@fcahealthcare.com
Web: www.franklincox.com,
www.fcahealthcare.com

Summary: Contingency, contract and executive search firm. Full service, generalist placements. Fully automated, e-cruitment. Value added services include outplacement services and on-line training.

Key Contact - Specialty:
Ms. Tammy Riley, President - *Administration, Healthcare, Physicians, Professional services, Psychiatry*
Ms. Calanrda Willingham, Executive Placement Specialist - *Administration, Finance, Healthcare, Management*

Salary Minimum: $50,000

Functions: Generalist (All), Healthcare

Industries: Generalist (All), Healthcare, Hospitals

A C Coy Company

400 Technology Dr
Canonsburg, PA 15317-9560
(724) 514-4444
(800) 784-5773
Fax: (724) 514-1111
Email: target@accoy.com
Web: www.accoy.com

Summary: Specializing in IT and engineering professionals. Our senior staff has technical recruiting and placement experience operating through the ups and downs of the business cycles since inception.

Key Contact - Specialty:
Mr. Frank J. Yocca, Principal
Mr. John S. Yocca, Principal - *Computers, Database (Warehousing), ERP, Information Systems, Information Technology*

Salary Minimum: $50,000

Functions: Senior Mgmt., Middle Mgmt., IT, MIS Mgmt., Systems Analysis, Systems Dev., Systems Implem., Systems Support, Network Admin., DB Admin.

Industries: Generalist (All)

The CPI Group Inc

PO Box 828
Columbus, MS 39703-0828
(662) 328-1042
Fax: (662) 329-1017
Email: msmith1@cpi-group.com
Web: www.cpi-group.com

Summary: We develop staffing and HR solutions for companies. Our focus is on engineering, management and IT, primarily within the manufacturing sector. We also have clients within telecom and finance.

Key Contact - Specialty:
Mr. Mark Smith, President - *Management, Marketing*

Salary Minimum: $25,000

Functions: Generalist (All)

Industries: Manufacturing, Banking, Accounting, HR Services, Telecoms, Network Infrastructure, Aerospace, Software, HR SW

Branches:
500 Russell St Ste 9
Starkville, MS 39759-5411
(662) 320-4466
Fax: (662) 320-4558
Key Contact - Specialty:
Mr. Truman Abbe, Branch Manager - *Staffing*

CPI Human Resources Solutions Inc

5203 Maverick Dr
Austin, TX 78727-5721
(512) 335-9347
Fax: (512) 335-9357
Email: info@cpipartners.com
Web: www.cpipartners.com

Summary: We specialize in providing human resources solutions to pre-IPO companies in the internet, software, and telecommunication industries.

Key Contact - Specialty:
Mr. Erik Chyten, President - *Finance*
Mrs. Dawn Chyten, Vice President - *Human resources*
Mr. Jan Jensen, Vice President - *Human resources, Organizational development*

Functions: Generalist (All)

Industries: Mgmt. Consulting, HR Services, Media, Advertising, New Media, Telecoms, Software

CPO Recruiting Group (Cresta, Phifer & Osadchuk)

PO Box 1741
Horsham, PA 19044-6741
(215) 672-6400
(215) 672-8538
Fax: (215) 672-8539
Email: info@cporecruiting.com
Web: www.cporecruiting.com

Summary: Our firm has successfully developed a reputable network for connecting IT, engineering, scientific and business specialists with Fortune 500 companies and other leading growth firms. We are able to provide our clients with many years of collective professional experience.

Key Contact - Specialty:
Ms. Michelle Cresta, Partner - *Banking, Computers (Programming, Software), Information Technology, Loans*
Ms. Jen Phifer, Partner - *Middle management, Systems, Systems (Analysts, Integration), Technical (Management)*

Functions: Generalist (All)

Industries: Generalist (All)

CPS Inc

1 Westbrook Corporate Ctr Ste 600
Westchester, IL 60154-5712
(708) 562-0001
(708) 836-0386
Fax: (708) 531-8368
Email: info@cps4jobs.com
Web: www.cps4jobs.com

Summary: Dynamic technical firm employing over 60 specialized recruiters. Consistently placing the top 20 percent of applicants. Divisional into 13 distinct marketplaces: engineering, sales & marketing, production supervision, etc.

Key Contact - Specialty:
Mr. H. Douglas Christiansen, President
Ms. Lee Romano, Secretary, Treasurer, VP, Admin - *Temporary*
Ms. Renee Mydlach, Manager - *Engineering*

Mr. Rich Brandeis, Division Manager - *Chemical, Engineering*
Mr. Dale Graham, Division Manager, Sales & Marketing
Mr. Pat Kilcoyne, Manager, Actuarial Division
Mr. David Schueneman, Manager - *Advertising*
Mr. Dan Tovrog, Manager
Ms. Natalie Sanders, Manager - *Finance*
Ms. Arlene Gasparro, Support Staff Manager
Ms. Julie Riley, Special Projects Coordinator
Ms. Marge Prendergast, Support Staff
Ms. Pat Dalton, Support Staff

Salary Minimum: $25,000

Functions: Generalist (All), Mfg., Materials, Sales & Mktg., Benefits, IT, R&D, Engineering

Industries: Generalist (All), Transportation, Misc. Financial, Media, Packaging, Insurance, Software

Branches:
130 W Lincoln Hwy
DeKalb, IL 60115-3610
(815) 756-1221
Fax: (815) 756-1350
Email: lab@cps4jobs.com
Key Contact - Specialty:
Mr. Jim Clark, Branch Manager

50 Federal St Ste 301
Boston, MA 02110-2509
(617) 368-3550
Fax: (617) 368-3562
Email: boston@cps4jobs.com
Key Contact - Specialty:
Ms. Mary O'Connel, Manager

CPUSearch

13612 Midway Rd Ste 333
Dallas, TX 75244-4309
(972) 233-1773
Fax: (972) 233-9619
Email: zipzap@cpusearch.com
Web: www.cpusearch.com

Summary: We specialize in pharmaceutical positions from senior management to entry level.

Key Contact - Specialty:
Mr. V.J. Zapotocky, Owner - *Healthcare*
Mr. Mark Allen, Operations Manager - *Healthcare*

Salary Minimum: $70,000

Functions: Physicians, Allied Health

Industries: Pharm Svcs., Hospitals

Susan Craig Associates Inc

371 Berkeley St
Toronto, ON M5A 2X8
Canada
(416) 960-5062
(888) 289-2614
Fax: (416) 960-6467
Email: susan@susancraig.com
Web: www.susancraig.com

Summary: We specialize in physician and physician executive search.

Key Contact - Specialty:
Ms. Susan Craig, MA, President

Functions: Physicians, Health Admin.

Industries: Generalist (All), Healthcare, Hospitals

Crandall Associates Inc

44 S Bayles Ave Ste 316
Port Washington, NY 11050-3765
(516) 767-6800
Fax: (516) 767-6980

Email: wendy@crandallassociates.com
Web: www.crandallassociates.com

Summary: We fill positions for all functions in direct marketing and emarketing including marketing, management, database, operations, telesales management and creative.

Key Contact - Specialty:
Ms. Wendy Weber, President

Salary Minimum: $50,000

Functions: Direct Mktg.

Industries: Generalist (All)

Creative Financial Staffing

1 Beacon St Fl 26
Boston, MA 02108-3106
(617) 880-7600
Fax: (617) 753-6016
Email: amccarthy@cfstaffing.com
Web: www.cfstaffing.com

Summary: Temp, permanent, and temp-to-permanent accounting & finance placement. We have an extensive network acros the U.S.

Key Contact - Specialty:
Mr. Daniel Casey, President
Mr. Bruce Gobdel, Chairman - *Finance*

Functions: Finance

Industries: Finance, Accounting

Affiliates:
Atkinson & Company Ltd
Albuquerque, NM

Lane Gorman Trubitt L L P
Dallas, TX

Branches:
60 Spear St Fl 4
San Francisco, CA 94105-1509
(415) 394-9888
Fax: (415) 421-2976
Email: ashinn@hoodstrong.com
Key Contact - Specialty:
Ms. Candice Warren, Consultant, Marketing
Ms. Alison Shinn

1600 Broadway Ste 2500
Denver, CO 80202-4921
(303) 830-0971
Fax: (303) 861-5261
Email: kileyb@cfs-co.com
Key Contact - Specialty:
Mr. Dan Long

PO Box 272000
West Hartford, CT 06127-2000
(860) 561-6850
Fax: (860) 521-9241
Email: kbrault@blumshapiro.com
Key Contact - Specialty:
Ms. Tarah Lelli, Area Manager

14750 NW 77th Ct Ste 200
Hialeah, FL 33016-1507
(305) 557-1924
Fax: (305) 557-0547
Email: hreyes@cfstaffingflorida.com
Key Contact - Specialty:
Ms. Jean Marie Allen

480 N Orlando Ave Ste 221
Winter Park, FL 32789-2918
(407) 539-0980
Fax: (407) 539-1828
Email: jhoppe@cfstaffingflorida.com
Key Contact - Specialty:
Ms. Megan Lynch, Regional Director

5565 Glenridge Connector NE Ste 200
Atlanta, GA 30342-4782
(404) 898-8247
Fax: (404) 898-7540
Email: denise.reid@hawcpa.com
Key Contact - Specialty:
Mr. John Gress

1000 Jorie Blvd Ste 250
Oak Brook, IL 60523-2233
(630) 371-1200
Fax: (630) 371-1201
Email: cfs_career@crowechizek.com
Key Contact - Specialty:
Mr. Gary Gadzinski

PO Box 40977
Indianapolis, IN 46240-0977
(317) 706-2600
Fax: (317) 706-2660
Email: asigman@crowechizek.com
Key Contact - Specialty:
Ms. Audra Sigman

340 Columbia St Ste 105
South Bend, IN 46601-2339
(219) 236-7600
Fax: (219) 239-7878
Email: sforrester@crowechizek.com
Key Contact - Specialty:
Mr. Mike Niedbalski

400 Locust St Ste 640
Des Moines, IA 50309-2354
(515) 558-6648
Fax: (515) 471-5241
Email: jett.judkins@rsmi.com
Key Contact - Specialty:
Mr. Joe Anzalone, Regional Director

140 Wood Rd Ste 104
Braintree, MA 02184-2512
(781) 356-6775
Fax: (781) 848-8559
Email: esandler@cfstaffing.com
Key Contact - Specialty:
Ms. Maryellen Kessinger

7900 Xerxes Ave S Ste 2400
Bloomington, MN 55431-1152
(952) 835-1344
Fax: (952) 835-5845
Email: lhuggett@virchowkrause.com
Key Contact - Specialty:
Ms. Laura Huggett

424 Main St Rm 707
Buffalo, NY 14202-3507
(716) 842-0939
Fax: (716) 856-3644
Email: resume@cfsbuffalo.com
Key Contact - Specialty:
Mr. Ron Soluri

111 W 40th St Fl 12
New York, NY 10018-2510
(212) 302-4567
Fax: (212) 302-1832
Key Contact - Specialty:
Mr. Phil Dubinsky

388 S Main St Ste 403
Akron, OH 44311-4407
(330) 237-0100
Fax: (330) 237-1730
Key Contact - Specialty:
Ms. Tamra Emmett, Search Consultant
Mr. Chris Guest, Search Consultant
Ms. Susan Davies, Search Consultant

4505 Stephens Cir NW Ste 200
Canton, OH 44718-3629
(330) 490-2175
Fax: (330) 497-8383

Key Contact - Specialty:
Ms. Teresa Bennett

6133 Rockside Rd Ste 403
Independence, OH 44131-2244
(216) 674-4200
Fax: (216) 674-4201
Key Contact - Specialty:
Ms. Evelyn Hronec

250 E Wilson Bridge Rd
Worthington, OH 43085-2323
(614) 343-7800
Fax: (614) 343-7808
Email: girwin@crowechizek.com
Key Contact - Specialty:
Mr. Gary Irwin

416 Ave Ponce de Leon Ste 1400
San Juan, PR 00918-3421
(787) 756-7597
Fax: (787) 753-1880
Email: privera@cfstaffingpr.com
Key Contact - Specialty:
Mr. Pedro Rivera

5718 Westheimer Rd Ste 800
Houston, TX 77057-5758
(713) 260-5238
Fax: (832) 251-8311
Email: tll@fittsroberts.com
Key Contact - Specialty:
Ms. Tori Logan, Recruiter

1801 Robert Fulton Dr
Reston, VA 20191-5461
(703) 758-3517
Email: ed.barrow@rsmi.com
Key Contact - Specialty:
Mr. Ed Barrow

PO Box 7398
Madison, WI 53707-7398
(608) 249-3180
Fax: (608) 249-1411
Email: cfs@virchowkrause.com
Key Contact - Specialty:
Ms. Laura Braendle

115 S 84th St Ste 400
Milwaukee, WI 53214-1475
(414) 777-5505
Fax: (414) 777-5555
Email: tjames@virchowkrause.com
Key Contact - Specialty:
Ms. Tonnia James, Executive Recruiter

Mariano Escobedo 396-203
Col Nueva Anzures
11590 Mexico City, DF
Mexico
55 5203 2761
Fax: 55 5203 9766
Email: cfsmexic@prodigy.net.mx
Key Contact - Specialty:
Mr. Enrique Hambleton

Creative HR Solutions

PO Box 1966
Stone Mountain, GA 30086-1966
(678) 938-3770
Email: jgross07@aol.com

Summary: We are a multicultural organization providing services in the areas of executive/technical search, HR management, business development, diversity training and outplacement.

Key Contact - Specialty:
Mr. Jerry Gross, Partner
Mr. Tim Duckett, Partner - *Financial*
Mr. Solomon Tedla, Principal - *Financial*

Salary Minimum: $35,000

Functions: Generalist (All), Senior Mgmt., Admin. Svcs., Staffing, Training, Systems Analysis, Systems Support, Minorities/Diversity
Industries: Generalist (All), Test, Measure Equip., Hospitality, Telecoms, Defense, Software

The Creative Network Inc

1325 SE Tech Center Dr Ste 190
Vancouver, WA 98683-5555
(360) 604-0802
Email: jessica@creativenetworkinc.com
Web: www.creativenetworkinc.com

Summary: We are a professional recruiting firm dedicated to enhancing the growth and development of candidates and client companies to achieve an exceptional and successful working partnership. Our firm has established itself as a search firm loyal to its clients and candidates. Our dedication and ethical approach has resulted in our reputation as a highly productive and successful search firm.

Key Contact - Specialty:
Ms. Jessica Goursolas, Vice President
Ms. Gail Czech, President
Ms. Nancy Ford, Senior Consultant

Salary Minimum: $50,000

Functions: Senior Mgmt., Product Dev., Purchasing, Packaging, Sales & Mktg., Advertising, Mktg. Research, Mktg. Mgmt., Sales Mgmt., Direct Mktg.
Industries: Manufacturing, Food, Bev., Tobacco, Textiles, Apparel, Soap, Perf., Cosmtcs., Consumer Elect., Misc. Mfg., Consumer Goods

The Creative Placement Agency LLC

13 N Main St
Norwalk, CT 06854-2702
(203) 838-7772
Fax: (203) 854-0700
Email: kheine@creativeplacement.com
Web: www.creativeplacement.com

Summary: We have been attracting and placing the best talent across all creative industries throughout the tri-state area. We work hand-in-hand with our clients, to ensure we match the right candidate with the talent, professionalism and experience our clients are looking for.

Key Contact - Specialty:
Mr. Karl Heine, Principal - *Biomedical, Biopharmaceutical, Biotechnology, Medical (Devices), Pharmaceutical*

Salary Minimum: $35,000

Functions: Sales & Mktg., Graphic Designers
Industries: Advertising, Publishing, New Media

Creative Search Affiliates

PO Box 2929
Palm Beach, FL 33480-2929
(561) 371-8385
(561) 659-3747
Email: resnickcsa@aol.com
Web: www.csaffiliates.com

Summary: We specialize in all phases of brokerage, banking, corporate finance, money management, pension, research analysts and p/mgr local and regional contacts. Stock brokers - retail and institutional.

Key Contact - Specialty:
Dr. A. Allan Resnick, Senior Partner & Founder
Mr. Harvey Wayne, Associate Vice President

Salary Minimum: $50,000

Functions: Generalist (All), M&A

Industries: Generalist (All), Invest. Banking, Brokers, Venture Cap., Misc. Financial

Credit Resource Group

3901 Northampton Way
Tampa, FL 33618-8443
(813) 817-7154
Email: brian@riley.net
Web: www.creditresourcegroup.com

Summary: Specialize in the credit, collection and receivables function for domestic and international companies. Our executive experience with leading issuers gives us a unique perspective in finding exceptional talent and providing you with candidates that are a cut above. Contingent and retained services, performance guarantee.

Key Contact - Specialty:
Mr. Brian Riley, Managing Partner

Functions: Management, Middle Mgmt., Sales & Mktg.

Industries: Finance, Banking, Misc. Financial, Mgmt. Consulting, Call Centers, Non-Classifiable

Criterion Executive Search Inc

550 N Reo St Ste 101
Tampa, FL 33609-1033
(813) 286-2000
Email: info@cesfl.com
Web: www.criterionsearch.com

Summary: We are a contingency firm consisting of professional recruiters with corporate experience in their fields. Our specialties include: audit, accounting & finance, healthcare, IT, engineering, insurance, legal, manufacturing and medical devices

Key Contact - Specialty:
Mr. Richard James, President

Functions: Generalist (All), Management, Materials, Purchasing, Packaging, Allied Health, Benefits, Finance, Engineering, Attorneys

Industries: Generalist (All), Manufacturing, Finance, Legal, Accounting, Mgmt. Consulting, HR Services, Packaging, Insurance, Healthcare, Hospitals, Physical Therapy, Occupational Therapy

Critical Path Inc

110 Fort Couch Rd Ste 3
Pittsburgh, PA 15241-1030
(412) 851-4144
Fax: (412) 851-5409
Email: info@criticalpathinc.net
Web: www.criticalpathinc.net

Summary: A professional recruitment firm providing retained and exclusive searches to clients in the pharmaceutical and biotechnology industries. Primary areas of experience are life science, regulatory, R&D, project management, informatics and executive management and executive positions.

Key Contact - Specialty:
Ms. Karen L. Baldwin, President
Mr. Drew Fiorentini, Vice President

Salary Minimum: $85,000

Functions: Generalist (All)

Industries: Pharm Svcs., E-commerce, IT Implementation, ERP SW, Security SW, System SW, Biotech/Life Sciences

Cromark International Inc

PO Box 878
Erin, ON N0B 1T0
Canada
(416) 657-2886
(888) 899-9090
Fax: (519) 833-9955
Email: resumes@cromark.com
Web: www.cromark.com

Summary: Automotive, transportation and distribution industry specialists to manufacturers, dealers, suppliers, finance sources, marketing/advertising firms in recruitment and management consulting.

Key Contact - Specialty:
Mr. Clive Crowe, Chief Executive Officer - *Management*

Functions: Generalist (All), Management, Board Members, Advertising, Mktg. Research, HR Mgmt., CFOs, Budgeting, Mgmt. Consultants

Industries: Manufacturing, Motor Vehicles, Transportation, Wholesale, Retail, Finance, Misc. Financial, Logistics Svcs., Supply Chain Mgmt, Travel, Advertising, Publishing, New Media, Defense, Haz. Waste

Cross Country Consultants Inc

111 Warren Rd Ste 4B
Cockeysville, MD 21030-3368
(410) 666-1100
Fax: (410) 666-1119
Email: crosscountrycons@aol.com
Web: www.ccchothobs.com

Summary: Professional recruiters specializing in engineering, logistics, manufacturing, telecom and sales. Engineering disciplines: plastics, metal products, electronics, chemical process, consumer products and mechanical engineering.

Key Contact - Specialty:
Mr. Sheldon Gottesfeld, President - *Engineering*
Mr. Bob Nemecek, Recruiter, Sales & Marketing - *Accounting, Marketing, Sales*

Salary Minimum: $30,000

Functions: Generalist (All)

Industries: Lumber, Furniture, Chemicals, Plastics, Rubber, Metal Products, Consumer Goods, Accounting, HR Services, Logistics Svcs., Defense

Crown International Consulting LLC

5741 Berryton Ct
Norcross, GA 30092-2050
(888) 917-9264
Fax: (888) 917-9264
Email: mburg@prodigy.net
Web: www.crownic.com

Summary: A professional recruiting and consulting firm that specializes in the credit industry.

Key Contact - Specialty:
Mr. Mike Burgess, President

Salary Minimum: $50,000

Functions: Management, Middle Mgmt., Sales & Mktg., Direct Mktg., HR Mgmt., Finance, Credit, Risk Mgmt.

Industries: Finance, Banking, Legal, Accounting, HR Services, Call Centers, Software

CRS

(also known as Construction Recruiting Services)
1141 Montreat Rd
Black Mountain, NC 28711-3231
(828) 699-2292
Fax: (828) 669-2287
Email: aforester@crsjob.com
Web: www.crsjob.com

Summary: We work within the construction industry, consistently delivering the highest-quality candidates for mid-tier executive, professional and technical positions to clients both large and small, in the top construction markets. The management recruiters division comprises the most powerful search and recruitment organization in the top growth markets.

Key Contact - Specialty:
Mr. Avery Forester, President & Chief Executive Officer
Ms. Julie Jarrett, Director, Administrations
Mrs. Joanne Nikolski, Account Executive - *Construction*
Mr. Eric Jones, Account Executive - *Construction*
Mr. Pierre LeBlanc, Account Executive - *Construction*

Functions: Management, Senior Mgmt., Sales & Mktg., Finance

Industries: Construction

Jim Crumpley & Associates

1200 E Woodhurst Dr Ste B400
Springfield, MO 65804-3779
(417) 882-7555
Fax: (417) 882-8555
Email: recruiter@crumpleyjobs.com
Web: www.crumpleyjobs.com

Summary: Retained and contingency search and placement of technical, scientific and engineering personnel for the pharmaceutical and medical device industry to include engineering, QA/C, validation, technical services, R&D, manufacturing supervision/management, supply chain and allied areas.

Key Contact - Specialty:
Mr. Jim Crumpley, Owner - *Pharmaceutical*

Salary Minimum: $40,000

Functions: Generalist (All), Product Dev., Production, Plant Mgmt., Quality, Materials Plng., R&D, Engineering

Industries: Generalist (All), Drugs Mfg., Medical Devices

Crutchfield Associates Inc

1000 Saint Andrews Rd Ste D
Columbia, SC 29210-3103
(803) 772-6152
Fax: (803) 798-4004
Email: bob@crutchfieldassociates.com
Web: www.crutchfieldassociates.com

Summary: We combine old-fashioned proven techniques with today's latest technological tools to find superstars who make an immediate contribution for our clients.

Key Contact - Specialty:
Mr. Bob Crutchfield, Owner & President - *Human resources, Management*

Salary Minimum: $30,000

Functions: Generalist (All), Board Members, Senior Mgmt., Admin. Svcs., Mktg. Research, Sales Mgmt., Customer Svc., Benefits, Training

Industries: Generalist (All), Printing, Medical Devices, Metal Products, Computer Equip., Misc. Mfg., Banking, Non-profits, Pharm Svcs., Legal, Accounting, HR Services, Telecoms, Call Centers, Wireless, Insurance, Software, Hospitals

CSI America

(formerly known as Custom Staffing Inc)
3520 Holiday Dr Ste C
New Orleans, LA 70114
(504) 367-1110
Fax: (504) 362-8838
Email: dcs@csi-america.com
Web: www.csi-america.com

Summary: We are a national search firm handling senior management and management positions in the following areas: technical, operational, financial, medical, legal, materials, and oil & gas. Our mission is making "Pinpoint Placements". We partner with national and international client companies in building top-caliber staff.

Key Contact - Specialty:
Ms. Donna C. Sphar, President - *Biomedical, Biotechnology, Management, Senior management*
Mr. Asa Sphar, III, PhD, Vice President - *Accounting, Controllers, Engineering, Information Technology, Psychiatry*

Salary Minimum: $70,000

Functions: Management, Senior Mgmt., Materials, MIS Mgmt.

Industries: Generalist (All), Oil & Gas, Wholesale, Retail, Non-profits, Legal, Accounting, IT Implementation, Engineering Svcs., Healthcare

CTEW Executive Personnel Services Inc

1207-409 Granville St
United Kingdom Bldg
Vancouver, BC V6C 1T2
Canada
(604) 682-3218
Fax: (604) 683-3211
Email: resumes@ctewgroup.com
Web: www.ctewgroup.com

Summary: We are a full-service search firm servicing clients with executive, managerial and supervisory recruiting assignments across all industry sectors.

Key Contact - Specialty:
Mr. Stan Dahl, Recruiter - *Environmental, Technical*
Ms. Hayley Lau, Group Manager - *Executives*
Mr. Jaspreet Walia, Recruiter - *Information Technology*

Salary Minimum: $40,000

Functions: Generalist (All), Senior Mgmt., Sales Mgmt., Systems Implem., Mgmt. Consultants

Industries: Generalist (All), Manufacturing, Misc. Financial, Higher Ed., Hospitality, Environmental Svcs., Software, Biotech/Life Sciences

CTR Group

PO Box 12177
Newport News, VA 23612-2177
(757) 686-3566
Fax: (757) 686-3567
Email: stevens@ctrc.com
Web: www.ctrc.com

Summary: A true full-service firm, excelling in permanent placement, contract labor and project/temp staffing. Focus on locating top talent for executive, middle management, medical, engineering and light industrial openings.

Key Contact - Specialty:
Mr. Steven Sheppard, Manager, Recruiting
Services Marketing - *Human resources,
Information Technology*

Functions: Generalist (All)

Industries: Generalist (All), Energy, Utilities,
Manufacturing, Wholesale, Finance,
Communications, Government, Aerospace,
Software, Healthcare

The Culver Group

(Culver Careers)
6610 Flanders Dr
San Diego, CA 92121-2976
(858) 587-4804 x220
Email: thill@culvercareers.com
Web: www.culvercareers.com

Summary: We specialize in sales and sales
management recruiting in a wide variety of
different sales industries. We work nationwide
with many of the Fortune 1000 companies along
with smaller to mid size firms as well.

Key Contact - Specialty:
Mr. Timothy J. Culver, Owner & Founder
Mr. Mike Hobbs, President
Mr. Ted Hill, Vice President, Sales -
Pharmaceutical, Sales
Mr. John Weaver, Chief Operating Officer -
Computers (Software), Sales

Functions: Sales & Mktg.

Industries: Drugs Mfg., Pharm Svcs.,
Biotech/Life Sciences

Branches:
1201 S Alma School Rd Ste 5000
Mesa, AZ 85210-2012
(480) 615-6565
Email: echambers@culvercareers.com
Key Contact - Specialty:
Ms. Elouise Chambers, Managing Director

1420 Harbor Bay Pkwy Ste 135
Alameda, CA 94502-7097
(510) 749-7910
Email: jholiday@culvercareers.com
Key Contact - Specialty:
Ms. Jennifer Holiday, Managing Director

1 Pointe Dr Ste 580
Brea, CA 92821-6305
(714) 990-4459
Email: tsullivan@culvercareers.com
Key Contact - Specialty:
Ms. Tami Sullivan, Vice President

1901 Camino Vida Roble Ste 201
Carlsbad, CA 92008-6561
(760) 431-0394
Email: acalvin@culvercareers.com
Key Contact - Specialty:
Ms. Amy Calvin, Managing Director
Ms. Megan McLaughlin, Managing Director

2221 Rosecrans Ave Ste 101
El Segundo, CA 90245-4935
(310) 643-2880
Email: gkaszacs@culvercareers.com
Key Contact - Specialty:
Mr. George Kaszacs, Managing Director

1810 Gateway Dr Ste 140
Foster City, CA 94404-2470
(650) 356-1100
Fax: (650) 356-1111
Email: gfagin@culvercareers.com
Key Contact - Specialty:
Ms. Gina Fagin, Managing Director

19700 Fairchild Ste 146
Irvine, CA 92612-2527
(949) 476-3224
Fax: (949) 476-8725
Email: bnarasaki@culvercareers.com
Key Contact - Specialty:
Mr. B. Narasaki, Branch Manager

3900 Kilroy Airport Way Ste 260
Long Beach, CA 90806-6819
(562) 427-0069
Fax: (562) 427-3506
Email: swells@culvercareers.com
Key Contact - Specialty:
Ms. Susan Hartman, Managing Director

5994 W Las Positas Blvd Ste 111
Pleasanton, CA 94588-8525
(925) 416-9400
Email: dwayland@culvercareers.com
Key Contact - Specialty:
Ms. Diane Wayland, Vice President

8599 Haven Ave Ste 205
Rancho Cucamonga, CA 91730-4849
(909) 989-3333
Fax: (909) 989-3962
Email: bschoch@culvercareers.com
Key Contact - Specialty:
Mr. Brian Schoch, Managing Director

1650 Spruce St Ste 104
Riverside, CA 92507-7403
(909) 276-1500
Fax: (909) 276-1600
Email: nmiller@culvercareers.com
Key Contact - Specialty:
Ms. Nadine Miller, Managing Director

1545 River Park Dr Ste 530
Sacramento, CA 95815-4693
(916) 923-4444
Email: awilliams@culvercareers.com
Key Contact - Specialty:
Ms. April Williams, Managing Director

9645 Granite Ridge Dr Ste 210
San Diego, CA 92123-2660
(858) 278-7680
Fax: (858) 278-2312
Email: cwitak@culvercareers.com
Key Contact - Specialty:
Ms. Cindy Witak, Senior Managing Director

22 Battery St Ste 888
San Francisco, CA 94111-5522
(415) 956-9911
Email: jsolari@culvercareers.com
Key Contact - Specialty:
Ms. Jennifer Solari, Branch Manager

2107 N Broadway Ste 105
Santa Ana, CA 92706-2631
(714) 558-6829
Fax: (714) 543-4607
Email: msmalstig@culvercareers.com
Key Contact - Specialty:
Ms. Meri Smalstig, Senior Managing Director

970 W 190th St Ste 970
Torrance, CA 90502-1070
(310) 756-0966
Fax: (310) 756-0969
Email: cdevereux@culvercareers.com
Key Contact - Specialty:
Ms. Catherine Devereux, Regional Vice President
Ms. Anna Powell, Managing Director

21031 Ventura Blvd Ste 920
Woodland Hills, CA 91364-6516
(818) 593-4960
Fax: (818) 593-4959
Email: mcoyle@culvercareers.com

Key Contact - Specialty:
Mr. Marshall Coyle, Managing Director

515 Double Eagle Ct Ste 202
Reno, NV 89521-2958
(775) 850-1422
Fax: (775) 850-2727
Email: lholder@culvercareers.com
Key Contact - Specialty:
Ms. Laura Holder, Managing Director

Cumberland Group Inc

608 S Washington St Ste 107
Naperville, IL 60540-6663
(630) 416-9494
Fax: (630) 416-3250
Email: jvogus@cumberlandgroup.net
Web: www.cumberlandgroup.net

Summary: We provide executive search for sales,
management and marketing for industrial
companies. We place a strong emphasis on capital
equipment and metals industry.

Key Contact - Specialty:
Mr. Jerry Vogus, President - *Metals*

Salary Minimum: $45,000

Functions: Automation, Sales & Mktg.

Industries: Manufacturing, Metal Products,
Machine, Appliance, Robotics

Frank Cuomo & Associates Inc

111 Brook St
Scarsdale, NY 10583-5143
(914) 723-8001
Fax: (914) 472-0507

Summary: Broad range of services to include
executive search and recruitment for service and
manufacturing companies. Particular emphasis on
sales, marketing, engineering, general
management and manufacturing management.

Key Contact - Specialty:
Mr. Frank Cuomo, President

Salary Minimum: $40,000

Functions: Generalist (All)

Industries: Energy, Utilities, Construction, Metal
Products, Test, Measure Equip., Environmental
Svcs., Haz. Waste

Curphey & Malkin Associates Inc

13011 W Washington Blvd
Los Angeles, CA 90066-5123
(310) 822-7555 x104
Fax: (310) 305-0467
Email: nancy@candm.com
Web: www.candm.com

Summary: We've been helping high-tech
companies grow by assessing clients' culture,
personality and staffing needs. Our clients include
global companies, start-up ventures and emerging
growth businesses looking for high-tech sales &
marketing talent. Positions include C-level, sales,
presales technical product marketing &
management and consulting. Candidates must
have prior high-tech experience.

Key Contact - Specialty:
Ms. Nancy Malkin, Partner - *Computers
(Sales,Software), High technology, Product
management/development, Technical
(Management)*

Salary Minimum: $100,000

Functions: Management, Sales & Mktg., Mktg.
Mgmt., Sales Mgmt., Mgmt. Consultants

Industries: New Media, Communications,
Software, Database SW, Development SW,
Doc. Mgmt., Production SW, ERP SW, Industry

Specific SW, Mfg. SW, Marketing SW, Networking, Comm. SW, Security SW, System SW

The Curran Group

1350 Treat Blvd Ste 260
Walnut Creek, CA 94597-2194
(925) 943-6060
(800) 955-7557
Email: mike@curransearch.com
Web: www.curransearch.com

Summary: Executive search firm with a focus on financial services, technology, and packaging.

Key Contact - Specialty:
Mr. Michael Curran, President - *Financial services, Technology*
Ms. Ina Miller, Director
Ms. Jeannie Gambino-Mark, Director
Mr. Peter Banchieri, Director, Software Practice
Ms. Susan Jetter, Senior Search Consultant
Mr. Ian Turner, Senior Search Consultant
Mr. Shawn Perry, Search Consultant

Salary Minimum: $85,000

Functions: Generalist (All), Sales Reps.

Industries: Printing, Medical Devices, Plastics, Rubber, Finance, Banking, Invest. Banking, Brokers, Venture Cap., Mutual/Hedge Funds, Misc. Financial, Packaging, Software, Marketing SW

The Currier-Winn Company Inc

147 Westgate Dr
Wheeling, WV 26003-4957
(304) 242-0106
Email: resumeservices@currierwinn.com
Web: www.currierwinn.com

Summary: Clients are only Fortune 200 firms in plastics, metal and computer hardware and software industries. We recruit for management, engineering and professional positions.

Key Contact - Specialty:
Mr. E.H. Bauzenberger, III, President

Salary Minimum: $45,000

Functions: Generalist (All), Management, Board Members, Senior Mgmt., Mfg., Product Dev.

Industries: Generalist (All), Manufacturing, Food, Bev., Tobacco, Printing, Chemicals, Drugs Mfg., Medical Devices, Plastics, Rubber, Paints, Petro. Products, Leather, Stone, Glass, Metal Products, Machine, Appliance, Motor Vehicles, Consumer Elect., Misc. Mfg., Electronic, Elec. Components, Robotics, Architectural Svcs., Accounting, HR Services, Accounting SW, ERP SW, HR SW

Tony Curtis & Associates

900-45 Sheppard Ave E
North York, ON M2N 5W9
Canada
(416) 224-0500
Fax: (905) 294-3349
Email: info@employmentinfashion.com
Web: www.employmentinfashion.com

Summary: We specialize in fashion industry professionals such as sales/marketing, graphics, buyers/sourcing/buyers retail, production domestic or import, merchandisers/designers and any other position related to the apparel industry.

Key Contact - Specialty:
Mr. Tony Curtis, President - *Sales*
Mr. Howard Curtis, Vice President, Sales - *Sales*

Functions: Management, Middle Mgmt., Admin. Svcs., Mfg., Production, Materials, Sales & Mktg., Finance

Industries: Textiles, Apparel, Leather, Stone, Glass, Wholesale, Retail

Custom Search Consultants Inc

24861 Avenida Libre
Lake Forest, CA 92630-2102
(949) 608-0813
Fax: (949) 608-0274
Web: www.customsearchconsultants.com

Summary: Our firm provides a unique blend of human capital management services specializing in the finance and accounting professions. Our sole purpose is to create quality win-win employment situations and build long-term relationships with our clients.

Key Contact - Specialty:
Mrs. Pam Andrus, CPA, President - *Accounting, Controllers, Finance, Financial, Healthcare*

Functions: Finance

Industries: Generalist (All)

The Cutting Edge

1201 Broadway Rm 904
New York, NY 10001-5405
(646) 935-1920
Fax: (646) 935-1923
Email: betsi@cuttingedgejobs.com
Web: www.cuttingedgejobs.com

Summary: We specialize in placing sales, marketing and business development executives at brick and mortar firms addressing eCommerce needs, Internet, technology and biotechnology companies.

Key Contact - Specialty:
Ms. Betsi Rosen, President & Chief Executive Officer - *New media*

Functions: Senior Mgmt., Sales & Mktg., Mktg. Research, Mktg. Mgmt., Sales Mgmt., Direct Mktg., Customer Svc., PR, Finance, Graphic Designers

Industries: Finance, Invest. Banking, Venture Cap., Accounting, Hospitality, Media, Advertising, Publishing, New Media, Software, Healthcare

CVPartners Inc

444 Spear St Ste 213
San Francisco, CA 94105-1693
(415) 543-8600
Fax: (877) 590-6286
Email: kgray@cvpartnersinc.com
Web: www.cvpartnersinc.com

Summary: Our firm specializes in finance/accounting on a permanent and contract basis.

Key Contact - Specialty:
Mr. Kent Gray, CPA, Managing Partner
Ms. Michelle Crowe, CPA, Recruiter
Mr. Juzer Essabhoy, CPA, Recruiter
Ms. Ann King, CPA, Recruiter
Ms. Jessica Fette, Recruiter
Ms. Aron Walker, CPA, Recruiter
Ms. Patricia McNamara, Recruiter
Mr. Ian Casey, Recruiter
Ms. Donna MacDonald, CPA, Recruiter
Ms. Jonelle Gachter, Recruiter
Ms. Patricia Redington, Recruiter

Salary Minimum: $50,000

Functions: Finance, CFOs, Budgeting, Cash Mgmt., Credit, Taxes, M&A, Risk Mgmt.

Industries: Generalist (All), Manufacturing, Semiconductors, Retail, Finance, Banking, Communications, Real Estate, Software, Biotech/Life Sciences

Branches:
2131 Landings Dr
Mountain View, CA 94043-0843
(650) 625-9600
Email: kgray@cvpartnersinc.com
Key Contact - Specialty:
Ms. Nancy Baltzer, Recruiter
Mr. Scott Hopkins, CPA, Recruiter
Mr. Tyler Hubbs, Recruiter
Mr. Sanford Collins, CPA, Recruiter
Ms. Honore Siri, Recruiter

CyberCoders Inc

320 Goddard Ste 100
Irvine, CA 92618-4612
(949) 885-5151
Fax: (949) 885-5150
Email: info@cybercoders.com
Web: www.cybercoders.com

Summary: We excel in all segments of professional recruiting nationwide. Sales, executive, technical, financial, accounting, engineering, construction and operational positions across all industries. We only hire experienced recruiters who are masters in their field of expertise.

Key Contact - Specialty:
Mr. Lance Miller, Chief Executive Officer
Ms. Heidi Golledge, Executive Vice President

Salary Minimum: $50,000

Functions: Generalist (All)

Industries: Generalist (All), Wholesale, Retail, Full Service Restaurants, Media, Communications, Real Estate, Software, Biotech/Life Sciences, Healthcare

Cyberna Associates Ltd

750-999 Boul de Maisonneuve O
Place Canada Trust
Montreal, QC H3A 3L4
Canada
(514) 843-8349
Fax: (514) 843-6993
Email: wbrown@optioncyberna.com
Web: www.optioncyberna.com

Summary: A recruitment and search, executive contracting, outsourcing and consulting organization, providing innovative and customized programs to meet client needs.

Key Contact - Specialty:
Ms. Wanda Brown, Vice President & General Manager

Salary Minimum: $50,000

Functions: Management, Middle Mgmt., Materials, Distribution, Healthcare, Mktg. Mgmt., HR Mgmt., Benefits, Staffing, Finance

Industries: Generalist (All), Drugs Mfg., Wholesale, Pharm Svcs., Logistics Svcs.

Cyr Associates Inc

177 Worcester St Ste 303
Wellesley Hills, MA 02481-5515
(781) 235-5900
Fax: (781) 239-0140
Email: cyrinc@mindspring.com
Web: www.cyrassociates.com

Summary: Our firm recruits for client companies in consumer goods and direct marketing including consumer and business-to-business catalog. We have expertise in: footwear, apparel, textiles, food, giftware, arts & crafts, toys, collectibles, home decor, accessories, cosmetics, fragrances and medical devices.

Key Contact - Specialty:
Mr. Maury N. Cyr, President - *Direct marketing*
Ms. Emily Mittman, Office Manager

Salary Minimum: $40,000

Functions: Mfg., Materials, Sales & Mktg., Int'l.

Industries: Manufacturing, Food, Bev., Tobacco, Textiles, Apparel, Lumber, Furniture, Soap, Perf., Cosmtcs., Drugs Mfg., Medical Devices, Plastics, Rubber, Consumer Elect., Misc. Mfg., Wholesale, Services, Advertising, Publishing, Packaging, Development SW, Mfg. SW

D & M Associates

245 Cedar Blvd Ste 100
Pittsburgh, PA 15228-1315
(412) 343-4892
Fax: (412) 343-4925

Summary: Specializing in marketing, advertising, banking, real estate, construction, and non-profits.

Key Contact - Specialty:
Mr. David Stobbe, President
Ms. Mickey Stobbe, Principal

Salary Minimum: $40,000

Functions: Senior Mgmt., Middle Mgmt., Advertising, Mktg. Mgmt., Minorities/Diversity, Non-profits, Graphic Designers

Industries: Construction, Banking, Media, Advertising, Publishing, Government, Real Estate

D&B Recruiting LLC

PO Box 260512
Highlands Ranch, CO 80163-0512
(720) 733-1067
Fax: (303) 663-4536
Email: jrd@dbrecruiting.com
Web: www.dbrecruiting.com

Summary: Our recruiting team consists of top performing, senior level recruiters with national and international experience. Our team has years of professional staffing industry expertise and award winning experience. Our professional recruiters specialize in the search for and placement of all level positions, in most industries.

Key Contact - Specialty:
Mr. Joseph Derringer, Manager

Functions: Generalist (All)

Industries: Generalist (All)

J P D'Anna & Associates

5 Grandview Ave Apt 103
Pittsburgh, PA 15211-1648
(412) 390-0214
Email: jdanna@comcast.net

Summary: We are consultants in executive search assisting client organizations in identifying and attracting qualified professionals and mid to upper-level managers for specific opportunities.

Key Contact - Specialty:
Mr. Joe D'Anna

Salary Minimum: $50,000

Functions: Generalist (All), Senior Mgmt.

Industries: Generalist (All), Construction, Real Estate

d. Diversified Services

30150 Telegraph Rd Ste 215
Bingham Farms, MI 48025-4519
(248) 633-0033
Fax: (248) 633-0030
Email: shenes@jobs4you.com
Web: www.jobs4you.com

Summary: We are a fast growing technical staffing company that does contract and direct placements. Our specialties include the following disciplines: engineering, CAD, healthcare, IT, sales and Technicians.

Key Contact - Specialty:
Mr. Stephen Henes, President

Salary Minimum: $50,000

Functions: Generalist (All), Management, Board Members, Middle Mgmt., Nurses, Systems Analysis, Network Admin., Engineering

Industries: Generalist (All), Plastics, Rubber, Machine, Appliance, Motor Vehicles, Computer Equip., Test, Measure Equip., Misc. Mfg., Electronic, Elec. Components, Robotics, Telecoms, Call Centers, Digital, Wireless, Fiber Optic, Software, Database SW, Development SW, ERP SW, Industry Specific SW, Mfg. SW, Networking, Comm. SW, System SW, Healthcare, Hospitals, Long-term/Home Care, Physical Therapy, Occupational Therapy

Daher & Associates Insurance Search Specialists Inc

5311 Kirby Dr Ste 200
Houston, TX 77005-1339
(713) 520-8261
(800) 458-9176
Fax: (713) 520-0526
Email: resume@daherinc.com
Web: www.daherinc.com

Summary: Insurance executive search and consultants specializing in commercial P&C, employee benefits, risk management and life executive benefits.

Key Contact - Specialty:
Miss Liz Daher, President & Founder
Mr. Marc Puppo, Senior Consultant Operations Manager
Miss Shannon Price, Recruiter

Salary Minimum: $100,000

Functions: Generalist (All), Senior Mgmt., Sales & Mktg.

Industries: Insurance, Casualty, Claims, Life, Commercial, Re-Insurance

Charles Dahl Group Inc

77 13th Ave NE Ste 209
Minneapolis, MN 55413-1067
(612) 331-7777
Fax: (612) 331-7778
Email: cdahl@cdahlgroup.com
Web: www.cdassoc.com

Summary: Specialize in legal, R&D, high-technology and bio-technology/gene sequencing industries. Concentration in diversity.

Key Contact - Specialty:
Mr. Charles Dahl, President - *CEOs, CIOs, Diversity, International*
Mr. Thomas Dunlap, Vice President - *Engineering, MIS, Sales*
Ms. Mary Ellen Dahl, Vice President - *Healthcare*

Salary Minimum: $50,000

Functions: Board Members, Sales Mgmt., Systems Implem., R&D, Engineering, Minorities/Diversity

Industries: Medical Devices, Computer Equip., Legal, Packaging, Software, Biotech/Life Sciences, Healthcare

The DAKO Group

2966 Industrial Row Dr
Troy, MI 48084-7040
(248) 655-0100
(800) 434-3256
Fax: (248) 655-0101
Email: recruiting@dakogroup.com
Web: www.dakogroup.com

Summary: We specialize in long-term contractual and permanent placement of technical professionals for the automotive and IT industries.

Key Contact - Specialty:
Mr. Anthony J. Lioi, Director, Recruiting - *Engineering*

Functions: Mfg., Product Dev., Production, Quality, Materials, HR Mgmt., IT, Engineering

Industries: Generalist (All), Chemicals, Plastics, Rubber, Motor Vehicles, Computer Equip., Test, Measure Equip., Mgmt. Consulting, HR Services, Aerospace, Packaging, Software, HR SW

Daley Consulting & Search

3765 Marice Ct
Concord, CA 94518-1609
(925) 798-3866
Fax: (925) 674-9939
Email: mdaley@dpsearch.com
Web: www.dpsearch.com

Summary: We specialize in the recruiting and placement of data processing and MIS/IT professionals for our clients. Our candidates' expertise includes everything from a two-year programmer level of experience up to and including, MIS executive-level management.

Key Contact - Specialty:
Mr. Michael F. Daley, Owner & Recruiter - *Computers (Software), Database, Database (Administration), Information Systems, Information Technology*

Salary Minimum: $50,000

Functions: IT

Industries: Generalist (All)

Dalton Management Consultants Ltd

1139 Indian Mound Dr
Milford, OH 45150-9600
(513) 831-6735
Fax: (513) 831-6735
Email: evonnedalton@aol.com

Summary: Our firm places human recources management, benefits, staffing and training professionals in all industries.

Key Contact - Specialty:
Ms. Evonne Dalton, President - *Human resources*

Salary Minimum: $75,000

Functions: HR Mgmt., Benefits, Staffing, Training

Industries: Generalist (All)

Damon & Associates Inc

5716 Portsmouth Ln
Dallas, TX 75224-4973
(972) 381-9055
Email: damonoffice@sbcglobal.net

Summary: Sales and sales management: medical, consumer, industrial, software and hardware, contract furniture, office products, IT, telecom and LAN/WAN.

Key Contact - Specialty:
Mr. Richard E. Damon, President - *Sales*
Mr. H.M. Hailey, Vice President, Operations - *Sales*

Salary Minimum: $30,000

Functions: Senior Mgmt., Healthcare, Sales & Mktg., IT

Industries: Generalist (All), Lumber, Furniture, Healthcare

Dangerfield & Associates

7700 San Felipe St Ste 490
Houston, TX 77063-1630
(832) 476-8728
Fax: (713) 456-2477
Email: w.dangerfield@deaus.com
Web: www.deaus.com

Summary: We are a retained and contingency based recruiting firm that places mid to upper level executives in the retail and restaurant industry.

Key Contact - Specialty:
Mr. Will Dangerfield, Principal

Salary Minimum: $35,000

Functions: Generalist (All)

Industries: Construction, Retail, Hospitality, Hotels, Resorts, Clubs, Restaurants, Quick Service Restaurants, Full Service Restaurants, Real Estate

Joseph Daniels & Associates Inc

653 Coates Ln
King of Prussia, PA 19406-2559
(610) 270-0605
Email: dfahy@josephdaniels.com
Web: www.josephdaniels.com

Summary: Search and placement firm that specializes in the accounting and finance sector. Service fees are paid by employer companies and are very competitive in the Philadelphia market place.

Key Contact - Specialty:
Mr. Daniel J. Fahy, Jr., CPC, President - *Accounting, Accounting (Big 4,Public), Audits, Tax*

Functions: Finance, CFOs, Taxes

Industries: Generalist (All)

R Dann & Associates LLC

633 S Danyell Dr
Chandler, AZ 85225-2256
(312) 276-8117
(866) 757-0523
Email: jdougherty@rdann.com
Web: www.rdann.com

Summary: We recruit qualified professionals uniquely suited for the insurance corporate cultures and business environments.

Key Contact - Specialty:
Mr. Russell Dann, Chairman/Chief Executive Officer - *Physicians*
Ms. Juanita Dougherty, President/Chief Operating Officer
Ms. Marion Fern, Vice President, Marketing

Salary Minimum: $50,000

Functions: Generalist (All)

Industries: Finance, Banking, Services, Legal, Insurance, Healthcare

Dapexs Consultants Inc

5109 W Genesee St
Camillus, NY 13031-2352
(315) 484-9300
Fax: (315) 484-9330
Email: employment@dapexs.com
Web: www.dapexs.com

Summary: Search and placement specialists in MIS, IT, software & hardware engineering, finance/accounting and other technical specialties. We search, screen, select and present only fully qualified candidates. Our exclusive search plan is tailored to fit specific client needs. Also place professionals on contract basis.

Key Contact - Specialty:
Mr. Peter J. Leofsky, President

Salary Minimum: $30,000

Functions: Generalist (All), Finance, IT, MIS Mgmt., Systems Analysis, Systems Dev., Systems Implem., Network Admin., DB Admin., Engineering

Industries: Generalist (All)

Dare Human Resources Corp

1750-275 Slater St
Ottawa, ON K1P 5H9
Canada
(613) 238-3273
Fax: (613) 238-9532
Email: resume@darehr.com
Web: www.darehr.com

Summary: Providing leading-edge HR and technical solutions catered to meet the specific needs of each company we service. Some key strengths include: executive search, technical recruitment, project management and accredited HR consultants.

Key Contact - Specialty:
Ms. Jocelyne Vitanza, President & Chief Executive Officer - *Engineering, Financial*
Ms. Alison Shipley, Comptroller
Mr. Andrew Ross, Manager, Business Operations - *Administration, Staffing*
Ms. Edith Lèsperance, Recruiter, Human Resources - *Administration, Government*
Ms. Susan Riley, Financial Assistant - *Finance*
Mr. Jacques Guilini, Account Manager - *Government, Information Technology*
Ms. Melodie Shonfield, Senior Recruitment Officer - *Clerical*
Ms. Melissa Roy, Recruitment & Administrative Support - *Technical*

Functions: Generalist (All)

Industries: Legal, Mgmt. Consulting, HR Services, IT Implementation, Higher Ed.

Data Career Center Inc

PO Box 59337
Chicago, IL 60659-0337
(773) 381-6200
Fax: (773) 381-9719
Email: datacareercenter@ameritech.net

Summary: We are specialists in the placement of IT and telecom personnel.

Key Contact - Specialty:
Mr. Larry Chaplik, President

Functions: Generalist (All), Middle Mgmt., MIS Mgmt., Systems Analysis, Systems Support, Network Admin., DB Admin.

Industries: E-commerce, IT Implementation, Call Centers, Network Infrastructure, Software, Database SW, Development SW

Data Force

626 N Park Ave
Indianapolis, IN 46204-1615
(317) 636-9900
(800) 837-9902
Fax: (317) 686-6384
Email: hotjobs@searchforceinc.com
Web: www.searchforceinc.com

Summary: We are a contingency and retained search firm serving IT, engineering, healthcare, accounting, and finance industries.

Key Contact - Specialty:
Mr. Shawn Miller, President & Chief Executive Officer

Salary Minimum: $40,000

Functions: Generalist (All), Healthcare, IT

Industries: Generalist (All), Finance, Engineering Svcs., Software, Healthcare, Dental

Data Search Network Inc

21301 Powerline Rd Ste 104
Boca Raton, FL 33433-2389
(561) 347-6421
Fax: (561) 347-6429
Email: careers@dsninc.com
Web: www.dsninc.com

Summary: Information systems firm serving wide range of clients. All consultants are principals with direct involvement in the search. Many years of experience in IS search.

Key Contact - Specialty:
Mr. Ken Gross, Managing Director

Salary Minimum: $75,000

Functions: IT, MIS Mgmt., Systems Dev., Systems Implem., Systems Support, DB Admin.

Industries: Generalist (All)

Branches:
24 Lyons Pl Ste 206
Westwood, NJ 07675-1819
(201) 358-1300
Fax: (201) 664-0693
Email: cmonte@dsninc.com
Key Contact - Specialty:
Ms. Claire Monte, Vice President, Northeast Region

The DataFinders Group® Inc

25 E Spring Valley Ave Ste 300
Maywood, NJ 07607-2150
(201) 845-7700
Fax: (201) 845-7365
Email: info@datafinders.net
Web: www.datafinders.net

Summary: A search firm specializing in the IT/data/tele-processing & healthcare industries in sales, sales management, marketing, field support and traditional end-user staff consulting/technical/programming positions on both a permanent and temp basis.

Key Contact - Specialty:
Mr. Thomas J. Credidio, Vice President
Mr. Peter A. Warns, President

Salary Minimum: $25,000

Functions: Sales & Mktg., Mktg. Mgmt., Sales Mgmt., IT, Network Admin.

Industries: Drugs Mfg., Medical Devices, Computer Equip., Pharm Svcs., Mgmt. Consulting, IT Implementation, Telecoms, Call Centers, Software, Database SW, ERP SW, HR SW, Networking, Comm. SW, Security SW, System SW, Healthcare

Branches:
4813 Hanging Moss Ln
Sarasota, FL 34238-3314
(941) 926-1181
Email: info@datafinders.net
Key Contact - Specialty:
Ms. Marilyn Marconi, Regional Manager

Datamatics Management Services Inc

330 New Brunswick Ave
Fords, NJ 08863-2230
(732) 738-9600
(732) 738-8500
Fax: (732) 738-9603
Email: nch@datamaticsinc.com
Web: www.datamaticsinc.com

Summary: Specialists in service related industries, general management, HR, data processing, IS, labor relations and training. Placement concerns center on organization fit within existing management structures, evaluating job requirements and formulation position specifications.

Key Contact - Specialty:
Mr. Norman C. Heinle, Jr., President
Mr. R. Kevin Heinle, Vice President

Salary Minimum: $75,000

Functions: Generalist (All)

Industries: Generalist (All)

Dataware Consulting Inc

78 De Quincy Blvd
North York, ON M3H 1Y7
Canada
(416) 784-4322
Email: it@datawareconsulting.com
Web: www.datawareconsulting.com

Summary: We provide contract, permanent and temp IT personnel ranging from junior programmers to VP level managers, including system administrators, database administrators, network engineers, hardware engineers, business analysts, architects, programmer & system analysts, tech support/help desk analysts, testers, technical writers and trainers.

Key Contact - Specialty:
Mr. Eric Eivin

Functions: Management, IT, Systems Analysis, Systems Dev., Systems Implem., Systems Support, Network Admin., DB Admin.

Industries: Generalist (All)

Alan N Daum & Associates Inc

6241 Riverside Dr
Dublin, OH 43017-5068
(614) 793-1200
(800) 933-3002
Fax: (614) 766-9644
Email: info@adaum.com
Web: www.adaum.com

Summary: Experience recruiting only process control engineers. We have a database of thousands of process control engineers.

Key Contact - Specialty:
Mr. Alan N. Daum, President

Salary Minimum: $55,000

Functions: Automation

Industries: Energy, Utilities, Manufacturing, Food, Bev., Tobacco, Paper, Chemicals, Soap, Perf., Cosmtcs., Drugs Mfg., Plastics, Rubber, Paints, Petro. Products, Test, Measure Equip.

Davco Resources LLC

PO Box 984
Voorhees, NJ 08043-0984
(856) 719-9100
Fax: (732) 783-0219
Email: info@davcoresources.com
Web: www.davcoresources.com

Summary: We are a healthcare recruitment firm servicing clients that provide products or services to hospitals, physician offices, veterinary, biotechnology and life science markets. Positions include all levels of sales & marketing, scientific, regulatory, logistics, senior and executive levels.

Key Contact - Specialty:
Ms. Nancy Davis, Principal

Salary Minimum: $50,000

Functions: Senior Mgmt., Sales & Mktg.

Industries: Biotech/Life Sciences, Healthcare, Hospitals

Branches:
99 Simms Dr
Annapolis, MD 21401-2262
(410) 268-7780
Key Contact - Specialty:
Mrs. Terry Reno-Benda

The David Wood Company

PO Box 87875
Vancouver, WA 98687-7875
(360) 260-0979
Fax: (360) 253-5292
Email: dwood@powerindustrycareers.com
Web: www.powerindustrycareers.com

Summary: Specialize in recruiting talent for the power generation industry.

Key Contact - Specialty:
Mr. David Wood, CPC, President

Functions: Generalist (All)

Industries: Energy, Utilities

Davidson, Laird & Associates Inc

29260 Franklin Rd Apt 418
Southfield, MI 48034-1197
(248) 358-2160
Email: meri@davidson-laird.com

Summary: We have an excellent reputation for long-term retention of our candidates with our clients. We attribute that to our team approach to matching and full-service placement with our clients. We service the automotive industry.

Key Contact - Specialty:
Ms. Meri Laird Jones, President - *Automotive*
Ms. Lori Laird, Managing Partner - *Engineering, Manufacturing*

Salary Minimum: $55,000

Functions: Generalist (All), Product Dev., Production, Automation, Plant Mgmt., Quality, Purchasing, Engineering, Process

Industries: Generalist (All), Plastics, Rubber, Motor Vehicles

Branches:
14406 Willow Grove Cir
Louisville, KY 40245-5160
(502) 749-4480
Key Contact - Specialty:
Ms. Meri Laird

DaVinci International Inc

24 E Greenway Plz Ste 1110
Houston, TX 77046-2412
(713) 439-0400
Fax: (713) 439-7489

Email: sharon.berglund@dvii.net
Web: www.dvii.net

Summary: We are a human capital management firm that has recognized that our corporate clients' success depends on the ability to secure highly specialized human capital for projects that have significant shareholder value. We place key members of management as both permanent additions and consultants who work on mission critical projects.

Key Contact - Specialty:
Ms. Sharon Berglund, Partner - *Financial*
Mr. Steven Tatar, Partner - *Tax*

Salary Minimum: $75,000

Functions: Finance

Industries: Energy, Utilities, Manufacturing

T A Davis & Associates Inc

604 Green Bay Rd
Kenilworth, IL 60043-1052
(847) 256-8900
Fax: (847) 256-8955
Email: lynnr@tadavis.com
Web: www.tadavis.com

Summary: Specializing in executive search in the restaurant, hotel, resort, and food service industries.

Key Contact - Specialty:
Mr. Thomas Davis, President

Salary Minimum: $60,000

Functions: Generalist (All)

Industries: Hospitality, Hotels, Resorts, Clubs, Restaurants, Quick Service Restaurants, Full Service Restaurants, Inst./Industrial Food Svc., Entertainment, Recreation, Sports, Travel

Dawn Davis & Associates

227 N Swall Dr
Beverly Hills, CA 90211-1712
(310) 271-4000
Fax: (310) 279-1112
Email: info@dawndavissearch.com
Web: www.dawndavissearch.com

Summary: Attorney search firm handling permanent placements of groups, partners and associates. We guide attorneys towards their career goals and assist firms in finding the best candidates. Our consultative philosophy emphasizes our ability to treat each candidate and each search uniquely; with genuine interest and focus.

Key Contact - Specialty:
Ms. Dawn Davis, President
Ms. Sigal McCarley, Recruiter

Functions: Attorneys

Industries: Generalist (All)

Carolyn Davis Associates Inc

70 W Red Oak Ln
White Plains, NY 10604-3602
(914) 697-7540
Email: careers@carolyndavis.net
Web: www.carolyndavis.net

Summary: We specialize in the recruitment and placement of property & casualty, life, health and pension professionals. Our commitment to excellence combined with integrity, respect for confidentiality, experience and knowledge of the insurance industry assures a successful search.

Key Contact - Specialty:
Ms. Carolyn Davis, CPC, President

Functions: Generalist (All)

Industries: Insurance, Casualty, Claims, Life, Commercial, Re-Insurance

Donna Davis Associates

2050 Center Ave Ste 550
Fort Lee, NJ 07024-4911
(201) 592-6000
Fax: (201) 592-5961
Email: donna@donnadavis.com
Web: www.donnadavisassociates.com

Summary: We are a recruiting firm exclusively dedicated to placing mid and senior-level human resources professionals.

Key Contact - Specialty:
Ms. Donna Davis, President - *Human resources*

Salary Minimum: $50,000

Functions: Generalist (All), Senior Mgmt., Middle Mgmt., HR Mgmt., Benefits, Staffing, Training

Industries: Generalist (All), HR Services

Davis O'Neill & Ross Search Partners

830 S Knight Ave
Park Ridge, IL 60068-4441
(847) 692-2255
Fax: (847) 692-2256
Email: rgullo@search-partners.net
Web: www.search-partners.net

Summary: We serve law firms and corporations in securing partners, practice groups and experienced attorneys. We focus on identifying our clients' specific needs based on their growth objective and we fulfill those needs with established lawyers who have proven history of success. Specific and focused, we seek out, recruit and place partners and practice groups with portable business.

Key Contact - Specialty:
Mr. Ross Gullo, Partner
Mr. Michael Davis, Partner - *Legal, Legal (Attorneys)*

Salary Minimum: $1,000,000

Functions: Board Members

Industries: Non-profits, Legal

Branches:
3211 Red Oak Dr
Eagan, MN 55121-2337
(651) 330-9028
Email: joneil@search-partners.net
Key Contact - Specialty:
Mr. John O'Neill, Esq., Partner

Bert Davis Publishing Placement Consultants

425 Madison Ave Fl 14
New York, NY 10017-1110
(212) 838-4000
Fax: (212) 935-3291
Email: info@bertdavis.com
Web: www.bertdavis.com

Summary: A leading executive placement firm specializing in publishing, publication communication, information and electronic media fields.

Key Contact - Specialty:
Ms. Wendy Baker, Senior Vice President
Mr. Larry Eidelberg, Senior Vice President - *Technology*
Ms. Linda Rascher, Vice President - *Financial*

Salary Minimum: $50,000

Functions: Generalist (All), Management, Senior Mgmt., Product Dev., Sales & Mktg., Finance, IT

Industries: Generalist (All), Advertising, Publishing, New Media, Software

Davis-Burns Group

900 Old Roswell Lakes Pkwy Ste 130
Roswell, GA 30076-8664
(770) 650-0056
Fax: (770) 650-5960
Email: resumes@davis-burns.com
Web: www.davis-burns.com

Summary: We are a full service corporate placement firm. Some industry specifics include construction, manufacturing, automotive, accounting, legal, property management and IT.

Key Contact - Specialty:
Ms. Lori Burns, President

Salary Minimum: $65,000

Functions: Management, Admin. Svcs., Mfg., Production, HR Mgmt., Finance, IT

Industries: Generalist (All), Printing, Medical Devices, Metal Products, Misc. Mfg., HR SW, Mfg. SW, Biotech/Life Sciences

Paul Day & Associates (TM)

5020 Celbridge Pl
Raleigh, NC 27613-6206
(919) 845-3307
Fax: (919) 846-8782
Email: pda@nc.rr.com
Web: www.pauldayassociates.com

Summary: An executive search and technical recruiting firm, specializing in recruiting engineers and executives for industries in engineering/information technology/aerospace/aircraft.

Key Contact - Specialty:
Mr. Paul Gomez, President - *Accounting, Administration, Aerospace, Communications, Engineering*
Ms. Donna Day, Vice President - *Administration, Computers (Software), Engineering*

Salary Minimum: $40,000

Functions: Mfg., IT, Engineering

Industries: Energy, Utilities, Computer Equip., Misc. Mfg., Robotics, Semiconductors, Consumer Goods, Telecoms, Digital, Wireless, Network Infrastructure, Government, Defense, Aerospace, Software, Development SW, Industry Specific SW, Networking, Comm. SW, System SW

DCA Professional Search

175 Georgian Dr
Coppell, TX 75019-6281
(214) 626-0149
Fax: (972) 745-1616
Email: info@dcaprosearch.com
Web: www.dcaprosearch.com

Summary: Executive search firm specializing in the area of Hispanic and advertising professionals in all areas of an advertising agency such as: account services, media, creative, promotions, account planning, research and public relations. In addition we also specialize in Hispanic marketing professionals on the client side for every industry. We also offer outplacement services at all levels.

Key Contact - Specialty:
Ms. Doris Aguirre, President

Salary Minimum: $40,000

Functions: Board Members, Middle Mgmt., Advertising, Mktg. Mgmt., PR, Minorities/Diversity

Industries: Advertising

DDS Resources Inc

207 Chesterfield Towne Ctr
Chesterfield, MO 63005-1257
(636) 536-6653
(877) 337-0563
Fax: (636) 536-6667
Email: info@ddsresources.com
Web: www.ddsresources.com

Summary: We are a nationwide dental recruitment firm specializing in the placement of dentists. We specialize in finding full-time practice opportunities for dentists throughout the United States. We are experienced dental consultants who will work closely with candidates throughout the entire job-hunting process. We offer complete recruitment solutions for both employers and the professionals.

Key Contact - Specialty:
Ms. Krista Holloway, Recruiter

Functions: Generalist (All)

Industries: Healthcare, Dental

The Deacon Group

8155 Annsbury Dr Ste 101
Shelby Township, MI 48316-1913
(586) 992-9700
Fax: (586) 992-9723
Email: main@deacongroup.com
Web: www.deacongroup.com

Summary: We are committed to finding the top candidates in IT (pre and post sales only) and sales for the enterprise software vendor environment. Our staff has the experience to serve both clients and candidates. But our distinguished tradition is in providing career solutions that fit.

Key Contact - Specialty:
Mr. Robert Drohan, President - *Sales*
Ms. Patti Schmidt, Senior Account Executive - *Sales*
Ms. Sandra J. Casey, Director, Internet Strategies - *Accounting (Bookkeeping), Computers (Software)*

Salary Minimum: $80,000

Functions: Senior Mgmt., Sales Mgmt.

Industries: IT Implementation, Supply Chain Mgmt, Software, Database SW, ERP SW, Industry Specific SW, Mfg. SW, Security SW, System SW

Affiliates:
Avant Solutions Inc
Decatur, AL

Tonia Deal Consultants Inc

77 Milford Dr
Hudson, OH 44236-2781
(330) 655-3610
Email: gregallen@tdcsupplychain.com
Web: www.toniadealconsultants.com

Summary: Premiere Recruiting Firm in supply chain management, purchasing/procurement, logistics and executive operations nationwide.

Key Contact - Specialty:
Mr. Greg Allen, Manager, Recruiting - *Logistics, Procurement, Purchasing, Six Sigma, Supply Chain*

Salary Minimum: $75,000

Functions: Materials, Purchasing, Materials Plng., Distribution

Industries: Generalist (All)

Deare & Associates Inc

7760 France Ave S Ste 1100
Minneapolis, MN 55435-5930
(952) 403-9700
Email: info@deare.com
Web: www.deare.com

Summary: Our reputation is a result of our exclusive working relationships with our highly valued clients and our successful acquisitions of top performing executives. Professionalism, confidentiality, integrity, commitment and results orientation are the foundation of our search process and the building blocks of our business relationships.

Key Contact - Specialty:
Mr. Richard Deare, President

Functions: Senior Mgmt., Middle Mgmt., Sales Mgmt., Sales Reps., HR Mgmt., Staffing, IT, Mgmt. Consultants

Industries: Generalist (All), Retail, Services, HR Services, IT Implementation, Hospitality, Communications, Software, Biotech/Life Sciences, Healthcare

Debbon Recruiting Group Inc

PO Box 510323
Saint Louis, MO 63151-0323
(314) 846-9101
Email: debbongroup@earthlink.net

Summary: Recruiting specialization in technical, a staff and line management position for food and pharmaceutical industries has resulted in industry wide contacts allowing for timely response to individual situations.

Key Contact - Specialty:
Mr. John Zipfel, President - *Food, Pharmaceutical*

Salary Minimum: $40,000

Functions: Mfg., Plant Mgmt., Quality, Materials, HR Mgmt., Engineering

Industries: Food, Bev., Tobacco, Chemicals, Soap, Perf., Cosmtcs., Drugs Mfg.

DeBellis Catherine & Morreale

350 Essjay Rd Ste 302
Williamsville, NY 14221-8200
(716) 632-1500
Fax: (716) 632-8844
Email: mdebellis@dcmstaffing.com
Web: www.dcmstaffing.com

Summary: We are a search firm covering the professional areas of: accounting/finance, banking, insurance, sales/marketing, engineering/manufacturing, food manufacturing, HR, healthcare, construction management, legal and IT. We represent companies of every size. Most of our searches are engaged on a partial retained basis.

Key Contact - Specialty:
Mr. Michael DeBellis, Jr., Partner

Salary Minimum: $50,000

Functions: Generalist (All), Management, Admin. Svcs., Mfg., Nurses, Sales & Mktg., Sales Mgmt., HR Mgmt., Finance, IT

Industries: Generalist (All), Construction, Manufacturing, Food, Bev., Tobacco, Printing, Chemicals, Medical Devices, Plastics, Rubber, Test, Measure Equip., Electronic, Elec. Components, Finance, Banking, Legal, Accounting, Environmental Svcs., Packaging, Insurance, Software, Biotech/Life Sciences, Healthcare, Hospitals, Long-term/Home Care, Physical Therapy, Occupational Therapy

DEC Health Care Personnel

(also known as AMDG Inc)
2555 E Chapman Ave Ste 210
Fullerton, CA 92831-3617
(714) 681-7430
Fax: (714) 681-7431
Email: info@decpersonnel.com
Web: www.decpersonnel.com

Summary: Staffing and recruitment exclusively for the medical industry specializing in: management, x-ray (CRT & Ltd), insurance billing/collection, medical assistants (F/O & B/O), nurses (clinical & administrative: RN & LVN), etc. Experienced & certified placement recruiters including the 2006 CSP Orange County Staffing Professional of the Year!

Key Contact - Specialty:
Miss Angelica Arias, CAC, CSP, Placement Recruiter - *Clinical, Dental, Healthcare, Hospital, Medical*
Ms. Faith Sparks, Administrative Manager - *Administration, Dental, Healthcare, Human resources, Medical*
Mrs. Christy Mora, CAC, Placement Recruiter - *Clinical, Dental, Healthcare, HMOs, Medical*

Functions: Management, Middle Mgmt., Admin. Svcs., Healthcare, Nurses, Allied Health, Health Admin., Sales & Mktg., Sales Reps., HR Mgmt.

Industries: Biotech/Life Sciences, Healthcare, Hospitals, Long-term/Home Care, Dental, Physical Therapy, Occupational Therapy, Women's

Branches:
5301 S Superstition Mountain Dr Ste 104 PMB 36
Gold Canyon, AZ 85218-1917
(866) 681-7430
Email: dskullr@decpersonnel.com
Key Contact - Specialty:
Ms. Diane Skullr, CTS

DeCaster Associates

1346 Wren Ln
Green Bay, WI 54313-6402
(920) 499-6005
Fax: (920) 499-6023
Email: pdecaster@sbcglobal.net

Summary: We offer professional search and recruiting services for corporations and law firms. Focused in experienced attorneys (all practice areas) and executive management.

Key Contact - Specialty:
Mr. Paul DeCaster, Principal

Salary Minimum: $75,000

Functions: Legal

Industries: Generalist (All)

Dedeke & Associates

9319 S Vandalia Ave
Tulsa, OK 74137-3703
(918) 491-1181
Fax: (918) 491-9989
Email: bdedeke@dedekeandassociates.com
Web: www.dedekeandassociates.com

Summary: We are an executive search firm that offers professional search services carefully targeted to the specific needs of our clients. We specialize in middle to senior management searches but often perform searches in technical disciplines as requested by our clients. We have over 30 years of search experience. We specialize in identifying high potential, proactive executives, managers and practitioners who can bring added value to your organization.

Key Contact - Specialty:
Mr. Bob Dedeke, Principal - *Senior management*

Salary Minimum: $60,000

Functions: Generalist (All), Management

Industries: Generalist (All), Oil & Gas, Plastics, Rubber, Metal Products, Machine, Appliance, Consumer Elect., Architectural Svcs., Accounting, Haz. Waste, Aerospace

Deeco International

PO Box 57033
Salt Lake City, UT 84157-0033
(801) 261-3326
(800) 742-8219
Fax: (801) 261-3955
Email: deecoinc@att.net
Web: www.deecointernational.com

Summary: Specialize in the medical and pharmaceutical industries.

Key Contact - Specialty:
Ms. Dee McBride, President
Miss Tammy McBride, Executive Recruiter - *Pharmaceutical, Sales*

Functions: Generalist (All), Senior Mgmt., Middle Mgmt., Product Dev., Mktg. Research, Mktg. Mgmt., Sales Mgmt., R&D

Industries: Generalist (All), Drugs Mfg., Medical Devices, Computer Equip., Pharm Svcs., Biotech/Life Sciences, Healthcare

Defense Recruiters LLC

46 W Culver St
Phoenix, AZ 85003-1228
(866) 205-1257
(602) 263-7805
Fax: (602) 234-7937
Email: cz@defenserecruiters.com
Web: www.defenserecruiters.com

Summary: We specialize in the global search and placement of defense and security professionals. We are experts in counterintelligence and counterterrorism. The majority of our candidates possess active security clearances issued by the Department of Defense and work within the US Intelligence community. We place contractors as well as candidates seeking permanent positions in the public and private sectors.

Key Contact - Specialty:
Ms. Claudia Zwick, President

Salary Minimum: $90,000

Functions: Management, Middle Mgmt., Sales & Mktg., Mktg. Mgmt., Sales Reps., IT, Mgmt. Consultants, Homeland Security

Industries: Mgmt. Consulting, Government, Defense, Homeland Security, Environmental Svcs., Aerospace, Industry Specific SW, Security SW, System SW

DEL Technical Services Inc

310 S Hale St
Wheaton, IL 60187-5220
(630) 588-3000
Fax: (630) 588-0333
Email: coneill@deltech.com
Web: www.deltech.com

Summary: Skill match, a proven process used to match the critical success factors of your ideal candidate with over 100,000 personnel that are not in the job market.

Key Contact - Specialty:
Mr. Chris O'Neill, President - *Technical, Technicians*
Mr. Kristen O'Neill, Recruiter - *Physicians*

Salary Minimum: $25,000

Functions: Generalist (All), Production, IT, Engineering, Specialized Svcs., Technicians

Industries: Generalist (All), Energy, Utilities, Construction, Manufacturing, Haz. Waste, Software

Delacore Resources

116 Oak Ln SE Ste 101
Hutchinson, MN 55350-3239
(320) 587-4420
(800) 967-2711
Fax: (320) 587-7252
Email: delacore@hutchtel.net
Web: www.mnrecruiter.com

Summary: Our firm has two divisions, physician recruiting (including most subspecialty areas) and allied healthcare professions.

Key Contact - Specialty:
Mr. Verne Meyer, Principal
Ms. Dianne Pasco, Recruiter

Salary Minimum: $70,000

Functions: Healthcare, Physicians

Industries: Healthcare

DeLacy & Associates

346 Ironwood Cir
Roseville, CA 95678-1056
(916) 773-1981
Fax: (916) 773-6497
Email: lacyde@surewest.net
Web: www.delacyassociates.net

Summary: Executive recruiting firm specializing in pharmaceutical, biotechnology, and medical device sales.

Key Contact - Specialty:
Mr. Bruna DeLacy, Principal - *Biotechnology, Medical (Devices), Pharmaceutical*

Functions: Healthcare

Industries: Medical Devices, Pharm Svcs., Biotech/Life Sciences

DeLalla - Fried Associates

279 E 44th St Apt 12J
New York, NY 10017-4308
(212) 370-4031
Email: delallafried@aol.com

Summary: We are a boutique firm specializing in the consumer packaged goods and cosmetic industries. We offer contingency and retained searches. The firm provides executive talent on a full time basis. Two divisions: one dedicated to consumer packaged goods and H&BA, one dedicated to cosmetic and H&BA.

Key Contact - Specialty:
Ms. Barbara DeLalla, Partner - *Consumer (Packaged Goods)*

Salary Minimum: $60,000

Functions: Product Dev., Sales & Mktg., Mktg. Research, Mktg. Mgmt., PR

Industries: Food, Bev., Tobacco, Soap, Perf., Cosmtcs., Consumer Goods

Branches:
201 E 77th St Apt 4D
New York, NY 10021-2081
(212) 249-8635
Email: annfrieddf@aol.com

Key Contact - Specialty:
Ms. Ann Fried, Partner - *Cosmetics*

Delta Crown Executive Search

PO Box 1779
Sequim, WA 98382-1779
(360) 681-5238
Fax: (360) 681-5199
Email: frank@deltacrownsearch.com
Web: www.deltacrownsearch.com

Summary: Searches focusing on all disciplines related to commercial real estate development, ownership and management. We serve retail and hospitality chains, office and industrial property owners, developers, general contracting/engineering firms, A&E firms, REITs, asset/property management firms, etc.

Key Contact - Specialty:
Mr. Frank Willett, President

Functions: Management, Architects, Bldg. Contractors, Attorneys

Industries: Wholesale, Retail, Architectural Svcs., Hospitality, Hotels, Resorts, Clubs, Restaurants, Quick Service Restaurants, Full Service Restaurants, Real Estate, Property/Facility Mgmt.

Delta Medical Search Associates

844 Brookpark Rd
Marion, OH 43302-6812
(614) 878-0550
Email: associates@deltasearch.com
Web: www.deltasearch.com

Summary: We provide recruitment of administrative, management and advanced clinical positions for hospitals, cancer centers, clinics and private practices. We specialize in oncology including physicists, dosimetrists, nurse practitioners, CNSs, oncology administrators. Each of our account executives has a medical background to better understand and service your needs.

Key Contact - Specialty:
Ms. Marilyn Wallace, CPC, PRC, President - *Healthcare, Hospital, Physicians*

Salary Minimum: $65,000

Functions: Senior Mgmt., Middle Mgmt., Healthcare, Physicians, Nurses, Allied Health, Health Admin.

Industries: Healthcare, Hospitals

Delta ProSearch

PO Box 267
Delta, PA 17314-0267
(717) 456-7172
(800) 753-6693
Fax: (717) 456-7593
Email: jobs@deltaprosearch.com
Web: www.deltaprosearch.com

Summary: We are experienced healthcare professionals with a good knowledge of the industry. Our high standards emphasize quality service, choice referrals and client satisfaction. We specialize in pharmaceutical and other allied healthcare recruiting.

Key Contact - Specialty:
Mr. John Banister, Jr., President

Salary Minimum: $50,000

Functions: Healthcare, Allied Health

Industries: Pharm Svcs., Hospitals

Delta Staffing

6100 Dixie Hwy Ste B
Clarkston, MI 48346-3496
(866) 3933582
(248) 623-6696
Email: brad@delta-staffing.com
Web: delta-staffing.com

Summary: Our firm invented a precision hiring system based on the principles of Six Sigma, and our results speak for themselves. Our staff of expert recruiters is up to any task.

Key Contact - Specialty:
Mr. Brad McKouen, President
Mr. Nick Gudowski, Senior Recruiter - *Design, Electrical, Engineering, Mechanical, Technicians*

Salary Minimum: $50,000

Functions: Generalist (All), Engineering

Industries: Plastics, Rubber, Electronic, Elec. Components, Robotics, Transportation

DeMatteo Associates

PO Box 13955
Albany, NY 12212-3955
(800) 477-8158
(518) 867-3900
Email: rob@dematteoassociates.com
Web: www.dematteoassociates.com

Summary: Nationwide Professional Search & Placement Services in Engineering, Manufacturing, Sales, Marketing and Management.

Key Contact - Specialty:
Ms. Robena DeMatteo, CSAM, President - *Sales*
Mr. Robert Natowitz, Executive Recruiter - *Paper, Plastics*
Mr. Ryan Flatt, Manager, Research

Functions: Board Members, Mfg., R&D, Engineering

Industries: Manufacturing, Paper, Printing, Drugs Mfg., Medical Devices, Plastics, Rubber, Metal Products, Pharm Svcs., Engineering Svcs., New Media, Defense, Packaging, Software

Denson & Associates Inc

1007 Main St
Bastrop, TX 78602-3396
(512) 321-5979
Email: mike@densonsearch.com
Web: www.densonsearch.com

Summary: Provide search services primarily to the exploration and production industry - management, operations, geoscience, engineering and R&D.

Key Contact - Specialty:
Ms. Jennifer Dowell - *Food*

Salary Minimum: $75,000

Functions: Generalist (All), Middle Mgmt., Production, Plant Mgmt., R&D, Engineering, Mgmt. Consultants, Int'l.

Industries: Generalist (All), Energy, Utilities

Branches:
819 Merrick Dr
Sugar Land, TX 77478-3743
(281) 494-2130
(281) 997-6875
Email: jeff@densonsearch.com

Key Contact - Specialty:
Mr. Mike Denson, President

Deosystems LLC
21 Candlewyck Ter
Portland, ME 04102-1515
(207) 879-1039
Fax: (207) 879-1045
Email: info@deosystems.com
Web: www.deosystems.com

Summary: We help clients achieve their corporate goals by effectively fulfilling their staffing needs on a contingency, retained or project basis. Our focus is on life sciences markets. We concentrate on placing regulatory, quality control and assurance, scientist and clinical trials professionals.

Key Contact - Specialty:
Mr. Ed de Oliveira, Founder
Mr. Dana Costigan, Recruiter

Salary Minimum: $50,000

Functions: Healthcare

Industries: Biotech/Life Sciences

Mee Derby & Company
4836 Rugby Ave
Bethesda, MD 20814-3019
(301) 656-3555
(800) 633-3372
Fax: (301) 320-7786
Email: recruiters@meederby.com
Web: www.meederby.com

Summary: We are an established, executive search firm specializing in placing professionals in staffing, professional services and human capital outsourcing.

Key Contact - Specialty:
Ms. Robin Mee, President - *Professional services*
Ms. Eliza Deang, Manager, Recruiting
Ms. Cindy Hall, Executive Recruiter, South East Region - *Healthcare, Hospital, Marketing, Medical, Physicians*
Ms. Lori Siets, Executive Recruiter, Western Region - *Healthcare, Hospital, Marketing, Medical, Physicians*
Ms. Betsy Grady, Executive Recruiter, Mid Atlantic Region - *Healthcare, Hospital, Marketing, Medical, Physicians*
Mr. Brooks Stockmon, Executive Recruiter, North East Region - *Healthcare, Hospital, Marketing, Medical, Physicians*
Ms. Alyse Parrino, Executive Recruiter, Western Region - *Healthcare, Hospital, Marketing, Medical, Physicians*

Functions: Senior Mgmt., Middle Mgmt., Sales Mgmt., Sales Reps., Staffing, IT

Industries: Services, Mgmt. Consulting, HR Services, E-commerce, IT Implementation

Descheneaux Insurance Recruiters Ltd
503-570 Granville St
Vancouver, BC V6C 3P1
Canada
(604) 669-9787
Fax: (604) 688-2130
Email: info@insuranceheadhunters.com
Web: www.insuranceheadhunters.com

Summary: A placement agency catering exclusively to the insurance industry, recruiting and hiring at all levels of executive, technical, sales and support staff. We bring talent and opportunity together.

Key Contact - Specialty:
Ms. Pat Descheneaux, President - *Insurance (Casualty,Claims,Health,Life,Reinsurance)*
Ms. Tiffany Chiu, Recruiter - *Insurance, Insurance (Casualty,Claims,Health,Reinsurance)*
Ms. Hayley Martin, Executive Assistant - *Insurance (Casualty,Claims,Health,Life,Reinsurance)*

Functions: Generalist (All)

Industries: Insurance

Design Profiles
1133 4th St
Sarasota, FL 34236-4870
(941) 330-2288
Email: info@designprofiles.com

Summary: We deliver the right people to those companies on the cutting-edge in the apparel, textile and home furnishing industries. Our proven track record is built upon a foundation of experience in the retail, mail order and wholesale markets.

Key Contact - Specialty:
Ms. Cheryl Burns-Noble, Owner

Salary Minimum: $50,000

Functions: Eng. Design

Industries: Textiles, Apparel

Devoto & Associates Inc
303 Twin Dolphin Dr Ste 600
San Carlos, CA 94065-1422
(650) 593-8205
(650) 632-4424
Fax: (650) 593-8206
Email: admin@devotoassociates.com
Web: www.devotoassociates.com

Summary: We specialize in placing sales & marketing professionals in software and internet related companies.

Key Contact - Specialty:
Ms. Andrea Devoto, Founder
Mr. Jeffrey Devoto, MBA, Managing Director

Salary Minimum: $100,000

Functions: Sales & Mktg., Mktg. Mgmt., Sales Mgmt.

Industries: Wireless, Network Infrastructure, Software, Database SW, Development SW, ERP SW, HR SW, Industry Specific SW, Networking, Comm. SW, Security SW, System SW

DFG Executive Search
269 Hamilton St #1
Worcester, MA 01604-2208
(508) 754-3451
Fax: (508) 754-1367
Email: delores.george@verizon.net
Web: www.dfgexecutivesearch.com

Summary: We staff positions that embrace virtually every discipline in the business organization.

Key Contact - Specialty:
Ms. Delores F. George, CPC, Owner & Executive Recruiter - *Engineering, Storage, Systems*

Functions: Generalist (All), Management, IT, MIS Mgmt., Systems Analysis, Systems Dev., Systems Implem., Engineering

Industries: Generalist (All), Medical Devices, Electronic, Elec. Components, Pharm Svcs., Accounting, Mgmt. Consulting, Engineering Svcs., Fiber Optic, Network Infrastructure, RF/Microwave, Networking, Comm. SW

D G A Personnel
2691 E Oakland Park Blvd Ste 201
Fort Lauderdale, FL 33306-1658
(954) 561-1771
Fax: (954) 561-1772
Email: dgagroup@aol.com
Web: www.dgagroup.com

Summary: A specialty is providing bilingual and multilingual candidates (on any level) able to travel to Latin America for operations based in South Florida. Our client base is comprised mainly of Fortune 500 and large to mid-sized private companies.

Key Contact - Specialty:
Mr. David Grant, President - *Finance*
Mr. Paul Brown, Vice President - *Sales*

Salary Minimum: $50,000

Functions: Int'l.

Industries: Manufacturing, Drugs Mfg., Medical Devices, Plastics, Rubber, Finance, Banking, Accounting, HR Services

Dialogue Consulting Group
782 Bayliss Dr Ste C
Marietta, GA 30068-4707
(770) 579-6050
(770) 579-5557
Fax: (240) 536-4072
Email: resumes@dcghire.com
Web: www.softwarerecruiter.com

Summary: From the beginning, we have specialized as software sales recruiters. For those executive candidates outside our market segment, we provide paid direct representation. We also provide both print and seminar versions of our proprietary marketing strategy program for transition candidates as part of a series.

Key Contact - Specialty:
Mr. Bruce Dreyfus, Managing Partner - *Computers (Software), Sales*

Salary Minimum: $75,000

Functions: Generalist (All), Sales & Mktg., Sales Mgmt.

Industries: Mgmt. Consulting, Software, Accounting SW, Database SW, Doc. Mgmt., Production SW, ERP SW, HR SW, Industry Specific SW, Mfg. SW, Marketing SW, Security SW

Dialogue Partners Inc
119 S Main St Ste 500
Memphis, TN 38103-3659
(901) 726-9800
(901) 219-3387
Fax: (901) 726-9803
Email: mbruno@dialoguepartners.com
Web: www.dialoguepartners.com

Summary: We are a boutique recruiting and consulting firm serving the contact center/customer care industry. We help HR professionals and hiring authorities in call centers and related organizations nationwide identify and hire high performing, specialized talent for key management positions throughout the enterprise.

Key Contact - Specialty:
Mr. Michael Bruno, Managing Principal

Salary Minimum: $75,000

Functions: Generalist (All)

Industries: Call Centers

Diamond Management Consultants

10051 Weathersfield Dr
Mentor, OH 44060-6843
(440) 358-1572
(440) 358-1570
Email: jillross@sap-dmc.com
Web: www.dmcjobs.com

Summary: We are a recruitment firm specializing in the permanent and contract placement of technical and managerial professionals. Our areas of expertise envelope the manufacturing sectors including automotive and general manufacturing. We also recruit in the high-technology sectors as well as the consumer product industries.

Key Contact - Specialty:
Ms. Jill Ross, President - *Automotive, High technology, Manufacturing, Quality*
Mr. David Wible, Director, Recruitment - *Aerospace, Automotive, Capital goods, Information Technology, Machining*

Salary Minimum: $55,000

Functions: Generalist (All), Engineering

Industries: Generalist (All), Manufacturing, Medical Devices, Motor Vehicles, Engineering Svcs., Supply Chain Mgmt, Government, Defense

Diamond Tax Recruiting

488 Fashion Ave Ph 12F
New York, NY 10018-6809
(212) 695-4220
Fax: (212) 695-4053
Email: steven@diamondtax.com
Web: diamondtax.com

Summary: Provision of contingency and retained search experience with a specialization within the tax profession. We have had a demonstrated record of success while maintaining the highest degree of professionalism.

Key Contact - Specialty:
Mr. Steven Hunter, President

Salary Minimum: $75,000

Functions: Taxes

Industries: Generalist (All)

DiBari & Associates

10113 San Remo Pl
Wake Forest, NC 27587-1622
(919) 303-5222
Fax: (866) 362-9800
Email: career@dibari.net
Web: www.dibari.net

Summary: We are a staffing and consulting firm specializing in the recruiting and placement of healthcare and advanced technology professionals. We are proven leaders in high-technology executive search. We are an innovative and progressive executive search firm representing high profile companies. We are a state-of-the-art company utilizing automated databases and an extensive, continually updated candidate database.

Key Contact - Specialty:
Mr. Francis DiBari, Executive Director - *Healthcare, Information Technology, Medical, Medical (Devices), Physicians*
Ms. Bettina Candelore, Managing Partner

Salary Minimum: $50,000

Functions: Senior Mgmt., Healthcare, Physicians, Sales Mgmt., MIS Mgmt.

Industries: Medical Devices, Computer Equip., IT Implementation, Communications, Telecoms,

Software, Security SW, Biotech/Life Sciences, Healthcare, Hospitals, Long-term/Home Care

Diener & Associates Inc

40485 Murrieta Hot Springs Rd Ste 180
Murrieta, CA 92563-6406
(909) 304-9288
Fax: (909) 304-9255
Email: info@dienersearch.com
Web: www.dienersearch.com

Summary: We are an executive search firm that not only fill search positions, we actively find positions for candidates as well. With many years of experience we offer a complete package.

Key Contact - Specialty:
Mr. Joel Diener, President

Salary Minimum: $30,000

Functions: Management, Mfg., Purchasing, Healthcare, Sales & Mktg., Finance, R&D, Engineering, Legal, Int'l.

Industries: Generalist (All), Energy, Utilities, Construction, Media, Communications, Aerospace, Packaging, Insurance, Real Estate, Software, Biotech/Life Sciences

Digital Action Inc

8 E Germantown Pike Ste 200
Plymouth Meeting, PA 19462-1531
(610) 941-0700
(866) 941-0700
Email: kjdiamond@digital-action.com
Web: www.digital-action.com

Summary: Our mission is to help client companies achieve leadership positions within the emerging technology, healthcare and pharmaceutical markets by leveraging our experience and relationships in order to both identify and assist in hiring exceptional individuals.

Key Contact - Specialty:
Mr. Ken Diamond, President
Ms. Cathy Kita, Managing Director
Ms. Leslie McCue, Vice President
Mr. Timothy Cousounis, Vice President, Healthcare Practice
Ms. Jodi Kaelin, Senior Consultant - *Healthcare, Pharmaceutical*

Salary Minimum: $50,000

Functions: Generalist (All)

Industries: Printing, Medical Devices, Pharm Svcs., Mgmt. Consulting, E-commerce, Digital, Packaging, Software, Healthcare, Hospitals

Digital Recruiters Inc

3760 Sixes Rd Ste 126
Canton, GA 30114-8195
(770) 262-8221
(888) 447-3911
Email: admin@digitalrecruiters.com
Web: www.digitalrecruiters.com

Summary: Woman-owned niche firm offering contract/permanent/contingency/retained search to the cable, telecom and high-technology industries. Specialties are delivering the hard-to-find candidate.

Key Contact - Specialty:
Ms. Terri Dewey, Associate Recruiter - *Cable, Call centers, Communications, General management, Technical*
Mr. Mark Pritchett, Associate Recruiter - *Cable, Diversity, New media, Staffing, Wireless*

Salary Minimum: $80,000

Functions: Generalist (All), Management, Staffing, Systems Implem., Technicians

Industries: IT Implementation, Communications, Telecoms, Call Centers, Telephony, Digital, Wireless, Fiber Optic, RF/Microwave, Database SW, Development SW, Industry Specific SW, Networking, Comm. SW, System SW

Branches:
5023 W 120th Ave Ste 262
Broomfield, CO 80020-5606
(888) 447-3911
Email: co.admin@digitalrecruiters.com
Key Contact - Specialty:
Ms. Valerie Hudgins, Director, Technical Recruiting - *Cable, Communications, Engineering, Telecommunications, Wireless*

Dimensional Resources

698 Harvest Rd
Valparaiso, IN 46383-6800
(219) 531-7325
Fax: (219) 531-7326
Email: edjames@netnitco.net
Web: www.dimensionalresources.com

Summary: Full service, retained/contingency, with specialization in the rotational molding process.

Key Contact - Specialty:
Mr. Ed James, Consultant

Functions: Generalist (All)

Industries: Generalist (All), Plastics, Rubber

Dimensions Professional Search

605 Lynndale Ct Ste E
Greenville, NC 27858-5449
(252) 355-7495
Fax: (252) 355-1865
Email: office@ncplastics.com
Web: www.ncplastics.com

Summary: We specialize in plastics/chemicals, more specifically: injection molding, thermoforming, vacuum forming, blow molding, injection blow, extrusion, co-extrusion, sheet, blown film, resins, compounding, technical, engineering, maintenance, production, quality and management.

Key Contact - Specialty:
Mr. Ed Belcher, CPC, Owner & President
Mr. Jeff van Schoyck, CPC, Manager & Senior Consultant
Mr. Ken Goldman, CPC, Senior Consultant
Mr. Rick Hess, Senior Technical Recruiter
Mr. William Paramore, Technical Recruiter - *Engineering, Maintenance, Manufacturing, Plastics, Thermoforming*
Mr. Gene Guernsey, Senior Technical Recruiter

Functions: Mfg., Plant Mgmt.

Industries: Food, Bev., Tobacco, Textiles, Apparel, Plastics, Rubber, Paints, Petro. Products

E P Dine Inc

115 E 57th St Ste 1230
New York, NY 10022-2116
(212) 355-6182
Fax: (212) 755-8486
Email: lbecker@epdine.com
Web: www.epdine.com

Summary: Specializing in the placement of general counsel, partners and other senior legal professionals as well as merger of law firms and practices. Concentrating in major industries including financial, telecom, technology, chemical, advertising, and consumer products.

Key Contact - Specialty:
Ms. Laurie Becker, President
Ms. Melissa Collery

Ms. Rosemary Moukad
Ms. Amy Echelman
Ms. Joanna Davis
Ms. Nancy H. Green, Esq.
Ms. Sandra Leibow, Esq.
Ms. Michele Jawin, Esq.

Functions: Generalist (All), Legal, Attorneys

Industries: Generalist (All), Legal

Direct Guarantee Staffing

494 Longwood Dr.
Buffalo Grove, IL 60089-3225
(847) 215-8812
Fax: (847) 358-7862
Email: denise@directguarantee.com

Summary: Specializing in Marketing mid-upper management within the healthcare, manufacturing and consumer products industries.

Key Contact - Specialty:
Ms. Denise Sage, President

Functions: Management, Admin. Svcs.

Industries: Generalist (All), Food, Bev., Tobacco, Accounting, Hospitality, Advertising, Healthcare

Direct Hire from Bennett Frost

6465 N Palm Ave Ste 101
Fresno, CA 93704-1085
(559) 449-0444
Fax: (559) 449-0457
Email: info@bfps.com
Web: www.bfdirecthire.com

Summary: We have established partnerships with area businesses and industries of all kinds. Our recruiters use a wide variety of resources to attract top-quality candidates to fill the staffing needs of our clients.

Key Contact - Specialty:
Ms. Cathy Frost, President
Ms. Heidi Horton, Recruiter - *Management*
Ms. Kathy Seiler, Area Manager, Human Resources
Mr. Tom Spradling, Controller
Ms. Laura Jackson, Office Manager, Visalia

Functions: Generalist (All)

Industries: Agri., Forestry, Mining, Misc. Mfg., Banking, Non-profits, Legal, Accounting, Mgmt. Consulting, HR Services

Direct Mail Jobs LLC

244 Hartford Ave
Newington, CT 06111-2077
(860) 667-0515
Fax: (860) 667-1453
Web: www.directmailjobs.com

Summary: Niche recruiting firm specializing exclusively in servicing clients in the direct mail and direct marketing industry.

Key Contact - Specialty:
Ms. Julie Abraham, Chief Executive Officer
Ms. Susan Hughes, Director, Recruiting
Ms. Shirley Edbrooke, Recruiter

Salary Minimum: $40,000

Functions: Sales & Mktg., Direct Mktg.

Industries: Advertising, Publishing

Direct Marketing Resources Inc

PO Box 900
Matthews, NC 28106-0900
(704) 845-5890
Fax: (704) 845-5899
Email: inbox@dmresources.com
Web: www.dmresources.com

Summary: Search firm specializing exclusively in the direct marketing industry. Functional areas include CRM, database marketing, research & analysis, account management, product management and creative.

Key Contact - Specialty:
Mr. Dan Sullivan, President - *Direct marketing*
Ms. Stephanie Alder, Partner - *Creative*

Salary Minimum: $60,000

Functions: Direct Mktg.

Industries: Retail, Finance, Services, Hospitality, Media, Communications, Insurance, Software, Healthcare

Branches:
6 Hawthorne Ct
Cherry Hill, NJ 08003-2272
(856) 489-3427
Fax: (856) 424-6829
Email: beverly@dmresources.com
Key Contact - Specialty:
Ms. Beverly Bingham

2729 Gaston Gate
Mount Pleasant, SC 29466-7927
(843) 849-7215
Email: dawn@dmresources.com
Key Contact - Specialty:
Ms. Dawn Darcy, Senior Parnter

Direct Marketing Solutions

1972 US Highway 60 E
Salem, KY 42078-9365
(270) 988-4888
(800) 815-0063
Fax: (270) 988-4887
Email: ingala@vci.net
Web: www.dirmktsolutions.com

Summary: Recruit and place direct marketing sales, sales support and marketing professionals. Specialize in production firms: DP service bureaus, letter shops, full-service firms, direct response advertising agencies and database marketing firms.

Key Contact - Specialty:
Mr. Thomas A. Ingala, President - *Direct marketing*

Functions: Sales & Mktg., Advertising, Mktg. Research, Mktg. Mgmt., Sales Mgmt., Direct Mktg., Sales Reps.

Industries: Printing, Non-profits, Advertising, Database SW, Doc. Mgmt., Production SW

Direct Recruiters Inc

24100 Chagrin Blvd Ste 450
Beachwood, OH 44122-5552
(216) 464-5570
Fax: (216) 464-7567
Email: shel@directrecruiters.com
Web: www.directrecruiters.com

Summary: Our firm provides employment solutions to the specialty practices of supply chain, AIDC, mobile wireless computing, labels, printing systems, paper, adhesives, packaging and material handling. We successfully match top-qualified professionals in management, sales, marketing and tech support with exceptional career opportunities.

Key Contact - Specialty:
Mr. Sheldon Myeroff, CPC, President
Ms. Gina Petrello-Pray, Vice President - *Adhesives, Paper*
Mr. Daniel Charney, Director, Packaging & Material Handling
Mr. David Peterson, Executive Recruiter

Salary Minimum: $40,000

Functions: Management, Senior Mgmt., Middle Mgmt., Sales & Mktg., Mktg. Mgmt., Sales Mgmt., Sales Reps.

Industries: Manufacturing, Printing, Wireless, Packaging, Software

Discovery Personnel Inc

PO Box 1228
Burnsville, MN 55337-0228
(800) 459-1940
(952) 431-2500
Fax: (952) 431-2512
Email: jim@discoverypersonnel.com
Web: www.discoverypersonnel.com

Summary: We are a technical recruiting firm specializing in the placement of manufacturing and technical executives, managers, supervisors, scientists, engineers, technicians and salespeople for the plastics industry. Our placements include all areas of industry that relate to the plastics industry, for example: automotive parts, medical packaging, custom molding, plastic house-wares, electronics, plastic toys, computers, plastic bottles, etc.

Key Contact - Specialty:
Ms. Lisa Carpenter, Technical Recruiter - *Management, Manufacturing, Molding, Molding (Blown,Injection)*
Mr. Jim Heilman, Technical Recruiter - *Film, Manufacturing, Molding, Molding (Blown,Injection)*

Salary Minimum: $30,000

Functions: Management, Mfg., Packaging, Sales & Mktg., Engineering, Technicians, Design

Industries: Medical Devices, Plastics, Rubber

Branches:
PO Box 4272
Springfield, MO 65808-4272
(800) 459-1940
Fax: (877) 431-2512
Email: jim@discoverypersonnel.com
Key Contact - Specialty:
Mr. Jim Heilman, Technical Recruiter

Discovery Solutions

51 E Jarrettsville Rd
Forest Hill, MD 21050-1631
(410) 838-4557
(410) 838-2110
Fax: (410) 838-1240
Email: diane.ranney@discoverysolutionsllc.com
Web: www.discoverysolutionsllc.com

Summary: We specialize in the nationwide placement of experienced pharmaceutical and biotechnology professionals. We have worked searches in all aspects of the industry including: management, administrative/legal, human resources, information, systems, validation, maintenance, regulatory, clinical, quality, research, development, engineering, manufacturing, and sales/marketing.

Key Contact - Specialty:
Mr. David Mossburg, Partner & Manager, Business Development - *Biopharmaceutical, Biotechnology, Pharmaceutical*
Mrs. Diane Ranney, Senior Recruiting Manager, Partner - *Biopharmaceutical, Biotechnology, Pharmaceutical*
Ms. Shawna Brinkerhoff, Manager, Finance & Partner - *Biopharmaceutical, Biotechnology, Pharmaceutical*
Mrs. Jessica Vocke, Associate Recruiter - *Biopharmaceutical, Biotechnology, Pharmaceutical*
Ms. Dannielle Gibbs, Administrative Assistant - *Biopharmaceutical, Biotechnology, Pharmaceutical*

Functions: Generalist (All), Management, Mfg., Product Dev., Automation, Quality, Sales & Mktg., HR Mgmt., R&D, Engineering

Industries: Drugs Mfg., Biotech/Life Sciences

Distribution Recruiters

2221 Peachtree Rd NE Ste D
Atlanta, GA 30309-1133
(770) 471-1979
Email: russ@distributionrecruiters.com
Web: www.distributionrecruiters.com

Summary: We are an executive search firm specializing in distribution, transportation and logistics. Engaged exclusively in the recruitment and selection of executive and management professionals.

Key Contact - Specialty:
Mr. Russ Baker, President

Salary Minimum: $40,000

Functions: Senior Mgmt., Distribution

Industries: Generalist (All), Food, Bev., Tobacco, Consumer Goods, Transportation, Wholesale, Retail, Logistics Svcs., Inst./Industrial Food Svc., Packaging

Diversified Group

1710 Douglas Dr N Ste 103
Golden Valley, MN 55422-4397
(763) 546-8255
Fax: (763) 546-4106
Email: dei@4employment.org
Web: www.4employment.org

Summary: We are an outsource HR firm that specializes in recruiting, consulting and testing for small to medium-sized businesses.

Key Contact - Specialty:
Mr. Mike Duthoy, President

Functions: Generalist (All)

Industries: Construction, Manufacturing, Accounting, HR Services, Advertising, Publishing, Packaging, Software

Diversified Technical

5959 West Loop S Ste 590
Bellaire, TX 77401-2419
(713) 785-1144
Email: jobs@diversified-technical.com
Web: www.diversified-technical.com

Summary: We are an executive search firm, affiliated with over 350 other recruiters. We specialize in all industries/professions including HR, engineering, management, quality, IT/computer, finance, chemist/scientist, environmental, automotive, manufacturing and many more.

Key Contact - Specialty:
Mr. D. Morgan, Owner

Salary Minimum: $40,000

Functions: Generalist (All)

Industries: Manufacturing, Finance, Accounting, Telecoms, Environmental Svcs., Aerospace, Packaging, Software

Diversity Central LLC

215 Collins St
Hartford, CT 06105-1552
(860) 727-8695
Email: barrydgreen@comcast.net

Summary: We specialize in placing minority professionals into mid-level to executive-level positions. The major focus is Black, Hispanic, Native American and women professionals across a variety of skills.

Key Contact - Specialty:
Mr. Barry Green, President

Salary Minimum: $50,000

Functions: Generalist (All), Management, Mfg., Sales & Mktg., HR Mgmt., Finance, IT, Engineering

Industries: Generalist (All), Manufacturing, Finance, Media, Aerospace, Software

Dixie Search Associates

(a division of The Fill Corp)
670 Village Trce NE Bldg 19D
Marietta, GA 30067-4064
(770) 850-0250
Fax: (770) 850-9295
Email: dsa@dixiesearch.com
Web: www.dixiesearch.com

Summary: We are a search firm working exclusively in the food, beverage and hospitality industries. Search services are unique and broad based in all facets of the industries served.

Key Contact - Specialty:
Mr. Clifford G. Fill, CPC, President - *Food*
Ms. Ellyn H. Fill, Senior Vice President - *Food*
Ms. Valarie Berekashvili, CPC, Director, Research & Recruiting - *Food, Hospitality*

Salary Minimum: $35,000

Functions: Generalist (All), Sales Mgmt., Hotel Mgmt.

Industries: Manufacturing, Food, Bev., Tobacco, Soap, Perf., Cosmtcs., Wholesale, Retail, Hospitality, Hotels, Resorts, Clubs, Restaurants, Quick Service Restaurants, Full Service Restaurants, Inst./Industrial Food Svc., Entertainment, Recreation, Sports, Packaging

DLR Associates

381 Broadway Apt 4F
Dobbs Ferry, NY 10522-1732
(914) 693-9165
Fax: (914) 479-0193
Email: dave@dlrassociates.biz

Summary: We place legal and compliance professionals at all levels of experience. We serve banks, broker dealers, hedge funds, investment advisors, and other financial services industries, large and small.

Key Contact - Specialty:
Mr. David L. Reitman, President - *Finance*
Ms. Donna Roses, Director, Administrative Affairs

Salary Minimum: $40,000

Functions: Senior Mgmt., Middle Mgmt., Legal, Attorneys

Industries: Finance, Banking, Invest. Banking, Brokers, Legal

DMN & Associates

PO Box 748
Harrison, TN 37341-0748
(423) 344-8203
(423) 344-8203
Email: dneal1247@capssoftware.com

Summary: Search and recruitment for the medical device industry.

Key Contact - Specialty:
Mr. Denton Neal, Owner

Salary Minimum: $50,000

Functions: Generalist (All), Product Dev., Quality, Sales & Mktg., Mktg. Research, Mktg. Mgmt., Sales Mgmt.

Industries: Medical Devices

DNA Executive Search LLC

36 Davey Dr
West Orange, NJ 07052-2176
(973) 669-0411
Email: dnaexecutivesearch@comcast.net
Web: www.dnaexecutivesearch.com

Summary: Ours is a client-focused boutique search firm supporting most industry and functional areas. Our strategic approach allows clients to focus on their core business while keeping a pulse on the marketplace.

Key Contact - Specialty:
Ms. Diane Nash Abrahams, Managing Director

Functions: Management, Senior Mgmt., Mktg. Mgmt., Sales Mgmt.

Industries: Generalist (All)

DNA Search Inc

16133 Ventura Blvd Ste 805
Encino, CA 91436-2409
(818) 986-6300
(800) 434-8687
Fax: (818) 981-1105
Email: inquire@dnasrch.com
Web: www.dnasrch.com

Summary: We specialize in healthcare and bioscience and have continued to build our extensive database with only the finest talent in the industry.

Key Contact - Specialty:
Mr. Daniel Levy, Chief Executive Officer - *Accounting, Biotechnology, Finance, Long term care, Medical*
Ms. Laurie Oceguera, Director, Marketing

Salary Minimum: $60,000

Functions: Generalist (All), Nurses, Health Admin., Mktg. Research, Sales Mgmt., CFOs, IT, Network Admin.

Industries: Generalist (All), Medical Devices, Pharm Svcs., Mgmt. Consulting, HR Services, Hospitality, Healthcare

Doctor's Choice Inc

2610 Little John Cir
Cumming, GA 30040-2882
(770) 475-0504
Fax: (770) 884-6168
Email: drchoice@mindspring.com

Summary: Permanent placement of health care professionals primarily in the private practice setting within the Atlanta, Georgia market. Specific searches for other health care businesses and organizations within same territory.

Key Contact - Specialty:
Ms. Sheree McGuire, CPC, Certified Personnel Consultant - *Medical*

Functions: Healthcare, Nurses, Health Admin.

Industries: Healthcare, Hospitals, Long-term/Home Care, Women's

Doctors' Corner Personnel Services

3855 Pacific Coast Hwy Ste 8
Torrance, CA 90505-5963
(310) 373-0931
Fax: (310) 373-7914
Email: doctorscornerpersonnel@atchealthcare.com
Web: www.doctorscornerpersonnel.com

Summary: We provide temp help and permanent staffing to the healthcare industry. We primarily staff medical & dental offices, groups and hospitals.

Key Contact - Specialty:
Mr. Gregorius Balk, President

Salary Minimum: $25,000

Functions: Generalist (All)

Industries: Healthcare

M T Donaldson Associates Inc

18 Narrowbrook Ct
Manalapan, NJ 07726-8966
(732) 761-9715
Fax: (732) 761-9718
Email: mtdon@optonline.net

Summary: Specialize in the cosmetic, HBA, household, chemical, and pharmaceutical industry primarily.

Key Contact - Specialty:
Mr. Sol Premisler, President - *Manufacturing*

Functions: Generalist (All), Product Dev., Production, Quality, Purchasing, Materials Plng., Packaging, Engineering

Industries: Generalist (All), Food, Bev., Tobacco, Chemicals, Soap, Perf., Cosmtcs., Drugs Mfg., Misc. Mfg., Packaging

The Donnelly Group-Sales Recruiters Inc

12536 Glenlea Dr
Maryland Heights, MO 63043-2840
(314) 469-6400
Fax: (561) 258-3187
Email: dan@donnellysearch.com
Web: www.donnellysearch.com

Summary: Specializes in sales & marketing positions. Experience through sales management levels. Focus industries are pharmaceuticals, biotechnology, medical, business to business, industrial and high technology. We listen to client needs and only send qualified, pre-screened candidates.

Key Contact - Specialty:
Mr. Dan Donnelly, Recruiter & Owner - *Industrial, Pharmaceutical, Sales*
Mr. Barry P. Sullivan, Recruiter, Consumer & Indutrial Sales - *Consumer, Consumer (Packaged Goods), Home health*

Salary Minimum: $45,000

Functions: Generalist (All), Sales & Mktg., Sales Mgmt.

Industries: Generalist (All), Manufacturing, Paper, Printing, Drugs Mfg., Medical Devices, Plastics, Rubber, Metal Products, Machine, Appliance, Pharm Svcs., Telecoms, Software, Industry Specific SW

The Dorfman Group

12005 E Mission Ln
Scottsdale, AZ 85259-6029
(480) 860-8820
Fax: (480) 860-0888
Email: mikef@thedorfmangroup.com
Web: www.thedorfmangroup.com

Summary: A national executive search and recruitment firm specializing in the material handling, logistics and supply chain industries. We recruit candidates at the regional and national levels.

Key Contact - Specialty:
Mr. Michael Flamer, Vice President - *Logistics*

Salary Minimum: $60,000

Functions: Senior Mgmt., Middle Mgmt., Automation, Distribution, Sales Mgmt., Systems Implem., Engineering

Industries: Manufacturing, Misc. Mfg., Robotics, Wholesale, Engineering Svcs., Logistics Svcs., Supply Chain Mgmt., ERP SW, Industry Specific SW, System SW

Dorigan & Associates

PO Box 802
Lake Oswego, OR 97034-0134
(503) 635-8565
Email: condor1@dorigan.com
Web: www.dorigan.com

Summary: Executive recruiters to US and International organizations. Special emphasis on software/emerging technology and call center management.

Key Contact - Specialty:
Ms. Connie Dorigan, President & Owner

Salary Minimum: $80,000

Functions: Management, Senior Mgmt., Quality, Customer Svc., Engineering

Industries: Venture Cap., Services, Engineering Svcs., Telecoms, Call Centers, Software, Networking, Comm. SW

The Dorries Group LLC

PO Box 2901
Burleson, TX 76097-2901
(817) 295-8486
Fax: (817) 887-2165
Email: juliea@dorriesgroup.com
Web: www.dorriesgroup.com

Summary: Executive recruiters in the waste and equipment industry.

Key Contact - Specialty:
Mr. Mark Dorries, Owner - *Equipment*
Mrs. Julie Alexander, Recruiter & Office Manager

Functions: Generalist (All)

Industries: Manufacturing, Motor Vehicles, Transportation, Equip Svcs., Engineering Svcs., Environmental Svcs., Haz. Waste, Non-Classifiable

Dorst Information Services Inc

99 Tulip Ave Ste 405
Floral Park, NY 11001-1974
(516) 775-0500
(516) 697-1175
Email: info@dorstsearch.com
Web: www.dorstsearch.com

Summary: A technology search firm supplying middle and senior global sales and systems management to: vendor software, consulting, hardware, networking and internet corporations throughout the USA; and consultants, architects and business development execs for large to small start-ups. Includes companies with vertical market expertise in financial services (banking, brokerage, insurance).

Key Contact - Specialty:
Mr. Martin J. Dorst, President - *Consulting, Hardware, Professional services, Telecommunications*

Salary Minimum: $150,000

Functions: Middle Mgmt., Sales & Mktg.

Industries: Computer Equip., Mgmt. Consulting, Software, Database SW, Networking, Comm. SW

Dougherty & Associates Inc

41 Sutter St
PMB 1228
San Francisco, CA 94104-4905
(415) 773-8280
Fax: (415) 704-3266
Email: jobs@lawsearch-sf.com
Web: www.lawsearch-sf.com

Summary: We offer placement of attorneys in law firms and corporate law departments with emphasis on high technology.

Key Contact - Specialty:
Ms. Deborah J. Dougherty, President

Functions: Legal

Industries: New Media, Telecoms, Real Estate, Software, Biotech/Life Sciences

Douglas Associates Inc

4444 W Riverside Dr Ste 204
Burbank, CA 91505-4048
(818) 842-2477
Fax: (818) 842-3874
Email: info@daisearch.com
Web: www.daisearch.com

Summary: We are a search firm specializing in retail. We handle positions in merchandising, planning, design, buying, product development/sourcing, HR, field (store) management, MIS, visual merchandising, marketing/advertising, logistics and distribution/warehouse.

Key Contact - Specialty:
Ms. Leslie Klein, Owner & President - *Retail*

Salary Minimum: $45,000

Functions: Generalist (All), Middle Mgmt., Product Dev., Purchasing, Distribution, Sales Mgmt., Staffing

Industries: Generalist (All), Textiles, Apparel, Transportation, Retail, HR Services, Logistics Svcs., Advertising, HR SW

Steven Douglas Associates

(an EMA Partners International company)
3040 Universal Blvd Ste 190
Weston, FL 33331-3529
(954) 385-8595
(305) 381-8100
Fax: (954) 385-1414
Email: sabrina@stevendouglas.com
Web: www.stevendouglas.com

Summary: Commitments to proactively search - identify and most importantly, attract - the best-qualified individual for the client's positions.

Key Contact - Specialty:
Mr. Mark Sadovnick, Executive Vice President - *Financial*
Mr. Steve Sadaka, President - *Financial*
Mr. Steve Kalisher, Senior Vice President
Ms. Cindy Hernandez, Vice President

Salary Minimum: $75,000

Functions: Generalist (All), Board Members, Senior Mgmt., Mktg. Mgmt., CFOs, Budgeting, Taxes, M&A, MIS Mgmt.

Industries: Generalist (All), Invest. Banking, Accounting, HR Services, Real Estate, Healthcare

Scott Douglas Inc

16968 Obsidian Dr Ste 101
Ramona, CA 92065-6839
(760) 788-5560
Fax: (760) 788-5506
Email: mmagic@cox.net

Summary: Boutique firm specializing in actuarial, managed care/bio-technology research scientists, CRAs and lab management/finance and financial engineering professionals. We provide research, account management and candidate screening, profiles and other services.

Key Contact - Specialty:
Mr. Michael F. Magic, President

Salary Minimum: $50,000

Functions: Generalist (All), Senior Mgmt., Actuaries

Industries: Finance, Invest. Banking, Venture Cap., Insurance, Biotech/Life Sciences

Douillard & Associates Inc

2451 Cumberland Pkwy Ste 3340
Atlanta, GA 30339-6157
(770) 803-3010
Fax: (770) 804-2006
Email: cdouillard@dai-us.com
Web: www.dai-us.com

Summary: We understand your most valuable assets are the people with whom you are surrounded. Our foundation is built on the unbreakable principle that success is achieved by acquiring and keeping the right people. We identify, recruit, and attract the best talent to your interviewing process.

Key Contact - Specialty:
Mr. Christ Douillard, President

Functions: Sales & Mktg.

Industries: Medical Devices, Advertising, Marketing SW, Biotech/Life Sciences, Healthcare, Hospitals

Dow Consultants International

370 Lexington Ave Rm 1407
New York, NY 10017-6583
(212) 953-4800
Fax: (212) 953-3611

Summary: We are a contingency and retainer-based search firm specializing in mid to senior-level assignments in investment and commercial banking as well as capital markets.

Key Contact - Specialty:
Mr. Ian James Dow, President

Salary Minimum: $75,000

Functions: M&A, Risk Mgmt.

Industries: Banking, Invest. Banking

Dowd Group Inc

60 Grange Ave Fl 2
Fair Haven, NJ 07704-3004
(732) 747-8100
Fax: (732) 842-0597
Email: recruiters@dowdgroup.com
Web: www.dowdgroup.com

Summary: We specialize in telecom and data storage solutions. Candidates include management professionals, sales executives, subject matter experts and sales engineers.

Key Contact - Specialty:
Mr. Charlie Dowd, Recruiter - *Call centers, Computers, Disaster planning & recovery, Storage, Telecommunications*

Functions: Senior Mgmt., Sales & Mktg., Sales Mgmt., Sales Reps., MIS Mgmt., Hardware

Industries: Computer Equip., Test, Measure Equip., Services, Communications, Telecoms, Call Centers, Telephony, Digital, Wireless, Fiber Optic, Network Infrastructure, Government, Software, Doc. Mgmt., Production SW

Patricia Dowd Inc

5001 Oceanaire St
Oxnard, CA 93035-2818
(805) 985-8243
Fax: (805) 382-0773
Email: pdowd@pdisearch.com
Web: www.pdisearch.com

Summary: We were the first recruiters to specialize in database marketing. Our specialty has evolved into CRM, knowledge-based marketing and most recently with the addition of Hispanic direct marketing. Our focus is on all disciplines of database marketing, direct marketing, strategic marketing & planning, program management, product marketing, analysts, professional services and client service providers.

Key Contact - Specialty:
Ms. Patricia Dowd, President
Mrs. Holly M. Tibbles, Executive Recruiter - *Analysts, Database, Direct marketing, Diversity, Product management/development*

Salary Minimum: $80,000

Functions: Generalist (All), Management, Sales & Mktg., Direct Mktg.

Industries: Generalist (All), Motor Vehicles, Banking, Misc. Financial, Mgmt. Consulting, E-commerce, Media, Advertising, Publishing, New Media, Digital, Database SW, Marketing SW

CS Dowling Executive Services

(also known as Dow-Tech Associates and Zaccaria Int'l Inc)
1700 State Route 23 Ste 100
Wayne, NJ 07470-7537
(973) 696-8000
(888) 236-9832
Fax: (973) 696-1964
Email: info@dow-tech.com
Web: www.dow-tech.com

Summary: We provide executive-level search and selection in the HVAC, energy services and retail industries. Positions focus on director, VP, GM, CEO, COO, sales and operations.

Key Contact - Specialty:
Mr. Chris Dowling, President - *HVAC*

Salary Minimum: $65,000

Functions: Management, Board Members, Senior Mgmt., Mktg. Mgmt., Sales Mgmt., Engineering

Industries: Generalist (All)

Downing & Downing Inc

8800 Tyler Blvd
Mentor, OH 44060-4361
(440) 255-1177
Fax: (440) 255-1877
Email: info@downing-downing.com
Web: www.downing-downing.com

Summary: With many years of loss prevention and recruiting experience, we offer an effective network of individuals in the retail loss prevention (security), safety, risk management and audit industries.

Key Contact - Specialty:
Mr. Gus Downing, Chief Executive Officer
Mr. Gene Smith, President

Salary Minimum: $25,000

Functions: Management, Middle Mgmt., Risk Mgmt., Security Personnel, Health & Safety

Industries: Retail

Downing Search Group

9930 Johnnycake Ridge Rd Ste 3F
Mentor, OH 44060-6762
(440) 352-7599
Fax: (440) 352-7564
Email: bill@downingsearch.com

Summary: We specialize in medical sales and sales management positions as well as clinical sales support.

Key Contact - Specialty:
Mr. William Downing, Owner & Medical Specialist
Mr. Mark Downing, Medical Recruiter

Salary Minimum: $50,000

Functions: Sales & Mktg., Sales Mgmt.

Industries: Medical Devices, Pharm Svcs., Healthcare, Long-term/Home Care, Women's

Downing Teal Inc

(an affiliate of C J Stafford & Associates)
650 S Cherry St Ste 525
Denver, CO 80246-1826
(303) 321-3844
Fax: (303) 321-3551
Email: apply@downingteal.com
Web: www.downingteal.com

Summary: Our firm is one of the world's leading global recruiting firms with a specialty in the mining, oil & gas and construction industries.

Key Contact - Specialty:
Mr. Leigh Freeman, General Manager
Mr. Steve Rosene, Manager, Houston

Salary Minimum: $50,000

Functions: Senior Mgmt.

Industries: Agri., Forestry, Mining, Energy, Utilities, Oil & Gas, Metal Products

Downs Associates

PO Box 22835
Little Rock, AR 72221-2835
(501) 868-7117
Email: gtdowns@downssearch.com
Web: www.downssearch.com

Summary: Contingency search firm specializing in engineering, manufacturing, safety & health and supply chain management opportunities on a nationwide basis. Affiliate offices nationwide.

Key Contact - Specialty:
Mr. Greg Downs, CPC, Owner - *Engineering, Manufacturing*

Salary Minimum: $45,000

Functions: Mfg., Product Dev., Production, Automation, Quality, Materials, Purchasing, Distribution, Engineering, Health & Safety

Industries: Generalist (All), Manufacturing, Food, Bev., Tobacco, Paper, Chemicals, Soap, Perf., Cosmtcs., Medical Devices, Plastics, Rubber, Paints, Petro. Products, Metal Products, Machine, Appliance, Motor Vehicles, Computer Equip., Consumer Elect., Misc. Mfg., Electronic, Elec. Components, Robotics, Consumer Goods, Packaging

Doyen Metallurgical

618 Brighton Ct Ste B
Rolla, MO 65401-3956
(573) 364-0020
Fax: (573) 341-9120
Email: mdoyen@rollanet.org

Summary: Specializing in the placement and recruiting of engineers, managers and executives for the primary and fabricated light metals industry, with particular emphasis in the fields of

aluminum metallurgy, quality and technical sales & marketing.

Key Contact - Specialty:
Mr. Mike Doyen, President - *Engineering, Manufacturing*

Salary Minimum: $50,000

Functions: Mfg., Quality, Sales & Mktg., Sales Mgmt., Engineering, Health & Safety

Industries: Metal Products

DP Resources
2443 Avalon Ct Ste 100
Aurora, IL 60503-8574
(630) 585-6731
(888) 637-5300
Fax: (630) 585-0198
Email: dkainpaul@dpresources.net
Web: www.dpresources.net

Summary: Our firm is a recruitment-consulting firm. We specialize in the placement of consultants and full time employees within the following industries: retail, banking, engineering, IT consulting, ISPs, software development, manufacturing, healthcare, eCommerce and telecom.

Key Contact - Specialty:
Ms. Danielle Kain-Paul, Partner, Recruitment

Salary Minimum: $30,000

Functions: Generalist (All), Senior Mgmt.

Industries: Generalist (All)

Drake Executive Search
9434 N 134th East Ave Ste 111
Owasso, OK 74055-4721
(918) 272-2608
Fax: (918) 272-2612
Email: linda@drakeexecutivesearch.com
Web: www.drakeexecutivesearch.com

Summary: Recruiting for the hospitality industry.

Key Contact - Specialty:
Ms. Linda Drake, President

Salary Minimum: $50,000

Functions: Board Members, Senior Mgmt., Middle Mgmt., Mktg. Mgmt., Sales Mgmt., HR Mgmt., Training, CFOs, Int'l.

Industries: Generalist (All), Hotels, Resorts, Clubs, Restaurants, Quick Service Restaurants, Full Service Restaurants, Inst./Industrial Food Svc., Entertainment, Recreation

Drayton & Associates
5982 Ethan Dr
Burlington, KY 41005-6527
(513) 324-5510
Email: jbdrayton@insightbb.com

Summary: Our principal has many years of HR management experience with major retailers and years of successful consulting and recruiting experience serving the retail industry.

Key Contact - Specialty:
Mr. J. Bradley Drayton, SPHR, President

Salary Minimum: $50,000

Functions: Generalist (All), Management, HR Mgmt., Finance

Industries: Generalist (All), Retail

Dream Team International
PO Box 5179
Lancaster, PA 17606-5179
(717) 560-9455
Fax: (717) 569-7173

Email: info@dreamteamsales.com
Web: www.dreamteamrecruiters.com

Summary: A professional, technical and executive search firm specializing in sales, engineering, R&D, quality and manufacturing specialists in the agriculture, food, beverage and building products industries.

Key Contact - Specialty:
Mr. Bill Morgan, Manager

Functions: Mfg., Product Dev., Quality, Sales & Mktg., Sales Reps.

Industries: Construction, Manufacturing, Food, Bev., Tobacco, Lumber, Furniture, Printing, Chemicals, IT Implementation, Inst./Industrial Food Svc.

Ralph C Dressler, CPC
1930 Marlton Pike E Ste T
Cherry Hill, NJ 08003-4217
(856) 489-4010
Email: ralphdcpc@aol.com

Summary: Our organization provides the level of services of retained search on a contingency basis. The goal is to perpetuate relationships by striving to make mutually successful long-term matches.

Key Contact - Specialty:
Mr. Ralph C. Dressler, Principal - *Consulting, Healthcare, Pharmaceutical*

Functions: Healthcare, IT, MIS Mgmt., Systems Analysis, Systems Dev., Systems Implem., Systems Support, Network Admin., DB Admin.

Industries: Generalist (All)

Drum Associates Inc
150 Broadway Fl 23
New York, NY 10038-4403
(212) 233-7550
Email: kcaliolo@drum2000.com
Web: www.drumassociates.com

Summary: Our firm has performed job searches for top financial institutions and multinational corporations in the areas of finance, accounting, corporate credit, asset management, technology, sales & marketing and corporate services. We work closely with the senior management and HR in our client organizations to identify outstanding individuals for a broad spectrum of leadership positions from staff assignments to chief executives.

Key Contact - Specialty:
Mr. Brian Drum, President
Ms. Carly Drum, Director
Ms. Cathy Galan, Director - *Credit*
Mr. Joe Pinto, Director - *Financial services*
Ms. Kristin E. Caliolo, Director, Marketing & Operations - *Advertising, Marketing*
Mrs. Stephanie Walsh, Director - *Wall Street*

Salary Minimum: $75,000

Functions: Generalist (All), Management, Board Members, Middle Mgmt., Mktg. Mgmt., Finance, Cash Mgmt., MIS Mgmt.

Industries: Finance, Banking, Invest. Banking, Brokers, Mutual/Hedge Funds, Misc. Financial, Non-profits, Accounting, HR Services, IT Implementation, Supply Chain Mgmt, Media, Communications, Real Estate, Property/Facility Mgmt., Software, Accounting SW, Hospitals

Drummond Associates Inc
519 Westfield Ave
Westfield, NJ 07090-3374
(908) 789-1221
Fax: (908) 789-1222
Email: chetdas@aol.com

Summary: We serve Wall Street firms, money center banks and financial consulting firms. Our coverage includes middle upper-level positions in capital markets including: corporate finance, asset management, technology and related.

Key Contact - Specialty:
Mr. Chester A. Fienberg, President - *Consulting*
Mr. Donald Mochwart, Vice President - *Capital markets, Operations*

Salary Minimum: $40,000

Functions: Generalist (All), Finance

Industries: Finance, Banking, Invest. Banking, Brokers, Venture Cap., Misc. Financial, Services, Accounting, Mgmt. Consulting

Druthers Agency Inc
13323 W Washington Blvd Ste 301
Los Angeles, CA 90066-5164
(310) 827-4140
(888) 378-8437
Fax: (310) 827-4143
Email: info@druthersagency.com
Web: www.druthersagency.com

Summary: We are an executive search services firm exclusively for long-term care and senior housing environments. Additionally, we provide consultation and training on recruitment and retention practices.

Key Contact - Specialty:
Mr. Jeffrey Harris, President

Functions: Senior Mgmt.

Industries: Healthcare, Long-term/Home Care

Dukas Associates
236 Payson Rd
Belmont, MA 02478-2877
(617) 484-9268
Fax: (617) 484-8607
Email: dukassoc@aol.com

Summary: We are a precise customized recruitment service specializing in senior biotechnology marketing and technical personnel; bi-coastal knowledge of companies, personnel and industry trends.

Key Contact - Specialty:
Mr. Theodore Dukas, President - *Biotechnology, Sales*

Salary Minimum: $50,000

Functions: Generalist (All), Product Dev., Mktg. Research, Mktg. Mgmt., Sales Mgmt., R&D, Engineering, Int'l.

Industries: Generalist (All), Chemicals, Drugs Mfg., Medical Devices, Test, Measure Equip., Biotech/Life Sciences

Dumont, Sampson & Lodge
(formerly known as Market Niche Consulting)
10224 E Minnesota Ave
Sun Lakes, AZ 85248-6882
(480) 802-9529
Email: rsamp@rsamp.biz

Summary: We are a firm specializing in the recruitment of architects, civil, structural, geotechnical and environmental engineers and construction management professionals.

Key Contact - Specialty:
Mr. Ron Sampson, Principal

Salary Minimum: $60,000

Functions: Generalist (All), Management, Engineering, Geotechnical, Structural, Eng. Design, Environmentalists, Architects

Industries: Agri., Forestry, Mining, Energy, Utilities, Construction, Transportation, Government, Defense, Environmental Svcs.

Bruce R Duncan & Associates

1005-8 King St E
Royal Bank Building
Toronto, ON M5C 1B5
Canada
(416) 361-1451
(416) 642-6455
Fax: (416) 361-1225
Email: staff@bruceduncan.com
Web: www.bruceduncan.com

Summary: We are an executive search firm who specializes in accounting/finance and sales/marketing.

Key Contact - Specialty:
Mrs. Joan Perry, President - *Finance, Management*

Salary Minimum: $50,000

Functions: Management

Industries: Generalist (All)

The Duncan-O'Dell Group Inc

PO Box 1161
La Porte, TX 77572-1161
(281) 470-1881
Email: dog1@sprintmail.com

Summary: Area of primary focus is manufacturing and sales of rotating equipment and industrial automation equipment. Also work in the heavy off road equipment manufacturing sector in engineering, sales, service and after market parts. In addition, we have specialists for recruiting and staffing in all human resources disciplines.

Key Contact - Specialty:
Mr. James E. Hall, Managing Partner - *Manufacturing, Metals*

Salary Minimum: $50,000

Functions: Management, Mfg.

Industries: Generalist (All), Manufacturing, Metal Products

Dunhill Personnel of Fort Wayne Inc

9918 Coldwater Rd
Fort Wayne, IN 46825-2040
(260) 489-5966
Fax: (260) 489-6120
Email: charlie@dunhillfw.com
Web: www.dunhillfortwayne.com

Summary: We have experience in providing salaried individuals for manufacturing plants. Specialize in the food and food packaging industry.

Key Contact - Specialty:
Mr. Charlie Davis, President
Mr. Larry Tackett, Recruiter - *High technology*

Salary Minimum: $30,000

Functions: Generalist (All), Production, Automation, Plant Mgmt., Quality, Productivity, HR Mgmt., Engineering

Industries: Food, Bev., Tobacco, Chemicals, Soap, Perf., Cosmtcs., Drugs Mfg.

Dunhill Personnel Search

41 Mohegan Ln
Rye Brook, NY 10573-1431
(914) 934-0801
Fax: (914) 934-0825
Email: headhunterone@att.net
Web: www.dunhillsearch.net

Summary: We deliver a prompt selection of over quota sales performers with checkable track records at no cost to you - unless you hire.

Key Contact - Specialty:
Mr. Tom Horn, Vice President, Sales Division
Mr. Robert J. Morris, Recruiter

Salary Minimum: $70,000

Functions: Generalist (All), Sales Mgmt.

Industries: Computer Equip., IT Implementation, Call Centers, Software, Database SW, Doc. Mgmt., Production SW, ERP SW, Security SW

Dunhill Professional Search

9190 Priority Way W Dr Ste 201
Indianapolis, IN 46240-1437
(317) 818-4900
(317) 818-9373
Fax: (317) 818-4910
Email: laura.arive@dunhillstaff.com
Web: www.dunhillstaff.com

Summary: A franchise network of executive recruiting franchise offices (more than 100 locations), specializing in many disciplines.

Key Contact - Specialty:
Mr. Robert Freeman, Chief Financial Officer
Mr. Rick Munzesheimer, Vice President, Franchise Development
Ms. Laura Arive, Vice President, Operations

Salary Minimum: $25,000

Functions: Generalist (All), Mfg., Healthcare, Sales & Mktg., HR Mgmt., Finance, IT, Engineering

Industries: Generalist (All), Energy, Utilities, Manufacturing, Transportation, Wholesale, Finance, Services, Media

Branches:
2080 S Bascom Ave Ste B
Campbell, CA 95008-3287
(408) 369-1900
Fax: (408) 369-8709
Email: jobs@dunhillprof.com
Key Contact - Specialty:
Mr. Gary Yuhara, President

15375 Barranca Pkwy Ste K104
Irvine, CA 92618-2211
(949) 341-0616
Fax: (949) 341-0619
Email: dunhillirvine@attglobal.net
Key Contact - Specialty:
Mr. Michael Lamanna, President

225 State St Ste 101
New London, CT 06320-6357
(860) 444-9057
Fax: (860) 444-9060
Email: resume@stoningtonsearch.com
Key Contact - Specialty:
Mr. Gary Avalone, President

850 N Main Street Ext Ste 1D1
Wallingford, CT 06492-2456
(203) 949-2000
Fax: (203) 949-2008
Email: resume@dsswallingford.com
Key Contact - Specialty:
Ms. Sasha Sundhar, Branch Manager
Ms. Teresa Pagan, Staffing Coordinator

PO Box 4165
Alpharetta, GA 30023-4165
(770) 495-3570
Fax: (770) 814-2221
Email: dunhillatlanta@bellsouth.net
Key Contact - Specialty:
Mr. Mark Zorin, President

211 W Wacker Dr Ste 1220
Chicago, IL 60606-1379
(312) 346-0933
Fax: (312) 346-0837
Email: chicago@dunhillstaff.com
Key Contact - Specialty:
Mr. Paul T. Kinderis, Manager, Chicago Area
Ms. Mary Menet, Senior Staffing Specialist - *Accounting, Banking, Financial services, Insurance*
Ms. Mary Jane Evans, Senior Staffing Specialist - *Accounting, Insurance, Legal*

8365 Keystone Xing Ste 105
Indianapolis, IN 46240-2685
(317) 594-1477
Email: indyne@dunhillstaff.com

PO Box 3001
Iowa City, IA 52244-3001
(319) 354-1407
Fax: (319) 354-1715
Email: lwsdunhill@yahoo.com
Key Contact - Specialty:
Mr. Lee Stannard, President

414 Hungerford Dr Ste 252
Rockville, MD 20850-4125
(301) 424-0450
Fax: (301) 762-4694
Email: dunhillmd@msn.com
Key Contact - Specialty:
Ms. Rosa Harper, President
Mr. Stuart Harper, Vice President

584 Delaware Ave Ste 101
Buffalo, NY 14202-1203
(716) 885-3576
Fax: (716) 885-3594
Email: buffalo@dunhillstaff.com
Key Contact - Specialty:
Ms. Alison B. Zubin, Branch Manager

775 Park Ave Ste 255
Huntington, NY 11743-7538
(631) 421-9500
Fax: (631) 421-9700
Email: joe@dunsearch.com
Key Contact - Specialty:
Mr. Joseph Lawless, CPC, President

PO Box 528
Pittsford, NY 14534-0528
(585) 377-7880
Fax: (585) 377-7972
Email: search3535@aol.com
Key Contact - Specialty:
Mr. Jack Tanner, President

PO Box 1347
41 Bogart Ave
Port Washington, NY 11050-7347
(516) 883-1172
Fax: (516) 767-0526
Email: nnewby@mindspring.com
Key Contact - Specialty:
Mr. Neville Newby, President

7831 Spinnaker Bay Dr
Sherrills Ford, NC 28673-9290
(828) 478-7000
Fax: (828) 478-9083
Email: lakeheadhunter@aol.com
Key Contact - Specialty:
Mr. Tom Barbeau, President

3947B Market St
Wilmington, NC 28403-1403
(910) 251-3450
Fax: (910) 251-3447
Email: recruiter@capefeardunhill.com
Key Contact - Specialty:
Mr. Chris Gibbons, President

247 N Broadway Ste 205
Edmond, OK 73034-3776
(405) 341-0990
Fax: (405) 341-0997
Email: ehs@safetyrecruiters.com
Key Contact - Specialty:
Mr. Dennis Garton, President

7666 E 61st St Ste 120
Tulsa, OK 74133-1129
(918) 252-4434
Fax: (918) 252-4498
Email: dunhilltulsa@aol.com
Key Contact - Specialty:
Mr. Curtis Reid, President

233 E Lancaster Ave Ste 303
Ardmore, PA 19003-2321
(610) 642-2223
Fax: (610) 642-2347
Email: phillydunhill@aol.com
Key Contact - Specialty:
Mr. Alan Trager, President

224 Nazareth Pike Unit 16
Bethlehem, PA 18020-9080
(610) 746-5066
Fax: (610) 746-5799
Email: dunjobs@fast.net
Key Contact - Specialty:
Ms. Mary Jo Stofflet, President
Mr. Jeffrey Stofflet, Vice President
Ms. Toni Ceraul, Consultant

2330A W 38th St
Erie, PA 16506-4564
(814) 836-9379
Fax: (814) 836-0890
Email: bazimmer@dunhillsearcherie.com
Key Contact - Specialty:
Ms. Beth Zimmer, President
Mr. Kerry Zimmer, Chief Executive Officer

14881 Quorum Dr Ste 150
Dallas, TX 75254-7005
(972) 503-2400
Fax: (972) 503-2404
Email: dallasn@dunhillstaff.com
Key Contact - Specialty:
Mrs. Anne Lebaron, Director, Southwestern
  Regional
Mrs. Heather Haynes, Branch Manager
Ms. Deborah Davis, Professional Search
  Consultant
Mrs. Linda Baier, Staffing Consultant

11259 Southwest Fwy
Houston, TX 77031-3603
(281) 921-4445
Fax: (281) 921-4450
Email: mw@dunhillhsw.com
Key Contact - Specialty:
Mr. Mike Wilcoxson, President
Mr. Elias Zinn, Chief Executive Officer

336 S Jefferson St
Green Bay, WI 54301-4523
(920) 432-2977
Fax: (920) 432-2038
Key Contact - Specialty:
Mr. Kramer Rock, President

2300 N Mayfair Rd Ste 220
Milwaukee, WI 53226-1503
(414) 771-1399
Fax: (414) 771-3920
Email: mayfair@dunhillstaff.com

Key Contact - Specialty:
Ms. Glenna Cose, CPC, Branch Manager

Dunhill Professional Search of Oakland

3732 Mt Diablo Blvd Ste 375
Lafayette, CA 94549-3625
(925) 283-5300
(925) 283-5003
Fax: (925) 283-5310
Email: jtierney@dunhilloak.com
Web: www.dunhillstaff.com

Summary: We work hard to find a custom fit
between the position you need to fill and the
person to fill it. We work with technical/engineers
in high technology operation positions. We work
with leading consumer companies in food and
beverage. We also work with electronic companies
in all areas of plant management including sales &
marketing. We have extensive success among
contingency and retained search assignments.

Key Contact - Specialty:
Mr. John F. Tierney, President
Mr. Leon B. Steffensen, Vice President

Salary Minimum: $50,000

Functions: Generalist (All), Management, Senior
Mgmt., Mfg., Materials, Mktg. Research,
Engineering

Industries: Generalist (All), Manufacturing, Food,
Bev., Tobacco

Dunhill Professional Search of Stockton

1803 W March Ln Ste M
Stockton, CA 95207-6414
(209) 474-7591
Fax: (209) 474-8249
Email: barney@dunhillstockton.com
Web: www.dunhillstockton.com

Summary: We have extensive industry contacts,
are part of a search network and provide recruiting
professionals who understand your business and
match the right people with the right tasks.
Whether it's filling a full time position or finding a
contractor for a short term assignment, you need
qualified people stepping in, solving problems and
producing results, fast.

Key Contact - Specialty:
Mr. Barney Kramer, President - *Accounting,
Banking
(Commercial,Corporate,Mortgage,Retail)*

Salary Minimum: $40,000

Functions: Management, Senior Mgmt., Middle
Mgmt.

Industries: Banking, Accounting

Dunhill Professional Search of Los Angeles

20550 Wells Dr
Woodland Hills, CA 91364-3434
(818) 710-7622
Email: rrcech@aol.com
Web: www.dunhill-la.com

Summary: We have extensive experience in
recruiting.

Key Contact - Specialty:
Mr. Raymond R. Cech, President -
  Environmental, Real estate, Sales

Salary Minimum: $75,000

Functions: Generalist (All), Senior Mgmt.,
Middle Mgmt., Product Dev., Sales & Mktg.,
Mktg. Mgmt., Sales Mgmt.

Industries: Generalist (All), E-commerce,
Communications, Telephony, Digital, Wireless,
Fiber Optic, Software, Database SW, Doc.
Mgmt., Production SW, ERP SW

Dunhill Professional Search of Englewood

1941 S Xanadu Way
Aurora, CO 80014-4310
(303) 755-7466
Fax: (303) 755-7081
Email: jllippe@att.net

Summary: Contingency search, primarily for
middle management positions such as engineering,
production, quality, R&D and distribution, in
process manufacturing industries specifically food,
beverage, and cosmetics.

Key Contact - Specialty:
Mr. John L. Lippe, President - *Manufacturing*

Salary Minimum: $50,000

Functions: Mfg., Production, Plant Mgmt.,
Quality, Process

Industries: Manufacturing, Food, Bev., Tobacco,
Soap, Perf., Cosmtcs.

Dunhill Professional Search of Ft. Collins

2120 S College Ave Ste 3
Fort Collins, CO 80525-1465
(970) 221-5630
Fax: (970) 495-1917
Email: dfc@frii.com

Summary: We are a privately owned and managed
firm specializing in commercial banking officers,
microelectronics design engineers, and wire and
cable industry personnel. Our small size allows us
to provide more individual attention to our clients
and candidates.

Key Contact - Specialty:
Mr. Jerold Lyons, MBA, President
Mr. Jack Donahue, Recruiter, Microelectronics

Salary Minimum: $30,000

Functions: Mfg., Finance, Engineering

Industries: Consumer Goods, Banking,
Telephony, Fiber Optic, Network Infrastructure

Dunhill Professional Search of Stuart

PO Box 806
Hobe Sound, FL 33475-0806
(772) 545-1955
Email: dunpro@adelphia.net

Summary: We are a national recruitment firm
specializing in the permanent placement of top
professionals in the healthcare, engineering,
manufacturing, information technology and
petro/chemical industries. Our partnering structure
puts the power and resources of a national
company to work for you with a personalized one-
on-one service.

Key Contact - Specialty:
Mr. Ralph DeMiranda, Manager & Senior
  Consultant - *Engineering, Healthcare,
  Information Technology, Manufacturing,
  Petrochemical*
Ms. Janice A. Dolynny, Senior Consultant -
  *Engineering, Healthcare, Human resources,
  Manufacturing, Petrochemical*

Salary Minimum: $50,000

Functions: Generalist (All)

Industries: Energy, Utilities, Oil & Gas, Manufacturing, Chemicals, Services, Pharm Svcs., Engineering Svcs., Healthcare, Hospitals, Long-term/Home Care

Dunhill Professional Search of W Atlanta

1949 Brownridge Dr NE
Marietta, GA 30062-2673
(770) 952-0007
Fax: (770) 952-9422
Email: recruiter@dunhillatlanta.com
Web: www.dunhillatlanta.com

Summary: Technical specialist in manufacturing industry, supply chain management, materials management, engineering and HR. Effectively use team recruiting with closely networked offices for fast response.

Key Contact - Specialty:
Mr. Jon D. Harvill, CPC, Managing Director - *Materials, Purchasing, Technical*

Salary Minimum: $40,000

Functions: Senior Mgmt., Middle Mgmt., Mfg., Product Dev., Production, Automation, Plant Mgmt., Materials, Purchasing, Materials Plng.

Industries: Manufacturing, Misc. Mfg., Consumer Goods, Transportation, Wholesale, Mgmt. Consulting, HR Services, Engineering Svcs., Logistics Svcs., Supply Chain Mgmt, Aerospace, Packaging, Non-Classifiable

Dunhill Professional Search of Hawaii

1247 Kailua Rd Ste D
Pali Center
Kailua, HI 96734-4364
(808) 524-2550
Fax: (808) 533-2196
Email: dunhill@dunhillhawaii.com
Web: www.dunhillstaff.com

Summary: Permanent placement, temp placement and professional contract staffing of experienced and qualified individuals for client companies and associations in engineering, accounting, data processing, audit, construction fields, technical and sales.

Key Contact - Specialty:
Ms. Nadine Stollenmaier, President - *Engineering, Technical*
Mr. James Stollenmaier, Vice President
Mr. Henry Sotelo, Corporate Secretary - *Engineering, Technical*
Mr. Randy Muth, Manager

Salary Minimum: $22,000

Functions: Generalist (All), Management, Production, Sales & Mktg., Finance, IT, Engineering, Int'l.

Industries: Generalist (All), Computer Equip., Accounting, IT Implementation, Telecoms, Accounting SW

Dunhill Professional Search of Sandpoint

559 Berry Hl
Cocolalla, ID 83813-9506
(208) 265-2651
(800) 536-8935
Fax: (270) 626-4068
Email: kc@dps-sandpoint.com
Web: www.dps-sandpoint.com

Summary: We specialize in hospital, retail and industry pharmaceutical and pharmaceutical operations management placements.

Key Contact - Specialty:
Mr. Keith Cutter, President

Salary Minimum: $80,000

Functions: Management, Healthcare

Industries: Pharm Svcs., Hospitals, Long-term/Home Care

Dunhill Professional Search of Rolling Meadows

PO Box 1781
Palatine, IL 60078-1781
(847) 991-8127
Fax: (847) 991-8137
Email: rkunke@starnetwx.net

Summary: Our president has many years of experience as a hiring manager. He understands technology, terminology, etc. We are part of a network of many franchise offices. We have years of experience in IT recruiting.

Key Contact - Specialty:
Mr. Russ Kunke, President

Salary Minimum: $50,000

Functions: IT, MIS Mgmt., Systems Analysis, Systems Dev., Systems Implem., Systems Support, Network Admin., DB Admin.

Industries: Generalist (All)

Dunhill Professional Search of Indianapolis

950 N Meridian St Ste 110
Indianapolis, IN 46204-1018
(317) 237-7878
Fax: (317) 237-7874
Email: indydwtn@dunhillstaff.com
Web: www.dunhillstaff.com

Summary: We specialize in the placement of computer IS professionals on a permanent as well as a contract basis.

Key Contact - Specialty:
Mr. Kristaan Kane, Technical Consultant

Functions: Generalist (All), Admin. Svcs.

Industries: Generalist (All), Software

Dunhill Executive Search of Brown County

PO Box 1068
Nashville, IN 47448-1068
(812) 988-1944
Fax: (812) 988-1944
Email: geowrogers@earthlink.net

Summary: We actively participate with other franchise offices in the exchange of both applicants and job opportunities, which gives a greater exposure of the marketable applicant and a greater potential for us to complete a search for the manufacturer.

Key Contact - Specialty:
Ms. S.L. Rogers, Proprietor - *Automotive, Engineering, Manufacturing*

Salary Minimum: $50,000

Functions: Mfg., Engineering

Industries: Generalist (All)

Dunhill Professional Search of Joplin

531 N Van Hoorebeke Rd
Joplin, MO 64801-9342
(417) 624-6552

Email: dunhill@joplin.com

Summary: Specialize in the recruitment of chemical, mechanical and electrical engineers for the chemical and related industries.

Key Contact - Specialty:
Mr. Mark Lickteig, President

Salary Minimum: $55,000

Functions: Engineering

Industries: Chemicals, Electronic, Elec. Components

Dunhill Professional Search of South Charlotte

10801 Johnston Rd Ste 211
Charlotte, NC 28226-0920
(704) 544-8556
(888) 407-1275
Fax: (704) 544-8158
Email: hauger@dpscharlotte.com
Web: www.dpscharlotte.com

Summary: We specialize in the real estate, relocation, mortgage and financial industries. We place all positions, including senior level executives. We have experience in the real estate, mortgage, relocation and financial industries. Discreet and professional.

Key Contact - Specialty:
Mr. Harvey Auger, President
Mr. Chip Auger, Vice President

Salary Minimum: $50,000

Functions: Generalist (All), Management, Senior Mgmt., Middle Mgmt., Sales & Mktg., Sales Mgmt.

Industries: Construction, Transportation, Finance, Banking, Invest. Banking, Brokers, Venture Cap., Mutual/Hedge Funds, Misc. Financial, Entertainment, Communications, Real Estate, Property/Facility Mgmt., Non-Classifiable

Dunhill Professional Search of Cincinnati

11270 Terwilligers Valley Ln Ste 101
Cincinnati, OH 45249-2739
(513) 769-9675
(888) 769-9675
Fax: (887) 485-7687
Email: dunofc@dunhill-usa.com
Web: www.dunhill-usa.com

Summary: We are a contingency and retained search firm, but will also handle contracts. We specialize in logistics, material handling, engineering and insurance.

Key Contact - Specialty:
Mr. Michael D. Green, Chief Executive Officer - *Financial, Logistics*
Ms. Judith C. Green, President
Mr. Michael Havens, Vice President - *Engineering, Food*

Salary Minimum: $30,000

Functions: Generalist (All)

Industries: Construction, Manufacturing, Food, Bev., Tobacco, Paper, Plastics, Rubber, Misc. Mfg., Retail, Finance, Misc. Financial, Insurance

Dunhill Professional Search of Greenwood

200 Greenville St
Abbeville, SC 29620-1756
(864) 366-5555
Email: dunhill@wctel.net

Summary: We provide professional recruiting for wire and cable industry. We recruit engineers and

all levels of management in manufacturing and administrative environments.

Key Contact - Specialty:
Mr. Hal Freese, President - *Cable, Plastics*

Salary Minimum: $40,000

Functions: Generalist (All), Mfg., Product Dev., Engineering

Industries: Generalist (All), Plastics, Rubber, Metal Products, Electronic, Elec. Components, Telecoms, Fiber Optic

Dunhill Staffing Systems of Charleston

1459 Stuart Engals Blvd Unit 300
Mount Pleasant, SC 29464-3600
(843) 375-0031
Email: ngw@dunhillsc.com
Web: www.dunhillsc.com

Summary: We place engineering, finance, sales, and administrative professional with our region's leading companies. All services are confidential, professional, and provided on a contingency basis.

Key Contact - Specialty:
Mr. Neil Whitman, CPC, President - *Construction, Engineering, Environmental, Manufacturing*
Ms. Katie Whitman, CPC, Vice President - *Engineering, Environmental, Insurance, Manufacturing, Real estate*
Ms. Susan George, Consultant - *Sales*
Ms. Holly Frielinghaus, Researcher

Functions: Generalist (All), Management, Sales & Mktg., Engineering

Industries: Generalist (All), Manufacturing, Electronic, Elec. Components, Consumer Goods

Dunhill Professional Search of Memphis

5120 Stage Rd Ste 2
Stage Woods Office Park
Memphis, TN 38134-3164
(901) 386-2500
Web:
www.dunhillstaff.com/office.cfm?office_ID=52

Summary: Our firm is a contingency recruiting of degreed engineering, manufacturing, and distribution candidates.

Key Contact - Specialty:
Mr. Eugene Rhodes, President
Mr. Mike Rhodes, Consultant

Salary Minimum: $35,000

Functions: Mfg., Distribution, Engineering

Industries: Generalist (All), Mfg. SW

Dunhill Professional Search of Austin

9600 Great Hills Trl Ste 150W
Austin, TX 78759-6303
(512) 795-9059
Fax: (512) 343-2759
Email: drh@dunhillaustin.com
Web: www.dunhillaustin.com

Summary: Our firm helps companies in the semiconductor & communication industries hire mid to senior level sales, marketing and engineering talent to achieve their business objectives.

Key Contact - Specialty:
Mr. Douglas Harrington, President
Mr. Tucker Stipe, Vice President
Mr. Jason LaFountain, Senior Consultant - *Electronics, Embedded microprocessor, Engineering, Semiconductors, Technical*

Functions: Sales & Mktg., Engineering, Eng. Design

Industries: Computer Equip., Consumer Elect., Electronic, Elec. Components, Semiconductors, Telecoms, Wireless, Fiber Optic, Network Infrastructure

Dunhill Professional Search of Corpus Christi Inc

4455 S Padre Island Dr Ste 102
Corpus Christi, TX 78411-5125
(361) 225-2580
(800) 277-3690
Fax: (361) 225-3888
Email: info@dunhillsearchcorpus.com
Web: www.dunhillsearchcorpus.com

Summary: We are a search firm specializing in the placement of engineering professionals within the HVAC/R and oil & gas industries. We also specialize in the placement of sales professionals within the office solutions/equipment and light industrial equipment industries.

Key Contact - Specialty:
Mr. Jesse G. Montalvo, President - *Sales*
Mr. Wayne Skinner, Senior Consultant - *Manufacturing*
Mr. Jeff Volling, Consultant - *Manufacturing*
Ms. Alana Gates, Consultant
Mr. Jim Heald, Consultant

Salary Minimum: $40,000

Functions: Management, Product Dev., Sales & Mktg.

Industries: Medical Devices, Metal Products, Machine, Appliance, Misc. Mfg., Electronic, Elec. Components, Pharm. Svcs., Equip. Svcs., Engineering Svcs., Call Centers

Dunhill Professional Search of Houston NW

340 N Sam Houston Pkwy E Ste 285
Houston, TX 77060-3324
(281) 931-6400
Fax: (281) 931-0929
Email: search@dunhillhouston.com
Web: www.dunhillhouston.com

Summary: Contingency and retained executive search firm specializing in mid to senior level positions in the areas of accounting, finance, audit, tax, credit, treasury, operations management, manufacturing, engineering, technical and industrial services. National and international geographic scope. Highest confidentiality standards. Diligent commitment to excellence in service and client satisfaction.

Key Contact - Specialty:
Mr. Richard Rice, President

Salary Minimum: $50,000

Functions: Generalist (All), Mfg., Quality, Finance, CFOs, Budgeting, Credit, Taxes, Int'l.

Industries: Generalist (All), Agri., Forestry, Mining, Energy, Utilities, Oil & Gas, Construction, Food, Bev., Tobacco, Printing, Chemicals, Plastics, Rubber, Paints, Petro. Products, Metal Products

Dunhill Professional Search of Arlington

2912 W Park Row Dr
Pantego, TX 76013-2051
(817) 265-2291
Fax: (817) 265-2294
Email: jobs@dunhillsearch.com
Web: www.dunhillsearch.com

Summary: We specialize in audit and IS audit. We work with Fortune 500 clients as well as small- to medium- sized companies.

Key Contact - Specialty:
Mr. Jon Molkentine, President

Salary Minimum: $50,000

Functions: Finance, Risk Mgmt., Systems Implem.

Industries: Generalist (All)

Dunhill Professional Search of New Braunfels

14514 Majestic Prince St
San Antonio, TX 78248-1133
(210) 492-5435
Fax: (210) 492-5297
Email: wave@ev1.net

Summary: We place engineering professionals in the energy, utilities, manufacturing, transportation, HR services and hazardous waste industries.

Key Contact - Specialty:
Ms. Angella Woodard, CPC, President

Functions: Engineering

Industries: Energy, Utilities, Manufacturing, Transportation, HR Services, Haz. Waste

Dunhill Professional Search of Vermont

PO Box 204
Warren, VT 05674-0204
(802) 496-0115
Fax: (802) 496-0116
Email: dunhillvt@aol.com

Summary: Contingency and retainer search for accounting/financial/EDP audit professional. Work closely with Big 6 firms for referrals as well as major MBA schools, customized searches as required.

Key Contact - Specialty:
Mr. Herb Hauser, President & Treasurer - *Finance*
Ms. Renate Von Recklinghausen, Vice President - *Finance*

Salary Minimum: $35,000

Functions: Budgeting, Taxes, M&A

Industries: Finance

Dunhill Professional Search of Charleston

PO Box 547
Charleston, WV 25322-0547
(304) 340-4260
Fax: (304) 340-4262
Email: dunhillwv@ntelos.net
Web: www.dunhillsc.com

Summary: Recruitment services for healthcare industry. Job titles include laboratory, nursing, diagnostic, financial and rehab services. Our clients offer relocation and interview assistance.

Key Contact - Specialty:
Ms. Marsha Simpkins, President

Functions: Healthcare, Nurses, Allied Health

Industries: Healthcare, Hospitals, Long-term/Home Care, Physical Therapy, Occupational Therapy, Women's

The William Dunne Agency Inc

825C Merrimon Ave # 370
Asheville, NC 28804-2404
(828) 253-0990
Fax: (828) 253-0089

Email: resume.@williamdunneagency.com
Web: www.williamdunneagency.com

Summary: We specialize in the identification, screening and referral of qualified commercial finance personnel mainly in the field of asset-based lending. We place all levels from CEO to middle management, including auditors and operations personnel at various levels. Companies served: asset based lenders, mezzanine lenders, commercial banks, healthcare lenders, factoring lenders, media lenders and telecom lenders.

Key Contact - Specialty:
Mr. Darin G. Kohler, President

Functions: Generalist (All)

Industries: Finance, Banking

Dussick Management Associates

27 White Birch Rd
Madison, CT 06443-2077
(203) 245-9311
Fax: (203) 245-1648
Email: vince@dussick.com
Web: www.dussick.com

Summary: We specialize in the executive recruitment and placement of mid and senior level marketing management professionals as well as senior level promotion talent (sales/consumer) in the consumer package goods industry. Our Fortune Top 25 client base continually utilizes our services.

Key Contact - Specialty:
Mr. Vince Dussick - *Marketing, Sales*
Ms. Gayle Moran - *Marketing, Sales*
Ms. Carol Kinney - *Marketing, Sales*
Mr. Mike Piccione - *Marketing, Sales*

Salary Minimum: $75,000

Functions: Generalist (All), Senior Mgmt., Healthcare, Advertising, Mktg. Mgmt., Sales Mgmt., HR Mgmt., Int'l.

Industries: Generalist (All), Food, Bev., Tobacco, Textiles, Apparel, Soap, Perf., Cosmtcs., Drugs Mfg., Consumer Elect., Pharm Svcs.

Duval Search Associates LLC

3445 Seminole Trl Ste 230
Charlottesville, VA 22911-5637
(800) 659-5190
Fax: (434) 974-7037
Email: info@duvalsearch.com
Web: www.duvalsearch.com

Summary: Our firm focuses specifically on career placement for internal auditors, with a specialization in searches for IS auditors.

Key Contact - Specialty:
Mr. Derek Duval, CPC, President

Salary Minimum: $45,000

Functions: Finance, Risk Mgmt., IT

Industries: Generalist (All), Finance, Misc. Financial, Accounting, Security SW

Dynamic Executive Search

300-197 County Court Blvd
Brampton, ON L6W 4P6
Canada
(905) 796-0210
Fax: (905) 796-5251
Email: info@dynamicexecutive.ca
Web: www.dynamicexecutive.ca

Summary: We are a professional team, providing services in recruitment and HR consulting. We are dedicated to targeting your search through understanding your needs and customizing the search to meet them. Our client base includes start-up, large and Fortune 500 corporations.

Key Contact - Specialty:
Mrs. Sylvie Hyndman, President
Mrs. Nancy Weisner, Vice President

Salary Minimum: $50,000

Functions: Generalist (All), Distribution, Finance

Industries: Generalist (All), Manufacturing, Finance, Pharm Svcs., HR Services, Digital, Wireless, Fiber Optic, Healthcare

Dynamic Search Systems Inc

220 W Campus Dr Ste 201
Arlington Heights, IL 60004-1499
(847) 259-3444
Fax: (847) 259-3480
Email: resumes@dssjobs.com
Web: www.dssjobs.com

Summary: We place IT professionals including applications developers, programmers, programmer/analysts, systems analysts, project leaders/managers, application managers/directors, technical services/systems programmers, administrators covering operating systems, telecom and database.

Key Contact - Specialty:
Mr. Michael J. Brindise, CPC, Principal - *Computers, Database, Information Systems, Information Technology, Systems*

Salary Minimum: $25,000

Functions: IT

Industries: Generalist (All)

Dynamic Staffing Network

1200 Harger Rd Ste 600
Oak Brook, IL 60523-1820
(630) 572-9980
Fax: (630) 572-9892
Email: hr@dynastaff.com
Web: www.dynastaff.com

Summary: Our Recruiters have extensive exerience in the business. We strive to have our clients look forward to working with us again.

Key Contact - Specialty:
Mr. James Gilbert, President
Mr. Richard Bradley, CPC, Vice President
Mr. George Custer, Secretary & Treasurer - *Manufacturing*
Ms. Denise Armbruster, Recruiter
Ms. Tammy Dougherty, Recruiter
Ms. Christine Grudecki, Recruiter - *Engineering*

Functions: Generalist (All), Management, Mfg., Materials, Finance, IT, Engineering

Industries: Generalist (All)

E Insurance Group

10563 Greencrest Dr
Tampa, FL 33626-5200
(813) 926-0306
Fax: (813) 926-5393
Email: michael@einsgroup.com
Web: www.einsgroup.com

Summary: Our clients include insurance agencies/brokerage, carriers, consulting, managing general agencies/underwriters, and wholesalers. Placement activity includes broking, claims, management, marketing, programs, sales/sales management, service, underwriting, risk services, professional liabilities, employee benefits/health & welfare, medical malpractice and start-ups. Industry niches include construction, energy/marine, environmental, healthcare, mergers & acquisitions, oil/gas, etc.

Key Contact - Specialty:
Mr. Michael S. Evdemon, II, President - *Insurance*

(Casualty, Claims, Health, Reinsurance, Workers Compensation)

Salary Minimum: $65,000

Functions: Board Members, Senior Mgmt., Middle Mgmt., Healthcare, Sales & Mktg., Mktg. Mgmt., Sales Mgmt., Risk Mgmt., Mgmt. Consultants

Industries: Energy, Utilities, Oil & Gas, Construction, Insurance, Casualty, Claims, Commercial, Re-Insurance

E O Technical

57 North St Ste 320
Danbury, CT 06810-5628
(203) 797-2653
Fax: (203) 797-2657
Email: jeanette@employops.com
Web: www.employops.com

Summary: We are a female-owned operation open for one purpose: to serve our clients and our applicants.

Key Contact - Specialty:
Ms. Jeanette Petroski, Owner

Functions: Generalist (All), MIS Mgmt., R&D

Industries: Generalist (All), Plastics, Rubber, Banking, Pharm Svcs., Legal, HR Services, IT Implementation, Defense, Insurance, Biotech/Life Sciences, Healthcare

Branches:
755 Main St
Monroe, CT 06468-2830
(203) 455-8111
Fax: (203) 455-8112
Email: gary@employops.com
Key Contact - Specialty:
Mr. Gary Petroski - *Technical*

E&C Services Inc

1004 5th Ave Ste 200
Coraopolis, PA 15108-1885
(412) 865-0555
Fax: (412) 865-0560
Email: eric.gaber@eandcservices.com
Web: www.eandcservices.com

Summary: Our purpose is to offer engineering, construction and Real Estate organizations an executive search process that is directed by industry experts in a professional, ethical and goal oriented manner.

Key Contact - Specialty:
Mr. Eric Gaber, President
Mr. David Roberts, Director - *Construction*
Mr. David Oney, Director - *Construction, Engineering*
Mr. Frank Russell, Project Manager - *Capital markets, CFOs, Construction, Engineering*
Mr. Mark Maier, Director, Recruiting - *Construction, Engineering*
Mr. Bill Stewart, Project Manager - *CEOs, CFOs, Construction, Design, Engineering*
Mr. Tony Trovato, Director - *Construction, Engineering, Real estate*

Salary Minimum: $90,000

Functions: Generalist (All), Board Members, Senior Mgmt., CFOs

Industries: Energy, Utilities, Construction, Manufacturing, Finance, Real Estate, Biotech/Life Sciences

e-TransActions

11569 S Highway 6 Ste 146
Sugar Land, TX 77478-4932
(713) 927-6235
Fax: (281) 754-4746

Email: elena.tran@gmail.com

Summary: We are an executive and IT recruiting firm.

Key Contact - Specialty:
Ms. Elena Tran, Director - *Executives, Marketing, Sales*

Functions: Generalist (All)

Industries: IT Implementation

E/Search International

PO Box 408
West Suffield, CT 06093-0408
(860) 668-5848
(800) 300-0477
Email: bob@directcompetitor.com
Web: www.directcompetitor.com

Summary: We work for high technology companies with highly focused executive level needs. Our specialty is targeting and finding top executives and sales people with direct competitors of our client companies. Industry experience includes biotechnology, electronics, software, manufacturing, telecom and more.

Key Contact - Specialty:
Mr. Bob Rossow, President

Salary Minimum: $75,000

Functions: Generalist (All), Management, Senior Mgmt.

Industries: Manufacturing, Test, Measure Equip., Electronic, Elec. Components, Communications, Telecoms, Telephony, Wireless, Network Infrastructure, Software, ERP SW, Mfg. SW, Marketing SW, Networking, Comm. SW, System SW, Biotech/Life Sciences

Eagle Consulting Group Inc

(also known as EagleSearch)
12300 Ford Rd Ste 150
Dallas, TX 75234-7293
(972) 247-0990
Fax: (972) 247-4306
Email: mail@eaglesearch.net
Web: www.eaglesearch.net

Summary: Our mission is to always provide excellence in performance while assuring the highest standards of professionalism and to meld our candidate delivery systems to meet each client's expectations and corporate objectives.

Key Contact - Specialty:
Mr. William G. Mitchell, President & Managing Director - *Biopharmaceutical*

Salary Minimum: $65,000

Functions: Generalist (All), Senior Mgmt., Mfg., Production, Quality, Materials Plng., R&D, Engineering

Industries: Generalist (All), Manufacturing, Drugs Mfg., Pharm Svcs., Healthcare

J M Eagle Partners Ltd

PO Box 80174
Saukville, WI 53080-0174
(262) 377-8888 x240
(262) 242-1812
Fax: (262) 375-6677
Email: jmoses@seekcareers.com

Summary: We offer a vertical approach to medical industry search. Specialization: in-depth knowledge and reputation within diagnostic imaging (radiology manufacturers).

Key Contact - Specialty:
Mr. Jerry Moses, President

Functions: Generalist (All), Sales & Mktg.

Industries: Generalist (All), Drugs Mfg., Medical Devices, Pharm Svcs., Equip Svcs., Mgmt. Consulting, HR Services, Software, Mfg. SW, Marketing SW, Biotech/Life Sciences

Eagle Research Inc

373 US Highway 46
Fairfield, NJ 07004-2442
(973) 244-0992
Fax: (973) 244-1239
Email: eagle@eagleresearch.net
Web: www.eagleresearch.net

Summary: Specializing in the pharmaceutical, biotechnology, specialty pharma, and related industries with an emphasis in clinical pharmacology, clinical R&D, medical affairs/marketing, drug safety, project management, clinical operations, and other related supporting R&D.

Key Contact - Specialty:
Ms. Annette S. Baron, MBA, PA, President - *Biopharmaceutical, Biotechnology, Pharmaceutical, Physicians, Research & development*

Functions: Healthcare, Physicians, R&D

Industries: Drugs Mfg., Biotech/Life Sciences

Eagle Rock Consulting Group

PO Box 6451
Chesterfield, MO 63006-6451
(314) 878-0900
Email: resumes@eagle-rock-consulting.com
Web: www.eagle-rock-consulting.com

Summary: The bulk of our assignments are in the accounting and finance functions in all industries. We handle both contingent and retained searches depending upon the nature of the assignment. Assignments handled cover the full range of professional positions from senior accountant up through CFO.

Key Contact - Specialty:
Mr. Bill Geis, Managing Consultant - *Accounting*

Salary Minimum: $60,000

Functions: Finance

Industries: Generalist (All)

Eagle Technology Group Inc

11575 W Theodore Trecker Way
Milwaukee, WI 53214-1143
(800) 964-9675
Fax: (414) 453-9720
Email: info@eagleinc.net
Web: www.eagleinc.net

Summary: We are a recognized Future 50 company and have emerged as a leader in the placement of engineering, manufacturing and technical professionals.

Key Contact - Specialty:
Mr. Michael R. Hansen, Vice President, Finance

Functions: Generalist (All), Mfg., Automation, Materials, Packaging, IT, R&D, Engineering, Architects, Technicians

Industries: Generalist (All), Manufacturing, Finance, Government, Insurance, Software, Healthcare

Easley Resource Group Inc

333 S State St Ste V
Lake Oswego, OR 97034-3948
(503) 699-4067
Fax: (503) 699-5467
Email: contact@glassrecruiters.com
Web: www.glassrecruiters.com

Summary: We specialize in bringing together professionals and career opportunities within the primary and secondary glass/ceramics industry. We perform retained, contingency and contract assignments for many of the best companies in the industry. Our energies are directed toward locating and recruiting the finest talent for our client companies. We do this the old fashioned way. We simply know the glass industry better than anyone.

Key Contact - Specialty:
Ms. Jill Kohler-Easley, Principal & Recruiter

Functions: Generalist (All)

Industries: Manufacturing, Leather, Stone, Glass

The East Wing Group

1250 S Grove Ave Ste 200
Barrington, IL 60010-5011
(847) 381-0977
Fax: (847) 381-0955
Email: info@eastwingsearchgroup.com
Web: www.eastwingsearchgroup.com

Summary: Our firm places management and sales professionals in the packaging, plastics, building products, communications industries, construction, manufacturing, banking, venture capital, management consulting and packaging industries.

Key Contact - Specialty:
Mr. Russ Riendeau, Recruiter

Salary Minimum: $50,000

Functions: Management, Sales Mgmt., Direct Mktg., PR, Specialized Svcs., Mgmt. Consultants

Industries: Energy, Utilities, Construction, Manufacturing, Banking, Venture Cap., Mgmt. Consulting, Hospitality, Haz. Waste, Aerospace, Packaging

Eastwood Personnel Associates Inc

418 Partridge St
Franklin, MA 02038-1521
(508) 528-8111
Fax: (508) 528-1221
Email: rick@eastwoodassociates.com
Web: www.eastwoodassociates.com

Summary: We are a professional employment source serving commercial and savings banks throughout the Northeastern US. We specialize in the search and recruitment of executives in the areas of corporate/commercial lending, real estate lending, loan review, loan workout, credit administration, specialized lending, trust, private banking, retail banking and cash management.

Key Contact - Specialty:
Mr. Rick Hohenberger, President

Salary Minimum: $75,000

Functions: Sales & Mktg., Finance, Cash Mgmt., Credit, Risk Mgmt.

Industries: Banking, Invest. Banking

eAttorney

(a division of Martindale-Hubbell)
245 Peachtree Center Ave NE Ste 2415
Marquis One Tower
Atlanta, GA 30303-1243
(800) 378-6101
Fax: (404) 215-5408
Email: eattorneyinfo@martindale.com
Web: www.eattorney.com

Summary: Taking the place of a traditional search firm, we are a company that links hundreds of legal employers with thousands of individual attorneys and students confidentially via a secured website.

Key Contact - Specialty:
Mr. Samuel B. Kellett, Jr., Executive Vice President

Functions: Generalist (All), Attorneys

Industries: Generalist (All), Legal

EBS Northwest Inc

21616 230th St SE
Monroe, WA 98272-8004
(360) 863-0376
Fax: (360) 294-5082
Email: resume@ebs-northwest.com
Web: www.ebs-northwest.com

Summary: We are an executive search and recruiting services for the eLearning industry. We offer services for executive, management and sales placements, and functional placements.

Key Contact - Specialty:
Mrs. Jeanine K. Kern, President

Functions: Senior Mgmt., Middle Mgmt., Product Dev., Sales & Mktg., Sales Mgmt., Sales Reps., Training, IT, Systems Dev., Systems Implem.

Industries: IT Implementation, Software, Training SW

Eckler Personnel Network (EPN Inc)

PO Box 549
Woodstock, VT 05091-0549
(802) 457-1605
Fax: (802) 910-1017
Email: epn@sover.net

Summary: Regionalized search and contingency placement firm specializing in all levels of business software,IT professionals, related sales/marketing and support functions.

Key Contact - Specialty:
Mr. Geoffrey N. Eckler, President

Salary Minimum: $75,000

Functions: Generalist (All), Sales & Mktg., Sales Mgmt., IT, Systems Dev., Systems Implem., Systems Support, Network Admin., DB Admin., Mgmt. Consultants, Homeland Security

Industries: Generalist (All), Mgmt. Consulting, E-commerce, IT Implementation, PSA/ASP, Defense, Homeland Security, Software

ECS Medical Staffing

(a division of ECS Staffing LLC)
295 Madison Ave Rm 1830
New York, NY 10017-6380
(212) 972-0350
Fax: (212) 972-2359
Web: www.ecsmedical.com

Summary: We specialize in the recruitment and placement of medical professionals. We offer exceptional personal service for all those we assist, from the prospective candidate to the healthcare administrator. We provide both permanent and temporary placements.

Key Contact - Specialty:
Ms. Judith Faske, Managing Director

Functions: Healthcare

Industries: Generalist (All), Healthcare

The Edelstein Group

13 Newton Rd
Gaylordsville, CT 06755-1315
(860) 350-4301
Fax: (860) 210-7998
Email: sue@edelsteingroup.com
Web: www.edelsteingroup.com

Summary: We specialize in mid-level and senior management searches within advertising, and branding companies. Our primary focus is: account management, account planning, project management, branding and business development.

Key Contact - Specialty:
Ms. Sue Edelstein, President & Owner

Salary Minimum: $50,000

Functions: Generalist (All), Management, Senior Mgmt., Middle Mgmt., Advertising

Industries: Advertising, New Media, Marketing SW

Edge Recruiting Solutions Inc

13302 Millard Ave Ste 104
Omaha, NE 68137-1776
(402) 896-3343
Fax: (402) 896-3367
Email: abecker@edgerecruiters.com
Web: www.edgerecruiters.com

Summary: Medical and pharmaceutical: sales, marketing and management candidates.

Key Contact - Specialty:
Mr. Aaron Becker, President - *Business to business, Medical, Medical (Sales), Pharmaceutical, Sales*

Salary Minimum: $35,000

Functions: Sales & Mktg.

Industries: Drugs Mfg., Medical Devices

The Edge Resource Group

PO Box 457
Greensburg, PA 15601-0457
(724) 523-4795
Email: terg@verizon.net

Summary: Area of specialization: Senior-level Sales and Sales Support primarily focused on the Software and Technology sectors.

Key Contact - Specialty:
Ms. Diane Schoff, Principal - *MIS*

Salary Minimum: $70,000

Functions: Sales & Mktg., Sales Mgmt

Industries: E-commerce, IT Implementation, Software

The Edgewater Group Inc

Harborside Financial Ctr Plaza 5 Ste 2500
Jersey City, NJ 07311-1114
(201) 633-4700
Email: mark@ewatergroup.com
Web: www.edgewatergroup.com

Summary: We are an IT recruiting firm servicing technology professionals in the financial services, software, consulting and pharmaceutical industries.

Key Contact - Specialty:
Mr. Mark Dinowitz, President - *Database (Warehousing), Derivatives, Information Technology, Risk management, SAP*

Salary Minimum: $60,000

Functions: IT

Industries: Banking, Invest. Banking, Brokers, Mutual/Hedge Funds, Pharm Svcs., Database SW, Development SW, Industry Specific SW, Security SW, Training SW

Edwards & Associates

4015 Goshen Lake Dr S
Augusta, GA 30906-9112
(706) 793-3679
Email: lisa.edwards@earthlink.net

Summary: Our primary focus is in sales (generalist as well as pharmaceutical/medical). Our secondary focus is the staffing industry and general sales. Ideal candidate profile has a business product or service background, if not industry specific.

Key Contact - Specialty:
Ms. Lisa Edwards, Owner & President - *Business to business, Copiers, Medical (Sales), Pharmaceutical*
Mrs. Rachel E. Reese, Executive Search Assistant - *Business to business, Medical (Sales), Pharmaceutical, Real estate, Sales*

Salary Minimum: $55,000

Functions: Sales & Mktg., Sales Reps.

Industries: Drugs Mfg., Medical Devices, Pharm Svcs., Equip Svcs., Dental

Edwards & Kote Executive Search

2103 Cedar Cir
Carrollton, TX 75006-1923
(972) 416-1275
(972) 236-4962
Fax: (866) 845-1406
Email: bill@edkosearch.com
Web: www.edkosearch.com

Summary: Executive recruiters specializing in the placement of candidates in the consumer packaged goods industry.

Key Contact - Specialty:
Mr. Bill Preston

Salary Minimum: $50,000

Functions: Generalist (All)

Industries: Food, Bev., Tobacco

Edwards Consulting Firm Inc

2871D N Decatur Rd Ste 171
Decatur, GA 30033-5989
(404) 288-8824
(877) 288-8824
Email: info@edwardsconsultingfirm.com
Web: www.edwardsconsultingfirm.com

Summary: Our firm is a corporate talent search firm. We are a generalist firm recruiting mid-to-senior level management with expertise in a wide range of industries, functional and diversity search assignments nationwide.

Key Contact - Specialty:
Ms. Damali Edwards, Founder & Chief Executive Officer
Mr. Arlando Edwards, Partner & Vice President

Salary Minimum: $75,000

Functions: Senior Mgmt., Middle Mgmt., Admin. Svcs., Sales & Mktg., HR Mgmt., Finance, IT, MIS Mgmt., Engineering, Minorities/Diversity

Industries: Generalist (All)

Edwards Recruitment Inc

PO Box 410
6028 Sheridan Dr
Williamsville, NY 14231-0410
(716) 332-1064
Fax: (716) 631-5272
Email: liz@lizedwards.com
Web: www.lizedwards.com

Summary: Specializing in the credit card and consumer finance industries for all areas of operations, marketing, risk, credit, finance, process improvements and sales.

Key Contact - Specialty:
Ms. Liz Edwards, Owner - *Credit cards, Financial services, Loss Prevention, Marketing, Risk management*

Salary Minimum: $100,000

Functions: Generalist (All), Senior Mgmt., Middle Mgmt.

Industries: Finance, Banking

Edwards Search Group Inc
1804 Soscol Ave Ste 201
Napa, CA 94559-1384
(707) 253-9200
Fax: (707) 253-9222
Email: kenn@edwardssearch.com
Web: www.edwardssearchgroup.com

Summary: We are an established leader in the medical/healthcare contingency search and recruiting field. We fill management & sales positions with individuals specifically chosen to bring an impact to your corporation. Our client companies share the same commitment in the people they hire as we do in the people we recruit.

Key Contact - Specialty:
Mr. Kenn Edwards, President - *Pharmaceutical, Sales*
Mr. Russ Cipriani, Vice President
Mr. Greg Schmaltz, Senior Recruiter - *Sales*
Mrs. Eva Kelly, Market Development Manager - *Healthcare, Marketing, Medical, Medical (Sales), Research & development*
Mr. Jim Bonk, Senior Recruiter
Miss Brooke Baldwin, Recruiter
Mr. Bob Yanover, Recruiter
Ms. Jan Schweitz, Administrative Assistant

Salary Minimum: $50,000

Functions: Generalist (All), Management, Sales & Mktg.

Industries: Manufacturing, Drugs Mfg., Medical Devices, Pharm Svcs., Healthcare, Hospitals

EFCO Consultants Inc
3 The Balsams
Roslyn, NY 11576-1715
(516) 829-9200
Fax: (516) 484-7387
Email: nfells@efconet.com
Web: www.efconet.com

Summary: We specialize in the placement of IT professionals.

Key Contact - Specialty:
Mr. Norman Fells, President

Salary Minimum: $80,000

Functions: Management, Senior Mgmt., Middle Mgmt., Sales & Mktg., Mktg. Mgmt., Sales Mgmt., IT, Systems Implem., Systems Support, Mgmt. Consultants

Industries: Computer Equip., Mgmt. Consulting, Software

Branches:
200 E 72nd St Apt 7B
New York, NY 10021-4500
(212) 706-1995
Fax: (212) 202-6412
Email: fells@efconet.com
Key Contact - Specialty:
Mr. Jeffrey Fells, Vice President

Effective Placement Inc
1841-144 St
Surrey, BC V4A 7E8
Canada
(604) 341-1053

Email: marie-helene@effectiveplacement.com
Web: www.effectiveplacement.com

Summary: Executive recruitment and search firm known for the placement of key professionals within the areas of finance, IT, operations and sales & marketing. In addition we provide on-site assistance in the areas of salary, benefits, compensation administration, working conditions, employee relations, presentation of offers, defining position parameters and hiring criteria. We let you get back to your focus on the growth and profitability of your business.

Key Contact - Specialty:
Ms. Marie-Helene Sakowski, Principal - *Consumer, Consumer (Packaged Goods), Manufacturing, Manufacturing (Management), Professional services*

Functions: Management, Senior Mgmt., Middle Mgmt., Plant Mgmt., Sales & Mktg., Systems Implem.

Industries: Agri., Forestry, Mining, Energy, Utilities, Oil & Gas, Food, Bev., Tobacco, Mgmt. Consulting, HR Services, IT Implementation, Engineering Svcs., Packaging, Database SW, Development SW, ERP SW, HR SW

Eggers Consulting Company Inc
11272 Elm St
Omaha, NE 68144-4731
(402) 333-3480
Fax: (402) 333-9759
Email: admin@eggersconsulting.com
Web: www.eggersconsulting.com

Summary: Professional search and executive recruiting firm. Specializing in banking, IT, insurance, retail, healthcare, transportation & logistics and hospitality.

Key Contact - Specialty:
Mr. James W. Eggers, President
Mr. Raymond Hamilius, Manager - *Retail*
Ms. Ellen Hembertt, Treasurer & Vice President
Ms. L.D. Miller, Vice President
Mr. Randy Lyons, Vice President

Functions: Generalist (All), Sales Mgmt., Staffing, IT, MIS Mgmt., Network Admin., DB Admin.

Industries: Generalist (All), Medical Devices, Transportation, Retail, Banking, Hospitality, Insurance, Database SW, Healthcare

MJ Egy & Associates
1000 S 14th St
Terre Haute, IN 47807-4925
(812) 235-2588
Fax: (812) 235-2587
Email: egy@primarymetals.net
Web: www.primarymetals.net

Summary: Our firm specialize in the search and placement of professionals in the primary metals industry. Our goal is to provide quality service, fast and accurately, to our client companies.

Key Contact - Specialty:
Mr. Michael J. Egy, President - *CEOs, COOs, Foundries, Steel*
Ms. Lorene Olmos, Senior Executive Recruiter - *Engineering, Foundries, Maintenance, Metals, Steel*
Mr. Robert Drogus, Executive Recruiter - *Engineering, Facilities engineering, ISO 9000, Safety, Six Sigma*
Mr. Jeff Wisby, Data Base Administrator - *Engineering, Foundries, Maintenance, Metals, Steel*

Salary Minimum: $50,000

Functions: Senior Mgmt., Product Dev., Plant Mgmt., Quality, Purchasing, Sales & Mktg., Engineering, Process

Industries: Manufacturing, Metal Products

eHire
350 5th Ave Ste 4501
New York, NY 10118-4501
(212) 736-9544
Fax: (212) 736-9522
Email: jsabrin@ehire.com
Web: www.ehire.com

Summary: Our firm is a full service executive search firm with extensive experience. We offer sophisticated, aggressive, quality-oriented services and solutions to businesses, which enables them to compete in a changing world. Our services encompass both the personal touch as well as a strategic approach; that makes us their partner of choice.

Key Contact - Specialty:
Mr. Joe Sabrin, Executive Vice President & Founder

Salary Minimum: $30,000

Functions: Generalist (All), Management, IT

Industries: Generalist (All), Finance, Invest. Banking, Call Centers

Eisner LLP
750 3rd Ave
New York, NY 10017-2703
(212) 949-8700
(212) 891-8703
Fax: (212) 891-4100
Email: hr@eisnerllp.com
Web: www.eisnerllp.com

Summary: Senior executive searches, compensation and management consulting services for a wide range of companies including mid-sized companies, portfolio companies of venture capital and buyout firms, new US ventures of non-US based companies.

Key Contact - Specialty:
Mr. Richard Fisher, Partner
Mr. Richard A. Eisner, Managing Partner - *Biopharmaceutical, Healthcare, Management, Pharmaceutical, Sales*

Salary Minimum: $70,000

Functions: Generalist (All), Management, Mktg. Mgmt., HR Mgmt., Finance, IT, Mgmt. Consultants

Industries: Generalist (All), Accounting

Branches:
100 Campus Dr
Florham Park, NJ 07932-1020
(973) 593-7000
Fax: (973) 593-7070
Key Contact - Specialty:
Mr. Eli Hoffman, Recruiter

Eissler & Associates Inc
(formerly known as W Robert Eissler & Associates Inc)
26214 Oak Ridge Dr
Spring, TX 77380-1961
(281) 367-1052
Fax: (281) 292-6489
Email: eissler@eissler.com
Web: www.eissler.com

Summary: We provide recruiters for senior and middle-level sales, management and technical positions. We specialize in the valve, instrumentation, fluid power, electronics and oil & gas industries.

Key Contact - Specialty:
Mr. W. Robert Eissler, President & Recruiter - *Process equipment*
Ms. Marie Devaney, Recruiter - *Engineering, Gas, Oil*
Mr. Al Weaver, Recruiter - *Chemical, Process equipment*
Mr. Mark Eissler, Recruiter - *Electronics, Instrumentation*

Salary Minimum: $25,000

Functions: Management

Industries: Generalist (All)

The Eldridge Group Ltd

27864 Irma Lee Cir Ste 106
Lake Forest, IL 60045-5114
(847) 680-9090
Fax: (847) 680-4141
Email: davea@eldridgegroup.com
Web: www.eldridgegroup.com

Summary: Search firm with an extensive national network We concentrate on sales/sales management in consumer products, B2B, medical and industrial assignments.

Key Contact - Specialty:
Mr. David Eldridge Archibald, President & Owner - *Business to business, Consumer (Packaged Goods), Industrial, Management, Medical (Sales)*

Salary Minimum: $85,000

Functions: Sales Mgmt.

Industries: Food, Bev., Tobacco, Paper, Soap, Perf., Cosmtcs., Drugs Mfg., Medical Devices, Computer Equip., Consumer Elect., Services, Software, Healthcare

Electronic Search Inc

5105 Tollview Dr Ste 245
Rolling Meadows, IL 60008-3786
(847) 506-0700
(888) 356-3501
Fax: (847) 506-9999
Email: email@electronicsearch.com
Web: www.electronicsearch.com

Summary: Places high level executives and technical professionals in the computer and telecom industry. We place an emphasis on personal relationships and in providing the right personnel match.

Key Contact - Specialty:
Mr. Steve Eddington, President - *Business development*

Salary Minimum: $30,000

Functions: Generalist (All), IT, MIS Mgmt., Systems Analysis, Systems Dev., Systems Implem., Engineering, Int'l.

Industries: Generalist (All), Computer Equip., Misc. Financial, Mgmt. Consulting, Telecoms, Software

Branches:
990 Highland Dr Ste 212K
Solana Beach, CA 92075-3404
(858) 792-8108
(800) 355-5927
Fax: (858) 792-8121
Email: aborn@electronicsearch.com

Key Contact - Specialty:
Mr. Al Born, Recruiter

Elite Consultants Inc

976 Florida Central Pkwy Ste 112
Longwood, FL 32750-7572
(407) 831-3448
(888) 562-7324
Fax: (407) 260-1347
Email: elite@elite-eci.com
Web: www.elite-eci.com

Summary: We maintain a large network of engineers and clients; our resources enable us to quickly match our clients' need with the right expertise.

Key Contact - Specialty:
Mrs. Janeen Cepull, General Manager

Functions: Generalist (All), Systems Dev., Systems Implem., Systems Support, Network Admin., Engineering

Industries: Generalist (All), Telecoms, Software

Elite Placement Service Inc

17047 El Camino Real Ste 200
Houston, TX 77058-2643
(281) 990-8833
Fax: (281) 990-8885
Email: watson@eliteplacement.com
Web: www.eliteplacement.com

Summary: Our firm is an executive search firm that specializes in the placement of experienced IT management, marketing, HR and sales professionals.

Key Contact - Specialty:
Mrs. Michelle Watson, President

Salary Minimum: $45,000

Functions: Board Members, Senior Mgmt., Middle Mgmt., Product Dev., Sales Mgmt., HR Mgmt., IT, MIS Mgmt., DB Admin.

Industries: Generalist (All), Mgmt. Consulting, HR Services, E-commerce, IT Implementation, Software, Marketing SW, Networking, Comm. SW, Security SW, Biotech/Life Sciences

Elite Professional Solutions

29 Woodmont Rd
Melville, NY 11747-3320
(631) 643-1450
Fax: (631) 980-7976
Email: brogers@elite-ps.com
Web: www.elite-ps.com

Summary: We are a recruitment firm providing executive search services in the semiconductor and power electronics industries. Our search services specialize in senior and mid level management positions in the areas of sales, marketing, applications engineering, and business management.

Key Contact - Specialty:
Mr. Bryan Rogers, President

Salary Minimum: $100,000

Functions: Mktg. Mgmt., Sales Mgmt.

Industries: Semiconductors

Elite Search Consultants

31194 La Baya Dr Ste 200
Westlake Village, CA 91362-6430
(818) 707-7340
(800) 301-5993
Fax: (818) 707-8631
Email: iplaw@eliteconsultants.com
Web: www.eliteconsultants.com

Summary: We are an executive search firm specializing in the placement of intellectual property attorneys. We maintain a diverse listing of career opportunities from the nation's top intellectual property boutiques and general practice firms as well as Fortune 500 corporations and start-up companies.

Key Contact - Specialty:
Ms. Ellen Tamiyasu, Principal
Ms. Caroline Cameron, Principal

Functions: Generalist (All), Attorneys

Industries: Legal, Property/Facility Mgmt.

Elite Staffing Services Inc

(also known as Elite Recruiting Services, Inc.)
PO Box 910205
4445 Eastgate Mall Rd Fl 2
San Diego, CA 92191-0205
(858) 455-8300
Fax: (858) 455-8383
Email: resumes@elitestaffingsvc.com
Web: www.elitestaffingsvc.com

Summary: We are a global recruitment firm dedicated to uniting high caliber individuals with exceptional organizations in; accounting/finance, administrative, biotechnology/science/medical device, business development, executive management, HR, IT, investor relations, legal, marketing, packaging/manufacturing, PR, quality assurance/validation, real estate/building industry/architecture, software development, and technical/engineering.

Key Contact - Specialty:
Ms. Lisa DeBenedittis, Recruiter

Salary Minimum: $50,000

Functions: Management, Board Members, Senior Mgmt., Middle Mgmt., Plant Mgmt., HR Mgmt., Finance, CFOs, Taxes, R&D

Industries: Generalist (All), Energy, Utilities, Manufacturing, Drugs Mfg., Medical Devices, Finance, Misc. Financial, Services, Non-profits, Pharm Svcs., Legal, Accounting, Mgmt. Consulting, HR Services, Logistics Svcs., Supply Chain Mgmt., Communications, Packaging, Software, Accounting SW, Networking, Comm. SW, Biotech/Life Sciences

Gene Ellefson & Associates Inc

330 Town Center Dr Ste 304
Dearborn, MI 48126-2795
(313) 982-6000
Email: gene@geassoc.com

Summary: We specialize in recruiting and placing with automotive OEM tier I, II, systems/components suppliers. Positions include engineering, sales, program management, purchasing, HR, etc.

Key Contact - Specialty:
Mr. Gene Ellefson, President - *Automotive, Components, Engineering, Sales*

Salary Minimum: $75,000

Functions: Generalist (All)

Industries: Motor Vehicles

Ted Elliott & Associates

11455 El Camino Real, Ste 390
San Diego, CA 92130-3036
(858) 509-9000
Email: inquiries@elliottrecruiting.com
Web: www.elliottrecruiting.com

Summary: We specialize in the placement of finance and accounting professionals on a permanent basis. Our clients consist of technology, telecommunication, biotech,

manufacturing, and service companies, ranging from startup to Fortune 500 companies.

Key Contact - Specialty:
Mr. Ted M. Elliott, Principal
Mr. Raul N. Lamas, Director

Functions: Finance

Industries: Finance

Phil Ellis Associates Inc

PO Box 900
Wrightsville Beach, NC 28480-0900
(910) 256-9810
Fax: (910) 256-2771
Email: philellis@pellis.com
Web: www.pellis.com

Summary: Pharmaceutical, bio-technology, medical device search and recruiting.

Key Contact - Specialty:
Mr. Phil Ellis, President
Mr. Lee Douglas, Principal
Mr. John Lee, Principal - *Engineering, Operations, Quality*

Salary Minimum: $50,000

Functions: Generalist (All)

Industries: Chemicals, Drugs Mfg., Medical Devices, Biotech/Life Sciences

Ellis Career Consultants

1090 Broadway
West Long Branch, NJ 07764-1337
(732) 222-5333
Fax: (732) 222-2332
Email: info@elliscareer.com
Web: www.elliscareer.com

Summary: Placing executive, corporate, merchandising, distribution, financial, and senior field people in the retail industry. We have an excellent reputation in the diversity community.

Key Contact - Specialty:
Ms. Lisa Shapiro, President - *Retail*

Salary Minimum: $60,000

Functions: Board Members, Senior Mgmt., Product Dev., Purchasing, Distribution, Advertising, Mktg. Mgmt., Sales Mgmt., HR Mgmt., Finance

Industries: Textiles, Apparel, Wholesale, Retail

The Elmhurst Group (TEG)

4120 Douglas Blvd Ste 306 PMB 207
Granite Bay, CA 95746-5936
(916) 772-6720
Email: teg@elmhurstgroup.com
Web: www.elmhurstgroup.com

Summary: Our firm is focused on finding the people who bring the intellect, achievement, integrity and experience to harness technology and discovery in ways that drive a life sciences and technology organization forward. We place physicians, pharmacists and other healthcare professionals in a variety of client settings. We also work with companies involved in the creation, design, development, marketing or sales of software products or services.

Key Contact - Specialty:
Ms. Shari Miller, Principal

Functions: Senior Mgmt., Product Dev., Healthcare, Physicians, Allied Health, Sales & Mktg., IT, Systems Dev., Systems Implem., Mgmt. Consultants

Industries: Pharm Svcs., Mgmt. Consulting, IT Implementation, New Media, Software, Database SW, Development SW, Doc. Mgmt., Production SW, ERP SW, Industry Specific

SW, Security SW, System SW, Healthcare, Hospitals, Long-term/Home Care, Physical Therapy, Occupational Therapy, Women's

Emerging Healthcare Partners LLC

57 North St Ste 212
Danbury, CT 06810-5627
(203) 796-0060
Fax: (203) 796-0056
Email: info@emerginghp.com
Web: www.emerginghp.com

Summary: We are a retained executive search firm serving the healthcare industry. We specialize in providing executive search solutions and services to emerging & rapidly growing companies in the pharmaceutical/biotech and medical device industries. Our primary focus is to place executives in the commercialization disciplines and general management roles.

Key Contact - Specialty:
Mr. Greg Flanagan, President & Founder
Ms. Jill Wiebke, Senior Consultant - *Biomedical, Biopharmaceutical, Biotechnology, Pharmaceutical*

Salary Minimum: $100,000

Functions: Senior Mgmt., Healthcare, Sales & Mktg., Mktg. Research, Mktg. Mgmt., Sales Mgmt., M&A

Industries: Drugs Mfg., Medical Devices, Consumer Goods, Biotech/Life Sciences, Healthcare

Emerging Technology Services Inc

34 1/2 W Main St
Waconia, MN 55387-1020
(952) 442-4570
Email: hq@specializedrecruiters.com
Web: www.emergingtechnologyservices.com

Summary: We specialize in recruiting for DBA, data warehouse, data architecture and data administration professionals across the country on both direct and contract basis. We provide services for fortune 500 clients.

Key Contact - Specialty:
Mr. Kevin Kapaun, President

Salary Minimum: $60,000

Functions: IT, Systems Dev., DB Admin.

Industries: Generalist (All)

The Emeritus Group Inc

17159 W 13 Mile Rd
Southfield, MI 48076-1241
(248) 647-9763
Fax: (248) 647-9778
Email: jmobrien@emeritusinc.com
Web: www.emeritusinc.com

Summary: Executive recruiting experience in multiple industries, preference to the health care field. Trained presidents of search firms.

Key Contact - Specialty:
Mr. J. Michael O'Brien, President

Salary Minimum: $80,000

Functions: Senior Mgmt.

Industries: Manufacturing, Medical Devices, Services, Non-profits, Mgmt. Consulting, HR Services, Software, Database SW, HR SW, Healthcare

Emerson Personnel Group

1040 Kings Hwy N Ste 400
Cherry Hill, NJ 08034-1925
(856) 667-9180
(800) 875-9180
Fax: (856) 667-0064
Email: wce@emersonpersonnel.com
Web: www.emersonpersonnel.com

Summary: We provide permanent and temp staffing solutions for employers. We specialize in all areas of office support, administrative support, accounting, and human resources placement services.

Key Contact - Specialty:
Mr. William Emerson, Chief Executive Officer
Mr. Steve Emerson, President
Ms. Jill Kraus, Vice President, Emerson Accounting Group
Ms. Karmae Cipriotti, Human Resources Group & Corporate Coach

Salary Minimum: $45,000

Functions: Admin. Svcs., HR Mgmt., Finance

Industries: Generalist (All)

Emkay Assoc Ltd

4920 Hunting Hills Cir
Roanoke, VA 24018-8761
(540) 772-1030
Fax: (540) 772-2508
Email: marketing@emkayasociates.com
Web: www.emkayasociates.com

Summary: We focus in professional sales and sales management achievers. We also recruit management and operations personnel in other disciplines; industries include document management, direct marketing, printing and office equipment.

Key Contact - Specialty:
Mr. Edward Welch, President - *Advertising, Business to business, Computers (Sales), Direct marketing, Executives*
Ms. Lee DeMattia, Director

Salary Minimum: $50,000

Functions: Management, Sales & Mktg.

Industries: Paper, Printing, Medical Devices, Computer Equip., Pharm Svcs., Advertising, Publishing, Packaging

Emmerson Consultants International

4280 NW 61st Ct
Coconut Creek, FL 33073-3276
(954) 428-7388
Fax: (954) 425-0723
Email: frhoden@emmersonnet.com
Web: www.emmersonnet.com

Summary: Professional executive search consulting and executive recruiting firm specializing in IT systems, network, internet, eCommerce solutions and consumer products. The firm is emerging as one of the premier executive recruiting/IT consulting organizations with one of the largest databases of IT, HR, health, travel and female & minority executives.

Key Contact - Specialty:
Mr. Frank E. Rhoden, Jr., President

Salary Minimum: $50,000

Employ®

PO Box 2032
Media, PA 19063-9032
(610) 565-1573
Fax: (610) 565-1573

Summary: We uncover candidates that help your affirmative action, diversity, and EEO commitment. Providing you with qualified people of color, females, people with disabilities, and veterans for your candidate pool. Ninety-nine percent of our placements were not actively seeking other employment. Our clients needed their talent and we recruit talent.

Key Contact - Specialty:
Ms. Sayre Dixon, Owner & Operator

Salary Minimum: $45,000

Functions: Management

Industries: Drugs Mfg., Medical Devices, Computer Equip., Finance, Legal, Accounting, Insurance, Software, Biotech/Life Sciences, Healthcare

Employment Atlanta Staffing

3748 Rogers Cv
Duluth, GA 30096-2767
(404) 255-4201
Email: ed@employmentatlanta.com
Web: www.employmentatlanta.com

Summary: Employment agency and recruiter for accountants and financial professionals.

Key Contact - Specialty:
Mr. Ed Freeman, Partner
Mr. Ed Welborn, Recruiter, CPA - *Accounting, Accounting (Big 4,Bookkeeping,General,Public)*

Salary Minimum: $20,000

Functions: Finance, CFOs, Budgeting, Credit, Taxes

Industries: Generalist (All)

Employment Professionals LLC

309 Richmond Place Ste 150
Franklin, TN 37064-3290
(888) 705-4003
(615) 595-2771
Fax: (615) 523-8855
Email: info@employmentprofessionals.com
Web: www.employmentprofessionals.com

Summary: Full service retained and contingency search and placement of: CEOs, COOs, CFOs, controllers, senior executives, patient financial services, business office and admitting directors/managers; with healthcare provider organizations including: hospitals, physician practices, large clinics, ambulatory and psychiatric care facilities.

Key Contact - Specialty:
Mr. Brad Arnold, Managing Partner - *C-level, Executives, Healthcare, Hospital, Long term care*
Mr. Douglas Pittman - *Healthcare, Hospital, Management consulting*

Salary Minimum: $50,000

Functions: Management, Senior Mgmt., Middle Mgmt., CFOs

Industries: Healthcare, Hospitals

The Employment Solution

500-40 Holly St
Toronto, ON M4S 3C3
Canada
(416) 482-2420
(800) 818-4744
Fax: (416) 482-9282
Email: frankw@tes.net
Web: www.tes.net

Summary: Providing contract and permanent staffing: IT, engineering/technical and office services.

Key Contact - Specialty:
Mr. Frank A. Wilson, President
Mr. Steve Cook, Vice Presdient, IT Services - *Computers, Computers (Hardware,Networking,Programming,Software)*

Salary Minimum: $30,000

Branches:
4000 Westchase Blvd Ste 135
Raleigh, NC 27607-3943
(919) 832-8900
(866) 832-8900
Fax: (919) 832-8905
Key Contact - Specialty:
Mr. Eric Danzey, Branch Manager

3430 South Service Rd
Main Floor
Burlington, ON L7N 3T9
Canada
(905) 639-2600
(800) 818-4893
Fax: (905) 639-4998
Key Contact - Specialty:
Mr. Bill Docherty, Branch Manager - *Engineering*

705-1 City Centre Dr
City Centre Plaza Phase 1
Mississauga, ON L5B 1M2
Canada
(905) 272-4296
(800) 818-4895
Fax: (905) 272-1068
Email: sandraa@tes.net
Key Contact - Specialty:
Ms. Sandra Allmark

410-301 Moodie Dr
B D O Centre
Nepean, ON K2H 9C4
Canada
(613) 828-7887
(800) 818-5469
Fax: (613) 828-2729
Key Contact - Specialty:
Mr. Alex Welsh, Branch Manager

Employment Solutions Group Inc

9420 Towne Square Ave Ste 19
Cincinnati, OH 45242-6910
(513) 791-1614
Fax: (513) 791-4246
Email: chris@esgsearch.com
Web: www.esgsearch.com

Summary: We specialize in the search of professionals for both: "brick" (which includes: store and multi-unit management, merchandising, MIS, store planning, design, construction and visual merchandising) and "click" (which includes: eCommerce merchandising, marketing, web design and development) retailers and those who serve the retail industry.

Key Contact - Specialty:
Mr. Chris Albrecht, President - *Retail*

Salary Minimum: $50,000

Functions: Generalist (All), Management, Architects, Graphic Designers

Industries: Construction, Retail, Hospitality, New Media

Employment Solutions Inc

1422 W Main St Ste 101B
Lewisville, TX 75067-3387
(972) 221-5566
Fax: (972) 219-7154
Email: empsol@aol.com

Summary: Recruitment and placement of clerical and light industrial individuals.

Key Contact - Specialty:
Ms. Lynne Von Villas, Managing Director

Functions: Admin. Svcs., Mfg.

Industries: Generalist (All)

Endeavor Management Search Group Inc

10 N Martingale Rd Ste 400
Schaumburg, IL 60173-2411
(888) 705-5627
(847) 466-1012
Email: mark@endeavorsearch.com
Web: www.endeavorsearch.com

Summary: An executive search firm that specializes in the restaurant, hospitality, foodservice sales, retail services, foodservice distribution and construction industries. Progressive approach to the search process including online video interviewing and candidate profile assessments conducted

Key Contact - Specialty:
Mr. Mark Gray, President
Ms. Sarah Hatfield, CPC, Business Development, Retail & Sevices
Ms. Michele Slafkosky, Staff Recruiter, Restaurants, Sales - *Distribution, Food service, Hospitality, Restaurants, Sales*
Ms. Tammy Woziak, Staff Recruiter
Mr. Bob Steelbaughs, Staff Recruiter - *Food service, Groceries, Hospitality, Hotels, Restaurants*

Salary Minimum: $40,000

Functions: Management, Senior Mgmt., Middle Mgmt., Sales & Mktg., Sales Reps., HR Mgmt., Architects, Hospitality, Chefs

Industries: Construction, Manufacturing, Food, Bev., Tobacco, Retail, Architectural Svcs., Legal, Equip Svcs., Hospitality, Hotels, Resorts, Clubs, Restaurants, Quick Service Restaurants, Full Service Restaurants, Inst./Industrial Food Svc., Entertainment, Recreation, Travel, Real Estate, Property/Facility Mgmt.

Energy Executives Inc

527 Medearis Dr
Charlotte, NC 28211-6066
(704) 366-7981
Fax: (770) 564-5584
Email: lpeak@energyexecs.com
Web: www.energyexecs.com

Summary: We successfully apply the years of industry and technical experience gained by our founders and employees to effectively recruiting the highest quality talent possible for our clients. All of our recruiters have energy industry experience, in senior level sales & marketing roles. We place marketing, sales, engineering and IT professionals with clients in the energy industry.

Key Contact - Specialty:
Ms. Linda Peak, President - *Sales*

Salary Minimum: $55,000

Functions: Management, Board Members, Senior Mgmt., Middle Mgmt., Sales & Mktg., Mktg. Mgmt., Sales Mgmt., IT, Mgmt. Consultants

Industries: Energy, Utilities, Manufacturing, Software

Branches:
3530 Ashford Dunwoody Rd NE Ste 210
Atlanta, GA 30319-2002
(404) 236-0803
Fax: (404) 236-0869

Email: chyder@energyexecs.com
Key Contact - Specialty:
Mr. Chuck Hyder

Energy Placement Inc

44489 Town Center Way Ste D
Palm Desert, CA 92260-2789
(760) 837-3864
Fax: (760) 888-8947
Email: jglenn@energyplacement.com
Web: www.energyplacement.com

Summary: Executive recruiters, energy, utilities,
oil, gas, petroleum, petrochemical, financial
services, IT and other industries. Engineering
recruiters.

Key Contact - Specialty:
Mr. James Glenn, Director, Recruitment &
  Consulting

Functions: Generalist (All), Management, Board
  Members, Senior Mgmt., Engineering

Industries: Generalist (All)

Energy Recruiters Inc

(also known as ERI)
9240 Bonita Beach Rd SE Ste 1117
Bonita Springs, FL 34135-4250
(239) 949-3385
(800) 435-0685
Fax: (239) 949-3386
Email: admin@er-inc.com
Web: www.er-inc.com

Summary: We are an executive search and career
placement firm. We specialize in the placement of
candidates the various industries including, retail
and wholesale, technology, energy, consumer
products, financial services, and health care. Our
typical concentrations include positions in
executive office, operations, marketing,
engineering, technology, finance, procurement,
and human resources.

Key Contact - Specialty:
Mr. Chris McAuliffe, Founder, President & CEO
Mr. Jason McAuliffe, Vice President &
  Recruiting Consultant
Ms. Samantha Hall, Executive Assistant &
  Researcher

Salary Minimum: $75,000

Functions: Generalist (All), Mfg.

Industries: Energy, Utilities, Manufacturing,
  Chemicals, Drugs Mfg., Consumer Goods,
  Transportation, Wholesale, Retail, Finance,
  Banking, Pharm Svcs., Accounting, Healthcare

Energy Recruiting Specialists Inc

PO Box 566
Douglassville, PA 19518-0566
(610) 385-9560
Fax: (610) 385-9560
Email: energyspecialist@msn.com

Summary: Hold ethics and confidentiality in the
highest regard. Hardworking firm with a strong
contact base within the electric and gas industries.
Our main goal is to help candidates and clients
progress in the marketplace.

Key Contact - Specialty:
Mr. Michael DeFazio, President - *Energy,
  Engineering, Finance, Marketing*

Salary Minimum: $75,000

Functions: Generalist (All)

Industries: Energy, Utilities, Oil & Gas, Invest.
  Banking, Equip Svcs., Engineering Svcs.,
  Environmental Svcs.

The Engineering Connection

7650 Chippewa Rd Ste 310
Brecksville, OH 44141-2319
(440) 838-5008
Fax: (440) 838-5009
Email: konfal@engconn.com
Web: www.engconn.com

Summary: We are thorough and comprehensive in
examining the references and accomplishments of
our candidates and strive for the ideal match
between business and candidate. The result is a
placement which exceeds the expectations of the
business.

Key Contact - Specialty:
Mr. Edward W. Nishnic, President
Mrs. Jean Konfal, Manager, Business

Functions: Senior Mgmt., Engineering

Industries: Generalist (All), Energy, Utilities,
  Medical Devices, Electronic, Elec. Components,
  Robotics, Semiconductors, IT Implementation,
  Engineering Svcs., Fiber Optic, Database SW,
  Development SW

Engineering Journeys with Agent HR

4218 126th Pl NE
Marysville, WA 98271-8762
(360) 653-1712
Email: rvanblaricome@agenthr.com
Web: www.agenthr.com/rvanblaricome

Summary: We place Civil Engineers in Private
Consulting Companies nation-wide.

Key Contact - Specialty:
Mr. Royce Van Blaricome, Executive Recruiter

Functions: Management, Senior Mgmt., Middle
  Mgmt., Engineering, Geotechnical, Eng. Design,
  Mgmt. Consultants

Industries: Construction, Services, Engineering
  Svcs.

Engineering Resource Group Inc

101 Gibraltar Dr
Morris Plains, NJ 07950-1287
(973) 490-7000
Fax: (973) 490-1957
Email: bestnjjobs@aol.com
Web: www.engineeringresource.com

Summary: Specialize in professional recruiting of
electrical engineers, electronic engineers, software
engineers, systems engineers, mechanical
engineers and aerospace engineers. We recruit for
the aerospace, electronics, telecom, industrial and
defense markets.

Key Contact - Specialty:
Mr. Branko A. Terkovich, Director
Mr. James Z. Terkovich, Director - *Engineering*

Salary Minimum: $40,000

Functions: Generalist (All), Engineering

Industries: Generalist (All), Food, Bev., Tobacco,
  Drugs Mfg., Plastics, Rubber, Computer Equip.,
  Telecoms, Aerospace, Software

Engineering Solutions International

(also known as Engineering Geniuses
International)
341 S Meadows Ave
Manhattan Beach, CA 90266-6909
(310) 798-8044
Email: submit@engineeringsolutions.com
Web: www.engineeringsolutions.com

Summary: We specialize in the placement of
biotechnology, bioinformatics, neural net, optic

artificial intelligence, computer and engineering
professionals for R&D applications. We also place
executives.

Key Contact - Specialty:
Ms. Urania Van Applebaum, President
Ms. Lynda DesLandes, Recruiter

Salary Minimum: $50,000

Functions: Generalist (All), Production, Sales
  Mgmt., Systems Analysis, Systems Dev.,
  Network Admin., R&D, Engineering

Industries: Generalist (All), Chemicals,
  Engineering Svcs., Telecoms, Aerospace,
  Software, Biotech/Life Sciences, Healthcare

ENSEARCH Management Consultants

905 E Cotati Ave
Cotati, CA 94931-4099
(888) 667-5627
(707) 795-3800
Fax: (707) 795-6200
Email: inquiry@ensearch.com
Web: www.ensearch.com

Summary: Dedicated to the ethical recruitment of
advanced practice nurses within a safe and
confidential environment. Our specialty niche is
neonatal nursing; specifically Neonatal Nurse
Practitioners (NNPs).

Key Contact - Specialty:
Mr. Tim Mattis, Principal - *Healthcare*
Ms. Kim McCann, Office Manager

Salary Minimum: $50,000

Functions: Nurses

Industries: Healthcare, Hospitals, Women's

Enterprise Recruiting

PO Box 131777
Carlsbad, CA 92013-1777
(760) 944-8903
Email: john@enterpriserecruiting.net
Web: www.enterpriserecruiting.net

Summary: Our mission is to provide our clients
the top candidates. We specialize in sales &
marketing top performers. Through careful
research and a thorough evaluation of your
organization's needs and requirements, we
uncover the most appropriate prospects and refer
only top candidates that match your needs and
exceed your expectations.

Key Contact - Specialty:
Mr. John DeMaio, PPC, President - *Life Sciences*

Salary Minimum: $75,000

Functions: Management, Sales & Mktg., Mktg.
  Research, Sales Mgmt., Sales Reps.

Industries: Biotech/Life Sciences

Enterprise Search Associates

7031 Corporate Way Ste 102
Dayton, OH 45459-4262
(937) 438-8774
(800) 993-5499
Email: careers@daytonjobs.com
Web: www.daytonjobs.com

Summary: We specialize in information
technology positions.

Key Contact - Specialty:
Mr. Jeffrey Linck, Owner

Salary Minimum: $45,000

Functions: IT, MIS Mgmt., Systems Analysis,
  Systems Dev., Systems Implem., Systems
  Support, Network Admin., DB Admin.

Industries: Generalist (All)

The Entertainment Technology Source

PO Box 596
Petaluma, CA 94953-0596
(707) 773-1279
Email: malcolm@etsource.com
Web: www.etsource.com

Summary: Our firm was created to assist interactive entertainment software engineers of all levels with their careers. We offer industry specific technology management and leadership experience to provide unique placement and career development expertise.

Key Contact - Specialty:
Mr. Malcolm Johnson, Principal

Salary Minimum: $70,000

Functions: Systems Dev.

Industries: Entertainment SW, Networking, Comm. SW

Environmental, Health & Safety (EH&S) Search Associates Inc

PO Box 1325
Palm Harbor, FL 34682-1325
(727) 787-3225
(706) 353-6866
Email: careers@ehssearch.com
Web: www.ehssearch.com

Summary: We are a search firm that specializes exclusively in recruiting safety, occupational health and environmental professionals. We work with a select group of clients in the manufacturing and service sectors and conduct searches on a retained or engaged contingency basis.

Key Contact - Specialty:
Mr. Randy L. Williams, President - *Environmental, Loss Control, Loss Prevention, Risk management, Safety*
Mrs. Jane McDonald, Senior Search Professional - *Environmental, Loss Control, Loss Prevention, Risk management, Safety*

Salary Minimum: $80,000

Functions: Risk Mgmt., Environmentalists, Security Personnel, Health & Safety

Industries: Generalist (All)

Epic Search Partners

9 S Passaic Ave
Chatham, NJ 07928-2331
(973) 635-3745
Fax: (978) 635-3748
Email: peter@epicsearchpartners.com
Web: www.epicsearchpartners.com

Summary: Epic Search Partners is a Search Engine Marketing specialty group placing top professionals in the SEM sector. We place people in the following roles in both permanent and contracted arrangements: executive management, senior management, sales and sales management, marketing, account management, search engine marketing (SEM), search engine optimization (SEO), pay per click (PPC), paid search, organic search, natural search, and client services.

Key Contact - Specialty:
Mr. Peter Rouillard, Managing Director - *Marketing*
Mrs. Jennifer Rouillard, Managing Director - *Marketing, Technology*
Ms. Beth Slutsky, Porject Coordinator - *Marketing*

Salary Minimum: $40,000

Functions: Management, Product Dev., Sales & Mktg., Mktg. Mgmt., Direct Mktg., Customer Svc., Sales Reps., Systems Dev., Mgmt. Consultants, Graphic Designers

Industries: Generalist (All), Media, Advertising, New Media

Equate Executive Search Inc

1350 Broadway Rm 2500
New York, NY 10018-7802
(212) 736-0606
Fax: (212) 695-5992
Email: equate@att.net
Web: www.equatejobs.com

Summary: We are a small firm connected to a wide network of select corporations, academic institutions and recruiters. We have extensive personal experience working in the fields of IS and finance. We specialize in technology, financial and sales/marketing positions.

Key Contact - Specialty:
Mr. Harry Miller, President
Ms. Caryn Fox, Managing Director - *Sales*

Salary Minimum: $75,000

Functions: Generalist (All), Board Members, Senior Mgmt., Mktg. Mgmt., Sales Mgmt., Risk Mgmt., IT, Mgmt. Consultants

Industries: Generalist (All), Finance, Accounting, Mgmt. Consulting, IT Implementation, Network Infrastructure, Software, Security SW, System SW, Training SW

ErpErp.Com Inc.

333 Racetrack Rd NW Ste 102
Fort Walton Beach, FL 32547-4602
(850) 862-1466
Fax: (850) 314-6606
Email: info@erperp.com
Web: www.erperp.com

Summary: We are a recruiting firm specializing in matching professionals with expertise in Enterprise Resource Planning software (specifically the former JD Edwards software) to companies utilizing these skills.

Key Contact - Specialty:
Mr. Marvin Olson, Senior Staffing Specialist - *JD Edwards - Computers (Programming), Consulting, Information Technology, JD Edwards, Staffing*

Functions: IT, Systems Dev., Network Admin.

Industries: Construction, Manufacturing, Textiles, Apparel, Lumber, Furniture, Paper, Medical Devices, Non-profits, IT Implementation, Supply Chain Mgmt., Call Centers

Erspamer Associates

4010 W 65th St Ste 100
Edina, MN 55435-1726
(952) 925-3747
Fax: (952) 925-4022
Email: hdhuntre1@aol.com

Summary: We offer our medical technology clients a focused depth and breadth of premium caliber candidates that few can match. Technical and technical management positions for the medical device/technology industry are our specialty. We also serve: R&D, engineering, clinical and regulatory affairs, quality systems and manufacturing recruiting needs.

Key Contact - Specialty:
Mr. Roy C. Erspamer, Principal - *Technical*

Functions: Generalist (All)

Industries: Drugs Mfg., Medical Devices, Plastics, Rubber, Biotech/Life Sciences

ESC2000

2489 Lori Dr
York, PA 17404-1281
(717) 767-1729
Fax: (717) 505-8684
Email: esc2000@esc2000.com
Web: www.esc2000.com

Summary: We specialize in retail recruiting from the store manager level to corporate VP and COO. We provide our client companies with a low-cost alternative with proven results. We provide contingency-based search at a discounted fee.

Key Contact - Specialty:
Mr. Tom Russell

Functions: Management, Senior Mgmt., Middle Mgmt.

Industries: Retail

The Esquire Group

15 S 5th St Ste 1000
Minneapolis, MN 55402-1061
(612) 340-9068
(800) 755-7779
Fax: (612) 340-1218
Email: esquire@esquiregroup.com
Web: www.esquiregroup.com

Summary: Our firm is a legal search and consulting firm providing permanent and temporary staffing of attorneys, paralegals, legal secretaries, and document review staff. Our clients include leading law firms and in house corporate legal departments.

Key Contact - Specialty:
Ms. Patricia A. Comeford, Esq., President & Founder

Functions: Legal, Attorneys, Paralegals

Industries: Generalist (All), Legal

Branches:
15 S 5th St Ste 1000
Minneapolis, MN 55402-1061
(303) 278-1701
(800) 755-7779
Email: millies@esquiregroup.com
Key Contact - Specialty:
Mr. Timothy Mahoney, Esq., Chief Operating Officer
Ms. Millie Steketee, Business Development

Essential Solutions Inc

5300 Stevens Creek Blvd Ste 430
San Jose, CA 95129-1039
(408) 850-2500
Fax: (408) 985-1700
Email: info@esiweb.com
Web: www.esiweb.com

Summary: Specializing in the placement of key contributors in management, engineering and marketing & sales for emerging communications companies. Specializing in: wireless communications, networking, Internet, multi-media and system semiconductors.

Key Contact - Specialty:
Mr. Aaron C. Woo, Principal - *Engineering*
Mr. Scott Morales, Search Consultant - *Engineering*
Miss Carmen Jacinto, Search Consultant

Salary Minimum: $70,000

Functions: Management, Mfg., Sales & Mktg., R&D, Engineering

Industries: Generalist (All)

Estes Consulting Associates Inc

14 Martingale Way
Pawling, NY 12564-2166
(845) 855-0057
Fax: (845) 340-4000
Email: resumes@ecai.com
Web: www.ecai.com

Summary: We provide professional staffing and consulting with primary focus in internal audit, IT audit, security and other areas of technology, such as ERP, e-commerce, Internet and CRM. Permanent and contract services are available for diversified industries.

Key Contact - Specialty:
Mr. Jeffrey Estes, President
Ms. Melissa Katzman, Director
Mr. Stephen Langenhoven, Director, Technology Consulting - *Manufacturing*
Mr. Alex Joseph, Research Administration
Mr. Julius Dana, Research Associate

Salary Minimum: $60,000

Functions: Risk Mgmt., IT, Security Personnel

Industries: Generalist (All)

ETA Recruiting

190 Robert Speck Pky
Sherwood Business Centre
Mississauga, ON L4Z 3K3
Canada
(905) 566-1616
Email: careers@trgc.ca

Summary: Our firm offers temp, contract and permanent placement. We have three divisions: temp, contact centers and corporate services. Servicing junior to management levels.

Key Contact - Specialty:
Mr. Keith Turner, President

Functions: Generalist (All), Mfg., Materials, Sales & Mktg., Finance

Industries: Generalist (All), Consumer Elect., Transportation, Finance, Equip Svcs., HR Services, Telecoms

Allen Etcovitch Associates Ltd

(a PSA International firm)
1707-666 Rue Sherbrooke O
Edifice Executive Towers
Montreal, QC H3A 1E7
Canada
(514) 287-9933
Fax: (514) 287-9940
Email: cvs@etcovitch.ca
Web: www.etcovitch.ca

Summary: We are industrial psychologists offering English/French services in recruitment, organizational design, psychological assessment, compensation, career management and outplacement. Clientele: from small family-owned firms to multinationals.

Key Contact - Specialty:
Mr. Allen Etcovitch, President & Chief Executive Officer
Ms. Marie-José Demers, Vice President & Senior Consultant

Salary Minimum: $50,000

Functions: Generalist (All), Management

Industries: Food, Bev., Tobacco, Textiles, Apparel, Printing, Chemicals, Metal Products, Misc. Mfg.

Ethical Search Professional Ltd

100 N Etnyre Ave
Oregon, IL 61061-9402
(815) 732-4773
Email: admin@ethicalsearch.com
Web: www.ethicalsearch.com

Summary: Recruiters specializing in finding and placing technical professionals (engineers, production management and maintenance management) at all levels. We provide services to plant, technical and corporate settings. Our clients are mainly in the food, consumer products, pharmaceutical, paper, converting, chemical processing and related industries.

Key Contact - Specialty:
Mr. Jim Sullivan, President & Senior Account Manager - *Engineering*
Mr. Jason Sullivan, Senior Technical Recruiter & Account Mgr - *Engineering*
Ms. Gayle Sullivan, Administrative Manager

Salary Minimum: $40,000

Functions: Mfg., Production, Automation, Plant Mgmt., Packaging, Engineering, Minorities/Diversity

Industries: Manufacturing, Food, Bev., Tobacco, Paper, Printing, Chemicals, Soap, Perf., Cosmtcs., Drugs Mfg., Plastics, Rubber, Paints, Petro. Products, Packaging

Evans & James Executive Search

PO Box 862232
Marietta, GA 30062-0001
(770) 992-4299
Fax: (770) 992-4283
Email: james@evansandjames.com
Web: www.evansandjames.com

Summary: We have many years of experience specializing in the plastic, packaging and converting industries. We are capable of finding sales, management, engineering or manufacturing professionals for all our clients.

Key Contact - Specialty:
Mr. James Ingram, CPC

Salary Minimum: $55,000

Functions: Generalist (All), Mfg.

Industries: Manufacturing, Food, Bev., Tobacco, Paper, Chemicals, Medical Devices, Plastics, Rubber, Hospitality, Packaging

M Evans and Associates

1532 Graham Rd
Silver Lake, OH 44224-3030
(330) 686-0885
Fax: (330) 686-1427
Email: resume@m-evans.net
Web: www.m-evans.net

Summary: We specialize in the information technology industry, recruiting for management, sales and support candidates.

Key Contact - Specialty:
Mr. Frank Layman, Principal

Functions: Sales & Mktg.

Industries: Software, Accounting SW, Database SW, Development SW, Doc. Mgmt., Production SW, ERP SW, HR SW, Industry Specific SW, Mfg. SW, Networking, Comm. SW

Evans Transportation Search

312-16 The Links Rd
Old Yonge Court
North York, ON M2P 1T5
Canada
(416) 224-2277
Fax: (416) 229-1973

Summary: A tireless group of headhunters totally committed to recruiting the best talent available in air, ocean and road transportation. Logistics, traffic and distribution, our focus is on emerging growth companies.

Key Contact - Specialty:
Mr. Ray Evans, Director - *Transportation*

Salary Minimum: $50,000

Functions: Generalist (All)

Industries: Transportation

Everett Career Management Consultants Inc

PO Box 101805
Fort Worth, TX 76185-1805
(800) 297-1872
(817) 989-7400
Fax: (214) 853-5800
Email: ea2000@usa.net
Web: www.eaplus.com

Summary: We are a generalist search firm specializing in executive, managerial and professional assignments. We will split fees with reciprocal arrangement on most listings. Primary industries include financial services, mortgage banking, commercial banking, credit cards, etc. and all HR functions, i.e., compensation, benefits, recruiting, training, OD, OT, employee relations, labor relations, leadership, development and general HR consulting across all industry lines.

Key Contact - Specialty:
Ms. Julia Lockleer, President - *Aerospace, Defense, Electronics, Financial services*
Mr. Jim Everett, CMP, Director, Employment - *Electronics, Manufacturing, Telecommunications*

Salary Minimum: $65,000

Functions: Generalist (All), HR Mgmt.

Industries: Banking, Invest. Banking, Brokers, Venture Cap., Mutual/Hedge Funds, Misc. Financial, Services, Accounting, Mgmt. Consulting, HR Services, Insurance, Real Estate, HR SW

Evergreen & Company

160 Mouse Mill Rd
Westport, MA 02790-4124
(800) 828-6705
Fax: (508) 636-8633
Email: maukp@staffing.net
Web: www.evergreenconsultants.com

Summary: Search firm specializing in IT managers and specialists. Providing recruiting assistance to manufacturing, financial and service industries.

Key Contact - Specialty:
Ms. Patricia Mauk, Owner

Salary Minimum: $45,000

Functions: Generalist (All), IT, MIS Mgmt., Systems Dev., Systems Implem., Network Admin., DB Admin.

Industries: Generalist (All), IT Implementation, Network Infrastructure

Evers Legal Search

1910 S Federal St Unit B
Chicago, IL 60616-4517
(312) 225-1144
(888) 324-0154
Fax: (312) 225-2277
Email: mike@everslegal.com
Web: www.everslegal.com

Summary: Our firm is retained by companies of all sizes on a national basis to recruit general counsel and experienced senior staff attorneys for in-house legal departments.

Key Contact - Specialty:
Mr. Michael Evers, Founder

Salary Minimum: $100,000

Functions: Attorneys

Industries: Generalist (All), Legal

The Excel Group Inc

18430 Brookhurst St Ste 202B
Fountain Valley, CA 92708-6759
(714) 593-5927
Fax: (714) 593-6027
Email: consulting@xlg.com
Web: www.xlg.com

Summary: Specialize in sales, marketing and IT support recruitment across all experience levels for wireless technology, enterprise software, networking/connectivity and internet firms as well as advertising and public relations agency professionals. Large database of screened high technology professionals to meet your needs.

Key Contact - Specialty:
Mr. Frank J. Suwalski, President - *Sales*
Ms. Rebecca Sazegar, Managing Partner - *Finance, Management, Sales, Technology*

Salary Minimum: $60,000

Functions: Generalist (All), Board Members, Admin. Svcs., Sales & Mktg., Direct Mktg., PR, Sales Reps., HR Mgmt.

Industries: Generalist (All), Retail, Media, Advertising, New Media, Communications, Call Centers, Digital, Wireless, Insurance, Commercial, Software, Database SW, Development SW, Doc. Mgmt., Production SW, Entertainment SW, ERP SW, HR SW, Industry Specific SW, Marketing SW, Networking, Comm. SW, Security SW, System SW

Excel Human Resources Inc

300-102 Bank St
Ottawa, ON K1P 5N4
Canada
(613) 230-5393
Fax: (613) 230-1623
Email: excel@excelhr.com
Web: www.excelhr.com

Summary: We are a full-service recruiting firm specialized in recruiting/staffing of administrative, management, accounting and IT positions for the private and public sectors, on both a contract and permanent basis.

Key Contact - Specialty:
Mr. Toni Guimaraes, Founder
Ms. Kathryn Tremblay, Founder
Ms. Lisa Dickson, Recruiting & Marketing Strategist
Ms. Amy Murdock, Recruiting & Marketing Strategist - *Professional services*
Ms. Ameera Girgis, Recruiting & Placement Specialist - *Administration*
Ms. Joanne Armstrong, Coordinator, Accounting/Operations
Ms. Megan Graham, Manager, Quality

Ms. Brigitte Labelle, Recruiter
Ms. Anne Mortensen, Manager, Marketing Communications - *Dental, Emergency room, Healthcare, Home health, Hospital*

Functions: Admin. Svcs., Mktg. Mgmt., HR Mgmt., Finance, IT

Industries: Generalist (All)

Excel Recruiting Services

12105 W Center Rd #135
Omaha, NE 68144-6022
(402) 896-5050
Fax: (413) 451-6885
Email: beckyz@physicians-excel.com
Web: www.physicians-excel.com

Summary: Recruiting firm dedicated to the placement of exceptional medical professionals.

Key Contact - Specialty:
Ms. Becky Zeising, Physicians

Functions: Physicians, Nurses, Allied Health

Industries: Healthcare, Hospitals

Excel Unlimited

15915 Katy Fwy Ste 205
Houston, TX 77094-1700
(281) 398-7650
Email: resumes@excelunlimited.com
Web: www.excelunlimited.com

Summary: Executive healthcare recruiting for hospitals and medical centers.

Key Contact - Specialty:
Mr. James Higgins, FHFMA, President

Functions: Healthcare

Industries: Finance, Accounting, Healthcare, Hospitals

Exclusive Search

781 Beta Dr Ste N
Cleveland, OH 44143-2360
(440) 461-7900
(866) 447-3968
Fax: (440) 461-6986
Email: doug@hireunow.com
Web: www.hireunow.com

Summary: All fees paid by the employer. Most positions are technical (engineering/IS/data processing).

Key Contact - Specialty:
Mr. Robert Holzheimer, President
Mr. Doug McKinney, Senior Recruiter

Salary Minimum: $25,000

Functions: Generalist (All), Engineering

Industries: Generalist (All)

Exec-Links LLC

1870 Brookhaven Dr W
Allentown, PA 18103-9696
(610) 432-8004
(610) 349-6883
Email: rickslifka@fast.net
Web: www.exec-links.com

Summary: We specialize in transaction/payment processing industry as well as in golf; sales, sales management, product management, account managers, CFO, CCO, and CEO.

Key Contact - Specialty:
Mr. Rick Slifka, President & Chief Executive Officer - *Packaging, Sales, Senior management, Sports, Start-up companies*
Ms. Megan Slifka, Vice President, Business Development

Functions: Generalist (All), Management, Product Dev., Packaging, Sales & Mktg., Sales Reps.

Industries: Finance, Banking, Misc. Financial, E-commerce, Sports, Packaging

ExecFinders

PO Box 3997
Wilmington, DE 19807-0997
(302) 753-6480
(800) 769-6811
Fax: (302) 764-6028
Email: info@execfinders.com
Web: www.execfinders.com

Summary: Executive search services specializing in areas of finance, technology, sales, marketing and management. A resource for critical hiring services.

Key Contact - Specialty:
Ms. Lyn D. Fink, Partner

Functions: Generalist (All), Management, Senior Mgmt., Middle Mgmt., Product Dev., Sales & Mktg., Mktg. Mgmt., Sales Mgmt., Staffing, Finance

Industries: Generalist (All), Finance, Venture Cap., IT Implementation, Media, Telecoms, Insurance, Software, Biotech/Life Sciences, Healthcare

Execu-Tech Search Inc

3500 American Blvd W Ste 20
Minneapolis, MN 55431-4430
(952) 893-6915
Fax: (952) 896-3479

Summary: Extensive experience in executive and technical candidates within the following engineering sectors: mechanical product design, industrial electrical design, chemical engineering, civil/environmental and the consulting engineering industry.

Key Contact - Specialty:
Mr. Marv Kaiser, President - *Engineering, Manufacturing*
Mr. Greg Kaiser, Vice President - *Engineering*

Functions: Production, Plant Mgmt., Quality, Engineering

Industries: Construction, Manufacturing, Food, Bev., Tobacco, Chemicals, Drugs Mfg., Metal Products, Machine, Appliance, Packaging

The ExecuSearch Group

201 E 42nd St Fl 5
New York, NY 10017-5704
(212) 922-1001
Fax: (212) 972-0250
Email: nyoffice@execu-search.com
Web: www.execu-search.com

Summary: Professional recruitment firm, offering placement of qualified individuals from staff to C-level executives within the brokerage, communications, hedge funds, insurance, law, banking, retail, investment, consumer products, public accounting and non-profit industries. Our specialty divisions are accounting/finance, accounting support, financial services, graphics, HR, IT, legal staffing, office support and retained search.

Key Contact - Specialty:
Mr. Edward Fleischman, Partner
Mr. Gary Grossman, Partner
Mr. Mitchell Peskin, Partner - *Financial services*
Mr. Glenn Bernstein, Partner - *Temporary*

Salary Minimum: $30,000

Functions: Senior Mgmt., Admin. Svcs., Nurses, HR Mgmt., Finance, CFOs, Cash Mgmt., IT, Paralegals, Graphic Designers

Industries: Generalist (All), Manufacturing, Finance, Banking, Invest. Banking, Brokers, Venture Cap., Mutual/Hedge Funds, Misc. Financial, Services, Legal, Accounting, E-commerce, Advertising, Publishing, New Media, Insurance, Casualty, Claims, Life, Re-Insurance, Software, Healthcare, Hospitals, Long-term/Home Care, Occupational Therapy

Branches:
2700 Westchester Ave
Purchase, NY 10577-2547
(914) 653-9000
Fax: (914) 653-9001
Email: info@execu-search.com
Key Contact - Specialty:
Ms. Rachel Feder, Director - *Accounting, Accounting (Public), CFOs, Controllers, Tax*

Execumax

241 Deluna Rd SW
Fort Walton Beach, FL 32548-6509
(850) 301-3800
Email: jobs@execumax.com
Web: www.execumax.com

Summary: We are a diversity focused talent acquisition firm specializing in the consumer packaged goods industry. We specialize in manager, director and VP level opportunities with Fortune 500 companies, and our areas of expertise include HR, manufacturing, supply chain, sales, marketing and finance disciplines.

Key Contact - Specialty:
Mr. Ron Todd, President - *Food & beverage, Human resources, Logistics, Manufacturing, Minorities*
Ms. Brandy Rice, Leader, Human Resources, Finance & Legal - *Consumer, Finance, Logistics, Manufacturing, Minorities*

Salary Minimum: $65,000

Functions: Generalist (All), Mfg., Plant Mgmt.

Industries: Manufacturing, Food, Bev., Tobacco, Soap, Perf., Cosmtcs., Drugs Mfg., Consumer Elect., Consumer Goods, Transportation, Wholesale, Finance, Packaging

ExecuREP LLC

333 Conestoga St
River's Bend Complex
Windsor, CT 06095-2205
(860) 219-8888
Email: rep@execurep.com
Web: www.execurep.com

Summary: Specializing in confidential searches for IT and IS security executives; we are a one-person boutique firm. Experience in the IT, contingency placement and executive search industries, we specializes in mid- and senior-level searches in a variety of industries.

Key Contact - Specialty:
Mr. Robert E. Pudney, CPC, Owner - *CIOs, High technology, Information Systems, Information Technology, Senior management*

Salary Minimum: $100,000

Functions: IT, MIS Mgmt.

Industries: Generalist (All)

ExecuSearch

13895 E Placita Pezuna
Vail, AZ 85641-1400
(520) 647-3426
Fax: (520) 647-7868

Email: dee@execusearch1.com
Web: www.execusearch1.com

Summary: We are one of the industry's most specialized executive level property and asset management recruiting firms. We focus exclusively in shopping center and retail property management professionals such as: property managers, general managers, asset managers, regional managers, directors of property management and vice presidents and presidents of property management/operations companies.

Key Contact - Specialty:
Ms. Dee Pfeiffer, Principal

Salary Minimum: $60,000

Functions: Management

Industries: Real Estate

Execusearch

21 Mountainwood Dr
Glenville, NY 12302-4603
(518) 384-2036
Fax: (518) 384-1413
Email: esearch1@aol.com

Summary: Specializing in placement of sales & marketing professionals. Currently placing in telecom, medical/pharmaceutical, business products and financial services industries.

Key Contact - Specialty:
Mr. Mark A. Quinn, President - *Sales*

Salary Minimum: $30,000

Functions: Sales & Mktg., Mktg. Mgmt., Sales Mgmt., Sales Reps., Cash Mgmt.

Industries: Manufacturing, Drugs Mfg., Medical Devices, Banking, Brokers, Mutual/Hedge Funds, Misc. Financial, Telecoms, Network Infrastructure, Biotech/Life Sciences

ExecuSearch Staffing Solutions Inc

8466 Lockwood Ridge Rd # 315
Sarasota, FL 34243-2951
(941) 358-0505
(815) 836-0990
Fax: (941) 358-0101
Email: brenda@execusearch-inc.com
Web: www.execusearch-inc.com

Summary: We are an executive search and placement firm specializing in placing executives in logistics, manufacturing, engineering and retail positions. Our organization specializes in the retail, food, medical, industrial supply and transportation industries. We serve these disciplines: engineering, logistics/supply chain, manufacturing, buying/merchandising, distribution/transportation, sales/marketing, inventory management, and retail management.

Key Contact - Specialty:
Mrs. Brenda Gradl, President

Salary Minimum: $35,000

Functions: Management

Industries: Food, Bev., Tobacco, Drugs Mfg., Medical Devices, Transportation, Wholesale, Retail

ExecuSearch USA

PO Box 3990
Plant City, FL 33563-0017
(813) 659-9665
(800) 896-5912
Fax: (813) 759-6303
Email: info@execusearch.net
Web: www.execusearch.net

Summary: Executive recruiting firm specializing in the healthcare market. Clinical, sales, operations and reimbursement personnel at executive, managerial and staff levels.

Key Contact - Specialty:
Mrs. Donna Lester, President & Owner - *Healthcare*
Mr. Elvis K. Lester, Vice President & Owner - *Management, Telecommunications*

Functions: Generalist (All)

Industries: Finance, Banking, Pharm Svcs., Biotech/Life Sciences, Healthcare

ExecuSource Consultants Inc

PO Box 680746
Houston, TX 77268-0746
(281) 257-1340
Fax: (281) 655-9685
Email: search@execusourcejobs.com
Web: www.execusourcejobs.com

Summary: We are a nationally focused firm, dedicated to building solid client relationships through integrity, service and performance. Our concentration is on both mid and senior-level management positions for telecom and IT related clients, with particular emphasis on wireless technologies.

Key Contact - Specialty:
Mr. Chris Trapani, President & Chief Executive Officer
Ms. Delores Trapani, Vice President - *Telecommunications*

Salary Minimum: $50,000

Functions: Generalist (All)

Industries: Telecoms, Call Centers, Telephony, Digital, Wireless, Fiber Optic, Network Infrastructure, RF/Microwave, Industry Specific SW, Networking, Comm. SW

ExecuSource Inc

1117 Perimeter Ctr W Ste W514
Atlanta, GA 30338-5445
(770) 604-9030
Fax: (770) 604-9818
Email: info@execusource.jobs
Web: www.execusource.jobs

Summary: Our firm is the Atlanta market's leading professional recruitment firm for accounting and financial professionals. We specialize in placing highly qualified people, from staff to senior executive level, across all industries. Typical positions placed include: CFO, controller, tax, FP&A, audit, accounting manager, staff and senior accountants.

Key Contact - Specialty:
Mr. David Flax, CPA

Salary Minimum: $30,000

Functions: Finance, CFOs, Budgeting, Cash Mgmt., Credit, Taxes, M&A

Industries: Generalist (All)

Executec Recruiters

7491 N Federal Hwy Ste C5 # 218
Boca Raton, FL 33487-1658
(561) 330-3510
Fax: (561) 276-4518
Web: www.executecrecruiters.com

Summary: Our firm is an established professional recruitment and staffing firm. We provide exceptional service and expertise to deliver state of the art staffing solutions for our clients.

Key Contact - Specialty:
Ms. Debbie Krausert, Executive Recruiter & Recruiting Manager

Salary Minimum: $30,000

Functions: Generalist (All)

Industries: Generalist (All), Manufacturing, Wholesale, Finance, Media, Communications, Insurance, Real Estate, Software, Healthcare

Executec Search Agency Inc

3156 E Russell Rd
Las Vegas, NV 89120-3463
(702) 892-8010
(702) 892-8008
Email: chris@executecsearch.com
Web: www.executecsearch.com

Summary: We are a leader in placing persons in the scientific marketplace. We specialize in the placement of the following job positions: president/CEO, GM, service engineer, software engineer, marketing manager, application chemist, product manager, NSM design engineer, sales engineer and much more. Our scope of industries includes: biotechnology, analytical chemistry, environment, process, semiconductor and more.

Key Contact - Specialty:
Mr. Mark Moyer, President & Founder - *Biotechnology*
Mr. Chris Avron, Vice President, Key Accounts - *Biotechnology*

Salary Minimum: $30,000

Functions: Generalist (All), Senior Mgmt., Sales & Mktg.

Industries: Chemicals, Semiconductors, Software, Biotech/Life Sciences

Executech Resource Consultants

43 N Saginaw St
Pontiac, MI 48342-2153
(248) 332-3800
Fax: (248) 828-3344
Email: jbagnasco@executechjobs.com
Web: www.executechjobs.com

Summary: We are a leading staffing and employment services firm specializing in providing IS specialists, automotive engineering professionals, secretarial & clerical personnel and customer service associates.

Key Contact - Specialty:
Mr. Dave Palma, President - *Optics, Sales*
Mr. Jeff Bagnasco, Recruiter
Mr. Vincent Hester, Recruiter - *Mechanical*

Functions: Sales & Mktg., IT, Engineering

Industries: Generalist (All), Plastics, Rubber, Motor Vehicles, Computer Equip., Electronic, Elec. Components, IT Implementation, Fiber Optic, Software, Database SW, Development SW, Security SW, System SW

Executive Advantage

PO Box 20415
Bradenton, FL 34204-0415
(941) 747-8256
Email: recruiter@execadvantage.com
Web: www.execadvantage.com

Summary: Our firm specializes in upper level management positions with a general focus on the food manufacturing, beverage, and pharmaceutical sector. Our methodology is strongly rooted in defining the true needs of both client and candidate, and the utilization of our PR/marketing background to properly represent both.

Key Contact - Specialty:
Mr. Ken D'Amelio, Recruiter

Salary Minimum: $50,000

Functions: Generalist (All), Management

Industries: Generalist (All), Manufacturing, Food, Bev., Tobacco, Chemicals, Soap, Perf., Cosmtcs., Drugs Mfg., Medical Devices, Paints, Petro. Products, Transportation, Wholesale, Pharm Svcs., HR Services, Engineering Svcs., Packaging

Executive Alliance

425 New York Ave Ste 206
Huntington, NY 11743-3436
(631) 271-0574
Fax: (631) 271-1365
Email: info@execsallied.com
Web: www.executivealliancesearch.com

Summary: Retained and contingency search, specializing in financial services, credit, collections, financial and retail positions.

Key Contact - Specialty:
Mr. Gary Zelamsky, Principal

Salary Minimum: $50,000

Functions: Generalist (All), Management, Sales & Mktg., Customer Svc., Finance, CFOs, Cash Mgmt., Credit, Risk Mgmt., Engineering

Industries: Generalist (All)

Executive BioSearch

405 Via Chico Ste 8
Palos Verdes Estates, CA 90274-6818
(310) 378-1217
Email: mail@executivebiosearch.com
Web: www.executivebiosearch.com

Summary: Our firm is an executive search firm specializing in the scientific/bio-technology and diagnostic industries. We have extensive experience in the industry working for biomedical companies and executive search. Our areas of recruitment specialization are: senior management, corporate development, marketing, sales and applications support.

Key Contact - Specialty:
Ms. Marie Aragon, Principal

Functions: Generalist (All), Management, Sales & Mktg.

Industries: Medical Devices, Pharm Svcs., Software, Biotech/Life Sciences, Healthcare

Executive Career Search Inc

PO Box 621361
Oviedo, FL 32762-1361
(407) 366-5238
Fax: (407) 366-8537
Web: www.excsi.com

Summary: Specializes in consumer package goods sales and marketing mid-level to senior level positions.

Key Contact - Specialty:
Ms. Meredith Miller, President

Salary Minimum: $70,000

Functions: Sales & Mktg.

Industries: Consumer Goods

Executive Career Search

219 Loch Haven Dr
Williamsburg, VA 23188-7042
(757) 566-4600
Email: headhunter@widomaker.com

Summary: We are a recruiting firm for the construction materials industries, aggregates, asphalt, sand & gravel, concrete block, readi-mix concrete and cement. Secondary industry, heavy highway construction concrete and asphalt paving.

Key Contact - Specialty:
Mr. Charles H. Sillery, CPC, Owner & President - *Data processing, Engineering*

Functions: Mfg.

Industries: Agri., Forestry, Mining, Construction

Executive Career Strategies Inc

7900 N University Dr Ste 201
Tamarac, FL 33321-2100
(954) 720-9764
(800) 234-1362
Fax: (954) 720-6576
Email: info@ecsinsurancesearch.com
Web: www.ecsinsurancesearch.com

Summary: We specialize in the recruitment and placement of talented professionals within all areas of the property/casualty insurance industry. We take pride in our quality performance and high ethical standards.

Key Contact - Specialty:
Ms. Linda Daniel
Ms. Rena Moosa
Ms. Cindy LeMoine, CPCU
Ms. Jenean Meier, MBA

Salary Minimum: $40,000

Functions: Generalist (All)

Industries: Insurance

Executive Connection

8225 Brecksville Rd Ste 2
Brecksville, OH 44141-1362
(440) 838-5657
Fax: (440) 838-5668
Email: econnect@staffing.net
Web: www.executiveconnection.net

Summary: We are an executive/technical search firm specialists in the recruitment and placement of all disciplines in all manufacturing industries.

Key Contact - Specialty:
Mr. Steven C. Brandvold, President - *Engineering, Operations, Quality*
Ms. Ellen Williams, Senior Consultant

Salary Minimum: $40,000

Functions: Generalist (All), Middle Mgmt.

Industries: Generalist (All), Food, Bev., Tobacco, Paper, Plastics, Rubber, Paints, Petro. Products, Metal Products, Motor Vehicles, Misc. Mfg., Robotics, Accounting, Mgmt. Consulting, HR Services, Advertising

Executive Connections Inc

PO Box 1853
Lexington, NC 27293-1853
(336) 956-2002
Fax: (336) 956-2002
Email: ace@executiveconnections.net

Summary: Our firm works with manufacturing customers, primarily in the southeast. We have been successful in placing all levels of management from CEOs to production supervisors. We cover almost all engineering fields, namely ME, EE, IE and CHEM E.

Key Contact - Specialty:
Mr. Ace Ragan, President

Salary Minimum: $45,000

Functions: Management, Plant Mgmt., IT

Industries: Manufacturing

The Executive Consulting Group

6016 Valley Forge Dr
Houston, TX 77057-1934
(713) 686-9500
(281) 580-0700
Email: dgandin@houston.rr.com

Summary: We service all industries desiring a full range of accounting, tax, audit or financial talent. Our candidates are typically CPAs or MBAs with current or prior experience in public accounting, corporate accounting, corporate tax, corporate finance or financial analysis. Tax and financial reporting are two primary areas of specialization.

Key Contact - Specialty:
Mr. David L. Gandin, CPC, Partner - *Accounting, Accounting (Big 4,Bookkeeping,General,Public)*
Mr. Tim Staton, Partner - *Banking (Corporate,Investment,Merchant), Finance, Financial*

Salary Minimum: $45,000

Functions: Finance, CFOs, Budgeting, Taxes

Industries: Generalist (All)

Executive Direction Inc

847 Sansome St Fl 4
San Francisco, CA 94111-1529
(415) 394-5500
Fax: (415) 394-6888
Email: edi.sanfrancisco@exdir.com
Web: www.exdir.com

Summary: We specialize in search and placement of professionals in the areas of IT, software development and telecom for high-technology industries. We also do solution sourcing dealing with many projects and building a team to bring that project to completion.

Key Contact - Specialty:
Mr. Fred Naderi, President & Chief Executive Officer
Mr. Brad W. Blue, Manager

Salary Minimum: $80,000

Functions: Generalist (All), Management, CFOs, IT, MIS Mgmt., Systems Analysis, Systems Dev., Systems Implem., Systems Support, DB Admin.

Industries: Generalist (All), Software

Branches:
4025 E Chandler Blvd Ste 70-B8
Phoenix, AZ 85048-8867
(480) 664-0200
Fax: (480) 775-8481
Email: edi.phoenix@exdir.com
Key Contact - Specialty:
Mr. John Anderson, Manager

Executive Dynamics Inc (EDI)

2 James Brite Cir
Mahwah, NJ 07430-2527
(201) 327-9070
Fax: (201) 327-9071
Email: edi1@iglide.net

Summary: Experienced track record of placement of sales & marketing professionals in consumer packaged goods, pharmaceutical and marketing service companies. Confidential professional service.

Key Contact - Specialty:
Ms. Susan J. Wagner, President - *Sales*

Salary Minimum: $60,000

Functions: Sales & Mktg., Advertising, Mktg. Mgmt., Sales Mgmt., Direct Mktg.

Industries: Food, Bev., Tobacco, Soap, Perf., Cosmtcs., Drugs Mfg., Consumer Goods, Pharm Svcs., Mgmt. Consulting, Advertising

The Executive Exchange Corp

2517 Highway 35 Ste e103
Manasquan, NJ 08736-1912
(732) 223-6655
Fax: (732) 223-1162
Email: execexchan@aol.com
Web: www.theexecutiveexchange.com

Summary: We offer professional recruitment in information technology, consulting services, sales and recruiting. We have specialists in recruiting recruiters for computer services firms.

Key Contact - Specialty:
Ms. Elizabeth B. Glosser, CPC, Managing Director
Ms. Carolyn Smith, Director, Research

Salary Minimum: $45,000

Functions: Sales & Mktg., Sales Mgmt.

Industries: Computer Equip., Mgmt. Consulting, Software

The Executive Group

3276 Buford Dr Ste 104-242
Buford, GA 30519-5702
(770) 456-5892
Fax: (770) 573-0139
Email: info@theexecutivegrp.com
Web: www.theexecutivegrp.com

Summary: Located in Atlanta, Georgia - we specialize in conducting targeted searches, throughout the United States for Human Resources, Accounting, Executive Assistants, Financial Services, Marketing, Management & Sales.

Key Contact - Specialty:
Mrs. Cassandra Bolden, Director, Operations - *Accounting, Accounting (Bookkeeping), Financial services, Human resources, Marketing*

Functions: Senior Mgmt.

Industries: Generalist (All), Medical Devices, Semiconductors, Mutual/Hedge Funds, Accounting, HR Services, Hotels, Resorts, Clubs, Entertainment, Accounting SW

Executive Levels International

4938 Hampden Ln # 430
Bethesda, MD 20814-2914
(301) 320-3080
Fax: (301) 576-4484
Email: moreinfo@executivelevels.com
Web: www.executivelevels.com

Summary: Executive recruiters in information technology for all verticals and the sports industry to include sports teams, sports marketing, sporting goods and sports organizations. We specialize in managers, directors, VPs and above.

Key Contact - Specialty:
Ms. Robin Owens-Wright, President & Chief Executive Officer - *C-level, General management, Manufacturing (Management), Senior management, Sports*
Mr. Reno Wright, Chief Operating Officer

Functions: Management, Senior Mgmt., Mfg., Mktg. Mgmt., MIS Mgmt.

Industries: Hospitality, Sports, Media, Communications, Insurance, Software, Biotech/Life Sciences

Executive Medical Search

111 Pacifica Ste 250
Irvine, CA 92618-3311
(949) 770-9022
Fax: (949) 770-5658
Email: execumedsearch@yahoo.com
Web: www.executivemedicalsearch.com

Summary: We primarily specialize in the homecare, long-term care, hospice, assisted living and acute care positions. We place area COO, regional VP, VP Ops, VP nursing, VP sales & marketing, VP clinical services, PharmD, GMs, nurse managers and sales people.

Key Contact - Specialty:
Ms. Diana Brewer, CPC, President & Chief Executive Officer

Salary Minimum: $55,000

Functions: Senior Mgmt., Middle Mgmt., Healthcare, Nurses, Health Admin., Sales & Mktg., Sales Mgmt., CFOs

Industries: Healthcare, Hospitals, Long-term/Home Care, Physical Therapy, Occupational Therapy

Executive Network & Research Associates

1125 Farmington Ave
Farmington, CT 06032-1401
(860) 409-7550
Fax: (860) 409-7552
Email: info@executiveresearch.cc
Web: www.executivenetwork.biz

Summary: We are an executive search firm specializing in the wholesale apparel, retail, and pharmaceutical markets.

Key Contact - Specialty:
Mr. Jim Schmunk, Principal
Ms. Pat O'Connor, Principal
Ms. Margaret Williams, Manager, Pharmaceutical
Ms. Delia Ayer, Office Administrator
Ms. Barb Brewer, Administrator, Wholesale
Ms. Deb Gallo, Recruiter
Ms. Jennifer Fontanella, Recruiter
Ms. Christine Barton, Recruiter
Ms. Candice Curren, Recruiter
Ms. Rose Marie Howes, Recruiter, Pharmaceutical
Ms. Beth Brigham, Recruiter
Ms. Linda Teixeira, Recruiter
Ms. Rachael Mongillo, Recruiter - *Pharmaceutical, Retail, Wholesale*
Ms. Joanne Dibble, Recruiter
Ms. Marianne Sawicki, Recruiter
Ms. Kathleen Faragosa, Recruiter
Ms. Lisanne Markowitz, Recruiter
Ms. Barbara Kasner, Recruiter - *High technology, Information service, Information Systems, Information Technology, Systems (Integration)*

Functions: Sales Mgmt.

Industries: Textiles, Apparel, Wholesale, Retail, Pharm Svcs.

Executive Options Ltd

8707 Skokie Blvd Ste 300
Skokie, IL 60077-2281
(847) 933-8760
Fax: (847) 933-8766
Email: info@execoptions.com
Web: www.execoptions.com

Summary: Search and consulting firm specializing in the placement of professionals in consulting, interim and project assignments, as well as permanent part-time and full-time positions in all functions of an organization. Consulting services include management assessment and development in the areas of communications, leadership skills,

emotional intelligence and overall workforce effectiveness.

Key Contact - Specialty:
Mrs. Andrea Y. Meltzer, President

Salary Minimum: $40,000

Functions: Generalist (All)

Industries: Manufacturing, Finance, Banking, Invest. Banking, Services, Non-profits, Accounting, HR Services, Advertising, Healthcare

Executive Personnel Services Inc

2734 Chancellor Dr Ste 106
Crestview Hills, KY 41017-5409
(859) 331-5533
Fax: (859) 331-3494
Email: eps@fuse.net
Web: epsboblong.com

Summary: We are an executive recruiting and search firm. Primary focus of our firm is permanent positions from staff to executive levels in the Accounting and Finance professions.

Key Contact - Specialty:
Mr. Bob Long, President

Functions: Finance, Budgeting, Taxes

Industries: Generalist (All)

Executive Placement Consultants

PO Box 793
Northbrook, IL 60065-0793
(847) 298-6445
Email: mike@epc-chicago.com
Web: www.epc-chicago.com

Summary: Many years of experience in placing finance and accounting professionals. We now offer placement for RNs and LPNs in hospitals and nursing homes and home healthcare.

Key Contact - Specialty:
Mr. Michael Colman, President - *Finance, Human resources*

Salary Minimum: $50,000

Functions: Healthcare, HR Mgmt., Finance

Industries: Generalist (All)

Executive Placement Services

5901 Peachtree Dundwoody Rd NE Ste B480
Atlanta, GA 30328-7170
(770) 396-9114
(678) 443-2150
Email: recruiter@execplacement.com
Web: www.execplacement.com

Summary: Our firm fills middle and upper management positions in the retail industry (all departments) and sales/marketing positions in consumer packaged goods and the food Industries. We maintain long-term relationships with companies – large and small, public and private.

Key Contact - Specialty:
Mr. John J. Weiss, CPC, President
Mr. Howard Steele, Retail Director - *Retail*

Salary Minimum: $50,000

Functions: Generalist (All)

Industries: Consumer Goods, Retail

Branches:
PO Box 1140
Waldorf, MD 20604-1140
(301) 934-5457
Fax: (301) 609-6087

Key Contact - Specialty:
Mr. John Ehman - *Retail*

Executive Placement Associates

(also known as Retail Placement Associates)
6001 Montrose Rd Ste 702
Rockville, MD 20852-4873
(301) 231-8150
(800) 601-5627
Fax: (301) 881-2918
Email: recruiter@executive-placement.com
Web: www.retail-placement.com

Summary: Retail industry specialists for: merchandising, management, operations, warehousing, loss prevention and HR. IT industry specialists for contract and permanent technology professionals in all fields.

Key Contact - Specialty:
Mr. Mark J. Suss, President - *Advertising, Human resources, Retail*
Ms. Ilissa Suss, Vice President, Contract Placement Assoc
Mr. John Stafford, Senior Retail Consultant
Ms. Anne Sklar, Senior Retail Consultant
Ms. Linda Barnett, Senior Retail Consultant
Mr. John Frankovich, Regional Director & Senior Recruiter - *Retail*
Mr. Thom Lamm, Regional Director & Senior Recruiter
Ms. Martha Wagner, Administrative Manager
Mrs. Beth Berman, Associate Recruiter - *Management, Operations, Retail*
Ms. Vicki Schuck, Associate Recruiter - *Management, Operations, Retail*
Mrs. Shalini Rossett, Associate Recruiter, Contract Division - *High technology, Information service, Information Systems, Information Technology, Systems (Integration)*

Salary Minimum: $40,000

Functions: Generalist (All), IT

Industries: Generalist (All), Retail, HR Services, IT Implementation

Executive Pro Search Ltd

70 W Madison St Ste 1400
Chicago, IL 60602-4267
(312) 214-3131
Email: srw@execprosearch.com

Summary: Search practice covers corporate finance/capital markets including: leveraged/structured finance, merchant/investment banking, M&A, private equity, fund-to-funds, asset management, financial advisory, middle market lending and corporate banking, private banking and commercial real estate lending.

Key Contact - Specialty:
Mr. Stephen Wetzel, Partner
Mr. Terry Murphy, Partner

Salary Minimum: $50,000

Functions: Finance, Cash Mgmt., M&A

Industries: Banking, Invest. Banking, Venture Cap., Mutual/Hedge Funds, Misc. Financial, Mgmt. Consulting

Executive Recruiters

PO Box 3447
Vero Beach, FL 32961-0347
(772) 234-6266
Fax: (772) 234-0632
Email: miles@execrecruit.org
Web: www.execrecruit.org

Summary: We specialize in life insurance sales working with agents who, as a minimum, meet MDRT level of production.

Key Contact - Specialty:
Mr. Miles O'Brien, President

Salary Minimum: $50,000

Functions: Sales Mgmt.

Industries: Life

Executive Recruiters

600 108th Ave NE Ste 242
Bellevue, WA 98004-5110
(206) 447-7404
(425) 451-0233
Fax: (425) 451-8704
Email: info@executive-recruiters.com
Web: executive-recruiters.com

Summary: Professional recruiting firm specializing in enterprise software, wireless software, content, wireless carriers, entertainment, gaming, eCommerce, digital media, at senior and executive levels in all major disciplines.

Key Contact - Specialty:
Mr. Ron Butler, President & Chief Executive Officer
Mr. Jerry Taylor, General Manager - *Computers, Marketing, Product management/development, Sales, Wireless*
Mrs. Barbara Jordan, Senior Consultant - *High technology, Sales, Staffing, Telecommunications, Wireless*
Miss Norma Kraft, Senior Consultant - *Computers, Computers (Programming,Science,Software), Technical (Management)*

Salary Minimum: $100,000

Functions: Middle Mgmt., Product Dev., Mktg. Mgmt., Sales Mgmt., PR, CFOs, Systems Dev.

Industries: Finance, Invest. Banking, E-commerce, Media, Communications, Wireless, Network Infrastructure, Software, Development SW, Entertainment SW, Industry Specific SW, Marketing SW, Networking, Comm. SW, Security SW

Executive Recruiters Agency Inc

PO Box 21810
Little Rock, AR 72221-1810
(501) 224-7000
Fax: (501) 224-8534
Email: grogers@execrecruit.com
Web: www.execrecruit.com

Summary: We are dedicated to the delivery of staffing services of the highest quality. Our commitment is to provide our clients with extraordinary value, efficiency through the personal caring of our staff and modern technology.

Key Contact - Specialty:
Mr. Aaron Lubin, President

Salary Minimum: $45,000

Functions: Mfg., Product Dev.; Automation, Quality, Materials, Distribution, Sales & Mktg., HR Mgmt., Finance, Engineering

Industries: Generalist (All), Paper, Chemicals, Drugs Mfg., Medical Devices, Plastics, Rubber, Motor Vehicles, Computer Equip., Consumer Elect., Electronic, Elec. Components, Robotics, Accounting, Engineering Svcs., Digital, Packaging

Executive Recruiters International Inc

PO Box 2537
Birmingham, MI 48012-2537
(313) 961-6200
Fax: (248) 593-2545

Email: eriinc@execrecruiters.com
Web: www.execrecruiters.com

Summary: We recruit for the automotive OEM and tier suppliers, specializing in technical sales, engineering, purchasing, manufacturing and management for all world markets. We consult and recruit for board level positions for automotive, healthcare and computer companies. We also recruit management personnel for healthcare, property management, environmental, computer and finance industries.

Key Contact - Specialty:
Ms. Kathleen A. Sinclair, Recruiter

Salary Minimum: $40,000

Functions: Management, Board Members, Mfg., Materials, Sales & Mktg., HR Mgmt., Finance, IT, Engineering, Int'l.

Industries: Manufacturing, Chemicals, Plastics, Rubber, Paints, Petro. Products, Motor Vehicles, Test, Measure Equip., Misc. Mfg., Electronic, Elec. Components, Transportation, Finance, HR Services, E-commerce, Engineering Svcs., Hospitality, Media, Packaging, Real Estate, Healthcare, Hospitals

Executive Recruiters & Consultants LLC

267 Palos Verdes Dr W Apt 7
Palos Verdes Estates, CA 90274-1329
(310) 373-2343
Fax: (310) 373-6575
Email: deborah@erc-us.com
Web: www.erc-us.com

Summary: Recognized executive search and recruitment company that specializes in the recruitment of sales/sales support, marketing, management and HR professionals in computer software, technology solutions, consumer products and business-to-business services.

Key Contact - Specialty:
Ms. Deborah Teate-Banks, CRM

Functions: Management, Sales & Mktg., HR Mgmt., Minorities/Diversity

Industries: Food, Bev., Tobacco, Soap, Perf., Cosmtcs., Computer Equip., Consumer Elect., Consumer Goods, Transportation, Services, Non-profits, HR Services, IT Implementation, Software

Executive Recruiters Group

8775 Cloudleap Ct Ste P29
Columbia, MD 21045-3081
(410) 796-7764
(443) 562-6101
Fax: (410) 964-3109
Email: rdickey@executiverecruitersgroup.com
Web: www.executiverecruitersgroup.com

Summary: We are a contingency-based search firm, specializing in the recruitment of diversity sales & marketing candidates for the pharmaceutical, bio-technology, medical device, consumer package goods and IT industries. Our candidates range from entry level to senior management. Our partners have experience in the pharmaceutical, biotechnology and consumer packaged goods industry.

Key Contact - Specialty:
Mr. Ronald Dickey, Partner

Salary Minimum: $40,000

Functions: Sales & Mktg.

Industries: Generalist (All), Drugs Mfg., Medical Devices, Biotech/Life Sciences, Healthcare, Hospitals

Executive Recruiters

135 Albert St
London, ON N6A 1L9
Canada
(519) 652-2722
(800) 317-4473
Fax: (519) 679-3454
Email: execurec@sprint.ca

Summary: We specialize in permanent placement of senior management, sales, marketing and clinical personnel for the pharmaceutical and medical device marketplace.

Key Contact - Specialty:
Ms. Nancy Howett, Recruiter - *Logistics, Operations, Sales*

Functions: Sales & Mktg.

Industries: Drugs Mfg., Medical Devices, Computer Equip., Telecoms, Software, Biotech/Life Sciences, Healthcare

Executive Recruiting Associates

750 W Lake Cook Rd Ste 155
Buffalo Grove, IL 60089-2071
(847) 465-1020
Fax: (847) 465-1546
Email: info@erecruitusa.com
Web: www.erecruitusa.com

Summary: We are a Full service contingency firm, recruiting in a variety of industries. Extensive experience in business with proven track record. We provide quality, professionalism and work ethics.

Key Contact - Specialty:
Mr. Tom Malloy, Chief Executive Officer - *Management, Sales*
Ms. Wendy Epstein, Executive Recruiter
Ms. Joyce Natkin, Administrative Manager

Functions: Generalist (All)

Industries: Drugs Mfg., Plastics, Rubber, Metal Products, Machine, Appliance, Computer Equip., Consumer Elect., Misc. Mfg., Misc. Financial, Accounting, Telecoms

Executive Recruiting Solutions LLC

2500 Towering Ridge Ln
Florence, KY 41042-7847
(513) 564-8885
(866) 222-8214
Email: tkelly@crsrecruiters.com
Web: www.ersrecruiters.com

Summary: We specialize in locating the hard to find top-level people in the marketplace today. People are the core of every business. We find the right people to meet your organizational goals and blend with the company culture. Our goal is to find quality people that will enhance the company.

Key Contact - Specialty:
Mr. Tom Kelly, President
Ms. Anne Castleberry, Vice President

Salary Minimum: $30,000

Functions: Generalist (All), Management

Industries: Printing, Drugs Mfg., Medical Devices, Finance, Banking, Invest. Banking, Brokers, Pharm Svcs., Mgmt. Consulting, HR Services, Hospitals, Dental

Executive Recruiting Consultants

108 W 4th St Ste C
Dell Rapids, SD 57022-1009
(605) 428-6150
Fax: (605) 428-6151

Email: craig@werecruit.net
Web: www.us-recruiters.com/members/libis.html

Summary: We specialize in the recruiting and placement of individuals in accounting, finance, banking, HR and sales & marketing. Trust, professionalism, reliability and integrity are the principles that we live and work by. Independent, unbiased and objective, we recruit all levels of professional candidates. We build long-lasting relationships by partnering with our clients. We invest the time to understand our clients' business, culture and current business issues.

Key Contact - Specialty:
Mr. Craig Libis, President

Salary Minimum: $25,000

Functions: Board Members

Industries: Generalist (All), Energy, Utilities, Manufacturing, Lumber, Furniture, Consumer Goods, Finance, Banking, Accounting, Hospitality, Mfg. SW

Executive Recruitment Services Inc

1134 Leicester Ct
Wheaton, IL 60187-7709
(630) 871-8050
Email: cpgrecruiter@comcast.net

Summary: Marketing and sales recruitment for consumer products manufacturing companies with an emphasis toward food manufacturers.

Key Contact - Specialty:
Mr. Gayle Stinn, CRM, President

Salary Minimum: $80,000

Functions: Sales & Mktg., Mktg. Mgmt.

Industries: Food, Bev., Tobacco, Soap, Perf., Cosmtcs., Consumer Elect., Consumer Goods, Inst./Industrial Food Svc.

Executive Referral Services Inc

8770 W Bryn Mawr Ave Fl 710
Chicago, IL 60631-3780
(773) 693-6622
Fax: (773) 693-8466
Email: info@ers-online.com
Web: www.ers-online.com

Summary: Our network, impeccable references and complete commitment to our assignments have resulted in our reputation as the source for recruitment within the hotel, restaurant, retail, club, gaming, entertainment, construction and real estate industries.

Key Contact - Specialty:
Mr. Bruce Freier, CPC, President - *Amusement parks, Cruise management, Culinary, Hospitality, Retail*
Ms. Robyn Huber, Account Executive - *Construction, Finance, Food & beverage, Food service, Real estate*
Ms. Erika Wallenda, Account Executive - *Gaming, Hospitality, Hotels, Resorts, Restaurants*

Salary Minimum: $25,000

Functions: Generalist (All)

Industries: Retail, Services, Accounting, Hospitality, Real Estate

Executive Register Inc

34 Mill Plain Rd
Danbury, CT 06811-5140
(203) 743-5542
Fax: (203) 794-1689
Email: swilliams@exec-reg.com
Web: www.exec-reg.com

Summary: We have successful recruitment experience in the fields of IT, accounting/finance and engineering/manufacturing. We believe that today's search is for tomorrow's success.

Key Contact - Specialty:
Mr. J. Scott Williams, CPC, President
Mr. Larry V. Hirschauer, CPC, Director - *Engineering, Manufacturing*

Salary Minimum: $50,000

Functions: Middle Mgmt., Mfg., Finance, IT, Systems Dev., DB Admin., Engineering

Industries: Generalist (All)

Executive Registry

1910-1200 Av McGill College
Centre Capitol
Montreal, QC H3B 4G7
Canada
(514) 866-7981
Email: er@executive-registry.net
Web: www.executive-registry.net

Summary: We are full-service management recruiters.

Key Contact - Specialty:
Mr. Harvey N. Stewart, President - *Finance, General management, Real estate*
Mr. Christian Boucher, Recruiter
Mr. Yvan Lachance, Recruiter
Mr. Pascal Delisi, Recruiter
Mr. Don Y. Lee, CHRA, Recruiter
Ms. Lyne Groulx, CRHA, Recruiter
Mr. Erick McGee, CRHA, Recruiter
Mr. Robert Rivet, Recruiter
Mr. Steve Rothstein, Recruiter
Ms. Janet Presser, Recruiter
Mr. Eric Audet, CGA, Recruiter
Ms. Annie Giguere, CGA, Recruiter

Salary Minimum: $50,000

Functions: Generalist (All), Management, Mfg., Sales & Mktg., HR Mgmt., Finance, IT, Engineering

Industries: Generalist (All), Manufacturing, Retail, Services, Packaging, Real Estate

Executive Resource Associates

1612 Bay Breeze Dr
Virginia Beach, VA 23454-1446
(757) 481-6221
Email: davedavid@topechelon.com

Summary: We belong to a recruiting network of over 600 offices and cover most professional disciplines and industries. We are able to find and place qualified candidates for client companies in technical and management positions. We offer confidentiality, honesty and integrity that is necessary to place the right candidate in the right job. Making the best fit for both the candidate and the client company creates a win-win situation for all involved.

Key Contact - Specialty:
Mr. Dave N. David, Director - *Chemical, Defense, Engineering, Manufacturing, Plastics*

Functions: Management, Middle Mgmt., Mfg., Production, Plant Mgmt., Sales & Mktg., Mktg. Mgmt., Engineering

Industries: Generalist (All), Oil & Gas, Manufacturing, Paper, Chemicals, Soap, Perf., Cosmtcs., Drugs Mfg., Plastics, Rubber, Paints, Petro. Products, Finance, Accounting, Software, ERP SW, Marketing SW, Biotech/Life Sciences

Executive Resource Group

4311 Coronet Dr
Encino, CA 91316-4324
(818) 654-9800
Fax: (818) 654-9889
Email: devoraherg@cs.com

Summary: The firm is an executive search firm specializing in the insurance industry and insurance related eCommerce companies. Areas of expertise include carrier underwriting, loss control and claims, reinsurance, alternative risk, risk management, professional liability and agent/broker. We have successfully matched hundreds of candidates with growth companies.

Key Contact - Specialty:
Ms. Devorah Torres, President

Salary Minimum: $45,000

Functions: Generalist (All), Middle Mgmt.

Industries: Insurance, Casualty, Claims, Commercial, Re-Insurance

Executive Resource Group Inc

1330 Cedarpoint Ct Ste 201
Amelia, OH 45102-1383
(513) 947-1447
Email: kennedypub@executiveresource.net
Web: www.executiveresource.net

Summary: Specialize in the search of superior HR professionals for our client companies, placing candidates from mid-level up to VP status. We fulfill their needs through our knowledge of their company, products and industry.

Key Contact - Specialty:
Mr. John S. Vujcec, President

Salary Minimum: $70,000

Functions: HR Mgmt.

Industries: Manufacturing

Executive Resource Inc

PO Box 356
Hartland, WI 53029-0356
(262) 369-2540
Fax: (262) 369-2558
Email: duane@erijobs.com
Web: www.erijobs.com

Summary: A professional recruiting firm that specializes in identifying and evaluating those professionals that are in the top 20 percent of their field, based on skill level and academic achievement.

Key Contact - Specialty:
Mr. William H. Mitton, Executive Vice President - *Finance, Human resources*
Mr. Duane Strong, President - *Manufacturing*
Mr. Peter Lamb

Salary Minimum: $40,000

Functions: Generalist (All), Mfg., Materials, HR Mgmt., Finance, CFOs, Engineering

Industries: Generalist (All), Manufacturing, Lumber, Furniture, Paper, Medical Devices, Plastics, Rubber, Machine, Appliance, Finance

Executive Resource Systems

2717 E Killingsworth Ave
Orange, CA 92869-3224
(714) 744-4000
Email: brody@erscareers.com
Web: www.erscareers.com

Summary: We are your resource for professional level permanent and contract placements. Online with the world's largest recruiter network of affiliates, we specialize in the placement of accounting, engineering, finance, HR, sales and systems professionals. Many exclusive, retained searches.

Key Contact - Specialty:
Mr. Steve Brody, President - *Engineering, Finance, Human resources, Systems*

Salary Minimum: $50,000

Functions: Materials, Purchasing, HR Mgmt., Finance, CFOs, Budgeting, Credit, Taxes, Risk Mgmt., Engineering

Industries: Generalist (All), Energy, Utilities, Food, Bev., Tobacco, Medical Devices, Computer Equip., Finance, Accounting, Aerospace, Biotech/Life Sciences, Healthcare

Executive Resource Solutions, Inc

PO Box 47054
Minneapolis, MN 55447-0054
(952) 892-5789
Fax: (952) 516-5299
Email: peggi@ers-team.com
Web: www.ers-team.com

Summary: We focus on director and above levels for all job functions within the food, retail and human resource industries.

Key Contact - Specialty:
Ms. Peggi Tobais, Principal - *Consumer (Products), Distribution, Finance, Food, Human resources*
Ms. Julie Curtis, Principal - *Accounting (General), Executives, Groceries, Purchasing, Retail*

Salary Minimum: $70,000

Functions: Generalist (All)

Industries: Food, Bev., Tobacco, Textiles, Apparel, Consumer Goods, Wholesale, Retail, Packaging

Executive Resources

3816 Ingersoll Ave
Des Moines, IA 50312-3452
(515) 287-6880
Fax: (515) 255-9445
Email: iaexecres@aol.com
Web: www.executiveresourcesltd.com

Summary: No advertising. Pure search.

Key Contact - Specialty:
Ms. Gerry Mullane, President - *Manufacturing, Sales*

Functions: Generalist (All), Admin. Svcs., Product Dev., Production, Advertising, Mktg. Research, Budgeting

Industries: Generalist (All), Medical Devices, Plastics, Rubber, Paints, Petro. Products, Venture Cap., Accounting, Packaging

Executive Resources International

Poste restante 632 Succ Victoria
Montreal, QC H3Z 2Y7
Canada
(514) 935-3695
(800) 667-5928
Fax: (514) 931-2495
Email: eri@istar.ca

Summary: We are an executive search organization recruiting management and technical personnel for service in developing areas in North America.

Key Contact - Specialty:
Mr. G.P. Creighton, Principal
Mr. Michael E. Berger, Associate Emeritus

Salary Minimum: $50,000

Functions: Middle Mgmt., Finance, Engineering, Environmentalists, Architects

Industries: Agri., Forestry, Mining, Energy, Utilities, Construction, Finance, Misc. Financial, Services, Environmental Svcs., Haz. Waste

Executive Sales Search Inc

1815 Habersham Trce
Cumming, GA 30041-5982
(770) 889-9665
Fax: (770) 889-9350
Email: lindamende@earthlink.net

Summary: Our firm specializes in placing experienced Medical Sales Representatives and Medical Sales Managers with top caliber medical device companies.

Key Contact - Specialty:
Ms. Linda H. Mende, Owner & Recruiter - *Medical (Devices,Sales), Surgical*
Mrs. Stacey Mayes, Recruiter - *Medical (Devices,Sales)*

Functions: Sales & Mktg., Sales Mgmt., Sales Reps., Minorities/Diversity

Industries: Drugs Mfg., Medical Devices, Pharm Svcs., Healthcare, Dental, Women's

Executive Search

13807 Penn St
Whittier, CA 90602-1970
(562) 789-1107
Fax: (562) 789-0107
Email: execsearchinc@aol.com

Summary: We are a generalist agency and work with a variety of industries. We have clients in the food and poultry industry, medical device (class 3), plumbing manufacturers, technology, electronic warfare, consumer goods and manufacturing. We specialize in engineers, sales & marketing, restructuring & turnaround controllers, cost control accountants, director/VP, quality control, reliability manager or director, middle and senior executive management candidates.

Key Contact - Specialty:
Ms. Cheryl Johnson, Recruiter

Functions: Generalist (All), Management, Engineering

Industries: Generalist (All), Manufacturing, Food, Bev., Tobacco, Chemicals, Drugs Mfg., Medical Devices, Plastics, Rubber, Metal Products, Consumer Elect., Test, Measure Equip., Misc. Mfg., Electronic, Elec. Components, Consumer Goods, Digital, Wireless, Fiber Optic, Network Infrastructure

Executive Search Associates Inc

185 Alewife Brook Pkwy Ste 400
Cambridge, MA 02138-1107
(617) 497-4953
Fax: (617) 497-5005
Email: mail@esaexecsearch.com
Web: www.esaexecsearch.com

Summary: We are part of a large network and have many contacts in healthcare and managed care.

Key Contact - Specialty:
Mr. Arthur H. Coffin, President & Principal - *Managed care*

Functions: Generalist (All), Management, Physicians, Health Admin., Sales Mgmt., Direct Mktg., Customer Svc., CFOs, MIS Mgmt.

Industries: Generalist (All), Insurance, Healthcare, Hospitals, Long-term/Home Care

Executive Search Consultants

2108 Appaloosa Cir
Petaluma, CA 94954-4654
(707) 763-0100
Email: peg@escba.com
Web: www.escba.com

Summary: We concentrate on senior software product development positions. Our focus is on Internet, networking and wireless communications environments placing software and hardware developers and managers. We look for senior design, architect, management, director, CTO, and VP level candidates.

Key Contact - Specialty:
Ms. Peg Iversen Grubb, President

Salary Minimum: $85,000

Functions: Product Dev.

Industries: Computer Equip., Consumer Elect., Telecoms, Software

Executive Search Consultants Corp

8 S Michigan Ave Ste 1205
Chicago, IL 60603-3385
(312) 251-8400

Summary: Recruitment without delegation ensures high quality execution tailored to transform the ideal to tangible. Offering counsel in partnership with client, sharing observations and experience, building fidelity through commitment. Firm size affords full time and attention.

Key Contact - Specialty:
Mr. Jack Flynn, Manager
Mr. William Weatherstone, President
Ms. Sandy Kinney, Vice President - *Telecommunications*
Mr. Bill Williams, Senior Consultant - *Gas, Oil*
Mr. Joe Marcello, Senior Consultant - *Non-profit*
Mr. Brent O'Brien, Consultant - *Gas, Oil*

Salary Minimum: $50,000

Functions: Generalist (All), Senior Mgmt., Middle Mgmt., CFOs, Cash Mgmt., Risk Mgmt., Mgmt. Consultants, Non-profits

Industries: Generalist (All), Energy, Utilities, Broadcast, Film, Insurance

The Executive Search Corp

772 Central Ave
Kinston, NC 28504-6248
(252) 527-5900
Fax: (252) 527-5592
Email: mdaughety@esn.net
Web: www.pulpandpaperjobs.com

Summary: We have extensive experience in providing HR and staffing solutions to the pulp & paper industry. We are providers of all staffing solutions to client companies from retained and contingency search, to temp and outplacement. Emphasis is placed on retained search and staffing consulting.

Key Contact - Specialty:
Mr. J. Mac Daughety, President & Owner

Salary Minimum: $80,000

Functions: Mfg., Int'l.

Industries: Paper, Printing

Executive Search Group

1300 Weathervane Ln Ste 216
Akron, OH 44313-7990
(330) 867-7725
Email: searchgroup@mindspring.com

Summary: We are an executive placement firm specializing in the toy and gift industries. Client list includes numerous Fortune 500 companies. We have expertise in CEO and VP level searches. Firm offers personal service, is aggressive and ethical.

Key Contact - Specialty:
Mr. David E. Fitzgibbons, CPC, President - *Marketing, Sales*

Salary Minimum: $45,000

Functions: Senior Mgmt., Middle Mgmt., Mktg. Mgmt., Sales Mgmt.

Industries: Misc. Mfg., Non-Classifiable

Executive Search International (ESI)

733 N Magnolia Ave
Orlando, FL 32803-3835
(407) 926-6000
Fax: (407) 425-6245
Email: bwosgien@esiglobal.cc
Web: www.esiglobal.cc

Summary: We are an executive recruitment company serving the hospitality industry.

Key Contact - Specialty:
Mr. Bernd K. Wosgien, CHA, Chairman & Chief Executive Officer

Salary Minimum: $50,000

Functions: Generalist (All), Hospitality

Industries: Hospitality, Hotels, Resorts, Clubs, Restaurants, Full Service Restaurants

Executive Search International Inc

3033 W Parker Rd Ste 204
Plano, TX 75023-8029
(972) 424-4714
Fax: (972) 424-5314
Email: mail@esihbc.com
Web: www.esihbc.com

Summary: We are specialists in nonfood consumer packaged goods for manufacturers. Our key placement areas HBC-OTC products, beauty care-cosmetics plus general merchandise, nutritional products (both mass & health stores)-- North America & Int'l

Key Contact - Specialty:
Mr. Ed Nalley, CPC, President & Executive Recruiter - *Consumer (Packaged Goods), Cosmetics, Executives, Presidents, Sales*
Ms. Linda Rogers, Senior Research Manager - *Consumer (Marketing,Packaged Goods), Cosmetics, Middle management, Supply Chain*

Salary Minimum: $60,000

Functions: Management, Board Members, Senior Mgmt., Product Dev., Sales & Mktg., Mktg. Research, Sales Mgmt.

Industries: Food, Bev., Tobacco, Soap, Perf., Cosmtcs., Drugs Mfg., Medical Devices, Marketing SW

Executive Search Ltd

8374 Princeton Glendale Rd Ste 3
West Chester, OH 45069-5937
(513) 874-6901
(513) 714-1060
Fax: (513) 870-6348
Email: tcimino@executivesearch.net
Web: www.executivesearch.net

Summary: Seasoned account executives with extensive prior experience in manufacturing, engineering, marketing, printing, packaging, packaging equipment, HR, foundry, automotive,

capital equipment, food, pulp/paper, IS/IT, pharmaceutical sales and healthcare. Also provide expert witness services.

Key Contact - Specialty:
Mrs. Terry Cimino, Chief Executive Officer - *Regulatory, Research & development, Six sigma, Stamping, Strategic planning*
Mr. James J. Cimino, President - *CEOs, COOs*

Salary Minimum: $90,000

Functions: Generalist (All), Senior Mgmt., Middle Mgmt., Product Dev., Production, Quality, Materials, Packaging, Nurses, Sales & Mktg.

Industries: Generalist (All), Manufacturing, Food, Bev., Tobacco, Paper, Printing, Soap, Perf., Cosmtcs., Drugs Mfg., Medical Devices, Metal Products, Machine, Appliance, Motor Vehicles, Computer Equip., Consumer Elect., Misc. Mfg., Electronic, Elec. Components, Robotics, Consumer Goods, Finance, Pharm Svcs., Logistics Svcs., Supply Chain Mgmt, Communications, Telephony, Aerospace, Packaging, Insurance, Software, Database SW, Biotech/Life Sciences, Healthcare, Hospitals, Long-term/Home Care

Branches:
2240 W Woolbright Rd Ste 353
Boynton Beach, FL 33426-6395
(561) 734-3550
Email: bennett@bentleygrp.com

Executive Search Management Inc

PO Box 2881
2111 W Plum St Ste 388
Aurora, IL 60507-2881
(630) 859-2200
Fax: (630) 859-2668
Email: executivesearch@esm-aurora.com
Web: www.esm-aurora.com

Summary: Our firm has taken the latest approach to enhance the client/recruiter relationship. We have experienced steady growth every year due to our partnership agreements with many top companies, which provide the best opportunities for growth. Our associates specialize in the financial, IT, industrial, marketing, engineering and sales marketplace.

Key Contact - Specialty:
Ms. Kristina Erdrich, President & Account Executive - *Banking, Banking (Commercial,Corporate,Mortgage), Information Technology*
Mr. John Erdrich, Senior Account Manager - *Electrical, Industrial, Manufacturing, Manufacturing (Management), Sales*

Salary Minimum: $40,000

Functions: Management, Senior Mgmt.

Industries: Construction, Manufacturing, Medical Devices, Plastics, Rubber, Test, Measure Equip., Misc. Mfg., Electronic, Elec. Components, Finance, Banking, Services, Equip Svcs., Media, Telecoms, Real Estate, Software

Executive Search Network

2607 W Sunrise Dr
Phoenix, AZ 85041-9607
(602) 276-9030
Email: marysnow@executivesearchnetwork.com
Web: www.executivesearchnetwork.com

Summary: Targeting is our business. We work nationally and specialize in the recruitment of executives in direct marketing and sales promotional advertising. We place database marketing and CRM specialists, creatives,

production, management, account service and freelancers.

Key Contact - Specialty:
Ms. Mary E. Snow, Owner & Recruiter

Salary Minimum: $35,000

Functions: Direct Mktg.

Industries: Generalist (All)

Executive Search of New England Inc

131 Ocean St
South Portland, ME 04106-3649
(207) 741-4100
Fax: (207) 741-4110
Email: info@jobsesne.com
Web: www.nationaljobbank.com

Summary: We are one of the area's largest and most diverse search and recruiting firms. Our personnel consultants bring a wealth of experience to a select list of clients.

Key Contact - Specialty:
Mr. Robert L. Sloat, CPC, Partner - *Administration, Bakery, Banking, Convenience stores, Engineering*
Mr. Robert T. Thayer, Partner

Salary Minimum: $40,000

Functions: Generalist (All)

Industries: Generalist (All), Construction, Manufacturing, Food, Bev., Tobacco, Banking, Misc. Financial, Architectural Svcs., Legal, Advertising, Telecoms

Executive Search of America LLC

22700 Shore Center Dr
Euclid, OH 44123-1637
(216) 261-7400
Fax: (216) 289-1635
Email: jobs@execsearchamerica.com
Web: www.execsearchamerica.com

Summary: We place sales and technical candidates. We work some of the worlds largest companies; security software, telecom, CRM, eCommerce and other technology type companies.

Key Contact - Specialty:
Mr. Scott Carpenter, Vice President

Salary Minimum: $40,000

Functions: Generalist (All), Senior Mgmt., Sales & Mktg., Sales Mgmt., IT, Systems Dev., Network Admin., Engineering

Industries: Generalist (All), Consumer Elect., Test, Measure Equip., Banking, New Media, Telecoms, Call Centers, Wireless, Network Infrastructure, Networking, Comm. SW, Security SW

Branches:
3569 Normandy Cir
Oceanside, CA 92056-4922
(760) 295-7018
Fax: (760) 295-7019
Email: socha@earthlink.net

137 Midway Is
Clearwater Beach, FL 33767-2314
(727) 447-4295
Key Contact - Specialty:
Mr. Edward Carpenter

Executive Search Partners

37838 Turnberry Ct
Farmington Hills, MI 48331-2892
(248) 553-8905

Email: gerickson@execsearchpartners.com
Web: www.execsearchpartners.com

Summary: We are an executive search company that specializes in senior level IT positions. We also provide senior level IT professional on a contract basis.

Key Contact - Specialty:
Mr. Gary Erickson, Managing Partner
Mr. Gary Robertson, Partner - *Automotive, CIOs, Computers (Sales), Information Technology, Management consulting*
Mr. Larry Hamilton, Partner - *Automotive, CIOs, Computers (Sales), Information Technology, Management consulting*

Salary Minimum: $100,000

Functions: IT, MIS Mgmt., Mgmt. Consultants

Industries: Generalist (All), Mgmt. Consulting, E-commerce, IT Implementation, Software, Accounting SW, Database SW, Development SW, ERP SW, Mfg. SW

Executive Search Partners Inc

153 E Main St Ste 220
Columbus, OH 43215-5276
(614) 241-5559
Fax: (614) 241-5570
Email: espiker@search-partners.com
Web: www.search-partners.com

Summary: Recruit executives (all functions) for marketing communications firms. Traditional advertising, direct marketing, sales promotion, PR and corporate marketing.

Key Contact - Specialty:
Mr. Ed Spiker, Senior Parnter
Mr. Brooks Young, Senior Parnter

Functions: Generalist (All)

Industries: Generalist (All)

Executive Search Professionals Inc

3483 Greenfield Pl
Carmel, CA 93923-9415
(831) 625-6200

Key Contact - Specialty:
Ms. Fila Barnett, President

Salary Minimum: $50,000

Functions: Production

Industries: Banking, Misc. Financial

Executive Selections

526 Oakwood Blvd
New Braunfels, TX 78130-5253
(830) 629-6291
Email: execsel@satx.rr.com

Summary: Executive search for life insurance companies. Specialty is attorneys in the estate planning discipline. We are an executive search for life insurance companies. Specialty is attorneys in the estate planning discipline.

Key Contact - Specialty:
Mr. Jim K. Rice, Owner

Salary Minimum: $35,000

Functions: Management, Board Members, Mktg. Research

Industries: Legal, Insurance, Life

Executive Staffers

PO Box 670651
Dallas, TX 75367-0651
(214) 265-9343
Fax: (214) 265-9343

Email: info@executivestaffers.com
Web: www.executivestaffers.com

Summary: We are a recruitment solutions firm specializing in developing and executing customized solutions for securing highly specialized mid to senior level professionals for a variety of industries. Our dedicated divisions service the following areas of expertise: accounting, advertising, creative, healthcare, hospitality, HR, public relations, marketing & sales, technology and C-class executives.

Key Contact - Specialty:
Mr. Robert Rota, President

Salary Minimum: $50,000

Functions: Management, Board Members, Senior Mgmt., Middle Mgmt., Healthcare, Sales & Mktg., Direct Mktg., PR, HR Mgmt., Finance

Industries: Generalist (All), Energy, Utilities, Manufacturing, Finance, Services, HR Services, Hospitality, Media, Communications, Software, Healthcare

Executive Staffing Solutions

150 E Wilson Bridge Rd Ste 200
Worthington, OH 43085-2390
(614) 885-8490
Fax: (614) 847-8377
Email: aw@ess-ld.com

Summary: Health care recruiting firm specializing in the managed care and hospital industries. Also recruit for both finance and accounting positions in our local market.

Key Contact - Specialty:
Ms. Laurie Glowac, Senior Recruiter
Mr. Aaron Wandtke, CPC, Senior Parnter
Mr. Rick McDonald, CPC, Senior Recruiter
Miss Joanne Harvey, Senior Recruiter

Salary Minimum: $50,000

Functions: Generalist (All), Middle Mgmt., Healthcare

Industries: Generalist (All), Healthcare

Executive's Silent Partner Ltd

400 Reservoir Ave
Calart Tower
Providence, RI 02907-3565
(401) 461-5170
Fax: (401) 461-2370
Email: inquiry@espglobal.net
Web: www.espglobal.net

Summary: Known as a premier executive recruiter exclusively for the jewelry manufacturing and jewelry import/export industry. Regarded as confidant for this close-knit, yet large industry. All searches performed confidentially by owner/principal.

Key Contact - Specialty:
Mr. Edward A. Lemire, CPC, President & Executive Recruiter

Salary Minimum: $40,000

Functions: Management, Mfg., Purchasing, Materials Plng., Sales & Mktg., CFOs, M&A

Industries: Generalist (All)

Executive-jobs.com

4460 Redwood Hwy Ste 16E
San Rafael, CA 94903-1953
(415) 492-1117
Email: larry@executive-jobs.com
Web: www.executive-jobs.com

Summary: We recruit and place experienced sales & marketing oriented high-technology professionals. These professionals have titles such

as president, CEO, COO, VP, director, in-house counsel, account executive and manager.

Key Contact - Specialty:
Mr. Larry Powers

Salary Minimum: $75,000

Functions: Senior Mgmt., Middle Mgmt., Sales & Mktg., Mktg. Mgmt.

Industries: Computer Equip., Electronic, Elec. Components, Semiconductors, Equip Svcs., E-commerce, IT Implementation, PSA/ASP, Communications, Telecoms, Telephony, Software

Executivefit NA

PO Box 8
202 Strathmore Dr
Syracuse, NY 13207-0008
(315) 425-9025
Fax: (315) 424-9473
Email: tim@executivefit.com
Web: www.executivefit.com

Summary: We place emphasis on skilled professionals within Fortune 500 firms. Functional disciplines include first and second-level managers, directors and VP levels. Client firm profiles of candidates typically require an advanced degree and a minimum of eight years experience.

Key Contact - Specialty:
Mr. Tim Dermady, Principal & Managing Partner - *Computers (Software), Manufacturing, Telecommunications*

Salary Minimum: $75,000

Functions: Generalist (All), Mktg. Mgmt., Sales Mgmt., Systems Dev., DB Admin.

Industries: Generalist (All), Soap, Perf., Cosmtcs., Drugs Mfg., Computer Equip., Consumer Elect., Telecoms, Aerospace, Software

Executives by Sterling Inc

3545 S Tamarac Dr Ste 380
Denver, CO 80237-1432
(303) 934-7343
Email: art@executivesbysterling.com
Web: www.executivesbysterling.com

Summary: We will direct your management-level search and enhance your company's goals with our hospitality industry consulting expertise. We make sound placements by matching individual capabilities and goals with the specific needs of our clients' firms.

Key Contact - Specialty:
Mr. Art Mangual, Principal - *Hospitality*
Mr. Tom Mulholland, Principal - *Hospitality*

Salary Minimum: $50,000

Functions: Generalist (All), Management, Senior Mgmt., Middle Mgmt., Sales & Mktg., Sales Mgmt., Sales Reps., Hospitality, Hotel Mgmt., Chefs

Industries: Generalist (All), Services, Hospitality, Hotels, Resorts, Clubs

EXEK Recruiters Ltd

35 Flatt Rd
Rochester, NY 14623-2511
(585) 292-0550
Fax: (585) 292-5645
Email: exek@exek-recruiters.com
Web: www.exek-recruiters.com

Summary: We specialize in the placement of engineers, scientists, managers and technical personnel. Industries served: electro-optics, telecom, automation/capital equipment, electronics, automotive and aluminum. Our

services range from permanent, contracting and employer of record capabilities through contingency, container and retainer arrangements.

Key Contact - Specialty:
Mr. Larry Ploscowe, Vice President - *Computers (Software), Hardware*

Salary Minimum: $40,000

Functions: Board Members, Middle Mgmt., Mfg., Automation, Materials, Engineering

Industries: Metal Products, Machine, Appliance, Motor Vehicles, Computer Equip., Consumer Elect., Test, Measure Equip., Misc. Mfg., Electronic, Elec. Components, Digital, Fiber Optic, Network Infrastructure, Mfg. SW, Networking, Comm. SW

Exesolution Inc

100 W 57th St
New York, NY 10019-3302
(212) 957-1881
Fax: (212) 957-0515
Email: info@execsolution.com
Web: www.execsolution.com

Summary: Our firm specializes in executive search (executive, operational, financial, & strategic leadership; rainmakers and commodity traders) and wealth creation through facilitation of deal flow and commodity trading proposals (including currency transactions) through introductions to and from investors and brokers, sellers, and buyers.

Key Contact - Specialty:
Ms. Margaret G. Orem, Chief Executive Officer

Salary Minimum: $100,000

Functions: Senior Mgmt.

Industries: Generalist (All)

ExpatRepat Services Inc

3402 Kensington Dr
Abilene, TX 79605-6625
(325) 695-7844
Email: ers@expat-repat.com
Web: www.expat-repat.com

Summary: We serve multinational businesses: screening candidates for expatriation; facilitating host country cultural adjustment; coaching expatriates through in-country crises; and providing resources for the 'coming home' process of repatriation. Coaching business leaders to more effective leadership. Search and placement services to qualified candidates for leadership in profitable companies.

Key Contact - Specialty:
Dr. Robert E. Scott, President - *Banking, Compensation, Human resources, International*

Salary Minimum: $100,000

Functions: Int'l.

Industries: Generalist (All)

Expert Company

PO Box 641
202 Crooked Creek Road
Hampton, SC 29924-0641
(912) 656-4139
(800) 864-3710
Fax: (843) 863-7922
Email: smithld@expertco.com
Web: www.expertco.com

Summary: We specialize in the placement of IS professionals primarily in health care and health insurance environments. We are particularly involved in programmers and systems analysts in LAN platforms.

Key Contact - Specialty:
Mr. Larry Smith, Managing Partner - *Medical, Strategic planning, Systems (Integration), Technical, Technical (Management)*

Salary Minimum: $50,000

Functions: Systems Dev.

Industries: Software, Healthcare

Express Professional Staffing - RWJ & Associates

8516 NW Expressway St
Oklahoma City, OK 73162-6010
(888) 446-2856
(405) 840-5000
Fax: (405) 720-9390
Email: onlineinfo@expresspersonnel.com
Web: www.expressprofessional.com

Summary: We are one of the world's largest privately owned, full-service staffing firms. Employing more than 224,000 people annually, our client base extends through three countries and is represented by three divisions including temp staffing/evaluation and direct hire; contract and executive recruiting and placement; and customized workplace services.

Key Contact - Specialty:
Mr. Robert A. Funk, Founder

Functions: Generalist (All), Management, Mfg., Materials, Sales & Mktg., IT

Industries: Generalist (All), Manufacturing, Wholesale, Services, Media, Software

Branches:
4925 University Dr NW Ste 166
Huntsville, AL 35816-1880
(866) 721-5627
Fax: (256) 830-5102
Email:
mklambert@huntsvilleal.expresspersonnel.com
Key Contact - Specialty:
Ms. Reba Sulava

129 Church St Ste 403
New Haven, CT 06510-2052
(203) 848-6365
Fax: (203) 848-6369
Email:
chris.malloy@e1655.expresspersonnel.com
Key Contact - Specialty:
Mr. Chris Malloy

6807 W Commercial Blvd
Lauderhill, FL 33319-2116
(954) 721-2429
Fax: (954) 721-2542
Email: jean.goetz@expresspersonnel.com
Key Contact - Specialty:
Ms. Jean Goetz

712 W Taylor St
Griffin, GA 30223-2720
(877) 588-8218
Fax: (770) 227-1139
Email: geoff.voight@expresspersonnel.com
Key Contact - Specialty:
Mr. Geoff Voight

9539 Highway 92 Ste 140
Woodstock, GA 30188-3823
(770) 591-5985
Fax: (770) 928-8386
Email: bob.robinson@expresspersonnel.com
Key Contact - Specialty:
Mr. Robert Robinson

1714 G St
Lewiston, ID 83501-2021
(208) 743-6507
(208) 883-4855
Fax: (208) 743-6508
Email: tedi.roach@expresspersonnel.com
Key Contact - Specialty:
Mr. Tedi Roach, CTS, CPC

608 Eastgate St
Carbondale, IL 62901-3304
(618) 549-4404
Fax: (618) 549-8471
Email: sue.endres@expresspersonnel.com
Key Contact - Specialty:
Ms. Sue Endres

3000 Professional Dr
Springfield, IL 62703-5931
(217) 528-3000
Fax: (217) 528-3400
Email: charlie.blackburn@expresspersonnel.com
Key Contact - Specialty:
Mr. Charlie Blackburn

977 Lakeview Pkwy Ste 190
Vernon Hills, IL 60061-1429
(847) 816-8422
Email: marshall.claassen@expresspersonnel.com
Key Contact - Specialty:
Mr. Marshall Claassen

2229 S 3rd St
Terre Haute, IN 47802-3046
(812) 232-9090
Fax: (812) 232-9098
Email: andrea.mcpherson@expresspersonnel.com
Key Contact - Specialty:
Ms. Andrea McPherson

15707 Hall Rd
Macomb, MI 48044-3887
(810) 566-8400
Fax: (810) 566-7433
Email: joann.wiegand@expresspersonnel.com
Key Contact - Specialty:
Ms. JoAnn Wiegand

1707 W Big Beaver Rd Ste 100
Troy, MI 48084-3510
(248) 643-8900
Fax: (248) 205-7267
Email: troy@rwj.com
Key Contact - Specialty:
Mr. John Bower

7101 France Ave S
Edina, MN 55435-4221
(952) 915-2003
Fax: (952) 920-9527
Email: bob.sannerud@rwj.com
Key Contact - Specialty:
Mr. Robert Sannerud

812 S Elm Ave
Owatonna, MN 55060-4061
(507) 451-9396
Fax: (507) 455-0271
Email: rroberts@rwj.com
Key Contact - Specialty:
Ms. Betsy Lindgren

910 Main St Ste 101
Red Wing, MN 55066-2261
(651) 388-6331
Fax: (651) 388-1195
Email: jobs.redwingmn@expresspersonnel.com
Key Contact - Specialty:
Ms. Sharon McCord, Recruiter

2518 N Broadway
Rochester, MN 55906-3968
(507) 285-9270
Fax: (507) 529-9419

Email: stasler@rwj.com
Key Contact - Specialty:
Ms. Sheryl Tasler

709 Robert E Lee Dr
Tupelo, MS 38801-5537
(662) 842-5500
Fax: (662) 842-5971
Email: jean.parker@expresspersonnel.com
Key Contact - Specialty:
Ms. Jean Parker

601 Business Loop 70 W Ste 128
Columbia, MO 65203-2579
(573) 443-1800
Fax: (573) 499-4473
Email: melinda.finnegan@expresspersonnel.com
Key Contact - Specialty:
Ms. Melinda Finnegan

2045 S Waverly Ave
Springfield, MO 65804-2414
(417) 887-5900
Fax: (417) 882-7001
Email: nikki.sells@expresspersonnel.com
Key Contact - Specialty:
Ms. Nikki Sells

3316 Battleground Ave Ste G
Greensboro, NC 27410-2458
(336) 282-7901
Fax: (336) 282-7903
Email: cathy.bechtel@expresspersonnel.com
Key Contact - Specialty:
Ms. Cathy Bechtel

4766 Cornell Rd
Cincinnati, OH 45241-2414
(513) 489-7787
Fax: (513) 489-3069
Email: cdharris@cintioh.expresspersonnel.com
Key Contact - Specialty:
Mr. Chuck Harris, Owner

2741 Miamisburg Centerville Rd Ste 217
Dayton, OH 45459-3729
(937) 438-4932
Fax: (937) 435-8931
Key Contact - Specialty:
Mr Richard Kortjohn

6300 NW Expressway St
Oklahoma City, OK 73132-5128
(405) 720-4616
Email: oklahomacity@rwj.com
Key Contact - Specialty:
Ms. Sheila Lawrence

10816 E 71st St
Tulsa, OK 74133-2500
(918) 499-5900
Fax: (918) 499-2293
Email: ray.r@expresspersonnel.com
Key Contact - Specialty:
Mr. Ray Roberson

901 NW Carlon Ave Ste 3
Bend, OR 97701-2636
(541) 330-1585
Fax: (541) 330-5037
Email: cworrell-druliner@rwj.com
Key Contact - Specialty:
Ms. Connie Worrell-Druliner
Ms. Angela Gatewood, Professional Recruiter

10011 SE Division St Ste 101
Portland, OR 97266-1352
(503) 254-1200
Fax: (503) 254-1567
Email: richard.yoerk@expresspersonnel.com
Key Contact - Specialty:
Mr. Richard Yoerk

Email your resume to a targeted list of recruiters now at www.ExecutiveAgent.com/DER07

7401 SW Washo Ct Ste 200
Tualatin, OR 97062-8343
(503) 612-1414
Fax: (503) 612-1410
Email: johns@express-rwj.com
Key Contact - Specialty:
Mr. John Sullivan

1900 E Oltorf St Ste 106
Austin, TX 78741-4029
(512) 416-6666
Fax: (512) 416-8440
Email: jobs.saustintx@expresspersonnel.com
Key Contact - Specialty:
Mr. Bob Eskridge
Mr. Jon Hall

1405 W Adams Ave
Temple, TX 76504-2449
(254) 771-5595
Fax: (254) 773-5611
Email:
smgromacki@templetx.expresspersonnel.com
Key Contact - Specialty:
Mr. George Gromacki

1126 S Gold St Ste 102
Centralia, WA 98531-3768
(360) 330-9050
Fax: (360) 330-9060
Email: david.gibson@expresspersonnel.com
Key Contact - Specialty:
Mr. David Gibson

4015 Rucker Ave Ste B
Everett, WA 98201-4835
(425) 339-8400
Fax: (425) 252-9817
Email: kelly.hatfield@expresspersonnel.com
Key Contact - Specialty:
Ms. Elizabeth Shinn

19125 33rd Ave W Ste D
Lynnwood, WA 98036-4735
(425) 775-4903
Fax: (425) 778-3090
Email: donna.knutsen@expresspersonnel.com
Key Contact - Specialty:
Ms. Donna Knutsen

525 E College Way Ste F
Mount Vernon, WA 98273-5571
(360) 336-1980
Fax: (360) 336-1540
Email: tara.panek-bringle@expresspersonnel.com
Key Contact - Specialty:
Ms. Tara Panek-Bringle

4301 S Pine St Ste 160
Tacoma, WA 98409-7221
(253) 475-6855
Fax: (253) 472-0721
Email: jennifer.patrick@expresspersonnel.com
Key Contact - Specialty:
Ms. Jennifer Patrick

208-1175 Johnson St
The Centre
Coquitlam, BC V3B 7K1
Canada
(604) 944-8530
Fax: (604) 944-0897
Email: brad.braekevelt@expressprofessional.com
Key Contact - Specialty:
Mr. Brad Braekevelt

704-50 Queen St N
Commerce House
Kitchener, ON N2H 6P4
Canada
(519) 578-9030
Fax: (519) 578-1121
Email: carol.marttini@expressprofessional.com

Key Contact - Specialty:
Ms. Carol Marttini

100-150 Dufferin Ave
Richmond Court
London, ON N6A 5N6
Canada
(519) 672-2795
Fax: (519) 672-8870
Email: tjohns@rwj.com
Key Contact - Specialty:
Mr. Mike Johnson

eXsource Inc

2500 Nash St N Ste E
Wilson, NC 27896-1394
(252) 234-6101
Email: jobs@exsource-inc.com
Web: www.exsource-inc.com
Summary: Our firm provides nationwide search
services and contract placement services to
employers and provides nationwide job
opportunities to qualified professionals in many
industries via our network of over 300 affiliated
firms.
Key Contact - Specialty:
Mr. Samuel F. Domby, CPC, Principal -
*Accounting, Automotive, Banking, Call centers,
CFOs*

Salary Minimum: $50,000

Functions: Generalist (All), Management, Middle
Mgmt., Plant Mgmt., Packaging, Healthcare,
Nurses, Sales & Mktg., Sales Mgmt.

Industries: Generalist (All), Oil & Gas,
Manufacturing, Transportation, Finance,
Services, Hospitality, Communications,
Telecoms, Call Centers, Wireless, Defense,
Software, ERP SW, Networking, Comm. SW,
Healthcare, Hospitals, Long-term/Home Care,
Physical Therapy, Occupational Therapy,
Women's, Non-Classifiable

FLAG

7304 Denly Ct
Wilmington, NC 28411-9694
(910) 681-5002
Email: flag@flagsearch.com
Web: www.flagsearch.com
Summary: We specialize exclusively in the
lubricant, coolant, grease and fuel product
industries and serve all sized firms. Our specialty
is in any base stocks, additives and finished
products. We recruit for the industrial, retail,
commercial and automotive markets.

Key Contact - Specialty:
Mr. Tom Warren, Owner

Salary Minimum: $40,000

Functions: Generalist (All)

Industries: Generalist (All), Paints, Petro.
Products

F-O-R-T-U-N-E Personnel Consultants (FPC)

1140 Avenue of the Americas Fl 5
New York, NY 10036-5803
(212) 302-1141
(800) 886-7839
Fax: (212) 302-2422
Email: info@fpcnational.com
Web: www.fpcnational.com
Summary: An executive search organization
comprised of franchised offices serving more than
20 industries. Involved in all phases of recruitment
and permanent placement; offering services on
either a contingency or retainer basis. Inter-office

relationships foster greater opportunity for both
clients and candidates.
Key Contact - Specialty:
Mr. Rudy Schott, Founder & Chief Executive
Officer
Mr. Ron Herzog, President

Salary Minimum: $50,000

Functions: Senior Mgmt., Middle Mgmt., Plant
Mgmt., Quality, Materials, Purchasing,
Healthcare, Systems Analysis, Engineering,
Legal

Industries: Manufacturing, Chemicals, Drugs
Mfg., Medical Devices, Pharm Svcs., Legal, HR
Services, Law Enforcement, Engineering Svcs.,
Supply Chain Mgmt., Biotech/Life Sciences,
Healthcare

Branches:
208 Roper St
Mobile, AL 36604-2920
(251) 694-0174
Email: tom@fpcsearch.com
Key Contact - Specialty:
Mr. Tom Templeton, President

1060 W King St Ste E1
Cocoa, FL 32922-8616
(321) 639-0794
Email: successfulcareers@fpcmelbourne.com
Key Contact - Specialty:
Mr. Vinnie Morris, President
Allanier Morris, Vice President & Senior
Consultant

PO Box 112797
9220 Bonita Beach Rd Ste 106
Naples, FL 34108-0147
(239) 495-3100
Email: recruiter@fpcnaples.com
Key Contact - Specialty:
Mr. Ben Gidwani, President & Chief Executive
Officer

2175 S Tamiami Trl
Osprey, FL 34229-9696
(941) 966-6441
Fax: (941) 966-1912
Email: fpcvenice@packet.net
Key Contact - Specialty:
Mr. Jim Shirley, President

1724 E Grand Ave
Lindenhurst, IL 60046-7820
(847) 265-3412
Fax: (847) 265-3840
Email: john@fpclakevilla.com
Key Contact - Specialty:
Mr. John Foote, President - *Six sigma*
Ms. Gail Foote, Office Administrator

600 Mariners Plaza Dr Ste 609
Mandeville, LA 70448-6824
(866) 320-9804
Fax: (985) 674-2256
Email: bobb_fpc@bellsouth.net
Key Contact - Specialty:
Mr. Bob Beatty, Owner - *Engineering,
Information Systems, Pharmaceutical, Quality,
Research & development*
Mr. Paul Boss, Executive Recruiter - *Pharmacists*

42 Idlewild St
Bel Air, MD 21014-4107
(410) 893-0450
Fax: (410) 893-1121
Email: fcbelair@comcast.net
Key Contact - Specialty:
Mr. Gary Hicks, President
Ms. Joanne Hicks, Vice President

100 Corporate Pl Ste 200
Peabody, MA 01960-3809
(978) 535-9920
Email: awildes@fpcnbt.com
Key Contact - Specialty:
Aline Wildes, President

100 Corporate Pl Ste 200
Peabody, MA 01960-3809
(978) 535-9920
Fax: (978) 535-4482
Email: david@fpclex.com
Key Contact - Specialty:
Mr. David Mitchell, Owner

100 Corporate Pl Ste 200
Peabody, MA 01960-3809
(978) 535-9920
Email: jgenovese@fpcboston.com
Key Contact - Specialty:
Mr. Joseph Genovese, Owner

4248 Kalamazoo Ave SE Ste B
Grand Rapids, MI 49508-3645
(616) 281-2861
Fax: (616) 281-2856
Email: success@fpcgrandrapids.com
Key Contact - Specialty:
Mr. Norbert Dishinger, President
Mr. Matt Wenzel, Chief of Research -
   Automotive, Capital goods, Consumer,
   Consumer (Products), Engineering

3407 Berrywood Dr Ste 202
Columbia, MO 65201-6500
(573) 442-2450
Fax: (573) 442-6304
Email: fpccareers@aol.com
Key Contact - Specialty:
Mr. Steve Winner, President

300 Craig Rd Fl 2
Manalapan, NJ 07726-8742
(732) 866-8606
Key Contact - Specialty:
Ms. Sheryl Horowitz, Director - *Clinical,*
   Research

PO Box 1742
Pinehurst, NC 28370-1742
(910) 295-5111
Fax: (910) 295-4992
Email: resume@fpcpinehurst.com
Key Contact - Specialty:
Ms. Beverly Godleski, Owner
Mr. Charlie Godleski, Owner

29 N Market St Ste C
Selinsgrove, PA 17870-1924
(570) 374-6744
Email: fpchar@sunlink.net
Key Contact - Specialty:
Mr. David A. Lawer, President

149 Riverwalk Blvd Ste 15
Ridgeland, SC 29936-8191
(843) 645-6997
Email: sandi@fpcht.com
Key Contact - Specialty:
Ms. Sandra Dietrich

1140 36th St Ste 204
Ogden, UT 84403-2049
(801) 866-0770
Email: ron@enginejobs.com
Key Contact - Specialty:
Mr. Ron Hiniker, President

FPC of Decatur

1414 5th Ave SE Ste A
Decatur, AL 35601-4245
(256) 341-0400
Fax: (256) 341-0444

Email: fpcdecatur@earthlink.net
Web: www.fpxrecruiting.com

Summary: We have years of experience as HR
professionals, heavily focused on all aspects of
hiring and career development. We are especially
proud of our reputation for trust and integrity. We
specialize in but are not limited to the chemical
and general manufacturing industries.

Key Contact - Specialty:
Mr. David L. Harris, President - *Environmental,*
   Finance, Sales
Mr. Wade Harris, Vice President - *Logistics,*
   Purchasing
Ms. Marilyn Harris, Administrator
Ms. Leigh Anne Bolan, Administrative Assistant
Ms. Lisa Cherry, Professional Recruiter
Mr. Ward Harris, Professional Recruiter

Salary Minimum: $50,000

Functions: Generalist (All), Mfg., Plant Mgmt.

Industries: Chemicals, Plastics, Rubber, Paints,
   Petro. Products, Electronic, Elec. Components,
   Accounting, HR Services, Engineering Svcs.,
   Logistics Svcs., Supply Chain Mgmt

FPC of Huntsville

3311 Bob Wallace Ave SW Ste 204
Huntsville, AL 35805-4064
(256) 534-7282
Fax: (256) 534-7334
Email: careers@fpchuntsville.com
Web: www.fpchuntsville.com

Summary: Nationwide search and placement of
executives, managers and professionals within the
automotive and electronics industries.

Key Contact - Specialty:
Mr. Bob Langford, President - *Electronics, Sales*
Ms. Judy Langford, Office Manager
Mr. Matt Langford, CPA, Vice President -
   Accounting, Electronics, Engineering,
   Operations, Sales
Mr. Bob Henshaw, Executive Recruiter -
   Automotive, Human resources, Operations
Mr. Hugh Hanson, Executive Recruiter -
   Automotive, Metals, Plastics, Quality
Mr. Andrew Henshaw, Executive Recruiter -
   Automotive, Design, Engineering, Mechanical
Ms. Lynn Lamb, Executive Recruiter - *Materials,*
   Purchasing, Supply Chain
Ms. Anneta Simmons, Executive Recruiter -
   Automotive, Design, Electronics, Engineering

Salary Minimum: $40,000

Functions: Generalist (All), Management, Mfg.,
   Materials, Sales & Mktg., HR Mgmt., Finance,
   Engineering

Industries: Generalist (All), Medical Devices,
   Plastics, Rubber, Metal Products, Motor
   Vehicles, Computer Equip., Consumer Elect.,
   Test, Measure Equip., Electronic, Elec.
   Components, Robotics, Semiconductors,
   Accounting, Communications, Healthcare

FPC of East Bay

(also known as F-O-R-T-U-N-E Personnel
Consultants)
3201 Danville Blvd Ste 155
Alamo, CA 94507-1938
(925) 837-6060
(800) 291-9229
Fax: (925) 837-2710
Email: mike@fpcbay.net
Web: www.fpcbay.net

Summary: We work nationwide with experienced
professionals that are pre-screened in the
pharmaceutical, biotechnology and medical
devices industries. We specialize in scientific,
regulatory affairs, quality- QA & QC, clinical,

validation, engineering, Compliance and some
marketing. We place candidates with a minimum
of two years experience to director/VP/C-level
(CSO, COO, etc.)

Key Contact - Specialty:
Mr. Michael Mullery, President - *Pharmaceutical*

Salary Minimum: $55,000

Functions: Management, Senior Mgmt., Middle
   Mgmt., Product Dev., Plant Mgmt., Quality,
   R&D, Engineering, Eng. Design, Process

Industries: Drugs Mfg., Medical Devices, Pharm
   Svcs., Biotech/Life Sciences

FPC of Denver Inc

7800 S Elati St Ste 319
Littleton, CO 80120-4456
(303) 795-9210
Fax: (303) 795-9215
Email: mail@fpcdenver.com
Web: www.fpcdenver.com

Summary: We support the staffing needs of the
world's industry leaders. A member of one of the
oldest and most reputable executive search
organizations, we provide a personalized service
that is enhanced by the extensive network realized
through national affiliation.

Key Contact - Specialty:
Mr. Jan Dorfman, PE, President - *Biomedical,*
   Clinical, Engineering, Medical, Quality

Salary Minimum: $50,000

Functions: Senior Mgmt., Middle Mgmt., Mfg.,
   Product Dev., Automation, Quality, Materials,
   Sales & Mktg., R&D, Engineering

Industries: Manufacturing, Drugs Mfg., Medical
   Devices, Transportation, Communications,
   Aerospace, Biotech/Life Sciences

FPC of Greenwood Village

6901 S Pierce St Ste 100G
Littleton, CO 80128-7204
(303) 773-0047
Fax: (303) 773-0048
Email: resume@fpcgwv.com
Web: www.fpcgwv.com

Summary: Our objective is to excel in the
placement industry and to deliver results. We will
consult with clients and individuals for
accomplishments that are mutually beneficial. We
are focused on the consumer products industry
including food, beverage, pharmaceutical and
related industries and work all manufacturing
disciplines.

Key Contact - Specialty:
Ms. Vicki Pike, President

Salary Minimum: $50,000

Functions: Mfg., Product Dev., Production, Plant
   Mgmt., Quality, Purchasing, Materials Plng.,
   Distribution, R&D, Engineering

Industries: Food, Bev., Tobacco, Soap, Perf.,
   Cosmtcs., Drugs Mfg., Misc. Mfg., Packaging

FPC of Sarasota

4317 Rum Cay Pl
Sarasota, FL 34233-3834
(941) 378-5262
Email: recruit@fpcsarasota.com
Web: www.fpcsarasota.com

Summary: In manufacturing, we place
professionals at all levels in operations/production
management, materials, supply chain, logistics,
engineering, quality, and accounting/ finance. Our
recruiters are specialists focusing in these areas.
We have access to a national network of recruiters.

Email your resume to a targeted list of recruiters now at www.ExecutiveAgent.com/DER07

Key Contact - Specialty:
Mr. Arthur R. Grindlinger, President - *Logistics, Manufacturing (Management), Materials, Purchasing*
Mr. Brad Stephens, Director, Engineering Placement - *Engineering, Manufacturing, Quality*

Salary Minimum: $50,000

Functions: Senior Mgmt., Middle Mgmt., Production, Plant Mgmt., Quality, Materials, Purchasing, Materials Plng., Finance, Engineering

Industries: Manufacturing

FPC of Atlanta

3071 Peachtree Industrial Blvd Ste 210
Duluth, GA 30097-8607
(770) 246-9757
Fax: (770) 246-0526
Email: search@fpccareers.com
Web: www.fpccareers.com

Summary: Executive recruitment for manufacturing, engineering, quality, validation, regulatory affairs, R&D, product development, sensory, pharmaceuticals, medical device, food, personal care, cosmetics, home care, chemicals, plastics and electronics.

Key Contact - Specialty:
Mr. James M. Deavours, President
Mr. Greg Wood, Director, Executive Search - *Cosmetics, Engineering, Food & beverage, Manufacturing (Management)*
Mr. Ira Mann, Manager, Executive Search - *Biopharmaceutical, Medical (Devices), Pharmaceutical, Quality, Regulatory*

Salary Minimum: $60,000

Functions: Middle Mgmt., Mfg., Product Dev., Production, Automation, Plant Mgmt., Quality, Packaging, R&D, Engineering

Industries: Manufacturing, Food, Bev., Tobacco, Chemicals, Soap, Perf., Cosmtcs., Drugs Mfg., Medical Devices, Plastics, Rubber, Consumer Elect., Biotech/Life Sciences

FPC of Savannah

PO Box 8846
Savannah, GA 31412-8846
(912) 233-4556
Email: execsearch@fpcsav.com

Summary: We place professionals in manufacturing industries focusing on the following disciplines: purchasing, materials management, logistics, supply chain and operations.

Key Contact - Specialty:
Mr. Clark W. Smith, President & Owner - *Distribution, Executives, Logistics, Supply Chain, Transportation*
Mr. Shane Dixon, Vice President - *Capital goods, Logistics, Manufacturing (Management), Purchasing, Supply Chain*
Mr. Mort Shor, Vice President - *Capital goods, Management consulting, Manufacturing (Management), Senior management, Six Sigma*
Mr. Doug Schmidt, Vice President - *Aerospace, Consumer (Hard Goods), Materials, Procurement, Supply Chain*

Salary Minimum: $60,000

Functions: Generalist (All), Senior Mgmt., Production, Plant Mgmt., Quality, Materials, Purchasing, Int'l.

Industries: Generalist (All), Manufacturing, Textiles, Apparel, Paper, Metal Products, Machine, Appliance, Motor Vehicles, Computer

Equip., Consumer Elect., Electronic, Elec. Components

FPC of Boise

415 E Parkcenter Blvd Ste 106
Boise, ID 83706-6505
(208) 343-5190
(800) 783-5190
Fax: (208) 343-6067
Email: gen@fpcboise.com
Web: www.fpcnational.com/boise

Summary: We are composed of former senior executives from Fortune 500 companies. We specialize in manufacturing management, engineering, human resources, accounting, logistics and other top to middle management roles.

Key Contact - Specialty:
Ms. Sandra K. Bishop, SPHR, President - *Accounting, CEOs, CFOs, Human resources, Management*
Mr. Garn Christensen, Vice President - *Safety, Senior management, Six sigma, Technical, Technical (Management)*
Mr. Russ Thompson, Director, Pulp & Paper - *Engineering, Forest industry/products, Human resources, Maintenance, Management*
Ms. Janet Littley, Research Assistant - *Engineering, Maintenance, Manufacturing (Management), Paper, Technical (Management)*
Ms. Pamela Day, Director, Transportation and Logistics - *Logistics, Procurement, Purchasing, Supply Chain, Transportation*
Ms. Michelle Rauer, Director, Manufacturing
Ms. Debbie Nichols, Research Assistant - *Distribution, Logistics, Procurement, Purchasing, Supply Chain*

Salary Minimum: $65,000

Functions: Generalist (All), Management, Mfg., Plant Mgmt., Quality, Purchasing, Distribution, HR Mgmt., Finance, Engineering

Industries: Manufacturing, Lumber, Furniture, Paper, Misc. Mfg., Finance, Accounting, HR Services, Logistics Svcs., Supply Chain Mgmt., Packaging

FPC of Arlington Heights

825 E Golf Rd Ste 1146
Arlington Heights, IL 60005-5200
(847) 228-7205
Fax: (847) 228-7206
Email: marshall@fpcarlington.com
Web: www.fpcarlington.com

Summary: We are specialists in the automotive industry, focusing on engineering, purchasing and supply chain management professionals.

Key Contact - Specialty:
Mr. Marshall Antonio, President - *Automotive, Manufacturing, Materials, Purchasing, Quality*
Ms. Melanie Hildebrandt, Vice President & Recruiter
Mr. Brandon Burton, Vice President & Recruiter
Ms. Lisa Mysliwiec, Vice President & Office Manager

Salary Minimum: $40,000

Functions: Generalist (All), Board Members, Senior Mgmt., Plant Mgmt., Quality, Purchasing, Engineering

Industries: Generalist (All), Motor Vehicles, Advertising

FPC of Hinsdale

115 E 1st St Ste 2E
Hinsdale, IL 60521-4258
(630) 920-1952
Fax: (630) 920-0793

Email: fpc@fpc-hinsdale.com
Web: www.fpc-hinsdale.com

Summary: Principal has extensive experience as financial professional with Fortune 50 manufacturers. Providing finance/accounting, HR and supply chain management professionals up through the executive-level for manufacturing and distribution companies.

Key Contact - Specialty:
Mr. Robert J. Kalember, Jr., President
Mr. David Franzone, Director, HR, Accounting & Finance
Mr. James Rybowiak, Director, Supply Chain Management - *Manufacturing, Materials, Purchasing*

Salary Minimum: $50,000

Functions: Production, Materials, Purchasing, Distribution, HR Mgmt., Benefits, Training, Finance, CFOs, Budgeting

Industries: Generalist (All), Manufacturing, Transportation, Wholesale, Media, Publishing, Aerospace, Packaging

FPC of Mount Vernon

201 Main St Ste D
Mount Vernon, IN 47620-1839
(812) 838-1607
Fax: (812) 838-1918
Email: fortmtv@sbcglobal.net

Summary: We are part of a national executive search franchise comprised of independently owned and operated offices. We are involved in all phases of recruitment and permanent placement offering services on either a contingency or retainer basis. Our primary focus is in accounting/finance and supply chain.

Key Contact - Specialty:
Mr. Al Gmutza, President

Salary Minimum: $40,000

Functions: Materials, Purchasing, Materials Plng., Distribution, Finance, CFOs, Budgeting, Cash Mgmt., M&A

Industries: Generalist (All), Energy, Utilities, Finance, Banking, Accounting

FPC of SW Indiana

201 Main St Ste A
Mount Vernon, IN 47620-1839
(812) 838-6636
Fax: (812) 838-6648
Email: fpc@evansville.net

Summary: The owner has many years of experience in the engineering, manufacturing and materials management areas in the chemical and plastics industries with four Fortune 50 companies.

Key Contact - Specialty:
Mr. Gary Fox, Owner
Ms. Keely Winiger, Recruiter - *Construction*

Salary Minimum: $55,000

Functions: Generalist (All)

Industries: Paper, Chemicals, Soap, Perf., Cosmtcs., Drugs Mfg., Plastics, Rubber, Paints, Petro. Products, Metal Products, Packaging

FPC of South Bend

52303 Emmons Rd Ste 27
Georgetown Center
South Bend, IN 46637-4288
(574) 273-3188
Fax: (574) 273-3887
Email: mike@fpcsouthbend.com
Web: www.fpcsouthbend.com

Summary: We are part of a network of recruitment offices specializing in executive and middle management personnel. Our office focuses solely in the placement of engineering, quality and supply chain professionals in the automotive and pharmaceutical industries. We conduct retained, container and contingency search assignments.

Key Contact - Specialty:
Mr. Michael Petras, III, President - *Engineering, Manufacturing, Manufacturing (Management), Quality, Sales*
Mr. Mark A. Petras, Vice President - *Engineering, Materials, Purchasing, Quality*
Mr. Matthew S. Petras, Executive Recruiter - *Engineering, Quality, Staffing, Temporary*
Mr. Alex Furioso, Executive Recruiter

Functions: Board Members, Senior Mgmt., Middle Mgmt., Quality, Purchasing

Industries: Food, Bev., Tobacco, Drugs Mfg., Motor Vehicles, Aerospace, Biotech/Life Sciences

FPC of Cedar Rapids

208 Collins Rd NE Ste 204
Cedar Rapids, IA 52402-3166
(319) 373-1163
Fax: (319) 373-1696
Email: careers@fpccr.com
Web: www.fpcnational.com/cedarrapids

Summary: We specialize in placement of professionals and executives in the areas of: sales, marketing, finance, HR, engineering and operations in the electronics industries, including: audio, wireless, aerospace/avionics, automotive electronics, electronic components, test & measurement and power supplies.

Key Contact - Specialty:
Mr. John Buckeridge, President - *ATE, Electronics, Finance, Marketing, Sales*
Ms. Elizabeth Buckeridge, President - *Electrical, Electronics, Embedded microprocessor, Engineering, Operations*
Ms. Christina Djerf, Executive, Business Development - *Electronics, Marketing, Sales*
Ms. Julia Byerly, Administrator

Salary Minimum: $50,000

Functions: Mfg., Quality, Materials, Sales & Mktg., Finance, Engineering

Industries: Consumer Elect., Test, Measure Equip., Electronic, Elec. Components, Semiconductors, Telecoms, Digital, Wireless, Fiber Optic, RF/Microwave, Aerospace

FPC of Bangor

PO BOX 612
Farmington, ME 04938-0612
(207) 778-2456
Fax: (207) 778-2676
Email: info@fpcbangor.com
Web: www.fpcbangor.com

Summary: We are a female owned executive recruiting firm specializing in management recruiting for the pulp & paper, chemical, packaging, and food and beverage industries. Our industry experience and affiliation makes us unique. We can advise on resume preparation, available career opportunities, interview strategies and career planning.

Key Contact - Specialty:
Ms. Gilly Hitchcock, Owner - *Sales*
Ms. Leisa Clark, Recruiting Specialist - *Converting*
Mr. Mike Luciano, Recruiter - *Food & beverage, Human resources, Manufacturing (Management), Paper, Quality*

Functions: Generalist (All)

Industries: Construction, Paper, Chemicals

FPC of Severna Park

PO Box 1538
Severna Park, MD 21146-8538
(410) 544-5151
Email: jobs@fpcspark.com
Web: www.fpcspark.com

Summary: Our firm has successfully assisted our client companies in meeting their recruiting needs with capable, qualified candidates. Our consultants place professionals nationwide on a contingency or retained search basis. Our recruiters specialize in: engineering, process control, HR, operations management, IS, materials management/purchasing for the pulp and paper industry only.

Key Contact - Specialty:
Mr. Ray Williams, Owner & President
Ms. Karen Williams, Owner & Vice President

Salary Minimum: $60,000

Functions: Generalist (All)

Industries: Paper

FPC of Topsfield

458 Boston St Ste 2P
Topsfield, MA 01983-1261
(978) 887-2032
Fax: (978) 887-2336
Email: plastics@topsfpc.com
Web: www.topsfpc.com

Summary: Recruiting for general management, engineering, operations and sales executives exclusively in the plastics and specialty chemical industries. Each recruiter has a particular expertise that allows very focused search capability.

Key Contact - Specialty:
Mr. James E. Slate, President - *Plastics*
Mr. John Mercier, Director - *Plastics*

Salary Minimum: $70,000

Functions: Management, Mfg., Quality, Sales & Mktg., R&D, Engineering

Industries: Paper, Chemicals, Plastics, Rubber, Paints, Petro. Products

FPC of Bloomfield

838 W Long Lake Rd Ste 230
Bloomfield Hills, MI 48302-2071
(248) 642-9383
Fax: (248) 642-9575
Email: exec1@ix.netcom.com
Web: www.fpcnational.com/bloomfield

Summary: As specialists in their industry and discipline, our search consultants possess in-depth knowledge of the business and resources available. Our searches are therefore focused, achieving results quickly and efficiently.

Key Contact - Specialty:
Mr. Karl Zimmermann, President - *Manufacturing, Purchasing, Quality*

Salary Minimum: $40,000

Functions: Management, Middle Mgmt., Production, Plant Mgmt., Quality, Purchasing, Materials Plng., Distribution

Industries: Metal Products, Machine, Appliance, Motor Vehicles, Computer Equip., Consumer Elect., Test, Measure Equip., Misc. Mfg., Electronic, Elec. Components, Transportation

FPC of Troy

(also known as F-O-R-T-U-N-E Personnel Consultants of Troy)
560 Kirts Blvd Ste 102
Troy, MI 48084-4141
(248) 244-9646
Fax: (248) 244-8568
Email: mdubeck@fpctroy.com
Web: www.fpctroy.com

Summary: We are a well respected executive search firm specializing in the placement of manufacturing, finance, engineering and healthcare professionals. The firm was established as a specialized health care provider. Our primary focus has been specialized searches in support of manufacturing firms' targeted personnel needs.

Key Contact - Specialty:
Mr. Michael Dubeck, President
Mr. Russell Chalmers, Executive Recruiter - *Engineering, Manufacturing*
Mr. Lanson Lee, Office Manager - *Logistics, Purchasing*
Ms. Catherine Whicker, Executive Recruiter - *Purchasing*
Ms. Bina Menon, Executive Recruiter - *Finance, Information Technology*
Ms. Debra Hunter, Executive Recruiter - *Healthcare, Manufacturing*
Ms. Jodi Knittel, Executive Director Business Development - *Engineering*

Salary Minimum: $40,000

Functions: Generalist (All), Mfg., Production, Plant Mgmt., Materials, Healthcare, Finance, CFOs, Engineering, Specialized Svcs.

Industries: Generalist (All), Manufacturing, Plastics, Rubber, Paints, Petro. Products, Metal Products, Motor Vehicles, Test, Measure Equip., Mgmt. Consulting, Packaging, Healthcare

FPC of St Louis

(also known as F-O-R-T-U-N-E Personnel Consultants of St. Lou)
1023 Executive Parkway Dr Ste 11
Creve Coeur, MO 63141-6323
(314) 205-1818
Email: careers@fpcstlouis.com
Web: www.fpcstlouis.com

Summary: We have set a distinguished standard for leadership, integrity and quality in recruitment. We provide prompt, efficient and confidential searches and present only qualified professional, management and executive candidates.

Key Contact - Specialty:
Mr. Craig Schultz, President - *Automotive, Equipment*
Mrs. Sandy Schultz, Vice President

Salary Minimum: $40,000

Functions: Middle Mgmt., Mfg., Production, Plant Mgmt., Quality, Productivity, Materials, Purchasing, HR Mgmt., Engineering

Industries: Manufacturing, Food, Bev., Tobacco, Lumber, Furniture, Medical Devices, Plastics, Rubber, Metal Products, Machine, Appliance, Motor Vehicles, Computer Equip., Misc. Mfg.

FPC of SW Missouri

5309 S Farm Road 135
Springfield, MO 65810-1904
(417) 887-6737
Fax: (417) 887-6955
Email: info@fpcswmo.com
Web: www.fpcswmo.com

Summary: Specializing in engineering, quality and technical sales at all levels and operations/production/supply chain management.

Our candidates are thoroughly screened and interviewed prior to presentation to our clients. References available.

Key Contact - Specialty:
Mr. Bill Belle Isle, President - *Engineering, Manufacturing*
Ms. Patrice Belle Isle, Vice President - *Accounting, Engineering, Human resources, Manufacturing, Quality*

Salary Minimum: $40,000

Functions: Management, Product Dev., Production, Plant Mgmt., Quality, Materials, Distribution, Sales & Mktg., Finance, Engineering

Industries: Manufacturing, Food, Bev., Tobacco, Drugs Mfg., Medical Devices, Plastics, Rubber, Metal Products, Machine, Appliance, Motor Vehicles, Consumer Elect., Test, Measure Equip., Electronic, Elec. Components, Biotech/Life Sciences

FPC of Bozeman

101 E Main St Ste F
Bozeman, MT 59715-4796
(406) 585-1332
Fax: (406) 585-2255
Email: kate@fpcbozeman.com

Summary: Recruiting firm specializing in all disciplines within the medical device, pharmaceutical and biotechnology industries.

Key Contact - Specialty:
Ms. Kate Regan Ciari, President & General Manager - *Engineering, Pharmaceutical, Sales*

Salary Minimum: $50,000

Functions: Generalist (All), Quality, R&D, Engineering

Industries: Generalist (All), Drugs Mfg., Medical Devices, Pharm Svcs., Logistics Svcs., Packaging, Biotech/Life Sciences

FPC of Nashua

505 W Hollis St Ste 208
Nashua, NH 03062-1387
(603) 880-4900
Fax: (603) 880-8861
Email: mail@fpcnashua.com
Web: www.fpcnashua.com

Summary: We are specialists in the biotechnology, pharmaceutical and medical device industries with a special emphasis on regulatory affairs, quality assurance, quality control, clinical affairs, validation, formulations, analytical chemistry and process development.

Key Contact - Specialty:
Mr. Norman J. Oppenheim, President - *Biotechnology, Medical (Devices), Pharmaceutical*
Mr. Chuck Lynch, Vice President - *Biopharmaceutical, Biotechnology, Pharmaceutical*

Salary Minimum: $60,000

Functions: Product Dev., Production, Quality, DB Admin., Engineering

Industries: Drugs Mfg., Medical Devices, Biotech/Life Sciences

FPC of Shore Region

571 W Lake Ave Ste 1
Bay Head, NJ 08742-5000
(732) 714-7600
Fax: (732) 714-7607
Email: fpc@comcast.net

Summary: A leading recruiter specializing in executive and professional level placement within

high-technology electronics, contract electronics manufacturing, general manufacturing, computer, medical, aerospace, DoD, homeland security, telecom and pharmaceutical industries.

Key Contact - Specialty:
Mr. Jim Kenny, President & Chief Executive Officer

Salary Minimum: $80,000

Functions: Generalist (All)

Industries: Misc. Mfg., Electronic, Elec. Components, Semiconductors, Telecoms, Digital, Wireless, Fiber Optic, RF/Microwave, Defense, Aerospace

FPC of Somerset

971 US Highway 202 N
Branchburg, NJ 08876-3757
(908) 218-0700
Fax: (908) 218-5055
Email: info@fpcsomerset.com
Web: www.fpcsomerset.com

Summary: We are a search firm dedicated to recruiting the best candidates for professional, middle management and executive positions in the pharmaceutical, medical device and biotechnological industries. We find pharmaceutical jobs, biotechnology jobs and medical device jobs for qualified candidates. Confidential searches.

Key Contact - Specialty:
Mr. Joe Jiuliano, CPC, President - *Research & development*
Ms. Margaret Jiuliano, Owner

Functions: Board Members, Senior Mgmt., Middle Mgmt., Product Dev., Quality, Purchasing, R&D

Industries: Drugs Mfg., Medical Devices, Pharm Svcs., Biotech/Life Sciences

FPC of Bergen County

275 N Franklin Tpke Ste 220
Ramsey, NJ 07446-2812
(201) 327-8252
Fax: (201) 327-2721
Email: mail@fpcbergencounty.com
Web: www.fpcbergencounty.com

Summary: Specialists in tech, mid and senior-level in pharmaceutical, biotechnology and medical device industries. Areas of specialization include QA, quality engineering, engineering, R&D, regulatory affairs, clinical affairs, QC, microbiology, scientific, manufacturing and statistics. Also specialists in mid and senior management in purchasing materials management and operations across all industries.

Key Contact - Specialty:
Mr. Howard G. Klein, CPC, President - *Biotechnology, Pharmaceutical*

Salary Minimum: $50,000

Functions: Senior Mgmt., Product Dev., Production, Automation, Quality, Materials, Mktg. Research, Mktg. Mgmt., R&D, Engineering

Industries: Generalist (All), Drugs Mfg., Medical Devices

FPC of Rockland County Inc

790 Grange Rd
Teaneck, NJ 07666-4237
(201) 907-0066
Fax: (201) 907-0057
Email: m.axelrod@verizon.net
Web: www.fpcnational.com/rocklandcounty

Summary: We provide nationwide search and placement of quality assurance, manufacturing and product design engineers and management personnel in the mechanical and electromechanical industries, especially in consumer products, aerospace and automotive. Services are available on a contingency as well as a retained search basis. All fees are client (company) paid.

Key Contact - Specialty:
Mr. Mark H. Axelrod, President - *Engineering, Management, Quality*

Salary Minimum: $50,000

Functions: Board Members, Middle Mgmt., Mfg., Product Dev., Quality, Staffing, Engineering

Industries: Manufacturing, Metal Products, Machine, Appliance, Motor Vehicles, Consumer Elect., Misc. Mfg.

FPC of Passaic County

41 Vreeland Ave Ste 26
Totowa, NJ 07512-1100
(973) 812-9819
Fax: (973) 812-9821
Email: stan@fpcpassaic.com
Web: www.fpcpassaic.com

Summary: This office, part of a nationwide franchise network, specializes in placing: sales, quality and purchasing/materials professionals within FDA regulated companies. Our primary focus is with medical device, biotechnology and pharmaceutical companies. We are constantly searching for exceptional talent to fill middle and upper management positions.

Key Contact - Specialty:
Mr. Stan Goldberg, President

Salary Minimum: $40,000

Functions: Quality, Materials, Purchasing, Packaging, Sales Mgmt., Sales Reps.

Industries: Generalist (All), Manufacturing, Drugs Mfg., Medical Devices, Pharm Svcs., Biotech/Life Sciences

FPC of Greensboro

445 Dolley Madison Rd Ste 412
Greensboro, NC 27410-5167
(336) 852-4455
Fax: (336) 854-9188
Email: info@fpcgboro.com
Web: www.fpcgboro.com

Summary: We provide executive and middle management retainer/contingent recruiting in supply chain management, plant management, focus factory managers, purchasing, quality management, Six Sigma, engineering management, logistics, transportation, distribution and 3PL professionals.

Key Contact - Specialty:
Mr. Bill Martin, President - *Operations*
Mr. Bill Markham, Director, Recruitment Practice - *Finance, Human resources*
Mr. Rich Bremer, Director, Supply Chain - *Logistics*
Mr. Chris Osl, Director, Supply Chain - *Purchasing*
Mr. Terry Kiger, Director, Six Sigma - *Engineering, Quality*

Salary Minimum: $40,000

Functions: Management, Mfg., Plant Mgmt., Quality, Materials, Purchasing, Materials Plng., HR Mgmt., Finance, Engineering

Industries: Generalist (All), Energy, Utilities, Manufacturing, Transportation

FPC of Charlotte

PO Box 460
Pineville, NC 28134-0460
(704) 889-1100
Fax: (704) 889-1109
Email: results@fpccharlotte.com
Web: www.fpccharlotte.com

Summary: Our firm provides executive recruitment services in searches for professionals in the medical device, pharmaceutical, biotechnology & metal forming and assembly manufacturing industries. Our consultants are all degreed at the bachelor/masters level and have industry work experience. We perform both contingency and retained searches.

Key Contact - Specialty:
Mr. David B. Griffith, President

Salary Minimum: $60,000

Functions: Senior Mgmt., Mfg., Product Dev., Plant Mgmt., Quality, Materials, Purchasing, R&D, Engineering

Industries: Drugs Mfg., Medical Devices, Plastics, Rubber, Metal Products, Machine, Appliance, Misc. Mfg., Electronic, Elec. Components, Fiber Optic, Aerospace, Packaging, Biotech/Life Sciences

FPC of Raleigh

7200 Stonehenge Dr Ste 305
Raleigh, NC 27613-1620
(919) 848-9929
Fax: (919) 848-1062
Email: david.singer@fpcraleigh.com
Web: www.fpcraleigh.com

Summary: With over 25 consultants specializing in a variety of disciplines, we have demonstrated that we can effectively handle all salaried staffing needs for our client firms.

Key Contact - Specialty:
Mr. Stan Deckelbaum, Chief Executive Officer - *Electronics, Hardware*
Mr. Rick Deckelbaum, President & Chief Operating Officer - *CEOs, Presidents*
Mr. Randy A. Cagan, CPC, Senior Vice President & Partner - *Engineering, Management, Manufacturing*
Mr. C.C. (Jay) Brown, Senior Vice President & Partner - *Converting*
Mr. David L. Singer, CPC, Senior Vice President & Partner - *Purchasing*
Mr. Richard D. Gorberg, CPC, Senior Vice President & Partner - *Marketing, Product management/development, Telecommunications, Wireless*

Salary Minimum: $40,000

Functions: Management, Senior Mgmt., Mfg., Materials, Healthcare, Sales & Mktg., HR Mgmt., Finance, Engineering, Legal

Industries: Generalist (All), Manufacturing, Food, Bev., Tobacco, Textiles, Apparel, Paper, Soap, Perf., Cosmtcs., Drugs Mfg., Medical Devices, Finance, Venture Cap., Misc. Financial, Pharm Svcs., Accounting, HR Services, E-commerce, Communications, Aerospace, Packaging, Software, Mfg. SW, Marketing SW, Biotech/Life Sciences, Healthcare

FPC of Cincinnati

4355 Ferguson Dr Ste 220
Cincinnati, OH 45245-5146
(513) 943-9095
Fax: (513) 943-9180
Email: fpccin@one.net
Web: www.fpcnational.com/cincinnati

Summary: Our firm focuses on serving manufacturing companies within the appliance, automotive, capital equipment, consumer products, continuous process, heavy equipment, machine tool and power systems industries. We focus on recruiting in engineering, operations, supply chain, purchasing, logistics, supplier quality, finance & accounting, HR and sales management positions for our clients.

Key Contact - Specialty:
Mr. James Pilcher, President & Owner - *Operations*
Mr. Mark Kuehling, Director, Supply Management, Purchasing - *Logistics, Manufacturing (Management), Procurement, Purchasing, Supply Chain*
Mr. Jamie Behm, Maintenance, Metallurgy, & Manufacturing - *Maintenance, Manufacturing, Materials, Safety*

Salary Minimum: $45,000

Functions: Generalist (All)

Industries: Manufacturing, Paper, Soap, Perf., Cosmtcs., Metal Products, Machine, Appliance, Motor Vehicles, Test, Measure Equip., Electronic, Elec. Components, Consumer Goods

FPC of Portland

311 B Ave Ste M
Lake Oswego, OR 97034-3071
(503) 675-7271
Fax: (503) 675-4560
Email: jobs@fpcportland.com
Web: www.fpcportland.com

Summary: We specialize in engineering, manufacturing and accounting/finance placements in the following industries: plastics & packaging, energy, mining, construction and automotive.

Key Contact - Specialty:
Mr. Mark Vague, Owner & President - *Automotive*

Salary Minimum: $60,000

Functions: Mfg., Finance, Engineering

Industries: Generalist (All), Food, Bev., Tobacco, Paper, Chemicals, Medical Devices, Motor Vehicles, Packaging

FPC of Philadelphia

PO Box 59
Huntingdon Valley, PA 19006-0059
(215) 914-1000
Fax: (215) 914-1021
Email: johnwille@johnwille.com
Web: www.johnwille.com

Summary: Our firm places actuaries in the financial industry.

Key Contact - Specialty:
Mr. John Wille, President

Salary Minimum: $40,000

Functions: Actuaries

Industries: Misc. Financial

FPC of Fort Washington

801 Old York Rd Ste 309
Jenkintown, PA 19046-1611
(215) 885-2500
Fax: (267) 287-1237
Email: search1@fpcftwash.com
Web: www.fpcftwash.com

Summary: We provide placement of attorneys, senior executives and other professionals for the insurance and investment industries. Other specialties include partnerships, associate placements and mergers in law firms.

Key Contact - Specialty:
Ms. Suzanne S. Richards, President - *Executives, Financial services, Insurance, Legal*

Functions: Legal, Attorneys

Industries: Generalist (All), Invest. Banking, Brokers, Mutual/Hedge Funds, Misc. Financial, Life, Re-Insurance

FPC of Abington

1410 W Street Rd
Warminster, PA 18974-3140
(215) 675-3100
Fax: (215) 675-3080
Email: search@fpcpharma.com

Summary: We provide senior level executive search primarily in pharmaceutical, biotechnology and CRO industries. We have highly knowledgeable, seasoned consultants that specialize in regulatory, clinical operations, biostatistics, data management, business development, manufacturing, engineering, project management and molecular biology.

Key Contact - Specialty:
Mr. Michael Strand, President - *Biopharmaceutical, Biotechnology, Business development, Clinical, Engineering*
Ms. Lauren Adams, Vice President, Pharmaceutical Services - *Biopharmaceutical, Biotechnology, Business development, Clinical, Pharmaceutical*
Mr. Larry Smith, Vice President, Regulatory Affairs & QA - *Biopharmaceutical, Biotechnology, Pharmaceutical, Quality, Regulatory*
Ms. Dawn Watson, Vice President, Clinical Operations - *Biotechnology, Pharmaceutical, Research, Research & development*
Mr. Clayton Doering, Vice President, Data Services - *Biopharmaceutical, Biotechnology, Clinical, Pharmaceutical, Research*

Salary Minimum: $80,000

Functions: Senior Mgmt., R&D, Int'l.

Industries: Generalist (All), Drugs Mfg., Finance, Pharm Svcs., Packaging, Biotech/Life Sciences

FPC of Providence

2843 S County Trl
East Greenwich, RI 02818-1728
(401) 885-8900
Fax: (401) 885-8901
Email: resume@fpcpro.com
Web: www.fpcpro.com

Summary: We specialize in all disciplines in the plastics, chemicals, paper, packaging, industrial gases, pharmaceuticals, bio-technology and medical device industries.

Key Contact - Specialty:
Mr. Eric Kniager, President
Mrs. Denise Kniager, Vice President - *Packaging*

Salary Minimum: $60,000

Functions: Mfg., Product Dev., Quality, Packaging, Sales & Mktg., R&D

Industries: Manufacturing, Paper, Printing, Chemicals, Drugs Mfg., Medical Devices, Plastics, Rubber, Metal Products, Motor Vehicles, Robotics, Packaging, Biotech/Life Sciences

FPC of Anderson

2006 N Main St
Anderson, SC 29621-3869
(864) 226-5322
Email: daryl@fpcsearch.com
Web: www.fpcsearch.com

Summary: Focus on R&D through manufacturing including formulations, analytical chemistry, quality/regulatory compliance, engineering operations and sales for pharmaceutical & medical device industries.

Key Contact - Specialty:
Mr. Daryl Kress, President - *Pharmaceutical*

Salary Minimum: $50,000

Functions: Generalist (All)

Industries: Chemicals, Drugs Mfg., Medical Devices, Pharm Svcs., Biotech/Life Sciences, Healthcare

FPC of Columbia

108 Columbia Northeast Dr Ste H
Columbia, SC 29223-6433
(803) 788-8877
Fax: (803) 788-1509
Email: generalinfo@fpccolumbia.com
Web: www.fpccolumbia.com

Summary: Specializing in the recruitment for and placement of middle management and executive positions in the manufacturing and distribution arenas, we can quickly find the technically qualified, state-of-the-art professional needed by your company.

Key Contact - Specialty:
Mr. Robert Thompson, Owner & Vice President & General Manager
Mr. Lentz Ivey, Owner & Vice President
Mr. Dan Ladrech, Owner & Vice President

Salary Minimum: $60,000

Functions: Management, Mfg.

Industries: Manufacturing, Chemicals, Plastics, Rubber, Metal Products, Machine, Appliance, Computer Equip., Consumer Elect., Misc. Mfg.

FPC of Greenville

25 Woods Lake Rd Ste 307
Greenville, SC 29607-2762
(864) 241-7700
Fax: (864) 241-7704
Email: fpcgrev@mindspring.com
Web: www.fpcnational.com

Summary: We are an executive placement (search) company. We search for the specific candidates, (quality, validation and engineering) in the pharmaceutical and biotech industry only, according to the company's specific requirements.

Key Contact - Specialty:
Mr. Alvin Dahl, President - *Pharmaceutical*

Salary Minimum: $50,000

Functions: Management, Senior Mgmt., Mfg., Automation, Plant Mgmt., Quality, Packaging, MIS Mgmt.

Industries: Food, Bev., Tobacco, Chemicals, Drugs Mfg., Medical Devices, Pharm Svcs., Aerospace, Insurance, Biotech/Life Sciences, Healthcare

FPC of Hilton Head

52 New Orleans Rd Ste 201
Hilton Head Island, SC 29928-4780
(843) 842-7221
Fax: (843) 842-7205
Email: recruit@fpchh.com
Web: www.fpchh.com

Summary: We are dedicated to the medical device, pharmaceutical, biotechnology, and CRO industries. Within these industries each recruiter has their own specialty: QA, QC, regulatory affairs, clinical affairs, R&D, manufacturing engineering, and business development & marketing. We have developed an extensive

network of candidates and companies. Our office works with industry leaders, as well as exciting startup companies.

Key Contact - Specialty:
Mr. David J. Ducharme, President - *Diagnostics, Medical, Medical (Devices), Pharmaceutical*
Ms. Donne G. Paine, RN, Vice President - *Biotechnology, Medical, Medical (Devices), Pharmaceutical*
Mrs. Rose Cofield, Office Manager, Research Recruiter - *Medical (Devices), Orthopedics, Pharmaceutical, Quality, Supply Chain*
Mr. Anthony Rizza, Recruiter - *Logistics, Medical (Devices), Pharmaceutical, Purchasing, Supply Chain*

Salary Minimum: $50,000

Functions: Generalist (All), Middle Mgmt., Product Dev., Production, Quality, Purchasing, Nurses, Mktg. Mgmt.

Industries: Drugs Mfg., Medical Devices, Plastics, Rubber, Pharm Svcs., Logistics Svcs., Supply Chain Mgmt, Biotech/Life Sciences

FPC of Chattanooga

5726 Marlin Rd Ste 100
Chattanooga, TN 37411-5666
(423) 855-0444
Fax: (423) 892-0083
Email: fortchatt@aol.com

Summary: We are a strong, fast-paced office dedicated to filling every job order and placing every applicant.

Key Contact - Specialty:
Mr. David W. Dickson, President - *Human resources, Manufacturing*
Ms. Brenda Hays, Owner - *Apparel*

Salary Minimum: $25,000

Functions: Generalist (All), Middle Mgmt., Production, Plant Mgmt., Purchasing, Distribution, Staffing, Engineering

Industries: Generalist (All), Textiles, Apparel, Plastics, Rubber, Metal Products, Machine, Appliance, Consumer Elect., Transportation, HR Services

FPC of Nashville

1099 Ridgecrest Dr
Kingston Springs, TN 37082-9761
(615) 952-9855
Email: tomo1@bellsouth.net

Summary: We provide recruiting services for manufacturing firms specializing in operational management, HR, engineering, QA, materials management and accounting.

Key Contact - Specialty:
Mr. Tom Oglesby, President - *Engineering, Operations*

Salary Minimum: $40,000

Functions: Generalist (All), Mfg.

Industries: Plastics, Rubber, Metal Products, Machine, Appliance, Motor Vehicles, Consumer Elect., Misc. Mfg., Electronic, Elec. Components, Robotics, Transportation, Finance

FPC of Concord

9827 Cogdill Rd Ste 4
Knoxville, TN 37932-3376
(865) 966-4002
Fax: (865) 966-4004
Email: harry@fpcconcord.com
Web: www.fpcconcord.com

Summary: We are a professional recruiting firm specializing in the placement of manufacturing and healthcare professionals.

Key Contact - Specialty:
Mr. Harry DeNardo, President

Salary Minimum: $40,000

Functions: Mfg., Quality, Physicians, Engineering

Industries: Generalist (All), Chemicals, Paints, Petro. Products, Leather, Stone, Glass, Metal Products

FPC of North Dallas

1545 W Mockingbird Ln Ste 1020
Dallas, TX 75235-5072
(214) 634-3929
(800) 618-3929
Fax: (214) 634-7741
Email: info@fpcndallas.com
Web: www.fpcndallas.com

Summary: We offer quick response to both client and candidate needs with many years of combined industry experience in medical device, pharmaceutical and general manufacturing.

Key Contact - Specialty:
Mr. Philip H. Pritchett, President & Owner - *Pharmaceutical*

Salary Minimum: $40,000

Functions: Product Dev., Mktg. Mgmt., Sales Mgmt., Engineering

Industries: Medical Devices

FPC of Houston

2555 Central Pkwy
Houston, TX 77092-7716
(713) 680-9132
Fax: (713) 680-1737
Email: info@fpchouston.com
Web: www.fpchouston.com

Summary: Specialize in Plastics, Chemicals Refining and Oil & Gas Industries. Assignments include specialized Professionals to Senior Management.

Key Contact - Specialty:
Mr. Robert M. Shanley, President
Ms. Suzanne M. Shanley, Vice President

Salary Minimum: $40,000

Functions: Board Members, Mfg., Product Dev., Sales & Mktg., HR Mgmt., Finance, R&D, Engineering

Industries: Manufacturing, Textiles, Apparel, Paper, Chemicals, Drugs Mfg., Plastics, Rubber, Paints, Petro. Products, Logistics Svcs., Supply Chain Mgmt

FPC of Virginia Highlands

RR 1 Box 132
Millboro, VA 24460-9529
(540) 925-2430
Fax: (540) 925-2434
Email: fpcvh@fpcvh.com
Web: www.fpcvh.com

Summary: We specialize in placement of middle management professionals in purchasing, materials, logistics, supply chain, and supplier quality.

Key Contact - Specialty:
Ms. Jean Howell, President - *Purchasing*
Mr. David Herscher, Director
Mr. Sandy Taylor, Director - *Research*
Ms. Sarah Irwin, Director - *Research*

Salary Minimum: $35,000

Functions: Materials

Industries: Manufacturing

FPC of Fairfax

1114 Fairfax Pike Ste 3
White Post, VA 22663-1803
(540) 868-0026
Fax: (540) 8680395
Email: resumes@fpcfairfax.com
Web: www.fpcfairfax.com

Summary: Established and emerging
organizations turn to our expertise for executive
staffing. With a long history and a franchise
network of many offices, we can provide talent
from across the market.

Key Contact - Specialty:
Mr. John Abbene, President - *Distribution,
Logistics, Materials, Purchasing*
Ms. Sandra Abbene, Vice President -
Engineering, Human resources

Salary Minimum: $40,000

Functions: Management, Senior Mgmt., Mfg.,
Production, Materials, Engineering,
Minorities/Diversity

Industries: Manufacturing, Food, Bev., Tobacco,
Chemicals, Soap, Perf., Cosmtcs., Plastics,
Rubber, Paints, Petro. Products, Metal Products,
Machine, Appliance, Computer Equip., Misc.
Mfg., Electronic, Elec. Components,
Semiconductors, HR Services, Engineering
Svcs., Logistics Svcs., Aerospace, Packaging

FPC of Williamsburg

3206 Ironbound Rd Ste D
Williamsburg, VA 23188-2452
(757) 220-0900
Fax: (757) 220-3099
Email: fpcw@verizon.net
Web: www.fpcnational.com

Summary: Executive and technical recruiting firm
specializing in the wood products manufacturing
industries such as residential and office furniture,
store fixtures, kitchen cabinets and millwork. We
place manufacturing management and engineers
up through the VP level positions. We specialize
in candidates and companies, which possess
knowledge and experience with Lean
manufacturing practices.

Key Contact - Specialty:
Mr. Walt Fowler, President

Salary Minimum: $50,000

Functions: Generalist (All)

Industries: Lumber, Furniture

FPC of East Seattle

95 S Tobin St Ste 202
Renton, WA 98057-5324
(425) 687-9889
Fax: (425) 687-9669
Email: info@fpc-eastseattle.com
Web: www.fpc-eastseattle.com

Summary: We are an executive search firm
specializing in the off-road heavy equipment,
mobile hydraulics, lawn & garden equipment,
power hand tools, automotive, bio-technology and
medical equipment industries. We work on
building relationships with our customer and at the
same time providing satisfaction to the candidates
we represent. Fostering a 'win-win' situation is our
focus.

Key Contact - Specialty:
Mr. Daniel Y. Chin, President & Recruiter
Mr. Zed Chin, Recruiter - *Pharmaceutical*
Mr. Danny Ventler, Research Associate

Salary Minimum: $45,000

Functions: Generalist (All), Middle Mgmt., Mfg.,
Materials, Engineering

Industries: Generalist (All), Agri., Forestry,
Mining, Construction, Medical Devices,
Machine, Appliance

Fabian Associates Inc

521 5th Ave Fl 17
New York, NY 10175-1799
(212) 697-9460
Fax: (212) 697-9488
Email: jfab@erols.com

Summary: President has extensive experience in
accounting and finance, having worked for 15
years in Fortune 500 companies. She is also a
CPA and MBA and has many contacts in Fortune
companies as well as in the financial services
industry.

Key Contact - Specialty:
Ms. Jeanne Fabian, President - *Direct marketing*

Salary Minimum: $50,000

Functions: Plant Mgmt., Distribution, Physicians,
Direct Mktg., Finance, Budgeting, Cash Mgmt.,
M&A, Risk Mgmt., Systems Dev.

Industries: Generalist (All), Chemicals, Invest.
Banking, Entertainment, Telecoms,
Entertainment SW, Hospitals

Factor Ten Executive Search

1300 Bristol St N Ste 175
Newport Beach, CA 92660-8929
(949) 474-2300
Fax: (949) 606-9960
Email: info@factor-ten.com
Web: www.factor-ten.com

Summary: For over a decade, Factor Ten has been
a specialty recruiting firm bringing together the
best companies in Southern California with the
most qualified employees. We offer specialized
recruiting services for finance and accounting
professionals only. Our high-performance
accounting and finance recruiting services enable
our clients to be more effective filling open
positions with qualified professionals more
quickly than they do on their own.

Key Contact - Specialty:
Mr. John Dyer, Executive Recruiter - *Accounting
(Big 4,General), Audits, Finance, Tax*
Mr. Michael Shenouda, Recruiter - *Accounting
(Big 4,General), Audits, Finance, Tax*
Ms. Marni Ellison-Albios, Recruiter - *Accounting
(Big 4,General), Audits, Finance, Tax*

Salary Minimum: $45,000

Functions: Management, Finance, CFOs,
Budgeting, Taxes, M&A, Risk Mgmt.

Industries: Generalist (All)

FAI

PO Box 200248
Denver, CO 80220-0248
(303) 388-8486
Fax: (303) 355-4213
Email: fgary12@aol.com

Summary: We are a generalist search firm
specializing in the Printing Industry. We will split
fees.

Key Contact - Specialty:
Mr. Gary Franklin, Chief Executive Officer

Salary Minimum: $35,000

Functions: Generalist (All), Senior Mgmt., Sales
& Mktg., Finance, Attorneys

Industries: Generalist (All), Printing, Brokers

Falcon Search Inc

1255 Waterwitch Cove Cir
Orlando, FL 32806-7852
(407) 852-6202

Summary: Executive search servicing internal
audit professionals.

Key Contact - Specialty:
Mr. Tom Gresosky, President

Salary Minimum: $100,000

Functions: Finance

Industries: Generalist (All)

Fallon & Company

PO Box 2268
New York, NY 10021-0055
(212) 692-0208
Email: info@fallonandcompany.com
Web: www.fallonandcompany.com

Summary: We specialize in executive placement
within the financial services industry. We
personally meet with and thoroughly interview all
candidates and are committed to the long view of
what is best for the client.

Key Contact - Specialty:
Mr. Michael E. Fallon, Managing Director -
Capital markets, Investment
Ms. Kathryn Jackson, Director, Research
Ms. Kathryn Fallon, Senior Recruiter

Functions: Generalist (All), Middle Mgmt.

Industries: Finance, Banking, Invest. Banking,
Brokers, Venture Cap., Mutual/Hedge Funds,
Misc. Financial, Non-profits, Accounting,
Publishing, New Media, Broadcast, Film

Fament Inc

505 Acton Rd
Columbus, OH 43214-3309
(614) 261-0552
Email: fament@famentinc.com
Web: www.famentinc.com

Summary: One of Midwest's oldest insurance
recruiting firm assisting companies, agencies,
brokers and banks with mid to top-management
level personnel needs.

Key Contact - Specialty:
Mr. Marty Shuherk

Salary Minimum: $95,000

Functions: Sales Mgmt.

Industries: Insurance

Dorothy W Farnath & Associates Inc

104 Centre Blvd Ste B
Marlton, NJ 08053-4130
(856) 810-2200
Email: info@farnath.com
Web: www.farnath.com

Summary: Specialize in recruitment for all
positions within the clinical and biotechnology
markets. Our skills in identifying qualified
candidates are enhanced by our strong technical
education and expertise. We have an exceptional
reputation, consistent ethical standards, and
excellent references.

Key Contact - Specialty:
Ms. Dorothy W. Farnath, President
Dr. Martin Praino, Executive Specialist,
Biotechnology
Mr. Frederick R. Clemens, Associate, Clinical
Specialist
Ms. Barbara N. Toren, Associate, Clinical
Specialist

Ms. Jane Meyers, Associate Biomedical
Specialist
Ms. Angie Lambrou, Associate - *Biotechnology,
Diagnostics, Direct marketing, Sales, Senior
management*
Mr. Dennis L. Kochanik, Associate, Biomedical
Specialist - *Biotechnology, Diagnostics*
Ms. Jean P. Zych, Associate, Clinical Specialist -
Clinical, Diagnostics

Functions: Generalist (All), Senior Mgmt.,
Middle Mgmt., Automation, Sales & Mktg.,
Mktg. Mgmt., Sales Mgmt., IT

Industries: Drugs Mfg., Medical Devices, Pharm
Svcs., Biotech/Life Sciences, Healthcare,
Hospitals

Faro Consultants International

2740 Chain Bridge Rd Ste 1007
Vienna, VA 22181-5378
(703) 281-1122
Email: george@farosearch.com
Web: www.farosearch.com

Summary: We offer specialized recruiting in
compensation and employee benefits consulting,
consulting actuaries and attorneys specializing in
ERISA and employee benefits law. We are experts
at identifying consulting and legal talent inside
and outside of consulting and law firms. We
conduct extensive searches in these specialties on
a contingency basis for those clients who qualify.

Key Contact - Specialty:
Mr. George Amato, President
Ms. Susan Lee Moe, Vice President
Ms. Nancy Moe, Vice President, Recruiting

Salary Minimum: $100,000

Functions: Benefits, Actuaries, Pension/Ret.
Planning, Mgmt. Consultants, Attorneys

Industries: Legal, Mgmt. Consulting, HR
Services, Compliance, Insurance, Healthcare

Fast Switch Ltd

37 W Bridge St Ste 200
Dublin, OH 43017-2117
(614) 336-3690
Fax: (614) 336-3695
Email: mark_pukita@fastswitch.com

Summary: Our clients get only highly qualified
candidates because of this; this saves them time
and expense. We provide retained search services
for both our retained and contingency clients.

Key Contact - Specialty:
Mr. Mark Pukita, Managing Director - *General
management, High technology, Sales*
Ms. Kimberly A. Triplett, Principal - *High
technology, Sales, Telecommunications*
Ms. Lin Hutaff, Principal - *Computers
(Hardware,Software), Information Technology,
Sales, Technical (Management)*

Salary Minimum: $60,000

Functions: Sales & Mktg., IT, MIS Mgmt.,
Systems Analysis, Systems Dev., Systems
Implem., Systems Support, Network Admin.,
DB Admin., Mgmt. Consultants

Industries: Generalist (All), Computer Equip.,
Mgmt. Consulting, New Media, Telecoms,
Software

Fast-Track Recruiters

2222 NE 22nd Ave
Cape Coral, FL 33909-4643
(239) 458-6722
Fax: (516) 706-7516
Email: atclark@earthlink.net
Web: www.fast-trackrecruiters.com

Summary: An elite team of seasoned veteran
recruiters, dedicated to seeking out exceptional
candidates and propelling their career to the next
level. We are experienced in a broad range of
industries and have contacts with all of the
Fortune 5000 companies. When you work with us,
you work with a team committed to putting you on
the fast track to success.

Key Contact - Specialty:
Mr. A. Clark, President & Chief Executive
Officer - *Finance, Sales, Technology*

Salary Minimum: $65,000

Functions: Generalist (All), Management, Senior
Mgmt.

Industries: Generalist (All)

A E Feldman Associates Inc

445 Northern Blvd Ste 10
Great Neck, NY 11021-4804
(516) 719-7900
Fax: (516) 719-7910
Email: cschwam@aefeldman.com
Web: www.aefeldman.com

Summary: We are a woman-owned executive
search and recruitment firm specializing in the
financial, legal, communications & technology
(media, internet, cable TV, telecom, mobile, IT)
industries. We recruit in the U.S. and overseas in
all areas and functions of these industries
including middle to board level management,
security clearances; separate diversity practice.

Key Contact - Specialty:
Ms. Carol Schwam, MBA, Chief Executive
Officer - *Banking (Investment), Finance,
Management consulting, Risk management,
Telecommunications*
Mr. Mitchell Feldman, President - *Accounting, C-
level, Financial services, Information
Technology, Telecommunications*

Salary Minimum: $50,000

Functions: Generalist (All)

Industries: Finance, Banking, Invest. Banking,
Legal, Accounting, Mgmt. Consulting,
Communications, Telecoms, Wireless, Software

FEP Search Group

(a division of Future Executive Personnel Ltd)
800-425 University Ave
Thompson Building
Toronto, ON M5G 1T6
Canada
(416) 979-7575
(888) 636-4802
Fax: (416) 979-3030
Email: staff@fepsearchgroup.com
Web: www.fepsearchgroup.com

Summary: We have assisted clients by placing
thousands of professionals with diverse
background and experience within their
organizations. We have successfully placed
numerous highly qualified candidates in leading
companies, and have established a rock-solid
reputation as one of North America's most
competent, aggressive and resource rich search
firms.

Key Contact - Specialty:
Mr. Mike Mehta, President

Salary Minimum: $40,000

Functions: Management, Mfg., Materials,
Purchasing, Packaging, Sales & Mktg., Finance,
IT, Engineering

Industries: Manufacturing, Food, Bev., Tobacco,
Transportation, Finance, Banking, Invest.
Banking, Venture Cap., Aerospace, Packaging,
Software, Biotech/Life Sciences

Branches:
800 W El Camino Real Ste 180
Mountain View, CA 94040-2586
(650) 903-2262
(888) 636-4802
Email: staff@fepsearchgroup.com

300 International Dr Ste 100
Williamsville, NY 14221-5783
(716) 626-3451
(888) 636-4802
Fax: (716) 626-3001
Email: staff@fepsearchgroup.com
Key Contact - Specialty:
Mr. Angel Mehta

Fergus Partnership Consulting Inc

1325 Avenue of the Americas Ste 2302
New York, NY 10019-6059
(212) 767-1775
Email: ny@ferguslex.com
Web: www.ferguslex.com

Summary: We successfully conduct attorney
searches at all levels with a particular
specialization in partner and senior level positions
for global law firms and corporations. In addition,
we assist law firms in the acquisition of practice
groups and in expansion of law offices.

Key Contact - Specialty:
Ms. Jean M.H. Fergus, Esq., Principal

Salary Minimum: $100,000

Functions: Legal

Industries: Banking, Invest. Banking, Venture
Cap., Non-Classifiable

Ferris & Associates LLC

1008 Norton Dr
Papillion, NE 68046-7007
(402) 758-9093
Fax: (402) 758-9093
Email: bob@fa.coxatwork.com

Summary: Professional permanent and
contracting search services specializing in MIS,
sales, management and marketing. Offer many
years of corporate business management
experience.

Key Contact - Specialty:
Mr. Robert M. Ferris, Jr., Owner - *Sales*

Salary Minimum: $40,000

Functions: Generalist (All), Management, Sales
& Mktg., IT, MIS Mgmt., Systems Analysis,
Systems Dev., Network Admin.

Industries: Generalist (All), Banking, Mgmt.
Consulting

Guild Fetridge Acoustical Search Inc

520 White Plains Rd Ste 500
Tarrytown, NY 10591-5118
(914) 467-7851
Email: gfacoustic@aol.com

Summary: We are specialists in acoustics,
vibration, noise control, HVAC, audio and audio-
visual for engineering, scientific, sales &
marketing and management functions.

Key Contact - Specialty:
Mr. Guild Fetridge, President - *Acoustics, HVAC*
Mr. Justin Fetridge, Consultant

Salary Minimum: $60,000

Functions: Generalist (All)

Industries: Machine, Appliance, Motor Vehicles,
Misc. Mfg., Defense

FGP International - Find Great People

150 Executive Center Dr Ste B82
Greenville, SC 29615-6503
(864) 297-0000
(800) 638-1661
Fax: (864) 297-0114
Email: contactus@findgreatpeople.com
Web: www.findgreatpeople.com

Summary: With offices in Greenville and Columbia, South Carolina, we find great people for specialized positions. Internationally, the professional recruiting division focuses in IT, retail, manufacturing/engineering, health care/medical field, accounting and finance industries. In South Carolina, the professional staffing division works in IT, accounting/finance and office support.

Key Contact - Specialty:
Mr. John Uprichard, President - *Accounting, Apparel, Healthcare, Information Technology, Manufacturing*
Mr. Steve Hall, CPC, CSP, Director, Professional Recruitment - *Accounting, Apparel, Healthcare, Information Technology, Manufacturing (Management)*
Mr. Eddie Payne, Division Manager, Professional Staffing - *Accounting (General), Administration, Finance, Human resources*
Ms. Beth Beard, Division Manager, Technology Staffing - *Computers, Computers (Networking,Programming,Software), Information Technology*

Salary Minimum: $60,000

Functions: Generalist (All)

Industries: Manufacturing, Retail, Finance, Accounting, HR Services, IT Implementation, Engineering Svcs., Software, Healthcare

Finance & Accounting Search Team (FAST)

655 Craig Rd Ste 244
Saint Louis, MO 63141-7170
(314) 371-3278
(877) 998-3278
Fax: (314) 426-4499
Email: info@fastsearch1.com
Web: www.fastsearch1.com

Summary: We specialize in placing accounting and finance professionals in permanent positions, however we also work on temp and contract positions. In addition, we have an IT division that places both permanent employees and contractors.

Key Contact - Specialty:
Mr. Mike Brenner, President
Ms. Michelle Dunski, CPA, Director, Recruiting
Ms. Yoanna Park-Haynes, Director, Information Technology Recruit

Functions: Finance, Budgeting, Cash Mgmt., Credit, Taxes, IT, Systems Analysis, Systems Dev., Systems Implem., Network Admin.

Industries: Generalist (All)

FinanceStaff Inc

300 Frank H Ogawa Plz Ste 210
Oakland, CA 94612-2038
(510) 465-6070
Email: info@financestaff.com
Web: www.financestaff.com

Summary: We provide recruiting, consulting and temporary staffing in accounting and finance. Positions range from CFO and VP of finance to controller, accounting manager and financial analyst.

Key Contact - Specialty:
Ms. Linda Carlton, CPA, President & Chief Executive Officer
Ms. Patricia Dedekian, Manager, Recruiting
Ms. Danielle Hayes, Manager, Recruiting
Mr. James Thomas, Contract Staffing Manager

Salary Minimum: $45,000

Functions: Finance, CFOs, Budgeting, Credit, Taxes, M&A, Systems Implem.

Industries: Generalist (All)

Financial Connections Company

5008 Andrea Ave
Annandale, VA 22003-4105
(703) 425-4240
Fax: (703) 323-6919
Email: m6272@erols.com
Web: users.erols.com/m6272/index.htm

Summary: The founder of our firm has many years of management experience in the life insurance and securities fields in addition to numerous certifications in the fields, namely a CLU, CHFC and FLMI.

Key Contact - Specialty:
Mr. David A. Richard, National Director - *Financial services, Securities*

Salary Minimum: $50,000

Functions: Generalist (All)

Industries: Banking, Invest. Banking, Brokers, Legal, Insurance

Financial Edge Executive Resources

5550 Cascade Rd SE Ste 200
Grand Rapids, MI 49546-6480
(616) 956-2981
Fax: (616) 464-4359
Email: info@fin-edge.com
Web: www.fin-edge.com

Summary: Our firm specializes in providing professional accounting and finance personnel on both a permanent and project basis.

Key Contact - Specialty:
Mr. Bill Benson, Managing Partner - *Aerospace, Automotive*
Mr. Joe LaLonde, Managing Director
Mr. Jon Koski, Senior Associate
Mr. Todd Hanson, Senior Associate - *Accounting, C-level, CFOs, Controllers, Finance*
Mr. Rob Mojsej, Senior Associate - *Accounting, Financial*
Ms. Leslie Cummings, Senior Associate - *Accounting, Finance*

Salary Minimum: $60,000

Functions: Generalist (All)

Industries: Finance, Accounting

Financial Executive Search

(an Ajilon company)
1921 Palomar Oaks Way Ste 205
Carlsbad, CA 92008-6524
(760) 431-7770
Fax: (760) 431-3709
Email: carlsbad@ajilonfinance.com
Web: www.ajilonfinance.com

Summary: Specializing in placement of accounting and financial professionals.

Key Contact - Specialty:
Ms. Tina Fox, Staffing Manager
Ms. Brenda Klein, Account Manager

Functions: Generalist (All), CFOs, Budgeting, Cash Mgmt., Credit, Taxes, M&A

Industries: Generalist (All), Manufacturing, Finance, Media, Software, Biotech/Life Sciences

Financial Executive Search

(an Ajilon company)
3424 Peachtree Rd NE Ste 125
Atlanta, GA 30326-1123
(404) 261-4800
Fax: (404) 233-1853
Email: atlanta@ajilonfinance.com
Web: www.ajilonfinance.com

Summary: We are a company specializing in the placement of accounting and financial professionals on both a temp and permanent basis with positions ranging from entry level to CFO.

Key Contact - Specialty:
Mrs. Sherry Pontious, Branch Vice President - *Accounting*

Functions: Finance, CFOs, Budgeting

Industries: Generalist (All)

Financial Executive Search

(an Ajilon company)
250 E 5th St Ste 450
Cincinnati, OH 45202-4173
(513) 381-4545
Fax: (513) 381-4672
Email: cincinnati@ajilonfinance.com
Web: www.ajilonfinance.com

Summary: We work with the top companies and candidates in the accounting and finance field. We are an organization that meets all of its candidates face to face before presenting them to a client.

Key Contact - Specialty:
Mr. Eric Roth, CPA, Executive Recruiter - *Finance*

Salary Minimum: $30,000

Functions: CFOs, Budgeting, Cash Mgmt., Credit, Taxes, M&A, Risk Mgmt.

Industries: Generalist (All)

Financial Placements

PO Box 29156
Shawnee Mission, KS 66201-9156
(913) 261-7000
(800) 336-1120
Email: info@banknews.com
Web: www.banknews.com

Summary: We specialize in banking.

Key Contact - Specialty:
Mr. Ray Makalous, Director, Banking Services
Mr. Mike Wall, Search Manager

Functions: Management, Board Members, Senior Mgmt., Middle Mgmt., Sales Mgmt., CFOs, Budgeting, Cash Mgmt.

Industries: Banking, Invest. Banking

Financial Recruiters

1125 Barrington Rdg
Richmond, IN 47374-7191
(800) 445-1793
Email: finrecruiter@usit.net
Web: bill.hrpanel.com

Summary: We place bankers in new and challenging positions. Commercial lending and management are our specialties. We do not forward information without your approval. Company is operated by a banker with many years of experience.

Key Contact - Specialty:
Mr. Bill Kozlowski, President

Salary Minimum: $50,000

Functions: Generalist (All), Middle Mgmt.

Industries: Banking

Financial Resource Associates Inc

105 W Orange St
Altamonte Springs, FL 32714-2538
(407) 869-7000
Fax: (407) 682-7291
Email: frasearch@frasearch.com

Summary: We are a national executive search firm specializing in the recruitment and placement of middle and senior management executives for banks, mortgage companies, savings & loans, real estate industry and other financial institutions throughout the country.

Key Contact - Specialty:
Mr. John Cannavino, President
Mr. Matthew J. Cannavino, Senior Vice President
Ms. Suzanne S. Perez, Vice President, Marketing

Salary Minimum: $50,000

Functions: Generalist (All), Finance, CFOs, Budgeting, Cash Mgmt., Credit, Taxes, M&A, Risk Mgmt.

Industries: Finance, Banking, Invest. Banking, Brokers, Venture Cap., Mutual/Hedge Funds, Misc. Financial

Financial Search Associates

8585 E Hartford Dr Ste 106
Scottsdale, AZ 85255-5472
(480) 505-4050
Fax: (480) 505-4051
Email: info@financialsearchassociates.com
Web: www.financialsearchassociates.com

Summary: Financial Search Associates (FSA) is a boutique executive search firm that specializes in placing the finest accounting and financial professionals nationwide. The firm's mission statement provides a strong foundation and reflects their vision. FSA's mission is to be a leading executive search firm that matches talented financial candidates with outstanding organizations. FSA provides inclusive career guidance to candidates and comprehensive employment solutions to clientele delivered with integrity and a passion for excellence.

Key Contact - Specialty:
Mr. Steve Gabbay, Partner
Ms. Paige Miller, Partner

Salary Minimum: $75,000

Functions: Finance, CFOs, Budgeting, Cash Mgmt., Taxes

Industries: Generalist (All)

Financial Services Recruiting

2418 Home Orchard Dr
Springfield, OH 45503-2338
(937) 390-9741
Email: recruiters@e-cruiters.net
Web: www.e-cruiters.net

Summary: Our firm specializes in efficiently locating, on contingency fee basis, the very best candidates for placement in all types of jobs in every type of financial services company. Try us. Remember there's no cost to your firm unless you hire one of our candidates and our services are guaranteed.

Key Contact - Specialty:
Mr. John J. Walsh, President - *Banking, Finance, Financial services, Insurance, Securities*
Ms. Bonnie D. Behrend, Partner - *Brokerage, Executives, MBAs, Securities, Wall Street*

Salary Minimum: $40,000

Functions: Generalist (All), Senior Mgmt., Sales Reps.

Industries: Finance, Banking, Brokers, Mutual/Hedge Funds, Misc. Financial, Pharm Svcs., Hospitality, Hotels, Resorts, Clubs, Insurance, Casualty, Life, Commercial, Re-Insurance

FINANCIALJobs.com

(also known as CPAjobs.com)
481 El Jina Ln
Ojai, CA 93023-9303
(805) 640-1849
Email: muller@financialjobs.com
Web: www.FINANCIALjobs.com, www.CPAjobs.com

Summary: Our websites and recruiting services feature accounting and finance jobs at all career levels, from accounting staff to financial analysts, CEOs and hundreds of other categories. We are part of a nationwide network of 2,000 recruiters, and our websites feature job advertisements that allow candidates to contact interested companies directly.

Key Contact - Specialty:
Mr. Michael Muller, Executive Recruiter - *Accounting, Accounting (Big 4,General,Public), Audits*

Salary Minimum: $40,000

Functions: Board Members, Senior Mgmt., Middle Mgmt., Finance, CFOs, Budgeting, Cash Mgmt., Credit, Taxes, M&A

Industries: Generalist (All), Manufacturing, Services, Accounting, Mgmt. Consulting, Hospitality

FinancialPeople LLC

1231 Delaware Ave Ste 1
Buffalo, NY 14209-1436
(716) 883-0771
Fax: (716) 883-0776
Email: jdaily@cpstaffing.com
Web: www.cpstaffing.com

Summary: Specialize in accounting, banking, finance and human recources.

Key Contact - Specialty:
Mr. John Daily, CMA

Salary Minimum: $30,000

Functions: Generalist (All), Benefits, Staffing, CFOs, Budgeting, Cash Mgmt., Credit, Taxes

Industries: Generalist (All), Misc. Mfg., Banking, Accounting, Broadcast, Film, Healthcare

Finders-Seekers Inc

1600 Heritage Lndg Ste 112C
Saint Peters, MO 63303-8490
(636) 922-5222
(800) 636-2999
Fax: (636) 498-6579
Email: evd@finderseekers.com
Web: www.finderseekers.com

Summary: Executive recruiter for sales & marketing positions within consumer packaged goods (food, beverage, drug) manufacturing companies. We place a special emphasis in category management and strategic partnering.

Key Contact - Specialty:
Mr. Ed Van Deventer, Director
Mr. John Larry, Owner & Manager

Salary Minimum: $50,000

Functions: Sales & Mktg.

Industries: Food, Bev., Tobacco, Soap, Perf., Cosmtcs., Industry Specific SW

Finesse Personnel Associates - Direct Placement Division

11030 Arrow Rte Ste 204
Rancho Cucamonga, CA 91730-4837
(909) 980-3392
Fax: (909) 980-4081
Email: email@finessepersonnel.com
Web: www.finessepersonnel.com

Summary: We are a regional firm specializing in managerial and executive placement.

Key Contact - Specialty:
Mr. Douglas Suchecki, Manager, Direct Placement

Salary Minimum: $40,000

Functions: Generalist (All), Middle Mgmt.

Industries: Manufacturing, Food, Bev., Tobacco, Transportation, Wholesale, Retail, Finance, Hospitality, Packaging

Branches:
555 5th St Ste 220
Santa Rosa, CA 95401-6342
(707) 579-2980
Fax: (707) 579-2788
Email: santarosajobs@finessepersonnel.com
Key Contact - Specialty:
Ms. Sara Cullins, Regional Manager

2701 NW Vaughn St Ste 473
Portland, OR 97210-5365
(503) 248-9392
Fax: (503) 248-9445
Email: portlandjobs@finessepersonnel.com
Key Contact - Specialty:
Ms. Linda Parthemer, Manager

Finn Associates LLC

6830 ELM St
Mc Lean, VA 22101-3874
(703) 442-7337
Fax: (703) 442-3877
Email: finnsearch@aol.com
Web: www.finnschneider.com

Summary: Place partners and associates in all legal specialty areas. Advise on law firm mergers and opening of branch offices. Firm has a national and international referral network.

Key Contact - Specialty:
Ms. Jacquelyn Finn, Owner

Functions: Legal

Industries: Banking, Invest. Banking, Venture Cap., Legal, Telecoms, Government, Aerospace, Real Estate, Biotech/Life Sciences, Healthcare

FinneyTaylor Consulting Group

200-602 11 Ave SW
Sun Rise Square
Calgary, AB T2R 1J8
Canada
(403) 264-4001
Fax: (403) 264-4057
Email: mailbox@finney-taylor.com
Web: www.finney-taylor.com

Summary: We are an information technology staffing solutions provider that assists clients in meeting their staffing demands. Our clients are companies that need mid to senior level IT professionals and they include over 50 of Canada's biggest firms.

Key Contact - Specialty:
Mr. Ian Giles, Account Manager - *CIOs, Information Technology*

Functions: IT

Industries: Generalist (All), Services

Fipp Associates Inc

PO Box 495
Plainsboro, NJ 08536-0495
(609) 799-2488
Fax: (609) 799-2998
Email: fippinc@att.net

Summary: We are a boutique contingency recruiting firm that specializes in the placement of marketing, direct marketing and advertising account service professionals. We also focus on these disciplines in the pharmaceutical and medical equipment industries.

Key Contact - Specialty:
Mr. Steve Fippinger, President - *Interactive, New media*

Functions: Advertising, Mktg. Mgmt.

Industries: Media, Advertising

Firm Advice Inc

1746 N St NW
Washington, DC 20036-2907
(202) 861-7707
Fax: (202) 861-7708
Email: mlegg@firmadvice.com
Web: www.firmadvice.com

Summary: We hold true to our name: we provide firm advice to law firms and corporations on their legal staffing needs. Our staff understands the legal environment and its demands. We search for and provide to our clients only top quality attorneys.

Key Contact - Specialty:
Ms. Mary W. Legg, President & General Counsel
Ms. Monika A. Paris, Recruiter
Ms. Yvonne Lee, Director, Recruiting, Finance & Admin

Functions: Attorneys

Industries: Legal

First Attorney Consultants Ltd

3356 W 95th St
Evergreen Park, IL 60805-2236
(708) 425-5515
Web: www.facltd.com

Summary: We are dedicated to the placement of attorneys at law firms and businesses across the United States and overseas. Our clients range from the largest international law firms to small boutiques, and from Fortune 500 companies to entrepreneurial start-ups.

Key Contact - Specialty:
Mr. Joseph Marovitch, President
Mr. Aaron Borowski, Senior Consultant - *Consulting*

Salary Minimum: $80,000

Functions: Attorneys

Industries: Legal

First Call Associates Inc (FCA)

PO Box 810994
Boca Raton, FL 33481-0994
(561) 994-5480
Fax: (561) 994-5490
Email: contactus@firstcallassociates.com
Web: www.firstcallassociates.com

Summary: Our firm offers high quality international search capabilities. The firm's search strength is in the wholesale and retail areas of energy related commodities trading and marketing. We also serve clients in the following industries: banking & finance, environmental, healthcare, insurance, manufacturing, natural resources and utilities.

Key Contact - Specialty:
Ms. Audrey Cullen Davis, CPC, Partner
Mr. Michael Davis, CPC, Partner
Mr. Adrian Clark, Director

Salary Minimum: $80,000

Functions: Generalist (All)

Industries: Oil & Gas, Chemicals, Metal Products, Finance, Legal, Accounting, Communications, Insurance, Healthcare, Non-Classifiable

First Call Professional Services

6960 Hillsdale Ct
Indianapolis, IN 46250-2040
(317) 596-3254
Fax: (317) 596-3284
Email: jkolumbus@fcqs.com

Summary: We provide contingency and retained search services. Our specialties include: engineering, manufacturing management, HR, accounting/finance and sales/marketing.

Key Contact - Specialty:
Mr. Jack Kolumbus, Senior Recruiter - *Engineering, Sales*

Salary Minimum: $50,000

Functions: Generalist (All), Senior Mgmt., Middle Mgmt., Mfg., Sales & Mktg., HR Mgmt., Finance, IT, Engineering, Int'l.

Industries: Generalist (All), Manufacturing, Medical Devices, Plastics, Rubber, Metal Products, Machine, Appliance, Motor Vehicles, Misc. Mfg., Accounting, Packaging

First Choice Placement Company

(also known as Janet & J C Newcomb)
560 Cherokee Rdg
Athens, GA 30606-1826
(706) 549-2758
Fax: (706) 549-8556
Email: firstchoiceplacement@hotmail.com

Summary: Specializing in the placement of engineers, allied medical professionals and nursing professionals.

Key Contact - Specialty:
Mr. J.C. Newcomb, Managing Partner

Salary Minimum: $40,000

Functions: Healthcare, Nurses, Engineering, Attorneys

Industries: Architectural Svcs., Legal, Engineering Svcs., Environmental Svcs., Healthcare, Hospitals, Physical Therapy, Occupational Therapy

First Coast Personnel Inc

9767 Beauclerc Ter
Jacksonville, FL 32257-5706
(904) 886-2471
Fax: (904) 739-9136
Email: bobpepple@fcpjax.com
Web: www.fcpjax.com

Summary: We are a nationwide leader in the recruitment and placement of middle management and executive-level personnel with major corporations throughout the country. We specialize in engineers, quality, manufacturing and strategic sourcing and supply professionals.

Key Contact - Specialty:
Mr. Bob Pepple, President

Salary Minimum: $40,000

Functions: Generalist (All), Management, Mfg., Quality, Materials, Purchasing, Distribution, Engineering

Industries: Generalist (All), Manufacturing, Plastics, Rubber, Motor Vehicles, Electronic, Elec. Components, Transportation, Communications, Fiber Optic, Packaging, Software

First Search America Inc

PO Box 85
Ardmore, TN 38449-0085
(256) 423-8800
Fax: (256) 423-6470
Email: firstsearch@ardmore.net

Summary: We recruit and place experienced, degreed individuals in food processing including poultry, pork and red meat processing industries. We specialize in general management, sales/marketing, production, R&D, technical services and all salaried positions. There is never a fee charged to the applicant.

Key Contact - Specialty:
Mr. Jim Fowler, President

Salary Minimum: $35,000

Functions: Generalist (All), Senior Mgmt., Middle Mgmt., Admin. Svcs., Mfg., Mktg. Mgmt., Sales Mgmt., R&D

Industries: Agri., Forestry, Mining, Food, Bev., Tobacco, Drugs Mfg.

Branches:
24778 Wolf Bay Ter
Orange Beach, AL 36561-3846
(888) 288-3243
Email: firstsearch@bellsouth.net
Key Contact - Specialty:
Ms. Lori Stevens, Senior Consultant

First Search Inc

1480 Renaissance Dr Ste 416
Park Ridge, IL 60068-1355
(847) 759-0001
Fax: (847) 759-0737
Email: alkatz@firstsearch.com
Web: www.firstsearch.com

Summary: Recruiters specializing in the construction industry with an emphasis on senior level management (vice-president and director levels), construction superintendents, construction managers, project managers as well as professional civil engineering in land development. Management professionals are placed in the residential as well as commercial aspects of construction.

Key Contact - Specialty:
Mr. Al Katz

Salary Minimum: $35,000

Functions: Generalist (All), Senior Mgmt., Engineering

Industries: Energy, Utilities, Oil & Gas, Construction, Computer Equip., Electronic, Elec. Components, Semiconductors, Telecoms, Wireless, Property/Facility Mgmt.

Fischer & Crane Associates

965 N Nob Hill Rd Ste 308
Plantation, FL 33324-1078
(954) 916-1280
(866) 437-2589
Email: kennedyinfobase@fischer-crane.com
Web: www.fischer-crane.com

Summary: Our firm recruits and places scientists, engineers and executives with three plus years industry experience whom their peers review as tops in their field. Industries include: pharmaceutical, biotechnology, medical device, research equipment & supplies and diagnostic tests and equipment

Key Contact - Specialty:
Ms. Katherine Fischer, Director, Biomedical
Search

Salary Minimum: $60,000

Functions: Generalist (All), Board Members,
Allied Health

Industries: Generalist (All), Drugs Mfg.,
Biotech/Life Sciences

Fishel & Bocker HR Associates Inc

4636 E University Dr Ste 255
Phoenix, AZ 85034-7499
(602) 266-5600
Fax: (602) 266-5656
Email: fbocker@fishelhr.com
Web: www.fishelhr.com

Summary: Many years as a leading, full-service,
contingency search firm recruiting for various
industries in the areas of HR, engineering,
management, financial and other professional and
technical disciplines.

Key Contact - Specialty:
Mr. Fred Bocker, President & Chief Executive
Officer

Salary Minimum: $45,000

Functions: HR Mgmt.

Industries: Generalist (All)

Jack Stuart Fisher Associates

PO Box 835
Lakewood, NJ 08701-0835
(732) 367-4950
Email: jsfheadhunter@juno.com

Summary: We are a full-service search for
scientists mostly in biotechnology and
pharmaceutical companies. Involved with starting
new companies in biotechnology, defense and
scientific areas.

Key Contact - Specialty:
Mr. Jack S. Fisher, Principal - *Pharmaceutical*

Salary Minimum: $60,000

Functions: Management, Senior Mgmt., Middle
Mgmt.

Industries: Drugs Mfg., Pharm Svcs., Software,
Biotech/Life Sciences

Fisher-Todd Associates

122 E 42nd St Rm 320
New York, NY 10168-0300
(212) 986-9052
(212) 557-5000
Fax: (212) 661-7897
Email: fishertodd@winstonstaffing.com
Web: www.winstonresources.com

Summary: We recruit at mid to senior-levels of
management within functional specialties in a
wide variety of industries. We build long-term
relationships by bringing professionalism and
expertise to the recruitment process. Specialties
include: product & services marketing
management, sales, sales management, market
research, sales promotion, corporate
communications, HR-generalists & specialists,
purchasing and facilities management.

Key Contact - Specialty:
Mr. Ronald Franz, Principal & Vice Principal -
Communications, Human resources

Salary Minimum: $50,000

Functions: Product Dev., Purchasing, Sales &
Mktg., Mktg. Research, Mktg. Mgmt., Direct
Mktg., HR Mgmt., Benefits, Staffing, Training

Industries: Generalist (All)

Fitzpatrick & Associates

6187 Sorrento Ave NW
Canton, OH 44718-3752
(330) 497-8994
Email: fitz@fitzpatrickcareers.com
Web: www.fitzpatrickcareers.com

Summary: Technical search and recruitment firm
specializing in the datacom, telecom and
semiconductor industries. We recruit hardware
(board level, FPGA/ASIC, full custom, mixed
signal & analog/RF IC), software (embedded, real-
time, firmware, device driver, protocols, etc.).

Key Contact - Specialty:
Mr. James Fitzpatrick, Principal - *Computers
(Software), Hardware*

Salary Minimum: $65,000

Functions: Generalist (All), Product Dev.,
Packaging, Engineering, Hardware

Industries: Communications, Telecoms, Call
Centers, Telephony, Digital, Wireless, Fiber
Optic, Network Infrastructure, RF/Microwave,
Packaging, Software, Development SW,
Industry Specific SW, Networking, Comm. SW,
System SW

FL USA Recruiters

8601 SW 146th St
Village of Palmetto Bay, FL 33158-1442
(305) 232-6322
Email: bruce@fl4usa.com
Web: www.fl4usa.com

Summary: We work with staffing professionals
throughout the country ensuring the application of
industry knowledge in solving staffing needs.

Key Contact - Specialty:
Mr. Bruce Bonnough, Owner & Manager -
*Aerospace, Engineering, Management, Safety,
Six sigma*
Mr. Edward Bailey - *Management, Minorities,
Restaurants, Telecommunications*

Functions: Generalist (All)

Industries: Energy, Utilities, Manufacturing,
Services, Hospitality, Communications,
Government, Software, Non-Classifiable

Flesher & Associates Inc

445 S San Antonio Rd Ste 102
Los Altos, CA 94022-3638
(650) 917-9900
Email: info@flesher.com
Web: www.flesher.com

Summary: We are an executive search firm
specializing in building strategic communications
teams for high-technology corporations and
agencies. Includes mid and senior-level
management searches.

Key Contact - Specialty:
Ms. Susan Flesher, President - *High technology,
Public relations*

Salary Minimum: $90,000

Functions: Management, PR

Industries: Media, Communications, Telecoms,
Software

CR Fletcher Associates Inc

126 N Salina St
Syracuse, NY 13202-1059
(315) 471-1000
Fax: (315) 471-6500
Email: sharon.ryan@crfletcher.com
Web: www.crfletcher.com

Summary: Full service recruiting firm offering
executive search, contract, temp or temp to hire
placement. We offer placement in the following
specialties: accounting/finance, sales/marketing,
IT, administrative and clerical.

Key Contact - Specialty:
Ms. Carol Fletcher, President & Chief Executive
Officer - *Sales*
Mr. Thomas Fletcher, President, Contract &Temp
Division - *Clerical*
Ms. Sharon Ryan, Recruiter

Salary Minimum: $40,000

Functions: Generalist (All), Admin. Svcs., Sales
& Mktg.

Industries: Generalist (All), Finance, Accounting,
IT Implementation

Susan Fletcher Attorney Employment Services

501 Grant St Ste 450
Union Trust Building
Pittsburgh, PA 15219-4414
(412) 281-6609
Fax: (412) 281-2949
Email: sufletcher@sflawjobs.com
Web: www.sflawjobs.com

Summary: Experience as law school placement
director and legal search consultant. Will supply
references from client employers and candidates
placed.

Key Contact - Specialty:
Ms. Susan Fletcher, Recruiter

Functions: Legal

Industries: Generalist (All), Manufacturing,
Legal, Accounting

Flex Execs Management Solutions

645 Executive Dr
Willowbrook, IL 60527-5603
(630) 655-0563
Fax: (630) 655-0564
Email: info@flexexecs.com
Web: www.flexexecs.com

Summary: We provide executive search for senior
and middle management experts on a full-time or
interim basis in the fields of HR, finance &
accounting and senior management. We are a
certified Women's Business Enterprise.

Key Contact - Specialty:
Ms. Karen Murphy, Managing Partner - *Finance,
Human resources, Middle management,
Operations, Senior management*
Ms. Kris Swanson, Managing Partner - *Finance,
Human resources, Middle management,
Operations, Senior management*

Salary Minimum: $75,000

Functions: Management, Senior Mgmt., HR
Mgmt., Finance

Industries: Generalist (All), Finance, Mgmt.
Consulting, Development SW, HR SW

Flexible Resources Inc

78 Harvard Ave Ste 315
Stamford, CT 06902-5548
(203) 351-1180
Fax: (203) 351-1185
Email: ct@flexibleresources.com
Web: www.flexibleresources.com

Summary: We provide placement of highly qualified professionals in flexible work arrangements, i.e. permanent part-time, job sharing, telecommuting and interim management staffing.

Key Contact - Specialty:
Ms. Laurie Young, Principal

Salary Minimum: $30,000

Functions: Generalist (All), Management, Purchasing, Sales & Mktg., HR Mgmt., Finance, IT, Mgmt. Consultants

Industries: Generalist (All), Manufacturing, Finance, Services, Media, Software, Healthcare

Branches:
542 Hopmeadow St Ste 222
Simsbury, CT 06070-2415
(860) 651-5299
Fax: (860) 651-5964
Email: hartford@flexibleresources.com
Key Contact - Specialty:
Ms. Susan Glasspiegel
Ms. Susan Rietano-Davey

175 Olde Half Day Rd Ste 100-18
Lincolnshire, IL 60069-3082
(847) 478-9556
Fax: (847) 478-9665
Email: chicago@flexibleresources.com
Key Contact - Specialty:
Ms. Gayle Pervos, Co-Director
Ms. Katie Turner, Co-Director

124 Little Falls Rd Ste E
Fairfield, NJ 07004-2132
(973) 439-9200
Fax: (973) 439-9209
Email: nj@flexibleresources.com
Key Contact - Specialty:
Ms. Tracey Austin

Flores Financial Services

314 Sage St
Lake Geneva, WI 53147-1931
(262) 248-2771
Fax: (262) 248-2562
Email: info@rflores.com
Web: www.floresfinancialservices.com

Summary: One of the leaders in executive recruiting for international bankers. We provide a full range of executive search consulting services to international financial institutions and corporations.

Key Contact - Specialty:
Mr. Robert Flores, President
Ms. Mary Herman, Director
Mr. Jeff Horner, Vice President, Consulting
Ms. Sally Kasper, Administrative Assistant

Salary Minimum: $30,000

Functions: Mfg., Finance

Industries: Finance, Banking, Invest. Banking, Venture Cap., Mutual/Hedge Funds, Misc. Financial

FMK Staffing Services LLC

83 Western Hwy
West Nyack, NY 10994-2619
(845) 353-2518

Email: resume@fmkstaffing.com
Web: www.fmkstaffing.com

Summary: Specialized recruitment of mid and senior-level technology executives with a strong track record, vision and capabilities who bring above average business acumen to the table. We focus on mid-career individuals responsible for: IT management, related development and operations personnel, pharmaceutical with background in R&D, bioinformatics and sales, mid and senior level personnel involved in technical sales.

Key Contact - Specialty:
Mr. Bob Kalinowski, Managing Partner
Ms. Roz McKinnon, Partner
Ms. Karen Wiegand, Partner

Salary Minimum: $90,000

Functions: Management, Healthcare, Sales Mgmt., IT, MIS Mgmt., Systems Dev., Systems Implem., Network Admin., DB Admin., Engineering

Industries: Generalist (All), Drugs Mfg., Medical Devices, Services, HR Services, E-commerce, IT Implementation, Communications, Network Infrastructure, Software, Biotech/Life Sciences

David Fockler & Associates Inc

25944 Paseo Estribo Ste 100
Monterey, CA 93940-6664
(831) 649-6666
Fax: (831) 649-0600
Email: dave@fockler.com
Web: www.fockler.com

Summary: Sales, marketing and manufacturing management positions for food (both retail and food service): consumer products, HBC, foodservice equipment and food ingredient manufacturers. Mid-management to lower upper-management.

Key Contact - Specialty:
Mr. David B. Fockler, Principal

Salary Minimum: $50,000

Functions: Management, Middle Mgmt., Mfg., Sales & Mktg., Advertising, Mktg. Research, Mktg. Mgmt., Sales Mgmt.

Industries: Manufacturing, Food, Bev., Tobacco, Textiles, Apparel, Soap, Perf., Cosmtcs., Drugs Mfg., Computer Equip., Consumer Elect., Consumer Goods, Software, Database SW, Development SW, Marketing SW

Branches:
1038 Bayview Ave Ste B
Pacific Grove, CA 93950-2418
(831) 621-3902
Email: dancounts@fockler.com
Key Contact - Specialty:
Mr. Dan Counts, Partner - *Computers (Hardware,Programming,Sales,Software), Sales*

940 S River Rd
Naperville, IL 60540-0315
(630) 428-4112
Fax: (630) 428-3201
Email: steve@fockler.com
Key Contact - Specialty:
Mr. Stephen A. Swan, Senior Partner - *Consumer, Cosmetics, Housewares, Marketing, Sales*

Focus Executive Search

2852 Anthony Ln S
Minneapolis, MN 55418-3233
(612) 706-4444
Fax: (612) 706-0544
Email: resume@focusexecutivesearch.com
Web: www.focusexecutivesearch.com

Summary: We excel at partnering with food, packaging, medical device and building product

industry companies. Offer an understanding of the industries we serve for timely and successful targeted searches. Recruiters all have previous hands on management experience in their industry specialization. Established client base of leading and emerging companies through a consultative partnering recruiting approach that produces top quality candidates.

Key Contact - Specialty:
Mr. Tim McLafferty, President - *Bakery, Dairy, Food, Food service*
Mr. Tim Schultz, Vice President
Mr. Tony Misura, Division Manager - *Lumber, Millwork*
Mr. Nicholas Kallenbach, Manager, Research
Ms. Gayle Holt, Administrative Manager

Salary Minimum: $50,000

Functions: Generalist (All), Mfg., Product Dev., Purchasing, Sales & Mktg.

Industries: Construction, Manufacturing, Food, Bev., Tobacco, Lumber, Furniture, Paper, Printing, Chemicals, Medical Devices, Plastics, Rubber, Metal Products, Transportation, Wholesale, Pharm Svcs., HR Services, Inst./Industrial Food Svc., Packaging

Focus Search Group

29528 Pebble Beach Dr
Sun City, CA 92586-3146
(951) 301-7036
Email: billk@focussearchgroup.com
Web: www.focussearchgroup.com

Summary: Principal has extensive experience in the hospitality field, with a special focus on hotels, restaurants and gaming industry. Strength of company relies on ability to penetrate competitive companies to contact candidates for its client's positions.

Key Contact - Specialty:
Mr. William J. Kresich, President - *Gaming, Hospitality, Hotels, Resorts, Restaurants*

Salary Minimum: $85,000

Functions: Senior Mgmt., Middle Mgmt., Mktg. Mgmt., Staffing, CFOs, MIS Mgmt., Hospitality, Hotel Mgmt., Chefs

Industries: Hospitality, Hotels, Resorts, Clubs, Restaurants, Quick Service Restaurants, Full Service Restaurants

FocusTeam

4159 Interdale Way
Palo Alto, CA 94306-3953
(650) 858-8318
Email: nikesh@focusteam.com
Web: www.focusteam.com

Summary: Boutique executive search firm providing services to internet, software, financial services, IT, network, telecom, and storage industries. Expertise in recruiting and pre-qualifying passive software engineering and leadership professionals.

Key Contact - Specialty:
Mr. Nikesh Mistry, Engineering & Leadership Recruiter - *Computers (Networking,Programming,Software), Information Systems, Internet*

Functions: Management, Middle Mgmt., Product Dev., IT, MIS Mgmt., Systems Dev.

Industries: Computer Equip., Banking, E-commerce, IT Implementation, Communications, Telecoms, Wireless, Network Infrastructure, Software, Database SW, Development SW, ERP SW, Mfg. SW, Marketing SW, Networking, Comm. SW, Security SW, System SW

Food Management Search

235 State St Apt 326
Springfield, MA 01103-1749
(413) 732-2666
Fax: (413) 732-6466
Email: recruiters@foodmanagementsearch.com
Web: www.foodmanagementsearch.com

Summary: Contingency firm specializing in recruiting food industry, management and technical career professionals in the areas of food manufacturing, supermarket and distribution, food service, restaurant, culinary, hotel food & beverage and CPG sales & marketing.

Key Contact - Specialty:
Mr. Joseph V. Cresci, President - *Consumer (Packaged Goods), Distribution, Food, Manufacturing, Supermarkets*

Salary Minimum: $75,000

Functions: Management, Senior Mgmt., Plant Mgmt., Purchasing, Mktg. Mgmt., Sales Mgmt., HR Mgmt., Finance, Engineering, Int'l.

Industries: Manufacturing, Food, Bev., Tobacco, Consumer Goods, Wholesale, Retail, Hospitality, Hotels, Resorts, Clubs, Restaurants, Quick Service Restaurants, Full Service Restaurants, Inst./Industrial Food Svc., Entertainment, Recreation

FOODPRO Recruiters Inc

14526 Jones Maltsberger Rd Ste 210
San Antonio, TX 78247-3749
(210) 494-9272
Fax: (210) 494-9662
Email: msoulek@foodprorecruiters.com
Web: www.foodprorecruiters.com

Summary: Our firm specializes in food, pharmaceutical and consumer products manufacturing recruitment. Candidates without experience in these areas should not apply. We work on projects for engineers, supervisors, quality control, operations, R&D, logistics, distribution, maintenance, etc.

Key Contact - Specialty:
Mr. Michael Soulek, President & General Manager - *Food, Pharmaceutical*

Salary Minimum: $50,000

Functions: Generalist (All), Mfg., Product Dev., Production, Plant Mgmt., Quality, Distribution, Packaging, Engineering, Minorities/Diversity

Industries: Manufacturing, Food, Bev., Tobacco, Medical Devices, Consumer Goods, Packaging

Forbes & Company Executive Search

7088 Stonebridge Rd
Newburgh, IN 47630-1706
(812) 853-9325
Fax: (812) 853-2841
Email: kforbes@aol.com
Web: www.jobsforadpros.com

Summary: We provide executive search and professional staffing in a broad range of industries with special emphasis in advertising, advertising agencies and marketing disciplines.

Key Contact - Specialty:
Mr. Kenneth P. Forbes, President - *Advertising*
Ms. Kay Koob Forbes, Vice President - *Advertising, Market research, Media*

Salary Minimum: $30,000

Functions: Generalist (All), Management

Industries: Printing, Advertising, Publishing, New Media, Broadcast, Film

Forbes & Gunn Consultants Ltd

505-1168 Hamilton St
Vancouver, BC V6B 2S2
Canada
(604) 484-4715
Fax: (604) 648-8480
Email: info@forbes-gunn.com
Web: www.forbes-gunn.com

Summary: Our firm specializes in IT recruiting and contract consulting. We do permanent, contract to hire, and contractor only

Key Contact - Specialty:
Mr. David Crouch, Executive Recruiter - *Computers (Software), Consulting*

Salary Minimum: $25,000

Functions: Generalist (All), Board Members

Industries: E-commerce, IT Implementation, Telecoms, Telephony, Digital, Wireless, Network Infrastructure, Software, Database SW, Development SW

Forbes Worldwide

468 N Camden Dr
Beverly Hills, CA 90210-4507
(310) 859-1396
Email:
internationheadquarters@forbesworldwide.com
Web: forbesworldwide.com

Summary: We are the premier executive search and consulting firm providing global solutions. Our firm is a frontrunner in recruitment for some of the world's most prestigious and sought-after companies including Global 1000, Euro Top 500, Fortune 500 and Inc. 500 Elite.

Key Contact - Specialty:
Mr. Charles Forbes

Salary Minimum: $100,000

Functions: Senior Mgmt.

Industries: Generalist (All), Manufacturing, Paper, Electronic, Elec. Components, Semiconductors, Media, Communications, Software, Biotech/Life Sciences, Healthcare

Ford & Associates Inc

808 Green Bay Trl
Myrtle Beach, SC 29577-2630
(843) 497-5350
Email: fordsearch@msn.com
Web: www.fordsearch.com

Summary: We are a confidential recruiting & search firm servicing the hospitality; commercial bakery, food & meat processing; retail; medical services; as well as the textile, plastics, metal assembly, OEM, and fabrication manufacturing industries. Within manufacturing we recruit engineers, operations management and staff professionals. We do not recruit in information technology.

Key Contact - Specialty:
Mr. Travis Ford, President
Mrs. Merlin B. Ford, Consultant

Salary Minimum: $45,000

Functions: Management, Mfg., Product Dev., Production, Plant Mgmt., Materials, HR Mgmt., Finance, Engineering, Textile/Fashion

Industries: Generalist (All), Manufacturing, Food, Bev., Tobacco, Textiles, Apparel, Chemicals, Drugs Mfg., Medical Devices, Plastics, Rubber, Metal Products, Machine, Appliance, Motor Vehicles, Consumer Goods, Retail, Services, Accounting, Engineering Svcs., Supply Chain Mgmt, Hospitality, Restaurants, Environmental Svcs., Packaging, Healthcare

Forest People International Search Ltd

800-1100 Melville St
SunLife Plaza
Vancouver, BC V6E 4A6
Canada
(604) 669-5635
Fax: (604) 684-4972
Email: people@forestpeople.com
Web: www.forestpeople.com

Summary: We are a personnel recruiting firm, serving all sectors of the forest industry. We recruit executive, operational management, professional, and technical personnel for a large client group of forest industry companies. We offer competent, cost effective recruiting services by knowledgeable forest industry specialists.

Key Contact - Specialty:
Mr. Ronald J. Hogg, President - *Forest industry/products, Senior management*
Mr. Bill Waschuk, Senior Consultant - *Forest industry/products*

Functions: Generalist (All)

Industries: Agri., Forestry, Mining

Forrest Edwards Group Ltd

12 E 41st St Fl 3
New York, NY 10017-7206
(212) 986-3600
Fax: (212) 557-2753
Email: info@forrestedwards.com
Web: www.forrestedwards.com

Summary: IT executive search, selection and strategic resourcing services including outsourcing and project management.

Key Contact - Specialty:
Mr. Thomas Edwards, President
Mr. Mark Hermansen, Manager, Client Services

Salary Minimum: $100,000

Functions: IT

Industries: Generalist (All)

A W Forrester Company

7310 W McNab Rd Ste 207
Tamarac, FL 33321-5328
(954) 722-7554
Fax: (954) 722-8821
Email: info@awforrester.com
Web: www.awforrester.com

Summary: We are a full-service executive search firm that accepts both contingency and retained search assignments. Our areas of specialty include health care, insurance, actuarial, underwriting and employee benefits.

Key Contact - Specialty:
Mr. Ken Forrester, Managing Director
Mr. Keneth Moore, Recruiter
Mr. Scott Fairbrother, Recruiter

Salary Minimum: $40,000

Functions: Senior Mgmt., HR Mgmt., Benefits, Mgmt. Consultants

Industries: Mgmt. Consulting, HR Services, Insurance, HR SW, Healthcare

Forsyte Associates Inc

129 Hampton Rd , Ste 2
Sharon, MA 02067-3203
(781) 344-8600
Fax: (617) 848-8947
Email: recruiters@forsyte.com
Web: www.forsyte.net (employers)
www.forsyte.com (candidates)

Summary: We specialize in executive search and recruiting services for the application software and IT industries, with a focus in sales and management positions. We offer in-depth knowledge of these industries and an extensive national network of qualified sales, management and C-level executives as well as technical sales consultants.

Key Contact - Specialty:
Mr. Mark Wolbarst, President & Principal Executive Recruit - *Computers (Software), CRM, ERP, Executives, Sales*
Ms. Lynn Reale, Website & Database Management - *Business to business, Computers (Software), Database (Administration), E-business, High technology*
Mr. David Wolbarst, Executive Recruiter - *Computers (Software), CRM, Information Technology, Professional services, Sales*
Mr. Michael Johnson, Executive Recruiter - *Business to business, Computers (Sales), E-business, Information Technology, Sales*

Salary Minimum: $60,000

Functions: Management, Senior Mgmt., Sales & Mktg., Mktg. Mgmt., Sales Mgmt., Sales Reps., e-HR, IT

Industries: HR Services, E-commerce, IT Implementation, Software, Accounting SW, Database SW, ERP SW, HR SW, Industry Specific SW, Mfg. SW, Networking, Comm. SW, Security SW, System SW

The Fortus Group

(also known as Dialysis Recruiting Specialists)
181 Genesee St Ste 600
Utica, NY 13501-2172
(315) 768-3322
(888) 387-3625
Fax: (315) 768-4349
Email: mauriz@dialysisjobs.com
Web: www.dialysisrecruiting.com

Summary: We are the dialysis-recruiting specialists and are committed to the highest standard of locating, recruiting and placing renal professionals at all levels of employment both clinically and in business.

Key Contact - Specialty:
Mr. Michael Maurizio, President
Mr. Cesar Puzon, Account Executive
Ms. Jennifer Viti, Account Executive
Mr. Andrew Lawrence, Operations Manager
Mr. Victor Gerace, Account Executive
Mr. James Mineo, Account Executive
Ms. Kelly Winder, Account Executive
Ms. Jessie Cerminaro, Account Executive - *Finance, Tax*
Mr. John Paoni, Account Executive
Mr. Michael Caiola, Project Coordinator
Ms. Barbara Mariano, Account Executive

Functions: Healthcare

Industries: Services, Healthcare, Hospitals, Long-term/Home Care

Forum Personnel Inc

260 Madison Ave Ste 200
New York, NY 10016-2401
(212) 687-4050
Email: info@forumper.com
Web: www.forumpersonnel.com

Summary: Areas of specialization include accounting, finance, HR, marketing/sales and IT. We offer permanent and temp consultant placement.

Key Contact - Specialty:
Mr. Frank Fusaro, President

Salary Minimum: $30,000

Functions: Generalist (All), Advertising, Mktg. Research, Benefits, Staffing, CFOs, Cash Mgmt., MIS Mgmt.

Industries: Generalist (All), Misc. Mfg., Finance, Accounting, Media, Advertising

Foster & Associates

PO Box 343
Watertown, WI 53094-0343
(920) 206-6030
Fax: (920) 206-6029
Web: www.jdfoster.net

Summary: Foster & Associates recognizes that your company's most important investment for future growth lies in locating and hiring only capable, talented people. Foster & Associates are specialists in the recruitment and placement of professionals within the Chemical Industry. We specialize in placing top quality people in Sales, Marketing, Manufacturing, Engineering, Research & Development, and Executive Level positions. We are committed to finding the right person for each position at every level, to help your company exceed its business goals.

Key Contact - Specialty:
Mr. J. D. Foster, Owner & Operator

Functions: Senior Mgmt.

Industries: Chemicals

The Foster McKay Group

30 Vreeland Rd
Florham Park, NJ 07932-1904
(973) 966-0909
Fax: (973) 966-6925
Email: careers@fostermckaynj.com
Web: www.fostermckay.com

Summary: We recruit on assignments, contingency and retained, within corporate finance, strategic planning, financial planning and analysis, corporate development, treasury, accounting and reporting, management consulting, internal audit and tax.

Key Contact - Specialty:
Mr. Allen Galorenzo, Vice President - *Finance*

Salary Minimum: $60,000

Functions: Senior Mgmt., Finance, CFOs, Budgeting, Cash Mgmt., Taxes, M&A

Industries: Generalist (All)

Foster, McMillan & Company

(a division of Intromation Inc)
24W500 Maple Ave Ste 209
Naperville, IL 60540-6057
(630) 778-7081
(800) 942-2378
Fax: (630) 778-7092
Email: petershea@fostermcmillan.com
Web: www.fostermcmillan.com

Summary: Placement limited exclusively to attorneys with our clients which include law firms and corporations.

Key Contact - Specialty:
Mr. Eugene B. Shea, President
Mr. Peter E. Shea, Vice President
Ms. Patricia A. Sarlas, Vice President

Functions: Legal

Industries: Legal

Foundation Networks

1604 8th Ave S
Nashville, TN 37203-5061
(650) 331-1962
Email: john@foundation-networks.net
Web: www.foundation-networks.net

Summary: Our firm is a professional staffing firm for executives and technical engineering roles in technology based companies. We focus on senior engineering roles in the software and hardware space and management level opportunities in product marketing/management and technical sales roles.

Key Contact - Specialty:
Mr. John Owen, President & Chief Executive Officer

Functions: Senior Mgmt., Engineering

Industries: Computer Equip., Electronic, Elec. Components, Semiconductors, E-commerce, Telephony, Digital, Wireless, Fiber Optic, Network Infrastructure, Database SW, Development SW, Entertainment SW, ERP SW, Networking, Comm. SW, Security SW, System SW

Fox Interlink Partners

PO Box 575
Pine, CO 80470-0575
(303) 838-1900
Email: foxip@earthlink.net

Summary: We offer permanent placement recruitment. Our firm specializes in wireless communications, telecommunications, and the medical industry. We place middle to upper level management. We place talent in several arenas to include sales, marketing, engineering, finance, HR, customer service & operations.

Key Contact - Specialty:
Ms. Cheryl Fox, President - *Medical, Medical (Devices,Sales), Telecommunications, Wireless*

Salary Minimum: $40,000

Functions: Management, Senior Mgmt., Middle Mgmt., Sales & Mktg., Advertising, Mktg. Mgmt., Sales Mgmt., HR Mgmt., Finance, CFOs

Industries: Medical Devices, Consumer Elect., Communications, Telecoms, Call Centers, Wireless

J R Fox Recruiters

PO Box 938
New Monmouth, NJ 07748-0938
(732) 671-7540
Fax: (732) 957-0139
Email: jrfoxrecruiters@comcast.net

Summary: Specializes in sales, marketing and operations positions for manufacturers and distributors in the pet product industry. We place the positions ranging from sales reps to CEOs.

Key Contact - Specialty:
Ms. J.R. Fox, President

Functions: Generalist (All), Senior Mgmt., Middle Mgmt., Product Dev., Purchasing, Sales & Mktg., Mktg. Mgmt., Sales Mgmt., Sales Reps.

Industries: Misc. Mfg., Non-Classifiable

FoxLight Ltd

20150 Tarawild Ct
Prunedale, CA 93907-1411
(831) 663-2999
Fax: (831) 663-1155
Email: paul@foxlight.com
Web: www.foxlight.com

Summary: We approach all of our projects in a systematic manner. Our recruiters work with your staff to establishing a map of your firms staffing efforts using the following steps: analysis, action, evaluation, follow-up and follow-through.

Key Contact - Specialty:
Mr. Paul Seaman, President
Ms. Candice Masters, Executive Recruiter

Functions: Generalist (All)

Industries: Engineering Svcs., Call Centers, Telephony, Accounting SW, Database SW, Development SW, Doc. Mgmt., Production SW, ERP SW, System SW, Biotech/Life Sciences

FPC of Fort Lauderdale

900 Bayberry Point Dr
Plantation, FL 33324-3507
(954) 473-9900
Fax: (954) 237-3143
Email: search@fpclauderdale.com

Summary: We offer recruiting and placement services for the pharmaceutical and biotechnology industries.

Key Contact - Specialty:
Mr. David Skiles, President
Ms. Karen Skiles, Vice President

Salary Minimum: $50,000

Functions: Generalist (All), Senior Mgmt., Middle Mgmt., Product Dev., Production, Quality, Sales & Mktg., Mktg. Mgmt., Sales Mgmt., R&D

Industries: Drugs Mfg., Pharm Svcs., Biotech/Life Sciences

FPC/Fortune of San Antonio

10924 Vance Jackson Rd Ste 303K
San Antonio, TX 78230-2559
(210) 690-9797
(800) 886-2608
Fax: (210) 696-6909
Email: fpcsat@fpcsat.com
Web: www.fpcsat.com

Summary: Our expertise has been assisting manufacturing/engineering professionals to build their careers, by recruiting and placing senior management to engineers, primarily in the medical, pharmaceutical, bio-technology, automotive, process and consumer products industries.

Key Contact - Specialty:
Mr. Jim Morrisey, CPC, Chief Executive Officer & President - *Biotechnology, Medical (Devices), Pharmaceutical, Quality, Regulatory*
Mr. Greg Buschmann, CPC, PHR, Vice President, Ops & Dir, Prcs Ind & HR - *Chemical, Engineering, Human resources, Manufacturing, Operations*
Mr. Warren Larson, Director, Medical Dvc, QA, RA & Engr - *Engineering, Manufacturing, Medical (Devices), Quality, Regulatory*
Mr. George Rodarte, Director, Maquiladora Recruiting - *Engineering, International, Manufacturing, Quality, Supply Chain*
Mr. Chris Kulvik, Director, Pharml & Biotech Recruiting - *Biotechnology, Engineering, Manufacturing, Pharmaceutical, Quality*

Salary Minimum: $50,000

Functions: Management, Middle Mgmt., Mfg., Product Dev., Automation, Plant Mgmt., Quality, HR Mgmt., Engineering

Industries: Manufacturing, Chemicals, Drugs Mfg., Medical Devices, Plastics, Rubber, Metal Products, Machine, Appliance, Motor Vehicles, Computer Equip., Consumer Elect., Test, Measure Equip., Misc. Mfg., Electronic, Elec. Components, Consumer Goods

Franchise Search Inc

48 Burd St Ste 101
Nyack, NY 10960-3225
(845) 727-4103
Fax: (845) 727-3918
Email: info@franchise-search.com
Web: www.franchise-search.com

Summary: We are a search firm dedicated exclusively to franchising. We represent only franchisor clients and we place only professional franchise management candidates in franchise sales, operations, training, marketing, legal, financial, real estate, construction and international development.

Key Contact - Specialty:
Mr. Douglas T. Kushell, President - *Hospitality*

Salary Minimum: $50,000

Functions: Generalist (All), Senior Mgmt., Middle Mgmt., Int'l.

Industries: Generalist (All), Hospitality, Real Estate, Non-Classifiable

Franklin Associates Inc

2061 SE Pyramid Rd
Port Saint Lucie, FL 34952-5827
(772) 219-0406
Fax: (772) 219-0860
Email: employ011@bellsouth.net

Summary: We are a boutique executive search firm with a national client base. A former VP of HR founded our firm and we are highly specialized and hands-on. Our industry specialties include real estate & development, hospitality, utilities, environmental services and financial services. Our functional specialties are HR, sales & marketing, finance and operations.

Key Contact - Specialty:
Mr. Frank (Bud) Gardner, Managing Partner - *Environmental, Finance, Hospitality, Human resources, Real estate*
Ms. Linda Brann, Vice President - *Hospitality*

Salary Minimum: $75,000

Functions: Generalist (All), Management, Senior Mgmt., Sales & Mktg., Sales Mgmt., HR Mgmt., Finance

Industries: Generalist (All), Energy, Utilities, Construction, Medical Devices, Motor Vehicles, Transportation, Banking, Accounting, Mgmt. Consulting, Hospitality, Hotels, Resorts, Clubs, Haz. Waste, Real Estate, Biotech/Life Sciences

The Franklin Career Group

51 Depot Rd Ste 200
Harwich, MA 02645-3341
(508) 430-9959
Fax: (978) 945-7871
Email: info@franklincareers.com
Web: www.franklincareers.com

Summary: We are an executive search firm that specializes in IT, operations and professional services. We also have a network of European affiliates. Our clients range from emerging companies to Fortune 500.

Key Contact - Specialty:
Mr. Frank A. Mainero, President & Chief Executive Officer - *Advertising, AS/400, Automotive, Banking (Commercial), Boards of Directors*
Mr. Luke Cantella, Principal & Senior Consultant - *Call centers, Computers (Software), Database, Database (Administration,Warehousing)*
Ms. Cathy McCoy, Founding Principal & VP, Recruiting - *Consumer (Marketing), Information Technology, Sales, Senior management*

Salary Minimum: $750,000

Functions: Management, Sales & Mktg., Mktg. Mgmt., Sales Mgmt., Sales Reps., HR Mgmt., Systems Dev., Systems Implem., DB Admin., Mgmt. Consultants

Industries: Manufacturing, Food, Bev., Tobacco, Drugs Mfg., Computer Equip., Consumer Goods, Banking, Mgmt. Consulting, Logistics Svcs., Supply Chain Mgmt., Advertising, Database SW, Development SW

Branches:
6863 Southport Dr
Boynton Beach, FL 33437-6915
(561) 735-7188
Key Contact - Specialty:
Mr. Ron Frates

3743 Sawgrass Dr
Titusville, FL 32780-5488
(321) 385-2157
Key Contact - Specialty:
Ms. Georgia Buckley, Consulting Director

3206 Fox Squirrel Ln
Valrico, FL 33594-8249
(813) 571-9636
Key Contact - Specialty:
Ms. Kathy Kanehl, Supervising Search Consultant

2101 Arden Dr
Monroe, NC 28112-6423
(704) 283-9378
Email: tharrill@franklincareers.com
Key Contact - Specialty:
Mr. Thirby Harrill, Senior Consultant

10606 Mount Tipton
San Antonio, TX 78213-1628
Key Contact - Specialty:
Mr. Troy Morlan, Senior Consultant - *401(K), Information Technology, Insurance, International, Marketing*

Franklin International Search Inc

PO Box 2566
Framingham, MA 01703-2566
(508) 788-1511
(508) 877-7103
Fax: (508) 788-1818
Email: franintl@rcn.com

Summary: We provide recruitment of technical/engineering, sales/marketing, manufacturing and quality control personnel for the aerospace/defense, optical networking/DWDM systems & components, semiconductor laser devices, optics/thin films, MEMS/MOEMS, data/telecom, OSS software, and data storage/recording fields.

Key Contact - Specialty:
Mr. Stanley L. Shindler, President - *Telecommunications, Wireless*

Salary Minimum: $80,000

Functions: Management, Board Members

Industries: Medical Devices, Test, Measure Equip., Semiconductors, Telecoms, Telephony, Wireless, Fiber Optic, Defense, Homeland Security, Aerospace, Networking, Comm. SW

Frazee Recruiting Consultants Inc

2351 Energy Dr Ste 1100
Baton Rouge, LA 70808-2618
(225) 231-7880
Fax: (225) 291-7887
Email: info@frazeerecruit.com
Web: www.frazeerecruit.com

Summary: We offer contingency search for accounting, IT, engineering, management and sales positions. We also offer contract and temp staffing in a variety of professional job categories.

Key Contact - Specialty:
Ms. Marianne Frazee, President & Owner - *Engineering*
Mr. Jeff Pruitt, Recruiter
Ms. Susie Hoffpauir, Recruiter

Salary Minimum: $22,000

Functions: Generalist (All), Mfg., Sales & Mktg., Finance, IT, Engineering

Industries: Generalist (All), Finance

Fred Stuart Consulting/Personnel Services

5855 E Naples Plz Ste 114
Long Beach, CA 90803-5077
(562) 439-0921
(888) 782-1384
Fax: (562) 439-4040
Email: resumes@fredstuart.com
Web: www.fredstuart.com

Summary: Our emphasis is in the employment and recruiting of IT professionals. We have also placed individuals with experience in HR, finance, accounting, general management, engineering, architecture, sales/marketing, etc. This may be accomplished by search, contingency or hourly projects. We have also provided services in the management of office buildings including renting space, maintaining facilities, remodeling and accounting support.

Key Contact - Specialty:
Mr. Fred Stuart, Owner

Salary Minimum: $20,000

Functions: Senior Mgmt., IT

Industries: Generalist (All), Non-profits, Accounting, Mgmt. Consulting, E-commerce, IT Implementation, PSA/ASP, Software, HR SW, Biotech/Life Sciences, Healthcare

Freeman Enterprises

10704 Marabou Ct
Raleigh, NC 27614-9052
(919) 846-1088
(919) 846-0993
Fax: (919) 676-5054
Email: lynnefreeman@nc.rr.com
Web: www.freeman-ent.com

Summary: We specialize in professional liability insurance positions. Claims, underwriting, marketing and risk management are the primary functional areas. Medical malpractice accounts for more than half of all placements. Other product lines: miscellaneous errors and omissions (E&O), directors and officers (D&O), employment practices liability (EPL), dental, lawyers (LPL), real estate, architects and engineers (A&E).

Key Contact - Specialty:
Ms. Lynne Freeman, Owner
Ms. Jackie Bullington, Vice President

Salary Minimum: $50,000

Functions: Generalist (All), Management, Senior Mgmt., Middle Mgmt., Product Dev., Nurses, Sales & Mktg., Risk Mgmt.

Industries: Insurance

Fresquez & Associates

PO Box 721238
San Diego, CA 92172-1238
(858) 538-4424
(858) 414-7564
Fax: (858) 538-4449

Email: ernesto@fresquez.com
Web: www.fresquez.com

Summary: Search firm that specializes in the recruitment of minority/diversity professionals, particularly strong in Hispanic community for bilingual professionals in accounting, auditing, finance, sales, marketing, management, HR, IT and engineering.

Key Contact - Specialty:
Mr. Ernesto Fresquez, Principal
Ms. Jeanette Acosta, Principal Consultant - *Banking (Investment), Biotechnology, Capital markets, Change management, Executives*

Salary Minimum: $50,000

Functions: Sales & Mktg., HR Mgmt., IT, Minorities/Diversity

Industries: Generalist (All)

Frey & Sher Associates Inc

1600 Prince St
Alexandria, VA 22314-2835
(703) 524-6500
Fax: (703) 524-6578
Email: info@freysher.com
Web: www.freysher.com

Summary: Attorney search specialists placing permanent lawyers in law firms, corporations, privately held business and government agencies. Advise law firms on merger and acquisition activity.

Key Contact - Specialty:
Ms. Florence Frey, Principal
Ms. Eileen Sher, Principal
Ms. Kate Gibbons, Managing Recruiter - *Communications, Management*
Ms. Patty Oldham, Recruiter

Salary Minimum: $130,000

Functions: Legal

Industries: Legal

Fristoe & Carleton Inc

77 Milford Dr
Hudson, OH 44236-2781
(330) 655-3535
Fax: (330) 655-3585
Email: fristcarl@adjob.com
Web: www.adjob.com

Summary: We are an executive search firm with extensive experience placing people in advertising agencies, public relations firms and sales promotion companies. Our principals worked extensively in the business so we have an excellent understanding of agency requirements whether it is account management, media, creative, public relations, direct, etc.

Key Contact - Specialty:
Mr. Jack Fristoe, President
Mr. Bob Carleton, Executive Vice President
Ms. Jill Grimm, Executive Recruiter
Ms. Tami Tam, Executive Recruiter

Salary Minimum: $30,000

Functions: Senior Mgmt., PR, Graphic Designers

Industries: Advertising

Peter Froehlich & Company

PO Box 339
Weatherford, TX 76086-0339
(800) 742-4947
Fax: (817) 594-1337
Email: pfsearch@flash.net
Web: www.flash.net/~pfsearch

Summary: Specializing in all levels of management positions for all disciplines within

the cable television and telecom industry. Clientele include operators and manufacturers.

Key Contact - Specialty:
Mr. Peter Froehlich, Chief Executive Officer
Ms. Karen Egeland, Office Manager
Mr. Mike Pask, Senior Consultant
Mr. Noel Egeland, Senior Consultant
Ms. Valerie Howard, Consultant

Functions: Generalist (All)

Industries: Media, Communications, Telecoms, Call Centers, Telephony, Digital, Wireless, Fiber Optic, Network Infrastructure

Front Line Solutions

6165 Lehman Dr Ste 203
Colorado Springs, CO 80918-5406
(719) 593-8232
(866) 357-5627
Email: mikemyers@flsolutions.net
Web: www.flsolutions.net

Summary: We are a direct placement and contract recruiting firm, specializing in placing prior military, DoD, defense and high-technology candidates.

Key Contact - Specialty:
Mr. Mike Myers, Owner
Mr. Edward Jones, Owner
Mr. Richard Harrold, Owner

Functions: Generalist (All), Management

Industries: Generalist (All), Computer Equip., Consumer Elect., Electronic, Elec. Components

The Fry Group Inc

369 Lexington Ave
New York, NY 10017-6506
(212) 557-0011
Email: folks@frygroup.com
Web: www.frygroup.com

Summary: Public relations, corporate communications, investor relations and marketing communications. Executive and middle management recruitment.

Key Contact - Specialty:
Mr. John M. Fry, CPC, President - *Public relations*

Salary Minimum: $35,000

Functions: PR

Industries: Generalist (All)

FSA Inc

6166 Talmadge Run NW
Acworth, GA 30101-9501
(770) 966-1101
Fax: (770) 966-1103
Email: info@fsasearch.com
Web: www.fsasearch.com

Summary: Executive search consultants to the property and casualty insurance industry. Specializing in actuaries and product managers.

Key Contact - Specialty:
Mr. Ron Biagini, CPC, President - *Actuarial, Insurance (Casualty, Property), Product management/development*

Salary Minimum: $75,000

Functions: Product Dev., Actuaries

Industries: Insurance, Casualty, Commercial, Re-Insurance

Fulcrum Search Science Inc

702-85 Richmond St W
Federal Building
Toronto, ON M5H 2C9
Canada
(416) 847-4990
(866) 409-4990
Fax: (416) 350-9600
Email: info@fulcrumsearchscience.com
Web: www.fulcrumsearchscience.com

Summary: We are a full-service search firm
covering finance/accounting, sales/marketing,
engineering/technical and general management
functions.

Key Contact - Specialty:
Mr. Bruce McAlpine, President

Salary Minimum: $55,000

Functions: Generalist (All)

Industries: Generalist (All)

S L Fults & Associates

14803 Hoya Ct Ste 201
Houston, TX 77070-2258
(281) 320-8315
Email: mail@slfults.com
Web: www.slfults.com

Summary: Executive search firm specializing in
e-business, IT to include: database analysts,
software development architects and project
management implementation specialists.

Key Contact - Specialty:
Ms. Sharon Fults

Salary Minimum: $65,000

Functions: IT

Industries: Accounting, Mgmt. Consulting, E-
commerce, IT Implementation, Network
Infrastructure, Software, Database SW,
Development SW, ERP SW, Security SW

Future Employment Service Inc

(also known as Sedona Staffing Services)
3392 Hillcrest Rd
Dubuque, IA 52002-3901
(563) 556-3040
Fax: (563) 556-3041
Email: carolt@careerpros.com
Web: www.careerpros.com

Summary: Women owned business with offices in
Iowa, Kansas, and Wisconsin. Full-service staffing
firm specializing in manufacturing professionals in
the areas of accounting, HR, engineers, supply
chain, biotechnology, and biotech sales.
Professional search and placement as well as
temporary staffing at all levels and disciplines.

Key Contact - Specialty:
Ms. Carol A. Townsend, CPC, President -
Engineering, Human resources, Operations

Salary Minimum: $35,000

Functions: Generalist (All), Mfg.

Industries: Generalist (All), Chemicals, Drugs
Mfg., Medical Devices, Plastics, Rubber, Misc.
Mfg., Accounting, HR Services, Environmental
Svcs., Biotech/Life Sciences

Branches:
3409 Cedar Heights Dr
Cedar Falls, IA 50613-6227
(319) 268-9204
Fax: (319) 268-9208
Email: job.cedarfalls@careerpros.com
Key Contact - Specialty:
Mr. Bryan Burton, Manager

2333 Blairs Ferry Rd NE
Cedar Rapids, IA 52402-1918
(319) 378-4487
Fax: (319) 378-4489
Email: crjobs@careerpros.com
Key Contact - Specialty:
Ms. Sharon Dralle, Area Manager - *Call centers,
Clerical, Industrial, Manufacturing*

2418 Virginia Ave
Clinton, IA 52732-7214
(563) 243-6788
Email: clinton@careerpros.com
Key Contact - Specialty:
Ms. Lori Susie, Manager - *Clerical, Industrial,
Manufacturing, Middle management, Office*

108 S Main St
Maquoketa, IA 52060-3034
(319) 652-5699
Fax: (319) 652-4206
Email: maquoketa@careerpros.com
Key Contact - Specialty:
Ms. Carri Gilson, Manager - *Clerical, Industrial,
Manufacturing, Sales*

330 Junction Rd
Madison, WI 53717-2612
(608) 664-9977
Fax: (608) 664-9978
Email: madison@careerpros.com
Key Contact - Specialty:
Ms. Carol Semenas, Manager

Futures Search Inc

1 Hampton Rd Unit 301
Exeter, NH 03833-4856
(603) 775-7800
Fax: (603) 775-7900
Email: info@futuressearch.com
Web: www.futuressearch.com

Summary: We specialize exclusively in the food
and consumer products industries to include food
service sales and marketing, consumer products,
manufacturing, and supermarket merchandising,
wholesalers and operations.

Key Contact - Specialty:
Mr. Thomas P. Colacchio, President - *Food
service, Sales*
Mr. Richard J. Mazzola, Vice President -
Supermarkets

Salary Minimum: $40,000

Functions: Generalist (All), Distribution, Sales &
Mktg., Mktg. Mgmt., Sales Mgmt., Direct
Mktg., Sales Reps., Finance, MIS Mgmt.,
Minorities/Diversity

Industries: Generalist (All), Food, Bev., Tobacco,
Hospitality

Gables Search Group Inc

37721 Vine St Ste 1
Willoughby, OH 44094-6256
(440) 951-9990
(800) 508-4225
Fax: (440) 951-9991
Email: info@gablessearch.com
Web: www.gablessearch.com

Summary: Our firm is a national employment
placement firm specializing in the areas of
accounting/finance, legal, management,
sales/marketing and technical personnel. Our
company can place an individual on a permanent
or temporary basis.

Key Contact - Specialty:
Mr. Michael Stuck, President - *Controllers,
Information Technology, Legal (Attorneys),
Management, Sales*
Mr. Lee Fierman, Senior Account Executive

Mr. Joe Rossi, Senior Recruiter - *Accounting
(General), Computers (Programming),
Engineering, Information Technology, Sales*
Mr. Keith Hawkins, Account Executive -
*Accounting, Banking (Mortgage), Information
Technology, Management, Safety*
Ms. Juli Williamson, Administrative Assistant -
*Executives, Food, Management, Marketing,
Sales*
Ms. Bonnie Kasik, Account Executive -
*Accounting, Executives, Finance, Human
resources, Sales*
Ms. Jan Bobo, Recruiter - *Accounting
(Bookkeeping), Administration, Information
Technology, Legal, Marketing*
Mr. Nathan Melamed, Sales Representative -
*Accounting, Engineering, Finance, Information
Technology, Legal*

Salary Minimum: $30,000

Functions: Generalist (All)

Industries: Construction, Manufacturing, Finance,
Services, Legal, Accounting, HR Services,
Telecoms, Call Centers, Software

The Gabor Group

1653 Merriman Rd Ste 211
Akron, OH 44313-5276
(330) 315-0126
Fax: (330) 865-9222
Email: kgi@gwis.com

Summary: We conduct executive search on a
contingency or retained basis for technical,
management and executive personnel. We
specialize in purchasing, sourcing, commodity
management, materials management, supply
chain, quality, Six Sigma and operations
management in manufacturing & service
industries.

Key Contact - Specialty:
Mr. Robert A. Gabor, President - *Human
resources, Purchasing, Quality*

Salary Minimum: $60,000

Functions: Senior Mgmt., Middle Mgmt., Mfg.,
Plant Mgmt., Quality, Materials, Purchasing,
Materials Plng.

Industries: Manufacturing, Printing, Medical
Devices, Plastics, Rubber, Metal Products,
Machine, Appliance, Motor Vehicles, Computer
Equip., Consumer Elect., Misc. Mfg.,
Electronic, Elec. Components, Consumer
Goods, Transportation, HR Services, Publishing,
Aerospace, Mfg. SW, Biotech/Life Sciences

Gabriel & Associates Inc

6630 Calico Woods Ln
Houston, TX 77041-7281
(713) 849-9412
Email: info@gabrielhr.com
Web: www.gabrielhr.com

Summary: We are a national executive recruiting
firm focused on the unique needs of financial
advisors nationwide. We have made placements
with some of the most selective employers on
Wall Street, including financial advisors,
producing sales managers, branch managers, sales
assistants and experienced trainees.

Key Contact - Specialty:
Ms. Heather Gabriel, PHR, President & Chief
Executive Officer - *Banking, Brokerage,
Finance, Financial services, Wall Street*
Mr. Jeff Cadieux, Vice President, Recruiting -
*Banking, Brokerage, Finance, Financial
services, Wall Street*
Mr. Damon Henson, Senior Recruiter - *Banking,
Brokerage, Finance, Financial services, Wall
Street*

Functions: Finance

Industries: Brokers

Gabriele & Company

2 Emery Rd
Bedford, MA 01730-1061
(781) 276-7999
Email: leslie@gabrieleandcompany.com
Web: www.gabrieleandcompany.com

Summary: We are recruiters for manufacturing and materials.

Key Contact - Specialty:
Ms. Leslie Gabriele, President - *Manufacturing, Materials*

Salary Minimum: $65,000

Functions: Mfg., Production, Quality, Materials, Purchasing, Materials Plng.

Industries: Generalist (All)

Galaxy Management Group

2 Penn Plz Rm 1500
New York, NY 10121-1590
(212) 292-5049
Email: info@galaxymgt.com
Web: www.galaxymgt.com

Summary: Ours is a full service executive recruiting firm. We offer permanent placement services, contract consulting services, right to hire consulting services, and career counseling and outplacement services.

Key Contact - Specialty:
Mr. James Sullivan, President
Ms. Maureen McManus, Executive Recruiter
Ms. Maureen King, Executive Recruiter

Salary Minimum: $50,000

Functions: Generalist (All), Sales & Mktg., IT

Industries: Generalist (All), Finance, Banking, Invest. Banking, Brokers, Mutual/Hedge Funds, Misc. Financial, Advertising, Publishing, New Media, Broadcast, Film, Accounting SW, Database SW, Development SW, HR SW, Industry Specific SW, Mfg. SW, Marketing SW, Networking, Comm. SW, Security SW, System SW

Galileo Search LLC

1140 Hightower Trl Ste 201
Atlanta, GA 30350-2988
(770) 552-2035 x101
Fax: (770) 552-2031
Email: healthjobs@galileosearch.com
Web: www.galileosearch.com

Summary: Our Clients: Outstanding Healthcare Professionals; Hospitals (100 - 1000+ beds); Long-Term Acute Care Facilities; Healthcare Organizations; Medical Device Companies; Fortune 500 Corporations Our Services: Recruitment / Permanent Placement; Specialized Search; Interim / Temporary Staffing Areas of Expertise: Acute Care Infection Control & Epidemiology; Clinical Microbiology / Laboratory; Clinical Nurse Specialists(CNS); Quality, Risk Management & Performance Improvement; Radiology / Diagnostic Imaging; Respiratory / Physical / Occupational Therapists; RN Clinical Nurse Management -

Key Contact - Specialty:
Mr. Jim Brown, President & Chief Talent Officer - *Healthcare, Medical, Medical (Devices,Sales)*
Mr. Edmund Rudell, Manager, Business Development & Search - *Healthcare, Medical, Medical (Devices,Sales)*

Functions: Healthcare, Nurses, Allied Health

Industries; Healthcare, Hospitals, Long-term/Home Care, Physical Therapy, Occupational Therapy

Gallant Search Group Inc (GSG)

PO Box 20086 RPO Byron
431 Boler Rd
London, ON N6K 4G6
Canada
(888) 663-1070
Fax: (888) 663-1074
Email: gallant@automotivecareers.com
Web: www.automotivecareers.com

Summary: Agency works with the automotive parts manufacturing community. No fee charged to applicants. Many years of success to offer all clients. We are an expert recruiter for materials, plant management, engineering, product design and quality.

Key Contact - Specialty:
Mr. Andrew Gallant, President

Salary Minimum: $50,000

Functions: Management, Middle Mgmt., Mfg., Product Dev., Production, Quality, Materials, Engineering

Industries: Manufacturing, Plastics, Rubber, Metal Products, Motor Vehicles, Consumer Elect., Misc. Mfg., Aerospace

Gallin Associates Inc

2777 Meadowview Ct
Tarpon Springs, FL 34688-7366
(727) 944-3300
Email: gallin@gallinassociates.com
Web: www.gallinassociates.com

Summary: We provide specialists in technical and managerial search for the chemical process, electronics, telecom and computer equipment semiconductor industries.

Key Contact - Specialty:
Mr. Lawrence Gallin, President - *Engineering, Management*

Salary Minimum: $50,000

Functions: Generalist (All)

Industries: Chemicals, Plastics, Rubber, Paints, Petro. Products

Branches:
1784 Alamanda Dr
Naples, FL 34102-5017
(239) 403-9210
Fax: (941) 403-9209
Email: stepler@gallinassociates.com
Key Contact - Specialty:
Mr. Paul Stepler, President - *Telecommunications*

Galloway & Associates Search Consultants Inc

1414-633 Bay St
Horizon On Bay
Toronto, ON M5G 2G4
Canada
(416) 969-8989
Email: glenn@gallowaysearch.com
Web: www.gallowaysearch.com

Summary: We have an engineer on staff and MIS experts, excellent business references, professional and thorough approach to searches.

Key Contact - Specialty:
Mr. Glenn Galloway, President
Ms. Catherine Pavlovich, Recruitment Professional

Salary Minimum: $50,000

Functions: Materials

Industries: Metal Products, Brokers, Telecoms, Aerospace, Packaging, Software

Gamen Group

804 S Main St Ste 3
Stowe, VT 05672-4650
(802) 253-0838
(888) 568-5727
Fax: (802) 253-7174
Email: nancygold@gamengroup.com
Web: www.gamengroup.com

Summary: Our firm specializes in the placement of management consultants with technology expertise. We focus on helping IT professionals in specific areas: ERP, (SAP & PeopleSoft), data warehouse/business intelligence, and enterprise application integration, architecture & network services, and web development.

Key Contact - Specialty:
Ms. Nancy Gold, President
Mr. Jeff Gauthier, Recruiter - *ERP, Information Technology, Management consulting, SAP*

Salary Minimum: $80,000

Functions: Mgmt. Consultants

Industries: Mgmt. Consulting, IT Implementation, Software, Database SW, Doc. Mgmt., Production SW, Entertainment SW, ERP SW, Industry Specific SW, Networking, Comm. SW, Security SW

GameRecruiter.com

401 E Las Olas Blvd Ste 130
Fort Lauderdale, FL 33301-2211
(866) 358-4263 x105
Fax: (866) 358-4219
Email: marc@gamerecruiter.com
Web: www.gamerecruiter.com

Summary: Staffed by game industry professionals who have been re-trained to recruit. We focus on the wireless, console, and PC interactive multimedia video games industry.

Key Contact - Specialty:
Mr. Marc Mencher, President

Functions: Management, Senior Mgmt, Middle Mgmt., Product Dev., Sales & Mktg., Mktg. Mgmt., Sales Mgmt., PR, Systems Dev., Graphic Designers

Industries: Entertainment, Entertainment SW

The Gammill Group Inc

9200 Worthington Rd Ste 101
Westerville, OH 43082-7802
(614) 848-7726
Fax: (614) 848-7738
Email: bgammill@gammillgroup.com
Web: www.gammillgroup.com

Summary: This firm is regarded for its service - taking a partnering approach to executive search; quality - consistently locating the best professionals and speed - agility in responding to customer's needs.

Key Contact - Specialty:
Mr. Robert A. Gammill, President
Mr. Michael Adams, Senior Executive Recruiter, Healthcare - *Accounting, Finance, HMOs, Hospital, Sales*
Mr. Jim Parsons, Senior Associate - *Accounting, Clinical, Finance, Hospital*

Salary Minimum: $40,000

Functions: Generalist (All), Management, Healthcare, Health Admin., Mktg. Mgmt., Sales Mgmt., CFOs, Systems Analysis, DB Admin.

Industries: Generalist (All), IT Implementation, Insurance, Healthcare, Hospitals

Gandin & Associates Inc

5518 Pinewood Springs Dr
Houston, TX 77066-2719
(281) 580-0700
Email: david_gandin@alumni.utexas.net

Summary: We service clients from all industries desiring professionals with accounting, tax, audit or financial experience. Many of our candidates are CPAs or MBAs with current or prior experience in public accounting, corporate accounting, corporate tax, corporate finance or financial analysis. Tax and financial reporting are two primary areas of specialization.

Key Contact - Specialty:
Mr. David L. Gandin, CPC, President -
*Accounting (Big
4,Bookkeeping,General,Public), Tax*

Salary Minimum: $45,000

Functions: Finance, CFOs, Budgeting, Taxes

Industries: Generalist (All)

Garb Jaffe & Associates Legal Placement LLC

12100 Wilshire Blvd Ste M90
Los Angeles, CA 90025-7100
(310) 207-0727
Fax: (310) 207-0470
Email: evejaffe@garbjaffe.com
Web: www.garbjaffe.com

Summary: Our firm is a legal placement firm, an industry leader that specializes in placing both partners and associates within law firms and corporations. All of our active recruiters are attorneys that graduated from top law schools. We work exclusively with attorneys.

Key Contact - Specialty:
Ms. Eve Jaffe, President
Ms. Sheila Garb, Vice President

Salary Minimum: $50,000

Functions: Attorneys

Industries: Generalist (All)

Branches:
2460 Grivel Pl
Tustin, CA 92782-1469
(714) 544-6622
Email: almersel@garbjaffe.com
Key Contact - Specialty:
Ms. Andrea Mersel, Executive Vice President

The Garret Group

23272 Mill Creek Dr Ste 260W
Laguna Hills, CA 92653-1657
(949) 215-7933
Fax: (949) 215-6836
Email: info@thegarretgroup.com
Web: www.thegarretgroup.com

Summary: We are dedicated to delivering professional recruiting solutions with emphasis on detail and integrity. Our aim is to consistently exceed client expectations, while recognizing our responsibility to assist candidates with individual career goals and objectives.

Key Contact - Specialty:
Ms. Marie Cravey, Principal

Functions: Generalist (All)

Industries: Computer Equip., Electronic, Elec. Components, Semiconductors, Consumer Goods, Services, Communications, Insurance, Software, Entertainment SW

The Garrison Organization

14225 University Ave Ste 206
Waukee, IA 50263-8294
(515) 309-4442
Fax: (509) 479-1213
Email: info@garrisonorg.com
Web: www.garrisonorg.com

Summary: Our firm is a retained executive search and selection firm serving the insurance and financial services industries.

Key Contact - Specialty:
Mr. Ed Garrison, President & Chief Executive Officer - *Financial services, Insurance (Life)*
Mr. Cory Garrison, Managing Partner - *Financial services, Insurance, Insurance (Life), Wholesale*
Mr. Jeff Garrison, JD, AIC, Managing Partner - *Insurance (Casualty,Claims,Property,Workers Compensation), Underwriting*
Ms. Mandy VanMaanen, Associate - *Insurance (Health,Property,Workers Compensation), Underwriting, Wholesale*

Salary Minimum: $50,000

Functions: Senior Mgmt., Middle Mgmt., Sales & Mktg., Mktg. Mgmt., Sales Mgmt., Mgmt. Consultants, Attorneys

Industries: Insurance, Casualty, Claims, Life, Commercial

Branches:
36 Washington St
Denver, CO 80203-4205
(303) 883-8279
Email: rgarrison@garrisonorg.com
Key Contact - Specialty:
Mr. Randy Garrison, CLU, Managing Partner - *Financial services, Insurance (Life)*

Garrison, Phillips & Israel Executive Search

1600 Bay Dr Ste 1000
Pleasantville, NJ 08232-2912
(609) 641-7945
Fax: (609) 641-7947
Email: gpisearch@aol.com
Web: biznet.maximizer.com/gpisearch

Summary: Our firm's practice is limited to the hospitality industry. We serve the nation's premiere hotels, resorts, conference centers, casino hotels, spas and CVBs. Recognized for impeccable ethical standards our award winning team thrives on solving our clients needs in highly competitive and tight markets.

Key Contact - Specialty:
Mr. Gary Israel, Managing Partner

Salary Minimum: $35,000

Functions: Senior Mgmt., Middle Mgmt., Sales & Mktg.

Industries: Hospitality

Richard Gast & Associates Ltd

20992 Bake Pkwy Ste 104
Lake Forest, CA 92630-2170
(949) 472-1130
Fax: (949) 472-0403
Email: dick@rgaltd.com
Web: www.rgaltd.com

Summary: We are a leader in the recruitment and placement of HR professionals. Serve a diversified clientele including many Fortune 500 corporations. Manage HR database of 25,000 plus.

Key Contact - Specialty:
Mr. Richard Gast, President - *Human resources*

Salary Minimum: $50,000

Functions: Generalist (All), HR Mgmt., Benefits, Staffing, Training

Industries: Generalist (All), Energy, Utilities, Manufacturing, Finance, Services, Insurance, Software

Gateway Group Personnel

1770 Kirby Pkwy Ste 216
Memphis, TN 38138-7405
(901) 756-6050
Fax: (901) 756-8445
Email: garen@gatewaypersonnel.com
Web: www.gatewaypersonnel.com

Summary: Contingent search firm with functional specialty in accounting, finance, auditing and banking. Serve Fortune 500 clients down through closely held entities.

Key Contact - Specialty:
Mr. Charles G. Haddad, Treasurer
Mr. Garen D. Haddad, Vice President - *Accounting, Accounting (Big 4,General), Banking, Finance*

Salary Minimum: $45,000

Functions: Management, Admin. Svcs., Sales Reps., Finance, CFOs, Budgeting, Architects

Industries: Generalist (All), Accounting

Gateway Strategy Group Inc

1153 Forest Ave
Bronx, NY 10456-5403
(212) 991-5536
Fax: (212) 876-8942
Email: gtwystrgygrp@aol.com
Web: www.gatewaystrategygroup.com

Summary: Our firm's mission is to open the channel of employment opportunity to qualified candidates. We attract, hire, and retain top talent. Even if you are satisfied with your present employment firm, it's always advisable to consider other staffing alternatives. Choosing the right placement firm will guarantee you a selection of the best candidates available for the position you wish filled.

Key Contact - Specialty:
Mr. Nelson Delerme, President - *Computers (Sales), Financial services, Healthcare, Investor relations, Systems (Analysts)*

Functions: Middle Mgmt., Nurses, Customer Svc., Finance, IT, Systems Support

Industries: Finance, Banking, Invest. Banking, Brokers, Mutual/Hedge Funds, Misc. Financial, Non-profits, Legal, Accounting, Call Centers, Network Infrastructure, Accounting SW, Database SW, Development SW, Doc. Mgmt., Production SW, Healthcare, Hospitals, Physical Therapy

Gatti & Associates

266 Main St Ste 21
Medfield, MA 02052-2019
(508) 359-4153
Fax: (508) 359-5902
Email: info@gattihr.com
Web: www.gattihr.com

Summary: Specialists in the placement of HR practitioners such as generalists, employment, compensation & benefits, training & development, college relations, EEO/AA, employee/labor relations or HRIS professionals in all industries.

Key Contact - Specialty:
Mr. Robert D. Gatti, President
Ms. Judith Banker, Principal
Mr. Richard Fleming, Vice President
Ms. Janet Mullert, Vice President
Ms. Irene Brousell, Vice President

Salary Minimum: $75,000

Functions: HR Mgmt., Benefits, Staffing, Training

Industries: Generalist (All)

GCB Executive Search

3653 Canton Rd Ste 106
Marietta, GA 30066-7601
(770) 517-9017
Fax: (770) 517-9016
Email: rcrtr@bellsouth.net
Web: www.gcbrcrtr.net

Summary: Real estate and healthcare finance are areas of specialization, both debt and equity. All structured finance, all debt-side analysis and business development.

Key Contact - Specialty:
Mr. G. Craig Baker, Proprietor - *Financial services*

Salary Minimum: $40,000

Functions: Generalist (All)

Industries: Finance, Banking, Invest. Banking, Venture Cap., Misc. Financial, Real Estate, Healthcare

Geller Braun & White Inc

PO Box 480113
Los Angeles, CA 90048-1113
(323) 965-8558
Email: hgeller@gbwscarch.com

Summary: We are a boutique recruiting firm specializing in executive placements in the high-technology, bio-technology, consumer products and manufacturing industries.

Key Contact - Specialty:
Mr. Henry Geller - *Hospitality*

Functions: Generalist (All)

Industries: Manufacturing, Medical Devices, Computer Equip., Consumer Elect., Electronic, Elec. Components, Semiconductors, HR Services, E-commerce, Telecoms, Biotech/Life Sciences

Gemini Executive Search Inc

11819 Coralberry Ct
Fort Wayne, IN 46814-4503
(260) 672-9785
Fax: (708) 401-1555
Email: afking1@hotmail.com
Web: www.geminies.com

Summary: We are a contingency search firm specializing in the permanent placement of middle to upper-management within the long-term healthcare and retirement living industries. Included is skilled nursing, independent and assisted living, continuing care retirement communities and alzheimer's.

Key Contact - Specialty:
Ms. Adrienne F. King, President

Salary Minimum: $45,000

Functions: Management, Senior Mgmt., Healthcare, Sales & Mktg., HR Mgmt., Finance, IT, MIS Mgmt., Mgmt. Consultants, Architects

Industries: Hospitality, Healthcare, Long-term/Home Care

General Search and Recruitment

209 W Jackson Blvd Ste 804
Chicago, IL 60606-6935
(312) 922-6664
Email: donna@gsr4you.com
Web: www.gsr4you.com

Summary: Our firm is committed to fulfilling the professional and executive staffing needs of our clients.

Key Contact - Specialty:
Mr. Mike McDonough, President

Functions: Generalist (All), Management, Board Members, Senior Mgmt., Middle Mgmt., Sales & Mktg., Mktg. Mgmt., Benefits, Finance

Industries: Insurance

Genesis Global Recruiting Inc

3350 SW 148th Ave Ste 110
Miramar, FL 33027-3237
(954) 433-5397
(800) 780-2232
Fax: (954) 433-8142
Email: tmeredith@genesis-global.com
Web: www.genesis-global.com

Summary: Our firm offers retained and contingency executive search services. We offer professional permanent placement within a multitude of various industries and a variety of different levels of positions.

Key Contact - Specialty:
Mr. Thomas Meredith, President & Chief Executive Officer
Ms. Anna Church-Meredith, Managing Partner - *Entertainment, Sales*
Ms. Deborah Johnson, Senior Executive Recruiter - *Information Technology, Management, Sales*

Salary Minimum: $24,000

Functions: Generalist (All)

Industries: Generalist (All), Manufacturing, Motor Vehicles, Finance, Services, Hospitality, Media, Communications, Insurance, Software

The Genesis Group

880 Lee St Ste 212
Des Plaines, IL 60016-6424
(847) 390-9968
Email: ewsiii@earthlink.net

Summary: Executive search for the financial services industry.

Key Contact - Specialty:
Mr. Edward W. Schnabel, III, President

Salary Minimum: $50,000

Functions: Generalist (All), Finance

Industries: Generalist (All), Banking, Invest. Banking, Venture Cap., Mutual/Hedge Funds, Misc. Financial

Genesis Recruiting

PO Box 2388
Granite Bay, CA 95746-2388
(916) 543-5363
Fax: (916) 660-1580
Email: genesisrec@aol.com

Summary: Specialize in placements of R&D professionals, technical service and process engineering. Typical placements are product development, technical service, applications chemistry, materials research, quality, analytical, and product characterizations. Senior management to entry level, all degrees, BS, MS and PhD. Specialties include adhesives, coatings, composites, ceramics, films, inks, paints, packaging and resins.

Key Contact - Specialty:
Mr. Jerry Kleames, Principal

Salary Minimum: $50,000

Functions: Generalist (All), Management, Product Dev., Quality, Materials, Packaging, Mktg. Research, R&D, Engineering, Process

Industries: Generalist (All), Paper, Printing, Chemicals, Medical Devices, Plastics, Rubber, Paints, Petro. Products, Fiber Optic, Packaging

Genesis Research

1520 Whetstone Ct
Wildwood, MO 63038-1356
(636) 273-6797
Fax: (636) 273-6799
Email: genesis211@earthlink.net
Web: www.genesisresearch.com

Summary: We are a contingency search/placement firm specializing in engineering, technical sales, marketing, management, technical service, R&D, plant engineering and management positions in the chemical, petroleum refining, metal finishing, metal working, water treatment, lubrication and power generation industry.

Key Contact - Specialty:
Mr. Dennis Lasini, Search Specialist - *Chemical, Refining*

Salary Minimum: $40,000

Functions: Product Dev., Production, Plant Mgmt., Sales & Mktg., Mktg. Mgmt., Sales Mgmt., Sales Reps., R&D, Engineering, Process

Industries: Energy, Utilities, Oil & Gas, Paper, Chemicals, Plastics, Rubber, Paints, Petro. Products, Metal Products, Test, Measure Equip.

Genie Matthews & Associates

1310 Raeford Rd Ste 4
Fayetteville, NC 28305-5026
(910) 484-4101
Fax: (910) 484-3272
Email: genie@gmarecruiters.com
Web: www.gmarecruiters.com

Summary: Specialized professional recruiting for industrial clients on a national basis. Industries include chemicals, pharmaceuticals, biotechnology, medical devices/products, polymers, plastics, aircraft and transportation. Positions include: engineering, chemists, scientists, management, financial/accounting, material/supply chain and sales.

Key Contact - Specialty:
Ms. Genie Matthews, President

Salary Minimum: $65,000

Functions: Production, Sales & Mktg., HR Mgmt., R&D, Engineering

Industries: Agri., Forestry, Mining, Manufacturing, Food, Bev., Tobacco, Chemicals, Soap, Perf., Cosmtcs., Drugs Mfg., Medical Devices, Plastics, Rubber, Paints, Petro. Products, Leather, Stone, Glass, Electronic, Elec. Components, Biotech/Life Sciences

Gent & Associates Inc

170 State St Ste 200
Los Altos, CA 94022-2831
(650) 917-9566
Email: info@gent-jobs.com
Web: www.gent-jobs.com

Summary: We are one of the leading executive search firms dedicated to providing available and experienced professionals. We have developed deep-rooted relationships with following industries: high technology, professional services, manufacturing, health care, biotechnology and pharmaceutical.

Key Contact - Specialty:
Mr. Gary Daugenti, Partner

Salary Minimum: $100,000

Functions: Management, Board Members

Industries: Manufacturing, Drugs Mfg., Medical Devices, Computer Equip., Retail, Finance, Mgmt. Consulting, E-commerce, IT Implementation, Communications, RF/Microwave, Government, Software, Biotech/Life Sciences

Robert George & Associates

2068 Rainbow Ave N Ste 765
Lake Havasu City, AZ 86403-4815
(928) 854-2828
Email: rga@frontiernet.net
Web: www.robgeo.com

Summary: Specialize in the recruitment, outplacement, contracting and alternate staffing of selective telecom and data processing personnel.

Key Contact - Specialty:
Mr. Fred Krafcik, CPC, Owner - *MIS, Telecommunications*

Salary Minimum: $50,000

Functions: Generalist (All), Management, Systems Analysis, Systems Dev., Systems Implem., Engineering

Industries: Generalist (All), Mgmt. Consulting, E-commerce, Engineering Svcs., Communications, Telecoms, Telephony, Digital, Wireless, Network Infrastructure, RF/Microwave, Database SW, Development SW, Mfg. SW, Networking, Comm. SW, Security SW

Gerdes & Associates

1300 Nicollet Ave Ste 3042
Minneapolis, MN 55403-2699
(612) 335-3553
Fax: (612) 335-3552
Email: rgerdes@att.com

Summary: We are recruiters for art directors, copywriters and designers for advertising agencies and companies.

Key Contact - Specialty:
Mr. Richard Gerdes, President

Salary Minimum: $25,000

Functions: Graphic Designers

Industries: Advertising

GFI Professional Staffing Services

127 Washington St
Keene, NH 03431-3106
(603) 357-3116
Fax: (603) 357-7818
Email: skendall@gfijobs.com
Web: www.gfijobs.com

Summary: We place the top 10 percent of talent, from entry level to the top tier of management, for a select group of corporations and businesses in New Hampshire and Vermont.

Key Contact - Specialty:
Ms. Susan V. Kendall, CPC, Chief Executive Officer - *Accounting, Banking, Insurance, Manufacturing, Sales*

Salary Minimum: $35,000

Functions: Generalist (All), Management, Admin. Svcs., Production, Plant Mgmt., Sales Mgmt., Customer Svc., Finance, Engineering

Industries: Generalist (All), Construction, Manufacturing, Lumber, Furniture, Paper, Chemicals, Medical Devices, Metal Products, Test, Measure Equip., Wholesale, Finance, Services, Accounting, HR Services, Engineering Svcs., Insurance, Casualty, Re-Insurance, Healthcare

GH&I Recruiting LLC

1200 Ashwood Pkwy Ste 300
Atlanta, GA 30338-4747
(770) 352-9374
Email: candidate@ghi-recruiting.com
Web: www.ghi-recruiting.com

Summary: We have access to leading CPAs, lawyers and financial experts who have helped build our network of talented professionals and hiring companies. We specialize in the placement of management level professionals in accounting and finance.

Key Contact - Specialty:
Ms. Lori Greene, Director, Recruiting

Functions: Management, Sales & Mktg., Mktg. Mgmt., Sales Mgmt., Finance, Taxes

Industries: Generalist (All), Finance, Accounting

GHP Consultants Inc

PO Box 1152
Colleyville, TX 76034-1152
(817) 318-7690
Fax: (817) 545-4981
Web: www.ghpconsultants.com

Summary: We specialize recruiting and placing insurance and legal professionals in the Dallas/Fort Worth Metroplex, Houston, across Texas and the United States.

Key Contact - Specialty:
Mr. Geoff Parr, Recruiter
Mr. James Crowley, Recruiter

Functions: Management, Board Members, Senior Mgmt.

Industries: Legal, Insurance, Casualty, Claims, Commercial, Re-Insurance

Gibson & Associates Inc

999 3rd Ave Ste 3800
Seattle, WA 98104-4023
(206) 224-3782
Fax: (425) 401-1153
Email: cj@gibsonasso.com
Web: www.gibsonasso.com

Summary: Financial executive recruiting firm specializing in CPAs.

Key Contact - Specialty:
Ms. Kristy Gibson, CPA, President
Ms. Carolyn Johnson, Vice President

Salary Minimum: $50,000

Functions: Senior Mgmt., Finance, CFOs, Budgeting, Cash Mgmt.

Industries: Generalist (All)

Gibson Technology & Engineering Associates

PO Box 1668
Marietta, GA 30061-1668
(770) 565-3433
Fax: (770) 565-2655
Email: ehs@gtea.net

Summary: This firm specializes in identifying and recruiting high-achieving candidates in the fields of safety, environmental, industrial hygiene and ergonomics. Principal owner is a safety professional, management consultant and experienced search executive.

Key Contact - Specialty:
Mr. Charles Gibson, CSP, Consultant

Functions: Management, Health & Safety

Industries: Agri., Forestry, Mining, Energy, Utilities, Construction, Manufacturing, Transportation, Wholesale, Retail, Aerospace, Packaging, Insurance

Gilbert Consulting Services Inc

PO Box 2226
Pismo Beach, CA 93448-2226
(805) 481-5105
Fax: (805) 481-7982
Email: keith@gcservices.com
Web: www.gcservices.com

Summary: Our firm is an award winning search firm. We are currently on contract with dozens of the elite electronics, defense, nuclear, energy and high technology companies. We specialize in the electronics, manufacturing, electronic design software, defense electronics, nuclear power, energy, printed circuit board, and semiconductor industries.

Key Contact - Specialty:
Mr. Keith A. Gilbert, President - *Electronics, Manufacturing*
Ms. Mary Gilbert, Manager

Functions: Generalist (All)

Industries: Generalist (All), Energy, Utilities, Machine, Appliance, Test, Measure Equip., Electronic, Elec. Components, Consumer Goods, Defense

Joe Giles Staffing Company

18105 Parkside St Ste 14
Detroit, MI 48221-2792
(313) 864-0022
Fax: (313) 864-8351
Email: gilesjobs@msn.com
Web: www.joegilesstaffing.com

Summary: Placement areas: we recruit and staff in healthcare and medical placement. We place physicians, pharmacists, RNs, CRNAs, medical physics, radiation oncology physics, physician assistant and nuclear medical technologists. The main areas of emphasis are to hospitals, clinics, retail, long-term, and pharmaceutical companies. We are the leader in direct-hire and contract placement of healthcare and medical professionals.

Key Contact - Specialty:
Mr. Joe L. Giles, Owner - *Engineering*
Ms. Valerie Gamache, Recruiter - *Engineering*

Salary Minimum: $50,000

Functions: Healthcare, Physicians, Nurses

Industries: Generalist (All), Pharm Svcs., Healthcare

Gillard Associates

202 Bussey St
The Gillard Building
Dedham, MA 02026-2512
(781) 329-4731
Fax: (781) 329-1357
Email: gillard@gillardlegal.com

Summary: We are a legal placement firm. We place attorneys, paralegals and legal secretaries. We follow strict ethical guidelines; firm founded to serve legal community.

Key Contact - Specialty:
Ms. Cheryl A. Gillard, President - *Legal*

Functions: Attorneys, Paralegals

Industries: Generalist (All)

D Gillespie & Associates Inc

207 Poplar Ave
Devon, PA 19333-1390
(610) 971-2074
Email: dgillassoc@comcast.net

Summary: We are focused on retained and high-level contingency search assignments. We specialized in IS/IT, sales & marketing and finance, with emphasis on small to mid-sized companies in the technology sector. Most of our clients would fall in the Fortune 500-1000 category or start-up/early phase.

Key Contact - Specialty:
Mr. David D. Gillespie, President & Principal - *General management*

Salary Minimum: $80,000

Functions: Senior Mgmt., Middle Mgmt., Sales & Mktg., IT

Industries: Manufacturing, Finance, Services, Mgmt. Consulting, E-commerce, IT Implementation, Communications, Network Infrastructure, Insurance, Software, ERP SW, Networking, Comm. SW, Biotech/Life Sciences, Healthcare

JP Gilmore & Associates

1387 Fairport Rd Ste 560
Fairport, NY 14450-2002
(585) 388-3110 x120
Email: jpg@jpgilmore.com
Web: jpgilmore.com

Summary: Our firm is an executive search firm that specializes in recruiting engineers, technical professionals, and sales and marketing executives for the semiconductor, microprocessor and software industries. Dedicated to the technology sector; the firm has several exclusive relationships with the most prominent companies in the technology sector.

Key Contact - Specialty:
Mr. John Gilmore, Director

Salary Minimum: $80,000

Functions: Engineering

Industries: Computer Equip., Consumer Elect., Test, Measure Equip., Electronic, Elec. Components, Digital, Wireless, RF/Microwave

Gimbel & Associates

201 NE 2nd St
Fort Lauderdale, FL 33301-1037
(954) 525-7000
Fax: (954) 525-7300
Email: mgimbel@gimbel.net

Summary: Low profile, established, respected, successful firm. Our firm has an excellent ability to recruit and place strong talent.

Key Contact - Specialty:
Mr. Mike Gimbel, President

Salary Minimum: $45,000

Functions: Generalist (All), Healthcare, Finance, CFOs, Cash Mgmt., Taxes, M&A, IT, Mgmt. Consultants, Attorneys

Industries: Generalist (All), Banking, Accounting, Mgmt. Consulting, Hospitality, Telecoms

GK & K Associates

1409 Hunters Branch Rd
Antioch, TN 37013-5110
(615) 333-7782
Fax: (615) 333-6656
Email: rfeldser@bellsouth.net

Summary: An experienced and proven recruitment/placement firm that specializes in the healthcare industry. We create a partnership with our clients that enhances the total recruiting efforts.

Key Contact - Specialty:
Mr. Richard J. Feldser, President - *Healthcare, Hospital, Human resources, Management consulting*

Functions: Generalist (All), Healthcare

Industries: Mgmt. Consulting, HR Services, Healthcare, Hospitals, Long-term/Home Care

Lawrence Glaser Associates Inc

505 S Lenola Rd Ste 128
Moorestown, NJ 08057-1549
(856) 778-9500
Fax: (856) 778-4390
Email: larryg@lgasearch.com
Web: www.lgasearch.com

Summary: We offer executive recruitment for sales and marketing managers in grocery, food, consumer, beverage, confectionary, non-food, HBC, and consumer durable products categories, including various services that are sold specifically into those industries.

Key Contact - Specialty:
Mr. Larry Glaser, President - *Consumer, Consumer (Packaged Goods), Food & beverage, Groceries, Sales*
Ms. Arlene Blumenthal, Systems Coordinator - *Food, Food & beverage, Groceries, Hardware, Housewares*
Ms. Nancy King, Researcher

Salary Minimum: $85,000

Functions: Sales & Mktg., Mktg. Mgmt., Sales Mgmt.

Industries: Food, Bev., Tobacco, Textiles, Apparel, Lumber, Furniture, Paper, Soap, Perf., Cosmtcs., Leather, Stone, Glass, Consumer Elect., Mgmt. Consulting, Advertising, Telecoms, Marketing SW

J H Glass & Associates

(also known as Glass Associates Achievers Inc, a Glasford Int)
PO Box 1015
Bala Cynwyd, PA 19004-5015
(215) 877-0101
(610) 975-0400
Email: info@glassassociates.com
Web: www.glassassociates.com

Summary: Executive search consultants with specialties in health care, finance, electronics, building products, manufacturing, fabrication, IT, pharmaceuticals, medical and engineering. We specialize in management and executive leadership. We are known for technological expertise and profound influence in sales & marketing. We also provide staff development and evaluation and other HR functions.

Key Contact - Specialty:
Mr. Jay H. Glass, President
Mr. David F. Simons, Vice President - *Building products*
Mr. Hal Gorden, Director - *Electronics*
Mr. James Stambaum, General Management
Mr. Larry Leighter, General Management, Financial
Ms. Ellen Worth, Manufacturing & Human Resources

Salary Minimum: $60,000

Functions: Management, Senior Mgmt., Mfg., Quality, Productivity, Materials, Physicians, Sales & Mktg., Sales Mgmt., Direct Mktg.

Industries: Construction, Drugs Mfg., Medical Devices, Plastics, Rubber, Leather, Stone, Glass, Metal Products, Electronic, Elec. Components, Robotics, Consumer Goods, Wholesale, Finance, Invest. Banking, Brokers, Venture Cap., Misc. Financial, Non-profits, Architectural

Svcs., Pharm Svcs., Mgmt. Consulting, HR Services, IT Implementation, Engineering Svcs., Logistics Svcs., Telecoms, RF/Microwave, Defense, Compliance, Aerospace, Database SW, Development SW, ERP SW, HR SW, Healthcare, Hospitals, Long-term/Home Care, Physical Therapy, Occupational Therapy

Branches:
290 Avon Rd
Devon, PA 19333-1360
(610) 975-0400

The Glennon Group

N25W23314 Paul Rd
Pewaukee, WI 53072-4060
(314) 542-6133
Email: tgg@sbcglobal.net

Summary: Specializes in mid to senior level searches in a variety of industries. We work on a combination of retained and contingency searches.

Key Contact - Specialty:
Mr. William G. Mueller, Owner

Salary Minimum: $75,000

Functions: Management

Industries: Construction, Manufacturing, Lumber, Furniture, Drugs Mfg., Medical Devices, Banking, Equip Svcs., Engineering Svcs., Logistics Svcs., Packaging

The GlenOaks Group Inc

10607 Taylor Farm Ct Ste 100
Prospect, KY 40059-9580
(502) 412-8774
Fax: (502) 412-1883
Email: jobs@glenoaksgroup.com
Web: www.glenoaksgroup.com

Summary: We are executive search consultants specializing in the recruitment of senior level sales & marketing personnel in the telecom and IT industry sectors.

Key Contact - Specialty:
Mr. John Siewertsen, President - *Telecommunications*
Mr. Roger Harris, Executive Search Consultant
Ms. Janice Smith, Executive Vice President - *Internet*

Salary Minimum: $75,000

Functions: Generalist (All)

Industries: Medical Devices, Computer Equip., Test, Measure Equip., New Media, Communications, Software, Networking, Comm. SW, Security SW, Biotech/Life Sciences

Global Career Services Inc

555 5th Ave Fl 8
New York, NY 10017-9266
(212) 599-6769
Fax: (212) 599-4684
Email: info@globalcareers.com
Web: www.globalcareers.com

Summary: We are one of the oldest targeted recruitment portals on the internet. We offer targeted search capabilities for both employers and job seekers in a number of vertical specialties. These include: accounting, finance, healthcare, legal services and transportation. We offer free trials subscriptions to new subscribers.

Key Contact - Specialty:
Mr. Frank Jones, Chairman

Salary Minimum: $25,000

Functions: Mfg., Materials, Healthcare, Sales & Mktg., HR Mgmt., Finance, IT, Engineering, Legal, Hospitality

Industries: Generalist (All)

Branches:
1 Dock St Ste 412
Stamford, CT 06902-5897
(203) 327-5700
Fax: (203) 353-1305
Email: tragland@globalcareers.com
Key Contact - Specialty:
Mr. William Cerynik, Managing Director

Global Consulting Group Inc

195 Main St N
Markham, ON L3P 1Y4
Canada
(905) 472-9677
Email: infoweb@globalrecruit.com
Web: www.globalrecruit.com

Summary: We are a technology recruitment firm with affiliated groups to service the specialized needs of clients in IT, sales/marketing, engineering, scientific, and executive search requirements.

Key Contact - Specialty:
Ms. Patricia Conlin, President - *Executives, HVAC, Information Technology, Marketing, Sales*
Ms. Nancy Chapman, Director, Strategic Accounts - *Environmental, Executives, Information Technology, Real estate, Sales*
Mr. Ron Beck, Director, Client Services - *Engineering, Executives, Information Technology*
Mr. Bill Johnson, Director, Operations
Ms. Gail Chambers, Manager, Recruitment - *Biopharmaceutical, Information Technology, Marketing, Pharmaceutical, Sales*
Ms. Shelley Millman, Manager, Client Services - *Embedded microprocessor, Engineering, Information Technology*
Mr. Asif Nakhuda, Senior Consultant, IT & Technology

Functions: Generalist (All), Board Members, Senior Mgmt., Sales & Mktg., IT, MIS Mgmt., Systems Dev., Engineering

Industries: Generalist (All), Finance, IT Implementation, Telecoms, Call Centers, Wireless, Property/Facility Mgmt., Software, Development SW, ERP SW, HR SW, Marketing SW, Networking, Comm. SW, Biotech/Life Sciences

Global Derivatives Search (GDS)

(also known as Capital Markets Executive Search Inc)
3646 E Ray Rd Ste 16 PMB 1658
Phoenix, AZ 85044-7116
(480) 706-8735
Fax: (480) 706-9310
Email: cmes@gds-usa.com
Web: www.gds-usa.com

Summary: We are an executive search agency specializing in the placement of financial experts working in the major money centers and markets. We dedicate our business to servicing a select number of leading firms with a focus on sell-side banks engaged in capital markets, treasury and securities businesses. Product support is in foreign exchange, fixed income and equity.

Key Contact - Specialty:
Mr. Kenny Blonder, President - *Financial services*

Salary Minimum: $75,000

Functions: Middle Mgmt.

Industries: Finance, Banking, Invest. Banking, Brokers, Mutual/Hedge Funds, Misc. Financial

Branches:
4065 Quakerbridge Rd Ste 101
Princeton Junction, NJ 08550-5200
(609) 919-0250
Fax: (480) 706-9310
Email: cmes@gds-usa.com
Key Contact - Specialty:
Mr. David Diamond, Chief Financial Officer & Treasurer - *Financial services*

Global Edge Recruiting Associates LLC

(formerly known as Global Edge Recruiting)
475 Mockingbird Rdg
Rogersville, MO 65742-9700
(417) 753-7070
(877) 370-2462
Fax: (816) 222-0830
Email: jobs@globaledgerecruiting.com
Web: www.globaledgerecruiting.com

Summary: We are a premier employment source dedicated to locating top sales talent for companies selling medical or pharmaceutical products, devices, or services. We are an executive search firm specializing in pharmaceutical, medical device, biotechnology and health care industries. We provide nationwide recruitment for sales, marketing and executive level positions.

Key Contact - Specialty:
Ms. Denise Wilkerson, Director, Recruiting

Functions: Sales Mgmt.

Industries: Drugs Mfg., Medical Devices, Pharm Svcs., Biotech/Life Sciences

Global HealthCare Services Inc (GHS)

10147 Royalton Rd Ste I
North Royalton, OH 44133-4462
(800) 808-7297
(440) 663-7071
Email: info@ghsrecruiting.com
Web: www.ghsrecruiting.com

Summary: We are a permanent placement firm retained directly by hospitals and other healthcare entities seeking to locate and hire highly skilled permanent, full-time employees. We specialize in the healthcare industry and remain industry leaders in the recruitment and placement of healthcare professionals. We recruit for all healthcare based positions including staff nurses and allied health, management, administration, and more.

Key Contact - Specialty:
Mr. Roy Munk, President - *Healthcare, Hospital*
Ms. Danielle Folliett, Vice President, Recruiting
Mr. Tom Cavalli, Recruitment Manager
Mr. Roger Rollins, Recruiter - *Healthcare, Hospital*
Mr. Rob Becker, Recruiter
Mr. Joe Tracey, Recruiter
Mr. Damien Bowman, Recruiter

Functions: Management, Healthcare, Physicians, Nurses, Allied Health, Risk Mgmt.

Industries: Pharm Svcs., Healthcare, Hospitals, Long-term/Home Care, Physical Therapy, Occupational Therapy, Women's

Global Network Recruiting LLC (GNR)

349 W Commercial St Ste 3030
East Rochester, NY 14445-2414
(888) 338-9087
Fax: (877) 366-0847

Email: jobs@globalnetr.com
Web: www.globalnetr.com

Summary: 'Engineers working with Engineers.' We are engineers, so we understand technology, which means you get presented the right opportunities. We service the high technology sector: semiconductors, computers/peripherals, wireless, defense, to medical products. We're most successful representing and placing engineers who are developing or managing the design.

Key Contact - Specialty:
Mr. Mike DeLaney, Owner & Partner
Mr. Kurt Phelps, Owner & Partner - *Engineering*

Salary Minimum: $75,000

Functions: Engineering

Industries: Computer Equip., Consumer Elect., Test, Measure Equip., Electronic, Elec. Components, Semiconductors, Communications, RF/Microwave, Defense, System SW

Global Recruiters Network

2001 Butterfield Rd Ste 102
Downers Grove, IL 60515-1595
(630) 663-1900
Fax: (630) 663-1919
Email: brad@grncorp.net
Web: www.grncorp.com

Summary: We are a rapidly growing network that offers management, technical, professional and executive search services to the corporate community. We specialize in identifying, attracting and placing top talent for our clients. Our company was developed to bring quality service, integrity and strong relationships to the forefront of franchise staffing.

Key Contact - Specialty:
Mr. Bradford A. Baiocchi, Chief Executive Officer & President
Mr. Jerry Hill, Vice President, Francise Ops & Training
Mr. Bob Angell, Vice Chairman
Mr. Steve Fogelgren, Vice President, Field Operations
Mr. John J. Israel, Vice President, Customer Service
Ms. Jolie Wilson, Vice President, Business Development
Mr. Glen A. Louthan, Executive Vice President & CFO & COO
Mr. Mark J. Baiocchi, Executive Vice President & Gen Col & CAO
Mr. Jerry O. Williams, Chairman

Salary Minimum: $50,000

Functions: Generalist (All)

Industries: Generalist (All)

Global Recruiters Network

8720 Castle Creek Parkway East Dr Ste 112
Indianapolis, IN 46250-4315
(317) 842-8114
Fax: (317) 842-8115
Email: nharris@grnindynorth.com
Web: www.grnindynorth.com

Summary: We are part of a rapidly growing network of executive search professionals. We currently serve four markets: Information Technology, Manufacturing, Construction and Financial Services Industries.

Key Contact - Specialty:
Mr. Nathan Harris, Search Consultant

Functions: Finance, Bldg. Contractors

Industries: Construction, Finance, Banking, Invest. Banking

Global Recruiters of Oak Brook Inc

1211 W 22nd St Ste 426
Oak Brook, IL 60523-2122
(630) 586-5000
Fax: (630) 586-5001
Email: dbaranski@grnoakbrook.com
Web: www.grnoakbrook.com

Summary: Our firm places managers in the investment banking/brokerage, banking, venture capital, accounting, software, insurance, food services and construction industries.

Key Contact - Specialty:
Mr. David Baranski, President & Founder -
  Banking
Ms. Toni Sieve, Managing Director

Salary Minimum: $40,000

Functions: Management, Cash Mgmt.

Industries: Construction, Banking, Invest. Banking, Brokers, Venture Cap., Mutual/Hedge Funds, Misc. Financial, Accounting, Insurance, Software

Global Recruiters of Indianapolis

77 S Girls School Rd Ste 105
Indianapolis, IN 46231-1170
(317) 244-7900
Email: bpatterson@grnindy.com
Web: www.grnindy.com

Summary: We perform searches for the pharmaceutical, biotechnology, healthcare and banking industry's most recognized companies. Our expertise includes: sales, business development, product managers, clinical research, regulatory affairs and medical affairs. Our association with our nationwide network of offices supports our search capability.

Key Contact - Specialty:
Ms. Brenda Patterson, CSAM, President
Mr. Gary Brown, General Manager
Mr. Pat Alberico, Search Consultant - *Banking*

Functions: Generalist (All), Product Dev., Quality, Physicians

Industries: Drugs Mfg., Medical Devices, Hospitals

Global Recruiters of Cape Cod

800 Falmouth Rd Ste 201B
Mashpee, MA 02649-3300
(508) 539-7000
Fax: (508) 539-9119
Email: mhagan@grncapecod.com
Web: www.grncapecod.com

Summary: We are a premier recruitment service specializing in real estate, construction, manufacturing, sales, marketing and financial services. We offer management, technical, professional and executive search services to the corporate community. Our goal is to provide our clients and candidates with superior quality recruitment services. We maintain the highest degree of integrity, confidentiality and professionalism.

Key Contact - Specialty:
Mr. Matthew Hagan, Senior Vice President
Mr. Francis (Bid) Hagan, Jr., President & Owner

Salary Minimum: $60,000

Functions: Management, Mfg.

Industries: Generalist (All), Construction, Finance, Real Estate

Global Recruiters of Milwaukee

735 N Water St Ste 830
Milwaukee, WI 53202-4104
(414) 226-1400
Fax: (414) 226-1401
Email: mklee@grnmilwaukee.com
Web: www.grnmilwaukee.com

Summary: We specialize in executive placement of management, sales and technical professionals to the packaging, printing, construction, insurance and financial industries.

Key Contact - Specialty:
Mr. Michael Klee, President - *Converting, Distribution, Insurance, Packaging, Sales*
Mr. Tony Novinska, Search Consultant - *Equipment, Field engineering, Packaging, Robotics, Sales*
Mr. Gary Wood, Search Consultant - *Converting, Engineering, Field engineering, Printing, Research & development*
Ms. Tamara Van Krey, Search Consultant - *Cement/concrete, Construction, General contractors, Real estate*
Mr. Kevin Moran, Search Consultant - *Field engineering, Manufacturing, Packaging, Process equipment, Sales*
Mr. Kerry Herro, Researcher - *Administration, Field engineering, Packaging, Printing*

Salary Minimum: $50,000

Functions: Management, Product Dev., Production, Plant Mgmt., Sales & Mktg., R&D, Engineering

Industries: Construction, Manufacturing, Paper, Printing, Machine, Appliance, Test, Measure Equip., Misc. Mfg., Robotics, Equip Svcs., Engineering Svcs., Supply Chain Mgmt, Packaging, Insurance, Casualty, Life, Mfg. SW

Global Recruiting Solutions

PO Box 235
201 E Main Ave
Frazee, MN 56544-0235
(888) 334-6142
(218) 334-6142
Fax: (218) 334-6144
Email: brian@globalrecruitingsolutions.com
Web: www.globalrecruitingsolutions.com

Summary: We are a recognized world leader in recruiting, executive search and turnkey staffing for agriculture, value-added Ag processing, ethanol, bio-diesel, renewable energy, food processing and farm management.

Key Contact - Specialty:
Mr. Brian B. Bigger, President - *Energy, Food*
Ms. DeeAnn Haase, Manager, Marketing

Salary Minimum: $40,000

Functions: Generalist (All), Management, Mfg., Materials, Sales & Mktg., HR Mgmt., Finance, Engineering

Industries: Generalist (All), Agri., Forestry, Mining, Energy, Utilities, Oil & Gas, Construction, Manufacturing, Food, Bev., Tobacco, Chemicals, Drugs Mfg., Engineering Svcs., Mfg. SW, Marketing SW, Biotech/Life Sciences

Global Search Network

118 S Fremont Ave
Tampa, FL 33606-1703
(813) 832-8300
(800) 254-3398
Fax: (813) 250-0280
Email: gsn@globalsearchnetwork.com
Web: www.globalsearchnetwork.com

Summary: Our firm has established success in the recruiting of personnel and has achieved a remarkable growth record by providing top quality service to both its client companies and its candidates. We specialize in food and beverage industry personnel, focusing on the manufacturing, distribution & logistics, sales, and finance roles found in the F & B industry.

Key Contact - Specialty:
Mr. Eric Busser, Executive Recruiter
Ms. Jeannie Hunn, Office & Research Manager
Ms. Andi Gillis, Executive Recruiter
Ms. Tammy Knapp, Executive Recruiter

Functions: Generalist (All)

Industries: Food, Bev., Tobacco, Plastics, Rubber, Consumer Goods

Global Telecommunications Inc

101 Pepper Bush St Ste 800
Shavano Park, TX 78231-1416
(210) 354-1111
Fax: (210) 493-0773
Email: globaltinc@aol.com

Summary: We are an executive search firm serving client companies in the telecommunication industry (i.e.: software, cable, solution consulting, wireless, global security, CLECs, internet and call-center). Specializing in middle to upper level executive management positions within sales, marketing and operations.

Key Contact - Specialty:
Mr. Robert S. Ott, President - *Cable, Internet, Wireless*

Functions: Senior Mgmt., Middle Mgmt., Product Dev., Sales & Mktg., Mktg. Research, Minorities/Diversity

Industries: Services, Telecoms, Call Centers, Telephony, Digital, Wireless, Fiber Optic, Network Infrastructure, Software

GlobalQuest Group

12 E Greenway Plz Ste 1100
Houston, TX 77046-1201
(713) 964 4007
Email: ron@globalquestgrp.com
Web: www.globalquestgrp.com

Summary: We are a confidential, custom-tailored, attention-to-detail professionalism resulting in solutions to complex recruiting problems.

Key Contact - Specialty:
Mr. Ronald J. Hakim, President - *Marketing, Operations, Sales*

Salary Minimum: $50,000

Functions: Sales & Mktg.

Industries: Generalist (All)

Jackie Glover Associates Inc

1 Glenlake Pkwy NE Ste 700
Atlanta, GA 30328-3496
(404) 250-1538
Fax: (404) 250-1222
Email: jackie@jga.net

Summary: Recruiter specializing in the permanent placement of office support staff (i.e. receptionists, administrative assistants, executive assistants and office managers).

Key Contact - Specialty:
Ms. Jackie Glover, CPC, Recruiter

Salary Minimum: $25,000

Functions: Admin. Svcs.

Industries: Construction, Misc. Financial, Services, Accounting, E-commerce, Insurance, Casualty, Real Estate

GM and Associates

5501 Independence Pkwy Ste 308
Plano, TX 75023-5461
(972) 618-3999
Email: georgemartin@gm-a.net
Web: www.gm-a.net

Summary: We are an executive search firm that offers contingency and retainer search for permanent placements. We place mostly mid to senior level professionals within the engineering industry (all types)... Civil Engineers, manufacturing, high tech, etc.

Key Contact - Specialty:
Mr. George Martin, Principal

Salary Minimum: $50,000

Functions: Engineering

Industries: Transportation, Architectural Svcs., Software, System SW

GMR Associates Inc

(also known as Genesis Healthcare Consultants)
10200 Larwin Ave Unit 2
Chatsworth, CA 91311-7492
(818) 885-6186
Fax: (818) 885-6197
Email: info@storkjobs.com
Web: www.storkjobs.com

Summary: We are a consulting firm specializing in recruitment of women's health care providers. This includes: OB/GYN physicians and sub-specialists, OB nurse practitioners and certified nurse midwives.

Key Contact - Specialty:
Mr. Dave Burton - *Healthcare, Physicians*

Functions: Physicians

Industries: Healthcare

Gnodde Associates

128 N Lincoln St
Hinsdale, IL 60521-3439
(630) 887-9510
Fax: (630) 887-9531
Email: gnoddeassociates@comcast.net
Web: www.gnoddeassociates.com

Summary: We conduct contingency searches for banks and financial institutions. Areas of specialization include commercial & commercial real estate lending, private banking & wealth management, personal trust, cash management banking and retail banking.

Key Contact - Specialty:
Mr. R. Dirk Gnodde, Owner - *Financial services*

Salary Minimum: $40,000

Functions: Generalist (All)

Industries: Banking

Goalline Technology Inc

15 Whitcomb Rd
East Windsor, NJ 08520-4736
(609) 371-2684
Email: info@goallinetechnology.com
Web: www.goallinetechnology.com

Summary: We are a full service staffing and recruiting company. We specialize in technology and sales recruiting and staffing permanent or contract/temporary.

Key Contact - Specialty:
Mr. Bob DAmbrosia, President

Functions: Sales & Mktg., IT, Systems Implem.

Industries: Generalist (All)

Godfrey Personnel

300 W Adams St Ste 612
Chicago, IL 60606-5194
(312) 236-4455
Fax: (312) 580-6292
Email: jobs@godfreypersonnel.com
Web: www.godfreypersonnel.com

Summary: Our specialty is recruitment and placement of insurance personnel from technical to senior management; i.e., underwriters, actuaries, claims adjusters (all lines), accounting, customer service reps, risk manager and loss control.

Key Contact - Specialty:
Mr. James R. Godfrey, President - *Executives, Technical*

Salary Minimum: $25,000

Functions: Generalist (All)

Industries: Insurance

Godshall Staffing

(also known as Godshall & Godshall Personnel Consultants Inc)
PO Box 1984
310 University Rdg
Greenville, SC 29602-1984
(864) 242-3491
Fax: (864) 370-9753
Email: staffing@godshallstaffing.com
Web: www.godshallstaffing.com

Summary: Our firm handles placement for candidates in the following areas: financial/accounting/banking, purchasing, HR, administrative, administrative management, non-clinical medical, manufacturing & industrial management and textile & apparel.

Key Contact - Specialty:
Mr. Wayne Godshall, CEC, President & Chief Executive Officer
Ms. Julie Godshall Brown, PHR, Vice President

Functions: Int'l.

Industries: Generalist (All)

Barry M Gold & Co LLC

2402 Michelson Dr Ste 225
Irvine, CA 92612-1346
(949) 660-5677
Fax: (949) 660-5611
Email: bmgco@insurancerecruiting.com
Web: www.insurancerecruiting.com

Summary: Our firm is an award winning executive search firm for the business insurance and benefits professional. Our principal is an acclaimed award winner.

Key Contact - Specialty:
Mr. Barry M. Gold, CAC, Managing Partner - *Benefits*
Mrs. Judith M. Trainor, Partner - *Management, Sales*
Mrs. Joyce L. Gold, Partner - *Insurance*

Salary Minimum: $40,000

Functions: Senior Mgmt., Sales & Mktg., Benefits

Industries: Insurance, Commercial

Goldbeck Recruiting Inc

(also known as Goldbeck Wireless Recruiting)
510-475 Georgia St W
British Columbia Turf Building
Vancouver, BC V6B 4M9
Canada
(604) 684-1428
(877) 684-1428
Fax: (604) 684-1429
Email: contact@goldbeck.com
Web: www.goldbeck.com

Summary: Our firm specializes in the recruitment and placement of professionals to companies in every major industry, whether they are Fortune 500, mid-size or start-up operations. We provide staffing services to a wide range of industries, including the high technology sector. Whether you are looking for employees or employment, we can meet your needs.

Key Contact - Specialty:
Mr. Henry Goldbeck, President
Ms. Karen Chan, MA, Manager, Marketing

Salary Minimum: $40,000

Functions: Generalist (All), Middle Mgmt., Automation, Plant Mgmt., Purchasing, Materials Plng., Mktg. Mgmt., Sales Mgmt., Engineering, Bldg. Contractors

Industries: Generalist (All), Agri., Forestry, Mining, Energy, Utilities, Construction, Manufacturing, Food, Bev., Tobacco, Lumber, Furniture, Paper, Transportation, Services, Communications, Telecoms, Telephony, Digital, Wireless, Fiber Optic, RF/Microwave, Software

Barry Goldberg & Associates Inc

1801 Avenue of the Stars Ste 934
Los Angeles, CA 90067-5803
(310) 277-5800
Fax: (310) 277-7944
Email: barrygoldberg@barrygoldberg.com
Web: www.centerset.com/bga/

Summary: Placement of partners and associates at the nation's leading law firms.

Key Contact - Specialty:
Mr. Barry Goldberg, President & Founder
Ms. Deanna Gerber, Recruiter
Ms. Sherry Glaser, Recruiter
Mr. Allen Mixon, CPA, Recruiter - *C-level, Information Technology, Marketing, Sales*

Salary Minimum: $75,000

Functions: Attorneys

Industries: Legal

Joseph Goldring & Associates Inc

7434 Glengrove Dr
Bloomfield Hills, MI 48301-3870
(248) 851-3727
Fax: (248) 851-3728
Email: jga@jobprofessionals.com
Web: www.jobprofessionals.com

Summary: We are an independent search organization devoted to providing confidential service on a contingency basis. Main areas are accounting/finance, engineering, information services and medical/healthcare.

Key Contact - Specialty:
Mr. Joe Goldring, President

Salary Minimum: $30,000

Functions: Management

Industries: Generalist (All)

David Gomez & Associates Inc

20 N Clark St Fl 29
Chicago, IL 60602-5096
(312) 346-5525
Fax: (312) 279-2077
Email: info@dgai.com
Web: www.dgai.com

Summary: We are a human capital solutions firm specializing in diversity. Our company provides retained search solutions in various industries.

Key Contact - Specialty:
Mr. David P. Gomez, Founder, Chairman & CEO
Ms. Petrina Rauzi, Chief Financial Officer -
CFOs, Compliance, Diversity, Finance, Six Sigma

Functions: Management

Industries: Generalist (All), Brokers, Misc. Financial, Non-profits, Accounting, HR Services, Hotels, Resorts, Clubs, Telephony, Network Infrastructure, Accounting SW

The Gordon Scott Group

(also known as Search Research Associates Inc)
400 W Cummings Park Ste 6900
Woburn, MA 01801-6518
(781) 939-5959
Fax: (781) 939-5962
Email: gordon@gordonscottassoc.com
Web: www.gordonscottassoc.com

Summary: We recruit in the real estate industry.

Key Contact - Specialty:
Mr. Gordon Scott, President - *Real estate*
Mr. Richard Gerding, CPC, Senior Associate -
Real estate
Mr. Mark Digby, Associate - *Real estate*

Salary Minimum: $50,000

Functions: Management

Industries: Construction, Real Estate, Property/Facility Mgmt.

The Gorge Group

PO Box 361
Corbett, OR 97019-0361
(503) 695-6020
Fax: (503) 695-6027
Email: mrhoward@gorgegroup.com
Web: www.gorgegroup.com

Summary: Our focus is on community banking, credit unions and the financial services industries. We recruit and place CEOs, CFOs, chief credit officers, IT, loan officers and other key personnel for the banking and credit union industries. If our client company needs to have a position filled, we will recruit for that position.

Key Contact - Specialty:
Mr. M.R. Howard, General Manager
Ms. Judy Howard, Director, Financial Services Division
Mrs. Peggy Vaughn, Associate, Recruiting -
Banking
Mr. Scott Orth, Associate, Recruiting - *Banking*

Functions: Management, Senior Mgmt., Middle Mgmt., Mktg. Research, Mktg. Mgmt., CFOs, Cash Mgmt., IT, MIS Mgmt.

Industries: Finance, Banking

Branches:
8629 20th St SE
Everett, WA 98205-2316
(425) 397-4717
Fax: (425) 397-4715
Email: mickh@gorgegroup.com

Key Contact - Specialty:
Mr. Mick Howard, Business Unit Manager -
Banking

GoStaffIT Recruiting

(a division of Strategic Marketing Ventures Inc)
8262 Lees Ridge Rd
Warrenton, VA 20186-8741
(540) 349-8888
Fax: (540) 349-8889
Email: matkins@gostaffit.com
Web: www.gostaffit.com

Summary: Our firm specializes in executive searches and executive coaching. A typical executive search includes: directors, CEOs, presidents, chief legal officers (general counsels), CFOs and chief marketing officers. Executive coaching includes: executive analysis, resumes, letters, research, marketing, submissions, interviewing and negotiations.

Key Contact - Specialty:
Mr. Michael Atkins, Chief Executive Officer

Salary Minimum: $100,000

Functions: Management, Sales & Mktg., IT, MIS Mgmt., Systems Analysis, Systems Dev., Systems Implem., Systems Support, Network Admin., DB Admin.

Industries: Finance, Banking, Invest. Banking, Venture Cap., E-commerce, IT Implementation, Software, Development SW, Industry Specific SW, Marketing SW

Government Contract Solutions Inc

1604 Spring Hill Rd Ste 400
Vienna, VA 22182-7510
(703) 749-2223
Fax: (703) 749-2244
Email: resume@gcsinfo.com
Web: www.gcsinfo.com

Summary: Our firm specializes in the temp and permanent placement of contracts, procurement, pricing, and financial personnel. We work with junior to executive-level candidates

Key Contact - Specialty:
Mr. Aaron McElroy, Senior Recruiter -
Procurement
Ms. Patti Price, Manager, Recruiting -
Procurement

Salary Minimum: $35,000

Functions: Generalist (All), Admin. Svcs., Purchasing, CFOs, Budgeting, Mgmt. Consultants

Industries: Generalist (All), Misc. Financial, Accounting, Mgmt. Consulting, Defense, Aerospace, Software

Gowdy Consultants

12059 Starcrest Dr
San Antonio, TX 78247-4350
(210) 499-4444
Fax: (210) 499-4676
Email: gowdycts@abcglobal.net

Summary: We specialize in sales and sales management.

Key Contact - Specialty:
Ms. Olga M. Gowdy, Owner
Ms. Kristi B. Mayer, Recruiter, Construction -
Consulting, Finance

Functions: Health Admin., Sales & Mktg., Sales Mgmt., Minorities/Diversity

Industries: Generalist (All), Construction, Manufacturing, Medical Devices, Transportation, Services, Pharm Svcs., Legal, E-

commerce, Media, Advertising, Communications, Telecoms, Government, Software, Marketing SW, Networking, Comm. SW, Biotech/Life Sciences, Healthcare, Hospitals

Grady Levkov & Company

580 Broadway Rm 1100
New York, NY 10012-3294
(212) 925-0900
Fax: (212) 925-0200
Email: info@gradylevkov.com
Web: www.gradylevkov.com

Summary: We are a boutique recruiting firm that focuses on searches in finance and technology. We are leaders in the recruiting industry with long-standing client relationships and a proven track record of hundreds of successful placements. Our firm's major clients include some of the country's leading banks, brokerages, asset managers, hedge funds, consultancies, software publishers and media producers.

Key Contact - Specialty:
Mr. Troy Grady, Managing Director
Mr. Joshua Levkov, Managing Director

Functions: Finance, Cash Mgmt., Credit, Risk Mgmt., IT, Systems Dev., Systems Support, Network Admin., DB Admin., Systems

Industries: Generalist (All), Finance, Banking, Invest. Banking, Mutual/Hedge Funds, Software

Grafton Executive Search

1001 W Southern Ave Ste 114
Mesa, AZ 85210-4912
(480) 833-3400
Fax: (480) 323-2220
Email: candidate@graftonsearch.com
Web: www.graftonsearch.com

Summary: Specializing in the contingency recruitment of corporate sales and c-level professionals, on a retained model.

Key Contact - Specialty:
Mr. Ryan Eberhard, President
Mr. Mark Hamade, Practice Leader, Consulting
Mr. Casey Neese, Practice Leader, Optics - *High technology, Opthalmics, Optics, Sales*
Mrs. Teri Amyx, Practice Leader, Finance -
Accounting, Asset management, Banking, Banking (Commercial, Corporate)
Mr. Vill Geist, Practice Leader, Healthcare -
Healthcare, HMOs, Hospital, Insurance (Health), Sales

Salary Minimum: $50,000

Functions: Sales & Mktg.

Industries: Finance, Services, Media, Communications, Packaging, Software, Database SW, Healthcare, Hospitals, Long-term/Home Care

Branches:
7007 College Blvd Ste 250
Overland Park, KS 66211-2437
(913) 498-0701
Email: candidate@graftonsearch.com
Key Contact - Specialty:
Mr. Richard Carroll, Chief Executive Officer

Graham Search Group Inc

1205 N 18th St Ste 215
Monroe, LA 71201-5462
(318) 361-2090
Fax: (318) 361-9747
Email: grahamsearchgroup@medicjobs.net
Web: www.medicjobs.net

Summary: We do confidential executive placements in the healthcare industry, including

nurses. We recruit in all areas of management for our clients, which include hospitals, clinics and surgery centers.

Key Contact - Specialty:
Ms. Beverly Doles Graham, Chief Executive Officer - *Healthcare*
Ms. Susan Crawford, Executive Recruiter

Functions: Healthcare, Physicians, Nurses, Allied Health, Health Admin.

Industries: Healthcare, Hospitals, Long-term/Home Care, Women's

Granite Solutions Groupe Inc

PO Box 3399
312 Main Street
Suite 202
Diamond Springs, CA 95619-3399
(888) 220-3524
Fax: (888) 244-1150
Email: info@granitesolutionsgroupe.com
Web: www.granitesolutionsgroupe.com

Summary: Granite Solutions Groupe provides superior contract consultant and direct hire placement services for the Financial Services and IT industries. We deploy the resources you need, when you need them to ensure success in the delivery of complex financial and enterprise applications.

Key Contact - Specialty:
Mr. Dan L'Abbe, Founder, Chairman & President - *Capital markets, COOs, Investment management, Product management/development, Supply Chain*
Mr. John Henning, Managing Director, Business Development - *Banking (Investment), CIOs, Derivatives, Information Technology, Technical (Management)*
Ms. Ann Bauer, Vice President, Operations

Salary Minimum: $100,000

Functions: Generalist (All), Management, Senior Mgmt., Middle Mgmt., Product Dev.

Industries: Finance, Banking, Invest. Banking, Brokers, Misc. Financial, Software, Database SW, Development SW, Networking, Comm. SW, System SW

Martin Grant Associates Inc

65 Franklin St
Boston, MA 02110-1303
(617) 357-5380
Fax: (617) 482-6581
Email: martingrant@msn.com
Web: www.insurancecareersearch.com

Summary: We are one of the leading insurance placement firm specializing in all levels of property/casualty, life/health/pension and risk management placement.

Key Contact - Specialty:
Mr. Barry Davis, CPC, President - *Insurance*
Ms. Diana Gazzolo, CPC, Vice President - *Insurance*

Salary Minimum: $25,000

Functions: Generalist (All)

Industries: Insurance

Grant-Franks & Associates

496 Kings Hwy N Ste 125
Cherry Hill, NJ 08034-1019
(856) 779-8844
Fax: (856) 779-0898

Summary: Our firm provides recruitment services to small and mid-size companies in a variety of industries.

Key Contact - Specialty:
Ms. Lee Grant, PHR

Salary Minimum: $30,000

Functions: Generalist (All), Materials, Sales & Mktg., HR Mgmt., Finance

Industries: Generalist (All), Construction, Transportation, Finance, Packaging, Insurance

Graphic Arts Marketing Associates Inc

3533 Deepwood Dr
Lambertville, MI 48144-9686
(734) 854-5225
(734) 854-5226
Fax: (734) 854-5224
Email: graphicama@aol.com

Summary: Placement in advertising, merchandising, printing, public relations and marketing covering all functions from general management, account executives, production, creative and media.

Key Contact - Specialty:
Mr. Roger Crawford, President - *Advertising, Marketing*
Ms. Jacqueline Crawford, Vice President - *Advertising, Creative*

Salary Minimum: $30,000

Functions: Sales & Mktg., Advertising, Mktg. Research, Mktg. Mgmt., Direct Mktg., PR, IT, Graphic Designers

Industries: Generalist (All), Media, Advertising, Publishing, New Media, Broadcast, Film, Communications, Marketing SW, Networking, Comm. SW

Graphic Resources & Associates Inc

2265 Roswell Rd Ste 100
Marietta, GA 30062-2980
(770) 509-2295
Email: jgoro@graphicresources.com
Web: www.graphicresources.com

Summary: We are a national recruiting firm specializing in the printing and packaging industry. We have attainted the status of certified personnel consultant (CPC). All positions require extensive experience in the printing/packaging industry.

Key Contact - Specialty:
Mr. Jeffrey Goro, CPC, President

Functions: Senior Mgmt., Middle Mgmt., Plant Mgmt., Quality, Packaging, Sales & Mktg., Mktg. Mgmt., Sales Mgmt., Customer Svc., Graphic Designers

Industries: Printing, Packaging

Graphic Search Associates

PO Box 373
Newtown Square, PA 19073-0373
(610) 359-1234
(800) 342-1777
Fax: (610) 353-8120
Email: info@graphsrch.com
Web: www.graphsrch.com

Summary: Recruiters for the graphic arts industry specializing in staff support, manufacturing, sales, marketing and general management opportunities.

Key Contact - Specialty:
Mr. Roger W. Linde, President - *Senior management*

Salary Minimum: $35,000

Functions: Generalist (All)

Industries: Manufacturing, Printing

Grauss & Company

2430 Canyon Lakes Dr
San Ramon, CA 94582-4929
(925) 735-8333
Email: debra@grauss.com
Web: www.grauss.com

Summary: We are a niche recruitment firm serving the investment community and construction industry. We specialize in investment banking, management and institutional brokerage. We have direct experience in the industry and service all levels, placing individuals from administrative to managing directors. We also consult in IT within the investment community.

Key Contact - Specialty:
Mr. Bryan J. Grauss, Senior Recruiter - *Construction, Engineering, Excavation, General contractors, Highways*

Salary Minimum: $40,000

Functions: Finance, Engineering, Bldg. Contractors

Industries: Generalist (All), Construction, Invest. Banking, Brokers, Mutual/Hedge Funds, Misc. Financial, Engineering Svcs.

Branches:
425 Market St
San Francisco, CA 94105-2406
(415) 777-5656
Key Contact - Specialty:
Ms. Debra Grauss

Great Work! Employment Services

572 W Market St Ste 4
Akron, OH 44303-1858
(330) 535-3800
Fax: (330) 761-3607
Email: apply@greatwork.cc
Web: www.greatwork.cc

Summary: We are in the business of helping progressive, growing companies and forward-thinking, motivated professionals find each other. Our professional search division provides confidential recruiting and career management in technology, insurance, management and engineering disciplines.

Key Contact - Specialty:
Ms. Tia Ramlow, President
Mr. Todd Kennedy, CTS, Manager, Sales - *Distribution, Engineering, Factories, Industrial, Information Technology*

Functions: Sales & Mktg.

Industries: Call Centers

Branches:
273 Wooster Rd N Unit 1A
Barberton, OH 44203-2310
(330) 848-0247

4313 Avondale Ln NW
Canton, OH 44708-1669
(330) 479-0758

9088 Superior Ave Ste 103
Streetsboro, OH 44241-5699
(330) 626-0500

Ben Greco Associates Inc

445 S Figueroa St Ste 2700
Los Angeles, CA 90071-1632
(213) 612-7766
Fax: (213) 612-7767
Email: bengreco@bengreco.com

Summary: Focus upon financial executives. Provide a personal, direct, efficient and confidential process to identify and recruit a quality executive with high performance standards who will make an immediate contribution and have long-term potential for the client company.

Key Contact - Specialty:
Mr. Ben Greco, Director - *Finance*

Salary Minimum: $75,000

Functions: Finance

Industries: Generalist (All)

Greene & Hauck

5 Powderhouse Ln
Sherborn, MA 01770-1316
(508) 655-1210
Fax: (508) 655-2139
Email: timgreene6@cs.com
Web: www.greeneandco.com

Summary: We are experienced in search services for banking and financial executives. We also work with investment management companies.

Key Contact - Specialty:
Mr. Timothy G. Greene, Principal
Mr. Bruce A. Hauck, Principal

Salary Minimum: $65,000

Functions: Finance

Industries: Banking, Invest. Banking

The Greene Group

PO Box 625
Pleasant Garden, NC 27313-0625
(336) 674-5345
Fax: (336) 674-5937
Email: billgreene@triad.rr.com
Web: www.thegreengroupltd.com

Summary: We are an executive and management search firm specializing in the kitchen cabinet, wood products and furniture industries. Other services include interim management, outplacement services and contract services.

Key Contact - Specialty:
Mr. William Greene, President & Owner - *Furniture, Millwork*
Mr. John Ibsen, Vice President, Operations - *Furniture, Millwork*
Mrs. Sharon Greene, Secretary & Treasurer
Mr. Bill Marlowe, Senior Recruiter - *Furniture, Millwork*

Salary Minimum: $45,000

Functions: Management, Senior Mgmt., Mfg., Product Dev., Plant Mgmt., Mktg. Research, CFOs, Credit, Engineering

Industries: Lumber, Furniture, Leather, Stone, Glass, Metal Products

Greene-Levin-Snyder LLC

150 E 58th St Fl 16
New York, NY 10155-0002
(212) 752-5200
Fax: (212) 752-8245
Email: search@glslsg.com
Web: www.glslsg.com

Summary: We place exclusively attorneys at all levels and our clients are major corporations, financial institutions and top-tier law firms. Twelve search professionals provide years of search expertise. Our assignments include retained general counsel and partner searches.

Key Contact - Specialty:
Ms. Karin L. Greene
Ms. Alisa F. Levin, Esq.
Ms. Susan Kurz Snyder, Esq.

Functions: Legal, Attorneys

Industries: Generalist (All), Manufacturing, Finance, Banking, Invest. Banking, Brokers, Media, Insurance

Greenline Group

1675 E Main St Ste 234
Kent, OH 44240-5818
(888) 350-3371
Fax: (888) 350-0234
Email: mark@greenlinegroup.net
Web: www.greenlinegroup.net

Summary: We are an executive search firm that is focused on the printed circuit board industry, semiconductor industry & construction management(NV). We have successfully served large, medium and small clients in our market.

Key Contact - Specialty:
Mr. Mike Thomas, Partner
Mr. Mark Meszar, Recruiter

Salary Minimum: $45,000

Functions: Senior Mgmt., Middle Mgmt., Plant Mgmt., Quality, Sales & Mktg., HR Mgmt., CFOs, Engineering, Mgmt. Consultants, Health & Safety

Industries: Construction, Manufacturing, Chemicals, Consumer Elect., Test, Measure Equip., Electronic, Elec. Components, Semiconductors, Consumer Goods, RF/Microwave, Aerospace

Greenwich Search Partners LLC

43 Hillcrest Park Rd
Old Greenwich, CT 06870-1020
(203) 637-2260
Email: gsp01@attglobal.net

Summary: Every individual associated with us has been a senior manager in a computer firm. We perform searches in the manner we preferred when we were hiring managers.

Key Contact - Specialty:
Mr. Robert Frishman, Principal - *Consulting, Marketing*
Ms. M. Susan Jones, Principal

Salary Minimum: $90,000

Functions: Senior Mgmt., Middle Mgmt., Sales & Mktg., Mktg. Mgmt., Sales Mgmt., Systems Implem.

Industries: Computer Equip., Mgmt. Consulting, Software

Gregg & Associates

1159 Highway 25
Gallatin, TN 37066
(615) 230-9482
Fax: (615) 296-4140
Email: fgregg@bellsouth.net

Summary: We specialize in finding the best skills set to fill key business positions in manufacturing for consumer and automotive product industries throughout the United States. We place special emphasis on identifying engineering and management talent that adds maximum value and provide a unique partnering experience for our clients.

Key Contact - Specialty:
Mr. Frank Gregg, President & Owner

Salary Minimum: $40,000

Functions: Generalist (All)

Industries: Generalist (All), Food, Bev., Tobacco, Drugs Mfg., Plastics, Rubber, Paints, Petro. Products, Metal Products, Machine, Appliance, Consumer Elect., Misc. Mfg., Accounting

Greyhorse Search Consultants Inc (GSC)

117 Lee Castleberry Rd Ste 100
Dawsonville, GA 30534-3781
(706) 216-3838
Fax: (801) 640-8951
Email: re@g-s.cc
Web: www.g-s.cc

Summary: Our firm provides professional search services with the focused goal of identifying and attracting top talent to our client's organizations. Our clients include leaders of corporate America. We have developed an analytical search methodology that identifies and attracts top industry talent to our clients. Our focus is executives, sales management, sales, and sales engineers.

Key Contact - Specialty:
Mr. Robert Edwards, President

Functions: Board Members, Senior Mgmt., Middle Mgmt., Sales & Mktg., Sales Mgmt.

Industries: Electronic, Elec. Components, Communications, Telecoms, Telephony, Digital, Wireless, Fiber Optic, Network Infrastructure, Networking, Comm. SW

GreyLee Professionals Inc

PO Box 1602
Goose Creek, SC 29445-1602
(843) 764-0006
(877) 473-9533
Email: itcareers@greylee.com
Web: www.greylee.com

Summary: We provide executive recruiting services with specialization in IT. We also provide options for direct hire, contract and contract to hire.

Key Contact - Specialty:
Ms. Chrys Rogge, President & Recruiting Consultant

Functions: IT, MIS Mgmt., Systems Analysis, Systems Dev., Systems Implem., Systems Support, Network Admin., DB Admin.

Industries: Generalist (All), Manufacturing, Services, E-commerce, IT Implementation, New Media, Communications, Telecoms, Network Infrastructure, Software, Accounting SW, Database SW, Development SW, ERP SW, HR SW, Industry Specific SW, Networking, Comm. SW, Security SW, System SW

The Griffin Group Inc

707 Sinclair Cir
Brentwood, TN 37027-3002
(615) 371-9257
Fax: (413) 803-9367
Email: griffingrp@comcast.net
Web: thesourcealliance.com

Summary: An executive search organization that specializes in the packaging industry and represents many of the industry's key raw material, converters, equipment, and actual producers of those using packaging products. This area covers the food, beverage, consumer, flexible, and equipment industry.

Key Contact - Specialty:
Mr. C. Griffin Jones, President - *Packaging*

Salary Minimum: $75,000

Functions: Generalist (All), Management, Senior Mgmt.

Industries: Generalist (All), Food, Bev., Tobacco, Paper, Printing, Plastics, Rubber, Metal Products, Consumer Goods, Engineering Svcs., Packaging

The Griffin Group

PO Box 71
Bridgewater, VA 22812-0071
(540) 828-2365
(888) 235-2365
Fax: (540) 828-2851
Email: info@thegriffingroup.cc
Web: www.thegriffingroup.cc

Summary: We are an executive search firm and recruitment services provider with over a decade of experience in the executive search. We provide recruitment services for the service industries.

Key Contact - Specialty:
Ms. Deana A. Griffin, President - *Human resources, Operations, Sales, Technical*

Salary Minimum: $40,000

Functions: Generalist (All), Management, Senior Mgmt., Plant Mgmt., Sales & Mktg., Sales Mgmt., Sales Reps., CFOs, Textile/Fashion

Industries: Textiles, Apparel

Griffiths & Associates

PO Box 13854
Akron, OH 44334-3854
(330) 865-9660

Summary: We offer personalized search and recruiting services to our clients for the hard to find engineering, technical and manufacturing professionals. With our extensive recruiting experience, we know where to search for the high quality candidate needed in today's competitive business climate.

Key Contact - Specialty:
Mr. Bob Griffiths, President - *Distribution, Engineering, Human resources, Manufacturing, Purchasing*

Salary Minimum: $50,000

Functions: Middle Mgmt., Mfg., Product Dev., Production, Automation, Plant Mgmt., Quality, Materials, Sales Mgmt., Engineering

Industries: Manufacturing, Food, Bev., Tobacco, Chemicals, Medical Devices, Plastics, Rubber, Paints, Petro. Products, Metal Products, Machine, Appliance, Motor Vehicles, Computer Equip., Consumer Elect., Test, Measure Equip., Electronic, Elec. Components, Aerospace, Packaging

Grobard & Associates Inc

230 Ridge Bluff Ln
Suwanee, GA 30024-3543
(770) 271-1828
Fax: (770) 271-4026
Email: e.grobard@grobardassociates.com
Web: www.grobardassociates.com

Summary: Our staff has extensive experience in the executive recruiting industry. We specialize in sales & marketing in, but not limited to: medical, pharmaceutical, medical equipment, medical devices, printing industry sales and industrial sales.

Key Contact - Specialty:
Mrs. Eileen Grobard, President & Recruiter - *Pharmaceutical*
Mr. Cy Grobard, Vice President, Operations
Mr. Milt Feinson, Senior Recruiter
Ms. Lynne Virion, Insurance Specialist - *Finance, Human resources, Manufacturing, Marketing*

Functions: Mfg., Materials Plng., Healthcare, Sales & Mktg.

Industries: Generalist (All), Printing, Medical Devices, Pharm Svcs., Commercial

Groenekamp & Associates

PO Box 2308
Beverly Hills, CA 90213-2308
(310) 855-0119
Fax: (310) 855-0110
Email: bill@hrwag.com
Web: www.hrwag.com

Summary: Executive search and professional staffing in broad range of industries. Also offer wide range of management consulting in HR.

Key Contact - Specialty:
Mr. William A. Groenekamp, President

Salary Minimum: $75,000

Functions: Generalist (All)

Industries: Generalist (All)

J B Groner Executive Search LLC

PO Box 101
Claymont, DE 19703-0101
(302) 792-9228
Fax: (610) 497-5500
Email: jbgroner@comcast.net
Web: www.execjobsearch.com

Summary: Specializing in senior corporate executives, CEOs, COOs, CFOs, senior accountants, trade association, non-profit executives, engineering managers and executives, IT managers and executives, CIOs, CTOs, HR executives, sales executives and accountants.

Key Contact - Specialty:
Mr. James B. Groner, President - *Technical*

Salary Minimum: $55,000

Functions: Generalist (All), Management

Industries: Energy, Utilities, Manufacturing, Chemicals, Drugs Mfg., Medical Devices, Computer Equip., Finance, Services, Non-profits, Accounting, Logistics Svcs., Supply Chain Mgmt., Media, Telecoms, Insurance, Software, ERP SW, HR SW, Biotech/Life Sciences, Healthcare

Gros Executive Recruiters

1616 Westgate Cir
Brentwood, TN 37027-8019
(800) 283-5643
(615) 661-4568
Web: www.PlasticsJOBS.com ;
www.PackagingPeople.com

Summary: Serving companies and individuals as the marketplace of professional career opportunities in packaging and plastics. Sales, management and technical jobs in injection molding, extrusion, film, sheet, bags, flexible packaging, blow molding, thermoforming, resin, color, compounding, labels and labeling, moldmaking, rotomolding and rotational molding, pultrusion, and machinery for these processes.

Key Contact - Specialty:
Mr. Dennis Gros, CPC, President - *Packaging, Plastics*
Mr. George Shaw, Account Manager - *Plastics*

Salary Minimum: $60,000

Functions: Generalist (All), Mfg., Materials

Industries: Manufacturing, Medical Devices, Plastics, Rubber, Machine, Appliance, Motor Vehicles, Computer Equip., Packaging

Group W Partners Inc

28W181 Belleau Dr
Winfield, IL 60190-1723
(630) 562-3363
Fax: (630) 231-6442
Email: steve@groupwpartners.com
Web: www.groupwpartners.com

Summary: Our firm specializes in recruiting and placing top performing sales & marketing professionals in the transaction services and eCommerce industries, including credit cards, debit cards, stored value cards electronic bill presentment and/or payment and other related services.

Key Contact - Specialty:
Mr. Steve Wade
Ms. Sandy Wade

Salary Minimum: $60,000

Functions: Sales & Mktg.

Industries: Banking, Misc. Financial, Mgmt. Consulting, Software, Doc. Mgmt., Production SW

GRS Global Recruitment Solutions

71 Prince Charles Dr
North York, ON M6A 2H4
Canada
(416) 789-4868
(416) 244-2402 x117
Fax: (416) 789-4868
Email: info@grsglobal.com
Web: www.grsglobal.com

Summary: A professional recruitment firm specializing in the pharmaceutical, biotechnology and IT industries. Our two senior partners possess extensive combined experience in the recruitment industry. Backed by a team of professional, courteous and knowledgeable recruitment professionals, we provide exceptional recruitment services to both clients and candidates.

Key Contact - Specialty:
Mr. Warren Shapiro, Partner - *Biotechnology, Pharmaceutical*
Mr. Larry Goldberg, Partner

Functions: Generalist (All)

Industries: Drugs Mfg., Medical Devices, Computer Equip., Equip Svcs., Software, Biotech/Life Sciences

Grupo Balmaseda

77 Franklin St Fl 3
Boston, MA 02110-1510
(888) 225-6273
(617) 522-0901
Fax: (617) 695-3299
Email: info@grupobalmaseda.com
Web: www.grupobalmaseda.com

Summary: Grupo Balmaseda is an Executive Recruiting firm wich specializes in placing Hispanic/Latino bilingual and bicultural candidates within diversity-oriented majority corporations.Our recruiting firm offers you a full service solution for best-in-class DIVERSITY candidates.This is our passion and exclusive area of expertise.As generalists, Grupo offers such candidates in all industries universities and governments at mid to senior levels.

Key Contact - Specialty:
Mr. Rene Balmaseda, Managing Director
Mr. Russell Meyer, Director, Information Systems
Ms. Cecilia Hernandez, Senior Associate, Recruiting

Salary Minimum: $70,000

Functions: Generalist (All)

Industries: Generalist (All)

GSP International

90 Woodbridge Ctr Dr Ste 110
Woodbridge, NJ 07095-1142
(732) 602-0100 x13
Fax: (732) 602-0108
Email: ekaye@gspintl.com
Web: www.gspintl.com

Summary: An executive search and placement firm specializing in the accounting and finance professions.

Key Contact - Specialty:
Mr. Edward Kaye, Senior Partner - *Accounting*
Mr. Tony Glennon, Managing Partner - *Accounting*
Mr. John Sicilia, Managing Partner - *Accounting*
Mr. Ray Pirre, Managing Partner - *Accounting*

Salary Minimum: $30,000

Functions: Finance

Industries: Generalist (All)

Nadine Guber & Associates Inc

575 Lexington Ave Rm 410
Regent Bus
New York, NY 10022-6106
(212) 572-9630
Fax: (212) 572-9635
Email: guberassociates@mindspring.com

Summary: We specialize in the placement of advertising agency account management and corporate marketing management executives. Our professionals utilize their experience, extensive database and understanding of clients' cultures to identify uniquely qualified candidates.

Key Contact - Specialty:
Ms. Nadine B. Guber, President - *Advertising, Marketing*

Salary Minimum: $50,000

Functions: Mktg. Mgmt.

Industries: Advertising, New Media

Michael R Guerin Company

16368 Avenida Suavidad
San Diego, CA 92128-3214
(858) 675-0395
Fax: (858) 675-0393
Email: mrgco1192@yahoo.com

Summary: We perform confidential search and consulting for senior management, sales, marketing and engineering professionals within the high technology/software/financial services/healthcare industries. Entire search conducted by principal who has performed as a senior level manager within the area of specialization.

Key Contact - Specialty:
Mr. Michael R. Guerin, President - *Computers (Software), Healthcare, Telecommunications*

Salary Minimum: $70,000

Functions: Senior Mgmt., Middle Mgmt., Product Dev., Healthcare, Mktg. Mgmt., Sales Mgmt., Engineering

Industries: Generalist (All), Computer Equip., Test, Measure Equip., Equip Svcs., Telecoms, Software

Guidarelli Associates Inc

4472 Winding Ln
Stevensville, MI 49127-9330
(269) 429-7001
Fax: (269) 429-7001
Email: shelley@guidarelli.com
Web: www.guidarelli.com

Summary: A long history of interaction with leading CPG companies and executives. High speed, technology driven networking to 20,000 targeted candidates. Specialties are; brand marketing, sales, category management, marketing research, trade marketing, marketing services. We are candidate friendly and corporate driven.

Key Contact - Specialty:
Ms. Shelley Guidarelli, President
Ms. Louann Gardner, Assistant to President

Salary Minimum: $60,000

Functions: Sales & Mktg.

Industries: Food, Bev., Tobacco, Soap, Perf., Cosmtcs., Consumer Goods

The GullGroup Executive Search

203 Yacht Club Dr
Rockwall, TX 75032-5735
(972) 772-0582
(972) 772-0583
Fax: (972) 772-0587
Email: gullgrp@swbell.net
Web: www.gullgroup.com

Summary: We specialize in hard-to-find candidates in the following areas: mortgage banking (residential and commercial), banking and financial services, Six Sigma, insurance industry (including P&C, reinsurance, health and life). We recruit highly experienced professionals on the sales and the operational side of the business including vice presidents and C-level executive officers.

Key Contact - Specialty:
Mr. James A. Ryan, Chief Executive Officer
Ms. Betty Ryan, Chief Operating Officer

Salary Minimum: $50,000

Functions: Senior Mgmt.

Industries: Finance, Banking, Accounting, Supply Chain Mgmt., Wireless, Insurance, Casualty, Claims, Life, Re-Insurance

The Gumbinner Company

509 Madison Ave Rm 708
New York, NY 10022-5567
(212) 688-0129
Email: paul@gumbinnercompany.com

Summary: We offer professional recruitment by advertising people for advertising people. We provide services for advertising account management from account executives to presidents. Also we staff for media and account planning executives at all levels and client side advertising executives as well.

Key Contact - Specialty:
Mr. Paul S. Gumbinner, President

Salary Minimum: $50,000

Functions: Generalist (All), Middle Mgmt., Advertising, Direct Mktg.

Industries: Generalist (All), Advertising, New Media

Gunther Group LLC

20 N Wacker Dr Ste 1920
Chicago, IL 60606-3001
(312) 629-4900
Fax: (312) 629-4901
Email: info@gunthergroup.com
Web: www.gunthergroup.com

Summary: Our firm specializes in the search and placement of talented lawyers. We place partners and associates at top law firms and companies. Importantly, all of our recruiters have been practicing attorneys and understand issues specific to attorneys. We work diligently to get to know our clients and candidates so that each placement has the best chance of success.

Key Contact - Specialty:
Mr. Art Gunther, President & Founder
Ms. Sandy Raitt, Recruiter, Legal
Ms. Shelley Dunck, Recruiter, Legal
Ms. Christine Lyons, Recruiter, Legal
Ms. Brooke Hillman, Recruiter, Legal - *Human resources*

Functions: Attorneys

Industries: Legal

H & H Consultants Inc

419 S Sharon Amity Rd Ste A
Charlotte, NC 28211-2884
(704) 442-0737
Fax: (704) 442-0766
Email: bhonour@msn.com

Summary: Extensive knowledge of the construction industry working with the top negotiated general contractors, many years as in-house HR specialist. Top 10 contractor provides insight into operation of a construction company.

Key Contact - Specialty:
Mr. Robert Honour, Principal - *Construction*

Functions: Generalist (All)

Industries: Construction

H & S Personnel

32 2nd St Ste F
Raritan, NJ 08869-1812
(908) 231-0880
Fax: (908) 707-1055
Email: ehughes@hugh-pod.com
Web: www.hugh-pod.com

Summary: Our executive and middle management recruiting experience has given us the insight necessary to provide excellence in professional recruiting, an excellence which has become our trademark in the field of personnel placement. Working closely with clients on both search and contingency assignments, we utilize our expertise gained from association with many diverse industries to recruit on a national level.

Key Contact - Specialty:
Mr. Edward Hughes, President

Salary Minimum: $50,000

Functions: Quality, Sales & Mktg., HR Mgmt., Finance, R&D

Industries: Generalist (All), Drugs Mfg., Medical Devices, Pharm Svcs.

H R Solutions Inc

125 N Main St Ste 201
Saint Charles, MO 63301-2800
(636) 916-3399
Fax: (636) 916-3058
Email: hrsol@inlink.com

Summary: Principals have combined total experience of many years of recruiting mid-management and executive-level candidates. Principals have prior work experience in their respective specializations.

Key Contact - Specialty:
Mr. Robert J. Keymer, President - *Hospitality*
Mr. James McDaniel, Division Vice President - *Home health*
Mr. Jason Wagenknecht, Division Vice President - *Hospitality*

Salary Minimum: $50,000

Functions: Generalist (All), Board Members, Senior Mgmt., Middle Mgmt., Sales & Mktg., CFOs, IT

Industries: Generalist (All), Pharm Svcs., Hospitality, Healthcare

The H S Group Inc

2611 Libal St
Green Bay, WI 54301-2865
(920) 432-7444
Fax: (920) 436-2966
Email: recruiters3@thehsgroup.com
Web: www.thehsgroup.com

Summary: Our firm has extensive experience in managerial and executive recruiting. We recruit in all industries for mid and senior level management and high-end technical positions. We cover most disciplines including: IS/IT, accounting & finance, operations, engineering, HR, sales & marketing, logistics, purchasing, board members and executives.

Key Contact - Specialty:
Mr. Jock Seal, Executive Recruiter & Owner
Mr. Jeff Lasee, Director, Recruiting - *Finance, Human resources, Marketing, Operations, Sales*

Salary Minimum: $50,000

Functions: Generalist (All)

Industries: Accounting, HR Services, IT Implementation

H T Associates

3030 W Salt Creek Ln Ste 121
Arlington Heights, IL 60005-5000
(847) 577-0300
(800) 482-0040
Fax: (847) 577-8131
Email: htassociates@htassociates.com
Web: www.htassociates.com

Summary: Our firm specializes in the placement of IT, accounting/finance and HR professionals. We continue to assist many of our market's premier employers seeking to locate qualified professional talent. Our firm is the proud recipient of the Malcolm Baldrige National Quality Award for outstanding service and ethical practices. We are proficient in recruiting for virtually all experience levels.

Key Contact - Specialty:
Mr. Stephen Higgins, President
Mr. Robert Tabrosky, Jr., Treasurer - *Human resources*

Salary Minimum: $40,000

Functions: Generalist (All), Board Members, IT

Industries: Generalist (All), Finance, Accounting, HR Services, IT Implementation

H T Prof Executive Search (High Tech Professionals)

2775 S Main St NW Ste G
Kennesaw, GA 30144-3557
(770) 420-7440
Fax: (770) 234-4160
Email: info@htprof.com
Web: www.htprof.com

Summary: We are an executive/technical search firm specializing in IT and telecommunication. We are also developing practices in the area of spatial/GIS/security and biotechnology.

Key Contact - Specialty:
Mr. Todd S. Porter, President

Salary Minimum: $75,000

Functions: Generalist (All), Sales & Mktg., IT, DB Admin.

Industries: Generalist (All), Communications, Software, Biotech/Life Sciences

H.E.A.T. Resources & STAT Medical Professionals

1915 Huguenot Rd Ste 304
Richmond, VA 23235-4315
(804) 378-7222
Email: tom@heatresources.com
Web: www.heatresources.com

Summary: Established to serve the needs of our clients through identifying the top talent of today that will allow their growth for tomorrow. We work in many industries including the health and medical community. We have been very successful in fulfilling the needs and objectives of many clients.

Key Contact - Specialty:
Mr. Tom Hodges, Managing Director

Functions: Board Members

Industries: Generalist (All), Defense, Healthcare, Hospitals, Long-term/Home Care, Physical Therapy, Occupational Therapy

J.C. Haase Consulting LLC

PO Box 10
Waldwick, NJ 07463-0010
(201) 444-5119
Fax: (201) 251-2582
Email: jchaase@netrealm.com
Web: www.jchaase.com

Summary: We specialize in recruiting professional personnel for both high technology companies and non-profit organizations in the medical, tele/data communications, IT industries, and hi-tech industrial manufacturing areas.

Key Contact - Specialty:
Ms. Jean Haase, Founder
Mr. Andrew Haase, Sales

Salary Minimum: $58,000

Functions: Healthcare, Sales & Mktg., Mktg. Mgmt., Sales Mgmt., Architects, Technicians

Industries: Manufacturing, Medical Devices, Plastics, Rubber, Computer Equip., Consumer Elect., Test, Measure Equip., Misc. Mfg., Electronic, Elec. Components, Robotics, Architectural Svcs., Pharm Svcs., Mgmt. Consulting, Telecoms, Telephony, Digital, Network Infrastructure, RF/Microwave, Hospitals

Russ Hadick & Associates Inc

77 W Elmwood Dr Ste 100
Dayton, OH 45459-4266
(937) 439-7700
Fax: (937) 439-7705
Email: rhadick@rharecruiters.com
Web: www.rharecruiters.com

Summary: We interview, reference check and verify degrees before our customers ever see our clients. We've been in business many years. All of our people held top management positions before coming into recruiting.

Key Contact - Specialty:
Mr. Bob Hadick, President - *Engineering, Management*
Mr. Ron Toke, Vice President, Technical Sales - *Engineering*
Mr. Todd Mikesell, Vice President, Banking Sales

Salary Minimum: $45,000

Functions: Generalist (All), Middle Mgmt.

Industries: Generalist (All), Manufacturing, Plastics, Rubber, Metal Products, Machine, Appliance, Robotics, Finance, Banking, Engineering Svcs., Defense, Software

Hadley Associates Inc

116 Ridgedale Ave
Florham Park, NJ 07932-1724
(973) 377-9177
Fax: (973) 377-9223
Email: thadleyassoc@aol.com

Summary: Search capabilities exclusively for the pharmaceutical, biotechnology, medical device and related healthcare industries. Areas of expertise include: regulatory affairs, QA/QC and clinical research.

Key Contact - Specialty:
Mr. Thomas M. Hadley, President - *Healthcare*

Functions: Quality, R&D, Engineering

Industries: Drugs Mfg., Medical Devices, Pharm Svcs., Biotech/Life Sciences, Healthcare

Halbrecht & Company

PO Box 2601
Fairfax, VA 22031-0601
(703) 359-2880
Fax: (703) 359-2933
Email: tomm@halbrecht.com
Web: www.halbrecht.com

Summary: We are proud of our reputation for assisting our clients in identifying and selecting superior business professionals dedicated to excellence rather than the merely qualified technician. Areas of expertise: IT, quantitative business professionals, management consultants, eCommerce and B2B.

Key Contact - Specialty:
Mr. Thomas J. Maltby, Partner
Mr. Thomas Kubiak, Partner
Mr. Dick Gibowicz - *Financial services*

Salary Minimum: $40,000

Functions: IT, Mgmt. Consultants

Industries: Generalist (All), Wholesale, Retail, Mgmt. Consulting, Telecoms, Software

William Halderson Associates Inc

PO Box 20056
Saint Simons Island, GA 31522-8056
(912) 638-8430
Email: bill@haldersonsearch.com
Web: www.haldersonsearch.com

Summary: We have specializations in the pharmaceutical, biotechnology and medical device industries. Contingency and retained searches including startup sales forces, medical science liaisons, middle and upper level management in sales & marketing, R&D, financial, quality control and quality assurance. Placement of CFOs, COOs, CEOs and CIOs is a primary function. Provide interim contract employees in each of these areas.

Key Contact - Specialty:
Mr. William Halderson, President - *Biotechnology, Healthcare, Medical (Devices), Middle management, Pharmaceutical*
Ms. Dot Werner, Associate - *Pharmaceutical*
Ms. Janice Wright, Associate
Ms. Carollynn Bouma, Associate - *Medical, Medical (Devices), Pharmaceutical*

Salary Minimum: $60,000

Functions: Generalist (All), Board Members, Senior Mgmt., Middle Mgmt., Healthcare, Mktg. Mgmt., Sales Mgmt., CFOs, R&D, Int'l.

Industries: Generalist (All), Drugs Mfg., Medical Devices, Pharm Svcs., Biotech/Life Sciences, Healthcare, Long-term/Home Care, Dental, Women's

Hale & Associates

PO Box 6941
New Orleans, LA 70174-6941
(504) 394-2956
Fax: (504) 391-3256
Email: jobs@hale-associateshome.com
Web: www.hale-associateshome.com

Summary: Our firm specializes in the recruitment of executive staff, clinical and non-clinical management positions for hospitals, healthcare systems and health related corporations.

Key Contact - Specialty:
Mr. Leonard Hale, Principal
Mr. Mike Johnson, Consultant - *Healthcare*
Ms. Victoria Turner, Consultant - *Healthcare*
Ms. Karen Shaffer, Consultant - *Healthcare*
Ms. Jennifer Johnson, Consultant - *Healthcare*

Salary Minimum: $45,000

Functions: Management, Board Members, Senior Mgmt., Physicians, Nurses, Benefits, Staffing, MIS Mgmt., Systems Analysis, Systems Dev.

Industries: Healthcare, Hospitals, Dental, Physical Therapy, Occupational Therapy, Women's

Don Hall & Associates

(also known as The Millwork Network)
617 Catalina Dr
Waco, TX 76712-3740
(254) 772-0420
(800) 999-0420
Fax: (254) 772-1333
Email: dhall@hot.rr.com
Web: www.millworknetwork.com

Summary: Our firm provides placement services to manufacturers, distributors and retailers of windows, doors, stairs, moldings, cabinets and related building materials. We only accept candidates who have experience in the millwork and building material fields for placements.

Key Contact - Specialty:
Mr. Don Hall, Owner - *Millwork*
Ms. Joann Hall, Co-Owner - *Millwork*
Mr. Arthur Haaker, Associate - *Building products, Human resources, HVAC, Millwork, Molding*

Salary Minimum: $20,000

Functions: Generalist (All)

Industries: Lumber, Furniture

Hall Management Group Inc

(also known as Lennon Search Associates)
611 W Union St
Morganton, NC 28655-4344
(828) 433-7058
(770) 534-5568
Email: bill@lennonsearch.com
Web: www.lennonsearch.com

Summary: Our president has extensive recruiting experience as a manufacturing and technology specialist in pharmaceuticals, medical devices, bioinformatics and biosciences. New business includes a partnership providing contracted CEO, CFO, CIOs for venture capitalists, IPO and turnaround needs of bioscience and healthcare product companies.

Key Contact - Specialty:
Mr. Bill Lennon, CPC, Owner & President - *Engineering, Information Technology, Management, Manufacturing, Quality*

Salary Minimum: $75,000

Functions: Generalist (All), Management, Senior Mgmt., Mfg., Quality, HR Mgmt., Finance, IT, Engineering

Industries: Generalist (All), Manufacturing, Food, Bev., Tobacco, Soap, Perf., Cosmtcs., Drugs Mfg., Medical Devices, Plastics, Rubber, Machine, Appliance, Accounting, Biotech/Life Sciences

Hallman Group Inc

4528 W KL Ave
Kalamazoo, MI 49006-5724
(269) 353-6835
Email: nancyhall@hallmangroup.com
Web: www.hallmangroup.com

Summary: We are a search firm specializing in various disciplines such as IT, quality assurance, quality control and R&D. We focus in specific industries, such as pharmaceutical, health care, manufacturing and banking. We thoroughly pre-screen and qualify our candidates and companies. We do not advertise but work off of our reputation. Executive retained and contingency search is our specialty.

Key Contact - Specialty:
Ms. Nancy L. Hall, President
Mr. Kenneth Killman, Vice President

Salary Minimum: $45,000

Functions: Management, Senior Mgmt., Middle Mgmt., Production, Quality, Physicians

Industries: Drugs Mfg., Medical Devices, Plastics, Rubber, Pharm Svcs., Software

Hamilton Grey Technology Search

250 Kenilworth Ave
Glen Ellyn, IL 60137-5325
(630) 858-4900
Fax: (630) 858-4912
Email: fbaron@hamgrey.com
Web: www.hamiltongrey.com

Summary: We specialize in the recruitment and placement of professionals with expertise in Information Technology throughout the United States on a permanent, temporary, and temp-to-hire basis. Our client list includes some of the most respected North American based firms, spreading throughout a full range of industries including financial, manufacturing, healthcare and pharmaceutical, transportation, retail, food services, etc.

Key Contact - Specialty:
Mr. Frank Baron, Manager, ERP Practice - *Information Technology, SAP*

Functions: Generalist (All), Senior Mgmt., Middle Mgmt., MIS Mgmt., Systems Analysis, Systems Dev., Systems Implem., Systems Support, Network Admin., DB Admin.

Industries: Generalist (All), Manufacturing, Transportation, Finance, Hospitality, Packaging, Insurance, Software, Database SW, Development SW, Doc. Mgmt., Production SW, ERP SW, HR SW, Industry Specific SW, Mfg. SW, Marketing SW, Networking, Comm. SW, Security SW, Healthcare

Hamilton Group Executive Search Inc

(formerly known as Dunhill Professional Search of Vancouver)
400-1681 Chestnut St
Vancouver, BC V6J 4M6
Canada
(604) 739-0100
Email: dunvan@shaw.ca

Summary: We are an executive search firm specializing in the placement of proven high achievers in sales, engineering and finance.

Key Contact - Specialty:
Mr. Peter Hamilton, President

Salary Minimum: $75,000

Functions: Senior Mgmt., Middle Mgmt.

Industries: Generalist (All), Food, Bev., Tobacco, Banking, Invest. Banking, Hotels, Resorts, Clubs, Telecoms, Haz. Waste

Stan Hamlet Associates Inc

274 Madison Ave Rm 1801
New York, NY 10016-0701
(212) 685-4884
Fax: (212) 685-8891
Email: sh@stanhamlet.com
Web: www.stanhamlet.com

Summary: We are a middle management recruiting firm specializing in accounting, audit, finance, tax, human recources, and systems.

Key Contact - Specialty:
Mr. Stan Hamlet, President
Mr. Ben Kramer, Vice President
Mr. Gregg David, Vice President

Salary Minimum: $50,000

Functions: Finance

Industries: Generalist (All), Food, Bev., Tobacco, Finance, Invest. Banking, Mutual/Hedge Funds, Misc. Financial, Entertainment, Advertising, Insurance, Real Estate

Hammer Haley

1580 Lincoln St Ste 1280
Denver, CO 80203-1529
(877) 764-4289
Email: mgozon@hammerhaley.com
Web: www.hammerhaley.com

Summary: Candidate base: top 20 MBA's currently working at tier-one management consulting or one position removed on client side. The 'Candidate Elite' seeking corporate 'strategy' roles. Positions filled: SVP, VP, Dir, Mgr - corporate development, strategy, strategic planning, M&A, internal consulting, product management, supply-chain.

Key Contact - Specialty:
Mr. Michael Gozon, Managing Partner
Mr. Chris Todd, Managing Partner

Functions: Mgmt. Consultants

Industries: Mgmt. Consulting

Hanna & Associates Inc

7710 N Union Blvd Ste 202
Colorado Springs, CO 80920-4085
(719) 266-5575
Fax: (719) 266-1823
Email: hanna@ahanna.com
Web: www.ahanna.com

Summary: Our firm specializes in the architectural and engineering fields at senior level positions. You must be PE or AIA registered to be considered an active candidate. We charge no fees to our candidate. All resumes are held in the strictest of confidence.

Key Contact - Specialty:
Mr. Al Hanna, Principal - *Engineering*

Salary Minimum: $50,000

Functions: Engineering, Architects

Industries: Architectural Svcs., K-12 Ed., Higher Ed., Engineering Svcs.

The Hanna Group

12140 Fowlers Mill Rd
Chardon, OH 44024-9315
(440) 285-2468
Fax: (440) 285-2066
Email: hanna@hannagroup.com
Web: www.hannagroup.com

Summary: Mid to upper-level management search in manufacturing, engineering, finance, HR and sales/marketing. We offer specific expertise in commercial vehicle, construction, agricultural equipment, heavy capital equipment, automotive, and allied industry.

Key Contact - Specialty:
Mr. M.A. (Jack) Hanna, Jr., President -
 Engineering, Finance, Sales
Ms. U.T. Hanna, Secretary

Salary Minimum: $50,000

Functions: Management, Mfg., Materials, Sales & Mktg., HR Mgmt., Finance, Engineering, Architects, Attorneys, Int'l.

Industries: Construction, Manufacturing, Transportation, Advertising, Environmental Svcs., Aerospace

Hanover Partners

60 Lewis Wharf
The Pilot House
Boston, MA 02110-3903
(617) 742-4222
Email: bedick@hanovercareers.com

Summary: We specialize in placing professionals of all levels within the accounting and finance disciplines. Our industry expertise spans several sectors including financial services, investment banking, biotechnology, software and high-technology manufacturing.

Key Contact - Specialty:
Ms. Beth Edick, Principal - *Executives*

Functions: Generalist (All)

Industries: Energy, Utilities, Drugs Mfg., Medical Devices, Venture Cap., Mutual/Hedge Funds, Communications, Real Estate, Software, Biotech/Life Sciences, Healthcare

Harbeck Associates Inc

2003 Claremont Cc Cmn
Normal, IL 61761-5275
(309) 452-5773
Fax: (309) 454-2332
Email: bill@harbeckassociates.com
Web: www.greatsalesjobs.com

Summary: We are a sales and executive recruiting firm specializing in the pharmaceutical, biotechnology and medical equipment industries. We help our clients staff their sales and sales management positions.

Key Contact - Specialty:
Ms. Lori Harbeck, President
Mr. Bill Baracani, Vice President -
 Pharmaceutical

Salary Minimum: $40,000

Functions: Generalist (All)

Industries: Drugs Mfg., Medical Devices, Biotech/Life Sciences, Healthcare

Harbor Consultants International Inc

PO Box 221616
Chantilly, VA 20153-1616
(703) 352-1888
Email: harbor_resumes@attglobal.net

Summary: We are a well established and highly regarded executive search firm specializing in the legal industry. We are recognized by the nation's leading law firms for our ability to attract top legal talent. We are especially adept at matching individual style with firm culture insuring long term relationships.

Key Contact - Specialty:
Mr. Frank Ojeda
Ms. Georgette Kohler

Functions: Legal, Attorneys

Industries: Generalist (All), Legal

Harbrowe Inc

PO Box 1240
Marion, MT 59925-1240
(877) 964-7301
Fax: (406) 854-2320
Email: j@harbrowe.com
Web: www.harbrowe.com

Summary: Recruiting for bio-technology/pharmaceutical sales and management.

Key Contact - Specialty:
Ms. Joanne LeBow, President - *Pharmaceutical*

Functions: Generalist (All), Management, Sales & Mktg.

Industries: Drugs Mfg., Pharm Svcs., Biotech/Life Sciences, Healthcare, Hospitals

Harcourt & Associates

10180 101 St NW
Manulife Place
Edmonton, AB T5J 3S4
Canada
(780) 425-5555
Fax: (780) 990-1891
Email: recruiter@harcourt.ca
Web: www.harcourt.ca

Summary: We provide staff and contract recruiting services. Area of recruitment: executive search, technical/engineering, insurance, accounting, office support and sales & marketing.

Key Contact - Specialty:
Ms. Judy Harcourt, CPC, President
Ms. Barbara Perkins, CPC, Vice President
Mr. Peter Harcourt, CPC, Chairman & Manager
 Technical Division - *Engineering,*
 Manufacturing

Functions: Generalist (All), Senior Mgmt., Mfg., Materials, Sales & Mktg., Finance, IT, Engineering

Industries: Generalist (All), Agri., Forestry, Mining, Energy, Utilities, Construction, Chemicals, Metal Products, Computer Equip.

Hardage Group

PO Box 208
Dyersburg, TN 38025-0208
(731) 285-3120
(800) 929-5970
Fax: (731) 286-6329
Email: hardage@ecsis.net
Web: www.hardagegroup.com

Summary: Principals are seasoned HR professionals with extensive executive recruiting experience. Primarily focused on union-free manufacturing environments in the functional areas of HR, finance, engineering and general management.

Key Contact - Specialty:
Mr. Phillip Hardage, CPC, Owner & Counselor -
 Engineering, Finance, Human resources, Steel

Ms. Grace Phelps, CPC, Counselor - *Food,*
 Human resources, Printing, Retail
Ms. Patsy Reasons, CPC, Counselor - *Automotive,*
 Food, Safety

Salary Minimum: $40,000

Functions: Mfg., Production, Automation, HR Mgmt., Finance

Industries: Generalist (All), Manufacturing, Food, Bev., Tobacco, Printing, Plastics, Rubber, Metal Products, Machine, Appliance, Motor Vehicles, Misc. Mfg., HR Services

Harder Consulting Inc

8303 N Mopac Expy Ste 270C
Austin, TX 78759-8351
(512) 479-0000
Fax: (512) 372-9900
Email: jobs@harderconsulting.com
Web: www.harderconsulting.com

Summary: Placement firm specializing in finance and accounting and human resources. Industries of specialization include technology, manufacturing, semiconductor, telecom, public accounting and services.

Key Contact - Specialty:
Ms. Elizabeth Harder, CPA, CPC, President -
 Accounting, Controllers, Finance,
 Manufacturing, Technology
Mr. Pete R. Farias, CPC, Manager, Recruiting -
 Accounting, Accounting (General),
 Comptrollers, Controllers, Finance

Salary Minimum: $40,000

Functions: Finance, Budgeting

Industries: Generalist (All), Manufacturing, Computer Equip., Test, Measure Equip., Misc. Mfg., Semiconductors, Finance, Services, Accounting, Advertising, Software

HardHatJobs Inc

(also known as Construction Executive Search)
1200 Executive Dr E Ste 127A
Richardson, TX 75081-2263
(972) 808-9200
(972) 808-9201
Email: bill@hardhatjobs.com
Web: www.hardhatjobs.com

Summary: We specialize in direct hire permanent, and temporary professional services contract staffing of senior executives and middle management, construction professionals, business managers, contractors and office administrators, human resources and safety professionals in the general contracting and construction management industries. Construction Executive Search sources and identifies C-level and Senior Management officers for commercial contractors via private emails.

Key Contact - Specialty:
Mr. Bill Stynetski, CPC, President - *Architecture,*
 C-level, Construction, Engineering,
 Management
Ms. Lynn S. Taylor, Manager, College Recruiting
 - *Architecture, Construction, Engineering,*
 General contractors, Highways

Functions: Management, Senior Mgmt., Middle Mgmt.

Industries: Construction

Robert Harkins Associates Inc

PO Box 547
Mount Gretna, PA 17064-0547
(717) 272-2503
Email: info@harkinsassoc.com
Web: www.harkinsassoc.com

Summary: The firm offers contingency, retained search and contract professional placement services in accounting, finance, engineering, manufacturing, logistics and HR.

Key Contact - Specialty:
Mr. Robert E. Harkins, CPC, President - *Engineering, Human resources, Manufacturing*

Salary Minimum: $40,000

Functions: Generalist (All)

Industries: Generalist (All), Printing, Chemicals, Medical Devices, Plastics, Rubber, Metal Products, Motor Vehicles, Electronic, Elec. Components, Robotics, Consumer Goods

The Harlan Group Inc

8624 Old Marsh Way
Montgomery, AL 36117-7414
(334) 279-7007
Fax: (334) 279-7940
Email: info@foodrecruiters.net
Web: www.Foodrecruiters.net

Summary: We place qualified candidates in salaried positions within all areas of food and beverage manufacturing and logistics industries. With extensive years of experience, we feel we have a strong understanding of these industries.

Key Contact - Specialty:
Ms. Lana K. Morris, CPC, President - *Accounting, Production, Purchasing, Research & development, Safety*
Mr. Harry G. Morris, CPC, Executive Vice President - *Finance, Manufacturing (Management), Quality, Research & development, Sales*
Ms. Debbie Bates, Search Assistant - *Food, Food & beverage, Manufacturing*
Mr. Chris Morris, CPC, Executive Recruiter & Consultant - *Bakery, Food, Food & beverage, Maintenance, Manufacturing*

Salary Minimum: $30,000

Functions: Mfg., Product Dev., Production, Plant Mgmt., Quality, Materials, Purchasing, Sales & Mktg., Finance, R&D

Industries: Food, Bev., Tobacco, Packaging

Harper Associates

31000 Northwestern Hwy Ste 240
Farmington Hills, MI 48334-2564
(248) 932-1170
Fax: (248) 932-1214
Email: resumes@harperjobs.com
Web: www.harperjobs.com

Summary: Hospitality management recruitment specialists for hotels, restaurants, resorts, country clubs and food service management companies. Searches are also conducted in healthcare.

Key Contact - Specialty:
Mr. Bennett Schwartz, President - *Hospitality*
Ms. Cindy Krainen, Vice President - *Hospitality*

Functions: Generalist (All), Middle Mgmt., Nurses, Health Admin., Mktg. Mgmt., Sales Mgmt., IT, Non-profits

Industries: Generalist (All), Retail, Non-profits, Hospitality, Healthcare

Harper Hewes Inc

1473 Calkins Rd
Pittsford, NY 14534-2545
(585) 321-1700
Fax: (585) 321-1707
Email: dharper@harperhewes.com
Web: www.harperhewes.com

Summary: We have a proven track record in providing qualified, hirable candidates who meet

or exceed our clients' expectations. We specialize in filling critical and sensitive positions requiring the ideal balance of technical expertise and interpersonal skills. Our industry focus includes: IT solutions & services, bio-technology/bioinformatics, financial services, management consulting, IT consulting and HR. Our interim executive division focuses on short term, shared or project based positions.

Key Contact - Specialty:
Ms. Deborah Harper, President - *C-level, Consulting, Sales, Senior management, Temporary*
Mr. David Miller, Vice President - *C-level, Senior management, Temporary*

Salary Minimum: $75,000

Functions: Senior Mgmt., Middle Mgmt., Sales & Mktg., Mktg. Mgmt., Sales Mgmt., Direct Mktg., HR Mgmt., Benefits, IT, Mgmt. Consultants

Industries: Generalist (All), Computer Equip., Finance, Mgmt. Consulting, HR Services, E-commerce, IT Implementation, Communications, Call Centers, Software, Biotech/Life Sciences

Bob Harrington Associates

214 Hillstone Pl # B
Jamestown, NC 27282-2000
(336) 454-1500
Fax: (336) 454-6011
Email: resumes@bobharringtonassociates.com
Web: www.bobharringtonassociates.com

Summary: We are specialists in printing, packaging and related industries with primary emphasis on labels.

Key Contact - Specialty:
Mr. Bob Harrington, CPC, President

Salary Minimum: $50,000

Functions: Generalist (All), Management, Senior Mgmt., Mfg.

Industries: Construction, Textiles, Apparel, Lumber, Furniture, Paper, Printing, Chemicals, Plastics, Rubber, Paints, Petro. Products, Computer Equip., Packaging

Harrington, O'Brien & Conway International

27 N Wacker Rm 660
Chicago, IL 60606-2800
Email: aconway@webmailoutlet.com

Summary: General management positions for most industries with some concentration within medical.

Key Contact - Specialty:
Mr. Andy G. Conway, Principal
Mr. Charles Harrington, II, Principal - *Biomedical*
Mr. James O'Brien, Principal - *Emergency room*

Salary Minimum: $60,000

Functions: Management, Nurses, Allied Health, HR Mgmt.

Industries: Generalist (All), Drugs Mfg., Medical Devices, Biotech/Life Sciences, Healthcare

Susan Harris & Associates

606 Post Rd E Ste 1 PMB 613
Westport, CT 06880-4540
(203) 227-5700
Fax: (203) 227-5688
Email: jobs@susanharris.com
Web: www.susanharris.com

Summary: We specialize in the placement of marketing, promotion and sales executives with a special emphasis on promotion agency executives.

Key Contact - Specialty:
Ms. Susan Harris, President

Salary Minimum: $30,000

Functions: Generalist (All)

Industries: Advertising

Jeff Harris & Associates

1959 Peace Haven Rd Ste 302
Winston Salem, NC 27106-4850
(800) 660-5640
Fax: (805) 435-3659
Email: info@jeffharrisassociates.com
Web: www.jeffharrisassociates.com

Summary: We are a full service executive recruiting and consulting firm that specializes in the healthcare industry. Our approach marries the professional, consultative environment of retained search firms with the flexibility of contingency search. At the heart of our efforts is a collaborative approach aimed at building strong successful management teams for our clients as well as dynamic and strategic career advancement for our candidates.

Key Contact - Specialty:
Mr. Jeff Harris, President - *Assisted living, Executives, Healthcare, Hospitality, Long term care*
Ms. Mary Poole, Senior Recruiter - *Assisted living, Healthcare, Home health, Long term care, Managed care*
Mr. Nick Bierman, Recruiter - *Healthcare, Home health, Hospital, Long term care*
Ms. Mia Mercado, Recruiter - *Assisted living, Healthcare, Long term care*
Ms. Jody Bierman, Recruiter - *Home health, Hospital, Hospitality, Long term care*

Salary Minimum: $60,000

Functions: Generalist (All), Management, Senior Mgmt., Middle Mgmt., Healthcare, Nurses, Allied Health, Health Admin., Sales & Mktg., Mktg. Research

Industries: Non-profits, Hotels, Resorts, Clubs, Property/Facility Mgmt., Healthcare, Hospitals, Long-term/Home Care

Branches:
23679 Calabasas Rd Ste 117
Calabasas, CA 91302-1502
(800) 660-5640
Email: info@jeffharrisassociates.com
Key Contact - Specialty:
Mr. Robert Batkovic, Senior Recruiter - *Assisted living, Hospital, Hospitality, Long term care*

Harris McCully Associates Inc

99 Park Ave Fl 18
New York, NY 10016-1601
(212) 983-1400
Fax: (212) 983-1451
Email: info@harrismccully.com
Web: www.harrismccully.com

Summary: We are a contingency and retainer-based search firm specializing in the placement of middle to senior-level professionals. Our forte is in financial services and luxury goods, yet we work with diverse industries and multiple disciplines.

Key Contact - Specialty:
Mr. Alan Harris, Chief Executive Officer & President
Mr. Ron Hamara, Chief Operating Officer & Sr VP

Salary Minimum: $75,000

Functions: Generalist (All), Management, HR Mgmt., Finance, IT, Int'l.

Industries: Generalist (All), Textiles, Apparel, Banking, Invest. Banking, Brokers, Venture Cap., Misc. Financial, Hospitality

Harris Personnel Resources

2425 W Pioneer Pkwy Ste 204
Pantego, TX 76013-6044
(817) 265-9190
Fax: (817) 543-3155
Email: veharris@imagin.net
Web: www.fullcareerservices.com

Summary: A full service search firm providing direct hire, contracting and temp-to-hire in most professional disciplines.

Key Contact - Specialty:
Ms. Vera E. Harris, Owner

Functions: Middle Mgmt., Mfg., Production, Plant Mgmt., Engineering

Industries: Plastics, Rubber, Paints, Petro. Products, Metal Products, Machine, Appliance, Motor Vehicles, Consumer Elect., Test, Measure Equip., Misc. Mfg., Robotics

Kenneth Harris Recruiting Group

1950 Butler Pike
PMB 222
Conshohocken, PA 19428-1202
(610) 940-3855
(888) 282-4118
Fax: (610) 940-3944
Email: khrg@khrg.com
Web: www.jobperfect.com

Summary: One of the premier national executive search firms exclusively dedicated to the recruitment of actuaries, underwriters, claims professionals, risk managers, retail & wholesale brokers and senior management for the property & casualty and healthcare insurance and reinsurance industries.

Key Contact - Specialty:
Mr. David Rubinstein, President - *Actuarial, CEOs, CFOs, Insurance (Casualty,Claims)*
Mr. Mark Abraham, Vice President - *Accounting, Actuarial, CEOs, CFOs, COOs*
Ms. Jessica Hoing, Underwriting Recruiting Specialist - *Insurance, Insurance (Casualty,Claims,Health,Life)*
Ms. Wendie Bender, Executive Search Associate - *Actuarial, Healthcare, Insurance (Casualty,Claims,Health)*

Salary Minimum: $75,000

Functions: Senior Mgmt., Sales & Mktg., HR Mgmt., Finance, Risk Mgmt., Actuaries, MIS Mgmt.

Industries: Insurance, Casualty, Claims, Life, Commercial, Re-Insurance

Career Partners International/Harrison & Associates

207-131 John St S
Hamilton, ON L8N 2C3
Canada
(905) 527-0631
(905) 527-3032
Email: info@cpi-hamilton.ca
Web: www.cpiworld.com

Summary: Providing outstanding HR services. An ethical, confidential and personal approach has earned a well deserved reputation for professionalism and quality results. Recruit for executive, managerial, professional, engineering and senior technical positions in both the private and public sectors.

Key Contact - Specialty:
Mr. Fred Hopkinson, CHRP, President
Mr. Peter Soderquest, Senior Associate
Ms. Leigh Kras, Consultant

Functions: Generalist (All)

Industries: Generalist (All), Manufacturing, Accounting, Mgmt. Consulting, HR Services, Hospitals

Harrison Consulting Group Inc

2660 Townsgate Rd Ste 160B
Westlake Village, CA 91361-5750
(805) 449-7250
Fax: (805) 449-7230
Email: doug@harrisonsearch.com
Web: www.harrisonsearch.com

Summary: Professional recruiters creating winning business relationships for permanent and temporary tax professionals.

Key Contact - Specialty:
Mr. Douglas Harrison Grue, President - *Tax*

Salary Minimum: $45,000

Functions: Taxes

Industries: Generalist (All)

The Harrison Group

PO Box 743
Milltown, NJ 08850-0743
(732) 249-6777
Fax: (732) 249-9108
Email: scott@harrisongroup.com
Web: www.harrisongroup.com

Summary: We are a technical search firm that focuses our recruiting efforts primarily in the following industries: pharmaceutical, cosmetics/personal care and chemical. We place candidates in the following areas: chemists (analytical R&D, QC, product development and tech services), engineering (chemical, packaging and industrial), regulatory affairs, regulatory compliance and quality. We perform searches on both a contingency and retained basis.

Key Contact - Specialty:
Mr. Scott W. Szur

Functions: Quality, R&D, Engineering

Industries: Chemicals, Soap, Perf., Cosmtcs., Drugs Mfg., Pharm Svcs.

Harrison Moore Inc

16009 Orchard Cir
Omaha, NE 68135-1068
(402) 861-0555
Fax: (312) 873-3895
Email: cmcley@cox.net

Summary: Specialty in the foundry and machining industries: management, production, operations, quality, technical, tooling, sales, metallurgy, plant engineering and maintenance.

Key Contact - Specialty:
Mr. Curt McLey, President

Functions: Management, Mfg., Product Dev., Production, Plant Mgmt., Quality, Productivity, Materials, Purchasing, Sales & Mktg.

Industries: Metal Products

Donald L Hart & Associates

604-3 Church St
Toronto, ON M5E 1M2
Canada
(416) 862-7104
Email: info@dlhart.com
Web: www.dlhart.com

Summary: We conduct professional IT recruiting in the areas of executive management personnel, key line sales personnel, marketing, program & project management, technical specialists and engineers. Our fields of expertise include: communication, systems & networks, graphics, applications software, professional services, web design and XML/HTML.

Key Contact - Specialty:
Mr. Donald L. Hart

Functions: Sales & Mktg., IT, Systems Analysis, Systems Dev., Systems Implem., Network Admin., DB Admin., Engineering, Environmentalists

Industries: Oil & Gas, Construction, Manufacturing, Test, Measure Equip., Electronic, Elec. Components, E-commerce, IT Implementation, PSA/ASP, Telephony, Network Infrastructure, Environmental Svcs., Haz. Waste, Database SW, ERP SW, Networking, Comm. SW, Security SW, System SW

Hart & Company

219 E 69th St Apt 7J
New York, NY 10021-5455
(212) 585-4000
Fax: (212) 585-1294
Email: gghart@aol.com
Web: www.hartandcompany.com

Summary: We are an executive recruiting organization with focus on the consumer-advertising agency and corporate communications industries. Agency positions are in all levels of account management, account planning, media and research. Client side includes advertising and marketing specialists.

Key Contact - Specialty:
Mr. Gerry Hart

Salary Minimum: $30,000

Functions: Management, Advertising, Mktg. Mgmt.

Industries: Advertising, New Media, Broadcast, Film, Marketing SW

Hartman & Company

535 Yale Ave
Claremont, CA 91711-4342
(909) 621-0117
Email: hartman@uia.net

Summary: Area of specialty is the recruitment and placement of mid and senior-level executives in the forest products, building materials and hard lines industries. Retail, wholesale and manufacturing arenas are served.

Key Contact - Specialty:
Mr. Dan Hartman, President

Functions: Generalist (All), Management, Senior Mgmt., Middle Mgmt.

Industries: Generalist (All), Agri., Forestry, Mining, Construction, Lumber, Furniture, Paper, Transportation, Wholesale, Retail, Marketing SW

Hartman Greene & Wells

1827 Jefferson Pl NW
Washington, DC 20036-2557
(202) 223-7644
(301) 775-2147
Email: zgreene@hartmangreene.com
Web: www.hartmangreene.com

Summary: Our greatest strength is providing qualified candidates both expeditiously and confidentially in the legal community. Our success is due to our personal touch. We only place in our

local area so that we know our clients and meet with our candidates.

Key Contact - Specialty:
Ms. Zina L. Greene, President

Functions: Attorneys

Industries: Legal

Harvco Consulting
7500 S Spalding Lake Dr
Atlanta, GA 30350-1043
(770) 913-0802
Email: atlantamri@mindspring.com

Summary: Specializing in technology start-ups, high-technology development, manufacturing, software, CRM/ERP, e-commerce and international applications. We have foundations in water technology, pulp & paper, building products, packaging, packaging systems, process sterilization for food & beverage and logistics/distribution. Primary disciplines include strategic business change, new product/business development, operations management and executive leadership.

Key Contact - Specialty:
Mr. John K. Harvey, President - *Building products, Logistics*

Salary Minimum: $75,000

Functions: Generalist (All), Product Dev., Packaging, Mktg. Mgmt., Finance, Engineering, Int'l.

Industries: Manufacturing, Food, Bev., Tobacco, Lumber, Furniture, Paper, Printing, Chemicals, Medical Devices, Plastics, Rubber, Metal Products, Test, Measure Equip., Electronic, Elec. Components, Transportation, Finance, Services, Non-profits, HR Services, E-commerce, Communications, Wireless, Packaging, Software, ERP SW, Marketing SW

Harwood & Harwood Inc
PO Box 1926
Blowing Rock, NC 28605-1926
(828) 295-9933
Fax: (828) 295-7290
Email: dharwood@harwoodsearch.com
Web: www.harwoodsearch.com

Summary: Our firm is an executive search firm serving the commercial banking, mortgage banking, real estate and legal industries. Our practice has earned the reputation as a premier recruiting firm for the financial services and legal industries by providing exceptional service and knowledgeable consultation to our clients.

Key Contact - Specialty:
Mr. David Harwood, CPC, President
Mr. Graham Harwood, CPC, Chief Executive Officer
Mr. Rick Tobin, Senior Associate
Mr. Web Alexander, Associate
Mr. George Burdell, Associate

Salary Minimum: $40,000

Functions: Generalist (All), Management, Senior Mgmt., Middle Mgmt., Sales & Mktg., HR Mgmt., Finance, Risk Mgmt., MIS Mgmt., Legal

Industries: Finance, Banking, Misc. Financial

Harwood Allen Associates
3615 Belgray Dr NW
Kennesaw, GA 30152-6995
(678) 290-1300
Fax: (707)
Email: mark@harwoodallen.com
Web: www.harwoodallen.com

Summary: We are a full-service recruiting firm. We have companies identify and hire exceptional talent in sales, marketing, product management, professional services and engineering. Our market focus includes: next generation communications, software & systems.

Key Contact - Specialty:
Mr. Mark Hill, Managing Partner - *Communications, Computers (Networking), Information Systems, Start-up companies, Telecommunications*
Ms. Les Newman, Recruiter - *Communications, Computers (Networking), High technology, Information Systems, Wireless*

Salary Minimum: $100,000

Functions: Management, Senior Mgmt., Middle Mgmt., Product Dev., Sales & Mktg., MIS Mgmt., Engineering

Industries: Telecoms, Telephony, Digital, Wireless, Fiber Optic, Network Infrastructure, Database SW, Development SW, ERP SW, Networking, Comm. SW, Security SW, System SW

Branches:
1301 Capital of Texas Hwy Ste A13
Austin, TX 78746-6574
(678) 290-1300

Hastings & Hastings
1001 Brickell Bay Dr Ste 2902
Miami, FL 33131-4903
(305) 374-2255
Fax: (305) 374-6417
Email: info@hastingsonline.com
Web: www.hastingsonline.com

Summary: We have grown to become a highly respected industry leader in placement and staffing with a well known reputation for excellence. We have continued to increase the services offered by adding a state of the art computer system, executive placement, a temp-to-permanent department and a temp division.

Key Contact - Specialty:
Ms. Lee Roberts, Senior Vice President
Ms Jill Brinkley, Vice President
Ms. Tina Rogers, Account Executive - *Finance, Marketing*
Ms. Claudia Perry, Account Executive

Functions: Generalist (All), Management, Sales & Mktg., HR Mgmt., Finance, IT

Industries: Generalist (All), Manufacturing, Finance, Services, Media, Software

Frank W Hastings
693A Rose Hollow Dr
Yardley, PA 19067-6333
(215) 321-0299
Email: fhastings2@verizon.net

Summary: We have been in the recruiting business for an extensive number of years. We hold membership in a network of several hundred recruiting firms, which is an invaluable service to applicants and employers by assuring success in their search.

Key Contact - Specialty:
Mr. Frank W. Hastings, President & Owner - *Accounting, Administration, Data processing, Manufacturing, Sales*

Salary Minimum: $50,000

Functions: Middle Mgmt., Admin. Svcs., Mfg., Materials, Sales & Mktg., HR Mgmt., Finance, IT, Engineering, Legal

Industries: Generalist (All)

Robert W Havener Associates Inc
2408 Chatau Ct
Fallston, MD 21047-2318
(410) 893-0256
Fax: (410) 420-8125
Email: havenerr@verizon.net

Summary: We have been specializing in the printing and packaging industry since inception. We place presidents, VPs, production management, sales and production positions.

Key Contact - Specialty:
Mr. Robert W. Havener, President - *Management, Printing*
Mr. Robert E. Hammock, Vice President - *Printing, Production*

Salary Minimum: $40,000

Functions: Senior Mgmt., Middle Mgmt., Plant Mgmt., Quality, Sales Mgmt., HR Mgmt.

Industries: Printing, Packaging

Phyllis Hawkins & Associates Inc
7601 N Central Ave Unit 5
Phoenix, AZ 85020-4080
(602) 263-0248
Fax: (602) 678-1564
Email: phyllis@azlawsearch.com
Web: www.azlawsearch.com

Summary: We conduct attorney searches for law firms and corporations. Our staff has an in-depth knowledge of the legal communities in our area and substantial experience in legal recruitment.

Key Contact - Specialty:
Ms. Phyllis Hawkins, President

Salary Minimum: $120,000

Functions: Legal, Attorneys

Industries: Generalist (All), Non-Classifiable

Michael J Hawkins Inc
1615 W Colonial Pkwy
Inverness, IL 60067-4732
(847) 705-5400
Fax: (847) 705-9065
Email: mikehawkins@mjhawkinsinc.com
Web: www.mjhawkinsinc.com

Summary: We are one of the nation's leading executive search organizations specializing in the supply segment of the food service industry. Search limited to general management, sales, marketing, engineering and manufacturing executives.

Key Contact - Specialty:
Mr. Michael J. Hawkins, CFSP, President - *Food, Food service*

Salary Minimum: $50,000

Functions: Senior Mgmt., Mfg.

Industries: Manufacturing, Paper, Chemicals

Haydon Legal Search
5225 Old Orchard Rd Ste 8
Skokie, IL 60077-1027
(847) 965-8222
Fax: (847) 965-1447
Email: haydonlegal@aol.com
Web: www.haydonlegal.com

Summary: Our founder, specializing in attorney search and placement, is recognized for providing exceptional recruiting services to law firms and corporate legal departments.

Key Contact - Specialty:
Ms. Meredith Haydon, Principal

Functions: Attorneys

Industries: Legal

Hayman Daugherty Associates Inc

5105 Old Ellis Pt
Roswell, GA 30076-5705
(800) 765-0432
(770) 772-4558
Fax: (800) 782-4999
Email: info@haymandaugherty.com
Web: www.haymandaugherty.com

Summary: We specialize in building relationships. Our consultants are geographically and specialty divided which allows them to enjoy a high-level of expertise. We understand your needs and can help you accomplish your goals.

Key Contact - Specialty:
Ms. Kimberly J. Daugherty-Hill, Chief Executive Officer
Ms. Karen Wink, Chief Operating Officer

Salary Minimum: $100,000

Functions: Physicians

Industries: Non-Classifiable

Hayward Simone Associates Inc

119 W 23rd St Ste 406
New York, NY 10011-6369
(212) 989-3003
Fax: (212) 989-3004
Email: hsa@haysim.com
Web: www.haywardsimone.com

Summary: Our areas of expertise include emerging technologies, management and IT consulting, systems development and integration; application implementation, deployment and business process planning.

Key Contact - Specialty:
Mr. Morris Green, Partner & Co-Founder
Ms. Judith Karpel, Partner & Co-Founder

Functions: IT

Industries: Finance, Banking, Misc. Financial, E-commerce, IT Implementation, Network Infrastructure, Government, Software

Lynn Hazan & Associates Inc

55 E Washington St Ste 715
Chicago, IL 60602-2842
(312) 863-5401
(312) 863-5402
Fax: (312) 960-9660
Email: lynn@lhazan.com
Web: www.lhazan.com

Summary: Specialties: marketing, communications and consulting. Values relationship marketing with candidates and clients. Clients include: PR and ad agencies, corporations, consulting firms and non-profits. Positions in corporate communications, marketing communications, PR, marketing, interactive, DM, editorial, art direction, graphic design, web content/design, copywriting, product management and account management.

Key Contact - Specialty:
Ms. Lynn Hazan, President - *Communications, Marketing*

Functions: Product Dev., Healthcare, Sales & Mktg., Advertising, Mktg. Research, Mktg. Mgmt., Direct Mktg., PR, Graphic Designers

Industries: Food, Bev., Tobacco, Computer Equip., Consumer Elect., Finance, Services, Non-profits, Pharm Svcs., Legal, Mgmt. Consulting, Higher Ed., Hospitality, Media, Advertising, Publishing, New Media, Packaging, Insurance, Real Estate, Software, Biotech/Life Sciences, Healthcare

Hazard, Young, Attea & Associates Ltd

1151 Waukegan Rd Ste 200
Glenview, IL 60025-3074
(847) 724-8465
Email: office@hyasearch.com
Web: www.hyasupersearches.com

Summary: We are an executive search services and management consulting with special emphasis on school districts, higher education.

Key Contact - Specialty:
Dr. William Attea, Managing Partner

Functions: Senior Mgmt., Middle Mgmt.

Industries: Higher Ed.

The HBC Group Inc

370 Lexington Ave Rm 2200
New York, NY 10017-6573
(212) 661-8300
Fax: (212) 661-8308
Email: norman@hbcgroupinc.com
Web: www.hbcgroupinc.com

Summary: We provide executive search for the banking industry. We specialize in risk management positions - capital markets credit risk management, market risk management, operational risk management and corporate credit.

Key Contact - Specialty:
Mr. Norman Gershgorn
Mr. Peter Herzog

Salary Minimum: $50,000

Functions: Middle Mgmt.

Industries: Banking

HCI Corp

28 S 5th St
Geneva, IL 60134-2111
(630) 208-3100
Fax: (630) 208-3111
Web: www.hci-search.com

Summary: What we offer is the ability to locate, screen and recruit the best possible candidates that fit your stringent criteria. This eliminates many of the risks involved in the hiring process along with finding the top candidates who may not be actively looking.

Key Contact - Specialty:
Mr. Frank Cianchetti, President - *Healthcare*
Mr. Kevin Joy - *Bakery*
Mr. Richard Smith
Mr. Wade Kawahara - *Chemical*
Mr. Bud Mulcahy
Mr. Mark Carlson

Functions: Generalist (All), Senior Mgmt., Production, Plant Mgmt., Sales & Mktg., Engineering, Int'l.

Industries: Generalist (All), Medical Devices, Biotech/Life Sciences, Healthcare

HDB Incorporated

PO Box 1612
Manchester, MO 63011-1312
(636) 391-7799
Email: kwolfe@hdbinc.com
Web: www.hdbinc.com

Summary: Our philosophy is simple: provide quality service to our client companies and candidates by setting standards of excellence through the commitment of our talents, expertise and resources.

Key Contact - Specialty:
Ms. Kathryn Davis Wolfe, CPC, President & Chief Executive Officer - *SAP*

Salary Minimum: $65,000

HDJ & Associates Inc

PO Box 252
Wexford, PA 15090-0252
(724) 933-3130
Fax: (724) 933-3119
Email: info@hdjassociates.com
Web: www.hdjassociates.com

Summary: We offer dedicated, personalized employment and search solutions to companies throughout the United States. Our team brings over 50 years of combined experience in sales, consulting and recruiting to your firm, putting our team head and shoulders above other search firms. Our permanent employment options include customized retainer searches, flexible container searches and basic contingency searches.

Key Contact - Specialty:
Ms. Hayley D. Jameson, President
Mr. Gary Napotnik, Managing Director - *Computers (Software), COOs, Information Technology, Manufacturing (Management), Sales*

Salary Minimum: $50,000

Functions: Generalist (All)

Industries: Generalist (All)

Headhunters Executive Search Inc

242 Washington Ave Ste H
Nutley, NJ 07110-1956
(973) 667-2799
Email: medsalesplus@aol.com

Summary: We recruit and place sales reps and management primarily in medical products and pharmaceuticals. Our secondary placement is in consumer sales.

Key Contact - Specialty:
Ms. Maria Mosca, President - *Marketing*
Ms. Elaine Jones, Vice President - *Marketing*

Salary Minimum: $80,000

Functions: Sales Mgmt.

Industries: Drugs Mfg., Medical Devices, Pharm Svcs., Biotech/Life Sciences, Healthcare

Health Care Dimensions

7330 S Alton Way Ste C
Centennial, CO 80112-2318
(800) 373-3401
(303) 814-8821
Fax: (303) 814-8832
Email: info@healthcaredimensions.com
Web: www.healthcaredimensions.com

Summary: We are the leaders in executive search for the eldercare continuum. We recruit top-level professionals for the most progressive long term care and senior living service companies in the country. Over the years we have developed an unparalleled network of contacts and resources. No other search firm can make this claim and back it up with a proven track record. We are ready to act quickly and discreetly on your behalf.

Key Contact - Specialty:
Ms. Angie Fetter, President & Managing Partner - *Assisted living, Healthcare, Long term care*
Mr. Bob Fetter, Managing Partner - *Assisted living, Healthcare, Long term care*

Salary Minimum: $50,000

Functions: Generalist (All)

Industries: Long-term/Home Care

Health Care Recruiting

61052 Ladera Rd Ste 400
Bend, OR 97702-9501
(541) 382-1732
Email: hcrjim@hcrecruit.com
Web: www.hcrecruit.com

Summary: We recruit for healthcare providers, physicians and midlevels. Our firm has recruited physicians and midlevels, worked extensively with client hospitals and clinics and worked ethically and confidentially on each and every search.

Key Contact - Specialty:
Mr. Jim Ransom

Salary Minimum: $100,000

Functions: Healthcare, Physicians

Industries: Healthcare

Health Search Inc

4175 E La Palma Ave Ste 125
Anaheim, CA 92807-1829
(714) 854-0100
Fax: (714) 854-0111
Email: jeff@health-search.net
Web: www.health-search.net

Summary: A search firm which conducts management level searches in the administrative, financial and clinical areas within the hospital, home health, managed care and medical group sectors of the healthcare industry.

Key Contact - Specialty:
Mr. Jeffrey Robbins, President - *Healthcare*
Ms. Fabiola Thomas, Executive Recruiter - *Healthcare*
Mr. Rick Wootton, Executive Recruiter - *Healthcare*
Ms. Barbara Carol, Director, Research - *Healthcare*
Ms. Alison Materassi, Research Associate
Mr. Jerry Schneider, Consultant - *Healthcare*
Mr. Donald Amaral, Advisor - *Healthcare*
Dr. Robert Landman, MD, Advisor, Medical - *Healthcare*

Salary Minimum: $75,000

Functions: Generalist (All), Management, Middle Mgmt., Healthcare

Industries: Healthcare, Hospitals, Long-term/Home Care

HealthCare Concepts

266 S Front St Ste 206
Memphis, TN 38103-3803
(800) 442-4346
(901) 527-7701
Fax: (901) 529-9101
Email: susan@healthcareconcepts.com
Web: www.healthcareconcepts.com

Summary: One of the nation's oldest executive search firms dedicated to serving the home health industry. Other specialty areas include long-term care, hospice, rehab and acute care. A full range of executive search services including interim management and additional consulting are available.

Key Contact - Specialty:
Ms. Laurel Reisman, President - *Home health*

Functions: Senior Mgmt., Healthcare

Industries: Generalist (All), Healthcare, Hospitals, Long-term/Home Care

HealthCare Recruiters International • Dallas

5220 Spring Valley Rd Ste 40
Dallas, TX 75254-1955
(972) 661-0055
(800) 380-9725 x 210
Email: andrea.forray@hcrnetwork.com
Web: www.healthcarerecruiters.com

Summary: We are an exclusive healthcare executive search firm emphasizing sales, sales management and clinical management opportunities. Candidates must currently be employed in medical/product sales or be a clinical candidate

Key Contact - Specialty:
Ms. Andrea Forray, RN, Manager, Business Development

Salary Minimum: $75,000

Functions: Management, Senior Mgmt., Nurses, Sales & Mktg.

Industries: Drugs Mfg., Medical Devices, Pharm Svcs., Insurance, Biotech/Life Sciences, Healthcare, Hospitals, Long-term/Home Care

Branches:
4500 Black Rock Rd Ste 102
Hampstead, MD 21074-2634
(410) 239-6464
Fax: (410) 374-5887
Email: midatlantic@hcrnetwork.com
Key Contact - Specialty:
Mr. Keith Graham

15400 S Outer 40 Ste 100
Chesterfield, MO 63017-2063
(636) 530-1030
Fax: (636) 530-1039
Email: stlouis@hcrnetwork.com
Key Contact - Specialty:
Mr. Dan Bemus

5321 S Sheridan Rd Ste 5
Tulsa, OK 74145-7509
(918) 828-7789
Fax: (918) 828-9008
Email: heartland@hcrnetwork.com

5220 Spring Valley Rd Ste 40
Dallas, TX 75254-3099
(972) 661-0055
Email: andrea.forray@hcrnetwork.com
Key Contact - Specialty:
Ms. Andrea Forray, RN, Manager, Business Development

12946 Dairy Ashford Rd Ste 460
Sugar Land, TX 77478-3277
(281) 340-2700
Fax: (281) 340-2720
Email: houston@hcrnetwork.com
Key Contact - Specialty:
Mr. James Tipton, President

HealthCare Recruiters International • Alabama

1945 Hoover Ct Ste 205
Birmingham, AL 35226-3606
(205) 979-9840
Email: alabama@hcrnetwork.com
Web: www.hcrnetwork.com

Summary: Recruit healthcare professionals in all areas; sales, sales support, marketing, management, field service engineers and pharmaceutical. Primary focus is sales, sales support, marketing, sales management and marketing management. Primary industries are IS, capitol equipment, medical, surgical, and pharmaceutical

Key Contact - Specialty:
Mr. Frank Y. Johnson, President
Mrs. Coleen Johnson, Office Manager
Mr. Sean Johnson, Recruiter & Researcher
Mr. Richard Coleman, Recruiter - *Management, Pharmaceutical, Sales*

Salary Minimum: $35,000

Functions: Senior Mgmt., Product Dev., Healthcare, Allied Health, Sales & Mktg., Mktg. Mgmt., Sales Mgmt., Sales Reps., IT

Industries: Drugs Mfg., Medical Devices, Computer Equip., Pharm Svcs., Software, Biotech/Life Sciences, Healthcare, Hospitals, Long-term/Home Care, Dental, Physical Therapy

HealthCare Recruiters International • San Diego

701 Palomar Airport Rd Ste 300
Carlsbad, CA 92011-1028
(760) 931-4790
Fax: (858) 777-3508
Email: sandiego@hcrnetwork.com
Web: www.hcrjobs.com

Summary: We provide executive-level medical and biotechnology recruitment. We do not place any entry-level positions, but do place both medical and biotechnology sales and marketing professionals.

Key Contact - Specialty:
Ms. Judy Thurmond, Owner & President

Salary Minimum: $50,000

Functions: Management, Senior Mgmt., Middle Mgmt., Product Dev., Sales & Mktg., Sales Reps., R&D

Industries: Drugs Mfg., Medical Devices, Pharm Svcs., Biotech/Life Sciences, Healthcare, Hospitals, Long-term/Home Care

HealthCare Recruiters International • Bay Area

220 Montgomery St Ste 969
San Francisco, CA 94104-3403
(415) 773-0333
Fax: (415) 773-0331
Email: bayarea@hcrnetwork.com
Web: www.hcrnetwork.com

Summary: We are one of the largest healthcare recruiting franchises. All areas of healthcare, executive, IS, surgery, sales, engineering, pharmaceutical and diagnostic.

Key Contact - Specialty:
Ms. Linda Rosen, Recruiter

Functions: Generalist (All)

Industries: Manufacturing, Finance, Pharm Svcs., IT Implementation, Biotech/Life Sciences, Healthcare

HealthCare Recruiters International • Los Angeles

15300 Ventura Blvd Ste 207
Sherman Oaks, CA 91403-5824
(818) 981-9510
Fax: (818) 981-9523
Email: la@hcrnetwork.com
Web: www.healthcarerecruiters.com

Summary: Medical search firm specialized in pharmaceutical, biotechnology, medical products, services and allied healthcare. All organizational departments/levels. Fortune 500 to venture capital.

Key Contact - Specialty:
Ms. Deborah Wilson, Vice President, Operations

Ms. Rita Montgomery, Vice President, Business Development - *Biotechnology, Pharmaceutical*
Mr. Michael Montgomery, Senior Account Executive

Functions: Generalist (All), Management, Mfg., Materials, Sales & Mktg., IT, R&D, Engineering

Industries: Drugs Mfg., Medical Devices, Pharm Svcs., Biotech/Life Sciences, Healthcare, Hospitals, Long-term/Home Care

HealthCare Recruiters International • Orange County

41877 Enterprise Cir N Ste 200O
Temecula, CA 92590-5628
(951) 296-6278
Email: orangecounty@hcrnetwork.com
Web: www.hcrnetwork.com

Summary: We provide services for network of sales, marketing and management specializing only in healthcare.

Key Contact - Specialty:
Ms. Carol Raia, President
Mr. Tony Raia, Chief Financial Officer

Functions: Generalist (All), Sales & Mktg.

Industries: Drugs Mfg., Medical Devices, Biotech/Life Sciences, Healthcare

HealthCare Recruiters International • Rockies

6860 S Yosemite Ct Ste 2000
Centennial, CO 80112-1448
(303) 779-8570
Email: rmoore@hcrrockies.com
Web: www.hcrrockies.com

Summary: We are an executive placement firm specializing in the toy and gift industries. Client list includes numerous Fortune 500 companies. Our firm as expertise in CEO and VP level searches. Firm offers personal service, is aggressive and ethical.

Key Contact - Specialty:
Mr. Richard Moore, President - *Diagnostics*

Salary Minimum: $40,000

Functions: Sales & Mktg.

Industries: Drugs Mfg., Medical Devices, Pharm Svcs., Biotech/Life Sciences, Healthcare, Hospitals, Long-term/Home Care, Dental

HealthCare Recruiters International • Central FL

2708 Alt 19 Ste 601
Palm Harbor, FL 34683-2644
(727) 467-9620
Fax: (727) 467-9249
Email: tampa@hcrnetwork.com
Web: www.hcrnintl.com

Summary: We recruit exclusively within the medical industry. We work for companies that manufacture and distribute medical supplies, IT, capital equipment, pharmaceuticals, as well as organizations that provide services to the health care market or are providers of health care services and other related companies. Our searches include all levels of sales, marketing, management and service providers.

Key Contact - Specialty:
Mr. Thomas C. McKone, III, President - *Home health, Hospital, Information Systems, Information Technology, Insurance*

Functions: Management, Senior Mgmt., Product Dev., Healthcare, Health Admin., Sales &

Mktg., Mktg. Mgmt., Sales Mgmt., Sales Reps., IT

Industries: Drugs Mfg., Medical Devices, Test, Measure Equip., Robotics, Pharm Svcs., IT Implementation, Communications, Call Centers, Software, Industry Specific SW, Marketing SW, Biotech/Life Sciences, Healthcare, Hospitals, Long-term/Home Care, Dental, Physical Therapy, Occupational Therapy, Women's

HealthCare Recruiters International • Indiana

233 E High St
Mooresville, IN 46158-1639
(317) 834-2400
Email: indiana@hcrnetwork.com
Web: www.hcrnetwork.com

Summary: We are all healthcare professionals who understand the needs of the industry.

Key Contact - Specialty:
Mr. John A. Clark, President & Chief Executive Officer

Functions: Healthcare, Sales & Mktg.

Industries: Generalist (All), Pharm Svcs., Biotech/Life Sciences, Healthcare, Hospitals, Long-term/Home Care, Dental, Physical Therapy, Occupational Therapy

HealthCare Recruiters International • New Orleans

3500 N Causeway Blvd Ste 1472
Metairie, LA 70002-3525
(504) 838-8875
Email: neworleans@hcrnetwork.com
Web: www.hcrnetwork.com

Summary: Specializing in medical sales, sales management and allied health positions in healthcare.

Key Contact - Specialty:
Mr. Vic Palazola, President - *Healthcare*

Functions: Product Dev., Allied Health, Sales & Mktg., Sales Mgmt., Sales Reps., MIS Mgmt.

Industries: Generalist (All), Drugs Mfg., Medical Devices, Robotics, Pharm Svcs., Software, Healthcare

HealthCare Recruiters International • Mid America

10920 NW Ambassador Dr Ste 320
Kansas City, MO 64153-1235
(816) 891-7778
Fax: (816) 891-7377
Email: midamerica@hcrnetwork.com

Summary: We are an executive recruiting firm specializing in the health care industry.

Key Contact - Specialty:
Ms. Karen Wonderly, President
Ms. Ann Supple, Account Executive - *Medical (Devices,Sales), Sales*
Mr. Brian Barbeau, Account Executive - *Pharmaceutical, Sales*

Functions: Generalist (All), Management, Mfg., Sales & Mktg., Mktg. Research, Mktg. Mgmt., Sales Mgmt., IT, R&D

Industries: Drugs Mfg., Medical Devices, Pharm Svcs., Equip Svcs., Mgmt. Consulting, Healthcare, Hospitals, Long-term/Home Care

HealthCare Recruiters International • Philadelphia

496 Kings Hwy N Ste 121
Cherry Hill, NJ 08034-1017
(856) 482-8545
Fax: (856) 482-8540
Email: frank.rosamilia@hcrnetwork.com
Web: www.hcrintlphila.com

Summary: Executive search firm specializing in healthcare positions.

Key Contact - Specialty:
Mr. Frank Rosamilia, President

Functions: Generalist (All), Senior Mgmt., Quality, Nurses, Advertising, Sales Mgmt., CFOs, IT, MIS Mgmt., Engineering

Industries: Drugs Mfg., Computer Equip., Biotech/Life Sciences, Healthcare

HealthCare Recruiters International • NY/NJ

55 Harristown Rd
Glen Rock, NJ 07452-3313
(201) 670-9800
Fax: (201) 670-1908
Email: nynj@hcrnetwork.com

Summary: Our mission is to help companies and medical facilities grow and succeed by providing the best professionals in the healthcare field. We are wholly dedicated to the healthcare industry.

Key Contact - Specialty:
Mr. Harold B. Conant, President - *Pharmaceutical, Senior management*
Ms. Ann M. Moore, Vice President - *Managed care*
Ms. Iris L. Fisher, Vice President - *Marketing, Sales, Technical*

Functions: Management, Senior Mgmt., Middle Mgmt., Product Dev., Sales & Mktg., Mktg. Research, Mktg. Mgmt., Sales Mgmt., IT

Industries: Drugs Mfg., Medical Devices, Pharm Svcs., Software, Biotech/Life Sciences, Healthcare, Hospitals, Long-term/Home Care, Dental, Physical Therapy

HealthCare Recruiters International • New York

455 Electronics Pkwy Ste 208
Liverpool, NY 13088-6052
(315) 701-0265
Fax: (315) 453-9525
Email: newyork@hcrnetwork.com
Web: www.hcrnetwork.com

Summary: We are an executive recruitment for medical, surgical, pharmaceutical, biotechnology and clinical based positions. We offer services for executive management, sales, marketing, clinical specialists and clinical professionals. We place high-end sales & marketing positions.

Key Contact - Specialty:
Mr. Dean McNitt, President - *Healthcare*

Functions: Healthcare

Industries: Chemicals, Drugs Mfg., Medical Devices, Computer Equip., Services, Pharm Svcs., Equip Svcs., Software, Biotech/Life Sciences, Healthcare

HealthCare Recruiters International • Carolinas

535 Keisler Dr Ste 202
Cary, NC 27518-9308
(919) 858-7017
Fax: (919) 858-7018

Email: carolinas@hcrnetwork.com
Web: www.healthcarerecruiters.com

Summary: Our franchise is wholly dedicated to serving the health care industry. Our mission is to help companies and medical facilities grow and succeed by providing them with the best professionals in the health care field.

Key Contact - Specialty:
Ms. Suzette Wood, President & Owner

Functions: Management, Board Members, Senior Mgmt., Middle Mgmt., Mfg., Product Dev.

Industries: Pharm Svcs., Biotech/Life Sciences, Healthcare, Hospitals, Long-term/Home Care

HealthCare Recruiters International • Cincinnati Inc

10 N Locust St Ste C1
Oxford, OH 45056-1182
(513) 523-8004
Fax: (513) 523-9004
Email: ohio@hcrnetwork.com
Web: www.hcrnetwork.com

Summary: We specialize in working with medical manufacturers, managed care organizations, hospitals and other health care facilities, providing the expertise they need to employee at executive levels, manufacturing, R&D, sales & marketing, as well as other positions.

Key Contact - Specialty:
Mr. Steve Darby, CPC, President - *Healthcare*

Functions: Healthcare

Industries: Drugs Mfg., Medical Devices, Pharm Svcs., Accounting, Mgmt. Consulting, HR Services, Biotech/Life Sciences, Healthcare

HealthCare Recruiters International • Pittsburgh

428 Forbes Ave Ste 600
Lawyers Building
Pittsburgh, PA 15219-1621
(412) 261-2244
(800) 875-5339
Fax: (412) 261-3577
Email: pittsburgh@hcrnetwork.com
Web: www.hcrnetwork.com

Summary: We are part of a national network of over 30 offices across the country serving the healthcare industry. Linked by our client candidate referral system database we help companies and medical facilities find the best professionals in a confidential manner.

Key Contact - Specialty:
Ms. Helen Lynch, President & Owner

Functions: Generalist (All), Healthcare, Sales & Mktg., R&D, Engineering, Minorities/Diversity, Technicians, Int'l.

Industries: Generalist (All), Drugs Mfg., Medical Devices, Pharm Svcs., Insurance, Biotech/Life Sciences, Healthcare

HealthCare Professional Group

356 New Byhalia Rd Ste 2
Collierville, TN 38017-3742
(901) 853-6696
Fax: (901) 853-1137
Email: info@hcpg.net
Web: www.hcpg.net

Summary: Our firm evolved from a network of offices focused on recruiting sales reps in the medical industry to a boutique search firm specializing in recruiting services in pharmaceutical services and health care professionals. We also offer value added HR consulting services.

Key Contact - Specialty:
Mr. Jeb Blanchard, Owner - *Healthcare*

Functions: Generalist (All), Management, Sales & Mktg.

Industries: Drugs Mfg., Pharm Svcs., HR Services, Call Centers, Healthcare, Hospitals, Long-term/Home Care

HealthCare Recruiters International • Northwest

321 Parkplace Ctr Ste G116
Kirkland, WA 98033-6202
(425) 576-5115
Fax: (425) 576-5225
Email: northwest@hcrnetwork.com
Web: www.hcrintl.com

Summary: Provides customized professional and executive recruiting services to match a healthcare company's unique personnel needs with qualified candidates to build a winning team.

Key Contact - Specialty:
Mr. David C. Garland, President & Owner - *Healthcare*

Salary Minimum: $30,000

Functions: Generalist (All), Management, Middle Mgmt., Allied Health, Sales & Mktg.

Industries: Drugs Mfg., Medical Devices, Pharm Svcs., Biotech/Life Sciences, Healthcare, Hospitals, Long-term/Home Care

HealthCare Resources & Technologies

215 Throckmorton Ave
Mill Valley, CA 94941-2761
(415) 381-4051
Fax: (415) 381-4772
Email: rfowler8@yahoo.com
Web: www.hcrt.us

Summary: HCR&T's primary focus is healthcare on the business side. Clients are health plans, health systems, consulting firms, PBMs, GPOs, Informatics groups and other niche healthcare and technology companies. The consultant and candidate network is nationwide and comprised of healthcare professionals with diverse, in-depth expertise in a variety of functional disciplines to meet the needs of the healthcare industry.

Key Contact - Specialty:
Ms. Randee Fowler, Principal & Recruiter
Ms. Nancy Mills-Smith, Senior Recruiting Consultant - *Accounting (Big 4), Healthcare, Information Systems, Information Technology, Management consulting*

Functions: Systems Implem., Mgmt. Consultants

Industries: IT Implementation, Healthcare

HealthCare Search Associates

11565 Laurel Canyon Blvd Ste 208
San Fernando, CA 91340-4651
(818) 838-1311
Fax: (818) 838-2010
Email: rasksearch@aol.com

Summary: We recruit healthcare professionals at the C, VP, director, and manager levels in all areas of operations (finance, managed care, medical management, claims, contracting, business development, sales, marketing, IT, etc.) for health care organizations nationally. Listed as one of the most effective firms in Southern California specializing in healthcare recruiting.

Key Contact - Specialty:
Mr. John Raskin, Director, Account Services - *Healthcare*

Salary Minimum: $40,000

Functions: Generalist (All)

Industries: Healthcare

Branches:
12304 Santa Monica Blvd Ste 220
Los Angeles, CA 90025-2587
(310) 207-0979
Fax: (310) 207-3437
Email: drscorner@personnel.com
Key Contact - Specialty:
Mr. Greg Balk, Office Manager

HealthExec Search Consultants Inc

PO Box 2363
Darien, IL 60561-7363
(630) 960-9690
Email: healthexecjobs@aol.com
Web: www.healthexecjobs.com

Summary: Our search expertise for mid to upper level managers, consultants and clinical professionals crosses all functional areas in healthcare. Our clients include managed care, medical supply, e-commerce, pharmaceutical, biotechnology and healthcare consulting organizations. We also conduct searches in traditional healthcare delivery systems, hospitals, physician practices and healthcare associations.

Key Contact - Specialty:
Ms. Julie Marshall

Salary Minimum: $50,000

Functions: Management, Healthcare, Physicians, Nurses, Health Admin., Sales & Mktg., Finance

Industries: Healthcare

HealthMatch Services

1712 Mayflower Dr
Richardson, TX 75081-4603
(972) 301-9994
Email: healthmatch@comcast.net
Web: www.healthmatchservices.com

Summary: Specializing in the recruitment of physicians in all medical specialties for opportunities located nationwide.

Key Contact - Specialty:
Ms. Le Filler, Owner & President
Mr. Jerry Filler, Vice President, Marketing - *Physicians*

Functions: Management, Physicians

Industries: Healthcare, Hospitals

HealthSearch Associates

PO Box 3262
LaVale, MD 21504-3262
(301) 722-0328
(301) 996-4077
Email: ted-schneider@verizon.net

Summary: We offer full life cycle recruiting to most health care organizations. Searches are for mid level and senior management in operations, clinical, finance, IT, HR, marketing and fund raising. Management consulting services include staffing long-term recruitment projects, advertising/media development & management, recruitment process development and improvement, and interim HR leadership.

Key Contact - Specialty:
Mr. Ted Schneider, Executive Recruiter

Salary Minimum: $75,000

Functions: Senior Mgmt., Middle Mgmt., Physicians, Nurses, Allied Health, Health Admin., HR Mgmt., CFOs, MIS Mgmt., Mgmt. Consultants

Industries: Insurance, Healthcare

Email your resume to a targeted list of recruiters now at www.ExecutiveAgent.com/DER07

The Healthsearch Group Inc

109 Croton Ave
Ossining, NY 10562-4219
(914) 941-6107
Fax: (914) 941-1748
Email: resume@healthsearchgroup.com
Web: www.healthsearchgroup.com

Summary: We are one of the largest recruiting
companies in the Northeast with a healthcare
specialty. We pride ourselves on the service we
provide our clients and the effectiveness of our
search process.

Key Contact - Specialty:
Mr. Alan Gordon, President
Mr. Jeff Gordon, Vice President - *Finance*
Ms. Teresa Bierce, Office Manager

Salary Minimum: $40,000

Functions: Healthcare

Industries: Hospitals, Long-term/Home Care

HealthSearch USA

5150 N 16th St Ste B232
Phoenix, AZ 85016-3990
(602) 266-4777
(800) 899-2200
Fax: (602) 650-0664
Email: info@healthsearchusa.com
Web: www.healthsearchusa.com

Summary: We are a physician search firm. We
specialize in permanent and locum tenens. We
have expertise in both retained/targeted search and
contingency and can provide a very high level of
service.

Key Contact - Specialty:
Mr. Steven Silverstein, MBA, President & Chief
Executive Officer

Functions: Physicians

Industries: Healthcare, Hospitals

E M Heath & Company

233 Needham St
Newton, MA 02464-1573
(617) 527-8839
Fax: (617) 527-0116
Email: mheath@emheath.com
Web: www.emheath.com

Summary: Our firm offers a comprehensive
service, which includes retained search,
contingency search and contracting for financial,
marketing and engineering positions.

Key Contact - Specialty:
Ms. Myrna Heath, CPC, Managing Director -
Engineering, Finance, Marketing

Salary Minimum: $75,000

Functions: Senior Mgmt., Product Dev.,
Production, Healthcare, Sales & Mktg., Finance,
CFOs, Budgeting, IT, Engineering

Industries: Manufacturing, Chemicals, Banking,
Misc. Financial, Publishing, Telecoms, Digital,
Fiber Optic, Network Infrastructure, Mfg. SW,
Marketing SW, Networking, Comm. SW,
Biotech/Life Sciences, Healthcare, Hospitals,
Physical Therapy, Occupational Therapy

HEC Group

400-69 John St S
Hamilton, ON L8N 2B9
Canada
(905) 527-7761
Fax: (905) 527-9937
Email: hec@hec-group.com
Web: www.hec-group.com

Summary: Major areas of expertise include
manufacturing, automotive and high technology.

Key Contact - Specialty:
Mr. Robert Leek, President - *Technical*

Salary Minimum: $35,000

Functions: Generalist (All), Management, Mfg.,
Sales & Mktg., HR Mgmt., Finance,
Engineering

Industries: Generalist (All), Food, Bev., Tobacco,
Chemicals, Drugs Mfg., Plastics, Rubber, Metal
Products, Machine, Appliance, Motor Vehicles,
Aerospace, Software

Thomas E Hedefine Associates

21 Ardagh St
Toronto, ON M6S 1Y2
Canada
(416) 207-3303
Email: tom@hedefine.ca

Summary: We provide recruitment activities for
leasing finance companies' asset based lenders
from line marketing, risk management and senior
management positions.

Key Contact - Specialty:
Mr. Thomas E. Hedefine, President
Dr. Kathleen P. Shea, Vice President - *Finance*

Salary Minimum: $40,000

Functions: Generalist (All), Credit, M&A, Risk
Mgmt.

Industries: Generalist (All), Finance, Banking,
Invest. Banking, Venture Cap., Misc. Financial,
Equip Svcs.

Hedlund Corp

1555 N Dearborn Pkwy Ste 1800
Chicago, IL 60610-1448
(312) 755-1400
Email: dhedlund@hedlundcorp.com
Web: www.hedlundcorp.com

Summary: Management search firm specialized in
professional services including consulting, legal,
and accounting.

Key Contact - Specialty:
Mr. David Hedlund, President
Ms. Peggy Meller, Senior Recruiter
Ms. Ingrid Ramos, Senior Recruiter
Ms. Marianne Grierson, Senior Recruiter
Ms. Katherine McGown, Research Assistant

Salary Minimum: $70,000

Functions: Generalist (All)

Industries: Mgmt. Consulting

Jay Heino Company LLC

444 Merrick Rd Ste 112
Lynbrook, NY 11563-2400
(212) 279-6780
Email: jayheino@netzero.net

Summary: Tax placement specialists. We have
both retainer and contingency. Clients are in:
financial industry-investment banking, tax
transactions/products, brokerage, hedge funds and
real estate. We provide services for
telecommunications, manufacturing (all types),
etc., public accounting and law firms. Our success
rate is excellent.

Key Contact - Specialty:
Mr. Jay J. Heino, President - *Tax*

Salary Minimum: $80,000

Functions: Taxes

Industries: Construction, Manufacturing,
Transportation, Retail, Finance, Services,
Media, Communications, Insurance

Heller, Kil Associates Inc

2060 S Halifax Dr
Daytona Beach, FL 32118-5206
(904) 761-5100
Fax: (904) 761-7206
Email: phillip.heller@hellerkil.com
Web: www.hellerkil.com

Summary: Executive search and professional
staffing to the automotive and heavy duty truck
parts/components industries specializing in sales,
marketing, engineering, quality and manufacturing
management to the GM and presidential level.

Key Contact - Specialty:
Mr. Phillip Heller, President - *General
management, Marketing, Sales*

Salary Minimum: $50,000

Functions: Generalist (All), Management, Mfg.,
Plant Mgmt., Quality, Sales & Mktg., M&A,
Engineering

Industries: Motor Vehicles

Branches:
306 Robert Dr
Normal, IL 61761-4310
(309) 454-7077
Fax: (309) 454-8227
Email: larryshapiro@insightbb.com
Key Contact - Specialty:
Mr. Larry Shapiro - *Engineering*

Neal Helsel & Associates Inc

(also known as Career Search Group)
PO Box 1476
Largo, FL 33779-1476
(727) 585-0980
Fax: (727) 584-6323
Email: careersearchgroup@yahoo.com

Summary: We have many years of recruiting
experience in the medical device industry,
including sales, marketing and upper level
management.

Key Contact - Specialty:
Mr. Neal Helsel, Owner - *Biomedical,
Biotechnology, Medical, Medical
(Devices,Sales)*
Mr. Tony Manatine - *Biotechnology, Dental,
Medical (Devices,Sales), Orthopedics*
Mr. Brett Searles - *Biotechnology, Medical
(Devices,Sales), Opthalmics, Orthopedics*

Functions: Management, Sales & Mktg., Sales
Mgmt.

Industries: Medical Devices, Marketing SW,
Biotech/Life Sciences, Healthcare, Hospitals,
Dental

Hemingway Solutions Inc

2102 Business Center Dr Ste 130
Irvine, CA 92612-1001
(949) 253-4620
Fax: (949) 721-1243
Email: lara@hemingwaysolutions.com
Web: www.hemingwaysolutions.com

Summary: We provide executive search, contract
services and temporaries serving the accounting
and finance professions. We also supply
comprehensive accounting testing software to
search, temp firms and internal recruiting
departments.

Key Contact - Specialty:
Ms. Dolores Lara, CPA, President

Salary Minimum: $35,000

Functions: Generalist (All), CFOs, Budgeting,
Credit, M&A, Risk Mgmt.

Industries: Generalist (All), Finance, Accounting

Kay Henry Associates

1200 Bustleton Pike Ste 5
Feasterville Trevose, PA 19053-4108
(215) 355-1600
Email: smiller@kayhenry.com
Web: www.melarden.com

Summary: All areas advertising (creative and account), public relations and marketing as they apply to agencies and corporations including direct marketing, pharmaceutical, marcom, ag chem. and animal health.

Key Contact - Specialty:
Ms. Shelley Miller, CPC, President - *Advertising, Marketing, Public relations*

Salary Minimum: $30,000

Functions: Generalist (All), Management, Board Members, Advertising, Mktg. Mgmt., PR

Industries: Generalist (All), HR Services, Advertising, Publishing, New Media

Henry Executive Recruiting, Inc

307 N Day St # 2
Orange, NJ 07050-2833
(770) 312-2773
Email: nhenry@henryrecruiting.com
Web: www.henryrecruiting.com

Summary: We are a search firm that recruits sales & business development executives & non-executives for the direct marketing, advertising, and online media industries.

Key Contact - Specialty:
Ms. Natasha Henry, President

Salary Minimum: $60,000

Functions: Senior Mgmt., Sales & Mktg., Advertising, Mktg. Research, Mktg. Mgmt., Sales Mgmt., Direct Mktg., Sales Reps., IT

Industries: Advertising, Publishing, New Media, Database SW

Henson Partners

(formerly known as Henson Enterprises Inc)
16733 E Palisades Blvd Ste 101
Fountain Hills, AZ 85268-8322
(480) 816-9911
(866) 898-9911
Fax: (480) 816-9966
Email: inquiry@hensonpartners.com
Web: www.hensonpartners.com

Summary: Dedicated to developing lasting relationships with our client companies through performance, integrity and professionalism. Our specialists generate enhanced results due to their direct experience and extensive knowledge of select industries. Search focus and expertise includes executive-level assignments in a variety of functional areas for the food and consumer products industries.

Key Contact - Specialty:
Mr. Jeff Henson, President & General Manager
Mr. Steve Williams, Director, Business Development - *Accounting, CFOs, Consulting, Controllers*
Mr. Calvin J. DeVoll, Executive Recruiter

Salary Minimum: $75,000

Functions: Generalist (All), Management, Senior Mgmt., Mfg., Production, Plant Mgmt., Quality, Sales & Mktg., Mktg. Mgmt., Sales Mgmt.

Industries: Manufacturing, Food, Bev., Tobacco, Consumer Elect., Consumer Goods

Heritage Search Group Inc

258 SW Lake Forest Way
Port Saint Lucie, FL 34986-1770
(772) 336-9020
Fax: (772) 340-5803
Email: heritage@adelphia.net

Summary: Specialize in consumer packaged goods marketing and/or related fields. We offer different and unique positions. We typically deal with normally small to medium sized companies. Also place high caliber people in consulting firms, small to medium, in all disciplines.

Key Contact - Specialty:
Mr. Philip Tripician, President - *Marketing*

Salary Minimum: $65,000

Functions: Generalist (All), Middle Mgmt., Sales & Mktg., Advertising, Mktg. Research, Mktg. Mgmt., Sales Mgmt., Minorities/Diversity

Industries: Generalist (All), Food, Bev., Tobacco, Paper, Chemicals, Soap, Perf., Cosmtcs., Drugs Mfg., Mgmt. Consulting, Hospitality

Branches:
7932 S Cedar St
Littleton, CO 80120-4431
(303) 347-0273
Fax: (303) 795-2143
Key Contact - Specialty:
Mr. Don Harper, Manager

Herrerias & Associates

5 Hamilton Lndg Ste 110
Novato, CA 94949-8263
(415) 721-7001
Fax: (415) 721-7003
Email: recruit@herrerias.com
Web: www.herrerias.com

Summary: We are one of the San Francisco Bay Area's premier executive search and leadership development firms. We provide recruiting and coaching for finance and accounting professionals in senior and middle level management positions.

Key Contact - Specialty:
Mr. Paul Herrerias, CPA, Founder & Executive Director
Ms. Mary Richardson, Senior Consultant
Mr. Patrick Fleck, CPA, MBA, Senior Associate
Ms. Danielle Herrerias, MA, Office Manager
Miss Teresa Rabenberg, MBA, Research Consultant - *Research, Technology*
Ms. Anne E. Taylor, Research Associate - *Administration, Office (Administration), Real estate*
Ms. Carrie Resing, Coordinator, Marketing - *Administration, Marketing*
Ms. Laura Ferracane, Technical Writer

Salary Minimum: $75,000

Functions: Generalist (All), Board Members, Sales & Mktg., HR Mgmt., Finance, Mgmt. Consultants

Industries: Accounting, E-commerce, Advertising, New Media, Telecoms, Software, Biotech/Life Sciences

The Herring Group

600 Pine Forest Dr Ste 130
Maumelle, AR 72113-6909
(501) 851-1234
(501) 851-2962
Fax: (501) 851-7753
Email: helpdesk@herringgroup.net
Web: www.herringgroup.net

Summary: We are a recruiter search firm, which has extensive experience in the placement of executives and professionals, ranging from key supervisory positions to VP and president levels.

Key Contact - Specialty:
Mr. Mike Tolleson, Executive Vice President - *Distribution, Logistics, Manufacturing, Transportation*
Mr. Tony Horne, Senior Vice President - *Distribution, Logistics, Manufacturing, Retail, Transportation*
Mr. Dan Ferguson, President - *Change management, Distribution, Logistics, Management consulting, Retail*
Mr. Bill Herring, Chairman - *Distribution, Logistics, Retail, Transportation*

Salary Minimum: $40,000

Functions: Senior Mgmt., Purchasing, Materials Plng., Distribution, Sales Mgmt., HR Mgmt., CFOs

Industries: Manufacturing, Transportation, Retail, E-commerce, Engineering Svcs., Logistics Svcs.

J D Hersey & Associates

1695 Old Henderson Rd
Columbus, OH 43220-3656
(614) 459-4555
Email: info@jdhersey.com
Web: www.jdhersey.com

Summary: We specialize in the recruitment of professionals within the CRM (customer relationship management), call/contact center, retailing, and real estate industries. A typical search targets mid to senior-level executives in sales, marketing, operations, or merchandising. Our dedication and professionalism has fostered many long-term relationships.

Key Contact - Specialty:
Mr. Jeffrey D. Hersey, President

Salary Minimum: $75,000

Functions: Senior Mgmt., Middle Mgmt., Purchasing, Distribution, Sales & Mktg., Mktg. Research, Customer Svc.

Industries: Computer Equip., Consumer Elect., Wholesale, Retail, Services, Mgmt. Consulting, Logistics Svcs., Supply Chain Mgmt, Hospitality, Media, New Media, Call Centers, Real Estate, Property/Facility Mgmt., Software

Hertner, Block & Associates Inc

15485 Eagle Nest Ln Ste 110
Hialeah, FL 33014-2221
(305) 556-8882
Fax: (305) 556-5650
Email: hhertner@legalrecruiting.com
Web: www.legalrecruiting.com

Summary: Our firm dedicates their services to the legal staffing needs for partners, associates and mergers of law firms, in addition to, general counsel and staff counsel for corporations.

Key Contact - Specialty:
Mr. Herbert H. Hertner, President - *Consulting, Legal (Attorneys)*
Mr. David J. Block, Esq., JD, Vice President - *Consulting, Legal (Attorneys)*
Mrs. Danielle G. Bowser, Esq., JD, Consultant - *Consulting, Legal (Attorneys)*
Mr. Richard S. Lubliner, Esq., JD, Consultant - *Consulting, Legal (Attorneys)*
Mrs. Pamela S. Spalter, Esq., JD, Consultant - *Consulting, Legal (Attorneys)*

Salary Minimum: $75,000

Functions: Legal

Industries: Generalist (All)

Email your resume to a targeted list of recruiters now at www.ExecutiveAgent.com/DER07

Hessel Associates Inc

70 W Red Oak Ln
White Plains, NY 10604-3602
(914) 697-7522
Fax: (914) 697-7524
Email: haisearch@aol.com
Web: www.haisearch.com

Summary: We are an experienced team of personnel consultants specializing in the recruitment of financial, marketing and IT professionals with particular emphasis on the financial services industries including banking, brokerage and insurance.

Key Contact - Specialty:
Mr. Jeffrey J. Hessel, Principal
Ms. Susan Miller, Vice President

Salary Minimum: $50,000

Functions: Generalist (All), Finance, CFOs, Budgeting, Cash Mgmt., M&A, Risk Mgmt., Mgmt. Consultants

Industries: Generalist (All), Manufacturing, Finance, Banking, Invest. Banking, Brokers, Misc. Financial, Insurance

Hewitt Partners International, Management Consultants Inc

7150 E Camelback Rd Ste 305
Scottsdale, AZ 85251-1278
(602) 996-1500
Fax: (602) 996-5100
Email: resume@hewittpartners.com
Web: www.hewittpartners.com

Summary: Since our inception, our firm has been a recognized leader in the area of healthcare consulting and executive search. Since then, we have strived to deliver some of the most innovative and client–focused executive search solutions in the healthcare industry. Today, our firm is recognized by our clients as one of the most quality focused and client-centered executive search firms in the industry.

Key Contact - Specialty:
Mr. Peter D. Hewitt, President - *Healthcare*
Mrs. Diane Bell Fontaine, Vice President - *Healthcare, Information service*
Mrs. Mary Ann Doran, RN, Consultant, Management - *HMOs, Hospital, Managed care*

Functions: Generalist (All), Healthcare

Industries: Generalist (All), Insurance, Claims, Healthcare, Hospitals, Long-term/Home Care, Dental

Hi-Tek Dynamics Inc

PO Box 892398
Temecula, CA 92589-2398
(951) 676-1230
Email: ginny@hitekdynamics.com
Web: www.hitekdynamics.com

Summary: Exclusive recruiters to the healthcare and bio-technology markets. Sales, marketing, management, R&D and upper management positions.

Key Contact - Specialty:
Ms. Ginny Geier-Mulhern, President & Senior Partner - *Biotechnology, Business development*
Ms. Trudy Giese, Senior Partner & Vice President
Ms. Leslie Geier, Director, Corporate Sales
Mr. Mitch Giese, Director, Sales

Salary Minimum: $50,000

Functions: Senior Mgmt., Sales & Mktg., R&D

Industries: Drugs Mfg., Medical Devices, Biotech/Life Sciences, Healthcare

Hidde & Associates

427 S Boston Ave Ste 913
Philtower Building
Tulsa, OK 74103-4114
(918) 749-1530
(800) 538-8516
Fax: (918) 587-7007
Email: mail@hiddeassociates.com
Web: www.hiddeassociates.com

Summary: Provide retained and contingency executive searches for management, marketing, sales, IT and finance. In addition, provide outplacement services and consulting services to a diverse client base.

Key Contact - Specialty:
Mr. Robert Hidde, Partner - *Finance, Management, Marketing, Sales*
Ms. Victoria Reynolds-Hidde, Partner - *Finance, Management, Marketing*
Ms. Leah Hidde-Gregory, Senior Transition Counselor - *Senior management*

Salary Minimum: $75,000

Functions: Generalist (All), Management, Sales & Mktg.

Industries: Generalist (All), Finance, HR Services, IT Implementation

Higbee Associates Inc

112 Rowayton Ave
Norwalk, CT 06853-1400
(203) 853-7600
(727) 384-4185
Fax: (203) 855-2426
Email: rhigbee@netaxis.com
Web: www.higbeeassociates.com

Summary: Specialist to the consulting industry at senior-level. Financial services, telecom, healthcare, insurance, pharmaceutical as it relates to strategy, operations and IT. ERP systems (PeopleSoft).

Key Contact - Specialty:
Mr. R.W. Higbee, President
Mr. Robert Lawrence, Senior Vice President

Salary Minimum: $75,000

Functions: Mgmt. Consultants

Industries: Medical Devices, Consumer Elect., Finance, Banking, Mgmt. Consulting, Biotech/Life Sciences, Healthcare

B W Higgins Inc

6828 Alnwick Ct
Indianapolis, IN 46220-4304
(317) 842-6346
Email: bwhinc@aol.com
Web: www.bwhiggins.com

Summary: An established and recognized search firm dedicated to all facets of the commercial insurance industry, i.e., carrier, brokerage, reinsurance, alternative risk, corporate risk management and eInsurance.

Key Contact - Specialty:
Mr. Bruce W. Higgins, Principal

Salary Minimum: $100,000

Functions: Generalist (All)

Industries: Insurance

High Road Personnel of Burlington

562 Maple Ave
Burlington, ON L7S 1M6
Canada
(905) 632-5870

Email: resumes@highroadpersonnel.com
Web: www.highroadpersonnel.com

Summary: Placement agency for permanent, contract & temp personnel: administrative, accounting, technical and payroll service.

Key Contact - Specialty:
Ms. Connie Mussell, President
Ms. Libby Mussell, Office Manager

Functions: Generalist (All), Management, Admin. Svcs., Plant Mgmt., Purchasing, Customer Svc., HR Mgmt., Finance, Legal

Industries: Generalist (All), Manufacturing, Finance, Services, Legal, Accounting, HR Services, Environmental Svcs., Insurance, Property/Facility Mgmt.

High Tech Opportunities Inc

264B N Broadway Ste 206
Salem, NH 03079-2180
(603) 893-9486
Fax: (603) 893-9492
Email: ron@hightechnh.com
Web: www.hightechopportunities.com

Summary: Our firm specializes in recruiting for electronic design automation, semiconductor, microprocessor design and computer hardware professionals.

Key Contact - Specialty:
Mr. Ron Cooper, CPC, President - *Design, Sales*
Mr. Michael Buckley
Mr. Ross Cooper, Recruiter - *Electronics, Engineering*

Salary Minimum: $80,000

Functions: Sales & Mktg., Engineering

Industries: Generalist (All), Electronic, Elec. Components, Semiconductors, Digital, Wireless, Network Infrastructure

High Tech Recruiters

220 2nd St # 2
Langley, WA 98260-8664
(360) 579-1314
(800) 644-9164
Fax: (888) 944-0426
Email: lynnl@htr.bz
Web: www.hightechrecruiters.com

Summary: We provide executive search and senior management placement. We believe in finding, hiring and retaining the right employees. We provide employee loyalty building and leadership team building process and services.

Key Contact - Specialty:
Ms. Lynn Launer, Founder & President

Salary Minimum: $80,000

Functions: Management

Industries: Database SW, Development SW, Doc. Mgmt., Production SW, Entertainment SW, ERP SW, Industry Specific SW, Marketing SW, Networking, Comm. SW, Security SW, System SW

High Tech Staffing Group

3112 SE 197th Ct
Camas, WA 98607-8803
(503) 780-3210
Email: careers@htsg.com
Web: www.htsg.com

Summary: We specialize in recruiting job seekers for Information Technology, software and hardware, RFID and medical device. We offer candidates and client companies' personal service, confidentiality and the most ethical, professional standards. Our clients' range from Fortune 500 companies to start-ups and our growth has resulted

from establishing relationships and gaining a thorough understanding of their needs, priorities and expectations.

Key Contact - Specialty:
Mr. Frank Michael Odia, President

Salary Minimum: $65,000

Functions: Generalist (All)

Industries: Drugs Mfg., Medical Devices, Computer Equip., Test, Measure Equip., Electronic, Elec. Components, Robotics, Semiconductors, Software, Biotech/Life Sciences

High Technology Recruiters Inc
PO Box 1905
Rockville, MD 20849-1905
(301) 315-8910
Email: bob@hitechrecruiters.net
Web: www.hitechrecruiters.net

Summary: Our firm specializes in network related IT fields including data communications, internet/intranet, e-commerce and telecom. We focus on staffing positions at all levels for sales, tech support, professional services and marketing positions nationwide.

Key Contact - Specialty:
Mr. Bob Bryer, President - *Networking, Sales*

Functions: Sales & Mktg., Sales Mgmt.

Industries: Computer Equip., Communications, Telecoms, Call Centers, Digital, Wireless, Fiber Optic, Network Infrastructure, RF/Microwave, Software, Doc. Mgmt., Production SW, Networking, Comm. SW, Security SW, System SW

High-Tech Professionals
PO Box 421175
San Diego, CA 92142-1175
(858) 560-8331
Email: contact@hightechpros.com
Web: www.hightechpros.com

Summary: We are a recruiting and staffing firm for permanent, temporary and contract positions. Our specialization is in computer, engineering, and IT. We work with software engineers, hardware engineers, executive level personnel, quality assurance engineers and testers, technical writers, program and project managers, and other computer and high technology professionals.

Key Contact - Specialty:
Ms. Denise Lidell, President

Salary Minimum: $50,000

Functions: Management, Mfg., Sales & Mktg., IT, MIS Mgmt., Systems Dev., DB Admin., R&D, Engineering, Design

Industries: Computer Equip., Consumer Elect., Test, Measure Equip., Misc. Mfg., Electronic, Elec. Components, Robotics, Semiconductors, IT Implementation, Media, Communications, Wireless, Software, Database SW, Development SW, Biotech/Life Sciences

Branches:
1635 SW Pheasant Dr
Beaverton, OR 97006-3811
(858) 560-8331

Higher Ground Associates
PO Box 827
Bryn Mawr, PA 19010-0827
(610) 581-7884
Fax: (801) 697-4891
Email: cathy@highergroundassoc.com
Web: www.highergroundassoc.com

Summary: Our firm provides timely and relevant research support to the executive search and business communities. Drawing on our internal proficiency, along with a variety of specialized outsourced resources, our strength lies in the ability to cut to the chase - quickly synthesizing large amounts of information from a variety of sources and crystallizing it into a valuable, effective approach to candidate, career and business development.

Key Contact - Specialty:
Ms. Catherine Palma, Founder

Salary Minimum: $90,000

Functions: Generalist (All)

Industries: Generalist (All)

Highland & Associates
3830 Valley Centre Dr Ste 705
PMB 646
San Diego, CA 92130-3307
(858) 794-1782
Fax: (858) 794-8209
Email: highlandandassoc@aol.com
Web: www.highlandandassociates.com

Summary: We have many years of experience in the commercial real estate industry. Specializing in real estate directors, construction, asset & property management, leasing, finance, and administration positions.

Key Contact - Specialty:
Ms. Maryjo Highland, Partner - *Real estate*

Salary Minimum: $40,000

Functions: Generalist (All), Senior Mgmt., Admin. Svcs.

Industries: Generalist (All), Construction, Real Estate

Hilleren & Associates Inc
3800 American Blvd W Ste 880
Minneapolis, MN 55431-4423
(952) 956-9090
Fax: (952) 956-9009
Email: jerry@hilleren.com
Web: www.hilleren.com

Summary: We are a search firm specializing in the building of superior sales & marketing teams. Our greatest expertise is with medical and pharmaceutical manufacturers.

Key Contact - Specialty:
Mr. Jerry Hilleren, President
Mr. Jim Colaizy, Director - *Pharmaceutical, Sales*
Ms. Maria Guertin, Consultant - *Pharmaceutical, Sales*

Salary Minimum: $70,000

Functions: Sales & Mktg., Sales Reps.

Industries: Biotech/Life Sciences, Healthcare, Hospitals, Long-term/Home Care

Hintz Associates
196 Prospect Ave
Valhalla, NY 10595-1831
(914) 761-4227
Fax: (914) 948-8630
Email: geohintz@aol.com

Summary: Our specialties are cost reduction analysts and external consultants as well as sales persons who have sold management consulting services. Our assignments include consultants who specialize in supply chain management, methods improvement and Kanban, Lean manufacturing techniques and industrial engineering.

Key Contact - Specialty:
Mr. George Hintz, President
Mr. George Jefferies, Vice President
Ms. DeAnne Cerreta, Research Coordinator
Ms. Dorothy DiMaggio, Administration

Salary Minimum: $45,000

Functions: Mgmt. Consultants

Industries: Mgmt. Consulting

The Hire Alternative
10755 Scripps Poway Pkwy
San Diego, CA 92131-3924
(858) 792-3535
Fax: (858) 695-6223
Email: recruiter@thehirealternative.com
Web: www.thehirealternative.com

Summary: Placing Finance, Accounting, Human Resources professionals (mid to senior and executive levels) on a contingency and retainer basis

Key Contact - Specialty:
Ms. Cindy Cremona, Principal

Salary Minimum: $100,000

Functions: Finance

Industries: Generalist (All), Biotech/Life Sciences

Hire Impact Inc
17603 E Peakview Ave
Aurora, CO 80016-3151
(303) 400-8958
Fax: (303) 496-7000
Email: jackie@hireimpact.com
Web: www.hireimpact.com

Summary: We provide nationwide placement of sales, recruiting, and management professionals for select IT services clients. We place regional vice presidents, area and branch managers, sales and recruiting managers, practice directors and managers, business development directors, national account managers, and account executives and recruiters. We also provide mergers and acquisitions support.

Key Contact - Specialty:
Ms. Jacqueline R. Nairne, President & Chief Executive Officer - *Information Technology, Management, Sales*

Functions: Sales & Mktg., Sales Mgmt., Sales Reps.

Industries: Services, E-commerce, IT Implementation, Software, Development SW

Hire Integrity
1982 N Fork Cir
Elgin, IL 60123-2667
(847) 289-0338
Fax: (847) 289-0338
Email: jobrien@hireintegrity.com
Web: www.hireintegrity.com

Summary: We specialize in the printing and graphic arts industry on a national basis. Our focus is on placing middle management, executive management, sales and sales management in printing, packaging and related industries. We also consult with companies in Personal Dynametrics Program's (PDP) behavioral work style profiling, to maximize employee and prospective employees' unique strengths.

Key Contact - Specialty:
Mr. Jack O'Brien, President

Functions: Management

Industries: Printing, Misc. Mfg., Publishing, New Media, Packaging, Doc. Mgmt., Production SW, Industry Specific SW

Hire Options Inc

70 W 40th St Fl 9
New York, NY 10018-2622
(212) 867-8383
(212) 867-8080
Email: mary@hireoptions.com
Web: www.hireoptions.com

Summary: Innovative recruiting and development company with a focus on sales, marketing, and engineering expertise.

Key Contact - Specialty:
Ms. Mary Louise Pernod, Founder - *E-business, Financial services, Human resources, Management, Sales*

Functions: Sales Reps.

Industries: Generalist (All), Media, Advertising, Publishing, New Media, Broadcast, Film, Telecoms, Call Centers, Digital, Wireless

Hire Precision Partners LLC

174 Holland Rd
Sussex, NJ 07461-2837
(973) 875-1980
Email: kevincurley@hireprecision.com
Web: www.hireprecision.com

Summary: A Recruitment Process Outsourcing firm focusing on sales, sales management and engineering positions in the fields of IT, healthcare and financial services.

Key Contact - Specialty:
Mr. Kevin Curley, Partner - *Banking (Corporate), Computers (Software), Financial services, Information Systems, Information Technology*
Mr. Frank Kijak, Partner - *Computers, ERP, Information Technology, Sales, Technology*

Salary Minimum: $75,000

Functions: Sales & Mktg., Sales Mgmt., Sales Reps.

Industries: Finance, Banking, Wireless, Software, Database SW, Doc. Mgmt., Production SW, ERP SW, Industry Specific SW, Mfg. SW, Networking, Comm. SW, Security SW, System SW, Training SW, Biotech/Life Sciences, Healthcare

Hire Solutions Recruiting

336 Valley View Rd
Springfield, PA 19064-2616
(610) 328-9744
Fax: (215) 827-5559
Email: sharp@hire-solutions.com
Web: www.hire-solutions.com

Summary: Full executive placement firm specializing in the hospitality, foodservice and lodging industries throughout the USA. Focus on mid-management to senior staff in the areas of operations, sales and marketing.

Key Contact - Specialty:
Ms. Johanne Sermania, Owner & Senior Recruiter

Salary Minimum: $60,000

Functions: Senior Mgmt., Middle Mgmt., Sales & Mktg.

Industries: Architectural Svcs., K-12 Ed., Higher Ed., Hospitality, Hotels, Resorts, Clubs, Restaurants, Quick Service Restaurants, Full Service Restaurants, Inst./Industrial Food Svc., Entertainment, Recreation, Environmental Svcs., Healthcare

HireKnowledge

100 Boylston St Ste 1070
Boston, MA 02116-4685
(617) 350-3033
Fax: (617) 350-3076
Email: boston1@hireknowledge.com
Web: www.hireknowledge.com

Summary: We are a staffing firm that specializes in the placement of high-end marketing, creative and technical professionals.

Key Contact - Specialty:
Mr. Damien Rocherolle, Vice President

Functions: IT, Systems Support, Graphic Designers

Industries: Generalist (All)

HireMinds LLC

222 3rd St Ste 350
Cambridge, MA 02142-1188
(617) 252-0606
Fax: (617) 252-0808
Email: minds@hireminds.com
Web: www.hireminds.com

Summary: Our firm, one of the leading specialty staffing firms in the area, specializes in the hottest disciplines, including biotechnology/scientific, high technology and creative/media. With our refined focus, our firm has the ability to service your needs more completely than any other staffing firm in the industry.

Key Contact - Specialty:
Mr. David Hayes, President

Salary Minimum: $35,000

Functions: Generalist (All)

Industries: Medical Devices, Pharm Svcs., E-commerce, IT Implementation, Recreation, Media, New Media, Software, Biotech/Life Sciences, Healthcare

HireStrategy

11730 Plaza America Dr Ste 340
Reston, VA 20190-4748
(703) 547-6700
Fax: (703) 707-1836
Email: paul@hirestrategy.com
Web: www.hirestrategy.com

Summary: We are a full service professional staffing firm providing: consulting services, permanent placement, and executive search solutions for companies and career management in the technology, sales, finance and accounting professions. Our customers include Fortune 500, middle market and emerging growth companies across diverse industries.

Key Contact - Specialty:
Mr. Paul Villella, President & Chief Executive Officer
Mr. Hector Velez, Vice President - *Sales, Technology*
Mr. Chris Owen, Vice President - *Accounting*

Salary Minimum: $50,000

Functions: Generalist (All), Board Members, Senior Mgmt., Middle Mgmt., Sales Mgmt., CFOs, Taxes, MIS Mgmt., Systems Dev., Systems Implem.

Industries: Generalist (All), Construction, Food, Bev., Tobacco, Finance, Mgmt. Consulting, HR Services, E-commerce, IT Implementation, Hospitality, Communications, Telecoms, Digital, Wireless, Network Infrastructure, Government, Software, Accounting SW, Database SW, Development SW, Security SW

Branches:
2020 K St NW Ste 7550
Washington, DC 20006-1806
(202) 857-6555
Key Contact - Specialty:
Mr. Tom Whitehead

Hiring Solutions Inc

201 N Washington Sq Ste 810
Lansing, MI 48933-1323
(517) 347-0590
Fax: (517) 347-1243
Email: hsinc@hiringsolutionsinc.com
Web: www.hiringsolutionsinc.com

Summary: Our firm specializes in executive search, recruitment assessment and HR consulting. We offer a variety of instruments, tests and assessment tools used for pre-employment screening, management development and employee training. We can audit your employment function to determine whether your company's recruitment, selection and placement functions are being performed in the most effective and cost-efficient manner.

Key Contact - Specialty:
Ms. Sandra K. Soltysiak, Director, Executive Search
Ms. Kathy V. Tungate, Search Consultant

Functions: Generalist (All)

Industries: Generalist (All)

Ruth Hirsch Associates Inc

201 E 66th St Apt 7C
New York, NY 10021-6455
(212) 396-0200
Fax: (212) 396-0679
Email: info@ruthhirschassociates.com
Web: www.ruthhirschassociates.com

Summary: We are a specialty firm limited to the placement of Owner's Representatives, Senior Facilities Managers, Interior Designers and Registered Architects.

Key Contact - Specialty:
Ms. Ruth Hirsch, President - *Interior design*

Salary Minimum: $65,000

Functions: Architects

Industries: Construction

Hite Executive Recruiting

PO Box 844
Altoona, PA 16603-0844
(814) 942-3248
Fax: (814) 942-8991
Email: dhite@hiterecruiting.com
Web: www.hiterecruiting.com

Summary: Generalist executive recruiting firm specializing in placing HR personnel and all other professional mid level management positions to executive level positions in all industries.

Key Contact - Specialty:
Mr. David Hite, Owner

Salary Minimum: $35,000

Functions: Management, Quality, Purchasing, Direct Mktg., HR Mgmt., Benefits, CFOs, Architects, Hotel Mgmt., Chefs

Industries: Generalist (All), Oil & Gas, Manufacturing, Food, Bev., Tobacco, Services

HITS Hi-Tech Staffing

333 Cobalt Way Ste 107
Sunnyvale, CA 94085-5404
(877) 224-3367
(408) 226-3367

Email: hits@hitechstaffing.com
Web: www.hitechstaffing.com

Summary: We help you attract top, mission-critical talent in a short period of time. Contract and permanent.

Key Contact - Specialty:
Mr. L.E. Duncan, Managing Partner

Functions: Generalist (All), Senior Mgmt.

Industries: Generalist (All), Semiconductors, Finance, Banking, Invest. Banking, Misc. Financial, Non-profits, Pharm Svcs., Telecoms, Database SW, Development SW, Doc. Mgmt., Production SW, ERP SW

HM Associates
2 Electronics Ave
Danvers, MA 01923-1071
(978) 762-7474
(508) 299-8175
Email: hmackenzie@hmassc.com
Web: www.hmassc.com

Summary: We provide HR consulting. We offer retained and contingency search, candidate development and contract recruiting services to the high technology and healthcare industries.

Key Contact - Specialty:
Mr. Hugh MacKenzie, CPC, President - *Computers (Software), Hardware, Marketing, Telecommunications*

Salary Minimum: $50,000

Functions: Generalist (All), Product Dev., Automation, Nurses, Hardware

Industries: Manufacturing, Computer Equip., Consumer Elect., Test, Measure Equip., Electronic, Elec. Components, Semiconductors, Misc. Financial, Communications, Digital, Wireless, Fiber Optic, RF/Microwave, Defense, Aerospace, Software, Database SW, Development SW, Industry Specific SW, Networking, Comm. SW, Security SW, System SW, Healthcare, Hospitals, Long-term/Home Care, Physical Therapy

HMR Inc
PO Box 970023
Boca Raton, FL 33497-0023
(561) 852-1891
Fax: (561) 852-6447
Email: jobsbyhmr@aol.com
Web: www.hospitalityjobsbyhmr.com

Summary: Our firm specializes on placements in the markets of hotels, restaurants, clubs, and some healthcare facilities.

Key Contact - Specialty:
Mr. Ron Stevens, President - *Hospitality*
Ms. Liz Stevens, Vice President, Secretary & Treasurer

Salary Minimum: $25,000

Functions: Management

Industries: Hospitality

HNH Partners Inc
10461 Mill Run Cir Ste 855
Owings Mills, MD 21117-5518
(443) 548-5000
Fax: (443) 548-5005
Email: info@hnhpartners.com
Web: www.hnhpartners.com

Summary: HNH Partners is a contingent executive search firm. While we are generalist firm, a large percent of our business comes from the financial services sector.

Key Contact - Specialty:
Mr. Cory Holmes, Managing Director - *Banking, Capital markets, Financial services, Mergers & acquisitions, Research*
Ms. Erin K. Holmes, Managing Director - *Banking, Energy, Financial services, Human resources, Research*

Salary Minimum: $75,000

Functions: Senior Mgmt.

Industries: Banking, Invest. Banking

Hobson Associates
PO Box 278
1781 Highland Ave Ste 201
Cheshire, CT 06410-0278
(203) 272-0227
Fax: (203) 272-1237
Email: hobson@hobsonassoc.com
Web: www.hobsonassoc.com

Summary: We are a premier boutique executive search firm whose unique process provides significant value to our clients. One specific focus of ours is sales/business development professionals for high technology IT clients. Our other initiative targets the life sciences, specifically pharmaceuticals, CRO, bioengineering & medical devices.

Key Contact - Specialty:
Mr. Danny Cahill, CPC, President - *Engineering*
Ms. Lisa Iannone, CPC, Vice President - *High technology, Sales*
Mr. Vern Chanski, CPC, Senior Partner & Chief Business Officer - *Biomedical, Biotechnology, C-level, Life Sciences, Medical (Devices)*
Mr. Tim Flanagan, Senior Parnter - *C-level, High technology, Manufacturing, Middle management, Senior management*
Ms. Beth Schneider, Senior Parnter - *Computers (Software), Financial services, High technology*

Salary Minimum: $50,000

Functions: Generalist (All), Mktg. Research, IT

Industries: Generalist (All), Manufacturing, Medical Devices, Computer Equip., Misc. Mfg., Consumer Goods, Mgmt. Consulting, New Media, Wireless, Software, Development SW, Doc. Mgmt., Production SW, Entertainment SW, ERP SW, Security SW, Biotech/Life Sciences

Hoffman Partnership Group Inc
15 Huntington Ct
Williamsville, NY 14221-5309
(716) 632-3379
(800) 540-4443
Fax: (815) 377-3673
Email: bhoffman@hpgrecruit.com
Web: www.hpgrecruit.com

Summary: We create long-term client partnerships to consistently fill opportunities in consumer packaged goods (beverage, food and HBA). We are a female-owned company (WBENC certified) and have expertise in national searches in customer team leadership, category management, trade marketing, DSD operational management, national accounts and general management. Typical searches are in the $80,000-160,000 base salary range.

Key Contact - Specialty:
Mr. Bradley D. Hoffman, President - *Sales*
Ms. Lisa M. Hoffman, Chief Executive Officer - *Sales*

Salary Minimum: $75,000

Functions: Sales & Mktg., Sales Mgmt.

Industries: Food, Bev., Tobacco, Paper, Soap, Perf., Cosmtcs., Consumer Goods, Inst./Industrial Food Svc., Advertising

Hoffman Recruiters
115 Broad St Ste 6
Boston, MA 02110-3032
(617) 535-3700
(888) 333-8595
Fax: (617) 535-3300
Email: contact@hrecruiters.com
Web: www.hrecruiters.com

Summary: We are a confidential recruiting service that is free for candidates. Our top priority is being able to understand each clients needs in order to recognize the right candidates immediately.

Key Contact - Specialty:
Mr. Judd A. Hoffman, President
Mr. Danko Fatovic, Chief Executive Officer

Functions: Senior Mgmt., Sales Mgmt., CFOs, MIS Mgmt., Systems Analysis, Systems Implem., DB Admin.

Industries: Generalist (All)

Holampco International
5825 Ellsworth Ave
Pittsburgh, PA 15232-1707
(412) 954-0000
(800) 875-6268
Fax: (412) 954-0030
Email: patti@hlcinternational.com

Summary: Our name, a combination of our two principals, is our personal signature to distinguish and passionately pursue excellence in partnering with you to attract the top talent. We are a professional executive search firm specializing in the building materials, glass and ceramic industries.

Key Contact - Specialty:
Ms. Patti Lampl, Managing Partner
Mr. Gary Holupka, Managing Partner
Mr. Bruce Wertz, Senior Level Account Executive

Holbrook & Associates
2 E 11th St Ste 115
Edmond, OK 73034-3990
(405) 341-9559
Email: hasearch@sbcglobal.net

Summary: Specialize in the oil & gas industry, food/beverage, automotive, chemical and pharmaceutical industries. Pipeline engineers, integrity engineers, production supervisors/managers, engineers, quality and validation.

Key Contact - Specialty:
Mr. Phillip Holbrook, Owner

Salary Minimum: $60,000

Functions: Generalist (All), Management

Industries: Generalist (All), Energy, Utilities, Oil & Gas, Manufacturing, Food, Bev., Tobacco, Chemicals, Soap, Perf., Cosmtcs., Drugs Mfg., Medical Devices, Machine, Appliance, Motor Vehicles, Computer Equip.

Holden & Harlan Associates Inc
PO Box 91
Flossmoor, IL 60422-0091
(708) 799-4447
Fax: (708) 799-4461
Email: info@actuarialrecruiting.com
Web: www.actuarialrecruiting.com

Summary: We provide executive recruiting and specialize in property/casualty, life, health and

pension actuaries, placing in insurance companies and consulting & brokerage firms. Retained searches available as well as online job listings for the entire insurance industry.

Key Contact - Specialty:
Mr. Jerry Hayes, President
Mrs. Mara Hayes, Corporate Secretary
Mr. Holden Hayes, Vice President

Salary Minimum: $45,000

Functions: CFOs, Actuaries

Industries: Generalist (All), Insurance

Holland & Associates Ltd

2345 York Rd Ste 300
The Harvest Building
Timonium, MD 21093-2283
(410) 308-1300
Email: resume@hollandcpasearch.com
Web: www.hollandcpasearch.com

Summary: We are dedicated exclusively to providing financial and accounting search and recruitment services to Big 4 and large local CPA firms. We pride ourselves in locating the top talent in public accounting, proven performers with advanced degrees and outstanding credentials.

Key Contact - Specialty:
Mr. Ray Holland, President - *Finance*

Salary Minimum: $50,000

Functions: Taxes

Industries: Accounting

Holland Search

(a division of Holland Group)
237 W Northfield Blvd Ste 200
Murfreesboro, TN 37129-0531
(615) 890-9895
Web: www.thehollandgroup.com

Summary: We are a division of a full-service agency. Other parts of the agency offer temp employment and training/consulting.

Key Contact - Specialty:
Ms. Karen Thrasher

Salary Minimum: $40,000

Functions: Generalist (All), Management, Mfg., Materials, HR Mgmt., Finance, IT, Engineering

Industries: Generalist (All), Finance

David J Hollinger Associates Inc

(also known as Hollinger Jobs)
1075 Easton Ave Ste 2
Tower 3
Somerset, NJ 08873-1648
(732) 247-5656
Fax: (732) 247-5989
Email: jobs@hollingerjobs.com
Web: www.hollingerjobs.com

Summary: Our firm provides exceptional recruiting and search services dedicated to the insurance industry. We secure the top P&C and benefits talent available for our clients which include: agencies, brokers, carriers both reinsurance & primary, TPA's, wholesalers, MGA's, risk management group's and consultants.

Key Contact - Specialty:
Mr. John R. Huttner, President

Salary Minimum: $60,000

Functions: Generalist (All), Risk Mgmt.

Industries: Insurance, Casualty, Claims, Life, Commercial, Re-Insurance

Hollister

75 State St Fl 9
Boston, MA 02109-1822
(617) 654-0200
Fax: (617) 695-3807
Web: www.hollisterinc.com

Summary: We are a leading full-service, privately owned recruiting firm. We have distinguished ourselves in the crowded staffing business by concentrating on a fundamental concept, which is to build and maintain respectful, productive relationships. We offer full-time and supplemental/contract placement within the areas of: accounting and finance, administrative, financial services and technology.

Key Contact - Specialty:
Ms. Kip Hollister, President & Chief Executive Officer
Mr. David Tomer, Vice President
Ms. Nancy Doyle, Director, Accounting & Finance
Mr. Mike Gorman, Director, Contract IT
Mr. Tom Finn, Director, Technology

Functions: Generalist (All), Senior Mgmt., CFOs, Cash Mgmt., Systems Implem., Systems Support, Network Admin., DB Admin.

Industries: Generalist (All), Invest. Banking, Brokers, Misc. Financial, Accounting, New Media

Branches:
5 Burlington Woods Ste 101
Burlington, MA 01803-4571
(781) 237-2424
Fax: (781) 229-4388
Key Contact - Specialty:
Ms. Annie Smith, Marketing

Holloway, Schulz & Partners

1500-1188 Georgia St W
Georgia Place
Vancouver, BC V6E 4A2
Canada
(604) 688-9595
Fax: (604) 688-3608
Email: info@recruiters.com
Web: www.recruiters.com

Summary: Professional recruitment firm and search firm with consultants specializing in various disciplines. Searches are conducted on both a contingency and retainer basis.

Key Contact - Specialty:
Mr. Malcolm McGowan, Partner
Mr. Clive Holloway, Partner
Mr. Bill Schulz, Partner - *General management*
Ms. Dawn A. Longshaw, Senior Associate
Ms. Lorna Court, Senior Associate
Ms. Gabrielle Hawkins, Consultant

Salary Minimum: $40,000

Functions: Generalist (All), Management, Mfg., Materials, Sales & Mktg., HR Mgmt., Finance, IT

Industries: Generalist (All), Construction, Manufacturing, Transportation, Finance, Services, Software

Melinda Holm & Associates

750 N Orleans St Ste 407
Chicago, IL 60610-3549
(312) 654-9391
Fax: (312) 654-9392
Email: info@mhajobs.com
Web: www.mhajobs.com

Summary: Melinda Holm & Associates is a woman-owned staffing consultancy and executive recruitment firm which specializes in marketing,

advertising, public relations and communications at all levels. All MHA recruiters have marketing and advertising agency backgrounds. MHA leverages this hands-on experience to target, recruit, and screen talent to actively manage the entire process of hiring. MHA employs a personalized and proactive methodology to contribute to the long-term success of each company.

Key Contact - Specialty:
Mrs. Lisa Casper, Vice President, Senior Recruiter - *Advertising, CEOs, Communications, Consulting, Consumer*
Mrs. Melinda Holm-Peterson, President - *Advertising, Business to business, CEOs, Communications, Consumer (Hard Goods)*
Miss Shari Rosen, Vice President, Senior Recrutier - *Advertising, Communications, Consumer (Durables,Hard Goods,Marketing)*

Functions: Advertising, Mktg. Mgmt.

Industries: Generalist (All), Food, Bev., Tobacco, Consumer Goods, Media, Advertising, New Media, Communications, Packaging, Healthcare

Michael Holm and Associates Inc

2050 75th St
Woodridge, IL 60517-2307
(630) 663-1195
Fax: (630) 663-1198
Email: recruit@holmandassociates.com.
Web: www.holmandassociates.com

Summary: We are executive search and placement firm specializing in the food and baking industry. Our areas of expertise are sales / marketing, executive, R&D / QA, production, engineering, sanitation, and distribution nationwide.

Key Contact - Specialty:
Mr. Paul Sharp, Vice President

Functions: Generalist (All)

Industries: Manufacturing, Food, Bev., Tobacco, Engineering Svcs., Inst./Industrial Food Svc.

Katherine Holt Enterprises Ltd

27 Broadbridge Dr
Scarborough, ON M1C 3K5
Canada
(416) 208-0139
Fax: (416) 208-0141
Email: kholtltd@idirect.com

Summary: Specializing in property management, administration and general insurance.

Key Contact - Specialty:
Ms. Katherine Holt, Principal - *Admtnistration, Finance, Property management*
Ms. Margaret Rooney, Senior Consultant - *Property management*

Salary Minimum: $40,000

Functions: Management, Board Members, Middle Mgmt., Admin. Svcs., Finance

Industries: Construction, Insurance, Real Estate, Property/Facility Mgmt.

Home Health & Hospital Recruiters Inc

2858 Johnson Ferry Rd Ste 250
Marietta, GA 30062-8321
(770) 993-2828
Fax: (770) 993-6448
Email: barry@hhhr.net
Web: www.hhhr.net

Summary: We specialize in the recruitment of home healthcare, hospice, hospital, assisted living and long-term care professionals. In addition, we also do interim management and consulting.

Key Contact - Specialty:
Mr. Barry P. Savransky, President
Mr. Alan Savransky, Vice President

Salary Minimum: $35,000

Functions: Generalist (All), Board Members, Senior Mgmt., Middle Mgmt., Healthcare, Nurses, Health Admin., CFOs, M&A

Industries: Generalist (All), Healthcare, Hospitals, Long-term/Home Care

Fred Hood & Associates Inc
24671 Dry Canyon Cold Creek Rd
Calabasas, CA 91302-3212
(818) 222-6222
Fax: (818) 222-4445
Email: fred@fredhood.com
Web: www.fredhood.com

Summary: We locate outstanding marketing, sales, operations, warehouse and category management for the beverage and food industries.

Key Contact - Specialty:
Mr. Fred L. Hood, President - *Distribution, Sales, Transportation*
Ms. Randi Tomlimson, Account Executive
Ms. Courtney Hood, Account Executive
Ms. Cheryl Ellis, Recruiter
Mr. Maurice Moore, Recruiter
Mr. Ken Bill, Recruiter
Ms. Barbara Van Sluyters, Coach - *Banking (Mortgage), Financial services, Wall Street*

Salary Minimum: $50,000

Functions: Generalist (All), Senior Mgmt., Middle Mgmt., Distribution, Sales Mgmt., PR, Cash Mgmt., MIS Mgmt.

Industries: Generalist (All), Food, Bev., Tobacco

J G Hood Associates
PO Box 2667
Westport, CT 06880-0667
(203) 226-1126
(203) 866-0763
Email: jghood@optonline.net

Summary: We are a full service search firm specializing in logistics & supply chain, technical, engineering, manufacturing, engineering, IT, HR, financial and marketing/sales professionals. Clients include top Fortune and private companies, including consumer product manufacturing, high technology, software, healthcare and pharmaceuticals.

Key Contact - Specialty:
Ms. Joyce G. Hood, Owner & President

Salary Minimum: $45,000

Functions: Generalist (All), Middle Mgmt., Product Dev., Production, Quality, Purchasing, Materials Plng.

Industries: Generalist (All), Manufacturing, Plastics, Rubber, Leather, Stone, Glass, Metal Products, Machine, Appliance, Consumer Elect., Test, Measure Equip., Misc. Mfg., Electronic, Elec. Components, Consumer Goods, E-commerce

Hope Resource Partners Inc
(also known as Tri-Force Recruiting Specialists)
8522 Rail Fence Rd
Fort Wayne, IN 46835-4494
(260) 486-7182
Email: triforce@triforce.com
Web: www.triforce.com

Summary: As recruiting specialists, we provide quality service by utilizing structured methods. Submitted candidates have the required skills, want the position and they hit the salary target.

Both direct and contract service available. IT professionals, engineers, HR and technical sales.

Key Contact - Specialty:
Mr. John F. Hope, CPC, President - *Engineering, Information Technology*

Salary Minimum: $45,000

Functions: Generalist (All), Sales & Mktg., HR Mgmt., IT, Engineering

Industries: Generalist (All), Manufacturing, Medical Devices, Plastics, Rubber, Computer Equip., Electronic, Elec. Components, Banking, Engineering Svcs., Software

Hope Technical Assoc
735 Granger Hollow Rd
North Bennington, VT 05257-9788
(802) 442-3708
Fax: (802) 442-3750
Email: ctteasdale@aol.com

Summary: We are an executive search and recruitment firm specializing in the automation, process control and industrial marketplaces. Our business is assisting major manufacturers locate and place key personnel in technical sales & marketing positions.

Key Contact - Specialty:
Ms. Catherine Teasdale, CRM, Recruiter

Salary Minimum: $70,000

Functions: Sales & Mktg.

Industries: Manufacturing, Test, Measure Equip., Electronic, Elec. Components, Semiconductors

Hopkins & Company Inc
411 Massachusetts Ave
Acton, MA 01720-3739
(978) 263-7899
(978) 263-5422
Email: nancy@hopkins.com
Web: www.hopkins.com

Summary: We create technology growth and change through recruiting and coordinating talent partnerships in the technology arena. Our specialties are: software, storage/backup, business continuity, biotechnology, and technology consulting.

Key Contact - Specialty:
Ms. Nancy Hopkins Kramer, President & Senior Consultant - *Biotechnology, Executives, High technology, Senior management, Start-up companies*
Mr. Alan H. Kramer, Esq., Vice President, Operations - *Business development*

Salary Minimum: $90,000

Functions: Generalist (All), Management

Industries: IT Implementation, Communications, Network Infrastructure, Software, Development SW, ERP SW, Industry Specific SW, Networking, Comm. SW, Security SW, System SW, Biotech/Life Sciences

The Horizon Group
2001 Marcus Ave Ste E240
New Hyde Park, NY 11042-1011
(516) 358-4141
Fax: (516) 358-7133
Email: abanks@horizong.com
Web: www.horizong.com

Summary: Our firm is an executive search firm and human resources management consulting company. We conduct retainer and contingency search activities both domestically and internationally, and are divided into three core business units: taxable fixed income, global derivatives, and IT.

Key Contact - Specialty:
Mr. Arthur Banks, Managing Partner - *CIOs, Information Systems, Information Technology*
Mr. David Grossman, President
Mr. Tom Angello, Vice President
Mr. Sal Petrara, Vice President - *Computers (Programming,Software), Database (Administration), E-business, Information Technology*

Salary Minimum: $75,000

Functions: Senior Mgmt., Middle Mgmt., Cash Mgmt., MIS Mgmt.

Industries: Brokers, Venture Cap., Mutual/Hedge Funds, Misc. Financial, Services, E-commerce, IT Implementation, Healthcare, Hospitals, Long-term/Home Care

Horizon Medical Search of NH
8 Grenada Cir
Nashua, NH 03062-1429
(877) 598-6611
(603) 598-6611
Fax: (603) 598-6622
Email: horizonmed@aol.com

Summary: We are a contingency search firm that specializes in assisting physicians to locate practice opportunities. All fees are employer paid - no cost to candidates. All communications are confidential.

Key Contact - Specialty:
Mrs. Sabine G. DuBois, President - *Hospital, Pharmacists, Physicians, Psychiatry*
Mr. Joseph W. DuBois, Jr., Consultant - *Physicians*
Mr. Anthony G. DuBois, Vice President, Marketing - *Pharmacists*

Salary Minimum: $100,000

Functions: Physicians

Industries: Healthcare

Horizons Healthcare Inc
146 W Boylston Dr
Worcester, MA 01606-2799
(508) 459-5005
Email: info@diamondstaffinginc.com
Web: www.horizonshealthcare.com

Summary: We are a boutique firm specializing in placing sales professionals in the Internet and telecom infrastructure industry, for example service providers, networking hardware and software. The founder has working experience directly in the industry, enabling us to provide our clients with insight and contacts to efficiently address their search requirements in this market.

Key Contact - Specialty:
Ms. Christine Lauzon

Salary Minimum: $100,000

Functions: Nurses, Allied Health

Industries: Pharm Svcs., Insurance, Biotech/Life Sciences, Healthcare, Hospitals, Long-term/Home Care, Physical Therapy, Occupational Therapy, Women's

Horizons Unlimited
9385 Tenaya Way
Kelseyville, CA 95451-9645
(800) 748-5269

Summary: We place sales, technical service, licensing and technical positions in the chemical and petroleum industries, including: catalyst, process additives, additives, water treatment, adsorbents, alumna, surfactants and process simulation.

Key Contact - Specialty:
Mr. Bruce Van Buskirk, Owner

Functions: Generalist (All)

Industries: Chemicals

Horton Group Inc

204 S Beverly Dr Ste 109
Beverly Hills, CA 90212-3800
(310) 777-6600
Fax: (310) 777-6606
Email: art@hortongroupinc.com
Web: www.hortongroupinc.com

Summary: We are recruiters in the securities
industry serving stock brokerage and money
management firms. We place stockbrokers, branch
managers, regional directors, buy/sell side analysts
and portfolio managers.

Key Contact - Specialty:
Ms. Elayne Horton, President
Mr. Arthur Horton, Chief Financial Officer

Salary Minimum: $100,000

Functions: Risk Mgmt., Actuaries, Pension/Ret.
Planning

Industries: Finance, Banking, Invest. Banking,
Brokers, Venture Cap., Mutual/Hedge Funds,
Misc. Financial, Insurance, Casualty, Life

Hospitality International

23 W 73rd St Ste 100
New York, NY 10023-3104
(212) 769-8800
Fax: (212) 769-2138
Email: jar@hospitalityinternational.com
Web: www.hospitalityinternational.com

Summary: We are a executive search firm
providing our clients with mid to senior level
management and sales professionals. We have a
hospitality industry focus that includes: hotels,
restaurants, catering, on site foodservice (for
business, education and health care), private clubs,
hospitality related technology, and support
services.

Key Contact - Specialty:
Mr. Joseph A. Radice, President - *Food service,
Hotels, Restaurants*

Salary Minimum: $50,000

Functions: Generalist (All)

Industries: Hospitality

Hotel Executive Placement Inc

6 Wellhaven Cir Apt 1338
Owings Mills, MD 21117-5269
(410) 356-8903
Fax: (410) 356-8905
Email: info@hoteljobsnetwork.com
Web: www.heprecruiting.com

Summary: We are a search and recruiting firm
covering all management personnel in the
hospitality industry. All placements are on a
contingency basis.

Key Contact - Specialty:
Mr. Adam Hardie

Salary Minimum: $35,000

Functions: Hospitality

Industries: Hospitality

Hotel Executive Search & Consulting

6565 West Loop S Ste 510
Bellaire, TX 77401-3504
(713) 660-0008
Fax: (713) 660-0009

Email: kenherst@ahotelrecruiter.com
Web: www.ahotelrecruiter.com

Summary: We have extensive experience
providing middle and upper-management to the
lodging industry.

Key Contact - Specialty:
Mr. Kenneth L. Herst, MHS, Owner - *Hotels,
Resorts*

Salary Minimum: $40,000

Functions: Board Members, Senior Mgmt., Sales
Mgmt., Finance, Hospitality, Hotel Mgmt., Int'l.

Industries: Hospitality, Hotels, Resorts, Clubs,
Restaurants, Quick Service Restaurants, Full
Service Restaurants, Inst./Industrial Food Svc.,
Recreation, Sports, Travel, Property/Facility
Mgmt.

Hotel Recruiting Concepts

45 W Prospect Ave Ste 1515
Cleveland, OH 44115-1039
(216) 430-1228
(216) 430-1272
Fax: (775) 307-2554
Email: resumes@recruitingconcepts.com
Web: www.recruitingconcepts.com

Summary: We provide hotel management
placement service and are offering opportunities
for experienced hotel management professionals
seeking to further advance their careers. See our
website for a listing of current career opportunities
and to apply online. We pay rewards for referral
candidates.

Key Contact - Specialty:
Mr. Frank J. Sotet, III, Director, Recruiting &
Relocation - *Food & beverage, Hotels, Real
estate, Resorts, Restaurants*

Salary Minimum: $35,000

Functions: Generalist (All), Management, Board
Members, Senior Mgmt., Middle Mgmt., Sales
& Mktg., Sales Mgmt., Customer Svc., HR
Mgmt.

Industries: Services, Hospitality, Hotels, Resorts,
Clubs, Restaurants, Quick Service Restaurants,
Full Service Restaurants, Inst./Industrial Food
Svc., Property/Facility Mgmt.

Houk Services Executive Recruiters

7201 W Vickery Blvd Ste 214
Fort Worth, TX 76116-9038
(817) 738-4777
Fax: (817) 738-4767
Email: dhouk@airmail.net
Web: www.houkservices.com

Summary: Our firm specializes in operations
management (manufacturing, supply chain,
logistics, engineering, HR and environmental),
finance and accounting (CFO, VP of finance,
controller, senior accountant and staff
accountant)and sales.

Key Contact - Specialty:
Mr. David Houk, CPC, Principal & Chief
Executive Officer - *Finance, Operations*
Ms. Sherry Hughes, Vice President

Salary Minimum: $55,000

Functions: Management, Finance

Industries: Manufacturing, Plastics, Rubber,
Robotics, Architectural Svcs., Accounting,
Mgmt. Consulting, HR Services, Engineering
Svcs., Logistics Svcs., Supply Chain Mgmt,
Defense, Environmental Svcs., Aerospace

Houser Martin Morris

110 110th Ave NE Ste 580
Bellevue, WA 98004-5854
(425) 453-2700
Fax: (425) 453-8726
Email: recruitr@houser.com
Web: www.houser.com

Summary: Professional recruiting and search
consultants providing recruiting and search
expertise in a variety of key disciplines for your
company.

Key Contact - Specialty:
Mr. Robert Holert, President
Mr. Josef Verner, Senior Vice President
Ms. Victoria Harris, Principal
Mr. Peter Biege, General Manager
Ms. Jerilyn Shearer, Director, Factory
Automation

Salary Minimum: $50,000

Functions: Generalist (All), Board Members,
Senior Mgmt., Mfg., Sales Mgmt., Finance, IT,
Engineering, Attorneys

Industries: Generalist (All), Manufacturing, Test,
Measure Equip., Robotics, Transportation,
Finance, Non-profits, Legal, Accounting, HR
Services, Property/Facility Mgmt., Software

Jan Howard Associates Ltd

115-220 Yonge St
Toronto Eaton Centre Gallery
Toronto, ON M5B 2H1
Canada
(416) 598-1775
Fax: (416) 598-0363
Email: janhoward@vif.com

Summary: We are a full-line agency. We also
recruit for technical and specialized personnel and
contract positions.

Key Contact - Specialty:
Ms. Jan Howard, President

Salary Minimum: $28,000

Functions: Generalist (All), Middle Mgmt.,
Admin. Svcs., Advertising, Mktg. Research,
MIS Mgmt., Network Admin., Legal

Industries: Generalist (All), Misc. Financial,
Legal, Advertising, New Media

Howard Team & Associates

3080 Valmont Rd Ste 220
Boulder, CO 80301-2152
(303) 443-6656
Fax: (303) 443-6676
Email: ghoward@ha-team.com

Summary: We are technical recruiters specializing
in healthcare, information technology, medical
imaging, and data storage personnel.

Key Contact - Specialty:
Mr. Gale Howard, President

Salary Minimum: $50,000

Functions: Management, IT, MIS Mgmt.,
Systems Analysis, Systems Dev., Systems
Implem., Systems Support, Network Admin.,
DB Admin.

Industries: Healthcare

Howard, Williams & Rahaim Inc

105 S Narcissus Ave Ste 806
West Palm Beach, FL 33401-5530
(561) 833-4888
Fax: (561) 833-2343
Email: jwilliams@hwrlegal.com
Web: www.hwrlegal.com

Summary: Have specialized in the recruitment of lawyers, at all levels, on behalf of law firm and corporation clients. Acquired recruiting firm that specializes in legal support i.e. paralegals, legal secretary, etc.

Key Contact - Specialty:
Mr. John Williams, President
Mr. Richard D. Rahaim, Partner
Ms. Christine Bernier, Administrator
Mr. Tim Williams, Consultant, Legal Search - *Intellectual property*
Ms. Cindy Hallman, Consultant, Legal Search
Mr. Craig Deitch, Consultant, Legal Search

Salary Minimum: $60,000

Functions: Generalist (All), Attorneys, Paralegals

Industries: Generalist (All), Legal, Accounting

Howard-Sloan Professional Search

1140 Avenue of the Americas
New York, NY 10036-5803
(212) 704-0444
(800) 221-1326
Fax: (212) 869-7999
Email: info@howardsloan.com
Web: www.howardsloan.com

Summary: Our clientele includes law firms, corporations and financial institutions. Areas of specialization in the law include bankruptcy, corporate, environmental, intellectual property, labor/employment, litigation, real estate, tax/ERISA/trusts & estates, partners and law firm mergers. Our financial search division specializes in the placement of accounting, compliance, financial, risk, tax, and treasury professionals.

Key Contact - Specialty:
Mr. Mitchell Berger, Chief Executive Officer

Salary Minimum: $75,000

Functions: Senior Mgmt., Finance, CFOs, Taxes, M&A, Risk Mgmt., IT, Engineering, Legal, Paralegals

Industries: Generalist (All)

EJ Howe & Associates

PO Box 1284
Barrington, IL 60011-1284
(847) 381-0303
Email: betsy@ejhowe.com
Web: www.ejhowe.com

Summary: Recruiting for the computer software industry, technology, banking, manufacturing, consulting, medical and financial. Job opportunities are: sales, sales engineer, engineer, pre-sales consultant, project management, systems analyst, manager, senior manager, consultant, operations management and product development.

Key Contact - Specialty:
Ms. Elizabeth Howe, Principal

Salary Minimum: $75,000

Functions: Mfg., Product Dev., Sales & Mktg., Sales Mgmt., Engineering, Mgmt. Consultants

Industries: Food, Bev., Tobacco, Lumber, Furniture, Banking, Services, Logistics Svcs., Supply Chain Mgmt., Telecoms, Call Centers, Software, Accounting SW, Database SW, Development SW, Doc. Mgmt., Production SW, Healthcare

Robert Howe & Associates

PO Box 450867
Atlanta, GA 31145-0867
(770) 270-1211

Summary: Representing small to large manufacturing and service companies, in recruiting at mid-upper-level management positions.

Key Contact - Specialty:
Mr. Robert W. Hamill, President - *Construction, Healthcare, Hospitality, Manufacturing*

Salary Minimum: $60,000

Functions: Generalist (All)

Industries: Construction, Manufacturing, Hospitality, Healthcare

HR Advantage Inc

PO Box 10319
Burke, VA 22009-0319
(703) 978-6028
Fax: (703) 832-8539
Email: jobs@hradvantageinc.net
Web: www.hradvantageinc.com

Summary: Placement agency specializing in recruiting executives and professionals in start-up to large firms with clients in the high technology, telecom, wireless, legal, financial, government contracting and professional services fields. Recruits in marketing, public relations, sales, finance, legal, HR operations, international and customer service.

Key Contact - Specialty:
Ms. Julie B. Rana, President - *Telecommunications*

Salary Minimum: $50,000

Functions: HR Mgmt.

Industries: Mgmt. Consulting, HR Services, Media

HR Connections

6000 N Shore Dr
West Bloomfield, MI 48324-2141
(248) 366-6000
Fax: (248) 366-6001
Email: dshapiro@hrjobs.com
Web: www.hrconnections.com

Summary: At HR Connections, we match the best HR people with the best HR jobs. For the last 13 years we have connected outstanding HR professionals with outstanding career opportunities within the Fortune 500, nationwide. View our current openings at www.HRConnections.com

Key Contact - Specialty:
Ms. Debbie Shapiro, President

Salary Minimum: $60,000

Functions: HR Mgmt., Benefits, Staffing, Training

Industries: Generalist (All)

HR Remedies LLC

6201 La Pas Trl Ste 220
Indianapolis, IN 46268-2513
(317) 290-1919
Web: www.hrremedies.com

Summary: Premier comprehensive executive search, human resources consulting/outsourcing and outplacement firm. Founded by a former human resources executive and small business owner, clients are given personalized solutions whether a start-up or a Fortune 500. There is a reason why we are a preferred vendor to numerous employer's of choice, partner with us and find out why.

Key Contact - Specialty:
Mr. Robert Sanders, SPHR - *Construction, Diversity, Management, Packaging, Printing*

Functions: Generalist (All)

Industries: Construction, Manufacturing, Transportation, Finance, Services, Packaging, Insurance, Software, Biotech/Life Sciences, Healthcare

HR Systems Inc

5942 Gleneagles Cir
San Jose, CA 95138-2370
(408) 781-1214
Email: rick@hrsystemsnet.com
Web: www.hrsystemsnet.com

Summary: A retainer based search firm with many years of experience in helping corporate America identify, attract and retain top notch executive and professional talent in a variety of industries and markets.

Key Contact - Specialty:
Mr. Rick Sondhi, President - *Healthcare, Human resources, Marketing, Sales, Transportation*

Functions: Generalist (All)

Industries: Generalist (All)

Hreshko Consulting Group

850 US Highway One
North Brunswick, NJ 08902-3312
(732) 545-9000
Fax: (732) 545-0080
Email: info@hcgusa.com
Web: www.hcgusa.com

Summary: Our firm offers executive assessments, detailed candidate evaluations and competitive market intelligence among other unique executive search services. Our committment to client satisfaction is the foundation of our firm.

Key Contact - Specialty:
Mr. Frank M. Hreshko, Managing Director - *Accounting, C-level, CFOs, Closely-held business, Mergers & acquisitions*
Mr. John C. Diefenbach, Director, Pharmaceutical & Manufacturing - *Accounting, Biopharmaceutical, Finance, International, Pharmaceutical*
Mr. Michael Francis, Director, Financial Services - *Financial services*
Mr. Joseph Talarico, Director, Information Technology - *Computers, Computers (Hardware,Networking,Sales,Software)*
Ms. Deborah Hardgrove, National Account Manager - *Biopharmaceutical, Clinical, Equipment, Pharmaceutical, Sales*
Mr. Mina Kelada, Account Manager - *Biotechnology, Business development, Financial, Medical (Devices), Pharmaceutical*
Ms. Karen Narlis, Account Manager - *Accounting, Biopharmaceutical, C-level, Closely-held business, Professional services*
Mr. Bill Fell, Senior Consultant - *Sales*
Ms. Christina Marie, Consultant
Ms. Toni Milazzo, Research Analyst
Ms. Olga Vignuolo, Director, Research

Salary Minimum: $50,000

Functions: Generalist (All)

Industries: Manufacturing, Drugs Mfg., Finance, Services, Pharm Svcs., Accounting, Mgmt. Consulting, HR Services, Biotech/Life Sciences, Healthcare

HRQuest

(a division of Canis Major Inc)
PO Box 742
Carmel, IN 46082-0742
(317) 581-8880
Fax: (317) 581-8856
Email: cla@hrquest.com
Web: www.agencycsr.com

Summary: Specializing in all levels of insurance agency and brokerage positions. For our clients; customized, direct recruitment of candidates with a very high level of client service on both the property & casualty and life & health sides of the insurance industry. For our candidates; a hub of information about professional opportunities in the insurance industry.

Key Contact - Specialty:
Ms. Carol Albright, CPC

Functions: Generalist (All), Risk Mgmt.

Industries: Generalist (All), Insurance

HTSS Executive Search

1119 W Hamilton St
Allentown, PA 18101-1014
(610) 432-4161
(888) 711-4877
Fax: (610) 432-5409
Email: lsnyder@howellsstaffing.com
Web: www.htssexecutive.com

Summary: We pay personal attention to your job search. We will advertise, perform custom searches, match personality to recruit the best people for your management team. Call us for all your recruiting needs - top management, professional, IS or technical. We are a WBENC certified company.

Key Contact - Specialty:
Ms. Pat Howells, President
Ms. Jean Gerhart, Executive Recruiter
Ms. Lori Snyder, Director, Marketing & Recruiting
Ms. Kristy Howells, Communications

Salary Minimum: $35,000

Functions: Generalist (All)

Industries: Restaurants, Long-term/Home Care

Ricci Lee Hubbart Associates Inc

20660 Stevens Creek Blvd Ste 177
Cupertino, CA 95014-2120
(408) 725-1242
Fax: (408) 716-2704
Email: susan@riccilee.com
Web: www.riccilee.com

Summary: Specializing in the recruitment and placement of stellar marketing professionals.

Key Contact - Specialty:
Ms. Susan Hubbart, President & Chief Executive Officer - *Advertising, Marketing, Public relations*

Salary Minimum: $100,000

Functions: Advertising, Mktg. Mgmt., Direct Mktg., PR

Industries: Computer Equip., Consumer Elect., Consumer Goods, Finance, Banking, Non-profits, E-commerce, Travel, Advertising, New Media, Software

Hudson Associates Inc

PO Box 28449
Chattanooga, TN 37424-8449
(765) 649-1133
Email: ghudson@hudsonassociates.net
Web: www.hudsonassociates.net

Summary: We are a small, highly specialized firm handling L&H and specialized P&C insurance positions. We are very active in the placement of attorneys within advanced marketing specialty area, as well as sales & marketing individuals.

Key Contact - Specialty:
Mr. George A. Hudson, Managing Director

Salary Minimum: $70,000

Functions: Management, Board Members, Middle Mgmt., Mktg. Mgmt., Sales Mgmt., Direct Mktg., Training, CFOs, Taxes, Legal

Industries: Insurance

Huffman Associates LLC

111 W Main St
Applied Technology Center
Bay Shore, NY 11706-8313
(631) 969-3600
(877) 969-3600
Email: info@huffmanassociates.com
Web: www.huffmanassociates.com

Summary: We are national executive search consultants. Our expertise ranges from management to senior management level. We concentrate in financial services, banking, mortgage banking, mortgage servicing, IT, e-business & software firms. Functional expertise in Risk Mgnt, Finance, Accounting, Treasury, Capital Markets, IT, HR, Sales, Operations.

Key Contact - Specialty:
Mr. Michael W. Huffman, CPC, President & Chief Executive Officer - *Finance, Financial services, Middle management, Operations, Risk management*

Salary Minimum: $150,000

Functions: Senior Mgmt., Middle Mgmt., Health Admin., Finance, Cash Mgmt., Risk Mgmt., IT, MIS Mgmt.

Industries: Generalist (All), Banking, Invest. Banking, Venture Cap., Mutual/Hedge Funds, Misc. Financial, Industry Specific SW

Hufford Associates

3 Pembrook Ct
Bolingbrook, IL 60440-1692
(630) 378-0005
Fax: (630) 378-0008
Email: craig@huffordassociates.com
Web: www.huffordassociates.com

Summary: We specialize in discreet search and consulting assignments designed to help our clients identify and hire the executive and technology professionals needed to drive their success. Our expertise lies in identifying talent and enhancing careers for professionals in research and development, engineering, marketing, sales, information technology and manufacturing.

Key Contact - Specialty:
Mr. Craig Hufford, President

Salary Minimum: $80,000

Functions: Management, Middle Mgmt., Sales & Mktg., Mktg. Research, Mktg. Mgmt., R&D, Engineering

Industries: Medical Devices, Computer Equip., Consumer Elect., Test, Measure Equip., Electronic, Elec. Components, Mgmt. Consulting, Communications, Telecoms, Telephony, Digital, Wireless, Fiber Optic, Network Infrastructure, RF/Microwave, Software, Development SW, Networking, Comm. SW

Hughes & Associates International Inc

3737 Government Blvd Ste 304B
Mobile, AL 36693-4361
(251) 661-8888
Email: timohughes@aol.com
Web: www.hughesandassoc.com

Summary: We provide recruiting of engineers for Fortune 500 companies and companies who serve those companies, mainly in the chemical, petrochemical, refining, pulp & paper and other manufacturing industries.

Key Contact - Specialty:
Mr. Tim Hughes, President - *Chemical, Petrochemical, Refining*

Salary Minimum: $48,000

Functions: Engineering

Industries: Energy, Utilities, Food, Bev., Tobacco, Textiles, Apparel, Paper, Printing, Chemicals, Plastics, Rubber, Paints, Petro. Products, Consumer Elect.

Hughes & Wilden Associates

3935 Old William Penn Hwy
Murrysville, PA 15668-1854
(724) 733-1130
Fax: (724) 733-1136
Email: rogerhw@alltel.net

Summary: Transportation, distribution and supply chain management is our specialty.

Key Contact - Specialty:
Mr. Roger Sulkowski, Partner - *Distribution, Logistics, Transportation*
Ms. Saundra Stupar, Administration Assistant
Mr. Robert Amato, Associate - *Supply Chain, Traffic, Transportation*

Salary Minimum: $50,000

Functions: Materials, Purchasing, Distribution

Industries: Transportation

Hughes Consultants LLC

999 Peachtree St NE Ste 2670
Atlanta, GA 30309-4484
(404) 879-5070
Fax: (404) 879-5075
Email: inquiry@hughesconsultants.com
Web: www.hughesconsultants.com

Summary: Our firm dedicates itself to serving the search and consulting needs of the legal community. We fill positions from associates to partners, from staff attorneys to general counsels. Our clients are a diverse group of law firms and corporations.

Key Contact - Specialty:
Ms. Melba Hughes, President
Ms. Tanya Cunningham, Managing Director
Mr. Neil Gottenberg, Managing Director

Functions: Attorneys

Industries: Generalist (All)

Branches:
330 Madison Ave Fl 9
New York, NY 10017-5001
(646) 495-5315
Fax: (404) 879-5075
Email: inquiry@hughes-consultants.com
Key Contact - Specialty:
Ms. Ilene Rosh

Hulst Consulting Group Inc

1799 Pennsylvania St Ste 200
Denver, CO 80203-1310
(303) 837-8274
Fax: (303) 837-8275
Email: steve@hcgsearch.com
Web: www.hcgsearch.com

Summary: We offer accounting, financial, human recources and IT executive searches.

Key Contact - Specialty:
Mr. Jack Hulst, President
Mr. Steve Hulst, Consultant

Functions: HR Mgmt., Finance, IT

Industries: Generalist (All)

Human Capital International Inc

17651 Jamestown Way
Lutz, FL 33558-7706
(813) 960-8404
Fax: (813) 908-5354
Email: cfsa@humancapitalintl.com
Web: www.humancapitalintl.com

Summary: Our firm's founder has recruited talent for many years and is the author of a number of books on the recruitment process. Fulfillment of hundreds of executive positions through client focused executive search.

Key Contact - Specialty:
Mr. Douglas Kosarek, President & Senior Partner

Salary Minimum: $60,000

Functions: Generalist (All), Senior Mgmt., Sales Reps., Bldg. Contractors

Industries: Generalist (All), Construction, Finance, Banking, Accounting, Insurance, Real Estate

Human Capital Resources Inc

290 Dr Martin Luther King Jr St N Ste 202
Saint Petersburg, FL 33705-1586
(727) 898-0212
Fax: (727) 898-0314
Email: resume@humancap.com
Web: www.humancap.com

Summary: We specialize in the need for professionals in the financial services marketplace. Our clients include banks, third party marketing firm, product manufacturers and broker/dealers.

Key Contact - Specialty:
Mr. Paul A. Werlin, President - *Financial services, Mutual funds*
Mr. John Donovan, Vice President - *Financial services*

Functions: Generalist (All), Sales & Mktg.

Industries: Finance, Banking, Invest. Banking, Brokers, Mutual/Hedge Funds, Misc. Financial

Human Resource Bureau

2932 Perla
Newport Beach, CA 92660-3529
(949) 660-7966
Fax: (949) 660-0562

Summary: Executive search firm dealing with management of all types: attorneys, engineers, etc.

Key Contact - Specialty:
Ms. Joyce Newberry, Vice President
Mr. Pat Brogan, Principal - *Management*

Salary Minimum: $80,000

Functions: Generalist (All), Management

Industries: Generalist (All), Manufacturing, Services, Legal, Mgmt. Consulting, Advertising, New Media, Communications, Telecoms, Software, Mfg. SW, Marketing SW, Training SW, Biotech/Life Sciences, Healthcare, Non-Classifiable

Human Resource Management Inc

PO Box 361225
Birmingham, AL 35236-1225
(205) 978-7198
(866) 947-2727
Fax: (205) 978-7616
Email: info@hrmasap.com
Web: www.hrmasap.com

Summary: We are a generalist human resource management consultancy successfully providing contingency and retained search services nationwide. The firm is acclaimed for its innovative research recruiting services offered on a retained or ad hoc hourly rate basis.

Key Contact - Specialty:
Mr. Charles Wilkinson, SPHR, Chief Executive Officer
Ms. Roberta Willard, Director, Search Services

Salary Minimum: $45,000

Functions: Senior Mgmt., Middle Mgmt., Mfg., Healthcare, Physicians, Sales & Mktg., HR Mgmt., Finance

Industries: Generalist (All), Healthcare

Human Resources Management Hawaii Inc

PO Box 398
Aiea, HI 96701-0398
(808) 536-3438
Email: hrmhelinski@msn.com

Summary: Our personal careers reflect successful work experience in administration, management, engineering and IT. We therefore can better understand your staffing needs and save you time to do what you do best.

Key Contact - Specialty:
Mr. Mike Elinski, President - *Financial*

Salary Minimum: $70,000

Functions: HR Mgmt., CFOs, IT, Engineering, Mgmt: Consultants

Industries: Generalist (All)

E F Humay Associates

PO Box 173
Fairview Village, PA 19409-0173
(610) 275-1559
(610) 275-8320
Fax: (610) 275-3485
Email: gene@efhumay.com
Web: www.efhumay.com

Summary: Recruit for manufacturers and distributors of construction and mining equipment (road, bridge, mining, etc.) in positions for sales, marketing, parts, service, engineering and all management positions.

Key Contact - Specialty:
Mr. Gene Humay, President - *Manufacturing, Marketing, Sales*
Mrs. Jane Humay, Operations Manager - *Manufacturing, Marketing, Sales*
Mr. Jon Humay, Vice President

Salary Minimum: $50,000

Functions: Generalist (All), Management, Board Members, Senior Mgmt., Mktg. Mgmt.

Industries: Agri., Forestry, Mining, Energy, Utilities, Construction, Manufacturing, Wholesale, Retail

Leigh Hunt & Associates Inc

8970 SW 122nd Pl Apt 112
Miami, FL 33186-4110
(305) 598-2803
Email: lhunt@leighhunt.com
Web: www.leighhunt.com

Summary: We maintain a database of over 5,000 plus companies and 6,000 plus candidates in polyurethane, paints and coatings industry that is an invaluable resource for job search, recruitment and placement. The right chemistry between candidate and company equals success.

Key Contact - Specialty:
Leigh Hunt, Owner & President

Salary Minimum: $40,000

Functions: Middle Mgmt., Product Dev., Sales & Mktg., Mktg. Research

Industries: Construction, Manufacturing, Chemicals, Plastics, Rubber, Paints, Petro. Products

Hunt For Executives

90 Tupper Rd
Sandwich, MA 02563-1872
(508) 833-4868
Fax: (508) 833-9691
Email: info@huntforexecutives.com
Web: www.huntforexecutives.com

Summary: We are a recruiting firm focusing on upper-level management and executive positions. We also serve mid-level professionals in many disciplines who are on career paths leading to upper-level responsibilities.

Key Contact - Specialty:
Ms. Mary Hunt, President
Mrs. Joanne Mazar, Director, Executive Recruiting - *Accounting, Banking, Financial services, Human resources, Staffing*

Functions: Senior Mgmt.

Industries: Generalist (All)

Hunt Ltd

727 Raritan Rd Ste 103
Clark, NJ 07066-2241
(732) 499-7711
Fax: (732) 499-4718
Email: info@huntltd.com
Web: www.huntltd.com

Summary: Our staff is made up of former distribution executives. Company specializes primarily in distribution/transportation opportunities.

Key Contact - Specialty:
Mr. Alex Metz, CPC, President - *Distribution, Logistics*

Salary Minimum: $45,000

Functions: Generalist (All), Senior Mgmt., Middle Mgmt., Materials, Purchasing, Materials Plng., Distribution

Industries: Generalist (All), Food, Bev., Tobacco, Textiles, Apparel, Paper, Chemicals, Soap, Perf., Cosmtcs., Drugs Mfg., Medical Devices, Plastics, Rubber, Paints, Petro. Products, Machine, Appliance, Computer Equip., Retail

Hunter & Michaels Executive Search

7502 Greenville Ave Ste 500
Dallas, TX 75231-3812
(214) 750-4666
Fax: (214) 750-4476
Email: ray@hunterm.com

Summary: We are specialists in the consumer packaged goods industry. We only place candidates that have a minimum of 10 years selling experience to the mass, food & drug channels of trade. Our specialty is placing qualified candidates that sell to the mass channel of trade.

Key Contact - Specialty:
Mr. Ray Smuland, President
Mr. Jason Smuland, Account Executive

Salary Minimum: $90,000

Functions: Sales & Mktg.

Industries: Food, Bev., Tobacco, Soap, Perf., Cosmtcs., Drugs Mfg., Consumer Elect.

The Hunter Group

(also known as BTI Financial)
600 Grant St Ste 500
Denver, CO 80203-3527
(303) 861-0405
Fax: (303) 861-0377

Summary: Our firm is made up of only experienced recruiters with combined recruiting experience specializing in banking, mortgage, finance, accounting, HR, sales/marketing and IT.

Key Contact - Specialty:
Mr. Greg Garvis, Chief Executive Officer
Ms. Lori Johnson, Executive Search Consultant - *Finance, Sales, Technical*

Salary Minimum: $35,000

Functions: Generalist (All), Cash Mgmt.

Industries: Generalist (All), Finance, Banking, Brokers, Services, Advertising, Telecoms, Wireless, Fiber Optic, Marketing SW, Networking, Comm. SW

The Hunter Group

1605 Green Pine Ct
Raleigh, NC 27614-9777
(919) 676-5900
Email: martha@hunts4u.com
Web: www.hunts4u.com

Summary: Executive and management level recruiters with emphasis on rapid response recruiting. Client driven and targeted, with special expertise in locating and placing top talent at senior and executive levels; partnering with startups; and providing creative & cost effective recruiting solutions at all levels. Incentive based/results driven.

Key Contact - Specialty:
Ms. Martha Lempicke
Mr. Todd Lempicke

Salary Minimum: $75,000

Functions: Generalist (All), Senior Mgmt.

Industries: Generalist (All), Services

T H Hunter Inc

815 Nicollet Mall Ste 210
Minneapolis, MN 55402-2523
(612) 339-0530
Fax: (612) 339-1937
Email: rbeller@thhunter.com
Web: www.thhunter.com

Summary: Generalist firm specializing in client oriented custom tailored searches, focusing on active recruiting of the best possible candidates.

Key Contact - Specialty:
Mr. Robert S. Beller, Executive Director

Salary Minimum: $50,000

Functions: Generalist (All), Management, Sales & Mktg., HR Mgmt., Finance, Credit, IT

Industries: Generalist (All), Finance, Accounting, Telecoms, Software, Healthcare

The Hunter Search Group Inc

8070 Beechmont Ave
Cincinnati, OH 45255-3145
(513) 474-0777
Fax: (513) 474-2777
Email: bbrown@huntersearch.net
Web: www.huntersearch.net

Summary: We are an executive search firm providing professional recruiting services on a national basis. Our focus is on the construction industry and related disciplines. Candidates are typically involved in architecture, engineering, construction management and real estate development.

Key Contact - Specialty:
Mr. Bob Brown, President

Salary Minimum: $50,000

Functions: Generalist (All), Management

Industries: Generalist (All), Construction, Architectural Svcs., Engineering Svcs.

Huntley Associates Inc

PO Box 868144
Plano, TX 75086-8144
(972) 599-0100
Fax: (972) 599-0300
Email: jobs@huntley.com
Web: www.huntley.com

Summary: Corporate consultants engaged in business development of commercial real estate investment, business process outsourcing, executive recruiting and the provision of contract consulting professionals.

Key Contact - Specialty:
Mr. David E. Huntley, CPC, President & Chief Executive Officer - *Business development, CRM, ERP, Information Technology, Telecommunications*
Ms. Sophie Huntley, Administration Manager - *Business development, Information Technology, International*

Salary Minimum: $75,000

Functions: Generalist (All), Middle Mgmt., Plant Mgmt., Materials, IT, Systems Dev., DB Admin., Engineering, Health & Safety, Design

Industries: Generalist (All), Manufacturing, Semiconductors, Communications, Telecoms, Digital, Aerospace, Software

Cathy L Hurless Executive Recruiting

6101 Fredericksburg Ln
Madison, WI 53718-8266
(608) 222-5300
(608) 575-1577
Fax: (608) 222-7463
Email: churless@charter.net
Web: www.cathyhurless.com

Summary: Executive media recruiter/advertising industry. Advertising agencies, media management firms, media planning/buying executives.

Key Contact - Specialty:
Ms. Cathy Hurless, President & Executive Recruiter - *Media*
Ms. Robin Peterson, Executive Recruiter - *Media*
Ms. Nancy Kromm, Executive Recruiter - *Media*
Ms. Marie Mednansky, Executive Recruiter - *Media*

Salary Minimum: $35,000

Functions: Generalist (All), Advertising

Industries: Media, Advertising, New Media

LM Hurley & Associates

PO Box 711691
San Diego, CA 92171-1691
(858) 277-8282
Email: info@lmhurley.com
Web: www.lmhurley.com

Summary: We are an executive recruiting firm that specializes in the placement of high caliber candidates, ranging from mid-level management to executive, within the long-term care and assisted living industry only. Applicants must have direct industry experience.

Key Contact - Specialty:
Ms. Lauren Gavit, President

Functions: Management, Board Members, Middle Mgmt., Healthcare, Nurses

Industries: Healthcare, Hospitals, Long-term/Home Care

Huston, Reed & Associates

Spartina Ct
Hilton Head Island, SC 29928-2935
(843) 671-4171
Email: hustonreed@aol.com
Web: www.jobsinprinting.com

Summary: We recruit for sheet-fed and web offset printers who produce magazines, catalogs, general commercial work, retail inserts, direct mail and books. We partner with our clients to identify candidates for all printing positions, including president, senior management, middle management, sales, customer service, prepress, scheduling/planning, mailing, distribution, pressroom and bindery operators.

Key Contact - Specialty:
Ms. Cindy Reed, President - *Printing*

Salary Minimum: $30,000

Functions: Management, Senior Mgmt., Middle Mgmt., Mfg., Production, Plant Mgmt., Quality, Sales & Mktg., Customer Svc., Sales Reps.

Industries: Printing

Hutchinson Group Inc

107-150 Consumers Rd
North York, ON M2J 1P9
Canada
(416) 499-6621
Fax: (416) 499-7953
Email: info@hutchgroup.com
Web: www.hutchgroup.com

Summary: Our firm has provided services to a diverse client community, both not-for-profit and corporate. We provide search services at all levels of an organization including executive, general management, IT, sales and administration. Whether permanent or contract we can provide the right people for our clients' needs.

Key Contact - Specialty:
Mr. H. David Hutchinson, President

Salary Minimum: $30,000

Functions: Generalist (All)

Industries: Generalist (All)

P F Hutton & Associates

4016 Old Sturbridge Dr
Apex, NC 27539-9799
(919) 662-3799
Fax: (919) 772-8681
Email: info@pfhutton.com
Web: www.pfhutton.com

Summary: Our firm provides professional staffing to a wide range of client companies. We are established; top producing, high energy recruiters and managers who possess a high degree of integrity. We can assist your organization in building a powerful team. We specialize in staffing management positions in administration, marketing, finance and information systems.

Key Contact - Specialty:
Ms. Pam Hutton, President

Functions: Generalist (All), HR Mgmt.

Industries: Energy, Utilities, Banking, Invest. Banking, Misc. Financial, Non-profits, Accounting, HR Services, Insurance, Casualty, Claims, Life, Commercial, Re-Insurance, Accounting SW

The Hutton Group Inc

1855 Bridgepointe Cir Unit 23
Vero Beach, FL 32967-6839
(772) 770-1787
Fax: (772) 365-7766
Email: contact@huttongrouphc.com
Web: www.huttongrouphc.com

Summary: Search and placement for healthcare executives and consultants for consulting firms, integrated health systems/hospitals, managed care organizations and software companies.

Key Contact - Specialty:
Ms. M. Joan Hutton, President & Chief Executive Officer - *Managed care, Physicians*

Salary Minimum: $50,000

Functions: Quality, Health Admin., Finance, CFOs, Budgeting, M&A, Risk Mgmt., Mgmt. Consultants

Industries: Healthcare, Hospitals

HW HealthFinders Inc

4450 Titleist Dr Ste 200
Fernandina Beach, FL 32034-5342
(904) 321-2448
Fax: (904) 321-5644
Email: bwhren@hwhealthfinders.com
Web: www.hwhealthfinders.com

Summary: We specialize in sales and operational positions ranging from executive positions to local operational staff and territorial sales positions for companies in the health care industry ranging from pharmaceutical and biotechnology companies, medical supply and device companies, clinical research, long term care, allied health professionals and hospitals.

Key Contact - Specialty:
Mr. Bob Whren, Managing Partner
Mr. Bruce Hackley, Managing Partner

Salary Minimum: $60,000

Functions: Management, Senior Mgmt., Middle Mgmt., Healthcare, Nurses, Allied Health, Sales & Mktg., Mktg. Mgmt., Sales Mgmt., Sales Reps.

Industries: Drugs Mfg., Medical Devices, Services, Non-profits, Pharm Svcs., Mgmt. Consulting, Biotech/Life Sciences, Healthcare, Hospitals, Long-term/Home Care, Physical Therapy, Occupational Therapy, Women's

Hyland Bay Executive Search LLC

1929 W Lone Cactus Dr Ste 6
Phoenix, AZ 85027-2634
(602) 381-1177
(800) 382-1177
Fax: (623) 869-0095
Email: hylandbay@hylandbay.com
Web: www.hylandbay.com

Summary: Searches performed for the real estate industry only. Handle all corporate positions in the home building industry including master planned communities. Able to place both inexperienced and experienced sales, sales management and construction professionals in sales & marketing positions with new home builders.

Key Contact - Specialty:
Mr. Richard Scott, President

Ms. Bette Finger, Chief Operating Officer
Ms. Diana Bass, Vice President, Executive Recruiting

Salary Minimum: $20,000

Functions: Sales Mgmt.

Industries: Real Estate

Ian Martin Limited

(formerly known as The 500 Staffing Services Inc)
465 Morden Rd
Floor 2
Oakville, ON L6K 3W6
Canada
(905) 815-1600 x2236
(800) 567-9675
Fax: (905) 815-1624
Email: bullock@ianmartin.com
Web: www.ianmartin.com

Summary: Our executive search division offers professional and management search capabilities within the following industry sectors: pharmaceutical, biotechnology & medical/surgical, business-to-business and industrial/technical.

Key Contact - Specialty:
Mr. Terrence Bullock, General Manager - *Computers, Professional services, Staffing, Systems, Technology*
Mr. Don Solar, Recruiter
Mr. Trevor Rudd, Recruiter

Salary Minimum: $75,000

Functions: Management, Middle Mgmt., Mfg., Product Dev., Production, Automation, Plant Mgmt., Sales & Mktg., MIS Mgmt., Systems

Industries: Generalist (All), Drugs Mfg., Medical Devices, Motor Vehicles, Telephony, Wireless, ERP SW, Mfg. SW, Biotech/Life Sciences

Branches:
510-138 4 Ave SE
First Street Plaza
Calgary, AB T2G 4Z6
Canada
(403) 262-2600
Email: robinson@the500.com
Key Contact - Specialty:
Ms. Rose Robinson

101-72 Victoria St S
Kitchener, ON N2G 4Y9
Canada
(519) 568-8300
Email: coulis@ianmartin.com
Key Contact - Specialty:
Ms. Cynthia Coulis

203-275 Slater St
Ottawa, ON K1P 5H9
Canada
(613) 237-0155
Fax: (613) 237-2070
Email: oconnor@ianmartin.com
Key Contact - Specialty:
Mr. Matt O'Connor

IC Solutions

1420-5650 Yonge St
The Xerox Tower
North York, ON M2M 4G3
Canada
(416) 238-4414
Fax: (416) 222-7738
Email: sarah@ic-solutions.ca
Web: www.ic-solutions.ca

Summary: Whether you need a premium staffing solution, a business consulting solution, or have basic staffing needs like temporary placement, we can help. For companies of any size that need

deployment of specialized business or IT project management expertise - we have the solutions that fit! We deliver excellent search services, with a focus on Sales, Marketing, IT and logisitics and additional à la carte service options to clients with wide-ranging placement requirements.

Key Contact - Specialty:
Ms. Sarah Canzano, President - *Finance, Information Technology, Marketing, Sales, Telecommunications*

Salary Minimum: $40,000

Functions: Generalist (All), Sales Reps.

Industries: Construction, Manufacturing, Soap, Perf., Cosmtcs., Transportation, Finance, IT Implementation, Communications, Telecoms, Wireless, Insurance, Software, Marketing SW, Security SW

IDC Executive Search

100 2nd Ave N Ste 130
Saint Petersburg, FL 33701-3337
(727) 898-6900
Fax: (727) 898-6920
Email: info@idcexec.com
Web: www.idcexec.com

Summary: We are a full-service executive search firm strictly in the power industry. We have the experience and contacts to match your background to the right position. We have a new additional emphasis in healthcare and senior living.

Key Contact - Specialty:
Mr. Marc Granet, President
Ms. Andrea Granet, Office Manager
Mr. Terry Trimmer, Vice President - *Emergency room, Medical, Operating rooms, Respiratory therapy, Subacute healthcare*

Salary Minimum: $75,000

Functions: Generalist (All), Healthcare

Industries: Energy, Utilities, Oil & Gas, Healthcare, Hospitals, Long-term/Home Care

IES (Individual Employment Services)

1 New Hampshire Ave Ste 125
Portsmouth, NH 03801-2907
(603) 570-4850
Email: iesjobs2@verizon.net

Summary: We successfully identify/recruit quality people for quality companies. We offer strict confidentiality at all times and strive for long term matches between client accounts and candidates.

Key Contact - Specialty:
Ms. Anita Labell, Principal
Mr. James Otis, Principal

Salary Minimum: $75,000

Functions: Senior Mgmt., Sales & Mktg., HR Mgmt., Benefits, Finance, CFOs, IT

Industries: Manufacturing, Finance, Insurance

iHeadHunt

PO Box 4355
Winter Park, FL 32793-4355
(407) 379-1003
Fax: (407) 379-0170
Email: careers@iheadhunt.cc
Web: www.iheadhunt.cc

Summary: Our firm specializes in contingent and retained search for the accounting, financial and technology industries. Providing the right people for the right job is the foundation of our business. We find the best employees with leading edge and traditional recruiting practices. Our accounting and finance team serves the Florida market

exclusively; and our ERP and technology team works on a nationwide basis.

Key Contact - Specialty:
Mr. Christian Sieg, CPC, Vice President, Recruiting - *C-level, CFOs, Comptrollers, Controllers, Financial*
Mr. Peter Lofgren, CPC, Vice President, Recruiting - *BAAN, Client/server, Computers, Computers (Automation,Programming)*
Mr. James Mitchell, CPC, Vice President, Recruiting - *Information service, Information Systems, Information Technology, SAP, Technology*
Mr. Vina Dang, Director, SAP Technology Services - *Information Systems, Information Technology, SAP*
Mr. Alan Hain, CPC, Senior Recruiter - *C-level, CFOs, Comptrollers, Controllers, Financial*
Ms. Debbie White, Account Manager - *Information Systems, Information Technology, SAP*
Mr. Jerry Daniele, Director, Recruiting - *JD Edwards, Outsourcing, PeopleSoft, Technical, Technical (Management)*

Salary Minimum: $35,000

Functions: Management, Finance, CFOs, Cash Mgmt., IT

Industries: Generalist (All), Construction, Finance, Misc. Financial, Accounting, IT Implementation, Hospitality, Accounting SW, ERP SW, Mfg. SW

ILS-Information Connection Inc

10426 Main St
Thonotosassa, FL 33592-8303
(888) 983-0209
Fax: (813) 982-1848
Email: beverly.flanders@verizon.net
Web: www.placementalternatives.com

Summary: We specialize in the healthcare industry.

Key Contact - Specialty:
Ms. Beverly Flanders, President - *Healthcare, Information Technology, Insurance, Managed care, Medical*

Functions: Generalist (All)

Industries: Insurance, Casualty, Claims, Commercial, Healthcare, Hospitals, Long-term/Home Care

Impact Executive Placement

5900 Westslope Dr
Austin, TX 78731-3655
(512) 453-4000
(877) 453-4530
Fax: (512) 374-1705
Email: jobs@impact-ep.com
Web: www.impact-ep.com

Summary: Our firm specializes in the battery and fuel cell industries.

Key Contact - Specialty:
Mr. Arnie Allen, Owner

Functions: Generalist (All), Management, Board Members, Senior Mgmt., Product Dev., Production, Sales & Mktg., R&D, Engineering

Industries: Energy, Utilities, Manufacturing, Misc. Mfg., Engineering Svcs., Non-Classifiable

Impact Personnel Services

PO Box 4081
Brandon, MS 39047-4081
(601) 992-1591
Fax: (601) 992-5037
Email: staffing@att.net

Summary: We are a full service, executive recruitment firm specializing in the placement of engineering, manufacturing and industrial personnel. Whether you are a hiring manager seeking to fill employment opportunities or a job seeker looking for a new career, we will offer you a customized plan to assist you in achieving your goals.

Key Contact - Specialty:
Ms. Jan Prystupa, President

Functions: Generalist (All)

Industries: Energy, Utilities, Construction, Manufacturing, Misc. Mfg., Electronic, Elec. Components, Equip Svcs., HR Services, Packaging, HR SW, Mfg. SW

Impact Resource Group, Inc

PO Box 20315
Roanoke, VA 24018-0032
(540) 343-1565
Fax: (540) 343-1566
Email: keith@impactrg.com
Web: www.impactrg.com

Summary: We specialize in the placement of sales and sales management professionals in the dental, dental implant and medical device fields.

Key Contact - Specialty:
Mr. Keith A. Ghaphery, CPC, President - *Dental, Medical, Medical (Devices), Sales*
Mrs. Melissa Ghaphery, Vice President - *Dental, Healthcare, Medical, Medical (Devices,Sales)*
Ms. Jayne Rydzak, Research Specialist - *Dental, Healthcare, Medical, Medical (Devices,Sales)*

Salary Minimum: $50,000

Functions: Board Members, Sales & Mktg.

Industries: Biotech/Life Sciences, Healthcare, Hospitals, Dental

Impact Source Inc

334 E Lake Rd Ste 218
Palm Harbor, FL 34685-2427
(727) 772-6499
Email: impacts@tampabay.rr.com

Summary: Great people make great companies. We help our clients find those great people. Industry specialization: building-product and industrial manufacturers. People specialization: sales/marketing - all levels. Operations - all management levels.

Key Contact - Specialty:
Mr. John E. Sattler, President - *Building products, Management, Marketing, Product management/development, Sales*

Salary Minimum: $55,000

Functions: Management, Senior Mgmt., Plant Mgmt., Distribution, Sales & Mktg., Mktg. Mgmt., Sales Mgmt.

Industries: Manufacturing, Lumber, Furniture, Paper, Chemicals, Plastics, Rubber, Paints, Petro. Products, Leather, Stone, Glass, Metal Products, Machine, Appliance, Services, Supply Chain Mgmt

Impex Services Inc

184 S Livingston Ave #9181
Livingston, NJ 07039-3063
(973) 994-2728
Email: elie@resumme.com
Web: www.resumme.com

Summary: Operated by sales and applications engineers, we are in the business of performing search and evaluation of those who excel in sales and marketing related positions within software and technology based products and services.

Key Contact - Specialty:
Mr. Elie Klachkin, MS, JCTC, President

Salary Minimum: $75,000

Functions: Management, Middle Mgmt., Product Dev., Sales & Mktg.

Industries: Manufacturing, Drugs Mfg., Medical Devices, Computer Equip., Consumer Elect., Test, Measure Equip., Robotics, Semiconductors, Communications, Software

Independent Resource Systems Inc

28222 Agoura Rd Ste 201
Agoura Hills, CA 91301-2412
(818) 865-3150
Fax: (818) 865-3155
Email: speth@irsystems.com
Web: www.irsystems.com

Summary: Search and placement for high-technology industry from Individual contributors to Executive management. Engineering, Sales and Marketing.

Key Contact - Specialty:
Mr. Don Speth, President - *High technology*

Salary Minimum: $75,000

Functions: Generalist (All), Management, Board Members, Middle Mgmt., Product Dev., Sales & Mktg., Mktg. Research, Systems Dev., Engineering, Architects

Industries: Computer Equip., Semiconductors, Venture Cap., Pharm Svcs., Mgmt. Consulting, HR Services, New Media, Broadcast, Film, Telecoms, Software, Database SW, Development SW, ERP SW, Industry Specific SW, Networking, Comm. SW, Security SW, Biotech/Life Sciences

IndustrySalesPros/Schaper Associates

525 Highland Blvd Ste 116
Coatesville, PA 19320-5810
(866) 384-9117
(800) 557-1674
Fax: (610) 380-8973
Email: admin@industrysalespros.com
Web: www.industrysalespros.com

Summary: We are a recruiting firm specializing in the placement of industrial sales & marketing professionals specific to the mechanical, electrical, electronic component markets, for example: motors, drives, motion, process, power transmission, HVAC, etc.

Key Contact - Specialty:
Mr. Walter Brod, Senior Account Manager - *Energy, Facilities engineering, Factories (Automation), General contractors, Home and building controls*
Mrs. Karen Schaper, President - *Energy, HVAC*

Salary Minimum: $50,000

Functions: Generalist (All), Sales & Mktg., Mktg. Mgmt., Sales Mgmt.

Industries: Energy, Utilities, Construction, Manufacturing, Machine, Appliance, Test, Measure Equip., Misc. Mfg., Electronic, Elec. Components, Robotics, Marketing SW

Infinity Business Solutions

2629 River Trace Ct
Birmingham, AL 35243-2243
(205) 520-4711
Fax: (205) 977-4176
Email: infinityllc1@bellsouth.net
Web: unlimited-possibilities.biz

Summary: Executive search and leadership development firm that specializes recruiting and consulting in the restaurant, retail, food service and food manufacturing industries.

Key Contact - Specialty:
Mr. Alton Shields, President

Salary Minimum: $75,000

Functions: Senior Mgmt.

Industries: Manufacturing, Food, Bev., Tobacco, Retail, Hospitality, Restaurants, Packaging

Influence Networks

800 N Circle Dr
Vestal, NY 13850-3141
(607) 330-0703
Fax: (702) 922-8421
Email: rstoddard@influencenetworks.com
Web: www.influencenetworks.com

Summary: Specialists in medical devices, semiconductor, optics and nanotechnology.

Key Contact - Specialty:
Ms. Rachael Stoddard, Founder & Principal Officer - *Product management/development, Research & development, Semiconductors, Technical (Management), Technology*
Mr. Evan Grubb, Managing Director - *Engineering, Management, Medical (Devices, Sales)*

Functions: Generalist (All)

Industries: Medical Devices, Electronic, Elec. Components, Semiconductors, Communications, Telecoms, Wireless, Fiber Optic

Information Technology Search

PO Box 317
Chadds Ford, PA 19317-0317
(610) 388-0587
(302) 369-4124
Email: aitken@400search.com

Summary: We are AS/400 niche specialists. We perform highly technical searches for ERP implementation specialists, directors of IT and the staff that reports to them. The staff that we place may include application programmers, AS/400 tech support pros and LAN/WAN engineers and/or administrators. We also place data architects, security experts and CIOs.

Key Contact - Specialty:
Ms. Carol Aitken, CPC, President

Salary Minimum: $60,000

Functions: IT, MIS Mgmt., Systems Analysis, Systems Dev., Systems Implem., Systems Support, Network Admin., DB Admin.

Industries: Generalist (All)

Information Technology Recruiting Ltd (ITR Ltd)

100-200 Consumers Rd
North York, ON M2J 4R4
Canada
(416) 502-3400
(888) 414-7324
Email: resumes@itrlimited.com
Web: www.itrlimited.com

Summary: We offer permanent and contract placement in the IT field. We place programmers, software developers, architects, web designers, project managers, business analysts, manager, director, and CEO positions. Our website offers real time listings. Confidentiality is assured, resumes are never submitted without the prior consent of the candidate.

Key Contact - Specialty:
Mr. Fernao Ferreira, Financial Analyst/Director
Mr. Keith Taylor, Executive Consultant
Mr. David Newman, Architect & Administrator, Network & Sys

Salary Minimum: $45,000

Functions: IT, Systems Analysis, Systems Dev., Systems Implem., Systems Support, Network Admin., DB Admin.

Industries: Generalist (All)

InfoTech Search

2308 Warm Springs St
Mesquite, TX 75149-1968
(972) 285-7544
(214) 638-0058
Email: haroldharrison@earthlink.net

Summary: Provide recruitment of CIO, IT management, data architects, database administration, data warehouse, ERP Specialists, web/eCommerce developers and senior technical personnel.

Key Contact - Specialty:
Mr. Harold M. Harrison, Owner

Salary Minimum: $80,000

Functions: IT, MIS Mgmt., Systems Analysis, Systems Dev., Systems Implem., Systems Support, DB Admin.

Industries: Generalist (All), Oil & Gas, Computer Equip., Banking, Mutual/Hedge Funds, Publishing, Telecoms, Wireless, Database SW, ERP SW, Hospitals

Ingman + Ingman

13024 Marshall Rd SE
Tenino, WA 98589-9417
(360) 264-5248
(360) 264-5249
Email: jeff@ingmancompany.com
Web: www.ingmancompany.com

Summary: We match truly exceptional civil/structural engineers including geotechnical, transportation, environmental, water and marine to their highest and best fit.

Key Contact - Specialty:
Ms. Sharon Ingman, Owner
Mr. Jeff Ingman, Partner

Salary Minimum: $50,000

Functions: Management, Engineering

Industries: Engineering Svcs.

Meredith Ingram Ltd

55 W Goethe St Apt 1225
Chicago, IL 60610-2233
(312) 640-0002
(312) 640-0005
Fax: (312) 640-1376
Email: ingrammere@aol.com

Summary: An executive recruiting firm whose principal has had many years of executive sales & marketing management experience with national brands and private label in the grocery industry.

Key Contact - Specialty:
Ms. Meredith Ingram, Principal - *Manufacturing, Sales*

Salary Minimum: $50,000

Functions: Purchasing, Sales & Mktg., Mktg. Research, Mktg. Mgmt., Sales Reps.

Industries: Generalist (All), Manufacturing, Food, Bev., Tobacco, Paper, Soap, Perf., Cosmtcs., Drugs Mfg., Paints, Petro. Products, Mgmt. Consulting

Inner Circle Consulting Group Inc

80 Davids Dr Ste 1
Hauppauge, NY 11788-2002
(631) 952-8966
Fax: (631) 952-8965
Email: janety@innercirclegroup.com
Web: www.innercirclegroup.com

Summary: We are a permanent employment service. We specialize in the business of searching and recruiting the most qualified candidates in a variety of markets. Founded on the principles that integrity goes along way, we take the time to listen to the needs of both the client and candidate to create the perfect match.

Key Contact - Specialty:
Ms. Janet Yudewitz, President

Salary Minimum: $25,000

Functions: Generalist (All), Management

Industries: Generalist (All)

Innovative Healthcare Services Inc

4119 Windermere Dr
Lithonia, GA 30038-4129
(678) 518-9206
Fax: (678) 518-9255
Email: adickey232@yahoo.com

Summary: We specialize in healthcare, medical care, insurance, medical equipment, pharmaceuticals, and technology.

Key Contact - Specialty:
Ms. Avis D. Dickey, President & Chief Executive Officer - *Healthcare*

Salary Minimum: $50,000

Functions: Generalist (All), Management, Healthcare, Sales & Mktg., Finance, IT, Specialized Svcs.

Industries: Generalist (All), Medical Devices, Pharm Svcs., Healthcare

Innovative Medical Recruiting LLC

221 Gum Bayou Ln
Slidell, LA 70461-1671
(985) 641-8817
Fax: (419) 791-8747
Email: dale@innomedical.com
Web: www.innomedical.com

Summary: Our firm specializes in the U.S. placement of healthcare professionals within the medical, pharmaceutical and bio-technology industries.

Key Contact - Specialty:
Mr. Dale Busbee, Owner - *Biopharmaceutical, Medical, Pharmaceutical*

Salary Minimum: $50,000

Functions: Generalist (All), Management, Senior Mgmt., Middle Mgmt., Healthcare, Sales & Mktg., Sales Mgmt.

Industries: Drugs Mfg., Medical Devices, Pharm Svcs., Biotech/Life Sciences, Healthcare

InSite Search

(a division of Chaves & Associates)
22 Crescent Rd
Westport, CT 06880-4542
(203) 222-2222
Fax: (203) 341-8844
Email: gen@insitesearch.com
Web: www.insitesearch.com

Summary: Computer software development and corporate MIS specialties including Internet, object oriented, database, technologies and consulting.

Key Contact - Specialty:
Mr. Victor Chaves, Chairman of the Board
Mr. Daniel Brown, Director
Mr. Timothy Zack, Director

Salary Minimum: $50,000

Functions: IT, MIS Mgmt., Systems Analysis, Systems Dev., Systems Implem., Systems Support, Network Admin., DB Admin.

Industries: Finance, Invest. Banking, Telecoms, Software, Biotech/Life Sciences

Branches:
31 Washington Ave
North Haven, CT 06473-2310
(203) 315-2966
Fax: (203) 234-9776
Email: jake@insitesearch.com
Key Contact - Specialty:
Mr. Jason Israel

50 Main St Ste 1017
White Plains, NY 10606-1900
(914) 682-6822
Fax: (914) 682-6888
Key Contact - Specialty:
Mr. Stephen Ozyck, Senior Parnter

The Insource Group

12221 Merit Dr Ste 1000
Dallas, TX 75251-2243
(972) 881-1313
Email: career@insourcegroup.com
Web: www.insourcegroup.com

Summary: We specialize in providing technology professionals for full time and consulting positions. Successful searches and capabilities range from individual contributor through VP/CTO/CIO searches.

Key Contact - Specialty:
Mr. Jim Thompason, President
Mr. Wayne Rampey, Vice President
Mr. Steven Raab, Vice President

Salary Minimum: $50,000

Functions: Generalist (All), Sales & Mktg., IT, MIS Mgmt., Systems Analysis, Systems Dev., Systems Implem., Systems Support

Industries: Software, Database SW, Development SW, ERP SW, Industry Specific SW

Insurance Career Center Inc

PO Box 370365
West Hartford, CT 06137-0365
(860) 523-5880
Fax: (860) 523-0149
Email: linda@insurancecareercenter.com

Summary: Recruit and place experienced insurance personnel mainly in property and casualty positions.

Key Contact - Specialty:
Ms. Linda Kiner, President

Salary Minimum: $25,000

Functions: Generalist (All)

Industries: Insurance

Insurance Personnel Resources Inc

8097 Roswell Rd Bldg B
Atlanta, GA 30350-6160
(770) 730-0701
Fax: (770) 730-0703

Email: blerch@mindspring.com
Web: www.insurancepersonnel.net

Summary: We offer recruitment and placement of only experienced insurance personnel at all levels and functions countrywide. Our specialties are in both personal and commercial lines of the property/casualty insurance business. Recruitment and placement in companies, agents, brokers, TPA's, and affiliated insurance firms.

Key Contact - Specialty:
Mr. Brent Lerch, President & Principal

Salary Minimum: $30,000

Functions: Generalist (All), Management, Senior Mgmt.

Industries: Insurance, Casualty, Claims, Commercial, Re-Insurance

Insurance Recruiting Specialists

2880 Russell Rd
Ostrander, OH 43061-9406
(740) 666-1212
Email: sbarker@insight.rr.com
Web: www.irsohio.com

Summary: We specialize in the recruitment of underwriting, marketing, claims and loss control personnel. We are a small, specialized firm, which tailors the search to meet the client's needs. We can only work with candidates that have insurance industry backgrounds.

Key Contact - Specialty:
Mr. Steve Barker, Owner

Salary Minimum: $35,000

Functions: Generalist (All)

Industries: Generalist (All), Insurance

Insurance Search

(also known as Rainbow Personnel)
PO Box 7354
Spring, TX 77387-7354
(281) 367-0137
(281) 367-3742
Fax: (281) 367-3842
Email: rainbowjobs@pdq.net
Web: www.rainbowjobs.com

Summary: We offer property and casualty insurance positions. Only represent applicants with experience from the insurance industry.

Key Contact - Specialty:
Mr. Bert Dionne, CPC, President
Ms. Wanda Hodges, CPC, Consultant

Salary Minimum: $30,000

Functions: Generalist (All), Management, Middle Mgmt., Admin. Svcs., Sales & Mktg., Customer Svc., Sales Reps., Finance, Risk Mgmt., Actuaries

Industries: Oil & Gas, Construction, Insurance, Casualty, Claims, Life, Commercial, Re-Insurance, Real Estate

Insurance Staffing Consultants

1288 Columbus Ave Ste 280
San Francisco, CA 94133-1302
(415) 351-1811
Fax: (415) 441-6110
Email: brucem@pacbell.net
Web: www.insurancestaffing.net

Summary: We are a specialized search firm specifically for the property and casualty insurance industry (underwriting, claims, loss control and brokerage).

Key Contact - Specialty:
Mr. Bruce Marx, Consultant, Recruiting

Salary Minimum: $70,000

Functions: Generalist (All), Management, Senior Mgmt., Middle Mgmt., Mktg. Research, Sales & Mktg., Risk Mgmt., Mgmt. Consultants

Industries: Generalist (All), Insurance, Casualty, Claims, Commercial, Re-Insurance

The Insurance Staffing Group

50 Salem St Bldg B
Lynnfield, MA 01940-2622
(781) 246-6786
Fax: (781) 246-6788
Email: jobs@insurancestaffing.com
Web: www.insurancestaffing.com

Summary: Our firm credits its success to the fact that every member of the placement staff has considerable experience in all areas of insurance and financial services.

Key Contact - Specialty:
Mr. Thomas F. Goode, President - *Financial services*

Salary Minimum: $30,000

Functions: Generalist (All)

Industries: Insurance, Healthcare

Integra IT Partners Inc

802-40 Eglinton Ave E
Toronto, ON M4P 3A2
Canada
(416) 487-3301
Fax: (416) 440-4025
Email: recruiting@integrait.com
Web: www.integrait.com

Summary: We are committed to establishing and maintaining staffing partnerships based on integrity and trust, specifically in the IT area. We strive to be a valued business partner by consistently presenting career opportunities to our candidates and providing staffing solutions to our clients.

Key Contact - Specialty:
Mr. Walter Jakowlew, President - *Information Technology*
Ms. Robyn Merizzi, Vice President - *Information Technology*

Functions: IT

Industries: Generalist (All)

Integra Personnel Inc

(an Alliance Partnership International company)
PO Box 55324
Shoreline, WA 98155-0324
(206) 365-7794
Fax: (206) 365-1375
Email: jobs@integrapersonnel.cc
Web: integrapersonnel.cc

Summary: Our firm places insurance and financial professionals from mid-level up to executive level (P&C, benefits and life/financial services). Client companies include agencies, brokers, wholesalers, carriers and some private industry (loss control, risk management, etc.).

Key Contact - Specialty:
Ms. Marlaine Kirsch Aly, Founder & Managing Principal

Salary Minimum: $50,000

Functions: Generalist (All)

Industries: Brokers, Misc. Financial, Accounting, Insurance, Casualty, Claims, Life, Commercial, Re-Insurance

Integrated Management Solutions

39 Broadway Rm 1601
New York, NY 10006-3082
(212) 509-7800
Fax: (212) 202-6061
Email: hr@intman.com

Summary: Our firm serves the needs of the financial services community with special emphasis on operations, accounting, regulatory, finance, sales, research and trading areas.

Key Contact - Specialty:
Mr. Howard Spindel, Senior Managing Director - *Financial services*
Mr. Michael E. Stupay, Senior Managing Director - *Financial services*

Salary Minimum: $36,000

Functions: Generalist (All), Management, Finance, IT, Mgmt. Consultants

Industries: Generalist (All), Banking, Invest. Banking, Brokers, Venture Cap., Misc. Financial, Accounting, Mgmt. Consulting

Integrated Staffing Solutions LLC

12750 Honeysuckle Cir
Eustace, TX 75124-6110
(214) 435-5181
Fax: (267) 224-5181
Email: integratedstaffllc@sbcglobal.net

Summary: Professional staffing solutions.

Key Contact - Specialty:
Ms. Amy Marable, Managing Partner

Functions: Management

Industries: Supply Chain Mgmt, Database SW, Development SW

Integrity Personnel Inc

914 164th St SE Ste B12
PMB 445
Mill Creek, WA 98012-6339
(425) 741-7334
Fax: (425) 741-3115
Email: info@integritypersonnelinc.com
Web: www.integritypersonnelinc.com

Summary: Dedicated to the needs of the healthcare, medical, and life science industries, we specialize in searches for professionals at the staff, supervisor, manager, director, and administrator levels. Our energies are directed toward locating and recruiting the finest talent for our client companies.

Key Contact - Specialty:
Ms. Terri Wilson, President

Functions: Healthcare

Industries: Generalist (All), Pharm Svcs., Mgmt. Consulting, Insurance, Healthcare, Hospitals, Long-term/Home Care, Physical Therapy, Occupational Therapy, Women's

Integrity Recruiting & Consulting

6414 Suttondale Rd
Huntley, IL 60142-9596
(847) 669-6723
(978) 387-5452
Fax: (847) 669-1062
Email: tom@sales-recruiting.net
Web: www.sales-recruiting.net

Summary: Management and field positions in sales, operations and customer service, focused in the business services industry.

Key Contact - Specialty:
Mr. Tom Siciliano, President - *Business development, Executives, General management, Sales*
Mr. Thom Kelly, Executive Vice President - *Business to business, Change management, General management, Sales, Transportation*

Salary Minimum: $60,000

Functions: Management, Senior Mgmt., Distribution, Sales & Mktg., Sales Mgmt., Sales Reps., Security Personnel, Textile/Fashion

Industries: Generalist (All), Textiles, Apparel, Wholesale, Equip Svcs., Mgmt. Consulting, Logistics Svcs., Hospitality, Inst./Industrial Food Svc., Entertainment, Haz. Waste, Commercial, Industry Specific SW, Non-Classifiable

Intelegra Inc

PO Box 505
Far Hills, NJ 07931-0505
(908) 876-5900
Fax: (908) 876-1788
Email: jpalmer111@intelegra.com
Web: www.intelegra.com

Summary: Our company provides technical help for the IT marketplace including technical sales people, system engineers, programmers, project managers and CIOs.

Key Contact - Specialty:
Mr. John A. Palmer, Recruiter

Salary Minimum: $50,000

Functions: IT, MIS Mgmt.

Industries: E-commerce, IT Implementation, PSA/ASP, Communications, Call Centers, Telephony, Digital, Wireless, Network Infrastructure, Software, Database SW, Development SW, Doc. Mgmt., Production SW, ERP SW, Marketing SW, Networking, Comm. SW, Security SW

Intelli-Source LLC

5850 San Felipe St Ste 500
Houston, TX 77057-8003
(713) 861-8656
(866) 861-8656
Fax: (713) 861-8660
Email: info@intelli-source.com
Web: www.intelli-source.com

Summary: Full service recruiting firm focusing on critical need and strategic positions in health care.

Key Contact - Specialty:
Mr. Richard Garza, President
Mr. Rick Whitley, Vice President
Ms. Nicole Badgett-Nau, Health Care Services Director
Mr. Douglas Hord, Director, Operations
Mr. Lance Arrendale, Manager, Marketing

Salary Minimum: $70,000

Functions: Generalist (All)

Industries: Energy, Utilities, Oil & Gas, Chemicals, Plastics, Rubber, Paints, Petro. Products, Pharm Svcs., HR Services, Aerospace, Hospitals, Physical Therapy

Branches:
5956 Sherry Ln Ste 1000
Dallas, TX 75225-8021
(214) 764-0854
(888) 300-4520
Email: info@intelli-source.com

Key Contact - Specialty:
Mr. Michael Bocox, Marketing Representative

IntelliSearch

2301 Ohio Dr Ste 260
Plano, TX 75093-3944
(972) 985-0300
Fax: (972) 985-3111
Email: brad@intellisearchjobs.com
Web: www.intellisearchjobs.com

Summary: We provide nationally recognized executive search and recruiting services to the mortgage banking and financial services industries. Our partnership with our clients, combined with our technical knowledge of the industries we serve, has allowed us to develop a national network of long term, high quality clients and candidates.

Key Contact - Specialty:
Mr. Bradford J. Hopson, President

Salary Minimum: $50,000

Functions: Generalist (All), Management

Industries: Finance, Banking, Misc. Financial

IntelliSource Inc

PO Box 8215
Radnor, PA 19087-8215
(610) 617-8873
Email: info@gotflex.com
Web: www.gotflex.com

Summary: With the knowledge of and being retained by growth-oriented companies. Ability to expertly advise candidates of strong career moves within IT. Our clients look for strong technical knowledge along with rapid career growth.

Key Contact - Specialty:
Ms. Carolyn Dougherty, CPC, President

Salary Minimum: $60,000

Functions: IT, MIS Mgmt.

Industries: Generalist (All), Food, Bev., Tobacco, Banking, Misc. Financial, Non-profits, Pharm Svcs., IT Implementation, Defense

Inteqna

1212-333 Seymour St
Price Waterhouse Building
Vancouver, BC V6B 5A6
Canada
(604) 683-6400
Fax: (604) 683-6440
Email: vancouver@inteqna.com
Web: www.inteqna.com

Summary: Our firm meets the highest standards in our industry and is a source of value and competitive advantage to our clients. We are leaders in the IT placement industry and maintain the highest regard for people, integrity and customer satisfaction.

Key Contact - Specialty:
Ms. Jennifer Rigal, Consultant - *Computers (Software), High technology*

Salary Minimum: $45,000

Functions: IT

Industries: Software

Inter-Regional Executive Search (IRES)

12 Southdown Dr
Lafayette, NJ 07848-3023
(973) 300-1010
Email: frankr@iresinc.com
Web: www.iresinc.com

Summary: We specialize in professional positions in all areas of insurance. Underwriters for property and casualty, surety, fidelity, and D&O. Also accounting, marketing and finance.

Key Contact - Specialty:
Mr. Frank G. Risalvato, President & Chief Executive Officer
Ms. Deb Lynn, Vice President, Sales Recruiting
Ms. Randi Moore, Regional Finance Recruiting Director - *Credit, Finance, Tax, Treasury*

Salary Minimum: $75,000

Functions: Management, Senior Mgmt., Middle Mgmt., Product Dev., Finance

Industries: Generalist (All), Consumer Elect., Misc. Mfg., Electronic, Elec. Components, Consumer Goods, Services, Accounting, Telecoms, Telephony, Digital, Fiber Optic, Network Infrastructure, Insurance, Casualty, Claims, Life, Commercial, Re-Insurance

Interactive Legal Search

51 Eagle Lake Ct Apt 23
San Ramon, CA 94582-4861
(925) 968-9083
(800) 211-1513
Fax: (925) 968-9084
Email: gcils@aol.com
Web: www.interactivelegalsearch.com

Summary: Recruit attorneys for multinational corporations and law firms. Specializing in the field of technology, we conduct searches in the areas of IP, new ventures, strategic alliances, JVs, marketing and distribution.

Key Contact - Specialty:
Ms. Gay Carter, President - *Intellectual property, Mergers & acquisitions*

Salary Minimum: $110,000

Functions: Legal, Attorneys, Paralegals

Industries: Generalist (All), Electronic, Elec. Components, Misc. Financial, Legal, E-commerce, Entertainment, Communications, Digital, Wireless, Network Infrastructure, Software, Database SW, Development SW, Networking, Comm. SW

Interactive Search Associates

2949 W Germantown Pike
Norristown, PA 19403-1035
(610) 630-3670
Fax: (610) 630-3678
Email: jzs@jobswitch.com
Web: www.zerkle.com

Summary: We are an executive search firm that has been in business many years with account executives specializing in sales, financial, administrative, technical, insurance, EDP, chemical, retail and healthcare areas.

Key Contact - Specialty:
Mr. John P. Zerkle, Sr., President - *General contractors, Loss Prevention, Management, Marketing, Pharmaceutical*

Salary Minimum: $50,000

Functions: Senior Mgmt., Sales & Mktg., R&D

Industries: Construction, Chemicals, Retail, Finance, Pharm Svcs., Logistics Svcs., Insurance, Real Estate, Healthcare

InterCom Management

310-56 The Esplanade
Greey Building
Toronto, ON M5E 1A7
Canada
(416) 364-5338
Fax: (416) 690-3365

Email: intercom@intercomjobs.ca
Web: www.intercomjobs.ca

Summary: Executive search firm specializing in marketing, advertising and direct marketing for full-time and contract needs.

Key Contact - Specialty:
Mr. Harry Teitelbaum, President - *Advertising, Marketing*

Salary Minimum: $40,000

Functions: Generalist (All), Sales & Mktg., Advertising, Mktg. Research, Mktg. Mgmt., Direct Mktg.

Industries: Generalist (All), Manufacturing, Food, Bev., Tobacco, Finance, Banking, Misc. Financial, Media, Advertising

International Consulting Services Inc

541 Castlewood Ln
Buffalo Grove, IL 60089-1617
(847) 537-1611
Fax: (847) 541-1899
Email: headhunter@interlync.com

Summary: We recruit design, research, development and science professionals. Electronics engineering, applied physics, scientific software, nanotechnology, quantum systems and systems engineering. Candidates range from contributor to VP. Industries served include instrumentation, control, medical, robotics, opto-electronics, semiconductor, laser, telecom, x-ray, defense, space and consumer.

Key Contact - Specialty:
Mr. Peter A. Sendler, President - *Management*

Salary Minimum: $75,000

Functions: Management, Product Dev., Automation, Healthcare, R&D, Engineering

Industries: Generalist (All), Medical Devices, Motor Vehicles, Computer Equip., Consumer Elect., Test, Measure Equip., Electronic, Elec. Components, Robotics, Semiconductors, Consumer Goods, Telecoms, Telephony, Digital, Wireless, RF/Microwave, Defense, Aerospace, Software, Industry Specific SW, Biotech/Life Sciences, Healthcare, Non-Classifiable

International Market Recruiters

55 W 39th St Fl 9
New York, NY 10018-3803
(212) 819-9100
Fax: (212) 354-9476
Email: recruiters@goimr.com
Web: www.goimr.com

Summary: We specialize in both permanent and temp placements in the financial service industries. We have earned a reputation for excellence in finding staff that resolve current situations, as well as becoming important decision makers for our clients.

Key Contact - Specialty:
Mr. Joseph M. Sullivan, President - *Financial services*

Functions: Generalist (All), Cash Mgmt., Risk Mgmt., Systems Support

Industries: Generalist (All), Banking, Invest. Banking, Brokers, Misc. Financial

Branches:
112 S Tryon St
Charlotte, NC 28284-2191
(704) 334-1044
Fax: (704) 334-1011
Email: charl@goimr.com

Key Contact - Specialty:
Mr. James Marchetti - *Financial services*

1800 John F Kennedy Blvd
Philadelphia, PA 19103-7421
(215) 981-0488
Fax: (215) 981-0988
Email: philly@goimr.com
Key Contact - Specialty:
Mr. Douglas Wong - *Financial services*

International Pro Sourcing Inc

407 Executive Dr
Langhorne, PA 19047-8003
(215) 968-7666
Fax: (215) 968-7667
Email: admin@prosourcing.com
Web: www.prosourcing.com

Summary: We are highly ethical contingency recruiters specializing in the placement of thoroughly screened and qualified candidates in high technology, pharmaceutical and medical sales positions for top notch US companies.

Key Contact - Specialty:
Ms. Joan Gallagher, Owner & Vice President - *Sales*
Ms. Kelly Gallagher, Owner & President - *Sales*

Functions: Sales & Mktg., Mktg. Research, Mktg. Mgmt., Sales Mgmt., Systems Dev., Systems Implem., Network Admin.

Industries: Generalist (All), Drugs Mfg., Medical Devices, Telecoms, Healthcare

International Search Consultants

7650 S McClintock Dr Ste 103
Tempe, AZ 85284-1673
(888) 866-7276
Fax: (888) 866-6625
Email: annr@iscjobs.com
Web: www.iscjobs.com

Summary: We are an elite group of seasoned professionals who specialize in high caliber sales and sales management people. We have long standing relationships with a number of clients.

Key Contact - Specialty:
Ms. Ann E. Zaslow-Rethaber, President & Chief Executive Officer

Salary Minimum: $50,000

Functions: Sales & Mktg., Sales Mgmt.

Industries: Printing, Machine, Appliance, Pharm Svcs., Equip Svcs., HR Services, Hospitality

International Search Consultants

30827 Mainmast Dr
Agoura Hills, CA 91301-1937
(818) 706-2635
Fax: (818) 706-1358
Email: george@isccnc.com
Web: www.isccnc.com

Summary: Specializing in the placement of sales, service and applications people in the CNC machine tool industry.

Key Contact - Specialty:
Mr. George Schortz

Salary Minimum: $40,000

Functions: Management, Senior Mgmt., Middle Mgmt., Automation, Sales & Mktg., Sales Mgmt.

Industries: Manufacturing, Metal Products, Machine, Appliance, Test, Measure Equip., Misc. Mfg.

International Staffing Consultants Inc

17310 Red Hill Ave Ste 140
Irvine, CA 92614-5635
(949) 255-5857
Fax: (949) 767-5959
Email: iscinc@iscworld.com
Web: www.iscworld.com

Summary: Global staffing of technical and professional levels for small private firms to large foreign and domestic governments and many of the world's largest private employers. Specialties include engineering, manufacturing, defense, aircraft, computers, electronics, architecture, construction, power, oil & gas, refinery, chemical, O&M, petrochemical, mining, airports, highways, water treatment facilities, etc.

Key Contact - Specialty:
Mr. James R. Gettys, President - *Business development, Engineering*

Salary Minimum: $50,000

Functions: Senior Mgmt., HR Mgmt., Benefits, Staffing, Training, Finance, Int'l.

Industries: Generalist (All), Energy, Utilities, Oil & Gas, Construction, Finance, Banking, Misc. Financial, Architectural Svcs., Accounting, HR Services, Engineering Svcs.

International Technical Resources

314 Ridge Rd
Jupiter, FL 33477-9655
(800) 975-1110
(561) 449-6779
Email: terryff@earthlink.net
Web: www.itrservices.com

Summary: Two division firm, one dedicated to mid-upper-level, outsourcing, HRO, consulting and software development professionals, one division dedicated to sales, marketing and implementation professionals. We pride ourselves on being extremely confidential and thorough.

Key Contact - Specialty:
Mr. Terry L. Funk, President

Salary Minimum: $75,000

Functions: Board Members, Mktg. Research, Mktg. Mgmt., Sales Mgmt., Systems Analysis, Systems Dev., Systems Implem.

Industries: Generalist (All)

Intrepid Executive Search

21 La Purisima
Rancho Santa Margarita, CA 92688-3108
(949) 713-4600
Fax: (949) 713-4601
Email: ecrane@intrepidsearch.com
Web: www.intrepidsearch.com

Summary: Search firm specializing in delivering top talent in the technology field. We place high profile sales, marketing, product development, R&D, product marketing/management candidates at individual contributor, manager, director, VP and EVP level. Examples of tech industries covered: computer software/services: data integration, data management, business intelligence, security, high-trust integration, etc.

Key Contact - Specialty:
Mrs. Elaine Crane, Managing Partner - *Research*

Salary Minimum: $100,000

Functions: Senior Mgmt., Middle Mgmt., Product Dev., Sales & Mktg.

Industries: Mgmt. Consulting, E-commerce, IT Implementation, Communications, Telephony, Digital, Wireless, Network Infrastructure, Software, Accounting SW, Database SW, Development SW, Doc. Mgmt., Production SW, Marketing SW, Networking, Comm. SW, Security SW, System SW, Biotech/Life Sciences

IPOND LLC

66 Bovet Rd Ste 353
San Mateo, CA 94402-3147
(650) 513-8902
Fax: (650) 578-1715
Email: info@ipond.com
Web: www.ipond.com

Summary: Delivers real time talent for contract, contract to hire and perm placements and offshore call center consultancy.

Key Contact - Specialty:
Mr. Ravi Sharma, President

Salary Minimum: $50,000

Functions: Generalist (All), IT, MIS Mgmt., Systems Analysis, Systems Dev., Systems Implem., Systems Support, Network Admin., DB Admin.

Industries: Generalist (All), Software, Database SW, Development SW, Doc. Mgmt., Production SW, ERP SW, HR SW, Industry Specific SW, Mfg. SW, Security SW, System SW

IRC Partners

7 Woodland Ave
Larchmont, NY 10538-3134
(914) 833-8890
Email: ircpartners@yahoo.com

Summary: A boutique firm specializing in searches within the finance, marketing and legal disciplines.

Key Contact - Specialty:
Mr. Irv Cohen, Managing Partner - *Finance, Marketing*

Salary Minimum: $75,000

Functions: Management, Advertising, Mktg. Research, Mktg. Mgmt., Direct Mktg., HR Mgmt., Finance, Specialized Svcs., Minorities/Diversity

Industries: Manufacturing, Food, Bev., Tobacco, Finance, Legal, HR Services, Media, Advertising

Irvine Search Partners

2349 Camino Rey
Fullerton, CA 92833-1308
(714) 870-1344
Email: gilriley@earthlink.net

Summary: We place IT professionals in a full range of positions, including: sales, marketing, technical and consulting. Our clients include some of the major consulting and software organizations in the country.

Key Contact - Specialty:
Mr. Gil Riley, Partner - *Computers, Computers (Software), Consulting, Networking*

Salary Minimum: $80,000

Functions: Generalist (All), Middle Mgmt.

Industries: Services, Mgmt. Consulting, E-commerce, IT Implementation, Communications, Network Infrastructure, Software, Accounting SW, Database SW, Development SW, Doc. Mgmt., Production SW, Industry Specific SW, Mfg. SW, Networking, Comm. SW

Joan Isbister Consultants

350 W 20th St
New York, NY 10011-3348
(212) 243-8733
Fax: (212) 255-3395
Email: jisbister@nyc.rr.com

Summary: Graphics and printing industries specialists; professional searches in management, marketing, and sales.

Key Contact - Specialty:
Ms. Joan Isbister, President

Salary Minimum: $50,000

Functions: Management, Sales Mgmt., Sales Reps.

Industries: Paper, Printing

ISC Executive Search Inc

124 College St
Asheville, NC 28801-3037
(828) 253-2828
Fax: (866) 468-4869
Email: thurman@iscexecutivesearch.com
Web: www.iscexecutivesearch.com

Summary: Specialists in infrastructure development, including commercial construction, architecture, and engineering.

Key Contact - Specialty:
Mr. Thurman Williams, President

Salary Minimum: $60,000

Functions: Management

Industries: Construction, Architectural Svcs., Engineering Svcs.

Branches:
PO Box 9587
Truckee, CA 96162-7587
(530) 550-7417
Email: bill@hunt1.com
Key Contact - Specialty:
Mr. Bill Voegele, Managing Director, Western Region

ISC of Atlanta

(a division of International Career Continuation Inc)
4350 Georgetown Sq Ste 707
Atlanta, GA 30338-6234
(770) 458-4180
(800) 290-0177
Fax: (770) 458-4131
Email: iscatl@iscatl.com
Web: www.iscatl.com

Summary: Successfully meeting the challenges of our changing industry while striving to do business in a friendly and fair way, we push towards gaining the respect and confidence of our clients, candidates and colleagues.

Key Contact - Specialty:
Mr. Arthur Kwapisz, President - *Operations, Sales, Technology*
Mr. William A. Konrad, Vice President - *Accounting*
Ms. Kathy Russell, Search Consultant - *Accounting*
Mr. Joseph Kessler, Search Consultant - *Accounting, Operations, Technology*
Ms. Donna Mulder, Researcher - *Sales*
Mr. Jonathan Kay, Search Consultant - *Audits, Finance, Regulatory*

Salary Minimum: $40,000

Functions: Generalist (All), Senior Mgmt., Middle Mgmt., Plant Mgmt., Productivity, Sales Mgmt., Finance, R&D, Engineering

Industries: Generalist (All), Energy, Utilities, Food, Bev., Tobacco, Chemicals, Drugs Mfg., Medical Devices, Plastics, Rubber, Misc. Mfg., Retail, Finance, Pharm Svcs., Accounting, Mgmt. Consulting, HR Services, Compliance

ISC of Houston

440 Benmar Dr Ste 2120
Houston, TX 77060-3169
(281) 847-0050
Fax: (281) 847-1357
Email: kburke@ischouston.com
Web: www.ischouston.com

Summary: We understand and speak the language of the healthcare and home building industry. Through our network and superior reputation, we can complete assignments in a timely and cost effective manner.

Key Contact - Specialty:
Ms. Karen Burke, President - *Healthcare*
Mr. Bob Bennett, Vice President

Salary Minimum: $40,000

Functions: Generalist (All), Management, Senior Mgmt., Middle Mgmt., Admin. Svcs., Purchasing, Mktg. Mgmt., Sales Mgmt., Finance, CFOs

Industries: Generalist (All), Construction, Manufacturing, Misc. Financial, Non-profits, Accounting, Mgmt. Consulting, Real Estate, Healthcare, Hospitals, Long-term/Home Care

ISOTEC Management Inc

101-200 Adelaide St W
Toronto, ON M5H 1W7
Canada
(416) 868-0100
Fax: (416) 868-6292
Email: info@isotecmgt.com
Web: www.isotecmgt.com

Summary: Our firm provides professional, results-oriented staffing solutions to clients with IT recruitment needs. We are committed to providing total customer service to our client companies. We work closely with a select number of growth-oriented companies enabling us to concentrate our resources on specific hiring projects. This approach allows us to identify and represent candidates that excel in their field.

Key Contact - Specialty:
Mr. Michael Riall, President

Salary Minimum: $40,000

Functions: Risk Mgmt., IT, MIS Mgmt., Systems Analysis, Systems Dev., Systems Implem., Systems Support, Network Admin., DB Admin., Mgmt. Consultants

Industries: Generalist (All)

Ann Israel & Associates Inc

730 5th Ave Ste 900
New York, NY 10019-4105
(212) 659-7730
Email: aisrael@annisrael.com
Web: www.attorneysearch.com

Summary: Serving the legal community with broad range of services to law firms and corporations including lateral placements of partners/associates, mergers/acquisitions of practice groups and management advisory services.

Key Contact - Specialty:
Ms. Ann M. Israel, President - *Legal (Attorneys,Lawyers)*
Ms. Colleen M. Williams, Esq. - *Legal (Attorneys,Lawyers)*

Salary Minimum: $100,000

Functions: Attorneys

Industries: Legal

IT Intellect Inc

1026 Towne Lake Hls E
Woodstock, GA 30189-2510
(770) 926-7869
Fax: (208) 988-7869
Email: christine@itintellect.net
Web: www.itintellect.net

Summary: Recruiting company involved in the placement of IT professionals from programmers to CIOs, both permanent and contract. Main focus is on ERP systems and mid to senior/executive management roles.

Key Contact - Specialty:
Mrs. Christine Bell, President

Salary Minimum: $80,000

Functions: Board Members, IT

Industries: Generalist (All)

IT Jazz

8101 E Prentice Ave Ste 910
Greenwood Village, CO 80111-2937
(303) 683-8696
Email: info@itjazz.com
Web: www.itjazz.com

Summary: Our firm is a team of search professionals dedicated to serving companies seeking technology executives and practitioners across all industries. We have been delivering inspired talent as a technology and executive search firm offering retained, contingency and outsourced recruitment services. We've earned our reputation by bringing together top technology, sales, and management talent with top companies; enabling them both to succeed.

Key Contact - Specialty:
Ms. Debra Gerring, Managing Partner - *Business to business, CIOs, Client/server, Computers (Networking,Programming)*

Salary Minimum: $90,000

Functions: Senior Mgmt., IT

Industries: Communications, Software

IT Management Partners Inc

4790 Irvine Blvd Ste 105
Irvine, CA 92620-1998
(714) 679-9548
Email: hr@itmpinc.com
Web: www.itmpinc.com

Summary: Our firm specializes in helping senior management executives reduce business' operating costs by tying technology usage to strategic and tactical business objectives. As a complement to an existing HR department, we work diligently to identify and place highly qualified candidates on short and long term assignments.

Key Contact - Specialty:
Mr. Bruce Mccullough, President & Chief Executive Officer

Salary Minimum: $100,000

Functions: MIS Mgmt.

Industries: Generalist (All), Manufacturing, Retail, Finance, Services, Accounting SW, Healthcare

IT Resources

PO Box 305
Lexington, MA 02420-0003
(781) 863-2661

Email: staffing@it-resources.com
Web: www.it-resources.com

Summary: Specializes in managers and implementers of leading edge IT, MIS and software in business environment - client server architecture, LAN/WAN, web-based applications and eCommerce.

Key Contact - Specialty:
Mr. Ken Loomis, Owner - *MIS*

Salary Minimum: $40,000

Functions: MIS Mgmt., Systems Analysis, Systems Dev., Systems Implem., Systems Support, Network Admin., DB Admin.

Industries: Generalist (All)

IT Resources Ltd

10-25 Valleywood Dr
Markham, ON L3R 5L9
Canada
(905) 415-1800
(877) 415-1800
Fax: (905) 415-8111
Email: resumes@itrgroup.com
Web: www.itrgroup.com

Summary: Our firm specializes in supplying quality contract and permanent IT staff to leading corporations. Our clientele range from growing entrepreneurial firms to major Fortune 500 companies such as banking & financial services, software, consulting companies and many more. We have an excellent reputation for building long lasting and rewarding relationships with clients and IT professionals alike.

Key Contact - Specialty:
Ms. Victoria Greco, President
Mr. John Danells, Vice President, Finance
Ms. Janet Simpson, Operations Manager

Functions: IT

Industries: Generalist (All)

IT Services

PO Box 327
Weatogue, CT 06089-0327
(860) 658-7900
Email: info@itservicesusa.com
Web: www.itservicesusa.com

Summary: Our firm is an executive IT search firm that specializes in permanent placement of software and hardware engineers, architects, sales and management of IT departments.

Key Contact - Specialty:
Mr. Larry Rubin, CPC, Executive Recruiter - *Telecommunications*
Mrs. Kristina DiMartino, Executive Recruiter - *Computers (Software), Information Technology*
Mr. Dan Ludwig, Executive Recruiter - *CRM, ERP*

Salary Minimum: $50,000

Functions: Senior Mgmt., Middle Mgmt., IT, Systems Dev., Systems Implem.

Industries: Generalist (All), Finance, E-commerce, IT Implementation, Telecoms, Fiber Optic, Network Infrastructure, Insurance, Database SW, Development SW, ERP SW, HR SW

itbRecruiting

1744 Oak Ave
Northbrook, IL 60062-5461
(847) 919-6204
Fax: (847) 572-0881
Email: info@itbrecruiting.com
Web: www.itbrecruiting.com

Summary: ITB Recruiting specializes in the recruitment of Sales and Sales Management professionals, with a concentration in advertising, software and web based technology sectors. This includes, but is not limited to: web based solution providers; pre-employment technology and screening companies; consulting and payroll and tax firms; human capital process management firms; outplacement companies; and software firms. Due to our national network of sales executives and recruiters from coast to coast, we can tap resources of top performing sales professionals across the nation.

Key Contact - Specialty:
Mr. Andy Roane, Principal - *.com, Advertising, Business development, Internet, Sales*
Mr. Jim Miller, Managing Partner - *.com, Advertising, Business development, E-business, Sales*
Mr. Samuel Montgomery, Director, Recruiting - *.com, Advertising, Internet, Sales, Technology*

Salary Minimum: $60,000

Functions: Sales & Mktg.

Industries: HR Services, Media, Advertising, New Media, Broadcast, Film, Software, ERP SW, HR SW, Networking, Comm. SW, Security SW

ITech Consulting Partners LLC

30 Church Hill Rd Ste 7
Newtown, CT 06470-1658
(203) 270-0051
Fax: (203) 270-0071
Email: john@itechcp.com
Web: www.itechcp.com

Summary: Specializing in the placement of IT professionals including IT management, project managers, application developers, systems analysts, DBA's, system programmers, and web designers. We also provide IT professionals on a contract basis to support in e-business solutions, mainframe application development, database & systems administration, data warehouse design, development and reporting.

Key Contact - Specialty:
Mr. John Barry, President

Salary Minimum: $50,000

Functions: Senior Mgmt., Healthcare, IT, MIS Mgmt., Systems Analysis, Systems Dev., Systems Implem., Network Admin., DB Admin.

Industries: Generalist (All), Drugs Mfg., Insurance

ITS Technologies Inc

6629 W Central Ave
Toledo, OH 43617-1098
(419) 842-2100
(800) 432-6607
Fax: (419) 841-7852
Email: cfelgner@wehireengineers.com
Web: www.wehireengineers.com

Summary: Technical staffing firm that specializes in all areas of engineering.

Key Contact - Specialty:
Mr. Chad Felgner, CPC, Senior Technical Recruiter
Mr. David Gignac, Recruiter

Salary Minimum: $40,000

Functions: Engineering

Industries: Generalist (All), Food, Bev., Tobacco, Textiles, Apparel, Lumber, Furniture, Soap, Perf., Cosmtcs., Drugs Mfg., Medical Devices, Plastics, Rubber, Computer Equip., Electronic, Elec. Components

Ives & Associates Inc

2931 E Dublin Granville Rd Ste 140
Columbus, OH 43231-2002
(614) 839-0202
Fax: (614) 839-0203
Email: phyllis@ivesearch.com
Web: www.executivesearchusa.com

Summary: We endeavor to form a partnership with our clients. By working together we can find that individual who will fit within our clients particular corporate culture.

Key Contact - Specialty:
Ms. Phyllis E. Ives, Chief Executive Officer - *Human resources, Marketing*
Mr. Jay Canowitz, President

Salary Minimum: $75,000

Functions: Generalist (All), Purchasing, Mktg. Research, HR Mgmt., Finance

Industries: Manufacturing, Food, Bev., Tobacco, Textiles, Apparel, Paper, Soap, Perf., Cosmtcs., Drugs Mfg., Medical Devices, Consumer Elect., Retail, Finance, Banking, Mgmt. Consulting, HR Services, Media, Advertising, New Media, Telephony, Wireless, Healthcare

J & C Nationwide Inc

3000 Old Alabama Rd Ste 119
PMB 608
Alpharetta, GA 30022-8555
(800) 272-2707
Fax: (800) 936-4562
Email: connect@jcnationwide.com
Web: www.jcnationwide.com

Summary: Placing physicians, allied health professionals in hospitals, group practices, HMOs and other healthcare settings in both permanent and locum tenens positions.

Key Contact - Specialty:
Mr. William Goldstein, Chief Executive Officer
Ms. Sandra Garrett, President
Mr. Karl Sander, Sr., Senior Vice President, Operations
Mr. Edward McEachern, Vice President, Marketing - *CEOs, Communications, Executives, Telecommunications, Wireless*

Functions: Healthcare, Physicians, Allied Health

Industries: Healthcare

Branches:
2880 Slater Rd Ste 110
Morrisville, NC 27560-6400
(919) 572-9266
(800) 841-2291
Fax: (919) 493-7763
Email: connect@jcnationwide.com
Key Contact - Specialty:
Ms. Beth Starkey, Vice President

406 W South Jordan Pkwy Ste 600
South Jordan, UT 84095-3943
(801) 293-8575
(800) 809-9990
Fax: (801) 293-8647
Email: connect@jcnationwide.com
Key Contact - Specialty:
Mr. Randy Weikle, Vice President - *Networking*

J & D Resources Inc

6410 Poplar Ave Ste 151
Memphis, TN 38119-4860
(901) 753-0500
Fax: (901) 753-0550
Email: jdrmail@jdresources.com
Web: www.jdresources.com

Summary: We present only the most qualified applicants for your review. We ensure that these

individuals are interested in the opportunity you have to offer. Our overall commitment is to you - to find the people that will contribute to your success.

Key Contact - Specialty:
Ms. Jill T. Herrin, CPC, President
Mr. Danny L. McKinney, CPC, Vice President

Salary Minimum: $25,000

Functions: IT

Industries: Generalist (All), Paper, Wholesale, Banking, Hotels, Resorts, Clubs

Ron Jackson & Associates

210 Morning Springs Walk
Fairburn, GA 30213-3495
(770) 719-2228
Email: rjacksonandassoc@prodigy.net

Summary: Our combined experience, which includes search and staffing at all levels, gives us the ability to provide superior service to our clients. In addition to our expert handling of a variety of assignments, we are able to provide access to top quality contract technical recruiters. We also offer access to a broad range of diversity candidates.

Key Contact - Specialty:
Mr. Ron Jackson, President

Salary Minimum: $50,000

Functions: Generalist (All), Management, Board Members, Middle Mgmt., Admin. Svcs.

Industries: Generalist (All), Manufacturing, Food, Bev., Tobacco, Textiles, Apparel, Printing, Soap, Perf., Cosmtcs., Drugs Mfg., Medical Devices, Consumer Goods, Transportation, Retail, Non-profits, Accounting, Mgmt. Consulting, HR Services, Logistics Svcs., Supply Chain Mgmt, Quick Service Restaurants, Telecoms, Government, Accounting SW, Healthcare, Hospitals

Jackson Roth Associates

54813 US Highway 275
Norfolk, NE 68701-1407
(800) 772-8033
Fax: (402) 379-7756
Email: jacksonroth@stantonwb.net

Summary: Full service radiology, nursing, allied health, healthcare administration and IT contingency search and contracting in all sub-specialties. Many years of professional recruiting/placement experience.

Key Contact - Specialty:
Ms. Nancy Ulbert, CPC, Senior Search Manager & Owner

Functions: Healthcare, Nurses, Allied Health, IT, Systems Analysis, Systems Dev., Systems Implem., Systems Support, Network Admin., DB Admin.

Industries: Generalist (All), Hospitals

The Jacobson Group

120 S La Salle St Ste 1410
Chicago, IL 60603-3579
(312) 726-1578
(800) 466-1578
Fax: (312) 726-2295
Email: info@jacobsonline.com
Web: www.jacobsononline.com

Summary: We specialize in professional and human capital services for the insurance, healthcare and financial service sectors. We provide the industry talent-driven solutions with bottom-line results. Our extensive portfolio of services includes executive search, professional

recruiting, interim staffing, specialized project support, consulting and operations outsourcing.

Key Contact - Specialty:
Mr. Gregory P. Jacobson, Co-Chief Executive Officer - *Boards of Directors, C-level, Executives, Financial services, Healthcare*
Mr. Rick Jacobson, Co-Chief Executive Officer - *Financial services, Healthcare, Insurance, Managed care*
Mr. Michael Loiacano, Senior Vice President - *Actuarial, Consulting, Executives, Financial services, Healthcare*
Mr. Jack J. Johnsey, Senior Vice President - *Financial services, Healthcare, Insurance, Interim, Managed care*

Salary Minimum: $30,000

Functions: Generalist (All), Board Members, Senior Mgmt., Middle Mgmt., Sales & Mktg., HR Mgmt., Finance, Risk Mgmt., Actuaries, MIS Mgmt.

Industries: Finance, Insurance, Healthcare

Branches:
1600 Parkwood Cir SE Ste 350
Atlanta, GA 30339-2147
(770) 952-3877
Fax: (770) 952-0061
Email: atlanta@jacobsononline.com
Key Contact - Specialty:
Mr. Marty Murphy, Senior Vice President - *Actuarial, Financial services, Healthcare, Insurance, Managed care*

233 Needham St Ste 300
Newton, MA 02464-1502
(866) 462-6712
Email: boston@jacobsononline.com
Key Contact - Specialty:
Ms. Susan Henry, Senior Vice President - *Financial services, Healthcare, Insurance, Interim, Managed care*

111 Westport Plz Ste 600
Saint Louis, MO 63146-3015
(800) 293-7139
Email: stlouis@jacobsononline.com
Key Contact - Specialty:
Mr. Ryan Schmidt, National Accounts Sales Manager - *Financial services, Healthcare, Insurance, Interim, Managed care*

1901 Rickety Ln Ste 115
Tyler, TX 75703-1700
(903) 581-9477
Fax: (903) 581-9479
Email: dallas@jacobsononline.com
Key Contact - Specialty:
Mr. Todd Gable, Consultant - *Financial services, Healthcare, Insurance, Managed care*

K Jaeger & Associates

60 Thoreau St Ste 300
Concord, MA 01742-2456
(978) 369-3352
Fax: (978) 369-0757
Email: kjaeger2@earthlink.net

Summary: We offer retained and contingency search with a difference. Our thorough, consultative approach ensures efficient solutions to: sales, marketing, engineering, line and staff searches. Our clients are suppliers of mechanical & electro-mechanical products, controls and capital equipment sold to industrial markets.

Key Contact - Specialty:
Mr. Karl Schoellkopf, Managing Director - *Industrial*

Mr. Peter Herrup, Associate - *Administration, Advertising, Banking (Investment), Boards of Directors, Brokerage*
Mr. Robert Bachman, Associate - *Machining, Petrochemical, Power, Sales, Supply Chain*

Salary Minimum: $50,000

Functions: Generalist (All)

Industries: Energy, Utilities, Construction, Manufacturing, Services, Non-profits, Higher Ed., Media, Real Estate

James & Richards

1017 W Park Dr
Midland, MI 48640-4276
(989) 839-4949
Fax: (989) 839-4023
Email: jwd49@aol.com
Web: www.jamesandrichards.com

Summary: Experienced chemists and engineers at all levels for chemical and allied industries. Pharmaceutical, specialty chemistry, plastics, etc.

Key Contact - Specialty:
Mr. John W. Dreyer, Recruiter
Mr. Richard C. Lamos, Recruiter

Salary Minimum: $50,000

Functions: Middle Mgmt., Mfg., Product Dev., Production, Plant Mgmt., Quality, Materials, R&D, Engineering

Industries: Chemicals, Soap, Perf., Cosmtcs., Drugs Mfg., Plastics, Rubber, Paints, Petro. Products

Lawrence James Associates of Florida

8795 W McNab Rd Ste 202
Tamarac, FL 33321-3255
(954) 721-6100
Fax: (954) 726-3555
Email: lawrencejames@mindspring.com
Web: www.lawrence-james.com

Summary: An executive search firm specializing in the supermarket and retail industry for many years with relationships in the industry enabling us to identify quickly client and candidates that excel.

Key Contact - Specialty:
Mr. Leonard Okyn, President

Functions: Management, Senior Mgmt., Admin. Svcs., Distribution, Sales & Mktg., HR Mgmt., Finance, CFOs, Minorities/Diversity

Industries: Wholesale, Retail

Victoria James Executive Search Inc

17 North Ave
Norwalk, CT 06851-3800
(203) 750-8838
Fax: (203) 750-8831
Email: vjames@victoriajames.com
Web: www.victoriajames.com

Summary: Provide mid to senior-level executive search services to the direct marketing and Internet communities. We are committed to ensuring exceptional search solutions for candidates and client companies.

Key Contact - Specialty:
Ms. Victoria James, President - *Direct marketing, Internet*

Salary Minimum: $70,000

Functions: Generalist (All)

Industries: Non-profits, Mgmt. Consulting, E-commerce, Advertising, Publishing, New

Media, Call Centers, Marketing SW, Non-Classifiable

The Jameson Group

287 S Robertson Blvd Ste 474
Beverly Hills, CA 90211-2810
(310) 289-5085
Fax: (310) 289-5086
Email: jbj@thejamesongroup.com
Web: www.thejamesongroup.com

Summary: We specialize in partner and group placements and law firm mergers.

Key Contact - Specialty:
Mr. John B. Jameson, Partner

Salary Minimum: $100,000

Functions: Attorneys

Industries: Legal

Janus Career Service

(also known as Janus Recruiting)
157 E New England Ave Ste 240
Winter Park, FL 32789-7006
(407) 628-1090
(407) 628-5249
Fax: (407) 628-5115
Email: jan@janusrecruiting.com
Web: www.janusrecruiting.com

Summary: We are an executive search firm with specializations in account execs, restaurant/hospitality, loan officers, mortgage branch managers, entry-level managers, sales and sales managers. We want to be your resource for quality candidates.

Key Contact - Specialty:
Ms. Jan Leach, CG, President - *Sales*
Mr. Victor Soto, Office Manager & Program - *Computers (Science)*

Functions: Generalist (All), Senior Mgmt.

Industries: Generalist (All), Manufacturing, Machine, Appliance, Wholesale, Retail, Finance, Banking, Invest. Banking, Brokers, Misc. Financial, Engineering Svcs., Hospitality, Restaurants, Call Centers, Insurance, Life

Jaques and Associates LLC

22030 Robinsway
Mattawan, MI 49071-9730
(269) 668-4979
(269) 598-6364
Fax: (269) 668-3649
Email: bill@jaquesandassociates.com
Web: www.jaquesandassociates.com

Summary: We specialize in the permanent, full-time placement of professionals in the financial services, HR and IT fields.

Key Contact - Specialty:
Mr. William Jaques, President

Salary Minimum: $40,000

Functions: Generalist (All), Management, Middle Mgmt.

Industries: Generalist (All), Finance, Banking, Invest. Banking, Brokers, Misc. Financial, Accounting, HR Services, IT Implementation

Jaral Consultants Inc

PO Box 498
Springfield, NJ 07081-0498
(973) 564-9236
Fax: (973) 379-1275

Summary: We specialize in placing in the following areas; fashion including designers, production, sales and all other technical and professional specialties specific to the fashion

industry. Presidents and other top executives are our primary placements.

Key Contact - Specialty:
Mr. Joseph Morgan, Recruiter

Salary Minimum: $50,000

Functions: Generalist (All), Product Dev., Production, Sales Mgmt., HR Mgmt., CFOs, IT, MIS Mgmt., Engineering, Int'l.

Industries: Manufacturing, Textiles, Apparel, Drugs Mfg., Electronic, Elec. Components, Wholesale, Retail, Pharm Svcs., Mgmt. Consulting, Hospitality, New Media, Telecoms, Software, Biotech/Life Sciences, Healthcare

Jatinen & Associates

2124 Main St Ste 170
Huntington Beach, CA 92648-6450
(714) 960-9082
Fax: (714) 960-1772
Email: djatinen@verizon.net

Summary: We recruit solely for the title insurance and escrow industry. Work all levels of management and senior technical positions.

Key Contact - Specialty:
Mr. Dave Jatinen, Owner

Salary Minimum: $40,000

Functions: Generalist (All)

Industries: Insurance, Real Estate

John Jay & Co

500 Route 1 Ste 4
Yarmouth, ME 04096-4712
(207) 846-7611
Fax: (207) 846-9211
Email: jhotchkss@aol.com

Summary: Small, boutique firm with a very personalized approach. Offers particular expertise in HR search and can provide HR consulting services as well.

Key Contact - Specialty:
Mr. Jay Hotchkiss, CMC, SPHR, President

Salary Minimum: $45,000

Functions: Generalist (All), Senior Mgmt., Plant Mgmt., HR Mgmt., Finance, R&D, Mgmt. Consultants

Industries: Generalist (All), Misc. Mfg., Finance, HR Services, Hospitality, Biotech/Life Sciences, Healthcare

JBN & Associates LLC

5010 E Shea Blvd Ste B222
Scottsdale, AZ 85254-4574
(480) 344-2822
Fax: (480) 344-2830
Email: kathy@jbnassociates.com
Web: www.jbnassociates.com

Summary: Executive search in land development; homebuilding and commercial construction. Placing executive management including accounting and finance.

Key Contact - Specialty:
Ms. Kathy Garcia-Colace, Founder & Managing Partner
Ms. Melissa Groen, Executive Recruiter - *Construction*
Mr. Matt Lissy, Executive Recruiter - *CEOs, Construction, COOs, Executives*
Mr. Michael Marchese, Executive Recruiter

Salary Minimum: $60,000

Functions: Generalist (All)

Industries: Construction, Property/Facility Mgmt.

JCL & Associates

PO Box 9541
Panama City Beach, FL 32417-9541
(850) 230-1888

Summary: Many years experience in private placement. Highly specialized in men's, women's, children's knitwear and intimate apparel from sales/marketing, manufacturing/sourcing, financial and product development/design.

Key Contact - Specialty:
Ms. Judy Lee, CPC, President

Salary Minimum: $30,000

Functions: Generalist (All), Senior Mgmt., Product Dev., Plant Mgmt., Distribution, Mktg. Research, Sales Mgmt., CFOs, MIS Mgmt.

Industries: Generalist (All), Textiles, Apparel

JDC Associates

300 Wheeler Rd Ste 104
Hauppauge, NY 11788-4300
(631) 231-8581
Fax: (631) 231-8011
Email: jdcassoc@optonline.net

Summary: Professional recruiting firm committed to identifying and isolating only the top 10 percent proven documented performers in the Pharmaceutical & Medical Sales industry. Their success is due to their creativity, versatility and commitment to excellence in the marketplace.

Key Contact - Specialty:
Ms. Lori Boyle, President - *Sales*

Functions: Generalist (All), Sales & Mktg., Sales Mgmt., Sales Reps.

Industries: Generalist (All), Drugs Mfg., Medical Devices, Accounting, Healthcare

Jefferson Ross Assocs Inc

1500 John F Kennedy Blvd Ste 312
Philadelphia, PA 19102-1872
(215) 564-5322
Fax: (215) 587-0766
Email: jeffross@cwl-inc.com

Summary: Executive search assignments for professional/technical and mid-management individuals in financial, insurance, healthcare, IS and computer services industries. Extensive years of experience in professional recruitment and search.

Key Contact - Specialty:
Mr. Craig Z. Cole, President

Salary Minimum: $50,000

Functions: Generalist (All), Management, Sales & Mktg., Sales Mgmt., HR Mgmt., Finance, IT

Industries: Generalist (All), Finance, Insurance, Software, Healthcare

JenKim International Ltd Inc

7040 W Palmetto Park Rd Ste 2
Boca Raton, FL 33433-3461
(954) 427-6962
Fax: (954) 427-0021
Email: bob_norton@bellsouth.net

Summary: We are a highly skilled and professional recruiting/search firm providing expert advice and assistance to those professionals seeking to advance their careers in the computer or telecom industry.

Key Contact - Specialty:
Mr. Robert W. Norton, President - *Telecommunications*
Mrs. Jennifer Johnson, Associate Recruiter - *Telecommunications*

Salary Minimum: $40,000

Functions: Board Members, Senior Mgmt., Middle Mgmt., Sales & Mktg., Mktg. Mgmt., Sales Mgmt., Engineering

Industries: Computer Equip., Test, Measure Equip., Semiconductors, Services, Equip Svcs., Mgmt. Consulting, HR Services, Media, Telecoms, Call Centers, Telephony, Wireless, Government, Defense, ERP SW

Edward Jennings Professional Search

25 S Main St Ste 179
Yardley, PA 19067-1527
(215) 428-3430
Fax: (215) 689-2729
Email: careers@edwardjenningsps.com
Web: www.edwardjenningsps.com

Summary: Our firm specializes in permanent placement services. We maintain specialty desks in: IT, telecomm, engineering, sales & marketing, food & beverage manufacturing and production as well as executive search. With the understanding derived from our extensive interview process, we act in your best interests in achieving all of your employee/employer objectives.

Key Contact - Specialty:
Ms. Karen Russo, Partner - *Advertising, Consumer (Marketing, Packaged Goods), Food, Manufacturing*
Mr. Anthony Russo, Partner - *Consumer, Consumer (Packaged Goods), Engineering, Executives, Marketing*

Salary Minimum: $40,000

Functions: Mfg., Sales & Mktg.

Industries: Food, Bev., Tobacco, Advertising, Government, Software

Jericho HR Group

PO Box 1701
Dallas, TX 75221-1701
(917) 254-4421
(214) 329-4323
Fax: (972) 463-0960
Email: jobs@jerichohr.com
Web: www.jerichohr.com

Summary: Picking the right executive search firm can be challenging. You want a firm that has experience, industry knowledge, and, of course, innovative ideas. We have the background and knowledge to help you or your company succeed. Whether you are a client company looking for great associates or candidates who need to be marketed to the top companies, we know how to get the job done.

Key Contact - Specialty:
Mr. Josh Slimmer, Principal - *Banking, Human resources, Information Technology, International, Staffing*
Ms. Joann Stokes, Partner - *Human resources, Pharmaceutical, Restaurants, Sales, Supply Chain*

Salary Minimum: $50,000

Functions: Generalist (All), Senior Mgmt., Healthcare, Sales & Mktg., HR Mgmt., Staffing, Finance, IT, Mgmt. Consultants, Int'l.

Industries: Generalist (All)

Jerome & Co

211 Culver Blvd Ste R
Playa del Rey, CA 90293-7776
(310) 305-1812
Fax: (310) 305-8678

Summary: Our clients are manufacturing companies in Southern California. We recruit presidents/GMs, directors of operations, engineering, materials, quality assurance, HR and CFOs/controllers. No marketing/sales or IT searches

Key Contact - Specialty:
Mr. Gerald E. Jerome, President

Salary Minimum: $70,000

Functions: Management, Senior Mgmt., Mfg., Plant Mgmt., Quality, Materials, CFOs, Engineering

Industries: Manufacturing

JFK Search

7013 Ximines Ln N
Osseo, MN 55369-7642
(612) 332-8082
(763) 424-7170
Email: jkmsp@comcast.net
Web: www.jfksearch.com

Summary: Specialist in advertising and public relations agency account service recruiting, network with many other recruiters.

Key Contact - Specialty:
Mr. James Kessler, President - *Advertising*

Functions: Senior Mgmt., Advertising, PR

Industries: Advertising

Jhirad Consulting Inc

914 164th St SE Ste B12
PMB 221
Mill Creek, WA 98012-6339
(212) 202-7567
Email: resume@jhirad.com
Web: www.jhirad.com

Summary: We are the executive search firm for companies mining exceptional talent in: mathematics, physics, derivatives, quantitative finance, trading, fixed income, currencies, commodities, equities and software engineering. Our global network of prestigious clients and top performing candidates is unparalleled.

Key Contact - Specialty:
Mr. Ephraim Jhirad, President - *Computers, Finance*
Ms. Ellen Jhirad, Director - *Computers, Finance, Financial*

Functions: Generalist (All), Management

Industries: Finance, Banking, Invest. Banking, Brokers, Venture Cap., Mutual/Hedge Funds, Misc. Financial, Software, Database SW, Development SW, System SW

JHL

1296 Dealy Ln
Napa, CA 94559-9706
(707) 935-1771
Fax: (707) 935-9596
Email: jhlindellco@earthlink.net

Summary: We specialize in executive and managerial recruitment and selection exclusively within the real estate development, construction and home building industries.

Key Contact - Specialty:
Mr. John H. Lindell, Recruiter

Functions: Generalist (All), Management

Industries: Construction, Real Estate

J Jireh & Associates Inc

PO Box 10158
Burbank, CA 91510-0158
(818) 361-7188

Email: info@j-jireh.com
Web: www.j-jireh.com

Summary: Our firm provides technical staffing and consulting services. We assist our clients to identify, acquire and retain highly qualified technical professionals and simultaneously achieve cost cutting, time saving service management results. Our goal is to provide our customers with flexible high quality services, solutions and highly skilled technical personnel, while also providing maximum value for HR and recruiting budgets.

Key Contact - Specialty:
Mr. Frank Liggett, President & Chief Executive Officer

Salary Minimum: $40,000

Functions: IT, MIS Mgmt., Systems Dev., Systems Implem,, Systems Support, Network Admin., DB Admin., Engineering

Industries: Generalist (All), Semiconductors, IT Implementation, Communications, Software

JK Executive Search

219 E Kanawha Ave
Columbus, OH 43214-1209
(614) 431-7292
Fax: (614) 431-8966
Email: jeff@jkexecutivesearch.com
Web: www.jkexecutivesearch.com

Summary: Executive search & placement specializing in construction (residential, commercial, specialty and building products). Mid to upper level management positions.

Key Contact - Specialty:
Mr. Jeff Kristoff, Executive Recruiter - *Engineering, Healthcare, Manufacturing, Operations*

Salary Minimum: $50,000

Functions: Generalist (All)

Industries: Construction

JL Healthcare Associates

(formerly known as JL Healthcare Executives)
7245 Redden Way NE
Lanesville, IN 47136-8101
(866) 762-5797
Fax: (309) 214-0557
Email: main@jlhealthcareassociates.com
Web: www.jlhealthcareassociates.com

Summary: Our firm is a national contingency and retained healthcare staffing firm that specializes in locum tenens, travel, per diem, and permanent placement.

Key Contact - Specialty:
Ms. Jeri Lyskowinski, Chief Executive Officer & President

Functions: Senior Mgmt., Healthcare

Industries: Drugs Mfg., Medical Devices, Pharm Svcs., Biotech/Life Sciences, Healthcare, Hospitals, Long-term/Home Care, Physical Therapy, Occupational Therapy

JMA Technologies Inc

2870 Regency Ct
Clearwater, FL 33759-1431
(727) 796-1393
Fax: (727) 724-8598
Email: jim@jmatech.net
Web: www.jmatech.net

Summary: Our firm is a professional services and executive search firm and is a privately held company whose principal staff provides computer based service solutions. Our firm specializes in contract and permanent placement along with

contract recruiting, with an emphasis on IT, marketing, accounting, sales, management, engineering, manufacturing and outsourcing strategy.

Key Contact - Specialty:
Mr. James Meyer, President

Salary Minimum: $32,000

Functions: Generalist (All), Management, Finance, IT

Industries: Generalist (All), Manufacturing, Accounting, Mgmt. Consulting, IT Implementation, Aerospace, Software, Healthcare

JOB-BORN Solutions

76 3rd Concession Rd
RR 1
Pickering, ON L1V 2P8
Canada
(519) 586-9607
Email: maryann@jobbornsolutions.com
Web: www.jobbornsolutions.com

Summary: We specialize in the insurance industry only. In addition to recruiting top quality insurance personnel, we are a proactive agency, actively marketing exceptional insurance candidates whom we have isolated and evaluated.

Key Contact - Specialty:
Mrs. Mary Ann Vaughn, CPC, President - *Insurance*

Salary Minimum: $125,000

Functions: Generalist (All)

Industries: Generalist (All), Insurance, Casualty, Claims, Commercial, Re-Insurance

The John Lawrence Group Inc

26111 W 14 Mile Rd Ste LL1
Franklin, MI 48025-1169
(248) 932-7770
Fax: (248) 932-7774
Email: jlgcareer@aol.com

Summary: Specialists in the search, recruitment and placement of professionals to the printing and prepress industries. Managers: operations, plant, sales, pressroom, prepress, bindery, fulfillment, financial, customer service, estimating, production, HR, mailing/distribution, etc. We are also very active in placing sales reps.

Key Contact - Specialty:
Mr. John Mason, Partner
Mr. Lawrence Swider, Partner

Salary Minimum: $50,000

Functions: Management

Industries: Printing

Paul Johnson & Associates Inc

402 Office Park Dr Ste 100
Birmingham, AL 35223-2435
(205) 871-6510
Web: www.pauljohnsonsearch.com/

Summary: We are a boutique executive search firm that specializes in recruiting leadership talent, mostly on a retained basis. We are generalists, conducting searches for management team members. Most of our work outside Birmingham is for manufacturing and distribution companies. Positions include plant manager, general manager, operations manager, VP operations, supply chain director, division controller.

Key Contact - Specialty:
Mr. Paul R. Johnson, President

Salary Minimum: $80,000

Functions: Senior Mgmt., Mfg., Materials, Sales & Mktg., HR Mgmt., CFOs, MIS Mgmt.

Industries: Generalist (All)

Verne Johnson & Associates Inc

444 Stone Rd
Pittsford, NY 14534-2854
(585) 249-5044
Fax: (585) 249-5072
Email: vjsearch@frontiernet.net
Web: www.vernejohnsonassociates.com

Summary: We are an executive search firm specializing in mid-level and senior level management personnel. Business sectors served include packaging converting, plastic films and resins, food and pharmaceutical industries.

Key Contact - Specialty:
Mr. Verne Johnson, President - *Packaging, Plastics, Printing*

Salary Minimum: $80,000

Functions: Management, Mfg., Product Dev., Sales & Mktg., Engineering

Industries: Plastics, Rubber, Packaging, Healthcare, Hospitals

Gil Johnson & Associates

304 Fairfax Dr
Allen, TX 75013-3605
(214) 750-2084
Email: giljohniii@aol.com

Summary: Executive search, consulting/training and outplacement firm with strong presence and specialization in the healthcare. The firm does retained and contingency work, provides outplacement services and management consulting and recruiter training.

Key Contact - Specialty:
Mr. Gil Johnson, CPC, President - *Healthcare*

Salary Minimum: $100,000

Functions: Senior Mgmt., Healthcare, Physicians, Allied Health

Industries: Pharm Svcs., Accounting, Mgmt. Consulting, HR Services, Higher Ed., Engineering Svcs., Government, Defense, Property/Facility Mgmt., Accounting SW, Mfg. SW, Healthcare, Hospitals, Long-term/Home Care, Physical Therapy

K E Johnson Associates

4213-187th Pl SE
Issaquah, WA 98027-9746
(425) 747-4559

Summary: We staff for all scientific fields and technical disciplines for PhD, engineering and executive type placements. Specializing in high-technology/computer related technologies and services.

Key Contact - Specialty:
Mr. Karl Johnson, Chief Executive, Agent & Owner - *High technology, Research & development*

Salary Minimum: $60,000

Functions: Board Members, Senior Mgmt., Product Dev., Mktg. Research, IT, Systems Dev., R&D, Engineering

Industries: Generalist (All), Construction, Manufacturing, Chemicals, Medical Devices, Computer Equip., Test, Measure Equip., Electronic, Elec. Components, Transportation, Finance, IT Implementation, Media, Communications, Government, Aerospace, Software, Biotech/Life Sciences, Healthcare

Johnson Associates Inc

114 N Hale St
Wheaton, IL 60187-5152
(630) 690-9200
Fax: (630) 690-9910
Email: info@jasearch.com
Web: www.jasearch.com

Summary: Our firm specializes nationally and exclusively in the food distribution and food manufacturing industries. We provide our clients with the best senior level talent in all functional areas: Executive management, sales, operations, finance, purchasing, R&D, quality, production, HR and MIS. Please, only executives with extensive food industry experience should apply.

Key Contact - Specialty:
Mr. Scott Johnson, President
Mr. John Carrigg, Manager
Ms. Mary Johnson, Vice President
Mr. Don Huston, Manager, Food Manufacturing Division

Salary Minimum: $80,000

Functions: Management, Senior Mgmt., Mfg., Production, Plant Mgmt., Purchasing, Distribution, Sales Mgmt., HR Mgmt., Finance

Industries: Food, Bev., Tobacco

Clifton Johnson Associates Inc

3824 Northern Pike Ste 725
Monroeville, PA 15146-2143
(412) 856 8000
Fax: (412) 856-8026
Email: cj@cliftonjohnson.com
Web: www.cliftonjohnson.com

Summary: We specialize in the fields of engineering, manufacturing, programming, computer systems (software & hardware), technical sales, as well as most professional management areas.

Key Contact - Specialty:
Mr. Cliff Johnson, President

Salary Minimum: $45,000

Functions: Generalist (All), Management

Industries: Generalist (All), Food, Bev., Tobacco, Chemicals, Drugs Mfg., Medical Devices, Plastics, Rubber, Metal Products, Machine, Appliance, Motor Vehicles, Misc. Mfg., Electronic, Elec. Components

Johnson Brown Associates Inc

7416 Sargent Rd
Indianapolis, IN 46256-2175
(317) 849-0500
Email: danbrown@topechelon.com

Summary: We are a responsive traditional recruiting firm conducting dedicated searches within the manufacturing sector, emphasizing close working relationships and an in depth understanding of our clients' industries and operations. Specialties include operations & manufacturing management, supply chain, quality & engineering.

Key Contact - Specialty:
Mr. Daniel P. Brown, Partner
Mr. John Kimbrough Johnson, Partner

Salary Minimum: $50,000

Functions: Mfg., Materials, HR Mgmt., Engineering

Industries: Generalist (All), Manufacturing, Medical Devices, Plastics, Rubber, Metal Products, Machine, Appliance, Motor Vehicles, Consumer Elect., Test, Measure Equip., Misc. Mfg., Electronic, Elec. Components, Aerospace

Johnson Personnel Company

1639 N Alpine Rd
Rockford, IL 61107-1449
(815) 964-0840
Email: darrell@johnsonpersonnel.com
Web: www.johnsonpersonnel.com

Summary: Many years of recruitment in product/manufacturing/quality/industrial/electrical engineering, operations, EHS, supply chain/procurement, HR, IT, accounting, and technical sales & marketing.

Key Contact - Specialty:
Mr. Darrell Johnson

Salary Minimum: $40,000

Functions: Generalist (All), Middle Mgmt., Product Dev., Mktg. Research, HR Mgmt.

Industries: Manufacturing, Food, Bev., Tobacco, Paper, Chemicals, Drugs Mfg., Plastics, Rubber, Metal Products, Machine, Appliance, Motor Vehicles, Computer Equip., Consumer Elect., Test, Measure Equip., Misc. Mfg., Telecoms

The Jonathan Group

170 Timber Ridge Rd
Drasco, AR 72530-9414
(501) 825-7876
Email: denny@groupjonathan.com
Web: www.groupjonathan.com

Summary: Our firm has recruiting experience with successful and timely results. Long term relationships are our forte.

Key Contact - Specialty:
Mr. Denny Brubaker, Recruiter - *Computers, Semiconductors, Technology, Wireless*
Mr. Jonathan Brubaker, Vice President - *Accounting*
Mr. Stan Witt, Recruiter - *Accounting, Automation, Design, Industrial, Manufacturing*
Ms. Cindy Hicks, Recruiter - *Management, Manufacturing, Supply Chain, Telecommunications, Wireless*
Mr. Ken Larsen, Recruiter - *C-level, Marketing, Medical, Operations, Research & development*
Mr. Paul Berry, Recruiter - *Computers, Electronics, Medical, Quality, Regulatory*

Salary Minimum: $25,000

Functions: Generalist (All)

Industries: Manufacturing, Electronic, Elec. Components, Finance, Accounting, IT Implementation, Communications, Aerospace, Software, Biotech/Life Sciences, Healthcare

J Joseph & Associates

3766 Fishcreek Rd
Stow, OH 44224-4379
(330) 676-0522
Fax: (330) 676-9522
Email: wecare@jjosephrecruiter.com
Web: www.jjosephrecruiter.com

Summary: Our firm specializes in field sales staffing. Our clients are exclusive to us.

Key Contact - Specialty:
Mr. Scott Raymont, President - *Sales*
Ms. Carolyn James, Vice President, Operations - *Sales*

Salary Minimum: $35,000

Functions: Generalist (All), Production, Sales & Mktg., Advertising, Mktg. Research, MIS Mgmt., Systems Analysis, Engineering

Industries: Generalist (All), Paper, Printing, Medical Devices, Computer Equip.

Joseph Associates Inc

229 Main St
Huntington, NY 11743-6933
(631) 351-5805
Fax: (631) 421-4123
Email: inquiries@jaexecutivesearch.com
Web: www.jaexecutivesearch.com

Summary: We specialize in areas where IT and the pharmaceutical industry converge: SAS programming, informatics (bioinformatics & cheminformatics), computational chemistry & biology, drug discovery (R&D PhD level scientist), statistics and biostatistics & data warehousing. We also place engineers and marketing specialists in the medical device industry. The top tier talent that we identify enables our clients to succeed and excel in this competitive business world.

Key Contact - Specialty:
Mr. Joseph Nakelski, President
Mrs. Denise Milano-Sprung, Vice President, Search Services
Mr. Jeff Axel, Managing Director

Salary Minimum: $75,000

Functions: Production, Healthcare, MIS Mgmt., Systems Analysis, Systems Dev., Network Admin., DB Admin., R&D

Industries: Generalist (All), Manufacturing, Drugs Mfg., Medical Devices, Services, HR Services, Software, Database SW, Marketing SW, Networking, Comm. SW, Security SW, Biotech/Life Sciences, Healthcare, Hospitals

Branches:
330 Washington Blvd Ste 509
Marina del Rey, CA 90292-5146
(310) 306-4556
Fax: (310) 306-4707
Email: mike@jaexecutivesearch.com

Joseph Consulting Inc

216 S Park Ave
Winter Park, FL 32789-7021
(407) 628-7073
Fax: (407) 628-7074
Email: mcgee@josephconsulting.com
Web: www.josephconsulting.com

Summary: We are a consulting and recruiting firm specializing in providing IT, sales, finance, engineering, management and executive level solutions on a contract or direct placement basis.

Key Contact - Specialty:
Mr. Jerry McGee, President & Chief Executive Officer - *Finance, Management, Sales*
Ms. Lisa Schweitzer, Recruiter, Internet

Salary Minimum: $50,000

Functions: Generalist (All)

Industries: Energy, Utilities, Finance, Services, Communications, Aerospace, Insurance, Real Estate, Software, Biotech/Life Sciences, Healthcare

Joslin & Associates Ltd

900 Intracoastal Dr Apt 24
Fort Lauderdale, FL 33304-3643
(954) 873-3487
Email: joslinltd@earthlink.net

Summary: Optimizing opportunities for individuals and organizations with scientific or technical orientation in the pharmaceutical industry, including: formulation and product development, scale-up and TS, anal, DDS, engineering, project mgt., quality, regulatory, and licensing. Extensive personal industry research and executive experience.

Key Contact - Specialty:
Dr. Robert S. Joslin, PhD, Consultant - *Adhesives, Analysts, Biomaterials, Engineering, Mergers & acquisitions*

Salary Minimum: $70,000

Functions: Senior Mgmt., Middle Mgmt., Mfg., Product Dev., Quality, Healthcare, R&D, Engineering

Industries: Drugs Mfg., Pharm Svcs.

Branches:
291 Deer Trail Ct Apt C
Lake Barrington, IL 60010-1773
(847) 304-1100
Email: joslinltd@earthlink.net

JP Morgan Chase

1111 Polaris Pkwy
Columbus, OH 43240-7001
(614) 248-7216
(614) 266-2776
Email: susan.x.asmo@jpmchase.com
Web: www.jpmchase.com

Summary: We are a leading global financial services firm and serve millions of consumers in the United States and many of the world's most prominent corporate, institutional and government clients.

Key Contact - Specialty:
Ms. Susan Asmo, Executive Recruiter

Salary Minimum: $50,000

Functions: Sales & Mktg.

Industries: Venture Cap., Misc. Financial

JPM International

26034 Acero
Mission Viejo, CA 92691-2768
(949) 699-4300
(800) 685-7856
Fax: (949) 699-4333
Email: leslieo@jpmintl.com
Web: www.jpmintl.com

Summary: We are a HR consulting firm specializing in the staffing/retention of all permanent employees hired into an organization. Through our partnership between the client, and us we achieve a full understanding of your company's needs, corporate cultures, goals and objectives.

Key Contact - Specialty:
Ms. Melissa Hannigan, Managing Partner - *Healthcare*
Ms. Lesley Graham, Managing Partner - *Telecommunications*
Ms. Trish Ryan, Managing Partner - *Senior management*

Salary Minimum: $75,000

Functions: Generalist (All)

Industries: Textiles, Apparel, Medical Devices, Invest. Banking, Venture Cap., Telecoms, Call Centers, Wireless

JRG Partners Inc

18 Lyman St Ste 1B
Westborough, MA 01581-1431
(508) 366-9862
Fax: (508) 366-4411
Email: jim@jrgpartners.com
Web: www.jrgpartners.com

Summary: Executive search and sales staffing company focused on technology and venture companies. Specialties include software, storage, communications and services.

Key Contact - Specialty:
Mr. Jim Gaudette, Founder & President

Salary Minimum: $100,000

Functions: Generalist (All)

Industries: Venture Cap., Communications, Software

JRG-USA Recruiting Inc

PO BOX 152911
Austin, TX 78715-2911
(512) 292-9755
(512) 587-3148
Email: jim@jrgcareers.com
Web: www.jrgcareers.com

Summary: JRG-USA Recruiting offers over 25 years of proven recruiting and leadership excellence. Our focused recruiting platform is universal to any industry. Our highly qualified recruiting staff is able to meet the staffing needs of companies regardless of what industry.

Key Contact - Specialty:
Mr. James Harrison, President - *Aerospace, Automotive, Aviation, Biomedical, Biopharmaceutical*
Mr. Luis Gonzales, Vice President - *Manufacturing*

Functions: Management, Mfg., Packaging, Sales Reps., Engineering, Technicians

Industries: Generalist (All), Energy, Utilities, Oil & Gas, Construction, Manufacturing, Semiconductors, Transportation, Services, Communications, Aerospace, Packaging

JRW & Associates

204 Powtan Dr
Lynchburg, VA 24502-5542
(434) 239-7141
Fax: (503) 210-7380
Email: jrwassociates@verizon.net

Summary: Our company has developed many contacts over the years. This enriches our base and allows us to present the most qualified candidates possible in our disciplines. From engineers or healthcare to data processing or computer, we have the sources.

Key Contact - Specialty:
Mr. Rick Warren, Owner

Functions: Generalist (All), Mfg., Production, Healthcare, Nurses, Training, IT, Systems Dev., Systems Support, Network Admin.

Industries: Generalist (All), Manufacturing, Paper, Chemicals, Plastics, Rubber, Paints, Petro. Products, E-commerce, IT Implementation, Higher Ed., Communications, Software, Healthcare, Hospitals

JT Associates

89 Comstock Hill Rd
New Canaan, CT 06840-5219
(203) 563-9565
Email: jtassoc@optonline.net

Summary: We are a contingency/retainer search firm specializing energy trading.

Key Contact - Specialty:
Mr. Joe Fazio, Partner
Ms. Mary Ellen Calderone, Partner

Salary Minimum: $50,000

Functions: Management

Industries: Energy, Utilities

Judge Inc
2500 Northwinds Pkwy Ste 300
Alpharetta, GA 30004-2247
(678) 297-0800
(877) 844-9189
Fax: (800) 303-6572
Email: jlw@judge.com
Web: www.judgeinc.com

Summary: Our firm is a powerhouse of food
industry recruiting with deep contacts in retail,
wholesale, manufacturing, sales/marketing and
distribution. We offer a wide-area-networked
database, real-time in all offices for maximum
exposure and total team concept.

Key Contact - Specialty:
Mr. Jason L. Wickline, CPC, Division Vice
President - *Distribution*

Salary Minimum: $30,000

Functions: Management, Senior Mgmt., Plant
Mgmt., Purchasing, Distribution, Sales & Mktg.,
HR Mgmt., Finance

Industries: Manufacturing, Food, Bev., Tobacco,
Soap, Perf., Cosmtcs., Drugs Mfg.,
Transportation, Wholesale, Retail

Branches:
7077 Bonneval Rd Ste 420
Jacksonville, FL 32216-6017
(904) 998-8200
Fax: (904) 998-0966
Email: jacksonvillejobs@judge.com
Key Contact - Specialty:
Mr. Steve Green, Division Vice President

500 N West Shore Blvd Ste 950
Tampa, FL 33609-5002
(813) 877-7000
Fax: (813) 286-0668
Email: tampajobs@inc.judge.com
Key Contact - Specialty:
Ms. Tina Gannon, Division Vice President

105 Fieldcrest Ave Ste 4D
Edison, NJ 08837-3628
(732) 346-9100
Fax: (732) 346-0188
Email: edisonjobs@inc.judge.com
Key Contact - Specialty:
Mr. Bob Posluszny, Division Vice President

300 Conshohocken State Rd Ste 300
West Conshohocken, PA 19428-3801
(610) 667-7700
Fax: (610) 667-1058
Email: jobs@inc.judge.com
Key Contact - Specialty:
Mr. Bill Gladstone, President

700 Highlander Blvd Ste 410
Arlington, TX 76015-4329
(817) 557-5511
Fax: (817) 557-0693
Email: arlingtonjobs@inc.judge.com
Key Contact - Specialty:
Mr. Gene Goodwin, Branch Manager

Juno Systems Inc
405 Lexington Ave Rm 4900
New York, NY 10174-4900
(212) 681-1430
Email: newyork@junosystems.com
Web: www.junosystems.com

Summary: We recruit executives for all areas and
IT professionals. We specialize in understanding
cross-cultural issues in addition to technical
competencies.

Key Contact - Specialty:
Ms. Mary J. Kuric, President

Functions: Generalist (All), MIS Mgmt., Systems
Analysis, Systems Dev., Systems Implem.,
Systems Support, Network Admin., DB Admin.

Industries: Generalist (All), Finance, Media,
Insurance, Software

Jurasek Associates Inc
PO Box 1302
Easton, MA 02334-1302
(508) 230-7260
(877) 859-2010
Fax: (877) 859-2010
Email: joe@jurasekassociates.com
Web: www.jurasekassociates.com

Summary: With extensive years in the recruitment
industry we offer a full line of search and
unbundled search services. We work with
companies ranging in size from small start-ups to
the more established or larger area firms.

Key Contact - Specialty:
Mr. Joseph W. Jurasek, President - *Computers
(Hardware,Programming), Defense,
Engineering, Technical*

Salary Minimum: $90,000

Functions: Middle Mgmt., Engineering

Industries: Computer Equip., Consumer Elect.,
Electronic, Elec. Components, Semiconductors,
RF/Microwave, Defense, Development SW

Juris Placements Inc
600 Germantown Pike
Lafayette Hill, PA 19444-1800
(610) 825-7751
(646) 519-7481
Fax: (215) 689-1442
Email: info@jurisplacements.com
Web: www.jurisplacements.com

Summary: We are a national search firm that
specializes in the recruitment and placement of
attorneys - lateral associates, partners and counsel.
We assist groups as well as individuals.

Key Contact - Specialty:
Mr. Mitchell Satalof, Chief Executive Officer
Mr. Steve Becker, Senior Recruiter - *Human
resources, Legal, Legal (Lawyers)*
Mr. Irving Seldin, Senior Recruiter - *Human
resources, Legal, Legal (Lawyers)*
Ms. Gabrielle Rossi, Administrator -
Administration

Salary Minimum: $100,000

Functions: Legal, Attorneys

Industries: Generalist (All), Energy, Utilities,
Services, Legal, Media, Communications,
Environmental Svcs., Real Estate, Software,
Biotech/Life Sciences, Healthcare

Juris Resources
33 Office Park Rd Unit A PMB 103
Hilton Head Island, SC 29928-4660
(843) 341-3004
Fax: (843) 340-2004
Email: info@jurisresources.com
Web: www.jurisresources.com

Summary: Our firm provides consulting,
recruiting and project staffing services to Fortune
500 companies and Top 100 law firms. All of our
consultants are attorneys with impressive real-
world accomplishments.

Key Contact - Specialty:
Mr. P. Jeffrey North, Managing Partner

Salary Minimum: $90,000

Functions: Attorneys

Industries: Generalist (All)

Just Management Services Inc
701 Enterprise Rd E Ste 805
Safety Harbor, FL 34695-5342
(727) 726-4000
(800) 544-5878
Fax: (727) 725-4966
Email: info@justmgt.com
Web: www.justmgt.com

Summary: Broad range of executive search
services to the apparel, home furnishings and
textile industries including: manufacturing, sales,
design, merchandising, import co-ordination and
sourcing.

Key Contact - Specialty:
Mr. Jim Just, Chairman
Ms. Susan Just, President - *Apparel, Metals,
Plastics, Textiles*

Salary Minimum: $40,000

Functions: Generalist (All), Management, Senior
Mgmt., Mfg., Product Dev., Production

Industries: Textiles, Apparel, Plastics, Rubber

A H Justice Search Consultants
(also known as Newman-Johnson-King Inc)
PO Box 729
Rockport, TX 78381-0729
(361) 727-1582
(361) 790-5959
Fax: (361) 727-1583
Email: jack@njksearch.com
Web: www.ahjustice.com

Summary: We have a history of providing ethical,
professional and effective service to firms and
candidates. Our concentration of recruitment effort
is in the engineering and science disciplines
involved in the oil & gas, petrochemical and oil
refining industries.

Key Contact - Specialty:
Mr. Jack King, III, BSME, MBA, President -
Engineering, Gas, Refineries, Refining, Science
Ms. Joan Peterson, Senior Consultant - *Chemical,
Engineering, Gas, Oil, Petrochemical*

Salary Minimum: $50,000

Functions: Mfg.

Industries: Energy, Utilities, Oil & Gas,
Manufacturing, Chemicals, Plastics, Rubber,
Paints, Petro. Products

JWC Associates
7 Thoreau Dr
Manalapan, NJ 07726-3715
(732) 792-2933
Fax: (732) 792-2936
Email: jwchh500@aol.com

Summary: Our clients include pharmaceutical,
medical device and biotechnology companies. We
concentrate our efforts in the areas following.
Marketing: product management, market research
and business development. Product development:
engineers and scientists. Operations: plant
management, production, quality assurance,
quality control and regulatory affairs.

Key Contact - Specialty:
Mr. John Colantoni, President - *Marketing,
Product management/development, Production*
Ms. Marie Lubrano, Recruiter

Salary Minimum: $60,000

Functions: Product Dev., Production, Plant
Mgmt., Quality, Healthcare, Sales & Mktg., HR
Mgmt., CFOs, R&D, Engineering

Industries: Generalist (All), Chemicals, Drugs
Mfg., Medical Devices, Pharm Svcs.

JWR Associates

13109 Fieldstone Rd
Keller, TX 76248-1742
(817) 481-0800
Email: jwrassociates@attglobal.net

Summary: IT recruiting specialists.

Key Contact - Specialty:
Mr. John W. Reinmiller, Principal

Salary Minimum: $100,000

Functions: Senior Mgmt., Middle Mgmt., Mktg.
Mgmt., Sales Mgmt., MIS Mgmt., Systems
Dev., Systems Support, Network Admin., DB
Admin.

Industries: Generalist (All), Oil & Gas, Computer
Equip., Mgmt. Consulting, IT Implementation,
Telecoms, Wireless, Software

K&M International Inc

1307 W 6th St Ste 220C
Corona, CA 92882-3168
(909) 279-6600
Fax: (909) 279-6620
Email: info@kandminternational.com
Web: www.kmcorporate.com

Summary: Our extensive database search
capabilities allow our consultants to target and
market our candidate's background and provide
our clients with top-notch employees.

Key Contact - Specialty:
Mr. Paul Kuch, Managing Consultant - *Finance*
Mr. Chris Miller, Managing Consultant - *Business
development, Strategic planning*

Salary Minimum: $30,000

Functions: Generalist (All), Purchasing, CFOs,
Budgeting, Credit, Taxes, Systems Support,
Mgmt. Consultants

Industries: Generalist (All), Manufacturing,
Wholesale, Finance, Accounting, Aerospace,
Accounting SW, Biotech/Life Sciences

Kaas Employment Services

425 2nd St SE Ste 610
Cedar Rapids, IA 52401-1816
(319) 366-1731
Fax: (319) 366-1402
Email: kpearson@kaas-emp.com

Summary: Contingency search and placement
firm specializing in professional, technical,
manufacturing, and engineering.

Key Contact - Specialty:
Ms. Kathy J. Pearson, Owner

Salary Minimum: $50,000

Functions: Generalist (All), Management, Senior
Mgmt., Admin. Svcs., Mfg.

Industries: Generalist (All), Manufacturing

Kabana Corp

PO Box 930785
49175 W Pontiac Trail
Wixom, MI 48393-0785
(248) 926-6427
Email: kabana@mich.com
Web: www.kabana.com

Summary: We perform retainer employer paid
executive search and recruitment services to
capital equipment, automotive OEM, aftermarket,
commercial, off road, motor sport, recreation
vehicle and marine production parts suppliers
industries and other industries. Our primary client
contacts include presidents, vice presidents,
human resource, plant, quality, purchasing,
materials, engineering and sales managers.

Key Contact - Specialty:
Mr. Steven E. Kabanuk, Executive Recruiter
Mrs. Marilyn Johnson, Office Manager

Salary Minimum: $45,000

Functions: Management, Mfg., Materials,
Purchasing, Sales & Mktg., Sales Mgmt., HR
Mgmt., Engineering, Minorities/Diversity, Int'l.

Industries: Plastics, Rubber, Paints, Petro.
Products, Motor Vehicles

KABL Ability Network

(a division of Syntre Corp)
1727 State St
Santa Barbara, CA 93101-2521
(805) 563-2398
(800) 432-5225
Email: 432kabl@msn.com

Summary: We are a network of recruiters
specializing in top management of small
companies, primarily high technology and
telecom. We place for both permanent and temp.

Key Contact - Specialty:
Mr. Brad Naegle, President

Salary Minimum: $100,000

Functions: Senior Mgmt.

Industries: Computer Equip., Telecoms, Software

Kaczmar & Associates

PO Box 1344
Doylestown, PA 18901-0119
(215) 766-3800
Fax: (215) 766-3591
Email: kaczmar@kaczmar.com
Web: www.kaczmar.com

Summary: We specialize in placing senior-level
sales and pre and post-sales consulting support
professionals with top 500 independent software
vendors, pre-IPO software vendors and IT services
firms.

Key Contact - Specialty:
Mr. Michael A. Kaczmar, Principal

Functions: Sales Mgmt., IT

Industries: Software

Richard Kader & Associates

6777 Engle Rd Ste A
Cleveland, OH 44130-7953
(440) 891-1700
Email: resumes@kaderonline.com
Web: www.kaderonline.com

Summary: Financial services: specializing in
investment management, investment research and
investment banking in all the major financial
capitals and in the emerging markets.

Key Contact - Specialty:
Mr. Richard H. Kader, President
Mr. Vern Sponseller, Vice President - *Financial*
Ms. Mamie Rudd, Vice President
Mr. Art DeLong, Vice President
Ms. Kate Christian, Vice President
Mr. Mark Woods, Vice President
Ms. Michele Carpenter, Associate Recruiter
Mr. Cliff Stenzel, Associate Recruiter
Ms. Kay Scarp, Associate Recruiter
Ms. Paulette Chalfant, Associate Recruiter

Salary Minimum: $40,000

Functions: Generalist (All)

Industries: Generalist (All), Manufacturing

Robert Kaestner & Associates

3047 Flat Rock Pl # 3
Land O Lakes, FL 34639-4581
(813) 996-5664
Fax: (813) 996-5934
Email: robkae@gte.net
Web: www.kaestner.com

Summary: This professional contingency and
retained search firm is devoted to serving the
office furniture and office supply industries at all
disciplines. We cater to the search needs of
manufacturers as well as dealers and distributors.

Key Contact - Specialty:
Mr. Bob Kaestner, Principal
Ms. Pat Kaye, Associate - *Interior design*

Salary Minimum: $50,000

Functions: Generalist (All)

Industries: Lumber, Furniture, Wholesale

Kain Management Group LLC

1650 Borel Pl Ste 125
San Mateo, CA 94402-3507
(650) 627-9919
Fax: (425) 928-3429
Email: syd@kainmg.com
Web: www.kainmg.com

Summary: We are a retained executive search
firm with a specialized concentration in recruiting
technical resources, sales professionals and
executive management. We service clients in the
high technology, research and consulting
industries. Our client base ranges from regional
providers to Fortune 500 companies.

Key Contact - Specialty:
Mr. Syd Kain, President
Mr. Josh Lopez, Executive Recruiter - *Computers
(Networking,Software), Sales, Senior
management, Technology*
Mr. John Colasanto

Salary Minimum: $90,000

Functions: Board Members, Senior Mgmt.,
Product Dev., Sales & Mktg., Sales Mgmt., IT

Industries: Computer Equip., Services, Mgmt.
Consulting, E-commerce, IT Implementation,
Media, Communications, Software, Biotech/Life
Sciences

Kaiser Whitney Staffing International

59 Elm St
New Haven, CT 06510-2047
(203) 562-0511
Fax: (203) 562-2637
Email: dkaiser@kaiserwhitney.com
Web: www.kaiserwhitney.com

Summary: American companies expanding
abroad and foreign companies coming to the USA
find their mid-level managers, sales/marketing,
accounting/finance and legal staff through us.
Office support staff and bilingual candidates are
also areas of specialization.

Key Contact - Specialty:
Mr. Donald J. Kaiser, President - *Biotechnology,
Human resources, Legal, Legal (Attorneys),
Marketing*
Mr. James Kaiser, General Manager & Director
International - *Business development,
Engineering, Environmental, Human resources,
Sales*
Mrs. Gina Criscuolo, CPA, Recruiter, Certified
Public Accountant - *Accounting, Accounting
(General), Finance, SAP, Tax*
Ms. Elaine Kaiser, Vice President & Dir, Temp &
Legal Div. - *Administration, Clerical, Legal,
Office (Support), Temporary*

Mr. Jack Kaiser, Recruiter - *Biotechnology, Human resources, International*
Mrs. Kim Zarra, Recruiter, Legal & Staffing Division - *Administration, Legal*
Mrs. Irene Kaiser, Vice President - *Administration, Human resources, Office (Services), Retail*

Salary Minimum: $30,000

Functions: Senior Mgmt., Middle Mgmt., Admin. Svcs., Plant Mgmt., Sales & Mktg., Finance, CFOs, Taxes, Legal, Int'l.

Industries: Generalist (All), Energy, Utilities, Construction, Manufacturing, Food, Bev., Tobacco, Medical Devices, Computer Equip., Transportation, Finance, Services, Legal, Mgmt. Consulting, Hospitality, Advertising, Telecoms, Environmental Svcs., Aerospace, Software, Biotech/Life Sciences, Healthcare

Kaleidoscope

3828 Karen Lynn Dr
Glendale, CA 91206-1218
(818) 790-9222
(818) 790-9223
Fax: (818) 790-9225
Email: astrid@kscope-search.com
Web: www.kscope-search.com

Summary: Our mission is to be a provider of highly specialized search techniques, recognized for commitment to our clients and for the delivery of excellent service.

Key Contact - Specialty:
Ms. Astrid Grey, Principal
Ms. Cindy Orozco, Principal

Functions: Generalist (All), Senior Mgmt., Middle Mgmt., Admin. Svcs., Direct Mktg., HR Mgmt., Finance

Industries: Finance, Banking, Invest. Banking, Venture Cap., Misc. Financial, Accounting, HR Services, Advertising, New Media, Non-Classifiable

Lisa Kalus & Associates Inc

80 Broad St Fl 5
New York, NY 10004-2257
(212) 837-7889
Email: resumes@lisakalus.com
Web: www.lisakalus.com

Summary: We are a recruitment firm specializing in construction, engineering, and real estate personnel.

Key Contact - Specialty:
Ms. Lisa Kalus, President - *Construction, Engineering*

Salary Minimum: $35,000

Functions: Engineering

Industries: Construction, Architectural Svcs., Real Estate

Kalvert Associates

PO Box 1394
Sugar Land, TX 77487-1394
(281) 438-2410
Email: akalvert@kalvertassociates.com
Web: www.kalvertassociates.com

Summary: Provides human capital acquisition solutions to the premier companies in the petroleum refining industry. The firm has worked closely with candidates and companies to complete search engagements in The United States, Latin America, Europe, the Middle East, and Asia

Key Contact - Specialty:
Mr. Arthur Kalvert, Consultant, Recruitment

Salary Minimum: $80,000

Functions: Generalist (All)

Industries: Energy, Utilities, Oil & Gas

Kames & Associates Inc

PO Box 3342
Annapolis, MD 21403-0342
(410) 990-0780
Fax: (410) 990-0784
Email: rkames@kames.com
Web: www.kames.com

Summary: Our professional recruiting service specializes in high technology, IT, software & systems engineering, defense, intelligence, IT, telecom, COMINT and SIGINT areas. We specialize in disciplines from the working-level to senior-management, sales, marketing and executive-management.

Key Contact - Specialty:
Mr. Robert Kames, President

Salary Minimum: $75,000

Functions: Generalist (All), Management, Sales & Mktg., Systems Dev.

Industries: Digital, Network Infrastructure, Government, Defense, Aerospace, Software, Development SW

Kamp & Associates

PO Box 222
Davidson, NC 28036-0222
(704) 892-5922
Email: dbkstar@aol.com

Summary: We specialize in talent acquisition, assessment, advancement, and retention across industries and disciplines.

Key Contact - Specialty:
Mr. Douglas B. Kamp, President - *Engineering, Manufacturing, Marketing*

Functions: Generalist (All)

Industries: Generalist (All)

Kane & Associates Inc

3027 Marina Bay Dr Ste 211
League City, TX 77573-2889
(281) 326-5263
Email: bernie@jobmenu.com
Web: www.jobmenu.com

Summary: We perform searches for a variety of functions and industries. We specialize in the financial and engineering areas. Industries include energy, banking, manufacturing and Oil & Gas.

Key Contact - Specialty:
Mr. Bernie Kane, President - *Accounting (Big 4,General), CFOs, Controllers, Financial*
Mr. Michael Kane, Vice President - *Power*
Mr. Greg Green, Partner - *Accounting (Big 4,General), Chemical, Engineering, Financial*
Mr. James Warren, Partner - *Banking, Banking (Commercial,Corporate,Investment)*
Mr. Robert Drenker, Partner - *Chemical, Energy, Engineering, Environmental, Manufacturing*
Mr. Marc Holdaway, Partner - *Engineering*
Mr. Tyler Cornelius, Senior Consultant - *Banking (Commercial,Corporate,Investment)*

Salary Minimum: $50,000

Functions: Generalist (All), Health & Safety

Industries: Energy, Utilities, Manufacturing, Paper, Chemicals, Plastics, Rubber, Paints, Petro. Products, Brokers, Misc. Financial, Services, Accounting, HR Services, Telecoms, Mfg. SW

Kapp & Associates

PO Box 103
Greenville, SC 29602-0103
(864) 250-0123
Fax: (864) 250-0127
Email: dfkapp@mindspring.com

Summary: We complete very specialized, confidential or otherwise challenging searches, from the first level through senior executives, primarily for manufacturing and distribution corporations. We utilize classical search techniques to identify and directly approach top performers, both for contingent and retained searches.

Key Contact - Specialty:
Mr. Donald Kapp, President

Salary Minimum: $50,000

Functions: Generalist (All)

Industries: Manufacturing

Karis Partners

645 Executive Dr
Willowbrook, IL 60527-5603
(630) 325-8881
Web: www.karispartners.com

Summary: Karis Partners offers leading corporations a flexible, customized approach to executive search including Contingent, Commitment Based and Retained. Karis Partners places managers and executive-level individuals in the following industries: Manufacturing, Healthcare, Distribution, Financial Services, Pharmaceutical, Not-for-profit organizations. Karis Partners is an affiliate of Flex Execs Management Solutions.

Key Contact - Specialty:
Ms. Karen Murphy, Managing Partner
Ms. Marianne M. Orland, Executive Search Consultant - *CFOs, Controllers, Executives, Management, Marketing*
Ms. Shannon Ross, Executive Search Consultant - *Benefits, Compensation, Human resources, Middle management, Organizational development*
Ms. Terri Conroy, Executive Search Consultant - *Executives, Healthcare, Hospital, Pharmacists, Senior management*
Ms. Janiece Durham, Executive Search Consultant - *Executives, Healthcare, Hospital, Middle management, Pharmacists*

Salary Minimum: $80,000

Functions: Generalist (All), Management, Healthcare, Allied Health, Mktg. Mgmt., HR Mgmt., Benefits, CFOs

Industries: Generalist (All), Manufacturing, Food, Bev., Tobacco, Services, HR Services, Healthcare, Hospitals

Karlyn Group

(also known as Karlyn Fashion Recruiters)
210 Sylvan Ave
Englewood Cliffs, NJ 07632-2524
(201) 871-9800
Fax: (201) 894-1186
Email: rloikits@karlyn.com
Web: www.karlyn.com

Summary: Services offered primarily on a contingency basis in all areas of management, fashion, office support, legal, logistics and sales positions.

Key Contact - Specialty:
Ms. Regina Loikits, Owner - *Management*

Salary Minimum: $40,000

Functions: Generalist (All)

Industries: Textiles, Apparel, Services, Legal, Packaging, Insurance

Branches:
450 Fashion Ave Fl 46
New York, NY 10123-0103
(212) 947-3399
Email: info@karlyn.com
Key Contact - Specialty:
Ms. Cathryn Liggio, Director

Karp & Associates
931 N State Road 434 Ste 1201
Altamonte Springs, FL 32714-7050
(407) 292-4637
Fax: (407) 294-1695
Email: lindakarp3@aol.com
Summary: We have had many years in pharmaceutical/medical sales, management and marketing recruiting. The owner personally has a clinical background in nursing as well as medical sales and management experience.
Key Contact - Specialty:
Ms. Linda S. Karp, President & Owner -
Management
Functions: Management, Product Dev., Healthcare, Physicians, Nurses, Sales & Mktg., Sales Mgmt., HR Mgmt., Int'l.
Industries: Drugs Mfg., Medical Devices, Pharm Svcs., Biotech/Life Sciences, Healthcare

Karras Personnel Inc
2 Central Ave
Madison, NJ 07940-1864
(973) 966-6800
Email: karraspersonnel@mindspring.com
Web: karraspersonnel.home.mindspring.com
Summary: HR recruiting and placement for professionals providing solutions for: generalist, staffing, talent management, succession planning, employee relations, organizational development, training & development, compensation, benefits, HRIS, EEO/Affirmative Action and labor relations.
Key Contact - Specialty:
Mr. Bill Karras, Recruiter, Human Resources -
Human resources
Salary Minimum: $35,000
Functions: Board Members, HR Mgmt., Benefits, Staffing, Training
Industries: Generalist (All), Manufacturing, Food, Bev., Tobacco, Chemicals, Drugs Mfg., Medical Devices, Consumer Elect., Consumer Goods, Pharm Svcs., HR Services, Publishing, Telecoms

Kass/Abell & Associates
10780 Santa Monica Blvd Ste 200
Los Angeles, CA 90025-7614
(310) 475-4666
(415) 788-5719
Fax: (310) 475-0485
Email: attyplcmnt@kassabell.com
Web: www.kassabell.com
Summary: We have recruited and placed attorneys for corporate law departments and law firms. We are networked nationwide to assist attorneys wishing to relocate.
Key Contact - Specialty:
Mr. Peter J. Redgrove, Principal
Functions: Legal
Industries: Generalist (All), Legal

Kasten Management
(formerly known as FPC of Redondo Beach)
2223 Ruhland Ave Ste B
Redondo Beach, CA 90278-2401
(310) 371-7170
Fax: (425) 928-0901
Email: kastenmgt@aol.com
Summary: Technical positions in medical device, pharmaceutical and bio-technology industries, including engineering, R&D, manufacturing management, quality assurance, quality control and regulatory.
Key Contact - Specialty:
Mr. Marc Kasten, President - *Biotechnology, Pharmaceutical*
Salary Minimum: $50,000
Functions: Management, Board Members, Senior Mgmt., Middle Mgmt., Mfg., Materials Plng., Packaging, R&D, Engineering
Industries: Generalist (All), Manufacturing, Drugs Mfg., Medical Devices, Plastics, Rubber, Packaging

The Katonah Group Inc
33 Flying Point Rd Ste 203
Southampton, NY 11968-5279
(631) 287-9001
Email: info@katonahgroup.com
Web: www.katonahgroup.com
Summary: Our firm specializes in executive recruiting for life sciences (genomic & proteomic instrumentation), bioinformatics, cheminformatics, medical device, clinical diagnostics and scientific/analytical instrumentation companies. Our clients range from Fortune 500 to well-funded start-ups and our emphasis is on the establishment of long term relationships based on the development of a thorough understanding of our clients' needs, priorities and expectations.
Key Contact - Specialty:
Mr. Diederik Thiers, President
Salary Minimum: $75,000
Functions: Generalist (All)
Industries: Drugs Mfg., Medical Devices, Biotech/Life Sciences

The Katz Company Inc
15210 Amberly Dr Apt 1121
Tampa, FL 33647-2190
(813) 903-8750
(800) 398-8034
Fax: (813) 903-1765
Email: katzco@tampabay.rr.com
Web: www.thekatzco.com
Summary: An emergency medicine recruiting and consulting firm.
Key Contact - Specialty:
Ms. Barbara Katz
Salary Minimum: $150,000
Functions: Physicians
Industries: Healthcare

The Kaufman Agency
23681 Candlewood Way
West Hills, CA 91307-1311
(818) 587-9118
Fax: (818) 587-9121
Email: patrice@thekaufmanagency.com
Web: www.thekaufmanagency.com/
Summary: Our firm has specialists with many years experience in executive search for all professional and support levels of insurance industry positions, both temporary and permanent.

The wants and needs of each party are carefully matched to facilitate the decision making process.
Key Contact - Specialty:
Ms. Patrice Kaufman, Owner
Functions: Generalist (All), Management, Board Members
Industries: Insurance, Casualty, Claims, Life, Commercial, Re-Insurance

Jim Kay & Associates Inc
132 Ridge Ave Ste C
Bloomingdale, IL 60108-2963
(630) 825-1500
Fax: (630) 825-3919
Email: careers@jimkayassociates.com
Web: www.jimkayassociates.com
Summary: Cost effective, timely recruiting backed by a long history of client satisfaction in both retained and contingency search assignments. Specialization in high technology that includes semiconductor, telecom, and communications market places. We work from all levels from executive down to the individual contributor.
Key Contact - Specialty:
Mr. Jim Kay, President
Mr. Brian Pahl, Executive Vice President -
Acoustics, High technology, Medical (Devices), Semiconductors, Technical (Management)
Salary Minimum: $80,000
Functions: Generalist (All), Senior Mgmt., Middle Mgmt., Product Dev., CFOs, Systems Dev., R&D, Engineering
Industries: Generalist (All), Computer Equip., Consumer Elect., Misc. Mfg., Telecoms, Software

Kay Concepts Inc
1411 Norris Way
Tarpon Springs, FL 34688-9117
(800) 879-5850
Fax: (800) 879-5828
Email: info@kayconcepts.com
Web: www.kayconcepts.com
Summary: We are a full service firm specializing in pharmaceutical recruitment, architectural, and engineering.
Key Contact - Specialty:
Ms. Heidi Kay, CPC, President - *Manufacturing, Marketing*
Functions: Quality, Healthcare, Sales & Mktg., Mktg. Mgmt., IT, Systems Dev., Engineering
Industries: Software, Healthcare

The Kay Group of 5th Ave
350 5th Ave Ste 2205
New York, NY 10118-2391
(212) 947-4646
Email: kayrecruit@att.net
Web: thekaygroup.com
Summary: We are professional placement specialists, dedicated to making the right match. We focus on client/candidate chemistry and long term growth.
Key Contact - Specialty:
Mr. Bernard A. Feinberg, President
Mr. Joseph Kay, Consultant
Salary Minimum: $40,000
Functions: Senior Mgmt., Middle Mgmt., Healthcare, Advertising, Direct Mktg., PR, Finance, CFOs, Mgmt. Consultants
Industries: Metal Products, Legal, Mgmt. Consulting, Advertising, Publishing, New Media

KCS Search Group

100 West Rd Ste 300
Towson, MD 21204-2370
(410) 494-6595
Email: kcs@kcssearchgroup.com

Summary: Our firm specializes in the placement of sales, sales management, marketing and pre-sales professionals in the IT industry. Our firm conducts searches through a trusted network of affiliate firms.

Key Contact - Specialty:
Ms. Kathleen Stone, President

Salary Minimum: $75,000

Functions: Sales & Mktg.

Industries: Computer Equip., Software, Accounting SW, Database SW, Doc. Mgmt., Production SW, ERP SW, HR SW, Mfg. SW, Security SW, Training SW

KDK Associates LLC

575 Waterford Dr
Lake Zurich, IL 60047-2995
(847) 726-2902
Fax: (847) 726-2903
Email: kdkassociates@aol.com
Web: www.kdkassociates.com

Summary: Service oriented sales & marketing management recruiting firm specializing in the needs of consumer and business-to-business companies. We will take time to understand your company's goals and management needs.

Key Contact - Specialty:
Mr. Michael J. Neises, Recruiter, Management

Salary Minimum: $50,000

Functions: Materials, Sales & Mktg.

Industries: Generalist (All), Manufacturing, Wholesale, Retail, Finance, Services, Hospitality, Media, Communications, Packaging, Software

Keena Staffing Services

2 Progress Blvd
Queensbury, NY 12804-3202
(518) 793-9825
Fax: (518) 793-0224
Email: staff@keena.com
Web: www.keena.com

Summary: We handle all positions in the manufacturing sector, including production, quality control, logistics, distribution, HR, accounting and sales.

Key Contact - Specialty:
Ms. Connie Gerarde, Co-Founder & President - Finance

Salary Minimum: $50,000

Functions: Mfg.

Industries: Manufacturing

Wm. Kellogg and Associates Inc

(formerly known as Kellogg, Rottman & Associates)
388 Market St Ste 400
San Francisco, CA 94111-5313
(415) 296-2530
Fax: (415) 296-2580
Email: wkassociates@msn.com
Web: www.wkassociatesinc.com

Summary: Our firm specializes in mid-level to senior level searches within the financial services (banks, broker-dealers, investment companies and registered investment advisors) and consumer packaged goods industries.

Key Contact - Specialty:
Mr. Bill Kellogg, Owner

Salary Minimum: $65,000

Functions: Generalist (All)

Industries: Food, Bev., Tobacco, Banking, Invest. Banking, Brokers, Venture Cap., Mutual/Hedge Funds, Misc. Financial, Mgmt. Consulting, Packaging, Accounting SW

Jack Kelly & Partners LLC

210 E 60th St FL 2
New York, NY 10022-1461
(212) 754-2424
Fax: (212) 754-2442
Email: janet@jkandp.com
Web: www.jkandp.com

Summary: We are a premier consulting firm specializing in permanent placement for; design, architecture, 'to the trade' home furnishings and allied hospitality industries. A thorough understanding of the staffing needs of interior design firms, architecture firms, design center showrooms and their manufacturers, art and antique galleries, and allied hospitality industries allows us to serve a broad base of the country's most elite firms.

Key Contact - Specialty:
Mr. Jack Kelly, Owner
Ms. Janet Roda, Executive Director - *Furniture, Hospitality, Kitchen, Marketing, Sales*
Mr. Billy Clark - *Accounting, Administration*
Mr. Andrew Griffin - *Architecture, Design*
Mr. Patrick Kyle - *Architecture, Design*
Mr. Justin White - *Architecture, Design*

Salary Minimum: $100,000

Functions: Senior Mgmt., Middle Mgmt., Admin. Svcs., Sales & Mktg., Mktg. Mgmt., Customer Svc., Sales Reps., Architects, Design, Hospitality

Industries: Generalist (All), Lumber, Furniture, Wholesale, Non-Classifiable

Kerry-Ben Kelly Executive Search

9835 E Sidewinder Trl
Scottsdale, AZ 85262-4400
(480) 575-6987
Email: kbksearch@aol.com

Summary: Business experience as an executive for leading retailers. We build relationships with clients and candidates.

Key Contact - Specialty:
Mr. Kerry-Ben Kelly, Owner - *Business to business, Healthcare, Hospitality, Retail, Wholesale*

Salary Minimum: $40,000

Functions: Management, Senior Mgmt., Middle Mgmt., Sales & Mktg., Mktg. Mgmt., Sales Mgmt., HR Mgmt., Finance

Industries: Generalist (All), Computer Equip., Consumer Elect., Wholesale, Retail, Communications, Call Centers, Digital, Wireless, Healthcare

Kelly Financial Resources

3333 N Mayfair Rd
Milwaukee, WI 53222-3219
(414) 290-9503
Fax: (414) 290-9531
Email: rick_haagensen@kellyservices.com
Web: www.kellyfinancial.com

Summary: We locate, evaluate and place in direct hire positions: accounting/finance professionals with leading employers. We work with the senior accountant to the CFO. We have a staff that provides senior level project/temp projects for candidates between jobs.

Key Contact - Specialty:
Mr. Rick Haagensen, Senior Financial Recruiter

Salary Minimum: $40,000

Functions: Generalist (All)

Industries: Food, Bev., Tobacco, Metal Products, Misc. Mfg., Finance, Banking, Mutual/Hedge Funds, Misc. Financial, Accounting

Kelly Law Registry

(a Kelly Services company)
90 State House Sq Fl 12
Hartford, CT 06103-3702
(860) 247-7440
Fax: (860) 548-7740
Email: klr17w1@kellylawregistry.com
Web: www.kellylawregistry.com

Summary: Full-service placement firm engaged in the permanent placement of general counsel, in-house counsel and paralegals and temp placement of attorneys and paralegals and legal teams for document reviews/due diligence.

Key Contact - Specialty:
Mr. Mark Davies, Managing Director

Functions: Generalist (All), Legal, Attorneys, Paralegals

Industries: Generalist (All), Legal

Kemper Associates

680 N Lake Shore Dr Apt 1408
Chicago, IL 60611-4484
(312) 944-6551
(312) 944-2835
Fax: (928) 222-4247
Email: kemperassoc@hotmail.com
Web: www.kemperassociates.net

Summary: We are an executive search firm (both retained and contingency) specializing in searches in A-V, video and business meetings/events production. Some positions available: sales account executives, video editors and performance improvement designers.

Key Contact - Specialty:
Mr. Phillip H. Kemper, Owner

Functions: Management

Industries: Hospitality, Broadcast, Film, Entertainment SW

Kenan Soper Bryant Ltd

936 W 4th St Ste 300
Winston Salem, NC 27101-2564
(336) 777-8777
Email: info@ksbconsulting.com

Summary: Our firm specializes in executive search, technology search & consulting, and search in the financial, accounting, marketing and technical sales fields. We service a diverse client base across business sectors such as technology, manufacturing, distribution and service (financial, medical, advertising, etc.).

Key Contact - Specialty:
Mr. David Bryant, Principal
Mr. Brian Soper, Principal
Mr. Bo Kenan, Principal

Functions: Sales & Mktg., Finance, IT

Industries: Generalist (All), Banking, Accounting

Kendall & Davis Company Inc

11325 Concord Village Ave
Saint Louis, MO 63123-6905
(314) 843-8838
(866) 675-3755
Fax: (314) 843-2262
Email: info@kendallanddavis.com
Web: www.kendallanddavis.com

Summary: To bring communities, hospitals and groups together with the appropriate physician, in a manner that is effective and rewarding for all parties.

Key Contact - Specialty:
Mr. James C. Kendall, President & Chief Executive Officer - *Physicians*

Functions: Generalist (All), Physicians

Industries: Healthcare, Hospitals

Kendall Placement Group (KPG)

14528 S Outer 40 Ste 444
Chesterfield, MO 63017-5743
(314) 985-1100
(877) 574-5627
Email: mike.kendall@kpginc.com
Web: www.kpginc.com

Summary: Our firm specializes in providing the regions top technology centers with IT consulting and staffing services.

Key Contact - Specialty:
Mr. Mike Kendall, President & Chief Executive Officer
Mr. David Hill, Manager, Finance
Ms. Debra Wannstedt, Operations Manager
Mr. Greg Wallen, Manager, Sales
Ms. Laurie Wilson, Manager, Recruiting

Salary Minimum: $45,000

Functions: IT

Industries: Generalist (All)

Branches:
2300 Main St Fl 9
Two Pershing Square
Kansas City, MO 64108-2408
(816) 448-3158
Fax: (816) 448-3794
Email: tony.taylor@kpginc.com
Key Contact - Specialty:
Mr. Tony Taylor, Recruiter

Kenmore Executives Inc

PO Box 66
Boca Raton, FL 33429-0066
(561) 392-0700
Fax: (561) 750-0818
Email: inquiries@kenmoreexecutives.com
Web: www.kenmoreexecutives.com

Summary: Specializing in the placement of management consultants with consulting firms and internal consulting organizations experienced in the implementation of concepts supporting business re-engineering, Lean manufacturing, change management, downsizing, supply chain management, management development, total quality management and strategic planning.

Key Contact - Specialty:
Ms. Marilyn Orr, Principal
Mr. Steven LoPrete, Principal
Mr. Joseph LoPrete, Principal

Salary Minimum: $60,000

Functions: Mfg., Productivity, Materials, Sales Mgmt., Training, Finance, IT, MIS Mgmt., Mgmt. Consultants

Industries: Generalist (All), Mgmt. Consulting

Kennison & Associates Inc

21 Custom House St Ste 710
Boston, MA 02110-3525
(617) 478-2888
(617) 478-2222
Email: info@kennisonassociates.com
Web: www.kennisonassociates.com

Summary: We earn the fee. Specialized and experienced. We provide a no-nonsense approach to filling your sensitive and important positions. Honesty, integrity and professionalism practiced.

Key Contact - Specialty:
Ms. Jane Kennison, Founder
Mr. Peter O'Connor, Principal
Ms. Kim Armstrong, Consultant
Ms. Lisa Clifford, Consultant
Mr. Kevin McNeal, Consultant - *Pharmaceutical*

Salary Minimum: $25,000

Functions: Generalist (All)

Industries: Generalist (All)

Kerr & Company Executive Search

13330 Noel Rd Apt 133
Dallas, TX 75240-5084
(214) 459-4455
Email: laura@hunt4exec.com

Summary: We are a generalist firm assisting clients in a broad range of industries. We are extremely client-centered and work primarily on retained/exclusive searches, but also conduct contingency searches on an exclusive basis.

Key Contact - Specialty:
Ms. Laura K. Weaver, President - *Accounting (Public), Architecture, Capital markets, Engineering, Hotels*

Salary Minimum: $65,000

Functions: Senior Mgmt., Finance, CFOs, Engineering, Specialized Svcs., Architects

Industries: Generalist (All), Construction, Printing, Finance, Brokers, Services, Architectural Svcs., IT Implementation, Higher Ed., Hotels, Resorts, Clubs, Telecoms, Call Centers, Wireless, Network Infrastructure, Real Estate, Software

Kerr Executive Recruiting

1439 Fulbright Ave
Redlands, CA 92373-4937
(909) 798-5377
Fax: (909) 798-5377
Email: john_kerr@eee.org

Summary: We have experience in specialty plastics recruiting and significant personal major management background experience. Normally retained and contingent searches can be realistically scheduled.

Key Contact - Specialty:
Mr. John B. Kerr, Jr., President & Owner - *Plastics, Rubber*

Salary Minimum: $70,000

Functions: Generalist (All), Middle Mgmt., Product Dev., Plant Mgmt., Productivity, Finance, Engineering, Technicians

Industries: Generalist (All), Manufacturing, Plastics, Rubber, Packaging

Kersey & Associates Inc

513 Usdasdi Dr
Brevard, NC 28712-7473
(828) 966-9030
Fax: (828) 966-9032

Email: davidkersey@topechelon.com
Web: www.kersey.com

Summary: We are a retained/contingency professional search firm doing consulting, contracting and direct hire placements. Our specialties are IT, Finance and Management

Key Contact - Specialty:
Mr. David Kersey, President

Salary Minimum: $45,000

Functions: Finance, IT, MIS Mgmt.

Industries: Generalist (All), Manufacturing, Development SW

Blair Kershaw Associates

1903 W 8th St
Erie, PA 16505-4936
(814) 454-5872
Fax: (814) 452-4598

Summary: We recruit for manufacturing, engineering, financial, medical, and management people.

Key Contact - Specialty:
Mr. Blair Kershaw, President - *Engineering, Finance, Management, Manufacturing*

Salary Minimum: $40,000

Functions: Generalist (All), Middle Mgmt., Mfg., Product Dev., Production, Quality, CFOs, Engineering

Industries: Generalist (All), Food, Bev., Tobacco, Plastics, Rubber, Metal Products, Machine, Appliance, Misc. Mfg.

Franklin Key Associates

831 Washington St
Franklin, MA 02038-3323
(508) 520-3500
Fax: (508) 520-3535
Email: bob@franklinkey.com
Web: www.franklinkey.com

Summary: We are a premier IS search and placement firm. We provide executive search, professional placement and staffing consulting. We believe that just meeting our clients' needs is ordinary; we strive to exceed expectations through a strong team approach that aligns the goals of everyone involved. We work with those who aim to be the best at what they do, because our clients ask us to be the best at what we do.

Key Contact - Specialty:
Mr. Robert Norton, Jr., CSP, Principal

Salary Minimum: $50,000

Functions: Board Members, Senior Mgmt., IT, MIS Mgmt., Systems Dev., Systems Implem., Systems Support, Network Admin., DB Admin.

Industries: Computer Equip., Misc. Mfg., Invest. Banking, Mutual/Hedge Funds, Mgmt. Consulting, E-commerce, IT Implementation, Telecoms, Call Centers, Wireless, Network Infrastructure, Software, Accounting SW, Database SW, Development SW, ERP SW, Mfg. SW, Marketing SW, Networking, Comm. SW, Security SW, System SW

Key Corporate Services LLC

9746 Olympia Dr
Fishers, IN 46037-8759
(317) 598-9450
Email: dkerns@keycorporateservices.com
Web: www.keycorporateservices.com

Summary: Recruitment within the chemical, life science, manufacturing and commercial construction industries.

Key Contact - Specialty:
Mr. David Kerns, Partner - *Biopharmaceutical, Biotechnology, Business development, Chemical, Life Sciences*
Mr. Jeff Wilson, Partner - *Construction, Manufacturing*
Mrs. Diane Wessel, National Account Manager - *Construction, General contractors*

Salary Minimum: $50,000

Functions: Plant Mgmt., Quality, Sales & Mktg., Sales Mgmt., Sales Reps., HR Mgmt.

Industries: Construction, Manufacturing, Chemicals, Soap, Perf., Cosmtcs., Drugs Mfg., Plastics, Rubber, Paints, Petro. Products

Key Employment

45 Sapphire Ln
Franklin Park, NJ 08823-1642
(732) 422-0240
Email: gsilberger@aol.com

Summary: We offer search and recruiting for engineering, administration, manufacturing, laboratory, technical sales & marketing. Clients include chemical, power engineering, cogeneration, plastics, electrical, electro mechanical, petroleum, environmental, pulp and paper industries.

Key Contact - Specialty:
Mr. Gary Silberger, President - *Sales*

Salary Minimum: $40,000

Functions: Senior Mgmt., Plant Mgmt., Purchasing, Materials Plng., Mktg. Research, Mktg. Mgmt., Engineering

Industries: Generalist (All), Energy, Utilities, Construction, Food, Bev., Tobacco, Printing, Chemicals, Paints, Petro. Products, Consumer Elect., Advertising

Key Recruit Inc

PO Box 1531
Voorhees, NJ 08043-7531
(856) 772-0830
Fax: (908) 325-0357
Email: andrewy@keyrecruit.com
Web: www.keyrecruit.com

Summary: We are recognized as a leading recruiting firm specializing in the search and selection of senior level management for the biopharmaceutical, biotech, and biomedical device industry. Our specialty is delivering highly qualified pre-screened professionals for your regulatory and clinical affairs, Q.A., Q.C., research & development, business development, sales & marketing, and manufacturing & operations openings.

Key Contact - Specialty:
Mr. Andrew Youngelson, Director, Recruitment

Functions: Senior Mgmt.

Industries: Medical Devices, Venture Cap., Pharm Svcs., Engineering Svcs., Biotech/Life Sciences, Healthcare

Key Recruiters

3390 Peachtree Rd NE Ste 1000
Atlanta, GA 30326-1108
(404) 233-8366
(770) 422-1783
Fax: (770) 422-0940
Email: keyjobs@bellsouth.net
Web: www.keyrecruitersonline.com

Summary: We have experience in executive recruiting and corporate staffing, operations, sales, management and IT.

Key Contact - Specialty:
Ms. Pattie Atkinson

Functions: Generalist (All), Management, Board Members, Senior Mgmt.

Industries: Generalist (All)

Keysearch International

PO Box 910370
Saint George, UT 84791-0370
(435) 634-1196
Fax: (435) 634-1195
Email: keysearch@keysearch.net
Web: www.keysearch.net

Summary: We are an executive search firm specializing in the transportation industry, with a merger and acquisition division.

Key Contact - Specialty:
Ms. Deborah L. Keys, President

Salary Minimum: $65,000

Functions: Generalist (All), Senior Mgmt.

Industries: Transportation, Services

Kforce

1001 E Palm Ave
Tampa, FL 33605-3551
(813) 552-5000
(888) 663-3626
Fax: (813) 552-2493
Email: kforce@kforce.com
Web: www.kforce.com

Summary: We are a publicly traded full-service specialty staffing firm providing flexible and permanent staffing solutions for organizations and career management for individuals in the specialty skill areas of IT, finance & accounting, pharmaceutical, healthcare and scientific.

Key Contact - Specialty:
Mr. David L. Dunkel, Chairman & Chief Executive Officer
Mr. William L. Sanders, President
Mr. Joseph J. Liberatore, Chief Financial Officer
Ms. Shannon Brannigan, Recruiter

Functions: Generalist (All), Management, Healthcare, HR Mgmt., Finance, CFOs, IT, Engineering

Industries: Generalist (All), Textiles, Apparel, Paper, Drugs Mfg., Medical Devices, Paints, Petro. Products, Retail, Finance, Banking, Invest. Banking, Brokers, Venture Cap., Misc. Financial, Non-profits, Pharm Svcs., Legal, Accounting, Equip Svcs., Mgmt. Consulting, HR Services, IT Implementation, Higher Ed., Hospitality, Call Centers, Network Infrastructure, Insurance, Software, Networking, Comm. SW, Biotech/Life Sciences, Healthcare, Hospitals, Long-term/Home Care, Women's

Branches:
97 E Brokaw Rd Ste 130
San Jose, CA 95112-4209
(408) 487-2800
(408) 501-1600
Fax: (408) 436-1842
Key Contact - Specialty:
Ms. Michelle Pletkin, Recruiter - *Finance*

6303 Blue Lagoon Dr Ste 135
Miami, FL 33126-6022
(786) 388-3290
Fax: (786) 3883292
Key Contact - Specialty:
Mr. Rich Raniere, Recruiter

4170 Ashford Dunwoody Rd NE Ste 285
Atlanta, GA 30319-1400
(404) 459-2300
Fax: (404) 459-2301

Key Contact - Specialty:
Ms. Christy Brooks, Recruiter

440 S Lasalle St Ste 3904
Chicago, IL 60605-5029
(888) 913-0111
Fax: (312) 913-1180
Key Contact - Specialty:
Ms. Crystal Schroeder

111 Monument Cir Ste 4540
Indianapolis, IN 46204-5103
(317) 656-2700
Fax: (317) 682-6100
Key Contact - Specialty:
Mr. Greg Bell, Recruiter

120 E Baltimore St Ste 2121
Baltimore, MD 21202-1617
(410) 454-1500
Fax: (410) 727-6808
Key Contact - Specialty:
Ms. Michele Kavanagh, Recruiter

350 5th Ave Ste 1700
New York, NY 10118-1700
(212) 883-7300
Fax: (212) 953-3504
Key Contact - Specialty:
Ms. Adele Chodorow, Recruiter - *Finance*

709 Westchester Ave Ste L3
White Plains, NY 10604-3171
(914) 640-1100
Fax: (914) 251-9565
Key Contact - Specialty:
Mr. Mark Davison, Recruiter - *Finance*

3 Summit Park Dr Ste 550
Independence, OH 44131-6902
(216) 643-8100
Fax: (216) 328-5909
Key Contact - Specialty:
Mr. Kurt Lang

KGA Inc

1320 Greenway Ter Apt 1
Brookfield, WI 53005-6917
(262) 786-5209
Fax: (262) 786-7961
Email: k.gunkel@usa.net

Summary: Extensive experience exclusively recruiting and placing HR professionals. Specialize in all HR placements of candidates with three years or more experience, to include compensation, benefits, staffing, training & development, as well as HR management up to and including VP level for all industries.

Key Contact - Specialty:
Mr. Keith J. Gunkel, President - *Human resources*

Salary Minimum: $50,000

Functions: HR Mgmt.

Industries: HR Services

Ki-Tech Executive Search

955 N 400 W Bldg 10
North Salt Lake, UT 84054-2616
(888) 283-0399
(801) 517-3602
Email: staff@ki-tech.com
Web: www.ki-tech.com

Summary: We are an elite small firm specializing in high-technology placement, information technology, aerospace/defense, electronics, IC design, biotechnology, marketing and technical sales professionals both management and hands-on contributors; software/hardware engineers, sales, product marketing and management. We

place senior management, technical, mid-level to executive placement.

Key Contact - Specialty:
Mr. James Mellos, President & Principal - *High technology, Presidents, Senior management*
Dr. Thomas Bakehorn, Vice President - *CEOs, CIOs, Marketing, Sales, Senior management*
Ms. Angelica Bailey, Recruiter - *Aerospace, Computers (Software), Defense, Engineering, Technical*
Mr. Bruce Waltz, Technical Recruiter - *Aerospace, Defense, Networking, Telecommunications*
Mr. Craig Taylor, Technical Recruiter - *Computers (Software), Engineering, Technical*

Salary Minimum: $50,000

Functions: Management, Senior Mgmt., Product Dev., Sales & Mktg., IT, Systems Dev., Engineering, Eng. Design, Design, Int'l.

Industries: Generalist (All), Medical Devices, Computer Equip., Consumer Elect., Misc. Mfg., Electronic, Elec. Components, Robotics, Semiconductors, Consumer Goods, Engineering Svcs., Communications, Telecoms, Digital, Wireless, Fiber Optic, Network Infrastructure, RF/Microwave, Defense, Homeland Security, Aerospace, Software, Accounting SW, Industry Specific SW, Networking, Comm. SW, Security SW, System SW

The Kidder Group Inc

217 E Stone Ave Ste 21
Greenville, SC 29609-5655
(864) 271-8880
Fax: (877) 473-3151
Email: mail@thekiddergroup.com
Web: www.thekiddergroup.com

Summary: We are a professional recruiting firm that concentrate on working with companies in the Southeastern United States and specialize in recruiting professionals with a background in manufacturing and expertise in the fields of executives, engineering, quality, management, human resources, finance, accounting, sales, supply chain management, information systems, and technology.

Key Contact - Specialty:
Mr. Garrett Tompkins, President & Chief Executive Officer
Ms. Kim Tompkins, Vice President - *Marketing*
Dr. Dale Tompkins, Director, Engineering Consulting Div - *Engineering*
Mr. Bill Conway, Recruiter, Licensed Professional - *Manufacturing (Management)*
Mr. John Moore, Professional Recruiter - *Electronics, Engineering, Materials, Quality, Research & development*
Ms. Carin Meerdink, Professional Recruiter - *Accounting (General), Engineering, Finance, Management, Quality*

Salary Minimum: $45,000

Functions: Generalist (All), Mfg., Product Dev., Production, Automation, Quality, Purchasing, Engineering

Industries: Generalist (All), Manufacturing, Machine, Appliance, Computer Equip., Test, Measure Equip., Finance, Brokers, Accounting, HR Services, Packaging

Kimball Personnel Sales Recruiters

2 Cross Rd
Hubbardston, MA 01452-1615
(508) 829-8849
Fax: (508) 829-4862

Summary: Staffing and recruitment of sales personnel for the telecom, office products, copier, medical, industrial, engineering, computer, retail-service, communications and insurance industries.

Key Contact - Specialty:
Mr. John Kimball, CPC, Owner - *Sales*

Functions: Generalist (All), Healthcare, Sales & Mktg., Sales Mgmt., Customer Svc.

Industries: Generalist (All), Media, Telecoms, Insurance

Kimmel & Associates Inc

25 Page Ave
Asheville, NC 28801-2707
(828) 251-9900
Fax: (828) 251-9955
Email: kimmel@kimmel.com
Web: www.kimmel.com

Summary: We specialize in helping companies and advancing the careers of professionals, from entry level to CEO, in construction, real estate development, solid waste, distribution, transportation and freight forwarding. We have worked diligently to know these industries and the people who drive them forward.

Key Contact - Specialty:
Mr. Joe W. Kimmel, President - *Construction*

Salary Minimum: $35,000

Functions: Management, Senior Mgmt., Distribution, Sales & Mktg., HR Mgmt., Finance, CFOs, Engineering

Industries: Generalist (All), Energy, Utilities, Construction, Manufacturing, Transportation, Architectural Svcs., Logistics Svcs., Supply Chain Mgmt., Real Estate

Kincaid Group Inc (KGI)

11230 West Ave Ste 1105
San Antonio, TX 78213-1359
(210) 308-9221
Email: kincaid@kincaidgroup.com
Web: www.kincaidgroup.com

Summary: We are a search consulting firm specializing in healthcare and executive placement. We assist organizations throughout the entire process of personnel activities from recruiting and training to termination and outplacement.

Key Contact - Specialty:
Mr. Raymond W. Kincaid, President

Functions: Generalist (All), Senior Mgmt., Healthcare

Industries: Generalist (All), Banking, Misc. Financial, Accounting, Mgmt. Consulting, HR Services, Healthcare, Non-Classifiable

Kinetix Talent Solutions

115 Perimeter Center Pl NE Ste 1045
Atlanta, GA 30346-1245
(770) 390-8360
Fax: (770) 390-8369
Email: recruit@kinetixhr.com
Web: www.kinetixhr.com

Summary: Our firm provides professional staffing and recruiting services in the following practice areas: human resources, information technology, accounting & finance and administrative & customer service on a national basis.

Key Contact - Specialty:
Ms. Shannon Russo, Chief Executive Officer
Mr. Timothy Barchie, Chief Financial Officer - *Accounting, Accounting (Public), Administration, Audits, C-level*

Salary Minimum: $50,000

Functions: Generalist (All)

Industries: Generalist (All)

Branches:
200 Galleria Pkwy SE Ste 260
Atlanta, GA 30339-5962
(770) 988-8484
Email: recruit@kinetixhr.com
Key Contact - Specialty:
Ms. Kimberly Hunt, Operations Manager - *Administration, Finance, Human resources, Information Technology, Non-profit*

Michael King Associates Inc

600 3rd Ave Fl 25
New York, NY 10016-1908
(212) 687-5490
(800) 367-3157
Fax: (212) 599-5323
Email: mka@michaelking.com
Web: www.michaelking.com

Summary: Specializes in making matches between significant Wall Street producers and premier financial firms.

Key Contact - Specialty:
Mr. Michael King, President
Ms. Dolores Bullard, Managing Partner

Functions: Management, Senior Mgmt., Sales & Mktg., Cash Mgmt.

Industries: Retail, Finance, Invest. Banking, Brokers

Michael D. King

PO Box 1208
Helotes, TX 78023-1208
(210) 695-5223
Email: king@michaeldking.com
Web: www.michaeldking.com

Summary: Nationwide executive recruiter with over 26 years of networking experience, specializing in professional search and placement. Areas of expertise include manufacturing operations, quality engineering, logistics, facilities, administration, and human resources.

Key Contact - Specialty:
Mr. Michael D. King, Recruiter

Functions: Plant Mgmt.

Industries: Manufacturing, Paper, Plastics, Rubber, Paints, Petro. Products, Machine, Appliance, Motor Vehicles, Finance

The Kinsa Group

9875 S Franklin Dr
Franklin, WI 53132-8895
(800) 403-3663
(414) 421-2000
Fax: (414) 421-6000
Email: recruiter@kinsa.com
Web: www.kinsa.com

Summary: A large search firm dedicated to the food, beverage and nutraceutical/pharmaceutical industries offering diverse search options and discipline experts.

Key Contact - Specialty:
Mr. Charles M. Nolan

Salary Minimum: $60,000

Functions: Generalist (All)

Industries: Manufacturing, Food, Bev., Tobacco, Drugs Mfg., Biotech/Life Sciences

Kirby/Bates Associates LLC
(formerly known as Bates & Associates)
1 Bala Ave Ste 234
Bala Cynwyd, PA 19004-3207
(610) 667-1800
Fax: (610) 660-9408
Email: corporate@kirbybates.com
Web: www.kirbybates.com

Summary: Ours is a national healthcare consulting firm committed to strengthening the patient care infrastructure through executive search, interim management and consulting services, all focused on nursing and patient care services.

Key Contact - Specialty:
Ms. Karen Kirby, RN, MSN, President & Chief Executive Officer
Ms. Pam DeCampli, RN, MSN, Vice President
Ms. Kathy Sherman, RN, MSN, Senior Search Consultant
Ms. Peggy Loughery, RN, Search Consultant - *Consulting*
Ms. Michele Murphy, Executive Assistant

Salary Minimum: $100,000

Functions: Healthcare, Nurses, Health Admin., Staffing

Industries: Mgmt. Consulting, Healthcare, Hospitals

The Kirdonn Sales Pros
(also known as Sales Pros Inc)
106 W 11th St Ste 1520
Kansas City, MO 64105-1806
(816) 474-0700
Fax: (816) 474-0702
Email: salespros@comcast.net
Web: www.kirdonn.com

Summary: Presence placing sales, sales management, marketing pros specializing in telecom, high-technology, medical, pharm consumer, industrial, advertising, office products and builder trades.

Key Contact - Specialty:
Mr. Jim Panus, CPC, President - *Sales*
Mr. Jay Panus, Vice President
Mr. Scott Richlin, Vice President
Mr. Jaime Panus, Vice President

Functions: Generalist (All), Senior Mgmt., Sales & Mktg.

Industries: Manufacturing, Food, Bev., Tobacco, Printing, Consumer Elect., Transportation, Finance, Services, Hospitality, Media, Packaging, Software, Biotech/Life Sciences, Healthcare

LC Kirk & Company
400 E Monroe Ave
Saint Louis, MO 63122-6336
(800) 708-2096
Fax: (314) 966-3454
Email: brian@lckirk.com
Web: www.lckirk.com

Summary: We are a proactive search and placement firm. Using a team approach, we access our network of relationships in order to deliver the most highly qualified candidates in a particular market. We use personal interaction with clients and candidates in order to obtain the information required for successful executive search.

Key Contact - Specialty:
Mr. Brian Kirk, Partner
Ms. Meghan Kirk, Recruiter
Mr. Jake Corrigan, Partner - *Financial services, Healthcare, Investment management, Private equity, Technology*

Functions: Senior Mgmt., Product Dev., Sales & Mktg., Sales Mgmt., Direct Mktg., Sales Reps.

Industries: Invest. Banking, Mutual/Hedge Funds

Kirkbride Associates Inc
3020 Issaquah Pine Lake Rd SE
PMB 72
Sammamish, WA 98075-7253
(425) 557-4602
(888) 764-9782
Fax: (425) 391-6991
Email: bobk@isomedia.com
Web: www.kirkbrideassoc.com

Summary: HVAC/R, building controls, senior/executive management, sales & marketing, project management, engineering, facility management, energy, general construction, electrical contracting, fire/life/safety and security.

Key Contact - Specialty:
Mr. Robert Kirkbride, Senior Partner - *Energy, Engineering, Marketing, Sales*
Mr. Greg Waters, Senior Partner
Mr. Al Gross, Recruiter - *Engineering, Sales*

Salary Minimum: $45,000

Functions: Board Members, Automation, Sales & Mktg., Engineering

Industries: Energy, Utilities, Construction, Services, Engineering Svcs., Property/Facility Mgmt., Marketing SW, Security SW, Non-Classifiable

Kistenmacher Recruiters of Dallas
6336 Greenville Ave Ste D
Dallas, TX 75206-1303
(214) 234-0909
Fax: (214) 722-1309
Email: doris.k@earthlink.net

Summary: We are involved with making permanent placements and have been active in placing candidates since 1976. Incorporated in the state of Texas since 1985. We focus in Manufacturing & Industrial for Upper Management caliber candidates with off-shore experience. Hands on expereince in providing candidates in oil & gas, utilities and foundries. In conjunction with augmentation there are constructiom companies whom we provide technical and management candidates.

Key Contact - Specialty:
Mrs. Doris Kistenmacher, President & Recruiter - *Consumer, Consumer (Packaged Goods), Cosmetics, Food & beverage, Medical*

Functions: Management, Mfg.

Industries: Medical Devices, Plastics, Rubber, Metal Products, Test, Measure Equip., Misc. Mfg., Electronic, Elec. Components

KLA Search Inc
708 Florsheim Dr
Libertyville, IL 60048-5001
(847) 438-1830
Fax: (866) 435-6339
Email: klasearch@klasearch.com
Web: www.klasearch.com

Summary: Retail search firm.

Key Contact - Specialty:
Ms. Kelly L. Anderson-Singer, CPC, President - *Retail*

Salary Minimum: $40,000

Functions: Generalist (All)

Industries: Retail

KLR Placement Services
951 N Main St
Providence, RI 02904-5759
(401) 274-2001
Fax: (401) 831-4018
Email: thebestpeople@klrplacement.com
Web: www.klrplacement.com

Summary: We specialize in the placement of accounting/financial and information technology professionals. We have significant experience in the financial and technology fields, we offer many opportunities to the candidate as well as the employer. Our goal is to add value to the recruiting process by working as a business partner with our clients. Each member of our team strives to exceed client expectations in all instances, by stressing timely, personalized service. Our experience and complete commitment to quality sets us apart from our competition.

Key Contact - Specialty:
Mr. Jason Medeiros, Director, Recruiting - *Accounting, Administration, CFOs, Controllers, Operations*

Salary Minimum: $75,000

Functions: Senior Mgmt.

Industries: Manufacturing, Food, Bev., Tobacco, Medical Devices, Consumer Goods, Retail, Finance, Non-profits, Entertainment, Sports, New Media

KMC Resources Inc
PO Box 90248
Austin, TX 78709-0248
(512) 288-9708
Fax: (512) 288-1979
Email: resume@kmcresources.com
Web: www.kmcresources.com

Summary: A recruiting, placement and outplacement service agency specializing in the following industries: finance, accounting, law, healthcare administration and physician & nursing recruitment, restaurant operations & management, and foodservice operations, sales & management. We are skilled in the recruitment of senior positions in those fields. We also place COOs, regional VPs and other operations and sales executives in the restaurant and foodservice industries.

Key Contact - Specialty:
Mr. Kevin Cromack, President

Functions: Physicians, Sales Mgmt., HR Mgmt., CFOs

Industries: Restaurants, Quick Service Restaurants, Healthcare, Hospitals

Joyce C Knauff & Associates
PO Box 624
Wilmette, IL 60091-0624
(847) 251-7284
Fax: (847) 251-6945
Email: joyce@jckassociates.com
Web: www.jckassociates.com

Summary: We are a search firm specializing in the infromation technology function of corporations and consulting firms.

Key Contact - Specialty:
Ms. Joyce C. Knauff, President - *MIS*

Salary Minimum: $60,000

Functions: MIS Mgmt., Systems Analysis, Systems Dev., Systems Implem., Systems Support, Specialized Svcs.

Industries: Generalist (All)

Dennis J Knox & Company

PO Box 4221
San Dimas, CA 91773-8221
(909) 599-9632
Fax: (949) 255-9046
Email: dennisknox@usa.net

Summary: We specialize in real estate
development and construction, architecture/design
nationwide. Our emphasis is commercial, retail,
residential and restaurant construction, however
we are also expanding our service into mixed-use
and high-rises. We also cover finance/accounting
professionals within the industry designations

Key Contact - Specialty:
Mr. Dennis Knox, Managing Principal

Salary Minimum: $65,000

Functions: Management, Board Members, Senior
Mgmt., Middle Mgmt., Finance, CFOs,
Budgeting, Taxes, M&A, Bldg. Contractors

Industries: Construction, Finance, Banking,
Invest. Banking, Misc. Financial, Accounting,
Hospitality, Quick Service Restaurants,
Entertainment, Real Estate, Property/Facility
Mgmt.

Koa Networks Inc

1017 El Camino Real # 300
Redwood City, CA 94063-1691
(650) 474-1300
Fax: (650) 474-1301
Email: tom@koa-networks.com
Web: koa-networks.com

Summary: Specialists in the wireless field, both
hardware and software engineers.

Key Contact - Specialty:
Mr. Tom Hanson, Team Leader

Functions: Generalist (All), Engineering

Industries: Computer Equip., Consumer Elect.,
Semiconductors, Telecoms, Digital, Wireless,
Fiber Optic, Network Infrastructure,
RF/Microwave, Software, Development SW,
Security SW, System SW

Koerner & Associates Inc

750 Old Hickory Blvd
Nashville, TN 37209-5110
(615) 371-6162
Fax: (615) 371-6172
Email: pkoerner@koernerassociates.com
Web: www.koernerassociates.com

Summary: We specialize in the search and
placement of attorneys. As one of the first attorney
search firms in our state, we take pride in our
professionalism and ethical manner of doing
business. We place attorneys for law firms,
corporations and financial institutions.

Key Contact - Specialty:
Ms. Pam L. Koerner, President

Salary Minimum: $50,000

Functions: Attorneys

Industries: Generalist (All)

Koll-Fairfield LLC

(also known as Z. Headhunters LLC)
397 Post Rd
Darien, CT 06820-3647
(203) 655-5001
Fax: (203) 656-2667
Email: careers@kfsearch.com
Web: www.kfsearch.com

Summary: We are a full-service boutique
recruiting firm offering contingency and variations
of retained search options to the accounting,

finance and IT community. We are a firm
dedicated to providing high quality candidates for
staffing solutions and quick results.

Key Contact - Specialty:
Mr. Richard Champagne, Principal - *Accounting,
Accounting (Big 4,General), Finance, Financial*
Mr. Bruce Stalowicz, Principal - *Accounting (Big
4,General), Finance, Financial*
Mr. Thomas McCabe, PMP, CSSMB, Director,
IS & IT Recruiting - *Information Systems,
Information Technology, Quality, Six Sigma,
Technical (Management)*

Salary Minimum: $80,000

Functions: Finance, CFOs, Budgeting, IT, MIS
Mgmt., Systems Implem.

Industries: Generalist (All)

Michael Kosmetos & Associates Inc

333 Babbitt Rd Ste 300
Cleveland, OH 44123-1636
(216) 261-1950
Fax: (216) 261-9796

Summary: Our staff is non-commissioned and we
approach projects as a search team. With many
years of combined experience this team approach
allows us to be expeditious and extremely
thorough.

Key Contact - Specialty:
Mr. Michael Kosmetos, President - *Retail*

Salary Minimum: $35,000

Functions: Senior Mgmt., Middle Mgmt.,
Distribution, HR Mgmt.

Industries: Retail

Dana Kowen Associates

PO Box 547308
Orlando, FL 32854-7308
(407) 246-1502
Fax: (407) 210-0464
Email: resumes@dkarecruiting.com
Web: www.dkarecruiting.com

Summary: We are an executive search and
recruitment firm specializing in the identification,
evaluation and placement of uniquely talented
sales professionals. We are committed to
providing the highest quality and caliber of
services. We focus on establishing long term
relationships with both employers and candidates
in lieu of quick placements.

Key Contact - Specialty:
Ms. Dana Kowen, President

Salary Minimum: $75,000

Functions: Sales & Mktg.

Industries: Printing, Publishing

Kozlin Associates Inc

9280 Transit Rd
East Amherst, NY 14051-1622
(716) 634-5955
Fax: (716) 626-0549
Email: jeffk@kozlin.com
Web: www.kozlin.com

Summary: Our company is a contingency/retained
search firm serving the manufacturing industry.
Our firm conducts research for all types of
engineers, as well as mid to upper-level managers.

Key Contact - Specialty:
Mr. Jeffrey M. Kozlin, President
Mr. Brian Weber, Recruiter

Salary Minimum: $40,000

Functions: Mfg.

Industries: Generalist (All)

KP Consulting Inc.

1703 Middletown Rd
Glen Mills, PA 19342-1908
(610) 459-2226
Fax: (610) 361-9585
Email: recruiter@kpconsultinginc.com
Web: www.kpconsultinginc.com

Summary: Our firm offers consulting and
recruiting services for the pharmaceutical/bio-
technology community with particular expertise in
the quality, compliance, regulatory and validation
sector.

Key Contact - Specialty:
Mr. Peter Alex

Salary Minimum: $75,000

Functions: Generalist (All), Engineering

Industries: Medical Devices, Pharm Svcs.,
Biotech/Life Sciences

Mary Kraft & Associates Inc

1447 York Rd Ste 601
Galleria Towers
Lutherville/Baltimore, MD 21093-6034
(410) 296-0655
Fax: (410) 324-4350
Email: marykraft@marykraft.com
Web: www.marykraft.com

Summary: We are full service staffing company
specializing in the recruiting and placement of
permanent, temporary to permanent, temporary
staffing. We provide our services to various clients
including healthcare, legal, financial, commercial,
service, and professional industries.We constantly
strives to match the right candidate with the right
job opportunity.Certified Woman/owned
company.

Key Contact - Specialty:
Ms. Mary Kraft, Founder & President

Salary Minimum: $30,000

Functions: Admin. Svcs.

Industries: Generalist (All)

Kratec Company

62 Wildwood Dr
Troy, MI 48085-1582
(248) 879-5560
Fax: (248) 879-0175
Email: resume@kratec.com
Web: www.kratec.com

Summary: We are an executive search firm
specializing in the computer, IT, Internet,
consulting and healthcare industries. We
specialize in executive level management, sales,
sales management, pre/post sales support, project
management and consultants. We are a permanent
placement company.

Key Contact - Specialty:
Mr. William Krajewski, Owner & President

Salary Minimum: $85,000

Functions: Generalist (All), Management, Senior
Mgmt., Sales Mgmt., Mgmt. Consultants

Industries: Generalist (All), Computer Equip.,
Semiconductors, Mgmt. Consulting, E-
commerce, IT Implementation, Supply Chain
Mgmt, Telecoms, Call Centers, Network
Infrastructure, Accounting SW, Database SW,
Development SW, Doc. Mgmt., Production SW,
Entertainment SW, ERP SW, HR SW, Industry
Specific SW, Mfg. SW, Networking, Comm.
SW, Security SW, System SW, Healthcare

Peter J Kratimenos Associates

PO Box 6037
Plymouth, MA 02362-6037
(508) 830-0079
Fax: (508) 830-4627
Email: pk@kratimenos.com
Web: www.kratimenos.com

Summary: We specialize in both retainer and contingency placement of all technical disciplines associated with pharmaceutical, bio-technology, manufacturing and life sciences. Our clients include some of the top Fortune 500 companies in the world. Confidentiality is guaranteed.

Key Contact - Specialty:
Mr. Peter J. Kratimenos, President -
Manufacturing, Metals, Pharmaceutical

Functions: Generalist (All)

Industries: Manufacturing, Chemicals, Drugs Mfg., Medical Devices, Pharm Svcs., Biotech/Life Sciences

Krauss Legal Search

73 Lexington St
Auburndale, MA 02466-1356
(617) 244-4459
Fax: (206) 984-3949
Email: krausslegal.search@verizon.net

Summary: We specialize in permanent placement of associate and partner-level attorneys at law firms and companies.

Key Contact - Specialty:
Mr. Steven Krauss, Principal

Salary Minimum: $100,000

Functions: Attorneys

Industries: Legal

Kressenberg Associates

1112 E Copeland Rd Ste 340
Arlington, TX 76011-4991
(817) 226-8990
(800) 551-5361
Fax: (817) 226-8999
Email: sammyc@kressenberg.attbbs.com
Web: www.kressenbergassociates.com

Summary: We are a boutique executive search firm conducting search assignments on an exclusive basis. Our specialties include trucking and automobile dealerships, veterinary medicine, retail management, and capital equipment for the semiconductor industry.

Key Contact - Specialty:
Ms. Sammye Jo Kressenberg, President -
Managed care, Sales

Salary Minimum: $50,000

Functions: Senior Mgmt., Middle Mgmt., Nurses, Health Admin., Sales Mgmt., HR Mgmt., Benefits, CFOs, Engineering

Industries: Generalist (All), Motor Vehicles, Computer Equip., Test, Measure Equip., Misc. Mfg., Electronic, Elec. Components, Semiconductors, Consumer Goods, Retail, Accounting, Mgmt. Consulting, Healthcare, Long-term/Home Care

Kreuzberger|Associates

(formerly known as Kreuzberger & Associates)
1000 4th St Ste 150
San Rafael, CA 94901-3115
(415) 459-2300
Fax: (415) 459-2471
Email: info@kreuzberger.com
Web: www.kreuzberger.com

Summary: We serve as a strategic staffing partner to clients and candidates. We are the experts in financial executive search and contract staffing. Our track record speaks for itself.

Key Contact - Specialty:
Mr. Neil L. Kreuzberger, CPA, President -
Financial services, Private equity, Technology, Telecommunications, Venture capital
Ms. Keri A. Pon, Vice President

Salary Minimum: $80,000

Functions: Management, Senior Mgmt., Finance, CFOs, Budgeting, Cash Mgmt., Credit, Taxes, M&A, Risk Mgmt.

Industries: Manufacturing, Retail, Finance, Services, Hospitality, Communications, Insurance, Real Estate, Software, Biotech/Life Sciences, Healthcare

Branches:
115 Sansome St Ste 1200
San Francisco, CA 94104-3630
(415) 398-3995
Fax: (415) 459-2471
Email: info@kreuzberger.com

Todd L Krueger & Associates

PO Box 1289
Seattle, WA 98111-1289
(425) 776-9247
(206) 406-8708
Email: tlkrueger2003@yahoo.com

Summary: We provide expertise assisting all size companies in staffing their corporate tax and accounting departments. Additionally, assist public accounting firms in recruiting specialized and experienced audit and tax personnel.

Key Contact - Specialty:
Mr. Todd L. Krueger, President & Owner -
Finance, Tax

Salary Minimum: $25,000

Functions: Generalist (All), Board Members, CFOs, Budgeting, Cash Mgmt., Taxes, Mgmt. Consultants

Industries: Generalist (All), Accounting, Equip Svcs., Mgmt. Consulting, Hospitality

KTP Executive Search

2275 Huntington Dr Ste 446
San Marino, CA 91108-2640
(866) 411-8963
Email: resume@ktpsearch.com
Web: www.ktpsearch.com

Summary: Our firm completes searches for some of the most prestigious financial institutions in the USA & Canada. Within the financial services industry, our experience spans across consumer banks, registered investment advisors, broker dealers, hedge fund and insurance and mutual fund companies. Our specialty is sales, marketing, management and compliance.

Key Contact - Specialty:
Mr. Tarin Yankovich, Principal - *Asset management, Banking (Investment), Financial services, Investment management, Securities*

Salary Minimum: $150,000

Functions: Sales & Mktg.

Industries: Banking, Brokers, Mutual/Hedge Funds

KTR A Search Firm

4540 Aspen Lake Dr Ste 206
Brunswick, OH 44212-4567
(330) 225-6100

Email: ktr@topechelon.com
Web: www.elevatorrecruiter.com

Summary: Our firm is a search firm dedicated to the elevator industry. Our philosophy is simple: tell the truth and recruit in a professional manner for its client companies and candidates. From hands-on engineers to Sales Reps to Executives, we service the entire elevator industry.

Key Contact - Specialty:
Mr. Vincent M. Kirkwood, President, Account Manager & Recruiter

Salary Minimum: $50,000

Functions: Senior Mgmt., Product Dev., Sales & Mktg.

Industries: Manufacturing, Equip Svcs.

Kuhn Med-Tech Inc

27128 Paseo Espada Ste B623
San Juan Capistrano, CA 92675-6709
(949) 496-3500
Fax: (949) 496-1716
Email: der@kuhnmed-tech.com
Web: www.kuhnmed-tech.com

Summary: Serving medical device and biotechnology industries. Exclusive contingency and retainers; positions secured for engineers, scientists, marketing/sales and senior management professionals for Fortune 500 companies and exciting start-up ventures.

Key Contact - Specialty:
Mr. Larry A. Kuhn, President - *Biomaterials, Biomedical, Biotechnology, Medical, Medical (Devices)*
Mr. Otis Archie, Jr., Vice President - *Electrical, Executives, Sales*

Salary Minimum: $50,000

Functions: Generalist (All), Management, Senior Mgmt., Mfg., Product Dev., Healthcare, Sales & Mktg., Staffing, R&D, Engineering

Industries: Generalist (All), Drugs Mfg., Medical Devices, Plastics, Rubber, Finance, Venture Cap., Misc. Financial, Services, HR Services, Engineering Svcs., Software, Development SW, Biotech/Life Sciences, Healthcare, Dental

Kunin Associates

900 SE 3rd Ave Ste 204
Fort Lauderdale, FL 33316-1118
(954) 467-9575
(305) 358-7977
Fax: (954) 467-9585
Email: jkunin@kuninassociates.com
Web: www.kuninassociates.com

Summary: We are a professional recruiting firm specializing in the placement of accounting, financial and bookkeeping personnel. We provide personalized service to our clients and deal directly with many of the finest public accounting firms and companies.

Key Contact - Specialty:
Ms. Jo-Anne Kunin, CPA, President - *Accounting*

Salary Minimum: $25,000

Functions: Middle Mgmt., CFOs, Budgeting, Cash Mgmt., Credit, Taxes, M&A, Risk Mgmt.

Industries: Generalist (All)

D Kunkle & Associates

PO Box 184
Barrington, IL 60011-0184
(847) 540-8651
Email: denise.kunkle@att.net

Summary: We bring technical and management experience to the search field. The unique

perspective we have gained in building organizations within major consumer packaged goods businesses ensures a more knowledgeable approach and superior search results.

Key Contact - Specialty:
Ms. Denise Kunkle, President

Salary Minimum: $40,000

Functions: Product Dev., Quality, Purchasing, Packaging, Engineering, Graphic Designers

Industries: Food, Bev., Tobacco, Soap, Perf., Cosmtcs., Drugs Mfg., Medical Devices, Packaging

Kurtz Pro-Search Inc

PO Box 4213
Warren, NJ 07059-0213
(908) 647-7789

Summary: We provide services for highly skilled computer industry sales or tech support candidates with software, hardware or services experience are recruited by this firm.

Key Contact - Specialty:
Mr. Sheldon I. Kurtz, President - *Networking, Telecommunications*

Salary Minimum: $75,000

Functions: Sales & Mktg., Sales Mgmt., MIS Mgmt., Systems Analysis, Systems Dev., Systems Implem., Systems Support, Mgmt. Consultants

Industries: Computer Equip., Mgmt. Consulting, New Media, Telecoms, Telephony, Network Infrastructure, Software

Kutcher Tax Careers Inc

37 Saw Mill River Rd Ste 1
Hawthorne, NY 10532-1548
(914) 592-6887
Fax: (914) 592-0441
Email: kutcher@taxcareers.com
Web: www.taxcareers.com

Summary: We are a niche-oriented recruiting firm that specializes exclusively in the tax area. Our detailed web site allows clients and candidates to submit their confidential information online as well as view sampling of placements made, client references/testimonials, principal's background and other pertinent items.

Key Contact - Specialty:
Mr. Howard Kutcher, CPA, MS, President

Salary Minimum: $40,000

Functions: Taxes

Industries: Generalist (All)

Kutt Inc

2336 Canyon Blvd Ste 202
Boulder, CO 80302-5653
(303) 440-4100
(303) 440-6111
Fax: (303) 440-9582
Email: info@kuttinc.com
Web: www.kuttinc.com

Summary: Executive search and recruiting firm serving the printing industry only; all levels of positions filled.

Key Contact - Specialty:
Mr. David Huff, Part Owner - *Printing*
Mr. Greg Neighbors, Part Owner - *Printing*

Salary Minimum: $40,000

Functions: Generalist (All)

Industries: Printing

Kuttnauer Search Group Inc

234 Midtown Dr
Traverse City, MI 49684-5751
(231) 922-9380
Fax: (269) 395-9380
Email: curtis@kuttnauer.com
Web: www.kuttnauer.com

Summary: Our firm specializes in the placement of full-time sales executives and sales professionals in the IT industry. Client companies are hardware, software and services organizations.

Key Contact - Specialty:
Mr. Curtis D. Kuttnauer, President
Ms. Kris Brown, Director, Research - *Computers (Hardware,Sales,Software), Sales, Technology*
Ms. Jennifer B. Lett, Researcher
Ms. Sandi K. Sullivan, Researcher

Salary Minimum: $100,000

Functions: Senior Mgmt., Sales & Mktg., Sales Mgmt., IT

Industries: Computer Equip., Equip Svcs., E-commerce, IT Implementation, PSA/ASP, Software

Niles Kvistad & Company

(formerly known as Daggett & Kvistad)
3015 Hopyard Rd Ste S
Pleasanton, CA 94588-5259
(925) 484-9050
Fax: (925) 484-9052
Email: nkvistad@nksearch.com

Summary: We specialize in the semiconductor, semiconductor capital equipment markets. Our assignments range from senior general management positions to functional manager positions.

Key Contact - Specialty:
Mr. Niles K. Kvistad, Owner

Salary Minimum: $80,000

Functions: Generalist (All), Middle Mgmt., Mfg., Product Dev., Automation, Quality, Materials, Sales & Mktg., Engineering

Industries: Computer Equip., Test, Measure Equip., Misc. Mfg., Electronic, Elec. Components, Equip Svcs., Digital, Fiber Optic, Software, Development SW, Industry Specific SW, Marketing SW

Gregory Kyle & Associates Inc

PO Box 901
Concord, NC 28026-0901
(704) 786-1231
Fax: (704) 795-3942
Email: gp@gregorykyleandassociates.com
Web: www.gregorykyleandassociates.com

Summary: We are an executive search firm specializing in professional recruitment and HR solutions for manufacturers. We conduct contingency and retained search assignments for degreed manufacturing professionals for Fortune 500 client companies.

Key Contact - Specialty:
Mr. Greg Picarella, President - *Manufacturing*

Salary Minimum: $50,000

Functions: Management, Mfg., Materials, Sales & Mktg., HR Mgmt., Finance, Engineering

Industries: Manufacturing

L & L Associates

PO Box 541
Brea, CA 92822-0541
(714) 990-5525
Email: alangold@sbcglobal.net

Summary: We are a contingency search firm specializing in the recruitment for "high-technology" companies.

Key Contact - Specialty:
Mr. Alan Gold, Owner - *Technical*

Salary Minimum: $25,000

Functions: Generalist (All), Management, Board Members, Senior Mgmt., Mfg., Product Dev., Engineering

Industries: Generalist (All), Manufacturing, Food, Bev., Tobacco, Drugs Mfg., Medical Devices, Plastics, Rubber, Paints, Petro. Products, Metal Products, Machine, Appliance, Motor Vehicles, Computer Equip., Consumer Elect., Test, Measure Equip., Misc. Mfg., Electronic, Elec. Components, Semiconductors, Consumer Goods, Engineering Svcs., Logistics Svcs., Supply Chain Mgmt., Telecoms, Digital, Aerospace, Software

La Vista Resources

1000 Abernathy Rd NE Ste 1000
Atlanta, GA 30328-5651
(770) 481-7300
Fax: (770) 481-7301
Email: kcoleman@lavistaresources.com
Web: www.lavistaresources.com

Summary: We specialize in professional level staffing both in contract and direct hire primarily in four areas: accounting & finance, IT, HR, administration and creative services.

Key Contact - Specialty:
Ms. Kelly Coleman, Client Services Manager - *Information Technology*
Mr. John Pope, Executive Account Manager

Functions: Board Members, Mfg., Sales & Mktg., HR Mgmt., Finance, IT

Industries: Generalist (All), Energy, Utilities, Manufacturing, Transportation, Wholesale, Finance, Services, IT Implementation, Media, Communications, Packaging, Insurance, Real Estate, Software, Healthcare, Hospitals, Non-Classifiable

Paul Labine & Associates

979 Avenida Pico Unit K PMB 230
San Clemente, CA 92673-3916
(949) 429-6726
Email: plabine@att.net
Web: www.search-consultants-inc.com

Summary: We recruit sales engineers, sales managers, marketing managers, technical experts and executives with chemistry or chemical engineering degrees.

Key Contact - Specialty:
Dr. Paul Labine, President - *Sales, Technical*

Salary Minimum: $50,000

Functions: Generalist (All), Sales Mgmt.

Industries: Chemicals, Drugs Mfg., Medical Devices, Biotech/Life Sciences

LaCosta & Associates International Inc

9988 Hibert St Ste 201
San Diego, CA 92131-2480
(858) 860-1222
Fax: (858) 860-1221
Email: paul@lacostasearch.com
Web: www.lacostasearch.com

Summary: We offer a variety of people development and recruiting services in the wireless/telecom/internet space industries, specializing in marketing, engineering, IT, customer service, sales management, executive

and general management. Also provided are retained and retained contingent searches to find HR and finance professionals across all industries.

Key Contact - Specialty:
Mr. Paul LaCosta, President
Mr. Doug Smith, Senior Account Manager
Mr. Steve Holman, Senior Account Manager
Ms. Vanessa Peek, Administrative Assistant

Salary Minimum: $50,000

Functions: Board Members, Senior Mgmt., Sales & Mktg., Customer Svc., HR Mgmt., Training, CFOs, MIS Mgmt., Engineering, Int'l.

Industries: E-commerce, Wireless

Lahey Consulting LLC

PO Box 395
Delmar, NY 12054-0395
(518) 439-4285
Fax: (518) 439-5795
Email: info@laheyconsulting.com
Web: www.laheyconsulting.com

Summary: Our sole focus is bringing classically trained marketing professionals and consumer products companies together. Our candidate and client networks are heavily concentrated within traditional consumer packaged goods industries. We perform both contingency and retained searches, depending on the level of the open position(s).

Key Contact - Specialty:
Mr. Stephen H. Lahey, President

Functions: Mktg. Mgmt.

Industries: Food, Bev., Tobacco, Soap, Perf., Cosmtcs., Medical Devices, Consumer Elect., Misc. Mfg., Consumer Goods, Hotels, Resorts, Clubs, Quick Service Restaurants, Sports, Non-Classifiable

Laing Group Executive Recruiting

305-1371 Harwood St
Vancouver, BC V6E 1S6
Canada
(604) 331-0426
Fax: (604) 605-0429
Email: janice@laingjobs.com
Web: www.laingjobs.com

Summary: The Laing Group focuses on recruiting business-to-business executive level sales, marketing and business development professionals in software and other high-tech sectors.

Key Contact - Specialty:
Ms. Janice Laing, Senior Account Manager

Functions: Sales & Mktg., Mktg. Mgmt., Sales Mgmt., Sales Reps., Systems Implem., Mgmt. Consultants

Industries: Software, Accounting SW, Database SW, Development SW, Doc. Mgmt., Production SW, ERP SW, HR SW, Industry Specific SW, Mfg. SW, Marketing SW, Networking, Comm. SW, Security SW

Gregory Laka & Company

11 E Adams St Ste 1000
Chicago, IL 60603-6318
(312) 922-7100
Fax: (312) 922-7199
Email: chicago@laka.com
Web: www.laka.com

Summary: Search in all areas of IT having a retainer and a contingency division.

Key Contact - Specialty:
Mr. Gregory Laka, Chief Executive Officer
Mr. Gregory David, President, Chicago Operations

Salary Minimum: $50,000

Functions: IT

Industries: Generalist (All)

Lam Associates

1860 Ala Moana Blvd Apt 1900G
Honolulu, HI 96815-1639
(808) 947-9815
Email: lamdocs@aol.com
Web: www.mdopenings.com

Summary: We are a service-oriented, employer-paid recruiting agency placing full-time and locum tenens positions. We specialize in physician and healthcare search. Your search is strictly confidential. We have affiliations with several recruiting networks and a longstanding membership in the Hawaii Chamber of Commerce. We have the experience and the connections to locate the best opportunity for you.

Key Contact - Specialty:
Ms. Pat Lambrecht, General Manager

Salary Minimum: $40,000

Functions: Physicians, Nurses

Industries: Healthcare, Hospitals

LaMorte Search Associates Inc

4412 Woodfield Blvd
Boca Raton, FL 33434-5304
(561) 997-1100
(800) 422-6306
Fax: (561) 997-1103
Email: lamortesearch@aol.com
Web: www.lamortesearch.com

Summary: Specializing exclusively in the insurance industry. Provide recruitment for the insurance company, insurance brokerage and risk management community.

Key Contact - Specialty:
Mr. William LaMorte, President
Ms. Michelle LaMorte, Executive Vice President

Salary Minimum: $75,000

Functions: Generalist (All), Management, Middle Mgmt., Risk Mgmt.

Industries: Insurance, Casualty, Claims

Lancaster Associates Inc

35 W High St
Somerville, NJ 08876-2114
(908) 526-5440
Fax: (908) 526-1992
Email: laura@somersetalliance.net

Summary: Small professional organization specializing in pre-screened candidates in all levels of applications, software systems and senior-level management. Heavy need for eCommerce/Internet and data warehousing professionals. Provide consultants with the right to hire.

Key Contact - Specialty:
Mr. Raymond F. Lancaster, Jr., Recruiter
Ms. Laura Rudbart, Recruiter

Salary Minimum: $80,000

Functions: IT

Industries: Chemicals, Drugs Mfg., Medical Devices, Mgmt. Consulting, Software, Biotech/Life Sciences

E J Lance Management Associates Inc

60 E 42nd St Rm 1165
New York, NY 10165-1165
(212) 490-9600
Fax: (212) 490-7282

Summary: Experienced professionals, many with MBAs. All candidates are personally screened. Client names are confidential. Average completion time for assignments is three to four weeks.

Key Contact - Specialty:
Ms. Elizabeth Killingsworth, Partner
Mr. Elliot Zgodny, Partner

Salary Minimum: $40,000

Functions: Generalist (All), Cash Mgmt., M&A

Industries: Invest. Banking

Landon Accounting Personnel

2551 Oscar Johnson Dr Ste A
North Charleston, SC 29405-6884
(843) 745-0220
Fax: (843) 745-0870
Email: jobs@landonservices.com
Web: www.landonservices.com

Summary: Our firm specializes in the direct placement of accounting and financial professionals.

Key Contact - Specialty:
Mr. Roger Davis, President

Functions: Finance

Industries: Generalist (All)

Landsman Foodservice.Net

2403 Logan Rd
Owings Mills, MD 21117-2311
(410) 342-5263
Fax: (410) 3426249
Email: jeff@lfsn.com
Web: www.lfsn.com

Summary: Food service manufacturing and distribution and Corporate Foodservice executives only need apply. We provide consultative recruitment services having expertise in all areas within food service. We place all functional areas of management with food service distributors and manufacturers alike. Retained and contingency recruitment firm. We also provide industry specific management consulting in sales and logistics.

Key Contact - Specialty:
Mr. Jeffrey B. Landsman, President

Salary Minimum: $80,000

Functions: Management, Distribution, Sales & Mktg.

Industries: Food, Bev., Tobacco, Transportation, Wholesale, Hospitality, Hotels, Resorts, Clubs, Restaurants, Quick Service Restaurants, Full Service Restaurants, Inst./Industrial Food Svc.

Lane Consulting LLC

4 W Red Oak Ln
West Harrison, NY 10604-3603
(914) 468-0100
Fax: (914) 468-0101
Web: www.laneconsult.com

Summary: Financial executive search firm.

Key Contact - Specialty:
Mr. David E. Lane, CPC, President
Mr. Robert L. Minton, Manager, Recruitment - *Accounting (Big 4), Finance, Financial, Financial services*

Mr. Todd Spring, Manager, Financial Services - *Accounting, Accounting (Big 4), Finance*
Ms. Zoe Devita, Manager - *Accounting, Finance*
Ms. Stephanie Lane, Financial Recruiter - *Accounting, Finance*

Salary Minimum: $100,000

Functions: Management, Senior Mgmt., Middle Mgmt., Finance, M&A

Industries: Manufacturing, Food, Bev., Tobacco, Consumer Goods, Finance, Mutual/Hedge Funds, Hotels, Resorts, Clubs, Media, Advertising, Publishing, New Media, Broadcast, Film, Communications, Telephony, Digital, Insurance, Software, Doc. Mgmt., Production SW

The Lane Group

735 N Water St Ste 1228
Milwaukee, WI 53202-4105
(414) 226-2400
Fax: (414) 226-2421
Email: info@thelanegroup.net
Web: www.thelanegroup.net

Summary: Executive search firm.

Key Contact - Specialty:
Mr. Douglas Lane, President - *Advertising, Consulting, Marketing, Senior management*
Mr. Steve Tewes, Vice President - *Advertising, Marketing, Sales*
Mr. Chris Spahn, Vice President - *Retail, Sales*
Mr. Sean O'Byrne, Account Executive - *Marketing, Sales*
Ms. Cheryl D'Amico, Project Manager
Mr. Thomas Stark, National Account Director
Ms. Tana Crivello, Account Executive

Salary Minimum: $40,000

Functions: Senior Mgmt., Advertising, Mktg. Mgmt., Sales Mgmt., Direct Mktg., Sales Reps., Finance, Cash Mgmt., Mgmt. Consultants, Legal

Industries: Generalist (All), Energy, Utilities, Manufacturing, Food, Bev., Tobacco, Printing, Soap, Perf., Cosmtcs., Drugs Mfg., Medical Devices, Computer Equip., Consumer Elect., Consumer Goods, Wholesale, Retail, Finance, Banking, Invest. Banking, Brokers, Venture Cap., Mutual/Hedge Funds, Misc. Financial, Services, Legal, Accounting, Mgmt. Consulting, Sports, Media, Advertising, Communications, Telephony, Compliance, Casualty, Life, Software, Training SW, Healthcare

Lange & Associates Inc

499 Bristol Dr
Wabash, IN 46992-1037
(260) 563-7402
Fax: (260) 563-7894
Email: langeassoc@ctlnet.com

Summary: We are experts in matching people and opportunities. We recruit all disciplines and specialize in rubber, plastics, metals and electronics. We place a large concentration in the automotive arena.

Key Contact - Specialty:
Mr. Jim Lange, President
Mr. Jack Lange, Vice President

Salary Minimum: $30,000

Functions: Management, Mfg., Materials, HR Mgmt., R&D, Engineering, Environmentalists

Industries: Manufacturing, Chemicals, Plastics, Rubber, Metal Products, HR Services, Aerospace

The Langford Search Inc

PO Box 536
Pelham, AL 35124-0536
(205) 621-6000
Fax: (205) 620-3555
Email: tlsearch@aol.com
Web: www.langfordsearch.com

Summary: We seek first to understand our client's business, then both the hard and soft skills required of a successful candidate. We present for consideration only those candidates that possess both.

Key Contact - Specialty:
Mr. K.R. Dick Langford, Chief Executive Officer - *General management*
Ms. Ann S. Langford, President

Functions: Generalist (All), CFOs

Industries: Generalist (All), Banking, Accounting, IT Implementation, Accounting SW

Lanken-Saunders Group

3061 Greyfield Pl SE
Marietta, GA 30067-5529
(770) 952-7530
Fax: (770) 952-6252
Email: jlanken@aol.com
Web: www.lankensaunders.com

Summary: We place a specific expertise in logistics, transportation, warehousing, distribution positions and requirements. Retained by fortune listed transportation companies. Full-service search firm including training and HR projects.

Key Contact - Specialty:
Mr. Joel Lanken, President - *Finance, Human resources, Logistics, Operations, Sales*
Mr. Bud Wallen, Director - *Marketing, Operations, Sales*
Mr. Wayne Saunders, Vice President - *Human resources, Training*
Mr. Sam Herman, Vice President - *Transportation*

Salary Minimum: $50,000

Functions: Generalist (All), Management, Senior Mgmt.

Industries: Generalist (All), Transportation, Wholesale, Retail, Finance, Services, HR Services, Logistics Svcs., Supply Chain Mgmt., Real Estate

Lannick Associates

3402-20 Queen St W
Cadillac Fairview Tower
Toronto, ON M5H 3R3
Canada
(416) 340-1500
Fax: (416) 340-1344
Email: lannick@lannick.com
Web: www.lannick.com

Summary: We are premier search firm in the accounting and finance field. Specialists in the recruitment of chartered accountants, CGAs, CMAs and MBAs for some of the world's biggest and best-respected public companies, to new dot-com start-ups.

Key Contact - Specialty:
Mr. Lance Osborne, President
Ms. Wendy Fox, Director, Research
Ms. Janet McAlpine, Director, Information Integration
Ms. Marie Werlick, Director, Admin & Project Management
Mr. Kevin Brockie, CA, Senior Associate
Ms. Vanessa Bryant, Senior Associate
Ms. Marilyn Eddy, CA, Senior Associate
Ms. Joanne Elek, Senior Associate

Ms. Daphne Fernandes, Senior Associate
Ms. Cathy Logue, CA, Senior Associate
Ms. Sheriza Perabtani, CA, Senior Associate
Ms. Kathy Steffan, Controller

Salary Minimum: $60,000

Functions: Board Members, Senior Mgmt., Middle Mgmt., Finance, CFOs, Budgeting, Cash Mgmt., Taxes, M&A, Risk Mgmt.

Industries: Generalist (All), Finance

Larmee Executive Search

9040 Executive Park Dr Ste 251
Knoxville, TN 37923-4629
(865) 531-9125
Email: dtlarmee@earthlink.net
Web: larmeerecruiting.com

Summary: Specializing in the banking/mortgage-banking arena with an emphasis on wholesale and correspondent lending.

Key Contact - Specialty:
Mr. Talmon Larmee, President

Functions: Sales Mgmt.

Industries: Finance, Banking

Robert Larned Associates Inc

1 Columbus Ctr Ste 600
Virginia Beach, VA 23462-6760
(757) 498-2700
Fax: (270) 675-4035
Email: rlabob@aol.com
Web: www.rlastaffing.com

Summary: We recruit for our Fortune 1000 clients to find top talent leaving the military, including junior military officers and technically rated enlisted personnel, as well as former military officers and engineers with industry experience.

Key Contact - Specialty:
Mr. Robert T. Larned, President

Salary Minimum: $50,000

Functions: Middle Mgmt., Mfg., Production, Sales Mgmt., IT, Technicians

Industries: Energy, Utilities, Manufacturing, Food, Bev., Tobacco, Printing, Chemicals, Soap, Perf., Cosmtcs., Metal Products, Machine, Appliance, Computer Equip., Telecoms, Defense, Aerospace, Packaging, Software

Jack B Larsen & Associates Inc

334 W 8th St
Erie, PA 16502-1411
(800) 239-5737
Fax: (800) 239-5736
Email: jbl@velocity.net
Web: www.jblhires.com

Summary: Full scope recruiting firm handling permanent career opportunities. All engineering disciplines plus HR, sales/sales management, IT, QC/QA, manufacturing mgmt, purchasing, and general management.

Key Contact - Specialty:
Mr. Jack B. Larsen, CPC, Chief Executive Officer

Salary Minimum: $50,000

Functions: Generalist (All), Mfg., Production, Distribution, Sales Mgmt., Benefits, Systems Analysis, Engineering

Industries: Generalist (All), Food, Bev., Tobacco, Plastics, Rubber, Metal Products, Machine, Appliance, Misc. Mfg., Electronic, Elec. Components, Non-profits, Telecoms, Hospitals, Long-term/Home Care

Larson, Katz & Young Inc

PO Box 44
Aldie, VA 20105-0044
(703) 327-1151
Fax: (703) 327-1161
Email: info@lkyi.com
Web: www.lkyi.com

Summary: Search firm for healthcare systems
vendors specializing in installations, support,
product marketing, sales and sales management.

Key Contact - Specialty:
Ms. Marcia Hall, President

Salary Minimum: $50,000

Functions: Generalist (All), Middle Mgmt.,
Product Dev., Healthcare, Nurses, Sales &
Mktg., Mktg. Mgmt., Sales Reps., IT, Systems
Implem.

Industries: Pharm Svcs., IT Implementation,
Software, Healthcare

LAS Executive Search LLC

3 Blueberry Ln
Staten Island, NY 10312-6419
(718) 317-7777
Email: info@lassearch.com
Web: www.lasmanagement.com

Summary: We are executive search specialists in
recruitment & placement of IT auditors &
information security professionals at all levels of
management. Corporate clients include large
accounting/consulting, security product & testing
organizations, successful financial service
companies, entertainment, manufacturing,
energy/utility, consumer products & high-
technology firms.

Key Contact - Specialty:
Mr. Tom DeAngelo, Director

Salary Minimum: $75,000

Functions: Generalist (All), Management, Board
Members

Industries: Manufacturing, Computer Equip.,
Finance, Services, Hospitality, Entertainment,
New Media, Broadcast, Film, Communications,
Telecoms, Defense, Aerospace, Insurance,
Software, ERP SW, Networking, Comm. SW,
Security SW, System SW

P Frank Lassiter & Co Inc

PO Box 29367
Richmond, VA 23242-0367
(804) 440-5761
Email: dpsricva@msn.com

Summary: Recruiting trust officers, trust
investment officers, private banking officers and
trust sales officers.

Key Contact - Specialty:
Mr. P. Frank Lassiter, President

Salary Minimum: $50,000

Functions: Middle Mgmt.

Industries: Banking, Invest. Banking, Brokers,
Mutual/Hedge Funds, Misc. Financial, Services

The Laudi Group Inc

300-12 Mercer St
Toronto, ON M5V 1H3
Canada
(416) 934-9500
Fax: (416) 935-0025
Email: info@laudigroup.com
Web: www.laudigroup.com

Summary: Executive search firm for emerging
sectors, executive search for emerging technology

companies, help organizations recruit senior
executives for key management positions.

Key Contact - Specialty:
Mr. Chris Ramsay, Principal
Mr. Mario Laudi, Founder

Salary Minimum: $80,000

Functions: Management, Sales & Mktg., HR
Mgmt., Finance, Engineering

Industries: Generalist (All)

The Lawner Group

33 Main St Ste 203
Nashua, NH 03064-2776
(603) 595-3388
Fax: (603) 595-3370
Email: info@thelawnergroup.com
Web: www.thelawnergroup.com

Summary: Ours blend of management consulting
and executive search specialties focuses on the
long-term business relationship and success of our
clients. We specialize in matching the most
qualified candidates with the most appropriate
positions, creating a productive and positive
environment for both employer and employee. We
offer our clients further value by providing advice
and intensive guidance for both the employer and
the career seeker.

Key Contact - Specialty:
Mr. Harvey Lawner, President

Salary Minimum: $100,000

Functions: Generalist (All)

Industries: Communications, Software,
Biotech/Life Sciences

Lawrence Personnel

(also known as Lawrence International)
1000 Valley Forge Cir Ste 110
King of Prussia, PA 19406-4527
(610) 783-5400
Fax: (610) 783-6008
Email: lawpers@staffing.net
Web: www.lawrencepersonnel.com

Summary: Our practice is limited to specific
searches and international opportunities. We offer
retained and contingency searches.

Key Contact - Specialty:
Mr. Larry Goldberg, CPC, General Manager
Mr. Conrad Anson, Manager, International
Searches

Salary Minimum: $50,000

Functions: Generalist (All), Quality

Industries: Generalist (All), Manufacturing,
Communications, Telecoms, Call Centers,
Telephony, Digital, Wireless, Fiber Optic,
Network Infrastructure

Lawrence-Balakonis & Associates Inc

PO Box 888241
Atlanta, GA 30356-0241
(770) 587-2342
Fax: (770) 587-5002
Email: balakonisnassoc@mindspring.com

Summary: Highly regarded executive search
consulting firm specializing in the consumer
packaged goods industry, with a primary focus on
sales & marketing mid and senior-level
management positions in the grocery products
industry.

Key Contact - Specialty:
Mr. Charles L. Balakonis, President - *Marketing,
Sales*

Mr. J. Robert Lawrence, Executive Vice President
- *Senior management*
Ms. Linda Roberts, Vice President, Research

Salary Minimum: $70,000

Functions: Generalist (All), Management, Senior
Mgmt., Middle Mgmt., Plant Mgmt., Sales &
Mktg., Sales Mgmt.

Industries: Generalist (All), Food, Bev., Tobacco,
Paper, Soap, Perf., Cosmtcs., Drugs Mfg., Misc.
Mfg.

The Lawson Group Inc

PO Box 7491
Hilton Head Island, SC 29938-7491
(843) 842-4949
Fax: (843) 842-7650
Email: email@lawsongroup.com
Web: www.lawsongroup.com

Summary: We believe American industry is past
the need for good people; today the best people are
needed. Through our methods of locating and
screening people, we are dedicated to that end. We
understand the importance of making the right fit
for both company and individual.

Key Contact - Specialty:
Mr. John W. Lawson, President
Ms. Mary Bjong, Vice President
Mr. Buddy Perkins, Vice President, Business
Development

Functions: Generalist (All), Management, Board
Members, Packaging, Specialized Svcs.

Industries: Paper, Printing, Packaging

LCS International Inc (LCSI)

12140 Larchgate Dr
Dallas, TX 75243-5053
(972) 690-1131
Fax: (972) 690-3107
Email: info@lcs-intl.com
Web: www.lcs-intl.com

Summary: Our firm helps hiring authorities find
exceptional candidates. We go beyond experience
and skills matching to people matching. Our
process is thorough and we respect the
confidentiality of our clients and candidates in the
search process. We recruit qualified professionals
for senior-level positions and support staff. We
help employers with their most difficult searches
by providing contingency, retained and contract
placements with assured results.

Key Contact - Specialty:
Ms. Donna M. Lanners, Recruiter & Prof Search
Consultant - *C-level, E-business, Engineering,
Manufacturing, Operations*

Salary Minimum: $50,000

Functions: Management, Board Members, Senior
Mgmt., Middle Mgmt., Admin. Svcs., Plant
Mgmt., Quality, HR Mgmt., CFOs, Engineering

Industries: Construction, Manufacturing

Leader Institute Inc

(also known as Peoplestaff)
1225 Johnson Ferry Rd Ste 300
Marietta, GA 30068-2769
(770) 321-1231
Fax: (801) 382-2452
Email: inquiry@peoplestaff.com
Web: www.peoplestaff.com

Summary: IT specialists applying search
techniques to the object oriented markets for CIO
searches.

Key Contact - Specialty:
Mr. Richard Zabor, President - *Data processing,
Oracle, PeopleSoft*

Salary Minimum: $60,000

Functions: Senior Mgmt., IT, MIS Mgmt., Systems Analysis, Systems Dev., Systems Implem., Systems Support, DB Admin.

Industries: Generalist (All), E-commerce, IT Implementation, Software, Accounting SW, Database SW, Development SW, ERP SW, HR SW, Industry Specific SW, Mfg. SW

Leader Network

241 Harding Ct
York, PA 17403-2739
(717) 845-6927
Fax: (717) 854-7079

Summary: We are a contingency search-executive, technical, aluminum and steel industries.

Key Contact - Specialty:
Ms. D. June Leader, Owner - *Steel, Technical*

Functions: Generalist (All), Senior Mgmt., Middle Mgmt., Production, Automation, Sales Mgmt., CFOs, Engineering

Industries: Generalist (All), Metal Products

Leaders IT Recruitment

PO Box 67002
Lincoln, NE 68506-7002
(402) 441-9340
(800) 575-7716
Email: kinga@leadersusa.com
Web: www.leadersusa.com

Summary: Specializing in recruitment of all types of IT professionals from entry level to executive level. We have frequently placed sales professionals and filled senior non-technical positions, which are more functional in nature but still deal with technology.

Key Contact - Specialty:
Ms. Kinga A. Wilson, President & Owner

Salary Minimum: $25,000

Functions: Generalist (All), Management, MIS Mgmt., Systems Analysis, Systems Dev., Systems Implem., Systems Support, Network Admin., DB Admin.

Industries: Generalist (All), Non-profits, E-commerce, IT Implementation, Media, Communications, Software, Database SW, Development SW, Networking, Comm. SW, System SW, Non-Classifiable

Leaders Professional Recruiting Inc

554 Jacksonville Dr
Jacksonville, FL 32250-3813
(800) 359-5323
(904) 246-7500
Fax: (904) 246-7565
Email: leaders@leadersinc.com
Web: www.leadersinc.com

Summary: We are committed to placing the finest individuals in exciting careers with companies leading their respective industries. We look for the proven, degreed leader who can apply his or her skills in fulfilling our client company's most challenging needs.

Key Contact - Specialty:
Mr. Tom Quinn, President & Chief Executive Officer
Mr. Buddy Webster, Chief Financial Officer & Vice President
Mr. David Purcell, National Sales Director
Mr. Pat Lemoine, Regional Recruiter
Mr. Pete Mooren, Regional Recruiter
Mrs. Ingrid Lynch, Regional Recruiter

Mr. Ben McGraw, Recruiter, Marine
Mr. Steve Jones, Regional Recruiter
Ms. Gina Miller, Recruiter, Sales & Conf Coordinator
Mrs. Sheryl Quinn, Sales Representative
Mrs. Tina Webster, Sales Representative
Ms. Jill Yarbrough, Administrative Specialist

Functions: Generalist (All)

Industries: Generalist (All)

Leading Edge Consulting Inc

13763 Fiji Way
Marina del Rey, CA 90292-6989
(310) 822-7557
Fax: (310) 827-9772
Email: susan@leadingedgejobs.com
Web: www.leadingedgejobs.com

Summary: We are specialists in information technology consulting and placement of executives and technical information technology professionals.

Key Contact - Specialty:
Ms. Susan Brainin-Martin, President

Functions: Senior Mgmt., IT

Industries: Generalist (All)

Lear & Associates Inc

1235 N Orange Ave Ste 202
Orlando, FL 32804-6411
(407) 645-4611
Fax: (407) 898-0444
Email: insurance@learsearch.com
Web: www.learsearch.com

Summary: Our goal is to treat your insurance career as our own. We have built relationships with CEOs, VPs, HR and managers of top insurance entities. We are committed to presenting these insurance opportunities to you in a professional, ethical and confidential manner. Our strengths include underwriting, claims and loss control careers at all levels. On the broker/agency side, we search for producers, account managers and CSRs.

Key Contact - Specialty:
Mr. Roger Lear, President - *Insurance, Insurance (Casualty,Claims,Property,Workers Compensation)*
Ms. Jenny Boyd, Senior Recruiting Officer - *Insurance, Insurance (Casualty,Claims,Workers Compensation), Underwriting*
Mrs. Sharon Frawley, Director, Marketing - *Insurance, Insurance (Casualty,Claims,Property,Workers Compensation)*
Mr. Kevin Rowlinson, Vice President, Recruiting - *Insurance (Casualty,Claims,Property,Workers Compensation), Underwriting*
Ms. Margaret Lockwood, Senior Executive Search Consultant - *Insurance, Insurance (Casualty,Claims,Property,Workers Compensation)*

Salary Minimum: $33,000

Functions: Generalist (All), HR Mgmt., Finance, CFOs, Risk Mgmt., MIS Mgmt.

Industries: Generalist (All), Hospitality, Insurance, Casualty, Claims, Commercial, Re-Insurance, Healthcare

Lechner & Associates Inc

7737 Holiday Dr
Sarasota, FL 34231-5313
(941) 923-3671
Fax: (941) 923-3675
Email: lechner@lechner.net
Web: www.lechner.net

Summary: Actuarial search for traditional and non-traditional actuarial roles. Retainer and contingency services.

Key Contact - Specialty:
Mrs. Lisa M. Bull, President
Dr. David B. Lechner, Advisor

Salary Minimum: $70,000

Functions: Generalist (All)

Industries: Generalist (All)

Susan Lee & Associates

PO Box 387
Chanhassen, MN 55317-0387
(952) 897-1170
Email: susan@susanlee.com
Web: www.susanlee.com

Summary: We specialize in the printing and graphics arts technology industry. All the recruiters come from the printing industry and understand the technology. We find the very best candidates.

Key Contact - Specialty:
Ms. Susan Lee, President

Functions: Generalist (All)

Industries: Paper, Printing, Advertising, Publishing, Packaging

Albert G Lee Associates

106 Greenwood Ave
Rumford, RI 02916-1935
(401) 434-7614
Email: aglee@aol.com

Summary: Practice specializing in pharmaceutical, biotechnology, technical; engineering, medical, clinical and MIS; operations, research, marketing: consumer, retail and high technology; finance: banking, real estate, accounting and taxes; and HR: benefits, compensation and employee relations.

Key Contact - Specialty:
Mr. Albert G. Lee, Chief Executive Officer - *Pharmaceutical, Research & development, Technical*

Salary Minimum: $60,000

Functions: Generalist (All), Management, Production, Healthcare, Mktg. Mgmt., Budgeting, MIS Mgmt., R&D, Engineering

Industries: Generalist (All), Drugs Mfg., Computer Equip., Retail, Pharm Svcs., Biotech/Life Sciences, Healthcare

Vincent Lee Associates

91 Fallon Ave
Elmont, NY 11003-3605
(516) 775-8551
Email: vincentleeassoc@att.net

Summary: We place an emphasis on accounting, banking, finance, marketing, insurance (property/casualty) and HR professionals executive search through VP.

Key Contact - Specialty:
Mr. Vincent Lee, President
Mr. Brian Lee, Vice President
Ms. Sheryl Baxter, Vice President
Ms. Judy Johnson, Vice President
Ms. Linda Monte, Associate Vice President

Salary Minimum: $25,000

Functions: Generalist (All), HR Mgmt.

Industries: Generalist (All), Finance, Banking, Services, Accounting, Insurance

Henry J Lee

PO Box 1140
Stratford, CT 06615-8640
(203) 293-5988
Email: hlee1952@hotmail.com

Summary: Independent executive recruiter with
full life cycle staffing. College recruiting, IT,
sales, telcom and diversity sourcing on site or
virtual.

Key Contact - Specialty:
Mr. Henry Lee

Salary Minimum: $35,000

Functions: Generalist (All)

Industries: Generalist (All), Energy, Utilities,
Pharm Svcs., HR Services, Communications,
Call Centers, Wireless, Network Infrastructure,
Software, Healthcare

Leeds and Leeds

PO Box 54
Brentwood, TN 37024-0054
(615) 371-1119
Fax: (615) 371-1225
Email: info@leedsandleeds.com
Web: www.leedsandleeds.com

Summary: We provide professional and efficient
service to life insurance, health insurance and
managed care organizations, assisting with their
recruiting needs.

Key Contact - Specialty:
Mr. Gerald I. Leeds, Principal

Salary Minimum: $50,000

Functions: Generalist (All), Middle Mgmt.

Industries: Insurance, Life

Legal Career Group LLC

87 Madison Springs Dr
Madison, CT 06443-2419
(203) 318-8146
Fax: (203) 318-8147
Email: nancy@legalcareergroup.com

Summary: Provide career counseling and
placement services exclusively to the legal
community, working with attorneys at all levels
throughout the United States and abroad. Resume
preparation service also available. Information
held in strictest confidence.

Key Contact - Specialty:
Ms. Nancy L. Roberts, Consultant, Legal
Placement - *Legal (Attorneys,Lawyers)*
Ms. Tina Saroka, Consultant, Legal Placement -
Legal (Attorneys,Lawyers)

Functions: Attorneys

Industries: Legal

The Legal Group

15485 Eagle Nest Ln Ste 110
Miami Lakes, FL 33014-2221
(305) 556-2110
Fax: (305) 556-8895
Email: allevin@bellsouth.net
Web: www.thelegalgroup.net

Summary: Legal search firm specializing in the
temporary and permanent placement of high-level
legal positions including attorneys, paralegals,
CFOs, CEOs and legal administrators.

Key Contact - Specialty:
Ms. Amy Levin, Managing Director
Mrs. Ayleen Gonzalez, Executive Legal Assistant

Salary Minimum: $35,000

Functions: Legal

Industries: Generalist (All), Construction,
Finance, Banking, Defense, Compliance,
Commercial, Re-Insurance, Real Estate

Legal Liaisons Ltd

1516 W Lake St Ste 303
Citadel Building
Minneapolis, MN 55408-2554
(612) 827-5165
Fax: (612) 823-1280
Email: resumes@legalliaisons.com
Web: www.legalliaisons.com

Summary: We are a national legal consulting and
recruiting firm for large law firms and Fortune 500
corporations to small enterprises and boutique law
firms. We staff permanent and temporary positions
for administrators, attorneys of all levels and other
legal professionals. We are engaged as a legal
talent scout, experienced professionals are
encouraged to inquire about opportunities.

Key Contact - Specialty:
Ms. Jodi L. Standke, President
Mr. Thomas Stephan, Esq., Vice President &
General Counsel

Functions: M&A, Risk Mgmt., Legal, Attorneys,
Paralegals

Industries: Generalist (All), Transportation,
Wholesale, Retail, Finance, Non-profits, Legal,
Media, Communications, Insurance, Re-
Insurance, Real Estate, Software, Biotech/Life
Sciences

Legal Network Inc

2151 Michelson Dr Ste 135
Irvine, CA 92612-1311
(949) 752-8800
Fax: (949) 752-9126
Email: legalnetwork@legalnetwork.cc
Web: www.legalnetwork.cc

Summary: Our network of candidates provides a
valuable resource for most law-related search
requests.

Key Contact - Specialty:
Ms. Carole Wampole, President
Mr. Daniel Wampole, General Manager

Functions: Generalist (All), Customer Svc.,
Systems Support, Network Admin., Legal,
Attorneys, Paralegals

Industries: Generalist (All), Legal, HR Services

Legal Search Associates Inc

6701 W 64th St Ste 302
Overland Park, KS 66202-4091
(913) 722-3500
Email: tbashor@jdhunter.com
Web: www.jdhunter.com

Summary: We recruit attorneys for law firms and
corporations. From general counsel positions to
staff attorneys or young associates to partners, we
have a proven track record of finding the best
candidates available.

Key Contact - Specialty:
Dr. Terry Bashor, President

Salary Minimum: $60,000

Functions: Legal, Attorneys

Industries: Generalist (All), Legal

Lehman & Associates Inc

1910 N 172nd Cir
Omaha, NE 68118-2897
(402) 763-8099
Fax: (402) 763-8098
Email: howard.lehman@cox.net

Summary: Specializing in the placement of IT
(programmers, network admin., database
administrators, web developers, etc.)
professionals. Also placing healthcare (nurses,
pharmacists, physical/respiratory therapists,
nuclear med., etc.) professionals.

Key Contact - Specialty:
Mr. Howard Lehman

Functions: Generalist (All), Product Dev., IT

Industries: Generalist (All), Database SW,
Development SW, ERP SW, HR SW, Industry
Specific SW, Networking, Comm. SW,
Healthcare, Hospitals, Physical Therapy

Ken Leiner Associates

11510 Georgia Ave Ste 105
Wheaton, MD 20902-1958
(301) 933-8800
Email: ken@itsearch.com
Web: www.itsearch.com

Summary: Our firm focuses on recruiting all
levels of sales, marketing, and technical talent for
the IT industry. Our clients include software and
systems vendors, integrators and consulting firms.
We work on a contingency or retainer basis and
have helped small and large technology companies
succeed in the marketplace.

Key Contact - Specialty:
Mr. Ken Leiner, President
Mr. Frank Munero, Vice President

Salary Minimum: $60,000

Functions: Sales & Mktg., IT, R&D, Engineering,
Specialized Svcs., Minorities/Diversity

Industries: Mgmt. Consulting, E-commerce, IT
Implementation, Telecoms, Network
Infrastructure, Government, Defense, Homeland
Security, Software, Database SW, Development
SW, ERP SW, HR SW, Networking, Comm.
SW, Security SW, System SW

Leitner Sarch Consultants

34 S Broadway Ste 102
White Plains, NY 10601-4432
(914) 682-4000
Email: info@leitnersarch.com
Web: www.leitnersarch.com

Summary: We specialize in retail sales, sales
management, and branch management within the
financial services industry.

Key Contact - Specialty:
Mr. Daniel Sarch, President
Mr. Jordan Schultz, Vice President
Mr. Steve Rappaport, Vice President
Ms. Elana Friedland, Associate - *Cable,
Computers (Software), Financial services,
Networking*

Salary Minimum: $80,000

Functions: Sales & Mktg.

Industries: Brokers, Misc. Financial

Leland Roberts Inc

900 American Blvd E Ste 104
Bloomington, MN 55420-1393
(952) 854-0441
Fax: (952) 814-9820
Email: information@lelandroberts.com
Web: www.lelandroberts.com

Summary: We are an executive search firm
specializing in the technical placement field. We
help professionals find the best environment for
ensuring satisfaction with their position. Our goal
is to create the best working relationship between
the professional and the company. We speak to
our hiring managers and HR professionals to find

out what kind of environment the candidate would be working in. We then find what our candidates needs are for the best fit.

Key Contact - Specialty:
Mr. Dwight Simpson, President
Mr. James Rose, Senior Recruiter

Functions: Management, HR Mgmt., IT, Systems Analysis, Systems Dev., Systems Implem., Systems Support, Network Admin., Engineering

Industries: Generalist (All), Finance, Services, HR Services, IT Implementation, Communications, Telecoms, Software, Accounting SW, ERP SW, HR SW, Industry Specific SW

Lema & Associates Inc

4 Bell Ln
Burlington, NJ 08016-5145
(609) 386-0944
Fax: (609) 386-0684
Email: customerservice@lema-and-associates.com
Web: www.lema-and-associates.com

Summary: A Recruiting and Placement Firm specializing in bilingual (English/Spanish) Professionals in US and Latin-America.

Key Contact - Specialty:
Mr. Mark Lema, President
Mrs. Rocio Rodriguez-Lema, Recruiter
Mr. Pablo Lema, Recruiter

Salary Minimum: $40,000

Functions: Minorities/Diversity

Industries: Generalist (All)

F P Lennon Associates

996 Old Eagle School Rd Ste 1102
Wayne, PA 19087-1806
(610) 687-8000
(888) 536-6667
Fax: (610) 687-8035
Web: www.fplennon.com

Summary: We are recognized as an industry leader in software sales and software consulting recruiting within the CRM, ERP, supply chain and B2B software industry.

Key Contact - Specialty:
Mr. Frank P. Lennon, President
Mr. Herbert Hutchinson, Senior Vice President

Salary Minimum: $80,000

Functions: Management

Industries: Database SW, Development SW, Doc. Mgmt., Production SW, ERP SW, HR SW, Industry Specific SW, Mfg. SW, Marketing SW, Networking, Comm. SW

Level A Inc

212-277 George St N
Peterborough, ON K9J 3G9
Canada
(705) 749-1919
Email: info@levela.net
Web: www.levela.net

Summary: We provide recruiting strategies & services to companies requiring personnel in administrative, finance, technical and key management/executive positions. Additional services include confidential advertising & candidate pre-qualification, reference checks, interview facilities & assistance, HR consulting, team building and skill validation.

Key Contact - Specialty:
Ms. Susan Blazey, Client Services - *Finance, Marketing, Office, Office (Administration), Staffing*
Ms. Kathy Pyle, President

Salary Minimum: $40,000

Functions: Generalist (All), Management, Senior Mgmt., Admin. Svcs., Mfg., Production, Healthcare, Sales & Mktg., Staffing

Industries: Generalist (All), Finance, Call Centers, Network Infrastructure, Defense, HR SW, Long-term/Home Care

The Levton Group Inc

140 Symington Ave
Toronto, ON M6P 3W4
Canada
(416) 532-0161
Fax: (416) 532-5832
Email: info@levton.com
Web: www.levton.com

Summary: The firm offers recruitment and other HR services on an hourly rated basis. Our strengths include senior clerical, accounting at all levels, computer professionals and management.

Key Contact - Specialty:
Mr. Nick Breaks, Principal

Salary Minimum: $25,000

Functions: Generalist (All)

Industries: Generalist (All)

Hal Levy & Associates

186 Mohonk Rd
High Falls, NY 12440-5229
(845) 687-4400
Fax: (845) 687-4401
Email: hal@hallevy.com
Web: www.hallevy.com

Summary: We are an executive search firm specializing in advertising direct response. We place people in direct marketing, advertising and new media.

Key Contact - Specialty:
Mr. Hal Levy, President
Ms. Eve Levy, Partner

Salary Minimum: $25,000

Functions: Generalist (All), Advertising, Mktg. Mgmt., Direct Mktg., Graphic Designers

Industries: Generalist (All), Advertising, Publishing, New Media

Branches:
500 5th Ave Ste 2700
New York, NY 10110-2799
(212) 686-4444

Lexington Software Inc

555 5th Ave Fl 14
New York, NY 10017-9257
(212) 376-7386
(646) 283-1377
Fax: (212) 986-5316
Email: lillian@lextn.com
Web: www.lexingtonsoftware.com

Summary: Our firm is an executive search organization serving the financial services industry for specific financial experience in risk management, derivatives, quantitative disciplines and technology-driven trading strategies.

Key Contact - Specialty:
Mr. John Rountree, BA, MBA, MS, Principal - *Banking, Derivatives, High technology, Mathematics, Risk management*

Ms. Jennifer Foster, BA, MA, EdD, Principal - *Administration, Competitive intelligence, Legal, Management, Training*
Ms. Lillian Lippencott, BA, Principal - *Accounting, Banking, Investment, Operations, Risk management*

Salary Minimum: $75,000

Functions: Finance, Taxes, Risk Mgmt., IT, Systems Analysis, Systems Dev.

Industries: Finance, Banking, Invest. Banking, Brokers, Mutual/Hedge Funds, Misc. Financial

The Liberty Group

(formerly known as Liberty Executive Search)
7500 San Felipe St Ste 950
Houston, TX 77063-1786
(713) 961-7666
Fax: (713) 961-1811
Email: info@thelibertygroup.com
Web: www.thelibertygroup.com

Summary: We are an executive search firm which specializes in the real estate, banking and mortgage industries. Additionally, our sister company provides contract IT professionals.

Key Contact - Specialty:
Mr. Rick McCain, CPC, Vice President
Mr. Louis de Ybarrondo, Partner, Liberty IT

Functions: Senior Mgmt., Middle Mgmt., Sales & Mktg., Sales Mgmt., Finance, Cash Mgmt., M&A

Industries: Real Estate

Pat Licata & Associates

5001 Weston Pkwy Ste 104
Cary, NC 27513-2316
(919) 653-1180
Fax: (919) 653-1199
Email: pat@patlicata.com
Web: www.patlicata.com

Summary: We are specialists in medical and pharmaceutical sales and sales management.

Key Contact - Specialty:
Ms. Pat Licata, President
Mr. Sam Licata, Chief Financial Officer

Salary Minimum: $40,000

Functions: Generalist (All), Sales & Mktg., Mktg. Mgmt., Sales Mgmt., Sales Reps., Minorities/Diversity

Industries: Generalist (All), Drugs Mfg., Medical Devices, Pharm Svcs., Equip Svcs., Biotech/Life Sciences, Healthcare, Hospitals, Dental, Women's

Lieberman-Nelson Inc

311 1st Ave N Ste 503
Minneapolis, MN 55401-3601
(612) 338-2432
Fax: (612) 332-8860
Email: l-n@lieberman-nelson.com
Web: www.lieberman-nelson.com

Summary: We are a full-service national legal search firm, placing full time attorneys exclusively.

Key Contact - Specialty:
Mr. Howard Lieberman
Ms. Nancy Nelson

Functions: Legal

Industries: Generalist (All)

LifeLine Solutions Inc
3949 Old Post Rd
Charlestown, RI 02813-2513
(401) 213-6416
(401) 207-1792
Email: paul@mylifeline.com
Web: www.mylifeline.com

Summary: A contract recruitment and sourcing company specializing in healthcare software, technical services, employer services (BPO, PEO) and high tech sales and marketing.

Key Contact - Specialty:
Mr. Paul Smith, President - *Communications, Computers (Software), Healthcare, Sales, Technical (Management)*

Salary Minimum: $50,000

Functions: Middle Mgmt., Sales & Mktg., HR Mgmt.

Industries: Generalist (All), Drugs Mfg., Plastics, Rubber, Computer Equip., Consumer Elect., Semiconductors, Misc. Financial, Pharm Svcs., Mgmt. Consulting, HR Services, Supply Chain Mgmt, Communications, Call Centers, Defense, Software, Database SW, Development SW, Doc. Mgmt., Production SW, Healthcare, Hospitals

LifeStyle Resources
(a JaNiece Rush company)
23 W 36th St Fl 4B
New York, NY 10018-7695
(212) 947-9792
Fax: (212) 736-9115
Email: mail@sterlinglifestyle.com
Web: www.sterlinglifestyle.com

Summary: We are a boutique search firm that caters to the personal service needs of the rich and sometimes famous. Butlers, personal assistants, private yacht & aircraft staff, executive & celebrity protection and household staff. We also provide concierge and temp services.

Key Contact - Specialty:
Ms. JaNiece Rush, President

Salary Minimum: $35,000

Functions: Senior Mgmt.

Industries: Non-Classifiable

Lighthouse Recruiting, LLC
40 Tower Ln
Avon, CT 06001-4222
(800) 838-0602
Fax: (860) 678-1711
Email: mharol@lighthouserecruiting.com
Web: www.lighthouserecruiting.com

Summary: We are an executive recruiting firm specializing in health care, engineering and retail sales professionals. We work on both a retained basis and contingency. Our team is comprised of highly trained and skilled recruiting professionals with extensive professional recruiting experience.

Key Contact - Specialty:
Mr. Mark Harol, Managing Partner
Mr. Jon Harol, Executive Recruiter HealthCare
Mr. Bill Tamburro, Executive Recruiter
Mrs. Chris Harol, CPC, Executive Recruiter

Salary Minimum: $40,000

Functions: Healthcare

Industries: Healthcare, Hospitals

J B Linde & Associates
1116 Rock Creek Elementary School Dr
O Fallon, MO 63366-7577
(636) 281-8040
Fax: (636) 281-8049
Email: rkessler@jblinde.com

Summary: We are a technical, management and executive recruiting in the manufacturing arena. Metal working industry i.e.; machining, stamping, welding, etc.

Key Contact - Specialty:
Mr. Roy Kessler, Owner - *Engineering*

Salary Minimum: $50,000

Functions: Management, Board Members, Senior Mgmt., Middle Mgmt., Mfg., Product Dev., Production, Automation, Plant Mgmt., Technicians

Industries: Metal Products, Machine, Appliance, Misc. Mfg.

Ginger Lindsey & Associates Inc
PO Box 2264
Coppell, TX 75019-8264
(972) 304-1089
Fax: (972) 304-0983
Email: ginger@glindsey.com
Web: www.glindsey.com

Summary: Specialize in mid to senior-level placements in market research with an emphasis on the high technology, telecom, financial services and packaged goods industries.

Key Contact - Specialty:
Ms. Ginger Lindsey, President - *Competitive intelligence, Market research*

Salary Minimum: $50,000

Functions: Mktg. Research

Industries: Food, Bev., Tobacco, Consumer Elect., Consumer Goods, Advertising

Lineal Recruiting Services
46 Copper Kettle Rd
Trumbull, CT 06611-5061
(203) 386-1091
(877) 386-1091
Fax: (203) 386-9788
Email: lisalineal@lineal.com
Web: www.lineal.com

Summary: Technical placement of sales, service, management and hourly exclusively in the electronic & electrical power and rotating apparatus industries, emphasizing service and repair of motors, controls, switchgear, UPS, transformers, drives, etc.

Key Contact - Specialty:
Ms. Lisa Lineal, Owner

Functions: Plant Mgmt., Sales Mgmt., Customer Svc., Engineering, Technicians

Industries: Energy, Utilities, Manufacturing, Test, Measure Equip., Misc. Mfg., Electronic, Elec. Components, Services, Equip Svcs., Engineering Svcs., Non-Classifiable

Link Executive Search
527 W Loveland Ave
Loveland, OH 45140-2323
(513) 683-8807
Fax: (513) 683-8826
Email: linkup@cinci.rr.com
Web: www.linkexecsearch.com

Summary: Years of successful packaging industry recruiting goes into discreet and confidential retained or contingency searches for executive leadership in the packaging and RFID industry

segments. Candidate screening, testing, reference checks, negotiations, background checks and more.

Key Contact - Specialty:
Mr. Steven Link, President

Salary Minimum: $60,000

Functions: Generalist (All), Management, Board Members, Senior Mgmt., Middle Mgmt., Sales & Mktg., Sales Mgmt., IT, Eng. Design, Process

Industries: Food, Bev., Tobacco, Paper, Printing, Drugs Mfg., IT Implementation, Supply Chain Mgmt, RF/Microwave, Packaging, Security SW, Hospitals

Lloyd, Martin & Associates
7127 Mexico Rd Ste 162
Saint Peters, MO 63376-5400
(314) 594-4040
(877) 428-3890
Email: fred@careersincomputers.com
Web: www.careersincomputers.com

Summary: We are an executive search firm specializing in information security and IT audit.

Key Contact - Specialty:
Mr. Fred Lloyd, Owner

Functions: IT

Industries: Generalist (All)

Lloyd Staffing
445 Broadhollow Rd Ste 119
Melville, NY 11747-3601
(631) 777-7600
(888) 292-6678
Fax: (800) 622-9324
Email: info@lloydstaffing.com
Web: www.lloydstaffing.com

Summary: We are a retained search and contingency placement service with extensive experience in many specialties, providing access to the highest quality candidates and positions. We are an industry leader in accounting, banking, life sciences, HR, sales & marketing, legal, architecture/engineering and IT/e-media.

Key Contact - Specialty:
Mr. Merrill Banks, CPC, President & Chief Executive Officer - *General management*
Mr. Keith Banks, CTS, Executive Vice President
Ms. Kay Lackmann, CTS, Senior Vice President
Mr. Vincent Albanese, CPA, Chief Financial Officer
Mr. Jon Hein, CIO
Ms. Nancy Schuman, CTS, Vice President, Marketing

Salary Minimum: $50,000

Functions: Generalist (All)

Industries: Banking, Services, Architectural Svcs., Accounting, HR Services, Media, Communications, Software, Marketing SW, Biotech/Life Sciences

Branches:
19601 Hamilton Ave
Torrance, CA 90502-1309
(310) 523-4320
Fax: (310) 523-4369
Email: torrance@lloydstaffing.com

140 Sherman St Fl 5
Fairfield, CT 06824-5849
(203) 254-9700
(866) 414-9700
Fax: (203) 319-7260
Key Contact - Specialty:
Ms. Barbara Grispo

1 Atlantic St Ste 701
Stamford, CT 06901-2407
(203) 353-8687
Fax: (203) 353-8802
Key Contact - Specialty:
Mr. Joe Grispo

8751 W Broward Blvd Ste 202
Plantation, FL 33324-2630
(954) 916-5044
Fax: (954) 916-8380
Key Contact - Specialty:
Mr. Marc Lester
Mr. Charles Rosenthal, Director

9501 Princess Palm Ave Ste 101
Tampa, FL 33619-8344
(813) 630-9000
Fax: (813) 630-4248
Key Contact - Specialty:
Ms. Jacquelyn Garvin

1777 Reisterstown Rd Ste 288
Baltimore, MD 21208-1344
(410) 486-1400
Fax: (410) 486-1282
Key Contact - Specialty:
Ms. Arlene Carmel, RN

1099 Wall St W Ste 390
Lyndhurst, NJ 07071-3617
(201) 935-7313
Fax: (201) 935-1401
Key Contact - Specialty:
Mr. Steve Joerg

3799 US Highway 46 Ste 203
Parsippany, NJ 07054-1060
(973) 394-1005
Fax: (973) 394-0302

1010 Northern Blvd Ste 234
Great Neck, NY 11021-5306
(516) 466-6670
Fax: (516) 466-6028
Email: work@lloydstaffing.com

4250 Veterans Memorial Hwy Ste 1100
Holbrook, NY 11741-4037
(631) 630-3400
Email: work@lloydstaffing.com

58 W 40th St Fl 14
New York, NY 10018-2635
(212) 354-8787
Email: work@lloydstaffing.com
Key Contact - Specialty:
Ms. Elisha Hashimoto, Staffing Specialist
Mr. Stuart Baran, MD, Financial Services

200 Main St
Blakely, PA 18447-1241
(570) 383-4100
Key Contact - Specialty:
Mr. Tim Brownell

LMB Associates

1468 Sunnyside Ave
Highland Park, IL 60035-2751
(847) 831-5990
Email: info@lmbassociates.com
Web: www.lmbassociates.com

Summary: Professional and executive search
specializing in IS.

Key Contact - Specialty:
Ms. Lorena M. Blonsky, President

Salary Minimum: $40,000

Functions: IT

Industries: Generalist (All)

LMC Group LLC

4 John St Bldg B
Morristown, NJ 07960-4287
(973) 292-0440
(570) 588-8007
Fax: (973) 292-6550
Email: alawton@lmc-grp.com
Web: www.lmc-grp.com

Summary: Retained/high-level contingency
executive search, outsourcing and management
consulting firm, specializing in the sales,
marketing, operations, product management,
project management and technology disciplines
within the financial services industry.

Key Contact - Specialty:
Mr. Alan Lawton, Managing Member, Partner -
    *Banking, Brokerage, Capital markets,
    Compliance, Marketing*
Mr. Ray Medina, Member & Partner - *Analysts,
    Banking, Banking (Mortgage), Brokerage,
    Compliance*

Salary Minimum: $70,000

Functions: Management, Product Dev., Mktg.
    Mgmt., Sales Mgmt., IT, Int'l.

Industries: Finance, Banking, Invest. Banking,
    Brokers, Venture Cap., Mutual/Hedge Funds,
    Misc. Financial, Services, Accounting, E-
    commerce, IT Implementation, Software,
    Accounting SW, Database SW, Development
    SW

LNH & Associates Inc

152 Sandy Hill Ranch Rd
Elgin, TX 78621-5618
(512) 426-1297
Fax: (707) 224-8899
Email: lnh@crnjobs.com
Web: www.crnjobs.com

Summary: We recruit for the construction
industry and specialize in highway, airport, bridge,
wastewater treatment and heavy civil construction.

Key Contact - Specialty:
Ms. Linda Hunt, President

Salary Minimum: $40,000

Functions: Generalist (All)

Industries: Construction

Lock & Associates

902-10 Four Seasons Pl
Burnhamthorpe Square
Etobicoke, ON M9B 6H7
Canada
(416) 626-8383
Fax: (416) 626-6609
Email: info@lock-associates.com
Web: www.lock-associates.com

Summary: Your partner in professional search.

Key Contact - Specialty:
Mr. Richard Lock, President
Mr. Peter Zukow, General Manager

Functions: Middle Mgmt., Production, Plant
    Mgmt., Purchasing, Distribution, Sales & Mktg.,
    Mktg. Mgmt., Sales Mgmt., HR Mgmt.,
    Engineering

Industries: Generalist (All)

Branches:
1770-1040 Georgia St W
The Grosvenor Building
Vancouver, BC V6E 4H1
Canada
(604) 669-8806
Fax: (604) 669-5385

Key Contact - Specialty:
Mr. Bruce MacDonald

1106-201 Portage Ave
T D Centre
Winnipeg, MB R3B 3K6
Canada
(204) 987-3744
Fax: (204) 987-3745
Key Contact - Specialty:
Mr. Gary Mattocks

650-633 Main St
Carson Building
Moncton, NB E1C 9X9
Canada
(506) 398-7835
Fax: (506) 389-7801
Key Contact - Specialty:
Mr. Greg O'Brien

100 Queen St
Ottawa, ON K1P 1J9
Canada
(613) 751-4450
Fax: (613) 566-7036
Email: mvilleneuve@lock-associates.com
Key Contact - Specialty:
Mr. Michael Villeneuve

3020-1800 Av McGill College
Place Montreal Trust Edifidce A
Montreal, QC H3A 3J6
Canada
(514) 866-2121
Fax: (514) 866-5257
Key Contact - Specialty:
Mr. Luc Cossette

480-410 22nd St E
Saskatoon Square
Saskatoon, SK S7K 5T6
Canada
(306) 244-2000
Fax: (306) 244-0087
Key Contact - Specialty:
Mr. Ray Beaudry

Locus Inc

PO Box 930
New Haven, WV 25265-0930
(304) 882-2483
Fax: (304) 882-2217
Email: doglady1@frontiernet.net

Summary: Recruit to specific openings
emphasizing quality over quantity. Like to work
directly with engineering managers and personnel
to ensure all requirements are considered.

Key Contact - Specialty:
Ms. Nancy S. Wainwright, President - *Technical*

Salary Minimum: $20,000

Functions: Generalist (All), Middle Mgmt., Mfg.,
    Engineering

Industries: Generalist (All), Metal Products,
    Machine, Appliance, Motor Vehicles, Misc.
    Mfg., Aerospace

LogiPros LLC

63 Beaverbrook Rd
Lincoln Park, NJ 07035-1440
(973) 696-1100
(800) 300-7609
Email: search@logipros.com
Web: www.logipros.com

Summary: We are a nationwide recruiting
organization specializing in the placement of
executives and middle management for the
logistics and supply chain industry. We also

provide interim executives for consulting, project implementation or temporary expertise.

Key Contact - Specialty:
Mr. Al Cheli, Vice President
Ms. Shelley Safian, Vice President - *Supply Chain*
Ms. June Rudd, Research Administration - *Supply Chain*

Functions: Management, Board Members, Senior Mgmt., Middle Mgmt., Admin. Svcs., Materials, Purchasing, Materials Plng., Distribution, Customer Svc.

Industries: Wholesale, Retail, Engineering Svcs., Logistics Svcs., Supply Chain Mgmt, Call Centers

Branches:
112 Kaiser Ln
Longwood, FL 32750-4100
(800) 300-7609
Key Contact - Specialty:
Ms. Shelly Safian, Vice President, Business Development

Logix Co

1601 Trapelo Rd Ste 230
Waltham, MA 02451-7359
(781) 890-0500
Fax: (781) 890-3535
Email: logix@logixinc.com
Web: www.logixinc.com

Summary: Our seasoned consulting staff is highly specialized in the search and selection of computer professionals and scientists ensuring maximum results in a quick, effective and professional manner.

Key Contact - Specialty:
Mr. David M. Zell, President

Salary Minimum: $65,000

Functions: Generalist (All), Sales & Mktg., IT, R&D

Industries: Insurance, Software, Biotech/Life Sciences

Logue & Rice Inc

(a division of Accounting Principals Inc)
8200 Greensboro Dr Ste 1175
Mc Lean, VA 22102-3872
(703) 761-7001
Fax: (703) 761-4248
Web: www.logueandrice.com

Summary: Our firm provides executive and management search that provide contingent and retained services for corporate and non-profit clients. We staff a full range from executives to professionals leaving Big 4 accounting firms.

Key Contact - Specialty:
Mr. Marc Zeid, Managing Director

Salary Minimum: $35,000

Functions: Generalist (All), Management, HR Mgmt., Finance, IT, Mgmt. Consultants

Industries: Generalist (All), Finance, Banking, Mgmt. Consulting, Hospitality, Communications, Telecoms, Real Estate, Software, Accounting SW, Biotech/Life Sciences

London Executive Consultants Inc

(also known as OEM Search International)
1420-380 Wellington St
Canada Trust Tower B
London, ON N6A 5B5
Canada
(519) 434-9167
Fax: (519) 434-6318
Email: info@londonexecutive.com
Web: www.londonexecutive.com

Summary: We are a well-established retainer/contingency search firm that works with branch/plant manufacturing companies requiring senior manufacturing and engineering personnel.

Key Contact - Specialty:
Mr. Paul Nelson, President - *Engineering, Technical*

Salary Minimum: $40,000

Functions: Generalist (All), Mfg., Materials, Sales & Mktg., HR Mgmt., Finance, IT, Engineering

Industries: Generalist (All), Manufacturing, Transportation, Environmental Svcs., Aerospace, Packaging

Longo Associates

454 Las Gallinas Ave Ste 258
San Rafael, CA 94903-3618
(415) 472-1400
(530) 582-0414
Email: rlongo@longo.com
Web: www.longo.com

Summary: We are an executive search and technical recruiting firm, with a high-technology focus, state-of-the-art computer-based technology, professional approach and successful track record.

Key Contact - Specialty:
Mr. Roger Longo, Principal

Functions: Generalist (All), Management

Industries: Generalist (All), Computer Equip., Consumer Elect., Test, Measure Equip., Electronic, Elec. Components, New Media, Communications, Security SW, System SW

Lordan Associates

602 Lime Ave Apt 502
Clearwater, FL 33756-5241
(727) 441-4803
Fax: (650) 745-1381
Email: mail@lordanassociates.com
Web: www.lordanassociates.com

Summary: Our firm specializes in the recruitment of professionals in the e-business, eCommerce, application software and EDI sectors, including sales, marketing, support and development professionals.

Key Contact - Specialty:
Ms. Susan Lordan, President

Functions: Board Members, Senior Mgmt., Middle Mgmt., Product Dev., Sales & Mktg., Mktg. Mgmt., Sales Mgmt., Training, Systems Dev., Systems Implem.

Industries: E-commerce, IT Implementation, PSA/ASP, Software, Accounting SW, Doc. Mgmt., Production SW, ERP SW, HR SW, Industry Specific SW, Mfg. SW, Marketing SW

Lorenc Group International LLC

4720 Salisbury Rd Ste 19
Jacksonville, FL 32256-6101
(904) 493-6042
Email: lorencgroup@attbi.com
Web: www.lorencgroup.com

Summary: Our firm is a leading edge client driven company focused on timely delivery of candidates. Our executive recruitment division is ready to serve your needs. We operate on either a retained basis or contingent basis. We have the industry experience and depth required to deliver the results you expect. We pride ourselves in professionalism, discretion and integrity.

Key Contact - Specialty:
Mr. Dick Lorenc, President - *Financial services, Healthcare*

Salary Minimum: $80,000

Functions: Generalist (All)

Industries: Generalist (All), Pharm Svcs., Accounting, Insurance, Casualty, Claims, Life, Commercial, Re-Insurance, Hospitals

Lost Dutchman Search

1140 Fall River Ct
Estes Park, CO 80517-9101
(970) 586-7676
Email: jkd@lostdutchmansearch.com
Web: www.lostdutchmansearch.com

Summary: We are dedicated exclusively to serving the recruitment and placement needs of our client insurance companies, brokers, MGA's, TPA's, MGU's and agencies. Lost Dutchman Search, established in 1992, is a national recruiting firm dedicated to the searching out and placement of exceptional insurance candidates. We have recruiters specializing in tax, audit, finance, accounting, commercial underwriting, actuarial, personal lines sales & marketing, reinsurance and claims. Mining for talent in the insurance industry!

Key Contact - Specialty:
Ms. Jeanine Drahota, Principal - *Accounting, Audits, Insurance, Tax*
Mr. Michael McCoy, General Recruiter
Ms. Mary Slattery, Commercial Underwriting Specialist
Mr. John Snyder, Actuarial Recruiter

Salary Minimum: $60,000

Functions: Board Members

Industries: Generalist (All), Insurance

J Louis Lynn Inc

PO Box 3373
Monument, CO 80132-3373
(719) 495-6863
Email: jmitten@jlouislynn.com
Web: www.jlouislynn.com

Summary: Concentrating on executive and senior executive roles for a variety of clients located in both the USA and abroad.

Key Contact - Specialty:
Mr. Jeffrey Mitten, President

Salary Minimum: $50,000

Functions: Generalist (All)

Industries: Manufacturing, Transportation, Wholesale, Retail, Logistics Svcs., Supply Chain Mgmt, Real Estate

Lovell & Associates Inc

105-300 North Queen St
Etobicoke, ON M9C 5K4
Canada
(416) 620-4155
Fax: (416) 620-9474
Email: info@lovellinc.ca
Web: www.lovellinc.ca

Summary: We are committed to performance excellence and are driven by the desire to become one of the most successful search firms in our

providence. As true generalists, we focus on relationship building and long-term partnering.

Key Contact - Specialty:
Mr. Andrée Lovell, CPC, President

Salary Minimum: $40,000

Functions: Product Dev., Materials Plng., Allied Health, Cash Mgmt., MIS Mgmt., R&D, Engineering, Graphic Designers

Industries: Manufacturing, Food, Bev., Tobacco, Textiles, Apparel, Lumber, Furniture, Paper, Printing, Chemicals, Soap, Perf., Cosmtcs., Drugs Mfg., Medical Devices, Metal Products, Retail, Finance, Services, Pharm Svcs., Equip Svcs., Mgmt. Consulting, HR Services, Packaging

Branches:
22-260 Holiday Inn Dr
Cambridge, ON N3C 4E8
Canada
(519) 651-1004
Fax: (519) 651-2083
Email: careers@conlov.com
Key Contact - Specialty:
Mr. Barry Connors, Vice President

LSI Manufacturing Solutions

PO Box 1044
Brunswick, OH 44212-8544
(330) 273-1002
Fax: (330) 225-3985
Email: lsi@lsijobs.com
Web: www.lsijobs.com

Summary: We specialize in placing engineering, management and quality professional candidates within the Swiss CNC and screw machine industry, producing medical device, automotive and aerospace components.

Key Contact - Specialty:
Mr. Lance Solak, President

Salary Minimum: $50,000

Functions: Board Members, Mfg.

Industries: Manufacturing, Medical Devices, Metal Products, Machine, Appliance, Engineering Svcs.

LTS Partners

1112 Elizabeth Ave
Naperville, IL 60540-5721
(630) 961-3331
Fax: (630) 961-9921
Email: mward@ltspartners.com
Web: www.ltspartners.com

Summary: Our firm places candidates in the technology leasing, sales and IS industries. Job placements are in: technology leasing sales, mid & senior level sales management, credit analysis, credit management, financial analysis, collections, accounting management & controllers and sales/pre-sales engineers.

Key Contact - Specialty:
Ms. Madeleine Ward, Partner - *Financial services, Leasing*
Mr. Stephen Rawls, Partner

Salary Minimum: $60,000

Functions: Management, Cash Mgmt., Risk Mgmt., Systems Dev.

Industries: Generalist (All), Finance, Banking, Invest. Banking, Misc. Financial, Equip Svcs., IT Implementation, Software

Lucas and Associates

4700 Falls Of Neuse Rd Ste 140
Raleigh, NC 27609-6278
(919) 647-9771
Email: joe@lucasandassociates.com
Web: www.lucasandassociates.com

Summary: Our firm conducts executive search nationally in the areas of accounting/finance and human resources

Key Contact - Specialty:
Mr. Joe Lucas, President
Mr. Toni Colon, Executive Recruiter

Salary Minimum: $75,000

Functions: Generalist (All)

Industries: Generalist (All), Finance, HR Services

Lucas Group

3384 Peachtree Rd NE Ste 700
Atlanta, GA 30326-1171
(404) 239-5620
Fax: (404) 260-7290
Email: info@lucasgroup.com
Web: www.lucasgroup.com

Summary: For more than three decades, we have built a reputation for quality service. As our company has grown and increased its reach, we have maintained a commitment to high performance and unsurpassed industry knowledge.

Key Contact - Specialty:
Ms. Guinevere Hayes, Manager, eCommerce Marketing
Mr. Art Lucas, President & Chief Executive Officer
Mr. Richard M. Bruno, Chief Financial Officer

Salary Minimum: $50,000

Functions: Generalist (All), Management, Mfg., Sales & Mktg., HR Mgmt., Finance, IT, Engineering, Attorneys, Paralegals

Industries: Generalist (All), Energy, Utilities, Construction, Manufacturing, Food, Bev., Tobacco, Chemicals, Medical Devices, Plastics, Rubber, Paints, Petro. Products, Misc. Mfg., Transportation, Retail, Finance, Invest. Banking, Misc. Financial, Services, Legal, Accounting, Mgmt. Consulting, HR Services, E-commerce, IT Implementation, Hospitality, Restaurants, Entertainment, Media, Advertising, Telecoms, Call Centers, Government, Defense, Aerospace, Packaging, Insurance, Real Estate, Software, Biotech/Life Sciences

Branches:
2231 E Camelback Rd Ste 317
Phoenix, AZ 85016-3447
(602) 954-1325
Fax: (602) 954-9594
Key Contact - Specialty:
Ms. Kerry Witherbee, Managing Partner

9100 Wilshire Blvd Ste 312E
Beverly Hills, CA 90212-3419
(310) 275-2920
Key Contact - Specialty:
Mr. Robert Wiener, Managing Partner

2600 Michelson Dr Ste 1550
Irvine, CA 92612-6531
(949) 660-9450
Fax: (949) 660-0126
Key Contact - Specialty:
Mr. Anthony P. Tommarello
Lee Cohen

5405 Morehouse Dr Ste 100
San Diego, CA 92121-4723
(858) 457-2005
Fax: (858) 558-0704

Key Contact - Specialty:
Mr. Scott Faurot, Managing Partner

2000 S Colorado Blvd Ste 2-660
Denver, CO 80222-7928
(303) 512-0600
Key Contact - Specialty:
Ms. Lisa Decker, Managing Partner

1200 G St NW Ste 800
Washington, DC 20005-6705
Key Contact - Specialty:
Mr. Tom Williamson, III, Managing Partner - *Legal, Legal (Attorneys,Lawyers)*

PO Box 1691
Aiea, HI 96701-7691
(808) 488-1390
Key Contact - Specialty:
Mr. Neil Voje

105 W Adams St Ste 2900
Chicago, IL 60603-6229
(312) 357-1160
Key Contact - Specialty:
Mr. Victor Palumbo

441 Lexington Ave Fl 18
New York, NY 10017-3924
(212) 599-2200
Fax: (212) 599-2014
Key Contact - Specialty:
Mr. Neil Handwerker

5001 Spring Valley Rd Ste 200E
Dallas, TX 75244-3916
(972) 490-0011
Fax: (972) 991-4144
Key Contact - Specialty:
Ms. Andrea Jennings, Division Director
Mr. Bryan Zawikowski, Division Director
Mr. Ira Bershad, Managing Partner

2 Riverway Ste 400
Houston, TX 77056-1971
(713) 864-5588
Fax: (713) 599-1657
Key Contact - Specialty:
Mr. Bill Kuchar, Managing Partner

585 Grove St Ste 120
Herndon, VA 20170-4791
(703) 456-0330
Fax: (703) 456-0337
Key Contact - Specialty:
Mr. Paul Fierszt, Managing Partner

Ludwig & Associates Inc

1005 Wagner Ct
Harrison City, PA 15636-1448
(724) 744-4949
Email: hr@ludwig-recruit.com
Web: www.ludwig-recruit.com

Summary: The key principal has many years of experience as a sales manager in the consumer products industry. The firm specializes in placing sales & marketing professionals with major consumer product companies.

Key Contact - Specialty:
Mr. Bob Ludwig, President - *Consumer, Consumer (Marketing,Packaged Goods,Products), Sales*

Salary Minimum: $50,000

Functions: Sales & Mktg.

Industries: Food, Bev., Tobacco

LUSSIER Executive Search Inc

PO Box 427 Stn 1st Can Place
1800-130 King St W
Toronto, ON M5X 1E3
Canada
(416) 860-6236
Email: info@lussiersearch.ca
Web: www.lussiersearch.ca

Summary: Ours is a registered Ontario
Corporation that specializes in the search and
recruitment of risk management, quantitative
analytics, finance, and accounting specialists in
the financial services sector. Clients include major
Canadian and foreign-owned financial institutions
in banking, wealth management, capital markets,
brokerage, pension fund and investment
management. Our mission is to find the right fit
for that essential addition to your team.

Key Contact - Specialty:
Ms. Héléne Lussier, President & Founder

Salary Minimum: $80,000

Functions: Generalist (All)

Industries: Banking, Invest. Banking, Brokers

Lutz Associates

9 Stephen St
Manchester, CT 06040-4430
(860) 647-9338
Email: lutzassociates@cox.net

Summary: Executive search and placement:
engineering, scientists, manufacturing and
marketing. Specializing in consumer products,
medical devices, electronics, rotating machinery,
office equipment, CAD/CAM, CIM and AI.

Key Contact - Specialty:
Mr. Allen Lutz, Owner - *Engineering*

Salary Minimum: $35,000

Functions: Management, Mfg., Materials, Mktg.
Mgmt., R&D, Engineering

Industries: Medical Devices, Plastics, Rubber,
Metal Products, Machine, Appliance, Consumer
Elect., Misc. Mfg., Robotics, Consumer Goods,
Aerospace, Software, Biotech/Life Sciences

Lybrook Associates Inc

PO Box 741
Bristol, RI 02809-0999
(401) 254-5840
Fax: (401) 253-7626
Email: recruiting@lybrook.com
Web: www.lybrook.com

Summary: We recruit chemists, chemical
engineers, biotechnology, pharmaceutical &
polymer/plastics engineers, scientists, managers &
executives for R&D, product development,
analytical, process, manufacturing, engineering,
QA/QC, technical service and sales/marketing
positions. We work with industries that hire
people with expertise in the above skills.

Key Contact - Specialty:
Ms. Karen Lybrook, President & Senior Partner -
*Biotechnology, Chemical, Coatings,
Instrumentation, Pharmaceutical*
Mr. David Lybrook - *Engineering,
Environmental, Plastics, Sales*

Salary Minimum: $30,000

Functions: Management, Senior Mgmt., Product
Dev., Quality, R&D, Engineering,
Environmentalists

Industries: Manufacturing, Food, Bev., Tobacco,
Textiles, Apparel, Chemicals, Soap, Perf.,
Cosmtcs., Drugs Mfg., Medical Devices,
Plastics, Rubber, Paints, Petro. Products, Test,
Measure Equip., Engineering Svcs.,
Environmental Svcs., Packaging, Biotech/Life
Sciences, Healthcare, Non-Classifiable

The LYNN Group HLF Inc

PO Box 158793
Nashville, TN 37215-8793
(615) 340-0800
Fax: (615) 467-5533
Email: heather@thelynngroup.com
Web: www.thelynngroup.com

Summary: We are a small firm performing both
retained and contingency searches for mid-level
and upper-management. We pride ourselves on
our hard work, reputation and ethical contributions
to the building industry (commercial developers,
architects and construction firms).

Key Contact - Specialty:
Ms. Heather Lynn Fike, President - *Entertainment*

Salary Minimum: $50,000

Functions: Generalist (All), Management, Sales
& Mktg., Architects

Industries: Generalist (All), Construction,
Hospitality, Real Estate, Healthcare

Paul Lynner & Associates

PO Box 118
Simpsonville, MD 21150-0118
(410) 531-9141
Fax: (410) 531-9141
Email: paul@lynner.biz
Web: www.lynner.biz

Summary: We are a premier telecommunication
sales & marketing recruiting organization with
extensive recruiting experience. We specialize in
supplying industry professionals to the providers
of networking hardware and software for the
public network environment.

Key Contact - Specialty:
Mr. Paul Lynner, President

Salary Minimum: $70,000

Functions: Generalist (All), Sales & Mktg.

Industries: Communications, Telecoms,
Telephony, Digital, Wireless, Fiber Optic,
Network Infrastructure, RF/Microwave

Lynx Inc

35 Bedford St Ste 3
Lexington, MA 02420-1538
(781) 274-6400
Fax: (781) 274-6300
Email: resumes@lynxinc.com
Web: www.lynxinc.com

Summary: Contingency search and placement
specializing in software engineering and related IT
positions in and around the greater Boston,
Southern NH and Rhode Island areas

Key Contact - Specialty:
Mr. Philip J. Hurd, President & Founder -
Computers (Software)
Ms. Sophia Navickas, Founder & Vice President -
Computers (Software)

Functions: IT

Industries: Generalist (All)

Corey Lyons & Associates

5125 S Kipling St Ste 210
Littleton, CO 80127-1736
(303) 933-3282
Email: coreylyons@aol.com

Summary: I work in the employee benefits
consulting industry. I place consultants, attorneys
and actuaries who deal with retirement plans,
executive compensation and healthcare issues. My
clients are the national accounting firms, actuarial
consulting firms, law firms and financial services
companies on a national basis.

Key Contact - Specialty:
Mr. Corey Lyons, Owner - *Benefits*

Functions: Benefits, M&A, Risk Mgmt.,
Actuaries, Pension/Ret. Planning, Legal,
Attorneys, Paralegals

Industries: Legal, Accounting, Mgmt. Consulting,
HR Services

Lyons & Associates Inc

7815 Loch Glen Dr
Village of Lakewood, IL 60014-3317
(815) 477-9292
Fax: (815) 477-9296

Summary: With a staff extensively experienced in
the graphics arts industry. We provide detailed,
thorough service to the printing and allied
industries.

Key Contact - Specialty:
Mr. Kent T. Lyons, President

Salary Minimum: $45,000

Functions: Generalist (All)

Industries: Printing

Lyons Pruitt International Inc

164 E Main St
Macungie, PA 18062-1311
(610) 966-1500
Email: search@lyonspruitt.com
Web: www.lyonspruitt.com

Summary: We have been providing executive
search services of the highest caliber. We
specialize in identifying exceptional professionals
with a verifiable track record of performance and
accomplishment.

Key Contact - Specialty:
Mr. Jim Pruitt, President

Salary Minimum: $80,000

Functions: Generalist (All), Senior Mgmt.,
Production, Sales Mgmt., CFOs, Cash Mgmt.,
Risk Mgmt., MIS Mgmt.

Industries: Generalist (All), Banking, Invest.
Banking, Venture Cap., Mutual/Hedge Funds,
Accounting, Mgmt. Consulting, New Media,
Software, Accounting SW

LZ Consulting Inc

PO Box 1644
Grand Rapids, MI 49501-1644
(616) 538-0510
(616) 538-1918
Email: lee@lzconsulting.com
Web: www.lzconsulting.com

Summary: Permanent placement, contingency and
retained search agency.

Key Contact - Specialty:
Mr. Lee Zeidler, President
Ms. Kathy Huizenga, Vice President - *Financial,
Manufacturing, Skilled trades*

Functions: IT, Engineering

Industries: Generalist (All)

M & M Associates Inc

11765 West Ave Ste 285
San Antonio, TX 78216-2559
(210) 340-8772
Fax: (210) 344-2080
Email: physicianjobs@md-jobs.com
Web: www.md-jobs.com

Summary: We are a physicians exclusive recruitment and placement firm for hospitals, medical groups, private practices, and universities.

Key Contact - Specialty:
Mr. Leonard N. Marino, President

Salary Minimum: $100,000

Functions: Physicians

Industries: Healthcare, Hospitals, Women's

M K & Associates

309 E Brady St
Butler, PA 16001-4895
(724) 285-7474
Fax: (724) 285-8339
Email: info@mkandassoc.com
Web: www.mkandassoc.com

Summary: Our recruiting firm has been placing top talented individuals throughout the food manufacturing industry.

Key Contact - Specialty:
Mr. John G. Mossman, Partner - *Food*
Ms. Maureen Knowlson, Partner - *Food*

Salary Minimum: $35,000

Functions: Senior Mgmt., Middle Mgmt., Product Dev., Production, Plant Mgmt., Quality, Distribution, Packaging, R&D, Engineering

Industries: Food, Bev., Tobacco

MacInnis Ward & Associates Inc

551 5th Ave Ste 3300
New York, NY 10176-0001
(212) 808-8080
Fax: (212) 808-8088
Email: info@macinnisward.com
Web: www.macinnisward.com

Summary: We provide a uniquely responsive, highly personalized approach to servicing the needs of our clients and candidates. Our clients include some of the most prestigious owners/developers, REITS, pension fund advisors, management companies and opportunity funds.

Key Contact - Specialty:
Ms. Mary A. Ward, President

Functions: Management

Industries: Accounting, Real Estate

Macro Resources

68 E Wacker Pl Ste 400
Chicago, IL 60601-7205
(312) 849-9100
Fax: (312) 849-9120
Email: frank@macroresources.com
Web: www.macroresources.com

Summary: We specialize in recruiting IT professionals. Software engineers, Java developers, DBAs, Internet developers, network administrators and security engineers to name a few. We also place staff temps.

Key Contact - Specialty:
Mr. Frank Roti, President

Salary Minimum: $50,000

Functions: IT, MIS Mgmt., Systems Analysis, Systems Dev., Systems Implem., Network Admin., DB Admin.

Industries: Generalist (All), Brokers, Services, E-commerce, IT Implementation, New Media, Telecoms, Wireless, Network Infrastructure, Software, Database SW, Development SW, Networking, Comm. SW, Security SW, System SW

Macrosearch Inc

11711 SE 8th St Ste 215
Bellevue, WA 98005-3543
(425) 641-7252
Fax: (425) 641-0969
Email: macro@macrosearch.com
Web: www.macrosearch.com

Summary: We are a personnel resource in high-technology career recruiting and placement.

Key Contact - Specialty:
Ms. Marjie Peterson, President & Chief Executive Officer - *High technology, Sales*
Mr. Howard Lazzarini, Executive Recruiter - *High technology*

Functions: Generalist (All), MIS Mgmt., Systems Analysis, Systems Dev., Systems Implem., Systems Support, Network Admin., DB Admin.

Industries: Generalist (All), Software

Magellan Search Partners

PO Box 862
Worthington, OH 43085-0862
(614) 846-7503
Fax: (614) 474-5680
Email: info@magellansp.com
Web: www.magellansp.com

Summary: Our core purpose is to discover and deliver talent to organizations that share in our unwavering commitment to excellence in staffing. With this philosophy it is our core purpose to enhance organizational success by securing individuals that excel in their talents and abilities.

Key Contact - Specialty:
Mr. Rob Zedeker, Managing Partner

Salary Minimum: $75,000

Functions: HR Mgmt., Staffing, Training, MIS Mgmt.

Industries: Generalist (All), Manufacturing, Retail, Finance, Services, Hospitality

The Magenta Group

27031 La Paja Ln Ste 500
Mission Viejo, CA 92691-6024
(949) 582-0600
Fax: (949) 582-2921
Email: mgnta@aol.com

Summary: As professionals in the graphic arts industry, besides helping clients with search and recruitment efforts, we help clients with general business trends, employment trends, comparative salary levels, benefit and relocation package comparisons as well as mergers & acquisitions.

Key Contact - Specialty:
Mr. Wayne Link, General Manager - *Printing*

Salary Minimum: $40,000

Functions: Generalist (All)

Industries: Printing, Publishing, New Media

Magna Search Inc

7946 Sunburst Ter
Lake Worth, FL 33467-7066
(561) 967-3211
Email: magnas@i-2000.com
Web: www.magnasearch.com

Summary: Executive search recruiters specializing in the HVAC, controls, energy management, energy services, building automation systems, facilities management and public accounting industries.

Key Contact - Specialty:
Ms. Billie Weiss, President
Mr. Howard Kay, Executive Vice President

Functions: Generalist (All), Technicians, Bldg. Contractors

Industries: Energy, Utilities, Construction, Manufacturing, Test, Measure Equip., Misc. Mfg., Electronic, Elec. Components, Banking, Invest. Banking, Brokers, Misc. Financial, Accounting, Engineering Svcs., Government, Healthcare

Magnum Search

1000 E Golfhurst Ave
Mount Prospect, IL 60056-4323
(847) 577-0007

Summary: HR management level experience with emphasis in search and recruiting for the metal fabrication and electronics industries.

Key Contact - Specialty:
Mr. Arthur N. Kristufek, President

Salary Minimum: $35,000

Functions: Generalist (All), Mfg., Materials, Sales & Mktg., HR Mgmt., Staffing, Mgmt. Consultants

Industries: Generalist (All), Paper, Plastics, Rubber, Metal Products, Machine, Appliance, Consumer Elect., Law Enforcement

Major Legal Services LLC

1111 Chester Ave Ste 510
Cleveland, OH 44114-3516
(216) 579-9782
Fax: (216) 579-1662
Email: dennis@majorlegalservices.com
Web: www.majorlegalservices.com

Summary: We are specialists in permanent and temporary (contract) recruiting of attorneys, paralegals, managers, administrators, secretaries and other support staff. Our client base is law firms and corporate legal departments in Ohio and throughout the Midwest.

Key Contact - Specialty:
Mr. Dennis J. Foster, President
Ms. Deborah L. Peters, Esq., Director, Recruiting
Ms. Sally Goodwin, Esq., LLB, LLM, Recruiter, Legal
Ms. Lesley Shiels, Recruiter, Legal

Functions: Legal, Attorneys, Paralegals

Industries: Generalist (All), Legal, Healthcare

Branches:
310 Grant St Ste 1
1 Oxford Ctr
Pittsburgh, PA 15219-2210
(412) 577-4010
Email: shari@majorlegalservices.com
Key Contact - Specialty:
Ms. Shari Paglia, Esq., Recruiter, Legal - *Legal, Legal (Attorneys,Lawyers), Staffing*
Ms. Juliana Werner, Recruiter, Legal - *Legal, Legal (Attorneys,Lawyers), Staffing*

Major, Lindsey & Africa

(formerly known as Major, Hagen, & Africa)
938 B St
San Rafael, CA 94901-3005
(415) 485-5121
(877) 482-1010
Email: sanrafael@mlaglobal.com
Web: www.mlaglobal.com

Summary: We place lawyers in organizations where having the absolute best lawyer for the job makes a difference. We've earned recognition for our track record of successful placements throughout the world. Combining experience with local personalized service, our recruiters are dedicated to intimately understanding our clients' and candidates' needs, finding the best match

between those needs and maintaining the highest level of professionalism and confidentiality.

Key Contact - Specialty:
Mr. Carter Brown, Chief Executive Officer
Mr. Joseph Beson, Chief Financial Officer
Mr. Robert Major, Partner
Mr. Chuck Fanning, Partner
Mr. Andy Sywak, Recruiter

Functions: Attorneys

Industries: Generalist (All), Legal

Branches:
801 S Figueroa St Ste 1100
Los Angeles, CA 90017-5503
(213) 689-0700
Email: losangeles@mlaglobal.com
Key Contact - Specialty:
Ms. Gigi Birchfield, Managing Partner

437 Lytton Ave Ste 201
Palo Alto, CA 94301-1533
(650) 853-1010
Email: paloalto@mlaglobal.com
Key Contact - Specialty:
Ms. Kimberly Fullerton, Managing Partner

600 B St Ste 2230
San Diego, CA 92101-4529
(619) 230-0450
Email: sandiego@mlaglobal.com
Key Contact - Specialty:
Ms. Catherine Rogers, Managing Director
Ms. Deborah Ben-Canaan, Managing Director

500 Washington St Ste 500
San Francisco, CA 94111-2914
(415) 956-1010
Email: sanfrancisco@mlaglobal.com
Key Contact - Specialty:
Ms. Martha Fay Africa
Ms. Nicole S. Lipman, Managing Director
Mr. Andrew E. Burrows, Managing Director
Ms. Jill Nissen, Managing Director
Mr. Chuck Fanning

601 13th St NW Ste 950 S
Washington, DC 20005-6817
(202) 628-0660
Email: washingtondc@mlaglobal.com
Key Contact - Specialty:
Mr. Jeffrey Lowe, Senior Managing Director

1355 Peachtree St NE Ste 1125
Atlanta, GA 30309-4902
(404) 875-1070
Email: atlanta@mlaglobal.com
Key Contact - Specialty:
Mr. Robert T. Graff, Senior Managing Director

35 E Wacker Dr Ste 2150
Chicago, IL 60601-2204
(312) 372-1010
Email: chicago@mlaglobal.com
Key Contact - Specialty:
Ms. Miriam J. Frank, Partner

260 Franklin St Ste 920
Boston, MA 02110-3146
(617) 345-4080
Email: boston@mlaglobal.com
Key Contact - Specialty:
Mr. Richards Gordon, Managing Partner - *Legal (Attorneys)*
Mr. Brion Bickerton, Partner - *Legal (Attorneys)*

551 5th Ave Fl 22
New York, NY 10176-2299
(212) 421-1011
Email: newyork@mlaglobal.com
Key Contact - Specialty:
Mr. Jonathan Lindsey, Managing Partner

1600 Market St Ste 1705
Philadelphia, PA 19103-7205
(215) 636-9802
Email: philadelphia@mlaglobal.com
Key Contact - Specialty:
Mr. Adam Stone, Managing Director

6836 Bee Cave Rd Ste 262
Austin, TX 78746-5079
(512) 533-9600
Email: austin@mlaglobal.com
Key Contact - Specialty:
Mrs. Carrie Trabue, Managing Director

100 Highland Park Vlg Fl 2
Dallas, TX 75205-2720
(214) 378-1010
Email: dallas@mlaglobal.com
Key Contact - Specialty:
Ms. Kelly Noblin, Managing Director - *Energy*

300 Main St Ste 200
Houston, TX 77002-1852
(713) 222-8140
Email: houston@mlaglobal.com
Key Contact - Specialty:
Mr. B. Cory Hawryluk, Senior Managing Director

2025 1st Ave Ste 400
Seattle, WA 98121-2100
(206) 218-1010
Email: seattle@mlaglobal.com
Key Contact - Specialty:
Ms. Karen Andersen, Senior Managing Director

205 E Wisconsin Ave Ste 205
Milwaukee, WI 53202-4207
(414) 272-1010
Email: milwaukee@mlaglobal.com
Key Contact - Specialty:
Mr. Mark Jungers, Managing Director

Debra Malbin Associates
270 W End Ave Apt 7S
New York, NY 10023-2624
(212) 501-9288
Email: dmaresume@aol.com
Web: www.debramalbinassociates.com
Summary: Our firm has the unique ability to understand and service the needs of the wholesale and retail fashion apparel industry. We have a distinctive vision and sense of integrity, enabling us to create successful partnerships benefiting both our clients and search candidates. We have placed candidates on all professional levels, with an emphasis on mid to senior management.

Key Contact - Specialty:
Ms. Debra Malbin, President - *Apparel*
Ms. Jill Ehrenberg, Senior Vice President
Ms. Marie Colletta, Vice President

Salary Minimum: $85,000

Functions: Senior Mgmt., Middle Mgmt., Product Dev.

Industries: Textiles, Apparel

Management Advisors International Inc
PO Box 3708
Hickory, NC 28603-3708
(828) 324-5772
Fax: (828) 324-4831
Email: bill@maisearch.com
Web: www.maisearch.com
Summary: We are a management consulting firm specializing in executive search/professional placement for the mortgage banking, commercial banking, capital markets, securities, thrift, and real estate finance.

Key Contact - Specialty:
Mr. William J. Castell, Jr., President

Salary Minimum: $80,000

Functions: Senior Mgmt., Nurses

Industries: Banking, Invest. Banking, Brokers, Mgmt. Consulting, Biotech/Life Sciences, Healthcare, Hospitals, Long-term/Home Care, Physical Therapy, Occupational Therapy, Women's

Branches:
2101 Rexford Rd Ste 119E
Charlotte, NC 28211-3454
(704) 521-9595
Email: msieck@maisearch.com
Key Contact - Specialty:
Ms. Serena Brock, President, Healthcare Division - *Healthcare, Home health, Medical, Occupational therapy, Physicians*
Ms. Mary Sieck, Branch Manager - *Compliance*

Management Consultants
15 Old Saybrook Dr
Greensboro, NC 27455-2724
(336) 540-9549
Fax: (336) 540-9434
Email: mancon@manageconsult.com
Web: www.manageconsult.com
Summary: We are an experienced and tested nationwide executive search and recruit firm specializing in supplying clients with management, technical, administrative and sales personnel. Our account executives place quality candidates with top clients in the automotive, plastics, textiles, telecom, optics, medical device, pharmaceutical and non-woven industries.

Key Contact - Specialty:
Ms. Marsha Willcox, President - *Automotive, Sales, Telecommunications, Textiles*
Ms. Sandra Ricketts, Office Manager

Functions: Generalist (All)

Industries: Generalist (All), Textiles, Apparel, Drugs Mfg., Medical Devices, Motor Vehicles, Electronic, Elec. Components, Pharm Svcs., Fiber Optic, Industry Specific SW, Biotech/Life Sciences

Management Decision Systems Inc (MDSI)
466 Kinderkamack Rd
Oradell, NJ 07649-1536
(201) 986-1200
Fax: (201) 986-1210
Email: amy@mdsisearch.com
Web: www.mdsisearch.com
Summary: We are data processing sales specialists. We focus on sales, sales management and pre-sales positions within the computer vendor community.

Key Contact - Specialty:
Mr. Brian Mahoney, President - *Sales*
Mr. Angelo Messina, Vice President
Mr. Richard Deakmann, Vice President - *Sales*
Mr. Victor Delray, Vice President - *Sales*

Salary Minimum: $50,000

Functions: Generalist (All), Sales Mgmt.

Industries: Generalist (All), Software

Management Group of America Inc
250 Passaic Ave Ste 210
Fairfield, NJ 07004-2518
(973) 808-3300
Fax: (973) 882-9284

Email: mgainc@aol.com
Web: www.mgainc.net

Summary: We are a consulting firm providing a complete range of services through our various divisions fulfilling the unique staffing needs of the insurance industry. The key factors for our success are experience, commitment, confidentiality and professionalism. We continually strive to maintain these factors and apply them to all aspects of our business.

Key Contact - Specialty:
Mr. James Byrne, President

Salary Minimum: $25,000

Functions: Generalist (All)

Industries: Insurance, Casualty, Claims, Life, Commercial, Re-Insurance

Management One Consultants

501-1200 Bay St
Toronto, ON M5R 2A5
Canada
(416) 961-6100
Fax: (416) 961-7018

Summary: Our strength is developing long-term relationships with top-notch clients and candidates. You always deal with the partners. We represent our clients in the marketplace in the most professional manner.

Key Contact - Specialty:
Mr. Frank Edelberg, President - *Marketing*
Ms. Dana Stewart - *Marketing*

Salary Minimum: $60,000

Functions: Mktg. Research, Mktg. Mgmt., Direct Mktg., Mgmt. Consultants

Industries: Generalist (All)

Management Recruiters International Inc (MRI)

(a subsidiary of CDI Corp)
200 Public Sq Ste 3100
Cleveland, OH 44114-2311
(216) 696-1122
(800) 875-4000
Fax: (216) 696-3221
Email: allen.salikof@brillantpeople.com
Web: www.mrinetwork.com

Summary: Search and recruitment for mid to senior management and professionals. Also provides interim staffing, assessment programs and international capability and videoconferencing services. Full range of staffing services.

Key Contact - Specialty:
Mr. Allen B. Salikof, President & Chief Executive Officer
Mr. Steve Mills, Chief Operating Officer
Mr. Phil Calamia, Chief Financial Officer
Mr. Donald L. Goldman, Vice President & General Counsel
Mr. Gary P. Williams, Vice President, Franchise Sales
Mr. Kevin O'Connor, Director, Human Resources

Salary Minimum: $45,000

Functions: Generalist (All)

Industries: Generalist (All)

Branches:
2 Metroplex Dr Ste 305
Birmingham, AL 35209
(205) 802-7377

Email: admin@mrbirmingham.com
Key Contact - Specialty:
Mr. Jim Emison
Ms. Karyn Uptain - *Banking, Banking (Commercial,Corporate,Retail), Financial services*

1428 Weatherly Rd SE Ste 204
Huntsville, AL 35803-1181
(256) 882-5011
Fax: (256) 882-5015
Email: rdavidson@midsouthconsultant.com
Key Contact - Specialty:
Mr. Bob Davidson

273 Azalea Rd Ste 1-104
Mobile, AL 36609-1924
(251) 342-8811
Fax: (334) 342-8817
Email: geraldg@sc-mobile.com
Key Contact - Specialty:
Mr. Gerald Grovenstein, Manager

2214 Executive Park Dr
Opelika, AL 36801-6062
(334) 749-4941
Fax: (334) 749-4914
Email: jobs@mrauburn.com
Key Contact - Specialty:
Mr. Tom Bennett, Account Executive
Mr. Richard Harlan, Accounts Executive
Ms. Angel Holladay, Administrative Assistant
Mr. David Strickland
Ms. Meg Parrish

1225 E Intl Airport Rd
Anchorage, AK 99518-1412
(907) 646-2300
Fax: (907) 646-2330
Email: mra@mr-anchorage.com
Key Contact - Specialty:
Keld Andersen

4710 Business Park Blvd Ste 18
Anchorage, AK 99503-7100
(907) 336-8595
Fax: (907) 336-8596
Email: jwilke@vortexgrp.com
Key Contact - Specialty:
Mr. James Wilke

154 E Redoubt Ave
Soldotna, AK 99669-8012
(907) 260-6433
(800) 474-5633
Fax: (907) 260-6460
Email: aaron@mrsca.com
Key Contact - Specialty:
Mr. Aaron Morse, Manager - *Banking (Commercial), Engineering*
Ms. Jeannine Morse, President
Mr. Walt Deal, Manager - *Engineering*
Mr. Matthew Morse, Manager
Mr. Kayda Nichols, Account Executive

PO Box 397
Payson, AZ 85547-0397
(928) 474-0005
Fax: (928) 474-1084
Email: careers@mripayson.com
Key Contact - Specialty:
Ms. Teresa Phillips, Co-Manager
Mr. Bob Phillips, Co-Manager

3404 W Cheryl Dr Ste A152
Phoenix, AZ 85051-9614
(602) 843-2790
Fax: (602) 843-2796
Email: mruck@mriphoenix.com
Key Contact - Specialty:
Mr. Michael Ruck

4800 N Scottsdale Rd Ste 2800
Scottsdale, AZ 85251-7634
(480) 941-2395
Fax: (480) 941-1430
Email: todd@govig.com
Key Contact - Specialty:
Mr. Dick A. Govig, Chairman
Mr. Todd Govig, President
Ms. Dianna LoDolce, Division Manager - *Sales*
Mr. Todd Wells, Account Executive - *Sales*
Mr. Terry Mahan, Account Executive - *Sales*
Mr. Mark VanderArk, Account Executive - *Sales*
Ms. Daniela Iwanski, Account Executive - *Sales*
Ms. Bobbi Moss, CSAM, Vicer President & Division Manager
Ms. Lois Berman, CSAM, Vice President
Ms. Bess Cadwell, CSAM, Vice President
Ms. Jacque Linaman, CSAM, Vice President
Ms. Jennifer Mitteer, CSAM, Vice President
Ms. Sharon Jochens, Account Executive
Mr. Brad Francis, CPA, Account Executive
Mr. Sheridan Bristow, Project Coordinator
Ms. Jana Halsne, Project Administrator
Ms. Jennie Miller, Project Coordinator
Ms. Marina Volpian, Project Coordinator
Ms. Terry Shaw, Project Coordinator
Ms. Diana Cota, Project Coordinator
Mr. Anthony Bell, Account Executive - *Biotechnology, Pharmaceutical*
Ms. Pat Throgmorton, Division Manager
Ms. Barbara Burns, Vice President
Ms. Julie Mead, Account Executive
Ms. Alicia Weitzel, Account Executive
Mr. Jeff Baker, CSAM, Division Manager & Vice President - *Plastics*
Mr. Brent Larson, Senior Account Executive - *Plastics*
Mr. John Lowery, Account Executive - *Plastics*
Mr. Matt des Tombes, Account Executive - *Plastics*
Mr. David Williams, Account Executive - *Plastics*
Ms. Karen Teetzel, Vice President
Mr. Barry Weeter, Vice President - *Technology*
Ms. Laura Roberts, Project Coordinator - *Technology*
Ms. Alison Drumm, CSAM, Vice President - *Healthcare*
Mr. Neil Hefta, CSAM, Vice President - *Healthcare*
Ms. Melissa Urich, Project Coordinator - *Healthcare*
Mr. Marc Fredrick, Account Executive - *Healthcare*
Mr. Will Donaldson, Account Executive - *Healthcare*
Ms. Stephanie Scher, Account Executive - *Healthcare*
Ms. Pam Harrison, Project Coordinator - *Healthcare*
Ms. Jackie McKelvey, Project Coordinator - *Healthcare*
Mr. Mike Todd, Senior Account Executive

6992 E Broadway Blvd
Tucson, AZ 85710-2803
(520) 529-0750
Fax: (520) 529-0931
Email: brian@mrtucsonnorth.com
Key Contact - Specialty:
Mr. Brian Bee

102 N First St
Rogers, AR 72756-6657
(479) 621-0706
Fax: (479) 621-9753
Email: resumes@mrirogers.com
Key Contact - Specialty:
Mr. Al McEwen, Manager
Mr. Morrie Brown, Recruiter
Ms. Sharla Gaither, Recruiter
Ms. Debbie McEwen, Manager
Mr. Shaun McEwen, Recruiter

Ms. Robbin Rose, Manager
JB Smith, Recruiter
Mr. David Whittlesey, Recruiter
Stacey Wingate, Recruiter

4501 E La Palma Ste 130
Anaheim, CA 92807-1998
(714) 970-1113
Email: rv@theocrecruiters.com
Key Contact - Specialty:
Mr. Rich Vandermey, President

188 Quail Run
Aptos Hills, CA 95076-9565
(831) 722-7900
Fax: (831) 722-7999
Email: dehaptos@hotmail.com
Key Contact - Specialty:
Ms. Cathy Henderson, Certified Sr Account
   Manager - *Construction*
Mr. Dale Henderson, Manager

7615 Morro Rd
Atascadero, CA 93422-4433
(805) 226-7613
Fax: (805) 466-0785
Email: glangston@mri-paso.com
Key Contact - Specialty:
Mr. Gary Langston

2382 Faraday Ave Ste 110
Carlsbad, CA 92008-7219
(760) 602-0204
Fax: (760) 602-0905
Email: john@sagemri.com
Key Contact - Specialty:
Mr. John Stankiewicz, Managing Director -
   Accounting, Finance
Mr. Matt Serafin, Account Executive -
   Accounting, Finance
Ms. Jennifer Lacefield, Researcher - *Accounting,*
   Finance
Mr. Chris John, Researcher - *Accounting, Finance*
Ms. Jan Rebecca, Administrative Assistant -
   Accounting

197 N Sunnyside Ave Ste 100
Clovis, CA 93611-0578
(559) 299-2600
Fax: (559) 325-3739
Email: rp@mrilincolnpartners.com
Key Contact - Specialty:
Mr. Rob Porcella, President
Mr. Kade Hudson, Senior Account Executive

55 Shaw Ave Ste 105
Clovis, CA 93612-3819
(559) 325-3990
Fax: (559) 325-3991
Email: recruit@mri-hart.com
Key Contact - Specialty:
Mr. Michael Hart

202 Cousteau Pl Ste 190
Davis, CA 95618-7719
(530) 297-5400
Fax: (530) 297-5401
Email: david@healthcareis.com
Key Contact - Specialty:
Mr. Dave Kushan, CSAM, Manager

2222 Francisco Dr Ste 430
El Dorado Hills, CA 95762-3765
(916) 939-9780
Fax: (916) 939-9785
Email: stan@mrifoodjobs.com
Key Contact - Specialty:
Mr. Stan Gardner, Manager

30092 Ivy Glenn Dr Ste 210
Laguna Niguel, CA 92677-5027
(949) 429-8813
Fax: (949) 429-8815
Email: spencer@mrisearchlight.com

Key Contact - Specialty:
Mr. Spencer Hermann, Manager

444 W Ocean Blvd Ste 1102
Long Beach, CA 90802-4519
(562) 432-5905
Fax: (562) 432-5935
Email: greid@reidmri.com
Key Contact - Specialty:
Mr. George Reid

111 N Sepulveda Blvd Ste 325
Manhattan Beach, CA 90266-6849
(310) 318-2931
Fax: (310) 318-2731
Email: trent.overholt@losangelesmri.com
Key Contact - Specialty:
Mr. Trent Overholt, Manager

27285 Las Ramblas Ste 147
Mission Viejo, CA 92691-8543
(949) 367-1095
Email: resume@mrmvc.com
Key Contact - Specialty:
Mr. Mark A Graban, President

1109 Jefferson St
Napa, CA 94559-2416
(707) 257-4430
Fax: (707) 257-2325
Email: lszmidt@sbcglobal.net
Key Contact - Specialty:
Les Szmidt, President - *Biomaterials, Biomedical,*
   Biopharmaceutical, Biotechnology, Medical
   (Devices)

22362 Gilberto Ste 110
Rancho Santa Margarita, CA 92688-2142
(949) 459-7000
Fax: (949) 459-7855
Email: info@greaterjob.com
Key Contact - Specialty:
Mr. Mark Myers

2151 River Plaza Dr Ste 308
Sacramento, CA 95833-4133
(916) 239-3700
Email: info@connectpointsg.com
Key Contact - Specialty:
Mr. Curtis Cetraro, Manager
Ms. Traci Cetraro, Manager

5500 Madison Ave Ste A
Sacramento, CA 95841-3149
(916) 334-7800
Fax: (916) 334-5800
Email: mrsacnorth@earthlink.net
Key Contact - Specialty:
Mr. Tom Kelly

2312 Bethards Dr Ste 7
Santa Rosa, CA 95405-9004
(707) 575-3699
Fax: (707) 575-3644
Email: info@scsantarosa.com
Key Contact - Specialty:
Mr. Russ Maney, Manager

25134 Rye Canyon Loop Ste 360
Valencia, CA 91355-5075
(661) 775-9999
Fax: (661) 775-9925
Email: john.broderick@mrivalencia.com
Key Contact - Specialty:
Mr. John Broderick

208 W Main St Ste 10
Visalia, CA 93291-6262
(559) 741-7900
Fax: (559) 741-7909
Email: recruit@theworks.com
Key Contact - Specialty:
Mr. Jim Ely, Manager

165 Lennon Ln Ste 102
Walnut Creek, CA 94598-2490
(925) 932-1045
Email: george@gbrsmith.com
Key Contact - Specialty:
Mr. George Smith, Founder and President

31822 Village Center Rd Ste 205
Westlake Village, CA 91361-4329
(818) 991-4410
Fax: (818) 991-4680
Email: azia@mri-la.com
Key Contact - Specialty:
Ali Zia

20300 Ventura Blvd Ste 380
Woodland Hills, CA 91364-0919
(818) 712-9930
Fax: (818) 712-9975
Email: resume@mriwh.com
Key Contact - Specialty:
Mr. Eman Talei
Mr. Kevin Javaheri

3639 E Arapahoe Rd Ste 210
Centennial, CO 80122-2071
(888) 320-5511
Email: resume@mridenversouth.com
Key Contact - Specialty:
Mr. Cliff Heller, Senior Partner
Ms. Gunnel Kramer, Senior Partner

1825 Austin Bluffs Pkwy Ste 200
Colorado Springs, CO 80918-7861
(719) 389-0600
Fax: (303) 265-9681
Email: resume@jobsmr.com
Key Contact - Specialty:
Mr. Brent Kiepke, Manager

925 S Broadway Ste 222
Cortez, CO 81321-4033
(970) 564-8585
Email: jgreenmeier@mrcortez.com
Key Contact - Specialty:
Mr. John Grenmeier, Founder and Managing
   Partner

3560 Evergreen Pkwy Ste 104
Evergreen, CO 80439-7761
(303) 679-6079
(800) 933-5250
Fax: (303) 679-6080
Email: jak@mridenver.com
Key Contact - Specialty:
Mr. John Kirschner

PO Box 841
Glenwood Springs, CO 81602-0841
(970) 947-9740
(866) 990-5550
Fax: (970) 947-9778
Email: klammey@elkpeaks.com
Key Contact - Specialty:
Mr. Keith Lammey

5441 Boeing Dr Ste 101
Loveland, CO 80538-8855
(970) 612-0801
Email: steve@mrfortcollins.com
Key Contact - Specialty:
Mr. Steve Betros, Owner & Managing Partner

30 Wall St
Coventry, CT 06238-3143
(860) 742-5130
Email: rlewis@frontlinerecruiters.com
Key Contact - Specialty:
Mr. Rich Lewis, Founder and President

75 Glen Rd Ste G2
Sandy Hook, CT 06482-1176
(203) 364-1871
Fax: (203) 426-8259

Email your resume to a targeted list of recruiters now at www.ExecutiveAgent.com/DER07

Email: dmcevoy@mrnewtown.net
Key Contact - Specialty:
Mr. Dick McEvoy

427 Bridgeport Ave
Shelton, CT 06484-5361
(203) 926-1200
Email: jbgurn@mricoastalgroup.com
Key Contact - Specialty:
Mr. Jim Gurn, President

196 Danbury Rd
Wilton, CT 06897-4029
(203) 761-1288
Fax: (203) 761-1258
Email: andy@scwilton.com
Key Contact - Specialty:
Mr. Andy E. Pratt, Manager

396 Danbury Rd Ste A
Wilton, CT 06897-2024
(203) 761-1342
Email: jobs@mriwestport.com
Key Contact - Specialty:
Mr. Rob Merkle, President

17585 Nassau Commons Blvd Ste 2
Lewes, DE 19958-6286
(302) 645-5600
Email: resumes@mrisussex.com
Key Contact - Specialty:
Mr. Steven B Howerton, President

2500 Quantum Lakes Dr Ste 203
Boynton Beach, FL 33426-8323
(561) 369-4481
Email: info@kenzakgroup.com
Key Contact - Specialty:
Mr. Brian M. Moskowitz, President

1201 6th Ave W Ste 321
Bradenton, FL 34205-7428
(941) 744-0944
Fax: (941) 744-5013
Email: jeffdentz@thedentzgroup.com
Key Contact - Specialty:
Mr. Jeff Dentz

2918 Miracle Pkwy
Cape Coral, FL 33914-3862
(239) 542-2745
Fax: (239) 542-2746
Email: topjob999@aol.com
Key Contact - Specialty:
Mr. Virgil L. Metcalf, Manager

2100 Ponce De Leon Blvd Ste 1045
Coral Gables, FL 33134-5241
(305) 445-7073
Fax: (305) 445-7375
Email: ddavis@mricgn.com
Key Contact - Specialty:
Mr. David Davis

210 N University Dr Ste 204
Coral Springs, FL 33071-7339
(954) 344-9222
Email: srupert@mrcoralsprings.com
Key Contact - Specialty:
Mr. Scott Rupert, Manager

5926 NW 122nd Dr
Coral Springs, FL 33076-1940
(954) 331-1096
Email: adam@mrisearchmax.com
Key Contact - Specialty:
Mr. Adam Dalva, Manager

9900 W Sample Rd Ste 407
Coral Springs, FL 33065-4079
(954) 340-8000
Fax: (954) 340-8300
Email: scijobs@bellsouth.net

Key Contact - Specialty:
Mr. Frank Braile, Jr., Manager
Mr. Andrew Skolnik

5367 Ortega Blvd Ste 300
Jacksonville, FL 32210-8447
(904) 981-0553
Fax: (904) 981-0539
Email: mnixon@mrjaxwest.com
Key Contact - Specialty:
Mr. Mike Nixon
Ms. Annette Nixon

270 S Central Blvd Ste 103
Jupiter, FL 33458-8816
(561) 744-1891
Email: mjewett@aliantgroup.com
Key Contact - Specialty:
Mr. Michael Jewett, Manager

1300 3rd St S Ste 301A
Naples, FL 34102-7239
(239) 261-8800
Fax: (239) 261-7551
Key Contact - Specialty:
Mr. Dan R. Ressler, Manager

4077 Tamiami Trail N Ste D201
Naples, FL 34103-3594
(239) 403-9218
Fax: (866) 403-9219
Email: jadmonius@jpworksolutions.com
Key Contact - Specialty:
Mr. James Admonius, Founder and President

809 Walkerbilt Rd Ste 2
Naples, FL 34110-1511
(239) 596-7280
Fax: (239) 596-1552
Email: dave@morisey-dart.com
Key Contact - Specialty:
Mr. David Dart
Ms. Linda Morisey

6014 US Highway 19 Ste 502
New Port Richey, FL 34652-2549
(727) 815-0901
Fax: (727) 815-0903
Email: rrussick@mrwestpasco.com
Key Contact - Specialty:
Ms. Ronda Russick

3751 Maguire Blvd Ste 221
Orlando, FL 32803-3011
(407) 898-4440
Email: careers@mriorlando.com
Key Contact - Specialty:
Ms. Paula Rutledge, Managing Director

7680 Unversal Blvd Ste 424
Orlando, FL 32819-8958
(407) 352-0113
Email: rick@nicholsesg.com
Key Contact - Specialty:
Mr. Rick Kleinschmidt, Managing Director
Mr. Steve Nichols, Managing Director
Ms. Lindsay Testa, Project Coordinator

124 N Nova Rd Ste 108
Ormond Beach, FL 32174-5122
(386) 677-2955
Email: scmrifla@aol.com
Key Contact - Specialty:
Jere Chambers, Founder and President

PO Box 19193
Panama City Beach, FL 32417-1093
(850) 235-3591
Email: executiverecruiter@att.net
Key Contact - Specialty:
Mr. Panama Charlie, Manager

117 W Alexander St Ste 307
Plant City, FL 33563-7155
(813) 754-6340
Fax: (813) 754-7557
Email: davezaring@pharmaceuticalchemist.com
Key Contact - Specialty:
Mr. David Zaring

101 N Riverside Dr Ste 208
Pompano Beach, FL 33062-5011
(954) 788-2699
Email: priddel@scpompanobeach.com
Key Contact - Specialty:
Ms. Pam Riddell, Founder and Managing Partner
Ms. Michelle Walsh, President
Mr. Nick Satek, Office Manager

9500 Koger Blvd N Ste 203
Saint Petersburg, FL 33702-2466
(727) 577-2116
Fax: (727) 576-5594
Email: phil@mrigulfcoast.com
Key Contact - Specialty:
Mr. Philip Petrillo
Mr. Matt Frushell

11110 W Oakland Park Blvd Ste 308
Sunrise, FL 33351-6808
(954) 509-9000
Email: mmaier@topcalibersearch.com
Key Contact - Specialty:
Mr. J Michael Maier, Managing Partner

743 E Tennessee St
Tallahassee, FL 32308-4913
(850) 656-8444
Fax: (850) 942-2793
Email: kitte@mrrecruiter.com
Key Contact - Specialty:
Ms. Kitte H. Carter, Manager

10500 University Center Dr Ste 110
Tampa, FL 33612-6419
(813) 972-0012
Email: carl@madici.com
Key Contact - Specialty:
Mr. Carl Will, Founder and Managing Partner

14502 N Dale Mabry Hwy Ste 200
Tampa, FL 33618-2040
(813) 265-3400
Email: resumes@e2recruiting.com
Key Contact - Specialty:
Ms. Kimberly Dachelet, President
Mr. Gary Jacobs, Managing Partner

16590 N Dale Mabry Hwy
Tampa, FL 33618-1325
(813) 265-8789
Fax: (813) 265-8902
Email: mri@tampabay.rr.com
Key Contact - Specialty:
Mr. James Carow

PO Box 5067
Tampa, FL 33675-5067
(813) 645-4224
Fax: (813) 645-4850
Email: alan@mriginn.com
Key Contact - Specialty:
Mr. Alan Ginn

2645 Exec Park Dr Ste 141
Weston, FL 33331-3624
(954) 385-3122
Fax: (954) 385-5186
Email: suzanne@mriweston.com
Key Contact - Specialty:
Mr. Ray George
Ms. Sue George

PO Box 590
1122 Monticello St Ste 16
Covington, GA 30015-0590
(770) 787-9056
Fax: (770) 787-7105
Email: rholt@mrcovington.com
Key Contact - Specialty:
Mr. Richard Holt

3700 Crestwood Pkwy NW Ste 320
Duluth, GA 30096-5585
(770) 925-0540
Key Contact - Specialty:
Lena Riggs, Manager

112 Governors Sq Ste B
Fayetteville, GA 30215-4864
(770) 632-0703
(770) 632-0804
Fax: (770) 632-0709
Email: rickreder@bellsouth.net
Key Contact - Specialty:
Mr. Rick Reder, President & Managing Owner -
  Consumer (Products), Executives,
  Manufacturing (Management), Marketing, Sales

5272 Bowman Springs Trl
Flowery Branch, GA 30542-5192
(770) 965-6750
Fax: (770) 965-6751
Email: wgbrownlee@charter.net
Key Contact - Specialty:
Mr. William Brownlee, Owner & Manager

5755 Ridgewater Cir
Gainesville, GA 30506-2389
(678) 343-2742
Email: ken@defenseplacements.com
Key Contact - Specialty:
Mr. Ken Setzer, Owner
Ms. Cindie Reddington, Project Coordinator

2935 Haynes Club Cir Set 101
Grayson, GA 30017-2848
(770) 982-0043
Email: judy.nixon@jnxpartners.com
Key Contact - Specialty:
Ms. Judy Nixon, Founder and President
Ms. Sandra Jordon, Account Executive

1165 Winborn Trl
Kennesaw, GA 30152-6965
(770) 590-1057
Email: susan@scherersolutions.com
Key Contact - Specialty:
Ms. Susan Scherer, Founder and Managing
  Partner

190 Camden Hill Rd Ste D
Lawrenceville, GA 30045-2448
(678) 377-9944
Fax: (678) 377-9912
Email: skip.freeman@hiretowin.com
Key Contact - Specialty:
Mr. Skip Freeman, President - *Chemical,*
  Engineering, Food & beverage, HVAC, Sales
Mr. Ed Cardon, Account Executive, Civil
  Engineering - *Bridges, Engineering, Highways,*
  Traffic, Transportation
Mr. Duane Hill, Account Executive, IT - *AS/400,*
  Database (Administration), ERP, Information
  Technology, SAP
Mr. Henry Gauthier, Search Consultant, Civil
  Engineering - *Bridges, Engineering, Traffic,*
  Travel, Utilities
Ms. Marie Nease, Search Consultant, Food &
  Beverage - *Business development, Consumer*
  (Packaged Goods), Food & beverage, Food
  service, Sales

1507 Johnson Ferry Rd Ste 175
Marietta, GA 30062-6438
(770) 565-8440

Email: info@tragergroup.com
Key Contact - Specialty:
Mr. Steve Trager, Founder and President

3535 Roswell Rd Ste 19
Marietta, GA 30062-6252
(678) 560-9078
Fax: (678) 560-9079
Email: rhollis5@bellsouth.net
Key Contact - Specialty:
Mr. Ron Hollis, Manager

118 S 2nd Ave
Mc Rae, GA 31055-1539
(229) 868-5001
Fax: (229) 868-6603
Email: rgraves@mrimcrae.com
Key Contact - Specialty:
Mr. Ron Graves, Manager

406 Line Creek Dr Ste B
Peachtree City, GA 30269-5647
(770) 486-0603
Fax: (770) 631-7684
Email: mgmrecr@fdn.com
Key Contact - Specialty:
Mr. Ronald L. Wise, Manager

PO Box 1455
Perry, GA 31069-1455
(478) 988-4444
Fax: (501) 423-7254
Email: twentz.mrmg@mindspring.com
Key Contact - Specialty:
Mr. Terry M. Wentz, Manager

1201 Macy Dr
Roswell, GA 30076-6350
(770) 645-6009
Fax: (770) 645-0988
Email: tilden@roswellgroup.com
Key Contact - Specialty:
Mr. Tilden Martin, Jr.
Ms. Sue Martin, Manager

45 W Crossville Rd Ste 514
Roswell, GA 30075-2964
(770) 650-0835
Fax: (770) 650-0836
Email: mderby@scroswell.com
Key Contact - Specialty:
Ms. Cheryl Derby
Mr. Michael Derby
Ms. Dorothy Minecci, Executive Recruiter

5000 Research Ct Ste 600
Suwanee, GA 30024-6605
(770) 495-0040
Fax: (770) 495-9049
Email: rpw@wcgsearch.com
Key Contact - Specialty:
Mr. Russ Wilson, Managing Director
Mr. Griff Martin, Director, Healthcare -
  Healthcare, Home health, Management,
  Medical (Sales), Sales
Mr. Moua T. Xiong, Executive, Pharmacy
  Account - *Hospital, Management, Medical,*
  Pharmacists
Mr. Lao Thao, Account Executive - *Healthcare,*
  Home health, Management, Sales
Violy Aludo David, Account Executive -
  Healthcare, Home health, Marketing, Medical
  (Devices), Sales

208 Creekstone Rdg
Woodstock, GA 30188-3732
(770) 592-9550
Fax: (770) 924-6206
Email: dralston@mriwoodstock.com
Key Contact - Specialty:
Mr. Doug O. Ralston, Manager

65-1158 Mamalahoa Hwy
Kamuela, HI 96743-8442
(808) 885-8621
Email: mrpr@hawaii.rr.com
Key Contact - Specialty:
Mr. Mark Copperthite, Manager

2449 S Vista Ave Ste A
Boise, ID 83705-4152
(208) 336-6770
Fax: (208) 336-2499
Email: resumes@mriboise.com
Key Contact - Specialty:
Mr. Craig R. Alexander, President & General
  Manager
Mr. Jamie Griffin, Account Executive
Mr. John Sears, Account Executive - *Dairy*
Mr. Kevin Veon, Account Executive
Ms. Selbi Board, Project Coordinator
Ms. Angela Shippy, Administrative Assistant

1621 N 3rd St Ste 900
Coeur D Alene, ID 83814-3385
(208) 667-7555
Fax: (208) 667-7030
Email: btravis@mrifcda.com
Key Contact - Specialty:
Mr. Brent Travis, Managing Director

495 North Commons Dr Ste 140
Aurora, IL 60504-8216
(630) 692-7970
Email: info@orchardsearch.com
Key Contact - Specialty:
Mr. Nik Veerachat, Managing Partner
Mr. Marlin L Walgrave, Founding Partner

707 N East St Ste 4
Bloomington, IL 61701-8115
(309) 829-6000
Fax: (309) 827-3023
Email: scbloom@scbloomington.com
Key Contact - Specialty:
Ms. Lyn M. Edwards, Co-Owner & Manager
Mr. Jack O. Edwards, Co-Owner & Manager

205 W Wacker Dr Ste 1000
Chicago, IL 60606-1454
(312) 666-9506
Fax: (312) 666-9560
Email: danm@mrchicagoloop.com
Key Contact - Specialty:
Mr. Dan Meikle

35 W Acorn Ln
Lake in the Hills, IL 60156-4804
(847) 658-7503
Email: resumes@mrialgonquin.com
Key Contact - Specialty:
Mr. Tom Molaski, Manager

479 E Business Ctr Dr Ste 104
Mount Prospect, IL 60056-6037
(847) 298-8780
Fax: (413) 793-0896
Email: plastic@plastics-careers.com
Key Contact - Specialty:
Mr. Tom A. DiDuca, Manager
Ms. Nancy DiDuca, Manager - *Plastics*

1641 Valencia Way
Mundelein, IL 60060-4828
(847) 837-1413
Fax: (847) 281-2228
Email: mike@northlakemri.com
Key Contact - Specialty:
Mr. Michael Santiago

211 Landmark Dr Ste B5
Normal, IL 61761-6165
(309) 452-1844
Fax: (309) 452-0403

Email: mrbloom@mribloomington.com
Key Contact - Specialty:
Mr. Alan Snedden, Manager

191 Waukegan Rd Ste 104
Northfield, IL 60093-2744
(847) 446-7737
Fax: (847) 446-0990
Email: info@om5anddaystar.com
Key Contact - Specialty:
Ms. Lynne Goldberg, Owner

1075 Eastgate Dr Ste 4
O Fallon, IL 62269-3742
(618) 624-8435
Fax: (618) 624-8491
Email: tmorris@mristl.com
Key Contact - Specialty:
Mr. Tim Morris

800 E Northweste Hwy Ste 323
Palatine, IL 60074-6519
(847) 776-3703
Email: victor@mrpalatine.com
Key Contact - Specialty:
Mr. Victor Kairelis, President

PO Box 425
6601 Main St
Union, IL 60180-0425
(815) 923-2500
Email: clintk@mvp4u.biz
Key Contact - Specialty:
Mr. Clint Kenner, Founder and Managing
 Director

303 Alexandria Pike Ste A
Anderson, IN 46012-2950
(765) 649-8380
(866) 948-7487
Email: ddasher@team-whiteriver.com
Key Contact - Specialty:
Mr. Dale Dasher, Managing Director -
 Engineering, Facilities engineering, Logistics,
 Manufacturing, Skilled trades
Mr. Andrew McDonald, Account Executive,
 Office Manager - *Consumer (Products), Food,*
 Food & beverage
Ms. Donna Oliver, Account Executive

11009 Turnberry Pl
Fort Wayne, IN 46814-9325
(260) 625-6501
Fax: (260) 625-4745
Email: mri@mrifortwayne.com
Key Contact - Specialty:
Mr. Harold Rudin, Executive Director -
 Automotive, Industrial, Rubber
Mrs. Myra Rudin, Managing Director -
 Automotive, Rubber

1502 Magnavox Way Ste 245
Fort Wayne, IN 46804-1555
(260) 435-3880
(866) 353-5821
Fax: (260) 435-3885
Email: ddostal@midwest-headhunters.com
Key Contact - Specialty:
Mr. Derek Dostal

340 Northpoint Ave Ste B
Huntington, IN 46750-8449
(260) 359-1755
Email: resumes@hartandhartinc.com
Key Contact - Specialty:
Mr. Steve Hart, President
Mr. Charlie Hart

PO Box 664
Indianapolis, IN 46206-0664
(317) 823-1044
Fax: (317) 823-6595

Email: mburton@level5search.com
Key Contact - Specialty:
Mr. Don Truetken

941 State St Ste 5
New Albany, IN 47150-4727
(812) 945-4595
Key Contact - Specialty:
Ms. Kimberly J Cook, Account Executive
Ms. Kathy Fautz, Account Executive

105 S 10th St
Noblesville, IN 46060-2832
(317) 776-3100
Email: info@jtjgroup.com
Key Contact - Specialty:
Mr. Thomas R Hinkley, Managing Director
Mr. Thomas C Erickson, Director, Healthcare
Mr. Joshua A Orendi, Account Executive
Ms. Megan B Cahill, Office Manager

2519 E Main St Ste 101
Richmond, IN 47374-5869
(765) 935-3356
Email: managementrecruiters@mr-richmond.com
Key Contact - Specialty:
Rande Martin, Manager

1455 W Oak St Ste B
Zionsville, IN 46077-1899
(317) 733-9644
Fax: (317) 733-9614
Email: mirz@mriz.net
Key Contact - Specialty:
Mr. Jim D. Rheude, Manager
Mr. Frank Pruce, Associate Partner

150 1st Ave NE Ste 400
Cedar Rapids, IA 52401-1110
(319) 366-8441
Fax: (319) 366-1103
Email: info@mricr.com
Key Contact - Specialty:
Ms. Cynthia Lyness

383 Collins Rd NE Ste 101
Cedar Rapids, IA 52402-3147
(319) 743-9830
Fax: (319) 294-8882
Email: info@llbexecutivepartners.com
Key Contact - Specialty:
Mrs. Lydia Brown, Managing Director
Mrs. Mary Abel, Account Executive
Mrs. Terri Hunter, Account Executive
Mrs. Brenda Stratton, Account Executive
Ms. Jodi Siamis, Recruiter - *Healthcare*

411 3rd St SE Ste 580
Cedar Rapids, IA 52401-1811
(319) 362-4500
(877) 392-0951
Fax: (319) 362-3088
Email: mgreubel@insuranceoccupations.com
Key Contact - Specialty:
Mr. Marty Greubel

4403 1st Ave SE Ste 306
Cedar Rapids, IA 52402-3221
(319) 743-0150
Fax: (319) 743-0911
Email: doren@corridorsales.net
Key Contact - Specialty:
Doren Kuster
Ms. Lori Palm, Manager
Mr. Joe Wimp, Project Coordinator

PO Box 52
Clear Lake, IA 50428-0052
(641) 357-8717
Email: brent@mriclearlake.com
Key Contact - Specialty:
Mr. Brent Biermann, President & Manager
Ms. Brenda Biermann, Vice President
Mr. Eric Bookmeyer, Senior Account Executive

Mr. Stephen Biermann, Project Coordinator
Mr. Stan Horsfall, Project Coordinator
Ms. Jennifer Leet, Administrative Assistant

325 E Washington St Ste 200
Iowa City, IA 52240-3959
(319) 339-7526
Email: resumes@rbmri.com
Key Contact - Specialty:
Mr. Robert R Brown, President

355 N 1st Ave
Iowa City, IA 52245-3618
(319) 351-5300
Email: cfuller@fullerrecruitment.com
Key Contact - Specialty:
Mr. Curt Fuller, Founder and Managing Partner

PO Box 175
Oakdale, IA 52319-0175
(319) 545-7110
Fax: (319) 545-7107
Email: info@mriowacity.com
Key Contact - Specialty:
Mr. John Lehnst, President - *Agriculture,*
 Biotechnology, Research & development, Sales,
 Senior management

7300 W 110th St Fl 7
Overland Park, KS 66210-2330
(913) 693-4570
Fax: (913) 693-4572
Email: officeinfo@mri-ks.com
Key Contact - Specialty:
Mr. Scott McLeroy

9401 Indian Creek Pkwy Ste 920
Overland Park, KS 66210-2020
(913) 661-9200
Fax: (913) 661-9030
Email: rbelcher@mrikc.com
Key Contact - Specialty:
Mr. Danny Buda, Jr., General Manager
Mr. Robert Belcher, CSAM, Senior Industrial
 Specialist - *Industrial, Sales, Technical*

6427 W Highway 146 Ste 6
Crestwood, KY 40014-9516
(502) 241-6165
Fax: (502) 241-5524
Email: george@mrcrestwood.com
Key Contact - Specialty:
Mr. George Ratterman, Executive Recruiter -
 Biotechnology, Pharmaceutical

103 Wind Haven Dr Ste 201
Nicholasville, KY 40356-8026
(859) 296-1605
(800) 273-7128
Fax: (859) 296-1602
Email: jlorenz@mrnicholasville.com
Key Contact - Specialty:
Mr. John Lorenz

2237 S Acadian Thruway Ste 707
Baton Rouge, LA 70808-2371
(225) 928-2212
Fax: (225) 928-1109
Email: gfell@pharmacyjobs.com
Key Contact - Specialty:
Mr. Gregory L. Fell, Manager
Mr. Steve Winkler, Senior Account Executive
Mr. Patrick Stutes, Senior Account Executive

PO Box 6605
3527 Ridgelake Dr
Metairie, LA 70009-6605
(504) 831-7333
Fax: (504) 838-9009
Email: info@mrineworleans.com
Key Contact - Specialty:
Mr. Edward N. Ameen, General Manager
Mr. Paul M. Luce, CSAM, Manager

2083 West St Ste 5A
Annapolis, MD 21401-3030
(410) 841-6600
Fax: (410) 841-6600
Email: resumeresume@hotmail.com
Key Contact - Specialty:
Mr. John Czajkowski, Manager

575 S Charles St Ste 401
Baltimore, MD 21201-2484
(410) 727-5750
Fax: (410) 727-1253
Email: sbraun@salesconsultants.org
Key Contact - Specialty:
Mr. Steven R. Braun, Manager

7500 Harford Rd
Baltimore, MD 21234-6902
(410) 593-9888
Fax: (410) 254-2585
Email: rondangelo@aol.com
Key Contact - Specialty:
Mr. Ronald D'Angelo

10320 Little Patuxent Pkwy Ste 203
Columbia, MD 21044-3343
(410) 997-2600
Fax: (410) 997-9206
Email: mthielen@stazagroup.com
Key Contact - Specialty:
Mr. Mark Thielen

3179 Braverton St Ste 203
Edgewater, MD 21037-2667
(410) 956-2800
Fax: (410) 956-0100
Email: wryon@scannapolis.com
Key Contact - Specialty:
Mr. Bill Ryon, President
Mrs. Beverly Ryon, Chief Financial Officer
Mrs. Monic Edwards, Consultant

3179 Braverton St Ste 203
Edgewater, MD 21037-2667
(410) 267-0469
Email: mgkuehn@mredgewater.com
Key Contact - Specialty:
Mr. Michael Kuehn, Manager

3807 Grosvenor Dr
Ellicott City, MD 21042-4939
(410) 992-4900
Fax: (410) 461-8155
Email: sccolmd@earthlink.net
Key Contact - Specialty:
Mr. David Rubin

2240 Northwood Dr
Salisbury, MD 21801-8811
(877) 300-3430
Fax: (410) 737-2665
Email: bullis.michael@gmail.com
Key Contact - Specialty:
Mr. Fred J. Puente, Manager
Mr. Michael Bullis, Manager

12200 Tech Rd Ste 335
Silver Spring, MD 20904-1961
(301) 625-5600
Fax: (301) 625-0138
Email: sim@mr-themeyersgroup.com
Key Contact - Specialty:
Mr. Stuart Meyers
Mr. Ronald Morton, MPA, CBHE, Vice
  President, Healthcare Division

508 Beaumont Rd Ste 1D
Silver Spring, MD 20904-1076
(301) 388-0940
Email: thummel@erols.com
Key Contact - Specialty:
Mr. Thomas F. Hummel, Manager

PO Box 420
180 State Rd Ste 5L
Sagamore Beach, MA 02562-0420
(508) 888-8704
Fax: (508) 888-9265
Email: sciofcc@adelphia.net
Key Contact - Specialty:
Mr. Edward T. Cahan, Manager

PO Box 83
315 Main St
West Dennis, MA 02670-0083
(508) 394-9700
Email: info@dennispartners.com
Key Contact - Specialty:
Mr. Brandan Sweeney, Manager

30 Capital Dr
Unit R
West Springfield, MA 01089-1364
(413) 693-0320
Email: bobf@robertssearch.com
Key Contact - Specialty:
Mr. Bob Francoeur, Founder and President

28 Michigan Ave E
Battle Creek, MI 49017-4010
(269) 968-5440
Fax: (269) 968-5443
Email: kellie@jamesclayton.com
Key Contact - Specialty:
Mr. Mark Maire, Managing Director

9067 US Highway 31 Ste 205
Berrien Springs, MI 49103-1664
(269) 471-5000
Fax: (269) 471-5545
Email: robert@rmlittle.com
Key Contact - Specialty:
Mr. Robert Little

PO Box 525
1511 S Main St
Eaton Rapids, MI 48827-0525
(517) 663-4595
Fax: (517) 663-4614
Email: mri@tlgworldwide.com
Key Contact - Specialty:
Ms. Jane Latham

33730 Freedom Rd Ste D
Farmington, MI 48335-4718
(248) 478-7100
Fax: (248) 478-7101
Email: chris@sc-southoakland.com
Key Contact - Specialty:
Mr. Chris Paige

228 Washington Ave
Grand Haven, MI 49417-1357
(616) 844-0073
Fax: (616) 844-7332
Email: info@mrottawa.com
Key Contact - Specialty:
Mr. Bruce Bradford-Royle

146 Monroe Center St NW Ste 1426
Grand Rapids, MI 49503-2823
(616) 336-8484
Fax: (616) 988-0872
Email: solutions@mirgr.com
Key Contact - Specialty:
Mr. Hunter Judson

PO Box 294
Higgins Lake, MI 48627-0294
(989) 275-1600
Fax: (989) 422-5738
Email: mrnc@voyager.net
Key Contact - Specialty:
Mr. Timothy Harris

400 136th Ave Ste 206
Holland, MI 49424-2903
(616) 396-2620
Fax: (616) 396-9465
Email: reb@mriholland.com
Key Contact - Specialty:
Mr. Robert E. Bakker, CSAM, Manager

2491 Cedar Park Dr
Holt, MI 48842-2184
(517) 694-1153
Fax: (517) 694-6502
Email: mrilansing@comcast.net
Key Contact - Specialty:
Mr. John A. Peterson, Co-Manager
Ms. Priscilla J. Peterson, Co-Manager
Mr. John A. Peterson, II, Operations Manager -
  Automotive, C-level, Engineering, Food,
  Manufacturing (Management)
Mrs. Amy D. Stokes, Support Services Manager -
  General management, Human resources,
  Insurance, Legal, Office (Administration)

3073 Shirley Dr
Jackson, MI 49201-7010
(517) 841-1336
Fax: (517) 841-1345
Email: don@mrjackson.com
Key Contact - Specialty:
Mr. Don Bills, Manager

912 Centennial Way Ste 340
Lansing, MI 48917-8246
(517) 323-4404
Fax: (517) 323-8083
Email: jeffyeagersearch@sbcglobal.net
Key Contact - Specialty:
Mr. Jeffrey A. Yeager, CSAM, Manager

1567 Putnam Cir
Midland, MI 48640-8401
(989) 835-7408
Fax: (989) 839-9267
Email: darin@mrimidland.com
Key Contact - Specialty:
Mr. Darin Lacoursiere

PO Box 1185
521 Union St
Traverse City, MI 49685-1185
(616) 935-4000
Email: sctc12@sbcglobal.net
Key Contact - Specialty:
Mr. E.J. Eckert, III, Manager

755 W Big Beaver Rd Ste 410
Troy, MI 48084-4903
(248) 764-4200
Fax: (248) 764-4242
Email: troygroup@mrtroy.com
Key Contact - Specialty:
Mr. Ed J. Moeller, Manager

570 W 78th St Ste 2001
Chanhassen, MN 55317-9676
(952) 443-1836
Fax: (952) 443-2243
Email: harris.c@mrimtg.com
Key Contact - Specialty:
Mr. Chuck Harris

3147 Superior Dr NW Ste 100
Rochester, MN 55901-2973
(507) 536-4510
Fax: (507) 536-4511
Email: rdennis@weatherhillsgroup.com
Key Contact - Specialty:
Mr. Randy Dennis, Managing Director
Mr. Mark Wernstrom, Executive Search
  Consultant - *Biomedical, Biopharmaceutical,*
  Biotechnology, Quality, Regulatory

174 Clarkson Rd Ste 140
Ballwin, MO 63011-2277
(636) 256-2624
Fax: (636) 256-2644
Email: steve@mrwildwood.com
Key Contact - Specialty:
Mr. Steve Howes

14323 S Outer 40 Ste 102M
Chesterfield, MO 63017-5734
(314) 542-6178
Fax: (314) 542-6183
Email: lnelson@mrstlouis.com
Key Contact - Specialty:
Mr. Larry Nelson

200 Long Rd Ste 220
Chesterfield, MO 63005-1200
(636) 532-6055
Fax: (636) 532-5221
Email: tscheff@mrclarkson.com
Key Contact - Specialty:
Mr. Ted Scheff

200 Fabricator Dr
Fenton, MO 63026-2914
(636) 349-4455
Fax: (636) 326-4207
Email: mrwcstl@swbell.net
Key Contact - Specialty:
Mr. Edward Travis, General Manager
Mr. Glenwood Alley, Manager

PO Box 1148
198 Lakota Dr
Linn Creek, MO 65052-1148
(573) 365-1040
Fax: (573) 346-0046
Email: bob@mri-camdenton.com
Key Contact - Specialty:
Ms. Judy H. Hodgson, Co-Owner & Manager
Mr. Robert D. Hodgson, Co-Owner & Manager

201 N Main St Ste 215
Saint Charles, MO 63301-2878
(636) 940-7444
Fax: (636) 940-7555
Email: mewhite@stlnet.com
Key Contact - Specialty:
Mr. Martin White, Manager

PO Box 853
Saint Charles, MO 63302-0853
(636) 724-0668
Fax: (636) 724-0669
Email: denise@carriganassociates.com
Key Contact - Specialty:
Ms. Denise Carrigan

1807 E Edgewood St Ste B
Springfield, MO 65804-3831
(417) 882-6220
Fax: (417) 882-7855
Email: rod@mrspringfield.com
Key Contact - Specialty:
Mr. Rod Panyik, Manager

4218 W Charleston Blvd
Las Vegas, NV 89102-1625
(702) 215-2630
Fax: (702) 215-2631
Email: todd@mri-lasvegas.com
Key Contact - Specialty:
Mr. Todd Enerson
Mr. Tom Enerson

PO Box 774
Hampton Falls, NH 03844-0774
(603) 926-1130
Fax: (603) 929-9007
Email: scottpower@appledoreassociates.com
Key Contact - Specialty:
Mr. Scott Power

1106 Hooksett Rd
Hooksett, NH 03106-1000
(603) 626-8400
Fax: (603) 626-1288
Email: jhncote@aol.com
Key Contact - Specialty:
Mr. John J. Cote, Manager

727 Raritan Rd Ste 101
Clark, NJ 07066-2241
(732) 381-9292
Fax: (732) 381-1680
Email: rpanzarasa@mriclark.com
Key Contact - Specialty:
Mr. Richard Panzarasa

12 Minneakoning Rd Ste 2
Flemington, NJ 08822-5729
(908) 237-1450
Fax: (908) 284-2302
Email: gdweigle@ctr-pt.com
Key Contact - Specialty:
Mr. Gregory Weigle

200 Munsonhurst Rd Ste 104
Franklin, NJ 07416-1811
(973) 823-1888
Fax: (973) 823-1620
Email: lance@retailplacement.com
Key Contact - Specialty:
Mr. Lance M. Incitti, Manager

855 Bloomfield Ave Ste 205
Glen Ridge, NJ 07028-1307
(973) 259-9990
Fax: (973) 259-9988
Email: mpotters@glenmontgroup.com
Key Contact - Specialty:
Mr. Michael Potters
Ms. Kate Potters

19 Tanner St
Haddonfield, NJ 08033-2403
(856) 428-2233
Fax: (856) 428-7733
Email: rkelly@erols.com
Key Contact - Specialty:
Mr. Leroy Kelly

PO Box 244
Hope, NJ 07844-0244
(908) 459-5798
Fax: (908) 459-4672
Email: mrinw@epix.net
Key Contact - Specialty:
Mr. Henry Magnusen

30 Lance Rd Ste 100
Lebanon, NJ 08833-5005
(908) 439-9211
Fax: (908) 439-9677
Email: rb@schunterdon.com
Key Contact - Specialty:
Mr. Robert Balseiro, Managing Partner

150 River Rd Ste H
Montville, NJ 07045-8922
(973) 316-9371
Fax: (973) 316-9373
Email: kit@capssoftware.com

1900 State Route 35 Ste 300
Oakhurst, NJ 07755-2758
(732) 663-0020
Fax: (732) 663-1399
Email: swallach@mrjobsearch.com
Key Contact - Specialty:
Mr. Steve Wallach

1719 State Rt 10 Ste 114
Parsippany, NJ 07054-4537
(973) 359-8858
Fax: (973) 359-9878
Email: johnperry@mriparsippany.com

Key Contact - Specialty:
Mr. John Perry

750 Hamburg Tpke Ste 203
Pompton Lakes, NJ 07068-1452
(973) 831-7778
Email: mrdaz@home.com
Key Contact - Specialty:
Mr. David Zawicki

145 N Franklin Tpke Ste 207
Ramsey, NJ 07446-1634
(888) 774-2268
(201) 934-9988
Email: mrutman@mriftc.com
Key Contact - Specialty:
Mr. Merrill Rutman

166 Patterson Ave Ste 5
Shrewsbury, NJ 07702-4166
(732) 450-1555
Fax: (732) 450-1665
Email: brian.baker@mrshrewsbury.com
Key Contact - Specialty:
Mr. Brian Baker

360 Sycamore Ave
Shrewsbury, NJ 07702-4513
(732) 530-8585
Fax: (732) 219-0306
Email: greakle@aol.com
Key Contact - Specialty:
Mr. Richard Eakle

75 W High St Fl 1
Somerville, NJ 08876-2114
(908) 541-9600
Fax: (908) 541-9660
Email: mf@mrsomerville.com
Key Contact - Specialty:
Mr. Michael Fuchs

376 Lafayette Rd Ste 200
Sparta, NJ 07871-3560
(973) 579-5555
Fax: (973) 579-2220
Email: stascom@stascomtech.com
Key Contact - Specialty:
Mr. Harvey Bass

151 Fries Mill Rd Ste 503B
Turnersville, NJ 08012-2016
(856) 228-4200
Fax: (856) 228-3333
Email: joelynch@thesearchpros.com
Key Contact - Specialty:
Mr. Joseph Lynch
Ms. Karen Lynch

1101 Laurel Oak Rd Ste 140
Voorhees, NJ 08043-4322
(856) 309-5306
Fax: (856) 309-5307
Email: dingram@mrivoorhees.com
Key Contact - Specialty:
Mr. Dan Ingram

422 Medico Ln Ste B
Santa Fe, NM 87505-4786
(505) 982-5445
Fax: (505) 982-7170
Email: wmiller@mri-santafe.com
Key Contact - Specialty:
Mr. Bill Miller, Manager

8555 Main St Ste 308
Buffalo, NY 14221-7456
(716) 631-3100
Fax: (716) 631-3140
Email: rea@scbuffalo.com
Key Contact - Specialty:
Mr. Robert Artis

6080 Jericho Tpke Ste 201
Commack, NY 11725-2808
(631) 462-6669
Fax: (631) 462-6969
Email: brianf@proactivesearch.com
Key Contact - Specialty:
Mr. Brian Feldman
Mr. Scott Bergman

8 Shetland Ct
Dix Hills, NY 11746-6163
(631) 864-2650
Fax: (631) 777-2714
Email: bob@brandonbecker.com
Key Contact - Specialty:
Mr. Robert Levitt

PO Box 532
Goshen, NY 10924-0532
(845) 294-5881
Fax: (631) 331-2814
Email: recruiters@hvc.rr.com
Key Contact - Specialty:
Mr. Domenick Patti
Ms. Barbara Patti

2537 Route 52 Ste 14
Hopewell Junction, NY 12533-3231
(845) 227-3161
Fax: (845) 227-3439
Email: tdamewood@mrmidhudvalley.com
Key Contact - Specialty:
Mr. Tom Damewood

33 Walt Whitman Rd Ste 107
Huntington Station, NY 11746-3673
(516) 385-0633
Fax: (516) 385-0759
Email: bob@brandonbecker.com
Key Contact - Specialty:
Mr. Robert Levitt

145 Pinelawn Rd Ste 345N
Melville, NY 11747-3123
(631) 777-2710
Fax: (631) 777-2714
Email: harris.cohen@princetonone.com
Key Contact - Specialty:
Mr. Harris Cohen, Managing Partner

535 Broadhollow Rd Ste A5
Melville, NY 11747-3701
(631) 752-6800
Fax: (631) 752-7574
Email: scott@stratstaff.com
Key Contact - Specialty:
Mr. Scott Bergman

347 E 58th St Apt 1R
New York, NY 10022-2253
(212) 223-2876
Fax: (425) 928-3424
Email: dib@mrmsp.com
Key Contact - Specialty:
Mr. Dave Broad

60 Madison Ave Ste 911A
New York, NY 10010-1674
(212) 251-0100
Fax: (212) 251-0768
Email: arthur.young@recruiter.com
Key Contact - Specialty:
Ms. Marcia Clarke, Manager
Mr. Arthur Young

225 Main St Ste 204
Northport, NY 11768-1787
(516) 261-0400
Fax: (516) 261-0400
Email: joe@mullingsgroup.com
Key Contact - Specialty:
Mr. Joseph Mullings

PO Box 237
Ogdensburg, NY 13669-0237
(315) 393-9460
Fax: (315) 393-9466
Email: mrslc@twcny.rr.com
Key Contact - Specialty:
Mr. Gary Scott

2031 Middle Rd
Oneida, NY 13421-4189
(315) 339-6342
Fax: (315) 339-6415
Email: mri@twcny.rr.com
Key Contact - Specialty:
Mr. Jim Szczerba

1721 Black River Blvd N Ste 205
Rome, NY 13440-2447
(315) 339-6342
Fax: (315) 339-6415
Key Contact - Specialty:
Mr. Carl Tardugno, Manager

204 Charlotte Hwy Ste H
Asheville, NC 28803-8681
(828) 296-1988
Fax: (828) 296-1987
Email: rspeight@mrbf.com
Key Contact - Specialty:
Mr. Rick Speight

PO Box 2376
Banner Elk, NC 28604-2376
(828) 963-5345
Fax: (828) 963-5345
Email: cwh43@skybest.com
Key Contact - Specialty:
Ms. Carroll Hickman

PO Box 1405
104 E College Ave
Boiling Springs, NC 28017-1405
(704) 434-0211
Fax: (704) 434-0211
Email: mrishelby@bellsouth.net
Key Contact - Specialty:
Mr. David Holland

PO Box 699
Bunn, NC 27508-0699
(919) 269-6612
Fax: (919) 269-9963
Email: mgtrecruiters@mindspring.com
Key Contact - Specialty:
Mr. Daniel Cone

3440 Toringdon Way Ste 200
Charlotte, NC 28277-3191
(704) 944-9800
Fax: (704) 944-8098
Email: tnear@nearassociates.com
Key Contact - Specialty:
Mr. Thomas Near, General Manager
Mr. Dave Camp, Manager

9101 Southern Pine Blvd Ste 290
Charlotte, NC 28273-5531
(704) 676-9290
Fax: (704) 676-9261
Email: gcromwell@cromwellgroup-mri.com
Key Contact - Specialty:
Mr. Gerry Cromwell, President & Founder -
    Property management
Mr. Jeff Harr, Senior Associate - *Property
    management*
Mr. Scott Gleason, Senior Account Executive -
    Property management
Mr. Donnie Solesbee, Account Executive -
    Property management

2554 Lewisville Clemmons Rd Ste 302
Clemmons, NC 27012-8749
(336) 766-4750 x204
(800) 585-5368 x204
Fax: (336) 766-4751
Email: wes@mrisc.com
Key Contact - Specialty:
Mr. Wes McCracken, Manager

1738 Hillandale Rd Ste 204
Durham, NC 27705-3046
(919) 416-9300
Fax: (919) 416-9333
Email: slr@scdurham.com
Key Contact - Specialty:
Ms. Sharon Reed
Mr. Mike Reed

5102 Durham Chapel Hill Blvd Ste 204
Durham, NC 27707-3394
(919) 489-6521
Fax: (919) 493-4611
Email: jmartin@mri-durham.com
Key Contact - Specialty:
Mr. Arthur Deberry, Manager
Mr. Stuart Hirsch, Account Executive

6011 Fayetteville Rd Ste 203
Durham, NC 27713-6248
(919) 572-2292
Fax: (919) 572-6556
Email: rsb@mri-rtp.com
Key Contact - Specialty:
Mr. Robert Bradley, Manager

500 S Allen Rd Unit 11
Flat Rock, NC 28731-9472
(828) 697-8228
Fax: (828) 697-8223
Email: tom@mr-hendersonville.com
Key Contact - Specialty:
Mr. Thomas W. Legg, President - *Adhesives,
    BSME, Business development, Chemical,
    Coatings*
Mr. Ronald M. Buono, Vice President - *Business
    development, Design, Engineering,
    Flexographic printing, General management*

620 S Elm St Ste 308A
Greensboro, NC 27406-1371
(336) 691-5744
Fax: (770) 234-5744
Email: bpbarnes@bellsouth.net
Key Contact - Specialty:
Mr. Bruce Barnes

148 New River Dr
Hertford, NC 27944-8141
(252) 426-2270
Fax: (252) 426-2270
Email: john@mritomsriver.com
Key Contact - Specialty:
Mr. John Hoepfner, President

835 Highland Ave SE
Hickory, NC 28602-1140
(828) 324-2020
Fax: (828) 324-6895
Email: scottv@mrihky.com
Key Contact - Specialty:
Mr. Scott Volz, General Manager
Mr. Bill Gaillard, CSAM, Manager

PO Box 6077
Hickory, NC 28603-6077
(828) 495-8233
Fax: (828) 495-7431
Email: byron@mrbethlehem.com
Key Contact - Specialty:
Mr. Byron L. King, Manager

2411 Penny Rd Ste 101
High Point, NC 27265-8124
(336) 883-4433
Fax: (336) 884-4433
Email: scihp@northstate.net
Key Contact - Specialty:
Mr. John Thomas Bunton, III

16419 Northcross Dr Ste D
Huntersville, NC 28078-5007
(704) 895-5525
Fax: (704) 895-5526
Email: inquiries@mri-usa.com
Key Contact - Specialty:
Mr. Hardy McConnell, Manager

PO Box 8
101 N Main St Ste 201
Louisburg, NC 27549-0008
(919) 496-2153
Fax: (919) 496-1417
Email: dperry@ncol.net
Key Contact - Specialty:
Mr. Darrell L. Perry, Jr., Manager

256 Raceway Dr Ste 3A
Mooresville, NC 28117-6514
(704) 664-4997
Fax: (704) 664-0841
Email: johnyapp@mrmooresville.com
Key Contact - Specialty:
Mr. Hugh L. Sykes, Manager

235 E Independence Blvd
Mount Airy, NC 27030-3855
(336) 786-4212
Fax: (336) 786-8415
Email: marc@mriofgranitecity.com
Key Contact - Specialty:
Mr. Marc Pumerantz

PO Box 4834
180 Westgate Dr
Pinehurst, NC 28374-4834
(910) 215-9933
Fax: (910) 215-9934
Email: papergirloffice@nc.rr.com
Key Contact - Specialty:
Mr. Doug Wright, General Manager
Ms. Anne B. Wright, Manager

120 N Franklin St Ste J
Rocky Mount, NC 27804-5448
(252) 446-3456
Fax: (252) 446-3556
Email: dsew32@earthlink.net
Key Contact - Specialty:
Mr. Danny Sewell

PO Box 2464
Shelby, NC 28151-2464
(704) 480-7889
Fax: (704) 480-7890
Email: mangrec@carolina.rr.com
Key Contact - Specialty:
Mr. Rex Whicker
Mr. Skip Almond

117 N Center St
Statesville, NC 28677-5255
(704) 971-9890
Fax: (704) 873-4559
Email: neilcoleman@mristatesville.com
Key Contact - Specialty:
Mr. Neil F. Coleman, Manager

1404 Wall Rd Ste 300
Wake Forest, NC 27587-7470
(919) 554-0783
Fax: (919) 554-9585
Email: darrell@alliance-exec.com
Key Contact - Specialty:
Mr. Darrell Boness

6309 Boathouse Rd Ste 100
Wilmington, NC 28403-3576
(910) 395-5516
Fax: (910) 395-5476
Email: pkester@cs.com
Key Contact - Specialty:
Mr. Paul Kester

150 E Firetower Rd Ste D
Winterville, NC 28590-8330
(252) 439-0966
Fax: (252) 439-0977
Email: gtaylor@mriwin.com
Key Contact - Specialty:
Mr. Gene Taylor, Manager

PO Box 1092
Fargo, ND 58107-1092
(218) 238-5123
Email: mrfargo@loretel.net
Key Contact - Specialty:
Mr. Joe Allen, President - *Manufacturing*

23611 Chagrin Blvd Ste 380
Beachwood, OH 44122-5540
(216) 591-0002
Fax: (253) 550-9715
Email: mykol@geristaff.com
Key Contact - Specialty:
Mr. Michael Greenwald

866 E Franklin St Ste C
Centerville, OH 45459-5608
(937) 438-0041
Fax: (937) 438-3782
Email: gap@mrctv.com
Key Contact - Specialty:
Mr. George Plotner

6690 Beta Dr Ste 100
Cleveland, OH 44143-2359
(440) 684-6150
Fax: (440) 684-6153
Email: twesley@mrifluidpower.com
Key Contact - Specialty:
Mr. Terry R. Wesley, Manager

9700 Rockside Rd Ste 100
Cleveland, OH 44125-6264
(440) 642-5788
Fax: (216) 642-5933
Email: mfd1000@aol.com
Key Contact - Specialty:
Mr. Paul F. Montigny, General Manager
Mr. Robert E. Jacobson, Manager

1041 Dublin Rd Ste 101
Columbus, OH 43215-1141
(614) 481-0000
Fax: (208) 474-0919
Email: fhs@simmondsgroup.com
Key Contact - Specialty:
Mr. Rick Simmonds

2460 Northwest Blvd
Columbus, OH 43221-3868
(614) 486-1388
Fax: (614) 486-3005
Email: cwatkins@mriohio.com
Key Contact - Specialty:
Mr. Chris Watkins
Mr. Greg Watkins

8930 Commerce Loop Dr
Columbus, OH 43240-2124
(614) 433-7254
Fax: (614) 433-7458
Key Contact - Specialty:
Mr. Larry Coburn

5450 Frantz Rd Ste 240
Dublin, OH 43016-4135
(614) 799-4000
Fax: (614) 799-4343

Email: bwayne@mridelta.com
Key Contact - Specialty:
Mr. Rob Wayne

6025 Dixie Hwy Ste 200
Fairfield, OH 45014-4253
(513) 682-4020
Fax: (513) 682-4030
Email: mri@one.net
Key Contact - Specialty:
Mr. Joseph J. Bierschwal, Manager

3880 Broadway
Grove City, OH 43123-2207
(614) 277-9255
Fax: (614) 277-9265
Email: mlykins@mricgc.com
Key Contact - Specialty:
Mr. Matt Lykins - *Apparel, Architecture,
Construction, Distribution, Facilities
engineering*

591 Boston Mills Rd Ste 600
Hudson, OH 44236-1197
(330) 656-0935
Email: smiller@schudson.com
Key Contact - Specialty:
Mr. Scott Miller
Ms. Kathy Spitalieri, Office Manager - *Market
research, Marketing*

PO Box 31495
Independence, OH 44131-0495
(216) 621-5522
Fax: (216) 621-5740
Email: mricleveland1@ameritech.net
Key Contact - Specialty:
Ms. Monica Rio, Manager

PO Box 2970
North Canton, OH 44720-0970
(330) 497-0122
Email: mikec@mrnc.com
Key Contact - Specialty:
Mr. Mike Collins, Account Executive
Ms. Ginny Collins, Vice President
Mr. Jim Shelton, Account Executive

10104 Brewster Ln Ste 150
Powell, OH 43065-7579
(614) 336-3637
Fax: (614) 336-3638
Email: kjk@mri-usa-search.com
Key Contact - Specialty:
Mr. Ken Kessler

6200 SOM Center Rd Ste D25
Solon, OH 44139-2946
(440) 498-1655
Fax: (440) 498-3145
Email: bsnyder@mrsolon.com
Key Contact - Specialty:
Mr. Bill Snyder, Managing Partner
Mrs. Jennifer Meyer, Managing Partner

8972 Darrow Rd Ste 302A
Twinsburg, OH 44087-2199
(330) 405-0400
Fax: (330) 405-0405
Email: apetersen@elitesearch.cc
Key Contact - Specialty:
Mr. Phil Slive

1531 Boettler Rd Ste A
Uniontown, OH 44685-7765
(330) 899-0802
Fax: (330) 899-0804
Email: donna@mrigreen.com
Key Contact - Specialty:
Ms. Donna Jordon
Mr. Mike Long

1 Park Center Dr Ste 305A
Wadsworth, OH 44281-7913
(877) 334-0285
Fax: (330) 334-2617
Email: serman@4whitetiger.com
Key Contact - Specialty:
Mr. Stanley Erman, President - *Fastener, Manufacturing, Metals, Supply Chain, Venture capital*
Mr. Kevin Cleary, Account Executive - *Computers (Sales), Defense, Information service, Information Systems, Information Technology*
Mr. Steve Yurick, Account Manager - *Information Technology*
Ms. Gloria Wozniak, Account Manager - *Banking (Commercial, Corporate, Mortgage), Capital markets, Wall Street*
Mr. Donald Hanna, Account Executive - *Environmental*
Mr. Daniel Wismar, CPC, Account Manager - *Construction, Environmental, Manufacturing*

7364 Kingsgate Way
West Chester, OH 45069-2450
(513) 755-6060
Fax: (513) 755-6161
Email: info@barcodejobs.com
Key Contact - Specialty:
Mr. Jonathan Bartos, Owner & Manager

8080 Beckett Center Dr Ste 103
West Chester, OH 45069-5028
(513) 860-3233
Fax: (513) 860-9799
Email: tom.shull@mri-br.com
Key Contact - Specialty:
Mr. Thomas Shull

24651 Center Ridge Rd Ste 325
Westlake, OH 44145-5694
(440) 617-0550
Fax: (440) 617-0553
Email: jling@mr-westlake.com
Key Contact - Specialty:
Mr. John Ling

38210 Glenn Ave
Willoughby, OH 44094-7808
(440) 953-9559
Fax: (440) 953-9944
Email: hbugos@tcgco.com
Key Contact - Specialty:
Mr. Thomas Christopher, Owner & Account Executive
Ms. Paula Christopher

40 Kinsey Rd
Xenia, OH 45385-1520
(937) 427-7222
Fax: (937) 427-7227
Email: timshelton@earthlink.net
Key Contact - Specialty:
Mr. Tim Shelton, Co-Manager
Mr. Jeff Milam, Co-Manager

2500 S Broadway Ste 320
Edmond, OK 73013-4040
(405) 340-0222
Fax: (405) 715-1119
Email: dmorris@career-searches.com
Key Contact - Specialty:
Mr. Dave Morris

1412 NW Sheridan Rd Ste C
Lawton, OK 73505-3903
(580) 351-1155
Fax: (580) 355-0125
Email: adouglas@mrlawton.com
Key Contact - Specialty:
Mr. Andrew Douglas

205 NW 63rd St Ste 390
Oklahoma City, OK 73116-8253
(405) 607-2425
Fax: (405) 607-2428
Email: steve@mriokcnorth.com
Key Contact - Specialty:
Mr. Steve Kinney, Manager

5801 E 41st St Ste 440
Tulsa, OK 74135-5614
(918) 663-3744
Fax: (918) 663-1783
Email: twolters@mritulsa.com
Key Contact - Specialty:
Mr. Tony Wolters

563 SW 13th St Ste 101
Bend, OR 97702-3156
(541) 382-9779
Fax: (541) 382-9772
Email: info@pangaeatek.com
Key Contact - Specialty:
Mr. Rob Schluter, Manager

1405 Coventry Rd
Allentown, PA 18104-2005
(610) 398-8600
Fax: (610) 740-9224
Email: mrlehigh@profcareer.com
Key Contact - Specialty:
Mr. Denny P. Farkas, Manager

2141 Downyflake Ln
Allentown, PA 18103-4774
(610) 797-8863
Fax: (610) 797-8873
Email: recruiter@mriallentown.com
Key Contact - Specialty:
Mr. Gary Filko, Manager

3466 Progress Dr Ste 218
Bensalem, PA 19020-5814
(215) 245-0515
Fax: (215) 245-6850
Email: bbagnell@pinnaclerecruiters.com
Key Contact - Specialty:
Mr. Robert Bagnell

1104 Fernwood Ave Ste 402
Camp Hill, PA 17011-6903
(717) 737-7500
Fax: (717) 737-7400
Email: resume@hotsalesjobs.com
Key Contact - Specialty:
Mr. Doug Miller

PO Box 648
Chinchilla, PA 18410-0648
(570) 587-9909
Fax: (570) 587-9910
Email: mros@mros.com
Key Contact - Specialty:
Mr. Victor Kochmer, Co-Manager
Ms. Sheila Kochmer, Co-Manager

PO Box 1108
Dingmans Ferry, PA 18328-1108
(570) 828-6428
Fax: (570) 828-1002
Email: mrisc@careersearches.com
Key Contact - Specialty:
Ms. Nancy Pitcher

PO Box 866
Fogelsville, PA 18051-0866
(610) 336-4599
Fax: (610) 336-4447
Email: cousinmarc@enter.net
Key Contact - Specialty:
Mr. Marc Sablow

428 Pennsylvania Ave Fl 2
Fort Washington, PA 19034-3413
(215) 793-9444
Fax: (215) 793-9451
Email: jobinfo@mrmontco.com
Key Contact - Specialty:
Ms. Sandra Teichman, Co-Manager
Mr. Mark Teichman, Co-Manager

55 Pierce Ln Ste 202
Montoursville, PA 17754-8326
(570) 368-2277
Fax: (570) 368-7586
Email: heltmr@suscom.net
Key Contact - Specialty:
Mr. Wally A. Helt, Manager

171 W Lancaster Ave Ste 200
Paoli, PA 19301-1775
(610) 993-9530
Fax: (610) 993-9740
Email: rkmri@comcast.net
Key Contact - Specialty:
Mr. Rick Knoll

325 Chestnut St Ste 1106
Philadelphia, PA 19106-2611
(215) 829-1900
Fax: (215) 829-1919
Email: mail@mriphiladelphia.net
Key Contact - Specialty:
Mr. Thomas A. Lucas, Manager

2589 Washington Rd Ste 435
Pittsburgh, PA 15241-2573
(412) 831-7290
Fax: (412) 831-7298
Email: resume@gomri.com
Key Contact - Specialty:
Mr. Jim Gallagher, Co-Manager
Ms. Sallie Gallagher, Co-Manager
Mr. Mark M. Wawrzeniak, Co-Manager

300 Weyman Rd Ste 200
Pittsburgh, PA 15236-1520
(412) 885-5222
Fax: (412) 885-2181
Email: mrpitsth@aol.com
Key Contact - Specialty:
Mr. Andrew Hallam

525 Plymouth Rd Ste 300
Plymouth Meeting, PA 19462-1640
(610) 834-9979
Fax: (610) 834-9976
Email: dkurtz@mripm.com
Key Contact - Specialty:
Mr. David Kurtz

446 N Claude A Lord Blvd Ste 2
Pottsville, PA 17901-2706
(570) 624-7050
Email: jhoffman@hoffman-group.com
Key Contact - Specialty:
Mr. John Hoffman, Managing Partner - *Computers (Software), Healthcare, Pharmaceutical*
Mr. Rob Hoffman

100 Northpointe Cir Ste 303
Seven Fields, PA 16046-7851
(724) 742-2300
Fax: (724) 742-2315
Email: laura.connelly@thehenleygrp.com
Key Contact - Specialty:
Ms. Laura Connelly

165 S Memorial Hwy Ste 2C
Shavertown, PA 18708-1418
(570) 696-5558
Fax: (570) 696-5562
Email: cme@mri-wilkesbarre.com
Key Contact - Specialty:
Mr. Charles Eckman

PO Box 879
Skippack, PA 19474-0879
(610) 584-8882
Fax: (610) 584-8801
Email: rebecca@mripower.com
Key Contact - Specialty:
Mr. Bob Eschenbach, Manager

PO Box 640
Spring House, PA 19477-0640
(215) 283-1800
Fax: (215) 283-2999
Email: mereisner@merwingroup.com
Key Contact - Specialty:
Mr. Mark Reisner, Managing Director
Ms. Nicole Freilich, Administrative Associate

RR 3 Box 3089
Stroudsburg, PA 18360-9321
(570) 629-7300
Fax: (570) 629-7378
Email: kwalls@sctannersville.com
Key Contact - Specialty:
Mr. Keith Von Zup, Managing Director
Ms. Danielle Gentile, Account Executive
Mrs. Kathy Walls, Office Manager

PO Box 1222
East Greenwich, RI 02818-0966
(401) 886-4606
Fax: (401) 885-1754
Email: rcalvano@scnewport.com
Key Contact - Specialty:
Mr. Bob Calvano

PO Box 730
Aiken, SC 29802-0730
(803) 648-1361
Fax: (803) 642-5114
Email: glasspeople@bellsouth.net
Key Contact - Specialty:
Mr. Michael Hardwick, Managing Partner -
  Building products
Mr. Leo Tatarenchik, Partner
Mr. Robert Barnett, Partner
Mr. Guy Hill, Partner
Mr. David Johnson, Partner - *Automotive*
Mr. Len Kane, Partner - *Plastics*

1064 Gardner Rd Ste 112B
Charleston, SC 29407-5746
(843) 329-0404
Fax: (843) 329-0408
Email: seanless@mrjohnsisland.com
Key Contact - Specialty:
Mr. Sean Less

137 Main St
Chester, SC 29706-1884
(803) 581-3100
Fax: (803) 385-2735
Email: gloria@wgpeople.com
Key Contact - Specialty:
Ms. Gloria Kellerhals
Ms. Tiffany Thomasson, Project Coordinator

2800 Bush River Rd Ste 4
Columbia, SC 29210-5662
(803) 772-0300
Fax: (803) 772-4600
Email: mrilex@btitelecom.net
Key Contact - Specialty:
Mr. Roger Hall, Co-Manager
Ms. Debbie Hall, Co-Manager

1057 521 Corporate Ctr Dr Ste 175
Fort Mill, SC 29715-7166
(803) 548-8140
Fax: (803) 548-8141
Email: jrw@mrilanco.com
Key Contact - Specialty:
Mr. Joachim Woerner

1203 Two Island Ct Unit 103A
Mount Pleasant, SC 29466-7405
(843) 849-8080
Fax: (843) 849-7070
Email: joe@salesconsultantsinc.com
Key Contact - Specialty:
Mr. Joe D. Rigter, Co-Manager
Ms. Kay H. Rigter, Co-Manager

1473 Stuart Engals Blvd
Mount Pleasant, SC 29464-3379
(864) 216-6565
Fax: (843) 216-6566
Email: warrengroup1@msn.com
Key Contact - Specialty:
Mr. Patrick Warren

266 W Coleman Blvd Ste 102
Mount Pleasant, SC 29464-5651
(843) 856-0544
Fax: (843) 856-0547
Email: jim@theheadhunter.com
Key Contact - Specialty:
Mr. James L. Dooley, CSAM, Manager

313 Commerce Dr Ste B
Pawleys Island, SC 29585-6052
(843) 979-1674
Fax: (843) 979-0687
Email: lynnmiller@sc.rr.com
Key Contact - Specialty:
Ms. Lynn Miller

101 E Main St
Pickens, SC 29671-2346
(864) 878-1113
Fax: (864) 878-1410
Email: eparris@mripickens.com
Key Contact - Specialty:
Mr. Ed Parris, Jr., Manager

100 Confederate Dr
Franklin, TN 37064-3817
(615) 656-2410
Fax: (615) 656-2413
Email: rbehrends@mrisc-coolsprings.com
Key Contact - Specialty:
Mr. Robert Behrends, President

236 Public Sq Ste 201
Franklin, TN 37064-2520
(615) 791-4391
Fax: (615) 791-4769
Email: rhmarriott@earthlink.net
Key Contact - Specialty:
Mr. Roger Marriott

PO Box 6662
Kingsport, TN 37663-1662
(423) 239-8270
Fax: (423) 952-0999
Key Contact - Specialty:
Mr. Keith Dawson

9815 Cogdill Rd Ste 6
Knoxville, TN 37932-3375
(865) 671-0511
Fax: (865) 671-0577
Email: gabie@mrconcord.com
Key Contact - Specialty:
Mr. Ray McLeroy

1800 S Rutherford Blvd Ste 103
Murfreesboro, TN 37130-5996
(615) 890-7623
Fax: (615) 890-9511
Email: tomhyde@mrisearch.com
Key Contact - Specialty:
Mr. Tom G. Hyde, Manager
Mr. Yukari Ishii

8800 Mountbatten Cir
Austin, TX 78730-3003
(512) 347-1600
Fax: (512) 327-4972
Email: davidb@mrina.com
Key Contact - Specialty:
Mr. David Byrne

600 S Denton Tap Rd Ste 145
Coppell, TX 75019-4561
(972) 745-8500
Email: ken@naishgroup.com
Key Contact - Specialty:
Mr. Ken Naish

5646 Milton St Ste 427
Dallas, TX 75206-3932
(214) 378-5476
Fax: (214) 378-5159
Email: maxtonkon@mriparkcities.com
Key Contact - Specialty:
Mr. Max Tonkon

6006 N Mesa St Ste 408
El Paso, TX 79912-4623
(915) 833-8211
Fax: (915) 833-8254
Email: mrielpaso@aol.com
Key Contact - Specialty:
Ms. Victoria A. Lummus, Co-Manager
Ms. Cindy L. Capanna, Co-Manager

1172 Country Club Ln
Fort Worth, TX 76112-2303
(817) 457-9995
Fax: (817) 457-9998
Email: gary@gr-morris.com
Key Contact - Specialty:
Mr. Gary Morris, President

102 N Shiloh Rd Ste 306
Garland, TX 75042-6695
(972) 485-4388
Fax: (972) 485-0267
Email: tomhern@msn.com
Key Contact - Specialty:
Mr. Tom Hern

8432 Sterling St Ste 202
Irving, TX 75063-2585
(972) 929-2222
Fax: (972) 929-2223
Email: jobs@itts.com
Key Contact - Specialty:
Ms. Alicia Smith

9901 Valley Ranch Pkwy E Ste 2000
Irving, TX 75063-6787
(866) 837-0025
Fax: (817) 416-5749
Email: jrademacher@mrirving.com
Key Contact - Specialty:
Mr. Joe Rademacher

20501 Katy Fwy Ste 214
Katy, TX 77450-1942
(281) 599-9177
Fax: (281) 599-0507
Email: glombard@mrkaty.com
Key Contact - Specialty:
Mr. Gary Lombard

1202 Richardson Dr Ste 112
Richardson, TX 75080-4611
(972) 669-3999
Fax: (972) 669-4737
Email: lpm@mrrichardson.com
Key Contact - Specialty:
Mr. Lawrence McClung

7550 W IH 10 Ste 300
San Antonio, TX 78229-5810
(210) 525-1800
Fax: (210) 525-9633

Email: sam@mrgoicoechea.com
Key Contact - Specialty:
Mr. Sam Goicoechea, Co-Manager
Ms. Lydia Goicoechea, Co-Manager

759 E 800 N
Orem, UT 84097-4242
(801) 434-9265
Fax: (801) 434-9535
Email: scprovo@scprovo.com
Key Contact - Specialty:
Mr. Jerry Johnson

1762 Prospector Ave Ste B
Park City, UT 84060-7499
(435) 647-5670
Fax: (435) 647-3958
Email: gesty@prospectorgroup.com
Key Contact - Specialty:
Mr. Gregory C. Esty, Co-Manager
Ms. Janet S. Esty, Co-Manager

1700 N Moore St Ste 1005
Arlington, VA 22209-1901
(703) 351-1300
Fax: (703) 351-1562
Email: rbranch@mriarlington.com
Key Contact - Specialty:
Mr. Roger Branch

PO Box 8347
Charlottesville, VA 22906-8347
(434) 293-0800
Fax: (434) 293-0813
Email: jobs@insurance-positions.com
Key Contact - Specialty:
Mr. James Metzgar

13343 Regal Crest Dr
Clifton, VA 20124-0981
(703) 766-0393
Fax: (703) 467-9115
Email: chris@mri-reston.com
Key Contact - Specialty:
Mr. Chris Garcia, Co-Manager
Ms. Linda Garcia, Co-Manager

10560 Main St Ste 407
Fairfax, VA 22030-7174
(703) 766-3000
Fax: (703) 766-3006
Email: rhoughton@mrfairfax.com
Key Contact - Specialty:
Mr. Rob Houghton, Managing Partner

212 Starling Ave Ste 201
Martinsville, VA 24112-3844
(276) 632-2355
Fax: (276) 632-0153
Email: herschel@neocom.net
Key Contact - Specialty:
Mr. Herschel Gurley, President

PO Box 450
Pulaski, VA 24301-0450
(540) 980-3100
Fax: (540) 980-3300
Email: nrvctr@adelphia.net
Key Contact - Specialty:
Mr. Ed J. Beckett, Manager
Mr. Chuck Morris, Account Executive
Mr. Gene Stewart, Account Executive

6802 Paragon Pl Ste 430
Richmond, VA 23230-1655
(804) 285-2071
Fax: (804) 282-4990
Email: jays@richgroupusa.com
Key Contact - Specialty:
Mr. Jay S. Schwartz, Manager

389 Edwin Dr
Virginia Beach, VA 23462-4548
(757) 490-0331
Fax: (757) 490-0129
Email: jobs@murpheygroup.com
Key Contact - Specialty:
Mr. James F. Murphey, Manager

104 Bypass Rd Ste 203
Williamsburg, VA 23185-3001
(757) 345-2494
Fax: (757) 345-2507
Email: tim@mriyorktown.com
Key Contact - Specialty:
Mr. Timothy Saumier

356 McLaws Cir Ste 3
Williamsburg, VA 23185-6345
(757) 229-6475
Fax: (757) 229-6495
Email: apolson@mricolonialgroup.com
Key Contact - Specialty:
Mr. Al Polson, President

376 McLaws Cir Ste 1
Williamsburg, VA 23185-5648
(757) 345-3755
Email: ken@defenseplacements.com
Key Contact - Specialty:
Mr. Ken Selzer

4957 Lakemont Blvd SE Ste C4-184
Bellevue, WA 98006-7801
(425) 557-4202
Fax: (866) 415-8161
Email: infomrb@mrbellevue.com
Key Contact - Specialty:
Mr. Fred Novick - *Healthcare, Pharmaceutical,
Telecommunications*

4819 33rd Ave W
Everett, WA 98203-1341
(425) 238-4149
Fax: (425) 303-0495
Email: careers@mreverett.com
Key Contact - Specialty:
Mr. John McElroy, PE, Manager

2709 Jahn Ave NW Ste H11
Gig Harbor, WA 98335-7995
(253) 858-9991
Fax: (253) 858-5140
Email: tacomamr@aol.com
Key Contact - Specialty:
Mr. Dennis R. Johnson, Manager

1610 Grover St Ste B5
Lynden, WA 98264-1539
(360) 354-1100
Email: dkorthuis@mrlynden.com
Key Contact - Specialty:
Mr. Don Korthuis

19105 36th Ave W Ste 211
Lynnwood, WA 98036-5760
(425) 778-1212
Fax: (425) 778-7840
Email: budnaff@mri-lynnwood.com
Key Contact - Specialty:
Mr. Robert Naff, Owner - *Construction,
Environmental*

2633A Parkmont Ln SW Ste B
Olympia, WA 98502-5751
(360) 357-9996
(877) 357-9996
Fax: (360) 357-9998
Email: dudley.pitchford@gte.net
Key Contact - Specialty:
Mr. Jim J. Pitchford, Manager

8195 166th Ave NE Ste 201
Redmond, WA 98052-3960
(425) 883-1313
Fax: (425) 883-8103
Email: wzbitnoff@earthlink.net
Key Contact - Specialty:
Mr. Bill Zbitnoff - *Transportation*

117 Judith Dr
Charleston, WV 25312-1102
(304) 344-5632
Fax: (304) 382-0448
Email: mrcharwv@aol.com
Key Contact - Specialty:
Mr. Anthony P. Oliverio, Manager

1818 Listravia Ave Ste A
Morgantown, WV 26505-6318
(304) 296-9800
Fax: (304) 296-2193
Email: mriray@adelphia.net
Key Contact - Specialty:
Mr. Raymond Wood, Manager

101 W Edison Ave Ste 224
Appleton, WI 54915-1390
(920) 830-8080
Fax: (920) 830-8090
Email: mail@scappleton.com
Key Contact - Specialty:
Mr. Jay Rhodes

3500 E Destination Dr
Appleton, WI 54915-7305
(920) 996-9700
Fax: (920) 996-9701
Email: sharon@ergmri.com
Key Contact - Specialty:
Mrs. Sharon K. Hulce, CSAM, President & Chief
Executive Officer - *Business development, C-
level, Construction, Hospital, Non-profit*
Mrs. Mary Harp-Jirschele, Chief Operating
Officer - *Boards of Directors, C-level,
Communications, COOs, Non-profit*
Ms. Donna Hartman, Chief Financial Officer
Mrs. Mary Wettstein, Assistant Vice President -
*Banking
(Commercial,Investment,Mortgage,Retail),
Investment*
Mr. Mike Kinderman, Assistant Vice President -
Healthcare, Home health, Hospital, Medical
Ms. Ragan Cheney, Esq., Director, Professional
Services - *Accounting, Human resources, Legal,
Legal (Attorneys), Marketing*
Mr. Tim Eichstaedt, Director, Construction
Services - *Construction, Design, General
contractors, Product management/development*
Mr. Rich Hedman, Director, Construction
Services - *Construction, General contractors*

15800 W Bluemound Rd Ste 160
Brookfield, WI 53005-6003
(262) 754-0600
Email: jluzar@scbrookfield.com
Key Contact - Specialty:
Mr. Jim Luzar

5576 State Road 50 Ste F
Delavan, WI 53115-4237
(262) 740-9000
Fax: (262) 740-9100
Email: info@mri-salesconsultants.com
Key Contact - Specialty:
Mr. Joseph Almburg, Jr.
Ms. Lori Almburg

1245 Cheyenne Ave Ste 102
Grafton, WI 53024-9323
(262) 387-7777
Fax: (262) 387-7770
Email: msharbuno@mrigrafton.com
Key Contact - Specialty:
Ms. Marinie Harris

PO Box 12708
Green Bay, WI 54307-2708
(920) 434-8770
Fax: (920) 434-9155
Email: sc@mrijobs.com
Key Contact - Specialty:
Mr. Garland E. Ross, Manager

772 W Main St Ste 202
Lake Geneva, WI 53147-1835
(262) 348-0100
Fax: (262) 348-0200
Email: mrlakegeneva@genevaonline.com
Key Contact - Specialty:
Mr. Gary Cook

2701 University Ave Stop 2 # 387
Madison, WI 53705-3700
(608) 238-6040
Email: pwilliams@mr-shorewood-hills.com
Key Contact - Specialty:
Ms. Patricia (Pat) Williams

207 S 4th Ave
Sturgeon Bay, WI 54235-2205
(920) 746-6740
Key Contact - Specialty:
Mr. David Maier

5420 Yellowstone Rd Unit 6
Cheyenne, WY 82009-4156
(307) 775-9900
Email: regina@thefitzgeraldgroup.com
Key Contact - Specialty:
Ms. Regina Fitzgerald
Mr. Rex Washburn

Alborada 124 suite 801 Parques Del Pedregal
14010 Mexico City, DF
Mexico
55 5606 8202
Email: mexicocity@mrimexico.com
Key Contact - Specialty:
Mr. Sergio Albores, Principal - *Accounting, Automotive, Electronics, Engineering, Food & beverage*

MRI ERP Services

(an affiliate of MRI)
108 N Bayview St
Fairhope, AL 36532-2505
(800) 799-8272
(800) 499-9060
Fax: (251) 929-2706
Email: jwbrock@erpservices.com
Web: www.erpservices.com

Summary: Specialized in placement on AS/400, RPG, COBOL programmer/analysts and C++ programmer/analysts in all functions. Also, MIS in all above functions.

Key Contact - Specialty:
Mr. James Brock, Manager
Ms. Angie Lewis, Personnel Consultant

Salary Minimum: $18,000

Functions: Mfg., Systems Dev.

Industries: Generalist (All)

SC of Huntsville

(an affiliate of MRI)
190 Lime Quarry Rd Ste 220
Madison, AL 35758-8976
(256) 464-9570
Email: billmay@hiwaay.net

Summary: Retained and contingency executive search firm specializing in the paper, plastic, and packaging industries.

Key Contact - Specialty:
Mr. William May, President - *Paper, Plastics*

Salary Minimum: $40,000

Functions: Generalist (All), Packaging

Industries: Generalist (All), Paper, Printing, Plastics, Rubber, Packaging

MR of Flagstaff

(an affiliate of MRI)
1515 N Main St Ste A-1
Flagstaff, AZ 86004-4923
(928) 213-1000
Fax: (928) 213-1001
Email: bp@mriflagstaff.com
Web: www.mriflagstaff.com

Summary: We are a professional staffing firm specializing in software, hardware, internet portal, professional development and publishing in the educational (K12 and higher education) and e-learning market. We focus on sales, marketing, training and business development positions from the CXO level on down.

Key Contact - Specialty:
Mr. Brian Petersen, Owner & President
Ms. Hope DeMello, Administrative Assistant

Functions: Senior Mgmt., Middle Mgmt., Sales & Mktg., Mktg. Research, Mktg. Mgmt., Sales Mgmt., Training

Industries: Services, Non-profits, Higher Ed., Publishing, Government, Software, Industry Specific SW, Training SW

The De Angelis Group

(an affiliate of MRI)
7950 E Redfield Rd Ste 280
Scottsdale, AZ 85260-6952
(480) 609-4868
(877) 416-0377
Email: info@thedeangelisgroup.com
Web: www.thedeangelisgroup.com

Summary: Our firm's team of recruiters is a dynamic group of very successful people some with prior experience as a recruiter and others who were recruited directly out of the medical device arena to join the team. The common denominator is that they all have relevant experience that is germane to the industry, commitment to integrity and excellence.

Key Contact - Specialty:
Mr. Drue De Angelis
Mr. Chad McCormick

Functions: Generalist (All)

Industries: Drugs Mfg., Medical Devices, Biotech/Life Sciences

SC of Northwest Arkansas

(an affiliate of MRI)
1 W Mountain St
Fayetteville, AR 72701-6068
(479) 521-9700
Fax: (479) 521-9770
Email: denver@leasingcareers.com
Web: www.leasingcareers.com

Summary: Our firm targets, recruits and delivers high-impact talent for the equipment leasing industry.

Key Contact - Specialty:
Mr. Denver Wilson, President

Functions: Generalist (All), Sales Mgmt., Sales Reps.

Industries: Finance, Services

MR of Little Rock

(an affiliate of MRI)
PO Box 22894
Little Rock, AR 72221-2894
(501) 224-0801
Email: noel.hall@search-team.com
Web: www.search-team.com

Summary: We are a hybrid search firm working with client firms to attract key administrative, managerial and technical professionals for engineering, construction, manufacturing, and food processing specialties.

Key Contact - Specialty:
Mr. Noel K. Hall, President

Salary Minimum: $50,000

Functions: Management, Product Dev., Production, Quality, Sales & Mktg., Finance, IT, Engineering, Geotechnical

Industries: Construction, Manufacturing, Food, Bev., Tobacco, Architectural Svcs., Accounting, Engineering Svcs., Environmental Svcs., Haz. Waste

MR of Templeton

(an affiliate of MRI)
7350 El Camino Real Ste 204
Atascadero, CA 93422-4655
(805) 460-0800
Fax: (805) 460-0860
Email: info@mrtempleton.com
Web: www.mrtempleton.com

Summary: We are a full service search and recruiting firm specializing in mid to senior level positions in biotechnology/pharmaceuticals; civil engineering design and banking.

Key Contact - Specialty:
Mr. Wayne Caruthers

Functions: Generalist (All)

Industries: Drugs Mfg., Medical Devices, Banking, Invest. Banking, Services, Architectural Svcs.

MR of Benicia

(an affiliate of MRI)
701 Southampton Rd Ste 106
Benicia, CA 94510-2076
(707) 747-7000
Fax: (707) 747-7008
Email: jlc@mrbenicia.com
Web: www.mrbenicia.com

Summary: We are a full-service executive search and placement firm specializing in the recruitment and placement of low to upper-level management, engineers, logistics and manufacturing personnel. Industry specialties include food & beverage, consumer products, manufacturing and logistics.

Key Contact - Specialty:
Mr. Jeffery L. Cundick, General Manager - *Food & beverage, Manufacturing*

Salary Minimum: $35,000

Functions: Generalist (All), Mfg.

Industries: Food, Bev., Tobacco, Soap, Perf., Cosmtcs.

MR of Berkeley

(an affiliate of MRI)
2150 Shattuck Ave Ste 407
Berkeley, CA 94704-1347
(510) 486-8100
Fax: (510) 486-8189
Email: rhoward@mrberkeley.com
Web: www.mrberkeley.com

Summary: We are a full-service executive placement firm that has been successfully meeting the staffing needs of employers and placing top candidates. Each of our account managers brings many years of professional experience in their industry specialties.

Key Contact - Specialty:
Mr. Richard H. Howard, Managing Director

Salary Minimum: $70,000

Functions: Management

Industries: Consumer Goods, Finance, Banking, Brokers, Misc. Financial, Logistics Svcs., Supply Chain Mgmt, Hospitality, Restaurants, Full Service Restaurants

---

MR of Chico

(also known as Barsuglia Enterprises Inc)
2060 Talbert Dr Ste 120
Chico, CA 95928-7689
(530) 892-9898
Fax: (530) 892-8668
Email: execusrch@msn.com
Web: www.mrichico.com

Summary: Our firm provides a broad range of executive and management search services for companies and candidates. Our account executives are experts in their industry specialties. They understand the trends in your industry and how they impact your unique staffing challenges.

Key Contact - Specialty:
Mr. Barry R. Barsuglia, President

Salary Minimum: $100,000

Functions: Generalist (All)

Industries: Food, Bev., Tobacco, Chemicals, Soap, Perf., Cosmtcs., Drugs Mfg., Medical Devices, Metal Products, Misc. Mfg.

---

www.medicaljobs.net

(also known as SC of Chico)
55 Independence Cir Ste 108
Chico, CA 95973-4909
(530) 892-8880
(888) 734-1949
Email: kl@medicaljobs.net
Web: www.medicaljobs.net

Summary: We specialize in placing and recruiting individuals who are in current medical device sales or current pharmaceutical sales.

Key Contact - Specialty:
Mrs. Carol Johnson, President & CSAM
Mr. K.L. Johnson, Vice President - *Research & development*
Ms. Lisa Hall, Office Manager

Functions: Sales & Mktg., Sales Mgmt., Sales Reps.

Industries: Drugs Mfg., Medical Devices, Biotech/Life Sciences

---

MR of North Fresno

(an affiliate of MRI)
375 Woodworth Ave Ste 104
Clovis, CA 93612-1060
(559) 297-5900
(800) 795-8060
Fax: (559) 297-5330
Email: info@mrinf.com
Web: www.mrinf.com

Summary: This office, a franchisee of one of the largest search networks, specializes in health care, which includes: acute hospitals, clinics, surgery centers, rehab, psych and skilled nursing management or specialty positions. Also, another industry is manufacturing including plastics, chemicals, film and medical devices.

Key Contact - Specialty:
Ms. Kay Lemon
Mr. Greg Lemon, Account Executive - *Healthcare*
Mrs. Roben Kennedy, Account Executive - *Healthcare*
Mrs. Stefanie Blanco, Senior Recruiting Specialist - *Healthcare*

Salary Minimum: $60,000

Functions: Management

Industries: Healthcare, Hospitals, Long-term/Home Care

MR of Clovis

(an affiliate of MRI)
777 Minnewawa Ave
Clovis, CA 93612-1729
(559) 299-7992
Fax: (559) 299-2167
Email: food2@pacbell.net
Web: www.mrinetwork.com

Summary: We specialize in the successful search and placement of supervisors, managers and executives in the food & beverage processing industry.

Key Contact - Specialty:
Mr. Gary Hendrickson, General Manager

Salary Minimum: $40,000

Functions: Management

Industries: Food, Bev., Tobacco

MR of Dana Point

(an affiliate of MRI)
24681 La Plz Ste 280
Dana Point, CA 92629-2567
(949) 443-2800
Fax: (949) 443-2806
Email: info@mridp.com
Web: www.mridp.com

Summary: We make companies and executives successful by finding and attracting the people they need. Our firm specializes in transportation, logistics, warehousing & distribution, medical & healthcare software, construction and manufacturing. We perform contingency and priority searches nationally with video conferencing and personality profile capabilities.

Key Contact - Specialty:
Mr. Todd Provost, General Manager - *Logistics, Supply Chain, Traffic, Transportation*

Salary Minimum: $30,000

Functions: Management, Sales & Mktg., Finance, Specialized Svcs.

Industries: Generalist (All), Construction, Manufacturing, Chemicals, Transportation, Finance, Accounting, Logistics Svcs., Supply Chain Mgmt, Software, Healthcare

---

MR of Fresno

(an affiliate of MRI)
5715 N West Ave Ste 101
Fresno, CA 93711-2366
(559) 432-3700
(800) 881-4139
Fax: (559) 432-9937
Email: rj1@mri-fresno.com
Web: www.mri-fresno.com

Summary: Our firm specializes in heavy commercial construction, software sales, energy eng, accounting, hospital & nursing, pharmacy, radiology, banking, mortgage lending, food processing industry, IS, call centers, pharmaceutical sales, medical representative, consumer district managers, buyers, bio-

---

technology research chemists, insurance and cyber programmers.

Key Contact - Specialty:
Mr. Ron L. Johnson, General Manager & President - *Managed care, Sales*
Mrs. Donna Johnson, Controller, Treasurer & Vice President
Mr. Scott D. Johnson, CSAM, Team Leader, Food Processing
Mrs. Tina Roberts, CSAM, Team Leader, Hospital Nursing
Mrs. Renee Peschel, Administrative Manager
Mr. Greg K. Johnson, Construction Team Leader

Functions: Purchasing, Distribution, Benefits, Training, CFOs, MIS Mgmt., Network Admin.

Industries: Generalist (All)

The Everest Group

(an affiliate of MRI)
211 S Glendora Ave Ste C
Glendora, CA 91741-3455
(626) 963-4503
Email: careers@mrglendora.com
Web: www.mrglendora.com

Summary: We specialize in placing senior level (manager to c-level) management in the functional areas of logistics, supply chain, transportation, distribution, warehousing, etc., across a broad span of industries.

Key Contact - Specialty:
Mr. Matthew Albanese, Principal
Mr. Dennis Teschler, National Account Executive
Mr. Anthony Duncan, National Account Executive
Ms. April Starkey, Executive Assistant & Proj Coordinator

Functions: Senior Mgmt., Product Dev., Materials, Purchasing, Distribution, CFOs

Industries: Generalist (All), Consumer Goods, Transportation, Pharm Svcs., Logistics Svcs., Supply Chain Mgmt, Biotech/Life Sciences

---

Retail Search Group

(an affiliate of MRI)
360 Sierra College Dr Ste 120
Grass Valley, CA 95945-5088
(530) 432-1966
Fax: (530) 432-3606
Email: gerald@retailsearchgroup.com
Web: www.retailsearchgroup.com

Summary: We are an executive search practice with highly experienced business executives with backgrounds in IT, telecom, MIS, and sales management.

Key Contact - Specialty:
Mr. Gerald Mitchell, President & Chief Executive Officer

Salary Minimum: $40,000

Functions: Generalist (All), Management, Senior Mgmt., Middle Mgmt., Purchasing, Distribution, HR Mgmt., Finance, CFOs, MIS Mgmt.

Industries: Retail

MR of Huntington Beach

(an affiliate of MRI)
18672 Florida St Ste 302B
Huntington Beach, CA 92648-1992
(714) 843-6433
Fax: (714) 843-6993
Email: resume@hbmri.com
Web: www.hbmri.com

Summary: Our firm specializes in international technology, financial, medical, logistics, consumer products, food, and restaurants/hospitality.

Key Contact - Specialty:
Ms. Peggy Smith, Recruiter

Functions: Senior Mgmt., Middle Mgmt., Distribution, Finance, CFOs, Budgeting, Cash Mgmt., M&A, IT, MIS Mgmt.

Industries: Generalist (All), Food, Bev., Tobacco, Drugs Mfg., Medical Devices, Finance, Services, Hospitality, Software, Biotech/Life Sciences, Healthcare

MR Biotech

(an affiliate of MRI)
700 Larkspur Landing Cir Ste 175
Larkspur, CA 94939-1754
(415) 461-2084
Email: mark@mrbiotech.com
Web: www.mrbiotech.com

Summary: Our specialty is in the bio-technology industry. We have specialists in research, development, engineering, quality, manufacturing, clinical, regulatory, business development and marketing.

Key Contact - Specialty:
Mr. Mark Hoffman, Owner - *Biotechnology*

Salary Minimum: $50,000

Functions: Generalist (All), Management, Middle Mgmt., Product Dev., Automation

Industries: Generalist (All), Drugs Mfg., Medical Devices, Pharm Svcs., Biotech/Life Sciences

MR of Menlo Park

(an affiliate of MRI)
869 El Camino Real
Menlo Park, CA 94025-4807
(650) 617-9440
Email: bms@mriresources.com
Web: www.mriresources.com

Summary: Today, unprecedented changes are transforming every aspect of how people work and how companies hire. Our mission is to provide staffing solutions specifically designed to meet the unique challenges these changes have created for your company.

Key Contact - Specialty:
Mr. Bruce Solomon, Manager, President

Functions: Management, Middle Mgmt., Healthcare, Nurses, Sales & Mktg., Mktg. Mgmt., Sales Mgmt., Engineering

Industries: Paper, Printing, Medical Devices, Consumer Elect., Test, Measure Equip., Misc. Mfg., Electronic, Elec. Components, Robotics, Semiconductors, Consumer Goods, Wholesale, Retail, Finance, Invest. Banking, Mutual/Hedge Funds, Misc. Financial, Non-profits, Publishing, Digital, Wireless, Fiber Optic, Network Infrastructure, Real Estate, Property/Facility Mgmt., Software, Healthcare, Hospitals, Long-term/Home Care, Dental, Non-Classifiable

MR of Monterey

(an affiliate of MRI)
479 Pacific St Ste 7
Monterey, CA 93940-2716
(831) 649-0737
Fax: (831) 649-0253

Summary: We are a search firm specializing in surgical and emergency nursing management with clients nationwide.

Key Contact - Specialty:
Mr. Richard J. Kashinsky, General Manager - *Healthcare, Surgical*

Salary Minimum: $60,000

Functions: Generalist (All), Nurses, Health Admin.

Industries: Generalist (All), Healthcare

SC of Palo Alto

(an affiliate of MRI)
2680 Bayshore Pkwy Ste 304
Mountain View, CA 94043-1020
(650) 237-9097
(888) 774-2268
Fax: (650) 237-9086
Email: dwhite@scpaloalto.com
Web: www.scpaloalto.com

Summary: We are a successful executive search firm specializing in high performance sales & marketing professionals in the software and communications industries.

Key Contact - Specialty:
Mr. David White, President

Functions: Sales & Mktg.

Industries: E-commerce, IT Implementation, Telecoms, Telephony, Digital, Wireless, Fiber Optic, Network Infrastructure

Principal Resource Group

(an affiliate of MRI)
313 Railroad Ave Ste 203
Nevada City, CA 95959-2851
(530) 478-6478
(888) 832-1057
Fax: (530) 478-6477
Email: engsearch@prgnc.com
Web: www.prgnc.com

Summary: We are an executive recruiting firm with two primary areas of focus; engineering and healthcare. Our engineering division is focused on civil engineering, including water/wastewater, structural, transportation, land development and related professions. Our health care division is focused on physicians, hospital administrators and mid-level practitioners.

Key Contact - Specialty:
Mr. Pat Havard, Owner & Manager - *Engineering*
Mr. Mark Vieaux, Account Manager - *Consulting, Engineering*
Ms. Cynthia Keck, Account Manager - *Consulting, Engineering*
Ms. Mary Wernette, Account Manager - *Consulting, Engineering*
Mr. Tom Herbert, Account Manager
Ms. Kathleen Feeley, Account Manager - *Engineering*
Ms. Pamela Norr, Account Manager - *Healthcare*
Ms. Diane Correll, Account Executive - *Healthcare, Long term care*

Salary Minimum: $60,000

Functions: Physicians, Engineering

Industries: Construction, Architectural Svcs., Engineering Svcs., Healthcare, Hospitals, Long-term/Home Care, Occupational Therapy

SC of Newport Beach

(an affiliate of MRI)
4120 Birch St Ste 106
Newport Beach, CA 92660-2228
(949) 622-0232
Fax: (949) 622-0240
Web: www.mrinetwork.com

Summary: Our firm is part of one of the largest recruiting franchise in the industry. We specialize in the recruitment of qualified personnel in the biotechnology, medical, legal, construction, manufacturing, financial services and engineering services industries. We work with clients throughout the market to attract qualified individuals for their staffing needs.

Key Contact - Specialty:
Mr. Ray Stockstill

Salary Minimum: $125,000

Functions: Generalist (All), Attorneys

Industries: Construction, Manufacturing, Finance, Services, Pharm Svcs., Legal, Accounting, Engineering Svcs., Aerospace, Biotech/Life Sciences, Healthcare

The Oceanside Group

(also known as SC of Oceanside/San Diego)
1213 S Pacific St
Oceanside, CA 92054-4933
(760) 744-0090
Fax: (760) 744-0708
Email: careers@careermatching.com
Web: www.careermatching.com

Summary: We specialize in the placement of top sales SE, consultants, and sales management professionals in the high-technology software arena.

Key Contact - Specialty:
Mr. Robert Enright, Owner & General Manager
Mrs. Linda Taylor, Administration - *Business to business, Computers, Computers (Software), CRM, ERP*

Salary Minimum: $150,000

Functions: Senior Mgmt., Mfg., Sales & Mktg., Mktg. Mgmt., Sales Mgmt.

Industries: E-commerce, IT Implementation, PSA/ASP, New Media, Wireless, Network Infrastructure, Software, Accounting SW, Database SW, Development SW, Doc. Mgmt., Production SW, ERP SW, HR SW, Industry Specific SW, Marketing SW, Networking, Comm. SW, Security SW, Training SW

MR of Pleasanton

(an affiliate of MRI)
1989A Santa Rita Rd Ste 275
Pleasanton, CA 94566-4727
(925) 462-8579
Fax: (925) 462-0208
Email: confidential@mricareers.com
Web: www.mricareers.com

Summary: Presidents club office: confidential contingency and retained search. Specializing in the recruitment of transportation, logistics, distribution and software (TMS,WMS,SCS) professionals.

Key Contact - Specialty:
Mr. Michael T. Machi, General Manager - *Distribution, Logistics, Management, Transportation*

Salary Minimum: $45,000

Functions: Generalist (All), Management, Distribution, Sales & Mktg., Sales Mgmt., Finance

Industries: Generalist (All), Plastics, Rubber, Transportation, Retail, Accounting, HR Services, Logistics Svcs., Software

MR of Redlands

(an affiliate of MRI)
19 E Citrus Ave Ste 201
Redlands, CA 92373-4742
(909) 335-2055
Fax: (909) 792-4194
Email: maurice@mrredlands.com
Web: www.mrredlands.com

Summary: We are a recruiting firm for construction, engineering and architecture. Recruiting for permanent positions and executive temp placement.

Key Contact - Specialty:
Mr. Maurice R. Meyers, President - *Architecture, Construction, Engineering*

Salary Minimum: $40,000

Functions: Generalist (All)

Industries: Construction, Architectural Svcs., Engineering Svcs.

SC of Sacramento

(an affiliate of MRI)
2999 Douglas Blvd Ste 334
Roseville, CA 95661-3839
(916) 677-7700
Fax: (916) 677-7710
Email: resumes@scsacramento.com
Web: www.scsacramento.com

Summary: We are a franchise of one of the country's largest recruiter of sales and sales management personnel with more than 160 offices serving every business market. Using this network of recruiters, we can locate the most highly trained candidate.

Key Contact - Specialty:
Mr. Ron Whitney, Owner & Manager - *Building products, Computers, Industrial*

Salary Minimum: $30,000

Functions: Generalist (All), Sales Mgmt., Sales Reps.

Industries: Generalist (All), Construction, Manufacturing, Consumer Goods, Banking

WorldBridge Partners of California

(an affiliate of MRI)
3721 Douglas Blvd Ste 350
Roseville, CA 95661-4254
(916) 781-8110
Fax: (916) 781-8110
Email: dave@worldbridgepartners.com
Web: www.worldbridgepartners.com

Summary: Our team of professionals is your single source for high technology recruiting of executive, technical, and sales & marketing talent. We specialize in the enterprise software, wireless, IT services, and telecom industries with other practices focusing on construction, banking and other financial services industries.

Key Contact - Specialty:
Mr. David Sanders, President - *Financial services*
Ms. Lorena Stanley, Vice President

Salary Minimum: $80,000

Functions: Management, Senior Mgmt., Sales & Mktg., Mktg. Mgmt., Sales Mgmt., CFOs, IT

Industries: Generalist (All), Brokers, Communications, Telecoms, Wireless, Network Infrastructure, Software, ERP SW, Networking, Comm. SW, Security SW

MR of Sacramento

(an affiliate of MRI)
1451 River Park Dr Ste 130
Sacramento, CA 95815-4518
(916) 565-2700
(800) 434-6877
Fax: (916) 565-2828
Email: mrwebres@mrsacramento.com
Web: www.mrsacramento.com

Summary: Our specialties include power & energy, mortgage banking, manufacturing, construction and accounting & finance. Our differentiator is our value added services, which include video-conferencing, specialized assessment tools and executive VIP packaging.

Key Contact - Specialty:
Mr. Karl Dinse, President - *Energy*
Ms. Elizabeth Dinse, Vice President - *Energy*

Salary Minimum: $50,000

Functions: Generalist (All)

Industries: Energy, Utilities, Construction, Manufacturing, Finance, Banking, Services, Accounting, HR Services

MR/SC of San Diego

(an affiliate of MRI)
9455 Ridgehaven Ct Ste 100
San Diego, CA 92123-1647
(858) 565-6600
Email: kennedy@mrisandiego.com
Web: www.mrisandiego.com

Summary: We recruit Architects and other technical and industrial professionals.

Key Contact - Specialty:
Mr. Harvey J. Baron, President

Salary Minimum: $30,000

Functions: Architects

Industries: Architectural Svcs.

MR/SC San Francisco Bay Area

(an affiliate of MRI)
3 Waters Park Dr Ste 222
San Mateo, CA 94403-1169
(650) 548-4800
Fax: (650) 655-6724
Email: admin@mrica.com
Web: www.mrica.com

Summary: Dedicated to conducting comprehensive candidate searches, customized to meet specific hiring needs. Specialize in placing qualified candidates within biotechnology sales, healthcare management, construction management, retail management, the food and food service industry and training, consulting, business services, high technology sales.

Key Contact - Specialty:
Mr. Michael T. Shaffer, CSM, CSAM, President - *Consumer, Food & beverage, Food service*
Mr. Brian Waller, CSAM, Vice President, Bioscience, Sales - *Biotechnology, Industrial, Sales*
Ms. Roberta Wright, CSAM, Vice President, Construction Management - *Construction*

Salary Minimum: $50,000

Functions: Generalist (All), Management, Product Dev., Sales Mgmt.

Industries: Generalist (All), Construction, Food, Bev., Tobacco, Consumer Goods, Wholesale, Retail, Mgmt. Consulting, Digital, Biotech/Life Sciences, Healthcare, Hospitals

MR of Santa Ana

(an affiliate of MRI)
2700 N Main St Ste 600
Santa Ana, CA 92705-6667
(714) 565-0010
(888) 654-0070
Fax: (714) 565-0020
Email: admin@socalmri.com
Web: www.socalmri.com

Summary: Our firm offers search and recruitment services in engineering and manufacturing in the following industries: medical device, aeronautical, automotive, machinery and metal fabrication.

Key Contact - Specialty:
Mr. Ray Burch, President - *Aerospace, Engineering, Manufacturing, Quality*
Ms. Caroline Burch, Account Manager - *Biotechnology, Engineering, Manufacturing, Medical, Quality*

Functions: Generalist (All)

Industries: Generalist (All), Manufacturing, Medical Devices, Metal Products, Electronic, Elec. Components, RF/Microwave, Aerospace

Intellenet LLC

(also known as MR of Santa Cruz)
303 Potrero St Ste 42-205
Santa Cruz, CA 95060-2780
(831) 425-5251
Fax: (831) 425-5430
Email: vb1@got.net
Web: www.techheadhunter.com

Summary: We specialize in placing exceptional sales and sales engineering talent with system software vendors. Desk specialties include data security, storage, systems, network and application management.

Key Contact - Specialty:
Mr. Tom Crahen, Manager

Salary Minimum: $70,000

Functions: Sales & Mktg., Sales Mgmt.

Industries: Wireless, Network Infrastructure, Database SW, Doc. Mgmt., Production SW, Networking, Comm. SW, Security SW, System SW

Amberg Consulting Group

(an affiliate of MRI)
777 S Highway 101 Ste 210
Solana Beach, CA 92075-2624
(858) 259-7877
Fax: (858) 259-7845
Email: acg@acgjobs.com
Web: www.acgjobs.com

Summary: Our firm serves clients in a variety of manufacturing industries including: construction, industrial and agricultural machinery, as well as automotive, plastics and metal related components. In order to provide the best selection of fully qualified candidates, our research, recruitment and selection procedures are generally conducted on a national level.

Key Contact - Specialty:
Mr. Arthur Amberg, President
Ms. Katrina Henderson, Research Consultant

Functions: Management, Mfg., Materials, Engineering

Industries: Manufacturing, Plastics, Rubber, Metal Products, Machine, Appliance, Motor Vehicles, Test, Measure Equip., Misc. Mfg., Industry Specific SW, Mfg. SW, Marketing SW

MR of Thousand Oaks

(an affiliate of MRI)
100 E Thousand Oaks Blvd Ste 115
Thousand Oaks, CA 91360-8172
(805) 497-4708
Fax: (805) 497-4718
Email: clientservices@mri-to.com
Web: www.mri-to.com

Summary: We focus on retail. Our clients needs seem to be specific to replenishment, buying, merchandising, and catalog development both online and hard copies. We are successful in identifying exceptional top candidates.

Key Contact - Specialty:

Ms. Mickey Kampsen, President & Account Executive - *E-business, Finance, Human resources, Sales*

Salary Minimum: $80,000

Functions: Senior Mgmt., Middle Mgmt.

Industries: Generalist (All), Retail, Finance, Services, Pharm Svcs., HR Services, E-commerce, Media, Communications, Software, HR SW, Training SW, Biotech/Life Sciences, Healthcare

R & J Arnold & Associates

(also known as MR of Broomfield Inc)
PO Box 2279
Boulder, CO 80306-2279
(717) 464-8536
Fax: (717) 464-8537
Email: r-j-arnold-assoc@att.net

Summary: We have earned a very solid reputation for surfacing qualified professionals who meet our clients' clinical/technical, philosophical and personality needs. Over 50 percent placed remain with the client over three years.

Key Contact - Specialty:

Ms. Janet N. Arnold, Partner - *Healthcare*
Mr. Robert W. Arnold, Partner

Functions: Generalist (All), Senior Mgmt., Middle Mgmt., Physicians, Nurses, Health Admin., MIS Mgmt.

Industries: Generalist (All), Healthcare, Hospitals

MR of Boulder

(an affiliate of MRI)
4885 Riverbend Rd Ste F
Boulder, CO 80301-2617
(303) 447-9900
Fax: (303) 447-9536
Email: windy@mrboulder.com
Web: www.mrboulder.com

Summary: We specialize in finding key personnel for companies in the areas of: financial consulting services - specifically litigation support, business recovery and valuations; and RF microwave and wireless communications - primarily the equipment providers. Within our areas of specialization we work with Fortune 500 firms as well as smaller stable and/or fast-growth companies.

Key Contact - Specialty:

Ms. Windy Bradfield, Certified Senior Account Manager
Mr. Rich Bradfield, Manager

Functions: Generalist (All), Senior Mgmt.

Industries: Finance, Engineering Svcs., RF/Microwave

MR of Colorado

(an affiliate of MRI)
6855 S Havana St Ste 650
Centennial, CO 80112-3868
(303) 799-8188
(800) 408-0045
Fax: (303) 799-0711
Email: resume@mricolorado.com
Web: www.mricolorado.com

Summary: With extensive executive recruiting experience, we've conducted searches over a vast range of industries & positions. We specialize in the following areas: nurse management, radiology, food & beverage manufacturing and production, banking, and construction. All supervisor to CEO level positions. Large multinational companies to small regional based organizations.

Key Contact - Specialty:

Mr. Kent Milius, Chief Executive Officer - *Food & beverage, Healthcare, Senior management*
Mrs. Lynne Milius, Administrative Vice 'President
Mr. Sean Milius, Chief Operating Officer & President - *Management*

Salary Minimum: $30,000

Functions: Generalist (All), Production, Nurses, Allied Health, Health Admin., Finance, Engineering

Industries: Generalist (All), Energy, Utilities, Construction, Food, Bev., Tobacco, Medical Devices, Banking, Legal, Biotech/Life Sciences, Healthcare

MR of Colorado Springs

(an affiliate of MRI)
13 S Tejon St Ste 305
Colorado Springs, CO 80903-1524
(719) 575-0500
Fax: (719) 575-0505
Email: info@mrcosprings.com
Web: www.mrcosprings.com

Summary: Contingency search, with an emphasis on technical positions in the following areas: gas & electric utilities, IT, telecom and manufacturing engineering (especially plastics).

Key Contact - Specialty:

Mr. Mark Merriman, Owner & Manager
Mr. Jack Merriman, Owner - *Energy*
Mr. Glenn S. Waugh, Recruiter
Mr. Ray Haley, Recruiter
Mr. Owen Olsen, Recruiter
Mr. Jim Griffin, Recruiter
Ms. Sharon Douglas, Administrative Assistant
Ms. Sherrill Reed, Administrative Assistant

Salary Minimum: $40,000

Functions: Generalist (All)

Industries: Generalist (All), Energy, Utilities, Manufacturing, Food, Bev., Tobacco, Plastics, Rubber, Paints, Petro. Products, Computer Equip., Misc. Mfg., Mgmt. Consulting, HR Services

MR of Denver-Downtown

(an affiliate of MRI)
928 S Cove Way
Denver, CO 80209-5110
(303) 765-4404
Fax: (303) 765-4432
Email: k.k.haynes@worldnet.att.net
Web: www.hvacmri.com

Summary: We specialize in the HVAC industry and related industries.

Key Contact - Specialty:

Mr. Kurt Haynes, Owner

Salary Minimum: $65,000

Functions: Sales & Mktg.

Industries: Construction, Equip Svcs.

Wise Executive Resources

(an affiliate of MRI)
3081 Bergen Peak Dr Ste 215
Evergreen, CO 80439-2224
(303) 679-3590
Email: talent@wiseexecutiveresources.com
Web: www.wiseexecutiveresources.com

Summary: Our mission is to provide executive search, staffing and consulting services specifically designed to meet the unique challenges in our dynamic business environment. We are a network affiliate of the world's leading global provider of executive recruiting services with offices worldwide. We specialize in transportation, distribution and logistics talent.

Key Contact - Specialty:

Mr. David Wise, President - *Distribution, Logistics, Transportation*

Salary Minimum: $50,000

Functions: Generalist (All), Senior Mgmt.

Industries: Generalist (All), Transportation, Wholesale, Services, Equip Svcs., Mgmt. Consulting, Logistics Svcs., Supply Chain Mgmt

MJM Global Search

(an affiliate of MRI)
2195 N Highway 83 Ste 17
Franktown, CO 80116-9600
(303) 660-0766
(800) 839-0393
Fax: (303) 660-0065
Email: marcie@jmjmglobalsearch.com
Web: www.mjmglobalsearch.com

Summary: Our professional practice encompasses all functional areas of high technology including executive leadership, sales and technical recruiting. Our clients rely on our capabilities to fill critical openings in the following industries: aerospace, eCommerce, high-tech, software, IT, semiconductor, MEMS, telecommunications, wireless, and temporary/contract placements.

Key Contact - Specialty:

Ms. Margie Cohen, Partner - *BSME, Computers (Hardware,Networking,Programming,Software)*
Mr. James Harlan, Partner - *Aerospace, Business development, Business to business, C-level, CEOs*
Ms. Marcie Norman, Partner - *Advertising, Business development, Computers (Sales), Consulting, Consumer (Packaged Goods)*

Salary Minimum: $50,000

Functions: Generalist (All), Mfg., Sales & Mktg., IT

Industries: Manufacturing, Computer Equip., Consumer Elect., Misc. Mfg., Electronic, Elec. Components, Semiconductors, Consumer Goods, Services, E-commerce, Media, Communications, Network Infrastructure, RF/Microwave, Government, Defense, Aerospace, Software, Database SW, Development SW, Industry Specific SW, Mfg. SW, Marketing SW, Networking, Comm. SW, Security SW, System SW

The Alpine Group

(an affiliate of MRI)
2764 Compass Dr Ste 238
Grand Junction, CO 81506-8746
(970) 241-4043
Fax: (970) 241-4395
Email: admin@alpinesearch.net
Web: www.alpinesearch.net

Summary: Our firm recruits exclusively on the commercial side of the bio-pharmaceutical, medical device and life science industries. We help progressive employers locate and hire top tier sales, marketing and business development professionals who want to make a significant impact on the growth of an organization.

Key Contact - Specialty:

Mr. Dave Murphy, Owner & Manager
Ms. Kim Whittaker-Golden, Vice President, Medical Affairs Recruit - *Pharmaceutical*

Mr. Brad Saelens, Executive Recruiter -
*Biopharmaceutical, Biotechnology,
Pharmaceutical*
Mr. Jason Lewis, Executive Recruiter -
*Biopharmaceutical, Pharmaceutical, Quality,
Regulatory*

Salary Minimum: $45,000

Functions: Generalist (All)

Industries: Drugs Mfg., Medical Devices, Pharm
Svcs., Biotech/Life Sciences

MR of Denver-Golden Hill

(an affiliate of MRI)
7114 W Jefferson Ave Ste 213
Lakewood, CO 80235-2309
(303) 233-8600
Fax: (303) 233-8479
Email: lori@mrigold.com

Summary: We are specialists in the fields of
medical device production & manufacturing and
custom industrial markets. Our search
assignments include: management, engineering,
project management, design, and sales positions.

Key Contact - Specialty:
Mr. Rodney D. Bonner, General Manager -
Manufacturing, Medical (Devices)
Mrs. Lori Williams, Senior Search & Recruiting
Specialist - *Manufacturing, Medical (Devices)*

Salary Minimum: $60,000

Functions: Product Dev., Automation,
Engineering

Industries: Manufacturing, Medical Devices,
Machine, Appliance, Packaging, Mfg. SW

MR of Highlands Ranch

(an affiliate of MRI)
10240 Sweet Rock Ct Ste 110
Parker, CO 80134-9160
(303) 805-7491
Fax: (303) 805-7492
Email: dshaw@thehighlandsgroup.net

Summary: We concentrate on placing talented and
successful executives, managers and technical
professionals with leading manufacturers from
coast to coast at the plant, divisional or corporate
level.

Key Contact - Specialty:
Mr. Darryl C. Shaw, Manager

Salary Minimum: $65,000

Functions: Management, Senior Mgmt.,
Production, Plant Mgmt., Engineering

Industries: Lumber, Furniture, Chemicals,
Plastics, Rubber, Paints, Petro. Products,
Leather, Stone, Glass, Metal Products, Machine,
Appliance, Misc. Mfg.

JRP Group

(also known as MR of Denver-Lodo)
PO Box 1699
Silverthorne, CO 80498-1699
(970) 668-4800
Fax: (970) 668-4807
Email: admin@jrpgroup.net
Web: www.jrpgroup.net

Summary: Our firm specializes in the restaurant,
retail, hospitality and casino industries as well as
industries which support those business sectors
such as construction, real estate, financial services
and engineering. We handle positions in the mid to
upper level management range.

Key Contact - Specialty:
Mr. John Paulus

Salary Minimum: $50,000

Functions: Management, Sales & Mktg.,
Advertising, Customer Svc., PR, HR Mgmt.,
Finance

Industries: Retail, Hospitality, Hotels, Resorts,
Clubs, Restaurants

SC of Westminster

(an affiliate of MRI)
8774 Yates Dr Ste 325
Westminster, CO 80031-6962
(720) 542-0500
(877) 551-0570
Fax: (720) 542-0600
Email: info@scwconsulting.com
Web: www.scwconsulting.com

Summary: We specialize in placing top
management, marketing, sales and technical talent.
We provide search and recruiting services for
electronic security industry and healthcare
information systems.

Key Contact - Specialty:
Mr. Thomas Verzuh, President - *Information
Systems, Manufacturing, Product
management/development, Sales*

Functions: Generalist (All), Senior Mgmt.,
Middle Mgmt., Healthcare, Sales & Mktg.,
Sales Mgmt., Security Personnel

Industries: Generalist (All), Database SW,
Industry Specific SW, Healthcare, Non-
Classifiable

Brower Group

(an affiliate of MRI)
40 Tower Ln
Avon, CT 06001-4222
(860) 676-8400
Fax: (860) 676-2500
Email: resume@browergroup.com
Web: www.browergroup.com

Summary: We are an executive search and
recruiting firm for the financial services, retail,
health care, insurance and legal industries.

Key Contact - Specialty:
Mr. Patrick M. Slater, President - *Banking,
Financial services, Retail, Trust*

Salary Minimum: $75,000

Functions: Generalist (All)

Industries: Retail, Finance, Legal, Insurance,
Healthcare

The Hudson Consulting Group LLC

(also know as WorldBridge Partners)
500 Winding Brook Dr
Glastonbury, CT 06033-4336
(860) 652-8660
Email: mgionta@hudsongrp.com
Web: www.hudsongrp.com

Summary: Specialize in computer networking
LAN/WAN sales/marketing. Additionally, the e-
learning and corporate education market is
covered extensively. In the construction market we
focus on uncovering professional talent in the
commercial markets. The Firm works largely on
retained projects from senior-level management
through field sales and engineering. Fulfillment
time averages 60 to 90 days.

Key Contact - Specialty:
Mr. Michael Gionta, President

Salary Minimum: $75,000

Functions: Management, Sales & Mktg.

Industries: Construction, E-commerce, IT
Implementation, Higher Ed., Telecoms, Digital,
Wireless, Fiber Optic, Network Infrastructure,
RF/Microwave, ERP SW, Networking, Comm.
SW, Security SW, Training SW

MR of Milford

(an affiliate of MRI)
61 Cherry St
Milford, CT 06460-8902
(203) 876-8755
Email: mrimlfd@aol.com

Summary: We are specialists in executive, R&D,
manufacturing, operations, engineering and
scientific recruitment for the biotechnology,
medical device & diagnostics, pharmaceutical and
analytical instrumentation industries.

Key Contact - Specialty:
Ms. Sandra L. Stratman, Senior Parnter -
Biotechnology, Diagnostics, Pharmaceutical
Ms. Sandra Campbell, Senior Parnter -
Pharmaceutical

Salary Minimum: $50,000

Functions: Generalist (All)

Industries: Drugs Mfg., Medical Devices, Pharm
Svcs., Biotech/Life Sciences

The Cowser Group

(an affiliate of MRI)
39 Locust Ave Ste 205
New Canaan, CT 06840-4783
(203) 966-5800
Fax: (203) 966-2562
Email: hr@mricowser.com
Web: www.mricowser.com

Summary: Our firm strives to develop and
maintain long term professional relationships with
our clients. We believe in a business relationship
based on hard work, cooperation, integrity, trust
and professionalism. We are an executive search
and recruiting firm specializing in the market
research industry.

Key Contact - Specialty:
Ms. Stephanie Cowser

Functions: Generalist (All), Mktg. Research

Industries: Soap, Perf., Cosmtcs., Consumer
Goods, Retail, Advertising

The Lewis Group

116 Washington Ave Ste 3
North Haven, CT 06473-1721
(203) 876-4949
Fax: (203) 876-4959
Web: www.lewgrp.com

Summary: We place audit, IT audit and financial
professionals.

Key Contact - Specialty:
Mr. Fred Raley, President

Functions: Finance

Industries: Generalist (All)

The Performance Group Inc

(also known as SC of Stamford-Darien)
111 Prospect St Ste 410
Stamford, CT 06901-1208
(203) 327-3270
Fax: (203) 327-6578
Email: jburt@perfgroup.net

Summary: We specialize in B2B services
industries: sales, marketing, sales management,
and general management positions.

Key Contact - Specialty:
Mr. James M. Burt, Managing Director

Salary Minimum: $70,000

Functions: Sales & Mktg., Training, Mgmt. Consultants

Industries: Generalist (All), Mgmt. Consulting, HR Services, Software

MR of Stamford

(an affiliate of MRI)
45 Church St Ste 301
Stamford, CT 06906-1734
(203) 356-9999
Fax: (203) 356-9717
Email: mris@internetcrossings.com
Web: www.internetcrossings.com

Summary: Our firm specializes in telecom, biotechnology, pharmaceuticals and financial positions. We place all levels from mid-senior management in sales, marketing, operations, engineering, IT, scientists, business development, sales positions and financial positions. We conduct razor-sharp searches on retained or contingency basis. Known for meeting deadlines; we provide maximum ongoing client support. We are very strong in placing senior management positions.

Key Contact - Specialty:
Mr. Alex Walker, President - *Biotechnology, C-level, CEOs, Pharmaceutical, Telecommunications*
Mr. Kevin Palisi, Director - *Biopharmaceutical, Biotechnology, Boards of Directors, CFOs, Pharmaceutical*
Ms. Lisa Walker, RN, MSN, Executive Search Consultant - *Biomedical, Biopharmaceutical, Biotechnology, Pharmaceutical, Sales*
Mr. Peter Lee, Contract Staffing Manager - *C-level, CFOs, CIOs, Information Technology, Telecommunications*

Salary Minimum: $100,000

Functions: Senior Mgmt.

Industries: Medical Devices, Pharm Svcs., Legal, E-commerce, IT Implementation, Telecoms, Wireless, Fiber Optic, Biotech/Life Sciences

MR of Winsted

(also known as Wireless Careers / RFID Careers)
PO Box 1017
Winsted, CT 06098-8017
(860) 738-5035
Fax: (860) 738-5039
Email: jjb@wirelesscareers.com
Web: www.wirelesscareers.com

Summary: We are seasoned executive recruiters focused in the wireless and wire-line industries, providing intelligent global staffing solutions in operations, sales & marketing and engineering within the RF infrastructure integration industry.

Key Contact - Specialty:
Mr. Jack Bourque, President

Salary Minimum: $80,000

Functions: Generalist (All), Management, Board Members, Senior Mgmt., Materials Plng., Sales & Mktg., Mktg. Research, Sales Mgmt., Systems Implem., Engineering

Industries: Electronic, Elec. Components, Logistics Svcs., Supply Chain Mgmt, Communications, Telecoms, Digital, Wireless, Fiber Optic, Network Infrastructure, RF/Microwave, Homeland Security, Security SW

MR of Bonita Springs

(an affiliate of MRI)
9240 Bonita Beach Rd SE Ste 3307
Bonita Springs, FL 34135-4252
(239) 495-7885
Fax: (239) 495-7686

Email: career@mriheadhunter.com
Web: www.mriheadhunter.com

Summary: While maintaining a level of professionalism and integrity unsurpassed in recruiting, we are dedicated to the successful placement of qualified professionals within the energy/utility industry. Our technical expertise and world-class service ensures the mutual satisfaction of our candidates and clients resulting in a significant number of long-term relationships.

Key Contact - Specialty:
Mr. Gary F. Shearer, BSCE, President - *Engineering, Management consulting*

Salary Minimum: $75,000

Functions: Generalist (All), Management, Board Members, Senior Mgmt., Middle Mgmt., Sales & Mktg., Sales Mgmt., Risk Mgmt., Systems Analysis, Engineering

Industries: Energy, Utilities, Construction, Mgmt. Consulting

MR of Anna Maria Island

(an affiliate of MRI)
3655 Cortez Rd W Ste 90
Bradenton, FL 34210-3147
(941) 756-3001
Fax: (941) 756-0027
Email: roster@mriflorida.com
Web: www.mriflorida.com

Summary: We are highly-specialized in placement to the technical areas of paper, food ingredient, product development, R&D, production and technical sales/marketing.

Key Contact - Specialty:
Mr. R. Rush Oster, President - *Food, Paper, Pharmaceutical, Steel*
Mr. Eric Lucas, Paper Industry Specialist

Salary Minimum: $40,000

Functions: Product Dev., Production, Mktg. Research, Sales Mgmt., CFOs, Mgmt. Consultants

Industries: Food, Bev., Tobacco, Paper, Printing

Galileo Group LLC

(an affiliate of MRI)
2520 NE Coachman Rd
Clearwater, FL 33765-1803
(727) 447-8610
Fax: (727) 447-8620
Email: si@g-legal.com
Web: www.g-legal.com

Summary: We are specialists who recruit in retained and contingency searches in the legal industry for firms and companies. This includes any opportunities for partners, associates and general counsel for all practice areas.

Key Contact - Specialty:
Mr. Ken Candela, Executive Director
Ms. Sandy Imerman, Executive Director

Salary Minimum: $55,000

Functions: Legal, Attorneys, Paralegals

Industries: Generalist (All)

SC of Ft Lauderdale

(an affiliate of MRI)
3000 NE 30th Pl Ste 408
Fort Lauderdale, FL 33306-1905
(954) 772-5100
Fax: (954) 772-0777
Email: resume@mri-sc-usa.com
Web: www.mri-sc-usa.com

Summary: We specialize in sales, sales management, marketing and executive placement.

We concentrate in the medical, pharmaceutical, pharmacy, data processing, consumer goods & spirits, packaging-designers and folding carton industries.

Key Contact - Specialty:
Mr. Jeffrey A. Taylor, Vice President & General Manager - *Building products, Construction, Sales, Six Sigma, Surgical*
Mr. Greg Peterson, President - *Business to business, Computers (Hardware), Consumer (Products), Food & beverage, Liquor*
Mr. Eric Olson, Senior Recruiter - *Pharmacists*
Ms. Sabina Zetrenne, Senior Recruiter - *Design, Manufacturing, Packaging*

Salary Minimum: $30,000

Functions: Generalist (All), Management, Middle Mgmt., Packaging, Nurses, Health Admin., Mktg. Mgmt., Sales Mgmt., Sales Reps., Architects

Industries: Generalist (All), Construction, Manufacturing, Food, Bev., Tobacco, Paper, Soap, Perf., Cosmtcs., Drugs Mfg., Medical Devices, Misc. Mfg., Consumer Goods, Wholesale, Finance, Invest. Banking, Services, Pharm Svcs., Mgmt. Consulting, Supply Chain Mgmt, Packaging, Real Estate, Biotech/Life Sciences, Healthcare, Hospitals, Long-term/Home Care, Dental, Physical Therapy, Occupational Therapy, Women's, Non-Classifiable

SC of Lee County

(an affiliate of MRI)
16521 San Carlos Blvd Ste 103C
Fort Myers, FL 33908-5245
(239) 278-4997
Fax: (239) 278-1380
Email: ted@sclee.net

Summary: We focus our recruiting efforts in two specialties; financial services in banking, mortgage lending & title services and telecom data sales/management.

Key Contact - Specialty:
Mr. Ted Lyke, President - *Banking, Banking (Commercial), Internet, Sales, Telecommunications*

Salary Minimum: $30,000

Functions: Sales Mgmt., Sales Reps., Finance

Industries: Banking, Invest. Banking, Misc. Financial, Telecoms, Telephony, Digital, Wireless, Fiber Optic, Network Infrastructure, Commercial

answerQuest Executive Search

(also known as MR of Hollywood)
1055 S Federal Hwy
Hollywood, FL 33020-6025
(954) 961-1101
Fax: (954) 342-8888
Email: info@answerquest.net
Web: www.answerquest.net

Summary: Our firm is a leader in identifying and delivering top business development talent in sales, retail and homeland security. In addition we specialize in the retail area (buyers and planners) and homeland security sales executives. By utilizing state of the art tools, such as video conferencing, skill assessment surveys and behavioral based interviewing, we help you make the right decisions about your company's most important asset, which is it's people.

Key Contact - Specialty:
Mr. Paul Silitsky, Managing Partner
Mr. Martin Schwartz, Practice Leader - *Sales*
Mr. Noel Glacer, Practice Leader
Ms. Karyn Rogers, Practice Leader - *Retail*

Salary Minimum: $50,000

Functions: Management, Sales & Mktg., Security Personnel

Industries: Electronic, Elec. Components, Retail, Brokers, Mgmt. Consulting, HR Services, E-commerce, IT Implementation, Wireless, Defense, Homeland Security, Software, Security SW, Healthcare

MR of Jacksonville

(an affiliate of MRI)
12708 San Jose Blvd Ste 1A
Jacksonville, FL 32223-2600
(904) 260-4444
Fax: (904) 260-4666
Email: packmann@fdn.com
Web: www.mrijax.com

Summary: We are a contingency search and recruiting firm specializing in sales and technical positions primarily in the capital equipment packaging machinery industry including automation and robotics. Our secondary interest is in the railway and passenger transit industries. We are experts in placement of medium to high-level candidates with machinery backgrounds.

Key Contact - Specialty:
Mr. Robert E. Lee, President - *Factories, Field engineering, Robotics, Technical, Technical (Management)*
Mrs. Barbara A. Lee, Administrator - *Administration, Automation, Bar coding, Robotics, Thermoforming*

Salary Minimum: $35,000

Functions: Generalist (All), Management, Mfg., Sales & Mktg., Sales Mgmt., Engineering

Industries: Generalist (All), Misc. Mfg., Robotics, Packaging

The Duval Group

(an affiliate of MRI)
9471 Baymeadows Rd Ste 204
Jacksonville, FL 32256-7935
(904) 737-5770
Fax: (904) 737-7927
Email: resume@duvalgroup.com
Web: www.duvalgroup.com

Summary: We are active in the permanent placement of consulting engineers within transportation and traffic design (not logistics) disciplines. We are also very active in placing professionals in the design, manufacture and marketing and sales of industrial machinery.

Key Contact - Specialty:
Mr. Joe Tucker, CSAM, Manager

Salary Minimum: $45,000

Functions: Generalist (All)

Industries: Energy, Utilities, Manufacturing, Metal Products, Machine, Appliance, Equip Svcs.

The Hansen Group Inc

(also known as MR of Jacksonville-South)
3840-1 Williamsburg Park Blvd
Jacksonville, FL 32257-9245
(904) 448-5200
Fax: (904) 448-1418
Email: admin@hansengroupinc.com
Web: www.hansengroupinc.com

Summary: This independently owned franchise provides high caliber talent in metal and steel manufacturing. Our exclusive database contains 43,000 companies and 18,000 candidate resumes.

Key Contact - Specialty:
Mr. Charles A. Hansen, President

Mr. Terry Bullock, Project Coordinator
Mr. Jon Law, Account Manager, Sales
Mr. Jay Pence, Manager - *Advertising, Public relations*

Functions: Management, Senior Mgmt., Mfg., Quality, Materials, Purchasing, Sales & Mktg., Sales Reps., Structural, Eng. Design

Industries: Metal Products

MR of Jensen Beach

(an affiliate of MRI)
3332 NE Sugarhill Ave
Jensen Beach, FL 34957-3750
(772) 334-8633
Fax: (772) 334-4145
Email: dwl2@adelphia.net

Summary: We recruit and place top talent with firms that provide hardware and software solutions across the supply chain. We work with material handling, factory automation and distribution/logistics firms on the hardware side. Our IT/software clients include firms that provide CRM, ERP, MRP, WMS and transportation/logistics related solutions. We work with manufacturers, distributors and integrators and are part of a large contingency placement organization.

Key Contact - Specialty:
Mr. Douglas W. Lane, President & Owner - *Sales, Telecommunications*

Salary Minimum: $60,000

Functions: Generalist (All), Sales & Mktg.

Industries: Misc. Mfg., Robotics, Engineering Svcs., Logistics Svcs., Supply Chain Mgmt, Telecoms, Software, ERP SW, Industry Specific SW, Mfg. SW

Bay Resources Inc

(also known as MR of Lutz)
PO Box 2686
Lutz, FL 33548-2686
(813) 948-6880
Fax: (813) 948-6881
Email: bayresources@bayresources.biz
Web: www.bayresources.biz

Summary: We are an interim and permanent professional placement agency.

Key Contact - Specialty:
Mr. Bill Rainey, President

Salary Minimum: $50,000

Functions: Generalist (All)

Industries: Food, Bev., Tobacco, Drugs Mfg., Retail, Accounting, Mgmt. Consulting, Hospitality, Full Service Restaurants

Priority Search International Inc

(an affiliate of MRI)
1101 N Lake Destiny Rd Ste 200
Maitland, FL 32751-7120
(407) 660-0089
Fax: (407) 660-2066
Email: tbrown@prioritysearch.com
Web: www.prioritysearch.com

Summary: Our tenured staff of industry professionals offers client companies flexible search solutions in six distinct practice areas.

Key Contact - Specialty:
Mr. Tom Brown, Co-Manager
Ms. Arlene Brown, Co-Manager

Salary Minimum: $35,000

Functions: Generalist (All), Board Members, Senior Mgmt., Middle Mgmt., Sales Reps., CFOs

Industries: Generalist (All), Agri., Forestry, Mining, Construction, Misc. Financial, Services, Legal, Accounting, Mgmt. Consulting, K-12 Ed., Higher Ed., Publishing, Industry Specific SW, Marketing SW

MR of Melbourne

(also known as The Atlantic Group)
1600 Sarno Rd Ste 212
Melbourne, FL 32935-4993
(321) 951-7644
Fax: (321) 951-4235
Email: larryc@mrirecruiter.com
Web: www.mrirecruiter.com

Summary: Specializing in: engineering in mobile equipment, satellite/broadcasting engineers, radio/TV/cable sales professionals, financial in health care, DON long term health care, hospitality, high technology, storage, sales executives

Key Contact - Specialty:
Mr. Lawrence K. Cinco, President

Functions: Generalist (All), Management, Mfg., Plant Mgmt., Healthcare, Sales & Mktg., Sales Mgmt., Finance, CFOs, Engineering

Industries: Generalist (All), Agri., Forestry, Mining, Manufacturing, Metal Products, Machine, Appliance, Motor Vehicles, Misc. Mfg., Transportation, Finance, Services, Accounting, Engineering Svcs., Media, Broadcast, Film, Communications, RF/Microwave, Environmental Svcs., Aerospace, Insurance, Software, Industry Specific SW, Biotech/Life Sciences, Healthcare, Hospitals, Long-term/Home Care

MR of Miami North

(an affiliate of MRI)
815 NW 57th Ave Ste 145
Miami, FL 33126-2073
(305) 264-4212 x302
Fax: (305) 264-4251
Email: mrmiami@mrmiami.com
Web: www.mrmiami.com

Summary: Specializing in confidential search and recruiting assignments for executives, managers and professionals in: manufacturing, engineering, pulp & paper, finance/accounting, administration, sales, marketing, information technology, supply chain/logistics, construction, international trade and other industries and functions.

Key Contact - Specialty:
Mr. Del Diaz, President - *Engineering, General management*

Functions: Generalist (All)

Industries: Generalist (All), Construction, Manufacturing, Paper, Finance, Services, Accounting, Advertising, Aerospace, Software

MR of Santa Rosa

(an affiliate of MRI)
6088 Berryhill Rd
Milton, FL 32570-5062
(850) 626-3303
Fax: (850) 626-3448
Email: info@santarosamri.com
Web: www.santarosamri.com

Summary: Retainer and contingency firm specializing in healthcare, managed care, and pharmaceutical industries.

Key Contact - Specialty:
Mr. John E. Brand, Chief Executive Officer
Ms. Karen M. Brand, Vice President
Mr. Ivan Garcia, Chief Financial Officer - *Physicians*

Salary Minimum: $60,000

Email your resume to a targeted list of recruiters now at www.ExecutiveAgent.com/DER07

Functions: Generalist (All), Management

Industries: Generalist (All), Drugs Mfg., Medical Devices, Pharm Svcs., Healthcare, Hospitals, Long-term/Home Care, Physical Therapy, Occupational Therapy, Women's, Non-Classifiable

MR of Lake County

(an affiliate of MRI)
1117 N Donnelly St
Mount Dora, FL 32757-4259
(352) 383-7101
(800) 856-1941
Fax: (352) 383-7103
Email: roger@mrilakecounty.com
Web: www.mrilakecounty.com

Summary: We are manufacturing specialists-production, engineering, management, quality control, technical and sales. We place particular emphasis in plastics, food processing, transportation equipment, medical manufacturing, pharmaceuticals, chemicals and electronic components.

Key Contact - Specialty:
Mr. Roger M. Holloway, Owner & Manager - *Plastics*
Ms. Linda Holloway, Co-Manager

Salary Minimum: $25,000

Functions: Generalist (All), Middle Mgmt., Product Dev., Production, Plant Mgmt., Quality, Engineering, Technicians

Industries: Generalist (All), Food, Bev., Tobacco, Chemicals, Soap, Perf., Cosmtcs., Drugs Mfg., Medical Devices, Plastics, Rubber, Metal Products, Motor Vehicles, Misc. Mfg., Electronic, Elec. Components, Semiconductors, Mfg. SW

SC of The Emerald Coast

(an affiliate of MRI)
4400 E Highway 20 Ste 407
Niceville, FL 32578-9735
(850) 897-2800
Fax: (850) 897-3055
Email: sales@sc-emeraldcoast.com
Web: www.sc-emeraldcoast.com

Summary: We specialize in consumer packaged goods (CPG) brand marketing, category management, customer/trade marketing, and high level sales opportunities with Fortune 1000 companies in the domestic US. With extensive experience in CPG on our account executive desks, we provide our clients some of the best talent available at the time of their need in the industry.

Key Contact - Specialty:
Mr. Tim Stapleton, President - *Groceries, Management, Medical (Devices), Sales, Senior management*
Ms. Susan McLeay, Director, CPG - *Consumer (Packaged Goods,Products), Marketing, Middle management, Sales*
Mrs. Janie Stapleton, Manager, Administration
Mrs. Kandy Cherry, Administration, Bookeeper - *Accounting (Bookkeeping)*

Salary Minimum: $48,000

Functions: Management, Senior Mgmt., Middle Mgmt., Sales & Mktg.

Industries: Food, Bev., Tobacco, Paper, Soap, Perf., Cosmtcs., Medical Devices, Consumer Goods, Inst./Industrial Food Svc., ERP SW

The DeSantis Group

(an affiliate of MRI)
760 US Highway 1 Ste 304
North Palm Beach, FL 33408-4424
(561) 694-0011
Web: www.mrinetwork.com

Summary: Our office specializes in the aerospace, automotive, medical device, transportation, civil engineering, building materials, and environmental services.

Key Contact - Specialty:
Mr. Victor Desantis, President - *Aerospace, Automotive, Steel, Transportation*
Mr. Nick DeSantis, Account Executive - *Telecommunications*
Ms. Joey DeSantis, Account Executive - *Aviation*
Ms. Ramona DeSantis, Office Manager
Mrs. Lindy DeSantis, Vice President
Mr. Doug Durham, Account Executive - *Aerospace, Banking (Retail), Transportation*
Miss Stefanie Karp, Account Executive

Salary Minimum: $50,000

Functions: Generalist (All)

Industries: Manufacturing, Transportation, E-commerce, IT Implementation, Hospitality, Telecoms, Environmental Svcs., Aerospace, Packaging, Mfg. SW

MR/SC of Tampa North

(an affiliate of MRI)
8517 Gunn Hwy
Odessa, FL 33556-3207
(813) 264-7165
(800) 878-7165
Fax: (813) 968-6450
Email: gary@mrtampanorth.com
Web: www.mrtampanorth.com

Summary: We specialize in executive search and placement. We work in all industries and place individuals from administrative to CEO, president, etc. The industries that we work in include: telecom, medical, biotechnology, residential/commercial construction, finance, building supplies, hospitality and food & beverage.

Key Contact - Specialty:
Mr. Gary King, President - *CEOs, CFOs, Finance, Financial, Telecommunications*
Mr. Stephen Fox, Vice President, Sales Manager - *CEOs, CFOs, Consumer (Packaged Goods,Products), Executives*
Mrs. Jackie Rademaker, Vice President - *Administration, C-level, Call centers, Information Technology, Medical (Devices)*

Salary Minimum: $40,000

Functions: Generalist (All), Mfg.

Industries: Construction, Food, Bev., Tobacco, Drugs Mfg., Medical Devices, Consumer Elect., Consumer Goods, Banking, Misc. Financial, Pharm Svcs., Hospitality, Telecoms, Wireless, Biotech/Life Sciences, Healthcare, Hospitals

MR of Pensacola

(an affiliate of MRI)
603A E Government St
Pensacola, FL 32502-6135
(850) 434-6500
Fax: (850) 434-9911
Email: jbraxton@mriplastics.com
Web: www.mriplastics.com

Summary: We provide upper-level sales, technical and manufacturing management recruitment in the plastic industry. Our emphasis is in the injection molding segment of the industry.

Key Contact - Specialty:
Mr. Ken Kirchgessner, Founder - *Plastics*
Mr. Jody Braxton, Managing Partner - *Plastics*
Cale Bowling, Accounting Executive

Salary Minimum: $50,000

Functions: Management, Board Members, Middle Mgmt., Product Dev., Production, Plant Mgmt., Quality, Productivity, Sales Mgmt., Engineering

Industries: Plastics, Rubber

SC of Plantation

(an affiliate of MRI)
150 S Pine Island Rd Ste 560
Plantation, FL 33324-2676
(954) 475-2525
Fax: (954) 475-9383
Email: info@scplantation.com
Web: www.scplantation.com

Summary: Our firm places sales & marketing professionals in the software and hospital industries.

Key Contact - Specialty:
Ms. Jennifer Blank, Recruiter, Internet
Mr. Cliff Bass, Manager
Ms. Christina Martin, Manager

Functions: Sales & Mktg.

Industries: Database SW, Doc. Mgmt., Production SW, Hospitals

TopGrading Solutions

(also known as MR of St. Lucie County)
756 SE Port St Lucie Blvd
Port Saint Lucie, FL 34984-5262
(772) 871-1100
Fax: (206) 984-1563
Email: admin@topgradingsolutions.com
Web: www.topgradingsolutions.com

Summary: Sales & marketing reps, management, executives, tech support, consultants, CEOs working with ERP, SAP, POS, CRM, e-retailing and card payment systems who market their products to the retail industry. We place attorneys with the AM 300 law firms. We place an emphasis on intellectual property and tax issues. CPG sales & marketing professionals

Key Contact - Specialty:
Mr. Larry J. Breault, Managing Partner - *CEOs, Executives*
Mr. Ed Schmitt, Project Manager, Payment Systems
Mr. Dave Camp, Practice Manager, Store Systems & Suppl - *Marketing, Retail, Sales, Supermarkets, Wireless*
Mr. Lawrence Lebofsky, Practice Manager, Technical Support - *Banking, Banking (Merchant,Retail), Credit cards, Risk management*
Mr. Brad Davis, Practice Manager, CPG Sales & Marketing - *Consumer, Marketing, Sales, Seafood*
Mr. Rick Stevens, JD, Practice Manager, Legal - *Intellectual property, Staffing*
Ms. Kristin Howells, JD, Practice Manager, Legal, Tax - *Legal, Legal (Attorneys,Lawyers), Staffing, Tax*
Mr. Andrew Palmese, Project Coordinator - *Banking, Convenience stores, Credit cards, Retail, Supermarkets*
Ms. Meredith C. Breault, Vice President, Administration

Salary Minimum: $50,000

Functions: Board Members, Senior Mgmt., Middle Mgmt., Product Dev., Sales & Mktg., Mktg. Research, Mktg. Mgmt., Sales Mgmt., IT, Legal

Industries: Retail, Finance, Services, Supply Chain Mgmt, Hospitality, Restaurants, Wireless, Software, Industry Specific SW, Marketing SW

MR of Clearwater

(an affiliate of MRI)
531 Main St Ste F
Safety Harbor, FL 34695-3558
(727) 791-3277
Fax: (727) 446-7732

Summary: We specialize in these specific areas: packaging (both corrugated manufacturing and plastic), health care (any position within the four walls of a hospital), and IT.

Key Contact - Specialty:
Mr. Tim Tuttle, Owner
Ms. Cheryle Tuttle, Co-Owner - *Human resources*

Salary Minimum: $40,000

Functions: Management, Nurses

Industries: Packaging, Healthcare, Hospitals

SC of Sarasota

(an affiliate of MRI)
1343 Main St Ste 600
Sarasota, FL 34236-5630
(941) 365-5151
Fax: (941) 365-1869
Email: office@scsarasota.com
Web: www.scsarasota.com

Summary: Our firm recruits mid to senior level manufacturing, engineering and sales & marketing executives in commercial, industrial and consumer products.

Key Contact - Specialty:
Ms. Rose Castellano, Managing Partner
Mr. Donald A. Mattran, General Manager

Functions: Senior Mgmt., Product Dev., Production, Materials, Packaging, Sales & Mktg., Mktg. Mgmt., Sales Mgmt.

Industries: Food, Bev., Tobacco, Textiles, Apparel, Lumber, Furniture, Soap, Perf., Cosmtcs., Machine, Appliance, Motor Vehicles, Consumer Elect., Test, Measure Equip., Publishing, Packaging

Beneva Group

(an affiliate of MRI)
7202 Beneva Rd
Sarasota, FL 34238-2806
(941) 953-3500
Fax: (941) 953-3544
Email: info@benevagroup.com
Web: www.benevagroup.com

Summary: Industry experts in aerospace, broadband communications, engineering, plastics and packaging staff our firm. Our mission is to be the preferred source of executive and professional staffing solutions, while providing career opportunities for superior candidates.

Key Contact - Specialty:
Mr. Charles Fridley, President - *Adhesives, Manufacturing (Management), Packaging, Plastics, Six Sigma*
Ms. Terri Fridley, Vice President
Mr. Dennis Akers, Account Executive - *Communications, High technology, Telecommunications, Wireless*
Dr. Nina Morozova, Recruiter & Project Coordinator - *Aerospace, Engineering, Optics, Plastics, Six Sigma*
Mr. Jeffrey P. Adams, Recruiter & Project Coordinator - *Engineering, Operations, Packaging, Plastics, Sales*
Ms. Kristen M. Riley, Operations Administrator - *Adhesives, Packaging, Plastics*

Salary Minimum: $70,000

Functions: Generalist (All), Management, Senior Mgmt., Middle Mgmt., Mfg., Quality, Sales & Mktg., Sales Mgmt., Engineering, Minorities/Diversity

Industries: Manufacturing, Paper, Printing, Chemicals, Medical Devices, Plastics, Rubber, Electronic, Elec. Components, Supply Chain Mgmt, Telecoms, Wireless, Network Infrastructure, Aerospace, Packaging

JL Reynolds & Associates Inc

(an affiliate of MRI)
10001 NW 50th St Ste 202
Sunrise, FL 33351-8093
(954) 747-4340
Fax: (954) 747-4342
Email: info@jlreynolds.com
Web: www.jlreynolds.com

Summary: We are executive recruiters placing pharmacists and pharmacy directors into hospital and long term care facilities.

Key Contact - Specialty:
Mr. Jay Reynolds, President & Chief Executive Officer

Functions: Healthcare, Allied Health

Industries: Hospitals, Long-term/Home Care, Physical Therapy

The Bayside Group

(an affiliate of MRI)
400 N Ashley Dr Ste 1725
Tampa, FL 33602-4337
(813) 229-0545
Fax: (813) 229-0785
Email: resume@mrretail.com
Web: www.mrretail.com

Summary: We specialize in all areas of the retail, catalog, eCommerce and manufacturing industries. Our emphasis is within corporate and mid to upper level management positions. Our business is people.

Key Contact - Specialty:
Mr. Larry Scofield, President & Owner - *Retail*
Mrs. Nancy Scofield, Vice President

Salary Minimum: $75,000

Functions: Generalist (All), Middle Mgmt., Distribution, Mktg. Research, Training, Budgeting, Systems Dev., Architects

Industries: Generalist (All), Food, Bev., Tobacco, Textiles, Apparel, Wholesale, Retail, E-commerce

SC of St Petersburg

(an affiliate of MRI)
275 104th Ave Ste A
Treasure Island, FL 33706-4826
(727) 367-8787
Fax: (727) 367-8532
Email: scstpete1g@netscape.net

Summary: We deal with laboratories and banks.

Key Contact - Specialty:
Ms. Christine Copas, Account Executive
Ms. Roxianna Garret, Account Executive - *Business development, Investment*

Salary Minimum: $50,000

Functions: Healthcare, Sales & Mktg.

Industries: Medical Devices, Banking, Invest. Banking, Brokers, Misc. Financial

Peterson Consulting Group Inc

(an affiliate of MRI)
80 Royal Palm Pt Ste 300
Vero Beach, FL 32960-4228
(772) 794-0371
(800) 269-7319
Fax: (772) 778-2688
Email: diana@onlinepcg.com
Web: www.onlinepcg.com

Summary: We are the leader in permanent placement in the building products industry, for example: roofing, contracting, concrete, manufacturing and engineering, more specifically mechanical, structural, civil and electrical, We meet our commitment to clients. The key to our success is service, integrity and honesty.

Key Contact - Specialty:
Mr. David A. Peterson, President & Chief Executive Officer - *Building products*
Ms. Diana K. Peterson, Chief Financial Officer & Vice President - *Building products*

Salary Minimum: $30,000

Functions: Generalist (All)

Industries: Generalist (All)

Executive Staffing Inc

18001 Old Cutler Rd Ste 401
Village of Palmetto Bay, FL 33157-6434
(305) 253-0098
Fax: (305) 253-0940
Email: dm3@cxccstaff.com
Web: www.execstaff.com

Summary: Our company is an international executive search firm that specializes in the placement of management, marketing and business development candidates within the IT, bio-technology, telecommunication, medical, consumer, securities and financial industries.

Key Contact - Specialty:
Mr. Dennis McCarthy, President

Functions: Management, Senior Mgmt., Middle Mgmt., Mktg. Research, Mktg. Mgmt.

Industries: Retail, Finance, Communications, Telecoms, Software, Healthcare

MR of The Northern Palm Beaches

(an affiliate of MRI)
8895 N Military Trl Ste 301B
West Palm Beach, FL 33410-6239
(561) 622-8110
Fax: (561) 622-8440
Email: jim@mrimarketing.com
Web: www.mrimarketing.com

Summary: Our mission - executive searches in marketing communications (advertising, promotion, public relations, printing and publishing). We provide market research and strategic planning for corporate and agency clients.

Key Contact - Specialty:
Mr. James R. Kissel, Managing Director - *E-business, Market research, Marketing, Public relations, Strategic planning*
Mrs. Linda Kissel, Vice President, Office Manager
Mr. Brian J. Kissel, Search Consultant
Mr. James Wolan, Search Consultant - *Advertising, Marketing*
Mr. Greg Ganoff, Search Consultant - *Advertising, E-business, Marketing, Sales*

Salary Minimum: $50,000

Functions: Advertising, Mktg. Mgmt.

Industries: Consumer Goods, Retail, E-commerce, Hospitality, Travel, Advertising

Park Avenue Group Inc

(an affiliate of MRI)
230 S New York Ave Ste 200
Winter Park, FL 32789-4244
(407) 629-2424
Fax: (407) 629-6424
Email: admin@parkavegrp.com
Web: www.parkavegrp.com

Summary: Our firm specializes in the financial services, beverage, biomedical/pharmaceutical and construction industries, including; banking: commercial lending, securities, private banking and trust; CRM sales: project management, and sales engineers; R&D research: government regulations, sales and service; and construction positions at all levels.

Key Contact - Specialty:
Ms. Stacy L. Ethun, President & Chief Executive Officer - *Financial services*
Mr. Marc Stevens, Director, Sales - *Biomedical, Biopharmaceutical, Biotechnology, Pharmaceutical*
Mr. Jesse Olinger, Account Executive - *Banking (Commercial,Corporate,Investment,Mortgage,R etail)*
Ms. Jill Goldsmith, Recruiter - *Banking (Corporate,Investment,Merchant,Mortgage,Reta il)*
Mr. Carlos Burbano, Recruiter - *Banking (Corporate,Investment,Merchant,Mortgage,Reta il)*
Mr. Glenn Hatfield, Account Executive - *Medical (Devices)*
Mr. Rod Hedrick, Account Executive - *Banking*
Mr. Drew Gaynair, Recruiter - *Banking*

Salary Minimum: $50,000

Functions: Generalist (All), Management, Senior Mgmt., Middle Mgmt., Sales & Mktg., Sales Mgmt., Staffing, Cash Mgmt., Mgmt. Consultants

Industries: Construction, Finance, Banking, Invest. Banking, Brokers, Venture Cap., Mutual/Hedge Funds, Misc. Financial, Pharm Svcs., Telecoms, Call Centers, Telephony, Biotech/Life Sciences

MR of Atlanta Windward

(an affiliate of MRI)
12705 Century Dr Unit D
Alpharetta, GA 30004-8378
(678) 566-6640
Email: resumes@mriatlanta.com
Web: www.mriatlanta.com

Summary: Areas of particular expertise are supply chain management and sales & marketing of supply chain/ERP software.

Key Contact - Specialty:
Mr. Bart Heres, CSAM, General Manager & Practice Leader - *C-level, CEOs, Consulting, Consumer (Products), COOs*
Mr. Chris Pass, Practice Leader, Tech Sales & Mktg - *Business development, Computers (Software), CRM, E-business, ERP*

Salary Minimum: $50,000

Functions: Management, Senior Mgmt., Materials, Purchasing, Materials Plng., Distribution, Sales & Mktg., Mktg. Mgmt., Sales Mgmt., Mgmt. Consultants

Industries: Manufacturing, Food, Bev., Tobacco, Computer Equip., Consumer Elect., Test, Measure Equip., Misc. Mfg., Electronic, Elec. Components, Semiconductors, Consumer Goods, Transportation, Wholesale, Mgmt. Consulting, IT Implementation, Logistics Svcs.,

Supply Chain Mgmt, Call Centers, Software, Marketing SW

SelectQuest

(an affiliate of MRI)
4305 State Bridge Rd Ste 103
Alpharetta, GA 30022-4470
(770) 619-0060
Fax: (770) 619-0061
Email: opportunities@selectquest.com
Web: www.selectquest.com

Summary: Our clients include companies in the following segments: software sales & sales management, commercial banking and technical positions. As an industry-specialized search firm, we understand the intricacies of our clients' business and the challenges and issues surrounding the technology & banking industries.

Key Contact - Specialty:
Mr. Nick Barillas, President
Ms. Mary Morris, Principal

Salary Minimum: $70,000

Functions: Generalist (All), Senior Mgmt.

Industries: Banking, IT Implementation, Wireless, Network Infrastructure, Accounting SW, Database SW, Development SW, Doc. Mgmt., Production SW, ERP SW, HR SW, Industry Specific SW, Mfg. SW, Security SW, System SW

MR of Atlanta Perimeter Center

(an affiliate of MRI)
1536 Dunwoody Village Pkwy Ste 225
Atlanta, GA 30338-4166
(770) 392-4800
Fax: (770) 392-9600
Email: admin@mriapc.com

Summary: Executive search firm specializing in consumer based marketing, marketing research, business development, agricultural processing and chemical engineering.

Key Contact - Specialty:
Mr. Thomas Fischgrund, President
Mr. David Ball, Search Consultant
Mr. Al Silva, Search Consultant
Ms. Jody Rendell, Search Consultant

Functions: Sales & Mktg., Mktg. Research, Mktg. Mgmt., Engineering

Industries: Generalist (All), Agri., Forestry, Mining, Food, Bev., Tobacco

The Dunwoody Group

(an affiliate of MRI)
20 Perimeter Park Dr Ste 101
Atlanta, GA 30341-1326
(770) 455-1958
Fax: (770) 455-6529
Email: resumes@dunwoodygroup.com
Web: www.dunwoodygroup.com

Summary: We are a large search and recruiting company with a particular strength in healthcare and nursing, finance, retail, biotechnology, pharmaceutical, food services, administration, food and general manufacturing.

Key Contact - Specialty:
Mr. Arthur Katz, President - *Healthcare, Manufacturing, Robotics*

Salary Minimum: $70,000

Functions: Board Members, Senior Mgmt., Middle Mgmt.

Industries: Generalist (All), Manufacturing, Drugs Mfg., Robotics, Retail, Finance, Pharm Svcs., Accounting, Quick Service Restaurants,

Full Service Restaurants, Biotech/Life Sciences, Healthcare, Hospitals

The Blass Group Inc

(an affiliate of MRI)
1303 Hightower Trl Ste 150
Atlanta, GA 30350-2986
(770) 668-0000
Fax: (770) 668-0999
Email: info@theblassgroup.com
Web: www.theblassgroup.com

Summary: Our firm is an executive search and management recruiting firm that has assisted companies of all sizes in the recruitment and selection of top talent from around the nation. We serve any marketing, sales, technology or operations staff in the equipment leasing industry. Additionally, we place sales professionals in the software industry.

Key Contact - Specialty:
Mr. Benjamin Sillins, President & Director, Spc Finance Pract - *Financial services*
Mr. Jim Johnson, Director, Software Practice
Ms. Michelle Jacobowitz, Director, Accounting

Functions: Board Members, Senior Mgmt., Middle Mgmt., Sales & Mktg., Finance, Attorneys

Industries: Generalist (All), Finance, Banking, Legal, Equip Svcs., Biotech/Life Sciences, Healthcare

MR of Cartersville

(an affiliate of MRI)
20 Felton Pl Ste B
Cartersville, GA 30120-2152
(770) 607-6630
(800) 607-9380
Fax: (770) 607-6638
Email: mrcareers@mrcartersville.com
Web: www.mrcartersville.com

Summary: We specialize in placing proven winners in all areas of the interior furnishings industry, in both commercial and residential environments. We have a long history with major companies. Our experience helps us understand your needs in all functions of your business. From sales & marketing to manufacturing and engineering, we get results.

Key Contact - Specialty:
Mr. Rick Elliot, Manager
Mr. Dustin Ford, Account Executive - *Business development, Sales*
Ms. Teresa Simpson, Account Executive
Ms. Debbie Sleight, Project Coordinator
Ms. Dawn Perkins, Office Manager
Ms. Kim Tibbetts, Recruiter

Functions: Generalist (All), Sales & Mktg.

Industries: Textiles, Apparel, Lumber, Furniture

MR of Dalton

(an affiliate of MRI)
PO Box 289
Cohutta, GA 30710-0289
(706) 694-8805
(706) 694-8804
Fax: (706) 694-8815
Email: mrga@charter.net

Summary: Specializing in management and technical areas of the apparel and plastics industries.

Key Contact - Specialty:
Ms. Verna F. Webb, Co-Manager
Mr. Donald W. Webb, Co-Manager

Salary Minimum: $25,000

Functions: Generalist (All), Management, Senior Mgmt., Middle Mgmt.

Industries: Generalist (All), Textiles, Apparel, Plastics, Rubber, Metal Products, Misc. Mfg.

MR of Atlanta-Lanier

(an affiliate of MRI)
6498 Namon Wallace Dr
Cumming, GA 30040-8576
(770) 592-8389
Fax: (770) 886-9022
Email: sbuck@mrifinance.com
Web: www.mrifinance.com

Summary: We are an executive search firm specializing in the commercial finance industry. We recruit primarily in the asset based lending, factoring, leveraged finance, bank commercial, corporate and business banking areas. We do retained, engaged and contingent searches and have completed searches for many of the leading financial services and banking organizations.

Key Contact - Specialty:
Mr. Steve Buck, President
Mr. Joseph Souder, Managing Director

Salary Minimum: $45,000

Functions: Generalist (All), Middle Mgmt.

Industries: Banking, Misc. Financial

The SearchLogix Group

2950 Cherokee St NW Ste 900
Kennesaw, GA 30144-6505
(770) 517-2660
Email: manager@searchlogixgroup.com
Web: www.searchlogixgroup.com

Summary: We are a full-service executive search and consulting firm. We specialize in logistics, supply chain, multi-channel marketing, retail, eCcommerce, interactive marketing, software, telecom, manufacturing, e-learning, medical device, distribution, transportation, retail, sales and marketing.

Key Contact - Specialty:
Mr. Brett M. Stevens, President - *Computers (Software), Consulting*
Ms. Gina O'Leary, General Manager - *Logistics*

Salary Minimum: $55,000

Functions: Generalist (All), Management, Mfg., Plant Mgmt., Materials, Purchasing, Materials Plng., Distribution, Sales & Mktg., Mgmt. Consultants

Industries: Generalist (All), Retail, Logistics Svcs., Software, ERP SW, Marketing SW

MR of Atlanta West

(an affiliate of MRI)
4260 Bankhead Hwy Ste A
Lithia Springs, GA 30122-1752
(770) 948-5560
Fax: (770) 948-5762
Email: steve@mraw.net

Summary: We specialize in placing sales, marketing and senior managers who have experience with consumer goods manufacturers or manufacturers of flexible plastic packaging film. We have the largest network of offices and recruiters to provide more job opportunities and quality candidates.

Key Contact - Specialty:
Mr. Steve Kendall, Manager
Ms. Theresa Swofford, Manager

Salary Minimum: $100,000

Functions: Senior Mgmt., Middle Mgmt., Plant Mgmt., Packaging, Mktg. Mgmt., Sales Mgmt.

Industries: Soap, Perf., Cosmtcs., Drugs Mfg., Plastics, Rubber, Consumer Goods, Packaging

MR of Roswell West

(an affiliate of MRI)
920 Holcomb Bridge Rd Ste 450
Roswell, GA 30076-4382
(770) 649-8778
Email: rnugent@mrirw.com
Web: www.medevicejobs.com

Summary: Our firm specializes in placing candidates in the medical device industry only. Our focus is in marketing, sales, regulatory affairs, quality, engineering, manufacturing and operations.

Key Contact - Specialty:
Mr. Randolph L. Nugent, Principal
Mr. Dan Shilt, Account Manager
Mr. Toby Blank, Account Manager
Ms. Rosa Phillips, Account Manager

Salary Minimum: $60,000

Functions: Healthcare

Industries: Medical Devices

CJ Walsh Group

(an affiliate of MRI)
11113 Houze Rd Ste 200
Roswell, GA 30076-1495
(770) 642-1230
Fax: (770) 642-6247
Email: info@cjwalshgroup.com
Web: www.cjwalshgroup.com

Summary: The principals of our firm have experience in the property and casualty insurance industry in various; underwriting, underwriting management, risk management, marketing and senior management positions. We specialize in retained, engaged and contingency searches in all technical and management positions within the property and casualty insurance field, including agents and brokers.

Key Contact - Specialty:
Mr. Jim Walsh, Managing Director - *Marketing, Middle management, Risk management, Senior management*
Mr. Lance B. Polikov, Director, Sales
Ms. Christine Walsh, AIC, Senior Executive Consultant

Salary Minimum: $70,000

Functions: Generalist (All), Management, Senior Mgmt.

Industries: Insurance, Casualty, Claims, Commercial, Re-Insurance

MR of Golden Isles

(an affiliate of MRI)
2465 Demere Rd Ste 208
Saint Simons Island, GA 31522-1630
(912) 634-0087
Fax: (912) 634-2391
Email: satlalla@firstrecruiters.com
Web: www.firstrecruiters.com

Summary: We are a search/placement organization that seeks to build strategic partnerships with clients. We work best in this environment. We terminate relationships with clients and candidates when partnerships are not possible. We strive for the best in all.

Key Contact - Specialty:
Mr. Sat Lalla, Director
Mr. John Harper, Executive Search Consultant - *Logistics, Materials, Procurement, Supply Chain, Transportation*

Functions: Generalist (All)

Industries: Food, Bev., Tobacco, Paper, Chemicals

MR of Savannah

(an affiliate of MRI)
306 E 41st St
Savannah, GA 31401-9129
(912) 232-0132
Fax: (912) 232-0136
Email: manager@expertsearches.com
Web: www.expertsearches.com

Summary: Our clients give us high praise for our consultative approach and our thorough pre-screening of candidates. Our highest priorities are saving our clients' time and finding the right match for our candidates.

Key Contact - Specialty:
Mr. Ron McElhaney, Managing Partner - *Plastics*
Mr. Ron McElhaney, Jr., Partner - *Chemical, Consumer (Packaged Goods), Food & beverage, Pharmaceutical, Sales*

Salary Minimum: $60,000

Functions: Generalist (All)

Industries: Food, Bev., Tobacco, Chemicals, Drugs Mfg., Plastics, Rubber, Paints, Petro. Products, Misc. Mfg.

MR of Atlanta-Peachtree North

(an affiliate of MRI)
3235 S Cherokee Ln Ste 1210
Woodstock, GA 30188-4461
(404) 221-1021
Fax: (678) 238-0379
Email: tom@mriatl.com
Web: www.mriatl.com

Summary: We are a franchise provider of staffing solutions specializing in the medical, pharmaceutical and IT professions.

Key Contact - Specialty:
Mr. Thomas A. Jayroe, Manager - *Pharmaceutical, Sales*
Mr. Rick Blackwell, Account Executive

Functions: Generalist (All), Mktg. Research, Mktg. Mgmt., Sales Mgmt., MIS Mgmt., Systems Analysis, Systems Implem., Technicians

Industries: Generalist (All), Software, Marketing SW, Healthcare

MR/SC of Honolulu

(an affiliate of MRI)
733 Bishop St Ste 1475
Honolulu, HI 96813-4083
(808) 533-3282
Fax: (808) 599-4760
Email: mail@mrihonolulu.com
Web: www.mrihonolulu.com

Summary: We place sales, sales support marketing and sales management. We also place people in hightechnology positions.

Key Contact - Specialty:
Mr. Don Bishop, Executive, Sales Account
Mr. Dale Dudas, Office Manager
Mr. Kawika Morse, Project Coordinator - *Management*

Salary Minimum: $30,000

Functions: Generalist (All)

Industries: Pharm Svcs., Accounting, Logistics Svcs., Hotels, Resorts, Clubs, Telecoms, Telephony, Digital, Haz. Waste, Insurance, Marketing SW

Email your resume to a targeted list of recruiters now at www.ExecutiveAgent.com/DER07

MR/SC of Arlington Heights

(an affiliate of MRI)
5 E College Dr Ste 202
Arlington Heights, IL 60004-1963
(847) 590-8880
Fax: (847) 590-0847
Email: mri@jobwish.com
Web: www.jobwish.com

Summary: Placing sales, product, marketing and sales management talent. We provide project management and HR capital solutions. We are also serving Engineering, technical services and other manufacturing needs for both a local market as well as global needs for our client companies.

Key Contact - Specialty:
Mr. Steve Briody, General Manager
Mr. Mark Gillespie, CSAM, Team Leader, Consumer - *Food & beverage*
Mr. Chris Hillman, CSAM, Team Leader, Industrial

Salary Minimum: $35,000

Functions: Generalist (All), Management, Sales & Mktg.

Industries: Manufacturing, Food, Bev., Tobacco, Medical Devices, Plastics, Rubber, Machine, Appliance, Motor Vehicles, Consumer Elect., Test, Measure Equip., Wholesale, Packaging, Insurance, Casualty, Claims, Life, Commercial, Re-Insurance, Marketing SW, Biotech/Life Sciences, Healthcare, Long-term/Home Care

MR of Barrington

(an affiliate of MRI)
417 N Hough St
Barrington, IL 60010-3034
(847) 382-5544
Fax: (847) 382-5591
Email: hvacjobs@mribarrington.com
Web: www.mribarrington.com

Summary: Our firm is focused on professionals in the HVAC, refrigeration, air conditioning, energy services, building automation systems, facilities management, general contracting, mechanical & electrical contracting and consulting engineering industries.

Key Contact - Specialty:
Mr. Gary T. Polvere, President
Mr. Jon Difatta, Manager, Sales Support - *Construction, Engineering, General contractors, HVAC, Mechanical*
Mr. Paul Odom, Account Executive - *BSME, Construction, Engineering, Transportation*
Mr. John Olszewski, Account Executive - *Construction, General contractors*
Mr. Bob Williams, Executive Search Consultant

Salary Minimum: $40,000

Functions: Management, Senior Mgmt., Sales Mgmt., Engineering

Industries: Energy, Utilities, Construction

The Myers Group Inc

(an affiliate of MRI)
7 Heritage Dr
Bourbonnais, IL 60914-2514
(815) 929-1900
Fax: (815) 929-0900
Email: tom.m@myersgroupinc.com
Web: www.myersgroupinc.com

Summary: We are a professional executive search firm focused on recruiting and placing professionals in logistics, engineering, banking, food & beverage, food scientists, household goods companies and relocation companies. Our dedicated professional recruiters are very thorough and maintain confidentiality at all times. We are

an award-winning firm and we work with today's leading companies that share our philosophy that 'the company with the best talent wins.'

Key Contact - Specialty:
Mr. Tom Myers, President & Chief Executive Officer
Mrs. Donna Meredith, Account Executive - *Aerospace, Engineering, Machining*
Mrs. Sandra Frenzke, CSAM, Business Unit Manager - *Culinary, Food, Food & beverage*
Ms. Lisa Gentry, Recruiter - *Culinary, Food & beverage*
Mrs. Gail Myers, Vice President - *General management*
Ms. Sandra Sims, Account Executive - *Banking (Commercial,Corporate,Investment,Merchant,R etail)*
Ms. Ashlee Hickory, Office Manager - *General management*
Mrs. Sue Jacobson, Account Executive - *Transportation*
Mrs. Kathy Anderson, Project Co-ordinator - *Administration, C-level, Financial services, Management*

Salary Minimum: $75,000

Functions: Generalist (All), Management, Senior Mgmt., Middle Mgmt., Product Dev., Plant Mgmt., Distribution, Sales & Mktg., Chefs

Industries: Generalist (All), Manufacturing, Food, Bev., Tobacco, Soap, Perf., Cosmtcs., Drugs Mfg., Metal Products, Consumer Elect., Misc. Mfg., Transportation, Wholesale, Retail, Mgmt. Consulting, E-commerce, Engineering Svcs., Logistics Svcs., Hotels, Resorts, Clubs, Restaurants, Inst./Industrial Food Svc., Aerospace

MR of Chicago-Michigan Ave

(an affiliate of MRI)
625 N Michigan Ave Ste 430
Chicago, IL 60611-3172
(312) 279-0140
Fax: (312) 279-0141
Email: office@jobsagent.com
Web: www.jobsagent.com

Summary: Our firm specializes in staffing solutions for sales, technical, manufacturing and administrative positions in plastics and packaging, and in many other industries as well. We do an excellent job understanding our assignments and candidates. We ask a lot of questions and listen carefully. We also provide comprehensive testing to help align personalities of candidates and requirements of the job.

Key Contact - Specialty:
Mr. Dick Post, President - *Plastics*

Salary Minimum: $50,000

Functions: Middle Mgmt., Product Dev., Production, Plant Mgmt., Quality, Productivity, Purchasing, Packaging, Sales & Mktg.

Industries: Generalist (All), Manufacturing, Food, Bev., Tobacco, Paper, Chemicals, Drugs Mfg., Plastics, Rubber, Services, Supply Chain Mgmt., Packaging

WorldBridge Partners

(an affiliate of MRI)
815 W Van Buren St Ste 309
Chicago, IL 60607-3568
(312) 733-4700
Fax: (312) 733-9769
Email: jack@sc-chicago.com
Web: www.sc-chicago.com

Summary: We specialize in the recruitment of telecom and data communications sales and sales support professionals. It is our philosophy that it

takes world-class talent to run world-class organizations.

Key Contact - Specialty:
Mr. Jack W. Downing, Managing Partner - *Telecommunications*

Salary Minimum: $75,000

Functions: Board Members, Senior Mgmt., Middle Mgmt., Sales Mgmt., Systems Support

Industries: Energy, Utilities, Brokers, Telecoms, Call Centers, Telephony, Wireless, Fiber Optic, Network Infrastructure, Networking, Comm. SW, Biotech/Life Sciences

OSG Global

(an affiliate of MRI)
1400 E Touhy Ave Ste 160
Des Plaines, IL 60018-3338
(847) 954-8000
(800) 940-7532
Fax: (847) 297-8744
Email: jobs@mr-ohare.com
Web: www.mr-ohare.com

Summary: Our firm has provided customized effective worldwide client search and recruitment representation. Our practices are focused in IT, bio-informatics, regulatory affairs, life sciences, accounting, finance, audit, tax, insurance, and sales & marketing.

Key Contact - Specialty:
Mr. Richard A. Kurz, President
Mr. Charles Bretz, Director - *Accounting, Biotechnology, Information Systems, Insurance, Regulatory*
Ms. Shena Barlas-Swartz, Director - *Information Systems, Information Technology*
Ms. Debra Teed, Director - *Accounting, Accounting (General), Finance, Financial services*

Salary Minimum: $100,000

Functions: Healthcare, Finance, CFOs, Budgeting, Taxes, IT, Systems Implem., Network Admin., DB Admin.

Industries: Generalist (All), Manufacturing, Transportation, Finance, Banking, Invest. Banking, Brokers, Venture Cap., Mutual/Hedge Funds, Misc. Financial, Services, Hospitality, Communications, Environmental Svcs., Packaging, Insurance, Software, Database SW, Development SW, Doc. Mgmt., Production SW, ERP SW, HR SW, Networking, Comm. SW, Security SW, System SW, Biotech/Life Sciences, Healthcare, Non-Classifiable

MR of Elgin

(an affiliate of MRI)
472 N McLean Blvd Ste 202
Elgin, IL 60123-3274
(847) 697-2201
Email: ron_reeves@mrelgin.com
Web: www.mrelgin.com

Summary: Our major areas of specialization are: accounting & finance, retail, trade show exhibits, point of purchase, banking and Hospital Executive and OT & PT

Key Contact - Specialty:
Mr. Ronald C. Reeves, Managing Partner
Mr. Bart Daly, Partner
Mr. Jason Stotlar, CPC, Partner
Mr. Mike Reeves, Partner
Ms. Cynthia Wade, Partner

Salary Minimum: $75,000

Functions: Management, Nurses, Finance, Credit, Eng. Design, Architects, Design

Industries: Generalist (All), Construction, Lumber, Furniture, Retail, Finance, Banking,

Misc. Financial, Architectural Svcs., Accounting, Engineering Svcs., Hospitals, Physical Therapy, Occupational Therapy

Barrington Search Group

(also known as SC of Barrington)
5140 Castaway Ln Ste 100
Hoffman Estates, IL 60010-5511
(847) 202-7088
Email: resume@barringtonsearch.com
Web: www.barringtonsearch.com

Summary: Our firm specializes in the construction and building materials industries. Our partners include general contractors, real estate developers, specialty contractors and architectural and engineering firms who specialize in general building and civil projects. We place candidates in management/professional positions including project management, field operations, estimating/pre-construction, business development, accounting/finance and engineering.

Key Contact - Specialty:
Mr. Curtis L. Baer, MBA, President

Salary Minimum: $50,000

Functions: Senior Mgmt., Middle Mgmt., Sales Mgmt., Sales Reps., Finance, Bldg. Contractors

Industries: Construction, Manufacturing, Lumber, Furniture, Wholesale

MR of Lake Forest

(an affiliate of MRI)
272 Market Sq Ste 2714
Lake Forest, IL 60045-1866
(847) 604-9000
Fax: (847) 604-9020
Email: jobs@mrilf.com
Web: www.mrilf.com

Summary: Our office has extensive experience in the medical device and biotechnology industry. Of the offices within our franchise, we are one of the top producing offices in medical device placements. We do placements in regulatory affairs, quality, clinical, R&D and engineering arenas.

Key Contact - Specialty:
Mr. Harry J. Cunneff, President - *Biotechnology, Clinical, Quality, Regulatory*
Ms. Sandra Cunneff, Vice President
Ms. Laurie Cunneff, Account Executive

Salary Minimum: $60,000

Functions: Senior Mgmt., Middle Mgmt., Mfg., Product Dev., Quality, R&D, Engineering

Industries: Drugs Mfg., Medical Devices, Biotech/Life Sciences

MR of Chicago Northwest

(an affiliate of MRI)
1 1st Bank Plz Ste 300
Lake Zurich, IL 60047-3109
(847) 550-1300
Fax: (847) 550-1314
Email: it@mrchicago.com
Web: www.mrchicago.com

Summary: We pride ourselves in evaluating top sales, executive management and consulting talent in the performance improvement, IT, healthcare/biotech and printing industries.

Key Contact - Specialty:
Mr. Gary L. Bozza, President & Executive Director - *Business development, Consulting, Healthcare, Printing, Sales*
Mr. Bryan Cole, Account Executive

Salary Minimum: $50,000

Functions: Sales & Mktg., Sales Reps.

Industries: Printing, Services, Mgmt. Consulting, Logistics Svcs., Call Centers, ERP SW, Biotech/Life Sciences, Healthcare

MR of Mattoon

(an affiliate of MRI)
PO Box 461
Mattoon, IL 61938-0461
(217) 235-9393
Fax: (217) 235-9396
Web: www.mrinet.com

Summary: We are a globally active search firm that is highly specialized to the flavor and fragrance industry.

Key Contact - Specialty:
Mr. David W. Tolle, President

Salary Minimum: $100,000

Functions: R&D

Industries: Food, Bev., Tobacco, Non-Classifiable

MR of Chicago Far West

(an affiliate of MRI)
564 S Washington St Ste 203
Naperville, IL 60540-6674
(630) 305-0200
Fax: (630) 305-0273
Email: mrchicagofw@jobsforsuccess.com
Web: www.jobsforsuccess.com

Summary: Our firm specializes in placing professionals in the manufacturing, materials, sales & marketing, HR management, finance, engineering, non-profit and architectural industries.

Key Contact - Specialty:
Mr. Marc Chaifetz, Co-Manager
Ms. Sherri Chaifetz, Co-Manager
Mr. Benjamin Crockett, Account Executive - *Manufacturing*
Mr. Joseph Oczak, Account Executive - *Manufacturing*

Salary Minimum: $50,000

Functions: Generalist (All), Mfg., Materials, Sales & Mktg., HR Mgmt., Finance, Engineering, Minorities/Diversity, Non-profits, Architects

Industries: Generalist (All), Manufacturing, Food, Bev., Tobacco, Textiles, Apparel, Lumber, Furniture, Paper, Soap, Perf., Cosmtcs., Drugs Mfg., Leather, Stone, Glass, Machine, Appliance, Consumer Elect., Transportation, Retail, Finance, Services, Non-profits, Architectural Svcs., Engineering Svcs., Haz. Waste, Real Estate, Property/Facility Mgmt.

Park Consultants Inc

899 Skokie Blvd Ste 510
Northbrook, IL 60062-4025
(847) 559-7000
Fax: (847) 559-0077
Email: resumes@parkconsultants.com
Web: www.parkconsultants.com

Summary: Search consultants in the medical device and pharmaceutical industries. Working with senior level management in the areas of marketing, corporate accounts, regulatory affairs, clinical research and sales management.

Key Contact - Specialty:
Ms. Sally Salzer, Co-Manager
Ms. Gayle Galloway, Co-Manager

Functions: Senior Mgmt., Middle Mgmt., Healthcare

Industries: Healthcare

The Miller Resource Group

(an affiliate of MRI)
1415 W 22nd St Ste 725
Oak Brook, IL 60523-8422
(630) 990-8233
Fax: (630) 990-2973
Email: garym@millerresource.com
Web: www.millerresource.com

Summary: We have been serving clients with a consistent, conscientious approach that they value and appreciate since the beginning. We help our clients find growth-oriented people, primarily in mid to senior management functions. We also have a sales project staffing capability where we help companies build and/or upgrade entire sales organizations.

Key Contact - Specialty:
Mr. Gary L. Miller, President & Owner
Ms. Martha Kroodsma, Manager, Training & Development

Salary Minimum: $60,000

Functions: Generalist (All)

Industries: Generalist (All)

SC of Chicago South

(an affiliate of MRI)
PO Box 268
Palos Heights, IL 60463-0268
(708) 489-5336
Email: frontdesk@card-recruiter.com
Web: www.card-recruiter.com

Summary: We focus on the card industries - credit, debit, stored value, smart card and loyalty card to ensure that the best talent in their industry is with the best companies in their industry.

Key Contact - Specialty:
Ms. Judie Collins, CSAM, Principal - *Credit cards, Market research, Marketing, Risk management, Sales*

Salary Minimum: $40,000

Functions: Sales & Mktg., Risk Mgmt.

Industries: Banking, Misc. Financial, Mgmt. Consulting, Database SW

MR of Cherry Valley

(an affiliate of MRI)
PO Box 590
Rockford, IL 61105-0590
(815) 399-1942
Fax: (815) 399-2750
Email: mcarter@mrcherryvalley.com
Web: www.mrcherryvalley.com

Summary: We are committed to being the preferred and pre-eminent provider of executive search for executives, VPs, directors and senior management. Our success is a direct reflection of the superior service and optimal support we provide to our customers. We are committed to helping them achieve their professional and financial objectives.

Key Contact - Specialty:
Mr. D. Michael Carter, Owner
Mr. Walter J. Masnyk, Recruiter - *Automotive, Hardware*

Salary Minimum: $65,000

Functions: Generalist (All)

Industries: Plastics, Rubber, Metal Products, Misc. Mfg., Electronic, Elec. Components, Banking, Packaging

MR of St Charles

(an affiliate of MRI)
318 S 2nd St
Saint Charles, IL 60174-2817
(630) 377-6466
Email: jobs@stcsearch.com
Web: www.stcsearch.com

Summary: Our firm specialty is management positions including HR, banking, accounting, engineering, IT, logistics, supply chain, purchasing, quality, manufacturing, educational sales and general sales.

Key Contact - Specialty:
Mr. Daniel C. Lasse, President - *Manufacturing, Training*
Mr. Alex Goloff, Senior Account Executive
Mr. Tom Tawney, Senior Account Executive
Mr. Rodger Macy, Senior Account Executive

Salary Minimum: $45,000

Functions: Generalist (All), Mfg., Quality, Purchasing, Sales & Mktg., HR Mgmt., Finance, IT

Industries: Generalist (All), Agri., Forestry, Mining, Manufacturing, Food, Bev., Tobacco, Metal Products, Machine, Appliance, Motor Vehicles, Misc. Mfg., Transportation, Wholesale, Banking, Brokers, Services, Accounting, Mgmt. Consulting, HR Services, Call Centers, Environmental Svcs., Haz. Waste, Insurance, Software, Healthcare

The McHenry Group

(an affiliate of MRI)
PO Box 425
Union, IL 60180-0425
(815) 923-2500
Fax: (815) 923-2587
Email: mvp@mvp4u.biz
Web: www.mvp4u.biz

Summary: We provide search and recruitment for the software vendor industry. Our principals possess extensive years of experience within this industry in senior management capacities prior to creating this executive search practice.

Key Contact - Specialty:
Mr. Dan Grant, President
Ms. Beth Major, Project Director
Mr. Dan Moriarty, Senior Project Coordinator
Mr. Jeff Wilson, Vice President

Functions: Generalist (All), Senior Mgmt., Mktg. Mgmt., Sales Mgmt., CFOs, MIS Mgmt., Systems Implem.

Industries: Generalist (All), Software, Healthcare

MR/SC of Indianapolis North

(an affiliate of MRI)
11611 N Meridian St Ste 650
Carmel, IN 46032-7149
(317) 582-0202
Fax: (317) 582-0303
Email: info@mrindianapolis.com
Web: www.mrindianapolis.com

Summary: Outstanding success in identifying top talent and meeting corporate America's total staffing needs.

Key Contact - Specialty:
Mr. George V. Ceryak, Co-Owner
Mr. David J. Oberting, Co-Owner
Mr. Chad Peddycord, Partner
Mr. Garth Young, Managing Partner

Salary Minimum: $20,000

Functions: Generalist (All), Senior Mgmt., Mfg., Sales & Mktg., Mktg. Research, Finance, IT, R&D

Industries: Generalist (All), Construction, Manufacturing, Retail, Finance, Media, Communications, Real Estate, Software, Biotech/Life Sciences, Healthcare

MR of Columbus

(an affiliate of MRI)
PO Box 2234
Columbus, IN 47202-2234
(812) 372-5500
Fax: (812) 372-8292
Email: mike@mrcols.com
Web: www.mrcols.com

Summary: We are an executive search firm specializing in banking, financial, MIS and manufacturing.

Key Contact - Specialty:
Mr. J. Michael Percifield, Owner & Manager

Salary Minimum: $50,000

Functions: Generalist (All), Product Dev., Plant Mgmt., Productivity, Health Admin., Systems Implem., Network Admin., Engineering

Industries: Generalist (All), Misc. Mfg., Banking, Invest. Banking, Brokers, Insurance

MR of Evansville

(an affiliate of MRI)
101 Plaza East Blvd Ste 312
Evansville, IN 47715-2871
(812) 477-5886
Fax: (812) 477-5887
Email: tboyle@mrievansville.com

Summary: Our firm places professionals in the lumber, furniture, medical devices, plastics, rubber, metal products, machine, appliance, motor vehicles, consumer electronics, electrical components, robotics and transportation industries.

Key Contact - Specialty:
Mr. Thomas Boyle, Recruiter

Salary Minimum: $50,000

Functions: Generalist (All)

Industries: Lumber, Furniture, Medical Devices, Plastics, Rubber, Metal Products, Machine, Appliance, Motor Vehicles, Consumer Elect., Electronic, Elec. Components, Robotics, Transportation

MR of Newburgh

(an affiliate of MRI)
8844 Ruffian Ln Ste A
Newburgh, IN 47630-3404
(812) 842-1000
Fax: (812) 842-4000
Email: careers@mrnewburgh.com
Web: www.mrnewburgh.com

Summary: We specialize in the recruitment of executives and management for banking, finance, manufacturing, engineering and health care. We operate under contingency or retained search. Our account executives each have extensive experience in their respective industry or the business industry in general.

Key Contact - Specialty:
Mr. M. Lynn Cooper, President - *Finance*
Mr. Dan Oates, Partner & Vice President - *Engineering, Manufacturing*
Mr. Brandon C. Cooper, Manager, Banking Team

Functions: Generalist (All), Management, Mfg., Healthcare, Finance, Engineering

Industries: Generalist (All), Manufacturing, Plastics, Rubber, Motor Vehicles, Misc. Mfg., Electronic, Elec. Components, Finance, Banking, Brokers, Misc. Financial, Services,

Non-profits, Architectural Svcs., Accounting, Mgmt. Consulting, HR Services, Engineering Svcs., Insurance, HR SW, Marketing SW, Healthcare, Hospitals, Long-term/Home Care, Physical Therapy, Occupational Therapy, Women's

MR of Noblesville-Indianapolis Northeast

(an affiliate of MRI)
15229 Herriman Blvd
Noblesville, IN 46060-4230
(317) 773-4323
Fax: (317) 773-9744
Email: mail@mriweb.com
Web: www.mriweb.com

Summary: We are a contingency/retained recruiting firm primarily placing engineers, supervisors, managers, sales engineers, sales management and VPs, in general manufacturing, technical sales and construction. Main industries include: biotechnology, construction, distribution, healthcare (radiology and therapy) HVAC, pharmaceutical, sales and transportation.

Key Contact - Specialty:
Mr. H. Peter Isenberg, Managing Partner
Ms. Elizabeth Searle, Partner

Salary Minimum: $45,000

Functions: Generalist (All), Product Dev., Production, Plant Mgmt., Quality, Materials Plng., Sales Mgmt., Engineering

Industries: Generalist (All), Construction, Manufacturing, Food, Bev., Tobacco, Drugs Mfg., Paints, Petro. Products, Metal Products, Machine, Appliance, Motor Vehicles, Misc. Mfg., Healthcare

The Lake City Group

(an affiliate of MRI)
102 S Buffalo St
Warsaw, IN 46580-2801
(574) 371-2525
Fax: (574) 371-2535
Email: gb3@lakecitygroup.com
Web: www.lakecitygroup.com

Summary: Our firm is a global executive search firm specializing in staffing solutions for the medical device, pharmaceutical, biotechnology and dental industries. Our practice focus includes positions at all levels of research and product development, clinical and regulatory affairs, quality, manufacturing operations, IT, marketing, sales, logistics and distribution.

Key Contact - Specialty:
Mr. George Brennan, III

Functions: Management, Board Members, Product Dev., Packaging, Sales & Mktg., Sales Mgmt., IT, R&D, Engineering, Int'l.

Industries: Manufacturing, Drugs Mfg., Medical Devices, Plastics, Rubber, Metal Products, Computer Equip., Test, Measure Equip., Electronic, Elec. Components, IT Implementation, Packaging, Software, Development SW, Industry Specific SW, Mfg. SW, Marketing SW, Biotech/Life Sciences, Dental

Cyclone Staffing Solutions

(an affiliate of MRI)
PO Box 840
589 Hwy 71 S
Arnolds Park, IA 51331-0840
(712) 332-2011
Fax: (712) 332-2051
Email: jayson@nationaljobs.net

Summary: We are an executive recruiting firm specializing in the placement of professionals in general manufacturing and the food manufacturing market with an emphasis in engineering and accounting. We offer pre-interview counseling, feedback after the interview, and help negotiating offers and acceptances for new positions.

Key Contact - Specialty:
Mr. Jayson Wollmuth, Owner - *Engineering*

Functions: Mfg., Purchasing, Materials Plng., Finance, Engineering

Industries: Generalist (All), Manufacturing

SC of Riverside

(an affiliate of MRI)
300 W Broadway Ste 36
Council Bluffs, IA 51503-9056
(712) 325-6884
Fax: (712) 325-6691
Email: receivable@scriverside.com
Web: www.scriverside.com

Summary: We are a search and recruitment specialists to the collection industry.

Key Contact - Specialty:
Mr. Jim Finocchiaro, President

Functions: Generalist (All)

Industries: Non-Classifiable

MR of Fairfield

(an affiliate of MRI)
100 S 6th St
Fairfield, IA 52556-3334
(641) 469-5811
(800) 499-5811
Email: mrf@lisco.com

Summary: Experienced, professional staff dedicated to middle and upper-management contingency placement in supply chain management, IT, manufacturing, engineering and HR functions.

Key Contact - Specialty:
Mr. Mark Soth, Manager - *Human resources*
Ms. Dawna Burnett, Account Executive - *Engineering, Manufacturing*
Ms. Maureen Boehm, Account Executive
Mr. Jay Gardner, Account Executive - *Food, Sales*

Salary Minimum: $50,000

Functions: Generalist (All), Management, Mfg., Distribution, Sales & Mktg., HR Mgmt., MIS Mgmt., Systems Analysis, Systems Implem., Engineering

Industries: Generalist (All), Manufacturing, Food, Bev., Tobacco, Lumber, Furniture, Computer Equip., Transportation, Logistics Svcs., Telecoms, ERP SW

MR of Siouxland

(an affiliate of MRI)
4617 Morningside Ave
Sioux City, IA 51106-2943
(712) 276-8454
Fax: (712) 276-8453
Email: mriscjr@mcleodusa.net

Summary: We are a complete search, reference checks, and personality profiles. In commercial construction (PM's supers estimators) metal buildings (sales, engineers) HR banking (comm.'s lenders)

Key Contact - Specialty:
Mr. James A. Rupert, President - *Banking, Banking (Commercial), Manufacturing, Manufacturing (Management)*

Ms. Patty Grace, Account Executive - *Construction, Engineering, Manufacturing, Metals, Sales*
Mr. Doug Strohbeen, Account Executive - *Construction, Engineering*
Ms. Janet Roepke, Admin Assistant & Project Coordinator - *Banking (Commercial), Construction, Engineering, General contractors, Human resources*
Mr. Ron R. Rohlena, Account Executive - *Construction*

Salary Minimum: $38,000

Functions: Management, Middle Mgmt., Structural, Bldg. Contractors, Design

Industries: Construction, Food, Bev., Tobacco, Metal Products, Healthcare

Vermillion Group

(an affiliate of MRI)
1801 25th St
West Des Moines, IA 50266-1416
(515) 224-9142
Email: mri@vermilliongroup.com
Web: www.vermilliongroup.com

Summary: We are one of the largest executive search firms in the area, focusing on: broadband/cable, construction, contract/subcontract management, data storage, data storage sales, energy & utilities, engineering, healthcare, information technologies, insurance & financial services, software sales, and telephony sales/telecom.

Key Contact - Specialty:
Mr. Michael Vermillion, President
Mr. Russ Tessman, Division Manager - *Healthcare, Information Systems, Information Technology, Pharmacists, Technology*
Mr. Brian Keith, Division Manager - *Construction, Engineering, Environmental, Industrial, Natural resources*
Mr. Ken Dickerson, Division Manager - *General contractors, Government, Information service, Medical (Sales), Sales*
Mr. Jim Roth, Division Manager - *Business development, Financial services*

Salary Minimum: $50,000

Functions: Generalist (All)

Industries: Pharm Svcs., IT Implementation, Engineering Svcs., Government, Insurance, Life, Software, Healthcare, Non-Classifiable

MR of Williamsburg

(an affiliate of MRI)
PO Box 1136
Williamsburg, IA 52361-1136
(319) 668-2881
Fax: (319) 668-1404
Email: info@wburgcareers.com
Web: www.wburgcareers.com

Summary: We are engineering specialists with an emphasis in manufacturing, senior-level positions, production, operation, management, quality and HR.

Key Contact - Specialty:
Ms. Lori Stecker, Owner & Account Executive - *Engineering, Human resources, Industrial, Manufacturing, Mechanical*

Functions: Mfg., Production, Plant Mgmt., Packaging, Engineering, Non-profits

Industries: Construction, Manufacturing, Plastics, Rubber, Metal Products, Machine, Appliance, Motor Vehicles, Misc. Mfg., Packaging

MR of Fort Scott

(an affiliate of MRI)
PO Box 5020
Fort Scott, KS 66701-5020
(620) 223-3133
(888) 846-6960
Email: mri@prorecruit.com
Web: www.prorecruit.com

Summary: We are a highly specialized firm serving the printing industry. Our firm places 100 to 150 printing professionals annually. Integrity is first, fulfillment second. Positions filled: sales reps, sales managers, plant managers, COOs, etc.

Key Contact - Specialty:
Mr. Tom Byler, Account Executive
Mr. Trent Styles, Account Executive
Ms. Vicky O'Bryan, Project Coordinator
Ms. Nancy Jackson, Project Coordinator

Salary Minimum: $30,000

Functions: Generalist (All), Senior Mgmt., Middle Mgmt., Product Dev., Plant Mgmt., Sales Mgmt., Customer Svc.

Industries: Generalist (All), Paper, Printing, Publishing

The Howard Group Inc

(an affiliate of MRI)
7450 W 130th St Ste 100
Overland Park, KS 66213-2685
(913) 663-2323
Fax: (913) 663 2424
Email: bhoward@thehowardgroup.com
Web: www.thehowardgroup.com

Summary: We are a national award-winning firm with dedicated practices in insurance (employee benefits and managed care), pension and retirement planning, property/casualty insurance, provider and payor technology.

Key Contact - Specialty:
Mr. Brian E. Howard, President

Salary Minimum: $50,000

Functions: Sales & Mktg., Sales Mgmt.

Industries: Finance, Banking, Mutual/Hedge Funds, Misc. Financial, Insurance, Casualty, Claims, Life, Commercial, Re-Insurance, Software, Database SW, Doc. Mgmt., Production SW, Industry Specific SW

Grimes Legal Inc

8264 Louisville Rd
Bowling Green, KY 42101-8041
(270) 782-3820
(800) 875-3820
Fax: (270) 782-3985
Email: info@grimeslegal.com
Web: www.grimeslegal.com

Summary: We recruit and place attorneys only as a legal search and placement agency.

Key Contact - Specialty:
Mr. G.D. Grimes, President & Manager
Ms. Nancy C. Grimes, Vice President & Secretary
Ms. Tonya Johnson, Office Administrator

Functions: Generalist (All), Attorneys

Industries: Generalist (All), Legal

MR of Lexington

(an affiliate of MRI)
1999 Richmond Rd Ste 2B
Lexington, KY 40502-1200
(859) 269-7227
Email: kts@mrlex.com
Web: www.mrlex.com

Summary: We are an executive search firm specializing primarily in all aspects of manufacturing with an emphasis on the automotive industry, paints & coatings and property & casualty insurance. Positions range from engineers with three to five years experience to president/CEO.

Key Contact - Specialty:
Mr. Kent T. Simpson, Manager
Mr. Edward Gridley, Recruiter
Mr. Clark Kidwell, Recruiter
Mr. Daniel Lindblade, Recruiter
Mr. Meredith M. Willis, Jr., Recruiter
Ms. Denise Zimmerman, Recruiter

Salary Minimum: $45,000

Functions: Mfg., Actuaries

Industries: Plastics, Rubber, Paints, Petro. Products, Motor Vehicles, Misc. Mfg., Insurance, Casualty, Claims, Commercial, Re-Insurance

MR of Prospect

(also know as WorldBridge Partners)
12935 W Highway 42
Prospect, KY 40059-9107
(502) 292-0010
Fax: (502) 292-0090
Email: dwallace@mrprospect.com
Web: www.mrprospect.com

Summary: Our firm focuses on pharmaceutical and nutritional sales & marketing searches. We particularly focus on the nephrology and dialysis markets.

Key Contact - Specialty:
Mr. David Wallace, President
Mrs. Tawnya Clark-Evans, Account Executive
Ms. Robin Shartzer, Executive Recruiter
Mr. Tim Valentino, Director, Contract Staffing
Ms. Tonya Lynam, Executive Recruiter

Salary Minimum: $50,000

Functions: Generalist (All)

Industries: Pharm Svcs., Biotech/Life Sciences, Healthcare, Hospitals, Long-term/Home Care

MR of Danville

(an affiliate of MRI)
140 Stonecrest Rd Ste 202
Shelbyville, KY 40065-8144
(502) 633-4002
Fax: (502) 633-4944
Email: rob@mriky.com
Web: www.mriky.com

Summary: Specialize in electrical, mechanical, process & quality engineers, and departmental managers in general metalworking.

Key Contact - Specialty:
Mr. Robert P. DiLuca, Owner & General Manager
Mr. Nick Kihlman, Account Executive
Ms. Susan DiLuca, Office Administrator
Ms. Staci Garlough, Administrative Assistant

Salary Minimum: $30,000

Functions: Generalist (All), Product Dev., Production, Automation, Plant Mgmt., Quality, Engineering

Industries: Generalist (All), Plastics, Rubber, Metal Products, Machine, Appliance, Motor Vehicles, Test, Measure Equip.

MR of Monroe

(an affiliate of MRI)
3124 Kilpatrick Blvd
Monroe, LA 71201-5156
(318) 322-2200
Fax: (318) 322-4745
Email: general@mrmonroe.com
Web: www.mrmonroe.com

Summary: We offer prompt response in slating candidates for key positions, discount moving rates and special mortgage program if relocation is desired/required. Additional services include executive temp placement and personality profiling. We specialize in building products, banking, engineering & construction and general manufacturing.

Key Contact - Specialty:
Mr. Bruce Hursey, President - *Building products*

Salary Minimum: $40,000

Functions: Mfg., Production, Plant Mgmt., Mktg. Mgmt., Sales Mgmt., HR Mgmt., Engineering

Industries: Generalist (All), Construction, Food, Bev., Tobacco, Lumber, Furniture, Plastics, Rubber, Metal Products, Banking

The McLain Group

(an affiliate of MRI)
710 Apple St
Norco, LA 70079-2424
(985) 725-0290
Fax: (985) 725-0608
Email: info@mrinow.com
Web: www.mrinow.com

Summary: We bring together the best in the electrical power and petrol-chemical industries.

Key Contact - Specialty:
Mr. Tom McLain
Ms. Donna Champagne
Mr. Ray Burski

Salary Minimum: $50,000

Functions: Generalist (All)

Industries: Energy, Utilities

SC of Alexandria

(an affiliate of MRI)
PO Box 611
511 Melody Dr
Oakdale, LA 71463-0611
(318) 561-2882
Fax: (413) 740-8535
Email: salesconsultants@aol.com

Summary: Our firm places board members, senior management, middle management and sales & marketing professionals in all industries.

Key Contact - Specialty:
Ms. Markay Dunn, President - *Furniture, Printing*

Functions: Generalist (All), Board Members, Senior Mgmt., Middle Mgmt., Sales & Mktg., Mktg. Research, Mktg. Mgmt., Sales Mgmt.

Industries: Generalist (All), Manufacturing, Lumber, Furniture, Paper, Printing, Plastics, Rubber, Metal Products, Consumer Elect., Misc. Mfg., Wholesale, Pharm Svcs., Packaging, Insurance, Healthcare

Magee Resource Group

(an affiliate of MRI)
920 Pierremont Rd Ste 515
Shreveport, LA 71106-2050
(318) 865-8411
Fax: (318) 861-3411
Email: cmagee@mageeresource.com
Web: www.mageeresource.com

Summary: We are the premier staffing, and contract human capital resource for SAP, IT, healthcare, manufacturing, and construction.

Key Contact - Specialty:
Ms. Gerri Magee, Chief Operating Officer & Executive VP
Mr. Charles Magee, President & Chief Executive Officer
Mr. Shay Hoosier, Director, Performance Development
Mr. Bart Bordelon, Division Sales Manager, Healthcare
Mr. Jeff Roach, Director, Client & Sales Development

Salary Minimum: $60,000

Functions: Generalist (All), Management, Senior Mgmt., Mfg., Healthcare, IT, MIS Mgmt.

Industries: Generalist (All), Construction, Manufacturing, Textiles, Apparel, Chemicals, Plastics, Rubber, Paints, Petro. Products, Machine, Appliance, Motor Vehicles, Misc. Mfg., Transportation, Wholesale, Retail, Finance, Banking, Services, Pharm Svcs., Hospitality, Communications, Software, Database SW, Development SW, Mfg. SW, Biotech/Life Sciences, Healthcare, Hospitals, Long-term/Home Care, Occupational Therapy, Non-Classifiable

MR of Saint Tammany

(an affiliate of MRI)
202 Village Cir Ste 3
Slidell, LA 70458-5374
(985) 847-1900
Email: jpecot@jobscenter.com
Web: www.jobscenter.com

Summary: We are specialists in the career fields we represent and provide fulfillment to your needs in a most professional and timely manner. Our team provides expertise in many industry functional and geographical specialties. Our goal is aiding clients in developing their human capital through recruiting and assessing executives.

Key Contact - Specialty:
Mr. Jack L. Pecot, President
Mr. Darrel E. Clark, Account Executive
Ms. Victoria Verges, Office Manager

Functions: Middle Mgmt., Engineering

Industries: Manufacturing, IT Implementation, Software

Executive Search Group Inc

(an affiliate of MRI)
2145 Post Rd
Wells, ME 04090-4769
(207) 646-9200
Fax: (207) 221-1230
Email: psmith@executivesg.com
Web: www.executivesg.com

Summary: We focus in the banking, healthcare and information technology sectors. We provide contingency, engaged and retained services to our clients on a national basis.

Key Contact - Specialty:
Mr. Pete Smith, President - *Sales, SAP, Start-up companies, Supply Chain, Systems (Integration)*
Mr. Carll Wilkinson, Search Consultant - *Sales, SAP, Senior management, Systems (Integration), Wireless*

Salary Minimum: $75,000

Functions: Senior Mgmt., Middle Mgmt., Sales & Mktg., Mktg. Mgmt., Sales Mgmt., Sales Reps.

Industries: Computer Equip., Finance, Banking, Invest. Banking, Brokers, Venture Cap., Mutual/Hedge Funds, Misc. Financial, Services,

E-commerce, IT Implementation, PSA/ASP, New Media, Communications, Wireless, Network Infrastructure, Software, Database SW, Doc. Mgmt., Production SW, ERP SW, HR SW, Mfg. SW, Networking, Comm. SW, Security SW, Training SW, Healthcare

MR of Columbia

(also known as PlasticJobSource.com)
8850 Columbia 100 Pkwy Ste 214
Columbia, MD 21045-2376
(410) 309-6590
(800) 267-1226
Fax: (410) 309-6595
Email: jobs@plasticjobsource.com
Web: www.plasticjobsource.com

Summary: We are the leading plastic recruitment firm in the nation. We provide job opportunities for professionals in plastics and packaging manufacturing. We serve the appliance, automotive, medical, consumer, industrial, high technology, packaging, cosmetic and food & beverage industries. Our website listings are updated weekly.

Key Contact - Specialty:
Mr. Randolph Reyes, General Manager & Senior Recruiter - *Product management/development*
Mr. Jim Feehan, Project Coordinator
Mr. Ed McGill, Project Coordinator - *Production*
Ms. Renee Reyes, Recruiter

Functions: Management, Board Members, Mfg.

Industries: Manufacturing, Food, Bev., Tobacco, Lumber, Furniture, Medical Devices, Plastics, Rubber, Motor Vehicles, Computer Equip., Consumer Elect., Transportation, Packaging

MR of Frederick

(an affiliate of MRI)
4 N East St
Frederick, MD 21701-5601
(301) 663-0600
(301) 831-4414
Email: paw@mrifrederick.com
Web: www.mrifrederick.com

Summary: Specialize in working with any company, any level, within the healthcare, pharmaceutical and medical equipment industries, IS and administrative areas.

Key Contact - Specialty:
Mrs. Pat Webb, Manager

Functions: Admin. Svcs., Mfg., Quality

Industries: Drugs Mfg., Medical Devices, Misc. Mfg., Electronic, Elec. Components, Robotics, Semiconductors, Pharm Svcs., HR Services, IT Implementation, Digital, Wireless, Network Infrastructure, RF/Microwave, Packaging, Property/Facility Mgmt., ERP SW, Biotech/Life Sciences

MR of Gaithersburg

(an affiliate of MRI)
963 Russell Ave Ste A
Gaithersburg, MD 20879-3287
(240) 631-7730
(877) 631-7730
Fax: (240) 631-7731
Email: esbeebe@mrigaithersburg.com
Web: www.mrigaithersburg.com

Summary: Our firm is a customer focused executive, management and technical search and staffing firm. Candidates and clients choose us because of the professional and ethical service we offer. Our search consultants have a reputation as industry experts and our specialties include the following areas: federal business development and sales, federal contracting and systems integration,

technology sales (commercial), IT, finance and administration.

Key Contact - Specialty:
Mr. Eric S. Beebe, President - *Sales*

Salary Minimum: $100,000

Functions: Management, Senior Mgmt., Sales & Mktg., IT, MIS Mgmt., DB Admin., R&D

Industries: Food, Bev., Tobacco, Consumer Elect., Test, Measure Equip., Electronic, Elec. Components, Services, Non-profits, Accounting, Equip Svcs., Mgmt. Consulting, HR Services, E-commerce, IT Implementation, Call Centers, Wireless, Fiber Optic, Network Infrastructure, Government, Defense, Software, Development SW, Doc. Mgmt., Production SW, ERP SW, Biotech/Life Sciences, Healthcare

MR of the BWI Corridor

(an affiliate of MRI)
7240 Parkway Dr Ste 150
Hanover, MD 21076-1378
(410) 712-0770
Fax: (410) 712-0510
Email: mribwi@recruitergurus.com
Web: www.recruitergurus.com

Summary: Providing full search and placement of permanent and interim talent within IT/IS including high performance computing, software, healthcare, chemical, electronics, power, energy and engineering. Specializing in management, engineering, R&D, manufacturing quality and sales/marketing level positions.

Key Contact - Specialty:
Mr. Lee Stubberfield, President
Ms. Kiaran Buckley, Office Manager
Mr. Jay Daley, Account Executive - *Computers, Computers (Software), Energy, Power*
Ms. Lynn Rodens, Account Executive - *Computers, Computers (Software), Information service, Information Technology*
Mr. Christopher Pukalski, Account Executive - *Computers, Information service, Information Systems, Information Technology*
Mr. Gilbert Weber, Account Executive - *Healthcare*
Mr. Steve Dawson, Account Executive - *BSME, Chemical, Engineering, Manufacturing, Mechanical*
Mr. David Haffner, Account Executive - *Healthcare, Home health, Hospital*
Mr. Bob Durbin, Account Executive - *Food, Food & beverage, Food service*

Salary Minimum: $40,000

Functions: Management, Mfg., Sales & Mktg., IT, R&D, Engineering, Int'l.

Industries: Energy, Utilities, Food, Bev., Tobacco, Chemicals, Medical Devices, Plastics, Rubber, Electronic, Elec. Components, Communications, Telecoms, Government, Software, Healthcare, Long-term/Home Care

Rockville Recruiter.com

(an affiliate of MRI)
15717 Crabbs Branch Way Ste 202C
Rockville, MD 20855-6652
(301) 948-7470
Fax: (301) 947-7475
Email: mrr@rockvillerecruiter.com
Web: www.rockvillerecruiter.com

Summary: We are The 36 month Guarantee Recruiting Company. If you are looking for an opportunity to be a recruiter or you are a hiring manager frustrated with the results of your current process, you should contact us. If your company is growing, you are exactly what this new type of recruiting is geared for.

Key Contact - Specialty:
Mr. Robert Moore, Regional Vice President
Mr. Carlton Powell, Recruiter - *Brokerage*

Functions: Generalist (All), Management, Middle Mgmt., Plant Mgmt., Distribution, HR Mgmt., IT, Engineering, Minorities/Diversity

Industries: Generalist (All), Food, Bev., Tobacco, Textiles, Apparel, Wholesale, Retail, Pharm Svcs., HR Services, Logistics Svcs., Biotech/Life Sciences, Women's

The Washington Group

(also known as MR of Washington)
12520 Prosperity Dr Ste 320
Silver Spring, MD 20904-1664
(301) 625-5100
(877) 625-5100
Fax: (301) 625-3001
Email: info@mr-twg.com
Web: www.mriwashington.com

Summary: Specialize in the industries of marketing, managed care & healthcare, pharmaceuticals, accounting & finance, marketing research and IT.

Key Contact - Specialty:
Mr. Frank S. Black, Jr., President - *Marketing*
Ms. Barbara Silver, Senior Account Manager - *Managed care*
Mr. Kevin Hughes, Vice President, Marketing Research
Ms. Marsha Levey, Vice President, Sales & Operations
Mr. Dennis Mauro-Huse, Account Director
Mr. John Marty, Account Director
Ms. Rhonds Henderson, Account Executive
Mr. Robert Bennett, Account Executive
Ms. Marilyn Oskard, Senior Account Executive
Ms. Sarah Bowman, Director, Legal Division
Hsinyu Yu, Account Executive, Legal Division

Functions: Generalist (All), Healthcare, Health Admin., Mktg. Research, Taxes, IT

Industries: Generalist (All), Pharm Svcs., Accounting, Mgmt. Consulting, Healthcare

MR/SC of Baltimore-Timonium

(an affiliate of MRI)
9515 Deereco Rd Ste 900
Timonium, MD 21093-2160
(410) 252-6616
(866) 277-4049
Fax: (410) 252-7076
Email: info@mribaltimore.com
Web: www.mribaltimore.com

Summary: We have the people and the processes to guarantee results. Put our unprecedented success to work for you. Our office provides centralized search and recruitment services through a vast network of offices, among the largest in the world. Harness our power and centralize recruiting efforts with one point of contact.

Key Contact - Specialty:
Ms. Linda A. Burton, President & Chief Executive Officer
Mr. Jeff Burton, Chief Financial Officer
Ms. Tracy Carroll, Vice President, Operations
Mr. Mike Adkins, National Account Manager
Ms. Heather Bradshaw, Project Manager

Functions: Senior Mgmt., Admin. Svcs., Mfg., Product Dev., Health Admin., Sales & Mktg., HR Mgmt., Finance, Engineering

Industries: Generalist (All), Manufacturing, Food, Bev., Tobacco, Drugs Mfg., Medical Devices, Plastics, Rubber, Test, Measure Equip., Misc. Mfg., Consumer Goods, Finance, Services, Packaging, Insurance, Real Estate, Biotech/Life Sciences

SC of Boston

(an affiliate of MRI)
790 Turnpike St
Andover, MA 01810-1072
(978) 475-5500
Fax: (978) 475-9116
Email: rstockard@scboston.com
Web: www.scboston.com

Summary: Our firm places sales & marketing professionals in the biotechnology and healthcare industries.

Key Contact - Specialty:
Mr. Robert G. Stockard, Chief Executive Officer
Ms. Maria Massaro, President

Functions: Sales & Mktg.

Industries: Biotech/Life Sciences, Healthcare

The Boston Group

(an affiliate of MRI)
607 Boylston St Ste 700
Boston, MA 02116-3614
(617) 262-5050 x116
Fax: (617) 421-9630
Email: jnehiley@mri-boston.com
Web: www.mri-boston.com

Summary: We have offered retained and contingency search with over 80 recruiters working in varied industries and specialties.

Key Contact - Specialty:
Mr. Jack Mohan, Chief Executive Officer
Mr. Jack J. Nehiley, Senior Vice President & General Manager
Mr. Arthur Greenfield, Senior Vice President, Finance
Ms. Monique Kenney, Vice President, Technology & Admin
Ms. Lauren O'Donnell, Manager, Corporate Administration
Ms. Kelly Warren, Administrative Assistant

Functions: Generalist (All)

Industries: Generalist (All), Construction, Food, Bev., Tobacco, Plastics, Rubber, Metal Products, Computer Equip., Misc. Mfg., Banking, Misc. Financial, Legal

Branches:
1500 Main St Ste 2008
Springfield, MA 01115-1000
(413) 781-1550
Fax: (413) 731-6566
Email: springfield@mri-boston.com
Key Contact - Specialty:
Mr. William Williams, Account Executive

2000 W Park Dr
Westborough, MA 01581-3923
(508) 366-9900
Fax: (508) 898-9982
Email: westboro@mri-boston.com
Key Contact - Specialty:
Ms. Irene Garrity, General Manager
Mr. Philip Bartley, Executive Recruiter

4 Bedford Farms Dr
Bedford, NH 03110-6528
(603) 669-9800
Email: bedford@mri-boston.com
Key Contact - Specialty:
Mr. Michael Bacon, Senior Vice President & General Manager

101 Dyer St Ste 500
Providence, RI 02903-3908
(401) 274-2810
Fax: (401) 274-6440
Email: providence@mri-boston.com

Key Contact - Specialty:
Mr. Stephen W. Morse, General Manager
Mr. Kevin Lavalla, Account Executive - *Legal*

SC of Brockton

(an affiliate of MRI)
220 Boylston St
Chestnut Hill, MA 02467-2077
(617) 969-9953
Fax: (617) 969-9701
Email: mfeinsonsc@aol.com

Summary: Specializing in sales & marketing with a large network of offices.

Key Contact - Specialty:
Mr. Milton M. Feinson, President

Functions: Sales & Mktg., Mktg. Mgmt., Sales Mgmt.

Industries: Generalist (All)

SC of Falmouth

(an affiliate of MRI)
PO Box 2049
North Falmouth, MA 02556-8049
(508) 564-4567
Fax: (508) 564-4567
Email: careers@scfalmouth.com
Web: www.scfalmouth.com

Summary: We are a full service recruiting and placement firm; contingent, priority and retained, operating nationally. Industry specialties include: executive placements across industries including C- and VP-levels. Consulting, IT sales, outsourcing & software services, pharmaceutical, biotechnology and retail.

Key Contact - Specialty:
Ms. Pamela Alden
Mr. Thomas Fitzpatrick, Partner

Salary Minimum: $70,000

Functions: Generalist (All)

Industries: Drugs Mfg., Medical Devices, Non-profits, Mgmt. Consulting, IT Implementation, Database SW, Doc. Mgmt., Production SW, ERP SW, Biotech/Life Sciences, Hospitals

SC of Wellesley

(an affiliate of MRI)
888 Worcester St Ste 95
Wellesley, MA 02482-3736
(781) 235-7700
Fax: (781) 237-7207
Email: scwellesley@scwellesley.com
Web: www.scwellesley.com

Summary: We are committed to offering honest and confidential recruiting services. We take pride in our ability to understand our assignment, conduct a successful confidential search and evaluate candidates in a competent and professional manner.

Key Contact - Specialty:
Mrs. Susan Durante, President

Functions: Sales & Mktg., Mktg. Mgmt.

Industries: Generalist (All)

Variant Partners

(an affiliate of MRI)
24 Frank Lloyd Wright Dr
Ann Arbor, MI 48105-9755
(734) 769-1720
Fax: (734) 769-0035
Email: info@vpartners.com
Web: www.vpartners.com

Summary: We are dedicated to building your business. We have extensive experience developing and delivering custom recruiting

solutions. We match impact players with opportunities and clients that desire them through the use of our proprietary recruitment approach.

Key Contact - Specialty:
Mr. Sam Sarafa, President
Mr. David Sarafa, Vice President
Mr. Dennis Sarafa, Vice President - *Construction, Database (Warehousing), Information Systems, Information Technology, Retail*
Ms. Rosemary Sarafa, Vice President
Ms. Stephanie Krupp, Account Director - *Energy, Legal (Attorneys,Lawyers)*
Ms. Carol LaBelle, Senior Account Executive - *Accounting, Accounting (Big 4,General), Finance, Tax*
Mr. Chris Behmer, Account Director - *Manufacturing, Manufacturing (Management), Quality*
Ms. Corina Eliason, Account Director - *Building products, Kitchen, Office (Administration,Support)*
Ms. Hilary Fletcher, Sr. Account Executive - *Accounting, Administration, Construction*
Mr. Jim Miles, Senior Account Executive - *Automotive, Engineering, Manufacturing, Manufacturing (Management)*
Ms. Lorie Thom, Account Executive - *Automotive, Engineering*
Mr. Mark Case, Account Executive - *Database (Warehousing), E-business, Information Systems, Information Technology, Retail*
Ms. Nancy Plane, Account Executive - *Construction*
Mr. Rob Michalowski, Account Director - *Banking, Banking (Commercial,Corporate,Investment,Retail)*
Mr. Ron Bell, Account Director - *Accounting, Accounting (Big 4,General,Public), Finance*
Mr. Bob Frazier, Account Executive - *Banking, Banking (Commercial,Corporate,Investment,Retail)*
Ms. Debbie Noetzel, Account Executive - *Electronics, Embedded microprocessor, Engineering*
Mr. Don Slankster, Account Executive - *Building products, Construction*

Functions: Generalist (All), Admin. Svcs., Engineering, Attorneys

Industries: Generalist (All), Energy, Utilities, Construction, Manufacturing, Motor Vehicles, Banking, Invest. Banking, Software, Healthcare, Non-Classifiable

SC of Auburn Hills

(an affiliate of MRI)
2601 Cambridge Ct Ste 204
Auburn Hills, MI 48326-2574
(248) 373-7177
Fax: (248) 373-7759
Email: scah@scauburnhills.com
Web: www.scauburnhills.com

Summary: We are a full service executive search firm specializing in sales, sales management, marketing, engineering, engineering management and quality positions. We cover a number of industries including: automotive, industrial, pharmaceutical, environmental & facilities management services, software, medical, intangibles, building and consumer products.

Key Contact - Specialty:
Mr. Boe Embrey, President - *Automotive, Engineering, Pharmaceutical, Sales*

Functions: Management, Senior Mgmt., Sales & Mktg., Sales Mgmt., Engineering

Industries: Generalist (All), Motor Vehicles, Misc. Mfg., Robotics

MR/SC of Birmingham

(an affiliate of MRI)
30700 Telegraph Rd Ste 3650
Bingham Farms, MI 48025-4527
(248) 6477766
Email: bbinke@recruiters-mri.com
Web: www.recruiters-mri.com

Summary: We are an executive search firm serving the construction industry as well as finance and accounting in a verity of industries. Our practice areas serve companies across a wide spectrum of positions. These areas include but are not limited to Project Management, Estimating, Superintendents, and Financial etc.

Key Contact - Specialty:
Mr. Brian Binke, President

Salary Minimum: $40,000

Functions: Senior Mgmt., Middle Mgmt., Sales & Mktg., Sales Mgmt., Finance, Structural, Bldg. Contractors

Industries: Generalist (All), Construction, Manufacturing, Retail, Finance, Banking, Services, Communications, Software, Non-Classifiable

Dublin Group

(also known as SC of Bloomfield Hills)
4111 Andover Rd Ste 120W
Bloomfield Hills, MI 48302-1931
(248) 594-0880
(800) 992-5986
Fax: (248) 594-5993
Email: dublingroup@usa.net

Summary: Recruiting firm specializing in powdered metal, steel, abrasives and cutting tools. Positions that we recruit for are sales and engineering, especially degreed metallurgists.

Key Contact - Specialty:
Mr. Gerry Anger, President - *Engineering, Sales*
Mr. Tom Kilkenney, Co-Manager

Salary Minimum: $40,000

Functions: Sales & Mktg.

Industries: Manufacturing, Metal Products, Machine, Appliance, Misc. Mfg., Engineering Svcs.

MR of East Detroit-Farmington Hills

(an affiliate of MRI)
34405 W 12 Mile Rd Ste 115
Farmington Hills, MI 48331-5626
(248) 324-2100
Fax: (248) 324-2101
Email: info@mridetroit.com
Web: www.mridetroit.com

Summary: Our firm specializes in Administration, Accounting & Sales.

Key Contact - Specialty:
Ms. Debra Lawson, President & General Manager - *Clerical*

Functions: Admin. Svcs.

Industries: Generalist (All)

SC of Grand Rapids

(an affiliate of MRI)
900 E Paris Ave SE Ste 301
Grand Rapids, MI 49546-3676
(616) 940-3900
Email: marissas@scgrandrapids.com
Web: www.scgrandrapids.com

Summary: We are an executive search firm specializing in recruiting sales professionals for the contract furniture, building products and industrial industries. We successfully work to find the right person for the right job.

Key Contact - Specialty:
Ms. Marissa Sturtevant, Manager, Human Resources - *Building products, Cement/concrete, Coatings, Composites, Design*

Functions: Senior Mgmt., Sales & Mktg., Sales Mgmt., Sales Reps., Design

Industries: Textiles, Apparel, Lumber, Furniture, Architectural Svcs.

JL Blake Inc

(an affiliate of MRI)
5380 Holiday Ter
Kalamazoo, MI 49009-2154
(269) 372-8007
Fax: (269) 372-8388
Email: mgb@jlblake.com
Web: www.jlblake.com

Summary: Recruiting company specializing in industrial sales and marketing specifically industrial instrumentation, controls and automation

Key Contact - Specialty:
Mr. Mark Bielecki, CSM, President - *Automation, Industrial, Instrumentation, Marketing, Sales*
Mr. Tim Kane, CSAM, Account Executive - *Automation, Industrial, Instrumentation, Marketing, Sales*

Functions: Sales Mgmt.

Industries: Electronic, Elec. Components, Robotics

MR of Kalamazoo

(an affiliate of MRI)
4021 W Main St Ste 200
Kalamazoo, MI 49006-3706
(269) 381-1153
Fax: (269) 381-8031
Email: info@mrikazoo.com
Web: www.mrikazoo.com

Summary: Executive search and recruiting firm working within the areas of manufacturing & engineering, specializing in plastics, pulp & paper, packaging, construction management, IT and industrial sales. Applicants need at least three to five years experience in specific industries.

Key Contact - Specialty:
Dr. M.J. Tessin, President
Mr. Norm Grosse, Operations Manager

Salary Minimum: $45,000

Functions: Generalist (All), Mfg.

Industries: Construction, Manufacturing, Paper, Plastics, Rubber, Metal Products, Misc. Mfg., E-commerce, IT Implementation, Engineering Svcs., Packaging

MR/SC of Laurel Park

(an affiliate of MRI)
17177 N Laurel Park Dr Ste 256
Livonia, MI 48152-3951
(734) 542-9099
(734) 542-1454
Fax: (734) 542-9098
Email: chrisa@capmri.com
Web: www.capmri.com

Summary: We offer client firms in-depth working knowledge of these industries: food processing, equipment & supply manufacturing, medical device manufacturing, and pharmaceutical and biotechnology for the following functions: sales, marketing, new product development, brand management, food science/technology, engineering, plant management, regulatory, clinical, R&D quality control and quality assurance.

Key Contact - Specialty:
Mr. Chris Arnold, President & Chief Executive Officer
Ms. Molle Kabodian, Managing Partner

Salary Minimum: $65,000

Functions: Senior Mgmt., Product Dev., Healthcare, Mktg. Mgmt., Sales Mgmt.

Industries: Generalist (All), Manufacturing, Food, Bev., Tobacco, Textiles, Apparel, Paper, Chemicals, Medical Devices, Plastics, Rubber, Machine, Appliance, Wholesale, Retail, Mfg. SW, Marketing SW

MR of Muskegon

(an affiliate of MRI)
427 Seminole Rd Ste 104
Muskegon, MI 49444-3747
(231) 830-8400
Fax: (231) 830-8500
Email: mrmuskegon@i2k.com

Summary: Our account executives know your business. We are industry specialists with a combined recruiting expertise and are qualified to handle the most difficult assignments.

Key Contact - Specialty:
Mr. John R. Mitchell, Jr., Manager

Functions: Middle Mgmt., Production, Plant Mgmt., Purchasing, Mktg. Mgmt., CFOs, Engineering

Industries: Lumber, Furniture, Printing, Plastics, Rubber, Metal Products, Motor Vehicles, Misc. Mfg., Accounting, HR Services, Law Enforcement

MR of Plymouth

(an affiliate of MRI)
41000 7 Mile Rd Ste 230
Northville, MI 48167-2664
(248) 465-0800
Fax: (248) 465-0801
Email: info@mrplymouth.com
Web: www.mrplymouth.com

Summary: Our firm specializes in plastics, chemicals, adhesive/sealants, coatings, inks, polymers, pharmaceuticals and biotechnology industries. We place the top 20 to 25 percent of talent available with our clients.

Key Contact - Specialty:
Mr. Joseph Boelter, President
Mr. Angelo Kircos, Project Coordinator
Mr. Ryan Leslie, Project Coordinator
Mr. Danny A. Kovacs, Account Executive
Mr. Anthony Leighton, Account Executive
Ms. Mary Rabban, Account Executive

Salary Minimum: $45,000

Functions: Generalist (All)

Industries: Energy, Utilities, Printing, Chemicals, Soap, Perf., Cosmtcs., Drugs Mfg., Medical Devices, Plastics, Rubber, Paints, Petro. Products, Misc. Mfg., Biotech/Life Sciences

SC Novi

(an affiliate of MRI)
41800 W 11 Mile Rd Ste 215
Novi, MI 48375-1818
(248) 305-9727
Email: info@scnovi.com
Web: www.scnovi.com

Summary: We are part of a large executive search franchise. Our office specializes in industrial sales, placing candidates in both sales and sales management positions.

Key Contact - Specialty:
Mr. James Guerrera, President
Mr. Scott Henderson, Account Executive
Mr. Stephen Nehez, Jr., Account Executive
Mr. Jeffrey J. Valentine, Project Recruiter
Mr. Todd M. Broski, Project Recruiter
Ms. Ashley King, Project Recruiter
Ms. Melinda Epperson, Office Researcher - *Pharmaceutical*

Functions: Sales & Mktg., Sales Mgmt.

Industries: Generalist (All), Manufacturing

Angott Search Group

(also known as MR of North Oakland County)
2530 S Rochester Rd
Rochester Hills, MI 48307-3817
(248) 299-1900
Email: info@asgteam.com
Web: www.asgteam.com

Summary: Dedicated to helping our clients address their professional staffing needs. We are part of the largest search and recruitment franchise organization with many offices.

Key Contact - Specialty:
Mr. Mark Angott, President
Mrs. Kathleen Riley

Salary Minimum: $25,000

Functions: Generalist (All), Management

Industries: Manufacturing, Retail, Finance, Banking, Brokers, Non-profits, Accounting, Equip Svcs., HR Services, IT Implementation, Engineering Svcs., Advertising, Software

SC of Detroit

(an affiliate of MRI)
29777 Telegraph Rd Ste 2260
Southfield, MI 48034-7651
(248) 352-9200
Fax: (248) 352-9374
Email: info@scjob.com
Web: www.scjob.com

Summary: We are an executive search firm specializing in placing sales executives in the chemical, medical devices, industrial, paper and plastic industries. We promise quick turn around on qualified candidates, which lower the cost per hire.

Key Contact - Specialty:
Mr. Tom Hoy, General Manager - *Automotive, Chemical*
Ms. Maureen Haney, Account Executive - *Chemical*
Mr. Eurick Ellison, Account Executive - *Industrial*

Functions: Product Dev., Healthcare, Health Admin., Sales & Mktg., Sales Mgmt., Sales Reps., R&D

Industries: Paper, Chemicals, Drugs Mfg., Medical Devices, Plastics, Rubber, Paints, Petro. Products, Pharm Svcs., Biotech/Life Sciences, Healthcare, Hospitals

MR of Traverse City

(an affiliate of MRI)
3622 Veterans Dr Ste 1
Traverse City, MI 49684-4580
(231) 947-8000
Fax: (231) 922-9481
Email: resumes@mritc.net
Web: www.mritc.net

Summary: We provide a focused industry expertise that enables us to locate, qualify and present the most qualified candidates in the areas of automotive, IT, manufacturing, technology sales, telecom and construction. We service

corporations seeking qualified individuals or someone considering a career change; contact us for a confidential analysis of your goals or objectives.

Key Contact - Specialty:
Ms. Mary J. Barker, CSAM, Manager
Mr. Doug Barker, Co-Owner & Recruiter - *Construction*
Mr. David Grabe, Recruiter - *Engineering, Manufacturing, Technical*
Ms. Shawna McLeod Batcha, Recruiter - *Automotive*
Mr. Robert Banks, Jr., Recruiter
Mrs. Rita Melotti, Recruiter - *Manufacturing*
Mr. Mario De Carolis, Recruiter - *PeopleSoft*
Mr. Daniel McKean, Recruiter
Mr. Chris McKenna, Recruiter

Salary Minimum: $35,000

Functions: Generalist (All), Mfg., Product Dev., Sales Mgmt., IT, Engineering

Industries: Construction, Manufacturing, Leather, Stone, Glass, Metal Products, Motor Vehicles, Consumer Elect., Electronic, Elec. Components, Finance, E-commerce, IT Implementation, Communications, Packaging, Insurance, Software, Doc. Mgmt., Production SW, ERP SW, Industry Specific SW, Biotech/Life Sciences, Healthcare, Non-Classifiable

MR of Northern Lakes

(also known as Binder Consulting Group)
11476 County Road 34 NW
Alexandria, MN 56308-9725
(320) 846-5270
(612) 419-3278
Email: michael@mrnortherlakes.com
Web: www.mrnortherlakes.com

Summary: We fill executive and staff recruiting needs for manufacturing companies. Extensive years of personal professional experience in management and finance functions including many years as a university finance professor.

Key Contact - Specialty:
Mr. Michael Binder, Owner & Recruiter

Functions: Generalist (All), Finance

Industries: Manufacturing, Finance, Banking

MR of Bloomington

(also known as Pengilly Group)
9217 17th Ave S Ste 206
Bloomington, MN 55425-2371
(952) 948-0280
(888) 948-6300
Email: mr@pengilly.com
Web: www.pengilly.com

Summary: We are a search firm working in the banking, finance, accounting, manufacturing and sales (industrial, technical, software)areas; superior personal service. We get the job done. We welcome your inquiry. We are part of the MRI Network

Key Contact - Specialty:
Mr. Dale Gustafson, JD, Manager - *Executives, Information Technology, Legal, Manufacturing, Sales*
Mr. Bob Klaus, Account Executive - *Banking, Banking (Commercial)*

Salary Minimum: $50,000

Functions: Senior Mgmt., Middle Mgmt., Production, Sales & Mktg., Sales Mgmt., Benefits, Finance, IT, MIS Mgmt.

Industries: Generalist (All), Printing, Machine, Appliance, Computer Equip., Misc. Mfg., Banking, Legal, Accounting, Software

MR of Burnsville

(an affiliate of MRI)
PO Box 2099
Burnsville, MN 55337-0040
(952) 736-9540
Fax: (952) 736-9539
Email: info@mrijobs.net
Web: www.mrijobs.net

Summary: We specialize in placing high quality candidates for sales into the packaging machinery industry.

Key Contact - Specialty:
Mr. Daniel Bessinger

Functions: Sales Mgmt.

Industries: Packaging

SC of Chaska

(an affiliate of MRI)
320 N Walnut St
Chaska, MN 55318-2046
(952) 496-3030
(952) 368-0024
Fax: (952) 368-0099
Email: mike@scchaska.com
Web: www.scchaska.com

Summary: Recruiting specialists that provide clients with an expertise in finding top people in the printing and pharmaceutical industries.

Key Contact - Specialty:
Mr. Michael Smith, President
Ms. Andrea Smith, Vice President
Mr. Jami Menden, Account Executive
Mr. Dirk Gasterland, Account Executive
Ms. Karen Andler, Account Executive

Functions: Generalist (All)

Industries: Printing, Drugs Mfg., Banking, Pharm Svcs.

MR of Eagan

(an affiliate of MRI)
4460 Erin Dr
Eagan, MN 55122-2357
(651) 365-0444
Fax: (651) 365-0111
Email: jhorn@mreagan.com
Web: www.mreagan.com

Summary: We specialize in the pharmaceutical, allied health care, medical device, IT, food industries and contract staffing. Our research, recruitment and selection procedures are generally conducted on a national level. We strive to develop and maintain long-term, professional relationships with our clients.

Key Contact - Specialty:
Mr. R. Jeff Von Horn, President
Mr. Robert H. Horn, Managing Partner
Mr. Jeremy Jackson, Senior Account Executive
Ms. Colleen Murphy, Office Manager
Ms. Shelli Jackson, Senior Recruiter

Functions: Generalist (All), Admin. Svcs., Plant Mgmt., Direct Mktg., Customer Svc., Finance, IT, Systems Analysis, DB Admin., Engineering

Industries: Generalist (All), Manufacturing, Food, Bev., Tobacco, Medical Devices, Pharm Svcs., Healthcare

MR of Rochester

(an affiliate of MRI)
1652 Greenview Dr SW Ste 600
Rochester, MN 55902-4285
(507) 282-2400
Fax: (507) 282-1308
Email: mrrocmn@ismidwest.com
Web: www.ismidwest.com

Summary: We specialize in IS and food & beverage industries. Most of our positions are technical or mid-level management; i.e. programmer, network administrator, data base administrator, production supervisor, quality or safety manager.

Key Contact - Specialty:
Mr. John Harris, Owner & Manager
Ms. Ellen Newman, Account Executive
Mr. Randy Eckerson, Account Executive

Functions: Middle Mgmt., Mfg., Production, Plant Mgmt., Quality, IT, Systems Analysis, Systems Dev., Systems Implem., R&D

Industries: Generalist (All), Food, Bev., Tobacco

MR of Salem Corner

(an affiliate of MRI)
1530 Greenview Dr SW Ste 201
Rochester, MN 55902-4327
(507) 536-0350
Fax: (507) 536-0349
Email: recruiters2@woodhunter.com
Web: www.woodhunter.com

Summary: Specialized in the wood products industry as a whole and all management and executive positions. Focused in: furniture, kitchen cabinets & bath, architectural millwork, lumber, components, trusses, industrial panels, decorative laminates, fixtures & displays, manufactured homes, doors & windows, sawmills and building products.

Key Contact - Specialty:
Mr. Bill E. Risma, Owner & Manager
Mr. Eric A.G. Bookmeyer, Account Executive

Functions: Generalist (All)

Industries: Construction, Manufacturing, Lumber, Furniture

MR of Shakopee

(an affiliate of MRI)
2235 Park Ridge Dr
Shakopee, MN 55379-2711
(952) 402-0379
Fax: (802) 609-9803
Email: mrshakope@msn.com
Web: www.mrinet.com

Summary: We are a full-service recruiting firm that specializes in the telecom industry exclusively.

Key Contact - Specialty:
Mr. Michael Brown, Manager

Functions: Senior Mgmt., Middle Mgmt., Sales & Mktg., IT, Engineering

Industries: Telecoms

MR of Minnetonka

(an affiliate of MRI)
4000 Shoreline Dr
Spring Park, MN 55384-9656
(952) 471-3013
Fax: (952) 471-3014
Email: karel.mri@mchsi.com

Summary: Our firm works with client companies in the pharmaceutical, biotechnology, medical device, and managed healthcare industries. We identify qualified candidates for positions in senior management to mid level management, including specialized technical positions; and assist in the hiring process.

Key Contact - Specialty:
Mr. Karel Van Langen, General Manager - *General management, Telecommunications*

Salary Minimum: $75,000

Functions: Generalist (All)

Industries: Drugs Mfg., Medical Devices, Biotech/Life Sciences, Healthcare

MR of Winona

(an affiliate of MRI)
1600 Gilmore Ave Ste 100
Winona, MN 55987-2172
(507) 452-2700
(877) 452-2700
Fax: (507) 452-2722
Email: jimc@mrwinona.com
Web: www.mrwinona.com

Summary: We provide staffing services for the high technology, telecommunications, banking/finance and contact center industries. We have a history of hands on experience in each industry we represent which makes us uniquely qualified to select and present candidates of the highest quality in our areas of specialty.

Key Contact - Specialty:
Mr. Jim Crigler, President
Mr. Kevin Kaufman, Account Executive - *Banking (Mortgage), Financial services, Leasing, Loans, Real estate*
Mr. Ernie Culp, Global Technology Recruiter - *ATM, C-level, CRM, Defense, Disaster planning & recovery*
Mrs. Nancy Strelow, Account Executive - *CRM, General management, Information Technology, Marketing, Sales*
Mr. J.D. Oelke, Practice Leader, HighTech & Contact Ctr - *Information Technology, Management, Networking, Professional services, Telecommunications*

Salary Minimum: $60,000

Functions: Generalist (All), Management, Senior Mgmt., Middle Mgmt., Sales & Mktg., CFOs, Network Admin., Engineering

Industries: Generalist (All), Telecoms

MR of Central Mississippi-Jackson

(an affiliate of MRI)
1985 Lakcland Dr Ste 100
Jackson, MS 39216-5024
(601) 366-4488
Fax: (601) 366-4699
Email: jwgmr1@juno.com
Web: www.mrinet.com

Summary: A contingency search firm engaged in the placement of professional staff personnel.

Key Contact - Specialty:
Mr. J.W. Gardner, General Manager

Functions: Generalist (All), Board Members, Mfg., Product Dev.

Industries: Generalist (All), Textiles, Apparel, Lumber, Furniture, Paper, Accounting, Aerospace, Software

MR of Rankin Company

(an affiliate of MRI)
2506 Lakeland Dr Ste 305
Jackson, MS 39232-7640
(601) 936-7900
Fax: (601) 936-9004
Email: mrvanwick@aol.com

Summary: We service the food, beverage, pharmaceutical and consumer goods industries. The positions that we place include all manufacturing, including engineering, production management, QA, logistics, etc. for plant and corporate environments. In addition, we place R&D, scientists, planners and any supply chain professionals. We service from entry to executive.

Key Contact - Specialty:
Mr. Mike Van Wick, President - *Engineering, Technical*

Salary Minimum: $50,000

Functions: Mfg.

Industries: Food, Bev., Tobacco, Soap, Perf., Cosmtcs., Drugs Mfg., Consumer Elect.

SC of St. Louis

(an affiliate of MRI)
1415 Elbridge Payne Rd Ste 105
Chesterfield, MO 63017-8522
(636) 537-5295
Fax: (636) 537-9201
Email: resume@scstlouis.com
Web: www.scstlouis.com

Summary: We specialize in the placement of top sales, sales management and marketing talent. Our industry specialties include automotive, building products, consumer products, consumer hardware, housewares, retail, franchising and all areas of marketing, such as product management and marketing services.

Key Contact - Specialty:
Mr. Don Borgschulte, General Manager & Owner
Ms. Cindy Lorenz, Director, Recruiting
Ms. Mary Stickler, Director
Mr. Christopher Sievers, Account Executive
Ms. Kim Carlson, Administrative Manager
Mr. Joe Lynett, Account Executive
Mr. Darbi Riddle, Director

Salary Minimum: $50,000

Functions: Product Dev., Sales & Mktg., Sales Mgmt.

Industries: Food, Bev., Tobacco, Textiles, Apparel, Lumber, Furniture, Plastics, Rubber, Leather, Stone, Glass, Motor Vehicles, Computer Equip., Consumer Elect., Higher Ed., Publishing

MR of Lake Saint Louis

(an affiliate of MRI)
1101 Edgewater Pt
Lake Saint Louis, MO 63367-2906
(636) 625-1780
Fax: (636) 625-1788
Email: email@mrilsl.com
Web: www.mrilsl.com

Summary: We provide executive search and placement.

Key Contact - Specialty:
Mr. Jeff Fairchild, CSAM, Owner & President - *Plastics*

Salary Minimum: $30,000

Functions: Management, Mfg., Product Dev., Materials, Distribution, Engineering, Technicians

Industries: Medical Devices, Plastics, Rubber, Retail, Engineering Svcs., Packaging

MR of Laurie

(an affiliate of MRI)
PO Box 1509
Laurie, MO 65038-1509
(573) 374-9338
Fax: (573) 374-7745
Email: mcartella@charter.net
Web: www.ozarkgroup.com

Summary: Our office serves both the manufacturing and electronics industries.

Key Contact - Specialty:
Mr. Mike Cartella, Co-Manager
Ms. Janet Cartella, Co-Manager

Functions: Middle Mgmt., Mfg., Quality, Materials, Engineering

Industries: Computer Equip., Consumer Elect., Misc. Mfg., Electronic, Elec. Components

Westport One

(an affiliate of MRI)
11701 Borman Dr Ste 250
Saint Louis, MO 63146-4199
(314) 991-4355
(877) 709-8784
Fax: (314) 991-9586
Email: mr@westportone.com
Web: www.westportone.com

Summary: Full service executive search firm. Client-paid fees only. Our account executives specialize in the industries of: insurance, software sales, construction, engineering and banking.

Key Contact - Specialty:
Mr. Phil L. Bertsch, Chief Executive Officer & General Mgr
Mr. Chris Heinz, Operations & Training Manager
Mr. Rob Hunter, Manager
Mr. James Maxwell, Manager

Salary Minimum: $30,000

Functions: Management

Industries: Energy, Utilities, Food, Bev., Tobacco, Machine, Appliance, Banking, Brokers, Mutual/Hedge Funds, Misc. Financial, Legal, Development SW, Biotech/Life Sciences

MR of Omaha

(also know as WorldBridge Partners)
4885 S 118th St Ste 200
Omaha, NE 68137-2239
(402) 397-8320
(800) 825-8620
Fax: (402) 397-6322
Email: info@mriomaha.com
Web: www.mriomaha.com

Summary: We specialize in the areas of engineering, insurance, IT, pension & financial services, medical devices, 401k, food production management and managed care professionals.

Key Contact - Specialty:
Mr. Todd Dawson, CSAM, President - *Engineering, Financial services, Information Technology*
Ms. Allyson Bradin, Team Leader
Mr. Craig Koehler, Team Leader
Ms. Gloria Breese, Team Leader

Salary Minimum: $30,000

Functions: Management

Industries: Food, Bev., Tobacco, Brokers, Venture Cap., Mutual/Hedge Funds, Insurance, Casualty, Claims, Life, Software, Accounting SW

PowerBrokers LLC

(an affiliate of MRI)
12635 Izard St
Omaha, NE 68154-1241
(402) 498-8981
Fax: (402) 445-9736
Email: efisher@powerbrokersllc.com
Web: www.powerbrokersllc.com

Summary: Middle to senior level executives with technical and management experience in the power industry. Focus on all areas of the electric utility and natural gas industries emphasizing wholesale & retail sales & marketing, energy traders, quantitative analyst, risk management and individuals in asset acquisition and development.

Key Contact - Specialty:
Mr. Earl Fisher, Jr., Principal & Director - *Energy, Power*

Salary Minimum: $70,000

Functions: Generalist (All), Mktg. Research, Mktg. Mgmt., Sales Mgmt., Risk Mgmt., Engineering, Legal

Industries: Generalist (All), Energy, Utilities, Misc. Financial, Legal

Branches:
10836 W Beloit Pl
Denver, CO 80227-2625
(303) 716-2987
Fax: (303) 716-3426
Email: kate@powerbrokersllc.com
Key Contact - Specialty:
Ms. Kate Szablya, Principal

PO Box 263
Newark, DE 19715-0263
(302) 983-8899
Fax: (302) 369-3999
Email: rfodge@powerbrokersllc.com
Key Contact - Specialty:
Mr. Robert Fodge, Principal

MR of Lake Tahoe

(an affiliate of MRI)
1179 Fairview Dr Ste A
Carson City, NV 89701-7871
(775) 884-4700
Fax: (775) 884-4776
Email: jcargill@searchpros.net
Web: www.searchpros.net

Summary: We specialize in sourcing impact candidates, including sales, management and executive in transportation/logistics, and staff, management, and executive in healthcare/hospitals. Our reputation is solid, and our references are outstanding. Retained and contingency searches at competitive rates.

Key Contact - Specialty:
Mr. Jim Cargill, Owner & General Manager - *Distribution, Logistics, Transportation*
Mr. David C. Bailey, Senior Account Manager - *Distribution, Logistics, Transportation*
Ms. Tracy Glenn, Account Executive - *Emergency room, Healthcare, Hospital, Operating rooms, Surgical*

Salary Minimum: $50,000

Functions: Generalist (All), Management, Senior Mgmt., Middle Mgmt., Purchasing, Distribution, Nurses, Allied Health, HR Mgmt.

Industries: Transportation, Logistics Svcs., Healthcare, Hospitals, Physical Therapy, Occupational Therapy

MEI Search Consultants

(an affiliate of MRI)
272 Main St
Keene, NH 03431-4144
(603) 357-5000
Fax: (603) 357-5005
Email: contactus@meisearch.net
Web: www.meisearch.net

Summary: We focus on recruiting for outdoor power equipment manufacturers, in the functions of engineering, supply chain, finance, sales & marketing, EH&S, and human resources.

Key Contact - Specialty:
Mr. Robert C. Meissner, Jr., CSAM, Owner & General Manager - *Business development, Equipment, International, Marketing, Sales*
Ms. Emily St. Pierre, Administration Manager - *Equipment, Manufacturing, Power*

Ms. Shannon Sullivan, Administration Manager - *BSME, Design, Engineering, Quality*
Ms. Lisa Carpenter, Supply Chain Recruiting Specialist - *Materials, Procurement, Purchasing, Supply Chain*
Ms. Katie Corliss, Professional Services Recruiter - *Accounting, Environmental, Finance, Human resources, Safety*
Ms. Jennifer Chabott, Recruiter, Sales & Marketing - *Business development, Equipment, Marketing, Sales*
Ms. Leslie Lazarus, Recruiting Specialist, Sales & Marketing
Mr. Silas W. Caranna, Account Executive - *Sales*

Salary Minimum: $50,000

Functions: Quality, Materials, Purchasing, Mktg. Mgmt., Sales Mgmt., HR Mgmt., Budgeting, Eng. Design, Process, Int'l.

Industries: Agri., Forestry, Mining, Construction, Metal Products, Machine, Appliance

SC of Nashua-Manchester

(an affiliate of MRI)
165 Steinmetz Dr
Manchester, NH 03104-1830
(603) 629-0052
Email: salesconsultants-nash-man@att.net

Summary: We specialize in recruiting and placing sales, sales management, marketing, executive management (president, vice president, CFO, CEO, COO) computers, banking, industrial, medical, pharmaceutical, bio-technology and insurance people in permanent and temp positions. Our staff is expertly trained and each is well versed in the industries they represent, enabling them to talk your language and understand your needs.

Key Contact - Specialty:
Mr. Sheldon S. Baron, Manager - *Computers, Sales*

Salary Minimum: $25,000

Functions: Generalist (All), Management, Board Members, Middle Mgmt., Plant Mgmt., Sales & Mktg., Sales Mgmt., Finance

Industries: Generalist (All), Manufacturing, Food, Bev., Tobacco, Textiles, Apparel, Lumber, Furniture, Paper, Printing, Chemicals, Soap, Perf., Cosmtcs., Drugs Mfg., Medical Devices, Metal Products, Machine, Appliance, Computer Equip., Consumer Elect., Misc. Mfg., Electronic, Elec. Components, Consumer Goods, Wholesale, Retail, Finance, Banking, Services, Communications, Telecoms, Environmental Svcs., Accounting SW, Database SW, Biotech/Life Sciences, Hospitals

SC on Elm

(an affiliate of MRI)
1087 Elm St Ste 404
Manchester, NH 03101-1849
(603) 666-4466
Fax: (603) 666-5588
Email: jrichards@mriscelm.com
Web: www.scneedham.com

Summary: We specialize in the recruitment of product development, buying and operations professionals for national catalog companies and specialty and department store chains. The companies we serve have a diverse range of products from collectibles and gifts to apparel and accessories for men, women and children.

Key Contact - Specialty:
Mr. James Richards, Jr., President
Ms. Leslie Richards, Vice President, Administration
Ms. Mary Johansen, Executive Assistant
Mr. Jack Leflar, Account Executive

Salary Minimum: $50,000

Functions: Senior Mgmt., Specialized Svcs.

Industries: Retail

MR of Bay Head

(an affiliate of MRI)
106 Bridge Ave Ste 3
Bayhead Commons
Bay Head, NJ 08742-5073
(732) 714-1300
Fax: (732) 714-1311
Email: recruiter@mrielectrical.com
Web: www.mrielectrical.com

Summary: Our firm specializes in all jobs (except clerical) in: electrical, electronics, factory automation, process controls, hardware, software and services. We provide services for sales, marketing, engineering, manufacturing, service and management.

Key Contact - Specialty:
Mr. Robert P. Ceresi, General Manager - *Electrical, Electronics*
Ms. Carole Ceresi, Co-Manager - *Electrical, Electronics*

Salary Minimum: $40,000

Functions: Management, Board Members, Middle Mgmt., Mfg., Sales & Mktg., Systems Dev., Systems Implem., R&D, Engineering

Industries: Machine, Appliance, Computer Equip., Test, Measure Equip., Misc. Mfg., Electronic, Elec. Components, Robotics, Semiconductors, Equip Svcs.

MR of Hillsborough

971 US Highway 202 N Ste 7
Branchburg, NJ 08876-3757
(908) 722-3525
Fax: (908) 722-3253
Email: vincea@mrhillsborough.com
Web: www.mrhillsborough.com

Summary: We are a full service search firm specializing in the recruitment of executive and mid-level management positions for the construction and retail industries as well as logistics and supply chain. Specialty, general merchandise, food and automotive. Retained and contingency fee basis.

Key Contact - Specialty:
Mr. Vince Albrecht, President - *Retail, Supermarkets, Supply Chain, Traffic, Transportation*
Mrs. Bobbie Albrecht, Vice President - *Building products, Construction, Engineering, Retail, Supply Chain*

Functions: Generalist (All), Management

Industries: Generalist (All)

MR of Bedminster

(an affiliate of MRI)
971 US Highway 202 N Ste 6
Branchburg, NJ 08876-3757
(908) 541-9223
Fax: (908) 541-9230
Email: alhauser@prodigy.net
Web: www.mrinetwork.com

Summary: With the extensive reach of a large network, we have a strong referral and support infrastructure. Our office is individually-owned, enabling us to provide our clients with customized, personalized attention on their staffing assignments.

Key Contact - Specialty:
Mr. Al Hauser, SPHR, President - *General management, Human resources, Middle management, Retail, Telecommunications*
Ms. Trish Lewis, Account Executive - *Consumer (Products), General management, Retail*

Salary Minimum: $50,000

Functions: Generalist (All), Management, HR Mgmt.

Industries: Generalist (All), Retail

MR/SC of Bridgewater

(an affiliate of MRI)
991 US Highway 22 Ste 106
Bridgewater, NJ 08807-2957
(908) 725-2595
Fax: (908) 725-0439
Email: jobs@mrbridgewater.com
Web: www.mrbridgewater.com

Summary: We are committed to establishing a partnership with our clients. We are a premier provider of innovative and intelligent staffing solutions.

Key Contact - Specialty:
Mr. Barry S. Smith, President
Mr. Mark Egner, Director, Sales & Operations

Functions: Management, Middle Mgmt., Admin. Svcs.

Industries: Food, Bev., Tobacco, Brokers, Non-profits, Pharm Svcs., Legal, Accounting, Equip Svcs., HR Services, Insurance

SC of Cherry Hill

(an affiliate of MRI)
600 Kings Hwy N Ste 2
Cherry Hill, NJ 08034-1505
(856) 338-0400
(386) 677-2955
Fax: (386) 677-3605
Email: sccherryhill@aol.com
Web: www.brilliantpeople.com

Summary: Our office places sales & marketing professionals at all levels. We specialize in the consumer products industry (i.e.: packaged goods, food, beverages, HBC, hardware/tools, soft goods, hard goods, durables, furniture, bedding, case goods, appliances and accessories). We have many high-profile client companies in the CP and durable goods industries.

Key Contact - Specialty:
Mr. Jere Chambers, President & General Manager

Salary Minimum: $50,000

Functions: Sales & Mktg., Mktg. Mgmt., Sales Mgmt., Sales Reps.

Industries: Generalist (All), Food, Bev., Tobacco, Textiles, Apparel, Lumber, Furniture, Soap, Perf., Cosmtcs., Machine, Appliance, Consumer Elect., Consumer Goods, Wholesale, Retail

MR of Fairfield

(an affiliate of MRI)
271 US Highway 46 Ste D206
Fairfield, NJ 07004-2432
(973) 575-6660
Fax: (973) 575-9669
Email: mparker@mriscience.com
Web: www.brilliantpeople.com

Summary: We serve the pharmaceutical and medical device industries.

Key Contact - Specialty:
Mr. Mario Parker

Functions: Management, Quality, Sales & Mktg., R&D

Industries: Drugs Mfg., Medical Devices

SC of Essex County

(an affiliate of MRI)
30 Two Bridges Rd Ste 270
Fairfield, NJ 07004-1547
(973) 227-8292
Fax: (973) 575-4901
Email: sci@sci-intl.com
Web: www.sci-intl.com

Summary: We are top-level IT executive consulting and software/solutions sales search specialists.

Key Contact - Specialty:
Ms. Debbie Seminerio, Co-Manager

Functions: Board Members, Senior Mgmt., Middle Mgmt., Sales Mgmt., Mgmt. Consultants

Industries: Mgmt. Consulting, E-commerce, New Media, Telecoms, Software, ERP SW

Talbot Associates Inc

(also known as MR of Medford NJ)
30 Jackson Rd Ste C4
Medford, NJ 08055-9281
(609) 654-9109
Fax: (609) 654-9166
Email: wnt@talbotassociates.com
Web: www.talbotassociates.com

Summary: We are a nationwide search firm specializing exclusively in the recruitment of technical, engineering, regulatory, and scientific personnel for the pharmaceutical and biopharmaceutical community.

Key Contact - Specialty:
Mr. Norman Talbot, President - *Biopharmaceutical, Pharmaceutical*

Salary Minimum: $75,000

Functions: Management, Senior Mgmt., Middle Mgmt., Plant Mgmt., Quality, R&D, Engineering

Industries: Drugs Mfg., Medical Devices, Biotech/Life Sciences

MR of Edison

(an affiliate of MRI)
276 Main St
Metuchen, NJ 08840-2453
(732) 767-1025
Fax: (732) 767-1218
Email: nancy@mriedison.com
Web: www.mriedison.com

Summary: We have many years of direct, hands-on engineering experience and specialize in placing engineers, engineering management, quality, validation people in the pharmaceutical, and biotechnology industries.

Key Contact - Specialty:
Mr. Frank Noorani, President
Ms. Seema Bhatt, Recruiter - *Automation, Biotechnology, Engineering, Pharmaceutical, Quality*
Mrs. Maj Hudda, Office Manager
Ms. Priya Krishnan, Recruiter - *Biopharmaceutical, Biotechnology, Engineering, Manufacturing, Pharmaceutical*

Salary Minimum: $40,000

Functions: Senior Mgmt., Mfg., Production, Automation, Plant Mgmt., Quality, Materials, Packaging, Engineering

Industries: Chemicals, Drugs Mfg., Medical Devices, Pharm Svcs., Packaging, Biotech/Life Sciences

MR of Short Hills

(an affiliate of MRI)
181 Millburn Ave
Millburn, NJ 07041-1811
(973) 379-4020
(877) 379-4020
Fax: (973) 379-2699
Email: recruiter@mrishorthills.com
Web: www.mrishorthills.com

Summary: Our firm strives to be the premier
executive search practice providing ethical,
customized and efficient hiring processes. Our
team of experienced search specialists delivers a
high quality responsive solution by balancing the
needs of companies and individuals. Our services
are intended to enhance the lives of the individuals
and the businesses we touch.

Key Contact - Specialty:
Mr. Martin Nicoll, Managing Director
Mr. Bob Henches, Director, Professional Services
Ms. Sharon Nicoll, Recruiter, Internet

Salary Minimum: $50,000

Functions: Generalist (All), Middle Mgmt., Sales
& Mktg., Sales Mgmt., Customer Svc.

Industries: Generalist (All), Banking, Mgmt.
Consulting, E-commerce, IT Implementation,
Communications, Telecoms, Software,
Biotech/Life Sciences

The Harrington Group

(an affiliate of MRI)
1 High Street Ct
Morristown, NJ 07960-6861
(864) 585-5850
Fax: (864) 596-1037
Email: chip@harringtongroup.net
Web: www.hgus.com

Summary: Our mission is to be a high integrity
executive search and recruiting organization, who
specializes in the placement of professionals for
the insurance and consulting industry.

Key Contact - Specialty:
Mr. T. Paul Harrington, President
Mrs. Renee Neal, Account Executive
Mr. Robert Rivers, Account Executive

Salary Minimum: $75,000

Functions: Generalist (All), Sales & Mktg., Sales
Mgmt.

Industries: Generalist (All), Mgmt. Consulting,
HR Services, E-commerce, IT Implementation,
Insurance, Casualty, Commercial, Re-Insurance,
Real Estate, ERP SW, Security SW, System
SW, Training SW

MR of Bordentown

(an affiliate of MRI)
1200 S Church St Ste 1
Mount Laurel, NJ 08054-2936
(856) 727-0005
Email: rrr.mri@att.net

Summary: Search for management consulting
firms for utility industry: utilities and energy
firms.

Key Contact - Specialty:
Mr. Randy R. Ruschak, Managing Director -
Energy, Management consulting, Utilities

Salary Minimum: $50,000

Functions: Generalist (All), Middle Mgmt.,
Mgmt. Consultants

Industries: Generalist (All), Energy, Utilities,
Insurance

MR of Union County

(also known as Office Mates 5)
1100 Springfield Ave
Mountainside, NJ 07092-2906
(908) 789-9400
(908) 789-8805
Fax: (908) 789-8845
Email: mriunion@mriunion.com
Web: www.mriunion.com

Summary: Our past success is a direct reflection
of our commitment to the companies we serve.
Only by providing the necessary support and
services required by our clients will we become
'Partners in Profit' for the future.

Key Contact - Specialty:
Mr. Ro Malfetti, Managing Partner
Mr. Jim Malfetti, Managing Partner

Salary Minimum: $25,000

Functions: Generalist (All), Admin. Svcs., Sales
& Mktg., Risk Mgmt.

Industries: Construction, Manufacturing,
Consumer Elect., Wholesale, Finance, Banking,
Invest. Banking, Venture Cap., Services, Equip
Svcs., HR Services, Hospitality, Media,
Communications, Aerospace, Packaging,
Insurance, Real Estate, Software, Accounting
SW

MR of New Brunswick

(an affiliate of MRI)
46 Bayard St Ste 209
New Brunswick, NJ 08901-2152
(732) 246-1212
Fax: (732) 246-1241
Email: rjones@iteamsearch.com
Web: www.iteamsearch.com

Summary: Our firm specializes in the
identification and qualification of outstanding
talent and opportunities in the IT industry. Our
clients rely on us for our ability to uncover
exceptional IT professionals and present them for
consideration. Similarly, our contacts value the
marketplace information we are able to provide.
These relationships are established over time and
the first step is getting acquainted.

Key Contact - Specialty:
Mr. Randy Jones, Vice President
Mr. Michael Rose, President

Salary Minimum: $50,000

Functions: Generalist (All)

Industries: IT Implementation

BrainWorks Inc

(an affiliate of MRI)
139 South St Ste 104
New Providence, NJ 07974-1999
(908) 771-0600
Fax: (908) 771-0779
Email: bw@brainworksinc.com
Web: www.brainworksinc.com

Summary: Executive search firm specializing in
consumer package goods, direct marketing,
Technology sales and pharmaceuticals.

Key Contact - Specialty:
Mr. Andrew S. Miller, President

Salary Minimum: $50,000

Functions: Generalist (All), Management, Sales
& Mktg., Mktg. Research, Direct Mktg., Credit,
Risk Mgmt., IT, R&D

Industries: Generalist (All), Food, Bev., Tobacco,
Soap, Perf., Cosmtcs., Drugs Mfg., Software,
Database SW, Development SW, Doc. Mgmt.,
Production SW, ERP SW, Industry Specific

SW, Mfg. SW, Networking, Comm. SW,
Biotech/Life Sciences

SC of Northern Jersey

(an affiliate of MRI)
11 E Oak St
Oakland, NJ 07436-2721
(201) 651-9200
Fax: (201) 651-1330
Email: whs@scnorthjersey.com
Web: www.scnorthjersey.com

Summary: We specialize in finding sales, sales
management and marketing professionals with
proven track records of success.

Key Contact - Specialty:
Mr. William Soodsma, President - *Sales*
Ms. Christine Conerly, Project Coordinator,
Consumer Industry
Mr. Neal Bruce, National Account Executive
Ms. Nancy Bruining, Project Coordinator

Functions: Generalist (All), Senior Mgmt.,
Advertising, Mktg. Research, Mktg. Mgmt.,
Sales Mgmt.

Industries: Generalist (All)

SC of Morris County

(an affiliate of MRI)
364 Parsippany Rd Ste 8B
Parsippany, NJ 07054-5110
(973) 887-3838
Fax: (973) 887-2304
Email: scmorris@marketing-sales.com
Web: www.marketing-sales.com

Summary: We specialize in sales and sales
management and secondarily in marketing. Our
expertise extends to the functional scientific areas
of R&D, QC, Product Application and Regulatory.
We focus in market areas related to engineering
services, chemicals (including flavors, personal
care, and pharmaceuticals), process equipment,
and consumer packaged goods & foods.

Key Contact - Specialty:
Mr. Ernie Bivona, President
Mr. Slater Isenberg, Recruiter
Mr. Nicholas Leno, Recruiter
Ms. Gloria Vega, Recruiter
Mr. Robert Vernicek, Recruiter

Salary Minimum: $30,000

Functions: Quality, Sales & Mktg., Mktg.
Research, Sales Mgmt., R&D

Industries: Construction, Food, Bev., Tobacco,
Chemicals, Soap, Perf., Cosmtcs., Drugs Mfg.,
Consumer Elect., Consumer Goods,
Architectural Svcs., Mgmt. Consulting,
Engineering Svcs.

SC of Middlesex County

(an affiliate of MRI)
10 Corporate Pl S Ste 106
Piscataway, NJ 08854-6148
(732) 981-8008
Fax: (732) 981-1187
Email: info@scmiddlesex.com
Web: www.scmiddlesex.com

Summary: Our office specializes in the packaging
industry; Focusing on the corrugated box sector.
We concentrate in sales, sales management,
marketing, production, operations, general
management and corporate level positions in the
industry.

Key Contact - Specialty:
Mr. James K. Malloy, President

Salary Minimum: $50,000

Functions: Generalist (All)

Industries: Paper, Packaging

Davalyn Corporation

(also known as SC of Hudson County)
1240 Sussex Turnpike Ste B
Randolph, NJ 07869-2944
(973) 895-5330
(800) 797-5228
Fax: (973) 895-5502
Email: manager@davalyncorp.com
Web: www.davalyncorp.com

Summary: Annually awarded the industry's top honors, we bring you a distinguished history of professional experience. Our family of staffing solutions has a proven record of success and is at the heart of a philosophy that has helped us earn a reputation as one of the most dependable firms in the business.

Key Contact - Specialty:
Mr. Richard K. Sinay, President

Functions: Generalist (All)

Industries: Food, Bev., Tobacco, Drugs Mfg., Robotics, Consumer Goods, Pharm Svcs.

The Metier Group

(also known as MR of Ridgewood)
10 Garber Sq Ste 7
Ridgewood, NJ 07450-3129
(201) 612-8805
Fax: (201) 612-6630
Email: resume@metiergroup.biz
Web: www.metiergroup.biz

Summary: We recognize that your people are one of the most critical factors contributing to your organizations success. Our mission is to recruit talented professionals at all levels that will ensure your company or firm surpasses its objectives. Our team consists of executive recruiters and consultants who were previously employed in the consumer products, legal, publishing, retail, services, and non-profit and insurance industries.

Key Contact - Specialty:
Ms. Wendy Larkin, Managing Partner -
  Consumer (Products), Food & beverage, Human resources, Marketing, Sales
Mr. Steve Larkin, Managing Partner - *Consumer (Packaged Goods,Products), Executives, Marketing, Sales*
Ms. Barbara Kalish, JD, Executive Search Consultant - *Human resources, Legal, Legal (Attorneys,Lawyers)*

Salary Minimum: $85,000

Functions: Senior Mgmt., Middle Mgmt., Product Dev., Sales & Mktg., Mktg. Research, Mktg. Mgmt., Sales Mgmt., HR Mgmt., Benefits, Legal

Industries: Generalist (All), Manufacturing, Food, Bev., Tobacco, Textiles, Apparel, Soap, Perf., Cosmtcs., Machine, Appliance, Computer Equip., Consumer Elect., Misc. Mfg., Consumer Goods, Finance, Services, Legal, Hospitality, Media, Communications, Biotech/Life Sciences, Healthcare, Non-Classifiable

MR of Northern Monmouth County

(an affiliate of MRI)
1129 Broad St Ste 8
Shrewsbury, NJ 07702-4333
(732) 578-0100
Fax: (732) 578-1800
Email: jobs@mrienergy.com
Web: www.mrienergy.com

Summary: We offer executive recruitment for the energy industry and for the optical communications, photonics and semiconductor industries.

Key Contact - Specialty:
Mr. Robert E. Goehring, Managing Partner
Mr. Todd J. Goehring, Managing Partner
Mr. Michael L. Jukofsky, Business Unit Manager

Functions: Engineering

Industries: Energy, Utilities, Construction, Manufacturing, Telecoms, Digital, Fiber Optic

MR of Stanhope

(an affiliate of MRI)
4 Waterloo Rd
Stanhope, NJ 07874-2653
(973) 691-2020
Fax: (973) 691-0728
Email: max@recruiter.com
Web: www.ittrade.com

Summary: Our focus is to place sales executives who develop, design, sell and implement next generation, complex enterprise technologies, which empower Fortune 500 companies to compete in today's market

Key Contact - Specialty:
Mr. Arthur L. Young, Managing Director
Ms. Janet Joyce, Director

Salary Minimum: $90,000

Functions: Middle Mgmt., Sales & Mktg., IT, Systems Implem.

Industries: Communications, Digital, Wireless, Network Infrastructure, Software, Database SW, Marketing SW, Networking, Comm. SW, Security SW

SC of Summit

(also known as Remus Klimaski & Associates)
86 Summit Ave
Summit, NJ 07901-3647
(908) 522-0700
Fax: (908) 522-0785
Email: mri-sc-summit@verizon.net

Summary: Specializing in process machinery and equipment sales & marketing (especially pumps) to the petroleum, chemical, petrochemical, power, pharmaceutical, food and other process industries.

Key Contact - Specialty:
Mr. Remus J. Klimaski, CSAM, Manager

Salary Minimum: $50,000

Functions: Sales & Mktg., Engineering

Industries: Oil & Gas, Construction, Manufacturing, Food, Bev., Tobacco, Paper, Chemicals, Drugs Mfg., Paints, Petro. Products, Equip Svcs., Engineering Svcs.

MR of Wayne

40 Galesi Dr Ste 17
Wayne, NJ 07470-4844
(973) 812-7200
Fax: (973) 812-7270
Email: joemriwayne@earthlink.net
Web: www.mr-waynenj.com

Summary: Our firm is dedicated to conducting candidate searches, which are customized to meet your specific hiring needs. We specialize in placing candidates within the food, beverage, natural foods, consumer products, and point of purchase/display/fixtures industries.

Key Contact - Specialty:
Mr. Joe A. Herrmann, President - *Consumer (Marketing,Packaged Goods,Products), Controllers, Cosmetics*

Ms. Kim Stillman, Project Coordinator -
  Accounting, Consumer (Products), Food, Food & beverage, Food service
Mrs. Maryanne Macaluso, Project Coordinator
Ms. Gabrielle Broderek, Account Executive -
  Accounting, Administration, Clerical, Sales

Salary Minimum: $40,000

Functions: Generalist (All)

Industries: Generalist (All), Manufacturing, Food, Bev., Tobacco, Plastics, Rubber, Consumer Goods

MR of Woodbridge

(an affiliate of MRI)
1 Woodbridge Ctr Ste 700
Woodbridge, NJ 07095-1160
(732) 636-9000
Fax: (732) 636-5000
Email: renu@mriwoodbridge.com
Web: www.mriwoodbridge.com

Summary: Our firm is a supplier of temp and permanent, executive and technical personnel staffing services.

Key Contact - Specialty:
Mrs. Rama Jiandani, Manager

Functions: Generalist (All)

Industries: Energy, Utilities, Drugs Mfg., Electronic, Elec. Components, Banking, E-commerce, IT Implementation, Advertising, Fiber Optic, Software, Biotech/Life Sciences

MR of The Sandias

(an affiliate of MRI)
10400 Academy Rd NE Ste 204
Albuquerque, NM 87111-7370
(505) 292-9800
Email: don@hireimpactplayers.com
Web: www.hireimpactplayers.com

Summary: Recruitment and placement of finance/banking, food & beverage management, commercial construction management, engineering, technology, healthcare information technology, insurance, and sales professionals nationwide.

Key Contact - Specialty:
Mr. Don Ancona, President & Owner

Salary Minimum: $50,000

Functions: Management, Senior Mgmt., Middle Mgmt., Sales Mgmt., Sales Reps.

Industries: Construction, Retail, Finance, Banking, Architectural Svcs., Engineering Svcs., Restaurants, Quick Service Restaurants, Full Service Restaurants

MR of Albuquerque

(an affiliate of MRI)
2500 Louisiana Blvd NE Ste 506
Albuquerque, NM 87110-4319
(505) 346-4700
Fax: (505) 346-4701
Email: eg@mrialbq.com
Web: www.mrialbq.com

Summary: Our firm is an award winning search and recruitment firm specializing in several industries.

Key Contact - Specialty:
Mr. Tom J. Schneider, Manager

Functions: Management, Middle Mgmt., Mfg., Production, Plant Mgmt., Quality, Sales & Mktg., HR Mgmt.

Industries: Food, Bev., Tobacco, Chemicals, Soap, Perf., Cosmtcs., Drugs Mfg., Medical Devices, Plastics, Rubber, Machine, Appliance,

Computer Equip., Consumer Elect., Test, Measure Equip., Electronic, Elec. Components, Robotics, Consumer Goods, HR Services

SC of Albuquerque

(an affiliate of MRI)
11005 Spain Rd NE Ste 3
Albuquerque, NM 87111-1899
(505) 323-7300
Email: jt@mrisales.com
Web: www.mrisales.com

Summary: We specialize in top legal talent for law firms and corporate companies. We recruit attorneys and paralegals only.

Key Contact - Specialty:
Ms. Judith Terry, Manager

Salary Minimum: $80,000

Functions: Attorneys, Paralegals

Industries: Legal

MR of Broome County

(an affiliate of MRI)
20 Hawley St Ste 605W
West Tower
Binghamton, NY 13901-3210
(607) 722-2243
(800) 805-1581
Fax: (607) 722-2456
Email: mrbroome@therecruiters.com
Web: www.therecruiters.com

Summary: We are experts in IT, sales & marketing and finance, professionally trained in the art of search and recruitment. We are solution oriented and understand the problems, needs and expectations of your functional executives and organizations.

Key Contact - Specialty:
Mr. Mark Wallace, President - *Finance, Sales*

Salary Minimum: $30,000

Functions: Management, Mfg., Product Dev., Finance, IT, Engineering

Industries: Generalist (All), Manufacturing, Food, Bev., Tobacco, Textiles, Apparel, Lumber, Furniture, Paper, Printing, Plastics, Rubber, Consumer Elect., Misc. Mfg., Consumer Goods, Services, Non-profits, Accounting, IT Implementation, Higher Ed., Communications, Network Infrastructure, Packaging, Software, Mfg. SW, System SW

StraussGroup Inc

(also known as MR of Williamsville)
8203 Main St Ste 2
Buffalo, NY 14221-6051
(716) 631-3200
Fax: (716) 631-3222
Email: randy@straussgroup.com
Web: www.straussgroup.com

Summary: We are a focused national search firm specializing in the placement of top professionals in the financial services, mortgage banking, health care, engineering, technology and insurance industries.

Key Contact - Specialty:
Mr. Randy Strauss, Managing Partner - *Banking (Investment,Mortgage,Retail), Financial services, Human resources*
Mr. Daniel Myers, Managing Partner - *Banking (Commercial,Investment,Merchant,Retail)*
Mr. Daniel Weinreib, Division Director - *Healthcare, Home health, Hospital*
Ms. Jill Gregory, Account Executive

Salary Minimum: $100,000

Functions: Generalist (All), Board Members, Finance

Industries: Misc. Mfg., Finance, Banking, Invest. Banking, Brokers, Venture Cap., Mutual/Hedge Funds, Misc. Financial, HR Services, Software, Healthcare, Hospitals

SC of Syracuse

(an affiliate of MRI)
212 Highbridge St Ste B
Fayetteville, NY 13066-1979
(315) 637-0619
Fax: (315) 637-0621
Email: mri.sc@verizon.net

Summary: Our firm is an executive recruiter that specializes in sales and sales management.

Key Contact - Specialty:
Mr. Douglas L. Welker, Manager - *Sales*

Functions: Sales & Mktg., Sales Mgmt.

Industries: Generalist (All), Medical Devices, Pharm Svcs., Database SW

MR of Orange County

(an affiliate of MRI)
PO Box 1530
Greenwood Lake, NY 10925-1530
(845) 477-9509
(973) 625-4822
Fax: (973) 625-8117
Email: mriny@warwick.net

Summary: We are confidential, honest professionals. We are committed to the pursuit of excellence with integrity and standards that put us ahead of our competitors.

Key Contact - Specialty:
Ms. Carolyn A. Chermak, President - *Engineering*
Mr. Charles Chermak, Vice President - *Energy, Engineering, Environmental, Geology, Transportation*

Functions: Generalist (All), Engineering, Environmentalists

Industries: Generalist (All), Energy, Utilities, Construction, Manufacturing, Architectural Svcs., Legal, Engineering Svcs., Compliance, Environmental Svcs., Haz. Waste

The Rachman Group

(also known as MR of Huntington)
33 Walt Whitman Rd Ste 232
Huntington Station, NY 11746-4293
(631) 547-5464
Fax: (631) 547-5465
Email: info@mrhuntington.com
Web: www.mrhuntington.com

Summary: We specialize in senior sales positions, executive and management positions that are focused in sales. We work with companies on a retained and/or exclusive relationship. Our desk focus is outsourcing, CRM, imaging, on demand print, legal technologies, consulting companies and document management positions. We were recently awarded as one of the fastest growing recruitment firms within our franchise.

Key Contact - Specialty:
Mr. Scott Rachman, Managing Partner
Ms. Fran Zeiler, Director, Recruiting - *Business development, Sales, Technology, Telecommunications*

Salary Minimum: $60,000

Functions: Senior Mgmt., Sales & Mktg., Sales Mgmt.

Industries: Printing, Services, Legal, Equip Svcs., Mgmt. Consulting, HR Services, Call Centers, Software, Non-Classifiable

Fairway Consulting Group

(an affiliate of MRI)
300 Merrick Rd Ste 404
Lynbrook, NY 11563-2522
(516) 596-2800
Email: krw@jobsrecruiting.com
Web: www.jobsrecruiting.com

Summary: We are a leading executive search firm dedicated to the pharmaceutical, biotechnology and medical device industries. We fill middle management to senior executive positions in marketing, market research, business development, sales operations, clinical development, medical affairs, managed care, regulatory affairs, QA, and more.

Key Contact - Specialty:
Mr. John Wiener, Chief Executive Officer - *Biopharmaceutical, Biotechnology, Medical (Devices), Pharmaceutical*

Functions: Senior Mgmt., Product Dev., Quality, Physicians, Sales & Mktg., Mktg. Research, Mktg. Mgmt., Sales Reps., R&D

Industries: Drugs Mfg., Medical Devices, Pharm Svcs., Biotech/Life Sciences

Merraine Group Inc

(also known as MR of Rockland County)
1 Executive Blvd Ste 110A
Montebello, NY 10901-4156
(845) 357-3355
(845) 362-4260
Fax: (845) 357-3393
Email: information@merrainegroup.com
Web: www.merraine.com

Summary: An executive search firm specializing in the healthcare, financial services and printing industries. Clients include leading hospitals, nursing homes, banks, brokerages, printers and publishers. Woman owned business.

Key Contact - Specialty:
Ms. Meredith J. Gantshar, President & Chief Executive Officer
Mr. David J. Gantshar, Executive Director
Ms. Barbara Ratner, Vice President, Career Development - *Biotechnology, Business development, Marketing, Pharmaceutical, Physicians*

Salary Minimum: $40,000

Functions: Management, Senior Mgmt., Middle Mgmt., Admin. Svcs., Mfg., Healthcare, Physicians, Nurses, Allied Health, Sales & Mktg.

Industries: Printing, Publishing, Healthcare, Hospitals, Long-term/Home Care, Dental, Physical Therapy, Occupational Therapy, Women's

MR of Gramercy

(an affiliate of MRI)
200 Park Ave S Ste 1510
New York, NY 10003-1522
(212) 505-5530
Email: admin1@quik.com
Web: www.managementrecruitersny.com

Summary: We are specialists in mid - executive level placement and consummate professionals, committed to the pursuit of excellence with uncompromising integrity.

Key Contact - Specialty:
Mr. Stephen D. Schwartz, President - *Advertising, Communications, Marketing*

Salary Minimum: $35,000

Functions: Generalist (All), Sales & Mktg., Advertising, Mktg. Research, Mktg. Mgmt., Sales Mgmt., Direct Mktg., PR

Industries: Generalist (All), Pharm Svcs., Media, Advertising, Publishing, New Media, Telecoms, Healthcare

MR of Manhattan on Broadway

(an affiliate of MRI)
350 7th Ave
New York, NY 10001-5013
(212) 974-7676
Fax: (212) 974-8585
Email: info@mrusa.com
Web: www.mrusa.com

Summary: We are part of the largest and most successful executive search and recruitment organizations offering permanent executive search services.

Key Contact - Specialty:
Mr. Richard Cohen, President - *Marketing*

Salary Minimum: $65,000

Functions: Generalist (All), Board Members, Middle Mgmt., Sales & Mktg., Mktg. Mgmt., Sales Mgmt., Direct Mktg., Sales Reps., Credit, Risk Mgmt.

Industries: Generalist (All), Banking, Accounting, Media, Advertising, Broadcast, Film, Call Centers, Telephony

MR/SC of Rochester

(an affiliate of MRI)
16 W Main St Ste 225
Rochester, NY 14614-1604
(585) 454-2440
Fax: (585) 454-4092
Email: jannesi@yahoo.com
Web: www.mrinet.com

Summary: Recruit engineering, manufacturing, quality and support candidates. Recruit pharmaceutical, medical sales and management candidates.

Key Contact - Specialty:
Mr. Jerry Annesi, Manager
Mr. Mark Simmons, Account Executive
Mr. Dan McLaughlin, BSBA, Account Executive

Salary Minimum: $50,000

Functions: Mfg., Production, Sales & Mktg.

Industries: Medical Devices, Metal Products, Machine, Appliance, Test, Measure Equip., Misc. Mfg., Pharm Svcs., Engineering Svcs., Logistics Svcs., Supply Chain Mgmt., Biotech/Life Sciences, Healthcare

Saratoga Source LLC

(an affiliate of MRI)
444 Broadway Ste 202
Saratoga Springs, NY 12866-2260
(518) 583-4500
Fax: (518) 583-2775
Email: jim@thesaratogasource.com
Web: www.thesaratogasource.com

Summary: We specialize in executive search and all functions in the following market segments: manufacturing, business consulting, fuel cells, physical security, alternate power and electronics.

Key Contact - Specialty:
Mr. Jim Pabis, President - *Engineering*

Functions: Generalist (All), Senior Mgmt., Middle Mgmt., Sales Mgmt., Customer Svc., CFOs, MIS Mgmt., Engineering, Mgmt. Consultants

Industries: Generalist (All), Chemicals, Misc. Mfg., Mgmt. Consulting, Security SW

The Hampton Group

(also known as MR of The Hamptons)
33 Flying Point Rd
Southampton, NY 11968-5248
(631) 287-3330
Fax: (631) 287-5610
Email: hamptongrp@hamptongrp.com
Web: www.hamptongrp.com

Summary: We are an executive search firm specializing in placing mid and senior level management in the medical, pharmaceutical and biotechnology industries. Our knowledge of the marketplace and database profiles of candidates and companies enables us to quickly target and identify contacts that closely match specific profiles.

Key Contact - Specialty:
Ms. Belle Lareau, Partner - *Biotechnology, Diagnostics, Pharmaceutical*
Mr. Gerard Lareau, Partner - *Biotechnology*
Ms. Beverly Norindr, Senior Account Executive
Ms. Virginia Kearns, Senior Account Executive - *Biopharmaceutical, Biotechnology, Pharmaceutical, Physicians, Psychiatry*
Mr. Harold Thiers, Account Executive - *Biopharmaceutical, Biotechnology, Medical, Medical (Devices), Pharmaceutical*
Ms. Minerva Perez, Account Executive - *Biopharmaceutical, Biotechnology, Medical, Pharmaceutical*
Mr. Ronnie Apfel, Account Executive - *Biopharmaceutical, Biotechnology, Business development, Marketing, Pharmaceutical*

Salary Minimum: $60,000

Functions: Management, Senior Mgmt., Mfg., Product Dev., Quality, Physicians, Sales & Mktg., Mktg. Research, Engineering

Industries: Drugs Mfg., Pharm Svcs., Biotech/Life Sciences

MR of Kingston

(an affiliate of MRI)
PO Box 386
Stone Ridge, NY 12484-0386
(845) 687-4739
Email: bobmrik@attglobal.net

Summary: The industries that we specialize in are chemical and pharmaceutical raw materials. We place positions in R&D, sales & marketing only in above industries.

Key Contact - Specialty:
Mr. Robert A. Mackenzie, CSAM, CPC, President - *Chemical, Executives, Marketing, Sales*

Salary Minimum: $75,000

Functions: Sales & Mktg., R&D

Industries: Chemicals, Paints, Petro. Products

MR of Woodbury

(an affiliate of MRI)
100 Crossways Park Dr W Ste 208
Woodbury, NY 11797-2012
(516) 364-9290
Fax: (516) 364-4478
Email: mrcareers@mrcareers.com
Web: www.mrcareers.com

Summary: Specialize in placing middle and senior management personnel in pharmaceutical, medical device, data processing, banking and consumer products.

Key Contact - Specialty:
Mr. Bill Jose, General Manager
Mr. Warren Kornfeld, Vice President

Mr. Chris Callahan, Account Manager
Mr. Ed Abinette, Executive Recruiter, Consumer Goods & Bu

Salary Minimum: $35,000

Functions: Generalist (All), Physicians, Mktg. Mgmt., Sales Mgmt., MIS Mgmt., Systems Analysis, Systems Dev., R&D

Industries: Generalist (All), Drugs Mfg., Medical Devices, Consumer Elect., Pharm Svcs., Insurance, Software

SC of Asheville

(an affiliate of MRI)
204 Charlotte Hwy Ste H
Asheville, NC 28803-8681
(828) 296-1986
Fax: (828) 296-1987
Email: info@searchexecs.com
Web: www.searchexecs.com

Summary: We specialize in helping companies in educational, technical, and professional publishing locate qualified personnel to meet their staffing needs, both in the sales/sales management and editorial/management areas.

Key Contact - Specialty:
Mr. Walter Dinteman, President
Mr. Jim Brown, Administrative Assistant - *Publishing*

Functions: Generalist (All)

Industries: Publishing

MR of Gastonia North

(an affiliate of MRI)
32 N Main St
Belmont, NC 28012-3162
(704) 825-0383
(877) 825-0383
Fax: (704) 825-0386
Email: search@kissfrog.com
Web: www.kissfrog.com

Summary: We specialize in medical device engineering, sales & marketing. The positions that we place are in project management, R&D/QA,QE,QC/ & manufacturing engineers. We place from technical level through engineering or sales & marketing management.

Key Contact - Specialty:
Ms. Mary Deal, Vice President
Mr. Randall Bormann, Vice President
Mr. Chuck Deal, Recruiter
Mrs. Susan Bormann, Secretary

Salary Minimum: $50,000

Functions: Management, Middle Mgmt., Mfg., Product Dev., Quality, Materials, Sales & Mktg., R&D, Engineering

Industries: Manufacturing, Medical Devices, Plastics, Rubber, Metal Products, Engineering Svcs.

MR of Burlington

(an affiliate of MRI)
2966 S Church St Ste 303
Burlington, NC 27215-5108
(336) 584-1295
Email: resume@mriburlington.com
Web: www.mriburlington.com

Summary: Providing technical, engineering, production and quality resources to clients in the specialty materials (i.e. chemicals, plastics, rubber and polymers) and the web processing (i.e. paper, film, tape, label and converting) industries.

Key Contact - Specialty:
Mr. Dick Pike, Owner & Manager - *Plastics*

Salary Minimum: $30,000

Functions: Management, Product Dev., Plant Mgmt., Quality, Engineering

Industries: Printing, Chemicals, Plastics, Rubber, Paints, Petro. Products

SC of Raleigh

(an affiliate of MRI)
107 Edinburgh South Dr Ste 213
Cary, NC 27511-6454
(919) 460-9595
Fax: (919) 460-0642
Email: rmc@mrirecruiter.net
Web: www.mrirecruiter.net

Summary: Office specialties: medical/pharmaceutical, packaging industry, industrial, instrumentation, insurance and advertising-nationally and all technical sales.

Key Contact - Specialty:
Mr. Mike Carfley, Chief Executive Officer & Mng Director
Ms. Susan Carfley, Owner & Business Manager

Salary Minimum: $70,000

Functions: Generalist (All), Management, Senior Mgmt., Sales Mgmt.

Industries: Manufacturing, Computer Equip., Test, Measure Equip., Services, Pharm Svcs., Equip Svcs., Mgmt. Consulting, HR Services, Media, Advertising, Telecoms, Software, Biotech/Life Sciences

The Biras Creek Group

(also known as SC of Chatham County)
11312 US Highway 15 501 N Ste 107
Chapel Hill, NC 27517-6377
(888) 774-2268
(919) 928-0082
Fax: (919) 928-0160
Email: sales@e-searchteam.com
Web: www.go2bcg.com

Summary: Our firm places senior management, middle management, clinical, R&D, regulatory, quality, business development and marketing professionals in the biotechnology/life sciences industry.

Key Contact - Specialty:
Mr. James Kessler, Managing Partner - *Aviation, Biotechnology, Pharmaceutical*
Ms. Betty Myers, Managing Partner - *Biopharmaceutical, Biotechnology, Pharmaceutical*

Functions: Generalist (All), Senior Mgmt., Middle Mgmt., Mfg., Product Dev., Quality, Sales & Mktg., Systems

Industries: Medical Devices, Aerospace, Software, Biotech/Life Sciences

MR of Chapel Hill

(also known as Day-Wrenn LLC)
88 VilCom Ctr Ste 185
Chapel Hill, NC 27514-1492
(919) 928-1101
Email: rice@mrchapelhill.com
Web: www.mrchapelhill.com

Summary: We utilize the network's proprietary approach Accelerated Recruitment approach to find the key individual who can make a positive impact on an entire team. Our proprietary Accelerated Recruitment approach is a customized combination of our streamlined methodology and the knowledge of our industry experts, from all over the world, designed specifically to help you target your next impact player and deliver them at the pace your business demands.

Key Contact - Specialty:
Mr. M. Rice Day, Jr., President & Chief Executive Officer - *Building products, Forest industry/products, Hardware, Lumber, Management*
Mr. Scott Oback, Vice President, Manufacturing Staffing - *Manufacturing, Plastics, Purchasing, Quality, Technical (Management)*
Mrs. Teri Pinheiro, Vice President, Biotech Pharma Staffing - *Biomedical, Biopharmaceutical, Biotechnology, Business development*
Mr. Charles Hipp, Vice President, Construction Staffing - *Construction, General contractors, General management, Management*
Ms. Peggy Britt, Vice President, Legal Staffing - *Executives, Intellectual property, Legal, Legal (Attorneys,Lawyers)*
Mr. Shaun O'Hara, Vice President, Financial Staffing - *Accounting, Accounting (Public), Asset management, CFOs*

Salary Minimum: $50,000

Functions: Senior Mgmt., Middle Mgmt., Plant Mgmt., Quality, Materials, Purchasing, Sales & Mktg., Sales Mgmt.

Industries: Agri., Forestry, Mining, Manufacturing, Lumber, Furniture, Plastics, Rubber, Paints, Petro. Products, Metal Products, Motor Vehicles, Misc. Mfg., Misc. Financial, Services, Supply Chain Mgmt

MR of Charlotte East

(an affiliate of MRI)
2101 Sardis Rd N Ste 102
Charlotte, NC 28227-7713
(704) 849-9200
Fax: (704) 849-9207
Email: frankq@makegooddecisions.com
Web: www.makegooddecisions.com

Summary: Specialize in pharmaceuticals, biologics, and medical devices. All medical affairs, regulatory and quality assurance. We provide services for executive level, vice president, director and manager. MD, PhD, RN, and MBA.

Key Contact - Specialty:
Mr. Frank A. Quinn, CSAM, General Manager
Ms. Peggy Quinn, Manager

Salary Minimum: $75,000

Functions: Management, Senior Mgmt., Middle Mgmt., Quality, Engineering

Industries: Drugs Mfg., Pharm Svcs., Biotech/Life Sciences

SC of Concord

(an affiliate of MRI)
254 Church St NE
Concord, NC 28025-4737
(704) 786-0700
Fax: (704) 782-1356
Email: britt@scconcord.com
Web: www.scconcord.com

Summary: Permanent placement search firm for companies that are re-engineering or adding specific industry expertise. Special IT skills in all phases of marketing and sales.

Key Contact - Specialty:
Mr. A.B. Pearson, PhD, Co-Founder
Ms. Anna Lee Pearson, MA, Co-Founder
Ms. Sherri Holiday, Executive Assistant
Mr. Britt Leatherman, President & Chief Executive Officer

Salary Minimum: $100,000

Functions: Sales & Mktg.

Industries: E-commerce, IT Implementation, Software, ERP SW, Networking, Comm. SW

MR of Davidson

(an affiliate of MRI)
710 Northeast Dr Ste 8
Davidson, NC 28036-7424
(704) 896-8890
Fax: (704) 896-8933
Email: joebubenzer@mrdavidson.com
Web: www.mrdavidson.com

Summary: Our firm specializes in all positions within the building products industry, including but not limited to: windows, doors, cabinets, shutters, siding, decking, etc.

Key Contact - Specialty:
Mr. Joe Bubenzer, Owner

Salary Minimum: $45,000

Functions: Engineering

Industries: Lumber, Furniture

MR of Enfield

(an affiliate of MRI)
111 N Railroad St
Enfield, NC 27823-1334
(252) 445-4251
Fax: (703) 852-4440
Email: search2@mindspring.com

Summary: Our firm, part of the world's largest search franchise, specializes in the paper and plastic packaging industry, covering the areas of plastic film and plastic foam extrusion, as well as converting, coating, laminating, flexographic and rotogravure printing.

Key Contact - Specialty:
Mr. Marvin G. Snook, Co-Manager
Ms. Maria P. Snook, Co-Manager

Functions: Senior Mgmt., Middle Mgmt., Mfg., Materials, Sales & Mktg.

Industries: Paper, Plastics, Rubber

MR of Fayetteville

(an affiliate of MRI)
951 S McPherson Church Rd Ste 105
Fayetteville, NC 28303-5383
(910) 483-2555
Fax: (910) 483-6524
Email: john.semmes@mrfayetteville.com
Web: www.mrfayetteville.com

Summary: We specialize in key account development in all areas of manufacturing operations: engineering, quality, design, electrical, mechanical, financial, HR and management and operating in various industries including appliances, motors, electronics and automotives.

Key Contact - Specialty:
Mr. John R. Semmes, Owner & President
Ms. Colleen Hodges, Operations Manager
Pat Hinson, Account Executive
Mr. Brian Grewe, Account Executive
Ms. Temperance Frey, Administrative Assistant

Salary Minimum: $30,000

Functions: Generalist (All), Mfg., Product Dev., Production, Plant Mgmt., Quality, Materials, HR Mgmt., Finance, Engineering

Industries: Manufacturing

SC of High Point West

(an affiliate of MRI)
175 Northpoint Ave Ste 106
High Point, NC 27262-7741
(336) 869-8700
Fax: (336) 869-8719

Email: schpw@northstate.net
Web: www.schighpoint.com

Summary: We are part of a large franchise system with teams specializing in technical and technical sales for the specialty and fine chemical industry.

Key Contact - Specialty:
Dr. Jim Stowers, Managing Director - *Chemical*

Salary Minimum: $50,000

Functions: Generalist (All)

Industries: Chemicals, Soap, Perf., Cosmtcs., Drugs Mfg.

MR of High Point North

(also known as The Everhart Group)
2121 Eastchester Dr Ste 101
High Point, NC 27265-1535
(336) 841-0123
Fax: (336) 841-0047
Email: greg@mreverhart.com
Web: www.mreverhart.com

Summary: Our firm focuses on the pharmaceutical industry and specializes in the functional areas of R&D, manufacturing and operations, regulatory affairs and compliance, quality assurance, quality control, validation and engineering.

Key Contact - Specialty:
Mr. Gregory Everhart, Managing Partner - *Manufacturing*
Mrs. Peggy Miller, Research Administrator - *Pharmaceutical*

Salary Minimum: $60,000

Functions: Generalist (All), Senior Mgmt., Middle Mgmt., Product Dev., Quality, Materials Plng., Distribution, Sales & Mktg., R&D, Engineering

Industries: Drugs Mfg., Pharm Svcs., Biotech/Life Sciences

MR of Charlotte North

(an affiliate of MRI)
103 Commerce Center Dr Ste 102
Huntersville, NC 28078-5803
(704) 947-0660
Fax: (704) 947-0705
Email: csherard@mrcn.com
Web: www.mrcn.com

Summary: Our firm specializes in HR and management consulting executive search. Our key functional areas include compensation, HR systems, HR strategy, customer relationship management, change management and IT.

Key Contact - Specialty:
Mr. Lawrence Duke, Owner - *Human resources, Management consulting*

Functions: HR Mgmt., Benefits, Training, MIS Mgmt., Systems Dev., Systems Support, Mgmt. Consultants

Industries: Generalist (All)

MR/SC of Jamestown

(an affiliate of MRI)
205A Hillstone Pl
Jamestown, NC 27282-2000
(336) 841-2050
Fax: (336) 841-2062
Email: mac@mribiotech.com
Web: www.mribiotech.com

Summary: We work exclusively with biotechnology clients.

Key Contact - Specialty:
Mr. Allen MacEntyre, President - *Biopharmaceutical, Biotechnology, Executives, Pharmaceutical, Senior management*

Functions: Generalist (All)

Industries: Biotech/Life Sciences

MR of Kannapolis

(an affiliate of MRI)
1787 Old Earnhardt Rd
Kannapolis, NC 28083-8023
(704) 938-6144
Fax: (704) 938-3480
Email: mrkannapolis@mrkannapolis.com
Web: www.mrkannapolis.com

Summary: Offering a full range of recruiting services. Specialties include IS, construction and healthcare.

Key Contact - Specialty:
Mr. T.H. Whitley, Manager

Functions: Management, Production, Automation, Nurses, Sales & Mktg., IT, Technicians

Industries: Generalist (All), Construction, Manufacturing, Computer Equip., Telecoms, Software, Healthcare, Hospitals

MR of Kings Mountain

(an affiliate of MRI)
PO Box 1969
Kings Mountain, NC 28086-1969
(704) 739-4401
Fax: (704) 739-0544
Email: lee@mrikingsmountain.com
Web: www.mrikingsmountain.com

Summary: We are an executive search firm and HR service organization dedicated to being your preeminent provider of HR and staffing solutions. We excel at locating, attracting, screening and making available the very best candidates for our clients needs. We have professionals who take a personalized approach to recruiting.

Key Contact - Specialty:
Mr. Lee Sherrill, Vice President, Business Development
Mrs. Johann Sherrill, Business Development, Industrial Admin
Mr. Tony Chapman, PE, Manufacturing Specialist - *Engineering, Environmental*
Mrs. Patsy Ledford, Healthcare Specialist - *Diagnostics, Hospital, Medical*

Functions: Generalist (All), Senior Mgmt., Mfg., Quality

Industries: Manufacturing, Drugs Mfg., Plastics, Rubber, Metal Products, Machine, Appliance, Motor Vehicles, Computer Equip., Consumer Elect., Misc. Mfg., Electronic, Elec. Components, Environmental Svcs., Aerospace, Hospitals

MR of Kinston

(an affiliate of MRI)
PO Box 219
Kinston, NC 28502-0219
(252) 527-9191
Fax: (252) 527-3625
Email: aturner@mrkinston.com
Web: www.mrkinston.com

Summary: Our firm has 5 account executives and a manager with many years of combined experience in recruiting engineering, manufacturing, and supply chain professionals.

Key Contact - Specialty:
Mr. Al W. Turner, President

Mr. Bob Thomas, CSAM, Account Manager - *Design, Mechanical*
Ms. Linda Gervasi, Account Manager - *BSME, Consumer (Durables,Marketing), Design*
Mr. Joey Smith, Account Manager - *BSME, Capital goods, Design, Engineering, Manufacturing*
Ms. Christina Riley, Account Manager - *Materials, Procurement, Purchasing, Supply Chain*

Salary Minimum: $40,000

Functions: Middle Mgmt., Mfg.

Industries: Plastics, Rubber, Metal Products, Machine, Appliance, Motor Vehicles, Computer Equip., Consumer Elect., Test, Measure Equip., Misc. Mfg., Electronic, Elec. Components

MR of Rockingham County

(an affiliate of MRI)
106 E Decatur St Ste A
Madison, NC 27025-1906
(336) 427-6153
Fax: (336) 427-6154
Email: jobs@mrrock.biz

Summary: We are recruiters specializing in textiles and general manufacturing. We staff all types of professionals and mid to upper management.

Key Contact - Specialty:
Mr. Gerald Summerlin, Manager

Functions: Generalist (All), Nurses

Industries: Generalist (All), Food, Bev., Tobacco, Textiles, Apparel, Plastics, Rubber, Metal Products, Misc. Mfg., Pharm Svcs., Accounting, Mgmt. Consulting

MR of Monroe

(an affiliate of MRI)
3513 W Highway 74 Ste A
Monroe, NC 28110-8441
(704) 291-7731
Fax: (704) 291-9689
Email: pirwin@mrimonroenc.com

Summary: We recruit in the food for operations, quality, engineering, maintenance and safety supervisors and managers for Fortune 500 food manufacturers. We believe in building strong relationships with clients to better serve their needs.

Key Contact - Specialty:
Mr. Phil Irwin, General Manager - *Food, Food & beverage, Operations, Quality, Technical*
Ms. Cathy Irwin, Manager - *Metals*

Salary Minimum: $50,000

Functions: Generalist (All)

Industries: Food, Bev., Tobacco, Consumer Goods

MR of Durham South

(an affiliate of MRI)
5920 S Miami Blvd Ste 203
Morrisville, NC 27560-8305
(919) 806-0990
Fax: (919) 806-0085
Email: loribb@mrdurham.com
Web: www.mrdurham.com

Summary: We are a retained, engaged and contingency search firm. We provide exceptional service to our clients through our industry knowledge, work ethic, and network of contacts and affiliations. Our repeat business speaks for our higher standards with both our clients and candidates.

Key Contact - Specialty:
Ms. Lori Bush, President - *C-level, Controllers, Electronics, Engineering, Human resources*
Mr. Jack Bush, Vice President, Operations - *Power, Sales, Semiconductors, Senior management, Technical (Management)*
Mr. William C. Eatherly, Account Executive - *Banking, Biotechnology, C-level, CEOs, CFOs*
Mr. Tom Carey, Account Executive - *Construction, Flexographic printing, Printing, Sales, Senior management*
Mr. Janathan A. Hesselink, Account Executive - *Accounting, CFOs, Controllers, Information Systems, Information Technology*
Mr. Steve Kozlow, Project Manager - *Components, Electrical, Electronics, Research & development, Semiconductors*
Ms. Susan Gidley, Internet Research - *Accounting, Information Systems, Information Technology, Internet, MIS*

Salary Minimum: $60,000

Functions: Management, Senior Mgmt., Production, Quality, Materials, Sales & Mktg., Mktg. Research, Finance, R&D, Engineering

Industries: Construction, Manufacturing, Printing, Chemicals, Drugs Mfg., Plastics, Rubber, Metal Products, Computer Equip., Consumer Elect., Test, Measure Equip., Misc. Mfg., Electronic, Elec. Components, Robotics, Semiconductors, Consumer Goods, Finance, Banking, Accounting, HR Services, Telecoms, Network Infrastructure, RF/Microwave, Defense, Packaging, Software, Biotech/Life Sciences

MR of Mount Airy

(an affiliate of MRI)
107 W Independence Blvd Ste B
Mount Airy, NC 27030-3589
(336) 719-2250
(888) 240-9255
Fax: (336) 719-2350
Email: mrmtairy@mvp-recruiters.com
Web: www.mvp-recruiters.com

Summary: Our search firm specializes in banking and manufacturing/electronics. We cover all functions within banking at the staff and management level. Within manufacturing/electronics, we cover R&D, engineering product, quality, manufacturing, manufacturing support functions in the semi-conductor and electronic passive components industry.

Key Contact - Specialty:
Mr. Donald F. Hackett, Owner & Manager - *Manufacturing*

Salary Minimum: $55,000

Functions: Generalist (All), Management, Board Members, Senior Mgmt., Middle Mgmt., Product Dev.

Industries: Manufacturing, Electronic, Elec. Components, Semiconductors, Banking, Brokers

The Eatman Group

(also known as MR of New Bern)
2807 Neuse Blvd Ste 3
New Bern, NC 28562-2816
(252) 633-1900
(888) 767-9772
Fax: (252) 633-3121
Email: mrinewbern@mrinewbern.com
Web: www.mrinewbern.com

Summary: Our firm recruits mainly in the manufacturing arena. We place CFOs, HR professionals, QC engineers - auditors, managers and accounting positions.

Key Contact - Specialty:
Mr. Fred Eatman, Manager

Functions: Generalist (All), Management, Board Members, Mfg., Production, HR Mgmt.

Industries: Generalist (All), Manufacturing, Food, Bev., Tobacco, Drugs Mfg., Medical Devices, Plastics, Rubber, Paints, Petro. Products, Metal Products, Motor Vehicles, Computer Equip., Misc. Mfg., Fiber Optic, Accounting SW, ERP SW, HR SW, Industry Specific SW, Mfg. SW

MR of Raleigh

(an affiliate of MRI)
5171 Glenwood Ave Ste 350
Raleigh, NC 27612-3266
(919) 781-0400
Email: recruiter@mriraleigh.com
Web: www.mriraleigh.com

Summary: We are an executive search firm focusing on management positions in four specialty practices: global life sciences, healthcare, construction, and manufacturing/engineering. Specifically: accounting/finance, automotive, aviation, bio-technology/pharmaceuticals/medical devices, construction, healthcare, engineering, manufacturing, materials, petrochemicals, quality, R&D and sales/marketing.

Key Contact - Specialty:
Ms. Linda Stanley, Managing Director - *Construction, Engineering, Healthcare, Manufacturing, Pharmaceutical*

Salary Minimum: $60,000

Functions: Generalist (All), Middle Mgmt.

Industries: Oil & Gas, Construction, Manufacturing, Drugs Mfg., Plastics, Rubber, Motor Vehicles, Engineering Svcs., Biotech/Life Sciences, Healthcare, Hospitals

MR of Person County

(an affiliate of MRI)
PO Box 1354
Roxboro, NC 27573-1354
(336) 597-4000
Fax: (336) 597-4011
Email: mri-person@mriofpersoncounty.com
Web: www.mriofpersoncounty.com

Summary: We specialize in plastics, automotive, furniture, engineering, manufacturing, quality, and materials management.

Key Contact - Specialty:
Mr. Don Buckner
Mrs. Angie Craven
Ms. Nichole Perkins

Functions: Mfg., Quality, Materials, Engineering

Industries: Lumber, Furniture, Plastics, Rubber, Motor Vehicles

SC of Wrightsville Beach

(also known as The Harriman Group)
1318 Military Cutoff Rd
Wilmington, NC 28405-3632
(910) 686-2848
Fax: (910) 686-2818
Email: scottharriman@earthlink.net

Summary: Our firm is a diverse recruiting organization with a long history of experience in the general manufacturing, lighting, power protection, quality, automotive, and pharmaceutical industries. We are also one of the only recruiting organizations with an industrial psychologist on staff to assist our clients with their candidate assessment needs.

Key Contact - Specialty:
Mr. Scott Harriman

Salary Minimum: $40,000

Functions: Generalist (All)

Industries: Generalist (All), Manufacturing, Plastics, Rubber, Metal Products, Misc. Mfg., Electronic, Elec. Components, HR SW, Mfg. SW, Biotech/Life Sciences, Healthcare

MR of Wilmington

(an affiliate of MRI)
4024 Oleander Dr Ste 1B
Wilmington, NC 28403-6814
(910) 791-2999
Email: harrylb@bellsouth.net

Summary: Each account executive is grounded in two fundamentals: professionalism and recruiting within a specific industry group which is his/her desk specialty.

Key Contact - Specialty:
Mr. Harry L. Bargholz, SPHR

Salary Minimum: $50,000

Functions: Generalist (All), HR Mgmt., Benefits, Staffing, Training

Industries: Generalist (All), Manufacturing, Food, Bev., Tobacco, Drugs Mfg., Medical Devices, Motor Vehicles, Services, HR Services

MR of Winston-Salem

(an affiliate of MRI)
PO Box 17054
Winston Salem, NC 27116-7054
(336) 723-0484
(800) 513-5305
Fax: (336) 723-0841
Email: search@mriws.com
Web: www.mriws.com

Summary: Providing management, technical and executive recruiting services in supply chain/RFID, sourcing/procurement, finance/accounting, food/nutrition, nutraceutical, pharmaceutical, biotechnology, chemical, environmental and safety.

Key Contact - Specialty:
Mr. Mike Jones, Managing Partner & Owner - *E-business, Executives, Procurement, Purchasing, Supply Chain*
Mrs. Judy Jones, Managing Partner & Owner - *Accounting, CFOs, Controllers, E-business, Supply Chain*
Mr. Ken White, Certified Senior Account Manager - *Chemical, Engineering, Environmental, Pharmaceutical, Safety*

Salary Minimum: $60,000

Functions: Generalist (All), Management, Mfg., Materials, Purchasing, HR Mgmt., Finance, Engineering, Health & Safety, Int'l.

Industries: Generalist (All), Manufacturing, Food, Bev., Tobacco, Chemicals, Drugs Mfg., Misc. Mfg., Consumer Goods, Finance, Misc. Financial, Accounting, E-commerce, Engineering Svcs., Logistics Svcs., Supply Chain Mgmt., Environmental Svcs., ERP SW, Biotech/Life Sciences

MR of Akron

(an affiliate of MRI)
544 White Pond Dr Ste A
Akron, OH 44320-1141
(330) 867-2900
Fax: (330) 867-3830
Email: info@mrakron.com
Web: www.mrakron.com

Summary: For many years, our clients have relied on us to locate, identify and attract top candidates in the plastic and rubber industries. We offer retained, engaged and contingency search services.

Key Contact - Specialty:
Mr. Mike Gerst, President - *Maintenance, Manufacturing, Molding, Plastics*
Mr. Tom Gerst, Partner - *Manufacturing, Molding, Plastics*
Mr. Art Smucker
Mr. Robert Dixon

Salary Minimum: $40,000

Functions: Generalist (All), Engineering

Industries: Generalist (All), Plastics, Rubber, Paints, Petro. Products

MR of Moreland Hills Inc

(also known as The Moreland Group)
23215 Commerce Park Ste 210
Beachwood, OH 44122-5843
(216) 591-0600
Email: info@mriresults.com
Web: www.mriresults.com

Summary: We specialize in bringing 'A' level impact players to companies in direct marketing, database marketing and e-marketing. Our clients are companies that recognize the value of hard to find, top performing, recruited candidates, and appreciate the value of a professional recruiter who knows their industry.

Key Contact - Specialty:
Mr. Jeff Rothman, Manager - *Direct marketing, Printing, Sales*
Ms. Lisa Ballard, Recruiting Specialist - *Direct marketing, Printing, Sales*
Mr. Scott Reed, Account Executive - *CRM, Direct marketing, Marketing, Printing, Sales*

Salary Minimum: $50,000

Functions: Senior Mgmt., Sales & Mktg., Mktg. Mgmt., Direct Mktg., Sales Reps.

Industries: Generalist (All), Non-profits, Pharm Svcs., Advertising, New Media, Marketing SW

SC of Broadview Heights

(an affiliate of MRI)
3505 E Royalton Rd Ste 170
Broadview Heights, OH 44147-2989
(440) 546-9154
Fax: (440) 546-9389
Email: bdoherty@scbroadviewheights.com

Summary: We specialize in financial services from a sales perspective primarily banking, equipment leasing and stock brokerage.

Key Contact - Specialty:
Mr. Brian Doherty, CSAM, Manager

Salary Minimum: $50,000

Functions: Sales Mgmt.

Industries: Finance, Banking

MR of Cleveland Southwest

(an affiliate of MRI)
PO Box 178
Brunswick, OH 44212-0178
(330) 273-4300
Fax: (330) 273-2862
Email: contactmri@aol.com
Web: www.mrinet.com

Summary: We specialize in photonics, fiber optics, electronics, finance and accounting, primary metals, engineering and manufacturing management.

Key Contact - Specialty:
Mr. Robert A. Boal, Manager

Salary Minimum: $80,000

Functions: Senior Mgmt., Middle Mgmt., Product Dev., Production, Plant Mgmt., Quality, Finance, Taxes, R&D, Engineering

Industries: Generalist (All), Manufacturing, Plastics, Rubber, Metal Products, Consumer Elect., Test, Measure Equip., Misc. Mfg., Finance, Banking, Accounting, Hospitality, Telecoms

MR of Chagrin Falls

(an affiliate of MRI)
PO Box 446
Chagrin Falls, OH 44022-0446
(440) 247-7350
Fax: (440) 247-7715
Email: gary@mricf.com
Web: www.mricf.com

Summary: Our firm is a top executive search firm dedicated to serving in the HVAC, air conditioning, temperature controls, consulting engineering, mechanical contracting, architectural engineering, pharmaceutical, accounting, industrial equipment sales, fluid power, software & hardware, and logistics/distribution/supply chain industries. Our services are provided with the utmost consultative professionalism, confidentiality and innovation.

Key Contact - Specialty:
Mr. Gary Gardiner, President - *HVAC*
Ms. Denise Szuhay, Administrative Assistant

Salary Minimum: $60,000

Functions: Generalist (All), Sales Reps., Engineering

Industries: Energy, Utilities, Construction, Manufacturing, Test, Measure Equip., Engineering Svcs., Haz. Waste, Packaging, Software

MR/SC of Cincinnati-Sharonville

(an affiliate of MRI)
4050 Executive Park Dr Ste 125
Cincinnati, OH 45241-2091
(513) 769-4747
Fax: (513) 769-0471
Email: resumes@mricinci.com
Web: www.mricinci.com

Summary: Retained/contingency executive search firm specializing in general management, manufacturing, engineering, finance/accounting and sales/marketing in paper, labels, packaging, printing, publishing, building products, furniture, office products, commercial construction, architectural, food/food processing, chemical, plastics, biotech/medical device industries.

Key Contact - Specialty:
Mr. William E. O'Reilly, President & Chief Executive Officer - *Paper, Printing, Publishing*

Salary Minimum: $40,000

Functions: Management, Board Members, Senior Mgmt., Middle Mgmt., Plant Mgmt., Quality, Packaging, Mktg. Mgmt., Sales Mgmt., Engineering

Industries: Generalist (All), Construction, Food, Bev., Tobacco, Lumber, Furniture, Paper, Printing, Chemicals, Plastics, Rubber, Supply Chain Mgmt., Inst./Industrial Food Svc., Biotech/Life Sciences

MR of Cincinnati

(an affiliate of MRI)
8 E 4th St
Cincinnati, OH 45202-3702
(513) 651-5500
Fax: (513) 651-3298
Email: careers@mricincy.com
Web: www.mricincy.com

Summary: Our account executives have received numerous national awards from our corporate office.

Key Contact - Specialty:
Mr. Joseph B. McCullough, President
Ms. Kathy Schiess, Vice President - *Clerical*
Mr. Joe Mehl, Operations Manager - *Engineering*
Ms. Beth Simminger, Director, Marketing
Mr. Anthony D'eramo

Functions: Generalist (All), Mfg., Sales & Mktg., HR Mgmt., Finance, IT, Engineering

Industries: Generalist (All), Manufacturing, Finance, Services

Quinlan & Associates Inc

(an affiliate of MRI)
10101 Alliance Rd Ste 195
Cincinnati, OH 45242-4715
(513) 985-9000
Fax: (513) 985-0975
Email: info@qnasearch.com
Web: www.qnasearch.com

Summary: With years of combined industry experience, we understand your hiring needs from a strategic perspective. Trust your staffing needs to us; we can provide a focused and knowledgeable industry search.

Key Contact - Specialty:
Mr. Bill Quinlan, President

Salary Minimum: $50,000

Functions: Generalist (All)

Industries: Food, Bev., Tobacco, Plastics, Rubber

Beechmont Consulting Group

(also known as SC of Clermont County Inc)
1010 Ohio Pike Ste C1
Cincinnati, OH 45245-2300
(513) 947-0922
Fax: (513) 947-0959
Email: info@bcgpharma.com
Web: www.bcgpharma.com

Summary: We are a full service staffing firm that has been successfully meeting the crucial staffing needs of the pharmaceutical industry from development to clinical trials, through manufacturing. Our efforts focus on the technical, scientific, management and executive disciplines of the pharmaceutical and biopharmaceutical industries.

Key Contact - Specialty:
Ms. Janet Murphy, President
Mr. Dennis Murphy, Vice President
Mr. Joe Doyle, Operations Manager
Ms. Maria Goble, Account Manager
Mr. Russ Darrow, Account Manager

Functions: Management, Mfg., Product Dev., Quality, Sales & Mktg., R&D, Engineering

Industries: Drugs Mfg., Pharm Svcs., Biotech/Life Sciences

MR/SC of Dayton

(also known as Noble Staffing Solutions)
333 W 1st St Ste 515
Dayton, OH 45402-5008
(937) 228-8271
Fax: (937) 228-2620
Email: info@mridayton.com
Web: www.mridayton.com

Summary: We are one of the largest professional placement service in the world.

Key Contact - Specialty:
Dr. Gerald R. Kotler, President - *Engineering*
Mr. Jeff Noble, CSP, Chief Executive Officer
Mr. Bob Snyder, Account Executive - *Manufacturing*
Ms. Susan Ehlenbach, Account Executive - *Manufacturing*
Mr. Mike Saxon, Account Executive

Salary Minimum: $55,000

Functions: Mfg., Product Dev., Production, Plant Mgmt., Quality, Productivity, Materials, Purchasing, Materials Plng., Engineering

Industries: Generalist (All), Manufacturing, Plastics, Rubber, Metal Products, Machine, Appliance, Motor Vehicles, Consumer Elect., Test, Measure Equip., Misc. Mfg., Electronic, Elec. Components, Consumer Goods, Aerospace

MRI Executive Solutions

(an affiliate of MRI)
3505 Embassy Pkwy Ste 200
Fairlawn, OH 44333-8358
(330) 666-3354
Fax: (330) 666-5655
Email: jchadbourne@mriexecutivesolutions.com
Web: www.mriexecutivesolutions.com

Summary: Our business is people. Meeting the needs of clients ranging from private, regional providers to globally recognized public corporations. We have assisted top talent in career transitions from executive leadership at the C-level to VPs, directors and managers in a variety of functional areas. We have the experience, resources and comprehensive knowledge to exceed your expectations in a wide array of specializations.

Key Contact - Specialty:
Mr. Jim Chadbourne, Managing Partner - *Logistics, Transportation*
Mr. Scott Chadbourne, Managing Director

Salary Minimum: $30,000

Functions: Generalist (All), Management, Board Members, Senior Mgmt., Middle Mgmt., Mfg., Production, Plant Mgmt., Materials, Purchasing

Industries: Generalist (All), Manufacturing, Food, Bev., Tobacco, Drugs Mfg., Medical Devices, Plastics, Rubber, Computer Equip., Transportation, Wholesale, Retail, Mgmt. Consulting, E-commerce, Defense, Haz. Waste, Aerospace, Biotech/Life Sciences

MR of Hudson

(an affiliate of MRI)
45 Milford Dr Ste 12
Hudson, OH 44236-2750
(330) 650-2300
Email: careers@mrihudson.com
Web: www.mrihudson.com

Summary: We are an executive search, recruiting and consulting firm. We specialize in the general industrial and manufacturing markets. Our industry experienced executive recruiters specialize in conducting confidential searches to fill openings with qualified candidates.

Key Contact - Specialty:
Mr. Jim Gorian, Owner & President - *Engineering, Industrial, Manufacturing (Management), Operations, Six Sigma*
Mrs. Gail Gorian, Office Manager - *Industrial, Manufacturing (Management)*
Mr. Hank Archer, Executive Search Consultant - *Industrial, Manufacturing (Management), Packaging*

Functions: Generalist (All)

Industries: Manufacturing, Plastics, Rubber, Metal Products, Motor Vehicles, Test, Measure Equip., Electronic, Elec. Components, Semiconductors, Engineering Svcs., Supply Chain Mgmt

MR of Massillon

(an affiliate of MRI)
2200 Wales Ave NW Ste 211
Massillon, OH 44646-2395
(330) 834-0600
Fax: (330) 834-0601
Email: jobs@mrmassillon.com
Web: www.mrmassillon.com

Summary: We are an executive search firm specializing in the placement of accounting/audit/finance,banking insurance human resources, manufacturing professional and hospitality.

Key Contact - Specialty:
Mr. David Reliford, President

Salary Minimum: $40,000

Functions: Management, Middle Mgmt., Admin. Svcs., Finance

Industries: Manufacturing, Food, Bev., Tobacco, Medical Devices, Finance, Banking, Misc. Financial, Accounting, HR Services, Hospitality, Restaurants, Quick Service Restaurants, Full Service Restaurants, Inst./Industrial Food Svc., Insurance

MR of Cleveland Northeast

(an affiliate of MRI)
8039 Broadmoor Rd Ste 20
Mentor, OH 44060-7577
(440) 946-2355
Fax: (440) 946-5488
Email: mri@mrilake.net

Summary: We specialize in the banking industry exclusively.

Key Contact - Specialty:
Mr. Ronald Sterling, General Manager
Ms. Cheryl Sterling, Manager

Salary Minimum: $45,000

Functions: Generalist (All), Management

Industries: Banking

MR of Sidney

(also known as Uniacke & Associates)
113 N Ohio Ave Ste 400
Sidney, OH 45365-2749
(937) 497-7080
Fax: (937) 497-7061
Email: dkmilanese@earthlink.net
Web: www.uniacke-associates.com

Summary: Our years of experience in the food industry offers an insider's perspective beneficial to your company by focusing on your total company needs relative to personality, company atmosphere and skill sets.

Key Contact - Specialty:
Mr. Keith J. Uniacke, President
Ms. Diane Milanese, Vice President - *Food*

Salary Minimum: $65,000

Functions: Management, Product Dev., Production, Plant Mgmt., Quality, Sales & Mktg., R&D

Industries: Food, Bev., Tobacco, Consumer Goods, Engineering Svcs., Restaurants, Inst./Industrial Food Svc., Marketing SW

The Kent Group Inc

(also known as MR of Northwest Ohio)
3450 W Central Ave Ste 360
Toledo, OH 43606-1418
(419) 537-1100
Fax: (419) 537-8730
Email: gfruchtman@kent-group.com
Web: www.kent-group.com

Summary: We are a full service firm, emphasizing search in the following industries: steel, steel tube and pipe, insurance, automotive, glass and food. We work vertically within these areas, placing talent in engineering, supervision, sales and management. We are part of a vast national network.

Key Contact - Specialty:
Mr. Gary Fruchtman, President - *Automotive, Steel*
Mr. Sam Balber, Account Manager - *Insurance, Insurance (Casualty,Property)*
Mr. Bill Lane, Account Manager - *Bakery, Food, Food & beverage, Manufacturing*
Mr. Roger Starr, Account Manager - *Automotive*
Mr. Mike Monus, Account Manager - *Building products*
Mr. Mike Rollins, Account Manager - *Engineering, Manufacturing, Manufacturing (Management), Operations*

Salary Minimum: $45,000

Functions: Generalist (All), Management, Mfg., Production, Systems Dev., Engineering

Industries: Generalist (All), Oil & Gas, Manufacturing, Food, Bev., Tobacco, Leather, Stone, Glass, Metal Products, Motor Vehicles, Misc. Mfg., Accounting, Insurance, Casualty, Commercial, Software, Biotech/Life Sciences

The Polaris Consulting Group

(an affiliate of MRI)
925 N State St Ste Q
Westerville, OH 43082-8023
(614) 865-1500
Fax: (614) 865-1600
Email: tcoan@polarisconsultinggroup.com
Web: www.polarisconsultinggroup.com

Summary: Mid and senior-level placements within retail focusing largely on product development, design, planning and merchandising.

Key Contact - Specialty:
Mr. Timothy Coan, Managing Director - *Apparel, Fashion, Product management/development, Retail, Textiles*

Functions: Generalist (All), Management, Senior Mgmt., Mfg., Product Dev., Purchasing, Packaging, Design, Graphic Designers, Textile/Fashion

Industries: Textiles, Apparel, Retail

MR of Columbus

(an affiliate of MRI)
4151 Executive Pkwy Ste 355
Westerville, OH 43081-3868
(614) 794-3200
Fax: (614) 794-3233
Email: careerpartners@mricolumbus.com
Web: www.mricolumbus.com

Summary: We are the number one contingency firm in Central Ohio. In our history, over 90 percent of our recruiters have earned acclaim showing our experience, tenure, professionalism and value to our clients. We can also provide administrative and operations staffing services.

Key Contact - Specialty:
Ms. Barbara Stoltz, President

Salary Minimum: $30,000

Functions: Senior Mgmt., Admin. Svcs., Customer Svc., Finance

Industries: Generalist (All), Accounting

MR of Westerville

(an affiliate of MRI)
480 Olde Worthington Rd Ste 125
Westerville, OH 43082-9493
(614) 794-5570
Fax: (614) 794-5575
Email: linda@mricareer.com
Web: www.mricareer.com

Summary: We are devoted to the permanent placement of management executives.

Key Contact - Specialty:
Ms. Linda LaCerva, President
Ms. Vickie Reynolds, Account Executive - *Healthcare*

Functions: Management, Senior Mgmt., Middle Mgmt., Healthcare, Nurses, Allied Health, HR Mgmt.

Industries: Healthcare, Hospitals, Long-term/Home Care, Physical Therapy, Occupational Therapy, Women's

MR of Youngstown

(an affiliate of MRI)
755 Boardman Canfield Rd Ste C3
Youngstown, OH 44512-4387
(330) 726-6100
Fax: (330) 707-0199
Email: dsomers@mrnetworking.com
Web: www.mrnetworking.com

Summary: Experienced executive recruiting firm specializing in MIS, LAN/WAN, client server as well as engineering, sales and manufacturing.

Key Contact - Specialty:
Mr. Donald A. Somers, President
Mr. Larry Proctor, Senior Account Manager
Ms. Lisa Fitzpatrick, Technical Consultant

Salary Minimum: $25,000

Functions: Generalist (All), MIS Mgmt., Systems Analysis, Systems Dev., Systems Implem., Systems Support, Network Admin., DB Admin.

Industries: Generalist (All), Finance, Banking, Telecoms, Software, Healthcare

MR of Edmond

(an affiliate of MRI)
1300 E 9th St Ste 4
Edmond, OK 73034-5760
(405) 348-5550
Fax: (405) 348-8808
Email: mri@mriedmond.com
Web: www.mriedmond.com

Summary: We provide a full range of employment services, from single searches for a key manager to major projects involving hundreds of assignments for a single-source client.

Key Contact - Specialty:
Mr. Craig S. Lyman, Manager

Functions: Management, Senior Mgmt.

Industries: Generalist (All), Construction, Architectural Svcs.

MR of Oklahoma City

(an affiliate of MRI)
3120 W Britton Rd Ste 200
Oklahoma City, OK 73120-2038
(405) 752-8848
Fax: (405) 752-8783
Email: gary@mriokc.com
Web: www.mriokc.com

Summary: We are recognized as one of the most tenured offices within our entire franchise family of offices.

Key Contact - Specialty:
Mr. Gary P. Roy, President

Salary Minimum: $30,000

Functions: Generalist (All), Sales Mgmt.

Industries: Construction, Plastics, Rubber, Venture Cap., Mutual/Hedge Funds, Misc. Financial, Engineering Svcs., Insurance, Long-term/Home Care

SC of Oklahoma City

(an affiliate of MRI)
5909 NW Expressway St
Oklahoma City, OK 73132-5161
(405) 721-6400
Fax: (405) 728-7128
Email: darla@scokc.com
Web: www.scokc.com

Summary: Specializing in sales, sales management and marketing positions for Fortune 500 Companies.

Key Contact - Specialty:
Ms. Darla Salisbury, Owner

Salary Minimum: $60,000

Functions: Healthcare, Sales Reps.

Industries: Drugs Mfg., Medical Devices

Wolters Search Group

(an affiliate of MRI)
5801 E 41st St Ste 440
Tulsa, OK 74135-5614
(918) 663-6744
Fax: (918) 663-1783
Email: info@wolterssearch.com
Web: www.wolterssearch.com

Summary: Our firm is part of one of the largest and most respected franchise staffing companies in the world. Our goal is to find the best talent for our client companies.

Key Contact - Specialty:
Mr. Tony A. Wolters, President & Owner
Mr. Bill Wetterman, Vice President, Training & Development
Ms. Ann Wolters, Vice President, Finance & Accounting
Mr. Audra Davidson, Vice President, Administration - *Engineering, Manufacturing, Operations, Retail*
Ms. Nina Lee, Senior Executive Recruiter
Mr. Mark Wolters, Senior Account Manager - *Gaming, Hospitality, Resorts, Restaurants, Retail*

Functions: Management

Industries: Generalist (All)

United Human Capital Solutions

(also known as SC of Lake Oswego)
1 Centerpointe Dr Ste 345
Lake Oswego, OR 97035-8656
(503) 443-6008
(503) 924-1755
Fax: (503) 443-6028
Email: talent@uhcsolutions.com
Web: www.uhcsolutions.com

Summary: Our firm is a team of inspired recruiting specialists. We believe remarkable employees are the secret to successful companies. We work with clients in the equipment leasing, banking, biotechnology and healthcare markets to provide them with the best candidates the industry offers.

Key Contact - Specialty:
Mr. Tim Mulvaney, President & Chief Executive Officer - *Pharmacists*

Mr. Joel Slenning, Vice President, Healthcare Services
Mr. Forest Denson, Search Consultant, Pharmacy - *Accounting, Banking, Biotechnology, Financial services, Pharmacists*
Mr. Glenn Wachter, Search Consultant

Salary Minimum: $30,000

Functions: Generalist (All), Healthcare

Industries: Finance, Banking, Biotech/Life Sciences, Healthcare, Hospitals

MR/SC of Portland

(an affiliate of MRI)
2020 Lloyd Ctr
Portland, OR 97232-1309
(503) 287-8701
Fax: (503) 282-4380
Email: jobs@mrportland.com
Web: www.mrportland.com

Summary: Our mission is to be the best at identifying, qualifying and delivering the best talent for our client companies.

Key Contact - Specialty:
Mr. Steven Ross, Managing Partner, President
Mr. Peter Monsantofils, Managing Partner, Treasurer
Mr. Christopher Johnson, Managing Partner, Sales & Training

Salary Minimum: $50,000

Functions: Management, Mfg., Physicians, Nurses, Health Admin., Sales & Mktg., HR Mgmt., Finance, R&D, Attorneys

Industries: Generalist (All), Construction, Manufacturing, Transportation, Wholesale, Retail, Finance, Pharm Svcs., Legal, Accounting, HR Services, Media, Communications, Accounting SW, HR SW, Biotech/Life Sciences, Healthcare, Hospitals

SC of La Costa

(an affiliate of MRI)
836 W Military Ave Ste 109
Roseburg, OR 97470-2977
(541) 440-6699
(541) 643-6699
Fax: (541) 646-2684
Email: jerry.jobs@gmail.com
Web: www.jerry.jobs@gmail.com

Summary: Our specialty is field management for retail nationwide covering all 50 states

Key Contact - Specialty:
Mr. Jerry Harris, Manager

Salary Minimum: $50,000

Functions: Management, Middle Mgmt.

Industries: Retail

Gladwyne Search Group Inc

(an affiliate of MRI)
44 W Lancaster Ave Ste 225
Ardmore, PA 19003-1350
(610) 642-1040
Fax: (610) 642-7360
Email: gsi@gladwynesearch.com
Web: www.gladwynesearch.com

Summary: We recognize the importance of the hiring process. The individual chosen must be able to accomplish the short term, as well as the long term goals of the organization within the confines of the company's resources. It is therefore, critical that the process be handled in an intelligent and expeditious manner in order to create this proper fit the first time.

Key Contact - Specialty:
Mr. Robert H. Eichman, Managing Director - *Consumer, Consumer (Durables,Marketing,Packaged Goods,Products)*
Ms. Addie Eichman, Executive Vice President, Operations - *Distribution, Engineering, Logistics, Six sigma*
Mr. Louis Crocetto, Account Executive - *Transportation*
Ms. Eleanor McCann, Account Manager - *Consumer, Consumer (Products), Distribution, Fashion, Retail*

Salary Minimum: $40,000

Functions: Generalist (All), Management, Senior Mgmt.

Industries: Manufacturing, Paper, Printing, Soap, Perf., Cosmtcs., Drugs Mfg., Transportation, Retail, Pharm Svcs., Mgmt. Consulting, Entertainment, Publishing, Packaging

MR of Bethlehem

(an affiliate of MRI)
1401 Easton Ave
Bethlehem, PA 18018-2618
(610) 974-9770
Email: mri@mribeth.com
Web: www.mribeth.com

Summary: Our specialties include the food industry and finance & accounting for a broad range of industries. Our food specialization is heavily oriented toward technical positions and includes processing, ingredients and food service. Finance and accounting includes mid to senior level professionals; e.g. COO, CFO, controllers, analysts, etc.

Key Contact - Specialty:
Mrs. Gayle A. McGeehan, President - *Food, Marketing, Operations, Packaging, Seafood*
Mrs. Christi Hunter, Account Executive - *Bakery, Engineering, Food & beverage, Quality, Research & development*
Ms. Debbie Goldberg, Account Executive - *Accounting, CFOs, Controllers, Finance, Retail*
Mr. Michael Solomon, Account Executive
Ms. Pat Conahan, Project Coordinator
Ms. Denise Witowski, Project Coordinator
Ms. Judy Campbell, Administrative Assistant

Salary Minimum: $60,000

Functions: Management, Board Members, Middle Mgmt., Packaging, Sales & Mktg., Engineering

Industries: Generalist (All), Food, Bev., Tobacco, Chemicals, Drugs Mfg., Retail, Finance, Accounting, Telecoms, Packaging, Non-Classifiable

SC of Harrisburg

(an affiliate of MRI)
225 S 19th St
Camp Hill, PA 17011-5500
(717) 731-8550
Fax: (717) 731-8729
Email: thomas@salesconsultants.net
Web: www.salesconsultants.net

Summary: We specialize in voice/data/video technologies in the executive, sales or marketing job titles.

Key Contact - Specialty:
Mr. Thomas M. Waite, President

Functions: Management, Sales & Mktg., IT

Industries: Generalist (All)

MR of Carlisle

(an affiliate of MRI)
21 State Ave Ste 103
Carlisle, PA 17013-4415
(717) 249-2626
(877) 222-7337
Fax: (717) 249-4843
Email: resume@mritcg.com
Web: www.mritcg.com

Summary: Our firm is nationally recognized as one of the top executive search firms dedicated to serving in the manufacturing, retail, insurance, banking, healthcare, financial services and distribution/logistics industries. Our services are provided with the utmost consultative professionalism, confidentiality and innovation.

Key Contact - Specialty:
Mr. Bert Wendeln, Owner & President
Ms. Margaret Christlieb, Director, Customer Service

Salary Minimum: $40,000

Functions: Generalist (All)

Industries: Manufacturing, Transportation, Retail, Finance, Accounting, Logistics Svcs., Insurance, Hospitals

MR of the Brandywine Valley

(an affiliate of MRI)
120 E Uwchlan Ave Ste 204
Exton, PA 19341-1275
(610) 524-1666
Email: bspillane@mribrandywine.com

Summary: Diverse office conducting searches in project management, engineering, accounting, internal audit and CFO/controller levels. Primary focus is electrical power generation, its design and distribution. Also focuses on defense industry, manufacturing home offices, chemical plants and other heavy industry such as air separation and steel.

Key Contact - Specialty:
Mr. Bill Spillane, Principal

Salary Minimum: $50,000

Functions: Generalist (All), Materials, Purchasing

Industries: Generalist (All), Energy, Utilities, Oil & Gas, Construction, Food, Bev., Tobacco, Paper, Metal Products, Machine, Appliance, Accounting, Equip Svcs., Mgmt. Consulting

MR of Cranberry

(an affiliate of MRI)
1310 Freedom Crider Rd
Freedom, PA 15042-9319
(724) 775-9030
Fax: (724) 775-9031
Email: skdawson@nauticom.net

Summary: Our focus is on finance and accounting executives in corporations from manager level to CFO level, as well as Big 4 placements. Additionally, we also work on searches for regional VPs, GMs and country heads.

Key Contact - Specialty:
Mr. Sanford Dawson

Salary Minimum: $70,000

Functions: Senior Mgmt., Middle Mgmt., Finance, CFOs, Int'l.

Industries: Generalist (All), Finance, Misc. Financial, Accounting

MR of Lancaster

(an affiliate of MRI)
1148 Elizabeth Ave Ste 10
Lancaster, PA 17601-4359
(717) 397-6444
Fax: (717) 397-6793
Email: mroflanc@infi.net
Web: www.mrlancpa.com

Summary: Our firm provides total staffing solutions. Our account executives specialize in HR, HR consulting and eHR/eBusiness HR.

Key Contact - Specialty:
Ms. Karen Rodebaugh, Executive Vice President & COO - *Human resources*
Mr. Thomas L. Rodebaugh, Jr., Managing Director

Functions: HR Mgmt.

Industries: Generalist (All), Mgmt. Consulting, HR Services

MR of Pittsburgh A-K Valley

(an affiliate of MRI)
2644 Leechburg Rd
Lower Burrell, PA 15068-3029
(724) 334-0400
Fax: (724) 334-0700
Email: info@mripit.com
Web: www.mripit.com

Summary: We specialize in the pharmaceutical, biotechnology and health care industries.

Key Contact - Specialty:
Mr. Frank Gigler, Managing Director - *Business development, Science*
Ms. Laurie Cario, Administrative Assistant
Mr. Kevin Krotine, Account Executive
Ms. Maureen Devine, Account Executive
Mr. Jesse Warnick, MBA, Account Executive - *Healthcare, Physicians*

Salary Minimum: $20,000

Functions: Management, Quality, Physicians, Allied Health, Mktg. Mgmt., Sales Mgmt., R&D

Industries: Drugs Mfg., Pharm Svcs., Biotech/Life Sciences, Healthcare, Hospitals, Long-term/Home Care

MR of Ambler-Philadelphia

(an affiliate of MRI)
716 N Bethlehem Pike Ste 201
Lower Gwynedd, PA 19002-2656
(215) 283-9799
Fax: (215) 283-9798
Email: hire@mribeach.com
Web: www.mribeach.com

Summary: We offer intelligent IT staffing solutions, including office support personnel.

Key Contact - Specialty:
Mr. Jeff Schonberg

Salary Minimum: $50,000

Functions: Generalist (All)

Industries: Generalist (All), Finance, Services, Non-profits, Accounting, E-commerce, Hospitality, Software

MR of McMurray

(also known as MR of Pittsburgh Southwest)
115 Hidden Valley Rd
McMurray, PA 15317-2603
(724) 942-4100
Fax: (724) 942-4111
Email: manager@chemicaljobs.com
Web: www.chemicaljobs.com

Summary: We recruit technical talent within the chemically related fields. We place BS/MS/PhD level chemists and chemical engineers up to the VP level.

Key Contact - Specialty:
Mr. Michael Fosnot, Managing Partner - *Technical*

Functions: Generalist (All)

Industries: Chemicals, Plastics, Rubber, Paints, Petro. Products

MR of Westmoreland County

(an affiliate of MRI)
3122 Carson Ave Ste 200
Murrysville, PA 15668-1815
(724) 325-4011
Fax: (724) 325-1760
Email: mriwc@mriwc.com
Web: www.mriwc.com

Summary: Chemical industry: sales, marketing, technical service, chemists, chemical management, production, manufacturing, process engineers, process development engineers and project engineers.

Key Contact - Specialty:
Mr. Frank Williamson, President

Salary Minimum: $40,000

Functions: Middle Mgmt., Mfg., Product Dev., Production, Sales Mgmt., Engineering

Industries: Manufacturing, Textiles, Apparel, Printing, Chemicals, Plastics, Rubber, Paints, Petro. Products

Newtown Consulting Group Inc

(an affiliate of MRI)
301 S State St
Newtown, PA 18940-1997
(215) 579-2450
(215) 579-5995
Email: info@mrinewtown.com
Web: www.mrinewtown.com

Summary: We are specialists in two areas. The first is in the recruiting of sales, sales management, marketing, underwriting, claims, training and general management personnel for the group life, group disability, group health, group managed care and group pension/retirement insurance industry. Secondly, we recruit in the executive benefits consulting (non-qualified retirement plans) arena.

Key Contact - Specialty:
Mr. James Plappert, President - *Benefits, Insurance, Insurance (Health,Life), Sales*

Salary Minimum: $35,000

Functions: Generalist (All), Management, Senior Mgmt., Middle Mgmt., Sales & Mktg., Mktg. Research, Mktg. Mgmt., Sales Mgmt., Mgmt. Consultants

Industries: Misc. Financial, Mgmt. Consulting, HR Services, Insurance

The Bishop Group

(an affiliate of MRI)
3415 W Chester Pike Ste 303
Newtown Square, PA 19073-4279
(610) 353-2705
Fax: (610) 356-8731
Email: sandy@thebishopgroup.com

Summary: We work in the electrical industry, including electrical controls, power products, various software products, wire & cable, and lighting. We also work in the process control industry; dcs, process instruments and analyzers. We place sales, product marketing, and engineering management, to general manager and president level.

Key Contact - Specialty:
Mr. Sandy Bishop, Manager - *Robotics, Sales*

Salary Minimum: $50,000

Functions: Mfg., Automation, Sales & Mktg.

Industries: Computer Equip., Misc. Mfg., Software, Mfg. SW

MR of Reading

(also known as StoneBridge Management, Inc)
2921 Windmill Rd
Reading, PA 19608-1678
(610) 670-8008
Fax: (610) 670-8009
Email: info@mrireading.com
Web: www.mrireading.com

Summary: Our firm offers permanent and contract staffing solutions in manufacturing management, engineering, logistics, sales, marketing, IT, construction, medical device, consumer products, food & beverage, biotechnology and insurance industries.

Key Contact - Specialty:
Mr. Jeff Burridge, President - *Entrepreneurs, Franchising, Medical, Sales, Start-up companies*
Mr. Tom Gervasi, Vice President
Mr. Jim Schuetz, Search Consultant - *Analysts, Logistics, Management, Materials, Purchasing*
Ms. Lonna Treichler, Search Consultant - *Consumer, Logistics, Manufacturing, Marketing, Sales*

Salary Minimum: $65,000

Functions: Senior Mgmt., Middle Mgmt., Mfg., Materials Plng., Healthcare, Sales & Mktg., R&D, Engineering

Industries: Generalist (All), Construction, Manufacturing, Drugs Mfg., Medical Devices, Consumer Goods, Services, Engineering Svcs., Logistics Svcs., Hospitality, Hotels, Resorts, Clubs, Insurance, Biotech/Life Sciences, Healthcare

MR of Pittsburgh West

(an affiliate of MRI)
2607 Nicholson Rd Ste 1100
Sewickley, PA 15143-8581
(724) 935-1774
Fax: (724) 935-1744
Email: pj@mripittsburghwest.com
Web: www.mripittsburghwest.com

Summary: Our firm places sales and sales management candidates with Fortune 200 companies. We specialize in medical devices, medical products and business-to-business services, for example, medical capital equipment sold into hospitals, leasing, credit card and information services.

Key Contact - Specialty:
Ms. P.J. Jones, CSAM, President & General Manager - *Sales*

Functions: Sales & Mktg., Sales Mgmt.

Industries: Generalist (All), Healthcare

MR of Pittsburgh North

(an affiliate of MRI)
PO Box 69
Sewickley, PA 15143-0069
(412) 741-5805
Fax: (412) 741-3801
Email: joni@mripitt.com
Web: www.mrpitt.com

Summary: Our specialties are electric utilities engineering, sub-station engineering, RF engineering, directors, operations, logistics, sales, consulting, medical devices, medical cardiac devices/diagnostics, capital equipment, marketing, medical informatics, electric utilities, engineering, and business development.

Key Contact - Specialty:
Mrs. Joni Lampl, President - *Biomedical, Biopharmaceutical, Biotechnology, C-level, Consumer (Packaged Goods)*
Mr. Richard Lampl, Vice President
Ms. Cheryl Burns, Administrative
Miss Abigail Dowling, Practice Leader, Electric Power Source - *C-level, CFOs, Distribution, Electrical, Engineering*
Mr. Steve Chamberlin, Practice Leader, Medical Imaging - *Medical (Sales)*
Mr. Keith Ziegler, CSMA, Practice Leader, Medical Diagnostics
Mr. Erich Curnow, Practice Leader, Medical Devices - *Medical (Devices)*
Mrs. Judith Higgins, Practice Leader, Packaging - *Consumer (Packaged Goods), Packaging*

Salary Minimum: $75,000

Functions: Generalist (All), Packaging, HR Mgmt., Benefits, Finance, MIS Mgmt., Systems Analysis, Systems Dev., Systems Implem., Systems Support

Industries: Generalist (All), Energy, Utilities, Construction, Manufacturing, Drugs Mfg., Medical Devices, Consumer Goods, E-commerce, IT Implementation, Engineering Svcs., Logistics Svcs., RF/Microwave, Government, Packaging, Insurance, Software, Database SW, Development SW, Doc. Mgmt., Production SW, ERP SW, HR SW, Industry Specific SW, Mfg. SW, Marketing SW, Networking, Comm. SW, Security SW, System SW, Healthcare, Hospitals

MR/SC of Southampton

(an affiliate of MRI)
928 Jaymor Rd Ste A200
Southampton, PA 18966-3841
(215) 364-7559
Fax: (215) 364-7579
Email: georgem@mriscs.com
Web: www.mriscs.com

Summary: We recruit management, sales & marketing talent for business process (BPO) & IT outsourcing (offshore/onshore), security technology & integration solutions (manufacturers, software developers & system integrators), financial services & banking technology solutions, document management & outsourcing and computer telephony (CTI), industries. Clients are global. Candidates are throughout the USA.

Key Contact - Specialty:
Mr. George McCafferty, Managing Partner
Ms. Dee McCafferty, Managing Partner, Operations
Mr. George Robert, Partner - *Business development, Business to business, Loss Prevention, Product management/development, Sales*
Ms. Cathy Fox, Partner
Mr. McCafferty

Salary Minimum: $65,000

Functions: Management, Sales & Mktg.

Industries: Electronic, Elec. Components, Finance, Communications, Software, Security SW, System SW

E W Dean Inc

(also known as MR of Pittsburgh-USC)
180 Warwick Dr Ste 10
Upper St Clair, PA 15241-1030
(412) 833-5833
Email: eric@ewdean.com
Web: www.ewdean.com

Summary: We provide domestic and international search and recruitment services for consulting engineering firms, architectural firms, and manufacturers.

Key Contact - Specialty:
Mr. Eric Dean, Jr., President

Salary Minimum: $48,000

MR of Bucks County

(an affiliate of MRI)
650 Louis Dr Ste 170
Warminster, PA 18974-2850
(215) 675-6440
(800) 606-6440
Fax: (215) 675-1446
Email: careers@mribc.com
Web: www.mribucks.com

Summary: Our industries include: banking, construction, food service & ingredients, real estate development and real estate finance.

Key Contact - Specialty:
Mr. Michael Mashack, President
Mr. Kevin McCann, CSAM, Vice President - *Bakery, Dairy, Financial services, Food, Food & beverage*
Ms. Rhoda Rogers, CSAM, Vice President, Real Estate Group - *CEOs, CFOs, COOs, Property management, Senior management*
Mr. Jonathan Sherby, Account Executive - *Analysts, Asset management, Controllers, Property management, Real estate*
Ms. Rosa Brazen, Account Executive - *Banking (Commercial,Mortgage), Finance, Financial services, Real estate*
Mr. Robert Sergeant, Account Executive - *Design, Electrical, Engineering, General contractors, HVAC*

Functions: Generalist (All)

Industries: Construction, Food, Bev., Tobacco, Banking, Invest. Banking, Brokers, Misc. Financial, Accounting, Real Estate, Property/Facility Mgmt.

Walker Forest

(also known as SC of King of Prussia)
997 Old Eagle School Rd Ste 209
Wayne, PA 19087-1706
(610) 989-8500
Fax: (610) 989-8501
Email: pdl@walkerforest.com
Web: www.walkerforest.com

Summary: Our mission is to improve the quality of your life. Our primary focus is on sales & marketing professionals in emerging and leading edge technology related companies.

Key Contact - Specialty:
Mr. Peter David Levitt, Partner - *Technology*
Mr. Philip Gardiner, CSAM, Senior Manager - *Healthcare*

Salary Minimum: $75,000

Functions: Generalist (All)

Industries: Computer Equip., Banking, Misc. Financial, Pharm Svcs., Mgmt. Consulting, E-commerce, Call Centers, Doc. Mgmt., Production SW, ERP SW, Marketing SW

SC of Chester County

(an affiliate of MRI)
22 N Darlington St Ste 201
West Chester, PA 19380-2911
(484) 905-5450
Email: springco@erols.com

Summary: We specialize in sales & marketing with a primary emphasis on the healthcare industry including: pharmaceutical, medical devices, bio-technology and oncology.

Key Contact - Specialty:
Mr. Mark W. Hetzel, Owner - *Pharmaceutical, Technology*

Functions: Generalist (All)

Industries: Drugs Mfg., Medical Devices, Pharm Svcs., Biotech/Life Sciences, Healthcare

MR of Willow Grove

(an affiliate of MRI)
2300 Computer Rd Ste C15
Willow Grove, PA 19090-1735
(215) 830-9211
Fax: (215) 830-9216
Email: fklein@mrwg.com
Web: www.mrwg.com

Summary: We are ranked as an "elite" office. We have successfully placed senior level professionals in Life Sciences as well as Information Technology. Keywords: pharma, clinical, CRO, software, business development, DMPK, Toxicology, Chemistry, HE/OR, Reg, QA.

Key Contact - Specialty:
Ms. Fern Klein, Co-Manager - *Computers (Software), Healthcare*
Mr. Robert Klein, Co-Manager
Mr. Jason Hersh, Co-Manager - *Biotechnology, Computers, Computers (Software), Sales*

Functions: Management, Senior Mgmt., Sales & Mktg.

Industries: Pharm Svcs., Software, ERP SW, HR SW, Mfg. SW, Marketing SW, Networking, Comm. SW, Security SW, System SW, Training SW, Biotech/Life Sciences

DJV Associates Inc

(an affiliate of MRI)
385 Oxford Valley Rd Ste 321
Yardley, PA 19067-7704
(215) 321-8800
Email: replies@djvassociates.com

Summary: We are an executive search firm focused on mid and senior-level management, sales professionals, management consultants and legal talent. We specialize in supply chain management/third party logistics, CRM, call centers/customer care, as well as business process outsourcing and health care. We also have a nationally recognized legal/attorney placement practice.

Key Contact - Specialty:
Mr. Derrick Vlad, President - *Business development, Call centers, Consulting, Logistics, Transportation*
Ms. Jill Arnstein, Esq., Director, Legal Services - *Legal, Legal (Attorneys,Lawyers)*

Salary Minimum: $75,000

Functions: Management, Sales & Mktg., Customer Svc., Mgmt. Consultants, Legal, Int'l.

Industries: Generalist (All), Energy, Utilities, Manufacturing, Medical Devices, Transportation, Finance, Banking, Invest. Banking, Mutual/Hedge Funds, Services, Legal, Mgmt. Consulting, Communications, Call Centers, Insurance, Software, Biotech/Life Sciences, Healthcare

MR of Puerto Rico

(an affiliate of MRI)
289 Ave Jesus T Pinero Ste 200
Urb Hyde Park
San Juan, PR 00927-3901
(787) 766-4020
(787) 766-4055
Email: recruiters@recruiters-pr.com
Web: www.managementrecruiterspr.com

Summary: We specialize in placing bilingual, bicultural Hispanic talent in the sales, manufacturing, finance and services industries. For years selective companies and executives have turned to us for professional results. As a premier office within the MRI network, we provide extended recruiting solutions world wide through our numerous affiliate offices.

Key Contact - Specialty:
Mr. Carlos R. Rodriguez, President - *C-level, Controllers, Finance, Insurance, Latin America*
Mr. Javier R. Rodriguez, CSAM, Vice President, Director, Operations - *Business to business, Consumer (Marketing), Latin America*
Mr. Carlos A. Rodriguez, Vice President, Senior Account Manager - *Latin America, Logistics, Marketing, Product management/development, Sales*

Salary Minimum: $20,000

Functions: Generalist (All), Management, Board Members

Industries: Generalist (All), Food, Bev., Tobacco, Chemicals, Drugs Mfg., Medical Devices, Plastics, Rubber, Wholesale, Retail, Finance, Logistics Svcs., Telephony, Biotech/Life Sciences

MR/SC of Rhode Island

(an affiliate of MRI)
2348 Post Rd Ste 101
Warwick, RI 02886-2262
(401) 737-3200
Fax: (401) 737-4322
Email: bestsalestalent@mrisales.net
Web: www.mrisales.net

Summary: Sales, sales management, and marketing search & recruitment.

Key Contact - Specialty:
Mr. Peter C. Cotton, President - *Marketing, Sales*

Salary Minimum: $30,000

Functions: Sales & Mktg.

Industries: Generalist (All)

MR of Anderson

(an affiliate of MRI)
PO Box 2874
Anderson, SC 29622-2874
(864) 225-1258
Fax: (864) 225-2332
Email: mrand@career-hunter.com
Web: www.career-hunter.com

Summary: Our firm specializes in permanent career placement in IT, pharmaceutical, bioinformatics, medical device and general manufacturing companies on a national basis. We will confidently meet your needs with professional attention and outstanding service that has always been our trademark.

Key Contact - Specialty:
Mr. Rod Pagan, General Manager
Mr. Jamie Riley, Account Executive
Mr. John Pagan, Operations & Accounts Manager

Functions: Generalist (All)

Industries: Manufacturing, Pharm Svcs., Biotech/Life Sciences

MR of Charleston

(an affiliate of MRI)
4 Carriage Ln Ste 301
Charleston, SC 29407-6050
(843) 556-6461
Fax: (843) 556-4803
Email: mr@search-jobs.com
Web: www.search-jobs.com

Summary: We specialize in the healthcare and manufacturing industries. We feel that the key to our success in serving our client companies and candidates is the expertise of our people. In healthcare we specialize in the administrative management of a variety of medical settings, from skilled nursing home administrators to hospital CEOs. In manufacturing we specialize in the areas of product, process, design, maintenance, quality and safety.

Key Contact - Specialty:
Mr. Bob Bean, Manager

Salary Minimum: $50,000

Functions: Mfg., Plant Mgmt., Healthcare, Engineering

Industries: Manufacturing, Paper, Plastics, Rubber, Metal Products, Machine, Appliance, Misc. Mfg., Hospitals, Long-term/Home Care

Columbus International Group

(also known as MR of Kiawah Island)
310 Broad St Apt 2F
Charleston, SC 29401-1257
(843) 973-3500
Email: info@columbusgroup.net
Web: www.columbusgroup.net

Summary: Our firm specializes in delivering customized, on-target searches, both on a retained or a contingency basis. Our interview-to-hire ratio consistently tracks at less than a four-to-one ratio in the IT and healthcare industries.

Key Contact - Specialty:
Mr. L.S. Carper, Managing Partner

Salary Minimum: $50,000

Functions: Nurses, Sales & Mktg., Sales Mgmt., Sales Reps., Mgmt. Consultants

Industries: Services, Mgmt. Consulting, Software, Hospitals, Women's

MR of Columbia

(an affiliate of MRI)
1512 Laurel St Fl 1
Columbia, SC 29201-2623
(803) 254-1334
Fax: (803) 254-1527
Email: recruiter@mricolumbia.com
Web: www.brilliantpeople.com

Summary: We specialize in healthcare, manufacturing, medical device industry, and upper level sales.

Key Contact - Specialty:
Mr. Robert Keen, Jr., Manager, Owner
Mr. John W.C. Brandon, Account Executive - *Sales*
Mr. Bobby Johnson, Account Executive
Mr. Jeff Stanley, Account Executive

Salary Minimum: $35,000

Functions: Healthcare, Sales & Mktg.

Industries: Generalist (All), Medical Devices, Pharm Svcs., Biotech/Life Sciences, Hospitals

The Forest Group

(an affiliate of MRI)
2711 Middleburg Dr Ste 313
Columbia, SC 29204-2486
(803) 758-5920
Email: bill@forestgrp.com
Web: www.forestgrp.com

Summary: We are an executive search firm that conducts searches for middle to upper management positions. We specialize in consulting engineering, architecture, manufacturing and banking.

Key Contact - Specialty:
Mr. William F. Duncan, President - *Engineering*

Salary Minimum: $50,000

Functions: Management, Middle Mgmt., Mfg., Plant Mgmt., Finance, Engineering, Bldg. Contractors, Design

Industries: Construction, Manufacturing, Plastics, Rubber, Metal Products, Machine, Appliance, Motor Vehicles, Consumer Elect., Test, Measure Equip., Electronic, Elec. Components, Robotics, Consumer Goods, Transportation, Finance, Banking, Invest. Banking, Brokers, Venture Cap., Mutual/Hedge Funds, Misc. Financial, Architectural Svcs., Mgmt. Consulting, Engineering Svcs., Environmental Svcs., Haz. Waste

MR of Florence

(an affiliate of MRI)
1224 W Evans St
Florence, SC 29501-3322
(843) 664-1112
Fax: (843) 673-2701
Email: jobs@mrflorence.com
Web: www.mrflorence.com

Summary: We identify, recruit and deliver manufacturing and manufacturing support managers, executives and technical professionals for clients who are or want to become world class manufacturers.

Key Contact - Specialty:
Mr. Alan Feimster, President - *Manufacturing*

Salary Minimum: $25,000

Functions: Mfg., Production, Materials

Industries: Manufacturing

FEB & Associates

(also known as MR of North Charleston)
131 Cherry Hill Ave
Goose Creek, SC 29445-5306
(843) 569-7981
Fax: (843) 797-2587
Email: fbabyak@febrecruiters.com

Summary: We are an office that supports manufacturing companies for technical, management, and professional positions.

Key Contact - Specialty:
Mr. Fran Babyak, President & Owner

Salary Minimum: $40,000

Functions: Generalist (All), Management, Mfg., Materials, Sales & Mktg., Finance, Engineering

Industries: Generalist (All), Drugs Mfg., Medical Devices, Metal Products, Machine, Appliance, Motor Vehicles, Consumer Elect., Test, Measure Equip., Misc. Mfg., Electronic, Elec. Components, Robotics, Semiconductors, Biotech/Life Sciences

The Newell Group

(also known as MR of Greer)
2082 Woodruff Rd Ste B
Greenville, SC 29607-5992
(864) 288-0011
Fax: (864) 288-5567
Email: dnewell@mgmttalent.com

Summary: We are an executive recruiting firm specializing in the retail management, insurance, banking and freight forwarding industries.

Key Contact - Specialty:
Mr. Dannie Newell, General Manager

Functions: Generalist (All)

Industries: Generalist (All), Retail, Accounting, Mgmt. Consulting, Insurance

MR of Greenville

(an affiliate of MRI)
150 Executive Center Dr Ste B127
Greenville, SC 29615-4532
(864) 370-2600
Fax: (864) 370-2611
Email: de@mrigreenvillesc.com
Web: www.mrigreenvillesc.com

Summary: We are specialists in finding and placing sales, sales management, marketing, construction and manufacturing management professionals.

Key Contact - Specialty:
Mr. Thomas Blackmon, President
Mr. M.D. Scarboro, President - *Automation, Electrical, Industrial*
Ms. Dee Scarboro

Salary Minimum: $50,000

Functions: Sales Mgmt., Engineering

Industries: Construction, Manufacturing, Lumber, Furniture, Paper, Chemicals, Plastics, Rubber, Metal Products, Machine, Appliance, Misc. Mfg.

MR of Orangeburg

(also known as The Carolina Recruiters Group)
2037 Saint Matthews Rd
Orangeburg, SC 29118-2036
(803) 531-4101
Fax: (803) 536-3714
Email: mro@carolinarecruiters.com
Web: www.carolinarecruiters.com

Summary: Our firm is an integral part of the world's largest executive search and recruitment franchise.

Key Contact - Specialty:
Mr. Ed Chewning, Jr., Account Manager
Mr. Dick B. Crawford, Account Manager
Ms. Lyn Dudarenke, Project Coordinator
Ms. Lindsay Crawford, Project Coordinator
Mr. Charles Hipp, Project Coordinator

Salary Minimum: $40,000

Functions: Management, Mfg., Production, Quality, HR Mgmt., Finance, Engineering

Industries: Manufacturing, Machine, Appliance, Motor Vehicles, Electronic, Elec. Components, Aerospace

SC of Orangeburg

(an affiliate of MRI)
PO Box 1578
Orangeburg, SC 29116-1578
(803) 536-4601
Fax: (803) 536-4401
Email: scoburg@msn.com

Summary: Our firm provides specialists in sales, sales management and marketing professionals.

Industry concentrations: electronics, electrical, industrial controls, robotics, automation, instrumentation, motion control, engraving, marking & etching, environmental, pumps, HVAC and industrial supplies.

Key Contact - Specialty:
Mr. Richard Jackson, President
Ms. Carolyn Jackson, Vice President

Salary Minimum: $25,000

Functions: Management, Board Members, Senior Mgmt., Middle Mgmt., Product Dev., Automation, Sales & Mktg., Sales Mgmt., Engineering

Industries: Generalist (All), Energy, Utilities, Medical Devices, Metal Products, Test, Measure Equip., Misc. Mfg., Electronic, Elec. Components, Robotics, Semiconductors, Engineering Svcs., Biotech/Life Sciences

MR of Powdersville

(an affiliate of MRI)
102 Commons Blvd Ste E
Piedmont, SC 29673-7766
(864) 855-8776
Fax: (864) 220-4243
Email: tbongi@bellsouth.net
Web: www.mritony.com

Summary: We specialize in the pharmaceutical and healthcare fields.

Key Contact - Specialty:
Mr. Tony Bongiovanni, Owner

Salary Minimum: $50,000

Functions: Mfg.

Industries: Pharm Svcs., Healthcare

MR of Myrtle Beach

(an affiliate of MRI)
1500 Highway 17 N Ste 308
Surfside Beach, SC 29575-6080
(843) 477-8800
Fax: (843) 477-8304
Email: contact@jobquestsite.com
Web: www.jobquestsite.com

Summary: We provide a superior recruiting service for corporate clients to aid in their growth and to provide candidates with the most rewarding career opportunities in their pursuit of excellence.

Key Contact - Specialty:
Mr. Mark E. Lewis, President - *Manufacturing*

Salary Minimum: $40,000

Functions: Generalist (All), Management, Production, Plant Mgmt., Quality, Materials, Mktg. Mgmt., Engineering

Industries: Generalist (All), Manufacturing, Food, Bev., Tobacco, Plastics, Rubber, Machine, Appliance, Motor Vehicles, Consumer Elect., Misc. Mfg., Transportation, Retail

MR of Travelers Rest

(an affiliate of MRI)
PO Box 639
Travelers Rest, SC 29690-0639
(864) 834-0643
Fax: (864) 834-0275
Email: gcmrtr@aol.com
Web: www.brilliantpeople.com

Summary: We are one of a vast number of franchised offices that are fully computerized with inter-office referral, executive search profile program, video conferencing centers and a custom designed IT program that optimizes information and communication flow within each office, between management recruiters offices and between individual offices and the business world.

Key Contact - Specialty:
Mr. Guy W. Carter, President
Ms. Gail Carter, Manager

Salary Minimum: $30,000

Functions: Management, Engineering

Industries: Manufacturing, Textiles, Apparel, Chemicals, Plastics, Rubber

MR of Sioux Falls

(an affiliate of MRI)
116 W 69th St Ste 200
Sioux Falls, SD 57108-6418
(605) 367-6939
(888) 693-6887
Fax: (605) 367-6940
Email: get@agoodjob.com
Web: www.agoodjob.com

Summary: Permanent and interim search and placement; executive, professional, management, technical, sales, and marketing.

Key Contact - Specialty:
Mr. David J. Good, Partner
Mr. Robert B. Good, Partner
Mr. Rick Bauermeister, Executive Recruiter
Ms. Pat Caldwell, Senior Account Manager
Mr. David Dierks, Account Executive - *Construction, Electrical, Engineering, General contractors, HVAC*

Salary Minimum: $30,000

Functions: Generalist (All)

Industries: Construction, Manufacturing, Finance, Services, Telecoms, Software

MR of Brentwood

(also known as Advantage One Executive Search)
231 Wilson Pike Cir Ste 204
Brentwood, TN 37027-5286
(615) 507-1717
Fax: (615) 507-1727
Email: lvaughn@advantage-search.com
Web: www.advantage-search.com

Summary: Our firm specializes in the pharmaceutical, bio-technology and medical/research equipment industries in the following areas: general management, sales & marketing, R&D, materials management, manufacturing, finance & accounting, regulatory affairs and IT/bio-informatics.

Key Contact - Specialty:
Mr. Larry Vaughn

Salary Minimum: $50,000

Functions: Management, Product Dev., Sales & Mktg., R&D

Industries: Biotech/Life Sciences

MR of Columbia

(an affiliate of MRI)
1129 Trotwood Ave Ste 11
Columbia, TN 38401-3046
(931) 388-5586
Email: dch@mritn.com
Web: www.mritn.com

Summary: We focus on management, administrative and technical recruiting for automotive and related manufacturing industries.

Key Contact - Specialty:
Mr. Douglas Holt, Manager - *Accounting, Automotive, Engineering, Maintenance, Supply Chain*
Ms. Marianne Stevick, Account Executive - *Accounting, Automotive, Engineering, Maintenance, Supply Chain*

Salary Minimum: $30,000

Functions: Generalist (All), Mfg., Plant Mgmt., Quality, Productivity, Materials, Engineering, Process

Industries: Manufacturing, Plastics, Rubber, Metal Products, Motor Vehicles, Electronic, Elec. Components, Robotics

MR of Cordova

(an affiliate of MRI)
1180 Vickery Ln Ste 4
Cordova, TN 38016-0629
(901) 432-1674
Fax: (901) 432-2674
Email: ehatcher@midsouth.rr.com
Web: www.mricordova.com

Summary: Our firm is an extremely aggressive search firm. We specialize in a variety of industries. Whether you are looking for entry-level professionals or executive caliber talent, we are the perfect place to spearhead your next search.

Key Contact - Specialty:
Mr. Eddy Hatcher, President - *Manufacturing*
Mr. Jason Martin, Account Executive
Mr. Josh Hatcher, Webmaster & Marketing Manager
Ms. Ann Roach
Ms. Jamie Miller
Mr. Jerry Brzowski

Functions: Generalist (All)

Industries: Generalist (All)

SalesHunter Inc

(an affiliate of MRI)
PO Box 38328
Germantown, TN 38183-0328
(901) 751-1995
Email: info@saleshunter.com
Web: www.saleshunter.com

Summary: Finding and placing sales talent is our only business.

Key Contact - Specialty:
Mr. Wayne Williams, President

Functions: Sales & Mktg.

Industries: Generalist (All)

MR of Chattanooga North

(an affiliate of MRI)
4808 Hixson Pike
Hixson, TN 37343-4416
(423) 877-4040
Fax: (423) 877-4466
Email: chub@inconfidence.com
Web: www.inconfidence.com

Summary: We are a professional search and recruiting firm specializing in accounting and technical positions in manufacturing. We also place data/com-tele/com sales positions.

Key Contact - Specialty:
Mr. Chub Ensminger, President & General Manager
Ms. Judy Kemp, Vice President, Recruiting
Mr. John Bates, Vice President, Recruiting

Salary Minimum: $50,000

Functions: Generalist (All), Mfg., Production, Plant Mgmt., Quality, Materials, Purchasing, Sales & Mktg., Sales Mgmt., Finance

Industries: Textiles, Apparel, Paper, Chemicals, Plastics, Rubber, Paints, Petro. Products, Metal Products, Machine, Appliance, Motor Vehicles, Computer Equip., Consumer Elect., Misc. Mfg., Electronic, Elec. Components, Accounting, Mgmt. Consulting, HR Services, Telecoms, Telephony, Digital, Wireless, Fiber Optic, Network Infrastructure

MR of Lenoir City

(an affiliate of MRI)
530 Highway 321 N Ste 303
Lenoir City, TN 37771-6407
(865) 986-3000
Fax: (865) 986-0874
Email: mrilc@aol.com

Summary: Specializing in recruitment within the manufacturing sector. Disciplines include engineering, production management and quality assurance. Industries include automotive, electric motors.

Key Contact - Specialty:
Mr. Ray S. Strobo, Manager

Functions: Mfg., Product Dev., Production, Automation, Plant Mgmt., Quality, Productivity, Engineering, Eng. Design, Hardware

Industries: Plastics, Rubber, Metal Products, Machine, Appliance, Motor Vehicles, Misc. Mfg., Robotics

MR of Bartlett

(an affiliate of MRI)
5158 Stage Rd Ste 130
Memphis, TN 38134-3116
(901) 888-2580
Fax: (901) 888-2581
Email: george@genmfg.com
Web: www.genmfg.com

Summary: Recruiting in the manufacturing industries, including engineering, operations, finance, HR, sales, accounting and purchasing.

Key Contact - Specialty:
Mr. George A. Harants, Manager - *Manufacturing, Middle management, Operations, Packaging, Production*
Ms. Debra Henderson, Account Executive - *Accounting, Accounting (Bookkeeping,General), Manufacturing, Manufacturing (Management)*

Salary Minimum: $40,000

Functions: Generalist (All), Production, Purchasing, HR Mgmt., CFOs, Engineering

Industries: Generalist (All), Manufacturing, Food, Bev., Tobacco, Paper, Accounting

MR of Nashville

(an affiliate of MRI)
4701 Trousdale Dr Ste 208
Nashville, TN 37220-1385
(615) 333-6067
Email: positions@mrnashville.com
Web: www.mrnashville.com

Summary: Healthcare industry specialists.

Key Contact - Specialty:
Mr. John W. Anderson, President - *Healthcare*

Functions: Generalist (All), Healthcare

Industries: Generalist (All), Healthcare

MR of Fort Worth-Arlington

(an affiliate of MRI)
1001 W Randol Mill Rd
Arlington, TX 76012-2513
(817) 469-6161
Fax: (817) 462-9155
Email: info@topcareers.com
Web: www.topcareers.com

Summary: We are a consistent leading mid-size management recruiters office. Our account managers specialize in placing: engineering, oil & gas, petroleum exploration & service, energy transmission, power marketing, health care, medical, manufacturing, food & beverage

manufacturing, printing and packaging professionals.

Key Contact - Specialty:
Mr. Robert J. Stoessel, CPC, General Manager - *Energy, Manufacturing*
Mr. Larry Laux, Manager - *Energy, Pipeline, Power, Refineries*

Salary Minimum: $50,000

Functions: Generalist (All), Management

Industries: Energy, Utilities, Oil & Gas, Construction, Food, Bev., Tobacco, Printing, Test, Measure Equip., Misc. Mfg., Electronic, Elec. Components, Equip Svcs., Logistics Svcs., Digital, Wireless, Fiber Optic, Database SW, Mfg. SW, Healthcare, Hospitals, Long-term/Home Care

SC of Austin

(an affiliate of MRI)
2301 S Capital of Texas Hwy Ste J101
Austin, TX 78746-7706
(512) 328-9955
Fax: (512) 328-8659
Email: dkilgore@vistasearchgroup.com
Web: www.vistasearchgroup.com

Summary: We specialize in placing individuals in the following industries: architectural/engineering consulting, airport consulting, banking, civil engineering, clinical research, and public relations.

Key Contact - Specialty:
Mr. C. Jay Middlebrook, President
Ms. Linda Middlebrook, Vice President

Functions: Middle Mgmt., Nurses, Sales Mgmt., PR, Eng. Design, Architects

Industries: Generalist (All), Banking, Pharm Svcs., Engineering Svcs.

MR of Bellaire

(an affiliate of MRI)
5116 Bissonnet St # 454
Bellaire, TX 77401-4007
(713) 668-8501
Email: marolda@mr-bellaire.com
Web: www.mr-bellaire.com

Summary: We perform both retained and contingency searches, focusing on consumer electronics, home automation, lighting, consumer products, and wireless industries. Our focus is in the sales/marketing, product managing and marketing, and engineering arenas.

Key Contact - Specialty:
Mr. Tony Marolda, Manager - *Consumer, Engineering, Home and building controls*
Mr. Bruce Crosthwait, Manager - *Acoustics, Marketing, Office (Products), Peripherals, Senior management*

Salary Minimum: $50,000

Functions: Management, Senior Mgmt., Mfg., Product Dev., Sales & Mktg., Mktg. Research, Mktg. Mgmt., Sales Mgmt., Sales Reps., Engineering

Industries: Generalist (All), Lumber, Furniture, Printing, Machine, Appliance, Computer Equip., Consumer Elect., Misc. Mfg., Electronic, Elec. Components, Consumer Goods, Wholesale, Hospitality, Entertainment, Publishing, New Media, Broadcast, Film, Communications, Telecoms, Digital, Wireless, RF/Microwave, Software, Mfg. SW

Graham Group

(an affiliate of MRI)
3740 N Josey Ln Ste 136
Carrollton, TX 75007-2502
(972) 939-8585

Email: sgraham@graphamgroupusa.com
Web: www.grahamgroupusa.com

Summary: Our firm offers recruitment solutions for an extensive and continuously growing list of companies in meeting their needs for world-class talent. Our team is dedicated to the recruitment of insurance professionals and is committed to the highest level of quality service and performance.

Key Contact - Specialty:
Mr. Shane Graham, Managing Partner
Mr. Bobby Graham, Managing Partner

Salary Minimum: $75,000

Functions: Management, Board Members, Senior Mgmt., Middle Mgmt., Admin. Svcs., Sales & Mktg., Sales Mgmt., Customer Svc., Sales Reps., Benefits

Industries: Insurance, Casualty, Claims, Life, Commercial, Re-Insurance

The Denson Group Inc

(also known as SC of Bradenton)
8972 Crighton Crossing Dr
Conroe, TX 77302-3479
(936) 494-2708
Email: info@densongroup.com
Web: www.densongroup.com

Summary: We specialize in marketing, sales management, engineering, QA, QC and regulatory affairs in the medical device industry.

Key Contact - Specialty:
Mr. Steve Denson, Founder
Mrs. Kip Denson, Co-Founder

Functions: Generalist (All)

Industries: Medical Devices

MR of Dallas

(an affiliate of MRI)
17950 Preston Rd Ste 980
Dallas, TX 75252-5637
(972) 788-1515
Fax: (972) 701-8242
Email: plineback@mridallas.com

Summary: Our firm is - part of the worldwide franchise - retainer and contingency - specializing in most job titles in construction, logistics, energy, IT, insurance, manufacturing, health care, financial services and various sales positions.

Key Contact - Specialty:
Mr. Robert Lineback, General Manager
Ms. Pam Lineback, Managing Director - *Construction, General management*

Salary Minimum: $60,000

Functions: Generalist (All)

Industries: Oil & Gas, Construction, Pharm Svcs., Legal, Accounting, E-commerce, Logistics Svcs., Insurance, Software, Healthcare

MR of Dallas North

(an affiliate of MRI)
15150 Preston Rd Ste 300
Dallas, TX 75248-4871
(972) 991-4500
Fax: (972) 858-7849
Email: mrdn@sprynet.com
Web: www.mrdn.biz

Summary: We are a firm with expertise in providing professionals in the areas of distribution and logistics, materials management, high-technology manufacturing management and HR & IT management. We also serve as the sales arm of a select group of clients in the dermatology industry.

Key Contact - Specialty:
Mr. George Buntrock, President - *Distribution, Logistics*

Salary Minimum: $50,000

Functions: Management, Plant Mgmt., Materials, Sales & Mktg., HR Mgmt., IT

Industries: Manufacturing, Misc. Mfg., Electronic, Elec. Components, Semiconductors, Transportation, Wholesale, Retail, Logistics Svcs., Supply Chain Mgmt, Non-Classifiable

SC of Dallas

(an affiliate of MRI)
3010 Lyndon B Johnson Fwy Ste 1470
Dallas, TX 75234-2735
(972) 488-9191
Fax: (972) 488-9090
Email: scdallas@scdallas.com
Web: www.scdallas.com

Summary: Extensive experience in professional sales/sales management/tech staffing. We are the top franchisee of one of the largest franchise companies in the world. Recognized for outstanding service to client industries; banking, travel, building materials, industrial, food, food service, SAP, and electronics.

Key Contact - Specialty:
Mr. Mark B. Rednick, President
Mrs. Anita Rednick, EP & Partner

Salary Minimum: $45,000

Functions: Generalist (All), Sales & Mktg., Sales Mgmt., Sales Reps.

Industries: Generalist (All), Construction, Manufacturing, Food, Bev., Tobacco, Electronic, Elec. Components, Semiconductors, Banking, Misc. Financial, Non-profits, Mgmt. Consulting, Logistics Svcs., Supply Chain Mgmt, Travel, ERP SW

Burt Moses Associates Inc

(also known as MR of Addison)
15400 Knoll Trail Dr Ste 230
Dallas, TX 75248-7022
(972) 702-0480
Fax: (972) 702-0482
Email: jobs@bmasearch.com
Web: www.bmasearch.com

Summary: We are an executive search firm for property and casualty insurance professionals. We place technical levels and higher. We are able to provide a vertical approach for our client companies. Each of our recruiting executives has solid insurance backgrounds with prior experience in the industry itself.

Key Contact - Specialty:
Mr. Burt Moses, CPCU, President & Chief Executive Officer
Mr. Curtis Powell, Senior Vice President
Mr. Bobby Lonergan, Vice President
Mrs. Lynne Moses, Vice President - *Insurance*

Salary Minimum: $50,000

Functions: Generalist (All), Management, Senior Mgmt., Middle Mgmt.

Industries: Insurance

Siter-Neubauer & Associates

(also known as MR of Fort Worth-Southwest)
5001 Byers Ave
Fort Worth, TX 76107-3625
(817) 989-9700
Fax: (817) 569-1126
Email: careers@mrifortworth.com
Web: www.mrifortworth.com

Summary: We provide executive recruitment focusing on telecom, IT, health care, civil, electrical, mechanical, architectural, software, hardware and embedded engineering, HR and banking.

Key Contact - Specialty:
Mr. Don Neubauer, Executive Vice President
Mr. Les Siter, President

Functions: Generalist (All), IT, Engineering

Industries: Generalist (All), Energy, Utilities, Construction, Manufacturing, Finance, Communications, Software, Healthcare

MR of Fort Worth-Downtown

(an affiliate of MRI)
500 W 7th St Unit 14
Fort Worth, TX 76102-4772
(817) 348-8900
Fax: (817) 348-8905
Email: info@mrifw.com
Web: www.mrifw.com

Summary: Our office specializes in providing high quality candidates for a variety of engineering, financial, management and sales & marketing positions in the following industries: aerospace, automotive, banking, biotechnology, construction, contract manufacturing, electronics, general manufacturing, and pharmaceutical.

Key Contact - Specialty:
Mr. Lee Shahwan, Managing Director

Functions: Mfg., Healthcare, Sales Mgmt., Engineering

Industries: Construction, Manufacturing, Drugs Mfg., Medical Devices, Computer Equip., Consumer Elect., Misc. Mfg., Electronic, Elec. Components, Robotics, Pharm Svcs., Engineering Svcs., Communications, RF/Microwave, Defense, Aerospace, Biotech/Life Sciences, Healthcare

Parkwood International

(an affiliate of MRI)
3550 Parkwood Blvd Ste 500
Frisco, TX 75034-1914
(972) 668-9855
Fax: (972) 668-9877
Email: admin@parkwoodintl.com
Web: www.parkwoodintl.com

Summary: Our firm provides permanent placement and contract staffing solutions and expertise in the following fields: consumer packaged goods, food & beverage, IT and telecom, industrial manufacturing, logistics & distribution, medical device sales & marketing, pharmaceutical sales, marketing and technical positions, packaging, finance & accounting, printing and pre-media, securities, chemicals.

Key Contact - Specialty:
Ms. Judy Daugherty, Chief Operating Officer, CSM - *Staffing*
Mr. Hal Daugherty, President, CSM - *Engineering, Finance, Human resources, Manufacturing, Manufacturing (Management)*
Mr. Alan Fine, Senior Search Consultant, CSAM - *Medical (Devices)*
Mr. Jeff Bailey, Senior Search Consultant, CSAM - *Medical, Medical (Devices,Sales)*
Ms. Donna Fine, Office Manager
Mr. Carl Gundlach, Senior Search Consultant, CSAM - *Manufacturing*
Mr. Etienne Joseph, III, Senior Search Consultant - *Medical, Medical (Devices)*
Ms. Racheal Donovan, Technical Manager
Mr. Reed Rogers, Senior Search Consultant - *Chemical, Manufacturing, Refineries*
Mr. Tim Wright, Senior Search Consultant, CSAM - *Accounting, Finance*

Mr. John Branson, Senior Search Consultant - *Film, Plastics*
Mr. Patrick Perry, Senior Search Consultant - *Printing*
Ms. Cara Harbour, Senior Search Consultant - *Pharmaceutical*
Ms. Sherri Kemp, Senior Search Consultant - *Pharmaceutical*
Mr. Frank Holt, Search Consultant - *Film, Plastics*
Mr. Joel Patterson, Search Consultant - *Accounting, Finance*
Ms. Christie Wright, Project Coordinator - *Medical (Devices)*
Mr. Jon Hoover, Search Consultant - *Pharmaceutical*
Mr. Allen Roulette, Search Consultant, Contract - *Information Systems, Information Technology, Telecommunications*
Mr. Nick Donovan, Search Consultant, Contract - *Information Systems, Information Technology, Telecommunications*
Mr. Nathan Hill, Search Consultant - *Information Systems, Information Technology*
Ms. Linda McEvoy, Administrative Assistant

Salary Minimum: $40,000

Functions: Generalist (All), Packaging, Healthcare, Nurses, Mktg. Mgmt., Sales Mgmt., Finance, IT, Engineering

Industries: Generalist (All), Manufacturing, Food, Bev., Tobacco, Printing, Chemicals, Drugs Mfg., Medical Devices, Finance, Pharm Svcs., Accounting, Engineering Svcs., Logistics Svcs., Packaging

MR of Houston West

(also known as Albrecht & Assoc Executive Search Consultants)
1360 Post Oak Blvd Ste 2015
Houston, TX 77056-3049
(713) 850-9850
Email: franke.albrecht@princetonsearch.com
Web: www.albrecht-assoc.com

Summary: We specialize in the pharmaceutical and bio-technology industries, as well as finance and accounting across industries. Our database includes virtually every company in these industries and we have an extensive network of clients and professionals in these organizations.

Key Contact - Specialty:
Ms. Franke M. Albrecht, President - *Biopharmaceutical, Biotechnology, Pharmaceutical*

Salary Minimum: $60,000

Functions: Generalist (All)

Industries: Drugs Mfg., Misc. Financial, Pharm Svcs., Accounting

SC of Houston

(an affiliate of MRI)
5075 Westheimer Rd Ste 790
Houston, TX 77056-5629
(713) 627-0880
Fax: (713) 622-7285
Email: jimd@schouston.com
Web: www.schouston.com

Summary: Single source HR services which include: custom search projects, permanent placement, interim executives, sales blitz management, videoconferencing, outplacement and relocation assistance/management.

Key Contact - Specialty:
Mr. Jim DeForest, President - *Chemical, Financial services, Plastics, Securities, Staffing*
Ms. Karene Jones, Vice President, Operations - *Financial services*

Mr. John Bradshaw, Vice President, Financial Services Div - *Financial services, Securities*
Mr. Rick Thwaites, CSAM, Certified Senior Account Manager - *Chemical, Coatings*
Mr. Dick Koob, Account Executive - *Packaging, Plastics*
Mr. Jeff Fox, Account Executive - *Business to business, Staffing*

Salary Minimum: $30,000

Functions: Generalist (All), Senior Mgmt., Mfg., Sales & Mktg., Benefits, Training, IT, Int'l.

Industries: Generalist (All), Manufacturing, Chemicals, Pharm Svcs., Law Enforcement, Publishing, Telecoms, Packaging

MR of Champions

(an affiliate of MRI)
3220 FM 1960 Rd W Ste A8
Houston, TX 77068-3109
(281) 580-6020
Fax: (914) 992-7766
Email: gakin@mrichampions.com
Web: www.mrichampions.com

Summary: Providing permanent placement, interim executive and outplacement services to clients needing candidates in sales engineering, manufacturing, cutting tools, mechanical & electrical engineering design, controls engineering and system integration.

Key Contact - Specialty:
Mr. Gary K. Akin, Manager
Ms. Nicola Akin, Co-Manager
Mr. Joe Slack, Account Executive

Salary Minimum: $35,000

Functions: Mfg., Product Dev., Production, Automation, Packaging, Sales & Mktg., Sales Mgmt., Systems Implem., Engineering

Industries: Manufacturing, Medical Devices, Metal Products, Misc. Mfg., Equip Svcs., Packaging

MR of LBJ Park-Dallas

(an affiliate of MRI)
400 E Royal Ln Ste 214
Irving, TX 75039-3512
(972) 488-1133 x101
Fax: (972) 488-1099
Email: info@mridfw.com
Web: www.mridfw.com

Summary: Our principal's background includes extensive experience in personnel recruiting, management, and training.

Key Contact - Specialty:
Mr. Ray Vlasek, President - *Technical*

Salary Minimum: $55,000

Functions: Generalist (All), Engineering

Industries: Construction, Chemicals, Metal Products, Machine, Appliance, Misc. Mfg., Architectural Svcs., Engineering Svcs., Telecoms, RF/Microwave, Aerospace, Healthcare

MR of Houston Northeast

(also known as LinGate Corp Inc)
1412A Stonehollow Dr
Kingwood, TX 77339-2493
(281) 359-7940
(800) 234-9316
Fax: (281) 359-7947
Email: lindak@mrihouston.com
Web: www.mrihouston.com

Summary: Our specialty divisions' partnered with all the leading companies in those industries to provide talented employees in technical,

managerial and executive positions. Our specialties include: lumber & building products, accounting/finance, architectural services, logistics and real estate. Our reputation in those industries is impeccable. We conduct retained and contingency searches for our client companies.

Key Contact - Specialty:
Ms. Linda Copeland, President
Mr. Gates Copeland, Vice President - *Forest industry/products*
Mr. Jeff Flowers, Account Executive - *Forest industry/products*
Ms. Susan Crusham, Account Executive - *Logistics*
Mr. Christopher Rowland, Account Executive
Ms. Amy Salsman, Account Executive - *Real estate*
Ms. Maria Wojciechowski, Account Executive - *Hospitality, Real estate*
Mr. Vernon Massey, Account Executive - *Building products*

Salary Minimum: $40,000

Functions: Generalist (All), Board Members, Senior Mgmt., Middle Mgmt., Finance, Architects

Industries: Generalist (All), Agri., Forestry, Mining, Construction, Lumber, Furniture, Paper, Medical Devices, Motor Vehicles, Wholesale, Retail, Finance, Banking, Invest. Banking, Accounting, HR Services, Insurance, Real Estate, Accounting SW, Development SW, Non-Classifiable

MR of Lewisville

(an affiliate of MRI)
1660 S Stemmons Fwy Ste 460
Lewisville, TX 75067-6392
(972) 434-9612
Fax: (972) 221-0268
Email: mrlrec@swbell.net
Web: www.mrlewisville.com

Summary: We have the employment solutions you need to thrive and grow, from permanent placement to flexible staffing to what we call 'right-fit services'. Our team specializes in matching highly qualified personnel with the special skills needed to solve client-staffing needs. Our project team knows the auto ID, printing, RF and industrial software solutions industries and the people in those industries.

Key Contact - Specialty:
Ms. Desni C. Kramer, General Manager - *Computers (Software)*

Salary Minimum: $50,000

Functions: Sales & Mktg.

Industries: Generalist (All)

MR of Keller

(an affiliate of MRI)
PO Box 822576
North Richland Hills, TX 76182-2576
(817) 237-0222
(817) 237-0223
Email: barbara@mreaglemountain.com
Web: www.mreaglemountain.com

Summary: Our firm recruits electrical engineers, mechanical engineers, controls engineers, maintenance managers, project engineers, process engineers, manufacturing engineers, industrial engineers, plant management operations management, applications engineers and sales engineers. Keywords/skills: manufacturing, operations, engineering, electrical, mechanical, sales and controls.

Key Contact - Specialty:
Ms. Barbara Baez

Salary Minimum: $60,000

Functions: Mfg.

Industries: Manufacturing, Food, Bev., Tobacco, Paper, Chemicals, Soap, Perf., Cosmtcs., Medical Devices, Plastics, Rubber, Paints, Petro. Products, Metal Products, Misc. Mfg.

The Jacob Group

(also known as MR of Preston Park)
2301 N Central Expy Ste 250
Plano, TX 75075-2586
(972) 422-3311
(800) 875-8546
Fax: (972) 422-4001
Email: solutions@jacobgroup.com
Web: www.jacobgroup.com

Summary: We are an executive search team specializing in all functional areas. We have special capability in large multiple hire projects.

Key Contact - Specialty:
Mr. Donald C. Jacob, Principal - *Human resources, Marketing, Operations, Sales*
Mr. Michael Patterson, Vice President
Mr. Craig Guidry, Vice President - *Human resources*
Mr. Jon Peterson, Vice President - *Food & beverage*

Salary Minimum: $50,000

Functions: Management, Mfg., Plant Mgmt., Materials, Sales & Mktg., HR Mgmt., Finance, Engineering, Hospitality, Hotel Mgmt.

Industries: Generalist (All), Banking

SC of San Antonio

(an affiliate of MRI)
8626 Tesoro Dr Ste 515
San Antonio, TX 78217-6217
(210) 805-0900
Fax: (210) 805-0904
Email: careers@scsanantonio.com
Web: www.scsanantonio.com

Summary: Whether you are an employer with critical staffing needs or a top-notch candidate seeking a new position, we can help you achieve your goals. We are dedicated to helping professionals advance their careers. Our mission is to develop long-term partnerships with our clients by providing world-class, value-added, human capital solutions. Professional, ethical, committed to quality, with a responsive and considerate attitude towards.

Key Contact - Specialty:
Mr. Chuck Wright, President
Ms. Vanessa Geck, Director, Research & Project Coordinator - *Energy*

Salary Minimum: $40,000

Functions: Generalist (All), Management, Sales & Mktg.

Industries: Food, Bev., Tobacco

MR of San Antonio

(an affiliate of MRI)
901 NE Loop 410 Ste 425
San Antonio, TX 78209-1307
(210) 829-8666
Fax: (210) 822-2218
Email: contact@mrisanantonio.com
Web: www.mrisanantonio.com

Summary: Additional client services include reduced rate moves, reduced rate mortgages, refinancing & closing costs and video conference network for interviewing (all financial services available to clients and candidates placed by us).

Key Contact - Specialty:
Mr. James L. Cornfoot, President
Mr. Scott Lane, Account Manager - *Food & beverage, Manufacturing, Manufacturing (Management), Production, Quality*
Ms. Lori Smith, Project Manager
Ms. Sarah Barrette, Project Coordinator - *Consumer (Packaged Goods,Products), Food & beverage, Marketing, Sales*

Salary Minimum: $70,000

Functions: Management, Middle Mgmt., Mfg., Production, Plant Mgmt., Quality, Distribution

Industries: Food, Bev., Tobacco, Motor Vehicles, Consumer Goods

---

MR of Dallas-Southlake

(an affiliate of MRI)
2535 E Southlake Blvd Ste 270
Southlake, TX 76092-6628
(817) 310-0606
Fax: (817) 310-0608
Email: tim@mriadvantage.com
Web: www.mriadvantage.com

Summary: We offer construction recruiting.

Key Contact - Specialty:
Mr. Timothy Matthews, President
Mr. Tim Spelts, Project Coordinator
Mr. Jeff Kenline, Account Executive
Mr. Tim Bernat, Account Executive
Mr. Chris Kenline, Researcher
Ms. Lynn Tipton, Administrative Assistant
Ms. Nicole Bernat, Executive Assistant - *Automotive, Engineering, Food & beverage, Manufacturing*

Functions: Generalist (All)

Industries: Construction

MR of Sugar Land

(an affiliate of MRI)
12919 Southwest Fwy Ste 100
Stafford, TX 77477-4104
(281) 240-0220
Fax: (281) 240-0880
Email: joan@mrfortbend.com

Summary: We are an executive search firm, specializing in the wood products industry. We work a vertical market in lumber, both hardwood and softwood, plywood, veneer, manufactured wood products and reconstituted wood products. We also handle placements in pulp, paper, packaging, and envelopes. We are always happy to hear from you whether you are a client company or candidate.

Key Contact - Specialty:
Mr. John R. Gandee, President - *Lumber, Millwork*
Ms. Joan C. Gandee, Vice President - *Lumber*
Mr. Don Hayes, Senior Search Consultant - *Paper*
Mr. Brad Gandee, Research Associate
Ms. Shayna Gandee, Project Coordinator - *Lumber, Millwork*

Salary Minimum: $30,000

Functions: Mfg., Sales & Mktg., HR Mgmt.

Industries: Lumber, Furniture, Paper, Packaging

MR of Ogden

(an affiliate of MRI)
533 26th St Ste 203B
Ogden, UT 84401-2459
(801) 621-1777
Fax: (801) 621-1788
Email: info@mrogden.com
Web: www.mrogden.com

Summary: We provide permanent and contract placement of technical and manufacturing individuals with an emphasis in HVAC, electric heat, appliance, trucks & tractors, power tools, wireless communication design, RF components, installation and sales & business development.

Key Contact - Specialty:
Mr. Jerry Manning, Owner & Manager - *Quality, Technical*
Mr. Rich Horwitz, Account Executive - *Biotechnology*
Mr. Scott Bexell, Account Executive
Mr. Andy Colbert, Administrative Assistant

Salary Minimum: $40,000

Functions: Generalist (All)

Industries: Manufacturing, Lumber, Furniture, Machine, Appliance, Test, Measure Equip., Misc. Mfg., Electronic, Elec. Components, Biotech/Life Sciences

---

MR of Provo

(an affiliate of MRI)
1933 N 1120 W
Provo, UT 84604-1044
(801) 375-0777
Fax: (801) 375-5757
Email: submit@jobsforpros.com
Web: www.jobsforpros.com

Summary: We are a search and recruiting firm specializing in commercial & investment banking, photonics, RF & microwave technology, automation, medical devices, bio-technology and pharmaceuticals & food manufacturing. Our recruiting focus is in the following disciplines: sales & business development, marketing, R&D, engineering, manufacturing, operations, quality assurance and clinical affairs.

Key Contact - Specialty:
Mr. Larry Massung, BSME, President
Mr. Nick Yama, Account Executive

Salary Minimum: $60,000

Functions: Generalist (All)

Industries: Food, Bev., Tobacco, Drugs Mfg., Medical Devices, Test, Measure Equip., Electronic, Elec. Components, Robotics, Banking, Invest. Banking, Communications, Biotech/Life Sciences

---

MR of Salt Lake City

(also known as Biostats Staffing)
1100 E 6600 S Ste 350
Salt Lake City, UT 84121-7400
(801) 264-9800
(800) 622-2085
Email: jobsusa@mrislc.com
Web: www.mrislc.com

Summary: Our search consultants are experts in their niches. We deliver impact players in the following areas: call centers, medical devices, commercial bankers in the Western US, biostatistics, and professionals in Utah.

Key Contact - Specialty:
Mr. Dirk A. Cotterell, President
Ms. Cary Jo Nieman, Researcher - *Banking, Biomedical, Call centers, Franchising, Pharmaceutical*
Mr. Micah Stanford, Senior Search Consultant

Salary Minimum: $70,000

Functions: Generalist (All), Quality, Sales & Mktg., R&D

Industries: Drugs Mfg., Medical Devices, Banking, Misc. Financial, Pharm Svcs., Mgmt. Consulting, HR Services, Logistics Svcs., Call Centers, Biotech/Life Sciences, Non-Classifiable

---

SC of Salt Lake City

(an affiliate of MRI)
1234 W South Jordan Pkwy Ste D100
South Jordan, UT 84095-4640
(801) 263-2400
Fax: (801) 302-9340
Email: admin@scslc.com
Web: www.scslc.com

Summary: We are specialists in the banking and application software worlds. Focusing on business development oriented professionals, from senior account executive to EVP, we bring the talent to you that can bring extraordinary returns in increased revenues, fees and profits.

Key Contact - Specialty:
Mr. Robert L. Hawks, Manager

Salary Minimum: $50,000

Functions: Middle Mgmt., Sales & Mktg., Mktg. Mgmt., Sales Mgmt.

Industries: Computer Equip., Banking, Software

MR of Burlington

(an affiliate of MRI)
PO Box 529
Hinesburg, VT 05461-0529
(802) 434-3000
Fax: (802) 329-2022
Email: mri@mri-vt.com
Web: www.mri-vt.com

Summary: Specialize in executive positions in finance nationally,compliance, banking, wealth management, retail & wholesale brokerage, consulting and insurance.

Key Contact - Specialty:
Mr. Alan Nyhan, Manager - *Banking (Commercial,Corporate,Investment)*
Mr. Paul Dawson, Recruiter - *Banking (Commercial,Corporate), Compliance, Investment management, Risk management*
Mrs. Nickie Dymon, Recruiter - *Banking (Commercial,Corporate,Investment,Mortgage), Finance*
Mr. Dave Barchard, Recruiter - *Banking, Banking (Commercial,Corporate,Investment), Capital markets*
Mr. Paul Toth - *Banking, Banking (Commercial,Corporate,Investment,Mortgage)*

Salary Minimum: $70,000

Functions: Generalist (All)

Industries: Banking, Invest. Banking, Brokers, Venture Cap., Mutual/Hedge Funds, Misc. Financial, Mgmt. Consulting

---

MR of Loudoun County South

(an affiliate of MRI)
PO Box 220685
Chantilly, VA 20153-6685
(703) 430-3700
Email: mri@cox.net
Web: www.mrloudoun.com

Summary: Complete HR services provider: permanent placement, outplacement assistance, management consulting, and relocation services offered to client companies.

Key Contact - Specialty:
Mr. Jerry Gilmore, General Manager

Salary Minimum: $50,000

Functions: Management, Middle Mgmt., Production, Plant Mgmt., Quality, Engineering, Environmentalists, Health & Safety

Industries: Energy, Utilities, Oil & Gas, Manufacturing, Chemicals, Soap, Perf., Cosmtcs., Drugs Mfg., Plastics, Rubber, Paints,

Petro. Products, Engineering Svcs., Environmental Svcs.

The Keswick Group

(an affiliate of MRI)
215 Wayles Ln Ste 100
Charlottesville, VA 22911-4661
(434) 220-4664
Fax: (434) 220-4676
Email: careers@keswickgroup.com

Summary: An executive search firm focused on the managed care, healthcare and healthcare consulting industries.

Key Contact - Specialty:
Mr. Paul Pascale

Functions: Generalist (All), Management, Senior Mgmt., Middle Mgmt., Healthcare, Nurses, Health Admin., HR Mgmt., Actuaries

Industries: Pharm Svcs., Legal, Accounting, Mgmt. Consulting, HR Services, Call Centers, Insurance, Casualty, Claims, Healthcare, Hospitals, Long-term/Home Care, Non-Classifiable

The Monticello Group

(also known as MR of Monticello)
590 Peter Jefferson Pkwy Ste 175
Charlottesville, VA 22911-4655
(434) 817-5300
Fax: (509) 695-8565
Email: info@mr-monticello.com
Web: www.mr-monticello.com

Summary: Our health care IT team specializes in providing staffing solutions in the placement of sales, implementation and revenue cycle management executives in the healthcare IT/software industry. TMG's long-term care/extended living team focus includes assisted and independent living clients.

Key Contact - Specialty:
Mr. Bill Anda
Ms. Stevia Anda

Salary Minimum: $50,000

Functions: Senior Mgmt., Healthcare, Nurses, Health Admin., Sales & Mktg., Sales Mgmt., Sales Reps., Systems Implem.

Industries: Software, Industry Specific SW, Healthcare, Long-term/Home Care

MR of Park Place

(an affiliate of MRI)
7524 Detwiller Dr
Clifton, VA 20124-2809
(703) 815-9300
Fax: (703) 365-9285
Email: resumes@mrparkplace.com

Summary: Executive search and recruitment in banking and financial services industry.

Key Contact - Specialty:
Mr. Michael Park
Ms. Jana Park

Salary Minimum: $100,000

Functions: Senior Mgmt., Middle Mgmt., Sales Mgmt., Finance, CFOs, Cash Mgmt., Credit, Risk Mgmt.

Industries: Finance, Banking, Invest. Banking, Misc. Financial

SC of Loudoun County

(an affiliate of MRI)
750 Miller Dr SE Ste F2
Leesburg, VA 20175-8916
(703) 777-0790
Fax: (703) 777-0791

Email: lparrotte@scnova.com

Summary: As a global leader in the staffing industry, we provide the proper training and advanced technological tools to support our search and recruitment specialists. We continually generate exceptional results by applying solution-based strategies tailored to the specific needs of our clients.

Key Contact - Specialty:
Mr. Larry Parrotte, President - *Aerospace, Aviation, Sales, Senior management*
Mr. Craig Hagberg, Account Executive - *Defense, Government, Military*
Ms. Laura Hall, Account Executive - *Medical (Devices,Sales)*
Ms. Jeanne Wolff, Account Executive - *Consumer (Durables,Marketing,Packaged Goods), Logistics*

Salary Minimum: $50,000

Functions: Senior Mgmt., Middle Mgmt., Quality, Distribution, Healthcare, Sales Mgmt., Sales Reps., Engineering, Mgmt. Consultants, Security Personnel

Industries: Drugs Mfg., Medical Devices, Transportation, Law Enforcement, Logistics Svcs., RF/Microwave, Defense, Aerospace, Software, Security SW

BlueFox Search Group

(also known as MR of Lynchburg)
2511 Memorial Ave Ste 202
Lynchburg, VA 24501-2657
(434) 528-1611
Fax: (434) 528-1617
Email: resumes@mrlynchburg.com
Web: www.brilliantpeople.com

Summary: The firm specializes primarily in the fields of finance & accounting and the technical aspects of manufacturing.

Key Contact - Specialty:
Mr. C. David Blue, Manager

Salary Minimum: $50,000

Functions: Mfg.

Industries: Generalist (All), Accounting

MR of McLean

(an affiliate of MRI)
6849 Old Dominion Dr Ste 225
Mc Lean, VA 22101-3705
(703) 442-4842
(800) 291-0642
Fax: (703) 356-8251
Email: alvisco@talenthunter.net
Web: www.talenthunter.net

Summary: We are members of the nation's number one contingency search firm with access to 1,000 offices. Specialty areas include IT, biotic/biotechnology engineering, market research, construction, sales, and business development.

Key Contact - Specialty:
Mr. Howard H. Reitkopp, President
Ms. Ellen L. Reitkopp, Secretary & Treasurer
Mr. Albert Visco, Vice President
Ms. May De la Rosa, Recruiter, PC
Mr. Anthony Cauterucci, Managing Director

Salary Minimum: $30,000

Functions: Generalist (All), Management, Sales & Mktg., Finance, IT, MIS Mgmt.

Industries: Generalist (All), Finance, Pharm Svcs., New Media, Software, Biotech/Life Sciences

MR of Piedmont

(an affiliate of MRI)
96 Garden Ln
Palmyra, VA 22963-4282
(434) 591-1028
(800) 976-1972
Fax: (434) 591-1139
Email: info@pharmarecruiting.com
Web: www.pharmarecruiting.com

Summary: We specialize in recruiting and placing sales, marketing, technical and management professionals in the medical and pharmaceutical industry.

Key Contact - Specialty:
Ms. Rebecca Leinen, President - *Marketing, Medical, Medical (Sales), Pharmaceutical, Sales*

Functions: Generalist (All), Sales & Mktg., Mktg. Research, Mktg. Mgmt., Sales Mgmt., Sales Reps., Minorities/Diversity

Industries: Generalist (All), Drugs Mfg., Medical Devices, Pharm Svcs., Biotech/Life Sciences, Healthcare, Long-term/Home Care, Dental

Executive Talent Search

(also known as SC of Roanoke)
2840 Hershberger Rd NW Ste G
Roanoke, VA 24017-1915
(540) 563-1688
Fax: (540) 563-1687
Email: mkcnncdy@executivetalentsearch.com
Web: www.executivetalentsearch.com

Summary: We are an independent recruiting firm with affiliations. We have two divisions, one that finds and places dentists and specialists in top practices across the country and one that does search and placement of world class talent in the following sectors: industrial capital equipment, manufacturing and security products and services.

Key Contact - Specialty:
Mr. Mark Kennedy, Owner

Functions: Generalist (All), Allied Health

Industries: Manufacturing, Security SW, Dental

MR of Roanoke

(an affiliate of MRI)
1950 Electric Rd Ste B
Roanoke, VA 24018-1621
(540) 989-1676
Fax: (540) 989-7556
Email: president@mriroanoke.com

Summary: We specialize in manufacturing, management, finance & accounting, paint and coatings and have extensive industry experience.

Key Contact - Specialty:
Mr. Paul S. Sharp, President - *Manufacturing, Sales, Technical*

Functions: Generalist (All)

Industries: Chemicals, Paints, Petro. Products

MR of Oakton

(an affiliate of MRI)
9794 Kedge Ct
Vienna, VA 22181-3206
(703) 242-7541
Fax: (703) 242-7543
Email: pfrogers@mroakton.com
Web: www.mroakton.com

Summary: We place senior executives (director and above), IS/IT sales, OSS sale, and pre-sales professionals.

Key Contact - Specialty:
Mr. Paul Rogers, President - *Sales*
Ms. Suzanne Rogers, Vice President & General Counsel

Functions: Board Members, Senior Mgmt., Sales & Mktg., IT

Industries: Generalist (All), New Media, Software

The Lakewood Group

(also known as MR of Lakewood-Tacoma)
6120 Main St SW Ste F
Lakewood, WA 98499-6504
(253) 582-8488
Email: diane@careers-nw.com
Web: www.careers-nw.com

Summary: We are an executive search & consulting firm focused on building strong, successful teams. Some specialty areas include: medical sales, medical device sales and medical supply manufacturers and distribution, healthcare IS, hospitality, logistics, information technology, general management. Looking for sales reps to national directors? – We'd love to help you!

Key Contact - Specialty:
Mr. Len Holmes, Managing Director
Ms. Laurie Cebula, Account Executive - *Medical (Devices,Sales)*
Mr. Jody Locklear, PhD, Business Development - *Hospitality, Information Technology, Logistics, Management*
Mr. Ryan Gegax, Account Executive - *Accounting, Administration, General management, Sales*
Ms. Lisa Yelvington, Project Manager - *Medical, Medical (Devices,Sales)*

Salary Minimum: $75,000

Functions: Generalist (All)

Industries: Medical Devices, Pharm Svcs., Logistics Svcs., Hotels, Resorts, Clubs

MR of Mercer Island

(an affiliate of MRI)
9725 SE 36th St Ste 312
Mercer Island, WA 98040-3840
(206) 232-0204
(206) 232-7051
Fax: (206) 232-6172
Email: denise@mrmi.com
Web: www.mrmi.com

Summary: We specialize in connectors, interconnect, semiconductor, footwear, apparel, nutrition, vitamin supplements, nutraceuticals, and hospitality.

Key Contact - Specialty:
Mr. Vince Holt, Owner & President
Mrs. Denise M. Holt, Office Manager - *Components, Fiber-optics, Footwear, Hospitality, Hotels*

Salary Minimum: $50,000

Functions: Generalist (All)

Industries: Food, Bev., Tobacco, Textiles, Apparel, Drugs Mfg., Consumer Elect., Electronic, Elec. Components, Hotels, Resorts, Clubs, Full Service Restaurants, Advertising, Biotech/Life Sciences

MR of Seattle

(an affiliate of MRI)
2510 Fairview Ave E
Seattle, WA 98102-3266
(206) 328-0936
(800) 237-6562
Fax: (206) 328-3256
Email: info@mriseattle.com
Web: www.mriseattle.com

Summary: We have professionals who specialize in high-technology, electronics, software, health & managed care, engineering, food, beverage, industrial, consumer products, marketing and retail.

Key Contact - Specialty:
Mr. Dan Jilka, General Manager - *Engineering*
Ms. Suzie Brown
Mr. Kevin P. Anderson
Ms. Ronda Clark, Managing Partner

Functions: Generalist (All), Senior Mgmt., Product Dev., Plant Mgmt., Health Admin., Mktg. Mgmt., R&D, Engineering

Industries: Generalist (All), Food, Bev., Tobacco, Medical Devices, Aerospace, Software, Biotech/Life Sciences, Healthcare

MR of Spokane

(an affiliate of MRI)
6607 N Ash St Ste 200
Spokane, WA 99208-4311
(509) 324-3333
Fax: (509) 324-3334
Email: usajobs@mrspokane.com
Web: www.mrspokane.com

Summary: We provide executive search specializing in the medical/healthcare/hospital, insurance, call center, sales, construction, IS, food production & processing, sales management, executive & management, bio-technology/pharmaceutical, packaging, franchise/business opportunity and telecom industries. We also work with entrepreneurial candidates looking to purchase a franchise or other business opportunity.

Key Contact - Specialty:
Mr. Dale Gilliam, President - *Sales*
Mrs. Toni Gilliam, Vice President
Ms. Nancy McMurray, Account Executive
Mr. Branson Jordan, Account Executive
Ms. Margot Cozza, Account Executive
Mr. Sam Hall, Account Executive
Ms. Sheri Perkins, Recruiter
Ms. Terri Fitch, Operations Manager

Salary Minimum: $40,000

Functions: Generalist (All), Management, Mfg., Healthcare, Sales & Mktg., Finance, IT, R&D

Industries: Generalist (All), Construction, Pharm Svcs., Call Centers, Insurance, Claims, Commercial, Biotech/Life Sciences, Healthcare, Hospitals

MR of Vancouver

(an affiliate of MRI)
700 Washington St Ste 508
Vancouver, WA 98660-3336
(360) 695-4688
(877) 695-4688
Fax: (360) 695-4384
Email: jpoloni@mrvancouver.com
Web: www.mrvancouver.com

Summary: Our firm specializes in the following industries: biotechnology, pharmaceutical, manufacturing, financial, insurance, media and retail. We work a vertical market. We have the ability to mobilize project teams to fulfill our clients' needs for multiple positions within time sensitive constraints. We work both retainer and contingency assignments.

Key Contact - Specialty:
Mr. James A. Poloni, Principal
Ms. Jennifer Poloni, Principal
Ms. Michelle Poloni, Recruiter
Ms. Denise Jennings, Recruiter
Ms. Barbara Vernon, Office Manager
Mr. Ramon Castaneda, Personnel Consultant

Salary Minimum: $65,000

Functions: Management, Senior Mgmt., Middle Mgmt., Product Dev., Quality, Sales & Mktg., R&D

Industries: Drugs Mfg., Medical Devices, Retail, Finance, Pharm Svcs., Media, Insurance, Biotech/Life Sciences, Healthcare

MR of Kanawha Valley

(an affiliate of MRI)
3006 Mount Vernon Rd Ste 1000
Premier Plaza
Hurricane, WV 25526-8865
(304) 757-4399
Fax: (304) 757-4398
Email: info@mrikv.com
Web: www.mrikv.com

Summary: We specialize in the recruitment of engineering and sales professionals in the MEP, HVAC, construction and DDC industries. The positions that we place are in sales, engineering and management.

Key Contact - Specialty:
Mr. Harry Ray, Jr., Managing Partner - *HVAC*
Ms. Lisa Ronk, Executive Administrative Assistant - *Engineering, HVAC, Mechanical*
Mr. John Rogers, Project Coordinator
Ms. Sue Ray, Project Coordinator

Functions: Management, Mfg.

Industries: Construction, Engineering Svcs.

MR of Morgantown

(an affiliate of MRI)
1714 Mileground Rd Ste 200
Morgantown, WV 26505-3753
(304) 284-8500
Fax: (304) 284-8985
Web: www.mrmorgantown.com

Summary: We currently specialize in recruiting for healthcare management positions in nursing (i.e. Director & Manager level nursing positions)

Key Contact - Specialty:
Ms. Vickie Adams, Owner & Manager
Ms. Sherry Henry, Administrative Assistant
Mr. Tim McVicker, Project Coordinator - *Healthcare*

Functions: Management, Board Members, Middle Mgmt., Admin. Svcs.

Industries: Healthcare

MR of Appleton

(also known as CompuSearch)
911 N Lynndale Dr Ste 1A
Appleton, WI 54914-3086
(920) 731-5221
Fax: (920) 731-9427
Email: mriappleton@mrappleton.com
Web: www.mrappleton.com

Summary: Offer the full range of placement services. Senior executive through all levels of technical, administrative and sales search. Search specialties include engineering & construction, film & packaging, printing, pulp & paper, general manufacturing, automotive, telecommunications, healthcare, MIS, finance & accounting and medical devices.

Key Contact - Specialty:
Mr. Russell V. Hanson, President

Salary Minimum: $45,000

Functions: Generalist (All), Management, Mfg.

Industries: Energy, Utilities, Construction, Food, Bev., Tobacco, Paper, Chemicals, Medical Devices, Metal Products, Motor Vehicles, Electronic, Elec. Components, Banking,

Accounting, IT Implementation, Supply Chain
Mgmt, Telecoms, Healthcare

MRI Milwaukee-West

(an affiliate of MRI)
13000 W Bluemound Rd Ste 310
Elm Grove, WI 53122-2650
(262) 797-7500
(800) 463-0298
Fax: (262) 797-7515
Email: mrmilw@ameritech.net
Web: www.mrmilw.com

Summary: Our firm is a management recruiting
affiliation firm, specializing in middle
management and professional people. We provide
services for most industries and services.

Key Contact - Specialty:
Mr. Peder Medtlie, President
Mr. Frank Hocker, Vice President

Salary Minimum: $35,000

Functions: Generalist (All), Senior Mgmt.,
Middle Mgmt., Quality, IT, MIS Mgmt.,
Systems Implem., Engineering

Industries: Generalist (All), Drugs Mfg.,
Accounting, Software

MR of Milwaukee South

(also known as Pasada Group)
5307 S 92nd St Ste 125
Hales Corners, WI 53130-1677
(414) 529-8020
Fax: (414) 529-8028
Email: careers@pasadagroup.com
Web: www.pasadagroup.com

Summary: Our mission is to serve clients' human
capital with a team of highly skilled, highly
respected, highly knowledgeable professionals.
Our firm begins with an understanding of our
clients' unique circumstances, strategies and
objectives. Areas of expertise: HR staffing
solutions, professional consulting network in:
executive compensation, global equity,
performance and rewards.

Key Contact - Specialty:
Mr Mark Simpson

Functions: HR Mgmt., Benefits, Mgmt.
Consultants

Industries: Generalist (All)

MR of Janesville

(an affiliate of MRI)
20 E Milwaukee St Ste 304
Janesville, WI 53545-3061
(608) 752-2125
Fax: (608) 752-2903
Email: csmith@mrjvl.com

Summary: Our firm has excellent recruiting
experience in automotive and general
manufacturing companies. We successfully place
people primarily in mid-top management roles in
engineering, operations quality and materials
roles. Our services include outplacement, video
conferencing and contract executive placement.

Key Contact - Specialty:
Ms. Carroll V. Smith, General Manager

Functions: Generalist (All), Senior Mgmt., Mfg.,
Quality, Materials, Purchasing

Industries: Lumber, Furniture, Paper, Printing,
Chemicals, Drugs Mfg., Medical Devices,
Plastics, Rubber, Metal Products, Machine,
Appliance, Motor Vehicles, Misc. Mfg.,
Electronic, Elec. Components, Semiconductors,
Consumer Goods, Transportation, Aerospace,
Packaging

MR of Lake Wisconsin

(an affiliate of MRI)
609A N Main St
Lodi, WI 53555-1232
(608) 592-2151
Fax: (608) 592-2133
Email: home@mrlakewi.com

Summary: We are an executive search firm,
focusing on technical and professional permanent
placements. We focus on the development of
client companies in the manufacturing and
industrial automation sectors, for whom we recruit
and place highly qualified candidates to support
their aggressive growth plans and significantly
enhance the careers of those candidates.

Key Contact - Specialty:
Mr. Merle Morack, Manager - *Computers,
Engineering, Manufacturing, Supply Chain,
Systems*

Salary Minimum: $50,000

Functions: Production, Automation, Finance,
CFOs, Budgeting, MIS Mgmt., Systems
Analysis, Systems Dev., Network Admin.,
Engineering

Industries: Manufacturing, Plastics, Rubber,
Metal Products, Machine, Appliance, Motor
Vehicles

MR of Madison

(an affiliate of MRI)
PO Box 14292
Madison, WI 53708-0292
(608) 442-6200
Email: pat@mrimadison.com
Web: www.mrimadison.com

Summary: We're an executive search firm focused
on meeting a company's individual cultural and
business needs. Industry focuses include
engineering and manufacturing of outdoor sports
and agricultural equipment.

Key Contact - Specialty:
Ms. Patricia Capanna, President - *Engineering,
Manufacturing, Product
management/development*
Mr. Gary Ellerman, SPHR, Managing Partner -
*Agriculture, Engineering, Manufacturing,
Manufacturing (Management)*

Salary Minimum: $40,000

Functions: Generalist (All), Management, Middle
Mgmt., Plant Mgmt., Quality, Engineering

Industries: Manufacturing, Metal Products,
Machine, Appliance, Motor Vehicles, Consumer
Elect., Misc. Mfg., Electronic, Elec.
Components, Transportation, Wholesale,
Banking, Communications, Aerospace, Industry
Specific SW, Mfg. SW

MR/SC of Madison

(an affiliate of MRI)
8000 Excelsior Dr Ste 401
Madison, WI 53717-1974
(608) 836-5566
(800) 887-4969
Fax: (608) 836-1906
Email: schultz@mriscmadison.com
Web: www.mriscmadison.com

Summary: Specialize in territory sales, sales
management, marketing, and senior management
for growth companies. Industries covered are
biotechnology, medical, scientific, healthcare,
professional liability, medical malpractice.

Key Contact - Specialty:
Mr. Bill Schultz, President - *Biotechnology,
Computers (Software)*

Salary Minimum: $50,000

Functions: Senior Mgmt., Middle Mgmt., Mktg.
Mgmt., Sales Mgmt., Sales Reps., Risk Mgmt.

Industries: Medical Devices, Architectural Svcs.,
Casualty, Claims, Life, Commercial, Re-
Insurance, Software, Biotech/Life Sciences,
Healthcare, Hospitals

MR/SC of Milwaukee-North

(also known as The Lawler Group)
1333 W Towne Square Rd
Mequon, WI 53092-5047
(262) 241-1600
Email: admin@lawlergroup.com
Web: www.lawlergroup.com

Summary: Nationwide, we recruit professional
managers and executives from a variety of
industries. Over 85 percent of our business is
repeat business, due to our tenured owner and
professionally trained team of recruiters.

Key Contact - Specialty:
Mr. Timothy M. Lawler, III, President -
*Engineering, Insurance, Legal, Manufacturing,
Sales*
Mr. Chris Lawler, Technology Services Manager
Mrs. Beth Culbertson, Account Executive -
*Electrical, Electrical motor, Industrial,
Marketing, Sales*
Mr. Gavin McNeil, Account Executive -
*Electronics, Engineering, Materials,
Procurement, Purchasing*
Mr. Jim Yee, CIC, Account Executive -
*Insurance, Insurance
(Casualty,Claims,Health,Life)*
Mrs. Ann Lawler, Director, Special Projects -
Advertising, Marketing
Mrs. Kim Koss, Office Manager
Mr. Kimberly Fejnas, Account Executive -
Industrial, Sales
Mr. Marty Oxman, Account Executive -
*Accounting, Accounting (Big 4,General,Public),
Finance*
Mr. Brian Mitchell, Account Executive -
Marketing, Sales

Functions: Generalist (All), Board Members,
Senior Mgmt., Middle Mgmt., Plant Mgmt.,
Sales & Mktg., Sales Mgmt., Finance, CFOs

Industries: Generalist (All), Manufacturing,
Legal, E-commerce, Insurance, Healthcare

MR of Milwaukee-Lakeshore

(an affiliate of MRI)
731 N Jackson St Ste 502
Milwaukee, WI 53202-4697
(414) 278-9778
(888) 378-9778
Fax: (414) 270-4520
Email: elizabeth@executivesearchpartners.com
Web: www.executivesearchpartners.com

Summary: We are dedicated to forming
partnerships with and between our corporate
clients and our candidates. Our executive search
division partners with management to provide
solutions for companies in all industries and
locations. Through our free agent marketing
organization we partner with professionals and
executives who are considered to be at the top of
their field.

Key Contact - Specialty:
Ms. Lisa Klug
Mr. Nicholas Curran

Functions: Management

Industries: Manufacturing, Finance, Banking,
Invest. Banking, Brokers, Venture Cap.,
Mutual/Hedge Funds, Misc. Financial

Worldbridge Partners of Milwaukee

(an affiliate of MRI)
11270 W Park Pl Ste 220
Milwaukee, WI 53224-3638
(414) 359-9494
Fax: (414) 359-9495
Email: careers@worldbridgepartners.com
Web: www.worldbridgepartners.com

Summary: Place middle and top management professionals in Industrial Sales, Engineering, Supply Chain Management, Banking and Insurance.

Key Contact - Specialty:
Mr. Greg Lee, President

Salary Minimum: $70,000

Functions: Management

Industries: Agri., Forestry, Mining, Manufacturing, Machine, Appliance, Motor Vehicles, Consumer Goods, Banking, Logistics Svcs., Supply Chain Mgmt, Casualty

Platinum Search Group Inc

(also known as MR of Stevens Point)
1117 County Road Db
Mosinee, WI 54455-8719
(715) 341-4900
Fax: (715) 341-4992
Email: brad@pointpartners.biz

Summary: Our firm concentrates on working with quality insurance organizations and accepts only the highest quality candidates. Our clients meet two criteria. They maintain the same commitment to excellence to their staff that we keep with the professionals we recruit; and two, that they possess a positive reputation in the industry.

Key Contact - Specialty:
Mr. Bradford L. Barick, President
Ms. Jennifer A. Swoboda, Account Executive - *Insurance (Casualty,Claims,Property,Reinsurance,Workers Compensation)*
Ms. Rita Dexter, Account Executive - *Insurance (Casualty,Claims,Property,Reinsurance,Workers Compensation)*

Salary Minimum: $75,000

Functions: Management, Senior Mgmt., Middle Mgmt., Product Dev., Sales & Mktg., Risk Mgmt.

Industries: Commercial

MR of New Glarus

(an affiliate of MRI)
PO Box 579
New Glarus, WI 53574-0579
(608) 442-0101
Fax: (608) 442-0303
Email: mri@recruitmed.net

Summary: Our office specializes in the recruitment of sales, management, marketing and application specialists in the medical device and equipment markets.

Key Contact - Specialty:
Mr. Gary Hooper, Managing Partner

Functions: Management, Senior Mgmt., Middle Mgmt., Sales & Mktg., Mktg. Mgmt., Sales Mgmt.

Industries: Medical Devices

The Nexus Group Inc

(also known as MR of Oconomowoc)
110 S Main St
Oconomowoc, WI 53066-5221
(262) 569-0800
Fax: (262) 569-0804
Email: resumes@nexusgrp.biz
Web: www.nexusgrp.biz

Summary: We are an executive search firm specializing in the chemical, plastic, and adhesive industries.

Key Contact - Specialty:
Mr. Dave Trepton, President

Functions: Generalist (All), Sales & Mktg., Sales Reps.

Industries: Food, Bev., Tobacco, Textiles, Apparel, Chemicals, Soap, Perf., Cosmtcs., Drugs Mfg., Plastics, Rubber, Paints, Petro. Products, HR Services

The Harbor Group of Port Washington

(also known as MR of Port Washington)
110 S Wisconsin St Ste 5
Port Washington, WI 53074-2248
(262) 268-5187
Fax: (262) 268-5192
Email: info@mriportwashington.com
Web: www.mriportwashington.com

Summary: Our firm's services include contingency, priority and retained search in the pharmaceutical, bio-technology and medical device industries.

Key Contact - Specialty:
Mr. Christopher Fox, Managing Director
Ms. Cathy Fox, Chief Financial Officer

Salary Minimum: $50,000

Functions: Middle Mgmt.

Industries: Drugs Mfg., Medical Devices

MR of Racine

(an affiliate of MRI)
8411 Corporate Dr Ste 100
Racine, WI 53406-3739
(262) 886-8000
Fax: (262) 886-7260
Email: info@mrracine.com
Web: www.mrracine.com

Summary: Our company is part of the world's largest recruiting organization. With our combined extensive recruiting experience, we know where talent is located and possess a thorough understanding of the job market. Our firm specializes in the placement of manufacturing, consumer products and financial services professionals.

Key Contact - Specialty:
Mr. John J. Henkel, Owner & President
Ms. Ellen L. Jante, CSAM, Director, Financial Services
Mrs. Jill Coates, Operations Manager
Ms. Barb Bouchard, Senior Account Manager
Mr. Dean Blake, Account Executive

Salary Minimum: $50,000

Functions: Management, Board Members, Mfg., Plant Mgmt., Purchasing, Cash Mgmt., Engineering

Industries: Generalist (All), Manufacturing, Medical Devices, Plastics, Rubber, Metal Products, Machine, Appliance, Misc. Mfg., Electronic, Elec. Components, Retail, Finance, Banking, Invest. Banking, Brokers, Misc. Financial

MR of Wausau

(an affiliate of MRI)
3309 Terrace Ct
Wausau, WI 54401-3952
(715) 842-1750
Fax: (715) 842-1741
Email: mriwausau@mriwausau.com
Web: www.mriwausau.com

Summary: Our office ranks in the top 5 percent of our franchisees group. We have a nationwide database of employers who have positions available and recruit candidates for these positions.

Key Contact - Specialty:
Ms. Laurie Prochnow, President & Account Executive
Mr. Ross McCullion, Senior Internet Researcher
Mr. Mark Salzer, Account Executive
Mr. Jim Finucan, Account Executive
Ms. Laura Jakubek, Account Executive
Ms. Jennifer Zinser, Account Executive
Ms. Sara Zenner, Account Executive
Mr. Keith Cohrs, Account Executive
Mr. Kevin Peterson, Account Executive
Mr. Cameron Saylor, Researcher, Internet
Mr. Adam Jaworski, Account Executive - *Banking (Corporate,Investment,Merchant,Mortgage,Retail)*
Ms. Monica Kummerfeldt, Account Executive - *Procurement, Sales, Technology*
Ms. Esther Martin - *Banking, Banking (Commercial,Corporate,Investment,Merchant)*
Ms. Irene Mroczenski, Account Executive - *Banking (Corporate,Investment,Merchant,Mortgage,Retail)*
Ms. Sarah Sheard, Project Coordinator - *Banking (Corporate,Investment,Merchant,Mortgage,Retail)*
Mr. John Yost, Account Executive - *Banking (Corporate,Investment,Merchant,Mortgage,Retail)*

Salary Minimum: $40,000

Functions: Generalist (All), MIS Mgmt., Systems Analysis, Systems Dev., Systems Implem., Systems Support, DB Admin.

Industries: Generalist (All), Finance, Banking, New Media, Network Infrastructure, Software

MR of Cheyenne

(an affiliate of MRI)
523 W 27th St Ste C
Cheyenne, WY 82001-3068
(307) 635-8731
Fax: (307) 635-6653
Email: mrwy@mrwy.net
Web: www.mrwy.net

Summary: We are a general executive search firm. Our areas of specialties include metal working manufacturing, power sports (motorcycle, ATV, PWC, marine, and snowmobile), and motor sports (racing, IRL, Formula 1, NASCAR, MotoGP, etc).

Key Contact - Specialty:
Mr. Anthony Cisneros, CSAM, President
Mrs. Carmen Cisneros, Vice President, Local Business
Mr. Guy Cleveland, Chief Operating Officer - *Apparel, Manufacturing, Manufacturing (Management), Marketing*
Mr. Samuel Sims - *Accounting, Banking, CEOs, CFOs, CIOs*

Functions: Generalist (All)

Industries: Manufacturing, Textiles, Apparel, Metal Products, Machine, Appliance, Motor

Vehicles, Healthcare, Hospitals, Long-term/Home Care

Trillium Talent Resource Group

(an affiliate of MRI)
99 Sheppard Ave W
North York, ON M2N 1M4
Canada
(416) 497-2624
(877) 722-8522
Fax: (416) 497-8491
Email: admin@trilliumhr.com
Web: www.trilliumhr.com

Summary: We provide recruitment solutions to the healthcare and supply chain (including manufacturing, distribution, retail and transportation) sectors. We recruit management and professional talent for our clients.

Key Contact - Specialty:
Ms. Poonam Kathuria, President
Mr. Robert Masters, Vice President

Functions: Management, Mfg., Distribution, Healthcare, Nurses, Allied Health, Advertising, Direct Mktg., Benefits, Staffing

Industries: Generalist (All), Manufacturing, Food, Bev., Tobacco, Textiles, Apparel, Paper, Printing, Drugs Mfg., Medical Devices, Plastics, Rubber, Leather, Stone, Glass, Metal Products, Machine, Appliance, Misc. Mfg., Transportation, Wholesale, Retail, Pharm Svcs., Mgmt. Consulting, HR Services, Packaging, Biotech/Life Sciences, Healthcare, Hospitals, Long-term/Home Care, Dental, Physical Therapy, Occupational Therapy

Branches:
204-99 Main St
Cambridge, ON N1R 1W1
Canada
(519) 620-9683
(800) 335-9668
Fax: (519) 620-9681
Email: thr@trilliumhr.com
Key Contact - Specialty:
Ms. Sabina Dinino, Manager

MR of Mexico

(an affiliate of MRI)
Domingo Diez 1589 Ste 121
Col El Empleado
62250 Cuernavaca, MOR
Mexico
77 7311 4045
Fax: 77 7311 4046
Email: mrimex@mrimex.com
Web: www.mrimex.com

Summary: Executive staffing consultants specializing in international corporations.

Key Contact - Specialty:
Mr. Carlos Kingwergs, Country Manager
Mr. Jens Hagedorn, Country Manager

Functions: Management, Senior Mgmt., Mfg., Sales & Mktg., Finance, CFOs, IT, Int'l.

Industries: Generalist (All)

Management Recruiting Group

21318 Via Colombard
Sonoma, CA 95476-8313
(707) 935-7777
Fax: (707) 939-1848
Email: john@hernandez-talentbank.com

Summary: We are a contingency recruiting firm focusing on the commercial banking industry.

Key Contact - Specialty:
Mr. John Hernandez, Owner
Salary Minimum: $40,000

Functions: Management, Sales & Mktg., HR Mgmt., Finance

Industries: Finance, Banking, Invest. Banking, Brokers, Venture Cap., Mutual/Hedge Funds, Misc. Financial

Management Resource Associates Inc

9044 Pine Springs Dr
Boca Raton, FL 33428-1455
(561) 852-5650
Fax: (561) 852-5650
Email: mra@gate.net

Summary: A dynamic middle to upper-management, management search firm, specializing in the high-technology industry and multi-nationals, with many years of corporate management and executive search experience.

Key Contact - Specialty:
Mr. Gerald Schneiderman, President & Managing Partner - *Accounting, Accounting (Big 4), Audits, CFOs, Human resources*

Salary Minimum: $75,000

Functions: HR Mgmt., Finance, Int'l.

Industries: Generalist (All)

Management Resource Group Inc

77 Bleecker St Apt 124
New York, NY 10012-1553
(212) 475 5327

Summary: We recruit all positions for entertainment and banking except system/IT and all industries in HR/training and development.

Key Contact - Specialty:
Mr. Matthew J. DeLuca, President - *Publishing*

Salary Minimum: $50,000

Functions: Generalist (All), Advertising, Mktg. Mgmt., Systems Support, Graphic Designers

Industries: Generalist (All), HR Services, Publishing, New Media

Management Resources Ltd

1500-250 6 Ave SW
Bow Valley Square 4
Calgary, AB T2P 3H7
Canada
(403) 233-2757
Email: mgmtres@telus.net

Summary: We are a technical and professional recruiting firm in the oil and gas industry. We focus on searching for outstanding petroleum engineers, explorations, landsmen, accountants and managers.

Key Contact - Specialty:
Mr. R.W. Michael, President

Salary Minimum: $60,000

Functions: Engineering

Industries: Oil & Gas

Management Search

202 S Cook St Ste 211
Barrington, IL 60010-4351
(847) 277-9200
Email: frankwol@core.com

Summary: We are a firm specializing in the functional areas of accounting and finance, supply chain, human resources, and healthcare for position levels ranging from middle to senior management.

Key Contact - Specialty:
Mr. Frank Wolowicz, President - *Accounting*
Ms. Kimberly A. Wolowicz, Operations Manager & Recruiter

Salary Minimum: $65,000

Functions: Materials, Healthcare, HR Mgmt., Finance

Industries: Generalist (All)

Management Search Associates

PO Box 460086
Aurora, CO 80046-0086
(303) 699-7501
Email: mgtsearcha@aol.com

Summary: Our core business is for technical, medical equipment and pharmaceutical, power generation equipment and manufacturing firms. We place presidents, VP in sales, finance, engineering and quality, directors of engineering, quality, sales, finance, controllers, accounting managers and engineers. We also place health care professionals.

Key Contact - Specialty:
Mr. Richard Crow, President
Mrs. Veronika F. Crow, Vice President

Salary Minimum: $60,000

Functions: Board Members, Senior Mgmt., Quality, Healthcare, Sales Mgmt., Finance, Budgeting, Engineering

Industries: Generalist (All), Energy, Utilities, Manufacturing, Drugs Mfg., Medical Devices, Machine, Appliance, Misc. Mfg., Electronic, Elec. Components, RF/Microwave, Healthcare, Non-Classifiable

Management Search Inc

117 S Cook St Ste 201
Barrington, IL 60010-4311
(847) 462-5980
Fax: (847) 462-5982
Email: steflink@ameritech.net

Summary: Fast, effective recruitment services. Strategic networking to provide Internet and communications companies with targeted executives, capital, strategic-alliance, and merger/acquisition opportunities.

Key Contact - Specialty:
Mr. Stefan Levy, President - *Internet, Venture capital*

Salary Minimum: $70,000

Functions: M&A

Industries: Venture Cap., Insurance

Management Search Inc

3013 NW 59th St Ste A1
Oklahoma City, OK 73112-4203
(405) 842-3173
Fax: (405) 842-8360
Email: dorwig@mgmtsearch.com
Web: www.mgmtsearch.com

Summary: Agriculture research and technical service positions, both agronomic and livestock. Agriculture sales and sales management positions.

Key Contact - Specialty:
Mr. David L. Orwig, President

Salary Minimum: $35,000

Functions: Generalist (All), Product Dev., Mktg. Research, Sales Mgmt., R&D

Industries: Generalist (All), Agri., Forestry, Mining, Food, Bev., Tobacco

Management Search Partners

15610 Aldersyde Dr
Shaker Heights, OH 44120-2502
(216) 751-0984
Fax: (216) 751-0009
Email: amyw@mspsearch.com

Summary: We recruit management and executive level professionals in the healthcare IT industry. Our focus is on: sales, marketing, product management, implementation and consulting positions. We are committed to understanding the business of our clients and developing an ongoing consultative relationship with them.

Key Contact - Specialty:
Ms. Amy Watts, President

Salary Minimum: $75,000

Functions: Generalist (All), Management, Product Dev., Sales & Mktg., Mktg. Mgmt., Sales Mgmt., Sales Reps.

Industries: Industry Specific SW

Management Services

PO Box 1804
Evans, GA 30809-1804
(706) 855-6205
Fax: (706) 855-7595
Email: jobs@managementservices.net
Web: www.managementservices.net

Summary: Recruiting agency specializing in poultry and meat processing.

Key Contact - Specialty:
Mr. Bob Leicht, Recruiter

Salary Minimum: $35,000

Functions: Generalist (All)

Industries: Food, Bev., Tobacco

Mancini Technical Recruiting

PO Box 27069
West Des Moines, IA 50265-9416
(515) 223-9555
Email: debbie@m-t-r.com
Web: www.m-t-r.com

Summary: We are a technical recruiting firm that assists companies in their staffing efforts. Our recent searches have included web developer, database administrator, network engineer, internet project manager, software engineer, web architect, technical manager, business analyst, and versant developer.

Key Contact - Specialty:
Ms. Deborah Mancini, Owner - *Computers (Software), High technology, Internet, New media*

Salary Minimum: $35,000

Functions: IT, MIS Mgmt., Systems Analysis, Systems Dev., Systems Implem., Systems Support, Network Admin., DB Admin.

Industries: Generalist (All), Services, HR Services, E-commerce, IT Implementation, Publishing, New Media, Telecoms, Insurance, Software, Database SW, Development SW, Networking, Comm. SW, Security SW, System SW, Training SW, Non-Classifiable

Mangieri/Hull Solutions LLC

1 Riverside Rd
Sandy Hook, CT 06482-1281
(203) 270-4800
Fax: (203) 270-4815
Email: cmangieri@mangierisolutions.com
Web: www.mhrecruiters.com

Summary: We produce top caliber people that ideally match your job descriptions and your company culture. Our specialty is the direct marketing industry, including call center operations, along with finance and accounting.

Key Contact - Specialty:
Mr. Christopher J. Mangieri, President - *Direct marketing, Finance, Market research, Marketing*
Mr. Thomas J. Hull, Partner - *Direct marketing, Finance, Market research, Marketing*
Mr. Nick Marsan, Director, Accounting, Finance Services
Mr. Frank Nicola, Executive Recruiter
Mr. Michael Fiorelli, Senior Executive Recruiter
Mr. Josh Gampel, Senior Executive Recruiter
Mr. Jamie Mitchell, Executive Recruiter
Mr. Ron Gallichio, Executive Recruiter
Ms. Kate Buess, Executive Recruiter
Mr. Christopher Taylor, Executive Recruiter
Ms. Kathy Egan, Office Manager

Salary Minimum: $50,000

Functions: Generalist (All), Advertising, Mktg. Research, Mktg. Mgmt., Direct Mktg., Customer Svc., Training, MIS Mgmt.

Industries: Generalist (All), Software, Healthcare

Manhattan Resources

1221 McKinney St Ste 2950
Houston, TX 77010-2035
(713) 980-1400
Fax: (713) 980-1405
Email: chris@manhattanresources.com
Web: www.manhattanresources.com

Summary: Executive Search specializing in Energy Trading & Marketing, Oil & Gas, Financial Services, Sales & Marketing, Accounting, Finance, Tax, Treasury and Credit. Offices in Houston, Chicago, New York and London

Key Contact - Specialty:
Mr. Chris B. Schoettelkotte, President & Chief Executive Officer
Mr. Steve McAleavy, Executive Vice President - *Boards of Directors, C-level, Energy, Power, Risk management*

Salary Minimum: $75,000

Functions: Management

Industries: Energy, Utilities, Oil & Gas, Chemicals, Plastics, Rubber, Banking, Invest. Banking, Misc. Financial, Logistics Svcs., Supply Chain Mgmt., HR SW

Mankuta Gallagher & Associates Inc

8333 W McNab Rd Ste 231
Tamarac, FL 33321-3203
(954) 720-9645
(800) 797-4276
Fax: (954) 720-5813
Email: info@mankutagallagher.com
Web: www.mankutagallagher.com

Summary: We are a client driven firm specializing in bio-technology, engineering, hospitality, restaurants and law.

Key Contact - Specialty:
Dr. Michael Gallagher, Managing Partner - *Biotechnology, Pharmaceutical*
Mr. Eric Mankuta, Managing Partner - *Biotechnology, Pharmaceutical*

Salary Minimum: $60,000

Functions: Management, Healthcare, R&D

Industries: Drugs Mfg., Retail, Hospitality, Biotech/Life Sciences, Healthcare

Manning Associates

4 Faneuil Hall Market Place
South Market, 4th Floor
Boston, MA 02109-6120
(617) 523-8866
Fax: (617) 722-8359
Email: kmanning@manningassociates.com
Web: www.manningassociates.com

Summary: We are a recruiting practice specializing in all areas of accounting and finance including, treasury, internal audit, tax and general accounting. We work with a large number of multi-national, middle market and eCommerce/internet start ups. We recruit qualified candidates from entry level accountants to CFOs.

Key Contact - Specialty:
Mr. Jack Manning, President - *Consulting, Finance, Systems*
Ms. Mary Manning, Manager - *Financial services, Healthcare, Manufacturing*

Salary Minimum: $30,000

Functions: Finance, CFOs, Budgeting, Cash Mgmt., Credit, Taxes, M&A, Risk Mgmt.

Industries: Generalist (All)

Branches:
1 S Market St Ste 4
Boston, MA 02109-6175
(617) 227-5115
Email: kmanning@manningassociates.com
Key Contact - Specialty:
Ms. Kelly Manning, Manager - *Healthcare*

Manning Search Group LLC

150 Saint Peters Centre Blvd Ste B
Saint Peters, MO 63376-1653
(636) 447-4900
Fax: (636) 447-1145
Email: roger@manningsearchgroup.com
Web: www.manningsearchgroup.com

Summary: Our firm is an executive search and recruitment permanent placement firm. We are heavily focused within the banking, healthcare services, industrial design & graphics, logistics & transportation management and medical manufacturing industries.

Key Contact - Specialty:
Mr. Roger Manning, President
Ms. Cathy Montgomery-Manning, Executive Search Consultant
Ms. Mary Foster, Administrative Assistant & Researcher

Salary Minimum: $75,000

Functions: Management

Industries: Wholesale, Retail, Banking, Brokers, Venture Cap., Pharm Svcs., Equip Svcs., Healthcare, Hospitals, Long-term/Home Care

Manpower Search

(also known as Manpower Professional)
3075 Governors Place Blvd Ste 200
Dayton, OH 45409-1333
(937) 293-0185
(937) 534-7417
Fax: (937) 643-7467
Email: marisa.wilt@na.manpower.com
Web: www.manpowerprofessional.com

Summary: Search Consultants for Manpower Professional are devoted exclusively to direct placement for professionals and executives. We fast-forward the hiring process by drawing on extensive field experience to locate and qualify talent within business industries including: Accounting/Finance, Engineering, IT and more. In 72 countries around the world, Manpower helps both companies and individuals navigate the ever-

changing world of work. 2005: Fortune's "Most Admired" 3rd year in a row. We have done business with 94% of the top 100 and 90% of the Global Fortune 500 companies.

Key Contact - Specialty:
Ms. Marisa Wilt, Search Consultant

Salary Minimum: $50,000

Functions: Generalist (All), Management, Senior Mgmt., Quality, Purchasing, Healthcare, Finance, IT, Engineering

Industries: Generalist (All), Energy, Utilities, Construction, Manufacturing, Textiles, Apparel, Medical Devices, Transportation, Wholesale, Finance, Services, HR Services, Engineering Svcs., RF/Microwave, Government, Defense, Aerospace, Packaging, Software, Healthcare

Manufacturing Resource Group LLC
1204 Main St Ste 209
Branford, CT 06405-3787
(860) 577-8056
(203) 506-4883
Fax: (860) 664-0533
Email: rgallentine@mfgresource.net

Summary: Partners are former CEO/COOs for technology-driven manufacturing and research organizations. Primary focus is placement of high skilled technical, managerial, engineering and research professionals in manufacturing, medical research and technical environment. Firm is also retained by a series of private equity companies to source senior personnel who are interested in leading "management buyouts" of the organizations for whom they work.

Key Contact - Specialty:
Mr. Richard A. Gallentine, President - *Human resources, Manufacturing*
Ms. Martha Roush, Vice President

Salary Minimum: $100,000

Functions: Management, Senior Mgmt.

Industries: Generalist (All), Manufacturing, Medical Devices, Plastics, Rubber, Metal Products, Transportation, Wholesale, Retail, Finance, Pharm Svcs., Mgmt. Consulting, Aerospace, Packaging, Biotech/Life Sciences, Healthcare

Manulogic Inc
2091 Kinridge Trl
Marietta, GA 30062-1883
(770) 509-7494
(800) 993-8973
Fax: (770) 565-9613
Email: manulogic@aol.com
Web: www.manulogic.com

Summary: We search for high technology candidates that specialize in sales, pre-sales, post-sales, product management, solution selling and marketing for software companies. We specialize in the following: process and discrete MRP, SCM, APS, B2B, ERP, WMS, CRM, EDI, business intelligence, e-commerce, data warehousing, HR/payroll, EPM, financials, transportation, logistics, energy, etc.

Key Contact - Specialty:
Ms. Marilyn Campbell, President

Salary Minimum: $80,000

Functions: Sales & Mktg., Sales Mgmt.

Industries: PSA/ASP, Accounting SW, Database SW, Development SW, Doc. Mgmt., Production SW, ERP SW, HR SW, Industry Specific SW, Mfg. SW, Marketing SW, Networking, Comm. SW

MARBL Consultants Inc
350 Bishops Way Ste 200
Brookfield, WI 53005-6221
(262) 796-6960
Fax: (262) 796-6970
Email: marblcons@aero.net

Summary: Client-driven organization committed to successfully completing a project in a timely manner. We are dedicated to excellence in five major areas: manufacturing, engineering, materials/purchasing/logistics, IT/MIS and HR.

Key Contact - Specialty:
Mr. Allan G. Adzima, President & Consultant - *Engineering, Logistics, Manufacturing, Materials, Purchasing*
Mr. Dennis J. Pradarelli, Administration, IT Sr Recruiting Manager - *Finance, MIS*
Ms. Diane Pruitt, Recruiter & Customer Service Manager

Salary Minimum: $45,000

Functions: Management, Mfg., Materials, Purchasing, HR Mgmt., Finance, IT, Engineering, Minorities/Diversity, Int'l.

Industries: Generalist (All), Manufacturing, Plastics, Rubber, Machine, Appliance, Motor Vehicles, Consumer Elect., Transportation, Retail, Finance, Accounting, Mgmt. Consulting, HR Services, Aerospace, Packaging, Software

Marc-Allen Associates Inc
7800 N Univ Dr Ste 202
Tamarac, FL 33321-2127
(954) 586-5866
(800) 342-8552
Fax: (954) 586-0588
Email: mike@marc-allen.com
Web: www.marc-allen.com

Summary: We are an executive search firm specializing in the placement of management talent in all divisions of the following industries: retail, technology, consumer products, manufacturing, and wholesale. We have the talent and experience to provide trusted creative solutions to the ongoing challenges of management recruitment and placement.

Key Contact - Specialty:
Mr. Mike Powell, President & Chief Executive Officer - *Middle management, Senior management, Supermarkets, Supply Chain, Wholesale*
Ms. Angi Tavares, MBA, Managing Director - *Marketing, Middle management, Retail, Senior management, Wholesale*
Ms. Diana Cohen, Executive Recruiter - *Middle management, Research, Retail, Wholesale*
Ms. Mary Powell, Manager, Administration - *Administration, Research*

Salary Minimum: $50,000

Functions: Management, Senior Mgmt., Middle Mgmt., Advertising, HR Mgmt., Finance, IT

Industries: Generalist (All), Consumer Goods, Transportation, Wholesale, Retail, Finance, Logistics Svcs., Supply Chain Mgmt., Advertising

MarCom Placements
236 Prune Tree Dr
Healdsburg, CA 95448-4336
(650) 329-9906
Fax: (650) 329-1912
Email: marcom@marcomjobs.com
Web: www.marcomjobs.com

Summary: Our firm is a contingency staffing agency that places marketing professionals into

the high-technology and medical device industries on a permanent or contract basis.

Key Contact - Specialty:
Ms. Kathleen McCaffrey, Owner - *Marketing*

Salary Minimum: $80,000

Functions: Mktg. Mgmt.

Industries: Wireless, Fiber Optic, Network Infrastructure, Software, Doc. Mgmt., Production SW, ERP SW, HR SW, Marketing SW, Networking, Comm. SW, Healthcare

Marconi Search Consultants Inc
PO Box 15304
Clearwater, FL 33766-5304
(727) 725-8282
Fax: (727) 723-3990
Email: marcon3481@aol.com

Summary: We are an executive recruiting to the insurance industry.

Key Contact - Specialty:
Mr. Mark Marconi, President
Mr. John Burniston, Recruiter & Consultant

Salary Minimum: $50,000

Functions: Management, Sales & Mktg., Benefits, Finance, CFOs, M&A, Risk Mgmt., MIS Mgmt.

Industries: Insurance

Marcus & Associates
358 Saw Mill River Rd
Millwood, NY 10546-1000
(914) 941-7100
Fax: (914) 941-8629
Email: info@marcusassoc.com
Web: www.marcusassoc.com

Summary: We are an executive search firm specializing in the pharmaceutical and biotechnology industries. We have expertise in searches from "bench to boardroom" for R&D, clinical & regulatory affairs, commercial operations and corporate staff.

Key Contact - Specialty:
Mr. Alvin B. Marcus, Chief Executive Officer
Ms. Denise Clements, President
Ms. Catherine McKenna, Senior Vice President & General Manager
Mr. Brian Harrington, Vice President, R&D Operations - *Research & development*
Ms. Randi Sperber, Senior Director, Regulatory Affairs
Mr. Christian Camp, Senior Director, Clinical Research
Mr. Joshua Marcus, Vice President, Business Development

Salary Minimum: $80,000

Functions: Generalist (All), Senior Mgmt.

Industries: Drugs Mfg., Medical Devices, Consumer Elect., Pharm Svcs., Biotech/Life Sciences, Healthcare

Marentz & Company
PO Box 926101
Houston, TX 77292-6101
(713) 856-9156
Fax: (713) 856-9188
Email: frankmar@marentzco.com
Web: www.marentzco.com

Summary: The ability to generate viable candidates from selected databases; industry networks and referrals allow our search consultants to provide the type of service demanded by the client. The firm offers flexible financial options for our search services and can be tailored to the needs of the client.

Key Contact - Specialty:
Mr. Frank Marentez, Vice President & General
  Manager - *Energy, Financial, Real estate, Sales*
Mr. Richard Ramirez, Vice President - *Financial,*
  Manufacturing, Real estate
Ms. Lily Campos, Associate - *Healthcare,*
  Hospitality
Mr. Jim Rand, Vice President - *Energy,*
  Engineering, Sales

Salary Minimum: $60,000

Functions: Generalist (All), Sales Mgmt., CFOs,
  Budgeting, Cash Mgmt., Taxes, Engineering

Industries: Generalist (All), Energy, Utilities, Oil
  & Gas, Construction, Food, Bev., Tobacco,
  Chemicals, Finance, Brokers, Accounting,
  Hospitality, Hotels, Resorts, Clubs, Insurance,
  Real Estate, Healthcare

Maresca & Associates

PO Box 235498
Honolulu, HI 96823-3508
(808) 545-7991
(808) 228-4372
Fax: (808) 394-1863
Email: smaresca@att.net

Summary: Our firm has served our market by
recruiting managers, executives, administrators,
financial controllers and operational expertise for
a variety of industries. We also have a
construction division where searches such as
project managers and estimators are conducted.

Key Contact - Specialty:
Ms. Shannon Maresca, Owner & Manager

Salary Minimum: $50,000

Functions: Generalist (All)

Industries: Generalist (All)

Margolin Consultants Inc

350 5th Ave Ste 2819
New York, NY 10118-2895
(212) 268-1940
Fax: (212) 268-2695
Email: margolinconsultants@hotmail.com

Summary: Executive search, product
development, market research, mergers &
acquisitions, venture capital and joint venture.

Key Contact - Specialty:
Mr. Efraim Margolin, President - *Management*

Salary Minimum: $50,000

Functions: Generalist (All), Middle Mgmt.,
  Product Dev., Production, Automation, Plant
  Mgmt., Sales Mgmt., Engineering

Industries: Generalist (All), Lumber, Furniture,
  Plastics, Rubber, Metal Products, Machine,
  Appliance, Telecoms, Packaging

Mark III Personnel Inc

5140 Morrowick Rd
Charlotte, NC 28226-7364
(704) 542-0553
Email: lamarkiii@aol.com

Summary: We staff all professional and
managerial positions. Focus areas are engineers,
chemists, quality professionals, materials/logistics
management, manmade fibers, textiles, medical
devices and pharmaceuticals.

Key Contact - Specialty:
Ms. Lindsay Allen, Jr. - *Engineering,*
  Environmental, Research & development

Salary Minimum: $40,000

Functions: Mfg., Materials, Healthcare, R&D,
  Engineering, Environmentalists

Industries: Textiles, Apparel, Chemicals, Medical
  Devices, Pharm Svcs., Environmental Svcs.

Markent Personnel Inc

PO Box 423
Portage, WI 53901-0423
(608) 742-7300
Fax: (608) 742-7737
Email: contactus@markentpersonnel.com
Web: www.markentpersonnel.com

Summary: Our firm specializes in servicing the
needs of manufacturing companies. We have
specialists in plastics, consumer products,
electronics, food processing, food processing
equipment and medical devices. As a recruiting
firm we are determined to satisfy all our clients'
professional hiring needs.

Key Contact - Specialty:
Mr. Thomas L. Udulutch, President - *Engineering*
Mr. Mark Udulutch, JD, Vice President -
  Engineering

Salary Minimum: $40,000

Functions: Generalist (All), Senior Mgmt., Mfg.,
  Product Dev., Quality, Purchasing, Engineering

Industries: Generalist (All), Manufacturing, Food,
  Bev., Tobacco, Paper, Printing, Chemicals,
  Medical Devices, Plastics, Rubber, Metal
  Products, Machine, Appliance, Motor Vehicles,
  Misc. Mfg., Electronic, Elec. Components,
  Consumer Goods, Biotech/Life Sciences

Marketing & Sales Resources Inc

6801 Lake Worth Rd Ste 126
Greenacres, FL 33467-2971
(561) 966-2800
Fax: (561) 434-4694
Email: msresources@bellsouth.net
Web: www.marketingsalesresources.com

Summary: Uniquely specialized in the recruitment
of mid and senior-level marketing and sales
management executives within the consumer
durables and industrial products markets.

Key Contact - Specialty:
Mr. Alan H. Gross, President
Ms. Tina Bass, Vice President

Salary Minimum: $80,000

Functions: Sales & Mktg., Mktg. Research, Mktg.
  Mgmt., Sales Mgmt.

Industries: Generalist (All), Manufacturing,
  Chemicals, Plastics, Rubber, Metal Products,
  Machine, Appliance, Consumer Elect., Test,
  Measure Equip.

Marketing Consultants Inc

3015 N Shepard Ave
Milwaukee, WI 53211-3437
(414) 962-6611
Email: carole@marketingrecruiters.com
Web: www.marketingrecruiters.com

Summary: Boutique search firm specializing in
CPG marketing professionals from sssistant levels
to vice presidents.

Key Contact - Specialty:
Ms. Carole Smolizer, President - *Marketin,)*
Mr. Gregory Fait, Vice President - *Marketing*

Salary Minimum: $50,000

Functions: Generalist (All), Management, Middle
  Mgmt., Advertising, Mktg. Research, Mktg.
  Mgmt., Minorities/Diversity, Int'l.

Industries: Generalist (All), Food, Bev., Tobacco,
  Paper, Soap, Perf., Cosmtcs., Drugs Mfg.,
  Consumer Goods, Media, Advertising

Marketing Recruiters Inc

PO Box 4098
Asheboro, NC 27204-4098
(336) 626-4009
Fax: (336) 626-5116
Email: mri@asheboro.com

Summary: We specialize in finding and placing
sales & marketing professionals. Our area of
expertise lies within the medical device industry.

Key Contact - Specialty:
Mr. Rass Bagley, President

Salary Minimum: $50,000

Functions: Sales Mgmt.

Industries: Medical Devices

Marketing Resources

PO Box 463
2 Smokerise Dr
Chelmsford, MA 01824-0463
(978) 256-8001
Email: mrcontact@comcast.net
Web: www.medjobs.com

Summary: Executive search and placement
services for marketing managers or specialists
with focus on medical technologies. Segments are
medical-surgical, clinical chemistry, patient
monitoring, cardiovascular, medical computer and
medical device companies.

Key Contact - Specialty:
Mr. Joseph D. Sheedy, President -
  Biopharmaceutical, Biotechnology, Medical,
  Medical (Sales), Middle management

Salary Minimum: $90,000

Functions: Middle Mgmt., Sales & Mktg., Mktg.
  Mgmt., Sales Mgmt.

Industries: Manufacturing, Drugs Mfg., Medical
  Devices, Test, Measure Equip., Electronic, Elec.
  Components, Venture Cap., Pharm Svcs.,
  Environmental Svcs., Software, Database SW,
  HR SW, Industry Specific SW, Mfg. SW,
  Marketing SW, Networking, Comm. SW,
  Biotech/Life Sciences, Healthcare, Hospitals,
  Non-Classifiable

MarketPro Inc

730 Peachtree St NE Ste 550
Atlanta, GA 30308-1238
(404) 222-9992
(866) 690-0069
Fax: (404) 222-9099
Email: mktpro@marketproinc.com
Web: www.marketproinc.com

Summary: Our firm specializes in placing mid to
senior level marketing executives in permanent
and contract opportunities. Our unique model
allows us to provide the best talent in the shortest
possible period of time.

Key Contact - Specialty:
Mr. Bob Van Rossum, President -
  Communications, Consumer, Direct marketing,
  Market research, Marketing
Mr. Brian Cornwell, Director, Business
  Development

Salary Minimum: $60,000

Functions: Generalist (All), Advertising, Mktg.
  Research, Mktg. Mgmt., Direct Mktg., PR,
  Minorities/Diversity

Industries: Generalist (All), Marketing SW

Marksmen Consultants

805 W Shepherds Ln
Santa Claus, IN 47579-6325
(812) 544-5200
(812) 544-5201
Fax: (812) 544-5202
Email: dvsearch@psci.net

Summary: We are on target with your staffing
needs. We are experienced in servicing the
aluminum extrusion industry providing: managers,
supervisors, engineers and technical specialists,
plant managers, extrusion, finishing and
fabrication managers & supervisors, die repair
specialists, maintenance, sales and sales managers.
Please note: If your experience does not include
aluminum extrusion, we will not be able to assist
with your job search.

Key Contact - Specialty:
Mr. Don Vogel, President

Salary Minimum: $30,000

Functions: Generalist (All), Management, Mfg.,
Materials, Sales & Mktg., HR Mgmt.,
Engineering

Industries: Generalist (All), Metal Products

Markwins International

22067 Ferrero
Walnut, CA 91789-5214
(909) 595-8898 x291
Email: yli@markwins.com
Web: markwins.com

Summary: We specialize in sales and marketing in
the cosmetics industry. We recruit experienced
professionals in product design, graphics, sales
and marketing.

Key Contact - Specialty:
Mr. Yuwie Li, Director, Marketing

Salary Minimum: $50,000

Functions: Sales & Mktg.

Industries: Generalist (All), Food, Bev., Tobacco,
Textiles, Apparel, Soap, Perf., Cosmtcs.,
Computer Equip., Consumer Goods, Wholesale,
Retail, Non-Classifiable

Marlen Company Inc

375 Sladen St
Dracut, MA 01826-3615
(978) 957-9634
Fax: (978) 957-4534
Email: marlencoinc@comcast.net
Web: www.ctrc.com/lenc

Summary: U.S. wide retained and contingency
search as well as contract. Practices include
healthcare, financial services, IT, DoD, computer
sciences, consultants, engineering, medical
devices, sciences, biotech, R&D, life & physical
sciences.

Key Contact - Specialty:
Mr. Len Costa, Owner
Mr. Charlie Duvall, Executive Recruiter
Mr. Steve Reynolds, Executive Recruiter

Salary Minimum: $90,000

Functions: Generalist (All)

Industries: Generalist (All), Manufacturing,
Finance, Mgmt. Consulting, Telecoms,
Government, Environmental Svcs., Software,
Biotech/Life Sciences, Healthcare

Marquis Management Inc

1901 Harrison St Ste 208
Hollywood, FL 33020-5017
(954) 925-5201

Email: info@marquismanagement.com
Web: www.marquismanagement.com

Summary: A leading executive search firm
serving the IT industry. We provide search
services for mid-senior level sales, marketing and
general management positions.

Key Contact - Specialty:
Mr. Tom P. Robinson, Managing Partner

Salary Minimum: $70,000

Functions: Generalist (All)

Industries: Mgmt. Consulting, IT Implementation,
Software, Database SW, ERP SW, Marketing
SW, Networking, Comm. SW, System SW,
Training SW

The Marr Roy Group (MRG)

402-8 Stavebank Rd
Mississauga, ON L5G 2T4
Canada
(905) 271-2710
(866) 222-2710
Fax: (905) 271-2783
Email: info@webmrg.com
Web: www.webmrg.com

Summary: We provide flexible staffing services
on both a permanent and contract basis and offer
search services on both a contingency and retained
basis. Our firm principally serves Global 2000
clients.

Key Contact - Specialty:
Mr. Steve Roy, Principal

Salary Minimum: $50,000

Functions: Generalist (All)

Industries: Banking, Venture Cap., Mgmt.
Consulting, E-commerce, New Media,
Telecoms, Digital, Wireless, Network
Infrastructure, Networking, Comm. SW

Karen Marshall Associates

7896 Ashley View Dr
Cincinnati, OH 45227-3951
(513) 561-4102

Summary: We are a recruiter, search and
placement of MIS professionals and executives.

Key Contact - Specialty:
Ms. Karen Marshall, President
Mr. Dennis Marshall, Vice President

Salary Minimum: $30,000

Functions: Distribution, IT, MIS Mgmt., Systems
Analysis, Systems Dev., Systems Implem.,
Systems Support, Network Admin., DB Admin.

Industries: Generalist (All), Transportation, Retail

Marshall Career Service Inc

6500 West Fwy Ste 200
Fort Worth, TX 76116-2112
(817) 737-2645
Email: careers@marshallcareerservice.com
Web: www.marshallcareerservice.com

Summary: We provide mid-management to
executive-level search and placements in
accounting, financial, engineering and operational
positions. Our clients are primarily manufacturing
and service related companies.

Key Contact - Specialty:
Mr. Jim Ashworth, CPC, Vice President
Mr. Rick Marshall, President

Salary Minimum: $55,000

Functions: Senior Mgmt., Middle Mgmt.,
Production, Plant Mgmt., Materials, Purchasing,
Finance, CFOs, Budgeting, Engineering

Industries: Generalist (All)

The Bob Marshall Group International

247 Bryans Dr Ste 100
McDonough, GA 30252-2513
(770) 898-5550
Fax: (706) 443-1146
Email: espro@bellsouth.net
Web: www.themarshallplan.org

Summary: We specialize in the healthcare
industry. We also place in the information security
area. We have extensive experience placing people
in technical, sales, marketing and administrative
positions within this industry.

Key Contact - Specialty:
Mr. Bob Marshall, CPC, CIPC, President

Salary Minimum: $75,000

Functions: Generalist (All), Management, Board
Members, Nurses

Industries: Government, Environmental Svcs.,
Software, Healthcare, Hospitals, Physical
Therapy, Women's

Marshall-Alan Associates Inc

5 W 37th St Rm 800
New York, NY 10018-5363
(212) 382-2440
Fax: (212) 764-5411
Email: alanm@marshallalan.com
Web: www.marshallalan.com

Summary: We are an executive search
organization specializing in the hotel, restaurant,
and food service industry.

Key Contact - Specialty:
Mr. Alan Massarsky, President - *Hospitality*
Ms. Joan Steinberg, Vice President - *Hospitality*
Mr. Kyrk Pappas, Vice President - *Hospitality*

Salary Minimum: $75,000

Functions: Generalist (All), Senior Mgmt.,
Middle Mgmt., Purchasing, Sales Mgmt.,
Training, CFOs, MIS Mgmt.

Industries: Hospitality, Hotels, Resorts, Clubs,
Restaurants

Mitchell Martin Inc

80 Wall St Ste 1215
New York, NY 10005-3604
(212) 943-1404
Fax: (212) 328-0964
Email: info@mitchellmartin.com
Web: www.itmmi.com

Summary: We are a full-service IT organization
servicing the contract and permanent staffing
needs of our clients throughout the tri-state area.
We also provide various healthcare providers with
nurses, PTs, OTs and SLPS on a contract and
permanent basis.

Key Contact - Specialty:
Mr. Gene Holtzman, President
Mr. Joseph Schimpf, Chief Operating Officer -
Finance
Mr. Michael Church, Vice President

Salary Minimum: $40,000

Functions: Admin. Svcs., Healthcare, Nurses, IT,
MIS Mgmt., Systems Analysis, Systems Dev.,
Systems Support, Network Admin., DB Admin.

Industries: Generalist (All), Physical Therapy,
Occupational Therapy

The Martwick Group Inc

61845 Ten Barr Rd
Bend, OR 97701-9314
(541) 318-5671

Email your resume to a targeted list of recruiters now at www.ExecutiveAgent.com/DER07

Email: gail@martwick.com
Web: www.martwick.com

Summary: We are a full-service executive search firm, specializing in the medical device industry. Our president has extensive experience in successful executive recruitment of marketing, engineering and manufacturing professionals in medical device and high technology companies.

Key Contact - Specialty:
Ms. Gail Martwick, President

Salary Minimum: $70,000

Functions: Mktg. Mgmt., Engineering

Industries: Manufacturing, Medical Devices

Marvel Consultant

28601 Chagrin Blvd Ste 670
Beachwood, OH 44122-4549
(216) 292-2855
Fax: (216) 292-7207
Email: recruiters@marvelconsultants.com
Web: www.marvelconsultants.com

Summary: Our company is a leading national recruiting firm uniquely qualified to identify and recruit outstanding candidates and superior talent for a broad spectrum of disciplines including: business, finance, accounting, legal, industrial, engineering, IT, medical, general management, banking, allied health, pharmaceutical, rubber & plastics, manufacturing and sales & marketing.

Key Contact - Specialty:
Mr. John Sowers, CPC, President
Mrs. Linda Sowers, Secretary
Mr. Eric C. Bergsman, CPC, Account Executive - *Marketing, Sales*
Mr. Marc Charney, CPC, Account Executive - *Plastics, Rubber*
Mr. Mark Kozell, Account Executive - *Legal, Legal (Attorneys,Lawyers)*
Mr. William Radke, CPC, Account Executive - *Distribution, Electronics, Factories, Factories (Automation), Fastener*
Mr. Dave Sevel, CPC, Account Executive - *Aerospace, Automation, Automotive, Biomedical, Biotechnology*
Mr. Jim Vaccarino, Account Executive - *Intellectual property, Legal, Legal (Attorneys,Lawyers)*
Mr. William B. Weiss, Esq., Legal Specialist
Mr. Lester Tavens, CPC, Medical Team Manager
Mr. Ken Bernstein, CPC, Account Executive - *Biomedical, Biopharmaceutical, Biotechnology, Clinical, Healthcare*
Mr. Monte Kushkin, Account Executive - *Emergency room, Hospital, Medical*
Mr. Brian Cayne, Account Executive - *Intellectual property, Legal, Legal (Attorneys,Lawyers)*
Mr. Robert Weiss, Account Executive - *Legal, Legal (Attorneys,Lawyers)*
Mr. Kevin Pierson, Account Executive - *Comptrollers, Controllers, Credit, Financial, Sales*
Mr. Michael Fieseler, Account Executive - *Information Technology, SAP, Systems (Analysts,Integration), Technology*

Functions: Generalist (All), Management, Board Members

Industries: Generalist (All), Manufacturing, Food, Bev., Tobacco, Chemicals, Plastics, Rubber, Paints, Petro. Products, Misc. Mfg., Finance, Pharm Svcs., Legal, Accounting, E-commerce, IT Implementation, Software, Healthcare

Dan Mask Associates

4250 Dumbarton Place
South Park
Charlotte, NC 28211-3410
(704) 366-8022
Email: dmask@bellsouth.net

Summary: Provide Career Development and Recruiting Services for $100K and above candidates

Key Contact - Specialty:
Mr. Dan Mask, CDFI, Recruiting & Career Development - *Financial services, Human resources, Sales, Senior management, Start-up companies*

Salary Minimum: $100,000

Functions: Sales & Mktg.

Industries: Finance, Banking, Misc. Financial, Non-Classifiable

The Maslow Media Group Inc

2134 Wisconsin Ave NW
Washington, DC 20007-2231
(202) 965-1100
Fax: (202) 965-6171
Email: lmaslow@maslowmedia.com
Web: www.maslowmedia.com

Summary: We provide payroll and staffing services specifically for the broadcast and multimedia Industry. Our purpose is to provide a centralized resource for outsourcing freelance and fulltime staffing, payroll, camera crews and production services.

Key Contact - Specialty:
Ms. Linda Maslow, Chief Executive Officer
Mr. Carl Neubecker, Vice President, Media Management Servs
Ms. Joan Fiddle, Vice President & Prod Mgr, Freelance Div - *Multimedia, Outsourcing, Staffing*

Functions: Generalist (All), Productivity

Industries: Media, New Media, Broadcast, Film

Mason Energy Services

34 Brushwood Ct
The Woodlands, TX 77380-3979
(281) 367-0357
Fax: (281) 298-5293
Email: info@masonenergy.com
Web: www.masonenergy.com

Summary: We specialize in the recruiting of geosciences professionals for the world-wide petroleum industry. We maintain an extensive data base professional candidates acquired through recruiting activities and our involvement in the oil & gas community. We have the resources to target professionals at major and independent petroleum companies and from other geographic regions.

Key Contact - Specialty:
Mr. William L. Mason, Owner

Functions: Board Members, Production

Industries: Energy, Utilities, Oil & Gas

Masterquest

5008 Saddlehorn Dr
Arlington, TX 76017-3923
(817) 561-4933
Fax: (817) 719-0059
Email: support@mquestrecruit.com
Web: www.mquestrecruit.com

Summary: We are a healthcare recruiting and consulting firm specializing in nurse practitioners, RNs, and healthcare managers. Our motto is 'Quest for the Best,' as we are always on a quest

for the best candidates and career opportunities and the best matches. We are members of Health Career Agents, a national network of healthcare recruiters that represent medical practitioners as their agent.

Key Contact - Specialty:
Ms. Elisa Juarez, President - *Clinical, Consulting, Direct marketing, Healthcare, Management*
Ms. Ellen J. Thompson, RN, Consultant - *Clinical, Consulting, Healthcare, Home health, Medical*
Ms. Sharon Akins, Consultant - *Consulting, Healthcare, Medical*
Mr. Sam Thompson, Researcher - *Healthcare, Medical, Research, Research & development*

Salary Minimum: $45,000

Functions: Generalist (All), Healthcare, Physicians

Industries: Healthcare, Hospitals, Long-term/Home Care, Women's

Masters Medical Search

3206 Mallard Cove Ln
Fort Wayne, IN 46804-2883
(260) 490-2808
Fax: (260) 969-0935
Email: phil@devicecareers.com
Web: www.devicecareers.com

Summary: We specialize in medical device industry placements with emphasis on marketing, engineering, clinical research, quality assurance, sales management and other leadership positions. Our clients include orthopedic/spine implant manufacturers and other segments of the surgical device arena.

Key Contact - Specialty:
Mr. Phil Mercier, President

Salary Minimum: $75,000

Functions: Generalist (All)

Industries: Medical Devices

Mathey Services

15170 Bethany Rd
Sycamore, IL 60178-8308
(815) 895-3846
Email: jam151@aol.com
Web: www.matheyservices.net

Summary: Executive recruiting, searching, screening and placement services provided to clients in the plastics, packaging and chemical industries. Specializing in the fields of sales & marketing, R&D, management and manufacturing.

Key Contact - Specialty:
Ms. Joyce Mathey, President - *Chemical, Packaging, Plastics*

Salary Minimum: $30,000

Functions: Generalist (All)

Industries: Chemicals, Plastics, Rubber, Packaging

Mathias Medical Search

7206 Capri St
Portage, MI 49002-9417
(269) 329-1153
(888) 355-4988
Fax: (413) 581-8025
Email: dmathias@mdjobsearch.com
Web: www.mdjobsearch.com

Summary: We are a contingency search firm with a focus on physician and mid-level practitioner recruitment. We are aware of opportunities and candidates covering a wide range of specialties and geographic locations.

Key Contact - Specialty:
Ms. Donna Mathias, President - *Physicians*

Functions: Generalist (All), Physicians

Industries: Generalist (All), Healthcare

Matrix Consultants Inc

PO Box 986
Wrightsville Beach, NC 28480-0986
(910) 256-8080
Fax: (910) 256-9500
Email: oj@pobox.com
Web: www.ojwomble.com

Summary: Specialize in recruiting and conducting searches in the food ingredient industry. We offer positions in research, sales & marketing to VP and presidents for the largest companies in the industry.

Key Contact - Specialty:
Mr. O.J. Womble, Vice President, Marketing - *Nutraceuticals*
Mr. Joe Marion, Director, Marketing
Mr. Bill Jordan, Executive Recruiter
Ms. Rebecca Charles, Executive Recruiter - *Food service, Nutraceuticals*

Salary Minimum: $65,000

Functions: Generalist (All), Board Members, Senior Mgmt., Middle Mgmt., Product Dev., Mktg. Mgmt., Sales Mgmt.

Industries: Generalist (All), Food, Bev., Tobacco, Chemicals, Biotech/Life Sciences

MATRIX Resources Inc

115 Perimeter Center Pl NE Ste 250
Atlanta, GA 30346-1285
(770) 677-2400
(800) 627-3533
Fax: (770) 668-0384
Email: matrixatl@matrixresources.com
Web: www.matrixresources.com

Summary: We are a premier IT staffing provider for both permanent placement and contract consulting positions. Our services range from a single direct hire placement or contract assignment to a customized managed services solution, utilizing our staffing experience and multiple strategic technology alliances.

Key Contact - Specialty:
Mr. Jim Huling, Chief Executive Officer - *C-level*
Mr. Tom Kapish, Vice President, Corporate Operations - *COOs*
Mr. Gary Wood, Vice President, Strategic Operations - *Staffing*
Ms. Shannon Brandon, Director, Sales - *Staffing*
Ms. Lisa Verde, Director, Recruiting - *Staffing*
Mr. Bill Hetherington, Director, Marketing - *Marketing*
Ms. Sandy Jess, Director, Human Resources - *Human resources*
Ms. Mary McAllister, Director, Administration - *Office (Administration)*
Mr. Robert Stovall, Director, Finance - *Finance*
Mr. Mark Marschke, Director, Information Technology - *Information Technology*

Salary Minimum: $25,000

Functions: Training, IT, MIS Mgmt., Systems Analysis, Systems Dev., Systems Implem., Systems Support, Network Admin., DB Admin.

Industries: Generalist (All)

Branches:
3800 Colonnade Pkwy Ste 430
Birmingham, AL 35243-3369
(866) 845-7005
(205) 314-5200
Fax: (205) 314-5350

Key Contact - Specialty:
Mr. Joe Perez, Director, Sales

4500 N 32nd St Ste 106
Phoenix, AZ 85018-3350
(877) 827-5223
(602) 522-3300
Fax: (602) 522-3499
Email: matrixphx@matrixresources.com
Key Contact - Specialty:
Mr. Paul Byerlein, Account Manager

90 Washington Valley Rd Ste 105
Bedminster, NJ 07921-2118
(888) 335-9860
(908) 719-8960
Fax: (866) 372-5971
Email: matrixnj@matrixresources.com
Key Contact - Specialty:
Mr. Don Palmer, Vice President, Field Operations

6047 Tyvola Glen Cir Ste 104
Charlotte, NC 28217-6436
(704) 426-1100
(704) 426-1117
Fax: (704) 426-1101
Email: matrixclt@matrixresources.com
Key Contact - Specialty:
Mr. Carl Rohsenberger

2803 Slater Rd Ste 105
Morrisville, NC 27560-9502
(800) 444-0965
(919) 653-1500
Fax: (919) 653-1550
Email: matrixrtp@matrixresources.com
Key Contact - Specialty:
Mr. Jim Murphy, Director, Sales

4851 Lyndon B Johnson Fwy Ste 700
Dallas, TX 75244-6078
(800) 522-0001
(972) 778-1800
Fax: (972) 980-4128
Email: matrixdal@matrixresources.com
Key Contact - Specialty:
Mr. Jon Davis, Director, Sales
Mr. Bob Fors, Director, Recruiting

G.P Mattocks & Associates Inc

5015 Country Club Dr N
Wilson, NC 27896-9123
(252) 399-0589
Fax: (252) 291-8467
Email: paul@gpmrecruiters.com
Web: www.gpmrecruiters.com

Summary: We are a privately owned and operated search firm working with our affiliates to search and recruit top candidates in the engineering and management fields.

Key Contact - Specialty:
Mr. Paul Mattocks, Owner & Recruiter - *Healthcare, Medical, Medical (Devices), MIS, Sales*
Mrs. Brenda Mattocks, Research & Data Input

Salary Minimum: $30,000

Functions: Management, Senior Mgmt.

Industries: Printing, Drugs Mfg., Medical Devices, Plastics, Rubber, Metal Products, Machine, Appliance, Motor Vehicles, Misc. Mfg., Electronic, Elec. Components, IT Implementation, Software, Accounting SW, Database SW, Development SW, Doc. Mgmt., Production SW, Biotech/Life Sciences, Healthcare

MAU Inc (Management Analysis & Utilization Inc)

501 Greene St
Augusta, GA 30901-4404
(706) 724-8367
(706) 823-2337
Fax: (706) 823-2388
Email: professionalresumes@mau.com
Web: www.mau.com

Summary: Our full spectrum HR & staffing services include: recruiting, screening, testing & assessment, professional placement, organizational development & training, outsourcing & outplacement, contract & temp staffing, medical, clerical, industrial, IT, office and professional. We also offer process analysis & design; production managed services and certified safety training.

Key Contact - Specialty:
Mr. Randall Hatcher, President
Ms. Lawrence Davis, Vice President

Functions: Generalist (All), Senior Mgmt., Admin. Svcs., Mfg., Nurses, HR Mgmt., Finance, IT, Engineering, Technicians

Industries: Generalist (All), Energy, Utilities, Manufacturing, Food, Bev., Tobacco, Textiles, Apparel, Paper, Printing, Chemicals, Drugs Mfg., Medical Devices, Metal Products, Machine, Appliance, Motor Vehicles, Consumer Elect., Misc. Mfg., Banking, Telecoms, Healthcare, Hospitals, Long-term/Home Care, Occupational Therapy

Branches:
230 Main St
Thomson, GA 30824-2617
(706) 595-5525
Fax: (706) 595-5780
Email: dhodges@mau.com
Key Contact - Specialty:
Mr. David Hodges, CTS, Manager

2800 S 25th Ave
Broadview, IL 60155-4532
(708) 450-8556
Fax: (708) 450-8580
Email: mborgen@mau.com
Key Contact - Specialty:
Mr. Mike Borgen, Manager

1034 Pine Log Rd
Aiken, SC 29803-7341
(803) 642-5255
Fax: (803) 642-5155
Email: nbanks@mau.com
Key Contact - Specialty:
Nat Banks, Manager

205A Concord Rd
Anderson, SC 29621-2731
(864) 225-0586
Fax: (864) 225-4570
Email: jbrown@mau.com
Key Contact - Specialty:
Ms. Jennifer Brown, Manager

5101 Ashley Phosphate Rd
Charleston, SC 29418-2832
(843) 767-7610
Fax: (843) 767-8270
Email: jsheehan@mau.com
Key Contact - Specialty:
Mr. Jim Sheehan, Manager

109 Pelham Commons Blvd
Greenville, SC 29615-4974
(864) 242-9460
Fax: (864) 987-0807
Email: bcallahan@mau.com

Key Contact - Specialty:
Mr. Brian Callahan, Manager

Maximum

230 Park Ave Rm 635
New York, NY 10169-0646
(212) 867-4646
Fax: (212) 682-4882
Email: mmc@maxmanhr.com
Web: www.maxmanhr.com

Summary: We are dedicated exclusively to HR placement. We place permanent, interim and entry level HR professionals in all HR disciplines.

Key Contact - Specialty:
Ms. Melissa Brophy, President - *Human resources*
Ms. Nancy Shield, Vice President - *Human resources*

Functions: Generalist (All), HR Mgmt., Benefits, Staffing, Training

Industries: Generalist (All)

MC Prosearch

851 Burlway Rd Ste 618
Burlingame, CA 94010-1715
(650) 340-0416
Fax: (650) 340-7156
Email: sonnymca@sbcglobal.net

Summary: We specialize in all types of sales positions.

Key Contact - Specialty:
Mr. Sonny Park, President - *Sales*

Functions: Sales & Mktg., Advertising, Mktg. Mgmt., Sales Mgmt.

Industries: Generalist (All), Construction, Manufacturing, Transportation, Communications, Software, Biotech/Life Sciences, Healthcare

The McAllister Group

5651 Silver Ridge Dr
Stone Mountain, GA 30087-2319
(770) 469-3843
Email: mgigroup@comcast.net

Summary: We offer an established base of clients, with whom we have had relationships. These clients engage us to identify candidates with hardware and home center industry experience in sales marketing and general management to manage business plans for big box retailers.

Key Contact - Specialty:
Mr. David McAllister, Managing Partner

Salary Minimum: $100,000

Functions: Management, Senior Mgmt., Middle Mgmt., Product Dev., Sales & Mktg., Mktg. Research, Mktg. Mgmt., Sales Reps.

Industries: Generalist (All), Agri., Forestry, Mining, Plastics, Rubber, Paints, Petro. Products, Consumer Elect., Consumer Goods, Retail, Supply Chain Mgmt, Sports, RF/Microwave, Homeland Security

The McCandlish Group

90 S High St Ste B
Dublin, OH 43017-1171
(614) 766-1800
Email: mike@mccandlishgroup.com
Web: www.mccandlishgroup.com

Summary: We are an executive search firm representing new technology originators and some of the finest companies in the world. Our interview/offer ratio is approximately 50 percent. We have many years of staffing experience and seek out opportunities with technology-based

growth firms. We only specialize in sales & marketing recruiting for numerous industries including the following: IT, software, manufacturing, healthcare, life sciences and telecom.

Key Contact - Specialty:
Mr. Mike McCandlish, President - *Healthcare, Manufacturing, Telecommunications*

Salary Minimum: $60,000

Functions: Senior Mgmt., Middle Mgmt., Mfg., Product Dev., Sales & Mktg., Mktg. Mgmt., Sales Mgmt., Sales Reps., MIS Mgmt., Engineering

Industries: Energy, Utilities, Construction, Manufacturing, Services, Entertainment, Communications, Telecoms, Software, Biotech/Life Sciences, Healthcare

McCanna Craig & Associates

PO Box 212161
Augusta, GA 30917-2161
(706) 863-8033
(803) 637-5447
Email: john@mccannacraig.com
Web: www.mccannacraig.com

Summary: Agency works with client companies in the chemical, automotive, pharmaceutical, food and beverage, biotech, medical device, plastics, rubber, consumer products and general manufacturing. Handle all positions technical, engineering and operations.

Key Contact - Specialty:
Mr. John Brumbaugh, President, CPC

Salary Minimum: $65,000

Functions: Senior Mgmt., Middle Mgmt., Mfg., Product Dev., Plant Mgmt., Productivity, Materials, Purchasing, Distribution, Physicians

Industries: Manufacturing, Food, Bev., Tobacco, Textiles, Apparel, Chemicals, Soap, Perf., Cosmtcs., Drugs Mfg., Medical Devices, Plastics, Rubber, Paints, Petro. Products, Machine, Appliance, Motor Vehicles, Consumer Goods, Healthcare, Hospitals

McCarthy-Komendera Associates

(also known as National BancSearch LLC)
2727 Prytania St Ste 6
New Orleans, LA 70130-5981
(504) 897-6688
Fax: (504) 891-0102
Email: info@nationalbanksearch.com
Web: www.nationalbanksearch.com

Summary: With integrity, credibility, and utmost confidentiality, we identify, profile and present only top-notch candidates matched to the needs of client companies and serve as an invaluable liaison during the sensitive hiring process.

Key Contact - Specialty:
Mr. Richard McCarthy, Owner & Manager - *Banking*
Ms. Stacy Komendera, Partner & Manager - *Executives, Finance, Financial, Information Technology, Operations*
Mr. Cade Cummings, Recruiter - *Banking*
Ms. Kera Johnson, Recruiter - *Banking*
Ms. Renee Kennedy, Recruiter & Administrator - *Banking, Executives, Financial*
Mr. David Ramsey, Recruiter - *Banking, Financial*

Functions: Generalist (All), Board Members, Finance, Cash Mgmt., M&A, IT

Industries: Generalist (All), Finance, Banking, Invest. Banking, Brokers, Venture Cap., Misc. Financial, Accounting, Mgmt. Consulting,

PSA/ASP, Hospitality, Hotels, Resorts, Clubs, Entertainment, Advertising, Call Centers, Real Estate, Marketing SW

The McClure Group Inc

1210 Bayshore Blvd
Indian Rocks Beach, FL 33785-2830
(727) 593-7163
Email: careers@mcclure-group.com
Web: www.mcclure-group.com

Summary: We are healthcare information systems (HIS) recruiting for permanent placement. Temp staffing for independent HIS consultants. Market intelligence and client satisfaction survey services. Clients are healthcare consulting companies, software vendors and providers.

Key Contact - Specialty:
Mr. Rob McClure, President & Owner

Salary Minimum: $75,000

Functions: Healthcare

Industries: IT Implementation

McCord Consulting Group Inc (MCG Inc)

4533 Pineview Dr NE
Cedar Rapids, IA 52402-1715
(319) 378-0077
Fax: (319) 378-1577
Email: sam@mccordgroup.com
Web: www.mccordgroup.com

Summary: We provide executive, engineering and company acquisition searches to the plastics industry. We represent companies ranging from small privately owned to Fortune 500.

Key Contact - Specialty:
Mr. Sam McCord, President & Chief Executive Officer
Mrs. Mary McCord, Vice President

Salary Minimum: $50,000

Functions: Management, Senior Mgmt., Middle Mgmt., Mfg., Production, Plant Mgmt., Quality, CFOs, M&A, Engineering

Industries: Manufacturing, Medical Devices, Plastics, Rubber, Metal Products, Machine, Appliance, Motor Vehicles, Computer Equip., Consumer Elect., Misc. Mfg., Electronic, Elec. Components, Packaging, Mfg. SW

McCormack Schreiber Legal Search Inc

150 N Wacker Dr Ste 1800
Chicago, IL 60606-1607
(312) 377-2000
(866) 819-4091
Fax: (312) 377-2001
Email: info@thelawrecruiters.com
Web: www.thelawrecruiters.com

Summary: We specialize in the placement of attorneys, including associates, partners, and practice groups, at large, mid-size and boutique law firms, and in-house counsel at local and national companies. We have law firm and in-house opportunities in a full range of legal practice areas.

Key Contact - Specialty:
Ms. Amy Leafe McCormack, Esq., Principal
Ms. Gay R. Schreiber, Esq., Principal
Ms. Nancy L. Carey, Esq.
Ms. Eynav S. Epstein, Esq.
Ms. Allison G. Hammer, Esq.
Ms. Denise R. Schwartz, Esq.
Ms. Sabrina C. Spitznagle, Esq.

Functions: Legal

Industries: Legal

The McCormick Group Inc

1440 Central Park Blvd Ste 207
Fredericksburg, VA 22401-4931
(540) 786-9777
Fax: (540) 786-9355
Email: tmg-corp@email.msn.com
Web: www.mccormickgroup.com

Summary: Established to become the most
effective executive search service in America:
offices in D.C. and Boston provide national
coverage.

Key Contact - Specialty:
Mr. William J. McCormick, Founder & Chief
  Executive Officer
Mr. Brian D. McCormick, Executive Vice
  President
Mr. W. Lyles Carr, III, Senior Vice President
Mr. Bill King, Vice President
Ms. Adrienne McCormick, Principal
Ms. Barbara Chamberlain, Controller

Salary Minimum: $50,000

Functions: Generalist (All), Mktg. Mgmt., Sales
Mgmt., HR Mgmt., MIS Mgmt., Systems Dev.,
Mgmt. Consultants, Attorneys

Industries: Generalist (All), Legal, Mgmt.
Consulting, HR Services, Media, Software

McCrea & Company Worldwide

8626 Hollis Ln #7
Brecksville, OH 44141-2032
(440) 526-1672
Email: mccreaworldwide@sbcglobal.net

Summary: We specialize in the recruitment of
Banking/Financial professionals, IT Auditors,
Internal Auditors, Risk and Assurance
Professionals

Key Contact - Specialty:
Mr. James McCrea, President - *Computers
(Software), Hardware*

Salary Minimum: $75,000

Functions: Middle Mgmt., Finance, IT, Systems
Analysis, Systems Dev., Systems Implem.,
Network Admin., DB Admin.

Industries: Generalist (All), Finance, Banking,
Architectural Svcs., Equip Svcs., E-commerce,
IT Implementation, Telecoms, Call Centers,
Telephony, Digital, Wireless, Fiber Optic,
Network Infrastructure, Database SW,
Development SW, Doc. Mgmt., Production SW,
ERP SW, Industry Specific SW, Networking,
Comm. SW, Security SW, System SW

The Paul McDaniel Company

PO Box 381672
Germantown, TN 38183-1672
(901) 757-9220
Fax: (901) 758-1111
Email: info@paulmcdaniel.com
Web: www.paulmcdaniel.com

Summary: We are successfully recruiting for
companies in categories previously listed. We
have an excellent industry reputation.

Key Contact - Specialty:
Mr. Paul McDaniel, Owner

Functions: Middle Mgmt.

Industries: Generalist (All), Wholesale, Retail

The McDermott Network LLP

32963 Neptune Bight
Nashotah, WI 53058-9523
(262) 367-2700
Fax: (262) 367-8811

Email: mcnetwrk@aol.com
Web:
www.members.aol.com/mcnet8808/mainie40.htm

Summary: We are your source for sales &
marketing employees in the food and beverage
industry, emphasizing supplier positions in the
beer, wine & spirits and non-alcoholic beverage
industry.

Key Contact - Specialty:
Mr. Bob McDermott, Recruiter - *Consumer,
  Consumer (Products), Distribution, Marketing,
  Sales*
Mr. Terri McDermott, Recruiter - *Consumer
  (Marketing,Products), Sales*

Salary Minimum: $40,000

Functions: Sales & Mktg.

Industries: Food, Bev., Tobacco

McDuffy-Edwards

3117 Medina Dr
Garland, TX 75041-4521
(972) 864-1174
(972)
Fax: (972) 864-4752
Email: tom@mcduffy-edwards.com
Web: www.mcduffy-edwards.com

Summary: Our firm recruits sales and technical
sales support professionals exclusively for the
information technology industry.

Key Contact - Specialty:
Mr. Tom Edwards, Owner - *Sales*

Salary Minimum: $60,000

Functions: Sales Mgmt., Customer Svc.

Industries: Computer Equip., Mgmt. Consulting,
Telecoms, Software

McGinnis & Associates

550 Water St Ste 1309
Jacksonville, FL 32202-5168
(904) 356-7337
Fax: (904) 356-7335
Email: recruite@aol.com

Summary: We place candidates in middle and
senior management accounting, tax and financial
positions.

Key Contact - Specialty:
Mr. Fred McGinnis

Salary Minimum: $50,000

Functions: Finance, CFOs, Taxes

Industries: Generalist (All)

McGowan Associates Inc

207 Overcreek Rd Ste 693
Phoenixville, PA 19460-1965
(610) 917-9913
Email: bamcgowan@att.net
Web: www.mcgowan-associates.com

Summary: As a food service recruitment company
we discover management, culinary and executive
talent for the hospitality and healthcare industries.
We focus on the candidates' professional skills and
competencies, as well as their sociability and
service quotients.

Key Contact - Specialty:
Mr. Brian A. McGowan, President - *Food service,
  Healthcare, Hospitality*

Salary Minimum: $30,000

Functions: Generalist (All), Management, Chefs

Industries: Hospitality, Hotels, Resorts, Clubs,
Restaurants, Full Service Restaurants

C A McInnis & Associates

203 Broad St Unit 7
Milford, CT 06460-4750
(203) 876-7110
Fax: (203) 783-1230
Email: carol@mcinnisinc.com
Web: www.mcinnisinc.com

Summary: We are an executive search firm
specializing in pharmaceutical permanent and
contract clinical research work of professionals.

Key Contact - Specialty:
Ms. Carol McInnis, President - *Pharmaceutical*

Functions: R&D, Engineering, Technicians

Industries: Drugs Mfg., Pharm Svcs.,
Biotech/Life Sciences

McInturff & Associates Inc

209 W Central St Ste 310
Natick, MA 01760-3716
(508) 653-4050
Fax: (508) 653-1418
Email: bob@mcinturff.com
Web: www.mcinturff.com

Summary: We've had many years of experience as
specialists in supply chain and manufacturing
management. Our firm is staffed by professionals
who bring in-depth knowledge to your unique
requirements.

Key Contact - Specialty:
Mr. Robert E. McInturff, President - *Logistics,
  Manufacturing, Materials*

Salary Minimum: $90,000

Functions: Mfg., Materials

Industries: Medical Devices, Plastics, Rubber,
Metal Products, Computer Equip.

The McIntyre Group

63 Glover Ave
Norwalk, CT 06850-1203
(203) 750-1111
Fax: (203) 750-1119
Email: mcintyre@themcintyregroup.com
Web: www.themcintyregroup.com

Summary: Our firm specializes in staffing for
both permanent and contract bases: accounting &
finance, executive assistants, legal secretaries,
sales & marketing, HR, customer service,
reception and clerical positions. We have built our
reputation on our ability to consistently offer key
career opportunities that meet our candidates'
criteria.

Key Contact - Specialty:
Ms. Leslie McIntyre-Tavella, President &
  Founder

Salary Minimum: $28,000

Functions: Admin. Svcs., Advertising, Finance,
IT

Industries: Generalist (All)

McIntyre Management Resources

1406-760 Mohawk Rd W
Chedoke Apts
Hamilton, ON L9C 6P6
Canada
(905) 574-6765
Email: mm@mcintyremgmt.com
Web: www.mcintyrejobs.com

Summary: Best known for our ability to partner
with clients, establishing in-depth, long-term
relationships. Relationships may be by industry
specialty or position/equipment specialty.

Key Contact - Specialty:
Ms. Marlene McIntyre, President

Salary Minimum: $40,000

Functions: Generalist (All), DB Admin.

Industries: Generalist (All), Manufacturing, Metal Products, Machine, Appliance, Motor Vehicles, Consumer Elect., Consumer Goods, HR Services, E-commerce, IT Implementation, Software, Database SW, ERP SW, Mfg. SW, Networking, Comm. SW, Security SW, System SW

McKinnon Management Group Inc

700-5160 Yonge St
Office Building
North York, ON M2N 6L9
Canada
(416) 250-6763
Fax: (416) 250-6916
Email: info@mckinnon.com
Web: www.mckinnon.com

Summary: We are an executive search firm focusing on leading edge business enterprise placing sales, marketing and healthcare professionals.

Key Contact - Specialty:
Mr. Greg McKinnon, President - *Sales*
Mr. Chris Bradshaw, Vice President - *High technology*

Functions: Generalist (All)

Industries: Misc. Financial, Pharm Svcs., E-commerce, IT Implementation, Advertising

The McKnight Group

1465 Post Rd E
Westport, CT 06880-5528
(203) 256-3570
(800) 575-2203
Fax: (203) 256-3574
Email: mcknightgroup@mail.com

Summary: We are executive search consultants with expertise in banking (i.e.: trust, new business development, commercial lending and more), financial services (i.e.: investment management, brokerage, risk and more), finance, accounting, tax and insurance. Our work involves wealth and risk management on all levels.

Key Contact - Specialty:
Mr. Richard F. McKnight, Managing Partner

Salary Minimum: $80,000

Functions: Generalist (All), Mktg. Mgmt., Sales Mgmt., Benefits, Taxes, M&A, Network Admin., DB Admin.

Industries: Generalist (All), Energy, Utilities, Machine, Appliance, Banking, Hospitality, Telecoms, Insurance

William K McLaughlin Associates Inc

PO Box 10308
Rochester, NY 14610-0308
(800) 728-1964
Fax: (585) 442-8587
Email: information@wkmclaughlin.com
Web: www.wkmclaughlin.com

Summary: We have assisted patent attorneys in finding positions with the leading law firms and corporations.

Key Contact - Specialty:
Mr. William K. McLaughlin, President
Mr. John F. McLaughlin, Vice President

Functions: Legal, Attorneys

Industries: Generalist (All), Legal

McLean Executive Consultants

888 3 St SW
Bankers Hall West Tower Floor 10
Calgary, AB T2P 5C5
Canada
(403) 270-8700
Email: info@mcleanexecutive.com
Web: www.mcleanexecutive.com

Summary: We are a premier marketing, sales and executive management recruiting company with expertise in healthcare, oil & gas, transportation/logistics and IT.

Key Contact - Specialty:
Mr. Mark Mooney, Director - *Business to business, Executives, Healthcare, Information Technology, Sales*
Mr. Robert Zagorsky, Director
Mr. Karl Fleurke, Consultant
Mr. Tom McMorrow, Consultant

Salary Minimum: $45,000

McMillan Associates Inc

4969 Alamanda Dr
Melbourne, Fl 32940-1433
(321) 254-4423
Email: jmcmillan@mcmillanassoc.com
Web: www.mcmillanassoc.com

Summary: We are an executive recruiting firm founded in 1968, specializes in placing degreed candidates within the Supply Chain to include materials management, purchasing, and logistics on a nationwide basis. We are continually recruiting candidates with knowledge of MRP, JIT, TQM, SPC, ISO standards, vendor quality, vendor certification, partnership agreements, and international sourcing.

Key Contact - Specialty:
Mr. John McMillan, Founder
Mrs. Donna McMillan, Founder

Salary Minimum: $50,000

Functions: Mfg., Materials, Purchasing, Distribution, Healthcare

Industries: Generalist (All), Food, Bev., Tobacco, Medical Devices, Motor Vehicles, Consumer Goods, Transportation, Wholesale, Logistics Svcs., Supply Chain Mgmt

McPherson Square Associates Inc

1025 Connecticut Ave NW Ste 1012
Washington, DC 20036-5417
(202) 737-8777
Web: www.msalegal.com

Summary: Specializing in placement of partners and groups with law firms and law firm mergers. We offer corporate legal placement.

Key Contact - Specialty:
Mr. Ronald G. Russell, President

Salary Minimum: $140,000

Functions: Legal, Attorneys

Industries: Generalist (All)

McSearch Personnel Consulting

4311 Oak Lawn Ave Ste 360
Dallas, TX 75219-2338
(214) 599-0171
Fax: (214) 599-0170
Email: info@mcsearch.com
Web: www.mcsearch.com

Summary: We are a recruiting firm specializing in banking, administrative support, accounting and HR positions.

Key Contact - Specialty:
Mr. Frank McLaughlin, CPC, Chairman of the Board - *Accounting, Administration, Banking, Clerical, Human resources*
Ms. Stephanie Struble, Manager, Client Solutions - *Accounting, Administration, Banking, Clerical, Human resources*

Salary Minimum: $20,000

Functions: Generalist (All)

Industries: Generalist (All)

Joseph J McTaggart

5710 Arapaho Dr
San Jose, CA 95123-3202
(408) 226-3203
Email: mct@jobmiracle.com
Web: www.joemctaggart.com

Summary: Solo practitioner. One-hundred percent search. No time limit guarantee. Candidate is guaranteed to earn you a profit or I replace. Specialty: GM and supporting high-level staff. Serving a potpourri of industries.

Key Contact - Specialty:
Mr. Joseph J. McTaggart, Owner - *Management*

Salary Minimum: $100,000

Functions: Management, Senior Mgmt.

Industries: Generalist (All), Electronic, Elec. Components, Misc. Financial, Advertising, Publishing, Life

MD Resources Inc

207 Chesterfield Towne Ctr
Chesterfield, MO 63005-1257
(636) 536-6656
(888) 669-1333
Fax: (636) 536-6667
Email: info@mdr-inc.com
Web: www.mdr-inc.com

Summary: We are a nationwide physician placement firm that specializes in the placement of resident and practicing physicians. We find excellent career opportunities for American and foreign physicians. We offer exceptional personal service for all those we assist, from the prospective candidate to the healthcare administrator.

Key Contact - Specialty:
Mr. Ed Taaffe, President

Functions: Management

Industries: Healthcare, Hospitals

MDR & Associates Inc

39 Audubon Trce
Saint Francisville, LA 70775-7319
(225) 614-1491
(800) 264-9701
Email: info@mdrandassociates.com
Web: www.mdrandassociates.com

Summary: We specialize in placing executives in the casino industry. We are very client oriented. We try to walk the extra mile to find the exact person described by the client. By doing this, we have developed a very good client list. Companies call us when they have a search. We treat both clients and candidates with equal respect.

Key Contact - Specialty:
Mr. Mel Robinson, President

Salary Minimum: $45,000

Functions: Senior Mgmt., Hospitality

Industries: Generalist (All), Hospitality, Hotels, Resorts, Clubs

Branches:
6930 Hilo Way
Diamondhead, MS 39525-3614
(228) 586-0699
Email: sonny@mdrandassociates.com
Key Contact - Specialty:
Mr. Sonny Fowler, Vice President

WH Meanor and Associates
PO Box 35036
Charlotte, NC 28235-5036
(704) 372-7640
Fax: (704) 372-7642
Email: crocha@whmeanor.com
Web: www.whmeanor.com

Summary: We are a minority-owned executive search and placement firm. Our focus is on executive-level placements, but we work with all levels based on our client's needs. Contract placement and training is also available.

Key Contact - Specialty:
Mrs. Cynthia Rocha, Vice President

Salary Minimum: $50,000

Functions: Senior Mgmt., Middle Mgmt., Mfg., Product Dev.

Industries: Generalist (All), Energy, Utilities, Construction, Manufacturing, Finance, Services, Media, Communications, Government, Defense, Aerospace, Software, Biotech/Life Sciences, Healthcare

Med Exec International
100 N Brand Blvd Ste 306
Glendale, CA 91203-2614
(818) 552-2036
(800) 507-5277
Fax: (928) 585-2036
Email: rosechristopher@medexecintl.com
Web: www.medexecintl.com

Summary: We provide customized search services to clients from the medical device and pharmaceutical industries that entrust their searches for regulatory affairs, clinical research and quality professionals to our care.

Key Contact - Specialty:
Ms. Rosemarie Christopher, Principal - *Pharmaceutical, Technical*
Mr. Lewie Casey, Administrative Assistant

Salary Minimum: $75,000

Functions: Board Members, Senior Mgmt., Middle Mgmt., Quality, Healthcare, Physicians

Industries: Drugs Mfg., Medical Devices, Electronic, Elec. Components, Pharm Svcs., Biotech/Life Sciences

Med Tracker Personnel Inc
261 W Causeway Approach
Mandeville, LA 70448-3032
(985) 727-3511
(800) 864-4776
Fax: (985) 727-0926
Email: info@medtrackerpersonnel.com
Web: www.medtrackerpersonnel.com

Summary: We are an executive medical recruitment search firm. We cover all areas of medical personnel. We specialize in physician and allied health.

Key Contact - Specialty:
Ms. Nikki Leimer, CPC, President
Mr. Adam Leimer, Senior Recruiter
Mr. Jay Gostisha, Senior Recruiter

Functions: Healthcare, Physicians

Industries: Non-profits, Healthcare, Hospitals, Long-term/Home Care, Dental, Physical Therapy, Occupational Therapy, Women's

Med-Ex Services
5000 Rockside Rd Ste 100
Independence, OH 44131-2141
(216) 573-1130
Fax: (216) 573-0727
Email: med-ex@stratos.net
Web: www.med-exservices.com

Summary: Permanent and temp medical/healthcare staffing with hospitals, clinics, doctors, dentists, labs, MCOs, PPOs, HMOs and more. If it's healthcare-related, we will fill the position.

Key Contact - Specialty:
Ms. Karin E. Deffler, CPC, President

Functions: Generalist (All), Healthcare, Physicians, Nurses, Allied Health, Health Admin., Mktg. Research, Sales Mgmt.

Industries: Generalist (All), Healthcare

Med-Search Recruiting Network Inc
15933 Clayton Rd Ste 100
Ballwin, MO 63011-2172
(636) 230-0717
(877) 897-5627
Fax: (636) 253-1269
Email: tim@medrecruiters.com
Web: www.medrecruiters.com

Summary: Our firm, the gateway to career success, is a dynamic search firm specializing in: the recruitment of sales, sales management, executive management and marketing professionals in the healthcare, medical pharmaceutical industries. We recruit on all levels vertically from entry level sales to VPs of sales & marketing.

Key Contact - Specialty:
Mr. Tim Charow, President

Functions: Management, Senior Mgmt., Sales & Mktg.

Industries: Chemicals, Soap, Perf., Cosmtcs., Misc. Mfg., Consumer Goods, IT Implementation, Biotech/Life Sciences, Healthcare

Medforce Inc
10600 Arrowhead Dr Ste 264
Fairfax, VA 22030-7306
(703) 691-7500
Fax: (703) 691-7404
Email: aplavin@medforce.com
Web: www.medforce.com

Summary: We are a premier medical staffing firm specializing in the career placement of nurses, pharmacists, rad techs, CT, MRI, nuclear medicine, RVT, CVT and ARDMS.

Key Contact - Specialty:
Ms. Avery Plavin, President

Salary Minimum: $35,000

Functions: Senior Mgmt., Healthcare

Industries: Pharm Svcs., Healthcare, Hospitals, Long-term/Home Care, Physical Therapy, Occupational Therapy, Women's

Media Management Resources Inc
31 Gulf Breeze Pkwy
Gulf Breeze, FL 32561-4461
(303) 290-9800
(850) 934-4880
Email: info@mediamanagement.com
Web: www.mediamanagement.com

Summary: Our firm is a respected executive search firm specializing in middle and upper-management serving select clients in telecom, new media and technology.

Key Contact - Specialty:
Mr. Michael S. Wein, Principal - *Interim, Management, Media, Technology, Telecommunications*
Mr. David Reiber, Vice President, Interim Services - *Telecommunications*

Salary Minimum: $75,000

Functions: Management, Board Members, Senior Mgmt., Middle Mgmt., Engineering, Mgmt. Consultants

Industries: Venture Cap., E-commerce, Entertainment, Media, New Media, Broadcast, Film, Communications, Telecoms, Telephony, Digital, Wireless, Fiber Optic, Network Infrastructure, Entertainment SW

Branches:
31B Gulf Breeze Pkwy
Gulf Breeze, FL 32561-4461
(850) 934-4880
Email: bwein@mediamanagement.com
Key Contact - Specialty:
Mr. William Wein, Principal - *Media, Technology, Telecommunications*

Media Recruiting Group Inc
1 Bridge St Ste P2
Irvington, NY 10533-1575
(914) 591-5511
Fax: (914) 591-8911
Email: info@mediarecruiting.com
Web: www.mediarecruiting.com

Summary: Our firm is one of the leading executive recruiters in magazine publishing for ad sales, marketing, promotion, research and circulation. Also leaders in other media, book publishing and direct marketing. Our expertise in the industry, integrity and long-term approach is unsurpassed, making us your recruiter of choice. Providing consistent, quality service, we have placed media candidates at all levels.

Key Contact - Specialty:
Mr. Steve Goldberg, Executive Vice President & Managing Ptnr - *Publishing*
Mrs. Risa Goldberg, President - *Publishing*

Salary Minimum: $50,000

Functions: Sales & Mktg., Advertising, Mktg. Mgmt., Sales Mgmt., Direct Mktg.

Industries: Advertising, Publishing, New Media

Medical & Executive Recruiters
24725 W 12 Mile Rd Ste 308
Southfield, MI 48034-8337
(248) 357-5373
Fax: (248) 357-5379
Email: mr1850@execrec.com

Summary: We place people in management and sales in the medical, electrical, engineering & manufacturing and consumer products areas.

Key Contact - Specialty:
Mr. Charles Greening - *Electrical, Manufacturing, Mechanical*

Functions: Middle Mgmt., Mfg., Materials, Physicians, Sales & Mktg., Benefits, Staffing, MIS Mgmt., Systems Dev.

Industries: Generalist (All)

Medical Executive Recruiters

1198 Melody Ln Ste 109
Roseville, CA 95678-5100
(916) 786-8615
Fax: (916) 786-8609
Email: medexec@pacbell.net

Summary: Our firm specializes in recruiting sales, sales management and marketing candidates for medical device and medical services companies.

Key Contact - Specialty:
Mr. John Cunningham, Owner & President - *Computers (Software)*

Salary Minimum: $50,000

Functions: Generalist (All), Quality, Mktg. Research, Mktg. Mgmt., Sales Mgmt.

Industries: Generalist (All), Drugs Mfg., Medical Devices, Software, Biotech/Life Sciences, Healthcare

Medical Executive Search Associates Inc

7464 E Ridge Point Rd
Tucson, AZ 85750-6263
(888) 884-2550
(520) 885-2552
Fax: (520) 885-2542
Email: wlp@mesaworldwide.com
Web: www.mesaworldwide.com

Summary: We have recruitment experience in the medical device, bio-technology, orthopedic and pharmaceutical industries.

Key Contact - Specialty:
Mr. William L. Piatkiewicz, President & General Manager - *Orthopedics*
Mrs. Mary Lou Piatkiewicz, Chief Financial Officer & Vice President - *Biotechnology, Orthopedics*

Salary Minimum: $50,000

Functions: Generalist (All)

Industries: Manufacturing, Drugs Mfg., Medical Devices, Packaging, Biotech/Life Sciences, Healthcare

Medical Innovations

PO Box 224
Orient, NY 11957-0224
(631) 323-3899
(631) 786-4457
Email: carolmartin2003@aol.com
Web: www.medicalinnovations.cc

Summary: Our specialty is placement in reputable healthcare manufacturers whose products are considered cutting edge technology. This is achieved only in an ethical, professional and compassionate process.

Key Contact - Specialty:
Ms. Carol Martin, President - *Management, Marketing, Product management/development*

Salary Minimum: $60,000

Functions: Sales & Mktg.

Industries: Drugs Mfg., Medical Devices, Healthcare

Medical Recruiters Inc

1401 S Brentwood Blvd Ste 750
Saint Louis, MO 63144-1437
(314) 222-4200
Fax: (314) 222-4211
Email: resumes@medrecinc.com

Summary: Specialists in medical sales and sales management placement.

Key Contact - Specialty:
Ms. Heidi Oberman, Recruitment Specialist
Ms. Denise Wottowa, Recruitment Specialist - *Clinical*
Ms. Natalie Skyberg, Medical Sales Recruiter
Ms. Sari Neudorf, Stategic Interview Consultant

Functions: Healthcare, Nurses, Sales Mgmt.

Industries: Drugs Mfg., Medical Devices, Pharm Svcs.

Medical Search Group

790 Turnpike St Ste 202
North Andover, MA 01845-6138
(978) 683-9800
Fax: (978) 683-8600
Email: admin@medicalsearchgroup.com
Web: www.medicalsearchgroup.com

Summary: We are recruiters specializing in medical and pharmaceutical sales with extensive experience in the industry.

Key Contact - Specialty:
Ms. Jean H. Khoury, CPC, President
Mr. Kevin J. Khoury, Vice President

Salary Minimum: $40,000

Functions: Sales & Mktg.

Industries: Drugs Mfg., Medical Devices, Pharm Svcs., Equip Svcs.

Medical Search of America Inc

PO Box 1716
Duluth, GA 30096-0030
(800) 523-1351
(770) 232-0530
Fax: (770) 232-0610
Email: chazsearch@earthlink.net

Summary: We are a multi-faceted health care search firm specializing in the location and placement of medical professionals - physician, executive, administrative, nursing, technical and allied health personnel.

Key Contact - Specialty:
Mr. Charles Sikes, President

Salary Minimum: $45,000

Functions: Healthcare, Physicians, Nurses, Allied Health, Health Admin.

Industries: Healthcare

Medical Search Solutions

(also known as Search Solutions)
2179 April Sound Ln
Frisco, TX 75034-1538
(972) 490-3778
Fax: (214) 705-6672
Email: msspennypeters@sbcglobal.net

Summary: We staff all positions in the medical field. Our specialty is staffing physician's offices on both the administrative and clinical sides. We also staff billing and insurance positions and place civil engineers locally and nationally.

Key Contact - Specialty:
Ms. D. Penny Peters, Recruiter

Functions: Generalist (All), Nurses, Engineering

Industries: Generalist (All), Energy, Utilities, Healthcare, Hospitals, Long-term/Home Care,

Dental, Physical Therapy, Occupational Therapy, Women's

Medicorp Inc

1101 Saint Peters Howell Rd
Saint Peters, MO 63376-5258
(636) 278-1700
(877) 295-7778
Fax: (636) 278-6080
Email: rjj@medicorpinc.com
Web: www.medicorpinc.com

Summary: We are a nationally recognized physician placement firm with a diverse clientele offering full time physician placement services. Our own in house sourcing team ensures fast matches and our consultants are specialists in their medical field. We recruit physicians only.

Key Contact - Specialty:
Mr. Jack Johnson, President & Chief Executive Officer - *Physicians*
Mr. Brad Bohannon, Director, Physician Recruitment
Ms. Laurie Baker, Administrative Assistant - *Human resources*

Salary Minimum: $120,000

Functions: Management, Middle Mgmt., Healthcare, Physicians, DB Admin.

Industries: Database SW, Healthcare, Hospitals, Long-term/Home Care, Dental, Physical Therapy, Occupational Therapy, Women's

MedIT Staff

(formerly known as EDP Staffing Solutions Inc)
PO Box 241033
Little Rock, AR 72223-0001
(501) 868-5283
(501) 258-5283
Email: mbean@meditstaff.com
Web: www.meditstaff.com

Summary: Our firm is committed to solving the staffing problems of our clients and meeting the career needs of our candidates by providing superior recruiting services. We accomplish this by utilizing our experience and knowledge of the marketplace, ongoing training and ethical practices. Our focus areas are IT and medical technology staffing.

Key Contact - Specialty:
Ms. Marjean Bean, CPC, President - *Information Technology*

Salary Minimum: $40,000

Functions: Allied Health, IT

Industries: Network Infrastructure, RF/Microwave, Software

Medpar Consulting

PO Box 78
Owings Mills, MD 21117-0078
(410) 998-9577
Email: dparker@medpar.com
Web: www.medpar.com

Summary: Our firm is a healthcare executive search firm.

Key Contact - Specialty:
Mr. David Parker, Managing Principal

Salary Minimum: $75,000

Functions: Management

Industries: Healthcare, Hospitals

Medpoint LLC

(formerly known as Proquest Inc)
10 E Washington St Apt 3G
Greenville, SC 29601-4817
(864) 527-5999
(800) 200-9292
Email: don@medpoint.com
Web: www.medpoint.com

Summary: We offer services to manufacturers of medical devices, pharmaceutical and biotechnology products. We specialize in the mid to senior level management positions in quality control, clinical affairs, research & development, manufacturing and engineering. We offer employment services in areas such as quality system audits and product approval submissions and engineering.

Key Contact - Specialty:
Mr. Donald Powell, MS, RPh, Chief Executive Officer & Founder - *Biomedical, Biopharmaceutical, Biotechnology, Clinical, Compliance*
Mr. Chuck Crumpton, President - *Biomaterials, Biomedical, Biotechnology, BSME, Clinical*

Salary Minimum: $70,000

Functions: Generalist (All), Quality, Healthcare

Industries: Drugs Mfg., Medical Devices, Plastics, Rubber, Test, Measure Equip., Misc. Mfg., Electronic, Elec. Components, Non-profits, HR Services, Biotech/Life Sciences

MedPoint Search LLC

PO Box 980043
4011 Garrott St
Houston, TX 77098-0043
(713) 524-4443
Fax: (713) 800-6831
Web: www.medpointsearch.com

Summary: We specialize in the recruitment and permanent placement of senior healthcare professionals. We offer exceptional personal service for all those we assist, and look forward to working together with you.

Key Contact - Specialty:
Mr. Brian Stutt, CPC, President - *Administration, Healthcare, Hospital, Medical, Senior management*
Ms. Tina Rose, MBA, Executive Search Consultant - *Administration, Healthcare, Hospital, Medical, Senior management*
Ms. Hannah Biondo, Executive Search Consultant - *Administration, Healthcare, Hospital, Medical, Senior management*

Functions: Senior Mgmt., Quality, Healthcare, Nurses, Health Admin., Sales & Mktg., CFOs, Risk Mgmt.

Industries: Generalist (All), Healthcare, Hospitals, Long-term/Home Care, Physical Therapy, Occupational Therapy, Women's

MedPro Personnel Inc

1935 Cliff Valley Way NE Ste 225
Atlanta, GA 30329-2435
(404) 633-8280
(800) 737-3101
Email: frontdesk@medpropersonnel.com
Web: www.medpropersonnel.com

Summary: We place medical personnel in hospitals, clinics and physician practices. We work with clerical and clinical staff in permanent, temp to hire and temp positions.

Key Contact - Specialty:
Ms. Marilyn Feingold, President & Chief Executive Officer

Functions: Generalist (All), Nurses, Health Admin.

Industries: Generalist (All), Healthcare

Affiliates:
AllStaff Technical
Atlanta, GA

MedQuest Associates

(also known as Health Industry Consultants Inc)
9250 E Costilla Ave Ste 600
Greenwood Village, CO 80112-3649
(303) 790-2009
Fax: (303) 790-2021
Email: judystiles@aol.com

Summary: Recruitment of sales & marketing professionals for medical device and pharmaceutical industries.

Key Contact - Specialty:
Ms. Judy Stiles, Director

Salary Minimum: $45,000

Functions: Generalist (All), Mktg. Research, Mktg. Mgmt., Sales Mgmt., Customer Svc., Sales Reps.

Industries: Generalist (All), Drugs Mfg., Medical Devices, Pharm Svcs., Biotech/Life Sciences

Medsearch

7530 Lucerne Dr
Middleburg Heights, OH 44130-6587
(440) 243-6363
Fax: (440) 243-9117
Email: webmaster@medsearchonline.com
Web: www.medsearchonline.com

Summary: We are the leader in providing comprehensive staffing solutions for our client hospitals, health care systems, long-term care facilities, pharmacies, insurance companies, clinics and private physician & dental practices.

Key Contact - Specialty:
Mr. Ralph Steeber, Chief Executive Officer

Salary Minimum: $50,000

Functions: Generalist (All), Sales & Mktg.

Industries: Generalist (All), Pharm Svcs., Engineering Svcs., Insurance, Biotech/Life Sciences, Healthcare, Hospitals, Long-term/Home Care, Dental, Physical Therapy, Occupational Therapy

MedSearch Resources Inc

1900 NW Corporate Blvd Ste 400 E
Boca Raton, FL 33431-8512
(561) 988-6866
Fax: (561) 988-6865
Email: info@medsearchresources.com
Web: www.medsearchresources.com

Summary: We are a retainer-based search and consulting firm serving the healthcare industry. Our clients include hospitals, physician practice management companies, hospital-based & private practice physician practice groups, outpatient diagnostic & imaging centers and medical marketing/research firms. We conduct searches including physicians, department heads, administrators and senior-level executive management.

Key Contact - Specialty:
Mr. Douglas I. Glick, President - *Executives, Physicians*

Salary Minimum: $50,000

Functions: Generalist (All), Senior Mgmt., Healthcare, Physicians, Allied Health

Industries: Drugs Mfg., Medical Devices, Non-profits, Pharm Svcs., Healthcare, Hospitals, Long-term/Home Care, Physical Therapy, Occupational Therapy

Medserve & Associates Inc

402 Phenita Point Dr
Millersville, MD 21108-1569
(888) 782-3337
(410) 923-5570
Fax: (410) 510-1346
Email: info@medserve.net
Web: www.medserve.net

Summary: We are a search and recruitment firm specializing in physician placements.

Key Contact - Specialty:
Mr. Sal Eren, Director, Placement - *Physicians*

Functions: Physicians, Nurses, Allied Health

Industries: Healthcare

MedSource Recruiters

1541 Seaside Rd SW
Ocean Isle Beach, NC 28469-5501
(910) 575-6060
(303) 814-2300
Email: mkurtic@medsource1.com

Summary: We are a very successful office specializing in marketing, R&D, regulatory affairs, manufacturing, QA, clinical research, sales, sales management, national accounts and training for medical device, pharmaceutical and bio-technology companies.

Key Contact - Specialty:
Mr. Marty Kurtic, President - *Engineering, Manufacturing, Marketing*

Functions: Generalist (All), Management, Middle Mgmt.

Industries: Drugs Mfg., Medical Devices, Pharm Svcs., Biotech/Life Sciences

Branches:
10162 Ridgegate Cir
Lone Tree, CO 80124-5538
(303) 814-2300
Email: headhunt1@msn.com
Key Contact - Specialty:
Mr. Brian Kurtic

Medstaff National Medical Staffing

PO Box 12525
Durham, NC 27709-2525
(919) 383-4075
Fax: (919) 382-2009
Email: akloehn@medstafflt.com
Web: www.medstafflt.com

Summary: Our firm places physicians in permanent and locum tenens (temp) positions. We specialize in anesthesiology, cardiology, dermatology, emergency medicine, family practice, general surgery, internal medicine, hospitals, obstetrics & gynecology, occupational medicine, pediatrics, radiology and others. Large enough to serve your needs...small enough to care.

Key Contact - Specialty:
Ms. Andrea Kloehn

Functions: Management, Healthcare, Physicians

Industries: Non-profits, Mgmt. Consulting, Travel, Government, Healthcare, Hospitals, Occupational Therapy, Women's

Medvec Resources Group / MSK East

(also known as Medvec Resources Group)
2745 Stiegler Rd
Valley City, OH 44280-9585
(330) 722-5171
Fax: (330) 722-7360
Email: recruiter@mrgcareers.com
Web: www.mrgcareers.com

Summary: Our executive search firm specializes in the screw machine, Swiss CNC turning, CNC machining, precision machining, cold heading, cold forming, metal forming, and precision metal machining jobs. Automotive, machine tool, electrical/electronic, tool manufacturing, medical fluid systems/valve, screw machine Swiss turn, connectors, manufacturing rep. firms, precision job shops and contract manufacturing.

Key Contact - Specialty:
Mr. Tom Medvec, Recruiter

Functions: Generalist (All), Board Members, Mfg.

Industries: Generalist (All), Manufacturing, Medical Devices, Metal Products, Motor Vehicles, Electronic, Elec. Components, Transportation, Engineering Svcs.

MedXec USA Inc

(also known as TempXec USA Inc)
1428 Tiki Ln
Lancaster, OH 43130-8731
(888) 784-1658
(740) 681-9920
Fax: (740) 681-9935
Email: dowling@medxecusa.com
Web: www.medxecusa.com

Summary: Ours is a premier recruiting firm to the staffing and healthcare industries. We specialize in all executive positions from sales to CEO's. We offer complete recruitment solutions for both companies and the professional.

Key Contact - Specialty:
Mrs. Connie Dowling, Chief Executive Officer & President - *Healthcare, Home health, Human resources, Insurance, Staffing*
Mrs. Nancy Burson, Division Director
Mrs. Lisa Hall, Executive Recruiter
Mrs. Cathy Shumaker, Executive Recruiter

Salary Minimum: $30,000

Functions: Generalist (All), Management, Healthcare, Sales & Mktg., HR Mgmt., Finance, IT

Industries: Healthcare

Mehta Consulting

PO Box 547
Dover, MA 02030-0547
(508) 785-2055
Fax: (508) 785-2994
Email: nkmehta@aol.com
Web: www.mehtaconsulting.com

Summary: A seasoned professional in the credit industry manages us. We specialize in collections, call center management, credit risk management and sales positions in the credit industry.

Key Contact - Specialty:
Mr. Narinder K. Mehta, President

Salary Minimum: $50,000

Functions: Generalist (All)

Industries: Finance, Banking

Mentor Associates Inc

34072 Violet Lantern St Ste C
Dana Point, CA 92629-2521
(949) 388-1720
Fax: (949) 388-1730
Web: www.saleslinks.com

Summary: We deliver first rate candidates and satisfied clients in the area of sales and marketing. We provide highly qualified field sales people and executives.

Key Contact - Specialty:
Ms. Amanda Hooper, Program Coordinator
Mr. Jack Carroll, Chief Executive Officer - *Consumer (Packaged Goods), Management, Marketing, Sales, Start-up companies*

Salary Minimum: $75,000

Functions: Management, Sales Mgmt., Sales Reps.

Industries: Generalist (All), Manufacturing, Finance, Services, HR Services, E-commerce, Software, Networking, Comm. SW

Meridian Legal Search/Legal Temps

25 W 43rd St Ste 700
New York, NY 10036-7414
(212) 354-9300
Fax: (212) 921-1127
Email: info@meridianlegal.com
Web: www.meridianlegal.com

Summary: Attorney staffing, permanent & contract, organization/corporate law firm, not-for-profit clients. Discreet representation of clients on a contingent or retainer basis. Computerized research and targeted recruiting of credentialed and high achieving attorney candidates at all levels resulting in an extremely high level of client satisfaction.

Key Contact - Specialty:
Mr. Joel Berger, Esq., President - *Legal (Attorneys,Lawyers)*
Mr. Will Mudloff, Senior Administrator - *Compliance, Legal (Lawyers)*

Salary Minimum: $50,000

Functions: Legal

Industries: Legal

Merit Consulting Inc

3948 Sunbeam Rd Ste 3
Jacksonville, FL 32257-8931
(904) 268-1695
Fax: (904) 268-6845
Email: dsmith@meritconsult.com
Web: www.meritconsult.com

Summary: A specialized executive search consultancy, with focus in mid-to-senior-level legal, operational, technical, sales, marketing, IT and financial recruitment. Special emphasis given to organizational assessment, career coaching, and transition management.

Key Contact - Specialty:
Mr. David C. Smith, President - *Engineering, Human resources, Marketing, Operations, Sales*
Mr. Arthur H. Rogove, Vice President - *Biotechnology, Chemical, Engineering, Packaging, Pharmaceutical*
Mr. Paul J. Consbruck, Esq., Vice President - *Intellectual property, Labor, Legal, Real estate, Tax*

Functions: Management, Mfg., Sales & Mktg., HR Mgmt., Finance, IT, R&D, Engineering, Legal

Industries: Printing, Chemicals, Drugs Mfg., Medical Devices, Plastics, Rubber, Paints, Petro.

Products, Pharm Svcs., Legal, Packaging, Biotech/Life Sciences

Merit Resource Group Inc

7950 Dublin Blvd Ste 205
Dublin, CA 94568-2937
(925) 828-4700
Fax: (925) 828-4796
Email: info@merithr.com
Web: www.merithr.com

Summary: Our focus is delivering HR management services, this includes regular full time and contract staffing of HR professionals. We also deliver a full spectrum of HR consulting services.

Key Contact - Specialty:
Mr. J.M. Burke, President
Ms. Cindy Kirkman, Client Services Manager
Ms. Patricia Maloney, Client Services Manager
Ms. Linda Tatum, Client Services Manager

Salary Minimum: $75,000

Functions: HR Mgmt., Benefits, Staffing, Training

Industries: Generalist (All)

Branches:
1290 Oakmead Pkwy Ste 105
Sunnyvale, CA 94085-4045
(408) 732-4300
Fax: (408) 732-4388
Key Contact - Specialty:
Ms. Anne Hausler, Client Services Manager
Ms. Tish Wallace, Client Services Manager

Merlin International Inc

PO Box 313
600 E Crescent Ave Ste 303
Ramsey, NJ 07446-0313
(201) 825-7220
Fax: (201) 825-7374
Email: merlin@merlininternational.biz
Web: www.merlin4u.com

Summary: We are a highly specialized firm. Devoted exclusively to all pharmaceutical and biotechnology, R&D. Clinical research physicians and staff. Pharmaceutical marketing and advertising services.

Key Contact - Specialty:
Mr. V. James Cinquina, Jr., Managing Partner - *Physicians*
Mr. Alan Fitzpatrick, Managing Partner - *Business development, Marketing*
Mr. Jim Stinson, Director
Mr. David Cinquina, Associate Director

Salary Minimum: $50,000

Functions: Generalist (All), Physicians, Advertising, Mktg. Research, Direct Mktg., R&D

Industries: Generalist (All), Drugs Mfg., Pharm Svcs., Advertising, Healthcare

Merlin Staffing

261 Madison Ave Fl 27
New York, NY 10016-2303
(212) 983-3533
Fax: (212) 972-1026
Email: info@merlinstaffing.com

Summary: Our firm is a full service staffing and training firm providing temporary help, temp-to-hire, direct hire and training services. We pride ourselves on maintaining ethical values combined with leading edge technology. People associate with us because we provide an atmosphere of respect and professionalism. Private interviews by appointment only.

Key Contact - Specialty:
Mr. Sal Bordonaro, Principal - *Accounting (General), Human resources, Legal, Office (Support), Training*

Functions: Middle Mgmt., Admin. Svcs., HR Mgmt., Staffing, Training, Finance, Network Admin., DB Admin., Legal, Paralegals

Industries: Generalist (All)

Metro Legal Search

733 3rd Ave Fl 21
New York, NY 10017-3221
(212) 557-9257
Fax: (212) 471-8633
Email: info@metrolegalsearch.com
Web: www.metrolegalsearch.com

Summary: Discreetly and professionally placing attorneys at all levels, from general counsel and staff attorneys at corporations and financial institutions to partners and associates at law firms. With a substantial portion of placements in-house, our firm represents investment and commercial banks as well companies in a wide range of industries including media, consumer products and technology.

Key Contact - Specialty:
Ms. Eileen Rosenberg, President

Functions: Legal

Industries: Generalist (All)

Metropolitan Personnal Inc

PO Box 641
Valley Forge, PA 19482-0641
(610) 933-4000
(610) 933-8402
Fax: (610) 933-4670
Email: eric@metropolitanpersonnel.com
Web: www.metropolitanpersonnel.com

Summary: Career placements and temporary help services provided, we are the areas leading independent personnel service. Leading companies count on our ability to understand their personnel needs and to recruit the best people - those with skills and dedication - those who get the job done.

Key Contact - Specialty:
Mr. Eric N.J. Rittenbaugh, CPC, CSP, Staffing Supervisor - *Administration, Advertising, Business to business, Human resources, Senior management*
Mr. Lawrence LaBoon, CPC, CSP, President & Chief Executive Officer - *Finance, Financial, Government, Senior management, Skilled trades*

Salary Minimum: $30,000

Functions: Management, Admin. Svcs., Packaging, Healthcare

Industries: Generalist (All), Manufacturing, Media, Packaging, Healthcare

Bert M Mezo & Associates Inc

1000-1235 Bay St
Scrivener Building
Toronto, ON M5R 3K4
Canada
(416) 944-0396

Summary: We provide a prompt, reliable service. Specializing in sales/marketing placements, primarily with high-technology focus.

Key Contact - Specialty:
Mr. Bert Mezo, President - *Sales*

Salary Minimum: $50,000

Functions: Generalist (All), Automation, Distribution, Mktg. Research, Mktg. Mgmt., Sales Mgmt., Systems Analysis, Systems Implem.

Industries: Generalist (All), Manufacturing, Medical Devices, Computer Equip., Consumer Elect., Test, Measure Equip., Robotics, Semiconductors, Transportation, Finance, Services, Communications, Telecoms, Wireless, Fiber Optic, Insurance, Software

MGA Executive Search

3000 Gulf To Bay Blvd Ste 503
Clearwater, FL 33759-4300
(727) 791-7890
(800) 642-4729
Fax: (727) 724-8039
Email: clearwater@mgatechnologies.com
Web: www.mgatechnologies.com

Summary: Our mission is to provide timely, high quality and cost effective contingency search services when undertaking nationwide MIS technical and managerial recruiting assignments for our clients.

Key Contact - Specialty:
Ms. Peggy Kivler, Director, Human Resources

Salary Minimum: $55,000

Functions: Generalist (All), MIS Mgmt., Systems Analysis, Systems Dev., Systems Implem., Systems Support

Industries: Generalist (All), Energy, Utilities, Misc. Mfg., Finance, Aerospace, Insurance, Healthcare

MGRM Associates Ltd

558 Columbine Ave
Lisle, IL 60532-2708
(630) 724-9458
Fax: (630) 724-9459
Email: logrecruiter@earthlink.net
Web: www.mgrmassociates.com

Summary: We specialize in all areas of logistics including senior management, international, customer service, fulfillment, business development, supply chain, third party, for hire carriers, rail, distribution, project management, warehousing, procurement, call centers operations and all related technologies. We primarily perform retained services, but do contingent as well.

Key Contact - Specialty:
Mr. Terrence R. McDorman, President - *Logistics, Transportation*

Salary Minimum: $75,000

Functions: Generalist (All), Management, Senior Mgmt., Middle Mgmt., Materials, Purchasing, Materials Plng., Distribution, Customer Svc.

Industries: Generalist (All), Energy, Utilities, Transportation, Logistics Svcs., Packaging

MH Executive Search Group

30617 US Highway 19 N Ste 502
Palm Harbor, FL 34684-4410
(727) 786-8877
Email: kp-pkgjobs@mhgroup.com
Web: www.mhgroup.com

Summary: We recruit qualified individuals with current experience in the packaging and flexographic industries in sales, marketing, plant management and general management personnel. We recruit in packaging and flexographic printing on packaging materials exclusively.

Key Contact - Specialty:
Mr. Mike Hochwalt, Senior Vice President - *Converting, Film, Flexographic printing, Marketing, Paper*
Mr. Lee Walt, Researcher - *Flexographic printing, Operations, Paper, Plastics*

Salary Minimum: $60,000

Functions: Middle Mgmt., Packaging, Sales & Mktg., Sales Reps.

Industries: Paper, Printing, Plastics, Rubber, Packaging

Michael Page International Inc

405 Lexington Ave Fl 28
New York, NY 10174-2899
(212) 661-4800
Fax: (212) 661-6622
Email: mpi.usa@michaelpage.com
Web: www.michaelpage.com

Summary: We are dedicated to providing an effective and professional recruitment service for the accounting, finance, banking & financial markets. Equipped with industry and cross-functional recruitment expertise, our consultants will facilitate contact with our prestigious network of global contacts and opportunities.

Key Contact - Specialty:
Mr. Gary James, Managing Director, N American Offices - *Finance*
Mr. Simon Lewis, Director, Banking & Financial Services - *Banking, Financial services*
Mr. Laurence Pengelly, Director, Finance & Accounting - *Accounting, Accounting (General, Public), CFOs, Finance*
Mr. Todd Bernard, Chief Financial Officer

Salary Minimum: $50,000

Functions: Senior Mgmt., Middle Mgmt., Finance, CFOs, Cash Mgmt., Credit, Taxes, M&A

Industries: Generalist (All), Energy, Utilities, Manufacturing, Food, Bev., Tobacco, Soap, Perf., Cosmtcs., Finance, Banking, Invest. Banking, Brokers, Venture Cap., Mutual/Hedge Funds, Misc. Financial, Pharm Svcs., Accounting, Mgmt. Consulting, HR Services, IT Implementation

Branches:
177 Broad St
Stamford, CT 06901-5003
(203) 905-5250
Fax: (203) 905-5299
Email: huwrothwell@michaelpage.com
Key Contact - Specialty:
Mr. Huw Rothwell, Manager - *Accounting, Accounting (Big 4, General, Public), Finance*

191 N Wacker Dr Ste 2865
Chicago, IL 60606-1919
(312) 263-7471
Fax: (312) 263-8469
Email: hugheverard@michaelpage.com
Key Contact - Specialty:
Mr. Hugh Everard, Managing Director, Midwest Region - *Accounting, Accounting (Big 4, General), CFOs, Finance*
Mr. Michael Pickens, CPA, Manager, Banking & Financial Services - *Accounting, Banking, Banking (Corporate, Investment), Financial services*

125 High St Fl 9
Boston, MA 02110-2704
(617) 428-3680
Fax: (617) 428-3793
Email: coalterpowers@michaelpage.com
Key Contact - Specialty:
Mr. David Martin, Manager, Banking & Financial Services
Mr. Coalter Powers, Consultant, Finance & Accounting - *Accounting, Accounting (Big 4, General), Finance*

99 Wood Ave S Fl 2
Iselin, NJ 08830-2734
(732) 623-4500
Fax: (732) 623-4212

Email your resume to a targeted list of recruiters now at www.ExecutiveAgent.com/DER07

Email: neilgalvin@michaelpage.com
Key Contact - Specialty:
Mr. Neil Galvin, Manager - *Finance*

John Michael Personnel Group Inc

PO Box 4437
Chattanooga, TN 37405-0437
(423) 756-6544
Fax: (423) 266-5334
Email: jmichaelpersonnel@comcast.net
Web: www.johnmichaelpersonnel.com

Summary: We are a national/international executive search firm specializing in the recruitment of supply chain professionals in the areas of strategic purchasing, materials management, logistics, plant management and continuous improvement management.

Key Contact - Specialty:
Mr. Emery J. Zobro, President

Salary Minimum: $80,000

Functions: Materials, Purchasing

Industries: Manufacturing, Logistics Svcs.

Michael Wayne Recruiters

59 St Marys Ln
Lindenhurst, IL 60046-4968
(847) 245-7100
Fax: (847) 245-7199
Email: mwrecruiters@sbcglobal.net
Web: www.michaelwaynerecruiters.com

Summary: Our firm offers a full range of services; preferred client status; contacts in retail, food service, manufacturing and wholesale food segments.

Key Contact - Specialty:
Mr. Irwin Goldman, President - *Retail, Wholesale*

Salary Minimum: $35,000

Functions: Generalist (All)

Industries: Food, Bev., Tobacco, Wholesale, Retail

Michael/Merrill

8909 W 101st Ter Apt 2
Overland Park, KS 66212-4218
(877) 341-6072
Fax: (913) 383-2962

Summary: We are a boutique search firm focusing on the placement of high achieving mid to senior level executives. We search the industry looking for people who meet our client's requirements, matching the candidates' requirements and preferences with our client's needs. We place candidates from middle management through senior-level management.

Key Contact - Specialty:
Mr. Wilson M. Liggett, owner

Salary Minimum: $35,000

Functions: Generalist (All)

Industries: Manufacturing, Transportation, Finance, Services, Packaging, Software

Lou Michaels Associates Inc

1230 Columbia Ave E
Battle Creek, MI 49014-5188
(269) 965-1486
Fax: (269) 965-2232
Email: lma@lmasearch.com
Web: www.lmasearch.com

Summary: Engineering and industrial management personnel/manufacturing industries, automotive, plastics, foundry, die cast, metal working, aerospace, electronics, machining, metal fabrication, stamping, primary metals, medical plastics and automotive plastics.

Key Contact - Specialty:
Mr. Lou Michaels, President - *Automotive, Engineering, Human resources, Machining, Manufacturing*
Mr. Chuck Winter, Recruiter, Industrial - *Automotive, Food & beverage, General management, Quality, Supply Chain*
Mrs. Sherry Fogel, Recruiter, Industrial - *Procurement, Purchasing, Quality, Re-engineering, Research & development*

Salary Minimum: $35,000

Functions: Generalist (All), Management, Mfg., Production, Materials, Sales & Mktg., HR Mgmt., Finance

Industries: Manufacturing, Food, Bev., Tobacco, Textiles, Apparel, Medical Devices, Plastics, Rubber, Metal Products, Machine, Appliance, Motor Vehicles, Consumer Elect., Misc. Mfg., Robotics, Aerospace, Packaging

Mid-America Placement Service Inc

1941 S 42nd St Ste 520
Omaha, NE 68105-2945
(402) 341-3338
Fax: (402) 341-6266
Email: ron@nejobs.net
Web: www.nejobs.net

Summary: We specialize in the screening and placement of experienced professionals. We pride ourselves in our professional approach and service both applicants and companies. Our reputation has been impeccable in the industry.

Key Contact - Specialty:
Mr. Ron Distransky, President - *Sales*

Salary Minimum: $18,000

Functions: Generalist (All), Management, Sales & Mktg., Sales Mgmt., HR Mgmt., Finance, IT, Engineering

Industries: Generalist (All), Computer Equip., Retail, Finance, Services, Hospitality, Hotels, Resorts, Clubs, Restaurants, Full Service Restaurants, Inst./Industrial Food Svc., Entertainment, Recreation, Sports, Travel, Media, Insurance

Midas Management Inc

PO Box 595
Sanibel, FL 33957-0595
(239) 395-2424
(203) 329-4060
Email: mmsearch@midasmgt.com
Web: www.midasmgt.com

Summary: We have always specialized in the placement of all levels of sales, sales support and sales management professionals in the computer software and hardware industry as well as IT consulting sales. We are based in Florida but do a great deal of work in the NY Metro area and the entire northeast, as well as throughout the United States. Our primary focus is on senior sales and management positions, selling consulting services and software applications.

Key Contact - Specialty:
Ms. Elaine Harris, Vice President, Operations

Salary Minimum: $70,000

Functions: Sales & Mktg., Sales Mgmt., IT, Mgmt. Consultants

Industries: Mgmt. Consulting, Software

Midland Consultants

7261 Engle Rd Ste 201
Cleveland, OH 44130-3479
(440) 234-1800
Fax: (440) 234-1758
Email: midland@midlandconsultants.com
Web: www.midlandconsultants.com

Summary: We service the entire rubber/chemical, plastic/packaging, building products, and manufacturing/metal industries.

Key Contact - Specialty:
Mr. Ron Eliason, CPC, Vice President - *Plastics*
Ms. Robin Graves, CPC, Account Executive - *Rubber*
Mr. Dave Suhy, Account Executive - *Manufacturing*
Mr. Matthew Skalski, Account Executive
Ms. Danielle T. Schade, Account Executive - *Human resources, Manufacturing (Management)*

Functions: Middle Mgmt., Mfg., Materials, Sales & Mktg., R&D, Engineering

Industries: Chemicals, Plastics, Rubber, Metal Products, Packaging

Midwest Headhunters Inc

PO Box 286
Marinette, WI 54143-0286
(800) 799-4520
Email: jim@midwestheadhunters.com
Web: www.midwestheadhunters.com

Summary: We are a full service search and placement firm specializing in professional manufacturing companies. Our philosophy: build a long-term working relationship with our clients; learn who they are and what they do; strive to help them attain their goals.

Key Contact - Specialty:
Mr. Jim Hipskind, CPC, Recruiter

Salary Minimum: $50,000

Functions: Generalist (All), Sales & Mktg.

Industries: Manufacturing, Food, Bev., Tobacco, Medical Devices, Plastics, Rubber, Metal Products, Machine, Appliance, Motor Vehicles, Misc. Mfg., Electronic, Elec. Components, Consumer Goods, Engineering Svcs.

Midwest Search Group LLC

13375 University Ave Ste 303
Clive, IA 50325-8248
(515) 453-2314
Fax: (515) 453-2315
Email: info@midwestsearchgroup.com
Web: www.midwestsearchgroup.com

Summary: Our team is comprised of professionals with extensive years of combined industry experience. Our core areas of specialization are: accounting & finance; banking, mortgage & credit; information technology and engineering.

Key Contact - Specialty:
Mr. Jim Bruno, Partner
Mr. John Blanchard, Partner
Mr. Joe Steer, Partner
Ms. Julie Blassl, Office Manager

Salary Minimum: $25,000

Functions: Generalist (All)

Industries: Finance, Banking, Invest. Banking, IT Implementation, Engineering Svcs., Software, Accounting SW, Database SW, Development SW, Doc. Mgmt., Production SW

Miera Consultants International

2403 San Mateo Blvd NE Ste W3
Albuquerque, NM 87110-4070
(505) 889-0456
Fax: (505) 889-3032
Email: miera@miera.com
Web: www.miera.com

Summary: We recruit exclusively for the healthcare industry including healthcare systems, hospitals, health maintenance organizations, clinics and long term care facilities.

Key Contact - Specialty:
Mr. Stephen P. Miera, Partner & National Account Director
Mr. Orlando Miera, CPA, Managing Partner & CFO
Mr. Paul O. Miera, II, Partner & National Account Director

Salary Minimum: $40,000

Functions: Generalist (All), Management

Industries: Accounting, Healthcare, Hospitals, Long-term/Home Care

George Mild Group Inc

3291 Morewood Rd
Fairlawn, OH 44333-3470
(330) 836-9191
Email: always_110@fastmail.fm

Summary: Our firm works in the polymers, petroleum, and glass fields with the emphasis on research and development, engineering, and chemistry.

Key Contact - Specialty:
Mr. George L. Mild, President
Mr. John Mild, Vice President

Functions: Product Dev., Sales & Mktg., R&D, Engineering

Industries: Chemicals, Plastics, Rubber, Paints, Petro. Products, Leather, Stone, Glass

Alan Miles & Associates Inc

1821 Wilshire Blvd Ste 550
Santa Monica, CA 90403-5668
(310) 829-9589
Fax: (310) 829-6771
Email: amiles@mileslawsearch.com
Web: www.mileslawsearch.com

Summary: Our firm is a legal search firm and we pride ourselves on our unique, successful approach to legal recruiting. We specialize in mergers, practice group and partner placements, while continuing to place highly qualified associates in various disciplines. We have had the privilege to facilitate some of the largest practice group placements in our area.

Key Contact - Specialty:
Mr. Alan Miles, Principal
Mr. William Vochoska, Recruiter
Ms. Nina Miles, Recruiter
Mr. Jeff L. Williams, Esq., Recruiter
Mr. Stephen Berger, Recruiter
Ms. Donna Balbin, Recruiter
Mr. Jason Yuen, Recruiter - *C-level, Industrial, Information Technology, Management consulting, Strategic planning*

Functions: Generalist (All), Attorneys

Industries: Generalist (All), Legal

J Miles Personnel Services

3029 E Sunshine St Ste A
Springfield, MO 65804-2054
(417) 882-5585
Fax: (417) 882-0656

Email: jmiles@jmiles.com
Web: www.jmiles.com

Summary: We are an independently owned and highly selective recruiting and placement firm specializing in the nationwide search, recruitment and placement of professionals in engineering, technical and manufacturing management positions within the food manufacturing and consumer products industries.

Key Contact - Specialty:
Ms. Jean Miles, Owner
Ms. Julie Alexander, Recruiter & Manager

Functions: Generalist (All)

Industries: Manufacturing, Food, Bev., Tobacco, Chemicals, Soap, Perf., Cosmtcs., Drugs Mfg., Medical Devices, Wholesale, Retail

Military2Civilian.com

(also known as Currie Career Coaching)
PO Box 1972
Orange Park, FL 32067-1972
(904) 215-2297
Email: ghcurrie@military2civilian.com
Web: www.military2civilian.com

Summary: Specialist in top quality transitioning junior and senior military officers, senior enlisted. Degreed, proven performers. Recruitment services are client corporation fee paid, free to the job candidate. Optional career transition coaching services are fee-based and candidate paid. Committed to professionalism, integrity and individual attention. Personal service oriented.

Key Contact - Specialty:
Mr. George Currie, MA, President & Senior Recruiter

Salary Minimum: $45,000

Functions: Generalist (All), Senior Mgmt., Middle Mgmt., Admin. Svcs., Mfg., Quality, Productivity, HR Mgmt., Training, Network Admin.

Industries: Generalist (All), Construction, Manufacturing, Transportation, Wholesale, Finance, Services, Communications, Government, Defense, Aerospace, Insurance, Software, Healthcare

Miller & Associates Inc

9036 NW 37th St
Polk City, IA 50226-2073
(888) 965-2727
(515) 965-5727
Email: rmiller@ag-careers.com
Web: www.ag-careers.com

Summary: We recruit quality candidates and list employment opportunities in the agriculture industry. We assist job placement in a variety of areas including agronomy, seed, feed, petroleum, animal health, grain and agricultural accounting.

Key Contact - Specialty:
Mr. Roger Miller, President

Functions: Senior Mgmt., Middle Mgmt., Production, Purchasing, Mktg. Mgmt., Sales Mgmt., Finance, IT

Industries: Agri., Forestry, Mining

Miller & Associates Inc

4436 Fuller Dr Ste 2
Eden, UT 84310-9830
(801) 745-1113
Fax: (801) 745-1190
Email: gkhansen@juno.com
Web: www.foldingcartonrecruiters.com

Summary: We serve the folding carton, label and printing industries.

Key Contact - Specialty:
Mr. Glain Hansen, President

Functions: Packaging

Industries: Printing, Packaging

Miller Jones Inc

13101 Preston Rd Ste 300
Dallas, TX 75240-5229
(972) 239-5322
Fax: (972) 239-7060
Email: millerjones@sbcglobal.net

Summary: Our firm does in excess of 100 placements annually. High-level (president, etc.), retained director-level and below and healthcare are fee contingent.

Key Contact - Specialty:
Mr. John Moffett, President
Mr. Mike Nunally

Salary Minimum: $70,000

Functions: Senior Mgmt., Healthcare, Sales & Mktg., Mktg. Research, Mktg. Mgmt., Sales Mgmt., Direct Mktg., HR Mgmt., Systems Implem., Network Admin.

Industries: Generalist (All), Software, Healthcare

Miller-Collins Associates Inc

4507 Furling Ln Ste 206
Destin, FL 32541-5342
(850) 650-4704
Fax: (850) 650-4706
Email: lisamiller@cox.net

Summary: We are financial and banking executive recruiters. Specializing in commercial finance.

Key Contact - Specialty:
Mrs. Sherry Miller-Collins, President
Ms. Lisa Miller, Senior Vice President

Salary Minimum: $40,000

Functions: Generalist (All), Finance

Industries: Finance, Banking, Misc. Financial, Accounting

MillerBlowers

201 E Kennedy Blvd Ste 950
Tampa, FL 33602-5826
(813) 224-9658
Fax: (813) 221-7491
Email: info@millerlawjobs.com
Web: www.millerlawjobs.com

Summary: We specialize exclusively in legal search, assisting law firms and corporations in associate, partner and in-house corporate placements.

Key Contact - Specialty:
Ms. Dixie Miller, President
Mr. David Pedreira, Attorney Search Consultant
Mr. Rob McFadden, Attorney Search Consultant - *Healthcare*

Functions: Legal, Attorneys

Industries: Generalist (All), Legal

Millstream Associates

3 Harrison St
Lawrence, MA 01843-1907
(978) 688-6102
(508) 870-3223
Fax: (978) 688-6103
Email: lisac@millstreamassociates.com
Web: www.millstreamassociates.com

Summary: Full service HR consulting firm specializing in contract and permanent placement and HR consulting nationwide. We specialize in

high tech industries such as electronics, telecommunications, capital equipment, engineering and manufacturing as well as HR professionals. Our HR consultants specialize in training, HRIS, benefits, administration, etc.

Key Contact - Specialty:
Mr. Richard Blatchford, Principal - *Computers (Hardware), Construction, Manufacturing, Semiconductors, Technical (Management)*
Ms. Lisa Cassinari, Senior Human Resources Consultant - *Administration, Electronics, Human resources, Information Technology, Operations*

Functions: Management, Senior Mgmt., Admin. Svcs., Mfg., Product Dev., HR Mgmt., Hardware, Systems, Mgmt. Consultants, Minorities/Diversity

Industries: Generalist (All), Manufacturing, Medical Devices, Computer Equip., Consumer Elect., Electronic, Elec. Components, Robotics, Semiconductors, HR Services, Communications, Aerospace, Software

Minority Executive Search Inc

PO Box 18063
2490 Lee Blvd Ste 301
Cleveland, OH 44118-0063
(216) 932-2022
Fax: (216) 932-7988
Email: info@minorityexecsearch.com
Web: www.minorityexecsearch.com

Summary: Specializing in women and minority job placements in the following fields: senior management, general management, IT, engineering (chemical, EE, ME, civil, etc.), sales/marketing, HR, finance/accounting, purchasing, manufacturing, logistics/distribution and legal. This ifs for profit and non-profit organizations.

Key Contact - Specialty:
Mr. Eral Burks, Chief Executive Officer & President

Salary Minimum: $50,000

Functions: Generalist (All), Management, Minorities/Diversity

Industries: Generalist (All), Energy, Utilities, Manufacturing, Transportation, Retail, Finance, Services, Hospitality, Communications, Government, Software

MIS Consultants

701-55 Eglinton Ave E
Toronto, ON M4P 1G8
Canada
(416) 489-4334
(800) 311-2828
Fax: (416) 489-0918
Email: jobs@misconsultants.ca
Web: www.misconsultants.ca

Summary: We do I.T. Recruitment and Consulting on a permanent and contract basis.

Key Contact - Specialty:
Mr. Eric Winters, President
Mrs. Judy Robinson, Corporate Administration

Functions: Sales & Mktg., Risk Mgmt., IT, Systems

Industries: Generalist (All), Computer Equip., Brokers, Venture Cap., Mutual/Hedge Funds, Misc. Financial, Services, Telecoms

Mission Search Inc

2203 N Lois Ave Ste 1225
Tampa, FL 33607-2390
(813) 870-9500
(800) 410-2009
Fax: (813) 870-9051
Email: info@missionsearch.org
Web: www.missionsearch.org

Summary: Our firm is a healthcare search and staffing firm founded on the principles of understanding the needs of our clients and candidates, developing methodologies to fulfill those needs and delivering on our promises and commitments to enhance our client organizations and our candidates' careers through the recruitment and placement of talented healthcare professionals. Please do not send your resume unless you are currently employed in the healthcare industry.

Key Contact - Specialty:
Mr. Steve Parzen, Executive Vice President & Principal
Mr. John Astrab, Founding Member
Mr. Pete Dominici, Chief Financial Officer
Mr. David Lowe, Vice President
Mr. John Randolph, Founder & Partner

Salary Minimum: $50,000

Functions: Generalist (All), Senior Mgmt., Finance

Industries: Generalist (All), Healthcare, Hospitals, Long-term/Home Care, Physical Therapy, Occupational Therapy, Women's

Branches:
400 Perimeter Center Ter NE Ste 900
Atlanta, GA 30346-1236
(770) 391-9090
Fax: (770) 391-9580
Email: info@faspros.com
Key Contact - Specialty:
Mr. Mike Zaremksi, Vice President
Mr. John Janowski, Founding Partner & Vice President - *Finance, Tax*

The Mitchell Group

4 Woodhaven Dr
New City, NY 10956-4417
(845) 638-2700
(800) 648-2435
Fax: (845) 708-6035
Email: info@actuary.tv
Web: www.actuary.tv

Summary: We have experience in recruiting actuaries within the life insurance, health insurance, managed care and pension fields.

Key Contact - Specialty:
Mr. Ken Mitchell, President

Functions: Generalist (All), Management, Senior Mgmt., Middle Mgmt., Sales Mgmt., HR Mgmt., Specialized Svcs., Mgmt. Consultants

Industries: Generalist (All), Energy, Utilities, Finance, Invest. Banking, Misc. Financial, Accounting, Mgmt. Consulting, HR Services, Insurance, Healthcare

MJF Associates

PO Box 132
Wallingford, CT 06492-0132
(203) 284-9878
Fax: (203) 284-9871
Email: mjfassoc@sbcglobal.net

Summary: We are a professional and technical search and placement firm. Accent is industrial, high technology, electronic, computer, mechanical, electrical, with sales, marketing,

management, engineering, and executive search disciplines.

Key Contact - Specialty:
Mr. Matt Furman, President - *Engineering, Management, Sales*

Salary Minimum: $30,000

Functions: Generalist (All), Sales Mgmt.

Industries: Generalist (All), Manufacturing, Electronic, Elec. Components, Equip Svcs., Engineering Svcs., Communications, RF/Microwave, Environmental Svcs., Aerospace, Packaging, Software

ML Recruiters

4710 Hanging Ivy Dr
Charlotte, NC 28215-5022
(704) 573-6566
Fax: (704) 573-6613
Email: mlrecruiters@hotmail.com
Web: www.mlrecruiters.com

Summary: We are an executive hospitality search firm that specializes in the recruitment and placement of senior and mid level hospitality executives for luxury resorts, hotels, casinos and country clubs.

Key Contact - Specialty:
Mr. Marvin Love, President

Salary Minimum: $50,000

Functions: Management, Hospitality

Industries: Hospitality, Hotels, Resorts, Clubs, Restaurants, Full Service Restaurants, Travel

ML&R Personnel Solutions LLC

401 Congress Ave Ste 1100
Austin, TX 78701-3788
(512) 370-3232
Fax: (512) 370-3250
Email: larchibald@mlrpc.com
Web: www.mlrpc.com

Summary: Our firm uses a consultative based approach to provide direct hire and project staffing solutions for our clients and candidates in the accounting and finance niche and finance, IT and business process consulting services. Our goal is to establish long term relationships built on trust and exceptional service so that the solutions we provide are beneficial to all involved parties.

Key Contact - Specialty:
Mr. Mark Wey, Director - *Consulting*

Salary Minimum: $50,000

Functions: Finance, CFOs, Budgeting, Taxes, M&A

Industries: Generalist (All)

MLA Resources Inc

PO Box 35115
Tulsa, OK 74153-0115
(918) 877-3202
Fax: (918) 877-3203
Email: mikeayling@mlaresources.com
Web: www.mlaresources.com

Summary: We are an executive and technical recruitment for the upstream oil and gas industry.

Key Contact - Specialty:
Mr. Michael L. Ayling, President - *Energy, Gas, Natural resources, Oil, Petrochemical*

Functions: Generalist (All), Management, Board Members, Senior Mgmt., Middle Mgmt., Production, Technicians

Industries: Energy, Utilities, Oil & Gas

MLA- Executive Search

(formerly known as MLA - Madeleine Lav &
Associates)
1270 Ellis Ave
Cambria, CA 93428-5956
(805) 927-3098
Fax: (805) 927-4138
Email: mlav333@aol.com

Summary: We have placed senior executives both
in corporate and in the field at premier retail and
food service companies in the country.

Key Contact - Specialty:
Ms. Madeleine Lav, President - *Food service,*
Retail

Salary Minimum: $50,000

Functions: Management, Middle Mgmt., Product
Dev., Distribution, HR Mgmt., Finance, CFOs

Industries: Food, Bev., Tobacco, Retail,
Restaurants, Real Estate

MLB Associates

1936 Saranac Ave Ste 2-300
Lake Placid, NY 12946-1171
(518) 523-2371
Email: info@mlbassociates.com
Web: www.mlbassociates.com

Summary: We specialize in recruiting and
assessing top-level direct marketing leaders who
have the experience, talent and drive to add long-
term value to their clients' competitive positions.

Key Contact - Specialty:
Ms. Robin Anthony, Vice President & Senior
Recruiter - *CRM, Database, Direct marketing,*
Interactive, Marketing
Ms. MaryLou Brown, President - *CRM,*
Database, Direct marketing, Interactive,
Marketing

Salary Minimum: $40,000

Functions: Mktg. Mgmt., Direct Mktg.

Industries: Generalist (All)

MMW International

PO Box 1116
Danville, CA 94526-8116
(925) 838-9163
Fax: (925) 215-2429
Email: info@mmwi.com
Web: www.mmwi.com

Summary: Our firm is an executive search and
technical recruiting firm. Our firm has been set up
to provide a highly specialized and tailored
recruitment service to the IT industry. Our
business is based on solid IT industry knowledge
and experience, combined with business and
recruitment skills.

Key Contact - Specialty:
Ms. Marie Minder, President
Mr. Nathaniel Harting, Senior Executive
Recruiter

Salary Minimum: $75,000

Functions: PR, Training, MIS Mgmt., Architects

Industries: Generalist (All)

Modicom Inc

1072 S De Anza Blvd Ste 339
San Jose, CA 95129-3500
(408) 873-7100
Fax: (408) 873-7101
Email: tony@modicom.com
Web: www.modicom.com

Summary: We are an executive search firm
specializing in the placement of software and
hardware engineers.

Key Contact - Specialty:
Mr. Tony Zammikiel, Director
Mr. Bobby Masak, Senior Technical Recruiter

Functions: R&D, Hardware

Industries: Telecoms, Call Centers, Telephony,
Digital, Wireless, Fiber Optic, Network
Infrastructure, RF/Microwave, Software,
Database SW, Development SW, Doc. Mgmt.,
Production SW, HR SW, Industry Specific SW,
Marketing SW, Networking, Comm. SW,
Security SW

Moffitt International Inc

3182 Sweeten Creek Rd
Asheville, NC 28803-2115
(828) 651-8550
Fax: (828) 651-8558
Email: resumes@emoffitt.com
Web: www.emoffitt.com

Summary: We are a research-based generalist
firm with strong market niches. We specialize in
Bio-med, legal, engineering, waste management,
construction and architecture.

Key Contact - Specialty:
Mr. Timothy D. Moffitt, President
Mr. G. Alan Folger, Vice President, Ops Mgr &
Director, A&E
Ms. Rita O'Brien, Director, Pharml, CRO,
Biotechnology - *Biotechnology, Pharmaceutical*
Mr. Bo Boling, Director - *Construction*
Mr. Brien Pierce, Director, Waste Management -
Accounting, Business development,
Comptrollers, Controllers, Executives

Functions: Generalist (All)

Industries: Pharm Svcs., Legal, Telecoms,
Biotech/Life Sciences

Branches:
6 Commerce Dr Ste 200
Cranford, NJ 07016-3515
(908) 709-1680
Fax: (908) 709-8946
Key Contact - Specialty:
Mr. Joseph W. Mrozek

Diedre Moire Corp Inc

510 Horizon Ctr
Robbinsville, NJ 08691-1907
(609) 584-9000
Fax: (609) 584-9575
Email: smr@diedremoire.com
Web: www.diedremoire.com

Summary: We are a retainer quality search
without the retainer. We have successfully
concluded over 4,000 searches. We love searching
for those highly technical professionals.

Key Contact - Specialty:
Mr. Stephen M. Reuning, CPC, President
Ms. Nicole Bakos, Engineer, IS
Mr. Laurence Chiaravallo, Practice Manager -
Biomedical, Biopharmaceutical
Mr. Scott Shanes, Consultant - *Biotechnology*
Mr. Stephen Casano, Practice Manager -
Biopharmaceutical
Mr. Bryan Grossman, Consultant
Mr. Carl Notter, Consultant - *Automation,*
Biopharmaceutical
Mr. David Eide, Group Leader
Mr. Gregory Foss, Practice Manager - *Insurance*
Mr. Winston Reuning, Information Coordinator
Mr. John Casey, Recruiter
Mr. Raymond Barnes, Recruiter
Dr. John G. Cavalli, FAPWCA, DPM, Recruiter -
Biopharmaceutical, Boards of Directors,
Clinical, Healthcare, Research & development

Mr. Robert S. Marrone, Recruiter - *Construction,*
Engineering, Facilities engineering, Highways
Mr. James A. Lockley, Recruiter - *Marketing,*
Sales

Functions: Generalist (All)

Industries: Manufacturing, Medical Devices, Test,
Measure Equip., Venture Cap., Pharm Svcs.,
New Media, Telecoms, Insurance, Software,
Biotech/Life Sciences

The Moisson Group Inc

750 Pipeline Ct Ste 100
Hurst, TX 76053-5758
(817) 268-0747
Fax: (817) 268-0776
Email: ccorrie@moissongrp.com
Web: www.themoissongroupinc.com

Summary: The firm specializes in recruiting
executives working in the investment management
arena. This includes sales & marketing executives,
consultants and portfolio managers. Our clients
include firms providing asset management
services to corporations, endowments,
foundations, pension funds and individuals. In
addition, we have practice areas including
construction, legal, and human resources.

Key Contact - Specialty:
Mr. Casey M. Corrie, President - *Asset*
management

Salary Minimum: $75,000

Functions: Sales Mgmt.

Industries: Construction, Banking, Invest.
Banking, Mutual/Hedge Funds, Legal, HR
Services, Marketing SW

Molecular Solutions Inc

1116 Miller Mountain Rd
Saluda, NC 28773-8677
(828) 859-5036
Email: mambos@molsol.com
Web: www.molsol.com

Summary: With extensive years of experience in
pharmaceutical research, we are the only executive
search firm, which can leverage technical
expertise and industry contacts to effectively
locate qualified computational scientists.

Key Contact - Specialty:
Dr. Allen Richon, President - *Biopharmaceutical,*
Biotechnology, Computers (Science),
Pharmaceutical, Research & development
Ms. Merry Ambos, Vice President -
Biopharmaceutical, Compensation, Competitive
intelligence, Pharmaceutical, Staffing

Salary Minimum: $80,000

Functions: Generalist (All), Board Members,
Senior Mgmt., Middle Mgmt., MIS Mgmt.,
Systems Dev., DB Admin., R&D

Industries: Generalist (All), Pharm Svcs.,
Biotech/Life Sciences

Momentum Search Group Inc

600 Anton Blvd Ste 1100
Costa Mesa, CA 92626-7100
(714) 371-4028
(949) 307-3133
Fax: (714) 371-4001
Email: mark@momentumsearchgroup.com
Web: www.momentumsearchgroup.com

Summary: We are a boutique search firm
specializing in filling management to executive
level accounting and finance positions

Key Contact - Specialty:
Mr. Mark McConnell, Search Consultant

Salary Minimum: $80,000

Functions: Management, Senior Mgmt., Middle Mgmt.

Industries: Finance

Vida Monahan Search

44 Hawick Dr
Shallotte, NC 28470-4556
(910) 575-8306
Email: info@vmsearch.com
Web: www.vmsearch.com

Summary: Our performance and staff help our clients attain their bottom line. We have successfully recruited, evaluated and recommended exceptional candidates to fill critical roles in our clients' organizations. We secure objective references on the candidates we recruit for partnership with our clients.

Key Contact - Specialty:
Mr. Jack Monahan, President
Mr. Darin Monahan, Vice President

Salary Minimum: $60,000

Functions: Generalist (All)

Industries: Generalist (All)

Monarch Systems

16 Greens Whisper
San Antonio, TX 78216-7805
(210) 494-3800
(210) 884-8326
Fax: (210) 434-3806
Email: richardking@satx.rr.com

Summary: Executive placement in the food, pharmaceutical and consumer packaged goods manufacturing industries. Discipline competencies in production/operations, engineering/maintenance, QA/QC, supply chain, and R&D.

Key Contact - Specialty:
Mr. Richard King, President

Functions: Mfg., Purchasing

Industries: Manufacturing, Food, Bev., Tobacco, Soap, Perf., Cosmtcs., Drugs Mfg., Medical Devices, Misc. Mfg., Consumer Goods, Transportation, Supply Chain Mgmt, Packaging, Mfg. SW

The Montgomery Group Inc

PO Box 30791
Knoxville, TN 37930-0791
(865) 693-0325
Fax: (865) 691-1900
Email: tmg@tmginckanox.com
Web: www.tmginckanox.com

Summary: We serve as consultants to agri-business and the food industry. Emphasis on recruiting the right person for the position. We have extensive industry experience.

Key Contact - Specialty:
Mr. Larry Suchomski, Executive Vice President & COO - *Operations, Sales*

Salary Minimum: $35,000

Functions: Generalist (All), Senior Mgmt., Plant Mgmt., Distribution, Mktg. Mgmt., Staffing, CFOs, R&D

Industries: Generalist (All), Agri., Forestry, Mining, Food, Bev., Tobacco

Montgomery Resources Inc

612 Howard St Lbby 100
San Francisco, CA 94105-3927
(415) 956-4242
Email: montres@montres.com
Web: www.montres.com

Summary: We are a recruitment firm for finance and accounting professionals for middle-management positions.

Key Contact - Specialty:
Mr. Roger A. Lee, Partner
Mr. Thomas K. McAteer, Partner

Salary Minimum: $60,000

Functions: Finance

Industries: Generalist (All), Manufacturing, Retail, Finance, Services, Communications, Real Estate, Software, Biotech/Life Sciences, Healthcare

James Moore & Associates

5150 El Camino Real Ste A26
Los Altos, CA 94022-1537
(650) 988-6600
Email: info@jamesmoore.com
Web: www.jamesmoore.com

Summary: Our search firm has experience in delivering well qualified computer professionals to a diverse mix of client companies.

Key Contact - Specialty:
Ms. Ann Mitchell, Director
Mr. Les Fenyves, Director
Mr. Rick Saxton, Senior Associate
Mr. Greg Pless, Senior Associate - *Healthcare*

Salary Minimum: $75,000

Functions: Generalist (All), MIS Mgmt., Systems Analysis, Systems Dev., Systems Implem., Systems Support, Network Admin., DB Admin.

Industries: Generalist (All), Computer Equip., Finance, Software, Biotech/Life Sciences, Healthcare

Larry Moore & Associates

18755 Lodestone Ct
Penn Valley, CA 95946-9019
(530) 432-8490
Fax: (781) 623-5550
Email: larrymoore@thegrid.net

Summary: Specialize in placements for the Information Systems/Information Technology industries in Northern California with emphasis in the San Francisco Bay area.

Key Contact - Specialty:
Mr. Larry W. Moore, President

Functions: Generalist (All), IT, Systems Analysis, Systems Dev., Systems Implem., Systems Support, Network Admin., DB Admin.

Industries: Generalist (All), Software

Mordue, Allen, Roberts, Bonney Ltd

PO Box 450
Gig Harbor, WA 98335-0450
(253) 851-5355
Email: mordue@marbl.com

Summary: We are a recruiting and placement firm for engineers, managers, directors and VPs specializing in the software, electronic and other high-technology industries.

Key Contact - Specialty:
Mr. Michael J. Mordue, President - *Computers (Software), High technology*
Ms. Sheila A. Schultz, Vice President - *Computers (Software)*

Salary Minimum: $80,000

Functions: MIS Mgmt., Systems Analysis, Systems Dev., R&D, Engineering

Industries: Medical Devices, Computer Equip., Test, Measure Equip., Software

MoreTech Consulting

113 Clover Dr
Hockessin, DE 19707-1306
(302) 234-4699
(877) 478-6595
Fax: (302) 234-2660
Email: info@moretechconsulting.com
Web: www.moretechconsulting.com

Summary: We have developed a tried and proven methodology to help our clients achieve their hiring goals. Through our relationship-based approach, we understand our clients' hiring needs and the selling features of their employment opportunity. This allows us to bring the most suitable candidates to the table in a timely manner.

Key Contact - Specialty:
Mr. Willard Ashmore, President
Mr. Eric Rupert, Vice President - *Business development*
Mr. Richard Collins, Principal Technical Recruiter

Salary Minimum: $50,000

Functions: Board Members, IT, MIS Mgmt., Systems Analysis

Industries: Generalist (All), Finance, Media, Communications, Telecoms, Call Centers, Telephony, Digital, Wireless, Fiber Optic, Network Infrastructure, Software, Security SW, System SW, Biotech/Life Sciences, Healthcare

Morgan & Associates

PO Box 379
Granby, MA 01033-0379
(413) 467-9156
Fax: (413) 467-3003
Email: employment@morgan-jobs.com
Web: www.morgan-jobs.com

Summary: We specialize in the manufacturing automation field including both mechanical and electronic automation companies.

Key Contact - Specialty:
Ms. Diane R. Morgan, Owner - *Automation*
Mr. Arthur Klebba, Consultant - *Automation*

Salary Minimum: $35,000

Functions: Mfg., Engineering

Industries: Manufacturing, Computer Equip., Test, Measure Equip., Misc. Mfg., Electronic, Elec. Components, Robotics, Semiconductors, Digital, Fiber Optic, RF/Microwave, Government, Defense, Aerospace, Software

The Morgan Group

PO Box 121153
Nashville, TN 37212-1153
(615) 665-1246
Fax: (615) 665-2925
Web: aafa.com

Summary: Accounting referrals from national and local CPA firms. Work with multi-national, publicly-held and private companies.

Key Contact - Specialty:
Mr. E. Allen Morgan, Managing Partner, MBA, Cornell Univ.

Salary Minimum: $50,000

Functions: Finance, CFOs, Budgeting, Cash Mgmt., Taxes, M&A

Industries: Generalist (All)

Morgan Hunter Corp

7600 W 110th St
Overland Park, KS 66210-2322
(913) 491-3434
Fax: (913) 409-1232

Email: jhellebusch@morganhunter.com
Web: www.morganhunter.com

Summary: We are a specialized contingency/retainer search firm.

Key Contact - Specialty:
Mr. Jerry Hellebusch, CPC, Owner & President

Salary Minimum: $30,000

Functions: Admin. Svcs., Sales & Mktg., Advertising, Mktg. Mgmt., Sales Mgmt., Finance, IT, Graphic Designers

Industries: Generalist (All), Computer Equip., Accounting, Advertising, New Media, Telecoms, Software

Morgan, Palmer, Morgan & Hill

(aka The Fleetwood Group, Inc.)
500 N Estrella Pkwy Ste B2
PMB 618
Goodyear, AZ 85338-4136
(206) 463-5721
(623) 533-4160
Email: mpmh@mpmhthefirm.com

Summary: We are a boutique global search firm specializing in the investment banking, private equity and restructuring sectors.

Key Contact - Specialty:
Mr. Warren Lee Hill, Jr., Senior Managing Partner

Salary Minimum: $125,000

Functions: Finance, M&A

Industries: Finance, Banking, Invest. Banking

Morgan Recruiting LLC

216 Alder Ct
Delaware, OH 43015-2775
(740) 363-2179
(614) 579-7550
Fax: (740) 363-2179
Email: polly@morganrecruiting.com
Web: www.morganrecruiting.com

Summary: Executive, technical and professional search specializing in placement of high-achievers in accounting, finance, IT and related disciplines. Focused on developing long-term, trust-based relationships with both employers and candidates.

Key Contact - Specialty:
Ms. Polly Morgan, CPC, Senior Recruiter, President - *Accounting, Finance, Information Systems, Information Technology, Senior management*

Salary Minimum: $35,000

Functions: Management, Quality, Finance, IT, DB Admin., Minorities/Diversity

Industries: Generalist (All), Manufacturing, Retail, Finance, Services, Accounting, IT Implementation, Communications, Call Centers, Network Infrastructure, Software, Development SW, ERP SW, Mfg. SW, Networking, Comm. SW, Security SW

Morgan Search LLC

233 Wilshire Blvd Ste 400
Santa Monica, CA 90401-1214
(310) 917-1066
Fax: (310) 458-1886
Email: jobs@morgansearch.com
Web: www.morgansearch.com

Summary: Executive recruiters specializing in the placement of market research professionals. Retained and contingency search options, all levels. Industries include: consumer packaged goods, pharmaceuticals, high technology, eCommerce, financial services, consulting,

advertising agencies and market research suppliers.

Key Contact - Specialty:
Ms. Karen Morgan, President
Ms. Allison Koeppe, Executive Recruiter
Ms. Rachel Hammelman, Executive Recruiter
Ms. Brenna Guthrie, Office Manager

Salary Minimum: $50,000

Functions: Mktg. Research

Industries: Generalist (All)

Morgan-Collier International LLC

PO Box 18128
Spartanburg, SC 29318-8128
(864) 579-0525
Fax: (864) 579-0526
Email: kacie@mcint.us
Web: www.mcint.us

Summary: We serve construction clients in two basic categories: 1) Precast/prestressed concrete producers involved in commercial/industrial construction of prisons, parking decks, stadiums, & bridges. Companies that serve precast such as suppliers and consulting engineers. 2) Commercial construction firms building projects of $3M and higher - military, healthcare and high-rise.

Key Contact - Specialty:
Ms. Kacie Morgan, President

Salary Minimum: $70,000

Functions: Management, Middle Mgmt., Plant Mgmt., Quality, Sales Mgmt., Engineering

Industries: Construction, Manufacturing

MorganSullivan, Inc.

1 E Main St Ste 206
Northborough, MA 01532-1662
(508) 439-9227
Fax: (508) 393-0076
Email: jpkreiss@morgansullivan.com
Web: www.morgansullivan.com

Summary: MorganSullivan is an Executive Search firm serving the Real Estate industry exclusively.

Key Contact - Specialty:
Mr. John Kreiss, President

Functions: Generalist (All)

Industries: Real Estate

Morgenstern International Inc

5970 SW 18th St Ste 240
Boca Raton, FL 33431-7197
(561) 620-8455
Fax: (561) 892-2472
Email: admin@attorney-search.com
Web: www.attorney-search.com

Summary: We have a reputation for helping clients recruit attorneys with superb reputations and practice experience. For law firm clients, we conduct strategic searches for partners and practice groups with significant portable practices, and advise on merger and acquisition matters. For corporate clients, we conduct searches for senior in-house attorneys, including general counsel.

Key Contact - Specialty:
Mr. Richard L. Morgenstern, Esq., President
Mr. Herrick A. Zeefe, Esq., Recruiter

Salary Minimum: $150,000

Functions: Legal, Attorneys

Industries: Generalist (All)

The Morley Group

6201 Corporate Dr Ste 200
Indianapolis, IN 46278-2943
(317) 879-4770
(317) 616-1748
Fax: (317) 879-4787
Email: smorley@themorleygroup.com
Web: www.themorleygroup.com

Summary: Recruiting, temp-direct and contract for engineering, accounting, healthcare, IT, administration/secretarial services. Other services include HR surrogacy, quality audit & certification, vendor management, resume preparation and competency testing.

Key Contact - Specialty:
Mr. Michael A. Morley, CPC, President
Ms. Sharon M. Morley, CPC, Vice President

Salary Minimum: $16,500

Functions: Generalist (All), Admin. Svcs., Mfg., Quality, Nurses, Allied Health, Finance, Eng. Design, Hardware, Legal

Industries: Generalist (All), Energy, Utilities, Construction, Manufacturing, Metal Products, Machine, Appliance, Motor Vehicles, Computer Equip., Transportation, Finance, Banking, Invest. Banking, Misc. Financial, Services, Legal, Equip Svcs., Mgmt. Consulting, Media, Software, Biotech/Life Sciences, Healthcare

Morris Executive Search

178 Myrtle Blvd
Larchmont, NY 10538-2040
(914) 834-6646
Fax: (914) 834-6643
Web: www.morrissearch.com

Summary: Ours is an executive recruitment firm based in New York. We provide permanent placement opportunities across most asset classes within financial services. Drawing on our industry experience, we form partnerships with our clients to achieve bottom-line results, the best possible candidate for the position. We believe the best fit means finding a candidate with the right personality as well as the relevant educational background, skills and experience.

Key Contact - Specialty:
Ms. Fran Morris, Principal

Salary Minimum: $100,000

Functions: Specialized Svcs.

Industries: Misc. Financial

Mortgage & Financial Personnel Services

23679 Calabasas Rd Ste 371
Calabasas, CA 91302-1502
(818) 591-8367
(800) 443-5627
Fax: (818) 591-7509
Email: jobs@mortgageandfinancial.com
Web: www.mortgageandfinancial.com

Summary: We have been providing the highest caliber of mortgage and lending professionals into financial firms since the start. We have upgraded our services to primarily concentrate on representing those mortgage professionals that are serious about improving their career paths by working with the best companies that the mortgage lending industry has to offer across the country.

Key Contact - Specialty:
Mr. Robert Sherman, President - *Banking, Banking (Mortgage), Financial services, Real estate*

Mr. Seth Jaffe, Executive Recruiter - *Banking (Corporate), Finance, Financial services, Loans, Real estate*
Ms. Susan Sherman, Vice President

Salary Minimum: $50,000

Functions: Generalist (All), Staffing

Industries: Generalist (All), Finance, Banking, Brokers, Misc. Financial, Real Estate

The Morton Group

5151 N 16th St Ste 234
Phoenix, AZ 85016-3920
(602) 279-5662
Fax: (602) 279-6215
Email: legaljobs@mortongrp.com
Web: www.mortongrp.com

Summary: We are the leading legal placement agency in Phoenix, Arizona specializing in direct hire, temp contract and temp-to-hire recruitment of attorneys, paralegals, legal secretaries, support staff and administrative assistants. HR support is provided to clients and career counseling to candidates.

Key Contact - Specialty:
Ms. Susan B. Morton, CPC, CTS, President

Functions: Admin. Svcs., Staffing, Legal, Attorneys, Paralegals

Industries: Generalist (All), Legal

Motion Medical Solutions Inc

601 W Spruce St Ste G
Missoula, MT 59802-4047
(406) 329-2668
Fax: (406) 329-2896
Email: info@betterjobs.com
Web: betterjobs.com

Summary: Small firm specializing in healthcare related professions. High quality perm and temp placements. We also provide consulting services for in-house recruiting departments. Owner has many years of professional recruiting experience.

Key Contact - Specialty:
Mr. John T. O'Conner, CPC

Functions: Physicians, Nurses, Allied Health, Health Admin.

Industries: Healthcare

MPA Associates

(a division of MPA Companies, LLC)
PO Box 2573
North Canton, OH 44720-0573
(330) 280-3432
Fax: (831) 301-9608
Email: mpa03@sbcglobal.net
Web: www.mpahire.com

Summary: Technical recruiter with a history of experience in the rubber, plastic, polymer and chemical industries. Search and recruiting assignments from a solid client company base with positions and candidates in R&D, engineering, manufacturing, technical and sales & marketing. Career transition and outplacement services available for salary and key hourly employees.

Key Contact - Specialty:
Mr. Mike Aquino, CPC, Owner & Technical Recruiter - *Chemical, Manufacturing, Plastics, Research & development, Rubber*
Ms. Michelle Copen, Manager, MPA Resumes

Salary Minimum: $60,000

Functions: Mfg., Product Dev., Production, Plant Mgmt., Materials, R&D, Engineering, Process

Industries: Manufacturing, Paper, Chemicals, Plastics, Rubber, Paints, Petro. Products, Metal

Products, Motor Vehicles, Semiconductors, Consumer Goods, Aerospace

MPC and Company

1910 Ala Moana Blvd Apt 9D
Honolulu, HI 96815-1815
(808) 945-2545
(808) 554-2545
Fax: (808) 949-2545
Email: sally@mpcandcompany.com
Web: www.mpcandcompany.com

Summary: We provide professional placement for various positions, including engineering, construction, health & safety, executive, healthcare, administrative, legal, accounting and general office, as well as any other positions that may be requested by our clients.

Key Contact - Specialty:
Ms. Sally Raade, Staffing Consultant

Functions: Generalist (All)

Industries: Generalist (All), Construction, Accounting, Engineering Svcs., Environmental Svcs., Healthcare

MRC - Management Resource Consulting

3809 Roanoke Dr
Garland, TX 75041-4951
(972) 926-4418
Email: rchapman@hrsearchmrc.com
Web: www.hrsearchmrc.com

Summary: As HR professionals (working HR exclusively) we are uniquely prepared to address your HR staffing needs.

Key Contact - Specialty:
Mr. Ralph Chapman, Senior Human Resources Consultant - *Human resources, Organizational development, Training*

Functions: HR Mgmt.

Industries: Generalist (All)

MSI International (Management Search Inc)

245 Peachtree Center Ave NE Ste 2500
Atlanta, GA 30303-1248
(404) 659-5050
(800) 511-0383
Fax: (404) 659-7139
Email: info@msi-intl.com
Web: www.msi-intl.com

Summary: Our recruiting fields include allied health, banking, sales, marketing, investment banking & financial services, legal, contract & permanent IT, construction, biomedical and engineering.

Key Contact - Specialty:
Mr. Eric J. Lindberg, President - *CEOs, Healthcare*
Mr. Michael DiDomenico, Vice President, Permanent Operations
Mr. Timothy Alderman, Vice President, Contract Operations
Mr. Doug Dershimer, General Manager

Salary Minimum: $30,000

Functions: Generalist (All), Senior Mgmt., Physicians, Nurses, Allied Health, IT, R&D, Int'l.

Industries: Generalist (All), Construction, Manufacturing, Banking, Invest. Banking, Biotech/Life Sciences, Healthcare

Branches:
4275 Executive Sq Ste 510
La Jolla, CA 92037-1477
(858) 552-6888
Fax: (858) 552-6891
Email: mca@n2.net
Key Contact - Specialty:
Mr. George Colberg, General Manager - *Biomedical*

1050 Crown Pointe Pkwy Ste 100
Atlanta, GA 30338-7701
(770) 394-2494
Fax: (770) 394-2251
Email: jim.watson@msi-intl.com
Key Contact - Specialty:
Mr. Jim Watson, CPC, General Manager - *Construction, Healthcare, Manufacturing*

6151 Powers Ferry Rd NW Ste 540
Atlanta, GA 30339-2951
(770) 850-6465
Fax: (770) 850-6468
Email: keith.colson@msi-intl.com
Key Contact - Specialty:
Mr. Keith Colson, General Manager - *Information Technology, Telecommunications*

1900 N 18th St Ste 306
Monroe, LA 71201-4455
(318) 324-0406
Fax: (318) 329-8188
Email: medical1@msi-monroe.com
Key Contact - Specialty:
Ms. Laurelle Williams, General Manager - *Healthcare, Physicians*

701 Poydras St Ste 3880
New Orleans, LA 70139-7918
(504) 522-6700
Fax: (504) 522-1998
Email: david.dietz@msi-intl.com
Key Contact - Specialty:
Mr. David Dietz, CPC, General Manager - *Healthcare, Physicians*

5215 N O'Connor Blvd
Irving, TX 75039-3707
(972) 869-3939
Fax: (972) 869-0085
Email: msi_mda@mindspring.com
Key Contact - Specialty:
Mr. Larry Klos, General Manager - *Healthcare, Information Technology*

3401 Custer Rd Ste 113
Plano, TX 75023-7546
(972) 758-0938
Fax: (972) 612-7444
Key Contact - Specialty:
Mr. Chris Wheeler, Manager

Mullin Company

2 Middleton Park Ln
Nashville, TN 37215-5321
(615) 305-3059
(615) 627-3519
Fax: (615) 221-1015
Email: mullinco@isdn.net
Web: www.construction-job.com

Summary: We are a recruiting firm that specializes in design and construction professionals for architects, engineers and the construction industry.

Key Contact - Specialty:
Mr. Dale H. Mullin, President

Salary Minimum: $65,000

Functions: Generalist (All), Senior Mgmt., Middle Mgmt., Admin. Svcs., Engineering, Architects

Industries: Generalist (All), Construction, Accounting, Hotels, Resorts, Clubs, Hospitals

The Multicultural Advantage
600 W Harvey St Apt A416
Philadelphia, PA 19144-4336
(215) 849-0946
Fax: (603) 806-7986
Email: tdemorsella@multiculturaladvantage.com
Web: www.tmaonline.net

Summary: We offer a number of highly effective and innovative diversity staffing and development services including placement, recruitment training, internet campaigns, recruitment program development, recruitment event coordination and multicultural communications tools.

Key Contact - Specialty:
Ms. Tracey DeMorsella, Managing Producer - *Diversity, Engineering, Marketing, Sales*

Functions: Generalist (All), Quality, Sales Mgmt., Staffing, Budgeting, Systems Analysis, Engineering, Minorities/Diversity

Industries: Generalist (All), Food, Bev., Tobacco, Chemicals, Soap, Perf., Cosmtcs., Drugs Mfg., Medical Devices, Software

Murdock & Associates
PO Box 162142
Austin, TX 78716-2142
(512) 329-5034
(512) 329-5034
Fax: (512) 732-2766
Email: kmurdock@kmurdock.com
Web: www.kmurdock.com

Summary: We specialize in sales, accounting and operations professionals for manufacturing industries.

Key Contact - Specialty:
Mr. Ken Murdock, Owner & President

Salary Minimum: $50,000

Functions: Generalist (All), Management, Board Members

Industries: Generalist (All), Manufacturing, Plastics, Rubber, Accounting, Mgmt. Consulting, Packaging, Accounting SW, Industry Specific SW, Mfg. SW

Kenneth Murphy & Associates
5112 Prince St
Halifax, NS B3J 1L3
Canada
(902) 425-4495
Fax: (902) 425-6691
Email: info@kma.ns.ca
Web: www.kma.ns.ca

Summary: We specialize in recruitment of IT professionals and executive search.

Key Contact - Specialty:
Mr. Ken Murphy, President
Ms. Karin Dobson, Recruiter

Salary Minimum: $50,000

Functions: Generalist (All), Management, Sales & Mktg., HR Mgmt., Finance, IT, Engineering

Industries: Generalist (All)

The Murphy Group
245 W Roosevelt Rd Ste 101
West Chicago, IL 60185-4819
(630) 639-5110
Fax: (630) 639-5113
Email: info@murphygroup.com
Web: www.murphygroup.com

Summary: We are a multi-disciplined firm in both search and temp/contract.

Key Contact - Specialty:
Mr. William Murphy, II, CPC, CIPC, President - *Information Technology, Sales*

Salary Minimum: $35,000

Functions: Generalist (All), Admin. Svcs., Health Admin., Sales Mgmt., Customer Svc., Benefits, MIS Mgmt., Network Admin.

Industries: Generalist (All), Manufacturing, Retail, Finance, Services, Media, Software

Murray & Tatro
2458 Creston Way
Los Angeles, CA 90068-2212
(323) 467-3553
Fax: (323) 467-3878
Email: murraytatro@cs.com

Summary: We place copywriters, art directors and creative directors at all levels for advertising agencies.

Key Contact - Specialty:
Ms. Marcia Murray, Owner
Mr. Richard Tatro, Partner

Functions: Advertising

Industries: Advertising

Musick & Associates
322 Cottonwood Creek Rd
Durango, CO 81301-6168
(970) 259-8647
Fax: (970) 259-8659
Email: stevem@professionalplacement.com
Web: www.professionalplacement.com

Summary: Contingency and retained firm specializing in accounting, finance, audit, tax, insurance, underwriting, claims

Key Contact - Specialty:
Mr. Stephen Musick, Principal - *Finance, Marketing, Tax*
Mrs. Diana Musick, Principal - *Finance, Operations, Tax*

Salary Minimum: $25,000

Functions: Generalist (All), Finance

Industries: Generalist (All), Energy, Utilities, Construction, Manufacturing, Wholesale, Retail, Finance, Hospitality, Media, Communications, Insurance, Casualty, Life, Commercial, Re-Insurance, Software

The MVP Group
150 Broadway Rm 2101
New York, NY 10038-4484
(212) 571-1833
Fax: (212) 393-1048
Email: jvalenti@mvpgroup.net
Web: www.mvpgroup.net

Summary: Our firm has been successfully serving the needs of financial service clients since it's founding. Our approach is to know our clients, most of whom have worked with the firm for years. The key to a successful search is to identify the specifications and understand the company culture in conjunction with managing the candidate process.

Key Contact - Specialty:
Mr. Joseph Valenti, Chief Executive Officer
Ms. Denise Moynihan Smith, Vice President - *Compliance, Credit*
Ms. Rosalie Langer, Vice President - *Brokerage*

Functions: Generalist (All), Management, Benefits, Staffing, Training, Finance, IT,

Systems Analysis, Systems Implem., Minorities/Diversity

Industries: Generalist (All), Finance, Banking, Invest. Banking, Brokers, Venture Cap., Mutual/Hedge Funds, Misc. Financial, Accounting, IT Implementation, Insurance

DDJ Myers Ltd
2303 N 44th St Ste 14-1740
Phoenix, AZ 85008-2497
(602) 840-9595
(800) 574-8877
Email: deedeem@ddjmyers.com
Web: www.ddjmyers.com

Summary: We provide recruiting, career and succession planning for financial and technology executives. Organizations use our services for internal and external searches, development and execution of career management processes and comprehensive succession plans.

Key Contact - Specialty:
Ms. Deedee Myers, President & Chief Executive Officer - *Finance*
Mr. Jim Rives, Senior Vice President - *Accounting (Big 4), Asset management, Banking, Banking (Commercial, Corporate)*

Functions: Generalist (All), Senior Mgmt., CFOs, Cash Mgmt., Risk Mgmt., IT

Industries: Transportation, Finance, Banking, Invest. Banking, Brokers, Equip Svcs., Mgmt. Consulting, HR Services

N2 Technologies
3790 El Camino Real Ste 400
Palo Alto, CA 94306-3314
(650) 493-1500
Fax: (650) 493-9263
Email: chris@n2tech.com
Web: www.n2tech.com

Summary: We are an executive search firm specializing in the placement of software engineers and developers.

Key Contact - Specialty:
Mr. Chris Lewis, Manager
Mr. Vernel Bakewell, Senior Technical Recruiter

Functions: Engineering

Industries: Generalist (All)

Nachman BioMedical
50 Church St
Cambridge, MA 02138-3726
(617) 492-8911
Email: phil@nachmanbiomedical.com
Web: www.nachmanbiomedical.com

Summary: Medical industry specialists: medical device, medical electronics, instrumentation, diagnostics, biotechnology and pharmaceuticals. Search practice focus is on VPs through program managers and experienced individual contributors. Skills include R&D, regulatory affairs, quality assurance, scale-up, manufacturing and marketing management.

Key Contact - Specialty:
Mr. Philip S. Nachman, President

Salary Minimum: $80,000

Functions: Management, Middle Mgmt., Product Dev., Production, Quality, Mktg. Research, Mktg. Mgmt., R&D, Engineering, Specialized Svcs.

Industries: Drugs Mfg., Medical Devices, Biotech/Life Sciences, Dental

Nagle & Associates Inc

PO Box 1
Fremont, IN 46737-0001
(260) 495-0491
Fax: (260) 495-7113
Email: j.jnagle@verizon.net

Summary: We are an executive search firm in the asset base lending/banking recruiting industry. We work with corporations and banks conducting searches for these positions: asset-based auditors, asset-based audit managers, credit managers, commercial lenders, calling officers, portfolio managers, credit analysts, underwriters, etc. All of these positions having asset based lending and banking experience in their backgrounds.

Key Contact - Specialty:
Ms. Jan Nagle, Owner
Mr. Daniel Nagle, Executive Recruiter

Functions: Generalist (All), Senior Mgmt., Mktg. Mgmt., Sales Mgmt., Finance, CFOs, Cash Mgmt., Credit, Risk Mgmt.

Industries: Finance, Banking

Nagle Company Inc

11514 N Port Washington Rd Ste 104
Mequon, WI 53092-3442
(262) 241-5350
Fax: (262) 241-5713
Email: nagleco@nagleco.com
Web: www.nagleco.com

Summary: Executive recruiting firm specializing in all areas of foundry employment.

Key Contact - Specialty:
Mr. Jim Nagle, CPC, President & Recruiter

Functions: Generalist (All)

Industries: Metal Products

Nail & Associates

1205 Johnson Ferry Rd Ste 136-186
Marietta, GA 30068-5401
(770) 565-2445
Email: nailassoc@aol.com

Summary: We are highly skilled in identifying and matching the culture with the candidate profile in an exceptionally timely manner. The net results are long-term placements on a consistent basis that offers a win-win solution for both the candidate and the employer.

Key Contact - Specialty:
Mr. Peter A. Nail, President - *Engineering, Research & development*

Salary Minimum: $40,000

Functions: Generalist (All), Automation, Quality, R&D

Industries: Food, Bev., Tobacco, Soap, Perf., Cosmtcs., Drugs Mfg., Consumer Goods, Packaging

NAP Executive Services Inc (Canada)

300-3101 Bathurst St
North York, ON M6A 2A6
Canada
(416) 949-8896
Email: toronto@fashion-career.com
Web: www.fashion-career.com

Summary: We specialize in recruiting at all levels within the apparel and textiles industries both at wholesale and retail. Our recruiters all have industry experience. All of our opportunities require fashion experience.

Key Contact - Specialty:
Mr. Steve Rothstein, President - *Apparel, Retail, Textiles*

Salary Minimum: $40,000

Functions: Generalist (All)

Industries: Textiles, Apparel, Wholesale, Retail

Branches:
904-1230 Av du Docteur-Penfield
Edifice Drummond McGregor
Montreal, QC H3G 1B5
Canada
(514) 592-8896
Email: montreal@fashion-career.com
Key Contact - Specialty:
Ms. Janet Presser

Delyse Nash & Associates

1754 Technology Dr Ste 102
San Jose, CA 95110-1320
(408) 998-3322
Fax: (408) 998-3318
Email: jobs@delysenash.com
Web: www.delysenash.com

Summary: We specialize in the recruitment and placement of finance/accounting and human resource professionals in small to medium size companies. Our philosophy is to work with a few select clients so that we can provide the exceptional services that our clients have come to expect.

Key Contact - Specialty:
Ms. Delyse Nash, President & Founder
Mrs. Louise Shelton, Director, Operations
Ms. Teresa Dykzeul, Manager, Recruiting
Mrs. Leah Quist, Manager, Officer & Recruiter
Mr. John Klusendorf, Account Executive
Ms. Diane Hillier, Account Executive
Ms. Marilyn Kanas, Account Executive
Mrs. Simone Roomer, Recruiter
Mr. Roy Bigge, Recruiter
Ms. Courtney Meyer, Recruiter - *Sales*

Salary Minimum: $80,000

Functions: Generalist (All), Senior Mgmt., Middle Mgmt., Finance

Industries: Accounting, HR Services

Nason & Nason

95 Merrick Way Ste 460
Coral Gables, FL 33134-5310
(305) 476-1000
Fax: (305) 372-9959
Email: main@nason-nason.com
Web: www.nason-nason.com

Summary: We are an executive recruiting firm specializing in financial services (banking, brokerage and insurance), as well as finance positions within multi-national corporations.

Key Contact - Specialty:
Mr. Dennis Nason, Managing Partner
Ms. Alexandra Nason-Aymerich, Senior Parnter - *Administration, Banking, Brokerage, Finance*
Mr. Dustin Nason, Senior Parnter - *Asset management, Banking, Finance*

Salary Minimum: $75,000

Functions: Generalist (All), Senior Mgmt., Middle Mgmt., Finance, CFOs, Risk Mgmt.

Industries: Generalist (All), Finance, Banking, Invest. Banking, Brokers, Mutual/Hedge Funds, Misc. Financial, Legal, Accounting, Mgmt. Consulting, Insurance, Property/Facility Mgmt.

Branches:
2875 S Ocean Blvd Ste 200
Palm Beach, FL 33480-5598
(561) 586-9919
Fax: (561) 586-9168
Email: dpinto18@bellsouth.net
Key Contact - Specialty:
Mr. David Pinto, Partner - *Finance*

NaTek Corp

27 Summerfield Ln
Saratoga Springs, NY 12866-5476
(518) 583-0456
Fax: (518) 583-0558
Email: mdillon@natek.com
Web: www.natek.com

Summary: We are an executive search firm specializing in the recruitment of technical professionals. We specialize in mid to upper-level search assignments with Fortune 1000 companies. Our focus covers engineering, operations, sales and all levels of management.

Key Contact - Specialty:
Mr. Mark Dillon, President - *Energy, Engineering, HVAC, Power, Sales*
Mr. Robert Bartone, Vice President, Sales
Mr. John Roche, Senior Recruiter - *Energy, Engineering, Environmental, Management, Sales*

Salary Minimum: $40,000

Functions: Mfg., Materials, Sales & Mktg., Sales Mgmt., HR Mgmt., Engineering

Industries: Energy, Utilities, Construction, Manufacturing, Paper, Drugs Mfg., Medical Devices, Plastics, Rubber, Consumer Elect., Test, Measure Equip., Services, Pharm Svcs., Equip Svcs., Mgmt. Consulting, HR Services, Government, Defense, Packaging, Healthcare

National Bank & Finance Executive Search

(also known as NBF Executive Search Inc)
1749 Via Allena
Oceanside, CA 92056-6216
(760) 630-3400
(760) 518-5857
Fax: (760) 630-2001
Email: bobbie@nbfsearch.com
Web: www.nbfsearch.com

Summary: Our firm specializes in the placement of banking and finance (non-bank) candidates from mid-level positions to CEO/president. Our main focus is commercial finance, asset-based lending, factoring, leasing, mortgage, retail and SBA.

Key Contact - Specialty:
Mr. Wayne Wedderien, Chief Executive Officer
Ms. Bobbie Back Wedderien, President - *Finance, Leasing*
Mr. Jim Farrell, Vice President & General Manager - *Finance*

Salary Minimum: $40,000

Functions: Sales & Mktg., HR Mgmt., Finance, IT, MIS Mgmt., Systems Dev., Attorneys

Industries: Wholesale, Retail, Finance, Banking, Invest. Banking, Venture Cap., Misc. Financial, Accounting, Real Estate

National Career Search

8060 E Gelding Dr Ste 103
Scottsdale, AZ 85260-6960
(480) 483-3968
Fax: (480) 905-0751
Email: ncs@ionet.net
Web: www.nationalcareersearch.com

Summary: We specifically specialize in: home healthcare, home infusion, home medical equipment, home respiratory therapy, hospice, long-term care, medical products, medical supply and medical device industries for manufacturers & distributors. We work on operational, sales, clinical, and financial positions.

Key Contact - Specialty:
Mr. Ben Krawetz, President - *Healthcare*

Functions: Generalist (All), Management, Senior Mgmt., Middle Mgmt., Healthcare, Nurses, Health Admin., Sales & Mktg., Sales Mgmt., Finance

Industries: Generalist (All), Healthcare, Long-term/Home Care

National Corporate Consultants Inc

409 E Cook Rd Ste 200
Fort Wayne, IN 46825-3656
(260) 489-0900
Fax: (260) 489-2699
Email: jcorya@hr-edge.com
Web: www.hr-edge.com

Summary: We are industry-experienced search consultants dedicated to assisting client organizations in identifying, qualifying and attracting managerial, technical and professional talent.

Key Contact - Specialty:
Mr. John Hursh, Managing Consultant
Mr. Tom Theard, Managing Consultant

Salary Minimum: $40,000

Functions: Plant Mgmt., Quality, Materials, Purchasing, Distribution, HR Mgmt., Engineering

Industries: Generalist (All), Manufacturing, Food, Bev., Tobacco, Plastics, Rubber, Metal Products, Motor Vehicles, Electronic, Elec. Components

National Discovery Inc

4 Yacht Club Dr Apt 212
Daphne, AL 36526-7191
(251) 626-7509
Fax: (251) 626-1035
Email: geverton@nationaldiscovery.com
Web: www.nationaldiscovery.com

Summary: We offer employment and job opportunities in the packaging industry.

Key Contact - Specialty:
Mr. Gary Everton, President

Salary Minimum: $60,000

Functions: Plant Mgmt., Packaging

Industries: Paper, Packaging

National Employment Solutions Inc

1635 Higdon Ferry Rd Ste C187
Hot Springs National Park, AR 71913-6913
(501) 455-5988
Email: cjsnes5988@comcast.net

Summary: Our firm focuses on providing the highest quality of support for the job seeker and service for the employer. We specialize in retained and contingency searches primarily working in the placement of individuals who are in sales or sales management. Main industries include banking, consumer products and finance.

Key Contact - Specialty:
Mr. Chris Samuel, President

Salary Minimum: $50,000

Functions: Management, Board Members, Senior Mgmt., Middle Mgmt., Mktg. Mgmt., Sales Mgmt., Sales Reps., Finance

Industries: Generalist (All), Manufacturing, Motor Vehicles, Consumer Goods, Banking

National Engineering Search

2445 NE Division St Ste 303
Bend, OR 97701-3568
(541) 317-4150
Email: nes@nes-llc.com
Web: www.nes-llc.com

Summary: We are a full-service engineering recruiting firm. Primary disciplines include geotechnical, structural, civil, transportation, wastewater, mining and environmental engineering.

Key Contact - Specialty:
Mr. Garry W. Todd, President

Salary Minimum: $55,000

Functions: Generalist (All), Geotechnical

Industries: Engineering Svcs., Environmental Svcs., Haz. Waste

National Executive

305-3200 Dufferin St
North York, ON M6A 3B2
Canada
(416) 256-0300
Fax: (416) 256-0035
Email: resume@national-executive.com
Web: www.national-executive.com

Summary: We specialize in the recruitment and placement of Engineering, Information Technology, and Computer professionals. Permanent and Contract personnel.

Key Contact - Specialty:
Mr. Don Cormier, Partner
Mr. Peter Ferrante, Partner

Salary Minimum: $35,000

Functions: Generalist (All), IT, Engineering

Industries: Manufacturing, Medical Devices, Computer Equip., Test, Measure Equip., Robotics, Semiconductors, Transportation, Retail, Finance, Services, E-commerce, Media, Communications, Telecoms, Defense, Aerospace, Insurance, Software, Biotech/Life Sciences, Healthcare

National Executive Resources Inc

8361 Sangre De Cristo Rd Ste 150
Littleton, CO 80127-4270
(303) 721-7672
(800) 886-7672
Fax: (800) 728-5797
Email: careers04@nerisearch.com
Web: www.nerisearch.com

Summary: The search work performed by our firm has included staff, engineer and management jobs/positions for the manufacturing, primary metals, secondary metals, aluminum, steel, ferrous, non-ferrous, minerals, engineering, mining, cement, aggregates, and chemical processing industries.

Key Contact - Specialty:
Mr. Alan Pike, President

Functions: Generalist (All), Management, Mfg.

Industries: Energy, Utilities, Construction, Manufacturing, Chemicals, Plastics, Rubber, Paints, Petro. Products, Metal Products, Misc. Mfg., Transportation

National Field Service Corp

162 Orange Ave
Suffern, NY 10901-6006
(845) 368-1600
(800) 368-1602
Fax: (845) 368-1989
Email: nfsco@aol.com
Web: www.nfsco.com

Summary: Our firm is a full service company that meets the technical needs of its client corporations. Our firm has placed qualified individuals in the telecom, IT and site acquisition industries and has developed a specialization in telecom requirements for both wire line as well as wireless companies.

Key Contact - Specialty:
Mr. Richard W. Avazian, President
Mr. Floyd Cole, Vice President - *Energy*
Mr. Philip L. Holt, Vice President - *Information Technology, MIS*
Ms. Margaret M. Forman, Secretary & Treasurer - *Administration, Data processing*
Mr. Robert M. Hayward, Director, Personnel & Staffing
Mr. Paul J. Piekara, Director, Telecom Operations
Ms. Lisa Saunders, Manager, Human Resources
Ms. Mary Ann Avazian, Recruiter - *Administration, Clerical*

Functions: MIS Mgmt., Systems Analysis, Systems Dev., Systems Implem., Systems Support, Network Admin., DB Admin., Engineering, Mgmt. Consultants

Industries: Computer Equip., Mgmt. Consulting, HR Services, Telecoms, Software

National Human Resource Group Inc (NHRG Inc)

PO Box 340940
2009 RR 620 N Ste 113
Austin, TX 78734-0016
(512) 328-4448
(888) 373-4810
Fax: (512) 328-1696
Email: info@nhrg.com
Web: www.nhrg.com

Summary: A full-service consulting company with extensive experience in the personnel industry. Our technical services division specializes in the placement of software and hardware engineering professionals.

Key Contact - Specialty:
Mr. Thomas Volick, Senior Vice President - *Computers (Software), Hardware*
Mr. Marc Byers, Recruiter - *Healthcare*

Salary Minimum: $60,000

Functions: Generalist (All), MIS Mgmt., Systems Analysis, Systems Dev., Systems Implem., Systems Support, Network Admin., DB Admin., Specialized Svcs.

Industries: Generalist (All), Computer Equip., Communications, Telecoms, Software

National Metal Services Corp

PO Box 39
Dyer, IN 46311-0039
(219) 322-4664
Fax: (219) 322-2957
Email: ntnlmtl@concentric.net
Web: www.concentric.net/~ntnlmtl

Key Contact - Specialty:
Mr. John V. Penrod, President - *Metals*
Mrs. Suzanne H. Penrod, Secretary & Treasurer
Ms. Eleanor Woods, Office Manager

Salary Minimum: $50,000

Functions: Management, Product Dev., Production, Plant Mgmt., Quality, Productivity, Materials, Purchasing, Mktg. Research, Sales Mgmt.

Industries: Metal Products

National Register Columbus Inc

550 Polaris Pkwy Ste 530
Westerville, OH 43082-7140
(614) 890-1200
Fax: (614) 890-1259
Email: sales@nrcols.com
Web: www.nrcols.com

Summary: We provide broad market sales search in the following areas: telecom, more specifically GAM, NAM, MAR and executive; IT software/hardware/services; medical/pharmaceutical; industrial; office products; publishing; and banking.

Key Contact - Specialty:
Mr. David Molnar, President - *Sales*

Functions: Generalist (All), Sales & Mktg., Sales Mgmt.

Industries: Medical Devices, Computer Equip., Finance, Banking, Services, IT Implementation, Publishing, Communications, Telecoms, Government, Software, Biotech/Life Sciences, Healthcare

National Resources Inc

23679 Calabasas Rd # 785
Calabasas, CA 91302-1502
(818) 703-1994
(818) 871-9603
Email: gene@nationalrecruiting.com
Web: www.nationalrecruiting.com

Summary: One of the areas largest search companies specializing in all disciplines in the IS area. We offer placement of both permanent and contract professionals.

Key Contact - Specialty:
Mr. Gene Jenkins

Salary Minimum: $75,000

Functions: IT, MIS Mgmt.

Industries: Mgmt. Consulting, E-commerce, IT Implementation, Logistics Svcs., Communications, Telecoms, Call Centers, Network Infrastructure, Software, Database SW

National Search Associates

2035 Corte del Nogal Ste 100
Carlsbad, CA 92011-1444
(760) 431-1115
Fax: (760) 431-0660
Email: philp@nsasearch.com
Web: www.nsasearch.com

Summary: We provide executive searches for pharmaceutical, biotechnology, biomedical, software development and telecom industries. Clients range from start-up companies to Fortune 500 corporations. Exceptional references provided.

Key Contact - Specialty:
Mr. Philip Peluso, President - *Biotechnology, Pharmaceutical*
Mr. Richard Cimicata, Vice President - *Biotechnology, Pharmaceutical*

Salary Minimum: $70,000

Functions: Generalist (All), R&D

Industries: Drugs Mfg., Medical Devices, Biotech/Life Sciences

National Search Committee

PO Box 551615
Jacksonville, FL 32255-1615
(904) 448-2000
Fax: (904) 448-2004
Email: nsc@mediaone.net
Web: www.nationalsearchcommittee.com

Summary: We perform retained and contingency search in the fields of finance, accounting, administration and technologies.

Key Contact - Specialty:
Mr. Daniel B. Miller, CPA, President & Chief Executive Officer
Ms. Elisabeth C. Buehler, Firm Administrator

Salary Minimum: $40,000

Functions: Finance, Taxes, IT

Industries: Generalist (All)

National Search Group Inc

800 Kings Hwy N Ste 505
Cherry Hill, NJ 08034-1511
(856) 321-1880
Fax: (856) 321-1244
Email: admin@nationalsearchgroup.com
Web: www.nationalsearchgroup.com

Summary: We are an executive search firm focused on the recruitment and placement of banking and legal professionals. Our recruiters engage in sourcing candidates for existing job orders and marketing services to potential clients.

Key Contact - Specialty:
Mrs. Rachel Evans, Principal

Functions: Legal, Attorneys

Industries: Generalist (All)

National Search Inc

2141 N University Dr Ste 396
Coral Springs, FL 33071-6134
(305) 795-6130
(800) 935-4355
Fax: (305) 675-5879
Email: info@nationalsearch.com
Web: www.nationalsearch.com

Summary: Established recruiting organization specializing in the healthcare and insurance industries, providing cost-effective, location-specific, retained search performance, on a contingency basis.

Key Contact - Specialty:
Mr. Amilcar Arevalo, President
Ms. Gail Colletta, Vice President

Salary Minimum: $40,000

Functions: Generalist (All), Management, Mfg., Healthcare, Sales & Mktg., HR Mgmt., CFOs, Risk Mgmt., Minorities/Diversity, Attorneys

Industries: Generalist (All), Brokers, Insurance, Healthcare

National Search Inc

PO Box 1732
Maple Grove, MN 55311-6732
(763) 420-6913
Fax: (763) 420-6413
Email: info@natlsearch.com
Web: www.natlsearch.com

Summary: Our firm specializes in placing people in the food/consumer packaged goods industry in sales & marketing. Within the food/CPG industry we work in the foodservice, retail and industrial segments. It is our policy to remain the strictest of confidence to all clients and candidates.

Key Contact - Specialty:
Ms. Jill Kitterman, President

Functions: Sales & Mktg., Mktg. Mgmt., Sales Mgmt., Sales Reps.

Industries: Agri., Forestry, Mining, Food, Bev., Tobacco, Soap, Perf., Cosmtcs.

National Staffing by Noelle & Associates

13701 Riverside Dr Ste 707
Sherman Oaks, CA 91423-2449
(818) 907-8660
Fax: (818) 905-1889
Email: info@natlstaffing.com
Web: www.natlstaffing.com

Summary: We specialize in placing medical and dental professionals, for example physicians, physician assistants, nurse practitioners, dentist, hygienists, RDAs and DAs.

Key Contact - Specialty:
Ms. Noelle Lea King, Owner - *Dental*

Functions: Generalist (All), Healthcare, Physicians, Nurses, Allied Health, Health Admin.

Industries: Generalist (All), Healthcare, Hospitals, Dental, Occupational Therapy

National Staffing Group Ltd

PO Box 31002
Independence, OH 44131-0002
(216) 524-7300
Email: kim@nsgl.com
Web: www.nsgl.com

Summary: Retained and contingency search services specializing in the automotive, power transmission, polymer and plastics industries.

Key Contact - Specialty:
Ms. Kim Barnett, President - *Automotive*

Salary Minimum: $50,000

Functions: Senior Mgmt., Middle Mgmt., Product Dev., Production, Plant Mgmt., Quality, Materials Plng., Sales & Mktg., Engineering, Int'l.

Industries: Plastics, Rubber, Metal Products, Machine, Appliance, Motor Vehicles

Nations Executive Recruiters

(also known as Nations Group Inc)
PO Box 5697
Glen Allen, VA 23058-5697
(804) 965-0084
Fax: (804) 965-2092
Email: nationsgroup@msn.com
Web: www.nationsgroupinc.com

Summary: Specializing in C-level sales consultative professionals, web-based knowledge management, digital content integration, senior sales-senior management-top executives, financial services, credit services & banking, database marketing/business intelligence, consumer information/database marketing, CRM, ERP, highly skilled-proven track record candidates, consultative sales/e-commerce, web-based content & online Internet and business development managers & national accounts.

Key Contact - Specialty:
Mr. Don Kirkpatrick, Officer & Senior Consultant - *Business development*

Salary Minimum: $50,000

Functions: Management, Senior Mgmt., Healthcare, Sales & Mktg.

Industries: Finance, Banking, Invest. Banking, Mutual/Hedge Funds, Pharm Svcs., Database SW, Healthcare

Nations Executive Search Group Inc

(also known as NES Group, Inc.)
217 Meadow View Ln
Queenstown, MD 21658-1235
(410) 827-0180
Email: rmilner@nesgroup.net
Web: www.nesgroup.net

Summary: We are a national search and
recruitment service for credit and marketing
technology solutions. Specializing in sales,
marketing, and business development executive
talent.

Key Contact - Specialty:
Mr. Robert B. Milner, Managing Partner -
*Business development, Business to business,
Consumer (Packaged Goods), Credit, Credit
cards*

Salary Minimum: $80,000

Functions: Board Members, Senior Mgmt.,
Middle Mgmt., Sales & Mktg., Mktg. Mgmt.,
Sales Mgmt.

Industries: Misc. Financial, Publishing, Software,
Database SW, Doc. Mgmt., Production SW,
Marketing SW

NationStaff Inc

41 E 11th St Fl 11
New York, NY 10003-4602
(212) 905-6290
Email: info@nationstaff.com
Web: www.nationstaff.com

Summary: Our firm offers executive search and
consulting services to the financial industry. Our
focus is financial technology. We have increased
specialization in online trading, fixed income,
equity, STP and shareholder services. We employ
a variety of search techniques including our
database and most importantly, the personal
network of hundreds of executives placed in the
past.

Key Contact - Specialty:
Mr. Guy Pickrell, Managing Director
Mr. Edward Guy, Managing Director

Salary Minimum: $80,000

Functions: IT, MIS Mgmt.

Industries: Banking, Invest. Banking, Brokers,
Venture Cap., Mutual/Hedge Funds, Misc.
Financial, Mgmt. Consulting, E-commerce, IT
Implementation, Software, Database SW,
Development SW

Nationwide Healthcare Staffing Inc

PO Box 930663
Norcross, GA 30003-0663
(770) 638-0496
Fax: (770) 638-0878
Email: nwhc1019@yahoo.com
Web: www.nwhc1019.com

Summary: Ours is a physician search and
placement firm. Clients and Candidates are treated
like royalty. We listen first ... before going to
work. Our goal is to achieve a balanced match for
Clients and Candidates. We are in the business to
provide medical facilities and health systems with
excellent skilled physicians who also possess an
agreeable nature.

Key Contact - Specialty:
Mr. Dee Russell, Director

Functions: Healthcare

Industries: Services, Mgmt. Consulting, HR
Services, Healthcare, Hospitals, Long-
term/Home Care, Physical Therapy,
Occupational Therapy

Nationwide Personnel Group

474 Elmwood Ave
Buffalo, NY 14222-2014
(716) 881-2144
Fax: (716) 881-0711
Email: gademsky@localnet.com
Web: www.nationwidepersonnel.com

Summary: We recruit and place computer and
engineering personnel with companies. Our
corporate clients range from Fortune 50 to small,
closely held and entrepreneurial. We are often
quoted in national publications as an authority on
the technical job market and frequently invited to
speak on career opportunities, interviewing and
resume preparation.

Key Contact - Specialty:
Mr. Mark Gademsky, CPC, President

Salary Minimum: $40,000

Functions: Generalist (All), Product Dev.,
Automation, IT, R&D, Engineering, Mgmt.
Consultants

Industries: Generalist (All), Non-Classifiable

Nationwide Personnel Placement Inc

PO Box 206
Loveland, OH 45140-0206
(513) 677-1998
Fax: (513) 683-9163
Email: moose-kopko@msn.com
Web:
www.angelfire.com/biz/personnel/index.html

Summary: Our principal has extensive years of
industrial experience in nine different firms,
including three Fortune 500 firms and many years
in the recruiting business, therefore he knows both
sides of the recruiting and placement business.

Key Contact - Specialty:
Mr. K. Michael Gowetski, President

Salary Minimum: $20,000

Functions: Generalist (All)

Industries: Generalist (All)

Nationwide Personnel Recruiting & Consulting Inc

20834 SW Martinazzi Ave
Tualatin, OR 97062-6318
(503) 692-4925
Fax: (503) 692-6764
Email: barbarab@barbara-nprc.com
Web: www.barbara-nprc.com

Summary: We are executive search specialists
serving the industrial marketplace in process
control engineering, sales, chemical,
environmental, automation, HMI, quality, sales
and mid to upper-level management.

Key Contact - Specialty:
Ms. Barbara A. Bodle, President - *High
technology, Instrumentation*
Mr. Darryl Bodle, Chief Financial Officer

Salary Minimum: $60,000

Functions: Generalist (All), Board Members,
Senior Mgmt., Middle Mgmt., Production,
Quality, Sales Mgmt., Engineering

Industries: Generalist (All), Chemicals, Test,
Measure Equip., Misc. Mfg.

Navigator Resources

64 E Uwchlan Ave Ste 236
Exton, PA 19341-1203
(610) 640-1300
Fax: (610) 640-1333
Email: rsrolis@navigatorresources.com
Web: www.navigatorresources.com

Summary: Our firm provides executive search and
related services to customers across a wide variety
of industries. We distinguish ourselves through
extraordinary responsiveness to our customers'
needs, through our energy and focus and through
the combined experience that we bring to each
assignment. Please allow us to demonstrate what
this difference can mean to you.

Key Contact - Specialty:
Mr. Robert B. Srolis, President & Chief
Executive Officer - *Financial services,
Healthcare, Managed care*

Functions: Generalist (All)

Industries: Drugs Mfg., Finance, Services, Pharm
Svcs., Mgmt. Consulting, Insurance,
Biotech/Life Sciences, Healthcare

Navin Group

200 Cordwainer Dr Ste 100
Norwell, MA 02061-1671
(781) 871-6770
(888) 837-1300
Fax: (781) 878-8703
Email: search@navingroup.com
Web: www.navingroup.com

Summary: Our firm does healthcare recruiting in
the provider, software vendor, and information
technology, and consulting marketplace.

Key Contact - Specialty:
Mr. John Haffty, President - *Consulting,
Healthcare, MIS, Operations*
Mr. Douglas MacLean, Vice President
Mr. Ken Shapiro, Recruiter
Ms. Melinda Morton, Recruiter, Clinical
Operations
Mr. Larry Guay, Recruiter
Mr. Scott Harrison, Recruiter
Ms. Sarah Gill, Recruiter
Ms. Carla Abate, Recruiter
Mr. Tony Kubica, Recruiter - *Clinical,
Operations*
Mr. Mercer VandenBurg, Recruiter - *Accounting,
Engineering, Executives, Labor, Manufacturing*

Functions: Generalist (All), Physicians, Nurses,
Allied Health, Health Admin., Sales Mgmt.

Industries: Generalist (All), Mgmt. Consulting,
Software, Healthcare

NCC Executive Search Consultants

(a subsidiary of National Careers Corp)
111 E Arrellaga St.
Santa Barbara, CA 93101-1903
(805) 963-0433
(800) 622-0431
Fax: (805) 730-1689
Email: resumes@nccx.com
Web: www.nccx.com

Summary: We offer full search service with
emphasis on senior technical and executive search.
Our firm specializes in senior staff and
management in high technology, software,
internet, biotechnology, financial, insurance,
healthcare, pharmaceutical/biotechnology, medical
devices, engineering and sales & marketing.

Key Contact - Specialty:
Mr. Gary Kravetz, Chief Executive Officer
Mr. Thom Henderson, Technical & Executive
    Recruiter - *Computers, Computers (Software),*
    Engineering, High technology, Sales
Ms. Nancy Speer, Senior Healthcare RN &
    Manager Recruiter - *Healthcare, Management*
Ms. Jill t'Sas, Dialysis RN & Executive Recruiter
    - *Executives, Healthcare, Medical (Devices)*
Ms. Lydia Cole, Senior Engineering Recruiter -
    Medical (Devices), Photonics, RF microwave,
    Semiconductors, Technical (Management)
Mr. Lonna Milton, Admin, Legal, Accounting,
    Exec Recruiter - *Accounting, Administration,*
    Banking, Executives, Insurance
Ms. Mary Lou Kravetz, Vice President, Research
    & Admin
Ms. Jeannine Serbanich, Controller

Salary Minimum: $40,000

Functions: Generalist (All)

Industries: Generalist (All)

Branches:
4601 Telephone Rd Ste 111
Ventura, CA 93003-5671
(805) 677-1680
(800) 639-3640
Fax: (805) 639-2015
Email: vs2@nccx.com
Key Contact - Specialty:
Ms. Dixie Vargas, Manager

NDB Associates Inc
1000 Grandview Ave Apt 904
Mount Washington, PA 15211-1357
(412) 488-0208
Fax: (412) 488-0207
Email: ndb1@ndbassociates.com

Summary: Our focus is cross-disciplinary,
integrated communications management within
the advertising and marketing sectors. Our agency
and individual service is grounded in
professionalism, integrity and discretion. The
director, possessing extensive agency account
management and corporate product marketing
experience, personally manages our firm.

Key Contact - Specialty:
Ms. Nancy Dolan-Brady, Director - *Advertising,*
    Marketing

Salary Minimum: $40,000

Functions: Management, Senior Mgmt., Middle
    Mgmt., Advertising, Mktg. Research, Mktg.
    Mgmt., Direct Mktg., PR, Graphic Designers

Industries: Generalist (All), Media, Advertising,
    New Media

NDS Associates Ltd
2774 S Ocean Blvd Apt 211
Palm Beach, FL 33480-5522
(561) 202-0968
Fax: (561) 282-3302
Email: nelson@ndsassoc.com
Web: www.ndsassoc.com

Summary: Global recruitment for the printed
circuit board manufacturing industry and related
supplier companies. General management, sales
management, marketing, product management,
quality control management and engineering.

Key Contact - Specialty:
Mr. Nelson Silverstein, President
Ms. Sue Kornfeld, Director, Recruitment

Salary Minimum: $75,000

Functions: Management, Middle Mgmt., Product
    Dev., Production, Quality, Sales & Mktg., Sales
    Mgmt., Engineering, Int'l.

Industries: Electronic, Elec. Components

Don Neal & Associates
2016 W Highway 66
Stroud, OK 74079-2801
(918) 968-2568
(800) 359-3990
Fax: (918) 968-2121
Email: dneal@brightok.net
Web: www.donneal.com

Summary: Our firm searches in the areas of
commercial bank, loan review, risk analysis,
underwriting, credit, compliance and agribusiness
credit review and relationship management.

Key Contact - Specialty:
Mr. Don Neal, President
Ms. Sharon Lawrence, Administrative Assistant -
    Banking (Commercial)

Salary Minimum: $65,000

Functions: Management, Middle Mgmt., Credit

Industries: Banking, Misc. Financial

Neal Management Inc
450 7th Ave Ste 923
New York, NY 10123-0101
(212) 686-1686
Fax: (212) 686-1590
Email: info@nealmanagement.com
Web: www.nealmanagement.com

Summary: We are a unique recruiting firm
specializing in the placement of high caliber
accounting and financial professionals geared
towards the financial service industry. We are a
market leader in permanent, long term consulting
and temp staffing.

Key Contact - Specialty:
Mr. Peter Tannenbaum, President
Mr. Howard Gold, Senior Recruiter
Mr. Steven Gordon, Senior Recruiter

Salary Minimum: $50,000

Functions: Management, Finance, Budgeting,
    Cash Mgmt.

Industries: Generalist (All), Finance, Banking,
    Invest. Banking, Brokers, Venture Cap.,
    Mutual/Hedge Funds, Accounting

Nelson & Associates
PO Box 2686
Kirkland, WA 98083-2686
(425) 823-0956
Email: nelson@foodrecruiter.com
Web: www.foodrecruiter.com

Summary: We are a consulting firm specializing
in the food manufacturing industry. We make it
our business to have a unique awareness of people
and activity that will benefit you.

Key Contact - Specialty:
Mr. Ken Nelson, Owner

Functions: Generalist (All), Board Members

Industries: Food, Bev., Tobacco

Beverly Nelson & Associates Inc
3187 Quiet Hills Dr Ste 200
Escondido, CA 92029-7305
(760) 480-8900
Fax: (760) 480-8973

Summary: We are an executive search firm
specializing in the placement of all levels of
personnel in the property/casualty insurance field
only.

Key Contact - Specialty:
Ms. Beverly M. Nelson, Owner

Salary Minimum: $40,000

Functions: Management, Technicians

Industries: Insurance, Casualty

Len Nelson & Associates Inc
11830 Greenwood Village Dr
San Antonio, TX 78249-3024
(210) 690-9191
Fax: (210) 690-3020
Email: lennelson@lensjobs.com
Web: www.lensjobs.com

Summary: Our firm works with other affiliates
and can market people in any location they prefer.

Key Contact - Specialty:
Mr. Len Nelson, President - *Computers*
    (Software), Electronics, Hardware,
    Manufacturing, Telecommunications

Salary Minimum: $30,000

Functions: Mfg., Product Dev., Production,
    Automation, Quality, Productivity, Materials,
    Materials Plng., Engineering,
    Minorities/Diversity

Industries: Medical Devices, Plastics, Rubber,
    Metal Products, Machine, Appliance, Motor
    Vehicles, Computer Equip., Telecoms, Defense,
    Aerospace, Packaging, Software

Nelson-McKay & Associates
(a division of Indika Inc)
3700 S Russell St Ste B110
Missoula, MT 59801-8759
(406) 542-4700
Fax: (406) 542-6602
Email: manschutz@nelsoncompanies.net.
Web: www.nelson-mckay.com

Summary: We are professional executive
recruiting search firm committed to excellence.
We enjoy a reputation for fairness, diligence and
ethical behavior. We emphasize developing long-
term relationships and partnerships with our
clients.

Key Contact - Specialty:
Mr. Gary Nelson, Owner
Mrs. Lynne Nelson, CSP, Owner - *Marketing,*
    Middle management, Sales, Staffing, Temporary
Mr. Dustin Harner, CSP, PEC - *Computers*
    (Networking), Legal, Office (Administration),
    Staffing, Temporary

Salary Minimum: $24,000

Functions: Generalist (All), Senior Mgmt., Mfg.,
    Distribution, Finance

Industries: Generalist (All), Agri., Forestry,
    Mining, Manufacturing, Food, Bev., Tobacco,
    Lumber, Furniture, Paper, Drugs Mfg., Medical
    Devices, Plastics, Rubber, Misc. Mfg.,
    Electronic, Elec. Components, Wholesale,
    Retail, Services, Legal, Accounting, Logistics
    Svcs., Communications, Networking, Comm.
    SW, Hospitals

NESCO Search
6140 Parkland Blvd
Mayfield Heights, OH 44124-6142
(440) 461-6000
Fax: (440) 449-3111
Email: webmaster@nescoresource.com
Web: www.nescoresource.com

Summary: Our forte is technical search. Sixty
percent of our business is in the engineering field
and 40 percent is in the IT industry.

Key Contact - Specialty:
J. Sarnese, Administrator

Salary Minimum: $40,000

Functions: Generalist (All), Middle Mgmt., Product Dev., Production, Automation, Plant Mgmt., IT, Engineering

Industries: Generalist (All), Plastics, Rubber, Metal Products, Machine, Appliance, Motor Vehicles, Consumer Elect., Misc. Mfg., Packaging

Net-Tel Search
40 Gardenville Pkwy W Ste 101
Buffalo, NY 14224-1387
(716) 824-5494
(866) 651-8377
Email: jobs@net-telsearch.com
Web: www.net-telsearch.com/

Summary: We are a national search firm specializing in telecom/networking/IT since 1980. We provide the best available candidates, both perm and contract, from technicians, analysts, engineers, architects to Sr level mgmt. Our client base is both end-users and vendors across many industries, including healthcare, manufacturing, banking, insurance, VARs, Interconnects, Telco companies, network service providers, cable, etc. Our firm president has always believed in the concept that "everyone wins"! Honesty, integrity, quality searches, and professionalism are what we offer.

Key Contact - Specialty:
Mr. Paul Sacca, President

Salary Minimum: $35,000

Functions: Senior Mgmt., Mktg. Research, Mktg. Mgmt., MIS Mgmt., Network Admin.

Industries: IT Implementation, Communications, Telecoms, Call Centers, Digital, Wireless, Fiber Optic, Network Infrastructure, RF/Microwave, Database SW, Development SW, ERP SW, Industry Specific SW, Networking, Comm. SW, Security SW, System SW

Netsoft
2727 Walsh Ave Ste 101
Santa Clara, CA 95051-0956
(408) 562-2080
Email: admin@netsoftsearch.com
Web: www.netsoftsearch.com

Summary: We service network infrastructure startups. Specializing in engineering, sales & marketing, and individual contributor to VP. We do not place entry-level positions.

Key Contact - Specialty:
Mr. Eric Thoreson, Co-Founder
Mr. Randy Prout, Co-Founder
Mr. Rick Raimondi, Managing Director, S California Ops

Salary Minimum: $60,000

Functions: Middle Mgmt., Product Dev., Mktg. Mgmt., Sales Mgmt., Engineering, Hardware, Systems

Industries: Semiconductors, Communications, Telecoms, Telephony, Digital, Wireless, Fiber Optic, Network Infrastructure, RF/Microwave, Database SW, Development SW, Doc. Mgmt., Production SW, Networking, Comm. SW, Security SW, System SW

Network Builders LLC
520 Kirkland Way Ste 202
Kirkland, WA 98033-6256
(425) 814-6121
Fax: (425) 650-7111
Email: inquiries@network-builders.com
Web: www.network-builders.com

Summary: We are an executive search firm that specializes in the search and placement of executive sales and sales management. Markets include: software applications, content management, business intelligence, eCommerce, internet, data storage, hardware, networking/security, telecom and system integration.

Key Contact - Specialty:
Mr. Doug Simonson, Founder

Functions: Sales & Mktg.

Industries: Media, Communications, Wireless, Software, Database SW, Development SW, ERP SW, Networking, Comm. SW, Security SW, System SW

The Network Corporate Search Personnel Inc
310-505 8 Ave SW
Shaw Building
Calgary, AB T2P 1G2
Canada
(403) 262-6630
(888) 262-2212
Fax: (403) 262-5150
Email: info@networksearch.net
Web: www.networksearch.net

Summary: A talented group of dynamic recruiters committed to servicing the IT and general insurance marketplace in a professional manner.

Key Contact - Specialty:
Ms. Pat Riddell, President
Ms. Kim McKay, Vice President

Salary Minimum: $40,000

Functions: IT

Industries: Insurance, Software

Network Dynamics Enterprises Inc
157 Fieldstone Dr
Morganville, NJ 07751-2048
(800) 677-5634
Email: walter@networkdynamics.com
Web: www.networkdynamics.com

Summary: We are a permanent placement executive search firm specializing in the placement of executive management, experienced sales executives and technical sales candidates. We service the software and technology services industry.

Key Contact - Specialty:
Mr. Mark O'Brien, Founder
Mr. Walter Zem, Managing Partner, Owner

Salary Minimum: $90,000

Functions: Senior Mgmt., Sales & Mktg., Sales Mgmt., Sales Reps., Systems Implem.

Industries: E-commerce, IT Implementation, PSA/ASP, Supply Chain Mgmt, Software, Accounting SW, Database SW, Development SW, ERP SW, HR SW, Mfg. SW, Marketing SW, Networking, Comm. SW, Security SW, System SW

Network Search Inc
1495 Yarmouth Ave
Boulder, CO 80304-0672
(303) 444-1714
Fax: (303) 440-3408
Email: info@networksearchinc.com
Web: www.networksearchinc.com

Summary: Specialize in high-technology start-ups, R&D, engineers.

Key Contact - Specialty:
Mr. Russell Agee, President

Salary Minimum: $65,000

Functions: Generalist (All), Board Members, Middle Mgmt., Systems Analysis, Systems Dev., Systems Implem., Network Admin., Engineering

Industries: Generalist (All), Aerospace, Software

Netzearch Consulting Inc
2831 N Oakland Forest Dr Apt 208
Oakland Park, FL 33309-6450
(954) 677-9492
Email: info@netzearch.com
Web: www.netzearch.com

Summary: Executive Search Services - We will help you attract and retain the top talent in your industry. We work with firms in a variety of industries including accounting & finance, information technology, sales, and sales management. Specialty area: Litigation Technology Solutions

Key Contact - Specialty:
Mr. David A. Netzer, Founder

Salary Minimum: $75,000

Functions: Sales & Mktg.

Industries: Legal, Accounting, HR Services, E-commerce, Network Infrastructure, Database SW, Doc. Mgmt., Production SW, ERP SW, Industry Specific SW

New Dimensions in Technology Inc
85 Lafayette St
Salem, MA 01970-3620
(978) 744-1010
Fax: (978) 7441011
Email: bk@ndt.com
Web: www.ndt.com

Summary: Our firm services early stage start-ups, mid-size and Global 2000 companies in need of technology and techno-business professionals. We specialize in the permanent placement of professionals in the areas of: software/hardware, IT, marketing/business development, consulting, and professional services.

Key Contact - Specialty:
Ms. Beverly A. Kahn, Founder & President - *Computers (Software), Defense, E-business, Engineering, Executives*
Mr. Laurence S. Kahn, Vice President, Recruiting - *Computers (Software), Consulting, Consumer (Marketing), E-business, Marketing*

Salary Minimum: $60,000

Functions: Generalist (All), Product Dev.

Industries: Finance, Mgmt. Consulting, IT Implementation, Defense, Homeland Security, Insurance, Software, Database SW, Development SW, Entertainment SW, ERP SW, Marketing SW, Networking, Comm. SW, Biotech/Life Sciences, Healthcare

New Level Partners LLC
182 Nassau St Ste 203
Princeton, NJ 08542-7000
(609) 430-2400
Fax: (609) 430-2288
Email: myfuture@newlevelpartners.com
Web: www.newlevelpartners.com

Summary: Engaged in executive search and HR consulting for selected industries. Specialize in difficult to find and quick turnaround assignments. Creative fee arrangements. Partners have senior level experience in both line and staff positions.

Key Contact - Specialty:
Mr. Mike McClellan, Partner

Mr. Bill Harwood, Partner
Ms. Nancy Langton, Partner

Salary Minimum: $60,000

Functions: Generalist (All)

Industries: Paper, Consumer Goods, Finance, Non-profits, Call Centers, Insurance, Casualty, Claims, Commercial, Re-Insurance

Newcomb-Desmond & Associates Inc

PO Box 201
Milford, OH 45150-0201
(513) 831-9522
Email: nda1@earthlink.net
Web: www.newcombdesmond.com

Summary: We are an aggressive national recruiting firm, broad client base, all resumes welcome. We work with management & executives in engineering & manufacturing, sale & marketing, human resources, finance and technology area.

Key Contact - Specialty:
Mr. Mike Desmond, President & Chief Operating Officer - *Information Technology, Manufacturing*
Mr. Dave Bash, Senior Recruiter - *Accounting, Finance, Financial services*

Salary Minimum: $45,000

Functions: Management, Middle Mgmt.

Industries: Manufacturing, Metal Products, Machine, Appliance, Motor Vehicles, Misc. Mfg., Engineering Svcs., Logistics Svcs., Aerospace, Packaging, Insurance, Software, System SW, Healthcare

Newman Hawkins Legal Search

31017 Westwood Rd
Farmington Hills, MI 48331-1469
(248) 661-8900
Fax: (248) 661-9018
Email: info@newmanhawkins.com
Web: www.newmanhawkins.com

Summary: Firm specializes in attorney placement. President practiced litigation at a prestigious law firm. We work with corporations and law firms to satisfy all attorney-hiring needs.

Key Contact - Specialty:
Ms. Nancy L. Newman, JD, President

Functions: Attorneys

Industries: Legal

Newman-Johnson-King Inc

PO Box 729
Rockport, TX 78381-0729
(361) 790-5959
Fax: (361) 790-5391
Email: jack@njksearch.com
Web: www.njksearch.com

Summary: Our firm has an extensive history of ethical, professional, effective service to firms and candidates. Concentration in the engineering disciplines involved in the petrochemical/oil & gas industry and IT and services arena.

Key Contact - Specialty:
Mr. Jack King, President - *Engineering, Manufacturing, Sales*

Salary Minimum: $40,000

Functions: Mfg., IT, R&D, Engineering

Industries: Generalist (All)

Newport Management

100 E Hartsdale Ave
Hartsdale, NY 10530-3207
(914) 725-5244
Email: newport@att.net

Summary: Specialize in sales, sales management, marketing and tech support in computer hardware, software and networking.

Key Contact - Specialty:
Mr. Kenneth Zeif, President

Salary Minimum: $50,000

Functions: Sales & Mktg., Sales Mgmt.

Industries: Computer Equip., Software

Newport Strategic Search Inc

332 Encinitas Blvd Ste 200
Encinitas, CA 92024-8706
(760) 944-1610
Fax: (760) 944-0075
Email: hr@newportsearch.com
Web: www.newportsearch.com

Summary: We are an executive search firm with divisions specializing in accounting & finance positions in various industries, and in real estate development, emphasizing both the production homebuilding and land development disciplines.

Key Contact - Specialty:
Mr. John Fitzpatrick, President - *Accounting (Big 4), Administration, Human resources, Interior design, Senior management*

Salary Minimum: $60,000

Functions: Generalist (All), Senior Mgmt., Healthcare, Finance, CFOs, Bldg. Contractors

Industries: Generalist (All), Construction, Accounting, HR Services, Healthcare

Next Iteration

426 Mahogany Walk
Newtown, PA 18940-4212
(888) 463-9848
(215) 579-1751
Fax: (215) 579-0578
Email: info@nextiteration.net
Web: www.nextiteration.net

Summary: Our firm provides human capital consulting and recruiting services in healthcare - physicians, nurses, allied health and medical system executive market segments in addition to serving the lifescience, biotech and pharmaceutical markets.

Key Contact - Specialty:
Lynden Kidd, President & Managing Partner
Mr. Jeffrey Marcinowski, MBA, Chief Operating Officer

Salary Minimum: $60,000

Functions: Management, Senior Mgmt., Middle Mgmt., Quality, Productivity, Healthcare, Physicians, Nurses, Allied Health, Health Admin.

Industries: Chemicals, Drugs Mfg., Medical Devices, Consumer Goods, Non-profits, Pharm Svcs., Legal, Mgmt. Consulting, HR Services, Biotech/Life Sciences, Healthcare, Hospitals, Women's

Next Step Group Inc

13990 Craig Way
Broomfield, CO 80020-6056
(303) 635-0101
Fax: (800) 867-0713
Email: info@4nextstep.com
Web: www.4nextstep.com

Summary: Specializing in placing senior sales and sales management professionals.

Key Contact - Specialty:
Mr. Glenn S. Davis, President - *Computers (Sales,Software), Consulting, CRM, ERP*
Mr. Jeffrey Spangler, Partner

Salary Minimum: $60,000

Functions: Management, Board Members, Sales & Mktg., Sales Mgmt., HR Mgmt., Training, IT, MIS Mgmt., Systems Implem., Systems Support

Industries: Brokers, Services, Mgmt. Consulting, HR Services, E-commerce, IT Implementation, Wireless, Software, ERP SW, Marketing SW, Training SW, Biotech/Life Sciences

Marc Nichols Associates Inc

205 Lexington Ave Fl 9
New York, NY 10016-6022
(212) 725-1750
Fax: (212) 725-1790
Email: basmoore@mna.com
Web: www.mna.com

Summary: Our firm includes 15 specialists, two generalists and a large research staff. Our departments include: banking, brokerage, investments, capital, emerging markets, MIS, accounting, EDP audit, marketing, sales, HR, compliance, telecom, and tax.

Key Contact - Specialty:
Mr. Marc Nichols, Senior Parnter
Mr. Bill Moore, Senior Parnter
Mr. Brian Gress, Vice President

Salary Minimum: $75,000

Functions: Management, Senior Mgmt., Middle Mgmt., Sales & Mktg., HR Mgmt., Finance, Taxes, Risk Mgmt., Mgmt. Consultants, Int'l.

Industries: Generalist (All), Finance, Banking, Invest. Banking, Brokers, Venture Cap., Misc. Financial, Services, IT Implementation, Telephony, Insurance, Accounting SW, HR SW, Marketing SW, Networking, Comm. SW

Ira Z Nitzberg

PO Box 60
Granite Springs, NY 10527-0060
(914) 245-9070
Fax: (914) 245-3743
Email: execrecruiter@bigfoot.com

Summary: We provide recruitment of data processing, healthcare and medical professionals in management, development and implementation in both the user and vendor environments. In the vendor environment we also place sales, marketing and support personnel.

Key Contact - Specialty:
Mr. Ira Z. Nitzberg, CDP, Owner
Ms. Shelly Heller, Senior Consultant

Functions: Generalist (All), Middle Mgmt., Physicians, Mktg. Mgmt., MIS Mgmt., Systems Analysis, Systems Dev., Mgmt. Consultants

Industries: Generalist (All), Drugs Mfg., Computer Equip., Pharm Svcs., Mgmt. Consulting, Telecoms, Network Infrastructure, Software, Database SW, Development SW, Marketing SW, Networking, Comm. SW, Security SW, System SW, Biotech/Life Sciences, Healthcare, Hospitals

J L Nixon Consulting Inc

3846 County Road 1147
Celeste, TX 75423-3528
(903) 568-4111
Fax: (206) 984-3804
Email: recruiters@jlnixon.com
Web: www.jlnixon.com

Summary: We are full service personnel consulting and executive search firm dedicated to the search and recruitment of professionals in the insurance and managed care industry. As industry specialists in property/casualty, life, accident & health insurance and managed care, our organization provides the most comprehensive array of services in the search business.

Key Contact - Specialty:
Mr. Jeffrey L. Nixon, CPC, President - *Brokerage, Insurance, Insurance (Casualty,Claims,Reinsurance)*

Salary Minimum: $45,000

Functions: Generalist (All)

Industries: Insurance, Casualty, Claims, Life, Commercial, Re-Insurance

NL Associates Inc
36 Mill Plain Rd Ste 211
Danbury, CT 06811-5111
(203) 744-3800
Fax: (203) 744-7100
Email: neil@nlassociates.com
Web: www.nlassociates.com

Summary: We place sales and marketing professionals nationally. Our client list includes many of the top fortune 1000 companies. We utilize special methods that allow us to find the right "fit" benefiting, both employee and employer.

Key Contact - Specialty:
Mr. Neil Liguori, President - *Sales*

Salary Minimum: $50,000

Functions: Board Members, Middle Mgmt., Sales & Mktg., Mktg. Mgmt., Sales Mgmt.

Industries: Generalist (All)

Branches:
25 Sunswept Dr
New Fairfield, CT 06812-4630
(203) 746-6060
Fax: (203) 746-5433
Email: neil@nlassociates.com
Key Contact - Specialty:
Mr. Erik Liguori
Ms. Susan Liguori

Noble & Associates Inc
444 E 75th St Apt 8B
New York, NY 10021-3444
(212) 838-7020
Fax: (888) 291-6496
Email: nobleinc@inch.com

Summary: Our firm specializes in marketing, advertising and corporate communications, including: direct marketing, product management, sports marketing, public relations, research, advertising account management, sales promotion, creative, new business, media, database marketing, general management and international.

Key Contact - Specialty:
Mr. Donald Noble, Principal

Salary Minimum: $50,000

Functions: Generalist (All)

Industries: Consumer Goods, Media, Advertising, New Media, Communications, Packaging

The Nolan Group
100 Pringle Ave Ste 250
Walnut Creek, CA 94596-7364
(925) 938-6700
Fax: (925) 938-7740
Email: resumes@thenolangroup.com
Web: www.thenolangroup.com

Summary: Executive search and consulting for accounting and finance professionals. Concentration at the controller, CFO and VP levels. IA, SOX, Treasury, SEC.

Key Contact - Specialty:
Ms. Nancy C. Nolan, President

Salary Minimum: $60,000

Functions: Generalist (All), Board Members, Middle Mgmt., Finance, CFOs, Budgeting, Cash Mgmt., M&A

Industries: Generalist (All), Construction, Manufacturing, Food, Bev., Tobacco, Drugs Mfg., Medical Devices, Retail, Finance, Misc. Financial, Accounting, Supply Chain Mgmt., Software, Accounting SW, Biotech/Life Sciences

Noll Human Resource Services
12905 W Dodge Rd
Noll Human Resources Building
Omaha, NE 68154-2145
(402) 334-9200
(800) 798-7736
Fax: (402) 334-7333
Email: bill@noll.com
Web: www.nolljobs.com

Summary: Experienced high integrity recruiters who get the job done in virtually every area of executive search.

Key Contact - Specialty:
Mr. William T. Noll, CPC, President
Ms. Peggy Noll, Recruiter - *Logistics, Retail, Sales*

Functions: Generalist (All), Packaging, Staffing

Industries: Generalist (All), Construction, Food, Bev., Tobacco, Banking, Architectural Svcs., Accounting, Engineering Svcs., Packaging, Insurance, Healthcare, Dental

Norgate Technology Inc
170 Old Country Rd Ste 311
Mineola, NY 11501-4310
(516) 248-0444
Fax: (516) 248-0488
Email: info@norgate.com
Web: www.norgate.com

Summary: Our firm provides technical search and recruiting of programmers and systems administrators specializing in Internet and client/server technologies. Java, UNIX/Solaris/HP-UX/AIX, Windows NT, object oriented technology, C++, Oracle, SQL Server, Sybase and DB2.

Key Contact - Specialty:
Mr. Lawrence J. Cohen, President - *Internet*

Salary Minimum: $35,000

Functions: Generalist (All), IT, MIS Mgmt., Systems Analysis, Systems Dev., Systems Implem., Systems Support, Network Admin., DB Admin.

Industries: Generalist (All), Finance, Software, Database SW, Development SW, Networking, Comm. SW

Normyle/Erstling Health Search Group
350 W Passaic St
Rochelle Park, NJ 07662-3073
(201) 843-6009
Fax: (201) 843-2060
Email: nehsg@medpharmsales.com
Web: www.medpharmsales.com

Summary: We recruit exclusively for sales reps, sales managers, marketing, and clinical specialists

for the pharmaceutical and medical device industries. We are professional, confidential and connected.

Key Contact - Specialty:
Mr. Charles D. Kreps, Managing Partner - *Biotechnology, Medical, Medical (Devices,Sales), Sales*
Ms. Janet Johnson, Recruiter - *Biotechnology, Medical (Devices,Sales), Pharmaceutical, Sales*
Ms. Helene Peck, Recruiter - *Biotechnology, Medical (Devices,Sales), Pharmaceutical, Sales*
Ms. Kelley Gray, Recruiter - *Home health, Medical (Devices,Sales), Pharmaceutical, Sales*
Ms. Terry Spiegel, Recruiter - *Biopharmaceutical, Biotechnology, Pharmaceutical, Sales*
Ms. Jan Post, Recruiter - *Biopharmaceutical, Biotechnology, Medical (Devices,Sales), Pharmaceutical*

Salary Minimum: $50,000

Functions: Healthcare, Nurses, Sales & Mktg., Mktg. Research, Mktg. Mgmt., Sales Mgmt., Sales Reps.

Industries: Drugs Mfg., Medical Devices, Pharm Svcs., Biotech/Life Sciences, Healthcare, Hospitals, Long-term/Home Care, Dental, Physical Therapy, Women's

Ronald Norris & Associates
8457 E Prairie Rd
Skokie, IL 60076-2809
(847) 679-6074

Summary: We have extensive experience in the concentration of equipment finance/leasing, asset base lending, and bank commercial lending.

Key Contact - Specialty:
Mr. Ronald Norris, Owner - *Leasing*

Salary Minimum: $25,000

Functions: Generalist (All), Middle Mgmt., Sales Mgmt., Credit

Industries: Generalist (All), Banking, Equip Svcs.

John B Norris & Associates Inc
PO Box 2068
Westminster, MD 21158-7058
(410) 876-0782
Fax: (410) 876-5551
Email: john@jbnorris.com
Web: www.jbnorris.com

Summary: A commitment to provide an acceptable candidate within four to six working days after placing a job order.

Key Contact - Specialty:
Mr. John B. Norris

Salary Minimum: $30,000

Functions: Generalist (All), Management, Mfg., Sales & Mktg., HR Mgmt., Finance, R&D, Engineering, Int'l.

Industries: Generalist (All), Food, Bev., Tobacco

Norris Agency
6112 Oakcrest Rd
Dallas, TX 75248-3853
(972) 701-0110
(888) 327-6971
Fax: (972) 701-0613
Email: headhunt@norrisagency.com

Summary: Certified personnel consultant. Executive searches within the food, beverage and consumer packaged goods industries.

Key Contact - Specialty:
Ms. Cathy A. Norris, CPC, Owner & Recruiter - *Science*

Salary Minimum: $60,000

Functions: Board Members, Senior Mgmt., Middle Mgmt., Product Dev., Quality, R&D

Industries: Food, Bev., Tobacco, Soap, Perf., Cosmtcs., Consumer Goods

NorTech Resources

86 Brookline Ave
Albany, NY 12203-1807
(518) 438-0111
Fax: (518) 438-0006
Email: info@nortechresources.com
Web: www.nortechresources.com

Summary: Our firm serves suppliers to: the adhesives, coatings, radiation curing, fine chemicals, thermoset polymer, pharmaceutical, and medical device industries; via contingency and retained searches for: chemists, chemical engineers, manufacturing managers, technical managers, technical service and sales & marketing people.

Key Contact - Specialty:
Mr. Michael T. Fahey, General Manager
Ms. Alexandra Itov, Administrative Assistant

Salary Minimum: $60,000

Functions: Management, Mfg., Product Dev., Sales & Mktg.

Industries: Printing, Chemicals, Soap, Perf., Cosmtcs., Drugs Mfg., Medical Devices, Plastics, Rubber, Paints, Petro. Products, Biotech/Life Sciences

North Coast Meridian Inc

PO Box 640
Pine Bush, NY 12566-0640
(585) 261-9053
Fax: (216) 274-9302
Email: ncmrecruiters@fcc.net
Web: www.ncmrecruiters.com

Summary: Technical recruiters specializing in manufacturing engineering, industrial engineering, process engineering and related disciplines. Operations and plant management, materials and logistics management, quality assurance and related. Contingency and retained search.

Key Contact - Specialty:
Mr. Charles F. Thomaschek, Recruiter - *Engineering, Manufacturing, Operations, Quality*

Salary Minimum: $40,000

Functions: Mfg., Materials, IT, Engineering, Technicians

Industries: Energy, Utilities, Manufacturing, Food, Bev., Tobacco, Chemicals, Metal Products, Machine, Appliance, Misc. Mfg., Equip Svcs., Aerospace, Packaging, Software

The North Peak Group

16208 Madison Ave
Cleveland, OH 44107-5619
(216) 221-8300
Email: northpeakgrp@aol.com

Summary: We are a national search firm concentrating in, but not limited to: IT, data processing, environmental, pharmaceutical, healthcare IS and engineering industries. We are affiliated with a group of the best search professionals nationwide. We have helped hundreds of clients and candidates find their 'perfect' match.

Key Contact - Specialty:
Mr. Matthew Bruns, President - *Engineering, Environmental, MIS*

Salary Minimum: $50,000

Functions: Senior Mgmt., Healthcare, Allied Health, MIS Mgmt., Systems Analysis, Systems Dev., Network Admin., DB Admin., Engineering

Industries: Generalist (All), Healthcare, Hospitals

Northland Employment Services

400 Highway 169 S Ste 450
Minneapolis, MN 55426-1130
(952) 541-1060
Fax: (952) 595-9878
Email: northland@jobsmn.com
Web: www.jobsmn.com

Summary: Specialist in IS, programming and systems analysts. We provide multidiscipline engineering placement in a broad range of technical fields. Financial executive search and interim placement.

Key Contact - Specialty:
Mr. David R. Gavin, President
Mr. Ned Lyons, Director, Engineering Staffing
Mr. Gary J. Nygaard, Vice President, Financial Search - *Data processing, Engineering, Technical*

Functions: Generalist (All)

Industries: Generalist (All)

Northstar International Insurance Recruiters Inc

10 James Thomas Rd
Malvern, PA 19355-1127
(610) 889-4800
(880) 521-5718
Fax: (610) 889-4802
Email: nstar@northstarjobs.com
Web: www.northstarjobs.com

Summary: We work exclusively in the property and casualty insurance industry. We have extensive experience in our two specialties/areas of concentration are actuarial, and predictive modeling/data mining.

Key Contact - Specialty:
Mr. Michael C. Crawford, President
Ms. Rita Gillen, Director, Actuarial
Ms. Eileen Fresta, Administrator

Functions: Generalist (All)

Industries: Insurance, Casualty, Commercial, Re-Insurance

NorthStar Technologies Inc

43 Beekman St Fl 3
New York, NY 10038-1536
(212) 267-4100
Fax: (212) 267-4468
Email: info@northstarplus.com
Web: www.northstarplus.com

Summary: We are a technology company, not just a recruiting firm. Besides our first-class recruiting practice, we also specialize in re-engineering, www/Internet development, mission-critical application development, management consulting, and systems integration.

Key Contact - Specialty:
Mr. Khurshed F. Birdie, President

Salary Minimum: $200,000

Functions: Generalist (All), Management, Senior Mgmt., MIS Mgmt., Systems Analysis, Systems Dev., Systems Implem., Systems Support, Network Admin., DB Admin.

Industries: Generalist (All), Banking, Invest. Banking, Brokers, Venture Cap., Mutual/Hedge Funds, Misc. Financial, Mgmt. Consulting, E-commerce, IT Implementation, New Media, Software

---

Novation Legal Placement Services

888 S Figueroa St Ste 170
Los Angeles, CA 90017-5454
(213) 892-0234
Fax: (213) 892-0682
Email: novation@novation-legal.com
Web: www.novation-legal.com

Summary: We place, on a temp and direct hire basis, legal professionals including attorneys, paralegals, legal secretaries & file clerks etc. Our specialties include: intellectual property, bankruptcy, corporate, litigation, health, labor, tax, ERISA and international.

Key Contact - Specialty:
Mr. Jonathan Perrelli, Branch Manager
Mr. Phil Prodehl, Recruiter
Mr. Kevin Meyer, Recruiter
Ms. Dai Meeks, Recruiter

Functions: Legal, Attorneys

Industries: Generalist (All), Legal

NRI Staffing Resources

1899 L St NW Ste 300
Washington, DC 20036-3819
(202) 466-4670
Fax: (202) 466-6593
Email: staffingdc@nri-staffing.com
Web: www.nri-staffing.com

Summary: We are a fully diversified staffing services firm. We specialize in five functional disciplines: accounting & finance, legal, healthcare, IT & technical, office support & administration and provide contingency search services, temp help services, contract staffing and temp-to-hire services in all five specialties. We have a reputation for excellence.

Key Contact - Specialty:
Mr. Robert D. Mulberger, CPC, President
Mr. Robert M. McClimans, CPA, CPC, Executive Vice President

Salary Minimum: $25,000

Functions: Generalist (All)

Industries: Banking, Misc. Financial, Non-profits, Legal, Accounting, Mgmt. Consulting, Call Centers, Software, Accounting SW, Healthcare

Branches:
734 15th St NW Ste 200
Washington, DC 20005-1041
(202) 628-3022
Fax: (202) 628-2838
Email: accountingdc@nri-staffing.com
Key Contact - Specialty:
Ms. Dori Konopka, General Manager - *Accounting, Legal*

1302 Concourse Dr Ste 203
Linthicum, MD 21090-1037
(410) 850-0730
Fax: (410) 850-5263
Email: baltimore@nri-staffing.com
Key Contact - Specialty:
Ms. Meredith Millet, General Manager - *Healthcare, Staffing*

11400 Rockville Pike Ste 820
Rockville, MD 20852-3054
(301) 230-0440
Fax: (301) 770-3198
Email: staffingmd@nri-staffing.com
Key Contact - Specialty:
Mr. John Giannone, General Manager - *Accounting*
Ms. Sonia Benson, General Manager - *Healthcare, Staffing*

7611 Little River Tpke Ste 402W
Annandale, VA 22003-2602
(703) 658-1705
Fax: (703) 658-1493
Email: annandale@nri-staffing.com
Key Contact - Specialty:
Mr. Matt Hoefling, General Manager -
Healthcare, Staffing

10780 Parkridge Blvd Ste 140
Reston, VA 20191-5454
(703) 391-8000
Fax: (703) 391-9091
Email: reston@nri-staffing.com
Key Contact - Specialty:
Ms. Adelle Correa, General Manager - *Staffing,
Technical*

Nstar

5412 Courseview Dr Ste 430
Mason, OH 45040-2355
(513) 459-0384
Fax: (513) 459-1325
Email: information@nstarsearch.com
Web: www.nstarsearch.com

Summary: We are specializing in recruiting
engineers, IT and manufacturing.

Key Contact - Specialty:
Mr. L.J. Hirnikel, President

Salary Minimum: $65,000

Functions: Mfg., IT, Engineering

Industries: Generalist (All), Electronic, Elec.
Components, Pharm Svcs., Digital, Wireless,
Environmental Svcs., Software, Database SW,
Networking, Comm. SW, Biotech/Life Sciences

Nunnelee & Associates Inc

628 Old Hickory Rd
Grenada, MS 38901-2727
(662) 623-9311
Fax: (662) 623-9303
Email: manufacturing@nunnelee.net

Summary: We provide staffing solutions for
manufacturing companies. We offer professional
experience in recruiting for leading manufacturing
companies.

Key Contact - Specialty:
Mr. Wayne Nunnelee, Owner & Manager -
*Accounting, Engineering, Human resources,
Manufacturing (Management), Product
management/development*

Salary Minimum: $50,000

Functions: Generalist (All), Management

Industries: Manufacturing, Lumber, Furniture,
Soap, Perf., Cosmtcs., Plastics, Rubber, Metal
Products, Machine, Appliance, Motor Vehicles,
Consumer Elect., Misc. Mfg., Consumer Goods

Nyborg-Dow Associates Inc

12781 Woodlake Rd
Grass Valley, CA 95949-9744
(530) 477-7817
Fax: (530) 477-0745
Email: marilyn@nydow.com
Web: www.nydow.com

Summary: Specializing in hardware and software
design engineers and management. Working with
a variety of start-ups and larger companies.
Networking, optical, routers, multimedia and a
variety of new technologies.

Key Contact - Specialty:
Ms. Marilyn Nyborg, Co-Owner
Ms. Georgia Dow, Co-Owner
Mr. Steven Russell, Recruiter

Salary Minimum: $80,000

Functions: Engineering
Industries: Software

NYCOR Search Inc

(also known as Nycor Technical Inc)
4930 W 77th St Ste 300
Minneapolis, MN 55435-4809
(952) 831-6444
(800) 675-6527
Fax: (952) 835-2883
Email: info@nycor.com
Web: www.nycor.com

Summary: We are a direct search and contract
staffing firm. We are a leader in technical staffing.
Our search teams specialize in: hardware,
software, engineering, biomedical, regulatory, IT,
manufacturing and finance & accounting at the
individual contributor, management and executive
levels.

Key Contact - Specialty:
Mr. John Nymark, President

Salary Minimum: $36,000

Functions: Management, Senior Mgmt., Middle
Mgmt., Product Dev., Finance, IT, R&D,
Engineering, Eng. Design, Hardware

Industries: Generalist (All), Food, Bev., Tobacco,
Medical Devices, Plastics, Rubber, Machine,
Appliance, Test, Measure Equip., Misc. Mfg.,
Electronic, Elec. Components, Robotics,
Transportation, Pharm Svcs., Accounting, E-
commerce, IT Implementation, Engineering
Svcs., Logistics Svcs., Telecoms, Call Centers,
Telephony, Digital, Wireless, Fiber Optic,
Government, Defense, Database SW,
Development SW, Doc. Mgmt., Production SW,
ERP SW, Networking, Comm. SW, Security
SW, System SW, Biotech/Life Sciences

O'Brien and Roof

6812 Caine Rd
Columbus, OH 43235-4233
(614) 766-8500
Fax: (614) 766-8505
Email: lindy@obrienroof.com
Web: www.obrienroof.com

Summary: We are a generalist firm whose
principals offer extensive years of recruiting
experience. Our searches conducted on either a
contingency or retainer basis. Over 80 percent of
our search assignments come from satisfied
clients.

Key Contact - Specialty:
Ms. Lindy O'Brien, President
Mr. Howard Roof, Chief Executive Officer
Mr. Tom Langsdon, Senior Search Consultant

Salary Minimum: $45,000

Functions: Generalist (All), Management, Sales
& Mktg., HR Mgmt., Finance

Industries: Generalist (All), Construction,
Manufacturing, Retail, Hospitality, Advertising,
Real Estate

O'Connell Group Inc

475 Danbury Rd
Wilton, CT 06897-2126
(203) 834-2900
Fax: (203) 834-2728
Email: search@oconnellgroup.com
Web: www.oconnellgroup.com

Summary: Our firm specializes in marketing and
marketing research disciplines in the consumer
and pharmaceutical industries.

Key Contact - Specialty:
Mr. Brian M. O'Connell, CPC, President -
Marketing, Research

Mr. Kenneth A. Dammeyer, CPC, Vice President
- *Marketing*
Mr. Hap Hoover, CPC, Vice President -
Marketing
Mr. Ronald K. Prestera, CPC, Vice President -
Research
Ms. Susan M. Murtha, Vice President - *Research*
Mr. Elton M Fowler, CPC, Vice President -
Marketing
Mr. James V. McConnell, Vice President -
Marketing
Mr. Robert P. Tansill, Vice President - *Marketing*
Ms. Virginia R. Stewart, Vice President - *Re-
engineering*
Ms. Katherine M. Epifano, Vice President -
Administration

Salary Minimum: $70,000

Functions: Mktg. Research, Mktg. Mgmt.

Industries: Food, Bev., Tobacco, Paper, Soap,
Perf., Cosmtcs., Drugs Mfg.

Branches:
9666 Olive Blvd Ste 796
Saint Louis, MO 63132-3026
(314) 997-3441
Fax: (314) 997-3931
Email: search@oconnellgroup.com
Key Contact - Specialty:
Ms. Kris S. Holmes, CPC, Vice President -
Marketing
Mr. Dixon A. Smith, CPC, Vice President -
Marketing
Ms. Joanne K. Abernathy, CPC, Vice President -
Research

425 N Avalon Rd
Winston Salem, NC 27104-2001
(336) 724-9932
Fax: (336) 725-6245
Email: search@oconnellgroup.com
Key Contact - Specialty:
Mr. Adnan H. Rukieh, Vice President - *Marketing*

O'Connor Resources

806 N 48th Ave Apt D
Omaha, NE 68132-2477
(402) 551-1001
Email: oconnor01@cox.net

Summary: Respected in managed care
development, marketing, operations, MIS; JVs
with providers, vendors, insurers and corporations.
We provide expertise in reorganization, mergers,
downsizing and management succession.

Key Contact - Specialty:
Mr. Rod O'Connor, President

Salary Minimum: $80,000

Functions: Generalist (All), Board Members,
Senior Mgmt., Middle Mgmt., Admin. Svcs.,
Health Admin., Mktg. Mgmt., Sales Mgmt.,
MIS Mgmt., Systems Implem.

Industries: Generalist (All), Drugs Mfg., Invest.
Banking, Venture Cap., Mgmt. Consulting, HR
Services, Media, New Media, Communications,
Telecoms, Call Centers, Telephony, Wireless,
Insurance, Software, Database SW, Healthcare,
Hospitals, Long-term/Home Care

O'Gorman & Company Inc

52 Cheever Pl
Brooklyn, NY 11231-3005
(917) 929-3478
Email: mog@ogormanandcompany.com
Web: www.ogormanandcompany.com

Summary: We are an executive search firm
specializing in corporate banking, capital markets
and asset management. Our focus is on senior
positions that require superior relationship

management, financial analysis, structuring and risk management skills.

Key Contact - Specialty:
Ms. Mary C. O'Gorman, President

Salary Minimum: $150,000

Functions: Management, Senior Mgmt., Middle Mgmt., Product Dev., Sales & Mktg., M&A, Risk Mgmt., Int'l.

Industries: Banking, Invest. Banking, Brokers, Mutual/Hedge Funds

O'Neill Group

PO Box 614
Lake Hopatcong, NJ 07849-0614
(973) 663-6634
(973) 663-5753
Fax: (973) 663-5301
Email: sheilas1@mindspring.com
Web: www.oneillgrp.com

Summary: We are an Executive Search Firm specializing in placement of senior management, outplacement consulting and contract payroll.

Key Contact - Specialty:
Ms. Sheila Manning, Executive Director - *Human resources*
Mr. John Waterhouse, Senior Vice President
Ms. Cindy Bergen, Director, Payroll
Ms. Barbara Conway, Vice President

Salary Minimum: $70,000

Functions: Generalist (All), Middle Mgmt., HR Mgmt., CFOs, Systems Analysis, Mgmt. Consultants, Minorities/Diversity, Int'l.

Industries: Generalist (All), Drugs Mfg., Consumer Elect., Pharm Svcs., Telecoms

O'Shea System Inc

(also known as O'Shea Personnel)
PO Box 2134
Aston, PA 19014-0134
(610) 364-3964
Fax: (610) 364-3962
Email: cptfjc@aol.com
Web: www.osheasystem.com

Summary: Being one of the oldest recruiting firms in the United States, we strive to recruit and place qualified personnel with commitment and integrity both locally and on a national basis. Areas of specialization include: Health Care (Physician), Actuarial, Benefits, Insurance, Financial.

Key Contact - Specialty:
Mr. Frank Comeau, CPC, President
Ms. Linda Trotter, Recruiter

Functions: Generalist (All), Physicians

Industries: Finance, Misc. Financial, HR Services, IT Implementation, Engineering Svcs., Call Centers, Software, Accounting SW, Healthcare, Hospitals, Long-term/Home Care, Physical Therapy

O'Sullivan Search Inc

401-2300 Yonge St
Yonge-Eglinton Centre
Toronto, ON M4P 1E4
Canada
(416) 481-2992
Fax: (416) 481-3424
Email: resumes@osullivansearch.com
Web: www.osullivansearch.com

Summary: Our mission statement: to put the right person in the right place at the right time.

Key Contact - Specialty:
Ms. Kathleen O'Sullivan, President

Salary Minimum: $22,000

Functions: Generalist (All), Admin. Svcs., Customer Svc., Staffing, Budgeting, Credit, Engineering

Industries: Generalist (All), Invest. Banking, Misc. Financial, Accounting, Insurance

Oberg & Associates

16475 Dallas Pkwy Ste 605
Addison, TX 75001-6817
(972) 239-3315
Fax: (972) 735-8096
Email: contact@obergassociates.com
Web: www.obergassociates.com

Summary: We have a systems-driven recruiting process that provides predictable results to our clients and candidates. We service the corrugated packaging industry.

Key Contact - Specialty:
Mr. Roy Oberg, Founder & Owner

Salary Minimum: $40,000

Functions: Generalist (All), Senior Mgmt., Middle Mgmt., Production, Plant Mgmt., Quality, Packaging, Sales Mgmt.

Industries: Generalist (All), Paper, Packaging

Objective Paradigm Inc

805 N Milwaukee Ave Ste 300
Chicago, IL 60622-4104
(646) 536-3111
(773) 572-6402
Fax: (270) 682-7251
Email: kkrumm@opstaffing.com
Web: www.opstaffing.com

Summary: We specialize in the contingency recruiting and contract staffing of IT talent for a variety of companies and industries.

Key Contact - Specialty:
Mr. Kevin Krumm, Managing Director

Salary Minimum: $75,000

Functions: Management, Senior Mgmt., Staffing, IT

Industries: Finance, Mgmt. Consulting, E-commerce, IT Implementation, Media, Insurance, Software, Database SW, Development SW, Doc. Mgmt., Production SW, ERP SW, Industry Specific SW, Security SW, System SW

Ocean Medical Inc

(formerly known as HeartBeat Medical, Inc.)
9140 Golfside Dr Ste 5N
Jacksonville, FL 32256-1805
(904) 730-9990
Fax: (904) 886-0033
Email: scott@oceanmedical.net
Web: www.oceanmedical.net

Summary: Executive search and recruitment in quality, regulatory and clinical along with R&D, manufacturing and operations for medical device start-ups and Fortune 500 companies. Focusing on cardiology, neurology, orthopedic, catheter, stent, implant and instruments.

Key Contact - Specialty:
Mr. Scott Bailey, President

Salary Minimum: $55,000

Functions: Senior Mgmt., Middle Mgmt., Mfg., Product Dev., Production, Quality, Healthcare, R&D, Engineering

Industries: Medical Devices

OceanSide Staffing

PO Box 324
Wareham, MA 02571-0324
(888) 456-2326
(508) 295-1717
Fax: (508) 295-5510
Email: myjonquil@aol.com
Web: www.oceansidestaffing.com

Summary: Our firm specializes in the permanent placement of ultrasound, vascular, echo techs, physical therapists, occupational therapists, respiratory therapists, RAD techs and dietitians.

Key Contact - Specialty:
Ms. Ann-Marie Bagley

Functions: Healthcare

Industries: Hospitals

Odell & Associates Inc

660 N Central Expy Ste 240
Plano, TX 75074-6869
(972) 458-7900
(800) 880-7900
Fax: (972) 233-1215
Email: odell@odellrecruits.com
Web: www.odellrecruits.com

Summary: We are a healthcare focused firm with extensive experience. We are consistently highly rated in local media. Our recruiting consultants are awarded top honors at personnel awards programs. We specialize in healthcare, accounting and healthcare technology.

Key Contact - Specialty:
Mr. Steve N. Odell, CPC, President

Salary Minimum: $30,000

Functions: Healthcare, Physicians, Nurses, Finance, Cash Mgmt., Taxes

Industries: Generalist (All), Insurance, Healthcare, Hospitals, Physical Therapy, Occupational Therapy

The Odella Group Inc

27068 La Paz Rd Ste 321
Aliso Viejo, CA 92656-3041
(949) 360-9997
Fax: (949) 360-9099
Email: careers@theodellagroup.com
Web: www.theodellagroup.com

Summary: Global provider of consulting, outsourcing and workforce management solutions and a recognized leader in organizational design, development and improvement. Specializing in the recruitment of mid-senior level positions for a broad spectrum of clients across multiple industries, disciplines and verticals. Expertise includes: outsourcing, call center, CRM, direct marketing, consumer electronics, technology and telecommunications.

Key Contact - Specialty:
Mrs. Lori Hall, President & Chief Executive Officer - *Call centers, CRM, Outsourcing, Technology, Telecommunications*
Mrs. Lori Trager, Executive Vice President & Partner - *Call centers, CRM, Direct marketing, Technology, Telecommunications*
Mr. Lyle Trager, Executive Vice President & Partner - *Communications, Computers (Software), Consumer (Products), Electronics, High technology*
Mr. Lance Hall, Partner & Vice President, Strtgc Sltns - *Entrepreneurs, Financial services, Real estate, Start-up companies, Venture capital*
Ms. Joelle Trager, Partner & Vice President, Call Ctr Sltns - *Call centers, Communications, Database, High technology, Outsourcing*

Mrs. Deb Miles, Partner & Vice President, Trilogy Sltns - *Human resources, Insurance, Retail, Staffing, Training*
Ms. Tina Komarnisky, Partner & Vice President, Creative Sltns - *Advertising, Creative, Media, Public relations, Travel*

Salary Minimum: $80,000

Functions: Generalist (All)

Industries: Computer Equip., Consumer Elect., Consumer Goods, Finance, Services, Telecoms, Call Centers, Wireless, Insurance, Software

Ohrmund Employment Group

W62N248 Washington Ave Ste 4
Cedarburg, WI 53012-2710
(262) 377-2731
Fax: (262) 546-0070
Email: greg@ohrmundgroup.com

Summary: Our firm specializes in supply chain and mechanical engineering professionals. We are client driven and will help our clients fill almost any position.

Key Contact - Specialty:
Mr. Gregory Ohrmund, President

Salary Minimum: $50,000

Functions: Senior Mgmt., Mfg., Production, Plant Mgmt., Materials, Purchasing, Materials Plng., Distribution, Healthcare, HR Mgmt.

Industries: Generalist (All), Healthcare

Olesky Associates Inc

310 Washington St Ste 201
Wellesley Hills, MA 02481-4949
(781) 235-4330
(800) 486-4330
Fax: (781) 239-1454
Email: info@olesky.com
Web: www.olesky.com

Summary: We offer over 3,100 physician jobs in all specialties. Permanent/locum positions, confidentiality insured.

Key Contact - Specialty:
Mr. Roy Olesky, President

Functions: Generalist (All), Physicians, Health Admin.

Industries: Generalist (All), HR Services, Healthcare

Oliveras & Company Inc

1605 John St Ste 109
Fort Lee, NJ 07024-2577
(201) 947-6662
Fax: (201) 451-2667
Email: wo@oliverascoinc.com
Web: www.oliverascoinc.com

Summary: We are a successful full-service national search firm specializing in the recruitment of attorneys, partners and mergers & acquisitions. We provide permanent and all temporary placements as well. Recruitment services are also provided for legal and non-legal support staff and all HR positions. Other specialized services include life career planning and development. [Member NALSC]

Key Contact - Specialty:
Ms. Wendy Oliveras, President & Chief Executive Officer - *Intellectual property, Legal, Mergers & acquisitions*

Functions: Admin. Svcs., HR Mgmt., Attorneys, Paralegals

Industries: Generalist (All), Legal, Biotech/Life Sciences

Omega Executive Search

1465 Northside Dr NW Ste 217
Atlanta, GA 30318-4239
(404) 873-2000
Fax: (404) 873-2006
Email: omega@hospitalitypros.com
Web: www.hospitalitypros.com

Summary: We specialize in searches for the hospitality industry (including, but not limited to, hotels, resorts, country clubs, casinos, restaurants, and food services).

Key Contact - Specialty:
Mr. Dave Dorries, President - *Hospitality*
Mr. David Zakin, Principal - *Hospitality*

Salary Minimum: $40,000

Functions: Management, Senior Mgmt., Sales & Mktg., Finance, Hospitality, Hotel Mgmt.

Industries: Hospitality, Hotels, Resorts, Clubs, Restaurants, Quick Service Restaurants, Full Service Restaurants, Inst./Industrial Food Svc., Entertainment, Recreation, Sports, Travel

Omega Search Inc

4425 Randolph Rd Ste 319
Charlotte, NC 28211-2377
(704) 364-8875
Fax: (704) 364-9290
Email: omegaemail@aol.com

Summary: With extensive years of executive recruitment experience, we are dedicated to being thorough and accomplishment-oriented as well as providing outstanding customer service in the search and recruitment of professionals.

Key Contact - Specialty:
Mr. Jeffrey M. Turk, President

Salary Minimum: $40,000

Functions: Quality, Mktg. Mgmt., HR Mgmt., Finance, Taxes, MIS Mgmt., R&D, Engineering, Legal, Attorneys

Industries: Generalist (All), Energy, Utilities, Food, Bev., Tobacco, Drugs Mfg., Medical Devices, Plastics, Rubber, Paints, Petro. Products, Machine, Appliance, Consumer Elect., Real Estate

Omega Systems LLC

PO Box 61417
Virginia Beach, VA 23466-1417
(757) 473-2378
Email: omegajobs@omegasystemsonline.com
Web: www.omegasystemsonline.com

Summary: Identify highest quality sales, marketing, engineering, manufacturing and service candidates for technical and high technology markets by capitalizing on in-depth industry knowledge and practical experience as former senior executive. Specialize in the semiconductor, instrumentation, industrial gas, chemical, vacuum, ultra-high vacuum, mechanical, welding, precision manufacturing and other high technology industries.

Key Contact - Specialty:
Mr. Daniel Lear, President - *Engineering, High technology, Marketing, Sales*

Salary Minimum: $40,000

Functions: Management, Senior Mgmt., Middle Mgmt., Automation, Sales Mgmt., Engineering, Minorities/Diversity, Technicians

Industries: Generalist (All), Energy, Utilities, Manufacturing, Chemicals, Plastics, Rubber, Paints, Petro. Products, Metal Products, Machine, Appliance, Robotics, Consumer Goods, Logistics Svcs., Supply Chain Mgmt., Non-Classifiable

OMNI Personnel Services

1313 Golf Course Cir
Lexington, KY 40517-3808
(859) 271-9701
Fax: (859) 271-9703
Email: opersserv@aol.com

Summary: Our firm specializes in executive search and HR consulting serving the coal & hard rock mining industry and general manufacturing to include automotive. We handle professional, technical and administrative, mid-level management to CEO level.

Key Contact - Specialty:
Mr. Norman L. Cornett, President.- *Technical*

Salary Minimum: $50,000

Functions: Generalist (All)

Industries: Generalist (All), Oil & Gas, Chemicals, Plastics, Rubber, Motor Vehicles

The Omni Recruiting Group Inc

6300 Powers Ferry Rd NW Ste 600-236
Atlanta, GA 30339-2961
(770) 988-0700
Fax: (770) 980-0700
Email: info@omnirecruiting.com
Web: www.omnirecruiting.com

Summary: We specialize in the placement of Staffing Industry Professionals.

Key Contact - Specialty:
Ms. Judy Paul, CPC, President - *Staffing*
Ms. Debra Skurski, Executive Recruiter - *Staffing*

Functions: Generalist (All), Management, Board Members, Senior Mgmt., Middle Mgmt., Sales & Mktg., Sales Mgmt., Sales Reps., Staffing, Mgmt. Consultants

Industries: Services, Mgmt. Consulting, HR Services

Omni Search Inc

5743 Corsa Ave Ste 123
Westlake Village, CA 91362-7310
(818) 707 4500
(800) 511-0587
Fax: (818) 707-4528
Email: omnisearch@omnisearchinc.com
Web: www.omnisearchinc.com

Summary: We are a recruiting firm specializing in long-term care, administrators, directors of nursing, nurse consultants and upper-level management personnel. We recognize your most urgent and consistent needs for quality staffing.

Key Contact - Specialty:
Mr. Lory Goldstein, President

Functions: Generalist (All), Nurses, Health Admin.

Industries: Generalist (All), Healthcare

OmniSearch Inc

334 E Lake Rd Ste 270
Palm Harbor, FL 34685-2427
(727) 789-4442
Fax: (727) 787-7743
Email: omni@omnisearch.biz
Web: www.omnisearch.biz

Summary: We have excellent, documented experience in pharmaceutical sales force expansion projects and pharmaceutical marketing experience from product and brand manager to marketing director.

Key Contact - Specialty:
Mr. Samuel Moyer, Vice President - *Sales*
Ms. Laurene F. Moyer, President - *Sales*

Salary Minimum: $50,000

Functions: Sales & Mktg.

Industries: Drugs Mfg., Medical Devices, Pharm Svcs., Biotech/Life Sciences

On Target Recruiting
813 Morningside Trl
Murphy, TX 75094-4368
(972) 461-0682
Fax: (972) 461-0679
Email: timgaffney@att.net
Web: www.ontargetrecruiting.com

Summary: A professional search firm, we specialize in the placement of sales & marketing professionals in consumer package goods, consumer electronics, home appliances and consumer durables industries. We place brand, category and trade marketing managers as well as field sales positions including directors, national accounts and VP level spots.

Key Contact - Specialty:
Mr. Tim Gaffney, President - *Sales*

Salary Minimum: $50,000

Functions: Middle Mgmt., Product Dev., Sales & Mktg., Advertising, Mktg. Mgmt., Sales Mgmt.

Industries: Food, Bev., Tobacco, Soap, Perf., Cosmtcs., Machine, Appliance, Computer Equip., Consumer Elect., Consumer Goods, Quick Service Restaurants, Inst./Industrial Food Svc., Advertising, Communications, Telecoms, Telephony, Wireless

One Source Managed Solutions
1 Hollycrest Dr Ste 101
Brick, NJ 08723-7536
(732) 451-0035
(732) 451-0035
Fax: (484) 450-5180
Email: vincentg@onesourcemanaged.com
Web: www.onesourcemanaged.com

Summary: We are a boutique recruiting management and contract recruiting consultancy. We provide cost effective solutions to our client companies that address their immediate and future staffing plans.

Key Contact - Specialty:
Mr. Vincent Graziano, Managing Director, Principal Consultant - *Technology, Telecommunications, Temporary, Venture capital, Wireless*

Salary Minimum: $80,000

Functions: Senior Mgmt.

Industries: Biotech/Life Sciences

oneBPO Inc
5178 Mowry Ave Ste 2125
Fremont, CA 94538-1046
(510) 794-6334
Fax: (510) 217-3928
Email: info@onebpo.com
Web: www.onebpo.com

Summary: We provide a suite of world class technology, HR and financial solutions. These offerings scale from a la carte services to comprehensive process oriented solutions. We also incorporate ongoing support for multiple practices under one vendor. This unique business model allows us to help clients save time, money and maintain a laser focus on their core business needs.

Key Contact - Specialty:
Mr. James Man Chin, Co-Founder & Chief Operating Officer
Mr. Mike Sarwari, Co-Founder & Chief Executive Officer
Mr. Glen Glazar, Director, Staffing Practice

Salary Minimum: $80,000

Functions: Management, Board Members, Senior Mgmt., Middle Mgmt., Sales & Mktg., Mktg. Mgmt., Sales Mgmt., IT, Systems Dev., Network Admin.

Industries: Generalist (All)

Onesource Professional Search
4075 Desoto St Ste A
Mandeville, LA 70471-1926
(985) 727-2060
Email: info@onesourcepros.com
Web: www.onesourcepros.com

Summary: Engineering, geoscience and tech support positions in the energy, civil & infrastructure, chemical and marine industries. Position level from staff engineer to VP.

Key Contact - Specialty:
Mr. Dave Mount, President, Mgr. Engineering/Tech Recr. - *Engineering, Geology, Highways, Oil, Refineries*
Mr. Henry Shurlds, Partner, Engineering & Tech Recruiter - *Energy, Engineering, Gas, Geology*

Salary Minimum: $60,000

Functions: Engineering

Industries: Energy, Utilities, Oil & Gas, Chemicals, Paints, Petro. Products, Transportation

Open Systems Technologies Inc
225 W 34th St Ste 1715
New York, NY 10122-1792
(212) 643-3100
Fax: (212) 643-4412
Email: info@opensystemstech.com
Web: www.opensystemstech.com

Summary: We are a specialized technical recruiting and consulting company that services the financial services community.

Key Contact - Specialty:
Mr. Harold Herling, Vice President
Mr. Steven Young, Principal

Salary Minimum: $55,000

Functions: Generalist (All), MIS Mgmt., Systems Analysis, Systems Dev., Systems Implem., Systems Support, Network Admin., DB Admin.

Industries: Generalist (All), Banking, Invest. Banking, Brokers, Misc. Financial, New Media, Software

Branches:
585 Stewart Ave Ste 536
Garden City, NY 11530-4701
(516) 357-9777
Fax: (516) 357-9676
Email: esultzer@opensystemstech.com
Key Contact - Specialty:
Mr. Eric Sultzer, Managing Director

Openbrier & Associates
PO Box 464
Glenshaw, PA 15116-0464
(412) 487-8534
Email: bobopenbrier@comcast.net
Web: www.openbrier.com

Summary: We have extensive experience in the recruiting business. Specialists in the recruitment of top caliber engineering/manufacturing, and executive talent for a broad spectrum of industries. Most recent assignments include Lean Manufacturing, Six Sigma and Diversity. Clients are mostly Fortune 500 companies.

Key Contact - Specialty:
Mr. Bob Openbrier, President

Salary Minimum: $50,000

Functions: Generalist (All), Board Members, Mfg.

Industries: Generalist (All), Energy, Utilities, Manufacturing, Medical Devices, Plastics, Rubber, Metal Products, Machine, Appliance, Motor Vehicles, Computer Equip., Consumer Elect., Misc. Mfg., Electronic, Elec. Components, Robotics, Engineering Svcs., Mfg. SW, Networking, Comm. SW

Opensoft Inc
201-322 King St W
Toronto, ON M5V 1J2
Canada
(416) 260-2656
Fax: (416) 260-5973
Email: info@osft.com
Web: www.osft.com

Summary: Our firm combines its highly ethical culture and values to provide high quality and responsive technology services to our clients. We focuses on helping IT organizations operate more productively and profitably through a full range of specialized project implementation products and services, including staff augmentation.

Key Contact - Specialty:
Mr. Jay Parmar, Director - *Capital markets, Consulting, Information Technology, Management consulting, Risk management*

Functions: IT

Industries: Banking, Invest. Banking, Venture Cap., Mgmt. Consulting, E-commerce, IT Implementation, New Media, Telephony, Wireless, Doc. Mgmt., Production SW

Opportunity Search Inc
PO Box 751
Olney, MD 20830-0751
(301) 924-4741
Fax: (301) 924-1318
Email: employers@oppsearch.com
Web: www.oppsearch.com

Summary: Our firm is a recruiting/search firm that has successfully placed hundreds of top-caliber professionals. Our primary emphasis is in the information technology(IT) field but during the past few years we have expanded our capabilities to include placement in the rfid, accounting, finance, sales, marketing areas. Our client base is primarily in the Maryland, Virginia, and Washington DC market but we have successfully filled positions with companies throughout the United States.

Key Contact - Specialty:
Mr. Marc Tappis, President

Functions: IT

Industries: Supply Chain Mgmt, Defense, Homeland Security, Database SW, Development SW, Security SW, System SW

Optimal Business Solutions
175 Georgian Dr
Coppell, TX 75019-6281
(972) 745-9089
Fax: (972) 745-1616
Email: resumes@obsworld.com
Web: www.obsworld.com

Summary: We are an executive search firm that places top executives in advertising, marketing, logistics and IT professions.

Key Contact - Specialty:
Mr. Jorge Aguirre, Managing Partner, Executive Search Team - *Procurement, SAP, Strategic planning, Supply Chain, Transportation*
Ms. Doris Aguirre, Managing Partner, Executive Search Team - *C-level, CEOs, Executives, Media, Middle management*

Salary Minimum: $60,000

Functions: Generalist (All), Senior Mgmt., Production, Distribution, Advertising, Mktg. Mgmt., Sales Reps., MIS Mgmt., Systems Implem.

Industries: Generalist (All), Manufacturing, Computer Equip., Transportation, Finance, Services, Mgmt. Consulting, IT Implementation, Engineering Svcs., Logistics Svcs., Supply Chain Mgmt, Media, Advertising, Publishing, New Media, Broadcast, Film, Software

Optimal Resources LLC

PO Box 1849
Bellaire, TX 77402-1849
(713) 666-2238
Fax: (713) 661-9972
Email: ori@wt.net

Summary: We are a management consulting/search recruiting firm. We engage to facilitate client company growth in a number of ways. We advise on and provide services related to building companies by units via mergers & acquisitions, strategic partnering and strategic unit acquisition; and we engage to recruit key executives, managers and professionals. Our clients are mostly technology-based companies ranging in size from post-startup to Fortune 100.

Key Contact - Specialty:
Dr. William Salathiel, PhD, MBA, President

Salary Minimum: $80,000

Functions: Generalist (All)

Industries: Generalist (All)

OPUS International Inc

1191 E Newport Center Dr PH E
Deerfield Beach, FL 33442-7708
(954) 428-3888
Fax: (954) 428-5470
Email: moira@foodscience.com
Web: www.foodscience.com

Summary: Our firm is both a contingency and retained search firm specializing in placing technical people in the food industry. Primarily, we place scientists with major food and food ingredients manufacturers in their R&D and quality assurance departments. The level of positions varies from senior scientists up to director and VP level.

Key Contact - Specialty:
Ms. Moira McGrath, President - *Food, Food & beverage, Food service, Quality, Research & development*
Mrs. Rosann Cook Sturm, Executive Recruiter - *Food, Food & beverage, Quality, Research & development*

Salary Minimum: $60,000

Functions: Product Dev., Quality, R&D

Industries: Food, Bev., Tobacco

Opus Marketing

23151 Moulton Pkwy
Laguna Hills, CA 92653-1206
(949) 581-0962
Fax: (949) 581-1497
Email: resumes@opusmarketing.com
Web: www.opusmarketing.com

Summary: We offer fully integrated staffing services including search plans, outplacement, hiring models and thorough screening of candidates. Our clients have cut turnover and improved new hire retention rates significantly.

Key Contact - Specialty:
Mr. Robert S. Kreisberg, President - *Professional services*

Salary Minimum: $40,000

Functions: Generalist (All), Sales Mgmt., Sales Reps., IT, Systems Support

Industries: Computer Equip., Telecoms, Software, Accounting SW, Database SW, Development SW, Doc. Mgmt., Production SW, Entertainment SW, ERP SW, HR SW, Industry Specific SW, Mfg. SW, Marketing SW, Networking, Comm. SW, Security SW

Oracle Recruiters

645 N Michigan Ave Ste 800
Chicago, IL 60611-2890
(773) 404-9300
Web: www.oraclerecruiters.com

Summary: Oracle Recruiters is a boutique search firm specializing in the placement of Oracle, PeopleSoft and JD Edwards candidates. Our international client base appreciates our one consultant per client approach.

Key Contact - Specialty:
Ms. Diane Cleary, Associate Director - *Computers (Software), Consulting, Oracle, PeopleSoft, Six Sigma*

Salary Minimum: $50,000

Functions: Generalist (All)

Industries: Generalist (All), Software, ERP SW, HR SW, Industry Specific SW, Mfg. SW, Marketing SW, Networking, Comm. SW, Security SW, System SW

The Origin Group LLC

124 N York St
Elmhurst, IL 60126-2865
(630) 782-0900 x12
(630) 782-0990
Email: recruiters@theorigingroup.com
Web: www.theorigingroup.com

Summary: Our firm specializes in permanent placement for professionals in the actuarial, employee benefit, HR and HR technology fields.

Key Contact - Specialty:
Mrs. Christine Sahlas, Principal - *Benefits*

Functions: Senior Mgmt., HR Mgmt., Benefits

Industries: Misc. Financial, Accounting, Mgmt. Consulting, HR Services, Insurance

Orion International Search Inc

60 E 42nd St Rm 3202
New York, NY 10165-3202
(212) 599-2170
Fax: (212) 599-2173
Email: info@nyc-orion.com
Web: www.nyc-orion.com

Summary: We are a global search and consulting organization founded by an attorney who had practiced law on Wall Street before turning to institutional equity sales with some of the largest international financial firms. Initially concentrating just on financial services, our firm has evolved with sub-specialties in corporate boards and CFOs.

Key Contact - Specialty:
Mr. John J. Palutis, JD, MBA, Principal - *Financial services*
Mr. John P. Tiernan, Managing Director

Salary Minimum: $100,000

Functions: Board Members, Product Dev., Sales & Mktg., Sales Mgmt., Finance, CFOs, M&A, Risk Mgmt., Attorneys, Int'l.

Industries: Energy, Utilities, Finance, Banking, Invest. Banking, Venture Cap., Mutual/Hedge Funds, Legal, Engineering Svcs., Insurance

Orion International

5511 Capital Center Dr Ste 216
Raleigh, NC 27606-3365
(919) 851-3309
Fax: (919) 851-7268
Web: www.orioninternational.com

Summary: Former military service members specializing in identifying the best talent leaving the services for career opportunities with leading companies.

Key Contact - Specialty:
Mr. Jim Tully, Chief Executive Officer & Co-Founder
Mr. Bill Laughlin, Co-Founder
Mr. Randy Nelson, Chief Financial Officer & Co-Founder

Salary Minimum: $35,000

Functions: Generalist (All), Production, Materials Plng., Sales Mgmt., Staffing, CFOs, MIS Mgmt., Technicians

Industries: Generalist (All), Construction, Drugs Mfg., Plastics, Rubber, Misc. Mfg., Misc. Financial, Aerospace, Healthcare

Branches:
9665 Chesapeake Dr Ste 450
San Diego, CA 92123-1354
(888) 756-7466
Email: sd@orioninternational.com
Key Contact - Specialty:
Mr. Brian Henry, Operations Manager
Mr. J.P. Sniffen
Mr. Mike Urcelay
Mr. Jay Koranda, Enlisted Candidates

10151 Deerwood Park Blvd Ste 200-105
Jacksonville, FL 32256-0564
(888) 674-6689
(888) 767-4660
Email: jac@orioninternational.com
Key Contact - Specialty:
Mr. Dave Catalano, Operations Manager

98-211 Pali Momi St Ste 504
Aiea, HI 96701-4328
(877) 451-9103
Email: hawaii@orioninternational.com
Key Contact - Specialty:
Mr. Wayne Dewees, Recruiter

4404 Barford Rd
Syracuse, NY 13215-1308
(800) 896-0024
Email: syr@orioninternational.com
Key Contact - Specialty:
Mr. Joe Brownell, Operations Manager
Ms. Monica Mclean

5412 Courseview Dr Ste 430
Mason, OH 45040-2355
(800) 324-2112
(800) 298-0432
Fax: (513) 459-9087
Email: cin@orioninternational.com
Key Contact - Specialty:
Mr. Ernest Burson, Operations Manager
Mr. Craig Stevens

143 4th Ave N
Franklin, TN 37064-2681
(888) 667-4667
Email: nas@orioninternational.com

Email your resume to a targeted list of recruiters now at www.ExecutiveAgent.com/DER07

Key Contact - Specialty:
Mr. Mark Whalls, Recruiter

1250 S Capital Of Texas Hwy Ste I270
West Lake Hills, TX 78746-4483
(512) 327-7111
(800) 336-7466
Fax: (512) 329-5444
Email: aus@orioninternational.com
Key Contact - Specialty:
Mr. Bob Berkholz, Operations Manager
Mr. Thomas Payne
Mr. Vearl Williams
Mr. Bill Key
Mr. James Harrison, Manager, Sales, SW Region

5800 Lake Wright Dr Ste 101
Norfolk, VA 23502-1804
(800) 544-1741
(800) 544-3787
Email: vb@orioninternational.com
Key Contact - Specialty:
Mr. Chris Hurst, Operations Manager
Mr. Stephen Norred

Orion Search Group Inc

152 Ambassador Dr
Red Bank, NJ 07701-2294
(800) 777-2902
(732) 219-1921
Fax: (732) 219-1921
Email: orionsearchgroup@comcast.net

Summary: We specialize in the property and
casualty insurance industry. We place candidates
in legal, claims, loss control, and premium audit
positions.

Key Contact - Specialty:
Ms. Mona George Myron, President
Mr. Ronald B. Myron, Vice President
Mr. Lowell Gannon, Vice President -
  Underwriting

Salary Minimum: $50,000

Functions: Generalist (All), Management, Senior
  Mgmt., Engineering, Legal, Attorneys

Industries: Generalist (All), Legal, Insurance,
  Casualty, Claims, Commercial, Re-Insurance

Kenneth Orth & Associates Ltd

310 Busse Hwy # 301
Park Ridge, IL 60068-3251
(847) 698-5184
Email: kenorth@sbcglobal.net

Summary: We are a full service staffing firm
providing nationwide support to candidates
looking for full-time direct hire positions to our
client companies. We work on hard to fill full-time
direct hire positions for client companies
nationwide.

Key Contact - Specialty:
Mr. Ken Orth, Staffing Solutions

Functions: Generalist (All)

Industries: Generalist (All)

OSI

PO Box 81092
Conyers, GA 30013-9092
(770) 760-7661
Email: tim@osijobs.com
Web: www.osijobs.com

Summary: Specialize in search and recruitment in
the food industry. We offer retained and
contingency search.

Key Contact - Specialty:
Mr. Tim Oliver, Senior Parnter - *Food*

Salary Minimum: $80,000

Functions: Generalist (All), Mfg.

Industries: Manufacturing, Food, Bev., Tobacco

Branches:
140 Raleigh St
Holly Springs, NC 27540-9043
(919) 557-5773
Fax: (919) 557-5108
Email: dave@osijobs.com
Key Contact - Specialty:
Mr. David Buergler - *Food*

Outsource Professionals

110 Barnard Pl NW
Atlanta, GA 30328-2010
(678) 297-0916
Fax: (678) 297-0197
Email: info@outsource-professionals.com
Web: www.outsource-professionals.com

Summary: Specialization on emerging growth
software companies with emphasis on
management, sales, technical and pre/post-sales
positions.

Key Contact - Specialty:
Ms. Lisa Ramsey, Partner - *Sales, Technical*
Mrs. Karen Moss, PHR, Partner - *Computers
  (Software)*

Salary Minimum: $50,000

Functions: Sales & Mktg., HR Mgmt., IT,
  Systems Dev., Systems Implem.

Industries: Services, Software

June L Owens & Associates LLC

PO Box 4521
Des Moines, IA 50305-4521
(515) 288-4907
Fax: (515) 288-1180
Email: info@juneowensassociates.com
Web: www.juneowensassociates.com

Summary: We are a generalist firm that recruits
diverse mid and senior-level management from all
industries.

Key Contact - Specialty:
Dr. June L. Owens, JD, President

Salary Minimum: $30,000

Functions: Generalist (All)

Industries: Finance, Non-profits, Pharm Svcs.,
  Legal, Accounting, HR Services, Media,
  Government, Insurance, Healthcare

The Oxbridge Group Ltd

2 Logan Sq
Philadelphia, PA 19103-2707
(215) 567-8800
Fax: (215) 567-8815
Email: info@oxbridgegroup.com
Web: www.oxbridgegroup.com

Summary: We target investment banks, venture
capital and private equity firms where we place
people from the analyst to managing director.

Key Contact - Specialty:
Ms. Nina E. Swift, President - *Financial services*
Ms. Marty M. Brady, Managing Director
Ms. Lauren E. Jones, Chief Operating Officer -
  Financial services
Ms. Julia Koenig Gilbert, Managing Director
Ms. Joanne Doyle Pauley, Managing Director
Ms. Michelle Pratt, Managing Director
Ms. Johanna Tyburski, Managing Director
Ms. Kimberly A. Little, Research Associate
Ms. Molly Blake, Associate
Ms. Lenore Borja, Associate
Ms. Demetra Kareman, Associate
Ms. Christiane Sabo, Associate

Salary Minimum: $100,000

Functions: Senior Mgmt., Cash Mgmt.

Industries: Generalist (All), Invest. Banking,
  Venture Cap.

Branches:
1901 Avenue of the Stars Ste 1075
Los Angeles, CA 90067-6037
(310) 785-0600
Fax: (310) 785-0680
Key Contact - Specialty:
Ms. Carlyn Henry, Consultant

150 E 52nd St Fl 23
New York, NY 10022-6247
(212) 980-0800
Fax: (212) 888-6062
Email: info@oxbridgegroup.com
Key Contact - Specialty:
Ms. Ann Kraftson, Consultant
Ms. Julia Gilbert, Consultant
Ms. Julie Prunier, Consultant

P & L Group Inc

366 N Broadway Ste 312
Jericho, NY 11753-2057
(516) 938-7337
Fax: (516) 939-2490
Email: hy@pandlgroup.net

Summary: Key strengths are in general
management, senior operations/manufacturing,
supply chain management (including purchasing
distribution and logistics), marketing, sales,
engineering, finance, quality assurance and HR.
Considerable success in start-ups and venture-
capital funded operations.

Key Contact - Specialty:
Mr. Hyman Livingston, President - *General
  management, Manufacturing, Marketing,
  Operations, Supply Chain*

Salary Minimum: $80,000

Functions: Mfg., Plant Mgmt., Materials,
  Purchasing, Distribution, Sales & Mktg.,
  Engineering

Industries: Generalist (All), Manufacturing,
  Electronic, Elec. Components, Services, Non-
  Classifiable

Pacific Bridge Inc

7315 Wisconsin Ave Ste 609E
Bethesda, MD 20814-3231
(301) 469-3400
Fax: (301) 469-3409
Email: info@pacificbridge.com
Web: www.pacificbridge.com

Summary: We are a recruiting company that
specializes in placing bilingual candidates.

Key Contact - Specialty:
Mr. Ames Gross, President

Functions: Int'l.

Industries: Generalist (All)

Pacific Recruiting

821D Eva St Ste 80
Montgomery, TX 77356-1808
(936) 597-6500
Fax: (936) 597-8095
Email: hdorland@ez2.net
Web: www.nirassn,com

Summary: Our firm has experience exclusively in
recruiting in the insurance industry. We have
access to openings and candidates on a nationwide
basis.

Key Contact - Specialty:
Mr. Harvey Dorland, President

Salary Minimum: $60,000

Functions: Generalist (All), Management, Senior Mgmt., Middle Mgmt.

Industries: Insurance

Pacific Search Consultants

2377 S El Camino Real Ste 201
San Clemente, CA 92672-3292
(949) 366-9000
Fax: (949) 366-9200
Email: arnold@speechtekjobs.com
Web: www.speechtekjobs.com

Summary: We focus on R&D and place in all levels of management, business development, marketing and product management in addressing the staffing needs of start-up ventures through Fortune 100 companies. Our emphasis has been in speech technology, computer telephony, performance engineering, data storage management systems, software engineering development, SQA/test, compilers, distributed systems, operating systems internals and networking/multi-modal communications.

Key Contact - Specialty:
Mr. Arnold L. Garlick, III, President

Salary Minimum: $60,000

Functions: Board Members, Systems Dev., R&D, Engineering

Industries: Software, Industry Specific SW

Pacific Search Group Inc

18375 Ventura Blvd Ste 427
Tarzana, CA 91356-4218
(818) 705-9990
(818) 705-9991
Fax: (818) 705-9993
Email: nickerpsg@aol.com

Summary: We are specialists in recruiting executives, consultants, CPAs, and other financial & MIS personnel for industry.

Key Contact - Specialty:
Mr. Nick Roberts, President - *CEOs, COOs, MIS*

Salary Minimum: $75,000

Functions: Generalist (All), Senior Mgmt., Finance, CFOs, Taxes, M&A, MIS Mgmt.

Industries: Generalist (All), Wholesale, Retail, Services, Hospitality, Media, Healthcare

Packaging Personnel Company Ltd

520 N Main St
Seymour, WI 54165-1023
(920) 833-9785
Fax: (920) 499-9512
Email: taylor@ppcltd.com
Web: www.ppcltd.com

Summary: We recruit exclusively for the packaging machinery industry, a narrow focus that allows us to help our client companies correctly identify and hire the best professionals for the job. With our extensive history in this unique specialty, we know "who's who" in the industry. We cover all disciplines: sales, marketing, engineering, manufacturing and technical services at all levels from entry to top management. We do retained searches for senior management positions.

Key Contact - Specialty:
Mr. Dick Taylor, President
Ms. Robin Huettl, Vice President

Salary Minimum: $40,000

Functions: Packaging

Industries: Machine, Appliance, Equip Svcs.

Packaging Resources

3317 Partipilo St
Mountain Home, AR 72653-5854
(870) 425-8807
Email: pcarveth@northarkansas.net
Web: www.packaging-resources.com

Summary: A search firm owned and operated by one individual who has been a packaging engineer or packaging manager for many years. Searches are conducted on a contingency basis for large consumer, food, pharmaceutical or medical companies for packaging professionals in R&D, operations and sales/marketing.

Key Contact - Specialty:
Mr. Peter Carveth, Business Owner

Salary Minimum: $35,000

Functions: Packaging, Engineering

Industries: Food, Bev., Tobacco, Drugs Mfg., Medical Devices, Plastics, Rubber, Paints, Petro. Products, Pharm Svcs., Packaging, Biotech/Life Sciences, Healthcare

PackStaff LLC

W1405 Beach Ct
Oostburg, WI 53070-1620
(920) 564-6361
Fax: (920) 564-6362
Email: jobs@packstaff.com
Web: www.packstaff.com

Summary: We are a search firm specializing in packaging engineers.

Key Contact - Specialty:
Mr. Walter Ellis, President

Salary Minimum: $40,000

Functions: Packaging

Industries: Generalist (All)

T Page & Associates

2905 Ranch Road 620 N
Austin, TX 78734-2208
(512) 263-5377
Fax: (512) 263 5783
Email: info@pageandassociates.net
Web: www.pageandassociates.net

Summary: We provide a significant advantage in identifying and attracting top talent by becoming an effective extension of the executive recruiting effort. We perform thorough assessments of our client's business organization, culture, goals and requirements. We strive to completely understand our client's specific search parameters.

Key Contact - Specialty:
Ms. Theresa Page, President - *Distribution, Logistics*
Ms. Yvonne Jones, Associate - *Engineering, Manufacturing*
Ms. Janet Rodriguez - *Distribution, Operations*
Mr. Clay Cooper, Principal

Salary Minimum: $50,000

Functions: Generalist (All), Production, Purchasing, Materials Plng., Distribution, Systems Implem., Engineering

Industries: Generalist (All), Food, Bev., Tobacco, Paper, Drugs Mfg., Computer Equip., Consumer Elect., Misc. Mfg., Retail

Janou Pakter Inc

5 W 19th St Fl 6
New York, NY 10011-4285
(212) 989-1288
Fax: (212) 989-9079
Email: info@jpakter.com
Web: www.janoupakter.com

Summary: We offer global, retainer and contingency executive recruiting and consulting for the design, fashion, publishing, corporate and advertising industries; for example: art direction, creative direction, graphic design, interactive new media, copy, marketing, account management and marketing.

Key Contact - Specialty:
Ms. Janou Pakter, President
Mr. Jerry Tavin, Vice President

Salary Minimum: $40,000

Functions: Generalist (All), Senior Mgmt., Advertising, Mktg. Research, PR, Architects, Graphic Designers, Int'l.

Industries: Generalist (All), Advertising, Publishing, New Media, Broadcast, Film

Lynne Palmer Executive Recruitment Inc

295 Madison Ave Rm 1002
New York, NY 10017-6340
(212) 883-0203
Fax: (212) 883-0149
Email: careers@lynnepalmerinc.com
Web: www.lynnepalmerinc.com

Summary: We offer retainer & contingency recruiting for all levels of the communications industry. Our clients includes major magazine, book and medical education companies in addition to related industries.

Key Contact - Specialty:
Ms. Susan Gordon, President

Functions: Generalist (All), Management, Admin. Svcs., Sales & Mktg., HR Mgmt., Graphic Designers

Industries: Food, Bev., Tobacco, HR Services, K-12 Ed., Higher Ed., Media, Advertising, Publishing, New Media, Communications

Palmer Group

(formerly known as Personnel Inc)
3737 Woodland Ave Ste 300
West Des Moines, IA 50266-1937
(515) 225-7000
Fax: (515) 224-4544
Email: gthomas@thepalmergroup.com
Web: www.thepalmergroup.com

Summary: We provide retained and contingent search services. Our search consultants are specialists with backgrounds in accounting & finance, sales & marketing, engineering, HR, office administration and IT.

Key Contact - Specialty:
Mr. Gregory Thomas, CPA, Director, Search Services
Mr. Austin Palmer, President
Mr. Jack T. Textor, Vice President
Ms. Traci Ellis, Manager, Business

Functions: Generalist (All)

Industries: Generalist (All)

Pan American Search Inc

600 Sunland Park Dr Ste 2-200
El Paso, TX 79912-5136
(915) 833-9991
Fax: (915) 833-9476
Email: resume@panamsearch.com
Web: www.panamsearch.com

Summary: We are an executive search firm specializing in off-shore manufacturing technical and professional management positions primarily up and down the U.S./Mexico border, Mexican interior and Latin America.

Key Contact - Specialty:
Ms. Stephanie Caviness, President

Salary Minimum: $60,000

Functions: Management, Senior Mgmt., Middle Mgmt., Admin. Svcs., Plant Mgmt., Quality, Materials, Purchasing

Industries: Manufacturing, Medical Devices, Plastics, Rubber, Metal Products, Machine, Appliance, Motor Vehicles, Computer Equip., Consumer Elect., Electronic, Elec. Components, Robotics, Consumer Goods

Florence Pape Legal Search Inc

216 13th St
Hoboken, NJ 07030-4435
(201) 798-0200
(800) 762-0096
Fax: (201) 798-9088
Email: fpape@fpls.com
Web: www.fpls.com

Summary: We specialize in the national placement of attorneys in law firms or corporations.

Key Contact - Specialty:
Ms. Florence Pape

Functions: Attorneys

Industries: Legal

Paper Industry Recruitment (PIR)

36 Main St
Gorham, ME 04038-1322
(207) 839-2633
Fax: (207) 839-2634
Email: mc@pirecruitment.com
Web: www.pirecruitment.com

Summary: We do senior-level searches for low up-front fees. We have extensive years of experience in paper industry recruiting. We also have a division, Pir Executive that searches for the very most senior management people in the paper industry.

Key Contact - Specialty:
Mr. Maynard G. Charron, Owner - *Paper*

Salary Minimum: $75,000

Functions: Generalist (All), Senior Mgmt., Product Dev., Plant Mgmt., Quality, Purchasing, Materials Plng., CFOs, Engineering

Industries: Paper

PAPSCO

312 Sterling Oaks Ln
Collierville, TN 38017-7062
(901) 336-4442
Fax: (901) 850-0608
Email: arens@usit.net

Summary: Our firm has over twenty years experience in executive recruitment. We serve most manufacturing processes. Our specialty is in medical product manufacturing, machining, and stamping. We offer complete recruitment solutions for both companies and the professionals.

Key Contact - Specialty:
Mr. Phil Arensberg, Owner
Mrs. Marilyn Arensberg, Systems Administrator

Salary Minimum: $40,000

Functions: Generalist (All)

Industries: Drugs Mfg., Medical Devices, Metal Products, Machine, Appliance, Motor Vehicles, Misc. Mfg.

Paquette Executive Search

104 Cheyney Dr
West Chester, PA 19382-7133
(610) 692-3911
Fax: (610) 692-5744
Email: paquettesearch@msn.com

Summary: We are a national search firm specializing in commercial printing, flexible packaging, converting, graphic arts, labels, envelopes, folding carton and corrugated paper industries.

Key Contact - Specialty:
Mr. Mark Paquette, CPC, President - *Printing*

Salary Minimum: $40,000

Functions: Generalist (All), Management, Senior Mgmt., Middle Mgmt., Mfg., Sales & Mktg.

Industries: Generalist (All), Paper, Printing, Media, Advertising, Publishing, Packaging

Paradigm Management Solutions Inc

270 The Kingsway
Humbertown Shopping Centre PMB 74541
Etobicoke, ON M9A 3T7
Canada
(905) 629-4990
Email: paradigm@pathcom.com
Web: www.keythinkers.ca

Summary: As a management consulting organization, being part of our clients' success is what drives us. Strategically blending our retainer and contingent search, selection and placement services, we deliver 21st century talent - the people who make your business successful.

Key Contact - Specialty:
Ms. Coralee Sheridan, President

Salary Minimum: $30,000

Functions: Management, Middle Mgmt., Healthcare, Finance, Budgeting, Cash Mgmt., Taxes, M&A, R&D, Int'l.

Industries: Generalist (All)

Paradigm Resources

2555 Taylor Rd
Ballwin, MO 63011-1862
(636) 273-1168
Fax: (636) 273-1168
Email: plawrence@paradigmresources.net
Web: www.paradigmresources.net

Summary: Healthcare consulting and recruiting firm, specializing in operational improvement, new business development and placing mid and senior level managers in the hospital setting.

Key Contact - Specialty:
Mr. Patrick Lawrence, President

Salary Minimum: $60,000

Functions: Management

Industries: Hospitals

Paragon Recruiting

17 W 10th St Ste 120
Holland, MI 49423-3189
(616) 494-0001
(888) 396-0394
Fax: (616) 494-0002
Email: foundit@paragonusa.com
Web: www.paragonusa.com

Summary: Our firm specializes in the placement of IT and engineering professionals.

Key Contact - Specialty:
Ms. Elizabeth Nielsen DeWilde, Principal - *Engineering*

Salary Minimum: $20,000

Functions: Generalist (All), IT, MIS Mgmt., Systems Analysis, Systems Dev., Systems Implem., Systems Support, Network Admin., DB Admin.

Industries: Generalist (All), Plastics, Rubber, Machine, Appliance, Motor Vehicles, Computer Equip., Misc. Mfg., Software

Carol Park

819 Walnut St
Kansas City, MO 64106-1818
(816) 421-1326
Fax: (816) 421-8226
Email: carol@carolpark.net
Web: www.nbn
jobs.com/mbrpages/prkwebpg.cfm

Summary: Our firm works only in the area of commercial banking.

Key Contact - Specialty:
Ms. Carol Park, Owner

Salary Minimum: $50,000

Functions: Finance

Industries: Banking

Parker & Lynch

(a division of Accounting Principals Inc)
1 Sansome St Ste 1895
San Francisco, CA 94104-4432
(415) 956-6700
Fax: (415) 956-5642
Email: sanfrancisco@parkerlynch.com
Web: www.parkerlynch.com

Summary: We specialize in the placement of finance and accounting professionals. Our clients range in size from start-ups to Fortune 500 organizations and cover all industries. Our geographic and functional specialization provides our clients and candidates with an unparalleled network of resources.

Key Contact - Specialty:
Ms. Chantelle Morrier, Vice President - *Accounting*
Mr. Montie Parker, Director - *Accounting*

Functions: Finance

Industries: Generalist (All)

Branches:
1050 Crown Pointe Pkwy Ste 1700
Atlanta, GA 30338-7704
(770) 671-9647
Fax: (770) 671-1341
Email: atlanta@parkerlynch.com
Key Contact - Specialty:
Mr. Patrick Myrick, Executive Director

14911 Quorum Dr Ste 120
Dallas, TX 75254-1401
(972) 661-5506
Email: northdallas@parkerlynch.com
Key Contact - Specialty:
Mr. Jason Flournoy, Executive Director

8200 Greensboro Dr Ste 1175
Mc Lean, VA 22102-3872
(703) 761-7001
Email: mclean@parkerlynch.com
Key Contact - Specialty:
Mr. Marc Zeid, Executive Director

Parker, McFadden & Associates

1581 Phoenix Blvd Ste 3
Atlanta, GA 30349-5538
(770) 991-0873
Fax: (770) 996-2455

Email: pma.info@parker-mcfadden.com
Web: www.parker-mcfadden.com

Summary: Our firm specializes in middle and senior management positions. We work with many of the Fortune 500 as well as other smaller public and private companies. Our expertise includes all phases of manufacturing, engineering, sales & marketing and other administrative areas.

Key Contact - Specialty:
Mr. Kenneth A. Parker, Principal
Mr. James R. McFadden, Principal
Mr. George McDaniel, Senior Recruiter
Mr. Craig A. McGaughey, Senior Recruiter

Salary Minimum: $50,000

Functions: Generalist (All), Management, Mfg., Production, Plant Mgmt., Materials, Purchasing, Engineering

Industries: Generalist (All), Metal Products, Machine, Appliance, Motor Vehicles, Misc. Mfg., Aerospace

Parkway Staffing Services

4601 NE 77th Ave Ste 350
Vancouver, WA 98662-6731
(866) 391-6374
(800) 761-2619
Fax: (360) 816-1559
Email: jreed@parkwaystaffing.com
Web: www.parkwaystaffing.com

Summary: Our firm is an executive search and professional staffing organization that focuses within the acute, LTAC, rehabilitation and skilled nursing and senior living segments of the healthcare industry.

Key Contact - Specialty:
Mr. Tony Perry, Managing Director - *Healthcare*
Mr. Joel Reed, Director
Mr. Matthew Warner, PHR, Branch Manager
Mr. Trish Boggess, Office Manager, Business

Salary Minimum: $40,000

Functions: Management, Nurses

Industries: Healthcare, Hospitals, Long-term/Home Care

Parkwood Consulting Intl LLC

8 N Nabby Rd
Danbury, CT 06811-3344
(203) 792-3563
(203) 792-4246
Email: basearcher@aol.com

Summary: Dedicated to excellence in technical and scientific search and recruiting for the pharmaceutical, biotechnology and Medical Device industries.

Key Contact - Specialty:
Mr. Bernard Apotheker, CPC, Recruiter

Salary Minimum: $50,000

Functions: Senior Mgmt., Middle Mgmt., Mfg., Product Dev., Quality, Physicians, R&D, Engineering, Process

Industries: Drugs Mfg., Medical Devices, Pharm Svcs., Biotech/Life Sciences

Parsons, Anderson & Gee Inc

44 Georgetown Ln
Fairport, NY 14450-3361
(716) 223-3770
(888) 586-8679
Fax: (716) 223-8536
Email: info@parandge.com
Web: www.parandge.com

Summary: Principal has worked for Fortune 25 Company as well as for small organization and has been responsible for internal recruitment. Additionally, principal is experienced in competency based interviewing and has extensive years in recruiting.

Key Contact - Specialty:
Mr. Arthur J. Fandel, President & Owner
Ms. Carole Fandel, Vice President, Administration

Salary Minimum: $35,000

Functions: Generalist (All)

Industries: Misc. Financial, Haz. Waste

Partners in Recruiting

PO Box 667
Belvidere, IL 61008-0667
(815) 885-2028
Fax: (815) 885-2048
Email: partnersir@aol.com

Summary: Specialists in the manufacturing industry, we will work with your agenda and complete our assignments in the shortest possible time; thus saving you time and money. We will recruit interested candidates from within your industry that can do the job and are ready to make a career move.

Key Contact - Specialty:
Ms. Diann Helnore, President & Technical Recruiting Manager - *Accounting, Engineering, Management, Manufacturing, Manufacturing (Management)*
Ms. Kim Helnore, Quality Assurance Account Manager - *Logistics, Production, Purchasing, Quality*
Mr. Douglas Helnore, Manager, Food & Beverage Service - *Food*
Ms. Dawn Wenzel, Account Manager, HR Management Training - *Administration, Human resources*
Mr. Lowell Clapp, Director, Executive Mgmt Search
Mr. Austin Davis, Executive Safety Director

Salary Minimum: $45,000

Functions: Generalist (All)

Industries: Generalist (All), Food, Bev., Tobacco, Chemicals, Medical Devices, Plastics, Rubber, Paints, Petro. Products, Metal Products, Machine, Appliance, Motor Vehicles, Test, Measure Equip.

Rick Pascal & Associates Inc

PO Box 543
Dept W
Fair Lawn, NJ 07410-0543
(201) 791-9541
Fax: (201) 791-1861
Email: info@packagecareers.com
Web: www.packagecareers.com

Summary: We focus exclusively on the packaging industry, conducting contingency and retainer searches for packaging engineers and developers, plus packaging related positions in sales and purchasing.

Key Contact - Specialty:
Mr. Rick Pascal, CPC, President - *Desig,), Packagin,)*

Salary Minimum: $60,000

Functions: Packaging

Industries: Food, Bev., Tobacco, Drugs Mfg., Medical Devices, Plastics, Rubber, Consumer Elect., Misc. Mfg., Packaging

Pascale & LaMorte LLC

391 Meadow St
Fairfield, CT 06824-5307
(203) 337-8155
Fax: (203) 337-8136
Email: pascale@pascale-lamorte.com
Web: www.pascale-lamorte.com

Summary: We specialize in financial, accounting and information technology recruitment for middle through executive management.

Key Contact - Specialty:
Mr. Ronald J. Pascale, Principal
Mr. Brian A. LaMorte, Principal
Mr. Kenneth M. Perec, Senior Vice President, Director

Salary Minimum: $75,000

Functions: Middle Mgmt., Finance, CFOs, Budgeting, Cash Mgmt., Taxes, IT, MIS Mgmt., Systems Analysis, Systems Implem.

Industries: Generalist (All), Accounting, Biotech/Life Sciences

Pasona Canada Inc

2040-130 Adelaide St W
Contintental Bank Building
Toronto, ON M5H 3P5
Canada
(416) 867-1162
Fax: (416) 867-1369
Email: jhaywood@pasona.com
Web: www.pasona.com

Summary: We specialize in placing individuals into Japan-related organizations. We provide bilingual and unilingual staff from entry level to senior management to such firms.

Key Contact - Specialty:
Ms. Joy Haywood, President
Ms. Fumie Wada, Branch Manager

Functions: Generalist (All)

Industries: Motor Vehicles, Consumer Elect., Misc. Mfg., Finance, Banking, Invest. Banking, Services, Accounting, HR Services, Aerospace

Paster & Associates

5556 Dayna Ct
New Orleans, LA 70124-1043
(504) 486-7080
Fax: (504) 486-4555
Email: sdpaster@aol.com

Summary: We do medical sales, pharmaceutical sales, sales management and marketing.

Key Contact - Specialty:
Mr. Steve Paster, President - *Pharmaceutical, Sales, Surgical*

Functions: Mktg. Research, Sales Mgmt.

Industries: Drugs Mfg., Medical Devices, Biotech/Life Sciences

Patch & Associates Inc

731 Market St Fl 6
San Francisco, CA 94103-2027
(415) 353-0272
Fax: (415) 503-3985
Email: info@patchassociates.com
Web: www.patchassociates.com

Summary: A full service search firm specializing in: public relations, marketing, corporate communications, and investor relations. We conduct executive searches for agencies and in house positions for firms in: technology, software, new media, consumer products, and financial services. We are a small agency with a large appetite for success.

Key Contact - Specialty:
Ms. Tracy Patch, Principal
Mr. Ronald H. Symansk, Recruiter

Functions: Generalist (All), Board Members,
Senior Mgmt., Middle Mgmt., Mktg. Research,
Mktg. Mgmt., PR

Industries: Generalist (All), Media, Advertising,
Publishing, New Media, Telecoms, Software

Pathfinders Health Search

5554 Reseda Blvd Ste 202
Tarzana, CA 91356-6211
(818) 758-8383
(800) 728-9912
Fax: (818) 758-8382
Email: info@pathfindershealth.com
Web: www.pathfindershealth.com

Summary: We provide placement of surgery nurse
managers.

Key Contact - Specialty:
Mr. Adam Silbar, General Manager
Ms. Debra Taylor, Director, Research Services
Mr. Stuart Silbar, Senior Account Executive -
Healthcare, Pharmaceutical

Salary Minimum: $50,000

Functions: Nurses, Health Admin.

Industries: Generalist (All)

PathSourcePartners

PO Box 2549
Nevada City, CA 95959-1950
(530) 272-4009
(800) 282-2086
Fax: (530) 274-9009
Email: recruiter1@pathsourcepartners.com
Web: www.pathsourcepartners.com

Summary: Executive recruiting firm specializing
in engineering, architectural, and construction
management services for healthcare, education
and science/technology facilities, sustainable
development projects and renewable energy
markets. Typical positions handled are technical
experts, senior managers and business executives.

Key Contact - Specialty:
Mr. David Jordan, Partner - *Built environments,
Construction, Design, Engineering,
Management*
Ms. Laurie Costenborder, Partner - *Biomedical,
Built environments, Design, Engineering,
Management*

Salary Minimum: $80,000

Functions: Senior Mgmt., Middle Mgmt.,
Engineering, Specialized Svcs., Architects

Industries: Construction, Architectural Svcs.,
Engineering Svcs., Biotech/Life Sciences

Patriot Associates

125 Strafford Ave Ste 300
Wayne, PA 19087-3337
(610) 687-7770
(610) 975-4589
Fax: (610) 687-7861
Email: tompatriot@aol.com
Web: www.members.aol.com/tompatriot

Summary: Firm specializes in
pharmaceutical/healthcare. Principal was a
recruitment manager for a major pharmaceutical
firm. We have strong contacts throughout the
industry and know and understand the language.
Specializes in medical liaison/clinical research.
We also have a unit that works with marketing in
the pharmaceutical industry.

Key Contact - Specialty:
Mr. Thomas Meltser, Principal

Salary Minimum: $40,000

Functions: Product Dev., Sales & Mktg., Mktg.
Research, Mktg. Mgmt., Sales Mgmt., Customer
Svc., Staffing, Training, Int'l.

Industries: Drugs Mfg., Pharm Svcs.,
Biotech/Life Sciences, Healthcare, Women's

Patterson Personnel

PO Box 101
Millersburg, OH 44654-0101
(330) 674-4040
Email: ppa709@adelphia.net
Web: www.pattersonpersonnel.com

Summary: Recruiting technical, managerial and
administrative personnel for manufacturing
companies.

Key Contact - Specialty:
Ms. Betty Patterson, Owner
Ms. Barb Swartenztruber, Assistant -
Administration

Salary Minimum: $40,000

Functions: Generalist (All), Admin. Svcs., IT

Industries: Generalist (All), Manufacturing,
Plastics, Rubber, Defense, Aerospace

Joel H Paul & Associates Inc

261 W 35th St Ste 400
New York, NY 10001-1902
(212) 564-6500
Fax: (212) 868-2671
Email: search@joelpaul.com
Web: www.joelpaul.com

Summary: We are an executive search firm
specializing in identifying executives, fundraisers,
directors, educators, etc. for non-profit
organizations.

Key Contact - Specialty:
Mr. Joel H. Paul, President - *Education,
Healthcare, Philanthropy*
Ms. Lillian Amcis, Senior Parnter - *Education,
Healthcare, Philanthropy*
Ms. Judy Magen, Vice President - *Education,
Healthcare, Philanthropy*

Salary Minimum: $60,000

Functions: Management, Board Members, Senior
Mgmt., Middle Mgmt., Health Admin., HR
Mgmt., CFOs, Non-profits

Industries: Non-profits, Mgmt. Consulting, K-12
Ed.

Joel Payne Associates

2880 E Flamingo Rd Ste E
Las Vegas, NV 89121-5223
(702) 733-1818
Fax: (702) 733-0102
Email: jpa@jpalasvegas.com
Web: www.jpalasvegas.com

Summary: We specialize in partner level attorneys
and groups. We also work in commercial
construction.

Key Contact - Specialty:
Mr. Joel Lalonde, Manager

Functions: Management, Attorneys

Industries: Generalist (All), Construction, Legal

Payton & Associates

210 Meidinger Tower
Louisville, KY 40202-4419
(502) 583-1530
Fax: (502) 587-6960
Email: apayton@paytonandassociates.com
Web: www.paytonandassociates.com

Summary: Our firm is committed to conducting
high quality searches. We recruit for senior
positions in law, finance, operations, HR and sales
& marketing.

Key Contact - Specialty:
Mr. Andrew J. Payton, President

Salary Minimum: $50,000

Functions: Generalist (All), Management, Sales
Mgmt., HR Mgmt., Finance, Non-profits,
Attorneys

Industries: Generalist (All), Energy, Utilities,
Manufacturing, Food, Bev., Tobacco,
Chemicals, Drugs Mfg., Medical Devices,
Insurance, Healthcare

PCI Staffing Solutions

11854 Lackland Rd
Saint Louis, MO 63146-4206
(314) 997-1212
Fax: (401) 712-6578
Email: info@tech-staffing.com
Web: www.tech-staffing.com

Summary: We are professional services staffing
firm providing contract, contract-to-hire and
direct-hire resources to companies looking for key
individuals. We serve industries like information
technology,finance, accounting, scientific,
engineering, instructional design, training as well
as client relations management.

Key Contact - Specialty:
Mr. Paul Van Dillen, President
Ms. Lisa Rokusek, Senior Staffing Specialist
Mr. Tony Lane, Senior Account Manager
Mr. John Engelmeyer, Chief Financial Officer -
Information Technology

Salary Minimum: $50,000

Functions: Generalist (All)

Industries: Generalist (All)

Peachtree Peopleware Inc

3530 Ashford Dunwoody Rd NE Ste 210
Atlanta, GA 30319-2002
(404) 252-5865
Fax: (404) 236-0869
Email: resume@ppwisearch.com
Web: www.ppwisearch.com

Summary: We use retained recruiting techniques
on a contingency fee basis to provide technical
recruiting services for high technology clients. We
place permanent and contract professionals in
software & hardware engineering and technical
marketing & sales positions. Our focus is on the
cable TV, energy and telecom industries.

Key Contact - Specialty:
Mr. Chuck Hyder, President - *Sales*
Mr. Burke Sisco, Vice President - *Computers
(Software)*
Ms. Linda Peak, Recruiter

Salary Minimum: $45,000

Functions: Generalist (All), IT

Industries: Telecoms, Wireless, Network
Infrastructure, Software, ERP SW, Networking,
Comm. SW

The Peak Organization

25 W 31st St Fl 12
New York, NY 10001-4413
(212) 947-6600
Fax: (212) 947-6780
Email: info@peakorg.com
Web: www.peakorg.com

Summary: We bring many years of experience in
the search field in the placement of mid to senior

level executives in the following disciplines: law, accounting & finance, marketing and IT.

Key Contact - Specialty:
Mr. Richard Eichenberg, CPC, President - *Finance, Marketing*

Salary Minimum: $50,000

Functions: Advertising, Mktg. Mgmt., Finance, Taxes, Risk Mgmt., IT, Systems Implem., Systems Support, Attorneys, Paralegals

Industries: Generalist (All)

Pearce & Associates
9218 Cypress Green Dr
Jacksonville, FL 32256-5512
(904) 739-1736
Fax: (904) 739-1746
Email: resume@pearcejobs.com
Web: www.pearcejobs.com

Summary: We are search and placement consultants recruiting sales professionals in B2B, IT-related products & services, e-business and telecom. We also handle management positions in the Big Box retail and P&C insurance industries.

Key Contact - Specialty:
Mr. Frank Pearce, Owner - *Business to business, Management, Sales, Staffing*
Ms. Lois Pearce, Owner - *Business to business, Sales*
Mrs. Faye Delaney, Administrative Assistant

Salary Minimum: $30,000

Functions: Sales & Mktg., Sales Mgmt., Staffing

Industries: Generalist (All), Mgmt. Consulting, HR Services, Telecoms

M A Pelle Associates Inc
PO Box 476
Huntington, NY 11743-0476
(631) 385-8925
Fax: (631) 385-5636
Email: mapelleinc@aol.com
Web: www.mapellestaffing.com

Summary: Technical recruiting specialists and also accept on-site recruiting assignments. We serve the following industries: banking, computer, IT, high-technology consumer electronics, aerospace/military defense electronics, semi-conductor and wireless & satellite telecom sectors.

Key Contact - Specialty:
Mr. Michael A. Pelle, President

Salary Minimum: $50,000

Functions: Generalist (All), Board Members, Middle Mgmt.

Industries: Computer Equip., Test, Measure Equip., Accounting, HR Services, IT Implementation, Telecoms, Digital, Wireless, Defense, Aerospace, Software, System SW

Pemberton & Associates
75 Market St Ste 301
Portland, ME 04101-5041
(207) 775-1772
(800) 406-1444
Fax: (207) 775-1983
Email: dpemberton@oldporthr.com
Web: www.oldporthr.com

Summary: Our firm operates in executive search and retention-based HR consulting services. Our search focus is in banking & finance, executive management and healthcare professionals (emphasis on psychiatric sector).

Key Contact - Specialty:
Mr. Theodore Pemberton, President

Salary Minimum: $60,000

Functions: Generalist (All), Management, Senior Mgmt., Healthcare

Industries: Generalist (All), Finance, Banking, Services, Non-profits, Accounting, HR Services, IT Implementation, Advertising, Network Infrastructure, Compliance, Software, Accounting SW, Database SW, Biotech/Life Sciences, Healthcare, Hospitals, Long-term/Home Care

Penn Search
997 Old Eagle School Rd Ste 1006
Wayne, PA 19087-1706
(610) 964-8820
Fax: (610) 964-8916
Web: www.pennsearch.com

Summary: We are a search firm working exclusively with accounting and financial professionals. We are industry generalists; functional specialists.

Key Contact - Specialty:
Mr. Charles DiGiovanni, President

Functions: Finance

Industries: Generalist (All)

Pennington Consulting Group
68 N Main St
Yardley, PA 19067-1410
(215) 493-8312
Fax: (215) 493-0664
Email: admin@pennningtonconsulting.com
Web: www.penningtonconsulting.com

Summary: We are an executive search and consulting firm specializing in wireless communications services.

Key Contact - Specialty:
Mr. Robert B. White, Founder & President
Ms. Elizabeth Ludlow, Vice President
Ms. Trish Ambrosio, Office Manager
Ms. Karen Britt, Account Executive

Functions: Generalist (All), HR Mgmt., Staffing

Industries: Generalist (All), Mgmt. Consulting, HR Services, Communications, Telecoms, Wireless

The Pennmor Group
25 Chestnut St Ste 107
Haddonfield, NJ 08033-1874
(856) 354-1414
Fax: (856) 354-7660
Email: info@pennmor.com
Web: www.pennmor.com

Summary: Experts in discreet one-on-one recruiting process. Specialty areas include all functions in HR, finance, operations, accounting and senior management. Known for our professional approach to clients and candidates and our long-term client relationships.

Key Contact - Specialty:
Mr. Anthony Trasatti, President - *Finance, Human resources, Marketing*
Ms. Jennifer Bartolomeo, Manager, Research - *Finance, Human resources, Marketing*

Salary Minimum: $75,000

Functions: Management, Sales & Mktg., HR Mgmt., Finance

Industries: Manufacturing, Finance, Services, Insurance

Pennswood Partners Inc
PO Box 6976
716 Park Rd N
Wyomissing, PA 19610-0976
(610) 375-8334
(866) 346-3737
Fax: (610) 375-6938
Email: info@pennswoodpartners.com
Web: www.pennswoodpartners.com

Summary: We are a management consulting firm whose mission is to serve manufacturers of industrial products in the building, expanding or strengthening of their rep networks. While our primary business activity is rep search, we also recruit sales management and business development talent for our clients, utilizing our large database of independent manufacturers' reps.

Key Contact - Specialty:
Mr. Roy Koppenhofer, Chairman
Mr. Gary Yeager, Jr., Manager, Rep Services
Ms. Jody Baver, Administrative Manager
Ms. Ellen Stubenvoll, Secretary - *CEOs, Executives, General management, Presidents, Senior management*

Salary Minimum: $50,000

Functions: Management, Senior Mgmt., Middle Mgmt., Mfg., Sales & Mktg., Mktg. Mgmt., Sales Mgmt., Sales Reps.

Industries: Manufacturing, Plastics, Rubber, Metal Products, Machine, Appliance, Misc. Mfg., Electronic, Elec. Components, Robotics, Semiconductors

People Consultants LLC
4885 Olde Towne Pkwy Ste 103
Marietta, GA 30068-5608
(770) 509-6811
Fax: (425) 944-8686
Email: fshackelford@mindspring.com
Web: www.peopleconsultants.com

Summary: We provide human resource consulting to any industry.

Key Contact - Specialty:
Mr. Fletcher Shackelford, Partner

Functions: Board Members, Senior Mgmt., Middle Mgmt., Direct Mktg., Customer Svc.

Industries: Generalist (All)

People Options LLC
44 Hickory Hill Rd
Wilton, CT 06897-1127
(203) 761-1201
Email: alan@peopleoptions.com
Web: www.peopleoptions.com

Summary: Our primary focus is recruiting the management team for growth organizations across most industries. General management, marketing, business development, sales, finance, HR and IT are our functional strengths.

Key Contact - Specialty:
Mr. Alan Nierenberg, CMC, Principal

Salary Minimum: $100,000

Functions: Generalist (All)

Industries: Generalist (All)

People Source LLC
307 Saddler Rd
Grasonville, MD 21638-1066
(410) 827-5882
Email: cap@hpasource.com
Web: www.peoplesourcellc.net

Summary: Our firm conducts searches in the functional areas of accounting & finance, sales,

operations and technical R&D. Our primary vertical markets are defense/aerospace, medical, high-technology and construction.

Key Contact - Specialty:
Mr. Carl Paladino, Principal

Salary Minimum: $50,000

Functions: Generalist (All)

Industries: Generalist (All)

PeopleSource Solutions

2840 Johnson Ferry Rd Ste 150
Marietta, GA 30062-8327
(770) 643-9990
Fax: (770) 643-0818
Email: manager@peoplesourcesolutions.com
Web: www.peoplesourcesolutions.com

Summary: We serve numerous industries and utilize the most technologically advanced systems found in the search and recruiting industry. Our software and e-commerce systems enable our staff to efficiently provide our customers with the most relevant and skilled candidates. Our recruiters are specialists in their respective industry segments.

Key Contact - Specialty:
Mr. Larry Dougherty, CPC, Managing Partner
Mrs. Shannon Curry, Partner
Ms. Debbie Davis, Partner
Mr. Chris Dean, Partner - *Distribution, Logistics*
Mr. Derek Bush, Director - *Distribution, Logistics*
Mr. Richard Dumont, Director - *Construction, HVAC, Mechanical*
Mr. Helgi Legi, Recruiter - *Logistics*
Mrs. Lisa Acton, Recruiter - *Manufacturing*
Mr. Doug Malcolm, Partner - *Consulting*
Mr. David Borel, Partner
Mr. David Case, Recruiter - *Consulting, Distribution, E-business, Logistics, Purchasing*

Salary Minimum: $45,000

Functions: Board Members, Senior Mgmt., Production, Plant Mgmt., Materials, Purchasing, Distribution, Engineering, Mgmt. Consultants

Industries: Generalist (All), Manufacturing, Soap, Perf., Cosmtcs., Drugs Mfg., Medical Devices, Wholesale, Retail, Pharm Svcs., Mgmt. Consulting, New Media, Haz. Waste, Aerospace, Packaging, Software, Biotech/Life Sciences, Healthcare

PeopleWare Technical Resources Inc

302 W Grand Ave Ste 4
El Segundo, CA 90245-5108
(310) 640-2406
Fax: (310) 640-2629
Email: peopleware@peoplewareinc.com
Web: www.peoplewareinc.com

Summary: We are dedicated to placing high quality IT professionals into contract and full-time positions. Our services focus on the development and support of applications and networks for either internal or commercial use. We specialize in Internet, client/server and micro system solutions.

Key Contact - Specialty:
Ms. Sheryl Rooker, President - *Information Technology*
Mr. Jeff Thaler, Chief Financial & Operating Officer - *Finance, Information Technology, Operations*
Ms. Valerie Vincent Taylor, Senior Account Executive - *Information Technology*
Ms. Yolanda Stedman, Manager, Human Resources - *Human resources*
Ms. Joanne Lin, Account Manager - *Information Technology*

Functions: IT

Industries: Network Infrastructure, Software, Accounting SW, Database SW, Development SW, Doc. Mgmt., Production SW, ERP SW, HR SW, Networking, Comm. SW, System SW

PERC Ltd

PO Box 15327
Phoenix, AZ 85060-5327
(800) 874-7246
(602) 553-9896
Fax: (602) 553-9897
Email: gordonstoa@qwest.net
Web: www.percaz.com

Summary: Change is constant. We offer strategic partnership in your search for qualified and competent candidates.

Key Contact - Specialty:
Mr. Gordon Stoa, Manager - *Food, Manufacturing*
Ms. Jackie Stoa, Vice President, Administration

Salary Minimum: $45,000

Functions: Generalist (All), Board Members

Industries: Agri., Forestry, Mining, Energy, Utilities, Construction, Manufacturing, Food, Bev., Tobacco, Chemicals, Misc. Mfg., Pharm Svcs., Mgmt. Consulting, Biotech/Life Sciences, Non-Classifiable

Permanent Search Group Inc/PSG Executive

304-4310 Sherwoodtowne Blvd
Mississauga, ON L4Z 4C4
Canada
(905) 276-2006
Fax: (905) 276-0258
Email: jobs@permanentsearch.com
Web: www.permanentsearch.com

Summary: We're a strategic recruitment firm focused on creating symbiotic associations between cutting edge companies and consummate candidates. Our diverse expertise enables us to scout talent for a spectrum of positions including: HR, sales, marketing, finance, corporate recruitment, operations, logistics and customer response.

Key Contact - Specialty:
Ms. Lisa Price, Partner
Ms. Lorrie Clark, Partner
Ms. Lori Forcione, Director, First Impressions
Mr. Chris Boyd, Manager, Sales Strategy
Ms. Sandra Gomes, Manager, Talent Acquisition
Ms. Grainne Walsh, Senior Associate
Ms. Rachelle Cushing, Associate
Ms. Magdalena Sorge, Associate
Ms. Trish O'Quinn, Associate
Ms. Elia Tio, Associate
Ms. Elaine DoRosario, Associate, Recruiting

Functions: Generalist (All), Management

Industries: Finance, HR Services, Logistics Svcs.

Permanent Solutions Inc

1500-4 Robert Speck Pky
Executive Centre
Mississauga, ON L4Z 1S1
Canada
(905) 566-5950
Email: resume@permanentsolutions.com
Web: www.permanentsolutions.com

Summary: We are a recruitment firm specializing in excelling corporate performance through identifying and isolating high achievers in management of sales/marketing, accounting/finance and HR.

Key Contact - Specialty:
Ms. Catherine Varga, President

Functions: Management, Middle Mgmt., Admin. Svcs.

Industries: Generalist (All), Manufacturing, Wholesale, Finance, Pharm Svcs., Accounting, Media, Telecoms, Insurance, Healthcare, Non-Classifiable

Permanent Staff Company Inc

28200 Orchard Lake Rd Ste 100
Farmington Hills, MI 48334-3761
(248) 737-5860
Fax: (248) 737-5886
Email: dmistura@ppcinconline.com
Web: www.personnelconsultants.com

Summary: We specialize in recruiting, technical, professional and management in accounting, marketing, engineering, technical, manufacturing, IT,administration,office support

Key Contact - Specialty:
Mr. Dan Mistura, President

Salary Minimum: $50,000

Functions: Management, Admin. Svcs., Mfg., HR Mgmt., IT

Industries: Generalist (All), Construction, Manufacturing, Plastics, Rubber, Metal Products, Motor Vehicles, Misc. Mfg., Transportation, Finance, Services, HR Services, IT Implementation, Engineering Svcs., Logistics Svcs., Packaging, Software, Mfg. SW, Marketing SW

Perry • Newton Associates

PO Box 1158
Rockville, MD 20849-1158
(301) 340-3360
Fax: (301) 340-3080
Email: executive_recruiters@perrynewton.com
Web: www.perrynewton.com

Summary: We provide retail search and placement, exclusively. We identify, recruit and place mid/upper level retailers. Positions that we work on include: director/VP of stores, district/regional management, HR executives, financial officers and merchants.

Key Contact - Specialty:
Mr. Dick Perry, President
Ms. Marje Newton, Senior Vice President

Salary Minimum: $40,000

Functions: Generalist (All), Management

Industries: Retail

David Perry Associates

525 Route 73 S Ste 201
Marlton, NJ 08053-9650
(856) 596-9400
Fax: (856) 596-9125
Email: davperas@att.net
Web: www.davidperryassociates.com

Summary: Mainly recruit and place candidates in the consumer packaged goods industry. In sales - anyone from key account manager to VP of sales. In marketing - brand managers to GMs.

Key Contact - Specialty:
Mr. Raymond Spadaro, President - *General management, Marketing, Sales*

Salary Minimum: $55,000

Functions: Senior Mgmt., Middle Mgmt., Sales & Mktg., Mktg. Research, Mktg. Mgmt., Sales Mgmt.

Industries: Food, Bev., Tobacco, Textiles, Apparel, Soap, Perf., Cosmtcs., Drugs Mfg., Consumer Elect., Misc. Mfg., Recreation

Fred Perry Associates

PO Box 680487
Houston, TX 77268-0487
(281) 350-2809
Fax: (281) 350-2894
Email: fred@fperry.com
Web: www.fperry.com

Summary: Experience recruiting for the nation's leading consulting engineering firms specializing in environmental and infrastructure.

Key Contact - Specialty:
Mr. Fred Perry, Executive Recruiter - *Consulting, Engineering*

Functions: Generalist (All)

Industries: Construction, Engineering Svcs., Environmental Svcs., Haz. Waste

Personalized Management Associates Inc

1950 Spectrum Cir SE Ste B310
Marietta, GA 30067-8473
(800) 466-7822
(770) 916-1668
Fax: (770) 916-1429
Email: david@pmasearch.com
Web: www.pmasearch.com

Summary: We are a executive search chain specializing in management in all industries, including; but not limited to: HR, management, marketing, manufacturing, retail, restaurant, real estate and franchising. We are retained and contingency.

Key Contact - Specialty:
Mr. David Hottle, CPC, Executive Vice President - *Middle management, Restaurants, Retail, Sales, Supermarkets*
Mr. Bill Lins, CPC, Executive Director, Operations

Salary Minimum: $45,000

Functions: Generalist (All)

Industries: Retail, HR Services, E-commerce, Hospitality, Hotels, Resorts, Clubs, Restaurants, Quick Service Restaurants, Full Service Restaurants, Inst./Industrial Food Svc., Entertainment

Branches:
225 Worcester Rd
Framingham, MA 01701-5355
(866) 473-8050
Fax: (508) 620-5805
Email: pmaboston@pmasearch.com
Key Contact - Specialty:
Ms. Jennifer Long, President - *Food & beverage, Hospitality, Management, Restaurants, Retail*
Mrs. Gretchen O'Brien, Vice President - *Food service, Hospitality, Hotels, Restaurants, Retail*

3000 United Founders Blvd
Oklahoma City, OK 73112-3958
(866) 842-2972
Fax: (405) 767-9162
Email: pmaoklahoma@pmasearch.com
Key Contact - Specialty:
Mrs. Teresa Hawkins, President - *Food service, Hospitality, Hotels, Restaurants, Retail*
Mr. David Hottle, Vice President - *Food service, Hospitality, Management, Restaurants, Retail*

Personnel Associates

140 McIntyre Rd
Cherryville, NC 28021-9314
(704) 480-7603

Summary: Executive search firm with expertise in minority recruitment serving the business professional through our nationwide network. Our office has experience in supporting operations, manufacturing, engineering and quality professionals.

Key Contact - Specialty:
Mr. Cliff Neighbors, President
Ms. Betty Neighbors
Ms. Chastity Tindall

Salary Minimum: $40,000

Functions: Generalist (All), Management, Mfg., Materials, Sales & Mktg., HR Mgmt., IT, Engineering

Industries: Generalist (All), Manufacturing, Finance, Media, Environmental Svcs., Packaging

Personnel Associates Inc

22433 Arbordale Ct
Murrieta, CA 92562-3089
(800) 733-5377
Email: sganz@uspublishingjobs.com
Web: www.uspublishingjobs.com

Summary: Searches conducted in most areas of publishing: specialize in acquisitions editorial and in sales/marketing for medical, college & professional and reference publishing. Work with some electronic publishing houses.

Key Contact - Specialty:
Mr. Steve Ganz, Recruiter - *Publishing*
Ms. Marjorie Crawford, Recruiter - *Publishing*

Salary Minimum: $35,000

Functions: Middle Mgmt., Sales & Mktg., Sales Reps.

Industries: Publishing

Personnel Associates Inc

120 E Washington St Ste 928
Syracuse, NY 13202-4010
(315) 422-0070
Fax: (315) 474-7293
Email: info@personnel-associates.com
Web: www.personnel-associates.com

Summary: We represent employers seeking high performing insurance professionals, managers and executives. Our clients are national and regional carriers, risk retention groups, third party administrators, national brokers, large regional agencies and risk management consulting firms.

Key Contact - Specialty:
Mr. Peter J. Baskin, CPC, President
Ms. Mary Beth Elmer, CPC, Vice President

Salary Minimum: $50,000

Functions: Generalist (All)

Industries: Insurance

Personnel Consultants

14042 NE 8th St Ste 201
Bellevue, WA 98007-4142
(425) 641-0657

Summary: Extensive experience specifically in the insurance industry.

Key Contact - Specialty:
Mr. Larry L. Dykes, MBA, JD, President

Salary Minimum: $35,000

Functions: Generalist (All), Risk Mgmt.

Industries: Finance, Insurance

Personnel Consulting Associates

7600 Jericho Tpke Ste 304
Woodbury, NY 11797-1705
(516) 364-1460
(800) 741-7199
Fax: (516) 364-2520
Email: joeslater@pcasearch.com
Web: www.pcasearch.com

Summary: We are an executive search firm serving the financial services industry. We've successfully completed searches for senior management and staff in commercial, retail & private banking, capital markets, risk, marketing, HR and accounting. Our consultants have industry expertise, a broad base of contacts and strong assessment skills.

Key Contact - Specialty:
Mr. Joseph Slater, Managing Principal - *Banking, Banking (Commercial,Corporate,Investment,Merchant)*
Mr. Adam Slater, Associate, Recruiting - *Banking (Commercial,Corporate,Merchant,Mortgage,Retail)*
Ms. Brenda Miller, Office Manager

Salary Minimum: $50,000

Functions: Generalist (All)

Industries: Finance, Banking, Invest. Banking, Misc. Financial, Mgmt. Consulting, HR Services, Advertising, Publishing

The Personnel Consulting Group

210 Baronne St Ste 922
New Orleans, LA 70112-4123
(800) 783-7533
(504) 581-7800
Fax: (504) 568-1222
Email: personnel@personnel-group.com
Web: www.personnel-group.com

Summary: We are placement specialists in accounting and finance, information technology, engineering, sales and marketing, human resources, and attorneys.

Key Contact - Specialty:
Mr. Frank Loria, CPC, President
Mr. Norman (Chip) Kerth, CPC, Manager - *Finance*

Functions: Sales & Mktg., Sales Mgmt., HR Mgmt., Finance, CFOs, IT, MIS Mgmt., Engineering, Attorneys, Paralegals

Industries: Generalist (All)

Personnel Inc

PO Box 1413
Huntsville, AL 35807-0413
(256) 536-4431
Fax: (256) 539-0583
Email: projobs1@bellsouth.net

Summary: Presently work with 34 agencies that met through networks. We specialize in engineering and manufacturing firms.

Key Contact - Specialty:
Mr. Bill Breen, President & Manager - *Engineering, Management*

Salary Minimum: $50,000

Functions: Generalist (All), Middle Mgmt., Production, Materials, HR Mgmt., IT, Engineering

Industries: Generalist (All), Manufacturing, Computer Equip., Misc. Mfg., Telecoms, Aerospace, Software

Personnel Management Resources

PO Box 1522
Manhattan, KS 66505-1522
(785) 776-6000
Fax: (785) 776-3178
Web: www.pmrjobs.com

Summary: We are a health care search firm specializing in physicians, nurse managers and pharmacists.

Key Contact - Specialty:
Mr. Clay Zapletal, President - *Healthcare*

Functions: Board Members, Physicians, Nurses, Allied Health, Health Admin.

Industries: Pharm Svcs., Healthcare, Hospitals, Long-term/Home Care, Physical Therapy, Occupational Therapy

Personnel Management Resources

PO Box 831
Carthage, MO 64836-0831
(800) 638-7501
Fax: (417) 358-4418
Email: pmrcareers@sbcglobal.net
Web: www.topmedicalcareers.com

Summary: Medical staffing firm placing healthcare professionals in hospitals and clinics.

Key Contact - Specialty:
Mr. Blake Zapletal, Account Executive

Personnel Management Group

300-1 Wesley Ave
Century Plaza
Winnipeg, MB R3C 4C6
Canada
(204) 982-1100
Fax: (204) 943-9535
Email: yvonne@pmg.mb.ca
Web: www.pmg.mb.ca

Summary: We have extensive experience in technical, manufacturing and logistics recruitment, including IT personnel in development & networks, accountants, all disciplines in engineering, manufacturing managers and supply chain specialists. Our service includes permanent placements and contract technical workers including project managers and IT specialists.

Key Contact - Specialty:
Ms. Yvonne Baert, Director & Owner - *Engineering, Manufacturing, Systems*
Mr. Robert A. Baert, Director & Owner - *Construction*
Ms. Cynthia Wharton, Recruiter, Logistics & Manufacturing - *Distribution, Logistics, Manufacturing, Transportation*

Salary Minimum: $40,000

Functions: Generalist (All), Mfg., Quality, Materials Plng., Distribution, HR Mgmt., CFOs, IT, Engineering

Industries: Generalist (All), Agri., Forestry, Mining, Energy, Utilities, Construction, Manufacturing, Transportation, Wholesale, Services, Packaging, Software

The Personnel Network Inc

PO Box 1426
Irmo, SC 29063-1426
(803) 781-2087
(803) 749-9355
Fax: (803) 732-7986
Email: chuckirmo@aol.com

Summary: Management and professional staff recruited confidentially in all areas of: manufacturing, public administration, marketing, hospitality, engineering, industrial, healthcare and environmental. Fax service on resumes for instant results.

Key Contact - Specialty:
Mr. Charles L. Larsen, Managing Director & EO - *Environmental, Hospitality, Industrial*
Mr. C. Lars Larsen, President - *Engineering*
Mr. James K. Larsen, Executive Vice President - *Industrial*
Ms. Sarah K. Hoechstetter, Associate Director - *Hospitality*
Mr. Carl L. Bullard, Manager, North Carolina - *Automotive, Hospitality*

Salary Minimum: $25,000

Functions: Generalist (All), Senior Mgmt., Middle Mgmt., Production, Allied Health, Engineering, Environmentalists, Graphic Designers

Industries: Generalist (All), Textiles, Apparel, HR Services, Hospitality, Entertainment, Media, Publishing, Government, Environmental Svcs., Healthcare

Personnel Search Ltd

883 Main St
Moncton, NB E1C 1G5
Canada
(506) 857-2156
Fax: (506) 857-9172
Email: pscareer@nbnet.nb.ca
Web: www.personnel-search.com

Summary: We search the industry looking for people who meet our client's requirements, matching the candidates' requirements and preferences with our client's needs. Our clients are large and medium sized companies in various industries. We provide cost effective services to meet the specific needs of each of our clients nationwide.

Key Contact - Specialty:
Ms. Lynn Breau, Recruiter

Functions: Generalist (All)

Industries: Generalist (All)

Personnel Solutions

15020 N Hayden Rd Ste 205
Scottsdale, AZ 85260-2552
(480) 946-0999
Email: rick@mymedicalrecruiter.com
Web: www.mymedicalrecruiter.com

Summary: Our firm specializes in recruiting nationally in the medical and pharmaceuticals sales market place.

Key Contact - Specialty:
Mr. Rick Spargo, President
Mr. Dan Kerr, Vice President, Recruiting Services

Functions: Sales Mgmt., Sales Reps.

Industries: Drugs Mfg., Medical Devices, Pharm Svcs., Biotech/Life Sciences, Healthcare, Hospitals, Long-term/Home Care, Dental

Personnel Unlimited/Executive Search

25 W Nora Ave
Spokane, WA 99205-4800
(509) 326-8880
Fax: (509) 326-0112
Email: gary@puinc.net
Web: www.puinc.net

Summary: We have exposure in all areas of employment. We have extensive experience providing executive searches for client companies.

Key Contact - Specialty:
Mr. Gary P. Desgrosellier, President - *Management*
Ms. Brandi McHenry, Executive Recruiter

Salary Minimum: $60,000

Functions: Management, Sales & Mktg., Sales Mgmt., Sales Reps.

Industries: Generalist (All), Food, Bev., Tobacco

J R Peterman Associates Inc

PO Box 3083
Stowe, VT 05672-3083
(802) 253-6304
Fax: (802) 253-6314
Email: peterman@jrpeterman.com
Web: www.jrpeterman.com

Summary: We specialize in life and health insurance, especially group, and employee benefits consulting. We work on a national basis, and do some international benefits recruiting. We recruit management and professionals in all disciplines including: underwriting, sales, claims, compliance, consultants, marketing, accounting, and administration/POS.

Key Contact - Specialty:
Mr. James R. Peterman, President
Mr. Jeremy K. Peterman, Director, Recruiting

Salary Minimum: $50,000

Functions: Generalist (All), Middle Mgmt., Sales Reps., Finance, Actuaries, Pension/Ret. Planning, Int'l.

Industries: Insurance, Claims, Life, Re-Insurance

Petro Staff International

510-706 7 Ave SW
Calgary, AB T2P 0Z1
Canada
(403) 266-8988
Fax: (403) 262-1310
Email: resumes@petro-staff.com
Web: www.petro-staff.com

Summary: We specialize in recruitment of professionals for international oil and gas companies as well as petroleum specialists. We also recruit IS and IT professionals, as well as medical personnel.

Key Contact - Specialty:
Mr. Iqbal E. Ali, Managing Director

Functions: Generalist (All), Management, Healthcare, HR Mgmt., Finance, IT, Engineering, Int'l.

Industries: Generalist (All), Energy, Utilities, Oil & Gas, Chemicals, Misc. Mfg., Aerospace, Software, Healthcare

Petruzzi Associates

PO Box 141
Scotch Plains, NJ 07076-0141
(908) 928-9083
Fax: (908) 928-9084
Email: vpetruzzi@comcast.net

Summary: In search of excellence for hard to find individuals in the areas of manufacturing, packaging, engineering, clinical data and marketing. We are primarily in the medical device, CRO, pharmaceutical, chemical and plastics industry.

Key Contact - Specialty:
Mr. Vincent J. Petruzzi, President - *Engineering, Manufacturing*

Salary Minimum: $40,000

Functions: Generalist (All), Management, Mfg., Materials, Mktg. Mgmt., Sales Mgmt., R&D, Engineering

Industries: Generalist (All), Chemicals, Soap, Perf., Cosmtcs., Drugs Mfg., Medical Devices, Plastics, Rubber, Paints, Petro. Products, Packaging

The Pettis Group Inc

903 Buckthorne Ct
Valparaiso, IN 46383-9788
(219) 464-2465
(866) 575-6932
Fax: (219) 477-4145
Email: johnpettis@thepettisgroup.com
Web: www.thepettisgroup.com

Summary: Our firm is a contingency search firm that focuses on industrial sales, marketing and sales management personnel. Our area of specialty is the material handling industry. Our personalized 16-step approach to each search assures our clients the right personnel for their specific needs, assures our candidates a secure career placement and assures our firm continued repeat business. Our interest is in earning your future business not just your initial order.

Key Contact - Specialty:
Mr. John A. Pettis, II, President

Salary Minimum: $50,000

Functions: Sales & Mktg.

Industries: Plastics, Rubber, Metal Products, Machine, Appliance, Test, Measure Equip., Misc. Mfg., Electronic, Elec. Components, Robotics, Government, Packaging

The Robert Pfaendler Company LLC

19800 Village Office Ct Ste 206
Bend, OR 97702-1813
(541) 389-4330
Fax: (541) 389-4331
Email: robert@robertpfaendler.com
Web: www.robertpfaendler.com

Summary: We offer only the highest code of professional and ethical standards.

Key Contact - Specialty:
Mr. Robert E. Pfaendler, President - *Banking (Commercial,Corporate,Retail), CEOs, CFOs*
Ms. Susan M. Koch, Administration & Office Manager - *Administration, Banking*
Mr. Richard J. Pliler, Senior Recruiting Consultant - *Banking, Banking (Commercial,Corporate,Retail), CFOs*
Mr. William A. Summerfield, Senior Recruiting Consultant - *Banking, Banking (Commercial,Corporate,Retail), CFOs*

Salary Minimum: $75,000

Functions: Generalist (All), Finance

Industries: Finance, Banking, Misc. Financial

PFS Financial

2028 S 8th St
Philadelphia, PA 19148-2422
(215) 661-0528
Fax: (215) 661-9266
Email: james_vines@excite.com

Key Contact - Specialty:
Mr. James Vines, District Manager

Functions: Sales Mgmt.

Industries: Generalist (All), Construction, Food, Bev., Tobacco, Transportation, Non-profits, Pharm Svcs., Equip Svcs., Mgmt. Consulting, Hospitality, Real Estate

Pharmaceutical Careers Inc

PO Box 124
Pleasantville, NY 10570-0124
(914) 769-1400
Fax: (914) 769-1496
Email: mail@pharmaceuticalcareers.com
Web: www.pharmaceuticalcareers.com

Summary: Employment recruiters to the pharmaceutical and biotechnology industries.

Key Contact - Specialty:
Mr. Tom Bramswig, Principal
Mr. John Clifford

Functions: HR Mgmt.

Industries: Pharm Svcs., Biotech/Life Sciences, Healthcare

Pharmaceutical Search Professionals Inc

311 N Sumneytown Pike Ste 1A
North Wales, PA 19454-2532
(215) 699-1900
(866) 670-7774
Fax: (215) 699-9189
Email: pspi@pspisearch.com
Web: www.pharmaceutical-search.com

Summary: We have earned an unprecedented reputation for placing MD, PhD and MBA level executives. Our clientele consists of the top pharmaceutical, biotechnology and medical device companies.

Key Contact - Specialty:
Mr. Tony M. Fischetti, Founder, President & CEO
Mr. John D. Wuko, Corporate Vice President - *CEOs*
Mr. David Graham, Corporate Vice President - *CEOs*

Functions: Generalist (All)

Industries: Pharm Svcs., Biotech/Life Sciences

PHD Conseil en Ressources Humaines Inc

2821-1 Place Ville-Marie
Immeuble Commercial
Montreal, QC H3B 4R4
Canada
(514) 861-7100
Fax: (514) 879-3281
Email: phdelisle@videotron.ca

Summary: We offer selection and recruitment of executives and seasoned professionals in information technology and information technology sales.

Key Contact - Specialty:
Mr. Pierre H. Delisle, President

Salary Minimum: $75,000

Functions: Generalist (All), Management, Mktg. Mgmt., Sales Mgmt., MIS Mgmt., Systems Analysis, Systems Implem., Network Admin., DB Admin.

Industries: Generalist (All), Agri., Forestry, Mining, Computer Equip., Consumer Elect., Equip Svcs., Mgmt. Consulting, E-commerce, IT Implementation, New Media, Telecoms, Call Centers, Telephony, Digital, Wireless, Network Infrastructure, Software

Phelps Personnel Associates

(also known as Strategic Recruiters Inc)
PO Box 26442
Greenville, SC 29616-1442
(864) 232-8139

Email: info@phelpspersonnel.com
Web: www.phelpspersonnel.com

Summary: We have extensive experience in recruiting for manufacturing clients. Our services are always company fee paid. We place permanent, engineering, technical, HR and other manufacturing support positions. Our client companies include automotive and consumer products, film, plastics, electro-mechanical and various metal working processes.

Key Contact - Specialty:
Mr. Dwight H. Smith, Jr., President - *Engineering, Human resources, Technical*
Mr. Dan Blakely

Salary Minimum: $40,000

Functions: Mfg., Product Dev., Plant Mgmt., Packaging, Sales Mgmt., HR Mgmt., Engineering, Graphic Designers

Industries: Manufacturing, Paper, Printing, Chemicals, Drugs Mfg., Plastics, Rubber, Paints, Petro. Products, Metal Products, Machine, Appliance, Motor Vehicles, Packaging

Phillips & Juarez Inc

10364 Triple Crown Ave Ste 100
Jacksonville, FL 32257-4791
(904) 260-2929
(888) 710-6565
Fax: (202) 478-0445
Email: dep@legalonesearch.com
Web: www.pjlegalsearch.com

Summary: We are a legal placement firm providing services to in-house and law firm clients and candidates. We provide in-house, client driven search capabilities for companies running the gamut from small regionals to Fortune 500s. Our private law firm placements tend to focus on the senior level attorney, practice group relocation and firm merger.

Key Contact - Specialty:
Mr. Donald E. Phillips, Recruiter

Functions: Board Members, Attorneys

Industries: Legal, Law Enforcement

Colin Phillips Group Inc

PO Box 4679
Boulder, CO 80306-4679
(303) 604-2116
Fax: (303) 604-2501
Email: info@colinphillips.com
Web: www.colinphillips.com

Summary: Our firm is a specialist in placing experienced sales & marketing, operations, engineering and human resources professionals in the high technology, manufacturing and service sectors.

Key Contact - Specialty:
Mr. Colin Frager, President

Salary Minimum: $75,000

Functions: Management, Mfg., Sales & Mktg., Advertising

Industries: Generalist (All), Manufacturing, Services, HR Services, Communications, Government, Aerospace, Packaging, Software

Phillips Personnel/Search

1675 Broadway Ste 2410
Denver, CO 80202-4624
(303) 893-1850
Email: phil@phillipspersonnel.com
Web: www.phillipspersonnel.com

Summary: Contingency and retained search - finance & accounting, sales & marketing, IT & IS,

engineering, production, administration and general & executive management.

Key Contact - Specialty:
Mr. Phil Heinschel, CPC, President - *Banking (Commercial), Distribution, Financial services, Human resources, Non-profit*
Mr. Bob Cunningham, Senior Technical Recruiter - *Energy, Engineering, Information Technology, Pipeline, Telecommunications*
Ms. Becky Wichern, Senior Sales & Marketing Recruiter - *Business development, Consumer (Marketing), Marketing, Sales*
Ms. Phyllis Jacques, Senior Administrative Recruiter - *Human resources, Legal, Non-profit, Office (Administration,Support)*

Salary Minimum: $55,000

Functions: Middle Mgmt., Admin. Svcs., Distribution, Sales & Mktg., Sales Mgmt., HR Mgmt., Finance, IT

Industries: Generalist (All), Metal Products, Electronic, Elec. Components, Semiconductors, Consumer Goods, Finance, Misc. Financial, Non-profits, Accounting, HR Services, Telecoms, Software

Richard Phillips Recruiting
1 Gerstle Ct
San Rafael, CA 94901-3600
(415) 721-7569

Summary: At our firm we provide executive and technical search and recruiting for small technology firms. We are generalists, handling positions in all departments, at any level.

Key Contact - Specialty:
Mr. Richard Phillips, Owner

Functions: Generalist (All)

Industries: Software

Phillips Resource Group
PO Box 5664
Greenville, SC 29606-5664
(864) 271-6350
Fax: (864) 271-8499
Email: info@sbphillips.com
Web: www.sbphillips.com

Summary: Industry specialists. Former officer level managers offer a high degree of client consciousness and business understanding supporting organization planning as well as executive search for all management and staff levels.

Key Contact - Specialty:
Mr. Sam B. Phillips, Jr.
Mr. Albert M. Hicks, President, Retained Search
Mr. C. Crawford Chavous, President - *Management consulting, Manufacturing (Management), Organizational development*
Mr. Jad Anthony, Executive Recruiter
Ms. Cam Donovan, Executive Recruiter - *Biopharmaceutical, Business to business, Hospital, Pharmaceutical, Sales*
Ms. Krista Matsumoto, Executive Recruiter

Salary Minimum: $30,000

Functions: Generalist (All), Management, Mfg., Healthcare, Sales & Mktg., Finance, IT, R&D, Engineering, Legal

Industries: Generalist (All), Textiles, Apparel, Paper, Chemicals, Plastics, Rubber, Machine, Appliance, Misc. Mfg., Banking

Branches:
PO Box 1495
Lancaster, SC 29721-1495
(800) 924-8279
Fax: (803) 285-7925
Email: plunkett@comporium.net

Key Contact - Specialty:
Mr. Mike Plunkett, Executive Recruiter - *Manufacturing, Manufacturing (Management)*

Phoenix Group International
PO Box 5690
Carefree, AZ 85377-5690
(480) 575-6636
(888) 208-8714
Fax: (480) 575-9365
Email: sflynn@phxgrpintl.com
Web: www.phxgrpintl.com

Summary: We are an executive recruiting firm specializing in placing analysts, associates, VPs, principals and partners in private equity firms, venture capital firms, hedge funds, and investment banks.

Key Contact - Specialty:
Mr. Stephen Flynn, Managing Director

Salary Minimum: $60,000

Functions: M&A

Industries: Invest. Banking, Venture Cap., Mutual/Hedge Funds

The Phoenix Health Search Group
PO Box 453
Ramsey, NJ 07446-0453
(201) 818-7355
Email: mail@phoenixhs92@aol.com
Web: www.phoenixhealthsearch.com

Summary: We provide professional executive-level search and recruitment of healthcare personnel, in the managed healthcare, medical devices, sub-acute healthcare services and pharmaceutical fields.

Key Contact - Specialty:
Mr. Gregory J. Erstling, Principal - *Administration, Management, Marketing, Sales*

Salary Minimum: $40,000

Functions: Middle Mgmt., Healthcare, Sales & Mktg.

Industries: Medical Devices, Pharm Svcs., Haz. Waste, Insurance, Life, Healthcare, Hospitals

Phoenix Partners Inc
6360 Glen Oaks Ln NE
Atlanta, GA 30328-4195
(404) 459-6995
Email: bobm@phoenixpartners.com
Web: www.phoenixpartners.com

Summary: We are a retained/contingency search firm specializing in corporate contracted searches for individuals who have focused their careers in the direct sales and support of computer software products and services. Our firm is involved in searches for software sales managers, sales reps, accounts executives, systems architects and software consultants.

Key Contact - Specialty:
Mr. Robert A. Martin, Managing Director - *Computers (Software)*

Salary Minimum: $150,000

Functions: Sales & Mktg.

Industries: Computer Equip., Software

Phoenix Search Group Inc
112 Sheppard Ave W
North York, ON M2N 1M5
Canada
(416) 221-5077
Fax: (416) 221-5059

Email: bruce@phoenixsearch.on.ca
Web: www.phoenixsearch.on.ca

Summary: We specialize globally in all disciplines. With a foundation grounded in the Greater Toronto Area. We have established a national reputation for accomplishing delicate recruiting assignments. The firm's extensive expertise as a full-service, specially-focused search firm has brought it considerable success, growth, and recognition.

Key Contact - Specialty:
Mr. Bruce Sturley, President

Salary Minimum: $45,000

Functions: Generalist (All)

Industries: Generalist (All)

Phoenix Technical Services Inc
5495 Fox Ridge Dr
West Bloomfield, MI 48322-2014
(248) 788-7671
Fax: (248) 788-7669
Email: resumes@ptscareers.com
Web: www.ptscareers.com

Summary: We specialize in engineering, technical and executive recruiting for the automotive and aerospace industries. We provide retained and contingent searches.

Key Contact - Specialty:
Mr. Louis Wassel, Vice President - *Automotive, Engineering*
Mr. Nimish Desai, President - *Automotive*

Salary Minimum: $50,000

Functions: Middle Mgmt., Mfg., Product Dev., Materials, R&D, Engineering, Minorities/Diversity

Industries: Manufacturing, Metal Products, Motor Vehicles, Electronic, Elec. Components, Transportation, Finance, Aerospace

Physician Recruiting Services Inc
15620 Manchester Rd Ste 9
Ellisville, MO 63011-2276
(636) 527-1884
(800) 872-2106
Fax: (636) 527-1841
Email: cmcprs1@aol.com

Summary: Our contingency firm provides a virtually risk free service to physicians, hospitals, medical groups, etc. assisting in matching physician staffing needs with appropriate candidates.

Key Contact - Specialty:
Mr. Chuck McMillan, Principal - *Physicians*

Salary Minimum: $100,000

Functions: Physicians

Industries: Healthcare, Hospitals, Long-term/Home Care

Physicians Search® Inc
18410 Irvine Blvd
Tustin, CA 92780
(714) 832-0230
(800) 748-6320
Fax: (714) 832-7858
Email: wally@physicianssearch.com
Web: www.physicianssearch.com

Summary: We are an established, reputable, ethical physician recruitment and medical practice brokerage firm serving clients in the healthcare industry for many years. We also do appraisals for medical practices.

Key Contact - Specialty:
Mr. Tom Fitterer, President - *Analysts,*
Brokerage, Sales

Salary Minimum: $100,000

Functions: Senior Mgmt., Nurses, Allied Health,
Health Admin., M&A

Industries: HR Services, Real Estate, Healthcare

Piedmont Group Inc

1316 W Chester Pike
West Chester, PA 19382-6425
(610) 998-0541
Email: bob@piedmontgroup.net
Web: www.piedmontgroup.net

Summary: Specializing in the chemical and petro
chemical industry. Staffing solutions in the areas
of management, engineering, research,
environmental, safety and sales & marketing.

Key Contact - Specialty:
Mr. Robert Meitz, President

Salary Minimum: $60,000

Functions: Generalist (All)

Industries: Manufacturing, Printing, Chemicals,
Soap, Perf., Cosmtcs., Drugs Mfg., Paints,
Petro. Products

J. Pimental & CO

13 Willard Pl
Plymouth, MA 02360-3441
(508) 747-5299
Fax: (508) 747-2950
Email: recruitjp@aol.com
Web: www.janepimental.com

Summary: Specializing in sales and sales
management for the medical device industry.
Clients include industry leaders and start-ups.

Key Contact - Specialty:
Miss Jane Pimental, CPC, Principal

Salary Minimum: $140,000

Functions: Healthcare, Sales & Mktg.

Industries: Food, Bev., Tobacco, Soap, Perf.,
Cosmtcs., Medical Devices, Biotech/Life
Sciences

Pinnacle CEO Recruiters

1740 E Ohio Ave
Denver, CO 80209-4533
(303) 339-0096
Fax: (303) 484-4860
Email: cmollman@ceo-recruiters.com
Web: www.ceo-recruiters.com

Summary: We are an executive search firm
focused exclusively on conducting CEO searches
for business services companies.

Key Contact - Specialty:
Mr. Chad Mollman, President - *CEOs*

Salary Minimum: $200,000

Functions: Senior Mgmt.

Industries: Finance, Misc. Financial, Services, HR
Services, IT Implementation, Higher Ed.,
Logistics Svcs., Media, Communications,
Healthcare

Pinnacle Executive Search

1051 County Line Rd Ste 105
Huntingdon Valley, PA 19006-1233
(215) 322-6960
Email: operations@pinnacle-es.com
Web: www.pinnacle-es.com

Summary: Our firm is one of the premier search
firms for both permanent placement and

contractual staffing of IT candidates. We
specialize in the placement of functional and
programmer experts for software in many systems.
We also place pharmaceutical biostatisticians,
SAS programmers and clinical data
associates/managers. We are a very cost-effective
alternative to the large consulting firms.

Key Contact - Specialty:
Mr. Bob Schneck, Director, Recruiting - *Oracle,*
PeopleSoft, SAP
Mr. Steve Hildebrand, Manager, Recruiting - *JD*
Edwards, Oracle, PeopleSoft, SAP
Mr. Robert Marks, Executive Recruiter - *Oracle,*
PeopleSoft, SAP
Mr. Steven Brennan, Executive Recruiter - *CRM,*
Oracle, PeopleSoft, Pharmaceutical, SAP

Salary Minimum: $50,000

Functions: Healthcare, Training, IT, Systems
Implem., Mgmt. Consultants

Industries: Pharm Svcs., Mgmt. Consulting, E-
commerce, IT Implementation, Database SW,
Development SW, Doc. Mgmt., Production SW,
ERP SW, Industry Specific SW, Mfg. SW,
Networking, Comm. SW, Security SW, System
SW, Training SW

Pinnacle Group

6 Greenleaf Woods Dr Unit 201
Portsmouth, NH 03801-5443
(603) 427-1700
(800) 308-7205
Fax: (603) 427-0526
Email: recruiter@pinnaclejobs.com
Web: www.pinnaclejobs.com

Summary: We are specialists in actuarial search
for annuity, life, health, property-casualty and
pension companies. Our client list includes some
of the nation's largest insurance, reinsurance and
consulting firms.

Key Contact - Specialty:
Mr. Thomas Miller, Principal

Salary Minimum: $40,000

Functions: Actuaries

Industries: Insurance

Pinnacle Group International

130 Water St Apt 12A
New York, NY 10005-1621
(212) 968-1200
(480) 488-4490
Email: dpalmieri@pinnaclegroup.com
Web: www.pinnaclegroup.com

Summary: Specialized executive recruiters
serving LBO and venture capital firms, mezzanine
& debt funds, investment & merchant banks and
fund of funds in successful searches from analyst
to partner level. Our personalized, contingency fee
driven approach to building businesses, one
relationship, one career at a time, has been the
hallmark of long, successful relationships and
attracted firms tired of a cookie-cutter approach to
a personal services business.

Key Contact - Specialty:
Mr. Joseph A. Logan, Managing Director
Ms. Denise Palmieri, Director, Client Relations

Salary Minimum: $50,000

Functions: Generalist (All), M&A

Industries: Generalist (All), Invest. Banking,
Venture Cap.

Branches:
80 Liberty Ship Way Ste 25
Sausalito, CA 94965-3300
(480) 488-4490
Email: mstraube@pinnaclegroup.com

Key Contact - Specialty:
Ms. Denise Palmieri, Director, Client Relations
Mr. Max Straube, Managing Director - *Banking*
(Investment), Private equity, Venture capital

Pinnacle Search & Recruit

26499 N 115th St
Scottsdale, AZ 85255-5737
(480) 495-0057
Email: pinnaclesearch@bigfoot.com

Summary: We are a contingency search firm
specializing in mid-upper level management
personnel across a wide variety of disciplines,
nationwide. There is never a fee to the candidates.

Key Contact - Specialty:
Mr. W.J. Marcoux, Vice President, Recruitment

Salary Minimum: $50,000

The Pinnacle Source Inc

5445 DTC Pkwy Ste 922
Greenwood Village, CO 80111-3054
(303) 796-9900
Fax: (303) 796-9901
Email: pinnacle@pinnso.com
Web: www.pinnaclesource.com

Summary: Our unique approach to executive
recruitment is supported by successful executive
search and placement experience. Our client
companies are high-technology industry leaders,
as well as start-up firms in the software/Internet
arena.

Key Contact - Specialty:
Mr. Jordan A. Greenberg, President -
Management, Sales

Salary Minimum: $65,000

Functions: Generalist (All), Sales & Mktg., Sales
Mgmt., MIS Mgmt., Systems Implem., Systems
Support

Industries: Generalist (All), Services,
Communications, Software, Database SW,
Development SW, ERP SW, HR SW, Mfg. SW,
Marketing SW, Security SW, System SW

Pioneer Executive Consultants

201-904 The East Mall
Toronto, ON M9B 6K2
Canada
(416) 620-5563
(416) 620-5376
Fax: (416) 620-5648
Email: pioneerexecutive@sympatico.ca
Web: www.pioneerexecutive.com

Summary: Full recruitment services to the
chemical, paint, adhesives, ink and building
materials industries in positions from general
management, plant management, R&D, quality,
engineering, sales and services.

Key Contact - Specialty:
Mr. Ed Gres, President - *Adhesives, Chemical,*
Paint
Mr. Paul Sinclair, Senior Consultant - *Adhesives,*
Chemical, Paint

Salary Minimum: $40,000

Functions: Generalist (All), Management, Mfg.,
Health & Safety

Industries: Manufacturing, Lumber, Furniture,
Printing, Chemicals, Plastics, Rubber, Paints,
Petro. Products, Accounting, HR Services,
Environmental Svcs., Haz. Waste, Packaging,
Biotech/Life Sciences

Pioneer Placement Inc

PO Box 434
Westfield, MA 01086-0434
(413) 568-2442
Fax: (413) 568-2444
Email: pionplac@vgernet.net
Web: www.pioneerplacement.com

Summary: Client companies receive the experience of a seasoned recruiter; yet the personal touch of the individual.

Key Contact - Specialty:
Mr. Nathan Rosenthal, CPC, President

Functions: Generalist (All), Benefits, Finance, Risk Mgmt., Legal

Industries: Generalist (All), Insurance

Pittleman & Associates

336 E 43rd St
New York, NY 10017-4801
(212) 370-9600
Fax: (212) 370-9608
Email: attysearch@pittlemanassociates.com
Web: www.pittlemanassociates.com

Summary: We specialize in placing attorneys at investment banks and corporations.

Key Contact - Specialty:
Mr. Steven Pittleman, Esq., President - *Management consulting*
Ms. Linda Pittleman, Esq., Chairman
Ms. Rona Gersten Berns, Esq., Recruiter
Mr. David Perez, Recruiter - *Legal, Legal (Attorneys,Lawyers)*
Mr. Alan Surchin, Esq., Recruiter - *Legal, Legal (Attorneys,Lawyers)*
Ms. Wendy Weitz, Recruiter
Ms. Anna Silva, Office Manager - *Administration*
Mr. Brian Manoff, Recruiter - *Legal*

Salary Minimum: $75,000

Functions: Legal, Attorneys

Industries: Invest. Banking, Legal

PJL & Associates

PO Box 6479
San Diego, CA 92166-0479
(619) 222-3722
Fax: (619) 223-2982
Email: pjlassociates@znet.com
Web: pjlandassociates.com

Summary: We specialize in assisting clients nationwide to fill key positions within the environmental, safety, and loss prevention professions. Our associates have worked in these industries and understand the skills and qualifications needed. That expertise, along with our comprehensive profile analysis, is instrumental in bringing together long-term successful partnerships.

Key Contact - Specialty:
Ms. Pamela Lynd, President - *Assets & liabilities, Compliance, Environmental, Fraud investigators, Loss Prevention*
Ms. Nancy Jalaty, National Director - *Asset management, Compliance, Environmental, Fraud investigators, Loss Prevention*

Functions: Sales Mgmt., Risk Mgmt., Engineering, Geotechnical, Specialized Svcs., Health & Safety

Industries: Generalist (All), Construction, Retail, Environmental Svcs., Haz. Waste

Placemart Personnel Service

80 Haines St
Lanoka Harbor, NJ 08734-2114
(732) 212-0144
(800) 394-7522
Fax: (732) 212-0145
Email: info@placemart.com
Web: www.placemart.com

Summary: Recruiting for technical and administrative positions in clinical research: including data management, statistics, medical writing, regulatory affairs, clinical research scientists and operations for medical product R&D.

Key Contact - Specialty:
Mr. William R. Kuhl, President - *Research & development*

Salary Minimum: $40,000

Functions: Healthcare, Physicians, R&D

Industries: Drugs Mfg., Medical Devices, Pharm Svcs., Biotech/Life Sciences, Healthcare

PlaceMeNow.com

3000 Whitney Ave Ste 122
Hamden, CT 06518-2353
(203) 389-6655
Fax: (203) 389-6878
Email: contactus@placemenow.com
Web: www.placemenow.com

Summary: Our firm is dedicated to finding the perfect job for the perfect IT professional. We don't try to be the biggest staffing company but we are the best, most thorough and most personal company.

Key Contact - Specialty:
Mr. Bob Allan, Account Director

Functions: Generalist (All)

Industries: Generalist (All)

Placement Group

736 6 Ave SW
Canada Life Tower Main Floor
Calgary, AB T2P 3T7
Canada
(403) 777-9000
Fax: (403) 777-9007
Email: resumes@pgstaff.com
Web: www.pgstaff.com

Summary: We are a full-service recruitment agency. We provide temp, permanent and contract staff in the areas of administration, accounting, data entry, management and marketing.

Key Contact - Specialty:
Ms. Judy Tidlund, Account Manager
Ms. Shelley Trenouth, Recruiter - *Middle management, Technical*

Functions: Generalist (All), Admin. Svcs., Plant Mgmt., Distribution, Customer Svc., Credit, Systems Support, Engineering

Industries: Generalist (All), Construction, Misc. Mfg., Transportation, Banking, Accounting, HR Services

Branches:
1027 Pandora Ave
Victoria, BC V8V 3P6
Canada
(250) 413-3111
(877) 413-3111
Email: victoria@pgstaff.com

Key Contact - Specialty:
Ms. Rose Arsenault, Manager, Placement Group

Placement Solutions

W270S3979 Heather Dr
Waukesha, WI 53189-6563
(262) 542-2250
Email: msshort@financerecruiting.com
Web: www.financerecruiting.com

Summary: Executive, managerial, professional positions in accounting and IS audit are specialties. All industries/businesses. We place CFOs, VPs, controllers, accounting managers, tax directors & managers, etc.

Key Contact - Specialty:
Ms. Mary Sue Short, Owner

Salary Minimum: $60,000

Functions: Management, Finance

Industries: Generalist (All), Finance, Misc. Financial, Accounting

Planet Earth Staffing

7668 El Camino Real Ste 104
Carlsbad, CA 92009-7932
(760) 634-2265
(760) 634-1991
Fax: (760) 634-1998
Email: paul@planetearthglobal.com
Web: www.planetearthgobal.com

Summary: Our firm provides premium full service staffing services, specializing in the strategic sourcing, assessment and hiring of the highest quality contract, contract to direct and direct hire personnel ranging from entry level employees to the most senior and experienced professionals. Whether you are searching for personnel for your company or a career for yourself - we will provide the solutions.

Key Contact - Specialty:
Mr. Paul Cevolani, President & Chief Executive Officer - *Human resources, Marketing, Sales*
Mr. Duane James, Executive Vice President, Business Dev
Ms. Alison Gross, Director, Marketing
Mr. Michael Danler, Chief Technology Officer

Functions: Generalist (All), Management, Mfg., Materials, Healthcare, Sales & Mktg., HR Mgmt., Finance, IT, Engineering

Industries: Generalist (All)

Branches:
PO Box 9
Elverta, CA 95626-0009
(800) 838-7665
Email: careers@planetearthglobal.com
Key Contact - Specialty:
Mr. Gary Slavit, Senior Eexecutive Vice President

3536 University Blvd N Ste 140
Jacksonville, FL 32277-2422
(800) 838-7665
Email: careers@planetearthglobal.com
Key Contact - Specialty:
Mr. Frank Albertini, Manager, Business Development

Platinum Search Consultants Inc

PO Box 3994
Scranton, PA 18505-0994
(570) 696-2830
Fax: (570) 696-2816
Email:
mwishniewski@platinumsearchconsultants.com
Web: www.platinumsearchconsultants.com

Summary: Our firm is a dynamic recruiting and placement service. Working with companies all across the country, we offer a full range of professional placement services for today's demanding workplace.

Key Contact - Specialty:
Mr. Mark Wishniewski, Senior Recruiting Consultant

Salary Minimum: $50,000

Functions: Senior Mgmt., Sales & Mktg., Sales Mgmt., Staffing, IT, MIS Mgmt., Engineering, Specialized Svcs., Hospitality

Industries: Generalist (All), Pharm Svcs., Mgmt. Consulting, IT Implementation, Hotels, Resorts, Clubs, Government, Software, Biotech/Life Sciences

PLC Associates
PO Box 3104
Guttenberg, NJ 07093-6104
(201) 854-4004
Fax: (201) 869-8611
Email: plcassoc@aol.com

Summary: Our primary services are executive search, diversity staffing and executive search research. We are a generalist firm specializing primarily in R&D, marketing, finance and IT positions.

Key Contact - Specialty:
Ms. Peggy L. Cave, President - *Diversity, Finance, Information Technology, Marketing, Minorities*

Salary Minimum: $40,000

Functions: Materials, Sales & Mktg., HR Mgmt., Finance, IT, R&D, Minorities/Diversity

Industries: Generalist (All), Food, Bev., Tobacco, Soap, Perf., Cosmtcs., Drugs Mfg., Medical Devices, Healthcare, Dental

The Thomas A Plihcik Company
2820 Lawndale Dr Ste 113
Greensboro, NC 27408-4127
(336) 282-3323
Email: tapcogso@bellsouth.net

Summary: We are a generalist firm with developed expertise in marketing searches. We serve a world-wide base of clients that range in size from small to Fortune 100. We also specialize in strategic organizational consulting.

Key Contact - Specialty:
Mr. Tom Plihcik, Owner & Manager

Functions: Generalist (All)

Industries: Generalist (All), Food, Bev., Tobacco, Textiles, Apparel, Wholesale, Non-profits, K-12 Ed., Logistics Svcs., Supply Chain Mgmt, Advertising, Marketing SW

PMJ & Associates
602-15 Toronto St
Strand House
Toronto, ON M5C 2E3
Canada
(416) 364-9997
Fax: (416) 364-8735
Email: allen@pmjpersonnel.com
Web: www.pmjpersonnel.com

Summary: Our firm is a fully qualified, highly professional organization with extensive experience in the personnel recruitment field. We specialize in one geographic area with our expertise in accounting/finance, insurance, bilingualism and IT, which enables us to have proper understanding of today's market.

Key Contact - Specialty:
Mr. Allen Fink, Manager - *Finance*
Ms. Miriam Frankel, Senior Consultant - *Credit*

Functions: Generalist (All), Board Members, Middle Mgmt., Budgeting, Cash Mgmt., Credit, Taxes, M&A, Systems Analysis

Industries: Generalist (All), Food, Bev., Tobacco, Finance, Brokers, Venture Cap., Mutual/Hedge Funds, Misc. Financial, Accounting, Mgmt. Consulting, Engineering Svcs., Logistics Svcs., Insurance, Claims, Re-Insurance, Accounting SW

PMR Search Consultants Inc
428B Osceola Ave
Jacksonville Beach, FL 32250-4077
(904) 270-0505
Fax: (904) 270-0520
Email: pgurtenstein@pmrsearch.com
Web: www.pmrsearch.com

Summary: We place attorneys in all disciplines of law. We handle associate and partner searches as well as firm mergers & acquisitions. We also specialize in placing health law attorneys.

Key Contact - Specialty:
Mr. Mark Rosenblum, Vice President
Mr. Peter Gurtenstein, President

Functions: Legal

Industries: Generalist (All), Drugs Mfg., Medical Devices, Pharm Svcs., Healthcare

Pam Pohly Associates
2707 Woodrow Ct Ste 100
Hays, KS 67601-1618
(785) 625-9790
Email: pam@pohly.com
Web: www.pohly.com

Summary: Healthcare firm provides executive search, interim management and consulting services. Recruit CEOs, CFOs, COOs and upper management candidates for permanent employment in medical centers and specialty hospitals. Interim management service provides CEO, CFO and service line leaders on temp basis. Consulting to hospitals for business planning, turnaround and start-up.

Key Contact - Specialty:
Ms. Pam Pohly, President

Functions: Management, Senior Mgmt., Admin. Svcs., Health Admin., Mktg. Mgmt., CFOs, Mgmt. Consultants

Industries: Healthcare

Bob Poline Associates Inc
11256 Vista Sorrento Pkwy Apt 202
San Diego, CA 92130-7633
(858) 481-3700
Fax: (858) 481-5187
Email: bob@polineassociates.com
Web: www.polineassociates.com

Summary: We make a total commitment to excellence in the shopping center/retail industry. We treasure our reputation and recognition for professional service, performance and client satisfaction.

Key Contact - Specialty:
Mr. Bob Poline, President

Salary Minimum: $50,000

Functions: Management, Senior Mgmt., Middle Mgmt., CFOs, Architects, Attorneys

Industries: Construction, Retail, Real Estate

Branches:
7 Ascot Mnr NW
Atlanta, GA 30327-4245
(770) 955-9306
Fax: (770) 988-0175
Email: rich@polineassociates.com
Key Contact - Specialty:
Mr. Rich Poline, President - *Construction, Legal, Real estate*

The Pollack Group
702-225 Metcalfe St
Kenson Building
Ottawa, ON K2P 1P9
Canada
(613) 238-2233
Fax: (613) 238-4407
Email: pollack.group@pollackgroup.com
Web: www.pollackgroup.com

Summary: Being in the center of high technology, we have been supplying top prospects to the country's best high-technology companies and all federal government departments.

Key Contact - Specialty:
Mr. Paul Pollack, President & Chief Executive Officer
Mr. Charles Durning, Director, Professional Services - *High technology*
Mr. Brian McKenna, Senior Recruiter
Ms. Colette Purchase, Senior Recruiter - *Technology*

Salary Minimum: $40,000

Functions: Generalist (All), Mktg. Mgmt., Sales Mgmt., Systems Analysis, Systems Dev., Systems Implem., Systems Support, Engineering

Industries: Generalist (All), HR Services, Aerospace, Software, Healthcare

Polymer Specialties Inc
(an affiliate of ExecuSearch Inc)
105 E Jefferson Blvd Ste 800
South Bend, IN 46601-1917
(574) 233-9353
(574) 386-1905
Email: mark@polymer-specialties.com
Web: www.polymer-specialties.com

Summary: We are a retained urethane industry search firm. We routinely handle CEO and other upper level management positions in polyurethane and other polymer areas. Our clients appreciate the extensive candidate information we provide which takes the guesswork out of hiring decisions.

Key Contact - Specialty:
Mr. Mark Timler, President - *Automation, Automotive, Chemical, Plastics*

Salary Minimum: $60,000

Functions: Generalist (All)

Industries: Chemicals, Plastics, Rubber

PontusOne LLC
55 Francisco St Ste 450
San Francisco, CA 94133-2113
(415) 362-9389
Email: info@pontusone.com
Web: www.pontusone.com

Summary: HR consulting and executive search for early-stage companies. HR recruiting, coaching and career consulting services. Executive education consulting and business development.

Key Contact - Specialty:
Mr. Steve Balogh, President & Chief Executive Officer

Mr. Tony Dunn, Director, Program Development
Ms. Rebecca Bonham, Recruiter - *Pharmaceutical*

Salary Minimum: $75,000

Functions: Management, Board Members, HR Mgmt.

Industries: Generalist (All)

Don V Poole & Associates Inc

7700 S Glencoe Way
Centennial, CO 80122-3815
(303) 721-6644
Fax: (303) 721-7724
Email: dvpoole@attglobal.net

Summary: We are specialists in the semiconductor equipment industries placing executives and middle management, sales & marketing professionals.

Key Contact - Specialty:
Mr. Don V. Poole, President - *Product management/development, Sales, Telecommunications*

Salary Minimum: $80,000

Functions: Management, Sales & Mktg., Engineering

Industries: Computer Equip., Test, Measure Equip., Electronic, Elec. Components

Jack Porter Associates Inc

24119 SE 18th Pl
Sammamish, WA 98075-8108
(425) 392-9252
Email: jackporterassocs@msn.com
Web: www.international-employment.net

Summary: We provide opportunities for foreign national professionals with international experience and native foreign language capability.

Key Contact - Specialty:
Mr. Jack Porter, President

Salary Minimum: $50,000

Functions: Generalist (All), Management, Engineering, Mgmt. Consultants, Int'l.

Industries: Generalist (All), Non-Classifiable

Porter Consulting Services Inc

4400 Old William Penn Hwy Ste 200
Monroeville, PA 15146-1480
(412) 380-7500
Email: info@porter-consulting.com
Web: www.porter-consulting.com

Summary: We specialize in national and international recruitment and placement of sales, marketing, management, executive-level, and technical support professionals. Our experience includes working with companies of all sizes, from Fortune 500 companies to start-ups. We work within a wide range of industries including information technology, business to business, telecommunications, medical, pharmaceutical, and legal.

Key Contact - Specialty:
Mr. William Porter, Founder & President
Mr. Patrick Wright, Director, Sales
Mr. Brian Porter, Director, Operations & Consultant
Mr. Bob Amato, Senior Consultant - *Industrial*
Mr. Art Floro, Senior Consultant - *Printing*
Mr. Orlando Brown, Senior Consultant
Ms. Lisa Sestak, Senior Recruiter - *Pharmaceutical*
Mrs. Nicole Nelson, Director, Finance & Administration
Ms. Tina Ioannou, Client Support & Business Development - *Healthcare*

Salary Minimum: $100,000

Functions: Senior Mgmt., Sales & Mktg., Sales Mgmt.

Industries: Manufacturing, Legal, Mgmt. Consulting, E-commerce, IT Implementation, Communications, Telecoms, Digital, Wireless, Software, Accounting SW, Database SW, Development SW, Doc. Mgmt., Production SW, Biotech/Life Sciences, Healthcare

The Porter Hamel Group Inc

565 Congress St Ste 203
Portland, ME 04101-3308
(207) 828-1134
Fax: (207) 828-1540
Email: phg@porterhamel.com
Web: www.porterhamel.com

Summary: Operations and technical recruiting from entry level to CEO for food manufacturing companies only.

Key Contact - Specialty:
Mr. Jeffrey C. Porter, President - *Operations, Technical*

Functions: Board Members, Mfg., Materials, HR Mgmt., R&D, Engineering

Industries: Manufacturing, Food, Bev., Tobacco, Soap, Perf., Cosmtcs., Drugs Mfg., Services, HR Services

Portfolio Placements & Resumes LLC

PO Box 2722
Westfield, NJ 07091-2722
(908) 654-0109
Email: michaelweinstock@portfolioplacements.com
Web: www.portfolioplacements.com

Summary: I place experienced & entry level candidates with over 150 portfolio/money management firms, hedge funds, 3rd party fund-of-funds and consultants. Positions include portfolio managers, research analysts, research assistants, portfolio administration, portfolio assistants, wrap fee specialists, sales & marketing associates/assistants, RFP specialists, performance/risk analysts, settlements, compliance, corporate actions/pricing, & systems administrators.

Key Contact - Specialty:
Mr. Michael A. Weinstock, Founder & President - *Asset management, Investment management, Mutual funds*

Salary Minimum: $40,000

Functions: Finance, Cash Mgmt., Risk Mgmt., IT

Industries: Mutual/Hedge Funds

Positions Inc

1 Faneuil Hall Market Pl Ste 500
South Market
Boston, MA 02109-6143
(617) 367-9200
Fax: (617) 367-4906
Email: opportunities@positionsinc.com
Web: www.positionsinc.com

Summary: Our firm has been one of the most successful executive recruiting firms in our area. Our success has resulted from our concern for our clients. We approach every client with the goal of a long-term relationship and repeat business based on high quality service and results.

Key Contact - Specialty:
Mr. Paul J. Sartori, President

Functions: Generalist (All), Admin. Svcs., Nurses, HR Mgmt., Finance, Engineering

Industries: Generalist (All), Manufacturing, Finance, Services, Hospitality, Real Estate, Software, Biotech/Life Sciences, Healthcare

Branches:
919 18th St NW Ste 230
Washington, DC 20006-5521
(202) 659-9270
Fax: (202) 659-9245
Email: jobs@positionsincwdc.com
Key Contact - Specialty:
Ms. Ellen Andrews, Managing Partner

Edward J Pospesil & Company LLC

221 Driftwood Ln
Guilford, CT 06437-1922
(203) 458-6566
Fax: (203) 458-6564
Email: ed@ejp.com
Web: www.ejp.com

Summary: Provide senior IT executive search. Clients range from Fortune 500 through mid-tier and entrepreneurial, across all industries. Extensive years IT executive search experience. Also mentor and coach senior IT executives.

Key Contact - Specialty:
Mr. Edward J. Pospesil, CPC, President - *CIOs, Competitive intelligence, Information Technology, MIS, Telecommunications*

Salary Minimum: $140,000

Functions: MIS Mgmt.

Industries: Generalist (All)

Power Recruiting Group

210 Phillips Pl
Orlando, FL 32806-1218
(407) 574-4874
Email: info@powerrecruiting.com
Web: www.powerrecruiting.com

Summary: We are an executive search firm devoted to the energy industry. We have the expertise and performance record needed to successfully marry employees to employers. Our recruiters have a solid background in the industry, so we understand the nuances of how an organization and its teams operate.

Key Contact - Specialty:
Mr. J. Michael Edwards, President - *Energy, Engineering, Executives, HVAC, Utilities*
Ms. Bonny Block-Edwards, Vice President - *Energy*
Mr. Stephen G. Yeater, Vice President - *Energy, Engineering, Military, Technicians, Utilities*

Functions: Generalist (All)

Industries: Energy, Utilities

Power Technology Associates Inc

1200 Providence Hwy
Sharon, MA 02067-1656
(781) 784-4200
Fax: (781) 784-4302
Email: info@powercareers.com
Web: www.powercareers.com

Summary: We specialize in the areas of power electronics, motion control, energy storage, lighting, RF, microwave and analog electronics.

Key Contact - Specialty:
Mr. Richard Cardarella, President
Ms. Julie A. Luciano, Systems Manager
Jynohn O'Connor, Office Administrator
Mr. Bob Chambers, Manager, Recruiting
Mr. Andy Kilgour, Manager, Recruiting
Ms. Holly Henderson, Manager, Recruiting

Ms. Kathy Kelley, Manager, Recruiting *Sales*
Mr. Bob Partridge, Manager, Recruiting -
  Engineering
Mr. Noah Sholes, Manager, Recruiting -
  Engineering
Mr. Mark van der Walde, Manager, Recruiting

Functions: Engineering

Industries: Manufacturing, Telecoms, Defense,
  Aerospace, Packaging, Software

PowerHour

1402 Cutter Ln
Park City, UT 84098-7531
(435) 615-8486
Fax: (435) 615-8670
Email: ernest@powerhour.com
Web: www.powerhour.com

Summary: We provide recruiting services for
sales/service organizations, publishing/advertising
sales teams and specialize in the multi-housing
industry.

Key Contact - Specialty:
Mr. Ernest Oriente, President & Chief Executive
  Officer

Salary Minimum: $80,000

Functions: Senior Mgmt., Sales & Mktg., Sales
  Mgmt.

Industries: Printing, Services, Mgmt. Consulting,
  Advertising, Publishing, New Media, Marketing
  SW, Training SW

Robert Powers & Associates

PO Box 1085
Placentia, CA 92871-1085
(714) 524-7279
Fax: (714) 524-8410

Summary: We are specialists in the restaurant,
hospitality and specialty retail industries. Cover
line, staff and executive management positions.

Key Contact - Specialty:
Mr. Robert Powers, CPC, President - *Hospitality*
Ms. Susan Powers, Vice President - *Hospitality*

Salary Minimum: $35,000

Functions: Generalist (All), Senior Mgmt.,
  Purchasing, Mktg. Research, Mktg. Mgmt., HR
  Mgmt., Finance, R&D, Minorities/Diversity,
  Hospitality

Industries: Food, Bev., Tobacco, Retail,
  Hospitality, Hotels, Resorts, Clubs, Restaurants,
  Quick Service Restaurants, Full Service
  Restaurants, Inst./Industrial Food Svc.

PPS Professional Personnel Services

1420 E Joppa Rd
Towson, MD 21286-5909
(410) 823-5630
(877) 777-5005
Fax: (410) 821-9423
Email: headhunter@ppsinfo.com
Web: www.ppsinfo.com

Summary: We are a technical recruitment firm
that specializes in all areas of infromation
technology, telecommunications, and sales.

Key Contact - Specialty:
Mr. Neal Fisher, President - *Telecommunications*
Mr. Jeff Klodzen, Account Manager
Ms. Lynn Eskite, Senior Recruiter, Information
  Technology
Mr. Brandon Lackey, Recruiter, Information
  Systems
Ms. Deborah Yake, Recruiter, Information
  Systems - *General management, Marketing,
  Sales*

Salary Minimum: $18,000

Functions: Generalist (All), IT

Industries: Generalist (All)

PR Talent

16168 Beach Blvd Ste 130
Huntington Beach, CA 92647-3831
(714) 375-9916
Fax: (714) 375-9535
Email: jdelulio@prtalent.com
Web: www.prtalent.com

Summary: Specializing in full-time and freelance
public relations talent.

Key Contact - Specialty:
Mr. Jim Delulio, President - *Public relations*

Salary Minimum: $35,000

Functions: PR

Industries: Generalist (All)

Branches:
941 Oneonta Dr
Los Angeles, CA 90065-4216
(323) 478-1821
Email: trobinson@prtalent.com
Key Contact - Specialty:
Ms. Talia Robinson, Vice President - *Public
  relations*

Practice Dynamics Inc

11222 Richmond Ave Ste 125
Houston, TX 77082-2700
(281) 531-0911
Fax: (281) 531-9014
Email: pdi@practice-dynamics.com

Summary: We provide services for all physician
specialties in the South, Southeast, Mid-Atlantic,
Southwest and Midwest. We have national
expertise in ORS, ONC, URO, RHU. Our firm
has many years of experience in medical practice
appraisals.

Key Contact - Specialty:
Ms. Karen M. Lovett, President - *Physicians*
Mr. John S. Harrison, Vice President

Functions: Physicians

Industries: Healthcare

PracticewiseMD

3500 DePauw Blvd Ste 1034
Indianapolis, IN 46268-1136
(317) 872-8900
(800) 995-2030
Fax: (317) 872-3045
Email: contact@practicewisemd.com
Web: www.practicewisemd.com

Summary: We are a national physician recruiting
and healthcare consulting firm comprised of
healthcare attorneys, practice management
consultants and physician recruiters. Our team of
professionals empowers both physicians seeking
superb opportunities and practices searching for
outstanding physicians with the choices,
information, and analysis necessary to make
critical career decisions competently and wisely.

Key Contact - Specialty:
Mr. Philip Anderson, Chief Executive Officer
Mr. William S. Spanglor, Esq., President &
  Consultant

Functions: Healthcare, Mgmt. Consultants

Industries: Generalist (All), Healthcare, Hospitals

P G Prager Search Associates Ltd

1979 Marcus Ave Ste 210
New Hyde Park, NY 11042-1022
(516) 294-4400
Fax: (516) 294-4443
Email: pgprager@att.net
Web: www.pgprager.com

Summary: One of the area's top recruitment firms
specializing in legal, financial, insurance and
general management, personalized service, no
candidate referred without a personal interview.
Substantial guarantee.

Key Contact - Specialty:
Mr. Michael B. Prager, President

Functions: Generalist (All), Senior Mgmt.,
  Admin. Svcs., Sales & Mktg., Mktg. Mgmt.,
  Sales Mgmt., Finance, Taxes, Legal, Attorneys

Industries: Generalist (All), Legal

Pragmatizm Inc

300-106 Front St E
Toronto, ON M5A 1E1
Canada
(416) 868-4767
Email: info@pragmatizm.com
Web: www.pragmatizm.com

Summary: IT staff augmentation firm -
contract/permanent/payrolling.

Key Contact - Specialty:
Mr. Victor Graziano, Partner

Functions: IT

Industries: Generalist (All)

The Prairie Group

1 Westbrook Corporate Ctr Ste 300
Westchester, IL 60154-5709
(708) 449-7710
Email: resumes@theprairiegroup.net

Summary: We provide top candidates for blue
chip clients in all areas of HR, corporate finance
and procurement (supply chain management).
Emphases on candidates that have demonstrated
the ability to add immediate value and grow
quickly. Frequently selected to recruit high
potential candidates due to our extensive network
of talented individuals.

Key Contact - Specialty:
Mr. James Kick, MBA, Principal - *Finance,
  Marketing, Procurement*
Mr. Romero Manzo, Principal - *Human resources*
Mr. Mark Scott, Principal - *Human resources*

Salary Minimum: $60,000

Functions: Purchasing, HR Mgmt., Finance

Industries: Generalist (All), Agri., Forestry,
  Mining, Food, Bev., Tobacco, Chemicals, Metal
  Products, Machine, Appliance, Motor Vehicles,
  Misc. Mfg., Electronic, Elec. Components,
  Finance, Banking, Invest. Banking, Misc.
  Financial, Accounting

PRC Advantage

6380 Wilshire Blvd Ste 1608
Los Angeles, CA 90048-5018
(323) 988-1188
Fax: (323) 908-8925
Email: prorecruit@earthlink.net
Web: www.professionalrecruitingconsultants.com

Summary: We are an executive recruiting firm
that provides management, technical, financial and
administrative pre-screened and reference checked
candidates for our clients. Our firm utilizes the
latest e-recruitment strategies and skills to source

high quality candidates beyond the internet job boards. We maintain confidentiality for clients and candidates alike.

Key Contact - Specialty:
Ms. Karen Smith, Manager
Ms. Stacey Dash, Recruiter
Ms. Jennifer James, Recruiter

Salary Minimum: $50,000

Functions: Generalist (All)

Industries: Generalist (All)

Precise Resource Inc

7400 Skyline Dr E Ste B
Columbus, OH 43235-2706
(614) 734-9680
Email: info@preciseresource.com
Web: www.preciseresource.com

Summary: With our assistance many Fortune 500 corporations enjoy attracting critical resources to join their ranks as dedicated contributors to their organization. By augmenting current in house human resources, we can bring objective, technically qualified, pre-screened resources directly to your hiring manager. With a strong focus on finding quality over quantity.

Key Contact - Specialty:
Ms. Janis Mitchell, Chief Executive Officer

Salary Minimum: $90,000

Functions: Generalist (All), Middle Mgmt., IT, MIS Mgmt.

Industries: Energy, Utilities, Finance, Banking, Services, Communications, Insurance, Casualty, Software, Security SW

Precision Placements Inc

PO Box 14245
Greensboro, NC 27415-4245
(888) 232-3038
Fax: (888) 989-9549
Email: info@textilejobs.com
Web: www.textilejobs.com

Summary: Our firm is an executive search firm specializing the apparel and textile industry. Our expertise is in mid to senior- level professionals in sales and marketing, manufacturing, engineering, and corporate management.

Key Contact - Specialty:
Mr. Ken Edwards, CPC, President

Functions: Generalist (All), Senior Mgmt., Middle Mgmt., Product Dev., Plant Mgmt., Sales & Mktg., Mktg. Mgmt., Sales Mgmt., Sales Reps., Textile/Fashion

Industries: Textiles, Apparel

Precision Search Group Inc

PO Box 131988
The Woodlands, TX 77393-1988
(936) 646-2076
Fax: (936) 646-5435
Email: psg@psg2000.com
Web: www.psg2000.com

Summary: We are an executive search exclusively for the IT marketplace. Positions include: sales, technical, marketing, managers, tech support, VP sales, branch/regional managers, project managers, network system engineers, etc.

Key Contact - Specialty:
Mr. Ken Lucas

Salary Minimum: $40,000

Functions: Generalist (All)

Industries: Software

Preferred Personnel

24 Smith Rd Ste 100
Midland, TX 79705-4406
(432) 684-5900
Fax: (432) 688-0516
Email: recruiters@preferred-personnel.com
Web: www.preferred-personnel.com

Summary: We provide executive recruiting in a broad range of industries, specializing in the oil and gas industry.

Key Contact - Specialty:
Mr. Larry Bledsoe, President
Ms. Paula Bledsoe, Vice President - *Accounting, Energy, Engineering, Geology, Oil*
Ms. Nancy Guisinger, Technical Recruiter - *Engineering*
Ms. Merlene Cox, Recruiter - *Accounting*
Mrs. Amy Houser, Recruiter - *Accounting, Administration, Human resources*

Functions: Generalist (All), Production, Materials, Purchasing, HR Mgmt., Finance, Engineering, Geotechnical, Health & Safety

Industries: Energy, Utilities, Oil & Gas, Finance, Banking, Media, Insurance, Accounting SW

Branches:
1330 Shady Bend Dr
Sugar Land, TX 77479-6923
(800) 531-3597
(281) 545-2288
Email: sue@preferred-personnel.com
Key Contact - Specialty:
Ms. Sue Hall, Executive Recruiter - *Environmental, Gas, Oil, Regulatory, Safety*

Preferred Professional Recruiters

PO Box 8747
Maumee, OH 43537-8747
(419) 865-2406
Fax: (419) 865-2409
Email: neilgreebe@aol.com
Web: www.preferred-recruiters.com

Summary: We specialize in accounting, computer/data processing, engineering, management personnel, sales & marketing, executives, technical and production supervisors in manufacturing.

Key Contact - Specialty:
Mr. Neil Greebe, CPC, Partner - *Manufacturing*

Salary Minimum: $40,000

Functions: Generalist (All), Management, Mfg., Materials, HR Mgmt., Finance, IT, Engineering

Industries: Generalist (All), Manufacturing, Chemicals, Plastics, Rubber, Metal Products, Machine, Appliance, Motor Vehicles, Computer Equip.

Premier Business Services

611 Quinby Ave
Wooster, OH 44691-2844
(330) 263-1300
Fax: (330) 263-9258
Email: jim@premierhrservices.com
Web: www.premierhrservices.com

Summary: We do professional recruiting search for airplane pilots, management, banking, finance executives, legal professionals and temp-to-hire clerical/office contract staffing. Also perform background checks on line www.premiersafe.com

Key Contact - Specialty:
Mr. James A. Babcock, President - *Engineering, General management, Operations*
Mrs. Cheryl Koch, Administration Assistant

Salary Minimum: $40,000

Functions: Generalist (All), Senior Mgmt., Middle Mgmt., Sales & Mktg., Customer Svc., Finance, CFOs, Engineering

Industries: Generalist (All), Finance, Banking, Invest. Banking, Misc. Financial, Legal, Accounting, HR Services, Insurance, Healthcare

Premier Careers Inc

PO Box 1215
Dunedin, FL 34697-1215
(727) 467-0220
(727) 467-0221
Email: jim@premiercareers.com
Web: premiercareers.com

Summary: We offer specialized service in selected fields, including the property & casualty, life insurance industries, accounting and sales organizations. Our success is achieved by establishing strong client relationships and; through well thought out, comprehensive candidate searches. Internet marketing and a large database of professionals add to our effectiveness.

Key Contact - Specialty:
Mr. James P. Roark, President - *Insurance, Risk management*
Mr. Bob Gobel, Senior Account Executive - *Insurance, Risk management*
Mr. Ben Galloway, Vice President - *Insurance, Risk management, Social work*
Mr. Doug Methvin, Senior Account Executive - *Audits, Insurance, Insurance (Casualty,Claims,Property)*

Salary Minimum: $40,000

Functions: Generalist (All), Finance

Industries: Generalist (All), Accounting, Insurance

Branches:
PO Box 660372
Atlanta, GA 30366-6972
(770) 452-7839
Email: chris@premiercareers.com
Key Contact - Specialty:
Mr. Chris Gaulden, Vice President

Premier Consulting

8400 E Prentice Ave Ste 1380
Greenwood Village, CO 80111-2925
(303) 779-1006
Fax: (303) 773-2191
Email: jan@premiersearch.com
Web: www.premiersearch.com

Summary: We place qualified people at all levels in IT and communications.

Key Contact - Specialty:
Ms. Jan Hanbery, President
Mrs. Jennifer Franks, Administrative Assistant

Functions: Senior Mgmt., Middle Mgmt., Sales Mgmt., IT, Systems Analysis, Systems Dev., Systems Implem., Systems Support, Network Admin.

Industries: Communications, Software

Premier Consulting Group of NY

12 Kildare Rd
Island Park, NY 11558-1026
(516) 670-9005
(212) 560-9004
Fax: (206) 201-6482
Email: info@nyconsulting.com
Web: www.nyconsulting.com

Summary: Our firm specializes in recruiting senior level technology professionals. Our expert recruiters will deliver the high-end people you need, when you need them. We are successful because we deliver. We consistently enhance our

clients' ability to make good hiring decisions. We build intimate relationships with our clients and take their business personally.

Key Contact - Specialty:
Mr. Ralitsa Sundquist, Vice President, Technical Recruiting

Functions: Management, Senior Mgmt., Middle Mgmt., Sales Mgmt., IT, Systems

Industries: Mgmt. Consulting, Communications, Network Infrastructure, Software, Database SW, Development SW, Doc. Mgmt., Production SW, Entertainment SW, ERP SW, Industry Specific SW, Networking, Comm. SW, Security SW, System SW

Premier Healthcare Recruiters Inc

5 Woodbury St Ste B
Dearborn, MI 48120-1048
(313) 441-6450
Fax: (313) 441-6460
Email: premierhealthcare@ameritech.net

Summary: We specialize in the professional recruitment of physicians for both clinical and administrative positions on a contingency basis.

Key Contact - Specialty:
Ms. Diana L. Watson, CPC, President - *Physicians*

Salary Minimum: $100,000

Functions: Physicians

Industries: Healthcare

Premier Placement Inc

PO Box 3436
Allentown, PA 18106-0436
(610) 395-9123
Email: premierad@mindspring.com
Web: www.premierplacement.com

Summary: We specialize in manufacturing: supply chain, production management, engineering, HR, finance, sales and IT.

Key Contact - Specialty:
Ms. Laura Schmieder, President - *Engineering, Manufacturing*

Functions: Mfg., Materials, Sales & Mktg., HR Mgmt., Engineering

Industries: Manufacturing, Packaging, Software, Biotech/Life Sciences

Premier Professional Search

3891 Willowwood St SW
Prior Lake, MN 55372-4301
(952) 447-0273
Fax: (952) 447-3897
Email: cheryl@ppsmn.com
Web: www.ppsmn.com

Summary: Our company is an executive search firm that specializes in recruiting and placement of mid to upper management in the hospitality and food industries, nationwide.

Key Contact - Specialty:
Ms. Cheryl Kormanik, President

Functions: Generalist (All), Management, Board Members

Industries: Manufacturing, Food, Bev., Tobacco, Hospitality, Hotels, Resorts, Clubs, Restaurants, Quick Service Restaurants, Full Service Restaurants, Inst./Industrial Food Svc.

Premier Search Inc

1440 Water View Dr W Unit 102
Largo, FL 33771-6400
(727) 518-6958
Fax: (817) 549-7749
Email: recruiting@premiersearchinc.com
Web: www.premiersearchinc.com

Summary: We specialize in sales, engineering, IT direct and contract staffing as well as assist job seekers with resume writing and interview consulting.

Key Contact - Specialty:
Ms. Melissa Beaudet, Founder

Salary Minimum: $50,000

Functions: Senior Mgmt., Sales & Mktg., Sales Mgmt., Sales Reps., IT, Engineering

Industries: Generalist (All)

Lloyd Prescott & Churchill Inc

24701 US Highway 19 N Ste 102
Clearwater, FL 33763-4086
(727) 797-5932
Fax: (727) 725-9406
Email: resume@lloydprescott.com
Web: www.lloydprescott.com

Summary: We are a generalist boutique firm providing executive, legal and professional search. We work nationwide and international on a retained and exclusive basis.

Key Contact - Specialty:
Mr. Kees A. Hulstein, Chief Executive Officer & Mng Partner

Salary Minimum: $100,000

Functions: Generalist (All), Senior Mgmt., Healthcare, Sales & Mktg., Sales Mgmt., HR Mgmt., CFOs, IT, Legal, Attorneys

Industries: Generalist (All), Manufacturing, Finance, Banking, Brokers, Legal, Supply Chain Mgmt., Insurance, Healthcare, Hospitals, Long-term/Home Care

Lloyd Prescott Associates Inc

24701 US Highway 19 N Ste 102
Clearwater, FL 33763-4086
(813) 881-1110
(800) 486-3463
Fax: (813) 889-8458
Email: headhunt7@lloydprescott.com
Web: www.lloydprescott.com

Summary: We are a generalist firm providing executive and professional search. Specializing in senior management, healthcare, legal, insurance, high technology, sales/marketing, finance/banking, manufacturing, consultants and food industry. Offering our clients the best and the brightest candidates in their field.

Key Contact - Specialty:
Mr. Sheldon M. Ginsberg, Managing Partner - *Senior management*
Mr. Manuel F. Gordon, Partner, Business Affairs - *Senior management*
Ms. Olga Nasthas, Vice President

Salary Minimum: $70,000

Functions: Generalist (All), Senior Mgmt., Middle Mgmt., Health Admin., MIS Mgmt., Engineering, Legal

Industries: Generalist (All), Drugs Mfg., Medical Devices, Banking, Mutual/Hedge Funds, Legal, Accounting, Casualty, Commercial, Re-Insurance

Prescott Legal Search Inc

3900 Essex Ln Ste 1110
Houston, TX 77027-5261
(713) 439-0911
Fax: (713) 439-1317
Web: www.prescottlegal.com

Summary: We are one of the largest legal recruiting firms in the region. Our staff includes 10 former practicing attorneys and we have a proprietary database containing confidential information on over 20,000 lawyers.

Key Contact - Specialty:
Mr. Larry W. Prescott, JD, President
Ms. Lauren Eaton Prescott, JD, Sales & Marketing
Mr. Stephen Mims, JD, Manager, Permanent Attorney Recruiter
Ms. Susan Pye, JD, Contract Attorney Recuiter
Mr. Tonda Hyde, Recruiter, Paralegal
Ms. Kristin Henley, JD, Recruiter, Permanent Attorney - *Legal*
Ms. Rose Hancock, Senior Vice President, Finance & Admin. - *Administration, CFOs, Executives, Human resources, Information Systems*

Functions: Nurses, Attorneys, Paralegals

Industries: Generalist (All)

Branches:
504 Lavaca St Ste 940
Austin, TX 78701-2854
(512) 482-9442
Fax: (512) 482-0020
Key Contact - Specialty:
Ms. M. Tish Hinojosa Elliott, JD
Ms. Jane Fields Pollard, JD
Ms. Courtney B. Sapire, JD
Ms. Mary Alice Naiser
Ms. Holly E. Coe
Ms. Judy Kirtley, RN

3102 Oak Lawn Ave Ste 700
Dallas, TX 75219-4293
(972) 210-2930
Fax: (214) 210-2989
Key Contact - Specialty:
Ms. Holly Sherman Pena, JD
Ms. Electra Harelson
Mr. Russell Newhouse, JD

Presley Consultants Inc

812 3rd St
Norco, CA 92860-2736
(951) 734-2237
(951) 429-1585
Fax: (951) 734-1775
Email: phil@presleyconsultants.com
Web: www.presleyconsultants.com

Summary: Executive search, recruitment specifically in the hospitality industries; exclusively client retained and primarily contingency; will conduct and have conducted retained search assignments.

Key Contact - Specialty:
Mr. Philip E. Presley, President & COO, Hospitality Div - *Finance, Food, General management, Operations, Sales*
Mr. Jason T. Presley, Vice President, Ops, Hospitality Div - *Food & beverage, Operations, Sales*
Ms. Linda C. Presley, Senior Vice President - *Finance*

Salary Minimum: $75,000

Functions: Generalist (All)

Industries: Services, Mgmt. Consulting, HR Services, Hospitality, Hotels, Resorts, Clubs, Restaurants, Quick Service Restaurants, Full Service Restaurants, Inst./Industrial Food Svc., Sports

Prestige Inc

PO Box 421
Reedsburg, WI 53959-0421
(608) 524-4032
Fax: (608) 524-8577
Email: prestige@rucls.net
Web: www.prestige-inc.com

Summary: Industry specialization affords us the opportunity to know the language, methods and personnel before we begin a search, eliminating many of the risks involved in the hiring process.

Key Contact - Specialty:
Mr. James A. Sammons, Managing Director

Salary Minimum: $50,000

Functions: Management, Product Dev., Plant Mgmt., Quality, Materials, Healthcare, Sales & Mktg., CFOs, Graphic Designers, Int'l.

Industries: Manufacturing, Transportation, Wholesale, Retail, Services, Media, Packaging, Healthcare

C Price & Associates

1114-111 Richmond St W
Toronto, ON M5H 2G4
Canada
(416) 362-1892
Fax: (416) 362-8084
Email: cprice@bellnet.ca
Web: cprice.ca

Summary: We are a senior executive search firm. We are known for successfully helping organizations of all sizes and types to recruit individuals and teams to build and manage profitable businesses. While we specialize in financial services our client base expands to a wide range of other industries.

Key Contact - Specialty:
Ms. Charlotte Price, Owner

Functions: Board Members, Middle Mgmt., Sales & Mktg., Mktg. Mgmt., HR Mgmt., Staffing, Finance, CFOs, Cash Mgmt., Systems

Industries: Generalist (All)

Branches:
130 W 15th St Apt 4E
New York, NY 10011-6793
(917) 742-4525
Key Contact - Specialty:
S. Grove

Prime Consulting International LLC

7 Pine Hill Ct (Ste 100)
Briarcliff Manor, NY 10510-1743
(914) 944-3131
Email: skoenig@pci-search.com
Web: pci-search.com

Summary: Complete staffing solutions, executive search and consulting services. Our expertise in sourcing experienced information technologists and risk management professionals at all levels for the capital markets. This includes software development, support and integration of front to back office systems for trading as well as, business intelligence systems, quantitative / analytical applications.

Key Contact - Specialty:
Mr. Stewart Koenig, Director, Executive Search Services

Salary Minimum: $100,000
Functions: Risk Mgmt., IT, MIS Mgmt.

Industries: Banking, Invest. Banking, Brokers, Venture Cap., Mutual/Hedge Funds, Misc. Financial, IT Implementation, Publishing, Database SW, Development SW, ERP SW, Networking, Comm. SW, Security SW, System SW

Prime Management Group Inc

365 Queens Ave
London, ON N6B 1X5
Canada
(519) 672-7710
Fax: (519) 672-5155
Email: jobs@pmg.on.ca
Web: www.pmg.on.ca

Summary: We are an executive search and recruitment firm specializing in the recruitment of professionals for both management and non-management positions. We encompass multiple areas of search and recruitment.

Key Contact - Specialty:
Ms. Kimberley Chesney, President

Functions: Management, Board Members, Senior Mgmt., Mfg., Sales & Mktg., HR Mgmt., Finance, IT, R&D, Int'l.

Industries: Generalist (All)

Branches:
260 Holiday Inn Dr
Cambridge, ON N3C 4E8
Canada
(519) 220-0310
Fax: (519) 220-0327
Email: jobs2@pmg.on.ca
Key Contact - Specialty:
Ms. Colleen Young, Senior Recruiter & Operations Manager

Prime Resource Associates Inc

PO Box 490
Brookfield, WI 53008-0490
(262) 860-1260
Fax: (262) 860-1264
Email: prime@powercom.net

Summary: Successful professional/technical recruiting and placement firm, specializing in durable goods manufacturing. Positions include entry level on up to executive level. We have expertise in engineering, manufacturing management, quality and sales & marketing.

Key Contact - Specialty:
Mr. Paul J. Schneider, President - *Engineering, Manufacturing, Technical*

Salary Minimum: $40,000

Functions: Generalist (All), Management, Mfg., Product Dev., Automation, Engineering

Industries: Manufacturing, Medical Devices, Plastics, Rubber, Metal Products, Machine, Appliance, Motor Vehicles, Computer Equip., Consumer Elect., Test, Measure Equip., Misc. Mfg., Electronic, Elec. Components, Robotics, Consumer Goods, Software

Primus Search

22 Trundy Rd
Cape Elizabeth, ME 04107-2819
(207) 741-9058
Email: primus10@main.rr.com
Web: www.primussearch.com

Summary: We are a recruiting agency that provides job placement to companies that provide healthcare/medical/surgical products (medical imaging equipment, medical devices, healthcare

software, medical equipment, medical supplies, etc.) to the healthcare market (hospitals, long term care facilities, HMOs, home care, medical offices, etc.).

Key Contact - Specialty:
Mr. Paul F. Moson, President
Mrs. Anne-Lise Moson, Vice President - *Sales*

Salary Minimum: $70,000

Functions: Senior Mgmt., Middle Mgmt., Mfg., Sales & Mktg.

Industries: Medical Devices, Industry Specific SW, Biotech/Life Sciences

Princetec Inc

40 W 25th St Fl 6
New York, NY 10010-2776
(212) 400-6100
Fax: (212) 206-8206
Email: info@princetec.com
Web: www.princetec.com

Summary: We are a leading staffing and IT consulting firm that provides strategic and creative technical resource solutions for some of the world's most successful future focused businesses. We provide highly qualified software engineers, internet/client-server developers/programmers, database experts, telecom engineers, embedded systems engineers and network engineers.

Key Contact - Specialty:
Mr. Raj Sajankila, Co-Founder - *Computers, Electronics*

Salary Minimum: $40,000

Functions: IT, Systems Dev., Systems Implem., Network Admin., DB Admin., Engineering

Industries: Generalist (All), Telecoms

Princeton Corp Consultants

420 W Baseline Rd Ste C
Claremont, CA 91711-1621
(909) 625-3007
Fax: (909) 621-0315
Email: sadams7727@aol.com
Web: www.princetonconsultants.com

Summary: We provide executive search to medical device and pharmaceutical companies. Primary candidates will be engineers, scientists, quality, regulatory, scientific, manufacturing and clinical.

Key Contact - Specialty:
Mr. Steve Adams, Senior Vice President - *Biotechnology*
Mrs. Rosalie Russell, Senior Director - *Administration, HMOs, Hospital*

Salary Minimum: $60,000

Functions: Management, Product Dev., Quality

Industries: Manufacturing, Drugs Mfg., Medical Devices, Plastics, Rubber, Pharm Svcs., IT Implementation, Engineering Svcs., Packaging, Mfg. SW, Biotech/Life Sciences, Healthcare, Hospitals, Long-term/Home Care

Branches:
940 S Coast Dr Ste 245
Costa Mesa, CA 92626-7799
(714) 513-5850
Email: sadams7727@aol.com

Key Contact - Specialty:
Ms. Carmen Hagevoort, Senior Director Operations

Princeton HR Consultants
211 Windsor Commons
East Windsor, NJ 08512-2526
(609) 918-1920
Fax: (609) 918-1920
Email: princetonhrconsultants@comcast.net
Web: www.princetonhrconsultants.com

Summary: We provide world class service while making each client feel as if they are our only client. Special rates available for first time clients.

Key Contact - Specialty:
Mr. Bob Mantz, Jr., President - *Accounting, Banking (Retail), C-level, Executives, Sales*

Salary Minimum: $60,000

Functions: Generalist (All), Senior Mgmt., Sales & Mktg.

Industries: Drugs Mfg., Medical Devices, Finance, Services, Pharm Svcs., Accounting, HR Services, Law Enforcement, Higher Ed., Hospitality, Telecoms, Biotech/Life Sciences, Healthcare

Princeton Legal Search Group LLC
116 Village Blvd Ste 200
Princeton, NJ 08540-5700
(609) 730-8240
Fax: (609) 730-8363
Email: dgarber@princetonlegal.com
Web: www.princetonlegal.com

Summary: We specialize in the permanent placement of exceptionally qualified attorneys in all practice areas with law firms and corporate legal departments throughout the United States.

Key Contact - Specialty:
Mr. David S. Garber, Esq., President & Founder

Functions: Attorneys

Industries: Generalist (All)

Principle Resources
5006 Navajo Dr
Frisco, TX 75034-1273
(469) 287-2649
Email: jamie@principleresources.com
Web: www.principleresources.com

Summary: We are a professional search firm focused on the placement of highly specialized individuals in the engineering, manufacturing and technical sales professions.

Key Contact - Specialty:
Ms. Jamie Honsaker, Owner

Salary Minimum: $50,000

Functions: Production, Materials, Engineering, Structural, Process, Architects

Industries: Construction, Manufacturing, Medical Devices, Metal Products, Machine, Appliance, Motor Vehicles, Computer Equip., Consumer Elect., Test, Measure Equip., Misc. Mfg., Electronic, Elec. Components, Robotics, Semiconductors, Consumer Goods, Architectural Svcs., Engineering Svcs., Communications

Priority Executive Search
14317 Ravenwood Ln
Tampa, FL 33618-2029
(813) 961-8074
Email: prioriti@ix.netcom.com
Web: www.healthexec.com

Summary: We dedicate our efforts on finding high quality candidates for key healthcare positions.

Key Contact - Specialty:
Mr. Rolf H. Kausch, Vice President
Mr. Ira Kausch, President - *Healthcare*

Salary Minimum: $20,000

Functions: Generalist (All), Board Members, Healthcare

Industries: Mgmt. Consulting, Healthcare, Hospitals, Long-term/Home Care, Physical Therapy, Occupational Therapy, Women's

Pritchett Associates Inc
PO Box 7341
Hicksville, NY 11802-7341
(516) 735-3765
Fax: (516) 735-3686
Email: jobs@hcrecruiters.com
Web: www.hcrecruiters.com

Summary: Specializes in conducting searches for the home health care industry. Emphasis on the recruitment of nurses, administrators, account executives, and other home health care professionals.

Key Contact - Specialty:
Mr. Dennis Barthmare, President
Ms. Lynn Barthmare, RN, Vice President

Functions: Generalist (All), Nurses

Industries: Generalist (All), Long-term/Home Care

Pro Search National Recruiting Services
216 W Pacific Ave Ste 104
Spokane, WA 99201-3661
(509) 363-1986
Fax: (509) 363-1987
Email: pat@prosearchnational.com

Summary: Our focus revolves around assisting our client companies in maintaining their sales and sales management teams. We approach this by establishing relationships with a national database of passive candidates who wish to be made aware of and considered for opportunities to take the next step in their career.

Key Contact - Specialty:
Mr. Patrick Bopray, Owner

Functions: Generalist (All), Sales & Mktg., Sales Mgmt., Sales Reps.

Industries: Construction, Manufacturing, Lumber, Furniture, Misc. Mfg., Consumer Goods, Wholesale, Retail

Pro Staffing Solutions
578 Hill Everhart Rd
Lexington, NC 27295-9137
(336) 243-5454
Fax: (336) 243-5453
Email: brad@prostaffingsolutions.net

Summary: We specialize in the placement of manufacturing professionals with an emphasis on both engineering, operations and supply chain professionals.

Key Contact - Specialty:
Mr. Brad Dach, President

Functions: Management, Senior Mgmt.

Industries: Generalist (All), Agri., Forestry, Mining, Construction, Manufacturing, Metal Products, Machine, Appliance

Pro-Tech Search Inc
113 E Douglas Ave Ste 200
Petersburg, IL 62675-1558
(217) 632-2299
Fax: (217) 632-3629
Email: kmccoy@pro-techsearch.com
Web: www.pro-techsearch.com

Summary: We are a Christian owned and operated full-service executive search and contract placement firm with expertise in the placement of information technology, accounting and engineering professionals at all levels. Our proven placement methodology matches high quality candidates and high caliber companies.

Key Contact - Specialty:
Mr. Karl McCoy, President - *Healthcare*

Salary Minimum: $30,000

Functions: Senior Mgmt., Middle Mgmt., Finance, IT, Engineering

Industries: Generalist (All)

Probus Executive Search
1961 Landings Dr
Mountain View, CA 94043-0806
(650) 960-3751
(650) 960-3757
Fax: (650) 960-0331
Email: jack@probus-exec.com
Web: www.probus-exec.com

Summary: Finance and accounting professionals for technology companies.

Key Contact - Specialty:
Mr. Jack McNeal, Partner - *Accounting*
Ms. Paulette Clements, Partner - *Accounting*

Salary Minimum: $60,000

Functions: Finance, CFOs, Budgeting, Cash Mgmt., Credit, M&A

Industries: Generalist (All), Manufacturing, Computer Equip., Electronic, Elec. Components, Consumer Goods, Finance, Communications, Digital, Network Infrastructure, Software, Networking, Comm. SW, System SW, Biotech/Life Sciences

Procom
605-2323 Yonge St
Toronto, ON M4P 2C9
Canada
(416) 483-0766
(800) 461-4878
Fax: (416) 483-8102
Web: www.procom.ca

Summary: We are one of the leading providers of full time and contract computer personnel in North America with over 100 clients in industries such as banking, automotive & software manufacturing, telecom, retail, insurance, transportation and oil refining.

Key Contact - Specialty:
Mr. Frank McCrea, President - *Information Technology*

Salary Minimum: $45,000

Functions: Generalist (All), MIS Mgmt., Systems Analysis, Systems Dev., Systems Implem., Systems Support, Network Admin., DB Admin.

Industries: Generalist (All), Transportation, Banking, Mgmt. Consulting, Insurance, Software

Branches:
275 Battery St Ste 950
San Francisco, CA 94111-3332
(415) 773-1873
(800) 231-1616
Fax: (415) 773-1833
Key Contact - Specialty:
Ms. Roberta D'Alois

3000 RDU Center Dr Ste 114
Morrisville, NC 27560-7664
(919) 840-0606
Fax: (919) 840-0777
Email: richardk@procomservices.com
Key Contact - Specialty:
Mr. Rich Kviring, Managing Director

801 E Campbell Rd Ste 375
Richardson, TX 75081-1894
(972) 234-6055
Fax: (972) 234-5661
Email: neilb@procomtexas.com
Key Contact - Specialty:
Mr. Neil Brooks, Managing Director

1800-250 6 Ave SW
Bow Valley Square 4
Calgary, AB T2P 3H7
Canada
(403) 571-7241
Fax: (403) 571-7195
Email: sallyd@procom.ca
Key Contact - Specialty:
Ms. Sally Drysdale, Managing Director

600-300 March Rd
Gateway Business Building 1
Kanata, ON K2K 2E2
Canada
(613) 270-9339
Fax: (613) 270-9449
Email: keithc@procom.ca
Key Contact - Specialty:
Mr. Keith Carter, Managing Director

226-871 Victoria St N
Executive Business Centre
Kitchener, ON N2B 3S4
Canada
(519) 885-4331
Fax: (519) 885-5308
Email: lukem@procom.ca
Key Contact - Specialty:
Mr. Luke Morrison

325-1440 Rue Sainte-Catherine O
Le 1440
Montreal, QC H3G 1R8
Canada
(514) 731-7224
(866) 662-7224
Fax: (514) 731-7244
Email: andrec@procom.ca
Key Contact - Specialty:
Mr. André Couillard

Procurement Resources

PO Box 778
Finksburg, MD 21048-0778
(410) 840-3692
Fax: (410) 840-3692
Email: procres@aol.com
Web: www.members.aol.com/procres/index.html

Summary: Specializing in the recruitment of
purchasing, logistics, materials and supply chain
professionals capable of meeting today's
challenges in supply chain management, global
sourcing and quality criteria.

Key Contact - Specialty:
Mr. John L. Cousins, Principal - *Distribution,*
Logistics, Purchasing

Salary Minimum: $50,000
Functions: Materials, Purchasing, Materials Plng.,
Distribution
Industries: Generalist (All)

Product Management Resources

44 E Parkwood Dr
Dayton, OH 45405-3423
(937) 277-1212
Email: mary_pmr@mindspring.com

Summary: We specialize in the permanent
placement of marketing, product management, and
product marketing professionals.

Key Contact - Specialty:
Ms. Mary Nurrenbrock, Owner

Salary Minimum: $75,000

Functions: Senior Mgmt., Middle Mgmt., Mktg.
Research, Mktg. Mgmt., Direct Mktg.

Industries: Food, Bev., Tobacco, Soap, Perf.,
Cosmtcs., Software, Accounting SW, Security
SW

Professional Career Solutions

3237 N 1050 E
Ogden, UT 84414-1724
(801) 605-0018
Fax: (801) 605-0018
Email: llarkin@procareersolutions.com
Web: www.procareersolutions.com

Summary: We focus our recruiting expertise on
the accounting, financial services and banking
industries. We are affiliated with a nation-wide
network of highly trained and successful
recruiters.

Key Contact - Specialty:
Mr. LaRon Larkin, Chief Executive Officer

Salary Minimum: $60,000

Functions: Generalist (All), Senior Mgmt.

Industries: Generalist (All), Finance, Banking,
Services, Accounting, Mgmt. Consulting, HR
Services

Professional Careers Inc

507 Rush Rd
Fayetteville, NC 28305-4917
(910) 323-3987
Email: vicki@procareer.com
Web: www.procareer.com

Summary: We specialize in IS and technology
positions. We handle opportunities for CIO,
director level, IS management, applications
software development, client server and network
(LAN/WAN/MAN) management. Additionally we
work the supply chain logistics / warehouse
management area. We target the development of
clients for long-term business relationships. We
guarantee the professionals that we place.

Key Contact - Specialty:
Ms. Vicki H. Sturgill, CPC, President & Recruiter
- *AS/400, Business to business, CIOs,*
Computers (Programming), Information
Technology

Salary Minimum: $60,000

Functions: IT, MIS Mgmt., Systems Analysis,
Systems Dev., Systems Implem., Network
Admin., DB Admin.

Industries: Generalist (All), IT Implementation

Professional Computer Resources Inc (PCR)

1500 South Blvd Ste 201B
Charlotte, NC 28203-4982
(704) 332-7226
(888) 727-2458
Fax: (704) 332-7288
Email: resumes@pcr.net
Web: www.pcr.net

Summary: Our recruiters place IT professionals
within the Internet/intranet, client server,
networking or specialty software areas on a full-
time and contract basis.

Key Contact - Specialty:
Mr. Christian Militello, President
Ms. Dianne C. Gold, Vice President, Finance &
Administration - *Capital markets*
Mr. Pat Hermsen, Consultant, Recruiting
Mr. Scott Haynes, Administration, Network
Mr. Bryant Hinnant, Recruiter

Salary Minimum: $65,000

Functions: Generalist (All), IT, MIS Mgmt.,
Systems Analysis, Systems Dev., Systems
Implem., Systems Support, Network Admin.,
DB Admin.

Industries: Generalist (All), Banking, Invest.
Banking, Brokers, Misc. Financial, Software,
Development SW

Professional Consulting Network Inc

595 Market St Ste 850
San Francisco, CA 94105-2855
(415) 777-4321
Fax: (415) 777-8632
Email: infosf@pcninc.com
Web: www.pcninc.com

Summary: We recruit for full time contract
positions. Employ consultants or represent
independent contractor for temp consulting
assignments in data processing/software
engineering assignments.

Key Contact - Specialty:
Mr. Peter Jozwik, Founder & Chief Executive
Officer
Mr. Heinz Bartesch, Director, Direct Hire,
Principal, Sales
Mr. Brooks Hoehn, Vice President, Sales
Mr. Gregory Krueger, Principal, Sales

Salary Minimum: $45,000

Functions: MIS Mgmt., Systems Analysis,
Systems Dev., Systems Implem., Systems
Support

Industries: Generalist (All)

Branches:
380 Interlocken Cres Ste 760
Broomfield, CO 80021-8025
(303) 316-7100
Fax: (720) 566-0729
Email: infoden@pcninc.com
Key Contact - Specialty:
Mr. Gregory Krueger, Principal

Professional Corporate Search Inc

99 Park Ave
New York, NY 10016-1601
(212) 213-3434
Fax: (212) 213-3433
Email: jobs@procorpsearch.com
Web: www.procorpsearch.com

Summary: We are an executive search firm
specializing in the placement of sales
professionals. We recruit for Fortune 100, 500 and

1000 corporations, as well as entrepreneurial growth companies involved in the expansion and development of top quality sales forces.

Key Contact - Specialty:
Mr. Errol Tucker, President - *Sales*

Salary Minimum: $40,000

Functions: Sales & Mktg., Sales Mgmt.

Industries: Generalist (All), Energy, Utilities, Manufacturing, Services, Hospitality, Telecoms, Software, Non-Classifiable

Branches:
207 E Redwood St Ste 510
Baltimore, MD 21202-3311
(410) 347-4848
Fax: (410) 347-1389
Email: jobs@procorpsearch.com
Key Contact - Specialty:
Ms. Sabine Pauyo-Tucker

Professional Engineering Technical Personnel Consultants

8504 Ragan Rd
Apex, NC 27502-9689
(919) 362-3944
Fax: (919) 362-3944
Email: rickbh@msn.com

Summary: Retained and contingency search provided for all disciplines and levels within the power electronics, industrial, motion, sensor and electronic industries.

Key Contact - Specialty:
Mr. Richard B. Huffman, Owner - *Electronics*

Salary Minimum: $35,000

Functions: Generalist (All), Product Dev.

Industries: Motor Vehicles, Computer Equip., Consumer Elect., Test, Measure Equip., Electronic, Elec. Components, Robotics, Consumer Goods, Equip Svcs., Telephony, Digital, Network Infrastructure, Development SW, Mfg. SW, Networking, Comm. SW

Professional Executive Recruiters Inc (PERI)

PO Box 864672
Plano, TX 75086-4672
(972) 509-5000
Fax: (972) 509-5001
Email: peri@pericorp.com
Web: www.pericorp.com

Summary: Extensive experiance in recruiting mid to executive-level personnel in the construction industry.

Key Contact - Specialty:
Mr. Ken Roberts, President

Functions: Generalist (All), Management, Senior Mgmt., Middle Mgmt., CFOs, Attorneys, Int'l.

Industries: Construction

Professional Outlook Inc

662 Butternut Dr
Holland, MI 49424-1508
(616) 738-9600
Email: info@professionaloutlook.com
Web: www.professionaloutlook.com

Summary: Professional search firm focusing on engineers and operations management for the chemical process industries, environmental, health & safety professionals and HR professionals.

Key Contact - Specialty:
Ms. Bethany Brevard-Harned, President & Senior Recruiter

Mr. John Zimmer, Manager & Senior Recruiter
Ms. Kelly Carroll, Senior Recruiter
Ms. Colleen Doerr, Senior Recruiter
Ms. Shelly Woodcock, Senior Recruiter
Mr. Scott Harned, Manager & Senior Recruiter
Ms. Kristine Martin, Recruiter Assistant
Ms. Debbie Hunkins, Senior Recruiter
Ms. Becky Kalsbeek, Senior Recruiter
Ms. Shannon Zimmer, Coordinator, Network
Ms. Jane Dowling, Assistant, Network
Ms. Susan Kendall, Research Coordinator - *Electrical, High technology, Sales*

Salary Minimum: $50,000

Functions: Middle Mgmt., Mfg., HR Mgmt., Benefits, Engineering, Environmentalists

Industries: Generalist (All), Energy, Utilities, Oil & Gas, Manufacturing, Food, Bev., Tobacco, Paper, Printing, Chemicals, Soap, Perf., Cosmtcs., Drugs Mfg., Medical Devices, Plastics, Rubber, Paints, Petro. Products, Environmental Svcs., Haz. Waste, HR SW, Biotech/Life Sciences

Professional Placement Associates Inc

287 Bowman Ave Ste 309
Purchase, NY 10577-2517
(914) 251-1000
Fax: (914) 251-1055
Email: lschachter@ppasearch.com
Web: www.ppasearch.com

Summary: We are a high quality firm with focused expertise in the healthcare field. Our client base includes: hospitals, nursing homes, home care agencies, managed care organizations, physician practices, faculty practice plans, etc. We render a highly personalized, intensive and cost effective service.

Key Contact - Specialty:
Ms. Laura J. Schachter, President - *Healthcare*

Salary Minimum: $50,000

Functions: Quality, Healthcare, Physicians, Nurses, Allied Health, Health Admin., HR Mgmt., MIS Mgmt., Engineering, Health & Safety

Industries: Healthcare, Hospitals, Long-term/Home Care, Physical Therapy, Occupational Therapy

The Professional Recruiting Center

305 SE 6th St
Cape Coral, FL 33990-1528
(239) 850-3592
(239) 573-7228
Fax: (239) 573-1807
Email: prcinfo@earthlink.net
Web: www.professionalrecruitingcenter.com

Summary: We are a contingency search firm serving clients throughout the United States. We identify qualified candidates for clients with mid- to senior-level professional, technical, and managerial positions. Areas of concentration include human resources, information technology & information systems, finance & accounting, engineering, business development, hospitality, and estate staffing.

Key Contact - Specialty:
Ms. Cheryl Hanson, Executive Partner
Ms. Rhonda Beitelschies, Executive Partner

Professional Recruiters

220 E 3900 S Ste 9
Salt Lake City, UT 84107-1575
(801) 268-9940
Fax: (801) 261-4584
Email: recruiter@icw.com
Web: www.recruitersslc.com

Summary: We are dedicated to addressing the need for quality placement services. As professionals, we concentrate on the placement requirements of businesses and refer only those individuals who are specifically qualified.

Key Contact - Specialty:
Ms. Lora Lea Mock, President - *Technology*
Ms. Clair Simpson, Recruiter
Ms. Franci Eisenborg, Recruiter - *Technology*
Ms. Lynda Moore, Recruiter - *Technology*
Mr. Brad Brian, Recruiter - *Technology*

Salary Minimum: $50,000

Functions: Generalist (All), Middle Mgmt., Mktg. Mgmt., Sales Mgmt., MIS Mgmt., Systems Analysis, Systems Dev., Systems Implem.

Industries: Generalist (All), Medical Devices, Computer Equip., Consumer Elect., Misc. Mfg., E-commerce, Telecoms, Telephony, Digital, Wireless, Software

Professional Recruiting Consultants Inc

3617A Silverside Rd
Wilmington, DE 19810-5101
(302) 479-9550
Fax: (302) 479-9560
Email: roger@prcstaffing.com
Web: www.prcstaffing.com

Summary: We are engaged in the business of identifying and recruiting qualified personnel for a variety of technical and non-technical disciplines at both the management and staff levels.

Key Contact - Specialty:
Mr. Roger Malatesta, President - *Engineering, Management, Purchasing*

Functions: Generalist (All), Management, Board Members, Senior Mgmt., Middle Mgmt., Mfg., Sales & Mktg., IT

Industries: Generalist (All), Oil & Gas, Chemicals, Medical Devices, Plastics, Rubber, Machine, Appliance, Test, Measure Equip., Misc. Mfg., IT Implementation, Communications, Biotech/Life Sciences

Professional Recruiting Offices Inc (PRO)

2558 Roosevelt St Ste 200
Carlsbad, CA 92008-1673
(760) 400-0123
Fax: (760) 400-0100
Email: info@proinc.com
Web: www.proinc.com

Summary: We are employee benefits and managed care executive search specialists. We have many years of combined executive search experience concentrating in the managed care and employee benefits areas.

Key Contact - Specialty:
Mr. Mark J. Schneekluth, President

Salary Minimum: $40,000

Functions: Sales & Mktg., Benefits, Pension/Ret. Planning

Industries: Services, Mgmt. Consulting, HR Services, Insurance, Life, Dental

Professional Recruiters Inc

705 1st St NE
Little Falls, MN 56345-2403
(320) 616-5849
(800) 594-8414
Email: bob@professionalrecruiters.com
Web: www.professionalrecruiters.com

Summary: Very strong track record of success recruiting technically oriented sales, marketing and sales/marketing management talent primarily for the industrial electrical, electronic and high-technology equipment markets.

Key Contact - Specialty:
Mr. Robert Reinitz, CRM, President & Founder

Salary Minimum: $60,000

Functions: Generalist (All), Board Members, Automation, Sales & Mktg., Advertising, Mktg. Research, Mktg. Mgmt., Sales Mgmt.

Industries: Computer Equip., Test, Measure Equip., Misc. Mfg., Electronic, Elec. Components, Robotics, Semiconductors, Equip Svcs., Engineering Svcs., Fiber Optic, Industry Specific SW, Mfg. SW, Marketing SW

Professional Recruiters Inc

40 S River Rd
Bedford, NH 03110-6719
(603) 644-0909
Email: tim@princorp.com
Web: www.princjobs.com

Summary: We are a search firm. We are comprised of defense, semiconductor, and commercial divisions which specialize in the search and placement of select professionals in the defense, public, and private sectors.

Key Contact - Specialty:
Mr. Timothy Moran, CPC, CIPC, Chief Executive Officer - *Computers (Hardware,Software), Defense, Engineering, Information Technology*

Professional Recruiting Partners LLC

118 Crystal Downs Ct
Chester, VA 23836-5785
(877) 276-2364
(866) 560-8003
Fax: (804) 530-1223
Email: contact@prp-llc.com
Web: www.prp-llc.com

Summary: We are independent medical recruiters. This husband and wife team is dedicated to helping qualified healthcare candidates find opportunities with excellent facilities.

Key Contact - Specialty:
Mr. Jim White, Member & Owner
Mrs. Kim White, Member & Owner

Functions: Healthcare

Industries: K-12 Ed., Government, Hospitals, Long-term/Home Care, Physical Therapy, Occupational Therapy, Women's

The Professional Sales Search Company Inc

12801 50th Avenue Ct NW
Gig Harbor, WA 98332-7874
(253) 851-3528
Fax: (253) 851-7505
Email: execadmin@psscinc.com
Web: www.psscinc.com

Summary: We provide quality, sales personnel staffing, executive search and sales management consulting services for corporate America.

Key Contact - Specialty:
Mr. Douglas R. Letts, Managing Partner - *Sales*

Salary Minimum: $75,000

Functions: Sales & Mktg.

Industries: Manufacturing, Transportation, Services, Communications, Software, Biotech/Life Sciences, Healthcare, Hospitals

Professional Search

521 Cambridge Dr
Muskegon, MI 49441-5011
(231) 798-3537
Fax: (231) 798-8062
Email: chip@professionalsearch.net
Web: www.professionalsearch.net

Summary: Our staff size, team approach and extensive resources enable us to offer recruiting services in a comprehensive range of areas. Our approach enables us to complete the assignment significantly faster than the industry average time.

Key Contact - Specialty:
Mr. George McKenzie, President
Mr. Chip Hall, Senior Account Executive - *Engineering, Metals, Quality, Technical, Technical (Management)*

Salary Minimum: $50,000

Functions: Generalist (All), Senior Mgmt.

Industries: Generalist (All), Construction, Manufacturing, Chemicals, Engineering Svcs.

Professional Search Centre Ltd

533 Capital Dr
Lake Zurich, IL 60047-6711
(847) 719-1200
Fax: (847) 719-1275
Email: contact.us@psc-usa.com
Web: www.psc-usa.com

Summary: We specialize in the placement of IT; sales, and FDA regulated industries. We fulfill our client's hiring needs by placing candidates on a direct basis. In the event a client needs a candidate for a short-term project, we work with our sister company, to fulfill that need.

Key Contact - Specialty:
Mr. Jerry S. Hirschel, CPC, President
Ms. Mia Hirschel
Ms. Holly Anichini
Ms. Sumona Ghosh

Salary Minimum: $40,000

Functions: IT, R&D

Industries: Biotech/Life Sciences

Professional Search Inc

PO Box 19908
San Diego, CA 92159-0908
(619) 697-2138
Fax: (619) 303-6578
Email: jobs@psiwest.com
Web: www.psiwest.com

Summary: Specializing exclusively in the placement of engineering, manufacturing, and software professionals.

Key Contact - Specialty:
Mr. Vernon Kleist, President

Salary Minimum: $50,000

Functions: Product Dev., Automation, Quality, Productivity, Packaging, Systems Dev., R&D, Engineering

Industries: Generalist (All), Medical Devices, Machine, Appliance, Computer Equip., Consumer Elect., Robotics, Digital, Wireless, RF/Microwave, System SW

Professional Search Inc

7909 S Monaco Ct
Centennial, CO 80112-3129
(303) 694-1210

Summary: We provide a professional approach and expert applicant selection for positions resulting in quality placements, thus eliminating costly interviewing for employers.

Key Contact - Specialty:
Mr. Lawrence M. Jock, President

Salary Minimum: $30,000

Functions: Generalist (All), Management, Mfg., Sales & Mktg., Finance, IT, Engineering

Industries: Generalist (All), Finance, Hospitality, Media, Environmental Svcs., Software

Professional Search

2111 Main Ave E
West Fargo, ND 58078-2216
(701) 235-3719
(800) 473-2512
Fax: (701) 235-7092
Email: ksolhjem@prosearchfargo.com

Summary: We specialize in engineering & manufacturing, healthcare, physicians, pharmacists, and finance.

Key Contact - Specialty:
Mr. Kent Hochgraber, President & Partner - *Accounting, Healthcare, Physicians*
Mrs. Karen Solhjem, Partner & Vice President - *Architecture, Engineering, Manufacturing*

Salary Minimum: $50,000

Functions: Management, Physicians, Finance, Engineering

Industries: Generalist (All), Metal Products, Machine, Appliance, Electronic, Elec. Components, Finance, Architectural Svcs., Pharm Svcs., Accounting, Engineering Svcs., Healthcare

Professional Support Inc

26 N Cayuga Rd
Williamsville, NY 14221-5408
(716) 634-0253
Fax: (716) 634-3083
Email: buffalo@psi4jobs.com
Web: www.psi4jobs.com

Summary: Executive recruiting (retainer and contingency search), in accounting and data processing (IT), disciplines; contract and rent-to-own programs, temp clerical & DP operational services; contract data processing (project) services, individual and group outplacement services, training programs, facilities planning and disaster recovery services.

Key Contact - Specialty:
Mr. Paul H. Eastmer, President - *Information Systems*
Mr. Gregory Eastmer, Director, Recruiting & Placement - *Information Systems, SAP*

Salary Minimum: $30,000

Functions: Generalist (All), Senior Mgmt., Staffing, Budgeting, M&A, Systems Dev., Systems Implem., Mgmt. Consultants

Industries: Generalist (All), Metal Products, Mgmt. Consulting, Software

Branches:
500 Helendale Rd Ste 190
Rochester, NY 14609-3193
(585) 654-7800
Email: rochester@psi4jobs.com

Key Contact - Specialty:
Mr. Edward Sandusky, Director, Account
Management - *Information Systems*

8225 Brecksville Rd Ste 3
PMB 107
Brecksville, OH 44141-1362
(440) 526-7650
Fax: (216) 526-6612
Email: clevelnd@psi4jobs.com
Key Contact - Specialty:
Mr. Richard Beldon, Senior Recruiter -
Information Systems

Professional Technical Search Inc

PO Box 132641
The Woodlands, TX 77393-2641
(936) 273-7700
(281) 558-3100
Email: resume@pts-us.net
Web: www.pts-us.net

Summary: We are a diverse recruiting firm,
providing you with experience, expertise and
service. We specialize in recruiting candidates of
all levels of geosciences and engineering
specialties.

Key Contact - Specialty:
Mr. Michael Geier, President
Ms. Kathleen Geier, Vice President
Mr. Andrew Geier, Vice President

Functions: Generalist (All), IT, MIS Mgmt.,
Systems Analysis, Systems Dev., Systems
Implem., Systems Support, Network Admin.,
DB Admin., Engineering

Industries: Generalist (All), Oil & Gas,
Construction, Computer Equip., IT
Implementation, Insurance, Software,
Accounting SW, Database SW, Development
SW, Doc. Mgmt., Production SW,
Entertainment SW

Professionals in Recruiting Company

1028 Cresthaven Rd Ste 207
Memphis, TN 38119-3850
(901) 685-2042

Summary: Any accepted search is handled in a
confidential, ethical and professional manner with
a vigorous and knowledgeable effort that promotes
the client company and a mutually beneficial
union with a candidate. We are strong in searches
for executives, especially medical directors.

Key Contact - Specialty:
Mr. James O. Murrell, Co-Owner - *Healthcare*
Ms. Maxine W. Murrell, Co-Owner

Salary Minimum: $40,000

Functions: Management, Healthcare, Physicians,
Nurses, Health Admin., Sales Mgmt., CFOs,
Actuaries, MIS Mgmt., Attorneys

Industries: Generalist (All), Sports, Insurance,
Healthcare

Professions Inc International

3600 Park 42 Dr Ste 125A
Cincinnati, OH 45241-4039
(513) 530-0909
Email: recruiters@professionsinc.com
Web: www.professionsinc.com

Summary: Our firm has the ability to identify and
attract high caliber talent on a global basis.
Working primarily on a retained search basis, we
are known for strong integrity and ethics with the
majority of new business a result of direct referral.

Key Contact - Specialty:
Mr. Carl Coco, Jr., CPC, Chairman & Chief
Executive Officer - *Diversity, Executives,
Management, Sales, Senior management*
Ms. Kim Valmore, CPC, President & Chief
Operating Officer - *Packaging, Sales, Senior
management*
Mr. Jeffrey Gies, CPC - *Banking
(Commercial,Investment,Mortgage,Retail)*
Mr. Michael Pfirrman, Account Manager,
Construction - *Bridges, Cement/concrete,
Construction, Highways, Steel*
Mr. Jerry Land, CPC, Senior Account Manager -
Accounting, Audits, Tax
Mr. Travis Barthelmas, Account Manager -
Executives, High technology, Management

Salary Minimum: $40,000

Functions: Senior Mgmt., Sales & Mktg.,
Minorities/Diversity

Industries: Manufacturing, Paper, Printing,
Finance, Banking, Invest. Banking, Misc.
Financial, Services, Supply Chain Mgmt,
Packaging, Industry Specific SW

Profile International USA Inc

184 E 75th St
New York, NY 10021-3228
(212) 717-4364
Fax: (212) 717-4366
Email: dvdl@pmsr.com
Web: www.pmsr.com

Summary: We are specialists in senior
management recruitment for the upscale hotel
industry. Units, as well as corporate positions are
handled.

Key Contact - Specialty:
Ms. Danielle van der Loos, Hospitality
Recruitment Consultant - *Restaurants*

Salary Minimum: $60,000

Functions: Generalist (All)

Industries: Hospitality, Hotels, Resorts, Clubs,
Restaurants

Profiler Digital Media Recruiters

1815 Holmby Ave Apt 401
Los Angeles, CA 90025-4982
(310) 446-8343
Email: bibs@profilerusa.com
Web: www.profilerusa.com

Summary: We specialize in the placement of sales
and marketing professionals within the interactive
advertising media space. We work with online
publishers, agencies and clients conducting
business on the Internet.

Key Contact - Specialty:
Ms. Bib Scott, Partner - *Marketing, Sales*
Ms. Kim Scott, Partner - *Marketing, Sales*
Ms. Pat Jacoby, Vice President - *Business
development, Marketing, Sales*

Salary Minimum: $40,000

Functions: Middle Mgmt., Sales & Mktg.,
Advertising

Industries: Media, Advertising, Publishing, New
Media, Broadcast, Film

Profiles Inc

6915 Rochester Rd Ste 300
Troy, MI 48085-1285
(248) 828-3700
Fax: (248) 828-3720
Email: info@profilesusa.com
Web: www.profilesusa.net

Summary: We are recruiters of sales,
management, technical and medical professionals.

Key Contact - Specialty:
Mr. Michael Wilson, President

Salary Minimum: $50,000

Functions: Management, Healthcare, Sales &
Mktg.

Industries: Generalist (All)

ProFinders Inc

PO Box 124
Orlando, FL 32802-0124
(407) 894-0840
Fax: (407) 894-5818
Email: sheri@profinders.com
Web: www.profinders.com

Summary: Specializing in the recruitment of sales,
marketing and operations professionals.

Key Contact - Specialty:
Mrs. Sheri Mitchell-Turner, President -
Marketing, Operations, Sales
Ms. Lori Smiles, Associate - *Marketing,
Operations, Sales*

Salary Minimum: $30,000

Functions: Sales & Mktg., Advertising, Mktg.
Research, Mktg. Mgmt., Sales Mgmt., Direct
Mktg., HR Mgmt.

Industries: Generalist (All)

Profitable Solutions Executive Search

2560 Country Side Dr
Orange Park, FL 32003-4949
(904) 215-3561
Email: info@jobwish.net
Web: www.jobwish.net

Summary: Our focus is consumer products,
specializing in sporting goods and fashion with a
strong emphasis on footwear manufacturing. We
recruit mid-to-upper level candidates in
management, sales, marketing, operations, design
and PD.

Key Contact - Specialty:
Ms. Susan Proffitt, President & Chief Executive
Officer - *Fashion, Footwear*

Salary Minimum: $75,000

Functions: Generalist (All)

Industries: Generalist (All), Manufacturing,
Textiles, Apparel, Leather, Stone, Glass,
Consumer Elect., Electronic, Elec. Components,
Consumer Goods, Wholesale, Retail, Supply
Chain Mgmt

Branches:
230 Mohawk Trl
Wayne, NJ 07470-5067
(973) 616-7954
Email: info@jobwish.net
Key Contact - Specialty:
Ms. R. S. Proffitt, Office Manager

Progressive Personnel

2218 Commerce Pkwy
Virginia Beach, VA 23454-4301
(757) 631-0372
Fax: (757) 631-2508
Email: cburd@progressivepersonnel.com
Web: www.progressivepersonnel.com

Summary: Specializing in recruiting restaurant
and hospitality managers in small privately owned
to large major corporate chains, nationwide. We've
also, recently set up and established an 'any and
all' utility for credit card and electronic financial
transactions that an owner or manager may need to
run a restaurant.

Key Contact - Specialty:
Mr. Craig Burd, MA, President

Salary Minimum: $35,000

Functions: Management, Sales Mgmt.,
Hospitality

Industries: Hospitality, Hotels, Resorts, Clubs,
Restaurants, Quick Service Restaurants, Full
Service Restaurants, Inst./Industrial Food Svc.,
Entertainment, Recreation, Sports, New Media

Branches:
PO Box 9972
Birmingham, AL 35220-0972
(205) 643-6955
Fax: (205) 815-8097
Email: hlarry@progressivepersonnel.com
Key Contact - Specialty:
H. Larry

PO Box 1421
Manassas, VA 20108-1421
(703) 367-0697
Fax: (703) 367-0408
Email: cgalloway@progressivepersonnel.com
Key Contact - Specialty:
Mr. Cliff Galloway, Recruiter, Management

Progressive Resources

1608 Calle Corte
Santa Barbara, CA 93101-4910
(805) 682-7884
Fax: (928) 752-8256
Email: sales@sbjobs.com
Web: www.sbjobs.com

Summary: Executive and technical recruiting
services.

Key Contact - Specialty:
Ms. Jill R. Tsas, Executive Recruiter - *Technical*

Salary Minimum: $50,000

Functions: Generalist (All), Management,
Production, IT, R&D, Engineering

Industries: Generalist (All), Medical Devices,
Computer Equip.

Progressive Search Associates

221 Boston Post Rd E Ste 250
Marlborough, MA 01752-3545
(508) 485-4430
Email: info@progressivesearch.com
Web: www.progressivesearch.com

Summary: We are a boutique firm specializing in
the search and placement of hard to find
individuals for technology related firms. Areas of
specialization include: software engineering, IT,
marketing and product management, customer
service, and sales. We've also formed a division
that focuses on the rapidly growing area of small
technology.

Key Contact - Specialty:
Mr. David Abrams, Managing Director

Salary Minimum: $50,000

Functions: Generalist (All), Sales Mgmt., IT

Industries: Food, Bev., Tobacco, Electronic, Elec.
Components, Mgmt. Consulting, E-commerce,
IT Implementation, Media, Advertising, New
Media, Broadcast, Film, Communications,
Software, Database SW, Development SW,
Marketing SW, Biotech/Life Sciences,
Healthcare

Project Hire Holdings Inc

1870 The Exchange SE Ste 100
Atlanta, GA 30339-2021
(770) 989-7303

Email: info@projecthire.com
Web: www.projecthire.com

Summary: Professional services and executive
search firm specializing in accounting, finance,
audit, and tax.

Key Contact - Specialty:
Mr. Dave Krier, Partner, JBII
Mr. Rick Stockfield, Managing Partner
Mr. Mike Veronesi, Managing Partner

Salary Minimum: $50,000

Functions: Finance

Industries: Finance, Accounting, Accounting SW

Proliance Group Inc

9972 Silver Maple Rd
Highlands Ranch, CO 80129-5469
(303) 683-4909
Email: resume@proliancegroup.com
Web: www.proliancegroup.com

Summary: Our firm is an executive search,
consulting, training and coaching firm. We
provide searches for high technology and
healthcare sales, sales management and executive
management as well as pre-hire and pre-interview
assessments, executive compatibly reports, sales
and leadership consulting, job search coaching,
sales coaching and keynote speaking.

Key Contact - Specialty:
Mr. David Suson, President

Salary Minimum: $70,000

Functions: Management, Senior Mgmt., Sales
Reps.

Industries: Generalist (All), Software

ProNet Inc

(also known as Starling and Associates)
677 WC Braswell Rd
Selma, NC 27576-6574
(919) 889-0852
Email: wrstarling@nc.rr.com

Summary: Recruiting in the data processing and
data communication industry, we provide
qualified candidates in a timely manner. Principals
have held sales & marketing positions with
Fortune 500 companies. Based upon the current
job market we are offering career coaching for
those people who have limited experience in
searching for a job.

Key Contact - Specialty:
Mr. Dick Starling, President

Salary Minimum: $60,000

Functions: Generalist (All), Mktg. Research,
Mktg. Mgmt., Sales Mgmt., CFOs, MIS Mgmt.,
Systems Dev.

Industries: Generalist (All), Computer Equip.,
Mgmt. Consulting, HR Services, E-commerce,
Communications, Telecoms, Telephony, Digital,
Wireless, Fiber Optic, Network Infrastructure,
RF/Microwave, Software, Networking, Comm.
SW

Proplacements Inc

24 N Oak St
Crystal Lake, IL 60014-4128
(815) 356-7900
Fax: (815) 356-7791
Email: info@proplacementsinc.com
Web: www.proplacementsinc.com

Summary: We are an insurance recruiting firm.
Our specialties include property, casualty, life,
health, carriers, brokers, agents and self-insureds,
underwriting, claims, producer, account managers,
actuaries, loss control and risk managers.

Key Contact - Specialty:
Ms. Sylvia Schafer

Functions: Generalist (All)

Industries: Insurance

ProSearch Inc

P O Box 7489
70 Center St Ste 3
Portland, ME 04112-7489
(207) 775-7600
Email: emckersie@psicareers.com
Web: www.psicareers.com

Summary: Small, high quality firm dedicated to
high ethics and confidentiality. Owner has
extensive years in the search and staffing industry
and the average recruiter experience with the firm
is five years. IT contract opportunities.

Key Contact - Specialty:
Mr. Edward S. McKersie, CPC, President &
Owner - *Finance, Marketing, Sales*
Ms. Andrea Brown, Director, Accounting,
Finance Recruiting
Mr. Gary Auger, Director, IT Staffing Services
Ms. Christy Hillman, Director, Temporary
Staffing Services
Ms. Rhiana Lippold, Manager, Temporary
Staffing Services
Ms. Mary Warren, Senior Recruiter
Ms. Sarah Davies, Senior Recruiter, IT
Mr. Todd Chamberlain, Recruiter, Information
Technology
Mr. Toni Leone, Office Manager

Salary Minimum: $25,000

Functions: Sales & Mktg., HR Mgmt., Finance,
IT

Industries: Generalist (All)

ProSearch International Inc

PO Box 590
Dunedin, FL 34697-0590
(727) 734-2466
Fax: (727) 734-7172
Email: prosearchint@earthlink.net

Summary: Our firm specializes in IT and
engineering contract and permanent placements.
We pride ourselves in our personal touch. Our
goal is to create a lasting relationship between
client and candidate.

Key Contact - Specialty:
Mr. Tommie Grayson, President

Salary Minimum: $55,000

Functions: Production, IT, MIS Mgmt., Systems
Analysis, Systems Dev., Systems Implem.,
Network Admin., Engineering

Industries: Generalist (All), Manufacturing

ProSearch Recruiting

2503 Sandycreek Dr
Westlake Village, CA 91361-5545
(818) 597-0300
Email: prosearchcareers@aol.com

Summary: We specialize in media, including
internet, print publishing, events & research
companies, advertising, broadcast and film. We
also serve the real estate industry. We attract
experienced and successful professionals in sales,
sales management, marketing, content, operations
and top management. Our extensive network and
years of publishing and recruiting experience
combine to give you the support you need.

Key Contact - Specialty:
Ms. Susan J. Curtis, President & Owner - *Internet, Publishing*
Ms. Suzanne Baird, Vice President, Research - *Editorial, Publishing*

Salary Minimum: $60,000

Functions: Management, Senior Mgmt., Middle Mgmt., Mktg. Mgmt., Sales Mgmt.

Industries: Venture Cap., Non-profits, Mgmt. Consulting, HR Services, K-12 Ed., Higher Ed., Media, Advertising, Publishing, New Media, Broadcast, Film, Wireless, Real Estate

Prospective Personnel Service Inc

PO Box 4727
Tulsa, OK 74159-0727
(918) 584-5000
Fax: (918) 584-5002
Email: bankrecruiter@cox.net

Summary: We are an executive search firm with experience specializing in professional level banking positions.

Key Contact - Specialty:
Ms. Linda Wilson, CPC, President & Owner - *Banking*

Functions: Generalist (All)

Industries: Banking

PROTECH Corporate Enterprises Inc.

(formerly known as PharmSearches)
271 Madison Ave Ste 1405
New York, NY 10016-1001
(212) 685-1400
Fax: (212) 685-4340
Email: bob@protechpharma.com
Web: www.protechpharma.com

Summary: We provide technical recruiting for the pharmaceutical, biotech and consumer health products industry. Specialties: manufacturing & packaging operations, engineering, QA, QC, regulatory affairs, and validation & qualification

Key Contact - Specialty:
Mr. Bob Brakel, President & Owner - *Engineering, Manufacturing, Technical*
Mr. Hansle Guichardo, Staffing Consultant
Ms. Jennifer Carrieri, Staffing Consultant

Salary Minimum: $60,000

Functions: Mfg., Plant Mgmt., Quality, Engineering

Industries: Drugs Mfg., Biotech/Life Sciences

Protocol Agency Inc

2659 Townsgate Rd Ste 203
Westlake Village, CA 91361-2774
(818) 706-1571
(805) 371-0069
Fax: (805) 371-0048
Email: wlv@protocolagency.com
Web: www.protocolagency.com

Summary: Search and selection firm specializing in contingency and retained placement of IT managers and programmers, accounting, financial, medical, HR and middle & upper-level management professionals.

Key Contact - Specialty:
Mr. Robert W. Sparks, President
Mr. Stuart Selter, Branch Manager - *Information Systems, Information Technology*

Salary Minimum: $40,000

Functions: Generalist (All), Senior Mgmt., Allied Health, Customer Svc., Training, CFOs, Network Admin., DB Admin.

Industries: Generalist (All), Manufacturing, Finance, Accounting, Haz. Waste, Real Estate, Healthcare

Branches:
16633 Ventura Blvd Ste 1440
Encino, CA 91436-1886
(818) 926-4200
(818) 926-4201
Fax: (818) 501-5828
Email: enc@protocolagency.com
Key Contact - Specialty:
Ms. Pamela Kriss-Calvino, Branch Manager - *Accounting (General), Data processing, Information Technology, Office (Support), Systems (Analysts)*

Providence Personnel Consultants

2404 4th St Ste 1
Cuyahoga Falls, OH 44221-2643
(330) 929-6431
Fax: (330) 929-4335
Email: ppconsult@aol.com
Web: www.providence-personnel.com

Summary: We are dedicated to assisting organizations in all phases of recruiting and staffing. We have both regional contacts and national resources that give us the ability to recruit for the most specialized positions. Our expertise has been developed through recruiting in fields including: manufacturing/engineering, IT, accounting/finance/banking/insurance, administrative/clerical, sales/marketing/advertising and HR.

Key Contact - Specialty:
Ms. Donna Early, CPC, President

Functions: Management, Mfg., Materials, Healthcare, Sales & Mktg., HR Mgmt., Finance, IT, Engineering, Specialized Svcs.

Industries: Generalist (All)

Provident Services

125 Valley Glen Ct
Greer, SC 29650-2566
(800) 507-2286
(864) 801-1440
Fax: (864) 801-1441
Email: career@provserv.com
Web: www.provserv.com

Summary: We recruit physicians, surgeons, psychiatrists, physician assistants, nurse practitioners, nurse managers, bio pharmaceutical, scientists, business, IT and more.

Key Contact - Specialty:
Ms. Laurie Radcliffe, President

Salary Minimum: $40,000

Functions: Management, Healthcare, Physicians, Nurses

Industries: Generalist (All), Robotics, Non-profits, Pharm Svcs., IT Implementation, Biotech/Life Sciences, Healthcare, Hospitals, Long-term/Home Care, Dental, Physical Therapy, Occupational Therapy, Women's, Non-Classifiable

PRY Resources Inc

PO Box 37507 RPO Malvern Town Ct
Scarborough, ON M1B 5P9
Canada
(416) 724-2829
Fax: (416) 724-6517
Email: pryresource@idirect.com

Summary: We are a recruitment and placement of permanent, contract and temp office support and IT personnel including software engineers from entry to management levels.

Key Contact - Specialty:
Ms. Ann Ragwen, Partner
Mr. Harry Yong, Partner

Functions: Generalist (All), Mfg., Sales & Mktg., HR Mgmt., Finance, IT, Engineering

Industries: Generalist (All), Manufacturing, Finance, Services, Media, Insurance, Software

Pryor Knowledge Recruiting Inc

PO Box 2773
La Crosse, WI 54602-2773
(608) 784-6278
Fax: (608) 784-6389
Email: lpryor@charter.net

Summary: We recruit for positions in sales, sales management, pre-sales engineering, product marketing as well as healthcare. Searches are conducted in pharmaceutical, medical, software, networking, telecom, services and consumer areas.

Key Contact - Specialty:
Ms. Laura Pryor, President

Functions: Generalist (All), Healthcare, Nurses, Allied Health, Mktg. Mgmt., Sales Mgmt., Sales Reps.

Industries: Drugs Mfg., Medical Devices, Computer Equip., Pharm Svcs., E-commerce, IT Implementation, Communications, Telecoms, Wireless, Network Infrastructure, Software, Database SW, Development SW, Doc. Mgmt., Production SW, ERP SW, Mfg. SW, Marketing SW, Networking, Comm. SW, Security SW, System SW, Hospitals, Dental

Pryor Personnel Agency Inc

(also known as Pryor Associates)
147 W Old Country Rd
Hicksville, NY 11801-4007
(516) 935-0100
(866) 622-8827
Fax: (516) 931-7842
Email: ppryor1578@aol.com
Web: www.ppryor.com

Summary: We have experience in placements in the insurance, actuarial and pension & employee benefits industry.

Key Contact - Specialty:
Ms. Patricia Pryor Bonica, President & Chief Executive Officer
Mr. Gerald O'Gorman, Secretary & Treasurer - *Risk management*
Ms. Pauline Reimer, ASA, Actuarial & Employee Benefits AE
Ms. Maureen Boehm, P&C Account Executive
Ms. Cathy Pryor, Executive, L&H Account - *Human resources*
Mr. Richard J. Pokorny, P&C Account Executive - *Brokerage*
Mr. Paul LaVacca, Claims Account Executive
Mr. Terry Breslau, Administrative Assistant
Mr. Osman Rahman, Administrative Assistant
Mr. Gene Mazzara, Bookkeeper

Salary Minimum: $25,000

Functions: Generalist (All), Middle Mgmt., Customer Svc., Benefits, Credit, Systems Analysis, Systems Dev.

Industries: Generalist (All), Insurance

PSP Agency

188 Montague St Ste 204
Brooklyn, NY 11201-3609
(718) 596-3786
(214) 739-0783
Email: pspagency@aol.com

Summary: Our firm specializes in targeting engineering, telecom and sales.

Key Contact - Specialty:
Ms. Angela D. Delors, President - *ATE, Automotive, BSME, Components, Consumer*
Mr. Arnold D. Harvey, Account Executive - *Mechanical, Medical, RF microwave, Sales, Six sigma*
Mr. James McFadden, Account Executive - *Medical, Quality, RF microwave, Semiconductors, Six sigma*
Mr. Alton Seymour, Account Executive - *Medical, RF microwave, Sales, Semiconductors, Six sigma*

Salary Minimum: $60,000

Functions: Management, Product Dev., Quality, Materials, Sales & Mktg., Systems Implem., Network Admin., DB Admin., Engineering, Technicians

Industries: Manufacturing, Drugs Mfg., Metal Products, Computer Equip., Test, Measure Equip., Pharm Svcs., Equip Svcs., Mgmt. Consulting, Telecoms, Software

PSW Group Executive Search & Placement

(formerly known as PSW Group)
PO Box 5222
Rock Island, IL 61204-5222
(309) 786-7850
(800) 210-6008
Email: pswresumes@mchsi.com
Web:
www.topechelon.com/obc/obc.asp?recruiterid=BQ
5501

Summary: Our firm specializes in senior executive and mid-management executive placements. Our specialties include: agriculture, engineering, health care, medical devices, IT, homeland security, hotels, hospitality, gaming, restaurant, non-profits, sales and call centers. We have the recruiting skills, industry knowledge, contacts and candidate network to fulfill your expectations.

Key Contact - Specialty:
Mr. Patrick Walsh, Partner - *Engineering, Hotels, Information Technology, Sales*
Ms. Susan Pells, Partner - *Accounting, Associations, Biotechnology, C-level, Finance*
Mr. Greg Runyard, Associate - *Middle management, Non-profit, Resorts, Restaurants, Senior management*

Salary Minimum: $30,000

Functions: Management, Mfg., Materials, Healthcare, Sales & Mktg., HR Mgmt., Finance, IT, Engineering, Hospitality

Industries: Generalist (All)

PsychPros Executive Search

2404 Auburn Ave
Cincinnati, OH 45219-2735
(513) 651-9500
(888) 651-8367
Fax: (513) 651-9558
Email: marilyn@psychpros.com
Web: www.psychpros.com

Summary: We are a search firm dedicated to the behavioral healthcare and social service industries. We place upper-level professionals such as presidents/CEO's, COO's, executive directors, CFO's, medical directors, clinical supervisors, and others into challenging positions. Customers include mental health, chemical dependency and social service organizations.

Key Contact - Specialty:
Ms. Holly Dorna, LPCC, MA, President & Chief Executive Officer - *Managed care, Psychiatry, Social work*
Mrs. Marilyn Tribbe, LSW, MA, Executive Search Consultant - *Managed care, Psychiatry, Social work*
Mrs. Cheryl Rapier, MA, Executive Search Consultant - *Managed care, Professional services, Psychiatry, Social work*

Salary Minimum: $65,000

Functions: Healthcare, Physicians, Nurses, Allied Health, Health Admin., Mgmt. Consultants

Industries: Non-profits, Healthcare, Hospitals, Long-term/Home Care

PTC Accounting and Finance Inc

300-1600 Steeles Ave W
Futurity Place
Concord, ON L4K 4M2
Canada
(905) 660-9550
(877) 303-9550
Email: info@ptcaccounting.com
Web: www.ptcaccounting.com

Summary: We are a leading provider of accounting and finance professionals as interim (i.e. contract or temp) resources for assignments, projects and open positions. We specialize in all levels of accountants, from one day to several years, provide responsive turnaround and work to our clients' budgets.

Key Contact - Specialty:
Mr. Bruce Singer, CA, Partner
Mr. Howard Maritzer, Partner
Mr. Ken Sugar, Partner
Ms. Heather Payne, Manager, Client Relations
Mr. Robert Fletcher, Manager, Client Relations

Functions: Finance

Industries: Generalist (All)

Publishing Search Solutions

PO Box 246
North Marshfield, MA 02059-0246
(781) 837-7959
Fax: (781) 837-5485
Email: mfoy@publishingseach.com
Web: www.publishingsearch.com

Summary: We are an executive search firm catering to book and magazine publishers primarily in the United States. The majority of our executive searches are for editorial talent at various levels from publisher to editor. The other part of our business concerns art, circulation and marketing executive placements.

Key Contact - Specialty:
Mr. Michael Foy, President

Salary Minimum: $35,000

Functions: Product Dev.

Industries: Media, Publishing, New Media, Communications

PulseHR Inc

1010-424 Queen St
Queen Towers Apts
Ottawa, ON K1R 5A8
Canada
(613) 231-6308
Fax: (613) 231-2900

Email: info@pulsehr.com
Web: www.pulsehr.com

Summary: Our firm is a recruitment agency specializing in the health sector. We recruit for medicine, nursing (including foreign-trained nurses), allied health, dentistry, and biotechnology.

Key Contact - Specialty:
Ms. Anna Tulchinsky, PhD, Principal, Co-Founder, Managing Director

Functions: Healthcare, Physicians, Nurses, Allied Health, Minorities/Diversity

Industries: Biotech/Life Sciences, Healthcare, Hospitals, Long-term/Home Care, Dental, Physical Therapy, Occupational Therapy, Women's

Pyramid Consulting Group LLC

1001 Avenue of the Americas Fl 4
New York, NY 10018-5476
(212) 790-9556
Fax: (212) 790-9557
Email: info@pyramidcg.net
Web: pyramidconsultinggroup.net

Summary: We offer expertise in the area of accounting & finance professional recruitment. Our clients include companies that cross a broad spectrum of industries including entertainment, retail, manufacturing, technology, financial services, hedge funds, pharmaceutical, advertising, publishing, consumer products, consulting, energy, real estate and public accounting.

Key Contact - Specialty:
Ms. Allyson Goodman, Managing Partner

Salary Minimum: $80,000

Q Biomedical Search

2901 W Shamrell Blvd Ste 101
Flagstaff, AZ 86001-9417
(928) 556-3097
(888) 811-0230
Fax: (928) 556-3084
Email: jobs@qbiomedical.com
Web: www.qbiomedical.com

Summary: We are a medical device recruiting firm specializing in the recruitment of medical device professionals. We mainly focus on any product/device associated with a class III implant (catheters, stents, guidewires and coils).

Key Contact - Specialty:
Mr. Dave Kasprzyk, Director, Technical Recruitment

Salary Minimum: $45,000

Functions: Healthcare, R&D

Industries: Plastics, Rubber, Engineering Svcs., Healthcare

QCI Technical Staffing

3970 New Vision Dr
Fort Wayne, IN 46845-1712
(260) 436-9797
Fax: (260) 436-6228
Email: resumes@qcitech.com
Web: www.qcitech.com

Summary: We primarily work in engineering (mfg, IE, process, product, controls, mechanical, SW, HW, electrical, chemical, bio-medical, etc.), IT and other professional (HR, accounting, production supervisors and plant manager) positions for our manufacturing clients. Management positions have included plant managers, engineering managers, director of international sales, etc.

Key Contact - Specialty:
Mr. Bill Quackenbush, CPC, CTS, President
Ms. Jennifer Fahlsing, Account Manager -
*Engineering, Information Technology,
Manufacturing, Manufacturing (Management),
Orthopedics*
Ms. Jennifer Gramling, Office Manager
Mr. John Sharkey, Recruiter
Ms. Regina Cannaday, Staffing Coordinator
Ms. Coffie Pippert, Staffing Coordinator
Mr. Larry Davidson, Staffing Coordinator,
Contract Division
Ms. April Cory, Support Staff - *Insurance, Office
(Support), Staffing, Underwriting*

Salary Minimum: $50,000

Functions: Generalist (All)

Industries: Medical Devices, Plastics, Rubber,
Metal Products, Machine, Appliance, Motor
Vehicles, Test, Measure Equip., Misc. Mfg.,
Electronic, Elec. Components, Accounting

Qualifind Inc

9635 Heinrich Hertz Dr Ste 6
San Diego, CA 92154-7918
(619) 661-2585
(619) 921-1795
Email: wcarter@quali-find.com
Web: www.quali-find.com

Summary: We are focused on mid to senior
management positions in accounting,
customs/regulatory compliance, engineering,
human resources, logistics, operations and supply
chain. We offer extensive access to bilingual
English/Spanish professionals, as well as multi-
lingual talent throughout the U.S., Mexico and
Canada. Our team has fluency in English, Spanish,
Japanese, French, German and Portuguese.

Key Contact - Specialty:
Mr. Warren R. Carter, Senior Managing Partner,
US - *Accounting (General), Human resources,
Manufacturing, Manufacturing (Management),
Supply Chain*

Salary Minimum: $40,000

Functions: Management, Senior Mgmt., Middle
Mgmt., Mfg., Production, Plant Mgmt.,
Materials, Purchasing, Distribution, HR Mgmt.

Industries: Generalist (All), Manufacturing,
Lumber, Furniture, Medical Devices, Plastics,
Rubber, Metal Products, Machine, Appliance,
Motor Vehicles, Computer Equip., Consumer
Elect., Misc. Mfg., Electronic, Elec.
Components, Consumer Goods, Accounting,
HR Services, IT Implementation, Engineering
Svcs., Logistics Svcs.

Branches:
11055 N 41st St
Phoenix, AZ 85028-2927
(602) 923-3387
(480) 390-5804
Email: dallday@quali-find.com
Key Contact - Specialty:
Mr. Doug Allday, Site Manager - *Computers
(Software), Construction, Distribution, General
management, Human resources*

7362 Remcon Cir
El Paso, TX 79912-1623
(915) 225-4044
(915) 203-2580
Email: mtovar@quali-find.com
Key Contact - Specialty:
Ms. Martha Tovar, Site Manager - *Distribution,
Diversity, Logistics, Purchasing, Quality*

Tizoz 387
Ciudad del Sol
Zapopan Jalisco
45050 Guadalajara, JAL
Mexico
33 3167 9439
Email: vibarra@quali-find.com
Key Contact - Specialty:
Ms. Veronica Ibarra, Site Manager - *Accounting,
Distribution, Engineering, Human resources,
Manufacturing (Management)*

Alfonso Napoles Gandara 50 Piso 4
Col. Pena Blanca Santa Fe
Col. Pena Blanca Santa Fe
01210 Mexico City, DF
Mexico
55 9171 1988
55 1794 5759
Email: libarra@quali-find.com
Key Contact - Specialty:
Ms. Lizette Ibarra, Site Manager - *Accounting
(Big 4,General), Benefits, Human resources,
Quality*

Fco. Javier Mina 1415-208
Zona Rio
22320 Tijuana, BJC
Mexico
(619) 421-7134
(619) 921-1798
Email: fespinosa@quali-find.com
Key Contact - Specialty:
Mr. Fernando Espinosa, Senior Managing
Partner, Mexico - *Engineering, General
management, Operations, Regulatory, Supply
Chain*

Quality Search

100 S Calumet Rd
Chesterton, IN 46304-2447
(219) 926-8202
Fax: (219) 926-3834
Email: jim@qsjobs.com
Web: www.qsjobs.com

Summary: We place/recruit technical/engineering
personnel for most manufacturing related firms.
Our specialization is packaging engineers, quality
control and manufacturing management.

Key Contact - Specialty:
Mr. James L. Jeselnick, President

Salary Minimum: $40,000

Functions: Generalist (All), Senior Mgmt.,
Production, Plant Mgmt., Productivity,
Packaging, Engineering

Industries: Generalist (All), Food, Bev., Tobacco,
Chemicals, Soap, Perf., Cosmtcs., Drugs Mfg.,
Medical Devices, Paints, Petro. Products,
Consumer Elect.

Quality Search Inc

PO Box 752294
Dayton, OH 45475-2294
(937) 433-0717
Email: bjohnson@qualitysearch.com
Web: www.qualitysearch.com

Summary: Sharply focused in serving individuals
with technical backgrounds: i.e. engineers, sales,
executives, in rubber & plastics, seals &
gasketing, motion control, hydraulics &
pneumatics, automation, pumps and filtration.

Key Contact - Specialty:
Mr. Robert J. Johnson, President - *Engineering,
Management, Sales*
Ms. Therese Martin

Salary Minimum: $45,000

Functions: Generalist (All), Management, Mfg.,
Product Dev., Automation, Quality, Sales &
Mktg., Sales Mgmt., Systems Analysis,
Engineering

Industries: Agri., Forestry, Mining, Medical
Devices, Plastics, Rubber, Metal Products,
Machine, Appliance, Motor Vehicles, Computer
Equip., Robotics

Quality Source Inc

14650 Detroit Ave Ste 120
Lakewood, OH 44107-4210
(216) 529-9911
Fax: (419) 715-0459
Email: dlscpc@aol.com
Web:
hometown.aol.com/qualitysourceinc/myhomepage
/index.html

Summary: Our firm performs professional search
and placement. We are networked with other top-
notch search firms giving us a broader range of
specialties but our main focus is legal.

Key Contact - Specialty:
Ms. Debra L. Stitt, CPC, Owner

Functions: Management, Admin. Svcs., HR
Mgmt., Finance, Legal, Paralegals

Industries: Generalist (All), Legal, Accounting

QualStaff Resources

6201 College Blvd Ste 200
Overland Park, KS 66211-2430
(913) 498-3434
Fax: (913) 498-8408
Email: webmaster@qualstaff.com
Web: www.qualstaff.com

Summary: Ours is a full-service provider of
employment solutions, from temporary
employment to direct placement of quality full-
time employees. We have a track record of
locating and recruiting top entry to executive level
professionals for our clients. We offer the
following four specialty placement divisions
through our professional search and staffing
services: accounting, office, tech and human
resources.

Key Contact - Specialty:
Mr. Andy Schroeder

Functions: Generalist (All), Management, Admin.
Svcs., HR Mgmt., Finance, IT, Engineering

Industries: Generalist (All)

Quantico Consulting LLC

PO Box 51716
Phoenix, AZ 85076-1716
(480) 598-5227
(928) 978-4316
Fax: (480) 598-5225
Email: jfarro.qcon@cox.net

Summary: We service the semiconductor
equipment and materials market, conducting
executive searches for general management, sales,
marketing, R&D, process engineering and field
service personnel.

Key Contact - Specialty:
Mr. Jerry Farro, Partner - *Sales, Technical*
Mr. William VanZanten, Partner - *Management
consulting, Manufacturing, Marketing, Sales,
Technical (Management)*

Functions: Generalist (All), Senior Mgmt.,
Middle Mgmt., Mfg., Sales & Mktg., IT, Int'l.

Industries: Computer Equip., Test, Measure
Equip., Electronic, Elec. Components,
Semiconductors, Software

Quantum Advantage Inc

16054 Sawyer Ranch Rd
Austin, TX 78737-8607
(512) 894-3695
(866) 734-5625
Fax: (512) 894-4432
Email: qai@austin.rr.com
Web: www.qaijobs.com

Summary: We specialize in recruiting and
permanent placement of technologists in all
modalities radiology in North America. Our
services include staffing: x-ray, CT, MRI,
mammography, ultrasonography, vascular,
echocardiology, cardiovascular, special
procedures, nuclear medicine, radiation therapy
and dosimetry.

Key Contact - Specialty:
Mr. Giles J. Andrews, Recruiter
Mrs. Antoinette Andrews, Recruiter

Salary Minimum: $35,000

Functions: Healthcare, Allied Health, Technicians

Industries: Healthcare, Hospitals

The Quantum Group

PO Box 1242
Ballwin, MO 63022-1242
(800) 216-1330
(636) 207-7887
Fax: (636) 207-7444
Email: quantmgrp@aol.com
Web: www.thequantumgrp.com

Summary: Specialization in placing salaried
personnel in manufacturing operations.

Key Contact - Specialty:
Mr. James G. Fitzgerald, President -
Manufacturing

Salary Minimum: $30,000

Functions: Generalist (All), Mfg., Production,
Plant Mgmt., Quality, HR Mgmt., CFOs,
Engineering

Industries: Generalist (All), Manufacturing,
Lumber, Furniture, Plastics, Rubber, Metal
Products, Machine, Appliance, HR Services,
Environmental Svcs.

Quantum Technology Recruiting Inc

1800-2000 Av McGill College
La Tour L' Industrielle-Vie
Montreal, QC H3A 3H3
Canada
(514) 842-5555
Fax: (514) 849-8846
Email: qtrny@quantum-qtr.com
Web: www.quantum-qtr.com

Summary: We are a recruitment firm specializing
in the placement of IT and technology
professionals. We are one of the country's largest,
privately held recruiting firm.

Key Contact - Specialty:
Mr. Tony Pittarelli

Functions: Staffing

Industries: Finance, Banking, Mgmt. Consulting,
New Media, Telecoms, Software

Branches:
420 Lexington Ave Rm 2600
New York, NY 10170-2609
(212) 972-1313
Fax: (212) 983-7087
Email: newyork@quantum-qtr.com
Key Contact - Specialty:
Mr. Michael Goldstein, Manager

950-55 University Ave
Uniwell Building
Toronto, ON M5J 2H7
Canada
(416) 366-3660
Fax: (416) 366-4363
Email: toronto@quantum-qtr.com
Key Contact - Specialty:
Mr. John Baglieri, Manager, Recruitment
Ms. Michela Syrie-Paul, Manager, Sales
Effectivenes

Questar Partners Inc

100 Winners Cir N Ste 160
Brentwood, TN 37027-1002
(615) 371-8800
Fax: (615) 371-8804
Email: mwharton@questarpartners.com
Web: www.questarpartners.com

Summary: We are a generalist firm working in the
areas of health care, manufacturing, engineering,
finance and IT on both a retained and a
contingency basis.

Key Contact - Specialty:
Ms. Melissa Wharton, President & Chief
Executive Officer

Functions: Generalist (All)

Industries: Construction, Manufacturing, Finance,
Legal, Mgmt. Consulting, IT Implementation,
Higher Ed., Media, Environmental Svcs.,
Healthcare

Questor Consultants Inc

2515 N Broad St
Colmar, PA 18915-9773
(215) 997-9262
Fax: (215) 997-9226
Email: sbevivino@questorconsultants.com
Web: www.questorconsultants.com

Summary: We are P/C insurance industry
specialists. Heavily specializing in claims,
marketing, and underwriting.

Key Contact - Specialty:
Mr. Sal Bevivino, President

Salary Minimum: $35,000

Functions: Management, Board Members, Risk
Mgmt.

Industries: Insurance, Casualty, Claims, Life,
Commercial, Re-Insurance

QuestPro Consultants LP

17300 Preston Rd Ste 350
Dallas, TX 75252-5799
(972) 960-1305
Fax: (972) 960-1357
Email: jobs@questpro.com
Web: www.questpro.com

Summary: Our firm is a human resources capital
firm focusing on the insurance industry. We
handle property & casualty, life & health and
managed care. Our firm services both large
international carriers and small regional agencies.
We handle claims, underwriting, sales/marketing,
loss control, systems, finance, and operations
positions.

Key Contact - Specialty:
Ms. Lauren Levinson, Partner
Mr. Kevin M. Burch, CPC, President & Chief
Executive Officer
Ms. Debbie Hubbell, Division Director

Salary Minimum: $30,000

Functions: Generalist (All), Board Members,
Senior Mgmt., Admin. Svcs., Nurses, HR
Mgmt., Risk Mgmt.

Industries: Generalist (All), Insurance, Casualty,
Claims, Life, Commercial, Re-Insurance,
Healthcare

Queue Systems

205-3100 Steeles Ave E
Markham, ON L3R 8T3
Canada
(905) 754-8000
Fax: (905) 754-8001
Email: staffing@queuesystems.net
Web: www.queuesystems.net

Summary: Are you unique? So are we. Our firm is
a small IT (contract and permanent) staffing firm,
with clients primarily in the greater Toronto area.
Our firm also has an IT consulting division
providing effective technology solutions so that
our clients benefit by valuable improvements in
productivity and profitability.

Key Contact - Specialty:
Mr. Paul Saunders, Vice President, Consulting
Services

Functions: Sales & Mktg., IT

Industries: Generalist (All), Software,
Development SW, Doc. Mgmt., Production SW,
ERP SW, HR SW, Industry Specific SW, Mfg.
SW, Marketing SW, Networking, Comm. SW,
System SW

Quidam Global

22609 NW Ashford Ct
Blue Springs, MO 64015-7331
(816) 224-9932
(816) 838-3892
Fax: (816) 224-2414
Email: quidam4exec@sbcglobal.net

Summary: A premier search firm specializing in
worldwide recruitment of professionals in
accounting, finance and tax. Dedicated to finding
the most accomplished leaders for both public and
private organizations. Demonstrated success in
working with executives across all industries and
business channels throughout North, Central and
South America, Europe and Asia.

Key Contact - Specialty:
Mrs. Lynn Thomas, Executive Consultant -
*Controllers, Executives, Financial, Tax,
Treasury*
Mrs. Lynna J. Sherlak-Thomas, Executive
Consultant - *Actuarial, Analysts, CFOs,
Controllers, Tax*

Salary Minimum: $80,000

Functions: Senior Mgmt., Middle Mgmt.,
Finance, CFOs, Budgeting, Taxes, M&A, Risk
Mgmt.

Industries: Generalist (All)

Martin Quinn Group Ltd

2211 W Ohio St
Chicago, IL 60612-1519
(312) 666-9960
(847) 386-6223
Email: kenbook@chicagotechjobs.com
Web: www.chicagotechjobs.com

Summary: We are executive recruiters in high-
technology and IT.

Key Contact - Specialty:
Mr. Quinn Dolan, President
Ms. Betsy Smith, Executive Recruiter

Salary Minimum: $50,000

Functions: IT

Industries: Generalist (All)

Quintal & Associates Human Resources Consultants Inc

(also known as Gen X Human Capital Inc)
301-133 Rue de la Commune O
Montreal, QC H2Y 2C7
Canada
(514) 284-7444
(866) 284-7444
Fax: (514) 284-9290
Email: administration@quintal.ca
Web: www.quintal.ca

Summary: Our firm specializes in the healthcare industry. Our clients such as the pharmaceutical, medical, biotechnology, diagnostic and genomic companies, rely on our expertise for their recruitment, organizational development and training needs. We also provide contractual employees through our human capital business unit.

Key Contact - Specialty:
Ms. Yves Quintal, President - *Biotechnology, Healthcare, Pharmaceutical, Presidents, Senior management*
Mrs. Nicole Paquin, Director, Administration
Mr. Roger Duchesne, Senior Consultant - *Diagnostics, Operating rooms, Pharmaceutical, Senior management, Surgical*
Miss Manon Tremblay, Senior Consultant - *Biopharmaceutical, Biotechnology, Diagnostics, Pharmaceutical, Surgical*
Mr. François Collin, Senior Consultant - *Biopharmaceutical, Comptrollers, Consumer (Packaged Goods), Field engineering, Medical (Sales)*

Salary Minimum: $50,000

Functions: Generalist (All), Senior Mgmt., Middle Mgmt., Product Dev., Production, Healthcare, Mktg. Mgmt., Sales Mgmt., HR Mgmt., R&D

Industries: Food, Bev., Tobacco, Printing, Chemicals, Soap, Perf., Cosmtcs., Drugs Mfg., Medical Devices, Pharm Svcs., Mgmt. Consulting, Advertising, Telecoms, Biotech/Life Sciences, Healthcare

Branches:
401-50 Burnhamthorpe Rd W
Sussex Centre
Mississauga, ON L5B 3C2
Canada
(905) 281-3337
Fax: (905) 281-8114
Email: smcbride@quintal.ca
Key Contact - Specialty:
Mr. Sean McBride, Managing Director - *Professional services, Purchasing, Regulatory, Research & development, Senior management*

Quiring Associates Inc

7267 Jessman Rd W Dr Apt C
Indianapolis, IN 46256-4193
(317) 841-7575 x4
Fax: (317) 577-8240
Email: patti@quiringassociates.com
Web: www.quiringassociates.com

Summary: We have strategic alliance partners across the country. Our firm specializes in permanent, full-time search.

Key Contact - Specialty:
Ms. Patti L. Quiring, CPC, President - *Healthcare, Human resources*

Salary Minimum: $25,000

Functions: Mfg., Healthcare, Physicians, Nurses, Allied Health, HR Mgmt., Staffing, Finance, Engineering

Industries: Generalist (All), Non-Classifiable

Quirk-Corporon & Associates Inc

1229 N Jackson St Unit 205
Milwaukee, WI 53202-2651
(414) 224-9399
(414) 271-8711
Fax: (414) 224-9472
Email: quirkrecruiters@sbcglobal.net
Web: www.quirkinsrecruiters.com

Summary: Recruit mid- and executive-level candidates for major insurance companies and national brokers. Primarily interested in insurance and financial institution candidates

Key Contact - Specialty:
Mr. Charles E. Corporon, President & Owner - *Financial*
Ms. Therese M. Quirk, Vice President - *Financial*

Salary Minimum: $30,000

Functions: Generalist (All)

Industries: Insurance, Casualty, Claims, Life, Commercial, Re-Insurance

R & K Associates Inc

1296 W Stacey Ln
Tempe, AZ 85284-5102
(480) 961-2983
Email: icrecruiter@mindspring.com
Web: www.icrecruiter.com

Summary: Specializing in high technology, the firm offers a cost effective alternative and short cycle times for searches. Experience handling large ramp ups is a key ingredient of experience and expertise.

Key Contact - Specialty:
Mr. Karl J. Reichardt, Principal & Owner - *Semiconductors*

Salary Minimum: $45,000

Functions: Generalist (All), Management, Mfg., Product Dev., Production, Automation

Industries: Medical Devices, Computer Equip., Test, Measure Equip., Electronic, Elec. Components, Semiconductors, Software, Database SW, Development SW, Industry Specific SW

R E P & Associates Inc

PO Box 55
Washington, NC 27889-0055
(252) 946-6643
Email: dick_rep@computerplacement.com
Web: www.computerplacement.com

Summary: Extensive experience in information technology combined with a long-standing history in recruiting expertise.

Key Contact - Specialty:
Mr. Richard Phelan, President
Ms. Betty Powers, Secretary & Treasurer
Ms. Sharon Sawyer, Senior Recruiter - *AS/400*

Salary Minimum: $50,000

Functions: Systems Analysis, Systems Dev., Systems Implem., Systems Support, Network Admin., DB Admin.

Industries: Generalist (All), Computer Equip., Electronic, Elec. Components, Call Centers, Network Infrastructure, Software

R J Associates

30 Glenn St
White Plains, NY 10603-3254
(914) 946-0278
Fax: (914) 946-2019
Email: info@rjsearch.com
Web: www.rjsearch.com

Summary: Complete staffing service for major corporate clients with consultants specializing by discipline.

Key Contact - Specialty:
Mr. Richard Birnbaum, Managing Director - *Finance, General management, Human resources, Operations, Senior management*
Mr. Michael Walters, Senior Vice President
Ms. Jeani Schaumann, Senior Consultant

Salary Minimum: $75,000

Functions: Generalist (All), Senior Mgmt., Mfg., Sales & Mktg., HR Mgmt., Finance, IT, R&D, Engineering, Attorneys

Industries: Generalist (All), Energy, Utilities, Manufacturing, Food, Bev., Tobacco, Soap, Perf., Cosmtcs., Drugs Mfg., Medical Devices, Test, Measure Equip., Finance, Publishing, Software, Biotech/Life Sciences, Healthcare

R&M Associates

2610 Sunset Dr SE
Lacey, WA 98503-3749
(360) 413-7605
Fax: (360) 747-0981
Email: ronkrenz@msn.com
Web: www.rmacareers.com

Summary: We are an executive search and professional recruitment organization devoted to meeting the critical staffing needs of our clients. Our founders are a team of professionals who share extensive years of recruiting experience between them.

Key Contact - Specialty:
Mr. Ron Krenz, President - *Printing*
Ms. Meri Masters, Director, IT Services & Vice President

Functions: Generalist (All)

Industries: Paper, Printing, Computer Equip., Finance, Banking, Packaging, Software, Industry Specific SW

R-Recruiter Staffing

131 Skowhegan Ct
San Jose, CA 95139-1250
(408) 362-0991
Email: stever@r-recruiter.com
Web: www.r-recruiter.com

Summary: Our firm specializes in the search and placement of civil, environmental, structural and transportation related professionals. In addition, we can provide candidates for construction projects ranging from residential to heavy industrial for both private and public projects. We pride ourselves on our ability to be flexible and strive to build lasting working relationships with our clients.

Key Contact - Specialty:
Mr. Stephen Reese, Owner

Salary Minimum: $100,000

Functions: Management, Engineering, Geotechnical, Structural, Eng. Design, Systems, Specialized Svcs., Environmentalists, Architects, Bldg. Contractors

Industries: Generalist (All), Energy, Utilities, Oil & Gas, Construction, Transportation, Engineering Svcs., Environmental Svcs.

R2 Staffing Inc

PO Box 3608
Barrington, IL 60011-3608
(847) 458-8500
Email: randys@r2staffing.com
Web: www.r2staffing.com

Summary: We specialize in development, sales and management positions associated with real-time, embedded systems software development. Additionally, we have significant expertise with client-server object-oriented software development. Our staff is comprised of engineers with real-world experience.

Key Contact - Specialty:
Mr. Randall E. Smith, President - *Management, Sales*

Salary Minimum: $80,000

Functions: Product Dev., Sales Mgmt., Systems Analysis, Systems Dev., Engineering, Eng. Design, Hardware, Systems

Industries: Medical Devices, Machine, Appliance, Motor Vehicles, Computer Equip., Consumer Elect., Test, Measure Equip., Electronic, Elec. Components, Robotics, Digital, Wireless, Defense, Aerospace, Development SW

Railey & Associates

5102 Westerham Pl
Houston, TX 77069-2041
(281) 444-4346

Summary: Legal only. All industries and law firms. All practice levels especially mid and upper echelons: associates, partners, legal administrators, attorneys and general counsel. Law firm mergers.

Key Contact - Specialty:
Mr. J. Larry Railey, President

Salary Minimum: $100,000

Functions: Attorneys

Industries: Generalist (All)

Raley & Associates Inc

7901 Grenezay Rd
Wilmington, NC 28411-8368
(910) 686-6034
(800) 350-7881
Fax: (910) 686-6046
Email: fraley3804@aol.com
Web: www.smart-office.net/4820

Summary: We specialize in recruiting technical and professional personnel in the manufacturing, fabrication, design & production of plastic, rubber & metal components and assemblies that possess the specific skills and experiences requested by our clients. We are an independent firm, networked with thousands of other recruiters for fast and effective service.

Key Contact - Specialty:
Mr. Frank Raley, CPC, Owner & President - *Manufacturing, Plastics*

Salary Minimum: $30,000

Functions: Mfg., Technicians

Industries: Generalist (All), Plastics, Rubber, Metal Products, Motor Vehicles, Computer Equip.

Ramer Search Consultants Inc

22 Mohawk Dr Fl 1
Livingston, NJ 07039-3112
(973) 422-0020
Fax: (973) 422-1210
Email: mramer@ramergroup.com
Web: www.ramergroup.com

Summary: Specializing in the financial services industry; commercial and private banking, portfolio and wealth management, and trust and estate services. Clients include leading banks and trust firms. The firm's president is a national trainer for the search industry.

Key Contact - Specialty:
Mr. Michael Ramer, Principal

Salary Minimum: $100,000

Functions: Senior Mgmt., Middle Mgmt., Sales & Mktg., Pension/Ret. Planning

Industries: Finance, Banking, Invest. Banking, Venture Cap., Mutual/Hedge Funds, Misc. Financial, Mgmt. Consulting

Bruce L Ramstad

PO Box 290518
Port Orange, FL 32129-0518
(386) 322-0348
Fax: (386) 322-0023
Email: bruce@ramstad.com
Web: www.ramstad.com

Summary: Totally candidate oriented. Provide engineering and manufacturing professionals for other recruiters in their disciplines.

Key Contact - Specialty:
Mr. Bruce L. Ramstad, Owner - *Engineering, Manufacturing*

Salary Minimum: $50,000

Functions: Middle Mgmt., Mfg., Product Dev., Production, Automation, Plant Mgmt., Quality

Industries: Manufacturing, Food, Bev., Tobacco, Paper, Chemicals, Drugs Mfg., Medical Devices, Plastics, Rubber, Metal Products, Machine, Appliance, Motor Vehicles, Consumer Elect., Misc. Mfg., Electronic, Elec. Components, Robotics, Consumer Goods

Rand-Curtis Resources

10611 N Indian Wells Dr
Fountain Hills, AZ 85268-5712
(480) 837-2100
Fax: (480) 837-9415
Email: judykopulos@aol.com

Summary: We have extensive experience in recruiting mid-to upper-level management for major restaurant companies, quick service and full-service. We offer integrity, experience and industry knowledge. We recruit for all functions within the industry.

Key Contact - Specialty:
Ms. Judy Kopulos, Owner - *Restaurants*

Salary Minimum: $65,000

Functions: Generalist (All), Management, Board Members, Senior Mgmt., Middle Mgmt., Staffing

Industries: Restaurants, Quick Service Restaurants, Full Service Restaurants

Lea Randolph & Associates Inc

(also known as LRA, Inc.)
2701 W 15th St #527
Plano, TX 75075-7523
(214) 982-9609
(615) 837-9990
Fax: (972) 424-2857
Email: troy@lra-recruiting.com
Web: www.lra-recruiting.com

Summary: Our company specializes in the professional recruitment of highly talented clinical and non-clinical healthcare personnel at the middle, upper and senior levels. We assist hospitals, home health & hospice agencies, senior living, long term care organizations and physician offices find outstanding talent. We provide contingent, retained and contract recruiting services.

Key Contact - Specialty:
Mrs. Lea Randolph, President & Owner - *Healthcare*

Salary Minimum: $40,000

Functions: Management, Senior Mgmt., Middle Mgmt., Quality, Healthcare, Physicians, Nurses, Allied Health, Health Admin., Sales & Mktg.

Industries: Generalist (All), Healthcare, Hospitals, Long-term/Home Care, Physical Therapy, Occupational Therapy, Non-Classifiable

Branches:
5543 Edmondson Pike Ste 147
Nashville, TN 37211-5808
(615) 837-9990
Fax: (972) 424-2857
Email: troyrandolph@hotmail.com
Key Contact - Specialty:
Mr. Troy Randolph, Partner - *Healthcare*

Rannou & Associates Inc

1900 The Exchange SE Ste 370
Atlanta, GA 30339-2050
(770) 956-8225
Email: pkgjob@bellsouth.net

Summary: Specialize in the packaging industry with heavy emphasis in the corrugated industry.

Key Contact - Specialty:
Mr. Glenn Charles, Executive Recruiter - *Packaging, Paper*
Ms. Loren Shayne, Executive Recruiter - *Converting, Packaging, Paper*
Mr. Frank Rannou, III, Recruiter - *Converting, Packaging, Paper*

Functions: Generalist (All), Packaging

Industries: Manufacturing, Paper, Printing

J E Ranta Associates

112 Washington St
Marblehead, MA 01945-3554
(781) 639-0788
Fax: (781) 631-9828
Email: eranta@erols.com
Web: www.erols.com/ranta

Summary: Contingency firm serving the IT needs of clients. Primary emphasis on software engineering and infrastructure opportunities at all levels especially in the web, e-commerce and networking areas. Extensive activity in end user computing, consulting, product development and support areas. Success of the firm has been built upon industry knowledge and relationships with key management level personnel.

Key Contact - Specialty:
Mr. Ed Ranta, Owner - *Telecommunications*

Salary Minimum: $60,000

Functions: Generalist (All), Management, IT, MIS Mgmt., Systems Analysis, Systems Dev., Systems Implem., Systems Support, Network Admin., DB Admin.

Industries: Generalist (All)

Harold L Rapp Associates

80 Hemlock Dr
Roslyn, NY 11576-2303
(516) 625-4341
Fax: (516) 625-4517
Email: hlrassoc@aol.com
Web: www.jewelryheadhunter.com

Summary: We are a recruitment of executives for the jewelry industry. Searches performed for wholesalers, importers and manufacturers of jewelry and watches.

Key Contact - Specialty:
Mr. Harold L. Rapp, President

Salary Minimum: $40,000

Functions: Generalist (All), Senior Mgmt., Middle Mgmt., Product Dev., Plant Mgmt., Mktg. Mgmt., Sales Mgmt., Customer Svc.

Industries: Generalist (All), Mgmt. Consulting, Non-Classifiable

Rasch & Associates Ltd

235 W 75th St Apt 10F
New York, NY 10023-1764
(212) 799-7134
Email: raschjf@aol.com

Summary: We are a contingency and retained search firm specializing within the financial services industry nationwide in the functional areas of credit, finance, lending, marketing, sales, operations and HR.

Key Contact - Specialty:
Ms. Judith Fredericks, President - *Credit, Finance, Human resources, Marketing*

Salary Minimum: $75,000

Functions: Generalist (All), Sales & Mktg., Direct Mktg., Customer Svc., Finance, Budgeting, Cash Mgmt., Credit, Risk Mgmt.

Industries: Consumer Goods, Finance, Banking

Vera L Rast Partners Inc (VLRPI)

2 N La Salle St Ste 1808
Chicago, IL 60602-4029
(312) 629-0339
Fax: (312) 629-0347
Email: vlrpi@vlrpilegalsearch.com
Web: www.vlrpilegalsearch.com

Summary: Legal search organization focused on lateral placement of attorneys for client law firms and corporations.

Key Contact - Specialty:
Ms. Vera L. Rast, President
Mr. Alex Trent, Consultant
Ms. Suzanne English Jones, Consultant

Functions: Legal

Industries: Generalist (All)

Joanne E Ratner Search

75 S Broadway Fl 4
White Plains, NY 10601-4413
(914) 304-4314
Fax: (914) 304-4315
Email: jobs@jrsearch.com
Web: www.jrsearch.com

Summary: Minority (female) owned boutique recruiting firm specializing in finance, marketing, management consulting and HR positions.

Key Contact - Specialty:
Ms. Joanne E. Ratner, President - *Finance, Marketing*

Salary Minimum: $75,000

Functions: Generalist (All), Senior Mgmt., Finance

Industries: Generalist (All), Consumer Elect., Finance, Banking, Invest. Banking, Non-profits, Hospitality, Advertising, Publishing, New Media, Broadcast, Film

Sharon Raymond Inc

16 Mark Ave
Hamburg, NY 14075-3817
(716) 649-9966
Email: sraymond@adelphia.net

Summary: Recruiter in health insurance, disease management, informatics, analytics, health care economics, contracting, medical directors, product development, sales, marketing and government programs. Certified women owned business.

Key Contact - Specialty:
Ms. Sharon Raymond, President

Salary Minimum: $85,000

Functions: Healthcare

Industries: Insurance, Healthcare

RaymondChase LLC

PO Box 30383
Raleigh, NC 27622-0383
(919) 786-9722
(800) 526-9570
Fax: (919) 882-9085
Email: jkr@raymondchase.com
Web: www.raymondchase.com

Summary: We are a multi-dimensional, client focused executive search firm that specializes in mid-level to executive level positions within the financial services sector.

Key Contact - Specialty:
Mr. John Raymond, President & Managing Partner

Salary Minimum: $65,000

Functions: Management

Industries: Finance, Banking, Invest. Banking, Brokers, Venture Cap., Mutual/Hedge Funds, Misc. Financial

Razzino Associates Inc

220 Kinderkamack Rd Ste E1
Westwood, NJ 07675-3601
(201) 722-3111
Fax: (201) 722-3113
Email: janelle@razzinoassociates.com

Summary: We are a boutique search firm offering the foremost in executive recruiting with a personal touch.

Key Contact - Specialty:
Ms. Janelle Razzino, Principal - *Finance, Telecommunications*

Salary Minimum: $75,000

Functions: Finance, IT

Industries: Manufacturing, Retail, Finance, Services, Mgmt. Consulting, Hospitality, Media, Telecoms, Insurance, Biotech/Life Sciences, Healthcare

RBW Associates

64723 Boonesborough Ct
Bend, OR 97701-8821
(541) 389-7500
(800) 385-3001
Fax: (541) 389-8046
Email: ray@rbwassoc.com
Web: www.rbwassoc.com

Summary: We are an executive search firm specializing in the pulp and paper, power, and other manufacturing industries, offering expedient and confidential service based on the highest professional ethics. Professional recruiting for industries' top 10 percent talent; management, technical, engineering/maintenance, administrative and sales.

Key Contact - Specialty:
Mr. Ray B. Wheeler, President

Salary Minimum: $40,000

Functions: Generalist (All), Senior Mgmt., Middle Mgmt., Mfg., Production, Plant Mgmt., Packaging, MIS Mgmt., Engineering

Industries: Agri., Forestry, Mining, Energy, Utilities, Construction, Lumber, Furniture, Paper, Printing, Chemicals, Packaging, Industry Specific SW

Branches:
204 San Mateo Dr
Hot Springs National Park, AR 71913-6719
(501) 525-3579
Fax: (501) 525-3579
Email: eutha1@cablelynx.com
Key Contact - Specialty:
Ms. Eutha Corder, Recruiter - *High technology, Lumber*

Rcm Technologies

2500 Mcclellan Blvd Ste 350
Pennsauken, NJ 08109-4617
(877) 726-0007
Fax: (856) 488-8833
Email: info@rcmt.com
Web: www.rcmt.com

Summary: We provide executive search and consulting services to the IT, pharmaceutical, nuclear, engineering and healthcare industries on retainer, contingency or consulting/contract.

Key Contact - Specialty:
Mr. Art Dell, Manager, Corporate Services

Functions: Generalist (All), Nurses, Allied Health, Systems Analysis, Systems Dev., Systems Implem., Network Admin., DB Admin.

Industries: Generalist (All), Pharm Svcs., Mgmt. Consulting, Engineering Svcs., Software, Healthcare

re-Source Net

37 Meade Ave
Hanover, PA 17331-3623
(717) 646-0007
Email: info@re-sourcenet.com
Web: www.re-sourcenet.com

Summary: Our firm is a highly selective contingency recruiting firm that specializes in search and placement of engineers, managers and sales personnel in the electronics and semiconductor industries.

Key Contact - Specialty:
Mr. Joel Ruths, Executive Search Consultant

Functions: Quality, Sales & Mktg., HR Mgmt., Engineering

Industries: Computer Equip., Consumer Elect., Test, Measure Equip., Electronic, Elec. Components, Semiconductors, Digital, Wireless, Fiber Optic, Network Infrastructure, RF/Microwave

Re:Search International LLC

500 N Commercial St
Manchester, NH 03101-1151
(603) 644-7800
Fax: (603) 644-5560
Email: search@cms-rsi.com
Web: www.cms-rsi.com

Summary: We are prominent global specialists in the footwear, sporting goods and active wear industries, searching in all specialties and disciplines.

Key Contact - Specialty:
Mr. Ken Snyder, President - *Apparel, Footwear*

Functions: Senior Mgmt., Production, Distribution, Sales & Mktg., Mktg. Research, Mktg. Mgmt., Sales Mgmt., CFOs, MIS Mgmt., Graphic Designers

Industries: Textiles, Apparel, Leather, Stone, Glass

Roberta Rea & Co Inc

4510 Executive Dr Plz 4
San Diego, CA 92121-3021
(858) 457-3566
Fax: (858) 457-4409
Email: roberta@robertareaco.com
Web: www.robertareaco.com

Summary: We are an executive search firm
specializing in the shopping center industry: real
estate and retail. Job placements are in the areas of
management, marketing, leasing and development.
On the retail side, we specialize in buyers, DMMs,
GMMs, directors, VPs, marketing, sourcing and
product development executives. We also
specialize in operations including district and
regional managers.

Key Contact - Specialty:
Ms. Shelle Orlansky, Executive Recruiter
Ms. Roberta Rea, Executive Recruiter
Mr. John McAuliffe, Recruiter
Mr. Chris Rollbusch, Recruiter
Ms. Pam Carmichael, Recruiter - *Retail*

Salary Minimum: $50,000

Functions: Generalist (All), Management, Senior
Mgmt., Product Dev., HR Mgmt., Staffing,
CFOs, Design, Textile/Fashion

Industries: Construction, Textiles, Apparel,
Wholesale, Retail, HR Services

ReadSource Ltd

8417 Kirkaldy Ct
Dublin, OH 43017-9730
(614) 764-8666
Email: readsource@columbus.rr.com
Web: www.thesourcealliance.com

Summary: We provide search services exclusively
to the packaging industry in a variety of
disciplines, including executive management,
sales & marketing, R&D, packaging engineering,
operations, and other areas.

Key Contact - Specialty:
Mr. William Read

Functions: Management, Senior Mgmt., Mfg.,
Product Dev., Plant Mgmt., Quality, Packaging,
Engineering

Industries: Packaging

ReadWaering Associates Inc

2817 Lebanon Pike Ste 207
Nashville, TN 37214-2585
(800) 489-3602
(800) 489-3602
Fax: (615) 369-3603
Email: jerryw@readwaering.com
Web: www.readwaering.com

Summary: We specialize in recruiting for the
life/health and managed care insurance industry.
Our areas of expertise include all the major
functional departments: accounting, actuarial,
auditing, claims, compliance, medical
management, provider relations, quality,
sales/marketing, underwriting, utilization, etc.

Key Contact - Specialty:
Mrs. Pamela Read-Lewis, President
Mr. Jerry H. Waering, Principal
Ms. Karen A. Gritton, Senior Recruiter
Ms. Krissa J. Zimmerman, Senior Recruiter
Ms. Angela D. Read, Recruiter

Functions: Generalist (All)

Industries: Insurance

Real Estate Executive Search Inc

PO Box 387
San Francisco, CA 94104-0387
(415) 398-4116
Email: jhavrees@aol.com

Summary: Our firm has extensive experience in
the retail industry.

Key Contact - Specialty:
Mr. J.A. Havens, President - *Management*

Salary Minimum: $40,000

Functions: Management

Industries: Real Estate

Recana Solutions

4925 Greenville Ave Ste 200
Dallas, TX 75206-0500
(214) 237-2938
Fax: (972) 306-0348
Email: info@recanausa.com
Web: www.recana.com

Summary: We are a full service, generalist firm
with an emphasis on building quality client
relationships through responsive, innovative and
customized recruitment services. Our goal is to
provide our clients with the Right People at the
Right Place at the Right Time.

Key Contact - Specialty:
Mr. Adam Stiles, President
Mr. Alex Stiles, Chief Financial Officer & VP,
Operations
Mr. Jack Williams, Vice President, Business
Development - *Business development, Business
to business, Human resources, Management,
Marketing*

Salary Minimum: $30,000

Functions: Management, Healthcare, Sales &
Mktg., HR Mgmt., Training, Finance, IT,
Engineering

Industries: Generalist (All)

Recruit America

10575 Katy Fwy Ste 300
Houston, TX 77024-1012
(713) 973-2525
Fax: (713) 973-8989
Email: contactus@recruitamerica.com
Web: www.recruitamerica.com

Summary: Our firm specializes in recruiting in the
restaurant & hospitality, supermarket, convenience
store, food manufacturing and distribution
industries.

Key Contact - Specialty:
Mr. Sid Nathan, Account Executive - *Culinary,
Food & beverage, Hospitality, Management,
Restaurants*
Mr. Art Pellenberg, Account Executive -
*Culinary, Distribution, Food, Manufacturing,
Research & development*
Mr. John Forney, Account Executive - *Bakery,
Convenience stores, Distribution, Groceries,
Supermarkets*

Functions: Management

Industries: Food, Bev., Tobacco, Retail, Supply
Chain Mgmt, Hospitality, Restaurants, Quick
Service Restaurants, Full Service Restaurants,
Inst./Industrial Food Svc., Recreation, Sports

Recruiter Pharma

(a division of ASSET Associates Inc)
10036 Sawgrass Dr W Ste 4
Ponte Vedra Beach, FL 32082-3565
(904) 273-2999
Fax: (904) 273-3070

Email: admin@recruiterpharma.com
Web: www.recruiterpharma.com

Summary: Specialize in recruitment and
concentrate exclusively in the pharmaceutical and
biopharmaceutical industries.

Key Contact - Specialty:
Mr. Marvin C. Lemons, General Partner -
Biotechnology
Mr. Al J. Marcel, General Partner - *Biotechnology*
Mr. Fred T. Icken, General Partner - *Marketing*

Salary Minimum: $65,000

Functions: Product Dev., Mktg. Research, Mktg.
Mgmt., Sales Mgmt., R&D, Specialized Svcs.,
Technicians

Industries: Drugs Mfg., Pharm Svcs.,
Biotech/Life Sciences

Recruiter Solutions International

(also known as Subs of Backtrack Inc)
8850 Tyler Blvd
Mentor, OH 44060-4361
(800) 992-3875
(440) 255-7457
Fax: (800) 992-3874
Email: tim@rsirecruiters.com
Web: www.rsirecruiters.com

Summary: We provide search and recruiting
services in a wide variety of industries at all
professional levels, including: sales, production
supervision and management, engineering,
financial and senior corporate executives. Our
specific areas of specialization include: forest
products, building products, packaging, plastics,
colorants & coatings and consumer products.

Key Contact - Specialty:
Mr. Robert Gandee, President
Mr. Jon Olson, Vice President - *Building
products, Forest industry/products, Furniture,
Lumber, Millwork*
Ms. Julie Freeman, Vice President - *Converting,
Industrial, Packaging, Plastics, Sales*
Mr. Daniel Regovich, Vice President - *Chemical,
Molding, Plastics, Thermoforming*
Mr. Tim Gandee, Vice President - *Coatings,
Composites, Film, Music, Plastics*
Mr. Larry Brill, Vice President - *Automotive,
Consumer (Durables,Products), Transportation*
Mr. Mike Pearlman, Vice President - *Capital
goods, Equipment, Industrial, Logistics,
Manufacturing*

Functions: Generalist (All), Management, Senior
Mgmt., Mfg., Production, Plant Mgmt., Sales &
Mktg., HR Mgmt., Finance, Engineering

Industries: Agri., Forestry, Mining, Lumber,
Furniture, Paper, Plastics, Rubber, Misc.
Financial, Accounting, Packaging, Accounting
SW

The Recruiters Advantage Inc

6800 Paragon Pl Ste 501
Richmond, VA 23230-1656
(804) 282-1044
Fax: (804) 282-2652
Email: recruiters@recruitingadvantage.com
Web: www.recruitingadvantage.com

Summary: We are specialists in recruiting legal
and medical/dental/healthcare professionals at all
levels and across all industries.

Key Contact - Specialty:
Mr. Steve Barley, CPA, CDP, President & Owner

Salary Minimum: $30,000

Functions: Healthcare, Physicians, Nurses, Allied
Health, Health Admin., Finance, Legal,
Attorneys, Paralegals

Industries: Generalist (All), Healthcare, Hospitals, Dental, Physical Therapy, Occupational Therapy

Recruiting & Consulting Professionals (RCP)

PO Box 8708
Phoenix, AZ 85066-8708
(877) 996-9953
Fax: (602) 232-2331
Email: excitingcareers@rcpintl.com
Web: www.rcpintl.com

Summary: We are an experienced search firm placing staff to VP level candidates within audit services. We specialize in the manufacturing and consumer product industries with secondary emphasis on computer technology, biotechnology, telecommunications, financial services and pharmaceutical businesses.

Key Contact - Specialty:
Ms. Lisa Martin, Recruiter & Consultant

Functions: Finance

Industries: Manufacturing, Food, Bev., Tobacco, Chemicals, Drugs Mfg., Medical Devices, Plastics, Rubber, Motor Vehicles, Computer Equip., Consumer Elect., Biotech/Life Sciences

Recruiting Associates of Amarillo

PO Box 8473
1616 S Kentucky Building C Ste 255
Amarillo, TX 79114-8473
(806) 353-9548
Fax: (806) 353-9540
Email: mrokey@recruitingassociates.com
Web: www.recruitingassociates.com

Summary: We are a professional recruiting and staffing service, both permanent and contract affiliations, reasonable fees.

Key Contact - Specialty:
Mr. Michael Rokey, CPC, Owner & Manager

Functions: Generalist (All), Systems Analysis, Systems Dev., Systems Implem., Systems Support, Network Admin., DB Admin., Engineering

Industries: Generalist (All), Metal Products, Machine, Appliance, Misc. Mfg., HR Services, Engineering Svcs., Software

Recruiting Choices

3973 Harts Mill Ln NE
Atlanta, GA 30319-1852
(404) 401-9047
Fax: (512) 233-2471
Email: info@recruitingchoices.com
Web: www.recruitingchoices.com

Summary: Experts at medium to large onsite contract recruiting projects. Reduce your overall recruiting costs with non-traditional contractual fee structures. Specializing in recruiting technical, sales/marketing, finance/accounting and HR talent. Post project DVDs provided with valuable reports and project data to assist with future recruitment needs. Nationwide strategic alliance partners.

Key Contact - Specialty:
Mr. Randy Shute, President
Mr. Eric Jaquith, Vice President

Salary Minimum: $60,000

Functions: Management, Senior Mgmt., Middle Mgmt., Sales & Mktg., HR Mgmt., Training, IT, Engineering, Hardware, Hospitality

Industries: Manufacturing, Computer Equip., Electronic, Elec. Components, Robotics, Semiconductors, Services, E-commerce, IT

Implementation, PSA/ASP, Hospitality, Hotels, Resorts, Clubs, Restaurants, Entertainment, New Media, Communications, Telephony, Wireless, Fiber Optic, RF/Microwave, Defense, Software, Networking, Comm. SW, Security SW, System SW, Training SW

Recruiting Executives Inc

PO Box 273107
Boca Raton, FL 33427-3107
(561) 289-1187
Email: bbeaver6@bellsouth.net
Web: www.recruitingexecutives.net

Summary: We are a very successful recruiting/search firm with many years of recruiting experience that conducts searches for all industries and for every type of discipline.

Key Contact - Specialty:
Mr. Robert W. Beaver, President & Owner

Salary Minimum: $70,000

Functions: Generalist (All), Management

Industries: Generalist (All)

The Recruiting Group Inc

96101 Bay View Dr
Amelia Island, FL 32034-6175
(914) 261-2211 x12
Fax: (904) 261-7555
Email: bwidnes@bestapplicants.com
Web: www.bestapplicants.com

Summary: We are a nationwide executive search firm specializing in sales, marketing, and human resources positions.

Key Contact - Specialty:
Mr. Bruce Widnes, President - *Management, Marketing, Sales*

Salary Minimum: $65,000

Functions: Management, Sales & Mktg., Sales Mgmt., Sales Reps., HR Mgmt., Benefits, Staffing

Industries: Generalist (All), Manufacturing, Food, Bev., Tobacco, Medical Devices, Plastics, Rubber, Machine, Appliance, Motor Vehicles, Misc. Mfg., Wholesale, Retail, Packaging

The Recruiting Group

5775 Wayzata Blvd Ste 925
Minneapolis, MN 55416-2673
(952) 544-1155
(800) 889-4595
Fax: (952) 546-2806
Email: joan@recruitads.com
Web: www.recruitinggroup.com

Summary: We are a custom search and placement for all levels of professionals in a variety of specialties.

Key Contact - Specialty:
Ms. Julie Valine, President

Functions: Management, Materials, Sales Mgmt., HR Mgmt., Finance, IT, Engineering

Industries: Generalist (All)

The Recruiting Leder Inc

4545 High Rock Ter
Marietta, GA 30066-1607
(770) 977-8783
(866) 977-8783
Fax: (770) 977-1174
Email: therecruitingleder@earthlink.net
Web: www.therecruitingleder.com

Summary: Recruiting management talent exclusively for the home furnishings industry.

Key Contact - Specialty:
Mr. Sam Leder, Chief Executive Officer & President - *Furniture, Management, Retail*

Functions: Management

Industries: Retail

Recruiting Management Associates

2977 Ygnacio Valley Rd Ste 175
Walnut Creek, CA 94598-3535
(925) 256-7313
Fax: (925) 256-7408
Email: info@rmitsearch.com
Web: www.rmitsearch.com

Summary: We are full-service executive recruiters specializing in IT, sales, marketing, business development and CXO level placements. We are a member of a worldwide network of alliance partners for extensive coverage of other disciplines and geos.

Key Contact - Specialty:
Mr. Ray MacDonald, Executive Recruiter

Salary Minimum: $75,000

Functions: Generalist (All)

Industries: Generalist (All), HR Services, Software

Recruiting Resources Inc

13813 Village Mill Dr
Midlothian, VA 23114-4381
(804) 794-1813
Email: recres@alcnet.com

Summary: Working closely with management and your personnel department, we can customize our services to ensure that the most qualified candidates are presented for your consideration.

Key Contact - Specialty:
Mr. Richard Baltimore, President - *Engineering, Manufacturing*

Functions: Generalist (All), Management, Mfg., Materials, Engineering

Industries: Manufacturing, Food, Bev., Tobacco, Textiles, Apparel, Lumber, Furniture, Chemicals, Plastics, Rubber, Metal Products, Machine, Appliance, Motor Vehicles, Misc. Mfg., Consumer Goods

Recruiting Services Group

(an Intertec-Consulting company)
18552 MacArthur Blvd Ste 100
Irvine, CA 92612-1235
(949) 425-1145
(949) 697-4418
Fax: (949) 831-2974
Email: marilynkruger@recruitingsg.com
Web: www.recruitingsg.com

Summary: Provide a total recruiting solution to any size organization. Services include, direct hire placement, sourcing & screening and contract recruiter needs.

Key Contact - Specialty:
Ms. Marilyn Kruger, General Manager

Salary Minimum: $50,000

Functions: Generalist (All)

Industries: Generalist (All), Energy, Utilities, Manufacturing, Finance, Services, Communications, Aerospace, Software, Biotech/Life Sciences, Healthcare

Recruiting Services International Inc

18 Villamoura
Laguna Niguel, CA 92677-8948
(949) 363-8149
Fax: (949) 363-8149
Email: info@recruitingservicesintl.com
Web: www.recruitingservicesintl.com

Summary: We use state-of-the-art recruiting research tools combined with innovative 21st century recruiting methods that yield fast results. We specialize in positions across science and technology and positions that require German language skills. We operate nationwide as well as within Europe and are connected to over 2,000 offices worldwide.

Key Contact - Specialty:
Ms. Jeanne Frese, President - *Biotechnology, Engineering, International, Research*

Functions: R&D, Engineering

Industries: Manufacturing, Chemicals, Drugs Mfg., Medical Devices, Machine, Appliance, Misc. Mfg., Electronic, Elec. Components, Robotics, Semiconductors, Biotech/Life Sciences

Recruiting Services Group Inc

3107 E Corporate Edge Dr
Germantown, TN 38138-7811
(901) 367-0778
Fax: (901) 367-0868
Email: resumes@rsghunt.com
Web: www.rsghunt.com

Summary: We are an executive search firm specializing in providing quality talent. The industries that we serve are: manufacturing, supply chain, logistics, HR, technology, and retail corporate operations. We focus on finding the best possible career match for both client and individual. Our firm is a certified WBE.

Key Contact - Specialty:
Ms. Whitney Hodges, President - *Distribution, Information Technology, Operations*
Ms. Anna Franks, Recruiter - *Executives, Logistics, Manufacturing, Manufacturing (Management), Senior management*

Salary Minimum: $60,000

Functions: Generalist (All), Management, Board Members, Senior Mgmt., Mfg., Materials, Distribution, Sales Mgmt., HR Mgmt., IT

Industries: Energy, Utilities, Manufacturing, Transportation, Accounting, HR Services, E-commerce, Engineering Svcs., Logistics Svcs., Defense, Aerospace, Software

Recruiting/Solutions

1070 Terrace Hill Cir
Westlake Village, CA 91362-5459
(818) 707-7610
Email: rice@sbcglobal.net

Summary: We are known for our ability to perform quickly for our clients. We will recruit and screen qualified candidates and present them to our clients in a timely manner. We complete all assignments.

Key Contact - Specialty:
Mr. Joel Rice, Senior Vice President

Salary Minimum: $50,000

Functions: Generalist (All), Management, Board Members, Senior Mgmt., Sales & Mktg., Mktg. Mgmt., Sales Mgmt.

Industries: Generalist (All), Food, Bev., Tobacco, Lumber, Furniture, Paper, Soap, Perf., Cosmtcs., Consumer Goods

The Recruitment Company

17 State St Fl 41
New York, NY 10004-1501
(212) 943-2023
Fax: (212) 943-8504
Email: gking@trcinternational.com
Web: www.trcny.com

Summary: We are a global provider of executive search and selection services specializing in the banking, finance, sales & marketing and IT sectors.

Key Contact - Specialty:
Mr. Graham King, Managing Director

Salary Minimum: $75,000

Functions: Management, Middle Mgmt., Finance

Industries: Energy, Utilities, Manufacturing, Finance, Banking, Invest. Banking, Brokers, Venture Cap., Services, Legal, Accounting, Entertainment, Media, Publishing, New Media, Communications, Digital, Software

Recruitment Resources Inc

2005 W Culver Ave Apt 25
Orange, CA 92868-4139
(714) 939-6417
(714) 978-7383
Email: rxsales@recruitmentresourcesinc.com
Web: www.recruitmentresourcesinc.com

Summary: We are an executive search firm that specializes in the placement of medical and pharmaceutical sales reps and managers.

Key Contact - Specialty:
Ms. Ruthie M. Ross, President - *Medical (Devices), Pharmaceutical*

Salary Minimum: $60,000

Functions: Sales & Mktg., Sales Mgmt.

Industries: Drugs Mfg., Medical Devices, Pharm Svcs.

Recruitment Specialists Inc

1001 Cromwell Bridge Rd Ste 200
Towson, MD 21286-3330
(410) 825-6186
(800) 7879669
Email: info@rsirecruit.com
Web: www.healthcareheadhunter.com

Summary: A nurse owned and operated firm with extensive years of experience recruiting mid-level and senior executives for healthcare organizations. Specialties: managed care organizations, healthcare systems, home health and sales management.

Key Contact - Specialty:
Ms. Roxanne Giannerini, President - *Healthcare*

Salary Minimum: $45,000

Functions: Healthcare, Nurses

Industries: Generalist (All), Healthcare

Recruitshop

(formerly known as National Career Connection)
52 N Urania Ave
Greensburg, PA 15601-2631
(724) 446-7287
Email: donalyn@recruitshop.com
Web: www.recruitshop.com

Summary: Contingency recruiter working to aide companies and candidates in the areas of sales/sales management and marketing. We specialize in B2B sales, pharmaceutical sales, medical sales, etc.

Key Contact - Specialty:
Ms. Donalyn Spisak, President - *Sales*

Functions: Sales & Mktg.

Industries: Generalist (All), Pharm Svcs., Advertising, Software

RecruitUSA

8834 Prichett Dr
Houston, TX 77096-2628
(713) 666-9993
Email: recruit@usa.net

Summary: We recruit experienced persons for engineering, marketing, manufacturing, human resources, and sales positions entrusted to us by our clients. We provide solutions to hire authorities.

Key Contact - Specialty:
Mr. Howard Frankel, President - *Computers (Software), HVAC, Legal (Attorneys), Marketing, Sales*
Ms. Marcia Frankel, Vice President - *Energy, Engineering, Human resources, Manufacturing (Management), Oracle*

Salary Minimum: $70,000

Functions: Generalist (All), Management, Senior Mgmt., Middle Mgmt., Admin. Svcs., Product Dev., Sales & Mktg., Mktg. Mgmt., Sales Mgmt.

Industries: Generalist (All), Energy, Utilities, Oil & Gas, Construction, Manufacturing, Chemicals, Paints, Petro. Products, Computer Equip., Electronic, Elec. Components, Semiconductors, Legal, Accounting, Equip Svcs., Mgmt. Consulting, HR Services, Law Enforcement, IT Implementation, Supply Chain Mgmt, Digital, Wireless, Network Infrastructure, Software, Accounting SW, Database SW, Development SW, Doc. Mgmt., Production SW, ERP SW, Industry Specific SW, Mfg. SW, Marketing SW, Security SW, System SW

Branches:
1005 Gravenstein Hwy N
Sebastopol, CA 95472-2811
(415) 336-4972
Email: margilevin@mac.com
Key Contact - Specialty:
Ms. Margi Levin, Recruiter - *Consulting, High technology, Information Technology, Marketing, Sales*

Red Rock Management

PO Box 2764
Reading, PA 19609-0764
(610) 927-3429
Fax: (720) 552-3999
Email: hr@redrockmanagement.biz
Web: www.redrockmanagement.biz

Summary: We are an executive recruiting firm that works with clientele and candidates nationwide. We specialize in the following: IS, healthcare, managed care, engineering, HR and actuarial sciences.

Key Contact - Specialty:
Mr. Fred Johnson, Senior Vice President, Recruiting

Salary Minimum: $50,000

Functions: Generalist (All), Management, Board Members, Senior Mgmt., Sales & Mktg., HR Mgmt., CFOs, Actuaries, IT, Engineering

Industries: Generalist (All), Energy, Utilities, Construction, Manufacturing, Drugs Mfg., Medical Devices, Computer Equip., Transportation, Finance, Banking, Services, HR Services, E-commerce, Engineering Svcs., Logistics Svcs., Communications, Government, Environmental Svcs., Aerospace, Insurance,

Software, Biotech/Life Sciences, Healthcare, Hospitals

P J Reda & Associates Inc
5555 Glenridge Connector NE Ste 200
Atlanta, GA 30342-4740
(404) 325-8812
Fax: (404) 325-8850
Email: predainc@mindspring.com
Web: www.pjredainc.com

Summary: We are a human resource consulting and executive search firm specializing in general through executive management (including operations and specialized technical positions) in the restaurant, hospitality, healthcare, medical and industries.

Key Contact - Specialty:
Ms. Pat Reda, President - *Biomedical, Biopharmaceutical, Healthcare, Hospitality, Hotels*

Salary Minimum: $50,000

Functions: Generalist (All), Board Members, Senior Mgmt., Middle Mgmt., Healthcare, Mktg. Mgmt., HR Mgmt., Hospitality

Industries: Pharm Svcs., HR Services, Hospitality, Hotels, Resorts, Clubs, Restaurants, Quick Service Restaurants, Full Service Restaurants, Inst./Industrial Food Svc., Biotech/Life Sciences, Healthcare, Hospitals

Redell Search Inc
6101 N Sheridan Rd Unit 31A
Chicago, IL 60660-6819
(773) 764-6100
Fax: (773) 764-6111
Email: john@redellsearch.com
Web: redellsearch.com

Summary: We specialize in doing recruitment for major IT consulting firms, software developers, IT consulting firms and hardware vendors.

Key Contact - Specialty:
Mr. John Redell, President

Functions: Board Members, Mfg., Sales & Mktg., IT, MIS Mgmt., Systems Implem., Mgmt. Consultants

Industries: Generalist (All), IT Implementation, Software, Accounting SW, Database SW, Development SW, ERP SW, HR SW, Industry Specific SW, Mfg. SW, Marketing SW, Networking, Comm. SW, Security SW, System SW

ReeseSource & Associates Ltd
306 Wendover Heights Cir
Charlotte, NC 28211-1349
(704) 362-6735
Fax: (270) 837-8961
Email: reesesource@carolina.rr.com
Web: www.thesourcealliance.com

Summary: Our president began a 32 year career in sales, marketing management and recruiting with Procter & Gamble. His plastics background evolved through expanding roles at General Electric Plastics, Rampart Products (now Printpack), Blessings Corp/Edison Plastics and OMNOVA Solutions. He focuses on flexible and rigid packaging for food and beverage applications.

Key Contact - Specialty:
Mr. David Reese, President

Salary Minimum: $75,000

Functions: Senior Mgmt., Middle Mgmt., Mfg., Product Dev., Plant Mgmt., Quality, Purchasing, Sales & Mktg., Sales Mgmt., Graphic Designers

Industries: Manufacturing, Food, Bev., Tobacco, Paper, Printing, Plastics, Rubber, Venture Cap., Packaging

Reeve & Associates
700 Canal St
Stamford, CT 06902-5921
(203) 328-3726
Email: mail@reevejobs.com
Web: www.reevejobs.com

Summary: We are a contingency search firm specializing in the market research function across all industries.

Key Contact - Specialty:
Mr. Philip Reeve, President - *Marketing*
Ms. Sara Reeve, Executive Recruiter
Ms. Lou Mollica, Executive Recruiter
Ms. Karen Nankil, Recruiter
Ms. Carolyn Davis, Recruiter - *Banking, Banking (Commercial), CFOs, Financial services, Trust*

Salary Minimum: $45,000

Functions: Middle Mgmt., Sales & Mktg., Mktg. Research

Industries: Generalist (All), Food, Bev., Tobacco

The Regency Group Ltd
256 N 115th St Ste 1
Omaha, NE 68154-2558
(402) 334-7255
Fax: (402) 334-7148
Email: resumes@regencygroup.com
Web: www.regencygroup.com

Summary: We are a performance based, executive search and recruiting firm whose services cover a variety of industries and positions. We primarily provide professional permanent placement services to area clients within the manufacturing and engineering sectors. We are also able to provide long term contract and other consulting services.

Key Contact - Specialty:
Mr. Dan J. Barrow, CPC, General Manager - *Telecommunications*

Salary Minimum: $30,000

Functions: Mfg., Product Dev., Production, Automation, Plant Mgmt., Quality, Productivity, Materials, Engineering

Industries: Generalist (All), Manufacturing, Food, Bev., Tobacco, Printing, Medical Devices, Plastics, Rubber, Paints, Petro. Products, Metal Products, Machine, Appliance, Motor Vehicles, Test, Measure Equip., Misc. Mfg., Electronic, Elec. Components, Robotics, Engineering Svcs., Supply Chain Mgmt

The Regent Group
2850 W Horizon Ridge Pkwy Ste 200
Henderson, NV 89052-4395
(702) 430-4600
Fax: (702) 430-4601
Email: glonas@theregentgroup.com
Web: www.theregentgroup.com

Summary: Our firm is a national executive search and consulting firm that provides leaders to companies within the insurance and risk management industries.

Key Contact - Specialty:
Mr. George Lonas, President - *Boards of Directors, Executives, Insurance (Casualty,Claims,Health)*
Ms. Barbara Anderson, Manager, Recruiting - *Insurance (Life,Property,Reinsurance,Workers Compensation), Risk management*

Ms. Angela Welch, Recruiting Specialist - *Insurance, Insurance (Claims,Health,Life,Workers Compensation)*
Ms. Sylvia Collins, Manager, Recruiting - *Boards of Directors, C-level, CEOs, CFOs, COOs*
Ms. Mary Smith, Manager, Recruiting - *Insurance (Casualty,Claims,Health,Life,Property)*

Salary Minimum: $50,000

Functions: Management, Board Members, Senior Mgmt., Middle Mgmt., Staffing, Risk Mgmt.

Industries: Generalist (All), Insurance, Casualty, Claims, Life, Commercial, Re-Insurance

Branches:
3960 Howard Hughes Pkwy Ste 500
Las Vegas, NV 89169-5988
(702) 990-3551
Fax: (702) 990-3552
Key Contact - Specialty:
Mr. Kimberly Ramos, Vice President - *Insurance (Life,Property,Reinsurance,Workers Compensation), Risk management*

David H Reid & Associates LLC
1 E Camelback Rd Ste 550
Phoenix, AZ 85012-1650
(602) 234-2010
Fax: (623) 572-7744
Email: dave@dreidassociates.com
Web: www.dreidassociates.com

Summary: On behalf of our clients, we recruit banking and financial services industry executives and professionals for management, executive and other specific positions. Through a network of select firms, we are able to recruit nationally for our clients to the benefit of our candidates.

Key Contact - Specialty:
Mr. David H. Reid, Managing Officer

Salary Minimum: $50,000

Functions: Generalist (All)

Industries: Finance, Banking

Reid & Company Executive Search LLC
500 Market St Unit 15
Portsmouth, NH 03801-3494
(603) 433-6222
Email: sonia@reidnco.com
Web: www.reidnco.com

Summary: Global search firm specializing in the footwear, accessories, apparel and sporting goods industries including both fashion and athletic product. We conduct searches in all functional areas.

Key Contact - Specialty:
Ms. Paula Reid, Founder & President
Mr. Mark Falvey, Search Consultant
Ms. Cathy Parker, Search Consultant
Ms. Sonia Mattson, Researcher & Search Consultant

Functions: Senior Mgmt., Middle Mgmt.

Industries: Textiles, Apparel, Wholesale, Retail

Reinecke & Associates
PO Box 1141
Secaucus, NJ 07096-1141
(201) 865-5935
Fax: (201) 865-6081
Email: reinecke@comcast.net

Summary: Specializing in the placements of senior managers and executives within the transportation and logistics industry.

Key Contact - Specialty:
Mr. Robert Schumann, President - *Transportation*

Salary Minimum: $35,000

Functions: Generalist (All), Middle Mgmt., Distribution, Sales Mgmt., CFOs, Credit, M&A, Int'l.

Industries: Generalist (All), Transportation, Accounting, Mgmt. Consulting

Reliant Search Inc

5335 Meadows Rd Ste 280
Lake Oswego, OR 97035-3150
(503) 598-0154
Fax: (503) 620-8963
Email: recruiter@reliantsearch.com
Web: www.reliantsearch.com

Summary: We are a boutique recruiting/staffing firm specializing in the direct-hire and temporary placement of professionals at all levels of accounting, finance, administrative and clerical positions.

Key Contact - Specialty:
Ms. Vaughna Cochenour, CPC, Principal & Executive Recruiter - *Accounting, Finance, Operations, Temporary*
Ms. Kristin D. Floyd, Manager, Business
Ms. Jenny Balisteri, Assistant, Recruiting
Ms. Crystal Mascorro, Assistant Recruiter - *Office (Administration), Temporary*

Functions: Admin. Svcs., Finance, CFOs

Industries: Generalist (All)

RemTech Business Solutions Inc

23097 Farmington Rd
Farmington, MI 48336-3981
(248) 426-6212
Fax: (248) 426-6216
Email: lcattermole@remtech-solutions.com
Web: www.remtech-solutions.com

Summary: Our firm offers clients the option of IT consultants, direct hire employees or outsourcing their projects to us. Our careful technical screening and personality analysis ensures high quality employees to match client specifications.

Key Contact - Specialty:
Mrs. Laura Cattermole, CPC, President & Chief Executive Officer

Salary Minimum: $45,000

Functions: IT, MIS Mgmt., Systems Analysis, Systems Dev., Systems Implem., Systems Support, Network Admin., DB Admin., Engineering

Industries: Generalist (All), Services, Mgmt. Consulting

The Renaissance Network Inc

495 Boylston St
Brookline, MA 02445-6000
(617) 264-6100
Fax: (617) 249-1631
Email: resume@ren-network.com
Web: www.ren-network.com

Summary: Ours is a small and highly focused search firm that specializes in the recruitment of sales and marketing professionals in information technology and professional services. We also conduct searches for executive level personnel in all management disciplines. We provide search and placement services nationally.

Key Contact - Specialty:
Ms. Lisa Sacchetti, Principal

Salary Minimum: $100,000

Functions: Management, Middle Mgmt., Sales & Mktg., Sales Mgmt., Sales Reps.

Industries: Generalist (All), Software

Renascent Solutions

PO Box 324
Kirkland, WA 98083-0324
(425) 605-8971
Email: dan@renascentsolutions.com
Web: www.renascentsolutions.com

Summary: Specializes in the recruitment and placement of high-technology sales & marketing professionals.

Key Contact - Specialty:
Mr. Daniel McLaughlin, President

Functions: Sales & Mktg.

Industries: Communications, Software

ReQuest People

700 Ackerman Rd Ste 390
Columbus, OH 43202-1559
(614) 267-7200
Fax: (614) 267-7595
Email: alan@requestpeople.com
Web: www.requestpeople.com

Summary: Specialize in accounting, financial, and IT recruiting.

Key Contact - Specialty:
Mr. Russell Sheets, President & Chief Executive Officer - *Tax*
Mr. Alan Wasserman, Resource Manager

Salary Minimum: $60,000

Functions: Finance, IT

Industries: Generalist (All), Telecoms, Call Centers, Telephony, Software, Database SW, Development SW, ERP SW, Networking, Comm. SW, Security SW, System SW

Request Technology LLC

200 E 5th Ave Ste 116
Naperville, IL 60563-3173
(630) 717-5865
Fax: (630) 717-1109
Email: admin@requesttechnology.com
Web: www.requesttechnology.com

Summary: Due to the industry experience of our entire staff and strong client relationships, we successfully fill over 80 percent of our available positions with a 98 percent retention ratio.

Key Contact - Specialty:
Mr. Richard W. Honquest, President

Functions: IT

Industries: Generalist (All)

Research Recruiters

PO Box 215
Mashpee, MA 02649-0215
(508) 477-8120
Email: lb@researchrecruiters.com
Web: www.researchrecruiters.com

Summary: We are an executive search firm focusing on the placement of equity research professionals. Our clients include investment and merchant banks, brokerage and asset management firms and independent and niche boutiques. Our specialization is placing equity research analysts and associates at all levels, supervisory analysts & editors, product managers, research strategists, portfolio/asset managers and directors of research.

Key Contact - Specialty:
Ms. Lorraine Barnicoat

Salary Minimum: $70,000

Functions: Finance

Industries: Invest. Banking

Resolution Staffing Inc

18062 FM 529 Rd Ste 150
Cypress, TX 77433-1168
(281) 345-0302
Fax: (832) 201-0694
Email: info@resolutionstaff.com
Web: www.resolutionstaff.com

Summary: Our firm is a specialist in the placement of administrative, accounting and IT contract and direct hire personnel. Additionally we place account executives, recruiters, branch managers, area managers, executive level position and other top talent within the staffing industry and related fields. We have additional expertise in HR and contract or corporate recruiting.

Key Contact - Specialty:
Mr. Vic Collins, Regional Vice President, Sales &·Mkt - *Accounting, Consulting, Information service, Sales, Staffing*

Functions: Generalist (All), Management, Admin. Svcs., Sales Mgmt., HR Mgmt., Staffing

Industries: Generalist (All), Oil & Gas, Finance, Accounting, HR Services, Law Enforcement, IT Implementation, Database SW, Development SW, Networking, Comm. SW, Security SW, System SW

Resource Consulting Services

113-190 Robert Speck Pky
Sherwood Business Centre
Mississauga, ON L4Z 3K3
Canada
(905) 272-5566
Fax: (905) 272-8246
Email: harmith@stn.net
Web: www.resourceconsultingservices.com

Summary: We are a HR company that deals in one stop shopping. Recruiting, T&D, outplacement, policy & procedures, business excellence & visioning programs, continuous improvement skill training, changing the operating practices for success, building business systems with an effective infrastructure, etc.

Key Contact - Specialty:
Mr. Dwight Smith, President - *Financial, Food & beverage, Food service, Franchising, Healthcare*
Mr. Nigel Southway, Principal Partner

Salary Minimum: $30,000

Functions: Generalist (All)

Industries: HR Services

Resource Management

177 Broad St Ste 1120
Stamford, CT 06901-2476
(203) 961-7000
Fax: (203) 961-7001
Email: recruit@rmginc.net
Web: www.rmginc.net

Summary: Our firm specializes in the recruitment of finance and accounting professionals. We have attracted numerous Fortune 500 companies, financial service organizations, public & privately held businesses and emerging entrepreneurial organizations. Our network of clients provides us with growing opportunities.

Key Contact - Specialty:
Mr. Denis LaPolice, President - *Finance*
Mr. Anthony Chioditti, Vice President
Mr. Kevin Cooke, Director
Mr. James Savoca, Manager
Mr. James F. Slemp, Senior Consultant

Mr. Brian Frederick, Senior Consultant
Ms. Lisa Lentine, Assistant Vice President
Mr. J. Matthew O'Brien, Consultant
Mr. Jonathan S. Gould, Consultant

Salary Minimum: $50,000

Functions: Generalist (All), Finance, CFOs, Budgeting, Cash Mgmt., Credit, Taxes, M&A, Risk Mgmt.

Industries: Generalist (All), Manufacturing, Finance, Services, Media, Real Estate

Resource Options Inc

31 Fremont St
Needham, MA 02494-2909
(781) 455-0224
Fax: (781) 455-7132
Email: info@resourceoptions.com
Web: www.resourceoptions.com

Summary: We are one of the area's fastest growing locally owned staffing firms specializing in the construction, engineering and environmental industries. A full service staffing solutions provider we were founded by experienced professionals whose knowledge of the industry and its players has made us the company that our market's best firms have come to count on. The cornerstone of our business is forming successful relationships between employers and employees.

Key Contact - Specialty:
Mr. Matthew Carlin, President
Ms. Marg Balcom, Executive Vice President
Ms. Patricia Wallace, Consultant, Recruitment

Salary Minimum: $30,000

Functions: Generalist (All)

Industries: Transportation, HR Services, Environmental Svcs.

Branches:
11 Harristown Rd
Glen Rock, NJ 07452-3319
(800) 505-4764
Email: info@resourceoptions.com
Key Contact - Specialty:
Mr. John Massey, Branch Manager

Resource Recruiting

547 Amherst St
Nashua, NH 03063-4000
(603) 595-2822
Fax: (603) 886-1822
Email: alan@resourcerecruiting.com
Web: www.resourcerecruiting.com

Summary: We are staffed with individuals experienced not only in recruiting, but with substantial experience in the disciplines they service. Our consultants conduct searches from staff-level to senior management.

Key Contact - Specialty:
Mr. Alan C. Etlinger, President - *Accounting, CFOs, Finance, Manufacturing (Management), Operations*
Mr. Robert C. Harrington, Executive Vice President - *Accounting, Accounting (Public), CFOs, Comptrollers, Finance*
Mr. Stephen R. Etlinger, Vice President - *Accounting, Finance, Marketing, Sales*
Ms. Nancy Baughman, Placement Director - *Accounting, Engineering, Finance, Human resources, Operations*

Functions: Sales & Mktg., Sales Mgmt., Finance, CFOs, Budgeting, Cash Mgmt., Credit, Taxes

Industries: Generalist (All)

Resource Services Inc

20 Crossways Park Dr N
Woodbury, NY 11797-2007
(516) 496-4100
Fax: (516) 496-4110
Email: jt@resourceservices.com
Web: www.resourceservices.com

Summary: We are an executive search firm with affiliations specializing in the placement of IT, biotechnology and communication professionals.

Key Contact - Specialty:
Mr. Joseph Trainor, Director
Ms. Mary Ann Trainor, President

Salary Minimum: $50,000

Functions: Generalist (All), Management, Senior Mgmt., IT, MIS Mgmt., Systems Analysis, Systems Dev., Systems Support, Network Admin., DB Admin.

Industries: Generalist (All), Computer Equip., Finance, Banking, Invest. Banking, Brokers, Venture Cap., Mutual/Hedge Funds, Misc. Financial, Hospitality, Telecoms, Telephony, Network Infrastructure, Software, Mfg. SW, Security SW, Biotech/Life Sciences

Resource360

7742 Spalding Dr Ste 422
Norcross, GA 30092-4207
(404) 377-1941
Fax: (770) 817-1183
Email: dmarsh@resource360.com
Web: www.resource360.com

Summary: We specialize in placing both full-time and contracting professionals in IT, finance/accounting and HR positions.

Key Contact - Specialty:
Mr. Martin Drucker, Chief Executive Officer
Mr. David Marsh, Sr., Division President

Salary Minimum: $30,000

Functions: Board Members, Senior Mgmt., Product Dev., HR Mgmt., Finance, IT, MIS Mgmt.

Industries: Generalist (All), Accounting SW, Database SW, Doc. Mgmt., Production SW

Resources in Food Inc

1007 N Main St
Columbia, IL 62236-1113
(618) 281-3100
Fax: (618) 281-3110
Email: cclark@rifood.com
Web: www.rifood.com

Summary: We are a placement firm dedicated solely to the food, beverage and hotel industry.

Key Contact - Specialty:
Mr. William F. Timmons, President
Mr. Kit Timmons, Vice President
Ms. Cheri Clark, Marketing

Salary Minimum: $35,000

Functions: Generalist (All), Management, Senior Mgmt., Middle Mgmt., Hospitality, Hotel Mgmt., Chefs

Industries: Food, Bev., Tobacco, Hospitality, Hotels, Resorts, Clubs, Restaurants, Quick Service Restaurants, Full Service Restaurants, Inst./Industrial Food Svc., Entertainment

Branches:
1438 W Broadway Rd Ste B260
Tempe, AZ 85282-1148
(480) 968-9200
Fax: (480) 968-0868
Email: riftempe@rifood.com

Key Contact - Specialty:
Ms. Melissa Kohlenberger - *Consumer, Manufacturing, Professional services, Technology, Telecommunications*

17985 Sky Park Cir Ste A
Irvine, CA 92614-6359
(949) 250-4916
Email: rifirvine@rifood.com
Key Contact - Specialty:
Ms. Cheri Clark - *Legal*

900 15th St NW Ste B
Washington, DC 20005-2501
(202) 464-3035
(877) 366-3444
Fax: (202) 326-0299
Email: rifwashingtondc@rifood.com
Key Contact - Specialty:
Mr. Jack Pogue, Regional Director
Ms. Colleen Jones, Recruiter

820 Maritime Ct
Bradenton, FL 34212-5244
(941) 744-5005
Fax: (941) 744-5150
Email: wtimmons@tampabay.rr.com
Key Contact - Specialty:
Mr. Bill Timmons, President

7680 Universal Blvd Ste 560
Orlando, FL 32819-8956
(407) 248-1066
Fax: (407) 248-1067
Email: riforlando@rifood.com
Key Contact - Specialty:
Ms. Jill Goldstein, Recruiter

1720 Peachtree St NW Ste 626
Atlanta, GA 30309-2450
(404) 897-5535
Fax: (404) 897-5454
Email: lparker@rifood.com
Key Contact - Specialty:
Mr. Les Parker, Recruiter

1260 Iroquois Ave Ste 304
Naperville, IL 60563-8549
(630) 357-7074
Fax: (630) 357-7548
Email: rifchicago@rifood.com
Key Contact - Specialty:
Mr. Jay Grimm, Recruiter
Mr. Paul Sassano, Recruiter
Mr. Michael Micek, Recruiter

23400 Michigan Ave Ste P32
Dearborn, MI 48124-1926
(313) 792-8300 x106
Fax: (313) 792-8305
Email: dmcmaster@rifood.com
Key Contact - Specialty:
Mr. Dave McMaster, Recruiter - *Food, Food & beverage, Food service, Hospitality, Restaurants*

10 S 5th St Ste 445
Minneapolis, MN 55402-1022
(612) 692-8030
Fax: (612) 692-8251
Email: rifminneapolis@rifood.com
Key Contact - Specialty:
Ms. Chris Opitz, Recruiter

4901 Main St Ste 230
Kansas City, MO 64112-2634
(816) 756-3233
Fax: (816) 561-0087
Email: rifkansascity@rifood.com
Key Contact - Specialty:
Mr. Carl Santoro, Franchise Owner
Mr. Phil Maicher, Recruiter
Ms. Amy Martin, Recruiter

222 S Central Ave Ste 202
Saint Louis, MO 63105-3509
(314) 727-0002
Fax: (314) 727-5590
Email: rifstlouis@rifood.com
Key Contact - Specialty:
Mr. Lary Beyer, Senior Recruiter

5900 Roche Dr Ste 550
Columbus, OH 43229-3283
(614) 841-0749
Fax: (614) 358-8301
Email: rifcolumbus@rifood.com
Key Contact - Specialty:
Mr. Alonso Pittsley, Recruiter

825 NE 20th Ave Ste 310
Portland, OR 97232-2275
(503) 232-8326
Fax: (503) 232-0273
Email: rifportland@rifood.com
Key Contact - Specialty:
Ms. Bonnie Pollock, Master Licensee

6060 N Central Expy Ste 425
Dallas, TX 75206-5280
(972) 980-4211
Fax: (972) 980-4292
Email: rifdallas@rifood.com
Key Contact - Specialty:
Ms. Debra Walsh, Senior Recruiter

10333 Northwest Fwy Ste 420
Houston, TX 77092-8218
(713) 957-2700
Email: rifhouston@rifood.com
Key Contact - Specialty:
Mr. Joe Casey

800 Dolorosa Ste 425
San Antonio, TX 78207-4506
(210) 220-1290
Fax: (210) 220-1296
Email: rifsanantonio@rifood.com
Key Contact - Specialty:
Mr. Jon Lark, Franchise Owner

The Response Companies

23 E 39th St
New York, NY 10016-0930
(212) 983-8870
Fax: (212) 983-9492
Email: bcohen@responseco.com
Web: www.responseco.com

Summary: We service the professional staffing arena in both permanent and temporary positions, specializing in accounting and finance, banking, mortgage banking, securities, compliance, legal, marketing and human resources.

Key Contact - Specialty:
Mr. Allen Gutterman, Chief Executive Officer
Mr. Ed Caliguiri, Chief Operating Officer

Salary Minimum: $75,000

Functions: Middle Mgmt., Healthcare, Sales & Mktg., HR Mgmt., Finance, Legal

Industries: Generalist (All), Banking, Invest. Banking, Mutual/Hedge Funds, Accounting, Mgmt. Consulting, Compliance, Hospitals, Long-term/Home Care, Physical Therapy, Occupational Therapy

Branches:
100 Prospect St Ste 201S
South Tower Plaza
Stamford, CT 06901-1642
(203) 316-2828

Key Contact - Specialty:
Mr. Barry Cohen

Retail Connection Inc

33 Newark Pompton Tpke
Riverdale, NJ 07457-1144
(973) 839-4599
(800) 770-4945
Fax: (973) 839-5199
Email: email@retailconnectioninc.com
Web: www.retailconnectioninc.com

Summary: We specialize in the recruitment and placement of retail executives. Positions include, regional, district & store management, buyers, allocators, planners, HR and loss prevention personnel.

Key Contact - Specialty:
Ms. Carole Thaller, President - *Retail*

Functions: Management, Middle Mgmt.

Industries: Retail

The Retail Network

272 Chauncy St Ste 8
Mansfield, MA 02048-1257
(508) 261-8764
Fax: (508) 339-5792
Email: retail@retailnetwork.com
Web: www.retailnetwork.com

Summary: Executive search firm specializing in search and placement for retail and retail related industries.

Key Contact - Specialty:
Mr. Gary Belastock, President

Salary Minimum: $30,000

Functions: Senior Mgmt., Middle Mgmt., Purchasing, Distribution, Direct Mktg., Training, CFOs

Industries: Retail

Retail Recruiters

2189 Silas Deane Hwy
Rocky Hill, CT 06067-2324
(860) 721-9550
Fax: (860) 257-8813
Email: careers@retailrecruitersusa.com
Web: www.retailrecruitersusa.com

Summary: We specialize in the placement of retail executives for the specialty, luxury, supermarket, big box, department and discount stores industry. Manufacturing assignments include product development, technical design, quality assurance and production sourcing.

Key Contact - Specialty:
Mr. Nathan Friedman, President

Functions: Management

Industries: Textiles, Apparel, Retail

RGA Associates Inc

465 California St Ste 1250
San Francisco, CA 94104-1849
(415) 397-4646
Fax: (415) 951-7979
Email: rga@rgatech.com
Web: www.rgatech.com

Summary: We provide the highest caliber of engineering, healthcare, life science and sales talent in the most cost effective and time efficient manner.

Key Contact - Specialty:
Mr. Richard Engelhardt, President - *Hardware*
Ms. Marguerite Bruchez, Vice President - *Computers (Software), Hardware*

Mr. Joseph Strate, Manager, Engineering Recruiting
Mr. John Polk Steward, Director, Consulting Services
Mr. Dave Seeley, Operations Manager
Mr. George Singer, Manager, Outsourcing Services - *Computers (Software), Engineering, International, Internet*

Salary Minimum: $80,000

Functions: Generalist (All), Management, Senior Mgmt., Nurses, Systems Dev., R&D, Engineering

Industries: Generalist (All), Semiconductors, Software, Database SW, Development SW, Doc. Mgmt., Production SW, ERP SW, Marketing SW, Networking, Comm. SW, Security SW, System SW, Biotech/Life Sciences, Healthcare, Hospitals

RGT Associates Inc

PO Box 1032
2 Greenleaf Woods Dr Unit 101
Portsmouth, NH 03802-1032
(603) 431-9500
Fax: (603) 431-6984
Email: recruitrgt@aol.com

Summary: We provide confidential, professional search and placement services for manufacturing and accounting management positions. The specialized services offered are most effective with small and medium-sized organizations and mid and senior-level management positions.

Key Contact - Specialty:
Mr. Bob Thiboutot, CPC, President & Recruiter
Mr. Michael Guenard, Recruiter - *Sales*

Salary Minimum: $45,000

Functions: Management, Middle Mgmt., Product Dev., Production, Plant Mgmt., Finance, R&D, Engineering

Industries: Manufacturing, Drugs Mfg., Medical Devices, Plastics, Rubber, Metal Products, Machine, Appliance, Computer Equip., Consumer Elect., Test, Measure Equip., Misc. Mfg., Electronic, Elec. Components

RHAssociates Inc

5911 Meadow Sweet Ln Ste 100
Shawnee, KS 66226-3605
(913) 422-0570
Email: recruiters@rha-staffing.com
Web: www.rha-staffing.com

Summary: Search firm specializing in retainer, container, contingency, contract, and employer of record placements.

Key Contact - Specialty:
Mr. Russell Hacker, President - *Information Technology*

Salary Minimum: $70,000

Functions: Senior Mgmt., Middle Mgmt., IT, MIS Mgmt., Engineering, Systems

Industries: Generalist (All), Manufacturing, Transportation, Finance, E-commerce, Government, Aerospace, Insurance, Software, Healthcare

Frank J Rich & Associates

14135 Palisades Dr
Poway, CA 92064-3841
(858) 513-9474
Fax: (858) 513-6381
Email: frank@fjrich.com
Web: www.fjrich.com

Summary: Full service executive recruiting and search firm, specializing in IT technology, call center, support and service professionals.

Key Contact - Specialty:
Mr. Frank J. Rich, President

Functions: Management

Industries: E-commerce, IT Implementation, Call Centers, Software

Jeff Rich Associates

67 Walnut Ave Ste 303
Clark, NJ 07066-1640
(732) 574-3888
Fax: (732) 574-1424
Email: jeffrich@clarknj.com
Web: www.clarknj.com/jeffrich

Summary: We develop a long lasting relationship with our clients that enable us to better understand the culture of each company and the personality of the management involved in the selection process for new employees.

Key Contact - Specialty:
Mr. Richard A. Thunberg, President

Salary Minimum: $40,000

Functions: Generalist (All), Finance, CFOs, Budgeting, Cash Mgmt., Credit, Taxes, M&A, Risk Mgmt.

Industries: Generalist (All)

Don Richard Associates Inc

(formerly known as Don Richard Associates of Tidewater)
6350 Center Dr Ste 112
Norfolk, VA 23502-4107
(757) 518-8600
Fax: (757) 518-9436
Email: donrich@donrichard.com
Web: www.donrichard.com

Summary: We have built a reputation for outstanding professionalism and quality service. The key to our long term success is founded in the caliber of our counselors and support staff. We are focused on the needs of our clients, as well as the desires of our candidates. As a result, our reputation for recruitment is unparalleled.

Key Contact - Specialty:
Mr. Ed Greene, CPA, President

Salary Minimum: $25,000

Functions: Generalist (All)

Industries: Finance, Accounting

Richard, Wayne & Roberts

24 E Greenway Plz Ste 1304
Houston, TX 77046-2486
(713) 629-6681
(800) 364-7979
Fax: (713) 623-2740
Web: www.rwr.com

Summary: We approach each recruiting assignment with a minimum three-member team, designating one recruiter as the principal contact for the client. Our mission is to be recognized as the leading recruiting firm in the industries and disciplines we serve.

Key Contact - Specialty:
Mr. Dick Weiss, CPC, Principal & Managing Partner
Mr. Neal Hirsch, CPC, Managing Partner
Ms. Alexis Cannon, CPC, Partner - *Accounting, Finance*
Mr. Mark Dremely, CPC, Partner - *Construction, Real estate*
Ms. Ruth Schlanger, CPC, Partner - *Legal*

Ms. Amy Adams, CPC, Partner - *Accounting, Clinical, Healthcare, Human resources*
Mr. Bobby Doyle, CPC, Partner - *Engineering*
Mrs. Nicole Seof, Partner - *Construction, Real estate*
Mr. Kenneth Mcqueen, CPC, Partner - *Engineering*

Salary Minimum: $40,000

Functions: Generalist (All)

Industries: Generalist (All)

Branches:
1423 Peachtree St
Jacksonville, FL 32207
(904) 379-0799
(800) 291-2949
Fax: (904) 291-0799
Key Contact - Specialty:
Mrs. Anna Colosimo, Manager, Executive Search

2203 Timberloch Pl Ste 250
Spring, TX 77380-1188
(281) 825-3052
(877) 477-1356
Fax: (281) 825-3061
Email: amya@rwr.com
Key Contact - Specialty:
Mrs. Amy Adam, Partner - *Healthcare, Human resources*

147 Finch Pl SW Ste 1
Bainbridge Island, WA 98110-4914
(800) 232-6943
(206) 855-9736
Fax: (206) 855-9746
Email: paulm@rwr.com
Key Contact - Specialty:
Mr. Paul McEwan, CPC, Executive Recruiter - *Marketing, Sales*

Terry Richards CPC

36 Public Sq Ste 105
Willoughby, OH 44094-7864
(440) 918-1800
Fax: (440) 975-1499
Email: trcpcrec@apk.net

Summary: We are an independent recruiting firm specializing in strategic leadership positions for a wide variety of manufacturing and distribution companies.

Key Contact - Specialty:
Mr. Terry Richards, CPC, Principal - *Distribution, Manufacturing*

Salary Minimum: $75,000

Functions: Generalist (All), Senior Mgmt., Middle Mgmt., Plant Mgmt., Quality, Purchasing, Materials Plng., Sales Mgmt., HR Mgmt., Finance

Industries: Manufacturing, Metal Products, Machine, Appliance, Motor Vehicles, Computer Equip., Consumer Elect., Misc. Mfg., Wholesale

Richardson & Farrell PC

1 SW Columbia St Ste 500
Portland, OR 97258-2006
(503) 295-5995
Email: tjfcpa@richardsonfarrell.com
Web: www.richardsonfarrell.com

Summary: Executive search firm specializing in accounting/finance, information technology, and sales/marketing recruiting.

Key Contact - Specialty:
Ms. Teresa J. Farrell, CPA, President - *Accounting, Finance, Sales*
Mr. Robert C. Richardson, CPA, Owner - *Accounting, Finance*
Ms. Jill Schroeder, Senior Executive Recruiter

Ms. Kristen Clark Fisher, MBA, Senior Executive Recruiter - *Finance*
Mr. Bruce T. Blanchard, Senior Executive Recruiter - *Finance, Marketing, Operations, Sales*

Salary Minimum: $60,000

Functions: Senior Mgmt., Sales & Mktg., Finance, CFOs, Budgeting, Taxes, IT, MIS Mgmt.

Industries: Generalist (All)

Branches:
601 Union St Ste 4200
Seattle, WA 98101-4036
(206) 499-3840
Fax: (503) 295-5939

The Richardson Group

10454 Stonebridge Blvd Ste 100
Boca Raton, FL 33498-6408
(561) 883-1734
Email: cr@trgstaffingsolutions.com
Web: www.trgstaffingsolutions.com

Summary: Provides a full compliment of economical HR services to companies and job seekers: contract, contingency, retained, outplacement, resume services, expert career counseling, coaching and business services. Specializing in all disciplines of wireless, telecommunications, DOD and the new technologies.

Key Contact - Specialty:
Ms. Carroll Richardson, President - *Business development, Finance, Product management/development, Wireless*

Salary Minimum: $84,000

Functions: Generalist (All), Management

Industries: Generalist (All), Test, Measure Equip., Electronic, Elec. Components, Robotics, Semiconductors, Misc. Financial, HR Services, Telecoms, Telephony, Digital, Wireless, Fiber Optic, Network Infrastructure, RF/Microwave, Defense

Jack Richman & Associates

PO Box 25412
Fort Lauderdale, FL 33320-5412
(305) 940-0721
(954) 389-9563
Fax: (954) 389-9572
Email: recruiter@floridatechjobs.com
Web: www.floridatechjobs.com

Summary: Our firm specializes exclusively in the IT industry. Multinational experience, as well as Spanish is preferred.

Key Contact - Specialty:
Mr. Jack Richman, Managing Partner - *Client/server, Telecommunications*
Ms. Gloria Newman, Senior Consultant - *Client/server*

Salary Minimum: $50,000

Functions: IT

Industries: Mgmt. Consulting, Software, Database SW, Development SW, Doc. Mgmt., Production SW, ERP SW, Mfg. SW, Networking, Comm. SW, Security SW

Richmond Associates

9 Pioneer St
Cooperstown, NY 13326-1022
(607) 547-9236
(607) 544-1031
Fax: (607) 441-1007
Email: jhulse@msn.com

Summary: We specialize in searching for and placing sales professionals and technical sales support professionals in software and hardware sales positions.

Key Contact - Specialty:
Ms. Jeanne Hulse, Consultant, Management
Mr. Rick Hulse, Consultant, Management

Salary Minimum: $65,000

Functions: Sales & Mktg.

Industries: Software, Doc. Mgmt., Production SW, ERP SW, HR SW, Industry Specific SW, Mfg. SW, Marketing SW, Networking, Comm. SW, Security SW, System SW

The Right Move Inc

10 Glenlake Pkwy NE Ste 130
Atlanta, GA 30328-3495
(770) 442-1993
Fax: (770) 720-1562
Email: trmassociates@trmcorp.com
Web: www.trmcorp.com

Summary: Permanent recruiting firm in the areas of information technology, sales, management, back office, and administrative.

Key Contact - Specialty:
Ms. Wendy White, President

Salary Minimum: $80,000

Functions: Management, Sales & Mktg.

Industries: IT Implementation

RightSource Inc

2616 S Peninsula Dr
Daytona Beach, FL 32118-5631
(386) 672-7282
Fax: (386) 767-2240
Email: info@rsi1.com
Web: www.rsi1.com

Summary: Executive search specialists for the food processing and ingredients industry exclusively.

Key Contact - Specialty:
Mr. Ronald Bynum, President
Ms. Susan Milavanovic, Executive Recruiter
Mr. Walter O'Brien, Executive Recruiter - *Culinary, Food, Research & development, Sales, Technical (Management)*

Salary Minimum: $50,000

Functions: Generalist (All), Management

Industries: Food, Bev., Tobacco, Soap, Perf., Cosmtcs., Pharm Svcs., Supply Chain Mgmt, Quick Service Restaurants, Full Service Restaurants, Inst./Industrial Food Svc.

Rincon Partners

8835 E Speedway Blvd Ste D
Tucson, AZ 85710-1844
(520) 722-7976
(888) 222-9549
Email: careers@rinconpartners.com
Web: www.rinconpartners.com

Summary: We are a technical search and recruitment firm, serving the semiconductor industry. We provide contract, temp-to-perm and direct placement services to our clients. Our expertise is centered on the IC design professional and the people that manage and support them. Whether you are looking for a new career opportunity or are a hiring manager seeking top technical talent, we can assist in all aspects of your staffing needs.

Key Contact - Specialty:
Mr. Ken MacFarlane, Senior Managing Partner
Mr. Ian MacFarlane, President

Functions: Product Dev., Engineering, Eng. Design

Industries: Semiconductors

Rita Technology Services

2502 N Rocky Point Dr Ste 180
Tampa, FL 33607-1450
(813) 289-3000
Fax: (813) 289-8173
Email: careers@ritatech.com
Web: www.ritatech.com

Summary: We are an IT search and consulting firm serving Tampa Bay, Orlando and Central Florida. Collectively our staff has over extensive years of IT recruiting experience. We provide contingency based search, vendor management and managed services.

Key Contact - Specialty:
Mr. Tom Byrne, Director, Staffing Services - *CIOs, Computers (Programming,Software), Information Technology, PeopleSoft*
Mr. John Holton, Director, Business Development

Functions: IT

Industries: Generalist (All)

Rittenhouse Executive Search Inc

1700 Benjamin Franklin Pkwy
The Windsor - Penthouse Suite
Philadelphia, PA 19103-2735
(215) 564-6007
(215) 564-6057
Fax: (215) 564-6051
Email: recruiter@ritsearch.com
Web: www.ritsearch.com

Summary: We specialize in the recruitment and permanent placement of accountants, financial professionals and attorneys. Clients include accounting firms, law firms and corporations.

Key Contact - Specialty:
Ms. Susan D. VanCola, CPA, Recruiter

Functions: Generalist (All), Legal, Attorneys

Industries: Generalist (All), Finance, Banking, Misc. Financial, Legal, Accounting

The Rivard Group

(also known as TRG Executive Search)
4306 Murfield Dr E
Bradenton, FL 34203-4094
(941) 727-6030
Fax: (941) 727-6031
Email: dick@rivardgroup.com
Web: www.rivardgroup.com

Summary: We specialize exclusively in the property and casualty insurance industry. We place mid to upper-level professionals/managers/executives in underwriting, claims, loss control, marketing, legal and financial on the company (standard, surplus and reinsurance) side as well as brokers, account executives and producers on the retail and wholesale brokerage side of the business.

Key Contact - Specialty:
Mr. Richard L. Rivard, President & Chief Executive Officer - *Insurance (Casualty,Claims,Property,Workers Compensation), Loss Control*
Mrs. Cheryl Rivard, Senior Vice President - *Insurance (Casualty,Claims,Property), Risk management, Underwriting*

Salary Minimum: $50,000

Functions: Generalist (All)

Industries: Insurance

River Glen Associates

33 Main St Ste 1
Newtown, CT 06470-2129
(203) 270-3400
Fax: (203) 270-3405
Email: davids@riverglen.net
Web: www.riverglen.net

Summary: Our firm is chartered with delivering superior talent who create real value and improve our clients' competitiveness through people. Our goal is to be a critical resource needed to build world-class organizations. We specialize in sales, marketing, business development and senior executive assignments.

Key Contact - Specialty:
Mr. David Sigovich, Managing Director - *Senior management*

Salary Minimum: $60,000

Functions: Senior Mgmt., Middle Mgmt., Sales & Mktg., IT, MIS Mgmt., Mgmt. Consultants, Hospitality

Industries: Manufacturing, Food, Bev., Tobacco, Soap, Perf., Cosmtcs., Computer Equip., Consumer Elect., Consumer Goods, Services, Mgmt. Consulting, E-commerce, IT Implementation, PSA/ASP, Recreation, New Media, Network Infrastructure, Defense, Software, Development SW, ERP SW, Security SW

River Region Executive Search Inc

4512 Reich St
Metairie, LA 70006-2240
(504) 831-4746
Fax: (504) 455-9975
Email: czamjahn@aol.com

Summary: Extensive years of experience in serving process industry employers. Previous chemical industry HR positions. Specialists in expanded foam packaging, polymers, plastics, chemicals, petrochemicals, refining and oil & gas service.

Key Contact - Specialty:
Mr. Charles J. Zamjahn, President - *Chemical, Manufacturing, Plastics, Refining*

Salary Minimum: $50,000

Functions: Management, Senior Mgmt., Middle Mgmt., Technicians

Industries: Oil & Gas, Chemicals, Packaging

River West Consultants Ltd

200 W Madison St Ste 2650
Chicago, IL 60606-3497
(312) 332-8300
Fax: (312) 332-8303
Email: info@riverwestconsultants.com
Web: www.riverwestconsultants.com

Summary: We are a legal search and consulting firm providing services in these areas to law firms and corporations. We place experienced attorneys, both at law firms and in-house and the merger of practice groups and firms.

Key Contact - Specialty:
Mr. Jeffrey M. Simon, Esq., Principal
Ms. Pamela J. Simon, Principal

Functions: Legal, Attorneys

Industries: Generalist (All)

Rivera Legal Search Inc

PO Box 63343
Los Angeles, CA 90063-0343
(323) 780-0000

Email: alrivera@jdhuntr.com
Web: www.jdhuntr.com

Summary: We recruit and place attorneys at all levels of experience. Clients include major law firms and corporations through out U.S. All inquiries held in strict confidence. All fees assumed by the employer.

Key Contact - Specialty:
Mr. Al Rivera, Managing Partner
Ms. Cecilia Arellano, Chief Operating Officier - *Business development, Communications, COOs, E-business*

Salary Minimum: $90,000

Functions: Generalist (All), Senior Mgmt., Legal, Attorneys

Industries: Generalist (All), Legal

RJ Associates

23730 Canzonet St
Woodland Hills, CA 91367-5843
(818) 715-7121
Fax: (818) 715-9438
Email: rja@socal.rr.com

Summary: Providing highly personalized professional search services within a wide array of industries for positions from CEO to financial analyst, from CIO to controller. Because we engage in a limited number of searches, we focus our full attention on each assignment. We are the names on the front door.

Key Contact - Specialty:
Ms. Judith Fischer, President - *Finance*
Mr. Ronald Fischer, Executive Vice President - *Finance*

Salary Minimum: $85,000

Functions: Management, Finance, CFOs, Budgeting, Cash Mgmt., Taxes, M&A, IT, MIS Mgmt.

Industries: Generalist (All)

RJR Associates

3563 Ridgewood Dr
Pittsburgh, PA 15235-5231
(412) 829-9511
Fax: (412) 824-6838
Email: bdevoe@adelphia.net

Summary: We are executive search firm specializing in recruiting, planning and consulting for commercial construction industry. We offer the client a professional and knowledgeable approach to recruitment needs and sources.

Key Contact - Specialty:
Mr. Robert DeVoe, President

Salary Minimum: $100,000

Functions: Generalist (All)

Industries: Energy, Utilities, Construction, Manufacturing, Finance, HR Services, Engineering Svcs., Real Estate, Property/Facility Mgmt.

RJS Associates Inc

10 Columbus Blvd
Hartford, CT 06106-1976
(860) 278-5840
Fax: (860) 522-8313
Email: rjs@rjsassoc.com
Web: www.rjsassoc.com

Summary: We are a search firm specializing in technical positions in the engineering, insurance, scientific, IS, finance, environmental, software, retail/grocery and distribution fields.

Key Contact - Specialty:
Mr. Richard Stewart, CPC, President - *Administration, Finance*
Mr. Brian Greer, CPC, Vice President - *Engineering*
Mr. Brad Earnest, CPC, Manager - *Engineering*
Mr. John Reever, CPC, Manager - *Finance*
Miss Jessica Duffy, Office Manager
Mrs. Amy Oler, Manager, Human Resources
Mr. Alan Gravelle, Manager, Network & Webmaster

Salary Minimum: $24,000

Functions: Generalist (All)

Industries: Construction, Chemicals, Drugs Mfg., Medical Devices, Plastics, Rubber, Metal Products, Machine, Appliance, Computer Equip., Accounting SW, Database SW

Branches:
4 Landmark Sq
Stamford, CT 06901-2502
(203) 967-8300
Fax: (203) 967-8400
Key Contact - Specialty:
Mr. Paul Smith, CPC, Manager

RKP Group Pharmaceutical and Biotech Search

(also known as RKP Group Pharmaceutical Search)
4543 Rutherford Way Ste 202
Dayton, MD 21036-1143
(443) 535-0044
Fax: (443) 535-0064
Email: rkpgroup@comcast.net
Web: www.rkpgroup.com

Summary: We provide R&D placements within the pharmaceutical and bio-technology industry at the scientist level through the executive scientist level. Fields of expertise are in immunology,toxicology and DMPK within drug discovery pre-clinical and drug development clinical.

Key Contact - Specialty:
Mr. Randall Pinato, General Manager
Dr. Neil Miller, PhD, Account Executive - *Biopharmaceutical, Pharmaceutical, Research & development*
Mr. John Wyatt, Account Executive - *Biopharmaceutical, Pharmaceutical, Research, Research & development*

Functions: Generalist (All), Management, Middle Mgmt., Healthcare, R&D

Industries: Generalist (All), Drugs Mfg., Medical Devices, Pharm Svcs., Biotech/Life Sciences, Healthcare

RNDatabase.com LLC

401 Main St Ste 207
Salem, NH 03079-2463
(866) 763-2822
(603) 898-7533
Fax: (603) 251-8414
Email: info@rndatabase.com
Web: www.rndatabase.com

Summary: We are one of the leading providers in healthcare recruiting and database development, specializing in hospice and home healthcare. Our goal is to ease your company's reliance on traditional costs associated with newspapers, internet job boards, sign-on bonuses and typical third party recruitment.

Key Contact - Specialty:
Mr. James Avanzino, President - *Emergency room, Healthcare, Home health, Hospital, Pharmacists*

Ms. Kerry Guanci, Account Manager - *Healthcare, Home health, Hospital*
Ms. Carolyn Avanzino, Account Manager - *Home health*
Ms. Sonia Capifali, Recruiter - *Healthcare, Home health, Hospital*
Ms. Eileen Harte, Recruiter - *Healthcare, Home health, Hospital*

Salary Minimum: $40,000

Functions: Generalist (All), Management, Board Members, Healthcare, Nurses, Health Admin.

Industries: Non-profits, Mgmt. Consulting, HR Services, Advertising, Development SW, HR SW, Marketing SW, Networking, Comm. SW, Training SW, Healthcare, Hospitals, Long-term/Home Care

Roberson & Company

PO Box 12222
Glendale, AZ 85318-2222
(623) 362-8855
(303) 410-6510
Fax: (623) 561-2369
Email: robersonco@cs.com
Web: www.recruiterpro.com

Summary: We are a full-service firm affiliated with member network, computer linked and are capable of the most specialized kinds of searches.

Key Contact - Specialty:
Mr. Charles A. Roberson, Director
Mr. Stephen D. Silvas, Director

Salary Minimum: $50,000

Functions: Generalist (All)

Industries: Generalist (All), Manufacturing, Transportation, Services, Telecoms, Fiber Optic, Packaging, Software, Mfg. SW, Healthcare

Bart Roberson & Company

1445 North Loop W Ste 800
Houston, TX 77008-1673
(713) 863-1445
Fax: (713) 863-1616
Email: bhr@bartroberson.com
Web: www.bartroberson.com

Summary: We encourage public accountants to contact us, engineering, specifically for energy, staffing, IT, sales & marketing, contingency, retainer, contract and international. Our firm is also now involved in mergers & acquisitions of CPA firms..

Key Contact - Specialty:
Mr. Barthell Roberson, Chairman - *Financial*
Mr. Boyd H. Rowland, President & Chief Executive Officer - *Power*

Functions: Senior Mgmt., Mktg. Mgmt., Finance, CFOs, M&A, MIS Mgmt., Engineering, Int'l.

Industries: Energy, Utilities, Oil & Gas, Construction, Manufacturing, Chemicals, Computer Equip., Transportation, Banking, Accounting, Engineering Svcs.

Eric Robert Associates Inc

363 7th Ave Fl 6
New York, NY 10001-3904
(212) 695-5900
Email: info@ericrobert.com
Web: www.ericrobert.com

Summary: We are a large established IT staffing company representing established financial institutions, eCommerce, advertising, insurance, banking and brokerage companies. We are involved at all levels from programmer through project manager to chief technology officer.

Key Contact - Specialty:
Mr. Robert Midoneck, Managing Partner - *Consulting, Information Technology*

Salary Minimum: $65,000

Functions: IT

Industries: Wholesale, Retail, Finance, Services, Hospitality, Media, Insurance, Real Estate, Software

Robert Sage & Associates

505 Avenue A NW Ste 310
Winter Haven, FL 33881-4636
(863) 299-9941
(800) 268-1765
Fax: (800) 480-4845
Email: mikesage@bellsouth.net
Web: www.robert-sage.com

Summary: A firm of professionals in niche industries: marine products, recreational vehicles, manufactured structures, medical devices, connectors, powder metal, rubber products, frozen foods, food processing, oil/gas downline, energy (wind, fossil fuels, gas, biomass and hydropower) and building products.

Key Contact - Specialty:
Mr. Robert Sage, President
Mr. Mark Sage, Vice President
Mr. David Chamberlain, National Director - *CEOs, COOs, Healthcare, Presidents, Senior management*

Salary Minimum: $50,000

Functions: Generalist (All), Minorities/Diversity

Industries: Generalist (All), Energy, Utilities, Oil & Gas, Food, Bev., Tobacco, Medical Devices, Plastics, Rubber, Metal Products, Motor Vehicles, Misc. Mfg., Semiconductors, Call Centers

Thomas Roberts & Company

PO Box 25733
Cleveland, OH 44125-0733
(216) 883-1245
Fax: (216) 883-0963
Email: trl@thomasroberts.com
Web: www.thomasroberts.com

Summary: By the diversity of our associates backgrounds (HR, sales, finance and manufacturing), we are able to work with clients and candidates on a more in depth level.

Key Contact - Specialty:
Mr. Tom Longano, CPC, President
Ms. Kathy Kosakowski, Partner

Salary Minimum: $60,000

Functions: Generalist (All), Sales & Mktg.

Industries: Manufacturing, Test, Measure Equip., Electronic, Elec. Components, Wholesale, Pharm Svcs., Equip Svcs., E-commerce, Publishing, New Media, Telecoms, Packaging, Software, Database SW

Roberts & Sellers Inc

3730 S Susan St Ste 120
Santa Ana, CA 92704-6960
(714) 435-0207
Fax: (714) 435-2853
Email: jobutler@rsinc.net
Web: www.rsinc.net

Summary: We are an executive search firm specializing in high-level engineering. Aerospace, high technology communication, telecom and other related industries. Executives and engineers are placed with our long-term clients.

Key Contact - Specialty:
Ms. Judy O. Butler, Vice President, Operations

Salary Minimum: $60,000

Functions: Generalist (All), Senior Mgmt., Engineering

Industries: Medical Devices, Test, Measure Equip., Misc. Mfg., Consumer Goods, Telecoms, Digital, Wireless, Fiber Optic, Network Infrastructure, RF/Microwave, Government, Defense, Aerospace, Software, HR SW, Industry Specific SW, Mfg. SW, Networking, Comm. SW, Security SW

Barry Robertson & Associates

1364 Anton Sq
Pickering, ON L1V 5T3
Canada
(905) 837-6570
Fax: (905) 420-6129
Email: barryrobertson@sympatico.ca

Summary: IT recruiting and placement company for both contract and permanent opportunities.

Key Contact - Specialty:
Mr. Barry Robertson, President - *Data processing*

Salary Minimum: $70,000

Functions: Sales & Mktg., HR Mgmt., IT

Industries: Generalist (All), HR Services, Call Centers

Robertson & Company Ltd

1104-1200 Bay St
Toronto, ON M5R 2A5
Canada
(416) 929-0226
Fax: (416) 929-5549
Email: davidr@robertsonandcompany.net
Web: www.robertsonandcompany.net

Summary: Our firm provides search, selection and research services to a wide range of client companies. We work with leaders in business, finance, not-for-profit and public sector organizations to help strengthen their environments and, in doing so, to meet strategic objectives. Our unique philosophy of thorough preparation and teamwork allows for consistently high results and satisfied clients.

Key Contact - Specialty:
Mr. Dave Robertson

Functions: Management, Sales & Mktg., Finance, Non-profits

Industries: Generalist (All)

Robins Consulting LLC

4345 Lindbergh Dr
Addison, TX 75001-4539
(214) 866-0122
Fax: (214) 722-1466
Email: info@robinsconsulting.com
Web: www.robinsconsulting.com

Summary: We are an experienced executive search firm devoted exclusively to the transportation, logistics, and supply chain industries. We pride ourselves on being industry insiders. We have an impeccable track record with prominent clients who work with us because we've proven our commitment to delivering exceptional results.

Key Contact - Specialty:
Mr. Craig Robins, President - *Brokerage, Consulting, Distribution, Executives, Logistics*
Mr. Anderw Carr, Vice President, Business Development - *AS/400, Management, Procurement, Sales, Traffic*

Mr. Shelly Berger, Senior Recruiter & Research Analyst - *Distribution, Logistics, Skilled trades, Traffic, Transportation*
Ms. Tasha Smith, Recruiter & Researcher - *Brokerage, Distribution, Freight, Logistics, Management*

Salary Minimum: $75,000

Functions: Generalist (All), Management

Industries: Transportation

The Robinson Group DA Ltd

2541 RFD
Long Grove, IL 60047-8330
(847) 438-0707
Email: robgrp@comcast.net

Summary: Large public accounting firms for tax departments specializing in state and local, international and federal.

Key Contact - Specialty:
Mr. Donald Alan Robinson, President

Salary Minimum: $60,000

Functions: Finance

Industries: Accounting

Rockport Professional Search

PO Box 1119
Rockport, TX 78381-1119
(361) 727-9797
(888) 974-7723
Fax: (361) 727-9494
Email: search@rockportsearch.com
Web: www.rockportsearch.com

Summary: We are a contingency search firm specializing in professional positions in the chemicals and polymers industry and in the food and beverage manufacturing and processing industry.

Key Contact - Specialty:
Mr. Jim Gunnin, Managing Partner - *Business development, Chemical, Food & beverage, Management, Petrochemical*
Ms. Barbara Gurtner, President - *Engineering, Food & beverage, Human resources, Management, Manufacturing (Management)*
Mr. Jimmie Krnavek, Production & Research Assistant - *Engineering, Food & beverage, Human resources, Maintenance, Manufacturing (Management)*
Ms. Elizabeth Lyons, Consultant - *Food & beverage, Human resources, Management, Manufacturing (Management), Organizational development*

Functions: Product Dev., Production, Plant Mgmt., Quality, Purchasing, Sales & Mktg., Mktg. Research, Mktg. Mgmt., Customer Svc., HR Mgmt.

Industries: Food, Bev., Tobacco, Chemicals, Plastics, Rubber

Rockwood Associates

PO Box 637
Spring Lake, NJ 07762-0637
(732) 681-2811
Fax: (732) 782-0203
Email: inquiry@rockwoodassociates.com
Web: www.rockwoodassociates.com

Summary: Our firm's functions are: sales, trading, finance, investment analytics and operations. Our industries are: natural gas marketers, refiners, utilities, bank/broker capital markets groups and commodity firms. Our products include: oil, gas, electricity, commodities, financial futures and derivatives.

Key Contact - Specialty:
Mr. Charles R. Bamford, Partner

Salary Minimum: $50,000

Functions: Generalist (All), Risk Mgmt.

Industries: Energy, Utilities, Banking

Rocky Mountain Recruiters Inc

2000 S Colorado Blvd Unit A
Denver, CO 80222-7912
(303) 296-2000
Fax: (303) 296-2223
Email: miket@rmrecruiters.com
Web: www.rmrecruiters.com

Summary: We specialize in placing accounting,
finance, petroleum, and mining professionals.

Key Contact - Specialty:
Mr. Michael Turner, President - *Accounting (Big
4), Finance*
Mr. Joe Sweeney, Senior Recruiter

Salary Minimum: $40,000

Functions: Management, Finance, Geotechnical

Industries: Generalist (All), Energy, Utilities, Oil
& Gas, Construction, Finance

J P Roddy Consultants

258 S 3rd St Ste 101
Philadelphia, PA 19106-3829
(215) 923-6770
Fax: (215) 923-6773
Email: jproddy@aol.com

Summary: Our firm's specialties are automotive
and transportation-related industries, also specialty
chemicals & other manufacturing type firms.
Positions at corporate tech centers include design,
engineering development, purchasing, materials,
and business management. We also place key
positions at manufacturing facilities such as plant
manager, quality, materials, manufacturing &
industrial engineering, and HR.

Key Contact - Specialty:
Mr. Jack P. Roddy, President & Owner -
Automotive, Plastics

Salary Minimum: $45,000

Functions: Middle Mgmt., Product Dev.,
Production, Automation, Plant Mgmt., Quality,
Productivity, Materials, R&D, Engineering

Industries: Plastics, Rubber, Motor Vehicles

J Rodgers & Associates

608 S Washington St Ste 207
Naperville, IL 60540-6657
(630) 961-9143
Fax: (877) 961-9143
Email: info@jrodgers.com
Web: www.jrodgers.com

Summary: Our firm is a boutique recruiting firm.
In keeping with the philosophy of vertical
specialization, our searches are limited to sales,
sales management, pre/post sales support and
marketing. Additionally, we recruit at the
executive level for start-up, pre-IPO companies.
The prime markets we service are printing
equipment, services, packaging, medical, IT and
business-to-business products.

Key Contact - Specialty:
Mr. Roger Bakken, Managing Partner - *Printing*
Ms. Sandy Marie, Recruiter

Salary Minimum: $45,000

Functions: Sales & Mktg.

Industries: Medical Devices, Mgmt. Consulting,
Telecoms, Packaging, Software, Doc. Mgmt.,
Production SW, ERP SW, HR SW, Industry
Specific SW, Security SW

Rodgers, Ramsey Inc

2450 Louisiana St Ste 400
MSC 503
Houston, TX 77006-2318
(713) 529-7010
Fax: (713) 529-2209
Email: gayle@rodgers-ramsey.com
Web: www.rodgers-ramsey.com

Summary: We specialize in employee benefits.
Pension/retirement, health and welfare
professionals are our bread and butter. We are well
known for discretion and results.

Key Contact - Specialty:
Ms. Gayle Rodgers

Salary Minimum: $60,000

Functions: Board Members, Benefits,
Pension/Ret. Planning

Industries: Finance, Invest. Banking, Brokers,
Mutual/Hedge Funds, HR Services, Insurance,
Healthcare

R A Rodriguez and Associates Inc

1326 Henry Brennan Dr
El Paso, TX 79936-6803
(915) 858-1676
Email: rarjobs@jobcareers.com
Web: www.jobcareers.com

Summary: Manufacturing executive search firm
specializing in the search and recruitment of
qualified individuals for manufacturing industries.
Confidentiality is absolutely guaranteed when
required.

Key Contact - Specialty:
Mr. Fred W. Smithson, CPC, Executive Vice
President - *International, Manufacturing*
Ms. Raquel Rodriguez Smithson, President -
International, Manufacturing

Salary Minimum: $40,000

Functions: Management, Senior Mgmt., Mfg.,
Production, Plant Mgmt., Quality, Materials, HR
Mgmt., Engineering, Minorities/Diversity

Industries: Manufacturing

Craig Roe & Associates LLC

3711 Ashley Way Ste A
Owings Mills, MD 21117-1429
(410) 654-6636
Fax: (410) 654-6630
Email: sylvia@craigroeassocs.com
Web: www.craigroeassocs.com

Summary: We assist clients in locating the best
sales talent in the marketplace. We match a
candidate's experience, ability and work ethic to
the requirements and culture of our client
companies.

Key Contact - Specialty:
Ms. Sylvia A. Roe, Vice President -
*Biotechnology, Healthcare, Pharmaceutical,
Sales*
Mr. Craig T. Roe, President - *Sales*

Salary Minimum: $50,000

Functions: Middle Mgmt., Mktg. Mgmt., Sales
Mgmt.

Industries: Drugs Mfg., Medical Devices, Pharm
Svcs., Biotech/Life Sciences, Healthcare

Roevin Technical People Ltd

2002-6860 Century Ave
Mississauga, ON L5N 2W5
Canada
(905) 826-4155
Fax: (905) 826-5336
Email: resumes@roevin.ca
Web: www.roevin.ca

Summary: We are specialists in temp hire and
placement of all levels and disciplines of technical
and engineering personnel.

Key Contact - Specialty:
Mr. Ian Wright, President

Functions: Generalist (All), Product Dev.,
Production, Automation, Plant Mgmt., Quality,
Productivity, Engineering

Industries: Generalist (All), Energy, Utilities,
Construction, Manufacturing, Chemicals, Drugs
Mfg., Plastics, Rubber

Branches:
1160-10303 Jasper Ave NW
Metropolitan Place
Edmonton, AB T5J 3N6
Canada
(780) 420-6232
Fax: (780) 423-3679
Email: edmonton@roevin.ca
Key Contact - Specialty:
Mr. David Shea

411-265 Front St N
265 North Front
Sarnia, ON N7T 7X1
Canada
(519) 383-6630
Fax: (519) 383-6631
Email: sarnia@roevin.ca
Key Contact - Specialty:
Mr. Steve Thomson, President
Ms. Melanie Thomson, Vice President

The Rogan Group Inc

20 Crossroads Dr Ste 115
Owings Mills, MD 21117-5480
(443) 394-8100
Fax: (443) 394-8102
Email: recruiting@rogangroup.com
Web: www.rogangroup.com

Summary: We are a recruiting firm specializing in
the risk and insurance management-recruiting
field. We have extensive insurance experience in
addition to search background. Specialty area
would include insurance brokerage production and
management positions.

Key Contact - Specialty:
Mr. Daniel Rogan, President
Mr. John McGraw, Account Manager
Ms. Janet Gunzelman, Senior Consultant
Mr. Leonard Levin, Senior Consultant
Ms. Barbara Vincent, Database Manager
Ms. Gaye Rogan, Research
Ms. Shell Simonson, Senior Consultant
Mr. Michael Gilbert, Senior Consultant
Mrs. Beth Carson, Senior Consultant -
Engineering, Marketing

Salary Minimum: $50,000

Functions: Generalist (All), Middle Mgmt.,
Health Admin., Sales & Mktg., Sales Mgmt.,
CFOs, M&A, MIS Mgmt.

Industries: Generalist (All), Banking, Misc.
Financial, Insurance, Healthcare

Branches:
19010 Peninsula Club Dr
Cornelius, NC 28031-5120
(704) 895-8488
Key Contact - Specialty:
Mr. Neil Huson, Senior Consultant

Gene Rogers Associates Inc

13211 SW 32nd Ct
Davie, FL 33330-4604
(954) 476-0221
(305) 476-0221
Fax: (954) 476-8437
Email: grogers190@aol.com
Web: www.generogers.com

Summary: We are specialists in banking, trust, investments and mortgages. Our professionals are eminently qualified to assist you in identifying key individuals needed for your organization or to assist those who are seeking a new career opportunity.

Key Contact - Specialty:
Ms. Rosa Rogers, Vice President - *International*
Ms. Adrianne Austin, Secretary
Mr. Gene Rogers, Jr., Vice President - *Banking, Banking (Commercial,Corporate,Investment,Merchant)*
Ms. Luz Lopez, Senior Associate - *Banking, Trust*
Mr. Gene Rogers, Sr., President - *Banking, Banking (Commercial,Corporate,Investment,Merchant)*

Salary Minimum: $25,000

Functions: Senior Mgmt., Mktg. Mgmt., HR Mgmt., Finance, Cash Mgmt., Pension/Ret. Planning, Int'l.

Industries: Banking, Invest. Banking, Brokers, Venture Cap., Mutual/Hedge Funds, Misc. Financial, Compliance

Branches:
444 Brickell Ave Ste 51-367
Miami, FL 33131-2403
(305) 476-0221
Fax: (954) 476-8437
Email: grogers190@aol.com
Key Contact - Specialty:
Mr. Gene Rogers

Rogers Employment Group Inc

PO Box 8878
Amarillo, TX 79114-8878
(806) 358-8676
(806) 358-7422
Fax: (806) 358-7473
Web: www.rogersemploymentgroup.com

Summary: Our firms are all under one roof to provide a full service agency.

Key Contact - Specialty:
Ms. Doris Rogers, President
Mr. Lee Studer, Manager, Sales - *Engineering, Industrial, Manufacturing, Wholesale*

Functions: Senior Mgmt., Mfg., Healthcare, Sales & Mktg., Finance, IT, Engineering, Non-profits, Legal

Industries: Generalist (All)

Roll International

7171 Helsem Bnd # 11
Dallas, TX 75230-1946
(972) 239-3800
Email: mroll@rollintl.com
Web: www.rollintl.com

Summary: We are specialist in board of director assignments. We also handle mid to upper-level executive ERP, supply chain management, customer relationship management, enterprise commerce management, private trading exchange, knowledge management recruitment encompassing leadership in operations, consulting, sales, marketing, implementation, software development and pre/post-IPO.

Key Contact - Specialty:
Mr. M.A. Roll, President - *International*

Salary Minimum: $60,000

Functions: Board Members, Senior Mgmt., Middle Mgmt., Materials Plng., Sales Mgmt., Finance, IT, Systems Analysis, Systems Implem., Mgmt. Consultants

Industries: Generalist (All), Venture Cap., Mgmt. Consulting, E-commerce, IT Implementation, PSA/ASP, Call Centers, Software, ERP SW

Rollins & Associates

4010 Watson Plaza Dr Ste 105
Lakewood, CA 90712-4035
(562) 421-6649
Fax: (562) 421-8918
Email: info@rollins-associates.com
Web: www.rollins-associates.com

Summary: We are global trade and logistics specialists. Searches have been conducted for importers/exporters including import/export compliance, logistics management, and support staff/bilingual employees. We also service customs brokerages, freight forwarders, ocean carriers, warehouse/distribution companies, and trucking companies. Searches are handled on a nationwide basis.

Key Contact - Specialty:
Ms. Joan E. Rollins, President - *Compliance, Exports, International, Logistics, Supply Chain*

Salary Minimum: $30,000

Functions: Management, Middle Mgmt., Purchasing, Distribution, Sales & Mktg., Finance

Industries: Textiles, Apparel, Drugs Mfg., Consumer Elect., Consumer Goods, Transportation, Wholesale, Accounting, Logistics Svcs., Supply Chain Mgmt

Romano McAvoy Associates Inc

872 Middle Country Rd
Saint James, NY 11780-3223
(631) 265-7878
(888) 316-6624
Fax: (631) 265-1252
Email: mike@mcavoysearch.com
Web: www.mcavoysearch.com

Summary: Networked with other quality and responsive recruiting firms with extensive job listing database.

Key Contact - Specialty:
Mr. Edward P. McAvoy, Vice President

Salary Minimum: $40,000

Functions: Generalist (All), Production, Quality, Purchasing, PR, Benefits, Systems Dev.

Industries: Generalist (All), Computer Equip., Consumer Elect., Aerospace, Software

Romeo Consulting

309 Fellowship Rd Ste 210
Mount Laurel, NJ 08054-1234
(856) 665-3466
(856) 642-4054
Email: promeo@romeoexecutivesearch.com
Web: www.romeoexecutivesearch.com

Summary: Our firm is nationwide, specializing in the recruitment and placement of middle to upper level professionals for the biotechnology and pharmaceutical industries. Our specialties include: clinical research, drug safety, medical affairs, regulatory affairs, QA/GCP compliance, marketing and drug discovery.

Key Contact - Specialty:
Mr. Paul C. Romeo, President - *Biotechnology, Pharmaceutical, Physicians, Research & development*

Salary Minimum: $100,000

Functions: Middle Mgmt., Product Dev., Quality, Physicians, Mktg. Mgmt., R&D

Industries: Drugs Mfg., Biotech/Life Sciences

Rooney Personnel Company

266 Elm St
Birmingham, MI 48009-6337
(248) 765-4073
(800) 755-5888
Fax: (248) 258-5671
Email: mikehri@yahoo.com
Web: www.careers-hri.com

Summary: Our firm has the technology to locate managers in any industry fast and affordably. We have extensive experience in recruiting successful candidates and retaining clients in the hospitality, restaurant, hotel, country club, golf and retail industries.

Key Contact - Specialty:
Mr. Michael Rooney, President - *Hospitality, Retail*
Mr. John Rooney - *Hospitality, Retail*
Mr. Ryan Rooney, Recruiter

Salary Minimum: $25,000

Functions: Generalist (All), Middle Mgmt., Mktg. Mgmt.

Industries: Generalist (All), Retail, Hospitality, Hotels, Resorts, Clubs, Restaurants

WR Rosato & Associates LLC

6 Commerce Dr Fl 3
Cranford, NJ 07016-3515
(908) 709-1133
Fax: (908) 709-1477
Email: wrrinc@aol.com
Web: www.wrrosato.com

Summary: We have search experience dedicated to the support of the investment banking, broker dealer and hedge fund community. We have expertise in information technology, quantitative analysis and risk management. Our firm places a specific emphasis on Derivative instruments.

Key Contact - Specialty:
Mr. William R. Rosato, Principal - *Financial services*
Mr. Frank M. Colasanto, Principal - *Financial services*
Mr. Jack Federman, Director, Research & Recruitment
Mrs. Andrea Maloney, Manager, Business

Salary Minimum: $150,000

Functions: Risk Mgmt., IT, MIS Mgmt.

Industries: Finance, Banking, Invest. Banking, Mutual/Hedge Funds, Misc. Financial

The Rose Search Group Inc

11353 Olde Turnbury Ct
Charlotte, NC 28277-6519
(704) 752-5100
(704) 752-5771
Email: jim.rosenberger@rosesearch.com
Web: www.rosesearch.com

Summary: Clinical and support management positions throughout the healthcare industry including physician placement management,

managed care, PHO/MSO, long-term care and hospitals.

Key Contact - Specialty:
Mr. Jim Rosenberger, President - *Healthcare*

Salary Minimum: $50,000

Functions: Generalist (All), Management, Healthcare

Industries: Medical Devices, Pharm Svcs., Healthcare, Hospitals, Long-term/Home Care, Dental, Physical Therapy, Occupational Therapy, Women's, Non-Classifiable

Susan Rosenstein Executive Search Limited

211 E Ontario St Ste 1575
Chicago, IL 60611-3297
(312) 266-7700
Email: info@srosenstein.com
Web: www.srosenstein.com

Summary: Our firm specializes in the recruitment of middle to senior level executives in the functional areas of marketing, marketing research, strategy, consumer promotions, marketing communications and public relations.

Key Contact - Specialty:
Ms. Susan Rosenstein, Owner & President - *Communications, Marketing*

Salary Minimum: $100,000

Functions: Middle Mgmt., Sales & Mktg., Mktg. Research, Mktg. Mgmt., Direct Mktg., PR

Industries: Generalist (All), Food, Bev., Tobacco, Soap, Perf., Cosmtcs., Consumer Goods, Services

Keith Ross & Associates Inc

490 E Roosevelt Rd Ste 203
West Chicago, IL 60185-3901
(630) 293-4000
Fax: (630) 293-9800
Email: lawyers@keithross.com
Web: www.keithross.com

Summary: We focus exclusively on the recruitment and placement of attorneys who specialize in intellectual property, patent, trademark and copyright law including litigation.

Key Contact - Specialty:
Mr. Keith Ross, President
Mr. Christian Vaughn, Director, Legal Search

Functions: Legal, Attorneys

Industries: Energy, Utilities, Manufacturing, Legal, Law Enforcement, Communications, Software, Biotech/Life Sciences, Healthcare

David Ross Associates Inc

231 North Ave W
Westfield, NJ 07090-1482
(908) 889-6459
Email: david_rien@hotmail.com

Summary: We specialize in the recruitment and placement of real estate investment management.

Key Contact - Specialty:
Mr. David Rien, President

Salary Minimum: $50,000

Functions: Generalist (All), IT, Systems Analysis, Systems Dev., Systems Implem., Systems Support, Network Admin., DB Admin.

Industries: Generalist (All), Invest. Banking, Real Estate

Ross Consulting International

630 Freedom Business Ctr Dr Ste 314
King of Prussia, PA 19406-1331
(610) 768-7735
Email: rossconsultingintl@erols.com
Web: www.rcisearch.com

Summary: We are a leading insurance and financial services executive search firm. Our insurance clients include group, individual, retirement and other businesses. Our recruiting concentration extends across all business areas.

Key Contact - Specialty:
Mr. Adam Ross, Managing Partner, Global Recruiting
Mr. Michael Blumberg, Manager, Candidate Research & Dev

Salary Minimum: $50,000

Functions: Generalist (All)

Industries: Finance, Banking, Invest. Banking, Brokers, Venture Cap., Misc. Financial, Services, Mgmt. Consulting, Insurance

Ross Personnel Consultants Inc

161 East Ave Ste 105
Norwalk, CT 06851-5710
(203) 866-2033
Email: info@rossconsultants.net
Web: www.rossconsultants.net

Summary: An executive search and recruiting firm specializing in sales, marketing, systems, training, field engineering and general management in the computer, telecom and copier industries.

Key Contact - Specialty:
Mr. Anthony J. Barca, President - *Sales*
Mrs. Tracy A. Franzen, Associate - *Sales*
Ms. Dana Tarzia, Research Specialist - *Sales*

Salary Minimum: $40,000

Functions: Product Dev., Sales & Mktg., Mktg. Mgmt., Sales Mgmt., Systems Dev.

Industries: Computer Equip.

Rossi & Associates Inc

1400-1500 Georgia St W
Crown Life Place
Vancouver, BC V6G 2Z6
Canada
(604) 683-3755
Email: hr@rossipeople.com
Web: www.rossipeople.com

Summary: We are specialists in the recruitment of business-to-business sales executives to a cross section of industries, including but not limited to IT, telecom and printing. Positions are from president to general business-to-business teams.

Key Contact - Specialty:
Ms. Donna Rossi, President - *Sales*

Salary Minimum: $40,000

Functions: Sales & Mktg., Sales Mgmt.

Industries: Construction, Computer Equip., Semiconductors, Media, Communications, Telecoms, Digital, Wireless, Network Infrastructure, Environmental Svcs., Software

Roster Technologies Inc

6209 Constitution Dr
Fort Wayne, IN 46804-1517
(260) 436-6330
Fax: (260) 432-7126
Email: roster1@rosternetwork.com
Web: www.rosternetwork.com

Summary: We are extremely automated and research driven. To assure constant quality, we use

and teach the Position Matrix (TM), which is a tool identifying, placing and evaluating employees.

Key Contact - Specialty:
Mr. Steve Trimarchi, Operations Manager
Mr. John King, President
Mr. Dennis Payne, Vice President
Mr. Martin Maisonneuve, Executive Recruiter

Functions: Generalist (All), Management, Mfg., HR Mgmt., Finance

Industries: Generalist (All)

Rostie & Associates Inc

1205-20 Bay St
WaterPark Place
Toronto, ON M5J 2N8
Canada
(416) 777-0780
Fax: (416) 777-0451
Email: rostie@rostie.com
Web: www.rostie.com

Summary: Our firm was formed to provide superior placement services for high technology companies requiring highly skilled professionals. We assist our client companies in their growth and success by maintaining a high standard of industry knowledge, along with practices and ethics that foster long term business relationships.

Key Contact - Specialty:
Ms. Cynthia Rostie, President

Salary Minimum: $50,000

Functions: Generalist (All)

Industries: Computer Equip., Consumer Elect., E-commerce, IT Implementation, Telecoms, Digital, Wireless, Fiber Optic, Network Infrastructure, Software

Branches:
28 9th St Apt 205
Medford, MA 02155-5140
(617) 350-6350
(800) 647-0780
Fax: (416) 777-0451
Email: rostie@rostie.com

Patricia Roth International

2682 NE 135th St
North Miami, FL 33181-3517
(305) 940-9130
Fax: (305) 940-8572
Email: rothint2@aol.com
Web: www.rothinternational.com

Summary: We are specific to the construction and mining equipment industries. Our experience in providing highly qualified personnel for the manufacturers and dealers, enables our clients to place the responsibility of locating their new employee in our hands.

Key Contact - Specialty:
Ms. Patricia Roth, President

Functions: Senior Mgmt., Middle Mgmt., Mktg. Mgmt., Sales Mgmt., CFOs, Engineering, Int'l.

Industries: Agri., Forestry, Mining, Construction

Roth Young

3087 Carson Ave
Murrysville, PA 15668-1814
(724) 733-5900
Fax: (724) 733-0183
Email: rothyoungpit@cs.com
Web: www.rothyoung.com

Summary: Specialists in healthcare, supermarket and hospitality industries. Healthcare placements: physicians.

Key Contact - Specialty:
Mr. Len Di Naples, President - *Healthcare, Hospitality*

Salary Minimum: $25,000

Functions: Generalist (All), Management, Senior Mgmt., Middle Mgmt.

Industries: Generalist (All), Food, Bev., Tobacco, Wholesale, Retail, Hospitality

Roth Young

(also known as DWS Inc)
PO Box 3307
305 111th Ave
Bellevue, WA 98009-3307
(425) 455-2141
(425) 455-2142
Fax: (425) 455-0067
Email: rothyoung@wolfenet.com
Web: www.rothyoung.com

Summary: Our commitment to excellence, understanding our clients business & staff requirements and creating a sphere of mutual respect, has enabled us to develop many long standing relationships with companies who appreciate the value of using recruiters for their top management positions.

Key Contact - Specialty:
Mr. David Salzberg, President - *Food, Hospitality, Manufacturing, Sales*
Mr. Robert Richardson, Vice President - *Financial services*

Salary Minimum: $40,000

Functions: Management, Senior Mgmt., Middle Mgmt., Plant Mgmt.

Industries: Generalist (All), Manufacturing, Food, Bev., Tobacco, Lumber, Furniture, Paper, Soap, Perf., Cosmtcs., Drugs Mfg., Paints, Petro. Products, Consumer Elect., Wholesale, Retail, Services, Non-profits, Accounting, Hospitality, Hotels, Resorts, Clubs, Restaurants, Quick Service Restaurants, Full Service Restaurants, Inst./Industrial Food Svc.

Roth Young Exec Search

(formerly known as Roth Young of Milwaukee)
5215 N Ironwood Ln Ste 201
Milwaukee, WI 53217-4908
(414) 962-7684
Fax: (414) 962-6261
Email: rothyoung@execpc.com
Web: www.rothyoungmilwaukee.com

Summary: We are a leading national executive search firm specializing exclusively in the recruitment and placement of executive, managerial and technical professionals within the food related industries to include food ingredients & technology, food manufacturing and food sales & marketing.

Key Contact - Specialty:
Mr. Thomas E. Brenneman, President & Chief Executive Officer - *Food, General management, Marketing, Sales, Technical*
Ms. Kay S. Boxer, Vice President - *Food, Marketing, Operations, Sales, Technical*

Salary Minimum: $50,000

Functions: Generalist (All), Management, Mfg., Materials, Sales & Mktg., HR Mgmt., R&D, Engineering

Industries: Generalist (All), Food, Bev., Tobacco, Non-Classifiable

Roth Young Jacksonville

(also known as AJ CONSULTANTS,INC.)
6 Live Oak Ln
Palm Coast, FL 32137-8003
(800) 821-9222
(386) 446-0237
Fax: (800) 339-3465
Email: acapece2@cfl.rr.com
Web: www.rothyoung.com

Summary: We are an executive search firm specializing in management positions in accounting, finance, retail, hospitality and food manufacturing.

Key Contact - Specialty:
Ms. Joyce Capece, President
Mr. Anthony F. Capece, Chief Executive Officer - *Finance, Hospitality, Retail*

Salary Minimum: $55,000

Functions: Generalist (All), Management, Senior Mgmt., Mktg. Research, Customer Svc., Finance

Industries: Construction, Manufacturing, Food, Bev., Tobacco, Textiles, Apparel, Wholesale, Retail, Finance, Banking, Pharm Svcs., Accounting, Mgmt. Consulting, HR Services, Hospitality, Hotels, Resorts, Clubs, Restaurants, Quick Service Restaurants, Full Service Restaurants

Roth Young of Houston

11999 Katy Fwy Ste 535
Houston, TX 77079-1612
(281) 368-8550
Fax: (281) 368-8560
Email: opportunity@rothyounghouston.com
Web: www.rothyounghouston.com

Summary: With extensive years in operation, we have grown to a staff of four recruiters and two recruiter assistants with operations in restaurant & hospitality, grocery wholesale & retail, retail (non-food) and food & beverage processing.

Key Contact - Specialty:
Mr. Ray Schorejs, Vice President
Mr. Bob O'Dell, Vice President - *Distribution, Retail, Supply Chain, Transportation*
Mr. Jim Hillier, Vice President - *Hospitality, Marketing, Restaurants*
Ms. Sherry Schorejs, Executive Assistant - *Distribution, Food service, Supply Chain, Transportation, Wholesale*

Salary Minimum: $50,000

Functions: Generalist (All), Senior Mgmt., Middle Mgmt., Distribution, Sales & Mktg.

Industries: Generalist (All), Food, Bev., Tobacco, Soap, Perf., Cosmtcs., Drugs Mfg., Consumer Goods, Transportation, Wholesale, Retail, Accounting, Hospitality, Restaurants, Inst./Industrial Food Svc., Advertising, Packaging

Roth Young of Long Island

PO Box 7365
Hicksville, NY 11802-7261
(516) 822-6000
Fax: (516) 822-6018
Email: careers@rothyoung-li.com
Web: www.rothyoung-li.com

Summary: Specialists in accounting, banking, food industry, healthcare, hospitality, HR, marketing, operations, retail, sales and technology.

Key Contact - Specialty:
Mr. George T. Jung, President - *Healthcare, Hospitality*

Functions: Senior Mgmt., Middle Mgmt., Mktg. Mgmt., Sales Mgmt., HR Mgmt., Finance

Industries: Food, Bev., Tobacco, Retail, Finance, Banking, Accounting, Hospitality, Communications, Telecoms, Software, Healthcare

Roth Young of Minneapolis

6212 Vernon Ct S
Minneapolis, MN 55436-1669
(952) 831-6655
Fax: (952) 831-7413
Email: info@rymn.com
Web: www.rymn.com

Summary: We are a nationwide recruiting franchise with offices coast-to-coast, filling professional and managerial positions in the retail and supermarket industries. Our highly trained and experienced recruiters specialize in the retail and supermarket industries. Not only do we refer qualified individuals, we also keep you apprised of industry trends.

Key Contact - Specialty:
Mr. Donald B. Spahr, President

Salary Minimum: $40,000

Functions: Generalist (All), Management, Product Dev., Purchasing, Distribution, Advertising, Sales Mgmt., Direct Mktg., HR Mgmt., Textile/Fashion

Industries: Wholesale, Retail

Roth Young of Philadelphia

188 Liberty Way
Woodbury, NJ 08096-6822
(856) 384-4774
Fax: (856) 384-8074
Email: rothyoungphl@comcast.net
Web: www.rothyoung.com

Summary: We are an executive recruiting firm specializing in all aspects of the food, hospitality and consumer packaged goods industry.

Key Contact - Specialty:
Mr. Paul Sundstrom, President - *Hospitality*
Mr. Andy Sundstrom, Director
Mr. Dieter Sievers, Director

Salary Minimum: $40,000

Functions: Generalist (All), Management, Mfg., Materials, Sales & Mktg., HR Mgmt., Finance, IT, Engineering

Industries: Food, Bev., Tobacco, Hospitality, Hotels, Resorts, Clubs, Restaurants

Rowland Mountain & Associates

2600 Century Pkwy NE Ste 120
Atlanta, GA 30345-3104
(404) 325-2189
Fax: (404) 321-1842
Email: mail@rmasales.com
Web: www.rmasales.com

Summary: Our firm has become an industry leader in sales and sales management recruitment consulting. The steadily increasing demand for our services is a result of our innovative use of leading edge technologies and a partnership driven, win-win business approach with our clients and candidates alike. We are committed to providing superior quality applicants and service to our clients while building a professional reputation and friendship with everyone we encounter.

Key Contact - Specialty:
Mr. Russell D. Mountain, CPC, President - *Marketing, Sales*
Ms. Tricia A. Mountain, CPC, Vice President - *Marketing, Sales*

Salary Minimum: $50,000

Functions: Sales & Mktg., Mktg. Mgmt., Sales Mgmt.

Industries: Generalist (All)

Rowlette Executive Search

6025 Frantz Rd
Dublin, OH 43017-1302
(614) 799-2311
Fax: (614) 799-0219
Email: prowlette@rowlette.net

Summary: Our firm specializes in the securities industry, with a major emphasis in recruiting investment brokers.

Key Contact - Specialty:
Ms. Patti S. Rowlette, President
Mr. Rob Blevins, Managing Director & EVP

Salary Minimum: $100,000

Functions: Generalist (All)

Industries: Brokers

Royal Associates & Royal Staffing Services

14011 Ventura Blvd Ste 214W
Sherman Oaks, CA 91423-5220
(818) 981-1080
Fax: (818) 981-1338
Email: consultants@royalstaff.com
Web: www.royalstaff.com

Summary: We have the capability, resources and experienced staff to successfully fill requirements for quality personnel. A state-of-the-art industry-specific search and retrieval system allows access to all employers stored in the database.

Key Contact - Specialty:
Ms. Gail Sullivan, Recruiter - *Human resources, Management*
Ms. Rosemarie Wolff, Recruiter

Salary Minimum: $45,000

Functions: Management, Mfg., Product Dev., Production, Materials, Purchasing, Health Admin., Sales & Mktg., HR Mgmt., Finance

Industries: Generalist (All)

Branches:
3625 E Thousand Oaks Blvd Ste 245
Westlake Village, CA 91362-3572
(805) 373-9909
(818) 889-8689
Fax: (805) 494-4365
Key Contact - Specialty:
Mr. Joe Cummings, Vice President

Royce Ashland Group Inc

1 Rossmoor Dr
Monroe Township, NJ 08831-1566
(609) 409-3601
Fax: (609) 409-3606
Email: royceashland@verizon.net
Web: www.royceashland.com

Summary: We have several divisions that represent major corporations throughout the USA who are looking for the following candidates: banking professionals, investment advisors, financial consultants, sales/marketing professionals, systems people, IT professionals, healthcare technologist and physicians.

Key Contact - Specialty:
Mr. Ronald Cali, CPC, President - *Printing*

Salary Minimum: $65,000

Functions: Management, Board Members, Healthcare, Sales & Mktg., IT

Industries: Printing, Computer Equip., Brokers, Mutual/Hedge Funds, Misc. Financial, Equip Svcs., Telecoms, Software, Healthcare

RS&A

(formerly known as Rathbun, Sapir & Associates)
PO Box 2337
Sedona, AZ 86339-2337
(928) 203-0074
Email: rsa@sedona.net

Summary: We work with client companies in the pharmaceutical, biopharma, API and medical diagnostics industries. Most often, our clients ask us to find the best-qualified candidates for scientific and executive positions in arenas such as R&D, pilot, regulatory, operations and clinical research.

Key Contact - Specialty:
Ms. Basirah N. Al'Basit, Managing Director - *Biopharmaceutical, Biotechnology, Quality, Research & development, Science*
Ms. Ann Rathbun

Salary Minimum: $50,000

Functions: Board Members, Middle Mgmt., Mfg., Product Dev., Quality, Physicians, Nurses, R&D, Engineering, Technicians

Industries: Chemicals, Drugs Mfg., Medical Devices, Pharm Svcs., Industry Specific SW, Mfg. SW, Biotech/Life Sciences, Non-Classifiable

RSM McGladrey Inc -South Florida HR Consulting

(formerly known as Berke-Durant Assoc)
100 NE 3rd Ave Ste 300
Fort Lauderdale, FL 33301-1193
(954) 462-6351
Fax: (954) 462-4607
Email: marilyndurant@rsmi.com
Web: www.rsmmcgladrey.com

Summary: Executive recruiting services: management positions specializing in HR, IT, finance, sales, marketing and customer service. Project recruiting - multiple positions and locations: customer service, call centers, sales; also, outplacement, coaching and HR consulting services.

Key Contact - Specialty:
Mr. Michael P. Berke, President - *Sales*
Ms. Marilyn C. Durant, SPHR, Chief Operating Officer & Vice President - *Human resources*

Salary Minimum: $50,000

Functions: Generalist (All), Management, Mktg. Mgmt., HR Mgmt., Finance

Industries: Generalist (All), Manufacturing, Retail, Finance, Services

Branches:
1555 Palm Beach Lakes Blvd Ste 1400
West Palm Beach, FL 33401-2327
(561) 712-4808
Key Contact - Specialty:
Ms. Kathleen O'Rourke

RSM Richter

(formerly known as Richter Professional Search)
1000-200 King St W
Sun Life Building
Toronto, ON M5H 3T4
Canada
(416) 932-8000
(888) 805-1793
Fax: (416) 932-6200
Email: torinfo@rsmrichter.com
Web: www.richter.ca

Summary: Specialize in the recruitment of financial, accounting and administrative personnel at all levels. Specialize in placing candidates in entrepreneurial environments.

Key Contact - Specialty:
Ms. Caroline Freedman, Director, Human Resources

Salary Minimum: $30,000

Functions: Senior Mgmt., Middle Mgmt., Admin. Svcs., HR Mgmt., Finance

Industries: Generalist (All), Accounting

RTR Associates Inc

12443 San Jose Blvd Ste 803
Jacksonville, FL 32223-8654
(904) 880-1122
Fax: (904) 880-1170
Email: reiss@rtrassociates.com
Web: www.rtrassociates.com

Summary: A contingency search firm that specializes in the homebuilding and real estate development industries. Positions filled include: executive management, construction, land acquisition/development, estimating, purchasing, sales, marketing, customer service, finance/accounting, office support, operations, warranty, and architecture/design.

Key Contact - Specialty:
Mr. Reiss Tatum, President & Chief Executive Officer - *C-level, Construction, Real estate*
Mr. Hank Heinold, Managing Director - *C-level, Construction, Real estate*
Mr. Gary Ackley, Executive Recruiter - *C-level, Construction, Real estate*
Mr. Luke Poynter, Associate, Recruiting - *Construction, Real estate*
Ms. Cathie Tatum, Director, Marketing - *Construction, Real estate*

Salary Minimum: $35,000

Functions: Generalist (All), Admin. Svcs.

Industries: Construction, Real Estate

RTX Inc

9000 E Nichols Ave Ste 140
Centennial, CO 80112-3406
(877) 904-1600
(303) 904-1600
Fax: (303) 904-1700
Email: contact@rtxstaffing.com
Web: www.rtx-inc.com

Summary: Our firm does quality-driven recruiting for engineering, design, construction management and related positions. We place key engineering talent within the petrochemical, pharmaceutical, bio-technologynical and power & utility markets. We place people on both a permanent and contract basis.

Key Contact - Specialty:
Ms. Cathie Wilkerson, Manager, Business Account & Recruiter - *Design, Engineering, Instrumentation, Safety*

Salary Minimum: $40,000

Functions: Production, Plant Mgmt., Quality, Engineering

Industries: Energy, Utilities, Oil & Gas, Construction, Food, Bev., Tobacco, Drugs Mfg., Pharm Svcs., Engineering Svcs., RF/Microwave, Government, Compliance, Biotech/Life Sciences

Ruderfer & Associates Inc

908 Pompton Ave Ste A2
Cedar Grove, NJ 07009-1263
(973) 857-2400
Fax: (973) 857-4343

Summary: We place manufacturing, healthcare, sales & marketing, HR management, finance, MIS management and R&D professionals in all industries.

Key Contact - Specialty:
Mr. Irwin A. Ruderfer, CPC, President
Ms. Nan Kanoff, Director, Physician & Biopharm
Mr. Richard Levy, Director, Financial & MIS
Ms. Alice Osur, Manager, Marketing
Mr. Harold Tapler, Recruiter - *Quality, Technical*
Dr. Louise Greenberg, Recruiter
Ms. Pauline Hamilton, Recruiter

Salary Minimum: $50,000

Functions: Generalist (All), Mfg., Healthcare, Sales & Mktg., HR Mgmt., Finance, MIS Mgmt., R&D

Industries: Generalist (All), Chemicals, Drugs Mfg., Medical Devices, Accounting, HR Services, Advertising, Biotech/Life Sciences

Susan Rudich

20 E 9th St
New York, NY 10003-5944
(212) 228-8126
(212) 989-7891

Summary: Extensive experience, lecturer, advisor art schools and associations. Former New York state sole textile placement specialist. There is a heavy emphasis on home furnishings as well.

Key Contact - Specialty:
Ms. Susan Rudich, President - *Design*

Salary Minimum: $25,000

Functions: Graphic Designers

Industries: Textiles, Apparel

Louis Rudzinsky Associates Inc

PO Box 640
Lexington, MA 02420-0006
(781) 862-6727
Fax: (781) 862-6868
Email: lra@lra.com
Web: www.lra.com

Summary: Our firm serves technology companies in optics, electronics, electro-optics, fiber optics, software, systems, solid state devices and instrumentation. Covering engineering, R&D, marketing, sales and general management.

Key Contact - Specialty:
Mr. Howard Rudzinsky, Senior Vice President - *Optics, Photonics*
Mr. Jeff Rudzinsky, Senior Vice President - *Computers (Software), Hardware, Systems*

Salary Minimum: $40,000

Functions: Generalist (All), Board Members, Product Dev., Production, Systems Analysis, Systems Dev., Systems Implem., R&D, Engineering

Industries: Generalist (All), Medical Devices, Computer Equip., Test, Measure Equip., Electronic, Elec. Components, Robotics, Semiconductors, Engineering Svcs., Fiber Optic, RF/Microwave, Defense, Software, Database SW, Development SW, Mfg. SW, Networking, Comm. SW, System SW

Thomas Ruff Company

1219 Morningside Dr
Manhattan Beach, CA 90266-4769
(310) 802-1496
Fax: (310) 802-1396
Email: sharilee@tomruff.com
Web: www.tomruff.com

Summary: Our firm specializes exclusively in pharmaceutical, biotechnology and medical sales, and sales management recruitment.

Key Contact - Specialty:
Ms. Sharon Patrick, Executive Recruiter, Southern Californa - *Biomedical, Medical (Devices,Sales), Pharmaceutical*
Ms. Tammy Rothschild, Executive Recruiter, Southern Californa - *Biomedical, Medical (Devices,Sales), Pharmaceutical*
Ms. Erica S. Basta, Executive Recruiter, Northern California - *Biomedical, Medical (Devices,Sales), Pharmaceutical*
Ms. Susan Kenner, National Accounts Recruiter - *Biomedical, Medical (Devices,Sales), Pharmaceutical*
Ms. Shari Lee Douglas, Operations Manager - *Operations*

Functions: Sales Mgmt., Sales Reps.

Industries: Drugs Mfg., Medical Devices, Pharm Svcs., Hospitals, Dental

Branches:
1 Market St Fl 36
San Francisco, CA 94105-1420
(415) 665-6611
Email: ericas@tomruff.com
Key Contact - Specialty:
Mr. Tom Ruff, President & Chief Executive Officer - *Biomedical, Biopharmaceutical, Medical (Devices,Sales), Pharmaceutical*

Rush Personnel Service

229 Coventry Ln
East Peoria, IL 61611-1820
(309) 699-4184
Email: randall@rushpersonnel.com
Web: www.rushpersonnel.com

Summary: We are a generalist supplying qualified, pre-screened candidates to select client companies to satisfy their management and technical needs.

Key Contact - Specialty:
Mr. Randall Rush, CPC, Owner

Salary Minimum: $35,000

Functions: Generalist (All)

Industries: Generalist (All)

The Russell Group

23 North Ave E
Cranford, NJ 07016-2196
(908) 709-1188
Fax: (908) 709-0959
Email: bill.russell@russellgrp.com
Web: www.russellgrp.com

Summary: Our firm is an executive search firm specializing in the placement of sales and sales management professionals in the pharmaceutical and medical industries. The firm is known for limiting their representation to only top tier companies and is likewise extremely selective in the candidates they represent.

Key Contact - Specialty:
Mr. William Russell, President

Salary Minimum: $40,000

Functions: Board Members, Sales & Mktg.

Industries: Generalist (All), Drugs Mfg., Medical Devices, Marketing SW, Biotech/Life Sciences, Healthcare

K Russo Associates Inc

300 Main St Ste 401
Stamford, CT 06901-3033
(203) 978-1004
Email: solutions@krussoassociates.com
Web: www.krussoassociates.com

Summary: We are a specialist firm focusing on executive search in the HR and public relations arena. The firm also offers HR consulting including competency modeling and organizational analysis.

Key Contact - Specialty:
Ms. Karen Russo, Principal - *Human resources, Marketing, Public relations*
Ms. Julie Wilson, Operations Manager
Ms. Kathleen Gallagher, Consultant, Recruiting - *Human resources*

Salary Minimum: $60,000

Functions: Generalist (All), PR, HR Mgmt., Benefits, Staffing, Training

Industries: Generalist (All), Manufacturing, Food, Bev., Tobacco, Finance, HR Services, Hospitality, Media, Advertising

RWK & Associates

PO Box 917523
Longwood, FL 32791-7523
(407) 774-9004
Fax: (407) 774-0966
Email: rwkassociates@mindspring.com

Summary: Experienced executive recruiter/researcher. We are generalists with special expertise in senior executive positions. Establishing relationships with colleagues in conducting research projects.

Key Contact - Specialty:
Ms. Rona Kaplan

Salary Minimum: $50,000

Functions: Generalist (All)

Industries: Construction, Chemicals, Drugs Mfg., Misc. Financial, Pharm Svcs., Accounting, HR Services, Insurance, Biotech/Life Sciences, Healthcare

Ryan Executive Search & Outplacement

2 Ave Ponce De Leon Ste 1615
San Juan, PR 00918-1620
(787) 766-1666
Fax: (787) 766-1467
Email: ryan@isla.net
Web: www.ryanrecruiters.com

Summary: We are a full-service recruiting firm of certified personnel consultants; executive search, headhunters, recruiters, management consultants, bilingual executives, outplacement, employment, occupation, jobs, work, service, positions, English/Spanish professionals, careers, candidates, hire, global experience, career change, benchmarking, personnel, outsourcing, technology, manufacturing, finance, HR, sales, marketing, nurses and engineers.

Key Contact - Specialty:
Ms. Evelyn Ryan, CPC, Chief Executive Officer - *Management*
Mr. Terence L. Ryan, President - *Sales*
Ms. Elisa Favale, CPC, Partner & Senior Employment Consultant - *Finance, Hospitality, Human resources*
Ms. Madeline Figueroa, Partner & Senior Consultant

Ms. Cathy Ryan, Vice President, Admin &
Employment Cnslt - *Administration, Computers,
Engineering, Manufacturing, Office
(Administration)*
Ms. Mildred Oliveras, Senior Engineering
Consultant

Salary Minimum: $20,000

Functions: Generalist (All), Management, Board
Members

Industries: Generalist (All)

The Ryan Group

PO Box 655
Waverly, PA 18471-0655
(570) 586-4566
Fax: (570) 586-4577
Email: don.ryan@theryangroup.org
Web: www.theryangroup.org

Summary: We are different from typical
'headhunters,' whose priority is solely the hiring
company. We balance the mutual needs of the
hiring company and the professional seeking a
new career opportunity.

Key Contact - Specialty:
Mr. Donald Ryan, President
Mr. Michael Rescigno, Principal

Salary Minimum: $35,000

Functions: Generalist (All), Board Members,
Middle Mgmt., Production, Finance

Industries: Manufacturing, Electronic, Elec.
Components, Banking, Misc. Financial,
Accounting, Mgmt. Consulting, HR Services, IT
Implementation, Engineering Svcs.,
Communications, Defense, Packaging,
Software, Accounting SW, Database SW, Mfg.
SW, Biotech/Life Sciences, Physical Therapy

Ryan, Miller & Associates

4601 Wilshire Blvd Ste 225
Los Angeles, CA 90010-3883
(323) 938-4768
Fax: (323) 857-7009
Email: ryanmiller@ryanmiller.com
Web: www.ryanmiller.com

Summary: We are an executive search firm
specializing in the recruitment of finance,
accounting and banking professionals.

Key Contact - Specialty:
Mr. Lee Ryan, President - *MBAs*
Mr. Michael O'Connell, Treasurer - *MBAs*

Salary Minimum: $60,000

Functions: Finance, CFOs, Budgeting, Cash
Mgmt., Taxes, M&A

Industries: Generalist (All), Banking,
Mutual/Hedge Funds, Accounting SW

Branches:
790 E Colorado Blvd Ste 506
Pasadena, CA 91101-2184
(626) 568-3100
Fax: (626) 568-3772
Key Contact - Specialty:
Mr. Roger Miller, President

Ryan-Allen & Associates Inc

PO Box 86865
28366 Crooked Oak Ln
San Diego, CA 92138-6865
(760) 751-8345
(858) 576-0737
Fax: (760) 751-8346
Email: michelle@ryan-allen.com
Web: www.ryan-allen.com

Summary: Our firm is an executive search
practice, concentrating in the recruitment of
accounting, finance, banking and human resource
professionals.

Key Contact - Specialty:
Mrs, Michelle Timm, CPC, Founding Principal

Functions: Generalist (All)

Industries: Finance, Banking, HR Services

Ryan-Allen & Associates

732 Devon Ct
San Diego, CA 92109-8005
(858) 576-0737
Email: sheila@ryan-allen.com

Summary: Specialize in the recruitment of
professionals in accounting, banking, finance and
human recources.

Key Contact - Specialty:
Ms. Sheila R. Hawley, CPC, President
Ms. Theresa Fulan, CAC, Executive Search
Consultant

Functions: Generalist (All), HR Mgmt., Finance,
CFOs

Industries: Generalist (All), Finance, Banking,
Accounting, HR SW

J Ryder Search

PO Box 241
White River Junction, VT 05001-0241
(802) 296-3732
Email: jpr@jrydersearch.com
Web: www.jrydersearch.com

Summary: Our firm places research scientists and
executives within the biotechnology industry.

Key Contact - Specialty:
Mr. Joseph Ryder, Owner

Salary Minimum: $65,000

Functions: Management, R&D

Industries: Biotech/Life Sciences

Ryman, Bell, Green & Michaels Inc

PO Box 421
Pattison, TX 77466-0421
(281) 375-8361
Fax: (281) 934-9188
Email: admin@rbgm.net
Web: www.rbgm.net

Summary: National and international search firm
representing Fortune 5000 and select law firms.

Key Contact - Specialty:
Mr. Phil Forman, President
Ms. Cindy Zator, Director, Financial Services

Salary Minimum: $150,000

Functions: Finance, Engineering, Geotechnical,
Process, Systems, Attorneys

Industries: Oil & Gas, Manufacturing, Finance,
Invest. Banking, Brokers, Legal

S Cunningham Inc

262 Dogwood View Ln
Suwanee, GA 30024-3922
(770) 831-1992
Email: sandycunningham@mindspring.com
Web: www.sandycunningham.com

Summary: Executive recruiter specializing in
payroll.

Key Contact - Specialty:
Ms. Sandy Cunningham, Recruiter

Salary Minimum: $50,000

Functions: Generalist (All)

Industries: Generalist (All)

S P Associates Inc

5950 Fairview Rd Ste 404
Charlotte, NC 28210-2103
(704) 643-7250
Fax: (704) 643-1249
Email: info@spassociates.com
Web: www.spassociates.com

Summary: All functions only in following
industries: textile & fibers, non-wovens,
packaging, pharmaceuticals, Beauty aids, medical
devices, engineering, and plastics.

Key Contact - Specialty:
Mr. Gabe C. Hill, III, President - *Composites,
Manufacturing, Research & development,
Technical, Textiles,*
Mr. Jim Walkup, Vice President - *Cosmetics,
Medical, Medical (Devices), Nutraceuticals,
Pharmaceutical*
Mr. Bert Giebel, Secretary & Treasurer - *Plastics*

Salary Minimum: $30,000

Functions: Generalist (All), Management, Senior
Mgmt.

Industries: Generalist (All), Manufacturing,
Textiles, Apparel, Paper, Printing, Chemicals,
Drugs Mfg., Medical Devices, Plastics, Rubber,
Paints, Petro. Products, Pharm Svcs., Packaging

S R & Associates

38285 Aberdeen Dr
Murrieta, CA 92562-9196
(949) 756-3271
Email: sraross@srassociatesinc.com
Web: www.srassociatesinc.com

Summary: We are a full service recruiting
corporation focused on high technology 'vendors'
only. We recruit for all sales levels within the
technology sector including pre-sales support
consultants and VP of sales. Additionally, we
recruit in the professional services sector,
including practice managers, implementation
managers and consultants.

Key Contact - Specialty:
Mr. Steve Ross, President & Founder

Salary Minimum: $75,000

Functions: Sales & Mktg., Sales Mgmt., MIS
Mgmt., Systems Implem.

Industries: Generalist (All), Manufacturing,
Computer Equip., Services, Mgmt. Consulting,
Communications, Software, Accounting SW,
Database SW, Development SW, Doc. Mgmt.,
Production SW, ERP SW, Industry Specific
SW, Mfg. SW, Biotech/Life Sciences

Sacks Legal Search

1735 Market St Ste A
Philadelphia, PA 19103-7502
(215) 790-1646
Email: ssacks@sackslegalsearch.com
Web: www.sackslegalsearch.com

Summary: Led by a licensed attorney with
experience placing attorneys in permanent
positions among law firms and corporations; we
pride ourselves on achieving client satisfaction
through principled, discreet, resourceful, timely
and cost effective service custom tailored for our
individual clients. We specialize in permanent
attorney placements.

Key Contact - Specialty:
Ms. Sabrina J. Sacks, Esq., President

Salary Minimum: $70,000

Functions: Attorneys

Industries: Legal

The Saddlebrook Group LLC

420 NW 11th Ave Unit 617
Portland, OR 97209-2962
(971) 544-0952
Fax: (971) 544-0953
Email: jobs@saddlebrookgroup.com
Web: www.saddlebrookgroup.com

Summary: We are an executive search firm focused on the medical device and medical products industries, with an emphasis on searches for sales & marketing executives, financial managers and GMs.

Key Contact - Specialty:
Mr. Michael Stringer, President

Salary Minimum: $75,000

Functions: Management, Sales & Mktg.

Industries: Biotech/Life Sciences, Healthcare, Hospitals, Physical Therapy, Occupational Therapy

Sage Employment Recruiters

127 E Windsor Ave Ste 8
Elkhart, IN 46514-5522
(574) 264-1126
Fax: (574) 264-1128
Email: sagesearch@aol.com

Summary: Industries with wheels, manufactured housing, marine, recreation vehicles, van conversion, truck/trailer body and the supply companies for these industries. Effective, discreet approach gets assignment accomplished in weeks not months.

Key Contact - Specialty:
Mr. John McGuire, Partner
Mr. Dean Garberick, Partner

Salary Minimum: $40,000

Functions: Generalist (All), Mfg., Materials, Sales Mgmt., Finance, IT, Mgmt. Consultants

Industries: Generalist (All), Metal Products, Motor Vehicles

Sales & Marketing Search

100 Cummings Ctr Ste 453H
Beverly, MA 01915-6132
(978) 921-8282
Fax: (978) 921-8283
Email: contactus@smsearch.com
Web: www.smsearch.com

Summary: We are a sales & marketing recruiting for product, service and technology companies.

Key Contact - Specialty:
Ms. Betsy Harper, Managing Partner & CEO
Mr. Donald Harper, Senior Consultant - *International*
Ms. Ana Gomes, Senior Recruiter

Salary Minimum: $60,000

Functions: Sales & Mktg.

Industries: Computer Equip., Software, Database SW, ERP SW, HR SW, Industry Specific SW, Mfg. SW, Marketing SW, Networking, Comm. SW, System SW

Sales Aces LLC

7777 Forest Ln Ste CA94 # 103
Dallas, TX 75230
(972) 569-9933
Fax: (972) 542-9901
Email: scott@salesaces.com
Web: www.salesaces.com

Summary: Our firm specializes in the recruitment of sales, sales management, sales support, and marketing professionals. Our firm has developed an extensive network of affiliate partners throughout the United States and Canada, giving us the ability to effectively serve our clients' staffing needs on a nationwide basis.

Key Contact - Specialty:
Mr. Scott Ritzmann, President

Functions: Sales & Mktg., Advertising, Mktg. Research, Mktg. Mgmt., Sales Mgmt., Direct Mktg., Customer Svc., PR, Sales Reps.

Industries: Drugs Mfg., Medical Devices, Consumer Goods, IT Implementation, Advertising, Publishing, New Media, Database SW, Development SW, Training SW

Sales Advantage

7805 SW 6th Ct
Plantation, FL 33324-3203
(954) 776-5554 x227
Fax: (954) 776-5855
Email: mbecker@beckerpro.com
Web: n/a

Summary: We target professionals in the top 20 percent of their respective fields to ensure that your company hires the candidate with the most positive impact on your bottom line.

Key Contact - Specialty:
Mr. Matt Becker, President - *Sales*

Salary Minimum: $50,000

Functions: Sales & Mktg.

Industries: Generalist (All), Insurance, Commercial

Sales Associates of America

2457 N Mayfair Rd Ste 200
Milwaukee, WI 53226-1405
(414) 774-9800
(414) 774-9804
Fax: (414) 774-9840
Email: jobs4you@saainc.com
Web: www.saainc.com

Summary: We specialize in sales & marketing individuals in the areas of consumer products, house-wares, builder's hardware, medical/pharmaceutical telecom, software, and office products.

Key Contact - Specialty:
Mr. Dennis Nefzer, Senior Recruitment Officer

Salary Minimum: $70,000

Functions: Sales & Mktg.

Industries: Food, Bev., Tobacco, Soap, Perf., Cosmtcs., Drugs Mfg., Paints, Petro. Products, Consumer Elect., Electronic, Elec. Components, Consumer Goods

Sales Executives Inc

33900 W 8 Mile Rd Ste 171
Farmington Hills, MI 48335-5204
(248) 615-0100
Email: dale@salesexecutives.com
Web: www.salesexecutives.com

Summary: We specialize in sales, marketing and sales management. Extensive experience in 'confidential' executive search.

Key Contact - Specialty:
Mr. Dale E. Statson, President
Mr. William Rabe, Founder & Senior Partner
Mr. Curt Stirzinger, Senior Parnter
Mr. Scott Statson - *Investment*

Salary Minimum: $50,000

Functions: Generalist (All), Healthcare, Sales Mgmt., Sales Reps.

Industries: Generalist (All), Manufacturing, Drugs Mfg., Medical Devices, Computer Equip., Telecoms, Wireless, Software

The Sales Group

3000 Northwoods Pkwy Ste 285
Norcross, GA 30071-4788
(678) 421-1950
Fax: (678) 421-9016
Web: www.salestalent.com

Summary: We are a full service recruiting agency specializing in placement of salespeople, sales managers, sales executives, and sales representatives for inside and outside sales. We have an extensive database of highly qualified salespeople in 28 different industries. We provide each client with the highest level of service.

Key Contact - Specialty:
Mr. Jack Scherer, President
Ms. Judy Scherer, Partner - *Marketing, Operations*
Ms. Theresa Brown, Recruiter

Functions: Sales & Mktg.

Industries: Energy, Utilities, Construction, Manufacturing, Banking, Services, Media, Communications, Packaging, Insurance, Software

Sales Management

3709 Osborne Dr
Warrenton, VA 20187-3913
(703) 478-0720
(888) 619-6606
Fax: (540) 349-9835
Email: wheatasoc@aol.com
Web: www.smgmt.com

Summary: We specialize in the recruitment of professional sales & marketing personnel. We have been affiliated for many years with a network of sales & marketing recruiters.

Key Contact - Specialty:
Mr. James B. Wheatley, MBA, President

Functions: Generalist (All)

Industries: Healthcare

Sales Management Resources Inc

24040 Camino Del Avion Ste A
MSC 177
Dana Point, CA 92629-4083
(949) 248-9429
Fax: (949) 248-8567
Email: smr@smrcareer.com
Web: www.smrcareer.com

Summary: We are an executive search firm that provides retained and contingency recruiting and consulting services to corporate consumer products industry clients. We specialize in mid-senior-level sales & marketing management positions.

Key Contact - Specialty:
Mr. Clancy Salway, President - *Sales*

Salary Minimum: $50,000

Functions: Sales & Mktg., Advertising, Mktg. Research, Mktg. Mgmt., Sales Mgmt., Direct Mktg.

Industries: Food, Bev., Tobacco, Textiles, Apparel, Soap, Perf., Cosmtcs., Drugs Mfg.

Sales Masters USA, Inc.

1412 Ventana Dr
Escondido, CA 92029-5519
(760) 746-0808
Email: scot@salesmastersinc.com
Web: www.salesmastersinc.com

Summary: We are an executive search
specializing in office equipment and high-tech
industries. Special emphasis on sales, sales
management and key accounts/major accounts
positions

Key Contact - Specialty:
Mr. Scot G. Stern, Managing Director - *CEOs,
Computers (Sales), Copiers, Executives, Sales*
Mr. Jack Signorelli, Senior Vice President -
CEOs, Copiers, Executives, Management, Sales
Ms. Norma Farley, Executive Recruiter -
Management, Office (Products), Sales
Ms. Carrie Cheryl, Recruiter - *Sales*

Salary Minimum: $20,000

Functions: Management, Senior Mgmt., Middle
Mgmt., Sales & Mktg., Sales Reps., Mgmt.
Consultants

Industries: Generalist (All), Equip Svcs.

Sales Medical Professionals

3945 SE 15th St Ste 101
Oklahoma City, OK 73115-2247
(405) 677-7872
Fax: (405) 672-5053
Email: medrxsales@juno.com

Summary: Contingency search firm specializing
in the medical field for sales reps of medical
equipment, implants, devices and supplies. We
also offer other non-medical sales on occasion.
We also help sales people transition from non-
medical to medical sales.

Key Contact - Specialty:
Mr. Dan Smith, Owner - *Healthcare, Sales*

Functions: Management, Healthcare, Sales &
Mktg., Sales Mgmt.

Industries: Generalist (All), Medical Devices,
Pharm Svcs., Biotech/Life Sciences, Healthcare

Sales Recruiters Inc

85 Stiles Rd Ste 104
Salem, NH 03079-4806
(603) 894-0007 x17
Fax: (603) 894-6666
Email: marilyn@salesrecruiters.com
Web: www.salesrecruiters.com

Summary: We are a job placement service that
recruits, screens and presents qualified sales
professionals to different types of organizations.
We offer a more comprehensive, personal
approach to recruiting.

Key Contact - Specialty:
Ms. Marilyn Jackson, CPC, CTS, Operations
Manager - *Advertising, Aerospace, Business
development, Business to business, C-level*

Salary Minimum: $20,000

Functions: Sales & Mktg.

Industries: Generalist (All)

Sales Recruiters International Ltd

2 Depot Plz Ste 303A
Bedford Hills, NY 10507-1834
(914) 244-9090
(800) 836-0881
Fax: (914) 244-3001
Email: info@salesrecruiters.net
Web: www.salesrecruiters.net

Summary: We have identified, recruited and
placed top sales, sales management and marketing
professionals for quality companies, where they
are recognized, developed and rewarded.

Key Contact - Specialty:
Ms. Jean Maxwell, CPC, President - *Marketing,
Sales*

Salary Minimum: $50,000

Functions: Sales & Mktg.

Industries: Food, Bev., Tobacco, Lumber,
Furniture, Printing, Soap, Perf., Cosmtcs.,
Consumer Goods, Architectural Svcs.,
Hospitality, Advertising

Sales Recruiters Network

N93W25118 Bittersweet Dr
Sussex, WI 53089-1064
(262) 628-9155
Email: becky@salesrecruitersnetwork.com
Web: www.salesrecruitersnetwork.com

Summary: Our firm specializes in recruiting and
placing the following: sales & marketing
professionals, IT, pharmaceutical, medical
devices, industrial and business products.

Key Contact - Specialty:
Mr. Jack Alexander, Recruiter
Ms. Becky Wheaton, Recruiter - *Business to
business, Copiers, Office (Products), Sales,
Technical*

Functions: Generalist (All)

Industries: Pharm Svcs., Equip Svcs., Publishing,
Telecoms, Digital, Wireless

Sales Recruiters of Oklahoma City

6803 S Western Ave Ste 305
Oklahoma City, OK 73139-1814
(405) 848-1536
Email: jr@salesrec.com
Web: www.salesrec.com

Summary: We are a search firm specializing in
outside sales. Industries include medical,
pharmaceutical, biotechnology, industrial, and
business products and services. We work with
Fortune 500 companies placing sales managers
and representatives.

Key Contact - Specialty:
Mr. J.R. Rimele, Lead Recruiter - *Biomedical,
Biopharmaceutical, Biotechnology, Medical
(Devices,Sales)*
Mr. Glen Johnson, Recruiter - *Sales*
Mr. Greg Johnson - *Sales*

Functions: Healthcare, Sales & Mktg., Sales
Reps.

Industries: Food, Bev., Tobacco, Lumber,
Furniture, Paper, Chemicals, Medical Devices,
Computer Equip., Pharm Svcs., Accounting,
Equip Svcs., Publishing, Biotech/Life Sciences,
Healthcare, Hospitals, Long-term/Home Care,
Dental, Physical Therapy, Occupational Therapy

Sales Recruiting Network

344 Mason Rd
Tarentum, PA 15084-3360
(724) 226-9900
Fax: (724) 226-2299
Email: cain@salesrecruitingnetwork.com
Web: www.srnweb.com

Summary: Our firm specializes in locating outside
sales and sales management (personnel and
positions) in consumer products, foodservice,
medical, pharmaceutical, industrial, and business-
to-business.

Key Contact - Specialty:
Mr. Douglas Cain, President - *Food service,
Industrial, Sales*

Salary Minimum: $40,000

Functions: Sales & Mktg., Sales Mgmt.

Industries: Generalist (All), Food, Bev., Tobacco,
Paper, Medical Devices, Consumer Goods,
Pharm Svcs., Inst./Industrial Food Svc.

Sales Search

17 Goodwill Ave
North York, ON M3H 1V5
Canada
(416) 636-3660
Email: salessearch@rogers.com
Web: www.salessearch-toronto.com

Summary: With many years of specialized sales,
marketing & related management search expertise,
we are known for saving valuable time and effort
in providing only qualified candidates for our
client companies.

Key Contact - Specialty:
Mr. Bob Glassberg, General Manager -
Management, Marketing, Sales

Functions: Sales & Mktg., Sales Mgmt.

Industries: Energy, Utilities, Construction,
Manufacturing, Wholesale, Services, Media,
Communications, Aerospace, Packaging,
Software, Biotech/Life Sciences

Sales Search Associates Inc

201 E Dundee Rd
Palatine, IL 60074-2806
(847) 358-7865
Fax: (847) 358-7862
Email: ssa@sales-search.com
Web: www.sales-search.com

Summary: Our firm specializes in search for sales,
marketing and management professionals.
Industries served include: business services,
consumer goods, capital equipment, software,
manufacturing, and other business to business
products.

Key Contact - Specialty:
Ms. Dianna Rudd

Salary Minimum: $50,000

Functions: Management, Packaging, Sales &
Mktg., Sales Reps.

Industries: Generalist (All), Construction,
Manufacturing, Food, Bev., Tobacco, Paper,
Printing, Soap, Perf., Cosmtcs., Drugs Mfg.,
Medical Devices, Plastics, Rubber,
Transportation, Wholesale, Services, Law
Enforcement, Hospitality, Media, Government,
Environmental Svcs., Packaging, Real Estate,
Software

Sales Solutions

PO Box 3557
Walnut Creek, CA 94598-0557
(925) 524-8900
Fax: (925) 524-8901
Email: salessol@sbcglobal.net

Summary: We specialize in the placement of
professionals in sales & marketing. Our primary
focus is in chemical and plastics industries. We
pay specific attention to industrial and specialty
gases.

Key Contact - Specialty:
Mr. Bill Schmeh, President - *Sales*

Salary Minimum: $50,000

Email your resume to a targeted list of recruiters now at www.ExecutiveAgent.com/DER07

Functions: Sales & Mktg., Sales Mgmt.

Industries: Generalist (All), Chemicals, Plastics, Rubber

Sales Source

331 Ushers Rd Ste 14
Ballston Lake, NY 12019-1591
(518) 877-6706
(800) 229-3093
Fax: (518) 877-8161
Email: home@salessource.net
Web: www.salessource.net

Summary: We are one of the oldest medical sales search firms in our area.

Key Contact - Specialty:
Mr. Clay Ward, Vice President
Mr. Bill Ward, Treasurer

Salary Minimum: $40,000

Functions: Sales Mgmt.

Industries: Drugs Mfg., Medical Devices, Computer Equip., Pharm Svcs., Telecoms, Software, Biotech/Life Sciences

Sales Talent Inc

270 3rd Ave Ste 200
Kirkland, WA 98033-6173
(425) 739-9979
Fax: (425) 828-3861
Email: yaffa@salestalentinc.com
Web: www.salestalentinc.com

Summary: Our firm specializes in the placement of sales professionals with companies that range from the hottest startups to the most respected blue chips. The searches range from entry level to experienced sales positions including sales management.

Key Contact - Specialty:
Mr. Yaffa Carlson, Vice President, Sales

Functions: Sales & Mktg., Sales Mgmt., Customer Svc.

Industries: Drugs Mfg., Computer Equip., Pharm Svcs., E-commerce, New Media, Telecoms, Software, Healthcare

Salesforce & Marshank

3294 Woodrow Way NE
Atlanta, GA 30319-2422
(404) 252-8566
Fax: (404) 942-0081
Email: fred@shankweiler.com
Web: www.shankweiler.com

Summary: We are an executive recruiting firm specializing in recruitment of personnel for: sales, sales management, mortgage management & staff, software and financial industry related.

Key Contact - Specialty:
Mr. Fred Shankweiler, President
Ms. Marilyn Y. Shankweiler, Co-Owner - *Computers (Software)*

Functions: Sales & Mktg., Sales Mgmt.

Industries: Food, Bev., Tobacco, Consumer Goods, Finance, Banking, Misc. Financial, E-commerce, Software

Salesrecruiter.biz

PO Box 923
Camp Hill, PA 17001-0923
(717) 796-1587
Email: salesrecruiter@comcast.net

Summary: A sales search firm for all areas of sales. Industrial sales specialists. We perform custom searches for industrial clients.

Key Contact - Specialty:
Mr. Bill Molin, Owner - *Sales*

Salary Minimum: $30,000

Functions: Sales & Mktg.

Industries: Construction, Manufacturing, Printing, Chemicals, Robotics, Engineering Svcs., Government, Defense, Biotech/Life Sciences, Non-Classifiable

Sampson Associates

4100 Redwood Rd Ste 359
Oakland, CA 94619-2363
(510) 531-4237
(650) 823-7963
Fax: (510) 531-2920
Email: hr@sampsonassociates.com
Web: www.sampsonassociates.com

Summary: Sales, technical and managerial search firm, our greatest asset and notable advantage is our network. We have assisted hundreds of companies to locate technical and sales professionals, management and executive men and women from virtually all fields.

Key Contact - Specialty:
Mr. James S. Sampson, President & Managing Director
Mr. Brian Sampson, Vice President, Product Services - *Management*

Salary Minimum: $75,000

Functions: Management, Board Members, Middle Mgmt., Sales & Mktg., Mktg. Research, Mktg. Mgmt., Systems Dev., Systems Implem., DB Admin., Architects

Industries: Computer Equip., Equip Svcs., Software, Biotech/Life Sciences, Healthcare

Sampson Medical Search

13234 Fiji Way Unit F
Marina del Rey, CA 90292-7061
(310) 305-8468
(310) 540-4617
Email: sms_resume@earthlink.net
Web: www.sampsonmed.com

Summary: We specialize in the pharmaceutical, biotech and device industries. Areas of expertise are: medical directors, CEO's, COO's, CFO's, regulatory affairs, project managers/directors, business development, data managers/directors, clinical operations, drug safety, clinical liaisons and CRA's.

Key Contact - Specialty:
Ms. Judie Sampson, President - *Business development, Regulatory*

Salary Minimum: $50,000

Functions: Healthcare

Industries: Generalist (All), Drugs Mfg., Medical Devices, Pharm Svcs., Packaging, Biotech/Life Sciences

Branches:
13200 W Monte Vista Dr
Goodyear, AZ 85338-2188
(602) 935-5993
Fax: (602) 935-5993
Key Contact - Specialty:
Mr. Robert Bauer, Operations Director - *Biotechnology, Pharmaceutical*

Norm Sanders Associates Inc

4 Bellevue Ave
Rumson, NJ 07760-1105
(732) 264-3700
Email: mail@normsanders.com
Web: www.normsanders.com

Summary: We are one of the leading firms recruiting CIOs, senior-level IS executives, technology leaders and consulting partners. We have in-depth capabilities to assess both business and technical acumen and utilize a database of senior-level IS talent.

Key Contact - Specialty:
Mr. Walter J. McGuigan, Jr., Managing Director
Mr. Louis B. Hughes, Principal
Mrs. Leslie Spencer, Office Manager

Salary Minimum: $225,000

Functions: Generalist (All), Senior Mgmt., Finance, Risk Mgmt., IT, MIS Mgmt.

Industries: Generalist (All), Transportation, Retail, Finance, Banking, Hospitality, Publishing

Sanderson Employment Service

2501 San Pedro Dr NE Ste 207
Albuquerque, NM 87110-4122
(505) 265-8827
Fax: (505) 268-5536
Email: sandersonq@aol.com
Web: www.sandersonemployment.com

Summary: We recruit and place civil, environmental, process, chemical, mechanical, design, structural, electrical, hardware & software engineers, IT professionals, manufacturing & production specialists, programmers, sales & marketing professionals as well as office support personnel.

Key Contact - Specialty:
Mr. Bill Sanderson, Recruiter - *Management*
Ms. Leah Baca - *Chemical*

Salary Minimum: $25,000

Functions: Systems Analysis, Systems Dev., Engineering, Structural, Bldg. Contractors

Industries: Energy, Utilities, Construction, Manufacturing, Test, Measure Equip., Pharm Svcs., Engineering Svcs., Fiber Optic, Network Infrastructure, RF/Microwave, Government, Defense, Environmental Svcs., Haz. Waste, Aerospace, Property/Facility Mgmt., Software, Database SW, Development SW, Doc. Mgmt., Production SW, Industry Specific SW, Security SW, System SW

Sanford Rose Associates - SRA International

(a franchisor of Sanford Rose Associates)
3737 Embassy Pkwy Ste 200
Akron, OH 44333-8369
(330) 670-9797
(800) 731-7724
Fax: (330) 670-9798
Email: hq@sanfordrose.com
Web: www.sanfordrose.com

Summary: We represent companies and institutions around the world in finding high-quality executives, managers and professionals for important position openings through our proprietary Dimensional Search® process.

Key Contact - Specialty:
Mr. George R. Snider, Jr., President & Chief Executive Officer
Mr. Douglas R. Rogers, Vice President, Operations
Mr. Scott Vollmer
Ms. Sherri Lemley

Salary Minimum: $75,000

Functions: Generalist (All), Management, Mfg., Healthcare, Sales & Mktg., Finance, IT, R&D, Engineering, Specialized Svcs.

Industries: Generalist (All), Construction, Manufacturing, Transportation, Finance, Services, Hospitality, Communications, Insurance, Healthcare

Sanford Rose Associates - Fairhope

22873 US Highway 98 Bldg I
Fairhope, AL 36532-3329
(251) 928-7072
Fax: (251) 928-7738
Email: sraprint@sanfordrose.com

Summary: Our firm specializes in the recruitment of senior-level executives and key managers for the print and packaging industries only. This includes: commercial printing, direct mail, publications, books, financial printing, folding cartons, flexible packaging, prime labels, shrink sleeves, business forms, envelopes and screen printing.

Key Contact - Specialty:
Mr. Paul Marquez, President
Mrs. Sonya Green, Search Consultant

Salary Minimum: $65,000

Functions: Management, Senior Mgmt., Mfg., Plant Mgmt., Sales & Mktg., Sales Mgmt., Direct Mktg., Customer Svc., CFOs, Legal

Industries: Printing, Packaging

Sanford Rose Associates - Corona

PO Box 78567
Corona, CA 92877-0152
(619) 482-2393
Email: kajohnson@sanfordrose.com
Web: www.sanfordrose.com/corona

Summary: Specializing in sales, marketing and operations within the safety, security, industrial and construction fields. We also do generalist work for selected clients.

Key Contact - Specialty:
Mr. Kirk Johnson, President - *Business development, Business to business, Industrial, Marketing, Middle management*

Salary Minimum: $60,000

Functions: Generalist (All)

Industries: Medical Devices, Metal Products, Test, Measure Equip., Logistics Svcs., Recreation, Sports, Call Centers, Defense, Homeland Security, Haz. Waste

Sanford Rose Associates - Rancho Bernardo

PO Box 300367
Escondido, CA 92030-0367
(800) 464-9417
(760) 432-8641
Email: mkmetz@sanfordrose.com
Web: www.sanfordrose.com/ranchobernardo

Summary: We are a search organization with offices worldwide. Industry expertise spans high technology, medical device and manufacturing clients with national searches in R&D, IT, operations, finance and engineering. We listen to our client's talent needs and identify high-performing candidates who best meet their corporate culture, education and experience requirements.

Key Contact - Specialty:
Ms. Melissa Metz, CPC, Managing Director - *Engineering, Finance, Manufacturing (Management), Medical (Devices), Technical (Management)*

D. E. Miller, Partner - *Field engineering, General management, High technology, Manufacturing (Management), Technical (Management)*
K. A. Johnson, CPC, Partner - *Engineering, Finance, Operations, Research & development, Sales*

Salary Minimum: $50,000

Functions: Senior Mgmt., Middle Mgmt.

Industries: Manufacturing, Food, Bev., Tobacco, Chemicals, Medical Devices, Semiconductors

Sanford Rose Associates - Sacramento

2701 Del Paso Rd Ste 130
Sacramento, CA 95835-2306
(916) 419-2092
Fax: (916) 419-9527
Email: sacramentoca@sanfordrose.com
Web: www.sanfordrose.com/sacramento

Summary: Our firm specializes in placing mid-level managers to senior-level executives in consumer products in all functions. We conduct custom searches on a contingency and retained basis. We focus on finding high quality candidates through our industry expertise, extensive network of professionals and commitment to clients. Not only do we identify candidates with the right skills and experience, we also match their individual style to the employer's corporate culture.

Key Contact - Specialty:
Ms. Debbie Roberts, President, Sales & Marketing
Mr. Robert Walker, Search Consultant
Mr. Juliet Leon, Research Coordinator
Ms. Kathy Johnson, Search Consultant

Salary Minimum: $50,000

Functions: Management, Mfg., Sales & Mktg., HR Mgmt.

Industries: Manufacturing, Food, Bev., Tobacco, Textiles, Apparel, Paper, Soap, Perf., Cosmtcs., Drugs Mfg., Machine, Appliance, Consumer Elect., Consumer Goods, Pharm Svcs., Mgmt. Consulting, HR Services, Logistics Svcs., Supply Chain Mgmt

Sanford Rose Associates - Temecula

31805 US Highway 79 S # 630
Temecula, CA 92592-8200
(951) 302-0668
Fax: (951) 526-2141
Email: bdudley@sratemecula.com
Web: www.sratemecula.com

Summary: We devote our practice to the biotechnology industry including devices, therapeutics, diagnostics and drug discovery. We also perform searches for senior HR professionals across all industry sectors.

Key Contact - Specialty:
Mr. Robert R. Dudley, CPC, President

Salary Minimum: $75,000

Functions: Management, Sales & Mktg., Mktg. Mgmt., HR Mgmt.

Industries: Generalist (All), Software, Biotech/Life Sciences

Sanford Rose Associates - Carlsbad

410 S Melrose Dr Ste 103
Vista, CA 92081-6607
(760) 643-4100
Fax: (760) 643-4101
Email: carlsbadca@sanfordrose.com
Web: www.sanfordrose.com/carlsbad

Summary: Our 'Five Star Office' specializes in the commercial and public works construction industries along with servicing select food and specialty chemicals clients. We operate as a valued partner and provide the highest level of professional recruiting services for a select group of clients that share our values of high integrity, industry knowledge and superior service.

Key Contact - Specialty:
Mr. David Miller, President - *Biotechnology, Chemical, Construction, Distribution, Food & beverage*
Ms. Alicia Anzalone, Vice President, Operations - *Chemical, Construction, Distribution, Food & beverage*
Ms. Donna Dickerson, Search Consultant - *Chemical, Construction, Distribution, Food & beverage*

Salary Minimum: $70,000

Functions: Generalist (All)

Industries: Construction, Manufacturing, Chemicals, Drugs Mfg., Medical Devices, Packaging

Sanford Rose Associates - Clearwater

2625 McCormick Dr Ste 103
Clearwater, FL 33759-1099
(727) 796-2201
Fax: (727) 793-0190
Email: mail@monroesearch.com
Web: www.monroesearch.com

Summary: Firm offers retained and contingency search assignment services for the pharmaceutical industry. With our computer database, industry network and the resources of other offices, we can move quickly to find highly qualified candidates.

Key Contact - Specialty:
Mr. Mark A. Soufleris, Managing Director - *Biopharmaceutical, Biotechnology, Healthcare, Pharmaceutical*
Ms. Ann Harrison, Senior Consultant
Ms. Judson Heinricher, Senior Consultant

Salary Minimum: $100,000

Functions: Senior Mgmt., Mfg., Product Dev., Sales & Mktg., HR Mgmt.

Industries: Drugs Mfg., Medical Devices, Pharm Svcs.

Sanford Rose Associates - Orlando

4767 New Broad St Ste 200
Orlando, FL 32814-6405
(407) 514-2635
Fax: (407) 514-2604
Email: sra-orl@sanfordrose.com
Web: www.sanfordrose.com

Summary: Our firm specializes in placing marketing, sales, engineering, and management professionals in the power quality, electronics, and electrical products industries.

Key Contact - Specialty:
Mr. James A. Roach, President - *Distribution, Electrical, Electronics, Manufacturing, Power*

Salary Minimum: $75,000

Functions: Generalist (All)

Industries: Manufacturing, Electronic, Elec. Components

Sanford Rose Associates - Norcross

9650 Ventana Way Ste 204
Alpharetta, GA 30022-6395
(770) 232-9900
Email: norcrossga@sanfordrose.com
Web: www.sanfordrose.com/norcross

Summary: We perform both contingency and retained searches in the telecom/technology and retail marketplaces, both in North America and internationally as well. Wireless is a particular focus. Mid to staff level general/senior management, sales/marketing, technical, finance, customer service and IT positions are areas of expertise.

Key Contact - Specialty:
Mr. Donald R. Patrick, CPC, President - *General management, Professional services, Retail, Senior management, Telecommunications*
Ms. Janet L. Patrick, Vice President - *Research*
Mr. J. Campbell O'Keeffe, Search Consultant - *Engineering, RF microwave, Technology, Telecommunications, Wireless*

Salary Minimum: $75,000

Functions: Generalist (All)

Industries: Retail, Communications, Telecoms, Call Centers, Telephony, Digital, Wireless, Fiber Optic, Network Infrastructure, RF/Microwave

Sanford Rose Associates - Athens

2500 W Broad St Ste 407
Athens, GA 30606-3440
(706) 548-3942
Fax: (706) 548-3786
Email: sraathens@aol.com

Summary: We are a custom recruiting for key manufacturing plant positions and division/staff management, QA, accounting, materials and engineers including, plant/IE/design/manufacturing/project/product.

Key Contact - Specialty:
Mr. Art Weiner, President - *Engineering, Technical*
Ms. Arlene Weiner - *Materials*
Mr. Ken Weiner, CPC, Executive Search Consultant & VP - *Engineering, Operations*

Salary Minimum: $50,000

Functions: Management, Senior Mgmt., Mfg., Product Dev., Plant Mgmt., Quality, Materials, HR Mgmt., Finance, Engineering

Industries: Manufacturing, Medical Devices, Plastics, Rubber, Metal Products, Machine, Appliance

Sanford Rose Associates - Crystal Lake

44 N Virginia St Ste 3B
Crystal Lake, IL 60014-4154
(815) 444-8382
Fax: (815) 444-8390
Email: info@careerfasttrack.com
Web: www.careerfasttrack.com

Summary: Our firm devotes its practice to serving the specialty chemicals, plastic packaging, food and legal professions. We are committed to providing our clients with candidates who will make a difference. It is our intent to develop long term, partnerships with each client by introducing exceptional candidates who fit the search profile, are pre-qualified by us and would enhance the organization.

Key Contact - Specialty:
Mr. Steven J. Burks, PhD, Chief Executive Officer
Mr. Gary Prindle, Senior Vice President
Ms. Laura Burks, Executive Recruiter
Mr. Gary Driscoll, PhD, Senior Vice President

Salary Minimum: $70,000

Functions: Generalist (All)

Industries: Generalist (All), Food, Bev., Tobacco, Chemicals, Soap, Perf., Cosmtcs., Plastics, Rubber, Paints, Petro. Products, Legal, Packaging

Sanford Rose Associates - Effingham

1901 S 4th St Ste 208
Effingham, IL 62401-4162
(217) 342-3928
Fax: (217) 347-7111
Email: sraeff@hotmail.com

Summary: We have experience and in-depth knowledge about printing and recruiting. Efficient searches are conducted resulting in timely placements.

Key Contact - Specialty:
Mr. Robert A. St. Denis, Owner & Director - *Printing*
Ms. Sherry St. Denis, Consultant - *Printing*
Mr. Albert Hemenway, Office Manager - *Printing*

Salary Minimum: $30,000

Functions: Generalist (All), Management

Industries: Generalist (All), Manufacturing, Printing

Sanford Rose Associates - Rockford

PO Box 15584
Loves Park, IL 61132-5584
(815) 636-0848
Email: dmwallace@sanfordrose.com

Summary: Industrial and capital equipment sales have been a recent focus. However our preference is work involving advanced manufacturing engineering, tooling, "Greenfield start-up" and industrial processes involving stamping, high-speed machining or plastic. Clients are utilizing high speed equipment, automation stamping, welding and assembly processes. Automotive (ILVS) in-line vehicle sequencing of modular assemblies.

Key Contact - Specialty:
Mr. Dennis M. Wallace

Salary Minimum: $50,000

Functions: Mfg., Production, Automation, Plant Mgmt., Productivity, Packaging, Sales Mgmt., Engineering, Minorities/Diversity

Industries: Generalist (All), Manufacturing, Medical Devices, Metal Products, Machine, Appliance, Motor Vehicles, Computer Equip., Consumer Elect., Misc. Mfg., Robotics, Consumer Goods, Transportation

Sanford Rose Associates - Carmel

408 S 9th St Ste 102
Noblesville, IN 46060-2734
(317) 776-3535
(800) 201-2463
Fax: (877) 801-6128
Email: sracarmel@aol.com
Web: www.sanfordrose.com/carmel

Summary: Recruiting services for executive, managerial and professional position openings in the property & casualty insurance industry.

Key Contact - Specialty:
Mr. Michael A. Nichipor, President & Chief Executive Officer - *Insurance, Insurance (Property)*

Salary Minimum: $50,000

Functions: Management, Senior Mgmt., Middle Mgmt., Sales & Mktg., HR Mgmt., Finance, CFOs, MIS Mgmt., Attorneys

Industries: Insurance, Casualty, Claims, Commercial, Re-Insurance

Sanford Rose Associates - Bardstown

101 Wetherby Ave
Bardstown, KY 40004-5707
(502) 350-3774
Fax: (502) 350-3779
Email: glcrawford@sanfordrose.com
Web: www.sanfordrose.com/bardstown

Summary: We devote our practice to the healthcare area, specializing in reimbursement revenue cycle and compliance. We conduct custom searches for executive, managerial and mid-to-upper level professional positions for our clients..

Key Contact - Specialty:
Ms. Gayle L. Crawford, Managing Director - *Healthcare*

Salary Minimum: $50,000

Functions: Healthcare

Industries: Accounting SW, Healthcare, Hospitals

Sanford Rose Associates - N Kentucky

7000 Houston Rd Ste 16
Florence, KY 41042-4882
(859) 647-6472
Fax: (859) 647-6942
Email: rjpremec@sanfordrose.com
Web: www.sanfordrose.com/nky

Summary: Director through senior level executives in the life sciences industries.

Key Contact - Specialty:
Mr. Richard J. Premec, Jr., President

Functions: Senior Mgmt., Middle Mgmt., Materials Plng., Distribution, Mktg. Research, Mktg. Mgmt., Sales Mgmt., CFOs, M&A, R&D

Industries: Drugs Mfg., Medical Devices, Test, Measure Equip., Pharm Svcs., Biotech/Life Sciences

Sanford Rose Associates - Louisville East

806 Stone Creek Pkwy Ste 10
Louisville, KY 40223-5394
(502) 426-4900
Fax: (502) 426-4313
Email: louisvilleky@sanfordrose.com
Web: www.sanfordrose.com/louisville

Summary: An executive search practice whose mission is to be the preferred provider to clients for custom recruiting services for critical executive, managerial, technical and professional position openings in the nutraceutical, pharma, coatings and allied products industries. Our practice focuses on coatings and allied products, dietary supplements, industrial organic chemicals, and general senior level management.

Key Contact - Specialty:
Mr. George S. Griffiths, President - *Coatings*

Salary Minimum: $80,000

Functions: Generalist (All)

Industries: Chemicals

Sanford Rose Associates - Paducah

371 Oakcrest Dr Ste 200
Paducah, KY 42001-6705
(270) 534-0074
Email: paducahresume@sanfordrose.com
Web: www.sanfordrose.com/paducah

Summary: We only conduct custom searches for executive, managerial and mid-to-upper level professional positions for our clients. To solve your complex search problems we listen carefully to understand your needs and take great pride in our ability to identify rare candidates, quickly.

Key Contact - Specialty:
Mr. Robert A. Bender, President - *Architecture, Chemical, Construction, Engineering, Environmental*
Ms. Teresa Bender, Vice President - *Architecture, Chemical, Construction, Engineering, Environmental*

Functions: Management, Senior Mgmt., Middle Mgmt., Plant Mgmt., Engineering, Eng. Design, Architects, Health & Safety

Industries: Construction, Chemicals, Drugs Mfg., Architectural Svcs., Mgmt. Consulting, Engineering Svcs., Environmental Svcs., Haz. Waste

Sanford Rose Associates - Portland

48 Free St
Portland, ME 04101-3952
(207) 775-1200
Fax: (207) 775-1212
Email: portlandme@sanfordrose.com
Web: www.sanfordrose.com/portlandmaine

Summary: This office devotes its practice primarily to legal/attorney recruitment. We successfully place attorneys all over the country with our corporate (in-house) clients at staff attorney levels up to general counsel and with law firms all over the country at both the associate and partner level. We also have expertise in placing senior level healthcare executives.

Key Contact - Specialty:
Mr. David Shapiro, President

Salary Minimum: $90,000

Functions: Healthcare, Legal, Attorneys

Industries: Generalist (All), Legal, Biotech/Life Sciences, Healthcare

Sanford Rose Associates - Annapolis

101 Log Canoe Cir Ste H
Stevensville, MD 21666-2106
(410) 604-3370
Fax: (410) 604-3432
Email: panorton@sanfordrose.com
Web: www.sanfordrose.com/annapolis

Summary: We provide a high quality candidate search and screening process aided by detailed candidate presentation formats. Our focus is on filling senior and critical leadership roles for global clients within the specialty chemical & formulated product industries. Search assignments are limited to retained and exclusive contingency searches.

Key Contact - Specialty:
Mr. Peter A. Norton, President, Search Consultant, Recruiting - *General management,*

Marketing, Research & development, Sales, Technical (Management)
Mrs. Chloe C. Norton, Research & Administrative Assistant - *Business development, Coatings, Manufacturing, Medical (Devices,Sales)*
Mrs. Eleni Mioduszewski, Executive Recruiter - *Adhesives, Chemical, Composites, Petrochemical, Plastics*
Ms. Tina M. Johnson, Recruiter & Research Assistant - *Converting, Manufacturing (Management), Marketing, Quality, Regulatory*
Ms. Tamara A. Ewald, Recruiter & Research Assistant - *Manufacturing, Medical (Devices), Start-up companies, Supply Chain, Technical (Management)*

Salary Minimum: $80,000

Functions: Generalist (All)

Industries: Generalist (All), Chemicals, Drugs Mfg., Medical Devices, Plastics, Rubber, Paints, Petro. Products, Mgmt. Consulting, Logistics Svcs., Packaging

Sanford Rose Associates - Boston South Shore

350 Lincoln St Ste 2400
Hingham, MA 02043-1579
(781) 740-2800
Email: knorgeot@sanfordrose.com

Summary: We serve the biotechnology, medical device and pharmaceutical industries by successfully completing searches at executive, management and supervisory levels for clinical research, quality, regulatory, drug safety, R&D, public relations/corporate communications, marketing finance/investor relations and project management.

Key Contact - Specialty:
Mr. Kevin Norgeot, Owner & Managing Director - *Biopharmaceutical, Clinical, Communications, Investor relations, Life Sciences*
Ms. Katelyn E. Clifford, Recruiter & Consultant, Researcher - *Biomedical, Biopharmaceutical, Communications, Life Sciences, Pharmaceutical*

Salary Minimum: $75,000

Functions: Management, Senior Mgmt., Product Dev., Quality, Physicians, Mktg. Mgmt., PR, CFOs, R&D

Industries: Chemicals, Drugs Mfg., Medical Devices, Plastics, Rubber, Pharm Svcs., Biotech/Life Sciences, Healthcare

Sanford Rose Associates - Andover

44 Carlton Ln
North Andover, MA 01845-5603
(978) 685-0160
Web: www.sanfordrose.com/andover

Summary: Our office specializes in the medical equipment and device markets. We conduct searches across all functional areas, and specialize in marketing, sales and business development management or executive positions.

Key Contact - Specialty:
Mr. Michael Ebert

Salary Minimum: $80,000

Functions: Management, Senior Mgmt., Sales & Mktg., Mktg. Mgmt., Sales Mgmt., Sales Reps.

Industries: Drugs Mfg., Medical Devices

Sanford Rose Associates - Traverse City

PO Box 156
Suttons Bay, MI 49682-0156
(616) 271-6100
Fax: (616) 271-6106
Email: trsheidler@sanfordrose.com

Summary: Professional Recruiters for: Facility Management, PACS (Picture Archiving & Communication System) RIS, Biomedical & Clinical Equipment Managers & Technicians

Key Contact - Specialty:
Mr. Thomas R. Sheidler, President

Functions: Generalist (All), Management, Production, Engineering

Industries: Generalist (All), Food, Bev., Tobacco, Medical Devices, IT Implementation, Engineering Svcs., Healthcare

Sanford Rose Associates - Lake Ann

120 Boardman Ave Ste H
Traverse City, MI 49684-5713
(231) 929-5189
(231) 929-0100
Fax: (231) 929-5049
Email: tjburby@sanfordrose.com
Web: www.sanfordrose.com/lakeann

Summary: We devote our practice to the consumer products area, specializing in house wares, health and beauty aids, and sporting goods. Our consultants have developed extensive experience within those markets. We conduct custom searches for executive, managerial and mid-to-upper level professional positions for our clients.

Key Contact - Specialty:
Mr. Thomas J. Burby, President - *Chemical, Manufacturing (Management), Molding (Injection), Packaging, Plastics*
Ms. Susan B. Burby, Senior Search Consultant - *Biomedical, Engineering, Equipment, Medical (Devices), Pharmaceutical*

Salary Minimum: $65,000

Functions: Management, Mfg., Product Dev., Quality, Packaging, Healthcare, Sales & Mktg., Engineering, Eng. Design

Industries: Manufacturing, Paper, Printing, Chemicals, Drugs Mfg., Medical Devices, Plastics, Rubber, Paints, Petro. Products, Metal Products, Consumer Goods, Packaging, Biotech/Life Sciences

Sanford Rose Associates - Wayne

1395 State Rt 23
Butler, NJ 07405-1732
(973) 492-5424
Email: waynesearch@sanfordrose.com
Web: www.sanfordrose.com/wayne

Summary: We are a full service executive search organization devoting our practice to all areas of: finance, accounting, general management, operations, technology and project management for all industries and sectors. We conduct custom searches only for executive, managerial, and mid to upper level professional positions.

Key Contact - Specialty:
Mr. Paul Feeney

Functions: Finance

Industries: Generalist (All)

Sanford Rose Associates - Amherst

5500 Main St Ste 201
Williamsville, NY 14221-6737
(716) 626-2265
(888) 860-6997
Fax: (716) 626-4997
Email: dparekh@sanfordrose.com
Web: www.sanfordrose.com/amherst

Summary: We conduct contingency and retainer searches for the manufacturing and transportation industries. Customized searches for executive and managerial staff are conducted globally.

Key Contact - Specialty:
Mr. Dinesh V. Parekh, CPC, President - *Automotive, Information Technology*

Salary Minimum: $75,000

Functions: Senior Mgmt., Middle Mgmt., Mfg., Production, Plant Mgmt., Purchasing, Mktg. Mgmt., Sales Mgmt.

Industries: Manufacturing, Motor Vehicles, Transportation, Biotech/Life Sciences

Sanford Rose Associates - Greensboro

2007 Yanceyville St Ste 12
Greensboro, NC 27405-5005
(336) 235-0707
Fax: (336) 235-0709
Email: djbassford@sanfordrose.com
Web: www.sanfordrose.com/greensboro

Summary: Our Greensboro office does recruitment of senior level executives, managers, and professionals for all industries. We specialize in the vehicular and manufacturing industries. Vehicular includes: automotive, truck, trailer, bus, RV, AG, and construction. Our mission, simply put, is to find those people who can make a difference.

Key Contact - Specialty:
Mr. Daniel J. Bassford, Owner & President - *Automotive, Manufacturing, Marketing, Sales*

Salary Minimum: $80,000

Functions: Senior Mgmt., Middle Mgmt., Mfg., Plant Mgmt., Quality, Sales & Mktg., Mktg. Mgmt., Sales Mgmt., Sales Reps.

Industries: Manufacturing, Medical Devices, Plastics, Rubber, Metal Products, Machine, Appliance, Motor Vehicles, Computer Equip., Test, Measure Equip., Misc. Mfg., Electronic, Elec. Components, Robotics, Transportation, Services, Hospitality

Sanford Rose Associates - Huntersville

PO Box 1096
Huntersville, NC 28070-1096
(704) 992-0116
Fax: (704) 992-0118
Email: lmhardy@sanfordrose.com
Web: www.sanfordrose.com/huntersville

Summary: Specialists in the food manufacturing industry at the managerial, professional, and executive levels

Key Contact - Specialty:
Mr. Lionel Hardy, CPC, President - *Manufacturing*

Salary Minimum: $70,000

Functions: Management, Mfg., Plant Mgmt., Materials, Finance, R&D, Engineering

Industries: Food, Bev., Tobacco

Sanford Rose Associates - Akron

265 S Main St Ste 200
Akron, OH 44308-1223
(330) 762-6211
(888) 333-3828
Fax: (330) 762-6161
Email: mail@sraoc.com
Web: www.sraoc.com

Summary: Worldwide service for employers involved with: aerospace, aircraft, avionics, defense, electronics, power/utilities, engineering consulting, architecture, civil and environmental. We provide a wide range of services including confidential executive searches, technical and professional recruiting, contract staffing and outplacement.

Key Contact - Specialty:
Mr. Douglas R. Eilertson, President - *Franchising, Healthcare, Hospital, Hospitality, Sports*
Mr. Sanford Rose, Chief Executive Officer
Mrs. Martha Harris, Senior Technical Recruiter - *Aerospace, Defense, Embedded microprocessor, Engineering, RF microwave*
Mr. Odell McLeod, Senior Technical Recruiter - *Power, Utilities*
Mr. Chris O'Donnell, Senior Technical Recruiter - *Construction, Energy, Power, Technicians, Utilities*
Mr. Michael Hinton, Executive Search Consultant - *Electrical, Engineering, Field engineering, Power, Technology*
Ms. Deborah Royse, Executive Search Consultant

Salary Minimum: $60,000

Functions: Management, Senior Mgmt., Mfg., Product Dev., Production, Quality, Materials, Finance, Engineering

Industries: Energy, Utilities, Electronic, Elec. Components, Telecoms, Defense, Aerospace

Sanford Rose Associates - Cincinnati East

431 Ohio Pike Ste 214
Cincinnati, OH 45255-3629
(513) 528-3400
Email: fniolet@sraceo.com
Web: www.sraceo.com

Summary: We pride ourselves on finding better candidates faster and moving people in the right direction in the life sciences, pharmaceutical and health care industries.

Key Contact - Specialty:
Mr. Frank Niolet, Managing Partner - *Biopharmaceutical, Biotechnology, Chemical, Nutraceuticals, Pharmaceutical*
Mr. Ted Sherman, Managing Partner - *Diagnostics, Freight, Medical, Medical (Devices), Pharmaceutical*

Salary Minimum: $70,000

Functions: Generalist (All)

Industries: Drugs Mfg., Medical Devices, Pharm Svcs., Logistics Svcs., Supply Chain Mgmt, Biotech/Life Sciences

Sanford Rose Associates - Orange

30799 Pinetree Rd Ste 129
Cleveland, OH 44124-5903
(440) 893-9408
(800) 939-0189
Email: orangeoh@sanfordrose.com
Web: www.sanfordrose.com/orange

Summary: We are a specialized executive search practice that focuses on the recruitment of senior management, sales, business development and

operations for healthcare it, financial services and healthcare business process outsourcing organizations throughout North America. We have the ability to find people who make a genuine difference in organizational performance.

Key Contact - Specialty:
Ms. Ginni Garner, CPC, Partner, Healthcare IT & Service Prac - *Medical (Sales), Outsourcing*

Salary Minimum: $80,000

Functions: Management, Senior Mgmt., Healthcare, Sales Mgmt.

Industries: Industry Specific SW, Hospitals

Sanford Rose Associates - Columbus North

5777 Frantz Rd Ste 150
Dublin, OH 43017-1885
(614) 734-9716
(800) 560-4984
Fax: (614) 273-0874
Email: bill@sracolumbus.com
Web: www.sracolumbus.com

Summary: We work on national as well as local openings. Our firm specializes in the areas of: MIS/EDP, computer hardware & software, finance, accounting, pharmaceutical and medical device sales. Appointment requested; unsolicited resumes accepted.

Key Contact - Specialty:
Mr. Bill Earhart, President

Functions: Generalist (All), Healthcare, Sales & Mktg., MIS Mgmt., Systems Analysis, Systems Dev., Systems Implem., Systems Support, Network Admin., DB Admin.

Industries: Generalist (All)

Sanford Rose Associates - Fairlawn

3200 W Market St Ste 110
Fairlawn, OH 44333-3324
(330) 865-4545
Fax: (330) 865-4544
Email: dlcreeger@aol.com

Summary: Our focus is on specialty & fine chemicals, plastics, rubber and related industries such as adhesives, plastic additives and personal care, for general management, marketing, sales, technical and engineering functions.

Key Contact - Specialty:
Mr. David Creeger, CPC, President - *Chemical, Plastics, Rubber*

Salary Minimum: $75,000

Functions: Management, Middle Mgmt., Product Dev., Sales & Mktg., Mktg. Research, Mktg. Mgmt., Sales Mgmt., Sales Reps., R&D, Engineering

Industries: Chemicals, Soap, Perf., Cosmtcs., Drugs Mfg., Plastics, Rubber, Paints, Petro. Products

Sanford Rose Associates - Hudson

70 W Streetsboro St Ste 109
Hudson, OH 44236-5110
(330) 653-3325
Fax: (330) 650-4801
Email: hudsonoh@sanfordrose.com
Web: www.sanfordrose.com/hudson

Summary: An executive search firm focused on the direct recruitment of executives and professionals for companies that process Chemicals and Specialty Materials. Our focus is on conducting custom recruiting efforts for senior

professional through Vice President level positions.

Key Contact - Specialty:
Mr. Allen Wass, President

Salary Minimum: $75,000

Functions: Generalist (All), Management

Industries: Textiles, Apparel, Paper, Printing, Chemicals, Soap, Perf., Cosmtcs., Plastics, Rubber, Paints, Petro. Products, Leather, Stone, Glass, Metal Products, Haz. Waste

Sanford Rose Associates - New Albany

1245 Whispering Meadow Ct Ste 100
New Albany, OH 43054-9557
(614) 939-1309
Email: jodicorrier@sranewalbany.com
Web: www.sranewalbany.com

Summary: We specialize in filling catastrophe modeling and catastrophe management positions at all levels.

Key Contact - Specialty:
Ms. Jodelle (Jodi) K. Corrier, President & Chief Executive Officer

Salary Minimum: $100,000

Functions: Generalist (All)

Industries: Insurance, Casualty, Claims, Commercial, Re-Insurance

Sanford Rose Associates - Portland

15280 NW Central Dr Ste 202-2
Portland, OR 97229-7807
(503) 614-1861
Email: srapdx@aol.com

Summary: We serve the following industries: food/beverage processing and consumer packaging.

Key Contact - Specialty:
Mr. Jack D. Stiles, Director
Mr. Timothy W. Stiles, Director

Salary Minimum: $60,000

Functions: Generalist (All), Product Dev., Production, Plant Mgmt., Quality, Materials, Distribution, Packaging, Sales Mgmt., R&D

Industries: Generalist (All), Food, Bev., Tobacco, Chemicals, Soap, Perf., Cosmtcs., Drugs Mfg., Packaging

Sanford Rose Associates - Philadelphia North

201 Woolston Dr Ste 2E1
Morrisville, PA 19067-5008
(215) 428-9121
(888) 568-9549
Fax: (215) 428-9121
Email: jfburns@sanfordrose.com
Web: www.sraphilly.com

Summary: Retained and exclusive contingent searches for commercial and technical professionals in the specialty chemical, fine chemical, and pharma chemical markets.

Key Contact - Specialty:
Mr. Joseph F. Burns

Salary Minimum: $80,000

Functions: Generalist (All)

Industries: Generalist (All), Oil & Gas, Chemicals, Soap, Perf., Cosmtcs., Drugs Mfg., Plastics, Rubber, Paints, Petro. Products

Sanford Rose Associates - Greenville

211 Century Dr Ste 106D
Greenville, SC 29607-1575
(864) 233-6100
Fax: (305) 946-2946
Email: greenvillesc@sanfordrose.com

Summary: We have extensive management experience helping world-class companies problem solve. We specialize in mid to upper level management in all functions of a manufacturing environment, including precision machining, automotive, plastics and automation.

Key Contact - Specialty:
Mr. Richard Witowski, CPC, President

Salary Minimum: $50,000

Functions: Generalist (All)

Industries: Manufacturing, Misc. Mfg.

Sanford Rose Associates - Santee

PO Box 1175
Santee, SC 29142-1175
(803) 854-0003
Fax: (803) 826-6385
Email: jpmalloy@sanfordrose.com
Web: www.sanfordrose.com/santee

Summary: We devote our practice to the manufacturing, printing, and construction industries. Our consultants have developed extensive experience within those markets to aid in locating difference makers. We conduct custom searches for executive, managerial and mid-to-upper level professional positions. We pride ourselves in our ability to identify the rare candidates who fit our client's specific needs.

Key Contact - Specialty:
Mr. John P. Malloy - *Aerospace, Automotive, C-level, HVAC, Manufacturing (Management)*
Mr. Jeremiah K. Truax - *Building products, Controllers, Engineering, Environmental, Finance*
Mr. Dan Challgren - *Automotive, Engineering, Manufacturing (Management)*
Mr. Tom Bradley - *Automotive, Construction, Human resources, Manufacturing (Management)*
Ms. Kathleen Truax

Functions: Senior Mgmt., Engineering, Health & Safety

Industries: Agri., Forestry, Mining, Construction, Manufacturing, Lumber, Furniture, Paper, Printing, Chemicals, Medical Devices, Plastics, Rubber, Leather, Stone, Glass, Metal Products, Machine, Appliance, Motor Vehicles, Misc. Mfg., Electronic, Elec. Components, Semiconductors, Environmental Svcs., Aerospace

Sanford Rose Associates - Nashville

9000 Church St E
Brentwood, TN 37027-5285
(615) 346-3000
Fax: (615) 346-3003
Email: sracareers@comcast.net
Web: www.sanfordrose.com/nashville

Summary: Management and general management positions in the printing, converting and print supply industries. Senior management positions are across all industries.

Key Contact - Specialty:
Mr. Terry Tringle, Managing Director - *Printing*

Salary Minimum: $75,000

Functions: Generalist (All)

Industries: Printing

Sanford Rose Associates - Middle Tennessee

509 Enon Springs Rd E
Smyrna, TN 37167-4486
(615) 220-5036
Fax: (615) 223-9004
Email: middletennessee@sanfordrose.com
Web: www.sanfordrose.com/middletennessee

Summary: Our company finds people who make a difference in every vertical of the retail industry. We serve our clients with extensive retail senior leadership experience. Our thorough, detailed and quality focused dimensional search process yields results for both the client and candidate.

Key Contact - Specialty:
Mr. Jeff D. Hagan, President - *Retail*
Ms. Crystal McLeod, Recruiting Specialist

Salary Minimum: $50,000

Functions: Management, Board Members, Senior Mgmt., Middle Mgmt.

Industries: Retail

Sanford Rose Associates - Madison

(also known as SRA-Madison)
105 S Main St
Lodi, WI 53555-1138
(608) 592-2700
Web: www.sanfordrose.com/madison

Summary: We are a premier executive search firm focused on the direct recruitment of executives and professionals in manufacturing and automation including food, beverage, consumer packaged goods (CPG), plastics and other industries. Our mission is simple and sincere; we want to be your preferred provider of staffing services. We are flexible to your needs.

Key Contact - Specialty:
Mr. William Boeger, PE, President - *Consumer (Packaged Goods), Food & beverage, Management, Manufacturing, Packaging*

Salary Minimum: $50,000

Functions: Management

Industries: Manufacturing, Food, Bev., Tobacco, Plastics, Rubber, Metal Products, Robotics, Consumer Goods, HR Services, Engineering Svcs., Packaging

Sanford Rose Associates - China

Level 8 Bank of America Tower
12 Harcourt Rd
Central Hong Kong
China
2588 3412
Email: bhsu@sanfordrose.com

Summary: Consumer goods, financial services, healthcare services, hospitality, industrial, life sciences, media, medical devices, retail, technology and not-for-profit.

Key Contact - Specialty:
Mr. Benjamin Hsu

Functions: Management

Industries: Manufacturing, Chemicals, Retail, Finance, Services, Telecoms, Biotech/Life Sciences

Sarver & Carruth Associates

3927 N 1st Ave
Durant, OK 74701-2539
(580) 931-0472
Fax: (580) 931-0473
Email: cjsarver@simplynet.net

Summary: We are an executive and technical recruitment firm dedicated to providing excellent service both to client companies and candidates.

Key Contact - Specialty:
Ms. Catherine J. Sarver, President - *Engineering*

Salary Minimum: $50,000

Functions: Senior Mgmt., Product Dev., Systems Implem., R&D, Engineering

Industries: Generalist (All), Computer Equip., Electronic, Elec. Components, Transportation, Defense

SawyerSearch

PO Box 681232
Franklin, TN 37068-1232
(615) 591-6511
Email: hsawyer@sawyersearch.com
Web: www.sawyersearch.com

Summary: Executive search for healthcare management. Hospital Administration, Physician Practice Management, & Administration Healthcare Operations.

Key Contact - Specialty:
Ms. Harriett Sawyer, Owner

Functions: Senior Mgmt., Middle Mgmt., Admin. Svcs., Distribution, Health Admin., Sales Mgmt., Sales Reps., HR Mgmt., Staffing

Industries: Pharm Svcs., Supply Chain Mgmt., Property/Facility Mgmt., Biotech/Life Sciences, Healthcare, Hospitals, Long-term/Home Care

Saxbury Recruiting

4450 California Pl Ste 362
Long Beach, CA 90807-2209
(562) 531-1820
Fax: (562) 531-1824
Email: susan@saxburyrecruiting.com
Web: www.saxburyrecruiting.com

Summary: We are a recruiting firm specializing in both IT and engineering professionals. Company goals are to provide the best possible service at a reasonable cost, and in a timely manner. Our candidates are gleaned from a specialized network of associates, and also from the use of modern technology.

Key Contact - Specialty:
Mrs. Susan Saxbury-Alvord

Salary Minimum: $30,000

Functions: Middle Mgmt., Mfg., Sales Reps., IT, Engineering

Industries: Generalist (All), Software, Development SW

S.C. International, Ltd

1315 Butterfield Rd Ste 224
Downers Grove, IL 60515-1080
(630) 963-3033
(800) 543-2553
Fax: (630) 963-3170
Email: search@scinternational.com
Web: www.scinternational.com

Summary: Specialists in insurance and employee benefits recruitment: actuaries, claims, underwriting and benefits consultants. Additionally healthcare professionals.

Key Contact - Specialty:
Mr. Scott Rollins, President

Salary Minimum: $40,000

Functions: Generalist (All), HR Mgmt.

Industries: Generalist (All), HR Services, Insurance, Healthcare

Schalekamp & Associates Inc

2608 W 102nd St
Minneapolis, MN 55431-3346
(952) 948-1948
Fax: (952) 948-9677
Email: paul@midwestinsurancejobs.com
Web: www.midwestinsurancejobs.com

Summary: Work exclusively in the insurance industry, both property & casualty and health.

Key Contact - Specialty:
Mr. Paul Schalekamp, President

Salary Minimum: $40,000

Functions: Generalist (All), Risk Mgmt.

Industries: Insurance, Casualty, Claims, Life

Scheer & Associates

1873 S Bellaire St Ste 900
Denver, CO 80222-4356
(303) 757-7357
Fax: (303) 692-0449
Email: rascheer@aol.com
Web: www.scheerandassociates.com

Summary: We specialize in sales and sales management.

Key Contact - Specialty:
Mr. Roger Scheer, President

Functions: Sales & Mktg.

Industries: Construction, Food, Bev., Tobacco, Lumber, Furniture, Printing, Chemicals, Drugs Mfg., Medical Devices, Plastics, Rubber, Paints, Petro. Products

Schick Professional Search Inc

PO Box 326
North Lima, OH 44452-0326
(330) 549-3961
Email: rschicksps@aol.com

Summary: We specialize in design engineers for electric motors, motor drives and mechanical & electronic design of high volume consumer products. An industry focus of aerospace, automotive and consumer products.

Key Contact - Specialty:
Mr. Rex Schick, CPC, President - *Technical*
Mr. Jon Schick, Senior Account Manager - *Technical*

Salary Minimum: $45,000

Functions: Product Dev., R&D, Engineering, Eng. Design, Hardware

Industries: Machine, Appliance, Motor Vehicles, Consumer Elect., Electronic, Elec. Components, Consumer Goods, Aerospace, Industry Specific SW, System SW

A D Schiff & Associates Ltd

869 Creek Bend Dr
Vernon Hills, IL 60061-3305
(847) 821-9220
Fax: (847) 821-9298
Email: adschiff@theramp.net

Summary: We have experience in the medical profession. We are search and recruitment consultants in all areas of healthcare; sales, eCommerce, marketing, executive, physician and management.

Key Contact - Specialty:
Ms. Arlene D. Schiff, President
Ms. Kim Feeny, Vice President

Functions: Generalist (All), Healthcare, Sales & Mktg.

Industries: Drugs Mfg., Medical Devices, Pharm Svcs., Equip Svcs., Advertising, Biotech/Life Sciences, Healthcare, Hospitals, Long-term/Home Care, Dental, Physical Therapy, Women's

Schlatter & Associates

388 Market St Ste 500
San Francisco, CA 94111-5313
(415) 433-8100
Fax: (415) 433-8100

Summary: We specialize in CFO, controller, financial, and accounting management positions.

Key Contact - Specialty:
Mr. Craig Schlatter, Managing Partner - *Finance, Systems*

Salary Minimum: $75,000

Functions: Generalist (All), Middle Mgmt., Finance, CFOs, Budgeting, Cash Mgmt., M&A, MIS Mgmt.

Industries: Generalist (All), Manufacturing, Retail, Finance, Services, Real Estate, Software, Biotech/Life Sciences

Schoales & Associates Inc

94 Marjoram Dr
Ajax, ON L1S 7P4
Canada
(416) 863-9978
Fax: (905) 426-9312
Email: mikeschoales@hotmail.com

Summary: We specialize in recruiting sales & marketing and administrative individuals primarily in the financial services industry. Other assignments have been successfully completed in similar disciplines.

Key Contact - Specialty:
Mr. Michael Schoales, President - *Financial services*
Ms. Gloria Schoales, Vice President

Functions: Sales & Mktg., Sales Mgmt., M&A

Industries: Finance, Venture Cap.

The Schoenwetter Recruiting Network LTD

PO Box 429
Crosslake, MN 56442-0429
(612) 851-0228
(877) 292-3990
Fax: (612) 851-0229
Email: admin@howigotintoinsurance.com
Web: www.howigotintoinsurance.com

Summary: Recruit and place primarily within the insurance and financial services industry (excluding banking).

Key Contact - Specialty:
Ms. Carrie Schoenwetter

Salary Minimum: $30,000

Functions: Generalist (All)

Industries: Insurance, Casualty, Claims, Life, Commercial, Re-Insurance

---

Don W Schooler & Associates Inc

4810 E Farm Road 132
Springfield, MO 65802-7298
(417) 831-0004
Fax: (417) 831-5101
Email: don@donschooler.com
Web: www.donschooler.com

Summary: Executive recruiting for banking, trust institutions and farm credit only. We fill all officer positions. Candidates must have experience in one of the above institutions.

Key Contact - Specialty:
Mr. Don W. Schooler, Owner

Salary Minimum: $40,000

Functions: Generalist (All), CFOs

Industries: Generalist (All), Banking, Misc. Financial

Schulenburg & Associates

1827 Powers Ferry Rd SE Ste 19-150
Atlanta, GA 30339-5696
(770) 948-2088
Fax: (208) 275-1822
Email: kathryn@schulenburg-assoc.com
Web: www.schulenburg-assoc.com

Summary: Recruiting business professionals for independent equity building opportunity.

Key Contact - Specialty:
Mr. Neil P. Schulenburg, President
Mrs. Kathryn Schulenburg, Vice President

Functions: Sales & Mktg.

Industries: Generalist (All)

G L Schwartz & Associates Inc

100 Arrow Way
Mineral Bluff, GA 30559-7655
(706) 492-4955
Email: glsainc@tds.net

Summary: We specialize in senior marketing and sales management for medical device manufacturers, management in companies that are outpatient clinical service providers and management of companies that sell equipment to research laboratories (not clinical laboratories).

Key Contact - Specialty:
Mr. Gary L. Schwartz, President - *Healthcare*
Ms. Beth O. Schwartz, Secretary & Treasurer - *Healthcare*

Functions: Management, Sales & Mktg.

Industries: Manufacturing, Medical Devices, Test, Measure Equip., Healthcare, Long-term/Home Care

Science Consultants LLC

5325 E 6th St
Tucson, AZ 85711-2340
(520) 790-3408
Fax: (520) 747-1956
Email: info@scienceconsultants.org
Web: www.scienceconsultants.org

Summary: We are a small, exclusive consultancy and search firm specializing in helping life science technology companies to identify and recruit key contributors in business and research. We have experience in a broad range of companies and technologies within the life sciences. We provide our clients with executive leadership solutions at the director, VP, president, CxO and board levels.

Key Contact - Specialty:
Mr. Eric S. Britten, President

Salary Minimum: $90,000

Functions: Management

Industries: Chemicals, Drugs Mfg., Medical Devices, Test, Measure Equip., Pharm Svcs., Mgmt. Consulting, HR Services, Defense, Homeland Security, Biotech/Life Sciences

Scientific Search

101 E Gate Dr
Cherry Hill, NJ 08034-2803
(856) 761-0900
Fax: (856) 761-0910
Email: joe@scientificsearch.com
Web: www.scientificsearch.com

Summary: We place technology, management and executive management professionals. Our areas of specialization include pharmaceutical & biotechnology, healthcare management, engineering & design, and information technology. From contract placements to direct placements and everything in between, we work with employers and technology professionals to find the perfect solution.

Key Contact - Specialty:
Mr. Joseph Peters, III, President - *Engineering*
Mr. David Trexler, Technical Recruiter - *Engineering*
Mr. Stuart Bergen, Director, Recruiting
Mr. Jim Jenkins, Director, New Business Development

Salary Minimum: $60,000

Functions: Management, Quality, Packaging, Sales Mgmt., MIS Mgmt., Systems Dev., R&D, Engineering

Industries: Generalist (All), Biotech/Life Sciences, Healthcare

SciTech Global

PO Box 13236
Research Triangle Park, NC 27709-3236
(919) 419-0445
Email: hr@scitechglobal.com
Web: www.scitechglobal.com

Summary: We are an executive search and human capital consulting firm focused on providing professional staff with pharmaceutical, biotechnology, financial services and software development backgrounds on a contract, contract-to-hire, or direct basis.

Key Contact - Specialty:
Ms. Gina Roper, Managing Partner - *Biopharmaceutical, Financial services, Information Technology, Legal (Attorneys), Pharmaceutical*

Salary Minimum: $60,000

Functions: Healthcare, Nurses, IT, Systems Analysis, Systems Dev., DB Admin., R&D

Industries: Drugs Mfg., Medical Devices, Pharm Svcs., Biotech/Life Sciences

J R Scott & Associates Ltd

(a division of Esquire Personnel Services Inc)
1 S Wacker Dr Ste 1616
Chicago, IL 60606-4616
(312) 795-4300
(312) 795-4400
Fax: (312) 795-4329
Email: m.bradley@esquirestaffing.com
Web: www.esquirestaffing.com

Summary: Our consultants have a history of locating and motivating some of the most prestigious professionals in the financial services arena including complete office staffing.

Key Contact - Specialty:
Mr. Sherwin J. Fischer, Chief Executive Officer - *Financial, Securities*
Mr. Mark Bradley, Director

Functions: Generalist (All), Board Members, Senior Mgmt., Mktg. Research, Sales Mgmt., Cash Mgmt., M&A, Risk Mgmt.

Industries: Generalist (All), Finance, Banking, Invest. Banking, Brokers, Venture Cap., Misc. Financial

C Scott & Associates Inc.

PO Box 427 Stn 1st Can Place
1800-130 King St W
Toronto, ON M5X 1E3
Canada
(416) 214-9822
Email: info@cscottinc.com
Web: www.cscottinc.com

Summary: We are an IT recruiting firm for the financial services industry.

Key Contact - Specialty:
Ms. C. Scott, President

Functions: IT, Systems Analysis, Systems Dev., Systems Implem., Network Admin.

Industries: Finance, Banking, Brokers, Misc. Financial

Devin Scott Associates

PO Box 4115
Pawleys Island, SC 29585-4115
(201) 346-0331
Email: rfedele@devinscottassociates.com
Web: www.devinscottassociates.com

Summary: Strong contacts for operational management and all staff support departments for the hospitality industry.

Key Contact - Specialty:
Mr. Rocco M. Fedele, President - *Hospitality, Restaurants*

Salary Minimum: $70,000

Functions: Generalist (All), Hospitality

Industries: Hospitality, Hotels, Resorts, Clubs, Restaurants, Quick Service Restaurants, Full Service Restaurants, Inst./Industrial Food Svc., Entertainment, Recreation, Sports, Travel

R L Scott Associates

(also known as National Healthcare Search)
451 FM 1148 Ste 4
Graham, TX 76450-5814
(940) 549-6777
Fax: (940) 549-6668
Email: rls@rlscottassociates.net
Web: www.rlscottassociates.net

Summary: We are a management search consulting firm specializing in executive recruitment for the hospital provider industry, with a subspecialty in behavioral medicine. The service provided is the recruiting, identifying, screening, referencing and recommendation of candidates for specified positions as defined by the hospital company.

Key Contact - Specialty:
Mr. R.L. (Randy) Scott, Owner & Principal

Salary Minimum: $60,000

Functions: Generalist (All), Management, Board Members, Middle Mgmt., Healthcare, Mktg. Mgmt., Sales Mgmt., HR Mgmt., MIS Mgmt.

Industries: Generalist (All), Healthcare, Hospitals

Robert Scott Associates

PO Box 486
Rancocas, NJ 08073-0486
(609) 835-2224
Email: robert_scott@verizon.net

Summary: Helping companies recruit the finest technically trained professionals in research, engineering, operations and maintenance.

Key Contact - Specialty:
Mr. Bob Scott, President - *Engineering, Human resources, Management, Operations*

Salary Minimum: $50,000

Functions: Generalist (All), Mfg.

Industries: Manufacturing, Paper, Chemicals, Drugs Mfg., Medical Devices, Plastics, Rubber, Metal Products, Consumer Elect., Test, Measure Equip., Misc. Mfg., Consumer Goods, Environmental Svcs., Aerospace, Software, Biotech/Life Sciences

Scott-Marlow Agency

(also known as California Recruiters.com, Inc)
206 N Signal St Ste D
Ojai, CA 93023-2656
(805) 646-5609
Fax: (805) 646-5230
Email: dkomaiko@scott-marlow.com
Web: www.scott-marlow.com

Summary: We are an executive and middle management search firm dedicated to the placement of financial and accounting personnel. We provide complete, objective information and a superior ability to understand the unique personalities of our client companies and applicants and match them accordingly.

Key Contact - Specialty:
Mr. Daniel Komaiko, Owner - *Finance*

Salary Minimum: $50,000

Functions: Finance

Industries: Generalist (All), Finance, Accounting

Scott-Thaler Associates Agency Inc

110 E 9th St Ste C277
Los Angeles, CA 90079-5277
(800) 968-1562
(213) 312-9312
Fax: (213) 312-9324
Email: careers@scott-thaler.com
Web: www.scott-thaler.com

Summary: We specialize in the fashion apparel, retail, accessories, footwear, luxury goods, beauty/cosmetics/HBA, home furnishings/gifts and transportation (freight brokers) industries. We offer extensive, specialized industry experience and a distinctively personalized approach to recruiting, in order to meet the immediate needs of the client and to establish a productive long-term relationship.

Key Contact - Specialty:
Mr. Brian D. Thaler, CES, CPC, President - *Apparel, Logistics, Retail*
Ms. Mary Oliva Soares, CAC, CSP, General Manager

Salary Minimum: $30,000

Functions: Materials, Sales & Mktg., HR Mgmt., Technicians, Graphic Designers

Industries: Manufacturing, Textiles, Apparel, Soap, Perf., Cosmtcs., Transportation, Wholesale, Retail

SCS & Associates

PO Box 2294
Chapel Hill, NC 27515-2294
(800) 733-3387
Fax: (919) 932-6900
Email: steve@scs-associates.com

Summary: We have a background in graphic arts and are successfully recruiting executives in the printing industry.

Key Contact - Specialty:
Mr. Steve Soltan, President - *Printing*

Salary Minimum: $40,000

Functions: Generalist (All), Management, Middle Mgmt., Admin. Svcs., Plant Mgmt., Sales Mgmt., Direct Mktg., Customer Svc., IT

Industries: Generalist (All), Printing, Packaging

Branches:
6538 Laurel Hill Blvd
Woodside, NY 11377-5851
(718) 651-6645
(718) 505-1888
Fax: (718) 505-1888
Email: brian@scs-associates.com
Key Contact - Specialty:
Mr. Brian Barsher, Manager

Seaport Recruiting Group

3438 Don Lorenzo Dr
Carlsbad, CA 92010-3925
(760) 431-8595
Fax: (760) 431-4748
Email: rfullerton@att.net

Summary: Recruitment of casualty actuaries at all levels of experience and exams for insurance companies, consulting & risk management firms, ISO, NCCI, AIPSO, CPA firms, DOI's, and industry. Fee paid by employer. We provide contingency or retained search.

Key Contact - Specialty:
Mr. Ralph Fullerton, Owner & Founder - *Actuarial*

Salary Minimum: $55,000

Search America Inc

105 Webster St Ste 6
Hanover, MA 02339-1227
(781) 871-9798
(800) 826-0317
Email: mike@search-america.com
Web: www.search-america.com

Summary: We offer retained and contingency recruitment for management consultants and business development professionals, at mid to senior levels - for software companies, consulting organizations and select innovative eCommerce companies.

Key Contact - Specialty:
Mr. Steve Lombardo, President
Mr. Michael Sullivan, Director, Recruitment
Ms. Liz Harris, Manager, Business Development

Salary Minimum: $90,000

Functions: Generalist (All), Senior Mgmt., Sales & Mktg., Mgmt. Consultants

Industries: Wholesale, Retail, Finance, Mgmt. Consulting, E-commerce, IT Implementation, Software, ERP SW, HR SW, Industry Specific SW, Mfg. SW, Marketing SW

Search Associates

PO Box 131
Eastwood, KY 40018-0131
(502) 245-2928
Fax: (502) 245-2923

Email: search@metaljobs.net
Web: www.metaljobs.net

Summary: We specialize in all aspects of steel, aluminum, copper and other primary metal industries including engineers, plant management, QA staff, and metallurgists; and all types of processes: casting, melting, rolling, extrusion, etc.

Key Contact - Specialty:
Mr. Bill Johnstone, Executive Recruiter
Ms. Glenda Smith, Executive Recruiter - *Engineering, Facilities engineering, Foundries, Industrial, Maintenance*
Mr. John Conrad, Executive Recruiter - *BSME, Engineering, Management, Manufacturing, Metals*

Functions: Middle Mgmt., Production, Plant Mgmt., Quality, Productivity, Engineering

Industries: Metal Products

Search Associates & Consultants LLC

10650 Culebra Rd Ste 104
San Antonio, TX 78251-4950
(888) 948-6810
Email: anita@sa-consultants.com
Web: www.sa-consultants.com

Summary: We specialize in the placement of mid to executive level in telecom, technical (IT), pharmaceutical, administrative, sales as well as diversity placements.

Key Contact - Specialty:
Ms. Anita Starks, CAC, President - *Pharmaceutical, Sales, Technical, Telecommunications*

Functions: Generalist (All), Minorities/Diversity

Industries: Energy, Utilities, Manufacturing, Services, Pharm Svcs., Mgmt. Consulting, IT Implementation, Hospitality, Hotels, Resorts, Clubs, Telecoms, Telephony, Government, Defense, Homeland Security, Healthcare, Women's

Search Associates Inc

5900 Sepulveda Blvd Ste 104
Sherman Oaks, CA 91411-2511
(818) 988-5600
(888) 442-7900
Fax: (818) 787-0110
Email: mail@swjobs.com
Web: www.saijobs.com

Summary: We specialize in IT, accounting & finance, architecture, workers comp, real estate development, property management, biotechnology, legal and engineering. We place professionals on a full-time basis as well as contract and temp.

Key Contact - Specialty:
Mr. Lee Woodward, Co-President - *Computers (Software)*
Mr. Bernard Sharf, Co-President - *Multimedia*

Salary Minimum: $50,000

Functions: Generalist (All), Mfg., IT, Systems Analysis, Engineering, Architects, Legal

Industries: Generalist (All), Misc. Financial, Architectural Svcs., Legal, Accounting, Casualty, Real Estate, Software, Development SW, Security SW, Biotech/Life Sciences

Search Bureau International

PO Box 377608
Chicago, IL 60637-7608
(708) 210-1834
Fax: (708) 210-1834
Email: bhu5450778@aol.com

Summary: We are a group of professionals who specialize in the areas of accounting, finance, engineering, insurance, HR management, data processing and marketing. We also provide outplacement service to Fortune 500 companies.

Key Contact - Specialty:
Mr. Reginald M. Hudson, President - *Finance, Human resources*

Salary Minimum: $50,000

Functions: Generalist (All), Senior Mgmt., Sales & Mktg., Mktg. Research, Mktg. Mgmt., Direct Mktg., HR Mgmt., Finance, IT, Textile/Fashion

Industries: Generalist (All)

The Search Center Inc

1155 Dairy Ashford St Ste 404
Houston, TX 77079-3012
(281) 589-8303
Fax: (281) 589-8425
Web: www.thesearchcenter.com

Summary: We specialize in oil, natural gas power, petroleum products, petrochemical, chemical, and plastics industries. We focus on professional sales, trading and senior executive management positions, with a strong emphasis in energy derivatives and trade finance.

Key Contact - Specialty:
Ms. Susan M. Magnani, President - *Energy*

Salary Minimum: $100,000

Functions: Senior Mgmt., Sales & Mktg.

Industries: Energy, Utilities, Chemicals, Plastics, Rubber, Banking, Invest. Banking, Brokers, Misc. Financial

The Search Committee

8 Westbury Rd
Lutherville, MD 21093-5536
(888) 732-6752
(410) 825-7811
Fax: (410) 825-9035
Email: search@comcast.net
Web: www.erols.com/secor

Summary: Our firm has spent many years in the medical industry. We provide a tailored fit, not a generic solution.

Key Contact - Specialty:
Mr. David B. Secor, President - *Healthcare*

Salary Minimum: $65,000

Functions: Generalist (All)

Industries: Healthcare

Search Consultants Inc

(formerly known as Central Pacific Ventures)
1078 Country Skies Ave
Las Vegas, NV 89123-5309
(949) 608-7312
Email: searchconsultantsinc@gmail.com

Summary: Five years of recruiting experience doing retained and contingency executive search. Middle Management to C-level.

Key Contact - Specialty:
Mr. Mark Reagan, Executive Search Consultant - *Construction, Legal, Technical, Technology, Wireless*

Salary Minimum: $75,000

Functions: Management, Senior Mgmt., Middle Mgmt., Structural, Mgmt. Consultants, Architects

Industries: Construction, Architectural Svcs., Engineering Svcs., Supply Chain Mgmt., Property/Facility Mgmt.

Search Consultants Inc

1 E Ridgewood Ave
Paramus, NJ 07652-3629
(201) 444-1770

Summary: Looking for guaranteed satisfaction in hiring a HR executive? For the record: many years of success; a very efficient and timely hiring process; virtually no relocation costs.

Key Contact - Specialty:
Mr. Walter Perog, President - *Human resources*

Salary Minimum: $65,000

Functions: Generalist (All), HR Mgmt., Benefits, Staffing, Training

Industries: Generalist (All)

Search Consultants International Inc

4545 Post Oak Place Dr Ste 208
Houston, TX 77027-3116
(713) 622-9188
Fax: (713) 622-9186
Email: info@searchconsultants.com
Web: www.searchconsultants.com

Summary: Our firm has extensive experience in mid and senior management executive search, with industry expertise in: energy (power & gas), risk management & quantitative analysis, environmental, health & safety (EHS), process safety/risk engineering, manufacturing (petrochemical/refining) and independent power/cogeneration (IPP).

Key Contact - Specialty:
Mr. S. Joseph Baker, CPC, President - *Energy, Power*
Mr. Michael Brentari, Vice President
Mr. Richard Fiore, Vice President
Mr. Lon McAllister, Senior Consultant
Ms. Judith M. Baker, Vice President & Controller & Finance

Salary Minimum: $75,000

Functions: Management, Senior Mgmt., Middle Mgmt., Mfg., Plant Mgmt., Risk Mgmt., Engineering, Environmentalists

Industries: Energy, Utilities, Manufacturing, Services, Mgmt. Consulting, Environmental Svcs.

Search Exec

PO Box 531
Macungie, PA 18062-0531
(610) 966-1060
Fax: (253) 660-1172
Email: rb@mysearchexec.com
Web: www.mysearchexec.com

Summary: Specializes in placing top talent in the financial services industry. Bank Presidents, CEO, CFO, COO, Underwriters, Investment banking, Commercial Real Estate, C&I, asset management, Development, Aquisitions, Commercial and Retail Banking, Property management, Small business administration,Internal Audit, SOX, Compliance, analysts, B2B, Business Development, etc...

Key Contact - Specialty:
Mrs. Rosa Blanco, President - *Analysts, Asset management, Banking, Banking (Commercial,Corporate)*

Functions: Management, Sales Reps.

Industries: Generalist (All), Finance, Banking, Invest. Banking, Brokers, Venture Cap., Mutual/Hedge Funds, Misc. Financial, Services, Hotels, Resorts, Clubs, Real Estate, Property/Facility Mgmt.

Search Experts Inc

10035 133rd St
Seminole, FL 33776-1545
(888) 365-0549
(888) 517-3459
Fax: (727) 517-3113
Email: mrc@searchexperts.com
Web: www.searchexperts.com

Summary: We are a multi-dimensional recruiting/training firm. Recruiting is focused in finance, HR, sales/marketing, engineering/science, administrative support and the health care industry. The firm is certified by Power Hiring to train all levels of management to interview, assess and recruit top talent.

Key Contact - Specialty:
Mr. Mike Coddington, Managing Partner - *Finance, Marketing*
Ms. Kaye Coddington, Managing Partner

Salary Minimum: $50,000

Functions: Healthcare, Finance

Industries: Finance, Healthcare

Branches:
99 LaRoche Ave
Harrington Park, NJ 07640-1808
(201) 784-6777
Key Contact - Specialty:
Ms. Charlotte A. Legg

Search Group International (SGI) LLC

105 N 4th St Ste 204
Coeur D Alene, ID 83814-2747
(208) 667-6604
(208) 769-7503
Fax: (208) 665-1346
Email: mail@searchgroupusa.com
Web: www.searchgroupusa.com

Summary: We are an innovator in search utilizing cutting edge search technologies. Serving Fortune 500 companies and entrepreneurial endeavors worldwide. Specialty practices include telecommunications and technology.

Key Contact - Specialty:
Mr. Dave A. Johnson, CPC, Chief Operating Officer & Sr Mng Consult - *Cellular, Emerging growth, Senior management, Telecommunications, Wireless*
Mr. Lee Johnson, Recruiter - *Telecommunications, Wireless*

Functions: Generalist (All), Senior Mgmt., Sales Mgmt., Engineering

Industries: Venture Cap., Communications, Telecoms, Call Centers, Telephony, Digital, Wireless, Fiber Optic, Network Infrastructure, RF/Microwave

Search Group Ltd

1500 Skokie Blvd Ste 106
Northbrook, IL 60062-4112
(847) 498-1569
Fax: (847) 498-1614
Email: ron@searchgp.com

Summary: A search firm dedicated to finding clients highly qualified candidates with the right combination of skills, talents, abilities and enthusiasm. We specialize in many functionalities including: accounting/finance, tax, technology, administrative, sales/marketing. Industry specializations include: hospitals, financial services/insurance, retail, legal, manufacturing, and consulting/professional services.

Key Contact - Specialty:
Mr. Ronald Shtulman, President

Functions: Generalist (All)

Industries: Generalist (All)

The Search Group

302 Caspian Ct
Edgewood, MD 21040-3612
(800) 296-8256
Fax: (301) 547-7076
Email: hruska@thesearchgroup.net
Web: www.thesearchgroup.net

Summary: We are a search practice working exclusively with the property and casualty insurance industry. During the past years, we have completed assignments for some of the top companies and brokers in the country.

Key Contact - Specialty:
Mr. Thomas Hruska, CPC, Managing Director

Salary Minimum: $50,000

Functions: Generalist (All)

Industries: Insurance, Casualty, Claims, Commercial, Re-Insurance

Search International LLC

100 Conestoga Dr Apt 196
Marlton, NJ 08053-1246
(856) 596-6679
Fax: (732) 838-0747
Email: recruiter@searchintl.net
Web: www.searchintl.net

Summary: We are an executive placement firm specializing in placing attorneys.

Key Contact - Specialty:
Mr. Arnold Keiser, Director, Recruiting

Functions: Attorneys, Paralegals

Industries: Legal

Search Leader Inc

5695 Cherokee Dr
Cleveland, OH 44124-3047
(440) 442-7777
Email: info@searchleaderusa.com
Web: searchleaderusa.com

Summary: We perform searches for mid and upper level positions primarily in the all industries, both a contingency and retainer basis. We also offer research services to our clients.

Key Contact - Specialty:
Mr. John J. Selvaggio, President

Salary Minimum: $35,000

Functions: Finance

Industries: Generalist (All)

Search Masters USA

4598 Hamlets Grove Dr
Sarasota, FL 34235-2269
(941) 351-7307
Email: searchmastersusa@yahoo.com

Summary: We are a specialized search and recruiting firm placing senior sales & marketing talent in food & medical diagnostics, microbiology, biotechnology, hospital equipment, lab equipment, doctor office clinics and commercial and research labs. We also place sales management, marketing and new business development.

Key Contact - Specialty:
Mr. Alex Stevenson, President - *Biomedical, Marketing, Sales*

Salary Minimum: $50,000

Functions: Board Members, Senior Mgmt., Middle Mgmt., Healthcare, Sales & Mktg., Mktg. Mgmt., Sales Mgmt.

Industries: Food, Bev., Tobacco, Chemicals, Drugs Mfg., Medical Devices, Pharm Svcs., Mfg. SW, Marketing SW, Biotech/Life Sciences, Healthcare, Hospitals, Dental, Physical Therapy, Occupational Therapy

Search Net

14 County Road 225
Glen, MS 38846-9516
(662) 427-9000
(662) 284-0284
Fax: (662) 427-9080
Email: jshullco@aol.com
Web: www.printingjobs.com

Summary: We are a premier search firm for the graphic arts and printing industries. We are targeting talent at all levels. We place CEO, sales, plant management and skilled craft persons. No search is too big or too small. We offer retained, modified retainer and contingency programs for your project(s).

Key Contact - Specialty:
Mr. John Shull, Owner & Recruiter - *Printing*

Functions: Generalist (All)

Industries: Paper, Printing, Publishing, HR SW, Industry Specific SW, Mfg. SW

The Search Network

5755 Oberlin Dr Ste 312
San Diego, CA 92121-4717
(858) 720-9578
Email: snet@engineerrecruiters.com
Web: www.engineerrecruiters.com

Summary: By placing excellent technical professionals, we have built strong lasting relationships with top high-technology firms in our local area. We find the best position to suit your needs. Confidentiality guaranteed.

Key Contact - Specialty:
Ms. Kaaren Liz Henderson, President - *High technology*

Salary Minimum: $30,000

Functions: Management, Engineering

Industries: Generalist (All), Manufacturing, Medical Devices, Computer Equip., Semiconductors, Wireless

Search North America Inc

PO Box 3577
Sunriver, OR 97707-0577
(503) 222-6461
(541) 593-2777
Fax: (503) 227-2804
Email: carlj@searchna.com
Web: www.searchna.com

Summary: To improve the future performance of our client companies in the forest products, pulp & paper, power generation and related industries, we locate and place results-oriented candidates.

Key Contact - Specialty:
Mr. Carl Jansen, President - *Forest industry/products*

Salary Minimum: $45,000

Functions: Senior Mgmt., Mfg., Sales & Mktg., CFOs, R&D, Engineering, Int'l.

Industries: Energy, Utilities, Lumber, Furniture, Paper

Search Orion Inc

850 Euclid Ave Ste 722
Cleveland, OH 44114-3304
(800) 921-0207
(216) 797-0570
Email: info@searchorion.com
Web: www.searchorion.com

Summary: Areas of expertise include; sales, marketing and executive management professionals for consumer products, houseware, lawn & garden, hardware and building materials industries. Contingency and retainer options, new client programs.

Key Contact - Specialty:
Mr. Sonny Verma
Ms. Peggy O'Grady

Salary Minimum: $75,000

Functions: Middle Mgmt., Sales & Mktg., Mktg. Mgmt., Sales Mgmt.

Industries: Food, Bev., Tobacco, Lumber, Furniture, Chemicals, Soap, Perf., Cosmtcs., Plastics, Rubber, Paints, Petro. Products, Leather, Stone, Glass, Metal Products, Machine, Appliance, Consumer Elect., Misc. Mfg., Electronic, Elec. Components, Consumer Goods, Wholesale, Retail

Search Personnel Inc

PO Box 88
Carolina, RI 02812-0088
(401) 213-6116
Fax: (401) 213-6117
Email: search@cox.net

Summary: Placement of professionals in engineering (including chemical engineering automation/process controls), IT, manufacturing, sales/marketing and finance. Provider of outplacement services and consultations.

Key Contact - Specialty:
Mr. Leo R. Lavoie, Principal

Salary Minimum: $30,000

Functions: Generalist (All), Production, Materials Plng., Sales Mgmt., Staffing, IT, Engineering

Industries: Generalist (All), Chemicals, Drugs Mfg., Plastics, Rubber, Software, Healthcare

Search Plus International

25882 Orchard Lake Rd Ste 207
Farmington Hills, MI 48336-1295
(248) 471-6110
Fax: (248) 471-6572
Email: spi@searchplusintl.com
Web: www.searchplusintl.com

Summary: With many years of experience in executive recruiting for corporations, our firm provides a complete human solution process with the flexibility of adapting to most industries.

Key Contact - Specialty:
Ms. Christine Greeneisen, President & Chief Executive Officer - *Engineering, Executives, Industrial, Manufacturing, Sales*

Salary Minimum: $90,000

Functions: Management, Senior Mgmt., Mfg., Materials, Distribution, Sales & Mktg., HR Mgmt., Finance, IT, Engineering

Industries: Generalist (All), Manufacturing, Plastics, Rubber, Motor Vehicles, Misc. Mfg., Electronic, Elec. Components, Transportation, Finance, IT Implementation, Aerospace, Software

Search Point LLC

296 Wellington Ave
Elk Grove Village, IL 60007-3406
(847) 952-7151
Fax: (847) 2785417
Email: mark@searchpointusa.com

Summary: With extensive experience, we are a executive search firm dedicated to helping exceptional organizations identify and attract top sales & marketing talent.

Key Contact - Specialty:
Mr. Steve Fried, Manager - *Sales*
Mr. Mark Rafferty, Manager - *Electrical, Electronics, Mechanical, Sales*

Salary Minimum: $50,000

Functions: Generalist (All), Sales & Mktg., Sales Mgmt.

Industries: Generalist (All), Energy, Utilities, Manufacturing, Food, Bev., Tobacco, Chemicals, Plastics, Rubber, Computer Equip., Test, Measure Equip., Misc. Mfg., Electronic, Elec. Components, Transportation, Services, Non-profits, Law Enforcement, Telecoms, Fiber Optic, Software, Doc. Mgmt., Production SW, Mfg. SW, Marketing SW, Non-Classifiable

Search Pro Inc

280 Clinton Pl
Hackensack, NJ 07601-2801
(201) 489-0908
Fax: (201) 342-3229
Email: searchpro@aol.com
Web: www.search-pro.com

Summary: Hospitality experienced executives with a broad scope of knowledge of your industry ready to serve you.

Key Contact - Specialty:
Ms. Pat Romero, President - *Executives, Middle management*
Ms. Vicky Farhi, Manager - *Culinary*

Salary Minimum: $25,000

Functions: Generalist (All), Management, Senior Mgmt., Middle Mgmt., Mktg. Research, HR Mgmt., CFOs

Industries: Generalist (All), Hospitality

Branches:
20173 Canyon View Dr
Canyon Country, CA 91351-5734
(661) 298-7008
Fax: (661) 298-7026
Email: searchpro@aol.com

Search Professionals Inc

PO Box 1900
Sandwich, MA 02563-7900
(508) 833-6161
(888) 703-4334
Fax: (508) 833-6106
Email: searchpros@searchprosinc.com
Web: www.searchprosinc.com

Summary: We specialize in retailing, mass merchants, specialty stores, discount, home centers, eCommerce, catalog, direct marketing, supply chain management, food retailing, department stores, logistics and supply chain.

Key Contact - Specialty:
Mr. Richard Barzelay, President - *Distribution, Retail*
Mr. Frank Tonini, Vice President - *Direct marketing, Retail*

Salary Minimum: $50,000

Functions: Generalist (All), Senior Mgmt., Middle Mgmt., Purchasing, Distribution, Direct Mktg.

Industries: Generalist (All), Textiles, Apparel, Transportation, Wholesale, Retail, Non-profits, E-commerce, Hospitality

Branches:
PO Box 16675
Surfside Beach, SC 29587-6675
(843) 215-2638
Fax: (843) 215-2642
Email: pmulln@aol.com
Key Contact - Specialty:
Mr. Paul Mullen - *Retail*

Search South Inc

PO Box 2224
Anniston, AL 36202-2224
(256) 237-1868
Fax: (256) 237-1850
Email: arthuryoung@searchsouth.com
Web: www.searchsouth.com

Summary: We provide professional, technical and management recruitment. We recruit primarily in accounting, engineering and manufacturing to include metal processing & fabrication, copper & steel tubing, automotive parts/assembly, energy, packaging, consumer products, copper wire and cable, composite material, CD/DVD, mobile equipment, distribution, environmental and food processing which includes poultry.

Key Contact - Specialty:
Mr. Arthur Young, President & Owner - *Distribution, Engineering, Manufacturing, Multimedia*
Ms. Lynn Higdon, Search Consultant - *Distribution, Engineering, Manufacturing*
Ms. Jamie Holland, Research & Sourcing Coordinator
Mrs. Patsy Young, Coordinator, NPA Network - *Automotive, Distribution*

Salary Minimum: $50,000

Functions: Generalist (All), Senior Mgmt., Middle Mgmt., Admin. Svcs., Mfg., Plant Mgmt., Quality, Distribution, CFOs, Engineering

Industries: Generalist (All), Energy, Utilities, Manufacturing, Paper, Chemicals, Metal Products, Machine, Appliance, Motor Vehicles, Misc. Mfg., Electronic, Elec. Components, Consumer Goods, Transportation, Finance, Accounting, Higher Ed., Packaging

Search Team One

10503 N Moore St
Syracuse, IN 46567-9554
(574) 457-8544
Fax: (574) 457-8543
Email: don@execsearchplus.com
Web: www.execsearchplus.com

Summary: We provide executive search, outplacement and contract services in engineering, management, telecommunication, manufacturing, data processing, banking, accounting and financial areas.

Key Contact - Specialty:
Mr. Donald G. Walker, President - *Engineering, Manufacturing, Materials, Quality*
Mr. Ron Klawitter, Search Consultant - *Computers, Engineering, Manufacturing, Manufacturing (Management), Quality*
Mr. Rick Kenniker, Senior Recruiter - *Design, Maintenance, Manufacturing (Management), Operations, Production*

Ms. Judy Kenniker, Recruiter - *Emergency room, Healthcare, Hospital, Medical, Operating rooms*
Ms. Beverly Newton, Senior Recruiter - *Biotechnology, Construction, Hospital, Medical, Medical (Sales)*

Salary Minimum: $40,000

Functions: Senior Mgmt., Product Dev., Production, Automation, Plant Mgmt., Quality, Purchasing, Materials Plng., Staffing, IT

Industries: Manufacturing, Plastics, Rubber, Metal Products, Machine, Appliance, Motor Vehicles, Computer Equip., Consumer Elect., Test, Measure Equip., Misc. Mfg., Electronic, Elec. Components, Robotics

Searchco

493 Whippers In Ct
Bloomfield Hills, MI 48304-3073
(877) 898-9880
Fax: (702) 973-4335
Email: dferris@searchco.net
Web: www.searchco.net

Summary: Provides executive search services for the world's leading companies. Works with individuals who are not actively seeking a new position. Often reaches the people who never have to answer a "help wanted" advertisement. Most placements are with candidates who are gainfully employed, but who utilize the firm to further their careers.

Key Contact - Specialty:
Dr. David A. Ferris, President - *Consulting, Information Technology, International, Legal, Senior management*
Mr. Stephen C. Clapper, Principal Consultant - *Defense, Engineering, Financial, Human resources, Sales*
Mr. Aaron T. Scogin, Principal Consultant - *Aerospace, Engineering, Healthcare, Manufacturing, Technology*
Mr. Lim Kokyun, Associate Consultant - *Financial, Hospitality, Mining, Oil, Paper*
Mr. Rosario DeLisi, Associate Consultant - *Computers, Computers (Programming), Consulting, Information Systems, Information Technology*

Salary Minimum: $75,000

Functions: Senior Mgmt., Healthcare, Physicians, Sales & Mktg., HR Mgmt., Finance, IT, Engineering, Legal, Int'l.

Industries: Generalist (All), Agri., Forestry, Mining, Energy, Utilities, Oil & Gas, Manufacturing, Paper, Drugs Mfg., Medical Devices, Computer Equip., Misc. Mfg., Consumer Goods, Banking, Invest. Banking, Brokers, Venture Cap., Mutual/Hedge Funds, Misc. Financial, Services, Pharm Svcs., Legal, Accounting, Mgmt. Consulting, HR Services, E-commerce, IT Implementation, Engineering Svcs., Supply Chain Mgmt., Entertainment, Communications, Call Centers, Digital, Wireless, Fiber Optic, RF/Microwave, Defense, Compliance, Aerospace, Software, Biotech/Life Sciences, Healthcare, Hospitals, Non-Classifiable

Searchlight Recruiters Inc

24338 El Toro Rd Ste E
Laguna Woods, CA 92637-2776
(949) 916-9880
Email: info@searchlightrecruiters.com
Web: www.searchlightrecruiters.com

Summary: We are an executive search firm specializing in placing people where healthcare and technology industries converge. From sales positions to the CIO, we work closely with our

customer to assist them in recruiting highly qualified and experienced professionals. We are a full service recruitment firm, providing either contingency or retained search. We also provide alternative staffing solutions such as contract staffing, temp-to-direct, and 1099 conversions.

Key Contact - Specialty:
Chris Cornwall, President & Chief Executive Officer

Salary Minimum: $50,000

Functions: Generalist (All), Admin. Svcs., Mktg. Mgmt., Systems Implem.

Industries: Generalist (All), New Media, Communications, Telecoms, Digital, Wireless, Fiber Optic, Network Infrastructure, Industry Specific SW, Biotech/Life Sciences, Healthcare, Hospitals

Searchmark Medical

8050 Beckett Center Dr Ste 326
West Chester, OH 45069-5045
(513) 772-7720
Fax: (815) 425-8981
Email: dls@searchmark.com
Web: www.searchmark.com

Summary: We provide recruiting services for the medical sales, sales management and marketing industry.

Key Contact - Specialty:
Mr. Dan Stiffler, President
Mr. Mike Hohman, Senior Medical Recruiter
Mr. Alan Smith, CPC, Director, Marketing Recruitment

Salary Minimum: $50,000

Functions: Sales & Mktg.

Industries: Drugs Mfg., Medical Devices

SearchNet

2211 Encinitas Blvd
Encinitas, CA 92024-4361
(760) 753-9922
Email: careers@searchnet.net
Web: www.searchnet.net

Summary: Our firm specializes in IT and software development related technical recruitment for our market area. We offer a refreshing, quality-oriented approach that puts the candidate's needs and requirements first to ensure good, long-lasting career matches.

Key Contact - Specialty:
Mr. Paul Korn, President
Ms. Danna Korn, Vice President

Functions: IT

Industries: Network Infrastructure, Database SW, Development SW, Doc. Mgmt., Production SW, Entertainment SW, ERP SW

SearchOne Inc

1202 Main St Ste 215
Little Rock, AR 72202-5057
(501) 224-8822
Fax: (501) 244-9508
Email: vickie@searchoneinc.com
Web: www.searchoneinc.com

Summary: We place candidates in accounting, finance, human recources, information technology, medical, and manufacturing management.

Key Contact - Specialty:
Ms. Vickie Hendrix-Siebenmorgen, CPC, President - *Accounting, Consumer (Products), Finance, Healthcare, Information Systems*

Ms. Kelly Slayden, CPC, Chief Operating Officer - *Accounting (General), Engineering, Finance, Healthcare, Human resources*
Ms. Jill Lambert, Recruiter - *Accounting (General), Chemical, Engineering, Information Technology, Manufacturing*

Salary Minimum: $40,000

Functions: Generalist (All), Management, Mfg., Healthcare, Finance, IT, Engineering

Industries: Generalist (All), Manufacturing, Misc. Financial

SearchPath International

1220 Huron Rd E Ste 4
Cleveland, OH 44115-1711
(216) 912-1500
Fax: (216) 658-9711
Email: aej@searchpath.com
Web: www.searchpath.com

Summary: We encourage collaboration of our franchises to offer world-class service in identifying top-tier players from the boardroom to the front line sales executive.

Key Contact - Specialty:
Mr. Thomas K. Johnston, President - *Healthcare, Staffing*
Ms. Amy Johnston, Vice President

Functions: Generalist (All), Management, Board Members, Senior Mgmt., Sales & Mktg., Sales Mgmt., CFOs, Risk Mgmt., MIS Mgmt.

Industries: Generalist (All), Banking, Brokers, HR Services, Hotels, Resorts, Clubs, Non-Classifiable

SearchPro Group of America Ltd

3500 DePauw Blvd Ste 2050
Indianapolis, IN 46268-6138
(317) 872-4960
Fax: (317) 879-1233
Email: mail@searchprogroup.com
Web: www.searchprogroup.com

Summary: We are an executive recruiting firm that specializes in medical, technical, manufacturing, financial and sales management positions. Company operates on a contingency and retained basis and offers executive search, outplacement and employee retention services.

Key Contact - Specialty:
Mr. Timothy P. Dugger, Owner - *Manufacturing*
Mr. Gregg Stephens, Operations Manager
Ms. Joan McAvoy, CPC, General Manager
Mr. Alan Karrfalt, Senior Account Executive - *Manufacturing, Metals, Plastics, Rubber*
Mr. Keith Noster, Senior Account Manager - *Finance, Managed care*
Mr. John Ugstad, Account Executive

Salary Minimum: $60,000

Functions: Board Members, Senior Mgmt., Mfg., Healthcare

Industries: Generalist (All), Manufacturing, Plastics, Rubber, Motor Vehicles, Electronic, Elec. Components, Transportation, Services, HR Services, Hospitality, Communications, Government, Software, Accounting SW, Healthcare, Hospitals, Long-term/Home Care, Dental, Physical Therapy, Occupational Therapy, Women's

SearchPro Inc

8206 Providence Rd Ste 1200 #400
Charlotte, NC 28277-9708
(704) 849-9092
Fax: (704) 849-9095
Email: mary@searchpro.com
Web: www.searchpro.com

Summary: Our search firm partners with over 55 banking specialty recruiters to offer a current database of premier talent. Our mission is to deliver exceptional confidential customer service. Our quality team goes the distance to meet your sensitive staffing needs.

Key Contact - Specialty:
Ms. Mary J. Mallett, CPC, CSP, Owner & President

Salary Minimum: $50,000

Functions: Generalist (All), Finance

Industries: Generalist (All), Finance, Banking, Invest. Banking, Brokers, Venture Cap., Misc. Financial

SearchStars Inc

46 Nelson Rd Ste B
Vestal, NY 13850-6121
(607) 748-5867
Email: searchstars@searchstars.com
Web: www.searchstars.com

Summary: We specialize in technical and professional staffing, direct & contract, payroll services, executive, engineering, healthcare, IT, financial and administrative. Retained, contingency and hourly based billing.

Key Contact - Specialty:
Mr. Frank Sommer, President

Salary Minimum: $70,000

Functions: Generalist (All), Board Members

Industries: Generalist (All), Manufacturing, Medical Devices, Computer Equip., Consumer Elect., Test, Measure Equip., Electronic, Elec. Components, Robotics, Consumer Goods, HR Services, Haz. Waste, Aerospace, Software, Development SW, Mfg. SW, Healthcare

Sears & Associates

16212 Bridlewood Cir
Delray Beach, FL 33445-6674
(561) 638-4750
Fax: (561) 637-6585
Email: jerrysears@aol.com
Web: www.mentoringpros.com

Summary: We mostly recruit senior attorneys for both law firms and in-house (corporate) positions. We also do some senior management and director recruiting for technology companies.

Key Contact - Specialty:
Mr. Jerry Sears, Principal

Salary Minimum: $80,000

Functions: Generalist (All), Board Members, Senior Mgmt., Admin. Svcs., Legal, Attorneys

Industries: Generalist (All), Services, Legal

DL Sears & Associates Inc

20 Lindstrom Rd
Morris Plains, NJ 07950-2407
(973) 285-0258
(201) 602-8988
Email: dlsears@optonline.net
Web: www.dlsears.com

Summary: Our executive search practice is focused on the investment management business segment, primarily in the New York, Boston and Philadelphia markets. We conduct searches for investment management professionals and teams. We also identify and assist with merger opportunities. Our services help grow the size and diversity of client firm assets under management (AUM).

Key Contact - Specialty:
Mr. David L. Sears, President - *General management, Product management/development, Technology*

Salary Minimum: $90,000

Functions: Senior Mgmt., Sales Mgmt.

Industries: Brokers, Mutual/Hedge Funds

Sears, West & Hutchins LLC

900 University Blvd N Ste 600
Jacksonville, FL 32211-5589
(904) 215-1103
(800) 557-1104
Fax: (904) 744-7893
Email: swhrlaw@yahoo.com
Web: www.swhlawyers.com

Summary: Our firm provides global practice development and merger specialists. Merger of law firms and/or placement of attorneys with law firms; associate and partner levels.

Key Contact - Specialty:
Mr. Doug Sears, Partner
Mr. Christopher West, Partner
Mr. Rob Hutchins, Partner

Salary Minimum: $70,000

Functions: M&A, Legal, Attorneys

Industries: Legal

SEC Services LLC

(also known as Sysgenix Resources)
1889 General George Patton Dr Ste 200
Franklin, TN 37067-6294
(615) 846-2200
Fax: (615) 846-2201
Email: recruiter@sysgenix.com
Web: www.sysgenix.com

Summary: We provide consulting and full time placement of IT professionals.

Key Contact - Specialty:
Mr. Rick Bellar, President
Mr. John Kepley, Director, Consulting Services

Functions: Mfg., Healthcare, IT

Industries: Generalist (All)

Seco & Zetto Associates Inc

587 Sierra Vista Ln
Valley Cottage, NY 10989-2713
(201) 784-0674
(845) 353-0662
Fax: (845) 348-0410
Email: szsearch@aol.com

Summary: We are specialists in keeping abreast of sudden or sensitive changes in the IT and Internet/telecom industries, while exhibiting an exceptionally rapid response time.

Key Contact - Specialty:
Mr. William M. Seco, President - *Management*
Ms. Kathryn Zetto, Executive Vice President - *Management*

Salary Minimum: $85,000

Functions: Management, Sales & Mktg., Sales Mgmt., IT, Systems Implem.

Industries: Mgmt. Consulting, PSA/ASP, Network Infrastructure, Software, Networking, Comm. SW

Security Management Resources Inc

19170 Springs Rd
Jeffersonton, VA 22724-1923
(540) 428-2020
Fax: (540) 349-3021

Email: corporate@smrgroup.com
Web: www.smrgroup.com

Summary: Exclusive corporate security search practice with niche market expertise focused on professional and executive level positions throughout the world. All principals and associates have significant senior level management experience leading and managing corporate security programs across a wide range of industries for leading global organizations.

Key Contact - Specialty:
Mr. Jerry J. Brennan, Managing Director
Mr. Mike Maddaloni, Senior Consultant

Salary Minimum: $75,000

Functions: Mgmt. Consultants, Homeland Security, Security Personnel

Industries: Generalist (All)

Affiliates:
Business Security Solution Inc
Hilton Head, SC

Ramsay Management Consulting
Suquamish, WA

Branches:
18950 US Highway 441 PMB 118
Mount Dora, FL 32757-6738
(352) 385-0739
Email: jay.crawford@smrgroup.com
Key Contact - Specialty:
Mr. Jay Crawford, CPP, Senior Consultant

Security Recruiters

(also known as Consultant Recruiter)
6842 N Park Manor Dr
Milwaukee, WI 53224-4636
(414) 975-5760
Fax: (267) 295-1884
Email: dwc@securityexecs.com
Web: www.securityexecs.com

Summary: We are focused security executives and information-security specialists. We have executive recruiting experience and a former information security consultant with extensive IT development and consulting experience directs our security recruiting.

Key Contact - Specialty:
Mr. Don Cornell, Principal
Mr. Eric Randall, Director, International Recruiting - *International*

Salary Minimum: $80,000

Functions: IT, Mgmt. Consultants

Industries: Banking, Mgmt. Consulting, Law Enforcement, Security SW

Laura Segal & Associates Inc

PO Box 12654
Charlotte, NC 28220-2654
(800) 757-8227
Email: lbradley@lawyer-placement.com
Web: www.lawyer-placement.com

Summary: Our firm is an attorney placement boutique for associates and partners. All searches are conducted by previously practicing attorneys with extensive contacts in the geographic regions and practice areas they serve. Searches are individually tailored to the abilities, needs and preferences of each candidate with strict emphasis on credibility and confidentiality.

Key Contact - Specialty:
Ms. Laura L. Bradley, Esq.

Functions: Attorneys

Industries: Generalist (All), Finance, Banking, Venture Cap., Mutual/Hedge Funds, Misc. Financial, Services, Legal

Segall & Associates Inc

611-220 Duncan Mill Rd
North York, ON M3B 3J5
Canada
(416) 492-7333
Email: resumes@segallassociates.com
Web: www.segallassociates.com

Summary: We focus on the placement of sales/marketing & business development candidates for our clients who are primarily in the technology & communications industries. Positions range from mid to executive level.

Key Contact - Specialty:
Ms. Rona Segall, President - *Communications, Computers (Software), Professional services, Telecommunications, Wireless*

Functions: Generalist (All)

Industries: IT Implementation, Media, New Media, Telecoms, Call Centers, Telephony, Wireless, Network Infrastructure, ERP SW, Healthcare

Select Medical Solutions

16303 Autumn View Terrace Dr
Ellisville, MO 63011-4744
(636) 405-0333
Fax: (636) 458-4657
Email: steve@selectmedicalsolutions.com

Summary: We are recruitment specialists for sales and sales management in medical device/products and pharmaceutical industries. Our insurance division specializes in placement within the industry for candidates with experience in claims, underwriting, loss prevention, premium audit, special investigative units (fraud), marketing, legal and sales.

Key Contact - Specialty:
Mr. Steve Huffman - *Medical, Medical (Sales), Pharmaceutical*
Ms. Amy Hood - *Medical, Medical (Sales), Pharmaceutical*
Ms. Cindy Roderique, Director, SMS Insurance Recruiting - *Insurance, Insurance (Casualty, Claims, Reinsurance, Workers Compensation)*

Salary Minimum: $30,000

Functions: Generalist (All), Management, Sales Mgmt., Sales Reps.

Industries: Drugs Mfg., Medical Devices, Pharm Svcs., Insurance, Casualty, Claims, Re-Insurance, Biotech/Life Sciences, Dental

Select Search

5 E College Dr Ste 200
Arlington Heights, IL 60004-1963
(847) 368-8900
Fax: (847) 368-8999
Email: rnasatir@selectsearch.com

Summary: We specialize in banking and accounting placements.

Key Contact - Specialty:
Mr. Richard Nasatir, President - *Computers, MIS*

Salary Minimum: $45,000

Functions: Automation, DB Admin.

Industries: Banking, Invest. Banking, Brokers, Venture Cap., Mutual/Hedge Funds

Selected Executives Inc

PO Box 380430
Cambridge, MA 02238-0430
(781) 933-1500
Fax: (617) 547-7333

Summary: Many years of experience, we specialize in diversity professionals and demonstrating that, with just a little extra effort, qualified diversity candidates can be identified for every key position.

Key Contact - Specialty:
Mr. Lee R. Sanborn, Jr., President
Mr. Jackson A. Brookins, Manager
Ms. K. Jane Lewis, Systems Manager
Ms. Suzanne S. Martin, Senior Counselor
Mr. Kenneth T. Dinklage, Vice President

Salary Minimum: $50,000

Functions: Generalist (All)

Industries: Generalist (All)

Selectis Corp

1539 N Douglas Ave Ste D
Arlington Heights, IL 60004-3901
(847) 454-1100
Email: selectis@selectis.com
Web: www.selectis.com

Summary: We provide high quality recruitment services and contractors for growing organizations with specialized, time critical requirements. Extensive research, recruiter expertise and urgency are involved in each project.

Key Contact - Specialty:
Mr. Frank Lutostanski, President - *Senior management*

Salary Minimum: $60,000

Functions: Production, Quality, Sales & Mktg., Sales Mgmt., IT

Industries: Generalist (All), Pharm Svcs., Insurance, Software, Development SW, Doc. Mgmt., Production SW

Selective Management Services Inc

PO Box 17008
Sarasota, FL 34276-0008
(941) 923-7114
Email: selectivemanagement@msn.com
Web: www.selectivemanagement.com

Summary: Recruiters, executive search and management consultants specializing in packaging and allied industries: corrugated box, folding cartons, paper, pharmaceuticals, plastics and printing.

Key Contact - Specialty:
Mr. Alan M. Schwartz, President - *Packaging*
Mr. Mark D. Steel, Senior Consultant - *Packaging*

Salary Minimum: $40,000

Functions: Generalist (All), Management, Senior Mgmt., Middle Mgmt., Plant Mgmt., Mktg. Mgmt., Sales Mgmt., CFOs, MIS Mgmt.

Industries: Generalist (All), Manufacturing, Paper, Printing, Plastics, Rubber, Packaging

Selective Recruiting Associates Inc

3605 Burbank Dr
Ann Arbor, MI 48105-2900
(734) 994-5632
Fax: (734) 996-8181
Email: recruiter@selectiverecruiting.com
Web: www.selectiverecruiting.com

Summary: Our client base includes the international automotive manufacturers and dozens of their suppliers. Additionally, we number scientific, high technology, environmental, medical and consumer products manufacturers among our active clients.

Key Contact - Specialty:
Ms. Gilda Bone, President & Chief Executive Officer - *Engineering*
Mr. Dave Calhoun, Executive Vice President

Salary Minimum: $40,000

Functions: Generalist (All), Mfg., Product Dev., Sales Mgmt., Engineering

Industries: Chemicals, Soap, Perf., Cosmtcs., Medical Devices, Plastics, Rubber, Metal Products, Machine, Appliance, Motor Vehicles, Computer Equip., Consumer Elect., Electronic, Elec. Components, Consumer Goods, Transportation

Selective Search Inc

(formerly known as MR of Sherwood)
1100 SW Wanamaker Rd Ste 7
Topeka, KS 66604-3805
(785) 273-6600
Fax: (785) 273-8455
Email: topjobs@ssius.net
Web: www.ssius.net

Summary: With many years of recruiting experience in our office, we are able to search out the top candidates available, pre-qualify, reference check and present the best of the best. Our desk specialties include: food processing (beef, pork and poultry), truss design and healthcare.

Key Contact - Specialty:
Ms. Carole J. Hawkins, President - *Assisted living*
Ms. Karen Rabe, Director, Food Processing Division - *Food, Food & beverage, Production*

Functions: Mfg., Production, Plant Mgmt., Quality, Healthcare, Health Admin.

Industries: Construction, Manufacturing, Food, Bev., Tobacco, Lumber, Furniture, Misc. Mfg., Architectural Svcs., Accounting, Mgmt. Consulting, HR Services, Engineering Svcs., Environmental Svcs., Mfg. SW, Healthcare, Hospitals, Long-term/Home Care, Physical Therapy, Occupational Therapy, Women's, Non-Classifiable

Selective Staffing

4905 N West Ave Ste 115
Fresno, CA 93705-0438
(559) 227-9100
(559) 227-9159
Fax: (559) 227-2950
Email: selectivestaffing_2000@yahoo.com

Summary: We have extensive experience in recruiting. We specialize in the Insurance Industry.

Key Contact - Specialty:
Ms. Jane Small, Principal

Salary Minimum: $30,000

Functions: Generalist (All), Management, Mfg., Healthcare, Sales & Mktg., Sales Mgmt., HR Mgmt., Finance, Attorneys

Industries: Generalist (All), Legal, Accounting, HR Services, IT Implementation, Insurance, Casualty, Claims, Commercial, Re-Insurance, Software, Healthcare

Sell & Associates Inc

511 Park St Fl 2
Columbus, OH 43215-2081
(614) 221-8199
Fax: (614) 221-0201

Email: jbliss@sellandassociates.com
Web: www.sellandassociates.com

Summary: We are an executive recruiting firm specializing in accounting, finance, banking and MIS. Our recruiters have significant experience in their respective fields and all are CPAs. Our services are available on a retainer basis.

Key Contact - Specialty:
Mr. Mark Sell, Founder & President
Mr. James Bliss, Partner & Vice President

Functions: Finance, CFOs, Budgeting, Cash Mgmt., Taxes, M&A, Risk Mgmt., MIS Mgmt.

Industries: Generalist (All), Construction, Finance, Banking, Invest. Banking, Accounting, Insurance, Real Estate, Software

Selman Associates Inc

PO Box 5747
Derwood, MD 20855-0747
(301) 519-7227
Email: mike@selmanassociates.com
Web: www.selmanassociates.com

Summary: Information technology sales recruiting. Strong specialty working with companies selling to the Federal government.

Key Contact - Specialty:
Mr. Mike Selman

Functions: Sales Mgmt., Sales Reps.

Industries: Services, Mgmt. Consulting, E-commerce, IT Implementation, Communications, Software

Seltzer Fontaine Beckwith

2999 Overland Ave Ste 120
Los Angeles, CA 90064-4256
(310) 839-6000
Fax: (310) 839-4408
Email: info@sfbsearch.com
Web: www.sfbsearch.com

Summary: We place individuals and groups of lawyers of all business-related law specialties in law firms, corporations and non-profit organizations. In addition, we facilitate law firm mergers and geographical expansion, and consult on a variety of issues facing the legal profession.

Key Contact - Specialty:
Ms. Valerie A. Fontaine, Partner - *Legal (Attorneys,Lawyers)*
Ms. Madeleine E. Seltzer, Partner - *Legal (Attorneys,Lawyers)*
Ms. Randy Beckwith, Partner - *Legal (Attorneys,Lawyers)*
Ms. Roberta Kass, Recruiter - *Legal (Attorneys,Lawyers)*
Ms. K.C. Victor, Recruiter - *Legal (Attorneys,Lawyers)*
Ms. Amber Handman, Recruiter - *Legal (Attorneys,Lawyers)*

Salary Minimum: $100,000

Functions: Attorneys

Industries: Legal

Senzo Research Corp

100 S Main St Ste 200
Doylestown, PA 18901-4882
(215) 345-0484
Fax: (215) 230-1830
Email: jacob@senzocorp.com
Web: www.senzocorp.com

Summary: Our firm is a 100 percent diversity-owned physician recruitment firm for the pharmaceutical and biotechnology industries. We provide contingency and retained search services, build diversity slates and facilitate contract

consultant placements. Our industry leading database with extensive accumulated contacts differentiates us from other firms.

Key Contact - Specialty:
Mr. Jacob Goldbas, Managing Director

Functions: Generalist (All), Healthcare, Physicians

Industries: Pharm Svcs., Biotech/Life Sciences

Sequoia Consulting, Inc.
920 Saratoga Ave Ste 106
San Jose, CA 95129-3403
(408) 244-2999
Fax: (408) 244-1431
Email: openings@sequoia-partners.com
Web: www.sequoia-partners.com

Summary: We are dedicated to finding the best people for your current employment needs. Our client companies see only very hirable candidates. We perform high quality search services specializing in the high-technology industry. We provide services to a select number of companies so that we can concentrate on our clients' needs.

Key Contact - Specialty:
Mr. Donald Fernandez, Founder & President - *Computers (Software)*
Mr. Scott Fernandez, Recruiter - *Professional services*

Functions: Management, Sales & Mktg., IT, R&D

Industries: Software, Database SW, Development SW, Doc. Mgmt., Production SW, ERP SW, Marketing SW, Networking, Comm. SW, Security SW, System SW

SFB Legal Search
725 5th Ave Fl 17
New York, NY 10022-2568
(212) 688-1128
Fax: (212) 688-1169
Email: inhouseresume@aol.com

Summary: We specialize in attorney placements within corporations, with substantial success in diversity legal hiring needs. Our principals have many combined years of experience, plus two part-time recruiters.

Key Contact - Specialty:
Ms. Stacia Foster Blake, President

Functions: Attorneys

Industries: Generalist (All)

SFG International
1700 Galloping Hill Rd
Kenilworth, NJ 07033-1303
(908) 272-9600
Email: brad@sfgsearch.com
Web: www.sfginternational.com

Summary: We specialize in the recruitment of sales & marketing individuals with a specialization in pharmaceutical, biotechnology, high technology, telecom and computer software.

Key Contact - Specialty:
Mr. Brad Shifrin, President - *Sales*
Miss Christine Poltorak, Director - *Pharmaceutical*
Mrs. Lois Shanker, Senior Director - *Sales*
Mr. Chris Dunn, Director - *Marketing, Sales*

Salary Minimum: $50,000

Functions: Sales & Mktg.

Industries: Drugs Mfg., Computer Equip., Consumer Elect., Invest. Banking, Services, Advertising, Telecoms, Packaging, Software, Biotech/Life Sciences

Shanklin and Associates
35 Sterncrest Dr
Chagrin Falls, OH 44022-1802
(440) 519-0441
Fax: (440) 519-0442
Email: jobs@techjobsearch.com
Web: www.techjobsearch.com

Summary: We are an independent search firm providing professional technical search and recruitment services on local and national levels for engineering and health and wellness professionals.

Key Contact - Specialty:
Ms. Joy Shanklin, President & Owner

Functions: Mfg., Product Dev., Healthcare, Engineering

Industries: Machine, Appliance, Consumer Elect., Test, Measure Equip., Misc. Mfg., Electronic, Elec. Components, Semiconductors, Consumer Goods, RF/Microwave, Biotech/Life Sciences, Healthcare, Hospitals, Long-term/Home Care, Physical Therapy, Occupational Therapy

Liz Shapiro Legal Search
210 W Rittenhouse Sq Ste 1900
Philadelphia, PA 19103-7250
(215) 893-6048
Fax: (215) 893-6088
Email: lshapiro@lsls.com
Web: www.lsls.com

Summary: Focusing on permanent attorney placements, our firm has found lawyers for clients as varied as national and international companies, entrepreneurial ventures and law firms ranging in size from large national, international and regional, to local and boutique practices.

Key Contact - Specialty:
Ms. Liz Shapiro, President
Ms. Liz Lorry, Recruiter

Functions: Attorneys

Industries: Legal

Sharp Executive Recruiters Corp
4918 E Longboat Blvd
Tampa, FL 33615-4226
(813) 855-0719
Email: corp@sharprecruiters.com
Web: www.sharprecruiters.com

Summary: Our firm specializes in the biotechnology, medical devices, pharmaceutical, scientific research and medical/physician specialty areas. We search and place executives, scientists, physicians (specialized) in all areas of these industries and professions.

Key Contact - Specialty:
Mr. Bruno Rizzato, Managing Director & Sr Search Consultant - *Executives, Physicians, Quality*

Functions: Management, Mfg., Product Dev., Quality, Materials, Healthcare, Physicians, Sales & Mktg., R&D

Industries: Food, Bev., Tobacco, Chemicals, Soap, Perf., Cosmtcs., Drugs Mfg., Medical Devices, Test, Measure Equip., Misc. Mfg., Robotics, Non-profits, Pharm Svcs., Mgmt. Consulting, Higher Ed., Defense, Environmental Svcs., Haz. Waste, Packaging, Biotech/Life Sciences, Healthcare, Hospitals, Non-Classifiable

Shaw Associates
11920 Fairway Lakes Dr Ste 2
Fort Myers, FL 33913-8337
(800) 875-7429
(239) 454-4414
Fax: (239) 454-4422
Email: resume@shawassociates.com
Web: www.shawassociates.com

Summary: Specializing in the pharmaceutical, biotechnology, and medical device industries.

Key Contact - Specialty:
Mr. Gregory Shaw, President
Mr. Brian Mistrot, Vice President
Mr. Mark Sallin, Vice President

Functions: Management, Product Dev., Quality, Physicians, R&D

Industries: Drugs Mfg., Medical Devices, Pharm Svcs., Biotech/Life Sciences

R Gordon Shaw
(also known as Permanent Staffing Solutions)
PO Box 91
Oakland, CA 94604-0091
(510) 536-6204
(613) 374-1940
Email: rita_gordon@rgordonshaw.com
Web: www.rgordonshaw.com

Summary: We specialize in Finance, HR and IT search and placement. We put to use recruitment and HR experience to provide the highest caliber of recruiting solutions for our customers. We pride ourselves on quality placements and tailored staffing solutions.

Key Contact - Specialty:
Ms. Rita Gordon, Principal - *Diversity, Engineering, Finance, Human resources, Information Technology*

Functions: Management, HR Mgmt., Finance, Cash Mgmt., IT

Industries: Generalist (All), Manufacturing, Finance, Banking, Invest. Banking, Brokers, Mutual/Hedge Funds, Misc. Financial, Accounting, Mgmt. Consulting, HR Services, Engineering Svcs., Media, Publishing, Government, Defense, Environmental Svcs.

John Shell Associates Inc
PO Box 23291
Columbia, SC 29224-3291
(803) 788-6619
Fax: (803) 788-1758
Email: mail@shellaccounting.com
Web: www.shellaccounting.com

Summary: Specialists in accounting and financial staffing.

Key Contact - Specialty:
Mr. John C. Shell, III, President - *Finance*
Ms. Kay H. Mayes, Executive Director, Shell Acct Temps - *Finance*

Salary Minimum: $30,000

Functions: Finance

Industries: Generalist (All)

Shelton Associates Inc
(formerly known as R W Apple & Associates)
PO Box 200
Manasquan, NJ 08736-0200
(732) 223-4305
Fax: (732) 223-4325
Email: services@sdshelton.com
Web: www.sdshelton.com

Summary: Executive search and HR services for the environmental and engineering consulting

industries. Concentrations include environmental engineering, hydrogeology, civil engineering, air pollution control, industrial hygiene, process development, water resources, and wastewater engineering.

Key Contact - Specialty:
Ms. Susan Shelton, President
Mrs. Melissa Ludemann, Associate
Mrs. Joanne Sunkimat, Associate
Ms. Diane C. Litchko, PHR, Associate

Salary Minimum: $30,000

Functions: Generalist (All), Management

Industries: Energy, Utilities, Oil & Gas, Construction, Chemicals, Transportation, Non-profits, Pharm Svcs., Mgmt. Consulting, HR Services, Engineering Svcs., Compliance, Environmental Svcs., Haz. Waste, Biotech/Life Sciences

Sherbrooke Associates Inc

727 Raritan Rd Ste 201B
Clark, NJ 07066-2241
(732) 382-5505
Fax: (732) 382-0052
Email: info@sa-jobs.com
Web: www.sa-jobs.com

Summary: Recruiting generalists with strengths in HBA and foods concentrating in marketing, sales, and engineering.

Key Contact - Specialty:
Ms. Patricia Quattrocchi, Manager, Research - *Biotechnology, Cosmetics, Engineering, Pharmaceutical, Sales*

Salary Minimum: $60,000

Functions: Generalist (All), Management

Industries: Food, Bev., Tobacco, Chemicals, Soap, Perf., Cosmtcs., Drugs Mfg., Medical Devices, Paints, Petro. Products, Metal Products

Shey-Harding Associates Inc

PO Box 67
Seal Beach, CA 90740-0067
(562) 799-8854
Email: info@shey-harding.com
Web: www.shey-harding.com

Summary: We specialize in recruiting for the transportation/logistics industries. We have an extensive database of expert, professional candidates and will conduct confidential searches to supply the best and brightest.

Key Contact - Specialty:
Mr. Michael W. Harding, President - *Logistics, Transportation*
Ms. Deborah Shey-Harding, Vice President
Mr. Jeff Dvonch, Recruiter
Ms. Susan S. Dvonch, Recruiter - *Logistics, Transportation*

Functions: Management, Materials, Purchasing, Distribution, Sales & Mktg., HR Mgmt., Finance, Credit, IT

Industries: Manufacturing, Transportation, Wholesale

Robert Shields & Associates

(also known as Technology Transfer Inc)
1560 W Bay Area Blvd Ste 200
Friendswood, TX 77546-2673
(281) 488-7961
(281) 679-1500
Fax: (281) 486-1496
Email: info@rsacorp.com
Web: www.itjobstoday.com

Summary: We are specialists in data processing and software engineering positions. We have

extensive contacts with established and start-up software vendors including Internet ASPs.

Key Contact - Specialty:
Mr. George F. Black, President
Mr. Richard Gross, Vice President
Ms. Jani Clemons, Vice President

Salary Minimum: $40,000

Functions: IT

Industries: Generalist (All)

Branches:
2470 Gray Falls Dr Ste 260
Houston, TX 77077-6514
(281) 679-1500
Fax: (281) 679-1508
Email: jkrupka@itjobstoday.com
Key Contact - Specialty:
Mr. Joe Krupka, Senior Counselor

Shiell & Associates

2040 N Causeway Blvd
Mandeville, LA 70471-3116
(985) 727-2958
Email: marc@shiellcareers.com
Web: www.shiellcareers.com

Summary: We specialize in the placement of sales, marketing and management professionals in the pharmaceutical and medical industries.

Key Contact - Specialty:
Mr. Marc Quiroz, Owner
Mr. Donald M. Shiell, Founder

Salary Minimum: $30,000

Functions: Generalist (All), Middle Mgmt., Sales Mgmt., Minorities/Diversity, Int'l.

Industries: Generalist (All), Pharm Svcs., Healthcare

Branches:
8408 Boxwood Dr
Tampa, FL 33615-4939
(813) 890-0393
Fax: (813) 882-9237
Email: phil@shiellcareers.com
Key Contact - Specialty:
Mr. Phil Stocton, Vice President

Shiloh Careers International Inc

PO Box 831
Brentwood, TN 37024-0831
(615) 373-3090
Email: maryann@shilohcareers.com
Web: www.shilohcareers.com

Summary: We have been successfully recruiting in the property and casualty insurance industry as well as Life & Health Actuaries.

Key Contact - Specialty:
Ms. Mary Ann Webber, President

Salary Minimum: $30,000

Functions: Generalist (All), Management, Middle Mgmt., Risk Mgmt.

Industries: Insurance, Casualty, Claims, Life, Commercial

Shoreline Digital

809 Cuesta Dr Ste B
Mountain View, CA 94040-3669
(650) 564-9400
Fax: (650) 564-9401
Email: jeff@shoredg.com
Web: www.shoredg.com

Summary: We are an executive search firm specializing in the placement of software engineers and developers.

Key Contact - Specialty:
Mr. Jeff Taylor, Manager

Functions: Engineering

Industries: Software, Database SW, Development SW, HR SW, Marketing SW, Networking, Comm. SW, System SW

Shoreline HealthCare Services

16030 Ventura Blvd Ste 235
Encino, CA 91436-4472
(818) 995-9720
Fax: (818) 995-9728
Email: job@shealthcare.com
Web: www.shealthcare.com

Summary: We are a medical executive search firm contracted by hospitals, clinics, assisted living facilities and medical management companies to fill their permanent positions. We place all levels of nurses, physicians, physical therapists, pharmaceutical and allied health professionals.

Key Contact - Specialty:
Mr. Miguel Cervantes, Manager

Functions: Healthcare, Nurses, Allied Health

Industries: Healthcare, Hospitals, Long-term/Home Care, Dental, Physical Therapy, Occupational Therapy, Women's, Non-Classifiable

ShortList

3420 St Kilda Ave
North Vancouver, BC V7N 2B1
Canada
(604) 988-2910
Fax: (604) 983-3601
Email: info@shortlist.ca
Web: www.shortlist.ca

Summary: Specialized expertise in the area of managerial and executive recruitment services strictly for the retail profession.

Key Contact - Specialty:
Mr. Paul Iannacone, President - *Retail*

Salary Minimum: $45,000

Functions: Management, Senior Mgmt., Middle Mgmt., Purchasing, Distribution, Advertising, Mktg. Mgmt., HR Mgmt., Finance, Hospitality

Industries: Retail, Restaurants

SHS Inc

711 De Lasalle Ct
Naperville, IL 60565-5361
(630) 718-1704
Fax: (630) 718-1709
Email: timj@shsinc.com
Web: www.shsinc.com

Summary: Our firm is a dynamic and progressive recruitment firm capable of handling either contingency or retainer search assignments. Our focus is in the biotechnology, pharmaceutical development, pharmaceutical advertising, continuing medical education and healthcare communications industries. Our consultants specialize in one or more of these industries.

Key Contact - Specialty:
Mr. Timothy Jadwin, CPC, President

Salary Minimum: $30,000

Functions: Generalist (All), Board Members

Industries: Drugs Mfg., Medical Devices, Pharm Svcs., Advertising, Publishing, New Media, Biotech/Life Sciences, Healthcare

SHS of Cherry Hill

496 Kings Hwy N Ste 125
Cherry Hill, NJ 08034-1019
(856) 779-9030
Fax: (856) 779-0898
Email: shs@shsofcherryhill.com
Web: www.shsofcherryhill.com

Summary: The firm provides recruiting services
on a contingency basis with specialization in
engineering/technical and manufacturing. A
database candidate system is utilized. The firm
was established many years ago.

Key Contact - Specialty:
Mr. Louis Kennedy - *Technical*

Salary Minimum: $30,000

Functions: Middle Mgmt., Mfg., Plant Mgmt.,
Engineering

Industries: Construction, Manufacturing, Food,
Bev., Tobacco, Paper, Chemicals, Drugs Mfg.,
Medical Devices, Metal Products, Machine,
Appliance, Motor Vehicles, Misc. Mfg.,
Wholesale, Services, Insurance

SHS TechStaffing

(a OneSource company)
1124 Highway 315
Wilkes Barre, PA 18702-6943
(570) 825-3411
Fax: (570) 825-7790
Email: contact@shstechstaffing.com
Web: www.shstechstaffing.com

Summary: Offering professional recruiting
services for direct hire and contract professionals.
We place an emphasis on IT, accounting and
engineering.

Key Contact - Specialty:
Mr. Nicholas J. Michalisin, Jr., Professional
Recruiter - *Engineering*
Mr. Reginald Thomas, Medical Technical
Recruiter - *Nutraceuticals, Pharmaceutical,
Physicians, Research, Technicians*
Mr. Charlie Davenport, Technical Recruiter

Salary Minimum: $40,000

Functions: Mfg., Materials, IT

Industries: Generalist (All), Manufacturing,
Printing, Chemicals, Drugs Mfg., Plastics,
Rubber, Metal Products, Computer Equip., Test,
Measure Equip., Biotech/Life Sciences,
Hospitals

The Shupack & Michaels Group Inc

27 Monmouth Dr Ste 277
East Northport, NY 11731-1332
(631) 757-4559
Fax: (631) 757-3880
Email: jshupack@shupackandmichaels.com
Web: www.shupackandmichaels.com

Summary: We are contingency and retainer
recruitment and placement of engineers at all
levels for consulting and A/E firms-
mechanical/HVAC, electrical, civil, structural,
architects, etc

Key Contact - Specialty:
Mr. Joseph Shupack, Founder - *Consulting*
Ms. Ellen Michaels, President - *Consulting*
Ms. Thea Richards, Executive Recruiter
Ms. Karen Duva, Recruiter
Ms. Jennifer Siani, Recruiter
Ms. Remzije Capric, Administrative Assistant

Functions: Engineering, Architects

Industries: Generalist (All), Energy, Utilities,
Construction, Transportation

Peter Siegel & Company

PO Box 920218
Needham, MA 02492-0003
(781) 455-9057
Fax: (781) 455-6246
Email: psiegco@aol.com

Summary: A candor, a personality and an
expertise that sources prospective employees to
complement the diverse corporate cultures of
clients represented.

Key Contact - Specialty:
Mr. Peter A. Siegel, President

Salary Minimum: $50,000

Functions: Generalist (All)

Industries: Retail

SignatureSoft Inc

6789 Mallee St
Carlsbad, CA 92011-5056
(619) 276-1539
(800) 999-8829
Fax: (619) 276-1754
Email: bob@signaturesoft.com
Web: www.signaturesoft.com

Summary: We are a full-service professional
search firm, specializing in the high-technology,
communications, networking and biotechnology
industries. Software and hardware engineering is
our main focus.

Key Contact - Specialty:
Mr. Bob DeGrasse, President - *Communications,
Engineering, Networking*

Salary Minimum: $50,000

Functions: Engineering, Hardware

Industries: Media, Communications, Telecoms,
Software

Silicon Executive Search Inc

46 Braemar Ave
Toronto, ON M5P 2L2
Canada
(416) 232-0600
Email: josie_erent@yahoo.com

Summary: Mid level to senior management level
specializing in the software, professional services,
engineering, manufacturing and pharmaceutical
industries. Specializing in mid-level and senior-
level executive positions including management.
Positions include senior executives, sales; direct &
channel, business development, pre/post sales
support positions including engineers and HR
professionals.

Key Contact - Specialty:
Ms. Josie Erent, President - *Computers
(Software), Professional services*

Functions: Senior Mgmt., Middle Mgmt., Sales &
Mktg., Sales Mgmt., Sales Reps., HR Mgmt.,
Finance, CFOs, MIS Mgmt., Engineering

Industries: Manufacturing, Drugs Mfg., Medical
Devices, Services, Communications, Software,
Biotech/Life Sciences

Silicon Talent Corp

1885 De La Cruz Blvd Ste 205
Santa Clara, CA 95050-3000
(408) 588-9800
Fax: (408) 492-1795
Email: contact@silicontalent.com
Web: www.silicontalent.com

Summary: We are a high technology recruiting
firm focusing on the engineering and marketing
functions within the software industry.

Key Contact - Specialty:
Ms. Linda Bozich, Executive Vice President
Engineering, Marketing
Mr. Joe Maxwell, President
Mr. Master Burnett, Director, Marketing -
Internet

Functions: Generalist (All), Middle Mgmt.

Industries: Generalist (All), New Media,
Telecoms, Wireless, Network Infrastructure,
Software, Entertainment SW, ERP SW,
Networking, Comm. SW, Security SW

Sill Technical Associates Inc

PO Box 898
Mechanicsburg, PA 17055-8898
(717) 691-6730
Fax: (717) 691-6873
Email: dsill1@aol.com

Summary: Our founder is a graduate engineer
(BSME) with many years of recruiting/placement
experience that practiced engineering for 15 years
before opening this employment service.

Key Contact - Specialty:
Mr. Darrell E. Sill, BSME, Manager -
Engineering

Functions: Management, Mfg., Product Dev.

Industries: Generalist (All), Medical Devices,
Plastics, Rubber, Electronic, Elec. Components,
RF/Microwave

Silver Associates

11925 Wilshire Blvd Ste 204
Los Angeles, CA 90025-6625
(310) 312-4820
Fax: (310) 312-1294
Email: susan@silverassociates.com
Web: www.silverassociates.com

Summary: Our experienced staff provides
executive search services for senior, middle and
staff positions in finance/accounting/tax/audit,
strategic planning, IT, sales/marketing, consulting,
HR, entertainment, internet/new media,
distribution, etc. We also provide recruiting and
event production and management services for
marketing and promotional events.

Key Contact - Specialty:
Ms. Susan Silver - *Entertainment, Finance,
Internet, New media*

Salary Minimum: $35,000

Functions: Generalist (All), Management, Sales
& Mktg., HR Mgmt., Finance, IT, Mgmt.
Consultants, Graphic Designers

Industries: Generalist (All), Manufacturing,
Finance, Services, Media, Communications,
Software

L A Silver Associates Inc

118 Horizon Vw
Colchester, VT 05446-6930
(802) 864-3396
Fax: (802) 864-9644
Email: lasilver@sprynet.com
Web: www.lasilver.com

Summary: We have specialized in providing
senior management for pre-IPO and post-IPO
software companies. We work closely with the VC
organization and executive management to ramp
up the company's results to achieve IPO status or
to expand its world wide sales results. We are
limited partners in two separate billion-dollar
venture capital organizations. Principals handle all
of our assignments. We handle pre and post IPO
(ISV) software only.

Key Contact - Specialty:
Mr. Lee Silver, President

Salary Minimum: $100,000
Functions: Generalist (All), Senior Mgmt.
Industries: Generalist (All), Software

Silverman & Associates

2640 Caminito Carino
La Jolla, CA 92037-4003
(858) 456-8589
Fax: (858) 456-8591
Email: info@silvermanandassociates.com
Web: www.silvermanandassociates.com

Summary: We serve shopping center developers and retailers. Specializing in retail real estate, leasing, development, legal, construction, financial and asset management. Principals bring extensive years of collective experience in the industry.

Key Contact - Specialty:
Ms. Beth Silverman, Partner - *Real estate*

Salary Minimum: $50,000

Functions: Generalist (All), Specialized Svcs.

Industries: Retail, Real Estate

D W Simpson & Company

1800 W Larchmont Ave
Chicago, IL 60613-2448
(312) 867-2300
Fax: (312) 951-8386
Email: actuaries@dwsimpson.com
Web: www.dwsimpson.com

Summary: Serving the actuarial profession and at all levels from student to fellow. We use a straightforward approach to meet the objectives of client companies and candidates.

Key Contact - Specialty:
Ms. Sally Ezra, Partner
Ms. Bethany Rave, Partner
Mr. Bob Morand, Partner
Mr. David Simpson, Managing Partner

Functions: Actuaries

Industries: Insurance

Simpson Associates

106 Central Park S Apt 3B
New York, NY 10019-1568
(212) 767-0006
Fax: (212) 767-0660
Email: simpsonassociates@msn.com
Web: www.simpsonassociates.com

Summary: We specialize in hard and soft-line specialty chains, catalogs, eCommerce, fashion/luxury retail and wholesale manufacturing businesses.

Key Contact - Specialty:
Ms. Terre Simpson, President
Ms. Susan Haubenstock, Vice President

Functions: Senior Mgmt., Middle Mgmt., Textile/Fashion

Industries: Textiles, Apparel

Arline Simpson Associates Inc

285 Passaic St
Hackensack, NJ 07601-2726
(201) 655-7477
Fax: (201) 655-7581
Email: arline@arlinesimpson.com
Web: www.asastaffing.com

Summary: Executive search; direct hire, temp, temp to hire, and contract staffing solutions; certified WBE (Women's Business Enterprise). Accountants, bookkeepers, administrative, HR, marketing, and IT. Specializing in the apparel, legal, retail, manufacturing and financial services industries.

Key Contact - Specialty:
Ms. Arline Simpson

Salary Minimum: $50,000

Functions: HR Mgmt., Finance, IT

Industries: Manufacturing, Retail, Finance, Legal, Accounting, HR Services, Advertising, Packaging, Real Estate, Marketing SW

Sims Executive Search LLC

1210 Red Orchard Ct Ste 200
O Fallon, MO 63368-8292
(636) 561-1516
Email: randy@simssearch.com
Web: www.simssearch.com

Summary: Executive search firm specializing in the areas of management, sales, and other related business skill sets. Vice president sales, sales rep., CMO, Vice President of HR, HR managers/generalist, recruiters, and staffing coordinators

Key Contact - Specialty:
Mr. Randy Sims, President

Salary Minimum: $50,000

Sinclair-Smith & Associates

3607 Rang Auclair
RR 1
Saint Polycarpe, QC J0P 1X0
Canada
(450) 265-3539
(450) 845-4208
Fax: (450) 265-4018
Email: sinclair@rocler.qc.ca
Web: www.sinclair-smithassoc.com

Summary: We recruit all levels of engineers in all industries and all functions. We specialize in multi-lingual engineers for overseas locations.

Key Contact - Specialty:
Mr. Michael Sinclair-Smith

Salary Minimum: $60,000

Functions: Middle Mgmt., Mfg., Product Dev., Production

Industries: Agri., Forestry, Mining, Energy, Utilities, Construction, Manufacturing

Marina Sirras & Associates LLC

420 Lexington Ave Rm 2545
New York, NY 10170-0022
(212) 490-0333
(800) 440-5490
Fax: (212) 490-2074
Email: info@lawseek.com
Web: www.lawseek.com

Summary: We specialize in placement of attorneys and administrators in law firms and corporations. Presently, we are actively recruiting candidates who are interested in working domestically as well as overseas.

Key Contact - Specialty:
Ms. Marina Sirras, Principal & Member
Ms. Jennifer Sirras Ray, Managing Director

Functions: Generalist (All), Attorneys

Industries: Generalist (All), Legal

Sissom & Associates

4204 Westgate Dr
Knoxville, TN 37921-1542
(865) 546-0645
Fax: (865) 546-0541
Email: csissom@comcast.net

Summary: We focus exclusively in HR and related areas including compensation, benefits, training and organizational development.

Key Contact - Specialty:
Mr. Chuck Sissom, Owner - *Human resources*

Salary Minimum: $45,000

Functions: HR Mgmt.

Industries: Generalist (All), Manufacturing

SJE Partners & Sandbox Management

11509 Bridgetender Dr
Richmond, VA 23233-1782
(804) 967-9048
Fax: (804) 762-4734
Email: steve@sjepartners.com
Web: www.sjepartners.com

Summary: Our mission is to help business leaders develop the people and organizational capabilities necessary to achieve both short term and long term objectives. We do this by focusing on three areas; finding the best talent, giving them a great place to work, and training them to be their best.

Key Contact - Specialty:
Mr. Steve Enright, President

Salary Minimum: $60,000

Functions: HR Mgmt., Benefits, Staffing, Training

Industries: Generalist (All)

Patricia Sklar & Associates Ltd

205 N Michigan Ave Ste 4120
Chicago, IL 60601-5925
(312) 467-4600
Fax: (312) 467-4664
Email: patricia@sklarsearch.com

Summary: We are dedicated exclusively to the communications industry. Our goal is to provide media organizations with knowledge and contacts. We recruit sales people, media buyers and media planning professionals.

Key Contact - Specialty:
Ms. Patricia Sklar, President - *Advertising, Communications*
Ms. Megan Bock, Associate
Ms. Victoria McLeod, Recruiter, Media

Functions: Advertising

Industries: Generalist (All)

Tom Sloan & Associates Inc

PO Box 50
Watertown, WI 53094-0050
(920) 261-8890
Fax: (920) 261-6357
Email: sloan@gdinet.com

Summary: We focus on food industry specialization, R&D, production management, engineering and sales/marketing. Industries: meat, dairy, canning/freezing, milling, baking, candy, fat/oils, beverage, food ingredient, snack foods, animal feed and supplements.

Key Contact - Specialty:
Mr. Tom Sloan, President - *Engineering*
Ms. Terri Sherman, Vice President

Salary Minimum: $25,000

Functions: Generalist (All), Management, Product Dev., Materials, Sales & Mktg., HR Mgmt., R&D, Engineering

Industries: Generalist (All), Food, Bev., Tobacco

Sloan & Associates PC

1769 Jamestown Rd
Williamsburg, VA 23185-2324
(757) 220-1111
Fax: (757) 220-1694

Email: general@sloansearch.com
Web: www.sloansearch.com

Summary: Our firm specializes in the consumer packaged goods industry. Our emphasis is on sales & marketing, mid and upper level management positions. Our sub-specialization by geography allows ultimate market penetration. Employment law, testing & assessment and compensation services are also available.

Key Contact - Specialty:
Mr. Mike Sloan, President
Mr. John Holland, Director, Western Area
Mr. Greg Wyenandt, Vice President & Southern Director - *Food & beverage*
Ms. Meghan Sloan, Director, Midwest Area
Mr. Steve Brecker, Director, Northeast Area

Salary Minimum: $50,000

Functions: Senior Mgmt., Sales & Mktg.

Industries: Food, Bev., Tobacco

Martha Sloane Consultants Ltd

500 5th Ave Ste 1130
New York, NY 10110-1102
(212) 269-7789
Email: msloane@marthasloane.com
Web: www.marthasloane.com

Summary: We recruit mid to senior-level editorial, marketing professionals, analysts and compliance officers for the financial services industry.

Key Contact - Specialty:
Ms. Martha E. Sloane, President - *Editorial, Financial services*

Salary Minimum: $85,000

Functions: Finance

Industries: Banking, Invest. Banking, Mutual/Hedge Funds, Misc. Financial, New Media, Compliance

J L Small Associates

312 N Burbank Dr
Hoover, AL 35226-1608
(205) 823-4545
Fax: (205) 979-8879

Summary: We are generalist specializing in engineering, accounting, manufacturing and HR. Pulp and paper is our main specialty.

Key Contact - Specialty:
Mr. Jim Small, Owner - *Manufacturing*

Salary Minimum: $35,000

Functions: Generalist (All), Mfg., Quality, Materials, HR Mgmt., CFOs, IT

Industries: Generalist (All), Construction, Manufacturing, Paper, Chemicals, Metal Products, Accounting, HR Services

SmartStaff Personnel

312 Springfield Ave
Berkeley Heights, NJ 07922-1277
(908) 508-0300
Fax: (908) 508-0323
Email: info@smartstaffpersonnel.com
Web: www.smartstaffpersonnel.com

Summary: Our firm is a temp staffing and full-time placement firm with specialties in the areas of accounting, finance, graphics, editorial, legal, HR, engineering, and general office support.

Key Contact - Specialty:
Mr. David Cantor, President

Salary Minimum: $30,000

Functions: Generalist (All)

Industries: Manufacturing, Finance, Legal, Accounting, HR Services, Advertising, Publishing, New Media, Software

SMC Search Associates LLC

52 Bates Rd
Merrimack, NH 03054-4504
(603) 429-9422
Email: schittenden@smcsearch.com

Summary: We are a technical search and placement firm specializing in IT: directors, software developers, software quality engineers, product managers, program and project managers as well as technical sales executives and sales engineers. We do both permanent and contract placements throughout the U.S.

Key Contact - Specialty:
Ms. Susan Chittenden, Principal - *Computers (Software), Engineering, Information Technology, Marketing, Product management/development*

Salary Minimum: $50,000

Functions: Generalist (All), Senior Mgmt.

Industries: E-commerce, IT Implementation, Telecoms, Wireless, Software, Database SW, Development SW, Doc. Mgmt., Production SW, ERP SW, Marketing SW

SMI Careers

1735 Buford Hwy Ste 215
Cumming, GA 30041-1268
(770) 205-3374
Fax: (678) 455-5227
Email: larry@proseeker.net
Web: www.smicareers.com

Summary: As a world-class firm, we help client companies both large and small find leadership and candidates find a place where they can shape tomorrow's business. As our company has grown, we have maintained a commitment to high performance. We offer candidates and client companies confidentiality, personal service and unsurpassed results.

Key Contact - Specialty:
Mr. Larry Schofield

Salary Minimum: $50,000

Functions: Generalist (All)

Industries: Generalist (All), Finance, Banking, Invest. Banking, Brokers, HR Services

Jeff Smith & Associates

54 Nate Nutting Rd
Groton, MA 01450-2026
(978) 448-8080
Fax: (978) 448-9992
Email: jeff@jsmithassoc.com
Web: www.jsmithassoc.com

Summary: Executive search and technical recruiting firm specializing in placing professionals in filtration, separations, water and wastewater treatment industries.

Key Contact - Specialty:
Mr. Jeff Smith, President

Salary Minimum: $75,000

Functions: Management, Senior Mgmt., Middle Mgmt., Product Dev., Sales & Mktg.

Industries: Energy, Utilities, Oil & Gas, Food, Bev., Tobacco, Chemicals, Drugs Mfg., Medical Devices, Test, Measure Equip., Semiconductors, Pharm Svcs., Environmental Svcs., Biotech/Life Sciences

Sylvia Smith & Associates

PO Box 829
Brandon, FL 33509-0829
(813) 689-2611
Fax: (813) 651-5446
Email: ssmith96@tampabay.rr.com

Summary: We are a nationwide placement agency. Our client companies pay all fees. Nationwide positions in quality managers/engineers, manufacturing managers/engineers black belt six sigma, plant managers, software embedded engineers, RF, civil, structural engineers, geotechnical, HR and purchasing.

Key Contact - Specialty:
Ms. Sylvia Smith, Owner - *Aerospace, Manufacturing*

Functions: Generalist (All)

Industries: Generalist (All)

Smith & Associates

3826 Monteith Dr Ste 300
Los Angeles, CA 90043-1747
(323) 295-8198
(800) 867-3932
Fax: (323) 293-9825
Email: darrell@searchsmith.com
Web: www.searchsmith.com

Summary: Our practice is established primarily along functional lines with special emphasis on mid and senior management to executive-level positions in sales, marketing, supply chain, finance, HR and general management.

Key Contact - Specialty:
Mr. Darrell G. Smith, President
Mr. Ron Higgins, Senior Associate & Exec Search Consult
Mr. D.J. Smith, Consultant
Ms. Angelik Lark, Consultant
Ms. Darlene Smith, Consultant
Mr. Brian Davis, Consultant

Salary Minimum: $75,000

Functions: Generalist (All), Materials, Healthcare, Sales & Mktg., Advertising, Mktg. Mgmt., Sales Mgmt., Finance, Minorities/Diversity

Industries: Generalist (All), Food, Bev., Tobacco, Soap, Perf., Cosmtcs., Computer Equip., Retail, Finance, Services, Hospitals, Physical Therapy, Occupational Therapy

Smith & Associates

123 Kings Ct
Savannah, GA 31406-6261
(800) 611-4043
(912) 354-7884
Fax: (801) 697-0593
Email: raysmith@technojobs.com
Web: www.technojobs.com

Summary: Recruitment and placement of computer IS professionals including programmers, analysts, developers, administrators and engineers. Particular emphasis on AS/400, web and client server experts. Primarily permanent placement, but increasing number of contract positions.

Key Contact - Specialty:
Mr. Ray E. Smith

Salary Minimum: $40,000

Functions: IT

Industries: Construction, Manufacturing, Transportation, Pharm Svcs., Telecoms, Aerospace, Packaging, Software

Email your resume to a targeted list of recruiters now at www.ExecutiveAgent.com/DER07

James F Smith & Associates
4651 Roswell Rd NE Ste B102
Atlanta, GA 30342-3054
(404) 256-6408
Email: jfsphd@yahoo.com

Summary: Consulting psychologists who provide executive search/recruiting services to their corporate clients.

Key Contact - Specialty:
Dr. James F. Smith

Salary Minimum: $50,000

Functions: Generalist (All), Senior Mgmt., Middle Mgmt., Plant Mgmt., Sales Mgmt., Mgmt. Consultants, Int'l.

Industries: Generalist (All), Metal Products, Misc. Mfg., Retail, Mgmt. Consulting, Hospitality, Defense

Peter A Smith & Associates
2390 Cal Young Rd
Eugene, OR 97401-5154
(541) 302-8100
Fax: (541) 302-6570
Email: petersmithsearch@comcast.net

Summary: Corporate and property level hospitality management and sales executives. Extensive years of industry experience in sales & marketing and operations. We place an emphasis on GM and sales positions. We have major hotel companies as clients.

Key Contact - Specialty:
Mr. Peter A. Smith, Principal - *Hospitality*

Salary Minimum: $50,000

Functions: Management, Sales & Mktg., Finance, Hotel Mgmt.

Industries: Hospitality, Hotels, Resorts, Clubs

J Harrington Smith Associates
PO Box 90065
Indianapolis, IN 46290-0065
(317) 251-0678
Email: jharringtonsmith@aol.com

Summary: We hire a range from human recources consultant to management.

Key Contact - Specialty:
Mr. James H. Smith, Principal - *Mining*

Salary Minimum: $60,000

Functions: Generalist (All), Management, Senior Mgmt., Middle Mgmt., Production, Materials, Engineering, Mgmt. Consultants, Environmentalists

Industries: Agri., Forestry, Mining, Construction, Paper, HR Services

Smith, Brown & Jones
7304 W 130th St Ste 300
Overland Park, KS 66213-2672
(913) 814-7770
(913) 814-7760
Fax: (913) 814-8440
Email: resume@smithbrownjones.com
Web: www.smithbrownjones.com

Summary: We are a food and agri-business recruiter.

Key Contact - Specialty:
Mr. Donald L. Smith, President
Mr. Jeff Hahn, Executive Recruiter - *Agriculture, Comptrollers, Engineering, Manufacturing, Quality*
Ms. Shelley Young, Treasurer - *Marketing, Sales*

Functions: Generalist (All), Production, Plant Mgmt., Mktg. Mgmt., CFOs, R&D, Int'l.

Industries: Generalist (All), Agri., Forestry, Mining, Manufacturing, Paper, Chemicals, Drugs Mfg., Consumer Goods, Finance, Legal, Environmental Svcs., Packaging, Biotech/Life Sciences

Branches:
4100 Belair Ln
Naples, FL 34103-3117
(941) 263-2548
Fax: (941) 263-4323

Smith Hanley Associates Inc
99 Park Ave
New York, NY 10016-1601
(212) 687-9696
Fax: (212) 818-9067
Email: thanley@smithhanley.com
Web: www.smithhanley.com

Summary: Retained and contingency recruitment concentrating on work in investment research, market research, fixed income analysis, corporate finance, technical services for financial service, consumer product, consulting firms, advertising agencies, insurance and risk management.

Key Contact - Specialty:
Mr. Thomas A. Hanley, Jr., Chief Executive Officer
Mr. Richard Wastrom, Partner - *Capital markets, Derivatives, Financial services, Investment management, Private equity*
Ms. Tracey Gmoser, Partner - *Pharmaceutical*

Salary Minimum: $50,000

Functions: Generalist (All), Distribution, Mktg. Research, Direct Mktg., M&A, Risk Mgmt., Mgmt. Consultants

Industries: Generalist (All), Drugs Mfg., Finance, Pharm Svcs., Accounting, Mgmt. Consulting, Advertising, Insurance

Branches:
107 Joan Dr
Fairfield, CT 06824-2234
(203) 319-4300
(888) 221-2900
Fax: (203) 319-4320
Key Contact - Specialty:
Mr. Andrew Davis - *Risk management*
Ms. Jacqueline Paige

200 W Madison St Ste 2110
Chicago, IL 60606-3444
(312) 629-2400
Fax: (312) 629-0615
Key Contact - Specialty:
Ms. Linda Burtch

Smith Professional Search
37000 Woodward Ave Ste 101
Bloomfield Hills, MI 48304-0923
(248) 540-8580
Fax: (248) 540-2136
Email: susan@smithprofessionalsearch.com
Web: www.smithprofessionalsearch.com

Summary: We specialize in the placement of HR professionals. Our emphasis is on quality service and the highest level of professionalism in the recruiting business. Our goal is to make the search process efficient, timely and to provide superior service.

Key Contact - Specialty:
Ms. Susan P. Smith, SPHR, Principal - *Human resources*

Salary Minimum: $50,000

Functions: HR Mgmt.

Industries: Generalist (All)

Smith Spencer Ltd
4565 Dressler Rd NW Ste 106
Canton, OH 44718-2576
(330) 491-0801
(330) 491-0802
Fax: (330) 491-0803
Email: ss@smithspencer.com
Web: www.smithspencer.com

Summary: Retained, contingency and contract search in manufacturing, engineering, IT, finance and transportation/logistics. Many years experience recruiting from the executive to the clerical level.

Key Contact - Specialty:
Mr. Todd Rimer, Senior Parnter
Mr. Mike Ziarko, Senior Parnter

Salary Minimum: $30,000

Functions: Generalist (All)

Industries: Energy, Utilities, Manufacturing, Transportation, Finance, Services, Insurance, Software, Biotech/Life Sciences, Healthcare

Dan Smolen Direct Search LLC
44 Lightfoot Dr
Stafford, VA 22554-8509
(703) 842-4348
Fax: (703) 842-4353
Email: dsmolen@dansmolen.com
Web: dansmolen.com

Summary: We focus on national-in-scope executive search exclusively for the direct marketing, interactive marketing, and consumer insights industries.

Key Contact - Specialty:
Mr. Dan Smolen, President - *Consumer, Database, Direct marketing, Interactive, Internet*

Salary Minimum: $70,000

Functions: Management

Industries: Mgmt. Consulting, Media, Advertising, Publishing, New Media

SMR Group Ltd
200 Sheffield St Ste 308
Mountainside, NJ 07092-2315
(800) 767-3340
Fax: (908) 789-2080
Email: rick@smrgroupltd.com
Web: www.smrgroupltd.com

Summary: Our mission is 'Recruiting Today's Business Leaders' for the sales, marketing and management needs of the pharmaceutical, biotechnology and medical products & services industries.

Key Contact - Specialty:
Mr. Richard Snowden, President - *Marketing, Pharmaceutical, Sales*

Functions: Management, Senior Mgmt., Sales & Mktg., Advertising, Mktg. Mgmt., Sales Mgmt., Sales Reps.

Industries: Drugs Mfg., Medical Devices, Pharm Svcs., Biotech/Life Sciences, Healthcare

Smythe Masterson & Judd Inc
551 Madison Ave Ste 1700
New York, NY 10022-3212
(212) 421-9630
Fax: (212) 421-9665
Email: info@smythemasterson.com
Web: www.smythemasterson.com

Summary: We are one of the nation's oldest, most established legal search firms. We engage in partner and associate placements, firm mergers

and practice group acquisitions. We also represent major companies and financial institutions.

Key Contact - Specialty:
Mr. Mark D.J. Henley, Managing Director, Law Firm Merger
Ms. Jessica C. Berman, Director
Mr. Ralph A. Blessey, Esq., Director
Mr. Brian Burlant, Esq., Director
Mr. Thomas C. Cromie, Director
Mr. Marc J. Fagin, Esq., Director
Ms. Linda A. Ginsberg, Esq., Director
Ms. Traci A. LaVallee, Esq., Director
Mrs. Amy S. Peluso, Esq., Director
Mr. Andrew I.R. Regan, Director

Salary Minimum: $90,000

Functions: Attorneys

Industries: Legal

Ron Snead Associates

15720 John J Delaney Dr Ste 300
Charlotte, NC 28277-1479
(704) 541-8844
Fax: (704) 542-5912
Email: ronsnead@aol.com
Web: www.yp.bellsouth.com/ronsnead

Summary: Our founder has extensive civilian and military recruiting experience.

Key Contact - Specialty:
Mr. Ronald B. Snead, Owner

Salary Minimum: $40,000

Functions: Generalist (All), Management, Senior Mgmt., Middle Mgmt., Sales & Mktg., Mktg. Mgmt., Sales Mgmt.

Industries: Generalist (All), Paper, Chemicals, Plastics, Rubber, Paints, Petro. Products, Machine, Appliance, Test, Measure Equip., Misc. Mfg.

Snelling Personnel of Summit

47 River Rd
Summit, NJ 07901-1426
(908) 273-6500
Email: eduncza@snellingsummit.com
Web: www.snelling.com/summit

Summary: Our firm actively shares your concerns, expectations and career goals. We conduct in-depth interviews with corporate clients' hiring managers to ensure long-term success. We only work with corporations with whom we have established personal relationships. This ensures expedited consideration by the companies who receive your resume.

Key Contact - Specialty:
Mr. Gary Frischman, Vice President
Mr. Don Muniz, Vice President - *Construction, Real estate*

Salary Minimum: $50,000

Functions: IT

Industries: Misc. Financial, IT Implementation, New Media, Telecoms, Telephony, Wireless, Fiber Optic, Network Infrastructure, Software, Biotech/Life Sciences

Snelling Personnel of Dallas

12801 N Central Expy Ste 600
Dallas, TX 75243-1725
(972) 934-9030
Fax: (972) 934-3639
Email: sbingham@algxmail.com
Web: www.snelling.com/northdallas

Summary: Our office specializes in placing sales professionals. Our particular focus is on sales engineers within the chemical and water treatment industries. Our office has been one of the most

successful within our franchise system and our recruiters have extensive combined experience.

Key Contact - Specialty:
Mr. Sam Bingham, CPC, Owner

Functions: Admin. Svcs., Sales & Mktg., Sales Mgmt., Engineering

Industries: Generalist (All), Energy, Utilities, Manufacturing, Paper, Chemicals, Plastics, Rubber, Paints, Petro. Products, Metal Products, Environmental Svcs., Industry Specific SW

Snelling Personnel Svcs

1813 University Dr NW Ste 101
Huntsville, AL 35801-5740
(256) 382-3000
Fax: (256) 382-6691
Email: gbarnes@snellinghsv.com
Web: www.snelling.com/huntsville

Summary: We are regarded as one of the premier recruiting firms in the Southeast.

Key Contact - Specialty:
Mr. George Barnes, Owner & Executive Recruiter - *Engineering, Sales, Technical*
Ms. Maureen Redler, Executive Recruiter
Mr. John Orton, Executive Recruiter
Ms. Selina Kingston, Manager, Business

Salary Minimum: $30,000

Functions: Senior Mgmt., Healthcare, Nurses, Finance, CFOs, IT, Engineering

Industries: Finance, Banking, Accounting, Engineering Svcs., Defense, Aerospace, Healthcare, Hospitals

Snelling Personnel Services

818 Connecticut Ave NW Ste 325
Washington, DC 20006-2731
(202) 833-6100
Email: parker@snellingmetro.com
Web: www.snelling.com/metro

Summary: Our firm is a leader in temp, contract and permanent placement for professionals in nearly all fields.

Key Contact - Specialty:
Mr. Anthony W. Parker, President
Mr. Rick Dolan, Personnel Manager
Mr. James Buchanan, Account Manager
Ms. Tabatha Briscoe, PMR

Functions: Management

Industries: Generalist (All)

Snelling Personnel Service

6555 NW 9th Ave Ste 203
Fort Lauderdale, FL 33309-2049
(954) 771-0090
Fax: (954) 771-8583
Email: ftlauderdale@snelling.com
Web: www.snelling.com/ftlauderdale

Summary: We are a professional recruitment service with recruiting specialists in construction management placement. We specialize in operations, superintendents, controller project managers, estimators, office management, executive administration contracts, administration, and job site secretaries. We also have a division that specializes in placing dental professionals.

Key Contact - Specialty:
Mr. K. Jerry Phillips, Manager
Ms. Vicki Hutchinson, Construction Recruiter - *Construction*
Ms. Heidi Casey, Administrative Manager
Ms. Gina Scaturro, Construction Recruiter - *Construction*

Ms. Shannon Horton, Recruiter - *Dental*
Zenobia Young, Account Manager - *Administration*

Salary Minimum: $50,000

Functions: Generalist (All), Management, Allied Health, CFOs, Engineering, Structural, Eng. Design, Architects, Bldg. Contractors, Design

Industries: Generalist (All), Construction, Manufacturing, Services, Media, Software, Dental

Snelling Personnel Services

236 N 5th St
Quincy, IL 62301-2918
(217) 222-7721
Fax: (217) 222-7995
Email: snelling@adams.net
Web: www.snelling.com/quincy

Summary: We are the right fit specialists. Our aim is to deliver workforce system solutions which consistently exceed expectations, thereby building lifetime business partnerships, while recognizing the responsibility we have in shaping the future of our candidates. We offer professional research, sourcing, recruiting, hiring for all of your staffing needs.

Key Contact - Specialty:
Mr. Tim Bonansinga, Owner, Manager & Recruiter

Salary Minimum: $35,000

Functions: Generalist (All), Management, Admin. Svcs., Legal, Attorneys, Paralegals

Industries: Generalist (All), Energy, Utilities, Non-profits, Legal, Law Enforcement, Government

Snelling Personnel Services

2931 Montvale Dr
Springfield, IL 62704-5480
(217) 698-4969
Fax: (217) 698-9496
Email: snelling@adams.net
Web: www.snelling.com/springfield

Summary: Full service recruiting and staffing firm. Focus on search and placement of professionals in law, management and regulatory affairs. Staffing services include full range of options including: recruiting, testing & assessment, evaluation, selection consulting and performance management.

Key Contact - Specialty:
Ms. Julie Bonansinga, Recruiter, Management

Salary Minimum: $50,000

Functions: Management, Legal, Paralegals

Industries: Generalist (All), Legal, Mgmt. Consulting

Snelling Personnel Services

80 Scenic Dr Ste 1
Freehold, NJ 07728-5211
(732) 431-2600
Fax: (732) 431-2811
Email: koleen@snellingnj.com
Web: www.snellingnj.com

Summary: We are an IT search firm specializing in the recruitment and placement of computer/networking professionals.

Key Contact - Specialty:
Mr. Frank Dalotto, General Manager

Functions: IT

Industries: E-commerce, IT Implementation, Marketing SW, Networking, Comm. SW

Email your resume to a targeted list of recruiters now at www.ExecutiveAgent.com/DER07

Snelling Personnel Services

150 Broadway Rm 902
New York, NY 10038-4394
(212) 331-9325
Fax: (212) 227-9803
Email: midtown@snelling.com
Web: www.snelling.com/midtown

Summary: We specialize in a variety of industries including: health care, travel, non-profit, cosmetics, advertising, investment banking and publishing.

Key Contact - Specialty:
Mr. Bret Portmann, Director, Staffing & Recruitment
Ms. Ayodele Correa, Operations Manager - *Engineering, Manufacturing, MIS, Sales*

Functions: Customer Svc., Finance, Legal

Industries: Finance, Banking, Invest. Banking, Brokers, Venture Cap., Mutual/Hedge Funds, Legal, Accounting, Communications, Call Centers

Snelling Personnel Services

7719 Wood Hollow Dr Ste 211
Austin, TX 78731-1634
(512) 345-4775
(512) 721-1993
Fax: (512) 345-5719
Email: search@snellingaustin.com
Web: www.snelling.com/austin

Summary: Our firm is a full-service staffing organization specializing in two general areas of employment. The first is the skilled office worker: this includes general clerks to administrative office management, customer service, technical communications and accounting. Second, executive search: specializing in sales, engineering and senior management professionals in software, telecommunication and the semiconductor industries.

Key Contact - Specialty:
Mr. J.D. Stewart, General Manager - *Information Systems, Information Technology, MIS, Networking, Technology*
Mrs. Patricia Stewart, Owner - *Accounting*

Salary Minimum: $50,000

Functions: Generalist (All)

Industries: Generalist (All), Manufacturing, Computer Equip., Semiconductors, Telecoms, Software

Snelling Search

PO Box 1627
Bentonville, AR 72712-1627
(479) 271-0505
Fax: (479) 271-0707
Email: balberson@snellingtrans.com
Web: www.snellingtrans.com

Summary: Transportation, distribution and logistics are our focus. Our process identifies and qualifies top percentile performers.

Key Contact - Specialty:
Mr. Neal Click, Principal & Managing Director - *Transportation*
Mr. Bob Alberson, CPC, Principal & General Manager - *Distribution, Logistics, Transportation*

Salary Minimum: $65,000

Functions: Generalist (All), Management

Industries: Transportation, Logistics Svcs.

Branches:
3 Abrahamson Ln
Bella Vista, AR 72714-5143
(479) 855-4022
Email: tbailey@snellingtrans.com
Key Contact - Specialty:
Mr. Tom Bailey, CPC, Recruiter

100 Lake Shore Dr Apt 303
Michigan City, IN 46360-2078
(219) 879-6923
Key Contact - Specialty:
Mr. John Vander Wagen, Recruiter - *Brokerage, Distribution, Logistics, Supply Chain, Transportation*

3217 Brush Creek Rd
Oklahoma City, OK 73120-1851
(405) 753-9620
Fax: (405) 753-9626
Email: nclick@snellingtrans.com

Snelling Search

2201 5th Ave Ste 5
Moline, IL 61265-1467
(309) 797-1101
Fax: (309) 797-7099
Email: snelling@snellingmoline.com
Web: www.snellingmoline.com

Summary: We are an established, award winning office, specializing in engineering, manufacturing, purchasing, IT and accounting. With many years in the recruiting business, we can meet your hiring and employment needs.

Key Contact - Specialty:
Mr. James V. Roeder, CPC, Vice President

Salary Minimum: $30,000

Functions: Generalist (All), Mfg., Materials, Purchasing, Sales & Mktg., Finance, IT

Industries: Generalist (All)

Snelling Search Recruiters

1813 University Dr NW
Huntsville, AL 35801-5700
(919) 876-0660
Fax: (919) 876-0355
Email: recruit2@mindspring.com
Web: www.recruit-search.com

Summary: We are successful, professional and experienced recruiters assisting qualified companies locating matched candidates that will contribute to their bottom line. We only work sales disciplines.

Key Contact - Specialty:
Mr. Robert J. Helfenbein, Sr., CPC, President
Ms. Cheryl Liles, CPC, Senior Recruiter - *Marketing, Sales*

Salary Minimum: $40,000

Functions: Sales Reps.

Industries: Generalist (All)

C Snow & Associates

1801-1 Yonge St
Telsec Business Centre
Toronto, ON M5E 1W7
Canada
(416) 465-8735
Fax: (416) 369-0515

Summary: With experience in the recruitment industry, we provide service of the highest integrity to professionals.

Key Contact - Specialty:
Ms. Christine Snow, President - *Marketing, Telecommunications*

Salary Minimum: $50,000

Functions: Generalist (All), Middle Mgmt., Mktg. Research, Mktg. Mgmt., Finance

Industries: Generalist (All), Food, Bev., Tobacco, Computer Equip., Misc. Financial, Telecoms, Software

Snyder Executive Search Inc

8840 Southampton Dr
Miramar, FL 33025-2718
(954) 436-2803
Email: alfredsnyder@bellsouth.net
Web: www.asnyder.com

Summary: We are executive recruiters specializing in the computer industry. We place computer, executives, marketing, sales reps, system engineers, business developers and software developers.

Key Contact - Specialty:
Ms. Phyllis Snyder, President
Mr. Alfred Snyder, Vice President

Salary Minimum: $75,000

Functions: Generalist (All), Senior Mgmt., Sales & Mktg., Mktg. Mgmt., Sales Mgmt., Sales Reps., IT, Systems Analysis, Systems Dev., DB Admin.

Industries: Computer Equip., Misc. Financial, IT Implementation, Engineering Svcs., Government, Defense, Software, Accounting SW, Database SW, Development SW, Doc. Mgmt., Production SW, ERP SW, HR SW, Industry Specific SW, Mfg. SW, Marketing SW, System SW

Andrea Sobel & Associates Inc

5316 Ventura Canyon Ave
Sherman Oaks, CA 91401-5923
(818) 788-3369
Email: andrea8087@aol.com

Summary: We have experience matching data processing professionals, including client/server, PC support, networking and mainframe to a variety of clients, including entertainment, new media, healthcare and banking.

Key Contact - Specialty:
Ms. Andrea Sobel, President

Functions: Generalist (All), Systems Analysis, Systems Dev., Systems Implem., Systems Support

Industries: Generalist (All), Banking, Hospitality, Network Infrastructure, Software, Database SW, Entertainment SW, ERP SW, Healthcare

Software Resource Consultants Inc

PO Box 38118
Germantown, TN 38183-0118
(901) 759-7225
Fax: (901) 759-1721
Email: info@onlinesrc.com
Web: www.onlinesrc.com

Summary: Specialized recruiting for IT, telecommunication industry, wireless technology and banking industry. Middle to senior management, programmers, analysts, engineers, development managers and business managers. Work closely with hiring organization to develop recruiting plan.

Key Contact - Specialty:
Ms. Pinakini Sheth, President - *Telecommunications*

Salary Minimum: $50,000

Functions: IT, R&D, Engineering, Specialized Svcs., Mgmt. Consultants

Industries: Generalist (All), Mgmt. Consulting, Software

Solaris Group

4277 N West Ave
Fresno, CA 93705-1407
(559) 447-9159
(559) 313-5270
Fax: (559) 221-4221
Email: ffj007@comcast.net,
debra@solarissearch.com
Web: www.solarissearch.com

Summary: Our firm is a specialized executive search firm, built to deliver excellence and complete searches in roughly half the time taken by most large search firms. We are a personal company that believes in face to face meeting and going with you on interviews. We would love the opportunity to work with you.

Key Contact - Specialty:
Mr. Fernando Flores, Jr., Owner - *Medical, Surgical*
Ms. Debra Morris, Assistant Recruiter - *Management, Medical, Surgical*

Salary Minimum: $135,000

Functions: Physicians

Industries: Construction, Finance, Banking, Architectural Svcs., Pharm Svcs., Accounting, Hospitality, Marketing SW, Hospitals, Women's

Phyllis Solomon Executive Search Inc

120 Sylvan Ave
Englewood Cliffs, NJ 07632-2501
(201) 947-8600
Fax: (201) 947-9894
Email: mail@solomonsearch.com
Web: www.solomonsearch.com

Summary: Our firm has expertise with pharmaceutical advertising, corporate marketing, medical education and creative services. We gear ourselves to isolate the top talent in the industry. We pride ourselves on an unparalleled record of customer satisfaction.

Key Contact - Specialty:
Ms. Phyllis Solomon, President - *Advertising, Marketing, Pharmaceutical*

Salary Minimum: $90,000

Functions: Physicians, Advertising, Mktg. Research, Mktg. Mgmt., Direct Mktg., PR

Industries: Generalist (All)

Solutions Worldwide Corporation

19360 Rinaldi St Ste 512
Porter Ranch, CA 91326-1607
(818) 366-1242
(800) 860-3112
Email: info@solutions-worldwide.com
Web: www.solutions-worldwide.com

Summary: Our firm is a contingency search/recruiting firm with extensive years of experience in sourcing and placing professionals with a variety of clients. Our main divisions are: supply chain - manufacturing, scientific, quality (QA/QC) and HR.

Key Contact - Specialty:
Ms. Tracey Virtue, Director - *Consumer, Manufacturing, Materials, Operations, Procurement*
Ms. Andrea Schoffstall, Director - *Biopharmaceutical, Consumer, Human resources, Quality, Science*

Salary Minimum: $30,000

Functions: Senior Mgmt., Quality, Materials, HR Mgmt., R&D

Industries: Manufacturing, Food, Bev., Tobacco, Textiles, Apparel, Soap, Perf., Cosmtcs., Drugs Mfg., Medical Devices, Machine, Appliance, Motor Vehicles, Misc. Mfg., Consumer Goods, Packaging, Biotech/Life Sciences

Somerset Group Inc

1375 Kings Hwy Ste 210
Fairfield, CT 06824-5318
(203) 334-3232
Fax: (203) 334-3233
Email: resumes@somersetgroup.com
Web: www.somersetgroup.com

Summary: We specialize in custom and syndicated marketing research. Clients consist of corporations, research suppliers and consulting firms. Industries include consumer packaged goods, pharmaceuticals, telecom, financial services, high technology, business-to-business and healthcare.

Key Contact - Specialty:
Mr. Richard Brenner, Managing Partner
Mr. Gregory King, Managing Partner

Salary Minimum: $50,000

Functions: Mktg. Research

Industries: Generalist (All), Manufacturing, Transportation, Retail, Finance, Hospitality, Media, Insurance, Software, Healthcare

Soundview Business Solutions Inc

40 Soundview Dr
Northport, NY 11768-1457
(631) 757-2936
Fax: (631) 262-8958
Email: info@soundviewbusinesssolutions.com
Web: www.soundviewexperience.com

Summary: We provide both retained and contingency search specializing in sales, marketing and management.

Key Contact - Specialty:
Mr. Jack Signorelli, President
Mr. Tim Alvarez, Senior Vice President
Mr. Phil Bartlett, Senior Vice President
Mr. Joe Viggiano, Senior Vice President

Functions: Senior Mgmt., Middle Mgmt., Sales Mgmt.

Industries: Generalist (All), Paper, Printing, Computer Equip., Electronic, Elec. Components, Pharm Svcs., Accounting, Equip Svcs., Mgmt. Consulting, HR Services, E-commerce, Digital, Software, Accounting SW, Doc. Mgmt., Production SW, ERP SW, HR SW, Marketing SW, Training SW

Branches:
15 Danbury Ln
Lake Hopatcong, NJ 07849-1116
(973) 663-8464
Key Contact - Specialty:
Mr. Don Walker, Senior Vice President

Source Consulting Group LLC

3613 W Pioneer Pkwy Ste B
Pantego, TX 76013-4517
(817) 277-3700
Fax: (817) 861-2307
Email: ronwallace@source-consulting.com
Web: www.source-consulting.com

Summary: We offer recruiting and consulting services to a variety of clients in the medical sales arena. Our clients range in size from, small

growth-oriented, closely held businesses to large national and multi-national organizations located in the United States, Canada and Europe. Our professionals bring over 30 years of working one-on-one with clients to understand their specific needs and implement targeted solutions. By taking this consultative approach, our team improves the client's staffing systems and practices and increases the effectiveness of the entire organization.

Key Contact - Specialty:
Mr. Ronald L. Wallace, Senior Partner & Chief Executive Officer

Functions: Middle Mgmt., Sales & Mktg., Mktg. Mgmt., Sales Mgmt., Sales Reps.

Industries: Drugs Mfg., Medical Devices, Biotech/Life Sciences, Healthcare, Hospitals

Source Executive Search | Consulting

(formerly known as PLA, Inc.)
1535 Dale Mabry Hwy Ste 103
Lutz, FL 33548-3001
(813) 909-4434
(866) 822-2330
Fax: (813) 949-9487
Email: info@sourceexecutive.com
Web: www.sourceexecutive.com

Summary: An executive search firm specializing in the placement of advertising and marketing professionals.

Key Contact - Specialty:
Ms. Kaarla A. McKenzie, President - *Advertising, Consumer (Marketing), Marketing*
Ms. Daire Goettler, Vice President - *Advertising, Consumer (Marketing), Marketing*

Functions: Advertising, Mktg. Research, Mktg. Mgmt., Direct Mktg., PR, Graphic Designers

Industries: Food, Bev., Tobacco, Soap, Perf., Cosmtcs., Consumer Goods, Retail, Non-profits, K-12 Ed., Hospitality, Hotels, Resorts, Clubs, Restaurants, Quick Service Restaurants, Entertainment, Travel, Media, Advertising, Communications

Source Medical

(formerly known as Source Medical & Focus Group)
680 Craig Rd Ste 300
Creve Coeur, MO 63141-7120
(800) 800-5664
(314) 989-0707
Fax: (800) 800-2661
Email: jhughes@source-medical.net
Web: www.source-medical.net

Summary: We are a search and recruitment firm specializing in placing physicians.

Key Contact - Specialty:
Mrs. Judy Hughes, Office Manager
Mr. Keith Long, Owner & Operator

Salary Minimum: $120,000

Functions: Generalist (All), Physicians

Industries: Healthcare, Hospitals, Long-term/Home Care, Non-Classifiable

Source One Solutions Inc

PO Box 41190
Brecksville, OH 44141-0190
(440) 717-2100
Fax: (440) 717-2101
Email: careers@mysource1.com
Web: www.mysource1.com

Summary: We use innovative marketing and career/opportunity matching strategies to improve

your level of performance. Our industry focus is the transportation, automotive, truck, and marine marketplace, with a specific emphasis on polymers/rubber/plastics, adhesives & sealants, interior components & systems, power train, chassis/suspension and the field of NVH/Acoustics.

Key Contact - Specialty:
Mr. John Demjanjuk, Jr., General Manager - *Acoustics, Adhesives, Automotive, Engineering, Executives*
Mr. Todd Lynch - *Automotive, Textiles*
Ms. Linda Vargo, President

Salary Minimum: $50,000

Functions: Generalist (All), Sales Reps.

Industries: Plastics, Rubber, Metal Products, Machine, Appliance, Motor Vehicles, Industry Specific SW, Mfg. SW

SourceWynds Executive Search

833 Chelsea Park Dr
Marietta, GA 30068-2460
(770) 973-2520
Fax: (770) 973-4795
Email: wynr@sourcewynds.com
Web: www.sourcewynds.com

Summary: We specialize in the recruitment of professional sales talent and executive candidates to vendor organizations serving the power, chemical, petrochemical, wastewater, process, pulp and paper, mining and biotechnology industries.

Key Contact - Specialty:
Mr. Wyn Robinson, President - *Chemical, Power*
Mr. Richard LaBarba, Director - *Power*

Salary Minimum: $75,000

Functions: Generalist (All), Management, Senior Mgmt., Sales & Mktg., Engineering, Int'l.

Industries: Energy, Utilities, Chemicals, Test, Measure Equip., Biotech/Life Sciences

Southern Chemical & Plastics Search

5035 Morton Ferry Cir Ste 100
Alpharetta, GA 30022-6622
(678) 893-0580
Email: recruiter@chemical-recruiter.com
Web: www.chemical-recruiter.com

Summary: We specialize in sales, sales management and marketing in the raw materials chemical and plastics industries. Our thorough and confidential searches within an industry enable us to process qualified individuals who meet the specific needs of the client.

Key Contact - Specialty:
Mr. Jim Allen, CSAM, Director - *Chemical, Composites, Materials, Pesticides, Plastics*
Mr. Robert Christian, Director - *Building products, Chemical, Construction, Environmental, Plastics*
Mr. Allan Hytowitz, CPC, CSAM, Director - *Adhesives, Chemical, Environmental, Plastics, Thermoforming*

Salary Minimum: $30,000

Functions: Mfg., Sales & Mktg., Mktg. Mgmt., Sales Mgmt., Engineering

Industries: Construction, Chemicals, Soap, Perf., Cosmtcs., Drugs Mfg., Medical Devices, Plastics, Rubber, Paints, Petro. Products, Packaging

Southern Medical Recruiters

15225 Leeward Dr Apt A1
Corpus Christi, TX 78418-8018
(361) 883-4469
(800) 531-3104
Fax: (361) 883-4425
Email: recruiter@southernmed.com
Web: www.southernmed.com

Summary: We have extensive experience in healthcare recruitment and specialize in CEO, CFO, CNO/CNE, nursing directors, business office directors, pharmaceutical, lab, radiology, ancillary, M.D./D.O.s, CRNA, nuclear, ultrasound, MRI, dietary, pediatrics, maternal child, LTC/skilled, rehab, psychiatric, staff RNs, nurses, critical care directors/emergency room, OB, dosimetry, radiation therapist, cardiovascular and cath lab.

Key Contact - Specialty:
Ms. Adela Guerrero-Dryden, President - *Healthcare*

Salary Minimum: $200,000

Functions: Generalist (All), Senior Mgmt., Healthcare, Physicians, Nurses, Allied Health, Health Admin.

Industries: Generalist (All), Medical Devices, Healthcare, Hospitals, Long-term/Home Care, Physical Therapy, Occupational Therapy, Women's

Southern Recruiters & Consultants Inc

PO Box 2745
Aiken, SC 29802-2745
(803) 648-7834
Email: recruiters@southernrecruiters.com
Web: www.southernrecruiters.com

Summary: We are in an award-winning firm dedicated to professional, ethical and long-term service for our candidates and client companies. We handle all disciplines in manufacturing - one stop shopping for client companies.

Key Contact - Specialty:
Mr. Ray Fehrenbach, CPC, President - *Accounting, Human resources, Information Technology*
Ms. Kelly Boik, Recruiter - *Food & beverage, HVAC, Logistics*
Mr. Andy Meek, Recruiter - *Environmental, Medical (Devices), Physicians, Plastics*
Mrs. Brittany Singleton, Recruiter - *Manufacturing, Metals, Paint*

Salary Minimum: $35,000

Functions: Generalist (All)

Industries: Manufacturing, Accounting, Equip Svcs., HR Services, Environmental Svcs., Haz. Waste, Aerospace, Packaging, Software, Biotech/Life Sciences

Southern Technical Recruiters

2640 Willard Dairy Rd Ste 100
High Point, NC 27265-8709
(336) 841-7999
Fax: (336) 841-8001
Email: recruiters@southerntechnical.com
Web: www.southerntechnical.com

Summary: We have many years of recruiting experience with particular emphasis in the engineering and technical fields. We specialize in engineering, manufacturing/operations, sales/marketing and international positions.

Key Contact - Specialty:
Mr. Bill Roberts, Owner & Technical Recruiter - *Engineering, General management, International, Manufacturing, Six Sigma*

Mr. Jim Heath, Technical Recruiter - *Capital goods, Engineering, International, Maintenance, Sales*
Mrs. Crystal McCall, Technical Recruiter - *Adhesives, Coatings, Engineering, Environmental, Manufacturing*
Mr. Scott Reynolds, Technical Recruiter - *Computers, Design, Engineering, Information Technology*

Salary Minimum: $45,000

Functions: Generalist (All), Mfg., Purchasing, Mktg. Mgmt., Sales Mgmt., Engineering

Industries: Generalist (All), Manufacturing

Southwest Search & Consulting Inc

4500 S Lakeshore Dr Ste 520
Tempe, AZ 85282-8344
(480) 838-0333
Fax: (480) 838-0368
Email: azjobs@azjobs.com
Web: www.azjobs.com

Summary: We are the largest recruiting firm in our area that specializes exclusively in IT. All of our recruiters are tenured, with at least ten years of experience each. Our client base includes top 50 companies in our state.

Key Contact - Specialty:
Ms. Marilyn McDannel, President

Salary Minimum: $40,000

Functions: MIS Mgmt., Systems Analysis, Systems Dev., Systems Implem., Systems Support, Network Admin., DB Admin.

Industries: Generalist (All)

Southwest Selective Search Inc

1600 Airport Fwy Ste 328
Bedford, TX 76022-6850
(817) 540-6195
Fax: (817) 545-1122
Email: swsearch@flash.net
Web: www.swselectivesearch.com

Summary: Our staff comes from the industries we serve. We take the time to fully understand your company and personnel needs to serve you better.

Key Contact - Specialty:
Mr. Paul Neir, President
Ms. Karla Neir, Vice President

Salary Minimum: $30,000

Functions: Generalist (All)

Industries: Services, Insurance, Casualty, Claims, Accounting SW

Southwest Technical Consultants Inc

615 N Nevada Ave
Colorado Springs, CO 80903-5004
(719) 473-5950
Fax: (719) 633-9932
Email: swtci@swtci.com
Web: www.swtci.com

Summary: Our firm provides both permanent placement and contract services to firms with technical staffing requirements. In addition, we offer contract technical recruiting services, available on an hourly, daily or monthly basis.

Key Contact - Specialty:
Ms. Linda Boedeker, President

Functions: Generalist (All)

Industries: Computer Equip., IT Implementation, Software

Southwestern Business Resources

2451 Atrium Way
Nashville, TN 37214-5102
(615) 391-2717
(800) 443-7977
Fax: (615) 231-4000
Email: info@thinkingahead.com
Web: www.thinkingahead.com

Summary: We recruit executive, middle management and contract labor for Fortune 100 companies and small private firms. The contract labor is for technical personnel.

Key Contact - Specialty:
Dr. Carl R. Roberts, PhD, President
Mr. Greg Boucher, Vice President
Mr. Guice Smith, Manager
Mr. Tim Knight, Manager

Salary Minimum: $50,000

Functions: Generalist (All), Sales Mgmt., CFOs, Budgeting, Systems Dev., Systems Support, Engineering, Mgmt. Consultants

Industries: Generalist (All), Manufacturing, Accounting, Equip Svcs., IT Implementation, Telecoms, Aerospace, Insurance, Software, Accounting SW, Healthcare

Branches:
2005 Concord Pike Fl 2
Wilmington, DE 19803-2983
(302) 425-0272
Fax: (302) 425-0277
Key Contact - Specialty:
Mr. Bill Hutchison, Business Unit Manager

1600 Parkwood Cir SE Ste 611
Atlanta, GA 30339-2119
(770) 635-1120
Fax: (770) 635-1110
Key Contact - Specialty:
Mr. Jeff Young, Manager

111 W Jackson Blvd Ste 1362
Chicago, IL 60604-3877
(312) 583-1931
Key Contact - Specialty:
Mr. Tim Spidel, Manager

1111 Military Cutoff Rd Ste 171
Wilmington, NC 28405-3686
(910) 509-3831
Fax: (910) 509-3832
Key Contact - Specialty:
Ms. Cathy Moll, Manager - *Healthcare*

11427 Reed Hartman Hwy
Cincinnati, OH 45241-2418
(513) 618-6410
Key Contact - Specialty:
Ms. Theresa Oldfield, Manager

Spear-Izzo Associates LLC

651 Holiday Dr Ste 300
Pittsburgh, PA 15220-2740
(412) 928-3290
Fax: (724) 940-1959
Email: info@siasearch.com
Web: www.siasearch.com

Summary: We specialize in recruiting only for the management consulting industry. We satisfy the hiring needs of both premier management consulting firms and the internal consulting divisions of leading corporations worldwide.

Key Contact - Specialty:
Mr. Kenneth Spear, Partner
Mr. Donald Wesley, Principal
Mr. Randall Lheureau, Principal

Salary Minimum: $45,000

Functions: Generalist (All), Mgmt. Consultants

Industries: Energy, Utilities, Manufacturing, Finance, Mgmt. Consulting, Hospitality, Communications, Insurance, Biotech/Life Sciences, Healthcare

Branches:
850 Dogwood Rd Ste A400
Lawrenceville, GA 30044-7221
(770) 279-8898
Fax: (770) 279-9110
Email: consultant@siasearch.com
Key Contact - Specialty:
Mr. Thomas M. Izzo, Partner
Mr. John Snellen, Principal

The Spearhead Group Inc

4615 Southwest Fwy Ste 470
Houston, TX 77027-7153
(713) 622-7171
Fax: (713) 622-7771
Email: vmccullo@spearheadgroup.com
Web: www.spearheadgroup.com

Summary: Our firm is an 8(a)/SDB, WBEA multiple service staffing and consulting firm with emphasis for IT, accounting and engineering disciplines. Many years of service in the staffing and consulting arena has enabled us to obtain an advanced level of expertise and skills in these fields.

Key Contact - Specialty:
Ms. Vikki McCullough, President

Functions: Middle Mgmt., HR Mgmt., Finance, IT, Systems Dev., Engineering, Hardware, Minorities/Diversity

Industries: Generalist (All), Software

Specialized Search Associates

15200 Jog Rd Ste 201
Delray Beach, FL 33446-1249
(561) 499-3711
(888) 405-2650
Fax: (561) 499-3770
Email: lm7780@aol.com

Summary: We specialize in the executive recruiting of engineers for the construction industry. We place in the areas of marketing, operations and sales. We provide services within the following areas of engineering: civil, structural, mechanical, electrical, process, environmental, bridges, roads & highways, airports, infrastructure, transit, etc.

Key Contact - Specialty:
Mr. Leonard Morris, President - *Engineering*

Salary Minimum: $90,000

Functions: Sales & Mktg., Structural, Eng. Design

Industries: Energy, Utilities, Construction, Semiconductors, Architectural Svcs., Engineering Svcs., Haz. Waste, Biotech/Life Sciences

Specialty Employment Services Inc

PO Box 567054
Atlanta, GA 31156-7054
(770) 350-0953
Email: ms@sesijobs.com
Web: www.sesijobs.com

Summary: We will place the best fit executives with our clients, based upon a thorough understanding of the organization and the position and will do so with appropriate attention to timeliness. With highly personalized service to our clients, we will execute our searches using the latest evaluation tools and search technologies.

Key Contact - Specialty:
Mr. Michael Siegel, President - *Chemical, Marketing, Sales, Technical*
Ms. Karen Cheng - *Chemical, Engineering, Research & development*

Salary Minimum: $40,000

Functions: Generalist (All), Management, Productivity, Sales & Mktg.

Industries: Generalist (All), Agri., Forestry, Mining, Energy, Utilities, Food, Bev., Tobacco, Paper, Chemicals, Soap, Perf., Cosmtcs., Drugs Mfg., Medical Devices, Plastics, Rubber, Electronic, Elec. Components, Semiconductors, Pharm Svcs., HR Services, Engineering Svcs., Logistics Svcs., Supply Chain Mgmt., Biotech/Life Sciences

SPECTRA Associates

PO Box 688
Stevensville, MT 59870-0688
(406) 369-1188
Email: jbarlow@spectra-assoc.com
Web: www.spectra-assoc.com

Summary: We are a full service executive search firm that specializes in recruiting for engineering markets. These markets include companies involved with manufacturing, production and engineering. Our firm provides recruiting and staffing solutions to companies that require highly specialized and technically qualified engineering talent.

Key Contact - Specialty:
Mr. James Barlow, Executive Recruiter

Salary Minimum: $60,000

Functions: Engineering

Industries: Manufacturing, Consumer Elect., Electronic, Elec. Components

The Spectrum Group

2961 Northfield Dr
Tarpon Springs, FL 34688-9122
(727) 943-1166
Fax: (727) 945-1638
Email: spectrum@usafoodjobs.com
Web: www.usafoodjobs.com

Summary: We are a premier executive placement company. We have been successful in enhancing the careers of food industry professionals. We specialize in all aspects of food manufacturing to include operations, production, engineering, maintenance, sanitation, food safety, quality assurance and R&D management. Over the years we have worked with both large corporations and smaller privately held companies; always with a commitment to excellence.

Key Contact - Specialty:
Mr. Arnie Holder, President

Salary Minimum: $50,000

Functions: Senior Mgmt., Middle Mgmt., Mfg., Product Dev., Production, Plant Mgmt., Quality, Distribution, Packaging, Engineering

Industries: Manufacturing, Food, Bev., Tobacco

Spectrum Retail Associates LLC

(also known as Retail Recruiters)
10 E Athens Ave Ste 200
Ardmore, PA 19003-2115
(610) 645-9520
Email: rrspectrum@rcn.com

Summary: Consultants are specialists in areas of retail, manufacturing, direct mail, catalog and

hospitality. Our searches are well known for our effectiveness and results.

Key Contact - Specialty:
Ms. Shirlee J. Berman, President - *Healthcare, Retail*

Functions: Generalist (All), Materials, Distribution, Sales & Mktg., HR Mgmt., Finance, MIS Mgmt., DB Admin., Graphic Designers

Industries: Generalist (All), Manufacturing, Retail

Spectrum Scientific Recruiters

666 Plainsboro Rd Ste 220
Plainsboro, NJ 08536-3004
(609) 936-8850
Fax: (609) 936-9344
Email: info@spectrumscientific.com
Web: www.spectrumscientific.com

Summary: Recruiters of pharmaceutical industry professionals for full time, permanent, and contract staffing positions. Primary areas of recruitment include: clinical drug development, clinical research, regulatory affairs, drug safety, pharmacoepidemiology, data management, biostatistics, medical affairs, outcomes research and quality assurance.

Key Contact - Specialty:
Mr. Scott Nagrod, President & Senior Recruiter

Salary Minimum: $65,000

Functions: Board Members, Senior Mgmt., Product Dev., Quality, Materials, Materials Plng., Physicians, Nurses, DB Admin., R&D

Industries: Drugs Mfg., Biotech/Life Sciences

Spectrum Search Agency Inc

60 E Highland Ave
Sierra Madre, CA 91024-1976
(626) 355-4066
Email: joe79@pacbell.net

Summary: Specializing in telephony sales and sales support.

Key Contact - Specialty:
Mr. Joe Florence, Owner

Salary Minimum: $85,000

Functions: Generalist (All), Sales & Mktg.

Industries: Telecoms

Spherion Professional Services

7900 Glades Rd Ste 520
Boca Raton, FL 33434-4105
(561) 477-6061
Fax: (561) 883-2782
Email: hilarycarman@spherion.com
Web: www.spherion.com

Summary: Our goal is to be your strategic partner, providing a consultative approach, impacting your growth and profitability. Our solutions are delivered through search-direct hire, contract and project staffing. Our dedicated practice areas of expertise include: finance & accounting, HR, technology, engineering & manufacturing, legal, sales & marketing and interim executives.

Key Contact - Specialty:
Mr. William J. Grubbs, Interim President
Mr. Hilary Carman, Branch Manager

Salary Minimum: $30,000

Functions: CFOs, Budgeting, Cash Mgmt., Credit, Taxes, M&A, Risk Mgmt.

Industries: Generalist (All)

Branches:
4343 N Scottsdale Rd Ste 365
Scottsdale, AZ 85251-3349
(480) 776-3300
Email: maryhennenfent@spherion.com
Key Contact - Specialty:
Mr. Sean Ebner, Managing Director
Ms. Mary Hennenfent

114 Pacifica Ct Ste 210
Irvine, CA 92618-3317
(949) 727-3205
Fax: (949) 727-8513
Email: tamicolclasure@spherion.com
Key Contact - Specialty:
Mr. Eric Coe, Branch Director
Ms. Tami Colclasure

3825 Hopyard Rd Ste 270
Pleasanton, CA 94588-2787
(925) 847-8500
Email: brianpugh@spherion.com
Key Contact - Specialty:
Mr. Brian Pugh

777 Campus Commons Ste 130
Sacramento, CA 95825-8343
(916) 561-5755
Email: bobvolk@spherion.com
Key Contact - Specialty:
Mr. Bob Volk

4660 La Jolla Village Dr Ste 910
San Diego, CA 92122-4608
(858) 458-9200
Fax: (858) 458-1830
Email: bobbinerini@spherion.com
Key Contact - Specialty:
Ms. Chauna Carallo, Branch Director - *Finance*
Ms. Bobbi Nerini

475 Sansome St Ste 770
San Francisco, CA 94111-3100
(415) 391-0200
Fax: (415) 391-0280
Email: stephaniezeppegno@spherion.com
Key Contact - Specialty:
Mr. Jack Phillips, Managing Director - *Finance*

970 W 190th St Ste 425
Torrance, CA 90502-1078
(310) 327-3558
Fax: (310) 327-1984
Email: tammyhawkins@spherion.com
Key Contact - Specialty:
Ms. Marcia Cordova, Branch Director
Ms. Tammy Hawkins

1050 17th St Ste 1450
Denver, CO 80265-1501
(303) 893-0146
(303) 825-1292
Email: rosalinhildreth@spherion.com
Key Contact - Specialty:
Mr. Larry Mills, Branch Director - *Finance*
Ms. Janice Lynge, Recruiter - *Hospitality*
Mr. Rosalin Hildreth

100 First Stamford Pl Ste 100
Stamford, CT 06902-6747
(203) 978-1200
Email: andrewgolden@spherion.com
Key Contact - Specialty:
Mr. Andrew Golden

111 Continental Dr Ste 407
Newark, DE 19713-4332
(302) 861-1060
Email: alexmeloro@spherion.com
Key Contact - Specialty:
Mr. Bill Evans, Managing Director
Mr. Alex Meloro

1120 G St NW Ste 1000
Washington, DC 20005-3892
(202) 737-0075
Fax: (202) 296-7387
Email: robparker@spherion.com
Key Contact - Specialty:
Mr. Rob Parker, Branch Director - *Finance*

7900 Glades Rd Ste 520
Boca Raton, FL 33434-4105
(561) 477-6044
Fax: (561) 883-2782
Email: andrewpober@spherion.com
Key Contact - Specialty:
Mr. Andrew Pober, Area Director - *Engineering, Finance, Manufacturing, Sales*

2050 Spectrum Blvd
Fort Lauderdale, FL 33309-3008
(954) 308-7600
Email: suetreney@spherion.com
Key Contact - Specialty:
Mr. Matthew Shore, Area Director - *Engineering, Finance, Manufacturing, Sales*
Ms. Sue Treney

10151 Deerwood Park Blvd Ste 200-250
Jacksonville, FL 32256-0589
(904) 287-0672
Email: robertbalazic@spherion.com
Key Contact - Specialty:
Ms. Sharon Manassa, Branch Director
Mr. Robert Balazic

101 Southhall Ln Ste 150
Maitland, FL 32751-7497
(407) 647-8117
Fax: (407) 647-5449
Email: johnspooner@spherion.com
Key Contact - Specialty:
Mr. Chris Garbow, Senior Search Consultant - *Sales*
Mr. John Spooner

701 Waterford Way Ste 720
Miami, FL 33126-4684
(305) 265-5300
Fax: (305) 265-5310
Email: kariowens@spherion.com
Key Contact - Specialty:
Mr. Robert Hensley, Branch Director - *Finance*
Ms. Kari Owens

3111 W Dr Martin Luther King Jr Blvd Ste 350
Tampa, FL 33607-6234
(813) 864-1111
Fax: (813) 864-1121
Email: brentshort@spherion.com
Key Contact - Specialty:
Mr. Michael Vigna, Area Director
Mr. Brent Short

925 N Point Pkwy
Alpharetta, GA 30005-5210
(678) 867-3000
Email: jeffclement@spherion.com
Key Contact - Specialty:
Ms. Stacy Bozarth, Managing Director
Mr. Jeff Clement

3379 Peachtree Rd NE Ste 925
Atlanta, GA 30326-1422
(404) 364-4660
Fax: (404) 364-4650
Email: gretchenselby@spherion.com
Key Contact - Specialty:
Ms. Gretchen Selby, Branch Director - *Finance*

11 S La Salle St Ste 2155
Chicago, IL 60603-1220
(312) 781-7220
Email: kimberlybradshaw@spherion.com
Key Contact - Specialty:
Mr. Michael Ruter, Branch Director

1 Pierce Pl Ste 550W
Itasca, IL 60143-3157
(630) 919-2999
Fax: (630) 919-2888
Email: tazstephens@spherion.com
Key Contact - Specialty:
Ms. Bridgette Chambers, Managing Director
Mr. Taz Stephens

510 E 96th St Ste 125
Indianapolis, IN 46240-3787
(317) 843-0464
Fax: (317) 843-0664
Email: mikejenkins@spherion.com
Key Contact - Specialty:
Mr. Steve Skillern, Branch Director
Mr. Mike Jenkins

6901 Vista Dr
West Des Moines, IA 50266-9309
(515) 221-0514
Email: tracyvaubel@spherion.com
Key Contact - Specialty:
Tracy Vaubel

151 West St Ste 201
Annapolis, MD 21401-2852
(410) 269-1092
Fax: (410) 269-1072
Email: melindafairchild@spherion.com
Key Contact - Specialty:
Mr. John Ruffini, Branch Director - *Finance*
Ms. Melinda Fairchild

120 E Baltimore St Ste 2220
Baltimore, MD 21202-1635
(410) 752-8367
Fax: (410) 752-5924
Email: craigwalker@spherion.com
Key Contact - Specialty:
Mr. Mike Bettick, Vice President

4550 Montgomery Ave Ste 325N
Bethesda, MD 20814-3341
(301) 654-0082
Fax: (301) 653-1455
Email: stevekerrigan@spherion.com
Key Contact - Specialty:
Mr. Steve Kerrigan, Branch Director

9891 Broken Land Pkwy Ste 401
Woodmere 2
Columbia, MD 21046-3006
(410) 772-2210
Fax: (410) 772-2212
Email: tomsabia@spherion.com
Key Contact - Specialty:
Mr. Tom Sabia, Branch Director

800 Boyleston St Ste 1425
Boston, MA 02199-8156
(617) 482-5996
Fax: (617) 482-5973
Email: gaylahensley@spherion.com
Key Contact - Specialty:
Ms. Gayla Hensley

100 E Big Beaver Rd Ste 103
Troy, MI 48083-1204
(419) 893-2400
Fax: (419) 893-2491
Email: loisogren@spherion.com
Key Contact - Specialty:
Ms. Lois Ogren, Managing Director

100 E Big Beaver Rd Ste 330
Troy, MI 48083-1213
(248) 689-5055
Fax: (248) 689-1730
Email: dougscott@spherion.com
Key Contact - Specialty:
Mr. Doug Scott, Branch Director - *Finance*

5601 Green Valley Dr Ste 200
Bloomington, MN 55437-1173
(952) 543-3300
Fax: (952) 595-7300
Email: terrineumann@spherion.com
Key Contact - Specialty:
Mr. Kris Lang-Shasky
Terri Newmann

80 S 8th St Ste 3939
Minneapolis, MN 55402-2256
(612) 313-7997
Fax: (612) 313-7999
Email: davidbell@spherion.com
Key Contact - Specialty:
Mr. David Bell, Branch Director - *Finance*

8880 Ward Pkwy
Kansas City, MO 64114-2700
(816) 753-4644
Fax: (816) 896-5709
Email: yasaminzadeh@spherion.com
Key Contact - Specialty:
Mr. Jeffrey Berger, Branch Director

1610 Des Peres Rd Ste 190
Saint Louis, MO 63131-1831
(314) 288-2100
Email: thomashoecker@spherion.com
Key Contact - Specialty:
Mr. Jim Broadley, Branch Director - *Finance*
Mr. Thomas Hoecker

1140 US Highway 22 Ste 310
Bridgewater, NJ 08807-2958
(908) 725-6600
Fax: (908) 725-0325
Email: katerossi@spherion.com
Key Contact - Specialty:
Mr. Al Derosa, Branch Director
Ms. Kate Rossi

126 Corporate Blvd
South Plainfield, NJ 07080-2408
(908) 822-2221
Email: istg-centraljersey@spherion.com
Key Contact - Specialty:
Mr. Sal Fanelli, Managing Director

350 Park Ave Fl 22
New York, NY 10022-6051
(212) 213-3600
Fax: (212) 965-9089
Email: johngramer@spherion.com
Key Contact - Specialty:
Mr. John Gramer, CPA, Branch Director
Mr. Donald Marotto, Staffing Services

40 Broad St Rm 700
New York, NY 10004-2932
(212) 480-2600
Email: lindadevivo@spherion.com
Key Contact - Specialty:
Mr. Tom Roach, Managing Director

1400 Old Country Rd Ste 411
Westbury, NY 11590-5119
(516) 876-9700
Fax: (516) 876-9754
Email: lindadevivo@spherion.com
Key Contact - Specialty:
Ms. Linda Devivo

6000 Fairview Rd Ste 550
Charlotte, NC 28210-2219
(704) 643-7822
Fax: (704) 643-7078
Email: charlottepsg@spherion.com
Key Contact - Specialty:
Mr. Brian Johnson, Branch Director
Ms. Charlotte PSG

5001 S Miami Blvd Ste 320
Durham, NC 27703-8526
(919) 474-8003
Fax: (919) 941-0073
Email: robertwilcox@spherion.com
Key Contact - Specialty:
Mr. Jeff Scolnick, Branch Director - *Finance*
Mr. Robert Wilcox

5151 Pfeiffer Rd Ste 120
Cincinnati, OH 45242-4854
(513) 792-6658
Fax: (513) 792-6850
Email: brendaschuttinger@spherion.com
Key Contact - Specialty:
Mr. Larry Hoelscher, Area Director - *Finance*
Ms. Sandra Terry, Executive Recruiter
Ms. Carrie Lockwood
Ms. Brenda Schuttinger

111 W Rich St Ste 210
Columbus, OH 43215-5252
(614) 786-7905
Email: mattwirkiowski@spherion.com
Key Contact - Specialty:
Ms. Patricia DiNunzio, Area Director
Ms. Matt Wirkiowski

7887 Washington Village Dr Ste 200
Dayton, OH 45459-3960
(937) 293-9644
Email: ericsedwick@spherion.com
Key Contact - Specialty:
Mr. Eric Sedwick, Branch Director - *Finance*

1745 Indian Wood Cir Ste 150
Maumee, OH 43537-4038
(419) 893-2400
Fax: (419) 893-2491
Email: scottgearig@spherion.com
Key Contact - Specialty:
Mr. Scott Gearig, Branch Director
Ms. Lois Ogren, Staffing Services

1150 1st Ave Ste 820
Park View Tower
King of Prussia, PA 19406-1338
(610) 337-0923
Fax: (610) 337-1147
Email: michaelboyle@spherion.com
Key Contact - Specialty:
Mr. Mike Boyle, Branch Director - *Finance*

1617 JFK Blvd
Philadelphia, PA 19103-1821
(215) 568-5899
Fax: (215) 568-5810
Email: michaeldonnelly@spherion.com
Key Contact - Specialty:
Mr. Michael Donnelly

651 Holiday Dr Ste 300
Foster Plaza 5
Pittsburgh, PA 15220-2740
(412) 281-6068
Email: heidinobie@spherion.com
Key Contact - Specialty:
Ms. Karen Cross - *Engineering, Medical
(Devices), Molding (Blown,Injection), Plastics*
Ms. Heidi Nobie

155 Westminster St Ste 1250
Providence, RI 02903-2008
(401) 272-1200
Fax: (401) 272-1201
Email: johno'leary@spherion.com
Key Contact - Specialty:
Mr. John O'Leary, Branch Director

110 West North St
Greenville, SC 29601-2779
(864) 676-9160
Fax: (864) 676-9164
Email: janjanas@spherion.com

Key Contact - Specialty:
Mr. Mark Crist, Branch Director
Ms. Jan Janas

3030 LBJ Fwy Ste 150
Dallas, TX 75234-7022
(972) 991-6800
Email: karenperson@spherion.com
Key Contact - Specialty:
Mr. David Davis, Branch Director

10111 Richmond Ave Ste 100
Houston, TX 77042-4217
(713) 273-7400
Fax: (713) 784-7709
Email: donlegate@spherion.com
Key Contact - Specialty:
Ms. Ann Blythe, Branch Director - *Engineering, Finance, Manufacturing, Sales*
Mr. Don Legate
Mr. Raye Seals, Recruiter - *Energy, Human resources, Natural resources, Utilities*
Mr. Felix Romero, Search Consultant
Ms. Lina Fayeseiler - *Finance*

9311 San Pedro Ave Ste 1450
San Antonio, TX 78216-4481
(210) 342-1220
Email: chadmacy@spherion.com
Key Contact - Specialty:
Ms. Karen Person, Managing Director
Mr. Chad Macy

1651 Old Meadow Rd Fl 6
Mc Lean, VA 22102-4311
(703) 917-7800
Email: alisiagenzler@spherion.com
Key Contact - Specialty:
Ms. Alisia Genzler, Managing Director

1750 Tysons Blvd Ste 260
Mc Lean, VA 22102-4228
(703) 790-1100
Fax: (703) 790-1123
Email: markhorning@spherion.com
Key Contact - Specialty:
Mr. Mark Horning, Branch Director

9020 Stony Point Pkwy Ste 175
Richmond, VA 23235-1946
(804) 320-0500
Fax: (804) 327-7409
Email: glenndubiel@spherion.com
Key Contact - Specialty:
Mr. Glenn Dubiel, Branch Director - *Finance*

Spherion Technology
120-440 Laurier Ave W
Bradson Business Centre
Ottawa, ON K1R 7X6
Canada
(905) 361-1550
Email: corporate@spherion.ca
Web: www.spherion.ca

Summary: We have extensive experience serving the private sector. With branches across the country, we are confident in our ability to meet all your professional services and recruitment needs. Our firm provides both superior customer service for specialized needs and comprehensive solutions for a variety of challenges; all offered through specialized offices.

Key Contact - Specialty:
Mr. Bernie Vogel, Vice President, Technology Group
Ms. Linda Paquette, Recruiter - *Computers (Software)*

Salary Minimum: $40,000

Functions: Sales Mgmt., IT, MIS Mgmt., Systems Dev., Systems Implem., DB Admin.

Industries: Manufacturing, Retail, Finance, Banking, Legal, E-commerce, IT Implementation, Communications, Telecoms, Telephony, Digital, Wireless, Government, Aerospace, Software, Accounting SW, Database SW, Development SW, ERP SW, Security SW, System SW, Biotech/Life Sciences

Branches:
414-214 King St W
General Electric Building
Toronto, ON M5H 3S6
Canada
(416) 506-0627
Fax: (416) 506-1519
Email: torontotech@spherion.ca
Key Contact - Specialty:
Mr. Kevin O'Rourke, Vice President, Technology Group

Kenn Spinrad Inc
PO Box 22526
Philadelphia, PA 19110-2526
(800) 373-0944
Fax: (800) 636-0944
Email: randy@spinrad.net
Web: www.spinrad.net

Summary: We are a contingency firm solely specializing in the sewn products and textile industries. Our focus is on production/manufacturing and sales positions in the sewn products and textile industries.

Key Contact - Specialty:
Ms. Sharon Spinrad, Vice President
Mr. Kenn Spinrad, Vice President
Mr. Randy Weinstock, President

Functions: Generalist (All), Management, Senior Mgmt., Middle Mgmt., Production, Plant Mgmt., Purchasing, Materials Plng.

Industries: Manufacturing, Textiles, Apparel, Lumber, Furniture, Leather, Stone, Glass, Metal Products, Machine, Appliance, Consumer Elect., Misc. Mfg., Transportation, Wholesale, Retail, HR Services, Engineering Svcs., Logistics Svcs., Government, Defense, Environmental Svcs., Haz. Waste

Toby Spitz Associates Inc
110 E 59th St Fl 29
New York, NY 10022-1325
(212) 319-0990
Fax: (212) 319-1555
Email: tobyspitz@jdsearch.com
Web: www.jdsearch.com

Summary: We place the following practice: corporate, regulatory, intellectual property, international, litigation, labor & employment, real estate, tax and benefits. Our clients are corporations and law firms.

Key Contact - Specialty:
Ms. Toby Spitz, President

Functions: Generalist (All), Attorneys

Industries: Generalist (All), Manufacturing, Finance, Legal, Biotech/Life Sciences, Healthcare

Spotlight Search
2250 E Imperial Hwy Ste 200
El Segundo, CA 90245-3508
(310) 563-2124
Email: jobs@spotlightjobs.net
Web: www.spotlightjobs.net

Summary: We are creating a new approach of fusing multi-disciplinary talent with emerging technology in the fields of entertainment, media and content distribution. We have worked in the industries of wireless, gaming, internet, video-on-

demand, digital rights management, music distribution, digital cinema and consumer electronics and services.

Key Contact - Specialty:
Ms. Terri Tiemann, CAC, CSP, President - *Convergence, Financial services*

Salary Minimum: $65,000

Functions: Management, Sales & Mktg., Mktg. Mgmt., HR Mgmt., Training, IT, Security Personnel

Industries: Banking, Mutual/Hedge Funds, E-commerce, Advertising, New Media, Broadcast, Film, Telecoms, Telephony, Digital, Wireless, Fiber Optic, RF/Microwave, Software, Database SW, Doc. Mgmt., Production SW, Entertainment SW, ERP SW, HR SW, Industry Specific SW, Security SW, Training SW

Sprout/Standish Inc
82 Palomino Ln Ste 503
Bedford, NH 03110-6448
(603) 622-0700
Fax: (603) 622-4172
Email: dclark@printquest.com
Web: www.printquest.com

Summary: We are a highly specialized firm dedicated to serving the printing, publishing and packaging industries only. Vertically and horizontally integrated, so as to allow complete coverage including senior executives, mid-management and top spots in the GAM top 100.

Key Contact - Specialty:
Mr. David A. Clark, Chairman & President - *Manufacturing, Printing, Sales*

Salary Minimum: $60,000

Functions: Senior Mgmt., Plant Mgmt., Quality, Sales & Mktg., Sales Mgmt., Direct Mktg., Sales Reps., CFOs

Industries: Printing, Packaging

Spyglass Search Inc
122 S Michigan St Ste 300
South Bend, IN 46601-1928
(574) 287-5701
Fax: (574) 287-5360
Email: joe@spyglasssearch.com
Web: www.spyglasssearch.com

Summary: Boutique executive search firm, specializing in accounting, finance and HR positions. Our focus is placed on a quality process and not on transactional volume.

Key Contact - Specialty:
Mr. Joseph Pozsgai, Partner - *Accounting, Finance*
Ms. Cynthia Strzelecki, Partner - *Accounting, Finance, Human resources*

Salary Minimum: $40,000

Functions: HR Mgmt., Finance, CFOs

Industries: Generalist (All)

Squires Resources Inc
1-301 Bryne Dr
Barrie, ON L4N 8V4
Canada
(705) 725-7660
(877) 435-0921
Fax: (705) 725-7665
Email: info@squiresresources.com
Web: www.squiresresources.com

Summary: We offer a unique insight into career opportunities available for specialists in the following industries: IT, insurance, risk management, banking, investment and other professionals.

Key Contact - Specialty:
Mr. Frank Squires, President - *Risk management*
Mr. David White, Consultant
Ms. Jocelyn Squires, Consultant
Ms. Rebekah d'Amboise, Consultant
Mr. Marcello Fracassi, Consultant - *Engineering, Information Technology*

Salary Minimum: $40,000

Functions: Sales & Mktg., Risk Mgmt., Actuaries, Systems Dev., Systems Implem., Systems Support, Network Admin., DB Admin., Technicians, Int'l.

Industries: Generalist (All), Food, Bev., Tobacco, Lumber, Furniture, Printing, Computer Equip., Retail, Banking, Invest. Banking, Mutual/Hedge Funds, E-commerce, IT Implementation, Hospitality, Telecoms, Telephony, Wireless, Network Infrastructure, Insurance, Re-Insurance, Doc. Mgmt., Production SW

Marcus St Jean

(formerly known as Judy Wald Partners Inc)
584 Broadway Rm 804
New York, NY 10012-5241
(212) 274-0277
Fax: (212) 274-0041
Email: info@marcustjean.com
Web: www.marcustjean.com

Summary: In continuing with our firms history, our two principals have created a new "brand" name in creative recruitment in advertising and marketing.

Key Contact - Specialty:
Ms. Catherine St. Jean, Partner & Chief Operating Officer
Ms. Anne-Marie Marcus, Partner & Chief Executive Officer

Functions: Advertising

Industries: Advertising, New Media

Staff Cure

524 Lackawanna Ave
Mayfield, PA 18433-1802
(570) 876-1991
Fax: (570) 876-4884
Email: info@staffcure.com
Web: www.staffcure.com

Summary: Staff Cure is a Healthcare Recruitment Firm specializing in the Permanent Placement of Physicians, Midlevel Practitioners, Nursing and Allied Health Professionals Nationwide.

Key Contact - Specialty:
Ms. Sabrina Andreas, President

Functions: Senior Mgmt., Healthcare, Physicians, Nurses, Allied Health, Health Admin.

Industries: Generalist (All), Non-profits, Pharm Svcs., Sports, Hospitals, Long-term/Home Care, Dental, Physical Therapy, Occupational Therapy, Women's, Non-Classifiable

Staff Resources Inc

PO Box 4557
Rock Hill, SC 29732-6557
(803) 366-0500
Fax: (803) 366-1021
Email: sri@srijobs.com
Web: www.srijobs.com

Summary: We specialize in manufacturing and all functions that support a manufacturing facility. Most all of our clients are Fortune 500 firms and have excellent benefits and relocation packages.

Key Contact - Specialty:
Mr. Dick Jordan, Senior Parnter - *Finance, Human resources, Manufacturing, Materials, Quality*

Ms. Carol Dodd, Research Assistant - *Engineering, Human resources, Manufacturing, Purchasing*
Mr. Ken Wells, Senior Recruiter

Salary Minimum: $25,000

Functions: Generalist (All), Materials

Industries: Manufacturing, Machine, Appliance, Transportation, Finance, Accounting, Equip Svcs., Mgmt. Consulting, HR Services, Hospitality, Telecoms, Packaging

Staff, Inc.

1550 Utica Ave S Ste 140
Minneapolis, MN 55416-3677
(952) 545-4000
Fax: (952) 546-0206
Email: gen@staffinc.com
Web: www.staffinc.com

Summary: Staffing firm specializing in insurance, healthcare and related business groups. We offer temp, temp-to-hire, direct hire and contract. We adhere to our motto "One Goal...Yours!"

Key Contact - Specialty:
Ms. Susan St. James, President & Owner - *Insurance (Claims,Health,Life,Reinsurance,Workers Compensation)*
Ms. Shari Rasmusson, Office Manager
Ms. Cristy Molter, Client Relations Manager

Functions: Senior Mgmt., Product Dev., Healthcare

Industries: Finance, Media, Communications, Insurance, Casualty, Claims, Life, Commercial, Re-Insurance, Healthcare

Staffing Authority

2117 Buffalo Rd Ste 213
Rochester, NY 14624-1507
(585) 413-4316
Fax: (585) 413-4343
Email: jobs@staffingauthority.com
Web: www.staffingauthority.com

Summary: We are a full service recruiting firm. From contingent and retained executive search to temporary staffing, temp-to-hire and direct placement, we partner with our clients to develop long term relationships. Our specialty areas include: engineering, information technology, healthcare, professional and executive search.

Key Contact - Specialty:
Mr. Chad Boehly, President - *Call centers, Engineering, Executives, Healthcare, Human resources*

Functions: Generalist (All), Senior Mgmt., Middle Mgmt., Admin. Svcs., Mfg., Production, Automation, Healthcare, HR Mgmt., Engineering

Industries: Generalist (All), Manufacturing, Machine, Appliance, Computer Equip., Test, Measure Equip., Misc. Mfg., Electronic, Elec. Components, Robotics, Finance, Services, Communications, Software, Biotech/Life Sciences, Healthcare

Staffing Services Inc

860 Biester Dr Ste 205
Belvidere, IL 61008-4053
(815) 547-7669
Fax: (815) 547-5697
Email: belvidere@staffingserv.com
Web: www.staffingserv.com

Summary: Expertise - Professionalism - Excellence

Key Contact - Specialty:
Mrs. Teresa Pesina, General Manager

Salary Minimum: $40,000

Functions: Generalist (All), Management

Industries: Manufacturing, Printing, Metal Products, Misc. Mfg., Electronic, Elec. Components, Legal, Accounting, Packaging

Branches:
1806 S Alpine Rd Ste B
Rockford, IL 61108-6471
(815) 227-5555
Email: debbie@staffingserv.com
Key Contact - Specialty:
Ms. Debbie Cantin, Branch Manager - *Administration, Clerical, Data processing, Database (Administration), Executives*

400 E Grant Ave Ste 312
Beloit, WI 53511-6200
(608) 363-0134
Fax: (608) 363-0174
Email: becky@staffingserv.com
Key Contact - Specialty:
Ms. Becky Lopez, Branch Manager - *Administration, CEOs, CFOs, Change management, Clerical*

Staffing Solutions USA Inc

(also known as Staffing Solutions USA Consulting Services, In)
51 E 42nd St Rm 810
New York, NY 10017-5404
(212) 972-5100
Fax: (212) 972-1377
Email: cliff@ssusa.com
Web: www.staffingsolutionsusa.com

Summary: Our firm is a full service staffing company covering the New York Tri-state Area, specializing in information technology and administrative support staffing. Our president has extensive experience placing technology professionals in positions with Fortune 1000 companies.

Key Contact - Specialty:
Mr. Cliff Shaw, President - *Information Technology*

Salary Minimum: $35,000

Functions: IT, MIS Mgmt., Systems Analysis, Systems Dev., Systems Implem., Systems Support, Network Admin., DB Admin., Hardware, Systems

Industries: Generalist (All)

Staffing USA

PO Box 310863
Birmingham, AL 35231-0863
(205) 648-2300
(800) 648-2301
Fax: (205) 648-4400
Email: staffingusa@charter.net
Web: www.staffingusa.net

Summary: Firm that specializes in IT, engineering and accountants.

Key Contact - Specialty:
Mrs. Mary Nell Blackburn, Owner - *Engineering*

Functions: Management, Finance, Budgeting, Taxes, IT, Engineering

Industries: Generalist (All), Energy, Utilities, Manufacturing, Finance, Banking, Accounting, E-commerce, IT Implementation, Communications, Telecoms, Network Infrastructure, Government, Environmental Svcs., Software

StaffWriters Plus

2150 Joshuas Path Ste 102
Hauppauge, NY 11788-4773
(631) 582-9000
Fax: (631) 582-8828
Email: info@staffwriters.com
Web: www.staffwriters.com

Summary: We offer access to the country's best
writers, editors and communicators in more than
350 highly specialized areas including marketing,
public relations, news media and corporate
communications and also use them to provide full
service marketing and custom publishing services
to major corporations.

Key Contact - Specialty:
Mr. George Giokas, President & Chief Executive
Officer
Mr. Andrew Sherman, Vice President

Functions: Admin. Svcs., Healthcare, Sales &
Mktg., Mktg. Research, Direct Mktg., PR,
Training, IT, Specialized Svcs., Graphic
Designers

Industries: Generalist (All), Media, Advertising,
Publishing, New Media, Broadcast, Film,
Hospitals

The Stanton Group Inc

374 E Marseilles St
Vernon Hills, IL 60061-4151
(847) 955-0540
Email: john.keister@stantongp.com
Web: www.stantongp.com

Summary: We specialize in the recruitment and
placement of engineering and technology
professionals in leadership roles. Our areas of
specialty include Six Sigma, software, systems
engineering, architecture, process improvement
(CMMI), quality, and nanotechnology. Our
principals have technical backgrounds in
engineering and mathematics.

Key Contact - Specialty:
Mr. John Keister, President & Founder -
*Computers (Software), Engineering, Research &
development, Systems, Technical (Management)*

Salary Minimum: $80,000

Functions: Management, Quality, R&D,
Engineering

Industries: Energy, Utilities, Manufacturing,
Transportation, Services, Communications,
Government, Defense, Aerospace, Software,
Biotech/Life Sciences

Star Recruiting Consultants LLC

819 W 4th St
Williamstown, WV 26187-1005
(740) 629-1283
Fax: (866) 877-4706
Email: src@star-recruiting.com
Web: www.star-recruiting.com

Summary: We are a specialized recruiting firm
that locates and places the highest caliber
candidates within multiple industries. Our firm
utilizes exclusive techniques and assets to ensure
successful placements of technical, government,
professional and executive fields. Our firm has the
ability to network worldwide allowing us to source
uniquely qualified candidates.

Key Contact - Specialty:
Mr. Dave Starcher, Owner

Salary Minimum: $50,000

Functions: Generalist (All)

Industries: Generalist (All)

Starbridge Group Inc

10801 Main St Ste 500
Fairfax, VA 22030-4744
(703) 691-3900
Fax: (703) 691-3999
Email: web@starbridgegroup.com
Web: www.starbridgegroup.com

Summary: Industry segmented specialization in
order to provide added value and expertise to our
clients. We aggressively deliver on our
commitments to our clients with high integrity and
professionalism. We specialize in permanent and
project based placement at mid to senior-level
professionals.

Key Contact - Specialty:
Mr. David Kurke, President
Ms. Kathleen Kurke, National Practice Leader
Dr. Gerry Sismore, Director, Services -
Consulting, Education, Multimedia, Training
Ms. Susan Miller, Executive Recruiter -
Consulting, Education, Training
Ms. Brenda Kaczmarek, Executive Recruiter
Mr. Matt Harris, Executive Recruiter
Ms. Suzanne Purdy, Executive Recruiter

Functions: Generalist (All), Senior Mgmt., Sales
& Mktg., Sales Mgmt., Training, Mgmt.
Consultants

Industries: Generalist (All), Services, Pharm
Svcs., Mgmt. Consulting, HR Services, E-
commerce, IT Implementation, PSA/ASP,
Higher Ed., HR SW, Training SW

StarDot PRG Inc

2020-633 6 Ave SW
Ford Tower
Calgary, AB T2P 2Y5
Canada
(403) 264-3897
Fax: (403) 264-3901
Email: info@stardotprg.com
Web: www.stardotprg.com

Summary: From our thousands of pre-screened IT
professionals, we provide a short list of qualified
people for your permanent or contract position.

Key Contact - Specialty:
Mr. Don Van Mierlo, President
Ms. Alice Matthews, Vice President, Recruiting
& Admin

Functions: Generalist (All), IT

Industries: Generalist (All)

Starpoint Solutions

115 Broadway Fl 2
New York, NY 10006-1644
(212) 962-1550
Email: info@starpoint,com
Web: www.starpoint.com

Summary: We have the people, technology and
experience to make your company thrive. We
provide world class enterprise wide consulting and
custom application and integration solutions. We
are privately held and have offices nationwide.

Key Contact - Specialty:
Mr. Jeffrey Najarian, Chairman

Functions: Generalist (All), MIS Mgmt., Systems
Analysis, Systems Dev., Systems Implem.,
Systems Support

Industries: Generalist (All), Finance, E-
commerce, IT Implementation, Media,
Communications, Software

Branches:
1 N La Salle St Ste 1425
Chicago, IL 60602-4481
(312) 726-7753

Email: info@starpoint.com
Key Contact - Specialty:
Mr. Dan Gish

10 High St Ste 650
Boston, MA 02110-1663
(617) 422-0226
Email: info@starpoint.com
Key Contact - Specialty:
Mr. Matthew Malvese
Mr. Thomas Farley, Recruiter

120 Wood Ave S Ste 400
Iselin, NJ 08830-2709
(732) 494-2210
Email: info@starpoint.com
Key Contact - Specialty:
Mr. Mark Alashaian

3333 Street Rd Ste 245
Bensalem, PA 19020-2042
(215) 245-0771
Email: info@starpoint.com
Key Contact - Specialty:
Mr. Arthur Farkas

5420 Lbj Fwy Ste 780
Dallas, TX 75240-6238
(972) 371-5679
Email: info@starpoint.com
Key Contact - Specialty:
Mr. Gary Raymond

8201 Greensboro Dr Ste 605
Mc Lean, VA 22102-3816
(703) 506-0789
Email: info@starpoint.com
Key Contact - Specialty:
Mr. Michael Michaelis

Marjorie Starr & Associates

PO Box 41024
Mesa, AZ 85274-1024
(480) 730-6050
Email: mstarr273@aol.com

Summary: We are proud to say that we have
assisted thousands of candidates and hundreds of
clients. Our mission is to bring higher quality and
a personal level of professional service to both our
clients and candidates.

Key Contact - Specialty:
Ms. Marjorie Starr, CPC - *Sales, Technical*

Functions: Generalist (All), Sales & Mktg.

Industries: Generalist (All), Services, Equip
Svcs., Telecoms, Telephony, Digital, Wireless,
Insurance, Software, Marketing SW

Fern G Stasiuk Executive Search Inc

PO Box 256
Baldwin Place, NY 10505-0256
(845) 621-2966
Email: fernfgs@bestweb.net
Web: www.bestweb.net/~fernfgs

Summary: Executive search specialists in the
telecom and emerging technologies industries. We
offer expertise in the identification and screening
of compliance, finance, legal, Sarbanes-Oxley
specialists, accounting, due diligence, sales,
marketing and general management talent.

Key Contact - Specialty:
Ms. Fern Stasiuk, President - *Telecommunications*

Salary Minimum: $90,000

Functions: Generalist (All)

Industries: Finance, Legal, Engineering Svcs.,
Telecoms, Telephony, Digital, Wireless,
Network Infrastructure, RF/Microwave

STAT Search

7 Colby Ct Ste 4
Bedford, NH 03110-6427
(603) 666-5500
(877) 623-5321
Fax: (603) 623-5322
Email: hunter@statsearch.com
Web: www.statsearch.com

Summary: We conduct confidential searches for sales, operations, and clinical executives for companies offering healthcare services and medical products. We listen to your needs and provide well screened candidates in an efficient and timely manner. These candidates are not only able to do your job, but want to do it, and are expected to thrive in your corporate culture.

Key Contact - Specialty:
Mrs. Dale Poklemba, MS, CPC, Principal & Founder - *C-level, Executives, Healthcare, Managed care, Medical (Sales)*
Mrs. Andrea Lampert, MBA, RN, Principal - *Clinical, Healthcare, Home health, Hospital*
Ms. Barbara Folb, MBA, CPC, RN, Principal - *Executives, Healthcare, Home health, Pharmacists, Procurement*
Ms. Paula Avriett, MS, SLP, Principal - *Clinical, Healthcare, Home health, Hospital*
Mrs. Laurie Loughney, LNHA, CALA, Principal - *Healthcare, Home health, Long term care, Management, Social work*

Salary Minimum: $60,000

Functions: Management, Board Members, Senior Mgmt., Middle Mgmt., Healthcare, Nurses, Allied Health, Health Admin., Mktg. Mgmt., CFOs

Industries: Generalist (All), Healthcare

Stebbins & Associates

520 N Lincoln Way Ste 7
Galt, CA 95632-8605
(209) 744-2003
Fax: (209) 744-7179
Email: stebbins@greenadvice.com
Web: www.greenadvice.com

Summary: We are an executive search firm serving clients in agri-business, waterworks, and lawn & garden industries.

Key Contact - Specialty:
Mr. Steve Stebbins, President - *Sales*

Salary Minimum: $50,000

Functions: Sales & Mktg.

Industries: Agri., Forestry, Mining

Steinfield & Associates LP

3333 Lee Pkwy Ste 600
Dallas, TX 75219-5117
(214) 220-0535
Fax: (214) 447-9524
Email: steinfield@airmail.net

Summary: We are an executive search firm specializing in the placement of management and executive-level finance, accounting, consulting, audit, tax and HR professionals.

Key Contact - Specialty:
Mr. David Steinfield, President - *Consulting, Finance, Human resources*

Salary Minimum: $75,000

Functions: HR Mgmt., Finance, CFOs, Budgeting, Cash Mgmt., Taxes, M&A, Mgmt. Consultants

Industries: Generalist (All), Finance, Accounting, Mgmt. Consulting, HR Services, Real Estate

The Stelton Group Inc

904 Oak Tree Ave Ste A
South Plainfield, NJ 07080-5126
(908) 757-9888
Fax: (908) 757-3179
Email: steltongroup@msn.com
Web: www.steltongroup.com

Summary: We are an industry specific recruiting of professional and executive candidates for all industries.

Key Contact - Specialty:
Mr. Al Lewis, President - *Engineering*
Ms. Cindy L. Slusser, Account Executive - *Information Technology*

Salary Minimum: $85,000

Functions: Generalist (All)

Industries: Generalist (All)

A Stephens & Associates LLC

PO Box 14154
Springfield, MO 65814-0154
(417) 886-4114
Fax: (417) 886-5962
Email: info@stephensrecruiters.com
Web: www.stephensrecruiters.com

Summary: Our firm is an executive search firm in the pharmaceutical, biotechnology and medical device industries. We develop effective recruitment strategies tailored to meet our client's specific needs.

Key Contact - Specialty:
Ms. Angela Stephens, President

Functions: Generalist (All), Board Members, Senior Mgmt., Middle Mgmt., Mktg. Research, Mktg. Mgmt., Sales Mgmt.

Industries: Generalist (All), Drugs Mfg., Medical Devices, Pharm Svcs., Advertising, Healthcare

Stephens International Recruiting Inc

97 Lakeshore Pl
Lakeview, AR 72642-9122
(870) 431-5485
Fax: (870) 431-5489
Email: info@bmets-usa.com
Web: www.bmets-usa.com

Summary: A healthcare recruiting firm of executive-level consultants with diverse experience and background in health care support services. Well-known for finding quality biomedical equipment, field service radiology/imaging technicians, managers, and executives. We provide full-service, executive-level recruitment services in all areas of health care: technical, management, clinical, and physician placement.

Key Contact - Specialty:
Ms. Cindy Stephens, Chief Executive Officer
Mr. Tim Hopkins, Vice President & Executive Recruiter - *Biomedical*

Salary Minimum: $50,000

Functions: Senior Mgmt., Healthcare, Physicians, Nurses, Allied Health, Health Admin., Technicians

Industries: Medical Devices, Misc. Mfg., Electronic, Elec. Components, Pharm Svcs., Government, Healthcare, Hospitals, Long-term/Home Care, Physical Therapy, Occupational Therapy, Women's

The Sterling Group

30352 Esperanza
Rancho Santa Margarita, CA 92688-2118
(949) 888-3030
Fax: (949) 888-3038
Email: mail@sterlinggroup.com
Web: www.sterlinggroup.com

Summary: A people solution provider, not just a search firm, that cares about developing long-term business relationships. Emphasis in senior to mid-level executives in information technology, finance, human resource, and bio-technology related disciplines.

Key Contact - Specialty:
Mr. Ron Henry, President
Ms. Lori LaFavre, Vice President, BioTech Division
Ms. Elaine Hobbins, Vice President, High Tech, Emerging Tech

Salary Minimum: $100,000

Functions: Senior Mgmt.

Industries: Generalist (All), Non-profits, Pharm Svcs., Accounting, Mgmt. Consulting, HR Services, IT Implementation, Call Centers, Software, Biotech/Life Sciences

Sterling Professional Search

1681 E Auburn Rd Ste C
Rochester Hills, MI 48307-5583
(248) 852-4900
Fax: (248) 852-9404
Email: fred@sterlingprosearch.com
Web: www.sterlingprosearch.com

Summary: We specialize in placing candidates in the tire and automotive community.

Key Contact - Specialty:
Ms. Sheila Stokes, Project Coordinator
Mr. Fred Melin, President & Chief Executive Officer - *Automotive*
Mr. Doug Carmean, Executive Search Specialist - *Automotive*
Mr. George Diamond, Executive Search Specialist - *Automotive*

Salary Minimum: $50,000

Functions: Middle Mgmt., Plant Mgmt., Quality, Materials, Purchasing

Industries: Plastics, Rubber, Paints, Petro. Products, Leather, Stone, Glass, Metal Products, Motor Vehicles, HR Services, Engineering Svcs., Logistics Svcs., Supply Chain Mgmt

Daniel Stern & Associates

10 Duff Rd Ste 215
Pittsburgh, PA 15235-3262
(412) 244-6434
(800) 438-2476
Fax: (800) 892-2781
Email: sternd@danielstern.com
Web: www.danielstern.com

Summary: We specialize in physician recruiting, healthcare administration and consulting services in emergency medicine, including practice enhancement, maximizing revenues, practice sales & acquisitions, contract development, negotiations and billing services.

Key Contact - Specialty:
Mr. Daniel Stern, President

Salary Minimum: $125,000

Functions: Physicians

Industries: Healthcare

Stern Professional Search

PO Box 50228
Saint Louis, MO 63105-5228
(312) 587-7777
Email: info@sternprosearch.com
Web: www.sternprosearch.com

Summary: Our firm specializes in the interior furnishings and design industry. We place sales and marketing, mid management and upper management. We also place architects and interior designers. Areas of expertise: furniture, textiles, carpeting, lighting, signage, and architectural hardware. Industries include: kitchen and bath, hospitality, health care, and residential furnishings.

Key Contact - Specialty:
Ms. Janet Grodsky, President - *Design, Furniture*
Ms. Cari O'Connor, Vice President

Salary Minimum: $50,000

Functions: Senior Mgmt., Middle Mgmt., Plant Mgmt., Sales & Mktg., Sales Mgmt., Architects, Graphic Designers

Industries: Manufacturing, Textiles, Apparel, Lumber, Furniture, Leather, Stone, Glass, Misc. Mfg.

Ron Stevens & Associates Inc

4501 Galloway Blvd
Bradenton, FL 34210-2949
(800) 458-1611
Email: rsa-inc@att.net

Summary: We are a contingency search firm concentrating in the recruitment and placement of mid and senior-level management executives for the chemical, petrochemical, utilities/energy and management consulting business.

Key Contact - Specialty:
Mr. Ron Stevens, President - *Technical*

Salary Minimum: $65,000

Functions: Management, Middle Mgmt., Sales & Mktg., Mktg. Mgmt., Int'l.

Industries: Generalist (All), Energy, Utilities, Oil & Gas, Manufacturing, Chemicals, Drugs Mfg., Plastics, Rubber, Paints, Petro. Products, Consumer Elect., Mgmt. Consulting, Mfg. SW, Marketing SW

The Stevens Group Executive Search Consultants

23679 Calabasas Rd Ste 512
Calabasas, CA 91302-1502
(818) 712-0242
Fax: (818) 712-0325
Email: stevensgroup@earthlink.net

Summary: Highly regarded boutique executive search practice committed to excellence and results. We are proud of our long-standing client and candidate relationships based on a high degree of integrity and personal involvement. One of the quickest response times and highest completion ratios in the industry. Reputation of integrity, honesty and service.

Key Contact - Specialty:
Ms. Martha Stevens, President

Salary Minimum: $50,000

Functions: Generalist (All), Management, Senior Mgmt., Middle Mgmt., Product Dev., Purchasing, Materials Plng., Packaging, Mktg. Mgmt., Finance

Industries: Manufacturing, Food, Bev., Tobacco, Soap, Perf., Cosmtcs., Drugs Mfg., Medical Devices, Metal Products, Computer Equip., Consumer Elect., Test, Measure Equip., Misc.

Mfg., Electronic, Elec. Components, Semiconductors, Consumer Goods, Finance, Accounting, E-commerce, Logistics Svcs., Supply Chain Mgmt, Packaging, Software, Biotech/Life Sciences

Stewart Associates

181 Windover Turn
Lancaster, PA 17601-5331
(717) 299-9242
Email: waltp@redrose.net

Summary: Broad range of recruiting services for the high-technology, commercial and defense sectors of the economy. Specializing in engineering and manufacturing management.

Key Contact - Specialty:
Mr. Walter S. Poyck, President - *Manufacturing*

Salary Minimum: $35,000

Functions: Management, Mfg., Materials, HR Mgmt., Finance, Risk Mgmt., R&D, Engineering

Industries: Generalist (All), Food, Bev., Tobacco, Chemicals, Metal Products, Motor Vehicles, Consumer Elect., Transportation

The Stewart Group

(a division of The Stewart Search Group Inc)
PO Box 2588
Ponte Vedra Beach, FL 32004-2588
(904) 285-6622
Fax: (904) 285-0076
Email: jim@stewartgroup.net
Web: www.stewartgroup.net

Summary: We provide services for pharmaceutical and medical recruitment in all departments. Mid to senior-level searches in most industries. Scientific and manufacturing placement in pharmaceutical and medical fields. Nursing & healthcare insurers.

Key Contact - Specialty:
Mr. James H. Stewart, President & Managing Director - *Clinical, Pharmaceutical, Regulatory*
Mr. Brian Stewart, Executive Search Consultant - *Marketing, Sales, Senior management*
Ms. Cathi Stewart, Recruiter - *Communications, Financial, Managed care, Sales*
Ms. Stephanie McCabe, Executive Search Consultant - *Engineering, Manufacturing, Regulatory*
Mrs. Colleen Frampton, Executive Search Consultant - *Information Systems, Information Technology, Technical, Technology, Telecommunications*
Mrs. Laurie Losee, Executive Search Consultant - *Healthcare, Hospital, Operating rooms*

Salary Minimum: $70,000

Functions: Generalist (All), Sales & Mktg.

Industries: Drugs Mfg., Medical Devices, Finance, Venture Cap., Services, Media, Broadcast, Film, Communications, Software, Biotech/Life Sciences, Healthcare

Stewart Search Advisors LLC

875 Greenland Rd Unit B8
Portsmouth, NH 03801-4162
(603) 430-2122
Fax: (603) 430-7339
Email: info@stewartsearch.com
Web: www.stewartsearch.com ,
www.actuarialfutures.com

Summary: We are dedicated to the placement of actuaries in life, annuity, disability, pension, investment, property & casualty and health careers. Our clients include the nation's leading insurance, reinsurance, consulting, investment and health companies.

Key Contact - Specialty:
Mr. William M. Stewart, Manager & Search Advisor
Ms. Susan Pearson Spaulding, Manager & Search Advisor

Functions: Generalist (All), Risk Mgmt., Actuaries

Industries: Generalist (All), Mutual/Hedge Funds, Insurance, Casualty, Life, Commercial, Re-Insurance

Stillwater Search

16656 Ventura Blvd Ste 204
Encino, CA 91436-4819
(818) 386-2110
Fax: (818) 386-2105
Email: stillwatersearch@sbcglobal.net

Summary: We specialize in placing sales professionals in the intangible/service industries such as financial services, information services, training & consulting, outsourcing, staffing, technical services, PEOs and legal services.

Key Contact - Specialty:
Ms. Suzi Martinez, President
Mr. David Kevoe, Vice President

Salary Minimum: $45,000

Functions: Board Members, Senior Mgmt., Sales Mgmt.

Industries: Generalist (All), Printing, Services, Legal, Accounting, Mgmt. Consulting, HR Services, Media, Insurance, Software, Training SW

StingRay Scientific

16030 Ventura Blvd Ste 235
Encino, CA 91436-4472
(818) 377-2590
Fax: (818) 377-2591
Email: info@stingraysci.com
Web: www.stingraysys.com

Summary: We are an executive search firm specializing in the placement of bio-technology & pharmaceutical scientists, chemists and professionals.

Key Contact - Specialty:
Mr. Patrick Ross, Manager

Functions: R&D

Industries: Pharm Svcs., Biotech/Life Sciences

StingRay Systems

1259 El Camino Real Ste 400
Menlo Park, CA 94025-4208
(650) 838-0310
Fax: (650) 838-0315
Email: mike@stingraysys.com
Web: www.stingraysys.com

Summary: Our firm is a professional technical search firm dedicated to meeting and exceeding the needs of our client companies as well as our candidates. We consistently provide a high level of professional service and integrity that is unparalleled in the industry. Our senior team of highly qualified recruiters is committed to providing you with the best service available.

Key Contact - Specialty:
Mr. Mike Pooley, Manager

Functions: R&D

Industries: Software, Accounting SW, Database SW, Development SW, Doc. Mgmt., Production SW, ERP SW, HR SW, Industry Specific SW, Mfg. SW, Marketing SW

Stoakley-Dudley Consultants Ltd
6547A Mississauga Rd
Mississauga, ON L5N 1A6
Canada
(905) 821-3455
Fax: (905) 821-3467
Email: stoakley@stoakley.com
Web: www.stoakley.com

Summary: We are an international high-technology search firm specializing in sales & marketing, engineering, hardware, software development, electronics, senior management and finance.

Key Contact - Specialty:
Mr. Ernie Stoakley, President - *RF microwave, Robotics, Semiconductors, Telecommunications, Wireless*
Mr. Reg Shortt, Consultant
Mr. Patrick Laforet, Consultant - *Manufacturing*
Ms. Deborah Milo, Consultant - *Automotive*
Mr. Don Christensen, Consultant - *Finance*
Mr. Trevor Stewart, Consultant - *Logistics*
Ms. Doris Torrans, Consultant - *Accounting, Accounting (Bookkeeping,General,Public), Comptrollers*
Mr. Bill MacLean, Consultant - *Database (Administration,Warehousing), E-business, ERP, Freight*

Salary Minimum: $40,000

Functions: Generalist (All)

Industries: Generalist (All)

Stone Legal Resources Group
100 Summer St Fl 10
Boston, MA 02110-2106
(617) 482-4100
(877) 529-5627
Fax: (617) 482-9601
Email: boston@stonelegal.com
Web: www.stonelegal.com

Summary: We are a leading East Coast firm devoted to the highest levels of placement for attorneys, paralegals and administrative support staff.

Key Contact - Specialty:
Ms. Karen Zelden, Vice President & National Acct Director

Functions: Senior Mgmt., Legal, Attorneys, Paralegals

Industries: Generalist (All), Construction, Retail, Legal

DM Stone Recruitment Solutions
100 Bush St Ste 750
San Francisco, CA 94104-3935
(415) 391-5151
Fax: (415) 391-5536
Email: mailbox@dmstone.com
Web: www.dmstone.com

Summary: We are a financial services specialist, serving clients in banking, brokerage, insurance, investment banking, asset management, accounting and IT. Providing temp, temp-to-hire and direct hire placement, from entry-level to executive management.

Key Contact - Specialty:
Mr. Dave M. Stone, President - *Financial services, Investment management, Trust*

Salary Minimum: $40,000

Functions: Admin. Svcs., Sales Mgmt., Customer Svc., Finance, CFOs, Budgeting, Cash Mgmt., Credit, Taxes, Legal

Industries: Generalist (All), Finance, Banking, Invest. Banking, Brokers, Venture Cap., Mutual/Hedge Funds, Misc. Financial

Susan Stoneberg Executive Search Inc
15200 163rd Pl NE
Woodinville, WA 98072-8942
(425) 487-1770
Email: slstoneberg@comcast.net
Web: www.us-recruiters.com/members/stoneberg.html

Summary: Executive placement of sales and sales management personnel in B2B products and services companies.

Key Contact - Specialty:
Ms. Susan Stoneberg, Principal

Functions: Management, Sales & Mktg.

Industries: Services, Mgmt. Consulting, HR Services, Media, Advertising, Publishing, New Media, Communications

StoneBridge Management Inc
(also known as Management Recruiters of Reading)
2921 Windmill Rd
Sinking Spring, PA 19608-1678
(610) 670-8008
Email: info@mrireading.com
Web: www.mrireading.com

Summary: Our firm is a network affiliate of one of the world's largest professional recruitment organizations. We operate in a number of major industries serving multi-national to small private companies. Consultants use the best practice methodology to assist them in researching, locating and securing the right person for each role. We offer retained and contingency search and contract staffing to fill short-term gaps.

Key Contact - Specialty:
Mr. Jeffrey Burridge, President - *Consulting, Franchising, Medical (Devices), Presidents, Senior management*

Salary Minimum: $65,000

Functions: Senior Mgmt., Middle Mgmt., Mfg., Materials, Sales & Mktg., Finance, R&D, Engineering, Specialized Svcs.

Industries: Construction, Manufacturing, Finance, Mgmt. Consulting, Engineering Svcs., Logistics Svcs., Supply Chain Mgmt, Hospitality, Insurance, Biotech/Life Sciences, Healthcare

Stoneburner Associates Inc
131 Terrace Trl W
Lake Quivira, KS 66217-8504
(913) 248-0066
Fax: (913) 248-0066
Email: sacareers@aol.com

Summary: We provide retained search or contingency placement in a wide variety of industries. Our emphasis is on high-technology firms and professionals. We offer a 90-day pro-rated guarantee.

Key Contact - Specialty:
Mr. Dwight T. Stoneburner, Owner - *Technical*

Salary Minimum: $45,000

Functions: Generalist (All)

Industries: Food, Bev., Tobacco, Drugs Mfg., Plastics, Rubber, Metal Products, Electronic, Elec. Components, IT Implementation, Fiber Optic, Software, Mfg. SW, Biotech/Life Sciences

The Stones River Group
2510 English Hill Dr
Murfreesboro, TN 37130-1432
(615) 494-1333
(615) 494-3291
Email: info@tsrgp.com
Web: under construction

Summary: We specialize in the metals fabrication industry placing top engineering and manufacturing management professionals. People create performance...performance creates profit...we create opportunities. Our mission is to be the preferred and pre-eminent provider of career placement solutions in our market. We provide only right-fit candidates to our clients and sought after clients to our candidates.

Key Contact - Specialty:
Mr. Wayne Moore, Managing Director - *Automotive, Engineering, Machining, Manufacturing, Metals*

Salary Minimum: $38,000

Functions: Generalist (All), Management, Middle Mgmt., Mfg., Product Dev., Production, Automation, Materials, Engineering

Industries: Metal Products, Machine, Appliance, Motor Vehicles, Computer Equip., Consumer Elect., Test, Measure Equip., Misc. Mfg., Electronic, Elec. Components

Stonington Associates
800 Summer St
Franklin, MA 02038-2340
(508) 541-8505
Fax: (508) 541-8303
Email: pmorton@stoningtonassoc.com
Web: www.stoningtonassoc.com

Summary: We support the professional staffing needs of commercial and community banks. We provide contingency and retained search services for our clients.

Key Contact - Specialty:
Mr. Philip A. Morton, President

Salary Minimum: $30,000

Functions: Generalist (All), Senior Mgmt., Middle Mgmt., Mktg. Mgmt., Staffing, CFOs, Cash Mgmt., Risk Mgmt.

Industries: Generalist (All), Banking, Venture Cap., Misc. Financial

Storevik Financial Search & Associates Inc
2658 Del Mar Heights Rd Ste 213
Del Mar, CA 92014-3100
(858) 792-0433
Fax: (858) 792-8443
Email: tstorev1@san.rr.com
Web: www.sfsacorp.com

Summary: We specialize in placement of professionals into major CPA and consulting firms. Preferred experience in litigation services/dispute analysis, insolvency, turnarounds, forensic/investigative, business valuations, financial or IS.

Key Contact - Specialty:
Mr. Terry R. Storevik, CPA, President
Mr. Matthew D. Storevik, Director

Salary Minimum: $50,000

Functions: Finance, Legal

Industries: Generalist (All), Services, Legal, Accounting, HR Services, Law Enforcement

Stradtman & Associates

(also known as StradtCo LLC)
3260 Keith Bridge RdSte 172
Cumming, GA 30041-3937
(706) 265-2277
Email: resumes@stradtco.com
Web: www.stradtco.com

Summary: Our company is an executive search and recruiting firm specializing in the automotive and metalworking manufacturing industries. We are proud to be the preferred hiring solution for many Fortune 500 companies while also representing some of the nations top manufacturing executives.

Key Contact - Specialty:
Mr. Rich Stradtman

Functions: Generalist (All)

Industries: Metal Products, Motor Vehicles

Suzanne Strange Enterprises Inc

PO Box 4889
Greenville, SC 29608-4889
(864) 246-1200
Fax: (864) 246-3492
Email: info@ceramics-personnel.com
Web: www.ceramics-personnel.com

Summary: We are a technical recruiting firm serving the ceramic industry. We specialize in placing the best ceramic engineers, materials engineers and other professionals with the finest companies in the country.

Key Contact - Specialty:
Mrs. Suzanne Strange, President & Recruiter

Functions: Mfg., Production, Plant Mgmt., Quality, Materials, Sales & Mktg., Engineering

Industries: Manufacturing, Misc. Mfg., Electronic, Elec. Components

StratAcuity Staffing Partners Inc

53A Green St
Portsmouth, NH 03801-3735
(603) 766-0600
Fax: (603) 766-0660
Web: www.stratacuity.com

Summary: Applying a strategic and focused approach, we have become recognized as a premier life sciences and healthcare permanent-placement staffing firm.

Key Contact - Specialty:
Mr. Patrick Marshall, Principal & General Partner
Mr. Robert Patten, Principal & General Partner

Salary Minimum: $38,000

Functions: Generalist (All)

Industries: Generalist (All), Chemicals, Drugs Mfg., Medical Devices, Robotics, Biotech/Life Sciences, Healthcare, Hospitals, Physical Therapy, Occupational Therapy

Strategic Associates Inc

PO Box 203278
Austin, TX 78720-3278
(512) 218-8222
Fax: (512) 218-8102
Email: sai@strategicassociates.com
Web: www.strategicassociates.com

Summary: Since its inception, our firm has focused on talent and opportunity in the nationwide manufacturing/supply chain/procurement marketplace in both industry and management consulting. This encompasses talent in operations (plant and corporate), supply chain, procurement, Six Sigma process improvement, engineering and information

technology. From senior support to management to executive levels.

Key Contact - Specialty:
Mr. Michael L. Goldman, CPC, President - *Diversity, Logistics, Management consulting, Manufacturing (Management), Operations*
Ms. Shirley Mehlenbacher, General Manager

Salary Minimum: $75,000

Functions: Management, Board Members, Senior Mgmt., Middle Mgmt.

Industries: Manufacturing, Medical Devices, Electronic, Elec. Components, Services, Mgmt. Consulting, IT Implementation, Logistics Svcs., Supply Chain Mgmt, Mfg. SW, Marketing SW, Biotech/Life Sciences

Strategic Partners LLC

1935 S Plum Grove Rd Ste 160
Palatine, IL 60067-7258
(847) 452-0433
Fax: (847) 991-9983
Email: info@strategic-partnersus.com
Web: strategic-partnersus.com

Summary: A nationally recognized management recruitment firm engaged in executive, sales, operations and engineering search assignments with an industry focus in managed services, outsourcing, facilities management and engineering. We serve the education, healthcare, manufacturing, commercial & industrial and service sector markets. Our unique process approach ensures that our clients receive superior customer service and exceptional candidates for each search assignment.

Key Contact - Specialty:
Mr. Robert A. Nash, President - *Engineering, Facilities engineering, Operations, Outsourcing, Sales*
Ms. Darci Wittke, Executive Director, Marketing - *Engineering, Facilities engineering, Management, Middle management, Operations*

Salary Minimum: $75,000

Functions: Senior Mgmt., Middle Mgmt., Sales Mgmt., Engineering

Industries: Manufacturing, Services, Higher Ed., Engineering Svcs., Property/Facility Mgmt., Healthcare

Strategic Placement Services Inc

880 Winter St Ste 130
Waltham Woods Corporate Center
Waltham, MA 02451-1465
(781) 890-2323
Fax: (781) 890-4350
Email: info@splacement.com
Web: www.splacement.com

Summary: Our firm is a privately held, full service financial search and staffing firm providing executive retained search, contingency placement and temp/contract employee services for the financial disciplines.

Key Contact - Specialty:
Mr. Lawrence C. Shumila, CPA, Co-Founder
Mr. Steven H. Lanzoni, Co-Founder

Salary Minimum: $50,000

Functions: Generalist (All), Finance

Industries: Generalist (All), Accounting

Strategic Resources Inc

23151 Moulton Pkwy
Laguna Hills, CA 92653-1206
(949) 458-7322
(800) 997-7322
Fax: (949) 855-1454

Email: ltl.srad@prodigy.net
Web: www.4strategic-search.info

Summary: Our firm is a highly responsive staffing agency which has developed a reputation for working with each client in developing programs that meet their individual needs, and providing the most qualified, pre-screened sales and technical professionals on a national basis to our client companies. Specialization: As an agency, we've always been 100% focused in the technology industry.

Key Contact - Specialty:
Mr. Lieschen Trumpf Lavine, President
Mr. Edward R. Lavine, Director, Business Development - *Technology, Telecommunications*

Functions: Generalist (All), Middle Mgmt., Sales & Mktg., Sales Mgmt., MIS Mgmt., Systems Support

Industries: Generalist (All), Computer Equip., Equip Svcs., E-commerce, IT Implementation, Engineering Svcs., New Media, Communications, Telephony, Digital, Wireless, Fiber Optic, Network Infrastructure, RF/Microwave, Software, Networking, Comm. SW, System SW

Strategic Resources Biotechnology & Medical Group

14059 SE 63rd St
Bellevue, WA 98006-4821
(425) 688-9807
Fax: (425) 747-4274
Email: info@srbmg.com
Web: www.srbmg.com

Summary: We are an executive search firm specializing in recruiting for biotechnology, medical and pharmaceutical industries. Typical candidates have three to five years of relevant industry experience. Sales, product managers, director to VP level.

Key Contact - Specialty:
Ms. Rena Roberts Bouchard, President - *Biotechnology*

Salary Minimum: $80,000

Functions: Generalist (All), Senior Mgmt., Middle Mgmt., Product Dev., Healthcare, Sales & Mktg., Mktg. Research, Mktg. Mgmt., Sales Mgmt.

Industries: Drugs Mfg., Medical Devices, Pharm Svcs., Biotech/Life Sciences, Healthcare

Strategic Resources

400 108th Ave NE Ste 620
Bellevue, WA 98004-5508
(425) 688-1151
Fax: (425) 732-2112
Email: corporate@strategicresources.com
Web: www.strategicresources.com

Summary: We are an international executive search firm with a variety of core practices including: advertising & public relations, finance, construction engineering & design, pharmaceuticals & life sciences, ethnic marketing, high technology (telecom, wireless, cable & satellite), sales & marketing and operations & senior management (C-level and board of director appointments).

Key Contact - Specialty:
Mr. Ted Warren, President & Senior Partner - *Advertising, Communications, Marketing, Pharmaceutical, Public relations*
Mr. Allen Barron, Senior Vice President, International Ser - *Consulting, International, Operations, Technology, Telecommunications*

Ms. Anne Marie Bachmann, PhD, Vice President, Life Sciences - *Biotechnology, Pharmaceutical, Product management/development*
Mr. Art Dreeben, Vice President, Consumer Products - *Apparel, Consumer, Textiles*
Ms. Ingrid Haiquel, Vice President, Ethnic Marketing - *Advertising, Consumer, Diversity, Marketing*
Ms. Karen Lang, Vice President, Engineering Design - *Architecture, Construction, Design, Engineering*
Ms. Carolyn Lindsley, Vice President, Finance & Operations - *Banking (Investment), CFOs, Finance, Logistics, Real estate*
Mr. Marcus Williams, Vice President, Finance & Accounting
Mr. James Young, Vice President, Med Device & Healthcare
Mr. Lee Trousdale, Vice President, Aerospace

Salary Minimum: $100,000

Functions: Generalist (All), Management

Industries: Generalist (All), Construction, Textiles, Apparel, Drugs Mfg., Medical Devices, Pharm Svcs., Accounting, Mgmt. Consulting, Advertising

Strategic Search Consultants

3450 W Central Ave Ste 232
Toledo, OH 43606-1417
(419) 324-2424
(888) 561-2424
Email: ken@ssc-online.com
Web: www.ssc-online.com

Summary: We provide elite companies access to IT's premiere talent in the electronic document/direct marketing and eCommerce/bill presentment and Internet content arenas.

Key Contact - Specialty:
Mr. Ken Leslie, President - *Direct marketing*

Functions: Generalist (All), Direct Mktg., MIS Mgmt., Systems Analysis, Systems Dev., Systems Implem., Systems Support, Mgmt. Consultants

Industries: Generalist (All), Printing, Computer Equip., Mgmt. Consulting, Software

Strategic Search Partners

PO Box 1176
Keller, TX 76244-1176
(817) 281-1282
Fax: (817) 281-4495
Email: info@searchssp.com
Web: www.searchssp.com

Summary: We offer high quality executive search work performed in the consumer products industry, for all functions plus supply chain, purchasing, global sourcing and logistics for Fortune 500 multi-plant manufacturing firms.

Key Contact - Specialty:
Mr. Frank J. Laux, President

Salary Minimum: $100,000

Functions: Generalist (All), Management, Board Members, Admin. Svcs.

Industries: Generalist (All), Food, Bev., Tobacco, Printing, Chemicals, Soap, Perf., Cosmtcs., Drugs Mfg., Plastics, Rubber, Leather, Stone, Glass, Metal Products, Machine, Appliance, Consumer Goods, HR Services, ERP SW, HR SW, Mfg. SW, Marketing SW

Strategic Services

10290 NE 12th St Apt E204
Bellevue, WA 98004-4282
(425) 269-7445
Fax: (702) 977-8116

Email: pkagan@mindspring.com

Summary: An executive search firm dedicated to the gaming industry: casinos, tribal casinos, analysts, attorneys, agencies and racing facilities.

Key Contact - Specialty:
Mr. Philip Kagan, President

Salary Minimum: $85,000

Functions: Senior Mgmt.

Industries: Hotels, Resorts, Clubs, Entertainment, Recreation

Strategic Staffing Solutions

5 Concourse Pkwy NE Ste 3000
Atlanta, GA 30328-7106
(800) 482-5204
(770) 399-8878
Fax: (800) 482-5643
Email: info@strategicstaffing.us
Web: www.strategicstaffing.us

Summary: We can save you the time consuming task of screening resumes and assist in filling critical executive level openings within your organization. Specialty areas include: information technology, accounting/finance, human resources, sales and marketing.

Key Contact - Specialty:
Mr. Dwayne L. Hairston, President & Chief Executive Officer - *Accounting, Biotechnology, Education, Financial services, Healthcare*

Salary Minimum: $100,000

Functions: Senior Mgmt.

Industries: Manufacturing, Finance, Services, Communications, Insurance, Software, Biotech/Life Sciences, Healthcare

Strategic Technology Resource

PO Box 3183
Dublin, OH 43016-0084
(614) 987-1247
Fax: (240) 358-4480
Email: info@hrgameplan.com
Web: www.hrgameplan.com

Summary: We are an executive search firm specializing in the placement of IT and telecom professionals. In addition to helping companies find the brightest and best candidates, we also help organizations retain and develop those new recruits with our HR technology consulting practice.

Key Contact - Specialty:
Mrs. Angela Walters, Principal

Salary Minimum: $40,000

Functions: Production, HR Mgmt., e-HR, Finance, IT, Engineering

Industries: Generalist (All), Construction, Biotech/Life Sciences

Strategic Workforce Solutions

500 5th Ave Ste 2520
New York, NY 10110-2502
(212) 944-9112
Fax: (212) 944-8448
Email: nycjobs@strategicworkforce.com
Web: www.strategicworkforce.com

Summary: We are a middle management search and staffing firm specializing in: HR, IT, legal, marketing, finance/investment banking and accounting. All of the managing directors at our firm have corporate experience relevant to their specialty giving them a unique understanding of the goals and requirements of our clients.

Key Contact - Specialty:
Mr. Jay Horowitz, Chief Executive Officer

Ms. Kristin Vickery, President
Mr. Patrick Lyons, Chief Financial Officer

Salary Minimum: $50,000

Functions: Sales & Mktg., HR Mgmt., Finance, CFOs, IT, Legal, Attorneys, Paralegals

Industries: Generalist (All)

Branches:
208 S La Salle St Ste 1250
Chicago, IL 60604-1322
(312) 541-9000
Fax: (312) 541-9002
Email: llupia@strategiclegal.com
Key Contact - Specialty:
Mrs. Mareile Cusack, Executive Managing Director
Ms. Lynette Lupia, Director, Recruitment

163 Madison Ave Ste 1
Morristown, NJ 07960-7324
(973) 285-4299
Fax: (973) 285-4290
Email: cgurry@strategiclegal.com
Key Contact - Specialty:
Ms. Chris Gurry, Managing Director

110 E 42nd St Rm 800
New York, NY 10017-8539
(212) 378-0700
(212) 944-9112
Fax: (212) 378-0780
Email: pgoodkind@strategicworkforce.com
Key Contact - Specialty:
Mr. Peter Goodkind, Principal
Mr. Stephen Horowitz, Principal
Ms. Patricia Amy, Vice President - *Financial services*
Mrs. Karen Isaacs, Managing Director
Mrs. Karen Peyser, Executive Vice President
Mrs. Lynn Anders, Vice President - *Sales*
Ms. Erin Wohlreich, Vice President - *Hospitality*
Mr. Richard Marx, Vice President - *Technology*

Strickstein Beckman Search

1801 Avenue of the Stars Ste 1420
Los Angeles, CA 90067-5899
(310) 287-2003
Fax: (310) 287-2009
Email: jrs@stricksteinbeckman.com
Web: www.stricksteinbeckman.com

Summary: Search firm in placing attorneys.

Key Contact - Specialty:
Ms. Jill Strickstein, Esq., Principal & Founder

Functions: Attorneys

Industries: Legal

The Strongest Link LLC

5239 Deerhurst Crescent Cir
Boca Raton, FL 33486-8534
(561) 417-7435
Fax: (561) 392-3259
Email: info@thestrongestlink.net
Web: www.thestrongestlink.net

Summary: Employment search agency focusing on IT and specializing in software vendors and professional services companies. We recruit business development, marketing, pre-sales support, software development and quality professionals.

Key Contact - Specialty:
Mr. John Kinstler, Recruiter

Salary Minimum: $30,000

Functions: Generalist (All), Management, Board Members

Industries: Manufacturing, Transportation, Retail, Finance, E-commerce, IT Implementation,

Hospitality, Communications, Network Infrastructure, Software, Accounting SW, Database SW, Development SW, Doc. Mgmt., Production SW, Entertainment SW, ERP SW, Mfg. SW, Marketing SW, Networking, Comm. SW, Security SW, Healthcare

The Studley Group

60 Walnut St
Wellesley Hills, MA 02481-2151
(781) 239-1666
Fax: (781) 237-5679
Email: studley@studleygroup.com
Web: www.studleygroup.com

Summary: We are a full service firm. We place special emphasis on technology, finance, health care and bio-technology industry.

Key Contact - Specialty:
Mr. Fred M. Studley, SPHR, Chairman & Chief Executive Officer - *Finance, Human resources, Manufacturing*
Mr. Brian Toland, Partner - *Finance, Technology*
Ms. Sandy W. Arthur, President, HRco

Salary Minimum: $75,000

Functions: Generalist (All), Board Members, Sales Reps., HR Mgmt., CFOs

Industries: Generalist (All)

Suber & McAuley Technical Search

461 Cochran Rd
Mount Lebanon, PA 15228-1253
(412) 323-0372
(412) 344-3336
Email: smts@aol.com
Web: www.subermcauley.com

Summary: Our firm is a technical contingency and retained search firm specializing in engineering, software, manufacturing, technical sales, information system and hardware design. We have many years of combined experience among both our partners.

Key Contact - Specialty:
Mr. John C. Suber, Senior Parnter

Salary Minimum: $50,000

Functions: Product Dev.

Industries: Medical Devices, Machine, Appliance, Electronic, Elec. Components, Pharm Svcs., Telecoms, Digital, Network Infrastructure, Software

Sullivan & Company

822 Montgomery Ave Ste 300
Narberth, PA 19072-1948
(610) 664-9000
Fax: (610) 664-8675
Email: ds@sullivancompany.com
Web: www.sullivancompany.com

Summary: We are a banking and financial services industry specialist firm with a track record of mid to senior-level recruitment. If you are looking for (or to fill) a banking or financial job in our market, this is the firm for you.

Key Contact - Specialty:
Mr. David Sullivan

Salary Minimum: $60,000

Functions: Middle Mgmt.

Industries: Banking, Invest. Banking, Venture Cap., Mgmt. Consulting, Real Estate

Summerfield Associates Inc

6555 Quince Rd Ste 525
Memphis, TN 38119-8225
(901) 753-7068
Fax: (901) 753-8947
Email: dsummerfield@summerfield.net
Web: www.summerfield.net

Summary: Our principals bring to our firm extensive experience in recruiting and consulting services. We consistently establish solid rapport with client companies by meeting their business goals and objectives. We are a recognized top producer in field.

Key Contact - Specialty:
Ms. Dotty Giusti, CPC, President - *Human resources*

Salary Minimum: $35,000

Functions: Generalist (All), Management

Industries: Generalist (All), Manufacturing, Lumber, Furniture, Paper, Printing, Drugs Mfg., Misc. Mfg., Legal, Accounting, Mgmt. Consulting, HR Services, E-commerce, IT Implementation, Telecoms, Software

Summit Group Consultants Inc

16 Voight Rd
Lafayette, NJ 07848-3132
(973) 875-3300
Email: garyp@nac.net

Summary: With many years of placement experience, we can assist with resumes, marketing techniques, interviewing preparation and salary issues, as well as career planning strategies.

Key Contact - Specialty:
Mr. Gary W. Pezzuti, Senior Parnter

Salary Minimum: $50,000

Functions: Management, Mfg., Production, Plant Mgmt., Materials, Purchasing, Materials Plng., Distribution, Packaging, Process

Industries: Manufacturing, Food, Bev., Tobacco, Chemicals, Soap, Perf., Cosmtcs., Drugs Mfg., Medical Devices, Plastics, Rubber, Paints, Petro. Products, Metal Products, Machine, Appliance, Test, Measure Equip., Misc. Mfg., Electronic, Elec. Components, Consumer Goods, Packaging

The Summit Group LLC

2118 Inwood Dr Ste 114
Fort Wayne, IN 46815-7124
(260) 497-7555
(800) 497-4567
Fax: (260) 497-7444
Email: info@summitna.com
Web: www.summitna.com

Summary: We specialize in the placement of manufacturing professionals with emphasis on quality, engineering, operations, and materials.

Key Contact - Specialty:
Mr. Steve Hillman, President

Salary Minimum: $50,000

Functions: Generalist (All), Board Members

Industries: Plastics, Rubber, Metal Products, Machine, Appliance, Motor Vehicles, Services, Engineering Svcs.

Sun Information Systems Inc

PO Box 1025
Huntersville, NC 28070-1025
(704) 655-9000
Fax: (704) 655-9900
Email: jobs@suninfosys.com
Web: www.suninfosys.com

Summary: International provider of IT executive recruitment and supplemental, contract services.

Key Contact - Specialty:
Mr. Tony Termini, Executive Vice President

Functions: Generalist (All), IT, Systems Analysis, Systems Dev., Systems Implem., Systems Support, Network Admin., DB Admin.

Industries: Generalist (All), Mgmt. Consulting, HR Services, IT Implementation

Sun Valley Search

PO Box 599
Ketchum, ID 83340-0599
(208) 725-5055
Fax: (208) 726-7591
Email: jobs@svsearch.com
Web: www.sunvalleysearch.com

Summary: We are industry specific recruiting only in the rotating equipment industries, pumps, compressors, turbines, seals and mixers with recruiters doing all positions within the industries.

Key Contact - Specialty:
Mr. Tom Lampl, Owner - *Equipment*

Salary Minimum: $40,000

Functions: Generalist (All), Management, Middle Mgmt.

Industries: Generalist (All), Machine, Appliance, Misc. Mfg.

Ron Sunshine Associates

2404 Clear Field Dr
Plano, TX 75025-5184
(214) 509-3778
Email: ron@ronsunshineassociates.com
Web: www.ronsunshineassociates.com

Summary: We are a firm that provides placement of middle and upper-management in all fields of manufacturing and engineering-metals, plastics and consumer goods.

Key Contact - Specialty:
Mr. Ron Sunshine, President - *Engineering, Manufacturing*
Ms. Barbara Blake - *Food*
Ms. Stacy Moscowitz, Vice President - *Human resources*

Salary Minimum: $50,000

Functions: Mfg.

Industries: Manufacturing, Medical Devices, Plastics, Rubber, Metal Products, Machine, Appliance, Motor Vehicles, Computer Equip., Consumer Elect., Misc. Mfg.

Survival Systems Staffing Inc

2149 Portola Rd
Ventura, CA 93003-7723
(805) 650-8888
Email: email@survivalsystems.com
Web: www.survivalsystems.com

Summary: We are an award winning search firm specializing in high technology electronics. Our areas of expertise include power conversion, motors, drives, semiconductors, electric vehicle, magnetics, photonics, lighting, batteries, fuel cell, information control technology, utility and telecom. We fill positions in engineering, sales, marketing, operations, manufacturing, quality, general management, CFOs and CEOs.

Key Contact - Specialty:
Mr. Dennis Nickerson, Principal - *CEOs, Engineering, Power, Semiconductors*
Ms. Sandy Schreiber - *CEOs, Electronics, Engineering, Semiconductors, Senior management*

Mr. Dick Gaines, Manager, Sales - *Electronics, Engineering, Management, Power, Semiconductors*
Ms. Brandee Jamma, Executive Director

Salary Minimum: $50,000

Functions: Generalist (All), Senior Mgmt., Product Dev., Quality, Mktg. Mgmt., Sales Mgmt., Systems Analysis, Engineering

Industries: Generalist (All), Energy, Utilities, Test, Measure Equip., Electronic, Elec. Components, Semiconductors, Mgmt. Consulting, Engineering Svcs., Telecoms, Digital, Wireless, Fiber Optic, RF/Microwave, Aerospace

Suvaalso Staffing Solutions

2455 Linwood St
Pickering, ON L1X 2N8
Canada
(905) 420-1842
Email: sunil.vaswani@suvaalso.com
Web: www.suvaalso.com

Summary: We are a Toronto based search firm that specializes in locating personnel for permanent positions in a variety of industries. Our main industries of expertise are finance, insurance, engineering, and IT.

Key Contact - Specialty:
Mr. Sunil Vaswani, Managing Partner

Salary Minimum: $50,000

Functions: Generalist (All)

Industries: Generalist (All)

Svenneby Corp

7307 S Waco St
Foxfield, CO 80016-1650
(303) 617-4481
Email: resumes@svenneby.com
Web: www.svenneby.com

Summary: We are an executive search firm specializing in building sales, marketing, and executive teams for small to medium sized software companies. We focus on enterprise software, engineering software, and corporate software industries including: ERP, CRM, SCM, storage, ILM, CAD, PDM, PLM, etc.

Key Contact - Specialty:
Mr. Peter Svenneby, Principal - *ERP, Storage*

Salary Minimum: $60,000

Functions: Management, Senior Mgmt., Sales & Mktg., Mktg. Research, Mktg. Mgmt., Sales Mgmt., Sales Reps.

Industries: Software, Database SW, Development SW, Doc. Mgmt., Production SW, ERP SW, HR SW, Industry Specific SW, Mfg. SW, Marketing SW, Security SW

The Swan Group

PO Box 620
Buckingham, PA 18912-0620
(215) 230-9612
(908) 526-5440
Email: barbara@swangroup.net
Web: www.swangroup.net

Summary: Search firm specializing in staffing the IT department. Have completed assignments for major pharmaceutical firms, consumer product companies and consulting firms that service the pharmaceutical industry. We fill director level positions and above in the IT department. We perform and have very happy customers.

Key Contact - Specialty:
Ms. Barbara Swan, CPC, Owner, Technical Recruiter - *Biopharmaceutical, Consulting,*

Information Technology, Life Sciences, Pharmaceutical

Salary Minimum: $100,000

Functions: IT, MIS Mgmt.

Industries: Chemicals, Drugs Mfg., Consumer Goods, Pharm Svcs., Mgmt. Consulting, Call Centers

Branches:
35 W High St
Somerville, NJ 08876-2114
(908) 526-5440
Email: steve@swangroup.net
Key Contact - Specialty:
Mr. Steve Swan, Associate

Swan Legal Search

11500 W Olympic Blvd Ste 370
Los Angeles, CA 90064-1527
(310) 445-5010
(888) 860-1154
Fax: (310) 445-0621
Email: info@swanlegal.com
Web: www.swanlegal.com

Summary: Our firm places attorneys with outstanding law firms and Fortune 500 corporations. We are comprised of former practicing attorneys, are dedicated to successful results and are committed to the utmost professional standards of integrity.

Key Contact - Specialty:
Ms. Delia K. Swan, Esq., Founder
Ms. Claudia T. Trevisan, Esq.
Ms. Elise K.Y. Lau, Esq.
Ms. Melinda A. Adams, Esq.

Functions: Attorneys

Industries: Legal

Swift & Associates LLC

PO Box 3335
Portland, ME 04104-3335
(207) 773-0330
Fax: (207) 773-7445
Email: inquiry@swiftassociates.com
Web: www.swiftassociates.com

Summary: We are a search firm specializing in national recruiting for northern New England employers. The firm has grown to serve a diverse client base, all of whom return to us for our highly customized and high value approach. We manage a very broad range of positions in diverse industries, many of which are at a critical growth stage.

Key Contact - Specialty:
Ms. Catherine Swift, President
Ms. Jessica S. Feinstein, Recruiter - *Entrepreneurs, Executives, General management, Human resources, Legal (Attorneys)*

Salary Minimum: $50,000

Functions: Management, Senior Mgmt., Middle Mgmt., Advertising, Mktg. Mgmt., Sales Mgmt., HR Mgmt., MIS Mgmt., Attorneys

Industries: Generalist (All), Energy, Utilities, Manufacturing, Food, Bev., Tobacco, Textiles, Apparel, Lumber, Furniture, Consumer Goods, Wholesale, Retail, Finance, Banking, Services, Non-profits, Pharm Svcs., Legal, E-commerce, Media, Communications, Insurance, Software, Biotech/Life Sciences, Healthcare, Hospitals

Synergy Search Ltd

3914 Miami Rd Ste 101
Cincinnati, OH 45227-3718
(513) 272-1000
Fax: (513) 272-1004
Email: synergysearch@email.com

Summary: A professional contingency search firm specializing in sales, manufacturing and operations positions within the packaging industry.

Key Contact - Specialty:
Mr. John W. Petru, Partner - *Management, Sales*
Mr. Garrett Levy, Partner - *Management, Manufacturing*

Functions: Generalist (All), Senior Mgmt., Production, Plant Mgmt., Quality, Sales Mgmt., Customer Svc., Graphic Designers

Industries: Generalist (All), Paper, Printing, Packaging

Synergy Search Partners Inc

11921 Freedom Dr Ste 550
Reston, VA 20190
(703) 481-9936
Fax: (703) 481-9938
Email: dhamilton@synergysearchpartners.com
Web: www.synergysearchpartners.com

Summary: We do senior/executive level recruiting for major technology, professional service firms, consulting firms and global 1000 companies.

Key Contact - Specialty:
Mr. Denman Hamilton, President
Mr. Sherman Hamilton, Senior Partner

Salary Minimum: $80,000

Functions: Management, Board Members, Senior Mgmt., Benefits, Finance, IT, MIS Mgmt., Systems Implem., Mgmt. Consultants, Minorities/Diversity

Industries: Energy, Utilities, Medical Devices, Transportation, Mgmt. Consulting, HR Services, E-commerce, IT Implementation, Logistics Svcs., Advertising, Communications, Telecoms, Government, Defense, Homeland Security, Environmental Svcs., Haz. Waste, Aerospace, Insurance, Software, Database SW, Security SW, Biotech/Life Sciences, Healthcare

Synergy Systems

8-600 Queens Quay W
Apartment Building
Toronto, ON M5V 3M3
Canada
(416) 597-2686
Email: synsys@sympatico.ca

Summary: Our firm is senior recruiters who know the computer vendor environment, both permanent and contract. Quick, discreet, professional service is our credo. Also recruit in pharmaceutical, biotechnologynical and medical device marketplace.

Key Contact - Specialty:
Mr. John Hall, Consultant

Salary Minimum: $65,000

Functions: Generalist (All), Senior Mgmt., Middle Mgmt., Mktg. Mgmt., Sales Mgmt., Systems Dev., Systems Implem., Systems Support

Industries: Generalist (All), Software

System 1 Search Inc

2200 Sunrise Blvd Ste 220
Gold River, CA 95670-4378
(916) 635-4800
Fax: (916) 635-4818
Email: search@system1.net
Web: www.system1.net

Summary: Our firm recruits sales, technical service, marketing and management professionals in health care. We are vertically integrated in all disciplines of the biotechnology, diagnostic and medical device industry.

Key Contact - Specialty:
Mr. Tom Duerr, President

Functions: Board Members

Industries: Biotech/Life Sciences, Healthcare, Hospitals

Branches:
2200 Sunrise Blvd Ste 220
Gold River, CA 95670-4378
(864) 627-0012
Fax: (864) 627-0013
Key Contact - Specialty:
Mr. Tony Bishop, Manager

396 San Diego Ave
Ventura, CA 93004-1185
(805) 659-6838
Fax: (805) 659-1437
Key Contact - Specialty:
Mr. Jim Patterson, Manager

System TWO Inc

7S505 Lynn Dr
Naperville, IL 60540-9577
(630) 717-2713
(630) 717-6500
Email: info@systemtwo.com
Web: www.systemtwo.com

Summary: Our firm focuses on the recruitment of specialized professionals. In order to provide you with the best services available, our commitment is to fully understand your specific position requirements, as well as your values and culture. Our experience spans a wide array of industries and disciplines. We are committed to quality, in our services to you and in the candidates we present. Additionally, we are members of an association of independent recruitment firms.

Key Contact - Specialty:
Ms. Vicki Starr, Vice President - *Engineering, Healthcare, Management, Manufacturing*
Mr. Thomas Wrona, President - *Sales*
Ms. Rebecca Madison, CMT, Recruiter - *Construction, Engineering, Environmental, Healthcare, Safety*

Salary Minimum: $50,000

Functions: Sales Mgmt., Training, Engineering

Industries: Agri., Forestry, Mining, Oil & Gas, Construction, Architectural Svcs., Mgmt. Consulting, HR Services, E-commerce, IT Implementation, Engineering Svcs., Call Centers, Haz. Waste, Real Estate, Accounting SW, Database SW, Development SW, Doc. Mgmt., Production SW, Training SW

Systems Careers

211 Sutter St Ste 607
San Francisco, CA 94108-4435
(415) 434-4770
Email: wayne_sarchett@msn.com

Summary: We provide a broad range of executive placement services in the computing industry in the areas of systems development, product development, software engineering, technical marketing, customer support, and QA management, consulting and hardware & software vendor professionals.

Key Contact - Specialty:
Mr. A. Wayne Sarchett, Principal - *Computers (Software), Consulting*

Salary Minimum: $120,000

Functions: Senior Mgmt., Middle Mgmt., Product Dev., Mktg. Research, Mktg. Mgmt., DB Admin., R&D, Engineering, Mgmt. Consultants, Architects

Industries: Software

Systems Personnel Group

968B Union Rd Ste 3
West Seneca, NY 14224-3438
(716) 677-2667
(888) 297-4825
Fax: (716) 677-0658
Email: staff@systemspersonnel.com
Web: www.systemspersonnel.com

Summary: Our firm provides IT and accounting & finance staffing on a direct or temp basis. We strive to differentiate ourselves by providing value added computer services and by thoroughly understanding our client's needs.

Key Contact - Specialty:
Mr. Jim Cipriani, Jr., President

Functions: Finance, IT

Industries: Generalist (All)

Systems Personnel Inc

115 W State St
Media, PA 19063-3200
(610) 565-8880
Email: info@systemspersonnelinc.com
Web: www.systemspersonnelinc.com

Summary: IT assignments across all industry segments and all technology. Additional focus on sales, marketing and HR disciplines.

Key Contact - Specialty:
Mr. James Doherty, Principal
Mr. Sam Porcelli, Vice President

Salary Minimum: $75,000

Functions: Generalist (All), Board Members, IT, MIS Mgmt., Systems Analysis, Systems Dev., Systems Implem., Systems Support, DB Admin.

Industries: Generalist (All), Network Infrastructure, Database SW, ERP SW, Networking, Comm. SW, Security SW

Systems Research Group

PO Box 230661
Encinitas, CA 92023-0661
(760) 436-1575
Email: career@systemsresearchgroup.com
Web: www.systemsresearchgroup.com

Summary: Specializes in placing executives, sales & marketing professionals with vendors of computer software and hardware. Industries include: large enterprise computing, supply chain, CRM, PLM, ERP and other vertical markets. We place executive staff, sales, marketing, application engineering and customer support professionals.

Key Contact - Specialty:
Mr. Stephen Gebler, President - *Sales*

Salary Minimum: $75,000

Functions: Generalist (All), Senior Mgmt., Middle Mgmt., Sales & Mktg., Mktg. Mgmt., Sales Mgmt.

Industries: Software, Doc. Mgmt., Production SW, ERP SW, Industry Specific SW, Mfg. SW, Security SW

Systems Research Group

235 E 5th St
Newport, KY 41071-1642
(859) 581-4000
Fax: (859) 581-6640
Email: info@srgrecruiting.com
Web: www.srgrecruiting.com

Summary: Our clients include the top architecture, engineering, and construction firms across the globe.

Key Contact - Specialty:
Mr. James Cole, President - *Architecture, Competitive intelligence, Construction, Engineering*

Functions: Engineering, Geotechnical, Structural, Architects, Bldg. Contractors

Industries: Generalist (All)

Systems Research Inc (SRI)

1250 Bank Dr
Schaumburg, IL 60173-6014
(847) 330-1222
(877) 774-0200
Fax: (847) 330-1411
Email: general@systemsresearchinc.com
Web: www.systemsresearchinc.com

Summary: Our firm is recognized and respected as a leader in providing industry with the HR resources to solve needs for executive, management and staff level positions in the areas of engineering, IT, finance and technical/manufacturing. We have succeeded in this venture due to our core philosophy of providing our clients with 100 percent satisfaction.

Key Contact - Specialty:
Mr. Dan Kuesis, President - *Engineering, Manufacturing, Materials, Technical*
Mr. Frank Agnello, Senior Account Manager - *Engineering, Manufacturing, Materials, Technical*
Mr. Art Hurley, Senior Account Manager - *Engineering, Manufacturing, Materials, Technical*
Mr. Rudy Albrecht, Senior Account Manager
Mr. Shawn Fier, Senior Account Manager
Ms. Maryn Elliott, Professional Recruiter - *Business development, Consulting, Outsourcing, Professional services, Sales*

Salary Minimum: $40,000

Functions: Generalist (All), Mfg., Materials, Finance, IT, Engineering, Architects, Technicians

Industries: Generalist (All), Manufacturing, Finance, Government, Aerospace, Packaging, Software

Branches:
1607 116th Ave NE Ste 101
Bellevue, WA 98004-3042
(877) 774-0200
Key Contact - Specialty:
Mr. Mark Johnson, Senior Account Manager

Systems Search

21 Portshire Dr
Lincolnshire, IL 60069-3325
(847) 374-9897
Email: ed@sysearch.com
Web: www.sysearch.com

Summary: We concentrate on client satisfaction, which has developed our reputation for excellence in recruiting personnel for Information Technology. We screen, interview and evaluate candidates and clients, to make sure you are getting the service and results you expect.

Key Contact - Specialty:
Mr. Edward Nathan, Principal

Salary Minimum: $40,000

Functions: Generalist (All)

Industries: E-commerce, IT Implementation, Software, Accounting SW, Database SW, Development SW, Doc. Mgmt., Production SW, ERP SW, Security SW, System SW

T E M Associates

PO Box 5243
De Pere, WI 54115-5243
(920) 339-8055
Fax: (920) 339-6177
Email: cmtm@execpc.com

Summary: Specialist in the pulp, paper and converting industry, consumer products and food industry.

Key Contact - Specialty:
Ms. Terri McCracken, President & Owner - *Paper*

Salary Minimum: $50,000

Functions: Generalist (All), Product Dev., Production, Plant Mgmt., Materials, Purchasing, Sales & Mktg., HR Mgmt., Finance, Engineering

Industries: Generalist (All), Food, Bev., Tobacco, Paper, Chemicals, Soap, Perf., Cosmtcs., Machine, Appliance, Packaging

T/MR

(also known as Technical /Management Resources)
310 Lorraine Dr
Pickerington, OH 43147-1239
(614) 837-8888
Email: techmgmtr@sprintmail.com

Summary: Took early retirement leaving as executive advisor. Specialties are manufacturing and processing operations. Over many years of operations have established strong contacts with other cooperative recruiters throughout United States.

Key Contact - Specialty:
Mr. Gordon S. Mead, President

Salary Minimum: $50,000

Functions: Management, Product Dev., Production, Automation, Plant Mgmt., Quality, Productivity, Materials Plng., Distribution, Eng. Design

Industries: Manufacturing, Plastics, Rubber, Metal Products, Machine, Appliance, Motor Vehicles, Misc. Mfg., Electronic, Elec. Components, Robotics, Consumer Goods, Transportation

TADA/Telecom and Data Associates

1214 Dandy Loop Rd
Yorktown, VA 23692-4538
(757) 377-3070
Email: telecomanddataassoc@cox.net

Summary: Contract Recruiting & Sourcing service in various industries, including hardware, software for telecommunications, data communications, and emerging technologies. Contract us by the job, the hour or the name.

Key Contact - Specialty:
Ms. Toni M. Buccarelli, Executive Recruiter & Owner - *Business development, Business to business, Computers (Sales), Executives, Sales*

Functions: Generalist (All), Sales Mgmt.

Industries: IT Implementation, Communications, Telecoms, Telephony, Digital, Wireless, Fiber Optic, Network Infrastructure, RF/Microwave, Doc. Mgmt., Production SW

Talent Asset Group LLC

1030 S Main St Ste 1
Cheshire, CT 06410-3482
(203) 439-7730
Fax: (203) 439-7736
Web: www.talentassetgroup.com

Summary: A national recruitment firm specializing in - Sales / Marketing Senior Execuive Searches Human Resources Consulting Finance

Key Contact - Specialty:
Mr. Jorge Colon, Founder & President
Ms. Marsha Goldberg, Consultant & Human Resources Generalist

Salary Minimum: $75,000

Functions: Senior Mgmt.

Industries: Generalist (All)

Talent Catch

1420 K St NW Ste 650
Washington, DC 20005-2516
(877) 255-7660
(202) 250-3985
Email: resumes@talentcatch.com
Web: www.talentcatch.com

Summary: Our firm provides executives and project managers across all functions and industries on a contract or permanent basis to Fortune 1000, middle-market and venture backed companies.

Key Contact - Specialty:
Ms. Parul Bhandari, Chief Executive Officer - *Consulting*

Salary Minimum: $40,000

Functions: Generalist (All), Management, Healthcare, Sales & Mktg., Finance, IT, Systems Implem., Mgmt. Consultants

Industries: Generalist (All), Finance, Mgmt. Consulting, Media, Telecoms, Software, Healthcare

Talent Chase Career Solutions (TCCS)

PO Box 2103
Waterloo, IA 50704-2103
(888) 520-8758
Fax: (319) 833-7573
Email: vashon@talentchase.net
Web: www.talentchase.net

Summary: We are an executive recruitment, research and Internet services company. We have proprietary technology that allows us to locate top talent quickly and efficiently. "Stop the chase... hire the catcher."

Key Contact - Specialty:
Ms. Vashon Borich, President

Salary Minimum: $50,000

Functions: Generalist (All)

Industries: Generalist (All), Manufacturing, Media, Communications, Environmental Svcs., Software

Talentude Search & Consulting

5328 Strawflower Dr. Ste B
Syracuse, NY 13212-1200
(315) 458-8382
Email: chuckb2@talentude.net
Web: www.talentude.net

Summary: We specialize in sales, marketing and purchasing at all levels of management. Our client base is composed of corporations and small businesses from a variety of industries.

Key Contact - Specialty:
Mr. Charles K. Bartlett, Principal & Owner - *Sales*

Salary Minimum: $40,000

Functions: Senior Mgmt., Mfg., Sales & Mktg., Mktg. Mgmt., Sales Mgmt.

Industries: Generalist (All)

Taligent Corporation

103 Providence Mine Rd Ste 201
Nevada City, CA 95959-2949
(530) 478-9300
Email: resumes@taligent.com
Web: www.taligent.com

Summary: We are an independent executive search firm specializing in the recruitment of first-tier, intelligent talent for a large number of growing, target market employers. We focus on providing value and delivering results every day. We believe that if we do our jobs with ethics and integrity, the business will take care of itself. In the process, we've built an extensive professional network of top, well-qualified talent, and exceptional career opportunities.

Key Contact - Specialty:
Mr. Cameron Hawley, President & Chief Executive Officer - *Computers (Sales,Science,Software), Healthcare, Instrumentation*

Salary Minimum: $50,000

Functions: Management, Product Dev., Quality, Healthcare, Physicians, Sales & Mktg., Mktg. Research, Mktg. Mgmt., Sales Mgmt., Sales Reps.

Industries: Generalist (All), Construction, Drugs Mfg., Medical Devices, Test, Measure Equip., Finance, Banking, Pharm Svcs., Telecoms, Software, Biotech/Life Sciences, Healthcare, Hospitals

Tallmadge & Hill Company

3700 Crestwood Pkwy NW Ste 320
Duluth, GA 30096-5585
(770) 925-2266
Fax: (770) 925-1090
Email: driggs@corpga.com
Web: www.corpga.com

Summary: Dedicated to improve our client's bottom line through customized staffing solutions.

Key Contact - Specialty:
Mr. David Riggs, President

Salary Minimum: $60,000

Functions: Board Members, Senior Mgmt., CFOs, Credit, M&A, Risk Mgmt.

Industries: Finance, Banking, Invest. Banking, Venture Cap., Misc. Financial, Services, Real Estate

Roy Talman & Associates Inc

150 S Wacker Dr Ste 2250
Chicago, IL 60606-4208
(312) 425-1300
Fax: (312) 425-0100
Email: resume@roytalman.com
Web: www.roytalman.com

Summary: We are a contingency technology search firm. We specialize in software and related information technology.

Key Contact - Specialty:
Mr. Ilya Talman, President - *Computers (Software), Financial*

Salary Minimum: $45,000

Functions: IT

Industries: Generalist (All)

TamingTurnover LLC

(formerly known as Corporate Tracs)
1825 Lockeway Dr Ste 206
Alpharetta, GA 30004-5930
(678) 990-4867
(678) 990-4864
Fax: (678) 669-9988
Email: mwood@tamingturnover.com
Web: www.tamingturnover.com

Summary: We are recruiting specialists in sales & marketing.

Key Contact - Specialty:
Mr. Marc Bailey, Chief Executive Officer
Mr. David Burks, Vice President, Business Development
Mr. Dan Kiefer, Senior Account Manager
Ms. Misty Wood, Account Manager

Functions: Sales & Mktg.

Industries: Generalist (All), Manufacturing, Media, Advertising, Publishing, New Media

Tangent Associates

PO Box 3054
Thousand Oaks, CA 91359-0054
(805) 496-2555
Email: tangentweb@aol.com

Summary: We are a successful, ethical search firm in all aspects of commercial banking led by an experienced recruiting team of former bank executive officers. Assignment-driven, we are matchmakers committed to developing long-term relationships.

Key Contact - Specialty:
Mr. Terry D. White

Salary Minimum: $50,000

Functions: Generalist (All)

Industries: Banking

S Tanner & Associates Inc

PO Box 91
Mount Forest, ON N0G 2L0
Canada
(519) 323-1474
Email: steve@tannerinc.net
Web: www.tannerinc.net

Summary: We specialize in engineering, operations management and logistics search. Our goal is quality searches, because quality is never an accident. It is always the result of high intentions, sincere effort, intelligent direction and skillful execution. It represents the wise choice of many alternatives.

Key Contact - Specialty:
Mr. Steve Tanner, President - *Engineering, Logistics, Management*

Salary Minimum: $35,000

Functions: Middle Mgmt., Production, Plant Mgmt., Quality, Materials, Purchasing, Materials Plng., Distribution, Packaging, Engineering

Industries: Manufacturing, Food, Bev., Tobacco, Textiles, Apparel, Lumber, Furniture, Chemicals, Soap, Perf., Cosmtcs., Drugs Mfg., Medical Devices, Paints, Petro. Products, Metal Products, Misc. Mfg., Transportation, Wholesale

Betty Tanner Executive Search Inc

5539 N Mesa St
El Paso, TX 79912-5422
(915) 587-5166
Fax: (915) 587-5167
Email: info@btsearch.com
Web: www.btsearch.com

Summary: Specializing in the manufacturing industry. Engineering, accounting, IT and the construction industry has been our expertise. We have specialized consultants which have become very specialized within their chosen disciplines.

Key Contact - Specialty:
Mr. Bruce Tanner, Co-Owner

Salary Minimum: $40,000

Functions: Management

Industries: Manufacturing, Finance, Engineering Svcs.

Tar Heel Recruiter Inc

PO Box 36454
Rock Hill, SC 29732-0507
(803) 233-1345 x221
(704) 644-3876 x221
Fax: (866) 394-5040
Email: wayne@tarheelrecruiter.com
Web: www.tarheelrecruiter.com

Summary: Executive search firm specializing in the appliance, HVAC, refrigeration, commercial restaurant equipment, and wholesale mortgage. In addition, we specialize in general manufacturing. We work in all aspects of manufacturing, including: operations, engineering, quality, material control, executive, sales and HR.

Key Contact - Specialty:
Mr. Wayne Miller, SRM, Senior Account Manager & Owner - *Consumer, Engineering, HVAC, Manufacturing, Manufacturing (Management)*
Mrs. Janice Miller, Project Coordinator - *BSME, Factories, Human resources, ISO 9000, Middle management*

Salary Minimum: $45,000

Functions: Generalist (All), Mfg.

Industries: Construction, Manufacturing, Metal Products, Machine, Appliance, Consumer Elect., Misc. Mfg., Consumer Goods

Target Pros Inc

80 Main St
West Orange, NJ 07052-5460
(973) 324-0900
Fax: (973) 324-0901
Email: jobs@targetpros.com
Web: www.targetpros.com

Summary: We are dedicated to serving the special needs of the health care industry by supplying motivated and highly qualified sales and marketing professionals in these specific areas: medical, pharmaceutical, biotech, and consumer products.

Key Contact - Specialty:
Mr. David Marshall, President - *Biotechnology, Medical, Medical (Sales), Pharmaceutical*

Salary Minimum: $75,000

Functions: Sales & Mktg., Mktg. Mgmt., Sales Mgmt., Sales Reps.

Industries: Pharm Svcs., Biotech/Life Sciences, Healthcare

Tavanese & Company Inc

1110 Druid Rd S
Clearwater, FL 33756-3818
(727) 441-2244
Email: info@tavanese.com
Web: www.tavanese.com

Summary: Retail and IT executive search company.

Key Contact - Specialty:
Mr. Dan Tavanese, Vice President, Operations
Mr. Stanley Tavanese, President - *Retail*

Salary Minimum: $40,000

Functions: Middle Mgmt.

Industries: Retail

Tax Advantage Personnel Inc

PO Box 1125
Harrison, TN 37341-1125
(866) 279-2386
Email: advantage@4caliber.com
Web: www.4caliber.com

Summary: Our firm meets the challenges of today's complex business environment. Ever-changing tax laws, legal issues, technology, market conditions and overall company performance are factors in nearly every decision. "Business as usual" is anything but. We recognize these challenges and we developed our services to support these needs. We offer clients financial professionals experienced in corporate tax.

Key Contact - Specialty:
Mr. Larry Barlow, President - *Tax*

Salary Minimum: $50,000

Functions: Taxes

Industries: Energy, Utilities, Manufacturing, Transportation, Retail, Finance, Services, Insurance, Real Estate, Software, Healthcare

Tax Recruitment Services

PO Box 647
White Plains, NY 10602-0647
(914) 789-6311
Fax: (914) 944-0879
Email: tax.recruit@verizon.net
Web: www.taxrecruitonline.com

Summary: We are one of the leading tax recruiting firms with a niche in servicing CPA firms and Fortune 1000 corporations by placing tax accountants and tax attorneys at all levels and functions.

Key Contact - Specialty:
Mr. Matt Sanders, Recruiter & Principal

Salary Minimum: $40,000

Functions: Taxes

Industries: Generalist (All)

TaxJobs.com

2205 Middle St Ste 207
Sullivans Island, SC 29482-9766
(843) 883-0100
(918) 955-4576
Fax: (843) 883-5200
Email: john@taxtalent.com
Web: www.taxjobs.com

Summary: We are an executive search firm specializing in the placement of tax professionals on a contract or interim basis. We also have a tax-exclusive job board and resume database.

Key Contact - Specialty:
Mr. John O'Neill, Director – *Tax*

Functions: Taxes
Industries: Generalist (All)

Terry Taylor & Associates
459 Bechman St
Springdale, PA 15144-1170
(724) 274-5627
Fax: (724) 274-5627
Email: tdtassoc@comcast.net

Summary: Our firm is a nationally recognized executive search consulting firm with many years in financial, litigation support, performance improvement and management IS recruitment. We specialize in recruitment and placement of experienced professionals in the consulting firm industry.

Key Contact - Specialty:
Mr. Terry Taylor, Vice President

Salary Minimum: $100,000

Functions: Senior Mgmt., Finance, IT, MIS Mgmt., Legal

Industries: Legal, Accounting, Mgmt. Consulting, E-commerce, IT Implementation

Peter R Taylor Associates Inc
PO Box 5582
Hanover, NH 03755-5582
(603) 643-5885
Email: peterrtaylor@aol.com

Summary: We specialize in corporate real estate executive search, retail chains, financial institutions, developers and industrial corporations.

Key Contact - Specialty:
Mr. Peter R. Taylor, President

Salary Minimum: $50,000

Functions: Generalist (All)

Industries: Real Estate

TCM Enterprises
3 Lyn Ct
Lutherville, MD 21093-5501
(410) 769-8120
Email: tmcpoyle@erols.com

Summary: Our clients include defense electronics, material scientists, meteorologists, shock physicists, chemical & environmental specialties, intelligent vehicle highway systems and experts in marketing and accounting/finance.

Key Contact - Specialty:
Mr. Thomas C. McPoyle, Jr., Principal

Functions: Generalist (All), Management, Materials, Sales & Mktg., IT, R&D, Engineering

Industries: Generalist (All), Manufacturing, Transportation, Accounting, Engineering Svcs., RF/Microwave, Defense, Environmental Svcs., Aerospace, Software

TDM & Associates
PO Box 797
Saint Joseph, IL 61873-0797
(217) 469-9400
Email: tim@tdm-assoc.com
Web: www.tdm-assoc.com

Summary: We are a boutique search firm with an excellent track record of recruiting and placing professional, technical and executive-level candidates. Our clients are primarily manufacturing based companies.

Key Contact - Specialty:
Mr. Tim Maupin, President

Salary Minimum: $40,000

Functions: Middle Mgmt., Materials, Mktg. Mgmt., Sales Mgmt., Engineering

Industries: Food, Bev., Tobacco, Printing, Chemicals, Plastics, Rubber, Paints, Petro. Products, Leather, Stone, Glass, Metal Products, Motor Vehicles, Consumer Elect., Consumer Goods

Branches:
PO Box 10294
Conway, AR 72034-0003
(501) 932-1541
Fax: (501) 932-1541
Email: julieb@tdm-assoc.com
Key Contact - Specialty:
Ms. Julie Blodgett, Search Consultant - *Engineering*

Team Place
1010 Wayne Ave Ste 890
Silver Spring, MD 20910-5665
(301) 565-3908
(800) 497-6767
Fax: (301) 565-3915
Email: 4jobs@teamplace.com
Web: www.teamplace.com

Summary: We are an executive search firm specializing in the recruitment of healthcare and pharmaceutical administrators, executives and physicians.

Key Contact - Specialty:
Ms. Elisabeth Peebles, President - *Research*
Mr. Rob Kaminski, Vice President, Bio-Research Division

Functions: Generalist (All), Senior Mgmt., Physicians, Health Admin., Sales Mgmt., CFOs

Industries: Generalist (All), Drugs Mfg., Medical Devices, Pharm Svcs., Mgmt. Consulting

Team-Stat Inc
3208 Dupont Ave S
Minneapolis, MN 55408-3512
(612) 825-0332
Email: tmelander@team-stat.com
Web: www.team-stat.com

Summary: We are a statistical warehouse providing statistical consulting, recruiting and other data analysis services. We have successfully placed statisticians in the fields of health care, biotechnology, R&D and marketing.

Key Contact - Specialty:
Mr. Todd E. Melander, President

Functions: Specialized Svcs.

Industries: Retail, Finance, Biotech/Life Sciences, Healthcare

TeboZandt Inc
56 Beach Hill Rd
Trumbull, CT 06611-1456
(203) 268-7670
Email: tzi@tebozandt.com
Web: www.tebozandt.com

Summary: An executive search firm focusing in management, sales, project management and technical architect positions in software sales, information technology and management consulting. Each member of our team has had direct information technology job experience, which provides our clients with the best service possible.

Key Contact - Specialty:
Ms. Violet Bliss, Managing Director - *Management*

Salary Minimum: $80,000

Functions: Generalist (All), Sales & Mktg., IT, MIS Mgmt.

Industries: Generalist (All), Mgmt. Consulting, E-commerce, IT Implementation, Software, Database SW, Development SW, Doc. Mgmt., Production SW, ERP SW, Mfg. SW, System SW

Tech Consulting
1316 12th St Apt 6
Santa Monica, CA 90401-2052
(727) 796-0635
Email: eejobs1@yahoo.com

Summary: We recruit for Fortune 500 companies and startups in the areas of telecom only, more specifically wireless & wire line, equipment and semiconductors. We only place in the areas of engineering and product management.

Key Contact - Specialty:
Mr. Mark Bavli, Manager - *Engineering, Telecommunications*

Salary Minimum: $50,000

Functions: R&D, Engineering

Industries: Telecoms, Digital, Wireless, Fiber Optic, Network Infrastructure, Networking, Comm. SW

Tech Law Recruiting Inc
521 S La Grange Rd Ste 104
La Grange, IL 60525-5633
(708) 482-1111
Fax: (708) 482-1112
Email: techlaw1@techlawcruiting.com
Web: www.techlawrecruiting.com

Summary: We specialize in the recruitment and placement of intellectual property law professionals.

Key Contact - Specialty:
Mr. Robert L. Ottoson, Principal
Mr. Chris Stevens

Salary Minimum: $90,000

Functions: Attorneys

Industries: Generalist (All)

Tech Search
2242 Bleckley Ct
Charlotte, NC 28270-1742
(888) 847-0788
(704) 846-3996
Fax: (704) 365-3735
Email: bob@tsearchinc.com
Web: www.tsearchinc.com

Summary: We specialize in nuclear and fossil fired power plant placement.

Key Contact - Specialty:
Mr. Bob Lindberg, Owner

Salary Minimum: $60,000

Functions: Generalist (All)

Industries: Oil & Gas, Construction

Tech Search Systems
PO Box 267
Southampton, MA 01073-0267
(413) 562-8685
Fax: (413) 562-8926
Email: info@techsearchsystems.com
Web: www.techsearchsystems.com

Summary: Our firm recruits for the capital equipment industry such as manufacturers of metal cutting machinery, metal fabricating machinery, packaging machinery. Searching specifically for candidates in: field service

installation, applications engineer, sales engineers, product managers and senior management positions.

Key Contact - Specialty:
Mr. Nicholas Boccio, President & Owner

Functions: Generalist (All)

Industries: Manufacturing, Textiles, Apparel, Lumber, Furniture, Paper, Metal Products, Machine, Appliance, Robotics

Techaid Inc

401-5165 Ch Queen-Mary
Edifice Queen Mary
Montreal, QC H3W 1X7
Canada
(514) 482-6790
(800) 341-6790
Fax: (514) 482-0324
Email: info@techaid.ca
Web: www.techaid.ca

Summary: We recruit and provide experienced technical staff on a temp or permanent basis. We are one of the longest established technical personnel agencies in our province with over 1,800 customers.

Key Contact - Specialty:
Mr. William F. Allen, President - *Engineering, Manufacturing*

Salary Minimum: $30,000

Functions: Mfg., Materials, IT, R&D, Engineering, Int'l.

Industries: Generalist (All)

TechHi Consultants Ltd

200-22 Frederick St
Oxlea Towers
Kitchener, ON N2H 6M6
Canada
(519) 749-1020
Fax: (519) 749-1070
Email: contact@techhi.com
Web: www.techhi.com

Summary: We specialize in high technology and automotive industries.

Key Contact - Specialty:
Mr. Jack Hougasian, General Manager

Functions: Generalist (All), Management, Mfg., Materials, Sales & Mktg., IT, R&D, Engineering

Industries: Generalist (All), Motor Vehicles, Computer Equip., Media, Aerospace, Software, Biotech/Life Sciences

Technical Connections Inc

11400 W Olympic Blvd Ste 700
Los Angeles, CA 90064-1582
(310) 479-8830
Fax: (310) 445-8726
Email: info@tci-la.com
Web: www.technicalconnections.com

Summary: We are one of the largest firms in our area specializing strictly in computer systems professionals including IT, software development and consulting. Staffed by computer professionals, we conduct face-to-face interviews with all candidates.

Key Contact - Specialty:
Mr. Peter MacKinnon, Chief Executive Officer
Ms. Rebecca Bailey, Director, Sales & Marketing

Salary Minimum: $35,000

Functions: Generalist (All), MIS Mgmt., Systems Analysis, Systems Dev., Systems Implem., Systems Support, Network Admin., DB Admin.

Industries: Generalist (All), Non-Classifiable

Technical Connection Inc

PO Box 1402
Burlington, VT 05402-1402
(802) 658-8324
Fax: (802) 658-0175
Email: vermontjobs@vttechjobs.com
Web: www.vttechjobs.com

Summary: Our recruiters place job seekers in professional and technical full time Vermont jobs. Additionally, we are able to offer technical contract employment, assigned to top companies in Vermont. We have over 18 years of experience in the professional staffing services industry. This experience has maximized our understanding of our corporate clients' staffing needs, helping us to attract the most qualified job candidates and put the right professional in the right job.

Key Contact - Specialty:
Mr. Chris Johnson, Recruiter
Ms. Kathie Cheney Taft, Recruiter

Functions: Middle Mgmt., Mfg.

Industries: Generalist (All), Finance, Architectural Svcs., Accounting, Mgmt. Consulting, HR Services, Defense, Homeland Security, ERP SW, HR SW, Industry Specific SW, Networking, Comm. SW

Technical Recruiting Consultants Inc

201 S Patton Ave
Arlington Heights, IL 60005-1657
(847) 394-1101

Summary: We are specialists in IS, engineering and manufacturing positions.

Key Contact - Specialty:
Mr. Dick Latimer, President - *Engineering, Manufacturing, MIS*

Salary Minimum: $50,000

Functions: MIS Mgmt., Systems Analysis, Systems Dev., Systems Implem., Systems Support

Industries: Generalist (All)

Technical Search Associates

20325 Center Ridge Rd Ste 622
Rocky River, OH 44116-3554
(440) 356-0880

Summary: We specialize in electrical, mechanical and manufacturing engineers in the electronics, automotive and aerospace industries. We also perform specialized searches per client requirements.

Key Contact - Specialty:
Mr. John M. Brunschwig - *Engineering*

Salary Minimum: $50,000

Functions: Product Dev., Engineering

Industries: Manufacturing, Motor Vehicles, Computer Equip., Consumer Elect., Electronic, Elec. Components, Defense, Aerospace, Software

Technical Service Consultants of Manitoba Ltd

3B-3380 Portage Ave
Winnipeg, MB R3K 0Z1
Canada
(204) 987-8080
Fax: (204) 987-8086
Email: tsc1@mts.net

Summary: We specialize in executive search, recruitment and outplacement services for the manufacturing and engineering sectors.

Key Contact - Specialty:
Mr. Brian Hayes, General Manager
Mr. Rick Tetreault, Associate

Salary Minimum: $40,000

Functions: Generalist (All)

Industries: Agri., Forestry, Mining, Manufacturing, Drugs Mfg., Medical Devices, Metal Products, Motor Vehicles, Misc. Mfg., Engineering Svcs., Supply Chain Mgmt, Aerospace

Technical Solutions Inc

12990 NW Sue St
Portland, OR 97229-5532
(503) 646-4704
Fax: (503) 646-2091
Email: info@tsi-pdx.com
Web: www.tsi-pdx.com

Summary: We provide recruiting services for computer professionals for direct hire or contract. We specialize in software & hardware engineers, test & QA and technical writers. We also provide off-site project development, including offshore development for a substantial cost saving.

Key Contact - Specialty:
Mr. Rajesh Jhunjhunwala, President
Mr. Barton J. Weaver, Chief Executive Officer

Salary Minimum: $40,000

Functions: Generalist (All), Systems Dev.

Industries: Medical Devices, Computer Equip., Test, Measure Equip., Semiconductors, Banking, Mgmt. Consulting, E-commerce, IT Implementation, Media, Aerospace, Software, Development SW, Networking, Comm. SW, Security SW, System SW

Technical Staffing Professionals LLC

8454 Carriage Hill Dr NE
Warren, OH 44484-1619
(330) 856-2758
Fax: (775) 796-8439
Email: techjobs@techstaffingpros.com
Web: www.techstaffingpros.com

Summary: We are an independent recruiting firm providing direct hire, contract and contract-to-perm employment options. We focus on sales, operations, engineering, and technical positions within manufacturing companies. Our experienced account executives find and present quality candidates and assist companies throughout the hiring and interviewing process.

Key Contact - Specialty:
Mr. Bruce Bille, President - *Aerospace, Automation, Energy, Engineering, Robotics*

Salary Minimum: $50,000

Functions: Management, Mfg., Automation, Engineering

Industries: Energy, Utilities, Manufacturing, Medical Devices, Metal Products, Machine, Appliance, Motor Vehicles, Electronic, Elec. Components, Robotics, Semiconductors, Aerospace, Packaging, Software, Biotech/Life Sciences

Technical Staffing Solutions

PO Box 1360
Frisco, TX 75034-0023
(972) 712-4411
Email: don@technicalstaffing.com
Web: www.technicalstaffing.com

Summary: Our agency recruits managers and experienced engineers and other technical professionals for employers in the petroleum refining and chemical industries.

Key Contact - Specialty:
Mr. Don J. Fink, CPC, President
Mr. Leighton Thetford, Recruiter

Salary Minimum: $65,000

Functions: Engineering, Geotechnical

Industries: Energy, Utilities, Oil & Gas

TechniSearch

PO Box 10235
Charlotte, NC 28212-5667
(704) 536-8776
Email: john@rcrtr.com
Web: www.rcrtr.com

Summary: Specializing in recruiting technical and management personnel in powder metallurgy, technical ceramics and carbides.

Key Contact - Specialty:
Mr. John Pflug, Owner

Salary Minimum: $30,000

Functions: Mfg., Product Dev., Production, Automation, Plant Mgmt., Quality, Materials, Engineering

Industries: Metal Products

TechNix Inc

100 Esgore Dr
North York, ON M5M 3S2
Canada
(416) 250-9195
Email: tnixon@technix.ca
Web: www.technix.ca

Summary: We are specialists in recruiting sales, marketing, pre/post-sales, senior architects, CTOs and executive management for technology vendors and IT consultancies.

Key Contact - Specialty:
Mr. Ted Nixon, President

Salary Minimum: $60,000

Functions: Management, Sales & Mktg., IT

Industries: Mgmt. Consulting, E-commerce, IT Implementation, Software, Accounting SW, Database SW, Development SW, Doc. Mgmt., Production SW, Entertainment SW, ERP SW, HR SW, Industry Specific SW, Mfg. SW, Marketing SW

Technoforce LLC

4 Knollwood Ter Ste 201
Randolph, NJ 07869-3012
(973) 328-1047
Email: robin@technoforce.com
Web: www.technoforce.com

Summary: We specialize in permanent and contract placement for e-commerce, high technology, pharmaceutical, hospitality, health and hospital industries. We place engineers, junior and senior programmers, web developers/designers, technical managers, e-commerce directors and strategic marketing managers. We also place accounting, banking, marketing, management and nursing professionals.

Key Contact - Specialty:
Ms. Robin Berg Tabakin, Managing Director

Salary Minimum: $25,000

Functions: Management, Healthcare, Nurses, Sales & Mktg., IT, Systems Dev., R&D, Engineering, Hotel Mgmt.

Industries: Generalist (All), Drugs Mfg., Medical Devices, Banking, Pharm Svcs., Hospitality, Hotels, Resorts, Clubs, Telephony, Digital, Wireless, Fiber Optic, Government, Defense, Aerospace, Insurance, Software, Development SW, Mfg. SW, Biotech/Life Sciences, Healthcare, Hospitals, Long-term/Home Care, Physical Therapy, Women's

Technology Data Resources

16 Knob Hill Rd
Madison, CT 06443-3345
(203) 318-1010
(888) 837-2990
Fax: (203) 318-1525
Email: contact-us@tdr.com
Web: www.tdr.com

Summary: Executive search consultants focused on sales related placements.

Key Contact - Specialty:
Mr. Michael Pagano, President

Salary Minimum: $30,000

Functions: Sales & Mktg., Sales Reps.

Industries: Generalist (All), Services, Communications, Software

Technology Search International

2107 N 1st St Ste 600
San Jose, CA 95131-2028
(408) 437-9500
Fax: (408) 437-1033
Email: info@tsearch.com
Web: www.tsearch.com

Summary: We are a high tech search and recruiting firm specializing predominantly in the placement of engineering professionals, ranging from the vice presidential level through senior individual contributors. Among our areas of strength: storage, networking, wireless computing, enterprise computing, embedded systems and computer security.

Key Contact - Specialty:
Mr. Alan Shapiro, President - *Senior management, Staffing, Start-up companies, Technology*
Mr. Matt Aberham, Manager - *Research & development, Staffing, Systems, Technical, Technology*

Salary Minimum: $100,000

Functions: Management, Middle Mgmt., Automation, Systems Dev.

Industries: E-commerce, Wireless, Software, Database SW, Development SW, Entertainment SW, ERP SW, Industry Specific SW, Marketing SW, Networking, Comm. SW, Security SW, System SW

Techsearch Services Inc

46 Wickford Pl
Madison, CT 06443-2071
(203) 318-1100
Fax: (203) 318-8800
Email: dtaft@snet.net
Web: www.techsearchservices.com

Summary: We are an executive recruiter of information/financial service professionals and traders for major investment companies/commercial banks. We place an emphasis on financial services community. We have particular expertise in the more analytical systems and business analysis.

Key Contact - Specialty:
Mr. David G. Taft, President

Salary Minimum: $75,000

Functions: Risk Mgmt., IT, Systems Dev.

Industries: Finance, Banking, Invest. Banking, Brokers, Mutual/Hedge Funds

Techstaff Inc

W177N9886 Rivercrest Dr Ste 100
Germantown, WI 53022-6407
(414) 359-4444
Fax: (414) 359-4949
Email: recruiter@techstaffwi.com
Web: www.techstaff.com

Summary: We specialize in the recruitment and placement of engineering and technical personnel.

Key Contact - Specialty:
Mr. Thomas Montgomery, Director, Placement - *Technical*
Ms. Susan Metzger, Coordinator, Recruiting - *Technical*

Salary Minimum: $35,000

Functions: Generalist (All), Mfg., Materials, HR Mgmt., Finance, IT, Engineering, Specialized Svcs.

Industries: Generalist (All), Medical Devices, Plastics, Rubber, Metal Products, Machine, Appliance, Consumer Elect., Misc. Mfg.

Branches:
4450 S Rural Rd Ste E126
Tempe, AZ 85282-7027
(480) 456-4050
Fax: (480) 456-4048
Email: recruiter@techstaffaz.com
Key Contact - Specialty:
Ms. Cindy Yetka, Branch Manager

500 E Esplanade Dr Ste 1200
Oxnard, CA 93036-0563
(262) 373-1318
Email: jleopold@techstaff.com
Key Contact - Specialty:
Mr. John Leopold, Branch Manager

4021 N Armenia Ave Ste 103
Tampa, FL 33607-1010
(813) 221-1222
Fax: (813) 221-6658
Email: recruiter@techstatttb.com
Key Contact - Specialty:
Mr. Adam Mainzer, Owner

804 E Park Ave Ste 109
Libertyville, IL 60048-2901
(847) 816-0500
Fax: (847) 816-0541
Email: recruiter@techstaffil.com
Key Contact - Specialty:
Mr. Steve Bauer

3625 Utica Ridge Rd
Bettendorf, IA 52722-1646
(563) 355-4400
Fax: (563) 355-0694
Email: recruiter@techstaffia.com
Key Contact - Specialty:
Mr. Scott Allen, Branch Manager

2150 44th St SE Ste 300
Grand Rapids, MI 49508-5094
(616) 827-3499
Fax: (616) 827-3944
Email: bill@techstaffmi.com
Key Contact - Specialty:
Mr. Bill Gansser, Owner

2670 S Ashland Ave
Green Bay, WI 54304-5300
(920) 498-9870
Email: ckahn@techstaff.com

Key Contact - Specialty:
Mr. Chris Kahn, Owner

Tecnix LLC
PO Box 240
Alpharetta, GA 30009-0240
(770) 751-7759
Email: info@tecnix.net
Web: www.tecnix.net

Summary: Our firm provides recruiting and knowledge management consulting services, to the medical device, diagnostic, pharmaceutical, optical, nanotechnology, biotechnology and related industries. In addition to recruiting and staffing, we can source and deliver the strategic contact you may need to successfully bring your product to market or project to completion.

Key Contact - Specialty:
Mr. Mario Martinez, CSIIIE, Managing Partner

Functions: Generalist (All), Senior Mgmt., Product Dev., Production, Engineering, Minorities/Diversity

Industries: Generalist (All), Manufacturing, Soap, Perf., Cosmtcs., Drugs Mfg., Medical Devices, Plastics, Rubber, Metal Products, Machine, Appliance, Invest. Banking, Venture Cap., Pharm Svcs., Defense, Packaging, Software, ERP SW, Mfg. SW, Biotech/Life Sciences, Dental, Non-Classifiable

Teeman, Perley, Gilmartin Inc
230 Park Ave Rm 2425
New York, NY 10169-2426
(212) 972-5544
Web: www.tpgsearch.com

Summary: We are a full-service executive search firm specializing in the financial community. Our expertise spans the breadth of Wall Street products including sales, trading, research and capital markets in both the equity and fixed income areas.

Key Contact - Specialty:
Ms. Susan S. Teeman, President
Ms. Ellen Perley, Partner
Ms. Marybeth Gilmartin, Partner

Functions: Generalist (All)

Industries: Finance

Tele-Solutions of Arizona Inc
7975 N Hayden Rd Ste A106
Scottsdale, AZ 85258-3261
(480) 483-1300
Fax: (480) 483-7221
Email: carole@telesolutionsearch.com
Web: www.telesolutionsearch.com

Summary: We are a search firm specializing in high technology, telecom and executive finance. We place contract, contract-to-perm and do permanent placement searches in the above industries.

Key Contact - Specialty:
Ms. Carole Wichansky, Owner & Manager - *Computers (Software), Engineering, Telecommunications*
Ms. Janice Robertson, Senior Recruiter - *Engineering, Hardware, Telecommunications*

Salary Minimum: $70,000

Functions: Senior Mgmt., Middle Mgmt., CFOs, Hardware

Industries: Semiconductors, Finance, Telecoms, Telephony, Digital, Wireless, Fiber Optic, Network Infrastructure, RF/Microwave, Software

Telecom Connections Inc
602 Golf Crest Ln Ste 200
Austin, TX 78734-4647
(512) 261-3290
Fax: (512) 261-3278
Email: gorr@telecomconnections.com
Web: www.telecomconnections.com

Summary: We specialize in placement of management through executive-level candidates primarily in wireless telecom companies. This includes sales & marketing, operations, telecom engineers and technical personnel. Our clients consist of wireless system operators, as well as suppliers to the industry.

Key Contact - Specialty:
Mr. George H. Orr, President

Salary Minimum: $75,000

Functions: Management, Senior Mgmt., Middle Mgmt., Mktg. Mgmt., Sales Mgmt., Engineering

Industries: Telecoms, Wireless

Telecom Recruiters Inc
12531 Lt Nichols Rd Ste 100
Fairfax, VA 22033-2433
(703) 620-4096
Fax: (703) 620-2973
Email: tom@telecom-recruiters.com
Web: www.telecom-recruiters.com

Summary: We specialize in providing telecom professionals to service providers for landline, wireless and call centers. In addition we conduct searches for telecommunication's manufacturers covering both hardware and software.

Key Contact - Specialty:
Mr. Thomas L. Fitzgerald, President - *Technical, Telecommunications*
Mr. Matthew A. Fitzgerald, Director - *Telecommunications*

Salary Minimum: $40,000

Functions: Generalist (All)

Industries: Telecoms

The Telecom Search Group
PO Box 326
Bella Vista, CA 96008-0326
(530) 549-5331
Fax: (530) 549-4168
Email: jobs@telecomsg.com
Web: www.telecomsg.com

Summary: We are a contingency search firm who specializes in the placement of contract and perm senior engineers and executive managers whose occupations are in the wireless, optical transport and CLEC telecom industries.

Key Contact - Specialty:
Mr. Randall Chambers, Owner - *Telecommunications*

Salary Minimum: $75,000

Functions: Management, Board Members, Senior Mgmt., Sales & Mktg., Training, CFOs, MIS Mgmt., Systems Implem., R&D, Engineering

Industries: Telecoms

Telem Adhesive Search Corp
PO Box 656
Owings Mills, MD 21117-0656
(410) 356-6200
Fax: (410) 356-5189
Email: telemadhesive@comcast.net
Web: www.adhesivesearch.com

Summary: We are one of the nation's preeminent search firms, satisfying the personnel needs of the adhesives, coatings and converting industries.

Key Contact - Specialty:
Mr. Peter B. Telem, President - *Adhesives, Coatings*

Salary Minimum: $50,000

Functions: Management, Product Dev., Production, Plant Mgmt., Quality, Materials, Packaging, Sales & Mktg., Mktg. Mgmt., Engineering

Industries: Manufacturing, Paper, Printing, Chemicals, Soap, Perf., Cosmtcs., Drugs Mfg., Medical Devices, Plastics, Rubber, Paints, Petro. Products, Packaging

TeleManagement Search
44 S Bayles Ave Ste 316
Port Washington, NY 11050-3765
(516) 767-6990
(312) 527-1166
Fax: (516) 767-6980
Email: connie@tmrecruiters.com
Web: www.tmrecruiters.com

Summary: We are an executive search firm dedicated to recruiting professional managerial inbound, outbound and customer service personnel. Recruit at all management levels including presidents, VPs, directors and managers.

Key Contact - Specialty:
Ms. Connie Caroli, President

Salary Minimum: $50,000

Functions: Direct Mktg., Customer Svc.

Industries: Generalist (All)

TeleQuest Communications Inc
PO Box 94
Mahwah, NJ 07430-0094
(845) 371-3500
Fax: (845) 371-3030
Email: client@telequestcom.com
Web: www.telequestcom.com

Summary: We are a telecom search firm specializing in all areas of telecom including voice, data, call centers and local and wide area networks. We place temp, permanent, sales and technical candidates at all levels.

Key Contact - Specialty:
Mr. Thomas Bartchak, President
Ms. Ellen Dansky, Vice President - *Telecommunications*

Salary Minimum: $40,000

Functions: Generalist (All), Management, Network Admin., Technicians

Industries: Mgmt. Consulting, IT Implementation, Communications, Telecoms, Call Centers, Telephony, Digital, Wireless, Fiber Optic, Network Infrastructure, RF/Microwave

Tell/Com Recruiters
800 Celebration Ave
Celebration, FL 34747-4999
(407) 566-2005
Fax: (407) 566-2006
Email: r@tellcom.com
Web: www.tellcom.com

Summary: We specialize in placements within the telecom industry in sales, engineering and management within voice processing, ACD, CDR, long distance, predictive dialing & video conferencing, CTI & voice over IP, as well as with leading interconnects and manufacturers of PBX and KEY systems.

Key Contact - Specialty:
Mr. Dennis F. Young, President - *Telecommunications*
Mr. Bob Bradford, Director, Sales

Salary Minimum: $50,000

Functions: Generalist (All), Mktg. Research, Mktg. Mgmt., Sales Mgmt.

Industries: Generalist (All), Telecoms, Software

Terik Company

2808 Avenida De Soto
Navarre, FL 32566-8806
(850) 939-4666
Fax: (850) 939-8423
Email: tomwilliams@mchsi.com

Summary: Our firm's specialties include the store fixture industry, both metal and wood. We work with the capital goods industry and finished metal products (automotive parts, hand tools, white goods, machine parts, etc.). We place mid to upper-level management.

Key Contact - Specialty:
Mr. Tom Williams, President

Salary Minimum: $50,000

Functions: Generalist (All), Management, Mfg., Materials, Purchasing, Sales & Mktg., Sales Mgmt., HR Mgmt., Finance, Engineering

Industries: Manufacturing, Lumber, Furniture, Metal Products, Machine, Appliance, Motor Vehicles, Misc. Mfg.

Terran Systems Professional Staffing Inc

3567 Benton St Ste 400
Santa Clara, CA 95051-4404
(408) 727-9000
Fax: (408) 727-9018
Email: terran@terransys.com
Web: www.terransys.com

Summary: We are an executive search firm specializing in the placement of software and hardware engineers.

Key Contact - Specialty:
Mr. Eric Williams, Manager

Functions: R&D, Engineering

Industries: Consumer Goods, Telecoms, Digital, Wireless, Network Infrastructure, RF/Microwave, Development SW, Networking, Comm. SW, System SW, Biotech/Life Sciences

Branches:
16030 Ventura Blvd Ste 235
Encino, CA 91436-4472
(818) 377-3770
Fax: (818) 377-3771
Email: terran@terransys.com
Key Contact - Specialty:
Ms. Susie Tabanyi

Terransoft Inc

16030 Ventura Blvd Ste 235
Encino, CA 91436
(818) 995-9245
Fax: (818) 995-9329

Summary: We are an executive search firm specializing in the placement of software engineers and developers in Silicon Valley/Northern California.

Key Contact - Specialty:
Ms. Susie Tabanyi, Administrator

Functions: IT

Industries: Software, Accounting SW, Database SW, Development SW, HR SW, Marketing SW, Networking, Comm. SW, System SW, Biotech/Life Sciences

Lee Terry & Associates Inc

PO Box 5427
San Mateo, CA 94402-0427
(650) 570-7913
Fax: (650) 572-1600
Email: leeterry@lterryrecruiter.com
Web: www.lterryrecruiter.com

Summary: We are specialists in executive search for homebuilders and land developers. Member of various building industry groups in our market.

Key Contact - Specialty:
Ms. Lee Terry, President

Functions: Generalist (All)

Industries: Construction, Real Estate

The Tetsell Group

1902 W Muirfield Ct
Anthem, AZ 85086-1800
(877) 371-0729
(623) 476-8022
Email: jill@tetsellgroup.com
Web: www.tetsellgroup.com

Summary: Property and casualty insurance specialists.

Key Contact - Specialty:
Ms. Jill M. Tetsell, CPCU, Owner
Mr. Dick Tetsell, Owner

Salary Minimum: $30,000

Functions: Generalist (All), Management

Industries: Generalist (All), Insurance

TFI

(formerly known as MR of Morris County)
17 Hanover Rd Ste 450
Florham Park, NJ 07932-1415
(973) 593-0400
Fax: (973) 593-0150

Summary: Specialty: building national remote sales teams for clients. Sales, tech support and marketing positions. Industry specialists: hardware and software data communications, telecom, broadband, data systems and converging technologies.

Key Contact - Specialty:
Ms. Susan M. Young, General Manager
Mr. Wayne Young, President

Salary Minimum: $75,000

Functions: Management, Senior Mgmt., Sales & Mktg., Mktg. Mgmt., Sales Mgmt., Direct Mktg.

Industries: Computer Equip., Test, Measure Equip., New Media, Broadcast, Film, Telecoms, Telephony, Digital, Wireless, Fiber Optic, Network Infrastructure, RF/Microwave, Software, Networking, Comm. SW, Security SW

The TGA Company

4605 Brandingshire Pl Ste 201
Fort Worth, TX 76133-6601
(817) 370-0865
Fax: (817) 292-6451
Email: trgreen@swbell.net

Summary: We handle contingency and retained searches for financial executives - all industries.

Key Contact - Specialty:
Mr. Thomas R. Green, President - *Finance*
Ms. Carolyn M. Byrne, Senior Associate - *Finance, MIS*
Mr. Thomas C. Green, Senior Associate - *Finance, Marketing, Sales*

Salary Minimum: $30,000

Functions: Taxes, M&A, Risk Mgmt., Systems Analysis, Systems Implem., Systems Support, Network Admin., DB Admin., Engineering

Industries: Generalist (All)

The Pagel Group

11981 Coopers Run
Strongsville, OH 44149-9260
(440) 878-0249
(216) 408-2101
Email: pagelsearch@hotmail.com

Summary: Retained and contingent legal recruiting with special emphasis in representation of law firm mergers and individuals who are interested in confidentially exploring partner-level opportunities. National practice, impeccable reputation, stellar references.

Key Contact - Specialty:
Ms. Lisa Pagel, President & Chief Executive Officer

Functions: Generalist (All), Management, Board Members, Senior Mgmt., M&A

Industries: Legal

Thinkpath Inc

201 Westcreek Blvd
ABB Body-In-White
Brampton, ON L6T 5S6
Canada
(905) 460-3040
Fax: (905) 460-3050
Email: jhenderson@thinkpath.com
Web: www.thinkpath.com

Summary: Our firm is an engineering services company offering a blended suite of engineering and design services, technical publishing and documentation, and on site engineering support to enhance the resource performance of our customers in the aerospace, automotive, defense, manufacturing and healthcare industries.

Key Contact - Specialty:
Mr. Declan French, President, CEO & Chairman
Ms. Kelly Hankinson, Chief Financial Officer

Salary Minimum: $45,000

Functions: IT, Engineering, Structural, Eng. Design, Process, Systems

Industries: Generalist (All), Manufacturing, Machine, Appliance, Robotics, Semiconductors, Engineering Svcs., Government, Aerospace, Healthcare

Branches:
1211 N West Shore Blvd Ste 410
Tampa, FL 33607-4605
(813) 636-8227
Fax: (813) 636-9059
Email: tampa@cadcaminc.com
Key Contact - Specialty:
Mr. Ed Godwin, Branch Manager

2505 Taylor Rd
Columbus, IN 47203-3102
(812) 376-8519
Fax: (812) 376-7530
Email: columbus@thinkpath.com
Key Contact - Specialty:
Mr. Jeff Anderson, Operations Manager

25840 Sherwood Ave
Warren, MI 48091-4160
(586) 754-2700
Fax: (586) 754-3700
Email: detroit@thinkpath.com
Key Contact - Specialty:
Mr. Rick Simon, Branch Manager

2800 E River Rd
Dayton, OH 45439-1538
(937) 643-4100
Fax: (973) 643-4110
Email: dayton@thinkpath.com
Key Contact - Specialty:
Mr. Robert Trick, Vice President, US Ops & Bus
  Development

Ursula Thomas & Associates, Inc

2111 Ras Ct
Snellville, GA 30078-2486
(770) 982-9551
(800) 691-7057
Fax: (770) 982-9552
Email: tursula@bellsouth.net

Summary: Recruitment assistance for board
certified, board eligible physicians, CRNA and
anesthesia assistants only.

Key Contact - Specialty:
Ms. Ursula Thomas

Functions: Physicians

Industries: Hospitals

Thomas & Associates

75817 Via Allegre
Indian Wells, CA 92210-8490
(760) 773-0717
Fax: (760) 862-9207
Email: thomas.associates@prodigy.net
Web: pages.prodigy.net/d.c.thomas

Summary: We are an executive staffing resource
for the telecom, IT, high technology and
pharmaceutical industries for engineering, sales &
marketing, financial and general management
disciplines.

Key Contact - Specialty:
Mr. Donald C. Thomas, Chairman - *High
  technology, Senior management*

Salary Minimum: $80,000

Functions: Generalist (All), Management, Board
  Members

Industries: Food, Bev., Tobacco, Textiles,
  Apparel, Medical Devices, Computer Equip.,
  Consumer Elect., Pharm Svcs., Mgmt.
  Consulting, HR Services, Hospitality, Telecoms,
  Real Estate, Software, Biotech/Life Sciences,
  Healthcare

Raymond Thomas & Associates

475 S Pressview Ave
Longwood, FL 32750-6851
(407) 774-8300
Fax: (407) 339-8591

Summary: Our firm has experience in metal
working industries along with experience in
executive recruiting specializing with machine
tool and related factory automation OEMs, as well
as users. We have an extensive network in mid-
upper to upper-levels of management.

Key Contact - Specialty:
Mr. Ray Huegel, Owner - *Machining*
Mr. Mark Leeser, Principal - *Machining*

Salary Minimum: $60,000

Functions: Generalist (All)

Industries: Metal Products, Machine, Appliance,
  Misc. Mfg.

Thomas & Associates of Michigan

PO Box 366
Union Pier, MI 49129-0366
(269) 469-5760
Fax: (269) 469-5774
Email: tomzonka@hotmail.com

Summary: We are a computerized affiliation with
an extensive network of recruiting firms. We fill
permanent, contract, and outplacement openings.

Key Contact - Specialty:
Mr. Thomas J. Zonka, President

Salary Minimum: $50,000

Functions: Management, Mfg., Materials, Sales &
  Mktg., Sales Mgmt., HR Mgmt., Finance, CFOs,
  IT, Engineering

Industries: Generalist (All), Manufacturing

Judy Thompson & Associates Financial Executive Search Inc

5080 Shoreham Pl Ste 204
San Diego, CA 92122-5932
(858) 452-1200
Fax: (858) 623-5910
Email: judy@jtaa.net
Web: www.jtaa.net

Summary: We specialize in recruiting experienced
degreed accounting/financial professionals for all
industries (excluding lending and operations for
financial institutions and financial sales) for San
Diego County companies.

Key Contact - Specialty:
Ms. Judy Thompson, President - *Accounting,
  CFOs, Controllers, Finance, Tax*
Mr. Ken Schmitt, Senior Director - *Accounting,
  Audits, CFOs, Controllers, Finance*
Mr. Brad Janik, Director - *Accounting, CFOs,
  Controllers, Finance*

Salary Minimum: $65,000

Functions: Finance, CFOs, Budgeting, Cash
  Mgmt., Credit, Taxes, M&A

Industries: Generalist (All), Accounting

Jeffrey Thompson Associates

PO Box 731
Rocky Hill, CT 06067-0731
(860) 721-7973

Summary: Boutique firm handling sales,
marketing, engineering and most other executive
level/management searches on a national basis.

Key Contact - Specialty:
Mr. Jeffrey Thompson, Owner - *Manufacturing,
  Marketing*

Functions: Generalist (All), Management

Industries: Generalist (All), Manufacturing, Metal
  Products, Consumer Elect., Misc. Mfg.,
  Hospitality, Hotels, Resorts, Clubs, Quick
  Service Restaurants

Rand Thompson Executive Search Consultants

261 Madison Ave
New York, NY 10016-2303
(212) 972-0090
Fax: (212) 370-0047
Email: jkelly@randthompson.com

Summary: We have grown and maintained
relationships with many firms rated #1 in their
respective industries. Currently 75 percent of
search assignments are completed with individuals
referred by satisfied applicants.

Key Contact - Specialty:
Mr. John Kelly, President - *Finance, Wall Street*
Mr. Harold Kost, Executive Vice President

Salary Minimum: $75,000

Functions: Management, Senior Mgmt., Middle
  Mgmt., Mfg., Materials, Sales & Mktg., HR
  Mgmt., Finance, IT, Legal

Industries: Generalist (All), Insurance

Thompson Recruiting Group

30 Burton Hills Blvd Ste 230
Nashville, TN 37215-6140
(866) 665-3518
Email: corey@trgcareers.com
Web: www.trgcareers.com

Summary: We are an executive search firm
specializing in the search and placement of
professionals.

Key Contact - Specialty:
Mr. Corey Pachciarz, Recruiter & Senior
  Consultant
Mr. Brett Thompson, CPC, Owner & President -
  *Business development, Healthcare,
  Management, Sales*

Functions: Management, Senior Mgmt., Middle
  Mgmt., Healthcare, Sales & Mktg., Mktg.
  Mgmt., Sales Mgmt., Sales Reps., Finance,
  Attorneys

Industries: Generalist (All), Manufacturing,
  Textiles, Apparel, Drugs Mfg., Medical
  Devices, Semiconductors, Consumer Goods,
  Retail, Finance, Services, Pharm Svcs., Legal,
  Accounting, HR Services, Hospitality, Hotels,
  Resorts, Clubs, Recreation, Media, Real Estate,
  Software, Biotech/Life Sciences, Healthcare,
  Hospitals, Long-term/Home Care, Dental

Thompson Search Consultants

410 Creek Bend Dr
Newark, DE 19711-3766
(302) 369-9960
Fax: (302) 369-9961
Email: brenda@thompsonsearchconsultants.com
Web: www.thompsonsearchconsultants.com

Summary: Our firm specializes on executive,
legal and financial placements - primarily for
corporations, law firms and financial institutions.

Key Contact - Specialty:
Ms. Brenda L. Thompson, Founder

Functions: Senior Mgmt., Finance, Legal

Industries: Finance, Legal

Thorek/Scott and Partners

702-67 Yonge St
Montreal Trust
Toronto, ON M5E 1J8
Canada
(416) 365-7561
(866) 365-7561
Fax: (416) 365-3240
Email: consult@thorekscott.com
Web: www.thorekscott.com

Summary: A leader in the field of executive
search, we successfully provide premiere talent
quickly and cost-effectively. Operating throughout
a wide array of service-based industries, including
financial services, marketing & sales, energy,
education, HR and entertainment & leisure, our
searches span the spectrum from senior executive
through middle management.

Key Contact - Specialty:
Mr. Michael Thorek, President
Mrs. Faye Thorek, Senior Consultant

Salary Minimum: $100,000

Functions: Senior Mgmt., Middle Mgmt., Admin. Svcs., Sales & Mktg., HR Mgmt., Benefits, Finance, CFOs, Risk Mgmt., Legal

Industries: Generalist (All)

Thorne Consulting Inc

649 N Highland Ave NE Apt 1
Atlanta, GA 30306-4561
(404) 873-3775
Fax: (404) 873-3705
Email: thorcon@mindspring.com
Web: www.thorneconsulting.com

Summary: We are a retained executive search and consulting firm. Client organizations (hospitals and related entities) seek our assistance to strategically fill their leadership and management staff vacancies. We develop "behavioral DNA profiles" to aid in the consistency and objectivity of selection and promotion decisions.

Key Contact - Specialty:
Mr. Richard Thorne, President - *Healthcare, Home health, Hospital, Long term care, Managed care*
Ms. Betsy Cagle, Client Executive - *HMOs, Home health, Hospital, Long term care, Managed care*

Salary Minimum: $75,000

Functions: Management, Board Members, Senior Mgmt., Middle Mgmt., Healthcare, Nurses, Health Admin., CFOs, Mgmt. Consultants

Industries: Generalist (All), Non-profits, Mgmt. Consulting, Healthcare, Hospitals, Long-term/Home Care, Women's

Thorsen Associates Inc

2020 Grand Ave
North Baldwin, NY 11510-2900
(516) 868-6500
Fax: (516) 868-7842
Email: info@thorsenassociates.com
Web: www.thorsenassociates.com

Summary: We are a contingency search firm specializing within the manufacturing market for management and engineering. Strong contacts with many years of experience in recruiting.

Key Contact - Specialty:
Mr. Peter Thorsen, President - *Engineering, Manufacturing, Supply Chain*

Salary Minimum: $35,000

Functions: Generalist (All)

Industries: Manufacturing, Medical Devices, Metal Products, Machine, Appliance, Computer Equip., Consumer Elect., Test, Measure Equip., Misc. Mfg., Electronic, Elec. Components, Consumer Goods

The Tidewater Group

115 Main St
Monroe, CT 06468-1662
(203) 459-2500
(727) 441-1305
Fax: (203) 459-8373
Email: john@tidewater.org
Web: www.tidewater.org

Summary: We are recruiters working for a diversified clientele. We have extensive recruiting experience.

Key Contact - Specialty:
Mr. John Wilson, Manager
Mr. Bill Jones, Director

Salary Minimum: $50,000

Functions: Generalist (All)

Industries: Generalist (All)

TMI FirstSearch

PO Box 806
Paoli, PA 19301-0806
(610) 722-9280 x20
(888) 292-3500
Fax: (610) 722-9241
Email: info@tmistaffing.com
Web: www.tmistaffing.com

Summary: Our firm specializes in biotechnology, telecom, and the related fields of IT, data storage and eCommerce. We identify mutually beneficial permanent and retained employment opportunities for both candidates and clients using our extensive experience, as well as our recruiting and placement skills.

Key Contact - Specialty:
Mr. William R. DePhillipo, President - *Telecommunications*

Salary Minimum: $45,000

Functions: Senior Mgmt., Middle Mgmt., Sales Mgmt., Direct Mktg., Customer Svc., IT, R&D, Technicians

Industries: Generalist (All), Communications, Telecoms, Telephony, Wireless, Fiber Optic, Network Infrastructure, Biotech/Life Sciences, Healthcare

TNG Global (The Nugget Group)

11 Crois Merton
Hampstead, QC H3X 1L5
Canada
(514) 931-8542 x202
Fax: (514) 931-8310
Email: inquiries@tngglobal.com
Web: www.tngglobal.com

Summary: We specialize in recruiting enterprise resource planning (ERP), customer relationship management (CRM) and eCommerce professionals.

Key Contact - Specialty:
Mr. Norman Gold, President
Ms. Nancy Gold, Vice President, Sales
Ms. Dayna Gedney, Recruiter - *Business development, Business to business*

Salary Minimum: $55,000

Functions: Generalist (All), MIS Mgmt., Systems Analysis, Systems Dev., Systems Implem., Systems Support, Network Admin., DB Admin.

Industries: Generalist (All), Energy, Utilities, Manufacturing, Finance, Services, Media, Software

The Toberson Group

884 Woods Mill Rd Ste 101
Ballwin, MO 63011-3657
(636) 891-9794
(800) 969-7952
Fax: (636) 891-9784
Email: info@toberson.com
Web: www.toberson.com

Summary: We are a contingency search firm. Our main areas of specialty include physicians and nurse practitioners.

Key Contact - Specialty:
Mr. James C. Anderson, Partner & Chief Executive Officer
Mr. Roger Toben, Partner & President
Mr. Michael Pranger, Vice President
Ms. Judy Hurley, Office Manager
Mr. John Conway, Recruiter - *Human resources*

Salary Minimum: $35,000

Functions: Healthcare, Physicians, Nurses

Industries: Healthcare

Tolfrey Group

PO Box 1982
El Cerrito, CA 94530-4982
(510) 315-0565
(510) 234-0090
Fax: (419) 818-1219
Email: resumes@tolfrey.com
Web: www.tolfrey.com

Summary: We specialize in world-class technology search. On the information technology side we are primarily ERP and CRM focused.

Key Contact - Specialty:
Mr. Grant Du Plooy, President - *CRM, ERP*

Salary Minimum: $60,000

Functions: Generalist (All), Systems Implem.

Industries: Robotics, HR Services, E-commerce, IT Implementation, Software, Development SW, ERP SW, HR SW, Industry Specific SW, Training SW, Healthcare

Tomass Executive Group Ltd

PO Box 601
New City, NY 10956-0601
(845) 639-9000
Fax: (845) 639-9043
Email: resume@tomassexecutive.com
Web: www.tegcareers.com

Summary: Our firm specializes in placing capital markets professionals. We place permanent, consultants, and temporaries.

Key Contact - Specialty:
Mr. Frank Tomass, President - *Finance, Operations, Wall Street*
Ms. Joanne Finochio, Executive Vice President - *Finance, Operations, Technology*

Salary Minimum: $40,000

Functions: Generalist (All), Middle Mgmt., Budgeting, M&A, Risk Mgmt., Systems Analysis, Systems Support, DB Admin.

Industries: Generalist (All), Finance, Banking, Invest. Banking, Brokers, Venture Cap., Mutual/Hedge Funds, Misc. Financial, Accounting, Mgmt. Consulting

Tomlinson Associates

401 N Michigan Ave Ste 1200
Chicago, IL 60611-4549
(312) 840-8250
Fax: (312) 840-8251
Email: tomlinsonassociates@msn.com

Summary: We are a boutique firm offering highly personalized service for reasonable fees, specializing in placing market research professionals. Clients include Fortune 500 manufacturers, global market research and consulting firms and advertising agencies.

Key Contact - Specialty:
Ms. Betsy Tomlinson, President - *Market research*

Salary Minimum: $75,000

Functions: Mktg. Research

Industries: Manufacturing, Food, Bev., Tobacco, Printing, Retail, Services, Architectural Svcs., Mgmt. Consulting, HR Services, Publishing, Healthcare

Tondorf & Associates Inc

720 Washington St
Hanover, MA 02339-2369
(781) 826-1440
Fax: (781) 826-2827
Email: tondorfasc@aol.com
Web: www.tondorf.com

Summary: We are an executive search and recruiting firm that focuses in the consumer products and healthcare industry. Specializing in category management and trade marketing positions that lead to future sales management positions.

Key Contact - Specialty:
Mr. Paul Tondorf, Jr., Principal - *Consumer (Marketing,Packaged Goods), Management, Medical (Devices), Pharmaceutical*
Mr. Jack Richard, Recruiter - *Financial services, Pharmaceutical, Sales*

Salary Minimum: $50,000

Functions: Healthcare, Sales & Mktg., Sales Mgmt., Sales Reps.

Industries: Food, Bev., Tobacco, Drugs Mfg., Medical Devices

Top of the World Inc

11770 Haynes Bridge Rd Ste 205 PMB 315
Alpharetta, GA 30004-1970
(678) 366-3430
Fax: (800) 639-1613
Email: info@topoftheworldjobs.com
Web: www.topoftheworldjobs.com

Summary: We are a full service professional search firm specializing in hospitality executives, medical professionals and IT. We listen to your needs and provide candidates in a timely manner. We will provide only the top candidates to your organization, thus avoiding the cycles of hiring, firing and laying off employees who don't quite fit into your organization.

Key Contact - Specialty:
Mr. Glenn Topps, Chief Executive Officer & Founder
Mr. Elijah Williams, President

Salary Minimum: $35,000

Functions: Management, Mfg.

Industries: Food, Bev., Tobacco, Paper, Soap, Perf., Cosmtcs., Medical Devices, Plastics, Rubber, Hospitality

Topaz Attorney Search

3 Regent St
Livingston, NJ 07039-1668
(973) 597-0500
Fax: (973) 597-1997
Email: info@topattorneys.com
Web: www.topattorneys.com

Summary: We provide premier attorney search for law firms and corporate legal departments in all disciplines and levels. Our clients range from large firms, boutiques and small corporations to the top international and Fortune 100 companies. Our specialties include: establishing/expanding corporate legal departments and branch offices of firms, law firm mergers and legal consulting services.

Key Contact - Specialty:
Ms. Ronni L. Gaines, Principal
Mr. Stewart Michaels, Principal - *Consulting, Mergers & acquisitions*
Ms. Pamela S. Frazer, Esq., Vice President, General Counsel

Salary Minimum: $80,000

Functions: Legal, Attorneys

Industries: Generalist (All)

Lisa Torres & Associates Inc

1550 Madruga Ave Ste 150
Coral Gables, FL 33146-3016
(305) 669-8600
Fax: (801) 730-0156

Email: torres@letusrecruit.com
Web: www.letusrecruit.com

Summary: We specialize in the executive recruitment and placement of mid and senior level executives. Our focus is in the areas of accounting/finance, sales/marketing, HR and general management. The firm assists regional and multinational corporations with their staffing needs. As executive recruitment specialists, we are able to provide customized services.

Key Contact - Specialty:
Ms. Lisa Torres, President

Salary Minimum: $50,000

Functions: Management, Sales & Mktg., HR Mgmt., Finance, Int'l.

Industries: Generalist (All)

Total Resource Solutions

1968 Crossland Rd
Clover, SC 29710-6426
(803) 222-9202
Fax: (803) 222-5683
Email: info@totalresourcesolutions.com
Web: www.totalresourcesolutions.com

Summary: Our firm has extensive engineering and leadership experience in multiple industries. We approach staffing with the knowledge that only hands-on experience brings. Proprietary job intake process; competent candidate prescreening. Retained or contingency searches. Focus on aerospace, automotive, motors, fluid power and motion control.

Key Contact - Specialty:
Ms. Karen Stumpf, President

Salary Minimum: $50,000

Functions: Generalist (All)

Industries: Manufacturing, Government, Defense, Aerospace

Toyjobs

(also known as CPR Group)
26 Park St Ste 2001
Montclair, NJ 07042-3443
(973) 744-0818
Email: tom@toyjobs.com
Web: www.toyjobs.com

Summary: The dominant recruiting firm in the toy and children's product industry

Key Contact - Specialty:
Mr. Thomas M. Keoughan, President

Salary Minimum: $60,000

Functions: Senior Mgmt., Product Dev., Purchasing, Mktg. Research, Sales Mgmt., Engineering, Graphic Designers

Industries: Wholesale

TPG & Associates

10619 Burgoyne Rd
Houston, TX 77042-2804
(713) 781-2010
Email: porter2010@geologist.com

Summary: We specialize in oil and gas exploration, production, refining & marketing, power generation, environmental, chemical, and also have worked aerospace, bio-technology, R&D, administrative and computer staff related to the above industries. We place some contractors.

Key Contact - Specialty:
Ms. Mary C. Porter, Principal - *Aerospace, Biotechnology*
Mr. Jim Porter, Recruiter

Salary Minimum: $60,000

Functions: Generalist (All), Engineering

Industries: Generalist (All), Energy, Utilities, Manufacturing, Transportation, Finance, Government, Environmental Svcs., Aerospace, Packaging, Software, Biotech/Life Sciences

TPR Group (Technical & Professional Recruiting)

PO Box 398
Gorham, ME 04038-0398
(207) 839-9810
(877) 490-0370
Fax: (207) 839-8557
Email: info@tprgroup.com
Web: www.tprgroup.com

Summary: Our firm works with a select group of leading companies who are searching for professionals who excel in engineering, accounting, IT, HR, medical and sales positions either in direct hire or contracting positions.

Key Contact - Specialty:
Ms. Cynthia Lebel, CPC, CTS, President - *Sales*
Mr. Lester Lebel, CPC, Vice President, Technical Recruiting Div - *Engineering, Information Technology*

Salary Minimum: $50,000

Functions: Management, Middle Mgmt., Plant Mgmt., Allied Health, Sales & Mktg., Sales Mgmt., HR Mgmt., Finance, IT, Engineering

Industries: Generalist (All)

Trace Executive Search

(a division of Trace Marketing Inc)
5560 Bee Ridge Rd Ste D5
Sarasota, FL 34233-1509
(941) 377-3700
(800) 798-7223
Fax: (941) 378-9015
Email: info@tracemarketing.com
Web: www.tracemarketing.com

Summary: We specialize in the senior housing industry including: independent senior housing, assisted living facilities, retirement communities, active adult communities, and long-term care. We are dedicated to conducting thorough searches for clients seeking top level candidates for executive positions in the retirement housing industry.

Key Contact - Specialty:
Ms. Betsy M. Hooper, Coordinator, Executive Search - *Database (Administration), Human resources, Information Technology, Research*
Ms. Tracy P. Lux, President - *Advertising, Consulting, Marketing, Strategic planning, Training*

Salary Minimum: $40,000

Functions: Senior Mgmt., Health Admin., Sales & Mktg., Mktg. Mgmt., Sales Mgmt., HR Mgmt., Finance, Specialized Svcs.

Industries: Property/Facility Mgmt., Industry Specific SW, Long-term/Home Care

Tracey-Auriema

19A Central St
Woodstock, VT 05091-1041
(802) 457-4200
Email: info@jaytracey.com
Web: www.jaytracey.com

Summary: We work with senior sales and marketing management, sales engineers, engineering management and engineering services for the industrial controls, factory automation, PLC/HMI/SCADA, MES, drives, power distribution and process control (DCS) industries.

Key Contact - Specialty:
Mr. Jay E. Tracey, Principal - *Automation, Plastics*
Mr. Mark H. Auriema, Principal - *Automation*

Salary Minimum: $75,000

Functions: Generalist (All), Senior Mgmt., Middle Mgmt., Automation, Mktg. Research, Mktg. Mgmt., Sales Mgmt., Engineering, Technicians

Industries: Generalist (All), Paper, Printing, Plastics, Rubber, Metal Products, Machine, Appliance, Computer Equip., Software

Trademark Recruiting Inc

101 E Kennedy Blvd Ste 1425
Tampa, FL 33602-5160
(813) 472-7200
Fax: (813) 472-7210
Email: croy@trademark1.net
Web: www.trademark1.net

Summary: With many years of recruiting experience, we specialize in IT, accounting and finance placements. We provide in-depth knowledge of our functional areas, personal interaction, an extensive network of qualified candidates and expertise in candidate evaluation and negotiation.

Key Contact - Specialty:
Mr. Michael C. Carideo, Partner
Mr. A. James Tagg, Partner
Mr. Bill Raferty, Senior Recruiter

Salary Minimum: $40,000

Functions: Generalist (All), Finance, IT

Industries: Generalist (All), Finance, Accounting, Mgmt. Consulting, HR Services, IT Implementation, Real Estate

Trans-United Consultants Ltd

110-3228 South Service Rd
Burlington, ON L7N 3H8
Canada
(905) 632-7176
Fax: (905) 632-5777
Email: tuc@trans-united.net
Web: www.trans-united.net

Summary: We specialize in the placement of contract and permanent engineering, design drafting/CAD, tech support, skilled trades and IT personnel.

Key Contact - Specialty:
Mr. Brian L. de Lottinville, Partner - *Engineering*
Mr. John L. Train, Partner - *Engineering*

Functions: Generalist (All), Product Dev., Production, Automation, Purchasing, Engineering

Industries: Generalist (All), Manufacturing, Environmental Svcs., Aerospace, Packaging

TransExec

PO Box 1499
La Jolla, CA 92038-1499
(858) 551-9230
Fax: (858) 551-9233
Email: resumes@trans-exec.com
Web: www.trans-exec.com

Summary: An executive search firm for the transportation industry.

Key Contact - Specialty:
Mr. Larry Christensen, Founder & President

Functions: Generalist (All)

Industries: Transportation

TranspacificGroup

9325 NE 135th Ln
Kirkland, WA 98034-1879
(425) 814-2646
Email: transpacific@comcast.net
Web: home.comcast.net/~transpacific

Summary: We specialize in placing M.D.'s, PhD's and PharmD's within Clinical R&D, Drug Safety and Medical Affairs within the pharmaceutical and biotech industries nationwide.

Key Contact - Specialty:
Mr. Tom O'Bremski, President & Executive Recruiter

Functions: Management

Industries: Biotech/Life Sciences

Travel Executive Search

(a division of Workstyles Inc)
5 Rose Ave
Great Neck, NY 11021-1530
(516) 829-8829
Email: tesintl@aol.com

Summary: We are executive recruitment specialists for the global travel industry: airlines, car rentals, motor coach, tours, corporate travel, hotel & resorts, retail, incentives, conventions & meetings, cruise companies, tourist offices, import & export, international, sports & entertainment, internet and eCommerce.

Key Contact - Specialty:
Ms. Karen Rubin, President - *Hospitality, Tourism, Transportation, Travel*

Salary Minimum: $30,000

Functions: Generalist (All), Management, Product Dev., Sales & Mktg., HR Mgmt., Finance, IT, Int'l.

Industries: Transportation, Finance, Hospitality, Media

The Travillian Group

550 American Ave Ste 203
King of Prussia, PA 19406-1441
(610) 768-2884
Fax: (610) 646-0809
Email: info@travilliangroup.com
Web: www.travilliangroup.com

Summary: Our firm is an executive recruiting firm for the financial services industry. We are an affiliate of a leading research and publishing company and recognized authority on financial institutions and utilities. We specialize in the placement of senior and mid-level executives in the commercial banking, specialty finance, insurance, real estate and energy industries, as well as with investment banks that serve them.

Key Contact - Specialty:
Mr. Peter Gray, Managing Partner
Mr. David Yancoskie, Managing Partner
Ms. Sarah Birdsong, Partner
Mr. Louis T. Steiner, Managing Director
Ms. Stephanie Baglio, Advisor
Mr. Mark Iozzi, Associate Recruiter

Functions: Management, Senior Mgmt., Middle Mgmt., HR Mgmt., Finance, CFOs

Industries: Finance

Travis & Associates

12596 E Wesley Ave
Aurora, CO 80014-1994
(720) 535-6433
Fax: (303) 632-1553
Email: victoria@travisandassociates.com
Web: www.statsearch.com

Summary: We are a full service executive search firm specializing in recruitment and placement of top talent. We focus on quality hospitals, for-profit and not-for-profit healthcare companies. One of our specialties is making sure there is a good fit between the candidate and the company for the long-term satisfaction and success of both parties. We receive high marks from candidates and clients alike in creating this powerful and successful synergy.

Key Contact - Specialty:
Ms. Victoria Travis, President - *Healthcare, Hospital, Management consulting, Medical*

Salary Minimum: $50,000

Functions: Middle Mgmt.

Industries: Mgmt. Consulting, Biotech/Life Sciences, Healthcare, Hospitals

Tri-Star Group Search LLC

630 Grove St
DeKalb, IL 60115-3864
(815) 758-6903
Email: tristargrpllc@aol.com

Summary: We specialize in the placement of HR, environmental health and safety professionals. All specialties are under the HR umbrella, in all industries. Additionally, we continue to do technical recruiting within manufacturing arena.

Key Contact - Specialty:
Mr. Tom Roff, Manager - *Human resources*

Salary Minimum: $30,000

Functions: Admin. Svcs., Product Dev., Plant Mgmt., Quality, HR Mgmt., Benefits, Staffing, Training, R&D, Minorities/Diversity

Industries: Generalist (All), Food, Bev., Tobacco, Paper, Printing, Chemicals, Soap, Perf., Cosmtcs., Drugs Mfg., Medical Devices, Plastics, Rubber, Paints, Petro. Products

Tri-Tech Associates Inc

40 Baldwin Rd
Parsippany, NJ 07054-2986
(973) 299-0055
Fax: (973) 299-0549
Email: tta@tritechnj.com
Web: www.tritechnj.com

Summary: We specialize in staffing in technical areas in manufacturing, pharmaceuticals, chemicals and electronics. We focus on product development, design, packaging, plant maintenance, QA/QC, materials management, production, IT and tech support. In addition, we have a contract assignments and payroll division.

Key Contact - Specialty:
Ms. Marlene Levitt, President
Ms. Marci Peister, Vice President, Operations
Mr. Eddie Kish, Technical Recruiter - *Biomedical, BSME, Chemical, Engineering, Manufacturing*
Ms. Florence Lucchesi, Technical Recruiter - *Accounting, Manufacturing, Manufacturing (Management), Office, Office (Administration)*

Salary Minimum: $40,000

Functions: Middle Mgmt., Mfg., Plant Mgmt., Quality, Materials, IT, Systems Dev., R&D, Engineering, Technicians

Industries: Manufacturing, Chemicals, Drugs Mfg., Medical Devices, Metal Products, Consumer Elect., Test, Measure Equip., Packaging, Software, Biotech/Life Sciences

Triad Consultants Inc

PO Box 717
West Caldwell, NJ 07007-0717
(973) 890-1655
Fax: (973) 890-9201
Email: triadconsultants@msn.com

Summary: We offer corporations and consulting firms the thoroughness and attention of retained search without advanced payment.

Key Contact - Specialty:
Mr. Jack Daudt, CPC, President - *Benefits, Compensation*

Salary Minimum: $70,000

Functions: Benefits, Mgmt. Consultants, Non-profits

Industries: Generalist (All), Banking, HR Services, Insurance

Triad Technology Group

10300 SW Greenburg Rd Ste 560
Portland, OR 97223-5466
(503) 293-9547
(866) 388-7423
Fax: (503) 293-9546
Email: triadjob@triadtechnology.com
Web: www.triadtechnology.com

Summary: We are an IT recruiting and contracting firm founded to provide a wide range of systems development and software engineering services including programming, relational database management system design, development and implementation and system integration.

Key Contact - Specialty:
Mr. Bruno C. Amicci, CPC, President & Chief Executive Officer
Mr. Jack Carpenter, Vice President & General Manager
Mr. Ed Pasco, Manager, Sales & Marketing
Mr. Richard Amicci, Manager, Accounts
Mr. Mark Folkard, Senior Resource Manager
Ms. Roslyn McFarland, Senior Resource Manager
Ms. Melanie Welker, Office Administrator - *Marketing, Media, Sales, Staffing, Technology*

Salary Minimum: $45,000

Functions: Generalist (All), IT, MIS Mgmt., Systems Analysis, Systems Dev., Systems Implem., Systems Support, DB Admin.

Industries: Generalist (All), Software

Triangle Technology

9050 N Capital Of Texas Hwy Ste 130
Austin, TX 78759-7256
(512) 498-9090
(877) 317-7446
Fax: (512) 498-9206
Email: info@triangletechnology.com
Web: www.triangletechnology.com

Summary: We are agents for the top technical talent. Our unique personal approach to technical staffing is focused on one goal...your goal.

Key Contact - Specialty:
Mr. Ray Schwitters, President
Mrs. Tiffany Howard, Principal
Mr. Jon Howard, Principal

Salary Minimum: $50,000

Functions: IT, Systems Analysis, Systems Dev., Systems Implem., Systems Support, Network Admin.

Industries: Communications, Software

Trillium Staffing Solutions

2323 Gull Rd Ste A
Kalamazoo, MI 49048-1400
(269) 345-4400
(269) 345-0150
Fax: (269) 345-9933
Email: klmz@trilliumstaffing.com
Web: www.trilliumstaffing.com

Summary: Our expanding executive recruiting division offers clients a broad recruiting network due to the support by our two technical contract companies and our many branch offices.

Key Contact - Specialty:
Ms. Carol Cosgriff, Professional Placement

Functions: Generalist (All), Management, Mfg., Sales & Mktg., Finance, IT, Engineering

Industries: Generalist (All), Manufacturing, Transportation

Branches:
3401 16th St
Moline, IL 61265-6046
(888) 695-4239
(309) 762-0045
Fax: (309) 762-0084
Key Contact - Specialty:
Ms. Liz Hartman, Recruiter

100 S Main St
Morton, IL 61550-2062
(309) 263-2277
Fax: (309) 263-5558
Email: morton@trilliumstaffing.com
Key Contact - Specialty:
Ms. Kathy Volmer

65 Patrick Dr Ste E
Bad Axe, MI 48413-9005
(989) 269-6923
Fax: (989) 269-8392
Email: badaxe@trilliumstaffing.com
Key Contact - Specialty:
Ms. Yvette Serrato, Area Manager
Ms. Joan Zemer, Account Representative

10524 Grand River Rd Ste 109
Brighton, MI 48116-9559
(810) 229-2033
Email: brighton@trilliumstaffing.com
Key Contact - Specialty:
Ms. Stephanie Pahl, Branch Manager
Ms. Kerie Dwyer, Staffing Consultant
Ms. Kristin Long, Staffing Consultant

114 W Harris St Ste B
Charlotte, MI 48813-2311
(989) 543-2023
Fax: (989) 543-5992
Email: charlotte@trilliumstaffing.com
Key Contact - Specialty:
Ms. Ginny Chase

836 E Bay St
East Tawas, MI 48730-1675
(989) 362-3452
Fax: (989) 362-6444
Email: tawas@trilliumstaffing.com
Key Contact - Specialty:
Ms. Carole Adams, Staffing Consultant

2222 S Linden Rd
Flint, MI 48532-5475
(810) 733-7180
Fax: (810) 733-2560
Email: flint@trilliumstaffing.com
Key Contact - Specialty:
Ms. Anne Magalski, Area Manager
Ms. Nicole Bixby, Staffing Consultant
Ms. Linda Niedecken, Staffing Consultant
Ms. Lisa Kolander, Staffing Consultant

255 28th St SE
Grand Rapids, MI 49548-1144
(616) 245-3300
Fax: (616) 245-3353
Key Contact - Specialty:
Mr. Mark Coisck

950 W Monroe St Ste 100
Jackson, MI 49202-2079
(517) 782-8231
Fax: (517) 782-9341
Email: jackson@trilliumstaffing.com
Key Contact - Specialty:
Ms. Judy Romanowski, Branch Manager

588 Olds St
Jonesville, MI 49250-9475
(616) 849-0062
Fax: (616) 849-0067
Email: jonesville@trilliumstaffing.com
Key Contact - Specialty:
Ms. Kathy O'Whene

558 S Main St Ste 3
Lapeer, MI 48446-2467
(810) 664-6688
Fax: (810) 664-1773
Email: lapeer@trilliumstaffing.com
Key Contact - Specialty:
Ms. Sherry Hemingway, Branch Manager
Ms. Lisa LeMieux, Account Representative
Ms. Jamie Swett, Staffing Consultant

422 E Michigan Ave
Marshall, MI 49068-1667
(616) 781-9727
Fax: (616) 781-7080
Email: marshall@trilliumstaffing.com
Key Contact - Specialty:
Ms. Cindy Fidler

901 E Indian St
Midland, MI 48640-5397
(517) 631-7851
Fax: (517) 631-5770
Email: midland@trilliumstaffing.com
Key Contact - Specialty:
Mr. Todd Johnroe, Branch Manager
Ms. Lisa Maxwell, Staffing Consultant
Ms. Melody Liverett, Staffing Consultant

1956 S 11th St
Niles, MI 49120-4059
(616) 684-6141
Fax: (616) 684-1677
Email: niles@trilliumstaffing.com
Key Contact - Specialty:
Ms. Cathie McIntyre

5375 Hampton Pl
Saginaw, MI 48604-9478
(989) 799-5960
Fax: (989) 799-8570
Email: saginaw@trilliumstaffing.com
Key Contact - Specialty:
Ms. Karen Gentle, Account Representative
Ms. Karen Musial, Staffing Consultant
Ms. Janie Thayer, Staffing Consultant

4055 W Dickman Rd Ste A
Springfield, MI 49015-1294
(616) 964-2225
Fax: (616) 964-9710
Email: battlecreek@trilliumstaffing.com
Key Contact - Specialty:
Ms. Cindi Liezert

912 W Chicago Rd
Sturgis, MI 49091-9701
(616) 651-9902
Fax: (616) 659-4886
Email: sturgis@trilliumstaffing.com
Key Contact - Specialty:
Ms. Lisa Stewart

844 Willard Dr
Green Bay, WI 54304-5265
(920) 498-9090
Fax: (920) 498-9095
Email: greenbay@trilliumstaffing.com
Key Contact - Specialty:
Mr. Tom Valeko

Trinity Group

Duncan Hill Rd Ste 219
Hendersonville, NC 28792-2714
(828) 698-8810
Fax: (828) 698-8552
Email: joe@trinitygroupusa.com
Web: www.trinitygroupusa.com

Summary: Trinity Group is an executive search
firm specializing in a broad spectrum of
disciplines, and is committed to a strong personal
involvement in the recruitment and placement of
A-Level professionals.

Key Contact - Specialty:
Mr. Joe Maxey, Managing Partner - *Engineering,
Executives, General management, Middle
management, Senior management*
Mr. Peter G. Neale, Manager, Recruiting -
*Capital goods, Engineering, Manufacturing,
Operations, Packaging*
Mr. David Walker, Senior Account Executive -
*Chemical, Engineering, Petrochemical, Plastics,
Refineries*

Salary Minimum: $50,000

Functions: Management, Senior Mgmt., Middle
Mgmt., Mfg., Plant Mgmt., Distribution,
Packaging, Finance, R&D, Engineering

Industries: Energy, Utilities, Oil & Gas,
Manufacturing, Chemicals, Plastics, Rubber,
Finance, Banking, Invest. Banking, Engineering
Svcs., Logistics Svcs., Supply Chain Mgmt,
Media, Packaging

Trinity Staffing Services

14100 San Pedro Ave Ste 420
San Antonio, TX 78232-4362
(210) 805-9920
Fax: (210) 805-9716
Email: jpjones@trinitystaffing.com
Web: www.trinitystaffing.com

Summary: We are a full service, independent,
locally owned recruiting service firm with six full
time professional recruiters working in a variety of
industrial classifications and occupations. Some of
our areas of specialization include defense related
industries, engineers, sales, IT, energy and
finance.

Key Contact - Specialty:
Mr. J.P. Jones, Principal
Ms. Shalon Tillotson, Account Manager
Mrs. Nellie Hernandez, Consultant, Workforce
Solutions - *Administration, Sales, Staffing*
Mrs. Connie Salas, Account Manager -
Manufacturing
Mrs. Kelly Allerheiligen, Account Manager
Mrs. Sue Jones, President

Salary Minimum: $40,000

Functions: Generalist (All)

Industries: Generalist (All), Oil & Gas,
Manufacturing, Finance, Services,
Communications, Call Centers, Defense,
Software

TriStaff Group

6336 Greenwich Dr Ste 100
San Diego, CA 92122-5922
(858) 453-1331
Fax: (858) 453-6022

Email: sandiego@tristaff.com
Web: www.tristaff.com

Summary: We utilize resources that are untapped
by conventional recruiting methods. We focus our
efforts on top performers who may not be actively
seeking a new position or answering employment
ads.

Key Contact - Specialty:
Mr. Gary van Eik, Chief Executive Officer
Mr. Richard Papike, President
Ms. Amy Moser, Vice President
Mr. Brett Lesser, Director, Recruiting
Ms. Kanani Moser, Director, Software
Recruitment
Ms. Susan Bernstein, Director, Software Recruit
and Marketing
Ms. Rhonda Lord, Director, Building Materials
Division
Mr. Alex Papike, Executive Recruiter
Mr. Chris Papike, Executive Recruiter
Ms. Melissa Lockwood, Consultant -
Engineering, Manufacturing

Functions: Generalist (All), Senior Mgmt.,
Physicians, Health Admin., CFOs, Systems
Analysis, Systems Dev., Engineering

Industries: Generalist (All), Computer Equip.,
Accounting, Mgmt. Consulting, Publishing,
Broadcast, Film, Healthcare

Branches:
3730 S Susan St Ste 100
Santa Ana, CA 92704-6959
(714) 513-9414
Fax: (714) 513-9417
Email: orangecounty@tristaff.com
Key Contact - Specialty:
Mr. Jason van Eik, Manager

The Truman Agency

13200 Crossroads Pkwy N Ste 470
City of Industry, CA 91746-3420
(562) 908-1233
Fax: (562) 908-1238
Email: jobs@trumanagency.com
Web: www.trumanagency.com

Summary: We offer confidential management
recruiting serving the manufacturing and
distribution industry sectors. Our strengths are in
administration, sales, accounting, plant/production
management, engineering and IT. A full service
agency, we can also provide administrative
support staff. Permanent placement and
contract/temp services are available.

Key Contact - Specialty:
Mr. Robert P. Zirbes, President

Salary Minimum: $30,000

Functions: Management, Mfg., Production,
Materials, Sales & Mktg., HR Mgmt., Finance,
IT

Industries: Generalist (All)

TSC Group

226-6 Lansing Sq
North York, ON M2J 1T5
Canada
(416) 494-6868
Fax: (416) 494-6171
Email: info@tscgroup.ca
Web: www.tscgroup.ca

Summary: We specialize in the placement of
technical and engineering related positions for
numerous types of organizations: manufacturing,
consulting engineering, government, construction,
automotive, etc.

Key Contact - Specialty:
Mr. Lesley Wieser
Mr. Bob Carro

Salary Minimum: $30,000

Functions: Mfg., Product Dev., Production, Plant
Mgmt., Quality, Purchasing, Sales & Mktg.,
R&D, Engineering, Architects

Industries: Generalist (All)

TSC Management Services Group Inc

(also known as Blue Marble Studios)
112 Wool St
Barrington, IL 60010-4503
(847) 381-0167
Fax: (847) 381-1977
Email: information@tscsearch.com
Web: www.tscsearch.com

Summary: We are a recruiting/search firm in the
entertainment/gaming industry. Contingency as
well as retained services. Our specialty is video
gaming; more specifically: coin-operated, PC,
home/console systems, wireless, Internet and
wagering.

Key Contact - Specialty:
Mr. Robert G. Stanton, Sr., President
Mr. Grant Stanton, Executive Vice President &
Secretary - *Gaming*
Ms. Gina Hess, Recruiter
Ms. Lisa Buechele, Recruiter
Mr. Steve Gotsis, Recruiter
Mr. Craig Sallas, Recruiter - *Diversity*

Salary Minimum: $50,000

Functions: Generalist (All)

Industries: Entertainment, Sports, Advertising,
Publishing, New Media, Broadcast, Film,
Wireless, Entertainment SW, Industry Specific
SW

TSI Group Inc.

(formerly known as TSI Group)
700-2630 Skymark Ave
Mississauga, ON L4W 5A4
Canada
(905) 629-3701
Fax: (905) 629-0799
Email: tsi@tsigroup.com
Web: www.tsigroup.com

Summary: We are a professional services firm
specializing in serving the needs of transportation
and logistics companies, as well as companies
with supply chain operations. Our services
include: recruitment, staffing, mergers &
acquisitions, training & development and advisory
services in supply chain, HR and general business
management issues.

Key Contact - Specialty:
Ms. Pamela Ruebusch, President & Chief
Executive Officer
Mr. Larry Dries, Chief Operating Officer

Salary Minimum: $40,000

Functions: Management, Production, Distribution

Industries: Agri., Forestry, Mining, Energy,
Utilities, Oil & Gas, Manufacturing, Food, Bev.,
Tobacco, Textiles, Apparel, Lumber, Furniture,
Chemicals, Transportation, Wholesale, Retail,
Mgmt. Consulting, HR Services, Logistics
Svcs., Packaging, ERP SW

TSS Consulting Ltd

2525 E Arizona Biltmore Cir Ste A114
Phoenix, AZ 85016-2146
(800) 489-2425
(602) 795-1047
Fax: (602) 795-0342
Email: resume@tss-consulting.com
Web: www.tss-consulting.com

Summary: We are a high-technology/executive recruitment firm with concentration in CAD/CAE, system software, semiconductor, government electronics, artificial intelligence and associated executive functions.

Key Contact - Specialty:
Mr. John R. McDonald, President - *Electronics, High technology*

Salary Minimum: $100,000

Functions: Generalist (All), Systems Dev., R&D, Engineering

Industries: Generalist (All), Computer Equip., Test, Measure Equip., Electronic, Elec. Components, Semiconductors, Digital, Wireless, RF/Microwave, Aerospace, Networking, Comm. SW

TSS Resources

8191 Glencree Pl
Dublin, OH 43016-9523
(614) 799-9300
Email: gberke@tssresources.com
Web: www.tssresources.com

Summary: We specialize in identifying and recruiting IT professionals. We are a group of technology executives with both the technical and management experience to accurately understand your staffing needs. Our industry- experienced staff provides an unusually high level of technical and interpersonal prequalification, so our clients see only the best candidates.

Key Contact - Specialty:
Ms. Ginny Berke, Managing Partner - *Telecommunications*

Salary Minimum: $50,000

Functions: Management, Senior Mgmt., Middle Mgmt., Sales & Mktg., IT, MIS Mgmt., Network Admin., Engineering, Eng. Design, Technicians

Industries: Generalist (All), Computer Equip., Banking, Equip Svcs., E-commerce, IT Implementation, PSA/ASP, Communications, Database SW, ERP SW, Networking, Comm. SW, Security SW

Tsunami Partners

66 Marston St
Medford, MA 02155-4469
(781) 395-2981
(617) 293-4345
Fax: (720) 834-6846
Email: dcoger@comcast.net
Web: www.tsunamipartners.net

Summary: We are an executive search firm that works on a retained or contingency basis. We have capabilities in high technology, financial services, biotechnology, industrial, manufacturing and service company assignments. Positions we have filled include CEO, President, CFO, CTO, SVP of Marketing, Sales and Engineering and the whole gamut of mid level and individual contributor positions.

Key Contact - Specialty:
Mr. Dal Coger, Contact Recruiter

Salary Minimum: $75,000

Functions: Management

Industries: Software, Accounting SW, Database SW, Doc. Mgmt., Production SW, ERP SW, HR SW, Mfg. SW, Marketing SW, Networking, Comm. SW, Security SW

Tumbiolo & Associates

2889 W Bainbridge Rd
San Diego, CA 92106-6074
(619) 224-1923
Fax: (619) 521-4890
Email: salesjob@cox.net

Summary: We offer executive search and recruitment services for clients and candidates in food industry and consumer goods. We place candidates in areas of sales and marketing. We offer the client a professional and knowledgeable approach to recruitment needs and sources.

Key Contact - Specialty:
Mrs. Lisa Tumbiolo, President

Functions: Sales & Mktg.

Industries: Food, Bev., Tobacco, Soap, Perf., Cosmtcs., Consumer Goods

Turnage Employment Service Group

1225 Breckenridge Dr Ste 206
Little Rock, AR 72205-1500
(501) 224-6870
(888) 264-6870
Fax: (501) 224-5709
Email: lindad@turnage-employment.com
Web: www.turnage-employment.com

Summary: We are the agency you can trust. Many of our client companies use us exclusively for all their staffing needs. Our goal is to provide quality service with a personalized approach; we will screen to exact specifications, saving your valuable time. We check references and test for specific openings.

Key Contact - Specialty:
Ms. Linda Dicus

Salary Minimum: $40,000

Functions: Management, Mfg., Production, Plant Mgmt., Healthcare, Physicians, Nurses, Allied Health, Sales & Mktg., Systems Dev.

Industries: Generalist (All), Misc. Mfg., Software, Healthcare, Dental, Physical Therapy, Occupational Therapy

Branches:
719 Front St
Conway, AR 72032-5421
(501) 327-6181
Fax: (501) 327-9376
Key Contact - Specialty:
Ms. Wanda Fields, Office Manager

425 E 4th St
Russellville, AR 72801-5218
(479) 967-4040
Email: turnage@cswnet.com
Key Contact - Specialty:
Mrs. Julia Light, Office Manager
Mrs. Michelle Brown, Counselor

J Q Turner & Associates Inc

PO Box 2195
Estes Park, CO 80517-2195
(970) 577-0789
Email: jim1@jqt.com
Web: www.jqt.com

Summary: We specialize placing people with a B.S., M.S., Ph.D., EE, ME or a physical/life science degree or technical professionals. We place in the following: R&D, process, manufacturing, quality, test, project, plant, for

electronics (ASICs), semiconductor, telecom, biomedical, mass storage, energetic materials, instrumentation, etc.

Key Contact - Specialty:
Mr. Jim Turner, President - *Engineering*

Salary Minimum: $50,000

Functions: Generalist (All), Process, Design

Industries: Manufacturing, Medical Devices, Plastics, Rubber, Machine, Appliance, Computer Equip., Consumer Elect., Test, Measure Equip., Communications, Digital, Wireless, Fiber Optic, Network Infrastructure, RF/Microwave, Software, Database SW, Development SW, Biotech/Life Sciences

Turning Point Inc

405 2nd St S Ste A
Safety Harbor, FL 34695-4014
(727) 725-8876
Email: mitch@tpisearch.com
Web: www.tpisearch.com

Summary: Our primary emphasis is currently on doing targeted executive search work and recruiting for various securities broker-dealers, insurance companies, and banks. We have additional interest and contacts in the asset management, non-profit, private banking/trust company arenas and with companies that are service and product vendors to the financial services industry.

Key Contact - Specialty:
Mr. Mitch Vigeveno, President - *Banking, Financial services, Insurance (Life), Investment, Securities*
Mr. Steve McQuinn, Vice President - *Banking, Banking (Investment), C-level, Financial services, Regulatory*
Mr. Jason Burke, Office Manager - *Office*

Salary Minimum: $75,000

Functions: Management, Sales & Mktg.

Industries: Banking, Invest. Banking, Brokers, Mutual/Hedge Funds, Misc. Financial, Non-profits, Insurance, Life

The Twin Oaks Team Inc

3604 Penhurst Pl
Raleigh, NC 27613-1226
(919) 870-5737
Fax: (919) 870-9464
Email: careers@twinoaksteam.com
Web: www.twinoaksteam.com

Summary: We recruit experienced sales, management and manufacturing candidates for sheet-fed and web offset, flexo and gravure printers, including pre press, press and bindery machine operators. Emergency consulting to solve problems that cause crisis for printing companies.

Key Contact - Specialty:
Mr. Stan Morse, President - *Printing*

Salary Minimum: $24,000

Functions: Senior Mgmt., Middle Mgmt., Plant Mgmt., Packaging, Sales & Mktg., HR Mgmt., CFOs, Engineering, Graphic Designers

Industries: Printing, Packaging

Tyler Search Consultants

400A Lake St
Ramsey, NJ 07446-1243
(201) 934-9880
Fax: (201) 934-9858
Email: careers@tylersearch.com
Web: www.tylersearch.com

Summary: We are dedicated to the, supply chain management, global trade, logistics and

transportation community. All of our recruiters are former supply chain professionals with a thorough understanding of our marketplace.

Key Contact - Specialty:
Mr. William Conroy, Executive Director - *Compliance, Distribution, Logistics, Supply Chain, Transportation*
Ms. Kristine Quick - *Compliance, Logistics, Purchasing, Supply Chain, Transportation*

Salary Minimum: $80,000

Functions: Management, Board Members, Senior Mgmt., Middle Mgmt., Mfg., Materials, Purchasing, Distribution, Sales Mgmt., Sales Reps.

Industries: Generalist (All), Manufacturing, Transportation, Logistics Svcs., Supply Chain Mgmt, Compliance

Uniquest International Consulting Inc

11015 N Dale Mabry Hwy Ste A
Tampa, FL 33618-3872
(813) 387-1000
Fax: (813) 387-3000
Email: info@uniquest.com
Web: www.uniquest.com

Summary: Our firm specializes in healthcare finance and administration. We enjoy an excellent reputation for comprehensive knowledge of the latest developments and trends. We have developed a proprietary database of over 50,000 healthcare individuals while forging strong relationships with many key people. We are the relationship healthcare recruiters.

Key Contact - Specialty:
Mr. Anthony F. Valone, President - *Healthcare*
Mr. Michael Valone, Vice President - *Healthcare*
Mr. Mike Pond, Senior Consultant - *Healthcare*
Mr. Marvin Falis, Senior Consultant - *Healthcare*
Ms. Judi Valone, Senior Consultant - *Healthcare*
Mr. Sandy Eastlick, Senior Consultant

Salary Minimum: $50,000

Functions: Senior Mgmt., Middle Mgmt., HR Mgmt., Finance, Cash Mgmt., Credit, Taxes, Mgmt. Consultants, Legal, Attorneys

Industries: Healthcare, Hospitals, Long-term/Home Care

Unisearch Search & Recruiting Inc

1651 E 4th St Ste 248
Santa Ana, CA 92701-5175
(714) 836-3600
Email: unisearch@sbcglobal.net

Summary: Executive search in the following industries: banking, finance, healthcare, legal, and plastics

Key Contact - Specialty:
Ms. Patricia Langdon, President - *Accounting, Asset management, CFOs, Controllers, Mergers & acquisitions*
Mr. Phillip DeMarks, Senior Account Executive - *Asset management, Banking, Banking (Commercial,Corporate,Investment)*
Mr. John Rhynerson, Senior Account Executive - *Intellectual property, Labor, Legal, Legal (Attorneys), Tax*
Ms. Susan Almond, Account Executive - *Manufacturing, Medical, Medical (Devices), Molding, Molding (Blown)*

Salary Minimum: $70,000

Functions: Management, Middle Mgmt., Production, Plant Mgmt., Healthcare, Sales & Mktg., Benefits, M&A, Attorneys

Industries: Paper, Printing, Medical Devices, Plastics, Rubber, Metal Products, Electronic, Elec. Components, Consumer Goods, Finance, Banking, Legal, Accounting, Mgmt. Consulting, Packaging, Healthcare, Hospitals, Long-term/Home Care, Occupational Therapy

Branches:
3318 Newport Dr
Lake Havasu City, AZ 86406-5558
(928) 680-6077
Email: jenrico@juno.com
Key Contact - Specialty:
Mr. James Enrico, Senior Account Executive & Branch Mgr

United Search

21 Market St
Onancock, VA 23417-1911
(757) 787-2332
Fax: (757) 787-2448
Email: usearch@intercom.net
Web: www.unitedsearch1.com

Summary: We are a professional, technical and executive search firm servicing clients in the chemical process, petroleum products, consumer products, pharmaceutical, bio-technology and custom engineered processing equipment industries. We specialize in uncovering professionals with expertise in chemical, mechanical, electrical and environmental engineering.

Key Contact - Specialty:
Mr. Ed Oswald, Director, Recruiting

Salary Minimum: $50,000

Functions: Mfg., Purchasing, Sales & Mktg., Engineering

Industries: Manufacturing, Food, Bev., Tobacco, Chemicals, Drugs Mfg., Medical Devices, Plastics, Rubber, Paints, Petro. Products, Metal Products, Misc. Mfg., Biotech/Life Sciences, Healthcare

United Search Associates

(also known as Health Network USA)
3201 Chimneyrock Dr
Plano, TX 75023-5621
(972) 519-0863
Fax: (972) 964-8696
Email: info@unitedsearch.com
Web: www.unitedsearch.com

Summary: We specialize in the placement of healthcare professionals. Clients include hospitals, clinics and other providers.

Key Contact - Specialty:
Mr. David J. Elliott, President - *Healthcare*
Ms. C.J. Elliott, Vice President - *Healthcare*

Salary Minimum: $40,000

Functions: Healthcare, Physicians, Nurses, Allied Health, Health Admin., HR Mgmt., CFOs

Industries: Generalist (All), Pharm Svcs., Healthcare, Hospitals, Physical Therapy, Occupational Therapy

Unlimited Nurse Search Inc

12520 High Bluff Dr Ste 140
San Diego, CA 92130-2061
(858) 350-3990
(800) 903-8532
Fax: (858) 350-3998
Email: ngruzd@unlimitednursesearch.com
Web: www.unlimitednursesearch.com

Summary: We are specialists in the placement of healthcare professionals into full time positions across the USA.

Key Contact - Specialty:
Mrs. Nadia Gruzd, President
Mr. John Yenney, Vice President
Mrs. Kim Aires, Director, Licensure & Immigration

Functions: Nurses

Industries: Hospitals, Long-term/Home Care, Physical Therapy, Occupational Therapy, Women's

Unlimited Resources

PO Box 6361
Lawrenceville, NJ 08648-0361
(609) 275-1986
Fax: (775) 806-7218
Email: info@urhire.com
Web: www.urhire.com

Summary: We have extensive experience in executive search for the retail and restaurant industries, and both the healthcare and IT sectors. We pride ourselves in providing best practice recruitment techniques to our corporate clients, large and small. We consult with them in a collaborative manner to ensure a search resulting in the recruitment and retention of the finest talent.

Key Contact - Specialty:
Ms. Alyson Parker, Managing Director

Functions: Middle Mgmt.

Industries: Generalist (All), Retail, Restaurants, Quick Service Restaurants, Full Service Restaurants

Uptheladder

290 Riverside Dr Apt 11A
New York, NY 10025-5277
(212) 222-6543
Fax: (212) 865-2008
Email: uptheladder@earthlink.net

Summary: Our firm performs executive searches, specializing in recruiting high level sales, marketing, technical & financial executives and managers for the financial call center, internet and software industries. Our candidates include high-level sales executives, all levels of management and key corporate personnel. Our philosophy is to develop a strong understanding of our clients needs and exceed their recruiting expectations.

Key Contact - Specialty:
Ms. Lucy Lasky, Chief Executive Officer

Salary Minimum: $45,000

Functions: Generalist (All)

Industries: Misc. Mfg., Banking, Invest. Banking, Misc. Financial, New Media, Broadcast, Film, Communications

The Urban Placement Service

PO Box 8040
Houston, TX 77288-8040
(713) 880-2211
Fax: (713) 880-5577
Email: urbanplacement@msn.com
Web: www.urbanplacement.com

Summary: Professional search: minority recruitment; accounting/finance, engineering, marketing/sales, production/logistics and HR.

Key Contact - Specialty:
Mr. Willie S. Bright, Owner

Salary Minimum: $50,000

Functions: Generalist (All), Mfg., Materials, Sales & Mktg., HR Mgmt., Finance, Engineering, Minorities/Diversity

Industries: Generalist (All), Manufacturing, Food, Bev., Tobacco, Chemicals, Drugs Mfg., Consumer Elect., Finance, Services, Pharm Svcs., Healthcare

Urpan Technologies Inc

341 Cobalt Way Ste 208
Sunnyvale, CA 94085-5405
(408) 245-0006
(408) 314-8997
Fax: (408) 245-5421
Email: pad@urpantech.com
Web: www.urpantech.com

Summary: Our firm is engaged in providing IT staffing, for the temp and permanent space, project staffing globally, as well provide market advisory services and software design, programming and testing services for the enterprise both on site and offshore. We can also provide permanent staffing at senior levels in IT as well as provide recruiting outsourcing services.

Key Contact - Specialty:
Mr. Pad N. Swami, President & Chief Executive Officer - *Information Technology, SAP*
Ms. Usha Padmanabhan, Director
Ms. Naveena Salla, Director, Resourcing - *CRM, Information Systems, Information Technology, Quality, SAP*

Salary Minimum: $40,000

Functions: Generalist (All), IT, Systems Analysis

Industries: Generalist (All), Energy, Utilities, Manufacturing, Retail, Finance, Services, Hospitality, Communications, Insurance, Software, Database SW, Development SW, Doc. Mgmt., Production SW, ERP SW, HR SW, Industry Specific SW, Mfg. SW, Networking, Comm. SW, Security SW, System SW, Healthcare, Non-Classifiable

US Gas/Search

PO Box 806
Claremore, OK 74018-0806
(918) 543-6000
Fax: (918) 543-6003
Email: keithl@ionet.net

Summary: We possess one of the finest networks of contacts, knowledge and ability of matching needs and talents in the gas industry today. This enables us to attract the very finest talent available and allows us to excel in gathering data important to your continued success.

Key Contact - Specialty:
Mr. Keith Louderback, Owner - *Marketing*

Salary Minimum: $70,000

Functions: Generalist (All), Senior Mgmt., Middle Mgmt., Mktg. Mgmt., Engineering

Industries: Generalist (All), Energy, Utilities

US Recruiting

6919 W Broward Blvd Ste 269
Plantation, FL 33317-2902
(954) 563-3230
(800) 916-9717
Fax: (954) 585-6349
Email: jason@usrecruiting.com
Web: www.usrecruiting.com

Summary: Executive search firm with specialties in property/casualty insurance, finance, sales and technology.

Key Contact - Specialty:
Mr. Jason Redman, President
Mr. Andy Kelly, Vice President

Functions: Generalist (All)

Industries: Banking, Brokers, Misc. Financial, Mgmt. Consulting, HR Services, Insurance, Casualty, Claims, Commercial, Re-Insurance

US Search LLC

712 W Broad St Ste 3
Falls Church, VA 22046-3222
(703) 448-1900
(800) 784-0099
Fax: (703) 448-1907
Email: info@ussearchllc.com
Web: www.ussearchllc.com

Summary: We provide industry specialized recruitment and are a search firm with a long history of experience delivering timely, discrete service. We provide effective service to our clients in all phases of the plastics and specialty materials industries. We have always believed that 'our clients are our best references'.

Key Contact - Specialty:
Mr. Arnie Hiller, President - *Plastics*

Salary Minimum: $60,000

Functions: Senior Mgmt., Mfg., Product Dev., Purchasing, Mktg. Mgmt., Sales Mgmt., R&D, Engineering

Industries: Generalist (All), Manufacturing, Chemicals, Plastics, Rubber, Paints, Petro. Products, Leather, Stone, Glass, Machine, Appliance, Packaging

US-Recruiters.com

(a division of RL Rystrom & Associates Inc)
11325 172nd St W
Lakeville, MN 55044-9325
(952) 435-6457
(612) 414-7072
Email: mail@rystrom.com
Web: www.us-recruiters.com

Summary: The nation's leading recruiters are members of our organization. We invite you to check out our posted jobs and submit your resume to our members by industry and or you can submit your resume to the candidate database.

Key Contact - Specialty:
Ms. Sally A. Geving, Vice President
Mr. Robert L. Rystrom, CRM, President & Chief Executive Officer

Salary Minimum: $60,000

Functions: Generalist (All), Middle Mgmt., Mktg. Research, Mktg. Mgmt.

Industries: Generalist (All), Computer Equip., Test, Measure Equip., Mgmt. Consulting, Software

USA Medical Placement Inc

3604 Date Palm Ave
McAllen, TX 78501-7901
(956) 631-3540
Fax: (956) 686-3540
Email: usamedpt@aol.com

Summary: We are a medical search firm specializing in administration, nursing and physicians. We treat each hospital or candidate with individual consideration. The degree of abilities, whether client or candidate, is a factor in our searches.

Key Contact - Specialty:
Ms. Patricia Tracy, President

Salary Minimum: $50,000

Functions: Physicians, Nurses

Industries: Healthcare, Hospitals

Valacon Inc

PO Box 6136
Altadena, CA 91003-6136
(626) 296-2751
Fax: (626) 296-2760
Email: info@valacon.com
Web: www.valacon.com

Summary: We are IT audit specialists. All our recruiters have relevant industry experience in addition to recruiting experience. We only present candidate approved resumes to clients.

Key Contact - Specialty:
Mr. Sandy Geffner, President

Salary Minimum: $40,000

Functions: Risk Mgmt.

Industries: Generalist (All)

Van Curan & Associates

PO Box 148
Prides Crossing, MA 01965-0148
(978) 922-4460
(978) 886-1812
Email: cdvc5@yahoo.com

Summary: We do retained and contingent executive and professional searches focused on the financial services industries, especially insurance and banking. We publish an insurance compensation survey annually.

Key Contact - Specialty:
Mr. Christopher D. Van Curan, Principal - *Financial services*
Mr. Frank Hoskin, Jr., CPCU, Senior Consultant

Salary Minimum: $75,000

Functions: Management, Senior Mgmt.

Industries: Finance, Banking, Non-profits, Insurance, Casualty, Claims, Life, Commercial, Re-Insurance

Van Popering McLogan Executive Search Inc (VPML Inc)

716 W Kilgore Rd
Kalamazoo, MI 49008-3612
(269) 344-0400
Fax: (269) 344-7476
Email: execsearch@vpml.com
Web: www.vpml.com

Summary: Our specialty is to serve all disciplines of the banking and financial services area. We also handle Accounting and Human Resources assignments.

Key Contact - Specialty:
Mr. Greg McLogan, Partner - *Financial services, Human resources*
Ms. Laura Van Popering, Partner - *Financial services, Human resources*

Salary Minimum: $50,000

Functions: Generalist (All), Management, Middle Mgmt., Product Dev., Sales Mgmt., HR Mgmt., Benefits, Attorneys

Industries: Finance, Banking, Accounting, HR Services

Dick Van Vliet & Associates

13405 Southwest Fwy Ste 115
Sugar Land, TX 77478-3559
(281) 265-8080
Email: dick@dickvanvliet.com
Web: www.dickvanvliet.com

Summary: We place accounting/financial professionals. Our client companies include Fortune 500 companies, Big 4, CPA firms as well

as growth industry and service companies. We meticulously over-screen applicants to insure a good match for our clients and for our candidates.

Key Contact - Specialty:
Mr. Dick Van Vliet, President - *Financial*

Salary Minimum: $35,000

Functions: Finance

Industries: Energy, Utilities, Oil & Gas, Construction, Manufacturing, Misc. Mfg., Services, Accounting

Van Zant Inc

9712 E Pershing Ave
Scottsdale, AZ 85260-4437
(480) 314-5750
Fax: (480) 314-1963
Email: infotech@primenet.com

Summary: Our firm specializes in IT, engineering technology, sales, marketing and high-level management positions. We offer clients and candidates the widest range of staffing services available anywhere in search, recruiting or employment agent business.

Key Contact - Specialty:
Mr. Mike Van Zant, Owner

Functions: Board Members, Senior Mgmt., Sales & Mktg., IT, MIS Mgmt., Systems Dev., Network Admin., DB Admin.

Industries: Generalist (All), Energy, Utilities, Drugs Mfg., Transportation, Banking, Brokers, Legal, Mgmt. Consulting, E commerce, IT Implementation, Advertising, Communications, Aerospace, Software, Healthcare, Dental

Van Zeeland Associates Inc

PO Box 188
Little Chute, WI 54140-0188
(920) 788-5222
Fax: (920) 788-5281
Email: gvze@gvze.com
Web: www.gvze.com

Summary: We are a direct placement staffing agency specializing in the placement of highly qualified sales/marketing professionals, engineers, upper-level management and executives within the electrical and mechanical industries.

Key Contact - Specialty:
Mr. Gary Van Zeeland, Founder & Placement Specialist
Ms. Kelly Koch, Placement Specialist
Ms. Penny Grissman, Placement Specialist

Functions: Generalist (All)

Industries: Test, Measure Equip., Misc. Mfg., Electronic, Elec. Components, Robotics

Vaughan & Company Executive Search Inc

59 Hidden Trl
Irvine, CA 92603-0212
(949) 623-3300
Fax: (949) 854-8027
Email: recruiters@vaughanandcompany.com
Web: www.vaughanandcompany.com

Summary: We offer search and placement services for professionals in the industrial sales & manufacturing, aviation, aerospace, overhaul & repair, semiconductor, electronics and other high-technology industries. We offer both contingency and retained services.

Key Contact - Specialty:
Mr. David B. Vaughan, President - *Aviation, Engineering, Industrial, Sales*

Ms. Julie Raab, Director, Major Accounts - *Aviation, Engineering, High technology, Industrial, Manufacturing*
Ms. Leah Magouirk, Executive Recruiter & Manager - *Aviation*

Salary Minimum: $75,000

Functions: Generalist (All), Senior Mgmt., Production, Sales Mgmt., Engineering

Industries: Generalist (All), Oil & Gas, Manufacturing, Plastics, Rubber, Metal Products, Misc. Mfg., Robotics, Semiconductors, Defense, Aerospace, Packaging

The Venor Group

961 Red Coat Farm Dr
Chalfont, PA 18914-4423
(215) 997-5960
Email: dgraham@venorgroup.com
Web: www.venorgroup.com

Summary: The Venor Group is an executive search firm focused on placing top talented healthcare/medical professionals in the Pharmaceutical and Biotechnology industries. Our areas of expertise include: Clinical Research & Development, Regulatory Affairs, Medical Affairs, Biostatistics and Quality

Key Contact - Specialty:
Mr. David Graham, Vice President, Executive Search

Functions: Healthcare

Industries: Drugs Mfg., Pharm Svcs., Biotech/Life Sciences

Venpro Consulting Inc

37 Rainbow Creek Way
North York, ON M2K 2T9
Canada
(416) 223-3341
Email: venpro@rogers.com

Summary: We work exclusively with software vendors. Our mission is to recruit quality sales professionals, specifically in the following job functions: sales, pre-sales support, and sales/marketing management.

Key Contact - Specialty:
Mr. Brian H. Campbell, President - *Sales*

Salary Minimum: $80,000

Functions: Sales & Mktg.

Industries: Database SW, Development SW, Doc. Mgmt., Production SW, Entertainment SW, ERP SW, HR SW, Mfg. SW, Marketing SW, Networking, Comm. SW

VerticalPath Recruiting Inc

6632 S 191st Pl Ste E101
Kent, WA 98032-2117
(425) 251-4940
(866) 760-4600
Fax: (425) 251-4945
Email: information@vertpath.com
Web: www.verticalpathrecruiting.com

Summary: Placement of contract and permanent personnel in IT, manufacturing, engineering, telecom, facilities and distribution. Specializing in placing former military candidates.

Key Contact - Specialty:
Mr. E. P. Pete Stiles, President
Ms. Charlene Young, Recruiter
Mr. Jim Barton, Recruiter
Ms. Stephanie Smiley, Recruiter - *Information Technology*
Ms. Amy Morrison, Candidate Coordinator

Salary Minimum: $45,000

Functions: Generalist (All), Board Members

Industries: Energy, Utilities, Oil & Gas, Construction, Manufacturing, Transportation, Services, IT Implementation, Communications, Government, Environmental Svcs., Aerospace

Verus Staffing Solutions LLC

2701 Tower Oaks Blvd Ste 201
Rockville, MD 20852-4239
(240) 221-2700
Fax: (240) 221-2722
Email: contact@verusstaffing.com
Web: www.verusstaffing.com

Summary: We are a permanent and contract recruiting firm that specializes in accounting and finance with a focus on tax and audit. We are comprised of very senior recruiters with extensive experience in relevant fields.

Key Contact - Specialty:
Ms. Stacy Birnbach, President - *Accounting, Accounting (Big 4,General,Public)*
Ms. Cathy Keith, Director, Sales & Operations - *Accounting, Accounting (Big 4,General,Public)*

Functions: Generalist (All), Senior Mgmt., Middle Mgmt.

Industries: Finance

The VET Recruiter

7822 E 96th Pl
Tulsa, OK 74133-6944
(918) 298-7025
(800) 436-0490
Email: stacy@thevetrecruiter.com
Web: www.thevetrecruiter.com

Summary: We are an executive search firm specializing in the veterinary, animal health and pet products industry. In addition to placing practicing veterinarians, chief of staffs and medical directors we place other professional level positions in all areas of the animal health industry including; management, regulatory affairs, research and development, sales and marketing.

Key Contact - Specialty:
Ms. Stacy Pursell, President - *Agriculture, Healthcare, Pharmaceutical, Physicians, Research & development*

Salary Minimum: $50,000

Functions: Generalist (All)

Industries: Non-Classifiable

ViLinks

660 Baker St
Costa Mesa, CA 92626-4428
(714) 708-8888
Fax: (253) 540-1926
Email: info@vilinks.com
Web: www.vilinks.com

Summary: We offer professional services, such as consulting, software, Internet and systems development & support. Our specialties are consultants, PSO, software engineering, marketing and tech support.

Key Contact - Specialty:
Mr. Richard Nelson, Principal - *Computers (Software), Consulting, Engineering, High technology, MIS*

Salary Minimum: $36,000

Functions: Engineering

Industries: Software

Villasenor & Associates

6546 San Vicente Blvd
Los Angeles, CA 90048-5340
(323) 936-4880
Fax: (323) 936-8066
Email: clickonlaw@aol.com

Summary: We specialize exclusively in placement of attorneys in law firms and corporations in the State of California. Our ability to successfully match qualified highly credentialed attorneys is the cornerstone of our highly successful search firm.

Key Contact - Specialty:
Mr. Hector Villasenor, Principal
Ms. Carole Howard, Principal

Salary Minimum: $85,000

Functions: Attorneys

Industries: Generalist (All), Legal

Vintage Resources Inc

11 E 44th St Rm 708
New York, NY 10017-0061
(212) 867-1001
Fax: (212) 490-9277
Email: careers@vintageresourcesinc.com
Web: www.vintageresourcesinc.com

Summary: Clients seeking a cost efficient, personalized approach from a select staff of recruitment professionals serving the advertising/direct marketing industries are encouraged to call us.

Key Contact - Specialty:
Mr. Perry Fishman, Vice President
Ms. Judy Fishman, Vice President

Salary Minimum: $30,000

Functions: Sales & Mktg., Advertising, Mktg. Research, Mktg. Mgmt., Direct Mktg.

Industries: Media, Advertising, Publishing, New Media, Broadcast, Film, Telecoms

Virtual HR Associates

23171 Heatherwood Ln
California, MD 20619-4125
(214) 437-4994
Email: lisa@virtualhra.com
Web: www.virtualhra.com

Summary: Our firm is an industry staffing leader in the K-12 educational publishing markets as well as the information technology sector. We have experience backed by training and certification in employment law and standard employment practices.

Key Contact - Specialty:
Ms. Lisa Mackie, CPC, Owner - *Accounting (Public), Education, Information Technology, Publishing, Sales*

Salary Minimum: $40,000

Functions: IT

Industries: Generalist (All)

Vision Group

1200 Pacific Coast Hwy Ste 201
Hermosa Beach, CA 90254-3955
(310) 937-7647
Fax: (310) 937-7849
Email: info@visionrg.com
Web: www.visionrg.com

Summary: Our firm specializes in placing top level talent in the following areas: sales, marketing, accounting, finance and asset management. We conduct searches on both a contingency and retained basis.

Key Contact - Specialty:
Ms. Shani Malcolm, Partner

Salary Minimum: $75,000

Functions: Generalist (All), Sales & Mktg., Sales Mgmt., Sales Reps.

Industries: Transportation, Finance, Invest. Banking, Services, Communications, Telecoms, Telephony, Network Infrastructure

Visions Personnel

33 Main St Ste 400
Nashua, NH 03064-2776
(603) 883-5897
Fax: (603) 889-9534
Email: careers@visionspersonnel.com
Web: www.visionspersonnel.com

Summary: We are a major force in placing qualified candidates in restaurant careers. We place staff in every sector of the restaurant industry from entry level management to senior corporate executives. We represent clients in all styles of restaurants; from quick serve, to casual theme and fine dining; our clients range from local independents to major national chains.

Key Contact - Specialty:
Mr. Steve Varrieur, President
Mr. Pete Greene, President
Ms. Maude Laurence, Vice President
Ms. Sharon Gannett, Office Manager
Mr. John Roemer, Vice President
Ms. Charlene Lambert, Vice President
Mr. Dan Dadoun, Staffing Manager
Ms. Susan Bullock, Staffing Manager
Ms. Denise Cerelli, Staffing Manager

Functions: Generalist (All)

Industries: Restaurants

Vista Partners Inc

10 S Latah St Ste 205
Boise, ID 83705-1563
(877) 266-6922
Fax: (208) 433-0626
Email: curt@vistapartners.net
Web: www.vistapartners.net

Summary: Ours is a nationally recognized recruiting firm, specializing in the healthcare and life science industries. We connect professionals with careers, maximizing experience and skill with opportunity. Being straightforward and easy to work with, we provide prompt and complete follow through. Our goal is to be your long-term recruiting solution.

Key Contact - Specialty:
Mr. Curt Broadsword, President
Mr. Jon Rider, Vice President

Functions: Generalist (All), Management, Board Members, Senior Mgmt., Middle Mgmt., Admin. Svcs., Product Dev., Quality, Healthcare, Physicians

Industries: Pharm Svcs., Biotech/Life Sciences, Healthcare, Hospitals

Vista Technology

800 Turnpike St Ste 300
North Andover, MA 01845-6156
(978) 686-2200
Fax: (978) 686-1313
Email: rich@vista-technology.com
Web: www.vista-technology.com

Summary: We are a contingency search firm specializing in the biotechnology/biopharmaceutical industry. Our client companies range from start-ups to well established companies. Our client candidates include research associates/scientists, clinical and medical affairs, informatics, quality and manufacturing scientists.

Key Contact - Specialty:
Mr. Richard Connors, Principal - *Biopharmaceutical, Biotechnology*

Salary Minimum: $40,000

Functions: Generalist (All)

Industries: Medical Devices, Pharm Svcs., Biotech/Life Sciences

Vital Staffing

40 Bassett St
Milton, MA 02186-5521
(617) 698-7269
Fax: (617) 698-7629
Email: info@vital-staffing.com
Web: www.vital-staffing.com

Summary: The growing medical staffing crisis has reached epidemic levels. We can help healthcare administrators cure this problem. Through our innovative programs and processes, we bring great candidates and great companies together.

Key Contact - Specialty:
Mr. Doug MacNeil, Vice President, Business Development
Mr. David Lucey, Vice President, Recruitment Services

Salary Minimum: $70,000

Functions: Senior Mgmt.

Industries: Invest. Banking, E-commerce, IT Implementation, Communications, Telecoms, Call Centers, Network Infrastructure, Healthcare, Hospitals, Long-term/Home Care

Beverly von Winckler & Assoc

1018 Lee St
Evanston, IL 60202-1716
(847) 869-6660
Fax: (847) 869-7574
Email: vonwinckler@earthlink.net

Summary: Our specialties include corporate communications, marketing, marketing communications, consulting, agencies, corporations, and suppliers. Form career long associations with both clients and candidates. Provide one-year guarantee on placements.

Key Contact - Specialty:
Ms. Beverly von Winckler, President - *Communications*

Functions: Sales & Mktg., Advertising, Mktg. Research, Mktg. Mgmt., Direct Mktg., PR, Graphic Designers

Industries: Generalist (All), Media, Advertising, Publishing

Vortechs Group

5011 Pine Creek Dr
Westerville, OH 43081-4849
(614) 899-6696
(877) 771-8324
Fax: (614) 898-9734
Email: glen@vtg.cc
Web: www.vtg.cc

Summary: Our firm seeks to place top technical talent in a company that is a fit both technically and culturally. We treat you with respect, listen to what you want and need, and will find your next career stepping stone in a timely fashion. We are dedicated to being honest and forthright in our placements, for the company's happiness and yours.

Key Contact - Specialty:
Mr. Glen Gardner, President
Ms. Karin Warner, Technical Recruiter

Ms. Bea Gardner, Technical Recruiter
Mr. Michael Elmer, Practice Manager, IT
  Supplier Management

Salary Minimum: $50,000

Functions: Board Members, MIS Mgmt.

Industries: Computer Equip., Banking, Mgmt.
  Consulting, Software, Database SW,
  Development SW, Doc. Mgmt., Production SW,
  ERP SW, HR SW, Networking, Comm. SW,
  Security SW, System SW

Wagner & Associates

200-360 Rue Saint-Francois-Xavier
Montreal, QC H2Y 2S8
Canada
(514) 842-5494
Fax: (514) 842-4529
Email: us@wagner.ca
Web: www.wagner.ca

Summary: Our recruitment specialty is IT,
computing and MIS professionals at all levels,
including: technical, more specifically SW
developers, database, networks, architects, QA and
tech support; and management, more specifically
projects, product, directors and VP.

Key Contact - Specialty:
Mr. Gabriel Wagner, President - *Information
  Technology*

Salary Minimum: $35,000

Functions: IT

Industries: Generalist (All)

Waldon Associates

1715 N West Shore Blvd Ste 460
Tampa, FL 33607-3914
(813) 289-0051
Fax: (813) 289-6004
Email: waldonassoc@waldon.fdn.com
Web: www.waldonassociates.com

Summary: Our knowledge of accounting,
bookkeeping, human resources, clerical & medical
administrative personnel enables us to test, screen
and qualify only the best candidates available. We
offer the most professional service and follow
through in our industry.

Key Contact - Specialty:
Mr. Jeffrey Waldon, President - *Management*
Ms. Maita Waldon, Vice President

Functions: Generalist (All), CFOs, Budgeting,
  Cash Mgmt., Credit, Taxes, M&A

Industries: Generalist (All), Finance, Misc.
  Financial, Accounting, Insurance, Real Estate,
  Healthcare

Waldorf Associates Inc

PO Box 887
Pacific Palisades, CA 90272-0887
(310) 230-4411
Email: mw@waldorf.org

Summary: Provide attorney and legal placement,
primarily partners and specialty practice groups,
for prominent law firms; career counseling and
development consulting services, including
presentation, interview and business development
skills; professional coaching; expert witness (e.g.,
labor/employment matters); and law firm
consulting and workshops on attorney hiring,
retention, marketing and other issues.

Key Contact - Specialty:
Mr. Michael Waldorf, JD, President - *Legal
  (Attorneys, Lawyers), Professional services*

Salary Minimum: $100,000

Functions: Management, Attorneys

Industries: Legal

Roy Walker & Associates Inc

2686 Regina Ave
Thousand Oaks, CA 91360-1609
(805) 492-3871
Fax: (805) 493-2701
Email: rwalker49@verizon.net
Web: www.nirassn.com

Summary: Executive search specializing in
insurance.

Key Contact - Specialty:
Mr. Roy Walker, Principal

Salary Minimum: $60,000

Functions: Management

Industries: Insurance, Casualty, Claims,
  Commercial, Re-Insurance

Walker & Associates

PO Box 526
Claysville, PA 15323-0626
(724) 225-3634
Fax: (724) 225-9482
Email: del@walkerbio.com
Web: www.bio-jobs.com

Summary: We provide contingent recruiting
services to the biotechnology industry, as well as
assist industry professionals in finding career
opportunities. We offer an online career search
website sponsored by our company.

Key Contact - Specialty:
Mr. Del Walker
Ms. Lauren Hathaway, BA, Recruiter -
  Biotechnology
Ms. Lori Wilkerson, BA, Manager

Salary Minimum: $20,000

Functions: Generalist (All)

Industries: Biotech/Life Sciences

Kelly Walker Associates

949 Forest Grove Dr
Dallas, TX 75218-2333
(214) 320-3006
Fax: (214) 324-5105
Email: kellywalker@kellywalker.com
Web: www.kellywalker.com

Summary: Manufacturers and distributors of
construction and mining equipment and fleets,
which use heavy equipment, utilize our specialized
knowledge of this industry to recruit world-class
managers.

Key Contact - Specialty:
Ms. Kelly Walker, President - *Construction,
  Industrial, Mining*
Mr. Jack Mears, Associate - *Construction, Mining*

Salary Minimum: $40,000

Functions: Management, Senior Mgmt.,
  Distribution, Sales & Mktg., Training

Industries: Agri., Forestry, Mining, Energy,
  Utilities, Construction, Wholesale, Equip Svcs.

Jarvis Walker Group

(a division of SKG)
30 Vreeland Rd
Florham Park, NJ 07932-1904
(973) 966-0900
Fax: (973) 966-6925
Email: careers@jwnj.com
Web: www.jarviswalker.com

Summary: Our firm specializes in the recruitment
of IT professionals. We have worked closely with
client companies to identify and recruit the highest
caliber candidates for challenging and rewarding
career opportunities.

Key Contact - Specialty:
Mr. Dan Jarvis, President
Mr. Jerry West, Senior Vice President

Salary Minimum: $90,000

Functions: IT, MIS Mgmt., Systems Analysis

Industries: Manufacturing, Food, Bev., Tobacco,
  Drugs Mfg., Consumer Elect., Finance, Invest.
  Banking, Pharm Svcs., E-commerce, IT
  Implementation, Publishing, Communications,
  Software, Biotech/Life Sciences, Healthcare

Walker Personnel Inc

3000 26th St Ste A
Metairie, LA 70002-6052
(504) 831-4767
Fax: (504) 831-2979

Summary: We specialize in property and casualty
insurance placement.

Key Contact - Specialty:
Ms. Linda G. Walker, CPC, President

Functions: Generalist (All)

Industries: Insurance

Wall Street Options LLC

53 W 36th St Rm 702
New York, NY 10018-7984
(212) 661-3738
Fax: (720) 384-1429
Email: steve.fleming@wsoll.com
Web: www.wsollc.com

Summary: Our firm recruits for hedge funds, fund
of funds and banks; specializing in accountants,
analysts, CFO, CIO, marketing, operations, PM,
programmers, PhD's / quants, research, sales,
traders and risk management.

Key Contact - Specialty:
Mr. Steve Fleming, Founding Partner
Mr. Kenneth Marma, Founding Partner

Salary Minimum: $100,000

Functions: Generalist (All)

Industries: Finance, Banking, Invest. Banking,
  Brokers, Venture Cap., Mutual/Hedge Funds,
  Misc. Financial, Accounting

Wallace Associates

PO Box 11294
Waterbury, CT 06703-0294
(203) 879-2011
Email: ggordon@wallacejobs.com
Web: www.wallacejobs.com

Summary: We provide personal consulting
experience throughout the United States. We
concentrate in the engineering, EDP and
manufacturing support disciplines up to and
including the executive level.

Key Contact - Specialty:
Mr. Gregory Gordon, Principal - *Automation,
  Electronics, Engineering, Manufacturing
  (Management), Medical (Devices)*

Salary Minimum: $50,000

Functions: Generalist (All), Management

Industries: Generalist (All), Manufacturing,
  Chemicals, Drugs Mfg., Medical Devices,
  Plastics, Rubber, Paints, Petro. Products, Motor
  Vehicles, Computer Equip., Electronic, Elec.
  Components, Packaging, Software

Denis P Walsh & Associates Inc

3823 Merrick St Ste 100
Houston, TX 77025-2425
(713) 839-7052
Email: deniswalsh@expertiselocator.com
Web: www.expertiselocator.com

Summary: We cover most functions, especially the oil and gas strategy consulting. We serve the heavy engineering and construction industries, rail, transit, refining, petrochemical, pulp & paper and power industries.

Key Contact - Specialty:
Mr. Denis P. Walsh, Jr., President - *Construction, Refining*

Salary Minimum: $40,000

Functions: Generalist (All), Management, Engineering

Industries: Generalist (All), Energy, Utilities, Oil & Gas, Construction, Mgmt. Consulting

Walter & Associates Inc

PO Box 3358
Olathe, KS 66063-3358
(913) 764-4930
(800) 236-4930
Fax: (913) 764-9381
Email: jpwalter@topechelon.com
Web: www.itopps.com

Summary: We are a professional search group, specializing in the successful placement of IT/ Information Systems Professionals. We focus the majority of our efforts in the ERP market. This includes all levels of technical, functional, management, & training needs. We locate individuals of outstanding character and qualifications on a nationwide basis.

Key Contact - Specialty:
Mr. Jerry P. Walter, President

Functions: IT

Industries: Generalist (All)

Walters & Associates LLC

2 Selfridge Rd
Bedford, MA 01730-2021
(781) 276-1776
Email: roywalters1@yahoo.com

Summary: We specialize in placing sales people, recruiters and management professionals exclusively in the staffing and consulting industry. We specialize in branch, area and regional level searches for staffing companies.

Key Contact - Specialty:
Mr. Roy Walters, Partner - *Staffing*

Salary Minimum: $50,000

Functions: Middle Mgmt., Sales & Mktg.

Industries: Legal, Mgmt. Consulting, HR Services, Sports

Robert Walters Associates Inc

7 Times Sq
New York, NY 10036-6524
(212) 704-9900
Fax: (212) 704-4312
Email: kurt.kraeger@robertwalters.com
Web: www.robertwalters.com

Summary: We are a financial recruitment firm specializing in all areas of finance.

Key Contact - Specialty:
Mr. Kurt H. Kraeger, President - *Energy, Finance*

Salary Minimum: $50,000

Functions: Management, Board Members, Senior Mgmt., Middle Mgmt., Finance, CFOs, Credit, M&A, Systems Implem., Mgmt. Consultants

Industries: Generalist (All), Manufacturing, Banking, Invest. Banking, Brokers, Mgmt. Consulting, Media, Real Estate

JR Walters Resources

PO Box 617
Saint Joseph, MI 49085-0617
(269) 925-3940
Email: jrwawa@jrwalters.com
Web: www.jrwalters.com

Summary: We are specialists in the placement of professionals in the architectural and engineering industry. We also offer positions through our partner agencies in all professional employment.

Key Contact - Specialty:
Ms. Joan R. Walters, CPC

Functions: Engineering, Environmentalists, Architects

Industries: Construction, Services

Ward & Ward International Recruiters & Consultants

(also known as AL Ward & Associates)
12180 N Yearling Cir
Hayden Lake, ID 83835-9884
(800) 800-6181
(208) 772-2209
Email: alward@imbris.net
Web: www.allward.com

Summary: Recruiting specializing in construction and architects.

Key Contact - Specialty:
Mr. Al L. Ward, Executive Recruiter - *Construction, Engineering*
Mrs. Gayle E. Ward, President

Salary Minimum: $50,000

Functions: Structural, Architects, Bldg. Contractors

Industries: Construction

Martha Ward Executive Search Inc

PO Box 2759
Amagansett, NY 11930-2759
(631) 267-3730
Fax: (631) 267-6335
Email: marketing@marthaward.com
Web: www.marthaward.com

Summary: Our firm has extensive experience and specializes in consumer products, marketing, and advertising.

Key Contact - Specialty:
Ms. Martha Ward, President - *Market research, Marketing*
Mr. Paul Poutouves, Vice President - *Advertising, Sales*
Mr. Eric Lane, Senior Executive Consultant

Salary Minimum: $70,000

Functions: Generalist (All), Board Members, Senior Mgmt., Middle Mgmt., Mktg. Research, Mktg. Mgmt., Sales Mgmt., Direct Mktg.

Industries: Generalist (All), Energy, Utilities, Food, Bev., Tobacco, Textiles, Apparel, Paper, Soap, Perf., Cosmtcs., Drugs Mfg., Metal Products, Advertising, Telecoms, Healthcare, Hospitals

Wardrup Associates

2508 Springpark Way Ste 300
Richardson, TX 75082-4620
(972) 437-9333
Fax: (972) 437-1208
Email: dwardrup@wardrup.com
Web: www.wardrup.com

Summary: Our firm offers retained/contingency search for qualified, experienced mid to senior management professionals to the nation's most business-aggressive established and emerging high technology companies. We specialize in computer hardware/software, telecom and IT/professional services with a focus on customer service, sales/marketing, operations and consulting.

Key Contact - Specialty:
Ms. Diane Wardrup, Principal

Functions: Generalist (All), Management, Board Members, Senior Mgmt.

Industries: Medical Devices, Computer Equip., Test, Measure Equip., Equip Svcs., Mgmt. Consulting, IT Implementation, Logistics Svcs., Supply Chain Mgmt., Telecoms, Call Centers, Telephony, Digital, Wireless, Fiber Optic, Network Infrastructure, Software, Marketing SW

Warner & Associates Inc

101 E College Ave
Westerville, OH 43081-1609
(614) 891-9003
Email: warnerassoc@netzero.net

Summary: We are a well established; owner managed firm offering customized and personal response to the needs of our clients. We specialize within most functional areas of manufacturing management.

Key Contact - Specialty:
Mr. Thomas P. Warner, President - *Manufacturing*

Salary Minimum: $40,000

Functions: Generalist (All)

Industries: Generalist (All), Manufacturing, Plastics, Rubber, Leather, Stone, Glass, Metal Products, Machine, Appliance, Motor Vehicles, Electronic, Elec. Components, Robotics

C D Warner & Associates

12 Davenport Dr
Downingtown, PA 19335-1883
(610) 458-8335
Email: doug@cdwarner.com
Web: www.cdwarner.com

Summary: We are an executive search firm specializing in IT and high technology computing; and focusing on management, specifically: CEOs, CIOs, CTOs, COOs, VPs, directors, marketing, sales and technical professionals. We have experience in many Industries such as insurance, banking, information technology, etc.

Key Contact - Specialty:
Mr. C. Douglas Warner, President - *Sales*
Mr. William D. Adams, Managing Partner, West Coast
Ms. Susan C. Warner, Vice President, Finance & Operations

Functions: Generalist (All), Senior Mgmt., Automation, Sales Mgmt., CFOs, IT, MIS Mgmt., Int'l.

Industries: Generalist (All), E-commerce, IT Implementation, Communications, Telecoms, Call Centers, Telephony, Digital, Wireless, Fiber Optic, Network Infrastructure, Software

Wasserman Associates Inc

19 Raisin Tree Cir
Pikesville, MD 21208-6365
(410) 486-4800
(800) 803-0011
Fax: (410) 486-7100
Email: careers@wassermanassociates.com
Web: www.wassermanassociates.com

Summary: We have extensive experience
specializing in consumer product sales and sales
support. Our emphasis is on food, drug, beverage,
health & beauty aids, OTC, personal care products
and general merchandise/non-food areas. We
place first level managers to VP-sales &
marketing. We also place trade marketing
managers, category managers and sales planning
managers.

Key Contact - Specialty:
Mr. Stan Wasserman, President - *Consumer
(Packaged Goods,Products), Food & beverage,
Sales*
Mr. Barry S. Levin, Vice President - *Consumer
(Durables,Packaged Goods,Products), Food &
beverage, Sales*
Ms. Lynn Orkin, Senior Account Executive &
Researcher

Salary Minimum: $75,000

Functions: Management, Sales & Mktg., Sales
Mgmt.

Industries: Food, Bev., Tobacco, Paper, Soap,
Perf., Cosmtcs., Drugs Mfg., Consumer Elect.,
Consumer Goods, Inst./Industrial Food Svc.

Waterbury Group Inc

275 N Main St
Springboro, OH 45066-9820
(937) 748-5319
Fax: (937) 748-5571
Email: jdo@waterburygroup.com
Web: www.waterburygroup.com

Summary: We are a client focused executive
search firm providing executive search services
for a broad range of clients. With experience in
most industries and virtually every functional
discipline, we provide our global clients with
quality, timely executive search services,

Key Contact - Specialty:
Mr. John O'Reilly, President - *Manufacturing,
Manufacturing (Management), Non-profit,
Retail, Senior management*
Mr. Greg Dunn, Vice President & Managing
Principal - *Manufacturing, Non-profit, Retail,
Robotics, Utilities*
Mr. Mark Simonetti, Managing Director -
*Automotive, Manufacturing, Manufacturing
(Management), Retail, Steel*
Mr. Richard Leever, Senior Consultant -
*Engineering, Human resources, Manufacturing,
Manufacturing (Management), Retail*
Mr. John Bringman, Senior Consultant -
*Engineering, Information Systems,
Management, Manufacturing, Manufacturing
(Management)*
Mr. Robert Hendricks, Senior Consultant -
*Foundries, Management, Manufacturing,
Manufacturing (Management), Metals*

Salary Minimum: $50,000

Functions: Generalist (All)

Industries: Energy, Utilities, Manufacturing,
Plastics, Rubber, Paints, Petro. Products, Metal
Products, Machine, Appliance, Motor Vehicles,
Computer Equip., Consumer Elect., Retail

Waterford Executive Group Ltd

1N141 County Farm Rd Ste 220
Winfield, IL 60190-2023
(630) 690-0055
Fax: (630) 690-5533
Email: info@waterfordgroup.com
Web: www.waterfordgroup.com

Summary: Our firm will fulfill our client's needs
via retainer or contingency arrangements with a
highly personalized and focused approach, mainly
in compensation and benefits consulting industry,
as well as corporate HR.

Key Contact - Specialty:
Mr. Patrick J. Atkinson, President -
Compensation, Human resources
Mr. Ted Tomei, Principal - *Change management,
Organizational development*
Ms. Joan Krings, Principal - *Benefits*

Salary Minimum: $40,000

Functions: HR Mgmt., Benefits, Actuaries,
Pension/Ret. Planning

Industries: Generalist (All)

Waterjobs

620 Violet St
Modesto, CA 95356-1420
(209) 529-5051
Fax: (209) 529-1878
Email: jim@waterjobs.com
Web: www.waterjobs.com

Summary: Recruiting agency for high purity
water and waste water systems and related
components.

Key Contact - Specialty:
Mr. Jim Ortman, Owner - *Biotechnology,
Pharmaceutical*

Salary Minimum: $35,000

Functions: Generalist (All), Mfg., Sales & Mktg.

Industries: Energy, Utilities, Construction,
Manufacturing, Food, Bev., Tobacco,
Chemicals, Metal Products, Test, Measure
Equip., Equip Svcs., Homeland Security,
Environmental Svcs., Haz. Waste, Biotech/Life
Sciences, Non-Classifiable

Watring & Associates Inc

402 E Roosevelt Rd Ste 210
Wheaton, IL 60187-5588
(630) 690-2707
Fax: (630) 690-2243
Email: email@watring.net
Web: www.watring.net

Summary: We conduct placement of all medical
pharmaceutical and biotechnology sales
marketing, management, engineering, including
R&D, quality control; also dealer sales forces and
clinical applications specialists.

Key Contact - Specialty:
Ms. Bernie Watring, President
Ms. Janet Blue, Associate - *Pharmaceutical,
Sales*

Functions: Physicians, Nurses, Sales & Mktg.,
Sales Mgmt., Training, Int'l.

Industries: Generalist (All)

The Watts Group

530 Wilshire Blvd Ste 200
Santa Monica, CA 90401-1422
(310) 395-3838
Fax: (310) 395-9188
Email: lindagw@aol.com

Summary: We are an executive search firm
specializing in advertising, marketing and

marketing communications. We have specialists in
account management/strategic planning/media and
creative. Our strength is in client service;
understanding both the business and culture of our
clients, and finding the talent that will help drive
future success.

Key Contact - Specialty:
Ms. Linda Watts, Owner & President
Ms. Marjorie Fulbright, Managing Director
Ms. Mary Flatlie, Executive Vice President
Ms. Lisa Coris, Executive Recruiter
Ms. Donna Siegel, Executive Recruiter - *Finance*

Functions: Senior Mgmt., Middle Mgmt.,
Advertising, Mktg. Mgmt.

Industries: Advertising, New Media

Wegner & Associates

11270 W Park Pl Ste 310
Milwaukee, WI 53224-3648
(414) 359-2333
Fax: (414) 359-2325
Email: cwegner@wegnerassoc.com

Summary: We specialize in upper and middle
management recruiting with particular emphasis in
financial, accounting and the MIS areas. Also do
extensive staff level recruiting in the accounting
and MIS areas. Also, we have an extensive HR
placement history.

Key Contact - Specialty:
Mr. Carl Wegner, CPA, President - *Financial,
General management*
Mr. Bob Schultz, Vice President - *MIS*
Ms. Nicole Manzeck, Director, Office
Administration
Mr. Carver Smith, CPA, SPHR, Vice President -
Finance

Salary Minimum: $35,000

Functions: Middle Mgmt., Finance, IT

Industries: Generalist (All)

David Weinfeld Group

PO Box 98719
Raleigh, NC 27624-8719
(919) 676-7828
Fax: (919) 676-7399
Email: david@weinfeldgroup.com
Web: www.weinfeldgroup.com

Summary: We specialize in customized
recruitment of key executives in sales, business
development, professional services, marketing,
engineering and management consultants in the
telecom, data com, networking and other related
applications including consulting functions and
software applications.

Key Contact - Specialty:
Mr. David C. Weinfeld, President - *Computers,
Computers (Software), Telecommunications*
Ms. Lauren Dunne, Research Assistant

Salary Minimum: $60,000

Functions: Generalist (All)

Industries: Consumer Goods, Mgmt. Consulting,
Telecoms, Digital, Wireless, Fiber Optic,
Defense, Development SW, Doc. Mgmt.,
Production SW

Weinman & Associates

7119 E Shea Blvd Ste 109
Scottsdale, AZ 85254-6107
(480) 483-2132
Fax: (480) 922-9248
Email: mweinman@primenet.com
Web: www.weinmanassociates.com

Summary: We are a full-service executive search
firm.

Email your resume to a targeted list of recruiters now at www.ExecutiveAgent.com/DER07

Key Contact - Specialty:
Ms. Mary Weinman, President - *Hospitality*
Ms. Robin Duncan, Vice President

Salary Minimum: $50,000

Functions: Generalist (All), Management, HR Mgmt., IT, MIS Mgmt., Specialized Svcs., Attorneys, Paralegals

Industries: Generalist (All), Construction, Finance, Services, Accounting, Hospitality

Weinpel Search Inc
PO Box 248
Riverdale, NJ 07457-0248
(973) 628-0858
Fax: (973) 694-7319
Email: weinpel@juno.com

Summary: We have technology staffing 'savvy'. We specialize in engineering (particularly aerospace/DoD) and most other functions with a technology content. Our staff members and most of our vendors are trained in technology that helps to assure professionalism with industry and candidates.

Key Contact - Specialty:
Mr. Charles J. Weinpel - *Computers (Software), Engineering, Science*

Salary Minimum: $75,000

Functions: Engineering

Industries: RF/Microwave, Defense, Aerospace

Weisberg Associates
2477 Church Ln
Willowood Business Campus
Kintnersville, PA 18930-9639
(610) 847-5999
Fax: (610) 847-8071
Email: allo@epix.net

Summary: Specialists in difficult to fill technical, engineering and operations management positions in industries engaged in design, manufacturing and sales. Our primary focus is in the Tier One/OEM automotive industry, particularly in the field of automotive plastics, including state of the art injection molding, RIM, highly automated robotic painting and plating of Class A plastic components.

Key Contact - Specialty:
Mr. Alan M. Weisberg, Principal - *Automotive, Engineering, Technical*

Salary Minimum: $50,000

Functions: Generalist (All), Automation

Industries: Generalist (All), Construction, Manufacturing, Plastics, Rubber, Paints, Petro. Products, Motor Vehicles, Consumer Elect., Misc. Mfg., Transportation, Property/Facility Mgmt.

Weiss & Associates Legal Search Inc
PO Box 915656
Longwood, FL 32791-5656
(407) 774-1212
Fax: (407) 880-9933
Email: lawhunter@aol.com

Summary: We are a legal search firm that specializes with experienced partners and associates for major law firms. In addition, we possess a sub-specialty involving experienced tax attorneys and 'key' tax professionals. We have earned a reputation for identifying and attracting outstanding candidates for our clients. Our clients consist of major multi-national corporations, prominent law firms in their respective cities and international accounting firms.

Key Contact - Specialty:
Mr. Terry M. Weiss, Esq., President

Salary Minimum: $125,000

Functions: Generalist (All), Board Members, Senior Mgmt., Taxes, M&A, Legal, Attorneys

Industries: Generalist (All), Manufacturing, Legal, Real Estate, Accounting SW, Biotech/Life Sciences, Healthcare

C Weiss Associates Inc
60 W 57th St
New York, NY 10019-3909
(212) 581-4040
Email: cweissinc@aol.com

Summary: We specialize in recruiting for consumer financial services. Our excellent research department is capable of handling unique assignments. Principal has a personal background in marketing, with an impressive career with a money center bank.

Key Contact - Specialty:
Ms. Cathy Weiss, President - *Direct marketing, Product management/development*

Salary Minimum: $40,000

Functions: Product Dev., Mktg. Mgmt., Direct Mktg.

Industries: Banking, Services, Advertising, New Media, Communications

Weitz & Associates
20914 Pacific Coast Hwy
Malibu, CA 90265-5218
(310) 456-5455
(310) 456-1856
Email: laweitz@amazingrecruiters.com
Web: www.amazingrecruiters.com

Summary: We are an executive search firm recruiting for private industry and public firms within the consumer products and interactive entertainment industries. We are proud to extend only the "highest standards of excellence" on representing only top firms. We source solely the very best and most highly qualified candidates and we want to offer them only the greatest of opportunities.

Key Contact - Specialty:
Mr. Larry A. Weitz, Principal - *Entertainment, Food & beverage, Sales*
Ms. Laurie R. Weitz, Principal - *Sales*
Mrs. Kimberly Till, Executive Recruitment
Ms. Toya Smith, Team Leader, Research

Salary Minimum: $75,000

Functions: Senior Mgmt., Middle Mgmt., Product Dev., Sales & Mktg., Sales Mgmt., HR Mgmt., Training, Finance, Mgmt. Consultants, Minorities/Diversity

Industries: Generalist (All), Food, Bev., Tobacco, Soap, Perf., Cosmtcs., Drugs Mfg., Consumer Goods, Mgmt. Consulting, HR Services, Entertainment, Advertising, Mfg. SW, Marketing SW

Welivers
92 Fletcher Pl
Mountain Home, AR 72653-6186
(877) 935-4837
Email: welivers@job4u.com

Summary: We specialize in IT and all related areas; sales, storage, telecommunication and consulting as well as engineering and medical. We network with over 400 recruiting firms.

Key Contact - Specialty:
Mr. Edward A. Weliver, Owner - *Human resources*
Ms. Billie S. Weliver, President

Salary Minimum: $35,000

Functions: Generalist (All), Healthcare, Staffing, MIS Mgmt., Systems Analysis, Systems Dev., Systems Implem., Systems Support, Network Admin.

Industries: Generalist (All), Computer Equip., Consumer Elect., New Media, Telecoms, Software, Healthcare

Branches:
243 Fieldcrest St
Ann Arbor, MI 48103-6421
(877) 935-4837
Key Contact - Specialty:
R.S. Weliver

Henry Welker & Associates
PO Box 530846
Livonia, MI 48153-0846
(734) 953-4900
Email: hwelker@twmi.rr.com

Summary: We specialize in management, IT, IS, HR, HR outsourcing, automotive engineering and automotive sales engineering.

Key Contact - Specialty:
Mr. Henry A. Welker, President

Salary Minimum: $50,000

Functions: Management, Senior Mgmt., Mfg., Materials, Sales Mgmt., HR Mgmt., IT, R&D, Engineering, Mgmt. Consultants

Industries: Generalist (All), Plastics, Rubber, Metal Products, Motor Vehicles, Computer Equip., Test, Measure Equip., Electronic, Elec. Components, Robotics, HR Services

Wellington Executive Search Inc
3162 Johnson Ferry Rd Ste 260
Marietta, GA 30062-7600
(770) 645-5799
(877) 207-4326
Fax: (770) 645-5749
Email: jobs@wellingtonsearch.com
Web: www.wellingtonsearch.com

Summary: We recruit for positions in R&D, product development, QC/QA, sales, marketing, production, operations, and customer service management. Entry level to VP and director level. We specialize in the area of food ingredients and related technologies. We are long time members and supporters of the IFT and the RCA.

Key Contact - Specialty:
Mr. Scott Wellington, President & Chief Executive Officer

Salary Minimum: $40,000

Functions: Mfg., Product Dev., Plant Mgmt., Quality, Sales & Mktg., Sales Mgmt., Sales Reps., R&D

Industries: Food, Bev., Tobacco, Chemicals, Soap, Perf., Cosmtcs., Drugs Mfg.

Wellington Thomas Ltd
5040 White Pine Cir NE
Saint Petersburg, FL 33703-6210
(800) 779-1233
(727) 522-0611
Fax: (727) 522-5912
Email: recruitment@wellingtonthomas.com
Web: www.wellingtonthomas.com

Summary: National recruitment firm which specializes in healthcare only. Company is noted

for its dedication to results oriented and ethical outcomes approach for both clients and candidates. Strong referral network throughout the US. Opportunities are in the clinical, operations, rehab therapy, pharmacy and sales; positions are corporate, regional or facility based.

Key Contact - Specialty:
Ms. Jean M. De Mange, Senior Consultant - *Healthcare*

Salary Minimum: $50,000

Functions: Generalist (All), Admin. Svcs., Healthcare, Nurses, Allied Health, Health Admin., Sales & Mktg.

Industries: Pharm Svcs., Healthcare, Hospitals, Long-term/Home Care, Physical Therapy, Occupational Therapy

Wells, Bradley & Associates Inc
520 Lake Elmo Ave N
Lake Elmo, MN 55042-9711
(651) 731-9202
(651) 430-2002
Email: kennedyinfo@wellsbradley.com
Web: www.wellsbradley.com

Summary: Our company specializes in the banking & credit card industry. Includes: alternative delivery, analytical positions, B2B, B2C, commercial banking, consumer finance, credit cards, credit management, decision technology, e-banking, e-commerce, executive management, payment systems, lending, private banking, retail banking, risk management, sales/marketing, statistics, treasury management, trust & investments and training & development.

Key Contact - Specialty:
Ms. Gillis Lindberg, Chief Executive Officer - *Banking, Banking (Commercial,Corporate,Mortgage,Retail)*
Ms. Sandy Bradley, CPC - *Banking, Banking (Commercial,Retail), Credit cards, Risk management*

Salary Minimum: $50,000

Functions: Board Members, Senior Mgmt., Middle Mgmt., Product Dev., Quality, Direct Mktg., Finance, CFOs, Cash Mgmt., Risk Mgmt.

Industries: Finance, Banking, Invest. Banking, Venture Cap., Mutual/Hedge Funds, Misc. Financial

R A Wells Company
107 N Lakeside Dr NW
Kennesaw, GA 30144-3094
(770) 424-8493
Fax: (770) 424-2724
Email: rawco@comcast.net

Summary: Our firm specializes in conducting search activity for clients in the plastic packaging industry. Send resume only if you have plastics experience in product development, management, design, sales, marketing, etc. You must always identify in the 'subject' column 'Plastics Experience' to prevent an email delete.

Key Contact - Specialty:
Mr. Robert A. Wells, Owner - *Plastics*

Salary Minimum: $35,000

Functions: Management, Mfg., Sales & Mktg., HR Mgmt., Benefits, IT, R&D, Engineering, Attorneys, Int'l.

Industries: Plastics, Rubber, Communications, Packaging

Werbin Associates Executive Search Inc
140 Riverside Dr Ste 10N
New York, NY 10024-2605
(212) 799-6111
Email: susan@werbins.com

Summary: Oriented towards assisting the computer, research, finance and management science professionals, technical management-all levels.

Key Contact - Specialty:
Ms. Susan Werbin, President - *Finance, Market research, Operations*

Functions: Management, Product Dev., Production, Sales & Mktg., Mktg. Research, HR Mgmt., Staffing, Finance, IT, R&D

Industries: Generalist (All), Energy, Utilities, Manufacturing, Computer Equip., Transportation, Finance, Banking, Invest. Banking, Services, Mgmt. Consulting, HR Services, Advertising, New Media, Communications, Telecoms, Insurance, Software, Database SW, Marketing SW, System SW

Michael West & Associates
PO Box 808
Downingtown, PA 19335-0808
(610) 692-9173
Fax: (610) 719-9984
Email: mike@michaelwestsearch.com
Web: www.michaelwestsearch.com

Summary: We are financial professionals who strongly believe in providing exceptional service to our clients. Our guiding principles are honesty, courtesy, respect and compassion for our clients and candidates. Our limited area of focus enables us to know the talented professionals within each niche and help our clients hire the best.

Key Contact - Specialty:
Mr. Mike Kershner, Chief Talent Officer - *Accounting (General), Finance, Financial services, Tax*

Salary Minimum: $50,000

Functions: Generalist (All)

Industries: Finance

West Coast Recruiting Inc
290 E Verdugo Ave Ste 204
Burbank, CA 91502-1342
(818) 556-6056
Fax: (818) 556-6102
Email: lprec@aol.com
Web: www.westcoastrecruiting.com

Summary: We are the preferred executive search organization in loss prevention and security for the nation's Fortune 500 companies. We have developed long lasting partnerships with the foremost loss prevention and security professionals within the retail and manufacturing industries.

Key Contact - Specialty:
Ms. Tracy A. Nini, President
Mr. Steven B. Nini, Vice President & General Manager

Salary Minimum: $40,000

Functions: Security Personnel

Industries: Manufacturing, Computer Equip., Retail, Non-profits, E-commerce, Logistics Svcs., Hospitality, Communications, Property/Facility Mgmt., Healthcare

Westcott Associates
27372 Young Dr
Laguna Niguel, CA 92677-3617
(949) 305-2741
Fax: (949) 625-7554
Email: info@westcott-associates.com
Web: www.westcott-associates.com

Summary: Need tax help? Tax staff up through tax director, we'll tap our deep resources and find the candidates who aren't responding to your ads but have the skills you need. We are highly effective calling into CPA firms, law firms and corporate tax departments. Finding the best in tax, one person at a time.

Key Contact - Specialty:
Mr. Chris Westcott

Salary Minimum: $50,000

Functions: Taxes

Industries: Generalist (All)

Western International Recruiters Inc
2550 N Thunderbird Cir Ste 205
Mesa, AZ 85215-1218
(800) 486-1757
(480) 777-0008
Fax: (480) 596-6888
Email: recruiters@westerninternational.com
Web: www.westerninternational.com

Summary: We are an insurance staffing firm providing full service staffing solutions to insurance carriers, TPAs, risk management firms, brokers and self-insureds. Our services include direct hire positions, contract and temp assignments, as well as special projects.

Key Contact - Specialty:
Ms. Dayne Hayes, President

Functions: Generalist (All), Senior Mgmt., Middle Mgmt., Admin. Svcs., Risk Mgmt., Actuaries

Industries: Insurance, Casualty, Claims, Commercial

Westover & Associates Inc
71 Walnut Ave
Atherton, CA 94027-3820
(650) 323-2607
(888) 978-6837
Email: info@westoverinc.com
Web: www.westoverinc.com

Summary: We specialize in thorough industry-wide searches for high-level sales, sales management, design, sourcing and product development positions in the home fashion industry.

Key Contact - Specialty:
Ms. Catherine Westover, CPC, President
Ms. Michelle Falk, Executive Vice President, Exec Recruit

Salary Minimum: $100,000

Functions: Management, Senior Mgmt., Product Dev.

Industries: Textiles, Apparel, Wholesale

Weterrings & Agnew Inc
132 Allens Creek Rd
Rochester, NY 14618-3302
(585) 241-9040
Fax: (585) 241-9044
Email: admin@weterrings.com
Web: www.weterrings.com

Summary: We provide professional recruitment services in all functional areas and across virtually all industry lines contingent and retained search.

Key Contact - Specialty:
Ms. Elaine J. McKenna, Partner
Mr. Thomas H. Quinn, Partner - *Marketing, Sales*
Mr. Charles F. Thomaschek, Technical Recruiting Manager - *Engineering, Manufacturing, Manufacturing (Management), Operations, Supply Chain*
Ms. Amy J. Koenig, Associate, Recruiting

Salary Minimum: $45,000

Functions: Generalist (All), Mfg., Plant Mgmt., Materials, Purchasing, Mktg. Research, Benefits, CFOs, MIS Mgmt., Engineering

Industries: Generalist (All), Energy, Utilities, Manufacturing, Food, Bev., Tobacco, Chemicals, Drugs Mfg., Medical Devices, Plastics, Rubber, Metal Products, Machine, Appliance, Consumer Elect., Test, Measure Equip., Misc. Mfg., Electronic, Elec. Components, Consumer Goods, Supply Chain Mgmt

Wharton-Lenox Executive Search

16 Maple St
Summit, NJ 07901-2136
(908) 608-1521
Fax: (908) 608-1519
Email: info@whartonlenox.com
Web: www.whartonlenox.com

Summary: We are a full-service executive search firm serving clients in the identification and hiring of exceptional professionals for development and fundraising positions with non-profit organizations. We are committed to finding and placing candidates whose professional and personality profiles match the needs and long-term goals of the client. We are equipped with an extensive database of high-level professionals.

Key Contact - Specialty:
Mr. Paul Leach, President - *Non-profit, Philanthropy*

Salary Minimum: $50,000

Functions: Management

Industries: Non-profits

Branches:
1101 Pennsylvania Ave NW Ste 700
Washington, DC 20004-2520
(877) 427-3616
Key Contact - Specialty:
Mr. Jarvis Jefferson, Vice President - *Accounting (Big 4), Human resources, Retail, Wholesale*

101 Federal St Ste 1900
Boston, MA 02110-1861
(877) 427-3616
Key Contact - Specialty:
Ms. Sara Angeletti, Vice President

Wheatley International Ltd

401 E 65th St
New York, NY 10021-6943
(212) 650-0181
Fax: (212) 639-9836
Email: wheatleypsa@aol.com

Summary: Our firm was established to furnish quality candidates to targeted segments of the financial community. We are a retained search firm and will only submit candidates who meet your requirements after thorough interviews in person, if geography permits. Our consultants have experience in finance, research and search.

Key Contact - Specialty:
Ms. Linda Wheatley, Principal - *Financial services*

Salary Minimum: $100,000

Functions: Management

Industries: Finance, Banking, Invest. Banking, Brokers, Venture Cap., Mutual/Hedge Funds, Misc. Financial, Services, Law Enforcement, Compliance

Kevin White & Associates

3740 Wembley Ln Ste 201
Lexington, KY 40515-1273
(859) 245-8000
Fax: (859) 201-1115
Email: kw@kwasearch.com
Web: www.kwasearch.com

Summary: We provide recruiting services for the manufacturing industry.

Key Contact - Specialty:
Mr. Kevin White, Executive Recruiter - *Manufacturing*

Salary Minimum: $50,000

Functions: Management, Middle Mgmt., Mfg., Production, Plant Mgmt., Quality, Materials Plng., HR Mgmt., Engineering

Industries: Manufacturing, Metal Products, Machine, Appliance, Motor Vehicles, Computer Equip., Misc. Mfg.

White/TemTech LLC

PO Box 3261
Shawnee Mission, KS 66203-0261
(913) 831-1821
Email: cwhite52@kc.rr.com

Summary: We are an executive search and staffing firm. We place management and executive professionals in many areas: accounting/finance; engineering; architectural & construction; manufacturing; sales & marketing. All industries including glass, plastics, chemical, automotive, environmental, heavy equipment, medical.

Key Contact - Specialty:
Ms. Carlene White, President

Salary Minimum: $50,000

Functions: Generalist (All), Management

Industries: Energy, Utilities, Construction, Manufacturing, Food, Bev., Tobacco, Lumber, Furniture, Soap, Perf., Cosmtcs., Leather, Stone, Glass, Machine, Appliance, Retail, Architectural Svcs., Hotels, Resorts, Clubs, Haz. Waste, Packaging, Healthcare

Robert Whitfield Associates

155 N Michigan Ave
Chicago, IL 60601-7511
(312) 938-9120
Fax: (312) 337-2172
Email: whitfieldassoc@aol.com
Web: www.robertwhitfieldassoc.com

Summary: We were founded in order to provide the legal profession with a full range of consulting services including retainer search, associate placement, management planning and marketing.

Key Contact - Specialty:
Mr. Robert Whitfield, Esq., President
Ms. Megan McKinney, Vice President

Salary Minimum: $125,000

Functions: Attorneys

Industries: Legal

The Whitney Smith Company Inc

301 Commerce St Ste 1950
Fort Worth, TX 76102-4184
(817) 877-4120
(817) 877-4314
Fax: (817) 877-3846
Email: dfarmer@whitneysmithco.com
Web: www.whitneysmithco.com

Summary: The firm specializes in recruiting and placement of executive and professionals in banking, financial services, HR, engineering, transportation, governmental, education, non-profits and sales/marketing.

Key Contact - Specialty:
Mr. David W. Farmer, Director, Recruiting - *Financial services, General management, Human resources*
Mr. Ben Perryman, Executive Search Consultant - *Financial services, Human resources*

Salary Minimum: $30,000

Functions: Management, Senior Mgmt., Mfg., Healthcare, Sales & Mktg., HR Mgmt., Finance, Engineering, Non-profits

Industries: Generalist (All), Transportation, Banking, Higher Ed., Government

Whittaker & Associates Inc

1000 Johnson Ferry Rd Ste B120
Marietta, GA 30068-2195
(678) 285-2222
Fax: (678) 285-0547
Email: jobs@whittakersearch.com
Web: www.whittakersearch.com

Summary: We specialize in the search and placement of managerial, supervisory and executive-level positions within the food industry with emphasis on dairy, meat, poultry, bakery ingredient and related products.

Key Contact - Specialty:
Mr. Arnold G. Whittaker, Chairman of the Board - *Dairy*
Mr. Brad Winkler, CPC, President - *Bakery*

Salary Minimum: $30,000

Functions: Senior Mgmt., Middle Mgmt., Product Dev., Production, Plant Mgmt., Quality, Distribution, Sales Mgmt., R&D, Engineering

Industries: Food, Bev., Tobacco

Joel H Wilensky Associates Inc

PO Box 155
Sudbury, MA 01776-0155
(978) 443-5176
Fax: (978) 443-3009
Email: jhwassoc@joelhwilensky.com
Web: www.joelhwilensky.com

Summary: The firm is a one-person contingency recruiting firm specializing in retail chain placement. Specific emphasis on corporate or home office placement (i.e. finance, IS, etc.).

Key Contact - Specialty:
Mr. Joel H. Wilensky, Executive Recruiter

Salary Minimum: $70,000

Functions: Generalist (All), Finance, CFOs, Taxes, IT, MIS Mgmt., Systems Dev.

Industries: Retail

WilliamCharles Executive Search

5550 Cascade Rd SE Ste 200
Grand Rapids, MI 49546-6480
(616) 464-4355
Fax: (616) 464-4359
Email: info@william charles.com
Web: www.william-charles.com

Summary: We are an executive level search firm that specializes in human recources, banking, finance, legal, and sales & marketing.

Key Contact - Specialty:
Mr. Bill Benson, Co-Founder & Partner
Mr. Chuck Smeester, Co-Founder & Partner - *Boards of Directors, CEOs, Executives, General management, Non-profit*
Mr. Brett Hoover, Senior Associate - *Banking, Banking (Commercial,Corporate,Investment,Merchant)*
Ms. Michele Bishop, Senior Associate - *Business development, C-level, Healthcare, Human resources, Legal (Attorneys)*
Ms. Vicki Legg, Senior Associate
Ms. Melanie VanDenHout, Research & Recruiting Specialist - *Human resources, Legal, Marketing, Office (Administration), Operations*

Salary Minimum: $60,000

Functions: Senior Mgmt.

Industries: Finance, Banking, Invest. Banking, Brokers, Non-profits, Legal, HR Services, Hospitals

John Williams & Associates

1309 Meadowild Dr
Round Rock, TX 78664-9322
(512) 990-9750
Fax: (512) 990-0543
Email: jwilliams401@aol.com

Summary: We are a full-service executive recruiting firm specializing in manufacturing operations, engineering, quality assurance and distribution/logistics disciplines, within the consumer food and beverage industries (both retained and exclusive contingency searches).

Key Contact - Specialty:
Mr. John G. Williams, President - *Engineering, Manufacturing*
Mrs. Alma Bustillos, Senior Associate

Functions: Generalist (All), Middle Mgmt., Plant Mgmt., Quality, Distribution, Engineering, Mgmt. Consultants, Minorities/Diversity

Industries: Generalist (All), Food, Bev., Tobacco, Soap, Perf., Cosmtcs., Drugs Mfg.

K L Williams & Associates

PO Box 5421
Auburn, CA 95604-5421
(530) 885-3693
Email: contact1@isearchbio.com
Web: www.isearchbio.com

Summary: We recruit mid to senior level sales, marketing, business development, marketing communications and some applications positions for the research laboratory market.

Key Contact - Specialty:
Ms. Kandi Williams, Owner

Functions: Sales & Mktg., R&D

Industries: Biotech/Life Sciences

Dick Williams & Associates

7901 Stoneridge Dr Ste 415
Pleasanton, CA 94588-3600
(925) 468-0304
Email: dick@dwasearch.com
Web: www.dwasearch.com

Summary: We are a dynamic, responsive, effective recruitment firm specializing in semiconductor capitol equipment, chemical, materials and related technology companies that include automation, motion control, bearings, linear motion, sensors and positioning systems. These positions include CEO, sales, marketing executives, process engineers & managers, ME,

EE, SW design engineers & managers, operations and service.

Key Contact - Specialty:
Mr. Dick Williams, President - *Process equipment, Sales*
Mr. Kenn Giles, Senior Executive Recruiter - *Process equipment, Sales*
Mr. Dave Lambert, Senior Executive Recruiter

Salary Minimum: $60,000

Functions: Senior Mgmt., Middle Mgmt., Automation, Sales & Mktg., Sales Mgmt., CFOs, Engineering

Industries: Computer Equip., Test, Measure Equip., Electronic, Elec. Components, Robotics, Semiconductors, RF/Microwave

Branches:
236 University Ave
Los Gatos, CA 95030-6013
(408) 354-7130
Email: semicons@verizon.net

Williams & Associates Inc

96 Cowley Ave
Etobicoke, ON M9B 2E5
Canada
(416) 626-9100
Fax: (416) 622-3205
Email: consultant@williamsandassociates.net
Web: www.williamsandassociates.net

Summary: Specializing in the industries involving exhibit & display, point-of-purchase, store fixtures, interiors, construction management, architectural consulting printing & pre-press, packaging, communications and custom fabrication.

Key Contact - Specialty:
Ms. Julianne Williams, President

Salary Minimum: $40,000

Functions: Generalist (All), Middle Mgmt.

Industries: Construction, Manufacturing, Printing, Plastics, Rubber, Metal Products, Misc. Mfg., Architectural Svcs., Media, Advertising, Packaging

The Williams Company

3844 W Beverly Dr
Dallas, TX 75209-5914
(214) 252-9333
Email: ssw26@aol.com

Summary: Our founder has extensive experience as a retail search consultant. We specialize in mid to upper-level retail management positions.

Key Contact - Specialty:
Ms. Sandra Williams, President & Owner - *Retail*

Salary Minimum: $50,000

Functions: Product Dev., Distribution, Advertising, Mktg. Research, Mktg. Mgmt., PR, HR Mgmt., Finance, CFOs, MIS Mgmt.

Industries: Retail

Williams Recruiting

10615 NE 47th Pl
Kirkland, WA 98033-7609
(425) 828-3956
(425) 869-7775
Fax: (425) 822-2356
Email: info@williamsrecruiting.com
Web: www.williamsrecruiting.com

Summary: We work with pharmaceutical and biotechnology companies. Functions within pharmaceutical and biotechnology are R&D, manufacturing & process development, regulatory

& clinical, quality, engineering, marketing and business development.

Key Contact - Specialty:
Ms. Gail Williams, President

Functions: Management, R&D

Industries: Drugs Mfg., Non-profits, Pharm Svcs., Biotech/Life Sciences

Williamsburg Group

PO Box 212
Dayton, NJ 08810-0212
(732) 329-3344
Fax: (732) 329-1620
Email: wgeileen@comcast.net
Web: www.williamsburgroup.com

Summary: Our reputation for success is built on pride, ethics, integrity and quality of service to our clients. Save valuable time and money by speaking to only our best candidates.

Key Contact - Specialty:
Ms. Eileen Levine, President - *Manufacturing, Technical*

Functions: Generalist (All), Product Dev., Production, Plant Mgmt., Quality, Purchasing, Packaging, R&D

Industries: Generalist (All), Chemicals, Soap, Perf., Cosmtcs., Drugs Mfg., Medical Devices, Plastics, Rubber, Metal Products, Misc. Mfg.

Willmott & Associates

922 Waltham St Ste 103
Lexington, MA 02421-8019
(781) 863-5400
Fax: (781) 863-8000
Email: willmott@willmott.com
Web: www.willmott.com

Summary: We are a HR consulting firm specializing in the search and placement of HR professionals both permanent and temp. We also provide fully customized talent acquisition solutions to organizations that need to implement new or compliment existing research/recruiting efforts.

Key Contact Specialty:
Mr. D. Clark Willmott, President - *Human resources*
Ms. Marilyn Dwyer, Recruiter - *Food & beverage, Human resources*

Salary Minimum: $60,000

Functions: Generalist (All), HR Mgmt., Benefits, Staffing, Training

Industries: Generalist (All)

Branches:
60 State St Lbby 7
Boston, MA 02109-1899
(617) 728-0990
Fax: (617) 728-0991
Key Contact - Specialty:
Ms. Joanne A. Lynch, Vice President, Contract Services

501 Islington St Ste 3
Portsmouth, NH 03801-4288
(603) 334-6663
(603) 334-6664
Fax: (603) 334-6688
Key Contact - Specialty:
Ms. Joyce Baldassare

95 Sockanosset Cross Rd Ste 107
Cranston, RI 02920-5559
(401) 943-5556
Fax: (401) 943-5575
Email: dzito@willmottri.com

Key Contact - Specialty:
Mr. David Zito, President

1660 International Dr Ste 400
Mc Lean, VA 22102-4855
(703) 287-0087
Fax: (703) 287-0085
Email: betsyf@willmott.com
Key Contact - Specialty:
Ms. Betsy Friedlander, President

N Willner & Company Inc

PO Box 746
Matawan, NJ 07747-0746
(732) 566-8882
Email: info@nwillner.com
Web: www.nwillner.com

Summary: We specialize in all areas of consumer marketing from the manager level thru VP/GM. Our strengths are in marketing management, sales promotion, marketing research and sales management.

Key Contact - Specialty:
Mr. Nathaniel Willner, President

Salary Minimum: $70,000

Functions: Sales & Mktg., Advertising, Mktg. Mgmt.

Industries: Food, Bev., Tobacco, Soap, Perf., Cosmtcs., Drugs Mfg., Consumer Elect., Misc. Mfg., Advertising

Willow, Wolff & Grace Co

(also known as MR of Palo Alto)
2479 E Bayshore Rd Ste 701
Palo Alto, CA 94303-3207
(650) 852-0667
Fax: (650) 852-0618
Email: hanako@wwgsearch.com
Web: www.wwgsearch.com

Summary: Our goal is to be recognized, respected and sought out by our clients as a valuable and essential member of and contributor to their staffing team.

Key Contact - Specialty:
Ms. Hanako Yanagi, JD, Partner - *Executives*
Mr. Richard Wolff, Managing Partner & Co-founder - *Executives, Management consulting*

Salary Minimum: $90,000

Functions: Generalist (All), Board Members, Senior Mgmt., Middle Mgmt., MIS Mgmt., Systems Analysis, Systems Implem., Attorneys

Industries: Generalist (All), Computer Equip., Transportation, Legal, E-commerce, Telecoms, Wireless, Software, ERP SW, Industry Specific SW, Mfg. SW

Willowbrook Employment Services Inc

3939 W Ridge Rd Ste A111
Erie, PA 16506-1884
(814) 835-4898
Fax: (814) 835-5275
Email: sue@willowbrookes.com
Web: www.willowbrookes.com

Summary: Executive recruiting nationally in varied industries. Specializing in locating hard to find candidates for difficult to fill positions. Excellence in customer service.

Key Contact - Specialty:
Ms. Sue Mckinney, Owner
Ms. Darlene Downey, Owner
Ms. Jen Davis, Secretary & Payroll Manager

Functions: Generalist (All)

Industries: Generalist (All)

Willstaff Inc

328 DeSiard St
Monroe, LA 71201-7429
(318) 324-8060
(318) 387-6090
Fax: (318) 324-9977
Email: willstaff@willstaff.net
Web: www.willstaff.net

Summary: Our trained and experienced group of staffing professionals has excelled in connecting skilled individuals with successful companies through working partnerships. Whether you are a business seeking solutions to your staffing needs or a talented individual searching for a rewarding job opportunity. We have the experience, information and skills to meet your individual needs.

Key Contact - Specialty:
Mr. Wayne Williamson, CPC, CTS, President & Chief Executive Officer
Ms. Mary Hendrix, Senior Vice President, Operations
Mr. Ross Johnson, CPC, Senior Vice President, Sales
Ms. Patti Mauney, CTS, Regional Vice President, Eastern Region
Ms. Sally Taylor, CTS, CPC, Regional Vice President, S Central Reg
Mr. Dave Wallace, Regional Vice President, Western Region
Ms. Kathy Williamson, Regional Vice President, Central Region
Ms. Christie Blue, CPA, Vice President & Controller
Mr. Ellis Lewis, CTS, Vice President & Receivables Management
Mr. Mark Daff, Director, Information Technology
Mr. Corby Reeves, Manager, Risk Management & Insurance
Ms. Aubrey Wood, Manager, Human Resources
Mr. John Taylor, Corporate Counsel
Ms. Dianne Barker, Executive Banking Recruiter - *Financial services, Human resources*
Ms. Sharlotte Parish

Functions: Middle Mgmt., Admin. Svcs., Distribution, Sales Mgmt., Customer Svc., HR Mgmt., Finance, Systems Dev., Engineering, Technicians

Industries: Agri., Forestry, Mining, Energy, Utilities, Construction, Manufacturing, Food, Bev., Tobacco, Transportation, Retail, Finance, Services, Legal, E-commerce, IT Implementation, Higher Ed., Hospitality, Media, Communications, Call Centers, Aerospace, Insurance, Software

Branches:
1500 Louisville Ave Ste 102
Monroe, LA 71201-6026
(318) 387-0099
Fax: (318) 361-0386
Email: monroe@willstaff.net
Key Contact - Specialty:
Mr. David Duffey, Manager

Wilson, Correll, Friedlander & Associates Inc

3135 State Road 580 Ste 13
Safety Harbor, FL 34695-4917
(727) 796-4955 x100
(877) 796-4955
Fax: (727) 796-4014
Email: wwilson@wcfanda.com
Web: www.sourcei.com

Summary: We are a search firm that specializes in the apparel, home furnishings and textile industry. Our consultants specialize in all levels of upper and mid-management, VP's, directors, sourcing, engineering, quality control, IT, design,

product development, production and logistics to name a few.
Key Contact - Specialty:
Mr. Wayne Wilson, President - *Apparel*
Ms. Lucie Campisi, Secretary & Treasurer
Ms. Cheri Boudreau, Director & Vice President, IT
Mr. Paul Correll, Jr., Vice President, Manufacturing - *Executives, Manufacturing*
Mr. John Bando, Director, Executive Search
Ms. Rhonda Smith, Administration
Mr. Tabin Talburt, Researcher

Salary Minimum: $50,000

Functions: Generalist (All), Senior Mgmt., Middle Mgmt., Mfg., Materials, Mktg. Mgmt., Sales Mgmt., IT, R&D, Engineering

Industries: Generalist (All), Textiles, Apparel, Retail

S R Wilson Inc

520 Mendocino Ave Ste 263
Santa Rosa, CA 95401-5257
(707) 571-5990
(707) 526-4411
Email: pams@sonic.net

Summary: We are historically strong in legal search (attorneys and top firm managers), telecommunication equipment industry (all management with emphasis on sales/marketing, engineers and top management) and the medical equipment industry placing CEO, COO, CFO and CTO. We are focused about 60 percent in legal, 25 percent in telecom and 15 percent in medical. Have also specialized in the optics/photonics industry. Also, banking operations placement.

Key Contact - Specialty:
Mr. Stoney Wilson, President
Ms. Pamela J. Wilson, Vice President

Salary Minimum: $45,000

Functions: CFOs, Budgeting, Cash Mgmt., Credit, Taxes, M&A, Risk Mgmt., Actuaries

Industries: Finance

Wilson Personnel Inc

134 Montford Ave
Asheville, NC 28801-2130
(828) 258-3900
Fax: (828) 258-3902
Email: wilsonpersonnel@ioa.com

Summary: We have been in business for many years in the recruitment and placement of engineers, technical and manufacturing management professionals. We have specialists in serving the manufacturing industries.

Key Contact - Specialty:
Mr. Kenneth Schapira, President - *Building products, Consumer (Hard Goods), Design, Mechanical, Technical (Management)*

Functions: Generalist (All), Middle Mgmt., Mfg., Materials, HR Mgmt., Engineering

Industries: Generalist (All), Manufacturing, Packaging, Non-Classifiable

The Wilson Stewart Group

540 Kenton Dr
Irmo, SC 29063-2192
(803) 260-4908
Email: js@wilsonstewartgroup.com

Summary: We provide expert recruitment services in the medical device industry. We perform executive searches for engineers, technical management, HR and senior executives. We work with Fortune 100 and 500 companies as well as up and coming bio-technology firms. Our success is

based on relationship development, trust and the ability to find the right fit for your company.

Key Contact - Specialty:
Mr. Jeff Stanley, Director, Development
Ms. Kelly Harrington, BA, Executive Recruiter - *Human resources*
Ms. Jill Warren, BS, Executive Recruiter
Mr. Tim Becknell, BS, Executive Recruiter

Salary Minimum: $50,000

Functions: Management, Senior Mgmt.

Industries: Medical Devices, Mgmt. Consulting, HR Services, Engineering Svcs., Biotech/Life Sciences

Wilson-Douglas-Jordan

1755 Park St Ste 200
Naperville, IL 60563-8404
(312) 782-0286
(630) 778-3838
Fax: (630) 983-0026
Email: wdjinc@aol.com

Summary: Our firm initially specialized in IT executive search and later broadened to include additional functional/executive areas. We provide retained/contingency search as well as outplacement services and contracted staffing. We have been a preferred search vendor to Big-4, product vendors, consulting firms and major Fortune-500 corporations spanning multiple industries.

Key Contact - Specialty:
Mr. John T. Wilson, President - *Management consulting*

Salary Minimum: $60,000

Functions: Senior Mgmt., IT, Systems Dev., Systems Implem.

Industries: Retail, Finance, Mgmt. Consulting, E-commerce, IT Implementation, Call Centers, Wireless, Insurance, Software, Accounting SW, Database SW, Development SW, ERP SW, System SW

Windsor Consultants Inc

13201 Northwest Fwy Ste 704
Houston, TX 77040-6025
(713) 460-0586
(866) 460-0586
Fax: (713) 460-0945
Email: windsor@wci78.com
Web: www.wci78.com

Summary: We are a top team of nine recruiters. We are highly successful in attorney placement nationwide as well as sales professionals in Texas. Both contingent fee and retained. All fees company paid.

Key Contact - Specialty:
Mr. Daniel Narsh, Chief Executive Officer - *Healthcare, Intellectual property*
Mr. Bruce Litvin, CPC, Manager, Legal Search
Mr. William Fraser, Manager, Sales Recruitment - *Sales*
Ms. Lynda Harris, Office Administrator - *Legal, Legal (Attorneys,Lawyers)*

Salary Minimum: $80,000

Functions: Generalist (All), Legal

Industries: Legal, Healthcare

Windsor Partners Inc

70 W Madison St Ste 1400
Chicago, IL 60602-4267
(312) 214-3760
Email: recruiter@windsorpartners.com

Summary: We recruit and place financial professionals for a diverse client base. Our search

engagements cross all financial functions. Our typical candidate has a postgraduate degree and usually started their career with a large CPA firm.

Key Contact - Specialty:
Mr. Alan S. Freemond, Jr., Principal - *Financial*

Salary Minimum: $70,000

Functions: Finance

Industries: Generalist (All)

Windsor Personnel & Executive Center

1319 Ouellette Ave
Windsor, ON N8X 1J6
Canada
(519) 258-9500
Fax: (519) 258-6478
Email: windsorpersonnel@on.aibn.com
Web: www.windsorpersonnel.com

Summary: Our focus is delivering qualified personnel in the following arenas; management, technical, administrative, sales, computer specialists, accounting, clerical, customer service representatives, bilingual CSRs and general labor.

Key Contact - Specialty:
Ms. Nancy O'Neill, Vice President, Sales & Marketing

Functions: Generalist (All), Management

Industries: Generalist (All), Motor Vehicles, Misc. Mfg., Mutual/Hedge Funds, Legal, Accounting, HR Services, E-commerce, IT Implementation, Engineering Svcs., Logistics Svcs., New Media, Call Centers, Software, Database SW

Windsor Southfield Service Co

6400 Farmington Rd Ste 105
West Bloomfield, MI 48322-2208
(248) 661-4174
Email: wssc82@att.net

Summary: Executive recruitment specializing in the food, pharmaceutical, medical, and retail industries.

Key Contact - Specialty:
Mr. Sam Skeegan, President - *Food, Pharmaceutical, Retail*

Salary Minimum: $60,000

Functions: Generalist (All), Board Members, Senior Mgmt., Materials, Mktg. Mgmt., IT, R&D, Engineering, Technicians

Industries: Manufacturing, Food, Bev., Tobacco, Chemicals, Drugs Mfg., Medical Devices, Pharm Svcs., Packaging, Software, Mfg. SW, Marketing SW, Biotech/Life Sciences, Healthcare

Windward Executive Search

1121 Hershey Dr
Marietta, GA 30062-4951
(770) 579-3877
Email: kennedy@hipotalent.net
Web: www.hipotalent.net

Summary: Retained search only for packaging and forest products related industries

Key Contact - Specialty:
Mr. Tom Arnette, President - *Executives, Forest industry/products, Human resources, Packaging, Paper*

Salary Minimum: $80,000

Functions: Generalist (All), Mfg.

Industries: Paper, Chemicals, Packaging

Winfield Associates Inc

53 Winter St
Weymouth, MA 02188-3367
(781) 337-1010
Fax: (781) 335-0089
Email: winfieldassociates@yahoo.com

Summary: We provide recruiting services for personnel in sales, marketing, general management, technical disciplines and regulatory affairs. The industries served are limited to manufacturers of medical and biotechnologynical products.

Key Contact - Specialty:
Mr. Carl W. Siegel, Owner

Salary Minimum: $40,000

Functions: Middle Mgmt., Product Dev., Production, Quality, Materials, Packaging, Mktg. Research, Mktg. Mgmt., Sales Mgmt.

Industries: Medical Devices

Winfield Scott Associates

140 Preston Executive Dr
Cary, NC 27513-8488
(919) 388-1915
(877) 767-0326
Fax: (919) 388-1916
Email: mscott@scottjobs.com

Summary: We specialize in experienced sales, design and manufacturing candidates in the corrugated box/POP display field. We focus on corrugated, folding carton, blister card and thermoforming.

Key Contact - Specialty:
Mr. Michael Scott, President

Functions: Generalist (All), Management, Senior Mgmt., Middle Mgmt., Sales & Mktg., Advertising, Mktg. Mgmt., Sales Mgmt., Eng. Design

Industries: Paper, Packaging

Wing Tips & Pumps Inc

PO Box 99580
Troy, MI 48099-9580
(248) 641-0980
Fax: (248) 641-0895
Email: wingtipsandpumps@comcast.net

Summary: We are a minority-owned executive search corporation emphasizing world-class service. We place executives in all areas.

Key Contact - Specialty:
Mr. Verba Lee Edwards, President & Chief Executive Officer - *Engineering, Finance, Human resources, Manufacturing*

Salary Minimum: $50,000

Functions: Generalist (All), Mfg., Plant Mgmt., Quality, Purchasing, Benefits, Cash Mgmt., Systems Dev., Engineering, Minorities/Diversity

Industries: Generalist (All), Plastics, Rubber, Motor Vehicles, Banking, Restaurants, Environmental Svcs., Packaging, Software

The Winn Group Inc

501 Lawrence Ave
Lawrence, KS 66049-4211
(785) 842-7111
(800) 844-9466
Fax: (785) 842-6333
Email: pam@thewinngroup.com
Web: www.thewinngroup.com

Summary: We are a sharply focused and selective recruiting practice limited exclusively to property and casualty actuaries.

Key Contact - Specialty:
Mr. James G. Winn, President

Salary Minimum: $50,000

Functions: Generalist (All), Actuaries

Industries: Insurance, Casualty

Branches:
4708 Wimbledon Dr
Lawrence, KS 66047-9301
(800) 337-5054
(785) 843-6001
Fax: (785) 843-6008
Email: pam@thewinngroup.com
Key Contact - Specialty:
Mr. Tom Heath, Vice President - *CEOs, CFOs, COOs, HMOs, Insurance*
Ms. Pamela A. Heath, Vice President

Winston & Green

111 W Washington St Ste 841
Chicago, IL 60602-2794
(312) 201-9777
Fax: (312) 201-9781
Email: lgreen@winstonandgreen.com
Web: www.winstonandgreen.com

Summary: We specialize in general counsel, senior corporate counsel and staff attorneys for corporations and law firms of all sizes. Law firm mergers & acquisitions. We conduct marketing and research studies for law firms. In addition, we consult with law firms on minority attorney retention and career development. We are committed to diversity programs.

Key Contact - Specialty:
Mr. Larry Green, President
Mr. Green

Salary Minimum: $80,000

Functions: Legal

Industries: Generalist (All), Communications, Telecoms, Insurance, Real Estate, Property/Facility Mgmt., Healthcare

Winter Wyman Co

950 Winter St Ste 3100
Waltham, MA 02451-1494
(781) 890-7000
Fax: (781) 890-3266
Email: global@winterwyman.com
Web: www.winterwyman.com

Summary: Professionals who are experienced in their specialty fields staff our contingency firm.

Key Contact - Specialty:
Mr. Kevin M. Steele, President

Salary Minimum: $40,000

Functions: Generalist (All), Sales & Mktg., Mktg. Mgmt., Sales Mgmt., Staffing, CFOs, Budgeting, MIS Mgmt., Systems Analysis

Industries: Generalist (All), Banking, Invest. Banking, Brokers, Misc. Financial, Accounting, E-commerce, IT Implementation, HR SW, Marketing SW

Branches:
75 Federal St Ste 720
Boston, MA 02110-1944
(617) 880-3000
Fax: (617) 880-3100
Email: boston@winterwyman.com
Key Contact - Specialty:
Mr. Ken Martin
Ms. Cheryl Simmons

405 Lexington Ave Fl 26
New York, NY 10174-2699
(888) 529-9300
Fax: (888) 321-5782

Email: newyork@winterwyman.com
Key Contact - Specialty:
Mr. Ian Ide - *Technology*
Mr. Jon Mazzocchi - *Accounting*

11921 Freedom Dr Ste 550
Reston, VA 20190-5635
(888) 986-6800
Email: dc@winterwyman.com
Key Contact - Specialty:
Mr. Mike Fitzgerald - *Technology*

Wisconsin Executive Search Group Ltd

2631 University Ave Ste 102
Madison, WI 53705-3774
(608) 231-5280
(608) 233-1759
Fax: (608) 231-5299
Email: jhr@wisexec.com
Web: www.wisexec.com

Summary: We specialize in banking, finance, engineering, manufacturing, utilities, eBusiness, business-to-business, insurance, healthcare, IT, retail and marketing.

Key Contact - Specialty:
Dr. John Richert, PhD, President
Mr. George Evers, Executive Recruiter - *Finance*
Mr. Michael Eisele, Vice President - *Business to business, Healthcare, Marketing*

Salary Minimum: $50,000

Functions: Management, Healthcare, Sales & Mktg., IT

Industries: Energy, Utilities, Manufacturing, Drugs Mfg., Retail, Finance, Banking, Pharm Svcs., E-commerce, Engineering Svcs., Advertising, Environmental Svcs., Insurance, Biotech/Life Sciences, Healthcare, Long-term/Home Care

Wise Men Consultants

1500 S Dairy Ashford St Ste 477
Houston, TX 77077-3861
(281) 497-5302
(281) 679-6740
Fax: (281) 679-6826
Email: recruiter@wisemen.net
Web: www.wisemen.net

Summary: IT staff augmentation; software development and system integration; offshore software development at considerable savings. A software product for supplier diversity departments to manage MWBE/HUB & 8A suppliers.

Key Contact - Specialty:
Mrs. Juhi Ahuja, President
Mr. Omprakash Ahuja, Vice President

Salary Minimum: $36,000

Functions: Product Dev., IT, MIS Mgmt., Systems Dev., Systems Implem., Network Admin., DB Admin., Mgmt. Consultants

Industries: Generalist (All), Mgmt. Consulting, Software

The Witt Group

PO Box 521281
Longwood, FL 32752-1281
(407) 324-4137
Fax: (407) 322-5172
Email: jwitt5@cfl.rr.com

Summary: We specialize in technical placements in the chemical industry. We have an excellent , ratio of offers to interviews.

Key Contact - Specialty:
Mr. Gerald E. Witt, President - *Sales, Technical*

Salary Minimum: $50,000

Functions: Management, Mfg., Product Dev., Plant Mgmt., Quality, Sales & Mktg., R&D, Engineering

Industries: Chemicals, Soap, Perf., Cosmtcs., Drugs Mfg., Plastics, Rubber, Paints, Petro. Products, Biotech/Life Sciences

WMD Inc

PO Box 123
Lenox, MA 01240-0123
(413) 637-8110

Summary: Our firm recruits, using experience within the areas of search. We understand both sides, from the company's viewpoint and the candidate's viewpoint.

Key Contact - Specialty:
Mr. Wayne Donelon, Senior Parnter - *Power*

Salary Minimum: $50,000

Functions: Management, Board Members, Senior Mgmt., Middle Mgmt., Mfg., Materials, Purchasing, Sales & Mktg., Engineering, Int'l.

Industries: Energy, Utilities, Equip Svcs.

L Wolf & Associates

3 Oriole Rd
New City, NY 10956-6313
(845) 634-1800
Email: larrywolf@optonline.net

Summary: We are an executive search firm specializing in accounting and finance. We have experience in the placement profession.

Key Contact - Specialty:
Mr. Lawrence Wolf, President

Salary Minimum: $70,000

Functions: Finance

Industries: Generalist (All)

Wood & Associates

17 Escalle Ln
Larkspur, CA 94939-1294
(415) 927-3112
Fax: (415) 927-3117
Email: mwood9775@sbcglobal.net

Summary: We specialize in the placement of civil, structural, environmental, and geo-technical engineering professionals.

Key Contact - Specialty:
Mr. Milo Wood, Owner - *Environmental*

Salary Minimum: $50,000

Functions: Engineering

Industries: Energy, Utilities, Construction, Transportation, Environmental Svcs., Haz. Waste

Wood Search & Consulting Inc

PO Box 92985
Southlake, TX 76092-0985
(817) 424-9162
Fax: (817) 251-9408
Email: woodconsulting@aol.com
Web: www.woodsearchandconsulting.com

Summary: We are a search firm and HR services provider that is based upon professional knowledge, responsiveness, integrity and guaranteed results. We specialize in: accounting, administration, construction, engineering, hospitality and sales. Our firm presents highly qualified candidates to our clients in a timely manner.

Key Contact - Specialty:
Ms. Dorothy Wood, President - *Management*

Functions: Generalist (All)

Industries: Generalist (All), Pharm Svcs., Legal, Accounting, Healthcare

Wood West & Partners Inc
700-1281 Georgia St W
Imperial Oil Building
Vancouver, BC V6E 3J7
Canada
(604) 682-3141
Fax: (604) 688-5749
Email: search@wood-west.com
Web: www.wood-west.com

Summary: We conduct executive search and recruitment for permanent and contract positions for managers and specialists in finance & banking, marketing & sales and engineering & manufacturing.

Key Contact - Specialty:
Mr. Ron Wood, BA, Principal - *Storage, Systems, Technology, Telecommunications, Wireless*
Mr. Fred West, PEng, Principal
Mr. John Jaye, Senior Consultant - *Investment management, Loans, Management, MBAs, Private equity*
Mr. Bal Gill, BA, Search Consultant - *Construction, Engineering, Environmental, Risk management*
Mr. Michael O'Brien, Search Consultant - *Information Technology, Systems, Telecommunications, Wireless*
Ms. Barb Goepel, Search Consultant - *Banking, Finance, Investment management*

Salary Minimum: $35,000

Functions: Management

Industries: Manufacturing, Computer Equip., Transportation, Banking, Invest. Banking, Accounting, Communications, Telecoms, Telephony, Environmental Svcs.

Woodlyn Partners Inc
281 Winter St Ste 305
Waltham, MA 02451-8715
(781) 890-6590
Email: info@woodlynpartners.com
Web: www.woodlynpartners.com

Summary: We are a contingency staffing firm with extensive combined experience, focusing exclusively on the search and placement of high technology sales & marketing professionals. Client companies can be found in enterprise software, telecom, data communications, eCommerce, internet, computer hardware and services.

Key Contact - Specialty:
Mr. Lee Hoffstein, Founding Partner
Ms. Sharon LoVan, Founding Partner
Mr. Mike Bernard, Founding Partner
Mr. Chris DeAnzeris, Partner
Mr. Ken Mossman, Partner - *Financial services, Management consulting, Professional services*

Functions: Sales & Mktg.

Industries: Communications, Software

Woodmoor Group Inc
PO Box 2938
Monument, CO 80132-2938
(719) 488-8589
Fax: (719) 488-9043
Email: woodmoor@woodmoor.com
Web: www.woodmoor.com

Summary: Experienced, energetic and tenacious, we conduct comprehensive searches with professionalism, always mindful that we are an extension of your company. We consider it a point of honor to complete every search assigned to us.

Key Contact - Specialty:
Mr. Ray N. Bedingfield, President - *Manufacturing*
Mr. Wendell Engle, Vice President - *Chemical*
Mr. Jeff Rose, Vice President
Mr. L.D. Williams, Vice President
Mr. Chris Petrucelli, Vice President

Salary Minimum: $60,000

Functions: Generalist (All)

Industries: Generalist (All)

Woodruff Associates
PO Box 25036
Seattle, WA 98165-1936
(206) 622-9634
Fax: (206) 622-4149
Email: rick@woodruffassociates.com
Web: www.woodruffassociates.com

Summary: We are a supermarket/wholesale, grocery/food service/consumer packaged goods recruiting firm for middle management and senior management. We have extensive recruiting experience with an outstanding track record with small, medium and large companies.

Key Contact - Specialty:
Mr. Rick Woodruff, President - *Supermarkets*

Salary Minimum: $60,000

Functions: Generalist (All)

Industries: Food, Bev., Tobacco, Soap, Perf., Cosmtcs., Wholesale, Retail, Pharm Svcs., Accounting, Logistics Svcs.

Jim Woodson & Associates Inc
1080 River Oaks Dr Ste B102
Jackson, MS 39232-9779
(601) 936-4037
Fax: (601) 936-4041
Email: jim@woodsonsearch.com

Summary: We recruit heavily in engineering and manufacturing to include metal fabrication, high volume assembly, machined products, consumer appliances, consumer electronics, automotive, electric motors and environmental. We also actively recruit accounting and financial people.

Key Contact - Specialty:
Mr. Jim Woodson, President

Salary Minimum: $40,000

Functions: Generalist (All), Management

Industries: Paper, Chemicals, Drugs Mfg., Medical Devices, Plastics, Rubber, Paints, Petro. Products, Metal Products, Machine, Appliance, Motor Vehicles, Misc. Mfg., Electronic, Elec. Components, Accounting

Wooldridge + Associates
12 E Greenway Plz Ste 1100
Houston, TX 77046-1201
(713) 521-2800
Fax: (713) 521-2865
Email: info@wooldridgeassociates.com
Web: www.wooldridgeassociates.com

Summary: Placement of attorneys at law firms and corporations.

Key Contact - Specialty:
Ms. Nancy K. Wooldridge

Functions: Staffing, Legal

Industries: Legal, HR Services

Chris Woolsey & Associates LLC
1949 E Sunshine St Ste 2-106
Springfield, MO 65804-1604
(417) 887-1229
Fax: (417) 888-2452
Email: cow@cwoolsey.com
Web: www.cwoolsey.com

Summary: We specialize in the placement of degreed professionals in the food and beverage manufacturing industry nationwide focusing on operations, engineering, maintenance, quality assurance, supply chain, HR, logistics, distribution, purchasing, etc.

Key Contact - Specialty:
Mr. Chris O. Woolsey, Principal - *Engineering, Maintenance, Operations*
Ms. Jackie Woolsey, Principal

Salary Minimum: $48,000

Functions: Generalist (All), Mfg.

Industries: Generalist (All), Food, Bev., Tobacco, Paper, Chemicals, Soap, Perf., Cosmtcs., Drugs Mfg.

Workforce Development Inc
(doing business as The Tarquinio Recruiting Group)
PO Box 722
Warrendale, PA 15095-0722
(724) 772-2000
Fax: (724) 772-2088
Email: job4you@nauticom.net
Web: www.tarquiniorecruiting.com

Summary: We are a national provider of permanent placement within the sales function of B2B selling organizations: positions include sales, sales and executive management, and pre-sales engineers.

Key Contact - Specialty:
Ms. Leslie Tarquinio, President
Mr. Alfred Tarquinio, Associate

Functions: Generalist (All), Sales & Mktg., Sales Mgmt., Technicians

Industries: Travel, Telecoms, Telephony, Digital, Fiber Optic, Network Infrastructure, Training SW

Workforce Solutions Group
22362 Gilberto Ste 205
Rancho Santa Margarita, CA 92688-2153
(949) 858-2230
Fax: (949) 858-2202
Email: pjung@workforcesolutionsgroup.com
Web: www.workforcesolutionsgroup.com

Summary: The human capital component of any organization is crucial. Attracting and hiring high caliber employees is a key element. Our firm combines the finest industry recruiters to secure and stabilize your workforce. With our extensive experience in human capital management, we are uniquely qualified to assist you with specialized placement services.

Key Contact - Specialty:
Ms. Colleen Jones, Chief Operating Officer - *Healthcare, Management, Sales, Staffing*
Mrs. Pamela Jung, Chief Executive Officer - *Healthcare, Sales, Staffing*

Salary Minimum: $45,000

Functions: Generalist (All), Management, Healthcare, Sales & Mktg., Sales Mgmt., Finance

Industries: Generalist (All), Construction, Finance, HR Services, Government, Environmental Svcs., Real Estate, Healthcare

Branches:
30021 Tomas
Rancho Santa Margarita, CA 92688-2128
(949) 766-6913
Fax: (949) 858-2202
Email: info@workforcesolutionsgroup.com
Key Contact - Specialty:
Ms. Irene Simpson, Manager, Recruiting -
  Healthcare, Sales

Workplace Solutions

616-268 Lakeshore Rd E
UPS Store
Oakville, ON L6J 7S4
Canada
(416) 410-0898
Fax: (905) 845-5548
Email: info@workplacesolutions.ca
Web: www.workplacesolutions.ca

Summary: Our firm was established with the view
to building trusting relationships with local
businesses and job seekers by providing a full
range of recruitment, training and HR services.
Our motto is "Common sense solutions for
complicated matters."

Key Contact - Specialty:
Ms. Lucille Conlon, President

Functions: Generalist (All)

Industries: Generalist (All), Manufacturing, Food,
  Bev., Tobacco, Transportation, Logistics Svcs.,
  Call Centers, Packaging

The Works

197 8th St
Charlestown, MA 02129-4208
(617) 241-0647
Fax: (617) 241-4904
Email: info@theworksnet.com
Web: www.theworksnet.com

Summary: We offer clients marketing, public
relations and creative talent on a freelance,
contract or permanent basis. We have expertise in
contingency, retained, temp and project based
consulting and search services.

Key Contact - Specialty:
Mr. Peter Eleftherio, Principal - *Marketing*
Ms. Alicia Recupero, Principal - *Marketing*
Ms. Melanie Lewis, Principal - *Marketing*

Functions: Senior Mgmt., Middle Mgmt., Product
  Dev., Advertising, Mktg. Research, Mktg.
  Mgmt., Direct Mktg., PR

Industries: Generalist (All), Drugs Mfg., Medical
  Devices, Consumer Elect., Finance, Venture
  Cap., Services, Mgmt. Consulting, Advertising,
  New Media, Communications, Telecoms,
  Software, Marketing SW

Worlco Computer Resources Inc

997 Old Eagle School Rd Ste 219
Wayne, PA 19087-1706
(610) 293-9070
Fax: (610) 293-1027
Email: parisi@worlco.com
Web: www.worlco.com

Summary: Our firm provides the full range of
recruiting, executive search and personnel
consulting services relating to Information
Technology professionals and executives. We
place IT consultants and undertake project
professional services assignments.

Key Contact - Specialty:
Mr. Frank Parisi, Managing Partner -
  Communications

Salary Minimum: $25,000

Functions: Generalist (All), Mktg. Mgmt., Sales
  Mgmt., IT, MIS Mgmt., Systems Analysis,
  Systems Implem., Systems Support

Industries: Generalist (All), Software

Branches:
901 Route 38
Cherry Hill, NJ 08002-2890
(856) 665-4700
Fax: (856) 665-8142
Email: hughes@worlco.com
Key Contact - Specialty:
Mr. Robert J. Hughes, Managing Partner

203 Plantation Dr
Southern Pines, NC 28387-2966
(910) 692-1378
Fax: (910) 692-1378
Email: jparisi@worlco.com
Key Contact - Specialty:
Mr. John Parisi, Senior Partner

World Search

2802 Carriage Ln
Springfield, OH 45505-4522
(937) 327-0667
Fax: (937) 327-0675
Email: world@erinet.com

Summary: We conduct contingency and retained
search, with emphasis in the engineering,
production management.

Key Contact - Specialty:
Mr. Thomas A. Baehl, President
Ms. Mary Kay Baehl, Vice President -
  Engineering

Salary Minimum: $40,000

Functions: Generalist (All), Management, Mfg.,
  Product Dev., Automation, Productivity, Sales
  Mgmt., Systems Analysis, Systems Implem.,
  Engineering

Industries: Generalist (All), Manufacturing,
  Printing, Plastics, Rubber, Metal Products,
  Machine, Appliance, Motor Vehicles, Robotics,
  Mgmt. Consulting, Engineering Svcs., Supply
  Chain Mgmt., Aerospace

Worldwide Executive Search

18101 Von Karman Ave Ste 330
Irvine, CA 92612-0146
(949) 388-4596
Email: info@worldwideexecsearch.com
Web: www.worldwideexecsearch.com

Summary: Our firm specializes in identifying
exceptional leaders within multiple industries. We
conduct both retained and contingency search
assignments with the highest level of integrity and
confidentiality. We offer speed of service, flexible
fee structure and a unconditional free replacement
guarantee.

Key Contact - Specialty:
Mr. Jim Ginther, President & Chief Executive
  Officer

Salary Minimum: $70,000

Functions: Management, Senior Mgmt., Middle
  Mgmt., Sales & Mktg., Sales Mgmt., CFOs

Industries: Generalist (All), Food, Bev., Tobacco,
  Retail, Finance, Accounting, Hospitality,
  Telecoms, Real Estate, Property/Facility Mgmt.,
  Software, Healthcare, Hospitals, Long-
  term/Home Care

Worldwide Medical Services

(also known as Bay Area Anesthesia Inc
TravelDoctor.com)
617 S State St
Ukiah, CA 95482-4912
(707) 462-9420
(800) 327-8362
Fax: (707) 462-5208
Email: locumnet@traveldoctor.com
Web: www.wwmedical.com

Summary: We place temp locum tenen
physicians, CRNA and mid-level clinicians for
anesthesiology and radiology. We have a large
proprietary database of over 150,000 clinicians,
many of whom are available for both permanent
and temp jobs and carry a multitude of medical
licenscs covering all states nationwide. We are an
official Federal GSA contractor for temp
physicians and CRNAS. We also assist in the
buy/sell of medical practices.

Key Contact - Specialty:
Mr. John Paju, President
Mr. Jack Sherwood, Radiology Recruitment
  Manager
Mr. John Lindsteadt, Manager, Anesthesia
  Recruitment
Mrs. Susan Bridwell, Government Contract
  Officer - *Surgical*

Salary Minimum: $100,000

Functions: Senior Mgmt., Admin. Svcs.,
  Healthcare, Physicians, Nurses, Allied Health,
  HR Mgmt., Int'l.

Industries: Mgmt. Consulting, HR Services,
  Travel, Government, Insurance, Healthcare,
  Hospitals, Non-Classifiable

Worldwide Resources Inc

7931 S Upham St
Littleton, CO 80128-5624
(303) 972-0609
Fax: (303) 973-8025
Email: davisb@qwest.net

Summary: We are a recruiting/search firm with
extensive experience placing FTE and contract IT
or engineering candidates. We provide our clients
and candidates with more options and diversity.
Many of our services are free - job posting,
resume critique and distribution, career
counseling, coaching, interview tips and salary
surveys to name a few. Personable, honest service
you can trust.

Key Contact - Specialty:
Mr. Bobby Davis, President

Functions: Quality, PR, Finance, IT, MIS Mgmt.,
  Systems Dev., Systems Implem., DB Admin.,
  Engineering, Process

Industries: Generalist (All), Construction,
  Manufacturing, Medical Devices, Computer
  Equip., Consumer Elect., Test, Measure Equip.,
  Misc. Mfg., Electronic, Elec. Components,
  Robotics, Semiconductors, Finance, Banking,
  Services, Supply Chain Mgmt,
  Communications, Telecoms, Government,
  Homeland Security, Aerospace, Insurance,
  Software, Database SW, Mfg. SW, Security SW

The Worth Group LLC

3850 Holcomb Bridge Rd Ste 110
Norcross, GA 30092-5220
(678) 421-9770
Fax: (678) 421-9773
Email: info@theworthgroup.com
Web: www.theworthgroup.com

Summary: Our firm is a retained and contingency
search firm focusing in the communications and
call center industries. Our clients range from start-

ups to Fortune 500 companies. Our applications include CTI, CRM, ERP, sales force automation, workforce management, e-commerce, internet, LAN/WAN and more. We place in executive level management, sales, sales support and tech support. Our successful performance has led to confidence and credibility among our clients.

Key Contact - Specialty:
Mr. Brett Buckwald, President

Salary Minimum: $75,000

Functions: Generalist (All), Management

Industries: Finance, Media, Telecoms, Software

Branches:
129 Broadway
Lynbrook, NY 11563-3281
(516) 887-8555
Fax: (516) 596-4987
Key Contact - Specialty:
Mr. Al Rosenblum - *Telecommunications*

Worthmore Inc

969 De Soto Ln Ste 201
Foster City, CA 94404-2927
(650) 341-4480
Fax: (650) 341-4417
Email: inquiry@worthmore.com
Web: www.worthmore.com

Summary: We are an executive consulting and coaching company offering a unique combination of consulting, coaching and search capabilities. We serve companies in the financial services industry with a focus on investment real estate, securities, portfolio management, collectibles, insurance, accounting/family office and research.

Key Contact - Specialty:
Mr. Kraig Rudinger, Vice President - *Capital markets, Financial services, Private equity, Real estate*

Salary Minimum: $950,000

Functions: Management

Industries: Finance, Non-profits, Legal, Accounting, Insurance, Real Estate, Accounting SW

Jay Wren & Associates

6355 Riverside Blvd Ste P
Sacramento, CA 95831-1143
(916) 394-2920
Email: cchasejaywren@msn.com
Web: www.jaywren.com

Summary: This firm has placed marketing managers, sales managers, sales support managers, product and brand managers with over 50 major consumer package goods companies and consumer package goods promotional, service and information companies.

Key Contact - Specialty:
Mr. Jay Wren, Owner

Salary Minimum: $50,000

Functions: Sales & Mktg., Mktg. Research, Direct Mktg.

Industries: Food, Bev., Tobacco, Soap, Perf., Cosmtcs., Drugs Mfg.

Arthur Wright & Associates Inc

12205 Old Big Bend Rd
Kirkwood, MO 63122-6803
(314) 822-7400
Fax: (314) 822-2553
Email: search@arthurwright.com

Summary: Recruiting specialists for the manufacturing industry. We cover all salary positions inside the manufacturing facility.

Key Contact - Specialty:
Mr. Craig S. Nowotny, President

Salary Minimum: $100,000

Functions: Mfg., Automation, Plant Mgmt., Materials Plng., Advertising, Training

Industries: Food, Bev., Tobacco, Lumber, Furniture, Printing, Soap, Perf., Cosmtcs., Medical Devices, Plastics, Rubber, Paints, Petro. Products, Metal Products, Machine, Appliance, Motor Vehicles, Misc. Mfg., Electronic, Elec. Components, Mfg. SW

Wright Associates

PO Box 3047
South Attleboro, MA 02703-0906
(508) 761-6354
Email: garywright@prodigy.net
Web: www.wrightassociates.org

Summary: We are a privately owned recruiting and executive search firm specializing in the high-technology industry. Management consulting services are also available. Specialized in all software, hardware, & IT positions from the technical level up through the VP level.

Key Contact - Specialty:
Mr. Gary Wright, President

Salary Minimum: $75,000

Functions: Generalist (All), Management, Senior Mgmt., Middle Mgmt., Customer Svc., IT, MIS Mgmt.

Industries: Computer Equip., Equip Svcs., Mgmt. Consulting, Call Centers, Telephony, Wireless, Software, Database SW, Development SW, Doc. Mgmt., Production SW, ERP SW, HR SW, Mfg. SW, System SW

Bob Wright Recruiting Inc

56 DeForest Rd
Wilton, CT 06897-1909
(203) 762-9046
Fax: (203) 762-5807
Email: bwri@optonline.net

Summary: Our principal has worked in direct marketing, sales promotion and business information industries. We specialize in placing new business development sales, general management, marketing and medical talent.

Key Contact - Specialty:
Mr. Bob Wright, President

Salary Minimum: $40,000

Functions: Management, Middle Mgmt., Sales & Mktg., Advertising, Mktg. Research, Mktg. Mgmt., Sales Mgmt., Direct Mktg., Customer Svc.

Industries: Advertising, New Media, Database SW, Development SW, Marketing SW

WSA Associates Restaurant Management Recruiting

5521 N Sierra Hermosa Ct Ste 101
Litchfield Park, AZ 85340-8386
(623) 935-0000
Fax: (623) 547-3836
Email: wsasearch@cox.net

Summary: We offer placement services in all areas of the restaurant industry specializing in operations, upper level management and HR. Other areas include: finance, training, site selection, construction and real estate.

Key Contact - Specialty:
Mr. Jeff Stone, Managing Partner

Salary Minimum: $35,000

Functions: Management, Senior Mgmt., Sales & Mktg., HR Mgmt., Staffing, Training, Finance, Risk Mgmt., Hospitality, Chefs

Industries: Restaurants, Quick Service Restaurants, Full Service Restaurants

John Wylie Associates Inc

1727 E 71st St
Tulsa, OK 74136-5108
(918) 496-2100
Email: jlwylie@sbcglobal.net

Summary: Management and Technical searches principally in oil, gas, and manufacturing in the South Central and Southwestern states.

Key Contact - Specialty:
Mr. John L. Wylie, President - *Technical*

Salary Minimum: $25,000

Functions: Generalist (All), Management, Mfg., Materials, HR Mgmt., IT, R&D, Engineering

Industries: Generalist (All), Energy, Utilities, Manufacturing, Environmental Svcs., Software

The Wylie Group Ltd

345 N Canal St Apt 1605
Chicago, IL 60606-1295
(312) 822-0333
Fax: (312) 454-1375
Email: wrw@wyliegroup.net

Summary: We focus on senior sales, sales management, national accounts, marketing, across a spectrum of industries.

Key Contact - Specialty:
Mr. William Wylie, President
Mr. Monet Stalle, Vice President, Research

Salary Minimum: $75,000

Functions: Generalist (All), Sales & Mktg., Mktg. Mgmt., Sales Mgmt.

Industries: Lumber, Furniture, Metal Products, Misc. Mfg., Mgmt. Consulting, Publishing

Dennis Wynn Associates Inc

PO Box 7100
Saint Petersburg, FL 33734-7100
(727) 823-2042
Email: denniswynn@msn.com

Summary: We are an IS recruitment specialist.

Key Contact - Specialty:
Mr. Dennis N. Wynn, President
Ms. Jean Wynn, Treasurer

Salary Minimum: $35,000

Functions: Generalist (All), MIS Mgmt., Systems Analysis, Systems Dev., Systems Implem., Systems Support, Network Admin., DB Admin.

Industries: Generalist (All), Software

X Staff

18 Washington St # 246
Canton, MA 02021-4004
(781) 251-0011
(866) 978-2331
Fax: (303) 766-9692
Email: dan@xstaff.com
Web: www.xstaff.com

Summary: We specialize in search and placement for information systems/technology and software engineering professionals throughout the Greater Boston region.

Key Contact - Specialty:
Mr. Dan Robitaille, CPC, Founder - *CIOs, Computers, Computers (Networking, Programming, Software)*

Functions: Generalist (All), MIS Mgmt.

Industries: Generalist (All), Medical Devices, Computer Equip., Consumer Goods, Finance, Services, Communications, Software, Biotech/Life Sciences, Healthcare

XH Consulting

4005 Howell Ferry Rd Ste 2500
Duluth, GA 30096-3124
(770) 497-0525
Email: webmistress@x-hunters.com
Web: www.x-hunters.com

Summary: Providing permanent placement and project consulting services. Focus on technical and management/executive area with strong diversity recruiting options.

Key Contact - Specialty:
Mr. James Marr, Account Manager

Salary Minimum: $50,000

Functions: Management, IT, Minorities/Diversity

Industries: Generalist (All)

XPE Incorporated

PO Box 158
Simi Valley, CA 93062-0158
(805) 579-6400
(866) 579-6400
Fax: (805) 579-6464
Email: info@xpe-inc.com
Web: www.xpe-inc.com

Summary: We are a professional services organization founded on the strategic importance of human capital management and a 'people first' orientation as a means to achieve significant revenue growth and market share capture that outpaces stakeholder expectations. We specialize in executive search, professional level permanent placement, interim executive management and strategic business consultation.

Key Contact - Specialty:
Mr. Todd McClure Cook, President & Chief Executive Officer

Functions: Management, Senior Mgmt., Healthcare, Physicians, Nurses, Allied Health

Industries: Pharm Svcs., K-12 Ed., Higher Ed., Healthcare, Hospitals, Long-term/Home Care, Dental, Physical Therapy, Occupational Therapy, Women's

Xycorp Inc

700-2 Sheppard Ave E
North York, ON M2N 5Y7
Canada
(416) 225-9900
Fax: (416) 225-9104
Email: info@xycorp.com
Web: www.xycorp.com

Summary: We specialize in the placement of IT professionals, both contract and permanent into both the vendor community and end users of information technology.

Key Contact - Specialty:
Mr. Chris Cullen, Manager, Customer Relationship
Mr. Frank Switt, Vice President, Sales

Salary Minimum: $30,000

Functions: Generalist (All), IT

Industries: Generalist (All), IT Implementation

The Yaiser Group

PO Box 665
Englewood, NJ 07631-0665
(201) 568-4745
Fax: (201) 894-0297
Email: dick.yaiser@verizon.net
Web: mysite.verizon.net/bizo58sa/

Summary: We are ethical, on target and waste neither our time nor yours in our efforts to identify proper candidates based upon your specifications.

Key Contact - Specialty:
Mr. Richard A. Yaiser, Senior Partner - *Medical (Devices), Pharmaceutical*

Salary Minimum: $40,000

Functions: Generalist (All), Mfg., Product Dev., Production, Quality, Allied Health, R&D, Engineering, Process, Specialized Svcs.

Industries: Drugs Mfg., Pharm Svcs.

York & Associates

929 38th Avenue Ct Ste 104D
Greeley, CO 80634-1546
(970) 352-3086
Fax: (970) 352-3087
Email: tyork@tyorkassociates.com

Summary: Focus is on mid-size construction companies, including commercial, industrial and public works companies. We provide the most thorough screening in the search industry. Clients interview only the perfect match candidates.

Key Contact - Specialty:
Ms. Teri F. York, President - *Construction*

Salary Minimum: $45,000

Functions: Management, Senior Mgmt., Middle Mgmt., Sales & Mktg., HR Mgmt., Finance, CFOs, Bldg. Contractors, Health & Safety

Industries: Construction

York & Associates LLC

51 N 3rd St Ste 409
Newark, OH 43055-5566
(888) 368-9675
Fax: (888) 486-2030
Email: jobs@yabanker.com
Web: www.yabanker.com

Summary: Executive recruiting firm specializing in the banking and financial services industry. Areas of expertise include but are not limited to: CEO, President, City Executive, CCO, CLO, CFO, Controller, Commercial Lender, Operations, Trust, Audit, and Credit.

Key Contact - Specialty:
Ms. Carrie E. York, CPC, President

Salary Minimum: $50,000

Functions: Generalist (All)

Industries: Banking

The York Group

3958 Rambla Orienta St
Malibu, CA 90265-5116
(310) 317-8568
Fax: (310) 317-8570
Email: yorkgrp@gte.net
Web: www.yorkgroup.com

Summary: We are an executive and agency search. Serving the healthcare industry and their corporate marketing and communications/medical education/advertising and public relations needs.

Key Contact - Specialty:
Ms. Karen York, Principal Consultant

Salary Minimum: $75,000

Functions: Management, Healthcare

Industries: Drugs Mfg., Medical Devices, Pharm Svcs., Advertising, Publishing, New Media, Marketing SW, Biotech/Life Sciences, Healthcare, Hospitals, Long-term/Home Care, Dental

Yorktowne Personnel Consultants Inc

103 E Market St
York, PA 17401-1277
(717) 843-0079
Fax: (717) 852-8797
Email: rgeiger@yorktownpc.com

Summary: We do all types of manufacturing involving engineering, management, supply chain, HR, financial & accounting, quality control, marketing, etc.

Key Contact - Specialty:
Mr. Roger Geiger, President

Salary Minimum: $50,000

Functions: Generalist (All)

Industries: Energy, Utilities, Construction, Food, Bev., Tobacco, Lumber, Furniture, Drugs Mfg., Plastics, Rubber, Paints, Petro. Products, Motor Vehicles, Transportation, HR Services

Yormak & Associates

5150 E Pacific Coast Hwy Ste 200
Long Beach, CA 90804-3399
(562) 494-7500
Fax: (562) 494-7501
Email: stuart@yormak.com

Summary: Recruitment firm serving the public accounting industry - including the Big 4, CPA firms, as well as private industry companies. We focus on placing highly qualified accounting and finance professionals in full-time regular positions.

Key Contact - Specialty:
Mr. Stuart I. Yormak, President - *Finance*

Salary Minimum: $30,000

Functions: Generalist (All), CFOs, Budgeting, Cash Mgmt., Credit, Taxes

Industries: Generalist (All), Finance, Hospitality, Broadcast, Film, Real Estate, Software, Healthcare

Jack Young Personnel Services

108 Wilson Pl
Plainview, NY 11803-2242
(516) 933-1234
Fax: (516) 933-1240
Email: huntres99@aol.com
Web: www.jackyoung.com

Summary: We are an executive search firm specializing in the automotive retail industry. We 'headhunt' for our clients' dealerships comprising every franchise product in stores ranging from the small 'Mom & Pop' to the large publicly traded consolidators. We place mission critical people in positions as CEOs, CFOs, GMs, controllers, service & parts directors, service managers, office managers, parts directors, GSMs, etc.

Key Contact - Specialty:
Mr. Jack Young, President & Founder
Ms. Peggy Matthaey, Senior Executive Recruiter

Functions: Senior Mgmt., Middle Mgmt., Sales Mgmt., Finance, CFOs

Industries: Motor Vehicles

Youngblood Associates

127 Lake Dr
Hendersonville, NC 28739-0944
(828) 698-3898
Email: rsy@youngbloodassoc.net
Web: www.youngbloodassoc.net

Summary: We specialize in providing quality recruitment consulting and search services specific to the field of investment management in the USA. We are dedicated to identifying high caliber professionals with the skills, experience and character appropriate to the needs of our clientele.

Key Contact - Specialty:
Mr. Robert Youngblood, President - *Asset management, Business development, CFOs, Consulting, Mutual funds*

Salary Minimum: $50,000

Functions: Senior Mgmt., Sales & Mktg., CFOs, Cash Mgmt., Mgmt. Consultants

Industries: Finance, Banking, Mutual/Hedge Funds, Misc. Financial

Youngman & Associates Inc

6304 Northwood Ave Apt 2
Saint Louis, MO 63105-2210
(314) 878-0228
Email: bankjobs@gabrielmail.com

Summary: We are an executive search firm with a history of service to the banking industry. We have enjoyed an excellent reputation for locating, recruiting and evaluating top industry talent for our clients, having conducted hundreds of successful searches for middle and upper level executives. As a result, we have established long-term partnerships with many of our clients.

Key Contact - Specialty:
Mr. Grant Youngman

Salary Minimum: $40,000

Functions: Generalist (All), Finance, Credit

Industries: Banking

Your Advantage Staffing Consultants Inc

426 Queen St W
Cambridge, ON N3C 1H1
Canada
(519) 651-2120
(888) 213-3375
Fax: (519) 651-2780
Email: info@transportjobs.net
Web: www.transportjobs.net

Summary: We offer significant expertise in the recruitment and selection of staff for the transportation, logistics and distribution industry throughout North America.

Key Contact - Specialty:
Ms. Lori Van Opstal, CPC, President - *Freight, Logistics, Safety, Supply Chain, Traffic*
Mrs. Christine Banfield, Executive Affiliate - *Traffic, Transportation*

Salary Minimum: $40,000

Functions: Generalist (All)

Industries: Transportation

YourNet International

7516 Rowland Rd NW
Edmonton, AB T6A 3W1
Canada
(780) 440-2300
Fax: (780) 490-6200
Email: brent@yournet.ca
Web: www.yournet.ca

Summary: Our firm is a multi-faceted telecom and technology consulting and staffing company, providing services to high-technology companies. Our mandate is to help our clients become 'top dogs' in their respective industries. Our specialty is emerging technologies and markets.

Key Contact - Specialty:
Mr. Brent Baim, President

Functions: Int'l.

Industries: Energy, Utilities, Electronic, Elec. Components, E-commerce, IT Implementation, Communications

Zackrison Associates Inc

PO Box 1843
Venice, FL 34284-1843
(941) 493-8211
Fax: (941) 493-1661
Email: zackrison@comcast.net
Web: www.zackrison.com

Summary: We are an executive recruiting firm specializing in the placement of physicians, clinical research professionals and other executives for the pharmaceutical and bio-technology industries.

Key Contact - Specialty:
Mr. Walter Zackrison, CPC, President - *Pharmaceutical*

Salary Minimum: $60,000

Functions: Physicians, HR Mgmt., R&D

Industries: Generalist (All), Drugs Mfg., Pharm Svcs.

RL Zapin Associates Inc

708 3rd Ave Fl 6
New York, NY 10017-4119
(212) 838-0807
Email: resumes@rlzapinassociates.com
Web: www.rlzapinassociates.com

Summary: Direct and database marketing specialists including marketing research, credit risk/policy, product/program marketing, loyalty/retention/acquisition/CRM, list management, database analysis, SAS, statistics and quantitative analysis.

Key Contact - Specialty:
Ms. Roni Zapin, President - *Credit cards, CRM, Database, Direct marketing, Marketing*
Ms. Lauren Kamens, Senior Recruiter - *Analysts, Database, Financial services, Market research, Mathematics*

Salary Minimum: $50,000

Functions: Middle Mgmt., Mktg. Research, Mktg. Mgmt., Direct Mktg., Credit, Risk Mgmt., MIS Mgmt.

Industries: Banking, Mgmt. Consulting, E-commerce, Entertainment, Advertising, Publishing, New Media, Insurance, Healthcare

Zeiger Associates LLC

5310 Zelzah Ave Apt 303
Encino, CA 91316-2276
(818) 222-0052
Fax: (818) 222-0232
Email: sazeiger@pacbell.net

Summary: We specialize in design, project, program and engineering, including: A&D, test, software, hardware, computer hard disk development, IC/ASIC design & development, SCSI engineering and management. We are specialists in disk drive and semiconductor executives and executive technical management, for example: president, CEO, COO, etc.

Key Contact - Specialty:
Mr. Stephen A. Zeiger, President
Mr. David Barkin Zeiger, Vice President

Salary Minimum: $45,000

Functions: Generalist (All), Board Members, Senior Mgmt., Middle Mgmt., MIS Mgmt., R&D, Engineering

Industries: Generalist (All), Computer Equip., Consumer Elect., Telecoms, Software

Zen Zen International Inc

385 St Mary Ave
Winnipeg, MB R3C 0N1
Canada
(204) 837-7943
Fax: (204) 837-4646
Email: zenzenmy@mb.sympatico.ca
Web: www.zenzen.ca

Summary: Our firm is specialists in recruitment and placement of IT professionals, accountants, management, and sales/marketing professionals. Secondary specialties include: engineers, merchandisers and HR management. We have expertise in apparel manufacturing/distribution/retail industry.

Key Contact - Specialty:
Mr. Michael Yakimishyn, President - *Engineering, Human resources, Sales*

Salary Minimum: $25,000

Functions: Management, Mfg., Healthcare, Sales & Mktg., Finance, IT

Industries: Generalist (All), Manufacturing, Textiles, Apparel, Lumber, Furniture, Wholesale, Retail, Accounting, Telecoms, Aerospace, Software, Healthcare

Zenner Consulting Group LLC

400 N Michigan Ave Ste 1220
Chicago, IL 60611-4101
(312) 645-0400
Fax: (312) 645-0200
Email: info@lawposition.com
Web: www.lawposition.com

Summary: We are comprised of five attorneys who practiced law at premier national firms, companies and public interest organizations.

Key Contact - Specialty:
Ms. Teri Zenner Toig, Esq., President

Functions: Generalist (All), Legal

Industries: Legal

Helen Ziegler & Associates Inc

2403-180 Dundas St W
Toronto, ON M5G 1Z8
Canada
(416) 977-6941
(800) 387-4616
Fax: (416) 977-6128
Email: hza@hziegler.com
Web: www.hziegler.com

Summary: We specialize in identifying hard-to-get candidates for challenging assignments and assessing their suitability for the given assignment.

Key Contact - Specialty:
Ms. Helen Ziegler, President

Salary Minimum: $36,000

Functions: Generalist (All), Senior Mgmt., Healthcare, Staffing, Int'l.

Industries: Generalist (All), Accounting, Healthcare

Zillifro & Associates

PO Box 1238
Manteo, NC 27954-1238
(252) 473-2021
Fax: (252) 473-5581
Email: zanda@zillifro.com
Web: www.zillifro.com

Summary: We have highly specialized experience and contacts. The hallmark on both sides of the equation is strong, personal relationships. Our focus is on understanding and filling needs. We are experts in recruiting for major chemical suppliers and are especially strong in serving the pulp & paper, water treatment, food additives & ingredients and other specialty niches. Our ethics and reputation are second to none.

Key Contact - Specialty:
Mr. W. Keith Zillifro, President

Salary Minimum: $50,000

Functions: Management, Product Dev., Quality, Sales & Mktg., Sales Mgmt., Sales Reps., HR Mgmt., R&D, Process, Int'l.

Industries: Chemicals

Zion Technologies Inc

PO Box 180584
Casselberry, FL 32718-0584
(407) 699-8080
Fax: (407) 699-8005
Email: services@ziontec.net
Web: www.ziontec.net

Summary: Our firm is a HR support firm that provides employment services for professionals in construction project management, the VP level of software for banking institutions, engineering and technical sales solutions.

Key Contact - Specialty:
Mr. Jim Stephanopoulos

Salary Minimum: $40,000

Functions: Management

Industries: Food, Bev., Tobacco, Restaurants, Telecoms, Hospitals, Physical Therapy

ZSA Legal Recruitment

1000-200 University Ave
Toronto, ON M5H 3C6
Canada
(416) 368-2051
(800) 401-9773
Fax: (416) 368-5699
Email: info@zsa.ca
Web: www.zsa.ca

Summary: We have offices across the country staffed by former practicing lawyers, law clerks and human relations specialists, all focused on their particular area of expertise. We offer a nationwide database of lawyers, law clerks and legal support staff. We assist law firms, large and small, as well as corporations.

Key Contact - Specialty:
Mr. Christopher Sweeney, President
Mr. Warren Bongard, Co-Founder & Vice President - *Legal (Lawyers)*
Ms. Carolyn Berger, Vice President & Director, Support Servs - *Administration, Legal, Management*
Ms. Susan Ann Kennedy, Manager & Senior Consultant - *Legal (Lawyers)*
Ms. Salima Alibhai, Senior Consultant - *Legal (Lawyers)*
Ms. Emily Lee, Senior Consultant - *Legal (Lawyers)*

Salary Minimum: $50,000

Functions: Generalist (All), M&A, Legal, Attorneys, Paralegals

Industries: Generalist (All), Invest. Banking, Legal, New Media

Branches:
1800-250 6 Ave SW
Bow Valley Square 4
Calgary, AB T2P 3H7
Canada
(403) 205-3444
Fax: (403) 205-3428
Key Contact - Specialty:
Ms. Caroline Carnerie, Director, Western Operations
Ms. Alison Bennett, Consultant - *Legal, Legal (Attorneys)*
Ms. Shannon Quinney, Consultant

1150-10180 101 St NW
Manulife Place
Edmonton, AB T5J 3S4
Canada
(780) 702-1000
Fax: (780) 701-5022
Key Contact - Specialty:
Mr. Brent Ludwig, Vice President & Director, ZSA-X - *Legal, Legal (Attorneys,Lawyers)*

300-1055 Hastings St W
Guinness Tower
Vancouver, BC V6E 2E9
Canada
(604) 681-0706
Fax: (604) 681-0566
Email: shacksel@zsa.ca
Key Contact - Specialty:
Ms. Stephanie Hacksel, Consultant
Ms. Siobhan Rea, Consultant

101-116 Lisgar St
Ottawa, ON K2P 0C2
Canada
(613) 232-8828
Fax: (613) 232-8887
Email: sfortier@zsa.ca
Key Contact - Specialty:
Ms. Sarah Fortier, Consultant - *Legal (Lawyers)*

2400-1000 Rue de la Gauchetiere O
Le 1000
Montreal, QC H3B 4W5
Canada
(514) 390-2300
Fax: (514) 390-2320
Email: info@zsa.ca
Key Contact - Specialty:
Ms. Dominique Tardif, Consultant - *Legal (Lawyers)*
Ms. Chantal Douillette, Consultant - *Legal, Legal (Attorneys,Lawyers)*

Zymac Inc

1B Commons Dr Unit 7
Londonderry, NH 03053-3442
(603) 537-0400
Fax: (603) 537-0114
Email: bmacleod@zymac.com
Web: www.zymac.com

Summary: Our firm provides a full suite of recruiting services: executive search, technology search and full-time or part-time contractor placement. Our focus is upon early stage technology companies within the software, IT services, semiconductor and communications business sector. We also support our clients in their fund raising and exit strategies.

Key Contact - Specialty:
Mr. Bob MacLeod, President
Mr. Brian Samolyk, Vice President - *Computers (Software), Storage, Venture capital*
Mr. Don Cummings, Vice President - *Optics, Photonics, Telecommunications*
Mr. Malcolm Widness, Senior Consultant - *Computers (Software), Venture capital*
Mr. Garrett MacLeod, Consultant - *Computers (Software)*

Salary Minimum: $80,000

Functions: Generalist (All), Senior Mgmt., Middle Mgmt., Mktg. Mgmt., Sales Mgmt., CFOs, Engineering

Industries: Generalist (All), Computer Equip., Telecoms, Software

Index by Functions

Firms with (R) are from the Retainer Section.
Firms with (C) are from the Contingency Section.

Basis of Functions Classification

This proprietary classification system was developed by Kennedy Information.

00.0	**GENERALIST (ALL FUNCTIONS)**	07.4	Credit & Collection
		07.5	Taxes
01.0	**MANAGEMENT**	07.6	Mergers & Acquisitions
01.1	Board Members/Directors	07.7	Risk Management
01.2	Senior Management *(e.g. CEO, COO, President,*	07.8	Actuaries
	General Manager)	07.9	Pension/Retirement Planning
01.3	Middle Management		
01.4	Administrative Services	08.0	**INFORMATION TECHNOLOGY**
		08.1	MIS Management *(e.g. CIO, VP-MIS)*
02.0	**MANUFACTURING**	08.2	Systems Analysis & Design
02.1	Product Development	08.3	Systems Development/Programming
02.2	Production Engineering, Planning, Scheduling &	08.4	Systems Integration/Implementation
	Control	08.5	Systems Support
02.3	Automation, Robotics	08.6	Network Administration
02.4	Plant Management	08.7	Database Administration
02.5	Quality		
02.6	Productivity	09.0	**RESEARCH & DEVELOPMENT/SCIENTISTS**
03.0	**MATERIALS MANAGEMENT**	10.0	**ENGINEERING**
03.1	Purchasing, Inventory Management	10.1	Geo-technical
03.2	Materials & Requirement Planning	10.2	Structural
03.3	Physical Distribution, Traffic & Transportation,	10.3	Design
	Logistics	10.4	Hardware
03.4	Packaging	10.5	Process
		10.6	Systems
04.0	**MEDICAL/HEALTHCARE**		
04.1	Physicians	11.0	**SPECIALIZED SERVICES**
04.2	Nurses	11.1	Management Consultants
04.3	Allied Health *(e.g. Chiropractors, Pharmacists,*	11.2	Minorities/Diversity
	Dentists, Therapists, Psychologists)	11.3	Fund-Raisers & Other Non-Profit Services
04.4	Administration	11.4	Environmentalists
		11.5	Architects
05.0	**SALES & MARKETING**	11.6	Technicians
05.1	Advertising, Sales Promotion	11.7	Building Contractors *(e.g. plumbers, electricians,*
05.2	Marketing & Product Research		*HVAC techs)*
05.3	Marketing Management	11.8	Security, Safety & Protective Services
05.4	Sales Management	11.9	Environmental, Health & Safety Professionals
05.5	Direct Mail, Marketing, Telemarketing		
05.6	Customer Service	12.0	**LEGAL**
05.7	Public Relations	12.1	Attorneys
05.8	Sales Representatives	12.2	Paralegals
06.0	**HUMAN RESOURCE MANAGEMENT**	13.0	**DESIGN**
06.1	Benefits, Compensation Planning, Total Rewards	13.1	Graphic Artists, Designers
06.2	Staffing & Selection	13.2	Textile/Fashion
06.3	Training, e-Learning, Distance Education		
06.4	e-HR	14.0	**HOSPITALITY, RESTAURANTS, CULINARY, HOTELS**
		14.1	Hotel Management
07.0	**FINANCE & ACCOUNTING**	14.2	Executive Chefs/Sous Chefs/Kitchen Managers
07.1	CFOs		
07.2	Budgeting, Cost Controls	15.0	**INTERNATIONAL GENERALIST**
07.3	Cash Management, Financing & Management of		
	Funds, Portfolios		

FUNCTIONS

FUNCTIONS

FUNCTIONS

FUNCTIONS

FUNCTIONS

01.0 Management

FUNCTIONS

FUNCTIONS

FUNCTIONS

FUNCTIONS

FUNCTIONS

01.2 Senior Management (e.g. CEO, COO, President, General Manager)

FUNCTIONS

FUNCTIONS

FUNCTIONS

FUNCTIONS

01.3 Middle Management

FUNCTIONS

FUNCTIONS

FUNCTIONS

02.0 Manufacturing

FUNCTIONS

02.1 Product Development

FUNCTIONS

02.2 Production Engineering, Planning, Scheduling & Control

FUNCTIONS

FUNCTIONS

02.6 Productivity

03.0 Materials Management

FUNCTIONS

03.1 Purchasing, Inventory Management

03.2 Materials & Requirement Planning

03.3 Physical Distribution, Traffic & Transportation, Logistics

FUNCTIONS

03.4 Packaging

04.0 Medical/Healthcare

FUNCTIONS

04.1 Physicians

04.2 Nurses

FUNCTIONS

04.3 Allied Health (e.g. Chiropractors, Pharmacists, Dentists, Therapists, Psychologists)

04.4 Administration

05.0 Sales & Marketing

FUNCTIONS

FUNCTIONS

FUNCTIONS

FUNCTIONS

05.1 Advertising, Sales Promotion

05.2 Marketing & Product Research

05.3 Marketing Management

05.4 Sales Management

FUNCTIONS

FUNCTIONS

05.5 Direct Mail, Marketing, Telemarketing

05.6 Customer Service

05.7 Public Relations

FUNCTIONS

05.8 Sales Representatives

FUNCTIONS

06.1 Benefits, Compensation Planning, Total Rewards

06.2 Staffing & Selection

FUNCTIONS

FUNCTIONS

FUNCTIONS

07.1 CFOs

FUNCTIONS

07.2 Budgeting, Cost Controls

FUNCTIONS

07.7 Risk Management

07.8 Actuaries

07.9 Pension/Retirement Planning

08.0 Information Technology

FUNCTIONS

FUNCTIONS

FUNCTIONS

08.2 Systems Analysis & Design

FUNCTIONS

08.4 Systems Integration / Implementation

08.5 Systems Support

08.6 Network Administration

08.7 Database Administration

FUNCTIONS

FUNCTIONS

10.0 Engineering

FUNCTIONS

10.1 Geo-technical

10.2 Structural

10.3 Design

10.4 Hardware

10.5 Process

FUNCTIONS

11.2 Minorities/Diversity

11.3 Fund-Raisers & Other Non-Profit Services

11.4 Environmentalists

11.5 Architects

FUNCTIONS

11.6 Technicians

11.7 Building Contractors (e.g. plumbers, electricians, HVAC techs)

11.8 Security, Safety & Protective Services

11.9 Environmental, Health & Safety Professionals

12.0 Legal

12.1 Attorneys

FUNCTIONS

12.2 Paralegals

13.0 Design

13.1 Graphic Designers

FUNCTIONS

Firms with (R) are from the Retainer Section.
Firms with (C) are from the Contingency Section.

Basis of Industries Classification

This proprietary classification system was developed by Kennedy Information.

0.00	**GENERALIST**	H.12	Securities & Commodities Brokers	L.00	**COMMUNICATIONS**
A.00	**AGRICULTURE, FORESTRY, FISHING, MINING**	H.13	Venture Capital	L.10	Telephone, Telecommunications
		H.14	Mutual/Hedge Funds	L.11	Call Centers
		H.15	Other Financial Services	L.12	Telephony
B.00	**ENERGY/UTILITIES**			L.13	Digital
B.10	Oil & Gas	I.00	**SERVICES**	L.14	Wireless
		I.10	Non-Profits, Museums, Galleries, Music/Arts, Libraries, Information Services, Membership	L.15	Fiber Optic
C.00	**CONSTRUCTION**			L.16	Network Infrastructure
D.00	**MANUFACTURING**			L.17	RF/Microwave
D.10	Food, Beverage, Tobacco & Kindred Products	I.11	Architectural Services	M.00	**PUBLIC ADMINISTRATION, GOVERNMENT**
D.11	Textile, Apparel, Related Products	I.12	Pharmaceutical (Other Than Manufacturing)		
D.12	Lumber, Wood, Furniture, Fixtures	I.13	Legal	M.10	Defense
		I.14	Accounting, Miscellaneous Business Services	M.11	Compliance
D.13	Paper & Allied Products			M.12	Homeland Security
D.14	Printing & Allied Industry	I.15	Equipment Services (Including Leasing)	N.00	**ENVIRONMENTAL SERVICES**
D.15	Chemicals & Allied Products				
D.16	Soap, Perfume, Cosmetics	I.16	Management Consulting	N.10	Hazardous Waste, Study, Cleanup
D.17	Drugs, Pharmaceuticals	I.17	Human Resource Services		
D.18	Medical Device & Instruments	I.18	Law Enforcement, Security	P.00	**AEROSPACE**
D.19	Plastics, Rubber Products	I.19	E-commerce	Q.00	**PACKAGING**
D.20	Paints, Allied Products, Petroleum Products	I.20	IT Implementation	R.00	**INSURANCE**
		I.21	Professional Services Automation/Application Services Providers	R.10	Casualty
D.21	Leather, Stone, Glass, Concrete, Clay Products			R.11	Claims
				R.12	Life
D.22	Primary & Fabricated Metal Products	I.22	K-12 Education	R.13	Commercial
		I.23	Higher Education	R.14	Re-Insurance
D.23	Industrial Machinery & Consumer Appliances	I.24	Engineering Services		
		I.25	Logistics	S.00	**REAL ESTATE**
D.24	Transportation Equipment (e.g. Automobiles)	I.26	Supply Chain Management Services	S.10	Property, Facility & Asset Management
D.25	Computer Equipment & Components	J.00	**HOSPITALITY**	T.00	**SOFTWARE**
		J.10	Hotels, Resorts, Clubs	T.10	Accounting Software
D.26	Consumer Electronics	J.11	Restaurants, Food & Beverage Services	T.11	Database Software
D.27	Test & Measurement Equipment			T.12	Development Software
		J.12	Quick Service Restaurants	T.13	Document Management, Production Software
D.28	Miscellaneous Manufacturing Industries	J.13	Full Service Restaurants		
		J.14	Institutional/Industrial Food Service	T.14	Entertainment Software
D.29	Electronic/Electrical Components			T.15	Enterprise Resource Planning Software
D.30	Robotics	J.15	Entertainment, Leisure, Amusement		
D.31	Semiconductors			T.16	Human Resource Software
D.32	Consumer Goods/Products	J.16	Recreation	T.17	Industry Specific Software
		J.17	Sports	T.18	Manufacturing Software
E.00	**TRANSPORTATION**	J.18	Travel	T.19	Marketing Software
F.00	**WHOLESALE TRADE**	K.00	**MEDIA**	T.20	Networking, Communications Software
G.00	**RETAIL TRADE**	K.10	Advertising, Public Relations		
		K.11	Publishing, Print Media	T.21	Security Software
H.00	**FINANCE**	K.12	New Media (e.g. Internet, Multimedia)	T.22	System Software
H.10	Commercial Banking			T.23	Training Software
H.11	Investment Banking	K.13	TV, Cable, Motion Pictures, Video, Radio		

INDUSTRIES

INDUSTRIES

INDUSTRIES

INDUSTRIES

INDUSTRIES

A.00 Agriculture, Forestry, Fishing, Mining

B.00 Energy/Utilities

INDUSTRIES

B.10 Oil & Gas

INDUSTRIES

C.00 Construction

INDUSTRIES

D.00 Manufacturing

INDUSTRIES

INDUSTRIES

INDUSTRIES

D.10 Food, Beverage, Tobacco & Kindred Products

INDUSTRIES

INDUSTRIES

INDUSTRIES

D.14 Printing & Allied Industry

D.15 Chemicals & Allied Products

INDUSTRIES

D.16 Soap, Perfume, Cosmetics

INDUSTRIES

D.17 Drugs, Pharmaceuticals

D.18 Medical Devices & Instruments

INDUSTRIES

D.19 Plastics, Rubber Products

INDUSTRIES

D.20 Paints, Allied Products, Petroleum Products

INDUSTRIES

D.21 Leather, Stone, Glass, Concrete, Clay Products

D.22 Primary & Fabricated Metal Products

D.23 Industrial Machinery & Consumer Appliances

INDUSTRIES

D.24 Transportation Equipment (e.g. Automobiles)

D.25 Computer Equipment & Components

INDUSTRIES

D.26 Consumer Electronics

D.27 Test & Measurement Equipment

INDUSTRIES

D.28 Miscellaneous Manufacturing Industries

INDUSTRIES

D.29 Electronic/Electrical Components

INDUSTRIES

D.30 Robotics

D.31 Semiconductors

INDUSTRIES

D.32 Consumer Goods/Products

E.00 Transportation

INDUSTRIES

F.00 Wholesale Trade

INDUSTRIES

G.00 Retail Trade

INDUSTRIES

H.00 Finance

INDUSTRIES

INDUSTRIES

INDUSTRIES

INDUSTRIES

H.11 Investment Banking

INDUSTRIES

H.12 Securities & Commodities Brokers

INDUSTRIES

H.14 Mutual/Hedge Funds

H.15 Other Financial Services

INDUSTRIES

I.00 Services

INDUSTRIES

INDUSTRIES

I.10 Non-Profits, Museums, Galleries, Music/Arts, Libraries, Information Services, Membership

INDUSTRIES

INDUSTRIES

I.13 Legal

I.14 Accounting, Miscellaneous Business Services

INDUSTRIES

INDUSTRIES

INDUSTRIES

I.17 Human Resource Services

INDUSTRIES

INDUSTRIES

I.18 Law Enforcement, Security

I.19 E-commerce

I.20 IT Implementation

INDUSTRIES

I.21 Professional Services Automation/Application Services Providers

I.22 K-12 Education

I.23 Higher Education

INDUSTRIES

I.24 Engineering Services

I.25 Logistics

INDUSTRIES

I.26 Supply Chain Management Services

INDUSTRIES

J.10 Hotels, Resorts, Clubs

J.11 Restaurants, Food & Beverage Services

J.12 Quick Service Restaurants

INDUSTRIES

J.16 Recreation

J.17 Sports

J.18 Travel

K.00 Media

INDUSTRIES

K.10 Advertising, Public Relations

INDUSTRIES

K.11 Publishing, Print Media

K.12 New Media (e.g. Internet, multimedia)

INDUSTRIES

K.13 TV, Cable, Motion Pictures, Video, Radio

L.00 Communications

INDUSTRIES

L.10 Telephone, Telecommunications

INDUSTRIES

INDUSTRIES

L.11 Call Centers

INDUSTRIES

L.14 Wireless

INDUSTRIES

L.15 Fiber Optic

L.16 Network Infrastructure

L.17 RF/Microwave

INDUSTRIES

M.00 Public Administration, Government

M.10 Defense

INDUSTRIES

M.11 Compliance

M.12 Homeland Security

N.00 Environmental Services

N.10 Hazardous Waste, Study, Cleanup

P.00 Aerospace

INDUSTRIES

R.00 Insurance

INDUSTRIES

R.10 Casualty

R.11 Claims

INDUSTRIES

INDUSTRIES

S.10 Property, Facility & Asset Management

T.00 Software

INDUSTRIES

INDUSTRIES

INDUSTRIES

T.10 Accounting Software

T.11 Database Software

INDUSTRIES

T.12 Development Software

INDUSTRIES

T.16 Human Resource Software

T.17 Industry Specific Software

INDUSTRIES

T.18 Manufacturing Software

INDUSTRIES

T.21 Security Software

T.22 System Software

INDUSTRIES

T.23 Training Software

U.00 Biotech & Life Sciences

INDUSTRIES

INDUSTRIES

V.00 Healthcare

INDUSTRIES

INDUSTRIES

V.10 Hospitals

INDUSTRIES

V.11 Long-term/Home Care

INDUSTRIES

INDUSTRIES

V.15 Women's

W.00 Non-Classifiable Industries

INDUSTRIES

Recruiter Specialties Index

Firms with (R) are from the Retainer Section.
Firms with (C) are from the Contingency Section.

This index allows individuals to pinpoint their particular area of specialization in addition to or in conjunction with what their firms have selected. It is a particularly helpful tool both for identifying individuals within the larger firms and when your need is very specific.

The categories were created by the recruiters themselves, without the constraints of established (but limited) indexes such as the Standard Industrial Classification. While this enabled us to collect deep and detailed data, it proved an ambitious task to corral into a logical index. We present it largely as it was collected; hence broad headings with several hundred entries appearing next to unique detailed ones with but a single entry.

To maximize the usefulness of this indexing approach, we encourage you to scan the master list with as many words as you can associate with your need. For example, Hospitality would produce a long list, but searches on Bakery, Food, Clubs, Food service, Hotels, Restaurants and Tourism might get you closer to a specific breakout of Hospitality.

In the index you will find the recruiter's name, his/her firm, whether firm operates on R (retainer) or C (contingency) basis, and page number. Please note minor categories are listed alphabetically under their major headings (for example: computer networking is listed under networking within computers).

.com	Retail	Compensation
Abrasives	Bar Coding	Competitive Intelligence
Accounting	Benefits	Compliance
Big 4	Biomaterials	Components
General	Biomedical	Composites
Public	Biopharmaceutical	Computers
Acoustics	Biotechnology	Automation
Actuarials	Board of Directors	Hardware
Adhesives	Bridges	Networking
Administration	Brokerage	Programming
Advertising	BME	Sales
Aerospace	Building Products	Science
Agriculture	Built Environments	Software
Amusement Parks	Business Development	Construction
Analysts	Business to Business	Consulting
Annuities	Buyout Firms	Consumer
Apparel	C-level	Durables
AS/400	Cable	Hard Goods
Asset Management	Call Centers	Marketing
Assisted Living	Capital Goods	Packaged goods
Associations	Capital Markets	Products
ATE	CEOs	Controllers
Audits	CFOs	Convenience Store
Automation	Change Management	Convergence
Automotive	Chemical	Converting
Aviation	CIOs	COOs
Bakery	Clerical	Copiers
Banking	Client/Server	Cosmetics
Commercial	Clinical	Creative
Corporate	Closely-held Business	Credit
Investment	Club	Credit Cards
Merchant	Coatings	CRM
Mortgage	Communications	Culinary

Petrochemical

Pharmaceutical

Pharmacists

Philanthropy

Photonics

Physicians

Plastics

Power

Presidents

Printing

Private Equity

Process Equipment

Procurement

Product Management/Development

Production

Professional services

Property Management

Psychiatry

Public Relations

Public Sector

Publishing

Purchasing

Quality

Re-engineering

Real Estate

Recreations

Refining

Regulatory

Research

Research & Development

Resorts

Respiratory Therapy

Restaurants

Retail

RF Microwave

Risk Management

Robotics

Rubber

Safety

Sales

SAP

Science

Seafood

Securities

Semiconductors

Senior Management

Six Sigma

Skilled Trades

Social Work

Sports

Staffing

Stamping

Start-up companies

Steel

Storage

Strategic Planning

Subacute Healthcare

Supermarkets

Supply Chain

Surgical

Systems
     Integration

Tax

Technical
     Management

Technicians

Technology

Telecommunications

Temporary

Textiles

Thermoforming

Tourism

Traffic

Training

Transportation

Travel

Treasury

Trust

Underwriting

Utilities

Venture Capital

Wall Street

Wholesale

Wireless

SPECIALTIES

Big 4

Bookkeeping

SPECIALTIES

Advertising

SPECIALTIES

SPECIALTIES

978 / THE DIRECTORY OF EXECUTIVE RECRUITERS

Commander, Charles, Heidrick & Struggles (R) 93
Cooper, William, The Rangeley Group (R) 171
Cuellar, Scott, Heidrick & Struggles (R) 93
Cushing, Daniel, Connexion Systems & Engineering (C) 312
Daratany, Ron, DMR Global Inc (R) 60
de Regt, John, Spencer Stuart (R) 198
DeSantis, Joey, The DeSantis Group (C) 478
Gardner, John, Heidrick & Struggles (R) 93
Gordy, Thomas, Harvard Group International (R) 91
Gregor, Joie, Heidrick & Struggles (R) 94
Hallagan, Robert, Heidrick & Struggles (R) 93
Harrison, James, JRG-USA Recruiting Inc (C) 432
Hauswirth, Jeffrey, Spencer Stuart (R) 199
Heid, Michele, Heidrick & Struggles (R) 94
Holden, Bradley, Heidrick & Struggles (R) 93
Jayne, Randy, Heidrick & Struggles (R) 94
Kessler, James, The Biras Creek Group (C) 498
Kirby, Joseph, Boyden (R) 25
Klein, Judy, Heidrick & Struggles (R) 94
MacEachern, David, Spencer Stuart (R) 198
Magouirk, Leah, Vaughan & Company Executive Search Inc (C) 661
McNamara, Timothy, Boyden (R) 24
Montesino, Jose, DMR Global Inc (R) 60
Moore, David, Heidrick & Struggles (R) 93
Nadeau, Robert, Spencer Stuart (R) 199
Ogden, Dayton, Spencer Stuart (R) 198
Parrotte, Larry, SC of Loudoun County (C) 513
Perman, Gary, Perma, Willits Langone Inc (R) 162
Raab, Julie, Vaughan & Company Executive Search Inc (C) 661
Sadick, Stuart, Heidrick & Struggles (R) 93
Vaughan, David, Vaughan & Company Executive Search Inc (C) 661
Visokey, Dale, Heidrick & Struggles (R) 93
Vourakis, Zan, ZanExec LLC (R) 228
Walburger, Gary, Spencer Stuart (R) 197
Wallace, Charles, Heidrick & Struggles (R) 94
White, Jonathan, Spencer Stuart (R) 198

BAAN

Lofgren, Peter, iHeadHunt (C) 420

Bakery

Bingham, Rick, Briant Associates Inc (R) 27
Comer, Margaret, BioPharmMed (R) 21
Forney, John, Recruit America (C) 586
Hunter, Christi, MR of Bethlehem (C) 504
Joy, Kevin, HCI Corp (C) 402
Lane, Bill, The Kent Group Inc (C) 502
McCann, Kevin, MR of Bucks County (C) 506
McLafferty, Tim, Focus Executive Search (C) 377
Morris, Chris, The Harlan Group Inc (C) 399
Myers, Scott, Corporate Search Consultants (C) 318
Sloat, Robert, Executive Search of New England Inc (C) 361
Winkler, Brad, Whittaker & Associates Inc (C) 668

Banking

Alberico, Pat, Global Recruiters of Indianapolis (C) 389
Amburgey, Rick, Socius Search LLC (R) 196
Amyx, Teri, Grafton Executive Search (C) 391
April, Kenneth, April International Inc (C) 258
Armstrong, Diane, McCracken & Partners Executive Search Inc (R) 142
Baranski, David, Global Recruiters of Oak Brook Inc (C) 389
Barchard, Dave, MR of Burlington (C) 512
Baugh, Pamela, Career Management Associates (C) 295
Beir, Diane, Fischer Group International Inc (R) 74
Berry, Sandy, Berry & Associates LLC (C) 274
Blanco, Rosa, Search Exec (C) 615
Bostick, Tim, Ray Partners Inc (R) 172
Bradley, Sandy, Wells, Bradley & Associates Inc (C) 667
Brinkley, Thomas, Coleman Lew & Associates Inc (R) 43
Bulmer, Robert, Alaska Executive Search Inc (C) 248
Butenschoen, Melissa, LarsonAllen Search LLC (R) 124
Cadieux, Jeff, Gabriel & Associates Inc (C) 382
Carrick, Jr., Kenneth, Coleman Lew & Associates Inc (R) 43
Carter, Van, Hudson Consulting Group (R) 102
Coleman, Carol, SPANUSA (R) 197
Conroy, Jane, McSherry & Associates 2 Inc (R) 143
Cresta, Michelle, CPO Recruiting Group (Cresta, Phifer & Osadchuk) (C) 320
Crocitto, Helene, Filcro Media Staffing (R) 73
Cummings, Cade, McCarthy-Komendera Associates (C) 524
Cunningham, Don, BancSearch Inc (C) 267
Cunningham, Maggie, BancSearch Inc (C) 267
Davis, Carolyn, Reeve & Associates (C) 589
Davis, Lori, Corporate Search Inc (C) 319
DeMarks, Phillip, Unisearch Search & Recruiting Inc (C) 659
Denson, Forest, United Human Capital Solutions (C) 503
Diamond, Judy, Allen Personnel (C) 250
Domby, Samuel, eXsource Inc (C) 364
Eatherly, William, MR of Durham South (C) 500
Eidlen, Heather, Adams Consulting Group LLC (C) 239
Erdrich, Kristina, Executive Search Management Inc (C) 361
Feit, Jennifer, J P Gleason Associates Inc (R) 82
Fende, Nicole, Allen Austin Executive Search Consultants (R) 13
Frazier, Bob, Variant Partners (C) 488
Frierson, Brenda, Renaissance Resources LLC (R) 175
Gabriel, Heather, Gabriel & Associates Inc (C) 382
Gaynair, Drew, Park Avenue Group Inc (C) 480
Geyer, Colleen, Corporate Consulting Associates Inc (C) 316
Ginley, Michael, The Lear Group Inc (R) 126
Goepel, Barb, Wood West & Partners Inc (C) 673
Goodson, Jr., W. Kenneth, DLG Associates Inc (R) 60
Grady, Dennis, Core Staffing Inc (C) 315
Graff, Thomas, The Hanover Consulting Group (R) 89
Greene, Ian, April International Inc (C) 258
Guilford, David, DLG Associates Inc (R) 60
Haddad, Garen, Gateway Group Personnel (C) 384
Hedrick, Rod, Park Avenue Group Inc (C) 480
Henson, Damon, Gabriel & Associates Inc (C) 382
Hirano, Keiko, April International Inc (C) 258
Holmes, Cory, HNH Partners Inc (C) 411
Holmes, Erin, HNH Partners Inc (C) 411
Hoover, Brett, WilliamCharles Executive Search (C) 669
Howard, Mick, The Gorge Group (C) 391
Huxtable, Robert, Socius Search LLC (R) 196
Johnson, Kera, McCarthy-Komendera Associates (C) 524
Joyce, Barbara, Cornell Global LLC (R) 48
Kane, Karen, Kaplan & Associates Inc (R) 115
Kang, Sumi, Choi & Burns LLC (R) 40
Kanzer, William, Kanzer Associates Inc (R) 115
Kelly, Peter, Highland Partners (R) 97
Kendall, Susan, GFI Professional Staffing Services (C) 386
Kennedy, Renee, McCarthy-Komendera Associates (C) 524
Kershner, Bruce, Kershner & Co (R) 117
Kiken, Mark, COBA Executive Search (R) 43
Klaus, Bob, MR of Bloomington (C) 490
Klein, Dara, Kaplan & Associates Inc (R) 115
Kobayashi, Noboru, Columbia Consulting Group (R) 44
Koch, Susan, The Robert Pfaendler Company LLC (C) 563
Lawton, Alan, LMC Group LLC (C) 452
Lebofsky, Lawrence, TopGrading Solutions (C) 478
Leinenbach, Stuart, Renaissance Resources LLC (R) 175
Lewis, Simon, Michael Page International Inc (C) 531
Lindberg, Gillis, Wells, Bradley & Associates Inc (C) 667
Linton, Leonard, Byron Leonard International Inc (R) 30
Lippencott, Lillian, Lexington Software Inc (C) 450
Locke, Jeffrey, Sterling Staffing (R) 202
Lopez, Luz, Gene Rogers Associates Inc (C) 598
LoPresto, Bob, Rusher, Loscavio & LoPresto (R) 181
Lyke, Ted, SC of Lee County (C) 476
Lysenko, Lisa, ALS Group (C) 251
Lysenko, Scott, ALS Group (C) 251
Madden, Francis, O'Shea, Divine & Company Inc (R) 154
Mallin, Ellen, Kaplan & Associates Inc (R) 115
Martin, Esther, MR of Wausau (C) 516
Mazar, Joanne, Hunt For Executives (C) 417
McCarthy, Richard, McCarthy-Komendera Associates (C) 524
McCrea, John, Bialla & Associates Inc (R) 20
McLaughlin, Frank, McSearch Personnel Consulting (C) 526
McNally, Glenna, Flynn, Hannock Inc (R) 75
McQuinn, Steve, Turning Point Inc (C) 658
Medina, Ray, LMC Group LLC (C) 452
Menet, Mary, Dunhill Professional Search of Chicago (C) 339
Michalowski, Rob, Variant Partners (C) 488
Milton, Lonna, NCC Executive Search Consultants (C) 544
Mitterwager, Jason, Epsen Fuller IMD Ineternational Search Group (R) 67
Morales, Carmen, Williger & Associates (R) 223
Nadherny, Pete, The Angus Group Ltd (R) 10
Nason, Dustin, Nason & Nason (C) 540
Nason-Aymerich, Alexandra, Nason & Nason (C) 540
Nassar, Brad, Martin Partners LLC (R) 139
Neese, Colleen, TowerHunter (R) 212
Nieman, Cary Jo, MR of Salt Lake City (C) 512
O'Malley, Kevin, Sterling Staffing (R) 202
Orth, Scott, The Gorge Group (C) 391
Owens, Jesse, Merle W Owens & Associates (R) 156
Palmese, Andrew, TopGrading Solutions (C) 478
Panski, Mandie, Corporate Consulting Associates Inc (C) 316
Pejril, Ronald, Williger & Associates (R) 223
Penfold, Bart, Rusher, Loscavio & LoPresto (R) 181
Peterson, Jason, Socius Search LLC (R) 196

The Directory of Executive Recruiters

SPECIALTIES

Lunsford, Kamron, Career Consultants Staffing Services Inc (C)....294
Lyons, Corey, Corey Lyons & Associates (C)....455
Marion, Pamela, Russillo/Gardner (R)....182
O'Brien May, Nancy, Human Capital Partners, LLC (R)....103
Plappert, James, Newtown Consulting Group Inc (C)....505
Price, Jennifer, Career Forum Inc (C)....294
Pugh, Robert, Chicago Consulting Partners Ltd (R)....39
Ross, Shannon, Karis Partners (C)....435
Sahlas, Christine, The Origin Group LLC (C)....553

Biomaterials

Crumpton, Chuck, Medpoint LLC (C)....529
Jackson, Rachel, Perma, Willits Langone Inc (R)....162
Joslin, Robert, Joslin & Associates Ltd (C)....432
Kuhn, Larry, Kuhn Med-Tech Inc (C)....443
Nelson, Regina, Dieck Group Inc (R)....58
Shelnut, James, Computer Technology Staffing (C)....311
Szmidt, Les, MR of Napa (C)....459

Biomedical

Ackerman, Esq., Corey, Cornerstone Search Group LLC (C)....315
Almoni, Yossi, Catalyx Group (R)....36
Barro, Arlene, Barro Global Search Inc (R)....15
Basilone, Maria, Command Consultants Inc (C)....309
Basta, Erica, Thomas Ruff Company (C)....602
Bernstein, Ken, Marvel Consultant (C)....522
Blank, Paula, Paula Blank International (R)....22
Burby, Susan, Sanford Rose Associates - Lake Ann (C)....609
Chanski, Vern, Hobson Associates (C)....411
Chiaravallo, Laurence, Diedre Moire Corp Inc (C)....535
Clifford, Katelyn, Sanford Rose Associates - Boston South Shore (C)....609
Colberg, George, MSI International (Management Search Inc) (C)....538
Conlan, Chris, Carlyle & Conlan Inc (R)....136
Costenborder, Laurie, PathSourcePartners (C)....558
Crumpton, Chuck, Medpoint LLC (C)....529
DiMascio, Suzette, Career Solutions International (C)....296
Dorfman, Jan, FPC of Denver Inc (C)....365
Eve, Jessica, Career Solutions International (C)....296
Fishel, Evan, Levin & Company Inc (R)....127
GIlbert, John, Epsen Fuller IMD Ineternational Search Group (R)....67
Harrington, II, Chris, Harrington, O'Brien and Conway International Inc (C)....399
Harrison, James, JRG-USA Recruiting Inc (C)....432
Hearn,, Bryan, BLH Recruiting (C)....278
Heine, Karl, The Creative Placement Agency LLC (C)....322
Helsel, Neal, Neal Helsel & Associates Inc (C)....406
Hopkins, Tim, Stephens International Recruiting Inc (C)....637
Kenner, Susan, Thomas Ruff Company (C)....602
Kish, Eddie, Tri-Tech Associates Inc (C)....655
Koellhoffer, Thomas, T J Koellhoffer & Associates (R)....120
Korban, Richard, Korban Associates (R)....120
Kuhn, Larry, Kuhn Med-Tech Inc (C)....443
Lampl, Joni, MR of Pittsburgh North (C)....505
Levin, Becky, Levin & Company Inc (R)....127
Miras, Cliff, Cornerstone Search Group LLC (C)....315
Nelson, Regina, Dieck Group Inc (R)....58
Nieman, Cary Jo, MR of Salt Lake City (C)....512
Patrick, Sharon, Thomas Ruff Company (C)....602
Pinheiro, Teri, MR of Chapel Hill (C)....498
Powell, Donald, Medpoint LLC (C)....529
Raz, Steve, Cornerstone Search Group LLC (C)....315
Reda, Pat, P J Reda & Associates Inc (C)....589
Reticker, Peter, Clinical One (C)....307
Richards, Christos, Levin & Company Inc (R)....127
Rimele, J.R., Sales Recruiters of Oklahoma City (C)....605
Robb, Molly, Horton International LLC (R)....101
Rothschild, Tammy, Thomas Ruff Company (C)....602
Ruff, Tom, Thomas Ruff & Associates, Inc. (C)....602
Salkin, Maureen, Levin & Company Inc (R)....127
Schepp, James, Lasher Associates (R)....124
Sevel, Dave, Marvel Consultant (C)....522
Sinatra, Rich, Socius Search LLC (R)....196
Smith, Scott, TowerHunter (R)....212
Sphar, Donna, CSI America (C)....323
Stevens, Marc, Park Avenue Group Inc (C)....480
Stevenson, Alex, Search Masters USA (C)....616
Szmidt, Les, MR of Napa (C)....459
Walker, Lisa, MR of Stamford (C)....476
Wegiel, Jason, Connexion Systems & Engineering (C)....312
Wernstrom, Mark, SC of Rochester (C)....463
Wiebke, Jill, Emerging Healthcare Partners LLC (C)....348

Biopharmaceutical

Ackerman, Esq., Corey, Cornerstone Search Group LLC (C)....315
Adams, Lauren, FPC of Abington (C)....369
Al'Basit, Basirah, RS&A (C)....601
Albrecht, Franke, MR of Houston West (C)....510
Almoni, Yossi, Catalyx Group (R)....36
Alorbi, Karl, Catalyx Group (R)....36
Ambos, Merry, Molecular Solutions Inc (C)....535
Apfel, Ronnie, The Hampton Group (C)....497
Barkley, Keith, Mackenzie Search (R)....132
Baron, Annette, Eagle Research Inc (C)....344
Bernstein, Ken, Marvel Consultant (C)....522
Boreham, Judy, Diversified Search Ray & Berndtson (R)....60
Briand, Paul, Briand Fiorella Search Inc (C)....284
Brinkerhoff, Shawna, Discovery Solutions (C)....334
Busbee, Dale, Innovative Medical Recruiting LLC (C)....421
Callaghan, Kathryn, Callaghan International Inc (R)....31
Campo, John, The CAMPO Group (C)....292
Casano, Stephen, Diedre Moire Corp Inc (C)....535
Cavalli, John, Diedre Moire Corp Inc (C)....535
Chambers, Gail, Global Consulting Group Inc (C)....388
Chiaravallo, Laurence, Diedre Moire Corp Inc (C)....535
Clark, Ellen, Clark Executive Search Inc (R)....42
Clifford, Katelyn, Sanford Rose Associates - Boston South Shore (C)....609
Collin, François, Quintal & Associates Human Resources Consultants Inc (C)....583
Connors, Richard, Vista Technology (C)....662
Cottone, Carol, Higgins Group Inc (R)....97
Crawford, Luke, Advanced Recruiters Inc (C)....241
Davis, Tamara, Levin & Company Inc (R)....127
DeMan, Denise, Bench International Search Inc (R)....18
DePui Martinsen, Nils, The Nema Group (R)....151
Diefenbach, John, Hreshko Consulting Group (C)....415
DiMascio, Suzette, Career Solutions International (C)....296
Doering, Clayton, FPC of Abington (C)....369
Donovan, Cam, Phillips Resource Group (C)....564
Eisner, Richard, Eisner LLP (C)....346
Eve, Jessica, Career Solutions International (C)....296
Fiorella, Nicole, Briand Fiorella Search Inc (C)....284
Fishel, Evan, Levin & Company Inc (R)....127
Foulkes, Janet, Bench International Search Inc (R)....19
Gadbois, Theresa, Search Masters International (R)....188
Gibbs, Dannielle, Discovery Solutions (C)....334
GIlbert, John, Epsen Fuller IMD Ineternational Search Group (R)....67
Hafter, Leslie, TWC (R)....214
Hardgrove, Deborah, Hreshko Consulting Group (C)....415
Harrison, James, JRG-USA Recruiting Inc (C)....432
Heine, Karl, The Creative Placement Agency LLC (C)....322
Higgins, Donna, Higgins Group Inc (R)....97
Israel, Dick, John Kurosky & Associates (R)....123
Kane, Karen, Kaplan & Associates Inc (R)....115
Kearns, Virginia, The Hampton Group (C)....497
Kerns, David, Key Corporate Services LLC (C)....439
Korban, Richard, Korban Associates (R)....120
Krishnan, Priya, MR of Edison (C)....493
Lampl, Joni, MR of Pittsburgh North (C)....505
Lewis, Jason, The Alpine Group (C)....475
Logue, Sara, Advanced Recruiters Inc (C)....241
Lynch, Chuck, FPC of Nashua (C)....368
MacEntyre, Allen, MR/SC of Jamestown (C)....499
MacNamara, Michael, Korban Associates (R)....120
Madden, Bridget, The Magellan Group (R)....133
Mancino, Gene, Mancino Burfield Edgerton (R)....138
Mann, Ira, FPC of Atlanta (C)....366
Maye, Carolyn, MC2 Executive Search (R)....141
McCallum, Fred, Bench International Search Inc (R)....19
McCormick, Kevin, TWC (R)....214
Michas, Spiro, The Cambridge Group Ltd (C)....291
Miles, James, Holohan Group Ltd (R)....100
Miller, Neil, RKP Group Pharmaceutical and Biotech Search (C)....595
Miras, Cliff, Cornerstone Search Group LLC (C)....315
Mitchell, William, Eagle Consulting Group Inc (C)....344
Mossburg, David, Discovery Solutions (C)....334
Myers, Betty, The Biras Creek Group (C)....498
Narlis, Karen, Hreshko Consulting Group (C)....415
Nelson, Regina, Dieck Group Inc (R)....58
Niolet, Frank, Sanford Rose Associates - Cincinnati East (C)....610
Norgeot, Kevin, Sanford Rose Associates - Boston South Shore (C)....609
Notter, Carl, Diedre Moire Corp Inc (C)....535
Palisi, Kevin, MR of Stamford (C)....476
Perez, Minerva, The Hampton Group (C)....497
Phillips, Norm, APP Consulting (C)....257
Pinheiro, Teri, MR of Chapel Hill (C)....498
Post, Jan, Normyle/Erstling Health Search Group (C)....547

SPECIALTIES

The Directory of Executive Recruiters

Biotechnology

Kreps, Charles, Normyle/Erstling Health
   Search Group (C)...........................547
Krishnan, Priya, MR of Edison (C)...........493
Kuhn, Larry, Kuhn Med-Tech Inc (C)............443
Kulvik, Chris, FPC/Fortune of San
   Antonio (C)...................................380
Laird, Jim, Ashton Tweed (R)................ 11
Lambrou, Angie, Dorothy W Farnath &
   Associates Inc (C)..........................372
Lampl, Joni, MR of Pittsburgh North (C).......505
Lareau, Belle, The Hampton Group (C)........497
Lareau, Gerard, The Hampton Group (C)......497
Leathers, Karen, The Chase Group Inc (R) 39
Lee, Donna, Lee Heagy & Company (R) 92
Leech, David, Strawn Arnold Leech &
   Ashpitz Inc (R)..............................205
Lehnst, John, MR of Iowa City (C)............462
Lemons, Marvin, Recruiter Pharma (C)........586
Levin, Becky, Levin & Company Inc (R)........127
Levy, Daniel, DNA Search Inc (C)............335
Logue, Sara, Advanced Recruiters Inc (C)....241
Lord, J. Scott, J S Lord & Company Inc
   (R)..130
Lurier, Amy, TechFind Inc (R).................209
Lybrook, Karen, Lybrook Associates Inc
   (C)..455
Lynch, Chuck, FPC of Nashua (C)............368
MacEntyre, Allen, MR/SC of Jamestown
   (C)..499
Manatine, Tony, Neal Helsel &
   Associates Inc (C)..........................406
Mancino, Gene, Mancino Burfield
   Edgerton (R).................................138
Mankuta, Eric, Mankuta Gallagher &
   Associates Inc (C)..........................518
Marcel, Al, Recruiter Pharma (C)............586
Marshall, David, Target Pros Inc (C) 646
Matteson, Jon, The Apollo Group (C).........257
Mazziota, Daniel, Ruth Sklar Associates
   Inc (R).......................................193
McCallister, Richard, Boyden (R)..............25
McCallum, Fred, Bench International
   Search Inc (R)............................... 19
McClanahan, Deb, BroadBand HR
   Consulting (C)...............................285
Michas, Spiro, The Cambridge Group Ltd
   (C)..291
Miles, James, Holohan Group Ltd (R)..........100
Miller, David, Sanford Rose Associates -
   Carlsbad (C).................................607
Miller, Shirley, Miller.Miller LLC (R).......147
Miras, Cliff, Cornerstone Search Group
   LLC (C).......................................315
Mitchell, John, Spencer Stuart (R)...........198
Montgomery, Rita, HealthCare Recruiters
   International • Los Angeles (C).............404
Moore, Vickie, Foster/Searing Ltd (R)........ 76
Morgan, Wyman, Infinity Resources LLC
   (R)..106
Morice, James, Conboy, Sur & Associates
   Inc (R)....................................... 45
Morrisey, Jim, FPC/Fortune of San
   Antonio (C)...................................380
Mossburg, David, Discovery Solutions
   (C)..334
Moyer, Mark, Executec Search Agency
   Inc (C).......................................355
Myers, Betty, The Biras Creek Group (C)......498
Nadeau, Liz, Bishop Executive Services
   LLC (C).......................................276
Nelson, Regina, Dieck Group Inc (R)............58
Newpoff, Brad, BeechTree Partners LLC
   (R)... 18
Newton, Beverly, Search Team One (C)........617
Niolet, Frank, Sanford Rose Associates -
   Cincinnati East (C)..........................610
O'Brien, Rita, Moffitt International Inc
   (C)..535
O'Brien-Kletti, Elke, Bishop Executive
   Services LLC (C).............................276
Oppenheim, Norman, FPC of Nashua (C)........368
Ortman, Jim, Waterjobs (C)....................665
Paine, Donne, FPC of Hilton Head (C) 370
Palisi, Kevin, MR of Stamford (C)............476

Parker, Donald, cFour Partners (R).............38
Peck, Helene, Normyle/Erstling Health
   Search Group (C)............................547
Pellicione, Maria, Hechkoff Executive
   Search Inc (C)............................... 92
Pells, Susan, PSW Group Executive
   Search & Placement (C)......................580
Peluso, Philip, National Search Associates
   (C)..542
Penfold, Bart, Rusher, Loscavio &
   LoPresto (R).................................181
Perez, Minerva, The Hampton Group (C)......497
Piatkiewicz, Mary Lou, Medical
   Executive Search Associates Inc (C) 528
Pieper, Lisa, Spencer Stuart (R)............198
Pinheiro, Teri, MR of Chapel Hill (C)........498
Porter, Mary, TPG & Associates (C)...........654
Post, Jan, Normyle/Erstling Health Search
   Group (C)....................................547
Poster, Lawrence, Catalyx Group (R)...........36
Powell, Donald, Medpoint LLC (C)............529
Quattrocchi, Patricia, Sherbrooke
   Associates Inc (C)..........................622
Quintal, Yves, Quintal & Associates
   Human Resources Consultants Inc (C) 583
Ranney, Diane, Discovery Solutions (C).......334
Ratner, Barbara, Merraine Group Inc (C)......496
Ratterman, George, MR of Crestwood (C)......462
Raz, Steve, Cornerstone Search Group
   LLC (C).......................................315
Reticker, Peter, Clinical One (C)............307
Richards, Christos, Levin & Company Inc
   (R)..127
Richon, Allen, Molecular Solutions Inc
   (C)..535
Ricker, Arlene, MC2 Executive Search
   (R)..141
Rimele, J.R., Sales Recruiters of
   Oklahoma City (C)...........................605
Robb, Molly, Horton International LLC
   (R)..101
Roberts Bouchard, Rena, Strategic
   Resources Biotechnology & Medical
   Group (C)....................................640
Robinson, Tom, Spencer Stuart (R)...........198
Roe, Sylvia, Craig Roe & Associates LLC
   (C)..597
Rogove, Arthur, Merit Consulting Inc (C).....530
Romeo, Paul, Romeo Consulting (C)...........598
Rutherford, Forbes, Rutherford
   International Executive Search Group
   Inc (R).......................................182
Ryan, Joseph, Epsen Fuller IMD
   International Search Group (R)............... 67
Rychlik, Bruce, J Robert Scott (R)...........187
Saelens, Brad, The Alpine Group (C)..........475
Salkin, Maureen, Levin & Company Inc
   (R)..127
Sartori, Paul, CHM Partners International
   LLC (R)....................................... 40
Schantz, Shawn, The Apollo Group (C).........257
Schepp, James, Lasher Associates (R) 124
Schultz, Bill, MR/SC of Madison (C)..........515
Schultz, Helen, DillonGray (R)................59
Searing, James, Foster/Searing Ltd (R)....... 76
Searles, Brett, Neal Helsel & Associates
   Inc (C).......................................406
Sevel, Dave, Marvel Consultant (C)...........522
Shanes, Scott, Diedre Moire Corp Inc (C).....535
Shapiro, Warren, GRS Global
   Recruitment Solutions (C)...................394
Sheedy, Joseph, Marketing Resources (C)......520
Sheweloff, William, McCray Sheweloff &
   Associates Inc (R)..........................142
Shiley, Bob, Brethet, Barnum &
   Associates Inc (C)..........................283
Shipherd, John, The Cassie-Shipherd
   Group (R).................................... 36
Sigmund, William, Bench International
   Search Inc (R).............................. 19
Sinatra, Rich, Socius Search LLC (R).........196
Smith, Larry, FPC of Abington (C)............369
Solomon, Neil, The Neil Michael Group
   Inc (R).......................................151

Soufleris, Mark, Sanford Rose Associates
   - Clearwater (C)............................607
Sphar, Donna, CSI America (C)..............323
Spiegel, Terry, Normyle/Erstling Health
   Search Group (C)............................547
St. Leger, Joe, Reaction Search
   International Inc (R).........................173
Stephenson, Jay, JG Consultants Inc (R).......111
Stevens, Marc, Park Avenue Group Inc
   (C)..480
Strand, Michael, FPC of Abington (C).........369
Stratman, Sandra, MR of Milford (C).........475
Strawn, William, Strawn Arnold Leech &
   Ashpitz Inc (R)..............................205
Szmidt, Les, MR of Napa (C)..................459
Thiers, Harold, The Hampton Group (C) 497
Thomas, Terry, Bialla & Associates Inc
   (R)... 20
Tinucci, Crystal, Search Masters
   International (R).............................188
Towne, Andrew, Hobbs & Towne Inc (R) 99
Tremblay, Manon, Quintal & Associates
   Human Resources Consultants Inc (C) 583
Vézina, Claude, Claude Vézina Conseil
   (R)... 42
Vinyard, Kiley, Advanced Recruiters Inc
   (C)..241
Vocke, Jessica, Discovery Solutions (C)......334
Walker, Alex, MR of Stamford (C)............476
Walker, Lisa, MR of Stamford (C)............476
Waller, Brian, MR/SC San Francisco Bay
   Area (C).....................................473
Warshafsky, Jordan, Ashton Tweed (R) 11
Waterfall, Clark, Boston Search (R) 24
Watkins, Robert, R J Watkins & Company
   Ltd (R).......................................218
Watson, Dawn, FPC of Abington (C) 369
Wegiel, Jason, Conncxion Systems &
   Engineering (C)..............................312
Welch, James, CHM Partners
   International LLC (R)........................ 40
Wernstrom, Mark, SC of Rochester (C).........463
Wheeler, Andrew, Diversified Search Ray
   & Berndtson (R)............................. 60
Wiebke, Jill, Emerging Healthcare
   Partners LLC (R).............................348
Wiener, John, Fairway Consulting Group
   (C)..496
Williams, Stephen, Bench International
   Search Inc (R)............................... 18
Yowe, Mark, Spencer Stuart (R)..............198
Zingaro, Ronald, Zingaro & Company (R) 230

Boards of Directors

Allred, J. Michael, Highland Partners (R)............97
Alorbi, Karl, Catalyx Group (R)...............36
Anderson, Kim, BoardWalk Consulting
   LLC (R)...................................... 22
Anderson, Ronni, Anderson Philips
   Associates (R)............................... 10
Arias, Jr., Victor, Heidrick & Struggles
   (R)... 94
Ballenger, Michael, Highland Partners (R) 97
Bellville, Maggie, CarterBaldwin (R)..............35
Bethmann, James, Highland Partners (R).........98
Biggins, J. Veronica, Heidrick &
   Struggles (R)................................ 93
Birch, Walter, CXO Executive Search Ltd
   (R)... 52
Bliley, Jerry, Spencer Stuart (R)............199
Blinkhorn, Ann, Spencer Stuart (R).........198
Boccuzi, Joseph, Spencer Stuart (R).........198
Boren, Susan, Spencer Stuart (R)...........198
Brack, Kelley, Heidrick & Struggles (R) 93
Bruce, Michael, Spencer Stuart (R) 197
Buckley, James, Spencer Stuart (R).........198
Bukowicz, John, Corporate Consulting
   Associates Inc (C)..........................316
Cavalli, John, Diedre Moire Corp Inc (C).....535
Chalk, Charles, Boyden (R).................. 25
Chen, Roger, Heidrick & Struggles (R) 94
Citrin, James, Spencer Stuart (R)...........198
Colbert, Brad, The Executive Network Inc
   (R)... 69

SPECIALTIES

Bridges

Brokerage

SPECIALTIES

Business to Business

Buyout Funds

C-Level

Cable

Call Centers

Capital Goods

Capital Markets

SPECIALTIES

SPECIALTIES

Compensation

Competitive Intelligence

Compliance

SPECIALTIES

SPECIALTIES

SPECIALTIES

Controllers

Convenience Stores

Convergence

Converting

COOs

SPECIALTIES

SPECIALTIES

White, Justin, Jack Kelly & Partners LLC
(C) 437
Wilkerson, Cathie, RTX Inc (C) 601
Witt, Stan, The Jonathan Group (C) 431
Wojcik, Carolyn, E A Hughes &
Company Inc (R) 103
Zetrenne, Sabina, SC of Ft Lauderdale (C) 476

Diagnostics

Allison, Ken, The Chase Group Inc (R) 39
Bowman, Mary, Bowman & Associates
Inc (R) 24
Ducharme, David, FPC of Hilton Head
(C) 370
Duchesne, Roger, Quintal & Associates
Human Resources Consultants Inc (C)...........583
Jagielo, Thomas, Martin Partners LLC (R).........139
Kazan, J. Neil, Kazan International Inc
(R) 116
Kochanik, Dennis, Dorothy W Farnath &
Associates Inc (C)..............................372
Kovach, Nancy, Korban Associates (R) 120
Lambrou, Angie, Dorothy W Farnath &
Associates Inc (C)..............................372
Lareau, Belle, The Hampton Group (C) 497
Leathers, Karen, The Chase Group Inc (R) 39
Ledford, Patsy, MR of Kings Mountain
(C) 499
Moore, Richard, HealthCare Recruiters
International • Rockies (C).....................404
Sartori, Paul, CHM Partners International
LLC (R) 40
Sherman, Ted, Sanford Rose Associates -
Cincinnati East (C) 610
Stratman, Sandra, MR of Milford (C)...............475
Tremblay, Manon, Quintal & Associates
Human Resources Consultants Inc (C)...........583
Vice, Michael, Denell-Archer
International Executive Search (R) 56
Zingaro, Ronald, Zingaro & Company (R).........230
Zych, Jean, Dorothy W Farnath &
Associates Inc (C)..............................372

Direct Marketing

Allard, Susan, Allard Associates Inc (C) 249
Anthony, Robin, MLB Associates (C)...............535
Baker, Heather, Bennett Wheelless Group
Ltd (R) 19
Ballard, Lisa, MR of Moreland Hills Inc
(C) 501
Banach-Osenni, Doris, The Brentwood
Group Inc (R) 27
Bates, Nina, Allard Associates Inc (C)............249
Bencin, Richard, Richard L Bencin &
Associates (R)................................... 19
Bennett, Neysa, Bennett Wheelless Group
Ltd (R) 19
Bernhart, Jerry, Bernhart Associates
Executive Search LLC (C)......................274
Bliss, Barbara, Barbara Bliss Co Ltd (C).........278
Brolin, Lawrence, DLB Associates (R) 60
Brown, MaryLou, MLB Associates (C) 535
Buffkin, Craig, Buffkin & Associates
LLC (R) 29
Candiotti, Lee, Bristol Associates Inc (C) 284
Carey, Peter, Peter N Carey & Associates
Inc (C) 297
Cyr, Maury, Cyr Associates Inc (C) 326
Daugherty, Sue, Allard Associates Inc (C).........249
Fabian, Jeanne, Fabian Associates Inc (C) 371
Finnigan Ellinger, Clare, Brentwood
International (R) 27
Fox, Lucie, Allard Associates Inc (C) 249
Hammond, Terry, TERHAM
Management Consultants (R)....................210
Hart, Laurie, Chad Management Group
(C) 301
Havas, Judy, Spencer Stuart (R)..................197
Hull, Thomas, Mangieri/Hull Solutions
LLC (C) 518
Ingala, Thomas, Direct Marketing
Solutions (C).....................................334

Jackowitz, Todd, Jackowitz & Company
Inc (R) 109
James, Victoria, Victoria James Executive
Search Inc (C)...................................428
Juarez, Elisa, Masterquest (C)....................522
Lambrou, Angie, Dorothy W Farnath &
Associates Inc (C)..............................372
Leslie, Ken, Strategic Search Consultants
(C) 641
Macan, Sandi, The Beam Group (R) 17
Maggiore, David, Richard L Bencin &
Associates (R) 19
Malloy, Brenda, Spencer Stuart (R)...............197
Mangieri, Christopher, Mangieri/Hull
Solutions LLC (C)...............................518
McClung, Margaret, The Resource Group
(R) 176
Mitchell, Brenda, A&S Resources
Staffing Inc (C)..................................233
Moore, Connie, C A Moore & Associates
Inc (R) 148
Nadherny, Christopher, Spencer Stuart (R).......197
Peragine, Ralph, The Resource Group (R) 176
Raz, Rita, Analytic Recruiting Inc (C) 254
Reed, Scott, MR of Moreland Hills Inc
(C) 501
Richardson, J. Rick, Spencer Stuart (R) 198
Ridenour, Suzanne, Ridenour &
Associates (R) 177
Rojas, Julie, Career Forum Inc (C)...............294
Rothman, Jeff, MR of Moreland Hills Inc
(C) 501
Schwartz, Matthew, MJS Executive
Search (R) 147
Smolen, Dan, Dan Smolen Direct Search
LLC (C) 626
Snyder, Thomas, Spencer Stuart (R)..............197
Sullivan, Dan, Direct Marketing
Resources Inc (C) 334
Tessler, Ivy, The Brentwood Group Inc
(R) 27
Tibbles, Holly, Patricia Dowd Inc (C)............337
Tonini, Frank, Search Professionals Inc
(C) 617
Trager, Lori, The Odella Group Inc (C) 550
Troyanos, Dennis, The Troyanos Group
Ltd (R) 213
Van Rossum, Bob, MarketPro Inc (C) 520
Weiner, Paula, Gould, McCoy, Chadick,
Ellig (R) 84
Weiss, Cathy, C Weiss Associates Inc (C).........666
Welch, Edward, Emkay Assoc Ltd (C) 348
Welch, Greg, Spencer Stuart (R) 197
Woodward, David, O'Keefe & Associates
Inc (R) 154
Zapin, Roni, RL Zapin Associates Inc (C) 677
Zwiff, Jeffrey, Aegis Consulting (R)................5

Disaster Planning & Recovery

Culp, Ernie, MR of Winona (C) 491
Dowd, Charlie, Dowd Group Inc (C) 337

Distribution

Abbene, John, FPC of Fairfax (C)..................371
Alberson, Bob, Snelling Search (C) 628
Allday, Doug, Qualifind Inc (C) 581
Anderson, Jim, Howard Clark Associates
(C) 305
Anderson, Wayne, Anderson Network
Group (C) 255
Anzalone, Alicia, Sanford Rose
Associates - Carlsbad (C) 607
Bailey, David, MR of Lake Tahoe (C) 492
Barzelay, Richard, Search Professionals
Inc (C) 617
Berger, Shelly, Robins Consulting LLC
(C) 596
Buntrock, George, MR of Dallas North
(C) 510
Bush, Derek, PeopleSource Solutions (C).........560
Campbell, Cheryl, Career Search
Associates (C) 296

Campbell, Dan, Campbell/Carlson LLC
(R).. 32
Carey, Harvey, Carion Resource Group
Inc (C)...297
Cargill, Jim, MR of Lake Tahoe (C) 492
Carter, Van, Hudson Consulting Group
(R)..102
Case, David, PeopleSource Solutions (C) 560
Conroy, William, Tyler Search
Consultants (C) 659
Cousins, John, Procurement Resources
(C) 574
Crawford, Luke, Advanced Recruiters Inc
(C) 241
Cresci, Joseph, Food Management Search
(C) 378
Currie, Ned, ABL Logistics Group LLC
(C) 235
Dean, Chris, PeopleSource Solutions (C)...........560
Dickerson, Donna, Sanford Rose
Associates - Carlsbad (C) 607
Dowling, Abigail, MR of Pittsburgh North
(C) 505
Eichman, Addie, Gladwyne Search Group
Inc (C)...504
Ferguson, Dan, The Herring Group (C) 407
Forney, John, Recruit America (C)................586
Goldsmith, Fred, Fred J Goldsmith
Associates (R) 83
Griffiths, Bob, Griffiths & Associates (C) 394
Heinschel, Phil, Phillips Personnel/Search
(C) 564
Herring, Bill, The Herring Group (C) 407
Higdon, Lynn, Search South Inc (C)...............617
Hodges, Whitney, Recruiting Services
Group Inc (C) 588
Hood, Fred, Fred Hood & Associates Inc
(C) 413
Horne, Tony, The Herring Group (C) 407
Ibarra, Veronica, Qualifind Inc (C) 581
Kennedy, Todd, Great Work!
Employment Services (C) 392
Klee, Michael, Global Recruiters of
Milwaukee (C) 389
Konnerth, Ted, Egret Consulting Group
(R).. 65
Lykins, Matt, MR of Columbus-Grove
City (C) 466
Machi, Michael, MR of Pleasanton (C) 472
Markt, John, Markt & Markworth Ltd (R) 138
Matté, Norman, Matté & Company Inc
(R)..140
McCann, Eleanor, Gladwyne Search
Group Inc (C) 504
McDermott, Bob, The McDermott
Network LLP (C) 525
McIntyre, Cookie Anne, The McIntyre
Company (C) 142
Metz, Alex, Hunt Ltd (C)..........................417
Miller, David, Sanford Rose Associates -
Carlsbad (C) 607
Nichols, Debbie, FPC of Boise (C) 366
O'Dell, Bob, Roth Young of Houston (C) 600
Page, Theresa, T Page & Associates (C)..........555
Pellenberg, Art, Recruit America (C)..............586
Perkins, R. Patrick, The Perkins Group
(R)..162
Pidek, Matthew, Corporate Consulting
Associates Inc (C) 316
Pollack, Fran, Ambiance Personnel Inc
(C) 252
Radke, William, Marvel Consultant (C) 522
Remillard, Brad, CJA Executive Search
(R).. 41
Richards, Terry, Terry Richards CPC (C) 593
Roach, James, Sanford Rose Associates -
Orlando (C) 607
Robins, Craig, Robins Consulting LLC
(C) 596
Rodriguez, Janet, T Page & Associates
(C) 555
Schorejs, Sherry, Roth Young of Houston
(C) 600

SPECIALTIES

Engineering

SPECIALTIES

SPECIALTIES

Entertainment

Entrepreneurs

Environmental

SPECIALTIES

SPECIALTIES

SPECIALTIES

SPECIALTIES

SPECIALTIES

Flexographic Printing

Floriculture

Food

Food & Beverage

Food Service

Footwear

Forest Industry/Products

Foundries

Franchising

Fraud Investigators

Freight

SPECIALTIES

Van Opstal, Lori, Your Advantage
Staffing Consultants Inc (C) 677

Furniture

Dunn, Markay, SC of Alexandria (C) 486
Graebner-Smith, Linda, Sloane &
Associates Inc (R) 137
Greene, William, The Greene Group (C) 393
Grodsky, Janet, Stern Professional Search
(C) 638
Ibsen, John, The Greene Group (C) 393
Leder, Sam, The Recruiting Leder Inc (C) 587
Marlowe, Bill, The Greene Group (C) 393
Olson, Jon, Recruiter Solutions
International (C) 586
Roda, Janet, Jack Kelly & Partners LLC
(C) 437
Wissler, Jim, Comprehensive Search (R) 45

Gaming

Allen, Marla, Allen & Associates Inc (C) 249
Bright, Jr., James, Bristol Associates Inc
(C) 284
Caracappa, Paula, Alfus Group Inc (R) 7
Farber, Lucy, Bristol Associates Inc (C) 284
Kresich, William, Focus Search Group
(C) 377
Latini, Rick, CasinoRecruiter.com (C) 299
Prager, Mitchell, Hospitality Career
Services (R) 101
Schostak, Glen, Korn/Ferry International
(R) 121
Stanton, Grant, TSC Management
Services Group Inc (C) 657
Wallenda, Erika, Executive Referral
Services Inc (C) 358
Weiswasser, Marc, CasinoRecruiter.com
(C) 299
Wolters, Mark, Wolters Search Group (C) 503
Wurster, Michael, HVS Executive Search
(R) 105

Gas

Aiken, Karen, Interchange Personnel Inc
(R) 108
Ayling, Michael, MLA Resources Inc (C) 534
Devaney, Marie, Eissler & Associates Inc
(C) 347
Hall, Sue, Preferred Personnel (C) 570
Hazlett, Kori, Career Forum Inc (C) 294
King, III, Jack, A H Justice Search
Consultants (C) 433
McCall - Baron, S. Caitlin, Allen Austin
Executive Search Consultants (R) 13
McKay, John, Korn/Ferry International
(R) 121
O'Brien, Brent, Executive Search
Consultants Corp (C) 360
Peterson, Joan, A H Justice Search
Consultants (C) 433
Shurlds, Henry, Onesource Professional
Search (C) 552
Williams, Bill, Executive Search
Consultants Corp (C) 360

General Contractors

Barker, Brad, Construction Resources
Group Inc (R) 46
Brod, Walter, IndustrySalesPros/Schaper
Associates (C) 420
Conroy, Daniel, Michael Latas &
Associates Inc (R) 125
Dickerson, Ken, Vermillion Group (C) 485
Dierks, David, MR of Sioux Falls (C) 508
Difatta, Jon, MR of Barrington (C) 482
Eichstaedt, Tim, MR of Menasha (C) 469
Foster, Kathie, Michael Latas &
Associates Inc (R) 125
Grauss, Bryan, Grauss & Company (C) 392
Grimes, Kent, MBA Management Inc (R) 141
Groom, Charles, Corporate Consulting
Group Inc (C) 316

Harris, Cheryl, Construction Resources
Group Inc (R) 46
Hedman, Rich, MR of Menasha (C) 469
Hipp, Charles, MR of Chapel Hill (C) 498
Jesberg, Gary, Michael Latas &
Associates Inc (R) 125
Leonard, William, Michael Latas &
Associates Inc (R) 125
O'Shea, Karen, G Adams Partners (R) 4
Olszewski, John, MR of Barrington (C) 482
Roepke, Janet, MR of Siouxland (C) 485
Sergeant, Robert, MR of Bucks County
(C) 506
Stockman, Ron, National Restaurant
Search Inc (R) 151
Taylor, Lynn, HardHatJobs Inc (C) 398
Van Krey, Tamara, Global Recruiters of
Milwaukee (C) 389
Wessel, Diane, Key Corporate Services
LLC (C) 439
Williams, Mike, ChaseAmerica Inc (R) 39
Zerkle, Sr., John, Interactive Search
Associates (C) 424

General Management

Aavik, Karl, Intrepid Consulting Group
(R) 109
Allday, Doug, Qualifind Inc (C) 581
Alman, Paul, Holland & Associates Inc
(R) 99
Ambruster, David, Renaissance Resources
LLC (R) 175
Ascher, Daniel, Denell-Archer
International Executive Search (R) 56
Avila Swartz, Janis, Berkhemer Clayton
Inc (R) 20
Babcock, James, Premier Business
Services (C) 570
Bachant, Arlene, A Greenstein &
Company (R) 85
Baker, Walter, Meridian Partners (R) 193
Balian-Mehren, Christina, Compass
Group Ltd (R) 44
Banks, Merrill, Lloyd Staffing (C) 451
Barton, Gary, Barton Associates Inc (R) 16
Bauman, Martin, Martin H Bauman
Associates LLC (R) 17
Beaudin, Elizabeth, Callan Associates Ltd
(R) 31
Bell, Julie, Page-Wheatcroft & Company
Ltd (R) 158
Bennett, Joan, Adams & Associates
International (R) 4
Beres, Robert, Bosch & Associates LLC
(R) 23
Bilotta, Christopher, Resource
Development Company Inc (R) 176
Birarda, Richard, JSG Group Management
Consultants (R) 114
Birnbaum, Richard, R J Associates (R) 583
Boland, Joseph, The Boland Group Inc
(R) 23
Bolen, Dan, Dan Bolen & Associates LLC
(C) 279
Bosch, Diane, Bosch & Associates LLC
(R) 23
Bosch, Eric, Bosch & Associates LLC (R) 23
Brenneman, Thomas, Roth Young Exec
Search (C) 600
Brolin, Lawrence, DLB Associates (R) 60
Brooks, Kathy, The Whyte Group Inc (R) 222
Brown, Arthur, James Mead & Co (R) 143
Buchholz, Edward, CareerTrac
Professional Group Inc (C) 297
Bulmer, Robert, Alaska Executive Search
Inc (C) 248
Buono, Ronald, MR of Hendersonville
(C) 465
Bush, William, Cook & Company (R) 47
Byrne, Joan, EFL Associates (R) 65
Callan, Jr., Robert, Callan Associates Ltd
(R) 31
Callan, Robert, Callan Associates Ltd (R) 31
Caplan, Shellie, Caplan Associates Inc (R) 33

Carpenter, Eric, Carpenter, Shackleton &
Company (R) 35
Caudill, Nancy, Aegis Consulting (R) 5
Chad, Rick, Chad Management Group (C) 301
Clayton, Fred, Berkhemer Clayton Inc (R) 20
Cloutier, E.J., American Executive
Management Inc (R) 8
Conroy, M.J., Conroy Ross Partners
Limited (R) 46
Cook, Patricia, Cook & Company (R) 47
Cowell, Roy, Cowell & Associates Ltd
(R) 50
Crowe, Thomas, Hunter, Rowan & Crowe
(R) 104
Cunningham, Sheila, Adams & Associates
International (R) 4
Custer, Bryce, The Custer Group (R) 52
Cyr, Randy, The Damase Group (R) 53
Daubenspeck, Rima, Daubenspeck and
Associates Ltd (R) 53
Davies, A. Gerry, Davies Park (R) 54
DeBaugh, David, PRAXIS Partners (R) 166
DeCoster, Steve, Martin Partners LLC (R) 139
Dee, Vincent, Hartsfield Advisors Inc (R) 91
Denney, Edward, Denney & Company Inc
(R) 56
Denney, Thomas, Denney & Company
Inc (R) 56
Despres, Raoul, Despres & Associates Inc
(R) 56
Dewey, Terri, Digital Recruiters Inc (C) 333
Diaz, Del, MR of Miami North (C) 477
Donnelly, John, Dise & Company Inc (R) 59
Doupe, S. Scott, Conroy Ross Partners
Limited (R) 46
Dukes, Ronald, Ronald Dukes Associates
LLC (R) 62
Earle, Holland, Executive Strategies Inc
(R) 71
England, Mark, JG Consultants Inc (R) 111
Espinosa, Fernando, Qualifind Inc (C) 581
Farmer, David, The Whitney Smith
Company Inc (C) 668
Farrell, Kelly, Ray & Berndtson/Lovas
Stanley (R) 172
Feinstein, Jessica, Swift & Associates
LLC (C) 643
Finley-Aguilera, Margot, Avondale
Search International Inc (R) 13
Fludd, Virgil, The Carvir Group Inc (C) 298
Flynn, Jerry, J G Flynn & Associates Inc
(R) 75
Foster, Dwight, FPA-US (R) 76
Franchot, Douglas, Franchot & Associates
Inc (R) 76
Garfield, John, Garfield & Associates (R) 79
Garmes, Kathryn, Prairie Resource Group
Inc (R) 166
Geddes, Murray, Murray Geddes &
Associates (R) 80
Gegax, Ryan, The Lakewood Group (C) 514
Getzkin, Helen, Stone Murphy (R) 204
Giesen, Al, Stone Murphy (R) 204
Gillespie, David, D Gillespie &
Associates Inc (C) 387
Ginley, Michael, The Lear Group Inc (R) 126
Glover, Russell, Shore Paralax LLC (R) 192
Gregg, Larry, The Lear Group Inc (R) 126
Gundersen, Steven, Gundersen Partners
LLC (R) 87
Hajek, Kathleen, Martin Partners LLC (R) 139
Hale, Maureen, Hale Associates (R) 88
Hamman, Cassie, Jacobs Scott Ltd (R) 110
Handley, Bill, The Apollo Group (C) 257
Hannock, Pamela, Flynn, Hannock Inc (R) 75
Harrison, Paula, TNS Partners Inc (R) 211
Hartig, David, The Angus Group Ltd (R) 10
Hartung, Chris, Waters Consulting Group
Inc (R) 218
Hastings, Jeff, Hastings & Associates Inc
(R) 91
Hauser, Al, MR of Bedminster (C) 493
Hedman, Kent, Hedman & Associates (R) 92

Heinze, David, Heinze & Associates Inc
(R)..95
Heller, Phillip, Heller, Kil Associates Inc
(C)..406
Hernandez, Dolores, Sanford Rose
Associates - Spain (R).......................185
Hickory, Ashlee, The Myers Group Inc
(C)..482
Hipp, Charles, MR of Chapel Hill (C)..........498
Hopkins, Chester, Handy Associates Corp
(R)..89
Hopkins, Edward, Shore Paralax LLC (R).........192
Jackson-Turner, Peggy, Nomadic
Consulting Inc (R)............................152
Joyce, Barbara, Cornell Global LLC (R)..........48
Kelly, Thom, Integrity Recruiting &
Consulting (C)..................................423
Kinsley, Richard, The Kinsley Group (R).........119
Kipson, Kip, Meticulum, Inc. (R)................145
Kleiman, Howard, Derhak Ireland &
Partners Inc (R)................................56
Knutson, David, The Knutson Group LLC
(R)..119
Koren, Michael, Koren, Rogers
Associates Inc (R)..............................120
Kristan, Robert, Kristan International Inc
(R)..123
Kurosky, John, John Kurosky &
Associates (R)..................................123
Lambert, Gerald, Lambert Group
International LLC (R)...........................123
Langford, K.R. Dick, The Langford
Search Inc (C)..................................446
Larkin, CorDell, Roberts & Ryan (R)............178
Lee, Kandy, Avant Solutions Inc (C)............265
Lehman, Neal, Sherwood Lehman
Massucco Inc (R)..............................191
Leslie, William, Riddle & McGrath LLC
(R)..177
Lewis, Trish, MR of Bedminster (C)............493
Lineback, Pam, MR of Dallas (R)...............509
Litchfield, Barbara, Litchfield & Willis
Inc (R)..129
Livingston, Hyman, P & L Group Inc (C)........554
Livingston, Peter, Livingston, Robert &
Co (R)..129
Marra, Jr., John, Marra Peters & Partners
(R)..139
Marshall, Dan, Dan Bolen & Associates
LLC (C)..279
Masin, Philip, Marra Peters & Partners
(R)..139
Mason, William, John Kurosky &
Associates (R)..................................123
Massucco, Harry, Sherwood Lehman
Massucco Inc (R)..............................191
Masterson, Louis, Louis Thomas
Masterson & Company (R)....................140
Matte, Richard, Matte Consulting Group
(R)..140
Mattes, Jr., Edward, The Ogdon
Partnership (R)..................................155
Maxey, Joe, Trinity Group (C)..................657
McCarthy, Deborah, The Whyte Group
Inc (R)..222
McElmeel, Joseph, Brooke Chase
Associates Inc (R)..............................28
McFadzean, Jr., James, Rusher, Loscavio
& LoPresto (R)..................................181
McGeady, John, Evenium (R)...................68
McNally, Glenna, Flynn, Hannock Inc (R)........75
McPolin, James, Advantage Partners Inc
(R)..5
Mead, James, James Mead & Co (R).............143
Miller, D., Sanford Rose Associates -
Rancho Bernardo (C)...........................607
Mittenthal, Robert, Roberts & Ryan (R).........178
Moorre, Deborah, Woessner & Associates
(R)..225
Morice, James, Conboy, Sur & Associates
Inc (R)..45
Morrill, Carolyn, Barrack Hill Partners
Inc (R)..15
Mruk, Edwin, Mruk & EMA Partners (R)........149

Murphy, Patrick, P J Murphy &
Associates Inc (R)..............................150
Myers, Gail, The Myers Group Inc (C)..........482
Nadherny, Pete, The Angus Group Ltd (R)........10
Neidhart, Cable, TNS Partners Inc (R)..........211
Neidhart, Craig, TNS Partners Inc (R)..........211
Nicholson, Philip, P J Nicholson &
Associates (R)..................................152
Norrie, Andrew, Ray & Berndtson/Lovas
Stanley (R)......................................172
Norton, Peter, Sanford Rose Associates -
Annapolis (C)..................................609
Owens-Wright, Robin, Executive Levels
International (R)................................356
Paley Zak, Susan, Dise & Company Inc
(R)..59
Patrick, Donald, Sanford Rose Associates
- Norcross (C)..................................608
Pawlusiak, Julie, Access/Resources Inc
(C)..236
Porter, Mike, TNS Partners Inc (R).............211
Presley, Philip, Presley Consultants Inc
(R)..571
Prod, Olga, Jay Gaines & Company Inc
(R)..79
Prusak, Conrad, Ethos Consulting Inc (R).........68
Pukita, Mark, Fast Switch Ltd (C)..............372
Ray, Marianne, Callan Associates Ltd (R)........31
Raymond, Allan, Stone Murphy (R)..............204
Renzenbrink, Paul, Satterfield &
Associates Inc (R)..............................186
Riddle, James, Riddle & McGrath LLC
(R)..177
Roberts, Bill, Southern Technical
Recruiters (R)..................................630
Robertson, Jim, J S Robertson - Retained
Search (R)......................................178
Romaniw, Michael, A la Carte
International Inc (R)............................3
Rooney, Joseph, Rooney Associates Inc
(R)..179
Rosenberg, Kevin, BridgeGate LLC (R)...........27
Runquist, Bill, Livingston, Robert & Co
(R)..129
Ryan, Lawrence, Roberts & Ryan (R)............178
Sarn, Jonathan, The Kinsley Group (R)..........119
Satterfield, Jr., Richard, Satterfield &
Associates Inc (R)..............................186
Schmidt, Paul, Martin Partners LLC (R).........139
Schulz, Bill, Holloway, Schulz & Partners
(R)..412
Schweiger, Michael, Search International
(R)..188
Sears, David, DL Sears & Associates Inc
(C)..619
Sebastian, Lynne, Cornell Global LLC (R).........48
Siciliano, Tom, Integrity Recruiting &
Consulting (C)..................................423
Slater, Marjorie, Logistics Management
Resources Inc (R)..............................130
Smayda, Anthony, BioQuest (R)..................21
Smeester, Chuck, WilliamCharles
Executive Search (R)...........................669
Snow, Thomas, The SearchAmerica
Group Inc (R)..................................189
Snyder, Luther, Conway & Greenwood
Inc (R)..46
Spadaro, Raymond, David Perry
Associates (C)..................................560
St-Louis, Michael, Matte Consulting
Group (R)..140
Staub, Jr., Robert, Staub, Warmbold &
Associates Inc (R)..............................202
Sted, Eric, The SearchAmerica Group Inc
(R)..189
Steele, Michael, Renaissance Resources
LLC (R)..175
Stewart, Harvey, Executive Registry (C)........359
Stokes, Amy, MR of Lansing (C)................463
Stoller, Richard, Heath/Norton Associates
Inc (R)..92
Strelow, Nancy, MR of Winona (C).............491
Stubenvoll, Ellen, Pennswood Partners Inc
(C)..559

Sucgang, Dante, Aegis Consulting (R)...........5
Symanski, Donald, Tierney Consulting
Group LLC (R)..................................211
Tabh, Roosevelt, Tabh & Associates (R).........207
Tancredi, Frank, Derhak Ireland &
Partners Inc (R)................................56
Taylor, Frederick, Ratliff & Taylor Inc
(R)..172
Toedtman, Dana, Resource Development
Company Inc (R)................................175
Toole, Thomas, MR of Laguna Hills-
Orange County (R)..............................134
Van Langen, Karel, MR of Minnetonka
(C)..491
Vangel, Peter, Access/Resources Inc (C).........236
Villareal, Morey, Villareal & Associates
Inc (R)..215
Vlcek, Thomas, Vlcek & Company Inc
(R)..216
Ward, Eileen, E K Ward & Associates (R)........217
Washington, Phyllis, BG & Associates
(C)..275
Wegner, Carl, Wegner & Associates (C).........665
Weidner, Jr., John, Cornell Global LLC
(R)..48
Wellman, Michael, Jefferson Partners
LLC (R)..111
White, Joseph, Sports Group International
(R)..199
Winter, Chuck, Lou Michaels Associates
Inc (C)..532
Wolf, Robert, CareerStrategies LLC (R)..........34
Wood, Michael, The Wood Group Inc (R)........226
Yake, Deborah, PPS Professional
Personnel Services (C)........................569
Zak, Adam, Adams & Associates
International (R)................................4

Geology

Bledsoe, Paula, Preferred Personnel (C).........570
Chermak, Charles, MR of Orange County
(C)..496
Davis, Christina, Brownson & Associates
LP (R)..29
Fishback, Joren, Derek Associates Inc (R).........56
Mount, Dave, Onesource Professional
Search (C)..552
Ray, Joel, Delta Services (R)...................55
Shurlds, Henry, Onesource Professional
Search (C)..552

Government

Affleck, John, The Executive Network Inc
(R)..69
Beezat, Robert, The PAR Group - Paul A
Reaume Ltd (R)..................................158
Bernard, G. Stevens, The PAR Group -
Paul A Reaume Ltd (R).........................158
Campbell, Margaret, Ray &
Berndtson/Lovas Stanley (R)..................172
Dalldorf, Charles, Wilcox, Miller &
Nelson (R)......................................223
Dickerson, Ken, Vermillion Group (C)..........485
Donald, Walter, The Executive Network
Inc (R)..69
Frederickson, Valerie, Valerie
Frederickson & Company (R)..................77
Grimes, William, Career Management
Associates (C)..................................295
Guilini, Jacques, Dare Human Resources
Corp (C)..327
Hagberg, Craig, SC of Loudoun County
(C)..513
Hagman, Gerald, The PAR Group - Paul
A Reaume Ltd (R)..............................158
Hobbs, Daniel, Boyden (R)......................25
Kerr, Mike, Davies Park (R)....................54
Kuhn, Gregory, The PAR Group - Paul A
Reaume Ltd (R)..................................158
LaBoon, Lawrence, Metropolitan
Personnal Inc (C)..............................531
Lèsperance, Edith, Dare Human
Resources Corp (C)............................327

SPECIALTIES

High Technology

SPECIALTIES

SPECIALTIES

SPECIALTIES

HVAC

Incentives

Industrial

SPECIALTIES

Information Service

Information Systems

SPECIALTIES

SPECIALTIES

Claims

Bender, Wendie, Kenneth Harris
Recruiting Group (C) 400
Boyd, Jenny, Lear & Associates Inc (C)............448
Chiu, Tiffany, Descheneaux Insurance
Recruiters Ltd (C).....................................332
Descheneaux, Pat, Descheneaux Insurance
Recruiters Ltd (C).....................................332
Dexter, Rita, Platinum Search Group Inc
(C) 516
Evdemon, II, Michael, E Insurance Group
(C) 343
Frawley, Sharon, Lear & Associates Inc
(C) 448
Garrison, Jeff, The Garrison Organization
(C)...384
Hoing, Jessica, Kenneth Harris Recruiting
Group (C)...400
Jacobs, James, MR/SC of Nassau (R)...............136
Lear, Roger, Lear & Associates Inc (C) 448
Lockwood, Margaret, Lear & Associates
Inc (C)...448
Lonas, George, The Regent Group (C)...............589
Martin, Hayley, Descheneaux Insurance
Recruiters Ltd (C)......................................332
Methvin, Doug, Premier Careers Inc (C).............570
Nixon, Jeffrey, J L Nixon Consulting Inc
(C) 547
Orlando, Joseph, Socius Search LLC (R) 196
Rivard, Cheryl, The Rivard Group (C)...............594
Rivard, Richard, The Rivard Group (C) 594
Roderique, Cindy, Select Medical
Solutions (C)..619
Rowlinson, Kevin, Lear & Associates Inc
(C) 448
Rubinstein, David, Kenneth Harris
Recruiting Group (C)..................................400
Smith, Mary, The Regent Group (C)..................589
St. James, Susan, Staff, Inc. (C) 635
Swoboda, Jennifer, Platinum Search
Group Inc (C) 516
Welch, Angela, The Regent Group (C) 589
Yee, Jim, MR/SC of Milwaukee-North
(C) 515

Health

Bender, Wendie, Kenneth Harris
Recruiting Group (C)..................................400
Brooks, Jim, Executive Solutions
International (R) 71
Chiu, Tiffany, Descheneaux Insurance
Recruiters Ltd (C).....................................332
Descheneaux, Pat, Descheneaux Insurance
Recruiters Ltd (C).....................................332
Elam, Kimarra, MR of Lincoln (R) 135
Evdemon, II, Michael, E Insurance Group
(C) 343
Geist, Vill, Grafton Executive Search (C).........391
Hoing, Jessica, Kenneth Harris Recruiting
Group (C)...400
Kauffman, Gail, The Madeira Group (R) 132
Lonas, George, The Regent Group (C)...............589
Martin, Hayley, Descheneaux Insurance
Recruiters Ltd (C).....................................332
Plappert, James, Newtown Consulting
Group Inc (C) 505
Smith, Mary, The Regent Group (C)..................589
St. James, Susan, Staff, Inc. (C) 635
VanMaanen, Mandy, The Garrison
Organization (C).......................................384
Welch, Angela, The Regent Group (C) 589
Yee, Jim, MR/SC of Milwaukee-North
(C) 515

Life

Affleck, John, The Executive Network Inc
(R) 69
Anderson, Barbara, The Regent Group (C) 589
Brooks, Jim, Executive Solutions
International (R) 71
Descheneaux, Pat, Descheneaux Insurance
Recruiters Ltd (C).....................................332
Elam, Kimarra, MR of Lincoln (R) 135

Garrison, Cory, The Garrison
Organization (C)..384
Garrison, Ed, The Garrison Organization
(C)..384
Garrison, Randy, The Garrison
Organization (C)..384
Hoing, Jessica, Kenneth Harris Recruiting
Group (C)...400
Hung, Elson, Rusher, Loscavio &
LoPresto (R) 181
Martin, Hayley, Descheneaux Insurance
Recruiters Ltd (C).....................................332
Orlando, Joseph, Socius Search LLC (R) 196
Plappert, James, Newtown Consulting
Group Inc (C) 505
Ramos, Kimberly, The Regent Group (C) 589
Smith, Mary, The Regent Group (C)..................589
St. James, Susan, Staff, Inc. (C)......................635
Vigeveno, Mitch, Turning Point Inc (C) 658
Welch, Angela, The Regent Group (C) 589
Yee, Jim, MR/SC of Milwaukee-North
(C) 515

Property

Anderson, Barbara, The Regent Group (C) 589
Balber, Sam, The Kent Group Inc (C)...............502
Biagini, Ron, FSA Inc (C) 381
Brooks, Jim, Executive Solutions
International (R) 71
Dexter, Rita, Platinum Search Group Inc
(C) 516
Frawley, Sharon, Lear & Associates Inc
(C) 448
Garrison, Jeff, The Garrison Organization
(C)..384
Jacobs, James, MR/SC of Nassau (R) 136
Lear, Roger, Lear & Associates Inc (C) 448
Lockwood, Margaret, Lear & Associates
Inc (C)...448
Methvin, Doug, Premier Careers Inc (C)...........570
Nichipor, Michael, Sanford Rose
Associates - Carmel (C).............................608
Ramos, Kimberly, The Regent Group (C) 589
Rivard, Cheryl, The Rivard Group (C)...............594
Rivard, Richard, The Rivard Group (C) 594
Rowlinson, Kevin, Lear & Associates Inc
(C) 448
Smith, Mary, The Regent Group (C)..................589
Swoboda, Jennifer, Platinum Search
Group Inc (C) 516
VanMaanen, Mandy, The Garrison
Organization (C)..384

Reinsurance

Anderson, Barbara, The Regent Group (C) 589
Brooks, Jim, Executive Solutions
International (R) 71
Chiu, Tiffany, Descheneaux Insurance
Recruiters Ltd (C).....................................332
Descheneaux, Pat, Descheneaux Insurance
Recruiters Ltd (C).....................................332
Dexter, Rita, Platinum Search Group Inc
(C) 516
Evdemon, II, Michael, E Insurance Group
(C) 343
Fernandez, Bruce, IR Search (R).....................109
Jacobs, James, MR/SC of Nassau (R) 136
Martin, Hayley, Descheneaux Insurance
Recruiters Ltd (C).....................................332
Nixon, Jeffrey, J L Nixon Consulting Inc
(C) 547
Ramos, Kimberly, The Regent Group (C) 589
Roderique, Cindy, Select Medical
Solutions (C) 619
St. James, Susan, Staff, Inc. (C) 635
Swoboda, Jennifer, Platinum Search
Group Inc (C) 516

Workers Compensation

Anderson, Barbara, The Regent Group (C) 589
Boyd, Jenny, Lear & Associates Inc (C) 448
Brooks, Jim, Executive Solutions
International (R) 71

Dexter, Rita, Platinum Search Group Inc
(C) 516
Evdemon, II, Michael, E Insurance Group
(C) 343
Frawley, Sharon, Lear & Associates Inc
(C) 448
Garrison, Jeff, The Garrison Organization
(C)..384
Lear, Roger, Lear & Associates Inc (C)............448
Lockwood, Margaret, Lear & Associates
Inc (C)...448
Ramos, Kimberly, The Regent Group (C).........589
Rivard, Richard, The Rivard Group (C) 594
Roderique, Cindy, Select Medical
Solutions (C) 619
Rowlinson, Kevin, Lear & Associates Inc
(C) 448
St. James, Susan, Staff, Inc. (C) 635
Swoboda, Jennifer, Platinum Search
Group Inc (C)...516
VanMaanen, Mandy, The Garrison
Organization (C) 384
Welch, Angela, The Regent Group (C) 589

Intellectual Property

Britt, Peggy, MR of Chapel Hill (C) 498
Caldwell, Kate, Caldwell Legal Recruiting
Consultants (C) 290
Carter, Gay, Interactive Legal Search (C).........424
Cayne, Brian, Marvel Consultant (C)...............522
Consbruck, Esq., Paul, Merit Consulting
Inc (C) 530
Farmaian, Mandy, ABA Search &
Staffing (C) 234
Fossett, Gary, John Michael Associates
(R)..145
Narsh, Daniel, Windsor Consultants Inc
(C)..671
Oliveras, Wendy, Oliveras & Company
Inc (C)...551
Rhynerson, John, Unisearch Search &
Recruiting Inc (C) 659
Stevens, Rick, TopGrading Solutions (C) 478
Toynbee, Brad, John Michael Associates
(R) 145
Vaccarino, Jim, Marvel Consultant (C)..............522
Williams, Tim, Howard, Williams &
Rahaim Inc (C)...415

Interactive

Anthony, Robin, MLB Associates (C) 535
Baker, Heather, Bennett Wheeless Group
Ltd (R) 19
Bennett, Neysa, Bennett Wheeless Group
Ltd (R) 19
Brown, MaryLou, MLB Associates (C)............535
Fippinger, Steve, Fipp Associates Inc (C).........375
Fixler, Eugene, Ariel Associates (R)................ 11
Scott, E. Ann, Scott Executive Search Inc
(R)..187
Smolen, Dan, Dan Smolen Direct Search
LLC (C) 626
Wexler, Rona, Ariel Associates (R) 11

Interim

Hannock, Pamela, Flynn, Hannock Inc (R).........75
Henry, Susan, The Jacobson Group (C) 428
Johnsey, Jack, The Jacobson Group (C)............428
Morgan, David, The Harris Consulting
Corp (R) 90
Schmidt, Ryan, The Jacobson Group (C)..........428
Sinclair, Keith, The Harris Consulting
Corp (R) 90
Wein, Michael, Media Management
Resources Inc (C)......................................527

Interior Design

Billy, Betty, Cameron Craig Group (R) 32
Cameron, Trey, Cameron Craig Group (R).........32
Craig, Karen, Cameron Craig Group (R) 32
Fitzpatrick, John, Newport Strategic
Search Inc (C) 546

SPECIALTIES

SPECIALTIES

Liquor

Loans

Logistics

Loss Control

Loss Prevention

Lumber

Machining

SPECIALTIES

Management Consulting

Hartung, Chris, Waters Consulting Group Inc (R) 218
Hayes, William, The Ransford Group (R) 171
Hechkoff, Robert, Hechkoff Executive Search Inc (R) 92
Hernandez, Dolores, Sanford Rose Associates - Spain (R) 185
Hildt, J. Bradley, Essex Consulting Group (R) 68
Hitchcock, Nancy, Hitchcock & Associates (R) 98
Kettinger, James, The Cooke Group Inc (R) 47
Kozik, Jerry, The Cooke Group Inc (R) 47
Liota, C., Murphy Partners International (R) 150
Lloyd, Gwyneth, The Lloyd Group (R) 129
Long, Janet, Integrity Search Inc (R).................108
MacLean, Jr., B.A. (Mackie), Diversified Search Ray & Berndtson (R) 60
Markworth, Jennifer, Markt & Markworth Ltd (R) 138
Meyer, Rick, Meyer Associates Inc (R) 145
Mills-Smith, Nancy, HealthCare Resources & Technologies (C) 405
Mossman, Ken, Woodlyn Partners Inc (C)......673
O'Neill, Jim, McSherry & Associates 2 Inc (R) 143
Parmar, Jay, Opensoft Inc (C) 552
Paul, Allan, Paul-Tittle Search Group (R) 160
Pejril, Ronald, Williger & Associates (R) 223
Pettingill, Christine, Columbia Consulting Group (R) 44
Picard, Daniel, Picard International Ltd (R) 164
Pittleman, Esq., Steven, Pittleman & Associates (C)........................566
Pittman, Douglas, Employment Professionals LLC (C)......................349
Preng, David, Preng & Associates (R) 166
Pugh, Robert, Chicago Consulting Partners Ltd (R) 39
Rhoten, Michele, Building Resources (C) 288
Ricker, Arlene, MC2 Executive Search (R) 141
Robertson, Gary, Executive Search Partners (C) 361
Ruschak, Randy, MR of Bordentown (C).........494
Rusher, Jr., William, Rusher, Loscavio & LoPresto (R) 181
Sartori, Paul, CHM Partners International LLC (R) 40
Schneider, George, The Cooke Group Inc (R) 47
Schumer, Rochelle, R & L Associates Ltd (R) 170
Schwam, Carol, A E Feldman Associates Inc (C) 372
Semyan, John, TNS Partners Inc (R).................211
Shearer, Gary, MR of Bonita Springs (C).........476
Shor, Mort, FPC of Savannah (C).................366
Smith, Gary, Smith, Scott & Associates (R) 195
Smith, Thomas, The Ransford Group (R).........171
Stevens, Ralph, Preng & Associates (R)............166
Stokes, Louis, Boyden (R) 25
Sucgang, Dante, Aegis Consulting (R) 5
Tittle, David, Paul-Tittle Search Group (R) 160
Travis, Victoria, Travis & Associates (C) 655
Ulrich, Mary Ann, D S Allen Associates (C) 250
VanZanten, William, Quantico Consulting LLC (C) 581
Waters, Rollie, Waters Consulting Group Inc (R) 218
Welch, James, CHM Partners International LLC (R) 40
Whittier, Richard, The Ransford Group (R) 171
Williams, Jeff, Fathom Human Capital Solutions (R) 72
Williger, David, Williger & Associates (R) 223

Wilson, John, Wilson-Douglas-Jordan (C).........671
Wolff, Richard, Willow, Wolff & Grace Co (C)...............................670
Yuen, Jason, Alan Miles & Associates Inc (C) 533

Manufacturing

Abrams, Burton, B J Abrams & Associates Inc (C)....................235
Acton, Lisa, PeopleSource Solutions (C) 560
Adam, Brandi, RSM McGladrey Inc (R)...........180
Adler, Louis, CJA Executive Search (R)............41
Adzima, Allan, MARBL Consultants Inc (C) 519
Agnello, Frank, Systems Research Inc (SRI) (C) 644
Alawan, Haider, Combined Resources Inc (R) 44
Allen, James, Continental Search Associates (C) 314
Allen, Joe, MR of Fargo (C) 466
Allen, William, Techaid Inc (C).................648
Almond, Susan, Unisearch Search & Recruiting Inc (C)......................659
Ambruster, David, Renaissance Resources LLC (R) 175
Anderson, Wayne, Anderson Network Group (C) 255
Antonio, Marshall, FPC of Arlington Heights (C) 366
Aquino, Mike, MPA Associates (C).................538
Askew, Thomas, Renaissance Resources LLC (R) 175
Austin, Brad, ATS Reliance Technical Group (C) 263
Baert, Yvonne, Personnel Management Group (C) 562
Baird, William, W G Baird & Associates (C) 266
Baker, Gary, Cochran, Cochran & Yale LLC (R) 43
Ballach, Allen, Allen Ballach Associates Inc (R) 14
Baltimore, Richard, Recruiting Resources Inc (C) 587
Balzer, Aniko, CAI Personnel Search Group (C) 290
Barbachano, Berenice, Barbachano International Inc (BIP) (C)...........268
Barnes, Richard, Barnes Development Group LLC (R).........................15
Bassford, Daniel, Sanford Rose Associates - Greensboro (C) 610
Bates, Debbie, The Harlan Group Inc (C) 399
Batista, Ana, Allen Personnel (C) 250
Bauman, Bobbi, BJB Associates (C).................277
Beaudin, Elizabeth, Callan Associates Ltd (R) 31
Becker, B. Hans, Hans Becker Associates LLC (C) 271
Becker, Ralph, Automation Technology Search (C) 264
Bedingfield, Ray, Woodmoor Group Inc (C) 673
Behm, Jamie, FPC of Cincinnati (C).................369
Behmer, Chris, Variant Partners (C) 488
Belle Isle, Bill, FPC of SW Missouri (C) 368
Belle Isle, Patrice, FPC of SW Missouri (C) 368
Berg, Eric, J N Adams & Associates Inc (C) 239
Bernat, Nicole, MR of Dallas-Southlake (C) 512
Bernstein, William, Concorde Search Associates (C) 312
Berol, Alec, Renaissance Resources LLC (R) 175
Beyer, Dan, Paradigm Technologies Inc (R) 158
Blatchford, Richard, Millstream Associates (C) 534
Blower, Aaron, Consumer Connection Inc (C) 313

Blythe, Ann, Spherion Professional Recruiting Group (C) 634
Boado, Manuel, SPANUSA (R) 197
Boeger, William, Sanford Rose Associates - Madison (C).....................611
Bolen, Dan, Dan Bolen & Associates LLC (C) 279
Bond, Paul, SeBA International LLC (R) 189
Bondi, Nikki, Advantage Partners Inc (R) 5
Bonner, Rodney, MR of Denver-Golden Hill (C) 475
Boruff, Fran, BranCo Search Inc (C) 282
Bos, John, Bos Business Consultants (C).........281
Boswell, Doug, Corporate Growth Specialists (C) 316
Brakel, Bob, PROTECH Corporate Enterprises Inc. (C) 579
Brauninger, John, AmeriPro Search Inc (C) 254
Bregman, Mark, Boyle Ogata Bregman (R) 25
Bringman, John, Waterbury Group Inc (C)......665
Briones, Christina, R A Briones & Company (C) 284
Burch, Caroline, MR of Santa Ana (C) 473
Burch, Ray, MR of Santa Ana (C) 473
Burnett, Dawna, MR of Fairfield (C) 485
Buschmann, Greg, FPC/Fortune of San Antonio (C) 380
Cagan, Randy, FPC of Raleigh (C) 369
Campbell, Dan, Campbell/Carlson LLC (R) 32
Capanna, Patricia, MR of Madison (C)............515
Caravello, Cindy, Capri Resource Group Inc (C) 293
Carey, Harvey, Carion Resource Group Inc (C) 297
Carpenter, Charles, Preng & Associates (R) 166
Carpenter, Lisa, Discovery Personnel Inc (C) 334
Carroll, Rebecca, CAI Personnel Search Group (C) 290
Carter, Van, Hudson Consulting Group (R) 102
Carter, Warren, Qualifind Inc (C) 581
Cary, Con, Cary & Associates (R) 36
Chalmers, Russell, FPC of Troy (C) 367
Chandler, Cynthia, Chandler Group (R) 38
Check, Andrew, AD Check Associates Inc (R) 39
Cherney, Mark, Resource Perspectives Inc (R) 176
Cherney, Steven, Resource Perspectives Inc (R) 176
Christine, Rich, R Christine Associates (C) 304
Christoffel, John, Stearns Group (R) 202
Cizek, John, Cizek Associates Inc (R) 41
Clark, Blair, Grasslands Group (C) 85
Clark, David, Sprout/Standish Inc (C) 634
Cleveland, Guy, MR of Cheyenne (C)............516
Close, Jr., E. Wade, Boyden (R) 25
Clothier, I.H. (Chip), Howe and Associates (R) 101
Colbert, Brad, The Executive Network Inc (R) 69
Cole, Dick, Auster Associates (R) 12
Collins, Peter, Collins & Associates (C) 309
Collins, Philip, Collins & Associates (C)............309
Conlan, Chris, Carlyle & Conlan Inc (R) 136
Conrad, John, Search Associates (C) 614
Cook, Dennis, Management Executive Services Associates Inc (MESA) (R)............134
Corcoran, Gary, GCI & Associates (R)............80
Correa, Ayodele, Snelling Personnel Services (C)..........................628
Correll, Jr., Paul, Wilson, Correll, Friedlander & Associates Inc (C) 670
Cox, Karen, The Westminster Group Inc (R) 221
Crane, Don, California Search Agency Inc (C) 290

SPECIALTIES

SPECIALTIES

Market Research

Marketing

SPECIALTIES

SPECIALTIES

Materials

Mathematics

MBAs

Mechanical

SPECIALTIES

1052 / THE DIRECTORY OF EXECUTIVE RECRUITERS

Vice, Michael, Denell-Archer International Executive Search (R) ... 56
Walkup, Jim, S P Associates Inc (C) ... 603
White, Laura, Affinity Options (C) ... 242
Williams, Jeff, Fathom Human Capital Solutions (R) ... 72
Xiong, Moua, Wilson Consulting Group (C) ... 461
Yelvington, Lisa, The Lakewood Group (C) ... 514

Devices

Ackerman, Esq., Corey, Cornerstone Search Group LLC (C) ... 315
Allen, James, Continental Search Associates (C) ... 314
Almond, Susan, Unisearch Search & Recruiting Inc (C) ... 659
Arbour, Lisa, Badon's Employment Inc (C) ... 266
Bailey, Jeff, Parkwood International (C) ... 510
Barrett, Bill, Barrett & Company Inc (C) ... 268
Basta, Erica, Thomas Ruff Company (C) ... 602
Beck, Steven, Beck/Eastwood Recruitment Solutions (C) ... 271
Bishop, Jim, Bishop Executive Services LLC (C) ... 276
Blumsack, Larry, Executive Resources International LLC (R) ... 70
Boccuzi, Joseph, Spencer Stuart (R) ... 198
Bonner, Rodney, MR of Denver-Golden Hill (C) ... 475
Bouma, Carollynn, William Halderson Associates Inc (C) ... 396
Brethet, Anne, Brethet, Barnum & Associates Inc (C) ... 283
Briand, Paul, Briand Fiorella Search Inc (C) ... 284
Brown, Jim, Galileo Search LLC (C) ... 383
Burby, Susan, Sanford Rose Associates - Lake Ann (C) ... 609
Burridge, Jeffrey, StoneBridge Management Inc (C) ... 639
Cebula, Laurie, The Lakewood Group (C) ... 514
Chandler, Brad, Chandler Group (R) ... 38
Chanski, Vern, Hobson Associates (C) ... 411
Chrzan, Phyllis, Brethet, Barnum & Associates Inc (C) ... 283
Cofield, Rose, FPC of Hilton Head (C) ... 370
Cole, Lydia, NCC Executive Search Consultants (C) ... 544
Coleman, Patricia, Spencer Stuart (R) ... 197
Conlan, Chris, Carlyle & Conlan Inc (R) ... 136
Crawford, Luke, Advanced Recruiters Inc (C) ... 241
Cross, Karen, Spherion Professional Recruiting Group (C) ... 633
Curnow, Erich, MR of Pittsburgh North (C) ... 505
David, Violy Aludo, Wilson Consulting Group (C) ... 461
Davis, Tamara, Levin & Company Inc (R) ... 127
Deendyal, Navin, Medical Device Recruiters Inc (R) ... 134
Deibel, Lori, Michael Dunford Associates LLC (R) ... 62
DeLacy, Bruna, DeLacy & Associates (C) ... 331
DiBari, Francis, DiBari & Associates (C) ... 333
Dreher, Beth Anne, Michael Dunford Associates LLC (R) ... 62
Ducharme, David, FPC of Hilton Head (C) ... 370
Dunford, Michael, Michael Dunford Associates LLC (R) ... 62
Earle, Paul, Spencer Stuart (R) ... 197
Ewald, Tamara, Sanford Rose Associates - Annapolis (C) ... 609
Falcone, Charles, Spencer Stuart (R) ... 197
Fine, Alan, Parkwood International (C) ... 510
Finn, James, The Garret Group (R) ... 80
Fiorella, Nicole, Briand Fiorella Search Inc (C) ... 284
Fox, Cheryl, Fox Interlink Partners (C) ... 379
Frankel, Brigitte, Spencer Stuart (R) ... 197
Gaspard, Keith, Diversified Search Ray & Berndtson (R) ... 60
Ghaphery, Keith, Impact Resource Group, Inc (C) ... 420
Ghaphery, Melissa, Impact Resource Group, Inc (C) ... 420
GIlbert, John, Epsen Fuller IMD Ineternational Search Group (R) ... 67
Gordon, Gregory, Wallace Associates (C) ... 663
Gray, Kelley, Normyle/Erstling Health Search Group (C) ... 547
Grubb, Evan, Influence Networks (C) ... 421
Halderson, William, William Halderson Associates Inc (C) ... 396
Hall, Laura, SC of Loudoun County (C) ... 513
Hancock, Mimi, Spencer Stuart (R) ... 198
Handley, Bill, The Apollo Group (C) ... 257
Harvey, Robert, Hudson Consulting Group (R) ... 102
Hatfield, Glenn, Park Avenue Group Inc (C) ... 480
Heine, Karl, The Creative Placement Agency LLC (C) ... 322
Heiser, Chuck, The Cassie-Shipherd Group (R) ... 36
Helsel, Neal, Neal Helsel & Associates Inc (C) ... 406
Holt, Carol, Bartholdi Partners (R) ... 16
Isaacson, Ira, Spencer Stuart (R) ... 198
Jarrett, Tom, Century Associates Inc (C) ... 301
Johasky, Eric, Medical Device Recruiters Inc (R) ... 134
Johnson, Janet, Normyle/Erstling Health Search Group (C) ... 547
Joseph, III, Etienne, Parkwood International (C) ... 510
Kelada, Mina, Hreshko Consulting Group (C) ... 415
Kenner, Susan, Thomas Ruff Company (C) ... 602
Klingsheim, Mark, Chandler Group (R) ... 38
Korban, Richard, Korban Associates (R) ... 120
Kovach, Nancy, Korban Associates (R) ... 120
Kreps, Charles, Normyle/Erstling Health Search Group (C) ... 547
Kuhn, Larry, Kuhn Med-Tech Inc (C) ... 443
Laird, Jim, Ashton Tweed (R) ... 11
Larson, Warren, FPC/Fortune of San Antonio (C) ... 380
Logue, Sara, Advanced Recruiters Inc (C) ... 241
Manatine, Tony, Neal Helsel & Associates Inc (C) ... 406
Mann, Ira, FPC of Atlanta (C) ... 366
Marlow, William, Straube Associates (R) ... 205
Matteson, Jon, The Apollo Group (C) ... 257
Mattocks, Paul, G P Mattocks & Associates Inc (C) ... 523
Mayes, Stacey, Executive Sales Search Inc (C) ... 360
Meek, Andy, Southern Recruiters & Consultants Inc (C) ... 630
Mende, Linda, Executive Sales Search Inc (C) ... 360
Metz, Melissa, Sanford Rose Associates - Rancho Bernardo (C) ... 607
Miras, Cliff, Cornerstone Search Group LLC (C) ... 315
Morrisey, Jim, FPC/Fortune of San Antonio (C) ... 380
Myhre, Jim, The Cassie-Shipherd Group (R) ... 36
Nadeau, Liz, Bishop Executive Services LLC (C) ... 276
Nickerson, Jill, Project Search Inc (R) ... 168
Norton, Chloe, Sanford Rose Associates - Annapolis (C) ... 609
O'Brien-Kletti, Elke, Bishop Executive Services LLC (C) ... 276
Ober, Shari, Banister International (R) ... 136
Oppenheim, Norman, FPC of Nashua (C) ... 368
Pahl, Brian, Jim Kay & Associates Inc (C) ... 436
Paine, Donne, FPC of Hilton Head (C) ... 370
Patrick, Sharon, Thomas Ruff Company (C) ... 602
Peck, Helene, Normyle/Erstling Health Search Group (C) ... 547
Phillips, Norm, APP Consulting (C) ... 257
Pieper, Lisa, Spencer Stuart (R) ... 198
Portillo, Rose, Corporate Search Associates (C) ... 318
Post, Jan, Normyle/Erstling Health Search Group (C) ... 547
Rademaker, Jackie, MR/SC of Tampa North (C) ... 478
Rimele, J.R., Sales Recruiters of Oklahoma City (C) ... 605
Rizza, Anthony, FPC of Hilton Head (C) ... 370
Robb, Molly, Horton International LLC (R) ... 101
Robinson, Tom, Spencer Stuart (R) ... 198
Rosenthal, Susan, S H Jacobs & Associates Inc (R) ... 110
Ross, Ruthie, Recruitment Resources Inc (C) ... 588
Rothschild, Tammy, Thomas Ruff Company (C) ... 602
Rudell, Edmund, Galileo Search LLC (C) ... 383
Ruff, Tom, Thomas Ruff & Associates, Inc. (C) ... 602
Ryan, Joseph, Epsen Fuller IMD Ineternational Search Group (R) ... 67
Rydzak, Jayne, Impact Resource Group, Inc (C) ... 420
Salkin, Maureen, Levin & Company Inc (R) ... 127
Scala, Joan, MC2 Executive Search (R) ... 141
Schantz, Shawn, The Apollo Group (C) ... 257
Searles, Brett, Neal Helsel & Associates Inc (C) ... 406
Sherman, Ted, Sanford Rose Associates - Cincinnati East (C) ... 610
Stapleton, Tim, SC of The Emerald Coast (C) ... 478
Supple, Ann, HealthCare Recruiters International • Mid America (C) ... 404
Szmidt, Les, MR of Napa (C) ... 459
t'Sas, Jill, NCC Executive Search Consultants (C) ... 544
Thiers, Harold, The Hampton Group (C) ... 497
Tondorf, Jr., Paul, Tondorf & Associates Inc (C) ... 654
Valle, Javier, Spencer Stuart (R) ... 199
Vinyard, Kiley, Advanced Recruiters Inc (C) ... 241
Walkup, Jim, S P Associates Inc (C) ... 603
Warshafsky, Jordan, Ashton Tweed (R) ... 11
Watkins, Robert, R J Watkins & Company Ltd (R) ... 218
Wheeler, Andrew, Diversified Search Ray & Berndtson (R) ... 60
Wiener, John, Fairway Consulting Group (C) ... 496
Williams, Lori, MR of Denver-Golden Hill (C) ... 475
Wright, Christie, Parkwood International (C) ... 510
Yaiser, Richard, The Yaiser Group (C) ... 676
Yelvington, Lisa, The Lakewood Group (C) ... 514
Yowe, Mark, Spencer Stuart (R) ... 198
Zinn, Michael, Michael D Zinn & Associates Inc (R) ... 230

Sales

Arbour, Lisa, Badon's Employment Inc (C) ... 266
Archibald, David Eldridge, The Eldridge Group Ltd (C) ... 347
Bailey, Jeff, Parkwood International (C) ... 510
Barrett, Bill, Barrett & Company Inc (C) ... 268
Basta, Erica, Thomas Ruff Company (C) ... 602
Beck, Steven, Beck/Eastwood Recruitment Solutions (C) ... 271
Becker, Aaron, Edge Recruiting Solutions Inc (C) ... 345
Bishop, Jim, Bishop Executive Services LLC (C) ... 276

The Directory of Executive Recruiters

Mergers & Acquisitions

Metals

Middle Management

Military

SPECIALTIES

Non-Profit

Nutraceuticals

OB/GYN

Occupational Therapy

SPECIALTIES

Opthalmics

Optics

Oracle

Organizational Development

Orthopedics

Outsourcing

SPECIALTIES

1058 / THE DIRECTORY OF EXECUTIVE RECRUITERS

Fiddle, Joan, The Maslow Media Group Inc (C) ... 522
Garner, Ginni, Sanford Rose Associates - Orange (C) ... 610
Hall, Lori, The Odella Group Inc (C) ... 550
Hay, Elaine, Campbell, Edgar Inc (C) ... 292
Kinney, Cynthia, Boyden (R) ... 25
Lane, David, Lane Partners, Inc. (R) ... 123
Murphy, Melissa, CMC Consultants Inc (C) ... 307
Nash, Robert, Strategic Partners LLC (C) ... 640
Oxemberg, John, Sanford Rose Associates - Spain (R) ... 185
Perrett, Lee, Talent Connections LLC (R) ... 207
Trager, Joelle, The Odella Group Inc (C) ... 550

Owner Reps

Sloane, Ronald, Sloane & Associates Inc (R) ... 137

Packaging

Adams, Jeffrey, Beneva Group (C) ... 479
Archer, Hank, MR of Hudson (C) ... 502
Arnette, Tom, Windward Executive Search (C) ... 671
Askew, Thomas, Renaissance Resources LLC (R) ... 175
Baker, Craig, JM & Company (R) ... 112
Boeger, William, Sanford Rose Associates - Madison (C) ... 611
Burby, Thomas, Sanford Rose Associates - Lake Ann (C) ... 609
Caprio, Jerry, Caprio & Associates Inc (R) ... 33
Caravello, Cindy, Capri Resource Group Inc (C) ... 293
Charles, Glenn, Rannou & Associates Inc (C) ... 584
Freeman, Julie, Recruiter Solutions International (C) ... 586
Fridley, Charles, Beneva Group (C) ... 479
Gros, Dennis, Gros Executive Recruiters (C) ... 394
Harants, George, MR of Bartlett (C) ... 509
Herro, Kerry, Global Recruiters of Milwaukee (C) ... 389
Higgins, Judith, MR of Pittsburgh North (C) ... 505
Johnson, Verne, Verne Johnson & Associates Inc (C) ... 431
Jones, C. Griffin, The Griffin Group Inc (C) ... 393
Kapela, Steven, BGR Technologies Inc (C) ... 275
Klee, Michael, Global Recruiters of Milwaukee (C) ... 389
Kniager, Denise, FPC of Providence (C) ... 369
Koob, Dick, SC of Houston (C) ... 511
Lane, David, Lane Partners, Inc. (R) ... 123
Lewis, Morris, BGR Technologies Inc (C) ... 275
Marshall, John, JM & Company (R) ... 112
Mathey, Joyce, Mathey Services (C) ... 522
McGeehan, Gayle, MR of Bethlehem (C) ... 504
McGinley, Jim, JM & Company (R) ... 112
Moran, Kevin, Global Recruiters of Milwaukee (C) ... 389
Neale, Peter, Trinity Group (C) ... 657
Novinska, Tony, Global Recruiters of Milwaukee (C) ... 389
Pascal, Rick, Rick Pascal & Associates Inc (C) ... 557
Rannou, III, Frank, Rannou & Associates Inc (C) ... 584
Riley, Kristen, Beneva Group (C) ... 479
Rogove, Arthur, Merit Consulting Inc (C) ... 530
Sanders, Robert, HR Remedies LLC (C) ... 415
Schwartz, Alan, Selective Management Services Inc (C) ... 620
Shayne, Loren, Rannou & Associates Inc (C) ... 584
Slifka, Rick, Exec-Links LLC (C) ... 353
Steel, Mark, Selective Management Services Inc (C) ... 620
Tewell, Hayden, JM & Company (R) ... 112
Valmore, Kim, Professions Inc International (C) ... 577
Vice, Michael, Denell-Archer International Executive Search (R) ... 56
Vowles, Dennis, BGR Technologies Inc (C) ... 275
Zetrenne, Sabina, SC of Ft Lauderdale (C) ... 476

Paint

Gres, Ed, Pioneer Executive Consultants (C) ... 565
Jentlie, Paul, Career Search Consultants LLC (C) ... 296
Mullen, James, Mullen Associates Inc (R) ... 149
Sinclair, Paul, Pioneer Executive Consultants (C) ... 565
Singleton, Brittany, Southern Recruiters & Consultants Inc (C) ... 630

Paper

Angell, Tryg, Tryg R Angell Ltd (C) ... 256
Argenio, Paul, Tierney Consulting Group LLC (R) ... 211
Arnette, Tom, Windward Executive Search (C) ... 671
Baker, Craig, JM & Company (R) ... 112
Charles, Glenn, Rannou & Associates Inc (C) ... 584
Charron, Maynard, Paper Industry Recruitment (PIR) (C) ... 556
Coffin, Susan, Spencer Stuart (R) ... 197
Froelich, K., Murphy Partners International (R) ... 150
Hayes, Don, MR of Sugar Land (C) ... 512
Hochwalt, Mike, MH Executive Search Group (C) ... 531
Kokyun, Lim, Searchco (C) ... 617
Littley, Janet, FPC of Boise (C) ... 366
Luciano, Mike, FPC of Bangor (C) ... 367
May, William, SC of Huntsville (C) ... 470
McCracken, Terri, T E M Associates (C) ... 645
Natowitz, Robert, DeMatteo Associates (C) ... 331
O'Reilly, William, MR/SC of Cincinnati-Sharonville (C) ... 501
Oster, R. Rush, MR of Anna Maria Island (C) ... 476
Petrello-Pray, Gina, Direct Recruiters Inc (C) ... 334
Rannou, III, Frank, Rannou & Associates Inc (C) ... 584
Shayne, Loren, Rannou & Associates Inc (C) ... 584
Tewell, Hayden, JM & Company (R) ... 112
Walt, Lee, MH Executive Search Group (C) ... 531

PeopleSoft

Brennan, Steven, Pinnacle Executive Search (C) ... 565
Byrne, Tom, Rita Technology Services (C) ... 594
Chapman, Mike, Connexion Systems & Engineering (C) ... 312
Cleary, Diane, Oracle Recruiters (C) ... 553
Daniele, Jerry, iHeadHunt (C) ... 420
De Carolis, Mario, MR of Traverse City (C) ... 490
Hildebrand, Steve, Pinnacle Executive Search (C) ... 565
Marks, Robert, Pinnacle Executive Search (C) ... 565
Schneck, Bob, Pinnacle Executive Search (C) ... 565
Zabor, Richard, Leader Institute Inc (C) ... 447

Peripherals

Crosthwait, Bruce, MR of Bellaire (C) ... 509
Hall, Dwight, The Landstone Group (R) ... 136

Pesticides

Allen, Jim, Southern Chemical & Plastics Search (C) ... 630

Petrochemical

Ayling, Michael, MLA Resources Inc (C) ... 534
Bachman, Robert, K Jaeger & Associates (C) ... 428
Carpenter, Charles, Preng & Associates (R) ... 166
DeMiranda, Ralph, Dunhill Professional Search of Stuart (C) ... 340
Dolynny, Janice, Dunhill Professional Search of Stuart (C) ... 340
Gunnin, Jim, Rockport Professional Search (C) ... 596
Hughes, Tim, Hughes & Associates International Inc (C) ... 416
Jansen, John, Delta Services (R) ... 55
Mioduszewski, Eleni, Sanford Rose Associates - Annapolis (C) ... 609
Peterson, Joan, A H Justice Search Consultants (C) ... 433
Ritchings, David, David Allen Associates (R) ... 7
Stover, Carl, Brownson & Associates LP (R) ... 29
Walker, David, Trinity Group (C) ... 657

Pharmaceutical

Ackerman, Esq., Corey, Cornerstone Search Group LLC (C) ... 315
Adams, Lauren, FPC of Abington (C) ... 369
Agriesti, Kay, Agriesti & Associates (C) ... 244
Ahrensdorf, Lee, Ahrensdorf & Associates (R) ... 6
Albrecht, Franke, MR of Houston West (C) ... 510
Allison, Ken, The Chase Group Inc (R) ... 39
Ambos, Merry, Molecular Solutions Inc (C) ... 535
Apfel, Ronnie, The Hampton Group (C) ... 497
Arnold, Jerome, Strawn Arnold Leech & Ashpitz Inc (R) ... 205
Ashpitz, Jeff, Strawn Arnold Leech & Ashpitz Inc (R) ... 205
Azzara, Robert, BioTech Solutions (C) ... 276
Babb, Richard, The Wilmington Group (R) ... 223
Bachmann, Anne Marie, Strategic Resources (C) ... 641
Baker, Chuck, Corporate Staffing Group Inc (R) ... 49
Baracani, Bill, Harbeck Associates Inc (C) ... 398
Barbeau, Brian, HealthCare Recruiters International • Mid America (C) ... 404
Baron, Annette, Eagle Research Inc (C) ... 344
Barrett, Bill, Barrett & Company Inc (C) ... 268
Barrientos, Manny, Manny Barrientos (C) ... 269
Basta, Erica, Thomas Ruff Company (C) ... 602
Bauer, Robert, Sampson Medical Search (C) ... 606
Beatty, Bob, FPC of Mandeville (C) ... 364
Becker, Aaron, Edge Recruiting Solutions Inc (C) ... 345
Bell, Anthony, MR of Scottsdale (C) ... 458
Bernstein, William, Concorde Search Associates (C) ... 312
Bhatt, Seema, MR of Edison (C) ... 493
Bishop, Jim, Bishop Executive Services LLC (C) ... 276
Blakslee, Jan, J Blakslee International Ltd (R) ... 22
Blank, Paula, Paula Blank International (R) ... 22
Blue, Janet, Watring & Associates Inc (C) ... 665
Boccuzi, Joseph, Spencer Stuart (R) ... 198
Bonham, Rebecca, PontusOne LLC (C) ... 568
Boreham, Judy, Diversified Search Ray & Berndtson (R) ... 60
Bornholdt, Elizabeth, Bornholdt Shivas & Friends Executive Recruiters (C) ... 281

The Directory of Executive Recruiters

SPECIALTIES

Pharmacists

Philanthropy

Photonics

Physicians

Pipeline

Plastics

SPECIALTIES

Power

Presidents

Printing

Private Equity

Process Equipment

Procurement

Product Management/Development

Production

Professional Service

SPECIALTIES

Public Sector

Boulware, Christine, The Boulware Group Inc (R) ... 24
Brimeyer, James, The Brimeyer Group Inc (R) ... 28
Campbell, Margaret, Ray & Berndtson/Lovas Stanley (R) ... 172
Dalldorf, Charles, Wilcox, Miller & Nelson (R) ... 223
Gentry, Cynthia, BoardWalk Consulting LLC (R) ... 22
Hartung, Chris, Waters Consulting Group Inc (R) ... 218
Keister, John, John Keister & Associates (R) ... 116
Litchfield, Barbara, Litchfield & Willis Inc (R) ... 129
Marshall, Robert, The Cooke Group Inc (R) ... 47
Pettway, Sam, BoardWalk Consulting LLC (R) ... 22
Tittle, David, Paul-Tittle Search Group (R) ... 160
Waters, Rollie, Waters Consulting Group Inc (R) ... 218

Publishing

Baird, Suzanne, ProSearch Recruiting (C) ... 579
Banach-Osenni, Doris, The Brentwood Group Inc (R) ... 27
Barro, Arlene, Barro Global Search Inc (R) ... 15
Bishop, Susan, Bishop Partners (R) ... 21
Blahnik, Mark, Trimarc Resources LLC (R) ... 213
Brown, Jim, SC of Asheville (C) ... 497
Corwen, Leonard, Leonard Corwen Corporate Recruiting Services (C) ... 319
Crawford, Marjorie, Personnel Associates Inc (C) ... 561
Curtis, Susan, ProSearch Recruiting (C) ... 579
DeLuca, Matthew, Management Resource Group Inc (C) ... 517
Eldredge, Peter, Boardroom Consultants (R) ... 22
Fixler, Eugene, Ariel Associates (R) ... 11
Gaines, Elizabeth, The Cheyenne Group (R) ... 39
Ganz, Steve, Personnel Associates Inc (C) ... 561
Goldberg, Risa, Media Recruiting Group Inc (C) ... 527
Goldberg, Steve, Media Recruiting Group Inc (C) ... 527
Grant, Michael, Zwell International (R) ... 230
Haygood, Holly, Bishop Partners (R) ... 21
Hubbard, Ted, K S Frary & Associates Inc (R) ... 77
Hughes, Cathy, The Ogdon Partnership (R) ... 155
Kanuit, Cathie, Brown, Bernardy, Van Remmen Inc (C) ... 285
Keklak, Mai, Cornell Group International Consulting Inc (R) ... 48
Koller, Jr., Edward, The Howard-Sloan-Koller Group (R) ... 101
Krumholz, Jill, Charleston Partners (R) ... 39
Lynch, Patrick, P J Lynch Associates (R) ... 131
Mackie, Lisa, Virtual HR Associates (C) ... 662
Masquelier, Sibyl, Executive Resource Group Inc (R) ... 70
Masserman, Bruce, Masserman & Associates Inc (R) ... 139
Mattes, Jr., Edward, The Ogdon Partnership (R) ... 155
O'Reilly, William, MR/SC of Cincinnati-Sharonville (C) ... 501
Ogdon, Kristin, The Ogdon Partnership (R) ... 155
Ogdon, Thomas, The Ogdon Partnership (R) ... 155
Pagana, Pat, The Brentwood Group Inc (R) ... 27
Protsik, Ralph, Boston Search (R) ... 24
Ross, Elsa, Gardner-Ross Associates Inc (R) ... 79
Sachs, Susan, Cornell Group International Consulting Inc (R) ... 48
Schneider, Thomas, WTW Associates Inc (R) ... 227
Schon, Jeff, The Cheyenne Group (R) ... 39
Timoney, Laura, Bishop Partners (R) ... 21
West, Cliff, Trimarc Resources LLC (R) ... 213
Wexler, Rona, Ariel Associates (R) ... 11

Purchasing

Abbene, John, FPC of Fairfax (C) ... 371
Abramson, Cheryl, Miller, Abramson & Company Inc (R) ... 146
Adzima, Allan, MARBL Consultants Inc (C) ... 519
Allen, Greg, Tonia Deal Consultants Inc (C) ... 329
Antonio, Marshall, FPC of Arlington Heights (C) ... 366
Beaudin, Elizabeth, Callan Associates Ltd (R) ... 31
Carpenter, Lisa, MEI Search Consultants (C) ... 492
Case, David, PeopleSource Solutions (C) ... 560
Cisar, Carl, The Cisar Group Inc (C) ... 304
Cousins, John, Procurement Resources (C) ... 574
Curtis, Julie, Executive Resource Solutions, Inc (C) ... 359
Day, Pamela, FPC of Boise (C) ... 366
Dixon, Shane, FPC of Savannah (C) ... 366
Dodd, Carol, Staff Resources Inc (C) ... 635
Eastwood, Gary, Beck/Eastwood Recruitment Solutions (C) ... 271
Fogel, Sherry, Lou Michaels Associates Inc (C) ... 532
Gabor, Robert, The Gabor Group (C) ... 382
Griffiths, Bob, Griffiths & Associates (C) ... 394
Grindlinger, Arthur, FPC of Sarasota (C) ... 366
Harris, Wade, FPC of Decatur (C) ... 365
Harvill, Jon, Dunhill Professional Search of W Atlanta (C) ... 341
Hay, Elaine, Campbell, Edgar Inc (C) ... 292
Helnore, Kim, Partners in Recruiting (C) ... 557
Howell, Jean, FPC of Virginia Highlands (C) ... 370
Jones, Mike, MR of Winston-Salem (C) ... 500
Kern, Jerry, ADOW Professionals (C) ... 240
Kuehling, Mark, FPC of Cincinnati (C) ... 369
Lamb, Lynn, FPC of Huntsville (C) ... 365
Lee, Lanson, FPC of Troy (C) ... 367
Lipe, Jerold, Compass Group Ltd (R) ... 45
Malatesta, Roger, Professional Recruiting Consultants Inc (C) ... 575
McBride, Sean, Quintal & Associates Human Resources Consultants Inc (C) ... 583
McNeil, Gavin, MR/SC of Milwaukee-North (C) ... 515
Morris, Lana, The Harlan Group Inc (C) ... 399
Nichols, Debbie, FPC of Boise (C) ... 366
Oback, Scott, MR of Chapel Hill (C) ... 498
Osl, Chris, FPC of Greensboro (C) ... 368
Petras, Mark, FPC of South Bend (C) ... 367
Quick, Kristine, Tyler Search Consultants (C) ... 659
Riley, Christina, MR of Kinston (C) ... 499
Rizza, Anthony, FPC of Hilton Head (C) ... 370
Rohan, Kevin, Cannon And Associates (C) ... 292
Roldan, Jorge, Barbachano International Inc (BIP) (C) ... 268
Rybowiak, James, FPC of Hinsdale (C) ... 366
Schuetz, Jim, MR of Reading (C) ... 505
Singer, David, FPC of Raleigh (C) ... 369
Slater, Marjorie, Logistics Management Resources Inc (R) ... 130
Staggs, Kristy, Byrnes & Rupkey Inc (C) ... 289
Tovar, Martha, Qualifind Inc (C) ... 581
Walker, Brett, Human Resources Personnel Agency (R) ... 103
Webb, James, CAI Personnel Search Group (C) ... 290
Whicker, Catherine, FPC of Troy (C) ... 367
Zimmermann, Karl, FPC of Bloomfield (C) ... 367

Quality

Al'Basit, Basirah, RS&A (C) ... 601
Antonio, Marshall, FPC of Arlington Heights (C) ... 366
Askew, Thomas, Renaissance Resources LLC (R) ... 175
Axelrod, Mark, FPC of Rockland County Inc (C) ... 368
Balzer, Aniko, CAI Personnel Search Group (C) ... 290
Beatty, Bob, FPC of Mandeville (C) ... 364
Behmer, Chris, Variant Partners (C) ... 488
Belle Isle, Patrice, FPC of SW Missouri (C) ... 368
Berg, Eric, J N Adams & Associates Inc (C) ... 239
Berry, Paul, The Jonathan Group (C) ... 431
Bhatt, Seema, MR of Edison (C) ... 493
Booton, Richard, TowerHunter (R) ... 212
Brandvold, Steven, Executive Connection (C) ... 355
Burch, Caroline, MR of Santa Ana (C) ... 473
Burch, Ray, MR of Santa Ana (C) ... 473
Cofield, Rose, FPC of Hilton Head (C) ... 370
Cook Sturm, Rosann, OPUS International Inc (C) ... 553
Cunneff, Harry, MR of Lake Forest (C) ... 483
Dorfman, Jan, FPC of Denver Inc (C) ... 365
Flynn, Christina, Empire International (R) ... 66
Fogel, Sherry, Lou Michaels Associates Inc (C) ... 532
Gabor, Robert, The Gabor Group (C) ... 382
Hahn, Jeff, Smith, Brown & Jones (C) ... 626
Hall, Chip, Professional Search (C) ... 576
Hanson, Hugh, FPC of Huntsville (C) ... 365
Hartwig, Mark, Search Masters International (R) ... 188
Helnore, Kim, Partners in Recruiting (C) ... 557
Holohan, Jr., Barth, Holohan Group Ltd (R) ... 100
Hunter, Christi, MR of Bethlehem (C) ... 504
Ibarra, Lizette, Qualifind Inc (C) ... 581
Irwin, Phil, MR of Monroe (C) ... 499
Johnson, Tina, Sanford Rose Associates - Annapolis (C) ... 609
Jordan, Dick, Staff Resources Inc (C) ... 635
Kiger, Terry, FPC of Greensboro (C) ... 368
Klawitter, Ron, Search Team One (C) ... 617
Kramer, Douglas, Michigan Consulting Group (R) ... 146
Krishnamurthy, Sumathy, CAI Personnel Search Group (C) ... 290
Kulvik, Chris, FPC/Fortune of San Antonio (C) ... 380
Lane, Scott, MR of San Antonio (C) ... 512
Larson, Warren, FPC/Fortune of San Antonio (C) ... 380
Lawry, William, W R Lawry Inc (R) ... 125
Lee, John, Phil Ellis Associates Inc (C) ... 348
Lennon, Bill, Hall Management Group Inc (C) ... 397
Lewis, Jason, The Alpine Group (C) ... 475
Lopez, Ricardo, Barbachano International Inc (BIP) (C) ... 268
Luciano, Mike, FPC of Bangor (C) ... 367
Mann, Ira, FPC of Atlanta (C) ... 366
Manning, Jerry, MR of Ogden (C) ... 512
Maye, Carolyn, MC2 Executive Search (R) ... 141
McCabe, Thomas, Koll-Fairfield LLC (C) ... 442
McDowell, Ron, Carnegie Resources Inc (C) ... 297
McFadden, James, PSP Agency (C) ... 580
McGrath, Moira, OPUS International Inc (C) ... 553
Meerdink, Carin, The Kidder Group Inc (C) ... 440
Moore, John, The Kidder Group Inc (C) ... 440
Morris, Harry, The Harlan Group Inc (C) ... 399

SPECIALTIES

The Directory of Executive Recruiters

SPECIALTIES

Resorts

Respiratory Therapy

Restaurants

Retail

RF Microwave

Risk Management

Robotics

Rubber

Safety

Sales

SPECIALTIES

SPECIALTIES

SPECIALTIES

SAP

Science

Seafood

Securities

SPECIALTIES

Six Sigma

Skilled Trades

Social Work

Sports

SPECIALTIES

SPECIALTIES

SPECIALTIES

Telecommunications

SPECIALTIES

SPECIALTIES

Geographical Index

Firms with (R) are from the Retainer Section.
Firms with (C) are from the Contingency Section.

This index is arranged alphabetically by state and then by city. Canada and Mexico follow the US entries.

GEOGRAPHIC

Victory Search Group (R) 215
Weinman & Associates (C) 665
Witt/Kieffer (R) 225

Sedona
RS&A (C) 601

Sun Lakes
Dumont, Sampson & Lodge (C) 338

Surprise
L Patrick & Steeple LLP (R) 160

Tempe
Boyden (R) 24
Civil Search International LLC (C) 304
International Search Consultants (C) 424
R & K Associates Inc (C) 583
Resources in Food Inc (C) 591
Southwest Search & Consulting Inc (C) 630
Techstaff Inc (C) 649

Tucson
Accounting & Finance Personnel Inc (C) 236
Computer Strategies Inc (C) 311
James Feerst & Associates Inc (R) 72
Management Recruiters International Inc
　(MRI) (C) 458
Medical Executive Search Associates Inc
　(C) 528
Rincon Partners (C) 594
Science Consultants LLC (C) 613

Vail
ExecuSearch (C) 354

Arkansas

Bella Vista
Snelling Search (C) 628

Bentonville
Builders Search Group LLC (C) 287
Snelling Search (C) 628

Conway
TDM & Associates (C) 647
Turnage Employment Service Group (C) 658

Drasco
The Jonathan Group (C) 431

Fayetteville
SC of Northwest Arkansas (C) 470

Hot Springs National Park
National Employment Solutions Inc (C) 541
RBW Associates (C) 585

Lakeview
Stephens International Recruiting Inc (C) 637

Little Rock
Alynco Inc (C) 252
Downs Associates (C) 337
Executive Recruiters Agency Inc (C) 357
Human Resources Personnel Agency (R) 103
MR of Little Rock (C) 470
MedIT Staff (C) 528
mfg/Search Inc (R) 145
The Rottman Group Inc (R) 180
SearchOne Inc (C) 618
Turnage Employment Service Group (C) 658

Maumelle
The Herring Group (C) 407

Mountain Home
Packaging Resources (C) 555
Welivers (C) 666

Norman
The Clertech Group Inc (C) 306

Rogers
Management Recruiters International Inc
　(MRI) (C) 458

Russellville
Turnage Employment Service Group (C) 658

California

Agoura Hills
Independent Resource Systems Inc (C) 420
International Search Consultants (C) 424

Alameda
The Culver Group (C) 324

Alamo
Crest Associates Inc (R) 50
FPC of East Bay (C) 365

Aliso Viejo
The Odella Group Inc (C) 550

Alta Loma
Forager (R) 75

Altadena
Valacon Inc (C) 660

Anaheim
Accounting Advantage (C) 236
ATA Healthcare Recruiters (C) 262
Health Search Inc (C) 403
Management Recruiters International Inc
　(MRI) (C) 459

Antioch
11th Hour Recruiting (C) 233

Aptos Hills
Management Recruiters International Inc
　(MRI) (C) 459

Arroyo Grande
Active Search and Placement (C) 239

Atascadero
Management Recruiters International Inc
　(MRI) (C) 459
MR of Templeton (C) 470

Atherton
Westover & Associates Inc (C) 667

Auburn
K L Williams & Associates (C) 669

Bakersfield
Search4um (R) 189

Bella Vista
The Telecom Search Group (C) 650

Benicia
MR of Benicia (C) 470

Berkeley
MR of Berkeley (C) 470
The Pacific Firm (R) 157

Beverly Hills
Alexander & Collins (C) 248
Bench International Search Inc (R) 18
Dawn Davis & Associates (C) 328
Elliot Group (R) 66
Fairfield (R) 72
Forbes Worldwide (C) 378
Groenekamp & Associates (C) 394
Horton Group Inc (C) 414
The Jameson Group (C) 428
Lucas Group (C) 454
Morgan Samuels Company LLC (R) 184

Bodega Bay
Nadzam & Associates (R) 150

Brea
The Culver Group (C) 324
L & L Associates (C) 444

Burbank
Ajilon Finance (C) 245
Douglas Associates Inc (C) 336
J Jireh & Associates Inc (C) 430
West Coast Recruiting Inc (C) 667

Burlingame
Accountants Inc (C) 236
Ames & Ames LLC (R) 9
Day & Associates (R) 54
Isaacson Miller Inc (R) 109
Kensington International (R) 117
MC Prosearch (C) 524
Trilogy Venture Search (R) 212

Calabasas
Jeff Harris & Associates (C) 399
Fred Hood & Associates Inc (C) 413
Mortgage & Financial Personnel Services
　(C) 537
National Resources Inc (C) 542
The Stevens Group Executive Search
　Consultants (C) 638

Camarillo
Adams & Associates (C) 239

Cambria
MLA- Executive Search (C) 535

Campbell
The Bradbury Group (R) 26
Dunhill Professional Search (C) 339
Duran Human Capital Partners Inc (R) 63
Howard Fischer Associates International
　Inc (R) 74
Horgan Splaine Partners (R) 100
Oxford Global Resources Inc (R) 157
The STS Group (R) 206
R J Watkins & Company Ltd (R) 218

Canyon Country
Leonard Corwen Corporate Recruiting
　Services (C) 319
Search Pro Inc (C) 617

Carlsbad
Akin & Associates (C) 248
Jeffrey Allan Company Inc (C) 249
BeechTree Partners LLC (R) 18

GEOGRAPHIC

Greenbrae
J Blakslee International Ltd (R) 21
Pierce & Crow (R) 164

Half Moon Bay
Colucci, Blendow & Johnson (R)...................... 44
HPI Executive Search & HR Consulting
   (R) 101

Healdsburg
MarCom Placements (C) 519

Hermosa Beach
Vision Group (C) 662

Hollywood
HRCG Inc (The Human Resource
   Consulting Group Inc) (R) 102

Huntington Beach
Bogle & Associates (C)......................................279
Corporate Careers Inc (C) 315
Custom Research Solutions (R)........................ 52
Jatinen & Associates (C)....................................429
MR of Huntington Beach (C)............................471
Ovca Associates Inc (R)....................................156
PR Talent (C) 569

Indian Wells
Ronald S Johnson Associates Inc (R) 113
DB Radden & Co Inc (R).................................170
Thomas & Associates (C) 652

Indio
Paschal•Murray Executive Search (R)................160

Irvine
Accounting Principals Ltd (C)...........................237
The Alicon Group Inc (C) 249
Asset Resource Inc (C) 261
Avestruz & Associates Inc (C)..........................265
Boyle Ogata Bregman (R)................................. 25
BridgeGate LLC (R) 27
California Executive Search Inc (C)...................290
California Search Agency Inc (C) 290
Castleton Consulting Inc (C) 299
S R Clarke Inc (C)..305
The Coelyn Group (R) 43
Compass Search Group LLC (C).......................309
Corporate DNA (C)..316
The Culver Group (C) 324
CyberCoders Inc (C) 325
DHR International (R)... 57
Diverse Connections (R)..................................... 59
Dunhill Professional Search (C) 339
Executive Medical Search (C)...........................356
Barry M Gold & Co LLC (C)............................390
Hemingway Solutions Inc (C)............................406
International Staffing Consultants Inc (C).........425
IT Management Partners Inc (C) 426
Korn/Ferry International (R) 121
John Kurosky & Associates (R) 123
Legal Network Inc (C) 449
Lucas Group (C) 454
MCS Associates (R)...143
Merritt, Hawkins & Associates (R) 144
The Millenia Group Inc (R)...............................146
Recruiting Services Group (C) 587
Resources in Food Inc (C) 591
Spencer Stuart (R)..197
Spherion Professional Services (C) 632
Vaughan & Company Executive Search
   Inc (C) 661
D L Weiss & Associates (R) 219
Witt/Kieffer (R) 225
Worldwide Executive Search (C).......................674

Kelseyville
Horizons Unlimited (C).......................................413

La Jolla
Ajilon Finance (C)..245
Don Allan Associates Inc (C).............................249
cFour Partners Worldwide (R)........................... 38
Alfred Daniels & Associates Inc (R)................. 53
ET Search Inc (R) 68
MSI International (Management Search
   Inc) (C) 538
Silverman & Associates (C) 624
TransExec (C)..655

La Palma
Accounting Principals Ltd (C) 237
Ajilon Finance (C) 245

Lafayette
CFOs2GO (C)...301
Dunhill Professional Search of Oakland
   (C) 340

Laguna Beach
Atlantic Pacific Group Inc (R) 12

Laguna Hills
CJA Executive Search (R) 41
The Garret Group (C)...384
Opus Marketing (C)..553
Strategic Resources Inc (C)...............................640
Victor White International (VWI) (R)...............221

Laguna Niguel
ACT (C)...238
Allen-Jeffers Associates (C) 250
DHR International (R).. 57
The Gobbell Company (R)................................. 83
Management Recruiters International Inc
   (MRI) (C) 459
Recruiting Services International Inc (C) 588
Strategic Alternatives Executive Search
   (R) 205
Westcott Associates (C).....................................667

Laguna Woods
Searchlight Recruiters Inc (C)...........................617

Lake Elsinore
Miller-Hall HRISearch (R) 147

Lake Forest
Custom Search Consultants Inc (C) 325
Richard Gast & Associates Ltd (C)...................384
MR of Laguna Hills-Orange County (R)...........134

Lakeport
California Management Search (C),...................290

Lakewood
Rollins & Associates (C)....................................598

Larkspur
Board Search Partners LLC (R) 22
Maczkov-Biosciences Inc (R)...........................132
MR Biotech (C)..472
Newlin Associates (R) 152
Oak Technology Partners LLC (R) 154
Schweichler Price & Partners Inc (R)................187
Wood & Associates (C) 672

Lodi
General Engineering Tectonics (R).................... 80

Lomita
Wayne S Chamberlain & Associates (C)...........302

Long Beach
Accounting Advantage (C) 237

The Culver Group (C)
The Culver Group (C)..324
Executives Unlimited Inc (R) 71
Fred Stuart Consulting/Personnel Services
   (C) 381
Hale & Estrada LLC (R).................................... 88
Evie Kreisler & Associates Inc (R)...................122
Management Recruiters International Inc
   (MRI) (C) 459
Saxbury Recruiting (C).......................................612
Yormak & Associates (C)...................................676

Los Altos
The Bauman Group (R) 17
Busch International (R).. 30
Flesher & Associates Inc (C) 376
Gent & Associates Inc (C) 385
Hockett Associates Inc (R)................................ 99
Karr Scheffel LLC (R).......................................115
James Moore & Associates (C)..........................536

Los Angeles
Accounting Advantage (C) 236
The Advocates Group Inc (C) 242
Ajilon Finance (C)..245
Allied Search Inc (C)...251
Avery James Inc (R) 13
Barro Global Search Inc (R) 15
Battalia Winston International (R) 16
Berkhemer Clayton Inc (R)................................ 19
BilingualPro (C) 276
BowersThomas (C)...281
Jerold Braun & Associates (C)...........................283
Brentwood International (R) 27
Bristol Associates Inc (C) 284
Carson-Thomas & Associates (R)...................... 35
The Cheyenne Group (R) 39
Chrisman & Company Inc (R)............................ 40
CJA Executive Search (R) 41
Clark Associates International Inc (C) 305
Commercial Programming Systems Inc
   (C) 309
Curphey & Malkin Associates Inc (C) 324
DHR International (R)... 57
Druthers Agency Inc (C) 338
Steve Ellis & Associates (R).............................. 66
ERx-Executive Recruitment in Healthcare
   Marketing & Comm (R) 67
Executive Careers Ltd (R) 68
Ferguson Partners Ltd (R)................................. 73
Garb Jaffe & Associates Legal Placement
   LLC (C) 384
Geller Braun & White Inc (C)...........................385
Barry Goldberg & Associates Inc (C) 390
Ben Greco Associates Inc (C) 392
Hampton Consulting, LLC (R) 89
HealthCare Search Associates (C) 405
Heidrick & Struggles (R)................................... 93
Hochman & Associates Inc (R) 99
HRCS (Human Resources Contract
   Services Inc) (R) 102
R I James Executive Search Consultants
   (R) 110
JobPlex Inc (R)...112
Kass/Abell & Associates (C) 436
Korn/Ferry International (R) 120
Larsen, Whitney, Blecksmith & Zilliacus,
   Inc. (R)...124
Levin & Company Inc (R) 127
Lipson & Co (R) 129
Major, Lindsey & Africa (C) 457
J Martin & Associates (R) 139
MAXIMUS Executive Search Services
   (R) 140
McCray Sheweloff & Associates Inc (R)..........142
Murray & Tatro (C)..539
NDH Search (R)...151
Novation Legal Placement Services (C) 548
The Oxbridge Group Ltd (C) 554
Poirier, Hoevel & Company (R) 165
PR Talent (C) 569
PRC Advantage (C)..569
Profiler Digital Media Recruiters (C)................577
Rivera Legal Search Inc (C) 594

GEOGRAPHIC

GEOGRAPHIC

GEOGRAPHIC

Faircastle Technology Group LLC (R) *71*
The Tidewater Group (C) *653*

New Canaan
Tom Bell & Associates (C) *272*
JT Associates (C) *432*
The Cowser Group (C) *475*
J D Walsh & Company (R) *216*

New Fairfield
The Burgess Group-Corporate Recruiters
   International Inc (C) *288*
NL Associates Inc (C) *547*

New Haven
Express Professional Staffing - RWJ &
   Associates (C) *363*
Heritage Partners International (R) *95*
Kaiser Whitney Staffing International (C) *434*

New London
Dunhill Professional Search (C) *339*

Newington
Direct Mail Jobs LLC (C) *334*
People Management SMD LLC (R) *161*

Newtown
ITech Consulting Partners LLC (C) *427*
River Glen Associates (C) *594*

North Haven
InSite Search (C) *422*
The Lewis Group (C) *475*

North Stonington
Gosselin Associates LLC (R) *84*

Norwalk
The Ayers Group (R) *14*
The Creative Placement Agency LLC (C) *322*
Harris Heery & Associates Inc (R) *90*
Higbee Associates Inc (C) *408*
Victoria James Executive Search Inc (C) *428*
The McIntyre Group (C) *525*
Plummer & Associates Inc (R) *164*
Ross Personnel Consultants Inc (C) *599*

Norwich
Chelsea Resources Inc (C) *303*
Staffing Consultants Inc (R) *200*

Old Greenwich
Garthwaite Partners International LLC (R) *80*
Greenwich Search Partners LLC (C) *393*

Ridgefield
Allen Austin Executive Search
   Consultants (R) *13*
Corporate Software Solutions LLC (C) *319*
P J Lynch Associates (R) *131*
Redden, Foy & Associates LLC (R) *173*

Rocky Hill
Matthews & Stephens Associates Inc (R) *140*
Retail Recruiters (C) *592*
Jeffrey Thompson Associates (C) *652*

Sandy Hook
Management Recruiters International Inc
   (MRI) (C) *459*
Mangieri/Hull Solutions LLC (C) *518*

Shelton
DAL Partners (R) *53*

Management Recruiters International Inc
   (MRI) (C) *460*

Simsbury
Flexible Resources Inc (C) *377*
W R Lawry Inc (R) *125*

Southbury
DHR International (R) *57*

Southport
Blackshaw, Olmstead, Lynch & Koenig
   (R) *21*
O'Keefe & Associates Inc (R) *154*
Ross & Company Inc (R) *180*

Stamford
Access Financial (C) *235*
Bonnell Associates Ltd (R) *23*
Burke & Associates (C) *288*
Cornell Group International Consulting
   Inc (R) *48*
Curran Partners Inc (R) *52*
DHR International (R) *57*
Flexible Resources Inc (C) *377*
Gilbert Tweed Associates Inc (R) *82*
Global Career Services Inc (C) *388*
Heidrick & Struggles (R) *93*
Highland Partners (R) *97*
InSearch Worldwide Corp (R) *107*
InteliSearch Inc (R) *108*
Jones Management Company (R) *113*
Korn/Ferry International (R) *121*
Lexington Associates (R) *128*
Lloyd Staffing (C) *452*
MR of Stamford (C) *476*
The Performance Group Inc (C) *475*
Michael Page International Inc (C) *531*
Morgan Howard Worldwide (R) *148*
Moyer, Sherwood Associates Inc (R) *149*
PRH Management Inc (R) *166*
Reeve & Associates (C) *589*
Resource Management (C) *590*
The Response Companies (C) *592*
RJS Associates Inc (C) *595*
K Russo Associates Inc (C) *602*
Slayton International (R) *194*
Spencer Stuart (R) *198*
Spherion Professional Services (C) *632*
Taylor, Rodgers & Associates LLC (R) *209*
Vojta & Associates (R) *216*

Stratford
Johnson & Company (R) *113*
Henry J Lee (C) *449*
Thorne, Brieger Associates Inc (R) *210*

Torrington
Blackwood Associates Inc (C) *277*

Trumbull
Tryg R Angell Ltd (C) *256*
Lineal Recruiting Services (C) *451*
TeboZandt Inc (C) *647*

Wallingford
Dunhill Professional Search (C) *339*
MJF Associates (C) *534*

Waterbury
Wallace Associates (C) *663*

Weatogue
IT Services (C) *426*

West Hartford
CBS (Compensation & Benefits Search)
   (C) *299*

Creative Financial Staffing (C) *321*
Flynn, Hannock Inc (R) *75*
Horton International LLC (R) *101*
Insurance Career Center Inc (C) *422*

West Haven
Harvard Aimes Group (R) *91*

West Suffield
E/Search International (C) *344*

Weston
The Aurora Group (C) *264*
Lynrow Associates LLC (R) *131*
Satterfield & Associates Inc (R) *186*

Westport
Barbara Bliss Co Ltd (C) *278*
Bond & Company (C) *280*
Cambridge Group (C) *291*
Caruthers & Company LLC (R) *36*
Rosemary Cass Ltd (R) *36*
Halbrecht Lieberman Associates Inc (R) *88*
Hamilton Partners (R) *88*
Susan Harris & Associates (C) *399*
J G Hood Associates (C) *413*
InSite Search (C) *421*
Karel & Company / Executive Search (R) *115*
Lambert Group International LLC (R) *123*
The McKnight Group (C) *526*
Barry Persky & Company Inc (R) *162*
Phase II Management (R) *163*
R/K International Inc (R) *170*
Frank A Rac & Associates (R) *170*
J Stroll Associates Inc (R) *205*
Ward Liebelt Associates Inc (R) *217*
Wheeler Associates (R) *221*

Wilton
Cornell Global LLC (R) *48*
Management Recruiters International Inc
   (MRI) (C) *460*
James Mead & Co (R) *143*
O'Connell Group Inc (C) *549*
People Options LLC (C) *559*
Bob Wright Recruiting Inc (C) *675*

Windsor
ExecuREP LLC (C) *354*

Winsted
MR of Winsted (C) *476*

Woodbury
W A Rutledge & Associates (R) *182*

Delaware

Claymont
J B Groner Executive Search LLC (C) *394*

Hockessin
MoreTech Consulting (C) *536*

Lewes
Management Recruiters International Inc
   (MRI) (C) *460*

Newark
PowerBrokers LLC (C) *492*
Spherion Professional Services (C) *632*
Thompson Search Consultants (C) *652*

Rehoboth Beach
The Helms International Group (R) *95*

GEOGRAPHIC

GEOGRAPHIC

GEOGRAPHIC

Stone Mountain
CBI Group Inc (R) 37
Creative HR Solutions (C) 322
The LeROI Group (R) 127
The McAllister Group (C) 524

Suwanee
The Corban Group (R) 48
Corporate Consulting Associates Inc (C) 316
Grobard & Associates Inc (C) 394
The Hunter Group Inc (R) 104
Management Recruiters International Inc
  (MRI) (C) 461
Rust & Associates Inc (R) 182
S Cunningham Inc (C) 603

Thomson
MAU Inc (Management Analysis &
  Utilization Inc) (C) 523

Tucker
Corporate Plus Ltd (C) 317

Woodstock
Express Professional Staffing - RWJ &
  Associates (C) 363
IT Intellect Inc (C) 426
Management Recruiters International Inc
  (MRI) (C) 461
MR of Atlanta-Peachtree North (C) 481

Hawaii

Aiea
Human Resources Management Hawaii
  Inc (C) 417
Lucas Group (C) 454
Orion International (C) 553

Honolulu
Executive Search World (R) 70
Lam Associates (C) 445
MR/SC of Honolulu (C) 481
Management Search & Consulting Inc (R) 137
Maresca & Associates (C) 520
MPC and Company (C) 538

Kailua
Dunhill Professional Search of Hawaii (C) 341

Kailua Kona
MBA Management Inc (R) 141

Kamuela
Management Recruiters International Inc
  (MRI) (C) 461

Kihei
R F Chapman & Company (C) 302

Idaho

Boise
FPC of Boise (C) 366
Management Recruiters International Inc
  (MRI) (C) 461
Vista Partners Inc (C) 662

Cocolalla
Dunhill Professional Search of Sandpoint
  (C) 341

Coeur D Alene
Management Recruiters International Inc
  (MRI) (C) 461

Search Group International (SGI) LLC
  (C) 615

Eagle
SMR Inc (R) 195

Hayden Lake
Ward & Ward International Recruiters &
  Consultants (C) 664

Ketchum
Sun Valley Search (C) 642

Lewiston
Express Professional Staffing - RWJ &
  Associates (C) 363

Illinois

Arlington Heights
BLH Recruiting (C) 278
Dynamic Search Systems Inc (C) 343
FPC of Arlington Heights (C) 366
H T Associates (C) 396
iScout Inc (R) 109
MR/SC of Arlington Heights (C) 482
Select Search (C) 619
Selectis Corp (C) 620
Technical Recruiting Consultants Inc (C) 648

Aurora
BA Search Group (C) 266
DP Resources (C) 338
Executive Search Management Inc (C) 361
Management Recruiters International Inc
  (MRI) (C) 461

Bannockburn
EFL Associates (R) 65

Barrington
Adams & Associates International (R) 4
Briant Associates Inc (R) 27
Carpenter, Shackleton & Company (R) 34
Despres & Associates Inc (R) 56
The East Wing Group (C) 344
EJ Howe & Associates (C) 415
D Kunkle & Associates (C) 443
MR of Barrington (C) 482
Management Search (C) 517
Management Search Inc (C) 517
R2 Staffing Inc (C) 583
The Remington Group (R) 174
TSC Management Services Group Inc (C) 657

Batavia
National Restaurant Search Inc (R) 151

Belvidere
Partners in Recruiting (C) 557
Staffing Services Inc (C) 635

Bloomingdale
Jim Kay & Associates Inc (C) 436

Bloomington
Adkisson Consultants Inc (R) 5
Management Recruiters International Inc
  (MRI) (C) 461

Bolingbrook
Hufford Associates (C) 416

Bourbonnais
The Myers Group Inc (C) 482

Broadview
MAU Inc (Management Analysis &
  Utilization Inc) (C) 523

Brookfield
David Rowe & Associates Inc (R) 180

Buffalo Grove
Direct Guarantee Staffing (C) 334
Executive Recruiting Associates (C) 358
Gossage Sager Associates LLC (R) 84
International Consulting Services Inc (C) 424
Smith & Partners Inc (R) 194
Staffing Now Inc (R) 200

Carbondale
Express Professional Staffing - RWJ &
  Associates (C) 363

Cary
J P Gleason Associates Inc (R) 82

Chicago
ADA Executive Search Inc (R) 4
G Adams Partners (R) 4
Ajilon Finance (C) 245
Audit Recruiters (C) 263
Baker Montgomery (R) 14
Bales Partners Inc (R) 14
Banner Professional Staffing (C) 267
Barrett Partners (C) 268
Battalia Winston International (R) 16
BCG Attorney Search (C) 270
BeechTree Partners LLC (R) 18
Gary S Bell Associates Inc (C) 272
T H Bender & Partners (R) 19
Bennett Wheeless Group Ltd (R) 19
Blackman Kallick Executive Search (R) 21
Blackshaw, Olmstead, Lynch & Koenig
  (R) 21
Bloom, Gross & Associates (C) 278
Blumenthal-Hart Ltd (R) 22
The Boulware Group Inc (R) 24
Boyden (R) 25
The Burling Group Ltd (R) 29
Business Systems of America Inc (R) 30
Capstone Consulting Group (R) 33
Cardwell Enterprises Inc (R) 33
Carlyle Group LTD (R) 34
Carpenter, Shackleton & Company (R) 35
Carrington & Carrington Ltd (R) 35
CBC Resources Inc (C) 299
CES Partners Ltd (R) 37
CFR Executive Search Inc (C) 301
Chase Hunter Group Inc (R) 39
Chicago Financial Search Inc (C) 303
Chicago Legal Search Ltd (C) 303
Chicagoland Recruiters (C) 303
CMC Consultants Inc (C) 307
Coffou Partners Inc (R) 43
Cook Associates (R) 47
Corporate Select International (C) 319
Data Career Center Inc (C) 327
Daubenspeck and Associates Ltd (R) 53
Patrick Delaney & Associates Inc (R) 55
DHR International (R) 56
Diamond Management Group Ltd (R) 58
Differential Partners (R) 58
Donahue/Patterson Associates (R) 61
James Drury Partners (R) 62
Ronald Dukes Associates LLC (R) 62
Dunhill Professional Search (C) 339
Early Cochran & Olson LLC (R) 63
Edward W Kelley & Partners, Ltd. (R) 64
Evers Legal Search (C) 353
Executive Pro Search Ltd (C) 357
Executive Referral Services Inc (C) 358
Executive Search Consultants Corp (C) 360
Ferguson Partners Ltd (R) 73
Gaines & Associates International Inc (R) 78
Garrett Search Partners LLC (R) 80

GEOGRAPHIC

GEOGRAPHIC

Lawrenceburg
Advanced Recruiting Techniques (C)................*241*

Michigan City
Brooks Placement Network (C)..........................*285*
Snelling Search (C)...*628*

Mishawaka
J Fabri Associates LLC (R)................................. *71*

Mooresville
HealthCare Recruiters International •
   Indiana (C)..*404*

Mount Vernon
FPC of Mount Vernon (C)................................*366*
FPC of SW Indiana (C)......................................*366*

Nashville
Dunhill Executive Search of Brown
   County (C)..*341*

New Albany
Management Recruiters International Inc
   (MRI) (C)..*462*

Newburgh
Forbes & Company Executive Search (C)..........*378*
MR of Newburgh (C)..*484*

Noblesville
Management Recruiters International Inc
   (MRI) (C)..*462*
MR of Noblesville-Indianapolis Northeast
   (C)...*484*
Sanford Rose Associates - Carmel (C)..............*608*

Richmond
Financial Recruiters (C).....................................*373*
Management Recruiters International Inc
   (MRI) (C)..*462*

Santa Claus
Marksmen Consultants (C)..................................*521*

South Bend
AmeriSearch Group Inc (C)...............................*254*
Creative Financial Staffing (C)..........................*321*
FPC of South Bend (C)......................................*366*
mfg/Search Inc (R)..*145*
Polymer Specialties Inc (C)...............................*567*
Spyglass Search Inc (C).....................................*634*

Syracuse
Search Team One (C)..*617*

Terre Haute
Corporate Search Consultants (C)......................*318*
MJ Egy & Associates (C)....................................*346*
Express Professional Staffing - RWJ &
   Associates (C)...*363*

Valparaiso
Dimensional Resources (C)................................*333*
The Pettis Group Inc (C).....................................*563*

Wabash
Lange & Associates Inc (C)................................*446*

Warsaw
The Lake City Group (C)....................................*484*

Zionsville
Management Recruiters International Inc
   (MRI) (C)..*462*

Iowa

Arnolds Park
Cyclone Staffing Solutions (C)..........................*484*

Bettendorf
Bryant Bureau Sales Recruiters (C)...................*286*
Techstaff Inc (C)..*649*
Triumph Consulting Inc (R)................................*213*

Cedar Falls
Future Employment Service Inc (C)...................*382*

Cedar Rapids
Cambridge Careers Inc (C)................................*291*
FPC of Cedar Rapids (C)....................................*367*
Future Employment Service Inc (C)...................*382*
Kaas Employment Services (C).........................*434*
Management Recruiters International Inc
   (MRI) (C)..*462*
McCord Consulting Group Inc (MCG Inc)
   (C)...*524*
Ray and Associates Inc (R)................................*172*
RSM McGladrey Inc (R).....................................*180*

Clear Lake
Management Recruiters International Inc
   (MRI) (C)..*462*

Clinton
Future Employment Service Inc (C)...................*382*

Clive
Agra Placements Ltd (C).....................................*243*
Career Search Associates (C)............................*296*
Midwest Search Group LLC (C).........................*532*

Council Bluffs
SC of Riverside (C)..*485*

Davenport
AGRI-associates, Inc. (C)..................................*243*
Management Resource Group Ltd (R)...............*137*

Des Moines
Creative Financial Staffing (C)..........................*321*
Executive Resources (C).....................................*359*
June L Owens & Associates LLC (C)................*554*
RSM McGladrey Inc (C).....................................*321*
RSM McGladrey Inc (R).....................................*180*

Dubuque
Future Employment Service Inc (C)...................*382*

Fairfield
MR of Fairfield (C)...*485*

Grinnell
Executive Recruiting & Search Consulting
   LLC (R)..*69*

Hiawatha
Management Resource Group Ltd (R)...............*137*

Iowa City
Dunhill Professional Search (C).........................*339*
Management Recruiters International Inc
   (MRI) (C)..*462*

Maquoketa
Future Employment Service Inc (C)...................*382*

Marion
The Humbert Group LLC (R)..............................*103*

Marshalltown
Andersen & Associates (C)................................*255*

Oakdale
Management Recruiters International Inc
   (MRI) (C)..*462*

Polk City
The Alliance Search Group Inc (C)....................*251*
Miller & Associates Inc (C)................................*533*

Robins
The Alliance Search Group Inc (C)....................*251*

Sioux City
MR of Siouxland (C)...*485*

Waterloo
Byrnes & Rupkey Inc (C)...................................*289*
Talent Chase Career Solutions (TCCS)
   (C)...*645*

Waukee
The Garrison Organization (C)..........................*384*

West Des Moines
Capstone Search Group (C)...............................*293*
Career Management Associates (C)...................*295*
Eyler Associates Inc (R).....................................*71*
Francis & Associates (R).....................................*76*
Hunter Search Group Inc (R).............................*104*
Vermillion Group (C)..*485*
Mancini Technical Recruiting (C)......................*518*
Palmer Group (C)...*555*
Spherion Professional Services (C)....................*633*
Staffing Now Inc (R)..*200*
Triumph Consulting Inc (R)................................*213*

Williamsburg
MR of Williamsburg (C)....................................*485*

Kansas

Andover
Agra Placements Ltd (C).....................................*243*

Fort Scott
MR of Fort Scott (C)..*485*

Hays
Pam Pohly Associates (C)..................................*567*

Lake Quivira
Stoneburner Associates Inc (C).........................*639*

Lawrence
The Winn Group Inc (C).....................................*671*
The Winn Group Inc (C).....................................*672*

Leawood
JobPlex Inc (R)..*112*

Manhattan
Personnel Management Resources (C)..............*562*

Olathe
Walter & Associates Inc (C)..............................*664*

GEOGRAPHIC

South Portland
Executive Search of New England Inc (C) *361*

Vinalhaven
Meticulum, Inc. (R)..*144*

Wells
Executive Search Group Inc (C)........................*486*

West Boothbay Harbor
Summit Partners Inc (R)....................................*206*

Yarmouth
John Jay & Co (C)..*429*

Maryland

Annapolis
BJB Associates (C)...*277*
Columbia Consulting Group (R) *44*
Davco Resources LLC (C) *328*
Kames & Associates Inc (C) *435*
Management Recruiters International Inc
  (MRI) (C)..*463*
Spherion Professional Services (C) *633*

Baltimore
Ajilon Finance (C) *246*
Bowie & Associates Inc (C)..............................*281*
Boyce Cunnane Inc (R)..................................... *24*
Boyden (R) *25*
Brandjes Associates (C).....................................*282*
Columbia Consulting Group (R) *44*
Computer Management Inc (C)..........................*311*
Continental Search & Outplacement Inc
  (C)...*314*
Kforce (C)..*439*
Kostmayer Associates Inc (R)...........................*121*
Lloyd Staffing (C)..*452*
Management Recruiters International Inc
  (MRI) (C)..*463*
Professional Corporate Search Inc (C) *575*
Spherion Professional Services (C) *633*
Stanton Chase International (R) *201*

Bel Air
Conboy, Sur & Associates Inc (R) *45*
F-O-R-T-U-N-E Personnel Consultants
  (FPC) (C)...*364*

Berlin
Brandywine Management Group (R) *26*

Bethesda
BG & Associates (C)...*275*
Mee Derby & Company (C)................................*332*
Arthur Diamond Associates Inc (R) *58*
Executive Levels International (C)....................*356*
Kershner & Co (R)..*117*
The Owens Group LLC (R).................................*156*
Pacific Bridge Inc (C) *554*
Security & Investigative Placement
  Consultants (R)...*190*
Spherion Professional Services (C) *633*
TEG Solutions (R) *210*
Witt/Kieffer (R) *225*

Brooklandville
Durakis Executive Search (R) *63*

California
Virtual HR Associates (C)..................................*662*

Catonsville
The Boland Group Inc (R) *23*

Chevy Chase
Krauthamer & Associates (R) *122*
Larsen & Lee Inc (R)..*124*
The Whyte Group Inc (R) *222*

Cockeysville
Cross Country Consultants Inc (C)....................*323*

Columbia
Christian & Timbers (R) *41*
Columbia Consulting Group (R) *44*
Executive Recruiters Group (C).........................*358*
Management Recruiters International Inc
  (MRI) (C)..*463*
MR of Columbia (C) *487*
Spherion Professional Services (C) *633*

Dayton
RKP Group Pharmaceutical and Biotech
  Search (C) *595*

Derwood
Selman Associates Inc (C) *620*

Edgewater
Management Recruiters International Inc
  (MRI) (C)..*463*

Edgewood
The Search Group (C)...*616*

Ellicott City
Management Recruiters International Inc
  (MRI) (C)..*463*

Fallston
Robert W Havener Associates Inc (C) *401*

Finksburg
Procurement Resources (C)................................*574*

Forest Hill
Discovery Solutions (C).....................................*334*
TEG Solutions (R) *210*

Frederick
MR of Frederick (C) *487*
Recruiting Solutions Worldwide LLC (R)..........*173*
Bill Young & Associates Inc (R) *228*

Gaithersburg
Association Executive Resources Group
  (R)...*12*
MR of Gaithersburg (C)......................................*487*

Grasonville
People Source LLC (C)......................................*559*

Hagerstown
Corporate Resources, Stevens Inc (C)...............*318*

Hampstead
Compass Run LLC (C) *309*
HealthCare Recruiters International •
  Dallas (C)...*403*

Hanover
MR of the BWI Corridor (C) *487*

Havre de Grace
Mackenzie Search (R).......................................*132*

Hunt Valley
The Hanover Consulting Group (R)....................*89*

LaVale
HealthSearch Associates (C)..............................*405*

Linthicum
NRI Staffing Resources (C) *548*

Lutherville
Brindisi Search (R) *28*
The Search Committee (C) *615*
TCM Enterprises (C) *647*

Lutherville/Baltimore
Mary Kraft & Associates Inc (C) *442*

Millersville
Medserve & Associates Inc (C) *529*

North Potomac
The Corporate Source Group Inc (R)..................*49*

Olney
Opportunity Search Inc (C)................................*552*

Owings Mills
HNH Partners Inc (C) *411*
Hotel Executive Placement Inc (C)....................*414*
Landsman Foodservice.Net (C) *445*
Medpar Consulting (C) *528*
Craig Roe & Associates LLC (C) *597*
The Rogan Group Inc (C) *597*
Telem Adhesive Search Corp (C) *650*

Pikesville
Wasserman Associates Inc (C) *665*

Queenstown
Nations Executive Search Group Inc (C) *543*

Rockville
ACSYS Inc (C)...*238*
Ajilon Finance (C) *246*
Dunhill Professional Search (C) *339*
Executive Placement Associates (C)..................*357*
High Technology Recruiters Inc (C).................*409*
JDG Associates Ltd (R) *110*
Rockville Recruiter.com (C)...............................*487*
NRI Staffing Resources (C) *548*
Perry · Newton Associates (C)...........................*560*
Resource Management Consultants (R)............*176*
Verus Staffing Solutions LLC (C) *661*

Salisbury
Management Recruiters International Inc
  (MRI) (C)..*463*

Severna Park
FPC of Severna Park (C) *367*
The Park Group & Associates Inc (R)..............*159*

Silver Spring
Management Recruiters International Inc
  (MRI) (C)..*463*
The Washington Group (C) *487*
Team Place (C)...*647*

Simpsonville
Paul Lynner & Associates (C) *455*

Stevensville
Sanford Rose Associates - Annapolis (C) *609*

GEOGRAPHIC

Groton
Jeff Smith & Associates (C) 625

Hanover
Search America Inc (C) 614
Tondorf & Associates Inc (C) 653

Harwich
The Franklin Career Group (C) 380

Hingham
AKS Associates Ltd (R) 6
Phillips, DiPisa & Associates Inc (R) 163
Sanford Rose Associates - Boston South
   Shore (C) 609
Springbrook Partners Inc (R) 199
Sullivan Associates (R) 206

Hubbardston
Kimball Personnel Sales Recruiters (C) 440

Lakeville
Edelman & Associates (R) 64

Lawrence
Millstream Associates (C) 533

Lenox
WMD Inc (C) 672

Leominster
Staffing Now Inc (R) 200

Lexington
Fitzgerald Associates (R) 74
IT Resources (C) 426
Lynx Inc (C) 455
Louis Rudzinsky Associates Inc (C) 602
Willmott & Associates (C) 669

Lynnfield
The Insurance Staffing Group (C) 422

Mansfield
The Retail Network (C) 592

Marblehead
K S Frary & Associates Inc (R) 77
J E Ranta Associates (C) 584
Taylor/Haley Search Partners LLC (R) 209

Marion
The Jeremiah Group LLC (R) 111

Marlborough
Progressive Search Associates (C) 578

Marshfield Hills
Resource Inc (R) 176

Marstons Mills
Access/Resources Inc (C) 236

Mashpee
Global Recruiters of Cape Cod (C) 389
Research Recruiters (C) 590

Medfield
Gatti & Associates (C) 384
J S Lord & Company Inc (R) 130
Prestonwood Associates (R) 166
Xavier Associates Inc (R) 227

Medford
Rostie & Associates Inc (C) 599
Tsunami Partners (C) 658

Mendon
Derek Associates Inc (R) 56

Milton
The Bray Group (R) 26
Vital Staffing (C) 662

Nahant
The Career Group Ltd (C) 294

Natick
McInturff & Associates Inc (C) 525
MD Parkin & Associates (R) 159
TechFind Inc (R) 209
The Yorkshire Group Ltd (R) 228
ZweigWhite (R) 230

Needham
Alexander, Wollman & Stark (R) 7
Resource Options Inc (C) 591
Peter Siegel & Company (C) 623
Trowbridge&Company Inc (R) 213

Needham Heights
Glou International Inc (R) 83

Newburyport
The Cassie Shipherd Group LLC (R) 36
Search International (R) 188

Newton
Barrack Hill Partners Inc (R) 15
Executive Search International (R) 70
E M Heath & Company (C) 406
The Jacobson Group (C) 428
Matlin Partners LLC (R) 140

Newton Center
Centre Street Associates Inc (C) 300
Alan Levine Associates (R) 127
Nagler Robins Partners (R) 150

Newton Lower Falls
Gustin Partners (R) 87

Norfolk
Heffelfinger Associates Inc (R) 92

North Andover
HRCG Inc (The Human Resource
   Consulting Group Inc) (R) 102
Medical Search Group (C) 528
Sanford Rose Associates - Andover (C) 609
Straube Associates (R) 205
Vista Technology (C) 662

North Falmouth
SC of Falmouth (C) 488

North Marshfield
Publishing Search Solutions (C) 580

Northampton
TalentFusion (R) 207

Northborough
Consumer Search Inc (C) 313
Kacevich, Lewis & Brown Inc (R) 114
MorganSullivan, Inc. (C) 537
SullivanKreiss, Inc. (R) 206

Norwell
Navin Group (C) 543

Norwood
A Greenstein & Company (R) 85

Osterville
The Kinlin Company Inc (R) 118
P•A•R• Associates Inc (R) 157

Peabody
F-O-R-T-U-N-E Personnel Consultants
   (FPC) (C) 365

Plymouth
Peter J Kratimenos Associates (C) 443
J. Pimental & CO (C) 565

Prides Crossing
Architechs (C) 259
Van Curan & Associates (C) 660

Quincy
Whitridge Associates Inc (R) 222

Rockland
Clin Force Inc (C) 306

Sagamore Beach
Management Recruiters International Inc
   (MRI) (C) 463

Salem
American Executive Management Inc (R) 8
New Dimensions in Technology Inc (C) 545

Sandwich
Hunt For Executives (C) 417
Search Professionals Inc (C) 617

Scituate
Bennett Yarger Associates (R) 19

Sharon
Forsyte Associates Inc (C) 378
Partridge Associates Inc (R) 160
Power Technology Associates Inc (C) 568
Stephen M Sonis Associates (R) 196

Sherborn
Greene & Hauck (C) 393

South Attleboro
Wright Associates (C) 675

South Hamilton
Kirk Palmer & Associates Inc (R) 158

Southampton
Tech Search Systems (C) 647

Southborough
Rusher, Loscavio & LoPresto (R) 181

Springfield
Douglas-Allen Inc (R) 61
Food Management Search (C) 378
The Boston Group (C) 488

Sudbury
Connexion Systems & Engineering (C) 312
Joel H Wilensky Associates Inc (C) 668

GEOGRAPHIC

Hillsdale
Advance Employment Inc (C) *241*

Holland
Management Recruiters International Inc
  (MRI) (C) *463*
Paragon Recruiting (C) *556*
Professional Outlook Inc (C)................... *575*

Holt
Management Recruiters International Inc
  (MRI) (C) *463*

Howell
Artemis HRC LLC (C)............................ *260*

Jackson
Advance Employment Inc (C) *241*
Management Recruiters International Inc
  (MRI) (C) *463*
Michigan Consulting Group (R)................... *146*
Trillium Staffing Solutions (C) *656*

Jonesville
Trillium Staffing Solutions (C) *656*

Kalamazoo
Advance Employment Inc (C) *241*
Cole's Paper Industry Recruiters Inc (C) ... *308*
Collins & Associates (C)........................... *308*
Hallman Group Inc (C) *397*
JL Blake Inc (C) *489*
MR of Kalamazoo (C)............................. *489*
Trillium Staffing Solutions (C) *656*
Van Popering McLogan Executive Search
  Inc (VPML Inc) (C) *660*

Lambertville
Graphic Arts Marketing Associates Inc
  (C) *392*

Lansing
Advance Employment Inc (C) *240*
Advance Employment Inc (C) *241*
Career Alternatives Executive Search (C) *293*
DHR International (R)............................. *57*
Hiring Solutions Inc (C)........................... *410*
Management Recruiters International Inc
  (MRI) (C) *463*

Lapeer
J E Lessner Associates Inc (R) *127*
Trillium Staffing Solutions (C) *656*

Livonia
Access/Resources Inc (C)........................ *236*
The Barton Group Inc (C) *269*
MR/SC of Laurel Park (C) *489*
Henry Welker & Associates (C)................... *666*

Macomb
Express Professional Staffing - RWJ &
  Associates (C)................................... *363*

Madison Heights
American Heritage Group Inc (C) *252*

Marshall
Trillium Staffing Solutions (C) *656*

Mattawan
Jaques and Associates LLC (C)................... *428*

Midland
James & Richards (C) *428*

Mount Pleasant
Advance Employment Inc (C) *241*

Muskegon
MR of Muskegon (C) *489*
Professional Search (C)........................... *576*

New Buffalo
Rovner & Associates Inc (R) *180*

Niles
Trillium Staffing Solutions (C) *656*

Northville
MR of Plymouth (C) *489*

Novi
Aegis Group Search Consultants LLC (R) *5*
SC Novi (C)....................................... *489*
Michigan Consulting Group (R)................... *146*

Pontiac
Executech Resource Consultants (C) *355*

Portage
Chadwell & Associates Inc (C) *302*
Mathias Medical Search (C)...................... *522*

Rochester Hills
Angott Search Group (C) *490*
Sterling Professional Search (C) *637*

Roseville
Bryant Bureau (C)................................ *286*

Saginaw
Trillium Staffing Solutions (C) *656*

Saint Clair Shores
Cars Group International (C) *298*

Saint Joseph
JR Walters Resources (C) *664*

Shelby Township
The Deacon Group (C).......................... *329*

Southfield
Ajilon Finance (C) *246*
Davidson, Laird & Associates Inc (C)............. *328*
The Emeritus Group Inc (C) *348*
Emplex Associates (R)........................... *66*
SC of Detroit (C)................................. *490*
Medical & Executive Recruiters (C) *527*

Springfield
Trillium Staffing Solutions (C) *656*

Sterling Heights
Administrative Employer Services (C).............. *240*
The Albo Group Inc (C)........................... *248*
Hans Becker Associates LLC (C) *271*

Stevensville
Guidarelli Associates Inc (C) *395*

Sturgis
Trillium Staffing Solutions (C) *656*

Suttons Bay
Sanford Rose Associates - Traverse City
  (C)... *609*

Three Rivers
Advance Employment Inc (C) *241*

Traverse City
Bogle & Associates (C) *279*
Kuttnauer Search Group Inc (C) *444*
Management Recruiters International Inc
  (MRI) (C).. *463*
MR of Traverse City (C).......................... *490*
Sanford Rose Associates - Lake Ann (C).......... *609*
SearchWide (R).................................. *189*

Troy
AJM Professional Services (C) *247*
The DAKO Group (C)............................ *326*
DHR International (R)............................ *57*
Express Professional Staffing - RWJ &
  Associates (C) *363*
FPC of Troy (C) *367*
Harvey Hohauser & Associates LLC (R).......... *99*
Kratec Company (C)............................. *442*
Management Recruiters International Inc
  (MRI) (C).. *463*
Michigan Consulting Group (R) *146*
Paradigm Technologies Inc (R) *158*
Profiles Inc (C) *577*
Seligman & Herrod (R) *190*
Spherion Professional Services (C)................. *633*
Wing Tips & Pumps Inc (C) *671*

Union Pier
Thomas & Associates of Michigan (C)............. *652*

Warren
Thinkpath Inc (C) *651*

West Bloomfield
Harmon/Watson/DeGross International
  (R)... *90*
HR Connections (C) *415*
Phoenix Technical Services Inc (C) *564*
Windsor Southfield Service Co (C) *671*

Wixom
Kabana Corp (C) *434*

Minnesota

Alexandria
MR of Northern Lakes (C)....................... *490*

Bloomington
Creative Financial Staffing (C)................... *321*
Leland Roberts Inc (C) *449*
MR of Bloomington (C) *490*
Spherion Professional Services (C).................. *633*

Burnsville
Discovery Personnel Inc (C)...................... *334*
MR of Burnsville (C)............................. *490*

Chanhassen
Ecruiters.net (R) *63*
Susan Lee & Associates (C) *448*
Management Recruiters International Inc
  (MRI) (C).. *463*
Yungner & Associates, LLC (R)................... *228*

Chaska
Bond Technologies (C)............................ *280*
SC of Chaska (C)................................. *490*

Mississippi

Missouri

GEOGRAPHIC

Chesterfield

Advanced Resources Group Inc (C) 241
Blonstein & Associates Executive
   Placement (C) 278
Boyden (R) 25
CareerStrategies LLC (R).................................. 34
DDS Resources Inc (C).....................................329
Eagle Rock Consulting Group (C).....................344
HealthCare Recruiters International •
   Dallas (C)..403
The Hindman Group Inc (R) 98
John & Powers Inc (R) 112
Kendall Placement Group (KPG) (C)...............438
Charles Luntz & Associates Inc (R) 131
Management Recruiters International Inc
   (MRI) (C)...464
SC of St. Louis (C)...491
MD Resources Inc (C) 526

Columbia

Express Professional Staffing - RWJ &
   Associates (C)..363
F-O-R-T-U-N-E Personnel Consultants
   (FPC) (C)..365

Creve Coeur

FPC of St Louis (C) 367
Source Medical (C)..629

Earth City

Application Design Group, Inc. (C) 258

Ellisville

Huey Enterprises Inc (R)...................................102
Physician Recruiting Services Inc (C) 564
Select Medical Solutions (C)..............................619

Fenton

Management Recruiters International Inc
   (MRI) (C) 464

Joplin

Computer Careers (C) 310
Dunhill Professional Search of Joplin (C) 341

Kansas City

AGRI-associates, Inc. (C) 243
Agri-Tech Personnel Inc (C) 243
Ajilon Finance (C) 246
BallResources (C)..267
Delphi Systems Ltd (R)...................................... 55
HealthCare Recruiters International • Mid
   America (C)..404
Huntress Real Estate Executive Search
   (R) 105
Kendall Placement Group (KPG) (C)...............438
The Kirdonn Sales Pros (C)...............................441
MSA Executive Search|Clark Consulting-
   Healthcare Group (R) 149
Carol Park (C)...556
Resources in Food Inc (C) 591
Spherion Professional Services (C) 633
Tryon & Heideman LLC (R)..............................213

Kirkwood

Arthur Wright & Associates Inc (C)..................675

Lake Saint Louis

MR of Lake Saint Louis (C)...............................491

Laurie

MR of Laurie (C) 491

Lees Summit

JobPlex Inc (R) 112
Pinnacle Executive Group Inc (R).....................164

Linn Creek

Management Recruiters International Inc
   (MRI) (C) 464

Manchester

Allen Consulting Group Inc (C) 250
HDB Incorporated (C) 402

Maryland Heights

The Donnelly Group-Sales Recruiters Inc
   (C) 336

O Fallon

J B Linde & Associates (C)................................451
Sims Executive Search LLC (C) 624

Rogersville

Global Edge Recruiting Associates LLC
   (C) 388

Rolla

Doyen Metallurgical (C) 337

Saint Charles

H R Solutions Inc (C) 395
Management Recruiters International Inc
   (MRI) (C) 464

Saint Louis

Aaron Consulting Inc (C)..................................233
Accounting Career Consultants (C)...................237
Ajilon Finance (C) 246
Bishop Partners LLC (C) 276
Bradford & Galt Inc (C) 282
Burchard & Associates Inc (C) 288
Capital Markets Recruiting Partners, Inc
   (C) 292
CareerConnections USA Inc (C) 296
Cejka Search (R)... 37
Debbon Recruiting Group Inc (C).....................330
DHR International (R) 57
Finance & Accounting Search Team
   (FAST) (C)...373
Grant Cooper & Associates Inc (R).................... 85
Annie Gray Associates Inc (R)........................... 85
Holohan Group Ltd (R)......................................100
Ingenium Partners Inc (R).................................106
The Jacobson Group (C) 428
Kendall & Davis Company Inc (C) 438
LC Kirk & Company (C) 441
Koppen & Associates LLC (R) 120
Michael Latas & Associates Inc (R)...................125
The Logan Group Inc (R)...................................129
Westport One (C)...492
Medical Recruiters Inc (C)................................528
Morton, McCorkle & Associates Inc (R) 148
O'Connell Group Inc (C)...................................549
PCI Staffing Solutions (C) 558
Powers Consultants Inc (R)...............................166
Resources in Food Inc (C) 592
The Sandler Group LLC (R)..............................184
Sanford Rose Associates - Florissant (R) 185
John Sibbald Associates Inc (R).........................192
Spherion Professional Services (C) 633
Stern Professional Search (C) 638
Witt/Kieffer (R) 225
Youngman & Associates Inc (C)........................677

Saint Peters

Finders-Seekers Inc (C) 374
Lloyd, Martin & Associates (C) 451
Manning Search Group LLC (C)........................518
Medicorp Inc (C) 528

Shell Knob

AIM Consultants (C) 244

Springfield

Jim Crumpley & Associates (C) 323
Discovery Personnel Inc (C)..............................334
Express Professional Staffing - RWJ &
   Associates (C)..363
FPC of SW Missouri (C) 367
Haggerman & Associates (R) 88
Management Recruiters International Inc
   (MRI) (C)..464
J Miles Personnel Services (C) 533
Don W Schooler & Associates Inc (C) 613
A Stephens & Associates LLC (C) 637
Chris Woolsey & Associates LLC (C)...............673

Wentzville

C and P Marketing Ltd (C) 289

Wildwood

Genesis Research (C)...385

Montana

Billings

David S Burt Associates (C)..............................288

Bozeman

FPC of Bozeman (C) 368

Kalispell

American Engineering Corp (C) 252

Marion

Harbrowe Inc (C)..398

Missoula

Motion Medical Solutions Inc (C) 538
Nelson-McKay & Associates (C).......................544

Ronan

American Engineering Corp (C) 252

Stevensville

SPECTRA Associates (C) 631

Nebraska

Kearney

Charles & Associates Inc (C).............................302

Lincoln

Berry & Associates (C)......................................274
Leaders IT Recruitment (C) 448
MR of Lincoln (R)...135

Norfolk

Jackson Roth Associates (C)..............................427

Omaha

Adams Inc (C) 239
AGRI-associates, Inc. (C) 243
AJ Associates (C) 244
Aureus Executive (C) 264
Edge Recruiting Solutions Inc (C) 345
Eggers Consulting Company Inc (C) 346
Excel Recruiting Services (C)............................353
Hansen Executive Search Inc (R) 90
Harrison Moore Inc (C) 400
Lehman & Associates Inc (C)............................449
MacArthur, Church & Keres (R) 131
MR of Omaha (C) 492
PowerBrokers LLC (C).......................................492
Mid-America Placement Service Inc (C) 532
Noll Human Resource Services (C) 547
O'Connor Resources (C)....................................549
The Regency Group Ltd (C) 589

GEOGRAPHIC

East Windsor
Goalline Technology Inc (C)...............................390
Princeton HR Consultants (C)............................573

Edison
ACSYS Inc (C)..238
Ajilon Finance (C)..246
Battalia Winston International (R)......................16
Judge Inc (C)..433

Emerson
Bryant Research (C)..286

Englewood
JBK Associates Inc (R)......................................110
The Yaiser Group (C)..676

Englewood Cliffs
Karlyn Group (C)..435
Phyllis Solomon Executive Search Inc (C)........629

Englishtown
Stewart/Laurence Associates Inc (R)................203

Fair Haven
Dowd Group Inc (C)..337
The Renascent Group LLC (R)..........................175

Fair Lawn
Rick Pascal & Associates Inc (C)......................557

Fairfield
Carter McKenzie Inc (C)....................................298
Eagle Research Inc (C).....................................344
Flexible Resources Inc (C)................................377
Management Group of America Inc (C)............457
MR of Fairfield (C)...493
SC of Essex County (C)....................................493

Far Hills
Intelegra Inc (C)..423

Flanders
The Comwell Company Inc (R)..........................45

Flemington
D S Allen Associates (C)...................................250
Management Recruiters International Inc
    (MRI) (C)...464

Florham Park
Frank E Allen & Associates Inc (C)..................249
Eisner LLP (C)...346
The Foster McKay Group (C)............................379
Hadley Associates Inc (C)................................396
TFI (C)..651
Jarvis Walker Group (C)...................................663

Fords
Datamatics Management Services Inc (C)..........328

Fort Lee
Donna Davis Associates (C)..............................329
Oliveras & Company Inc (C).............................551
The Stevenson Group (R)..................................203
Tschudin Inc (R)..214

Franklin
Management Recruiters International Inc
    (MRI) (C)...464

Franklin Park
Key Employment (C)...439

Freehold
Snelling Personnel Services (C)........................627

Glen Ridge
Management Recruiters International Inc
    (MRI) (C)...464

Glen Rock
HealthCare Recruiters International •
    NY/NJ (C)..404
Resource Options Inc (C).................................591

Green Brook
Trac One (R)..212

Guttenberg
PLC Associates (C)...567

Hackensack
Career Center Inc (C).......................................293
Search Pro Inc (C)...617
Arline Simpson Associates Inc (C)..................624

Haddonfield
David Allen Associates (R)..................................7
Management Recruiters International Inc
    (MRI) (C)...464
The Pennmor Group (C)...................................559
Stevens, Valentine & McKeever (R).................203

Harrington Park
Search Experts Inc (C).....................................615

Hasbrouck Heights
Carter Mckay (C)...298

Hightstown
Beacon Career Management, LLC (C)...............271

Hillsborough
Cannellos-Smartt Associates (R)........................32

Hillsdale
The Macdonald Group Inc (R)..........................132

Ho Ho Kus
Waveland International Inc (R).........................218

Hoboken
Florence Pape Legal Search Inc (C).................556

Hope
Management Recruiters International Inc
    (MRI) (C)...464

Howell
William Bell Associates Inc (C)........................272

Iselin
The Kleinstein Group (R).................................119
Michael Page International Inc (C)...................531
Starpoint Solutions (C)....................................636

Jersey City
Ajilon Finance (C)..246
The Edgewater Group Inc (C)...........................345

Kenilworth
SFG International (C).......................................621

Kinnelon
The Brentwood Group Inc (R)............................27

Lafayette
Inter-Regional Executive Search (IRES)
    (C)...423
Summit Group Consultants Inc (C)..................642

Lake Hiawatha
Besen Associates Inc (C)..................................274

Lake Hopatcong
O'Neill Group (C)..550
Soundview Business Solutions Inc (C).............629

Lakewood
Jack Stuart Fisher Associates (C).....................376

Lanoka Harbor
Placemart Personnel Service (C)......................566

Lawrenceville
Alexander Associates (R).....................................6
Carnegie Executive Search Inc (C)..................297
Ken Clark International (R)...............................42
Unlimited Resources (C)..................................659
Michael D Zinn & Associates Inc (R)..............230

Lebanon
Management Recruiters International Inc
    (MRI) (C)...464

Lincoln Park
LogiPros LLC (C)...452

Little Silver
Allen Thomas Associates Inc (C).....................250

Livingston
Impex Services Inc (C).....................................420
Ramer Search Consultants Inc (C)...................584
Topaz Attorney Search (C)...............................654

Long Valley
The Bonner Group (R)..23

Longport
Vogel Associates (R)...216

Lyndhurst
Lloyd Staffing (C)..452

Madison
Joseph R Burns & Associates Inc (R)..............29
Karras Personnel Inc (C).................................436

Mahwah
Butterfass, Pepe & MacCallan Inc (R)..............30
Executive Dynamics Inc (EDI) (C)..................356
TeleQuest Communications Inc (C).................650

Manalapan
M T Donaldson Associates Inc (C)...................336
F-O-R-T-U-N-E Personnel Consultants
    (FPC) (C)...365
JWC Associates (C)..433

Manasquan
CKR Associates LLC (C)...................................304
The Executive Exchange Corp (C)...................356
Shelton Associates Inc (C)..............................621

Marlton
Bonifield Associates (C)...................................280
Dorothy W Farnath & Associates Inc (C).........371
David Perry Associates (C)...............................560
Search International LLC (C)...........................616

GEOGRAPHIC

River Edge
J Burkey Associates (R) 29

Riverdale
Retail Connection Inc (C) 592
Weinpel Search Inc (C) 666

Robbinsville
Diedre Moire Corp Inc (C) 535

Rochelle Park
Normyle/Erstling Health Search Group
    (C) 547

Rumson
Charleston Partners (R) 39
Norm Sanders Associates Inc (C) 606

Rutherford
Corporate Information Systems Inc (C) 317

Saddle Brook
Ajilon Finance (C) 244
Cornell Group International Consulting
    Inc (R) 48

Saddle River
Robert Drexler Associates Inc (R) 62

Scotch Plains
Executives Unlimited Inc (R) 71
Petruzzi Associates (C) 562

Secaucus
Reinecke & Associates (C) 589
Robinson Consulting Group (R) 178

Shrewsbury
Management Recruiters International Inc
    (MRI) (C) 464
MR of Northern Monmouth County (C) 495

Skillman
PrincetonOne (R) 135

Somerset
David J Hollinger Associates Inc (C) 412

Somerville
Lancaster Associates Inc (C) 445
Management Recruiters International Inc
    (MRI) (C) 464
The Swan Group (C) 643

South Plainfield
Spherion Professional Services (C) 633
The Stelton Group Inc (C) 637

Sparta
Management Recruiters International Inc
    (MRI) (C) 464

Spring Lake
Rockwood Associates (C) 596

Springfield
Jaral Consultants Inc (C) 428
Marra Peters & Partners (R) 139

Stanhope
MR of Stanhope (C) 495

Summit
Boyden (R) 25
Corporate Search Technologies LLC (C) 319
The Governance Group Inc (R) 84
SC of Summit (C) 495
Snelling Personnel of Summit (C) 627
Wharton-Lenox Executive Search (C) 668

Sussex
Hire Precision Partners LLC (C) 410

Teaneck
FPC of Rockland County Inc (C) 368

Toms River
The Cassie Shipherd Group LLC (R) 36
Infinity Resources LLC (R) 106

Totowa
Raymond Alexander Associates (R) 6
FPC of Passaic County (C) 368

Turnersville
Barkbridge Staffing Group LLC (C) 268
Management Recruiters International Inc
    (MRI) (C) 464

Union
Brett Associates, LLC (C) 283
Career Center Inc (C) 293

Upper Saddle River
The Ward Group (R) 217

Verona
Asset Group Inc (R) 12

Voorhees
Davco Resources LLC (C) 328
Key Recruit Inc (C) 439
Management Recruiters International Inc
    (MRI) (C) 464

Waldwick
Advertising Recruitment Specialists (C) 242
J.C. Haase Consulting LLC (C) 396
Rosebud Research Inc (R) 179

Wall
Acquis Associates Inc (C) 238

Warren
Atlantic Management Resources Inc (C) 262
Kurtz Pro-Search Inc (C) 444

Wayne
Comforce Staffing Services (R) 44
CS Dowling Executive Services (C) 337
The Gogates Group Inc (R) 83
MR of Wayne (C) 495
Profitable Solutions Executive Search (C) 577

West Caldwell
Career Placement Network, LLC (C) 295
Triad Consultants Inc (C) 656

West Long Branch
Ellis Career Consultants (C) 348

West Orange
DNA Executive Search LLC (C) 335
Target Pros Inc (C) 646

Westfield
Drummond Associates Inc (C) 338
W N Garbarini & Associates (R) 79
Randy S Kahn & Associates (R) 114
Mancino Burfield Edgerton (R) 138
Portfolio Placements & Resumes LLC (C) 568
David Ross Associates Inc (C) 599
Tarnow Associates (R) 208

Westwood
Data Search Network Inc (C) 327
Razzino Associates Inc (C) 585

Whippany
Frank Palma Associates (R) 77

Woodbridge
AltcoSearch (C) 252
GSP International (C) 395
MR of Woodbridge (C) 495

Woodbury
Roth Young of Philadelphia (C) 600

Woodcliff Lake
Anderson Young and Associates Inc (C) 255

Wyckoff
The Human Resource Advantage Inc (R) 103

New Mexico

Albuquerque
ACC Consultants Inc (C) 235
High Desert Executive Search LLC (R) 97
MR of Albuquerque (C) 495
MR of The Sandias (C) 495
SC of Albuquerque (C) 496
Miera Consultants International (C) 533
Sanderson Employment Service (C) 606

Corrales
RLR Resources (R) 178

Santa Fe
Karel & Company / Executive Search (R) 115
Management Recruiters International Inc
    (MRI) (C) 464

New York

Albany
DeMatteo Associates (C) 331
NorTech Resources (C) 548

Amagansett
Martha Ward Executive Search Inc (C) 664

Amsterdam
Sheila Greco Associates LLC (R) 85

Armonk
APA Search Inc (R) 10

Babylon
IMA Search Inc (R) 105

Baldwin
AJC Search Associates Ltd (C) 244
WorldBridge Partners of New York (R) 136

Baldwin Place
Fern G Stasiuk Executive Search Inc (C) 636

GEOGRAPHIC

GEOGRAPHIC

Queensbury
Keena Staffing Services (C) *437*
The Mulshine Company Ltd (R) *149*

Rochester
ATS Reliance Technical Group (C) *263*
Cochran, Cochran & Yale LLC (R) *43*
Cook Partners International (C).......................*314*
EXEK Recruiters Ltd (C) *362*
MR/SC of Rochester (C) *497*
William K McLaughlin Associates Inc (C) *526*
Printlink (R)..*168*
Professional Support Inc (C) *576*
Scott Executive Search Inc (R)........................*187*
Staffing Authority (C) *635*
Weterrings & Agnew Inc (C) *667*

Rome
Management Recruiters International Inc
   (MRI) (C) *465*

Roslyn
EFCO Consultants Inc (C) *346*
Harold L Rapp Associates (C)...........................*584*

Rye
Bennett Yarger Associates (R) *19*
Conspectus Inc (R)..*46*

Rye Brook
Dunhill Personnel Search (C)............................*339*

Saint James
Romano McAvoy Associates Inc (C) *598*

Saratoga Springs
Lyons Associates (R) *131*
Saratoga Source LLC (C) *497*
Molloy Partners (R) *147*
NaTek Corp (C) *540*

Scarsdale
Adept Tech Recruiting Inc (C) *240*
Frank Cuomo & Associates Inc (C)....................*324*
Global Research Partnership Inc (R) *82*

Severance
Cadre Cache LLC (C) *290*

Shelter Island
Clark Executive Search Inc (R).........................*42*

Somers
Stanley Herz & Company (R) *96*

Southampton
The Katonah Group Inc (C)..............................*436*
The Hampton Group (C) *497*
Renaissance Unlimited Inc (R).........................*175*

Staten Island
LAS Executive Search LLC (C)........................*447*

Stone Ridge
MR of Kingston (C) *497*

Stony Point
New World Healthcare Solutions Inc (R)..........*151*

Suffern
National Field Service Corp (C)........................*541*

Syosset
Ames-O'Neill Associates Inc (C) *254*

Corporate Search Inc (C) *318*

Syracuse
Executivefit NA (C) *362*
CR Fletcher Associates Inc (C)..........................*376*
Orion International (C) *553*
Personnel Associates Inc (C) *561*
Talentude Search & Consulting (C) *645*

Tarrytown
Elliot Group (R)...*65*
Guild Fetridge Acoustical Search Inc (C) *372*

Utica
The Fortus Group (C).......................................*379*

Valhalla
Hintz Associates (C) *409*

Valley Cottage
Seco & Zetto Associates Inc (C) *619*
Lee H Walton & Associates (R).........................*217*

Vestal
Influence Networks (C)....................................*421*
SearchStars Inc (C) *618*

Victor
Access Tech Search (C) *236*

Wantagh
TEG Solutions (R) *210*

West Harrison
Lane Consulting LLC (C) *445*

West Nyack
FMK Staffing Services LLC (C) *377*

West Seneca
Systems Personnel Group (C) *644*

Westbury
Sharp Placement Professionals Inc (R) *191*
Spherion Professional Services (C) *633*

White Plains
Burke & Associates (C) *288*
Concorde Search Associates (C) *312*
Carolyn Davis Associates Inc (C) *328*
Hessel Associates Inc (C) *408*
InSite Search (C)..*422*
Kforce (C)..*439*
Koren, Rogers Associates Inc (R) *120*
Leitner Sarch Consultants (C) *449*
mfg/Search Inc (R)..*145*
R J Associates (C)..*583*
Joanne E Ratner Search (C) *585*
Tax Recruitment Services (C)............................*646*
Winthrop Partners (R)......................................*224*
Work&Partners LLC (R) *226*

Williamsville
Action Employment Resources (C)....................*238*
Briand Fiorella Search Inc (C) *284*
Cochran, Cochran & Yale LLC (R) *43*
Corporate Moves Inc (R)..................................*49*
DeBellis Catherine & Morreale (C) *330*
Edwards Recruitment Inc (C)............................*345*
Executive Dimensions (R) *68*
FEP Search Group (C) *372*
Hoffman Partnership Group Inc (C)..................*411*
Professional Support Inc (C) *576*
Sanford Rose Associates - Amherst (C) *610*

Woodbury
MR of Woodbury (C) *497*
Personnel Consulting Associates (C) *561*
Resource Services Inc (C)................................*591*

Woodside
SCS & Associates (C)......................................*614*

Yorktown Heights
Infinity Resources LLC (R) *106*

North Carolina

Apex
P F Hutton & Associates (C) *418*
Professional Engineering Technical
   Personnel Consultants (C) *575*

Arden
Asheville Search & Consulting (C)....................*261*
Parallax Ventures Inc (R) *158*

Asheboro
Marketing Recruiters Inc (C) *520*

Asheville
The Asheville Group (C) *260*
The Borton Wallace Company (R) *23*
Angeline Cadenhead Associates (C)..................*290*
Christopher Group Executive Search (C)...........*304*
The William Dunne Agency Inc (C) *342*
ISC Executive Search Inc (C) *425*
Kimmel & Associates Inc (C)...........................*440*
Management Recruiters International Inc
   (MRI) (C) *465*
SC of Asheville (C) *497*
mf Branch Associates, Inc. (R) *145*
Moffitt International Inc (C) *535*
Wilson Personnel Inc (C)................................*670*

Banner Elk
Management Recruiters International Inc
   (MRI) (C) *465*

Belmont
MR of Gastonia North (C) *497*

Black Mountain
CRS (C)..*323*

Blowing Rock
Harwood & Harwood Inc (C) *401*

Boiling Springs
Management Recruiters International Inc
   (MRI) (C) *465*

Brevard
Kersey & Associates Inc (C).............................*438*

Bunn
Management Recruiters International Inc
   (MRI) (C)...*465*

Burlington
MR of Burlington (C) *497*

Cary
The Albrecht Group (C)....................................*248*
Babson Professional Search Inc (C) *266*
Carter Mckay (C)..*298*
HealthCare Recruiters International •
   Carolinas (C)..*404*
Pat Licata & Associates (C)..............................*450*

GEOGRAPHIC

New Bern

Ocean Isle Beach

Pinehurst

Pineville

Pleasant Garden

Raleigh

Research Triangle Park

Rocky Mount

Roxboro

Saluda

Selma

Shallotte

Shelby

Sherrills Ford

Southern Pines

Statesville

Wake Forest

Washington

Welcome

Wilmington

Wilson

Winston Salem

Winterville

Wrightsville Beach

North Dakota

Fargo

West Fargo

Ohio

Akron

Amelia

Barberton

Bath

Bay Village

Beachwood

Blacklick

Brecksville

Broadview Heights

Brunswick

Canton

Carroll

Centerville

Chagrin Falls

Chardon

Cincinnati

GEOGRAPHIC

Patterson Personnel (C) *558*

New Albany
Sanford Rose Associates - New Albany
   (C) *611*

Newark
York & Associates LLC (C) *676*

North Bend
Satterfield & Associates Inc (R) *186*

North Canton
C G S Executive Search (C) *289*
Executive Directions & Pinnacle
   International (R) *69*
Management Recruiters International Inc
   (MRI) (C) *466*
MPA Associates (C) *538*

North Lima
Schick Professional Search Inc (C) *612*

North Olmsted
Ratliff & Taylor Inc (R) *172*

North Royalton
Global HealthCare Services Inc (GHS)
   (C) *388*

Ostrander
Deffet Group Inc (R) *55*
Insurance Recruiting Specialists (C) *422*

Oxford
HealthCare Recruiters International •
   Cincinnati Inc (C) *405*

Pickerington
Action International (C) *238*
Continental Search Associates (C) *314*
T/MR (C) *645*
TRS Associates (R) *213*

Poland
Elliot Group (R) *66*

Powell
Ahern Search Partners (R) *6*
Management Recruiters International Inc
   (MRI) (C) *466*
The McIntyre Company (R) *142*

Reynoldsburg
J W Barleycorn & Associates Inc (R) *15*

Richfield
Yetka Management Group (R) *227*

Rocky River
Technical Search Associates (C) *648*

Shaker Heights
Management Search Partners (C) *518*
H C Smith Ltd (R) *195*

Sidney
MR of Sidney (C) *502*

Silver Lake
M Evans and Associates (C) *352*

Solon
Management Recruiters International Inc
   (MRI) (C) *466*
Torch Group Inc (R) *211*

Springboro
Waterbury Group Inc (C) *665*

Springfield
Financial Services Recruiting (C) *374*
World Search (C) *674*

Stow
J Joseph & Associates (C) *431*

Streetsboro
Great Work! Employment Services (C) *392*

Strongsville
Combined Resources Inc (R) *44*
The SearchAmerica Group Inc (R) *189*
The Pagel Group (C) *651*

Toledo
Associated Staffing Services (C) *262*
BGR Technologies Inc (C) *275*
ITS Technologies Inc (C) *427*
The Kent Group Inc (C) *502*
Selection Resource Inc (R) *190*
Strategic Search Consultants (C) *641*
Waverly Partners LLC (R) *218*

Twinsburg
Management Recruiters International Inc
   (MRI) (C) *466*

Uniontown
Management Recruiters International Inc
   (MRI) (C) *466*

Valley City
Medvec Resources Group / MSK East (C) *530*

Wadsworth
C John Grom Executive Search Inc (R) *86*
Management Recruiters International Inc
   (MRI) (C) *467*

Warren
Technical Staffing Professionals LLC (C) *648*

West Chester
Executive Search Ltd (C) *360*
Management Recruiters International Inc
   (MRI) (C) *467*
Searchmark Medical (C) *618*

Westerville
The Gammill Group Inc (C) *383*
MR of Columbus (C) *502*
MR of Westerville (C) *503*
The Polaris Consulting Group (C) *502*
National Register Columbus Inc (C) *542*
Sanford Rose Associates - Westerville (R) *185*
Vortechs Group (C) *662*
Warner & Associates Inc (C) *664*

Westlake
DHR International (R) *58*
Harcor Quest & Associates (R) *90*
Management Recruiters International Inc
   (MRI) (C) *467*

Willoughby
Artgo Inc (R) *11*

Gables Search Group Inc (C) *382*
Management Recruiters International Inc
   (MRI) (C) *467*
Terry Richards CPC (C) *593*

Wooster
Premier Business Services (C) *570*

Worthington
Creative Financial Staffing (C) *322*
Executive Staffing Solutions (C) *362*
Hudepohl & Associates Inc (R) *102*
Magellan Search Partners (C) *456*

Xenia
Management Recruiters International Inc
   (MRI) (C) *467*

Yellow Springs
CM Executive Search, Inc. (C) *307*

Youngstown
The Callos Companies (C) *291*
Michael Latas & Associates Inc (R) *125*
MR of Youngstown (C) *503*

Oklahoma

Claremore
US Gas/Search (C) *660*

Durant
Sarver & Carruth Associates (C) *612*

Edmond
Dunhill Professional Search (C) *340*
Holbrook & Associates (C) *411*
Management Recruiters International Inc
   (MRI) (C) *467*
MR of Edmond (C) *503*

Lawton
Management Recruiters International Inc
   (MRI) (C) *467*

Oklahoma City
AmeriResource Group Inc (C) *254*
Joy Reed Belt Search Consultants Inc (C) *272*
Career Concepts Executive Options, Inc.
   (C) *294*
Express Professional Staffing - RWJ &
   Associates (C) *363*
James Farris Associates (R) *72*
Management Recruiters International Inc
   (MRI) (C) *467*
MR of Oklahoma City (C) *503*
SC of Oklahoma City (C) *503*
Management Search Inc (C) *517*
Personalized Management Associates Inc
   (C) *561*
Sales Medical Professionals (C) *605*
Sales Recruiters of Oklahoma City (C) *605*
Snelling Search (C) *628*

Owasso
Drake Executive Search (C) *338*

Shawnee
Wolf Gugler & Associates Ltd (R) *87*

Stroud
Don Neal & Associates (C) *544*

Tulsa
Accounting Principals Ltd (C) *237*
Ajilon Finance (C) *246*

GEOGRAPHIC

Dalton
Brandt Associates (C) 283

Delta
Delta ProSearch (C) 331

Devon
D Gillespie & Associates Inc (C) 386
J H Glass & Associates (C) 387

Dingmans Ferry
Management Recruiters International Inc
(MRI) (C) 467

Douglassville
Energy Recruiting Specialists Inc (C) 350

Downingtown
C D Warner & Associates (C) 664
Michael West & Associates (C) 667

Doylestown
Corporate Staffing Group Inc (R) 49
Gold Partners (R) 83
Handley Group Inc (R) 89
Kaczmar & Associates (C) 434
Mancino Burfield Edgerton (R) 138
George R Martin (R) 139
Senzo Research Corp (C) 620

Elkins Park
Atomic Personnel Inc (C) 262

Erie
Ann Bond Associates Inc (C) 280
DPSI Medical One (R) 61
Dunhill Professional Search (C) 340
Blair Kershaw Associates (C) 438
Jack B Larsen & Associates Inc (C) 446
Willowbrook Employment Services Inc
(C) 670

Exton
MR of the Brandywine Valley (C) 504
Navigator Resources (C) 543
Tower Consultants Ltd (R) 211

Fairview Village
E F Humay Associates (C) 417

Feasterville Trevose
The Bontempo Group Inc (C) 280
Churchill & Affiliates Inc (R) 41
Kay Henry Associates (C) 407

Fogelsville
Management Recruiters International Inc
(MRI) (C) 467

Fort Washington
Management Recruiters International Inc
(MRI) (C) 467
Salzmann Gay Associates Inc (R) 184

Freedom
MR of Cranberry (C) 504

Glen Mills
KP Consulting Inc. (C) 442

Glenshaw
Openbrier & Associates (C) 552

Greensburg
Dunn Associates (R) 63
The Edge Resource Group (C) 345
Recruitshop (C) 588

Hanover
re-Source Net (C) 585

Harrisburg
ACSYS Inc (C) 238

Harrison City
Ludwig & Associates Inc (C) 454

Haverford
DerrJones Inc (R) 56

Havertown
Amato & Associates LLC Insurance
Recruiters (C) 252

Horsham
CPO Recruiting Group (Cresta, Phifer &
Osadchuk) (C) 320

Huntingdon Valley
FPC of Philadelphia (C) 369
Pinnacle Executive Search (C) 565

Huntington Mills
The Madeira Group (R) 132

Jenkintown
Anita's Careers (C) 256
FPC of Fort Washington (C) 369
S H Jacobs & Associates Inc (R) 110

King Of Prussia
Ajilon Finance (C) 246
Joseph Daniels & Associates Inc (C) 327
JM & Company (R) 112
Lawrence Personnel (C) 447
Ross Consulting International (C) 599
Spherion Professional Services (C) 633
The Travillian Group (C) 655

Kintnersville
Weisberg Associates (C) 666

Lafayette Hill
Juris Placements Inc (C) 433

Lake Ariel
C P Consulting (R) 30

Lancaster
ACSYS Inc (C) 238
Dream Team International (C) 338
MR of Lancaster (C) 504
The Principal Group LLC (R) 167
QSPP Group (R) 169
Stewart Associates (C) 638
Charles Stickler Associates Inc (R) 203
Tandy, Morrison & LaTour LLC (R) 207

Langhorne
International Pro Sourcing Inc (C) 424

Lebanon
Corporate Image Group (C) 317

Ligonier
Fagan & Company (R) 71

Lords Valley
FPA-US (R) 76

Lower Burrell
MR of Pittsburgh A-K Valley (C) 504

Lower Gwynedd
MR of Ambler-Philadelphia (C) 504

Macungie
Lyons Pruitt International Inc (C) 455
Search Exec (C) 615

Malvern
Brandywine Consulting Group (R) 26
Northstar International Insurance
Recruiters Inc (C) 548

Manheim
Cowan Search Group (C) 320

Maple Glen
Search Innovations Inc (R) 188

Mayfield
Staff Cure (C) 635

Mcknight
The Cisar Group Inc (C) 304

McMurray
MR of McMurray (C) 504

Mechanicsburg
Sill Technical Associates Inc (C) 623

Media
R Christine Associates (C) 304
Employ® (C) 348
Fitzgibbon & Associates (R) 74
Integrity Search Inc (R) 108
Systems Personnel Inc (C) 644

Monroeville
Clifton Johnson Associates Inc (C) 431
Porter Consulting Services Inc (C) 568

Montoursville
Management Recruiters International Inc
(MRI) (C) 467

Morrisville
Sanford Rose Associates - Philadelphia
North (C) 611

Mount Gretna
Robert Harkins Associates Inc (C) 398

Mount Lebanon
Suber & McAuley Technical Search (C) 642

Mount Washington
NDB Associates Inc (C) 544

Murrysville
Hughes & Wilden Associates (C) 416
MR of Westmoreland County (C) 505
Roth Young (C) 599

Narberth
Sullivan & Company (C) 642

GEOGRAPHIC

GEOGRAPHIC

Texas

Abilene
ExpatRepat Services Inc (C) 362

Addison
Anthony Andrew LLC (R) 10
Oberg & Associates (C) 550
Page-Wheatcroft & Company Ltd (R)..............157
Robins Consulting LLC (C) 596
The Talon Group (R)..207
Top Gun Ventures LLC (R) 211

Allen
Gil Johnson & Associates (C) 431

Amarillo
Recruiting Associates of Amarillo (C) 587
Rogers Employment Group Inc (C)...................598

Anna
Corporate Search Consultants
  International (R) 49

Arlington
J Burke & Associates Inc (C) 288
Hedman & Associates (R) 92
Judge Inc (C)..433
Kressenberg Associates (C)...............................443
MR of Fort Worth-Arlington (C).......................509
Masterquest (C)..522
Thomas R Moore Executive Search LLC
  (R)..148
The Stevens Group (R)......................................203

Austin
The Adkins Group Inc (R) 5
J Arnold & Associates (C) 259
Browning Search Group (C)...............................285
Career Consultants Staffing Services Inc
  (C)..294
Cendea (R) 37
CPI Human Resources Solutions Inc (C)...........320
DHR International (R)...................................... 58
Dunhill Professional Search of Austin (C) 342
Elliot Group (R)... 66
The Enfield Company (R) 67
Express Professional Staffing - RWJ &
  Associates (C)..364
Greywolf Consulting Service Inc (R) 86
Harder Consulting Inc (C)................................398
Harwood Allen Associates (C)...........................401
Hunter-Stiles Associates (R) 105
Impact Executive Placement (C) 420
InterSource Executive Search Inc (R) 108
JRG-USA Recruiting Inc (C) 432
KMC Resources Inc (C)....................................441
Major, Lindsey & Africa (C)..............................457
Management Recruiters International Inc
  (MRI) (C) 468
SC of Austin (C)...509
ML&R Personnel Solutions LLC (C)..................534
Murdock & Associates (C).................................539
National Human Resource Group Inc
  (NHRG Inc) (C)..541
T Page & Associates (C) 555
Pedley-Richard & Associates Inc (R)..................160
Prescott Legal Search Inc (C)............................571
Quantum Advantage Inc (C)..............................582
Riley Grainger Executive Search (R) 177
Snelling Personnel Services (C) 628
Stanton Chase International (R) 201
Strategic Associates Inc (C) 640
Strawn Arnold Leech & Ashpitz Inc (R) 205
Technifind International (R)...............................209
Telecom Connections Inc (C)............................650
Triangle Technology (C)....................................656

Bastrop
Denson & Associates Inc (C) 331

Bedford
Merle W Owens & Associates (R) 156
Southwest Selective Search Inc (C) 630

Bellaire
Diversified Technical (C)...................................335
Hotel Executive Search & Consulting (C)..........414
MR of Bellaire (C)...509
Optimal Resources LLC (C) 553

Briarcliff
Zingaro & Company (R) 229

Buffalo
RWS Partners in Search (R)...............................183

Burleson
The Dorries Group LLC (C) 336

Carrollton
Edwards & Kote Executive Search (C) 345
Graham Group (C)...509

Celeste
J L Nixon Consulting Inc (C) 546

Colleyville
Executives Unlimited Inc (R)............................ 71
GHP Consultants Inc (C) 386

Conroe
The Denson Group Inc (C).................................509

Coppell
DCA Professional Search (C) 329
Ginger Lindsey & Associates Inc (C)..................451
Management Recruiters International Inc
  (MRI) (C)...468
Optimal Business Solutions (C) 552

Corpus Christi
Dunhill Professional Search of Corpus
  Christi Inc (C)..342
Southern Medical Recruiters (C)........................630

Cypress
Corporate Leads Inc (C)....................................317
Resolution Staffing Inc (C) 590

Dallas
The Arcus Group Inc (R) 10
Austin-McGregor (R)....................................... 13
AutoPeople (C)..265
R Gaines Baty Associates Inc (R) 16
Brigham Hill Consultancy (R) 28
Benavides Technical Staffing Inc (C) 287
Candidates on Demand Group Inc (R) 32
Carter Executive Search LLP (R)....................... 35
Corporate Search Partners (C)............................319
CPUSearch (C)..321
The CSO Board (R) 51
Damon & Associates Inc (C) 326
Andre David & Associates Inc (R)...................... 53
DHR International (R)...................................... 58
Dunhill Professional Search (C)........................340
Eagle Consulting Group Inc (C)........................344
Executive Staffers (C)......................................361
FPC of North Dallas (C)...................................370
Ferguson Partners Ltd (R)................................. 73
Fowler & Associates (R)................................... 76
HealthCare Recruiters International •
  Dallas (C) 403
Heidrick & Struggles (R) 94

Highland Partners (R)....................................... 97
HumCap LP (R)... 103
Hunter & Michaels Executive Search (C) 417
Hyde, Danforth & Company (R).......................105
The Insource Group (C) 422
Intelli-Source LLC (C) 423
Jericho HR Group (C).......................................429
JG Consultants Inc (R).....................................111
JobPlex Inc (R)..112
Kendrick Executive Resources Inc (R) 116
Kenzer Corp (R)... 117
Kerr & Company Executive Search (C) 438
Kistenmacher Recruiters of Dallas (C) 441
Korn/Ferry International (R)..............................121
LCS International Inc (LCSI) (C) 447
The Lloyd Group (R)..129
Lucas Group (C)..454
Major, Lindsey & Africa (C)..............................457
Burt Moses Associates Inc (C)...........................510
Management Recruiters International Inc
  (MRI) (C)...468
MR of Dallas (C)...509
MR of Dallas North (C)....................................509
MR of Frisco (R)...137
SC of Dallas (C)..510
MATRIX Resources Inc (C)..............................523
McSearch Personnel Consulting (C)...................526
Miller Jones Inc (C)...533
Norris Agency (C)..547
Olschwanger Partners LLC (R)..........................155
Parker & Lynch (C)..556
Pearson Partners International Inc (R) 160
Prescott Legal Search (C) 571
Prescott Legal Search Inc (C)............................571
QuestPro Consultants LP (C) 582
Recana Solutions (C)..586
Resources in Food Inc (C) 592
Roll International (C)..598
Russell Reynolds Associates Inc (R) 182
Sales Aces LLC (C)...604
Search America® (R) 188
SearchCom Inc (R) 189
Snelling Personnel of Dallas (C)........................627
Spencer Stuart (R) 199
Spherion Professional Services (C).....................634
Spilman & Associates Inc (R) 199
Stanton Chase International (R) 201
Starpoint Solutions (C) 636
Steinfield & Associates LP (C)...........................637
Synapse Human Resource Consulting
  Group (R) 207
Carl J Taylor & Company (R) 208
Taylor Winfield (R)...208
TNS Partners Inc (R) 211
Kelly Walker Associates (C) 663
Waters Consulting Group Inc (R) 218
Waveland International Inc (R)...........................218
Whitehouse Pimms (R).....................................221
The Williams Company (C)................................669
Witt/Kieffer (R) 225
Bruce G Woods Executive Search (R) 226
Egon Zehnder International Inc (R) 229

El Paso
R A Briones & Company (C).............................284
Corporate Search Associates (C) 318
Management Recruiters International Inc
  (MRI) (C)...468
Pan American Search Inc (C) 555
Qualifind Inc (C) 581
R A Rodriguez and Associates Inc (C) 597
Shasteen Medical Search (R) 191
Betty Tanner Executive Search Inc (C)...............646
Technifind International (R) 209

Elgin
LNH & Associates Inc (C).................................452

Euless
Drake & Andrews International (R).....................61

GEOGRAPHIC

GEOGRAPHIC

GEOGRAPHIC

Sturgeon Bay
Management Recruiters International Inc
(MRI) (C) 470

Sussex
Sales Recruiters Network (C)...........................605

Thiensville
Peck & Associates Ltd (R) 160

Wales
The Cooper Executive Search Group Inc
(R) 47

Watertown
Foster & Associates (C) 379
Tom Sloan & Associates Inc (C).......................624

Waukesha
Placement Solutions (C).................................566

Wausau
MR of Wausau (C)...516

West Bend
Egan & Associates Inc (R) 65

Whitewater
Wojdula & Associates Ltd (R) 225

Wyoming

Cheyenne
Management Recruiters International Inc
(MRI) (C) 470
MR of Cheyenne (C)..516

Canada

Alberta

Calgary
Ajilon Communications (C) 244
David Aplin Recruiting (C)................................257
ATS Reliance Technical Group (C) 263
Baldwin Executive Search Ltd (C)....................266
BOWEN (C) 281
Boyden (R) 25
Cenera Inc (R).. 37
Computer Horizons Canada (C) 310
Conroy Ross Partners Limited (R) 45
The Counsel Network (R) 50
Davies Park (R).. 54
FinneyTaylor Consulting Group (C) 374
Genesis Corporate Search Ltd (R)..................... 81
Ian Martin Limited (C)......................................419
Interchange Personnel Inc (R) 108
Korn/Ferry International (R) 121
Leader Search Inc (R) 125
MacKenzie Gray Management Inc (R)................132
Management Resources Ltd (C)........................517
McLean Executive Consultants (C)....................526
The Network Corporate Search Personnel
Inc (C)..545
Petro Staff International (C) 562
Placement Group (C)..566
Procom (C) 574
Staffing Strategists International (R) 200
StarDot PRG Inc (C)...636
Western Management Consultants (R) 220
ZSA Legal Recruitment (C) 678

Edmonton
David Aplin Recruiting (C)................................257
ATS Reliance Technical Group (C) 263

Conroy Ross Partners Limited (R) 46
Davies Park (R).. 54
A W Fraser & Associates (R)............................. 77
Harcourt & Associates (C)................................398
Prichard Kymen Inc (R)....................................167
Project Search Inc (R) 168
Roevin Technical People Ltd (C) 597
Slate Personnel Ltd (R)....................................194
YourNet International (C) 677
ZSA Legal Recruitment (C) 678

Lloydminster
Kennedy Personnel Solutions Inc (R) 116

British Columbia

Coquitlam
Express Professional Staffing - RWJ &
Associates (C) 364

Delta
Campbell, Edgar Inc (C) 291

Kelowna
J G Flynn & Associates Inc (R) 75

North Vancouver
ShortList (C)...622

Surrey
Effective Placement Inc (C) 346

Vancouver
Ajilon Finance (C) 247
David Aplin Recruiting (C)................................257
ATS Reliance Technical Group (C) 263
BeyondTech Solutions Inc (C)...........................275
The Cadman Consulting Group Inc (R)............... 30
The Caldwell Partners International (R)............... 31
Campbell, Edgar Inc (C) 291
Chapman & Associates (C)...............................302
Corporate Recruiters Ltd (C) 317
The Counsel Network (R) 49
CTEW Executive Personnel Services Inc
(C) 323
Descheneaux Insurance Recruiters Ltd (C) 332
Forbes & Gunn Consultants Ltd (C) 378
Forest People International Search Ltd (C) 378
Glazin/Sisco Executive Search
Consultants Inc (R).................................... 82
Goldbeck Recruiting Inc (C) 390
Hamilton Group Executive Search Inc (C)..........397
Holloway, Schulz & Partners (C).......................412
Inteqna (C)..423
David Warwick Kennedy & Associates
(R)...116
Korn/Ferry International (R) 121
Laing Group Executive Recruiting (C) 445
Lock & Associates (C)......................................452
Lyons Black & Associates Ltd (R).....................131
Pinton Forrest & Madden (R)............................164
PricewaterhouseCoopers Executive
Search (R) 167
Rossi & Associates Inc (C) 599
Savage Consultants Inc (R)..............................186
Western Management Consultants (R)...............220
Wood West & Partners Inc (C) 673
ZSA Legal Recruitment (C) 678

Victoria
The Executive Network Inc (R) 69
Jacobs Scott Ltd (R).......................................110
Placement Group (C)..566

Manitoba

Winnipeg
David Aplin Recruiting (C)................................257

The Harris Consulting Corp (R)......................... 90
Lock & Associates (C)......................................452
People First Executive Search (R) 161
Personnel Management Group (C)......................562
Technical Service Consultants of
Manitoba Ltd (C) 648
Zen Zen International Inc (C) 677

New Brunswick

Moncton
Concept II Employment Service (C).................311
Lock & Associates (C)......................................452
Personnel Search Ltd (C) 562

Nova Scotia

Bedford
Ajilon Communications (C)...............................244

Halifax
David Aplin Recruiting (C) 257
The Caldwell Partners International (R) 31
Gerald Walsh Associates Inc (R) 81
Kenneth Murphy & Associates (C)....................539
Staffing Strategists International (R).................200

Ontario

Ajax
Schoales & Associates Inc (C)..........................612

Ancaster
J P Anderson & Associates Inc (C)...................255

Barrie
Squires Resources Inc (C) 634

Brampton
Dynamic Executive Search (C)..........................343
Thinkpath Inc (C) 651

Burlington
Addison Kelly Ltd (R).. 4
Angus Employment Ltd (C)...............................256
ATS Reliance Technical Group (C) 263
The Burke Group (C)..288
CCT Inc Engineering Personnel (C) 300
The Employment Solution (C)...........................349
High Road Personnel of Burlington (C)............408
Trans-United Consultants Ltd (C).......................655

Cambridge
ATS Reliance Technical Group (C) 263
Lovell & Associates Inc (C) 454
Trillium Talent Resource Group (C)....................517
Prime Management Group Inc (C)......................572
Your Advantage Staffing Consultants Inc
(C) 677

Carlisle
James T Boyce & Associates (C)......................281

Concord
PTC Accounting and Finance Inc (C) 580

Erin
Cromark International Inc (C)..........................323

Etobicoke
Brunel Multec Canada Ltd (C).........................286
Derhak Ireland & Partners Inc (R) 56
Heidrick & Struggles (R) 94
Korn/Ferry International (R) 121
Lock & Associates (C)......................................452

GEOGRAPHIC

Firms Index

Firms with (R) are from the Retainer Section.
Firms with (C) are from the Contingency Section.

This is a master index of all firms listed.

FIRMS

FIRMS

FIRMS

FIRMS

FIRMS

FIRMS

FIRMS

FIRMS

FIRMS

FIRMS

FIRMS

FIRMS

NOTES

NOTES

NOTES

NOTES

NOTES

NOTES

NOTES